Features

114th Edition

Statistical Abstract of the United States 1994

Issued September 1994

U.S. Department of Commerce
Ronald H. Brown, Secretary
David J. Barram, Deputy Secretary

Economics and Statistics Administration
Everett M. Ehrlich, Under Secretary for Economic Affairs

BUREAU OF THE CENSUS
Harry A. Scarr, Acting Director

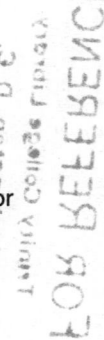

Economics and Statistics Administration
Everett M. Ehrlich, Under Secretary for Economic Affairs

BUREAU OF THE CENSUS
Harry A. Scarr, Acting Director
Jane A. Callen, Assistant Director for Communications

DATA USER SERVICES DIVISION
Jane A. Callen, Acting Chief

Acknowledgments

Glenn W. King, Chief, Statistical Compendia Staff, was responsible for general supervision and compilation of this volume under the direction of **Marie Argana. Lars B. Johanson** was responsible for technical supervision and coordination. Assisting in the research and analytical phases of assigned sections and in the developmental aspects of new tables were **Rosemary E. Clark, Edward C. Jagers** and **Rachael LaPorte Taylor.** The latter two were also responsible for content and preparation of graphics. **Geraldine W. Blackburn** provided primary editorial assistance. Other editorial assistance was rendered by **Kelvin Elmore, Patricia S. Lancaster, Catherine Lavender, Joyce Mori,** and **Marjorie M. Sproesser.**

The staff of the Administrative and Publications Services Division, **Walter C. Odom,** Chief, performed publication planning, editorial review, design, composition, and printing planning and procurement. **Patricia Heiston** provided publication coordination and editing. **Janet Sweeney** provided design and graphics services.

Library of Congress Card No. 4–18089

SUGGESTED CITATION

U.S. Bureau of the Census, *Statistical Abstract of the United States: 1994*
(114th edition.) Washington, DC, 1994

For sale by the U.S. Government Printing Office
Superintendent of Documents, Mail Stop: SSOP, Washington, DC 20402-9328
(Paper)   ISBN 0–16–045174–4
(Cloth)   ISBN 0–16–045173–6

213110

Preface

The *Statistical Abstract of the United States,* published since 1878, is the standard summary of statistics on the social, political, and economic organization of the United States. It is designed to serve as a convenient volume for statistical reference and as a guide to other statistical publications and sources. The latter function is served by the introductory text to each section, the source note appearing below each table, and Appendix I, which comprises the Guide to Sources of Statistics, the Guide to State Statistical Abstracts, and the Guide to Foreign Statistical Abstracts.

This volume includes a selection of data from many statistical publications, both government and private. Publications cited as sources usually contain additional statistical detail and more comprehensive discussions of definitions and concepts than can be presented here. Data not available in publications issued by the contributing agency but obtained from unpublished records are identified in the source notes as "unpublished data." More information on the subjects covered in the tables so noted may generally be obtained from the source.

Except as indicated, figures are for the United States as presently constituted. Although emphasis in the *Statistical Abstract* is primarily given to national data, many tables present data for regions and individual States and a smaller number for metropolitan areas and cities. Appendix II, Metropolitan Area Concepts and Components, presents explanatory text, a complete current listing and population data for metropolitan statistical areas (MSA's), the primary metropolitan statistical areas (PMSA's), and the consolidated metropolitan statistical areas (CMSA's) defined as of June 30, 1993. Table 42 in section 1 presents selected population characteristics for MSA's with population of 250,000 or more. Statistics for the Commonwealth of Puerto Rico and for outlying areas of the United States are included in many State tables and are supplemented by information in section 29. Additional information for States, cities, counties, metropolitan areas, and other small units, as well as more

historical data, are available in various supplements to the *Abstract* (see inside back cover).

Changes in this edition.—Subject matter content changes include new tables covering State population projections and household estimates for States, national health expenditures for States, persons without health insurance by State, persons with disability, college costs, crime victims, toxic chemical releases, leisure activities, 401(k) plans, employment projections, wealthholders, financial assets of households, venture capital, recording industry sales, airline screening, agriculture imports and exports, aquaculture, and manufacturing technology. (See Appendix VI, pp. 956-958 for a complete list of new tables introduced in this edition.) We have also consolidated the mining and forestry and fishing sections into one section titled "Natural Resources." In addition, Appendix III has been renamed "Limitations of the Data."

Statistics in this edition are generally for the most recent year or period available by late 1993. Special effort was made to include economic series which became available in early 1994 including series covering the labor force, the consumer price index, construction, and foreign trade. Each year almost 1,500 tables and charts are reviewed and evaluated; new tables and charts of current interest are added, continuing series are updated, and less timely data are condensed or eliminated. Text notes and appendices are revised as appropriate.

USA Statistics in Brief, 1994, a pocket-size pamphlet highlighting many statistical series in the *Abstract,* is available separately. Single copies can be obtained free from U.S. Bureau of the Census, Customer Services, Washington, DC 20233 (telephone 301-763-4100).

Historical statistics.—Specific headnote references in this *Abstract* link many tables to earlier data shown in *Historical Statistics of the United States, Colonial Times to 1970.* (See Appendix IV, pp. 951 and 952).

Statistics for States and metropolitan areas.—Data for States and metro areas may also be found in the *State and Metropolitan Area Data Book, 1991.*

Statistical reliability and responsibility.—The contents of this volume were taken from many sources. All data from either censuses and surveys or from administrative records are subject to error arising from a number of factors: Sampling variability (for statistics based on samples), reporting errors in the data for individual units, incomplete coverage, nonresponse, imputations, and processing error. (See also Appendix III, pp. 936–950). The Bureau of the Census cannot accept the responsibility for the accuracy or limitations of the data presented here, other than those for which it collects. The responsibility for selection of the material and for proper presentation, however, rests with the Bureau.

For additional information on data presented.—Please consult the source publications available in local libraries or write to the agency indicated in the source notes. Write to the Bureau of the Census only if it is cited as the source.

Suggestions and comments.—Users of the *Statistical Abstract* and its supplements (see inside back cover) are urged to make their data needs known for consideration in planning future editions. Suggestions and comments for improving coverage and presentation of data should be sent to the Director, U.S. Bureau of the Census, Washington, DC 20233.

STATISTICAL ABSTRACT USER SURVEY

Last year we included a postcard sized survey to get your feedback about current and potential products. By the end of May, 1,999 questionnaires had been returned and processed. Brief highlights include the following: 63% are interested in the CD-ROM version (which first became available with the 1993 edition of the Abstract); 38% are interested in individual sections on diskette; 35% are interested in updated tables by FAX; 41% of respondents were librarians and 29% research/analysts.

This year we have included a more extensive questionnaire, which we try to do every 5 years. Again, we would appreciate your taking the time to complete it so we can continue to assess our product mix and services. Please complete the survey and return it to us. If it is no longer in the book and you wish to obtain a copy, please write to U.S. Bureau of the Census, Statistical Compendia Staff, Washington, DC, 20233-8300, or call 301-763-5299.

Contents

[Numbers following subjects are page numbers]

Contents

APPROXIMATE CONVERSION MEASURES

[For assistance on metric usage, call or write the Office of Metric Programs, U.S. Department of Commerce, Washington, DC 20230 (301-975-3690)]

Symbol	When you know conventional	Multiply by	To find metric	Symbol
in	inch	2.54	centimeter	cm
ft	foot	30.48	centimeter	cm
yd	yard	0.91	meter	m
mi	mile	1.61	kilometer	km
in^2	square inch	6.45	square centimeter	cm^2
ft^2	square foot	0.09	square meter	m^2
yd^2	square yard	0.84	square meter	m^2
mi^2	square mile	2.59	square kilometer	km^2
	acre	0.41	hectare	ha
oz	ounce [1]	28.35	gram	g
lb	pound [1]	.45	kilograms	kg
oz (troy)	ounce [2]	31.10	gram	g
	short ton (2,000 lbs)	0.91	metric ton	t
	long ton (2,240 lbs)	1.02	metric ton	t
fl oz	fluid ounce	29.57	milliliter	mL
c	cup	0.24	liter	L
pt	pint	0.47	liter	L
qt	quart	0.95	liter	L
gal	gallon	3.78	liter	L
ft^3	cubic foot	0.03	cubic meter	m^3
yd^3	cubic yard	0.76	cubic meter	m^3
F	degrees Fahrenheit (subtract 32)	0.55	degrees Celsius	C

Symbol	When you know metric	Multiply by	To find conventional	Symbol
cm	centimeter	0.39	inch	in
cm	centimeter	0.33	foot	ft
m	meter	1.09	yard	yd
km	kilometer	0.62	mile	mi
cm^2	square centimeter	0.15	square inch	in^2
m^2	square meter	10.76	square foot	ft^2
m^2	square meter	1.20	square yard	yd^2
km^2	square kilometer	0.39	square mile	mi^2
ha	hectare	2.47	acre	
g	gram	.035	ounce [1]	oz
kg	kilogram	2.21	pounds	lb [1]
g	gram	.032	ounce [2]	oz (troy)
t	metric ton	1.10	short ton (2,000 lbs)	
t	metric ton	0.98	long ton (2,240 lbs)	
mL	milliliter	0.03	fluid ounce	fl oz
L	liter	4.24	cup	c
L	liter	2.13	pint (liquid)	pt
L	liter	1.05	quart (liquid)	qt
L	liter	0.26	gallon	gal
m^3	cubic meter	35.32	cubic foot	ft^3
m^3	cubic meter	1.32	cubic yard	yd^3
C	degrees Celsius	1.80	degrees Fahrenheit (after subtracting 32)	F

[1] For weighing ordinary commodities.   [2] For weighing precious metals, jewels, etc.

Example of table structure:

No. 586. State and Local Government Retirement Systems— Beneficiaries and Finances: 1980 to 1991

[In millions of dollars, except as indicated. For fiscal years closed during the 12 months ending June 30]

YEAR AND LEVEL OF GOVERNMENT	Number of beneficiaries (1,000)	RECEIPTS					BENEFITS AND WITHDRAWALS			Cash and security holdings
		Total	Employee contributions	Government contributions		Earnings on investments	Total	Benefits	Withdrawals	
				State	Local					
1980: All systems	(NA)	37,313	6,466	7,581	9,951	13,315	14,008	12,207	1,801	185,226
State-administered	(NA)	28,603	5,285	7,399	5,611	10,308	10,257	8,809	1,448	144,682
Locally administered	(NA)	8,710	1,180	181	4,340	3,008	3,752	3,399	353	40,544
1985: All systems	3,378	71,411	9,468	12,227	15,170	34,546	24,413	21,999	2,414	374,433
State-administered	2,661	55,960	7,901	11,976	8,944	27,139	18,230	16,183	2,047	296,951
Locally administered	716	15,451	1,567	251	6,226	7,407	6,183	5,816	367	77,481
1990: All systems	4,026	111,339	13,853	13,994	18,583	64,907	38,396	35,966	2,430	703,772
State-administered	3,232	89,162	11,648	13,964	11,538	52,012	29,603	27,562	2,041	565,641
Locally administered	794	22,177	2,205	32	7,045	12,895	8,793	8,404	389	138,131
1991: All systems	4,179	108,240	16,268	14,473	18,691	58,808	42,028	39,421	2,607	783,405
State-administered	3,357	85,576	12,563	14,455	11,553	47,006	32,323	30,167	2,156	630,551
Locally administered	822	22,664	3,705	18	7,138	11,803	9,706	9,255	451	152,854

NA Not available.

Source: U.S. Bureau of the Census, *Finances of Employee-Retirement Systems of State and Local Governments*, series GF, No. 2, annual.

Headnotes immediately below table titles provide information important for correct interpretation or evaluation of the table as a whole or for a major segment of it.

Footnotes below the bottom rule of tables give information relating to specific items or figures within the table.

Unit indicators show the *specified quantities* in which data items are presented. They are used for two primary reasons. Sometimes data are not available in absolute form and are estimates (as in the case of many surveys). In other cases we round the numbers in order to save space to show more data, as in the case above.

EXAMPLES OF UNIT INDICATOR INTERPRETATION FROM TABLE 586

Year	Item	Unit Indicator	Number shown	Multiplier
1991	Beneficiaries	Thousands	4,179	1,000
1991	Receipts	$ Millions	108,240	1,000,000

To Determine the Figure it Is Necessary to Multiply the Number Shown by the Unit Indicator:

Beneficiaries = 4,179 * 1,000 or 4,179,000 (over 4 million).
Receipts = 108,240 * 1,000,000 or 108,240,000,000 (over 108 billion).

When a table presents data with more than one unit indicator, they are found in the headnotes and column headings (shown above), spanner (table 53), stub (table 77), or unit column (table 76). When the data in a table are shown in the same unit indicator, it is shown in boldface as the first part of the headnote (table 2). If no unit indicator is shown, data presented are in absolute form (table 1).

Heavy vertical rules are used to separate independent sections of a table, as shown above, or in tables where the stub is continued into one or more additional columns (table 4).

Averages. An average is a single number or value that is often used to represent the "typical value" of a group of numbers. It is regarded as a measure of "location" or "central tendency" of a group of numbers.

The *arithmetic mean* is the type of average used most frequently. It is derived by summing the individual item values of a particular group and dividing the total by the number of items. The arithmetic mean is often referred to as simply the "mean" or "average."

The *median* of a group of numbers is the middle number or value when each item in the group is arranged according to size (lowest to highest or visa versa); it generally has the same number of items above it as well as below it. If there is an even number if items in the group, the median is taken to be the average of the two middle numbers.

Per capita (or per person) quantities. A per capita figure represents an average computed for every person in a specified group (or population). It is derived by taking the total for an item (such as income, taxes, or retail sales) and dividing it by the number of persons in the specified population.

Index numbers. An index number is the measure of difference or change, usually expressed as a percent, relating one quantity (the variable) of a specified kind to another quantity of the same kind. Index numbers are widely used to express changes in prices over periods of time but may also be used to express differences between related subjects for a single point in time.

To compute a price index, a base year or period is selected. The base year price (of the commodity or service) is then designated as the base or reference price to which the prices for other years or periods are related. Many price indexes use the year 1982 as the base year; in tables this is shown as "1982=100". A method of expressing the price relationship is: The price of a set of one or more items for a related year (e.g. 1990) **divided by** the price of the same set of items for the base year (e.g. 1982). The result multiplied by 100 provides the index number. When 100 is subtracted from the index number, the result equals the percent change in price from the base year.

Average annual percent change. Unless otherwise stated in the *Abstract* (as in Section 1, Population), average annual percent change is computed by use of a *compound interest formula*. This formula assumes that the rate of change is constant throughout a specified compounding period (one year for average annual rates of change). The formula is similar to that used to compute the balance of a savings account which receives compound interest. According to this formula, at the end of a compounding period the amount of accrued change (e.g. school enrollment or bank interest) is added to the amount which existed at the beginning the period. As a result, over time (e.g., with each year or quarter), the same rate of change is applied to a larger and larger figure.

The *exponential formula*, which is based on continuous compounding, is often used to measure population change. It is preferred by population experts because they view population and population-related subjects as changing without interruption, ever ongoing. Both exponential and compound interest formulas assume a constant rate of change. The former, however, applies the amount of change continuously to the base rather than at the end of each compounding period. When the average annual rates are small

(e.g., less than 5 percent) both formulas give virtually the same results. For an explanation of these two formulas as they relate to population, see U.S. Bureau of the Census, *The Methods and Materials of Demography,* vol. 2, 3d printing (rev.), 1975, pp. 372-381.

Current and constant dollars. Statistics in some tables in a number of sections are expressed in both current and constant dollars (see, for example, table 699 in section 14). Current dollar figures reflect actual prices or costs prevailing during the specified year(s). Constant dollar figures are estimates representing an effort to remove the effects of price changes from statistical series reported in dollar terms. In general, constant dollar series are derived by dividing current dollar estimates by the appropriate price index for the appropriate period (for example, the Consumer Price Index). The result is a series as it would presumably exist if prices were the same throughout, as in the base year—in other words as if the dollar had constant purchasing power. Any changes in this constant dollar series would reflect only changes in real volume of output, income, expenditures, or other measure.

Explanation of Symbols:

The following symbols, used in the tables throughout this book, are explained in condensed form in footnotes to the tables where they appear:

- Represents zero or rounds to less than half the unit of measurement shown.

B Base figure too small to meet statistical standards for reliability of a derived figure.

D Figure withheld to avoid disclosure pertaining to a specific organization or individual.

NA Data not enumerated, tabulated, or otherwise available separately.

NS Percent change irrelevant or insignificant.

S Figure does not meet publication standards for reasons other than that covered by symbol B, above.

X Figure not applicable because column heading and stub line make entry impossible, absurd, or meaningless.

Z Entry would amount to less than half the unit of measurement shown.

In many tables, details will not add to the totals shown because of rounding.

State Rankings

[When States share the same rank, the next lower rank is omitted. Because of rounded data, States may have identical values shown, but different ranks]

REGION, DIVISION, AND STATE	RESIDENT POPULATION [1]									
	Total, [2] 1993		Percent increase, [3] 1990-93		Total, [4] 2000		Percent increase, [4] 1990-2000		65 years old and over, [5] 1993	
	Number (1,000)	Rank	Percent	Rank	Number (1,000)	Rank	Percent	Rank	Percent	Rank
United States . . .	257,908	(X)	3.7	(X)	276,242	(X)	11.1	(X)	12.7	(X)
Northeast	51,355	(X)	1.1	(X)	51,884	(X)	2.1	(X)	14.0	(X)
New England	13,230	(X)	0.2	(X)	13,216	(X)	0.1	(X)	13.8	(X)
Maine	1,239	39	0.9	46	1,240	41	1.0	46	13.7	15
New Hampshire . .	1,125	41	1.4	42	1,165	42	5.0	41	11.9	34
Vermont	576	49	2.3	32	592	49	5.2	39	12.0	33
Massachusetts . . .	6,012	13	-0.1	47	5,950	15	-1.1	50	14.0	12
Rhode Island . . .	1,000	43	-0.3	48	998	43	-0.5	48	14.1	11
Connecticut	3,277	27	-0.3	48	3,271	29	-0.5	48	14.1	(X)
Middle Atlantic	38,125	(X)	1.4	(X)	38,668	(X)	2.8	(X)	13.1	22
New York	18,197	2	1.1	45	18,237	3	1.4	45	13.1	22
New Jersey	7,879	9	1.9	38	8,135	9	5.2	39	13.6	17
Pennsylvania	12,048	5	1.4	42	12,296	5	3.5	43	15.8	2
Midwest	61,070	(X)	2.3	(X)	63,836	(X)	7.0	(X)	13.2	(X)
East North Central . .	43,017	(X)	2.4	(X)	44,806	(X)	6.7	(X)	12.9	(X)
Ohio	11,091	7	2.3	32	11,453	7	5.6	37	13.3	21
Indiana	5,713	14	3.0	26	6,045	14	9.0	29	12.7	25
Illinois	11,697	6	2.3	32	12,168	6	6.5	34	12.6	27
Michigan	9,478	8	2.0	37	9,759	8	5.0	41	12.4	32
Wisconsin	5,038	18	3.0	26	5,381	18	10.0	26	13.4	20
West North Central .	18,054	(X)	2.2	(X)	19,030	(X)	7.8	(X)	14.0	(X)
Minnesota	4,517	20	3.3	24	4,824	20	10.3	25	12.6	28
Iowa	2,814	30	1.3	44	2,930	30	5.5	38	15.5	3
Missouri	5,234	16	2.3	32	5,437	17	6.3	35	14.2	10
North Dakota . . .	635	47	-0.6	50	643	48	0.7	47	14.8	7
South Dakota	715	45	2.8	28	770	45	10.6	24	14.7	8
Nebraska	1,607	37	1.8	39	1,704	37	8.0	31	14.2	9
Kansas	2,531	32	2.1	36	2,722	32	9.9	27	13.9	13
South	89,438	(X)	4.7	(X)	97,244	(X)	13.8	(X)	12.7	(X)
South Atlantic	45,738	(X)	5.0	(X)	50,005	(X)	14.8	(X)	13.6	(X)
Delaware	700	46	5.1	14	759	46	13.9	18	12.4	31
Maryland	4,965	19	3.8	21	5,322	19	11.3	22	11.1	41
Dist. of Columbia .	578	(X)	-4.7	(X)	537	(X)	-11.5	(X)	13.3	(X)
Virginia	6,491	12	4.9	16	7,048	12	13.9	18	11.0	43
West Virginia	1,820	35	1.5	41	1,840	35	2.6	44	15.3	5
North Carolina . . .	6,945	10	4.8	18	7,617	11	14.9	17	12.5	29
South Carolina . . .	3,643	25	4.5	19	3,932	26	12.8	21	11.7	36
Georgia	6,917	11	6.8	8	7,637	10	17.9	13	10.1	47
Florida	13,679	4	5.7	12	15,313	4	18.4	11	18.6	1
East South Central .	15,717	(X)	3.6	(X)	16,762	(X)	10.4	(X)	12.8	(X)
Kentucky	3,789	24	2.8	28	3,989	25	8.2	30	12.7	26
Tennessee	5,099	17	4.5	19	5,538	16	13.5	20	12.8	24
Alabama	4,187	22	3.6	23	4,485	21	11.0	23	13.0	23
Mississippi	2,643	31	2.7	30	2,750	31	6.9	33	12.5	30
West South Central .	27,983	(X)	4.8	(X)	30,477	(X)	14.1	(X)	11.2	(X)
Arkansas	2,424	33	3.1	25	2,578	33	9.7	28	15.0	6
Louisiana	4,295	21	1.8	39	4,478	22	6.1	36	11.3	39
Oklahoma	3,231	28	2.7	30	3,382	28	7.5	32	13.6	16
Texas	18,031	3	6.2	11	20,039	2	18.0	12	10.2	46
West	56,044	(X)	6.2	(X)	63,278	(X)	19.9	(X)	11.0	(X)
Mountain	14,776	(X)	8.2	(X)	16,890	(X)	23.7	(X)	11.3	(X)
Montana	839	44	5.1	14	920	44	15.1	15	13.4	18
Idaho	1,099	42	9.2	2	1,290	40	28.1	2	11.8	35
Wyoming	470	50	3.7	22	522	50	15.1	15	10.9	44
Colorado	3,566	26	8.2	4	4,059	24	23.2	6	10.0	48
New Mexico	1,616	36	6.7	9	1,823	36	20.3	8	11.0	42
Arizona	3,936	23	7.4	7	4,437	23	21.1	7	13.4	19
Utah	1,860	34	7.9	6	2,148	34	24.7	4	8.9	49
Nevada	1,389	38	15.6	1	1,691	38	40.7	1	11.1	40
Pacific	41,269	(X)	5.5	(X)	46,388	(X)	18.6	(X)	10.9	(X)
Washington	5,255	15	8.0	5	6,070	13	24.7	4	11.6	38
Oregon	3,032	29	6.7	9	3,404	27	19.8	9	13.8	14
California	31,211	1	4.9	16	34,888	1	17.2	14	10.6	45
Alaska	599	48	8.9	3	699	47	27.1	3	4.4	50
Hawaii	1,172	40	5.7	12	1,327	39	19.7	10	11.7	37

X Not applicable.   [1] Source: U.S. Bureau of the Census. As of July 1.   [2] See table 26.   [3] See table 27.   [4] Series A (the preferred series model). See table 34.   [5] See table 33.

[When States share the same rank, the next lower rank is omitted. Because of rounded data, States may have identical values shown, but different ranks]

REGION, DIVISION, AND STATE	RESIDENT POPULATION IN METRO AREAS, [1] 1992		BIRTH RATE PER 1,000 POPULATION, [2][3] 1991		INFANT MORTALITY RATE, [3][4] 1991		DEATH RATE PER 100,000 POPULATION, [3][5] 1991			
							Heart disease		Cancer	
	Percent	Rank	Rate	Rank	Rate	Rank	Rate	Rank	Rate	Rank
United States . . .	79.7	(X)	16.3	(X)	8.9	(X)	286	(X)	204	(X)
Northeast	89.4	(X)	(NA)	(X)	(NA)	(X)	(NA)	(X)	(NA)	(X)
New England	84.1	(X)	14.6	(X)	6.8	(X)	287	(X)	224	(X)
Maine	35.7	44	13.6	49	6.7	46	300	20	238	4
New Hampshire . .	59.4	34	14.8	35	6.1	48	246	35	203	30
Vermont	27.0	49	14.0	46	5.8	50	259	31	197	34
Massachusetts . . .	96.2	3	14.7	37	6.6	47	285	27	230	8
Rhode Island	93.6	5	14.7	37	8.0	34	323	11	236	6
Connecticut	95.7	4	14.8	35	7.4	42	291	24	214	19
Middle Atlantic	91.2	(X)	15.4	(X)	9.2	(X)	346	(X)	229	(X)
New York	91.7	8	16.2	15	9.4	15	353	4	213	21
New Jersey	100.0	1	15.6	21	8.7	27	301	19	234	7
Pennsylvania	84.8	10	14.1	45	9.1	20	363	3	251	3
Midwest	73.4	(X)	(NA)	(X)	(NA)	(X)	(NA)	(X)	(NA)	(X)
East North Central . .	79.5	(X)	15.7	(X)	9.8	(X)	305	(X)	213	(X)
Ohio	81.3	18	15.2	27	9.4	15	320	15	222	13
Indiana	71.6	23	15.3	25	9.1	20	299	21	214	18
Illinois	84.0	12	16.8	10	10.7	7	309	17	212	24
Michigan	82.7	15	16.0	18	10.4	9	295	22	206	28
Wisconsin	68.1	28	14.5	42	8.3	30	290	25	209	26
West North Central .	58.8	(X)	15.0	(X)	8.7	(X)	308	(X)	212	(X)
Minnesota	69.3	26	15.1	30	7.5	40	241	38	189	38
Iowa	43.8	40	13.9	48	8.0	34	346	7	228	11
Missouri	68.3	27	15.3	25	10.2	10	345	8	229	10
North Dakota	41.6	43	14.0	46	8.1	32	286	26	216	14
South Dakota	32.6	45	15.6	21	9.4	15	331	10	215	16
Nebraska	50.6	37	15.1	30	7.6	38	322	12	200	32
Kansas	54.6	36	15.2	27	8.9	23	301	18	206	27
South	74.2	(X)	(NA)	(X)	(NA)	(X)	(NA)	(X)	(NA)	(X)
South Atlantic	78.9	(X)	15.4	(X)	10.2	(X)	292	(X)	216	(X)
Delaware	82.7	16	16.5	13	11.8	1	283	28	224	12
Maryland	92.8	7	16.3	14	9.2	18	242	37	201	31
Dist. of Columbia .	100.0	(X)	19.7	(X)	21.0	(X)	312	(X)	259	(X)
Virginia	77.5	19	15.5	23	9.9	13	250	32	191	36
West Virginia	41.8	42	12.5	50	8.2	31	393	1	257	2
North Carolina . . .	66.3	32	15.2	27	10.8	6	281	29	198	33
South Carolina . . .	69.8	25	16.2	15	11.3	4	268	30	190	37
Georgia	67.7	30	16.7	11	11.4	2	249	34	175	41
Florida	93.0	6	14.6	39	9.0	22	348	5	260	1
East South Central . .	56.8	(X)	15.3	(X)	10.3	(X)	327	(X)	218	(X)
Kentucky	48.5	38	14.6	39	8.9	23	322	14	230	9
Tennessee	67.7	29	15.0	33	10.0	12	313	16	213	20
Alabama	67.4	31	15.4	24	11.2	5	322	13	216	15
Mississippi	30.7	46	16.7	11	11.4	2	372	2	213	22
West South Central .	76.4	(X)	17.4	(X)	8.5	(X)	261	(X)	186	(X)
Arkansas	44.7	39	15.0	33	10.2	10	346	6	236	5
Louisiana	75.0	21	17.0	9	10.5	8	293	23	209	25
Oklahoma	60.1	33	15.1	30	9.6	14	340	9	215	17
Texas	83.9	13	18.3	4	7.7	37	227	41	168	42
West	86.1	(X)	(NA)	(X)	(NA)	(X)	(NA)	(X)	(NA)	(X)
Mountain	70.6	(X)	17.3	(X)	8.1	(X)	208	(X)	165	(X)
Montana	24.0	50	14.2	44	7.0	45	241	39	203	29
Idaho	30.0	47	16.2	15	8.7	27	225	42	165	44
Wyoming	29.7	48	14.6	39	7.9	36	198	46	154	46
Colorado	81.8	17	15.9	19	8.9	23	182	47	154	45
New Mexico	56.0	35	18.0	6	8.1	32	200	45	152	47
Arizona	84.7	11	18.2	5	8.6	29	234	40	191	35
Utah	77.5	20	20.4	2	6.1	48	157	49	112	49
Nevada	84.8	9	17.2	8	9.2	18	250	33	186	39
Pacific	91.6	(X)	19.1	(X)	7.6	(X)	221	(X)	169	(X)
Washington	83.0	14	15.9	19	7.5	40	223	43	183	40
Oregon	70.0	24	14.5	42	7.3	44	246	35	213	23
California	96.7	2	20.1	3	7.6	38	222	44	165	43
Alaska	41.8	41	20.5	1	8.9	23	83	50	88	50
Hawaii	74.7	22	17.6	7	7.4	42	180	48	146	48

NA Not available. X Not applicable. [1] See table 41. Source: U.S. Bureau of the Census. [2] See table 93. [3] Source: U.S. National Center for Health Statistics. [4] See table 123. Represents deaths of infants under 1 year old per 1,000 live births, by place of residence. Excludes fetal deaths. [5] See table 129.

xiv   State Rankings

[When States share the same rank, the next lower rank is omitted. Because of rounded data, States may have identical values shown, but different ranks]

REGION, DIVISION, AND STATE	PERCENT OF PERSONS WITHOUT HEALTH INSURANCE,[1] 1990-92		COMMUNITY HOSPITALS,[2] 1992				PUBLIC SCHOOL ENROLLMENT, PERCENT INCREASE[5] 1990-93			
			Occupancy rate[3]		Average cost per patient per day[4]		Grades K-8		Grades 9-12	
	Percent	Rank	Rate	Rank	Dollars	Rank	Percent	Rank	Percent	Rank
United States . . .	14.2	(X)	65.6	(X)	820	(X)	4.1	(X)	4.8	(X)
Northeast	(NA)	(X)	77.9	(X)	(NA)	(X)	5.4	(X)	2.3	(X)
New England	(NA)	(X)	72.1	(X)	(NA)	(X)	8.3	(X)	1.7	(X)
Maine	11.1	34	68.2	11	674	37	5.0	16	5.1	22
New Hampshire . .	10.9	36	66.1	14	776	26	16.4	1	7.6	11
Vermont	10.6	38	65.0	18	726	33	4.4	17	4.4	26
Massachusetts . . .	10.1	41	72.3	8	937	10	8.4	11	-	49
Rhode Island	10.2	40	76.9	4	801	21	4.1	19	2.7	40
Connecticut	7.5	48	75.6	5	1,012	5	8.8	8	0.2	48
Middle Atlantic	(NA)	(X)	79.5	(X)	(NA)	(X)	4.3	(X)	2.5	(X)
New York	12.6	24	84.2	1	744	29	2.9	23	2.9	37
New Jersey	11.3	33	79.5	3	737	31	8.7	10	1.0	47
Pennsylvania	8.8	44	72.6	7	793	23	3.5	20	2.7	40
Midwest	(NA)	(X)	62.2	(X)	(NA)	(X)	0.8	(X)	4.8	(X)
East North Central . .	(NA)	(X)	63.0	(X)	(NA)	(X)	0.9	(X)	3.6	(X)
Ohio	10.5	39	61.0	32	875	15	0.9	31	3.0	36
Indiana	11.5	31	59.4	38	822	19	0.6	36	4.1	27
Illinois	11.8	30	64.9	19	849	16	0.6	36	3.8	30
Michigan	9.4	42	64.8	20	847	17	1.8	28	2.1	46
Wisconsin	7.9	47	63.9	22	674	38	0.1	38	6.9	14
West North Central .	(NA)	(X)	60.7	(X)	(NA)	(X)	0.4	(X)	7.5	(X)
Minnesota	8.8	44	66.6	13	618	42	2.5	25	9.1	5
Iowa	9.0	43	59.6	36	588	45	-6.3	47	6.6	16
Missouri	13.1	22	60.4	34	792	24	3.0	22	6.8	15
North Dakota	7.4	49	65.4	16	484	48	-3.5	42	6.4	17
South Dakota	12.2	27	62.1	26	457	50	0.9	31	8.8	8
Nebraska	8.7	46	56.3	43	600	44	-1.6	39	3.9	29
Kansas	11.0	35	54.2	47	661	39	1.3	30	9.1	5
South	(NA)	(X)	62.4	(X)	(NA)	(X)	3.9	(X)	3.7	(X)
South Atlantic	(NA)	(X)	66.2	(X)	(NA)	(X)	9.0	(X)	4.0	(X)
Delaware	12.7	23	70.2	10	920	12	8.8	8	7.2	12
Maryland	12.3	26	75.5	6	806	20	12.7	3	7.8	10
Dist. of Columbia . .	22.0	(X)	74.4	(X)	1,124	(X)	4.4	(X)	3.0	(X)
Virginia	15.5	14	65.8	15	774	27	11.5	5	4.7	25
West Virginia	15.0	16	64.4	21	655	40	-9.0	49	-2.4	50
North Carolina . . .	14.2	18	71.2	9	711	35	6.8	14	3.4	32
South Carolina . . .	15.4	15	67.9	12	782	25	3.3	21	5.2	21
Georgia	16.1	12	65.3	17	721	34	8.4	11	5.4	20
Florida	18.7	8	61.2	31	886	14	12.8	2	2.5	43
East South Central . .	(NA)	(X)	61.8	(X)	(NA)	(X)	-0.7	(X)	3.1	(X)
Kentucky	13.6	19	62.8	24	674	36	-5.5	46	3.8	30
Tennessee	13.6	19	61.9	29	796	22	2.3	26	2.9	37
Alabama	17.3	10	62.1	27	729	32	1.7	29	2.2	44
Mississippi.	19.3	5	59.6	37	516	46	-2.9	40	4.0	28
West South Central .	(NA)	(X)	57.0	(X)	(NA)	(X)	-0.3	(X)	3.5	(X)
Arkansas.	17.6	9	59.1	39	633	41	0.8	33	3.4	32
Louisiana	20.8	3	58.2	40	836	18	-3.3	41	2.2	44
Oklahoma	19.5	4	56.2	44	740	30	-4.0	43	5.1	22
Texas	21.9	1	56.3	42	933	11	0.8	33	3.4	32
West	(NA)	(X)	61.3	(X)	(NA)	(X)	6.7	(X)	8.7	(X)
Mountain	(NA)	(X)	59.1	(X)	(NA)	(X)	2.6	(X)	8.9	(X)
Montana	12.0	28	63.7	23	474	49	-4.7	45	2.9	37
Idaho	16.4	11	57.3	41	618	43	-6.9	48	7.0	13
Wyoming.	11.9	29	49.9	50	515	47	-9.8	50	2.6	42
Colorado.	12.4	25	61.6	30	904	13	2.9	23	5.6	19
New Mexico.	21.0	2	55.1	46	950	9	6.2	15	3.4	32
Arizona	15.8	13	60.2	35	1,051	3	10.6	6	11.3	3
Utah.	11.5	31	55.2	45	1,036	4	-4.3	44	15.1	2
Nevada.	19.3	5	60.4	33	952	8	8.1	13	16.7	1
Pacific	(NA)	(X)	62.2	(X)	(NA)	(X)	8.4	(X)	8.6	(X)
Washington	10.7	37	61.9	28	974	7	4.3	18	10.1	4
Oregon.	13.3	21	54.1	48	1,011	6	2.0	27	9.0	7
California.	19.0	7	62.5	25	1,134	1	9.7	7	8.5	9
Alaska	14.9	17	53.7	49	1,116	2	0.8	33	4.9	24
Hawaii	6.8	50	81.7	2	761	28	12.3	4	6.4	17

- Represents or rounds to zero.   NA Not available.   X Not applicable.   [1] See table 166. Source: U.S. Bureau of the Census.   [2] Source: American Hospital Association, Chicago, IL, (copyright).   [3] See table 180. Ratio of the number of inpatients receiving treatment each day to every 100 beds. Excludes newborns.   [4] See table 183. Average cost to community hospitals; based on total hospital expenses (payroll, employee benefits, professional fees, supplies, etc.)   [5] See table 242. Source: U.S. National Center for Education Statistics.

State Rankings

[When States share the same rank, the next lower rank is omitted. Because of rounded data, States may have identical values shown, but different ranks]

REGION, DIVISION, AND STATE	PUBLIC ELEMENTARY AND SECONDARY SCHOOL TEACHERS' AVERAGE SALARIES,[1] 1993		COLLEGE ENROLLMENT,[2] 1992				EDUCATIONAL ATTAINMENT,[3] 1990			
			Full-time		Minority		High school graduate or higher		Bachelor's degree or higher	
	Dollars	Rank	Percent	Rank	Percent	Rank	Percent	Rank	Percent	Rank
United States ...	35,000	(X)	56.3	(X)	21.8	(X)	75.2	(X)	20.3	(X)
Northeast	(NA)	(X)	60.6	(X)	18.5	(X)	76.2	(X)	22.8	(X)
New England	(NA)	(X)	60.0	(X)	11.6	(X)	79.3	(X)	25.6	(X)
Maine..........	30,300	29	55.9	35	4.3	49	78.8	18	18.8	27
New Hampshire ..	33,900	22	63.2	19	5.4	46	82.2	7	24.4	2
Vermont	34,800	19	67.2	10	5.4	46	80.8	12	24.4	
Massachusetts...	38,200	10	63.0	20	3.9	50	80.8	12	24.3	
Rhode Island	37,900	11	62.0	23	13.6	28	80.0	15	27.2	
Connecticut	48,300	1	50.0	43	9.9	35	72.0	40	21.3	17
Middle Atlantic	(NA)	(X)	60.8	(X)	13.8	27	79.2	17	27.2	1
New York	45,000	3	63.0	20	21.3	(X)	75.2	(X)	21.8	(X)
New Jersey	42,700	5	50.4	41	25.9	9	74.8	34	23.1	10
Pennsylvania	41,200	6	62.7	22	23.8	12	76.7	26	24.9	5
Midwest	(NA)	(X)	57.5	(X)	12.2	30	74.7	35	17.9	31
East North Central..	(NA)	(X)	56.2	(X)	13.6	(X)	77.1	(X)	18.4	(X)
Ohio.. .º.......	34,500	20	61.7	24	15.8	(X)	76.4	(X)	18.1	(X)
Indiana	35,100	17	65.3	14	11.7	32	75.7	30	17.0	39
Illinois........	38,600	9	50.1	42	9.6	36	75.6	31	15.6	45
Michigan	43,600	4	51.5	40	25.0	11	76.2	28	21.0	19
Wisconsin	35,900	14	60.3	26	14.9	25	76.8	25	17.4	36
West North Central .	(NA)	(X)	60.6	(X)	8.5	37	78.6	21	17.7	34
Minnesota	35,100	17	58.5	28	8.7	(X)	78.9	(X)	19.2	(X)
Iowa..	30,100	31	70.1	6	6.6	43	82.4	6	21.8	15
Missouri	29,400	35	56.8	31	6.4	44	80.1	13	16.9	40
North Dakota....	25,200	48	78.4	1	12.2	30	73.9	38	17.8	32
South Dakota....	24,300	50	69.5	7	7.0	41	76.7	26	18.1	30
Nebraska	28,800	39	56.1	34	7.4	39	77.1	24	17.2	38
Kansas	32,900	24	57.5	29	7.0	41	81.8	8	18.9	26
South	(NA)	(X)	59.1	(X)	10.3	33	81.3	10	21.1	18
South Atlantic	(NA)	(X)	56.4	(X)	24.4	(X)	71.3	(X)	18.7	(X)
Delaware.......	36,200	13	59.8	27	24.1	(X)	73.0	(X)	19.9	(X)
Maryland.......	38,800	8	46.3	46	15.7	23	77.5	23	21.4	16
Dist. of Columbia ..	38,700	(X)	61.4	(X)	26.5	8	78.4	22	26.5	4
Virginia........	32,300	25	56.3	32	38.8	(X)	73.1	(X)	33.3	(X)
West Virginia ...	30,300	29	67.5	9	20.9	17	75.2	32	24.5	6
North Carolina ...	29,300	36	61.7	24	5.3	48	66.0	48	12.3	50
South Carolina ...	29,200	37	64.4	15	22.3	15	70.0	42	17.4	36
Georgia........	30,100	31	66.2	13	23.3	13	68.3	43	16.6	41
Florida.........	31,200	27	48.3	45	25.8	10	70.9	41	19.3	25
East South Central..	(NA)	(X)	67.0	(X)	26.8	7	74.4	37	18.3	29
Kentucky	31,100	28	64.3	17	18.6	(X)	66.0	(X)	15.1	(X)
Tennessee	29,000	38	64.4	15	8.1	38	64.6	49	13.6	48
Alabama	27,000	44	67.2	10	16.8	21	67.1	45	16.0	43
Mississippi......	24,400	49	75.8	2	23.3	13	66.9	46	15.7	44
West South Central .	(NA)	(X)	59.0	(X)	29.2	5	64.3	50	14.7	47
Arkansas.......	27,400	42	70.3	5	28.2	(X)	71.3	(X)	18.7	(X)
Louisiana	27,600	40	70.4	4	16.6	22	66.3	47	13.3	49
Oklahoma	25,900	47	63.8	18	28.9	6	68.3	43	16.1	42
Texas.........	29,900	34	54.5	38	17.2	20	74.6	36	17.8	32
West	(NA)	(X)	48.0	(X)	31.4	4	72.1	39	20.3	22
Mountain	(NA)	(X)	52.8	(X)	29.8	(X)	78.6	(X)	22.7	(X)
Montana	27,600	40	74.9	3	17.5	(X)	80.8	(X)	21.4	(X)
Idaho	27,000	44	66.9	12	12.5	29	81.0	11	19.8	24
Wyoming.......	30,100	31	54.8	37	5.4	46	79.7	16	17.7	34
Colorado.......	33,500	23	52.5	39	7.1	40	83.0	5	18.8	27
New Mexico.....	26,500	46	49.7	44	15.4	24	84.4	3	27.0	3
Arizona........	31,400	26	44.9	47	38.9	2	75.1	33	20.4	21
Utah..........	27,200	43	68.1	8	21.5	16	78.7	20	20.3	22
Nevada........	34,100	21	33.1	50	5.6	45	85.1	2	22.3	14
Pacific	(NA)	(X)	46.2	(X)	18.3	18	78.8	18	15.3	46
Washington	35,800	16	57.4	30	34.4	(X)	77.8	(X)	23.1	(X)
Oregon........	35,900	14	56.2	33	14.5	26	83.8	4	22.9	12
California.......	40,000	7	43.6	48	10.2	34	81.5	9	20.6	20
Alaska	46,000	2	39.1	49	38.6	3	76.2	28	23.4	9
Hawaii	36,500	12	55.1	36	17.9	19	86.6	1	23.0	11
					63.8	1	80.1	13	22.9	12

NA Not available. X Not applicable [1] See table 245. Source: National Education Association, Washington, DC, (copyright). [2] See table 275. Source: U.S. National Center for Education Statistics. [3] See table 236. Source: U.S. Bureau of the Census. Persons 25 years old and over.

State Rankings

[When States share the same rank, the next lower rank is omitted. Because of rounded data, States may have identical values shown, but different ranks]

REGION, DIVISION, AND STATE	CRIME, 1992						SOCIAL SECURITY RECIPIENTS,[4] 1992		PUBLIC AID RECIPIENTS,[5] 1992	
	Violent crime rate per 100,000 population[1]		Federal and State prisoners, rate per 1,000 population[2]		Child abuse cases reported[3]					
	Rate	Rank	Rate	Rank	Number (1,000)	Rank	Percent	Rank	Percent	Rank
United States . . .	758	(X)	3.5	(X)	1,899	(X)	15.9	(X)	7.6	(X)
Northeast	731	(X)	2.7	(X)	283	(X)	17.0	(X)	7.5	(X)
New England	535	(X)	2.2	(X)	69	(X)	16.9	(X)	6.8	(X)
Maine	131	47	1.2	47	5	46	18.1	8	7.6	14
New Hampshire . .	126	48	1.6	43	7	44	15.4	36	3.4	49
Vermont	109	49	2.2	33	3	50	16.1	30	7.2	16
Massachusetts . . .	779	11	1.7	42	32	18	16.9	20	7.5	15
Rhode Island	395	34	2.8	24	8	42	18.6	6	8.0	12
Connecticut	495	31	3.5	13	14	35	16.7	22	6.0	31
Middle Atlantic . . .	800	(X)	2.9	(X)	214	(X)	17.1	(X)	7.8	(X)
New York	1,122	2	3.4	18	138	2	16.1	30	9.0	6
New Jersey	626	20	2.9	23	50	10	16.2	28	6.1	30
Pennsylvania	427	32	2.1	35	26	25	19.1	4	6.9	21
Midwest	607	(X)	2.8	(X)	440	(X)	16.7	(X)	7.2	(X)
East North Central .	671	(X)	3.1	(X)	308	(X)	16.4	(X)	7.8	(X)
Ohio	526	27	3.5	13	95	5	16.9	20	8.7	8
Indiana	508	30	2.5	28	39	14	16.6	25	5.0	41
Illinois	977	6	2.7	26	74	6	15.5	35	7.9	13
Michigan	770	12	4.1	9	52	8	16.4	27	9.0	7
Wisconsin	276	42	1.8	40	48	12	17.3	16	6.9	19
West North Central .	455	(X)	2.0	(X)	132	(X)	17.3	(X)	5.5	(X)
Minnesota	338	37	0.9	48	18	31	15.4	36	5.7	34
Iowa	278	41	1.6	43	19	30	19.0	5	5.0	39
Missouri	740	14	3.1	21	49	11	18.1	8	6.8	24
North Dakota	83	50	0.8	50	5	48	18.0	10	4.3	45
South Dakota	195	45	2.1	35	10	39	18.6	6	4.6	44
Nebraska	349	36	1.6	43	8	43	17.2	18	4.2	46
Kansas	511	28	2.4	30	22	28	16.7	22	4.6	43
South	810	(X)	3.7	(X)	623	(X)	16.3	(X)	7.3	(X)
South Atlantic	867	(X)	3.8	(X)	332	(X)	16.7	(X)	6.9	(X)
Delaware	621	22	5.9	1	5	47	16.2	28	5.2	38
Maryland	1,000	4	4.1	9	30	20	13.0	47	6.0	32
Dist. of Columbia	2,833	(X)	18.6	(X)	6	(X)	13.5	(X)	13.3	(X)
Virginia	375	35	3.3	20	36	16	13.8	42	4.8	42
West Virginia . . .	212	44	0.9	48	13	37	20.8	1	9.7	5
North Carolina . .	681	17	3.0	22	55	7	16.7	22	7.2	17
South Carolina . .	944	7	5.2	2	20	29	16.0	32	6.7	25
Georgia	733	15	3.7	11	51	9	13.8	42	8.5	10
Florida	1,207	1	3.6	12	116	3	17.7	13	9.0	6
East South Central .	672	(X)	3.1	(X)	113	(X)	18.0	(X)	9.8	(X)
Kentucky	535	25	2.8	24	36	15	18.0	10	9.8	4
Tennessee	746	13	2.4	30	31	19	17.3	16	8.6	9
Alabama	872	9	4.2	8	28	22	17.9	12	7.1	18
Mississippi	412	33	3.4	18	18	32	17.9	12	11.8	1
West South Central .	793	(X)	3.8	(X)	178	(X)	14.6	(X)	6.8	(X)
Arkansas	577	24	3.5	13	17	33	20.1	3	10.2	3
Louisiana	985	5	4.9	3	26	24	15.9	33	6.4	28
Oklahoma	623	21	4.6	5	24	27	17.2	18	6.3	29
Texas	806	10	3.5	13	111	4	13.1	45	8.5	7
West	864	(X)	3.2	(X)	552	(X)	13.4	(X)	8.5	(X)
Mountain	563	(X)	2.9	(X)	146	(X)	14.6	(X)	5.3	(X)
Montana	170	46	1.8	40	10	41	17.8	14	5.4	35
Idaho	281	40	2.1	35	12	38	15.6	34	3.2	50
Wyoming	320	38	2.3	32	3	49	14.2	41	5.0	37
Colorado	579	23	2.6	27	34	17	13.1	45	5.0	40
New Mexico	935	8	2.1	35	27	23	14.9	38	8.0	11
Arizona	671	18	4.3	7	29	21	16.6	25	6.4	27
Utah	291	39	1.5	46	16	34	11.3	49	3.8	47
Nevada	697	16	4.5	6	14	36	14.4	40	3.6	48
Pacific	970	(X)	3.2	(X)	407	(X)	13.0	(X)	9.7	(X)
Washington	535	25	1.9	39	40	13	14.5	39	6.9	20
Oregon	510	29	2.2	33	26	26	17.5	15	5.2	36
California	1,120	3	3.5	13	326	1	12.4	48	10.7	2
Alaska	660	19	4.9	3	10	40	6.3	50	6.7	26
Hawaii	258	43	2.5	28	5	45	13.4	44	5.9	33

X Not applicable.   [1] See table 303. Source: U.S. Federal Bureau of Investigation. Based on offenses known to police.   [2] See table 342. Source: U.S. Bureau of Justice Statistics.   [3] Based on reports alleging child abuse and neglect that were referred for investigation by child protective services. See table 337. Source: U.S. Department of Health and Human Services.   [4] See table 583. Source: U.S. Social Security Administration.   [5] See table 599. Source: U.S. Bureau of the Census. Recipients of Aid to Families with Dependent Children plus Supplemental Security Income as percent of resident population.

[When States share the same rank, the next lower rank is omitted. Because of rounded data, States may have identical values shown, but different ranks]

REGION, DIVISION, AND STATE	HAZARDOUS WASTE SITES,[1] 1993		FEDERAL FUNDS,[2] 1993							
			Total[3]		Defense[3]		Grants to State and local governments			
							Total[3]		Per person[4]	
	Number	Rank	Mil. dol.	Rank	Percent	Rank	Mil. dol.	Rank	Dollars	Rank
United States . . .	1,258	(X)	1,260,213	(X)	18.3	(X)	195,201	(X)	746	(X)
Northeast	386	(X)	250,215	(X)	12.1	(X)	47,565	(X)	926	(X)
New England	93	(X)	69,146	(X)	20.1	(X)	11,693	(X)	884	(X)
Maine	10	36	6,664	39	25.9	6	1,166	37	941	11
New Hampshire . .	17	23	4,128	45	15.2	26	652	46	579	47
Vermont	8	41	2,320	49	6.3	47	557	49	967	9
Massachusetts . . .	31	13	34,300	11	20.6	15	5,520	10	918	12
Rhode Island	12	29	5,287	41	15.5	24	1,107	39	1,107	5
Connecticut	15	24	16,447	26	21.3	11	2,691	24	821	16
Middle Atlantic	293	(X)	181,069	(X)	9.0	(X)	35,872	(X)	941	(X)
New York	85	4	87,442	2	7.4	43	21,166	2	1,163	3
New Jersey	109	1	35,885	10	11.7	34	6,189	9	786	18
Pennsylvania	99	2	57,742	5	9.7	38	8,517	4	707	24
Midwest	332	(X)	257,590	(X)	11.1	(X)	41,954	(X)	687	(X)
East North Central . .	222	(X)	171,396	(X)	9.0	(X)	29,344	(X)	682	(X)
Ohio	36	11	45,985	7	12.3	32	7,716	6	696	26
Indiana	33	12	22,111	18	13.0	31	3,732	15	653	36
Illinois	37	10	47,559	6	6.8	44	7,845	5	671	33
Michigan	76	5	36,830	9	6.4	46	6,654	8	702	25
Wisconsin	40	9	18,911	21	6.8	44	3,397	18	674	32
West North Central .	110	(X)	86,194	(X)	15.2	(X)	12,610	(X)	698	(X)
Minnesota	41	8	18,017	24	10.7	36	3,297	20	730	22
Iowa	20	19	12,131	31	4.9	49	1,737	33	617	44
Missouri	23	17	29,278	14	23.6	8	3,566	17	681	31
North Dakota	2	49	3,642	46	14.1	30	640	48	1,008	7
South Dakota	4	45	3,627	47	9.8	37	654	45	915	13
Nebraska	10	36	7,613	36	12.2	33	1,108	38	690	30
Kansas	10	36	11,886	32	15.4	25	1,608	34	635	42
South	293	(X)	448,269	(X)	20.7	(X)	61,711	(X)	690	(X)
South Atlantic	175	(X)	252,320	(X)	23.3	(X)	29,561	(X)	646	(X)
Delaware	19	21	2,833	48	14.6	27	455	50	650	38
Maryland	12	29	33,775	12	21.2	12	3,310	19	667	35
Dist. of Columbia .	-	(X)	20,250	(X)	14.0	(X)	1,961	(X)	3,392	(X)
Virginia	24	15	44,295	8	42.0	1	2,945	23	454	50
West Virginia	6	44	8,928	35	4.0	50	1,884	31	1,035	6
North Carolina . . .	22	18	27,210	15	19.3	18	4,498	12	648	39
South Carolina . . .	24	15	16,367	27	19.9	17	2,521	26	692	28
Georgia	13	27	30,139	13	27.2	4	4,408	13	637	41
Florida	55	6	68,523	4	18.6	20	7,579	7	554	48
East South Central . .	53	(X)	74,835	(X)	15.1	(X)	12,332	(X)	785	(X)
Kentucky	20	19	16,797	25	15.7	23	3,041	22	802	17
Tennessee	15	24	23,778	17	8.2	41	3,925	14	770	19
Alabama	14	26	21,180	19	19.0	19	3,081	21	736	21
Mississippi	4	45	13,080	29	20.8	14	2,285	27	864	14
West South Central .	65	(X)	121,114	(X)	18.7	(X)	19,818	(X)	708	(X)
Arkansas	12	29	10,843	34	9.4	39	1,855	32	765	20
Louisiana	12	29	20,204	20	14.3	28	4,817	11	1,122	4
Oklahoma	11	34	14,799	28	17.7	21	2,111	28	653	36
Texas	30	14	75,268	3	21.4	10	11,035	3	612	45
West	247	(X)	268,615	(X)	23.0	(X)	39,799	(X)	710	(X)
Mountain	74	(X)	72,377	(X)	19.7	(X)	10,411	(X)	705	(X)
Montana	8	41	4,376	44	7.6	42	831	42	990	8
Idaho	10	36	4,825	42	8.3	40	712	44	648	39
Wyoming	3	47	2,217	50	11.0	35	645	47	1,372	2
Colorado	18	22	18,159	23	26.6	5	2,109	29	592	46
New Mexico	11	34	11,197	33	16.9	22	1,534	35	949	10
Arizona	10	36	18,376	22	22.9	9	2,640	25	671	33
Utah	13	27	7,461	37	20.6	15	1,173	36	631	43
Nevada	1	50	5,766	40	14.3	28	767	43	552	49
Pacific	173	(X)	196,238	(X)	24.2	(X)	29,388	(X)	712	(X)
Washington	55	6	24,832	16	21.0	13	3,722	16	708	23
Oregon	12	29	12,379	30	5.1	48	2,099	30	692	28
California	95	3	147,364	1	25.0	7	21,635	1	693	27
Alaska	8	41	4,611	43	37.4	3	948	41	1,583	1
Hawaii	3	47	7,052	38	41.5	2	984	40	840	15

- Represents or rounds to zero.   X Not applicable.   [1] See table 372. Source: U.S. Environmental Protection Agency. [2] Source: U.S. Bureau of the Census.   [3] See table 518.   [4] See table 469.

State Rankings

[When States share the same rank, the next lower rank is omitted. Because of rounded data, States may have identical values shown, but different ranks]

REGION, DIVISION, AND STATE	CIVILIAN LABOR FORCE, [1] 1993						NONFARM EMPLOYMENT, [2] 1993			
	Male participation rate		Female participation rate		Unemployment rate		Services		Manufacturing	
	Rate	Rank	Rate	Rank	Percent	Rank	Percent	Rank	Percent	Rank
United States . . .	75.2	(X)	57.9	(X)	6.8	(X)	27.4	(X)	16.2	(X)
Northeast	73.7	(X)	56.3	(X)	7.2	(X)	30.4	(X)	15.6	(X)
New England	76.8	(X)	61.6	(X)	6.8	(X)	30.9	(X)	17.6	(X)
Maine.	72.3	40	60.8	23	7.9	3	25.8	26	17.6	20
New Hampshire . .	80.0	5	64.5	8	6.6	21	27.3	17	19.4	12
Vermont	77.7	13	66.4	2	5.4	35	28.8	12	16.9	23
Massachusetts. . .	76.4	23	60.3	26	6.9	20	33.5	2	16.0	26
Rhode Island	74.7	34	60.6	24	7.7	4	31.5	4	20.4	11
Connecticut	78.7	8	62.6	14	6.2	25	29.0	10	19.2	13
Middle Atlantic	72.6	(X)	54.5	(X)	7.4	(X)	30.3	(X)	14.9	(X)
New York	70.8	47	53.5	46	7.7	4	31.1	6	12.7	36
New Jersey	75.6	27	56.4	36	7.4	11	29.1	9	14.8	30
Pennsylvania	73.2	39	54.7	40	7.0	16	29.9	8	18.4	17
Midwest	77.0	(X)	60.4	(X)	6.0	(X)	25.7	(X)	19.8	(X)
East North Central. .	76.2	(X)	59.1	(X)	6.5	(X)	25.6	(X)	21.3	(X)
Ohio.	74.7	34	56.9	35	6.5	22	26.0	24	21.4	10
Indiana	77.7	13	59.6	28	5.3	37	21.7	45	24.7	3
Illinois.	76.9	19	59.4	30	7.4	11	27.6	15	17.5	21
Michigan	75.2	32	57.3	34	7.0	16	25.5	30	22.6	8
Wisconsin	78.4	11	65.9	4	4.7	44	24.7	35	23.2	6
West North Central .	78.7	(X)	63.7	(X)	4.9	(X)	26.1	(X)	16.6	(X)
Minnesota	81.0	4	66.7	1	5.1	40	27.4	16	18.1	18
Iowa.	81.8	1	65.1	6	4.0	47	24.9	32	18.5	16
Missouri	75.5	28	60.3	26	6.4	23	26.9	19	17.2	22
North Dakota. . . .	76.3	24	61.8	18	4.3	45	26.9	19	6.8	45
South Dakota. . . .	78.1	12	62.4	16	3.5	49	25.9	25	12.4	38
Nebraska	78.8	7	65.8	5	2.6	50	24.6	37	13.5	33
Kansas	78.6	9	63.6	10	5.0	41	23.7	39	16.1	24
South	74.4	(X)	57.2	(X)	6.5	(X)	25.9	(X)	15.9	(X)
South Atlantic	73.9	(X)	58.4	(X)	6.2	(X)	27.4	(X)	14.9	(X)
Delaware	77.5	17	62.7	13	5.3	37	25.7	27	18.8	15
Maryland.	76.8	21	64.6	7	6.2	25	31.2	5	8.5	43
Dist. of Columbia .	73.1	(X)	61.5	(X)	8.5	(X)	38.1	(X)	2.1	(X)
Virginia	76.9	19	62.5	15	5.0	41	27.3	17	13.9	31
West Virginia	66.0	50	45.0	50	10.8	1	25.5	30	12.7	36
North Carolina . . .	74.8	33	60.4	25	4.9	43	21.2	46	26.1	1
South Carolina . . .	76.8	21	57.9	33	7.5	7	21.2	46	23.8	5
Georgia	75.4	29	59.6	28	5.8	33	23.5	41	17.9	19
Florida	70.5	49	54.4	42	7.0	16	32.6	3	8.7	42
East South Central. .	72.0	(X)	54.5	(X)	6.4	(X)	22.8	(X)	22.2	(X)
Kentucky.	71.2	46	54.0	43	6.2	25	23.7	39	19.1	14
Tennessee	72.3	40	56.2	37	5.7	34	24.7	35	22.7	7
Alabama	72.2	42	53.6	45	7.5	7	21.2	46	22.4	9
Mississippi	72.1	43	52.9	48	6.3	24	19.6	50	25.5	2
West South Central .	76.5	(X)	56.8	(X)	6.9	(X)	25.2	(X)	14.0	(X)
Arkansas	72.0	44	55.2	39	6.2	25	22.2	44	24.6	4
Louisiana	70.8	47	50.2	49	7.4	11	24.9	32	11.3	39
Oklahoma	74.0	37	53.9	44	6.0	31	24.5	38	13.5	33
Texas	79.0	6	59.2	31	7.0	16	25.7	27	13.2	35
West	75.9	(X)	57.7	(X)	7.9	(X)	28.3	(X)	13.4	(X)
Mountain	76.0	(X)	59.2	(X)	5.8	(X)	28.8	(X)	10.2	(X)
Montana	74.5	36	61.3	20	6.0	31	26.8	21	7.0	44
Idaho	77.6	15	59.2	31	6.1	30	22.3	43	15.9	27
Wyoming	77.6	15	62.2	17	5.4	35	20.5	49	4.5	48
Colorado.	78.5	10	63.7	9	5.2	39	28.1	14	11.3	39
New Mexico.	73.5	38	54.6	41	7.5	7	26.8	21	6.8	45
Arizona	71.8	45	53.4	47	6.2	25	28.5	13	11.1	41
Utah.	81.2	2	63.5	11	3.9	48	26.2	23	13.6	32
Nevada.	77.3	18	62.8	12	7.2	14	43.9	1	4.4	49
Pacific	75.9	(X)	57.1	(X)	8.7	(X)	28.1	(X)	14.6	(X)
Washington	76.2	25	60.9	22	7.5	7	25.7	27	15.1	28
Oregon	75.4	29	61.1	21	7.2	14	24.9	32	16.1	24
California.	75.8	26	55.8	38	9.2	2	28.9	11	15.0	29
Alaska	81.2	2	66.2	3	7.6	6	22.5	42	6.8	45
Hawaii	75.4	29	61.8	18	4.2	46	30.3	7	3.5	50

X Not applicable. [1] See table 621. Source: U.S. Bureau of Labor Statistics. [2] See table 655. Source: U.S. Bureau of Labor Statistics.

[When States share the same rank, the next lower rank is omitted. Because of rounded data, States may have identical values shown, but different ranks]

REGION, DIVISION, AND STATE	GROSS STATE PRODUCT,[1][2] 1990		DISPOSABLE PERSONAL INCOME PER PERSON[2][3]				BUSINESS FAILURES PER 10,000 CONCERNS,[4] 1993		ENERGY EXPENDITURES PER PERSON,[5] 1991	
			Total, 1993		Percent change, 1990-93					
	Mil. dol.	Rank	Dollars	Rank	Percent	Rank	Rate	Rank	Dollars	Rank
United States ...	5,498,793	(X)	18,177	(X)	12.4	(X)	96	(X)	1,853	(X)
Northeast	1,247,080	(X)	20,753	(X)	11.9	(X)	(NA)	(X)	1,771	(X)
New England	327,196	(X)	20,867	(X)	10.8	(X)	100	(X)	1,826	(X)
Maine...........	23,267	42	16,898	29	12.2	34	76	26	2,057	10
New Hampshire ..	23,885	41	20,278	7	11.9	39	124	5	1,727	39
Vermont	11,228	50	17,076	28	12.2	34	62	34	1,930	17
Massachusetts...	153,928	10	20,985	3	10.9	44	121	6	1,767	36
Rhode Island ...	20,978	43	18,384	17	10.9	44	89	17	1,747	38
Connecticut	93,910	21	23,776	1	10.1	47	77	25	1,885	22
Middle Atlantic	919,884	(X)	20,713	(X)	12.3	(X)	94	(X)	1,752	(X)
New York	466,828	2	20,948	4	11.8	40	101	12	1,551	49
New Jersey	208,422	8	23,354	2	12.0	36	100	13	2,047	11
Pennsylvania	244,634	5	18,632	14	13.5	21	79	23	1,863	29
Midwest	1,264,262	(X)	17,713	(X)	13.0	(X)	(NA)	(X)	1,871	(X)
East North Central..	894,831	(X)	17,961	(X)	13.2	(X)	64	(X)	1,872	(X)
Ohio...........	222,126	7	17,180	25	12.7	31	63	33	1,928	18
Indiana	111,851	14	16,824	31	14.9	16	66	31	2,125	6
Illinois.........	272,197	4	19,648	10	12.8	30	49	42	1,863	29
Michigan	188,041	9	17,886	20	12.9	29	79	23	1,786	35
Wisconsin	100,617	18	17,196	24	14.3	18	71	29	1,645	45
West North Central .	369,431	(X)	17,122	(X)	12.4	(X)	59	(X)	1,869	(X)
Minnesota ..·...	100,005	19	17,907	19	12.0	36	52	40	1,714	41
Iowa...........	56,099	28	15,782	38	8.7	49	33	49	1,865	28
Missouri	103,674	17	17,158	26	12.5	32	70	30	1,821	32
North Dakota....	12,087	49	15,688	39	13.4	23	49	42	2,502	4
South Dakota....	13,078	47	15,981	35	13.2	27	47	44	1,804	33
Nebraska	33,375	34	17,416	23	13.5	21	57	37	1,942	15
Kansas	51,112	31	17,635	21	15.6	12	97	14	2,061	9
South	1,751,759	(X)	16,939	(X)	14.3	(X)	(NA)	(X)	2,002	(X)
South Atlantic	921,027	(X)	17,847	(X)	12.5	(X)	96	(X)	1,748	(X)
Delaware......	19,628	44	18,374	18	11.1	41	56	39	2,040	12
Maryland.......	108,570	16	20,552	5	9.9	48	95	15	1,657	44
Dist. of Columbia .	36,455	(X)	24,595	(X)	21.1	(X)	58	(X)	1,899	(X)
Virginia	141,658	11	18,762	13	11.1	41	87	19	1,758	37
West Virginia ...	28,312	38	14,552	47	16.6	6	64	32	2,081	8
North Carolina ...	141,149	12	16,421	34	15.3	14	62	34	1,871	27
South Carolina ...	63,756	27	15,071	42	13.1	28	42	46	1,921	20
Georgia........	136,875	13	16,871	30	13.3	24	138	3	1,884	23
Florida	244,624	6	18,513	16	12.0	36	121	6	1,533	50
East South Central..	273,106	(X)	15,414	(X)	16.7	(X)	77	(X)	1,931	(X)
Kentucky.......	67,492	25	15,010	44	16.3	7	81	21	1,936	16
Tennessee	95,447	20	16,705	33	16.7	5	88	18	1,872	26
Alabama.......	70,346	24	15,332	40	15.9	8	80	22	2,029	13
Mississippi.....	39,821	32	13,631	50	18.6	1	46	45	1,882	24
West South Central .	557,626	(X)	16,313	(X)	16.0	(X)	92	(X)	2,457	(X)
Arkansas.......	38,737	33	14,424	48	17.9	2	23	50	1,975	14
Louisiana	90,882	22	14,947	45	17.4	4	117	8	3,095	3
Oklahoma	56,019	29	15,060	43	13.3	24	57	37	1,888	21
Texas.........	371,988	3	17,116	27	15.8	9	102	10	2,471	5
West	1,235,690	(X)	18,297	(X)	9.9	(X)	(NA)	(X)	1,668	(X)
Mountain	271,254	(X)	16,567	(X)	14.1	(X)	100	(X)	1,796	(X)
Montana	13,331	46	15,128	41	17.9	2	42	46	2,096	7
Idaho	18,555	45	15,974	36	15.5	13	75	27	1,837	31
Wyoming	12,594	48	17,504	22	15.8	9	39	48	3,245	2
Colorado.......	71,470	23	18,628	15	14.8	17	102	10	1,603	47
New Mexico.	26,687	39	14,587	46	15.2	15	83	20	1,927	19
Arizona........	67,265	26	15,921	37	11.0	43	148	2	1,716	40
Utah..........	30,603	36	14,066	49	15.7	11	62	34	1,621	46
Nevada........	30,749	35	19,781	9	12.5	32	125	4	1,875	25
Pacific	964,436	(X)	18,916	(X)	8.8	(X)	148	(X)	1,623	(X)
Washington	109,362	15	19,290	11	14.2	19	105	9	1,714	41
Oregon........	55,426	30	16,731	32	13.7	20	74	28	1,714	41
California......	744,729	1	18,997	12	7.4	50	166	1	1,562	48
Alaska	26,270	40	20,306	6	10.6	46	52	40	3,249	1
Hawaii	28,649	37	20,038	8	13.3	24	95	15	1,793	34

NA Not available. X Not applicable. [1] See table 688. [2] Source: U.S. Bureau of Economic Analysis. [3] See table 697. [4] See table 847. Source: Dun & Bradstreet Corporation, New York, NY, (copyright). [5] See table 926. Source: U.S. Energy Information Administration.

State Rankings

[When States share the same rank, the next lower rank is omitted. Because of rounded data, States may have identical values shown, but different ranks]

REGION, DIVISION, AND STATE	MOTOR VEHICLES, 1992						HOUSING			
	Auto insurance, average expenditures per insured vehicle [1]		Deaths per 100 million vehicle miles [2]		Miles of travel per mile of road [3]		Starts, percent increase, [4] 1992-93		Existing home sales, percent increase, [5] 1992-93	
	Dollars	Rank	Rate	Rank	Number (1,000)	Rank	Percent	Rank	Percent	Rank
United States . . .	617	(X)	1.8	(X)	574	(X)	3.4	(X)	8.0	(X)
Northeast	(NA)	(X)	(NA)	(X)	(NA)	(X)	-2.4	(X)	(NA)	(X)
New England	(NA)	(X)	(NA)	(X)	(NA)	(X)	-3.3	(X)	(NA)	(X)
Maine	468	38	1.7	27	555	25	-8.9	48	12.6	13
New Hampshire . .	638	19	1.2	47	673	17	18.2	3	13.3	12
Vermont	484	35	1.6	31	429	32	-	29	15.8	7
Massachusetts . . .	860	4	1.0	50	1,391	5	-1.1	32	14.6	11
Rhode Island . . .	837	5	1.1	48	1,283	7	-3.2	40	10.0	18
Connecticut	878	3	1.1	48	1,325	6	-10.6	49	14.8	10
Middle Atlantic . .	(NA)	(X)	(NA)	(X)	(NA)	(X)	-2.1	(X)	(NA)	(X)
New York	799	7	1.6	31	981	10	-7.9	47	4.9	36
New Jersey	957	2	1.3	45	1,747	2	-1.1	32	5.2	35
Pennsylvania . . .	642	18	1.7	27	762	13	1.8	26	5.7	33
Midwest	(NA)	(X)	(NA)	(X)	(NA)	(X)	-1.4	(X)	(NA)	(X)
East North Central . .	(NA)	(X)	(NA)	(X)	(NA)	(X)	-1.7	(X)	(NA)	(X)
Ohio	503	31	1.5	37	835	12	-7.3	45	7.0	26
Indiana	497	32	1.6	31	620	21	0.3	28	18.9	3
Illinois	534	25	1.6	31	644	18	6.0	21	4.1	38
Michigan	661	15	1.5	37	714	14	-4.7	43	8.5	19
Wisconsin	492	34	1.4	40	433	31	-1.9	38	3.4	40
West North Central .	(NA)	(X)	(NA)	(X)	(NA)	(X)	-0.4	(X)	(NA)	(X)
Minnesota	566	21	1.4	40	317	36	-3.9	41	8.1	21
Iowa	379	46	1.8	23	212	43	-1.6	36	0.8	43
Missouri	493	33	1.9	19	440	30	3.3	24	7.7	24
North Dakota . . .	319	50	1.4	40	70	50	6.9	20	-0.8	44
South Dakota . . .	333	49	2.3	9	87	49	5.4	22	7.9	22
Nebraska	352	48	1.9	19	157	47	-1.2	34	3.6	39
Kansas	392	45	1.6	31	181	45	-0.9	31	16.2	6
South	(NA)	(X)	(NA)	(X)	(NA)	(X)	11.7	(X)	(NA)	(X)
South Atlantic	(NA)	(X)	(NA)	(X)	(NA)	(X)	10.9	(X)	(NA)	(X)
Delaware	745	8	2.1	17	1,150	8	8.6	15	-6.0	48
Maryland	702	10	1.6	31	1,445	4	8.5	16	6.4	29
Dist. of Columbia .	880	(X)	(NA)	(X)	3,600	(X)	-	(X)	-0.8	(X)
Virginia	503	30	1.3	45	932	11	7.2	19	2.9	41
West Virginia	557	22	2.5	4	471	29	10.3	13	-2.4	46
North Carolina . . .	448	41	2.4	5	703	15	13.3	9	15.5	8
South Carolina . . .	528	26	2.3	9	547	26	0.9	27	5.6	34
Georgia	514	28	1.8	23	702	16	7.5	18	(NA)	(X)
Florida	684	12	2.1	17	1,030	9	15.6	6	16.6	5
East South Central . .	(NA)	(X)	(NA)	(X)	(NA)	(X)	10.4	(X)	(NA)	(X)
Kentucky	473	37	2.3	9	529	27	5.4	22	5.8	32
Tennessee	478	36	2.4	5	588	22	10.2	14	17.9	4
Alabama	510	29	2.3	9	498	28	12.9	10	7.4	25
Mississippi	519	27	2.4	5	359	35	17.6	4	11.2	15
West South Central .	(NA)	(X)	(NA)	(X)	(NA)	(X)	15.4	(X)	(NA)	(X)
Arkansas	424	42	2.6	2	299	39	15.1	8	10.5	16
Louisiana	724	9	2.4	5	575	23	8.5	16	4.9	36
Oklahoma	448	40	1.8	23	313	37	19.5	2	6.8	27
Texas	646	17	1.9	19	557	24	16.1	5	6.6	28
West	(NA)	(X)	(NA)	(X)	(NA)	(X)	-3.1	(X)	(NA)	(X)
Mountain	(NA)	(X)	(NA)	(X)	(NA)	(X)	7.6	(X)	(NA)	(X)
Montana	393	44	2.2	16	121	48	2.9	25	-2.4	46
Idaho	402	43	2.3	9	183	44	-6.0	44	8.3	20
Wyoming	366	47	1.9	19	159	46	-	29	10.1	17
Colorado	653	16	1.8	23	371	34	20.4	1	15.0	9
New Mexico	543	23	2.7	1	303	38	-1.6	36	6.2	30
Arizona	667	14	2.3	9	625	20	11.1	12	20.2	1
Utah	463	39	1.7	27	379	33	15.6	6	-1.0	45
Nevada	673	13	2.3	9	237	42	-7.6	46	19.1	2
Pacific	(NA)	(X)	(NA)	(X)	(NA)	(X)	-10.4	(X)	(NA)	(X)
Washington	588	20	1.4	40	625	19	-4.2	42	6.2	30
Oregon	535	24	1.7	27	294	40	-3.0	39	12.0	14
California	800	6	1.4	40	1,563	3	-15.1	50	2.2	42
Alaska	685	11	2.6	2	271	41	12.5	11	(NA)	(X)
Hawaii	974	1	1.5	37	2,000	1	-1.5	35	7.8	23

- Represents or rounds to zero. NA Not available. X Not applicable. [1] See table 831. Source: National Association of Insurance Commissioners, Kansas City, MO, (copyright). [2] See table 1015. Source: National Safety Council, Itasca, IL, (copyright). [3] See table 1006. Source: U.S. Federal Highway Administration. [4] See table 1203. Source: National Association of Home Builders, Washington, DC. [5] See table 1210. Source: National Association of REALTORS, Washington, DC, (copyright).

State Rankings

[When States share the same rank, the next lower rank is omitted. Because of rounded data, States may have identical values shown, but different ranks]

REGION, DIVISION, AND STATE	FARM LAND, PERCENT INCREASE IN AVERAGE VALUE PER ACRE,[1] 1990-93		AVERAGE HOURLY EARNINGS OF PRODUCTION WORKERS IN MANUFACTURING,[2] 1993		RETAIL SALES PER HOUSEHOLD[3]				U.S. EXPORTS BY STATE OF ORIGIN, PERCENT CHANGE,[4] 1992-93	
					Total, 1992		Percent increase, 1991-92			
	Percent	Rank	Dollars	Rank	Dollars	Rank	Percent	Rank	Percent	Rank
United States . . .	4.8	(X)	11.76	(X)	20,710	(X)	6.5	(X)	3.3	(X)
Northeast	(NA)	(X)	(NA)	(X)	20,994	(X)	5.8	(X)	11.2	(X)
New England	(NA)	(X)	(NA)	(X)	22,662	(X)	1.9	(X)	3.6	(X)
Maine	-2.7	39	11.40	32	24,377	5	14.4	2	13.9	8
New Hampshire . .	-2.6	38	11.61	27	27,831	2	7.3	25	-1.4	37
Vermont	-2.7	39	11.81	25	23,571	8	13.8	4	2.1	30
Massachusetts . . .	-2.7	39	12.36	12	21,083	20	-8.7	50	0.2	35
Rhode Island	-2.7	39	10.22	41	19,330	39	8.9	21	3.9	27
Connecticut	-2.7	39	13.01	6	23,963	7	11.9	9	9.8	13
Middle Atlantic	(NA)	(X)	(NA)	(X)	20,403	(X)	7.4	(X)	14.8	(X)
New York	14.9	5	11.97	23	18,889	42	3.0	42	25.4	2
New Jersey	-2.1	37	12.98	7	23,987	6	7.0	28	3.7	28
Pennsylvania	-3.3	44	12.09	18	20,401	28	14.3	3	1.3	34
Midwest	(NA)	(X)	(NA)	(X)	20,704	(X)	7.9	(X)	8.8	(X)
East North Central . .	(NA)	(X)	(NA)	(X)	20,775	(X)	7.5	(X)	10.1	(X)
Ohio	5.2	23	14.05	2	19,463	37	5.0	32	6.1	22
Indiana	9.8	16	13.17	5	19,641	36	2.7	44	16.9	6
Illinois	8.2	17	12.04	19	22,192	10	10.6	18	7.2	18
Michigan	12.4	12	15.36	1	21,043	22	7.2	26	13.6	9
Wisconsin	16.1	2	12.17	17	21,253	17	11.6	13	9.7	14
West North Central .	(NA)	(X)	(NA)	(X)	20,539	(X)	8.7	(X)	3.8	(X)
Minnesota	11.3	13	12.23	14	20,968	23	0.2	47	1.5	32
Iowa	13.0	10	12.22	15	20,344	29	11.2	14	12.3	11
Missouri	5.3	21	11.54	28	20,599	25	12.4	8	-3.7	38
North Dakota	14.1	7	9.87	43	21,969	11	13.0	6	21.5	4
South Dakota	12.7	11	8.89	50	21,116	19	13.1	5	9.4	15
Nebraska	5.5	20	10.46	38	19,707	35	11.7	12	9.9	12
Kansas	6.9	19	11.99	21	19,891	34	10.9	17	6.1	22
South	(NA)	(X)	(NA)	(X)	20,160	(X)	6.4	(X)	-0.9	(X)
South Atlantic	(NA)	(X)	(NA)	(X)	20,704	(X)	7.1	(X)	-3.4	(X)
Delaware	4.6	24	13.31	4	24,473	4	2.4	46	-12.6	47
Maryland	4.2	27	12.83	8	21,121	18	4.3	36	12.8	10
Dist. of Columbia .	(X)	(X)	13.18	(X)	14,763	(X)	0.2	(X)	34.8	(X)
Virginia	-14.6	48	10.85	37	22,415	9	15.0	1	-7.5	42
West Virginia	13.5	8	12.27	13	15,299	50	3.5	39	-18.5	49
North Carolina . . .	4.4	26	9.80	44	19,326	40	8.2	23	-4.7	39
South Carolina . . .	-4.2	45	9.80	44	19,426	38	3.4	41	6.9	19
Georgia	-4.7	46	10.08	42	19,933	31	4.2	37	-10.8	44
Florida	-0.5	36	9.76	46	21,919	12	7.2	27	-1.3	36
East South Central . .	(NA)	(X)	(NA)	(X)	18,203	(X)	7.0	(X)	3.8	(X)
Kentucky	10.5	15	11.48	30	18,129	45	4.4	34	15.5	7
Tennessee	5.3	21	10.33	40	19,921	32	12.7	7	8.6	16
Alabama	2.9	31	10.36	39	17,808	46	4.0	38	-5.2	41
Mississippi	4.0	28	9.16	49	15,435	49	3.5	40	-14.1	48
West South Central .	(NA)	(X)	(NA)	(X)	20,356	(X)	4.9	(X)	0.2	(X)
Arkansas	1.2	32	9.36	48	17,194	47	-0.5	48	2.2	29
Louisiana	3.3	29	12.66	9	20,156	30	4.6	33	-11.0	45
Oklahoma	3.0	30	11.41	31	16,167	48	-3.1	49	5.7	24
Texas	-4.8	47	11.02	36	21,675	14	6.9	29	4.0	26
West	(NA)	(X)	(NA)	(X)	21,356	(X)	5.9	(X)	-0.2	(X)
Mountain	(NA)	(X)	(NA)	(X)	20,426	(X)	10.1	(X)	4.5	(X)
Montana	13.4	9	12.38	10	19,917	33	11.8	10	1.5	32
Idaho	4.5	25	11.88	24	18,416	44	9.3	20	4.3	25
Wyoming	-	35	11.54	28	18,480	43	11.7	11	-8.5	43
Colorado	7.0	18	12.02	20	20,326	16	11.0	16	18.2	5
New Mexico	14.8	6	9.74	47	19,132	41	11.1	15	22.0	3
Arizona	16.0	3	11.07	35	20,673	24	10.0	19	6.4	20
Utah	19.3	1	11.10	34	20,589	26	8.6	22	-12.5	46
Nevada	10.8	14	11.65	26	21,054	21	8.0	24	6.4	20
Pacific	(NA)	(X)	(NA)	(X)	21,697	(X)	4.6	(X)	-0.8	(X)
Washington	0.4	34	13.97	3	20,577	27	5.1	31	-5.1	40
Oregon	15.1	4	12.18	16	21,817	13	6.0	30	7.8	17
California	1.1	33	12.37	11	21,471	15	4.4	35	1.6	31
Alaska	(NA)	(X)	11.14	33	24,818	3	2.6	45	-21.4	50
Hawaii	(NA)	(X)	11.98	22	32,008	1	2.9	43	26.1	1

- Represents or rounds to zero. NA Not available. X Not applicable. [1] See table 1087. Source: U.S. Department of Agriculture. [2] See table 1238. Source: U.S. Bureau of Labor Statistics. [3] See table 1295. Source: Market Statistics, New York, NY, (copyright). [4] See table 1324. Source: U.S. Bureau of the Census.

Telephone Contacts List

To help *Abstract* users find more data and information about statistical publications, we are issuing this list of contacts for Federal agencies with major statistical programs. The intent is to give a single, first-contact point-of-entry for users of statistics. These agencies will provide general information on their statistical programs and publications, as well as specific information on how to order their publications.

Executive Office of the President
Office of Management and Budget
Administrator
Office of Information and Regulatory Affairs
Office of Management and Budget
Washington, DC 20503
Information: 202-395-3000
Publications: 202-395-7332

Department of Agriculture
Economic Research Service
Information Division
Economic Research Service
U.S. Department of Agriculture
Room 236
1301 New York Ave., N.W.
Washington, DC 20005-4788
Information and Publications: 202-219-0515
National Agricultural Statistics Service
National Agricultural Statistics Service
U.S. Department of Agriculture
14th St. and Independence Ave., S.W.
Washington, DC 20250
Information and Publications: 202-720-4020

Department of Commerce
U.S. Department of Commerce
Room 5058 Main Commerce
14th St. and Constitution Ave., N.W.
Washington, DC 20230
Newsroom: 202-482-4901
Bureau of the Census
Customer Services Branch
Data User Services Division
Bureau of the Census
U.S. Department of Commerce
Washington, DC 20233
Information and Publications: 301-763-4100
Bureau of Economic Analysis
Current Business Analysis Division, BE-53
Bureau of Economic Analysis
U.S. Department of Commerce
Washington, DC 20230
Information and Publications: 202-606-9900

Department of Commerce —Con.
International Trade Administration
Trade Statistics Division .
International Trade Administration
Room 2814 B
U.S. Department of Commerce
Washington, DC 20230
Information and Publications: 202-482-2185

National Oceanic and Atmospheric Administration
National Oceanic and Atmospheric Administration Library
U.S. Department of Commerce
1315 East-West Highway
2nd Floor
Silver Spring MD 20910
Library: 301-713-2600

Department of Defense
Department of Defense
Office of the Assistant to the Secretary of Defense (Public Affairs)
Attention: Directorate for Public Correspondence
The Pentagon, 2E777
Washington, DC 20301-1400
Information: 703-697-5737

Department of Education
Office of Information Services
Statistical Information Office
U.S. Department of Education
555 New Jersey Ave., N.W.
Washington, DC 20208-5641
Information and Publications: 202-219-1651;
1-800-424-1616

Department of Energy
Energy Information Administration
National Energy Information Center
Energy Information Administration
U.S. Department of Energy
Washington, DC 20585
Information and Publications: 202-586-8800

Department of Health and Human Services

Health Resources and Services Administration
Administrator for Health Resources and Services
Health Resources and Services Administration
U.S. Department of Health and Human Services
5600 Fishers Lane
42 Parklawn Building 14-05
Rockville, MD 20857
Publications: 301-443-2086

Substance Abuse Mental Health Services Administration
U.S. Department of Health and Human Services
5600 Fishers Lane
Room 12C105
Rockville, MD 20857
Information: 301-443-3783
Publications: 301-468-2600

Centers for Disease Control
Office of Information
Centers for Disease Control
21600 Clifton Road, N.E.
Atlanta, GA 30333
Public Inquiries: 404-639-3534

Health Care Financing Administration
Office of Public Affairs
Health Care Financing Administration
U.S. Department of Health and Human Services
Room 428H, Humphrey Building
200 Independence Ave., S.W.
Washington, DC 20201
Media Relations: 202-690-6145

National Center for Health Statistics
Scientific and Technical Information Branch
National Center for Health Statistics
U.S. Department of Health and Human Services
6525 Belcrest Rd. Rm. 1064
Hyattsville, MD 20782
Information and Publications: 301-436-8500

Social Security Administration
Publications Staff
Office of Research and Statistics
Social Security Administration
U.S. Department of Health and Human Services
Van Ness Centre, Room 209
4301 Connecticut Ave., N.W.
Washington, DC 20008
Information and Publications: 202-282-7138

Department of Housing and Urban Development

Assistant Secretary for Community Planning and Development
Office of the Assistant Secretary for Community Planning and Development
U.S. Department of Housing and Urban Development
451 7th St., S.W.
Washington, DC 20410-0555
Information: 202-708-2690
Publications: 301-251-5154

Department of the Interior

Bureau of Mines
Office of Public Information
Bureau of Mines
U.S. Department of the Interior .
Washington, DC 20241
Information: 202-501-9649
Publications: 202-501-9757

Geological Survey
Public Inquiries Office
Geological Survey
U.S. Department of the Interior
507 National Center
Reston, VA 22092
Information and Publications: 703-648-6892

Department of Justice

Bureau of Justice Statistics
Statistics Division
Bureau of Justice Statistics
U.S. Department of Justice
633 Indiana Ave., N.W.
Washington, DC 20531
Information and Publications: 202-307-6100

National Criminal Justice Reference Service
Box 6000
Rockville, MD 20850
Information and Publications: 301-251-5500
Publications: 1-800-732-3277

Federal Bureau of Investigation
National Crime Information Center
Federal Bureau of Investigation
U.S. Department of Justice
9th St. and Pennsylvania Ave., N.W.
Washington, DC 20535
Information and Publications: 202-324-3691
Publications: 202-324-5343

Immigration and Naturalization Service
Statistics Branch
Immigration and Naturalization Service
U.S. Department of Justice
425 I St., N.W.
Washington, DC 20536
Attention: Tariff Rm. 235
Information and Publications: 202-376-3066

Department of Labor

Bureau of Labor Statistics
Office of Publications and Information
Services
Bureau of Labor Statistics
U.S. Department of Labor
441 G St., N.W., Room 2831A
Washington, DC 20212
Information and Publications: 202-606-7828

Employment and Training Administration
Office of Public Information
Employment and Training Administration
U.S. Department of Labor
200 Constitution Ave., N.W., Room N4700 .
Information and Publications: 202-219-6871

Department of Transportation

Federal Aviation Administration
Public Inquiry Center
APA 200
Federal Aviation Administration
U.S. Department of Transportation
800 Independence Ave., S.W.
Washington, DC 20591
Information and Publications: 202-267-3484

Federal Highway Administration
Office of Public Affairs
Federal Highway Administration
U.S. Department of Transportation
400 7th St., S.W.
Washington, DC 20590
Information: 202-366-0660

National Highway Traffic Safety Administration
Office of Public Affairs
National Highway Traffic Safety
Administration
U.S. Department of Transportation
400 7th St., S.W.
Washington, DC 20590
Information: 202-366-0123
Publications: 202-366-2588

Department of the Treasury

Internal Revenue Service
Statistics of Income Division
Internal Revenue Service
U.S. Department of the Treasury
P.O. Box 2608
Washington, DC 20013
Information and Publications: 202-874-0410

Department of Veterans Affairs

Department of Veterans Affairs
Office of Public Affairs
Department of Veterans Affairs
810 Vermont Ave., N.W.
Washington, DC 20420
Information: 202-273-5700

Independent Agencies

Environmental Protection Agency
Public Information Center, Rm. 3404
Environmental Protection Agency
401 M St., S.W.
Washington, DC 20460
Information: 202-260-2080

Federal Reserve Board
Division of Research and Statistics
Federal Reserve Board
Washington, DC 20551
Information: 202-452-3301 .

National Science Foundation
Office of Public Information
National Science Foundation
4201 Wilson Boulevard.
Arlington Virginia 22230
Information: 703-306-1234
Publications: 703-306-1130

Securities and Exchange Commission
Office of Public Affairs
Securities and Exchange Commission
450 5th St., N.W.
Washington, DC 20549
Information: 202-272-3100
Publications: 202-272-7460

Population

This section presents statistics on the growth, distribution, and characteristics of the U.S. population. The principal source of these data is the Bureau of the Census, which conducts a decennial census of population, a monthly population survey, a program of population estimates and projections, and a number of other periodic surveys relating to population characteristics. For a list of relevant publications, see the Guide to Sources of Statistics in Appendix I.

Decennial censuses.—The U.S. Constitution provides for a census of the population every 10 years, primarily to establish a basis for apportionment of members of the House of Representatives among the States. For over a century after the first census in 1790, the census organization was a temporary one, created only for each decennial census. In 1902, the Bureau of the Census was established as a permanent Federal agency, responsible for enumerating the population and also for compiling statistics on other subjects.

The census of population is a complete count. That is, an attempt is made to account for every person, for each person's residence, and for other characteristics (sex, age, family relationships, etc.). Since the 1940 census, in addition to the complete count information, some data have been obtained from representative samples of the population. In the 1990 census, variable sampling rates were employed. For most of the country, one in every six households (about 17 percent) received the long form or sample questionnaire; in governmental units estimated to have fewer than 2,500 inhabitants, every other household (50 percent) received the sample questionnaire to enhance the reliability of sample data for small areas. Exact agreement is not to be expected between sample data and the complete census count. Sample data may be used with confidence where large numbers are involved and assumed to indicate trends and relationships where small numbers are involved.

Three different census counts for the resident population in 1970 are shown

203,211,926; 203,235,298; and 203,302,031. The first is the initial tabulated count, the second is the official count, and the third contains the latest revisions. Breakdowns of the revised count of 203,302,031 are not available for demographic characteristics and may not be available for some levels of geography. The complete count data from the 1980 and 1990 censuses shown in this edition are generally consistent with figures published in the 1980 and 1990 census final reports, series PC80-1-A and series 1990 CP-1, respectively.

Census data presented here have not been adjusted for underenumeration. Results from the evaluation program for the 1990 census indicate that the overall national undercount was between 1 and 2 percent—the estimate from the Post Enumeration Survey (PES) was 1.6 percent and the estimate from Demographic Analysis (DA) was 1.8 percent. Both the PES and DA estimates show disproportionately high undercounts for some demographic groups. For example, the PES estimates of percent net undercount for Blacks (4.4 percent), Hispanics (5.0 percent), and American Indians (4.5 percent) were higher than the estimated undercount of non-Hispanic Whites (0.7 percent). Historical DA estimates demonstrate that the overall undercount rate in the census has declined significantly over the past 50 years (from an estimated 5.4 percent in 1940 to 1.8 percent in 1990), yet the undercount of Blacks has remained disproportionately high.

Current Population Survey (CPS).— This is a monthly nationwide survey of a scientifically selected sample representing the noninstitutional civilian population. The sample is located in 729 areas comprising 1,973 counties, independent cities, and minor civil divisions with coverage in every State and the District of Columbia and is subject to sampling error. At the present time, about 60,000 occupied households are eligible for interview every month; of these between 4 and 5 percent are, for various reasons, unavailable for interview.

While the primary purpose of the CPS is to obtain monthly statistics on the labor force, it also serves as a vehicle for inquiries on other subjects. Using CPS data, the Bureau issues a series of publications under the general title of Current Population Reports, which cover population characteristics (series P20), consumer income (series P60), special studies (series P23), and other topics.

Estimates of population characteristics based on the CPS will not agree with the counts from the census because the CPS and the census use different procedures for collecting and processing the data for racial groups, the Hispanic population, and other topics. Caution should also be used when comparing estimates for 1980 and later, which reflect 1980 census-based population controls, to those for 1971 through 1979, which reflect 1970 census-based population controls. This change in population controls had relatively little impact on derived measures such as means, medians, and percent distribution, but did have a significant impact on levels.

Population estimates and projections.— National population estimates are derived by using decennial census data as benchmarks and data available from various agencies as follows: Births and deaths (National Center for Health Statistics); immigrants (Immigration and Naturalization Service); Armed Forces (Department of Defense and Department of Transportation); net movement between Puerto Rico and the U.S. mainland (Puerto Rico Planning Board); and Federal employees abroad (Office of Personnel Management and Department of Defense). Estimates for States and smaller areas are based on data series such as births and deaths, school statistics from State departments of

education and parochial school systems, and Federal income tax returns. These estimates contain estimated emigration of 160,000 per year since 1980 and net undocumented immigration of 200,000 per year. For further information, see Current Population Reports, P25-1095.

Data for the population by age for April 1, 1990, (shown in tables 13, 20, and 21) are modified counts. The review of detailed 1990 information indicated that respondents tended to provide their age as of the date of completion of the questionnaire, not their age as of April 1, 1990. In addition, there may have been a tendency for respondents to round up their age if they were close to having a birthday. A detailed explanation of the age modification procedure appears in 1990 Census of Population and Housing Data Paper Listing (CPH-L-74).

Population estimates and projections are published in the P25 series of Current Population Reports. These estimates and projections are generally consistent with official decennial census figures and do not reflect the amount of estimated census underenumeration. However, these estimates and projections by race have been modified and are not comparable to the census race categories (see section below under "race"). For details on methodology, see the sources cited below the individual tables.

The population projections for States, by single year of age, sex, race, and Hispanic origin prepared for July 1, 1993, to 2020 use the cohort-component method. This method requires separate assumptions for each component of population change: births, deaths, internal migration, and international migration. These components are produced and refined using various administrative records and census distributions. State estimates for 1992 are the starting points for these projections which are consistent with the national projections reported in the U.S. Bureau of the Census, Current Population Reports, series P25-1104. The four series of projections (see table 31) are based on different internal migration assumptions: 1) Series A, is the preferred series model and uses State-to-State migration observed from 1975-76 through 1991-92; 2) Series B, the economic model, uses the Bureau of

Economic Analysis employment projections; 3) Series C, the floating mean model, is the mean of the n most recent years for the n-th projection year; and 4) Series D, is the zero net internal migration assumption.

Immigration.—The principal source of immigration data is the *Statistical Yearbook of the Immigration and Naturalization Service,* published annually by the Immigration and Naturalization Service (INS), a unit of the Department of Justice. Immigration statistics are prepared from entry visas and change of immigration status forms. Immigrants are aliens admitted for legal permanent residence in the United States. The procedures for admission depend on whether the alien is residing inside or outside the United States at the time of application for permanent residence. Eligible aliens residing outside the United States are issued immigrant visas by the U.S. Department of State. Eligible aliens residing in the United States are allowed to change their status from temporary to permanent residence at INS district offices. The category, immigrant, includes persons who may have entered the United States as nonimmigrants or refugees, but who subsequently changed their status to that of a permanent resident. Nonresident aliens admitted to the United States for a temporary period are nonimmigrants (tables 7 and 422). Refugees are considered nonimmigrants when initially admitted into the United States, but are not included in nonimmigrant admission data. A refugee is any person who is outside his or her country of nationality who is unable or unwilling to return to that country because of persecution or a well-founded fear of persecution.

U.S. immigration law gives preferential immigration status to aliens who are related to certain U.S. citizens or legal permanent residents, aliens with needed job skills, or aliens who qualify as refugees. Immigration to the United States can be divided into two general categories: (1) those subject to the annual worldwide limitation, and (2) those exempt from it. The Immigration Act of 1990 established major revisions in the numerical limits and preference system regulating legal immigration. The numerical limits are imposed on visas issued and not on

admissions. The maximum number of visas allowed to be issued under the preference categories in 1992 was 366,000— 226,000 for family-sponsored immigrants and 140,000 for employment-based immigrants. There are nine categories among which the family-sponsored and employment-based immigrant visas are distributed, beginning in fiscal year 1991. The family-sponsored preferences are based on the alien's relationship with a U.S. citizen or legal permanent resident (see table 6). The employment-based preferences are: 1) priority workers (persons of extraordinary ability, outstanding professors and researchers, and certain multinational executives and managers); 2) professionals with advanced degrees or aliens with exceptional ability; 3) skilled workers, professionals without advanced degrees, and needed unskilled workers; 4) special immigrants; and 5) employment creation immigrants (investors). Within the overall limitations the per-country limit for independent countries is set to 7 percent of the total family and employment limits, while dependent areas are limited to 2 percent of the total. The 1992 limit allowed no more than 25,620 preference visas for any independent country and 7,320 for any dependency. Those exempt from the worldwide limitation include immediate relatives of U.S. citizens, refugees and asylees adjusting to permanent residence, and other various classes of special immigrants (see table 6).

The Refugee Act of 1980, effective April 1, 1980, provides for a uniform admission procedure for refugees of all countries, based on the United Nations' definition of refugees. Authorized admission ceilings are set annually by the President in consultation with Congress. After one year of residence in the United States, refugees are eligible for immigrant status.

The Immigration Reform and Control Act of 1986 (IRCA) allows two groups of illegal aliens to become temporary and then permanent residents of the United States: aliens who have been in the United States unlawfully since January 1, 1982 (legalization applicants), and aliens who were employed in seasonal agricultural work for a minimum period of time (Special Agricultural Worker (SAW) applicants). The application period for temporary residency for legalization applicants began on May 5, 1987, and ended on May 4, 1988, while the application period for SAW applicants began on June 1, 1987, and ended on November 30, 1988. Legalization applicants became eligible for permanent residence beginning in fiscal year 1989. Beginning 1989, immigrant data include temporary residents who were granted permanent residence under the legalization program of IRCA.

Metropolitan Areas (MA's).—The general concept of a metropolitan area is one of a core area containing a large population nucleus, together with adjacent communities that have a high degree of social and economic integration with that core. Metropolitan statistical areas (MSA's), consolidated metropolitan statistical areas (CMSA's), and primary metropolitan statistical areas (PMSA's) are defined by the Office of Management and Budget (OMB) as a standard for Federal agencies in the preparation and publication of statistics relating to metropolitan areas. The entire territory of the United States is classified as metropolitan (inside MSA's or CMSA's) or nonmetropolitan (outside MSA's or CMSA's). MSA's, CMSA's, and PMSA's are defined in terms of entire counties except in New England, where the definitions are in terms of cities and towns. The OMB also defines New England County Metropolitan Areas (NECMA's) which are county-based alternatives to the MSA's and CMSA's in the six New England States. From time to time, new MA's are created and the boundaries of others change. As a result, data for MA's over time may not be comparable and the analysis of historical trends must be made cautiously. For descriptive details and a listing of titles and components of MA's, see Appendix II.

Urban and rural.—According to the 1990 census definition, the urban population comprises all persons living in (a) places of 2,500 or more inhabitants incorporated as cities, villages, boroughs (except in Alaska and New York), and towns (except in the New England States, New York, and Wisconsin), but excluding those persons living in the rural portions of extended cities (places with low population density in one or more large parts of their area); (b) census designated places (previously termed unincorporated) of 2,500 or more inhabitants; and (c) other territory, incorporated or unincorporated, included in urbanized areas. An urbanized area comprises one or more places and the adjacent densely settled surrounding territory that together have a minimum population of 50,000 persons.

In all definitions, the population not classified as urban constitutes the rural population.

Residence.—In determining residence, the Bureau of the Census counts each person as an inhabitant of a usual place of residence (i.e., the place where one usually lives and sleeps). While this place is not necessarily a person's legal residence or voting residence, the use of these different bases of classification would produce the same results in the vast majority of cases.

Race.—The Bureau of the Census collects and publishes racial statistics as outlined in Statistical Policy Directive No. 15 issued by the U.S. Office of Management and Budget. This directive provides standards on ethnic and racial categories for statistical reporting to be used by all Federal agencies. According to the directive, the basic racial categories are American Indian or Alaska Native, Asian or Pacific Islander, Black, and White. (The directive identifies Hispanic origin as an ethnicity.) The concept of race the Bureau of the Census uses reflects self-identification by respondents; that is the individual's perception of his/her racial identity. The concept is not intended to reflect any biological or anthropological definition. Although the Bureau of the Census adheres to the overall guidelines of Directive No. 15, it recognizes that there are persons who do not identify with a specific racial group. The 1990 census race question includes an "Other race" category with provisions for a write-in entry. Furthermore, the Bureau of the Census recognizes that the categories of the race item include both racial and national origin or socio-cultural groups.

Differences between the 1990 census and earlier censuses affect the comparability of data for certain racial groups and American Indian tribes. The lack of comparability is due to changes in the way some respondents reported their race as well as changes in 1990 census procedures related to the racial classification. (For a fuller explanation, see *1990 Census of Population, Volume I, General Population Characteristics* (1990 CP-1)).

Data for the population by race for April 1, 1990, (shown in tables 11, 12, 17, 18, 20, and 21) are modified counts and are not comparable to the 1990 census race categories. These numbers were computed using 1990 census data by race which had been modified to be consistent with the race categories used in the reporting of vital statistics by the U.S. National Center for Health Statistics. A detailed explanation of the race modification procedure appears in *1990 Census of Population and Housing Data Paper Listing* (CPH-L-74).

In the CPS and other household sample surveys in which data are obtained through personal interview, respondents are asked to classify their race as: (1) White, (2) Black, (3) American Indian, Aleut, or Eskimo, or (4) Asian or Pacific Islander. The procedures for classifying persons of mixed races who could not provide a single response to the race question are generally similar to those used in the census.

Hispanic population.—In the 1990 census, the Bureau of the Census collected data on the Hispanic origin population in the United States by using a self-identification question. Persons of Spanish/Hispanic origin are those who classified themselves in one of the specific Hispanic origin categories listed on the questionnaire—Mexican, Puerto Rican, Cuban, or Other Spanish/Hispanic origin. The difference between the 1980 and the 1990 questionnaire was that in the 1980 census, a Hispanic origin question was used with prelisted categories for the largest Spanish origin groups and a residual Other Spanish/Hispanic category. For the 1990 census the questionnaire was modified by adding a space for the respondent to write-in the entry for the Other Spanish/Hispanic category. It

should be noted that Hispanic persons may be of any race.

In the CPS information on Hispanic persons is gathered by using a self-identification question. Persons classify themselves in one of the Hispanic categories in response to the question: "What is the origin or descent of each person in this household?" Hispanic persons in the CPS are persons who report themselves as Mexican-American, Chicano, Mexican, Puerto Rican, Cuban, Central or South American (Spanish countries), or other Hispanic origin.

Nativity.—The native population consists of all persons born in the United States, Puerto Rico, or an outlying area of the United States. It also includes persons born at sea or in a foreign country who have at least one American parent. All others are classified as "foreign born."

Mobility status.—The U.S. population is classified according to mobility status on the basis of a comparison between the place of residence of each individual at the time of the survey or census and the place of residence at a specified earlier date. Nonmovers are all persons who were living in the same house or apartment at the end of the period as at the beginning of the period. Movers are all persons who were living in a different house at the end of the period from that in which they were living at the beginning of the period. Movers from abroad include all persons, either citizens or aliens, whose place of residence was outside the United States at the beginning of the period; that is, in Puerto Rico, an outlying area under the jurisdiction of the United States, or a foreign country.

Living arrangements.—Living arrangements refer to residency in households or in group quarters. A "household" comprises all persons who occupy a "housing unit," that is, a house, an apartment or other group of rooms, or a single room that constitutes "separate living quarters." A household includes the related family members and all the unrelated persons, if any, such as lodgers, foster children, wards, or employees who share the housing unit. A person living alone or a group of unrelated persons sharing the same housing unit is also counted as a household. See text, section 25, Construction and Housing, for definition of housing unit.

All persons not living in households are classified as living in group quarters. These individuals may be institutionalized, e.g., under care or custody in juvenile facilities, jails, correctional centers, hospitals, or rest homes; or they may be residents in college dormitories, military barracks, rooming houses, etc. (see table 84).

Householder.—The householder is the first adult household member listed on the questionnaire. The instructions call for listing first the person (or one of the persons) in whose name the home is owned or rented. If a home is owned or rented jointly by a married couple, either the husband or the wife may be listed first. Prior to 1980, the husband was always considered the household head (householder) in married-couple households.

Family.—The term "family" refers to a group of two or more persons related by birth, marriage, or adoption and residing together in a household. A family includes among its members the householder.

Subfamily.—A subfamily consists of a married couple and their children, if any, or one parent with one or more never-married children under 18 years old living in a household. Subfamilies are divided into "related" and "unrelated" subfamilies. A related subfamily is related to, but does not include, the householder. Members of a related subfamily are also members of the family with whom they live. The number of related subfamilies, therefore, is not included in the count of families. An unrelated subfamily may include persons such as guests, lodgers, or resident employees and their spouses and/or children; none of whom is related to the householder.

Married couple.—A "married couple" is defined as a husband and wife living together in the same household, with or without children and other relatives.

Unrelated individuals.—"Unrelated individuals" are persons (other than inmates of institutions) who are not members of families or subfamilies.

Secondary individuals.—Secondary individuals are persons of any age who reside in a household, but are not related to the householder (except unrelated subfamily members). Persons who reside in group quarters are also secondary individuals. Examples of a secondary individual include (1) a guest, partner, roommate, or resident employee; (2) a foster child; or (3) a person residing in a rooming house, a halfway house, staff quarters at a hospital, or other type of group quarters.

Statistical reliability.—For a discussion of statistical collection and estimation, sampling procedures, and measures of statistical reliability applicable to Census Bureau data, see Appendix III.

Historical statistics.—Tabular headnotes provide cross-references, where applicable, to *Historical Statistics of the United States, Colonial Times to 1970.* See Appendix IV.

Figure 1.1
Projected Percent Change in State Populations: 1990 to 2000

Percent (U.S.=10.8)
Gain:
20.0 and over
10.0 to 19.9
0 to 9.9
Loss

Source: Chart prepared by U.S. Bureau of the Census. Based on preferred series A.
For data, see tables 26 and 34.

Population

No. 1. Population and Area: 1790 to 1990

[Area figures represent area on indicated date including in some cases considerable areas not then organized or settled, and not covered by the census. Total area figures for 1790 to 1970 have been recalculated on the basis of the remeasurement of States and counties for the 1980 census, but not on the basis of the 1990 census. The land and water area figures for past censuses have not been adjusted and are not strictly comparable with the total area data for comparable dates because the land areas were derived from different base data, and these values are known to have changed with the construction of reservoirs, draining of lakes, etc. Density figures are based on land area measurements as reported in earlier censuses]

CENSUS DATE	RESIDENT POPULATION				AREA (square miles)		
	Number	Per square mile of land area	Increase over preceding census		Total	Land	Water
			Number	Percent			
CONTERMINOUS U.S. [1]							
1790 (Aug. 2)	3,929,214	4.5	(X)	(X)	891,364	864,746	24,065
1800 (Aug. 4)	5,308,483	6.1	1,379,269	35.1	891,364	864,746	24,065
1810 (Aug. 6)	7,239,881	4.3	1,931,398	36.4	1,722,685	1,681,828	34,175
1820 (Aug. 7)	9,638,453	5.5	2,398,572	33.1	1,792,552	1,749,462	38,544
1830 (June 1)	12,866,020	7.4	3,227,567	33.5	1,792,552	1,749,462	38,544
1840 (June 1)	17,069,453	9.8	4,203,433	32.7	1,792,552	1,749,462	38,544
1850 (June 1)	23,191,876	7.9	6,122,423	35.9	2,991,655	2,940,042	52,705
1860 (June 1)	31,443,321	10.6	8,251,445	35.6	3,021,295	2,969,640	52,747
1870 (June 1)	[2]39,818,449	[2]13.4	8,375,128	26.6	3,021,295	2,969,640	52,747
1880 (June 1)	50,155,783	16.9	10,337,334	26.0	3,021,295	2,969,640	52,747
1890 (June 1)	62,947,714	21.2	12,791,931	25.5	3,021,295	2,969,640	52,747
1900 (June 1)	75,994,575	25.6	13,046,861	20.7	3,021,295	2,969,834	52,553
1910 (Apr. 15)	91,972,266	31.0	15,977,691	21.0	3,021,295	2,969,565	52,822
1920 (Jan. 1)	105,710,620	35.6	13,738,354	14.9	3,021,295	2,969,451	52,936
1930 (Apr. 1)	122,775,046	41.2	17,064,426	16.1	3,021,295	2,977,128	45,259
1940 (Apr. 1)	131,669,275	44.2	8,894,229	7.2	3,021,295	2,977,128	45,259
1950 (Apr. 1)	150,697,361	50.7	19,028,086	14.5	3,021,295	2,974,726	47,661
1960 (Apr. 1)	178,464,236	60.1	27,766,875	18.4	3,021,295	2,968,054	54,207
UNITED STATES							
1950 (Apr. 1)	151,325,798	42.6	19,161,229	14.5	3,618,770	3,552,206	63,005
1960 (Apr. 1)	179,323,175	50.6	27,997,377	18.5	3,618,770	3,540,911	[3]74,212
1970 (Apr. 1)	[3]203,302,031	[3]57.4	23,978,856	13.4	3,618,770	[3]3,540,023	[3]78,444
1980 (Apr. 1)	[4]226,542,199	64.0	23,240,168	11.4	3,618,770	3,539,289	79,481
1990 (Apr. 1)	248,709,873	70.3	22,167,674	9.8	3,732,396	3,536,338	[5]196,058

X Not applicable.   [1] Excludes Alaska and Hawaii.   [2] Revised to include adjustments for underenumeration in southern States; unrevised number is 38,558,371 (13.0 per square mile).   [3] Figures corrected after 1970 final reports were issued.   [4] Total population count has been revised since the 1980 census publications. Numbers by age, race, Hispanic origin, and sex have not been corrected.   [5] Comprises Great Lakes, inland, and coastal water. Data for prior years cover inland water only. For further explanation, see table 351.

Source: U.S. Bureau of the Census, *U.S. Census of Population: 1920 to 1990*, vol. I; and other reports and unpublished data. See also *Areas of the United States, 1940*, and *Area Measurement Reports, 1960*, series GE-20, No. 1.

No. 2. Population: 1950 to 1993

[In thousands, except percent. Estimates as of July 1. Total population includes Armed Forces abroad; civilian population excludes Armed Forces. For basis of estimates, see text, section 1. See also *Historical Statistics, Colonial Times to 1970*, series A 6-8]

YEAR	TOTAL		Resident population	Civilian population	YEAR	TOTAL		Resident population	Civilian population
	Population	Percent change				Population	Percent change		
1950	152,271	(X)	151,868	150,790	1972	209,896	1.08	209,284	207,511
1951	154,878	1.71	153,982	151,599	1973	211,909	0.96	211,357	209,600
1952	157,553	1.73	156,393	153,892	1974	213,854	0.92	213,342	211,636
1953	160,184	1.67	158,956	156,595	1975	215,973	0.99	215,465	213,789
1954	163,026	1.77	161,884	159,695	1976	218,035	0.95	217,563	215,894
1955	165,931	1.78	165,069	162,967	1977	220,239	1.01	219,760	218,106
1956	168,903	1.79	168,088	166,055	1978	222,585	1.06	222,095	220,467
1957	171,984	1.82	171,187	169,110	1979	225,055	1.11	224,567	222,969
1958	174,882	1.68	174,149	172,226	1980	227,726	1.19	227,225	225,621
1959	177,830	1.69	177,135	175,277	1981	229,966	0.98	229,466	227,818
1960	180,671	1.60	179,979	178,140	1982	232,188	0.97	231,664	229,995
1961	183,691	1.67	182,992	181,143	1983	234,307	0.91	233,792	232,097
1962	186,538	1.55	185,771	183,677	1984	236,348	0.87	235,825	234,110
1963	189,242	1.45	188,483	186,493	1985	238,466	0.90	237,924	236,219
1964	191,889	1.40	191,141	189,141	1986	240,651	0.92	240,133	238,412
1965	194,303	1.26	193,526	191,605	1987	242,804	0.89	242,289	240,550
1966	196,560	1.16	195,576	193,420	1988	245,021	0.91	244,499	242,817
1967	198,712	1.09	197,457	195,264	1989	247,342	0.95	246,819	245,131
1968	200,706	1.00	199,399	197,113	1990	249,908	1.04	249,399	247,759
1969	202,677	0.98	201,385	199,145	1991	252,648	1.10	252,137	250,526
1970	205,052	1.17	203,984	201,895	1992	255,458	1.11	255,078	253,493
1971	207,661	1.27	206,827	204,866	1993	258,245	1.09	257,908	256,436

X Not applicable.

Source: U.S. Bureau of the Census, *Current Population Reports*, P25-1045 and P25-1112.

Population Projections

9

No. 3. Resident Population Projections: 1993 to 2050

[In thousands. As of July 1. Each series shown assumes middle levels of fertility, life expectancy, and net immigration unless otherwise specified. Middle level components are shown in footnote 1]

YEAR	Middle series [1]	Lowest series [2]	Highest series [3]	FERTILITY Low	FERTILITY High	LIFE EXPECTANCY Low	LIFE EXPECTANCY High	NET IMMIGRATION Low	NET IMMIGRATION High
1993	257,927	257,670	258,157	257,927	257,927	257,882	257,961	257,715	258,123
1994	260,711	259,973	261,390	260,618	260,809	260,601	260,796	260,176	261,206
1995	263,434	262,051	264,715	263,218	263,661	263,238	263,587	262,461	264,334
1996	266,096	263,905	268,138	265,730	266,486	265,795	266,333	264,569	267,510
1997	268,702	265,647	271,568	268,159	269,289	268,278	269,039	266,608	270,642
1998	271,258	267,281	275,011	270,510	272,074	270,692	271,710	268,584	273,736
1999	273,769	268,816	278,472	272,790	274,849	273,044	274,352	270,502	276,798
2000	276,241	270,259	281,957	275,004	277,618	275,341	276,970	272,370	279,832
2005	288,286	276,316	299,941	285,341	291,687	286,204	289,893	281,230	294,847
2010	300,431	281,180	319,536	295,014	306,876	296,775	303,115	289,969	310,179
2015	313,116	285,680	340,794	304,744	323,322	307,564	317,037	299,078	326,220
2020	325,942	289,553	363,213	314,281	340,512	318,164	331,271	308,158	342,572
2025	338,338	292,092	386,595	322,935	358,130	327,988	345,299	316,609	358,687
2030	349,993	292,902	410,991	330,290	376,130	336,732	358,859	324,111	374,268
2040	371,505	290,351	463,579	341,584	414,144	351,769	384,846	336,797	404,142
2050	392,031	285,502	522,098	350,233	456,471	366,036	409,960	348,032	433,501

[1] Ultimate total fertility rate = 2,150; life expectancy in 2050 = 82.6 years; and annual net immigration = 880,000. These are middle level assumptions. For explanation of total fertility rate; see headnote, table 94. [2] Ultimate total fertility rate = 1,892; life expectancy in 2050 = 75.3 years; and annual net immigration = 350,000. These are lowest level assumptions. [3] Ultimate total fertility rate = 2,622; life expectancy in 2050 = 87.5 years; and annual net immigration = 1,370,000. These are highest level assumptions.

Source: U.S. Bureau of the Census, *Current Population Reports*, P25-1104.

No. 4. Components of Population Change, 1980 to 1992, and Projections, 1993 to 2050

[Resident population]

YEAR	Population at start of period (1,000)	Net increase [1] Total (1,000)	Net increase [1] Per-cent [2]	Natural increase Births (1,000)	Natural increase Deaths (1,000)	Net migration [3] (1,000)	Net growth rate [1]	Natural increase Birth rate	Natural increase Death rate	Net migration [3]
1980 [4]	226,546	1,900	0.8	2,743	1,463	724	11.1	16.0	8.6	4.2
1981	228,446	2,200	1.0	3,629	1,978	690	9.6	15.8	8.6	3.0
1982	230,645	2,157	0.9	3,681	1,975	595	9.3	15.9	8.5	2.6
1983	232,803	2,066	0.9	3,639	2,019	592	8.8	15.6	8.6	2.5
1984	234,868	2,070	0.9	3,669	2,039	589	8.8	15.6	8.6	2.5
1985	236,938	2,171	0.9	3,761	2,086	649	9.1	15.8	8.8	2.7
1986	239,109	2,158	0.9	3,757	2,105	661	9.0	15.6	8.8	2.8
1987	241,267	2,195	0.9	3,809	2,123	666	9.1	15.7	8.8	2.7
1988	243,462	2,243	0.9	3,910	2,168	662	9.2	16.0	8.9	2.7
1989	245,705	2,438	1.0	4,041	2,150	712	9.9	16.4	8.7	2.9
1990	248,143	2,549	1.0	4,148	2,152	[5]594	10.2	16.6	8.6	[5]2.4
1991	250,692	2,976	1.2	4,111	2,165	[5]1,030	11.8	16.3	8.6	[5]4.1
1992	253,667	2,888	1.1	4,087	2,166	967	11.3	16.0	8.5	3.8
PROJECTIONS [6]										
1993	256,504	2,815	1.1	4,086	2,152	880	10.9	15.8	8.3	3.4
1994	259,319	2,754	1.1	4,055	2,181	880	10.6	15.6	8.4	3.4
1995	262,073	2,693	1.0	4,024	2,211	880	10.2	15.3	8.4	3.3
1996	264,765	2,634	1.0	3,995	2,241	880	9.9	15.0	8.4	3.3
1997	267,399	2,581	1.0	3,971	2,270	880	9.6	14.8	8.4	3.3
1998	269,980	2,533	0.9	3,953	2,300	880	9.3	14.6	8.5	3.2
1999	272,513	2,492	0.9	3,941	2,329	880	9.1	14.4	8.5	3.2
2000	275,005	2,458	0.9	3,934	2,357	880	8.9	14.2	8.5	3.2
2005	287,092	2,391	0.8	3,990	2,479	880	8.3	13.8	8.6	3.1
2010	299,194	2,486	0.8	4,207	2,601	880	8.3	14.0	8.7	2.9
2015	311,833	2,570	0.8	4,420	2,730	880	8.2	14.1	8.7	2.8
2020	324,668	2,539	0.8	4,543	2,884	880	7.8	13.9	8.8	2.7
2025	337,126	2,408	0.7	4,607	3,079	880	7.1	13.6	9.1	2.6
2030	348,858	2,257	0.6	4,690	3,313	880	6.4	13.4	9.5	2.5
2040	370,466	2,074	0.6	4,989	3,795	880	5.6	13.4	10.2	2.4
2050	391,000	2,067	0.5	5,250	4,064	880	5.3	13.4	10.4	2.2

[1] Prior to April 1, 1990, includes "error of closure" (the amount necessary to make the components of change add to the net change between censuses), for which figures are not shown separately. [2] Percent of population at beginning of period. [3] Covers net international migration and movement of Armed Forces, federally affiliated civilian citizens, and their dependents. [4] Data are for period April 1 to December 31. [5] Data reflect movement of Armed Forces due to the Gulf War. [6] Based on middle series of assumptions. See footnote 1, table 3.

Source: U.S. Bureau of the Census, *Current Population Reports*, P25-1095 and P25-1104; and unpublished data.

No. 5. Immigration: 1901 to 1992

[In thousands, except rate. For fiscal years ending in year shown ; see text, section 9. For definition of immigrants, see text, section 1. Data represent immigrants admitted. Rates based on Bureau of the Census estimates as of July 1 for resident population through 1929, and for total population thereafter (excluding Alaska and Hawaii prior to 1959). See also *Historical Statistics, Colonial Times to 1970*, series C 89]

PERIOD	Number	Rate [1]	YEAR	Number	Rate [1]
1901 to 1910	8,795	10.4	1980	531	2.3
1911 to 1920	5,736	5.7	1985	570	2.4
1921 to 1930	4,107	3.5	1986	602	2.5
1931 to 1940	528	0.4	1987	602	2.5
1941 to 1950	1,035	0.7	1988	643	2.6
1951 to 1960	2,515	1.5	1989 [2]	1,091	4.4
1961 to 1970	3,322	1.7	1990 [2]	1,536	6.1
1971 to 1980	4,493	2.1	1991 [2]	1,827	7.2
1981 to 1990	7,338	3.1	1992 [2]	974	3.8

[1] Annual rate per 1,000 U.S. population. Rate computed by dividing sum of annual immigration totals by sum of annual U.S. population totals for same number of years. [2] Includes persons who were granted permanent residence under the legalization program of the Immigration Reform and Control Act of 1986.

No. 6. Immigrants Admitted, by Class of Admission: 1980 to 1992

[For fiscal year ending September 30. For definition of immigrants, see text, section 1. See also *Historical Statistics, Colonial Times to 1970*, series C 143-157]

CLASS OF ADMISSION	1980	1985	1989	1990	1991	1992
Immigrants, total	530,639	570,009	1,090,924	1,536,483	1,827,167	973,977
New arrivals	339,355	356,365	402,431	435,729	443,107	511,769
Adjustments	191,284	213,644	688,493	1,100,754	1,384,060	462,208
Preference immigrants, total	264,367	266,703	274,833	272,742	275,613	329,321
Family-sponsored immigrants, total	216,856	213,257	217,092	214,550	216,088	213,123
Unmarried sons/daughters of U.S. citizens and their children	5,668	9,319	13,259	15,861	15,385	12,486
Spouses, unmarried sons/daughters of alien residents, and their children	110,269	114,997	112,771	107,686	110,126	118,247
Married sons/daughters of U.S. citizens [1]	10,752	18,460	26,975	26,751	27,115	22,195
Brothers or sisters of U.S. citizens [1]	90,167	70,481	64,087	64,252	63,462	60,195
Employment-based immigrants, total	47,511	53,446	57,741	58,192	59,525	116,198
Priority workers [1]	(X)	(X)	(X)	(X)	(X)	5,456
Professionals with advanced degrees [1]	(X)	(X)	(X)	(X)	(X)	58,401
Skilled workers, professionals, unskilled workers [1]	(X)	(X)	(X)	(X)	(X)	47,568
Special immigrants [1]	3,142	2,551	4,986	4,463	4,576	4,063
Employment creation [1]	(X)	(X)	(X)	(X)	(X)	59
Professional or highly skilled immigrants [1] [2]	18,583	24,905	26,798	26,546	27,748	340
Needed skilled or unskilled workers [1] [2]	25,786	25,990	25,957	27,183	27,201	311
Immediate relatives	157,743	204,368	217,514	231,680	237,103	235,484
Spouses of U.S. citizens	96,854	129,790	125,744	125,426	125,397	128,396
Children of U.S. citizens	27,207	35,592	41,276	46,065	48,130	42,324
Orphans	5,139	9,286	7,948	7,088	9,008	6,536
Parents of U.S. citizens	33,682	38,986	50,494	60,189	63,576	64,764
Refugees and asylees	88,057	95,040	84,288	97,364	139,079	117,037
Cuban Refugee Act, Nov. 1966	6,021	14,288	5,206	5,730	5,486	5,365
Indochinese Refugee Act, Oct. 1977	22,497	166	40	33	22	29
Refugee-Parolee Act, Oct. 1978	46,058	3,766	381	153	69	82
Asylees, Refugee Act of 1980	1,250	5,000	5,145	4,937	22,664	10,658
Refugees, Refugee Act of 1980	(X)	71,820	73,516	86,511	110,838	100,902
Other refugees	12,231	-	-	-	-	1
Other immigrants	20,472	3,898	514,289	934,697	1,175,372	292,135
Children born abroad to resident aliens or subsequent to issuance of visa	4,059	3,508	2,806	2,630	2,516	2,116
Diversity Programs [3]	(X)	(X)	7,068	29,161	22,070	36,348
Amerasians (P.L. 100-202) [4]	(X)	(X)	8,589	13,059	16,010	17,253
Immigration Reform and Control Act of 1986 legalization adjustments	(X)	(X)	478,814	880,372	1,123,162	163,342
Legalization dependents [5]	(X)	(X)	(X)	(X)	(X)	52,272
Other	16,413	390	17,012	9,475	11,614	20,804

- Represents zero. X Not applicable. [1] Includes spouses and children. [2] Category was eliminated in 1992 by the Immigration Act of 1990. [3] Includes categories of immigrants admitted under three laws intended to diversify immigration: P.L. 99-603, P.L. 100-658, and P.L. 101-649. [4] Under Public Law 100-202 Amerasians are aliens born in Vietnam between January 1, 1962, and January 1, 1976, who were fathered by U.S. citizens. [5] Spouses and children of persons granted permanent resident status under provisions of the Immigration Reform and Control Act of 1986.

Source of tables 5 and 6: U.S. Immigration and Naturalization Service, *Statistical Yearbook*, annual.

No. 7. Nonimmigrants Admitted, by Class of Admission: 1985 to 1992

[In thousands, except as noted. For fiscal years ending Sept. 30; see text, section 9. Nonimmigrants are nonresident aliens (non-U.S. citizens) admitted to the United States for a temporary period. Excluded are border crossers, crewmen, and insular travelers. See also *Historical Statistics, Colonial Times to 1970*, series C 149-157]

CLASS OF ADMISSION	1985	1986	1987	1988	1989	1990	1991	1992
Nonimmigrants [1]	9,540	10,471	12,273	14,592	16,145	17,574	18,963	20,794
Temporary visitors, total	8,405	9,280	11,019	13,197	14,667	16,080	17,386	19,238
For pleasure	6,609	7,342	8,887	10,821	12,115	13,418	14,734	16,450
For business	1,797	1,938	2,132	2,376	2,553	2,661	2,652	2,788
Transit aliens [2]	237	244	264	299	293	306	364	346
Foreign government officials [3]	90	94	92	99	102	97	98	103
Treaty traders and investors [3]	97	104	114	126	140	148	155	152
Students [3]	286	288	289	338	361	355	314	275
Representatives to international organizations [3]	57	59	57	59	61	61	64	70
Temporary workers and trainees [4]	88	99	114	133	165	174	205	217
Registered nurses [5]	(X)	(X)	(X)	(X)	(X)	(X)	1	7
Specialty occupations [6]	(X)	(X)	(X)	(X)	(X)	(X)	117	110
Workers of distinguished merit or ability [7]	47	54	66	78	90	100	(X)	(X)
Performing services unavailable in U.S.	25	28	29	33	47	36	40	34
U.S.-Canada Free-Trade Agreement [8]	(X)	(X)	(X)	(X)	3	5	8	13
Spouses and children of workers and trainees	13	14	16	20	24	29	35	41
Representatives of foreign information media [3]	17	17	18	22	21	20	21	22
Exchange visitors [3]	141	163	183	203	217	215	224	232
NATO officials [3]	8	7	7	9	9	8	9	9
Fiances(ees) of U.S. citizens [9]	8	8	7	7	7	7	8	9
Intracompany transferees [3]	107	108	107	102	101	103	113	121
Parolees [10]	64	67	63	95	107	90	127	137
Refugees	68	51	67	80	101	110	100	123

X Not applicable.   [1] Includes nonimmigrants whose class of admission is unknown.   [2] Includes foreign government officials and their spouses and (unmarried minor or dependent) children, in transit.   [3] Includes spouses and children.   [4] Includes other classes of admission, not shown separately.   [5] Entries began October 1, 1990 (fiscal year 1991). Data for fiscal year 1991 are underreported; an unknown number of H1A entries were counted as H1B entries.   [6] Prior to October 1, 1991 (fiscal year 1992), H1B entries were termed "Distinguished merit or ability." Data for fiscal year 1991 are overreported; an unknown number of H1A entries were counted as H1B entries.   [7] Beginning 1992, as a result of the Immigration Act of 1990, the existing temporary worker and trainee classes of admission have been revised and new worker classes have been created.   [8] Entries under the U.S.-Canada Free-Trade Agreement began in January 1989.   [9] Includes children of fiances(ees) of U.S. citizens.   [10] Aliens allowed to enter the United States for a temporary period of time on emergency conditions or when the entry is determined to be in the public interest (e.g., witness in court).

No. 8. Immigrants, by Country of Birth: 1971 to 1992

[In thousands. For fiscal years ending in year shown; see text, section 9. For definition of immigrants, see text, section 1]

COUNTRY OF BIRTH	1971-80, total	1981-90, total	1991	1992	COUNTRY OF BIRTH	1971-80, total	1981-90, total	1991	1992
All countries	4,493.3	7,338.1	1,827.2	974.0	Philippines	360.2	495.3	63.6	61.0
Europe [1]	801.3	705.6	135.2	145.4	Syria	13.3	20.6	2.8	2.9
France	17.8	23.1	2.5	3.3	Thailand	44.1	64.4	7.4	7.1
Germany	66.0	70.1	6.5	9.9	Turkey	18.6	20.9	2.5	2.5
Greece	93.7	29.1	2.1	1.9	Vietnam	179.7	401.4	55.3	77.7
Ireland	14.1	32.8	4.8	12.2	North America [1]	1,645.0	3,125.0	1,211.0	384.0
Italy	130.1	32.9	2.6	2.6	Canada	114.8	119.2	13.5	15.2
Poland	43.6	97.4	19.2	25.5	Mexico	637.2	1,653.3	946.2	213.8
Portugal	104.5	40.0	4.5	2.7	Caribbean [1]	759.8	892.7	140.1	97.4
Romania [2]	17.5	38.9	8.1	6.5	Barbados	20.9	17.4	1.5	1.1
Soviet Union, former [2]	43.2	84.0	57.0	43.6	Cuba	276.8	159.2	10.3	11.8
Armenia	(NA)	(NA)	(NA)	6.1	Dominican Republic	148.0	251.8	41.4	42.0
Azerbaijan	(NA)	(NA)	(NA)	1.6	Haiti	58.7	140.2	47.5	11.0
Belarus	(NA)	(NA)	(NA)	3.2	Jamaica	142.0	213.8	23.8	18.9
Moldova	(NA)	(NA)	(NA)	1.7	Trinidad and Tobago	61.8	39.5	8.4	7.0
Russia	(NA)	(NA)	(NA)	8.9	Central America [1]	132.4	458.7	111.1	57.6
Ukraine	(NA)	(NA)	(NA)	14.4	El Salvador	34.4	214.6	47.4	26.2
Uzbekistan	(NA)	(NA)	(NA)	1.7	Guatemala	25.6	87.9	25.5	10.5
Spain	30.0	15.8	1.8	1.6	Honduras	17.2	49.5	11.5	6.6
United Kingdom	123.5	142.1	13.9	20.0	Nicaragua	13.0	44.1	17.8	8.9
Yugoslavia	42.1	19.2	2.7	2.6	Panama	22.7	29.0	4.2	2.8
Asia [1]	1,633.8	2,817.4	358.5	357.0	South America [1]	284.4	455.9	79.9	55.3
Afghanistan	2.0	26.6	2.9	2.7	Argentina	25.1	25.7	3.9	3.9
Cambodia	8.4	116.6	3.3	2.6	Brazil	13.7	23.7	8.1	4.8
China: Mainland	[3]202.5	[3]388.8	33.0	38.9	Chile	17.6	23.4	2.8	1.9
Taiwan	([3])	([3])	13.3	16.3	Colombia	77.6	124.4	19.7	13.2
Hong Kong	47.5	63.0	10.4	10.5	Ecuador	50.2	56.0	10.0	7.3
India	176.8	261.9	45.1	36.8	Guyana	47.5	95.4	11.7	9.1
Iran	46.2	154.8	19.6	13.2	Peru	29.1	64.4	16.2	9.9
Iraq	23.4	19.6	1.5	4.1	Africa [1]	91.5	192.3	36.2	27.1
Israel	26.6	36.3	4.2	5.1	Egypt	25.5	31.4	5.6	3.6
Japan	47.9	43.2	5.0	11.0	Ethiopia	(NA)	27.2	5.1	4.6
Jordan	29.6	32.6	4.3	4.0	Nigeria	8.8	35.3	7.9	4.6
Korea	272.0	338.8	26.5	19.4	Other countries [4]	37.3	41.9	6.3	5.2
Laos	22.6	145.6	10.0	8.7	Australia	14.3	13.9	1.7	2.2
Lebanon	33.8	41.6	6.0	5.8					
Pakistan	31.2	61.3	20.4	10.2					

NA Not available.   [1] Includes countries not shown separately.   [2] Includes other republics and unknown republics, not shown separately.   [3] Data for Taiwan included with China: Mainland.   [4] Includes New Zealand and unknown countries.

Source of tables 7 and 8: U.S. Immigration and Naturalization Service, *Statistical Yearbook*, annual; and releases.

No. 9. Immigrants Admitted as Permanent Residents Under Refugee Acts, by Country of Birth: 1971 to 1992

[For fiscal years ending in year shown; see text, section 9. Covers immigrants who were allowed to enter the United States under 1953 Refugee Relief Act and later acts; Hungarian parolees under July 1958 Act; refugee-escapee parolees under July 1960 Act; conditional entries by refugees under Oct. 1965 Act; Cuban parolees under Nov. 1966 Act; beginning 1978, Indochina refugees under Act of Oct. 1977; beginning 1980, refugee-parolees under the Act of Oct. 1978, and asylees under the Act of March 1980; and beginning 1981 refugees under the Act of March 1980]

COUNTRY OF BIRTH	1971-80, total	1981-90, total	1991	1992	COUNTRY OF BIRTH	1971-80, total	1981-90, total	1991	1992
Total	539,447	1,013,620	139,079	117,037	China [3]	13,760	7,928	625	894
Europe [1]	71,858	155,512	62,946	42,721	Hong Kong	3,468	1,916	75	193
Albania	395	353	75	539	Indonesia	222	1,385	12	13
Bulgaria	1,238	1,197	311	562	Iran	364	46,773	8,515	3,093
Czechoslovakia	3,646	8,204	659	319	Iraq	6,851	7,540	193	365
Germany	143	851	214	94	Laos	21,690	142,964	9,127	8,026
Greece	478	1,408	127	28	Lebanon	(NA)	1,271	318	140
Hungary	4,358	4,942	817	229	Malaysia	192	1,277	93	88
Italy	346	394	206	105	Pakistan	(NA)	666	166	129
Poland	5,882	33,889	4,205	1,512	Philippines	216	3,403	249	221
Romania	6,812	29,798	4,276	4,971	Syria	1,336	2,145	252	96
Soviet Union, former [2]	31,309	72,306	51,551	33,504	Thailand	1,241	30,259	3,603	4,048
Armenia	(NA)	(NA)	(NA)	479	Turkey	1,193	1,896	109	16
Azerbaijan	(NA)	(NA)	(NA)	1,551	Vietnam [1]	150,266	324,453	21,543	32,155
Belarus	(NA)	(NA)	(NA)	3,008	North America [1]	252,633	121,840	21,317	15,962
Moldova	(NA)	(NA)	(NA)	1,588	Cuba	251,514	113,367	7,953	9,919
Russia	(NA)	(NA)	(NA)	7,122	El Salvador	45	1,383	1,249	743
Ukraine	(NA)	(NA)	(NA)	13,347	Nicaragua	36	5,590	11,233	4,668
Uzbekistan	(NA)	(NA)	(NA)	1,550	South America [1]	1,244	1,976	320	442
Spain	5,317	736	96	50	Africa [1]	2,991	22,149	4,731	4,480
Yugoslavia	11,297	324	66	58	Egypt	1,473	426	52	18
Asia [1]	210,683	712,092	49,762	53,422	Ethiopia	1,307	18,542	3,582	3,268
Afghanistan	542	22,946	2,100	2,082	Sudan	(NA)	(NA)	(NA)	369
Cambodia	7,739	114,064	2,550	1,695	Other	38	51	3	10

NA Not available. [1] Includes other countries, not shown separately. [2] Includes other republics and unknown republics, not shown separately. [3] Covers Mainland and Taiwan.

Source: U.S. Immigration and Naturalization Service, *Statistical Yearbook*, annual; and releases.

No. 10. Immigrants Admitted, by Leading Country of Birth and State: 1992

[For year ending September 30. For definition of immigrants, see text, section 1]

REGION, DIVISION, AND STATE	Total [1]	Mexico	Vietnam	Philippines	REGION, DIVISION, AND STATE	Total [1]	Mexico	Vietnam	Philippines
U.S. [2]	973,977	213,802	77,735	61,022	DC	4,275	41	751	171
					VA	17,739	334	2,339	1,441
Northeast	252,187	2,878	9,254	11,088	WV	723	18	54	49
N.E.	38,261	273	3,068	1,017	NC	6,425	583	929	279
ME	847	15	103	65	SC	2,118	141	110	209
NH	1,250	15	97	38	GA	11,243	1,343	1,796	381
VT	668	4	186	14	FL	61,127	2,389	1,844	1,799
MA	22,231	101	2,102	417	E.S.C.	8,065	370	1,564	466
RI	2,920	17	65	76	KY	2,119	75	397	124
CT	10,345	121	515	407	TN	2,995	155	628	154
M.A.	213,926	2,605	6,186	10,071	AL	2,109	94	347	99
NY	149,399	1,809	2,810	5,484	MS	842	46	192	89
NJ	48,314	537	1,180	4,077	W.S.C.	83,949	40,124	8,873	2,525
PA	16,213	259	2,196	510	AR	1,039	168	157	64
Midwest	94,144	12,650	7,387	4,704	LA	4,230	118	1,321	194
E.N.C.	75,370	11,258	2,979	3,851	OK	3,147	537	726	150
OH	10,194	187	554	475	TX	75,533	39,301	6,669	2,117
IN	3,115	385	161	189	West	404,205	152,191	41,499	34,871
IL	43,532	9,861	1,174	2,467	Mountain	36,042	17,805	2,835	1,725
MI	14,268	423	902	555	MT	493	42	15	50
WI	4,261	402	188	165	ID	1,186	380	55	57
W.N.C.	18,774	1,392	4,408	853	WY	281	61	2	27
MN	6,851	195	1,189	218	CO	6,553	1,447	909	261
IA	2,228	234	738	112	NM	3,907	2,543	299	121
MO	4,250	171	1,057	257	AZ	15,792	10,779	892	420
ND	513	11	142	41	UT	2,744	425	491	103
SD	522	13	83	37	NV	5,086	2,128	172	686
NE	1,486	316	466	82	Pacific	368,163	134,386	38,664	33,146
KS	2,924	452	733	106	WA	15,861	1,239	3,179	1,624
South	212,106	45,662	19,523	8,263	OR	6,275	846	1,216	307
S.A.	120,092	5,168	9,086	5,272	CA	336,663	132,138	33,477	26,846
DE	1,034	82	69	51	AK	1,165	64	100	368
MD	15,408	237	1,194	892	HI	8,199	99	692	4,001

[1] Includes other countries, not shown separately. [2] Includes Guam, Puerto Rico, Northern Mariana Islands, Virgin Islands, and other or unknown areas not shown separately.

Source: U.S. Immigration and Naturalization Service, *Statistical Yearbook*, annual.

No. 11. Resident Population—Selected Characteristics, 1790 to 1992, and Projections, 1995 to 2050

[In thousands. See also *Historical Statistics, Colonial Times to 1970*, series A 73-81 and A 143-149]

DATE	SEX		RACE					Hispanic origin [1]
						Other		
	Male	Female	White	Black	Total	American Indians and Alaska Natives	Asian and Pacific Islanders	
1790 (Aug. 2) [2]	(NA)	(NA)	3,172	757	(NA)	(NA)	(NA)	(NA)
1800 (Aug. 4) [2]	(NA)	(NA)	4,306	1,002	(NA)	(NA)	(NA)	(NA)
1850 (June 1) [2]	11,838	11,354	19,553	3,639	(NA)	(NA)	(NA)	(NA)
1900 (June 1) [2]	38,816	37,178	66,809	8,834	351	(NA)	(NA)	(NA)
1910 (Apr. 15) [2]	47,332	44,640	81,732	9,828	413	(NA)	(NA)	(NA)
1920 (Jan. 1) [2]	53,900	51,810	94,821	10,463	427	(NA)	(NA)	(NA)
1930 (Apr. 1) [2]	62,137	60,638	110,287	11,891	597	(NA)	(NA)	(NA)
1940 (Apr. 1) [2]	66,062	65,608	118,215	12,866	589	(NA)	(NA)	(NA)
1950 (Apr. 1) [2]	74,833	75,864	134,942	15,042	713	(NA)	(NA)	(NA)
1950 (Apr. 1)......	75,187	76,139	135,150	15,045	1,131	(NA)	(NA)	(NA)
1960 (Apr. 1)......	88,331	90,992	158,832	18,872	1,620	(NA)	(NA)	(NA)
1970 (Apr. 1) [3]	98,926	104,309	178,098	22,581	2,557	(NA)	(NA)	(NA)
1980 (Apr. 1) [4][5]	110,053	116,493	194,713	26,683	5,150	1,420	3,729	14,609
1990 (Apr. 1) [4]	121,239	127,471	208,704	30,483	9,523	2,065	7,458	22,354
1991 (July 1) [6]	122,979	129,181	211,006	31,090	10,064	2,103	7,961	23,379
1992 (July 1) [6]	124,493	130,589	212,912	31,635	10,535	2,134	8,401	24,238
1995 (July 1) [7]	128,685	134,749	218,334	33,117	11,982	2,226	9,756	26,798
2000 (July 1) [7]	135,101	141,140	226,267	35,469	14,505	2,380	12,125	31,166
2005 (July 1) [7]	141,121	147,165	233,343	37,793	17,151	2,543	14,608	35,702
2010 (July 1) [7]	147,187	153,245	240,297	40,224	19,910	2,719	17,191	40,525
2015 (July 1) [7]	153,517	159,599	247,542	42,797	22,777	2,904	19,873	45,719
2020 (July 1) [7]	159,897	166,045	254,791	45,409	25,743	3,090	22,653	51,217
2025 (July 1) [7]	166,012	172,326	261,531	48,005	28,802	3,278	25,524	56,927
2050 (July 1) [7]	192,098	199,933	285,591	61,586	44,854	4,346	40,508	88,071

NA Not available. [1] Persons of Hispanic origin may be of any race. [2] Excludes Alaska and Hawaii. [3] The revised 1970 resident population count is 203,302,031; which incorporates changes due to errors found after tabulations were completed. The race and sex data shown here reflect the official 1970 census count; see text, section 1. [4] The race data shown have been modified; see text, section 1, for explanation. [5] See footnote 4, table 1. [6] Estimated. [7] Middle series projection; see table 3.

No. 12. Resident Population Characteristics—Percent Distribution and Median Age, 1850 to 1992, and Projections, 1995 to 2050

[In percent, except as indicated. For definition of median, see Guide to Tabular Presentation]

DATE	SEX		RACE			Hispanic origin [1]	Median age (years)
	Male	Female	White	Black	Other		
1850 (June 1) [2]	51.0	49.0	84.3	15.7	(NA)	(NA)	18.9
1900 (June 1) [2]	51.1	48.9	87.9	11.6	0.5	(NA)	22.9
1910 (Apr. 15) [2]	51.5	48.5	88.9	10.7	0.4	(NA)	24.1
1920 (Jan. 1) [2]	51.0	49.0	89.7	9.9	0.4	(NA)	25.3
1930 (Apr. 1) [2]	50.6	49.4	89.8	9.7	0.5	(NA)	26.4
1940 (Apr. 1) [2]	50.2	49.8	89.8	9.8	0.4	(NA)	29.0
1950 (Apr. 1) [2]	49.7	50.3	89.5	10.0	0.5	(NA)	30.2
1950 (Apr. 1)................	49.7	50.3	89.3	9.9	0.7	(NA)	30.2
1960 (Apr. 1)................	49.3	50.7	88.6	10.5	0.9	(NA)	29.5
1970 (Apr. 1)................	48.7	51.3	87.6	11.1	1.3	(NA)	28.0
1980 (Apr. 1) [3][4]	48.6	51.4	85.9	11.8	2.3	6.4	30.0
1990 (Apr. 1) [3]	48.7	51.3	83.9	12.3	3.8	9.0	32.8
1991 (July 1) [5]	48.8	51.2	83.7	12.3	4.0	9.3	33.1
1992 (July 1) [5]	48.8	51.2	83.5	12.4	4.1	9.5	33.4
1995 (July 1) [6]	48.8	51.2	82.9	12.6	4.5	10.2	34.0
2000 (July 1) [6]	48.9	51.1	81.9	12.8	5.3	11.3	35.5
2025 (July 1) [6]	49.1	50.9	77.3	14.2	8.5	16.8	38.1
2050 (July 1) [6]	49.0	51.0	72.8	15.7	11.4	22.5	39.0

NA Not available. [1] Persons of Hispanic origin may be of any race. [2] Excludes Alaska and Hawaii. [3] The race data shown have been modified; see text, section 1 for explanation. [4] See footnote 4, table 1. [5] Estimated. [6] Middle series projection; see table 3.

Source of tables 11 and 12: U.S. Bureau of the Census, *U.S. Census of Population: 1940*, vol. II, part 1, and vol. IV, part 1; *1950*, vol. II, part 1; *1960*, vol. I, part 1; *1970*, vol. I, part B; *Current Population Reports*, P25-1095 and P25-1104; and unpublished data.

No. 13. Resident Population, by Age and Sex: 1970 to 1992

[In thousands, except as indicated. 1970, 1980, and 1990 data are enumerated population as of April 1; data for other years are estimated population as of July 1. Excludes Armed Forces overseas. For definition of median, see Guide to Tabular Presentation. See also Historical Statistics, Colonial Times to 1970, series A119-134]

YEAR AND SEX	Total, all years	Under 5 years	5-9 years	10-14 years	15-19 years	20-24 years	25-29 years	30-34 years	35-39 years	40-44 years	45-49 years	50-54 years	55-59 years	60-64 years	65-74 years	75-84 years	85 years and over	5-13 years	14-17 years	18-24 years	Median age (yr.)
1970, total [1]	203,235	17,163	19,969	20,804	19,084	16,383	13,486	11,437	11,113	11,988	12,124	11,111	9,979	8,623	12,443	6,122	1,408	36,675	15,851	23,714	28.0
Male	98,926	8,750	10,175	10,598	9,641	7,925	6,626	5,599	5,416	5,823	5,855	5,351	4,769	4,030	5,440	2,437	489	18,687	8,069	11,583	26.8
Female	104,309	8,413	9,794	10,206	9,443	8,458	6,859	5,838	5,697	6,166	6,269	5,759	5,210	4,593	7,002	3,684	919	17,987	7,782	12,131	29.3
1980, total [2]	226,546	16,348	16,700	18,242	21,168	21,319	19,521	17,561	13,965	11,669	11,090	11,710	11,615	10,088	15,581	7,729	2,240	31,159	16,247	30,022	30.0
Male	110,053	8,362	8,539	9,316	10,755	10,663	9,705	8,677	6,862	5,708	5,388	5,621	5,482	4,670	6,757	2,867	682	15,923	8,298	15,054	28.8
Female	116,493	7,986	8,161	8,926	10,413	10,655	9,816	8,884	7,104	5,961	5,702	6,089	6,133	5,418	8,824	4,862	1,559	15,237	7,950	14,969	31.3
1981, total	229,466	16,893	16,060	18,300	20,541	21,663	20,169	18,731	14,366	12,028	10,985	11,595	11,554	10,359	15,890	7,982	2,349	30,711	15,609	30,245	30.3
1982, total	231,664	17,228	15,956	18,145	19,962	21,682	20,704	18,714	15,566	12,464	11,011	11,414	11,463	10,567	16,147	8,203	2,437	30,528	15,057	30,162	30.5
1983, total	233,792	17,547	16,053	17,869	19,388	21,632	21,141	19,067	16,117	13,150	11,201	11,155	11,457	10,655	16,414	8,429	2,518	30,279	14,740	29,922	30.8
1984, total	235,825	17,695	16,338	17,450	18,931	21,459	21,459	19,503	16,867	13,636	11,429	10,957	11,352	10,906	16,626	8,656	2,595	30,062	14,725	29,461	31.1
1985, total	237,924	17,842	16,665	17,027	18,727	21,265	21,671	20,025	17,604	14,087	11,606	10,854	11,229	10,859	16,858	8,890	2,667	29,893	14,888	28,902	31.4
1986, total	240,133	17,963	17,098	16,474	18,813	20,744	21,857	20,479	18,611	14,398	11,878	10,781	11,135	10,783	17,137	9,129	2,742	30,078	14,824	28,227	31.7
1987, total	242,289	18,052	17,430	16,377	18,698	20,192	21,739	20,984	18,619	15,608	12,294	10,802	10,968	10,791	17,426	9,376	2,823	30,502	14,502	27,356	32.0
1988, total	244,499	18,195	17,759	16,496	18,496	19,655	21,560	21,391	18,993	16,188	12,954	10,995	10,722	10,707	17,626	9,612	2,885	31,028	14,023	27,156	32.3
1989, total	246,819	18,508	17,917	16,797	18,133	19,258	21,328	21,676	19,455	16,960	13,421	11,212	10,534	10,625	17,864	9,850	2,968	31,413	13,536	26,942	32.6
1990, total [3]	248,710	18,758	18,035	17,060	17,882	19,132	21,327	21,833	19,846	17,589	13,744	11,313	10,487	10,626	18,045	10,012	3,021	31,826	13,340	26,942	32.8
Male	121,239	9,599	9,232	8,739	9,173	9,743	10,702	10,862	9,833	8,676	6,739	5,493	5,008	4,947	7,907	3,745	841	16,295	6,857	13,734	31.6
Female	127,471	9,159	8,803	8,322	8,709	9,389	10,625	10,971	10,013	8,913	7,004	5,820	5,479	5,679	10,139	6,267	2,180	15,532	6,483	13,208	34.0
1991, total	252,160	19,204	18,237	17,672	17,162	19,173	20,737	22,171	20,528	18,761	14,098	11,647	10,423	10,583	18,280	10,331	3,153	32,501	13,419	26,324	33.1
1992, total [3]	255,082	19,512	18,349	18,100	17,074	19,050	20,189	22,273	21,099	18,805	15,361	12,056	10,487	10,441	18,460	10,565	3,259	33,005	13,648	25,919	33.4
Male	124,493	9,986	9,396	9,271	8,762	9,706	10,140	11,107	10,481	9,287	7,541	5,858	5,022	4,891	8,126	4,010	909	16,901	7,016	13,217	32.2
Female	130,589	9,526	8,954	8,829	8,312	9,345	10,049	11,166	10,618	9,518	7,820	6,198	5,464	5,550	10,336	6,555	2,349	16,105	6,632	12,703	34.6
Percent:																					
1970 [2]	100.0	8.4	9.8	10.2	9.4	8.1	6.6	5.6	5.5	5.9	6.0	5.5	4.9	4.2	6.1	3.0	0.7	18.0	7.8	11.7	(X)
1980 [3]	100.0	7.2	7.4	8.1	9.3	9.4	8.6	7.8	6.2	5.2	4.9	5.2	5.1	4.5	6.9	3.4	1.0	13.8	7.2	13.3	(X)
1990 [3]	100.0	7.5	7.3	6.9	7.2	7.7	8.6	8.8	8.0	7.1	5.5	4.5	4.2	4.3	7.3	4.0	1.2	12.8	5.4	10.8	(X)
1992	100.0	7.6	7.2	7.1	6.7	7.5	7.9	8.7	8.3	7.4	6.0	4.7	4.1	4.1	7.2	4.1	1.3	12.9	5.4	10.2	(X)
Male	100.0	8.0	7.5	7.4	7.0	7.8	8.1	8.9	8.4	7.5	6.1	4.7	4.0	3.9	6.5	3.2	0.7	13.6	5.6	10.6	(X)
Female	100.0	7.3	6.9	6.8	6.4	7.2	7.7	8.6	8.1	7.3	6.0	4.7	4.2	4.2	7.9	5.0	1.8	12.3	5.1	9.7	(X)

X Not applicable. [1] Official count. The revised 1970 resident population count is 203,302,031; the difference of 66,733 is due to errors found after release of the official series. [2] See footnote 4, table 1. [3] The data shown have been modified from the official 1990 census counts. See text, section 1, for explanation.

Source: U.S. Bureau of the Census, Current Population Reports, P25-917 and P25-1095; and unpublished data.

No. 14. Ratio of Males to Females, by Age Group, 1950 to 1992, and Projections, 2000 and 2025

[Number of males per 100 females. Total resident population]

AGE	1950 (Apr. 1)	1960 (Apr. 1)	1970 (Apr. 1)	1980 (Apr. 1)	1990 (Apr. 1)	1992 (July 1)	PROJECTIONS [1] 2000 (July 1)	2025 (July 1)
All ages	98.6	97.1	94.8	94.5	95.1	95.3	95.7	96.3
Under 14 years	103.7	103.4	103.9	104.6	104.9	104.9	105.2	105.4
14 to 24 years	98.2	98.7	98.7	101.9	104.6	104.6	104.4	104.7
25 to 44 years	96.4	95.7	95.5	97.4	98.9	99.2	99.1	98.6
45 to 64 years	100.1	95.7	91.6	90.7	92.5	93.1	94.1	94.2
65 years and over. . . .	89.6	82.8	72.1	67.6	67.2	67.8	70.5	82.0

[1] Middle series projections; see table 3.

Source: U.S. Bureau of the Census, *U.S. Census of Population: 1950*, vol. II, part 1; *1960*, vol. I, part 1; *1970*, vol. I, part B; *Current Population Reports*, P25-1095 and P25-1104; and unpublished data.

No. 15. Resident Population, by Sex and Age: 1992

[In thousands, except as indicated. As of July 1. For derivation of estimates, see text, section 1]

AGE	Total	Male	Female	AGE	Total	Male	Female
Total	255,082	124,493	130,589	43 yrs. old	3,599	1,768	1,832
				44 yrs. old	3,728	1,849	1,879
Under 5 yrs. old	19,512	9,986	9,526	45 to 49 yrs. old.	15,361	7,541	7,820
Under 1 yr. old	3,984	2,039	1,945	45 yrs. old	3,912	1,933	1,978
1 yr. old	3,978	2,036	1,943	46 yrs. old	2,758	1,352	1,406
2 yrs. old	3,959	2,027	1,932	47 yrs. old	2,851	1,394	1,457
3 yrs. old	3,813	1,951	1,861	48 yrs. old	2,712	1,323	1,388
4 yrs. old	3,778	1,933	1,845	49 yrs. old	3,130	1,538	1,592
5 to 9 yrs. old	18,349	9,396	8,954				
5 yrs. old	3,722	1,906	1,816	50 to 54 yrs. old	12,056	5,858	6,198
6 yrs. old	3,705	1,897	1,808	50 yrs. old	2,663	1,299	1,363
7 yrs. old	3,697	1,891	1,805	51 yrs. old	2,436	1,186	1,250
8 yrs. old	3,450	1,766	1,684	52 yrs. old	2,328	1,131	1,197
9 yrs. old	3,776	1,936	1,840	53 yrs. old	2,316	1,122	1,194
				54 yrs. old	2,314	1,119	1,195
10 to 14 yrs. old.	18,100	9,271	8,829	55 to 59 yrs. old.	10,487	5,022	5,464
10 yrs. old	3,795	1,946	1,849	55 yrs. old	2,137	1,027	1,110
11 yrs. old	3,665	1,877	1,788	56 yrs. old	2,160	1,035	1,125
12 yrs. old	3,670	1,878	1,792	57 yrs. old	2,205	1,057	1,148
13 yrs. old	3,526	1,804	1,722	58 yrs. old	1,927	922	1,006
14 yrs. old	3,443	1,765	1,678	59 yrs. old	2,057	981	1,076
15 to 19 yrs. old.	17,074	8,762	8,312	60 to 64 yrs. old	10,441	4,891	5,550
15 yrs. old	3,448	1,769	1,679	60 yrs. old	2,026	949	1,077
16 yrs. old	3,317	1,707	1,610	61 yrs. old	2,075	977	1,098
17 yrs. old	3,440	1,775	1,665	62 yrs. old	2,085	981	1,103
18 yrs. old	3,304	1,693	1,611	63 yrs. old	2,081	976	1,104
19 yrs. old	3,565	1,818	1,747	64 yrs. old	2,175	1,007	1,168
				65 to 69 yrs. old.	9,977	4,475	5,503
20 to 24 yrs. old.	19,050	9,706	9,345	65 yrs. old	2,085	951	1,135
20 yrs. old	3,757	1,917	1,841	66 yrs. old	2,020	913	1,108
21 yrs. old	3,983	2,033	1,951	67 yrs. old	2,034	914	1,120
22 yrs. old	3,871	1,976	1,894	68 yrs. old	1,931	859	1,072
23 yrs. old	3,713	1,890	1,823	69 yrs. old	1,907	838	1,069
24 yrs. old	3,726	1,890	1,836				
25 to 29 yrs. old.	20,189	10,140	10,049	70 to 74 yrs. old	8,483	3,651	4,833
25 yrs. old	3,758	1,897	1,860	70 yrs. old	1,905	837	1,068
26 yrs. old	3,833	1,925	1,909	71 yrs. old	1,837	802	1,034
27 yrs. old	4,085	2,052	2,034	72 yrs. old	1,698	735	962
28 yrs. old	4,015	2,012	2,003	73 yrs. old	1,561	660	901
29 yrs. old	4,498	2,255	2,243	74 yrs. old	1,483	616	867
				75 to 79 yrs. old.	6,415	2,553	3,862
30 to 34 yrs. old.	22,273	11,107	11,166	75 yrs. old	1,419	584	834
30 yrs. old	4,487	2,242	2,245	76 yrs. old	1,344	548	796
31 yrs. old	4,405	2,196	2,208	77 yrs. old	1,283	511	772
32 yrs. old	4,452	2,220	2,232	78 yrs. old	1,221	474	748
33 yrs. old	4,379	2,173	2,205	79 yrs. old	1,147	436	712
34 yrs. old	4,551	2,275	2,275	80 to 84 yrs. old	4,150	1,457	2,693
35 to 39 yrs. old.	21,099	10,481	10,618	80 yrs. old	996	369	627
35 yrs. old	4,501	2,244	2,257	81 yrs. old	907	324	583
36 yrs. old	4,237	2,102	2,135	82 yrs. old	820	287	534
37 yrs. old	4,247	2,110	2,138	83 yrs. old	752	256	496
38 yrs. old	3,899	1,929	1,969	84 yrs. old	676	223	453
39 yrs. old	4,214	2,095	2,119	85 to 89 yrs. old	2,162	647	1,515
40 to 44 yrs. old.	18,805	9,287	9,518	90 to 94 yrs. old	834	207	627
40 yrs. old	4,011	1,986	2,025	95 to 99 yrs. old	217	46	172
41 yrs. old	3,753	1,851	1,902	100 yrs. old and over . .	45	10	35
42 yrs. old	3,713	1,834	1,880	Median age (yr.)	33.4	32.2	34.6

Source: U.S. Bureau of the Census, unpublished data.

Population

No. 16. Resident Population Projections, by Age and Sex: 1993 to 2050

[In thousands, except as indicated. As of July. See headnote, table 3]

YEAR	Total	Under 5 years	5 to 13 years	14 to 17 years	18 to 24 years	25 to 34 years	35 to 44 years	45 to 54 years	55 to 64 years	65 to 74 years	75 to 84 years	85 years and over
TOTAL												
Lowest series:												
1993	257,670	19,902	33,396	13,785	26,090	42,772	40,345	27,718	21,110	18,632	10,614	3,304
1994	259,973	19,998	33,800	14,048	25,741	42,095	41,195	28,946	21,089	18,816	10,812	3,431
1995	262,051	19,892	34,140	14,519	25,281	41,435	42,023	30,142	21,166	18,881	11,023	3,547
2000	270,259	18,034	35,869	15,564	25,306	37,286	44,565	35,813	23,370	18,217	12,132	4,101
2005	276,316	16,951	34,668	16,542	27,309	35,121	41,898	40,475	28,203	17,984	12,600	4,564
2010	281,180	16,653	32,100	16,425	29,005	35,934	37,703	42,833	33,422	19,933	12,115	5,055
2020	289,553	17,336	31,272	14,404	26,764	40,218	36,362	36,228	39,890	28,513	13,439	5,127
2030	292,902	16,519	31,773	14,792	25,260	36,593	40,553	34,921	33,656	33,800	19,228	5,808
2040	290,351	16,202	30,299	14,537	26,092	35,429	36,957	38,921	32,508	28,486	22,691	8,229
2050	285,502	16,250	30,174	13,986	24,920	36,106	35,791	35,443	36,185	27,665	19,088	9,894
Middle series:												
1993	257,927	19,917	33,425	13,802	26,133	42,822	40,371	27,736	21,128	18,650	10,628	3,315
1994	260,711	20,129	33,870	14,088	25,846	42,223	41,264	28,991	21,131	18,863	10,848	3,459
1995	263,434	20,181	34,262	14,591	25,465	41,670	42,150	30,224	21,241	18,963	11,087	3,598
2000	276,241	19,431	36,547	15,811	25,911	38,237	45,123	36,170	23,690	18,551	12,438	4,333
2005	288,286	19,333	36,843	16,947	28,238	36,792	43,075	41,219	28,870	18,623	13,265	5,082
2010	300,431	20,017	36,213	17,388	30,220	38,179	39,659	44,099	34,552	20,978	13,157	5,969
2020	325,942	21,957	38,701	17,119	30,456	43,553	39,662	38,885	42,262	30,910	15,480	6,959
2030	349,993	22,689	41,528	18,820	31,802	43,572	45,040	38,936	37,429	37,984	23,348	8,843
2040	371,505	23,978	43,069	19,747	34,510	46,127	45,134	44,224	37,701	33,968	29,206	13,840
2050	392,031	25,382	45,742	20,630	35,710	49,462	47,739	44,337	42,920	34,628	26,588	18,893
Highest series:												
1993	258,157	19,928	33,450	13,818	26,174	42,873	40,401	27,752	21,139	18,661	10,641	3,321
1994	261,390	20,259	33,935	14,127	25,947	42,353	41,341	29,029	21,161	18,887	10,877	3,475
1995	264,715	20,470	34,380	14,659	25,643	41,907	42,294	30,295	21,295	19,008	11,139	3,626
2000	281,957	20,938	37,206	16,045	26,498	39,198	45,797	36,501	23,910	18,733	12,649	4,483
2005	299,941	22,076	39,099	17,333	29,131	38,444	44,443	41,979	29,311	18,900	13,687	5,445
2010	319,536	24,108	40,756	18,331	31,383	40,358	41,772	45,470	35,322	21,586	13,805	6,644
2020	363,213	27,960	47,760	20,174	34,302	46,735	43,000	41,674	44,162	32,313	16,729	8,405
2030	410,991	31,472	54,296	23,745	39,423	50,832	49,467	42,984	40,729	40,776	25,855	11,410
2040	463,579	36,246	61,516	26,653	44,998	58,392	53,705	49,454	42,279	38,127	33,472	18,736
2050	522,098	41,404	70,680	30,400	50,494	65,872	61,394	53,662	48,751	40,095	32,028	27,318
MALE (middle series)												
1993	125,921	10,204	17,126	7,099	13,311	21,420	20,003	13,560	10,017	8,217	4,038	924
1994	127,318	10,316	17,353	7,244	13,159	21,118	20,458	14,174	10,035	8,344	4,150	965
1995	128,685	10,344	17,556	7,503	12,958	20,835	20,911	14,777	10,101	8,420	4,274	1,005
2000	135,101	9,958	18,738	8,129	13,177	19,059	22,425	17,692	11,321	8,385	4,980	1,238
2005	141,121	9,908	18,895	8,716	14,360	18,301	21,372	20,193	13,842	8,559	5,463	1,512
2010	147,187	10,262	18,575	8,949	15,382	18,991	19,620	21,631	16,603	9,744	5,574	1,855
2020	159,897	11,263	19,866	8,816	15,513	21,703	19,601	18,989	20,414	14,561	6,874	2,297
2030	171,690	11,635	21,312	9,691	16,197	21,721	22,294	18,988	18,008	18,081	10,643	3,122
2040	182,049	12,289	22,091	10,161	17,571	22,998	22,361	21,597	18,125	16,174	13,566	5,116
2050	192,098	13,008	23,460	10,614	18,181	24,675	23,681	21,690	20,696	16,552	12,446	7,094
FEMALE (middle series)												
1993	132,006	9,712	16,298	6,703	12,820	21,402	20,369	14,177	11,110	10,433	6,590	2,391
1994	133,393	9,813	16,514	6,843	12,687	21,107	20,806	14,816	11,097	10,517	6,698	2,494
1995	134,749	9,837	16,707	7,087	12,507	20,835	21,238	15,447	11,140	10,544	6,814	2,593
2000	141,140	9,473	17,811	7,681	12,734	19,178	22,697	18,477	12,369	10,166	7,458	3,095
2005	147,165	9,425	17,948	8,230	13,878	18,491	21,702	21,028	15,027	10,065	7,802	3,570
2010	153,245	9,756	17,637	8,438	14,839	19,188	20,038	22,468	17,949	11,235	7,583	4,114
2020	166,045	10,693	18,835	8,303	14,943	21,849	20,060	19,896	21,848	16,348	8,606	4,662
2030	178,303	11,054	20,216	9,131	15,606	21,851	22,746	19,947	19,421	19,903	12,705	5,721
2040	189,456	11,689	20,978	9,585	16,939	23,129	22,773	22,627	19,576	17,794	15,640	8,724
2050	199,933	12,374	22,282	10,016	17,530	24,787	24,057	22,647	22,224	18,076	14,141	11,799
PERCENT DISTRIBUTION (middle series)												
1995	100.0	7.7	13.0	5.4	10.1	16.6	15.7	10.8	8.2	7.2	4.1	1.3
2000	100.0	7.0	13.2	5.7	9.4	13.8	16.3	13.1	8.6	6.7	4.5	1.6
2005	100.0	6.7	12.8	5.9	9.8	12.8	14.9	14.3	10.0	6.5	4.6	1.8
2010	100.0	6.7	12.1	5.8	10.1	12.7	13.2	14.7	11.5	7.0	4.4	2.0
2020	100.0	6.7	11.9	5.3	9.3	13.4	12.2	11.9	13.0	9.5	4.7	2.1
2030	100.0	6.5	11.9	5.4	9.1	12.4	12.9	11.1	10.7	10.9	6.7	2.5
2040	100.0	6.5	11.6	5.3	9.3	12.4	12.1	11.9	10.1	9.1	7.9	3.7
2050	100.0	6.5	11.7	5.3	9.1	12.6	12.2	11.3	10.9	8.8	6.8	4.8

Source: U.S. Bureau of the Census, *Current Population Reports*, P25-1104.

No. 17. Resident Population, by Race, 1980 to 1992, and Projections, 1993 to 2050

[In thousands, except as indicated. As of July, except as indicated. These data are consistent with the 1980 and 1990 decennial enumerations and have been modified from the official census counts; see text, section 1 for explanation. See headnote, table 3]

YEAR	Total	White	Black	American Indian, Eskimo, Aleut	Asian, Pacific Islander
1980 (April) [1]	226,546	194,713	26,683	1,420	3,729
1980	227,225	195,185	26,771	1,433	3,837
1981	229,466	196,635	27,133	1,483	4,214
1982	231,664	198,037	27,508	1,537	4,581
1983	233,792	199,420	27,867	1,596	4,909
1984	235,825	200,708	28,212	1,656	5,249
1985	237,924	202,031	28,569	1,718	5,606
1986	240,133	203,430	28,942	1,783	5,978
1987	242,289	204,770	29,325	1,851	6,343
1988	244,499	206,129	29,723	1,923	6,724
1989	246,819	207,540	30,143	2,001	7,134
1990 (April)	248,710	208,704	30,483	2,065	7,458
1990	249,391	209,165	30,592	2,072	7,563
1991	252,160	211,006	31,090	2,103	7,961
1992	255,082	212,912	31,635	2,134	8,401
PROJECTIONS					
Lowest series:					
1993	257,670	214,600	32,113	2,165	8,792
1994	259,973	216,076	32,547	2,194	9,155
1995	262,051	217,381	32,954	2,222	9,493
2000	270,259	222,143	34,715	2,354	11,047
2005	276,316	225,080	36,175	2,480	12,581
2010	281,180	227,026	37,456	2,604	14,094
2020	289,553	229,790	39,735	2,837	17,191
2030	292,902	228,386	41,161	3,029	20,326
2040	290,351	222,048	41,828	3,191	23,284
2050	285,502	214,054	42,026	3,323	26,099
Middle series:					
1993	257,927	214,778	32,137	2,165	8,846
1994	260,711	216,586	32,631	2,196	9,298
1995	263,434	218,334	33,117	2,226	9,756
2000	276,241	226,267	35,469	2,380	12,125
2005	288,286	233,343	37,793	2,543	14,608
2010	300,431	240,297	40,224	2,719	17,191
2020	325,942	254,791	45,409	3,090	22,653
2030	349,993	267,457	50,596	3,473	28,467
2040	371,505	277,232	55,917	3,894	34,461
2050	392,031	285,591	61,586	4,346	40,508
Highest series:					
1993	258,157	214,928	32,166	2,165	8,899
1994	261,390	217,046	32,714	2,197	9,432
1995	264,715	219,210	33,274	2,228	10,002
2000	281,957	230,232	36,195	2,390	13,140
2005	299,941	241,516	39,314	2,569	16,541
2010	319,536	253,813	42,751	2,773	20,200
2020	363,213	281,304	50,475	3,223	28,212
2030	410,991	310,917	59,073	3,729	37,271
2040	463,579	342,960	68,767	4,336	47,516
2050	522,098	378,408	79,722	5,039	58,930
PERCENT DISTRIBUTION					
Middle series:					
1995	100.0	82.9	12.6	0.8	3.7
2000	100.0	81.9	12.8	0.9	4.4
2005	100.0	80.9	13.1	0.9	5.1
2010	100.0	80.0	13.4	0.9	5.7
2020	100.0	78.2	13.9	0.9	7.0
2030	100.0	76.4	14.5	1.0	8.1
2040	100.0	74.6	15.1	1.0	9.3
2050	100.0	72.8	15.7	1.1	10.3
PERCENT CHANGE (middle series)					
1993-2000	7.1	5.3	10.4	9.9	37.1
2000-2010	8.8	6.2	13.4	14.2	41.8
2010-2020	8.5	6.0	12.9	13.6	31.8
2020-2030	7.4	5.0	11.4	12.4	25.7
2030-2040	6.1	3.7	10.5	12.1	21.1
2040-2050	5.5	3.0	10.1	11.6	17.5

[1] See footnote 4, table 1.

Source: U.S. Bureau of the Census, Current Population Reports, P25-1095 and P25-1104; and unpublished data.

Population

No. 18. Resident Population, by Hispanic Origin Status, 1980 to 1992, and Projections, 1993 to 2050

[In thousands, except as indicated. As of **July**, except as indicated. These data are consistent with the 1980 and 1990 decennial enumerations and have been modified from the official census counts; see text, section 1, for explanation. See headnote, table 3. Minus sign (-) indicates decrease]

YEAR	Total	Hispanic origin [1]	NOT OF HISPANIC ORIGIN			
			White	Black	American Indian, Eskimo, Aleut	Asian, Pacific Islander
1980 (April) [2]	226,546	14,609	180,906	26,142	1,326	3,563
1980	227,225	14,869	181,140	26,215	1,336	3,665
1981	229,466	15,560	181,974	26,532	1,377	4,022
1982	231,664	16,240	182,782	26,856	1,420	4,367
1983	233,792	16,935	183,561	27,159	1,466	4,671
1984	235,825	17,640	184,243	27,444	1,512	4,986
1985	237,924	18,368	184,945	27,738	1,558	5,315
1986	240,133	19,154	185,678	28,040	1,606	5,655
1987	242,289	19,946	186,353	28,351	1,654	5,985
1988	244,499	20,786	187,012	28,669	1,703	6,329
1989	246,819	21,648	187,713	29,005	1,755	6,698
1990 (April)	248,710	22,354	188,300	29,273	1,796	6,988
1990	249,391	22,553	188,580	29,370	1,801	7,087
1991	252,160	23,379	189,674	29,820	1,826	7,461
1992	255,082	24,238	190,802	30,316	1,850	7,876
PROJECTIONS						
Lowest series:						
1993	257,670	25,011	191,786	30,750	1,876	8,247
1994	259,973	25,728	192,607	31,144	1,900	8,593
1995	262,051	26,402	193,295	31,514	1,924	8,915
2000	270,259	29,473	195,240	33,112	2,033	10,400
2005	276,316	32,373	195,520	34,419	2,137	11,867
2010	281,180	35,223	194,860	35,547	2,237	13,311
2020	289,553	41,235	192,130	37,503	2,424	16,261
2030	292,902	47,049	185,402	38,624	2,576	19,250
2040	290,351	52,450	174,123	39,009	2,704	22,066
2050	285,502	57,643	161,382	38,933	2,807	24,738
Middle series:						
1993	257,927	25,085	191,899	30,768	1,876	8,298
1994	260,711	25,939	192,932	31,212	1,902	8,727
1995	263,434	26,798	193,900	31,648	1,927	9,161
2000	276,241	31,166	197,872	33,741	2,055	11,407
2005	288,286	35,702	200,842	35,793	2,190	13,759
2010	300,431	40,525	203,441	37,930	2,336	16,199
2020	325,942	51,217	208,280	42,459	2,641	21,345
2030	349,993	62,810	210,480	46,934	2,960	26,810
2040	371,505	75,130	209,148	51,489	3,314	32,424
2050	392,031	88,071	205,849	56,346	3,701	38,064
Highest series:						
1993	258,157	25,156	191,985	30,792	1,876	8,347
1994	261,390	26,129	193,224	31,281	1,902	8,853
1995	264,715	27,150	194,465	31,779	1,929	9,392
2000	281,957	32,699	200,482	34,354	2,063	12,359
2005	299,941	38,767	206,306	37,089	2,210	15,569
2010	319,536	45,494	212,559	40,094	2,376	19,013
2020	363,213	61,104	226,025	46,813	2,741	26,530
2030	410,991	79,684	238,947	54,209	3,154	34,998
2040	463,579	101,872	251,077	62,453	3,647	44,529
2050	522,098	128,255	262,855	71,675	4,221	55,093
PERCENT DISTRIBUTION						
Middle series:						
1995	100.0	10.2	73.6	12.0	0.7	3.5
2000	100.0	11.3	71.6	12.2	0.7	4.1
2005	100.0	12.4	69.7	12.4	0.8	4.8
2010	100.0	13.5	67.7	12.6	0.8	5.4
2020	100.0	15.7	63.9	13.0	0.8	6.5
2030	100.0	17.9	60.1	13.4	0.8	7.7
2040	100.0	20.2	56.3	13.9	0.9	8.7
2050	100.0	22.5	52.5	14.4	0.9	9.7
PERCENT CHANGE (middle series)						
1993-2000	7.1	24.2	3.1	9.7	9.5	37.5
2000-2010	8.8	30.0	2.8	12.4	13.7	42.0
2010-2020	8.5	26.4	2.4	11.9	13.1	31.8
2020-2030	7.4	22.6	1.1	10.5	12.1	25.6
2030-2040	6.1	19.6	-0.6	9.7	12.0	20.9
2040-2050	5.5	17.2	-1.6	9.4	11.7	17.4

[1] Persons of Hispanic origin may be of any race.   [2] See footnote 4, table 1.

Source: U.S. Bureau of the Census, *Current Population Reports*, P25-1095 and P25-1104; and unpublished data.

No. 19. Components of Population Change, by Race and Hispanic Origin, 1980 to 1992, and Projections, 1995 and 2000

[Minus sign (-) indicates net outmigration]

YEAR	TOTAL (Jan. 1-Dec. 31) Population at start of period (1,000)	Net increase [1] Total (1,000)	Net increase Per-cent [2]	Natural increase Births (1,000)	Natural increase Deaths (1,000)	Net migra-tion [3] (1,000)	RATE PER 1,000 MIDYEAR POPULATION Net growth rate [1]	Natural increase Birth rate	Natural increase Death rate	Net migra-tion rate [3]
WHITE										
1980 [4]	194,713	1,270	0.7	2,203	1,277	429	8.6	15.0	8.7	2.9
1985	201,419	1,378	0.7	2,991	1,819	354	6.8	14.8	9.0	1.8
1990	208,376	1,664	0.8	3,265	1,859	[5]306	8.0	15.6	8.9	[5]1.5
1991	210,040	1,963	0.9	3,236	1,868	[5]595	9.3	15.3	8.9	[5]2.8
1992	212,003	1,874	0.9	3,201	1,871	544	8.8	15.0	8.8	2.6
Projections:[6]										
1995	217,460	1,718	0.8	3,128	1,892	482	7.9	14.3	8.7	2.2
2000	225,520	1,478	0.7	2,992	1,997	482	6.5	13.2	8.8	2.1
BLACK										
1980 [4]	26,683	289	1.1	445	173	62	14.4	22.1	8.6	3.1
1985	28,406	364	1.3	608	244	61	12.7	21.3	8.5	2.1
1990	30,377	426	1.4	692	264	[5]12	13.9	22.6	8.6	[5]0.4
1991	30,803	575	1.9	687	265	[5]153	18.5	22.1	8.5	[5]4.9
1992	31,378	536	1.7	693	263	107	17.0	21.9	8.3	3.4
Projections:[6]										
1995	32,874	483	1.5	685	283	81	14.6	20.7	8.5	2.4
2000	35,238	463	1.3	695	313	81	13.0	19.6	8.8	2.3
AMERICAN INDIAN, ESKIMO, ALEUT										
1980 [4]	1,420	38	2.7	28	9	1	35.3	26.2	4.8	0.5
1985	1,687	64	3.8	43	7	-	37.3	24.8	4.2	0.2
1990	2,044	43	2.1	42	9	[5]-1	20.6	20.1	4.2	[5]-0.4
1991	2,087	32	1.5	39	9	[5]2	15.3	18.6	4.2	[5]0.9
1992	2,119	31	1.5	39	9	1	14.7	18.5	4.1	0.4
Projections:[6]										
1995	2,211	30	1.4	40	10	-	13.7	17.9	4.4	0.1
2000	2,364	31	1.3	42	11	-	13.2	17.7	4.6	0.1
ASIAN, PACIFIC ISLANDER										
1980 [4]	3,729	302	8.1	67	8	232	103.4	22.9	2.9	79.3
1985	5,426	365	6.7	118	16	233	65.1	21.1	2.9	41.6
1990	7,345	416	5.7	149	20	[5]276	55.0	19.7	2.7	[5]36.5
1991	7,762	406	5.2	149	23	[5]280	51.0	18.7	2.8	[5]35.1
1992	8,168	446	5.5	154	23	315	53.1	18.3	2.8	37.5
Projections:[6]										
1995	9,527	461	4.8	170	26	317	47.2	17.5	2.7	32.5
2000	11,883	486	4.1	205	36	317	40.1	16.9	2.9	26.1
HISPANIC ORIGIN [7]										
1980 [4]	14,609	613	4.2	261	45	339	54.5	23.2	4.0	30.2
1985	17,997	763	4.2	415	73	302	41.6	22.6	4.0	16.4
1990	22,122	838	3.8	586	84	[5]292	37.1	26.0	3.7	[5]12.9
1991	22,960	836	3.6	624	88	[5]300	35.7	26.7	3.7	[5]12.8
1992	23,796	883	3.7	654	90	319	36.4	27.0	3.7	13.2
Projections:[6]										
1995	26,368	862	3.3	639	100	322	32.1	23.8	3.7	12.0
2000	30,723	888	2.9	690	125	322	28.5	22.1	4.0	10.3
WHITE, NON-HISPANIC										
1980 [4]	180,906	716	0.4	1,958	1,234	113	5.3	14.4	9.1	0.8
1985	184,649	729	0.4	2,607	1,750	82	3.9	14.1	9.5	0.4
1990	188,160	927	0.5	2,732	1,782	[5]45	4.9	14.5	9.5	[5]0.2
1991	189,087	1,206	0.6	2,669	1,787	[5]325	6.4	14.1	9.4	[5]1.7
1992	190,294	1,074	0.6	2,606	1,787	256	5.6	13.7	9.4	1.3
Projections:[6]										
1995	193,416	936	0.5	2,544	1,800	193	4.8	13.1	9.3	1.0
2000	197,525	674	0.3	2,363	1,882	193	3.4	11.9	9.5	1.0
BLACK, NON-HISPANIC										
1980 [4]	26,142	253	1.0	434	171	47	12.8	22.0	8.7	2.4
1985	27,607	297	1.1	588	241	42	10.7	21.2	8.7	1.5
1990	29,191	366	1.3	660	260	[5]-6	12.5	22.5	8.8	[5]-0.2
1991	29,557	527	1.8	652	261	[5]136	17.7	21.9	8.7	[5]4.6
1992	30,084	486	1.6	656	259	89	16.0	21.6	8.5	2.9
Projections:[6]										
1995	31,430	432	1.4	649	278	61	13.7	20.5	8.8	1.9
2000	33,536	410	1.2	655	307	61	12.1	19.4	9.1	1.8

- Represents or rounds to zero. [1] Prior to April 1, 1990, includes "error of closure" (the amount necessary to make the components of change add to the net change between censuses), for which figures are not shown separately. [2] Percent of population at beginning of period. [3] Covers net international migration and movement of Armed Forces, federally affiliated civilian citizens, and their dependents. [4] Represents data for period April 1, 1980, to December 31, 1980. [5] Data reflect movement of Armed Forces due to the Gulf War. [6] Based on middle series of assumptions. See footnote 1, table 3. [7] Persons of Hispanic origin may be of any race.

Source: U.S. Bureau of the Census, *Current Population Reports*, P25-1095 and P25-1104; and unpublished data.

No. 20. Resident Population, by Age and Race: 1980 to 1992

[In thousands, except percent. As of April, except 1992 as of July. See headnote, table 17 and, for 1980 data, footnote 4, table 1]

YEAR, SEX, AND RACE	Total, all years	Under 5 years	5-9 years	10-14 years	15-19 years	20-24 years	25-29 years	30-34 years	35-39 years	40-44 years	45-49 years	50-54 years	55-59 years	60-64 years	65-74 years	75-84 years	85 years and over	5-13 years	14-17 years	18-24 years
ALL RACES																				
1980	226,546	16,348	16,700	18,242	21,168	21,319	19,521	17,561	13,965	11,669	11,090	11,710	11,615	10,088	15,581	7,729	2,240	31,159	16,247	30,022
1990	248,710	18,758	18,035	17,060	17,882	19,132	21,328	21,833	19,846	17,589	13,744	11,313	10,487	10,625	18,045	10,012	3,021	31,826	13,340	26,942
1992	255,082	19,512	18,349	18,100	17,074	19,050	20,189	22,273	21,099	18,805	15,361	12,056	10,487	10,441	18,460	10,565	3,259	33,005	13,648	25,919
Male	124,493	9,986	9,396	9,271	8,762	9,706	10,140	11,107	10,481	9,287	7,541	5,858	5,022	4,891	8,126	4,010	909	16,901	7,016	13,217
Female	130,589	9,526	8,954	8,829	8,312	9,345	10,049	11,166	10,618	9,518	7,820	6,198	5,464	5,550	10,336	6,555	2,349	16,105	6,632	12,703
WHITE																				
1980	194,713	13,414	13,717	15,095	17,681	18,072	16,658	15,157	12,122	10,110	9,693	10,360	10,394	9,078	14,045	7,057	2,060	25,692	13,491	25,381
1990	208,704	14,960	14,502	13,670	14,351	15,637	17,638	18,190	16,652	15,001	11,826	9,744	9,131	9,381	16,175	9,084	2,761	25,557	10,664	21,939
1992	212,912	15,454	14,688	14,438	13,622	15,430	16,520	18,471	17,601	15,857	13,225	10,354	9,073	9,155	16,468	9,581	2,975	26,381	10,887	20,910
Male	104,344	7,928	7,538	7,416	7,010	7,905	8,370	9,308	8,837	7,919	6,555	5,078	4,391	4,335	7,292	3,642	821	13,543	5,610	10,716
Female	108,567	7,526	7,150	7,022	6,612	7,525	8,150	9,163	8,764	7,938	6,670	5,276	4,682	4,820	9,176	5,939	2,154	12,838	5,278	10,194
BLACK																				
1980	26,683	2,459	2,509	2,691	3,007	2,749	2,342	1,904	1,469	1,260	1,150	1,135	1,041	874	1,344	588	159	4,628	2,380	3,948
1990	30,483	2,939	2,711	2,629	2,714	2,655	2,780	2,718	2,359	1,882	1,413	1,178	1,041	972	1,498	772	223	4,837	2,056	3,816
1992	31,635	3,099	2,782	2,782	2,638	2,686	2,714	2,794	2,565	2,139	1,541	1,256	1,059	982	1,559	801	238	5,032	2,109	3,747
Male	14,990	1,568	1,410	1,408	1,335	1,321	1,296	1,308	1,197	989	703	565	467	423	644	287	70	2,549	1,072	1,853
Female	16,645	1,531	1,372	1,374	1,303	1,365	1,418	1,485	1,368	1,150	838	691	592	560	916	514	168	2,483	1,038	1,894
AMERICAN INDIAN, ESKIMO, ALEUT																				
1980	1,420	149	147	156	170	149	125	107	84	69	58	52	45	34	48	21	6	270	136	216
1990	2,065	220	209	197	191	179	188	181	157	132	99	79	64	53	73	34	9	368	152	256
1992	2,134	219	215	214	185	185	181	185	166	142	110	84	67	55	78	37	12	389	153	256
Male	1,059	111	109	108	94	97	92	91	81	69	53	40	32	26	34	15	4	196	78	133
Female	1,076	107	106	106	91	88	89	94	85	73	56	44	35	29	43	23	8	192	75	123
ASIAN, PACIFIC ISLANDER																				
1980	3,729	326	328	300	310	349	396	393	291	230	188	163	135	101	143	63	15	570	239	478
1990	7,458	638	612	564	626	661	722	745	678	574	405	312	252	220	300	122	29	1,063	469	931
1992	8,401	740	665	666	629	749	774	824	767	667	485	362	288	249	356	146	34	1,206	498	1,005
Male	4,100	379	338	338	323	383	382	400	366	311	230	174	133	107	155	66	14	613	257	513
Female	4,301	361	326	328	306	366	392	424	401	357	255	188	155	141	200	80	20	592	242	491
PERCENT																				
Total, 1992	100.0	7.6	7.2	7.1	6.7	7.5	7.9	8.7	8.7	7.4	6.0	4.7	4.1	4.1	7.2	4.1	1.3	12.9	5.4	10.2
White	100.0	7.3	6.9	6.8	6.4	7.2	7.8	8.7	8.3	7.4	6.2	4.9	4.3	4.3	7.7	4.5	1.4	12.4	5.1	9.8
Black	100.0	9.8	8.8	8.8	8.3	8.5	8.6	8.8	8.1	6.8	4.9	4.0	3.3	3.1	4.9	2.5	0.8	15.9	6.7	11.8
American Indian, Eskimo, Aleut	100.0	10.3	10.1	10.0	8.7	8.7	8.5	8.7	7.8	6.7	5.2	3.9	3.1	2.6	3.7	1.7	0.6	18.2	7.2	12.0
Asian, Pacific Islander	100.0	8.8	7.9	7.9	7.5	8.9	9.2	9.8	9.1	7.9	5.8	4.3	3.4	3.0	4.2	1.7	0.4	14.4	5.9	12.0

Source: U.S. Bureau of the Census, *Current Population Reports*, P25-1095; and unpublished data.

No. 21. Resident Population, by Age and Sex and Hispanic Origin: 1980 to 1992

[In thousands, except percent. As of April, except 1992 as of July. See headnote, table 17 and, for 1980 data, footnote 4, table 1. Hispanic persons may be of any race]

YEAR AND SEX	Total, all years	Under 5 years	5-9 years	10-14 years	15-19 years	20-24 years	25-29 years	30-34 years	35-39 years	40-44 years	45-49 years	50-54 years	55-59 years	60-64 years	65-74 years	75-84 years	85 years and over	5-13 years	14-17 years	18-24 years
HISPANIC ORIGIN																				
1980	14,609	1,663	1,537	1,475	1,606	1,586	1,376	1,129	854	712	622	564	454	321	457	203	49	2,715	1,251	2,240
1990	22,354	2,467	2,178	1,989	2,084	2,320	2,337	2,045	1,642	1,276	936	750	633	550	715	339	91	3,782	1,575	3,215
1992	24,238	2,809	2,325	2,169	2,071	2,344	2,447	2,268	1,867	1,460	1,084	824	681	595	812	376	110	4,083	1,633	3,189
Male	12,334	1,437	1,187	1,060	1,109	1,275	1,314	1,188	957	731	532	397	322	275	356	145	38	2,086	838	1,718
Female	11,904	1,372	1,138	1,060	997	1,069	1,133	1,080	910	728	552	427	359	320	457	231	71	1,998	795	1,471
NON-HISPANIC WHITE																				
1980	180,906	11,842	12,262	13,703	16,166	16,574	15,358	14,091	11,315	9,437	9,104	9,824	9,963	8,775	13,614	6,863	2,014	23,126	12,313	23,267
1990	188,300	12,721	12,516	11,854	12,447	13,522	15,508	16,332	15,162	13,839	10,971	9,057	8,548	8,871	15,511	8,767	2,675	22,106	9,225	19,008
1992	190,802	12,904	12,574	12,464	11,730	13,294	14,291	16,406	15,906	14,530	12,235	9,601	8,446	8,605	15,715	9,229	2,871	22,665	9,397	17,999
Male	93,084	6,624	6,459	6,406	6,029	6,741	7,172	8,224	7,967	7,253	6,069	4,715	4,094	4,080	6,961	3,507	785	11,645	4,845	9,146
Female	97,718	6,280	6,115	6,057	5,701	6,553	7,120	8,182	7,939	7,277	6,167	4,886	4,352	4,525	8,755	5,724	2,086	11,019	4,552	8,854
BLACK																				
1980	26,142	2,399	2,455	2,635	2,944	2,689	2,292	1,865	1,438	1,233	1,127	1,114	1,024	861	1,327	582	157	4,530	2,331	3,862
1990	29,273	2,799	2,597	2,525	2,605	2,528	2,649	2,600	2,265	1,811	1,362	1,137	1,008	945	1,465	757	219	4,639	1,976	3,640
1992	30,316	2,942	2,653	2,666	2,530	2,559	2,577	2,666	2,456	2,056	1,482	1,211	1,024	952	1,521	785	234	4,809	2,023	3,577
Male	14,324	1,487	1,344	1,349	1,279	1,253	1,224	1,242	1,141	948	674	544	451	409	628	282	69	2,435	1,028	1,763
Female	15,992	1,455	1,309	1,318	1,251	1,306	1,354	1,424	1,315	1,109	808	667	573	543	892	503	165	2,374	994	1,814
AMERICAN INDIAN, ESKIMO, ALEUT																				
1980	1,326	136	135	145	158	138	116	100	79	66	55	49	43	32	46	20	6	249	127	199
1990	1,796	185	179	170	165	151	160	156	138	117	90	72	58	48	68	31	9	317	131	217
1992	1,850	181	183	184	160	157	154	159	145	125	98	76	61	50	72	35	11	332	133	219
Male	911	92	93	93	81	81	77	77	70	60	48	36	29	23	32	14	4	168	68	112
Female	939	89	90	91	79	76	77	81	75	65	51	40	32	27	39	21	7	164	66	107
ASIAN, PACIFIC ISLANDER																				
1980	3,563	308	311	285	294	332	378	376	279	221	182	158	131	98	136	60	14	540	226	455
1990	6,988	586	566	522	581	611	673	700	640	545	384	297	240	210	287	116	27	984	436	862
1992	7,876	676	614	618	586	695	720	774	725	634	461	345	274	238	342	140	33	1,116	463	934
Male	3,839	346	313	314	301	355	354	375	346	295	219	166	127	102	150	64	13	567	238	477
Female	4,036	330	302	304	285	341	366	399	379	339	243	179	147	135	192	76	19	549	225	458
1992, PERCENT																				
Hispanic origin	100.0	11.6	9.6	8.9	8.5	9.7	10.1	9.4	7.7	6.0	4.5	3.4	2.8	2.5	3.4	1.6	0.5	16.8	6.7	13.2
Non-Hispanic:																				
White	100.0	6.8	6.6	6.5	6.1	7.0	7.5	8.6	8.3	7.6	6.4	5.0	4.4	4.5	8.2	4.8	1.5	11.9	4.9	9.4
Black	100.0	9.7	8.8	8.8	8.3	8.4	8.5	8.8	8.1	6.8	4.9	4.0	3.4	3.1	5.0	2.6	0.8	15.9	6.7	11.8
American Indian, Eskimo, Aleut	100.0	9.8	9.9	9.9	8.6	8.5	8.3	8.6	7.8	6.8	5.3	4.1	3.3	2.7	3.9	1.9	0.6	17.9	7.2	11.8
Asian, Pacific Islander	100.0	8.6	7.8	7.8	7.4	8.8	9.1	9.8	9.2	8.0	5.9	4.4	3.5	3.0	4.3	1.8	0.4	14.2	5.9	11.9

Source: U.S. Bureau of the Census, Current Population Reports, P25-1095; and unpublished data.

No. 22. Resident Population, by Race, Hispanic Origin, and Single Years of Age: 1992

[In thousands, except as indicated. As of July 1. Resident population. For derivation of estimates, see text, section 1]

AGE	Total	RACE				Hispanic origin [1]	NOT OF HISPANIC ORIGIN			
		White	Black	American Indian, Eskimo, Aleut	Asian, Pacific Islander		White	Black	American Indian, Eskimo, Aleut	Asian, Pacific Islander
Total	255,082	212,912	31,635	2,134	8,401	24,238	190,802	30,316	1,850	7,876
Under 5 yrs. old ..	19,512	15,454	3,099	219	740	2,809	12,904	2,942	181	676
Under 1 yr. old..	3,984	3,140	640	42	162	625	2,572	606	34	146
1 yr. old	3,978	3,157	623	41	157	594	2,616	592	33	143
2 yrs. old	3,959	3,146	623	46	144	564	2,634	591	38	132
3 yrs. old	3,813	3,016	613	46	139	518	2,547	582	38	127
4 yrs. old	3,778	2,995	601	44	138	509	2,535	571	37	127
5-9 yrs. old.....	18,349	14,688	2,782	215	665	2,325	12,574	2,653	183	614
5 yrs. old	3,722	2,967	579	43	133	485	2,527	551	36	122
6 yrs. old	3,705	2,973	557	43	132	478	2,538	531	36	122
7 yrs. old	3,697	2,967	555	43	132	463	2,545	530	36	122
8 yrs. old	3,450	2,764	516	41	128	431	2,372	493	35	119
9 yrs. old	3,776	3,017	574	45	140	467	2,592	548	39	130
10-14 yrs. old....	18,100	14,438	2,782	214	666	2,169	12,464	2,666	184	618
10 yrs. old.....	3,795	3,035	577	44	139	459	2,617	552	38	129
11 yrs. old.....	3,665	2,934	552	44	137	450	2,523	528	37	127
12 yrs. old.....	3,670	2,917	575	44	135	434	2,521	552	38	125
13 yrs. old.....	3,526	2,807	546	42	130	415	2,430	524	36	121
14 yrs. old....	3,443	2,746	532	40	125	410	2,373	510	35	116
15-19 yrs. old	17,074	13,622	2,638	185	629	2,068	11,730	2,530	160	586
15 yrs. old.....	3,448	2,741	544	39	124	407	2,370	522	34	115
16 yrs. old.....	3,317	2,649	509	37	122	403	2,281	488	32	113
17 yrs. old....	3,440	2,751	524	37	127	413	2,373	503	32	119
18 yrs. old.....	3,304	2,640	508	34	121	400	2,273	488	30	113
19 yrs. old.....	3,565	2,840	553	37	135	445	2,432	530	32	126
20-24 yrs. old	19,050	15,430	2,686	185	749	2,344	13,294	2,559	157	695
20 yrs. old.....	3,757	3,012	565	37	142	453	2,598	542	32	133
21 yrs. old.....	3,983	3,206	579	40	158	478	2,771	553	34	147
22 yrs. old.....	3,871	3,150	529	38	154	468	2,724	504	32	143
23 yrs. old.....	3,713	3,031	499	35	147	467	2,606	474	30	136
24 yrs. old.....	3,726	3,030	513	35	148	478	2,594	487	30	137
25-29 yrs. old	20,189	16,520	2,714	181	774	2,447	14,291	2,577	154	720
25 yrs. old....	3,758	3,065	512	36	146	482	2,626	486	30	135
26 yrs. old....	3,833	3,117	531	35	149	489	2,672	504	30	138
27 yrs. old....	4,085	3,343	551	37	155	496	2,890	523	31	145
28 yrs. old....	4,015	3,309	523	35	148	468	2,882	497	29	139
29 yrs. old....	4,498	3,686	597	40	175	512	3,221	567	34	164
30-34 yrs. old	22,273	18,471	2,794	185	824	2,268	16,406	2,666	159	774
30 yrs. old....	4,487	3,714	574	38	162	478	3,278	547	32	152
31 yrs. old....	4,405	3,652	549	37	167	474	3,219	523	32	156
32 yrs. old....	4,452	3,688	560	37	167	454	3,275	535	32	156
33 yrs. old....	4,379	3,640	543	35	161	427	3,250	519	31	151
34 yrs. old....	4,551	3,778	568	37	168	434	3,384	542	32	159
35-39 yrs. old	21,099	17,601	2,565	166	767	1,867	15,906	2,456	145	725
35 yrs. old....	4,501	3,743	560	36	163	410	3,371	536	31	153
36 yrs. old....	4,237	3,530	518	33	156	393	3,173	495	29	147
37 yrs. old....	4,247	3,535	523	33	156	378	3,192	501	29	147
38 yrs. old....	3,899	3,268	462	30	138	332	2,967	443	27	131
39 yrs. old.....	4,214	3,525	502	33	155	355	3,203	481	29	147
40-44 yrs. old	18,805	15,857	2,139	142	667	1,460	14,530	2,056	125	634
40 yrs. old....	4,011	3,371	468	31	141	321	3,080	449	27	133
41 yrs. old....	3,753	3,146	438	29	140	309	2,865	420	26	133
42 yrs. old....	3,713	3,121	430	28	134	291	2,857	414	24	128
43 yrs. old....	3,599	3,033	404	28	134	270	2,788	389	25	128
44 yrs. old....	3,728	3,186	399	26	118	269	2,941	384	23	112

See footnotes at end of table.

No. 22. Resident Population, by Race, Hispanic Origin, and Single Years of Age: 1992—Continued

[See headnote, page 22]

AGE	Total	RACE					NOT OF HISPANIC ORIGIN			
		White	Black	American Indian, Eskimo, Aleut	Asian, Pacific Islander	Hispanic origin [1]	White	Black	American Indian, Eskimo, Aleut	Asian, Pacific Islander
45-49 yrs. old	15,361	13,225	1,541	110	485	1,084	12,235	1,482	98	461
45 yrs. old.	3,912	3,399	373	26	114	260	3,162	359	23	108
46 yrs. old.	2,758	2,355	283	22	98	219	2,155	272	19	93
47 yrs. old.	2,851	2,422	308	22	99	210	2,230	296	19	94
48 yrs. old.	2,712	2,343	267	19	83	189	2,169	257	17	79
49 yrs. old.	3,130	2,706	310	22	91	206	2,519	299	20	87
50-54 yrs. old	12,056	10,354	1,256	84	362	824	9,601	1,211	76	345
50 yrs. old.	2,663	2,283	279	19	81	180	2,119	269	17	77
51 yrs. old.	2,436	2,095	249	17	76	170	1,939	240	16	72
52 yrs. old.	2,328	1,997	244	16	71	162	1,849	235	15	67
53 yrs. old.	2,316	1,994	240	16	67	158	1,849	231	14	64
54 yrs. old.	2,314	1,985	245	16	68	154	1,844	236	15	65
55-59 yrs. old	10,487	9,073	1,059	67	288	681	8,446	1,024	61	274
55 yrs. old.	2,137	1,830	228	15	64	142	1,700	221	13	61
56 yrs. old.	2,160	1,868	219	14	59	144	1,736	212	12	56
57 yrs. old.	2,205	1,912	221	14	58	144	1,779	213	13	56
58 yrs. old.	1,927	1,681	184	12	51	123	1,568	178	11	48
59 yrs. old.	2,057	1,781	207	13	57	128	1,663	200	12	54
60-64 yrs. old	10,441	9,155	982	55	249	595	8,605	952	50	238
60 yrs. old.	2,026	1,764	199	12	51	120	1,653	193	11	49
61 yrs. old.	2,075	1,819	194	11	51	124	1,705	188	10	48
62 yrs. old.	2,085	1,824	199	11	51	120	1,714	193	10	48
63 yrs. old.	2,081	1,835	188	10	47	116	1,727	183	9	45
64 yrs. old.	2,175	1,913	202	11	49	115	1,807	197	10	47
65-69 yrs. old	9,977	8,847	878	45	208	478	8,405	854	41	199
65 yrs. old.	2,085	1,830	199	10	46	105	1,734	193	9	44
66 yrs. old.	2,020	1,782	187	9	43	101	1,689	182	8	41
67 yrs. old.	2,034	1,808	177	9	41	97	1,718	172	8	39
68 yrs. old.	1,931	1,727	158	8	39	90	1,643	153	8	37
69 yrs. old.	1,907	1,701	158	8	39	86	1,621	154	8	38
70-74 yrs. old	8,483	7,621	681	33	148	334	7,311	666	31	142
70 yrs. old.	1,905	1,705	157	8	36	80	1,631	153	7	34
71 yrs. old.	1,837	1,650	147	7	33	75	1,580	143	7	31
72 yrs. old.	1,698	1,522	138	7	31	67	1,460	135	6	30
73 yrs. old.	1,561	1,406	123	6	26	58	1,352	121	6	25
74 yrs. old.	1,483	1,338	117	5	23	53	1,288	114	5	22
75-79 yrs. old	6,415	5,798	499	23	95	229	5,584	489	21	91
75 yrs. old.	1,419	1,281	111	5	22	50	1,235	109	5	21
76 yrs. old.	1,344	1,222	98	5	20	48	1,177	95	4	19
77 yrs. old.	1,284	1,162	97	5	20	46	1,119	95	4	19
78 yrs. old.	1,221	1,104	96	4	17	44	1,063	94	4	16
79 yrs. old.	1,148	1,029	98	5	16	42	990	96	4	16
80-84 yrs. old	4,150	3,783	302	14	51	147	3,646	296	13	48
80 yrs. old.	996	907	72	4	13	36	874	71	3	12
81 yrs. old.	907	825	67	3	11	33	794	66	3	11
82 yrs. old.	820	747	61	3	10	29	720	60	3	9
83 yrs. old.	752	689	51	2	9	26	665	50	2	8
84 yrs. old.	676	615	50	2	8	23	593	49	2	8
85-89 yrs. old	2,162	1,980	152	7	22	74	1,910	150	7	21
90-94 yrs. old	834	761	61	3	9	27	735	60	3	9
95-99 yrs. old	217	197	18	1	2	7	190	17	1	2
100 yrs. old and over	45	37	7	-	1	2	35	7	-	1
Median age (yr.) . .	33.4	34.4	28.5	26.4	29.9	25.8	35.5	28.6	27.0	30.2

- Represents or rounds to zero.   [1] Persons of Hispanic origin may be of any race.

Source: U.S. Bureau of the Census, unpublished data.

Population

No. 23. Projections of Resident Population, by Age, Sex, and Race: 1995 to 2025

[As of July 1. Data are for middle series; for assumptions, see table 3]

AGE, SEX, AND RACE	POPULATION (1,000)					PERCENT DISTRIBUTION		
	1995	2000	2005	2010	2025	2000	2010	2025
Total	**263,434**	**276,241**	**288,286**	**300,431**	**338,338**	**100.0**	**100.0**	**100.0**
Under 5 years old	20,181	19,431	19,333	20,017	22,372	7.0	6.7	6.6
5 to 13 years old	34,262	36,547	36,843	36,213	40,455	13.2	12.1	12.0
14 to 17 years old	14,591	15,811	16,947	17,388	17,897	5.7	5.8	5.3
18 to 24 years old	25,465	25,911	28,238	30,220	30,585	9.4	10.1	9.0
25 to 34 years old	41,670	38,237	36,792	38,179	44,299	13.8	12.7	13.1
35 to 44 years old	42,150	45,123	43,075	39,659	42,590	16.3	13.2	12.6
45 to 54 years old	30,224	36,170	41,219	44,099	37,534	13.1	14.7	11.1
55 to 64 years old	21,241	23,690	28,870	34,552	40,455	8.6	11.5	12.0
65 to 74 years old	18,963	18,551	18,623	20,978	35,361	6.7	7.0	10.5
75 to 84 years old	11,087	12,438	13,265	13,157	19,274	4.5	4.4	5.7
85 years old and over	3,598	4,333	5,082	5,969	7,515	1.6	2.0	2.2
Male	128,685	135,101	141,121	147,187	166,012	48.9	49.0	49.1
Female	134,749	141,140	147,165	153,245	172,326	51.1	51.0	50.9
White, total	**218,334**	**226,267**	**233,343**	**240,297**	**261,531**	**100.0**	**100.0**	**100.0**
Under 5 years old	15,841	14,945	14,587	14,893	16,117	6.6	6.2	6.2
5 to 13 years old	27,167	28,534	28,244	27,184	29,258	12.6	11.3	11.2
14 to 17 years old	11,544	12,409	13,078	13,203	12,874	5.5	5.5	4.9
18 to 24 years old	20,339	20,477	22,149	23,396	22,396	9.0	9.7	8.6
25 to 34 years old	34,027	30,534	28,900	29,715	33,202	13.5	12.4	12.7
35 to 44 years old	35,081	37,139	34,879	31,394	32,634	16.4	13.1	12.5
45 to 54 years old	25,852	30,535	34,313	36,330	29,259	13.5	15.1	11.2
55 to 64 years old	18,355	20,339	24,688	29,213	32,913	9.0	12.2	12.6
65 to 74 years old	16,822	16,220	16,058	17,998	29,634	7.2	7.5	11.3
75 to 84 years old	10,035	11,219	11,866	11,612	16,726	5.0	4.8	6.4
85 years old and over	3,271	3,917	4,581	5,357	6,518	1.7	2.2	2.5
Male	107,140	111,245	114,911	118,505	129,322	49.2	49.3	49.4
Female	111,195	115,022	118,433	121,792	132,209	50.8	50.7	50.6
Black, total	**33,117**	**35,469**	**37,793**	**40,224**	**48,005**	**100.0**	**100.0**	**100.0**
Under 5 years old	3,243	3,214	3,310	3,518	4,102	9.1	8.7	8.5
5 to 13 years old	5,285	5,836	6,025	6,114	7,238	16.5	15.2	15.1
14 to 17 years old	2,285	2,431	2,741	2,842	3,182	6.9	7.1	6.6
18 to 24 years old	3,764	3,900	4,222	4,687	5,140	11.0	11.7	10.7
25 to 34 years old	5,475	5,235	5,176	5,409	6,698	14.8	13.4	14.0
35 to 44 years old	5,088	5,610	5,506	5,268	5,933	15.8	13.1	12.4
45 to 54 years old	3,122	3,954	4,811	5,297	4,956	11.1	13.2	10.3
55 to 64 years old	2,124	2,370	2,880	3,654	4,858	6.7	9.1	10.1
65 to 74 years old	1,629	1,686	1,772	1,997	3,815	4.8	5.0	7.9
75 to 84 years old	835	907	981	1,025	1,547	2.6	2.5	3.2
85 years old and over	268	326	367	413	535	0.9	1.0	1.1
Male	15,697	16,802	17,886	19,027	22,713	47.4	47.3	47.3
Female	17,420	18,667	19,906	21,197	25,291	52.6	52.7	52.7
American Indian, Eskimo, Aleut, total	**2,226**	**2,380**	**2,543**	**2,719**	**3,278**	**100.0**	**100.0**	**100.0**
Under 5 years old	222	215	231	252	287	9.0	9.3	8.8
5 to 13 years old	410	428	420	435	533	18.0	16.0	16.3
14 to 17 years old	167	192	210	198	243	8.1	7.3	7.4
18 to 24 years old	256	271	312	342	364	11.4	12.6	11.1
25 to 34 years old	364	356	363	399	473	15.0	14.7	14.4
35 to 44 years old	327	352	345	340	432	14.8	12.5	13.2
45 to 54 years old	212	256	294	317	313	10.8	11.7	9.5
55 to 64 years old	129	149	180	218	268	6.3	8.0	8.2
65 to 74 years old	84	90	102	118	202	3.8	4.3	6.2
75 to 84 years old	41	50	58	63	104	2.1	2.3	3.2
85 years old and over	14	21	28	36	59	0.9	1.3	1.8
Male	1,103	1,177	1,256	1,342	1,614	49.5	49.4	49.2
Female	1,123	1,203	1,287	1,377	1,664	50.5	50.6	50.8
Asian, Pacific Islander, total	**9,756**	**12,125**	**14,608**	**17,191**	**25,524**	**100.0**	**100.0**	**100.0**
Under 5 years old	876	1,056	1,205	1,354	1,866	8.7	7.9	7.3
5 to 13 years old	1,400	1,751	2,153	2,479	3,425	14.4	14.4	13.4
14 to 17 years old	594	779	918	1,143	1,600	6.4	6.6	6.3
18 to 24 years old	1,105	1,262	1,553	1,795	2,685	10.4	10.4	10.5
25 to 34 years old	1,805	2,112	2,353	2,656	3,927	17.4	15.4	15.4
35 to 44 years old	1,655	2,023	2,344	2,657	3,591	16.7	15.5	14.1
45 to 54 years old	1,038	1,425	1,802	2,155	3,005	11.8	12.5	11.8
55 to 64 years old	633	833	1,120	1,468	2,417	6.9	8.5	9.5
65 to 74 years old	429	555	692	864	1,710	4.6	5.0	6.7
75 to 84 years old	178	261	360	458	897	2.2	2.7	3.5
85 years old and over	44	69	106	163	402	0.6	0.9	1.6
Male	4,745	5,877	7,068	8,312	12,363	48.5	48.4	48.4
Female	5,011	6,248	7,540	8,878	13,161	51.5	51.6	51.6

Source: U.S. Bureau of the Census, *Current Population Reports*, P25-1104.

No. 24. Projections of Hispanic and Non-Hispanic Populations, by Age and Sex: 1995 to 2025

[As of **July 1**. Resident population. Data are for middle series; for assumptions, see table 3]

AGE AND SEX	POPULATION (1,000)					PERCENT DISTRIBUTION		
	1995	2000	2005	2010	2025	2000	2010	2025
Hispanic origin, total [1]	**26,798**	**31,166**	**35,702**	**40,525**	**56,927**	**100.0**	**100.0**	**100.0**
Under 5 years old	3,090	3,293	3,579	3,983	5,337	10.6	9.8	9.4
5 to 13 years old	4,560	5,542	6,196	6,651	9,020	17.8	16.4	15.8
14 to 17 years old	1,817	2,102	2,582	2,909	3,750	6.7	7.2	6.6
18 to 24 years old	3,204	3,547	4,070	4,863	6,300	11.4	12.0	11.1
25 to 34 years old	5,021	5,145	5,301	5,834	8,464	16.5	14.4	14.9
35 to 44 years old	3,894	4,830	5,396	5,519	7,043	15.5	13.6	12.4
45 to 54 years old	2,274	3,046	3,930	4,828	5,668	9.8	11.9	10.0
55 to 64 years old	1,407	1,734	2,281	3,020	5,266	5.6	7.5	9.3
65 to 74 years old	955	1,137	1,333	1,637	3,609	3.6	4.0	6.3
75 to 84 years old	436	586	767	914	1,744	1.9	2.3	3.1
85 years old and over	141	203	267	367	725	0.7	0.9	1.3
Male	13,610	15,777	18,022	20,410	28,531	50.6	50.4	50.1
Female	13,188	15,388	17,679	20,115	28,396	49.4	49.6	49.9
Non-Hispanic White, total	**193,900**	**197,872**	**200,842**	**203,441**	**209,863**	**100.0**	**100.0**	**100.0**
Under 5 years old	13,020	11,936	11,326	11,273	11,267	6.0	5.5	5.4
5 to 13 years old	23,032	23,506	22,605	21,141	21,096	11.9	10.4	10.1
14 to 17 years old	9,892	10,507	10,751	10,564	9,494	5.3	5.2	4.5
18 to 24 years old	17,413	17,245	18,458	19,001	16,691	8.7	9.3	8.0
25 to 34 years old	29,455	25,852	24,077	24,421	25,531	13.1	12.0	12.2
35 to 44 years old	31,542	32,741	29,965	26,370	26,262	16.5	13.0	12.5
45 to 54 years old	23,777	27,760	30,735	31,928	24,094	14.0	15.7	11.5
55 to 64 years old	17,064	18,751	22,605	26,459	28,104	9.5	13.0	13.4
65 to 74 years old	15,938	15,174	14,837	16,503	26,348	7.7	8.1	12.6
75 to 84 years old	9,629	10,674	11,153	10,768	15,129	5.4	5.3	7.2
85 years old and over	3,138	3,726	4,331	5,013	5,846	1.9	2.5	2.8
Male	94,716	96,846	98,472	99,903	103,362	48.9	49.1	49.3
Female	99,184	101,025	102,370	103,538	106,501	51.1	50.9	50.7
Non-Hispanic Black, total	**31,648**	**33,741**	**35,793**	**37,930**	**44,705**	**100.0**	**100.0**	**100.0**
Under 5 years old	3,076	3,033	3,109	3,289	3,790	9.0	8.7	8.5
5 to 13 years old	5,027	5,519	5,678	5,735	6,704	16.4	15.1	15.0
14 to 17 years old	2,187	2,312	2,587	2,676	2,955	6.9	7.1	6.6
18 to 24 years old	3,593	3,705	3,990	4,400	4,769	11.0	11.6	10.7
25 to 34 years old	5,196	4,953	4,886	5,084	6,214	14.7	13.4	13.9
35 to 44 years old	4,863	5,338	5,207	4,967	5,526	15.8	13.1	12.4
45 to 54 years old	2,996	3,781	4,584	5,023	4,647	11.2	13.2	10.4
55 to 64 years old	2,049	2,274	2,752	3,480	4,561	6.7	9.2	10.2
65 to 74 years old	1,583	1,626	1,698	1,903	3,593	4.8	5.0	8.0
75 to 84 years old	814	880	945	978	1,447	2.6	2.6	3.2
85 years old and over	263	319	356	397	500	0.9	1.0	1.1
Male	14,958	15,939	16,891	17,890	21,089	47.2	47.2	47.2
Female	16,689	17,802	18,901	20,040	23,616	52.8	52.8	52.8
Non-Hispanic American Indian, Eskimo, Aleut, total	**1,927**	**2,055**	**2,190**	**2,336**	**2,796**	**100.0**	**100.0**	**100.0**
Under 5 years old	188	185	198	214	246	9.0	9.2	8.8
5 to 13 years old	347	361	359	372	453	17.6	15.9	16.2
14 to 17 years old	144	164	176	170	205	8.0	7.3	7.3
18 to 24 years old	222	232	265	286	310	11.3	12.2	11.1
25 to 34 years old	310	304	313	341	403	14.8	14.6	14.4
35 to 44 years old	284	302	293	290	363	14.7	12.4	13.0
45 to 54 years old	189	225	255	272	269	10.9	11.6	9.6
55 to 64 years old	117	134	161	191	226	6.5	8.2	8.1
65 to 74 years old	76	82	91	106	174	4.0	4.5	6.2
75 to 84 years old	38	46	53	58	92	2.2	2.5	3.3
85 years old and over	13	20	27	34	55	1.0	1.5	2.0
Male	948	1,010	1,075	1,146	1,370	49.1	49.1	49.0
Female	979	1,045	1,115	1,190	1,426	50.9	50.9	51.0
Non-Hispanic Asian, Pacific Islander, total	**9,161**	**11,407**	**13,759**	**16,199**	**24,046**	**100.0**	**100.0**	**100.0**
Under 5 years old	807	984	1,122	1,258	1,732	8.6	7.8	7.2
5 to 13 years old	1,295	1,617	2,006	2,314	3,184	14.2	14.3	13.2
14 to 17 years old	552	727	850	1,070	1,492	6.4	6.6	6.2
18 to 24 years old	1,034	1,181	1,454	1,670	2,515	10.4	10.3	10.5
25 to 34 years old	1,688	1,983	2,215	2,499	3,687	17.4	15.4	15.3
35 to 44 years old	1,567	1,914	2,214	2,513	3,394	16.8	15.5	14.1
45 to 54 years old	988	1,357	1,715	2,048	2,857	11.9	12.6	11.9
55 to 64 years old	604	795	1,071	1,403	2,298	7.0	8.7	9.6
65 to 74 years old	412	532	663	829	1,637	4.7	5.1	6.8
75 to 84 years old	170	251	346	441	861	2.2	2.7	3.6
85 years old and over	42	66	102	157	389	0.6	1.0	1.6
Male	4,453	5,529	6,660	7,838	11,660	48.5	48.4	48.5
Female	4,708	5,879	7,099	8,361	12,386	51.5	51.6	51.5

[1] Persons of Hispanic origin may be of any race.

Source: U.S. Bureau of the Census, *Current Population Reports*, P25-1104.

Population

No. 25. Centers of Population: 1790 to 1990

[The mean center of population is that point at which an imaginary flat, weightless, and rigid map of the United States would balance if weights of identical value were placed on it so that each weight represented the location of one person on the date of the census. The median center is located at the intersection of two median lines, a north–south line constructed so that half of the Nation's population lives east and half lives west of it, and an east–west line selected so that half of the Nation's population lives north and half lives south of it]

YEAR	MEDIAN CENTER		MEAN CENTER		
	Latitude-N	Longitude-W	Latitude-N	Longitude-W	Approximate location
1790 (August 2)	(NA)	(NA)	39 16 30	76 11 12	In Kent County, MD, 23 miles E of Baltimore
1850 (June 1) ..	(NA)	(NA)	38 59 00	81 19 00	In Wirt County, WV, 23 miles SE of Parkersburg
1900 (June 1) ..	40 03 32	84 49 01	39 09 36	85 48 54	In Bartholomew County, IN, 6 miles SE of Columbus
1950 (April 1) ..	40 00 12	84 56 51	38 50 21	88 09 33	In Richland County, IL, 8 miles NNW of Olney
1960 (April 1) ..	39 56 25	85 16 60	38 35 58	88 12 35	In Clinton County, IL, 6.5 miles NW of Centralia
1970 (April 1) ..	39 47 43	85 31 43	38 27 47	89 42 22	In St. Clair Country, IL, 5.3 miles ESE of Mascoutah
1980 (April 1) ..	39 18 60	86 08 15	38 08 13	90 34 26	In Jefferson Country, MO, .25 mile W of DeSoto
1990 (April 1) ..	38 57 55	86 31 53	37 52 20	91 12 55	In Crawford Country, MO, 10 miles SE of Steelville

NA Not available.
Source: U.S. Bureau of the Census, unpublished data.

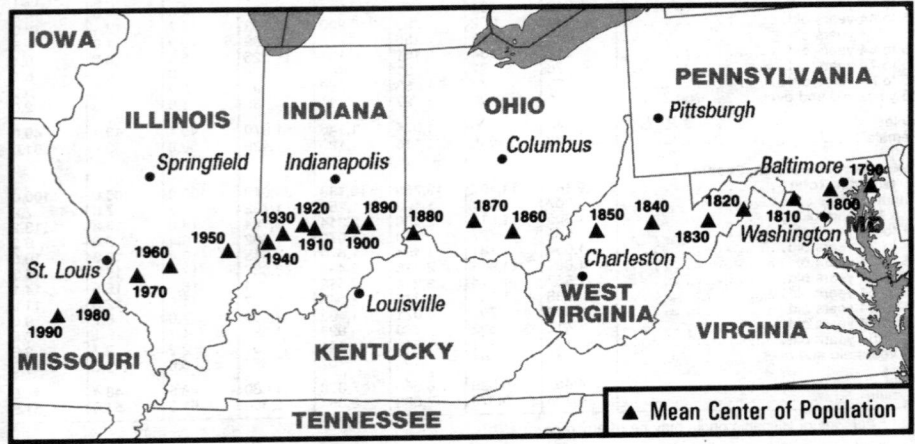

Source: U.S. Bureau of the Census, *1990 Census of Population and Housing, Population and Housing Unit Counts, United States* (1990 CPH-2-1).

No. 26. Resident Population—States: 1970 to 1993

[In thousands. As of **July 1**; except **1970, 1980, and 1990**, as of **April 1**. Insofar as possible, population shown for all years is that of present area of State. See *Historical Statistics, Colonial Times to 1970*, series A 172, for population by regions, and A 195 for population by States]

REGION, DIVISION, AND STATE	1970	1980 [1]	1985	1986	1987	1988	1989	1990	1991	1992	1993
U.S.	203,302	226,546	237,924	240,133	242,289	244,499	246,819	248,710	252,137	255,078	257,908
Northeast.	49,061	49,135	49,869	50,071	50,302	50,584	50,757	50,809	50,970	51,121	51,355
N.E.	11,848	12,348	12,741	12,833	12,951	13,085	13,182	13,207	13,201	13,196	13,230
ME.	994	1,125	1,163	1,170	1,185	1,204	1,220	1,228	1,236	1,236	1,239
NH.	738	921	.997	1,025	1,054	1,083	1,105	1,109	1,108	1,115	1,125
VT.	445	511	530	534	540	550	558	563	568	571	576
MA.	5,689	5,737	5,881	5,903	5,935	5,980	6,015	6,016	5,995	5,993	6,012
RI	950	947	969	977	990	996	1,001	1,003	1,004	1,001	1,000
CT	3,032	3,108	3,201	3,224	3,247	3,272	3,283	3,287	3,290	3,279	3,277
M.A.	37,213	36,787	37,128	37,238	37,350	37,499	37,575	37,602	37,769	37,925	38,125
NY	18,241	17,558	17,792	17,833	17,869	17,941	17,983	17,990	18,047	18,109	18,197
NJ	7,171	7,365	7,566	7,622	7,671	7,712	7,726	7,730	7,773	7,820	7,879
PA	11,801	11,864	11,771	11,783	11,811	11,846	11,866	11,882	11,949	11,995	12,048
Midwest	56,589	58,866	58,820	58,848	59,018	59,254	59,468	59,669	60,180	60,639	61,070
E.N.C.	40,262	41,682	41,418	41,455	41,590	41,721	41,873	42,009	42,392	42,719	43,017
OH.	10,657	10,798	10,735	10,730	10,760	10,799	10,829	10,847	10,940	11,021	11,091
IN	5,195	5,490	5,459	5,454	5,473	5,492	5,524	5,544	5,607	5,658	5,713
IL	11,110	11,427	11,400	11,387	11,391	11,390	11,410	11,431	11,525	11,613	11,697
MI	8,882	9,262	9,076	9,128	9,187	9,218	9,253	9,295	9,375	9,434	9,478
WI	4,418	4,706	4,748	4,756	4,778	4,822	4,857	4,892	4,947	4,993	5,038
W.N.C.	16,327	17,183	17,402	17,393	17,428	17,533	17,595	17,660	17,788	17,920	18,054
MN.	3,806	4,076	4,184	4,205	4,235	4,296	4,338	4,375	4,426	4,468	4,517
IA	2,825	2,914	2,830	2,792	2,767	2,768	2,771	2,777	2,790	2,803	2,814
MO	4,678	4,917	5,000	5,023	5,057	5,082	5,096	5,117	5,156	5,191	5,234
ND.	618	653	677	669	661	655	646	639	633	634	635
SD.	666	691	698	696	696	698	697	696	702	708	715
NE.	1,485	1,570	1,585	1,574	1,567	1,571	1,575	1,578	1,590	1,601	1,607
KS.	2,249	2,364	2,427	2,433	2,445	2,462	2,473	2,478	2,491	2,515	2,531
South.	62,812	75,372	81,409	82,428	83,208	83,890	84,700	85,446	86,920	88,185	89,438
S.A.	30,678	36,959	40,159	40,863	41,619	42,318	43,008	43,567	44,436	45,092	45,738
DE.	548	594	618	628	637	648	658	666	681	691	700
MD.	3,924	4,217	4,413	4,487	4,566	4,658	4,727	4,781	4,863	4,917	4,965
DC.	757	638	635	638	637	630	624	607	594	585	578
VA.	4,651	5,347	5,715	5,812	5,932	6,037	6,120	6,187	6,288	6,394	6,491
WV	1,744	1,950	1,907	1,882	1,858	1,830	1,807	1,793	1,799	1,809	1,820
NC.	5,084	5,882	6,254	6,322	6,404	6,481	6,565	6,629	6,749	6,836	6,945
SC.	2,591	3,122	3,303	3,343	3,381	3,412	3,457	3,487	3,561	3,603	3,643
GA.	4,588	5,463	5,963	6,085	6,208	6,316	6,411	6,478	6,628	6,773	6,917
FL.	6,791	9,746	11,351	11,668	11,997	12,306	12,638	12,938	13,273	13,483	13,679
E.S.C.	12,808	14,666	14,971	15,012	15,070	15,107	15,136	15,176	15,350	15,532	15,717
KY.	3,221	3,661	3,695	3,688	3,683	3,680	3,677	3,685	3,715	3,754	3,789
TN.	3,926	4,591	4,715	4,739	4,783	4,822	4,854	4,877	4,952	5,025	5,099
AL.	3,444	3,894	3,973	3,992	4,015	4,024	4,030	4,041	4,090	4,138	4,187
MS.	2,217	2,521	2,588	2,594	2,589	2,580	2,574	2,573	2,592	2,615	2,643
W.S.C.	19,326	23,747	26,279	26,553	26,518	26,466	26,556	26,703	27,134	27,561	27,983
AR.	1,923	2,286	2,327	2,332	2,342	2,343	2,346	2,351	2,371	2,394	2,424
LA.	3,645	4,206	4,408	4,407	4,344	4,289	4,253	4,220	4,244	4,279	4,295
OK.	2,559	3,025	3,271	3,253	3,210	3,167	3,150	3,146	3,168	3,205	3,231
TX.	11,199	14,229	16,273	16,561	16,622	16,667	16,807	16,987	17,352	17,683	18,031
West	34,838	43,172	47,827	48,786	49,762	50,770	51,894	52,786	54,066	55,133	56,044
Mountain.	8,289	11,373	12,741	12,952	13,145	13,303	13,498	13,659	14,021	14,379	14,776
MT.	694	787	822	814	805	800	800	799	807	822	839
ID	713	944	994	990	985	986	994	1,007	1,038	1,066	1,099
WY	332	470	500	496	477	465	458	454	458	465	470
CO.	2,210	2,890	3,209	3,237	3,260	3,262	3,276	3,294	3,370	3,465	3,566
NM.	1,017	1,303	1,438	1,463	1,479	1,490	1,504	1,515	1,547	1,582	1,616
AZ.	1,775	2,718	3,184	3,308	3,437	3,535	3,622	3,665	3,746	3,832	3,936
UT.	1,059	1,461	1,643	1,663	1,678	1,689	1,706	1,723	1,767	1,811	1,860
NV.	489	800	951	981	1,023	1,075	1,137	1,202	1,288	1,336	1,389
Pacific.	26,549	31,800	35,086	35,835	36,617	37,467	38,397	39,127	40,046	40,753	41,269
WA	3,413	4,132	4,400	4,453	4,532	4,640	4,746	4,867	5,016	5,143	5,255
OR.	2,092	2,633	2,673	2,684	2,701	2,741	2,791	2,842	2,919	2,972	3,032
CA.	19,971	23,668	26,441	27,102	27,777	28,464	29,218	29,760	30,407	30,895	31,211
AK.	303	402	532	544	539	542	547	550	569	588	599
HI	770	965	1,040	1,052	1,068	1,080	1,095	1,108	1,135	1,156	1,172

[1] See footnote 4, table 1.

Source: U.S. Bureau of the Census, *1990 Census of Population and Housing, Population and Housing Unit Counts* (CPH-2); *Current Population Reports*, P25-1106; and unpublished data.

No. 27. State Population—Rank, Percent Change, and Population Density: 1970 to 1993

[As of **April 1**, except **1993**, as of **July 1**. For area figures of States, see table 351. Minus sign (-) indicates decrease. See *Historical Statistics, Colonial Times to 1970*, series A 197]

REGION, DIVISION, AND STATE	RANK				PERCENT CHANGE			POPULATION PER SQ. MILE OF LAND AREA [1]	
	1970	1980	1990	1993	1970-80	1980-90	1990-93	1970	1993
U.S.	(X)	(X)	(X)	(X)	11.4	9.8	3.7	57.5	72.9
Northeast	(X)	(X)	(X)	(X)	0.2	3.4	1.1	302.3	316.5
N.E.	(X)	(X)	(X)	(X)	4.2	7.0	0.2	188.6	210.6
ME	38	38	38	39	13.2	9.2	0.9	32.2	40.2
NH	41	42	40	41	24.8	20.5	1.4	82.2	125.5
VT	48	48	48	49	15.0	10.0	2.3	48.1	62.2
MA	10	11	13	13	0.8	4.9	-0.1	725.8	767.1
RI	39	40	43	43	-0.3	5.9	-0.3	908.8	956.9
CT	24	25	27	27	2.5	5.8	-0.3	625.8	676.4
M.A.	(X)	(X)	(X)	(X)	-1.1	2.2	1.4	374.1	383.3
NY	2	2	2	2	-3.7	2.5	1.1	386.3	385.3
NJ	8	9	9	9	2.7	5.0	1.9	966.6	1,062.0
PA	3	4	5	5	0.5	0.1	1.4	263.3	268.8
Midwest	(X)	(X)	(X)	(X)	4.0	1.4	2.3	75.3	81.3
E.N.C	(X)	(X)	(X)	(X)	3.5	0.8	2.4	165.3	176.6
OH	6	6	7	7	1.3	0.5	2.3	260.2	270.8
IN	11	12	14	14	5.7	1.0	3.0	144.8	159.3
IL	5	5	6	6	2.8	(Z)	2.3	199.9	210.4
MI	7	8	8	8	4.3	0.4	2.0	156.3	166.8
WI	16	16	16	18	6.5	4.0	3.0	81.3	92.8
W.N.C	(X)	(X)	(X)	(X)	5.2	2.8	2.2	32.1	35.5
MN	19	21	20	20	7.1	7.3	3.3	47.8	56.7
IA	25	27	30	30	3.1	-4.7	1.3	50.6	50.4
MO	13	15	15	16	5.1	4.1	2.3	67.9	76.0
ND	45	46	47	47	5.7	-2.1	-0.6	9.0	9.2
SD	44	45	45	45	3.7	0.8	2.8	8.8	9.4
NE	35	35	36	37	5.7	0.5	1.8	19.3	20.9
KS	28	32	32	32	5.1	4.8	2.1	27.5	30.9
South	(X)	(X)	(X)	(X)	20.0	13.4	4.7	72.1	102.7
S.A.	(X)	(X)	(X)	(X)	20.5	17.9	5.0	115.2	171.8
DE	46	47	46	46	8.4	12.1	5.1	280.4	358.2
MD	18	18	19	19	7.5	13.4	3.8	401.4	507.9
DC	(X)	(X)	(X)	(X)	-15.6	-4.9	-4.7	12,404.4	9,482.8
VA	14	14	12	12	14.9	15.7	4.9	117.5	163.9
WV	34	34	34	35	11.8	-8.0	1.5	72.4	75.6
NC	12	10	10	10	15.7	12.7	4.8	104.4	142.6
SC	26	24	25	25	20.5	11.7	4.5	86.0	121.0
GA	15	13	11	11	19.1	18.6	6.8	79.2	119.4
FL	9	7	4	4	43.5	32.7	5.7	125.8	253.3
E.S.C.	(X)	(X)	(X)	(X)	14.5	3.5	3.6	71.7	88.0
KY	23	23	23	24	13.7	0.7	2.8	81.1	95.4
TN	17	17	17	17	16.9	6.2	4.5	95.2	123.7
AL	21	22	22	22	13.1	3.8	3.6	67.9	82.5
MS	29	31	31	31	13.7	2.1	2.7	47.3	56.3
W.S.C	(X)	(X)	(X)	(X)	22.9	12.4	4.8	45.3	65.7
AR	32	33	33	33	18.9	2.8	3.1	36.9	46.6
LA	20	19	21	21	15.4	0.3	1.8	83.7	98.6
OK	27	26	28	28	18.2	4.0	2.7	37.3	47.1
TX	4	3	3	3	27.1	19.4	6.2	42.8	68.8
West	(X)	(X)	(X)	(X)	23.9	22.3	6.2	19.9	32.0
Mountain	(X)	(X)	(X)	(X)	37.2	20.1	8.2	9.7	17.3
MT	43	44	44	44	13.3	1.6	5.1	4.8	5.8
ID	42	41	42	42	32.4	6.7	9.2	8.6	13.3
WY	49	49	50	50	41.3	-3.4	3.7	3.4	4.8
CO	30	28	26	26	30.8	14.0	8.2	21.3	34.4
NM	37	37	37	36	28.1	16.3	6.7	8.4	13.3
AZ	33	29	24	23	53.1	34.8	7.4	15.6	34.6
UT	36	36	35	34	37.9	17.9	7.9	12.9	22.6
NV	47	43	39	38	63.8	50.1	15.6	4.5	12.6
Pacific	(X)	(X)	(X)	(X)	19.8	23.0	5.5	29.7	46.1
WA	22	20	18	15	21.1	17.8	8.0	51.3	78.9
OR	31	30	29	29	25.9	7.9	6.7	21.8	31.6
CA	1	1	1	1	18.5	25.7	4.9	128.0	200.1
AK	50	50	49	48	32.8	36.9	8.9	0.5	1.1
HI	40	39	41	40	25.3	14.9	5.7	119.9	182.4

X Not applicable.   Z Less than 0.5 percent.   [1] Persons per square mile were calculated on the basis of land area data from the 1990 census.

Source: U.S. Bureau of the Census, *1990 Census of Population and Housing, Population and Housing Unit Counts* (CPH-2); and unpublished data.

No. 28. Components of Population Change—States: 1990 to 1993

[In thousands, except percent. Covers period April 1, 1990 to July 1, 1993]

REGION, DIVISION, AND STATE	NET CHANGE, 1990-93		Births	Deaths	NET MOVEMENT FROM ABROAD		Residual change [1]
	Number	Percent			International migration	Federal U.S. citizen	
United States ...	9,198	3.7	13,331	7,074	2,615	327	-
Northeast	545	1.1	2,511	1,550	705	19	-1,140
New England.......	23	0.2	628	377	102	7	-336
Maine...........	12	0.9	53	36	2	1	-10
New Hampshire....	16	1.4	53	28	3	-	-13
Vermont.........	13	2.3	26	15	2	-	1
Massachusetts.....	-4	-0.1	290	175	59	2	-180
Rhode Island......	-3	-0.3	49	32	6	1	-27
Connecticut.......	-10	-0.3	157	92	29	2	-107
Middle Atlantic	522	1.4	1,883	1,172	604	12	-804
New York.......	207	1.1	945	542	422	7	-624
New Jersey......	149	1.9	394	231	136	3	-153
Pennsylvania.....	167	1.4	544	399	46	2	-27
Midwest...........	1,402	2.3	3,013	1,751	280	26	-166
East North Central...	1,008	2.4	2,154	1,222	231	11	-167
Ohio	244	2.3	545	325	25	2	-3
Indiana.........	169	3.0	276	163	9	1	45
Illinois.........	267	2.3	628	335	144	6	-175
Michigan........	182	2.0	473	259	41	2	-75
Wisconsin.......	146	3.0	232	138	12	-	41
West North Central ..	394	2.2	859	529	49	14	1
Minnesota.......	142	3.3	217	114	17	1	23
Iowa	37	1.3	126	88	6	-	-6
Missouri........	117	2.3	251	165	12	3	16
North Dakota.....	-4	-0.6	29	19	1	2	-18
South Dakota	19	2.8	36	22	1	1	3
Nebraska	29	1.8	77	48	4	2	-6
Kansas.........	53	2.1	123	73	8	5	-10
South	3,992	4.7	4,544	2,510	601	174	1,182
South Atlantic.....	2,171	5.0	2,232	1,305	334	119	792
Delaware	34	5.1	36	19	3	1	13
Maryland	183	3.8	255	125	43	9	1
District of Columbia .	-28	-4.7	36	24	12	2	-54
Virginia.........	303	4.9	317	160	50	38	58
West Virginia.....	27	1.5	73	65	2	-	17
North Carolina....	317	4.8	335	192	14	23	136
South Carolina....	156	4.5	186	99	5	12	52
Georgia........	439	6.8	362	173	28	15	208
Florida	741	5.7	632	448	176	20	360
East South Central...	541	3.6	763	480	20	17	221
Kentucky	104	2.8	175	115	5	6	32
Tennessee	222	4.5	242	153	8	4	121
Alabama........	146	3.6	205	130	5	4	62
Mississippi	70	2.7	141	83	2	3	6
West South Central ..	1,280	4.8	1,549	724	247	38	169
Arkansas	74	3.1	115	82	2	1	36
Louisiana	76	1.8	234	123	11	6	-51
Oklahoma.......	86	2.7	156	99	8	6	15
Texas..........	1,045	6.2	1,043	419	226	25	169
West	3,258	6.2	3,263	1,264	1,028	108	124
Mountain.........	1,117	8.2	793	329	83	22	547
Montana........	40	5.1	38	23	1	1	24
Idaho..........	92	9.2	55	25	4	1	57
Wyoming	17	3.7	22	11	1	1	3
Colorado........	272	8.2	176	73	18	9	142
New Mexico	101	6.7	91	37	11	3	33
Arizona.........	271	7.4	220	97	30	5	114
Utah	137	7.9	120	31	7	1	40
Nevada	187	15.6	71	32	12	2	134
Pacific	2,141	5.5	2,470	935	945	85	-424
Washington......	389	8.0	258	121	37	12	202
Oregon.........	190	6.7	137	83	18	-	117
California	1,451	4.9	1,972	702	863	56	-739
Alaska	49	8.9	38	7	3	5	9
Hawaii	63	5.7	65	22	23	11	-14

- Represents or rounds to zero. [1] The bulk of residual change is internal (domestic) net migration, although the source has no reliable way to quantify it. The data are also affected by any inaccuracies in input data or variations in implementing the estimating method.

Source: U.S. Bureau of the Census, unpublished data.

Population

No. 29. U.S. Resident Population, by Region and Division: 1960 to 1993

[As of **April 1**; except **1985** and **1993**, as of **July 1**. For composition of divisions, see table 26]

REGION AND DIVISION	POPULATION (millions)						PERCENT DISTRIBUTION					
	1960	1970	1980	1985	1990	1993	1960	1970	1980	1985	1990	1993
United States.....	179.3	203.3	226.5	237.9	248.7	257.9	100.0	100.0	100.0	100.0	100.0	100.0
Northeast..........	44.7	49.1	49.1	49.9	50.8	51.4	24.9	24.1	21.7	21.0	20.4	19.9
New England.......	10.5	11.8	12.3	12.7	13.2	13.2	5.9	5.8	5.5	5.4	5.3	5.1
Middle Atlantic......	34.2	37.2	36.8	37.1	37.6	38.1	19.1	18.3	16.2	15.6	15.1	14.8
Midwest...........	51.6	56.6	58.9	58.8	59.7	61.1	28.8	27.8	26.0	24.7	24.0	23.7
East North Central....	36.2	40.3	41.7	41.4	42.0	43.0	20.2	19.8	18.4	17.4	16.9	16.7
West North Central ...	15.4	16.3	17.2	17.4	17.7	18.1	8.6	8.0	7.6	7.3	7.1	7.0
South.............	55.0	62.8	75.4	81.4	85.4	89.4	30.7	30.9	33.3	34.2	34.4	34.7
South Atlantic.......	26.0	30.7	37.0	40.2	43.6	45.7	14.5	15.1	16.3	16.9	17.5	17.7
East South Central ...	12.1	12.8	14.7	15.0	15.2	15.7	6.7	6.3	6.5	6.3	6.1	6.1
West South Central ...	17.0	19.3	23.7	26.3	26.7	28.0	9.5	9.5	10.5	11.0	10.7	10.8
West.............	28.1	34.8	43.2	47.8	52.8	56.0	15.6	17.1	19.1	20.1	21.2	21.7
Mountain..........	6.9	8.3	11.4	12.7	13.7	14.8	3.8	4.1	5.0	5.4	5.5	5.7
Pacific...........	21.2	26.5	31.8	35.1	39.1	41.3	11.8	13.1	14.0	14.7	15.7	16.0

Source: U.S. Bureau of the Census, *1990 Census of Population and Housing, Population and Housing Unit Counts* (CPH-2); and unpublished data.

No. 30. Resident Population, by Region, Race, and Hispanic Origin: 1990

[As of **April 1**. For composition of regions, see table 26]

RACE AND HISPANIC ORIGIN	POPULATION (1,000)					PERCENT DISTRIBUTION				
	United States	North-east	Midwest	South	West	United States	North-east	Midwest	South	West
Total...........	248,710	50,809	59,669	85,446	52,786	100.0	20.4	24.0	34.4	21.2
White..............	199,686	42,069	52,018	65,582	40,017	100.0	21.1	26.0	32.8	20.0
Black..............	29,986	5,613	5,716	15,829	2,828	100.0	18.7	19.1	52.8	9.4
American Indian, Eskimo, Aleut..............	1,959	125	338	563	933	100.0	6.4	17.2	28.7	47.6
American Indian......	1,878	122	334	557	866	100.0	6.5	17.8	29.7	46.1
Eskimo............	57	2	2	3	51	100.0	2.9	3.5	4.9	88.8
Aleut.............	24	2	2	3	17	100.0	8.1	8.1	11.5	72.3
Asian or Pacific Islander ..	7,274	1,335	768	1,122	4,048	100.0	18.4	10.6	15.4	55.7
Chinese	1,645	445	133	204	863	100.0	27.0	8.1	12.4	52.4
Filipino	1,407	143	113	159	991	100.0	10.2	8.1	11.3	70.5
Japanese	848	74	63	67	643	100.0	8.8	7.5	7.9	75.9
Asian Indian........	815	285	146	196	189	100.0	35.0	17.9	24.0	23.1
Korean	799	182	109	153	355	100.0	22.8	13.7	19.2	44.4
Vietnamese	615	61	52	169	334	100.0	9.8	8.5	27.4	54.3
Laotian	149	16	28	29	76	100.0	10.7	18.6	19.6	51.0
Cambodian	147	30	13	19	85	100.0	20.5	8.8	13.1	57.7
Thai	91	12	13	24	43	100.0	12.9	14.2	26.0	46.8
Hmong	90	2	37	2	50	100.0	1.9	41.3	1.8	55.0
Pakistani...........	81	28	15	22	17	100.0	34.3	18.9	26.5	20.4
Hawaiian..........	211	4	6	12	189	100.0	2.0	2.6	5.8	89.6
Samoan	63	2	2	4	55	100.0	2.4	3.6	6.4	87.6
Guamanian	49	4	3	8	34	100.0	7.3	6.4	16.8	69.5
Other Asian or Pacific Islander	263	49	34	54	126	100.0	18.5	12.9	20.6	48.0
Other races	9,805	1,667	829	2,350	4,960	100.0	17.0	8.5	24.0	50.6
Hispanic origin [1]	22,354	3,754	1,727	6,767	10,106	100.0	16.8	7.7	30.3	45.2
Mexican	13,496	175	1,153	4,344	7,824	100.0	1.3	8.5	32.2	58.0
Puerto Rican	2,728	1,872	258	406	192	100.0	68.6	9.4	14.9	7.0
Cuban............	1,044	184	37	735	88	100.0	17.6	3.5	70.5	8.5
Other Hispanic.......	5,086	1,524	279	1,282	2,002	100.0	30.0	5.5	25.2	39.4
Not of Hispanic origin....	226,356	47,055	57,942	78,679	42,680	100.0	20.8	25.6	34.8	18.9

[1] Persons of Hispanic origin may be of any race.

Source: U.S. Bureau of the Census, *1990 Census of Population, General Population Characteristics, United States* (CP-1-1).

No. 31. Annual Inmigration, Outmigration, and Net Migration for Regions: 1980 to 1992

[In thousands. As of **March**. For persons 1 year old and over. Excludes members of the Armed Forces except those living off post or with their families on post. Based on Current Population Survey; see text, section 1, and Appendix III. For composition of regions, see table 26. Minus sign (-) indicates net outmigration]

PERIOD	North-east	Mid-west	South	West	PERIOD	North-east	Mid-west	South	West
1980-81: Immigrants	464	650	1,377	871	**1988-89:** Inmigrants	370	777	1,318	791
Outmigrants	706	1,056	890	710	Outmigrants	714	703	1,071	637
Net internal migration	-242	-406	487	161	Net internal migration	-344	74	247	154
Movers from abroad	207	180	412	514	Movers from abroad	292	170	375	629
Net migration	-35	-226	899	675	Net migration	-52	244	622	783
1983-84: Immigrants	487	820	1,399	834	**1989-90:** Immigrants	461	908	1,428	964
Outmigrants	578	1,102	973	887	Outmigrants	758	1,024	1,198	781
Net internal migration	-91	-282	426	-53	Net internal migration	-297	-116	230	183
Movers from abroad	213	141	383	341	Movers from abroad	328	169	500	562
Net migration	122	-141	809	288	Net migration	30	53	730	745
1984-85: Immigrants	482	842	1,329	994	**1990-91:** Immigrants	346	782	1,421	835
Outmigrants	691	1,053	1,169	734	Outmigrants	932	797	987	668
Net internal migration	-209	-211	160	260	Net internal migration	-585	-15	433	167
Movers from abroad	228	168	532	499	Movers from abroad	209	208	351	617
Net migration	19	-43	692	759	Net migration	-376	193	784	784
1985-86: Immigrants	502	1,011	1,355	910	**1991-92:**				
Outmigrants	752	996	1,320	710	Total inmigrants	409	816	1,305	755
Net internal migration	-250	15	35	200	From Northeast	(X)	127	429	145
Movers from abroad	198	158	342	502	From Midwest	101	(X)	520	258
Net migration	-52	173	377	702	From South	255	473	(X)	352
1986-87: Immigrants	398	858	1,374	916	From West	53	216	356	(X)
Outmigrants	732	969	1,095	750	Total outmigrants	701	878	1,081	626
Net internal migration	-334	-111	279	166	To Northeast	(X)	101	255	53
Movers from abroad	214	193	277	458	To Midwest	127	(X)	473	216
Net migration	-120	82	556	624	To South	429	520	(X)	356
1987-88: Immigrants	430	715	1,338	613	To West	145	258	352	(X)
Outmigrants	671	818	886	721	Net internal migration	-292	-62	224	129
Net internal migration	-241	-103	452	-108	Movers from abroad	255	175	383	442
Movers from abroad	261	146	414	379	Net migration	-37	113	607	571
Net migration	20	43	866	271					

X Not applicable.

Source: U.S. Bureau of the Census, *Current Population Reports*, P20-473, and earlier reports.

No. 32. Mobility Status of the Population, by Selected Characteristics: 1992

[See headnote, table 31]

AGE AND REGION	Total (1,000)	Non-movers (same house in 1991)	Movers (different house in United States in 1991) Total	Same county	Different county Total	Same State	Different State	Movers from abroad
Total	247,380	83	17	11	6	3	3	1
1 to 4 years old	15,511	78	22	15	7	3	4	(Z)
5 to 9 years old	18,604	82	18	11	6	3	1	(Z)
10 to 14 years old	18,021	85	15	10	5	3	1	(Z)
15 to 19 years old	16,568	83	17	11	6	3	3	(Z)
20 to 24 years old	17,848	63	35	23	13	7	6	1
25 to 29 years old	20,132	67	32	21	11	6	6	1
30 to 44 years old	61,932	82	17	11	6	3	3	1
45 to 54 years old	27,023	89	10	6	4	2	2	1
55 to 64 years old	21,150	93	7	4	3	1	2	(Z)
65 to 74 years old	18,440	95	5	3	3	1	1	(Z)
75 years old and over	12,149	96	5	3	3	1	1	(Z)
Northeast	50,045	88	11	7	4	2	2	1
Midwest	59,471	84	16	10	5	3	2	1
South	84,701	81	18	11	7	4	4	(Z)
West	53,163	79	20	14	7	4	3	1

Z Less than 0.5 percent.

Source: U.S. Bureau of the Census, *Current Population Reports*, P20-473.

Population

No. 33. Resident Population, by Age and State: 1993

[In thousands, except percent. As of July 1. Includes Armed Forces stationed in area. See text, section 1 for basis of estimates. See *Historical Statistics, Colonial Times to 1970*, series A 204-209 for decennial census data]

REGION, DIVISION, AND STATE	Total	Under 5 years	5 to 17 years	18 to 24 years	25 to 34 years	35 to 44 years	45 to 54 years	55 to 64 years	65 to 74 years	75 to 84 years	85 years and over	Percent 65 years and over
U.S.	257,908	19,705	47,428	25,659	41,907	40,830	28,666	20,923	18,652	10,769	3,369	12.7
Northeast . . .	51,355	3,699	8,674	4,906	8,325	8,157	5,946	4,449	4,065	2,381	753	14.0
N.E	13,230	932	2,205	1,290	2,220	2,147	1,522	1,081	1,011	614	207	13.8
ME.	1,239	81	226	121	189	205	142	105	95	56	19	13.7
NH.	1,125	80	203	108	189	194	130	85	75	44	15	11.9
VT	576	39	105	62	90	99	67	45	38	23	8	12.0
MA.	6,012	428	965	602	1,053	960	678	485	462	283	97	14.0
RI.	1,000	71	164	105	162	155	108	81	86	52	17	15.5
CT	3,277	234	541	292	537	534	398	280	255	156	51	14.1
M.A.	38,125	2,767	6,469	3,616	6,105	6,010	4,424	3,368	3,053	1,767	546	14.1
NY	18,197	1,375	3,093	1,759	3,021	2,859	2,116	1,586	1,349	781	257	13.1
NJ	7,879	580	1,316	699	1,290	1,279	949	696	619	350	102	13.6
PA	12,048	812	2,060	1,158	1,794	1,872	1,359	1,086	1,085	635	187	15.8
Midwest	61,070	4,485	11,588	6,069	9,521	9,562	6,740	5,045	4,460	2,694	906	13.2
E.N.C.	43,017	3,185	8,059	4,323	6,766	6,770	4,808	3,573	3,126	1,824	583	12.9
OH.	11,091	806	2,053	1,108	1,698	1,739	1,251	956	853	476	151	13.3
IN.	5,713	406	1,063	610	885	893	647	480	411	239	77	12.7
IL	11,697	913	2,155	1,147	1,911	1,835	1,300	957	824	498	157	12.6
MI	9,478	705	1,801	967	1,487	1,511	1,067	770	676	378	116	12.4
WI	5,038	355	987	491	785	792	544	409	362	234	80	13.4
W.N.C.	18,054	1,300	3,529	1,746	2,755	2,792	1,932	1,473	1,334	870	323	14.0
MN.	4,517	333	895	420	733	733	489	345	298	197	73	12.6
IA.	2,814	190	544	279	402	422	300	241	226	152	58	15.5
MO.	5,234	375	988	505	802	795	581	447	401	251	89	14.2
ND.	635	44	128	66	95	97	61	50	47	34	13	14.8
SD.	715	55	153	69	100	105	69	58	55	37	14	14.7
NE	1,607	116	323	157	238	246	166	132	119	79	31	14.2
KS	2,531	186	498	250	385	393	265	201	186	121	46	13.9
South	89,438	6,734	16,489	9,155	14,420	13,967	9,955	7,358	6,546	3,699	1,115	12.7
S.A	45,738	3,321	7,898	4,523	7,432	7,197	5,230	3,909	3,616	2,025	587	13.6
DE	700	53	122	71	119	109	79	60	53	26	8	12.4
MD.	4,965	378	863	453	876	841	604	402	328	170	52	11.1
DC	578	40	75	64	116	93	65	47	43	25	8	13.3
VA	6,491	472	1,116	682	1,133	1,081	778	518	422	223	67	11.0
WV	1,820	108	326	195	245	286	213	169	159	92	28	15.3
NC	6,945	503	1,201	755	1,133	1,091	800	597	510	275	80	12.5
SC	3,643	275	677	406	584	568	409	297	259	132	35	11.7
GA	6,917	541	1,300	738	1,189	1,127	800	528	405	224	65	10.1
FL	13,679	952	2,217	1,160	2,037	2,000	1,481	1,292	1,436	858	245	18.6
E.S.C.	15,717	1,130	2,943	1,693	2,410	2,412	1,778	1,345	1,137	663	207	12.8
KY	3,789	261	710	404	587	590	432	322	271	159	52	12.7
TN	5,099	361	908	530	801	804	602	443	372	214	66	12.8
AL	4,187	301	776	454	638	639	470	365	311	180	54	13.0
MS	2,643	208	550	305	384	379	274	213	184	110	35	12.5
W.S.C	27,983	2,283	5,648	2,939	4,579	4,358	2,947	2,104	1,793	1,011	321	11.2
AR	2,424	172	463	247	344	351	272	213	200	124	39	15.0
LA	4,295	342	901	457	675	656	447	330	285	156	47	11.3
OK	3,231	235	634	332	481	488	353	268	244	146	50	13.6
TX	18,031	1,534	3,649	1,903	3,079	2,864	1,875	1,293	1,063	586	186	10.2
West	56,044	4,786	10,677	5,529	9,641	9,144	6,025	4,071	3,582	1,995	595	11.0
Mountain . .	14,776	1,198	3,010	1,481	2,360	2,365	1,572	1,113	981	542	155	11.3
MT	839	59	173	78	113	139	95	69	62	39	12	13.4
ID.	1,099	86	247	115	151	173	117	81	72	45	13	11.8
WY.	470	34	104	48	69	81	50	32	30	17	5	10.9
CO	3,566	268	670	346	603	645	412	264	209	112	37	10.0
NM.	1,616	137	344	159	247	256	171	126	104	57	16	11.0
AZ	3,936	325	745	389	637	594	405	313	310	174	46	13.4
UT	1,860	180	485	226	284	252	159	109	95	54	16	8.9
NV	1,389	110	242	120	256	225	164	118	101	44	10	11.1
Pacific. . . .	41,269	3,588	7,667	4,048	7,281	6,779	4,452	2,958	2,601	1,454	441	10.9
WA	5,255	396	997	492	857	909	606	387	347	203	62	11.6
OR	3,032	212	570	279	450	516	355	233	232	143	43	13.8
CA	31,211	2,830	5,764	3,102	5,669	5,041	3,293	2,210	1,921	1,060	323	10.6
AK	599	57	132	58	108	117	67	33	18	7	2	4.4
HI.	1,172	94	205	118	197	196	132	94	84	41	12	11.7

Source: U.S. Bureau of the Census, unpublished data.

No. 34. State Population Projections: 1995 to 2010

[In thousands. As of July 1. Series A, B, C, and D reflect different interstate migration assumptions. Series A is the preferred series model. For explanation of methodology, see text, section 1]

REGION, DIVISION, AND STATE	1995				2000				2010			
	Series A	Series B	Series C	Series D	Series A	Series B	Series C	Series D	Series A	Series B	Series C	Series D
U.S.	263,437	263,437	263,435	263,435	276,242	276,242	276,239	276,239	300,430	300,431	300,431	300,430
Northeast	51,441	52,123	51,465	52,507	51,884	53,210	52,329	54,582	53,301	55,102	54,225	58,183
N.E.	13,198	13,601	13,213	13,523	13,216	14,025	13,507	13,996	13,755	14,785	14,212	14,751
ME	1,236	1,276	1,242	1,250	1,240	1,323	1,288	1,270	1,309	1,413	1,375	1,300
NH	1,132	1,183	1,128	1,133	1,165	1,274	1,204	1,163	1,280	1,429	1,350	1,207
VT	579	593	580	581	592	623	605	596	623	675	644	620
MA	5,976	6,133	5,974	6,159	5,950	6,254	6,032	6,401	6,097	6,495	6,249	6,785
RI	1,001	1,031	1,004	1,029	998	1,060	1,022	1,065	1,034	1,115	1,072	1,126
CT.	3,274	3,385	3,285	3,371	3,271	3,491	3,356	3,501	3,412	3,658	3,522	3,713
M.A	38,243	38,522	38,252	38,984	38,668	39,185	38,822	40,586	39,546	40,317	40,013	43,432
NY.	18,178	18,319	18,184	18,795	18,237	18,504	18,321	19,838	18,546	18,856	18,799	21,761
NJ.	7,931	8,005	7,926	8,040	8,135	8,267	8,165	8,413	8,562	8,681	8,677	9,075
PA.	12,134	12,198	12,142	12,149	12,296	12,414	12,336	12,335	12,438	12,780	12,537	12,596
Midwest.	61,993	61,469	61,989	62,068	63,836	62,610	63,664	64,075	66,333	64,953	65,982	67,716
E.N.C	43,610	43,258	43,620	43,753	44,806	44,013	44,769	45,220	46,259	45,506	46,242	47,805
OH	11,203	11,103	11,203	11,209	11,453	11,238	11,430	11,479	11,659	11,500	11,661	11,913
IN	5,820	5,766	5,821	5,771	6,045	5,922	6,032	5,929	6,286	6,212	6,274	6,187
IL	11,853	11,770	11,855	11,991	12,168	11,974	12,153	12,533	12,652	12,424	12,621	13,541
MI	9,575	9,512	9,584	9,682	9,759	9,614	9,826	10,040	10,033	9,803	10,160	10,666
WI	5,159	5,107	5,157	5,100	5,381	5,265	5,328	5,239	5,629	5,567	5,526	5,498
W.N.C	18,383	18,211	18,369	18,315	19,030	18,597	18,895	18,855	20,074	19,447	19,740	19,911
MN	4,619	4,581	4,618	4,591	4,824	4,733	4,814	4,756	5,127	5,020	5,096	5,068
IA	2,861	2,834	2,859	2,851	2,930	2,867	2,885	2,912	2,981	2,946	2,868	3,032
MO	5,286	5,241	5,289	5,279	5,437	5,313	5,459	5,406	5,760	5,489	5,788	5,638
ND	637	634	634	647	643	633	622	663	676	642	626	698
SD.	735	720	732	725	770	737	750	749	815	781	786	805
NE.	1,644	1,626	1,644	1,635	1,704	1,660	1,681	1,680	1,793	1,742	1,734	1,773
KS.	2,601	2,575	2,593	2,587	2,722	2,654	2,684	2,689	2,922	2,827	2,842	2,897
South	91,728	91,387	91,705	90,684	97,244	96,576	96,931	94,503	107,385	106,120	106,852	101,445
S.A.	47,019	46,988	47,070	46,257	50,005	50,015	50,517	48,004	55,321	55,422	56,737	50,976
DE.	718	715	719	705	759	757	770	727	815	834	850	758
MD	5,078	5,081	5,089	5,081	5,322	5,334	5,420	5,334	5,782	5,762	6,008	5,763
DC.	559	564	559	608	537	545	549	640	577	545	584	697
VA.	6,646	6,645	6,644	6,570	7,048	7,060	7,106	6,854	7,728	7,760	7,902	7,318
WV	1,824	1,812	1,819	1,820	1,840	1,811	1,783	1,830	1,842	1,827	1,720	1,835
NC	7,150	7,130	7,143	6,980	7,617	7,588	7,616	7,169	8,341	8,416	8,455	7,438
SC.	3,732	3,727	3,743	3,688	3,932	3,924	3,976	3,808	4,311	4,287	4,378	3,998
GA	7,102	7,120	7,097	6,954	7,637	7,678	7,664	7,249	8,553	8,679	8,732	7,758
FL.	14,210	14,194	14,257	13,851	15,313	15,318	15,633	14,393	17,372	17,312	18,108	15,411
E.S.C	16,019	15,844	15,997	15,823	16,762	16,357	16,633	16,252	17,941	17,412	17,697	16,962
KY.	3,851	3,803	3,842	3,819	3,989	3,883	3,927	3,913	4,160	4,050	4,046	4,064
TN.	5,228	5,166	5,221	5,108	5,538	5,399	5,513	5,222	6,007	5,857	5,980	5,392
AL.	4,274	4,228	4,272	4,225	4,485	4,375	4,471	4,357	4,856	4,677	4,818	4,580
MS	2,666	2,647	2,662	2,671	2,750	2,700	2,722	2,760	2,918	2,828	2,853	2,926
W.S.C	28,690	28,555	28,638	28,604	30,477	30,204	29,781	30,247	34,123	33,286	32,418	33,507
AR.	2,468	2,456	2,462	2,434	2,578	2,557	2,546	2,489	2,782	2,751	2,716	2,592
LA.	4,359	4,334	4,346	4,407	4,478	4,424	4,343	4,592	4,808	4,604	4,471	4,947
OK	3,271	3,265	3,262	3,267	3,382	3,366	3,259	3,353	3,683	3,578	3,352	3,524
TX.	18,592	18,500	18,568	18,496	20,039	19,857	19,633	19,813	22,850	22,353	21,879	22,444
West	58,275	58,458	58,276	58,176	63,278	63,846	63,315	63,079	73,411	74,256	73,372	73,086
Mountain . . .	15,384	15,142	15,323	14,902	16,890	16,339	16,391	15,718	19,093	18,625	18,331	17,359
MT	862	851	855	837	920	894	867	859	996	993	899	906
ID	1,156	1,117	1,152	1,101	1,290	1,200	1,229	1,158	1,454	1,373	1,335	1,282
WY	487	484	484	477	522	512	483	495	596	571	491	534
CO	3,710	3,663	3,683	3,575	4,059	3,957	3,851	3,729	4,494	4,477	4,183	4,000
NM	1,676	1,658	1,670	1,641	1,823	1,780	1,776	1,737	2,082	2,005	2,009	1,939
AZ.	4,072	4,024	4,051	3,978	4,437	4,320	4,404	4,201	5,074	4,891	5,136	4,645
UT.	1,944	1,914	1,936	1,910	2,148	2,079	2,063	2,076	2,462	2,413	2,294	2,442
NV.	1,477	1,431	1,492	1,383	1,691	1,597	1,718	1,463	1,935	1,902	1,984	1,611
Pacific	42,891	43,316	42,953	43,274	46,388	47,507	46,924	47,361	54,318	55,631	55,041	55,727
WA	5,497	5,453	5,504	5,295	6,070	6,025	6,054	5,539	7,025	7,087	6,898	6,005
OR	3,141	3,105	3,147	3,045	3,404	3,340	3,396	3,151	3,876	3,812	3,753	3,360
CA.	32,398	32,892	32,450	33,097	34,888	36,062	35,490	36,689	41,085	42,255	42,075	44,076
AK.	634	642	631	618	699	732	658	666	781	880	754	769
HI	1,221	1,224	1,221	1,219	1,327	1,348	1,326	1,316	1,551	1,597	1,561	1,517

Source: U.S. Bureau of the Census, *Current Population Reports*, series P25-1111.

Population

No. 35. Population Projections, by Age—States: 1995 to 2010

[In thousands. As of July 1. Data shown are for series A, the preferred series model; for explanation of methodology, see text, section 1]

REGION, DIVISION, AND STATE	UNDER 18 YEARS			18 TO 44 YEARS			45 TO 64 YEARS			65 YEARS AND OVER		
	1995	2000	2010	1995	2000	2010	1995	2000	2010	1995	2000	2010
U.S.	69,036	71,789	73,619	109,288	109,274	108,058	51,468	59,860	78,651	33,655	35,324	40,099
Northeast	12,593	12,801	12,326	21,056	20,069	18,912	10,523	11,711	14,465	7,272	7,304	7,597
N.E.	3,187	3,191	3,045	5,503	5,154	4,902	2,667	3,018	3,830	1,842	1,853	1,977
ME	303	294	286	504	477	458	257	294	375	172	175	191
NH	288	288	285	482	464	457	228	273	372	135	141	165
VT	148	149	146	245	235	228	116	135	167	70	72	82
MA	1,418	1,420	1,317	2,530	2,358	2,226	1,184	1,329	1,672	844	842	881
RI	238	237	227	414	387	368	195	223	286	154	151	153
CT.	792	803	784	1,328	1,233	1,165	687	764	958	467	472	505
M.A	9,406	9,610	9,281	15,553	14,915	14,010	7,856	8,693	10,635	5,430	5,451	5,620
NY.	4,539	4,611	4,439	7,505	7,143	6,735	3,717	4,058	4,846	2,417	2,426	2,525
NJ	1,951	2,047	2,051	3,232	3,121	2,972	1,658	1,854	2,348	1,091	1,112	1,192
PA.	2,916	2,952	2,791	4,816	4,651	4,303	2,481	2,781	3,441	1,922	1,913	1,903
Midwest.	16,356	16,593	16,340	25,355	25,095	23,799	12,103	13,784	17,282	8,179	8,369	8,912
E.N.C	11,458	11,665	11,467	17,951	17,676	16,660	8,574	9,711	12,035	5,628	5,755	6,097
OH	2,873	2,891	2,778	4,567	4,483	4,159	2,253	2,532	3,103	1,509	1,547	1,618
IN	1,509	1,550	1,534	2,412	2,409	2,278	1,154	1,314	1,636	745	772	836
IL	3,126	3,206	3,198	4,930	4,857	4,640	2,303	2,592	3,225	1,496	1,513	1,589
MI	2,583	2,635	2,621	3,932	3,802	3,569	1,871	2,112	2,567	1,189	1,211	1,278
WI	1,367	1,383	1,336	2,110	2,125	2,014	993	1,161	1,504	689	712	776
W.N.C	4,898	4,928	4,873	7,404	7,419	7,139	3,529	4,073	5,247	2,551	2,614	2,815
MN	1,243	1,254	1,225	1,921	1,930	1,849	875	1,038	1,370	578	602	683
IA	743	736	705	1,125	1,128	1,061	556	627	767	438	439	449
MO	1,376	1,381	1,371	2,107	2,090	2,006	1,055	1,197	1,546	749	769	837
ND	170	164	163	259	254	250	115	133	170	93	94	93
SD.	211	216	218	285	292	284	132	155	203	105	107	111
NE.	449	452	448	656	663	649	309	354	447	231	236	248
KS.	706	725	743	1,051	1,062	1,040	487	569	744	357	367	394
South	23,875	24,901	25,688	37,959	38,346	37,992	18,090	21,274	28,647	11,809	12,724	15,055
S.A.	11,618	12,217	12,505	19,316	19,402	19,107	9,547	11,255	15,148	6,539	7,130	8,559
DE.	182	191	193	302	305	295	142	164	214	92	99	113
MD	1,317	1,405	1,453	2,159	2,124	2,077	1,033	1,192	1,551	568	602	701
DC.	109	99	102	263	248	261	112	117	142	76	73	72
VA.	1,654	1,745	1,780	2,907	2,923	2,879	1,343	1,576	2,101	742	803	967
WV	432	425	406	724	703	642	389	434	514	280	277	280
NC	1,758	1,862	1,879	3,023	3,045	2,978	1,462	1,713	2,284	908	997	1,199
SC.	980	1,013	1,036	1,569	1,570	1,548	740	867	1,152	443	481	575
GA.	1,909	2,030	2,125	3,080	3,153	3,161	1,387	1,656	2,269	726	798	998
FL.	3,277	3,447	3,531	5,289	5,331	5,266	2,939	3,536	4,921	2,704	3,000	3,654
E.S.C	4,157	4,275	4,305	6,574	6,606	6,352	3,232	3,714	4,824	2,058	2,167	2,459
KY.	983	996	982	1,598	1,594	1,490	779	890	1,125	491	509	563
TN.	1,295	1,343	1,343	2,173	2,209	2,151	1,090	1,269	1,674	671	717	839
AL.	1,125	1,183	1,233	1,732	1,736	1,691	858	975	1,264	560	591	667
MS	754	753	747	1,071	1,067	1,020	505	580	761	336	350	390
W.S.C	8,100	8,409	8,878	12,069	12,338	12,533	5,311	6,305	8,675	3,212	3,427	4,037
AR.	643	657	661	953	960	927	504	578	758	368	383	436
LA.	1,251	1,247	1,282	1,803	1,792	1,766	808	925	1,195	498	515	565
OK	870	875	900	1,313	1,314	1,312	648	739	969	441	454	502
TX.	5,336	5,630	6,035	8,000	8,272	8,528	3,351	4,063	5,753	1,905	2,075	2,534
West	16,212	17,494	19,265	24,918	25,764	27,355	10,752	13,091	18,257	6,395	6,927	8,535
Mountain	4,376	4,690	4,967	6,410	6,770	6,919	2,848	3,503	4,847	1,750	1,924	2,362
MT	233	242	250	343	356	357	172	203	260	114	117	130
ID	344	373	396	466	512	526	211	262	360	133	143	172
WY	141	145	162	207	218	235	89	108	144	51	51	54
CO	972	1,037	1,054	1,645	1,722	1,728	717	885	1,198	376	415	514
NM	500	540	588	679	705	734	311	374	515	185	204	247
AZ.	1,127	1,213	1,281	1,629	1,673	1,705	759	927	1,305	558	623	783
UT.	684	723	800	803	882	928	286	356	504	172	188	230
NV.	375	417	436	638	702	706	303	388	561	161	183	232
Pacific	11,836	12,804	14,298	18,508	18,994	20,434	7,904	9,588	13,410	4,645	5,003	6,173
WA	1,461	1,589	1,712	2,336	2,464	2,589	1,070	1,342	1,888	631	675	836
OR	811	869	945	1,279	1,328	1,400	631	773	1,026	421	434	504
CA.	9,048	9,779	11,008	14,061	14,327	15,494	5,867	7,077	9,978	3,422	3,704	4,605
AK.	201	221	239	300	319	342	105	129	163	28	31	38
HI	315	346	394	532	556	611	231	267	355	143	159	190

Source: U.S. Bureau of the Census, *Current Population Reports*, series P25-1111.

No. 36. Population Projections, by Race—States: 1995 to 2010

[In thousands. As of July 1. Data shown are for series A, the preferred series model; for explanation of methodology, see text, section 1]

REGION, DIVISION, AND STATE	WHITE			BLACK			AMERICAN INDIAN, ESKIMO, ALEUT			ASIAN, PACIFIC ISLANDER		
	1995	2000	2010	1995	2000	2010	1995	2000	2010	1995	2000	2010
U.S.	218,333	226,268	240,293	33,118	35,475	40,227	2,229	2,382	2,718	9,756	12,121	17,188
Northeast	43,381	43,218	43,268	6,263	6,570	7,267	118	108	98	1,678	1,989	2,669
N.E.	12,183	12,120	12,408	691	718	810	32	31	31	291	348	506
ME	1,217	1,220	1,283	5	5	5	6	6	6	8	9	14
NH	1,109	1,137	1,236	7	8	10	2	3	3	14	18	31
VT	570	582	609	2	3	4	2	2	2	4	5	9
MA	5,445	5,373	5,387	340	352	393	11	10	10	180	215	307
RI	927	917	933	44	46	51	4	4	4	25	31	46
CT	2,915	2,891	2,960	293	304	347	7	6	6	60	70	99
M.A	31,198	31,098	30,860	5,572	5,852	6,457	86	77	67	1,387	1,641	2,163
NY	14,025	13,819	13,542	3,249	3,391	3,705	57	50	43	846	977	1,257
NJ	6,405	6,445	6,526	1,156	1,242	1,434	14	13	11	356	435	591
PA	10,768	10,834	10,792	1,167	1,219	1,318	15	14	13	185	229	315
Midwest.	54,306	55,391	56,441	6,249	6,689	7,526	382	411	460	1,055	1,345	1,900
E.N.C	37,392	38,006	38,350	5,277	5,653	6,379	165	170	174	776	976	1,354
OH	9,806	9,943	9,948	1,253	1,335	1,483	22	22	22	122	152	206
IN	5,275	5,444	5,587	476	514	582	14	15	15	55	72	102
IL	9,603	9,713	9,801	1,843	1,957	2,181	23	22	21	383	476	648
MI	7,958	8,000	7,979	1,417	1,520	1,737	61	63	64	383	476	648
WI	4,750	4,906	5,035	288	327	396	45	48	52	76	100	145
W.N.C	16,914	17,385	18,091	972	1,036	1,147	217	241	286	279	369	546
MN	4,344	4,498	4,699	104	111	122	58	64	74	113	151	232
IA	2,763	2,816	2,841	57	65	78	8	8	8	33	41	53
MO	4,629	4,737	4,970	581	609	664	20	20	21	56	72	105
ND	600	601	622	4	4	5	28	31	37	5	7	11
SD	663	685	702	3	4	4	62	74	97	5	7	11
NE	1,550	1,598	1,669	64	69	76	14	15	16	17	22	31
KS	2,365	2,450	2,588	159	174	198	27	29	33	50	69	103
South	72,121	75,813	82,386	17,378	18,708	21,297	606	630	677	1,624	2,094	3,024
S.A.	35,962	37,772	40,805	9,960	10,868	12,615	185	194	208	911	1,173	1,691
DE	570	589	603	132	149	181	3	3	3	14	18	28
MD	3,500	3,546	3,631	1,368	1,514	1,776	13	13	14	196	249	361
DC	178	176	195	369	349	365	1	1	1	11	12	16
VA	5,127	5,367	5,743	1,284	1,391	1,592	15	15	15	220	275	378
WV	1,756	1,770	1,768	54	53	50	3	3	3	11	14	20
NC	5,378	5,682	6,125	1,594	1,715	1,916	90	98	109	88	123	190
SC	2,561	2,677	2,902	1,131	1,207	1,344	9	9	9	31	39	56
GA	5,025	5,346	5,857	1,955	2,139	2,485	13	12	12	109	140	199
FL	11,867	12,619	13,981	2,073	2,351	2,906	38	40	42	231	303	443
E.S.C	12,690	13,231	14,042	3,166	3,331	3,634	44	45	46	120	155	219
KY	3,535	3,646	3,769	286	307	345	6	6	6	24	30	40
TN	4,327	4,563	4,899	845	905	1,014	11	11	11	46	59	83
AL	3,140	3,284	3,529	1,083	1,139	1,243	18	18	19	33	44	65
MS	1,688	1,738	1,845	952	980	1,032	9	10	10	17	22	31
W.S.C	23,469	24,810	27,539	4,252	4,509	5,048	377	391	423	593	766	1,114
AR	2,047	2,139	2,311	386	395	412	15	17	18	20	27	41
LA	2,909	2,953	3,119	1,371	1,427	1,550	19	19	20	60	78	119
OK	2,699	2,770	2,979	244	251	269	276	290	320	52	71	115
TX	15,814	16,948	19,130	2,251	2,436	2,817	67	65	65	461	590	839
West	48,525	51,846	58,198	3,228	3,508	4,137	1,123	1,233	1,483	5,399	6,693	9,595
Mountain . . .	14,004	15,248	16,974	436	485	556	589	669	818	354	490	748
MT	798	847	908	2	2	3	55	62	74	6	8	12
ID	1,118	1,242	1,392	5	6	8	18	21	24	15	21	31
WY	467	498	564	4	5	5	12	14	17	4	6	9
CO	3,431	3,733	4,090	156	174	200	34	36	38	89	117	166
NM	1,460	1,574	1,760	32	33	35	159	181	231	25	35	56
AZ	3,606	3,894	4,379	123	131	143	251	285	348	91	127	204
UT	1,843	2,017	2,272	14	16	18	33	39	50	54	77	122
NV	1,281	1,443	1,609	100	118	144	27	31	36	70	99	148
Pacific	34,521	36,598	41,224	2,792	3,023	3,581	534	564	665	5,045	6,203	8,847
WA	4,915	5,360	6,071	164	174	187	101	112	131	318	424	635
OR	2,929	3,139	3,508	54	60	70	47	52	60	111	153	238
CA	25,701	26,987	30,357	2,512	2,719	3,245	277	276	314	3,908	4,906	7,169
AK	477	516	543	26	28	29	102	116	150	29	39	59
HI	499	596	745	36	42	50	7	8	10	679	681	746

Source: U.S. Bureau of the Census, *Current Population Reports*, series P25-1111.

No. 37. Population Projections, by Hispanic Origin Status—States: 1995 to 2010

[In thousands. As of July 1. Data shown are for series A, the preferred series model; for explanation of methodology, see text, section 1. Persons of Hispanic origin may be of any race]

REGION, DIVISION, AND STATE	HISPANIC ORIGIN			NOT OF HISPANIC ORIGIN		
	1995	2000	2010	1995	2000	2010
U.S.	26,797	31,164	40,526	236,640	245,078	259,904
Northeast	4,251	4,690	5,559	47,190	47,194	47,742
N.E.	684	796	1,035	12,514	12,420	12,720
ME	9	11	15	1,227	1,229	1,294
NH	13	16	24	1,119	1,149	1,256
VT	4	5	8	575	587	615
MA	342	394	510	5,634	5,556	5,587
RI	58	70	95	943	928	939
CT	258	300	383	3,016	2,971	3,029
M.A	3,567	3,894	4,524	34,676	34,774	35,022
NY	2,372	2,498	2,750	15,806	15,739	15,796
NJ	898	1,037	1,287	7,033	7,098	7,275
PA	297	359	487	11,837	11,937	11,951
Midwest......	2,103	2,479	3,284	59,890	61,357	63,049
E.N.C	1,738	2,037	2,683	41,872	42,769	43,576
OH	170	201	268	11,033	11,252	11,391
IN	122	145	197	5,698	5,900	6,089
IL	1,086	1,264	1,643	10,767	10,904	11,009
MI	242	283	375	9,333	9,476	9,658
WI	118	144	200	5,041	5,237	5,429
W.N.C	365	442	601	18,018	18,588	19,473
MN	68	83	116	4,551	4,741	5,011
IA	45	56	75	2,816	2,874	2,906
MO	71	82	108	5,215	5,355	5,652
ND	5	6	8	632	637	668
SD	7	9	11	728	761	804
NE	53	67	93	1,591	1,637	1,700
KS	116	139	190	2,485	2,583	2,732
South	8,259	9,752	12,944	83,469	87,492	94,441
S.A.	2,645	3,166	4,316	44,374	46,839	51,005
DE.	22	28	39	696	731	776
MD.	158	188	248	4,920	5,134	5,534
DC.	30	29	32	529	508	545
VA.	193	228	308	6,453	6,820	7,420
WV	10	12	16	1,814	1,828	1,826
NC	100	123	167	7,050	7,494	8,174
SC.	40	49	67	3,692	3,883	4,244
GA	144	176	237	6,958	7,461	8,316
FL.	1,948	2,333	3,202	12,262	12,980	14,170
E.S.C	112	132	176	15,907	16,630	17,765
KY.	23	26	34	3,828	3,963	4,126
TN.	42	51	67	5,186	5,487	5,940
AL.	29	35	49	4,245	4,450	4,807
MS	18	20	26	2,648	2,730	2,892
W.S.C	5,502	6,454	8,452	23,188	24,023	25,671
AR.	27	33	44	2,441	2,545	2,738
LA.	109	124	154	4,250	4,354	4,654
OK	106	124	160	3,165	3,258	3,523
TX.	5,260	6,173	8,094	13,332	13,866	14,756
West	12,184	14,243	18,739	46,091	49,035	54,672
Mountain ...	2,471	2,945	3,954	12,913	13,945	15,139
MT	15	17	22	847	903	974
ID	74	95	138	1,082	1,195	1,316
WY	31	36	45	456	486	551
CO	511	595	771	3,199	3,464	3,723
NM	686	792	1,024	990	1,031	1,058
AZ.	853	1,019	1,382	3,219	3,418	3,692
UT.	106	127	170	1,838	2,021	2,292
NV.	195	264	402	1,282	1,427	1,533
Pacific	9,713	11,298	14,785	33,178	35,090	39,533
WA	291	368	526	5,206	5,702	6,499
OR	151	189	265	2,990	3,215	3,611
CA	9,143	10,584	13,775	23,255	24,304	27,310
AK.	22	26	33	612	673	748
HI	106	131	186	1,115	1,196	1,365

Source: U.S. Bureau of the Census, Current Population Reports, series P25-1111.

No. 38. Population in Coastal Counties: 1960 to 1992

[Enumerated population as of **April 1**, except as indicated. Areas as defined by U.S. National Oceanic and Atmospheric Agency, 1992. Covers 672 counties and equivalent areas with at least 15 percent of their land area either in a coastal watershed or in a coastal cataloging unit]

YEAR	Total	COUNTIES IN COASTAL REGIONS					Balance of United States
		Total	Atlantic	Gulf of Mexico	Great Lakes	Pacific	
Land area, 1990 (1,000 sq. mi.)	3,536	888	148	114	115	510	2,649
POPULATION							
1960 (mil.).	179.3	94.5	44.5	8.4	23.7	17.9	84.8
1970 (mil.).	203.3	110.0	51.1	10.0	26.0	22.8	93.3
1980 (mil.).	226.5	119.8	53.7	13.1	26.0	27.0	106.7
1990 (mil.).	248.7	133.4	59.0	15.2	25.9	33.2	115.3
1992 (July 1)(mil.).	255.1	136.5	59.9	15.8	26.3	34.4	118.6
1960 (percent)	100	53	25	5	14	10	47
1970 (percent)	100	54	25	5	13	11	46
1980 (percent)	100	53	24	6	11	12	47
1990 (percent)	100	54	24	6	10	13	46
1992 (July 1)(percent)	100	54	24	6	10	14	46

Source: U.S. Bureau of the Census, *U.S. Census of Population: 1960* and *1970; 1980 Census of Population*, vol. 1, chapter A (PC80-1-A-1), *U.S. Summary; 1990 Census of Population and Housing* (CPH1); and unpublished data.

No. 39. Metropolitan and Nonmetropolitan Area Population: 1970 to 1992

[Metropolitan areas are as defined by U.S. Office of Management and Budget as of year shown, except as noted. See headnote, table 40]

ITEM	1970	1980 [1] (SMSA's)	MSA's AND CMSA's [2]		
			1980	1990	1992
Metropolitan areas: Number of areas	243	318	268	268	268
Population (1,000)	139,480	169,431	176,893	197,725	203,172
Percent change over previous year shown . .	[3]23.6	21.5	(X)	11.8	2.8
Percent of total U.S. population.	68.6	74.8	78.1	79.5	79.7
Land area, percent of U.S. land area.	10.9	16.0	19.0	19.0	19.0
Nonmetropolitan areas, population (1,000)	63,822	57,115	49,649	50,985	51,905

X Not applicable. [1] SMSA=standard metropolitan statistical area. Areas are as defined June 30, 1981. [2] Areas are as defined June 30, 1993. [3] Percent change from 1960.

Source: U.S. Bureau of the Census, *U.S. Census of Population: 1970; 1980 Census of Population*, vol. 1, chapter A (PC80-1-A) and *Supplementary Report, Metropolitan Statistical Areas* (PC80-S1-18); *1990 Census of Population and Housing, Supplementary Reports, Metropolitan Areas as Defined by the Office of Management and Budget, June 30, 1993* (1990 CPH-S-1-1); press release CB94-15; and unpublished data.

No. 40. Number and Population of Metropolitan Areas, by Population Size-Class in 1990: 1970 to 1990

[As of **April 1**. Data exclude Puerto Rico. CMSA=consolidated metropolitan statistical area. MSA=metropolitan statistical area. PMSA=primary metropolitan statistical area. Areas are as defined by U.S. Office of Management and Budget, June 30, 1993. For area definitions, see Appendix II. See also *Historical Statistics, Colonial Times to 1970*, series A 264-275]

LEVEL AND POPULATION SIZE-CLASS OF METROPOLITAN AREA IN 1990	CMSA's AND MSA's					MSA's AND PMSA's		
	Number, 1990	Popu-lation, 1970 (mil.)	Popu-lation, 1980 (mil.)	Population, 1990		Number, 1990	Population, 1990	
				Total (mil.)	Percent in each class		Total (mil.)	Percent in each class
Total, all metropolitan areas . . .	268	159.6	176.9	197.7	100	323	197.7	100
Level A (1,000,000 or more).	40	109.4	118.7	132.9	67	51	118.7	60
2,500,000 or more.	15	79.0	84.3	94.1	48	13	58.2	29
1,000,000 to 2,499,999	25	30.4	34.4	38.8	20	38	60.5	31
Level B (250,000 to 999,999)	96	35.5	41.2	46.4	23	119	56.9	29
500,000 to 999,999	33	18.2	21.4	24.3	12	41	29.4	15
250,000 to 499,999	63	17.3	19.8	22.0	11	78	27.5	14
Level C (100,000 to 249,999)	110	13.0	15.2	16.6	8	130	20.1	10
Level D (less than 100,000)	22	1.7	1.8	1.9	1	23	2.0	1

Source: U.S. Bureau of the Census, *1980 Census of Population, Supplementary Report, Metropolitan Statistical Areas* (PC80-S1-18); and *1990 Census of Population and Housing, Supplementary Reports, Metropolitan Areas as Defined by the Office of Management and Budget, June 30, 1993, (1990 CPH-S-1-1).*

No. 41. Metropolitan and Nonmetropolitan Population—States: 1980 to 1992

[As of **April 1**, except **1992**, as of **July**. Metropolitan refers to 250 metropolitan statistical areas and 18 consolidated metropolitan statistical areas as defined by U.S. Office of Management and Budget, June 30, 1993; nonmetropolitan is the area outside metropolitan areas; see Appendix II. Minus sign (-) indicates decrease]

REGION, DIVISION, AND STATE	METROPOLITAN POPULATION						NONMETROPOLITAN POPULATION					
	Total (1,000)			Percent change, 1980-92	Percent of State		Total (1,000)			Percent change, 1980-92	Percent of State	
	1980	1990	1992		1980	1992	1980	1990	1992		1980	1992
U.S.... .	176,893	197,725	203,172	14.9	78.1	79.7	49,649	50,985	51,905	4.5	21.9	20.3
Northeast ..	44,047	45,455	45,698	3.7	89.6	89.4	5,090	5,354	5,423	6.5	10.4	10.6
N.E	10,470	11,127	11,095	6.0	84.8	84.1	1,878	2,080	2,101	11.8	15.2	15.9
ME	405	443	441	9.0	36.0	35.7	721	785	795	10.4	64.0	64.3
NH	535	659	662	23.8	58.1	59.4	386	450	453	17.4	41.9	40.6
VT	133	152	154	15.9	26.0	27.0	378	411	417	10.2	74.0	73.0
MA	5,530	5,788	5,763	4.2	96.4	96.2	207	229	230	11.2	3.6	3.8
RI.....	886	938	937	5.8	93.5	93.6	61	65	64	5.1	6.5	6.4
CT	2,982	3,148	3,138	5.2	96.0	95.7	126	140	141	12.1	4.0	4.3
M.A	33,576	34,328	34,603	3.1	91.3	91.2	3,212	3,274	3,322	3.4	8.7	8.8
NY	16,144	16,515	16,613	2.9	91.9	91.7	1,414	1,475	1,497	5.9	8.1	8.3
NJ....	7,365	7,730	7,820	6.2	100.0	100.0	(X)	(X)	(X)	(X)	(X)	(X)
PA	10,067	10,083	10,170	1.0	84.8	84.8	1,798	1,799	1,825	1.5	15.2	15.2
Midwest ..	42,557	43,691	44,522	4.6	72.3	73.4	16,310	15,978	16,117	-1.2	27.7	26.6
E.N.C	33,031	33,391	33,976	2.9	79.2	79.5	8,652	8,618	8,743	1.1	20.8	20.5
OH	8,791	8,826	8,966	2.0	81.4	81.3	2,007	2,021	2,056	2.4	18.6	18.7
IN	3,885	3,962	4,052	4.3	70.8	71.6	1,605	1,582	1,606	(Z)	29.2	28.4
IL	9,461	9,574	9,757	3.1	82.8	84.0	1,967	1,857	1,856	-5.6	17.2	16.0
MI	7,719	7,698	7,799	1.0	83.3	82.7	1,543	1,598	1,635	5.9	16.7	17.3
WI....	3,176	3,331	3,402	7.1	67.5	68.1	1,530	1,561	1,591	4.0	32.5	31.9
W.N.C ...	9,526	10,300	10,546	10.7	55.4	58.8	7,658	7,360	7,374	-3.7	44.6	41.2
MN	2,674	3,011	3,096	15.8	65.6	69.3	1,402	1,364	1,372	-2.2	34.4	30.7
IA	1,198	1,200	1,228	2.5	41.1	43.8	1,716	1,577	1,575	-8.2	58.9	56.2
MO	3,314	3,491	3,543	6.9	67.4	68.3	1,603	1,626	1,647	2.8	32.6	31.7
ND	234	257	263	12.4	35.9	41.6	418	381	371	-11.4	64.1	58.4
SD	194	221	231	19.1	28.0	32.6	497	475	478	-3.9	72.0	67.4
NE	728	787	809	11.1	46.4	50.6	842	791	791	-6.0	53.6	49.4
KS	1,184	1,333	1,374	16.1	50.1	54.6	1,180	1,145	1,141	-3.3	49.9	45.4
South	53,634	63,092	65,463	22.1	71.2	74.2	21,733	22,354	22,722	4.5	28.8	25.8
S.A	28,226	34,294	35,599	26.1	76.4	78.9	8,732	9,273	9,493	8.7	23.6	21.1
DE	496	553	571	15.1	83.5	82.7	98	113	120	22.3	16.5	17.3
MD	3,920	4,439	4,563	16.4	93.0	92.8	297	343	354	19.1	7.0	7.2
DC	638	607	585	-8.3	100.0	100.0	(X)	(X)	(X)	(X)	(X)	(X)
VA	3,966	4,773	4,954	24.9	74.2	77.5	1,381	1,414	1,440	4.3	25.8	22.5
WV	796	748	756	-5.0	40.8	41.8	1,155	1,045	1,053	-8.8	59.2	58.2
NC	3,749	4,376	4,535	21.0	63.8	66.3	2,131	2,253	2,301	8.0	36.2	33.7
SC	2,114	2,423	2,514	18.9	67.8	69.8	1,006	1,064	1,089	8.2	32.2	30.2
GA	3,507	4,352	4,587	30.8	64.2	67.7	1,956	2,127	2,186	11.8	35.8	32.3
FL....	9,039	12,023	12,532	38.7	92.7	93.0	708	915	950	34.2	7.3	7.0
E.S.C	8,057	8,563	8,815	9.4	54.9	56.8	6,609	6,613	6,716	1.6	45.1	43.2
KY	1,735	1,780	1,820	4.9	47.4	48.5	1,925	1,906	1,934	0.5	52.6	51.5
TN	3,045	3,298	3,404	11.8	66.3	67.7	1,546	1,579	1,621	4.9	33.7	32.3
AL....	2,560	2,710	2,788	8.9	65.7	67.4	1,334	1,331	1,349	1.1	34.3	32.6
MS	776	776	803	12.1	28.4	30.7	1,805	1,798	1,812	0.4	71.6	69.3
W.S.C	17,351	20,235	21,048	21.3	73.1	76.4	6,392	6,468	6,513	1.9	26.9	23.6
AR	963	1,040	1,071	11.2	42.1	44.7	1,323	1,311	1,323	(Z)	57.9	55.3
LA....	3,125	3,160	3,210	2.7	74.3	75.0	1,082	1,060	1,069	-1.2	25.7	25.0
OK	1,724	1,870	1,927	11.7	57.0	60.1	1,301	1,276	1,278	-1.8	43.0	39.9
TX	11,539	14,166	14,840	28.6	81.1	83.9	2,686	2,821	2,842	5.8	18.9	16.1
West.....	36,655	45,487	47,490	29.6	84.9	86.1	6,516	7,299	7,643	17.3	15.1	13.9
Mountain .	7,645	9,605	10,155	32.8	67.2	70.6	3,726	4,054	4,225	13.4	32.8	29.4
MT	189	191	197	4.6	24.0	24.0	598	608	625	4.5	76.0	76.0
ID....	257	296	320	24.4	27.2	30.0	687	711	746	8.6	72.8	70.0
WY	141	134	138	-1.8	29.9	29.7	329	319	327	-0.7	70.1	70.3
CO	2,326	2,686	2,832	21.7	80.5	81.8	563	608	632	12.3	19.5	18.2
NM	675	842	886	31.3	51.8	56.0	628	673	696	10.7	48.2	44.0
AZ	2,264	3,106	3,244	43.3	83.3	84.7	453	559	588	29.9	16.7	15.3
UT	1,128	1,336	1,403	24.4	77.2	77.5	333	387	408	22.6	22.8	22.5
NV	666	1,014	1,134	70.3	83.2	84.8	135	188	203	50.5	16.8	15.2
Pacific ...	29,010	35,882	37,335	28.7	91.2	91.6	2,790	3,245	3,418	22.5	8.8	8.4
WA	3,366	4,036	4,270	26.8	81.5	83.0	766	830	873	14.0	18.5	17.0
OR	1,799	1,985	2,081	15.7	68.3	70.0	834	858	890	6.7	31.7	30.0
CA	22,907	28,799	29,875	30.4	96.8	96.7	760	961	1,021	34.3	3.2	3.3
AK	174	226	246	41.0	43.4	41.8	227	324	342	50.3	56.6	58.2
HI....	763	836	863	13.2	79.0	74.7	202	272	293	44.8	21.0	25.3

X Not applicable. Z Less than 0.05 percent.

Source: U.S. Bureau of the Census, *1990 Census of Population and Housing, Supplementary Reports, Metropolitan Areas as Defined by the Office of Management and Budget, June 30, 1993*, (1990 CPH-S-1-1); and unpublished data.

No. 42. Large Metropolitan Areas—Population: 1980 to 1992

[As of **April** 1, except **1992** as of **July** 1. Covers 18 consolidated metropolitan statistical areas (CMSA's), their 73 component primary metropolitan statistical areas (PMSA's), and the remaining 119 MSA's with 250,000 and over population in 1992 as defined by the U.S. Office of Management and Budget as of June 30, 1993. Rank based on unrounded figures for CMSA's and MSA's only. For definitions and components of all MA's and population of NECMA's (New England County Metropolitan Areas), see Appendix II. Minus sign (-) indicates decrease]

METROPOLITAN AREA	1980, total (1,000)	1990 Total (1,000)	1990 Under 18 yrs. old (percent)	1990 65 yrs. old and over (percent)	1992 Total (1,000)	1992 Rank	PERCENT CHANGE 1980-90	PERCENT CHANGE 1990-92
Albany-Schenectady-Troy, NY MSA	825	861	23.3	14.1	872	52	4.4	1.3
Albuquerque, NM MSA	485	589	27.1	10.4	616	63	21.4	4.6
Allentown-Bethlehem-Easton, PA MSA	551	595	22.9	15.5	606	66	8.0	1.9
Appleton-Oshkosh-Neenah, WI MSA	291	315	26.7	11.9	324	113	8.2	2.8
Atlanta, GA MSA	2,233	2,960	25.9	8.0	3,143	12	32.5	6.2
Augusta-Aiken, GA-SC MSA	363	415	27.9	10.0	444	81	14.2	6.8
Austin-San Marcos, TX MSA	585	846	25.6	7.8	901	49	44.6	6.5
Bakersfield, CA MSA	403	543	31.5	9.7	588	69	34.8	8.1
Baton Rouge, LA MSA	494	528	28.6	8.9	546	71	6.9	3.4
Beaumont-Port Arthur, TX MSA	373	361	27.6	13.1	370	101	-3.2	2.4
Biloxi-Gulfport-Pascagoula, MS MSA	300	312	28.3	10.6	324	114	4.1	3.7
Binghamton, NY MSA	263	264	24.0	14.2	266	133	0.4	0.5
Birmingham, AL MSA	815	840	25.4	13.1	859	54	3.0	2.2
Boise City, ID MSA	257	296	29.1	11.4	320	115	15.2	8.0
Boston-Worcester-Lawrence, MA-NH-ME-CT CMSA	5,122	5,455	22.7	12.7	5,439	7	6.5	-0.3
Boston, MA-NH PMSA	3,149	3,228	20.9	13.1	3,211	(X)	2.5	-0.5
Brockton, MA PMSA	225	236	26.0	11.1	236	(X)	5.1	-0.2
Fitchburg-Leominster, MA PMSA	125	138	24.7	13.8	137	(X)	10.5	-0.8
Lawrence, MA-NH PMSA	298	353	27.0	11.2	357	(X)	18.4	1.0
Lowell, MA-NH PMSA	249	281	26.0	9.7	283	(X)	12.5	0.9
Manchester, NH PMSA	146	174	25.3	11.2	175	(X)	18.9	0.5
Nashua, NH PMSA	134	168	26.5	8.3	171	(X)	25.4	1.9
New Bedford, MA PMSA	167	176	24.4	16.3	173	(X)	5.4	-1.3
Portsmouth-Rochester, NH-ME PMSA	189	223	23.4	11.6	219	(X)	18.0	-1.9
Worcester, MA-CT PMSA	439	478	24.0	14.2	477	(X)	8.9	-0.4
Brownsville-Harlingen-San Benito, TX MSA	210	260	35.3	10.6	279	126	24.0	7.1
Buffalo-Niagara Falls, NY MSA	1,243	1,189	23.6	13.6	1,194	34	-4.3	0.4
Canton-Massillon, OH MSA	404	394	25.3	14.4	399	95	-2.6	1.3
Charleston-North Charleston, SC MSA	430	507	27.6	8.6	529	72	17.8	4.3
Charleston, WV MSA	270	250	23.8	14.9	253	136	-7.1	1.1
Charlotte-Gastonia-Rock Hill, NC-SC MSA	971	1,162	24.7	10.9	1,212	33	19.6	4.3
Chattanooga, TN-GA MSA	418	424	24.7	13.0	431	85	1.6	1.5
Chicago-Gary-Kenosha, IL-IN-WI CMSA	8,115	8,240	26.1	11.4	8,410	3	1.5	2.1
Chicago, IL PMSA	7,246	7,411	25.9	11.3	7,561	(X)	2.3	2.0
Gary, IN PMSA	643	605	27.9	11.8	617	(X)	-5.9	2.0
Kankakee, IL PMSA	103	96	28.1	13.7	99	(X)	-6.5	2.8
Kenosha, WI PMSA	123	128	26.8	12.6	134	(X)	4.1	4.5
Cincinnati-Hamilton, OH-KY-IN CMSA	1,726	1,818	26.8	11.8	1,865	23	5.3	2.6
Cincinnati, OH-KY-IN PMSA	1,468	1,526	26.9	12.1	1,560	(X)	4.0	2.2
Hamilton-Middletown, OH PMSA	259	291	26.2	10.2	305	(X)	12.6	4.7
Cleveland-Akron, OH CMSA	2,938	2,860	24.9	13.9	2,890	14	-2.7	1.1
Akron, OH PMSA	660	658	24.4	12.9	669	(X)	-0.4	1.8
Cleveland-Lorain-Elyria, OH PMSA	2,278	2,202	25.1	14.2	2,221	(X)	-3.3	0.9
Colorado Springs, CO MSA	309	397	27.6	8.0	421	86	28.3	6.1
Columbia, SC MSA	410	453	25.0	9.3	472	78	10.6	4.1
Columbus, GA-AL MSA	255	261	26.9	10.7	270	130	2.4	3.6
Columbus, OH MSA	1,214	1,345	25.1	10.0	1,394	29	10.8	3.6
Corpus Christi, TX MSA	326	350	30.8	10.2	361	103	7.3	3.3
Dallas-Fort Worth, TX CMSA	3,046	4,037	27.2	8.3	4,215	9	32.5	4.4
Dallas, TX PMSA	2,055	2,676	27.1	8.1	2,795	(X)	30.2	4.4
Fort Worth-Arlington, TX PMSA	991	1,361	27.3	8.8	1,419	(X)	37.4	4.3
Davenport-Moline-Rock Island, IA-IL MSA	385	351	26.7	13.7	356	105	-8.8	1.5
Dayton-Springfield, OH MSA	942	951	25.3	12.4	962	46	1.0	1.1
Daytona Beach, FL MSA	270	399	19.7	23.0	422	87	48.1	5.6
Denver-Boulder-Greeley, CO CMSA	1,742	1,980	25.7	9.2	2,089	21	13.7	5.5
Boulder-Longmont, CO PMSA	190	225	23.0	7.6	238	(X)	18.8	5.7
Denver, CO PMSA	1,429	1,623	25.9	9.4	1,715	(X)	13.6	5.7
Greeley, CO PMSA	123	132	28.1	10.2	136	(X)	6.8	3.1
Des Moines, IA MSA	368	393	25.6	11.7	406	92	6.9	3.4
Detroit-Ann Arbor-Flint, MI CMSA	5,293	5,187	26.1	11.5	5,246	8	-2.0	1.1
Ann Arbor, MI PMSA	455	490	24.5	8.5	505	(X)	7.7	3.0
Detroit, MI PMSA	4,388	4,267	26.0	11.9	4,308	(X)	-2.8	1.0
Flint, MI PMSA	450	430	28.0	10.2	434	(X)	-4.4	0.7
El Paso, TX MSA	480	592	32.6	8.2	628	62	23.3	6.2
Erie, PA MSA	280	276	25.9	13.8	280	125	-1.5	1.5
Eugene-Springfield, OR MSA	275	283	24.5	13.1	291	122	2.8	2.8
Evansville-Henderson, IN-KY MSA	276	279	25.4	14.0	283	124	1.0	1.4
Fayetteville, NC MSA	247	275	28.0	6.1	277	127	11.1	1.0
Fort Myers-Cape Coral, FL MSA	205	335	19.6	24.8	352	107	63.3	5.1
Fort Pierce-Port St. Lucie, FL MSA	151	251	20.9	23.6	265	134	66.1	5.7
Fort Wayne, IN MSA	445	456	28.2	12.0	463	79	2.6	1.5
Fresno, CA MSA	578	756	31.3	10.6	805	56	30.8	6.5

See footnotes at end of table.

Population

No. 42. Metropolitan Areas—Population: 1980 to 1992—Continued

[See headnote, page 39]

METROPOLITAN AREA	1980, total (1,000)	1990			1992		PERCENT CHANGE	
		Total (1,000)	Under 18 yrs. old (percent)	65 yrs. old and over (percent)	Total (1,000)	Rank	1980-90	1990-92
Grand Rapids-Muskegon-Holland, MI MSA	841	938	28.6	11.1	964	45	11.5	2.8
Greensboro—Winston-Salem—High Point, NC MSA. .	951	1,050	22.9	12.4	1,078	39	10.5	2.7
Greenville-Spartanburg-Anderson, SC MSA	744	831	24.5	12.4	853	55	11.6	2.7
Harrisburg-Lebanon-Carlisle, PA MSA	556	588	23.4	13.9	601	68	5.7	2.3
Hartford, CT MSA	1,081	1,158	22.6	13.2	1,156	35	7.1	-0.2
Hickory-Morganton, NC MSA	270	292	23.8	12.2	299	120	8.1	2.3
Honolulu, HI MSA	763	836	24.5	11.0	863	53	9.7	3.2
Houston-Galveston-Brazoria, TX CMSA	3,118	3,731	28.9	7.3	3,962	10	19.6	6.2
Brazoria, TX PMSA	170	192	29.3	7.8	204	(X)	13.0	6.3
Galveston-Texas City, TX PMSA	196	217	27.6	10.5	228	(X)	11.1	4.9
Houston, TX PMSA.	2,753	3,322	28.9	7.1	3,530	(X)	20.7	6.3
Huntington-Ashland, WV-KY-OH MSA	336	313	24.5	14.4	315	117	-7.1	0.8
Huntsville, AL MSA	243	293	24.7	9.4	308	118	20.6	5.1
Indianapolis, IN MSA	1,306	1,380	26.2	11.4	1,424	28	5.7	3.2
Jackson, MS MSA	362	395	28.1	10.5	405	93	9.2	2.4
Jacksonville, FL MSA	722	907	26.0	10.9	953	47	25.5	5.1
Johnson City-Kingsport-Bristol, TN-VA MSA	434	436	22.3	14.6	445	80	0.6	2.0
Kalamazoo-Battle Creek, MI MSA.	421	429	25.9	11.8	436	83	2.1	1.6
Kansas City, MO-KS MSA	1,449	1,583	26.4	11.6	1,617	25	9.2	2.2
Killeen-Temple, TX MSA	215	255	28.2	8.0	255	135	19.0	-0.2
Knoxville, TN MSA.	546	586	22.9	13.4	610	65	7.2	4.2
Lafayette, LA MSA	331	345	30.6	10.0	353	106	4.3	2.4
Lakeland-Winter Haven, FL MSA	322	405	24.1	18.6	419	91	26.0	3.4
Lancaster, PA MSA	362	423	26.5	13.1	434	84	16.7	2.7
Lansing-East Lansing, MI MSA.	420	433	25.6	9.0	436	82	3.1	0.9
Las Vegas, NV-AZ MSA	528	853	24.3	11.6	971	43	61.5	13.9
Lexington, KY MSA	371	406	23.6	10.3	420	90	9.4	3.5
Little Rock-North Little Rock, AR MSA	474	513	26.5	11.4	526	73	8.1	2.5
Los Angeles-Riverside-Orange County, CA CMSA . .	11,498	14,532	26.6	9.8	15,048	2	26.4	3.6
Los Angeles-Long Beach, CA PMSA	7,477	8,863	26.2	9.7	9,054	(X)	18.5	2.1
Orange County, CA PMSA	1,933	2,411	24.4	9.2	2,485	(X)	24.7	3.1
Riverside-San Bernardino, CA PMSA	1,558	2,589	29.8	10.8	2,823	(X)	66.1	9.0
Ventura, CA PMSA	529	669	27.4	9.4	687	(X)	26.4	2.6
Louisville, KY-IN MSA.	954	949	25.3	12.6	968	44	-0.5	2.0
Macon, GA MSA	273	291	27.4	10.8	299	121	6.6	2.7
Madison, WI MSA	324	367	22.7	9.3	380	98	13.5	3.6
McAllen-Edinburg-Mission, TX MSA	283	384	36.6	10.0	421	89	35.4	9.8
Melbourne-Titusville-Palm Bay, FL MSA.	273	399	21.9	16.6	426	86	46.2	6.7
Memphis, TN-AR-MS MSA	939	1,007	27.9	10.4	1,034	40	7.3	2.6
Miami-Fort Lauderdale, FL CMSA	2,644	3,193	22.7	16.6	3,309	11	20.8	3.7
Fort Lauderdale, FL PMSA	1,018	1,255	20.4	20.8	1,301	(X)	23.3	3.6
Miami, FL PMSA.	1,626	1,937	24.2	14.0	2,008	(X)	19.2	3.7
Milwaukee-Racine, WI CMSA.	1,570	1,607	26.4	12.4	1,629	24	2.4	1.4
Milwaukee-Waukesha, WI PMSA	1,397	1,432	26.3	12.5	1,450	(X)	2.5	1.2
Racine, WI PMSA	173	175	27.8	12.0	180	(X)	1.1	2.6
Minneapolis-St. Paul, MN-WI MSA	2,198	2,539	26.4	9.8	2,618	15	15.5	3.1
Mobile, AL MSA	444	477	28.0	12.5	496	77	7.5	3.9
Modesto, CA MSA	266	371	30.6	10.8	395	96	39.3	6.7
Montgomery, AL MSA.	273	293	27.4	11.4	304	119	7.3	3.8
Nashville, TN MSA.	851	985	25.1	10.6	1,023	41	15.8	3.9
New London-Norwich, CT-RI MSA	273	291	23.6	12.5	284	123	6.5	-2.3
New Orleans, LA MSA	1,304	1,285	28.1	11.0	1,303	32	-1.5	1.4
New York-Northern New Jersey-Long Island, NY-NJ-CT-PA CMSA.	18,906	19,550	23.0	13.1	19,670	1	3.4	0.6
Bergen-Passaic, NJ PMSA	1,293	1,278	21.7	14.5	1,291	(X)	-1.1	1.0
Bridgeport, CT PMSA	439	444	23.2	14.7	443	(X)	1.2	-0.2
Danbury, CT PMSA.	175	194	24.3	10.0	196	(X)	10.3	1.5
Dutchess County, NY PMSA.	245	259	23.9	11.4	263	(X)	5.9	1.3
Jersey City, NJ PMSA	557	553	22.1	12.7	555	(X)	-0.7	0.3
Middlesex-Somerset-Hunterdon, NJ PMSA	886	1,020	21.9	11.3	1,047	(X)	15.1	2.6
Monmouth-Ocean, NJ PMSA	849	986	23.6	17.3	1,004	(X)	16.1	1.8
Nassau-Suffolk, NY PMSA	2,606	2,609	23.3	12.4	2,640	(X)	0.1	1.2
Newark, NJ PMSA	1,964	1,916	23.6	12.6	1,923	(X)	-2.4	0.4
Newburgh, NY-PA PMSA	278	336	27.4	10.9	348	(X)	20.8	3.8
New Haven-Meriden, CT PMSA	500	530	22.6	14.1	527	(X)	5.9	-0.6
New York, NY PMSA.	8,275	8,547	23.0	13.0	8,552	(X)	3.3	0.1
Stamford-Norwalk, CT PMSA	326	330	20.9	13.4	331	(X)	1.3	0.2
Trenton, NJ PMSA	308	326	22.5	13.0	328	(X)	5.8	0.6
Waterbury, CT PMSA	205	222	23.4	15.6	222	(X)	8.1	0.1
Norfolk-Virginia Beach-Newport News, VA-NC MSA. .	1,201	1,443	26.4	9.2	1,497	27	20.2	3.7
Oklahoma City, OK MSA	861	959	26.6	11.0	984	42	11.4	2.6
Omaha, NE-IA MSA	605	640	27.9	10.7	656	60	5.6	2.6
Orlando, FL MSA.	805	1,225	23.8	12.9	1,305	31	52.2	6.5
Pensacola, FL MSA	290	344	25.7	11.3	361	104	18.9	4.9
Peoria-Pekin, IL MSA	366	339	26.4	13.8	343	110	-7.3	1.0

See footnotes at end of table.

No. 42. Metropolitan Areas—Population: 1980 to 1992—Continued

[See headnote, page 39]

METROPOLITAN AREA	1980, total (1,000)	1990 Total (1,000)	1990 Under 18 yrs. old (per-cent)	1990 65 yrs. old and over (per-cent)	1992 Total (1,000)	1992 Rank	PERCENT CHANGE 1980-90	PERCENT CHANGE 1990-92
Philadelphia-Wilmington-Atlantic City, PA-NJ-DE-MD CMSA	5,649	5,893	24.4	13.5	5,939	6	4.3	0.8
Atlantic-Cape May, NJ PMSA	276	319	22.7	16.2	326	(X)	15.6	2.1
Philadelphia, PA-NJ PMSA	4,781	4,922	24.4	13.5	4,944	(X)	2.9	0.4
Vineland-Millville-Bridgeton, NJ PMSA	133	138	26.0	13.5	138	(X)	3.9	0.3
Wilmington-Newark, DE-MD PMSA	459	513	24.5	11.2	530	(X)	11.9	3.3
Phoenix-Mesa, AZ MSA	1,600	2,238	26.4	12.6	2,330	19	39.9	4.1
Pittsburgh, PA MSA	2,571	2,395	22.0	17.1	2,406	18	−6.9	0.5
Portland-Salem, OR-WA CMSA	1,584	1,793	25.8	12.4	1,897	22	13.3	5.8
Portland-Vancouver, OR-WA PMSA	1,334	1,515	25.7	12.0	1,605	(X)	13.6	5.9
Salem, OR PMSA	250	278	26.4	14.4	292	(X)	11.3	5.0
Providence-Fall River-Warwick, RI-MA MSA	1,077	1,134	22.8	15.1	1,131	36	5.4	−0.3
Provo-Orem, UT MSA	218	264	37.8	7.0	275	129	20.9	4.4
Raleigh-Durham-Chapel Hill, NC MSA	665	856	22.7	9.5	909	48	28.7	6.3
Reading, PA MSA	313	337	23.3	15.6	343	109	7.7	2.0
Reno, NV MSA	194	255	23.1	10.3	269	131	31.5	5.4
Richmond-Petersburg, VA MSA	761	866	24.3	11.3	896	51	13.7	3.5
Rochester, NY MSA	1,031	1,062	25.1	12.5	1,081	38	3.1	1.8
Rockford, IL MSA	326	330	26.5	12.8	340	111	1.2	3.0
Sacramento-Yolo, CA CMSA	1,100	1,481	26.2	10.8	1,563	26	34.7	5.6
Sacramento, CA PMSA	986	1,340	26.4	10.9	1,419	(X)	35.8	5.9
Yolo, CA PMSA	113	141	24.1	9.5	145	(X)	24.4	2.6
Saginaw-Bay City-Midland, MI MSA	422	399	27.5	12.1	403	94	−5.3	0.8
St. Louis, MO-IL MSA	2,414	2,493	26.3	12.8	2,519	17	3.3	1.0
Salinas, CA MSA	290	356	27.5	9.8	368	102	22.5	3.6
Salt Lake City-Ogden, UT MSA	910	1,072	35.6	8.4	1,128	37	17.8	5.2
San Antonio, TX MSA	1,089	1,325	29.0	10.3	1,379	30	21.7	4.1
San Diego, CA MSA	1,862	2,498	24.5	10.9	2,601	16	34.2	4.1
San Francisco-Oakland-San Jose, CA CMSA	5,368	6,253	23.1	11.1	6,410	5	16.5	2.5
Oakland, CA PMSA	1,762	2,083	24.3	10.7	2,148	(X)	18.2	3.1
San Francisco, CA PMSA	1,489	1,604	18.9	13.3	1,626	(X)	7.7	1.4
San Jose, CA PMSA	1,295	1,498	24.0	8.7	1,528	(X)	15.6	2.1
Santa Cruz-Watsonville, CA PMSA	188	230	23.8	11.3	231	(X)	22.1	0.5
Santa Rosa, CA PMSA	300	388	24.7	13.4	401	(X)	29.5	3.3
Vallejo-Fairfield-Napa, CA PMSA	334	451	27.4	10.2	475	(X)	34.9	5.3
Santa Barbara-Santa Maria-Lompoc, CA MSA	299	370	23.2	12.3	376	99	23.7	1.6
Sarasota-Bradenton, FL MSA	351	489	17.2	30.4	499	76	39.6	1.9
Savannah, GA MSA	231	258	27.2	11.9	267	132	11.8	3.6
Scranton—Wilkes-Barre—Hazleton, PA MSA	659	638	21.9	19.0	639	61	−3.2	-
Seattle-Tacoma-Bremerton, WA CMSA	2,409	2,970	25.0	10.8	3,131	13	23.3	5.4
Bremerton, WA PMSA	147	190	27.9	10.7	211	(X)	28.9	11.1
Olympia, WA PMSA	124	161	26.9	11.7	177	(X)	29.8	9.5
Seattle-Bellevue-Everett, WA PMSA	1,652	2,033	23.9	10.8	2,124	(X)	23.1	4.5
Tacoma, WA PMSA	486	586	27.2	10.5	620	(X)	20.7	5.7
Shreveport-Bossier City, LA MSA	377	376	28.6	12.7	374	100	−0.1	−0.6
South Bend, IN MSA	242	247	25.3	14.1	251	137	2.2	1.4
Spokane, WA MSA	342	361	26.4	13.3	381	97	5.7	5.5
Springfield, MA MSA	570	588	23.4	14.1	584	70	3.2	−0.6
Springfield, MO MSA	228	264	24.1	13.0	276	128	15.9	4.3
Stockton-Lodi, CA MSA	347	481	29.6	11.1	504	74	38.4	4.9
Syracuse, NY MSA	723	742	25.3	12.6	752	57	2.7	1.4
Tampa-St. Petersburg-Clearwater, FL MSA	1,614	2,068	20.4	21.6	2,107	20	28.2	1.9
Toledo, OH MSA	617	614	26.3	12.4	615	64	−0.4	0.2
Tucson, AZ MSA	531	667	24.9	13.7	690	59	25.5	3.5
Tulsa, OK MSA	657	709	26.8	11.6	732	58	7.9	3.2
Utica-Rome, NY MSA	320	317	24.5	15.7	318	116	−1.1	0.5
Visalia-Tulare-Porterville, CA MSA	246	312	33.1	10.8	331	112	26.9	6.1
Washington-Baltimore, DC-MD-VA-WV CMSA	5,791	6,727	23.9	9.9	6,920	4	16.2	2.9
Baltimore, MD PMSA	2,199	2,382	24.1	11.7	2,434	(X)	8.3	2.2
Hagerstown, MD PMSA	113	121	22.7	13.8	125	(X)	7.3	3.4
Washington, DC-MD-VA-WV PMSA	3,478	4,223	23.7	8.7	4,360	(X)	21.4	3.2
West Palm Beach-Boca Raton, FL MSA	577	864	19.6	24.3	901	50	49.7	4.3
Wichita, KS MSA	442	485	27.8	11.9	501	75	9.7	3.3
York, PA MSA	313	340	24.2	13.1	350	108	8.5	3.1
Youngstown-Warren, OH MSA	645	601	25.1	15.6	606	67	−6.8	0.8

- Represents or rounds to zero. X Not applicable.

Source: U.S. Bureau of the Census, *1990 Census of Population and Housing, Supplementary Reports, Metropolitan Areas as Defined by the Office of Management and Budget, June 30, 1993,* (1990 CPH-S-1-1); and unpublished data.

No. 43. 75 Largest Metropolitan Areas—Racial and Hispanic Origin Populations: 1990

[As of **April 1**. Areas as defined by U.S. Office of Management and Budget, June 30, 1993. For area definitions, see Appendix II]

METROPOLITAN AREA [1]	Total population (1,000)	PERCENT OF TOTAL METROPOLITAN POPULATION			
		Black	American Indian, Eskimo, Aleut	Asian and Pacific Islander	Hispanic origin [2]
New York-Northern New Jersey-Long Island, NY-NJ-CT-PA CMSA .	19,550	17.7	0.2	4.6	14.6
Los Angeles-Riverside-Orange County, CA CMSA	14,532	8.5	0.6	9.2	32.9
Chicago-Gary-Kenosha, IL-IN-WI CMSA	8,240	19.0	0.2	3.1	10.9
Washington-Baltimore, DC-MD-VA-WV CMSA	6,727	25.2	0.3	3.7	3.9
San Francisco-Oakland-San Jose, CA CMSA	6,253	8.6	0.7	14.8	15.5
Philadelphia-Wilmington-Atlantic City, PA-NJ-DE-MD CMSA . . .	5,893	18.4	0.2	2.0	3.8
Boston-Worcester-Lawrence, MA-NH-ME-CT CMSA	5,455	4.8	0.2	2.5	4.4
Detroit-Ann Arbor-Flint, MI CMSA	5,187	20.5	0.4	1.4	2.0
Dallas-Fort Worth, TX CMSA	4,037	14.0	0.5	2.4	13.0
Houston-Galveston-Brazoria, TX CMSA	3,731	17.9	0.3	3.5	20.7
Miami-Fort Lauderdale, FL CMSA	3,193	18.5	0.2	1.4	33.3
Seattle-Tacoma-Bremerton, WA CMSA	2,970	4.5	1.3	6.1	3.0
Atlanta, GA MSA	2,960	25.2	0.2	1.8	2.0
Cleveland-Akron, OH CMSA	2,860	15.6	0.2	1.0	1.9
Minneapolis-St. Paul, MN-WI MSA	2,539	3.5	1.0	2.6	1.5
San Diego, CA MSA	2,498	6.4	0.8	7.9	20.4
St. Louis, MO-IL MSA	2,493	17.0	0.2	1.0	1.1
Pittsburgh, PA MSA	2,395	7.5	0.1	0.7	0.6
Phoenix-Mesa, AZ MSA	2,238	3.5	2.2	1.6	17.0
Tampa-St. Petersburg-Clearwater, FL MSA	2,068	9.0	0.3	1.1	6.7
Denver-Boulder-Greeley, CO CMSA	1,980	5.0	0.7	2.2	12.8
Cincinnati-Hamilton, OH-KY-IN CMSA	1,818	11.2	0.1	0.8	0.5
Portland-Salem, OR-WA CMSA	1,793	2.5	1.0	3.2	4.0
Milwaukee-Racine, WI CMSA	1,607	13.3	0.5	1.2	3.8
Kansas City, MO-KS MSA	1,583	12.7	0.5	1.1	2.9
Sacramento-Yolo, CA CMSA	1,481	6.9	1.1	7.7	11.6
Norfolk-Virginia Beach-Newport News, VA-NC MSA	1,443	28.3	0.3	2.4	2.3
Indianapolis, IN MSA	1,380	13.2	0.2	0.8	0.9
Columbus, OH MSA	1,345	12.1	0.2	1.6	0.8
San Antonio, TX MSA	1,325	6.7	0.4	1.2	47.4
New Orleans, LA MSA	1,285	34.8	0.3	1.7	4.2
Orlando, FL MSA	1,225	12.0	0.3	1.7	8.2
Buffalo-Niagara Falls, NY MSA	1,189	10.3	0.6	0.9	2.0
Charlotte-Gastonia-Rock Hill, NC-SC MSA	1,162	19.9	0.4	1.0	0.9
Hartford, CT MSA	1,158	8.3	0.2	1.5	6.9
Providence-Fall River-Warwick, RI-MA MSA	1,134	3.3	0.3	1.8	4.2
Salt Lake City-Ogden, UT MSA	1,072	1.0	0.8	2.4	5.8
Rochester, NY MSA	1,062	8.9	0.3	1.3	3.0
Greensboro—Winston-Salem—High Point, NC MSA	1,050	19.3	0.3	0.7	0.7
Memphis, TN-AR-MS MSA	1,007	40.7	0.2	0.8	0.8
Nashville, TN MSA	985	15.5	0.2	1.0	0.8
Oklahoma City, OK MSA	959	10.5	4.8	1.9	3.6
Dayton-Springfield, OH MSA	951	13.3	0.2	1.0	0.8
Louisville, KY-IN MSA	949	12.9	0.2	0.6	0.6
Grand Rapids-Muskegon-Holland, MI MSA	938	6.9	0.6	0.9	3.1
Jacksonville, FL MSA	907	20.0	0.3	1.7	2.5
Richmond-Petersburg, VA MSA	866	29.2	0.3	1.4	1.1
West Palm Beach-Boca Raton, FL MSA	864	12.5	0.1	1.0	7.7
Albany-Schenectady-Troy, NY MSA	861	4.6	0.2	1.2	1.7
Raleigh-Durham-Chapel Hill, NC MSA	856	24.2	0.3	1.6	1.3
Las Vegas, NV-AZ MSA	853	8.4	1.1	3.1	10.4
Austin-San Marcos, TX MSA	846	9.4	0.4	2.2	20.9
Birmingham, AL MSA	840	28.7	0.2	0.5	0.4
Honolulu, HI MSA	836	3.1	0.4	63.0	6.8
Greenville-Spartanburg-Anderson, SC MSA	831	17.4	0.1	0.6	0.7
Fresno, CA MSA	756	4.8	1.1	7.7	35.3
Syracuse, NY MSA	742	5.7	0.6	1.1	1.4
Tulsa, OK MSA	709	8.2	6.8	0.9	2.1
Tucson, AZ MSA	667	3.1	3.0	1.8	24.5
Omaha, NE-IA MSA	640	8.0	0.5	1.0	2.6
Scranton—Wilkes-Barre—Hazleton, PA MSA	638	0.9	0.1	0.5	0.6
Toledo, OH MSA	614	11.4	0.2	1.0	3.3
Youngstown-Warren, OH MSA	601	9.4	0.2	0.4	1.3
Allentown-Bethlehem-Easton, PA MSA	595	2.0	0.1	1.1	4.6
El Paso, TX MSA	592	3.7	0.4	1.1	69.6
Albuquerque, NM MSA	589	2.5	5.1	1.4	37.1
Harrisburg-Lebanon-Carlisle, PA MSA	588	6.7	0.1	1.1	1.7
Springfield, MA MSA	588	6.3	0.2	1.4	8.5
Knoxville, TN MSA	586	6.1	0.2	0.8	0.5
Bakersfield, CA MSA	543	5.5	1.3	3.0	28.0
Baton Rouge, LA MSA	528	29.6	0.2	1.1	1.4
Little Rock-North Little Rock, AR MSA	513	19.9	0.4	0.7	0.8
Charleston-North Charleston, SC MSA	507	30.2	0.3	1.2	1.5
Sarasota-Bradenton, FL MSA	489	5.8	0.2	0.5	3.1
Wichita, KS MSA	485	7.6	1.1	1.9	4.1

[1] Metropolitan areas are shown in rank order of total population of consolidated metropolitan statistical areas (CMSA's) and metropolitan statistical areas (MSA's).　　[2] Persons of Hispanic origin may be of any race.

Source: U.S. Bureau of the Census, *1990 Census of Population and Housing, Supplementary Reports, Metropolitan Areas as Defined by the Office of Management and Budget, June 30, 1993*, (1990 CPH-S-1-1).

No. 44. Urban and Rural Population, 1960 to 1990, and by State, 1990

[In thousands, except percent. As of April 1. Resident population]

REGION, DIVISION, AND STATE	Total	URBAN Number	URBAN Percent	Rural	REGION, DIVISION, AND STATE	Total	URBAN Number	URBAN Percent	Rural
1960	179,323	125,269	69.9	54,054	MD	4,781	3,888	81.3	893
1970	¹203,212	149,647	73.6	53,565	DC	607	607	100.0	-
1980	²226,546	167,051	73.7	59,495	VA	6,187	4,293	69.4	1,894
1990, total	248,710	187,053	75.2	61,656	WV	1,793	648	36.1	1,145
Northeast	50,809	40,092	78.9	10,717	NC	6,629	3,338	50.4	3,291
N.E.	13,207	9,829	74.4	3,378	SC	3,487	1,905	54.6	1,581
ME	1,228	548	44.6	680	GA	6,478	4,097	63.2	2,381
NH	1,109	566	51.0	544	FL	12,938	10,967	84.8	1,971
VT	563	181	32.2	382	E.S.C	15,176	8,531	56.2	6,646
MA	6,016	5,070	84.3	947	KY	3,685	1,910	51.8	1,775
RI	1,003	863	86.0	140	TN	4,877	2,970	60.9	1,907
CT	3,287	2,602	79.1	686	AL	4,041	2,440	60.4	1,601
M.A.	37,602	30,263	80.5	7,340	MS	2,573	1,211	47.1	1,362
NY	17,990	15,164	84.3	2,826	W.S.C	26,703	19,894	74.5	6,808
NJ	7,730	6,910	89.4	820	AR	2,351	1,258	53.5	1,093
PA	11,882	8,188	68.9	3,693	LA	4,220	2,872	68.1	1,348
Midwest	59,669	42,774	71.7	16,894	OK	3,146	2,130	67.7	1,015
E.N.C.	42,009	31,074	74.0	10,935	TX	16,987	13,635	80.3	3,352
OH	10,847	8,039	74.1	2,808	West	52,786	45,531	86.3	7,255
IN	5,544	3,598	64.9	1,946	Mountain	13,659	10,881	79.7	2,777
IL	11,431	9,669	84.6	1,762	MT	799	420	52.5	379
MI	9,295	6,556	70.5	2,739	ID	1,007	578	57.4	429
WI	4,892	3,212	65.7	1,680	WY	454	295	65.0	159
W.N.C.	17,660	11,700	66.3	5,959	CO	3,294	2,716	82.4	579
MN	4,375	3,056	69.9	1,319	NM	1,515	1,106	73.0	409
IA	2,777	1,683	60.6	1,094	AZ	3,665	3,207	87.5	458
MO	5,117	3,516	68.7	1,601	UT	1,723	1,499	87.0	224
ND	639	340	53.3	298	NV	1,202	1,061	88.3	140
SD	696	348	50.0	348	Pacfic	39,127	34,650	88.6	4,477
NE	1,578	1,044	66.1	534	WA	4,867	3,718	76.4	1,149
KS	2,478	1,713	69.1	765	OR	2,842	2,003	70.5	839
South	85,446	58,656	68.6	26,790	CA	29,760	27,571	92.6	2,189
S.A.	43,567	30,231	69.4	13,336	AK	550	371	67.5	179
DE	666	487	73.0	180	HI	1,108	986	89.0	122

- Represents zero. ¹ The revised 1970 resident population count is 203,302,031; which incorporates changes due to errors found after tabulations were completed. ² Total population count has been revised since the 1980 census publications to 226,542,203.

Source: U.S. Bureau of the Census, *1990 Census of Population and Housing, Population and Housing Unit Counts* (1990 CPH-2).

No. 45. Incorporated Places, by Population Size: 1960 to 1990

POPULATION SIZE	NUMBER OF INCORPORATED PLACES				POPULATION (mil.)				PERCENT OF TOTAL			
	1960	1970	1980	1990	1960	1970	1980	1990	1960	1970	1980	1990
Total	18,088	18,666	19,097	19,290	115.9	131.9	140.3	152.9	100.0	100.0	100.0	100.0
1,000,000 or more	5	6	6	8	17.5	18.8	17.5	20.0	15.1	14.2	12.5	13.0
500,000 to 999,999	16	20	16	15	11.1	13.0	10.9	10.1	9.6	9.8	7.8	6.6
250,000 to 499,999	30	30	33	41	10.8	10.5	11.8	14.2	9.3	7.9	8.4	9.3
100,000 to 249,999	79	97	114	131	11.4	13.9	16.6	19.1	9.8	10.5	11.8	12.5
50,000 to 99,999	180	232	250	309	12.5	16.2	17.6	21.2	10.8	12.2	12.3	13.9
25,000 to 49,999	366	455	526	567	12.7	15.7	18.4	20.0	11.0	11.9	13.1	13.0
10,000 to 24,999	978	1,127	1,260	1,290	15.1	17.6	19.8	20.3	13.1	13.3	14.1	13.3
Under 10,000	16,434	16,699	16,892	16,929	24.9	26.4	28.0	28.2	21.5	20.0	20.0	18.4

Source: U.S. Bureau of the Census, *Census of Population: 1970, 1980,* and *1990,* vol. I.

No. 46. Cities With 100,000 or More Inhabitants in 1992—Population, 1980 to 1992, and Land Area, 1990

[**Population**: As of **April 1**; except **1992**, as of **July 1**. Data refer to boundaries in effect on January 1, 1990. Minus sign (-) indicates decrease]

			POPULATION							Land
		1990					1992			area,
			Percent—						Per-	1990
CITY	1980, total (1,000)	Total (1,000)	Black	American Indian, Eskimo, Aleut	Asian, Pacific Islander	His-panic [1]	Total (1,000)	Rank	cent change, 1990-92	(square miles)
Abilene, TX	98	107	7.0	0.4	1.3	15.5	108	179	1.4	103.1
Akron, OH	237	223	24.5	0.3	1.2	0.7	224	73	0.3	62.2
Albuquerque, NM	332	385	3.0	3.0	1.7	34.5	398	36	3.6	132.2
Alexandria, VA	103	111	21.9	0.3	4.2	9.7	113	169	1.8	15.3
Allentown, PA	104	105	5.0	0.2	1.3	11.7	106	186	1.3	17.7
Amarillo, TX	149	158	6.0	0.8	1.9	14.7	161	112	2.2	87.9
Anaheim, CA	219	266	2.5	0.5	9.4	31.4	274	58	2.9	44.3
Anchorage, AK	174	226	6.4	6.4	4.8	4.1	246	65	8.6	1,697.7
Ann Arbor, MI	108	110	9.0	0.4	7.7	2.6	110	176	0.2	25.9
Arlington, TX	160	262	8.4	0.5	3.9	8.9	276	57	5.4	93.0
Atlanta, GA	425	394	67.1	0.1	0.9	1.9	395	37	0.2	131.8
Aurora, CO	159	222	11.4	0.6	3.8	6.6	240	66	7.9	132.5
Aurora, IL	81	100	11.9	0.2	1.3	23.0	106	190	6.4	33.5
Austin, TX	346	466	12.4	0.4	3.0	23.0	492	25	5.7	217.8
Bakersfield, CA	106	175	9.4	1.1	3.6	20.5	188	88	7.5	91.8
Baltimore, MD	787	736	59.2	0.3	1.1	1.0	726	14	-1.3	80.8
Baton Rouge, LA	220	220	43.9	0.1	1.7	1.6	225	72	2.4	74.0
Beaumont, TX	118	114	41.3	0.2	1.7	4.3	115	161	1.0	80.1
Berkeley, CA	103	103	18.8	0.6	14.8	8.4	101	198	-1.6	10.5
Birmingham, AL	284	266	63.3	0.1	0.6	(Z)	265	63	-0.4	148.5
Boise City, ID	102	126	0.6	0.6	1.6	2.7	136	141	7.8	46.1
Boston, MA	563	574	25.6	0.3	5.3	10.8	552	20	-3.9	48.4
Bridgeport, CT	143	142	26.6	0.3	2.3	26.5	137	138	-3.3	16.0
Brownsville, TX	85	99	0.2	0.1	0.3	90.1	106	191	6.9	27.9
Buffalo, NY	358	328	30.7	0.8	1.0	4.9	323	50	-1.5	40.6
Cedar Rapids, IA	110	109	2.9	0.2	1.0	1.1	112	173	2.7	53.5
Chandler, AZ	30	91	2.6	1.2	2.4	17.3	100	200	10.6	47.6
Charlotte, NC	315	396	31.8	0.4	1.8	1.4	416	34	5.1	174.3
Chattanooga, TN	170	152	33.7	0.2	1.0	0.6	153	116	0.3	118.4
Chesapeake, VA	114	152	27.4	0.3	1.2	1.3	166	106	9.2	340.7
Chicago, IL	3,005	2,784	39.1	0.3	3.7	19.6	2,768	3	-0.5	227.2
Chula Vista, CA	84	135	4.6	0.6	8.9	37.3	145	123	7.1	29.0
Cincinnati, OH	385	364	37.9	0.2	1.1	0.7	364	46	0.1	77.2
Cleveland, OH	574	506	46.6	0.3	1.0	4.6	503	23	-0.6	77.0
Colorado Springs, CO	215	281	7.0	0.8	2.4	9.1	296	53	5.2	183.2
Columbus, GA	169	179	38.1	0.3	1.4	3.0	186	92	4.0	216.1
Columbus, OH	565	633	22.6	0.2	2.4	1.1	643	16	1.6	190.9
Concord, CA	104	111	2.4	0.7	8.7	11.5	113	171	1.2	29.5
Corpus Christi, TX	232	257	4.8	0.4	0.9	50.4	266	62	3.5	135.0
Dallas, TX	905	1,007	29.5	0.5	2.2	20.9	1,022	7	1.6	342.4
Dayton, OH	194	182	40.4	0.2	0.6	0.7	183	95	0.6	55.0
Denver, CO	493	468	12.8	1.2	2.4	23.0	484	27	3.5	153.3
Des Moines, IA	191	193	7.1	0.4	2.4	2.4	195	82	0.7	75.3
Detroit, MI	1,203	1,028	75.7	0.4	0.8	2.8	1,012	9	-1.5	138.7
Durham, NC	101	137	45.7	0.2	2.0	1.2	141	128	3.2	69.3
Elizabeth, NJ	106	110	19.8	0.3	2.7	39.1	108	180	-1.9	12.3
El Monte, CA	79	106	1.0	0.6	11.8	72.5	107	184	0.7	9.5
El Paso, TX	425	515	3.4	0.4	1.2	69.0	544	21	5.5	245.4
Erie, PA	119	109	12.0	0.2	0.5	2.4	109	177	0.5	22.0
Escondido, CA	64	109	1.5	0.8	3.7	23.4	113	168	4.2	35.6
Eugene, OR	106	113	1.3	0.9	3.5	2.7	116	160	2.9	38.0
Evansville, IN	130	126	9.5	0.2	0.6	0.6	128	146	1.0	40.7
Flint, MI	160	141	47.9	0.7	0.5	2.9	139	133	-1.0	33.8
Fort Lauderdale, FL	153	149	28.1	0.2	0.9	7.2	149	117	-0.6	31.4
Fort Wayne, IN	172	173	16.7	0.3	1.0	2.7	174	101	0.4	62.7
Fort Worth, TX	385	448	22.0	0.4	2.0	19.5	454	28	1.5	281.1
Fremont, CA	132	173	3.8	0.7	19.4	13.3	179	96	3.4	77.0
Fresno, CA	217	354	8.3	1.1	12.5	29.9	376	40	6.2	99.1
Fullerton, CA	102	114	2.2	0.5	12.2	21.3	115	162	1.2	22.1
Garden Grove, CA	123	143	1.5	0.6	20.5	23.5	146	119	2.0	17.9
Garland, TX	139	181	8.9	0.5	4.5	11.6	191	86	5.8	57.4
Gary, IN	152	117	80.6	0.2	0.2	5.7	117	158	(Z)	50.2
Glendale, AZ	97	148	3.0	0.9	2.1	15.5	156	113	5.4	52.2
Glendale, CA	139	180	1.3	0.3	14.1	21.0	178	97	-1.3	30.6
Grand Prairie, TX	71	100	9.7	0.8	3.0	20.5	104	193	4.9	68.5
Grand Rapids, MI	182	189	18.5	0.8	1.1	5.0	191	85	1.1	44.3
Green Bay, WI	88	96	0.5	2.5	2.3	1.1	100	199	4.1	43.8
Greensboro, NC	156	184	33.9	0.5	1.4	1.0	190	87	3.5	79.8

See footnotes at end of table.

No. 46. Cities With 100,000 or More Inhabitants in 1992—Population, 1980 to 1992, and Land Area, 1990—Continued

[See headnote, p. 44]

CITY	1980, total (1,000)	POPULATION 1990 Total (1,000)	1990 Percent— Black	1990 Percent— American Indian, Eskimo, Aleut	1990 Percent— Asian, Pacific Islander	1990 Percent— His-panic [1]	1992 Total (1,000)	1992 Rank	Per-cent change, 1990-92	Land area, 1990 (square miles)
Hampton, VA.	123	134	38.9	0.3	1.7	2.0	137	136	2.4	51.8
Hartford, CT	136	140	38.9	0.3	1.4	31.6	132	144	-5.5	17.3
Hayward, CA.	94	111	9.8	1.0	15.5	23.9	115	163	3.3	43.5
Hialeah, FL	145	188	1.9	0.1	0.5	87.6	192	84	2.0	19.2
Hollywood, FL	121	122	8.5	0.2	1.3	11.9	122	151	(Z)	27.3
Honolulu, HI [3]	365	365	1.3	0.3	70.5	4.6	371	43	1.7	85.7
Houston, TX	1,595	1,631	28.1	0.3	4.1	27.6	1,690	4	3.7	539.9
Huntington Beach, CA. . .	171	182	0.9	0.6	8.3	11.2	185	93	1.9	26.4
Huntsville, AL	143	160	24.4	0.5	2.1	1.2	163	109	2.2	164.4
Independence, MO.	112	112	1.4	0.6	1.0	2.0	113	170	0.4	78.2
Indianapolis, IN [2]	701	731	22.6	0.2	0.9	1.1	747	12	2.1	361.7
Inglewood, CA.	94	110	51.9	0.4	2.5	38.5	111	174	1.7	9.2
Irvine, CA	62	110	1.8	0.2	18.1	6.3	119	153	8.2	42.3
Irving, TX	110	155	7.5	0.6	4.6	16.3	161	111	4.0	67.6
Jackson, MS	203	197	55.7	0.1	0.5	0.4	196	80	-0.2	109.0
Jacksonville, FL [2]	541	635	25.2	0.3	1.9	2.6	661	15	4.1	758.7
Jersey City, NJ	224	229	29.7	0.3	11.4	24.2	229	71	(Z)	14.9
Kansas City, KS.	161	150	29.3	0.7	1.2	7.1	147	118	-2.2	107.8
Kansas City, MO	448	435	29.6	0.5	1.2	3.9	432	32	-0.8	311.5
Knoxville, TN.	175	165	15.8	0.2	1.0	0.7	167	105	1.3	77.2
Lakewood, CO.	114	126	1.0	0.7	1.9	9.1	126	148	-0.4	40.8
Lancaster, CA	48	97	7.4	0.9	3.7	15.2	106	188	9.1	88.8
Lansing, MI	130	127	18.6	1.0	1.8	7.9	127	147	-0.5	33.9
Laredo, TX	91	123	0.1	0.2	0.4	93.9	137	139	11.1	32.9
Las Vegas, NV.	165	258	11.4	0.9	3.6	12.5	296	54	14.4	83.3
Lexington-Fayette, KY. . .	204	225	13.4	0.2	1.6	1.1	233	70	3.2	284.5
Lincoln, NE	172	192	2.4	0.6	1.7	2.0	197	78	2.9	63.3
Little Rock, AR	159	176	34.0	0.3	0.9	0.8	177	99	0.6	102.9
Livonia, MI	105	101	0.3	0.2	1.3	1.3	101	197	0.5	35.7
Long Beach, CA.	361	429	13.7	0.6	13.6	23.6	439	31	2.2	50.0
Los Angeles, CA	2,969	3,485	14.0	0.5	9.8	39.9	3,490	2	0.1	469.3
Louisville, KY.	299	269	29.7	0.2	0.7	0.7	271	59	0.7	62.1
Lubbock, TX.	174	186	8.6	0.3	1.4	22.5	188	89	0.9	104.1
Macon, GA	117	107	52.2	0.1	0.4	0.6	107	183	0.6	47.9
Madison, WI	171	191	4.2	0.4	3.9	2.0	195	81	2.0	57.8
Memphis, TN.	646	610	54.8	0.2	0.8	0.7	610	18	(-Z)	256.0
Mesa, AZ	152	288	1.9	1.0	1.5	10.9	297	52	3.0	108.6
Mesquite, TX.	67	101	5.8	0.5	2.6	8.8	108	178	6.7	42.8
Miami, FL	347	359	27.4	0.2	0.6	62.5	367	44	2.4	35.6
Milwaukee, WI	636	628	30.5	0.9	1.9	6.3	617	17	-1.8	96.1
Minneapolis, MN	371	368	13.0	3.3	4.3	2.1	363	47	-1.5	54.9
Mobile, AL	200	196	38.9	0.2	1.0	1.0	202	77	2.9	118.0
Modesto, CA.	107	165	2.7	1.0	7.9	16.3	172	103	4.6	30.2
Montgomery, AL	178	187	42.3	0.2	0.7	0.8	192	83	2.7	135.0
Moreno Valley, CA.	(4)	119	13.8	0.7	6.6	22.9	132	143	11.2	49.1
Nashville-Davidson, TN [2].	456	488	24.3	0.2	1.4	0.9	495	24	1.4	473.3
Newark, NJ	329	275	58.5	0.2	1.2	26.1	268	61	-2.7	23.8
New Haven, CT.	126	130	36.1	0.3	2.4	13.2	124	150	-5.0	18.9
New Orleans, LA	558	497	61.9	0.2	1.9	3.5	490	26	-1.5	180.7
Newport News, VA.	145	170	33.6	0.3	2.3	2.8	177	98	4.3	68.3
New York, NY	7,072	7,323	28.7	0.4	7.0	24.4	7,312	1	-0.1	309.0
Bronx Borough	1,169	1,204	37.3	0.5	3.0	43.5	1,195	(X)	-0.8	42.0
Brooklyn Borough	2,231	2,301	37.9	0.3	4.8	20.1	2,286	(X)	-0.6	70.5
Manhattan Borough. . . .	1,428	1,488	22.0	0.4	7.4	26.0	1,489	(X)	0.1	28.4
Queens Borough. . . .	1,891	1,952	21.7	0.4	12.2	19.5	1,951	(X)	(-Z)	109.4
Staten Island Borough .	352	379	8.1	0.2	4.5	8.0	391	(X)	3.2	58.6
Norfolk, VA.	267	261	39.1	0.4	2.6	2.9	254	64	-2.9	53.8
Oakland, CA	339	372	43.9	0.6	14.8	13.9	373	42	0.3	56.1
Oceanside, CA	77	128	7.9	0.7	6.1	22.6	140	131	8.8	40.5
Oklahoma City, OK.	404	445	16.0	4.2	2.4	5.0	454	29	2.1	608.2
Omaha, NE.	314	336	13.1	0.7	1.0	3.1	340	48	1.2	100.7
Ontario, CA.	89	133	7.3	0.7	3.9	41.7	139	134	4.4	36.8
Orange, CA.	91	111	1.4	0.5	7.9	22.8	114	167	2.7	23.3
Orlando, FL.	128	165	26.9	0.3	1.6	8.7	174	100	5.8	67.3
Overland Park, KS	82	112	1.8	0.3	1.9	2.0	119	154	6.7	55.7
Oxnard, CA.	108	142	5.2	0.8	8.6	54.4	145	121	1.8	24.4
Pasadena, CA	118	132	19.0	0.4	8.1	27.3	133	142	0.8	23.0
Pasadena, TX	113	119	1.0	0.5	1.6	28.8	125	149	5.1	43.8
Paterson, NJ	138	141	36.0	0.3	1.4	41.0	139	132	-1.1	8.4
Peoria, IL	124	114	20.9	0.2	1.7	1.6	114	165	0.4	40.9
Philadelphia, PA.	1,688	1,586	39.9	0.2	2.7	5.6	1,553	5	-2.1	135.1
Phoenix, AZ	790	983	5.2	1.9	1.7	20.0	1,012	8	2.9	419.9
Pittsburgh, PA	424	370	25.8	0.2	1.6	0.9	367	45	-0.8	55.6
Plano, TX	72	129	4.1	0.3	4.0	6.2	142	126	10.4	66.3
Pomona, CA	93	132	14.4	0.6	6.7	51.3	140	129	6.6	22.8
Portland, OR	368	437	7.7	1.2	5.3	3.2	445	30	1.9	124.7
Portsmouth, VA	105	104	47.3	0.3	0.8	1.3	104	194	0.4	33.1
Providence, RI.	157	161	14.8	0.9	5.9	15.5	155	114	-3.3	18.5

See footnotes at end of table.

No. 46. Cities With 100,000 or More Inhabitants in 1992—Population, 1980 to 1992, and Land Area, 1990—Continued

[See headnote, p. 44]

CITY	1980, total (1,000)	POPULATION 1990 Total (1,000)	Black	American Indian, Eskimo, Aleut	Asian, Pacific Islander	Hispanic[1]	1992 Total (1,000)	Rank	Percent change, 1990-92	Land area, 1990 (square miles)
			Percent—							
Raleigh, NC	150	208	27.6	0.3	2.5	1.4	221	74	6.0	88.1
Rancho Cucamonga, CA	55	101	5.9	0.6	5.4	20.0	111	175	9.6	37.8
Reno, NV	101	134	2.9	1.4	4.9	11.1	140	130	4.5	57.5
Richmond, VA	219	203	55.2	0.2	0.9	0.9	202	76	-0.4	60.1
Riverside, CA	171	227	7.4	0.8	5.2	26.0	239	67	5.3	77.7
Rochester, NY	242	232	31.5	0.5	1.8	8.7	234	69	1.1	35.8
Rockford, IL	140	139	15.0	0.3	1.5	4.2	142	127	1.6	45.0
Sacramento, CA	276	369	15.3	1.2	15.0	16.2	383	39	3.6	96.3
St. Louis, MO	453	397	47.5	0.2	0.9	1.3	384	38	-3.3	61.9
St. Paul, MN	270	272	7.4	1.4	7.1	4.2	268	60	-1.5	52.8
St. Petersburg, FL	239	239	19.6	0.2	1.7	2.6	235	68	-1.4	59.2
Salem, OR	89	108	1.5	1.6	2.4	6.1	112	172	4.0	41.5
Salinas, CA	80	109	3.0	0.9	8.1	50.6	115	164	5.5	18.6
Salt Lake City, UT	163	160	1.7	1.6	4.7	9.7	166	107	3.7	109.0
San Antonio, TX	786	936	7.0	0.4	1.1	55.6	966	10	3.3	333.0
San Bernardino, CA	119	164	16.0	1.0	4.0	34.6	172	102	5.0	55.1
San Diego, CA	876	1,111	9.4	0.6	11.8	20.7	1,149	6	3.4	324.0
San Francisco, CA	679	724	10.9	0.5	29.1	13.9	729	13	0.7	46.7
San Jose, CA	629	782	4.7	0.7	19.5	26.6	801	11	2.4	171.3
Santa Ana, CA	204	294	2.6	0.5	9.7	65.2	288	55	-1.9	27.1
Santa Clarita, CA	(4)	111	1.5	0.6	4.2	13.4	119	155	7.3	40.5
Santa Rosa, CA	83	113	1.8	1.2	3.4	9.5	117	159	2.9	33.7
Savannah, GA	142	138	51.3	0.2	1.1	1.4	139	135	1.0	62.6
Scottsdale, AZ	89	130	0.8	0.6	1.2	4.8	137	137	5.3	184.4
Seattle, WA	494	516	10.1	1.4	11.8	3.6	520	22	0.6	83.9
Shreveport, LA	206	199	44.8	0.2	0.5	1.1	197	79	-0.9	98.6
Simi Valley, CA	78	100	1.5	0.6	5.5	12.7	104	196	3.6	33.0
Sioux Falls, SD	81	101	0.7	1.6	0.7	0.6	106	192	4.8	45.1
South Bend, IN	110	106	20.9	0.4	0.9	3.4	106	189	0.4	36.4
Spokane, WA	171	177	1.9	2.0	2.1	2.1	187	90	5.8	55.9
Springfield, IL	100	105	13.0	0.2	1.0	0.8	106	187	1.1	42.5
Springfield, MA	152	157	19.2	0.2	1.0	16.9	153	115	-2.2	32.1
Springfield, MO	133	140	2.5	0.7	0.9	1.0	145	120	3.5	68.0
Stamford, CT	102	108	17.8	0.1	2.6	9.8	108	181	-0.4	37.7
Sterling Heights, MI	109	118	0.4	0.2	2.9	1.1	118	157	0.4	36.6
Stockton, CA	150	211	9.6	1.0	22.8	25.0	220	75	4.1	52.6
Sunnyvale, CA	107	117	3.4	0.5	19.3	13.2	118	156	1.0	21.9
Syracuse, NY	170	164	20.3	1.3	2.2	2.9	163	110	-0.6	25.1
Tacoma, WA	159	177	11.4	2.0	6.9	3.8	184	94	4.1	48.1
Tallahassee, FL	82	125	29.1	0.2	1.8	3.0	130	145	4.5	63.3
Tampa, FL	272	280	25.0	0.3	1.4	15.0	285	56	1.7	108.7
Tempe, AZ	107	142	3.2	1.3	4.1	10.9	142	125	0.2	39.5
Thousand Oaks, CA	77	104	1.2	0.4	4.8	9.6	108	182	3.0	49.6
Toledo, OH	355	333	19.7	0.3	1.0	4.0	329	49	-1.1	80.6
Topeka, KS	119	120	10.6	1.3	0.8	5.8	120	152	0.3	55.2
Torrance, CA	130	133	1.5	0.4	21.9	10.1	136	140	1.9	20.5
Tucson, AZ	331	405	4.3	1.6	2.2	29.3	415	35	2.4	156.3
Tulsa, OK	361	367	13.6	4.7	1.4	2.6	375	41	2.2	183.5
Vallejo, CA	80	109	21.2	0.7	23.0	10.8	114	166	4.1	30.2
Virginia Beach, VA	262	393	13.9	0.4	4.3	3.1	417	33	6.1	248.3
Waco, TX	101	104	23.1	0.3	0.9	16.3	104	195	0.4	75.8
Warren, MI	161	145	0.7	0.5	1.3	1.1	142	124	-1.7	34.3
Washington, DC	638	607	65.8	0.2	1.8	5.4	585	19	-3.6	61.4
Waterbury, CT	103	109	13.0	0.3	0.7	13.4	107	185	-1.9	28.6
Wichita, KS	280	304	11.3	1.2	2.6	5.0	312	51	2.5	115.1
Winston-Salem, NC	132	143	39.3	0.2	0.8	0.9	145	122	0.9	71.1
Worcester, MA	162	170	4.5	0.3	2.8	9.6	163	108	-3.7	37.6
Yonkers, NY	195	188	14.1	0.2	3.0	16.7	186	91	-1.1	18.1

X Not applicable.   Z Less than .05 percent.   [1] Hispanic persons may be of any race.   [2] Represents the portion of a consolidated city that is not within one or more separately incorporated places.   [3] The population shown in this table is for the census designated place (CDP); the 1990 census population for the City and County of Honolulu is 836,231.   [4] Not incorporated.

Source: U.S. Bureau of the Census, *1980 Census of Population*, vol. 1, chapters A and B; *1990 Census of Population and Housing, Summary Population and Housing Characteristics*, (CPH-1); and press release CB94-15.

No. 47. Population 65 Years Old and Over, by Age Group and Sex, 1980 to 1992, and Projections, 2000

[As of **April**, except **1992** and **2000**, as of **July**. Projection based on middle series, see table 3]

AGE GROUP AND SEX	NUMBER (1,000)				PERCENT DISTRIBUTION			
	1980	1990	1992	2000, proj.	1980	1990	1992	2000, proj.
Persons 65 yrs. and over.....	25,549	31,079	32,285	35,322	100.0	100.0	100.0	100.0
65 to 69 years old	8,782	10,066	9,977	9,594	34.3	32.4	30.9	27.2
70 to 74 years old	6,798	7,980	8,483	8,957	26.6	25.7	26.3	25.4
75 to 79 years old	4,794	6,103	6,415	7,507	18.8	19.6	19.9	21.3
80 to 84 years old	2,935	3,909	4,150	4,931	11.5	12.6	12.9	14.0
85 years old and over	2,240	3,021	3,259	4,333	8.8	9.7	10.1	12.3
Males, 65 yrs. and over..........	10,305	12,493	13,045	14,603	100.0	100.0	100.0	100.0
65 to 69 years old.............	3,903	4,508	4,475	4,420	37.8	36.1	34.3	30.3
70 to 74 years old.............	2,854	3,399	3,651	3,965	27.7	27.2	28.0	27.2
75 to 79 years old.............	1,848	2,389	2,553	3,138	18.0	19.1	19.6	21.5
80 to 84 years old.............	1,019	1,356	1,457	1,842	9.9	10.9	11.2	12.6
85 years old and over	682	841	909	1,238	6.6	6.7	7.0	8.5
Females, 65 yrs. and over	15,245	18,586	19,240	20,719	100.0	100.0	100.0	100.0
65 to 69 years old.............	4,880	5,558	5,503	5,173	31.9	29.9	28.6	25.0
70 to 74 years old.............	3,945	4,580	4,833	4,993	25.9	24.6	25.1	24.1
75 to 79 years old.............	2,946	3,714	3,862	4,369	19.3	20.0	20.1	21.1
80 to 84 years old.............	1,916	2,553	2,693	3,089	12.6	13.7	14.0	14.9
85 years old and over	1,559	2,180	2,349	3,095	10.3	11.7	12.2	14.9

Source: U.S. Bureau of the Census, *Current Population Reports*, P25-1095 and P25-1104; and unpublished data.

No. 48. Persons 65 Years Old and Over—Characteristics, by Sex: 1980 to 1993

[As of **March, except as noted.** Covers civilian noninstitutional population. See headnote, table 49]

CHARACTERISTIC	TOTAL				MALE				FEMALE			
	1980	1985	1990	1993	1980	1985	1990	1993	1980	1985	1990	1993
Total [1] (million).............	24.2	26.8	29.6	30.9	9.9	11.0	12.3	12.8	14.2	15.8	17.2	18.0
White (million).................	21.9	24.2	26.5	27.5	9.0	9.9	11.0	11.4	12.9	14.3	15.4	16.1
Black (million)	2.0	2.2	2.5	2.7	0.8	0.9	1.0	1.1	1.2	1.3	1.5	1.6
Percent below poverty level [2].......	15.2	12.4	11.4	12.9	11.1	8.7	7.8	8.9	17.9	15.0	13.9	15.7
PERCENT DISTRIBUTION												
Marital status:												
Single......................	5.5	5.2	4.6	4.4	4.9	5.3	4.2	4.4	5.9	5.1	4.9	4.4
Married.....................	55.4	55.2	56.1	56.6	78.0	77.2	76.5	76.8	39.5	39.9	41.4	42.2
Spouse present.............	53.6	53.4	54.1	54.7	76.1	75.0	74.2	74.6	37.9	38.3	39.7	40.6
Spouse absent	1.8	1.8	2.0	1.9	1.9	2.2	2.3	2.2	1.7	1.6	1.7	1.6
Widowed...................	35.7	35.6	34.2	33.7	13.5	13.8	14.2	14.3	51.2	50.7	48.6	47.6
Divorced	3.5	4.0	5.0	5.3	3.6	3.7	5.0	4.5	3.4	4.3	5.1	5.8
Family status:												
In families [3]...............	67.6	67.3	66.7	67.5	83.0	82.4	81.9	81.6	56.8	56.7	55.8	57.4
Nonfamily householders........	31.2	31.1	31.9	31.2	15.7	15.4	16.6	16.4	42.0	42.1	42.8	41.7
Secondary individuals...........	1.2	1.6	1.4	1.3	1.3	2.2	1.5	1.9	1.1	1.1	1.4	0.9
Living arrangements:												
Living in household	99.8	99.6	99.7	99.9	99.9	99.5	99.9	99.9	99.7	99.6	99.5	99.9
Living alone..................	30.3	30.2	31.0	30.3	14.9	14.7	15.5	15.5	41.0	41.1	42.0	40.8
Spouse present	53.6	53.4	54.1	54.0	76.1	75.0	74.3	73.7	37.9	38.3	39.7	40.1
Living with someone else........	15.9	15.9	14.6	15.5	8.9	9.8	9.9	10.7	20.8	20.2	17.8	19.0
Not in household [4]...........	0.2	0.4	0.3	0.1	0.1	0.5	0.1	0.1	0.3	0.4	0.5	0.1
Years of school completed:												
8 years or less	43.1	35.4	28.5	24.1	45.3	37.2	30.0	25.0	41.6	34.1	27.5	23.5
1 to 3 years of high school	16.2	16.5	16.1	[5]15.6	15.5	15.7	15.7	[5]14.9	16.7	17.0	16.4	[5]16.1
4 years of high school	24.0	29.0	32.9	[6]34.2	21.4	26.4	29.0	[6]29.7	25.8	30.7	35.6	[6]37.4
1 to 3 years of college	8.2	9.8	10.9	[7]14.1	7.5	9.1	10.8	[7]14.3	8.6	10.3	11.0	[7]13.9
4 years or more of college	8.6	9.4	11.6	[8]12.0	10.3	11.5	14.5	[8]16.1	7.4	8.0	9.5	[8]9.0
Labor force participation: [9]												
Employed	12.2	10.4	11.5	10.9	18.4	15.3	15.9	15.1	7.8	7.0	8.4	7.9
Unemployed.................	0.4	0.3	0.4	0.4	0.6	0.5	0.5	0.5	0.3	0.2	0.3	0.3
Not in labor force	87.5	89.2	88.1	88.7	81.0	84.2	83.6	84.4	91.9	92.7	91.3	91.8

[1] Includes other races, not shown separately. [2] Poverty status based on income in preceding year. [3] Excludes those living in unrelated subfamilies. [4] In group quarters other than institutions. [5] Represents those who completed ninth to twelfth grade, but have no high school diploma. [6] High school graduate. [7] Some college or associate degree. [8] Bachelor's or advanced degree. [9] Annual averages of monthly figures. Source: U.S. Bureau of Labor Statistics, *Employment and Earnings*, January issues.

Source: Except as noted, U.S. Bureau of the Census, *Current Population Reports*, P20-450, and earlier reports; P60-185 and earlier reports; and unpublished data.

No. 49. Social and Economic Characteristics of the White and Black Populations: 1980 to 1993

[As of **March, except labor force status, annual average.** Excludes members of Armed Forces except those living off post or with their families on post. Based on Current Population Survey; see text, section 1, and Appendix III]

CHARACTERISTIC	NUMBER (1,000) White			Black			PERCENT DISTRIBUTION White		Black	
	1980	1990	1993	1980	1990	1993	1980	1993	1980	1993
Total persons	**191,905**	**206,983**	**211,955**	**26,033**	**30,392**	**32,036**	**100.0**	**100.0**	**100.0**	**100.0**
Under 5 years old	13,307	15,161	15,611	2,444	2,932	3,262	6.9	7.4	9.4	10.2
5 to 14 years old	28,828	28,405	29,543	5,190	5,546	5,837	15.0	13.9	19.9	18.2
15 to 44 years old	88,570	96,656	96,423	12,247	14,660	15,180	46.2	45.5	47.0	47.4
45 to 64 years old	39,302	40,282	42,876	4,112	4,766	5,098	20.5	20.2	15.8	15.9
65 years old and over.	21,898	26,479	27,501	2,040	2,487	2,660	11.4	13.0	7.8	8.3
YEARS OF SCHOOL COMPLETED										
Persons 25 years old and over	**114,763**	**134,687**	**139,019**	**12,927**	**16,751**	**17,786**	**100.0**	**100.0**	**100.0**	**100.0**
Elementary: 0 to 8 years.	18,739	14,131	12,189	3,559	2,701	2,183	16.3	8.8	27.5	12.3
High school: 1 to 3 years	15,064	14,080	[1]13,479	2,748	2,969	[1]3,079	13.1	[1]9.7	21.3	[1]17.3
4 years	43,149	52,449	[2]49,538	3,980	6,239	[2]6,451	37.6	[2]35.6	30.8	[2]36.3
College: 1 to 3 years	17,350	24,350	[3]32,428	1,618	2,952	[3]3,909	15.1	[3]23.3	12.5	[3]22.0
4 years or more.	20,460	29,677	[4]31,385	1,024	1,890	[4]2,164	17.8	[4]22.6	7.9	[4]12.2
LABOR FORCE STATUS [5]										
Civilians 16 years old and over	**146,122**	**160,415**	**163,921**	**17,824**	**21,300**	**22,329**	**100.0**	**100.0**	**100.0**	**100.0**
Civilian labor force	93,600	107,177	109,359	10,865	13,493	13,943	64.1	66.7	61.0	62.4
Employed	87,715	102,087	102,812	9,313	11,966	12,146	60.0	62.7	52.2	54.4
Unemployed	5,884	5,091	6,547	1,553	1,527	1,796	4.0	4.0	8.7	8.0
Unemployment rate [6]	6.3	4.7	6.0	14.3	11.3	12.9	(X)	(X)	(X)	(X)
Not in labor force.	52,523	53,237	54,562	6,959	7,808	8,386	35.9	33.3	39.0	37.6
FAMILY TYPE										
Total families. . . . . ,. . . .	**52,243**	**56,590**	**57,858**	**6,184**	**7,470**	**7,888**	**100.0**	**100.0**	**100.0**	**100.0**
With own children [7]. . . .	26,474	26,718	27,334	3,820	4,378	4,560	50.7	47.2	61.8	57.8
Married couple . . . ,.	44,751	46,981	47,601	3,433	3,750	3,748	85.7	82.3	55.5	47.5
With own children [7].	22,415	21,579	21,684	1,927	1,972	1,945	42.9	37.5	31.2	24.7
Female householder, no spouse present ,.	6,052	7,306	7,848	2,495	3,275	3,680	11.6	13.6	40.3	46.7
With own children [7].	3,558	4,199	4,552	1,793	2,232	2,434	6.8	7.9	29.0	30.9
Male householder, no spouse present . . ,. . . .	1,441	2,303	2,409	256	446	460	2.8	4.2	4.1	5.8
With own children [7].	500	939	1,098	99	173	182	1.0	1.9	1.6	2.3
FAMILY INCOME IN PREVIOUS YEAR IN CONSTANT (1992) DOLLARS										
Total families.	**52,243**	**56,590**	**57,858**	**6,184**	**7,470**	**7,888**	**100.0**	**100.0**	**100.0**	**100.0**
Less than $5,000.	952	1,240	1,547	424	691	888	1.8	2.7	6.9	11.3
$5,000 to $9,999	2,213	2,370	2,608	899	968	1,186	4.2	4.5	14.5	15.0
$10,000 to $14,999	3,239	3,567	3,842	803	968	933	6.2	6.6	13.0	11.8
$15,000 to $24,999	8,222	8,145	8,780	1,356	1,383	1,480	15.7	15.2	21.9	18.8
$25,000 to $34,999	8,416	8,377	8,826	861	1,021	1,028	16.1	15.3	13.9	13.0
$35,000 to $49,999	12,199	11,590	11,571	956	1,110	1,104	23.4	20.0	15.5	14.0
$50,000 or more	17,002	21,303	20,685	886	1,329	1,269	32.5	35.8	14.3	16.1
Median income (dol.) [8]	38,751	40,704	38,909	21,944	22,866	21,161	(X)	(X)	(X)	(X)
Families below poverty level [9] .	3,581	4,409	5,160	1,722	2,077	2,435	6.9	8.9	27.8	30.9
Persons below poverty level [9] .	17,214	20,785	24,523	8,050	9,302	10,613	9.0	11.6	31.0	33.3
HOUSING TENURE										
Total occupied units. . . .	**70,766**	**80,163**	**82,083**	**8,586**	**10,486**	**11,190**	**100.0**	**100.0**	**100.0**	**100.0**
Owner-occupied	49,913	54,094	55,915	4,173	4,445	4,726	70.5	68.1	48.6	42.2
Renter-occupied	19,581	24,685	24,785	4,257	5,862	6,235	27.7	30.2	49.6	55.7
No cash rent.	1,272	1,384	1,383	156	178	229	1.8	1.7	1.8	2.0

X Not applicable. [1] Represents those who completed ninth to twelfth grade, but have no high school diploma. [2] High school graduate. [3] Some college or associate degree. [4] Bachelor's or advanced degree. [5] Source: U.S. Bureau of Labor Statistics, *Employment and Earnings*, January issues. [6] Total unemployment as percent of civilian labor force. [7] Children under 18 years old. [8] For definition of median, see Guide to Tabular Presentation. [9] For explanation of poverty level, see text, section 14.

Source: Except as noted, U.S. Bureau of the Census, *Current Population Reports*, P20-471, and earlier reports; P60-184 and P60-185; and unpublished data.

No. 50. Social and Economic Characteristics of the Asian and Pacific Islander Population: 1990 and 1993

[As of **March**. Excludes members of Armed Forces except those living off post or with their families on post. Based on Current Population Survey; see text, section 1, and Appendix III]

CHARACTERISTIC	NUMBER (1,000)		PERCENT DISTRIBUTION	
	1990	1993	1990	1993
Total persons	**6,679**	**7,285**	**100.0**	**100.0**
Under 5 years old	602	629	9.0	8.6
5 to 14 years old	1,112	1,175	16.6	16.1
15 to 44 years old	3,345	3,618	50.1	49.7
45 to 64 years old	1,155	1,332	17.3	18.3
65 years old and over.	465	530	7.0	7.3
YEARS OF SCHOOL COMPLETED				
Persons 25 years old and over	**3,961**	**4,462**	**100.0**	**100.0**
Elementary: 0 to 8 years.	543	488	13.7	10.9
High school: 1 to 3 years	234	[1]217	5.9	[1]4.9
4 years	1,038	[2]1,113	26.2	[2]24.9
College: 1 to 3 years	568	[3]768	14.3	[3]17.2
4 years or more.	1,578	[4]1,874	39.9	[4]42.0
LABOR FORCE STATUS				
Civilians 16 years old and over	**4,849**	**5,355**	**100.0**	**100.0**
Civilian labor force.	3,216	3,498	66.3	65.3
Employed	3,079	3,297	63.5	61.6
Unemployed	136	201	2.8	3.8
Unemployment rate [5]	4.2	5.7	(X)	(X)
Not in labor force.	1,634	1,857	33.7	34.7
FAMILY TYPE				
Total families.	**1,531**	**1,662**	**100.0**	**100.0**
Married couple	1,256	1,335	82.1	80.3
Female householder, no spouse present	188	232	12.3	14.0
Male householder, no spouse present	86	95	5.6	5.7
FAMILY INCOME IN PREVIOUS YEAR IN CONSTANT (1992) DOLLARS				
Total families.	**1,531**	**1,662**	**100.0**	**100.0**
Less than $5,000.	(NA)	59	(NA)	3.5
$5,000 to $9,999	(NA)	97	(NA)	5.8
$10,000 to $14,999	(NA)	96	(NA)	5.8
$15,000 to $24,999	(NA)	190	(NA)	11.4
$25,000 to $34,999	(NA)	210	(NA)	12.6
$35,000 to $49,999	(NA)	330	(NA)	19.9
$50,000 or more	(NA)	680	(NA)	40.9
Families below poverty level [6]	182	200	11.9	12.0
Persons below poverty level [6]	939	912	14.1	12.5
HOUSING TENURE				
Total occupied units.	**1,988**	**2,118**	**100.0**	**100.0**
Owner-occupied	977	1,090	49.1	51.5
Renter-occupied	982	995	49.4	47.0
No cash rent.	30	33	1.5	1.6

NA Not available. X Not applicable. [1] Represents those who completed ninth to twelfth grade, but have no high school diploma. [2] High school graduate. [3] Some college or associate degree. [4] Bachelor's or advanced degree. [5] Total unemployment as percent of civilian labor force. [6] For explanation of poverty level, see text, section 14.

Source: U.S. Bureau of the Census, *Current Population Reports*, P20-459; and unpublished data.

No. 51. American Indian, Eskimo, and Aleut Population—Population Living Inside and Outside Identified Areas and Households, by Type: 1990

[In thousands. As of April 1. Households are based on race of householder]

IDENTIFIED AREA AND HOUSEHOLD TYPE	Total [1]	Oklahoma	California	Arizona	New Mexico	Alaska	Washington
Total population	1,959	252	242	204	134	86	81
Inside identified areas	739	207	14	142	88	48	22
American Indian areas	692	207	14	142	88	1	22
Reservations [2]	411	6	13	142	68	1	21
Trust lands [3]	26	(X)	(Z)	(Z)	19	(X)	1
Tribal Jurisdiction Statistical Areas [4]	201	201	(X)	(X)	(X)	(X)	(X)
Tribal Designated Statistical Areas [5]	54	(X)	(X)	(X)	(X)	(X)	(X)
Alaska Native Village Statistical Areas [6]	47	(X)	(X)	(X)	(X)	47	(X)
Outside identified areas	1,220	45	229	61	47	37	60
Total households	591	78	79	50	33	22	25
Family households	442	59	56	41	28	16	18
Married couple family	284	43	37	24	16	10	11
With related children	179	25	21	18	13	7	6
With no related children	104	18	15	6	4	2	4
Male householder, no spouse present	37	3	5	4	3	2	2
With related children	25	2	3	3	2	1	1
With no related children	12	1	2	1	1	1	(Z)
Female householder, no spouse present	121	13	15	13	8	5	6
With related children	94	9	11	10	6	4	5
With no related children	27	3	4	3	2	1	1
Nonfamily households	149	19	23	9	6	6	7
One person households	116	16	16	7	5	5	5
Two or more person households	33	2	7	2	1	1	2

X Not applicable. Area not located within this State.   Z Fewer than 500.   [1] Includes other States not shown separately. [2] Federal American Indian reservations are areas with boundaries established by treaty, statute, and/or executive or court order, and recognized by the Federal Government as territory in which American Indian tribes have jurisdiction. State reservations are lands held in trust by State governments for the use and benefit of a given tribe. [3] Property associated with a particular American Indian reservation or tribe, held in trust by the Federal Government. These lands are located outside of a reservation boundary. [4] Areas delineated by federally-recognized tribes in Oklahoma without a reservation, for which the Census Bureau tabulates data. [5] Areas delineated outside Oklahoma by federally- and State- recognized tribes without a land base or associated trust lands, to provide statistical areas for which the Census Bureau tabulates data. [6] Alaska Native villages constitute tribes, bands, clans, groups, villages, communities, or associations in Alaska that are recognized pursuant to the Alaska Native Claims Settlement Act of 1972.

Source: U.S. Bureau of the Census, *1990 Census of Population, General Population Characteristics, American Indian and Alaska Native Areas* (CP-1-1A); and unpublished data.

No. 52. Population Living on Selected Reservations and Trust Lands and American Indian Tribes With 10,000 or More American Indians: 1990

[As of April]

RESERVATION AND TRUST LANDS WITH 5,000 OR MORE AMERICAN INDIANS, ESKIMOS, AND ALEUTS	Total population	AMERICAN INDIANS, ESKIMOS, ALEUTS Number	Percent of total	AMERICAN INDIAN TRIBE	Number	Percent distribution
All reservation and trust lands	808,163	437,431	54.1	American Indian population, total [2]	1,878,285	100.0
Navajo and Trust Lands, AZ-NM-UT	148,451	143,405	96.6	Cherokee	308,132	16.4
Pine Ridge and Trust Lands, NE-SD	12,215	11,182	91.5	Navajo	219,198	11.7
Fort Apache, AZ	10,394	9,825	94.5	Chippewa	103,826	5.5
Gila River, AZ	9,540	9,116	95.6	Sioux [3]	103,255	5.5
Papago, AZ	8,730	8,480	97.1	Choctaw	82,299	4.4
Rosebud and Trust Lands, SD	9,696	8,043	83.0	Pueblo	52,939	2.8
San Carlos, AZ	7,294	7,110	97.5	Apache	50,051	2.7
Zuni Pueblo, AZ-NM	7,412	7,073	95.4	Iroquois [4]	49,038	2.6
Hopi and Trust Lands, AZ	7,360	7,061	95.9	Lumbee	48,444	2.6
Blackfeet, MT	8,549	7,025	82.2	Creek	43,550	2.3
Turtle Mountain and Trust Lands, ND-SD	7,106	6,772	95.3	Blackfoot	32,234	1.7
Yakima and Trust Lands, WA	27,668	6,307	22.8	Canadian and Latin American	22,379	1.2
Osage, OK [1]	41,645	6,161	14.8	Chickasaw	20,631	1.1
Fort Peck, MT	10,595	5,782	54.6	Potawatomi [4]	16,763	0.9
Wind River, WY	21,851	5,676	26.0	Tohono O'odham	16,041	0.9
Eastern Cherokee, NC	6,527	5,388	82.5	Pima	14,431	0.8
Flathead, MT	21,259	5,130	24.1	Tlingit	13,925	0.7
Cheyenne River, SD	7,743	5,100	65.9	Seminole	13,797	0.7
				Alaskan Athabaskans	13,738	0.7
				Cheyenne	11,456	0.6
				Comanche	11,322	0.6
				Paiute	11,142	0.6
				Puget Sound Salish	10,246	0.5

[1] The Osage Reservation is coextensive with Osage County. Data shown for the reservation are for the entire reservation. [2] Includes other American Indian tribes, not shown separately. [3] Any entry with the spelling "Siouan" was miscoded to Sioux in North Carolina. [4] Reporting and/or processing problems have affected the data for this tribe.

Source: U.S. Bureau of the Census, *1990 Census of Population, General Population Characteristics, American Indian and Alaska Native Areas* (CP-1-1A); and press release CB92-244.

No. 53. Social and Economic Characteristics of the Hispanic Population: 1993

[As of March, except labor force status, annual average. Excludes members of the Armed Forces except those living off post or with their families on post. Based on Current Population Survey; see text, section 1, and Appendix III]

CHARACTERISTIC	NUMBER (1,000)						PERCENT DISTRIBUTION					
	His-panic, total	Mexi-can	Puer-to Rican	Cuban	Central and South American	Other His-panic	His-panic, total	Mexi-can	Puer-to Rican	Cuban	Central and South American	Other His-panic
Total persons	**22,752**	**14,628**	**2,402**	**1,071**	**3,052**	**1,598**	**100.0**	**100.0**	**100.0**	**100.0**	**100.0**	**100.0**
Under 5 years old	2,523	1,787	251	49	304	133	11.1	12.2	10.4	4.6	10.0	8.3
5 to 14 years old	4,207	2,939	496	85	461	226	18.5	20.1	20.6	7.9	15.1	14.1
15 to 44 years old	11,529	7,447	1,162	429	1,732	759	50.7	50.9	48.4	40.1	56.7	47.5
45 to 64 years old	3,271	1,844	355	291	438	344	14.4	12.6	14.8	27.2	14.3	21.5
65 years old and over	1,222	612	138	218	119	135	5.4	4.2	5.7	20.3	3.9	8.4
EDUCATIONAL ATTAINMENT												
Persons 25 years old and over	**12,100**	**7,198**	**1,280**	**818**	**1,776**	**1,029**	**100.0**	**100.0**	**100.0**	**100.0**	**100.0**	**100.0**
High school graduate or higher	6,424	3,324	766	508	1,117	709	53.1	46.2	59.8	62.1	62.9	68.9
Bachelor's degree or higher	1,090	428	103	135	269	155	9.0	5.9	8.0	16.5	15.1	15.1
LABOR FORCE STATUS [1]												
Civilians 16 years old and over	**15,753**	**9,693**	**1,676**	**927**	**(NA)**	**(NA)**	**100.0**	**100.0**	**100.0**	**100.0**	**(NA)**	**(NA)**
Civilian labor force	10,377	6,499	950	554	(NA)	(NA)	65.9	67.0	56.7	59.8	(NA)	(NA)
Employed	9,272	5,805	828	511	(NA)	(NA)	58.9	59.9	49.4	55.1	(NA)	(NA)
Unemployed	1,104	693	122	43	(NA)	(NA)	7.0	7.1	7.3	4.6	(NA)	(NA)
Unemployment rate [2]	10.6	10.7	12.8	7.8	(NA)	(NA)	(X)	(X)	(X)	(X)	(NA)	(NA)
Not in labor force	5,377	3,194	725	373	(NA)	(NA)	34.1	33.0	43.3	40.2	(NA)	(NA)
FAMILY TYPE												
Total families	**5,318**	**3,210**	**653**	**309**	**751**	**395**	**100.0**	**100.0**	**100.0**	**100.0**	**100.0**	**100.0**
Married couple	3,674	2,320	349	235	510	261	69.1	72.3	53.4	76.1	67.9	66.0
Female householder, no spouse present	1,238	622	264	56	186	110	23.3	19.4	40.5	18.2	24.7	27.7
Male householder, no spouse present	407	269	40	18	56	25	7.7	8.4	6.2	5.7	7.4	6.3
FAMILY INCOME IN 1992												
Total families	**5,318**	**3,210**	**653**	**309**	**751**	**395**	**100.0**	**100.0**	**100.0**	**100.0**	**100.0**	**100**
Less than $5,000	320	178	60	14	45	23	6.0	5.5	9.2	4.5	6.0	5.8
$5,000 to $9,999	620	338	123	23	85	50	11.7	10.5	18.8	7.4	11.3	12.7
$10,000 to $14,999	671	423	70	29	116	32	12.6	13.2	10.7	9.4	15.4	8.1
$15,000 to $24,999	1,152	740	140	61	142	71	21.7	23.1	21.4	19.7	18.9	18.0
$25,000 to $34,999	865	550	89	47	124	53	16.3	17.1	13.6	15.2	16.5	13.4
$35,000 to $49,999	802	503	77	50	104	66	15.1	15.7	11.8	16.2	13.8	16.7
$50,000 or more	889	478	96	85	133	98	16.7	14.9	14.7	27.5	17.7	24.8
Median income (dol.) [3]	23,912	23,714	20,301	31,015	23,649	28,562	(X)	(X)	(X)	(X)	(X)	(X)
Families below poverty level [4]	1,395	847	212	47	203	86	26.2	26.4	32.5	15.4	27.0	21.7
Persons below poverty level [4]	6,655	4,404	874	194	815	368	29.3	30.1	36.5	18.1	26.7	23.1
HOUSING TENURE												
Total occupied units	**6,626**	**3,869**	**841**	**405**	**937**	**574**	**100.0**	**100.0**	**100.0**	**100.0**	**100.0**	**100.0**
Owner-occupied	2,654	1,708	197	215	239	294	40.0	44.2	23.4	53.0	25.6	51.2
Renter-occupied [5]	3,973	2,160	644	191	697	280	60.0	55.8	76.6	47.2	74.4	48.8

NA Not available. X Not applicable. [1] Source: U.S. Bureau of Labor Statistics, *Employment and Earnings*, January 1994. [2] Total unemployment as percent of civilian labor force. [3] For definition of median, see Guide to Tabular Presentation. [4] For explanation of poverty level, see text, section 14. [5] Includes no cash rent.

Source: Except as noted, U.S. Bureau of the Census, *Current Population Reports*, P20-475.

Population

No. 54. Native and Foreign-Born Population, by Place of Birth: 1920 to 1990

[In thousands, except percent. Beginning 1950, data are based on a sample from the census; for details, see text, section 1. See source for sampling variability. See also *Historical Statistics, Colonial Times to 1970*, series C 1-10]

YEAR	Total popula-tion	NATIVE POPULATION						FOREIGN-BORN	
		Total	Born in State of resi-dence	Born in other States	State of birth not reported	Born in outlying areas [1]	Born abroad or at sea of American parents	Number	Percent of total population
1920	105,711	91,790	71,071	20,274	314	38	93	13,921	13.2
1930	122,775	108,571	82,678	25,388	238	136	131	14,204	11.6
1940	131,669	120,074	92,610	26,906	280	157	122	11,595	8.8
1950	150,216	139,869	102,788	35,284	1,370	330	96	10,347	6.9
1960	178,467	168,806	118,802	44,264	4,526	817	397	9,661	5.4
1970	203,194	193,454	131,296	51,659	8,882	873	744	9,740	4.8
1980	226,546	212,466	144,871	65,452	(NA)	1,088	1,055	14,080	6.2
1990	248,710	228,943	153,685	72,011	(NA)	1,382	1,864	19,767	7.9

NA Not available.   [1] 1920-50, includes Alaska and Hawaii. Includes Puerto Rico.

No. 55. Foreign-Born Population, by Place of Birth: 1990

[In percent, except as indicated. As of April 1. Based on a sample and subject to sampling variability, see text, section 1]

PLACE OF BIRTH	Number (1,000)	Percent entered between 1980-90	Percent 65 years old and over	EDUCATION [1]		OCCUPATION OF EMPLOYED PERSONS [3]				Median household income in 1989 (dol.)
				High school gradu-ates	College gradu-ates [2]	Profes-sional specialty	Service occupa-tions	Opera-tors, fabrica-tors, laborers		
Total [4]	19,767	43.8	13.6	58.8	20.4	12.3	18.1	18.6	28,314
Europe [5]	4,017	17.9	31.4	63.5	18.0	15.4	14.5	12.8	30,892
France	119	29.4	18.6	82.0	31.9	21.6	15.8	6.1	33,165
Germany	712	11.2	27.3	75.9	19.1	16.3	13.3	8.8	30,652
Greece	177	12.8	18.8	50.0	14.8	10.8	22.7	11.9	33,500
Hungary	110	11.9	40.1	65.6	22.2	20.2	9.9	11.0	30,060
Ireland	170	19.4	35.1	63.9	14.6	17.1	19.5	8.8	31,562
Italy	581	6.4	40.2	39.3	8.6	8.5	17.2	18.3	29,369
Poland	388	30.0	39.4	58.1	16.3	11.9	18.1	19.7	26,948
Portugal	210	21.6	12.7	32.1	4.6	3.9	14.0	35.9	35,053
United Kingdom	640	24.1	26.6	81.3	23.1	20.8	10.6	5.8	34,339
Yugoslavia	142	15.8	25.3	52.6	13.7	10.6	18.6	18.8	32,352
Soviet Union [6]	334	39.4	40.5	64.0	27.1	20.1	11.9	11.0	19,125
Asia [5]	4,979	56.1	7.1	75.8	38.4	18.9	14.8	12.5	35,318
Cambodia	119	85.8	3.4	35.4	5.5	5.5	18.7	29.2	19,728
China	530	53.5	17.9	60.6	30.9	16.9	24.5	16.1	30,597
Hong Kong	147	44.3	1.9	83.3	46.8	22.5	12.2	7.2	42,033
India	450	55.7	3.9	87.2	64.9	34.0	6.2	8.5	48,320
Iran	211	49.6	6.1	86.7	50.6	24.0	9.3	6.3	35,836
Japan	290	52.7	6.2	86.4	35.0	17.6	16.9	7.4	34,999
Korea	568	56.1	5.3	80.1	34.4	13.3	15.0	13.0	30,147
Laos	172	76.4	3.5	37.8	5.1	4.4	15.5	41.1	19,671
Philippines	913	49.0	10.4	82.5	43.0	18.0	16.8	10.7	45,419
Taiwan	244	65.4	2.4	91.6	62.2	28.7	10.3	4.0	38,966
Thailand	107	55.7	1.1	74.1	33.2	14.2	26.6	14.4	31,815
Vietnam	543	61.8	3.3	58.9	15.9	10.7	15.6	20.8	30,039
Canada	745	16.6	33.7	72.6	22.1	21.1	9.5	8.3	30,186
Mexico	4,298	49.9	4.9	24.3	3.5	2.6	21.0	32.2	21,926
Caribbean [5]	1,938	40.4	12.0	56.9	13.6	10.5	21.4	17.8	26,621
Cuba	737	25.5	21.1	54.1	15.6	10.9	13.2	18.0	27,292
Dominican Republic	348	53.1	5.0	41.7	7.5	5.2	23.0	31.0	19,996
Haiti	225	58.9	4.3	57.6	11.8	9.1	33.9	20.5	25,454
Jamaica	334	46.3	7.8	67.9	14.9	13.2	26.4	11.2	30,599
Trinidad and Tobago	116	40.1	5.7	74.1	15.6	12.9	22.2	9.4	30,236
Central America [5]	1,134	67.4	4.1	45.7	8.5	4.5	29.8	24.3	24,509
El Salvador	465	75.2	2.6	32.7	4.6	2.4	34.1	26.8	23,533
Guatemala	226	68.3	2.7	37.5	5.8	3.3	31.3	27.6	24,362
Honduras	109	65.6	4.1	49.2	8.3	4.5	29.8	23.7	21,947
Nicaragua	169	74.0	4.6	58.8	14.6	5.0	23.2	24.2	24,944
South America [5]	1,037	52.1	5.6	71.3	20.0	11.4	21.0	17.9	31,129
Colombia	286	51.2	5.0	66.8	15.5	8.8	22.1	21.4	29,139
Ecuador	143	43.3	5.8	60.3	11.8	6.9	19.5	26.8	30,615
Guyana	121	60.3	6.3	69.5	15.8	11.6	19.1	12.8	34,243
Peru	144	60.8	5.2	78.6	21.0	10.0	24.1	18.5	30,465
Africa	364	59.3	4.1	87.9	47.1	22.1	16.4	11.7	30,907
Oceania	104	46.1	11.0	77.0	24.2	18.0	15.8	11.2	35,067

[1] For persons 25 years old and over.   [2] Bachelor's or advanced degree.   [3] For persons 16 years old and over.   [4] Includes persons whose place of birth was not reported.   [5] Includes other areas not shown separately.   [6] The former Soviet Union is now referred to as the following geopolitical entities: Armenia, Azerbaijan, Byelarus, Georgia, Kazakhstan, Kyrgyzstan, Moldova, Russia, Tajikistan, Turkmenistan, Ukraine, and Uzbekistan.

Source of tables 54 and 55: U.S. Bureau of the Census, *1970 Census of Population*, vol. II, PC(2)-2A; 1990 Census of Population and Housing Listing (1990 CPH-L-98 and 1990 CPH-L-121) and *1990 Census of Population, The Foreign-Born Population in the United States* (1990 CP-3-1).

No. 56. Population, by Selected Ancestry Group and Region: 1990

[As of **April 1**. Covers persons who reported single and multiple ancestry groups. Persons who reported a multiple ancestry group may be included in more than one category. Major classifications of ancestry groups do not represent strict geographic or cultural definitions. Based on a sample and subject to sampling variability; see text, section 1]

ANCESTRY GROUP	Total (1,000)	Northeast	Midwest	South	West
European: [1]					
Austrian	865	38	21	19	22
British	1,119	17	18	39	26
Croatian	544	21	43	20	16
Czech	1,296	10	52	22	16
Danish	1,635	9	34	12	45
Dutch	6,227	16	34	29	21
English	32,652	18	22	35	25
European	467	14	17	31	39
Finnish	659	14	47	11	27
French	10,321	26	26	29	20
German	57,947	17	39	25	19
Greek	1,110	37	23	21	19
Hungarian	1,582	36	32	17	16
Irish	38,736	24	25	33	17
Italian	14,665	51	17	17	15
Lithuanian	812	43	28	16	13
Norwegian	3,869	6	52	10	33
Polish	9,366	37	37	15	11
Portuguese	1,153	49	3	8	41
Russian	2,953	44	16	18	22
Scandinavian	679	8	33	15	45
Scotch-Irish	5,618	14	19	47	20
Scottish	5,394	20	21	33	26
Slovak	1,883	40	34	14	11
Swedish	4,681	14	40	14	32
Swiss	1,045	16	36	17	30
Ukrainian	741	51	22	14	13
Welsh	2,034	22	24	27	27
Yugoslavian	258	23	28	12	37

ANCESTRY GROUP	Total (1,000)	Northeast	Midwest	South	West
Central & South America [2] **and Spain:**					
Cuban	860	18	3	69	9
Dominican	506	86	1	10	2
Hispanic	1,113	13	6	31	50
Mexican	11,587	1	9	33	57
Puerto Rican	1,955	66	11	15	8
Salvadoran	499	13	2	23	62
Spanish	2,024	16	8	30	45
West Indian: [1]					
Jamaican	435	59	5	31	6
Asia:					
Asian Indian	570	32	19	26	24
Chinese	1,505	25	8	12	55
Filipino	1,451	10	9	13	68
Japanese	1,005	9	8	11	72
Korean	837	22	14	20	44
Vietnamese	536	9	8	28	54
North America:					
Acadian/Cajun	668	1	2	91	5
Afro-American	23,777	15	21	54	10
American Indian	8,708	9	22	47	23
American	12,396	10	18	61	11
Canadian	550	34	18	21	28
French Canadian	2,167	45	20	20	15
United States	644	16	18	53	13
White	1,800	7	13	53	28

[1] Non-Hispanic groups.   [2] Hispanic groups.

Source: U.S. Bureau of the Census, *1990 Census of Population, Supplementary Reports, Detailed Ancestry Groups for States* (1990 CP-S-1-2).

No. 57. Persons Speaking a Language Other Than English at Home, by Age and Language: 1990

[As of **April**. Based on a sample and subject to sampling variability]

AGE GROUP AND LANGUAGE SPOKEN AT HOME	Persons who speak language (1,000)	Percent who speak English less than "very well"
Persons 5 years old and over	230,446	(X)
Speak only English	198,601	(X)
Speak other language	31,845	43.9
Speak Spanish or Spanish Creole	17,345	47.9
Speak Asian or Pacific Island language	4,472	54.1
Speak other language	10,028	32.4
Persons 5 to 17 years old	45,342	(X)
Speak only English	39,020	(X)
Speak other language	6,323	37.8
Speak Spanish or Spanish Creole	4,168	39.3
Speak Asian or Pacific Island language	816	44.2
Speak other language	1,340	29.2
Persons 18 to 64 years old	153,908	(X)
Speak only English	132,200	(X)
Speak other language	21,708	45.1
Speak Spanish or Spanish Creole	12,121	49.6
Speak Asian or Pacific Island language	3,301	54.7
Speak other language	6,286	31.4
Persons 65 years old and over	31,195	(X)
Speak only English	27,381	(X)
Speak other language	3,814	47.2
Speak Spanish or Spanish Creole	1,057	62.3
Speak Asian or Pacific Island language	355	72.0
Speak other language	2,402	36.9

LANGUAGE	Persons, 5 years old and over who speak language (1,000)
Speak only English	198,601
Spanish	17,339
French	1,702
German	1,547
Italian	1,309
Chinese	1,249
Tagalog	843
Polish	723
Korean	626
Vietnamese	507
Portuguese	430
Japanese	428
Greek	388
Arabic	355
Hindi (Urdu)	331
Russian	242
Yiddish	213
Thai (Laotian)	206
Persian	202
French Creole	188
Armenian	150
Navaho	149
Hungarian	148
Hebrew	144
Dutch	143
Mon-Khmer (Cambodian)	127
Gujarathi	102

X Not applicable.

Source: U.S. Bureau of the Census, *1990 Census of Population and Housing Data Paper Listing* (CPH-L-133); and Summary Tape File 3C.

54   Population

No. 58. Foreign-Born Population, Leading Ancestry Groups, and Persons Speaking a Language Other Than English at Home—States: 1990

[As of **April**. Based on a sample and subject to sampling variability]

REGION, DIVISION, AND STATE	FOREIGN BORN POPULATION Number (1,000)	Percent of total population	Year of entry, 1980-90 (1,000)	ANCESTRY GROUPS Leading ancestry group — Group	Number (1,000)	Second leading group — Group	Number (1,000)	PERSON 5 YEARS OLD AND OVER SPEAKING LANGUAGE OTHER THAN ENGLISH Number (1,000)	Percent of total population
U.S...	**19,767**	**7.9**	**8,664**	**German . . . . .**	**57,947**	**Irish . . . .**	**38,736**	**31,845**	**13.8**
Northeast.	5,231	10.3	2,059	German	9,929	Irish.	9,420	7,824	16.5
N.E . . .	1,043	7.9	368	Irish.	2,949	English	2,330	1,703	13.9
ME . .	36	3.0	7	English	372	French.	224	105	9.2
NH . .	41	3.7	10	English	266	Irish.	232	89	8.7
VT . .	18	3.1	3	English	147	French.	133	30	5.8
MA . .	574	9.5	223	Irish.	1,571	English	921	852	15.2
RI . .	95	9.5	35	Irish.	214	Italian	199	159	17.0
CT . .	279	8.5	90	Italian	628	Irish.	614	466	15.2
M.A . . .	4,188	11.1	1,691	German	8,622	Irish.	6,471	6,122	17.5
NY . .	2,852	15.9	1,190	German	2,899	Italian	2,838	3,909	23.3
NJ . .	967	12.5	385	Italian	1,457	Irish.	1,415	1,406	19.5
PA . .	369	3.1	116	German	4,315	Irish.	2,256	807	7.3
Midwest . .	2,131	3.6	754	German	22,477	Irish.	9,643	3,921	7.1
E.N.C . .	1,783	4.2	608	German	14,776	Irish.	6,655	3,125	8.0
OH . .	260	2.4	71	German	4,068	Irish.	1,896	546	5.4
IN . .	94	1.7	31	German	2,085	Irish.	965	246	4.8
IL . .	952	8.3	371	German	3,326	Irish.	1,861	1,499	14.2
MI . .	355	3.8	94	German	2,666	Irish.	1,320	570	6.6
WI . .	122	2.5	41	German	2,631	Irish.	612	264	5.8
W.N.C. .	348	2.0	146	German	7,702	Irish.	2,988	796	4.9
MN . .	113	2.6	51	German	2,021	Norwegian . . .	757	227	5.6
IA . .	43	1.6	19	German	1,395	Irish.	527	100	3.9
MO . .	84	1.6	30	German	1,843	Irish.	1,038	178	3.8
ND . .	9	1.5	3	German	325	Norwegian . . .	189	47	7.9
SD . .	8	1.1	2	German	355	Norwegian . . .	106	42	6.5
NE . .	28	1.8	10	German	795	Irish.	272	70	4.8
KS . .	63	2.5	31	German	968	Irish.	436	132	5.7
South . . .	4,582	5.4	2,030	German	14,630	Irish.	12,951	8,670	10.9
S.A . . .	2,723	6.3	1,172	German	7,882	Afro-American.	7,106	3,708	9.1
DE . .	22	3.3	7	Irish.	139	German	138	42	6.9
MD . .	313	6.6	148	German	1,218	Afro-American.	966	395	8.9
DC . .	59	9.7	34	Afro-American.	315	German	39	71	12.5
VA . .	312	5.0	159	German	1,186	English	1,051	419	7.3
WV . .	16	0.9	4	German	469	Irish.	348	44	2.6
NC . .	115	1.7	52	Afro-American.	1,228	German	1,111	241	3.9
SC . .	50	1.4	18	Afro-American.	870	German	500	113	3.5
GA . .	173	2.7	90	Afro-American.	1,421	Irish.	971	285	4.8
FL . .	1,663	12.9	660	German	2,410	Irish.	1,899	2,098	17.3
E.S.C . .	157	1.0	65	Irish.	2,581	German	2,177	392	2.8
KY . .	34	0.9	14	German	798	Irish.	696	86	2.5
TN . .	59	1.2	26	Irish.	875	German	724	132	2.9
AL . .	44	1.1	18	Afro-American.	839	American . . .	687	108	2.9
MS . .	20	0.8	8	Afro-American.	775	Irish.	393	67	2.8
W.S.C. .	1,702	6.4	793	German	4,572	Irish.	3,993	4,569	18.6
AR . .	25	1.1	10	Irish.	464	German	400	61	2.8
LA . .	87	2.1	35	Afro-American.	1,097	French.	550	392	10.1
OK . .	65	2.1	30	German	714	Irish.	642	146	5.0
TX . .	1,524	9.0	718	Mexican	3,403	German	2,950	3,970	25.4
West	7,823	14.8	3,821	German	10,911	English	8,110	11,430	23.5
Mt	715	5.2	297	German	3,477	English	2,843	1,901	15.1
MT . .	14	1.7	3	German	285	Irish.	139	37	5.0
ID . . .	29	2.9	13	English	291	German	279	59	6.4
WY . .	8	1.7	2	German	158	English	101	24	5.7
CO . .	142	4.3	57	German	1,064	English	582	321	10.5
NM . .	81	5.3	31	German	234	Mexican	216	494	35.5
AZ . .	278	7.6	117	German	878	English	586	700	20.8
UT . .	59	3.4	26	English	750	German	299	120	7.8
NV . .	105	8.7	48	German	280	English	207	146	13.2
Pac . . .	7,108	18.2	3,524	German	7,433	Mexican	5,539	9,529	26.4
WA . .	322	6.6	129	German	1,390	English	897	403	9.0
OR . .	139	4.9	61	German	879	English	575	192	7.3
CA . .	6,459	21.7	3,256	Mexican	5,322	German	4,935	8,619	31.5
AK . .	25	4.5	11	German	127	English	77	60	12.1
HI . .	163	14.7	67	Japanese	262	Filipino	176	255	24.8

Source: U.S. Bureau of the Census, *1990 Census of Population and Housing, Summary Social, Economic, and Housing Characteristics, United States* (1990 CPH-5-1); *1990 Census of Population and Housing Listing* (1990 CPH-L-98); and *1990 Census of Population, Supplementary Reports, Detailed Ancestry Groups for States* (1990 CP-S-1-2).

No. 59. Marital Status of the Population, by Sex, Race, and Hispanic Origin: 1970 to 1993

[In millions, except percent. As of March, except as noted. Persons 18 years old and over. Excludes members of Armed Forces except those living off post or with their families on post. Except as noted, based on Current Population Survey, see text, section 1, and Appendix III. See *Historical Statistics, Colonial Times to 1970*, series A 160-171, for decennial data]

MARITAL STATUS, RACE, AND HISPANIC ORIGIN	TOTAL				MALE				FEMALE			
	1970	1980	1990	1993	1970	1980	1990	1993	1970	1980	1990	1993
Total [1]	132.5	159.5	181.8	187.1	62.5	75.7	86.9	89.7	70.0	83.8	95.0	97.4
Never married	21.4	32.3	40.4	42.3	11.8	18.0	22.4	23.6	9.6	14.3	17.9	18.6
Married	95.0	104.6	112.6	114.5	47.1	51.8	55.8	56.8	47.9	52.8	56.7	57.7
Widowed	11.8	12.7	13.8	13.7	2.1	2.0	2.3	2.5	9.7	10.8	11.5	11.2
Divorced	4.3	9.9	15.1	16.7	1.6	3.9	6.3	6.8	2.7	6.0	8.8	9.9
Percent of total	100.0	100.0	100.0	100.0	100.0	100.0	100.0	100.0	100.0	100.0	100.0	100.0
Never married	16.2	20.3	22.2	22.6	18.9	23.8	25.8	26.3	13.7	17.1	18.9	19.1
Married	71.7	65.5	61.9	61.2	75.3	68.4	64.3	63.4	68.5	63.0	59.7	59.2
Widowed	8.9	8.0	7.6	7.3	3.3	2.6	2.7	2.8	13.9	12.8	12.1	11.5
Divorced	3.2	6.2	8.3	8.9	2.5	5.2	7.2	7.6	3.9	7.1	9.3	10.1
Percent standardized for age: [2]												
Never married	14.1	16.5	20.6	22.0	16.5	18.7	23.3	24.9	12.1	14.5	18.2	19.4
Married	74.2	69.3	63.7	62.2	77.6	72.9	66.5	64.3	70.8	65.9	61.2	60.1
Widowed	8.3	7.6	6.9	6.7	3.3	2.7	2.7	3.1	13.0	12.1	10.8	10.0
Divorced	3.4	6.6	8.7	9.1	2.6	5.6	7.6	7.7	4.1	7.6	9.8	10.4
White, total	118.2	139.5	155.5	158.7	55.9	66.7	74.8	76.6	62.2	72.8	80.6	82.1
Never married	18.4	26.4	31.6	32.4	10.2	15.0	18.0	18.6	8.2	11.4	13.6	13.8
Married	85.8	93.8	99.5	100.9	42.7	46.7	49.5	50.3	43.1	47.1	49.9	50.6
Widowed	10.3	10.9	11.7	11.5	1.7	1.6	1.9	2.0	8.6	9.3	9.8	9.5
Divorced	3.7	8.3	12.6	14.0	1.3	3.4	5.4	5.8	2.3	5.0	7.3	8.2
Percent of total	100.0	100.0	100.0	100.0	100.0	100.0	100.0	100.0	100.0	100.0	100.0	100.0
Never married	15.6	18.9	20.3	20.4	18.2	22.5	24.1	24.3	13.2	15.7	16.9	16.8
Married	72.6	67.2	64.0	63.6	76.3	70.0	66.2	65.7	69.3	64.7	61.9	61.6
Widowed	8.7	7.8	7.5	7.2	3.1	2.5	2.6	2.6	13.8	12.8	12.2	11.6
Divorced	3.1	6.0	8.1	8.8	2.4	5.0	7.2	7.5	3.8	6.8	9.0	10.0
Black, total	13.0	16.6	20.3	21.3	5.9	7.4	9.1	9.6	7.1	9.2	11.2	11.7
Never married	2.7	5.1	7.1	8.0	1.4	2.5	3.5	3.9	1.2	2.5	3.6	4.1
Married	8.3	8.5	9.3	9.2	3.9	4.1	4.5	4.4	4.4	4.5	4.8	4.8
Widowed	1.4	1.6	1.7	1.8	0.3	0.3	0.3	0.4	1.1	1.3	1.4	1.4
Divorced	0.6	1.4	2.1	2.2	0.2	0.5	0.8	0.8	0.4	0.9	1.3	1.4
Percent of total	100.0	100.0	100.0	100.0	100.0	100.0	100.0	100.0	100.0	100.0	100.0	100.0
Never married	20.6	30.5	35.1	37.6	24.3	34.3	38.4	40.8	17.4	27.4	32.5	34.9
Married	64.1	51.4	45.8	43.4	66.9	54.6	49.2	46.1	61.7	48.7	43.0	41.1
Widowed	11.0	9.8	8.5	8.6	5.2	4.2	3.7	4.4	15.8	14.3	12.4	12.0
Divorced	4.4	8.4	10.6	10.5	3.6	7.0	8.8	8.6	5.0	9.5	12.0	12.0
Hispanic, [3] total	5.1	7.9	13.6	14.9	2.4	3.8	6.7	7.4	2.6	4.1	6.8	7.5
Never married	0.9	1.9	3.7	4.2	0.5	1.0	2.2	2.4	0.4	0.9	1.5	1.7
Married	3.6	5.2	8.4	9.0	1.8	2.5	4.1	4.4	1.8	2.6	4.3	4.6
Widowed	0.3	0.4	0.5	0.7	0.1	0.1	0.1	0.1	0.2	0.3	0.4	0.5
Divorced	0.2	0.5	1.0	1.1	0.1	0.2	0.4	0.5	0.1	0.3	0.6	0.6
Percent of total	100.0	100.0	100.0	100.0	100.0	100.0	100.0	100.0	100.0	100.0	100.0	100.0
Never married	18.6	24.1	27.2	27.9	21.2	27.3	32.1	32.5	16.2	21.1	22.5	23.3
Married	71.8	65.6	61.7	60.4	73.8	67.1	60.9	59.7	70.0	64.3	62.4	61.1
Widowed	5.6	4.4	4.0	4.4	2.3	1.6	1.5	1.7	8.7	7.1	6.5	7.0
Divorced	3.9	5.8	7.0	7.3	2.7	4.0	5.5	6.1	5.1	7.6	8.5	8.6

[1] Includes persons of other races, not shown separately. [2] 1960 age distribution used as standard; standardization improves comparability over time by removing effects of changes in age distribution of population. [3] Hispanic persons may be of any race. 1970 data as of April and based on census.

Source: U.S. Bureau of the Census, *1970 Census of Population*, vol. I, part 1, and *Current Population Reports*, P20-450, and earlier reports; and unpublished data.

No. 60. Marital Status of the Population, by Sex and Age: 1993

[As of **March**. **Persons 18 years old and over**. Excludes members of Armed Forces except those living off post or with their families on post. Based on Current Population Survey; see text, section 1, and Appendix III. See *Historical Statistics, Colonial Times to 1970*, series A 160-171, for decennial census data]

SEX AND AGE	NUMBER OF PERSONS (1,000)					PERCENT DISTRIBUTION				
	Total	Single	Married	Widowed	Divorced	Total	Single	Married	Widowed	Divorced
Male	**89,692**	**23,618**	**56,832**	**2,468**	**6,778**	**100.0**	**26.3**	**63.4**	**2.8**	**7.6**
18 to 19 years old	3,263	3,162	96	-	6	100.0	96.9	2.9	-	0.2
20 to 24 years old	8,786	7,113	1,575	7	91	100.0	81.0	17.9	0.1	1.0
25 to 29 years old	9,767	4,727	4,595	11	435	100.0	48.4	47.0	0.1	4.5
30 to 34 years old	11,089	3,333	6,919	15	822	100.0	30.1	62.4	0.1	7.4
35 to 39 years old	10,606	2,085	7,300	33	1,189	100.0	19.7	68.8	0.3	11.2
40 to 44 years old	9,298	1,008	7,091	51	1,148	100.0	10.8	76.3	0.5	12.3
45 to 54 years old	13,847	951	11,153	142	1,602	100.0	6.9	80.5	1.0	11.6
55 to 64 years old	10,205	670	8,251	380	904	100.0	6.6	80.9	3.7	8.9
65 to 74 years old	8,114	389	6,502	765	458	100.0	4.8	80.1	9.4	5.6
75 years old and over	4,717	180	3,350	1,064	124	100.0	3.8	71.0	22.6	2.6
Female	**97,441**	**18,639**	**57,708**	**11,214**	**9,880**	**100.0**	**19.1**	**59.2**	**11.5**	**10.1**
18 to 19 years old	3,244	2,918	312	-	14	100.0	90.0	9.6	-	0.4
20 to 24 years old	9,016	6,019	2,796	7	194	100.0	66.8	31.0	0.1	2.2
25 to 29 years old	9,836	3,258	5,765	25	789	100.0	33.1	58.6	0.3	8.0
30 to 34 years old	11,171	2,153	7,760	58	1,200	100.0	19.3	69.5	0.5	10.7
35 to 39 years old	10,861	1,362	8,010	121	1,367	100.0	12.5	73.8	1.1	12.6
40 to 44 years old	9,577	867	7,065	181	1,465	100.0	9.1	73.8	1.9	15.3
45 to 54 years old	14,655	798	10,760	648	2,448	100.0	5.4	73.4	4.4	16.7
55 to 64 years old	11,042	469	7,629	1,594	1,349	100.0	4.2	69.1	14.4	12.2
65 to 74 years old	10,249	376	5,537	3,607	728	100.0	3.7	54.0	35.2	7.1
75 years old and over	7,790	419	2,074	4,972	326	100.0	5.4	26.6	63.8	4.2

- Represents or rounds to zero.

No. 61. Unmarried Couples, by Selected Characteristics: 1970 to 1993

[In thousands. As of March. An "unmarried couple" is two unrelated adults of the opposite sex sharing the same household. See headnote, table 66]

PRESENCE OF CHILDREN AND AGE OF HOUSEHOLDER	1970	1980	1985	1990	1993
Unmarried couples, total	523	1,589	1,983	2,856	3,510
No children under 15 years old	327	1,159	1,380	1,966	2,274
Some children under 15 years old	196	431	603	891	1,236
Under 25 years old	55	411	425	596	714
25 to 44 years old	103	837	1,203	1,775	2,139
45 to 64 years old	186	221	239	358	491
65 years old and over	178	119	116	127	166

No. 62. Married Couples of Same or Mixed Races and Origins: 1970 to 1993

[In thousands. As of **March, except as noted. Persons 15 years old and over**. Persons of Hispanic origin may be of any race. Except as noted, based on Current Population Survey; see headnote, table 66]

RACE AND ORIGIN OF SPOUSES	1970 [1]	1980	1990	1993
Married couples, total	**44,598**	**49,714**	**53,256**	**54,199**
RACE				
Same race couples	43,922	48,264	50,889	51,437
White/White	40,578	44,910	47,202	47,782
Black/Black	3,344	3,354	3,687	3,655
Interracial couples	310	651	964	1,195
Black/White	65	167	211	242
Black husband/White wife	41	122	150	182
White husband/Black wife	24	45	61	60
White/other race [2]	233	450	720	920
Black/other race [2]	12	34	33	33
All other couples [2]	366	799	1,401	1,567
HISPANIC ORIGIN				
Hispanic/Hispanic	1,368	1,906	3,085	3,419
Hispanic/other origin (not Hispanic)	584	891	1,193	1,206
All other couples (not of Hispanic origin)	42,645	46,917	48,979	49,573

[1] As of April and based on Census of Population.   [2] Excluding White and Black.

Source of tables 60-62: U.S. Bureau of the Census, *Current Population Reports*, P20-450; and earlier reports; and unpublished data.

No. 63. Living Arrangements of Persons 15 Years Old and Over, by Selected Characteristics: 1993

[As of **March.** Based on Current Population Survey which includes members of Armed Forces living off post or with families on post, but excludes other Armed Forces; see text, section 1, and Appendix III]

AGE AND SEX	ALL RACES [1]					WHITE PERSONS PERCENT LIVING—			BLACK PERSONS PERCENT LIVING—		
	Total (1,000)	Percent living—				Alone	With spouse	With other relatives	Alone	With spouse	With other relatives
		Alone	With spouse	With other relatives	With nonrelatives						
Total	197,254	12	55	26	7	12	58	23	13	33	48
15 to 19 years old.	16,627	1	3	93	4	1	3	92	-	-	97
20 to 24 years old.	17,802	6	23	56	16	6	25	52	6	11	75
25 to 34 years old.	41,864	9	56	24	11	9	60	20	10	32	49
35 to 44 years old.	40,342	8	69	17	6	8	72	14	10	44	39
45 to 54 years old.	28,503	11	73	12	4	10	76	10	14	51	28
55 to 64 years old.	21,247	14	71	11	4	14	74	9	21	47	26
65 years old and over	30,870	30	55	13	2	30	56	11	33	39	25
65 to 74 years old	18,362	24	64	11	2	23	66	9	30	46	22
75 years old and over. . .	12,508	40	42	16	2	41	43	14	40	25	32
Male.	94,854	10	57	25	8	10	60	22	12	37	41
15 to 19 years old.	8,424	1	1	95	3	1	1	95	-	-	98
20 to 24 years old.	8,786	7	17	60	17	7	19	57	5	9	76
25 to 34 years old.	20,856	11	52	23	14	11	55	20	13	33	40
35 to 44 years old.	19,904	10	69	13	9	10	71	12	12	49	24
45 to 54 years old.	13,847	11	77	8	4	10	79	7	14	58	18
55 to 64 years old.	10,205	10	77	8	5	10	80	6	15	56	18
65 years old and over	12,832	16	75	7	3	15	76	6	24	57	15
65 to 74 years old	8,114	13	78	6	3	12	80	5	21	62	13
75 years old and over. . .	4,717	20	69	8	3	19	71	7	31	45	18
Female.	102,400	14	53	28	5	14	56	24	13	30	53
15 to 19 years old.	8,202	1	4	91	4	1	5	90	-	1	97
20 to 24 years old.	9,016	5	28	52	15	5	31	48	6	14	74
25 to 34 years old.	21,007	7	60	25	8	7	64	20	7	31	56
35 to 44 years old.	20,438	6	69	21	4	6	73	17	7	39	51
45 to 54 years old.	14,655	11	70	17	3	11	72	14	14	45	36
55 to 64 years old.	11,042	18	66	14	2	17	69	11	26	39	33
65 years old and over	18,038	41	41	17	2	41	42	15	39	26	32
65 to 74 years old	10,249	32	52	14	1	32	54	12	36	35	28
75 years old and over. . .	7,790	52	25	20	2	54	26	18	44	14	39

- Represents or rounds to zero.   [1] Includes other races not shown separately.

Source: U.S. Bureau of the Census, unpublished data.

No. 64. Living Arrangements of Young Adults: 1970 to 1993

[**1970** and **1980,** as of **April.** Beginning **1985,** as of **March** and based on Current Population Survey, see headnote, table 63]

LIVING ARRANGEMENTS AND SEX	PERSONS 18 TO 24 YEARS OLD					PERSONS 25 TO 34 YEARS OLD				
	1970	1980	1985	1990	1993	1970	1980	1985	1990	1993
Total (1,000)	22,357	29,122	27,844	25,310	24,309	24,566	36,796	40,857	43,240	41,863
Percent distribution:										
Child of householder [1]	47	48	54	53	53	8	9	11	12	12
Family householder or spouse . . .	38	29	24	22	22	83	72	68	65	63
Nonfamily householder	5	10	8	9	9	5	12	13	13	13
Other.	10	13	14	16	16	4	7	9	11	12
Male (1,000)	10,398	14,278	13,695	12,450	12,049	11,929	18,107	20,184	21,462	20,856
Percent distribution:										
Child of householder [1]	54	54	60	58	59	10	11	13	15	16
Family householder or spouse . . .	30	21	16	15	15	79	66	60	56	54
Nonfamily householder	5	11	10	10	11	7	15	16	16	16
Other.	10	13	14	17	16	4	8	11	13	14
Female (1,000)	11,959	14,844	14,149	12,860	12,260	12,637	18,689	20,673	21,779	21,007
Percent distribution:										
Child of householder [1]	41	43	48	48	47	7	7	8	8	9
Family householder or spouse . . .	45	36	32	30	29	86	78	76	73	72
Nonfamily householder	4	8	7	8	8	4	9	10	10	10
Other.	10	13	13	15	16	4	6	7	9	10

[1] Includes unmarried college students living in dormitories.
Source: U.S. Bureau of the Census, *1970* and *1980 Census of Population,* PC(2)-4B and *Current Population Reports,* P20-410 and P20-450; and unpublished data.

No. 65. Householder and Marital Status of Population, 15 Years Old and Over: 1993

[In thousands. As of March. See headnote, table 66]

HOUSEHOLDER AND MARITAL STATUS	Total, 15 yrs. and over	MALE					FEMALE				
		Total [1]	20 to 24 years	25 to 44 years	45 to 64 years	65 yr. and over	Total [1]	20 to 24 years	25 to 44 years	45 to 64 years	65 yr. and over
Total persons	197,254	94,854	8,786	40,760	24,052	12,832	102,400	9,016	41,445	25,697	18,038
Householder.	96,391	63,764	2,578	29,084	20,664	11,247	32,627	1,975	12,374	8,350	9,649
Never married	14,652	7,213	1,357	4,439	887	398	7,439	1,485	4,227	905	579
Married, spouse present . .	53,171	48,484	1,149	21,619	16,888	8,776	4,687	244	2,557	1,337	531
Married, spouse absent. .	4,425	1,617	29	790	591	204	2,807	143	1,647	774	230
Widowed	11,621	1,898	5	78	375	1,440	9,724	2	319	2,029	7,374
Divorced.	12,523	4,552	38	2,159	1,923	430	7,970	102	3,625	3,305	934
Not householder	100,863	31,090	6,208	11,677	3,389	1,584	69,773	7,040	29,071	17,347	8,389
Never married	37,657	21,562	5,756	6,714	735	170	16,095	4,535	3,414	363	215
Married, spouse present .	55,228	5,715	335	2,892	1,666	792	49,513	2,285	24,000	16,124	6,787
Married, spouse absent. .	1,778	1,016	63	605	257	80	762	124	394	154	62
Widowed	2,061	571	1	32	147	390	1,491	5	66	213	1,205
Divorced.	4,139	2,226	53	1,436	583	152	1,913	91	1,195	492	119

[1] Includes 15 to 19 year olds.

Source: U.S. Bureau of the Census, unpublished data.

No. 66. Households, Families, Subfamilies, Married Couples, and Unrelated Individuals: 1960 to 1993

[In thousands, except as indicated. As of March. Based on Current Population Survey; includes members of Armed Forces living off post or with their families on post, but excludes all other members of Armed Forces; see text, section 1, and Appendix III. For definition of terms, see text, section 1. Minus sign (-) indicates decrease. See also *Historical Statistics, Colonial Times to 1970*, series A 288-319]

TYPE OF UNIT	1960	1970	1975	1980	1985	1990	1992	1993	PERCENT CHANGE		
									1970-80	1980-90	1990-93
Households	52,799	63,401	71,120	80,776	86,789	93,347	95,669	96,391	27	16	3
Average size.	3.33	3.14	2.94	2.76	2.69	2.63	2.62	2.63	(X)	(X)	(X)
Family households	44,905	51,456	55,563	59,550	62,706	66,090	67,173	68,144	16	11	3
Married couple	39,254	44,728	46,951	49,112	50,350	52,317	52,457	53,171	10	7	2
Male householder [1]	1,228	1,228	1,485	1,733	2,228	2,884	3,025	3,026	41	66	5
Female householder [1]	4,422	5,500	7,127	8,705	10,129	10,890	11,692	11,947	58	25	10
Nonfamily households	7,895	11,945	15,557	21,226	24,082	27,257	28,496	28,247	78	28	4
Male householder	2,716	4,063	5,912	8,807	10,114	11,606	12,428	12,254	117	32	6
Female householder.	5,179	7,882	9,645	12,419	13,968	15,651	16,068	15,993	58	26	2
One person	6,896	10,851	13,939	18,296	20,602	22,999	23,974	23,642	69	26	3
Families.	45,111	51,586	55,712	59,550	62,706	66,090	67,173	68,144	15	11	3
Average size.	3.67	3.58	3.42	3.29	3.23	3.17	3.17	3.16	(X)	(X)	(X)
Married couple	39,329	44,755	46,971	49,112	50,350	52,317	52,457	53,171	10	7	2
Male householder [1]	1,275	1,239	1,499	1,733	2,228	2,884	3,025	3,026	40	66	5
Female householder [1]	4,507	5,591	7,242	8,705	10,129	10,890	11,692	11,947	56	25	10
Unrelated subfamilies	207	130	149	360	526	534	669	708	177	48	33
Married couple	75	27	20	20	46	68	92	83	(B)	(B)	(B)
Male reference persons [1] . .	47	11	14	36	85	45	55	68	(B)	(B)	(B)
Female reference persons [1] . .	85	91	115	304	395	421	523	557	234	39	32
Related subfamilies	1,514	1,150	1,349	1,150	2,228	2,403	2,559	2,671	-	109	11
Married couple	871	617	576	582	719	871	963	945	-6	50	8
Father-child [1]	115	48	69	54	116	153	134	170	(B)	(B)	11
Mother-child [1]	528	484	705	512	1,392	1,378	1,462	1,556	6	169	13
Married couples.	40,200	45,373	47,547	49,714	51,114	53,256	53,512	54,199	10	7	2
With own household	39,254	44,728	46,951	49,112	50,350	52,317	52,457	53,171	10	7	2
Without own household	946	645	596	602	764	939	1,055	1,028	-7	56	9
Percent without	2.4	1.4	1.3	1.2	1.5	1.8	2.0	1.9	(X)	(X)	(X)
Unrelated individuals	11,092	14,988	19,100	26,426	30,518	35,384	37,094	37,006	76	34	5
Nonfamily householders. . . .	7,895	11,945	15,557	21,226	24,082	27,257	28,496	28,247	78	28	4
Secondary individuals	3,198	3,043	3,543	5,200	6,436	8,127	8,598	8,759	71	56	8
Male	1,746	1,631	2,087	3,006	3,743	4,711	5,076	5,169	84	57	10
Female	1,451	1,412	1,456	2,194	2,693	3,416	3,522	3,589	55	56	5

- Represents or rounds to zero.   B Not shown; base less than 75,000.   X Not applicable.   [1] No spouse present.

Source: U.S. Bureau of the Census, *Current Population Reports*, P20-477.

No. 67. Households, 1980 to 1993, and Persons in Households, 1993, by Type of Household and Presence of Children

[As of **March**. Based on Current Population Survey; see headnote, table 66]

TYPE OF HOUSEHOLD AND PRESENCE OF CHILDREN	HOUSEHOLDS					PERSONS IN HOUSEHOLDS, 1993		Persons per house-hold, 1993
	Number (1,000)			Percent distribution		Num-ber (1,000)	Percent distribu-tion	
	1980	1990	1993	1980	1993			
Total households.	80,776	93,347	96,391	100	100	253,924	100	2.63
Family households	59,550	66,090	68,144	74	71	218,965	86	3.21
With own children under 18	31,022	32,289	33,257	38	35	130,542	51	3.93
Without own children under 18	28,528	33,801	34,887	35	36	88,423	35	2.53
Married couple family.	49,112	52,317	53,171	61	55	172,268	68	3.24
With own children under 18	24,961	24,537	24,707	31	26	102,581	40	4.15
Without own children under 18	24,151	27,780	28,464	30	30	69,687	27	2.45
Male householder, no spouse present. . .	1,733	2,884	3,026	2	3	9,395	4	3.11
With own children under 18	616	1,153	1,324	1	1	4,396	2	3.32
Without own children under 18	1,117	1,731	1,702	1	2	4,999	2	2.94
Female householder, no spouse present .	8,705	10,890	11,947	11	12	37,302	15	3.12
With own children under 18	5,445	6,599	7,226	7	7	23,565	9	3.26
Without own children under 18	3,261	4,290	4,721	4	5	13,737	5	2.91
Nonfamily households.	21,226	27,257	28,247	26	29	34,959	14	1.24
Living alone.	18,296	22,999	23,642	23	25	23,642	9	1.00
Male householder	8,807	11,606	12,254	11	13	16,448	6	1.34
Living alone.	6,966	9,049	9,436	9	10	9,436	4	1.00
Female householder	12,419	15,651	15,993	15	17	18,511	7	1.16
Living alone.	11,330	13,950	14,206	14	15	14,206	6	1.00

Source: U.S. Bureau of the Census, *Current Population Reports*, P20-477, and earlier reports.

No. 68. Household Characteristics, by Type of Household: 1993

[As of **March**. Based on Current Population Survey; see headnote, table 66. For composition of regions, see table 26]

CHARACTERISTIC	NUMBER OF HOUSEHOLDS (1,000)					PERCENT DISTRIBUTION				
	Total	Family households			Non-family house-holds	Total	Family households			Non-family house-holds
		Total [1]	Married couple	Female house-holder [2]			Total [1]	Married couple	Female house-holder [2]	
Total	96,391	68,144	53,171	11,947	28,247	100	100	100	100	100
Age of householder:										
15 to 24 years old	5,022	2,751	1,463	1,005	2,271	5	4	3	8	8
25 to 29 years old	8,614	5,932	4,210	1,342	2,682	9	9	8	11	9
30 to 34 years old	11,127	8,444	6,444	1,604	2,682	12	12	12	13	9
35 to 44 years old	21,718	17,569	13,521	3,269	4,148	23	26	25	27	15
45 to 54 years old	16,575	13,070	10,550	1,956	3,506	17	19	20	16	12
55 to 64 years old	12,438	9,117	7,674	1,179	3,321	13	13	14	10	12
65 to 74 years old	11,834	7,350	6,223	913	4,484	12	11	12	8	16
75 years old and over	9,061	3,911	3,083	679	5,151	9	6	6	6	18
Region:										
Northeast.	19,437	13,478	10,391	2,477	5,958	20	20	20	21	21
Midwest.	23,307	16,326	12,827	2,787	6,982	24	24	24	23	25
South	33,392	24,040	18,704	4,446	9,352	35	35	35	37	33
West.	20,255	14,299	11,249	2,237	5,956	21	21	21	19	21
Size of household:										
One person	23,642	(X)	(X)	(X)	23,642	25	(X)	(X)	(X)	84
Two persons	31,175	27,516	21,043	5,106	3,659	32	40	40	43	13
Three persons	16,895	16,264	11,703	3,657	631	18	24	22	31	2
Four persons	14,926	14,694	12,360	1,878	233	15	22	23	16	1
Five persons	6,357	6,294	5,378	745	63	7	9	10	6	(Z)
Six persons	2,180	2,168	1,789	299	12	2	3	3	3	(Z)
Seven persons or more . . .	1,215	1,208	898	261	7	1	2	2	2	(Z)
Marital status of householder:										
Never married (single)	14,652	4,117	(X)	3,037	10,534	15	6	(X)	25	37
Married, spouse present. . .	53,171	53,171	53,171	(X)	(X)	55	78	100	(X)	(X)
Married, spouse absent . . .	4,425	2,494	(X)	2,064	1,931	5	4	(X)	17	7
Widowed	11,621	2,856	(X)	2,418	8,765	12	4	(X)	20	31
Divorced	12,523	5,506	(X)	4,427	7,017	13	8	(X)	37	25
Tenure:										
Owner occupied	62,220	48,807	41,928	5,237	13,413	65	72	79	44	47
Renter occupied	34,171	19,336	11,243	6,710	14,835	35	28	21	56	53

X Not applicable.   Z Less than 0.5 percent.   [1] Includes male householder, no spouse present.   [2] No spouse present.

Source: U.S. Bureau of the Census, *Current Population Reports*, P60-184; and unpublished data.

No. 69. Households, by Age of Householder and Size of Household
1970 to 1993

[As of **March**. Based on Current Population Survey; see headnote, table 66. See also *Historical Statistics, Colonial Times to 1970*, series A 335-349]

AGE OF HOUSEHOLDER AND SIZE OF HOUSEHOLD	1970	1975	1980	1985	1990	1993 Total [1]	1993 White	1993 Black	1993 His-panic [2]
NUMBER (mil.)									
Total	**63.4**	**71.1**	**80.8**	**86.8**	**93.3**	**96.4**	**82.1**	**11.2**	**6.6**
Age of householder:									
15 to 24 years old [3]	4.4	5.8	6.6	5.4	5.1	5.0	4.1	0.7	0.6
25 to 29 years old	6.1	7.8	9.3	9.6	9.4	8.6	7.0	1.2	0.9
30 to 34 years old	5.6	7.1	9.3	10.4	11.0	11.1	9.2	1.5	1.0
35 to 44 years old	11.8	11.9	14.0	17.5	20.6	21.7	18.2	2.7	1.7
45 to 54 years old	12.2	12.9	12.7	12.6	14.5	16.6	14.2	1.8	1.1
55 to 64 years old	10.8	11.3	12.5	13.1	12.5	12.4	10.7	1.4	0.7
65 to 74 years old	7.7	8.9	10.1	10.9	11.7	11.8	10.4	1.2	0.5
75 years old and over.	4.8	5.4	6.4	7.3	8.4	9.1	8.2	0.7	0.2
One person	10.9	13.9	18.3	20.6	23.0	23.6	20.2	2.9	1.0
Male	3.5	4.9	7.0	7.9	9.0	9.4	7.9	1.2	0.5
Female	7.3	9.0	11.3	12.7	14.0	14.2	12.3	1.6	0.5
Two persons	18.3	21.8	25.3	27.4	30.1	31.2	27.5	2.9	1.5
Three persons	10.9	12.4	14.1	15.5	16.1	16.9	14.1	2.2	1.3
Four persons	10.0	11.1	12.7	13.6	14.5	14.9	12.6	1.7	1.3
Five persons	6.5	6.4	6.1	6.1	6.2	6.4	5.2	0.9	0.8
Six persons	3.5	3.1	2.5	2.3	2.1	2.2	1.6	0.4	0.4
Seven persons or more	3.2	2.5	1.8	1.3	1.3	1.2	0.9	0.2	0.4
PERCENT DISTRIBUTION									
Total	**100**	**100**	**100**	**100**	**100**	**100**	**100**	**100**	**100**
Age of householder:									
15 to 24 years old [3]	7	8	8	6	6	5	5	6	9
25 to 29 years old	10	11	12	11	10	9	9	11	13
30 to 34 years old	9	10	12	12	12	12	11	13	15
35 to 44 years old	19	17	17	20	22	23	22	24	25
45 to 54 years old	20	18	16	15	16	17	17	16	17
55 to 64 years old	17	16	16	15	13	13	13	13	11
65 to 74 years old	12	13	13	13	13	12	13	11	7
75 years old and over.	8	8	8	8	9	9	10	6	4
One person	17	20	23	24	25	24	25	26	15
Male	6	7	9	9	10	10	10	11	7
Female	12	13	14	15	15	15	15	15	8
Two persons	29	31	31	32	32	32	33	26	22
Three persons	17	17	18	18	17	18	17	19	20
Four persons	16	16	16	16	16	15	15	15	19
Five persons	10	9	8	7	7	7	6	8	12
Six persons	6	4	3	3	2	2	2	4	6
Seven persons or more	5	4	2	2	1	1	1	2	5

[1] Includes other races, not shown separately. [2] Hispanic persons may be of any race. [3] 1970 and 1975, persons 14 to 24 years old.

Source: U.S. Bureau of the Census, *Current Population Reports*, P20-477, and earlier reports.

No. 70. Households—States: 1970 to 1993

[As of **April** 1, except **beginning 1991**, as of **July** 1. Minus sign (-) indicates decrease]

REGION, DIVISION, AND STATE	NUMBER (1,000)						PERCENT CHANGE			PERSONS PER HOUSEHOLD		
	1970	1980	1990	1991	1992	1993	1970-80	1980-90	1990-93	1980	1990	1993
U.S.	**63,450**	**80,390**	**91,947**	**92,895**	**94,401**	**95,133**	**26.7**	**14.4**	**3.5**	**2.75**	**2.63**	**2.64**
Northeast . . .	**15,483**	**17,471**	**18,873**	**18,890**	**19,049**	**19,069**	**12.8**	**8.0**	**1.0**	**2.74**	**2.61**	**2.61**
N.E.	**3,645**	**4,362**	**4,943**	**4,941**	**4,971**	**4,973**	**19.7**	**13.3**	**0.6**	**2.74**	**2.58**	**2.57**
ME	303	395	465	470	473	472	30.5	17.7	1.5	2.75	2.56	2.55
NH	225	323	411	412	417	420	43.5	27.1	2.0	2.75	2.62	2.61
VT	132	178	211	212	215	217	35.0	18.1	2.9	2.75	2.57	2.56
MA	1,760	2,033	2,247	2,239	2,254	2,258	15.5	10.5	0.5	2.72	2.58	2.57
RI	292	339	378	377	377	376	16.0	11.6	-0.6	2.70	2.55	2.56
CT	933	1,094	1,230	1,231	1,235	1,231	17.2	12.5	-	2.76	2.59	2.58
M.A.	**11,837**	**13,109**	**13,930**	**13,949**	**14,078**	**14,096**	**10.7**	**6.3**	**1.2**	**2.74**	**2.62**	**2.63**
NY	5,914	6,340	6,639	6,629	6,683	6,691	7.2	4.7	0.8	2.70	2.63	2.64
NJ	2,218	2,549	2,795	2,806	2,839	2,849	14.9	9.7	1.9	2.84	2.70	2.71
PA	3,705	4,220	4,496	4,514	4,556	4,556	13.9	6.5	1.3	2.74	2.57	2.57
Midwest	**17,537**	**20,859**	**22,317**	**22,464**	**22,746**	**22,827**	**18.9**	**7.0**	**2.3**	**2.75**	**2.60**	**2.61**
E.N.C.	**12,383**	**14,654**	**15,597**	**15,720**	**15,926**	**15,986**	**18.3**	**6.4**	**2.5**	**2.78**	**2.63**	**2.62**
OH	3,289	3,834	4,088	4,122	4,177	4,185	16.5	6.6	2.4	2.76	2.59	2.59
IN	1,609	1,927	2,065	2,087	2,121	2,139	19.7	7.2	3.6	2.77	2.61	2.59
IL	3,502	4,045	4,202	4,226	4,277	4,290	15.5	3.9	2.1	2.76	2.65	2.66
MI	2,653	3,195	3,419	3,446	3,486	3,497	20.4	7.0	2.3	2.84	2.66	2.65
WI	1,329	1,652	1,822	1,839	1,864	1,875	24.3	10.3	2.9	2.77	2.61	2.62
W.N.C.	**5,154**	**6,205**	**6,720**	**6,744**	**6,820**	**6,841**	**20.4**	**8.3**	**1.8**	**2.68**	**2.55**	**2.56**
MN	1,154	1,445	1,648	1,664	1,687	1,697	25.2	14.0	3.0	2.74	2.58	2.59
IA	896	1,053	1,064	1,065	1,073	1,074	17.5	1.1	0.9	2.68	2.52	2.53
MO	1,521	1,793	1,961	1,966	1,988	1,996	17.9	9.4	1.8	2.67	2.54	2.55
ND	182	228	241	239	241	240	25.4	5.8	-0.2	2.75	2.55	2.54
SD	201	243	259	260	263	263	20.8	6.8	1.5	2.74	2.59	2.62
NE	474	571	602	604	609	610	20.6	5.4	1.2	2.66	2.54	2.56
KS	727	872	945	945	959	961	19.9	8.3	1.7	2.62	2.53	2.55
South	**19,258**	**26,486**	**31,822**	**32,282**	**32,895**	**33,262**	**37.5**	**20.1**	**4.5**	**2.77**	**2.61**	**2.62**
S.A.	**9,438**	**13,160**	**16,503**	**16,787**	**17,112**	**17,312**	**39.4**	**25.4**	**4.9**	**2.73**	**2.56**	**2.57**
DE	165	207	247	253	258	261	25.7	19.5	5.4	2.79	2.61	2.61
MD	1,175	1,461	1,749	1,777	1,807	1,822	24.3	19.7	4.2	2.82	2.67	2.66
DC	263	253	250	244	243	240	-3.6	-1.4	-3.7	2.40	2.26	2.24
VA	1,391	1,863	2,292	2,329	2,384	2,418	34.0	23.0	5.5	2.77	2.61	2.60
WV	547	686	689	690	697	699	25.4	0.3	1.5	2.79	2.55	2.55
NC	1,510	2,043	2,517	2,556	2,601	2,637	35.4	23.2	4.8	2.78	2.54	2.55
SC	734	1,030	1,258	1,283	1,307	1,321	40.3	22.1	5.0	2.93	2.68	2.67
GA	1,369	1,872	2,367	2,419	2,487	2,535	36.7	26.4	7.1	2.84	2.66	2.66
FL	2,285	3,744	5,135	5,235	5,328	5,381	63.9	37.1	4.8	2.55	2.46	2.49
E.S.C.	**3,868**	**5,051**	**5,652**	**5,707**	**5,807**	**5,856**	**30.6**	**11.9**	**3.6**	**2.83**	**2.62**	**2.62**
KY	984	1,263	1,380	1,389	1,411	1,420	28.4	9.2	2.9	2.82	2.60	2.60
TN	1,213	1,619	1,854	1,881	1,917	1,938	33.4	14.5	4.5	2.77	2.56	2.57
AL	1,034	1,342	1,507	1,521	1,549	1,565	29.8	12.3	3.9	2.84	2.62	2.62
MS	637	827	911	916	930	934	29.9	10.2	2.5	2.97	2.75	2.75
W.S.C.	**5,952**	**8,276**	**9,668**	**9,787**	**9,976**	**10,093**	**39.0**	**16.8**	**4.4**	**2.80**	**2.69**	**2.71**
AR	615	816	891	896	909	916	32.6	9.2	2.8	2.74	2.57	2.58
LA	1,052	1,412	1,499	1,507	1,528	1,529	34.2	6.2	2.0	2.91	2.74	2.74
OK	851	1,119	1,206	1,209	1,225	1,227	31.5	7.8	1.7	2.62	2.53	2.56
TX	3,434	4,929	6,071	6,175	6,315	6,420	43.5	23.2	5.8	2.82	2.73	2.75
West	**11,172**	**15,574**	**18,935**	**19,259**	**19,710**	**19,976**	**39.4**	**21.6**	**5.5**	**2.71**	**2.72**	**2.74**
Mountain . .	**2,518**	**3,986**	**5,033**	**5,146**	**5,300**	**5,432**	**58.3**	**26.3**	**7.9**	**2.79**	**2.65**	**2.66**
MT	217	284	306	309	316	320	30.6	7.9	4.4	2.70	2.53	2.55
ID	219	324	361	370	382	392	48.0	11.3	8.7	2.85	2.73	2.75
WY	105	166	169	170	172	173	58.3	1.9	2.7	2.78	2.63	2.65
CO	691	1,061	1,282	1,308	1,350	1,385	53.6	20.8	8.0	2.65	2.51	2.52
NM	289	441	543	552	567	577	52.6	22.9	6.3	2.90	2.74	2.75
AZ	539	957	1,369	1,392	1,429	1,467	77.5	43.0	7.2	2.79	2.62	2.63
UT	298	449	537	549	566	582	50.6	19.8	8.3	3.20	3.15	3.15
NV	160	304	466	496	517	537	90.1	53.2	15.1	2.59	2.53	2.54
Pacific	**8,653**	**11,587**	**13,902**	**14,113**	**14,411**	**14,543**	**33.9**	**20.0**	**4.6**	**2.68**	**2.74**	**2.77**
WA	1,106	1,541	1,872	1,919	1,975	2,009	39.3	21.5	7.3	2.61	2.53	2.56
OR	692	992	1,103	1,127	1,151	1,170	43.4	11.3	6.0	2.60	2.52	2.54
CA	6,574	8,630	10,381	10,507	10,707	10,779	31.3	20.3	3.8	2.68	2.79	2.82
AK	79	131	189	195	202	206	66.3	43.7	9.1	2.93	2.80	2.81
HI	203	294	356	366	375	379	44.8	21.2	6.4	3.15	3.01	2.99

- Represents or rounds to zero.

Source: U.S. Bureau of the Census, *Census of Population: 1970*; *1980 Census of Population*, vol. 1, chapter B; *1990 Census of Population, General Population Characteristics, United States* (1990 CP-1-1); and *Current Population Reports*, P25, forthcoming report.

No. 71. Family and Nonfamily Households, by Race, Hispanic Origin, and Type: 1970 to 1993

[As of **March**, except as noted. Based on Current Population Survey, except as noted; see headnote, table 66. See also *Historical Statistics, Colonial Times to 1970*, series A 292-295 and A 320-334]

RACE, HISPANIC ORIGIN, AND TYPE	NUMBER (1,000)					PERCENT DISTRIBUTION				
	1970	1980	1985	1990	1993	1970	1980	1985	1990	1993
TOTAL HOUSEHOLDS										
Total [1]	**63,401**	**80,776**	**86,789**	**93,347**	**96,391**	**100**	**100**	**100**	**100**	**100**
White	56,602	70,766	75,328	80,163	82,083	89	88	87	86	85
Black	6,223	8,586	9,480	10,486	11,190	10	11	11	11	12
Hispanic [2]	2,303	3,684	4,883	5,933	6,626	4	5	6	6	7
FAMILY HOUSEHOLDS										
White, total	**46,166**	**52,243**	**54,400**	**56,590**	**57,858**	**100**	**100**	**100**	**100**	**100**
Married couple	41,029	44,751	45,643	46,981	47,601	89	86	84	83	82
Male householder [3]	1,038	1,441	1,816	2,303	2,409	2	3	3	4	4
Female householder [3]	4,099	6,052	6,941	7,306	7,848	9	12	13	13	14
Black, total	**4,856**	**6,184**	**6,778**	**7,470**	**7,888**	**100**	**100**	**100**	**100**	**100**
Married couple	3,317	3,433	3,469	3,750	3,748	68	56	51	50	48
Male householder [3]	181	256	344	446	460	4	4	5	6	6
Female householder [3]	1,358	2,495	2,964	3,275	3,680	28	40	44	44	47
Asian or Pacific Islander, total [4]	**(NA)**	**818**	**(NA)**	**1,531**	**1,662**	**(NA)**	**100**	**(NA)**	**100**	**100**
Married couple	(NA)	691	(NA)	1,256	1,335	(NA)	84	(NA)	82	80
Male householder [3]	(NA)	39	(NA)	86	95	(NA)	5	(NA)	6	6
Female householder [3]	(NA)	88	(NA)	188	232	(NA)	11	(NA)	12	14
Hispanic, total [2]	**2,004**	**3,029**	**3,939**	**4,840**	**5,318**	**100**	**100**	**100**	**100**	**100**
Married couple	1,615	2,282	2,824	3,395	3,674	81	75	72	70	69
Male householder [3]	82	138	210	329	407	4	5	5	7	8
Female householder [3]	307	610	905	1,116	1,238	15	20	23	23	23
NONFAMILY HOUSEHOLDS										
White, total	**10,436**	**18,522**	**20,928**	**23,573**	**24,225**	**100**	**100**	**100**	**100**	**100**
Male householder	3,406	7,499	8,608	9,951	10,370	33	40	41	42	43
Female householder	7,030	11,023	12,320	13,622	13,856	67	60	59	58	57
Black, total	**1,367**	**2,402**	**2,703**	**3,015**	**3,302**	**100**	**100**	**100**	**100**	**100**
Male householder	564	1,146	1,244	1,313	1,484	41	48	46	44	45
Female householder	803	1,256	1,459	1,702	1,818	59	52	54	56	55
Hispanic, total [2]	**299**	**654**	**944**	**1,093**	**1,308**	**100**	**100**	**100**	**100**	**100**
Male householder	150	365	509	587	691	50	56	54	54	53
Female householder	148	289	435	506	617	49	44	46	46	47

NA Not available.　[1] Includes other races not shown separately.　[2] Hispanic persons may be of any race. 1970 data as of April.　[3] No spouse present.　[4] 1980 data as of April and are from 1980 Census of Population.
Source: U.S. Bureau of the Census, *Census of Population: 1970, Persons of Spanish Origin*, PC(2)-1C; and *Current Population Reports*, P20-477, and earlier reports.

No. 72. Family Groups with Children Under 18 Years Old, by Race and Hispanic Origin: 1970 to 1993

[As of **March**. Family groups comprise family households, related subfamilies, and unrelated subfamilies. Excludes members of Armed Forces except those living off post or with their families on post. Based on Current Population Survey; see text, section 1, and Appendix III]

RACE AND HISPANIC ORIGIN OF HOUSEHOLDER OR REFERENCE PERSON	NUMBER (1,000)				PERCENT DISTRIBUTION			
	1970	1980	1990	1993	1970	1980	1990	1993
All races, total [1]	**29,631**	**32,150**	**34,670**	**36,058**	**100**	**100**	**100**	**100**
Two-parent family groups	25,823	25,231	24,921	25,157	87	79	72	70
One-parent family groups	3,808	6,920	9,749	10,901	13	22	28	30
Maintained by mother	3,415	6,230	8,398	9,339	12	19	24	26
Maintained by father	393	690	1,351	1,562	1	2	4	4
White, total	**26,115**	**27,294**	**28,294**	**29,225**	**100**	**100**	**100**	**100**
Two-parent family groups	23,477	22,628	21,905	22,058	90	83	77	76
One-parent family groups	2,638	4,664	6,389	7,167	10	17	23	25
Maintained by mother	2,330	4,122	5,310	5,901	9	15	19	20
Maintained by father	307	542	1,079	1,265	1	2	4	4
Black, total	**3,219**	**4,074**	**5,087**	**5,364**	**100**	**100**	**100**	**100**
Two-parent family groups	2,071	1,961	2,006	1,987	64	48	39	37
One-parent family groups	1,148	2,114	3,081	3,377	36	52	61	63
Maintained by mother	1,063	1,984	2,860	3,135	33	49	56	58
Maintained by father	85	129	221	242	3	3	4	5
Hispanic, total [2]	**(NA)**	**2,194**	**3,429**	**3,838**	**(NA)**	**100**	**100**	**100**
Two-parent family groups	(NA)	1,626	2,289	2,494	(NA)	74	67	65
One-parent family groups	(NA)	568	1,140	1,344	(NA)	26	33	35
Maintained by mother	(NA)	526	1,003	1,157	(NA)	24	29	30
Maintained by father	(NA)	42	138	187	(NA)	2	4	5

NA Not available.　[1] Includes other races, not shown separately.　[2] Hispanic persons may be of any race.
Source: U.S. Bureau of the Census, *Current Population Reports*, P20-477, and earlier reports.

No. 73. Family Groups With Children Under 18 Years Old, by Type, Race and Hispanic Origin: 1993

[As of **March**. Excludes members of Armed Forces except those living off post or with their families on post. Based on Current Population Survey; see text, section 1, and Appendix III]

RACE OR HISPANIC ORIGIN OF HOUSEHOLDER OR REFERENCE PERSON	NUMBER (1,000)					PERCENT DISTRIBUTION				
	Total	Family house-holds	Subfamilies			Total	Family house-holds	Subfamilies		
			Total	Related	Unre-lated			Total	Related	Unre-lated
All races, total [1]	**36,058**	**33,257**	**2,801**	**2,136**	**666**	**100**	**100**	**100**	**100**	**100**
Two-parent family groups	25,157	24,707	450	410	40	70	74	16	19	6
One-parent family groups	10,901	8,550	2,351	1,726	625	30	26	84	81	94
Maintained by mother	9,339	7,226	2,113	1,556	557	26	22	75	73	84
Maintained by father	1,562	1,324	238	170	68	4	4	9	8	10
White, total	**29,225**	**27,335**	**1,889**	**1,326**	**563**	**100**	**100**	**100**	**100**	**100**
Two-parent family groups	22,058	21,686	372	337	35	76	79	20	25	6
One-parent family groups	7,167	5,649	1,517	989	528	25	21	80	75	94
Maintained by mother	5,901	4,552	1,350	878	472	20	17	72	66	84
Maintained by father	1,265	1,098	167	112	56	4	4	9	8	10
Black, total	**5,364**	**4,560**	**804**	**719**	**84**	**100**	**100**	**100**	**100**	**100**
Two-parent family groups	1,987	1,945	42	39	3	37	43	5	5	4
One-parent family groups	3,377	2,615	762	680	82	63	57	95	95	98
Maintained by mother	3,135	2,434	701	632	69	58	53	87	88	82
Maintained by father	242	182	61	49	12	5	4	8	7	14
Hispanic, total [2]	**3,838**	**3,345**	**492**	**382**	**110**	**100**	**100**	**100**	**100**	**100**
Two-parent family groups	2,494	2,355	139	120	18	65	70	28	31	16
One-parent family groups	1,344	990	354	262	92	35	30	72	69	84
Maintained by mother	1,157	830	327	242	85	30	25	67	63	77
Maintained by father	187	160	27	20	7	5	5	6	5	6

[1] Includes other races, not shown separately.   [2] Hispanic persons may be of any race.

Source: U.S. Bureau of the Census, *Current Population Reports*, P20-477.

No. 74. Families, by Size and Presence of Children: 1980 to 1993

[In thousands, except as indicated. As of **March**. Excludes members of Armed Forces except those living off post or with their families on post. Based on Current Population Survey; see text, section 1, and Appendix III. For definition of families, see text, section 1]

CHARACTERISTIC	NUMBER				PERCENT DISTRIBUTION			
	1980	1985	1990	1993	1980	1985	1990	1993
Total	**59,550**	**62,706**	**66,090**	**68,144**	**100**	**100**	**100**	**100**
Size of family:								
Two persons	23,461	25,349	27,606	28,612	39	40	42	42
Three persons	13,603	14,804	15,353	16,060	23	24	23	24
Four persons	12,372	13,259	14,026	14,306	21	21	21	21
Five persons	5,930	5,894	5,938	6,048	10	9	9	9
Six persons	2,461	2,175	1,997	2,039	4	4	3	3
Seven or more persons . .	1,723	1,225	1,170	1,079	3	2	2	2
Average per family	3.29	3.23	3.17	3.16	(X)	(X)	(X)	(X)
Own children under age 18:								
None	28,528	31,594	33,801	34,887	48	50	51	51
One	12,443	13,108	13,530	13,690	21	21	20	20
Two	11,470	11,645	12,263	12,804	19	19	19	19
Three	4,674	4,486	4,650	4,849	8	7	7	7
Four or more	2,435	1,873	1,846	1,914	4	3	3	3
Own children under age 6:								
None	46,063	48,505	50,905	52,576	77	77	77	77
One	9,441	9,677	10,304	10,554	16	15	16	15
Two or more	4,047	4,525	4,882	5,014	7	7	7	7

X Not applicable.

Source: U.S. Bureau of the Census, *Current Population Reports*, P20-477, and earlier reports.

No. 75. Families, by Number of Own Children Under 18 Years Old: 1970 to 1993

[Except as noted, as of **March** and based on Current Population Survey; see headnote, table 74. See also *Historical Statistics, Colonial Times to 1970*, series A 353-358]

RACE, HISPANIC ORIGIN, AND YEAR	NUMBER OF FAMILIES (1,000)					PERCENT DISTRIBUTION				
	Total	No children	One child	Two children	Three or more children	Total	No children	One child	Two children	Three or more children
ALL FAMILIES [1]										
1970	51,586	22,774	9,398	8,969	10,445	100	44	18	17	20
1980	59,550	28,528	12,443	11,470	7,109	100	48	21	19	12
1985	62,706	31,594	13,108	11,645	6,359	100	50	21	19	10
1990	66,090	33,801	13,530	12,263	6,496	100	51	20	19	10
1993	68,144	34,887	13,690	12,804	6,763	100	51	20	19	10
Married couple	53,171	28,464	9,466	10,007	5,234	100	54	18	19	10
Male householder [2]	3,026	1,702	799	397	128	100	56	26	13	4
Female householder [2]	11,947	4,721	3,425	2,400	1,400	100	40	29	20	12
WHITE FAMILIES										
1970	46,261	20,719	8,437	8,174	8,931	100	45	18	18	19
1980	52,243	25,769	10,727	9,977	5,769	100	49	21	19	11
1985	54,400	28,169	11,174	9,937	5,120	100	52	21	18	9
1990	56,590	29,872	11,186	10,342	5,191	100	53	20	18	9
1993	57,858	30,523	11,168	10,869	5,298	100	53	19	19	9
BLACK FAMILIES										
1970	4,887	1,903	858	726	1,401	100	39	18	15	29
1980	6,184	2,364	1,449	1,235	1,136	100	38	23	20	18
1985	6,778	2,887	1,579	1,330	982	100	43	23	20	15
1990	7,470	3,093	1,894	1,433	1,049	100	41	25	19	14
1993	7,888	3,327	1,937	1,452	1,172	100	42	25	18	15
HISPANIC FAMILIES [3]										
1970	2,004	597	390	388	629	100	30	20	19	31
1980	3,029	946	680	698	706	100	31	22	23	23
1985	3,939	1,337	904	865	833	100	34	23	22	21
1990	4,840	1,790	1,095	1,036	919	100	37	23	21	19
1993	5,318	1,973	1,223	1,155	967	100	37	23	22	18

[1] Includes other races, not shown separately.   [2] No spouse present.   [3] Hispanic persons may be of any race. 1970 Hispanic data as of April and based on Census of Population.

Source: U.S. Bureau of the Census, *U.S. Census of Population, 1970* (PC-2-4A), and *Current Population Reports*, P20-477, and earlier reports.

No. 76. Female Family Householders With No Spouse Present—Characteristics, by Race and Hispanic Origin: 1980 to 1993

[As of **March**. Covers persons 15 years old and over. Based on Current Population Survey; see headnote, table 74]

CHARACTERISTIC	Unit	WHITE			BLACK			HISPANIC ORIGIN [1]		
		1980	1990	1993	1980	1990	1993	1980	1990	1993
Female family householder	1,000	6,052	7,306	7,848	2,495	3,275	3,680	610	1,116	1,238
Marital status:										
Never married (single)	Percent	11	15	17	27	39	43	23	27	31
Married, spouse absent	Percent	17	16	16	29	21	20	32	29	26
Widowed	Percent	33	26	23	22	17	15	15	16	14
Divorced	Percent	40	43	44	22	23	22	30	29	28
Presence of children under 18:										
No own children	Percent	41	43	42	28	32	34	25	33	33
With own children	Percent	59	58	58	72	68	66	75	67	67

[1] Persons of Hispanic origin may be of any race.

Source: U.S. Bureau of the Census, *Current Population Reports*, P20-477, and earlier reports.

No. 77. Family Households With Own Children Under Age 18, by Type of Family, 1980 to 1993, and by Age of Householder, 1993

[As of **March**. Excludes members of Armed Forces except those living off post or with their families on post. Based on Current Population Survey; see text, section 1, and Appendix III]

FAMILY TYPE	1980	1990	1993						
			Total	15 to 24 years old	25 to 34 years old	35 to 44 years old	45 to 54 years old	55 to 64 years old	65 years old and over
NUMBER (1,000)									
Family households with children . . .	31,022	32,289	33,257	1,775	11,025	14,165	5,415	735	140
Married couple	24,961	24,537	24,707	789	7,836	10,923	4,426	618	115
Male householder [1]	616	1,153	1,324	118	426	508	231	37	3
Female householder [1]	5,445	6,599	7,226	869	2,762	2,735	758	79	22
PERCENT DISTRIBUTION									
Family households with children . . .	100	100	100	100	100	100	100	100	100
Married couple	81	76	74	44	71	77	82	84	82
Male householder [1]	2	4	4	7	4	4	4	5	2
Female householder [1]	18	20	22	49	25	19	14	11	16
HOUSEHOLDS WITH CHILDREN, AS A PERCENT OF ALL FAMILY HOUSEHOLDS, BY TYPE									
Family households with children, total	52	49	49	65	77	81	41	8	1
Married couple	51	47	46	54	74	81	42	8	1
Male householder [1]	36	40	44	42	55	65	41	14	1
Female householder [1]	63	61	60	86	94	84	39	7	1

[1] No spouse present.

Source: U.S. Bureau of the Census, *Current Population Reports*, P20-477, and earlier reports.

No. 78. Married Couple Family Households with Children: 1980 to 1990

[As of **June**. Covers only those married-couple families with at least one "own child" under age 18 living in their household. "Own children" are children of the householder and/or the householder's spouse. Each child who was the biological child of one of the parents but not of the other parent was classified as a stepchild. If one spouse adopted the biological child of the other spouse, the child was still considered to be a stepchild. Children who were the biological children of both parents were classified as biological children, while all "own" children who were not biological children of either of their parents were classified as adoptive children. Based on Current Population Survey; see text, section 1, and Appendix III]

TYPE OF FAMILY	NUMBER (1,000)			PERCENT DISTRIBUTION		
	1980	1985	1990	1980	1985	1990
Total	24,091	23,868	25,314	100.0	100.0	100.0
Biological [1]	19,037	18,470	19,253	79.0	77.4	76.1
Adoptive [2]	429	303	345	1.8	1.3	1.4
Biological mother-stepfather [3]	1,818	2,207	2,619	7.5	9.2	10.3
Biological father-stepmother [4]	171	180	152	0.7	0.8	0.6
Joint biological-step [5]	1,862	2,038	2,475	7.7	8.5	9.8
Joint biological-adoptive [6]	429	223	324	1.8	0.9	1.3
Joint step-adoptive [7]	12	15	8	-	0.1	-
Joint bio-step-adoptive [8]	25	29	-	0.1	0.1	-
Unknown [9]	309	403	137	1.3	1.7	0.5

- Represents or rounds to zero.   [1] All the own children were biological children of both parents.   [2] All the own children were adoptive children of both parents.   [3] All the own children were biological children of the mother and stepchildren of the father.   [4] All the own children were biological children of the father and stepchildren of the mother.   [5] At least one child was a biological child of both parents, at least one was a biological child of one parent and a stepchild of the other parent, and no other type of child was present; or a stepchild of each parent and no other type of child was present.   [6] At least one child was a biological child of both parents, at least one was an adopted child of both parents, and no other type of child was present.   [7] At least one child was a biological child of one parent and a stepchild of the other parent, at least one was an adopted child of both parents, and no other type of child was present.   [8] At least one child was a biological child of both parents, at least one was the biological child of one parent and the stepchild of the other, and at least one was an adopted child of both parents.   [9] At least one child had at least one parent for whom the nature of the relationship could not be designated.

Source: U.S. Bureau of the Census, *Current Population Reports*, P23-180.

Population

No. 79. Children Living With Biological, Step, and Adoptive Married-Couple Parents, by Race and Hispanic Origin of Mother: 1980 to 1990

[As of **June**. See headnote, table 78]

TYPE OF PARENT	ALL RACES [1]			WHITE			BLACK			His-panic [2] origin, 1990
	1980	1985	1990	1980	1985	1990	1980	1985	1990	
NUMBER (1,000)										
Own children under 18 years, total.	47,248	45,347	45,448	42,329	39,942	39,732	3,775	3,816	3,671	4,568
Biological mother and father	39,523	37,213	37,026	35,852	33,202	32,975	2,698	2,661	2,336	3,703
Biological mother-stepfather	5,355	6,049	6,643	4,362	4,918	5,258	877	952	1,149	699
Stepmother-biological father	727	740	608	664	676	549	46	50	38	38
Adoptive mother and father.	1,350	866	974	1,209	754	815	119	76	97	101
Unknown mother or father	293	479	197	242	391	135	35	77	51	27
PERCENT DISTRIBUTION										
Own children under 18 years, total.	100.0	100.0	100.0	100.0	100.0	100.0	100.0	100.0	100.0	100.0
Biological mother and father	83.7	82.1	81.5	84.7	83.1	83.0	71.5	69.7	63.6	81.1
Biological mother-stepfather	11.3	13.3	14.6	10.3	12.3	13.2	23.2	24.9	31.3	15.3
Stepmother-biological father	1.5	1.6	1.3	1.6	1.7	1.4	1.2	1.3	1.0	0.8
Adoptive mother and father.	2.9	1.9	2.1	2.9	1.9	2.1	3.1	2.0	2.6	2.2
Unknown mother or father	0.6	1.1	0.4	0.6	1.0	0.3	0.9	2.0	1.4	0.6

[1] Includes other races not shown separately.   [2] Persons of Hispanic origin may be of any race.

Source: U.S. Bureau of the Census, *Current Population Reports*, P23-180.

No. 80. Children Under 18 Years Old, by Presence of Parents: 1970 to 1993

[As of **March**. Excludes persons under 18 years old who maintained households or family groups. Based on Current Population Survey; see headnote, table 74]

RACE, HISPANIC ORIGIN, AND YEAR	Number (1,000)	PERCENT LIVING WITH—							
		Both parents	Mother only					Father only	Neither parent
			Total	Divorced	Married, spouse absent	Never married (single)	Wid-owed		
ALL RACES [1]									
1970	69,162	85	11	3	5	1	2	1	3
1980	63,427	77	18	8	6	3	2	2	4
1985	62,475	74	21	9	5	6	2	3	3
1990	64,137	73	22	8	5	7	2	3	3
1993	66,893	71	23	9	6	8	1	3	3
WHITE									
1970	58,790	90	8	3	3	(Z)	2	1	2
1980	52,242	83	14	7	4	1	2	2	2
1985	50,836	80	16	8	4	2	1	2	2
1990	51,390	79	16	8	4	3	1	3	2
1993	53,075	77	17	8	4	4	1	3	2
BLACK									
1970	9,422	59	30	5	16	4	4	2	10
1980	9,375	42	44	11	16	13	4	2	12
1985	9,479	40	51	11	12	25	3	3	7
1990	10,018	38	51	10	12	27	2	4	8
1993	10,660	36	54	10	12	31	1	3	7
HISPANIC [2]									
1970	[3]4,006	78	(NA)	(NA)	(NA)	(NA)	(NA)	(NA)	(NA)
1980	5,459	75	20	6	8	4	2	2	4
1985	6,057	68	27	7	11	7	2	2	3
1990	7,174	67	27	7	10	8	2	3	3
1993	7,776	65	28	7	8	11	1	4	4

NA Not available.   Z Less than 0.5 percent.   [1] Includes other races not shown separately.   [2] Hispanic persons may be of any race.   [3] All persons under 18 years old.

Source: U.S. Bureau of the Census, *Current Population Reports*, P20-450, and earlier reports; and unpublished data.

No. 81. Living Arrangements of Children Under 18 Years Old, by Selected Characteristic of Parent: 1993

[In thousands. As of March. Covers only those persons under 18 years old who are living with one or both parents. Characteristics are shown for the householder or reference person in married-couple situations. See also headnote, table 74]

CHARACTERISTIC OF PARENT	ALL RACES[1]				WHITE				BLACK				HISPANIC[2]			
	Total	Both parents	Mother only	Father only	Total	Both parents	Mother only	Father only	Total	Both parents	Mother only	Father only	Total	Both parents	Mother only	Father only
Children under 18 years old	65,052	47,181	15,586	2,286	52,106	40,996	9,256	1,854	9,875	3,796	5,757	322	7,489	5,017	2,176	296
Age:																
15 to 24 years old	3,807	1,300	2,301	207	2,478	1,110	1,217	152	1,204	149	1,021	34	678	279	354	46
25 to 29 years old	8,338	4,878	3,081	378	6,276	4,211	1,786	279	1,758	478	1,186	94	1,280	774	441	66
30 to 34 years old	14,497	10,402	3,645	450	11,683	9,184	2,143	356	2,237	770	1,401	67	1,729	1,168	514	48
35 to 39 years old	15,875	12,181	3,227	467	13,086	10,766	1,893	427	2,045	854	1,166	24	1,625	1,125	446	55
40 to 44 years old	12,625	10,146	2,098	381	10,426	8,754	1,360	312	1,481	779	654	48	1,150	879	252	19
45 to 54 years old	8,613	7,166	1,102	345	7,246	6,169	788	288	901	577	276	48	840	646	141	53
55 to 64 years old	1,097	945	100	53	763	673	52	37	214	164	43	7	155	123	25	8
65 years old and over	199	162	33	5	148	129	17	3	34	24	10	-	31	25	5	2
Educational attainment:																
Less than 9th grade	3,893	2,691	1,052	150	3,235	2,343	780	113	382	149	204	29	2,281	1,626	576	79
9th to 12th grade, no diploma	7,799	3,890	3,479	430	5,392	3,239	1,796	357	2,092	465	1,575	55	1,603	923	601	80
High school graduate[3]	22,519	15,638	5,964	916	17,534	13,486	3,311	737	4,171	1,557	2,479	135	1,993	1,285	640	69
Some college, no degree or associate degree	16,307	12,021	3,815	471	13,334	10,494	2,447	393	2,330	1,060	1,209	61	1,132	798	287	47
Bachelor's degree	9,332	8,188	939	205	8,060	7,239	669	152	639	379	221	39	331	249	61	21
Graduate or professional degree	5,202	4,752	337	113	4,552	4,196	253	103	261	189	69	4	148	137	12	-
Employment status:[4]																
In the civilian labor force	54,345	42,812	9,531	2,002	45,343	37,672	6,026	1,645	6,621	3,180	3,180	262	5,797	4,446	1,082	269
Employed	50,603	40,579	8,295	1,730	42,641	35,795	5,419	1,428	5,773	2,950	2,602	221	5,131	3,994	911	226
Both parents employed	25,885	25,885	(X)	(X)	22,613	22,613	(X)	(X)	2,086	2,086	(X)	(X)	2,017	2,017	(X)	(X)
Unemployed	3,742	2,233	1,236	273	2,702	1,877	607	218	848	230	577	41	666	452	171	43
Not in the labor force	9,751	3,417	6,055	279	6,069	2,632	3,230	206	3,066	428	2,578	61	1,611	490	1,094	27
Family income:																
Under $5,000	3,894	649	3,063	182	2,232	509	1,586	137	1,528	115	1,371	41	576	134	402	40
$5,000 to $9,999	5,177	1,314	3,588	273	3,009	1,014	1,789	202	1,928	209	1,666	53	1,010	365	593	52
$10,000 to $14,999	4,867	2,323	2,312	233	3,421	1,884	1,345	193	1,157	245	887	26	1,091	624	408	58
$15,000 to $24,999	9,346	5,955	2,869	522	7,209	4,965	1,832	414	1,716	698	930	88	1,675	1,215	392	68
$25,000 to $29,999	4,604	3,373	1,017	213	3,788	2,906	702	179	596	293	278	25	677	542	126	8
$30,000 to $39,999	8,832	7,270	1,247	315	7,504	6,371	868	265	938	569	334	35	868	711	114	43
$40,000 to $49,999	8,213	7,257	703	253	7,191	6,433	540	218	693	544	129	20	622	545	61	16
$50,000 and over	20,119	19,039	786	294	17,753	16,910	595	248	1,318	1,123	161	34	972	880	82	10
Tenure:[5]																
Owned	40,876	34,682	5,010	1,184	35,561	30,984	3,578	999	3,583	2,200	1,253	132	2,774	2,313	389	72
Rented	24,176	12,499	10,576	1,101	16,545	10,013	5,678	855	6,290	1,596	4,505	190	4,715	2,703	1,788	224

- Represents or rounds to zero.   X Not applicable.   [1] Includes other races, not shown separately.   [2] Persons of Hispanic origin may be of any race.   [3] Includes equivalency.   [4] Excludes children whose parent is in the Armed Forces.   [5] Refers to the tenure of the householder (who may or may not be the child's parent).

Source: U.S. Bureau of the Census, unpublished data.

Population

No. 82. Nonfamily Households, by Sex and Age of Householder: 1980 to 1993

[As of **March**. See headnote, table 74]

ITEM	MALE HOUSEHOLDER (1,000)					FEMALE HOUSEHOLDER (1,000)				
	Total	15 to 24 yr. old	25 to 44 yr. old	45 to 64 yr. old	65 yr. old and over	Total	15 to 24 yr. old	25 to 44 yr. old	45 to 64 yr. old	65 yr. old and over
1980, total	**8,807**	**1,567**	**3,854**	**1,822**	**1,565**	**12,419**	**1,189**	**2,198**	**3,048**	**5,983**
One person (living alone).	6,966	947	2,920	1,613	1,486	11,330	779	1,809	2,901	5,842
Nonrelatives present. . . .	1,841	620	934	209	79	1,089	410	389	147	141
1990, total	**11,606**	**1,236**	**5,780**	**2,536**	**2,053**	**15,651**	**1,032**	**3,697**	**3,545**	**7,377**
One person (living alone).	9,049	674	4,231	2,203	1,943	13,950	536	2,881	3,300	7,233
Nonrelatives present. . . .	2,557	560	1,551	334	112	1,701	497	817	245	143
Never married	5,844	1,175	3,689	696	285	4,382	976	2,406	510	491
Married [1]	1,117	28	513	391	187	794	15	261	320	198
Widowed	1,417	-	29	221	1,166	7,428	4	52	1,333	6,038
Divorced.	3,228	33	1,550	1,229	416	3,046	37	977	1,382	649
1993, total	**12,254**	**1,283**	**5,912**	**2,950**	**2,110**	**15,993**	**988**	**3,602**	**3,878**	**7,525**
One person (living alone).	9,436	665	4,254	2,522	1,994	14,206	521	2,764	3,559	7,361
Nonrelatives present. . . .	2,818	618	1,658	427	116	1,787	467	837	319	164
Never married	6,133	1,211	3,797	782	343	4,402	936	2,406	604	456
Married [1]	1,188	27	533	439	189	743	29	215	322	177
Widowed	1,460	5	24	243	1,188	7,305	-	60	1,129	6,117
Divorced.	3,474	39	1,559	1,486	390	3,543	23	921	1,824	775

- Represents or rounds to zero.   [1] No spouse present.

Source: U.S. Bureau of the Census, *Current Population Reports*, P20-450, and earlier reports; and unpublished data.

No. 83. Persons Living Alone, by Sex and Age: 1970 to 1993

[As of **March**. Based on Current Population Survey; see headnote, table 74]

SEX AND AGE	NUMBER OF PERSONS (1,000)					PERCENT DISTRIBUTION				
	1970	1980	1985	1990	1993	1970	1980	1985	1990	1993
Both sexes . , ...	**10,851**	**18,296**	**20,602**	**22,999**	**23,642**	**100**	**100**	**100**	**100**	**100**
15 to 24 years old [1]	556	1,726	1,324	1,210	1,186	5	9	6	5	5
25 to 34 years old	[2]1,604	[2]4,729	3,905	3,972	3,735	[2]15	[2]26	19	17	16
35 to 44 years old	[2]	[2]	2,322	3,138	3,286	[2]	[2]	11	14	14
45 to 64 years old	3,622	4,514	4,939	5,502	6,081	33	25	24	24	26
65 to 74 years old	2,815	3,851	4,130	4,350	4,330	26	21	20	19	18
75 years old and over	2,256	3,477	3,982	4,825	5,025	21	19	19	21	21
Male	**3,532**	**6,966**	**7,922**	**9,049**	**9,436**	**33**	**38**	**39**	**39**	**40**
15 to 24 years old [1]	274	947	750	674	665	3	5	4	3	3
25 to 34 years old	[2]933	[2]2,920	2,307	2,395	2,282	[2]9	[2]16	11	10	10
35 to 44 years old	[2]	[2]	1,406	1,836	1,972	[2]	[2]	7	8	8
45 to 64 years old	1,152	1,613	1,845	2,203	2,522	11	9	9	10	11
65 to 74 years old	611	775	868	1,042	1,046	6	4	4	5	4
75 years old and over	563	711	746	901	948	5	4	4	4	4
Female . . . . , ...	**7,319**	**11,330**	**12,680**	**13,950**	**14,206**	**68**	**62**	**62**	**61**	**60**
15 to 24 years old [1]	282	779	573	536	521	3	4	3	2	2
25 to 34 years old	[2]671	[2]1,809	1,598	1,578	1,451	[2]6	[2]10	8	7	6
35 to 44 years old	[2]	[2]	916	1,303	1,313	[2]	[2]	4	6	6
45 to 64 years old	2,470	2,901	3,095	3,300	3,559	23	16	15	14	15
65 to 74 years old	2,204	3,076	3,262	3,309	3,284	20	17	16	14	14
75 years old and over	1,693	2,766	3,236	3,924	4,078	16	15	16	17	17

[1] 1970, persons 14 to 24 years old.   [2] Data for persons 35 to 44 years old included with persons 25 to 34 years old.

Source: U.S. Bureau of the Census, *Current Population Reports*, P20-450, and earlier reports; and unpublished data.

No. 84. Population in Institutions and Other Group Quarters, by Type of Group Quarters and State: 1990

[As of **April** 1. See text, section 1, and Appendix III. See *Historical Statistics, Colonial Times to 1970*, series A 359-371, for inmates of institutions]

REGION, DIVISION, AND STATE	Group quarters population, total [1]	INSTITUTIONALIZED PERSONS				College dormitories	Military quarters	Emergency shelters for homeless persons [3]	Persons visible in street locations [3]
		Total [2]	Correctional institutions	Nursing homes	Juvenile institutions				
U.S....	6,697,744	3,334,018	1,115,111	1,772,032	104,200	1,953,558	589,700	178,638	49,734
Northeast ..	1,510,088	713,335	195,275	399,329	20,091	540,689	47,252	60,077	14,653
N.E	445,031	179,333	33,227	119,646	4,998	198,866	20,349	11,898	970
ME....	37,169	14,136	2,311	9,855	427	14,118	5,153	419	7
NH....	32,151	11,466	1,991	8,202	284	17,025	923	377	8
VT....	21,642	6,161	807	4,809	172	13,435	-	232	16
MA....	214,307	84,345	15,471	55,662	2,457	100,487	4,439	6,207	674
RI....	38,595	14,801	2,645	10,156	498	18,898	2,851	469	44
CT....	101,167	48,424	10,002	30,962	1,160	34,903	6,983	4,194	221
M.A	1,065,057	534,002	162,048	279,683	15,093	341,823	26,903	48,179	13,683
NY....	545,265	267,122	90,025	126,175	6,981	165,925	12,875	32,472	10,732
NJ....	171,368	92,670	29,093	47,054	2,343	43,711	10,102	7,470	1,639
PA....	348,424	174,210	42,930	106,454	5,769	132,187	3,926	8,237	1,312
Midwest ...	1,598,620	852,419	211,192	544,650	26,134	557,270	40,203	27,245	3,324
E.N.C ...	1,055,689	568,050	157,275	346,243	18,374	369,009	19,261	19,348	2,544
OH....	261,451	152,331	41,618	93,769	6,158	88,785	449	4,277	188
IN....	161,992	81,686	21,726	50,845	2,823	70,873	883	2,251	268
IL....	286,956	149,842	37,334	93,662	3,601	86,777	16,091	7,481	1,755
MI....	211,692	112,903	42,849	57,622	3,835	73,093	1,693	3,784	262
WI....	133,598	71,288	13,748	50,345	1,957	49,481	145	1,555	71
W.N.C ...	542,931	284,369	53,917	198,407	7,760	188,261	20,942	7,897	780
MN....	117,621	63,279	9,969	47,051	1,417	39,280	24	2,253	138
IA....	99,520	47,841	5,630	36,455	1,142	43,093	57	989	148
MO....	145,397	80,854	19,975	52,060	2,173	44,033	6,424	2,276	215
ND....	24,234	10,574	831	8,159	443	10,377	2,245	279	30
SD....	25,841	13,305	2,543	9,356	565	9,306	1,051	396	71
NE....	47,553	25,620	3,662	19,171	1,191	16,692	1,104	764	20
KS....	82,765	42,896	11,307	26,155	829	25,480	10,037	940	158
South	2,294,420	1,145,986	439,250	558,382	31,432	615,791	312,915	42,407	7,975
S.A	1,243,962	577,690	231,369	270,930	14,778	322,299	213,816	25,260	5,025
DE....	20,071	8,662	3,347	4,596	179	8,806	1,164	313	19
MD....	113,856	62,760	27,025	26,884	2,252	30,892	10,426	2,507	523
DC....	41,717	14,070	4,035	7,008	138	16,126	2,181	4,682	131
VA....	209,300	84,292	33,553	37,762	2,860	61,943	51,869	2,657	319
WV....	36,911	19,469	4,439	12,591	458	15,083	32	451	33
NC....	224,470	83,400	24,857	47,014	2,119	71,266	58,378	2,637	259
SC....	116,543	44,134	18,351	18,228	2,123	35,488	30,166	973	102
GA....	173,633	87,266	40,803	36,549	1,666	39,723	30,261	3,930	450
FL....	307,461	173,637	74,959	80,298	2,983	42,972	29,339	7,110	3,189
E.S.C	392,424	194,314	63,082	102,900	6,169	131,846	38,432	5,061	922
KY....	101,176	47,609	13,948	27,874	1,052	30,600	15,228	1,284	118
TN....	129,129	65,389	21,335	35,192	2,194	43,683	11,126	1,864	357
AL....	92,402	51,583	19,226	24,031	1,924	28,859	6,085	1,530	364
MS....	69,717	29,733	8,573	15,803	999	28,704	5,993	383	83
W.S.C	658,034	373,982	144,799	184,552	10,485	161,646	60,667	12,086	2,028
AR....	58,332	34,223	8,642	21,809	827	16,775	1,814	489	62
LA....	112,578	67,276	26,792	32,072	1,633	27,990	10,851	1,559	184
OK....	93,677	51,211	15,108	29,666	1,044	24,924	8,712	2,222	340
TX....	393,447	221,272	94,257	101,005	6,981	91,957	39,290	7,816	1,442
West	1,294,616	622,278	269,394	269,671	26,543	239,808	189,330	48,909	23,782
Mountain .	297,687	144,834	60,762	65,842	6,777	77,782	27,269	8,983	3,215
MT....	23,747	11,125	2,174	7,764	393	6,195	1,000	445	17
ID....	21,490	10,478	2,871	6,318	457	6,676	740	461	19
WY....	10,240	5,434	1,556	2,679	297	3,414	832	183	13
CO....	79,472	35,976	13,446	18,506	1,706	22,749	12,895	2,554	393
NM....	28,807	14,024	5,385	6,276	637	8,333	3,088	667	164
AZ....	80,683	41,508	22,636	14,472	1,751	18,459	6,071	2,735	1,897
UT....	29,048	12,739	4,252	6,222	901	10,156	1,046	925	276
NV....	24,200	13,550	8,442	3,605	635	1,800	1,597	1,013	436
Pacific ...	996,929	477,444	208,632	203,829	19,766	162,026	162,061	39,926	20,567
WA....	120,531	55,313	14,569	32,840	1,606	27,908	18,491	4,565	772
OR....	66,205	33,378	10,912	18,200	1,317	18,970	122	3,254	564
CA....	751,860	376,374	178,199	148,362	16,375	108,880	115,334	30,806	18,081
AK....	20,701	4,574	2,630	1,202	386	1,310	8,807	447	79
HI....	37,632	7,805	2,322	3,225	82	4,958	19,307	854	1,071

- Represents zero.   [1] Includes persons in other types of group quarters not shown separately.   [2] Includes other institutionalized persons not shown separately.   [3] Results reported from the enumeration of emergency shelters and visible in street locations are not (and were never intended to be) a count of the total population of homeless persons at the national, State, or local level. The data do not represent a complete count of the homeless population. Counts of persons in these two locations represent one of the Bureau's efforts to include homeless persons in the 1990 census.

Source: U.S. Bureau of the Census, *1990 Census of Population, General Population Characteristics* (CP-1).

No. 85. Religious Preference, Church Membership, and Attendance: 1957 to 1991

[In percent. Covers civilian noninstitutional population, 18 years old and over. Data represent averages of the combined results of several surveys during year. Data are subject to sampling variability, see source]

YEAR	RELIGIOUS PREFERENCE					Church/ synagogue members	Persons attending church/ synagogue [1]	AGE AND REGION	Church/ synagogue members, 1991
	Protestant	Catholic	Jewish	Other	None				
1957	66	26	3	1	3	[2]73	47	18-29 years old. . . .	60
1967	67	25	3	3	2	[3]73	43	30-49 years old. . . .	67
1975	62	27	2	4	6	71	41	50 years and over . .	76
1980	61	28	2	2	7	69	40	East [4]	69
1985	57	28	2	4	9	71	42	Midwest [5]	66
1990	56	25	2	6	11	65	40	South [6]	76
1991	56	25	2	6	11	68	42	West [7]	54

[1] Persons who attended a church or synagogue in the last seven days. [2] 1952 data. [3] 1965 data. [4] ME, NH, RI, NY, CT, VT, MA, NJ, PA, WV, DE, MD, and DC. [5] OH, IN, IL, MI, MN, WI, IA, ND, SD, KS, NE, and MO. [6] KY, TN, VA, NC, SC, GA, FL, AL, MS, TX, AR, OK, and LA. [7] AZ, NM, CO, NV, MT, ID, WY, UT, CA, WA, OR, AK, and HI.

Source: Princeton Religion Research Center, Princeton, NJ, "Emerging Trends," periodical. Based on surveys conducted by The Gallup Organization, Inc.

No. 86. Religious Bodies—Church Membership, 1960 to 1990, and Number of Churches, 1990

[Membership in thousands, except as indicated. See headnote, table 87. See also Historical Statistics, Colonial Times to 1970, series H 793-799]

RELIGIOUS BODY	MEMBERSHIP						Number of churches, 1990
	1960	1970	1975	1980	1985	1990	
Total	114,449	131,045	131,013	134,817	142,926	156,336	358,194
Members as percent of population [1]	64	63	61	59	60	63	(X)
Average members per local church	359	399	393	401	413	436	(X)
Buddhist Churches of America	20	100	60	60	100	19	67
Eastern Churches.	2,699	3,850	3,696	3,823	4,026	3,976	1,702
Jews [2]	5,367	5,870	6,115	5,920	5,835	5,981	3,416
Old Catholic, Polish National Catholic, and Armenian Churches.	590	848	846	924	1,024	950	441
The Roman Catholic Church	42,105	48,215	48,882	50,450	52,655	58,568	23,685
Protestants [3]	[4]63,669	71,713	71,043	73,479	79,096	86,684	327,717
Miscellaneous [5]	([4])	449	372	161	191	157	1,166

X Not applicable. [1] Based on Bureau of the Census estimated total population as of July 1. Estimates for 1980's reflect results of 1990 census. [2] Estimates of the Jewish community including those identified with Orthodox, Conservative and Reform synagogues or temples. [3] Includes nonprotestant bodies such as "Latter-day Saints" and "Jehovah's Witnesses." [4] Data for "Miscellaneous" included with Protestants. [5] Includes non-Christian bodies such as "Spiritualists," "Ethical Culture Movement," and "Unitarian-Universalists."

Source: National Council of the Churches of Christ in the United States of America, New York, NY, Yearbook of American and Canadian Churches, annual (copyright).

No. 87. Religious Bodies—Selected Data

[Represents latest information available from religious bodies with memberships of 60,000 or more; excludes a few groups giving no data. Not all groups follow same calendar year nor count membership in same way; some groups give only approximate figures. Roman Catholics count all baptized persons, including infants; Jewish statistics are estimates of the number of persons living in Jewish households including as a consequence of intermarriage, approximately 7.4 percent non-Jewish persons. Eastern Orthodox Churches include all persons in their nationality or cultural groups; most Protestant bodies count only persons who have attained full membership, and previous estimates have indicated that all but a minority of these are over 11 years of age; however, many Lutheran bodies and The Episcopal Church report all baptized persons, and not only those confirmed. Data which appear in italics are "noncurrent," i.e., they are reported for 1990 or earlier. All other data are "current" and were reported in 1991 or 1992]

RELIGIOUS BODY	Year reported	Churches reported	Membership (1,000)	Pastors serving parishes [1]	Sunday school enrollment [2] (1,000)
African Methodist Episcopal Church [3]	1991	(NA)	3,500	(NA)	(NA)
African Methodist Episcopal Zion Church	1991	3,000	1,200	2,500	50
American Baptist Association	1986	1,705	250	1,740	(NA)
American Baptist Churches in the U.S.A.	1991	5,862	1,528	5,346	323
Antiochian Orthodox Christian Archdiocese of North America, The . . .	1992	170	350	225	6
Apostolic Catholic Assyrian Church of the East, N. American Diocese .	1989	22	120	92	(NA)
Armenian Apostolic Church of America	1992	30	150	22	1
Assemblies of God.	1991	11,536	2,235	17,047	1,415
Bahai Faith	1992	1,700	110	(NA)	(NA)
Baptist General Conference.	1992	821	135	1,200	82
Baptist Missionary Association of America	1991	1,312	230	1,200	93

See footnotes at end of table.

No. 87. Religious Bodies—Selected Data—Continued

[See headnote, page 70]

RELIGIOUS BODY	Year reported	Churches reported	Member-ship (1,000)	Pastors serving par-ishes [1]	Sunday school enrollment [2] (1,000)
Christian and Missionary Alliance, The	1991	1,900	268	1,639	144
Christian Brethren (a.k.a. Plymouth Brethren)	1984	1,150	98	(NA)	(NA)
Christian Church (Disciples of Christ)	1991	4,031	1,023	3,729	304
Christian Churches and Churches of Christ	1988	5,579	1,071	5,525	(NA)
Christian Congregation, Inc., The	1991	1,447	111	1,447	47
Christian Methodist Episcopal Church	1983	2,340	719	2,340	(NA)
Christian Reformed Church in North America	1992	739	225	671	(NA)
Church of God (Anderson, IN)	1992	2,330	215	3,000	165
Church of God (Cleveland, TN)	1990	5,841	620	4,665	389
Church of God in Christ, The	1991	15,300	5,500	28,988	(NA)
Church of God in Christ, International, The	1982	300	200	700	(NA)
Church of God of Prophecy, The	1992	2,072	72	12,211	67
Church of Jesus Christ of Latter-day Saints, The	1991	9,468	4,336	28,404	3,486
Church of the Brethren	1990	1,095	148	1,084	(NA)
Church of the Nazarene	1991	5,172	574	4,416	860
Churches of Christ	1992	13,200	1,690	(NA)	(NA)
Community Churches, International Council of	1991	398	250	(NA)	(NA)
Congregational Christian Churches, National Association of	1992	405	90	600	(NA)
Conservative Baptist Association of America	1989	1,126	210	1,126	(NA)
Coptic Orthodox Church	1992	55	260	60	(NA)
Cumberland Presbyterian Church	1991	784	92	(NA)	45
Episcopal Church, The	1991	7,367	2,472	8,040	532
Evangelical Covenant Church, The	1991	596	90	542	78
Evangelical Free Church of America	1992	1,113	188	1,631	(NA)
Evangelical Lutheran Church in America	1991	11,074	5,245	9,929	1,113
Free Methodist Church of North America	1991	1,063	74	956	94
Free Will Baptists, National Association of	1991	2,495	209	2,800	46
Full Gospel Fellowship of Churches and Ministers International	1985	450	65	850	(NA)
General Association of Regular Baptist Churches	1992	1,532	160	(NA)	(NA)
General Baptists (General Association of)	1990	876	74	1,384	(NA)
Independent Fundamental Churches of America	1991	700	78	745	75
International Church of the Foursquare Gospel	1991	1,516	208	(NA)	38
International Pentecostal Holiness Church	1990	(NA)	132	(NA)	(NA)
Jehovah's Witnesses	1992	9,890	914	(NA)	(NA)
Jews [4]	1990	3,416	5,981	(NA)	(NA)
Lutheran Church - Missouri Synod, The	1991	5,364	2,607	5,417	668
Mennonite Church	1992	1,053	99	1,631	(NA)
National Baptist Convention of America	1987	2,500	3,500	(NA)	(NA)
National Baptist Convention, U.S.A., Inc.	1992	36,000	8,000	30,000	(NA)
National Missionary Baptist Convention of America	1992	(NA)	2,500	(NA)	(NA)
Old Order Amish Church	1992	876	79	(NA)	(NA)
Orthodox Church in America	1992	1,000	1,030	750	(NA)
Pentecostal Assemblies of the World [3]	1989	1,005	500	(NA)	(NA)
Pentecostal Church of God	1991	1,160	92	(NA)	(NA)
Presbyterian Church in America	1991	(NA)	234	(NA)	(NA)
Presbyterian Church (U.S.A.)	1991	11,468	3,778	10,042	1,141
Progressive National Baptist Convention, Inc.	1991	1,400	2,500	1,400	(NA)
Reformed Church in America	1991	967	341	926	110
Reorganized Church of Jesus Christ of Latter-day Saints	1992	1,001	150	16,742	(NA)
Roman Catholic Church, The	1991	19,971	58,267	(NA)	(NA)
Romanian Orthodox Episcopate of America	1990	37	65	37	2
Salvation Army, The	1991	1,151	446	2,710	108
Serbian Orthodox Church in the U.S.A. and Canada	1986	68	67	60	(NA)
Seventh-day Adventist Church	1991	4,229	733	2,312	395
Southern Baptist Convention	1991	36,168	15,232	38,700	8,178
Unitarian Universalist Association	1991	1,020	141	650	49
United Church of Christ	1991	6,301	1,584	4,581	413
United Methodist Church, The	1991	37,100	8,785	20,607	3,852
United Pentecostal Church International	1992	3,500	550	(NA)	(NA)
Wesleyan Church (USA), The	1992	1,612	114	1,755	(NA)
Wisconsin Evangelical Lutheran Synod	1990	1,211	420	1,167	49

NA Not available.   [1] Includes other pastors performing pastoral duties.   [2] Includes pupils, officers, and teachers.
[3] Figures obtained from the *Directory of African American Religious Bodies, 1991*.   [4] Estimate of size of Jewish community provided by American Jewish Yearbook. Estimates of the number of Jews holding membership in synagogues or temples of the four branches of Judaism amount to 4,750,000.

Source: National Council of the Churches of Christ in the United States of America, New York, NY, *Yearbook of American and Canadian Churches*, annual, (copyright).

No. 88. Religious Congregations—Summary: 1991

[Excludes Alaska and Hawaii. A religious congregation is a community of people who meet together for worship, for fellowship, and for service to their members and the larger communities in which they live. Excludes informal congregational groups that did not have an official meeting place, denominational organizations, religious charities, and religiously-owned or -affiliated institutions. Based on a sample survey of 1,003 congregations with telephones conducted by the source; for details, see source]

SIZE OF CONGREGATION	Number of congregations	AREAS OF ACTIVITY	Percent of all congregations providing support or service [4]	SOURCE OF REVENUE OR TYPE OF EXPENDITURE	Amount (mil. dol.)
Total	[1]**257,648**	Human services	91.7	**Revenues, total [9]**	**48,412**
Fewer than 100 members ..	[2]52,065	Recreation [5]	72.6	Individual giving	39,223
100-199 members	[3]70,464	Marriage counseling ..	70.5	Fees, charges for services	1,851
200-299 members	39,553	Family counseling	61.8	School tuition	1,352
300-399 members	23,521	Meal services [6]	50.1		
400-499 members	16,051	Single adults programs..	46.5	**Expenditures, total**	**47,648**
500-999 members	31,826	Health	89.5	Current operating [9]	34,183
1,000-1,999 members	15,451	Visitation and support [7] .	87.4	Wages, salaries	16,532
2,000 or more members ...	8,717	Alcohol/drug prevention .	47.3	Fringe benefits	3,696
		International	73.9	Supplies, services	10,400
Fewer than 100 nonmembers	136,513	Relief abroad	61.5	Donations [9]	6,626
100-199 nonmembers.....	63,956	Education &/or health ..	39.0	Within denomination	4,655
200-299 nonmembers....	20,883	Public benefit.	62.2	To other organizations	1,317
300-499 nonmembers....	12,150	Abortion activities [8]	41.8	Construction, capital improvements [10]	5,051
500 or more nonmembers ..	19,804	Education	53.3	Savings	1,788

[1] Includes those which don't know or did not answer. [2] Includes churches with fewer than 100 nonmembers. [3] Includes churches with fewer than 100 members but with 100 or more nonmembers. [4] Congregations could give multiple responses. [5] Includes camp programs and other youth programs. [6] Includes food kitchens. [7] Programs for sick and shut-ins. [8] Pro-life or pro-choice. [9] Includes other items, not shown separately. [10] Includes acquisition of real property.
Source: INDEPENDENT SECTOR, Washington, DC, *From Belief to Commitment: The Community Service Activities and Finances of Religious Congregations in the United States, 1993 Edition* (copyright).

No. 89. Christian Church Adherents, 1990, and Jewish Population, 1992—States

[Christian church adherents were defined as "all members, including full members, their children and the estimated number of other regular participants who are not considered as communicant, confirmed or full members." Data on Christian church adherents are based on reports of 133 church groupings and exclude 34 church bodies that reported more than 100,000 members to the *Yearbook of American and Canadian Churches*. The Jewish population includes Jews who define themselves as Jewish by religion as well as those who define themselves as Jewish in cultural terms. Data on Jewish population are based primarily on a compilation of individual estimates made by local Jewish federations. Additionally, most large communities have completed Jewish demographic surveys from which the Jewish population can be determined]

REGION, DIVISION, AND STATE	CHRISTIAN ADHERENTS, 1990		JEWISH POPULATION, 1992		REGION, DIVISION, AND STATE	CHRISTIAN ADHERENTS, 1990		JEWISH POPULATION, 1992	
	Number (1,000)	Percent of population [1]	Number (1,000)	Percent of population [1]		Number (1,000)	Percent of population [1]	Number (1,000)	Percent of population [1]
U.S. ...	**131,084**	**52.7**	**5,828**	**2.3**	DC. . .	349	57.5	25	4.2
					VA. . .	2,898	46.8	69	1.1
Northeast.	**28,692**	**56.5**	**2,828**	**5.5**	WV. . .	740	41.3	2	0.1
N.E.	**7,456**	**56.5**	**411**	**3.1**	NC. . .	3,962	59.8	18	0.3
ME. . .	439	35.8	8	0.6	SC. . .	2,149	61.6	8	0.2
NH. . .	431	38.9	7	0.6	GA. . .	3,659	56.5	75	1.1
VT. . .	232	41.2	6	1.0	FL. . .	5,106	39.5	599	4.5
MA. . .	3,666	60.9	275	4.6	**E.S.C.** ..	**9,844**	**64.9**	**39**	**0.3**
RI . . .	754	75.1	16	1.6	KY. . .	2,216	60.1	12	0.3
CT . . .	1,935	58.9	100	3.1	TN. . .	2,966	60.8	18	0.4
M.A. . . .	**21,235**	**56.5**	**2,416**	**6.4**	AL. . .	2,858	70.7	9	0.2
NY. . .	9,970	55.4	1,643	9.1	MS. . .	1,804	70.1	1	0.1
NJ. . .	4,305	55.7	443	5.7	**W.S.C.** ..	**17,267**	**64.7**	**132**	**0.5**
PA. . .	6,961	58.6	329	2.8	AR. . .	1,423	60.5	2	0.1
Midwest ..	**32,882**	**55.1**	**680**	**1.1**	LA. . .	2,959	70.1	16	0.4
E.N.C.	**22,220**	**52.9**	**557**	**1.3**	OK. . .	2,097	66.7	5	0.2
OH. . .	5,307	48.9	130	1.2	TX. . .	10,787	63.5	109	0.6
IN . . .	2,617	47.2	18	0.3	**West**	**21,141**	**40.1**	**1,133**	**2.1**
IL. . . .	6,591	57.7	268	2.3	**Mt.**	**6,434**	**47.1**	**154**	**1.1**
MI . . .	4,580	49.3	107	1.1	MT. . .	341	42.7	(Z)	0.1
WI . . .	3,125	63.9	35	0.7	ID . . .	507	50.4	(Z)	0.1
W.N.C. . .	**10,662**	**60.4**	**122**	**0.7**	WY . . .	216	47.6	(Z)	0.1
MN. . .	2,807	64.2	33	0.7	CO. . .	1,244	37.8	51	1.5
IA . . .	1,675	60.3	6	0.2	NM. . .	883	58.3	6	0.4
MO . . .	2,883	56.3	62	1.2	AZ. . .	1,505	41.1	72	1.9
ND. . .	484	75.8	1	0.1	UT. . .	1,371	79.6	3	0.2
SD. . .	474	68.1	(Z)	0.1	NV. . .	366	30.5	21	1.6
NE. . .	1,000	63.4	7	0.5	**Pac.**	**14,707**	**37.6**	**979**	**2.4**
KS. . .	1,341	54.1	14	0.6	WA . . .	1,580	32.5	33	0.7
South. . . .	**48,370**	**56.6**	**1,188**	**1.4**	OR. . .	903	31.8	17	0.6
S.A. . . .	**21,258**	**48.8**	**1,017**	**2.3**	CA. . .	11,665	39.2	920	3.0
DE. . .	297	44.6	9	1.4	AK. . .	175	31.8	2	0.4
MD. . .	2,101	43.9	212	4.4	HI . . .	384	34.6	7	0.6

Z Fewer than 500. [1] Based on U.S. Bureau of the Census data for resident population enumerated as of April 1, 1990, and estimated as of July 1, 1992.
Source: Christian church adherents—M. Bradley; N. Green, Jr.; D. Jones; M. Lynn; and L. McNeil; *Churches and Church Membership in the United States 1990*, Glenmary Research Center, Atlanta, GA, 1992 (copyright); Jewish population—American Jewish Committee and the Jewish Publication Society, New York, NY, *American Jewish Year Book, 1993* (copyright).

Vital Statistics

This section presents vital statistics data on births, deaths, abortions, fetal deaths, fertility, life expectancy, marriages, and divorces. Vital statistics are compiled for the country as a whole by the National Center for Health Statistics (NCHS) and published in its annual report, *Vital Statistics of the United States*, in certain reports of the *Vital and Health Statistics* series, and in the *Monthly Vital Statistics Report*. Reports in this field are also issued by the various State bureaus of vital statistics. Data on fertility, on age of persons at first marriage, and on marital status and marital history are compiled by the Bureau of the Census from its Current Population Survey (CPS; see text, section 1) and published in *Current Population Reports*, P20 series. Data on abortions are published by the Alan Guttmacher Institute, New York, NY in selected issues of *Family Planning Perspectives*.

Registration of vital events.—The registration of births, deaths, fetal deaths, and other vital events in the United States is primarily a State and local function. The civil laws of every State provide for a continuous and permanent birth- and death-registration system. Many States also provide for marriage- and divorce-registration systems. Vital events occurring to U.S. residents outside the United States are not included in the data.

Births and deaths.—The live-birth, death, and fetal-death statistics prepared by NCHS are based on vital records filed in the registration offices of all States, of New York City, and of the District of Columbia. The annual collection of death statistics on a national basis began in 1900 with a national death-registration area of 10 States and the District of Columbia; a similar annual collection of birth statistics for a national birth-registration area began in 1915, also with 10 reporting States and the District of Columbia. Since 1933, the birth- and death-registration areas have comprised the entire United States, including Alaska (beginning 1959) and Hawaii (beginning 1960). National statistics on fetal deaths were

In Brief

1992:

Births	4,084,000
Deaths	2,177,000
Marriages	2,362,000
Divorces	1,215,000

Acquired Immunodeficiency Syndrome deaths; 1982–92:

All ages	166,467
Under 5 years old	1,796
5 to 12 years old	373
13 to 29 years old	30,518
30 to 39 years old	75,023
40 to 49 years old	39,177
50 to 59 years old	13,493
60 years old and over	6,087

first compiled for 1918 and annually since 1922.

Prior to 1951, birth statistics came from a complete count of records received in the Public Health Service (now received in NCHS). From 1951 through 1971, they were based on a 50-percent sample of all registered births (except for a complete count in 1955 and a 20- to 50-percent sample in 1967). Beginning in 1972, they have been based on a complete count for States participating in the Vital Statistics Cooperative Program (VSCP) (for details, see the technical appendix in *Vital Statistics of the United States*) and on a 50-percent sample of all other areas. Beginning 1986 all reporting areas participated in the VSCP. Mortality data have been based on a complete count of records for each area (except for a 50-percent sample in 1972). Beginning in 1970, births to, and deaths of nonresident aliens of the United States and U.S. citizens outside the United States have been excluded from the data. Fetal deaths and deaths among Armed Forces abroad are excluded. Data based on samples are subject to sampling error; for details, see annual issues of *Vital Statistics of the United States*.

Mortality statistics by cause of death are compiled in accordance with World Health Organization regulations according to the *International Classification of Diseases* (ICD). The ICD is revised approximately every 10 years. The ninth revision of the ICD was employed beginning in 1979. Deaths for prior years were classified according to the revision of the ICD in use at the time. Each revision of the ICD introduces a number of discontinuities in mortality statistics; for a discussion of those between the eighth and ninth revisions of the ICD, see *Monthly Vital Statistics Report,* vol. 28, No. 11, supplement.

Some of the tables present age-adjusted death rates in addition to crude death rates. Age-adjusted death rates shown in this section were prepared using the direct method, in which age-specific death rates for a population of interest are applied to a standard population distributed by age. Age adjustment eliminates the differences in observed rates between points in time or among compared population groups that result from age differences in population composition.

Abortions.—The U.S. Centers for Disease Control (CDC) collects data on abortions annually from States which have a central health agency with a statewide reporting system. The Alan Guttmacher Institute, New York, NY also issues data on the number of abortions based on its own surveys of hospitals and physicians. The Guttmacher Institute also publishes data on the characteristics of abortions after adjusting CDC data for changes in the number of States reporting each year.

Fertility and life expectancy.—The total fertility rate, defined as the number of births that 1,000 women would have in their lifetime if, at each year of age, they experienced the birth rates occurring in the specified year, is compiled and published by NCHS. Other data relating to social and medical factors which affect fertility rates, such as contraceptive use and birth expectations, are collected and made available by both NCHS and the Bureau of the Census. NCHS figures are based on information in birth and fetal death certificates and on the periodic National Surveys of Family Growth; Bureau of the Census data are based on decennial censuses and the CPS.

Data on life expectancy, the average remaining lifetime in years for persons who attain a given age, are computed and published by NCHS. For details, see the

technical appendix in *Vital Statistics of the United States.*

Marriage and divorce.—The compilation of nationwide statistics on marriages and divorces in the United States began in 1887-88 when the National Office of Vital Statistics prepared estimates for the years 1867-86. Although periodic updates took place after 1888, marriage and divorce statistics were not collected and published annually until 1944 by that Office. In 1957 and 1958, respectively, the same Office established marriage- and divorce-registration areas. Beginning in 1957, the marriage-registration area comprised 30 States, plus Alaska, Hawaii, Puerto Rico, and the Virgin Islands; it currently includes 42 States and the District of Columbia. The divorce-registration area, starting in 1958 with 14 States, Alaska, Hawaii, and the Virgin Islands, currently includes a total of 31 States and the Virgin Islands. Procedures for estimating the number of marriages and divorces in the registration States are discussed in *Vital Statistics of the United States,* vol. III—*Marriage and Divorce.* Total counts of events for registration and nonregistration States are gathered by collecting already summarized data on marriages and divorces reported by State offices of vital statistics and by county offices of registration.

Another important source of data on marriage and divorce trends in the United States is the March supplement to the Current Population Survey conducted by the Bureau of the Census. For information on marital status, see section 1.

Vital statistics rates.—Except as noted, vital statistics rates computed by NCHS are based on decennial census population figures as of April 1 for 1940, 1950, 1960, 1970, 1980, and 1990; and on midyear population figures for other years, as estimated by the Bureau of the Census (see text, section 1).

Race.—Data by race for births, deaths, marriages, and divorces from NCHS are based on information contained in the certificates of registration. The Census Bureau's Current Population Survey obtains information on race by asking respondents to classify their race as: (1) White, (2) Black, (3) American Indian, Eskimo, or Aleut, or (4) Asian or Pacific Islander.

No. 90. Live Births, Deaths, Marriages, and Divorces: 1950 to 1992

[Prior to 1960, excludes Alaska and Hawaii. Beginning 1970, excludes births to, and deaths of nonresidents of the United States. See Appendix III. See also *Historical Statistics, Colonial Times to 1970*, series B 1-5, B 142, B 167, and B 216]

YEAR	NUMBER (1,000)					RATE PER 1,000 POPULATION				
	Births [1]	Deaths		Mar-riages [3]	Divor-ces [4]	Births [1]	Deaths		Mar-riages [3]	Divor-ces [4]
		Total	Infant [2]				Total	Infant [2]		
1950	3,632	1,452	104	1,667	385	24.1	9.6	29.2	11.1	2.6
1955	4,097	1,529	107	1,531	377	25.0	9.3	26.4	9.3	2.3
1957	4,300	1,633	112	1,518	381	25.3	9.6	26.3	8.9	2.2
1960	4,258	1,712	111	1,523	393	23.7	9.5	26.0	8.5	2.2
1965	3,760	1,828	93	1,800	479	19.4	9.4	24.7	9.3	2.5
1970	3,731	1,921	75	2,159	708	18.4	9.5	20.0	10.6	3.5
1971	3,556	1,928	68	2,190	773	17.2	9.3	19.1	10.6	3.7
1972	3,258	1,964	60	2,282	845	15.6	9.4	18.5	10.9	4.0
1973	3,137	1,973	56	2,284	915	14.8	9.3	17.7	10.8	4.3
1974	3,160	1,934	53	2,230	977	14.8	9.1	16.7	10.5	4.6
1975	3,144	1,893	51	2,153	1,036	14.6	8.8	16.1	10.0	4.8
1976	3,168	1,909	48	2,155	1,083	14.6	8.8	15.2	9.9	5.0
1977	3,327	1,900	47	2,178	1,091	15.1	8.6	14.1	9.9	5.0
1978	3,333	1,928	46	2,282	1,130	15.0	8.7	13.8	10.3	5.1
1979	3,494	1,914	46	2,331	1,181	15.6	8.5	13.1	10.4	5.3
1980	3,612	1,990	46	2,390	1,189	15.9	8.8	12.6	10.6	5.2
1981	3,629	1,978	43	2,422	1,213	15.8	8.6	11.9	10.6	5.3
1982	3,681	1,975	42	2,456	1,170	15.9	8.5	11.5	10.6	5.1
1983	3,639	2,019	41	2,446	1,158	15.6	8.6	11.2	10.5	5.0
1984	3,669	2,039	40	2,477	1,169	15.6	8.6	10.8	10.5	5.0
1985	3,761	2,086	40	2,413	1,190	15.8	8.8	10.6	10.1	5.0
1986	3,757	2,105	39	2,407	1,178	15.6	8.8	10.4	10.0	4.9
1987	3,809	2,123	38	2,403	1,166	15.7	8.8	10.1	9.9	4.8
1988	3,910	2,168	39	2,396	[5]1,167	16.0	8.9	10.0	9.8	4.8
1989	4,041	2,150	40	[5]2,404	[5]1,163	16.4	8.7	9.8	[5]9.7	[5]4.7
1990	4,158	2,148	38	[5]2,448	[5]1,175	16.7	8.6	9.2	[5]9.8	[5]4.7
1991	4,111	2,170	37	[5]2,371	[5]1,187	16.3	8.6	8.9	[5]9.4	[5]4.7
1992 [5]	4,084	2,177	34	2,362	1,215	16.0	8.5	8.5	9.3	4.8

[1] Prior to 1960, data adjusted for underregistration.   [2] Infants under 1 year, excluding fetal deaths; rates per 1,000 registered live births.   [3] Includes estimates for some States through 1965 and also for 1976 and 1977 and marriage licenses for some States for all years except 1973 and 1975. Beginning 1978, includes nonlicensed marriages in California.   [4] Includes reported annulments and some estimated State figures for all years.   [5] Preliminary.

Source: U.S. National Center for Health Statistics, *Vital Statistics of the United States*, annual, *Monthly Vital Statistics Report*; and unpublished data.

No. 91. Live Births and Deaths—20 Largest Metropolitan Areas: 1988

[Excludes births to and deaths of nonresidents of the United States. Data are by place of residence. Metropolitan statistical areas (MSA's), consolidated metropolitan statistical areas (CMSA's), and New England County Metropolitan Areas (NECMA's) are defined by the U.S. Office of Management and Budget as of December 31, 1992; see Appendix II for definitions and components]

METROPOLITAN AREA	NUMBER (1,000)			RATE PER 1,000 POPULATION		
	Births	Deaths		Births	Deaths	
		Total	Infant [1]		Total	Infant [1]
New York-Northern New Jersey-Long Island, NY-NJ-CT-PA CMSA/NECMA [2]	307,126	189,362	3,354	15.8	9.7	10.9
Los Angeles-Riverside-Orange County, CA CMSA	276,991	101,850	2,458	19.9	7.3	8.9
Chicago-Gary-Kenosha, IL-IN-WI CMSA	141,570	71,500	1,678	17.3	8.7	11.9
Washington-Baltimore, DC-MD-VA-WV CMSA	107,954	50,890	1,243	16.4	7.7	11.5
San Francisco-Oakland-San Jose, CA CMSA	99,474	47,356	774	16.3	7.8	7.8
Philadelphia-Wilmington-Atlantic City, PA-NJ-DE-MD CMSA	94,245	58,748	1,100	16.1	10.0	11.7
Boston-Brockton-Nashua, MA-NH NECMA	85,666	50,656	659	15.2	9.0	7.7
Detroit-Ann Arbor-Flint, MI CMSA	78,425	45,227	967	15.2	8.8	12.3
Dallas-Fort Worth, TX CMSA	74,017	25,596	654	18.9	6.5	8.8
Houston-Galveston-Brazoria, TX CMSA	67,130	22,579	644	18.7	6.3	9.6
Miami-Fort Lauderdale, FL CMSA	48,638	32,785	542	15.8	10.7	11.1
Seattle-Tacoma-Bremerton, WA CMSA	44,475	20,447	395	15.8	7.3	8.9
Atlanta, GA MSA	49,123	19,235	554	17.3	6.8	11.3
Cleveland-Akron, OH CMSA	42,012	27,524	463	14.7	9.6	11.0
Minneapolis-St. Paul, MN-WI MSA	41,436	16,896	322	16.8	6.8	7.8
San Diego, CA MSA	44,096	16,658	315	18.7	7.0	7.1
St. Louis, MO-IL MSA	40,097	23,302	390	16.1	9.4	9.7
Pittsburgh, PA MSA	30,134	27,206	260	12.5	11.3	8.6
Phoenix-Mesa, AZ MSA	40,216	16,315	398	18.6	7.5	9.9
Tampa-St. Petersburg-Clearwater, FL MSA	27,201	24,903	290	13.6	12.4	10.7

[1] Infants under 1 year, excluding fetal deaths; rates per 1,000 registered live births.   [2] Includes parts of New Haven County, CT, not in the CMSA; excludes parts of Litchfield and Middlesex Counties, CT, in the CMSA.

Source: U.S. National Center for Health Statistics, *Vital Statistics of the United States*, annual; and unpublished data.

Vital Statistics

No. 92. Births and Birth Rates: 1970 to 1991

[Births in thousands and by race of child, except as indicated. Excludes births to nonresidents of the United States. For population bases used to derive these data, see text, section 2, and Appendix III. See also *Historical Statistics, Colonial Times to 1970*, series B 1, B 5-10, and B 12-20]

ITEM	1970	1980	1983	1984	1985	1986	1987	1988	1989	1990	1991
Live births [1]	**3,731**	**3,612**	**3,639**	**3,669**	**3,761**	**3,757**	**3,809**	**3,910**	**4,041**	**4,158**	**4,111**
White	3,091	2,899	2,904	2,924	2,991	2,970	2,992	3,046	3,132	3,225	3,241
Black	572	590	586	593	608	621	642	672	709	725	683
Male	1,915	1,853	1,866	1,879	1,928	1,925	1,951	2,002	2,069	2,129	2,102
Female	1,816	1,760	1,773	1,790	1,833	1,832	1,858	1,907	1,971	2,029	2,009
Males per 100 females	106	105	105	105	105	105	105	105	105	105	105
Age of mother:											
Under 20 years old	656	562	499	480	478	472	473	489	518	533	532
20 to 24 years old	1,419	1,226	1,160	1,142	1,141	1,102	1,076	1,067	1,078	1,094	1,090
25 to 29 years old	995	1,108	1,148	1,166	1,201	1,200	1,216	1,239	1,263	1,277	1,220
30 to 34 years old	428	550	625	658	696	721	761	804	842	886	885
35 to 39 years old	180	141	180	196	214	230	248	270	294	318	331
40 years old or more	53	24	27	28	29	31	36	41	46	50	54
Age of father:											
Under 20 years old	189	137	116	109	108	105	105	111	120	129	130
20 to 24 years old	1,015	803	722	696	685	651	627	617	613	628	625
25 to 29 years old	1,085	1,082	1,070	1,067	1,081	1,059	1,053	1,055	1,056	1,060	1,007
30 to 34 years old	599	739	782	806	837	845	872	904	922	955	940
35 to 39 years old	298	275	335	356	381	398	413	431	451	474	478
40 years old or more	214	139	153	160	167	174	191	205	221	231	236
Age not stated	330	437	461	475	502	524	549	585	659	681	696
Birth rate per 1,000 population	**18.4**	**15.9**	**15.6**	**15.6**	**15.8**	**15.6**	**15.7**	**16.0**	**16.4**	**16.7**	**16.3**
White	17.4	14.9	14.6	14.6	14.8	14.6	14.6	14.8	15.1	15.5	15.4
Black	25.3	22.1	21.0	21.0	21.3	21.5	21.9	22.6	23.5	23.8	21.9
Male	19.4	16.8	16.4	16.4	16.7	16.5	16.5	16.8	17.2	17.6	17.1
Female	17.4	15.1	14.8	14.8	15.0	14.9	14.9	15.2	15.6	15.9	15.6
Plural birth ratio [2]	[3]18.1	19.3	20.3	20.3	21.0	21.6	22.0	22.4	23.0	23.3	23.9
White	[3]17.3	18.5	19.6	19.8	20.4	21.2	21.6	22.0	[4]22.5	[4]22.9	[4]23.4
Black	[3]22.8	24.1	24.5	24.2	25.3	24.9	25.4	25.8	[4]26.9	[4]27.0	[4]27.8
Birth rate per 1,000 women [5]	**87.9**	**68.4**	**65.8**	**65.4**	**66.2**	**65.4**	**65.7**	**67.2**	**69.2**	**70.9**	**69.6**
White [5]	84.1	64.7	62.4	62.2	63.0	61.9	62.0	63.0	64.7	66.9	67.0
Black [5]	115.4	88.1	81.7	81.4	82.2	82.4	83.8	86.6	90.4	91.9	85.2
Age of mother:											
10 to 14 years old	1.2	1.1	1.1	1.2	1.2	1.3	1.3	1.3	1.4	1.4	1.4
15 to 19 years old	68.3	53.0	51.4	50.6	51.0	50.2	50.6	53.0	57.3	59.9	62.1
20 to 24 years old	167.8	115.1	107.8	106.8	108.3	107.4	107.9	110.2	113.8	116.5	115.7
25 to 29 years old	145.1	112.9	108.5	108.7	111.0	109.8	111.6	114.4	117.6	120.2	118.2
30 to 34 years old	73.3	61.9	64.9	67.0	69.1	70.1	72.1	74.8	77.4	80.8	79.5
35 to 39 years old	31.7	19.8	22.0	22.9	24.0	24.4	26.3	28.1	29.9	31.7	32.0
40 to 44 years old	8.1	3.9	3.9	3.9	4.0	4.1	4.4	4.8	5.2	5.5	5.5
45 to 49 years old	0.5	0.2	0.2	0.2	0.2	0.2	0.2	0.2	0.2	0.2	0.2
Birth rate per 1,000 men [6]	**71.5**	**57.0**	**55.1**	**55.0**	**55.6**	**54.8**	**55.0**	**55.8**	**57.2**	**58.4**	**57.1**
White [6]	67.1	52.9	51.4	51.2	51.9	51.0	50.9	51.5	52.6	53.8	53.3
Black [6]	107.4	83.8	78.1	77.6	78.3	78.3	79.5	82.0	85.4	86.3	83.4
Age of father: [7]											
15 to 19 years old [8]	25.6	18.8	18.2	17.8	18.0	17.9	18.3	19.6	21.9	23.5	24.8
20 to 24 years old	146.6	92.0	82.7	80.7	81.2	80.3	80.5	82.4	85.4	88.0	88.0
25 to 29 years old	175.0	123.0	113.0	111.4	112.3	109.6	109.6	111.6	114.3	116.4	114.7
30 to 34 years old	112.3	91.0	89.0	89.9	91.1	90.3	91.2	93.1	94.8	97.8	95.1
35 to 39 years old	57.6	42.8	45.2	46.0	47.3	46.8	48.6	49.9	51.3	53.0	51.8
40 to 44 years old	24.9	17.1	17.4	17.8	18.1	18.3	19.0	19.9	20.4	21.0	20.2
45 to 49 years old	9.1	6.1	6.4	6.3	6.6	6.7	6.9	7.1	7.4	7.5	7.5
50 to 54 years old	3.1	2.2	2.3	2.4	2.5	2.6	2.6	2.7	2.7	2.8	2.7
55 years old and over	0.6	0.4	0.4	0.4	0.4	0.4	0.4	0.4	0.4	0.6	0.4

[1] Includes other races not shown separately. [2] Number of multiple births per 1,000 live births. [3] 1971. [4] Race of mother; data not directly comparable with prior years. [5] Per 1,000 women, 15 to 44 years old in specified group. The rate for *age of mother 45 to 49 years old* computed by relating births to mothers 45 years old and over to women 45 to 49 years old. [6] Rate computed by relating total births, regardless of age of father, to 1,000 men, 15 to 54 years old in specified group. [7] Rates by age of father computed using frequencies with age not stated distributed among all age groups. [8] Rate computed by relating births to fathers under 20 years of age to men 15 to 19 years old.

Source: U.S. National Center for Health Statistics, *Vital Statistics of the United States*, annual; *Monthly Vital Statistics Report*; and unpublished data.

No. 93. Live Births, by State: 1990 and 1991

[In thousands. Registered births. Excludes births to nonresidents of the United States. By race of child, except as indicated. See Appendix III]

DIVISION AND STATE	1990 All races[1]	1990 White	1990 Black	1990 Hispanic[2] Total	1990 Hispanic[2] Mexican	1991 All races[1]	1991 White	1991 Black	1991 Hispanic[2] Total	1991 Hispanic[2] Mexican
United States..	4,158.2	3,290.3	684.3	595.1	385.6	4,110.9	3,241.3	682.6	623.1	411.2
New England	201.2	178.4	16.8	15.5	0.6	192.6	170.4	16.4	0.1	(Z)
Maine	17.4	17.0	0.1	0.1	(Z)	16.8	16.4	0.1	0.1	(Z)
New Hampshire ..	17.6	17.3	0.1	(NA)	(NA)	16.3	16.1	0.1	(NA)	(NA)
Vermont	8.3	8.2	(Z)	(Z)	(Z)	8.0	7.9	(Z)	(Z)	(Z)
Massachusetts ...	92.7	79.9	9.0	8.4	0.3	88.2	76.0	8.7	8.5	0.2
Rhode Island	15.2	13.4	1.2	1.6	0.1	14.7	12.9	1.1	1.4	0.1
Connecticut	50.1	42.6	6.4	5.3	0.2	48.6	41.1	6.3	5.2	0.1
Middle Atlantic	591.8	458.6	112.0	75.7	5.1	582.9	449.4	111.7	(Z)	(Z)
New York	297.6	220.7	63.3	53.1	3.8	292.6	216.7	62.2	53.7	4.4
New Jersey	122.3	94.4	23.1	17.0	0.9	121.4	92.8	23.7	17.5	1.3
Pennsylvania	172.0	143.5	25.5	5.6	0.4	168.9	139.9	25.8	6.0	0.4
East North Central.	675.5	544.6	117.9	34.7	23.8	668.0	536.8	118.0	(NA)	(NA)
Ohio.........	166.9	139.2	26.0	2.4	1.0	165.8	137.7	26.4	2.6	1.1
Indiana	86.2	75.8	9.5	1.9	1.4	85.7	75.4	9.5	1.8	1.4
Illinois.........	195.8	147.2	43.3	24.2	17.7	194.2	145.5	43.2	25.7	19.3
Michigan	153.7	119.1	32.0	4.3	2.6	150.2	116.0	31.6	4.4	2.6
Wisconsin	72.9	63.3	7.2	1.9	1.2	72.1	62.3	7.2	2.0	1.3
West North Central.	270.3	239.0	22.1	5.6	4.1	266.4	234.3	22.3	(NA)	(NA)
Minnesota	68.0	62.0	2.6	1.1	0.8	67.1	60.6	2.8	1.3	0.9
Iowa	39.4	37.7	1.0	0.6	0.4	39.0	37.1	1.2	0.7	0.4
Missouri........	79.3	64.6	13.6	1.0	0.7	78.7	63.9	13.7	1.1	0.8
North Dakota	9.3	8.3	0.1	0.1	0.1	8.9	7.9	0.1	0.1	0.1
South Dakota....	11.0	9.2	0.1	0.1	0.1	10.9	9.1	0.1	0.1	0.1
Nebraska.......	24.4	22.4	1.4	0.8	0.5	24.0	22.0	1.3	1.0	0.7
Kansas	39.0	34.7	3.3	2.0	1.6	37.8	33.7	3.2	2.1	1.7
South Atlantic	700.3	483.9	201.4	39.4	8.9	686.3	470.1	200.6	(NA)	(NA)
Delaware.......	11.1	8.4	2.6	0.3	0.1	11.2	8.1	2.9	0.4	0.1
Maryland.......	80.2	52.4	24.9	2.5	0.5	79.2	51.1	25.0	2.5	0.4
Dist. of Columbia..	11.9	1.8	9.1	0.9	(Z)	11.8	1.6	9.2	0.9	(Z)
Virginia	99.4	72.3	23.9	3.5	0.6	97.4	70.3	23.8	3.7	0.7
West Virginia	22.6	21.6	0.9	0.1	(Z)	22.5	21.6	0.8	0.1	(Z)
North Carolina ...	104.5	71.2	30.8	1.8	1.0	102.4	69.3	30.4	1.8	1.1
South Carolina ...	58.6	35.6	22.4	0.6	0.3	57.6	34.6	22.5	0.6	0.3
Georgia........	112.7	70.6	40.5	2.3	1.3	110.3	68.3	40.3	2.6	1.6
Florida........	199.3	150.0	46.4	27.6	5.0	194.0	145.2	45.7	28.2	5.2
East South Central.	236.4	168.9	65.3	1.2	0.6	234.9	167.2	65.6	(NA)	(NA)
Kentucky.......	54.4	48.9	5.1	0.3	0.2	54.3	48.7	5.3	0.2	0.2
Tennessee......	75.0	56.6	17.6	0.4	0.2	74.5	56.0	17.8	0.5	0.3
Alabama	63.5	41.1	21.9	0.3	0.2	62.8	40.7	21.7	0.4	0.2
Mississippi	43.6	22.3	20.8	0.1	(Z)	43.2	21.9	20.8	0.1	0.1
West South Central.	472.7	372.7	86.7	117.2	103.5	473.2	372.2	87.0	(NA)	(NA)
Arkansas.......	36.5	27.5	8.5	0.4	0.2	35.5	26.8	8.3	0.4	0.3
Louisiana.......	72.2	41.3	29.7	0.9	0.2	72.2	40.6	30.4	0.9	0.2
Oklahoma	47.6	37.8	5.1	(NA)	(NA)	47.8	37.5	5.2	1.9	1.4
Texas	316.4	266.2	43.4	115.8	103.0	317.7	267.3	43.1	121.2	106.4
Mountain	242.8	216.4	8.3	48.7	31.8	242.8	216.3	8.4	(NA)	(NA)
Montana	11.6	10.0	(Z)	0.3	0.1	11.5	10.0	(Z)	0.3	0.1
Idaho	16.4	16.0	(Z)	1.4	1.2	16.8	16.3	0.1	1.5	1.2
Wyoming	7.0	6.6	0.1	0.5	0.3	6.7	6.3	0.1	0.5	0.3
Colorado	53.5	49.0	2.9	9.3	4.7	53.8	49.1	2.9	9.8	4.8
New Mexico.....	27.4	22.6	0.5	12.2	2.8	27.8	23.0	0.6	12.6	3.0
Arizona........	69.0	59.2	2.6	19.7	18.9	68.1	58.5	2.5	20.6	19.7
Utah.........	36.3	34.4	0.2	2.0	1.2	36.0	34.2	0.2	2.2	1.4
Nevada........	21.6	18.6	1.9	3.3	2.5	22.0	18.7	2.1	3.7	2.9
Pacific.........	767.2	627.8	54.0	257.0	207.2	763.9	624.5	52.9	(NA)	(NA)
Washington	79.3	70.7	2.9	5.7	3.9	79.7	70.6	3.1	6.5	4.6
Oregon	42.9	39.9	0.9	3.0	2.6	42.5	39.5	1.0	3.3	2.9
California.......	612.6	503.0	49.0	245.6	200.1	610.1	500.7	47.7	258.0	214.3
Alaska........	11.9	8.1	0.5	0.3	0.2	11.7	7.9	0.5	0.4	0.2
Hawaii........	20.5	5.2	0.7	2.4	0.3	19.9	5.9	0.6	2.2	0.3

NA Not available. Z Less than 50. [1] Includes other races not shown separately. [2] Persons of Hispanic origin may be of any race. Births by Hispanic origin of mother.

Source: U.S. National Center for Health Statistics, *Vital Statistics of the United States*, annual, and *Monthly Vital Statistics Report*.

No. 94. Total Fertility Rate and Intrinsic Rate of Natural Increase: 1960 to 1990

[Based on race of child and registered births only. Beginning 1970, excludes births to nonresidents of United States. The *total fertility rate* is the number of births that 1,000 women would have in their lifetime if, at each year of age, they experienced the birth rates occurring in the specified year. A total fertility rate of 2,110 represents "replacement level" fertility for the total population under current mortality conditions (assuming no net immigration). The *intrinsic rate of natural increase* is the rate that would eventually prevail if a population were to experience, at each year of age, the birth rates and death rates occurring in the specified year and if those rates remained unchanged over a long period of time. Minus sign (-) indicates decrease. See also Appendix III and *Historical Statistics, Colonial Times to 1970*, series B 11]

ANNUAL AVERAGE AND YEAR	TOTAL FERTILITY RATE			INTRINSIC RATE OF NATURAL INCREASE			ANNUAL AVERAGE AND YEAR	TOTAL FERTILITY RATE			INTRINSIC RATE OF NATURAL INCREASE		
	Total	White	Black and other	Total	White	Black and other		Total	White	Black and other	Total	White	Black and other
1960-64 ...	3,449	3,326	4,326	18.6	17.1	27.7	1977	1,790	1,703	2,279	-6.2	-8.1	3.2
1965-69 ...	2,622	2,512	3,362	8.2	6.4	18.6	1978	1,760	1,668	2,265	-6.8	-8.8	2.9
1970-74 ...	2,094	1,997	2,680	-0.7	-2.5	9.1	1979	1,808	1,716	2,310	-5.7	-7.7	3.8
1975-79 ...	1,774	1,685	2,270	-6.6	-8.5	3.0	1980	1,840	1,749	2,323	-5.1	-7.0	4.0
1980-84 ...	1,819	1,731	2,262	-5.4	-7.3	3.0	1981	1,815	1,726	2,275	-5.5	-7.4	3.3
1985-88 ...	1,870	1,769	2,339	-4.2	-6.3	4.3	1982	1,829	1,742	2,265	-5.2	-7.0	3.0
							1983	1,803	1,718	2,225	-5.7	-7.5	2.5
1970	2,480	2,385	3,067	6.0	4.5	14.4	1984	1,806	1,719	2,224	-5.6	-7.4	2.4
1971	2,267	2,161	2,920	2.6	0.8	12.6	1985	1,843	1,754	2,263	-4.8	-6.6	3.1
1972	2,010	1,907	2,628	-2.0	-3.9	8.6	1986	1,836	1,742	2,282	-4.9	-6.8	3.3
1973	1,879	1,783	2,443	-4.5	-6.5	5.7	1987	1,871	1,767	2,349	-4.2	-6.3	4.5
1974	1,835	1,749	2,339	-5.4	-7.2	4.0	1988	1,932	1,814	2,463	-3.0	-5.3	6.3
1975	1,774	1,686	2,276	-6.7	-8.6	3.0	1989	2,014	1,895	2,526	-1.4	-3.6	7.4
1976	1,738	1,652	2,223	-7.4	-9.3	2.1	1990	2,081	1,963	2,578	-1.0	-2.3	8.3

Source: U.S. National Center for Health Statistics, *Vital Statistics of the United States*, annual; and unpublished data.

No. 95. Projected Fertility Rates, by Race and Age Group: 1993 and 2010

[For definition of total fertility rate, see headnote, table 94. Birth rates represent live births per 1,000 women in age group indicated. Projections are based on middle fertility assumptions. For explanations of methodology, see text, section 1]

AGE GROUP	ALL RACES [1]		WHITE		BLACK		AMERICAN INDIAN, ESKIMO, ALEUT		ASIAN AND PACIFIC ISLANDERS		HISPANIC [2]	
	1993	2010	1993	2010	1993	2010	1993	2010	1993	2010	1993	2010
Total fertility rate ..	2,074	2,119	1,973	2,009	2,470	2,469	2,778	2,759	2,514	2,406	2,900	2,777
Birth rates:												
10 to 14 years old....	1.4	1.6	0.7	0.9	4.8	5.0	2.0	2.1	0.8	0.8	2.3	2.3
15 to 19 years old....	60.5	62.4	50.4	52.9	114.4	113.8	103.9	105.2	33.7	31.6	99.6	95.8
20 to 24 years old....	117.6	120.0	109.6	112.4	161.0	161.1	188.7	187.0	99.7	95.6	180.5	172.6
25 to 29 years old....	118.6	120.2	117.9	118.8	112.9	113.5	141.4	141.6	160.8	153.4	149.8	143.7
30 to 34 years old....	80.1	82.0	80.2	80.9	67.8	68.4	78.2	78.4	134.3	128.4	95.8	91.5
35 to 39 years old....	31.6	31.8	31.0	30.6	28.1	27.5	34.0	33.5	61.4	57.9	43.1	40.5
40 to 44 years old....	5.4	5.5	5.1	5.1	5.4	5.1	7.2	7.0	12.7	12.0	9.2	8.5
45 to 49 years old....	0.2	0.3	0.2	0.2	0.3	0.3	0.4	0.4	1.3	1.2	0.6	0.5

[1] Includes races not shown separately. [2] Persons of Hispanic origin may be of any race.

Source: U.S. Bureau of the Census, *Current Population Reports*, P25-1104.

No. 96. Birth Rates, by Live-Birth Order and Race: 1970 to 1991

[**Births per 1,000 women 15 to 44 years old in specified racial group.** Live-birth order refers to number of children born alive. Figures for births of order not stated are distributed. See also headnote, table 92, and *Historical Statistics, Colonial Times to 1970*, series B 20-27]

LIVE-BIRTH ORDER	ALL RACES [1]					WHITE					BLACK				
	1970	1980	1985	1990	1991	1970	1980	1985	1990	1991	1970	1980	1985	1990	1991
Total	87.9	68.4	66.3	70.9	69.6	84.1	64.7	63.2	66.9	67.0	115.4	88.1	82.4	91.9	85.2
First birth	34.2	29.5	27.6	29.0	28.3	32.9	28.4	26.6	27.8	27.8	43.3	35.2	32.5	34.6	31.5
Second birth	24.2	21.8	22.0	22.8	22.4	23.7	21.0	21.5	22.0	22.0	27.1	25.7	24.5	27.1	25.0
Third birth..........	13.6	10.3	10.4	11.7	11.4	13.3	9.5	9.7	10.8	10.8	16.1	14.5	14.0	16.4	15.4
Fourth birth..........	7.2	3.9	3.8	4.5	4.5	6.8	3.4	3.3	3.9	4.0	10.0	6.7	6.3	7.7	7.4
Fifth birth	3.8	1.5	1.4	1.7	1.7	3.4	1.3	1.1	1.4	1.4	6.4	3.0	2.7	3.3	3.3
Sixth and seventh	3.2	1.0	0.8	1.0	1.0	2.7	0.8	0.7	0.7	0.8	7.0	2.1	1.8	2.1	2.1
Eighth and over	1.8	0.4	0.3	0.3	0.3	1.2	0.3	0.2	0.2	0.2	5.6	0.9	0.6	0.6	0.6

[1] Includes other races not shown separately.

Source: U.S. National Center for Health Statistics, *Vital Statistics of the United States*, annual; and *Monthly Vital Statistics Reports*.

No. 97. Live Births, by Race and Type of Hispanic Origin—Selected Characteristics: 1990 and 1991

[Represents registered births. Excludes births to nonresidents of the United States. Data are based on Hispanic origin of mother and beginning 1990, race of mother. Prior to 1990, data are for race of child and are not comparable. Hispanic origin data are available from only 23 States and the District of Columbia in 1985 and 48 States and DC in 1990.]

RACE AND HISPANIC ORIGIN	NUMBER OF BIRTHS (1,000)		BIRTHS TO TEENAGE MOTHERS, PERCENT OF TOTAL		BIRTHS TO UNMARRIED MOTHERS, PERCENT OF TOTAL		PERCENT OF MOTHERS BEGINNING PRENATAL CARE DURING—				PERCENT OF BIRTHS WITH LOW BIRTH WEIGHT [1]	
							First trimester		Third trimester or no care			
	1990	1991	1990	1991	1990	1991	1990	1991	1990	1991	1990	1991
Total	4,158	4,111	12.8	12.9	26.6	28.0	74.2	76.2	6.0	5.8	7.0	7.1
White	3,290	3,241	10.9	11.0	16.9	18.0	77.7	79.5	4.9	4.7	5.7	5.8
Black	684	683	23.1	23.1	66.7	68.2	60.7	61.9	10.9	10.7	13.3	13.6
American Indian, Eskimo, Aleut .	39	39	19.5	20.3	53.6	55.3	57.9	59.9	12.9	12.2	6.1	6.2
Asian and Pacific Islander [2] ...	142	145	5.7	5.8	(NA)	(NA)	(NA)	(NA)	(NA)	(NA)	(NA)	(NA)
Filipino	26	26	6.1	6.1	15.9	16.8	77.1	77.1	4.5	5.0	7.3	7.3
Chinese	23	22	1.2	1.1	5.0	5.5	81.3	82.3	3.4	3.4	4.7	5.1
Japanese	9	9	2.9	2.7	9.6	9.8	87.0	87.7	2.9	2.5	6.2	5.9
Hawaiian.	6	6	18.4	18.1	45.0	45.0	65.8	68.1	8.7	7.5	7.2	6.7
Hispanic origin [3]	595	623	16.8	17.2	36.7	38.5	60.2	61.0	12.0	11.0	6.1	6.1
Mexican	386	411	17.7	18.1	33.3	35.3	57.8	58.7	13.2	12.2	5.5	5.6
Puerto Rican	59	60	21.7	21.7	55.9	57.5	63.5	65.0	10.6	9.1	9.0	9.4
Cuban	11	11	7.7	7.1	18.2	19.5	84.8	85.4	2.8	2.4	5.7	5.6
Central and South American. .	83	87	9.0	9.4	41.2	43.1	61.5	63.4	10.9	9.5	5.8	5.9

NA Not available. [1] Births less than 2,500 grams (5 lb.-8 oz.). [2] Includes other races not shown separately. [3] Hispanic persons may be of any race. Includes other types, not shown separately.

No. 98. Live Births, by Place of Delivery, Median and Low Birth Weight, and Prenatal Care: 1970 to 1991

[Represents registered births. Excludes births to nonresidents of the United States. For total number of births, see table 90. See Appendix III]

YEAR	BIRTHS ATTENDED (1,000)				MEDIAN BIRTH WEIGHT [3]			PERCENT OF BIRTHS WITH LOW BIRTH WEIGHT [5]			PERCENT OF BIRTHS BY PERIOD IN WHICH PRENATAL CARE BEGAN	
	In hospital [1]	Not in hospital			Total [4]	White	Black	Total [3]	White	Black	1st trimester	3d trimester or no prenatal care
		Physician	Midwife and other [2]									
1970	3,708	5	18	7 lb.-4 oz. . .	7 lb.-5 oz. . .	6 lb.-14 oz. .	7.9	6.8	13.9	68.0	7.9
1975	3,105	11	28	7 lb.-5 oz. . .	7 lb.-7 oz. . .	6 lb.-15 oz. .	7.4	6.3	13.1	72.4	6.0
1980	3,576	12	24	7 lb.-7 oz. . .	7 lb.-8 oz. . .	7 lb.-0 oz. . .	6.8	5.7	12.5	76.3	5.1
1985	3,722	10	29	7 lb.-7 oz. . .	7 lb.-9 oz. . .	7 lb.-0 oz. . .	6.8	5.6	12.4	76.2	5.7
1986	3,720	9	27	7 lb.-7 oz. . .	7 lb.-9 oz. . .	7 lb.-0 oz. . .	6.8	5.6	12.5	75.9	6.0
1987	3,774	8	27	7 lb.-7 oz. . .	7 lb.-9 oz. . .	7 lb.-0 oz. . .	6.9	5.7	12.7	76.0	6.1
1988	3,872	9	28	7 lb.-7 oz. . .	7 lb.-9 oz. . .	7 lb.-0 oz. . .	6.9	5.6	13.0	75.9	6.1
1989	3,991	13	22	7 lb.-7 oz. . .	7 lb.-8 oz. . .	6 lb.-15 oz. .	7.0	5.7	13.2	73.9	6.3
1990	4,110	14	21	7 lb.-7 oz. . .	7 lb.-8 oz. . .	7 lb.-0 oz. . .	7.0	5.7	13.3	74.2	6.0
1991	4,064	46	22	7 lb.-7 oz. . .	7 lb.-8 oz. . .	6 lb.-15 oz. .	7.1	5.8	13.6	76.2	5.8

[1] Includes all births in hospitals or institutions and in clinics. [2] Includes births with attendant not specified. [3] Beginning 1989, median birth weight based on race of mother; prior to 1989, based on race of child. [4] Includes other races not shown separately. [5] Through 1975, births of 2,500 grams (5 lb.-8 oz.) or less at birth; thereafter, less than 2,500 grams.

Source of tables 98 and 99: U.S. National Center for Health Statistics, Vital Statistics of the United States, annual; Monthly Vital Statistics Report; and unpublished data.

No. 99. Cesarean Section Deliveries, by Age of Mother: 1970 to 1992

[Based on data collected from the National Hospital Discharge Survey, a sample survey of hospital records of patients discharged in year shown; subject to sampling variability. Beginning 1988, comparisons with data for earlier years should be made with caution as estimates of change may reflect improvements in the 1988 design rather than true changes in hospital use]

AGE OF MOTHER	1970	1980	1985	1986	1987	1988	1989	1990	1991	1992
Number of cesarean deliveries (1,000)	195	619	877	906	953	933	938	945	933	921
Rate: Mothers, all ages [1]	5.5	16.5	22.7	24.1	24.4	24.7	23.8	23.5	23.5	23.6
Under 20 years	3.9	14.5	16.1	18.3	18.5	19.5	18.1	16.6	18.2	17.5
20 to 24 years	4.9	15.8	21.2	21.9	22.9	20.1	21.1	21.0	21.0	21.4
25 to 29 years	5.9	16.7	22.9	25.3	23.7	26.7	24.8	23.3	24.3	23.2
30 to 34 years	7.5	18.0	26.6	26.2	28.3	28.0	26.6	27.8	26.7	27.1
35 years and over	8.3	20.6	30.7	32.6	31.6	32.1	30.3	31.4	28.4	30.1

[1] Cesarean rates are the number of cesarean deliveries per 100 total deliveries for specified category.
Source: U.S. National Center for Health Statistics, unpublished data.

No. 100. Births to Unmarried Women, by Race of Child and Age of Mother: 1970 to 1991

[Excludes births to nonresidents of United States. Data for 1970 include estimates for States in which marital status data were not reported. Beginning in 1980, marital status is inferred from a comparison of the child's and parents' surnames on the birth certificate for those States that do not report on marital status. No estimates included for misstatements on birth records or failures to register births. See also Appendix III and *Historical Statistics, Colonial Times to 1970*, series B 28-35]

RACE OF CHILD AND AGE OF MOTHER	1970	1980	1985	1990	1991	RACE OF CHILD AND AGE OF MOTHER	1970	1980	1985	1990	1991
NUMBER (1,000)						20 to 24 years	32	36	36	35	35
Total live births [1]	398.7	665.7	828.2	1,165.4	1,213.8	25 to 29 years	10	15	18	20	19
White	175.1	320.1	433.0	647.4	707.5	30 to 34 years	5	6	8	10	10
Black	215.1	325.7	365.5	472.7	463.8	35 years and over	3	2	3	5	5
Under 15 years old	9.5	9.0	9.4	10.7	11.0	AS PERCENT OF ALL BIRTHS IN RACIAL GROUPS					
15 to 19 years old	190.4	262.8	270.9	350.0	357.5						
20 to 24 years old	126.7	237.3	300.4	403.9	429.1	Total [1]	11	18	22	28	30
25 to 29 years old	40.6	99.6	152.0	230.0	234.6	White	6	11	15	20	22
30 to 34 years old	19.1	41.0	67.3	118.2	123.9	Black	38	55	60	65	68
35 years old and over	12.4	16.1	28.2	52.7	57.7	BIRTH RATE [2]					
PERCENT DISTRIBUTION						Total [1][3]	26.4	29.4	32.8	43.8	45.2
						White [3]	13.9	17.6	21.8	31.8	34.6
Total [1]	100	100	100	100	100	Black [3]	95.5	82.9	79.0	93.9	189.5
White	44	48	52	56	58	15 to 19 years	22.4	27.6	31.4	42.5	44.8
Black	54	49	44	41	38	20 to 24 years	38.4	40.9	46.5	65.1	68.0
Under 15 years	2	1	1	1	1	25 to 29 years	37.0	34.0	39.9	56.0	56.5
15 to 19 years	48	40	33	30	29	30 to 34 years	27.1	21.1	25.2	37.6	38.1

[1] Includes other races not shown separately.   [2] Rate per 1,000 unmarried women (never-married, widowed, and divorced) estimated as of July 1.   [3] Covers women aged 15 to 44 years.

Source: U.S. National Center for Health Statistics, *Vital Statistics of the United States*, annual; *Monthly Vital Statistics Report*; and unpublished data.

No. 101. Low Birth Weight and Births to Teenage Mothers and to Unmarried Women—States: 1980 and 1991

[Represents registered births. Excludes births to nonresidents of the United States. Based on 100 percent of births in all States and the District of Columbia. See Appendix III]

DIVISION AND STATE	PERCENT OF BIRTHS WITH LOW BIRTH WEIGHT[1] 1980	1991	BIRTHS TO TEENAGE MOTHERS, PERCENT OF TOTAL 1980	1991	BIRTHS TO UNMARRIED WOMEN, PERCENT OF TOTAL 1980	1991
U.S.	6.8	7.1	15.6	12.9	18.4	29.2
N.E.	6.2	(NA)	11.6	(NA)	15.5	(NA)
ME	6.5	5.4	15.3	10.9	13.9	24.1
NH	5.4	4.9	10.7	7.1	11.0	17.1
VT	5.9	5.7	13.0	9.3	13.7	22.7
MA	6.1	5.9	10.7	8.0	15.7	24.7
RI	6.3	6.0	12.3	9.8	15.7	26.8
CT	6.7	6.9	11.4	8.2	[2]17.9	27.1
M.A.	7.1	(NA)	12.6	(NA)	21.3	(NA)
NY	7.4	7.9	11.8	9.2	[2]23.8	33.5
NJ	7.2	7.4	12.3	8.4	21.1	26.1
PA	6.5	7.3	13.9	10.8	17.7	29.9
E.N.C.	6.7	(NA)	15.2	(NA)	18.0	(NA)
OH	6.8	7.5	15.7	14.0	[2]17.8	30.5
IN	6.3	6.7	17.3	14.4	15.5	28.2
IL	7.2	7.8	15.7	13.0	22.5	32.3
MI	6.9	7.8	14.0	13.2	[2]16.2	26.6
WI	5.4	6.1	12.3	10.3	13.9	25.0
W.N.C.	5.7	(NA)	13.5	(NA)	13.1	(NA)
MN	5.1	5.3	10.4	8.1	11.4	22.0
IA	5.0	5.7	12.5	10.5	10.3	22.0
MO	6.6	7.5	16.9	14.4	17.6	29.9
ND	4.9	4.8	10.9	8.7	9.2	21.1
SD	5.1	5.4	13.5	11.0	13.4	24.7
NE	5.6	5.6	12.1	9.8	11.6	21.3
KS	5.8	6.2	15.0	12.2	12.3	22.4
S.A.	8.0	(NA)	18.3	(NA)	22.2	(NA)
DE	7.7	7.9	16.7	12.2	[2]24.2	32.0
MD	8.2	8.1	14.8	10.4	[2]25.2	30.3
DC	12.8	15.4	20.7	17.4	56.5	65.9
VA	7.5	7.2	15.5	11.5	19.2	27.3
WV	6.7	6.8	20.1	17.6	13.1	26.7
NC	7.9	8.4	19.2	16.2	19.0	30.9
SC	8.6	9.2	19.8	17.0	23.0	34.1
GA	8.6	8.6	20.7	16.7	23.2	33.8
FL	7.6	7.4	18.2	13.9	23.0	32.2
E.S.C.	7.8	(NA)	21.0	(NA)	20.9	(NA)
KY	6.8	7.2	21.1	17.4	15.1	25.4
TN	8.0	8.8	19.9	17.7	19.9	32.1
AL	7.9	8.7	20.6	18.5	22.2	31.5
MS	8.7	9.7	23.2	21.7	28.0	42.0
W.S.C.	7.3	(NA)	19.1	(NA)	15.8	(NA)
AR	7.6	8.2	21.6	19.9	20.5	29.1
LA	8.6	9.4	20.1	17.6	23.4	38.4
OK	6.8	6.6	19.6	17.2	14.0	27.2
TX	6.9	7.1	18.3	16.0	[2]13.3	17.9
Mountain	6.6	(NA)	14.3	(NA)	12.7	(NA)
MT	5.6	5.6	12.4	11.5	[2]12.5	25.0
ID	5.3	5.8	13.1	13.3	7.9	17.8
WY	7.3	7.0	15.5	14.0	8.2	22.1
CO	8.2	8.2	13.3	11.8	13.0	23.7
NM	7.6	7.1	18.2	16.5	16.1	38.1
AZ	6.2	6.4	16.5	14.8	18.7	34.6
UT	5.2	6.0	11.0	10.8	6.2	14.3
NV	6.6	7.2	15.4	12.9	[2]13.5	32.5
Pacific	5.8	(NA)	13.6	(NA)	19.6	(NA)
WA	5.1	5.1	12.5	10.8	13.6	25.1
OR	4.9	4.9	13.3	12.3	14.8	26.4
CA	5.9	5.8	13.9	11.8	[2]21.4	33.3
AK	5.4	4.7	11.8	10.5	15.1	26.4
HI	7.1	6.8	11.5	10.6	17.6	25.4

NA Not available.   [1] Less than 2,500 grams (5 pounds-8 ounces).   [2] Marital status of mother is inferred.

Source: U.S. National Center for Health Statistics, *Vital Statistics of the United States*, annual; and *Monthly Vital Statistics Report*.

No. 102. Women Who Have Had a Child in the Last Year, by Age: 1980 to 1992

[See headnote, table 103]

AGE OF MOTHER	WOMEN WHO HAD A CHILD IN LAST YEAR (1,000)			TOTAL BIRTHS PER 1,000 WOMEN			FIRST BIRTHS PER 1,000 WOMEN		
	1980	1990	1992	1980	1990	1992	1980	1990	1992
Total..........	3,247	3,913	3,688	71.1	67.0	62.9	28.5	26.4	24.8
15 to 29 years old [1]...	2,476	2,568	2,346	103.7	90.8	85.9	48.6	43.2	40.9
15 to 19 years old .	(NA)	338	311	(NA)	39.8	38.0	(NA)	30.1	27.9
20 to 24 years old [2].	1,396	1,038	940	96.6	113.4	103.4	(NA)	51.8	49.4
25 to 29 years old ..	1,081	1,192	1,094	114.8	112.1	109.0	(NA)	46.2	43.7
30 to 44 years old....	770	1,346	1,342	35.4	44.7	42.9	6.3	10.6	10.7
30 to 34 years old ..	519	892	856	60.0	80.4	76.1	(NA)	21.9	21.8
35 to 39 years old ..	192	377	404	26.9	37.3	38.0	(NA)	6.5	6.4
40 to 44 years old ..	59	77	82	9.9	8.6	8.7	(NA)	1.2	2.3

NA Not available. [1] For 1980-88, 18 to 29 years old. [2] For 1980-88, 18 to 24 years old.

Source: U.S. Bureau of the Census, *Current Population Reports*, P20-454; and unpublished data.

No. 103. Characteristics of Women Who Have Had a Child in the Last Year: 1992

[As of June. Covers civilian noninstitutional population. Since the number of women who had a birth during the 12-month period was tabulated and not the actual numbers of births, some small underestimation of fertility for this period may exist due to the omission of: (1) Multiple births, (2) Two or more live births spaced within the 12-month period (the woman is counted only once), (3) Women who had births in the period and who did not survive to the survey date, (4) Women who were in institutions and therefore not in the survey universe. These losses may be somewhat offset by the inclusion in the CPS of births to immigrants who did not have their children born in the United States and births to nonresident women. These births would not have been recorded in the vital registration system. Based on Current Population Survey (CPS); see text, section 1, and Appendix III]

CHARACTERISTIC	TOTAL, 15 TO 44 YEARS OLD			15 TO 29 YEARS OLD			30 TO 44 YEARS OLD		
	Num-ber of women (1,000)	Women who have had a child in the last year		Num-ber of women (1,000)	Women who have had a child in the last year		Num-ber of women (1,000)	Women who have had a child in the last year	
		Total births per 1,000 women	First births per 1,000 women		Total births per 1,000 women	First births per 1,000 women		Total births per 1,000 women	First births per 1,000 women
Total [1]..................	58,614	63	25	27,312	86	41	31,302	43	11
White.....................	48,157	62	25	22,102	82	41	26,056	44	11
Black.....................	8,017	69	22	4,070	106	39	3,947	31	5
Asian or Pacific Islander..........	1,827	64	26	832	69	30	996	59	16
Hispanic [2]	5,555	95	35	2,915	125	60	2,640	62	8
Currently married...............	31,878	88	32	9,209	176	80	22,668	52	13
Married, spouse present..........	29,531	90	33	8,338	180	84	21,193	54	14
Married, spouse absent [3]........	2,347	65	19	871	132	45	1,475	26	3
Widowed or divorced.............	5,383	27	10	973	75	31	4,409	16	5
Never married.................	21,354	35	17	17,129	38	20	4,225	22	5
Educational attainment:									
Less than high school...........	12,159	67	24	8,422	79	33	3,737	40	4
High school, 4 years...........	19,063	65	25	7,762	113	50	11,301	33	7
College: 1 or more years........	27,392	60	25	11,128	73	40	16,264	51	15
No degree.............	12,422	59	24	6,362	72	36	6,060	45	10
Associate degree	3,982	56	23	1,420	87	46	2,562	38	11
Bachelor's degree.......	8,173	65	27	2,864	70	44	5,310	63	18
Grad. or prof. degree......	2,814	55	30	482	65	48	2,332	53	27
Labor force status:									
Employed	38,139	45	19	15,906	61	32	22,233	34	11
Unemployed	3,849	69	31	2,418	88	45	1,432	37	9
Not in labor force.............	16,626	102	35	8,988	129	56	7,637	71	12
Occupation of employed women:									
Managerial-professional.........	9,923	47	22	2,918	68	43	7,005	38	13
Tech., sales, admin. support.......	16,818	47	21	7,602	58	32	9,216	37	12
Service workers.............	7,102	46	16	3,763	61	26	3,339	28	4
Farming, forestry, and fishing	512	44	10	207	78	25	306	21	-
Precision prod., craft, repair	738	44	19	238	54	29	500	39	14
Operators, fabricators, laborers.....	3,047	31	12	1,179	61	25	1,868	12	4
Family income: Under $10,000.......	7,500	95	29	4,426	133	47	3,074	41	3
$10,000 to $19,999.............	9,201	70	29	4,946	103	50	4,255	32	5
$20,000 to $24,999.............	4,964	66	27	2,480	100	47	2,484	33	7
$25,000 to $29,999.............	4,492	57	21	2,086	86	40	2,406	32	5
$30,000 to $34,999.............	4,631	61	22	2,078	89	41	2,553	37	6
$35,000 to $49,999.............	10,677	58	22	4,444	69	37	6,233	50	11
$50,000 to $74,999.............	8,821	53	24	3,407	54	34	5,414	52	18
$75,000 and over..............	5,259	43	21	2,053	29	20	3,205	52	21

- Represents or rounds to zero. [1] Includes women of other races and women with family income not reported, not shown separately. [2] Persons of Hispanic origin may be of any race. [3] Includes separated women.

Source: U.S. Bureau of the Census, *Current Population Reports*, P20-454; and unpublished data.

No. 104. Women Who Have Had a Child in the Last Year, by Age and Labor Force Status: 1980 to 1992

[See headnote, table 103]

YEAR	TOTAL, 18 TO 44 YEARS OLD			18 TO 29 YEARS OLD			30 TO 44 YEARS OLD		
	Number (1,000)	In the labor force		Number (1,000)	In the labor force		Number (1,000)	In the labor force	
		Number (1,000)	Percent		Number (1,000)	Percent		Number (1,000)	Percent
1980	3,247	1,233	38	2,476	947	38	770	287	37
1985	3,497	1,691	48	2,512	1,204	48	984	488	50
1986	3,625	1,805	50	2,452	1,185	48	1,174	620	53
1987	3,701	1,881	51	2,521	1,258	50	1,180	623	53
1988 [1]	3,667	1,866	51	2,384	1,177	49	1,283	688	54
1990 [1]	3,913	2,068	53	2,568	1,275	50	1,346	793	59
1992 [1]	3,688	1,985	54	2,346	1,182	50	1,342	802	60

[1] Lower age limit is 15 years old.
Source: U.S. Bureau of the Census, Current Population Reports, P20-454; and unpublished data.

No. 105. Childless Women and Children Ever Born, by Race, Age, and Marital Status: 1992

[See headnote, table 103]

CHARACTERISTIC	Total number of women (1,000)	WOMEN BY NUMBER OF CHILDREN EVER BORN (percent)				CHILDREN EVER BORN	
		Total	None	One	Two or more	Total number (1,000)	Per 1,000 women
ALL RACES [1]							
Women ever married	37,260	100	18	23	59	65,874	1,768
15 to 19 years old	339	100	44	46	10	228	673
20 to 24 years old	3,064	100	38	34	28	3,046	994
25 to 29 years old	6,780	100	28	30	43	9,237	1,362
30 to 34 years old	9,050	100	17	23	60	15,988	1,767
35 to 39 years old	9,337	100	12	19	69	18,866	2,020
40 to 44 years old	8,690	100	11	18	71	18,509	2,130
Women never married	21,354	100	81	10	9	7,440	348
15 to 19 years old	7,847	100	95	4	1	511	65
20 to 24 years old	6,023	100	80	13	7	1,827	303
25 to 29 years old	3,259	100	70	13	17	1,926	591
30 to 34 years old	2,199	100	64	15	22	1,728	786
35 to 39 years old	1,300	100	65	13	22	1,016	782
40 to 44 years old	726	100	75	11	15	433	596
WHITE							
Women ever married	32,165	100	19	23	58	55,482	1,725
15 to 19 years old	313	100	45	47	8	200	638
20 to 24 years old	2,708	100	40	35	26	2,546	940
25 to 29 years old	5,929	100	28	30	41	7,827	1,320
30 to 34 years old	7,799	100	17	23	60	13,650	1,750
35 to 39 years old	7,993	100	13	19	68	15,753	1,971
40 to 44 years old	7,422	100	12	17	72	15,507	2,089
Women never married	15,993	100	88	7	5	3,006	188
15 to 19 years old	6,191	100	96	3	1	272	44
20 to 24 years old	4,674	100	87	9	4	814	174
25 to 29 years old	2,287	100	80	10	10	832	364
30 to 34 years old	1,476	100	77	13	10	641	434
35 to 39 years old	837	100	82	8	10	307	367
40 to 44 years old	529	100	88	6	6	140	265
BLACK							
Women ever married	3,585	100	11	23	66	7,686	2,144
15 to 19 years old	16	100	(B)	(B)	(B)	16	(B)
20 to 24 years old	238	100	22	28	50	384	1,609
25 to 29 years old	608	100	19	27	54	1,072	1,763
30 to 34 years old	858	100	12	22	66	1,707	1,988
35 to 39 years old	934	100	7	22	71	2,255	2,416
40 to 44 years old	930	100	7	22	72	2,251	2,421
Women never married	4,432	100	53	20	27	4,215	951
15 to 19 years old	1,297	100	88	9	4	226	174
20 to 24 years old	1,097	100	47	29	23	966	881
25 to 29 years old	813	100	41	23	37	1,028	1,264
30 to 34 years old	634	100	31	21	49	1,039	1,639
35 to 39 years old	412	100	30	24	47	677	1,645
40 to 44 years old	179	100	34	26	41	278	1,555

B Base figure too small to meet statistical standards for reliability.   [1] Includes other races, not shown separately.
Source: U.S. Bureau of the Census, Current Population Reports, series P20; and unpublished data.

No. 106. Lifetime Births Expected per 1,000 Wives: 1971 to 1992
[See headnote, table 103]

YEAR	LIFETIME BIRTHS TO ALL WIVES [1] AGED—			LIFETIME BIRTHS TO WHITE WIVES AGED—			LIFETIME BIRTHS TO BLACK WIVES AGED—			LIFETIME BIRTHS TO HISPANIC [2] WIVES AGED—		
	18 to 24 yrs. old	25 to 29 yrs. old	30 to 34 yrs. old	18 to 24 yrs. old	25 to 29 yrs. old	30 to 34 yrs. old	18 to 24 yrs. old	25 to 29 yrs. old	30 to 34 yrs. old	18 to 24 yrs. old	25 to 29 yrs. old	30 to 34 yrs. old
1971....	2,375	2,619	2,989	2,353	2,577	2,936	2,623	3,112	3,714	(NA)	(NA)	(NA)
1975....	2,173	2,260	2,610	2,147	2,233	2,564	2,489	2,587	3,212	2,223	2,607	3,238
1980....	2,134	2,166	2,248	2,130	2,146	2,223	2,155	2,426	2,522	2,428	2,495	2,909
1985....	2,183	2,236	2,167	2,177	2,227	2,139	2,242	2,259	2,521	2,367	2,628	2,712
1990....	2,244	2,285	2,277	2,218	2,272	2,257	2,509	2,443	2,579	2,404	2,482	2,824
1992....	2,279	2,271	2,218	2,274	2,259	2,208	2,353	2,389	2,362	2,511	2,437	2,600

NA Not available. [1] Includes other races not shown separately. [2] Persons of Hispanic origin may be of any race.

No. 107. Lifetime Births Expected by Women, 18 to 34 Years Old, by Selected Characteristics: 1992
[As of **June.** Covers women in the civilian noninstitutional population. Based on Current Population Survey; see text, section 1, and Appendix III]

CHARACTERISTIC	Women reporting on birth expec- tations (1,000)	RATE PER 1,000 WOMEN			PERCENTAGE EXPECTING—	
		Births to date	Future births expected	Lifetime births expected	No lifetime births	No future births
Total [1]	24,223	1,135	963	2,098	9.3	48.3
White.	20,141	1,077	1,014	2,091	9.3	46.1
Black.	3,217	1,508	628	2,136	9.3	63.4
Hispanic [2].	2,357	1,493	838	2,331	5.7	51.4
Not a high school graduate	3,599	1,776	616	2,393	7.6	63.8
High school, 4 years............	8,760	1,325	718	2,043	9.0	57.9
College: 1 or more years..........	11,864	800	1,249	2,049	10.0	36.5
Some college, no degree	5,871	848	1,216	2,064	10.0	39.2
Associate degree	1,731	1,020	1,018	2,038	8.9	43.4
Bachelor's degree............	3,466	663	1,380	2,043	10.3	31.0
Graduate or professional degree ...	795	563	1,427	1,990	12.0	26.0
In labor force.................	17,834	929	1,069	1,998	10.5	44.1
Employed	16,130	903	1,077	1,980	10.7	43.6
Unemployed................	1,705	1,176	991	2,167	8.4	49.3
Not in labor force...............	6,389	1,710	667	2,377	6.0	60.1
Managerial and professional........	3,760	725	1,232	1,957	11.3	36.8
Technical, sales, and admin. support..	7,511	835	1,126	1,962	10.2	41.0
Service workers...............	3,127	1,097	974	2,071	9.5	48.2
Farming, forestry, and fishing......	198	1,426	972	2,398	14.1	55.5
Precision production, craft, and repair .	299	1,135	714	1,849	12.7	59.5
Operators, fabricators, and laborers. ..	1,235	1,223	675	1,897	13.5	62.4

[1] Includes other races not shown separately. [2] Persons of Hispanic origin may be of any race.
Source of tables 106 and 107: U.S. Bureau of the Census, *Current Population Reports*, series P20, unpublished data.

No. 108. Pregnancies, Number and Outcome: 1976 to 1988
[**Live births:** source of data is statistics of registered births published annually by National Center for Health Statistics (NCHS). **Induced abortions:** derived from published reports by the Alan Guttmacher Institute. **Fetal losses:** based on the National Survey of Family Growth conducted by NCHS]

YEAR	NUMBER (1,000)				RATE PER 1,000 WOMEN, 15 TO 44 YEARS OLD			
	Total	Live births	Induced abortions	Fetal losses	Total	Live births	Induced abortions	Fetal losses
1976	5,002	3,168	1,179	655	102.7	65.0	24.2	13.4
1977	5,331	3,327	1,317	687	107.0	66.8	26.4	13.8
1978	5,433	3,333	1,410	690	106.7	65.5	27.7	13.5
1979	5,714	3,494	1,498	722	109.9	67.2	28.8	13.9
1980	5,913	3,612	1,554	747	111.9	68.4	29.4	14.1
1981	5,958	3,629	1,577	751	110.7	67.4	29.3	14.0
1982	6,024	3,681	1,574	769	110.2	67.3	28.8	14.0
1983	5,975	3,639	1,575	761	108.0	65.8	28.5	13.8
1984	6,018	3,669	1,577	771	107.3	65.4	28.1	13.8
1985	6,144	3,761	1,589	795	108.2	66.2	28.0	14.0
1986	6,129	3,757	1,574	798	106.6	65.4	27.4	13.9
1987	6,183	3,809	1,559	815	106.7	65.7	26.9	14.1
1988	6,341	3,910	1,591	840	109.0	67.2	27.3	14.4

Source: U.S. National Center for Health Statistics, *Monthly Vital Statistics Report*, vol. 41, No. 6, Supplement.

No. 109. Pregnancies, by Outcome, Age of Woman, and Race: 1988
[See headnote, table 108]

ITEM	Total	Under 15 years old	15 to 19 years old	20 to 24 years old	25 to 29 years old	30 to 34 years old	35 to 39 years old	40 years old and over
NUMBER (1,000)								
Total, all pregnancies.	6,341	27	988	1,774	1,821	1,195	456	79
Live births.	3,910	11	478	1,067	1,239	804	270	41
Induced abortions.	1,591	14	393	520	347	197	96	24
Fetal losses	840	3	117	187	234	194	91	14
White, all pregnancies	4,698	11	673	1,270	1,406	927	350	59
Live births.	3,046	4	315	805	1,011	661	218	32
Induced abortions.	1,026	6	264	332	219	125	63	17
Fetal losses	626	2	94	133	177	141	69	10
Other races, all pregnancies	1,643	16	315	504	415	268	106	20
Live births.	863	7	163	263	229	142	52	9
Induced abortions.	565	8	129	187	129	72	33	7
Fetal losses	214	1	23	54	58	53	21	4
RATE PER 1,000 WOMEN								
Total, all pregnancies.	109.0	3.3	110.8	185.3	166.7	109.7	47.2	9.6
Live births.	67.2	1.3	53.6	111.5	113.4	73.7	27.9	5.0
Induced abortions.	27.3	1.7	44.0	54.2	31.8	18.1	9.9	3.0
Fetal losses	14.4	0.3	13.2	19.6	21.5	17.8	9.4	1.7
White, all pregnancies	97.2	1.8	93.4	161.7	155.3	102.2	43.2	8.4
Live births.	63.0	0.6	43.7	102.5	111.6	72.9	26.9	4.6
Induced abortions.	21.2	0.9	36.6	42.3	24.1	13.8	7.8	2.4
Fetal losses	13.0	0.2	13.1	16.9	19.5	15.5	8.5	1.5
Other races, all pregnancies	166.5	9.7	184.3	292.3	221.9	146.5	68.1	16.6
Live births.	87.5	4.0	95.3	152.3	122.3	77.8	33.4	7.3
Induced abortions.	57.3	4.9	75.5	108.5	68.8	39.6	21.0	6.2
Fetal losses	21.7	0.7	13.6	31.5	30.8	29.1	13.8	3.0
PERCENT DISTRIBUTION								
Total, all pregnancies.	100.0	100.0	100.0	100.0	100.0	100.0	100.0	100.0
Live births.	61.7	39.2	48.4	60.2	68.1	67.2	59.1	51.6
Induced abortions.	25.1	50.5	39.7	29.3	19.1	16.5	21.0	30.9
Fetal losses	13.3	10.3	11.9	10.6	12.9	16.2	19.9	17.4
White, all pregnancies	100.0	100.0	100.0	100.0	100.0	100.0	100.0	100.0
Live births.	64.8	35.6	46.9	63.4	71.9	71.3	62.2	54.1
Induced abortions.	21.8	50.2	39.2	26.2	15.6	13.5	18.1	28.7
Fetal losses	13.3	14.2	14.0	10.5	12.6	15.2	19.8	17.2
Other races, all pregnancies	100.0	100.0	100.0	100.0	100.0	100.0	100.0	100.0
Live births.	52.6	41.8	51.7	52.1	55.1	53.1	49.0	44.2
Induced abortions.	34.4	50.7	41.0	37.1	31.0	27.0	30.8	37.6
Fetal losses	13.1	7.5	7.4	10.8	13.9	19.9	20.2	18.2

Source: U.S. National Center for Health Statistics, *Monthly Vital Statistics Report*, vol. 41, No. 6.

No. 110. Contraceptive Use by Women, 15 to 44 Years Old: 1982 and 1988
[Based on the 1982 and 1988 National Survey of Family Growth; see Appendix III]

CONTRACEPTIVE STATUS AND METHOD	All women, 1982	1988 All women[1]	AGE 15-24 years	AGE 25-34 years	AGE 35-44 years	RACE White	RACE Black	MARITAL STATUS Never married	MARITAL STATUS Currently married	MARITAL STATUS Formerly married
All women (1,000).	54,099	57,900	18,592	21,726	17,582	47,077	7,679	21,058	29,147	7,695
PERCENT DISTRIBUTION										
Sterile	27.2	29.7	3.1	27.0	61.3	30.5	29.6	5.2	44.0	42.6
Surgically sterile	25.7	28.3	2.4	26.0	58.7	29.2	27.8	4.3	42.4	40.9
Noncontraceptively sterile [2] . . .	6.6	4.7	0.2	2.7	12.0	4.7	5.7	0.9	6.2	9.7
Contraceptively sterile [3]	19.0	23.6	2.2	23.3	46.7	24.5	22.1	3.4	36.2	31.3
Nonsurgically sterile [4].	1.5	1.4	0.7	0.9	2.7	1.3	1.8	1.0	1.6	1.7
Pregnant, postpartum	5.0	4.8	5.0	7.6	1.1	4.8	5.0	2.4	7.1	2.5
Seeking pregnancy	4.2	3.8	2.7	5.8	2.4	3.7	3.9	1.3	6.0	2.0
Other nonusers	26.9	25.0	45.7	16.7	13.5	23.8	26.9	52.5	4.8	26.6
Not sexually active [5]	19.5	19.0	37.9	10.3	8.5	18.1	16.7	43.5	0.3	19.5
Sexually active [5]	7.4	6.5	7.8	6.4	5.0	5.7	10.2	9.0	4.5	7.1
Nonsurgical contraceptors	36.7	36.7	43.5	43.0	21.6	37.2	34.6	38.5	38.1	26.3
Pill	15.6	18.5	29.7	21.6	3.0	18.4	21.6	24.7	15.1	14.5
IUD.	4.0	1.2	0.1	1.4	2.1	1.1	1.7	0.6	1.5	2.1
Diaphragm	4.5	3.5	1.3	4.8	4.1	3.8	1.1	2.1	4.6	3.0
Condom.	6.7	8.8	9.5	9.1	7.7	9.2	5.8	8.2	10.6	3.4
Foam	1.3	0.6	0.3	0.8	0.8	0.6	0.6	0.2	1.0	0.5
Rhythm [6]	2.2	1.4	0.6	1.7	1.8	1.4	1.2	0.6	2.1	1.1
Other methods [7]	2.5	2.6	2.0	3.6	2.2	2.5	2.6	2.1	3.2	1.7

[1] Includes other races, not shown separately.   [2] Persons who had sterilizing operation and who gave as one reason that they had medical problems with their female organs.   [3] Includes all other sterilization operations, and sterilization of the husband or current partner.   [4] Persons sterile from illness, accident, or congenital conditions.   [5] Those having intercourse in the last 3 months before the survey.   [6] Periodic abstinence and natural family planning.   [7] Withdrawal, douche, suppository, and less frequently used methods.

Source: U.S. National Center for Health Statistics, *Advance Data from Vital and Health Statistics*, No. 182.

No. 111. Abortions—Number, Rate, and Ratio, by Race: 1975 to 1992

[Refers to women 15 to 44 years old at time of abortion]

	ALL RACES				WHITE				BLACK AND OTHER			
	Women 15-44 years old (1,000)	Abortions			Women 15-44 years old (1,000)	Abortions			Women 15-44 years old (1,000)	Abortions		
YEAR		Num-ber (1,000)	Rate per 1,000 women	Ratio per 1,000 live births [1]		Num-ber (1,000)	Rate per 1,000 women	Ratio per 1,000 live births [1]		Num-ber (1,000)	Rate per 1,000 women	Ratio per 1,000 live births [1]
1975 ..	47,606	1,034	21.7	331	40,857	701	17.2	276	6,749	333	49.3	565
1978 ..	50,920	1,410	27.7	413	43,427	969	22.3	356	7,493	440	58.7	665
1979 ..	52,016	1,498	28.8	420	44,266	1,062	24.0	373	7,750	435	56.2	625
1980 ..	53,048	1,554	29.3	428	44,942	1,094	24.3	376	8,106	460	56.5	642
1981 ..	53,901	1,577	29.3	430	45,494	1,108	24.3	377	8,407	470	55.9	645
1982 ..	54,679	1,574	28.8	428	46,049	1,095	23.8	373	8,630	479	55.5	646
1983 [2] ..	55,340	1,575	28.5	436	46,506	1,084	23.3	376	8,834	491	55.5	670
1984 ..	56,061	1,577	28.1	423	47,023	1,087	23.1	366	9,038	491	54.3	646
1985 ..	56,754	1,589	28.0	422	47,512	1,076	22.6	360	9,242	513	55.5	659
1986 [2] ..	57,483	1,574	27.4	416	48,010	1,045	21.8	350	9,473	529	55.9	661
1987 ..	57,964	1,559	27.1	405	48,288	1,017	21.1	338	9,676	542	56.0	648
1988 ..	58,192	1,591	27.3	401	48,325	1,026	21.2	333	9,867	565	57.3	638
1989 [2] ..	58,365	1,557	26.8	380	48,104	1,006	20.9	309	10,261	561	54.7	650
1990 [2] ..	58,700	1,609	27.4	389	48,224	1,039	21.5	318	10,476	570	54.4	655
1991 ..	59,076	1,557	26.3	378	(NA)	(NA)	(NA)	(NA)	(NA)	(NA)	(NA)	(NA)
1992 ..	59,008	1,529	25.9	379	(NA)	(NA)	(NA)	(NA)	(NA)	(NA)	(NA)	(NA)

NA Not available. [1] Live births are those which occurred from July 1 of year shown through June 30 of the following year (to match time of conception with abortions). Births are classified by race of child 1972-1988, and by race of mother after 1988. [2] Total numbers of abortions in 1983 and 1986 have been estimated by interpolation; 1989 and 1990 have been estimated using trends in CDC data.

No. 112. Abortions, by Selected Characteristics: 1980 to 1990

[Number of abortions from surveys conducted by source; characteristics from the U.S. Centers for Disea abortion surveillance summaries, with adjustments for changes in States reporting data to the CDC each year]

CHARACTERISTIC	NUMBER (1,000)			PERCENT DISTRIBUTION			ABORTION RATIO [1]		
	1980	1985	1990 [1]	1980	1985	1990 [1]	1980	1985	1990 [1]
Total abortions	1,554	1,589	1,609	100	100	100	300	297	280
Age of woman:									
Less than 15 years old	15	17	13	1	1	1	607	624	515
15 to 19 years old	445	399	351	29	25	22	451	462	403
20 to 24 years old	549	548	532	35	35	33	310	328	328
25 to 29 years old	304	336	360	20	21	22	213	219	224
30 to 34 years old	153	181	216	10	11	13	213	203	196
35 to 39 years old	67	87	108	4	5	7	317	280	249
40 years old and over	21	21	29	1	1	2	461	409	354
Race of woman:									
White....................	1,094	1,076	1,039	70	68	65	274	265	241
Black and other	460	513	570	30	32	35	392	397	396
Marital status of woman:									
Married..................	320	281	284	21	18	18	98	88	88
Unmarried................	1,234	1,307	1,325	79	82	82	649	605	527
Number of prior live births:									
None....................	900	872	780	58	55	49	365	358	316
One.....................	305	349	396	20	22	25	208	219	230
Two.....................	216	240	280	14	15	17	283	288	292
Three...................	83	85	102	5	5	6	288	281	279
Four or more.............	51	43	50	3	3	3	251	230	223
Number of prior induced abortions:									
None....................	1,043	944	891	67	60	55	(NA)	(NA)	(NA)
One.....................	373	416	443	24	26	28	(NA)	(NA)	(NA)
Two or more	138	228	275	9	14	17	(NA)	(NA)	(NA)
Weeks of gestation: [2]									
Less than 9 weeks	800	811	850	52	51	53	(NA)	(NA)	(NA)
9 to 10 weeks	417	425	418	27	27	26	(NA)	(NA)	(NA)
11 to 12 weeks	202	198	185	13	12	12	(NA)	(NA)	(NA)
13 weeks or more	136	154	155	9	10	10	(NA)	(NA)	(NA)
One.....................	373	416	(NA)	24	26	(NA)	(NA)	(NA)	(NA)
Two or more	138	228	(NA)	9	14	(NA)	(NA)	(NA)	(NA)
Weeks of gestation: [2]									
Less than 9 weeks	800	811	(NA)	52	51	(NA)	(NA)	(NA)	(NA)
9 to 10 weeks	417	425	(NA)	27	27	(NA)	(NA)	(NA)	(NA)
11 to 12 weeks	202	198	(NA)	13	12	(NA)	(NA)	(NA)	(NA)
13 weeks or more	136	154	(NA)	9	10	(NA)	(NA)	(NA)	(NA)

NA Not available. [1] Number of abortions per 1,000 abortions and live births. Live births are those which occurred from July 1 of year shown through June 30 of the following year (to match time of conception with abortions). [2] Beginning 1985, data not exactly comparable with prior years because of a change in the method of calculation.

Source of tables 111 and 112: S.K. Henshaw and J. Van Vort, eds., *Abortion Factbook, 1992 Edition: Readings, Trends, and State and Local Data to 1988*, The Alan Guttmacher Institute, New York, NY, 1992 (copyright); S.K. Henshaw and J. Van Vort, *Abortion Services in the United States, 1991 and 1992; Family Perspectives, 26:100, 1994;* and unpublished data.

Vital Statistics

No. 113. Abortions—Number, Rate, and Abortion/Live Birth Ratio, by State: 1980 to 1992

[Number of abortions from surveys of hospitals, clinics, and physicians identified as providers of abortion services conducted by The Alan Guttmacher Institute. Abortion rates are computed per 1,000 women 15 to 44 years of age on **July 1** of specified year; abortion ratios are computed as the number of abortions per 1,000 live births from **July 1** of year shown to **June 30** of following year, by State of occurrence]

DIVISION, REGION, AND STATE	NUMBER OF ABORTIONS (1,000)			RATE PER 1,000 WOMEN, 15 TO 44 YEARS OLD			RATIO: ABORTIONS PER 1,000 LIVE BIRTHS		
	1980	1985	1992	1980	1985	1992	1980	1985	1992
United States	**1,554**	**1,589**	**1,529**	**29.3**	**28.0**	**25.9**	**428**	**422**	**379**
Northeast	**396**	**407**	**379**	**34.9**	**(NA)**	**32.1**	**604**	**(NA)**	**506**
New England	**84**	**85**	**78**	**28.9**	**28.6**	**25.2**	**530**	**504**	**429**
Maine	5	5	4	18.6	18.6	14.7	289	308	282
New Hampshire	5	7	4	21.1	29.0	14.6	347	419	269
Vermont	4	3	3	30.4	26.2	21.2	466	448	393
Massachusetts	46	40	41	33.5	29.3	28.4	609	533	472
Rhode Island	7	8	7	30.7	35.5	30.0	529	572	461
Connecticut	19	22	20	25.6	29.3	26.2	561	550	444
Middle Atlantic	**312**	**322**	**300**	**37.0**	**37.6**	**34.6**	**627**	**607**	**530**
New York	188	195	195	45.8	47.4	46.2	780	746	694
New Jersey	56	69	55	32.8	39.6	31.0	591	672	460
Pennsylvania	69	57	50	26.1	21.3	18.6	423	348	302
Midwest	**318**	**289**	**262**	**23.3**	**(NA)**	**18.9**	**336**	**(NA)**	**287**
East North Central	**243**	**221**	**205**	**24.9**	**22.1**	**20.7**	**369**	**356**	**313**
Ohio	67	57	50	26.8	22.4	19.5	397	357	294
Indiana	20	16	16	15.3	12.2	12.0	227	202	185
Illinois	69	65	68	25.9	23.8	25.4	374	372	361
Michigan	65	64	56	29.7	28.7	25.2	457	486	393
Wisconsin	22	18	15	20.1	15.7	13.6	292	246	223
West North Central	**75**	**68**	**57**	**19.2**	**16.7**	**14.3**	**260**	**252**	**221**
Minnesota	20	17	16	20.7	16.6	15.6	288	257	251
Iowa	9	10	7	14.3	15.0	11.4	195	248	185
Missouri	22	20	14	19.4	17.3	11.6	273	261	175
North Dakota	3	3	1	21.5	18.5	10.7	235	230	149
South Dakota	1	2	1	9.0	10.6	6.8	103	140	92
Nebraska	6	7	6	17.9	18.2	15.7	227	268	246
Kansas	14	10	13	25.6	18.2	22.4	343	264	353
South	**457**	**453**	**450**	**25.9**	**(NA)**	**22.0**	**369**	**(NA)**	**323**
South Atlantic	**255**	**257**	**269**	**29.4**	**27.1**	**25.9**	**462**	**429**	**397**
Delaware	4	5	6	25.9	30.9	35.2	395	451	502
Maryland	31	30	31	29.2	26.9	26.4	571	480	454
District of Columbia	29	24	21	168.3	145.9	138.4	1,569	1,186	1,104
Virginia	32	34	35	24.2	24.0	22.7	417	412	373
West Virginia	3	5	3	6.9	10.1	7.7	104	185	134
North Carolina	32	34	36	22.8	22.6	22.4	377	379	357
South Carolina	14	11	12	18.2	13.7	14.2	274	228	229
Georgia	38	38	40	28.4	26.1	24.0	395	397	350
Florida	74	77	85	35.5	31.8	30.0	547	465	438
East South Central	**65**	**57**	**54**	**19.2**	**15.8**	**14.9**	**271**	**258**	**228**
Kentucky	13	10	10	15.1	11.0	11.4	215	189	191
Tennessee	26	22	19	23.6	19.1	16.2	352	315	243
Alabama	21	19	17	23.1	20.2	18.2	331	333	277
Mississippi	6	6	8	10.6	9.7	12.4	132	142	176
West South Central	**137**	**139**	**127**	**24.5**	**21.8**	**19.6**	**308**	**290**	**266**
Arkansas	6	5	7	12.3	10.1	13.5	173	159	213
Louisiana	18	19	14	17.6	17.4	13.4	218	240	195
Oklahoma	11	13	9	16.4	17.1	12.5	221	269	193
Texas	102	101	97	30.0	25.5	23.1	367	320	297
West	**383**	**440**	**438**	**36.8**	**(NA)**	**34.1**	**486**	**(NA)**	**446**
Mountain	**68**	**75**	**70**	**25.0**	**23.6**	**21.0**	**302**	**316**	**280**
Montana	4	4	3	20.1	19.0	18.2	265	288	298
Idaho	3	3	2	12.7	11.1	7.2	141	155	97
Wyoming	1	1	-	9.5	7.9	4.3	107	125	74
Colorado	23	24	20	31.4	28.8	23.6	447	438	362
New Mexico	8	6	6	27.0	17.4	17.7	358	219	228
Arizona	16	22	21	25.0	29.9	24.1	310	373	295
Utah	4	4	4	12.3	11.1	9.3	97	116	104
Nevada	9	10	13	46.6	40.5	44.2	697	641	591
Pacific	**315**	**365**	**368**	**41.0**	**42.8**	**38.7**	**561**	**594**	**501**
Washington	37	31	33	37.5	28.0	27.7	522	458	447
Oregon	18	15	16	28.3	22.3	23.9	396	374	372
California	250	304	304	43.7	47.9	42.1	598	640	519
Alaska	2	4	2	17.9	27.7	16.5	196	283	222
Hawaii	8	11	12	34.4	43.7	46.0	441	611	617

NA Not available.

Source: S.K. Henshaw and J. Van Vort, eds., *Abortion Factbook, 1992 Edition: Readings, Trends, and State and Local Data to 1988*, The Alan Guttmacher Institute, New York, NY, 1992 (copyright); S.K. Henshaw and J. Vam Vort, *Abortion Services in the United States, 1991 and 1992*, Family Planning Perspectives, 26:100, 1994; and unpublished data.

No. 114. Expectation of Life at Birth, 1970 to 1992, and Projections, 1995 to 2010

[In years. Excludes deaths of nonresidents of the United States. See also *Historical Statistics, Colonial Times to 1970,* series B 107-115]

YEAR	TOTAL			WHITE			BLACK AND OTHER			BLACK		
	Total	Male	Female	Total	Male	Female	Total	Male	Female	Total	Male	Female
1970............	70.8	67.1	74.7	71.7	68.0	75.6	65.3	61.3	69.4	64.1	60.0	68.3
1975............	72.6	68.8	76.6	73.4	69.5	77.3	68.0	63.7	72.4	66.8	62.4	71.3
1980............	73.7	70.0	77.4	74.4	70.7	78.1	69.5	65.3	73.6	68.1	63.8	72.5
1981............	74.1	70.4	77.8	74.8	71.1	78.4	70.3	66.2	74.4	68.9	64.5	73.2
1982............	74.5	70.8	78.1	75.1	71.5	78.7	70.9	66.8	74.9	69.4	65.1	73.6
1983............	74.6	71.0	78.1	75.2	71.6	78.7	70.9	67.0	74.7	69.4	65.2	73.5
1984............	74.7	71.1	78.2	75.3	71.8	78.7	71.1	67.2	74.9	69.5	65.3	73.6
1985............	74.7	71.1	78.2	75.3	71.8	78.7	71.0	67.0	74.8	69.3	65.0	73.4
1986............	74.7	71.2	78.2	75.4	71.9	78.8	70.9	66.8	74.9	69.1	64.8	73.4
1987............	74.9	71.4	78.3	75.6	72.1	78.9	71.0	66.9	75.0	69.1	64.7	73.4
1988............	74.9	71.4	78.3	75.6	72.2	78.9	70.8	66.7	74.8	68.9	64.4	73.2
1989............	75.1	71.7	78.5	75.9	72.5	79.2	70.9	66.7	74.9	68.8	64.3	73.3
1990............	75.4	71.8	78.8	76.1	72.7	79.4	71.2	67.0	75.2	69.1	64.5	73.6
1991............	75.5	72.0	78.9	76.3	72.9	79.6	71.5	67.3	75.5	69.3	64.6	73.8
1992 prel.	75.7	72.3	79.0	76.5	73.2	79.7	71.8	67.8	75.6	69.8	65.5	73.9
Projections:[1] 1995 ...	76.3	72.8	79.7	77.0	73.7	80.3	72.5	68.2	76.8	70.3	65.8	74.8
2000 ...	76.7	73.2	80.2	77.6	74.3	80.9	72.9	68.3	77.5	70.2	65.3	75.1
2005 ...	77.3	73.8	80.7	78.2	74.9	81.4	73.6	69.1	78.1	70.7	65.9	75.5
2010 ...	77.9	74.5	81.3	78.8	75.6	82.0	74.3	69.9	78.7	71.3	66.5	76.0

[1] Based on middle mortality assumptions; for details, see source. Source: U.S. Bureau of the Census, *Current Population Reports,* P25-1104.

Source: Except as noted, U.S. National Center for Health Statistics, *Vital Statistics of the United States,* annual, and *Monthly Vital Statistics Reports.*

No. 115. Selected Life Table Values: 1979 to 1991

[See also *Historical Statistics, Colonial Times to 1970,* series B 116-125]

AGE AND SEX	TOTAL [1]			WHITE			BLACK		
	1979-1981	1990	1991	1979-1981	1990	1991	1979-1981	1990	1991
AVERAGE EXPECTATION OF LIFE IN YEARS									
At birth: Male............	70.1	71.8	72.0	70.8	72.7	72.9	64.1	64.5	64.6
Female..........	77.6	78.8	78.9	78.2	79.4	79.6	72.9	73.6	73.8
Age 20: Male............	51.9	53.3	53.4	52.5	54.0	54.1	46.4	46.7	46.9
Female..........	59.0	59.8	59.9	59.4	60.3	60.4	54.9	55.3	55.4
Age 40: Male............	33.6	35.1	35.3	34.0	35.6	35.8	29.5	30.1	30.3
Female..........	39.8	40.6	40.7	40.2	41.0	41.1	36.3	36.8	36.9
Age 50: Male............	25.0	26.4	26.6	25.3	26.7	26.9	22.0	22.5	22.7
Female..........	30.7	31.3	31.5	31.0	31.6	31.8	27.8	28.2	28.3
Age 65: Male............	14.2	15.1	15.3	14.3	15.2	15.4	13.3	13.2	13.4
Female..........	18.4	18.9	19.1	18.6	19.1	19.2	17.1	17.2	17.2
EXPECTED DEATHS PER 1,000 ALIVE AT SPECIFIED AGE [2]									
At birth: Male............	13.9	10.3	10.0	12.3	8.6	8.2	23.0	19.7	19.4
Female..........	11.2	8.2	7.8	9.7	6.6	6.3	19.3	16.3	15.7
Age 20: Male............	1.8	1.6	1.6	1.8	1.4	1.4	2.2	2.7	3.0
Female..........	0.6	0.5	0.5	0.6	0.5	0.5	0.7	0.7	0.8
Age 40: Male............	3.0	3.1	3.1	2.6	2.7	2.7	6.9	7.1	7.1
Female..........	1.6	1.4	1.4	1.4	1.2	1.2	3.2	3.1	3.1
Age 50: Male............	7.8	6.2	6.1	7.1	5.6	5.5	14.9	12.8	12.8
Female..........	4.2	3.5	3.5	3.8	3.2	3.1	7.7	6.6	6.5
Age 65: Male............	28.2	12.9	23.6	27.4	23.0	22.7	38.5	36.8	35.9
Female..........	14.3	13.5	13.3	13.6	12.8	12.7	21.6	21.4	20.7
NUMBER SURVIVING TO SPECIFIED AGE PER 1,000 BORN ALIVE									
Age 20: Male............	973	979	979	975	981	982	961	963	962
Female..........	982	986	986	984	988	988	972	976	977
Age 40: Male............	933	938	938	940	946	946	885	880	878
Female..........	965	971	971	969	975	975	941	944	944
Age 50: Male............	890	899	899	901	912	912	801	801	800
Female..........	941	950	950	947	957	957	896	904	904
Age 65: Male............	706	741	743	724	760	763	551	571	575
Female..........	835	851	852	848	864	865	733	751	755

[1] Includes other races not shown separately. [2] See footnote 1, table 117.
Source: U.S. National Center for Health Statistics, *U.S. Life Tables and Actuarial Tables, 1959-61, 1969-71, and 1979-81; Vital Statistics of the United States,* annual; and unpublished data.

No. 116. Expectation of Life and Expected Deaths, by Race, Sex, and Age: 1991

AGE IN 1990 (years)	EXPECTATION OF LIFE IN YEARS					EXPECTED DEATHS PER 1,000 ALIVE AT SPECIFIED AGE [1]				
	Total	White		Black		Total	White		Black	
		Male	Female	Male	Female		Male	Female	Male	Female
At birth	75.4	72.7	79.4	64.5	73.6	9.27	8.55	6.59	19.68	16.30
1	75.1	72.3	78.9	64.8	73.8	0.66	0.67	0.50	1.20	0.87
2	74.1	71.4	78.0	63.9	72.9	0.49	0.48	0.38	0.88	0.70
3	73.1	70.4	77.0	62.9	71.9	0.38	0.36	0.30	0.67	0.57
4	72.2	69.4	76.0	62.0	71.0	0.31	0.30	0.25	0.55	0.45
5	71.2	68.5	75.0	61.0	70.0	0.27	0.27	0.21	0.47	0.37
6	70.2	67.5	74.1	60.1	69.0	0.25	0.26	0.19	0.43	0.30
7	69.2	66.5	73.1	59.1	68.1	0.22	0.25	0.17	0.39	0.26
8	68.2	65.5	72.1	58.1	67.1	0.20	0.22	0.15	0.33	0.23
9	67.3	64.5	71.1	57.1	66.1	0.17	0.18	0.14	0.26	0.22
10	66.3	63.5	70.1	56.1	65.1	0.15	0.15	0.13	0.20	0.22
11	65.3	62.6	69.1	55.1	64.1	0.15	0.15	0.14	0.21	0.24
12	64.3	61.6	68.1	54.2	63.1	0.20	0.21	0.16	0.32	0.27
13	63.3	60.6	67.1	53.2	62.1	0.31	0.36	0.21	0.58	0.31
14	62.3	59.6	66.2	52.2	61.2	0.46	0.58	0.28	0.93	0.36
15	61.3	58.6	65.2	51.3	60.2	0.64	0.82	0.36	1.34	0.42
16	60.4	57.7	64.2	50.3	59.2	0.80	1.04	0.43	1.73	0.49
17	59.4	56.7	63.2	49.4	58.2	0.92	1.21	0.48	2.07	0.55
18	58.5	55.8	62.3	48.5	57.3	0.99	1.31	0.50	2.33	0.60
19	57.5	54.9	61.3	47.6	56.3	1.02	1.36	0.49	2.54	0.65
20	56.6	54.0	60.3	46.7	55.3	1.04	1.39	0.47	2.74	0.70
21	55.7	53.0	59.3	45.9	54.4	1.07	1.43	0.46	2.95	0.75
22	54.7	52.1	58.4	45.0	53.4	1.10	1.47	0.45	3.13	0.82
23	53.8	51.2	57.4	44.1	52.5	1.13	1.49	0.46	3.27	0.90
24	52.8	50.3	56.4	43.3	51.5	1.15	1.52	0.48	3.37	0.99
25	51.9	49.3	55.4	42.4	50.6	1.18	1.54	0.50	3.46	1.09
26	51.0	48.4	54.5	41.6	49.6	1.20	1.55	0.52	3.56	1.19
27	50.0	47.5	53.5	40.7	48.7	1.23	1.58	0.54	3.70	1.30
28	49.1	46.6	52.5	39.9	47.7	1.28	1.63	0.56	3.90	1.41
29	48.1	45.6	51.6	39.0	46.8	1.33	1.69	0.59	4.14	1.53
30	47.2	44.7	50.6	38.2	45.9	1.39	1.76	0.61	4.39	1.65
31	46.3	43.8	49.6	37.4	45.0	1.46	1.83	0.65	4.64	1.78
32	45.3	42.9	48.7	36.5	44.0	1.53	1.91	0.68	4.90	1.91
33	44.4	41.9	47.7	35.7	43.1	1.61	2.00	0.73	5.17	2.04
34	43.5	41.0	46.7	34.9	42.2	1.69	2.09	0.77	5.45	2.16
35	42.6	40.1	45.8	34.1	41.3	1.79	2.21	0.83	5.76	2.30
36	41.6	39.2	44.8	33.3	40.4	1.90	2.32	0.89	6.07	2.45
37	40.7	38.3	43.8	32.5	39.5	2.00	2.43	0.95	6.37	2.60
38	39.8	37.4	42.9	31.7	38.6	2.08	2.52	1.02	6.63	2.74
39	38.9	36.5	41.9	30.9	37.7	2.16	2.60	1.09	6.87	2.89
40	38.0	35.6	41.0	30.1	36.8	2.24	2.69	1.18	7.11	3.05
41	37.0	34.7	40.0	29.3	35.9	2.36	2.81	1.28	7.40	3.23
42	36.1	33.8	39.1	28.5	35.0	2.50	2.97	1.40	7.77	3.46
43	35.2	32.9	38.1	27.7	34.1	2.68	3.16	1.55	8.23	3.72
44	34.3	32.0	37.2	27.0	33.3	2.90	3.39	1.72	8.78	4.03
45	33.4	31.1	36.2	26.2	32.4	3.15	3.66	1.92	9.39	4.38
46	32.5	30.2	35.3	25.4	31.5	3.42	3.96	2.13	10.03	4.75
47	31.6	29.3	34.4	24.7	30.7	3.73	4.30	2.37	10.70	5.15
48	30.7	28.4	33.5	24.0	29.8	4.07	4.69	2.62	11.37	5.59
49	29.9	27.6	32.5	23.2	29.0	4.44	5.12	2.89	12.07	6.07
50	29.0	26.7	31.6	22.5	28.2	4.86	5.60	3.20	12.81	6.58
51	28.1	25.8	30.7	21.8	27.4	5.31	6.14	3.53	13.63	7.14
52	27.3	25.0	29.8	21.1	26.6	5.82	6.67	3.89	14.60	7.75
53	26.4	24.2	29.0	20.4	25.8	6.39	7.46	4.28	15.78	8.41
54	25.6	23.3	28.1	19.7	25.0	7.01	8.25	4.70	17.12	9.12
55	24.8	22.5	27.2	19.0	24.2	7.68	9.10	5.15	18.57	9.87
56	24.0	21.7	26.4	18.4	23.4	8.41	10.03	5.65	20.08	10.67
57	23.2	21.0	25.5	17.8	22.7	9.22	11.07	6.21	21.65	11.57
58	22.4	20.2	24.7	17.1	22.0	10.12	12.24	6.85	23.27	12.58
59	21.6	19.4	23.8	16.5	21.2	11.11	13.54	7.56	24.94	13.69
60	20.8	18.7	23.0	15.9	20.5	12.19	14.96	8.35	26.71	14.87
61	20.1	18.0	22.2	15.4	19.8	13.33	16.46	9.18	28.59	16.09
62	19.4	17.3	21.4	14.8	19.1	14.50	18.01	10.04	30.54	17.36
63	18.6	16.6	20.6	14.3	18.5	15.70	19.59	10.91	32.55	18.66
64	17.9	15.9	19.8	13.7	17.8	16.93	21.24	11.80	34.63	20.00
65	17.2	15.2	19.1	13.2	17.2	18.23	22.96	12.76	36.79	21.41
70	13.9	12.1	15.4	10.7	14.1	27.33	35.15	19.78	51.00	29.49
75	10.9	9.4	12.0	8.6	11.2	41.08	53.88	31.08	68.81	40.48
80	8.3	7.1	9.0	6.7	8.6	62.24	82.01	49.92	93.91	58.55
85 and over	6.1	5.2	6.4	5.0	6.3	1,000	1,000	1,000	1,000	1,000

[1] Based on the proportion of the cohort who are alive at the beginning of an indicated age interval who will die before reaching the end of that interval. For example, out of every 1,000 people alive and exactly 50 years old at the beginning of the period, between 4 and 5 (4.86) will die before reaching their 51st birthdays.

Source: U.S. National Center for Health Statistics, *Vital Statistics of the United States*, annual; and unpublished data.

No. 117. Deaths and Death Rates, by Sex and Race: 1970 to 1991

[Rates are per 1,000 population for specified groups. Excludes deaths of nonresidents of the United States and fetal deaths. For explanation of age-adjustment, see text, section 2. The standard population for this table is the total population of the United States enumerated in 1940. See Appendix III. See also *Historical Statistics, Colonial Times to 1970*, series B 167-173 and B 181-192]

SEX AND RACE	1970	1980	1982	1983	1984	1985	1986	1987	1988	1989	1990	1991
Deaths [1] (1,000)........	1,921	1,990	1,975	2,019	2,039	2,086	2,105	2,123	2,168	2,150	2,148	2,170
Male [1] (1,000)............	1,078	1,075	1,056	1,072	1,077	1,098	1,104	1,108	1,126	1,114	1,113	1,122
Female [1] (1,000)..........	843	915	918	947	963	989	1,001	1,015	1,042	1,036	1,035	1,048
White (1,000).............	1,682	1,739	1,729	1,766	1,782	1,819	1,831	1,843	1,877	1,854	1,853	1,869
Male (1,000)............	942	934	919	932	935	950	953	953	965	951	951	956
Female (1,000).........	740	805	810	834	847	869	879	890	911	903	902	912
Black (1,000).............	226	233	227	233	236	244	250	255	264	268	266	270
Male (1,000)............	128	130	126	128	129	134	137	140	144	146	145	147
Female (1,000).........	98	103	101	105	107	111	113	115	120	121	120	122
Death rates [1].........	9.5	8.8	8.5	8.6	8.6	8.8	8.8	8.8	8.8	8.7	8.6	8.6
Male [1]................	10.9	9.8	9.4	9.4	9.4	9.5	9.4	9.4	9.5	9.3	9.2	9.1
Female [1]................	8.1	7.9	7.7	7.9	7.9	8.1	8.1	8.2	8.3	8.2	8.1	8.1
White.................	9.5	8.9	8.7	8.9	8.9	9.0	9.0	9.0	9.1	8.9	8.9	8.9
Male...............	10.9	9.8	9.5	9.6	9.5	9.6	9.6	9.5	9.6	9.4	9.3	9.3
Female.............	8.1	8.1	8.0	8.2	8.2	8.4	8.4	8.5	8.7	8.5	8.5	8.5
Black................	10.0	8.8	8.2	8.4	8.4	8.5	8.6	8.7	8.9	8.9	8.8	8.6
Male...............	11.9	10.3	9.7	9.7	9.7	9.9	10.0	10.1	10.3	10.3	10.1	10.0
Female.............	8.3	7.3	7.0	7.2	7.2	7.3	7.4	7.5	7.6	7.6	7.5	7.4
Age-adjusted death rates [1]	7.1	5.9	5.5	5.5	5.5	5.5	5.5	5.4	5.4	5.4	5.3	5.2
Male [1]................	9.3	7.8	7.3	7.3	7.2	7.2	7.2	7.1	7.1	6.9	6.8	6.7
Female [1]................	5.3	4.3	4.1	4.1	4.1	4.1	4.1	4.0	4.1	4.0	3.9	3.9
White.................	6.8	5.6	5.3	5.3	5.3	5.2	5.2	5.1	5.1	5.0	4.9	4.9
Male...............	8.9	7.5	7.1	7.0	6.9	6.9	6.8	6.7	6.7	6.5	6.4	6.3
Female.............	5.0	4.1	3.9	3.9	3.9	3.9	3.9	3.8	3.9	3.8	3.7	3.7
Black................	10.4	8.4	7.8	7.9	7.8	7.9	8.0	8.0	8.1	8.1	7.9	7.8
Male...............	13.2	11.1	10.4	10.4	10.4	10.5	10.6	10.6	10.8	10.8	10.6	1.0
Female.............	8.1	6.3	5.9	6.0	5.9	5.9	5.9	5.9	6.0	5.9	5.8	5.8

[1] Includes other races, not shown separately.

Source: U.S. National Center for Health Statistics, *Vital Statistics of the United States*, annual; and *Monthly Vital Statistics Report*.

No. 118. Death Rates, by Age, Sex, and Race: 1970 to 1992

[Number of deaths per 100,000 population in specified group. See headnote, table 117]

SEX, YEAR, AND RACE	All ages [1]	Under 1 yr. old	1-4 yr. old	5-14 yr. old	15-24 yr. old	25-34 yr. old	35-44 yr. old	45-54 yr. old	55-64 yr. old	65-74 yr. old	75-84 yr. old	85 yr. old and over
MALE [2]												
1970..............	1,090	2,410	93	51	189	215	403	959	2,283	4,874	10,010	17,822
1980..............	977	1,429	73	37	172	196	299	767	1,815	4,105	8,817	18,801
1990 [3]...........	918	1,083	52	29	147	204	310	610	1,553	3,492	7,889	18,057
1991 [3]...........	912	1,024	52	29	148	204	312	605	1,525	3,439	7,689	17,800
1992 [3]...........	902	919	47	278	145	200	325	587	1,482	3,360	7,538	17,656
White: 1970........	1,087	2,113	84	48	171	177	344	883	2,203	4,810	10,099	18,552
1980	983	1,230	66	35	167	171	257	699	1,729	4,036	8,830	19,097
1990 [3]......	931	896	46	26	131	176	268	549	1,467	3,398	7,845	18,268
1991 [3]......	926	861	46	27	128	176	269	545	1,444	3,350	7,642	18,021
1992 [3]......	917	755	43	26	124	173	285	531	1,396	3,271	7,479	17,866
Black: 1970........	1,187	4,299	151	67	321	560	957	1,778	3,257	5,803	9,455	12,222
1980	1,034	2,587	111	47	209	407	690	1,480	2,873	5,131	9,232	16,099
1990 [3]......	1,008	2,112	86	41	252	431	700	1,261	2,618	4,946	9,130	16,955
1991 [3]......	999	1,957	88	42	278	426	702	1,257	2,534	4,851	9,013	16,664
1992 [3]......	980	1,830	68	41	271	413	683	1,186	2,512	4,761	9,035	17,014
FEMALE [2]												
1970..............	808	1,864	75	32	68	102	231	517	1,099	2,580	6,678	15,518
1980..............	785	1,142	55	24	58	76	159	413	934	2,145	5,440	14,747
1990 [3]...........	812	856	41	19	49	74	138	343	879	1,991	4,883	14,274
1991 [3]...........	811	804	43	18	50	74	139	339	873	1,977	4,801	14,067
1992 [3]...........	807	808	38	17	48	70	143	323	872	1,966	4,728	13,839
White: 1970........	813	1,615	66	30	62	84	193	463	1,015	2,471	6,699	15,980
1980	806	963	49	23	56	65	138	373	876	2,067	5,402	14,980
1990 [3]......	847	690	36	18	46	62	117	309	823	1,924	4,839	14,401
1991 [3]......	848	659	38	17	47	62	117	306	822	1,909	4,733	14,188
1992 [3]......	843	653	33	16	43	57	118	291	814	1,911	4,696	13,919
Black: 1970........	829	3,369	129	44	112	231	533	1,044	1,986	3,861	6,692	10,707
1980	733	2,124	84	31	71	150	324	768	1,561	3,057	6,212	12,367
1990 [3]......	748	1,736	68	28	69	160	299	639	1,453	2,866	5,688	13,310
1991 [3]......	745	1,581	71	26	73	159	304	633	1,400	2,854	5,707	13,259
1992 [3]......	741	1,601	63	26	72	155	318	619	1,458	2,700	5,529	13,719

[1] Includes unknown age.　[2] Includes other races not shown separately.　[3] Includes deaths of nonresidents. Based on a 10-percent sample of deaths.

Source: U.S. National Center for Health Statistics, *Vital Statistics of the United States*, annual; *Monthly Vital Statistics Report*; and unpublished data.

No. 119. Deaths and Death Rates, by State: 1980 to 1992

[By State of residence. Excludes deaths of nonresidents of the United States, except as noted. Caution should be used in comparing death rates by State; rates are affected by the population composition of the area. See also Appendix III]

DIVISION AND STATE	NUMBER OF DEATHS (1,000)							RATE PER 1,000 POPULATION [2]						
	1980	1985	1988	1989	1990	1991	1992, prel.[1]	1980	1985	1988	1989	1990	1991	1992, prel.[1]
United States . .	1,990	2,086	2,168	2,150	2,148	2,165	2,177	8.8	8.8	8.9	8.7	8.6	8.6	8.5
New England	115	118	120	116	115	112	116	9.3	9.3	9.2	8.8	8.7	8.5	8.8
Maine	11	11	12	11	11	11	11	9.6	9.8	9.6	9.2	9.0	8.9	8.8
New Hampshire . .	8	8	9	8	8	9	9	8.3	8.5	8.1	7.7	7.7	7.7	7.7
Vermont	5	5	5	5	5	5	5	9.0	8.8	8.5	8.2	8.2	8.0	8.3
Massachusetts . . .	55	56	56	54	53	51	54	9.6	9.5	9.4	9.0	8.8	8.6	9.1
Rhode Island	9	10	10	10	10	9	9	9.8	10.0	9.8	9.6	9.5	9.2	9.4
Connecticut	27	28	29	28	28	28	28	8.8	8.8	8.7	8.6	8.4	8.4	8.6
Middle Atlantic	365	367	376	367	361	360	359	9.9	9.9	10.0	9.8	9.6	9.5	9.5
New York	173	172	176	172	169	167	165	9.8	9.7	9.8	9.5	9.4	9.2	9.1
New Jersey	69	71	73	71	70	70	71	9.4	9.4	9.5	9.2	9.1	9.0	9.1
Pennsylvania	124	124	126	124	122	124	123	10.4	10.5	10.6	10.4	10.3	10.3	10.3
East North Central .	365	370	379	372	373	379	372	8.8	8.9	9.1	8.9	8.9	8.9	8.7
Ohio	98	99	100	98	99	99	10	9.1	9.2	9.3	9.1	9.1	9.1	9.0
Indiana	47	48	50	49	50	52	50	8.6	8.8	9.1	8.9	8.9	9.2	8.9
Illinois	103	102	105	103	103	105	102	9.0	9.0	9.2	9.1	9.0	9.1	8.7
Michigan	75	79	80	79	79	80	79	8.1	8.7	8.7	8.5	8.5	8.5	8.4
Wisconsin	41	41	43	42	43	44	42	8.7	8.7	8.9	8.7	8.7	8.8	8.3
West North Central.	159	162	164	161	161	164	164	9.2	9.3	9.4	9.2	9.1	9.2	9.0
Minnesota	33	35	35	34	35	35	35	8.2	8.3	8.3	7.9	7.9	8.0	7.8
Iowa	27	28	28	27	27	26	27	9.3	9.8	10.1	9.8	9.7	9.3	9.6
Missouri.	50	50	51	50	50	53	50	10.1	10.1	10.0	9.9	9.8	10.4	9.7
North Dakota	6	6	6	6	6	6	6	8.6	8.3	8.6	8.5	8.9	8.9	9.1
South Dakota	7	7	7	7	6	7	7	9.5	9.5	9.4	9.4	9.1	9.4	9.7
Nebraska.	14	15	15	15	15	15	15	9.2	9.4	9.5	9.4	9.4	9.2	9.2
Kansas	22	22	23	22	22	23	22	9.3	9.1	9.3	9.0	9.0	9.0	8.8
South Atlantic	330	364	389	391	392	397	404	8.9	9.1	9.2	9.1	9.0	8.9	9.0
Delaware.	5	5	6	6	6	6	6	8.5	8.9	8.9	8.9	8.7	8.6	8.6
Maryland	34	37	39	38	38	38	38	8.1	8.3	8.3	8.1	8.0	7.8	7.7
Dist. of Col.	7	7	8	8	7	7	7	11.1	11.0	12.2	12.3	12.0	11.7	11.2
Virginia	43	45	48	47	48	49	50	8.0	7.9	7.9	7.7	7.8	7.8	7.8
West Virginia	19	19	20	20	19	20	20	9.9	10.2	10.8	10.8	10.8	11.0	11.1
North Carolina . . .	48	53	58	57	57	59	59	8.2	8.5	8.9	8.8	8.6	8.7	8.7
South Carolina . . .	25	27	29	30	30	30	31	8.1	8.2	8.6	8.6	8.5	8.4	8.5
Georgia.	44	49	52	52	52	53	53	8.1	8.2	8.2	8.2	8.0	8.0	7.9
Florida.	105	121	131	133	134	135	140	10.7	10.7	10.6	10.5	10.4	10.2	10.4
East South Central .	134	140	145	145	146	144	147	9.1	9.4	9.6	9.6	9.6	9.4	9.5
Kentucky	34	35	36	35	35	35	35	9.2	9.4	9.7	9.6	9.5	9.5	9.4
Tennessee.	41	43	46	45	46	45	47	8.9	9.2	9.5	9.4	9.5	9.2	9.4
Alabama	36	38	39	39	39	38	40	9.1	9.5	9.7	9.7	9.7	9.3	9.6
Mississippi	24	25	25	25	25	26	25	9.4	9.5	9.6	9.9	9.8	9.9	9.7
West South Central.	195	209	215	217	218	222	224	8.2	8.0	8.1	8.2	8.2	8.2	8.1
Arkansas	23	24	25	25	25	24	25	9.9	10.4	10.6	10.5	10.5	10.2	10.5
Louisiana	36	37	38	38	38	38	37	8.5	8.4	8.8	8.9	8.9	9.0	8.7
Oklahoma	28	30	30	30	30	30	31	9.3	9.1	9.5	9.5	9.7	9.6	9.5
Texas	108	118	123	125	125	129	131	7.6	7.3	7.4	7.4	7.4	7.4	7.4
Mountain	80	88	95	95	97	99	103	7.0	6.9	7.1	7.1	7.1	7.1	7.2
Montana	7	7	7	7	7	7	7	8.5	8.2	8.5	8.4	8.6	8.7	8.7
Idaho	7	7	8	7	7	8	8	7.2	7.2	7.8	7.5	7.4	7.5	7.6
Wyoming	3	3	3	3	3	3	3	6.9	6.6	7.0	7.1	7.1	6.9	7.2
Colorado	19	20	21	21	22	22	23	6.6	6.3	6.5	6.5	6.6	6.6	6.5
New Mexico.	9	10	10	11	11	11	12	7.0	6.8	7.0	7.0	7.0	7.2	7.3
Arizona	21	25	28	28	29	29	31	7.9	7.7	7.8	7.8	7.9	7.8	8.0
Utah	8	9	9	9	9	9	10	5.6	5.5	5.5	5.4	5.3	5.2	5.5
Nevada	6	7	8	9	9	9	10	7.4	7.6	7.9	7.6	7.8	7.2	7.6
Pacific.	247	268	285	286	286	290	287	7.8	7.6	7.6	7.5	7.3	7.3	7.1
Washington	32	35	36	36	37	38	37	7.7	7.8	7.8	7.6	7.6	7.5	7.3
Oregon	22	24	25	25	25	25	26	8.3	8.9	9.1	8.9	8.8	8.6	8.7
California	187	202	215	217	214	219	215	7.9	7.6	7.6	7.4	7.2	7.2	7.0
Alaska.	2	2	2	2	2	2	2	4.3	3.9	3.8	3.8	4.0	3.8	3.8
Hawaii.	5	6	6	7	7	7	7	5.2	5.6	5.6	5.9	6.1	5.9	6.0

[1] Includes deaths of nonresidents.   [2] Rates based on enumerated resident population as of April 1 for 1980; and 1990; estimated resident population as of July 1 for all other years.

Source: U.S. National Center for Health Statistics, *Vital Statistics of the United States*, annual; and *Monthly Vital Statistics Report.*

No. 120. Infant, Maternal, and Neonatal Mortality Rates and Fetal Mortality Ratios, by Race: 1970 to 1991

[Deaths per 1,000 live births, except as noted. Excludes deaths of nonresidents of the United States. See also Appendix III and *Historical Statistics, Colonial Times to 1970*, series B 136-147]

ITEM	1970	1980	1981	1982	1983	1984	1985	1986	1987	1988	1989	1990	1991
Infant deaths [1]	20.0	12.6	11.9	11.5	11.2	10.8	10.3	10.4	10.1	10.0	9.8	9.2	8.9
White	17.8	11.0	10.5	10.1	9.7	9.4	9.3	8.9	8.6	8.5	8.2	7.6	7.3
Black and other.	30.9	19.1	17.8	17.3	16.8	16.1	15.8	15.7	15.4	15.0	15.2	15.5	15.1
Black	32.6	21.4	20.0	19.6	19.2	18.4	18.2	18.0	17.9	17.6	17.7	18.0	17.6
Maternal deaths [2]	21.5	9.2	8.5	7.9	8.0	7.8	7.8	7.2	6.6	8.4	7.9	8.2	7.9
White	14.4	6.7	6.3	5.8	5.9	5.4	5.2	4.9	5.1	5.9	5.6	5.4	5.8
Black and other.	55.9	19.8	17.3	16.4	16.3	16.9	18.1	16.0	12.0	17.4	16.5	19.1	15.6
Black	59.8	21.5	20.4	18.2	18.3	19.7	20.4	18.8	14.2	19.5	18.4	22.4	18.3
Fetal deaths [3]	14.2	9.2	9.0	8.9	8.5	8.2	7.9	7.7	7.7	7.5	7.5	7.5	(NA)
White	12.4	8.2	8.0	7.9	7.5	7.4	7.0	6.8	6.7	6.4	6.4	6.4	(NA)
Black and other.	22.6	13.4	12.8	12.7	12.4	11.5	11.3	11.2	11.5	11.4	11.4	11.7	(NA)
Neonatal deaths [4]	15.1	8.5	8.0	7.7	7.3	7.0	7.0	6.7	6.5	6.3	6.2	5.8	5.6
White	13.8	7.5	7.1	6.8	6.4	6.2	6.1	5.8	5.5	5.4	5.2	4.8	4.5
Black and other.	21.4	12.5	11.8	11.3	10.8	10.2	10.3	10.1	10.0	9.7	9.6	9.9	9.5
Black	22.8	14.1	13.4	13.1	12.4	11.8	12.1	11.7	11.7	11.5	11.3	11.6	11.2

NA Not available. [1] Represents deaths of infants under 1 year old, exclusive of fetal deaths. [2] Per 100,000 live births from deliveries and complications of pregnancy, childbirth, and the puerperium. Beginning 1979, deaths are classified according to the ninth revision of the *International Classification of Diseases;* earlier years classified according to the revision in use at the time; see text, section 2. [3] Includes only those deaths with stated or presumed period of gestation of 20 weeks or more. [4] Represents deaths of infants under 28 days old, exclusive of fetal deaths.

No. 121. Fetal and Infant Deaths—Number and Percent Distribution: 1970 to 1990

[State requirements for reporting of fetal deaths vary. Most States require reporting of fetal deaths of gestations of 20 weeks or more. There is substantial evidence that not all fetal deaths for which reporting is required are reported. For details of methodology, see Appendix III and source]

YEAR	NUMBER						PERCENT DISTRIBUTION					
		Fetal deaths		Infant deaths				Fetal deaths		Infant deaths		
	Total	Early [1]	Late [2]	Neonatal		Post-neo-natal [5]	Total	Early [1]	Late [2]	Neonatal		Post-neo-natal [5]
				Early [3]	Late [4]					Early [3]	Late [4]	
1970	127,628	17,170	35,791	50,821	5,458	18,388	100.0	13.5	28.0	39.8	4.3	14.4
1980	78,879	10754	22,599	25,492	5,126	14,908	100.0	13.6	28.7	32.3	6.5	18.9
1981	75,901	11126	21,470	24,384	4,737	14,184	100.0	14.7	28.3	32.1	6.2	18.7
1982	75,095	11,028	21,666	23,706	4,629	14,066	100.0	14.7	28.9	31.6	6.2	18.7
1983	71,379	10,933	19,819	22,315	4,192	14,120	100.0	15.3	27.8	31.3	5.9	19.8
1984	69,679	10,963	19,136	21,566	4,125	13,889	100.0	15.7	27.5	31.0	5.9	19.9
1985	69,691	10,958	18,703	21,865	4,314	13,851	100.0	15.7	26.8	31.4	6.2	19.9
1986	67,863	11,100	17,872	21,053	4,159	13,679	100.0	16.4	26.3	31.0	6.1	20.2
1987	67,757	11,656	17,693	20,471	4,156	13,781	100.0	17.2	26.1	30.2	6.1	20.3
1988	68,352	11,833	17,609	20,471	4,219	14,220	100.0	17.3	25.8	29.9	6.2	20.8
1989	70,124	12,397	18,072	20,796	4,372	14,487	100.0	17.7	25.8	29.7	6.2	20.7
1990	67,696	12,554	16,791	20,020	4,289	14,042	100.0	18.5	24.8	29.6	6.3	20.7

[1] 20-27 weeks gestation. [2] 28 weeks or more gestation. [3] Less than 7 days. [4] 7-27 days. [5] 28 days-11 months.

No. 122. Infant Deaths and Infant Mortality Rates, by Cause of Death: 1980 to 1991

[Excludes deaths of nonresidents of the United States. Deaths classified according to ninth revision of *International Classification of Diseases*. See also Appendix III]

CAUSE OF DEATH	NUMBER			PERCENT DISTRIBUTION			INFANT MORTALITY RATE [1]		
	1980	1990	1991	1980	1990	1991	1980	1990	1991
Total	45,526	38,351	36,766	100	100	100	12.6	9.2	8.9
Congenital anomalies	9,220	8,239	7,685	20	21	21	2.6	2.0	1.9
Sudden infant death syndrome	5,510	5,417	5,349	12	14	15	1.5	1.3	1.3
Respiratory distress syndrome	4,989	2,850	2,569	11	7	7	1.4	0.7	0.6
Disorders relating to short gestation and unspecified low birth weight	3,648	4,013	4,139	8	10	11	1.0	1.0	1.0
Newborn affected by maternal complications of pregnancy	1,572	1,655	1,536	4	4	4	0.4	0.4	0.4
Intrauterine hypoxia and birth asphyxia.	1,497	762	599	3	2	2	0.4	0.2	0.1
Infections specific to the perinatal period.	971	875	881	2	2	2	0.3	0.2	0.2
Accidents and adverse effects	1,166	930	961	3	2	3	0.3	0.2	0.2
Newborn affected by complications of placenta, cord, and membranes	985	975	962	2	3	3	0.3	0.2	0.2
Pneumonia and influenza.	1,012	634	607	2	2	2	0.3	0.2	0.1
All other causes.	14,956	12,001	11,478	33	31	31	4.1	2.9	2.8

[1] Deaths of infants under 1 year old per 1,000 live births.

Sources of tables 121-123: U.S. National Center for Health Statistics, *Vital Statistics of the United States*, annual, and *Monthly Vital Statistics Report;* and unpublished data.

No. 123. Infant Mortality Rates, by Race—States: 1980 to 1991

[Deaths per 1,000 live births, by place of residence. Represents deaths of infants under 1 year old, exclusive of fetal deaths. Excludes deaths of nonresidents of the United States. See Appendix III and *Historical Statistics, Colonial Times to 1970*, series B 143-147, for U.S. totals]

DIVISION AND STATE	TOTAL [1] 1980	TOTAL [1] 1990	TOTAL [1] 1991	WHITE 1980	WHITE 1990	BLACK 1980	BLACK 1990	DIVISION AND STATE	TOTAL [1] 1980	TOTAL [1] 1990	TOTAL [1] 1991	WHITE 1980	WHITE 1990	BLACK 1980	BLACK 1990
U.S.	12.6	9.2	8.9	11.0	7.7	21.4	17.0	VA...	13.6	10.2	9.9	11.9	7.5	19.8	18.8
N.E....	10.5	7.2	6.8	10.1	6.8	17.7	12.3	WV..	11.8	9.9	8.2	11.4	9.6	21.5	16.6
ME...	9.2	6.2	6.7	9.4	6.2	(NA)	6.1	NC...	14.5	10.6	10.8	12.1	8.3	20.0	16.0
NH...	9.9	7.1	6.1	9.9	7.2	[2]22.5	5.4	SC...	15.6	11.7	11.3	10.8	8.3	22.9	17.1
VT...	10.7	6.4	5.8	10.7	6.5	(NA)	(NA)	GA...	14.5	12.4	11.4	10.8	9.1	21.0	18.0
MA...	10.5	7.0	6.6	10.1	6.7	[2]16.8	10.4	FL...	14.6	9.6	9.0	11.8	7.6	22.8	16.2
RI ...	11.0	8.1	8.0	10.9	8.3	[2]17.4	9.7	E.S.C.	14.5	10.4	10.3	11.8	8.1	21.8	16.2
CT ...	11.2	7.9	7.4	10.2	6.6	19.1	16.0	KY...	12.9	8.5	8.9	12.0	8.0	22.0	13.6
M.A....	12.8	9.5	9.2	11.1	7.5	21.1	17.7	TN...	13.5	10.3	10.0	11.9	8.0	19.3	17.5
NY...	12.5	9.6	9.4	10.8	7.7	20.0	17.3	AL...	15.1	10.8	11.2	11.6	8.3	21.6	15.9
NJ...	12.5	9.0	8.7	10.3	6.8	21.9	17.3	MS...	17.0	12.1	11.4	11.1	8.5	23.7	16.1
PA...	13.2	9.6	9.1	11.9	7.8	23.1	18.8	W.S.C..	12.7	8.7	8.5	11.1	7.4	19.8	14.7
E.N.C ..	13.0	10.1	9.8	10.9	8.0	24.4	20.0	AR...	12.7	9.2	10.2	10.3	8.0	20.0	13.6
OH...	12.8	9.8	9.4	11.2	8.2	23.0	18.3	LA...	14.3	11.1	10.5	10.5	7.3	20.6	16.5
IN ...	11.9	9.6	9.1	10.5	8.9	23.4	16.0	OK...	12.7	9.2	9.6	12.1	9.4	21.8	13.2
IL...	14.8	10.7	10.7	11.7	7.7	26.3	21.5	TX...	12.2	8.1	7.7	11.2	7.1	18.8	13.9
MI ...	12.8	10.7	10.4	10.6	7.9	24.2	21.0	Mt....	11.0	8.6	8.1	10.7	8.3	19.5	15.0
WI ...	10.3	8.2	8.3	9.7	7.2	18.5	18.1	MT...	12.4	9.0	7.0	11.8	8.6	(NA)	13.3
W.N.C ..	11.3	8.4	8.7	10.5	7.5	21.3	17.3	ID...	10.7	8.7	8.7	10.7	8.7	(NA)	10.9
MN...	10.0	7.3	7.5	9.6	6.7	20.0	19.7	WY...	9.8	8.6	7.9	9.3	8.8	[2]25.9	(NA)
IA...	11.8	8.1	8.0	11.5	7.8	27.2	18.0	CO...	10.1	8.8	8.9	9.8	8.4	19.1	16.5
MO ...	12.4	9.4	10.2	11.1	7.8	20.7	17.5	NM...	11.5	9.0	8.1	11.3	9.3	[2]23.1	12.8
ND...	12.1	8.0	8.1	11.7	7.9	[2]27.5	(NA)	AZ...	12.4	8.8	8.6	11.8	8.2	18.4	16.7
SD...	10.9	10.1	9.4	9.0	8.6	(NA)	7.4	UT...	10.4	7.5	6.1	10.5	7.4	[2]27.3	13.0
NE...	11.5	8.3	7.6	10.7	7.2	25.2	16.8	NV...	10.7	8.4	9.2	10.0	8.1	20.6	12.5
KS...	10.4	8.4	8.9	9.5	7.7	20.6	15.4	Pac....	11.2	7.9	7.6	10.9	7.6	17.8	14.1
S.A....	14.5	10.7	10.2	11.6	8.0	21.6	17.4	WA...	11.8	7.8	7.5	11.5	7.6	16.4	14.5
DE...	13.9	10.1	11.8	9.8	7.3	27.9	19.4	OR...	12.2	8.3	7.3	12.2	8.1	[2]15.9	15.1
MD...	14.0	9.5	9.2	11.6	6.5	20.4	16.3	CA...	11.1	7.9	7.6	10.6	7.6	18.0	14.2
DC...	25.0	20.7	21.0	17.8	12.1	26.7	24.4	AK...	12.3	10.5	8.9	9.4	8.5	[2]19.5	11.2
								HI ...	10.3	6.7	7.4	11.6	5.1	[2]11.8	11.5

NA Not available.   [1] Includes other races, not shown separately.   [2] Based on a frequency of less than 20 infant deaths.

No. 124. Age-Adjusted Death Rates, by Selected Causes: 1980 to 1991

[Rates per 100,000 population. For explanation of age-adjustment, see text, section 2. The standard population for this table is the total population of the United States enumerated in 1940. See also headnote, table 125]

CAUSE OF DEATH	1980	1990	1991	CAUSE OF DEATH	1980	1990	1991
All causes	585.8	520.2	513.7	Pneumonia and influenza	12.9	14.0	13.4
				Pneumonia	12.4	13.7	13.2
Major cardiovascular diseases	256.0	189.8	185.0	Influenza..................	0.5	0.3	0.2
Diseases of heart	202.0	152.0	148.2				
Rheumatic fever and rheumatic heart disease.............	2.6	1.5	1.4	Diabetes mellitus...............	10.1	11.7	11.8
Hypertensive heart disease [1]	6.8	5.3	4.7	Suicide....................	11.4	11.5	11.4
Ischemic heart disease.......	149.8	102.6	99.1	Chronic liver disease and cirrhosis	12.2	8.6	8.3
Other diseases of endocardium ...	2.0	2.5	2.5	Nephritis, nephrotic syndrome, and			
All other forms of heart disease ...	40.8	40.1	39.9	nephrosis	4.5	4.3	4.3
Hypertension [1]	2.0	1.9	1.9	Homicide and legal intervention	10.8	10.2	10.9
Cerebrovascular diseases	40.8	27.7	26.8	Septicemia	2.6	4.1	4.1
Atherosclerosis..............	5.7	2.7	2.6	Other infectious and parasitic diseases .	1.8	12.0	13.3
Other	5.5	5.4	5.4	Benign neoplasms [4]	2.0	1.7	1.7
Malignancies [2]	132.8	135.0	134.5	Ulcer of stomach and duodenum	1.7	1.3	1.2
Of respiratory and intrathoracic organs..................	36.4	41.4	41.1	Hernia of abdominal cavity and intestinal obstruction [5]	1.4	1.1	1.1
Of digestive organs and peritoneum..	33.0	30.2	29.9	Anemias	0.9	0.9	0.9
Of genital organs	13.6	13.6	13.6	Cholelithiasis and other disorders of			
Of breast	12.5	12.7	12.4	gallbladder	0.8	0.6	0.5
Of urinary organs	5.2	5.1	5.1	Nutritional deficiencies	0.5	0.5	0.5
Leukemia	5.4	5.0	5.0	Infections of kidney	0.7	0.2	0.2
Accidents and adverse effects	42.3	32.5	31.0	Tuberculosis................	0.6	0.5	0.5
Motor vehicle	22.9	18.5	17.0	Meningitis.................	0.6	0.3	0.3
All other	19.5	14.0	13.9	Viral hepatitis	0.3	0.5	0.6
Chronic obstructive pulmonary diseases and allied conditions [3]	15.9	19.7	20.1	Acute bronchitis and bronchiolitis	0.2	0.1	0.1
Bronchitis, chronic and unspecified ..	1.0	0.8	0.8	Hyperplasia of prostate	0.2	0.1	0.1
Emphysema................	4.0	3.7	3.8	Symptoms, signs, and ill-defined			
Asthma...................	1.0	1.4	1.5	conditions.................	9.8	7.3	7.2
Other	9.9	13.7	14.1	All other causes	36.8	38.4	38.5

[1] With or without renal disease.   [2] Includes other types of malignancies not shown separately.   [3] Prior to 1980, data are shown for bronchitis, emphysema, and asthma.   [4] Includes neoplasms of unspecified nature; beginning 1980, also includes carcinoma in situ.   [5] Without mention of hernia.

Source of tables 123 and 124: U.S. National Center for Health Statistics, *Vital Statistics of the United States*, annual; *Monthly Vital Statistics Reports*; and unpublished data.

No. 125. Deaths and Death Rates, by Selected Causes: 1970 to 1992

[Excludes deaths of nonresidents of the United States, except as noted. Beginning 1979, deaths classified according to ninth revision of *Intern Classification of Diseases*; for earlier years, classified according to revision in use at that time. See also Appendix III and *Historical Statistics, Colonial Times to 1970*, series B 149-166]

CAUSE OF DEATH	DEATHS, (1,000					CRUDE DEATH RATE PER 100,000 POPULATION [2]				
	1970	1980	1990	1991	1992 [1]	1970	1980	1990	1991	1992 [1]
All causes	1,921.0	1,989.8	2,148.5	2,165.0	2177.0	945.3	878.3	863.8	858.5	853.3
Major cardiovascular diseases	1,008.0	988.5	916.0	913.4	915.4	496.0	436.4	368.3	362.2	358.8
Diseases of heart	735.5	761.1	720.1	718.1	720.5	362.0	336.0	289.5	284.8	282.5
Percent of total	38.3	38.3	33.5	33.2	33.1	38.3	38.3	33.5	33.2	33.1
Rheumatic fever and rheumatic heart disease.	14.9	7.8	6.0	6.0	6.0	7.3	3.5	2.4	2.4	2.3
Hypertensive heart disease [3]	15.0	24.8	23.4	24.1	25.3	7.4	10.9	9.5	9.5	(NA)
Ischemic heart disease	666.7	565.8	489.2	478.5	480.2	328.1	249.7	196.7	189.8	188.2
Other diseases of endocardium . . .	6.7	7.2	13.0	14.2	15.8	3.3	3.2	5.2	5.6	6.2
All other forms of heart disease . . .	32.3	155.5	188.4	195.3	193.3	15.9	68.7	75.8	77.5	75.8
Hypertension [3]	8.3	7.8	9.2	9.2	10.5	4.1	3.5	3.7	3.7	4.1
Cerebrovascular diseases	207.2	170.2	144.1	144.1	143.6	101.9	75.1	57.9	57.1	56.3
Atherosclerosis.	31.7	29.4	18.0	17.1	16.1	15.6	13.0	7.3	6.8	6.3
Other	25.3	20.0	24.6	24.9	24.6	12.5	8.8	9.9	9.9	9.7
Malignancies [4]	330.7	416.5	505.3	514.3	521.1	162.8	183.9	203.2	204.0	204.3
Percent of total	17.2	20.9	23.5	23.8	23.9	17.2	20.9	23.5	23.8	23.9
Of respiratory and intrathoracic organs.	69.5	108.5	146.4	148.8	155.0	34.2	47.9	58.9	59.0	60.7
Of digestive organs and peritoneum. .	94.7	110.6	120.8	120.4	121.4	46.6	48.8	48.6	47.8	47.6
Of genital organs	41.2	46.4	57.5	59.4	58.6	20.3	20.5	23.1	23.5	23.0
Of breast.	29.9	35.9	43.7	44.5	44.2	14.7	15.8	17.6	17.6	17.3
Of urinary organs	15.5	17.8	20.7	21.0	22.2	7.6	7.9	8.3	8.3	8.7
Leukemia	14.5	16.5	18.6	19.6	19.2	7.1	7.3	7.5	7.8	7.5
Accidents and adverse effects	114.6	105.7	92.0	91.7	86.3	56.4	46.7	37.0	36.4	33.8
Motor vehicle.	54.6	53.2	46.8	45.2	41.7	26.9	23.5	18.8	17.9	16.4
All other	60.0	52.5	45.2	46.5	44.6	29.5	23.3	18.2	18.4	17.5
Chronic obstructive pulmonary diseases and allied conditions [5]	30.9	56.1	86.7	89.1	91.4	15.2	24.7	34.9	35.3	35.8
Bronchitis, chronic and unspecified . .	5.8	3.7	3.6	4.0	4.2	2.9	1.6	1.4	1.6	1.6
Emphysema.	22.7	13.9	15.7	16.6	16.6	11.2	6.1	6.3	6.6	6.5
Asthma.	2.3	2.9	4.8	4.5	4.7	1.1	1.3	1.9	1.8	1.8
Other	(⁶)	35.6	62.6	64.1	66.0	(⁶)	15.7	25.2	25.4	25.9
Pneumonia and influenza	62.7	54.6	79.5	75.0	76.1	30.9	24.1	32.0	29.7	29.8
Pneumonia	59.0	51.9	77.4	74.0	74.9	29.0	22.9	31.1	29.3	29.3
Influenza	3.7	2.7	2.1	1.0	1.3	1.8	1.2	0.8	0.4	0.5
Diabetes mellitus	38.3	34.9	47.7	50.0	50.2	18.9	15.4	19.2	19.7	19.8
Suicide	23.5	26.9	30.9	30.2	29.8	11.6	11.9	12.4	12.0	11.7
Chronic liver disease and cirrhosis	31.4	30.6	25.8	24.7	24.8	15.5	13.5	10.4	9.8	9.7
Other infectious and parasitic diseases .	6.9	5.1	32.2	36.9	40.4	3.4	2.2	13.0	14.6	15.8
Homicide and legal intervention	16.8	24.3	24.9	27.4	26.6	8.3	10.7	10.0	10.9	10.4
Nephritis, nephrotic syndrome, and nephrosis	8.9	16.8	20.8	22.0	22.4	4.4	7.4	8.3	8.7	8.8
Septicemia	3.5	9.4	19.2	19.5	19.9	1.7	4.2	7.7	7.7	7.8
Certain conditions originating in the perinatal period	43.2	22.9	17.7	16.6	15.8	21.3	10.1	7.1	6.6	6.2
Congenital anomalies	16.8	13.9	13.1	11.8	12.4	8.3	6.2	5.3	4.7	4.9
Benign neoplasms [7]	4.8	6.2	6.8	7.0	6.5	2.4	2.7	2.7	2.8	2.5
Ulcer of stomach and duodenum	8.6	6.1	6.2	6.4	5.8	4.2	0.0	2.5	2.5	2.3
Hernia of abdominal cavity and intestinal obstruction [8]	7.2	5.4	5.8	5.8	6.2	3.6	2.4	2.3	2.3	2.4
Anemias.	3.4	3.2	4.1	4.2	4.0	1.7	1.4	1.6	1.6	1.6
Cholelithiasis and other disorders of gall bladder.	4.0	3.3	3.0	3.0	3.0	2.0	1.5	1.2	1.2	1.2
Nutritional deficiencies	2.5	2.4	3.0	3.2	3.1	1.2	1.0	1.2	1.3	1.2
Tuberculosis	5.2	2.0	1.8	1.7	1.4	2.6	0.9	0.7	0.7	0.5
Infections of kidney	8.2	2.7	1.3	1.3	1.2	4.0	1.2	0.5	0.5	0.5
Viral hepatitis	1.0	0.8	1.6	1.9	1.9	0.5	0.4	0.6	0.8	0.8
Meningitis.	1.7	1.4	1.0	0.7	0.7	0.8	0.6	0.4	0.3	0.3
Acute bronchitis and bronchiolitis	1.3	0.6	0.6	0.6	0.5	0.6	0.3	0.3	0.2	0.2
Hyperplasia of prostate.	2.2	0.8	0.5	0.3	0.4	1.1	0.3	0.2	0.1	0.1
Symptoms, signs, and ill-defined conditions	25.8	28.8	24.1	23.6	24.2	12.7	12.7	9.7	9.3	9.5
All other causes	108.8	120.0	172.9	178.3	181.0	53.5	53.0	69.5	70.7	70.9

NA Not available. [1] Based on a 10-percent sample of deaths. Includes deaths of nonresidents. [2] 1970, 1980, and 1990 based on resident population enumerated as of April 1. Other years based on resident population estimated as of July 1. [3] With or without renal disease. [4] Includes other types of malignancies not shown separately. [5] Prior to 1980, data are shown for bronchitis, emphysema, and asthma. [6] Included in "all other causes." Comparable data not available separately. [7] Includes neoplasms of unspecified nature; beginning 1980 also includes carcinoma in situ. [8] Without mention of hernia.

Source: U.S. National Center for Health Statistics, *Vital Statistics of the United States*, annual; *Monthly Vital Statistics Report*; and unpublished data.

No. 126. Deaths, by Selected Causes and Selected Characteristics: 1991

[In thousands. Excludes deaths of nonresidents of the United States. Deaths classified according to ninth revision of *International Classification of Diseases*. See also Appendix III]

AGE, SEX, AND RACE	Total [1]	Heart disease	Cancer	Accidents and adverse effects	Cerebrovascular diseases	Chronic obstructive pulmonary diseases [2]	Pneumonia, flu	Suicide	Chronic liver disease, cirrhosis	Diabetes mellitus	Homicide and legal intervention
ALL RACES [3]											
Both sexes, total [4]	**2,169.5**	**720.9**	**514.7**	**89.3**	**143.5**	**90.7**	**77.9**	**30.8**	**25.4**	**49.0**	**26.5**
Under 1 year old	36.8	0.7	0.1	1.0	0.2	0.1	0.6	-	(Z)	(Z)	0.4
1 to 4 years old	7.2	0.3	0.5	2.7	0.1	0.1	0.2	-	(Z)	(Z)	0.4
5 to 14 years old	8.5	0.3	1.1	3.7	0.1	0.1	0.1	0.3	(Z)	(Z)	0.5
15 to 24 years old	36.5	1.0	1.8	15.3	0.2	0.2	0.3	4.8	(Z)	0.1	8.2
25 to 34 years old	59.6	3.4	5.3	14.8	0.8	0.3	0.8	6.5	0.9	0.7	7.8
35 to 44 years old	88.1	12.4	16.9	11.8	2.5	0.7	1.4	5.8	3.6	1.6	4.6
45 to 54 years old	120.7	30.4	40.0	7.1	4.7	2.3	1.7	4.0	4.5	3.0	2.1
55 to 64 years old	248.1	75.0	94.2	6.6	9.7	10.4	3.7	3.2	6.0	7.0	1.2
65 to 74 years old	478.6	159.4	159.3	8.1	25.5	28.6	10.2	3.1	6.2	13.8	0.7
75 to 84 years old	607.5	228.9	139.4	10.1	49.4	33.7	24.6	2.4	3.5	14.7	0.4
85 years old and over	477.4	209.0	56.1	8.2	50.2	14.1	34.1	0.8	0.7	8.0	0.1
Male, total [4]	**1,121.7**	**360.0**	**272.4**	**59.7**	**56.7**	**50.5**	**36.2**	**24.8**	**16.3**	**21.1**	**20.8**
Under 1 year old	21.0	0.4	(Z)	0.6	0.1	(Z)	0.3	-	(Z)	-	0.2
1 to 4 years old	4.0	0.2	0.3	1.6	(Z)	(Z)	0.1	-	(Z)	(Z)	0.2
5 to 14 years old	5.3	0.2	0.7	2.5	(Z)	0.1	0.1	0.2	(Z)	(Z)	0.3
15 to 24 years old	27.5	0.6	1.1	11.5	0.1	0.1	0.2	4.1	(Z)	0.1	6.9
25 to 34 years old	43.7	2.3	2.6	11.6	0.4	0.2	0.5	5.4	0.5	0.4	6.2
35 to 44 years old	60.6	9.2	7.5	9.0	1.4	0.4	0.9	4.5	2.6	0.9	3.6
45 to 54 years old	76.0	22.5	20.0	5.2	2.6	1.2	1.1	3.0	3.2	1.7	1.6
55 to 64 years old	151.4	51.7	52.2	4.5	5.2	5.7	2.3	2.5	4.1	3.5	0.9
65 to 74 years old	275.9	97.8	89.9	4.9	13.1	16.2	6.0	2.5	3.7	6.4	0.5
75 to 84 years old	299.0	110.8	73.8	5.1	20.6	19.3	12.7	2.1	1.8	6.0	0.2
85 years old and over	156.8	64.0	24.3	3.1	13.1	7.3	12.1	0.6	0.3	2.3	(Z)
Female, total [4]	**1,047.9**	**361.0**	**242.3**	**29.6**	**86.8**	**40.2**	**41.6**	**6.0**	**9.2**	**27.9**	**5.7**
Under 1 year old	15.8	0.3	(Z)	0.4	0.1	(Z)	0.3	-	(Z)	(Z)	0.2
1 to 4 years old	3.2	0.2	0.2	1.1	(Z)	(Z)	0.1	-	(Z)	(Z)	0.2
5 to 14 years old	3.2	0.1	0.5	1.2	(Z)	(Z)	0.1	0.1	(Z)	(Z)	0.2
15 to 24 years old	8.9	0.3	0.7	3.7	0.1	0.1	0.1	0.7	(Z)	0.1	1.2
25 to 34 years old	15.9	1.1	2.7	3.2	0.4	0.2	0.3	1.2	0.3	0.3	1.6
35 to 44 years old	27.6	3.2	9.4	2.8	1.2	0.3	0.5	1.3	1.0	0.6	1.0
45 to 54 years old	44.6	7.8	20.0	1.9	2.2	1.2	0.7	1.0	1.3	1.4	0.5
55 to 64 years old	96.6	23.3	42.0	2.0	4.5	4.7	1.4	0.7	1.9	3.5	0.3
65 to 74 years old	202.8	61.6	69.4	3.2	12.4	12.3	4.3	0.6	2.5	7.5	0.2
75 to 84 years old	308.5	118.0	65.6	5.0	28.8	14.5	11.9	0.4	1.7	8.7	0.2
85 years old and over	320.6	145.0	31.8	5.1	37.0	6.8	22.1	0.1	0.4	5.8	0.1
WHITE											
Both sexes, total [4]	**1,868.9**	**636.8**	**450.0**	**74.4**	**123.7**	**84.0**	**69.3**	**28.0**	**21.4**	**39.6**	**12.8**
Under 1 year old	23.7	0.5	0.1	0.6	0.1	(Z)	0.3	-	(Z)	(Z)	0.2
1 to 4 years old	5.0	0.2	0.4	1.9	(Z)	(Z)	0.1	-	(Z)	(Z)	0.2
5 to 14 years old	6.3	0.2	0.9	2.7	0.1	0.1	0.1	0.2	(Z)	(Z)	0.3
15 to 24 years old	26.0	0.7	1.5	12.9	0.2	0.1	0.2	4.1	(Z)	0.1	3.2
25 to 34 years old	42.3	2.3	4.3	12.0	0.5	0.2	0.5	5.7	0.6	0.5	3.5
35 to 44 years old	64.0	9.0	13.4	9.2	1.6	0.4	0.9	5.3	2.6	1.1	2.4
45 to 54 years old	93.7	23.7	32.5	5.8	3.1	1.9	1.2	3.7	3.5	2.1	1.3
55 to 64 years old	205.3	61.8	80.2	5.4	7.1	9.3	3.0	3.0	5.1	5.2	0.7
65 to 74 years old	415.8	138.2	140.2	7.0	20.9	26.5	8.8	3.0	5.6	11.1	0.5
75 to 84 years old	546.6	206.6	125.2	9.2	43.8	32.0	22.3	2.3	3.2	12.4	0.3
85 years old and over	439.8	193.7	50.8	7.5	46.2	13.4	31.9	0.7	0.7	7.0	0.1
BLACK											
Both sexes, total [4]	**269.5**	**76.0**	**57.9**	**12.5**	**17.4**	**5.8**	**7.4**	**2.1**	**3.5**	**8.5**	**13.0**
Under 1 year old	12.0	2.2	(Z)	0.3	(Z)	(Z)	0.2	-	(Z)	-	0.2
1 to 4 years old	1.9	0.1	0.1	0.6	(Z)	(Z)	0.1	-	-	-	0.2
5 to 14 years old	1.9	0.8	0.2	0.8	(Z)	0.1	(Z)	(Z)	(Z)	(Z)	0.2
15 to 24 years old	9.3	0.3	0.3	1.9	(Z)	0.1	0.1	0.5	(Z)	(Z)	4.8
25 to 34 years old	15.7	1.0	0.9	2.3	0.3	0.1	0.3	0.6	0.2	0.2	4.0
35 to 44 years old	22.1	3.2	3.0	2.2	0.9	0.2	0.5	0.4	0.8	0.4	2.0
45 to 54 years old	24.4	6.2	6.5	1.1	1.4	0.5	0.5	0.2	0.8	0.8	0.7
55 to 64 years old	38.4	12.0	12.5	10.0	2.3	1.0	0.7	0.1	0.8	1.6	0.4
65 to 74 years old	56.4	19.3	17.1	10.0	4.0	1.8	1.2	0.1	0.6	2.5	0.3
75 to 84 years old	54.2	20.0	12.7	8.0	4.9	1.5	1.9	0.1	0.2	2.0	0.1
85 years old and over	33.1	13.6	4.7	0.6	3.4	0.6	1.8	(Z)	(Z)	1.0	(Z)

- Represents zero.   Z Fewer than 50.   [1] Includes other causes not shown separately.   [2] Includes allied conditions. [3] Includes other races not shown separately.   [4] Includes those deaths with age not stated.

Source: U.S. National Center for Health Statistics, *Vital Statistics of the United States*, annual.

No. 127. Deaths, by Age and Leading Cause: 1991

[Excludes deaths of nonresidents of the United States. Deaths classified according to ninth revision of *International Classification of Diseases.* See also Appendix III and *Historical Statistics, Colonial Times to 1970,* series B 149-166]

AGE AND LEADING CAUSE OF DEATH	NUMBER OF DEATHS			DEATH RATE PER 100,000 POPULATION		
	Total	Male	Female	Total	Male	Female
ALL AGES [1]						
All races [2]	2,169,518	1,121,665	1,047,853	860.3	912.1	811.0
White	1,868,904	956,497	912,407	886.2	926.2	847.7
Black	269,525	147,331	122,194	864.9	998.7	744.5
Leading causes of death:						
Heart disease	720,862	359,814	361,048	285.9	292.6	279.5
Malignant neoplasms (cancer)	514,657	272,380	242,277	204.1	221.5	187.5
Cerebrovascular disease (stroke)	143,481	56,714	86,767	56.9	46.1	67.2
Chronic obstructive pulmonary disease	90,650	50,485	40,165	35.9	41.1	31.2
Accidents	89,347	59,730	29,617	35.4	48.6	22.9
Motor vehicle	43,536	29,947	13,589	17.3	24.4	10.5
Pneumonia	77,860	36,214	41,646	30.9	29.4	32.2
Diabetes	48,951	21,096	27,855	19.4	17.2	21.6
Suicide	30,810	24,769	(NA)	12.2	20.1	(NA)
HIV infection [3]	29,555	26,046	(NA)	11.7	21.2	(NA)
Homicide and legal intervention	26,513	20,768	(NA)	10.5	16.9	(NA)
1 TO 4 YEARS OLD						
All causes	7,214	4,045	3,169	47.4	52.0	42.7
Leading causes of death:						
Accidents	2,665	1,566	1,099	17.5	20.1	14.8
Motor vehicle	902	491	411	5.9	6.3	5.5
Congenital anomalies	871	469	402	5.7	6.0	5.4
Malignant neoplasms (cancer)	526	288	238	3.5	3.7	3.2
Homicide and legal intervention	428	235	193	2.8	3.0	2.6
Heart disease	332	178	154	2.2	2.3	2.1
Pneumonia and influenza	207	125	82	1.4	1.6	1.1
5 TO 14 YEARS OLD						
All causes	8,479	5,272	3,207	23.6	28.7	18.3
Leading causes of death:						
Accidents	3,660	2,493	1,167	10.2	13.6	6.7
Malignant neoplasms (cancer)	1,106	650	456	3.1	3.5	2.6
Congenital anomalies	487	263	224	1.4	1.4	1.3
Homicide and legal intervention	519	337	182	1.4	1.8	1.0
Heart disease	281	151	130	0.8	0.8	0.7
Pneumonia and influenza	135	69	66	0.4	0.4	0.4
15 TO 24 YEARS OLD						
All causes	36,452	27,549	8,903	100.1	148.0	50.0
Leading causes of death:						
Accidents	15,278	11,534	3,744	42.0	62.0	21.0
Motor vehicle	11,664	8,468	3,196	32.0	45.5	18.0
Homicide and legal intervention	8,159	6,923	1,236	22.4	37.2	6.9
Suicide	4,751	4,073	678	13.1	21.9	3.8
Malignant neoplasms (cancer)	1,814	1,083	731	5.0	5.8	4.1
Heart disease	990	641	349	2.7	3.4	2.0
HIV infection [3]	613	452	161	1.7	2.4	0.9
25 TO 44 YEARS OLD						
All causes	147,750	104,261	43,489	179.9	255.2	105.3
Leading causes of death:						
Accidents	26,526	20,561	5,965	32.3	50.3	14.4
Motor vehicle	15,082	11,142	3,940	18.4	27.3	9.5
Malignant neoplasms (cancer)	22,228	10,164	12,064	27.1	24.9	29.2
HIV infection [3]	21,747	19,263	2,484	26.5	47.1	6.0
Heart disease	15,822	11,497	4,325	19.3	28.1	10.5
Homicide and legal intervention	12,372	9,770	2,602	15.1	23.9	6.3
Suicide	12,281	9,836	2,445	14.9	24.1	5.9
45 TO 64 YEARS OLD						
All causes	368,754	227,464	141,290	788.9	1,011.2	582.6
Leading causes of death:						
Malignant neoplasms (cancer)	134,117	72,193	61,924	286.9	320.9	255.4
Heart disease	105,359	74,258	31,101	225.4	330.1	128.3
Cerebrovascular (stroke)	14,464	7,791	6,673	30.9	34.6	27.5
Accidents	13,693	9,750	3,943	29.3	43.3	16.3
Motor vehicle	6,616	4,458	2,158	14.2	19.8	8.9
Chronic obstructive pulmonary disease	12,769	6,874	5,895	27.3	30.6	24.3
Chronic liver disease and cirrhosis	10,497	7,301	3,196	22.5	32.5	13.2
Diabetes	10,045	5,129	4,916	21.5	22.8	20.3
65 YEARS OLD AND OVER						
All causes	1,563,527	731,629	831,898	4,924.0	5,719.9	4,387.0
Leading causes of death:						
Heart disease	597,267	272,619	324,648	1,881.0	2,131.3	1,712.0
Malignant neoplasms (cancer)	354,768	187,944	166,824	1,117.3	1,469.3	879.7
Cerebrovascular (stroke)	125,139	46,887	78,252	394.1	366.6	412.7
Chronic obstructive pulmonary disease	76,412	42,814	33,598	240.6	334.7	177.2
Pneumonia and influenza	68,962	30,710	38,252	217.2	240.1	201.7
Diabetes	36,528	14,593	21,935	115.0	114.1	115.7
Accidents	26,444	13,163	13,281	83.3	102.9	70.0
Motor vehicle	7,044	3,956	3,088	22.2	30.9	16.3

[1] Includes those deaths with age not stated.   [2] Includes other races not shown separately.   [3] Human immunodeficiency virus.

Source: U.S. National Center for Health Statistics, *Vital Statistics of the United States,* annual; and unpublished data.

No. 128. Death Rates, by Selected Causes and Age: 1980 to 1991

[Deaths per 100,000 population in specified group. Except as noted, excludes deaths of nonresidents of the United States. See headnote, table 124]

YEAR, RACE, AND AGE	Total [1]	Heart disease	Malignant neoplasms	Accidents and adverse effects	Cerebrovascular diseases	Chronic obstructive pulmonary diseases [2]	Pneumonia, flu	Suicide	Chronic liver disease, cirrhosis	Diabetes mellitus	Homicide and legal intervention
ALL RACES [3]											
Both sexes:											
1980, age-adjusted . . .	585.8	336.0	183.9	46.7	75.1	24.7	24.1	11.9	13.5	15.4	10.7
1990, age-adjusted . . .	520.2	289.5	203.2	37.0	57.9	34.9	32.0	12.4	10.4	19.2	10.0
1991, age-adjusted . . .	513.7	285.9	204.1	35.4	56.9	35.9	30.9	12.2	10.1	19.4	10.5
15 to 24 years old . .	(NA)	2.7	5.0	42.0	0.6	0.6	0.7	13.1	0.1	0.3	22.4
25 to 34 years old . .	(NA)	8.0	12.4	34.5	1.9	0.8	1.8	15.2	2.0	1.5	18.2
35 to 44 years old . .	(NA)	31.6	43.1	29.9	6.4	1.7	3.7	14.7	9.1	4.0	11.6
45 to 54 years old . .	(NA)	118.0	155.1	27.7	18.3	9.1	6.8	15.5	17.3	11.8	8.2
55 to 64 years old . .	(NA)	357.0	448.4	31.2	46.4	49.7	17.8	15.4	28.8	33.4	5.5
65 to 74 years old . .	(NA)	872.0	871.6	44.5	139.6	156.3	55.9	16.9	34.0	75.7	4.0
75 to 84 years old . .	(NA)	2,219.1	1,351.6	98.3	479.4	327.0	238.5	23.5	33.4	142.3	4.2
85 years old and over	(NA)	6,613.4	1,773.9	258.4	1,587.7	446.9	1,080.5	24.0	23.1	253.8	4.1
Male:											
1980, age-adjusted	777.2	368.6	205.3	67.4	63.6	35.1	25.1	18.6	18.0	13.0	17.3
1990, age-adjusted	680.2	297.6	221.3	51.1	46.8	40.8	30.4	20.4	13.7	16.7	16.2
1991, age-adjusted	669.9	292.6	221.5	48.6	46.1	41.1	29.4	20.1	13.2	17.2	16.9
15 to 24 years old. . . .	(NA)	3.4	5.8	62.0	0.6	0.6	0.8	21.9	0.1	0.4	37.2
25 to 34 years old. . . .	(NA)	10.7	12.2	54.0	1.8	0.8	2.3	25.0	2.5	1.7	28.9
35 to 44 years old. . . .	(NA)	47.4	38.8	46.2	7.1	1.8	4.9	23.0	13.3	4.7	18.4
45 to 54 years old. . . .	(NA)	179.3	159.0	41.4	20.3	9.3	8.5	23.7	25.3	13.2	12.8
55 to 64 years old. . . .	(NA)	520.8	525.7	45.7	52.7	57.5	23.4	25.3	41.6	34.9	8.7
65 to 74 years old. . . .	(NA)	1,219.1	1,120.4	61.4	163.8	202.4	74.1	30.7	46.1	79.6	6.2
75 to 84 years old. . . .	(NA)	2,850.9	1,898.4	132.3	530.0	495.4	326.9	53.0	45.8	153.1	5.7
85 years old and over .	(NA)	7,262.4	2,753.3	350.6	1,491.3	830.8	1,368.7	69.7	34.3	256.2	5.6
Female:											
1980, age-adjusted	432.6	305.1	163.6	27.1	86.1	15.0	23.2	5.5	9.3	17.6	4.5
1990, age-adjusted	390.6	281.8	186.0	23.6	68.6	29.2	33.4	4.8	7.2	21.5	4.2
1991, age-adjusted	386.5	279.5	187.5	22.9	67.2	31.1	32.2	4.7	7.1	21.6	4.4
15 to 24 years old. . . .	(NA)	2.0	4.1	21.0	0.6	0.5	0.6	3.8	(NA)	0.3	6.9
25 to 34 years old. . . .	(NA)	5.3	12.6	14.9	2.0	0.7	1.3	5.4	1.5	1.4	7.5
35 to 44 years old. . . .	(NA)	16.0	47.2	13.9	5.8	1.7	2.5	6.5	5.0	3.2	5.0
45 to 54 years old. . . .	(NA)	59.5	151.3	14.6	16.4	8.9	5.1	7.6	9.7	10.4	3.8
55 to 64 years old. . . .	(NA)	210.0	379.1	18.2	40.7	42.7	12.8	6.5	17.3	32.0	2.6
65 to 74 years old. . . .	(NA)	600.6	676.9	31.3	120.7	120.2	41.7	6.0	24.6	72.6	2.4
75 to 84 years old. . . .	(NA)	1,836.9	1,020.7	77.8	448.8	225.1	185.0	5.7	26.0	135.7	3.4
85 years old and over .	(NA)	6,362.5	1,395.2	222.7	1,625.0	298.6	969.1	6.3	18.8	252.8	3.6
WHITE											
Both sexes:											
1980, age-adjusted . . .	559.4	350.8	189.0	46.3	76.3	26.9	24.8	12.7	13.0	14.8	7.0
1990, age-adjusted . . .	492.8	305.4	211.6	36.9	59.7	38.4	33.9	13.5	10.3	18.5	5.8
1991, age-adjusted . . .	486.8	301.9	213.1	35.3	58.7	39.8	32.8	13.3	10.1	18.8	6.1
Male:											
1980, age-adjusted	745.3	384.0	208.7	66.3	63.3	37.9	25.1	19.9	17.3	12.8	10.9
1990, age-adjusted	644.3	312.7	227.7	50.3	47.0	44.3	31.4	22.0	13.6	16.5	9.0
1991, age-adjusted	634.4	307.6	228.9	47.7	46.3	44.9	30.6	21.7	13.4	16.9	9.3
Female:											
1980, age-adjusted	411.1	319.2	170.3	27.2	88.8	16.4	24.6	5.9	8.8	16.8	3.2
1990, age-adjusted	369.9	298.4	196.1	24.0	71.8	32.8	36.3	5.3	7.1	20.5	2.8
1991, age-adjusted	366.3	296.5	198.0	23.4	70.5	35.0	35.0	5.2	7.1	20.6	3.0
BLACK											
Both sexes:											
1980, age-adjusted . . .	842.5	274.0	169.1	50.6	75.6	12.7	21.2	6.0	18.0	20.8	38.6
1990, age-adjusted . . .	789.2	246.4	187.2	40.7	57.1	18.6	24.8	6.9	12.3	26.6	39.8
1991, age-adjusted . . .	780.7	243.9	185.9	40.0	55.7	18.7	23.7	6.7	11.1	27.3	41.6
Male:											
1980, age-adjusted	1,112.8	301.0	205.5	77.1	73.1	19.3	26.9	10.3	24.0	16.0	66.6
1990, age-adjusted	1,061.3	256.8	221.9	60.7	53.1	25.2	28.9	12.0	16.6	21.1	69.2
1991, age-adjusted	1,048.8	253.9	217.5	59.8	52.1	24.5	26.7	12.1	14.5	22.1	72.0
Female:											
1980, age-adjusted	631.1	249.7	136.5	26.9	77.9	6.8	16.1	2.2	12.6	25.2	13.5
1990, age-adjusted	581.6	237.0	156.1	22.8	60.7	12.6	21.2	2.3	8.5	31.5	13.5
1991, age-adjusted	575.1	235.0	157.4	22.2	59.0	13.4	20.9	1.9	8.1	32.0	14.2

NA Not available.   [1] Includes other causes not shown separately.   [2] Includes allied conditions.   [3] Includes other races not shown separately.

Source: U.S. National Center for Health Statistics, *Vital Statistics of the United States*, annual; and *Monthly Vital Statistics Report*.

No. 129. Death Rates, by Cause—States: 1991

[Deaths per 100,000 resident population enumerated as of April 1. By place of residence. Excludes nonresidents of the United States. Causes of death classified according to ninth revision of *International Classification of Diseases*]

DIVISION AND STATE	Total[1]	Heart disease	Cancer	Cerebro-vascular diseases	Accidents and adverse effects	Chronic obstructive pulmonary diseases[2]	Pneumonia, flu	Diabetes mellitus	Suicide	Chronic liver disease and cirrhosis	Athero-sclerosis
U.S....	860.3	285.9	204.1	56.9	35.4	34.9	32.0	19.2	12.2	10.4	7.3
N.E........	869.1	286.5	223.6	53.6	25.5	34.2	35.4	19.0	9.8	10.5	7.1
ME......	909.0	299.8	237.8	53.7	32.4	45.8	32.9	19.9	14.3	8.9	9.5
NH......	761.4	246.4	203.0	50.4	26.4	34.3	24.7	17.9	11.8	9.9	8.0
VT......	804.8	258.7	197.0	46.7	30.9	39.3	36.3	19.2	16.2	10.5	5.0
MA......	885.2	285.4	230.2	54.5	23.4	33.0	38.5	20.4	8.2	11.2	6.9
RI......	936.1	323.4	236.1	56.5	28.2	36.0	28.7	22.1	8.2	10.1	11.2
CT......	851.7	290.6	214.0	53.2	24.8	30.5	36.1	15.5	10.0	10.0	5.1
M.A.......	954.8	345.7	229.4	53.6	29.9	33.2	36.5	21.3	9.2	11.2	5.8
NY......	927.8	353.1	213.2	47.5	28.6	31.6	41.2	15.8	8.8	11.5	5.5
NJ......	908.4	301.1	234.3	51.8	26.4	29.8	31.4	26.8	6.6	11.8	5.8
PA......	1,025.5	363.3	250.8	63.9	34.1	37.9	32.9	26.1	11.7	10.4	6.4
E.N.C......	890.2	305.1	212.8	59.2	33.7	35.1	31.8	22.1	11.4	10.2	8.1
OH......	915.9	319.9	221.5	56.2	33.2	39.0	28.8	25.3	11.3	9.1	8.1
IN......	893.9	299.4	214.4	64.2	36.9	38.0	30.0	21.8	12.5	7.5	10.4
IL......	902.0	309.0	211.5	59.5	33.1	33.1	34.8	19.8	10.3	11.8	6.8
MI......	853.8	294.7	205.5	55.3	32.4	32.4	30.9	21.7	12.2	12.1	8.7
WI......	870.6	289.5	208.7	66.9	34.7	32.8	35.4	21.9	11.6	8.1	7.8
W.N.C.....	915.1	308.3	212.0	67.0	38.3	39.3	38.5	18.9	12.5	7.2	10.4
MN......	796.7	241.0	189.3	64.4	33.2	32.8	33.4	15.7	11.5	6.7	8.2
IA......	978.6	345.7	227.5	74.9	39.5	42.6	44.0	20.7	12.0	6.7	15.2
MO......	986.5	344.8	228.8	66.3	42.0	41.5	39.8	21.3	13.8	8.2	8.2
ND......	878.1	285.5	215.6	69.3	32.4	34.9	30.7	24.7	11.7	8.1	15.8
SD......	945.1	331.2	215.2	65.1	43.4	38.9	36.5	17.2	13.5	7.2	8.2
NE......	924.4	322.4	200.0	68.2	38.0	47.0	43.3	16.2	12.0	5.9	14.2
KS......	902.0	301.3	206.2	63.8	38.8	38.9	38.1	18.4	12.4	6.9	9.9
S.A........	897.0	291.6	215.6	60.2	37.9	34.9	27.7	20.2	13.1	10.7	6.6
DE......	871.8	283.2	223.5	52.2	32.9	33.6	24.9	28.8	11.6	11.0	4.8
MD......	790.7	241.5	200.8	45.6	27.1	29.4	24.8	21.1	8.8	8.4	4.4
DC......	1,183.1	311.9	258.7	56.7	33.4	25.9	34.4	32.3	5.7	31.6	9.4
VA......	781.6	250.0	191.0	52.6	34.1	29.2	27.9	14.4	12.6	8.0	5.8
WV......	1,108.5	392.8	256.9	65.9	49.1	50.9	39.7	27.2	13.3	10.0	8.6
NC......	874.0	281.4	198.4	68.3	41.4	30.9	29.3	19.8	12.5	10.9	5.0
SC......	841.7	267.6	190.2	67.8	47.5	29.9	23.4	20.8	11.8	10.3	4.7
GA......	797.3	249.4	175.0	56.2	42.0	29.5	27.7	15.5	13.5	8.7	6.6
FL......	1,026.5	348.2	260.4	64.7	36.2	43.9	27.0	22.9	15.8	13.1	8.7
E.S.C......	960.3	327.4	217.9	67.3	49.3	38.3	33.9	19.9	13.1	9.7	7.0
KY......	952.0	321.6	229.9	63.1	45.3	42.2	36.7	21.7	13.2	8.6	6.2
TN......	935.0	312.8	213.4	68.8	44.4	38.2	34.8	18.7	13.4	10.5	8.3
AL......	979.8	322.2	215.5	68.7	53.9	37.5	30.3	21.5	13.2	10.7	7.0
MS......	990.1	371.6	213.0	68.1	56.8	34.2	33.8	17.1	12.5	8.2	5.5
W.S.C.....	811.8	260.7	185.6	55.4	39.3	31.7	28.2	21.6	13.0	9.1	7.3
AR......	1,056.0	346.0	236.4	89.9	51.8	44.2	38.5	22.0	11.9	8.7	6.9
LA......	900.4	292.6	208.9	57.2	42.0	29.0	24.0	28.8	13.1	8.6	7.6
OK......	953.5	340.4	214.8	64.5	44.6	42.6	41.0	16.1	13.9	7.9	12.0
TX......	730.8	226.7	167.5	48.6	35.9	29.0	25.4	20.7	13.0	9.4	6.5
Mountain ...	719.0	208.1	164.9	44.4	40.2	39.0	27.8	15.4	18.0	10.3	6.9
MT......	868.1	240.5	203.3	62.0	48.6	48.7	29.8	19.4	19.9	10.6	8.4
ID.......	742.9	225.0	164.9	54.8	44.3	37.7	31.0	17.0	15.9	5.1	6.8
WY......	686.7	197.8	153.9	43.9	46.5	44.1	27.8	14.6	18.9	8.6	5.5
CO......	668.9	181.7	154.2	40.4	35.4	39.5	28.4	12.3	16.7	9.0	8.3
NM......	728.0	199.9	151.9	41.3	56.3	35.2	23.0	21.1	18.3	15.3	7.3
AZ......	787.9	234.4	191.1	47.7	40.2	43.5	32.3	15.1	17.7	11.7	7.0
UT......	545.3	157.2	111.5	38.6	29.2	20.8	23.2	16.7	16.2	6.1	4.5
NV.......	775.9	249.8	186.1	37.2	37.9	47.9	21.7	12.7	24.8	14.1	5.3
Pacific......	715.5	220.8	169.2	52.0	32.2	33.7	31.7	12.4	12.6	12.0	7.3
WA......	738.8	223.1	183.2	56.0	32.5	39.9	28.9	15.8	13.8	8.5	9.0
OR......	856.1	246.4	212.6	66.7	37.3	45.1	34.6	16.7	15.5	9.4	11.2
CA......	708.6	222.0	165.1	50.6	31.3	32.4	32.6	11.3	12.2	13.1	6.9
AK.......	386.0	82.5	88.2	15.4	63.2	16.4	8.7	9.3	12.8	8.4	2.4
HI.......	600.0	180.4	146.2	49.6	25.0	19.6	26.2	15.2	9.4	6.8	2.1

[1] Includes other causes not shown separately.　　[2] Includes allied conditions.

Source: U.S. National Center for Health Statistics, *Monthly Vital Statistics Report;* and unpublished data.

No. 130. Acquired Immunodeficiency Syndrome (AIDS) Deaths, by Selected Characteristics: 1982 to 1992

[Data are shown by year of death and are subject to substantial retrospective changes. For data on AIDS cases reported, see table 206. Based on reporting by State health departments]

CHARACTERISTIC	NUMBER									PERCENT DISTRIBUTION	
	Total, 1982-1992 [1]	1985	1986	1987	1988	1989	1990	1991	1992	Total	1982-1992
Total [2]	166,467	6,682	11,537	15,451	19,657	26,157	28,060	30,593	22,675	100	100
Age:											
Under 5 years old......	1,796	96	127	223	246	277	290	248	192	1	1
5 to 12 years old	373	10	24	50	46	58	68	74	36	(Z)	(Z)
13 to 29 years old	30,518	1,329	2,286	3,012	3,794	4,801	5,021	5,292	3,809	18	17
30 to 39 years old	75,023	3,013	5,244	6,924	8,761	11,880	12,654	13,731	10,265	45	45
40 to 49 years old	39,177	1,396	2,469	3,285	4,326	6,063	6,825	7,743	5,855	24	26
50 to 59 years old	13,493	590	923	1,266	1,642	2,156	2,238	2,442	1,760	8	8
60 years old and over...	6,087	248	464	691	842	922	964	1,063	758	4	3
Sex:											
Male	148,863	6,177	10,557	13,921	17,551	23,394	24,936	27,048	20,110	89	89
Female.............	17,604	505	980	1,530	2,106	2,763	3,124	3,545	2,565	11	11
Race/ethnicity:											
White, non-Hispanic	92,007	3,981	6,871	8,717	10,694	14,219	15,384	16,609	12,323	56	55
Black, non-Hispanic	50,121	1,777	3,044	4,525	6,015	7,969	8,584	9,468	7,092	30	32
Hispanic.............	22,727	884	1,535	2,087	2,764	3,703	3,823	4,157	2,971	14	13

Z Less than 0.5 percent. [1] Includes deaths prior to 1982. [2] Includes other race/ethnicity groups not shown separately.

Source: U.S. Centers for Disease Control, Surveillance Report, annual.

No. 131. Death Rates From Heart Disease, by Sex and Age: 1970 to 1991

[**Deaths per 100,000 population in specified age groups.** Excludes deaths of nonresidents of the United States. Beginning 1980, deaths classified according to the ninth revision of the *International Classification of Diseases*. For earlier years, classified according to the revision in use at the time; see text, section 2. See Appendix III]

AGE AT DEATH AND SELECTED TYPE OF HEART DISEASE	MALE					FEMALE				
	1970	1980	1985	1990	1991	1970	1980	1985	1990	1991
Total U.S. rate [1]	422.5	368.6	342.8	297.6	292.6	304.5	305.1	304.3	281.8	279.5
25 to 34 years old	15.2	11.4	11.5	10.3	10.7	7.7	5.3	5.0	5.0	5.3
35 to 44 years old	103.2	68.7	58.4	48.1	47.4	32.2	21.4	18.3	15.1	16.0
45 to 54 years old	376.4	282.6	236.9	183.0	179.3	109.9	84.5	73.8	61.0	59.5
55 to 64 years old	987.2	746.8	651.9	537.3	520.8	351.6	272.1	250.3	215.7	210.0
65 to 74 years old	2,170.3	1,728.0	1,508.4	1,250.0	1,219.1	1,082.7	828.6	745.3	616.8	600.6
75 to 84 years old	4,534.8	3,834.3	3,498.0	2,968.2	2,850.9	3,120.8	2,497.0	2,245.2	1,893.8	1,836.9
85 years old and over........	8,426.2	8,752.7	8,123.7	7,418.4	7,262.4	7,591.8	7,350.5	6,935.7	6,478.1	6,362.5
Persons 45 to 54 years old:										
Ischemic heart	338.0	217.3	170.6	123.8	119.6	84.0	52.2	43.6	33.6	33.4
Rheumatic heart	11.4	3.1	1.9	1.1	1.0	10.6	4.3	2.8	1.9	1.8
Hypertensive heart [2]	4.6	8.3	8.5	7.6	8.0	4.0	5.5	4.7	4.3	4.0
Persons 55 to 64 years old:										
Ischemic heart	904.6	581.1	479.9	375.4	360.3	299.1	189.0	164.5	135.4	133.1
Rheumatic heart ..., ...	21.5	6.2	4.3	3.4	3.0	20.8	9.2	6.3	4.7	4.6
Hypertensive heart [2]	11.7	21.8	19.8	18.1	18.4	9.1	13.3	12.3	10.9	10.4
Persons 65 to 74 years old:										
Ischemic heart	2,010.0	1,355.5	1,130.9	898.5	870.2	978.0	605.3	514.7	415.2	398.9
Rheumatic heart	31.9	11.8	8.7	7.1	6.3	30.2	18.6	13.3	10.9	10.4
Hypertensive heart [2]	30.6	44.3	38.9	33.2	31.5	24.8	36.2	29.1	25.9	24.6
Persons 75 to 84 years old:										
Ischemic heart	4,222.7	2,953.7	2,544.2	2,129.6	2,032.3	2,866.3	1,842.7	1,530.3	1,287.6	1,236.9
Rheumatic heart .., ...	34.8	16.7	14.7	12.3	12.8	34.3	25.4	23.8	22.5	22.2
Hypertensive heart [2]	80.8	90.7	79.4	67.9	68.4	83.9	101.1	79.5	69.7	68.7
Persons 85 years old and over:										
Ischemic heart	7,781.5	6,501.6	5,748.1	5,120.7	4,964.5	6,951.5	5,280.6	4,711.0	4,257.8	4,145.9
Rheumatic heart	34.7	19.5	18.0	18.7	22.7	39.2	25.8	27.6	33.3	31.8
Hypertensive heart [2]	182.0	180.3	153.1	154.3	155.2	223.5	250.8	217.0	212.1	214.7

[1] Includes persons under 25 years old not shown separately. [2] With or without renal disease.

Source: U.S. National Center for Health Statistics, *Vital Statistics of the United States*, annual; and unpublished data.

No. 132. Death Rates From Cancer, by Sex and Age: 1970 to 1991

[Deaths per 100,000 population in the specified age groups. See headnote, table 131]

AGE AT DEATH AND SELECTED TYPE OF CANCER	MALE					FEMALE				
	1970	1980	1985	1990	1991	1970	1980	1985	1990	1991
Total [1]	182.1	205.3	213.4	221.3	221.5	144.4	163.6	175.7	186.0	187.5
25 to 34 years	16.3	13.4	13.2	12.6	12.2	16.7	14.0	13.2	12.6	12.6
35 to 44 years	53.0	44.0	42.4	38.5	38.8	65.6	53.1	49.2	48.1	47.2
45 to 54 years	183.5	188.7	175.2	162.5	159.0	181.5	171.8	165.3	155.5	151.3
55 to 64 years	511.8	520.8	536.9	532.9	525.7	343.2	361.7	381.8	375.2	379.1
65 to 74 years	1,006.8	1,093.2	1,105.2	1,122.2	1,120.4	557.9	607.1	645.3	677.4	676.9
75 to 84 years	1,588.3	1,790.5	1,839.7	1,914.4	1,898.4	891.9	903.1	937.8	1,010.3	1,020.7
85 years old and over	1,720.8	2,369.5	2,451.8	2,739.9	2,753.3	1,096.7	1,255.7	1,281.4	1,372.1	1,395.2
Persons, 35 to 44 years old:										
Respiratory, intrathoracic	17.0	12.6	10.6	9.1	8.6	6.5	6.8	5.8	5.4	5.5
Digestive organs, peritoneum . .	11.4	9.5	9.1	8.9	9.2	8.6	6.5	5.8	5.5	5.7
Breast	0.1	-	(B)	(B)	(B)	20.4	17.9	17.5	17.8	16.9
Genital organs	1.4	0.7	0.7	0.6	0.7	13.6	8.3	7.1	7.3	7.1
Lymphatic and hematopoietic tissues, excl. leukemia	5.6	4.3	4.6	4.5	5.1	3.2	2.4	2.3	2.1	2.2
Urinary organs	1.9	1.4	1.6	1.5	1.5	1.0	0.6	0.9	0.6	0.7
Lip, oral cavity, and pharynx . . .	1.7	1.8	1.4	1.3	1.3	0.7	0.5	0.6	0.3	0.3
Leukemia	3.4	3.2	3.0	2.5	2.3	2.8	2.6	2.1	2.2	2.0
Persons, 45 to 54 years old:										
Respiratory, intrathoracic	72.1	79.8	71.0	63.0	60.6	22.2	34.8	36.2	35.3	33.8
Digestive organs, peritoneum . .	45.9	44.3	41.9	40.4	38.2	32.5	27.8	25.9	23.3	22.3
Breast	0.4	0.2	0.3	0.3	(B)	52.6	48.1	47.1	45.4	44.3
Genital organs	3.4	3.4	3.2	2.9	3.0	34.4	24.1	20.6	19.4	18.4
Lymphatic and hematopoietic tissues, excl. leukemia	12.8	10.2	10.0	10.9	11.0	8.3	6.6	6.5	6.0	6.4
Urinary organs	8.0	7.4	7.5	7.2	7.1	3.5	3.3	3.1	2.9	3.0
Lip, oral cavity, and pharynx . . .	7.9	8.2	6.8	5.9	6.1	2.8	2.6	2.0	1.6	1.6
Leukemia	6.6	6.2	5.7	5.6	5.5	4.9	4.4	4.3	4.1	4.0
Persons, 55 to 64 years old:										
Respiratory, intrathoracic	202.3	223.8	233.6	232.6	226.0	38.9	74.5	94.5	107.6	107.0
Digestive organs, peritoneum . .	139.0	129.3	130.8	124.0	125.4	86.0	79.1	75.2	69.3	70.0
Breast	0.6	0.7	0.6	0.6	0.5	77.6	80.5	84.2	78.6	79.1
Genital organs	22.8	23.5	24.6	27.9	26.8	58.2	46.8	43.1	40.1	40.3
Lymphatic and hematopoietic tissues, excl. leukemia	27.1	24.4	25.3	27.2	26.7	17.7	16.8	17.6	16.7	18.1
Urinary organs	26.4	22.9	22.5	23.5	23.2	9.4	8.9	8.6	8.8	9.6
Lip, oral cavity, and pharynx . . .	20.1	17.9	16.0	16.2	14.7	6.2	6.0	5.4	4.7	5.3
Leukemia	15.4	14.7	14.7	14.7	14.6	9.0	9.3	9.2	8.8	9.1
Persons, 65 to 74 years old:										
Respiratory, intrathoracic	340.7	422.0	432.5	447.3	446.0	45.6	106.1	145.3	181.7	185.8
Digestive organs, peritoneum . . .	293.3	284.1	277.6	267.4	262.6	185.8	173.6	162.9	153.0	149.7
Breast	1.4	1.1	1.1	1.1	1.1	93.8	101.1	107.8	111.7	108.6
Genital organs	103.7	107.6	110.3	123.5	122.1	85.6	73.6	71.2	71.0	70.2
Lymphatic and hematopoietic tissues, excl. leukemia	50.3	48.1	53.2	56.8	57.9	34.6	34.4	36.6	39.5	41.1
Urinary organs	60.3	56.9	52.0	50.7	52.8	20.1	19.7	19.7	19.8	19.7
Lip, oral cavity, and pharynx . . .	26.8	25.4	24.2	21.5	20.6	6.7	8.8	8.6	8.3	7.8
Leukemia	35.3	35.3	34.7	36.0	36.1	19.3	18.7	19.2	18.8	19.3
Persons, 75 to 84 years old:										
Respiratory, intrathoracic	354.2	511.5	558.9	594.4	593.9	56.5	98.0	135.7	194.5	207.1
Digestive organs, peritoneum . .	507.5	496.6	476.1	468.0	454.1	353.3	326.3	308.7	293.3	290.0
Breast	2.7	2.1	2.3	1.6	1.7	127.4	126.4	136.2	146.3	145.1
Genital organs	299.4	315.4	321.3	358.5	363.5	104.9	95.7	92.7	95.3	94.8
Lymphatic and hematopoietic tissues, excl. leukemia	74.0	80.0	92.8	104.5	104.1	49.4	57.8	63.5	71.2	75.4
Urinary organs	112.2	112.4	106.1	107.5	103.5	44.0	37.4	36.4	38.5	38.5
Lip, oral cavity, and pharynx . . .	36.6	31.4	27.6	26.1	25.7	10.8	10.9	9.8	11.6	11.3
Leukemia	68.3	71.5	70.0	71.9	69.7	39.6	38.5	38.0	38.8	39.8
Persons, 85 years old and over:										
Respiratory, intrathoracic	215.3	386.3	457.3	538.0	552.1	56.5	96.3	104.2	142.8	154.4
Digestive organs, peritoneum . .	583.7	705.8	667.1	699.5	688.2	465.0	504.3	497.6	497.6	495.6
Breast	2.9	2.6	3.9	2.4	4.1	157.1	169.3	178.5	196.8	197.9
Genital organs	434.2	612.3	614.6	750.0	781.0	107.3	115.9	106.1	115.6	117.8
Lymphatic and hematopoietic tissues, excl. leukemia	58.1	93.2	114.8	140.5	140.7	41.7	63.0	73.7	90.0	92.8
Urinary organs	140.5	177.0	185.5	186.3	186.2	59.9	63.8	63.2	68.5	67.7
Lip, oral cavity, and pharynx . . .	47.0	40.2	32.7	37.4	31.9	19.2	16.0	16.0	17.5	17.1
Leukemia	83.3	117.1	114.8	116.0	111.7	50.9	61.1	63.9	65.0	70.0

- Represents zero. B Base figure too small to meet statistical standards for reliability of a derived figure. [1] Includes persons under 25 years of age and malignant neoplasms of other and unspecified sites, not shown separately.

Source: U.S. National Center for Health Statistics, *Vital Statistics of the United States*, annual; and unpublished data.

No. 133. Death Rates From Accidents and Violence: 1980 to 1991

[Rates are per 100,000 population. Excludes deaths of nonresidents of the United States. Beginning 1980, deaths classified according to the ninth revision of the *International Classification of Diseases*. For earlier years, classified according to the revisions in use at the time; see text, section 2. See Appendix III]

| CAUSE OF DEATH AND AGE | WHITE | | | | | | BLACK | | | | | |
| | Male | | | Female | | | Male | | | Female | | |
	1980	1990	1991	1980	1990	1991	1980	1990	1991	1980	1990	1991
Total [1]	97.1	81.2	78.7	36.3	32.1	31.5	154.0	142.0	143.9	42.6	38.6	38.4
Motor vehicle accidents	35.9	26.1	24.4	12.8	11.4	10.8	31.1	28.1	25.6	8.3	9.4	8.7
All other accidents	30.4	23.6	23.3	14.4	12.4	12.6	46.0	32.7	34.2	18.6	13.4	13.5
Suicide	19.9	22.0	21.7	5.9	5.3	5.2	10.3	12.0	12.1	2.2	2.3	1.9
Homicide	10.9	9.0	9.3	3.2	2.8	3.0	66.6	69.2	72.0	13.5	13.5	14.2
15 to 24 years old	138.6	107.3	104.2	37.3	30.5	31.2	162.0	208.0	231.9	35.0	34.9	37.0
25 to 34 years old	118.4	97.4	94.2	29.0	26.0	24.7	256.9	218.1	213.8	49.4	48.1	47.7
35 to 44 years old	94.1	82.3	78.5	29.2	24.4	23.5	218.1	176.6	171.8	43.2	38.5	40.0
45 to 54 years old	90.8	73.5	72.9	31.8	25.3	25.2	207.3	138.5	132.4	40.2	30.7	33.1
55 to 64 years old	92.3	79.5	75.6	33.8	29.4	26.6	188.5	129.9	124.7	47.3	36.1	32.5
65 years old and over	163.9	150.7	147.4	87.2	80.1	79.6	215.8	175.5	182.2	102.9	81.6	78.6
65 to 74 years old	116.7	99.7	94.8	46.4	40.5	39.0	182.2	141.8	142.6	68.7	50.4	48.1
75 to 84 years old	209.2	195.7	190.5	101.5	89.4	87.1	261.4	206.1	213.5	137.5	95.8	89.7
85 years old and over	438.5	428.3	433.3	268.1	232.4	234.8	379.2	359.1	373.9	235.7	213.0	209.8

[1] Includes persons under 15 years old, not shown separately.

No. 134. Deaths and Death Rates From Accidents, by Type: 1970 to 1991

[See headnote, table 133 and Appendix III. See also *Historical Statistics, Colonial Times to 1970*, series B 163-165]

| TYPE OF ACCIDENT | DEATHS (number) | | | | | RATE PER 100,000 POPULATION | | | | |
	1970	1980	1985	1990	1991	1970	1980	1985	1990	1991
Total	114,638	105,718	93,457	91,983	89,347	56.4	46.7	39.3	37.0	35.4
Motor vehicle accidents	54,633	53,172	45,901	46,814	43,536	26.9	23.5	19.3	18.8	17.3
Traffic	53,493	51,930	44,822	45,827	42,621	26.3	22.9	18.8	18.4	16.9
Nontraffic	1,140	1,242	1,079	987	915	0.6	0.5	0.5	0.4	0.4
Water-transport accidents	1,651	1,429	1,111	923	851	0.8	0.6	0.5	0.4	0.3
Air and space transport accidents	1,612	1,494	1,428	941	1,000	0.8	0.7	0.6	0.4	0.4
Railway accidents	852	632	551	663	651	0.4	0.3	0.2	0.3	0.3
Accidental falls	16,926	13,294	12,001	12,313	12,662	8.3	5.9	5.0	5.0	5.0
Fall from one level to another	4,798	3,743	3,365	3,194	3,291	2.4	1.7	1.4	1.3	1.3
Fall on the same level	828	415	411	499	474	0.4	0.2	0.2	0.2	0.2
Fracture, cause unspecified, and other unspecified falls	11,300	9,136	8,225	8,620	8,897	5.6	4.0	3.5	3.5	3.5
Accidental drowning	6,391	6,043	4,407	3,979	3,967	3.1	2.7	1.9	1.6	1.6
Accidents caused by—										
Fires and flames	6,718	5,822	4,938	4,175	4,120	3.3	2.6	2.1	1.7	1.6
Firearms	2,406	1,955	1,649	1,416	1,441	1.2	0.9	0.7	0.6	0.6
Electric current	1,140	1,095	802	670	626	0.6	0.5	0.3	0.3	0.2
Accidental poisoning by—										
Drugs and medicines	2,505	2,492	3,612	4,506	5,215	1.2	1.1	1.5	1.8	2.1
Other solid and liquid substances	1,174	597	479	549	483	0.6	0.3	0.2	0.2	0.2
Gases and vapors	1,620	1,242	1,079	748	736	0.8	0.5	0.5	0.3	0.3
Complications due to medical procedures	3,581	2437	2,674	2,669	2,473	1.8	1.1	1.1	1.1	1.0
Inhalation and ingestion of objects	2,753	3,249	3,551	3,303	3,240	1.4	1.5	1.5	1.3	1.3

No. 135. Suicides, by Sex and Method Used: 1970 to 1991

[Excludes deaths of nonresidents of the United States. Beginning 1979, deaths classified according to the ninth revision of the *International Classification of Diseases*. For earlier years, classified according to the revision in use at the time; see text, section 2. See also *Historical Statistics, Colonial Times to 1970*, series H 979-986]

| METHOD | MALE | | | | | | FEMALE | | | | | |
	1970	1980	1985	1989	1990	1991	1970	1980	1985	1989	1990	1991
Total	16,629	20,505	23,145	24,102	24,724	24,769	6,851	6,364	6,308	6,130	6,182	6,041
Firearms [1]	9,704	12,937	14,809	15,680	16,285	16,120	2,068	2,459	2,554	2,498	2,600	2,406
Percent of total	58	63	64	65	66	65	30	39	41	41	42	40
Poisoning [2]	3,299	2,997	3,319	3,211	3,221	3,316	3,285	2,456	2,385	2,232	2,203	2,228
Hanging and strangulation [3]	2,422	2,997	3,532	3,708	3,688	3,751	831	694	732	776	756	810
Other [4]	1,204	1,574	1,485	1,503	1,530	1,582	667	755	637	624	623	597

[1] Includes explosives in 1970.　　[2] Includes solids, liquids, and gases.　　[3] Includes suffocation.　　[4] Beginning 1980, includes explosives.

Source of tables 133-135: U.S. National Center for Health Statistics, *Vital Statistics of the United States*, annual; and unpublished data.

No. 136. Suicide Rates, by Sex, Race, and Age Group: 1980 to 1991

[See headnote, tables 128 and 133]

AGE	TOTAL [1]			MALE						FEMALE					
				White			Black			White			Black		
	1980	1990	1991	1980	1990	1991	1980	1990	1991	1980	1990	1991	1980	1990	1991
All ages [2]	11.9	12.4	12.2	19.9	22.0	21.7	10.3	12.0	12.1	5.9	5.3	5.2	2.2	2.3	1.9
10 to 14 years old. . . .	0.8	1.5	1.5	1.4	2.3	2.4	0.5	1.6	2.0	0.3	0.9	0.8	0.1	(B)	(B)
15 to 19 years old. . . .	8.5	11.1	11.0	15.0	19.3	19.1	5.6	11.5	12.2	3.3	4.0	4.2	1.6	1.9	(B)
20 to 24 years old. . . .	16.1	15.1	14.9	27.8	26.8	26.5	20.0	19.0	20.7	5.9	4.4	4.3	3.1	2.6	1.8
25 to 34 years old. . . .	16.0	15.2	15.2	25.6	25.6	26.1	21.8	21.9	21.1	7.5	6.0	5.8	4.1	3.7	3.3
35 to 44 years old. . . .	15.4	15.3	14.7	23.5	25.3	24.7	15.6	16.9	15.2	9.1	7.4	7.2	4.6	4.0	2.9
45 to 54 years old. . . .	15.9	14.8	15.5	24.2	24.8	25.3	12.0	14.8	14.3	10.2	7.5	8.3	2.8	3.2	3.0
55 to 64 years old. . . .	15.9	16.0	15.4	25.8	27.5	26.8	11.7	10.8	13.0	9.1	8.0	7.1	2.3	2.6	2.1
65 to 74 years over. . .	16.9	17.9	16.9	32.5	34.2	32.6	11.1	14.7	13.8	7.0	7.2	6.4	1.7	2.6	2.4
75 to 84 years over. . .	19.1	24.9	23.5	45.5	60.2	56.1	10.5	14.4	21.6	5.7	6.7	6.0	1.4	(B)	(B)
85 years and over. . . .	19.2	22.2	24.0	52.8	70.3	75.1	18.9	(B)	(B)	5.8	5.4	6.6	0.1	(B)	(B)

B Base figure too small to meet statistical standards for reliability of a derived figure. [1] Includes other races not shown separately. [2] Includes other age groups not shown separately.

Source: U.S. National Center for Health Statistics, *Monthly Vital Statistics Report;* and unpublished data.

No. 137. Firearm Mortality Among Children, Youth, and Young Adults, 1 to 34 Years Old: 1991

[**Death rate per 100,000 population.** Deaths classified according to the ninth revision of the *International Classification of Diseases*]

ITEM	Under 5 years old	5 to 9 years old	10 to 14 years old	15 to 19 years old	20 to 24 years old	25 to 29 years old	30 to 34 years old
MALE							
Total: White	0.5	0.5	4.6	29.1	34.6	29.0	26.0
Black	1.4	1.5	11.5	140.5	184.3	129.4	94.8
Accidents: White	0.1	0.3	1.6	2.9	1.6	1.0	0.8
Black	0.2	0.6	2.0	6.3	4.7	2.2	1.2
Suicide: White.	(X)	(X)	1.5	13.6	17.7	15.3	14.9
Black	(X)	(X)	1.1	9.0	14.4	13.4	10.5
Homicide: White	0.3	0.3	1.4	11.8	14.9	12.3	10.1
Black	1.1	0.9	8.2	123.6	164.4	113.4	82.9
FEMALE							
Total: White	0.4	0.3	1.0	4.6	5.1	4.9	5.5
Black	1.5	0.5	3.0	12.7	17.7	16.5	13.9
Accidents: White	0.1	0.1	0.1	0.2	0.2	0.1	0.1
Black	0.4	0.1	0.2	0.2	(X)	0.1	0.1
Suicide: White.	(X)	(X)	0.4	2.1	2.0	2.4	2.8
Black	(X)	(X)	0.1	0.8	0.7	1.9	0.7
Homicide: White	0.3	0.2	0.5	2.2	2.7	2.3	2.4
Black	1.1	0.4	2.7	11.2	16.8	14.4	13.1
Accidents: White	0.1	0.1	0.1	0.2	0.2	0.1	0.1
Black	0.4	0.1	0.2	0.2	(X)	0.1	0.1

X Not applicable.

Source: U.S. National Center for Health Statistics, *Advance Data from Vital and Health Statistics,* No. 231.

No. 138. Deaths—Life Years Lost and Mortality Costs, by Age, Sex, and Cause: 1991

[Life years lost: Number of years person would have lived in absence of death. **Mortality cost:** value of lifetime earnings lost by persons who die prematurely, discounted at 6 percent]

CHARACTER-ISTIC	Number of deaths (1,000)	LIFE YEARS LOST [1]		MORTALITY COST [2]		CHARACTER-ISTIC	Number of deaths (1,000)	LIFE YEARS LOST [1]		MORTALITY COST [2]	
		Total (1,000)	Per death	Total (mil.)	Per death			Total (1,000)	Per death	Total (mil.)	Per death
Total.	2,170	33,691	16	246,146	113,487	Heart disease .	360	4,241	12	32,277	89,724
Under 5 yrs. . .	44	3,253	74	10,936	248,650	Cancer.	272	3,653	13	30,108	110,541
5-14 yrs.	8	553	65	3,373	397,843	Cerebrovas-					
15-24 yrs. . . .	36	1,986	54	22,041	604,652	cular diseases	57	599	11	4,065	71,677
25-44 yrs.	148	5,925	40	90,936	615,469	Injuries.	60	2,074	35	26,674	447,384
45-64 yrs.	369	8,252	22	87,252	236,614	Other.	373	7,823	21	78,813	211,413
65 yrs. and over	1,564	13,722	9	31,608	20,216						
Heart disease .	721	8,056	11	45,686	63,386	**Female . . .**	1,048	15,301	15	74,209	70,829
Cancer.	515	7,628	15	53,403	103,768	Under 5 yrs. . .	19	1,473	78	4,166	220,107
Cerebrovas-						5-14 yrs.	3	223	70	1,103	343,954
cular diseases	143	1,505	10	7,354	51,258	15-24 yrs.	9	529	59	4,427	497,279
Injuries.	89	2,995	34	33,336	373,609	25-44 yrs.	43	1,896	44	20,368	468,351
Other.	701	13,508	19	106,368	151,893	45-64 yrs.	141	3,525	25	27,682	195,926
Male	1,122	18,390	16	171,937	153,347	65 yrs. and over	832	7,655	9	16,462	19,789
Under 5 yrs. . .	25	1,780	71	6,770	270,214	Heart disease .	361	3,814	11	13,408	37,140
5-14 yrs.	5	330	63	2,270	430,264	Cancer.	242	3,975	16	23,295	96,152
15-24 yrs.	28	1,457	53	17,614	639,352	Cerebrovas-					
25-44 yrs.	104	4,029	39	70,567	676,835	cular diseases	87	906	10	3,289	37,913
45-64 yrs.	227	4,727	21	59,570	261,887	Injuries.	30	921	31	6,662	225,033
65 yrs. and over	732	6,067	8	15,146	20,702	Other.	328	5,685	17	27,554	83,991

[1] Based on life expectancy at year of death.   [2] Cost estimates based on the person's age, sex, life expectancy at the time of death, labor force participation rates, annual earnings, value of homemaking services, and a 6-percent discount rate by which to convert to present worth the potential aggregate earnings lost over the years.
Source: Institute for Health and Aging, University of California, San Francisco, CA, unpublished data.

No. 139. Marriages and Divorces: 1970 to 1988

[See also *Historical Statistics, Colonial Times to 1970*, series B 214-217]

YEAR	MARRIAGES [1]						DIVORCES AND ANNULMENTS		
	Number (1,000)	Rate per 1,000 population					Number (1,000)	Rate per 1,000 population	
		Total	Men, 15 yrs. old and over	Women, 15 yrs. old and over	Unmarried women			Total	Married women, 15 yrs. old and over
					15 yrs. old and over	15 to 44 yrs. old			
1970	2,159	10.6	31.1	28.4	76.5	140.2	708	3.5	14.9
1975	2,153	10.0	27.9	25.6	66.9	118.5	1,036	4.8	20.3
1980	2,390	10.6	28.5	26.1	61.4	102.6	1,189	5.2	22.6
1981	2,422	10.6	28.4	26.1	61.7	103.1	1,213	5.3	22.6
1982	2,456	10.6	28.4	26.1	61.4	101.9	1,170	5.0	21.7
1983	2,446	10.5	28.0	25.7	59.9	99.3	1,158	4.9	21.3
1984	2,477	10.5	28.1	25.8	59.5	99.0	1,169	5.0	21.5
1985	2,413	10.1	26.9	24.8	57.0	94.9	1,190	5.0	21.7
1986	2,407	10.0	26.5	24.5	56.2	93.9	1,178	4.9	21.2
1987	2,403	9.9	26.2	24.2	55.7	92.4	1,166	4.8	20.8
1988	2,396	9.7	25.9	23.9	54.6	91.0	1,167	4.7	20.7

[1] Beginning 1980, includes nonlicensed marriages registered in California.

No. 140. Percent Distribution of Marriages, by Marriage Order: 1970 to 1988

[Excludes marriages with marriage order not stated. See headnote, table 142]

MARRIAGE ORDER	1970	1980	1981	1982	1983	1984	1985	1986	1987	1988
Total	100.0	100.0	100.0	100.0	100.0	100.0	100.0	100.0	100.0	100.0
First marriage of bride and groom	68.6	56.2	54.7	54.8	54.4	54.4	54.3	53.9	53.9	54.1
First marriage of bride, remarriage of groom . . .	7.6	11.3	11.8	11.6	11.6	11.5	11.5	11.3	11.3	11.1
Remarriage of bride, first marriage of groom . . .	7.3	9.8	10.1	10.3	10.5	10.7	10.9	11.2	11.3	11.4
Remarriage of bride and groom	16.5	22.7	23.4	23.3	23.5	23.4	23.4	23.6	23.5	23.4

Source of tables 139 and 140: U.S. National Center for Health Statistics, *Vital Statistics of the United States*, annual; *Monthly Vital Statistics Report;* and unpublished data.

No. 141. Percent Distribution of Marriages, by Age, Sex, and Previous Marital Status: 1980 to 1988

[Data cover marriage registration area; see text, section 2. Based on a sample and subject to sampling variability; for details, see source]

SEX AND PREVIOUS MARITAL STATUS	Total	Under 20 years old	20-24 years old	25-29 years old	30-34 years old	35-44 years old	45-64 years old	65 years old and over
WOMEN								
All marriages: [1]								
1980	100.0	21.1	37.1	18.7	9.3	7.8	5.0	1.0
1988	100.0	11.8	31.5	24.1	13.2	12.6	5.8	1.0
First marriages: [2]								
1980	100.0	30.4	47.3	16.0	4.0	1.6	0.6	0.1
1988	100.0	17.7	43.3	26.1	8.5	3.7	0.7	0.1
Remarriages: [2][3]								
1980	100.0	1.7	15.3	24.4	20.6	20.8	14.3	2.9
1988	100.0	0.7	9.1	20.5	21.9	29.5	15.4	2.8
Previously divorced: [4] 1980.	100.0	1.7	16.7	26.7	22.5	21.6	10.0	0.6
1988.	100.0	0.8	9.8	22.2	23.3	30.7	12.5	0.6
MEN								
All marriages: [1]								
1980	100.0	8.5	35.7	23.8	12.3	10.5	7.4	1.8
1988	100.0	4.5	26.9	27.2	15.8	15.1	8.6	1.9
First marriages: [2]								
1980	100.0	12.7	50.0	25.7	7.5	2.9	1.1	0.1
1988	100.0	6.9	38.7	33.9	13.6	5.8	1.1	0.1
Remarriages: [2][3]								
1980	100.0	0.2	7.2	20.1	21.9	25.6	20.0	5.1
1988	100.0	0.1	4.0	14.4	20.1	33.1	23.1	5.2
Previously divorced: [4] 1980.	100.0	0.2	7.7	21.7	24.1	27.7	17.3	1.4
1988.	100.0	0.1	4.3	15.6	21.8	35.3	21.3	1.6

[1] Includes marriage order not stated.   [2] Excludes data for Iowa.   [3] Includes remarriages of previously widowed.
[4] Excludes remarriages in Michigan, Ohio, and South Carolina.

No. 142. Marriage Rates and Median Age of Bride and Groom, by Previous Marital Status: 1970 to 1988

[Data cover marriage registration area; see text, section 2. Figures for previously divorced and previously widowed exclude data for Michigan and Ohio for all years, for South Carolina beginning 1975, and for the District of Columbia for 1970. Based on a sample and subject to sampling variability; for details, see source. For definition of median, see Guide to Tabular Presentation. See also *Historical Statistics, Colonial Times to 1970*, series A 158-159]

YEAR	MARRIAGE RATES [1]						MEDIAN AGE AT MARRIAGE (years)					
	Women			Men			Women			Men		
	Single	Divorced	Wid-owed	Single	Divorced	Wid-owed	First mar-riage	Remarriage		First mar-riage	Remarriage	
								Divorced	Widowed		Divorced	Widowed
1970	93.4	123.3	10.2	80.4	204.5	40.6	20.6	30.1	51.2	22.5	34.5	58.7
1975	75.9	117.2	8.3	61.5	189.8	40.4	20.8	30.2	52.4	22.7	33.6	59.4
1980	66.0	91.3	6.7	54.7	142.1	32.2	21.8	31.0	53.6	23.6	34.0	61.2
1985	61.5	81.8	5.7	50.1	121.6	27.7	23.0	32.8	54.6	24.8	36.1	62.7
1986	59.7	79.5	5.5	49.1	117.8	26.8	23.3	33.1	54.3	25.1	36.6	62.9
1987	58.9	80.7	5.4	48.8	115.7	26.1	23.6	33.3	53.9	25.3	36.7	62.8
1988	58.4	78.6	5.3	48.3	109.7	25.1	23.7	33.6	53.9	25.5	37.0	63.0

[1] Rate per 1,000 population 15 years old and over in specified group.

No. 143. Divorces and Annulments—Duration of Marriage, Age at Divorce, and Children Involved: 1970 to 1988

[Data cover divorce-registration area; see text, section 2. Based on a sample and subject to sampling variability; for details, see source. Median age computed on data by single years of age. See also *Historical Statistics, Colonial Times to 1970*, series B 218]

DURATION OF MARRIAGE, AGE AT DIVORCE, AND CHILDREN INVOLVED	1970	1975	1980	1981	1982	1983	1984	1985	1986	1987	1988
Median duration of marriage (years)	6.7	6.5	6.8	7.0	7.0	7.0	6.9	6.8	6.9	7.0	7.1
Median age at divorce:											
Men (years)	32.9	32.2	32.7	33.1	33.6	34.0	34.3	34.4	34.6	34.9	35.1
Women (years)	29.8	29.5	30.3	30.6	31.1	31.5	31.7	31.9	32.1	32.5	32.6
Estimated number of children involved											
in divorce (1,000)	870	1,123	1,174	1,180	1,108	1,091	1,081	1,091	1,064	1,038	1,044
Avg. number of children per decree	1.22	1.08	0.98	0.97	0.94	0.94	0.92	0.92	0.90	0.89	0.89
Rate per 1,000 children under 18 years of age.	12.5	16.7	17.3	18.7	17.6	17.4	17.2	17.3	16.8	16.3	16.4

Source of tables 141-143: U.S. National Center for Health Statistics of the United States, *Vital Statistics of the United States*, annual, *Monthly Vital Statistics Report*; and unpublished data.

No. 144. First Marriage Dissolution and Years Until Remarriage for Women, by Race and Hispanic Origin: 1988

[For women 15 to 44 years old. Based on 1988 National Survey of Family Growth; see Appendix III. Marriage dissolution includes death of spouse, separation because of marital discord, and divorce]

ITEM	Number (1,000)	YEARS UNTIL REMARRIAGE (cumulative percent)					
		All	1	2	3	4	5
ALL RACES [1]							
Year of dissolution of first marriage:							
All years	11,577	56.8	20.6	32.8	40.7	46.2	49.7
1980-84....................	3,504	47.5	16.3	28.1	36.4	[2]41.1	[2]45.4
1975-79....................	3,235	65.3	21.9	36.0	44.7	52.7	55.4
1970-74....................	1,887	83.2	24.9	38.6	47.9	56.4	61.2
1965-69....................	1,013	89.9	32.6	48.7	60.2	65.0	72.8
WHITE							
Year of dissolution of first marriage:							
All years	10,103	59.9	21.9	35.2	43.5	49.4	53.0
1980-84....................	3,030	51.4	18.2	31.1	40.3	[2]45.2	[2]49.8
1975-79....................	2,839	69.5	23.2	38.5	46.9	55.6	58.4
1970-74....................	1,622	87.5	24.9	39.8	49.8	59.3	64.3
1965-69....................	893	91.0	34.7	52.3	64.9	69.3	76.9
BLACK							
Year of dissolution of first marriage:							
All years	1,166	34.0	10.9	16.5	19.6	22.7	25.0
1980-84....................	380	19.7	[3]4.7	[3]10.6	[3]12.9	[2]14.8	[2]14.8
1975-79....................	301	32.3	[3]11.4	[3]15.6	18.5	22.2	24.9
1970-74....................	227	59.0	22.3	29.4	35.3	38.7	42.3
1965-69....................	98	81.2	[3]20.9	[3]27.3	[3]31.3	40.8	52.1
Hispanic, [4] all years	942	44.7	12.5	16.6	22.7	27.8	29.9

[1] Includes other races. [2] The percent having remarried is biased downward because the women had not completed the indicated number of years since dissolution of first marriage at the time of the survey. [3] Figure does not meet standard of reliability or precision. [4] Hispanic persons may be of any race.

Source: National Center for Health Statistics, *Advance Data from Vital and Health Statistics*, No. 194.

No. 145. Marriage Experience for Women, by Age and Race: 1980 and 1990

[In percent. As of June. Based on Current Population Survey; see text, section 1]

MARITAL STATUS AND AGE	ALL RACES		WHITE		BLACK		HISPANIC [1]	
	1980	1990	1980	1990	1980	1990	1980	1990
EVER MARRIED								
20 to 24 years old...............	49.5	38.5	52.2	41.3	33.3	23.5	55.4	45.8
25 to 29 years old...............	78.6	69.0	81.0	73.2	62.3	45.0	80.2	69.6
30 to 34 years old...............	89.9	82.2	91.6	85.6	77.9	61.1	88.3	83.0
35 to 39 years old...............	94.3	89.4	95.3	91.4	87.4	74.9	91.2	88.9
40 to 44 years old...............	95.1	92.0	95.8	93.4	89.7	82.1	94.2	92.8
45 to 49 years old...............	95.9	94.4	96.4	95.1	92.5	89.7	94.4	91.7
50 to 54 years old...............	95.3	95.5	95.8	96.1	92.1	91.9	95.0	91.8
DIVORCED AFTER FIRST MARRIAGE								
20 to 24 years old...............	14.2	12.5	14.7	12.8	10.5	9.6	9.4	6.8
25 to 29 years old...............	20.7	19.2	21.0	19.8	20.2	17.8	13.9	13.5
30 to 34 years old...............	26.2	28.1	25.8	28.6	31.4	26.6	21.1	19.9
35 to 39 years old...............	27.2	34.1	26.7	34.6	32.9	35.8	21.9	29.7
40 to 44 years old...............	26.1	35.8	25.5	35.2	33.7	45.1	19.7	26.6
45 to 49 years old...............	23.1	35.2	22.7	35.5	29.0	39.8	23.9	24.6
50 to 54 years old...............	21.8	29.5	21.0	28.5	29.0	39.2	22.5	22.9
REMARRIED AFTER DIVORCE								
20 to 24 years old...............	45.5	38.1	47.0	39.3	(B)	(B)	(B)	(B)
25 to 29 years old...............	53.4	51.8	56.4	52.8	27.9	44.4	(B)	49.5
30 to 34 years old...............	60.9	59.6	63.3	61.4	42.0	42.0	58.3	45.9
35 to 39 years old...............	64.9	65.0	66.9	66.5	50.6	54.0	45.2	51.2
40 to 44 years old...............	67.4	67.1	68.6	69.5	58.4	50.3	(B)	53.9
45 to 49 years old...............	69.2	65.9	70.4	67.2	62.7	55.0	(B)	51.0
50 to 54 years old...............	72.0	63.0	72.6	65.4	72.7	50.2	(B)	62.2
REDIVORCED AFTER REMARRIAGE								
20 to 24 years old...............	8.5	13.1	(NA)	(NA)	(NA)	(NA)	(NA)	(NA)
25 to 29 years old...............	15.6	17.8	(NA)	(NA)	(NA)	(NA)	(NA)	(NA)
30 to 34 years old...............	19.1	22.7	(NA)	(NA)	(NA)	(NA)	(NA)	(NA)
35 to 39 years old...............	24.7	28.5	(NA)	(NA)	(NA)	(NA)	(NA)	(NA)
40 to 44 years old...............	28.4	30.6	(NA)	(NA)	(NA)	(NA)	(NA)	(NA)
45 to 49 years old...............	25.1	36.4	(NA)	(NA)	(NA)	(NA)	(NA)	(NA)
50 to 54 years old...............	29.0	34.5	(NA)	(NA)	(NA)	(NA)	(NA)	(NA)

B Base is less than 75,000.   NA Not available.   [1] Persons of Hispanic origin may be of any race.

Source: U.S. Bureau of the Census, *Current Population Reports*, P23-180.

No. 146. Marriages and Divorces—Number and Rate, by State: 1980 to 1992

[By place of occurrence]

DIVISION AND STATE	MARRIAGES[1]						DIVORCES[3]					
	Number (1,000)			Rate per 1,000 population[2]			Number (1,000)			Rate per 1,000 population[2]		
	1980	1985	1992, prel.	1980	1985	1992, prel.	1980	1985	1992, prel.	1980	1985	1992, prel.
United States...	2,390.3	2,412.6	[4]2,362.0	10.6	10.1	[4]9.3	1,189.0	[5]1,190.0	1,215.0	5.2	[5]5.0	4.8
New England.......	106.3	114.3	104.4	8.6	9.0	7.9	49.0	49.9	44.7	4.0	3.9	3.4
Maine..........	12.0	12.2	11.2	10.7	10.5	9.1	6.2	6.1	5.9	5.5	5.2	4.8
New Hampshire....	9.3	11.4	8.8	10.0	11.4	7.9	5.3	4.9	5.5	5.7	4.9	5.0
Vermont.........	5.2	5.5	5.9	10.2	10.4	10.4	2.6	2.4	3.0	5.1	4.4	5.2
Massachusetts.....	46.3	49.8	42.2	8.1	8.6	7.0	17.9	21.6	16.7	3.1	3.7	2.8
Rhode Island.....	7.5	8.0	7.3	7.9	8.3	7.3	3.6	3.7	3.6	3.8	3.8	3.6
Connecticut......	26.0	27.3	28.9	8.4	8.6	8.8	13.5	11.2	10.1	4.3	3.5	3.1
Middle Atlantic.....	294.0	314.3	291.9	8.0	8.5	7.7	124.7	137.1	122.3	3.4	3.7	3.2
New York........	144.5	164.0	156.3	8.2	9.2	8.6	62.0	67.6	57.0	3.5	3.8	3.1
New Jersey.......	55.8	61.2	55.2	7.6	8.1	7.1	27.8	29.3	25.4	3.8	3.9	3.3
Pennsylvania.....	93.7	89.1	80.4	7.9	7.5	6.7	34.9	40.2	39.9	2.9	3.4	3.3
East North Central...	395.5	[6]362.2	343.9	9.5	[6]8.7	8.0	212.4	[6]192.6	[7]154.9	5.1	[6]4.6	[7]4.2
Ohio..........	99.8	[6]94.4	92.2	9.2	[6]8.8	8.4	58.8	[6]53.0	53.5	5.4	[6]4.9	4.9
Indiana.........	57.9	51.1	50.4	10.5	9.3	8.9	40.0	[6]35.3	(NA)	[6]7.3	[6]6.4	(NA)
Illinois..........	109.8	97.7	93.5	9.6	8.5	8.0	51.0	48.9	43.6	4.5	4.2	3.7
Michigan........	86.9	79.0	70.7	9.4	8.7	7.5	45.0	38.8	39.4	4.9	4.3	4.2
Wisconsin........	41.1	40.0	37.1	8.7	8.4	7.4	17.5	16.6	18.3	3.7	3.5	3.7
West North Central ..	173.7	158.3	146.7	10.1	9.0	8.2	79.6	74.3	77.9	4.6	4.2	4.3
Minnesota........	37.6	35.1	32.3	9.2	8.4	7.2	15.4	14.8	16.3	3.8	3.5	3.6
Iowa...........	27.5	24.6	22.1	9.4	8.5	7.9	11.9	10.5	11.0	4.1	3.7	3.9
Missouri.........	54.6	49.5	45.4	11.1	9.8	8.7	27.6	25.0	25.7	5.6	5.0	4.9
North Dakota.....	6.1	5.4	4.8	9.3	7.9	7.6	2.1	2.3	2.3	3.3	3.4	3.6
South Dakota	8.8	7.8	7.6	12.7	11.0	10.6	2.8	2.6	2.9	4.1	3.6	4.1
Nebraska	14.2	12.7	12.8	9.1	7.9	8.0	6.4	6.4	6.6	4.1	4.0	4.1
Kansas.........	24.8	23.3	21.7	10.5	9.5	8.6	13.4	12.8	13.2	5.7	5.2	5.2
South Atlantic......	413.1	438.8	438.1	11.2	10.9	9.7	206.3	210.5	238.9	5.6	5.2	5.3
Delaware	4.4	5.4	5.1	7.5	8.6	7.3	2.3	3.0	3.4	3.9	4.8	4.9
Maryland........	46.3	46.1	44.1	11.0	10.5	9.0	17.5	16.2	17.6	4.1	3.7	3.6
Dist. of Columbia ...	5.2	5.0	4.0	8.1	8.1	6.7	4.7	2.7	2.7	7.3	4.3	4.5
Virginia.........	60.2	66.5	69.7	11.3	11.7	10.9	23.6	24.1	29.7	4.4	4.2	4.7
West Virginia.....	17.4	14.6	12.3	8.9	7.5	6.8	10.3	9.9	9.9	5.3	5.1	5.4
North Carolina....	46.7	50.5	48.2	7.9	8.1	7.0	28.1	30.2	36.2	4.8	4.8	5.3
South Carolina....	53.9	52.8	53.3	17.3	15.8	14.8	13.6	13.5	15.9	4.4	4.0	4.4
Georgia	70.6	72.3	63.4	12.9	12.1	9.4	34.7	33.4	39.6	6.4	5.6	5.9
Florida	108.3	125.5	138.1	11.1	11.0	10.2	71.6	77.5	84.1	7.3	6.8	6.2
East South Central...	[6]168.8	171.8	184.1	[6]11.5	11.4	11.9	87.5	[6]86.2	99.8	[6]6.0	[6]5.7	6.4
Kentucky........	[6]32.7	46.0	49.9	[6]8.9	12.3	13.3	16.7	18.3	24.2	[6]4.6	4.9	6.4
Tennessee	59.2	55.0	70.9	12.9	11.5	14.1	30.2	29.9	33.9	6.6	6.3	6.8
Alabama........	49.0	46.1	40.5	12.6	11.5	9.8	26.7	25.0	27.0	6.9	6.2	6.5
Mississippi	27.9	24.8	22.8	11.1	9.5	8.7	13.8	[6]13.0	14.6	5.5	[6]5.0	5.6
West South Central ..	298.2	308.6	287.5	12.6	11.6	10.4	155.0	[6]160.9	[7]140.8	[6]6.5	(NA)	[7]6.1
Arkansas........	26.5	31.7	37.3	11.6	13.4	15.6	15.9	[6]16.5	18.4	[6]6.9	[7]7.0	7.7
Louisiana........	43.5	39.4	35.4	10.3	8.8	8.3	18.1	[7]17.6	(NA)	[6]4.3	(NA)	(NA)
Oklahoma.......	46.5	35.9	31.8	15.4	10.9	9.9	24.2	26.4	23.4	8.0	8.0	7.3
Texas..........	181.8	201.6	183.0	12.8	12.3	10.4	96.8	100.4	99.0	6.8	6.1	5.6
Mountain	241.7	233.7	243.7	21.3	18.3	16.9	86.1	89.9	[7]78.8	7.6	7.0	[7]5.5
Montana........	8.3	7.2	7.2	10.6	8.7	8.8	4.9	4.3	4.3	6.3	5.2	5.2
Idaho..........	13.4	12.3	14.5	14.2	12.2	13.5	6.6	6.2	6.7	7.0	6.2	6.3
Wyoming	6.9	5.4	4.9	14.6	10.6	10.5	4.0	3.8	3.2	8.5	7.5	6.9
Colorado........	34.9	[8]33.6	33.7	12.1	10.4	9.7	18.6	19.2	19.5	6.4	5.9	5.6
New Mexico	16.6	[9]15.5	13.0	12.8	[9]10.7	8.2	10.4	[10]13.2	9.7	8.0	[10]9.1	6.2
Arizona.........	30.2	35.7	36.4	11.1	11.2	9.5	19.9	21.2	25.6	7.3	6.6	6.7
Utah	17.0	17.5	19.9	11.6	10.6	11.0	7.8	8.8	9.7	5.3	5.3	5.3
Nevada.........	114.3	106.5	114.2	142.8	113.7	86.1	13.8	13.3	(NA)	17.3	14.2	(NA)
Pacific	298.8	310.6	[7]92.8	9.4	8.9	[7]9.4	187.9	188.5	[7]54.0	5.9	5.4	[7]5.5
Washington.......	47.7	43.8	45.1	11.6	9.9	8.8	28.6	26.3	29.4	6.9	5.4	5.7
Oregon. .,......	23.0	22.4	24.3	8.7	8.3	8.2	17.8	15.7	15.9	6.7	5.9	5.3
California [11]......	210.9	222.8	(NA)	8.9	8.5	(NA)	133.5	[12]137.5	(NA)	5.6	[12]5.2	(NA)
Alaska	5.4	6.2	5.7	13.3	11.8	9.8	3.5	4.0	3.7	8.8	7.7	6.3
Hawaii	11.9	15.4	17.6	12.3	14.7	15.2	4.4	4.9	5.0	4.6	4.6	4.3

NA Not available.　[1] Data are counts of marriages performed, except as noted.　[2] Based on total population residing in area; population enumerated as of April 1 for 1980; estimated as of July 1 for all other years.　[3] Includes annulments.　[4] Estimate for the United States is based on monthly reports adjusted for observed differences from final monthly figures. State figures are not adjusted in this manner.　[5] Estimated.　[6] Data are incomplete.　[7] Excludes figures for States shown below as not available.　[8] Includes divorce petitions filed for some counties.　[9] Premarital health forms issued.　[10] Divorce petitions filed.　[11] Marriage data include nonlicensed marriages registered.　[12] Data include legal separations.

Source: U.S. National Center for Health Statistics, *Vital Statistics of the United States*, annual; and *Monthly Vital Statistics Reports*.

Figure 3.1
Personal Health Care Expenses, Average Annual Percent Change: 1980 to 1991

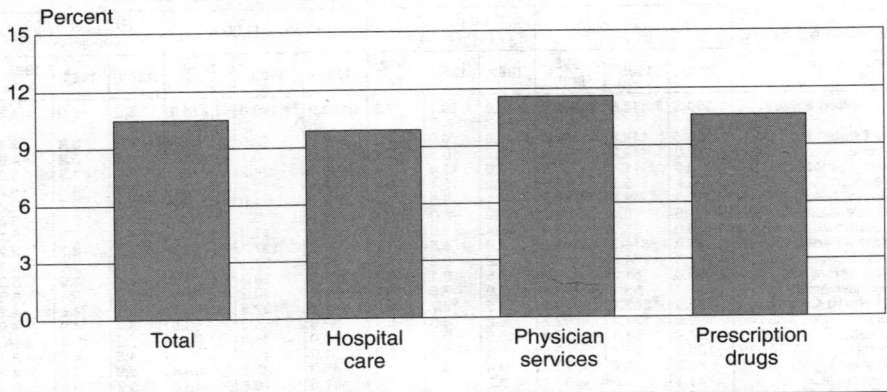

Figure 3.2
Consumer Price Indexes—Medical Services: 1970 to 1993

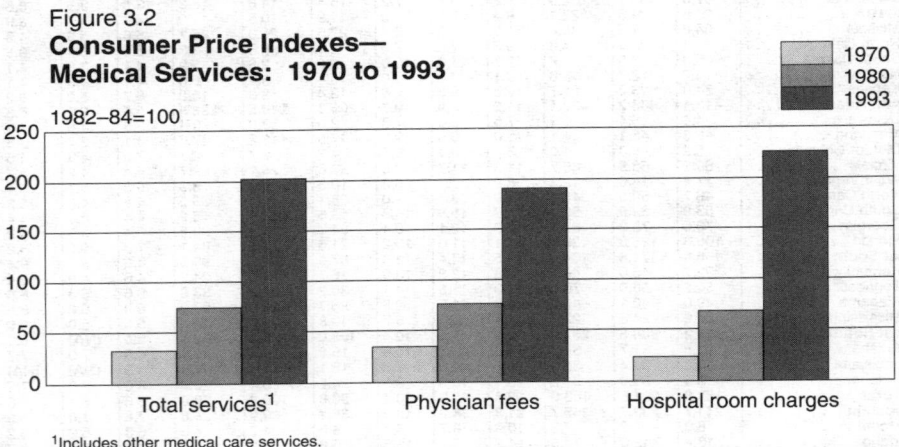

[1]Includes other medical care services.

Figure 3.3
Per Capita Food Consumption, by Selected Products: 1970 to 1992

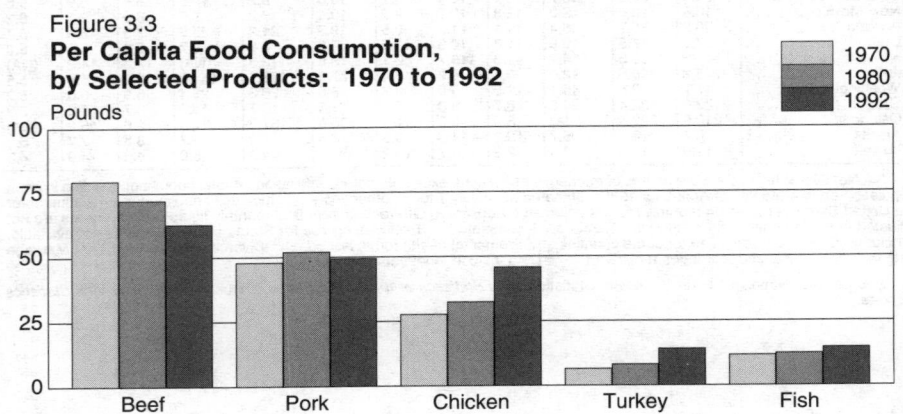

Source: Charts prepared by U.S. Bureau of the Census.
For figure 3.1 data, see table 150; figure 3.2 data, see table 163; figure 3.3 data, see table 220.

Health and Nutrition

This section presents statistics on health expenditures and insurance coverage, including Medicare and Medicaid; medical personnel; hospitals; nursing homes and other care facilities; incidence of acute and prevalence of chronic conditions; nutritional intake of the population; and food consumption. Summary statistics showing recent trends on health care and discussions of selected health issues are published annually by the U.S. National Center for Health Statistics (NCHS) in *Health, United States.* Data on national health expenditures, medical costs, and insurance coverage are compiled by the U.S. Health Care Financing Administration (HCFA) and appear in the quarterly *Health Care Financing Review* and in the *Annual Medicare Program Statistics* series. Statistics on health insurance are also collected by NCHS and are published in series 10 of *Vital and Health Statistics.* The Census Bureau also publishes data on insurance coverage in *Current Population Reports,* series P70. Statistics on health facilities are collected by NCHS and are published in series 14 of *Vital and Health Statistics.* Statistics on hospitals are published annually by the American Hospital Association, Chicago, IL, in *Hospital Statistics.* Primary sources for data on nutrition are the quarterly *National Food Review* and the annual *Food Consumption, Prices, and Expenditures,* both issued by the U.S. Department of Agriculture. NCHS also conducts periodic surveys of nutrient levels in the population, including estimates of food and nutrient intake, overweight and obesity, hypercholesterolemia, hypertension, and clinical signs of malnutrition.

National health expenditures.—HCFA compiles estimates of national health expenditures (NHE) to measure spending for health care in the United States. With the publication of the 1988 estimates, major revisions to the NHE back to 1960 have been incorporated into the accounts. The NHE accounts are structured to show spending by type of expenditure (i.e., hospital care, physician care, dental care, and other professional care; home health; drugs and other medical nondurables; vision products and other medical durables; nursing home care and other

In Brief

In 1992:
34 million with no health insurance.

Hospital surgeries—
percent outpatient:

1980	*16*
1992	*54*

Per capita consumption of chicken:

1980	*33 pounds*
1992	*46 pounds*

personal health expenditures; plus nonpersonal health expenditures for such items as public health, research, construction of medical facilities, and administration) and by source of funding (e.g., private health insurance, out-of-pocket payments, and a range of public programs including Medicare, Medicaid, and those operated by the Department of Veterans Affairs (VA)).

In all cases except private insurance (HCFA conducts its own survey of part of the health insurance industry), data used to estimate health expenditures come from existing sources which are tabulated for other purposes. The type of expenditure estimates rely upon statistics produced by such groups as the American Hospital Association, the Internal Revenue Service, the Department of Commerce, and the Department of Health and Human Services (HHS). Source of funding estimates are constructed using administrative and statistical records from the Medicare and Medicaid programs, the Department of Defense and VA medical programs, the Social Security Administration, Census Bureau's *Governmental Finances,* State and local governments, other HHS agencies, and other nongovernment sources. Detailed descriptions of sources and methods, along with the most recent analysis of health care expenditure estimates, are published in the *Health Care Financing Review's* annual article on national health expenditures.

Medicare and Medicaid.—Since July 1966, the Federal Medicare program has provided two coordinated plans for nearly all people age 65 and over: (1) A hospital insurance plan which covers hospital and related services and (2) a voluntary supplementary medical insurance plan, financed partially by monthly premiums paid by participants, which partly covers physicians' and related medical services. Such insurance also applies, since July 1973, to disabled beneficiaries of any age after 24 months of entitlement to cash benefits under the social security or railroad retirement programs and to persons with end stage renal disease.

Under Medicaid, all States offer basic health services to certain very poor people: Individuals who are pregnant, aged, disabled or blind, and families with dependent children. Medicaid eligibility is automatic for almost all cash welfare recipients in these States. Thirty-nine States also extend Medicaid to certain other persons who qualify, except for incomes above regular eligibility levels; those persons include those who have medical expenses which, when subtracted from their income, spend down to a State "medically needy" level or those who meet the higher "medically needy" income restrictions. Within Federal guidelines, each State determines its own Medicaid eligibility criteria and the health services to be provided under Medicaid. The cost of providing Medicaid services is jointly shared by the Federal Government and the States.

Health resources.—Hospital statistics based on data from the American Hospital Association's yearly survey are published annually in *Hospital Statistics,* and cover all hospitals accepted for registration by the Association. To be accepted for registration, a hospital must meet certain requirements relating to number of beds, construction, equipment, medical and nursing staff, patient care, clinical records, surgical and obstetrical facilities, diagnostic and treatment facilities, laboratory services, etc. Data obtained from NCHS cover all U.S. hospitals which meet certain criteria for inclusion. The criteria are published in *Vital and Health Statistics* reports, series 13. NCHS defines a hospital as a non-Federal short-term general or special facility with six or more inpatient beds with an average stay of less than 60 days.

Statistics on the demographic characteristics of persons employed in the health occupations are compiled by the U.S. Bureau of Labor Statistics and reported in *Employment and Earnings* (monthly) (see table 637, section 13). Data based on surveys of health personnel and utilization of health facilities providing long-term care, ambulatory care, and hospital care are presented in NCHS series 13 and series 14, *Data on Health Resources Utilization* and *Data on Health Resources: Manpower and Facilities.* Statistics on patient visits to health care providers, as reported in health interviews, appear in NCHS series 10, *National Health Interview Survey Data.*

The HCFA's *Health Care Financing Review* and *Health Care Financing Program Statistics* present data for hospitals and nursing homes as well as extended care facilities and home health agencies. These data are based on records of the Medicare program and differ from those of other sources because they are limited to facilities meeting Federal eligibility standards for participation in Medicare.

Data on patients in hospitals for the mentally ill and on mental health facilities are collected by the National Institute of Mental Health (NIMH) and appear in *Mental Health, U.S.,* the *Mental Health Statistics* reports, (series CN), and the Mental Health Statistical Note series.

Disability and illness.—General health statistics, including morbidity, disability, injuries, preventive care, and findings from physiological testing are collected by NCHS in its National Health Interview Survey and its National Health and Nutrition Examination Surveys and appear in *Vital and Health Statistics,* series 10 and 11, respectively. The Department of Labor compiles statistics on industrial injuries (see section 13). Annual incidence data on notifiable diseases are compiled by the Public Health Service (PHS) at its Centers for Disease Control in Atlanta, Georgia, and are published as a supplement to its *Morbidity and Mortality Weekly Report.* The list of diseases is revised annually and includes those which, by mutual agreement of the States and PHS, are communicable diseases of national importance.

Nutrition.—Statistics on annual per capita consumption of food and its nutrient value are estimated by the U.S. Department of Agriculture and published quarterly in *National Food Review.* Historical data can be found in *Food Consumption, Prices, and Expenditures,* issued annually.

Statistics on food insufficiency and food and nutrient intake are collected by NCHS to estimate the nation's population diet. NCHS also collects physical examination data to assess the population's nutritional status, including growth, overweight/obesity, nutritional deficiencies, and prevalence of nutrition-related

conditions, such as hypertension, hypercholesterolemia, and diabetes.

Statistical reliability.—For discussion of statistical collection, estimation, and sampling procedures and measures of reliability applicable to data from NCHS and HCFA, see Appendix III.

Historical statistics.—Tabular headnotes provide cross-references, where applicable, to *Historical Statistics of the United States, Colonial Times to 1970.* See Appendix IV.

No. 147. National Health Expenditures: 1960 to 1991

[Includes Puerto Rico and outlying areas]

YEAR	TOTAL[1]			HEALTH SERVICES AND SUPPLIES						
				Private					Public	
					Out-of-pocket payments		Insurance pre-miums[4] (bil.dol.)	Medical payments		
	Total (bil.dol.)	Per capita (dol.)	Percent of GDP[2]	Total[3] (bil.dol.)	Total (bil.dol.)	Percent of total private		Total (bil.dol.)	Medi-care (bil. dol.)	Public assis-tance (bil. dol.)
1960	27.1	143	5.3	19.8	13.3	67.5	5.9	5.7	–	0.5
1965	41.6	204	5.9	29.9	19.0	63.7	10.0	8.3	–	1.7
1970	74.4	346	7.4	44.1	25.6	58.0	16.7	24.9	7.6	6.3
1971	82.3	379	7.5	48.2	27.1	56.2	19.1	28.2	8.5	7.7
1972	92.3	421	7.6	54.0	29.8	55.2	21.9	31.8	9.3	8.9
1973	102.5	464	7.6	59.9	32.9	54.8	24.6	35.9	10.7	10.2
1974	116.1	521	8.0	66.1	35.6	53.8	27.8	42.8	13.5	11.9
1975	132.9	592	8.4	74.5	38.5	51.8	32.9	50.2	16.4	14.5
1976	152.2	672	8.6	86.3	42.5	49.2	39.7	56.9	19.8	16.4
1977	172.0	753	8.7	98.6	46.3	46.9	47.8	64.6	22.8	18.8
1978	193.7	840	8.7	110.4	50.2	45.5	55.0	73.6	26.8	20.9
1979	217.2	933	8.7	123.2	54.1	43.9	63.2	84.1	31.1	24.0
1980	250.1	1,064	9.2	140.7	59.5	42.3	73.4	98.1	37.5	28.0
1981	290.2	1,222	9.6	163.3	67.2	41.1	86.9	114.2	45.2	32.6
1982	326.1	1,359	10.4	185.2	74.2	40.1	100.5	127.0	52.6	34.5
1983	358.6	1,480	10.5	204.1	81.4	39.9	111.4	139.5	59.9	37.9
1984	389.6	1,592	10.3	223.3	87.7	39.3	123.7	150.8	65.9	40.7
1985	422.6	1,711	10.5	242.0	94.4	39.0	134.2	165.2	72.0	44.6
1986	454.9	1,824	10.7	259.2	100.9	38.9	143.8	179.7	76.8	48.3
1987	494.2	1,962	10.9	279.5	108.8	38.9	155.2	197.3	83.0	53.9
1988	546.1	2,146	11.1	311.1	118.5	38.1	175.3	215.1	90.5	58.2
1989	604.3	2,352	11.5	342.8	126.2	36.8	197.1	240.9	102.6	65.8
1990	675.0	2,601	12.2	380.7	136.5	35.9	222.2	271.7	110.7	79.7
1991	751.8	2,868	13.2	412.7	144.3	35.0	244.4	315.9	122.8	104.9

– Represents zero. [1] Includes medical research and medical facilities construction. [2] GDP=Gross domestic product; see table 686. [3] Includes other sources of funds not shown separately. [4] See footnote 2, table 148.

Source: U. S. Health Care Financing Administration, *Health Care Financing Review,* winter 1992.

No. 148. National Health Expenditures, by Type: 1970 to 1991

[In millions of dollars, except percent. Includes Puerto Rico and outlying areas. See also *Historical Statistics, Colonial Times to 1970*, series B 248-261]

TYPE OF EXPENDITURE	1970	1980	1985	1987	1988	1989	1990	1991
Total	**74,377**	**250,126**	**422,600**	**494,159**	**546,080**	**604,315**	**675,037**	**751,771**
Annual percent change [1]	12.3	15.1	8.5	8.6	10.5	10.7	11.7	11.4
Private expenditures.	**46,703**	**144,966**	**247,988**	**286,196**	**318,984**	**350,998**	**389,973**	**421,811**
Health services and supplies	44,148	140,736	242,000	279,542	311,147	342,787	380,707	412,708
Out-of-pocket payments	25,606	59,500	94,390	108,825	118,504	126,198	136,491	144,260
Insurance premiums [2]	16,743	73,407	134,197	155,220	175,325	197,069	222,167	244,367
Other	1,798	7,829	13,413	15,497	17,318	19,520	22,050	24,081
Medical research	215	274	501	725	744	801	843	910
Medical facilities construction	2,341	3,956	5,488	5,929	7,094	7,410	8,423	8,193
Public expenditures	**27,674**	**105,159**	**174,612**	**207,962**	**227,096**	**253,316**	**285,063**	**329,960**
Percent Federal of public	64.1	68.4	70.7	69.0	69.0	69.1	68.2	67.5
Health services and supplies	24,908	98,114	165,205	197,343	215,088	240,857	271,670	315,921
Medicare [3]	7,633	37,533	72,005	83,000	90,480	102,639	110,736	122,803
Public assistance medical payments [4]	6,310	28,007	44,585	53,870	58,185	65,848	79,685	104,941
Temporary disability insurance [5]	66	51	57	62	64	62	64
Workers' compensation (medical) [5]	1,409	5,177	8,036	10,757	12,353	14,447	16,388	17,793
Defense Dept. hospital, medical	1,784	4,346	7,634	9,303	9,766	10,376	11,661	12,809
Maternal, child health programs	425	892	1,262	1,607	1,694	1,794	1,895	1,999
Public health activities	1,385	7,219	12,306	14,600	16,571	18,938	21,976	24,533
Veterans' hospital, medical care	1,764	5,934	8,613	9,620	10,011	10,641	11,451	12,185
Medical vocational rehabilitation	158	298	401	468	500	523	555	593
State and local hospitals [6]	3,173	5,589	7,030	10,336	11,443	11,770	12,451	12,697
Other [7]	803	3,067	3,282	3,725	4,024	3,816	4,812	5,503
Medical research	1,741	5,170	7,294	8,304	9,596	10,184	11,016	11,674
Medical facilities construction	1,025	1,875	2,112	2,315	2,411	2,275	2,377	2,365

[1] Change from immediate prior year except for 1970, average annual change from 1965. For explanation of average annual percent change, see Guide to Tabular Presentation. [2] Covers insurance benefits and amount retained by insurance companies for expenses, additions to reserves, and profits (net cost of insurance). [3] Represents expenditures for benefits and administrative cost from Federal hospital and medical insurance trust funds under old-age, survivors, disability, and health insurance programs; see text, section 12. [4] Payments made directly to suppliers of medical care (primarily Medicaid). [5] Includes medical benefits paid under public law by private insurance carriers and self-insurers. [6] Expenditures not offset by other revenues. [7] Covers expenditures for Alcohol, Drug Abuse, and Mental Health Administration; Indian Health Service; school health and other programs.

Source: U.S. Health Care Financing Administration, *Health Care Financing Review*, winter 1992.

No. 149. National Health Expenditures, by Object: 1970 to 1991

[In billions of dollars. Includes Puerto Rico and outlying areas. See also *Historical Statistics, Colonial Times to 1970*, series B 221-235]

OBJECT OF EXPENDITURE	1970	1980	1985	1987	1988	1989	1990	1991
Total	**74.4**	**250.1**	**422.6**	**494.2**	**546.1**	**604.3**	**675.0**	**751.8**
Spent by—								
Consumers	42.3	132.9	228.6	264.0	293.8	323.3	358.7	388.6
Government	27.7	105.2	174.6	208.0	227.1	253.3	285.1	330.0
Other [1]	4.4	12.1	19.4	22.2	25.2	27.7	31.3	33.2
Spent for—								
Health services and supplies	69.1	238.9	407.2	476.9	526.2	583.6	652.4	728.6
Personal health care expenses	64.9	219.4	369.7	439.3	482.8	530.9	591.5	660.2
Hospital care	27.9	102.4	168.3	194.2	212.0	232.4	258.1	288.6
Physicians' services	13.6	41.9	74.0	93.0	105.1	116.1	128.8	142.0
Dentists' services	4.7	14.4	23.3	27.1	29.4	31.6	34.1	37.1
Other professional services [2]	1.5	8.7	16.6	21.1	23.8	27.1	30.7	35.8
Home health care	0.1	1.3	3.8	4.1	4.5	5.6	7.6	9.8
Drugs/other medical nondurables	8.8	21.6	36.2	43.2	46.3	50.5	55.6	60.7
Vision products/other med. durables [3]	2.0	4.6	7.1	9.1	10.1	10.4	11.7	12.4
Nursing home care	4.9	20.0	34.1	39.7	42.8	47.5	53.3	59.9
Other health services	1.4	4.6	6.4	7.8	8.7	9.8	11.5	14.0
Net cost of insurance and admin. [4]	2.8	12.2	25.2	23.0	26.9	33.8	38.9	43.9
Government public health activities	1.4	7.2	12.3	14.6	16.6	18.9	22.0	24.5
Medical research	2.0	5.4	7.8	9.0	10.3	11.0	11.9	12.6
Medical facilities construction	3.4	5.8	7.6	8.2	9.5	9.7	10.8	10.6

[1] Includes nonpatient revenues, privately funded construction, and industrial inplant. [2] Includes services of registered and practical nurses in private duty, visiting nurses, podiatrists, optometrists, physical therapists, clinical psychologists, chiropractors, naturopaths, and Christian Science practitioners. [3] Includes expenditures for eyeglasses, hearing aids, orthopedic appliances, artificial limbs, crutches, wheelchairs, etc. [4] Includes administrative expenses of federally financed health programs.

Source: U.S. Health Care Financing Administration, *Health Care Financing Review*, winter 1992.

No. 150. Health Care Expenditures, by State: 1980 and 1991

[Covers approximately 70 percent of U.S. personal health care expenditures. Data represent spending for services produced by each State's health care providers, as opposed to those consumed by State residents or supplied by State employers]

STATE	1980 (mil. dol.)				1991 (mil. dol.)				AVERAGE ANNUAL PERCENT CHANGE, 1980-91			
	Total	Hospital care	Physician services	Prescription drugs [1]	Total	Hospital care	Physician services	Prescription drugs [1]	Total	Hospital care	Physician services	Prescription drugs [1]
U.S.	158,452	101,247	45,156	12,049	473,320	286,053	150,891	36,377	10.5	9.9	11.6	10.6
Alabama	2,456	1,588	633	235	7,494	4,521	2,296	677	10.7	10.0	12.4	10.1
Alaska.	312	200	96	16	1,027	659	312	56	11.4	11.4	11.3	12.0
Arizona	1,857	1,087	647	123	6,420	3,615	2,321	483	11.9	11.5	12.3	13.3
Arkansas	1,271	743	375	153	3,968	2,359	1,241	368	10.9	11.1	11.5	8.3
California.	19,819	11,584	6,938	1,296	58,141	31,128	23,108	3,904	10.3	9.4	11.6	10.5
Colorado	1,948	1,218	603	127	6,100	3,614	2,122	364	10.9	10.4	12.1	10.0
Connecticut	2,155	1,392	590	174	6,844	4,089	2,236	520	11.1	10.3	12.9	10.5
Delaware.	396	258	113	25	1,379	800	488	91	12.0	10.8	14.2	12.4
Dist. of Columbia. .	1,254	985	237	32	3,400	2,641	666	93	9.5	9.4	9.8	10.3
Florida.	7,404	4,366	2,502	536	27,047	15,210	9,881	1,956	12.5	12.0	13.3	12.5
Georgia	3,420	2,139	987	294	12,476	7,603	3,902	971	12.5	12.2	13.3	11.5
Hawaii.	655	360	251	44	2,144	1,287	719	137	11.4	12.3	10.0	10.9
Idaho	426	242	141	44	1,282	762	397	123	10.5	11.0	9.9	9.8
Illinois	8,899	6,205	2,133	561	21,234	13,792	5,731	1,711	8.2	7.5	9.4	10.7
Indiana	3,332	2,123	904	305	9,749	6,024	2,890	835	10.3	9.9	11.1	9.6
Iowa	1,818	1,174	488	156	4,631	2,933	1,294	404	8.9	8.7	9.3	9.0
Kansas	1,675	1,084	464	128	4,307	2,545	1,404	358	9.0	8.1	10.6	9.8
Kentucky	2,010	1,223	561	225	6,362	3,908	1,814	639	11.0	11.1	11.3	10.0
Louisiana.	2,730	1,737	738	254	8,335	5,277	2,400	658	10.7	10.6	11.3	9.0
Maine	652	460	141	51	1,966	1,257	547	162	10.6	9.6	13.1	11.0
Maryland	3,091	2,033	833	226	9,323	5,210	3,284	829	10.6	8.9	13.3	12.6
Massachusetts . . .	4,892	3,630	971	290	14,402	9,097	4,244	1,061	10.3	8.7	14.3	12.5
Michigan	7,045	4,473	2,044	527	17,383	10,663	5,141	1,578	8.6	8.2	8.7	10.5
Minnesota	2,897	1,738	968	191	8,726	4,607	3,571	548	10.5	9.3	12.6	10.0
Mississippi	1,331	863	326	142	3,732	2,425	923	384	9.8	9.9	9.9	9.5
Missouri.	3,678	2,520	883	274	10,226	6,660	2,815	751	9.7	9.2	11.1	9.6
Montana	432	264	137	31	1,164	763	314	87	9.4	10.1	7.8	9.8
Nebraska.	1,035	678	277	80	2,794	1,789	779	227	9.5	9.2	9.9	9.9
Nevada.	632	385	210	36	2,274	1,195	945	135	12.4	10.8	14.7	12.6
New Hampshire . .	481	313	129	39	1,917	1,129	641	146	13.4	12.4	15.7	12.8
New Jersey	4,506	2,759	1,367	381	14,647	8,829	4,569	1,249	11.3	11.2	11.6	11.4
New Mexico	684	448	185	52	2,448	1,570	699	179	12.3	12.1	12.9	12.0
New York	13,423	9,552	3,051	820	38,533	25,345	10,611	2,577	10.1	9.3	12.0	11.0
North Carolina . . .	3,161	1,953	868	340	10,987	6,795	3,200	992	12.0	12.0	12.6	10.2
North Dakota	481	313	140	28	1,322	796	442	84	9.6	8.8	11.0	10.5
Ohio	7,561	4,798	2,157	607	20,335	12,628	6,094	1,613	9.4	9.2	9.9	9.3
Oklahoma	1,888	1,171	542	175	4,929	3,016	1,471	442	9.1	9.0	9.5	8.8
Oregon	1,646	923	597	125	4,597	2,562	1,738	297	9.8	9.7	10.2	8.2
Pennsylvania . . .	8,584	6,008	1,960	616	25,178	16,622	6,680	1,876	10.3	9.7	11.8	10.7
Rhode Island . . .	694	480	165	48	1,924	1,215	543	166	9.7	8.8	11.4	11.8
South Carolina . . .	1,527	972	402	154	5,547	3,614	1,455	479	12.4	12.7	12.4	10.9
South Dakota . . .	405	271	103	30	1,221	799	342	80	10.6	10.3	11.5	9.3
Tennessee.	3,149	2,015	846	288	9,948	6,239	2,865	844	11.0	10.8	11.7	10.3
Texas	9,368	5,520	3,000	848	30,222	18,086	9,754	2,382	11.2	11.4	11.3	9.8
Utah	751	452	245	54	2,539	1,510	822	207	11.7	11.6	11.6	13.0
Vermont	256	173	61	22	824	502	243	79	11.2	10.2	13.4	12.4
Virginia	3,235	2,068	892	275	10,825	6,407	3,464	955	11.6	10.8	13.1	12.0
Washington	2,510	1,390	908	212	8,486	4,581	3,336	568	11.7	11.4	12.6	9.4
West Virginia	1,268	825	327	116	3,229	2,000	900	329	8.9	8.4	9.6	10.0
Wisconsin	3,117	1,947	952	218	8,733	4,981	3,077	675	9.8	8.9	11.3	10.8
Wyoming	234	146	65	23	598	394	155	49	8.9	9.4	8.2	7.2

[1] Expenditures for retail purchases of prescription drugs.

Source: U.S. Health Care Financing Administration, Office of the Actuary: Data from the Office of National Health Statistics.

No. 151. Health Services and Supplies—Per Capita Consumer Expenditures, by Object: 1970 to 1991

[In dollars, except percent. Based on Social Security Administration estimates of total U.S. population as of July 1, including Armed Forces and Federal employees abroad and civilian population of outlying areas. Excludes research and construction. See also *Historical Statistics, Colonial Times to 1970*, series B 222-232]

OBJECT OF EXPENDITURE	1970	1975	1980	1985	1987	1988	1989	1990	1991
Total, national.	322	555	1,016	1,648	1,893	2,068	2,271	2,513	2,779
Annual percent change [1].	11.4	11.5	14.2	7.8	7.6	9.3	9.8	10.7	10.6
Hospital care	130	233	435	681	771	833	904	994	1,101
Physicians' services	63	104	178	299	369	413	452	496	542
Dentists' services	22	37	61	94	108	116	123	131	141
Other professional services [2]	7	16	37	67	84	93	105	118	137
Home health care	1	2	6	16	16	18	22	29	37
Drugs and other medical nondurables . . . . [2] . . .	41	58	92	146	171	182	196	214	231
Vision products and other medical durables [2] . . .	9	14	19	29	36	40	41	45	47
Nursing home care	23	44	85	138	157	168	185	205	229
Other health services . . . . [2] . . .	6	12	19	26	31	34	38	44	53
Net cost of insurance and administration [2]	13	23	52	102	91	106	131	150	167
Government public health activities	6	14	31	50	58	65	74	85	94
Total, private consumer [3].	197	318	565	925	1,048	1,155	1,258	1,382	1,482
Hospital care	56	100	182	277	310	340	370	403	425
Physicians' services	49	75	124	202	244	275	297	327	353
Dentists' services	21	35	58	92	105	113	120	128	137
Other professional services [2]	5	10	26	46	58	65	72	78	88
Home health care	(Z)	(Z)	1	3	3	3	4	6	8
Drugs and other medical nondurables . . . . [2] . . .	39	54	85	134	155	164	176	191	203
Vision products and other medical durables [2] . . .	9	13	17	23	28	31	31	34	34
Nursing home care	11	19	38	69	77	83	84	95	101
Net cost of insurance	7	14	35	81	68	80	103	119	134

Z Rounds to zero.   [1] Beginning 1980, change from immediate prior year. For 1975, average annual change from 1970, and for 1970, average annual change from 1965. For explanation of average annual percent change, see Guide to Tabular Presentation.   [2] See footnotes for corresponding objects in table 149.   [3] Represents out-of-pocket payments and private health insurance.

Source: U.S. Health Care Financing Administration, *Health Care Financing Review*, winter 1992.

No. 152. Personal Health Care—Third Party Payments and Private Consumer Expenditures: 1970 to 1991

[In billions of dollars, except percent. See headnote, table 153]

ITEM	1970	1975	1980	1985	1987	1988	1989	1990	1991
Personal health care expenditures.	64.9	116.6	219.4	369.7	439.3	482.8	530.9	591.5	660.2
Third party payments, total	39.3	78.0	159.9	275.3	330.5	364.3	404.7	455.0	516.0
Percent of personal health care	60.5	66.9	72.9	74.5	75.2	75.5	76.2	76.9	78.1
Private insurance payments	15.2	29.9	65.3	114.2	138.1	155.0	170.6	191.2	209.3
Government expenditures.	22.4	45.3	87.1	148.2	177.4	192.5	215.2	242.3	283.3
Other [1]	1.7	2.9	7.6	12.9	15.0	16.8	19.0	21.5	23.4
Private consumer expenditures [2]	40.8	68.4	124.8	208.6	246.9	273.5	296.8	327.7	353.5
Percent met by private insurance	37.2	43.7	52.3	54.7	55.9	56.7	57.5	58.4	59.2
Hospital care	12.1	22.4	42.8	68.4	78.1	86.6	95.1	104.7	111.4
Percent met by private insurance	79.2	80.4	87.5	87.1	88.9	88.0	88.6	90.1	91.1
Physicians' services.	10.6	16.8	29.2	49.8	61.6	70.0	76.4	84.8	92.5
Percent met by private insurance	45.1	54.5	61.5	67.7	69.1	70.2	70.5	71.6	72.2

[1] Includes nonpatient revenues and industrial inplant health services.   [2] Includes expenditures not shown separately. Represents out-of-pocket payments and private health insurance benefits. Excludes net cost of insurance.

Source: U.S. Health Care Financing Administration, *Health Care Financing Review*, winter 1992.

No. 153. Personal Health Care Expenditures, by Object and Source of Payment: 1991

[In millions of dollars, except as indicated. Includes Puerto Rico and outlying areas. Covers all expenditures for health services and supplies, except net cost of insurance and administration, government public health activities, and expenditures of philanthropic agencies for fund raising activities]

OBJECT OF PAYMENT	Total	Out of pocket payments	THIRD PARTY PAYMENTS				Private [2]
			Total	Private health insurance	Govern-ment	Other [1]	
Total..........................	660,217	144,260	515,957	209,265	283,252	23,440	376,965
Hospital care.....................	288,627	9,879	278,748	101,497	162,600	14,650	126,027
Physicians' services	141,985	25,728	116,257	66,770	49,435	52	92,550
Dentists' services..........	37,066	19,916	17,150	16,083	1,067	-	35,999
Other professional services [3]	35,823	9,668	26,154	13,344	8,371	4,439	27,451
Home health care...................	9,762	1,238	8,524	742	7,053	729	2,709
Drugs/other medical nondurables	60,674	44,329	16,345	9,000	7,345	-	53,328
Vision products/other med. durables [3]	12,361	7,654	4,707	1,187	3,520	-	8,841
Nursing home care.................	59,943	25,848	34,096	641	32,309	1,146	27,635
Other health services	13,976	-	13,976	-	11,552	2,424	2,424

- Represents or rounds to zero.   [1] Includes nonpatient revenues and industrial plant.   [2] Covers out-of-pocket payments, private health insurance, and other.   [3] See footnotes for corresponding items on table 149.

Source: U.S. Health Care Financing Administration, *Health Care Financing Review*, winter 1992.

No. 154. Government Expenditures for Health Services and Supplies: 1990 and 1991

[In millions of dollars. Includes Puerto Rico and outlying areas. Excludes medical research and construction]

YEAR AND TYPE OF SERVICE	Total [1]	Federal	State and local	Medi-care [2] (OASDHI)	Public assis-tance [3]	OTHER HEALTH SERVICES		
						Veterans	Defense Dept. [4]	Workers' compensa-tion [5]
1990, total [1]	271,670	184,079	87,591	110,736	79,685	11,451	11,661	16,388
Hospital care........	139,465	103,989	35,476	67,414	31,598	9,553	9,234	7,775
Physicians' services	44,038	34,890	9,148	29,717	5,765	11,451	1,466	6,479
Nursing home care....	27,552	17,001	10,551	2,421	24,086	1,045	-	-
Drugs and other medical nondurables........	6,083	2,981	3,102	-	5,651	10	83	304
Administration	7,407	4,681	2,726	2,275	3,698	41	159	1,056
Public health activities...	21,976	2,381	19,595	-	-	-	-	-
1991, total [1]	315,921	211,990	103,931	122,803	104,941	12,185	12,809	17,793
Hospital care........	162,600	119,150	43,451	73,306	46,227	10,137	10,132	8,421
Physicians' services	49,435	39,035	10,400	32,781	7,313	12,185	1,628	7,055
Nursing home care....	32,309	19,501	12,808	2,667	28,493	1,149	-	-
Drugs and other medical nondurables........	7,345	3,624	3,721	-	6,872	11	93	330
Administration	8,136	5,166	2,970	2,560	4,028	45	162	1,151
Public health activities...	24,533	2,687	21,846	-	-	-	-	-

- Represents zero.   [1] Includes other items not shown separately.   [2] Covers hospital and medical insurance payments and administrative costs under old-age, survivors, disability, and health insurance program.   [3] Covers Medicaid and other medical public assistance. Excludes funds paid into Medicare trust fund by States to cover premiums for public assistance recipients and medically indigent persons.   [4] Includes care for retirees and military dependents.   [5] Medical benefits.

Source: U.S. Health Care Financing Administration, *Health Care Financing Review*, winter 1992.

No. 155. Expenditures for Health Services and Supplies, by Type of Payer: 1970 to 1991

[In billions of dollars]

TYPE OF PAYER	1970	1975	1980	1985	1986	1987	1988	1989	1990	1991
Total expenditures.	69.1	124.7	238.9	407.2	438.9	476.9	526.2	583.6	652.4	728.6
Private....................	50.1	86.2	162.0	279.0	301.8	327.5	362.5	398.3	436.6	474.1
Business	13.7	27.8	64.3	113.5	125.9	131.8	151.0	167.0	187.9	205.4
Share of private health insurance premiums	9.8	19.9	47.9	83.9	92.2	95.0	110.9	122.8	140.2	152.7
Households [1]	35.0	55.9	90.8	153.6	163.1	181.9	196.1	213.8	228.9	247.0
Share of private health insurance premiums	6.0	9.9	16.6	30.0	30.9	37.5	37.7	42.7	46.6	52.2
Out-of-pocket spending.....	18.9	38.5	59.5	94.4	100.9	108.8	118.5	126.2	136.5	144.3
Nonpatient revenues [2]	1.5	2.5	7.0	12.0	12.9	13.8	15.4	17.5	19.8	21.7
Public..................	18.9	38.5	76.8	128.2	137.1	149.4	163.7	185.4	215.8	254.5
Federal government........	10.4	21.3	42.6	68.9	71.6	77.0	84.3	96.5	113.7	133.8
State/local government	8.5	17.2	34.2	59.3	65.5	72.4	79.4	88.8	102.1	120.7

[1] Includes other items not shown separately.   [2] Includes philanthropy.

Source: U.S. Health Care Financing Administration, *Health Care Financing Review*, spring 1993.

Health and Nutrition

No. 156. Medicare Program—Enrollment and Payments: 1970 to 1991

[Enrollment as of **July 1**; payments for calendar year. Benefit payments represent trust fund outlays. Includes Puerto Rico, outlying areas, and enrollees in foreign countries. See text, section 3, for explanation of coverage]

TYPE OF INSURANCE	Unit	1970	1975	1980	1985	1988	1989	1990	1991
HOSPITAL AND/OR MEDICAL INSURANCE									
Enrollment, total	1,000	20,491	24,959	28,478	31,083	32,980	33,579	34,203	34,870
Benefit payments	Mil. dol	7,099	15,588	35,699	70,527	86,487	98,305	108,707	118,778
HOSPITAL INSURANCE									
Enrollment, total	1,000	20,361	24,640	28,067	30,589	32,413	33,040	33,719	34,429
Persons 65 and over	1,000	20,361	22,472	25,104	27,683	29,312	29,869	30,464	31,043
Disabled persons [1]	1,000	(X)	2,168	2,963	2,907	3,101	3,171	3,255	3,385
Benefit payments	Mil. dol	5,124	11,315	25,064	47,580	52,517	60,011	66,239	71,549
MEDICAL INSURANCE									
Enrollment, total	1,000	19,584	23,904	27,400	29,989	31,617	32,099	32,629	33,237
Persons 65 and over	1,000	19,584	21,945	24,680	27,311	28,780	29,216	29,686	30,185
Disabled persons [1]	1,000	(X)	1,959	2,719	2,678	2,837	2,883	2,943	3,052
Benefit payments	Mil. dol	1,975	4,273	10,635	22,947	33,970	38,294	42,468	47,229

X Not applicable.   [1] Age under 65; includes persons enrolled because of end-stage renal disease (ESRD) only.

Source: U.S. Health Care Financing Administration. Published in U.S. Social Security Administration, *Annual Statistical Supplement* to the *Social Security Bulletin.*

No. 157. Medicare—Persons Served and Reimbursements: 1980 to 1991

[Persons served are enrollees who use covered services, incurred expenses greater than the applicable deductible amounts and for whom Medicare paid benefits. Reimbursements are amounts paid to providers for covered services. Excluded are retroactive adjustments resulting from end of fiscal year cost settlements and certain lump-sum interim payments. Also excluded are beneficiary (or third party payor) liabilities for applicable deductibles, coinsurance amounts, and charges for noncovered services. Includes data for enrollees living in outlying territories and foreign countries]

TYPE OF COVERAGE AND SERVICE	Unit	PERSONS 65 YEARS OLD AND OVER			DISABLED PERSONS [1]		
		1980	1990	1991	1980	1990	1991
Persons served, total [2]	1,000	16,271	24,809	25,190	1,760	2,390	2,466
Hospital insurance [2]	1,000	6,024	6,367	6,576	728	680	706
Inpatient hospital	1,000	5,951	5,906	6,052	721	644	666
Skilled-nursing services	1,000	248	615	648	9	23	23
Home health services [3]	1,000	675	1,818	2,082	51	122	141
Supplementary medical insurance [2]	1,000	16,099	24,687	25,053	1,723	2,365	2,439
Physicians' and other medical services	1,000	15,627	24,193	24,492	1,631	2,249	2,304
Outpatient services	1,000	6,629	14,055	14,787	909	1,496	1,583
Home health services [3]	1,000	302	38	32	25	-	-
Persons served per 1,000 enrollees, total [2]	Rate	638	802	800	594	734	729
Hospital insurance [2]	Rate	240	209	212	246	209	209
Inpatient hospital	Rate	237	194	195	243	198	197
Skilled-nursing services	Rate	10	20	21	3	7	7
Home health services [3]	Rate	27	60	67	17	38	42
Supplementary medical insurance [2]	Rate	652	832	830	634	804	799
Physicians' and other medical services	Rate	633	815	811	600	764	755
Outpatient services	Rate	269	474	490	334	508	519
Home health services [3]	Rate	12	1	1	9	-	-
Reimbursements, total	Mil. dol	29,134	88,778	98,384	4,478	11,239	12,503
Per person served	Dollars	1,791	3,578	3,906	2,544	4,703	5,070
Hospital insurance	Mil. dol	20,353	54,244	61,474	2,765	6,694	7,512
Inpatient hospital	Mil. dol	19,583	48,952	54,366	2,714	6,346	7,045
Skilled-nursing services	Mil. dol	331	1,886	2,151	13	85	87
Home health services [3]	Mil. dol	440	3,406	4,958	38	264	379
Supplementary medical insurance	Mil. dol	8,781	34,533	36,910	1,713	4,545	4,991
Physicians' and other medical services	Mil. dol	7,361	27,379	28,965	997	2,831	3,054
Outpatient services	Mil. dol	1,261	7,077	7,870	701	1,714	1,937
Home health services [3]	Mil. dol	159	78	76	16	-	-

- Represents or rounds to zero.   [1] Age under 65; includes persons enrolled because of end-stage renal disease (ESRD) only.   [2] Persons are counted once for each type of covered service used, but are not double counted in totals.   [3] Beginning 1982, a change in legislation resulted in virtually all home health services being paid under hospital insurance.

Source: U.S. Health Care Financing Administration, *Medicare Program Statistics*, annual; and unpublished data.

No. 158. Medicare—Utilization and Charges: 1970 to 1992

[Data reflect date expense was incurred based on bills submitted for payment and recorded in Health Care Financing Administration central records through May 1993. Includes Puerto Rico, Virgin Islands, Guam, other outlying areas, and enrollees in foreign countries]

ITEM	Unit	PERSONS 65 YEARS OLD AND OVER				DISABLED PERSONS [1]			
		1970	1980	1990	1992	1975	1980	1990	1992
Hospital inpatient care:									
Admissions [2]	1,000...	6,141	9,258	9,216	10,021	822	1,271	1,257	1,367
Per 1,000 enrollees [3]	Rate...	302	369	309	317	379	429	396	383
Covered days of care.	Millions.	79	98	82	84	9	13	11	11
Per 1,000 enrollees [3]	Rate...	3,902	3,885	2,702	2,654	4,198	4,549	3,464	3,082
Per admission	Days...	12.9	10.5	8.9	8.9	11.1	10.6	8.8	8.0
Hospital covered charges..	Mil. dol..	5,968	28,615	90,846	116,977	1,371	4,087	11,910	15,951
Per covered day.	Dollars..	75	293	1,104	1,395	151	303	1,057	1,395
Percent of covered charges reimbursed [4]	Percent..	78.0	70.0	47.5	50.4	73.6	68.6	46.5	50.4
Physician allowed charges [5]..	Mil. dol..	2,310	9,011	30,447	34,083	367	1,112	2,907	3,787
Percent reimbursed	Percent..	71.9	78.0	77.0	75.6	76.1	78.7	75.7	75.6

[1] Disabled persons under age 65 and persons enrolled solely because of end-stage renal disease.   [2] Beginning 1990, represents number of discharges and includes pass-through amounts, except for kidney acquisition.   [3] Based on Hospital Insurance (HI) enrollment as of July 1.   [4] Prior to 1990, billing reimbursements exclude: (1) PPS pass-through amounts for capital, direct medical education, kidney acquisitions, and bad debts by Medicare patients; (2) certain lump-sum interim payments. All years exclude retroactive adjustments resulting from end-of-fiscal year cost reports.   [5] Calendar year data.

Source: U.S. Health Care Financing Administration, unpublished data.

No. 159. Medicare and Medicaid—Summary, by State and Other Areas: 1992

[Data are preliminary estimates]

STATE AND AREA	MEDICARE		MEDICAID [3]		STATE AND AREA	MEDICARE		MEDICAID [3]	
	Enroll-ment [1] (1,000)	Pay-ments [2] (mil. dol.)	Recipi-ents [4] (1,000)	Pay-ments [5] (mil. dol.)		Enroll-ment [1] (1,000)	Pay-ments [2] (mil. dol.)	Recipi-ents [4] (1,000)	Pay-ments [5] (mil. dol.)
All areas ..	35,579	129,179	31,150	91,480	MT..........	123	307	60	217
U.S. [6] ...	34,853	128,520	30,251	91,317	NE..........	242	631	151	468
AL..........	606	2,100	467	1,056	NV..........	161	598	78	282
AK..........	28	82	58	187	NH..........	145	428	71	340
AZ..........	538	2,077	402	209	NJ..........	1,126	4,188	697	2,802
AR..........	404	1,309	321	885	NM..........	192	489	212	478
CA..........	3,421	15,653	4,486	8,692	NY..........	2,556	10,269	2,558	15,281
CO..........	382	1,242	259	814	NC..........	944	3,006	785	2,083
CT..........	483	1,953	316	1,663	ND..........	101	352	57	253
DE..........	93	267	61	219	OH..........	1,598	5,721	1,299	3,653
DC..........	78	1,112	109	499	OK..........	466	1,471	360	1,004
FL..........	2,455	10,361	1,538	3,518	OR..........	445	1,357	295	748
GA..........	771	2,864	864	2,149	PA..........	2,014	8,365	1,398	4,213
HI..........	136	404	100	270	RI..........	163	588	213	774
ID..........	139	300	87	275	SC..........	468	1,244	431	1,151
IL..........	1,574	5,565	1,313	4,070	SD..........	113	276	64	231
IN..........	789	2,455	507	2,225	TN..........	722	2,895	785	1,735
IA..........	465	1,242	279	855	TX..........	1,923	6,978	2,025	4,407
KS..........	373	1,161	227	620	UT..........	171	427	137	365
KY..........	554	1,788	583	1,543	VT..........	77	200	78	222
LA..........	551	2,318	702	2,479	VA..........	760	2,226	515	1,511
ME..........	190	514	162	642	WA..........	645	2,145	569	1,347
MD..........	567	2,262	377	1,612	WV..........	317	931	308	795
MA..........	895	3,780	686	3,248	WI..........	734	2,126	440	1,677
MI..........	1,282	4,642	1,129	2,802	WY..........	55	98	42	114
MN..........	606	1,943	406	1,750	PR	446	556	[8]85	158
MS..........	378	1,235	487	881	Outlying areas	8	5	[7]13	[7]5
MO	804	2,674	554	1,350	Foreign	271	(NA)	(X)	(X)

NA Not available.   X Not applicable.   [1] Hospital and/or medical insurance enrollment as of July 1.   [2] Benefit payments are for calendar year. Payments for "All areas" represent actual Trust Fund disbursements as shown in the 1990 Trustees Reports, and other actuarial data. Distribution by State is based on interim payment as reflected on claims for services rendered in 1989 and recorded in central office through December, 1990. Payments have been adjusted to include estimated PPS pass-through amounts, but exclude retroactive cost-based adjustments and administrative expenses. Data reflect State of residence of beneficiary.   [3] For fiscal year ending Sept. 30.   [4] Persons receiving Medicaid at any time during the year.   [5] Payments are for calendar year and represent disbursements from Federal hospital and medical insurance trust funds. Estimates of distribution by State based on preliminary billing data.   [6] Includes data for enrollees with residence unknown.   [7] Virgin Islands only.

Source: U.S. Health Care Financing Administration, unpublished data.

No. 160. Medicaid—Selected Utilization Measures: 1975 to 1992

[In thousands. For fiscal years ending in year shown. Includes Virgin Islands. See text, section 3]

MEASURE	1975	1980	1985	1988	1989	1990	1991	1992
General hospitals:								
Recipients discharged	2,336	2,255	2,390	2,640	2,701	3,261	3,638	3,709
Total days of care	22,941	24,089	29,562	24,022	22,754	27,471	28,998	28,776
Nursing facilities: [1]								
Total recipients	1,212	1,395	1,375	1,445	1,438	1,461	1,500	1,573
Total days of care	199,715	273,497	277,996	344,693	367,228	360,044	387,621	388,931
Intermediate care facilities: [2]								
Total recipients	69	121	147	145	147	146	146	151
Total days of care	9,060	250,124	47,324	46,825	50,276	49,730	50,223	50,916

[1] Includes skilled nursing facilities and intermediate care facilities for all other than the mentally retarded.   [2] Mentally retarded.

Source: U.S. Health Care Financing Administration, unpublished data.

No. 161. Medicaid—Selected Characteristics of Persons Covered: 1988 to 1992

[In thousands, except percent. Represents number of persons as of March of following year who were enrolled at any time in year shown. Person did not have to receive medical care paid for by Medicaid in order to be counted. See headnote, table 578]

POVERTY STATUS	1988	1990	1992							
			Total [1]	White	Black	His-panic [2]	Under 18 years old	18-44 years old	45-64 years old	65 years and over
Persons covered, total	20,674	24,160	28,411	18,046	8,860	4,976	14,329	8,645	2,521	2,914
Below poverty level	13,185	15,175	17,419	10,122	6,445	3,172	9,590	5,275	1,349	1,205
Above poverty level	7,489	8,985	10,992	7,924	2,415	1,804	4,739	3,370	1,172	1,709
Percent of population covered	8.5	9.7	11.2	8.5	27.8	21.9	21.4	8.1	5.1	9.4
Below poverty level	41.5	45.2	47.2	41.3	60.7	47.7	65.6	38.1	30.5	30.2
Above poverty level	3.5	4.2	5.1	4.2	11.3	11.2	9.1	3.6	2.6	6.4

[1] Includes other races not shown separately.   [2] Persons of Hispanic origin may be of any race.

Source: U.S. Bureau of the Census, Current Population Reports, P60-185, earlier reports; and unpublished data.

No. 162. Medicaid—Recipients and Payments: 1980 to 1992

[For fiscal year ending in year shown; see text, section 10. Includes Puerto Rico and outlying areas. Medical vendor payments are those made directly to suppliers of medical care]

BASIS OF ELIGIBILITY AND TYPE OF SERVICE	RECIPIENTS (1,000)					PAYMENTS (mil. dol.)				
	1980	1985	1990	1991	1992	1980	1985	1990	1991	1992
Total [1]	21,605	21,814	25,255	28,280	31,150	23,311	37,508	64,859	77,048	91,480
Age 65 and over	3,440	3,061	3,202	3,359	3,749	8,739	14,096	21,508	25,453	29,089
Blindness	92	80	83	85	84	124	249	434	475	530
Disabled [2]	2,819	2,937	3,635	3,983	4,402	7,497	13,203	23,969	27,798	33,474
AFDC [3] program	14,210	15,275	17,230	20,194	22,240	6,354	9,160	17,690	22,129	27,161
Other and unknown	1,499	1,214	1,105	658	675	596	798	1,257	1,193	1,226
Inpatient services in—										
General hospital	3,680	3,434	4,593	5,072	5,790	6,412	9,453	16,674	19,891	23,686
Mental hospital	66	60	92	65	77	775	1,192	1,714	2,010	2,200
Intermediate care facilities:										
Mentally retarded	121	147	147	146	151	1,989	4,731	7,354	7,680	8,552
Nursing facility services [4]	1,398	1,375	1,461	1,500	1,573	7,887	11,587	17,693	20,709	23,547
Physicians	13,765	14,387	17,078	19,321	21,683	1,875	2,346	4,018	4,952	6,122
Dental	4,652	4,672	4,552	5,209	5,717	462	458	593	710	853
Other practitioner	3,234	3,357	3,873	4,282	4,725	198	251	372	437	539
Outpatient hospital	9,705	10,072	12,370	14,137	15,167	1,101	1,789	3,324	4,283	5,296
Clinic	1,531	2,121	2,804	3,511	4,128	320	714	1,688	2,211	2,825
Laboratory [5]	3,212	6,354	8,959	10,505	11,850	121	337	721	897	1,040
Home health	392	535	719	813	926	332	1,120	3,404	4,101	4,888
Prescribed drugs	13,707	13,921	17,294	19,602	22,070	1,318	2,315	4,420	5,424	6,790
Family planning	1,129	1,636	1,752	2,185	2,559	81	195	265	359	504

[1] Recipient data do not add due to small number of recipients that are reported in more than one category. Includes recipients of, and payments for, other care not shown separately.   [2] Permanently and totally.   [3] Aid to families with dependent children. [4] Nursing facility services includes skilled nursing facility services and intermediate care facility services for all other than the mentally retarded.   [5] Includes radiological services.

Source: U.S. Health Care Financing Administration, Health Care Financing Review, quarterly.

No. 163. Consumer Price Indexes of Medical Care Prices: 1970 to 1993

[1982-1984 = 100. Indexes are annual averages of monthly data based on components of consumer price index for all urban consumers; for explanation, see text, section 15. See *Historical Statistics, Colonial Times to 1970*, series B 262-272 for similar data]

| YEAR | Medical care | MEDICAL CARE SERVICES | | | | | Medical care commodities[2] | ANNUAL PERCENT CHANGE[3] | | | | | |
| | | Total[1] | Professional services | | | Hospital room | | Medical care | Medical care services | | | | Medical care commodities[2] |
			Total[1]	Physicians	Dental				Total[1]	Physicians	Dental	Hospital room	
1970	34.0	32.3	37.0	34.5	39.2	23.6	46.5	6.6	7.0	7.5	5.7	12.9	2.4
1975	47.5	46.6	50.8	48.1	53.2	38.3	53.3	12.0	12.6	12.1	10.4	17.1	8.3
1980	74.9	74.8	77.9	76.5	78.9	68.0	75.4	11.0	11.3	10.5	11.9	13.1	9.3
1985	113.5	113.2	113.5	113.3	114.2	115.4	115.2	6.3	6.1	5.9	6.2	5.9	7.2
1986	122.0	121.9	120.8	121.5	120.6	122.3	122.8	7.5	7.7	7.2	5.6	6.0	6.6
1987	130.1	130.0	128.8	130.4	128.8	131.1	131.0	6.6	6.6	7.3	6.8	7.2	6.7
1988	138.6	138.3	137.5	139.8	137.5	143.3	139.9	6.5	6.4	7.2	6.8	9.3	6.8
1989	149.3	148.9	146.4	150.1	146.1	158.1	150.8	7.7	7.7	7.4	6.3	10.3	7.8
1990	162.8	162.7	156.1	160.8	155.8	175.4	163.4	9.0	9.3	7.1	6.6	10.9	8.4
1991	177.0	177.1	165.7	170.5	167.4	191.9	176.8	8.7	8.9	6.0	7.4	9.4	8.2
1992	190.1	190.5	175.8	181.2	178.7	208.7	188.1	7.4	7.6	6.3	6.8	8.8	6.4
1993	201.4	202.9	184.7	191.3	188.1	226.4	195.0	5.9	6.5	5.6	5.3	8.5	3.7

[1] Includes other services not shown separately. [2] Prior to 1980, covers drugs and prescriptions only. [3] Percent change from the immediate prior year.

Source: U.S. Bureau of Labor Statistics, *CPI Detailed Report*, January 1994; and unpublished data.

No. 164. Average Annual Expenditures per Consumer Unit for Health Care: 1984 to 1992

[In dollars, except percent. See text, section 14, and headnote, table 703. For composition of regions, see table 26]

| ITEM | HEALTH CARE, TOTAL | | Health insurance | Medical services | Drugs and medical supplies[1] | PERCENT DISTRIBUTION | | |
	Amount	Percent of total expenditures				Health insurance	Medical services	Drugs and medical supplies[1]
1984	1,049	4.8	370	454	225	35.3	43.3	21.4
1985	1,108	4.7	375	496	238	33.8	44.8	21.5
1986	1,135	4.8	371	502	261	32.7	44.2	23.0
1987	1,135	4.6	392	467	276	34.5	41.1	24.3
1988	1,298	5.0	474	529	294	36.5	40.8	22.7
1989	1,407	5.1	537	542	327	38.2	38.5	23.2
1990	1,480	5.2	581	562	337	39.3	38.0	22.8
1991	1,554	5.2	656	555	344	42.2	35.7	22.1
1992	**1,634**	**5.5**	**725**	**533**	**375**	**44.4**	**32.6**	**22.9**
Age of reference person:								
Under 25 years old	416	2.4	147	159	110	35.3	38.2	26.4
25 to 34 years old	1,053	3.6	463	406	183	44.0	38.6	17.4
35 to 44 years old	1,570	4.2	620	648	302	39.5	41.3	19.2
45 to 54 years old	1,646	4.4	657	585	403	39.9	35.5	24.5
55 to 64 years old	1,993	6.3	854	685	453	42.8	34.4	22.7
65 to 74 years old	2,487	10.9	1239	576	671	49.8	23.2	27.0
75 years old and over	2,460	13.8	1291	514	654	52.5	20.9	26.6
Race:								
White and other	1,743	5.6	765	579	399	43.9	33.2	22.9
Black	795	4.0	420	178	197	52.8	22.4	24.8
Region of residence:								
Northeast	1,653	5.3	741	540	372	44.8	32.7	22.5
Midwest	1,535	5.4	721	463	351	47.0	30.2	22.9
South	1,711	6.2	755	543	413	44.1	31.7	24.1
West	1,610	4.8	665	596	349	41.3	37.0	21.7
Size of consumer unit:								
One person	1,049	5.9	482	304	263	45.9	29.0	25.1
Two or more persons	1,874	5.4	825	627	422	44.0	33.5	22.5
Two persons	2,047	6.7	932	596	519	45.5	29.1	25.4
Three persons	1,760	5.0	775	608	377	44.0	34.5	21.4
Four persons	1,840	4.5	751	736	353	40.8	40.0	19.2
Five persons or more	1,570	4.1	685	587	298	43.6	37.4	19.0
Income before taxes:								
Complete income reporters[2]	1,654	5.4	728	546	380	44.0	33.0	23.0
Quintiles of income:								
Lowest 20 percent	964	7.6	435	276	253	45.1	28.6	26.2
Second 20 percent	1,507	7.8	711	383	413	47.2	25.4	27.4
Third 20 percent	1,655	6.2	790	469	395	47.7	28.3	23.9
Fourth 20 percent	1,883	5.2	833	675	374	44.2	35.8	19.9
Highest 20 percent	2,257	3.9	868	926	464	38.5	41.0	20.6
Incomplete reporters of income	1,517	5.8	712	451	354	46.9	29.7	23.3

[1] Includes prescription and nonprescription drugs. [2] A complete reporter is a consumer unit providing values for at least one of the major sources of income.

Source: Bureau of Labor Statistics, *Consumer Expenditure Survey*, annual.

Health and Nutrition

No. 165. Health Insurance Coverage Status, by Selected Characteristics: 1987 to 1992

[Persons as of following year for coverage in the year shown. Government health insurance includes Medicare, Medicaid, and military plans. Based on Current Population Survey; see text, section 1, and Appendix III]

CHARACTERISTIC	Total persons	NUMBER (mil.)						PERCENT			
		Covered by private or Government health insurance					Not covered by health insurance	Covered by private or Government health insurance			Not covered by health insurance
		Total [1]	Private		Government			Total [1]	Private	Medi-caid	
			Total	Group health [2]	Medi-care	Medi-caid					
1987	241.2	210.2	182.2	149.7	30.5	20.2	31.0	87.1	75.5	8.4	12.9
1988	243.7	211.0	182.0	150.9	30.9	20.7	32.7	86.6	74.7	8.5	13.4
1989	246.2	212.8	183.6	151.6	31.5	21.2	33.4	86.4	74.6	8.6	13.6
1990	248.9	214.2	182.1	150.2	32.3	24.3	34.7	86.1	73.2	9.7	13.9
1991	251.4	216.0	181.4	150.1	32.9	26.9	35.4	85.9	72.1	10.7	14.1
1992, total [3] **. . .**	**254.2**	**216.8**	**180.8**	**148.2**	**33.7**	**28.6**	**37.4**	**85.3**	**71.1**	**11.2**	**14.7**
Sex: Male	124.0	103.6	88.2	73.7	14.3	11.7	20.4	83.5	71.1	9.4	16.5
Female	130.2	113.2	92.6	74.5	19.3	16.9	17.0	86.9	71.1	13.0	13.1
Race: White	212.0	183.1	158.7	129.7	29.6	18.1	28.9	86.4	74.9	8.5	13.6
Black	32.0	25.6	15.7	13.3	3.3	8.9	6.4	79.9	49.0	27.9	20.1
Hispanic origin [4]	22.8	15.3	10.1	8.8	1.5	5.0	7.4	67.5	44.5	21.9	32.5
Age: Under 18 years.	67.1	58.8	46.5	39.8	0.1	14.5	8.3	87.6	69.3	21.6	12.4
18 to 24 years . . .	24.3	17.3	14.5	10.5	0.2	2.7	7.0	71.1	59.5	11.1	28.9
25 to 34 years . . .	41.9	33.1	28.8	26.0	0.6	3.7	8.7	79.1	68.8	8.8	20.9
35 to 44 years . . .	40.3	34.1	31.1	28.1	0.7	2.2	6.2	84.5	77.1	5.6	15.5
45 to 54 years . . .	28.5	24.5	22.6	20.1	0.7	1.3	4.0	86.0	79.2	4.6	14.0
55 to 64 years . . .	21.2	18.5	16.4	13.6	1.7	1.2	2.7	87.1	77.0	5.7	12.9
65 years and over .	30.9	30.5	20.9	10.1	29.7	2.9	0.4	98.8	67.7	9.4	1.2

[1] Includes other Government insurance, not shown separately. Persons with coverage counted only once in total, even though they may have been covered by more that one type of policy. [2] Related to employment of self or other family members. [3] Includes other races not shown separately. [4] Persons of Hispanic origin may be of any race.

Source: U.S. Bureau of the Census, March 1993 Supplement to the Current Population Survey, unpublished data.

No. 166. Persons Without Health Insurance, by State: 1990 to 1992

[In percent. Based on the Current Population Survey and subject to sampling error; see text, section 1, and Appendix III]

STATE	1992	Three-year average [1], 1990-92	STATE	1992	Three-year average [1], 1990-92
United States	14.7	14.2	Missouri	14.3	13.1
Alabama	16.6	17.3	Montana	9.3	12.0
Alaska	16.1	14.9	Nebraska	9.3	8.7
Arizona	14.9	15.8	Nevada	22.7	19.3
Arkansas	19.8	17.6	New Hampshire	12.6	10.9
California	19.3	19.0	New Jersey	13.0	11.3
Colorado	12.4	12.4	New Mexico	19.3	21.0
Connecticut	8.1	7.5	New York	13.5	12.6
Delaware	10.9	12.7	North Carolina	13.8	14.2
District of Columbia	21.3	22.0	North Dakota	8.3	7.4
Florida	19.5	18.7	Ohio	11.0	10.5
Georgia	19.0	16.1	Oklahoma	21.6	19.5
Hawaii	6.0	6.8	Oregon	13.2	13.3
Idaho.	16.3	16.4	Pennsylvania.	8.5	8.8
Illinois	12.9	11.8	Rhode Island	9.3	10.2
Indiana	10.9	11.5	South Carolina	17.0	15.4
Iowa	10.1	9.0	South Dakota	15.0	12.2
Kansas	10.8	11.0	Tennessee	13.6	13.6
Kentucky	14.6	13.6	Texas	22.4	21.9
Louisiana	22.1	20.8	Utah	11.7	11.5
Maine	11.1	11.1	Vermont	9.4	10.6
Maryland	11.2	12.3	Virginia	14.5	15.5
Massachusetts	10.4	10.1	Washington	10.2	10.7
Michigan	9.9	9.4	West Virginia.	15.4	15.0
Minnesota	8.1	8.8	Wisconsin.	9.0	7.9
Mississippi	19.2	19.3	Wyoming	11.8	11.9

[1] Three-year average is recommended when comparing rates between States to reduce somewhat the chances of misinterpreting differences and lessen the effect of sampling variability.

Source: U.S. Bureau of the Census, Current Population Reports, P60-184.

No.167. Health Insurance Coverage, by Selected Characteristic: 1987-89

[Data represent persons covered by Government or private health insurance coverage during a 28-month period, beginning October 1986. Based on Survey of Income and Program Participation. See text, section 14]

CHARACTERISTIC	All persons (mil.)	COVERED BY INSURANCE (mil.)				PERCENT COVERED BY INSURANCE			
		Government or private			Private for entire period	Government or private			Private for entire period
		For entire period	For part of the period	No coverage		For entire period	For part of the period	No coverage	
Total [1]	231.0	169.8	52.1	9.1	146.8	73.5	22.6	3.9	63.6
Under 18 years old	63.3	42.7	17.7	3.0	36.3	67.4	28.0	4.7	57.3
Under 6 years old	22.4	14.8	6.6	0.9	12.1	66.3	29.5	4.2	54.1
18 to 21 years old	13.6	6.6	6.2	0.8	6.1	48.9	45.6	5.6	44.6
22 to 24 years old	11.5	5.9	5.1	0.5	5.4	51.3	44.3	4.6	46.6
25 to 34 years old	41.4	28.9	10.8	1.7	26.8	69.8	26.1	4.1	64.6
35 to 44 years old	33.0	25.3	6.2	1.4	24.0	76.9	18.8	4.3	72.8
45 to 64 years old	43.5	35.8	6.0	1.7	32.7	82.4	13.8	3.9	75.2
65 years old and over	24.7	24.5	0.2	0.2	15.7	99.3	0.1	0.1	63.6
Male	111.5	80.2	26.6	4.7	71.0	71.9	23.9	4.2	63.7
Female	119.5	89.6	25.6	4.3	75.8	75.0	21.4	3.6	63.5
White	195.6	148.2	40.2	7.2	132.6	75.8	20.6	3.7	67.8
Black	27.8	16.7	9.7	1.4	10.5	60.2	34.9	4.9	37.8
Hispanic [2]	17.4	9.3	6.2	1.9	7.0	53.6	35.6	10.7	40.2
Educational attainment: [3]									
Less than 12 years	37.6	27.3	7.9	2.3	18.1	72.8	21.0	6.2	48.1
12 to 15 years	96.3	72.1	21.0	3.2	65.9	74.9	21.8	3.3	68.4
16 years or more	30.4	26.0	3.9	0.5	25.1	85.5	12.8	1.5	82.6
Work-status: [4]									
Worked entire 28 months—									
Full time	57.2	49.0	7.0	1.2	48.6	85.7	12.2	2.1	85.0
Part time	5.6	4.1	1.1	0.4	4.0	72.7	19.6	7.0	70.3
Had at least one work interruption	59.7	34.3	22.2	3.2	31.6	57.4	37.2	5.4	52.9

[1] Includes other races, not shown separately.   [2] Persons of Hispanic origin may be of any race.   [3] For persons 19 years old and over.   [4] For wage and salary workers.
Source: U.S. Bureau of the Census, *Current Population Reports*, P70-29; and unpublished data.

No. 168. Health Maintenance Organizations (HMO's): 1980 to 1992

[As of June 30, except as noted. Under the Health Maintenance Organization Act, an HMO must have four characteristics: (1) an organized system for providing health care in a geographic area, for which the HMO is responsible for providing or otherwise assuring its delivery; (2) an agreed upon set of basic and supplemental health maintenance and treatment services; (3) a voluntarily enrolled group of people; and (4) community rating. A staff HMO delivers services through a physician group controlled by the HMO unit. A group HMO contracts with one or more medical groups to provide services to members and generally provides all services except hospital care under one roof. A network HMO provides comprehensive health services to members in two or more distinct geographic areas. Individual practice association (IPA) HMO contracts with a physician organization that in turn contracts with individual physicians. IPA physicians provide care to HMO members from their private offices and continue to see their fee-for-service patients. An open-ended product line allows enrollees to receive services from health care providers outside the HMO network for additional out-of-pocket fee (typically a deductible and coinsurance are imposed)]

TYPE OF PRACTICE AND SIZE	1980	1985	1986	1987	1988	1989 (July 1)	1990 (July 1)	1991 (July 1)	1992 (Dec. 1)
NUMBER OF PLANS									
Total	236	393	595	662	[1]643	[1]590	[1]556	[1]559	[1]546
Staff	63	55	71	64	69	60	50	46	61
Group	76	71	86	74	69	66	62	55	55
Network	(NA)	86	93	107	93	93	82	68	88
I.P.A.	97	181	345	417	412	371	350	349	342
Mixed	(NA)	(NA)	(NA)	(NA)	(NA)	(NA)	12	41	(NA)
ENROLLMENT (1,000)									
Total	9,100	18,894	23,664	28,587	[2]31,366	[2]32,493	[2]33,622	[2]35,052	[2]41,382
Staff	1,673	2,686	3,136	3,079	4,276	3,997	3,577	3,425	5,602
Group	5,732	6,488	7,118	7,286	7,985	9,177	9,535	9,471	10,087
Network	(NA)	5,073	4,955	6,895	5,622	5,719	5,874	4,077	6,634
I.P.A.	1,694	4,646	8,454	11,327	13,483	13,598	13,879	13,984	19,059
Mixed	(NA)	(NA)	(NA)	(NA)	(NA)	(NA)	755	4,096	(NA)
HMO's WITH OPEN-ENDED PRODUCT LINE									
Number of plans	(X)	(X)	(X)	(X)	48	78	96	157	271
Enrollment (1,000)	(X)	(X)	(X)	(X)	482	703	1,041	1,430	1,588

NA Not available.   X Not applicable.   [1] Includes HMO's containing only open-ended members, not distributed by enrollment size.   [2] Excludes enrollees participating in open-ended plans.
Source: InterStudy, Excelsior, MN, *The InterStudy Competitive Edge*, 1992, vol. 2, No. 2, and earlier publications (copyright); and Group Health Association of America, Inc., Washington, DC, *1993 National Directory of HMO's*.

No. 169. Employment in the Health Service Industries: 1980 to 1993

[In thousands. See headnote table 656]

INDUSTRY	1987 SIC code [1]	1980	1985	1990	1991	1992	1993
Health services [2]	80	5,278	6,293	7,814	8,183	8,523	8,871
Offices and clinics of MD's	801	802	1,028	1,338	1,405	1,473	1,545
Offices and clinics of Dentist's	802	(NA)	439	513	528	542	563
Offices and clinics of other practitioners	804	96	165	277	304	327	354
Nursing and personal care facilities	805	997	1,198	1,415	1,493	1,543	1,615
Skilled nursing care facilities	8051	(NA)	791	989	1,067	1,099	1,151
Intermediate care facilities	8052	(NA)	(NA)	200	211	220	230
Other, n.e.c. [3]	8059	(NA)	(NA)	227	215	224	234
Hospitals	806	2,750	2,997	3,549	3,655	3,760	3,816
General medical and surgical hospitals	8062	(NA)	2,811	3,268	3,359	3,457	3,510
Psychiatric hospitals	8063	(NA)	59	104	106	103	101
Specialty hospitals, exc. psychiatric	8069	(NA)	126	176	190	199	206
Medical and dental laboratories	807	105	119	166	173	181	193
Home health care services	808	(NA)	152	291	345	402	474

NA Not available.   [1] Based on the 1987 Standard Industrial Classification code; see text, section 13.   [2] Includes other industries not shown separately.   [3] N.e.c. means not elsewhere classified.

Source: U.S. Bureau of Labor Statistics, Bulletins 2370 and 2429, and *Employment and Earnings*, monthly, March and June issues.

No. 170. Annual Receipts for the Health Service Industries: 1987 to 1992

[In millions of dollars. For employer establishments]

INDUSTRY	1987 SIC code [1]	1987	1988	1989	1990	1991	1992
TAXABLE FIRMS							
Health services [2]	80	182,289	203,827	220,088	244,517	262,745	285,040
Offices and clinics of MD's	801	90,462	100,837	107,461	116,962	124,456	134,986
Offices and clinics of Dentist's	802	24,017	25,642	27,127	28,785	29,993	32,878
Offices and clinics of Doctor's of Osteopathy	803	2,119	2,335	2,321	2,513	2,599	2,736
Offices and clinics of other practitioners [2]	804	10,340	12,167	12,795	14,802	15,628	17,323
Offices and clinics of Chiropractors	8041	3,275	3,984	4,420	4,828	4,986	5,787
Offices and clinics of Optometrists	8042	3,450	3,760	3,864	4,275	4,430	4,649
Offices and clinics of Podiatrists	8043	(NA)	(NA)	(NA)	1,689	1,826	1,961
Nursing and personal care facilities	805	20,063	21,361	23,349	26,446	28,848	30,726
Hospitals	806	19,720	22,625	24,674	28,309	30,743	33,058
General medical and surgical hospitals	8062	(NA)	(NA)	(NA)	21,788	23,683	25,753
Psychiatric hospitals	8063	(NA)	(NA)	(NA)	5,096	5,434	5,426
Specialty hospitals, exc. psychiatric	8069	(NA)	(NA)	(NA)	1,425	1,626	1,879
Medical and dental laboratories	807	7,114	8,119	8,933	9,872	10,527	11,115
Medical laboratories	8071	5,518	6,620	7,374	8,209	8,849	9,336
Dental laboratories	8072	1,596	1,499	1,559	1,663	1,678	1,779
Home health care services	808	(NA)	(NA)	(NA)	6,196	7,381	8,936
Miscellaneous allied services, n.e.c. [3]	809	(NA)	(NA)	(NA)	10,618	12,562	13,282
Kidney dialysis centers	8092	(NA)	(NA)	(NA)	1,272	1,505	1,877
Specialty outpatient facilities, n.e.c. [3]	8093	(NA)	(NA)	(NA)	5,258	6,426	6,395
TAX EXEMPT FIRMS							
Selected health services [2]	805, 6, 8, 9	(NA)	(NA)	(NA)	280,892	312,665	340,044
Offices and clinics of doctors of medicine	801	(NA)	(NA)	(NA)	11,794	13,492	15,143
Nursing and personal care facilities	805	8,201	8,633	8,844	9,303	10,471	11,736
Hospitals	806	(NA)	(NA)	(NA)	251,884	279,612	302,132
General medical and surgical hospitals	8062	(NA)	(NA)	(NA)	230,025	255,763	277,984
Psychiatric hospitals	8063	(NA)	(NA)	(NA)	9,515	9,907	9,450
Specialty hospitals, exc. psychiatric	8069	(NA)	(NA)	(NA)	12,344	13,942	14,698
Home health care services	808	(NA)	(NA)	(NA)	3,233	3,859	4,769
Miscellaneous allied services, n.e.c. [2][3]	809	(NA)	(NA)	(NA)	4,554	5,097	6,121
Kidney dialysis centers	8092	(NA)	(NA)	(NA)	347	406	455
Specialty outpatient facilities, n.e.c. [3]	8093	(NA)	(NA)	(NA)	3,018	3,289	3,806

NA Not available.   [1] Based on the 1987 Standard Industrial Classification code; see text, section 13.   [2] Includes other industries not shown separately.   [3] N.e.c. means not elsewhere classified.

Source: U.S. Bureau of the Census, Current Business Reports, *Service Annual Survey, BS/92*.

No. 171. Physicians, by Selected Activity: 1970 to 1992

[In thousands. Through 1985, as of Dec. 31; thereafter as of Jan. 1, except as noted. Includes Puerto Rico and outlying areas. See also *Historical Statistics, Colonial Times to 1970*, series B 275-280]

ACTIVITY	1970	1980	1985	1988	1989	1990	1992
Doctors of medicine, total	**334.0**	**467.7**	**552.7**	**585.6**	**600.8**	**615.4**	**653.1**
Professionally active	310.8	414.9	497.1	521.3	536.8	547.3	578.1
Place of medical education:							
U.S. medical graduates	256.4	333.3	392.0	410.3	423.2	432.9	451.7
Foreign medical graduates [1]	54.4	81.6	105.1	111.0	113.6	114.4	126.4
Sex: Male	289.5	370.2	425.3	(NA)	(NA)	454.0	471.1
Female	21.4	44.7	71.9	(NA)	(NA)	93.3	107.0
Active Non-Federal	281.3	397.1	475.6	499.6	516.4	526.8	558.9
Patient care	255.0	361.9	431.5	453.2	468.9	479.5	513.4
Office-based practice	188.9	271.3	329.0	337.5	350.1	359.9	387.9
General and family practice	50.8	47.8	53.9	55.1	56.3	57.6	58.6
Cardiovascular diseases	3.9	6.7	9.1	9.9	10.2	10.7	11.4
Dermatology	2.9	4.4	5.3	5.5	5.7	6.0	6.3
Gastroenterology	1.1	2.7	4.1	4.8	4.9	5.2	5.7
Internal medicine	23.0	40.5	52.7	55.5	56.9	57.8	65.1
Pediatrics	10.3	17.4	22.4	23.4	24.7	26.5	29.0
Pulmonary diseases	0.8	2.0	3.0	3.5	3.6	3.7	4.0
General surgery	18.1	22.4	24.7	23.7	24.7	24.5	24.9
Obstetrics and gynecology	13.8	19.5	23.5	24.3	25.2	25.5	27.1
Ophthalmology	7.6	10.6	12.2	12.5	12.8	13.1	13.7
Orthopedic surgery	6.5	10.7	13.0	13.5	14.1	14.2	15.8
Otolaryngology	3.9	5.3	5.8	6.0	6.2	6.4	6.6
Plastic surgery	1.2	2.4	3.3	3.5	3.6	3.8	4.0
Urological surgery	4.3	6.2	7.1	7.2	7.3	7.4	7.7
Anesthesiology	7.4	11.3	15.3	16.0	16.7	17.8	20.0
Diagnostic radiology	0.9	4.2	7.7	8.6	9.0	9.8	10.9
Emergency medicine	(NA)	(NA)	(NA)	7.6	8.0	8.4	9.4
Neurology	1.2	3.2	4.7	5.1	5.4	5.6	6.3
Pathology, anatomical/clinical	3.0	6.0	6.9	6.7	7.0	7.3	7.9
Psychiatry	10.1	15.9	18.5	18.7	19.6	20.0	21.8
Radiology	5.8	7.8	7.4	6.1	6.2	6.1	5.8
Other specialty	12.4	24.1	28.5	20.3	21.7	22.8	25.9
Hospital-based practice	66.1	90.6	102.5	115.7	118.8	119.6	125.5
Residents and interns	45.8	59.6	72.2	79.5	80.0	81.7	85.4
Full-time hospital staff	20.3	31.0	30.3	36.2	38.8	38.0	40.1
Other professional activity [2]	26.3	35.2	44.0	46.4	47.5	47.3	45.5
Federal	29.5	17.8	21.6	21.7	20.4	20.5	19.2
Patient care	23.5	14.6	17.3	16.9	15.6	15.6	14.7
Office-based practice	3.5	0.7	1.2	1.1	1.1	1.1	1.5
Hospital-based practice	20.0	13.9	16.1	15.8	14.4	14.6	13.2
Other professional activity [2]	6.0	3.2	4.3	4.8	4.8	4.8	4.6
Inactive/unknown address [3]	23.2	52.8	55.6	64.3	64.0	68.1	75.0
Doctors of osteopathy [4]	**14.3**	**18.8**	**24.0**	**28.3**	**29.6**	**30.9**	**33.5**
Medical and osteopathic schools [5]	110	141	142	142	142	142	141
Students [5]	42.6	70.1	73.2	71.9	71.6	72.0	73.5
Graduates [5]	8.8	16.2	17.8	17.5	17.5	17.2	17.1

NA Not available. [1] Foreign medical graduates received their medical education in schools outside the United States and Canada. [2] Includes medical teaching, administration, research, clinical fellows, and other. [3] Includes those not classified. [4] As of July. Total DO's. Source: American Osteopathic Association, Chicago, IL. [5] Number of schools and students as of fall; graduates for academic year ending in year shown. Based on data from annual surveys conducted by the Association of American Medical Colleges and the American Association of Colleges of Osteopathic Medicine. Source: See table 172.

Source: Except as noted, American Medical Association, Chicago, IL, *Physician Characteristics and Distribution in the U.S.*, annual (copyright).

No. 172. Dentists and Nurses: 1970 to 1992

[As of end of year, except as noted. Excludes Puerto Rico and outlying areas. See also *Historical Statistics, Colonial Times to 1970*, series B 281-290]

ITEM	Unit	1970	1975	1980	1985	1988	1989	1990	1991	1992
Dentists, number	1,000	116	127	141	156	164	168	[1]173	179	(NA)
Active (exc. in Federal service) [2]	1,000	96	107	121	136	142	144	148	150	(NA)
Rate per 100,000 population [3]	Rate	47	50	53	57	58	58	60	60	(NA)
Dental schools [4]	Number	53	59	60	60	58	58	56	55	55
Students [4]	1,000	16.6	20.8	22.8	19.6	17.1	16.2	16.0	15.9	16.0
Graduates [4]	1,000	3.7	5.0	5.3	5.4	4.6	4.3	4.2	4.0	3.9
Nurses, number (active registered)	1,000	750	961	1,273	1,538	1,648	1,679	1,715	1,758	1,853
Rate per 100,000 population [3]	Rate	368	446	560	644	670	676	690	697	726
Nursing programs [5]	Number	1,343	1,360	1,385	1,473	1,442	1,457	1,470	1,484	1,484
Students [5]	1,000	165	250	231	218	185	201	221	238	258
Graduates [5]	1,000	44	75	76	82	65	62	66	72	81

NA Not available. [1] Revised since originally published. [2] Source: American Dental Association, Bureau of Economic and Behavioral Research, Master Membership file and periodic censuses. [3] Based on Bureau of Census estimated resident population as of July 1. Estimates reflect revisions based on the 1990 Census of Population. [4] Number of schools and students as of fall; graduates for academic year ending in year shown. Based on data from the American Dental Association, Council on Dental Education, Annual Report on Dental Education. [5] Number of programs and students are as of October 15 and number of graduates are for academic year ending in year shown; from National League for Nursing, NLN Data Book, annual issues and State-Approved Schools of Nursing, RN, annual issues.

Source: Except as noted, U.S. Dept. of Health and Human Services, Health Resources and Services Administration, unpublished data. Prior to 1980, data were published by U.S. National Center for Health Statistics in *Health Resources Statistics*, annual.

No. 173. Active Non-Federal Physicians and Nurses, by State: 1992

[Nurses as of March; Physicians as of Jan. 1. Excludes doctors of osteopathy, Federally employed persons, and physicians with addresses unknown. Includes all physicians not classified according to activity status]

STATE	PHYSICIANS Total	Rate [1]	NURSES Total	Rate [1]	STATE	PHYSICIANS Total	Rate [1]	NURSES Total	Rate [1]
United States..	568,132	224	1,853,024	731	Missouri	10,722	207	42,035	812
Alabama.........	6,913	168	27,717	673	Montana.........	1,359	166	5,848	715
Alaska	748	133	3,583	637	Nebraska	2,964	187	13,257	834
Arizona..........	7,461	196	27,093	711	Nevada	1,928	145	7,135	538
Arkansas	3,855	161	14,001	587	New Hampshire....	2,324	209	10,743	964
California	73,713	241	173,973	568	New Jersey.......	20,277	260	64,519	827
Colorado.........	7,431	217	26,697	780	New Mexico	2,987	191	9,393	600
Connecticut.......	10,383	318	30,918	946	New York........	60,171	333	159,297	881
Delaware	1,420	207	6,137	894	North Carolina....	13,332	198	47,602	708
District of Columbia .	3,908	677	11,352	1,966	North Dakota.....	1,157	185	6,300	1,007
Florida..........	28,379	212	94,591	707	Ohio...........	22,709	206	89,799	816
Georgia	12,000	179	43,386	647	Oklahoma........	4,865	153	16,972	534
Hawaii	2,740	249	7,674	697	Oregon..........	6,246	210	23,992	808
Idaho...........	1,366	129	5,702	537	Pennsylvania.....	30,090	251	108,663	907
Illinois..........	26,395	228	93,069	804	Rhode Island.....	2,680	269	9,665	971
Indiana..........	9,318	165	39,602	700	South Carolina....	6,091	172	20,684	584
Iowa	4,393	157	25,838	922	South Dakota	1,062	151	6,828	973
Kansas..........	4,549	183	19,773	794	Tennessee	10,396	208	35,318	706
Kentucky........	6,644	178	24,552	659	Texas...........	31,374	179	92,810	528
Louisiana........	8,526	201	24,233	570	Utah	3,384	187	9,831	545
Maine...........	2,325	189	10,584	861	Vermont	1,503	263	5,199	910
Maryland	16,695	342	38,170	783	Virginia.........	13,366	215	42,519	684
Massachusetts....	21,129	353	63,751	1,066	Washington......	11,054	217	38,698	761
Michigan........	18,265	194	65,441	694	West Virginia.....	3,240	179	11,875	657
Minnesota.......	10,379	232	39,876	893	Wisconsin.......	9,733	195	39,883	799
Mississippi	3,539	136	13,415	516	Wyoming........	644	140	3,032	658

[1] Per 100,000 civilian population. Based on U.S. Bureau of the Census estimates as of July 1, 1992.

Source: Physicians: American Medical Association, Chicago, IL, *Physician Characteristics and Distribution in the U.S.*, annual (copyright); Nurses: U.S. Dept. of Health and Human Services, Health Resources and Services Administration, unpublished data.

No. 174. Physician and Dental Contacts, by Patient Characteristics: 1970 to 1992

[See headnote, table 201. Based on National Health Interview Survey; see Appendix III]

TYPE OF VISIT AND YEAR	TOTAL VISITS (mil.) Sex Male	Female	Race [1] White	Black	VISITS PER PERSON PER YEAR Sex Male	Female	Race [1] White	Black	Age (years) Under 5	5 to 17	18 to 24	25 to 44	45 to 64	65 and over
PHYSICIANS														
1970..........	396	531	832	87	4.1	5.1	4.8	3.9	[2]5.9	[3]2.9	[4]4.6	4.6	5.2	6.3
1980..........	426	610	903	115	4.0	5.4	4.8	4.5	[2]6.7	[3]3.2	[4]4.0	4.6	5.1	6.4
1983..........	470	694	1,018	126	4.3	5.8	5.2	4.6	[2]6.5	[3]3.2	[4]4.0	4.7	5.8	7.6
1985..........	498	733	1,074	132	4.4	6.1	5.4	4.7	[2]6.3	[3]3.1	[4]4.2	4.9	6.1	8.3
1986..........	515	756	1,110	131	4.5	6.2	5.5	4.6	6.3	3.3	4.2	4.7	6.6	9.1
1987..........	523	765	1,118	140	4.5	6.2	5.5	4.9	6.7	3.3	4.4	4.8	6.4	8.9
1988..........	530	774	1,139	136	4.5	6.2	5.6	4.6	7.0	3.4	3.8	5.1	6.1	8.7
1989..........	552	771	1,148	140	4.7	6.1	5.6	4.7	6.7	3.5	3.9	5.1	6.1	8.9
1990..........	558	806	1,178	148	4.7	6.4	5.7	4.9	6.9	3.2	4.3	5.1	6.4	9.2
1991..........	589	842	1,243	152	4.9	6.6	6.0	4.9	7.1	3.4	3.9	5.1	6.6	10.4
1992..........	624	889	1,286	181	5.1	6.9	6.1	5.8	6.9	3.5	4.1	5.4	7.2	10.6
DENTISTS														
1970..........	133	171	283	17	1.4	1.7	1.6	0.8	[2]0.5	[3]1.9	[4]1.8	1.7	1.5	1.1
1980..........	158	207	333	26	1.5	1.8	1.8	1.0	[2]0.5	[3]2.3	[4]1.6	1.7	1.8	1.4
1983..........	183	239	382	31	1.6	2.0	1.9	1.1	[2]0.5	[3]2.6	[4]1.6	1.9	2.0	1.5
1986..........	210	256	416	37	1.9	2.2	2.1	1.4	0.7	2.4	1.7	2.0	2.2	2.1
1989..........	221	271	441	34	1.9	2.2	2.2	1.2	0.5	2.4	1.6	2.0	2.4	2.0

[1] See footnote 2, table 201.　[2] Under 6 years.　[3] 6 to 17 years.　[4] 17 to 24 years.

Source: U.S. National Center for Health Statistics, *Vital and Health Statistics*, series 10, No. 189, and earlier reports; and unpublished data.

No. 175. Physician Contacts, by Place of Contact: 1992

[Based on the National Health Interview Survey; see Appendix III]

PATIENT CHARACTERISTIC	NUMBER (mil.)					VISITS PER PERSON				
	All places [1]	Tele-phone	Office	Hos-pital [2]	Other	All places [1]	Tele-phone	Office	Hos-pital [2]	Other
All persons [3]	1,513	181	834	222	266	6.0	0.7	3.3	0.9	1.1
AGE										
Under 5 years old.	136	20	80	19	16	6.9	1.0	4.1	1.0	0.8
5 to 17 years old	164	23	94	25	20	3.5	0.5	2.0	0.5	0.4
18 to 24 years old	101	11	48	19	22	4.1	0.4	2.0	0.8	0.9
25 to 44 years old	436	57	248	61	67	5.4	0.7	3.1	0.7	0.8
45 to 64 years old	349	42	191	55	59	7.2	0.9	3.9	1.1	1.2
65 to 74 years old	179	17	98	26	36	9.7	0.9	5.3	1.4	2.0
75 years old and over	149	12	74	16	46	12.1	1.0	6.0	1.3	3.7
SEX										
Male	624	66	338	106	110	5.1	0.5	2.8	0.9	0.9
Female.	889	115	496	115	156	6.9	0.9	3.8	0.9	1.2
RACE										
White.	1,286	161	728	174	216	6.1	0.8	3.5	0.8	1.0
Black	181	15	83	38	42	5.8	0.5	2.6	1.2	1.3
INCOME										
Under $10,000.	192	20	83	42	46	7.8	0.8	3.4	1.7	1.9
$10,000 to $19,999	255	30	128	42	53	6.6	0.8	3.3	1.1	1.4
$20,000 to $34,999	299	38	162	45	53	5.8	0.7	3.2	0.9	1.0
$35,000 or more	515	74	318	60	59	5.7	0.8	3.5	0.7	0.6

[1] Includes unknown place of contact. [2] Excludes contacts while an overnight patient in a hospital. [3] Includes other races and unknown income.

Source: U.S. National Center for Health Statistics, *Vital and Health Statistics*, series 10, No. 189.

No. 176. Medical Practice Characteristics, by Selected Specialty: 1985 to 1991

[**Dollar figures in thousands.** Based on a sample telephone survey of 4,000 non-Federal office and hospital based patient care physicians, excluding residents, with a response rate of 69.1 percent in 1990 and 66.7 percent in 1991. For details, see source. For definition of mean, see Guide to Tabular Presentation]

SPECIALTY	1985	1986	1987	1988	1989	1990	1991
MEAN PATIENT VISITS PER WEEK							
All physicians [1]	117.1	117.7	119.3	121.1	121.6	120.9	118.4
General/Family practice	138.1	139.2	138.3	145.6	143.0	146.0	144.4
Internal medicine.	105.2	111.1	114.5	113.0	117.9	112.0	110.7
Surgery	108.2	105.8	107.8	105.0	107.7	107.6	106.9
Pediatrics.	130.8	131.9	127.4	135.1	138.1	134.0	133.5
Obstetrics/Gynecology.	112.0	114.8	112.7	118.9	115.6	120.0	112.2
MEAN HOURS IN PATIENT CARE PER WEEK							
All physicians [1]	51.3	52.2	52.9	53.1	53.3	53.3	53.3
General/Family practice	53.6	53.3	53.7	54.4	54.4	55.0	54.7
Internal medicine.	52.4	54.0	56.0	56.2	56.8	55.7	56.3
Surgery	51.2	52.6	53.0	53.8	53.3	53.1	53.4
Pediatrics.	50.6	52.4	53.6	52.5	53.4	52.4	52.4
Obstetrics/Gynecology.	56.9	59.0	57.0	59.4	59.0	60.4	59.5
MEAN NET INCOME							
All physicians [1]	112.2	119.5	132.3	144.7	155.8	164.5	170.6
General/Family practice	77.9	80.3	91.5	94.6	95.9	102.7	111.5
Internal medicine.	102.0	109.4	121.8	130.9	146.5	152.5	149.6
Surgery	155.0	162.4	187.9	207.5	220.5	236.4	223.8
Pediatrics.	76.2	81.8	85.3	94.9	104.7	106.5	119.3
Obstetrics/Gynecology.	124.3	135.9	163.2	180.7	194.3	207.3	221.8
MEAN PROFESSIONAL EXPENSES							
All physicians [1]	102.7	118.4	123.7	140.8	148.4	150.0	168.4
General/Family practice	96.5	119.9	121.2	122.3	128.5	134.5	146.4
Internal medicine.	90.0	110.5	117.8	136.3	139.1	139.2	159.0
Surgery	135.7	148.6	164.7	188.2	203.2	201.0	215.6
Pediatrics.	87.3	93.2	100.2	115.3	132.5	138.0	145.4
Obstetrics/Gynecology.	131.9	149.5	173.2	189.6	197.4	212.6	236.2
MEAN LIABILITY PREMIUM							
All physicians [1]	10.5	12.8	15.0	15.9	15.5	14.5	14.9
General/Family practice	6.8	7.3	8.9	9.4	9.0	7.8	8.1
Internal medicine.	5.8	7.1	8.4	9.0	8.2	9.2	8.0
Surgery	16.6	21.3	24.5	26.5	25.8	22.8	22.5
Pediatrics.	4.7	6.3	7.1	9.3	7.8	7.8	8.4
Obstetrics/Gynecology.	23.5	29.3	35.3	35.3	35.3	37.0	34.9

[1] Includes other specialties not shown separately.

Source: American Medical Association, Chicago IL, *Socioeconomic Characteristics of Medical Practice*, annual (copyright).

No. 177. Hospital Registered Nursing Personnel—Summary: 1991

[In percent, except as indicated. Based on a sample of 6,852 U.S. short term acute care hospitals registered and unregistered by the American Hospital Association, with a response rate of 33.6 percent. For details see source. For an explanation of mean, see Guide to Tabular Presentation]

CHARACTERISTIC	1991	CHARACTERISTIC	1991
Full-time registered nurses per hospital (mean) [1] . . .	112.7	Registered nurse, full-time:	
		Lowest mean hourly wage paid.	13.31
LENGTH OF EMPLOYMENT AT HOSPITAL [2]		Highest mean hourly wage paid	18.74
		Mean hourly wage paid	16.11
Full-time: Less than 1 year	16.4		
1 year to less than 2 years	15.1	HOSPITAL STAFFING MECHANISMS [4]	
2 years to less than 5 years.	26.0		
5 years or more	42.5	Per-diem	31.2
		Float-pool [5]	21.2
Part-time: Less than 1 year	15.1	On-call	8.7
1 year to less than 2 years	14.3	Temporary nursing service	25.3
2 years to less than 5 years.	25.8	Other	13.6
5 years or more	44.8		
		HOSPITAL POSITION SCHEDULES [6]	
EDUCATIONAL ATTAINMENT [3]			
		Days only	29.6
Associate degree in nursing	37.3	Evenings only	17.3
Nursing diploma	27.9	Nights only.	17.1
Baccalaureate degree in nursing	30.8	Shifts: Day/evening	12.9
Master's degree in nursing or higher.	3.6	Day/night	8.4
		Evening/night	4.1
SALARY/WAGES (dol. per hr.) [2]		Rotate all	10.6
Full-time head nurse:		HOSPITAL BARGAINING STATUS	
Lowest mean annual salary paid.	16.53		
Highest mean annual salary paid	21.28	Organized for the purpose of collective bargaining . .	14.8

[1] Source: American Hospital Association, Chicago, IL, 1991 Human Resource Survey.   [2] Full-time: at least 35 hours worked per week. Part-time: less than 35 hours worked per week.   [3] Full-time only.   [4] Percent of positions with each mechanism. [5] In-house nursing staff personnel routinely assigned schedules who work different units in the institution according to the demands of variable patient volume and acuity levels.   [6] Percent of positions.

Source: Except as indicated, American Hospital Association, Chicago, IL, *Report of the Hospital Nursing Personnel Survey, 1991* (copyright).

No. 178. Hospitals and Nursing Homes—Summary Characteristics: 1971 to 1992

[Except as indicated, based on National Master Facility Inventory]

YEAR AND TYPE OF FACILITY	Total	FACILITIES UNDER—			FACILITIES WITH—			Resi-dents [2] (1,000)	Full-time employ-ees (1,000)
		Gov't. control	Propri-etary control	Non-profit control	Fewer than 25 beds [1]	25-74 beds	75 or more beds		
1971: All facilities.	29,682	4,178	18,091	7,413	8,902	10,959	9,821	2,262	3,007
Nursing homes [3]	22,004	1,368	17,049	3,587	8,266	8,259	5,479	1,076	568
Hospitals	7,678	2,810	1,042	3,826	636	2,700	4,342	1,186	2,439
1980: All facilities.	30,116	3,498	19,611	7,007	8,852	8,573	12,691	2,427	3,919
Nursing homes [3][4]	23,065	936	18,669	3,460	8,498	6,362	8,205	1,396	[5]798
Hospitals	7,051	2,562	942	3,547	354	2,211	4,486	1,031	3,121
1986: All facilities.	32,600	3,275	21,399	7,926	9,903	8,755	13,942	2,427	(NA)
All hospitals [6]	6,954	2,230	1,176	3,548	290	2,150	4,514	874	3,241
General.	5,956	1,871	829	3,256	259	1,849	3,848	690	2,871
Psychiatric	584	267	218	99	12	140	432	139	248
Chronic	44	30	4	10	-	6	38	13	21
Tuberculosis.	4	3	-	1	-	1	3	-	1
Nursing homes [3]	25,646	1,045	20,223	4,378	9,613	6,605	9,428	1,553	(NA)
1991: All facilities.	39,744	3,689	25,477	10,578	15,614	9,239	14,891	2,552	(NA)
All hospitals [6]	6,738	2,119	1,221	3,398	308	2,066	4,364	823	3,663
General.	5,535	1,762	688	3,085	272	1,645	3,618	661	3,276
Psychiatric	779	276	389	114	19	242	518	122	253
Chronic	30	24	2	4	-	5	25	10	17
Tuberculosis.	4	3	-	1	-	1	3	-	1
Nursing homes [3]	33,006	1,570	24,256	7,180	15,306	7,173	10,527	1,729	(NA)
1992: All hospitals [6]	6,639	2,060	1,189	3,390	312	2,035	4,292	802	3,723
General.	5,451	1,716	663	3,072	270	1,603	3,578	650	3,346
Psychiatric	762	266	378	118	23	253	486	113	242
Chronic	32	24	2	6	-	5	27	10	18
Tuberculosis.	4	3	-	1	-	2	2	-	1

- Represents or rounds to zero.   NA Not available.   [1] For hospitals, minimum of six beds; for nursing homes, minimum of three beds.   [2] Number of residents as of date of interview.   [3] See footnotes 1, 3, and 4, table 192.   [4] Includes 1978 data for Alaska and South Dakota.   [5] Estimated.   [6] Includes types not shown separately. Based on data from the American Hospital Association.

Source: U.S. National Center for Health Statistics, *Health Resources Statistics, 1971;* and unpublished data.

No. 179. Hospitals—Summary Characteristics: 1972 to 1992

[Covers hospitals accepted for registration by the American Hospital Association; see text, section 3. Short-term hospitals have an average patient stay of less than 30 days; long-term, an average stay of longer duration. Special hospitals include obstetrics and gynecology; eye, ear, nose, and throat; rehabilitation; orthopedic; and chronic and other special hospitals except psychiatric, tuberculosis, alcoholism, and chemical dependency hospitals. See also *Historical Statistics, Colonial Times to 1970*, series B 305-318, B 331-344, and B 413-422]

ITEM	1972	1980	1985	1987	1988	1989	1990	1991	1992
Number:									
All hospitals	7,061	6,965	6,872	6,821	6,780	6,720	6,649	6,634	6,539
With 100 beds or more	2,710	3,755	3,805	3,713	3,681	3,650	3,620	3,611	3,572
Non-Federal [1]	6,660	6,606	6,529	6,479	6,438	6,380	6,312	6,300	6,214
Community hospitals [2]	5,746	5,830	5,732	5,611	5,533	5,455	5,384	5,342	5,292
Nongovernmental nonprofit	3,301	3,322	3,349	3,274	3,242	3,220	3,191	3,175	3,173
For profit	738	730	805	828	790	769	749	738	723
State and local government	1,707	1,778	1,578	1,509	1,501	1,466	1,444	1,429	1,396
Long-term general and special	216	157	128	131	129	138	131	126	115
Psychiatric	529	534	610	684	726	741	757	800	774
Tuberculosis	72	11	7	5	4	4	4	4	4
Federal	401	359	343	342	342	340	337	334	325
Beds (1,000):									
All hospitals [3]	1,550	1,365	1,309	1,261	1,241	1,224	1,211	1,197	1,174
Rate per 1,000 population [4]	7.4	6.0	5.5	5.2	5.1	5.0	4.9	4.7	4.6
Beds per hospital	220	196	190	185	183	182	182	180	180
Non-Federal [1]	1,407	1,248	1,197	1,152	1,138	1,124	1,113	1,101	1,085
Community hospitals [2]	879	988	1,001	958	944	933	928	924	921
Rate per 1,000 population [4]	4.2	4.3	4.2	4.0	3.9	3.8	3.7	3.7	3.6
Nongovernmental nonprofit	617	692	707	673	666	660	657	656	656
For profit	57	87	104	106	103	103	102	100	99
State and local government	205	209	189	180	175	170	169	168	167
Long-term general and special	54	39	31	28	27	27	25	25	23
Psychiatric	457	215	169	165	163	160	158	150	139
Tuberculosis	13	2	1	1	(Z)	(Z)	(Z)	(Z)	(Z)
Federal	143	117	112	109	104	100	98	95	89
Occupancy rate: [5]									
All hospitals	78.0	77.7	69.5	69.2	69.6	69.7	69.7	69.1	68.7
Non-Federal [1]	78.0	77.4	68.9	68.7	69.1	69.3	69.4	68.8	68.0
Community hospitals [2]	75.4	75.6	64.8	64.9	65.7	66.2	66.7	66.1	65.6
Nongovernmental nonprofit	77.5	78.2	67.2	67.6	68.4	68.8	69.3	68.6	67.9
For profit	68.7	65.2	52.2	51.0	51.0	51.6	52.6	52.5	52.0
State and local government	71.0	71.1	62.9	63.1	63.9	64.9	65.3	64.4	64.7
Long-term general and special	83.0	85.9	88.5	87.2	87.5	86.6	85.9	84.9	84.5
Psychiatric	82.8	85.2	87.0	86.4	86.3	84.6	82.5	82.4	81.4
Tuberculosis	61.2	67.0	64.1	64.1	67.2	69.3	66.4	76.6	82.9
Federal	80.0	80.1	76.3	74.2	74.4	73.7	73.3	72.8	77.3
Expenses (bil. dol.): [6]									
All hospitals	32.7	91.9	153.3	178.7	196.7	214.9	234.9	258.5	282.5
Non-Federal [1]	30.0	84.0	141.0	165.0	182.1	199.8	219.6	241.7	264.3
Community hospitals [2]	25.5	76.9	130.5	152.6	168.7	184.9	203.7	225.0	248.1
Nongovernmental nonprofit	18.4	55.8	96.1	112.3	124.7	136.9	150.7	166.8	183.8
For profit	1.4	5.8	11.5	14.1	15.5	17.2	18.8	20.5	22.5
State and local government	5.7	15.2	22.9	26.2	28.5	30.8	34.2	37.7	41.8
Long-term general and special	0.7	1.2	1.9	2.2	2.3	2.5	2.7	2.9	2.7
Psychiatric	3.1	5.8	8.3	9.9	10.9	12.0	12.9	13.5	13.2
Tuberculosis	0.1	0.1	0.1	(Z)	(Z)	(Z)	0.1	(Z)	(Z)
Federal	3.1	7.9	12.3	13.7	14.6	15.1	15.2	16.8	18.2
Personnel (1,000): [7]									
All hospitals	2,671	3,492	3,625	3,742	3,840	3,937	4,063	4,165	4,236
Non-Federal [1]	2,439	3,213	3,326	3,445	3,545	3,648	3,760	3,864	3,929
Community hospitals [2]	2,051	2,873	2,997	3,114	3,205	3,303	3,420	3,535	3,620
Nongovernmental nonprofit	1,473	2,086	2,216	2,298	2,373	2,454	2,533	2,624	2,692
For profit	105	189	221	242	249	261	273	281	285
State and local government	473	598	561	573	583	589	614	630	643
Long-term general and special	63	56	58	55	54	56	55	55	49
Psychiatric	307	275	263	269	281	284	280	269	256
Tuberculosis	12	3	2	1	1	1	1	1	1
Federal	232	279	299	297	295	288	303	301	306
Personnel per 100 patients [7]	221	329	398	429	445	462	482	504	525
Outpatient visits (mil.)	219.2	263.0	282.1	310.7	336.2	352.2	368.2	387.7	417.9
Emergency	60.1	82.0	80.1	83.5	86.6	89.9	92.8	93.5	95.8
Closures	(NA)	73	59	93	106	80	63	67	60

NA Not available.   Z Less than 500 beds, $50 million, or 0.5 percent.   [1] Short term (average length of stay less than 30 days) general and special (e.g., obstetrics and gynecology; eye, ear, nose and throat; rehabilitation etc. except psychiatric, tuberculosis, alcoholism and chemical dependency). Includes hospital units of institutions.   [2] Excludes hospital units of institutions.   [3] Beginning 1988, number of beds at end of reporting period; prior years, average number in 12 month period.   [4] Based on Bureau of the Census estimated resident population as of July 1. Estimates reflect revisions based on the 1990 Census of Population.   [5] Ratio of average daily census to every 100 beds.   [6] Excludes new construction.   [7] Includes full-time equivalents of part-time personnel.

Source: American Hospital Association, Chicago, IL, *Hospital Statistics*, annual (copyright).

Health and Nutrition

No. 180. Community Hospitals—States and Puerto Rico: 1992

[For definition of community hospitals see footnotes 1 and 2, table 179. See also *Historical Statistics, Colonial Times to 1970*, series B 305-308 and B 359-362 for data on all hospitals]

REGION, DIVISION, AND STATE OR OTHER AREA	Number of hospitals	Beds (1,000)	Patients admitted (1,000)	Average daily census [1] (1,000)	Occupancy rate [2] (percent)	Personnel [3] (1,000)	Outpatient visits (mil.)
United States.....	5,292	921.3	31,033.6	604.4	65.6	3,619.8	348.5
Northeast............	790	203.2	6,954.5	158.3	77.9	864.3	88.8
New England........	230	43.7	1,638.5	31.5	72.1	204.8	23.3
Maine............	39	4.5	147.8	3.1	68.2	18.6	2.2
New Hampshire.....	27	3.4	116.3	2.3	66.1	14.2	1.6
Vermont...........	15	1.7	56.9	1.1	65.0	6.6	0.7
Massachusetts......	102	21.8	836.0	15.8	72.3	105.0	12.6
Rhode Island.......	12	3.1	131.2	2.4	76.9	15.3	1.4
Connecticut........	35	9.1	350.3	6.9	75.6	45.1	4.7
Middle Atlantic.......	560	159.6	5,316.0	126.8	79.5	659.5	65.6
New York.........	231	76.3	2,374.1	64.2	84.2	319.1	32.3
New Jersey........	97	31.3	1,124.2	24.9	79.5	118.9	10.7
Pennsylvania.......	232	52.0	1,817.7	37.7	72.6	221.5	22.6
Midwest.............	1,535	244.0	7,563.3	151.7	62.2	935.9	95.2
East North Central....	813	158.6	5,295.3	99.9	63.0	652.5	71.3
Ohio.............	192	42.1	1,438.3	25.7	61.0	176.3	18.9
Indiana...........	113	21.4	711.0	12.7	59.4	87.0	10.4
Illinois............	210	45.2	1,496.9	29.3	64.9	180.9	18.0
Michigan..........	170	31.6	1,061.9	20.5	64.8	142.7	17.1
Wisconsin.........	128	18.3	587.3	11.7	63.9	65.7	6.9
West North Central....	722	85.4	2,267.9	51.8	60.7	283.3	23.9
Minnesota.........	145	18.9	524.8	12.6	66.6	57.2	4.9
Iowa.............	121	13.9	363.6	8.3	59.6	45.4	5.0
Missouri...........	133	24.0	718.0	14.5	60.4	95.6	7.4
North Dakota.......	47	4.4	92.7	2.9	65.4	12.4	0.7
South Dakota.......	52	4.3	95.4	2.7	62.1	11.4	0.9
Nebraska..........	90	8.5	181.2	4.8	56.3	25.2	1.9
Kansas...........	134	11.5	292.2	6.3	54.2	36.2	3.2
South...............	1,990	329.6	11,058.5	205.8	62.4	1,233.0	96.6
South Atlantic.......	790	158.9	5,488.6	105.2	66.2	616.0	48.5
Delaware..........	8	2.1	82.4	1.5	70.2	10.6	1.1
Maryland..........	49	13.1	565.8	9.9	75.5	59.7	4.4
District of Columbia...	11	4.4	162.4	3.3	74.4	21.0	1.1
Virginia...........	98	19.6	700.1	12.9	65.8	75.5	6.3
West Virginia......	57	8.2	278.2	5.3	64.4	29.5	3.2
North Carolina.....	117	22.5	796.1	16.0	71.2	94.4	7.2
South Carolina.....	68	11.5	396.9	7.8	67.9	44.8	3.9
Georgia...........	159	26.4	861.3	17.2	65.3	95.8	7.8
Florida............	223	51.1	1,645.3	31.3	61.2	184.7	13.5
East South Central....	454	70.3	2,271.8	43.4	61.8	246.6	19.6
Kentucky..........	107	16.1	530.4	10.1	62.8	59.3	5.2
Tennessee.........	131	23.1	769.1	14.3	61.9	84.7	6.4
Alabama..........	116	18.6	603.9	11.5	62.1	65.1	5.4
Mississippi........	100	12.5	368.4	7.4	59.6	37.6	2.5
West South Central....	746	100.4	3,298.1	57.2	57.0	370.4	28.6
Arkansas..........	87	11.1	344.8	6.6	59.1	36.3	2.8
Louisiana..........	135	18.8	609.6	10.9	58.2	69.2	6.9
Oklahoma.........	110	11.9	372.6	6.7	56.2	44.0	2.7
Texas............	414	58.6	1,971.2	33.0	56.3	220.9	16.2
West................	977	144.5	5,457.3	88.6	61.3	586.7	67.9
Mountain............	352	41.5	1,443.6	24.5	59.1	158.3	17.5
Montana..........	53	4.4	102.0	2.8	63.7	12.2	1.1
Idaho............	41	3.4	100.1	1.9	57.3	11.4	1.5
Wyoming..........	26	2.2	46.0	1.1	49.9	5.9	0.6
Colorado..........	71	10.1	344.2	6.2	61.6	41.9	4.5
New Mexico........	38	4.2	155.8	2.3	55.1	17.7	2.3
Arizona...........	60	9.4	392.6	5.7	60.2	38.1	3.2
Utah.............	42	4.3	173.3	2.4	55.2	19.5	2.9
Nevada...........	21	3.6	129.6	2.2	60.4	11.6	1.4
Pacific.............	625	103.0	4,013.7	64.1	62.2	428.4	50.4
Washington........	90	12.0	500.9	7.4	61.9	54.0	6.7
Oregon...........	63	7.5	296.0	4.1	54.1	32.1	4.0
California..........	436	79.3	3,081.5	49.5	62.5	324.1	37.0
Alaska............	16	1.3	37.8	0.7	53.7	4.6	0.6
Hawaii............	20	2.9	97.5	2.4	81.7	13.6	2.0
Puerto Rico..........	51	9.2	400.0	5.8	70.6	27.0	3.1

[1] Inpatients receiving treatment each day; excludes newborn. [2] Ratio of average daily census to every 100 beds. [3] Includes full-time equivalents of part-time personnel.

Source: American Hospital Association, Chicago, IL, *Hospital Statistics, 1993-94* (copyright).

No. 181. Hospital Use Rates, by Type of Hospital: 1972 to 1992

[See also *Historical Statistics, Colonial Times to 1970*, series B 384-387]

TYPE OF HOSPITAL	1972	1980	1985	1988	1989	1990	1991	1992
Community hospitals: [1]								
Admissions per 1,000 population [2]	147	159	141	129	126	125	123	122
Admissions per bed	35	37	33	33	33	34	34	34
Average length of stay [3] (days)	7.9	7.6	7.1	7.2	7.2	7.2	7.2	7.1
Outpatient visits per admission	1.8	5.6	6.5	8.6	9.2	9.7	10.4	11.2
Outpatient visits per 1,000 population [2]	777	890	919	1,101	1,158	1,208	1,277	1,366
Surgical operations (million)	14.8	18.8	20.1	21.4	21.3	21.9	22.4	22.9
Number per admission	0.5	0.5	0.6	0.7	0.7	0.7	0.7	0.7
Non-Federal psychiatric:								
Admissions per 1,000 population [2]	2.8	2.5	2.5	2.8	2.9	2.9	2.9	2.9
Days in hospital per 1,000 population [2]	661	295	224	209	201	190	179	164

[1] For definition of community hospitals, see footnotes 1 and 2, table 179. [2] Based on Bureau of the Census estimated resident population as of July 1. Estimates reflect revisions based on the 1990 Census of Population. [3] Number of inpatient days divided by number of admissions.

Source: American Hospital Association, Chicago, IL, *Hospital Statistics*, annual (copyright); and unpublished data.

No. 182. Average Cost to Community Hospitals per Patient: 1970 to 1992

[In dollars, except percent. Covers non-Federal short-term general or special hospitals (excluding psychiatric or tuberculosis hospitals and, beginning 1975, hospital units of institutions). Total cost per patient based on total hospital expenses (payroll, employee benefits, professional fees, supplies, etc.). Data have been adjusted for outpatient visits]

TYPE OF EXPENSE AND HOSPITAL	1970	1975	1980	1985	1987	1988	1989	1990	1991	1992
Average cost per day, total	74	134	245	460	539	586	637	687	752	820
Annual percent change [1]	12.7	17.5	12.9	11.9	7.6	8.7	8.7	7.8	9.5	9.0
Nongovernmental nonprofit	75	133	246	463	544	591	642	692	758	828
For profit	71	133	257	500	585	649	708	752	820	889
State and local government	71	136	239	433	499	539	582	634	696	754
Average cost per stay, total	605	1,030	1,851	3,245	3,850	4,207	4,588	4,947	5,360	5,794
Nongovernmental nonprofit	615	1,040	1,902	3,307	3,914	4,273	4,649	5,001	5,393	5,809
For profit	486	876	1,676	3,033	3,617	4,023	4,406	4,727	5,134	5,548
State and local government	614	1,031	1,750	3,106	3,718	4,034	4,430	4,838	5,340	5,871

[1] Change from immediate prior year, except 1970, average annual change from 1965. For explanation of average annual change, see Guide to Tabular Presentation.

Source: American Hospital Association, Chicago, IL, *Hospital Statistics*, annual (copyright); and unpublished data.

No. 183. Average Cost to Community Hospitals per Patient, by State: 1990 to 1992

[In dollars. See headnote, table 182]

STATE	AVERAGE COST PER DAY			AVERAGE COST PER STAY			STATE	AVERAGE COST PER DAY			AVERAGE COST PER STAY		
	1990	1991	1992	1990	1991	1992		1990	1991	1992	1990	1991	1992
U.S.	687	752	820	4,947	5,360	5,794	MO	679	737	792	5,022	5,429	5,789
AL	588	637	729	4,175	4,455	5,080	MT	405	437	474	3,973	4,395	4,704
AK	1,070	1,130	1,116	6,249	6,448	7,456	NE	490	546	600	4,675	5,214	5,714
AZ	867	955	1,051	4,877	5,212	5,502	NV	854	907	952	5,511	5,883	5,778
AR	534	571	633	3,730	3,927	4,376	NH	671	713	776	4,544	4,995	5,480
CA	939	1,037	1,134	5,709	6,169	6,626	NJ	613	680	737	4,573	5,136	5,909
CO	725	801	904	5,209	5,449	5,933	NM	734	840	950	4,172	4,583	5,094
CT	825	910	1,012	6,238	6,696	7,241	NY	641	694	744	6,397	6,823	7,316
DE	771	845	920	5,112	5,748	6,123	NC	595	651	711	4,408	4,759	5,217
DC	995	1,038	1,124	7,876	7,743	8,218	ND	427	454	484	4,468	4,898	5,302
FL	769	836	886	5,312	5,831	6,092	OH	720	782	875	4,801	5,133	5,649
GA	630	652	721	4,303	4,677	5,238	OK	632	684	740	4,302	4,547	4,847
HI	638	686	761	6,048	6,553	6,876	OR	800	896	1,011	4,432	4,787	5,112
ID	547	565	618	3,701	4,026	4,346	PA	662	732	793	5,120	5,490	5,955
IL	717	770	849	5,253	5,570	6,048	RI	663	730	801	4,839	5,063	5,355
IN	667	745	822	4,390	4,879	5,305	SC	590	684	782	4,168	4,868	5,617
IA	495	538	588	4,135	4,527	4,920	SD	391	436	457	3,905	4,436	4,653
KS	532	585	661	4,161	4,548	5,115	TN	633	716	796	4,340	4,859	5,392
KY	563	616	674	3,762	4,216	4,652	TX	752	846	933	4,663	5,179	5,666
LA	701	764	836	4,575	5,044	5,457	UT	832	915	1,036	4,409	4,688	5,104
ME	574	617	674	4,604	4,867	5,142	VT	598	621	726	4,343	4,673	5,046
MD	678	740	806	4,640	4,835	5,139	VA	635	701	774	4,408	4,875	5,226
MA	788	880	937	5,709	6,086	6,381	WA	817	904	974	4,519	5,035	5,238
MI	716	792	847	5,358	5,750	5,899	WV	565	612	655	3,918	4,319	4,496
MN	536	582	618	4,782	5,035	5,456	WI	554	611	674	4,083	4,450	4,909
MS	439	479	516	3,116	3,454	3,807	WY	462	489	515	3,990	4,081	4,370

Source: American Hospital Association, Chicago, IL, *Hospital Statistics*, annual (copyright); and unpublished data.

No. 184. Facilities and Services Provided by Community Hospitals: 1992

[Community hospitals are non-Federal short-stay (average length stay fewer than 30 days) excluding hospital units of institutions. Data are for hospitals responding to that portion of the questionnaire 4,931 of a total of 5,292 community hospitals in 1992]

SERVICE	Hospitals with service	Percent of total	SERVICE	Hospitals with service	Percent of total
AIDS inpatient care	3,484	70.7	Outpatient surgery services	4,655	94.4
AIDS outpatient care	316	6.4	Patient representative services.	2,794	56.7
Adult day care program.	338	6.9	Psychiatric services:		
Angioplasty.	1,047	21.2	Emergency	1,708	34.6
Alcoholism/chemical dependency			Outpatient	1,081	21.9
outpatient services	1,037	21.0	Radiation therapy:		
Birthing rooms.	3,293	66.8	X-ray	966	19.6
Blood bank.	3,424	69.4	Megavoltage (mil. volts).	993	20.1
Cardiac catheterization.	1,545	31.3	Radio-active implants	1,247	25.3
Cardiac rehabilitation	2,342	47.5	Radio isotope facilities:		
Computed tomographic (CT) scanner . .	3,708	75.2	Diagnostic.	3,066	62.2
Emergency department.	4,530	91.9	Therapeutic	1,294	26.2
Extracorporeal shock wave			Rehabilitation outpatient		
lithotripter	410	8.3	department	2,711	55.0
Genetic counseling services	498	10.1	Reproductive health services	2,123	43.1
Geriatric services.	3,144	63.8	Therapy services:		
Hemodialysis	1,350	27.4	Occupational therapy services.	2,623	53.2
Histopathology laboratory	3,170	64.3	Physical therapy services	4,176	84.7
Home health services.	1,873	38.0	Recreational therapy services	1,704	34.6
Hospice	874	17.7	Respiratory therapy services.	4,483	90.9
Hospital auxiliary	4,071	82.6	Trauma center.	862	17.5
Magnetic resonance imaging (MRI). . . .	1,213	24.6	Ultrasound	4,183	84.8
Open-heart surgery facilities	891	18.1	Volunteer services department.	3,517	71.3
Organ tissue transplant.	581	11.8	Women's center	1,246	25.3

Source: American Hospital Association, Chicago, IL, *Hospital Statistics, 1993-94* and *1992 Annual Survey of Hospitals* (copyright).

No. 185. Hospital Utilization Rates: 1970 to 1992

[Represents estimates of inpatients discharged from noninstitutional, short-stay hospitals, exclusive of Federal hospitals. Excludes newborn infants. Based on sample data collected from the National Hospital Discharge Survey, a sample survey of hospital records of patients discharged in year shown; subject to sampling variability. For composition of regions, see table 26]

SELECTED CHARACTERISTIC	Patients discharged (1,000)	PATIENTS DISCHARGED PER 1,000 PERSONS [1]			DAYS OF CARE PER 1,000 PERSONS [1]			AVERAGE STAY (days)		
		Total	Male	Female	Total	Male	Female	Total	Male	Female
1970.	29,127	144	118	169	1,122	982	1,251	8.0	8.7	7.6
1980.	37,832	168	139	194	1,217	1,068	1,356	7.3	7.7	7.0
1985.	35,056	148	124	171	954	849	1,053	6.5	6.9	6.2
1986.	34,256	143	121	164	913	817	1,003	6.4	6.8	6.1
1987.	33,387	138	116	159	889	806	968	6.4	6.9	6.1
1988 [2]	31,146	128	107	147	834	757	907	6.5	7.1	6.2
1989 [2]	30,947	126	105	145	815	741	884	6.5	7.0	6.1
1990 [2]	30,788	124	102	144	792	704	875	6.4	6.9	6.1
1991 [2]	31,098	124	103	144	795	715	869	6.4	7.0	6.0
1992, [2] total	30,951	122	101	142	751	680	818	6.2	6.7	5.8
Age:										
Under 1 year old	822	206	232	179	1,292	1,531	1,041	6.3	6.6	5.8
1 to 4 years old	806	52	58	46	185	200	170	3.6	3.5	3.7
5 to 14 years old	904	25	26	24	117	120	114	4.7	4.6	4.8
15 to 24 years old	3,287	93	40	146	333	220	448	3.6	5.5	3.1
25 to 34 years old	4,615	110	53	166	461	346	574	4.2	6.5	3.5
35 to 44 years old	3,325	84	69	99	443	410	475	5.3	6.0	4.8
45 to 64 years old	6,329	131	135	128	827	863	794	6.3	6.4	6.2
65 to 74 years old	4,883	265	293	242	2,041	2,240	1,885	7.7	7.6	7.8
75 years old and over . . .	5,981	433	470	412	3,748	3,929	3,648	8.7	8.4	8.9
Region:										
Northeast	7,141	140	122	157	1,005	916	1,087	7.2	7.5	6.9
Midwest	7,121	118	99	135	725	665	781	6.2	6.7	5.8
South.	11,256	129	106	150	769	696	837	6.0	6.5	5.6
West	5,433	100	75	124	514	456	571	5.2	6.1	4.6

[1] Based on Bureau of the Census estimated civilian population as of July 1. Estimates for 1980-90 do not reflect revisions based on the 1990 Census of Population.   [2] Comparisons beginning 1988 with data for earlier years should be made with caution as estimates of change may reflect improvements in the design rather than true changes in hospital use.

Source: U.S. National Center for Health Statistics, *Vital and Health Statistics,* series 13; and unpublished data.

No. 186. Hospital Discharges and Days of Care: 1992

[See headnote, table 185]

AGE AND FIRST-LISTED DIAGNOSIS	DISCHARGES Number (1,000)	DISCHARGES Per 1,000 persons [1]	Days of care per 1,000 persons [1]	Average stay (days)	AGE AND FIRST-LISTED DIAGNOSIS	DISCHARGES Number (1,000)	DISCHARGES Per 1,000 persons [1]	Days of care per 1,000 persons [1]	Average stay (days)
MALE					**FEMALE**				
All ages [2]	12,406	100.8	679.7	6.7	**All ages [2]**	18,545	142.2	818.3	5.8
					Delivery	3,910	30.0	77.0	2.6
Diseases of heart	2,083	16.9	108.3	6.4	Diseases of heart	1,852	14.2	99.1	7.0
Malignant neoplasms	765	6.2	55.2	8.9	Malignant neoplasms	812	6.2	50.9	8.2
Pneumonia, all forms	535	4.3	37.1	8.5	Fractures, all sites	552	4.2	35.3	8.4
Fractures, all sites	465	3.8	26.3	7.0	Pneumonia, all forms	524	4.0	32.4	8.1
Psychoses	408	3.3	39.8	12.0					
					Under 15 years [2]	1,115	40.8	195.6	4.8
Under 15 years [2]	1,416	49.4	242.4	4.9	Pneumonia, all forms	89	3.3	15.9	4.9
Bronchitis, emphysema [3]	133	4.6	14.0	3.0	Acute respiratory infection	86	3.2	10.3	3.3
Acute respiratory infection	129	4.5	15.4	3.4	Bronchitis, emphysema [3]	70	2.6	7.3	2.8
Pneumonia, all forms	119	4.2	17.9	4.3	Congenital anomalies	59	2.2	14.1	6.5
Congenital anomalies	78	2.7	19.5	7.2	Noninfectious enteritis				
Fractures, all sites	59	2.1	9.5	4.6	of colitis	49	1.8	4.5	2.5
15 to 44 years [2]	3,162	54.4	328.8	6.0	15 to 44 years [2]	8,064	137.1	502.3	3.7
Psychoses	240	4.1	48.6	11.8	Delivery	3,895	66.2	169.8	2.6
Fractures, all sites	220	3.8	22.2	5.9	Psychoses	240	4.1	51.4	12.6
Diseases of heart	158	2.7	14.6	5.4	Pregnancy w/abortive outcome	177	3.0	5.9	2.0
Alcohol dependence syndrome	134	2.3	21.8	9.5	Benign neoplasms	171	2.9	10.8	3.7
Intervertebral disc disorders	120	2.1	7.2	3.5	Cholelithiasis	138	2.4	6.6	2.8
45 to 64 years [2]	3,135	134.7	862.9	6.4	45 to 64 years [2]	3,194	127.6	793.8	6.2
Diseases of heart	758	32.6	182.9	5.6	Diseases of heart	427	17.1	101.6	6.0
Malignant neoplasms	228	9.8	90.0	9.2	Malignant neoplasms	272	10.8	81.2	7.5
Cerebrovascular disease	95	4.1	35.6	8.8	Psychoses	118	4.7	65.7	13.9
Psychoses	89	3.8	46.1	12.1	Benign neoplasms	111	4.4	17.9	4.0
Pneumonia, all forms	82	3.5	30.4	8.6	Cholelithiasis	106	4.2	15.5	3.6
65 years old and older [2]	4,692	359.7	2,876.7	8.0	65 years old and older [2]	6,172	320.8	2,700.5	8.4
Diseases of heart	1,155	88.5	623.6	7.0	Diseases of heart	1,332	69.2	512.4	7.4
Malignant neoplasms	443	34.0	306.4	9.0	Malignant neoplasms	408	21.2	192.3	9.1
Pneumonia, all forms	264	20.2	215.8	10.7	Cerebrovascular disease	358	18.6	161.6	8.7
Cerebrovascular disease	265	20.3	180.3	8.9	Fractures, all sites	339	17.6	178.4	10.1
Hyperplasia of prostate	173	13.2	60.4	4.6	Pneumonia, all forms	292	15.2	144.1	9.5

[1] See footnote 1, table 185.   [2] Includes other first-listed diagnoses not shown separately.   [3] Includes asthma.

Source: U.S. National Center for Health Statistics, *Health, United States*, 1993; and unpublished data.

No. 187. Outpatient Surgery Performed in Hospitals: 1980 to 1992

TYPE OF HOSPITAL	1980	1985	1986	1987	1988	1989	1990	1991	1992
OUTPATIENT SURGERIES (1,000)									
All hospitals	3,198	7,309	8,705	9,758	10,586	10,953	11,678	12,209	12,849
Ownership:									
Non-Federal hospitals	3,063	6,984	8,272	9,145	10,038	10,362	11,085	11,724	12,316
Community hospitals [1]	3,054	6,951	8,247	9,126	10,028	10,351	11,070	11,712	12,308
Nongovernmental nonprofit	2,416	5,392	6,265	6,903	7,577	7,834	8,389	8,989	9,500
Federal hospitals	135	325	434	612	548	591	593	486	533
Size of hospital: 6 to 99 beds	354	752	966	1,146	1,229	1,241	1,303	1,366	1,464
100 to 199 beds	571	1,502	1,811	2,030	2,252	2,360	2,498	2,636	2,824
200 to 299 beds	630	1,521	1,836	2,023	2,297	2,383	2,543	2,695	2,790
300 to 499 beds	977	2,069	2,368	2,617	2,845	2,920	3,172	3,293	3,340
500 beds or more	666	1,465	1,725	1,942	1,963	2,049	2,162	2,220	2,431
OUTPATIENT SURGERIES AS PERCENT OF TOTAL									
All hospitals	16.4	34.5	40.3	44.2	47.0	48.7	50.6	52.1	53.6
Ownership:									
Non-Federal hospitals	16.3	34.5	40.3	43.9	46.8	48.5	50.5	52.3	53.8
Community hospitals [1]	16.3	34.6	40.3	43.8	46.8	48.5	50.5	52.3	53.8
Nongovernmental nonprofit	17.1	35.5	40.8	44.2	47.0	48.6	50.7	52.5	54.0
Federal hospitals	18.6	33.9	40.7	49.9	49.7	51.5	51.8	47.8	49.3
Size of hospital: 6 to 99 beds	17.9	36.5	44.7	49.4	52.8	54.1	56.2	58.7	61.1
100 to 199 beds	15.4	36.3	42.9	47.2	50.3	52.3	55.0	56.3	58.3
200 to 299 beds	16.7	36.4	42.0	45.7	49.2	50.7	52.9	54.6	55.3
300 to 499 beds	17.2	34.4	40.0	43.1	46.5	48.0	48.8	50.6	51.9
500 beds or more	15.1	30.4	35.2	39.2	39.6	41.6	43.9	44.4	46.5

[1] For definition of community hospital, see footnotes 1 and 2, table 179.

Source: American Hospital Association, Chicago, IL, *Hospital Statistics*, annual (copyright); and unpublished data from the Annual Survey of Hospitals.

No. 188. Procedures for Inpatients Discharged From Short-Stay Hospitals: 1980 to 1992

[Excludes newborn infants and discharges from Federal hospitals. See headnote, table 185]

SEX AND TYPE OF PROCEDURE	NUMBER OF PROCEDURES (1,000)				RATE PER 1,000 POPULATION [2]			
	1980	1985	1990 [1]	1992 [1]	1980	1985	1990 [1]	1992 [1]
Surgical procedures, total [3] [4]	24,494	24,799	23,051	23,253	108.6	104.6	92.4	91.7
MALE								
Total [3] [4]	8,505	8,805	8,538	8,646	78.1	76.8	70.6	70.2
Cardiac catheterization	228	439	620	636	2.1	3.8	5.1	5.2
Prostatectomy	335	367	364	353	3.1	3.2	3.0	2.9
Reduction of fracture [5]	325	339	300	311	3.0	3.0	2.5	2.5
Repair of inguinal hernia	483	370	181	121	4.4	3.2	1.5	1.0
FEMALE								
Total [3] [4]	15,989	15,994	14,513	14,607	137.1	130.6	113.0	112.0
Procedures to assist delivery [4]	2,391	2,494	2,491	2,441	20.5	20.4	19.4	18.7
Cesarean section....................	619	877	945	921	5.3	7.2	7.4	7.1
Repair of current obstetric laceration..........	355	548	795	790	3.0	4.5	6.2	6.1
Hysterectomy	649	670	591	580	5.6	5.5	4.6	4.4
Diagnostic and other nonsurgical procedures [4] [6]	6,918	11,961	17,455	19,381	30.7	50.5	70.0	76.5
MALE								
Total [4] [6]	3,386	5,889	7,378	8,149	31.1	51.4	61.0	66.2
Angiocardiography and arteriography [7]	355	693	1,051	1,060	3.3	6.0	8.7	8.6
CAT scan [8]........................	152	671	736	608	1.4	5.9	6.1	4.9
FEMALE								
Total [4] [6]	3,532	6,072	10,077	11,231	30.3	49.6	78.5	86.1
Diagnostic ultrasound	204	756	941	871	1.7	6.2	7.3	6.7
CAT scan [8]........................	154	707	770	658	1.3	5.8	6.0	5.0

[1] Comparisons beginning 1988 with data for earlier years should be made with caution as estimates of change may reflect improvements in the design rather than true changes in hospital use.   [2] Based on Bureau of the Census estimated civilian population as of July 1. Population estimates for the 1980's do not reflect revised estimates based on the 1990 Census of Population.   [3] Includes other types of surgical procedures not shown separately.   [4] Beginning in 1989, the definition of some surgical and diagnostic and other nonsurgical procedures was revised, causing a discontinuity in the trends for some totals. [5] Excluding skull, nose, and jaw.   [6] Includes other nonsurgical procedures not shown separately.   [7] Using contrast material. [8] Computerized axial tomography.

Source: U.S. National Center for Health Statistics, *Vital and Health Statistics*, series 13; and unpublished data.

No. 189. Live Births With Selected Obstetric Procedures Performed, by Age and Race of Mother: 1990

[Except as noted, for 49 States and DC. Excludes Oklahoma]

PROCEDURE AND RACE OF MOTHER	All births [1] (1,000)	Obstetric procedure reported (1,000)	RATE BY AGE OF MOTHER [2]							Births with procedure not stated (1,000)
			All ages	Under 20 years old	20 to 24 years old	25 to 29 years old	30 to 34 years old	35 to 39 years old	40 to 44 years old	
ALL RACES [3]										
Amniocentesis	4,110.6	133.9	33.4	13.8	16.5	19.3	33.1	156.3	193.9	103.8
Electronic fetal monitoring .	4,110.6	2,933.7	732.2	741.1	735.7	735.9	726.0	711.6	702.4	103.8
Induction of labor	4,110.6	382.0	95.3	81.6	92.1	99.7	98.9	100.6	104.7	103.8
Stimulation of labor	4,110.6	456.6	113.9	109.9	112.7	116.9	114.5	111.9	112.0	103.8
Tocolysis.	4,110.6	64.0	16.0	19.3	16.7	14.9	14.8	15.6	15.0	103.8
Ultrasound [4].	3,914.8	2,000.9	524.7	506.2	517.6	531	530.7	537.8	528.7	101.5
WHITE										
Amniocentesis	3,252.5	114.8	36.2	15.0	17.5	19.9	34.7	167.6	208.7	78.7
Electronic fetal monitoring .	3,252.5	2,342.3	738.0	746.9	741.2	742.4	732.7	717.4	708.9	78.7
Induction of labor	3,252.5	326.4	102.8	90.6	100.8	106.4	104.5	105.9	110.4	78.7
Stimulation of labor	3,252.5	371.5	117.0	114.1	116.1	119.5	117.0	114.8	115.4	78.7
Tocolysis.	3,252.5	49.6	15.6	19.1	16.4	14.6	14.6	15.5	14.9	78.7
Ultrasound [4].	3,105.2	1,627.8	537.5	523.6	531.2	542.4	541.0	547.7	538.7	77.1
BLACK										
Amniocentesis	679.2	12.6	19.1	11.2	13.0	16.0	22.4	81.8	108.3	20.8
Electronic fetal monitoring .	679.2	475.6	722.3	733.3	724.5	717.7	712.6	710.1	712.5	20.8
Induction of labor	679.2	44.1	67.0	62.3	63.6	68.9	73.1	79.5	88.6	20.8
Stimulation of labor	679.2	66.7	101.3	101.0	101.2	103.3	99.7	99.6	94.2	20.8
Tocolysis.	679.2	12.2	18.5	20.0	18.8	17.9	17.3	17.5	17.2	20.8
Ultrasound [4].	635.9	295.7	480.3	467.3	474.6	485.8	492.9	506.8	505.4	20.2

[1] Total number of births in areas reporting specified obstetric procedures.   [2] Rate per 1,000 live births with specified procedure.   [3] includes other races, not shown separately.   [4] Excludes Illinois.

Source: U.S. National Center for Health Statistics, *Monthly Vital Statistics Report*, vol. 42, No. 2, supplement.

No. 190. Organ Transplants and Grafts: 1981 to 1992

[As of end of year. Based on reports of procurement programs and transplant centers in the United States, except as noted]

PROCEDURE	NUMBER OF PROCEDURES							NUMBER OF CENTERS		Number of people waiting, 1992	1-year survival rates, 1990 (percent)
	1981	1985	1988	1989	1990	1991	1992	1981	1992		
Transplant:											
Heart........	62	719	1,647	1,673	1,996	2,125	2,172	8	163	2,693	[1]82
Liver........	26	602	1,680	2,160	2,534	2,954	3,059	1	109	2,318	[1]74
Kidney.......	4,883	7,695	9,123	8,890	9,433	9,949	10,210	157	244	22,445	[1]93
Heart-lung.....	5	30	74	67	52	51	48	(NA)	87	180	[1]53
Lung........	-	2	31	89	187	401	535	(NA)	83	967	[1]54
Pancreas/Islet cell........	(NA)	130	243	413	529	532	557	(NA)	109	125	[1]89
Cornea grafts [2]...	15,500	26,300	36,900	38,464	40,631	41,393	42,377	(NA)	[3]111	5,829	[4]95
Bone grafts	(NA)	(NA)	300,000	(NA)	350,000	350,000	350,000	(NA)	35	(NA)	(NA)
Skin grafts	(NA)	(NA)	5,200	(NA)	5,500	5,500	5,500	(NA)	25	(NA)	(NA)

- Represents zero.   NA Not available.   [1] One year patient survival rates for transplants performed between October 1, 1987, and December 31, 1989.   [2] Number of procedures and eye banks include Canada.   [3] Eye banks.   [4] Success rate.

Source: U.S. Department of Health and Human Services, Public Health Service, Division of Organ Transplantation; American Association of Tissue Banks, McLean, VA; and Eye Bank Association of America, Washington, DC; and unpublished data.

No. 191. Patients Discharged From Hospitals—Principal Source of Expected Payment, by Selected Characteristic: 1991

[Covers non-Federal short-stay hospitals. Discharges exclude newborn infants. Based on the National Hospital Discharge Survey. See headnote, table 185. For composition of regions, see table 26]

CHARACTERISTIC	Total discharges [1] (1,000)	PRINCIPAL SOURCE OF EXPECTED PAYMENT— PERCENT DISTRIBUTION								
		Private insurance	Government					Self-pay	No charge	Other [2]
			Medicare	Medicaid	Worker's compensation	Other				
AGE										
All ages	30,951	33.0	35.1	13.4	1.1	1.7	6.0	0.3	3.4	
Under 15 years old...........	2,531	42.6	1.5	36.8	(X)	2.5	5.7	0.9	5.2	
15 to 44 years old	11,227	47.0	4.1	21.9	1.6	2.8	8.9	0.5	5.0	
45 to 64 years old	6,329	54.8	14.7	9.3	1.4	2.2	6.7	0.4	4.3	
65 years old and over	10,864	3.6	86.8	1.5	0.6	0.2	2.8	([3])	0.9	
SEX										
Male, all ages.............	12,406	31.2	38.8	9.9	2.0	1.8	6.8	0.4	3.5	
Under 15 years old...........	1,416	42.8	1.2	36.9	(X)	2.6	5.5	1.0	5.2	
15 to 44 years old	3,162	43.3	8.2	13.3	4.5	3.5	13.1	0.9	5.5	
45 to 64 years old	3,135	53.9	16.7	7.4	2.0	2.0	6.7	0.4	4.5	
65 years old and over	4,692	4.3	85.5	1.3	0.8	0.3	2.8	([3])	1.0	
Female, all ages.............	18,545	34.2	32.5	15.7	0.5	1.7	5.5	0.3	3.4	
Under 15 years old...........	1,115	42.3	1.8	36.7	(X)	2.4	5.9	([3])	5.1	
15 to 44 years old	8,064	48.5	2.5	25.3	0.5	2.5	7.2	0.4	4.7	
45 to 64 years old	3,194	55.7	12.7	11.1	0.8	2.4	6.7	0.4	4.1	
65 years old and over	6,172	3.0	87.7	1.6	0.5	([3])	2.7	([3])	0.8	
RACE										
White.....................	20,018	35.0	38.5	9.1	1.2	1.3	5.0	0.2	3.2	
All other.................	4,820	24.4	21.5	27.1	1.1	2.5	9.5	1.2	3.9	
Not stated.................	6,113	33.2	34.4	16.7	0.9	2.4	6.7	3.0	3.7	
REGION										
Northeast	7,141	33.6	34.7	13.5	1.0	0.6	4.4	([3])	4.5	
Midwest	7,121	36.3	39.0	12.4	0.7	1.7	4.3	0.4	2.5	
South	11,256	33.5	38.1	13.8	1.1	2.4	6.0	0.6	1.8	
West	5,433	26.9	24.2	13.7	1.8	1.8	10.6	([3])	6.5	

X Not applicable.   [1] Includes discharges for whom expected source of payment was unknown.   [2] Includes all other nonprofit source of payment such as church, welfare, or United Way.   [3] Figure does not meet standards of reliability or precision.

Source: U.S. National Center for Health Statistics, unpublished data.

No. 192. Nursing and Related Care Facilities: 1971 to 1991

ITEM	Unit	1971	1973	1976	1978	1980	1982	1986	1991
Nursing and related care: [1]									
Facilities	Number	22,004	21,834	20,468	[2]18,722	[3]23,065	[4]25,849	[4]25,648	[4]33,006
Beds	1,000	1,202	1,328	1,415	[2]1,349	[3]1,537	[4]1,642	[4]1,709	[4]1,921
Resident patients	1,000	1,076	1,198	1,293	[2]1,240	[3]1,396	[4]1,493	[4]1,553	[4]1,729
Employees, full-time	1,000	568	636	653	[2]664	[3]798	(NA)	(NA)	(NA)
Per 1,000 patients	Rate	528	531	505	[2]535	[3]571	(NA)	(NA)	(NA)
Skilled nursing facilities [5]	Number	4,277	3,970	3,922	4,745	5,052	5,408	6,897	9,711
Beds	1,000	307	287	309	408	436	488	(NA)	570
Per 1,000 Medicare enrollees [6]	Rate	15.1	13.5	13.7	17.3	17.7	19.1	(NA)	16.9

NA Not available. [1] Covers nursing homes with three beds or more and all other places providing some form of nursing, personal, or domiciliary care; standards vary widely among States. Includes skilled nursing facilities. 1971-1984 based on National Master Facility Inventory. Some changes in data beginning 1976 may be due to dependence on State collection. 1986 data based on the 1986 Inventory of Long Term Care Places. Data may not be strictly comparable with previous years. 1991 based on National Health Provider Inventory; excludes board and care homes for the mentally retarded. [2] Includes 1976 data for California, District of Columbia, New York, and North Carolina. [3] Excludes hospital-based nursing homes and includes 1978 data for Alaska and South Dakota. [4] Excludes hospital-based nursing homes. [5] Source: Through 1976, U.S. Social Security Administration, *Health Insurance Statistics* and unpublished data. Beginning 1978, U.S. Health Care Financing Administration, *Medicare Participating Providers and Suppliers of Health Services, 1980;* and unpublished data. Covers facilities and beds certified for participation under Medicare as of mid-year. Includes facilities which have transfer agreements with one or more participating hospitals, and are engaged primarily in providing skilled nursing care and related services for the rehabilitation of injured, disabled, or sick persons. [6] Based on number of aged persons residing in United States who were enrolled in the Medicare hospital insurance program as of July 1 of year stated.

Source: Except as noted, U.S. National Center for Health Statistics, *Health Resources Statistics,* annual through 1976 and 1978; 1982, 1986, and 1991 *Advance Data from Vital and Health Statistics,* No. 111, No. 147, and No. 244; and unpublished data.

No. 193. Nursing and Related Care Facilities, by Selected Characteristics: 1991

[Excludes hospital-based nursing homes which numbered 767 with 51,897 residents in 1991. Based on the National Health Provider Inventor. For composition of regions, see table 26]

CHARACTERISTIC	TOTAL FACILITIES				NURSING HOMES [1]				BOARD AND CARE HOMES [2]			
	Homes	Beds (1,000)	Average number of beds	Occu-pancy rate	Homes	Beds (1,000)	Average number of beds	Occu-pancy rate	Homes	Beds (1,000)	Average number of beds	Occu-pancy rate
Total	33,006	1,921	58	90.0	14,744	1,559	106	91.5	18,262	362	20	83.6
REGION												
Northeast	5,834	414	71	93.5	2,654	328	124	95.3	3,180	86	27	86.6
Midwest	9,142	583	64	89.7	5,137	519	101	90.3	4,005	64	16	84.7
South	9,499	609	64	89.6	4,708	504	107	90.9	4,791	106	22	83.0
West	8,531	315	37	86.8	2,245	209	93	89.6	6,286	106	17	81.3
OWNERSHIP												
Government	1,570	113	72	92.3	725	100	138	93.5	845	13	16	83.8
Proprietary	24,256	1,349	56	89.0	10,522	1,087	103	90.6	13,734	262	19	82.6
Nonprofit	7,180	459	64	92.2	3,497	372	106	93.5	3,683	87	24	86.8
SIZE												
Fewer than 10 beds	10,025	53	5	83.9	165	1	5	81.6	9,860	52	5	83.9
10 to 24 beds	5,281	82	15	85.5	398	7	18	88.5	4,883	74	15	85.2
25 to 49 beds	3,381	124	37	87.9	1,590	61	39	91.1	1,791	62	35	84.9
50 to 74 beds	3,792	229	60	90.9	3,050	184	60	92.1	742	44	60	85.8
75 to 99 beds	2,795	245	88	90.2	2,401	211	88	91.2	394	34	86	83.6
100 to 199 beds	6,497	854	132	90.8	6,028	792	131	91.5	469	62	132	81.9
200 to 299 beds	941	217	231	90.1	846	196	231	91.4	95	22	228	79.0
300 to 499 beds	248	89	358	89.5	224	80	359	91.0	24	8	347	75.5
500 beds or more	46	29	633	90.8	42	26	625	92.1	4	3	721	78.8

[1] These facilities have three or more beds. [2] These facilities offer no nursing services and provide only personal care or supervisory care. Excludes board and care homes for the mentally retarded.

Source: U.S. National Center for Health Statistics, *Advance Data From Vital and Health Statistics,* No. 244; and unpublished data.

No. 194. Home Health and Hospice Care Agencies, by Selected Characteristics: 1991

[In percent, except total in thousands. Based on the 1992 National Home and Hospice Care Survey. Home health care is provided to individuals and families in their place of residence. Hospice care is available in both the home and inpatient settings. Agencies which provide both types of care are classified according to how the majority of their patients are cared for. See source for details. For composition of regions, see table 26]

ITEM	AGENCIES			CURRENT PATIENTS [1]			DISCHARGED PATIENTS [2]		
	Total	Home health agency	Hospice	Total	Home health agency	Hospice	Total	Home health agency	Hospice
Total (1,000)	8.0	7.0	1.0	1,284.2	1,237.1	47.2	3,273.3	3,066.3	207.0
PERCENT DISTRIBUTION									
Ownership:									
Proprietary	34.0	38.2	3.4	27.1	27.8	10.5	24.4	25.6	6.3
Voluntary nonprofit............	48.0	41.7	93.5	61.1	60.2	86.2	68.3	66.7	91.4
Government and other	18.0	20.1	3.1	11.7	12.1	3.3	7.3	7.7	2.4
Certification:									
Medicare	82.2	84.7	64.5	91.4	91.4	92.3	96.4	96.6	93.5
Medicaid	82.4	86.0	56.8	91.8	92.0	86.1	93.5	93.9	87.0
Region:									
Northeast..................	22.1	23.0	16.0	32.3	32.3	34.1	31.7	31.9	29.0
Midwest...................	29.8	29.5	31.7	21.0	21.1	19.7	19.5	19.3	21.5
South	33.9	34.1	32.5	34.2	34.2	33.0	29.2	29.2	30.4
West	14.2	13.5	19.8	12.5	12.4	13.2	19.6	19.6	19.1

[1] Patients on the rolls of the agency as of midnight the day prior to the survey.   [2] Patients removed from the rolls of the agency during the 12 months prior to the day of the survey.

Source: U.S. National Center for Health Statistics, *Vital and Health Statistics, Advance Data*, No. 235.

No. 195. Home Health and Hospice Care Patients, by Selected Characteristics: 1991

[See headnote, table 194]

ITEM	CURRENT PATIENTS [1]			DISCHARGED PATIENTS [2]		
	Total	Home health agency	Hospice	Total	Home health agency	Hospice
Total (1,000)	1,284.2	1,237.1	47.2	3,273.3	3,066.3	207.0
PERCENT DISTRIBUTION						
Age:						
Under 45 years old	11.0	11.1	6.3	12.2	12.6	6.5
45-54 years old	3.9	3.9	4.5	5.0	4.7	9.1
55-64 years old......................	9.0	9.0	10.3	8.0	7.7	12.5
65 years old and over.................	75.2	75.1	76.7	74.0	74.2	71.0
65-69 years old	10.6	10.5	14.3	11.4	11.2	14.0
70-74 years old	13.8	13.8	13.2	13.9	13.6	17.2
75-79 years old	16.5	16.5	17.7	17.6	17.7	15.5
80-84 years old	17.2	17.1	19.3	15.9	16.3	11.2
85 years old and over..............	17.1	17.3	12.3	15.2	15.3	13.2
Age unknown	0.9	0.9	(³)	0.8	0.8	(³)
Sex:						
Male	33.7	33.2	45.1	37.6	36.8	49.7
Female	66.3	66.8	54.9	62.4	63.2	50.3
Race:						
White	68.5	67.9	83.2	68.6	67.4	85.8
Black.........................	13.2	13.4	7.6	9.6	9.8	6.1
Other or unknown	18.3	18.7	9.2	21.8	22.8	8.1
Marital status at admission:						
Married	34.0	33.4	49.4	37.9	37.4	45.1
Widowed	35.4	35.5	34.3	31.7	31.5	33.9
Divorced or separated	4.7	4.7	5.0	5.0	4.6	11.2
Never married....................	11.9	12.1	6.5	11.9	12.3	5.7
Unknown	13.9	14.3	4.7	13.6	14.2	4.1

[1] Patients on the rolls of the agency as of midnight the day prior to the survey.   [2] Patients removed from the rolls of the agency during the 12 months prior to the day of the survey.   [3] Base figure too small to meet statistical standards of reliability for a derived figure.

Source: National Center for Health Statistics, *Vital and Health Statistics, Advance Data*, No. 235.

No. 196. Residential Facilities for Persons with Mental Retardation: 1970 to 1991

[For years ending **June 30**. Persons with mental retardation refers to those who have been so designated by State governments in the process of placing them into residential facilities]

ITEM	STATE OPERATED FACILITIES [1]					PRIVATE FACILITIES [3]			
	1970	1980 [2]	1985 [2]	1990 [2]	1991	1977	1982	1990	1991
Number of facilities [4]	190	394	881	1,321	1,477	10,219	14,605	41,588	45,309
Residents beginning of year	189,956	148,734	117,101	94,625	91,239	(NA)	(NA)	(NA)	(NA)
Admissions [5]	14,985	14,064	7,713	5,548	3,654	22,363	22,431	(NA)	(NA)
Deaths in institutions	3,496	2,142	1,537	1,100	1,077	891	920	(NA)	(NA)
Live releases [6]	14,702	16,225	10,310	7,620	5,541	12,384	12,999	(NA)	(NA)
Residents end of year	186,743	140,230	112,183	91,640	88,132	89,120	115,032	188,902	201,238
Rate per 100,000 population [7]	92.5	62.2	47.5	34.7	35.2	40.9	50.0	76.0	79.8
Average daily residents	187,897	136,304	111,791	92,729	88,841	(NA)	(NA)	(NA)	(NA)
Maintenance expenditures per day per average daily resident (dollars) [8]	13	68	122	196	193	[9]19	[9]37	(NA)	(NA)

NA Not available. [1] Data as submitted by many State agencies; figures reflect some estimates. Resident patients at the end of a year do not equal the number at the beginning of a succeeding year. Includes estimates for underreporting. [2] Includes data for 142 facilities in 1980, 121 facilities in 1985, and 108 in 1990 operated as mental hospitals or other facilities and which have residents with mental retardation. The average daily number of residents with mental retardation was 8,240 in 1980, 5,602 in 1985, and 1,487 in 1990. [3] A privately-operated living quarter which provides 24-hour, 7-days-a-week responsibility for room, board, and supervision of mentally retarded persons. Excludes single-family homes providing services to a relative; and nursing homes, boarding homes, and foster homes not formally licensed or contracted as mental retardation service providers. [4] Beginning 1985, reflects the development of a large number of community based State-operated facilities which were developed in the early 1980's. [5] Includes readmissions and excludes transfers. Excludes people entering newly opened facilities. [6] 1970, represents excess of residents released alive from facility over those returning to facility. Beginning 1980, total live releases. [7] Based on Bureau of the Census estimated civilian population as of July 1. Estimates reflect revisions based on 1990 Census of Population. [8] Reporting facilities only; includes salaries and wages, purchased provisions, fuel, light, water, etc. [9] Represents average daily reimbursement rate per resident.

Source: 1970 State-operated facilities: U.S. Office of Human Development Services, *Residents in Public Institutions for the Mentally Retarded*, annual, and unpublished data; later State-operated facilities and private facilities: Center for Residential Services and Community Living (CRSCL), Institute on Community Integration, UAP, University of Minnesota, Minneapolis, MN, Lakin, Blake, Prouty, Mamgam, and Bruininks, Report No. 38 and earlier reports and unpublished data.

No. 197. Mental Health Facilities—Summary, by Type of Facility: 1990

[Revised 1990 data. Facilities, beds and inpatients as of year-end 1990; other data are for calendar year or fiscal year ending in a month other than December since facilities are permitted to report on either a calendar or fiscal year basis. Excludes private psychiatric office practice and psychiatric service modes of all types in hospitals or outpatient clinics of Federal agencies other than U.S. Dept. of Veterans Affairs. Excludes data from Puerto Rico, Virgin Islands, Guam, and other territories]

TYPE OF FACILITY	Number of facilities	INPATIENT BEDS		INPATIENTS		Average daily inpatients (1,000)	Inpatient care episodes [2] (1,000)	EXPENDITURES		Patient care staff [4] (1,000)
		Total (1,000)	Rate [1]	Total (1,000)	Rate [1]			Total (mil. dol.)	Per capita [3] (dol.)	
Total	5,284	272.2	111.5	229.7	93.0	224.4	2,260.9	28,357	116.3	471.8
Mental hospitals:										
State and county	270	98.4	40.3	90.3	37.0	89.7	365.7	7,705	31.6	112.8
Private [5]	967	75.0	30.7	60.3	24.7	58.4	509.0	8,093	33.2	99.6
General hospitals [6]	1,674	53.5	21.9	38.3	15.7	38.6	997.6	4,662	19.1	80.7
Veterans Administration [7]	141	21.7	8.9	17.2	7.1	17.3	215.6	1,480	6.1	29.7
Free-standing psychiatric outpatient clinics [8]	743	(X)	(X)	(X)	(X)	(X)	(X)	671	2.8	14.3
Other [9]	1,489	23.6	9.7	23.6	8.5	20.4	173.0	5,746	23.5	134.7

X Not applicable. [1] Rate per 100,000 population. Based on Bureau of the Census estimated civilian population as of July 1. [2] "Inpatient care episodes" is defined as the number of residents in inpatient facilities at the beginning of the year plus the total additions to inpatient facilities during the year. [3] Based on Bureau of the Census estimated civilian population as of July 1. [4] Full-time equivalent. [5] Includes residential treatment centers for emotionally disturbed children. [6] Non-Federal hospitals with separate psychiatric services. [7] Includes U.S. Department of Veterans Affairs (VA) neuropsychiatric hospitals, VA general hospitals with separate psychiatric settings and VA freestanding psychiatric outpatient clinics. [8] Includes mental health facilities which provide only psychiatric outpatient services. [9] Includes other multiservice mental health facilities with two or more settings, which are not elsewhere classified, as well as freestanding partial care facilities which only provide psychiatric partial care services. Number of facilities, expenditures, and staff data also include freestanding psychiatric partial care facilities.

Source: U.S. Substance Abuse and Mental Health Services Administration, Center for Mental Health Services, unpublished data.

No. 198. Persons Injured, by Sex: 1970 to 1992

[Persons injured in millions. Covers civilian noninstitutional population and comprises incidents leading to restricted activity and/or medical attention. Beginning 1982, data not strictly comparable with other years. See headnote, table 201. Based on National Health Interview Survey; see Appendix III]

YEAR	PERSONS INJURED		RATE PER 100 POPULATION		AGE AND TYPE	PERSONS INJURED			RATE PER 100 POPULATION		
	Male	Female	Male	Female		Total	Male	Female	Total	Male	Female
1970 ..	31.8	24.2	33.0	23.3	1992, total [1] ..	59.6	32.8	26.8	23.7	26.8	20.7
1975 ..	39.4	32.5	39.1	30.0	Under 5 years.....	4.8	2.6	2.2	24.5	26.3	22.6
1980 ..	39.0	29.1	37.1	25.8	5 to 17 years	13.4	8.2	5.2	28.6	34.2	22.7
1983 ..	33.0	28.1	29.8	23.7	18 to 44 years	27.7	16.7	11.1	26.3	32.1	20.6
1984 ..	33.7	27.4	30.1	22.9	45 years and over..	13.6	5.2	8.4	17.1	14.5	19.4
1985 ..	34.6	28.0	30.6	23.1	Fractures [2]	7.8	4.6	3.2	3.1	3.7	2.5
1986 ..	34.0	28.4	29.8	23.3	Sprains and strains .	13.8	7.0	6.8	5.5	5.8	5.2
1987 ..	33.6	28.4	29.1	23.1	Open wounds and						
1988 ..	32.4	26.8	27.7	21.6	lacerations......	12.4	7.8	4.6	4.9	6.4	3.5
1989 ..	31.7	26.3	26.9	20.9	Contusions [3]	10.7	6.1	4.6	4.2	5.0	3.6
1990 ..	33.6	26.6	28.1	21.0	Other	15.0	7.3	7.6	5.9	6.0	5.9
1991 ..	32.2	27.5	26.7	21.5							

[1] Includes unknown place of accident not shown separately.   [2] Includes dislocations.   [3] Includes superficial injuries.

Source: U.S. National Center for Health Statistics, *Vital and Health Statistics,* series 10, No. 189, and earlier reports; and unpublished data.

No. 199. Injuries Associated With Consumer Products: 1990 and 1991

[For products associated with more than 16,000 injuries in 1991. Estimates calculated from a representative sample of hospitals with emergency treatment departments in the United States. Data are estimates of the number of emergency room treated cases nationwide associated with various products. Product involvement does not necessarily mean the product caused the accident. Products were selected from the U.S. Consumer Product Safety Commission's National Electronic Injury Surveillance System]

PRODUCT	1990	1991	PRODUCT	1990	1991
Home maintenance:			Housewares:		
Noncaustic cleaning equip. [1]	24,452	21,890	Cookware, pots, pans..........	32,971	34,868
Cleaning agents (except soap)....	40,475	38,397	Cutlery, knives, unpowered	446,318	448,525
Paints, solvents, lubricants	21,712	21,430	Drinking glasses	133,084	134,790
Misc. household chemicals	18,691	20,369	Scissors..................	26,966	30,973
			Small kitchen appliances........	43,571	40,952
Home workshop equipment:			Tableware and accessories	111,413	116,796
Power home tools, except saws ...	29,825	29,014	Misc. housewares	57,235	55,635
Power home workshop saws	93,722	94,076	General household appliances:		
Welding, soldering, cutting tools ...	19,359	19,368	Cooking ranges, ovens, etc	48,378	54,659
Workshop manual tools	118,068	118,799	Irons, clothes steamers........	17,393	18,120
Misc. workshop equipment	39,625	40,147	Refrigerators, freezers	35,227	31,741
			Washers, dryers	21,405	19,205
Yard and garden equipment:			Misc. household appliances......	30,959	30,532
Chains and saws	39,331	44,019			
Hand garden tools	35,327	38,796	Heating, cooling equipment: [4]		
Hatchets, axes	17,239	18,270	Chimneys, fireplaces	18,957	24,120
Lawn garden care equipment....	49,501	54,507	Fans (except stove)	19,240	21,126
Lawn mowers..............	77,373	76,133	Heating stoves, space heaters....	33,306	31,439
Other power lawn equipment.....	22,967	19,424	Pipes, heating and plumbing	23,272	21,238
Household packaging and containers:			Home entertainment equipment:		
Cans, other containers	216,726	209,407	Pet supplies, equipment	22,236	23,177
Glass bottles, jars	75,510	69,837	Sound recording equip [5]	44,211	42,678
Paper, cardboard, plastic products .	42,649	36,931	Television sets, stands	37,881	36,995
Home furnishing: [2]			Personal use items:		
Bathtub, shower structures	148,741	152,770	Cigarettes, lighters, fuels........	19,509	20,355
Beds, mattresses, pillows	352,113	362,790	Clothing	118,735	126,173
Carpets, rugs	92,950	97,784	Grooming devices	28,853	32,937
Chairs, sofas, sofa beds	369,403	381,024	Holders for personal items	16,954	16,550
Desks, cabinets, shelves, racks ...	206,689	210,188	Jewelry	49,004	49,891
Electric fixtures, lamps, equipment .	49,833	55,191	Paper money, coins	29,613	31,796
Ladders, stools	171,230	179,422	Pencils, pens, other desk supplies .	46,224	45,833
Mirrors, mirror glass	21,595	23,325	Razors, shavers, razor blades	46,765	43,916
Sinks, toilets...............	56,118	54,847	Sewing equipment	29,683	32,044
Tables...................	316,531	332,775			
Other misc. accessories	47,267	53,181	Sports and recreation equipment:		
			Bicycles, accessories	580,119	600,649
Home structures, construction: [3]			Exercise equipment	78,814	86,210
Cabinets or door hardware	21,987	22,946	Mopeds, minibikes, ATV's [6]	124,345	127,371
Ceilings, walls, inside panels	219,571	227,618	Nonpowder guns, BB's, pellets....	24,216	32,562
Counters, counter tops	29,651	33,748	Playground equipment	253,030	266,869
Fences	120,866	122,111	Skateboards...............	82,428	56,435
Glass doors, windows, panels	227,321	217,916	Toboggans, sleds, snow disks, etc .	28,510	38,282
Handrails, railings, banisters	42,225	40,765	Trampolines	32,554	38,823
Nails, carpet tacks, etc	253,874	241,859			
Nonglass doors, panels	345,458	336,790	Miscellaneous products:		
Porches, open side floors, etc	119,234	118,166	Dollies, carts..............	40,996	41,363
Stairs, ramps, landings, floors	1,711,986	1,693,175	Gasoline and diesel fuels	20,408	18,882
Window, door sills, frames.......	52,057	53,523	Nursery equipment	96,746	112,753
Misc. construction materials......	91,886	85,492	Toys	164,532	163,624

[1] Includes detergent.   [2] Includes accessories.   [3] Includes materials.   [4] Includes ventilating equipment.   [5] Includes reproducing equipment.   [6] All-terrain vehicles.

Source: National Safety Council, Itasca, IL, *Accident Facts,* annual (copyright).

No. 200. Costs of Accidents: 1992

[Covers costs for accidents in which deaths or disabling injuries beyond the day of the accident occurred, together with vehicle accidents and fires]

COST	AMOUNT (bil. dol.)					PERCENT DISTRIBUTION				
	Total [1]	Motor vehicle	Work	Home	Other	Total [1]	Motor vehicle	Work	Home	Other
Total	399.0	156.6	115.9	85.1	56.7	100.0	100.0	100.0	100.0	100.0
Wage and productivity losses [2] ...	211.2	60.6	62.5	53.1	39.4	52.9	38.7	53.9	62.4	69.5
Medical expense.	75.2	20.7	22.0	21.6	12.2	18.8	13.2	19.0	25.4	21.5
Administrative expenses [3].	46.9	35.2	14.5	1.7	1.1	11.8	22.5	12.5	2.0	1.9
Motor vehicle damage	38.1	38.1	3.4	(NA)	(NA)	9.5	24.3	2.9	(NA)	(NA)
Employer cost [4]	17.5	2.0	10.2	3.3	2.6	4.4	1.3	8.8	3.9	4.6
Fire loss	10.1	(NA)	3.3	5.4	1.4	2.5	(NA)	2.8	6.3	2.5

NA Not available.   [1] Excludes duplication between work and motor vehicle ($15.3 billion) in 1992.   [2] Actual loss of wages and household production, and the present value of future earnings lost.   [3] Includes the administrative cost of public and private insurance, and police and legal costs.   [4] Estimate of the uninsured costs incurred by employees, representing the money value of time lost by uninsured workers.

Source: National Safety Council, Itasca, IL, *Accident Facts, 1993* (copyright).

No. 201. Days of Disability, by Type and Selected Characteristics: 1970 to 1992

[Covers civilian noninstitutional population. Beginning 1985, the levels of estimates may not be comparable to estimates for 1970-1980 because the later data are based on a revised questionnaire and field procedures; for further information, see source. Based on National Health Interview Survey; see Appendix III. For composition of regions, see table 26]

ITEM	TOTAL DAYS OF DISABILITY (millions)						DAYS PER PERSON					
	1970	1980	1985	1990	1991	1992	1970	1980	1985	1990	1991	1992
Restricted-activity days [1] ..	2,913	4,165	3,453	3,669	3,996	4,096	14.6	19.1	14.8	14.9	16.1	16.3
Male	1,273	1,802	1,442	1,558	1,701	1,739	13.2	17.1	12.8	13.1	14.1	14.2
Female	1,640	2,363	2,011	2,111	2,296	2,357	15.8	21.0	16.6	16.7	17.9	18.2
White [2]	2,526	3,518	2,899	3,057	3,344	3,384	14.4	18.7	14.5	14.8	16.1	16.2
Black [2].	365	580	489	536	540	586	16.2	22.7	17.4	17.7	17.5	18.6
Hispanic [3]	(NA)	(NA)	228	(NA)	(NA)	(NA)	(NA)	(NA)	13.2	(NA)	(NA)	(NA)
Under 65 years	2,331	3,228	2,557	2,734	2,966	3,005	12.9	16.6	12.4	12.6	13.6	13.6
65 years and over	582	937	895	936	1,030	1,091	30.7	39.2	32.4	33.1	34.0	35.4
Northeast...........	709	862	689	656	658	684	14.5	17.9	13.8	13.2	13.1	13.7
Midwest...........	691	989	744	836	907	946	12.4	17.2	12.7	14.0	15.2	15.4
South	996	1,415	1,308	1,404	1,529	1,518	15.9	19.8	16.3	16.7	18.2	18.0
West.............	518	899	712	773	902	948	15.6	22.0	15.7	14.8	16.5	17.1
Family income:												
Under $10,000.	(NA)	(NA)	893	662	711	712	(NA)	(NA)	25.8	27.3	29.8	29.0
$10,000 to $19,999 ...	(NA)	(NA)	781	758	789	847	(NA)	(NA)	16.7	19.1	20.8	22.1
$20,000 to $34,999 ...	(NA)	(NA)	791	715	724	750	(NA)	(NA)	12.1	13.5	13.6	14.6
$35,000 or more	(NA)	(NA)	568	912	983	940	(NA)	(NA)	9.9	10.3	11.0	10.3
Bed-disability days [4]	1,222	1,520	1,436	1,521	1,613	1,585	6.1	7.0	6.1	6.2	6.5	6.3
Male	503	616	583	625	657	648	5.2	5.9	5.2	5.2	5.4	5.3
Female	720	904	852	896	956	938	6.9	8.0	7.1	7.1	7.5	7.3
Under 65 years	959	1,190	1,064	1,115	1,166	1,130	5.3	6.1	5.1	5.2	5.3	5.1
65 years and over	263	330	371	406	447	455	13.8	13.8	13.7	13.6	14.7	14.8
Work-loss days [5]	417	485	575	621	650	597	5.4	5.0	5.3	5.3	5.6	5.1
Male	243	271	287	303	313	280	5.0	4.9	4.8	4.7	4.9	4.4
Female	175	215	288	319	337	317	5.9	5.1	6.0	5.9	6.3	5.9
School-loss days [6]	222	204	217	212	237	215	4.9	5.3	4.8	4.6	5.1	4.6
Male	108	95	100	100	114	101	4.7	4.8	4.4	4.3	4.8	4.2
Female	114	109	117	112	123	114	5.1	5.7	5.3	5.0	5.5	5.0

NA Not available.   [1] A day when a person cuts down on his activities for more than half a day because of illness or injury. Includes bed-disability, work-loss, and school-loss days. Total includes other races and unknown income, not shown separately.   [2] Beginning 1980, race was determined by asking the household respondent to report his race. In earlier years the racial classification of respondents was determined by interviewer observation.   [3] Persons of Hispanic origin may be of any race.   [4] A day when a person stayed in bed more than half a day because of illness or injury. Includes those work-loss and school-loss days actually spent in bed.   [5] A day when a person lost more than a workday because of illness or injury. Computed for persons 17 years of age and over (beginning 1985, 18 years of age and over) in the currently employed population, defined as those who were working or had a job or business from which they were not on layoff during the 2-week period preceding the week of interview.   [6] Child's loss of more than half a school day because of illness or injury. Computed for children 6-16 years of age. Beginning 1985, children 5-17 years old.

Source: U.S. National Center for Health Statistics, *Vital and Health Statistics*, series 10, No. 189; and earlier reports and unpublished data.

No. 202. Persons With Disabilities: 1991-92

[Covers the civilian noninstitutional resident population and members of the Armed Forces living off post or with their families on post. The criteria for presence of disability varied by age. In general, a disability is considered a reduced ability to perform tasks one would normally do at a given stage in life. Based on the Survey of Income and Program Participation; for details, see source]

CHARACTERISTIC	PERSONS (1,000)			PERCENT DISTRIBUTION		
	Total	Male	Female	Total	Male	Female
All ages.	**251,796**	**122,692**	**129,104**	**100.0**	**100.0**	**100.0**
With a disability	48,936	22,916	26,020	19.4	18.7	20.2
Severe.	24,117	9,929	14,187	9.6	8.1	11.0
Not severe	24,819	12,987	11,833	9.9	10.6	9.2
PERSONS 15 YEARS OLD AND OVER						
Total	195,729	93,985	101,744	100.0	100.0	100.0
With a disability	46,023	21,040	24,982	23.5	22.4	24.6
Severe.	23,588	9,593	13,995	12.1	10.2	13.8
Not severe	22,435	11,447	10,987	11.5	12.2	10.8
With functional limitations	34,163	14,774	19,389	17.5	15.7	19.1
Has difficulty—						
Seeing words and letters	9,685	4,006	5,679	5.0	4.3	5.6
Hearing normal conversation	10,928	6,421	4,506	5.6	6.8	4.4
Having speech understood	2,284	1,316	968	1.2	1.4	1.0
Lifting or carrying 10 lbs.	16,205	5,218	10,987	8.3	5.6	10.8
Climbing stairs without resting	17,469	6,465	11,003	8.9	6.9	10.8
Walking three city blocks	17,319	6,653	10,665	8.9	7.1	10.5
Is unable to—						
See words and letters	1,590	661	929	0.8	0.7	0.9
Hear normal conversation	924	529	396	0.5	0.6	0.4
Have speech understood	237	141	95	0.1	0.2	0.1
Lift or carry 10 lbs.	7,734	2,375	5,359	4.0	2.5	5.3
Climb stairs without resting	9,116	3,277	5,839	4.7	3.5	5.7
Walk three city blocks	8,972	3,236	5,736	4.6	3.4	5.6
With limitations of activities of daily living	7,919	3,013	4,907	4.1	3.2	4.8
Has difficulty—						
Getting around inside the house.	3,664	1,376	2,288	1.9	1.5	2.3
Getting in/out of bed or a chair	5,280	2,006	3,274	2.7	2.1	3.2
Taking a bath or shower.	4,501	1,550	2,951	2.3	1.7	2.9
Dressing	3,234	1,262	1,971	1.7	1.3	1.9
Eating	1,077	437	640	0.6	0.5	0.6
Getting to or using the toilet	2,084	767	1,317	1.1	0.8	1.3
Needs personal assistance with—						
Getting around inside the house.	1,706	698	1,008	0.9	0.7	1.0
Getting in/out of bed or a chair	2,022	796	1,227	1.0	0.9	1.2
Taking a bath or shower.	2,718	1,028	1,691	1.4	1.1	1.7
Dressing	2,060	866	1,193	1.1	0.9	1.2
Eating	487	226	261	0.3	0.2	0.3
Getting to or using the toilet	1,157	477	680	0.6	0.5	0.7
With limitations of instrumental activities of daily living	11,694	4,601	7,093	6.0	4.9	7.0
Has difficulty—						
Going outside the home	7,809	2,759	5,050	4.0	2.9	5.0
Keeping track of money and bills	3,901	1,621	2,280	2.0	1.7	2.2
Preparing meals	4,530	1,699	2,831	2.3	1.8	2.8
Doing light housework	6,313	2,191	4,122	3.2	2.3	4.1
Using the telephone.	3,130	1,749	1,381	1.6	1.9	1.4
Needs personal assistance with—						
Going outside the home	6,011	2,017	3,994	3.1	2.2	3.9
Keeping track of money and bills	3,425	1,460	1,965	1.8	1.6	1.9
Preparing meals	3,685	1,447	2,238	1.9	1.5	2.2
Doing light housework	4,745	1,626	3,119	2.4	1.7	3.1
Using the telephone.	933	509	424	0.5	0.5	0.4

Source: U.S. Bureau of the Census, *Current Population Reports*, P70-33.

No. 203. Children Immunized Against Specified Diseases: 1991 and 1992

[In percent. Covers civilian noninstitutionalized population ages 19 months to 35 months. Based on estimates from the National Health Interview Survey. Excludes respondents with unknown or missing information. See Appendix III]

VACCINATION	1991, total	1992			
		Total	White	Black	Other
Diphtheria-tetanus-pertussis (DPT)/ diphtheria-tetanus:					
3+ doses	68.8	83.0	84.8	74.7	79.3
4+ doses	43.3	59.0	59.5	55.0	59.7
Polio: 3+ doses	53.2	72.4	74.1	62.7	75.5
Hib [1]: 3+ doses	1.7	28.2	29.1	25.5	23.0
Measles containing	82.0	82.5	83.6	77.9	79.9
3 DPT/3 polio/1 MMR [2]	50.0	68.7	70.0	60.2	71.9
4 DPT/3 polio/1 MMR [2][3]	37.0	55.3	55.9	50.9	57.5

[1] Haemophilus B.　[2] Measles, measles/rubella, measles/mumps, and measles/mumps/rubella.　[3] Up-to-date for age.

Source: U.S. Centers for Disease Control and Prevention, Atlanta, GA, the National Health Interview Survey.

No. 204. Specified Reportable Diseases—Cases Reported: 1970 to 1992

[Figures should be interpreted with caution. Although reporting of some of these diseases is incomplete, the figures are of value in indicating trends of disease incidence. Includes cases imported from outside the United States. See *Historical Statistics, Colonial Times to 1970*, series B 291-303, for related data]

DISEASE	1970	1980	1985	1987	1988	1989	1990	1991	1992
AIDS [1]	(NA)	(NA)	8,249	21,070	31,001	33,722	41,595	43,672	45,472
Amebiasis	2,888	5,271	4,433	3,123	2,860	3,217	3,328	2,989	2,942
Aseptic meningitis	6,480	8,028	10,619	11,487	7,234	10,274	11,852	14,526	12,223
Botulism [2]	12	89	122	82	84	89	92	114	91
Brucellosis (undulant fever)	213	183	153	129	96	95	85	104	105
Chickenpox (1,000)	(³)	190.9	178.2	213.2	192.9	185.4	173.1	147.1	158.4
Diphtheria	435	3	3	3	2	3	4	5	4
Encephalitis:									
Primary infectious [4]	1,580	1,362	1,376	1,418	882	981	1,341	1,021	774
Post infectious [4]	370	40	161	121	121	88	105	82	129
Haemophilius influenza	(³)	(³)	(³)	(³)	(³)	(³)	(³)	2,764	1,412
Hepatitis: B (serum) (1,000)	8.3	19.0	26.6	25.9	23.2	23.4	21.1	18.0	16.1
A (infectious) (1,000)	56.8	29.1	23.2	25.3	28.5	35.8	31.4	24.4	23.1
Unspecified (1,000)	(³)	11.9	5.5	3.1	2.5	2.3	1.7	1.3	0.9
Non-A, non-B (1,000)	(³)	(³)	4.2	3.0	2.6	2.5	2.6	3.6	6.0
Legionellosis	(³)	(³)	830	1,038	1,085	1,190	1,370	1,317	1,339
Leprosy (Hansen disease)	129	223	361	238	184	163	198	154	172
Leptospirosis	47	85	57	43	54	93	77	58	54
Lyme disease	(³)	(³)	(³)	(³)	(³)	(³)	(³)	9,465	9,895
Malaria	3,051	2,062	1,049	944	1,099	1,277	1,292	1,278	1,087
Measles (1,000)	47.4	13.5	2.8	3.7	3.4	18.2	27.8	9.6	2.2
Meningococcal infections	2,505	2,840	2,479	2,930	2,964	2,727	2,451	2,130	2,134
Mumps (1,000)	105.0	8.6	3.0	12.8	4.9	5.7	5.3	4.3	2.6
Pertussis [5] (1,000)	4.2	1.7	3.6	2.8	3.5	4.2	4.6	2.7	4.1
Plague	13	18	17	12	15	4	2	11	13
Poliomyelitis, acute	33	9	7	6	9	5	7	8	4
Psittacosis	35	124	119	98	114	116	113	94	92
Rabies, animal	3,224	6,421	5,565	4,658	4,651	4,724	4,826	6,910	8,589
Rabies, human	3	-	1	1	1	-	1	3	1
Rheumatic fever, acute [6]	3,227	432	90	141	158	144	108	127	75
Rubella [7] (1,000)	56.6	3.9	0.6	0.3	0.2	0.4	1.1	1.4	0.2
Salmonellosis [8] (1,000)	22.1	33.7	65.3	50.9	48.9	47.8	48.6	48.2	40.9
Shigellosis [9] (1,000)	13.8	19.0	17.1	23.9	30.6	25.0	27.1	23.5	23.9
Tetanus	148	95	83	48	53	53	64	57	45
Toxic-shock syndrome	(³)	(³)	384	372	390	400	322	280	244
Trichinosis	109	131	61	40	45	30	129	62	41
Tuberculosis [10] (1,000)	37.1	27.7	22.2	22.5	22.4	23.5	25.7	26.3	26.7
Tularemia	172	234	177	214	201	152	152	193	159
Typhoid fever	346	510	402	400	436	460	552	501	414
Typhus fever:									
Flea-borne (endemic-murine)	27	81	37	49	54	41	50	43	28
Tick-borne (Rocky Mt. spotted fever)	380	1,163	714	604	609	623	651	628	502
Venereal diseases (civilian cases):									
Gonorrhea (1,000)	600	1,004	911	781	720	733	690	620	501
Syphilis (1,000)	91	69	68	87	103	111	134	129	113
Other (1,000)	2.2	1.0	2.3	5.3	5.2	4.9	4.6	4.0	2.2

- Represents zero. NA Not available. [1] Acquired immunodeficiency syndrome was not a notifiable disease until 1984. Figures are shown for years in which cases were reported to the CDC. [2] Beginning in 1980, includes foodborne, infant, wound, and unspecified cases. [3] Disease was not notifiable. [4] Beginning 1980, reported data reflect new diagnostic categories. [5] Whooping cough. [6] Based on reports from States: 38 in 1970, 37 in 1980, 31 in 1985, 25 in 1987, 29 in 1988, 28 in 1989, 30 in 1990, 23 in 1991, and 26 in 1992. [7] German measles. [8] Excludes typhoid fever. [9] Bacillary dysentery. [10] Newly reported active cases. New diagnostic standards introduced in 1980.

Source: U.S. Centers for Disease Control and Prevention, Atlanta, GA, *Summary of Notifiable Diseases, United States, Morbidity and Mortality Weekly Report*, vol. 41, No. 55, September 1993.

No. 205. Selected Measures of Hospital Utilization for Patients Discharged With the Diagnosis of Human Immunodeficiency Virus (HIV): 1985 to 1992

[See headnote, table 185]

MEASURE OF UTILIZATION	Unit	1985	1988	1989	1990	1991	1992
Number of patients discharged [1]	1,000....	23	95	140	146	165	194
Rate of patient discharges [2]	Rate	1.0	3.9	5.7	5.9	6.6	7.6
Number of days of care	1,000....	387	1,277	1,731	2,188	2,108	2,136
Rate of days of care [2]	Rate	16.3	52.3	70.2	87.7	84.1	84.3
Average length of stay [3]	Days	17.1	13.4	12.4	14.9	12.8	11.0

[1] Comparisons beginning 1988 with data for earlier years should be made with caution as estimates of change may reflect improvements in the 1988 design rather than true changes in hospital use. [2] Per 10,000 population. Based on Bureau of the Census estimated civilian population as of July 1. Population estimates for the 1980's do not reflect revised estimates based on the 1990 Census of Population. [3] For similar data on all patients, see table 185.

Source: National Center for Health Statistics, *Vital and Health Statistics*, series 13.

No. 206. AIDS Cases Reported, by Patient Characteristic: 1981 to 1992

[Provisional. For cases reported in the year shown. For data on AIDS deaths, see table 130. Data are subject to retrospective changes and may differ from those data in table 204]

CHARACTERISTIC	NUMBER OF CASES									PERCENT DISTRIBUTION	
	Total	1981-1985	1986	1987	1988	1989	1990	1991	1992	1981-1985	1992
Total	244,939	15,564	13,147	21,088	30,719	33,595	41,653	43,701	45,472	100.0	100.0
Age:											
Under 5 years old. . .	3,265	203	155	266	443	494	580	521	603	1.3	1.3
5 to 12 years old . . .	765	22	28	56	128	102	143	146	140	0.1	0.3
13 to 29 years old . .	47,307	3,289	2,821	4,359	6,343	6,726	8,114	7,852	7,803	21.1	17.2
30 to 39 years old . .	112,084	7,302	6,100	9,617	14,118	15,524	18,944	19,954	20,525	46.9	45.1
40 to 49 years old . .	56,235	3,259	2,703	4,519	6,524	7,329	9,701	10,643	11,557	20.9	25.4
50 to 59 years old . .	17,835	1,167	964	1,562	2,146	2,413	2,934	3,246	3,403	7.5	7.5
Over 60 years old. . .	7,448	322	376	709	1,017	1,007	1,237	1,339	1,441	2.1	3.2
Sex:											
Male	217,141	14,466	12,099	19,256	27,435	29,942	36,770	38,013	39,160	92.9	86.1
Female..........	27,798	1,098	1,048	1,832	3,284	3,653	4,883	5,688	6,312	7.1	13.9
Race/ethnic group:											
White [1]	132,573	9,299	7,837	12,962	17,063	18,569	22,325	22,193	22,325	59.7	49.1
Black [1]..........	75,929	4,032	3,388	5,379	9,118	10,293	13,220	14,609	15,890	25.9	34.9
Hispanic	33,827	2,138	1,803	2,543	4,260	4,358	5,658	6,405	6,662	13.7	14.7
Other/unknown	2,610	95	119	204	278	375	450	494	595	0.6	1.3
Leading States: [2]											
New York	50,985	5,372	3,768	3,948	6,965	5,993	8,389	8,152	8,398	34.5	18.5
California	46,818	3,572	2,656	4,885	5,703	6,426	7,337	7,700	8,539	23.0	18.8
Florida	24,492	1,085	1,028	1,632	2,665	3,449	4,018	5,514	5,101	7.0	11.2
Texas...........	17,363	842	937	1,667	2,215	2,381	3,334	3,067	2,920	5.4	6.4
New Jersey.......	14,702	948	766	1,509	2,452	2,225	2,459	2,303	2,040	6.1	4.5
Illinois	8,229	345	346	629	987	1,132	1,276	1,602	1,912	2.2	4.2
Georgia	7,044	286	304	517	838	1,093	1,228	1,454	1,324	1.8	2.9
Pennsylvania.....	6,967	346	309	653	852	1,071	1,192	1,218	1,326	2.2	2.9
Maryland	5,307	236	188	457	544	713	996	969	1,204	1.5	2.6
Massachusetts.	5,177	297	282	452	710	752	842	967	875	1.9	1.9
District of Columbia .	4,118	291	227	464	494	493	734	709	706	1.9	1.6
Louisiana	3,794	177	165	336	401	508	703	794	710	1.1	1.6
Ohio	3,674	100	213	336	506	488	679	619	733	0.6	1.6
Virginia..........	3,525	176	160	242	348	392	744	679	784	1.1	1.7
Washington.......	3,404	175	168	324	342	526	746	572	551	1.1	1.2
Michigan.........	3,343	105	150	211	455	506	579	619	718	0.7	1.6
Missouri	3,192	85	74	238	411	442	580	654	708	0.5	1.6
Connecticut.......	3,079	171	175	252	412	431	425	567	646	1.1	1.4
North Carolina	2,854	89	81	209	276	444	571	600	584	0.6	1.3
Colorado.........	2,433	126	166	226	324	386	362	433	410	0.8	0.9
Arizona..........	1,943	78	78	214	275	321	309	282	386	0.5	0.8
Tennessee	1,864	25	72	72	329	266	341	351	408	0.2	0.9
South Carolina.....	1,785	56	58	84	174	327	360	335	391	0.4	0.9
Indiana..........	1,744	55	71	132	78	399	292	315	402	0.4	0.9
Alabama.........	1,702	40	33	153	211	214	239	375	437	0.3	1.0
Oregon..........	1,565	55	63	160	177	228	336	257	289	0.4	0.6
Percent of total...	94.4	97.2	95.4	94.9	94.9	94.1	93.8	94.1	93.5	(X)	(X)

X Not applicable.   [1] Non-Hispanic.   [2] States with at least 1,500 total cases reported through 1992.

Source: U.S. Centers for Disease Control and Prevention, Atlanta, GA, unpublished data.

No. 207. Acute Conditions, by Type: 1970 to 1992

[Covers civilian noninstitutional population. Estimates include only acute conditions which were medically attended or caused at least 1 day of restricted activity. Based on National Health Interview Survey; see Appendix III. See headnote, table 201. For composition of regions, see table 26]

YEAR AND CHARACTERISTIC	NUMBER OF CONDITIONS (mil.)					RATE PER 100 POPULATION				
	Infective and parasitic	Respiratory Common cold	Respiratory Influenza	Digestive system	Injuries	Infective and parasitic	Respiratory Common cold	Respiratory Influenza	Digestive system	Injuries
1970	48.2	(NA)	(NA)	23.0	59.2	24.1	(NA)	(NA)	11.5	29.6
1975	47.6	(NA)	(NA)	21.6	76.2	22.8	(NA)	(NA)	10.3	36.4
1980	53.6	(NA)	(NA)	24.9	72.7	24.6	(NA)	(NA)	11.4	33.4
1985	47.8	(NA)	(NA)	16.3	64.0	20.5	(NA)	(NA)	7.0	27.4
1990	51.7	61.5	106.8	13.0	60.1	21.0	25.0	43.4	5.3	24.4
1991	46.1	71.2	129.6	16.5	59.7	18.5	28.6	52.1	6.6	24.0
1992, total [1]	56.2	64.6	107.3	17.6	59.6	22.4	25.7	42.7	7.0	23.7
Under 5 years old	11.6	13.0	11.2	2.5	4.8	59.0	66.1	56.7	12.9	24.5
5 to 17 years old	21.2	16.6	27.7	4.3	13.4	45.2	35.4	59.1	9.2	28.6
18 to 24 years old	5.1	7.2	10.2	1.3	7.6	20.9	29.6	41.8	5.2	31.3
25 to 44 years old	13.2	17.2	37.2	4.7	20.1	16.2	21.1	45.7	5.8	24.8
45 to 64 years old	3.5	6.3	15.3	2.3	7.2	7.1	13.0	31.5	4.7	14.8
65 years old and over	1.8	4.4	5.9	2.5	6.4	5.8	14.2	19.1	8.0	20.9
Male	23.4	28.3	47.6	8.7	32.8	19.1	23.2	39.0	7.1	26.8
Female	32.9	36.3	59.7	8.9	26.8	25.4	28.1	46.2	6.9	20.7
White	48.6	54.3	95.5	14.2	51.2	23.2	25.9	45.6	6.8	24.5
Black	6.6	7.7	8.1	2.4	6.8	20.9	24.5	25.7	7.7	21.7
Northeast	12.2	12.7	16.4	3.1	10.3	24.4	25.5	32.8	6.1	20.6
Midwest	10.9	15.8	31.6	3.7	14.4	17.8	25.7	51.4	6.1	23.4
South	25.2	17.7	25.8	6.0	20.7	29.9	21.0	30.6	7.1	24.6
West	7.9	18.4	33.5	4.8	14.1	14.2	33.1	60.3	8.6	25.5
Family income:										
Under $10,000	6.3	9.2	12.1	1.9	6.2	25.6	37.7	49.5	7.6	25.3
$10,000 to $19,999	6.1	9.3	19.5	3.2	10.8	15.7	24.3	50.9	8.3	28.1
$20,000 to $34,999	13.3	11.7	22.4	3.8	12.6	25.9	22.8	43.7	7.5	24.6
$35,000 or more	22.8	24.7	36.7	6.0	20.7	25.0	27.1	40.2	6.6	22.7

NA Not available.   [1] Includes other races and unknown income not shown separately.

Source: U.S. National Center for Health Statistics, *Vital and Health Statistics*, series 10, No. 189, and earlier reports; and unpublished data.

No. 208. Prevalence of Selected Chronic Conditions, by Age and Sex: 1992

[Covers civilian noninstitutional population. Conditions classified according to ninth revision of International Classification of Diseases. Based on National Health Interview Survey. See headnote, table 201]

CHRONIC CONDITION	Conditions (1,000)	RATE [1]							
		Male				Female			
		Under 45 years old	45 to 64 years old	65 to 74 years old	75 years old and over	Under 45 years old	45 to 64 years old	65 to 74 years old	75 years old and over
Arthritis	33,317	26.1	199.2	364.8	417.2	42.2	315.9	508.7	611.2
Dermatitis, including eczema	10,146	32.6	32.1	33.5	37.9	48.6	50.1	49.0	24.8
Trouble with—									
Dry (itching) skin	5,383	14.5	19.8	25.4	35.3	20.7	31.5	34.3	49.1
Ingrown nails	6,273	21.6	26.1	28.3	[2]29.0	17.0	35.9	47.2	75.7
Corns and calluses	4,433	6.5	24.3	[2]13.9	44.4	11.2	41.4	51.2	58.9
Visual impairments	8,976	31.1	66.0	96.6	131.9	14.5	33.1	49.6	99.4
Cataracts	6,721	2.5	18.7	112.5	193.2	[2]1.7	32.3	137.1	245.2
Hearing impairments	23,777	44.3	216.2	322.3	452.7	30.4	96.9	204.3	392.9
Tinnitus	7,779	11.4	75.2	95.5	113.7	13.5	45.1	77.1	84.6
Deformities or orthopedic impairments	31,605	102.1	181.8	154.9	[2]85.8	100.5	167.4	167.1	243.0
Ulcer	4,408	11.1	23.2	38.4	[2]31.8	13.4	29.5	34.0	26.9
Hernia of abdominal cavity	5,228	11.5	39.0	61.5	64.8	6.5	34.1	57.4	67.5
Frequent indigestion	6,374	19.0	37.9	56.0	34.4	16.9	42.0	43.4	35.7
Frequent constipation	4,296	4.8	12.6	24.9	40.9	16.0	28.2	40.9	88.8
Diabetes	7,417	6.1	52.5	119.6	96.8	9.0	59.2	109.2	110.2
Migraine	10,627	26.0	18.4	[2]15.3	[2]8.4	60.8	80.6	35.4	21.7
Heart conditions	21,584	25.7	150.8	334.7	408.5	32.9	120.3	220.6	401.2
High blood pressure (Hypertension)	27,816	37.5	231.0	341.4	314.7	30.2	222.1	377.7	374.3
Varicose veins of lower extremities	7,281	5.3	26.7	34.3	56.3	24.2	76.9	84.4	101.0
Hemorrhoids	9,562	19.0	77.3	63.9	56.7	30.5	65.6	51.6	68.9
Chronic bronchitis	13,494	41.0	43.6	76.6	40.1	58.0	71.9	80.0	65.9
Asthma	12,375	50.7	32.4	28.9	35.7	53.5	56.6	55.9	32.8
Hay fever, allergic rhinitis without asthma	25,698	102.4	98.2	61.5	63.7	109.2	104.8	103.0	90.5
Chronic sinusitis	36,659	108.5	152.7	123.9	120.2	155.0	219.3	185.4	183.6

[1] Conditions per 1,000 persons.   [2] Figure does not meet standards of reliability or precision.

Source: U.S. National Center for Health Statistics, *Vital and Health Statistics*, series 10, No. 189, and earlier reports; and unpublished data.

No. 209. Substance Abuse Treatment Services: 1992

[As of **September 30.** Based on the National Drug and Alcoholism Treatment Unit Survey (NDATUS), a census of all known drug abuse and alcoholism treatment facilities in the United States. Data collected in cooperation with State agencies which defined what constitutes a facility for reporting purposes]

TYPE OF CARE AND LOCATION	Service locations reporting [1]	All clients	Drug abuse clients only	Alcoholism clients only	Clients with both problems	Clients with a drug problem [2]	Clients with an alcohol problem [3]
Total	9,483	794,755	214,736	290,040	289,979	504,715	580,019
TYPE OF CARE							
Detoxification: [4] Hospital inpatient . .	852	5,071	854	1,535	2,682	3,536	4,217
Free-standing residential.	586	6,020	1,143	2,469	2,408	3,551	4,877
Rehab/residential: [5]							
Hospital inpatient	636	8,540	933	2,410	5,197	6,130	7,607
Short-term—30 days or less	917	16,495	2,328	4,847	9,320	11,648	14,167
Long-term—over 30 days	2,147	58,158	14,797	9,544	33,817	48,614	43,361
Ambulatory: [6]							
Outpatient	6,306	649,317	180,882	256,256	212,179	393,061	468,435
Intensive outpatient [7]	2,135	44,801	8,893	12,463	23,445	32,338	35,908
Detoxification [8]	322	6,353	4,906	516	931	5,837	1,447
UNIT LOCATION							
Community mental health care	1,274	129,913	26,949	56,676	46,288	73,237	102,964
Free-standing nonresidential facility. . .	4,038	423,840	124,363	173,943	125,534	249,897	299,477
Hospital [9]	1,315	82,645	23,281	21,788	37,576	60,857	59,364
Correctional facility	239	24,746	4,408	2,447	17,891	22,299	20,338
Halfway house	800	16,945	2,216	4,939	9,790	12,006	14,729
Other residential facility	1,287	53,670	13,334	13,457	26,879	40,213	40,336
Other site	97	7,033	1,736	2,391	2,906	4,642	5,297
Multiple sites	212	32,827	5,652	11,880	15,295	20,947	27,175
Unknown	221	23,136	12,797	2,519	7,820	20,617	10,339

[1] Some units provide more than one type of treatment but are counted only once in the total.   [2] The sum of clients with a drug problem and clients with both diagnoses.   [3] The sum of clients with an alcohol problem and clients with both diagnoses.   [4] 24 hour care for the withdrawal and transition to ongoing treatment.   [5] Other than detoxification. Provides treatment services for dependency.   [6] Ambulatory care provides care in a nonresidential setting.   [7] "Intensive" outpatient involves at least 2 hours of treatment a day for 3 or more days a week.   [8] Less than 24 hour care.   [9] Includes general hospitals, alcoholism hospitals, mental/psychiatric hospitals, and other specialized hospitals.
Source: U.S. Substance Abuse and Mental Health Services Administration and U.S. Institute on Alcohol Abuse and Alcoholism, "Highlights from the National Drug and Alcoholism Treatment Unit Survey: 1992 and Selected Trends."

No. 210. Drug Use, by Type of Drug and Age Group: 1974 to 1992

[In percent. Current users are those who used drugs at least once within month prior to this study. Based on national samples of respondents residing in households. Subject to sampling variability; see source]

AGE AND TYPE OF DRUG	EVER USED					CURRENT USER				
	1974	1979	1985	1988	1992	1974	1979	1985	1988	1992
12 TO 17 YEARS OLD										
Marijuana	23.0	30.9	23.6	17.4	10.6	12.0	16.7	12.0	6.4	4.0
Cocaine	3.6	5.4	4.9	3.4	1.7	1.0	1.4	1.5	1.1	0.3
Inhalants	8.5	9.8	9.2	8.8	5.7	0.7	2.0	3.4	2.0	1.6
Hallucinogens	6.0	7.1	3.3	3.5	2.6	1.3	2.2	1.2	0.8	0.6
Heroin	1.0	0.5	(B)	0.6	0.2	(B)	(B)	(B)	(B)	0.1
Stimulants [1]	5.0	3.4	5.6	4.2	2.1	1.0	1.2	1.6	1.2	0.2
Sedatives [1]	5.0	3.2	4.1	2.3	1.5	1.0	1.1	1.0	0.6	0.4
Tranquilizers [1]	3.0	4.1	4.8	2.0	1.6	1.0	0.6	0.6	0.2	0.2
Analgesics [1]	(NA)	3.2	5.8	4.1	3.9	(NA)	0.6	0.9	0.9	0.8
Alcohol.	54.0	70.3	55.5	50.2	39.3	34.0	37.2	31.0	25.2	15.7
Cigarettes	52.0	54.1	45.2	42.3	33.7	25.0	12.1	15.3	11.8	9.6
18 TO 25 YEARS OLD										
Marijuana	52.7	68.2	60.3	56.4	48.1	25.2	35.4	21.8	15.5	11.0
Cocaine	12.7	27.5	25.2	19.7	15.8	3.1	9.3	7.6	4.5	1.8
Inhalants	9.2	16.5	12.4	12.5	9.8	(B)	1.2	0.8	1.7	0.8
Hallucinogens	16.6	25.1	11.3	13.8	13.4	2.5	4.4	1.9	1.9	1.3
Heroin	4.5	3.5	1.2	0.3	1.3	(B)	(B)	(B)	(B)	0.2
Stimulants [1]	17.0	18.2	17.1	11.3	6.8	3.7	3.5	3.7	2.4	0.7
Sedatives [1]	15.0	17.0	11.0	5.5	3.2	1.6	2.8	1.6	0.9	0.6
Tranquilizers [1]	10.0	15.8	12.0	7.8	6.8	1.2	2.1	1.6	1.0	0.6
Analgesics [1]	(NA)	11.8	11.3	9.4	8.7	(NA)	1.0	1.8	1.5	1.2
Alcohol.	81.6	95.3	92.6	90.3	86.3	69.3	75.9	71.4	65.3	59.2
Cigarettes	68.8	82.8	75.6	75.0	68.7	48.8	42.6	36.8	35.2	31.9
26 YEARS OLD AND OVER										
Marijuana	9.9	19.6	27.2	30.7	33.0	2.0	6.0	6.1	3.9	3.2
Cocaine	0.9	4.3	9.5	9.9	11.4	(B)	0.9	2.0	0.9	0.5
Inhalants	1.2	3.9	5.0	3.9	3.7	(B)	0.5	0.5	0.2	0.2
Hallucinogens	1.3	4.5	6.2	6.6	7.7	(B)	(B)	(B)	(B)	(B)
Heroin	0.5	1.0	1.1	1.1	0.9	(B)	(B)	(B)	(B)	(B)
Stimulants [1]	3.0	5.8	7.9	6.6	6.7	(B)	0.5	0.7	0.5	0.2
Sedatives [1]	2.0	3.5	5.2	3.3	3.8	(B)	(B)	0.6	0.3	0.3
Tranquilizers [1]	2.0	3.1	7.2	4.5	5.3	(B)	(B)	1.0	0.6	0.4
Analgesics [1]	(NA)	2.7	6.4	4.5	5.1	(NA)	(B)	0.9	0.4	0.7
Alcohol.	73.2	91.5	89.4	88.6	88.1	54.5	61.3	60.6	54.8	50.1
Cigarettes	65.4	83.0	80.5	79.6	76.3	39.1	36.9	32.8	29.8	27.4

B Base too small to meet statistical standards for reliability of a derived figure.   NA Not available.   [1] Nonmedical use; does not include over-the-counter drugs.
Source: U.S. Substance Abuse and Mental Health Services Administration, *National Household Survey on Drug Abuse: 1992.*

No. 211. Use of Selected Drugs, by Age of User: 1992

[In percent. See headnote, table 210. For composition of regions, see table 26]

SUBSTANCE AND AGE GROUP	Total [1]	SEX		RACE/ETHNICITY			REGION			
		Male	Female	White [2]	Black [2]	Hispanic	Northeast	Midwest	South	West
CURRENT USERS										
Cigarettes: Total	26.2	27.9	24.6	26.9	26.7	21.5	24.8	25.5	28.5	24.4
12 to 17 years old	9.6	9.6	9.5	11.6	3.2	7.4	8.2	11.3	9.7	8.4
18 to 25 years old	31.9	32.8	31.1	35.5	20.2	24.1	35.4	35.1	31.7	26.2
26 to 34 years old	33.7	35.4	32.1	35.3	33.5	24.4	32.2	35.3	36.1	29.6
35 years old and over	25.3	27.6	23.3	24.8	32.5	23.3	22.7	22.9	28.5	25.1
Alcohol: Total	47.8	55.9	40.4	49.7	39.8	45.0	52.9	49.2	41.7	52.2
12 to 17 years old	15.7	16.9	14.5	16.7	13.2	16.2	14.3	18.1	14.5	16.2
18 to 25 years old	59.2	65.6	53.0	62.9	50.9	52.8	67.2	60.3	55.4	57.8
26 to 34 years old	61.2	70.0	52.8	63.7	55.6	56.1	66.8	61.7	56.2	64.1
35 years old and over	46.5	56.1	38.0	47.8	37.2	44.9	51.1	48.5	38.4	53.4
Marijuana: Total	4.4	5.9	2.9	4.4	5.2	3.7	4.2	3.7	3.9	6.0
12 to 17 years old	4.0	4.6	3.5	4.1	3.4	4.8	2.9	4.7	3.2	5.7
18 to 25 years old	11.0	14.5	7.5	11.6	11.2	8.0	13.4	9.0	10.6	11.5
26 to 34 years old	8.2	11.0	5.5	8.8	8.2	5.6	9.1	5.9	7.7	10.8
35 years old and over	1.6	2.3	1.0	1.6	2.5	0.7	0.9	1.8	1.1	3.0
Cocaine: Total	0.6	0.9	0.4	0.5	1.0	1.2	0.8	0.6	0.4	0.8
12 to 17 years old	0.3	0.2	0.3	0.1	0.2	1.2	0.3	([3])	0.3	0.5
18 to 25 years old	1.8	2.9	0.8	2.0	1.4	1.8	2.4	2.2	1.1	2.3
26 to 34 years old	1.4	1.7	1.1	1.2	1.7	2.4	2.5	1.1	0.9	1.5
35 years old and over	0.2	0.3	0.1	0.1	0.8	0.4	0.1	0.2	0.2	0.3
Smokeless tobacco: Total	3.7	7.1	0.5	4.3	2.0	0.7	1.5	2.8	6.2	2.3
12 to 17 years old	2.6	4.8	0.3	3.6	0.4	0.3	1.1	2.7	4.1	1.2
18 to 25 years old	6.0	11.7	0.4	8.0	0.5	1.4	2.8	7.1	7.3	5.2
26 to 34 years old	3.9	7.6	0.3	4.7	1.3	1.4	2.2	3.3	5.8	2.7
35 years old and over	3.2	6.2	0.6	3.5	3.1	0.2	1.1	1.8	6.4	1.6
EVER USED										
Crack: Total	1.4	1.9	0.9	1.2	2.5	1.3	1.2	1.0	1.3	2.0
12 to 17 years old	0.6	0.7	0.6	0.7	0.4	1.0	0.6	0.2	0.9	0.7
18 to 25 years old	3.2	4.5	2.0	3.3	3.7	2.2	3.0	2.9	3.1	3.9
26 to 34 years old	3.3	4.6	2.1	3.1	5.6	2.5	3.7	2.0	3.1	4.6
35 years old and over	0.4	0.6	0.3	0.3	1.4	0.3	0.1	0.4	0.3	0.9
Inhalants: Total	4.8	6.5	3.2	5.3	2.1	4.4	4.8	4.3	4.4	5.9
12 to 17 years old	5.7	5.6	5.7	6.2	3.1	6.5	4.2	5.6	5.9	6.6
18 to 25 years old	9.8	12.0	7.7	11.7	2.8	6.6	10.2	9.7	8.5	11.7
26 to 34 years old	9.2	12.6	5.8	10.9	2.8	6.4	10.6	7.0	8.2	11.9
35 years old and over	2.0	3.2	0.9	2.2	1.3	1.7	1.9	2.0	1.8	2.3
Hallucinogens: Total	8.0	10.3	5.8	9.3	2.6	5.1	8.0	7.3	6.2	11.9
12 to 17 years old	2.6	2.4	2.9	3.2	0.2	2.8	2.4	1.7	2.3	4.4
18 to 25 years old	13.4	15.9	11.1	16.5	3.0	8.1	16.2	12.6	11.2	15.9
26 to 34 years old	15.6	19.6	11.7	19.2	3.7	8.4	17.4	14.8	13.0	19.2
35 years old and over	5.2	7.3	3.4	5.8	2.7	2.8	4.1	4.8	3.5	9.7
Stimulants: [4] Total	6.3	7.3	5.3	7.3	1.9	4.1	4.7	5.2	4.9	11.2
12 to 17 years old	2.1	1.7	2.5	2.2	1.3	2.4	1.3	1.3	2.6	2.7
18 to 25 years old	6.8	7.0	6.6	8.3	0.9	4.9	4.1	6.4	5.8	11.1
26 to 34 years old	11.9	14.3	9.6	14.4	3.1	7.0	10.6	8.1	12.0	17.0
35 years old and over	5.0	6.0	4.2	5.8	1.9	2.7	3.5	4.8	2.8	10.7
Sedatives: [4] Total	3.5	4.1	2.9	3.9	1.8	2.1	2.9	3.3	3.2	4.7
12 to 17 years old	1.5	0.9	2.1	1.5	1.1	1.5	0.9	1.2	2.0	1.3
18 to 25 years old	3.2	4.4	2.1	3.8	0.6	2.7	2.0	3.2	3.5	3.9
26 to 34 years old	6.3	7.8	4.9	7.6	3.3	3.0	6.2	5.0	7.8	5.4
35 years old and over	2.9	3.3	2.6	3.3	1.7	1.6	2.4	3.2	1.8	5.2
Tranquilizers: [4] Total	5.1	5.8	4.6	5.9	2.1	3.1	4.5	4.0	4.9	7.4
12 to 17 years old	1.6	1.5	1.6	1.7	0.8	0.8	1.5	1.1	1.9	1.6
18 to 25 years old	6.8	7.8	5.8	8.2	1.9	4.0	4.4	5.9	8.8	6.0
26 to 34 years old	9.0	10.6	7.4	10.8	4.0	4.4	9.2	5.6	11.4	8.3
35 years old and over	4.1	4.4	3.9	4.7	1.7	2.6	3.6	3.6	2.3	8.5
Analgesics: [4] Total	5.5	6.1	4.9	6.0	3.8	4.1	4.4	5.0	5.3	7.4
12 to 17 years old	3.9	3.3	4.6	3.7	4.3	3.9	2.4	3.9	4.4	4.4
18 to 25 years old	8.7	9.2	8.2	10.1	4.3	5.8	7.0	9.0	8.5	10.3
26 to 34 years old	10.0	11.6	8.6	11.5	6.8	6.0	9.4	8.2	10.5	11.7
35 years old and over	3.5	4.0	3.1	3.8	2.4	2.4	2.6	3.3	3.0	5.7

[1] Includes other races, not shown separately.   [2] Non-Hispanic.   [3] Low precision; no estimate reported.   [4] Nonmedical use; does not include over-the-counter drugs.

Source: U.S. Substance Abuse and Mental Health Services Administration, *National Household Survey on Drug Abuse, 1992.*

No. 212. Current Cigarette Smoking: 1965 to 1991

[In percent. A current smoker is a person who has smoked at least 100 cigarettes and who now smokes; includes occasional smokers. Excludes unknown smoking status. Based on the National Health Interview Survey; for details, see Appendix III]

SEX, AGE, AND RACE	1965	1974	1979	1983	1985	1987	1988	1990	1991
Total smokers, 18 years old and over	**42.4**	**37.1**	**33.5**	**32.1**	**30.1**	**28.8**	**28.1**	**25.5**	**25.6**
Male, total	51.9	43.1	37.5	35.1	32.6	31.2	30.8	28.4	28.1
18 to 24 years	54.1	42.1	35.0	32.9	28.0	28.2	25.5	26.6	23.5
25 to 34 years	60.7	50.5	43.9	38.8	38.2	34.8	36.2	31.6	32.8
35 to 44 years	58.2	51.0	41.8	41.0	37.6	36.6	36.5	34.5	33.1
45 to 64 years	51.9	42.6	39.3	35.9	33.4	33.5	31.3	29.3	29.3
65 years and over	28.5	24.8	20.9	22.0	19.6	17.2	18.0	14.6	15.1
White, total	51.1	41.9	36.8	34.5	31.7	30.5	30.1	28.0	27.4
18 to 24 years	53.0	40.8	34.3	32.5	28.4	29.2	26.7	27.4	25.1
25 to 34 years	60.1	49.5	43.6	38.6	37.3	33.8	35.4	31.6	32.1
35 to 44 years	57.3	50.1	41.3	40.8	36.6	36.2	35.8	33.5	32.1
45 to 64 years	51.3	41.2	38.3	35.0	32.1	32.4	30.0	28.7	28.0
65 years and over	27.7	24.3	20.5	20.6	18.9	16.0	16.9	13.7	13.7
Black, total	60.4	54.3	44.1	40.6	39.9	39.0	36.5	32.5	35.0
18 to 24 years	62.8	54.9	40.2	34.2	27.2	24.9	18.6	21.3	15.0
25 to 34 years	68.4	58.5	47.5	39.9	45.6	44.9	41.6	33.8	39.4
35 to 44 years	67.3	61.5	48.6	45.5	45.0	44.0	42.5	42.0	44.4
45 to 64 years	57.9	57.8	50.0	44.8	46.1	44.3	43.2	36.7	42.0
65 years and over	36.4	29.7	26.2	38.9	27.7	30.3	29.8	21.5	24.3
Female, total	33.9	32.1	29.9	29.5	27.9	26.5	25.7	22.8	23.5
18 to 24 years	38.1	34.1	33.8	35.5	30.4	26.1	26.3	22.5	22.4
25 to 34 years	43.7	38.8	33.7	32.6	32.0	31.8	31.3	28.2	28.4
35 to 44 years	43.7	39.8	37.0	33.8	31.5	29.6	27.8	24.8	27.6
45 to 64 years	32.0	33.4	30.7	31.0	29.9	28.6	27.7	24.8	24.6
65 years and over	9.6	12.0	13.2	13.1	13.5	13.7	12.8	11.5	12.0
White, total	34.0	31.7	30.1	29.4	27.7	26.7	25.7	23.4	23.7
18 to 24 years	38.4	34.0	34.5	36.5	31.8	27.8	27.5	25.4	25.1
25 to 34 years	43.4	38.6	34.1	32.2	32.0	31.9	31.0	28.5	28.4
35 to 44 years	43.9	39.3	37.2	34.8	31.0	29.2	28.3	25.0	27.0
45 to 64 years	32.7	33.0	30.6	30.6	29.7	29.0	27.7	25.4	25.3
65 years and over	9.8	12.3	13.8	13.2	13.3	13.9	12.6	11.5	12.1
Black, total	33.7	36.4	31.1	32.2	31.0	28.0	27.8	21.2	24.4
18 to 24 years	37.1	35.6	31.8	32.0	23.7	20.4	21.8	10.0	11.8
25 to 34 years	47.8	42.2	35.2	38.0	36.2	35.8	37.2	29.1	32.4
35 to 44 years	42.8	46.4	37.7	32.7	40.2	35.3	27.6	25.5	35.3
45 to 64 years	25.7	38.9	34.2	36.3	33.4	28.4	29.5	22.6	23.4
65 years and over	7.1	8.9	8.5	13.1	14.5	11.7	14.8	11.1	9.6

Source: U.S. National Center for Health Statistics, Health, United States, 1992.

No. 213. Cancer—Estimated New Cases, 1993, and Survival Rates, 1974-76 to 1983-89

[The 5-year relative survival rate, which is derived by adjusting the observed survival rate for expected mortality, represents the liklihood that a person will not die from causes directly related to their cancer within 5 years. Survival data shown are based on those patients diagnosed while residents of an area listed below during the time periods shown. Data are based on information collected as part of the National Cancer Institute's Surveillance, Epidemiology and End Results (SEER) program, a collection of population-based registries in Connecticut, New Mexico, Utah, Iowa, Hawaii, Atlanta, Detroit, Seattle-Puget Sound, and San Francisco-Oakland]

SITE	ESTIMATED NEW CASES,[1] 1993 (1,000)			5-YEAR RELATIVE SURVIVAL RATES (percent)							
				White				Black			
	Total	Male	Female	1974 -76	1977 -79	1980 -82	1983 -89	1974 -76	1977 -79	1980 -82	1983 -89
All sites[2]	1,170	600	570	50.2	50.7	51.5	54.5	38.7	38.8	39.1	39.4
Lung	170	100	70	11.0	12.0	12.0	13.4	11.3	11.0	12.1	11.2
Breast[3]	183	1	182	74.8	75.1	76.7	80.5	62.9	62.5	65.6	64.1
Colon	109	53	56	50.2	52.7	55.3	59.3	45.5	47.6	48.7	48.7
Prostate	165	165	(X)	67.6	71.7	74.0	79.4	57.7	61.9	63.9	64.4
Bladder	52	39	13	73.6	75.6	78.6	79.9	47.8	54.8	57.5	60.9
Rectum	43	24	19	48.6	50.4	52.7	57.5	41.6	37.7	37.7	45.2
Corpus uteri	31	(X)	31	88.6	86.1	82.5	84.6	60.4	57.8	53.6	55.5
Non-Hodgkin's lymphoma[4]	43	24	19	47.5	48.1	51.4	52.3	47.8	49.6	50.0	43.8
Oral cavity and pharynx	30	20	10	54.8	54.1	54.9	54.4	35.7	36.0	30.4	32.6
Leukemia[4]	29	17	13	34.5	37.2	37.5	38.7	31.1	30.1	31.5	30.4
Melanoma of skin	32	17	15	79.8	81.5	81.9	84.2	68.5	51.7	59.5	72.3
Pancreas	28	14	14	2.7	2.2	2.8	3.0	2.2	3.8	4.8	4.9
Kidney	27	17	10	51.5	50.6	50.7	55.7	48.6	52.4	55.1	51.1
Stomach	24	15	9	14.4	16.1	16.1	17.1	16.4	15.3	19.1	17.8
Ovary	22	(X)	22	36.2	37.5	38.6	40.2	40.7	39.5	37.3	40.2
Cervix uteri[5]	14	(X)	14	69.2	68.8	67.3	69.1	63.2	61.8	60.1	57.0

X Not applicable. [1] Estimates provided by American Cancer Society are based on rates from the National Cancer Institute's SEER program. [2] Includes other sites not shown separately. [3] Survival rates for female only. [4] All types combined. [5] Invasive cancer only.

Source: U.S. National Institutes of Health, National Cancer Institute, Cancer Statistics Review, annual.

Health and Nutrition

No. 214. Women—Selected Health Practices: 1990

[Based on the National Health Interview Survey and subject to sampling error; for details see source and Appendix III]

CHARACTERISTIC	POPULATION 18 YEARS AND OVER						POPULATION 35 YEARS AND OVER		
	Total (1,000)	Percent who—					Total (1,000)	Percent who had a mammogram	
		Had a breast exam [1]	Knew how to do BSE [2]	Did a BSE monthly [2][3]	Had a PAP smear [4]			Ever	In the past 3 years
Total [5]	**95,169**	**53.1**	**88.1**	**43.1**	**50.1**		**59,934**	**57.7**	**50.5**
Race:									
White..............	81,255	53.1	88.8	42.3	49.7		52,188	58.9	51.5
Black..............	11,212	55.3	86.0	50.9	54.3		6,282	51.3	44.9
Hispanic origin:									
Hispanic...........	7,709	50.4	74.7	44.1	49.1		3,704	49.4	42.3
Non-Hispanic	87,151	53.4	89.2	43.1	50.1		56,029	58.2	51.0
Marital status:									
Currently married......	58,398	55.8	90.6	44.5	53.5		38,074	61.5	55.0
Formerly married......	21,650	45.5	84.8	43.8	39.1		18,536	51.7	43.4
Never married.......	15,031	53.1	82.8	36.4	51.5		3,312	47.4	38.9
Educational attainment:									
Less than 12 years	20,326	43.0	76.9	43.9	37.9		14,714	44.9	37.4
12 years...........	38,634	52.2	89.7	43.6	49.6		24,234	59.0	51.8
More than 12 years	35,964	59.7	92.8	42.2	57.2		20,798	65.5	58.5
Income:									
Less than $10,000.....	11,930	45.5	80.0	42.2	41.0		7,203	40.9	32.7
$10,000 to $19,999	16,740	47.0	85.3	43.0	44.0		10,408	50.3	42.5
$20,000 to $34,999	20,445	53.0	90.6	42.3	50.1		11,948	58.9	52.0
$35,000 to $49,999	14,149	58.3	93.3	43.1	55.2		8,545	62.9	56.6
$50,000 or more	17,405	61.4	92.5	41.5	58.9		11,710	71.4	64.5

[1] In the past year by a professional.   [2] BSE=Breast self-examination.   [3] On average over the past year.   [4] In the past year.   [5] Includes persons whose characteristics are unknown.

Source: U.S. National Center for Health Statistics, *Health Promotion and Disease Prevention, United States 1990, Vital and Health Statistics,* series 10, No. 185.

No. 215. Personal Health Practices, by Selected Characteristic: 1990

[In percent, except total persons. For persons 18 years of age and over. See headnote, table 214]

CHARACTERISTIC	Total persons (1,000)	Eats breakfast [1]	Rarely snacks	Exercised regularly [2]	Had two or more drinks on any day [3]	Current smoker	20 percent or more above weight [4]
All persons [5]	**181,447**	**56.4**	**25.5**	**40.7**	**5.5**	**25.5**	**27.5**
Sex:							
Male..................	86,278	54.6	25.6	44.0	9.7	28.4	29.6
Female	95,169	58.0	25.4	37.7	1.7	22.8	25.6
Race:							
White	155,301	57.8	25.8	41.5	5.8	25.6	26.7
Black	20,248	46.9	22.7	34.3	4.3	26.2	38.0
Hispanic origin:							
Hispanic	14,314	52.5	29.3	34.9	4.6	23.0	27.6
Non-Hispanic	166,599	56.7	25.2	41.2	5.6	25.7	27.5
Marital status:							
Currently married..........	117,413	57.8	25.3	39.4	5.3	24.6	29.2
Formerly married..........	30,439	61.5	31.2	34.3	5.3	30.3	29.1
Never married............	33,413	46.9	20.9	51.3	6.6	24.3	19.8
Education level:							
Less than 12 years	38,367	58.6	26.9	25.9	5.1	31.8	32.7
12 years	69,405	52.6	24.0	37.0	5.9	29.6	28.6
More than 12 years	73,244	58.8	26.4	52.1	5.4	18.3	23.8
Income:							
Less than $10,000.........	18,469	54.1	27.6	32.9	4.8	31.6	29.3
$10,000 to $19,999	30,452	56.6	25.9	32.3	4.9	29.8	28.5
$20,000 to $34,999	40,216	55.2	25.1	40.5	5.8	26.9	28.2
$35,000 to $49,999	29,795	53.7	23.8	46.1	5.6	23.4	27.8
$50,000 or more	36,199	57.2	25.8	51.7	6.7	19.3	24.9

[1] Almost every day.   [2] Or played sports regularly.   [3] On average per day in the past 2 weeks.   [4] Above desirable weight. Based on 1983 Metropolitan Life Insurance Company standards. Height and weight data are self-reported.   [5] Includes persons whose characteristics are unknown.

Source: U.S. National Center for Health Statistics, *Health Promotion and Disease Prevention: United States, 1990, Vital and Health Statistics,* series 10, No. 185.

No. 216. Medical Device Implants, by Age, Sex, and Race: 1988
[In thousands, except percent. Based in the National Health Interview Survey; for details, see Appendix III]

DEVICE	Total [1]	PERCENT DISTRIBUTION							
		Age				Sex		Race	
		Under 18 years old	18-44 years old	45-64 years old	65 years old and over	Male	Female	White	Black
Artificial joints [2]	1,625	[3]0.6	13.0	24.6	61.7	39.9	60.1	92.3	6.2
Hip joints	816	[3]0.5	6.5	26.3	66.7	37.5	62.4	93.5	5.5
Knee joints	521	-	10.9	20.5	68.5	41.8	58.2	88.1	10.0
Fixation devices [4]	4,890	3.9	44.3	28.4	23.4	57.2	42.8	91.7	6.6
Head	351	[3]4.3	67.8	22.8	[3]5.4	57.3	42.7	93.2	[3]4.8
Torso	563	[3]5.3	49.6	31.8	13.3	62.7	37.5	92.2	[3]6.9
Upper extremities	646	[3]3.7	55.9	25.4	15.0	70.4	29.7	91.6	[3]5.6
Lower extremities	2,690	3.0	39.6	27.9	29.4	52.8	47.2	91.1	7.7
Other	622	[3]6.4	34.4	34.1	25.1	57.9	42.1	93.6	[3]3.7
Other devices:									
Ear vent tubes	1,494	[5]25.8	[6]27.0	[7]34.6	[8]12.6	39.9	61.1	92.3	[6]6.2
Silicone implants	620	[3]0.5	73.1	23.7	[3]2.9	8.2	91.8	97.6	[3]0.8
Breast implants	544	[3]0.6	73.0	24.1	[3]2.6	[3]2.0	98.0	98.5	-
Shunt or catheter	321	[3]4.3	24.3	22.1	[3]29.3	50.5	49.2	85.7	[3]12.5
Dental implants	275	[3]2.2	57.8	27.3	[3]12.7	56.4	43.6	93.8	[3]4.0
Heart valve	279	(NA)	[9]14.7	35.5	49.8	52.3	47.8	89.2	10.0
Pacemaker	460	(NA)	(NA)	[10]13.5	86.7	50.4	49.6	93.7	[3]5.2
Eye lens	3,765	(NA)	(NA)	[10]18.7	81.3	37.6	62.4	95.6	3.5

- Represents or rounds to zero. NA Not available. [1] Includes other races not shown separately. [2] Includes other devices not shown separately. [3] Figure does not meet standards of reliability or precision. [4] Includes sites unknown. Each device represents a single body part regardless of the number of pins, screws, nails, wires, rods, or plates. [5] Under 3 years old. [6] 3 to 5 years old. [7] 6 to 17 years old. [8] 18 years old and over. [9] Under 45 years old. [10] Under 65 years old.
Source: U.S. National Center for Health Statistics, *National Health Interview Survey*, 1988; unpublished data.

No. 217. Persons Using Devices or Features to Assist With Impairments, by Age: 1990
[In percent, except as indicated. For the civilian noninstitutionalized population. Based on the Current Population Survey; see text, section 1, and Appendix III]

DEVICE OR FEATURE	Total	Under 25 years old	25 to 44 years old	45 to 64 years old	65 to 74 years old	75 years old and over
Persons using assistive technology devices [1] (1,000)	13,128	1,048	2,228	3,022	2,756	4,073
Anatomical devices	28.4	61.7	61.4	34.8	14.1	6.8
Leg brace	6.6	19.9	12.9	6.9	3.5	1.5
Foot brace	1.4	6.8	2.0	1.0	1.1	[2]0.3
Arm brace	1.6	2.7	3.9	2.0	0.7	[2]0.3
Hand brace	1.6	2.7	4.2	2.1	0.8	[2]0.1
Neck brace	2.3	2.6	5.3	3.6	1.0	[2]0.4
Back brace	8.9	6.5	18.8	15.2	4.6	2.4
Other brace	6.5	[2]3.0	16.6	4.8	1.7	1.2
Artificial leg or foot	1.4	[2]0.8	1.3	2.1	1.7	0.9
Artificial arm or hand	0.3	1.1	[2]0.2	[2]0.3	[2]0.3	[2].
Mobility devices	48.8	22.9	27.3	45.8	52.1	67.2
Crutch	5.1	8.3	7.8	6.9	5.0	1.6
Cane or walking stick	33.5	3.0	14.3	33.5	37.4	49.3
Walker	12.9	3.2	3.2	9.1	12.7	23.5
Wheelchair	10.8	13.3	7.6	10.0	11.8	11.7
Scooter	0.5	[2]0.6	[2]0.5	[2]0.6	[2]0.7	[2]0.3
Other mobility devices	1.9	[2]1.7	1.3	2.2	2.1	2.1
Hearing devices	30.4	14.5	11.5	27.1	41.4	39.7
Hearing aid	28.8	14.1	10.2	24.6	40.0	38.3
TDD/TTY [3]	1.3	2.1	1.0	1.8	0.9	1.2
Special Alarm	0.6	[2]0.7	[2]0.8	0.8	[2]0.2	0.6
Other hearing devices	4.3	2.3	2.5	4.5	5.1	5.0
Source of payment [4]	100.0	100.0	100.0	100.0	100.0	100.0
Out-of-pocket	48.2	34.0	37.5	45.5	52.5	56.0
Third party	34.0	45.0	49.2	37.1	28.7	24.8
Combination	17.9	21.0	13.3	17.4	18.7	19.2
Persons using home accessibility features (1,000)	7,102	1,395	1,272	1,484	1,284	1,667
Ramps	29.7	41.4	36.0	32.8	25.0	16.0
Extra-wide doors	23.2	28.5	26.2	27.6	19.4	15.8
Elevator or stair lift	5.8	4.7	2.2	3.0	7.6	10.4
Hand rails	47.8	30.5	33.0	46.2	60.6	65.2
Raised toilet	18.6	9.0	10.5	19.2	21.5	30.3
Adaptive door locks	5.8	4.1	2.3	6.1	6.7	8.9
Lowered counters	3.4	3.7	3.7	4.0	1.7	3.7
Slip-resistant floors	3.0	2.9	3.2	5.3	1.9	1.6
Other features	22.5	22.4	24.6	23.3	22.8	19.8
Source of payment [4]	100.0	100.0	100.0	100.0	100.0	100.0
Out-of-pocket	77.5	76.1	77.9	74.6	81.6	78.1
Third party	15.2	17.9	15.4	16.1	11.7	15.0
Combination	7.3	6.0	6.7	9.3	6.8	6.9

- Represents or rounds to zero. [1] Includes other devices, not shown separately. Excludes any implanted devices, such as pacemakers. [2] Figure does not meet standards of reliability or precision. [3] TDD/TTY is a typewriter-like device for the deaf that communicates over telephone lines using text. [4] Excludes persons who indicated no payment or gift.
Source: U.S. National Center for Health Statistics, *Advance Data from Vital and Health Statistics*, No. 217, September 16, 1992.

No. 218. Cumulative Percent Distribution of Population, by Height and Sex: 1976-80

[For persons 18 to 74 years old. Height was measured without shoes. Based on sample and subject to sampling variability; see source]

HEIGHT	MALES						FEMALES					
	18-24 years	25-34 years	35-44 years	45-54 years	55-64 years	65-74 years	18-24 years	25-34 years	35-44 years	45-54 years	55-64 years	65-74 years
Percent under—												
4'8"	-	-	-	-	-	-	0.05	-	0.10	0.28	0.46	1.04
4'9"	-	-	-	-	-	-	0.43	0.23	0.34	0.35	1.07	2.27
4'10"	-	-	-	-	-	-	0.94	0.64	0.95	1.22	3.02	4.23
4'11"	-	-	-	-	-	-	2.22	1.65	1.94	4.20	6.43	9.33
5'	0.18	0.05	0.27	-	0.27	0.24	4.22	3.65	4.56	8.88	11.40	17.20
5'1"	0.18	0.31	0.34	0.19	0.72	1.22	9.13	8.60	7.75	16.16	19.70	29.00
5'2"	0.34	0.42	0.87	0.70	0.92	2.66	17.75	19.11	18.24	27.68	31.71	44.34
5'3"	0.61	0.54	2.07	1.50	2.78	5.97	29.06	32.96	33.11	39.83	45.87	59.15
5'4"	2.37	1.55	3.68	2.55	5.28	10.53	41.81	47.43	49.90	57.21	63.89	76.44
5'5"	3.85	4.36	6.36	5.72	9.29	18.31	58.09	61.36	63.88	70.47	77.44	86.97
5'6"	8.24	9.51	12.39	11.39	17.54	29.42	74.76	74.92	78.07	84.64	88.91	94.63
5'7"	16.18	15.25	17.63	21.24	29.10	41.63	85.37	85.65	87.95	91.21	94.56	97.86
5'8"	26.68	26.69	26.40	33.56	43.53	57.75	92.30	93.28	93.43	96.28	97.70	99.20
5'9"	38.89	39.68	42.52	50.39	58.21	69.96	96.23	97.19	97.18	98.17	99.36	99.81
5'10"	53.66	55.35	57.01	63.38	71.51	81.95	98.34	99.49	99.19	99.58	99.78	99.92
5'11"	68.25	69.67	70.70	76.94	83.09	89.59	99.38	99.68	99.39	99.84	99.81	100.00
6'	80.14	81.58	81.15	85.83	90.99	94.52	100.00	100.00	100.00	100.00	100.00	100.00
6'1"	88.54	89.95	90.04	93.43	96.28	97.82	100.00	100.00	100.00	100.00	100.00	100.00
6'2"	92.74	95.57	95.05	98.01	97.66	99.17	100.00	100.00	100.00	100.00	100.00	100.00
6'3"	96.17	97.98	97.82	99.35	98.90	99.86	100.00	100.00	100.00	100.00	100.00	100.00
6'4"	98.40	99.23	99.19	99.70	99.79	100.00	100.00	100.00	100.00	100.00	100.00	100.00

- Represents or rounds to zero.

Source: U.S. National Center for Health Statistics, *Vital and Health Statistics*, series 11, No. 238.

No. 219. Nutrition—Nutrients in Foods Available for Civilian Consumption per Capita per Day: 1950 to 1990

[Computed by the Human Nutrition Information Service (HNIS). Based on Economic Research Service (ERS) estimates of per capita quantities of food available for consumption from "Food Consumption, Prices, and Expenditures," on imputed consumption data for foods no longer reported by ERS, and on HNIS estimates of quantities of produce from home gardens. Food supply estimates do not reflect loss of food or nutrients from further marketing or home processing. Enrichment and fortification levels of iron, thiamin, riboflavin, niacin, vitamin A, vitamin B_6, vitamin B_{12}, and ascorbic acid are included. See *Historical Statistics, Colonial Times to 1970*, series G 851-856 for related details]

NUTRIENT	Unit	1950-59	1960-69	1970-79	1980-89	1990
Food energy	Calories	3,100	3,200	3,300	3,500	3,700
Carbohydrate	Grams	382	374	388	416	452
Protein	Grams	93	96	99	101	105
Total fat [1]	Grams	141	150	158	165	165
Saturated	Grams	60	62	59	60	59
Monounsaturated	Grams	57	61	64	66	67
Polyunsaturated	Grams	18	22	29	32	32
Cholesterol	Milligrams	510	490	460	440	410
Vitamin A	Micrograms RE [2]	1,310	1,320	1,530	1,460	1,420
Carotenes	Micrograms RE [2]	420	410	570	580	620
Vitamin E	Milligrams α-TE [3]	11.7	12.4	13.6	14.7	15.7
Vitamin C	Milligrams	101	96	110	112	105
Thiamin	Milligrams	1.9	2	2.2	2.4	2.5
Riboflavin	Milligrams	2.4	2.3	2.4	2.5	2.6
Niacin	Milligrams	20.4	21.8	24.6	26.6	27.9
Vitamin B_6	Milligrams	1.9	1.9	2.1	2.1	2.2
Folacin	Micrograms	306	289	294	294	296
Vitamin B_{12}	Micrograms	9.2	9.8	10.1	9.2	8.7
Calcium	Milligrams	940	880	860	880	920
Phosphorus	Milligrams	1,500	1,490	1,500	1,530	1,600
Magnesium	Milligrams	330	320	320	330	350
Iron	Milligrams	14.7	15	18.9	17.8	19.3
Zinc	Milligrams	11.9	12.2	12.6	12.6	12.7
Copper	Milligrams	1.7	1.6	1.6	1.7	1.7
Potassium	Milligrams	3,650	3,510	3,480	3,480	3,540

[1] Includes other types of fat not shown separately. [2] Retinol equivalents. [3] Alpha-Tocopherol equivalents.

Source: U.S. Dept. of Agriculture, Human Nutrition Information Service. Data published by Economic Research Service in *Food Consumption, Prices, and Expenditures*, annual; and *National Food Review*, quarterly.

No. 220. Per Capita Consumption of Major Food Commodities: 1970 to 1992

[In pounds, retail weight except as indicated. Consumption represents the residual after exports, nonfood use and ending stocks are subtracted from the sum of beginning stocks, domestic production, and imports. Based on Bureau of the Census estimated population. Estimates reflect revisions based on the 1990 Census of Population. For similar but unrevised data, see *Historical Statistics, Colonial Times to 1970*, series G 881-915]

COMMODITY	1970	1975	1980	1985	1989	1990	1991	1992
Red meat, total (boneless, trimmed weight) [1][2]	131.7	125.8	126.4	124.9	115.9	112.4	111.9	114.1
Beef	79.6	83.0	72.1	74.6	65.4	64.0	63.1	62.8
Veal	2.0	2.8	1.3	1.5	1.0	0.9	0.8	0.8
Lamb and mutton	2.1	1.3	1.0	1.1	1.1	1.1	1.0	1.0
Pork (excluding lard)	48.0	38.7	52.1	47.7	48.4	46.4	46.9	49.5
Fish and shellfish (edible weight) [3]	11.7	12.1	12.4	15.0	15.6	15.0	14.8	14.7
Fresh and frozen	6.9	7.5	7.8	9.7	10.2	9.6	9.6	9.8
Canned	4.4	4.2	4.3	5.0	5.1	5.1	4.9	4.6
Tuna	2.5	2.8	3.0	3.3	3.9	3.7	3.6	3.5
Cured	0.4	0.4	0.3	0.3	0.3	0.3	0.3	0.3
Poultry products: (boneless weight) [2][4]	33.8	32.9	40.6	45.2	53.6	55.9	58.0	60.1
Chicken	27.7	26.4	32.5	36.1	40.5	42.1	43.9	45.9
Turkey	6.4	6.5	8.1	9.1	13.1	13.8	14.1	14.2
Eggs (farm weight) (number)	309.0	276.0	271.0	255.0	236.0	233.0	233.0	234.0
Dairy products:								
Total (milk equivalent, milkfat basis) [5]	563.8	539.1	543.2	593.7	565.2	569.7	565.2	564.6
Fluid milk and cream [6]	275.1	261.4	245.6	241.0	236.4	233.4	233.1	230.8
Beverage milks	269.1	254.0	237.4	229.7	224.3	221.7	221.5	218.5
Plain whole milk	213.5	174.9	141.7	119.7	94.5	87.6	84.7	81.4
Plain lowfat milk	29.8	53.2	70.1	83.3	96.3	98.3	99.7	99.3
Plain skim milk	11.6	11.5	11.6	12.6	20.2	22.9	23.9	25.0
Flavored whole milk	5.6	6.3	4.7	3.7	3.1	2.8	2.7	2.7
Flavored lowfat and skim milks	3.0	3.3	5.3	6.0	6.5	6.6	6.8	6.9
Buttermilk	5.5	4.7	4.1	4.4	3.7	3.5	3.4	3.2
Yogurt (excl. frozen)	0.8	2.1	2.6	4.1	4.3	4.1	4.2	4.3
Cream [7]	3.8	3.3	3.4	4.4	4.8	4.6	4.6	4.8
Sour cream and dip	1.1	1.6	1.8	2.3	2.5	2.5	2.6	2.7
Condensed and evaporated milk:								
Whole milk	7.0	5.1	3.8	3.6	3.1	3.0	3.1	3.3
Skim milk	5.0	3.5	3.3	3.8	4.7	4.8	5.0	5.2
Cheese [8]	11.4	14.3	17.5	22.5	23.8	24.6	25.0	26.0
American	7.0	8.2	9.6	12.2	11.0	11.1	11.1	11.3
Cheddar	5.8	6.0	6.9	9.8	9.2	9.1	9.0	9.2
Italian	2.1	3.2	4.4	6.5	8.5	9.0	9.4	10.0
Mozzarella	1.2	2.1	3.0	4.6	6.4	6.9	7.2	7.7
Other [9]	2.3	2.9	3.4	3.9	4.3	4.6	4.6	4.7
Swiss	0.9	1.1	1.3	1.3	1.2	1.4	1.2	1.2
Cream and Neufchatel	0.6	0.7	1.0	1.2	1.6	1.7	1.8	2.0
Cottage cheese	5.2	4.6	4.5	4.1	3.6	3.4	3.3	3.1
Ice cream	17.8	18.6	17.5	18.1	16.1	15.8	16.3	16.4
Ice milk	7.7	7.6	7.1	6.9	8.4	7.7	7.4	7.1
Fats and oils:								
Total, fat content only [10]	52.6	52.6	57.2	64.3	60.4	62.2	63.8	65.6
Butter (product weight)	5.4	4.7	4.5	4.9	4.4	4.4	4.2	4.2
Margarine (product weight)	10.8	11.0	11.3	10.8	10.2	10.9	10.6	11.0
Lard (direct use)	4.6	3.2	2.6	1.8	1.8	1.9	1.7	1.7
Edible tallow (direct use)	(NA)	(NA)	1.1	1.9	0.3	0.6	1.4	2.4
Shortening	17.3	17.0	18.2	22.9	21.5	22.2	22.4	22.4
Salad and cooking oils	15.4	17.9	21.2	23.5	24.0	24.2	25.2	25.6
Other edible fats and oils	2.3	2.0	1.5	1.6	1.3	1.2	1.3	1.4
Flour and cereal products	135.3	138.8	144.6	156.1	175.4	183.5	185.4	187.0
Wheat flour [11]	110.9	114.5	116.9	124.7	129.6	135.8	136.5	138.3
Rye flour	1.2	1.0	0.7	0.7	0.6	0.6	0.6	0.6
Rice, milled [12]	6.7	7.6	9.4	9.0	15.2	16.2	16.8	16.8
Corn products	11.1	10.8	12.9	17.1	21.5	21.7	21.9	21.9
Oat products	4.4	4.1	3.7	3.7	7.5	8.2	8.6	8.5
Barley products	1.0	0.9	1.1	1.0	1.0	1.0	0.9	0.9
Caloric sweeteners, total [13]	122.6	117.9	123.9	131.3	137.3	140.7	141.7	143.3
Sugar, refined cane and beet	101.8	89.2	83.6	62.7	62.8	64.4	63.7	64.5
Corn sweeteners (dry weight)	19.3	27.4	39.0	67.2	73.1	74.9	76.6	77.4
Low-calorie sweeteners (sugar sweetness equivalent) [14]	5.8	6.1	7.7	18.1	20.3	22.2	24.3	(NA)
Saccharin	5.8	6.1	7.7	6.0	6.1	6.7	7.3	(NA)
Aspartame	-	-	-	12.1	14.2	15.5	17.0	(NA)
Other:								
Cocoa beans	3.9	3.2	3.4	4.6	4.9	5.4	5.7	5.7
Coffee (green beans)	13.6	12.2	10.3	10.5	10.1	10.3	10.5	10.6
Peanuts (shelled)	5.5	6.0	4.8	6.3	7.0	6.0	6.5	6.4
Tree nuts (shelled)	1.7	1.9	1.8	2.3	2.4	2.6	2.3	2.4

- Represents or rounds to zero. NA Not available. [1] Excludes edible offals. [2] Excludes shipments to Puerto Rico and the other U.S. possessions. [3] Excludes consumption from recreational fishing, approximately 3 to 4 pounds per capita. [4] Includes backs, necks, skin, and giblets. [5] Includes other products, not shown separately. [6] Fluid milk figures are aggregates of commercial sales and milk produced and consumed on farms. [7] Heavy cream, light cream, and half and half. [8] Excludes cottage, pot, and baker's cheese. [9] Includes other cheeses not shown separately. [10] The fat content of butter and margarine is 80 percent of product weight. [11] White, whole wheat, semolina, and durum flour. [12] For crop year beginning in previous year. [13] Dry weight. Includes edible syrups (maple, molasses, etc.) and honey not shown separately. [14] Assumes saccharin is 300 times as sweet as sugar and aspartame 200 times as sweet as sugar.

Source: U.S. Department of Agriculture, Economic Research Service, *Food Consumption, Prices, and Expenditures*, annual.

No. 221. Per Capita Utilization of Selected Commercially Produced Fresh Fruits and Vegetables: 1970 to 1992

[In pounds, farm weight. Domestic food use of fresh fruits and vegetables reflects the fresh-market share of commodity production plus imports and minus exports. All data are on a calendar year basis except for citrus fruits, October or November; apples, August; grapes and pears, July. See headnote, table 220]

COMMODITY	1970	1975	1980	1985	1988	1989	1990	1991	1992
Fresh fruits, total............	79.1	84.0	86.9	86.5	97.0	96.6	92.2	89.8	98.7
Noncitrus	50.3	55.0	60.8	65.1	71.7	73.1	70.8	70.8	74.4
Bananas	17.4	17.6	20.8	23.5	24.3	24.7	24.4	25.1	27.3
Apples	17.0	19.5	19.2	17.3	19.9	21.4	19.7	18.3	19.3
Grapes	2.9	3.6	4.0	6.8	7.7	7.9	7.9	7.3	7.2
Nectarines and peaches......	5.8	5.0	7.1	5.5	6.6	5.7	5.5	6.4	5.9
Pears	1.9	2.7	2.6	2.8	3.2	3.2	3.2	3.2	3.1
Strawberries.............	1.7	1.8	2.0	3.0	3.3	3.3	3.2	3.6	3.5
Pineapples..............	0.7	1.0	1.5	1.5	1.8	2.0	2.1	1.9	2.0
Plums and prunes..........	1.5	1.3	1.5	1.4	1.7	1.4	1.5	1.4	1.8
Other [1]	1.4	2.5	2.1	3.3	3.2	3.5	3.3	3.6	4.3
Citrus..................	28.8	28.9	26.0	21.4	25.3	23.5	21.3	19.0	24.3
Oranges	16.2	15.9	14.3	11.6	13.9	12.2	12.4	8.5	12.9
Grapefruit	8.2	8.3	7.3	5.5	6.6	6.6	4.4	5.8	5.9
Other [2]	4.4	4.7	4.4	4.3	4.8	4.7	4.5	4.7	5.5
Selected melons............	21.6	17.7	17.9	24.1	23.8	26.5	24.6	23.3	24.0
Watermelons.............	13.5	11.4	10.7	13.5	13.5	13.6	13.3	12.8	13.6
Cantaloups	7.2	5.2	5.8	8.5	7.9	10.4	9.2	8.7	8.5
Honeydews..............	0.9	1.1	1.4	2.1	2.3	2.5	2.1	1.9	1.9
Selected fresh vegetables........	88.1	88.6	92.5	103.0	111.5	115.5	113.3	110.4	109.3
Asparagus	0.4	0.4	0.3	0.5	0.6	0.6	0.6	0.6	0.6
Broccoli	0.5	1.0	1.4	2.6	3.8	3.8	3.4	3.1	3.4
Cabbage................	11.4	9.1	8.1	9.2	8.7	8.4	8.7	8.2	7.1
Carrots.................	6.0	6.4	6.2	6.5	7.2	7.9	8.0	7.5	8.1
Cauliflower	0.7	0.9	1.1	1.8	2.2	2.3	2.2	2.0	2.0
Celery	7.3	6.9	7.5	7.0	7.2	7.5	7.2	6.8	6.5
Corn	7.8	7.8	6.5	6.4	5.7	6.4	6.5	5.7	6.4
Cucumbers	2.8	2.8	3.9	4.4	4.8	4.8	4.7	4.6	4.9
Iceberg lettuce............	22.4	23.5	25.6	23.7	27.0	28.8	27.8	26.1	24.1
Onions	10.1	10.5	11.4	13.6	14.5	14.8	15.1	15.8	16.2
Snap beans..............	1.5	1.4	1.3	1.3	1.2	1.2	1.1	1.1	1.3
Green peppers	2.2	2.5	2.9	3.8	4.5	4.7	4.5	5.1	5.3
Tomatoes...............	12.1	12.0	12.8	14.9	16.8	16.8	15.5	15.4	14.4
Other fresh vegetables [3]	2.9	3.4	3.5	7.3	7.3	7.5	8.0	8.4	9.0
Potatoes..................	121.7	122.0	114.7	122.4	122.5	127.1	127.8	130.6	133.5
Fresh..................	61.8	52.6	51.1	46.3	49.6	50.0	45.9	46.9	48.7
For freezing.............	28.5	37.1	35.4	45.4	43.3	46.8	50.2	51.0	51.8
For chips/shoestrings.........	17.4	15.5	16.5	17.6	17.2	17.5	17.0	17.1	17.0
For dehydrating	12.0	14.7	9.8	11.2	10.4	10.8	12.8	13.9	14.1
For canning.	2.0	2.0	1.9	1.9	1.9	2.0	1.9	1.8	1.8
Sweet potatoes [4]	5.4	5.4	4.4	5.4	4.1	4.1	4.6	4.0	4.3
Mushrooms...............	1.3	1.9	2.7	3.6	3.5	3.6	3.7	3.6	3.4
For fresh	0.3	0.7	1.2	1.8	2.0	2.0	2.0	1.9	1.9
For processing...........	1.0	1.2	1.5	1.8	1.5	1.5	1.7	1.7	1.6

[1] Includes apricots, avocados, cherries, cranberries, figs, kiwifruit, mangos, olives, papayas, persimmons, and pomegranates.   [2] Includes tangerines, tangelos, lemons, and limes.   [3] Includes artichokes, garlic, and eggplant.   [4] Fresh and processed.

Source: U.S. Dept. of Agriculture, Economic Research Service, *Food Consumption, Prices and Expenditures,* annual; and unpublished data.

No. 222. Per Capita Consumption of Selected Beverages, by Type: 1970 to 1992

[In gallons. See headnote, table 220]

COMMODITY	1970	1975	1980	1985	1988	1989	1990	1991	1992
Nonalcoholic [1]................	95.8	103.0	106.4	109.0	114.3	116.8	118.4	119.2	119.2
Milk (plain and flavored)	31.3	29.5	27.6	26.7	25.8	26.0	25.7	25.7	25.3
Whole	25.5	21.1	17.0	14.3	12.3	11.3	10.5	10.2	9.8
Lowfat	4.4	7.1	9.2	10.9	11.6	12.3	12.6	12.7	12.7
Skim	1.3	1.3	1.3	1.5	1.9	2.3	2.6	2.8	2.9
Tea...................	6.8	7.5	7.3	7.1	7.0	6.9	6.8	6.9	7.0
Coffee.................	33.4	31.4	26.7	27.4	25.7	26.3	27.1	27.4	27.8
Bottled water	(NA)	(NA)	2.4	4.5	6.5	7.4	8.0	8.0	8.2
Soft drinks	24.3	28.2	35.0	35.7	41.6	42.5	44.0	43.9	44.1
Fruit juices.............	(NA)	6.4	7.4	7.6	7.7	7.7	6.8	7.3	6.8
Alcoholic (adult population)	35.7	39.7	42.8	40.7	39.8	39.1	40.0	37.8	37.4
Beer..................	30.6	33.9	36.6	34.6	34.3	33.9	34.9	33.2	32.7
Wine..................	2.2	2.7	3.2	3.5	3.2	3.1	2.9	2.7	2.7
Distilled spirits	3.0	3.1	3.0	2.6	2.2	2.2	2.2	2.0	2.0

NA Not available.   [1] Excludes vegetable juices.

Source: U.S. Dept. of Agriculture, Economic Research Service, *Food Consumption, Prices, and Expenditures,* annual; and unpublished data.

Education

This section presents data primarily concerning formal education as a whole, at various levels, and for public and private schools. Data shown relate to the school-age population and school enrollment, educational attainment, education personnel, and financial aspects of education. In addition, data are shown for libraries, computer usage in schools, and adult education. The chief sources are the decennial census of population and the Current Population Survey (CPS), both conducted by the Bureau of the Census (see text, section 1); annual, biennial, and other periodic surveys conducted by the National Center for Education Statistics, a part of the U.S. Department of Education; and surveys conducted by the National Education Association.

The censuses of population have included data on school enrollment since 1840 and on educational attainment since 1940. The CPS has reported on school enrollment annually since 1945 and on educational attainment periodically since 1947.

The National Center for Education Statistics is continuing the pattern of statistical studies and surveys conducted by the U.S. Office of Education since 1870. The annual *Digest of Education Statistics* provides summary data on pupils, staff, finances, including government expenditures, and organization at the elementary, secondary, and higher education levels. It is also a primary source for detailed information on Federal funds for education, projections of enrollment, graduates, and teachers. *The Condition of Education,* issued annually, presents a summary of information on education of particular interest to policymakers.

Other sources of data include special studies by the National Center for Education Statistics and annual or biennial reports of education agencies in individual States. The census of governments, conducted by the Bureau of the Census every 5 years (for the years ending in "2" and "7"), provides data on school district finances and State and local government

In Brief

The enrollment rate of 3 to 5 year olds in preprimary school:

1970	37 percent
1992	56 percent

Persons 25 years old and over completing college:

1970	11 percent
1993	22 percent

Elementary and secondary schools with microcomputers:

1985	78 percent
1993	97 percent

expenditures for education. Reports published by the Bureau of Labor Statistics contain data relating civilian labor force experience to educational attainment (see also tables 617, 618, 640, 650, and 651 in section 13).

Types and sources of data.—The statistics in this section are of two general types. One type, exemplified by data from the Bureau of the Census, is based on direct interviews with individuals to obtain information about their own and their family members' education. Data of this type relate to school enrollment and level of education attained, classified by age, sex, and other characteristics of the population. The school enrollment statistics reflect attendance or enrollment in any regular school within a given period; educational attainment statistics reflect the highest grade completed by an individual or, beginning in 1992, the highest diploma or degree received.

For enrollment data starting in October 1981, the CPS used 1980 census population controls; for years 1971 through 1980, 1970 census population controls had been used. This change had little impact on summary measures (e.g., medians) and proportional measures (e.g., enrollment rates); however, use of the controls may have significant impact on absolute numbers.

Beginning with data for 1986, a new edit and tabulation package for school enrollment has been introduced. The data produced increased the estimates of high school enrollment for 1986 by 200,000 and college enrollment by 300,000. See table 231 which presents both earlier and revised estimates. In other enrollment tables, revised estimates are shown. In 1988, a new edit and tabulation package was introduced for educational attainment data.

The second type, generally exemplified by data from the National Center for Education Statistics and the National Education Association, is based on reports from administrators of educational institutions and of State and local agencies having jurisdiction over education. Data of this type relate to enrollment, attendance, staff, and finances for the Nation, individual States, and local areas.

Unlike the National Center for Education Statistics, the Census Bureau does not regularly include specialized vocational, trade, business, or correspondence schools in its surveys. The National Center for Education Statistics includes nursery schools and kindergartens that are part of regular grade schools in their enrollment figures. The Census Bureau includes all nursery schools and kindergartens. At the higher education level, the statistics of both agencies are concerned with institutions granting degrees or offering work acceptable for degree-credit, such as junior colleges.

School attendance.—All States require that children attend school. While State laws vary as to the ages and circumstances of compulsory attendance, generally they require that formal schooling begin by age 6 and continue to age 16.

Schools.—The National Center for Education Statistics defines a *school* as "a division of the school system consisting of students composing one or more grade groups or other identifiable groups, organized as one unit with one or more teachers to give instruction of a defined type, and housed in a school plant of one or more buildings. More than one school may be housed in one school plant, as is the case when the elementary and secondary programs are housed in the same school plant."

Regular schools are those which advance a person toward a diploma or degree. They include public and private nursery schools, kindergartens, graded schools, colleges, universities, and professional schools.

Public schools are schools controlled and supported by local, State, or Federal governmental agencies; *private* schools are those controlled and supported mainly by religious organizations or by private persons or organizations.

The Bureau of the Census defines *elementary* schools as including grades 1 through 8; *high* schools as including grades 9 through 12; and *colleges* as including junior or community colleges, regular 4-year colleges, and universities and graduate or professional schools. Statistics reported by the National Center for Education Statistics and the National Education Association by type of organization, such as elementary level and secondary level, may not be strictly comparable with those from the Bureau of the Census because the grades included at the two levels vary, depending on the level assigned to the middle or junior high school by the local school systems.

School year.—Except as otherwise indicated in the tables, data refer to the school year which, for elementary and secondary schools, generally begins in September of the preceding year and ends in June of the year stated. For the most part, statistics concerning school finances are for a 12-month period, usually July 1 to June 30. Enrollment data generally refer to a specific point in time, such as fall, as indicated in the tables.

Statistical reliability.—For a discussion of statistical collection, estimation, and sampling procedures and measures of statistical reliability applicable to Census Bureau and the National Center for Education Statistics data, see Appendix III.

Historical statistics.—Tabular headnotes provide cross-references, where applicable, to *Historical Statistics of the United States, Colonial Times to 1970.* See Appendix IV.

No. 223. School Enrollment, 1955 to 1992, With Projections to 2004, and Number of Schools, 1955 to 1991

[In thousands. As of fall. See also *Historical Statistics, Colonial Times to 1970*, series H 421-429]

ITEM AND YEAR	TOTAL		ELEMENTARY [1]		SECONDARY		COLLEGE	
	Public	Private	Public	Private	Public	Private	Public	Private
Enrollment: [2]								
1955	32,164	5,777	22,159	3,800	8,521	800	[3]1,484	1,177
1965	46,039	8,251	26,604	4,900	15,465	1,400	3,970	1,951
1970	52,322	7,516	27,492	4,052	18,402	1,311	6,428	2,153
1975	53,655	7,350	25,656	3,700	19,164	1,300	8,835	2,350
1980	50,334	7,971	24,196	3,992	16,681	1,339	9,457	2,640
1983	48,935	8,497	23,635	4,315	15,617	1,400	9,683	2,782
1984	48,685	8,465	23,742	4,300	15,466	1,400	9,477	2,765
1985	48,901	8,325	24,135	4,195	15,287	1,362	9,479	2,768
1986	49,467	8,242	24,497	4,116	15,256	1,336	9,714	2,790
1987	49,981	8,272	25,215	4,232	14,793	1,247	9,973	2,793
1988	50,349	8,136	25,740	4,036	14,448	1,206	10,161	2,894
1989	51,121	8,316	26,408	4,162	14,135	1,193	10,578	2,961
1990	52,062	8,206	27,050	4,095	14,167	1,136	10,845	2,975
1991, est.	53,310	8,248	27,564	4,074	14,436	1,125	11,310	3,049
1992, est. [4]	53,884	8,479	27,784	4,212	14,712	1,163	11,388	3,104
1995, proj.	56,744	8,911	29,018	4,393	16,031	1,267	11,695	3,251
2000, proj.	60,453	9,421	31,027	4,688	17,318	1,379	12,108	3,354
2002, proj.	61,332	9,568	31,309	4,743	17,705	1,405	12,318	3,420
2003, proj.	61,645	9,616	31,273	4,758	18,007	1,421	12,365	3,437
2004, proj.	61,937	9,660	31,142	4,753	18,364	1,446	12,431	3,461
Schools: [5]								
1955	(X)	(X)	104.4	12.4	26.0	3.9	0.7	1.2
1965	(X)	(X)	73.2	15.3	26.6	4.6	0.8	1.4
1970	(X)	(X)	65.8	14.4	25.4	3.8	(NA)	(NA)
1976 [6]	(X)	(X)	62.6	16.4	25.4	5.9	1.5	1.6
1980	(X)	(X)	61.1	16.8	24.4	5.7	1.5	1.7
1986	(X)	(X)	60.8	(NA)	23.4	(NA)	1.5	1.9
1987 [7]	(X)	(X)	61.5	23.0	22.9	8.4	1.6	2.0
1988 [7]	(X)	(X)	61.5	(NA)	22.8	(NA)	1.6	2.0
1990 [7]	(X)	(X)	61.3	22.2	22.7	9.0	1.6	2.0
1991	(X)	(X)	61.7	22.6	22.6	(NA)	1.6	2.0

NA Not available. X Not applicable. [1] Enrollment includes kindergarten. [2] For regular schools. [3] Degree-credit enrollment only. [4] Higher education figures are preliminary. [5] Excludes schools not reported by level, such as special education. Schools with both elementary and secondary programs are included under elementary and also secondary. [6] Beginning 1976, branch campuses of college institutions counted separately. [7] Data for private elementary and secondary schools not comparable to figures for earlier years.

Source: U.S. National Center for Education Statistics, *Digest of Education Statistics*, annual, and *Projections of Education Statistics*, annual.

No. 224. School Expenditures, by Type of Control and Level of Instruction in Constant (1990-91) Dollars: 1960 to 1993

[In millions of dollars. For school years ending in year shown. Total expenditures for public elementary and secondary schools include current expenditures, interest on school debt and capital outlay. Data deflated by the Consumer Price Index, wage earners, and clerical workers through 1975; thereafter, all urban consumers, on a school year basis (supplied by the National Center for Education Statistics). See also Appendix III. See *Historical Statistics, Colonial Times to 1970*, series H 494, 499, and 500 for related but not comparable data, and H 513-519 for private schools]

YEAR	Total	ELEMENTARY AND SECONDARY SCHOOLS			COLLEGES AND UNIVERSITIES		
		Total	Public	Private [1]	Total	Public	Private [1]
1960	108,747	76,173	71,160	5,013	32,574	17,791	14,783
1970	242,696	153,091	144,228	8,863	89,605	57,552	32,053
1975	280,969	178,013	167,670	10,343	102,956	69,726	33,230
1980	285,706	177,954	165,534	12,420	107,752	71,474	36,279
1983	289,366	175,634	161,580	14,053	113,732	74,139	39,593
1984	300,768	182,884	167,753	15,131	117,884	76,475	41,410
1985	313,572	189,163	173,463	15,700	124,409	80,660	43,749
1986	331,645	199,121	182,876	16,245	132,524	86,231	46,293
1987	351,517	210,929	193,713	17,216	140,588	89,756	50,832
1988	362,270	217,333	199,645	17,687	144,937	92,320	52,618
1989	383,305	231,362	213,240	18,122	151,943	96,253	55,690
1990	402,950	242,891	223,696	19,195	160,059	102,403	57,657
1991, revised	414,093	248,333	228,933	19,400	165,760	105,631	60,128
1992, revised	427,263	256,146	235,894	20,251	171,117	108,232	62,885
1993 [1]	437,943	262,525	241,948	20,577	175,418	110,685	64,733

[1] Estimated.

Source: U.S. National Center for Education Statistics, *Digest Education Statistics*, annual.

Education

No. 225. School Enrollment, Faculty, Graduates, and Finances, With Projections: 1985 to 2003

[As of fall, except as indicated]

ITEM	Unit	1985	1990	1992, est. [1]	1993, proj.	1994, proj.	1995, proj.	2000, proj.	2003, proj.
ELEMENTARY AND SECONDARY SCHOOLS									
School-age population [2]	1,000...	44,782	45,311	46,655	47,226	47,958	48,854	52,358	53,384
School enrollment: Total	1,000...	44,979	46,448	47,871	48,925	49,819	50,709	54,412	55,459
Elementary	1,000...	28,330	31,145	31,996	32,577	32,956	33,411	35,715	36,031
Secondary	1,000...	16,649	15,304	15,875	16,348	16,863	17,298	18,697	19,428
Public, total	1,000...	39,422	41,217	42,496	43,454	44,254	45,049	48,345	49,280
Elementary	1,000...	24,135	27,050	27,784	28,297	28,623	29,018	31,027	31,273
Secondary	1,000...	15,287	14,167	14,712	15,157	15,631	16,031	17,318	18,007
Private, total	1,000...	5,557	5,232	5,375	5,471	5,565	5,660	6,067	6,179
Elementary	1,000...	4,195	4,095	4,212	4,280	4,333	4,393	4,688	4,758
Secondary	1,000...	1,362	1,137	1,163	1,191	1,232	1,267	1,379	1,421
Classroom teachers: Total	1,000...	2,549	2,753	2,814	2,838	2,890	2,950	3,179	3,268
Elementary	1,000...	1,483	1,680	1,738	1,752	1,736	1,768	1,903	1,943
Secondary	1,000...	1,066	1,073	1,076	1,087	1,155	1,181	1,276	1,325
Public, total	1,000...	2,206	2,398	2,451	2,474	2,520	2,572	2,772	2,851
Elementary	1,000...	1,237	1,426	1,478	1,491	1,476	1,504	1,618	1,653
Secondary	1,000...	969	972	973	984	1,044	1,068	1,154	1,198
Private, total	1,000...	343	355	363	364	371	378	407	418
Elementary	1,000...	246	254	260	261	260	265	285	291
Secondary	1,000...	97	101	103	103	111	113	122	127
High school graduates, total [3]	1,000...	2,643	2,505	2,534	[4]2,526	2,648	2,669	3,039	3,116
Public	1,000...	2,383	2,237	2,277	2,267	2,377	2,396	2,728	2,797
Public schools: [3]									
Average daily attendance (ADA)	1,000...	36,523	38,427	39,594	40,321	41,063	41,801	44,859	45,727
Constant (1990-91) dollars:									
Teachers' average salary	Dol.	32,011	34,172	34,316	34,632	35,388	36,330	37,995	38,572
Current school expenditures	Bil. dol.	174.2	208.0	219.8	228.4	238.9	249.1	290.1	(NA)
HIGHER EDUCATION									
Enrollment, total	1,000...	12,247	13,820	14,558	14,994	15,005	14,946	15,462	15,802
Male	1,000...	5,818	6,285	6,654	6,842	6,831	6,781	6,970	7,161
Full-time	1,000...	3,608	3,808	3,992	4,104	4,071	4,031	4,218	4,396
Part-time	1,000...	2,211	2,477	2,662	2,738	2,760	2,750	2,752	2,765
Female	1,000...	6,429	7,535	7,904	8,152	8,174	8,165	8,492	8,641
Full-time	1,000...	3,468	4,013	4,147	4,251	4,241	4,211	4,439	4,596
Part-time	1,000...	2,961	3,522	3,757	3,901	3,933	3,954	4,053	4,045
Public	1,000...	9,479	10,844	11,377	11,722	11,736	11,695	12,108	12,365
Four-year institutions	1,000...	5,210	5,848	6,139	6,318	6,308	6,270	6,489	6,666
Two-year institutions	1,000...	4,270	4,996	5,238	5,404	5,428	5,425	5,619	5,699
Private	1,000...	2,768	2,975	3,181	3,272	3,269	3,251	3,354	3,437
Four-year institutions	1,000...	2,506	2,731	2,921	3,005	3,002	2,985	3,074	3,150
Two-year institutions	1,000...	261	244	260	267	267	266	280	287
Undergraduate	1,000...	10,597	11,959	12,450	12,823	12,815	12,761	13,309	13,659
Graduate	1,000...	1,376	1,586	1,790	1,844	1,861	1,859	1,841	1,830
First-time professional	1,000...	274	274	318	327	329	326	312	313
Full-time equivalent	1,000...	8,943	9,984	10,455	10,751	10,726	10,661	11,112	11,449
Public	1,000...	6,668	7,558	7,872	8,098	8,082	8,036	8,389	8,641
Private	1,000...	2,276	2,426	2,583	2,653	2,644	2,625	2,723	2,808
Faculty, total	1,000...	715	840	880	890	875	889	952	(NA)
Public	1,000...	503	592	620	627	612	621	665	(NA)
Private	1,000...	212	248	260	263	264	268	288	(NA)
Degrees conferred, total [3]	1,000...	1,830	2,025	2,120	2,155	2,189	2,231	2,220	2,316
Associate's	1,000...	446	482	497	504	518	518	538	560
Bachelor's	1,000...	988	1,095	1,145	1,165	1,178	1,214	1,203	1,278
Master's	1,000...	289	337	364	370	377	383	364	363
Doctorate's	1,000...	34	39	40	41	41	41	41	41
First-professional	1,000...	74	72	74	75	75	75	74	74

NA Not available. [1] Higher education data are projections. [2] Population 5-17 years old. As of July. [3] For school year ending June the following year. [4] High school graduate data are early estimates.

Source: U.S. National Center for Education Statistics, *Digest of Education Statistics*, annual, and *Projections of Educational Statistics*, annual. 32.2

No. 226. Federal Funds for Education and Related Programs: 1991 to 1993

[In millions of dollars, except percent. For fiscal years ending in June. Figures represent on-budget funds]

LEVEL, AGENCY, AND PROGRAM	1991	1992	1993 [1]
Total, all programs	**57,595.7**	**61,474.0**	**68,448.0**
Percent of Federal budget outlays	4.4	4.5	4.9
Elementary/secondary education programs	**25,418.0**	**27,926.9**	**31,512.7**
Department of Education [2]	10,865.3	12,057.7	13,828.3
Grants for the disadvantaged	5,218.7	6,158.8	6,878.4
School improvement programs	1,375.9	1,514.9	1,719.0
Indian education	65.6	68.5	79.6
Education for the handicapped	2,174.4	2,243.3	2,761.6
Vocational and adult education	1,090.4	1,079.1	1,308.6
Department of Agriculture [2]	6,074.7	6,714.1	7,430.7
Child nutrition programs	5,537.0	6,127.0	6,841.3
Agricultural Marketing Service—commodities [3]	350.9	400.0	400.0
Department of Defense [2]	1,253.1	1,197.3	1,205.5
Overseas dependents schools	960.3	912.9	905.9
Section VI schools [4]	239.6	229.7	225.0
Department of Energy	15.7	15.2	14.7
Department of Health and Human Services	2,997.2	3,310.2	4,160.6
Head Start	1,951.8	2,201.8	2,776.3
Social security student benefits	499.7	514.2	551.1
Department of the Interior [2]	644.8	517.7	533.5
Mineral Leasing Act and other funds	166.7	167.9	162.0
Indian Education	477.5	349.2	370.5
Department of Justice	78.1	94.7	115.7
Inmate programs	76.3	92.8	112.6
Department of Labor	3,209.1	3,708.4	3,898.4
Job Corps	805.3	925.8	950.8
Department of Veterans Affairs	167.0	190.6	211.4
Vocational rehab for disabled veterans	161.1	184.5	205.5
Other agencies and programs	113.0	120.9	113.8
Higher education programs [2]	**14,703.6**	**14,378.2**	**17,031.2**
Department of Education [2]	12,002.8	11,323.6	13,813.3
Student financial assistance	6,333.8	7,071.4	7,551.9
Guaranteed student loans	4,781.9	3,253.6	5,044.5
Department of Agriculture	32.3	34.2	32.7
Department of Defense	665.1	680.2	648.1
Tuition assistance for military personnel	94.8	102.4	102.4
Service academies [5]	135.1	125.1	135.9
Senior ROTC	189.8	193.3	192.8
Professional development education	241.7	259.3	217.0
Department of Energy [2]	30.9	34.4	32.2

LEVEL, AGENCY, AND PROGRAM	1991	1992	1993 [1]
Department of Health and Human Services [2]	697.4	737.5	742.9
Health professions training programs	533.5	305.8	282.8
National Health Service Corps scholarships	48.8	58.7	73.4
National Institutes of Health training grants [6]	268.5	348.0	349.2
Department of the Interior	141.5	140.3	140.3
Shared revenues, Mineral Leasing Act and other receipts—estimated education share	74.4	69.0	69.0
Indian programs	67.1	71.3	71.4
Department of Transportation	46.6	54.0	54.9
Department of Veterans Affairs [2]	614.4	854.5	986.7
Post-Vietnam veterans	118.1	88.5	58.9
All-volunteer-force educational assistance	366.9	650.5	813.0
Other agencies and programs [2]	472.6	519.5	580.1
National Endowment for the Humanities	55.9	58.5	58.3
National Science Foundation	191.7	210.4	215.4
United States Information Agency	185.9	207.7	261.5
Other education programs [2]	**3,698.6**	**4,002.5**	**4,315.7**
Department of Education [2]	2,419.3	2,579.9	2,778.6
Administration	365.7	368.4	394.9
Libraries	142.6	214.9	168.8
Rehabilitative services and handicapped research	1,902.3	1,991.9	2,207.2
Department of Agriculture	382.3	400.4	409.7
Department of Health and Human Services	89.1	97.6	104.4
Department of Justice	30.5	34.5	28.3
Department of State	41.8	44.1	51.2
Department of the Treasury [2]	60.1	51.7	60.6
Other agencies and programs [2]	675.4	794.2	882.7
Agency for International Development	154.0	212.2	259.1
Library of Congress	279.7	296.0	331.1
National Endowment for the Arts	1.6	3.3	2.8
National Endowment for the Humanities	93.4	99.8	99.4
Research programs at universities and related institutions	**13,775.4**	**15,166.4**	**15,588.4**
Department of Agriculture	385.8	424.4	415.8
Department of Defense	1,789.1	2,243.2	2,116.2
Department of Energy	2,692.3	2,872.9	2,778.7
Department of Health and Human Services	5,686.4	6,021.1	6,319.3
National Aeronautics and Space Administration	1,270.1	1,404.8	1,424.5
National Science Foundation	1,546.8	1,698.5	1,972.6

[1] Estimated. [2] Includes other programs and agencies, not shown separately. [3] Purchased under Section 32 of the Act of August 1935 for use in child nutrition programs. [4] Includes stateside schools on military installations for free education of dependents. [5] Instructional costs only including academics, audiovisual, academic computer center, faculty training, military training, physical education, and libraries. [6] Beginning 1992, includes alcohol, drug abuse, and mental health training programs.

Source: U.S. National Center for Education Statistics, Digest of Education Statistics, 1993.

No. 227. School Expenditures, by Source of Funds in Constant (1990-91) Dollars: 1970 to 1991

[In billions of dollars. For school years ending in year shown. Includes nursery, kindergarten, and special programs when provided by school system. All nonpublic school data and all data beginning 1980 are estimated. Data are deflated by the Consumer Price Index. For 1970, for wage earners and clerical workers; beginning 1980, for all urban consumers, on a school year basis (supplied by the U.S. National Center for Education Statistics). Due to revised methodology, data for 1970 are not comparable to later years or to table 224]

SOURCE OF FUNDS AND CONTROL OF SCHOOL	1970	1980	1984	1985	1986	1987	1988	1989	1990	1991
Total	**249.5**	**285.7**	**300.8**	**313.6**	**331.6**	**351.5**	**362.3**	**383.3**	**403.0**	**414.1**
Federal	26.6	32.6	25.9	27.0	29.0	30.4	30.9	32.1	33.4	34.4
State	78.7	111.0	114.4	121.7	129.6	136.3	139.9	143.9	149.9	153.3
Local	80.2	74.6	79.1	80.2	83.6	88.4	91.6	101.8	103.0	105.3
All other	64.1	67.5	81.3	84.7	89.5	96.4	99.9	105.6	116.6	121.0
Public	201.3	237.0	244.3	254.1	269.1	283.5	292.0	309.5	326.1	334.6
Federal	20.6	25.6	19.4	20.0	21.3	21.7	22.1	23.1	24.2	24.9
State	78.4	110.2	113.7	120.9	128.7	135.2	138.6	142.4	148.5	151.8
Local	79.7	74.4	78.8	79.8	83.3	88.1	91.3	101.4	102.6	104.9
All other	22.7	26.9	32.3	33.3	35.8	38.5	40.0	42.5	50.8	53.0
Private	48.2	48.7	56.5	59.5	62.5	68.0	70.3	73.8	76.9	79.5
Federal	6.0	7.1	6.5	7.0	7.6	8.7	8.7	8.9	9.2	9.5
State and local	0.7	1.1	1.1	1.2	1.3	1.4	1.6	1.8	1.9	2.1
All other	41.4	40.6	49.0	51.4	53.7	57.9	59.9	63.1	65.8	68.0
Elementary and secondary	**162.0**	**177.9**	**182.9**	**189.2**	**199.1**	**210.9**	**217.3**	**231.4**	**242.9**	**248.3**
Federal	12.0	16.2	11.4	11.5	12.2	12.4	12.6	13.2	13.9	14.2
State	56.0	77.1	79.8	84.5	89.9	95.9	98.5	101.5	105.8	108.2
Local	76.9	71.7	76.0	76.9	80.2	84.8	87.9	97.9	98.8	100.9
All other	17.0	12.9	15.6	16.2	16.8	17.8	18.3	18.8	24.6	25.0
Public	145.3	165.6	167.8	173.5	182.9	193.7	199.6	213.2	223.7	228.9
Federal	12.0	16.2	11.4	11.5	12.2	12.4	12.6	13.2	13.7	14.2
State	56.0	77.1	79.8	84.5	89.9	95.9	98.5	101.5	105.8	108.2
Local	76.9	71.7	76.0	76.9	80.2	84.8	87.9	97.9	98.8	100.9
All other [1]	0.3	0.5	0.5	0.5	0.5	0.6	0.6	0.6	5.4	5.6
Private	16.7	12.4	15.1	15.7	16.2	17.2	17.7	18.1	19.2	19.4
Higher education	**87.5**	**107.8**	**117.9**	**124.5**	**132.5**	**140.6**	**144.9**	**151.9**	**160.1**	**165.8**
Federal	14.6	16.5	14.6	15.5	16.7	18.0	18.3	18.8	19.8	20.3
State	22.7	33.9	34.6	37.2	39.7	40.4	41.4	42.4	44.1	45.1
Local	3.2	3.0	3.1	3.3	3.4	3.6	3.7	4.0	4.2	4.4
All other	47.1	54.5	65.7	68.6	72.8	78.6	81.6	86.8	92.0	95.9
Public	56.0	71.5	76.5	80.7	86.2	89.8	92.3	96.3	102.4	105.6
Federal	8.5	9.4	8.0	8.5	9.1	9.3	9.5	9.9	10.6	10.8
State	22.4	33.1	33.9	36.4	38.8	39.2	40.1	40.9	42.7	43.5
Local	2.8	2.6	2.7	3.0	3.1	3.3	3.4	3.6	3.8	4.0
All other	22.4	26.4	31.9	32.8	35.3	37.9	39.4	41.9	45.4	47.4
Private	31.5	36.3	41.4	43.8	46.3	50.8	52.6	55.7	57.7	60.1
Federal	6.0	7.1	6.5	7.0	7.6	8.7	8.7	8.9	9.2	9.5
State and local	0.7	1.1	1.1	1.2	1.2	1.4	1.6	1.8	1.9	2.1
All other	24.8	28.2	33.9	35.6	37.5	40.7	42.2	44.9	46.6	48.6

[1] Beginning in 1989-90, includes all fees for transportation, books, and food services.

Source: U.S. National Center for Education Statistics, *Digest of Education Statistics*, annual.

No. 228. Enrollment in Public and Private Schools, by Control and Level, With Projections: 1970 to 2003

[In thousands. As of fall. Data are for regular day schools and exclude independent nursery schools and kindergartens, residential schools for exceptional children, subcollegiate departments of colleges, Federal schools for Indians, and federally operated schools on Federal installations. College data include degree-credit and nondegree-credit enrollment]

CONTROL OF SCHOOL AND LEVEL	1970	1980	1985	1988	1989	1990	1991, est.	1992, est.	1995, proj.	2000, proj.	2003, proj.
Total	**59,838**	**58,305**	**57,226**	**58,485**	**59,436**	**60,268**	**61,558**	**62,363**	**65,655**	**69,874**	**71,261**
Public	52,322	50,335	48,901	50,350	51,121	52,061	53,310	53,884	56,744	60,453	61,645
Private	7,516	7,971	8,325	8,136	8,316	8,206	8,248	8,479	8,911	9,421	9,616
Kindergarten through 8	36,610	31,639	31,229	32,535	33,314	33,973	34,544	35,031	36,668	39,129	39,713
Public	32,558	27,647	27,034	28,501	29,152	29,878	30,470	30,819	32,275	34,441	34,955
Private	4,052	3,992	4,195	4,036	4,162	4,095	4,074	4,212	4,393	4,688	4,758
Grades 9 through 12	14,647	14,570	13,750	12,896	12,583	12,475	12,655	12,841	14,041	15,283	15,746
Public	13,336	13,231	12,388	11,687	11,390	11,338	11,530	11,678	12,774	13,904	14,325
Private	1,311	1,339	1,362	1,206	1,193	1,137	1,125	1,163	1,267	1,379	1,421
College	8,581	12,097	12,247	13,055	13,539	13,820	14,359	[1]14,492	14,946	15,462	15,802
Public	6,428	9,457	9,479	10,161	10,578	10,845	11,310	11,388	11,695	12,108	12,365
Private	2,153	2,640	2,768	2,894	2,961	2,975	3,049	3,104	3,251	3,354	3,437

[1] Higher education figures are preliminary.

Source: U.S. Department of Education, National Center for Education Statistics, *Digest of Education Statistics*, annual; *Projections of Education Statistics*, annual; and unpublished data.

No. 229. School Enrollment, by Age, Race, and Hispanic Origin: 1970 to 1992

[As of October. Covers civilian noninstitutional population enrolled in nursery school and above. Based on Current Population Survey, see text, section 1. See *Historical Statistics, Colonial Times to 1970,* series H 442-476 for enrollment 5-34 years old]

AGE, RACE, AND HISPANIC ORIGIN	ENROLLMENT (1,000)						RATE					
	1970	1980	1985	1990	1991	1992	1970	1980	1985	1990	1991	1992
Total 3 to 34 years old [1]	60,357	57,348	58,013	60,588	61,276	62,084	56.4	49.7	48.3	50.2	50.7	51.4
3 and 4 years old	1,461	2,280	2,801	3,292	3,068	3,063	20.5	36.7	38.9	44.4	40.5	39.7
5 and 6 years old	7,000	5,853	6,697	7,207	7,178	7,252	89.5	95.7	96.1	96.5	95.4	95.5
7 to 13 years old	28,943	23,751	22,849	25,016	25,445	25,768	99.2	99.3	99.2	99.6	99.7	99.4
14 and 15 years old	7,869	7,282	7,362	6,555	6,634	6,861	98.1	98.2	98.1	99.0	98.8	99.1
16 and 17 years old	6,927	7,129	6,654	6,098	6,155	6,272	90.0	89.0	91.7	92.5	93.3	94.1
18 and 19 years old	3,322	3,788	3,716	4,044	3,969	4,012	47.7	46.4	51.6	57.3	59.6	61.4
20 and 21 years old	1,949	2,515	2,708	2,852	3,041	3,027	31.9	31.0	35.3	39.7	42.0	44.0
22 to 24 years old	1,410	1,931	2,068	2,231	2,365	2,577	14.9	16.3	16.9	21.0	22.2	23.7
25 to 29 years old	1,011	1,714	1,942	2,013	2,045	1,907	7.5	9.3	9.2	9.7	10.2	9.8
30 to 34 years old	466	1,105	1,218	1,281	1,377	1,344	4.2	6.4	6.1	5.8	6.2	6.1
35 years old and over	(NA)	1,290	1,766	2,439	2,620	2,473	(NA)	1.4	1.7	2.1	2.2	2.1
White: Total 3 to 34 years old	51,719	47,673	47,452	48,899	49,156	49,710	56.2	48.9	47.8	49.5	50.0	50.7
3 and 4 years old	1,181	1,844	2,250	2,700	2,502	2,473	19.9	36.3	38.6	44.9	41.3	40.1
5 and 6 years old	5,899	4,781	5,437	5,750	5,727	5,774	90.3	95.8	96.4	96.5	95.3	95.4
7 to 13 years old	24,564	19,585	18,464	20,076	20,325	20,551	99.2	99.2	99.3	99.6	99.6	99.3
14 and 15 years old	6,761	6,038	6,007	5,265	5,311	5,462	98.2	98.3	98.1	99.1	98.7	99.2
16 and 17 years old	6,008	5,937	5,449	4,858	4,902	4,982	90.6	88.6	91.6	92.5	93.3	94.2
18 and 19 years old	2,924	3,199	3,105	3,271	3,197	3,212	48.7	46.3	52.4	57.1	59.7	61.7
20 and 21 years old	1,750	2,206	2,318	2,402	2,517	2,530	33.1	31.9	36.1	41.0	43.2	45.3
22 to 24 years old	1,305	1,669	1,744	1,781	1,910	2,069	15.7	16.4	17.0	20.2	21.7	23.3
25 to 29 years old	910	1,473	1,635	1,706	1,646	1,553	7.7	9.2	9.2	9.9	9.9	9.6
30 to 34 years old	416	942	1,043	1,090	1,119	1,104	4.2	6.3	6.2	5.9	6.0	6.0
35 years old and over	(NA)	1,104	1,533	2,096	2,219	2,136	(NA)	1.3	1.7	2.1	2.2	2.1
Black: Total 3 to 34 years old	7,829	8,251	8,444	8,854	9,031	9,151	57.4	53.9	50.9	51.9	52.5	53.0
3 and 4 years old	250	371	469	452	428	446	22.7	38.2	42.7	41.6	37.2	38.6
5 and 6 years old	999	904	1,030	1,129	1,108	1,143	84.9	95.4	95.7	96.3	95.8	95.9
7 to 13 years old	3,998	3,598	3,549	3,832	3,941	3,926	99.3	99.4	99.1	99.8	99.8	99.5
14 and 15 years old	1,025	1,088	1,106	1,023	1,032	1,089	97.6	97.9	97.9	99.2	99.1	99.4
16 and 17 years old	837	1,047	994	962	959	994	85.7	90.6	91.7	91.7	91.7	93.0
18 and 19 years old	352	494	472	596	578	566	40.1	45.7	44.1	55.2	55.6	56.2
20 and 21 years old	174	242	298	305	329	335	22.8	23.4	27.7	28.4	30.0	33.3
22 to 24 years old	84	196	215	274	249	305	8.0	13.6	13.7	20.0	18.2	20.3
25 to 29 years old	68	187	192	162	229	203	4.8	8.8	7.4	6.1	8.7	7.9
30 to 34 years old	41	124	119	119	177	144	3.4	6.8	5.1	4.4	6.5	5.3
35 years old and over	(NA)	186	233	238	289	227	(NA)	1.8	1.9	2.1	2.5	1.9
Hispanic: [2] **Total 3 to 34 years old**	(NA)	4,263	5,070	6,073	6,306	6,598	(NA)	49.8	47.7	47.4	47.9	49.2
3 and 4 years old	(NA)	172	213	249	299	286	(NA)	28.5	27.0	29.8	30.6	28.8
5 and 6 years old	(NA)	491	662	835	850	896	(NA)	94.5	94.5	94.8	92.4	96.0
7 to 13 years old	(NA)	2,009	2,322	2,794	2,909	2,946	(NA)	99.2	99.0	99.4	99.7	99.3
14 and 15 years old	(NA)	568	606	739	732	774	(NA)	94.3	96.1	99.0	97.2	98.8
16 and 17 years old	(NA)	454	562	592	532	630	(NA)	81.8	84.5	85.4	82.6	87.2
18 and 19 years old	(NA)	226	238	329	394	418	(NA)	37.8	41.8	44.1	47.9	53.7
20 and 21 years old	(NA)	111	137	213	215	230	(NA)	19.5	24.0	27.2	26.4	30.1
22 to 24 years old	(NA)	93	125	121	144	176	(NA)	11.7	11.6	9.9	11.6	14.5
25 to 29 years old	(NA)	84	120	130	140	143	(NA)	6.9	6.6	6.3	6.9	6.7
30 to 34 years old	(NA)	54	83	72	93	100	(NA)	5.1	5.7	3.6	4.5	4.7
35 years old and over	(NA)	(NA)	(NA)	145	148	136	(NA)	(NA)	(NA)	2.1	2.0	1.8
Mexican: [2] **Total 3 to 34 years old**	(NA)	2,698	3,180	4,017	4,171	4,462	(NA)	49.0	47.5	46.8	47.7	48.9
3 and 4 years old	(NA)	104	137	165	215	159	(NA)	27.0	26.0	27.4	32.3	24.3
5 and 6 years old	(NA)	327	458	619	581	648	(NA)	93.2	95.3	94.7	92.1	95.9
7 to 13 years old	(NA)	1,378	1,526	1,815	1,957	2,081	(NA)	99.5	99.2	99.7	99.7	99.1
14 and 15 years old	(NA)	361	367	499	475	515	(NA)	92.1	97.7	99.5	97.6	98.7
16 and 17 years old	(NA)	257	358	403	351	418	(NA)	76.1	83.8	83.8	81.0	86.3
18 and 19 years old	(NA)	113	127	213	282	283	(NA)	32.0	35.2	40.9	47.0	50.6
20 and 21 years old	(NA)	55	61	121	132	134	(NA)	15.6	16.4	23.6	24.8	24.2
22 to 24 years old	(NA)	40	55	70	70	95	(NA)	7.5	7.8	8.3	8.2	11.9
25 to 29 years old	(NA)	41	56	64	61	74	(NA)	5.4	5.0	4.9	4.8	5.4
30 to 34 years old	(NA)	22	36	47	48	55	(NA)	3.3	4.5	3.6	3.7	3.9
35 years old and over	(NA)	(NA)	(NA)	81	89	91	(NA)	(NA)	(NA)	2.1	2.2	2.0

NA Not available.   [1] Includes other races, not shown separately.   [2] Persons of Hispanic origin may be of any race.

Source: U.S. Bureau of the Census, *Current Population Reports,* P20-474, and earlier reports.

No. 230. Enrollment in Public and Private Schools: 1960 to 1992

[In millions, except percent. As of October. For civilian noninstitutional population. For **1960**, 5 to 34 years old; for **1970 to 1985**, 3 to 34 years old; **beginning 1986**, for 3 years old and over]

YEAR	PUBLIC						PRIVATE					
	Total	Nur-sery	Kinder-garten	Ele-mentary	High School	College	Total	Nur-sery	Kinder-garten	Ele-mentary	High School	College
1960	39.0	(NA)	(¹)	27.5	9.2	2.3	7.2	(NA)	(¹)	4.9	1.0	1.3
1970	52.2	0.3	2.6	30.0	13.5	5.7	8.1	0.8	0.5	3.9	1.2	1.7
1975	52.8	0.6	2.9	27.2	14.5	7.7	8.2	1.2	0.5	3.3	1.2	2.0
1976	52.4	0.5	3.0	26.7	14.5	7.7	8.1	1.1	0.5	3.1	1.2	2.2
1977	51.6	0.6	2.7	26.0	14.5	7.9	8.4	1.1	0.5	3.3	1.2	2.3
1978	50.0	0.6	2.5	25.3	14.2	7.4	8.6	1.2	0.5	3.2	1.2	2.4
1979	50.0	0.6	2.6	24.8	14.0	7.7	8.2	1.2	0.4	3.1	1.1	2.3
1980	(NA)	0.6	2.7	24.4	(NA)	(NA)	(NA)	1.4	0.5	3.1	(NA)	(NA)
1981	49.7	0.7	2.6	24.8	13.5	8.2	8.7	1.4	0.5	3.0	1.1	2.6
1982	49.2	0.7	2.7	24.4	13.0	8.4	8.2	1.4	0.6	3.0	1.1	2.6
1983	48.7	0.8	2.7	24.2	12.8	8.2	9.0	1.5	0.7	3.0	1.2	2.6
1984	49.0	0.8	3.0	24.1	12.7	8.5	8.3	1.6	0.5	2.7	1.1	2.4
1985	49.0	0.9	3.2	23.8	12.8	8.4	9.0	1.6	0.6	3.1	1.2	2.5
1986 ²	51.2	0.8	3.4	24.2	13.0	9.8	9.4	1.7	0.6	3.0	1.2	2.9
1987 ²	51.7	0.8	3.4	24.8	12.7	10.0	8.9	1.7	0.6	2.8	1.1	2.8
1988 ²	52.2	0.9	3.4	25.5	12.2	10.3	8.9	1.8	0.5	2.8	1.0	2.8
1989 ²	52.5	0.9	3.3	25.9	12.1	10.3	8.9	1.9	0.6	2.7	0.8	2.9
1990 ²	53.8	1.2	3.3	26.6	11.9	10.7	9.2	2.2	0.6	2.7	0.9	2.9
1991 ²	54.5	1.1	3.5	26.6	12.2	11.1	9.4	1.8	0.6	3.0	1.0	3.0
1992 ²	55.0	1.1	3.5	27.1	12.3	11.1	9.4	1.8	0.6	3.1	1.0	3.0
Percent White:												
1960	85.7	(NA)	(¹)	84.3	88.2	92.2	95.7	(NA)	(¹)	95.3	96.7	96.3
1970	84.5	59.5	84.4	83.1	85.6	90.7	93.4	91.1	88.2	94.1	96.1	92.8
1980	(NA)	68.2	80.7	80.9	(NA)	(NA)	(NA)	89.0	87.0	90.7	(NA)	(NA)
1990	79.8	71.7	78.3	78.9	79.2	84.1	87.4	89.6	83.2	88.2	89.4	85.0
1991	79.3	74.0	78.3	78.6	78.4	82.8	86.7	89.0	81.8	87.9	88.8	84.3
1992	79.2	71.5	77.8	78.4	78.6	83.1	86.7	89	84.9	87.6	87.5	84.5

NA Not available.   ¹ Included in elementary school.   ² See table 272 for college enrollment 35 years old and over. Also data beginning 1986 based on a revised edit and tabulation package.

Source: U.S. Bureau of the Census, *Current Population Reports*, P20-474; and earlier reports.

No. 231. School Enrollment, by Sex and Level: 1960 to 1992

[In millions. As of Oct. For the civilian noninstitutional population. For **1960**, persons 5 to 34 years old; **1970-1979** 3 to 34 years old; **beginning 1980**, 3 years old and over. Elementary includes kindergarten and grades 1-8; high school, grades 9-12; and college, 2-year and 4-year colleges, universities, and graduate and professional schools. Data for college represent degree-credit enrollment]

YEAR	ALL LEVELS ¹			ELEMENTARY			HIGH SCHOOL			COLLEGE		
	Total	Male	Female	Total	Male	Female	Total	Male	Female	Total	Male	Female
1960	46.3	24.2	22.0	32.4	16.7	15.7	10.2	5.2	5.1	3.6	2.3	1.2
1970	60.4	31.4	28.9	37.1	19.0	18.1	14.7	7.4	7.3	7.4	4.4	3.0
1975	61.0	31.6	29.4	33.8	17.3	16.5	15.7	8.0	7.7	9.7	5.3	4.4
1976	60.5	31.2	29.3	33.3	17.0	16.2	15.7	8.1	7.7	10.0	5.3	4.7
1977	60.0	30.8	29.2	32.4	16.6	15.8	15.8	8.0	7.7	10.2	5.4	4.8
1978	58.6	30.1	28.6	31.5	16.1	15.3	15.5	7.8	7.6	9.8	5.1	4.7
1979	57.9	29.5	28.3	30.9	15.9	15.0	15.1	7.7	7.4	10.0	5.0	5.0
1980	58.6	29.6	29.1	30.6	15.8	14.9	14.6	7.3	7.3	11.4	5.4	6.0
1981 ²	58.4	29.5	28.9	30.1	15.5	14.7	14.4	7.3	7.1	11.8	5.6	6.2
1981 ³	59.9	30.3	29.6	31.0	15.9	15.0	14.7	7.5	7.3	12.1	5.8	6.3
1982	59.4	30.0	29.4	30.7	15.8	14.9	14.2	7.2	7.0	12.3	5.9	6.4
1983	59.3	30.1	29.2	30.6	15.7	14.8	14.1	7.1	7.0	12.4	6.0	6.3
1984	58.9	29.9	29.0	30.3	15.6	14.7	13.9	7.1	6.8	12.3	6.0	6.3
1985	59.8	30.0	29.7	30.7	15.7	15.0	14.1	7.2	6.9	12.5	5.9	6.6
1986	60.1	30.4	29.7	31.1	16.1	15.0	14.0	7.1	6.9	12.4	5.8	6.6
1986 ⁴	60.5	30.6	30.0	31.1	16.1	15.0	14.2	7.2	7.0	12.7	6.0	6.7
1987	60.6	30.7	29.9	31.6	16.3	15.3	13.8	7.0	6.8	12.7	6.0	6.7
1988	61.1	30.7	30.5	32.2	16.6	15.6	13.2	6.7	6.4	13.1	5.9	7.2
1989	61.5	30.8	30.7	32.5	16.7	15.8	12.9	6.6	6.3	13.2	6.0	7.2
1990	63.0	31.5	31.5	33.2	17.1	16.0	12.8	6.5	6.4	13.6	6.2	7.4
1991	63.9	32.1	31.8	33.8	17.3	16.4	13.1	6.8	6.4	14.1	6.4	7.6
1992	64.6	32.2	32.3	34.3	17.7	16.6	13.3	6.8	6.5	14.0	6.2	7.8

¹ Beginning 1970, includes nursery schools, not shown separately.   ² Based on 1970 population controls.   ³ Based on 1980 population controls.   ⁴ Revised. Data beginning 1986, based on a revised edit and tabulation package.

Source: U.S. Bureau of the Census, *Current Population Reports*, P20-474; and earlier reports.

No. 232. Educational Attainment, by Race and Ethnicity: 1960 to 1993

[In percent. For persons 25 years old and over. 1960, 1970, and 1980 as of April 1 and based on sample data from the censuses of population. Other years as of March and based on the Current Population Survey; see text, section 1, and Appendix III. See table 233 for data by sex]

YEAR	Total [1]	White	Black	Asian and Pacific Islander	HISPANIC [2]			
					Total [3]	Mexican	Puerto Rican	Cuban
COMPLETED 4 YEARS OF HIGH SCHOOL OR MORE								
1960.	41.1	43.2	20.1	(NA)	(NA)	(NA)	(NA)	(NA)
1965.	49.0	51.3	27.2	(NA)	(NA)	(NA)	(NA)	(NA)
1970.	52.3	54.5	31.4	(NA)	32.1	24.2	23.4	43.9
1975.	62.5	64.5	42.5	(NA)	37.9	31.0	28.7	51.7
1980.	66.5	68.8	51.2	(NA)	44.0	37.6	40.1	55.3
1985.	73.9	75.5	59.8	(NA)	47.9	41.9	46.3	51.1
1990.	77.6	79.1	66.2	80.4	50.8	44.1	55.5	63.5
1991.	78.4	79.9	66.7	81.8	51.3	43.6	58.0	61.0
1992 [4]	79.4	80.9	67.7	(NA)	52.6	45.2	60.5	62.0
1993 [4]	80.2	81.5	70.4	(NA)	53.1	46.2	59.8	62.1
COMPLETED 4 YEARS OF COLLEGE OR MORE								
1960.	7.7	8.1	3.1	(NA)	(NA)	(NA)	(NA)	(NA)
1965.	9.4	9.9	4.7	(NA)	(NA)	(NA)	(NA)	(NA)
1970.	10.7	11.3	4.4	(NA)	4.5	2.5	2.2	11.1
1975.	13.9	14.5	6.4	(NA)	(NA)	(NA)	(NA)	(NA)
1980.	16.2	17.1	8.4	(NA)	7.6	4.9	5.6	16.2
1985.	19.4	20.0	11.1	(NA)	8.5	5.5	7.0	13.7
1990.	21.3	22.0	11.3	39.9	9.2	5.4	9.7	20.2
1991.	21.4	22.2	11.5	39.1	9.7	6.2	10.1	18.5
1992 [4]	21.4	22.1	11.9	(NA)	9.3	6.1	8.4	18.4
1993 [4]	21.9	22.6	12.2	(NA)	9.0	5.9	8.0	16.5

NA Not available. [1] Includes other races, not shown separately. [2] Persons of Hispanic origin may be of any race. [3] Includes persons of other Hispanic origin, not shown separately. [4] Beginning 1992, persons high school graduates and those with a BA degree or higher.

Source: U.S. Bureau of the Census, *U.S. Census of Population, U.S. Summary,* PC80-1-C1 and *Current Population Reports* P20-455, P20-459, P20-462, P20-465RV, P20-475; and unpublished data.

No. 233. Educational Attainment, by Race, Ethnicity, and Sex: 1960 to 1993

[In percent. For persons 25 years old and over. 1960, 1970 and 1980 as of April 1 and based on sample data from the censuses of population. Other years as of March and based on the Current Population Survey; see text, section 1 and Appendix III. See table 232 for totals for both sexes]

YEAR	ALL RACES [1]		WHITE		BLACK		ASIAN AND PACIFIC ISLANDER		HISPANIC [2]	
	Male	Female	Male	Female	Male	Female	Male	Female	Male	Female
COMPLETED 4 YEARS OF HIGH SCHOOL OR MORE										
1960.	39.5	42.5	41.6	44.7	18.2	21.8	(NA)	(NA)	(NA)	(NA)
1965.	48.0	49.9	50.2	52.2	25.8	28.4	(NA)	(NA)	(NA)	(NA)
1970.	51.9	52.8	54.0	55.0	30.1	32.5	(NA)	(NA)	37.9	34.2
1975.	63.1	62.1	65.0	64.1	41.6	43.3	(NA)	(NA)	39.5	36.7
1980.	67.3	65.8	69.6	68.1	50.8	51.5	(NA)	(NA)	67.3	65.8
1985.	74.4	73.5	76.0	75.1	58.4	60.8	(NA)	(NA)	48.5	47.4
1990.	77.7	77.5	79.1	79.0	65.8	66.5	84.0	77.2	50.3	51.3
1991.	78.5	78.3	79.8	79.9	66.7	66.7	83.8	80.0	51.4	51.2
1992 [3]	79.7	79.2	81.1	80.7	67.0	68.2	(NA)	(NA)	53.7	51.5
1993 [3]	80.5	80.0	81.8	81.3	69.6	71.1	(NA)	(NA)	52.9	53.2
COMPLETED 4 YEARS OF COLLEGE OR MORE										
1960.	9.7	5.8	10.3	6.0	2.8	3.3	(NA)	(NA)	(NA)	(NA)
1965.	12.0	7.1	12.7	7.3	4.9	4.5	(NA)	(NA)	(NA)	(NA)
1970.	13.5	8.1	14.4	8.4	4.2	4.6	(NA)	(NA)	7.8	4.3
1975.	17.6	10.6	18.4	11.0	6.7	6.2	(NA)	(NA)	8.3	4.6
1980.	20.1	12.8	21.3	13.3	8.4	8.3	(NA)	(NA)	9.4	6.0
1985.	23.1	16.0	24.0	16.3	11.2	11.0	(NA)	(NA)	9.7	7.3
1990.	24.4	18.4	25.3	19.0	11.9	10.8	44.9	35.4	9.8	8.7
1991.	24.3	18.8	25.4	19.3	11.4	11.6	43.2	35.5	10.0	9.4
1992 [3]	24.3	18.6	25.2	19.1	11.9	12.0	(NA)	(NA)	10.2	8.5
1993 [3]	24.8	19.2	25.7	19.7	11.9	12.4	(NA)	(NA)	9.5	8.5

NA Not available. [1] Includes other races, not shown separately. [2] Persons of Hispanic origin may be of any race. [3] Beginning 1992, persons high school graduates and those with a BA degree or higher.

Source: U.S. Bureau of the Census, *U.S. Census of Population, 1960, 1970, and 1980, vol.1;* and *Current Population Reports* P20-459, P20-462, P20-475; and unpublished data.

No. 234. Years of School Completed, by Selected Characteristic: 1993

[For persons 25 years old and over. As of March. Based on Current Population Survey; see text, section 1, and Appendix III. For composition of regions, see table 26]

CHARACTERISTIC	Population (1,000)	PERCENT OF POPULATION—					
		Not a high school graduate	High school graduate	With some college, but no degree	With an associate's degree [1]	With a bachelor's degree	With an advanced degree
Total persons.	162,826	19.8	35.4	16.6	6.4	14.5	7.4
Age:							
25 to 34 years old.	41,864	13.1	35.9	19.2	7.9	18.6	5.2
35 to 44 years old.	40,342	11.4	34.0	19.6	8.3	17.6	9.1
45 to 54 years old.	28,503	15.3	35.8	17.1	6.5	14.1	11.2
55 to 64 years old.	21,247	25.7	37.9	13.3	4.4	10.9	7.7
65 to 74 years old.	18,362	34.2	37.5	11.9	3.3	8.5	4.7
75 years old or over	12,508	47.9	29.5	10.0	2.4	6.7	3.5
Sex: Male.	77,644	19.5	33.2	16.6	5.9	15.7	9.1
Female	85,181	20.0	37.4	16.6	6.8	13.5	5.7
Race: White	139,019	18.5	35.6	16.8	6.5	14.9	7.7
Black	17,786	29.6	36.3	16.7	5.3	8.8	3.4
Other	6,021	21.0	26.6	12.2	6.3	22.1	11.8
Hispanic origin: Hispanic	12,100	46.9	26.8	12.8	4.5	6.4	2.6
Non-Hispanic	150,726	17.6	36.1	17.0	6.5	15.2	7.7
Region: Northeast	33,609	18.5	37.9	13.0	6.4	15.3	9.0
Midwest.	38,506	17.9	39.9	16.1	6.1	13.4	6.6
South	55,957	23.3	34.3	16.7	5.8	13.4	6.6
West	34,753	17.5	29.6	20.6	7.6	16.8	7.9
Marital status:							
Never married.	23,046	18.1	31.2	16.7	6.8	19.3	7.9
Married spouse present	103,968	16.7	36.3	16.8	6.7	15.4	8.2
Married spouse absent.	5,791	30.3	34.0	17.7	4.8	9.4	3.8
Separated.	4,343	28.7	36.1	18.9	4.9	8.2	3.1
Widowed	13,668	44.6	33.3	10.3	3.0	5.9	2.8
Divorced	16,353	17.0	37.7	20.7	6.9	11.3	6.4
Civilian labor force status:							
Employed	100,152	11.1	34.8	18.5	7.8	18.1	9.8
Unemployed.	6,716	23.7	40.2	16.7	5.8	9.7	3.9
Not in the labor force.	55,268	35.3	35.9	13.1	3.8	8.6	3.3

[1] Includes vocational degrees.

Source: U.S. Bureau of the Census, unpublished data.

No. 235. Mean Monthly Income, by Highest Degree Earned: 1990

[For persons 18 years old and over. Based on the Survey of Income and Program Participation; see source for details]

CHARACTERISTIC	Total persons	LEVEL OF DEGREE								
		Not a high school graduate	High school graduate only	Some college, no degree	Voca-tional	Asso-ciate's	Bache-lor's	Master's	Profes-sional	Doc-torate
All persons	182,591	38,012	65,291	33,191	4,973	7,570	22,845	7,599	2,054	1,056
MEAN MONTHLY INCOME [1] (dol.)										
All persons [2]	1,599	856	1,357	1,545	1,568	1,879	2,489	3,211	5,554	4,545
Age: 18 to 24 years old. .	724	461	778	698	892	951	1,154	(B)	(B)	(B)
25 to 34 years old. . . .	1,546	859	1,340	1,529	1,392	1,639	2,154	2,478	3,310	(B)
35 to 44 years old. . . .	2,056	947	1,546	2,028	1,784	2,265	2,634	3,580	5,719	4,917
45 to 54 years old. . . .	2,148	1,064	1,790	2,140	1,781	2,357	3,510	3,512	7,597	4,625
55 to 64 years old. . . .	1,725	951	1,393	2,046	1,877	2,125	2,920	3,421	8,320	(B)
65 years old and over .	1,275	852	1,191	1,656	1,483	1,469	2,439	2,470	4,301	(B)
Sex: Male.	2,148	1,166	1,853	2,002	2,085	2,380	3,235	3,748	6,367	4,915
Female	1,096	579	943	1,115	1,290	1,425	1,698	2,614	3,070	3,162
Race: White	1,672	909	1,405	1,595	1,593	1,920	2,552	3,248	5,611	4,679
Black	1,070	652	1,009	1,204	1,170	1,595	2,002	2,786	(B)	(B)
Hispanic [3]	1,078	760	1,092	1,298	1,314	1,549	1,895	2,840	(B)	(B)

B Base figure too small to meet statistical standards for reliability of a derived figure.   [1] For definition of mean, see Guide to Tabular Presentation.   [2] Includes other races, not shown separately.   [3] Persons of Hispanic origin may be of any race.

Source: U.S. Bureau of the Census, Current Population Reports, P70-32.

No. 236. Educational Attainment—States: 1990

[As of **April 1. For persons 25 years old and over, except as indicated.** Based on the 1990 Census of Population; see text, section 1, and Appendix III]

STATE	Population (1,000)	PERCENT OF POPULATION—						
		Not a high school graduate	High school graduate	With some college, but no degree	With an associate's degree	With a bachelor's degree	With an advanced degree	Drop-outs [1]
United States	**158,868**	**24.8**	**30.0**	**18.7**	**6.2**	**13.1**	**7.2**	**11.2**
Alabama.	2,546	33.1	29.4	16.8	5.0	10.1	5.5	12.6
Alaska.	323	13.4	28.7	27.6	7.2	15.0	8.0	10.9
Arizona.	2,301	21.3	26.1	25.4	6.8	13.3	7.0	14.4
Arkansas	1,496	33.7	32.7	16.6	3.7	8.9	4.5	11.4
California	18,695	23.8	22.3	22.6	7.9	15.3	8.1	14.2
Colorado.	2,107	15.6	26.5	24.0	6.9	18.0	9.0	9.8
Connecticut.	2,199	20.8	29.5	15.9	6.6	16.2	11.0	9.0
Delaware	428	22.5	32.7	16.9	6.5	13.7	7.7	10.4
District of Columbia	409	26.9	21.2	15.6	3.1	16.1	17.2	13.9
Florida	8,887	25.6	30.1	19.4	6.6	12.0	6.3	14.3
Georgia	4,023	29.1	29.6	17.0	5.0	12.9	6.4	14.1
Hawaii	710	19.9	28.7	20.1	8.3	15.8	7.1	7.5
Idaho.	601	20.3	30.4	24.2	7.5	12.4	5.3	10.4
Illinois.	7,294	23.8	30.0	19.4	5.8	13.6	7.5	10.6
Indiana.	3,489	24.4	38.2	16.6	5.3	9.2	6.4	11.4
Iowa	1,777	19.9	38.5	17.0	7.7	11.7	5.2	6.6
Kansas.	1,566	18.7	32.8	21.9	5.4	14.1	7.0	8.7
Kentucky	2,334	35.4	31.8	15.2	4.1	8.1	5.5	13.3
Louisiana	2,537	31.7	31.7	17.2	3.3	10.5	5.6	12.5
Maine.	796	21.2	37.1	16.1	6.9	12.7	6.1	8.3
Maryland	3,123	21.6	28.1	18.6	5.2	15.6	10.9	10.9
Massachusetts.	3,962	20.0	29.7	15.8	7.2	16.6	10.6	8.5
Michigan.	5,843	23.2	32.3	20.4	6.7	10.9	6.4	10.0
Minnesota.	2,771	17.6	33.0	19.0	8.6	15.6	6.3	6.4
Mississippi	1,539	35.7	27.5	16.9	5.2	9.7	5.1	11.8
Missouri	3,292	26.1	33.1	18.4	4.5	11.7	6.1	11.4
Montana.	508	19.0	33.5	22.1	5.6	14.1	5.7	8.1
Nebraska	996	18.2	34.7	21.1	7.1	13.1	5.9	7.0
Nevada	790	21.2	31.5	25.8	6.2	10.1	5.2	15.2
New Hampshire	714	17.8	31.7	18.0	8.1	16.4	7.9	9.4
New Jersey.	5,166	23.3	31.1	15.5	5.2	16.0	8.8	9.6
New Mexico	923	24.9	28.7	20.9	5.0	12.1	8.3	11.7
New York	11,819	25.2	29.5	15.7	6.5	13.2	9.9	9.9
North Carolina.	4,253	30.0	29.0	16.8	6.8	12.0	5.4	12.5
North Dakota.	397	23.3	28.0	20.5	10.0	13.5	4.5	4.6
Ohio	6,925	24.3	36.3	17.0	5.3	11.1	5.9	8.9
Oklahoma.	1,995	25.4	30.5	21.3	5.0	11.8	6.0	10.4
Oregon.	1,855	18.5	28.9	25.0	6.9	13.6	7.0	11.8
Pennsylvania	7,873	25.3	38.6	12.9	5.2	11.3	6.6	9.1
Rhode Island.	659	28.0	29.5	15.0	6.3	13.5	7.8	11.1
South Carolina.	2,168	31.7	29.5	15.8	6.3	11.2	5.4	11.7
South Dakota	431	22.9	33.7	18.8	7.4	12.3	4.9	7.7
Tennessee	3,139	32.9	30.0	16.9	4.2	10.5	5.4	13.4
Texas.	10,311	27.9	25.6	21.1	5.2	13.9	6.5	12.9
Utah	897	14.9	27.2	27.9	7.8	15.4	6.8	8.7
Vermont	357	19.2	34.6	14.7	7.2	15.4	8.9	8.0
Virginia	3,975	24.8	26.6	18.5	5.5	15.4	9.1	10.0
Washington.	3,126	16.2	27.9	25.0	7.9	15.9	7.0	10.6
West Virginia	1,172	34.0	36.6	13.2	3.8	7.5	4.8	10.9
Wisconsin	3,094	21.4	37.1	16.7	7.1	12.1	5.6	7.1
Wyoming	278	17.0	33.2	24.2	6.9	13.1	5.7	6.9

[1] For persons 16 to 19 years old. A dropout is a person who is not in regular school and who has not completed the 12th grade or received a general equivalency degree.

Source: U.S. Bureau of the Census, *1990 Census of Population*, CPH-L-96.

No. 237. Preprimary School Enrollment—Summary: 1970 to 1992

[As of **October**. Civilian noninstitutional population. Includes public and nonpublic nursery school and kindergarten programs. Excludes 5 year olds enrolled in elementary school. Based on Current Population Survey; see text, section 1]

ITEM	1970	1975	1980	1985	1988	1989	1990	1991	1992
NUMBER OF CHILDREN (1,000)									
Population, 3 to 5 years old	10,949	10,183	9,284	10,733	10,994	11,038	11,207	11,370	11,544
Total enrolled [1]	4,104	4,954	4,878	5,865	5,977	6,026	6,659	6,334	6,403
Nursery	1,094	1,745	1,981	2,477	2,621	2,825	3,378	2,824	2,857
Public	332	570	628	846	852	930	1,202	996	1,074
Private	762	1,174	1,353	1,631	1,770	1,894	2,177	1,827	1,784
Kindergarten	3,010	3,211	2,897	3,388	3,356	3,201	3,281	3,510	3,546
Public	2,498	2,682	2,438	2,847	2,875	2,704	2,767	2,968	2,996
Private	511	528	459	541	481	496	513	543	550
White	3,443	4,105	3,994	4,757	4,891	4,911	5,389	5,104	5,137
Black	586	731	725	919	814	872	964	928	966
Hispanic [2]	(NA)	(NA)	370	496	544	520	642	675	728
3 years old	454	683	857	1,035	1,028	1,005	1,205	1,075	1,081
4 years old	1,007	1,418	1,423	1,765	1,768	1,882	2,086	1,993	1,982
5 years old	2,643	2,852	2,598	3,065	3,183	3,139	3,367	3,266	3,340
ENROLLMENT RATE									
Total enrolled [1]	37.5	48.6	52.5	54.6	54.4	54.6	59.4	55.7	55.5
White	37.8	48.6	52.7	54.7	55.4	55.0	59.7	56.2	55.8
Black	34.9	48.1	51.8	55.8	48.2	54.2	57.8	53.1	55.1
Hispanic [2]	(NA)	(NA)	43.3	43.3	44.2	41.6	49.0	46.4	48.4
3 years old	12.9	21.5	27.3	28.8	27.6	27.1	32.6	28.2	27.7
4 years old	27.8	40.5	46.3	49.1	49.1	51.0	56.0	53.0	52.1
5 years old	69.3	81.3	84.7	86.5	86.6	86.4	88.8	86.0	87.2

NA Not available.   [1] Includes races not shown separately.   [2] Persons of Hispanic origin may be of any race. The method of identifying Hispanic children was changed in 1980 from allocation based on status of mother to status reported for each child. The number of Hispanic children using the new method is larger.
Source: U.S. Bureau of the Census, *Current Population Reports*, P20-474.

No. 238. Preprimary School Enrollment, by Level of Enrollment and Labor Force Status of Mother: 1978 and 1992

[See headnote, table 237]

RACE AND LABOR FORCE STATUS	ALL CHILDREN (1,000)		PERCENT ENROLLED IN—							PERCENT NOT ENROLLED	
			Nursery school				Kindergarten				
			Total		Full day		Total		Full day, 1992		
	1978	1992	1978	1992	1978	1992	1978	1992		1978	1992
TOTAL [1]											
Children 3 to 5 years old	9,110	11,544	20.0	24.7	6.9	7.7	30.3	30.7	13.2	49.7	44.6
Living with mother	8,883	10,646	19.8	25.1	6.8	7.7	30.4	30.4	12.8	49.8	44.5
Mother in labor force	4,097	6,073	22.1	26.8	11.4	10.3	31.0	31.6	14.0	47.0	41.6
Employed	3,737	5,538	22.5	27.4	11.7	10.5	31.0	31.8	13.8	46.5	40.8
Full-time	2,446	3,746	22.3	26.3	15.2	13.3	31.2	31.4	14.5	46.5	42.3
Part-time	1,291	1,792	23.0	29.5	5.2	4.6	30.5	32.6	12.6	46.4	37.9
Unemployed	360	535	17.4	21.1	7.8	8.8	30.6	29.7	15.1	52.0	49.2
Mother not in labor force	4,786	4,573	17.9	22.7	2.9	4.1	29.9	28.8	11.3	52.2	48.5
WHITE											
Children 3 to 5 years old	7,460	9,213	19.5	25.5	5.2	6.4	30.1	30.2	11.6	50.5	44.3
Living with mother	7,301	8,631	19.4	26.0	5.1	6.6	30.1	30.2	11.6	50.5	43.8
Mother in labor force	3,235	4,899	21.1	28.1	9.2	9.3	30.4	30.8	12.2	48.5	41.1
Employed	3,014	4,557	21.3	28.7	9.4	9.7	30.7	30.9	12.2	48.0	40.4
Full-time	1,877	2,984	20.1	27.5	12.6	12.8	31.0	30.1	12.6	48.9	42.4
Part-time	1,137	1,575	23.3	31.0	4.1	4.0	30.2	32.3	11.6	46.5	36.7
Unemployed	220	340	17.9	20.3	6.4	3.5	27.1	30.3	12.1	55.0	49.4
Mother not in labor force	4,067	3,732	18.0	23.2	1.9	3.0	29.8	29.4	10.8	52.2	47.4
BLACK											
Children 3 to 5 years old	1,410	1,752	22.1	21.1	15.3	13.6	31.0	34.6	22.5	46.9	44.8
Living with mother	1,347	1,493	21.7	20.0	15.5	13.1	31.3	32.8	21.1	47.1	47.2
Mother in labor force	731	874	25.9	19.7	20.6	15.0	32.5	36.5	24.3	41.6	43.8
Employed	598	693	28.0	19.3	22.8	14.1	31.7	38.5	25.0	40.3	42.2
Full-time	469	556	29.6	19.1	24.8	14.6	32.0	38.5	24.8	38.4	42.4
Part-time	128	137	22.3	20.4	15.8	12.4	30.7	38.0	25.5	47.0	41.6
Unemployed	133	181	16.7	21.0	10.6	18.2	35.7	29.3	21.5	47.6	49.7
Mother not in labor force	616	620	16.6	20.5	9.4	10.5	29.8	27.6	16.6	53.5	51.9
HISPANIC [2]											
Children 3 to 5 years old	720	1,503	11.8	14.0	5.0	4.9	29.1	34.5	11.9	59.1	51.5
Living with mother	713	1,394	11.7	14.4	5.0	5.1	28.9	33.7	13.6	59.4	51.9
Mother in labor force	296	623	16.3	17.0	7.1	7.4	27.5	35.3	14.9	56.2	47.7
Employed	263	519	17.1	17.7	6.7	7.7	26.0	36.8	16.2	56.9	45.5
Full-time	196	385	16.9	19.0	7.5	9.9	25.9	36.9	14.8	57.2	44.1
Part-time	67	133	(B)	14.3	(B)	12.8	(B)	37.6	20.3	(B)	48.1
Unemployed	33	104	(B)	14.4	(B)	4.8	(B)	26.9	9.6	(B)	58.7
Mother not in labor force	417	771	8.4	12.3	3.5	3.2	29.9	32.4	12.3	61.7	55.3

B Base figure too small to meet statistical standards for reliability of derived figure.   [1] Includes races not shown separately.   [2] Persons of Hispanic origin may be of any race.
Source: U.S. Bureau of the Census, *Current Population Reports*, P20-474.

No. 239. Public Elementary and Secondary Schools—Summary: 1980 to 1993

[For school year ending in year shown, except as indicated. Data are estimates]

ITEM	Unit	1980	1985	1989	1990	1991	1992	1993
School districts, total.	Number .	16,044	15,812	15,530	15,449	15,439	15,360	15,218
ENROLLMENT								
Population 5-17 years old [1]	1,000. . .	48,041	44,788	45,052	44,948	45,311	45,923	46,654
Percent of resident population	Percent .	21.4	19.0	18.4	18.2	18.2	18.2	18.3
Fall enrollment [2]	1,000. . .	41,778	39,354	40,207	40,527	41,198	41,956	42,659
Percent of population 5-17 years old	Percent .	87.0	87.9	89.2	90.2	90.9	91.4	91.4
Elementary [3]	1,000. . .	24,397	23,830	25,752	26,397	27,075	27,582	28,008
Secondary [4]	1,000. . .	17,381	15,524	14,455	14,130	14,123	14,374	14,651
Average daily:								
Attendance (ADA)	1,000. . .	38,411	36,530	37,178	37,573	38,181	38,928	39,578
High school graduates	1,000. . .	2,762	2,424	2,468	2,327	2,232	2,233	2,249
INSTRUCTIONAL STAFF								
Total [5]	1,000. . .	2,521	2,473	2,652	2,685	2,745	2,764	2,811
Classroom teachers.	1,000. . .	2,211	2,175	2,324	2,362	2,409	2,431	2,464
Average salaries:								
Instructional staff.	Dollar . .	16,715	24,666	30,850	32,638	34,412	35,550	36,431
Classroom teachers.	Dollar . .	15,970	23,600	29,564	31,367	33,090	34,084	35,027
REVENUES								
Revenue receipts	Mil. dol. .	97,635	141,013	193,235	208,656	224,080	235,250	246,199
Federal	Mil. dol. .	9,020	9,533	12,342	13,184	14,180	15,703	16,973
State.	Mil. dol. .	47,929	69,107	93,796	100,787	107,970	111,784	115,168
Local	Mil. dol. .	40,686	62,373	87,096	94,685	101,931	107,763	114,058
Percent of total:								
Federal	Percent .	9.2	6.8	6.4	6.3	6.3	6.7	6.9
State.	Percent .	49.1	49.0	48.5	48.3	48.2	47.5	46.8
Local	Percent .	41.7	44.2	45.1	45.4	45.5	45.8	46.3
EXPENDITURES								
Total	Mil. dol. .	96,105	139,382	191,378	209,698	227,422	238,884	251,706
Current expenditures								
(day schools)	Mil. dol. .	85,661	127,230	171,527	186,583	200,963	210,358	220,604
Other current expenditures [6]	Mil. dol. .	1,859	2,109	3,146	3,341	3,683	4,653	5,438
Capital outlay	Mil. dol. .	6,504	7,529	13,310	16,012	18,289	18,935	19,896
Interest on school debt	Mil. dol. .	2,081	2,514	3,395	3,762	4,487	4,937	5,769
Percent of total:								
Current expenditures								
(day schools)	Percent .	89.1	91.3	89.8	89.0	88.4	88.1	87.6
Other current expenditures [6]	Percent .	1.9	1.5	1.5	1.6	1.6	1.9	2.2
Capital outlay	Percent .	6.8	5.4	6.9	7.6	8.0	7.9	7.9
Interest on school debt	Percent .	2.2	1.8	1.8	1.8	2.0	2.1	2.3
In current dollars:								
Revenue receipts per pupil enrolled	Dollar . .	2,337	3,583	4,806	5,149	5,439	5,607	5,771
Current expenditures per pupil enrolled	Dollar . .	2,050	3,233	4,266	4,604	4,878	5,014	5,171
In constant (1993) dollars: [7]								
Revenue receipts per pupil enrolled	Dollar . .	4,373	4,918	5,758	5,886	5,898	5,891	5,771
Current expenditures per pupil enrolled	Dollar . .	3,837	4,437	5,111	5,264	5,290	5,268	5,171

[1] Estimated resident population as of July 1 of the previous year. Estimates reflect revisions based on the 1990 Census of Population. [2] Fall enrollment of the previous year. [3] Kindergarten through grade 6. [4] Grades 7 through 12. [5] Full-time equivalent. [6] Current expenses for summer schools, adult education, post-high school vocational education, personnel retraining, etc., when operated by local school districts and not part of regular public elementary and secondary day-school program. [7] Compiled by U.S. Bureau of the Census. Deflated by the Consumer Price Index, all urban consumers (for school year) supplied by U.S. National Center for Education Statistics.

Source: Except as noted, National Education Association, Washington, DC, *Estimates of School Statistics*, annual (copyright); *Rankings of the States*, annual (copyright); and unpublished data.

Education

No. 240. Elementary and Secondary Schools—Enrollment and Teachers, With Projections, 1960 to 2004

[In thousands, except percent. As of fall. Schools are classified by type of organization, rather than by grade group; elementary includes kindergarten and secondary includes junior high]

ITEM	TOTAL			PUBLIC			PRIVATE [1]		
	Total	Elementary	Secondary	Total	Elementary	Secondary	Total	Elementary	Secondary
Enrollment: 1960....	42,181	29,150	13,031	36,281	24,350	11,931	5,900	4,800	1,100
1965	48,369	31,504	16,865	42,069	26,604	15,465	6,300	4,900	1,400
1970	51,257	31,544	19,713	45,894	27,492	18,402	5,363	4,052	1,311
1975	49,819	29,356	20,464	44,819	25,656	19,164	5,000	3,700	1,300
1980	46,208	28,188	18,020	40,877	24,196	16,681	5,331	3,992	1,339
1985	44,979	28,330	16,649	39,422	24,135	15,287	5,557	4,195	1,362
1989	45,898	30,570	15,328	40,543	26,408	14,135	5,355	4,162	1,193
1990	46,448	31,145	15,305	41,217	27,050	14,167	5,231	4,095	1,136
1991, est........	47,199	31,638	15,561	42,000	27,564	14,436	5,199	4,074	1,125
1992, est........	47,872	31,996	15,875	42,496	27,784	14,712	5,375	4,212	1,163
1993, proj.......	48,925	32,577	16,348	43,454	28,297	15,157	5,471	4,280	1,191
1994, proj.......	49,819	32,956	16,863	44,254	28,623	15,631	5,565	4,333	1,232
1995, proj.......	50,709	33,411	17,298	45,049	29,018	16,031	5,660	4,393	1,267
2000, proj.......	54,412	35,715	18,697	48,345	31,027	17,318	6,067	4,688	1,379
2003, proj.......	55,459	36,031	19,428	49,280	31,273	18,007	6,179	4,758	1,421
2004, proj.......	55,706	35,895	19,810	49,506	31,142	18,364	6,200	4,753	1,446
Teachers: 1960....	1,600	991	609	1,408	858	550	192	133	59
1965	1,933	1,112	822	1,710	965	746	223	147	76
1970	2,292	1,283	1,009	2,059	1,130	929	233	153	80
1975	2,453	1,353	1,100	2,198	1,181	1,017	255	172	83
1980	2,486	1,402	1,084	2,185	1,190	995	301	212	89
1985	2,549	1,483	1,066	2,206	1,237	969	343	246	97
1989	2,679	1,622	1,057	2,357	1,387	970	322	235	87
1990	2,753	1,680	1,073	2,398	1,426	972	356	254	101
1991, est........	2,787	1,713	1,074	2,432	1,459	973	355	254	101
1992, est........	2,814	1,738	1,076	2,451	1,478	973	363	260	103
1993, proj.......	2,838	1,752	1,086	2,474	1,491	984	364	261	103
1994, proj.......	2,890	1,736	1,155	2,520	1,476	1,044	370	260	111
1995, proj.......	2,950	1,768	1,181	2,572	1,504	1,068	378	265	113
2000, proj.......	3,179	1,903	1,276	2,772	1,618	1,154	407	285	122
2003, proj.......	3,268	1,943	1,325	2,851	1,653	1,198	418	291	127
2004, proj.......	3,296	1,949	1,347	2,875	1,658	1,218	420	292	129

[1] Data beginning 1970 are estimated.

Source: U.S. National Center for Education Statistics, *Digest of Education Statistics*, annual; and *Projections of Education Statistics*, annual.

No. 241. Public Elementary and Secondary Schools, by Type and Size of School: 1991-92

[Data reported by schools, rather than school districts]

ENROLLMENT SIZE OF SCHOOL	NUMBER OF SCHOOLS					ENROLLMENT (1,000)				
	Total	Elementary [1]	Secondary [2]	Combined [3]	Other [4]	Total	Elementary [1]	Secondary [2]	Combined [3]	Other [4]
Total.............	84,578	59,258	20,120	2,481	2,719	41,949	27,139	13,647	1,010	153
PERCENT DISTRIBUTION [5]										
Total.............	100.0	100.0	100.0	100.0	100.0	100.0	100.0	100.0	100.0	100.0
Under 100 students	8.8	6.2	11.8	27.2	57.0	0.9	0.7	0.9	3.0	15.7
100 to 199 students......	10.4	9.8	11.0	14.9	18.9	3.1	3.3	2.4	5.3	16.7
200 to 299 students......	11.7	12.7	9.1	9.8	9.5	5.8	7.0	3.3	6.0	14.7
300 to 399 students......	14.1	16.5	8.1	8.5	6.6	9.7	12.6	4.2	7.4	14.2
400 to 499 students......	13.5	15.9	7.6	9.3	2.1	12.0	15.5	5.1	10.3	6.0
500 to 599 students......	11.8	13.6	7.5	6.1	1.2	12.7	16.3	6.1	8.3	3.9
600 to 699 students......	8.6	9.5	6.6	5.4	1.2	10.9	13.4	6.3	8.5	4.7
700 to 799 students......	6.0	6.3	5.8	4.0	0.6	8.9	10.2	6.4	7.3	3.0
800 to 999 students......	6.8	6.1	9.2	6.1	1.3	11.9	11.7	12.2	13.3	7.0
1,000 to 1,499 students ...	5.8	3.2	13.7	6.1	1.3	13.8	8.1	24.7	17.6	9.3
1,500 to 1,999 students ...	1.7	0.3	5.8	1.7	0.3	5.6	1.0	14.6	7.2	3.5
2,000 to 2,999 students ...	0.9	(Z)	3.3	0.8	0.1	4.0	0.2	11.5	4.6	1.4
3,000 or more students....	0.1	(Z)	0.5	0.1	(Z)	0.8	(Z)	2.5	1.2	(Z)
Average enrollment	507	458	678	407	150	507	458	678	407	160

Z Represents or rounds to zero. [1] Includes schools beginning with grade 6 or below and with no grade higher than 8. [2] Includes schools with no grade lower than 7. [3] Includes schools with both elementary and secondary grades. [4] Includes special education, alternative, and other schools not classified by grade span. [5] Data for those schools reporting enrollment.

Source: U.S. National Center for Education Statistics, *Digest of Education Statistics*, annual.

No. 242. Public Elementary and Secondary School Enrollment With Projections, by State: 1980 to 1993

[In thousands, except rate. As of fall. Includes unclassified students. Data will not agree with national level projections presented in other tables due to revised projections at the national level]

| STATE | ENROLLMENT | | | | | | | | | | ENROLL-MENT RATE [1] | |
| | K through Grade 8 | | | | | Grades 9 through 12 | | | | | | |
	1980	1990	1991, est.	1992, proj.	1993, proj.	1980	1990	1991, est.	1992, proj.	1993, proj.	1980	1991, est.
U.S.	**27,647**	**29,878**	**30,470**	**30,663**	**31,091**	**13,231**	**11,338**	**11,530**	**11,587**	**11,880**	**86.5**	**91.5**
Alabama	528	527	526	533	536	231	195	196	197	199	87.6	93.0
Alaska	60	85	89	84	86	26	29	30	29	30	94.0	95.7
Arizona	357	479	490	513	530	157	161	167	172	179	88.9	93.9
Arkansas	310	314	315	316	316	138	123	123	125	127	90.3	96.2
California	2,730	3,615	3,720	3,850	3,967	1,347	1,336	1,387	1,410	1,449	88.0	92.6
Colorado	374	420	436	428	432	172	154	157	159	163	92.2	94.7
Connecticut	364	347	355	367	378	168	122	126	120	122	83.3	91.5
Delaware	62	73	75	76	79	37	27	28	29	29	79.5	88.1
District of Columbia	71	61	61	62	64	29	19	20	19	20	91.8	102.0
Florida	1,042	1,370	1,428	1,488	1,545	468	492	505	479	504	84.4	92.8
Georgia	742	849	868	898	920	327	303	309	310	319	86.9	94.3
Hawaii	110	123	127	133	138	55	49	48	49	52	83.4	87.4
Idaho	144	160	161	152	149	59	61	64	62	65	95.4	95.6
Illinois	1,335	1,310	1,328	1,305	1,318	649	512	520	521	531	82.6	87.6
Indiana	708	676	676	682	680	347	279	281	285	290	88.0	90.3
Iowa	351	345	348	330	323	183	139	143	145	148	88.4	92.4
Kansas	283	320	325	323	324	133	117	120	125	128	88.7	92.0
Kentucky	464	459	466	440	434	206	177	180	181	184	83.7	92.2
Louisiana	544	586	573	570	567	234	199	193	197	203	80.3	85.6
Maine	153	155	157	160	163	70	60	60	60	63	91.5	95.8
Maryland	493	527	543	571	594	258	188	193	196	203	83.9	89.2
Massachusetts	676	604	616	637	655	346	230	230	226	230	88.6	89.9
Michigan	1,227	1,145	1,157	1,161	1,166	570	440	434	440	449	90.1	89.9
Minnesota	482	546	557	558	559	272	211	217	222	230	87.2	91.0
Mississippi	330	372	370	362	361	147	131	134	135	136	79.6	92.0
Missouri	567	588	596	601	606	277	228	231	237	244	83.8	86.0
Montana	106	111	113	108	106	50	42	43	42	43	92.9	95.0
Nebraska	189	198	201	196	195	91	76	78	78	79	86.6	88.7
Nevada	101	150	158	158	162	49	51	54	56	60	93.4	96.3
New Hampshire	112	126	130	141	147	55	46	47	48	50	85.3	90.8
New Jersey	820	784	801	824	852	426	306	309	302	309	81.5	86.8
New Mexico	186	208	213	216	221	85	94	96	95	97	89.5	94.7
New York	1,838	1,828	1,862	1,854	1,881	1,033	770	782	779	793	80.8	87.3
North Carolina	786	783	795	815	836	343	304	303	306	314	90.0	94.7
North Dakota	77	85	85	83	82	40	33	33	34	35	85.9	93.2
Ohio	1,312	1,258	1,277	1,268	1,269	645	514	506	519	529	84.8	88.1
Oklahoma	399	425	432	415	408	179	154	156	158	162	92.9	95.3
Oregon	319	340	359	347	347	145	132	139	141	144	88.5	92.3
Pennsylvania	1,231	1,172	1,195	1,201	1,213	678	496	498	500	509	80.4	84.1
Rhode Island	98	102	104	105	106	51	37	38	37	38	79.7	88.3
South Carolina	426	452	456	462	467	193	170	171	174	179	88.1	94.1
South Dakota	86	95	96	96	96	42	34	35	36	37	87.4	91.4
Tennessee	602	598	605	608	612	252	226	229	227	233	87.8	94.5
Texas	2,049	2,511	2,575	2,516	2,532	851	872	889	892	902	92.4	98.6
Utah	250	325	327	316	311	93	122	129	133	140	98.2	97.7
Vermont	66	71	73	72	74	29	25	24	26	26	87.9	94.3
Virginia	703	728	741	782	812	307	270	275	274	283	90.7	94.4
Washington	515	613	633	632	639	242	227	237	240	250	91.0	93.2
West Virginia	270	224	222	210	204	113	98	99	95	96	92.6	97.0
Wisconsin	528	566	560	569	566	303	232	235	241	248	82.1	85.8
Wyoming	70	71	74	66	64	28	27	28	27	28	97.3	101.1

[1] Percent of persons 5-17 years old. 1980 based on enumerated resident population as of April 1; 1991 based on estimated resident population July 1.

Source: U.S. National Center for Education Statistics, *Digest of Education Statistics*, annual.

No. 243. Public Elementary and Secondary School Enrollment, by Grade: 1960 to 1991

[In thousands. 1960, for school year; thereafter, as of **fall** of year. Beginning 1970, kindergarten includes nursery schools. For 1960, enrollment figures are prorated and 12th grade includes postgraduates. See also *Historical Statistics, Colonial Times to 1970*, series H 420-424]

GRADE	1960	1970	1975	1980	1984	1985	1986	1987	1988	1989	1990	1991, est.
Pupils enrolled .	36,087	45,894	44,819	40,877	39,208	39,422	39,753	40,008	40,189	40,543	41,217	42,000
Kindergarten and grades 1-8	27,602	32,558	30,515	27,647	26,905	27,034	27,420	27,933	28,501	29,152	29,878	30,470
Kindergarten.	1,923	2,564	2,971	2,689	3,009	3,192	3,310	3,388	3,433	3,486	3,610	3,664
First	3,733	3,817	3,238	2,894	3,113	3,239	3,358	3,407	3,460	3,485	3,499	3,554
Second	3,436	3,654	3,027	2,800	2,904	2,941	3,054	3,173	3,223	3,289	3,327	3,359
Third	3,302	3,663	3,038	2,893	2,765	2,895	2,933	3,046	3,167	3,235	3,297	3,333
Fourth	3,146	3,675	3,112	3,107	2,772	2,771	2,896	2,938	3,051	3,182	3,248	3,312
Fifth	3,118	3,635	3,281	3,130	2,761	2,776	2,775	2,901	2,945	3,067	3,197	3,268
Sixth	3,070	3,598	3,476	3,038	2,831	2,789	2,806	2,811	2,937	2,987	3,110	3,238
Seventh	3,173	3,662	3,619	3,085	3,036	2,938	2,899	2,910	2,905	3,027	3,067	3,180
Eighth	2,701	3,601	3,636	3,086	3,186	2,982	2,870	2,839	2,853	2,853	2,979	3,020
Unclassified [1]	(X)	690	1,116	924	527	511	520	520	527	540	543	541
Grades 9-12	8,485	13,336	14,304	13,231	12,304	12,388	12,333	12,076	11,687	11,390	11,338	11,530
Ninth	2,412	3,654	3,879	3,377	3,441	3,439	3,256	3,143	3,106	3,141	3,169	3,310
Tenth	2,258	3,458	3,723	3,368	3,145	3,230	3,215	3,020	2,895	2,868	2,896	2,914
Eleventh	2,063	3,128	3,354	3,195	2,819	2,866	2,954	2,936	2,749	2,629	2,612	2,643
Twelfth	1,752	2,775	2,986	2,925	2,599	2,550	2,601	2,681	2,650	2,473	2,381	2,390
Unclassified [1]	(X)	321	362	366	300	303	308	296	288	279	282	273

X Not applicable. [1] Includes ungraded and special education.

Source: U.S. National Center for Education Statistics, *Digest of Education Statistics*, annual.

No. 244. Public Elementary and Secondary School Teachers—Selected Characteristics: 1990-91

[For school year. Based on survey and subject to sampling error; for details, see source. Excludes prekindergarten teachers. See table 258 for similar data on private school teachers]

CHARACTERISTIC	Unit	AGE				SEX		RACE/ETHNICITY		
		Under 30 years old	30 to 39 years old	40 to 49 years old	Over 50 years old	Male	Female	White [1]	Black [1]	Hispanic
Total teachers [2]	1,000 . .	312	731	1,002	514	719	1,840	2,214	212	87
Highest degree held:										
Bachelor's	Percent .	84.1	56.4	43.8	41.6	44.7	54.7	51.5	50.8	61.0
Master's	Percent .	14.4	39.1	48.8	49.9	47.0	40.1	42.7	42.1	32.9
Education specialist	Percent .	1.2	3.4	5.9	5.9	5.3	4.3	4.5	5.0	4.3
Doctorate	Percent .	-	0.4	1.0	1.4	1.3	0.6	0.7	1.3	0.9
Full-time teaching experience:										
Less than 3 years	Percent .	41.8	10.2	3.5	1.5	7.8	10.4	9.7	6.5	14.0
3 to 9 years	Percent .	58.1	38.7	16.3	7.3	19.9	28.4	26.3	20.0	33.4
10 to 20 years	Percent .	0.1	51.0	49.1	26.0	37.0	39.8	39.0	40.9	39.6
20 years or more	Percent .	(X)	0.1	31.1	65.2	35.3	21.4	25.1	32.8	13.1
Full-time teachers	1,000 . .	283	650	925	481	668	1,680	2,021	202	82
Earned income	Dol. . . .	24,918	30,108	36,083	38,614	37,874	31,870	33,611	33,539	32,907
Salary	Dol. . . .	22,779	27,918	33,690	36,333	33,360	30,476	31,293	31,579	30,743
Supplemental contract during school year:										
Teachers receiving	1,000 . .	122	231	313	122	354	435	703	49	25
Salary	Dol. . . .	1,675	2,045	1,914	2,088	2,663	1,357	1,977	1,664	1,709
Supplemental contract during summer:										
Teachers receiving.	1,000 . .	54	113	162	64	156	237	321	45	18
Salary	Dol. . . .	1,615	1,969	2,018	2,294	2,328	1,773	1,935	2,251	2,375
Teachers with nonschool employment:										
Teaching/tutoring	1,000 . .	13	30	47	20	39	71	95	8	5
Education related	1,000 . .	9	18	28	12	31	36	59	5	2
Not education related.	1,000 . .	33	63	91	42	130	99	204	16	5

- Represents or rounds to zero.   X Not applicable.   [1] Non-Hispanic.   [2] Includes teachers with no degrees and associates degrees, not shown separately.

Source: U.S. National Center for Education Statistics, *Digest of Education Statistics*, 1993.

No. 245. Public Elementary and Secondary Schools—Number and Average Salary of Classroom Teachers, 1960 to 1993, and by State, 1993

[Estimates for school year ending in **June** of year shown. Schools classified by type of organization rather than by grade-group; elementary includes kindergarten]

YEAR AND STATE	TEACHERS [1] (1,000)			AVG. SALARY ($1,000)			YEAR AND STATE	TEACHERS [1] (1,000)			AVG. SALARY ($1,000)		
	Total	Elementary	Secondary	All teachers	Elementary	Secondary		Total	Elementary	Secondary	All teachers	Elementary	Secondary
1960.....	1,355	834	521	5.0	4.8	5.3	LA......	45.6	31.5	14.1	27.6	27.6	27.6
1970.....	2,008	1,109	899	8.6	8.4	8.9	ME......	15.1	9.3	5.8	30.3	29.7	31.4
1975.....	2,171	1,169	1,001	11.7	11.3	12.0	MD......	43.4	25.3	18.1	38.8	37.5	39.9
1980.....	2,211	1,206	1,005	16.0	15.6	16.5	MA......	57.2	24.6	32.6	38.2	38.2	38.2
1984.....	2,144	1,189	955	21.9	21.5	22.6	MI......	82.4	57.4	25.0	43.6	43.6	43.6
1985.....	2,175	1,212	963	23.6	23.2	24.2	MN......	45.3	23.3	22.0	35.1	34.5	35.7
1986.....	2,215	1,242	973	25.2	24.7	25.8	MS......	28.0	17.3	10.7	24.4	24.0	24.9
1987.....	2,249	1,274	975	26.6	26.1	27.2	MO......	53.0	28.2	24.8	29.4	28.6	30.3
1988.....	2,282	1,308	974	28.0	27.5	28.8	MT......	10.1	6.7	3.4	27.6	27.4	27.9
1989.....	2,324	1,354	970	29.6	29.0	30.2	NE......	19.0	10.8	8.2	28.8	28.8	28.8
1990.....	2,362	1,390	972	31.4	30.8	32.0	NV......	12.0	7.2	4.8	34.1	33.4	35.2
1991.....	2,409	1,432	977	33.1	32.5	33.9	NH......	11.7	8.1	3.6	33.9	33.9	33.9
1992.....	2,431	1,465	966	34.1	33.5	34.8	NJ......	83.0	52.7	30.4	42.7	41.7	44.4
							NM......	17.3	12.1	5.2	26.5	26.1	27.0
1993, U.S.	**2,464**	**1,490**	**974**	**35.0**	**34.4**	**35.8**	NY......	184.3	92.1	92.2	45.0	43.4	46.6
AL......	41.7	22.5	19.3	27.0	27.0	27.0	NC......	66.0	40.3	25.7	29.3	29.2	29.4
AK......	7.2	5.1	2.1	46.0	46.0	46.0	ND......	7.8	5.1	2.7	25.2	25.2	25.2
AZ......	35.1	27.0	8.1	31.4	31.4	31.4	OH......	102.4	68.0	34.4	34.5	34.1	35.3
AR......	26.0	12.7	13.3	27.4	26.7	28.2	OK......	38.5	20.7	17.8	25.9	25.2	26.8
CA......	215.7	159.0	56.7	40.0	38.4	42.2	OR......	27.8	17.6	10.3	35.9	35.3	36.8
CO......	33.4	17.0	16.4	33.5	33.0	34.1	PA......	100.9	51.3	49.6	41.2	40.5	42.0
CT......	34.4	23.8	10.6	48.3	47.7	49.8	RI......	9.8	5.3	4.5	37.9	37.9	38.0
DE......	6.3	3.2	3.0	36.2	35.4	37.1	SC......	36.5	24.8	11.7	29.2	28.7	30.2
DC......	6.8	4.3	2.5	38.7	38.7	38.7	SD......	8.8	6.2	2.6	24.3	23.8	24.5
FL......	107.6	59.0	48.6	31.2	31.2	31.2	TN......	46.1	32.9	13.2	29.0	28.5	30.2
GA......	73.1	49.1	24.0	30.1	30.1	30.1	TX......	219.3	118.0	101.4	29.9	29.3	30.5
HI......	10.3	5.8	4.5	36.5	36.5	36.5	UT......	19.4	11.0	8.4	27.2	27.2	27.8
ID......	11.8	6.2	5.6	27.0	26.8	27.2	VT......	7.2	3.7	3.5	34.8	34.8	34.8
IL......	111.1	78.8	32.3	38.6	36.8	43.1	VA......	67.4	40.2	27.2	32.3	31.2	33.9
IN......	54.5	29.2	25.3	35.1	35.0	35.2	WA......	44.3	26.7	17.7	35.8	35.2	36.6
IA......	31.5	15.1	16.4	30.1	29.0	31.2	WV......	20.8	12.2	8.6	30.3	29.9	30.8
KS......	29.8	17.6	12.1	32.9	32.9	32.9	WI......	52.9	34.0	18.9	35.9	34.2	36.4
KY......	37.9	26.3	11.6	31.1	30.4	32.7	WY......	6.6	3.4	3.2	30.1	30.0	30.1

[1] Full-time equivalent.

Source: National Education Association, Washington, DC, *Estimates of School Statistics, 1992-93*, and earlier issues. (Copyright by the National Education Association. All rights reserved.)

No. 246. Average Starting Salaries of Public School Teachers Compared With Salaries in Private Industry, by Selected Position: 1975 to 1993

[Except as noted, salaries represent what corporations plan to offer graduates graduating in the year shown with bachelors' degrees. Based on a survey of approximately 200 companies]

ITEM AND POSITION	1975	1980	1985	1988	1989	1990	1991	1992	1993
SALARIES (dollars)									
Teachers [1].............	8,233	10,764	15,460	19,400	(NA)	20,486	21,481	22,171	22,505
College graduates:									
Engineering	12,744	20,136	26,880	29,856	30,852	32,304	34,236	34,620	35,004
Accounting............	11,880	15,720	20,628	25,140	25,908	27,408	27,924	28,404	28,020
Sales—marketing	10,344	15,936	20,616	23,484	27,768	27,828	26,580	26,532	28,536
Business administration ...	9,768	14,100	19,896	23,880	25,344	26,496	26,256	27,156	27,564
Liberal arts [2]	9,312	13,296	18,828	23,508	25,608	26,364	25,560	27,324	27,216
Chemistry	11,904	17,124	24,216	27,108	27,552	29,088	29,700	30,360	30,456
Mathematics—statistics ...	10,980	17,604	22,704	25,548	28,416	28,944	29,244	29,472	30,756
Economics—finance	10,212	14,472	20,964	23,928	25,812	26,712	26,424	27,708	28,584
Computer science	(NA)	17,712	24,156	26,904	28,608	29,100	30,924	30,888	31,164
INDEX (1975=100)									
Teachers [1].............	100	131	187	236	(NA)	249	261	269	273
College graduates:									
Engineering	100	158	211	234	242	253	268	271	275
Accounting............	100	132	174	212	218	230	235	239	236
Sales—marketing	100	154	199	227	268	269	257	256	276
Business administration ...	100	144	204	244	259	271	268	278	282
Liberal arts [2]	100	143	202	252	275	283	274	293	292
Chemistry	100	144	203	228	231	244	249	255	256
Mathematics—statistics ...	100	160	207	233	258	263	266	268	280
Economics—finance	100	142	205	234	252	261	258	271	280
Computer science [3].....	(NA)	125	171	190	202	205	218	217	218

NA Not available. [1] Estimate. Minimum mean salary. Source: National Education Association, Washington, DC, unpublished data. [2] Excludes Chemistry, Mathematics, Economics, and Computer Science. [3] Computer science index (1978=100).

Source: Except as noted, Northwestern University Placement Center, Evanston, IL, *The Northwestern University Lindquist-Endicott Report* (copyright).

No. 247. Average Salary and Wages Paid in Public School Systems: 1975 to 1993

[In dollars. For school year ending in year shown. Data reported by a stratified sample of school systems enrolling 300 or more pupils. Data represent unweighted means of average salaries paid school personnel reported by each school system]

POSITION	1975	1980	1985	1988	1989	1990	1991	1992	1993
ANNUAL SALARY									
Central office administrators:									
Superintendent (contract salary). . . .	30,338	39,344	56,954	68,147	71,190	75,425	79,874	83,342	85,120
Deputy/assoc. superintendent	30,074	37,440	52,877	63,872	66,214	69,623	72,428	76,796	77,057
Assistant superintendent	26,460	33,452	48,003	56,894	59,655	62,698	66,553	69,315	70,525
Administrators for—									
Finance and business	21,850	27,147	40,344	47,330	49,933	52,354	55,097	57,036	57,864
Instructional services	22,608	29,790	43,452	50,838	53,716	56,359	59,162	62,102	62,508
Public relations/information	21,470	24,021	35,287	41,305	43,402	44,926	47,938	50,625	50,622
Staff personnel services	21,470	29,623	44,182	51,421	53,972	56,344	59,271	62,269	62,162
Subject area supervisors	18,601	23,974	34,422	41,086	43,555	45,929	48,366	50,580	51,407
School building administrators:									
Principals:									
Elementary	19,061	25,165	36,452	43,664	45,909	48,431	51,453	53,856	54,905
Junior high/middle	21,136	27,625	39,650	47,078	49,427	52,163	55,083	57,504	58,620
Senior high	22,894	29,207	42,094	50,512	52,987	55,722	59,106	61,768	63,054
Assistant principals:									
Elementary	15,968	20,708	30,496	36,364	38,360	40,916	43,548	45,558	45,377
Junior high/middle	17,868	23,507	33,793	40,093	42,292	44,570	46,981	48,956	49,925
Senior high	18,939	24,816	35,491	41,839	44,002	46,486	49,009	51,318	52,348
Classroom teachers.	11,507	15,913	23,587	28,230	29,608	31,278	32,915	34,565	35,291
Auxiliary professional personnel:									
Counselors.	14,479	18,847	27,593	32,896	34,244	35,979	38,024	39,563	40,413
Librarians.	12,546	16,764	24,981	30,046	31,645	33,469	35,417	37,227	37,945
School nurses	10,673	13,788	19,944	23,692	24,804	26,090	27,713	28,721	29,555
Secretarial/clerical personnel:									
Central office:									
Secretaries/stenographers.	7,318	10,331	15,343	18,220	19,045	20,238	21,303	22,309	22,770
Accounting/payroll clerks	7,588	10,479	15,421	18,229	19,143	20,088	21,202	22,215	22,605
Clerk-typists	6,089	8,359	12,481	14,651	15,192	16,125	16,859	17,646	17,772
School building level:									
Secretaries/stenographers.	6,046	8,348	12,504	14,749	15,364	16,184	16,953	17,784	18,104
Library clerks.	5,052	6,778	9,911	11,234	11,751	12,151	12,696	13,347	13,311
HOURLY WAGE RATE									
Other support personnel:									
Teacher aides:									
Instructional	2.91	4.06	5.89	6.72	7.05	7.43	7.77	8.15	8.31
Noninstructional.	2.81	3.89	5.60	6.45	6.69	7.08	7.43	7.70	7.82
Custodians.	3.54	4.88	6.90	7.82	8.19	8.54	9.05	9.35	9.51
Cafeteria workers	2.61	3.78	5.42	6.23	6.56	6.77	7.19	7.39	7.56
Bus drivers.	3.75	5.21	7.27	8.31	8.78	9.21	9.52	10.04	10.15

Source: Educational Research Service, Arlington, VA, *National Survey of Salaries and Wages in Public Schools*, annual, vols. 2 and 3. (All rights reserved. Copyright.)

No. 248. Public School Employment: 1982 and 1992

[In thousands. Covers full-time employment. Excludes Hawaii. 1982 also excludes District of Columbia and New Jersey. 1982 based on sample survey of school districts with 250 or more students. 1992 based on sample survey of school districts with 100 or more employees; see source for sampling variability]

OCCUPATION	1982					1992				
	Total	Male	Female	White [1]	Black [1]	Total	Male	Female	White [1]	Black [1]
All occupations	3,082	1,063	2,019	2,498	432	3,376	948	2,428	2,643	494
Officials, administrators	41	31	10	36	3	44	27	17	37	5
Principals and assistant										
principals	90	72	19	76	11	93	56	37	74	14
Classroom teachers [2]	1,680	534	1,146	1,435	186	1,862	487	1,375	1,565	202
Elementary schools	798	129	669	667	98	930	123	807	770	108
Secondary schools.	706	363	343	619	67	693	312	381	598	67
Other professional staff	235	91	144	193	35	242	59	184	199	31
Teachers aides [3]	215	14	200	146	45	351	58	293	223	76
Clerical, secretarial staff.	210	4	206	177	19	236	6	231	187	27
Service workers [4]	611	316	295	434	132	547	255	292	360	138

[1] Excludes individuals of Hispanic origin.   [2] Includes other classroom teachers, not shown separately.   [3] Includes technicians.   [4] Includes craftworkers and laborers.

Source: U.S. Equal Employment Opportunity Commission, *Elementary-Secondary Staff Information (EEO-5)*, biennial.

No. 249. Public Elementary and Secondary School Price Indexes: 1975 to 1992

[1983=100. For years ending June 30. Reflects prices paid by public elementary-secondary schools. For explanation of average annual percent change, see Guide to Tabular Presentation]

YEAR	Index, total	PERSONNEL COMPENSATION				CONTRACTED SERVICES, SUPPLIES AND EQUIPMENT						
		Total	Professional salaries	Nonprofessional salaries	Fringe benefits	Total	Services	Supplies and materials	Equipment replacement	Library materials and textbooks	Utilities	Fixed costs
1975 ..	52.7	53.3	56.0	55.6	40.2	50.6	55.7	58.0	53.7	53.8	35.9	45.0
1980 ..	76.5	75.7	76.7	77.8	69.8	79.6	77.4	85.9	79.6	82.1	73.2	77.6
1981 ..	85.7	84.4	85.1	85.9	80.2	90.4	85.7	95.7	88.0	86.9	92.8	86.9
1982 ..	93.7	92.6	92.8	94.4	90.3	97.8	94.6	101.1	95.5	91.6	102.2	94.1
1983 ..	100.0	100.0	100.0	100.0	100.0	100.0	100.0	100.0	100.0	100.0	100.0	100.0
1984 ..	105.6	106.2	105.7	104.5	109.4	103.5	106.2	102.2	103.0	107.3	98.2	106.9
1985 ..	112.6	114.2	113.4	111.3	120.3	106.4	112.3	103.5	105.6	113.0	96.5	111.8
1986 ..	119.6	122.7	121.4	117.6	132.6	107.6	118.8	102.5	108.7	119.0	88.3	117.8
1987 ..	125.7	129.9	128.4	121.9	143.5	109.8	122.8	103.9	111.3	126.8	83.2	124.6
1988 ..	132.7	137.6	135.5	127.5	155.4	113.8	125.3	110.3	111.3	145.2	79.1	131.2
1989 ..	139.6	144.9	142.2	133.3	166.6	119.3	132.2	118.8	116.3	151.4	77.9	137.0
1990 ..	147.6	153.4	150.1	139.4	179.5	125.5	136.7	122.5	120.8	175.9	85.8	142.5
1991 ..	156.0	162.3	158.1	146.5	193.4	132.2	142.5	126.1	124.7	196.1	96.2	147.8
1992 ..	162.9	170.6	165.9	152.4	206.4	133.3	147.1	123.5	127.5	209.9	90.4	153.4

Source: Research Associates of Washington, Washington, DC, *Inflation Measures for Schools and Colleges*, annual (copyright).

No. 250. Finances of Public Elementary and Secondary School Systems, by Enrollment-Size Group: 1990-91

[In millions of dollars, except as indicated. Data are estimates subject to sampling variability. For details, see source. See also Appendix III]

ITEM	All school systems	ENROLLMENT SIZE						
		50,000 or more	25,000 to 49,999	15,000 to 24,999	7,500 to 14,999	5,000 to 7,499	3,000 to 4,999	Under 3,000
Enrollment, fall (1,000)	41,255	7,548	4,301	3,746	6,235	3,773	4,764	10,888
General revenue [1]	224,226	42,858	21,680	18,243	31,591	19,421	25,419	65,014
Intergovernmental	122,415	23,839	12,630	10,847	17,038	9,713	12,112	36,236
From Federal government	1,352	284	100	75	150	107	116	520
From States	118,050	23,356	12,193	10,532	16,523	9,367	11,633	34,445
Federal aid distributed by State governments	11,983	3,071	1,273	979	1,541	913	1,108	3,099
From local governments	3,013	199	337	239	364	239	363	1,271
From own sources	101,811	19,019	9,050	7,396	14,553	9,708	13,306	28,778
Taxes	69,147	9,283	6,152	5,072	10,017	7,149	9,713	21,759
Property	67,383	8,900	5,962	4,997	9,765	6,963	9,451	21,344
Contribution from parent government	19,135	7,548	1,541	1,046	2,464	1,355	1,995	3,186
Charges and miscellaneous	13,529	2,189	1,356	1,277	2,072	1,203	1,598	3,833
Current charges	6,353	1,168	646	579	959	560	731	1,711
School lunch sales	3,639	485	357	322	584	370	478	1,042
Interest earnings	3,584	527	352	324	529	335	428	1,089
Other	3,592	493	359	375	584	309	439	1,033
Employee-retirement revenue	1,007	793	203	11	-	(Z)	-	-
General expenditure [1]	226,803	43,962	22,310	18,601	32,088	19,568	25,730	64,544
Intergovernmental	604	24	31	53	107	64	99	226
Direct	226,199	43,938	22,279	18,548	31,981	19,503	25,632	64,318
Current operation	203,735	40,010	19,715	16,418	28,559	17,679	22,989	58,364
Salaries and wages	131,966	26,590	13,417	11,203	19,155	11,751	15,147	34,703
Capital outlay	18,607	3,322	2,131	1,769	2,811	1,489	2,149	4,936
Construction	11,153	1,944	1,184	1,079	1,783	874	1,383	2,906
Interest on debt	3,857	606	433	360	611	336	493	1,018
Employee-retirement expenditure	324	198	120	5	-	(Z)	-	-
Debt outstanding [2]	63,669	11,110	6,660	5,769	9,820	5,404	8,190	16,716
Long-term	60,521	11,043	6,519	5,664	9,279	5,105	7,559	15,351
Short-term	3,148	67	141	104	541	298	632	1,365
Long-term debt issued	12,806	2,251	1,460	1,245	2,076	1,008	1,510	3,257
Long-term debt retired	5,777	854	647	479	869	574	765	1,590
Cash and security holdings	50,909	10,177	6,016	3,649	5,854	3,734	5,060	16,419
Employee-retirement holdings	6,278	4,385	1,792	101	-	(Z)	-	(Z)

- Represents zero.   Z Rounds to zero.   [1] Excludes interschool system transactions.   [2] As of end of fiscal year.

Source: U.S. Bureau of the Census, *Public Education Finances: 1990-91*, GF/91-10.

Education

No. 251. Public Elementary and Secondary Estimated Finances, 1970 to 1993, and by State, 1993

[In millions of dollars, except as noted. For school years ending in June of year shown]

YEAR AND STATE	Total	RECEIPTS					EXPENDITURES				
		Revenue receipts				Non-revenue receipts[1]	Total[2]	Per capita[3] (dol.)	Current expenditures		
		Total	Source						Elementary and secondary day schools	Average per pupil in ADA[4]	
			Federal	State	Local					Amount (dol.)	Rank
1970.........	41,621	38,192	2,767	15,628	19,797	3,429	39,091	194	32,683	773	(X)
1975.........	66,319	63,047	5,089	27,472	30,486	3,273	62,340	292	53,333	1,286	(X)
1980.........	101,724	97,635	9,020	47,929	40,686	4,089	96,105	428	85,661	2,230	(X)
1985.........	146,976	141,013	9,533	69,107	62,373	5,963	139,382	591	127,230	3,483	(X)
1990.........	218,126	208,656	13,184	100,787	94,685	9,469	209,698	850	186,583	4,966	(X)
1992.........	250,993	235,250	15,703	111,783	107,763	15,743	238,884	947	210,358	5,404	(X)
1993, total..	**262,966**	**246,199**	**16,973**	**115,168**	**114,058**	**16,768**	**251,706**	**987**	**220,604**	**5,574**	**(X)**
Alabama......	2,716	2,605	351	1,687	568	111	2,865	692	2,580	3,779	49
Alaska	1,082	972	122	618	231	110	1,058	1,800	962	9,290	2
Arizona.......	3,784	3,325	285	1,421	1,619	459	3,508	915	2,641	4,140	44
Arkansas.....	2,046	1,879	186	1,175	518	168	1,825	762	1,578	3,838	48
California......	28,862	27,145	2,271	16,561	8,313	1,717	28,387	919	23,679	4,608	37
Colorado......	3,435	3,135	156	1,341	1,639	300	3,375	974	2,823	4,969	31
Connecticut.....	4,107	4,105	200	1,575	2,330	2	4,107	1,252	3,828	8,188	4
Delaware......	698	653	57	434	163	45	673	974	614	6,420	12
District of Columbia	622	590	75	-	515	32	621	1,061	572	7,998	5
Florida.......	12,032	11,236	948	5,505	4,783	796	11,645	864	9,641	5,303	27
Georgia.......	5,767	5,453	425	2,612	2,416	314	5,646	834	5,067	4,544	39
Hawaii	1,084	1,084	79	984	20	-	1,077	932	963	5,806	18
Idaho........	997	894	72	551	271	102	957	898	877	4,025	47
Illinois........	11,010	10,048	863	3,475	5,710	962	10,043	865	8,751	5,191	29
Indiana.......	5,805	5,696	284	2,976	2,436	109	5,821	1,029	4,975	5,641	20
Iowa.........	2,616	2,538	143	1,287	1,108	79	2,642	943	2,453	5,297	28
Kansas.......	2,572	2,364	130	1,179	1,056	208	2,575	1,024	2,255	5,459	25
Kentucky......	3,340	3,092	309	2,101	682	248	3,158	841	2,861	4,942	33
Louisiana	3,789	3,449	410	1,877	1,162	340	3,442	804	3,145	4,352	43
Maine........	1,357	1,277	93	652	531	80	1,357	1,098	1,224	6,162	15
Maryland......	4,997	4,841	270	1,988	2,582	156	4,932	1,003	4,494	6,447	11
Massachusetts...	5,762	5,738	348	1,943	3,447	25	5,470	913	5,164	6,505	9
Michigan......	11,409	10,733	616	3,446	6,671	677	10,896	1,155	9,438	6,402	13
Minnesota.....	5,129	4,694	200	2,367	2,127	435	5,022	1,124	4,096	5,572	22
Mississippi.....	1,915	1,811	313	957	541	104	1,769	676	1,604	3,390	50
Missouri	4,646	4,197	274	1,576	2,348	449	3,966	764	3,401	4,487	40
Montana......	836	827	74	323	430	9	868	1,056	776	5,348	26
Nebraska	1,408	1,400	85	587	728	7	1,449	905	1,307	4,950	32
Nevada.......	1,197	1,159	54	431	674	38	1,288	964	1,016	4,976	30
New Hampshire ..	1,114	1,094	31	90	973	20	1,021	916	936	5,619	21
New Jersey.....	10,989	10,888	373	4,661	5,854	101	10,569	1,351	10,281	9,712	1
New Mexico....	1,396	1,343	170	1,022	151	53	1,453	919	1,231	4,643	36
New York	24,504	22,504	1,320	8,884	12,300	2,000	22,917	1,265	20,375	8,525	3
North Carolina ...	5,697	5,470	412	3,516	1,542	226	5,594	818	4,979	4,810	35
North Dakota....	579	548	62	245	241	31	547	863	503	4,404	41
Ohio.........	11,355	10,155	600	4,110	5,445	1,200	11,289	1,024	9,598	5,963	16
Oklahoma.....	2,813	2,592	197	1,622	773	221	2,726	850	2,290	4,085	45
Oregon.......	3,201	2,944	192	1,107	1,646	257	3,382	1,138	2,931	6,240	14
Pennsylvania ...	15,728	13,771	646	5,951	7,174	1,957	13,148	1,096	12,311	7,748	6
Rhode Island....	904	904	46	324	534	-	904	903	875	6,649	8
South Carolina...	3,300	3,019	277	1,444	1,298	281	3,055	848	2,660	4,573	38
South Dakota....	638	602	70	161	371	37	627	885	552	4,359	42
Tennessee	3,489	3,311	351	1,572	1,387	178	3,333	663	3,170	4,033	46
Texas........	19,621	18,986	1,391	8,200	9,395	635	18,555	1,049	15,972	4,933	34
Utah.........	1,832	1,655	115	961	578	178	1,510	834	1,393	3,218	51
Vermont	697	677	34	220	423	19	684	1,197	640	7,172	7
Virginia.......	5,641	5,564	268	1,912	3,385	76	6,014	940	5,328	5,517	24
Washington.....	5,861	5,422	307	3,933	1,181	439	5,816	1,131	4,634	5,528	23
West Virginia....	1,926	1,860	147	1,248	465	66	1,890	1,045	1,671	5,689	19
Wisconsin	6,036	5,346	237	2,048	3,062	690	5,609	1,123	4,928	6,500	10
Wyoming......	625	605	35	309	261	20	621	1,336	558	5,932	17

- Represents or rounds to zero.   X Not applicable.   [1] Amount received by local education agencies from the sales of bonds and real property and equipment, loans, and proceeds from insurance adjustments.   [2] Includes interest on school debt and other current expenditures not shown above.   [3] Based on Bureau of the Census estimated resident population, as of July 1, the previous year. Estimates reflect revisions based on the 1990 Census of Population.   [4] Average daily attendance.

Source: National Education Association, Washington, DC, *Estimates of School Statistics*, annual (copyright); and unpublished data.

No. 252. Microcomputers for Student Instruction in Elementary and Secondary Schools: 1985 and 1993

[As of **fall for public schools; as of midwinter for private schools.** Public school data based on surveys of every school district and all public schools. Private school data based on surveys of all Catholic and private schools. For details, see source]

LEVEL	1984-85				1992-93			
	Total schools	Percent with micros	Number of micros [1]	Students per micro	Total schools	Percent with micros	Number of micros [1]	Students per micro
U.S. total.........	105,509	77.7	631,983	62.7	105,425	97.4	3,952,064	12.2
Public schools, total......	81,100	85.1	569,825	63.5	82,981	98.5	3,620,956	12.0
Elementary............	50,967	82.2	215,393	79.3	49,969	98.6	1,604,976	13.9
Middle/junior high.......	9,791	93.1	100,331	61.2	11,938	99.6	643,515	11.9
Senior high	15,152	94.6	228,726	51.5	14,137	99.5	1,124,492	9.7
K-12/other...........	5,190	70.3	25,375	45.8	6,937	86.6	247,973	10.1
Catholic schools, total......	9,463	63.4	28,427	73.5	8,385	97.8	166,537	15.3
Elementary...........	7,831	56.4	15,863	85.1	6,984	97.8	119,672	16.0
Secondary...........	1,481	87.0	12,147	57.8	1,249	97.9	43,936	13.6
K-12/other...........	151	46.4	417	(NA)	152	96.1	2,929	14.6
Other private schools, total ..	14,946	46.4	33,731	40.5	14,059	85.6	164,571	13.6
Elementary...........	8,226	45.1	13,400	42.7	7,176	85.8	67,033	14.9
Secondary...........	950	82.7	6,266	40.1	1,034	86.2	21,743	9.5
K-12/other...........	5,770	42.4	14,065	(NA)	5,849	85.1	75,795	13.7

NA Not available.　[1] Includes estimates for schools not reporting number of micros.

Source: Market Data Retrieval, Shelton, CT, unpublished data.

No. 253. Instructional Use of Computers in Elementary and Secondary Schools: 1985 to 1992

[Includes microcomputers and terminals used by students or teachers. Based on stratified, probability sample of 1,416 public, private, and parochial schools surveyed in spring 1989, and 571 surveyed in spring 1992. Represents all elementary and secondary schools in the United States, except preschools and those that have no grade 5 or higher]

ITEM	Unit	Total, 1985	Total, 1989	1992, BY GRADE LEVEL			
				Total	Grade 5	Grade 8	Grade 11
ALL SCHOOLS							
Computers used for instruction	1,000 ..	1,034	2,355	3,536	1,485	874	1,177
Schools using computers	Percent.	86	96	100	100	100	100
Schools with 15 or more computers	Percent.	24	57	80	77	75	96
SCHOOLS USING COMPUTERS FOR INSTRUCTION							
Mean [1] number of computers	Number.	10	26	37	28	31	65
Median [1]............................	Number.	8	19	25	23	24	47
Students per computer, median [1].............	Number.	42	20	14	15	14	10
Percent of all instructional computers in—							
Classrooms...........................	Percent.	37	36	37	41	28	33
Computer labs........................	Percent.	49	50	50	47	58	52
Other locations	Percent.	14	14	13	12	14	15
Percent of all instructional computers used—							
Usually every day.......................	Percent.	(NA)	71	(NA)	(NA)	(NA)	(NA)
Less than every week or not used at all	Percent.	(NA)	10	(NA)	(NA)	(NA)	(NA)
Median hours of use per week (in rooms with greatest number of computers) [1]	Number.	17	20	20	20	18	22
Percent of all student computer use: [2]							
Learning math........................	Percent.	(NA)	14	15	18	12	7
Word processing (how to use)	Percent.	(NA)	14	14	12	16	17
Keyboarding (how to)	Percent.	(NA)	13	14	13	15	14
Learning English	Percent.	(NA)	13	13	17	10	7
Programming........................	Percent.	(NA)	8	5	3	7	8
Recreational use	Percent.	(NA)	8	9	10	10	6
Tools, e.g., spreadsheets.................	Percent.	(NA)	7	6	4	8	12
Learning science	Percent.	(NA)	6	7	8	7	6
Learning social studies	Percent.	(NA)	5	7	9	6	3
Business education [3]...................	Percent.	(NA)	5	4	3	3	10
Industrial arts........................	Percent.	(NA)	3	2	1	3	6
Fine arts............................	Percent.	(NA)	2	2	2	2	2
Learning foreign languages	Percent.	(NA)	1	1	-	1	2
Other..............................	Percent.	(NA)	1	1	1	1	-

- Represents zero. NA Not available. [1] For definition of mean and median, see Guide to Tabular Presentation. [2] Estimates supplied by each school's technology coordinator. [3] Other than keyboarding or word processing instruction.

Source: University of Minnesota, MN, Department of Sociology, IEA Computers in Education Study.

No. 254. Technology in Public Schools: 1992 and 1993

[For school year ending in year shown. Based on surveys of school districts conducted in the spring and summer of the school year. For details, see source]

TECHNOLOGY	NUMBER			PERCENT OF TOTAL SCHOOLS	
	Total		Percent change, 1992-93		
	1992	1993		1992	1993
Schools with interactive videodisk players [1]	6,502	11,729	80	8	14
Elementary [2]	2,921	5,986	105	6	12
Junior high [3]	1,258	2,386	90	10	18
Senior high [4]	2,106	3,129	49	14	19
Students represented (1,000)	5,781	9,064	57	14	21
Schools with modems [1]	13,597	18,471	36	16	22
Elementary [2]	5,831	8,492	46	11	17
Junior high [3]	2,608	3,431	32	20	26
Senior high [4]	5,001	6,371	27	30	38
Students represented (1,000)	10,717	13,382	25	25	31
Schools with networks [1]	4,184	11,657	179	5	14
Elementary [2]	1,583	4,683	196	3	9
Junior high [3]	776	2,030	162	6	15
Senior high [4]	1,736	4,895	182	10	29
Students represented (1,000)	3,754	8,043	114	9	19
Schools with CD-ROM's [1]	5,706	11,021	93	7	13
Elementary [2]	1,897	4,457	135	4	9
Junior high [3]	1,231	2,326	89	9	17
Senior high [4]	2,543	4,168	64	15	25
Students represented (1,000)	5,298	8,534	61	12	20
Schools with satellite dishes [1]	1,129	8,812	681	1	11
Elementary [2]	351	2,988	751	1	6
Junior high [3]	166	1,503	805	1	11
Senior high [4]	606	4,292	608	4	26
Students represented (1,000)	1,906	4,668	145	4	11
Schools with cable [1]	(NA)	47,745	(X)	(X)	57
Elementary [2]	(NA)	27,923	(X)	(X)	54
Junior high [3]	(NA)	9,266	(X)	(X)	69
Senior high [4]	(NA)	10,296	(X)	(X)	62
Students represented (1,000)	(NA)	27,324	(X)	(X)	65

NA Not available.   X Not applicable.   [1] Includes schools for special education and adult education, not shown separately.
[2] Includes K-12, preschool, preschool through 3, K-6, and K-8.   [3] Includes schools with grade spans of 4-8, 7-8, and 7-9.
[4] Includes 7-12, 9-12, 10-12, vocational technical, and alternative high schools.

Source: Quality Education Data, Inc., Denver, CO, *Technology in Public Schools, 1991-92* and *1992-93.*

No. 255. Children and Youth With Disabilities in Educational Programs for the Disabled, by Type of Disability: 1980 to 1991

[For school year ending in year shown. For persons under 22 years old, except as noted. Represents children under 20 served under Chapter 1 of the Elementary and Secondary Education Act (ESEA), State Operated Programs (SOP), and children 3 to 21 served under Individuals with Disabilities Education Act, Part B (IDEA). Excludes outlying areas]

ITEM	1980	1985	1986	1987	1988 [1]	1989 [1]	1990 [1]	1991 [1]	1992 [1]
All conditions (1,000)	4,005	4,315	4,317	4,374	4,128	4,173	4,219	4,320	4,459
PERCENT DISTRIBUTION									
Learning disabled	31.9	42.4	43.1	43.6	47.0	47.8	48.6	49.3	50.1
Speech impaired	29.6	26.1	26.1	25.8	23.2	23.1	23.1	22.8	22.3
Mentally retarded	21.7	16.1	15.3	15.0	14.6	13.8	13.0	12.4	12.0
Emotionally disturbed	8.2	8.6	8.7	8.7	9.1	8.9	9.0	9.0	8.9
Hard of hearing and deaf	2.0	1.6	1.5	1.5	1.4	1.4	1.3	1.3	1.3
Orthopedically handicapped	1.6	1.3	1.3	1.3	1.1	1.1	1.1	1.1	1.1
Other health impaired	2.6	1.6	1.3	1.2	1.1	1.2	1.2	1.3	1.3
Visually handicapped	0.8	0.7	0.6	0.6	0.6	0.5	0.5	0.5	0.5
Multihandicapped	1.5	1.6	2.0	2.2	1.9	2.0	2.0	2.2	2.2
Deaf-blind	0.1	0.1	(Z)	(Z)	(Z)	(Z)	(Z)	(Z)	(Z)
Autism	(NA)	(NA)	(NA)	(NA)	(NA)	(NA)	(NA)	(NA)	0.1
Traumatic brain injury	(NA)	(NA)	(NA)	(NA)	(NA)	(NA)	(NA)	(NA)	(Z)

Z Less than .05 percent.   NA Not available.   [1] For children 6 to 21 years old; total number of children served under 22 years old was 4,494,280 in school year 1987-88, 4,568,118 in school year 1988-89, 4,640,969 in 1989-90, 4,761,742 in 1990-91, and 4,940,507 in 1991-92.

Source: U.S. Dept. of Education, Office of Special Education Programs, *Annual Report to Congress.*

No. 256. Children and Youth With Disabilities, by Age and Educational Environment: 1990

[For school year ending in year shown. Covers children 3 to 21 served under Chapter 1 of ESEA (SOP) and IDEA-B; see headnote, table 255]

ENVIRONMENT	NUMBER (1,000)					PERCENT DISTRIBUTION			
	Total	3-5 years old	6-11 years old	12-17 years old	18-21 years old	3-5 years old	6-11 years old	12-17 years old	18-21 years old
Total	4,567.8	356.3	2,221.1	1,761.1	229.4	100.0	100.0	100.0	100.0
Regular class [1]	1,493.2	159.5	936.4	359.7	37.6	44.8	42.2	20.4	16.4
Resource room [2]	1,620.0	42.6	741.3	761.3	74.8	12.0	33.4	43.2	32.6
Separate class [3]	1,146.3	98.9	460.0	512.3	75.0	27.8	20.7	29.1	32.7
Separate school facility:									
Public	159.5	25.9	44.8	63.8	25.0	7.3	2.0	3.6	10.9
Private	75.8	20.2	23.8	25.7	6.1	5.7	1.1	1.5	2.7
Separate residential facility:									
Public	28.9	1.1	6.1	15.6	6.1	0.3	0.3	0.9	2.7
Private	12.5	0.4	2.6	7.3	2.1	0.1	0.1	0.4	0.9
Correctional facility [4]	11.9	(NA)	(NA)	(NA)	(NA)	(NA)	(NA)	(NA)	(NA)
Home/hospital	31.6	7.6	5.9	15.4	2.6	2.1	0.3	0.9	1.1

NA Not available. [1] Receives special education and related services less than 21 percent of the school day. [2] Receives services between 21 and 60 percent of the school day. [3] Receives services for more than 60 percent of the school day. [4] Students in correctional institutions are also distributed by type of environment, but not duplicated in the total.
Source: U.S. Dept. of Education, Office of Special Education Programs, Data Analysis Systems (DANS), unpublished data.

No. 257. Catholic Elementary and Secondary Schools: 1960 to 1992

[As of October 1. Regular sessions only. See also Historical Statistics, Colonial Times to 1970, series H 535-544]

ITEM	Unit	1960	1970	1975	1980	1985	1988	1989	1990	1991	1992
Elementary schools. . . .	Number	10,501	9,362	8,340	8,043	7,806	7,501	7,395	7,291	7,239	7,174
Pupils enrolled	1,000. .	4,373	3,359	2,525	2,269	2,057	1,912	1,893	1,884	1,964	1,984
Teachers, total [1] . . .	1,000. .	108	112	99	97	97	94	94	91	109	110
Religious.	1,000. .	79	52	35	25	18	14	12	11	12	11
Lay	1,000. .	29	60	64	72	79	80	82	80	96	98
Secondary schools . . .	Number	2,392	1,981	1,653	1,516	1,430	1,362	1,324	1,296	1,269	1,249
Pupils enrolled	1,000. .	880	1,008	890	837	762	639	606	592	587	584
Teachers, total [1] . . .	1,000. .	44	54	50	49	50	44	43	40	44	45
Religious.	1,000. .	33	28	20	14	11	8	8	6	6	6
Lay	1,000. .	11	26	30	35	39	36	35	34	37	38

[1] Beginning 1991, includes part-time teachers.
Source: National Catholic Educational Association, (NCEA) Washington, DC; From the NCEA Data Bank—U.S. Catholic Schools 1967-1968, (copyright) and U.S. Catholic Elementary and Secondary Schools 1992-1993 Annual Statistical Report on Schools, Enrollment & Staffing, NCEA, annual (copyright); and NCEA/Ganley's Catholic Schools in America, 1993 edition, annual (copyright).

No. 258. Private Elementary and Secondary School Teachers—Selected Characteristics: 1990-91

[For school year. Based on survey and subject to sampling error; for details, see source. See table 244 for similar data on public school teachers]

CHARACTERISTIC	Unit	AGE				SEX		RACE/ETHNICITY		
		Under 30 years old	30 to 39 years old	40 to 49 years old	Over 50 years old	Male	Female	White [1]	Black [1]	Hispanic
Total teachers [2] . . .	1,000 . . .	68	105	115	67	82	275	329	9	12
Highest degree held:										
Bachelor's	Percent .	81.4	65.9	55.4	47.0	51.5	65.0	61.8	72.8	60.6
Master's	Percent .	9.8	23.5	33.4	38.7	35.3	24.5	27.3	21.7	22.1
Education specialist .	Percent .	0.8	2.3	3.7	4.8	4.0	2.6	3.0	1.0	1.7
Doctorate	Percent .	0.3	1.1	1.9	4.0	4.2	1.0	1.8	0.9	2.7
Full-time teaching experience:										
Less than 3 years. . .	Percent .	51.7	19.7	10.1	7.3	19.8	20.6	20.1	20.1	28.8
3 to 9 years	Percent .	48.0	45.4	31.3	10.0	30.7	35.8	34.8	39.1	31.6
10 to 20 years.	Percent .	0.2	34.8	44.7	27.5	30.4	29.9	30.3	25.4	25.3
20 years or more . . .	Percent .	-	0.1	13.8	55.2	19.0	13.7	14.9	15.4	14.2
Full-time teachers	1,000 . . .	61	86	98	55	70	231	277	9	9
Earned income	Dol. . . .	18,658	21,334	22,463	24,197	27,196	20,007	21,578	23,094	22,912
Salary	Dol. . . .	16,403	19,190	20,892	21,534	23,003	18,815	19,717	20,333	20,740

- Represents zero. [1] Non-Hispanic. [2] Includes teachers with no degrees and associates degrees, not shown separately.
Source: U.S. National Center for Education Statistics, Digest of Education Statistics, 1993.

Education

No. 259. Private Elementary and Secondary Schools—Enrollment and Tuition, by Orientation: 1991

[For school year ending in year shown. Based on survey and subject to sampling error; for details see source. Revised since originally published]

CHARACTERISTIC	ENROLLMENT (1,000)				SCHOOLS			
	Total	Catholic	Other religious	Non-sectarian	Total	Catholic	Other religious	Non-sectarian
Total	4,673.9	2,555.9	1,468.5	649.4	24,690	8,731	11,476	4,483
School enrollment:								
Less than 150 students..........	824.4	176.0	461.9	186.6	13,072	1,703	8,217	3,152
150 to 299 students	1,499.5	904.6	430.0	164.9	7,027	4,148	2,082	797
300 to 499 students	1,112.7	692.8	291.3	128.6	2,923	1,824	775	324
500 to 749 students	682.3	420.3	184.9	77.1	1,122	700	301	121
750 or more students	555.0	362.3	100.5	92.2	458	357	101	(B)
Percent minority students:								
Less than 5 percent	36.0	34.1	44.9	23.0	40.0	38.3	49.0	20.6
5 percent, less than 20 percent	31.9	29.6	31.5	41.9	28.8	28.3	25.8	37.5
20 percent, less than 50 percent. ...	17.6	17.9	14.1	24.6	16.9	15.5	14.9	24.8
50 percent or more.	14.5	18.4	9.5	10.4	14.2	17.9	10.3	17.2
Average annual tuition (dol.):								
Total	(X)	(X)	(X)	(X)	2,595	1,776	2,633	5,727
Elementary.	(X)	(X)	(X)	(X)	1,705	1,260	2,270	3,846
Secondary	(X)	(X)	(X)	(X)	3,649	3,007	4,070	8,061
Combined	(X)	(X)	(X)	(X)	3,853	(B)	2,711	6,257

B Base too small to meet statistical standards for reliability of a derived figure. X Not applicable.

Source: U.S. National Center for Education Statistics, *Digest of Education Statistics*, 1993.

No. 260. High School Dropouts, by Race and Hispanic Origin: 1973 to 1992

[In percent. As of October]

ITEM	1973	1975	1980	1984	1985	1986	1987 [1]	1988	1989	1990	1991	1992
EVENT DROPOUTS [2]												
Total [3]	6.3	5.8	6.0	5.0	5.2	4.3	4.1	4.8	4.5	4.0	4.0	4.3
White.	5.7	5.4	5.6	5.0	4.8	4.2	3.7	4.7	3.9	3.8	3.7	4.1
Male.	6.1	5.0	6.4	5.3	4.9	4.2	4.1	5.1	4.1	4.1	3.6	3.8
Female	5.3	5.8	4.9	4.6	4.7	4.1	3.4	4.3	3.8	3.5	3.8	4.4
Black.	10.1	8.7	8.3	5.8	7.7	4.7	6.4	6.3	7.7	5.1	6.2	4.9
Male.	12.0	8.3	8.0	6.2	8.3	4.8	6.2	6.7	6.9	4.1	5.5	3.3
Female	8.4	9.0	8.5	5.3	7.2	4.6	6.4	6.0	8.6	6.0	7.0	6.7
Hispanic [4].	10.0	10.9	11.5	10.9	9.7	11.9	5.6	10.5	7.7	8.0	7.3	7.9
Male.	7.9	10.1	16.9	12.2	9.3	11.7	5.0	12.3	7.6	8.7	10.4	5.8
Female	12.0	11.6	6.9	10.1	9.8	12.4	6.2	8.4	7.7	7.2	4.8	8.6
STATUS DROPOUTS [5]												
Total [3]	15.7	15.6	15.6	14.8	13.9	13.8	14.5	14.6	14.4	13.6	14.2	12.7
White.	14.2	13.9	14.4	14.1	13.5	13.5	14.2	14.2	14.1	13.5	14.2	12.2
Male.	13.8	13.5	15.7	15.1	14.7	14.6	15.1	15.4	15.4	14.2	15.4	13.3
Female	14.5	14.2	13.2	13.0	12.3	12.4	13.2	13.0	12.8	12.8	13.1	11.1
Black.	26.5	27.3	23.5	18.4	17.6	16.6	17.0	17.7	16.4	15.1	15.6	16.3
Male.	25.9	27.8	26.0	20.2	18.8	18.1	18.7	18.9	18.6	13.6	15.4	15.5
Female	27.1	26.9	21.5	17.0	16.6	15.8	15.4	16.6	14.5	16.2	15.8	17.1
Hispanic [4].	38.9	34.9	40.3	34.2	31.5	27.9	32.8	39.6	37.7	37.3	39.6	33.9
Male.	36.5	32.6	42.6	35.4	35.8	37.4	34.5	40.2	40.3	39.8	44.4	38.4
Female	41.3	36.8	38.1	33.2	27.0	31.1	30.8	38.8	35.0	34.5	34.5	29.6

[1] Beginning 1987 reflects new editing procedures for cases with missing data on school enrollment. [2] Percent of students who drop out in a single year without completing high school. For grades 10 to 12. [3] Includes other races, not shown separately. [4] Persons of Hispanic origin may be of any race. [5] Percent of the population who have not completed high school and are not enrolled, regardless of when they dropped out. For persons 18 to 24 years old.

Source: U.S. Bureau of the Census, *Current Population Reports*, P20-474.

No. 261. High School Dropouts by Age, Race, and Hispanic Origin: 1970 to 1992

[As of October. For persons 14 to 24 years old. See table 263 for definition of dropouts]

AGE AND RACE	NUMBER OF DROPOUTS (1,000)							PERCENT OF POPULATION			
	1970	1980	1985	1989	1990	1991	1992	1970	1980	1990	1992
Total dropouts [1][2]	**4,670**	**5,212**	**4,456**	**4,109**	**3,854**	**3,964**	**3,468**	**12.2**	**12.0**	**10.1**	**9.2**
16 to 17 years.	617	709	505	395	418	395	327	8.0	8.8	6.3	4.9
18 to 21 years.	2,138	2,578	2,095	2,128	1,921	1,960	1,722	16.4	15.8	13.4	12.8
22 to 24 years.	1,770	1,798	1,724	1,516	1,458	1,526	1,361	18.7	15.2	13.8	12.5
White [2]	3,577	4,169	3,583	3,314	3,127	3,229	2,703	10.8	11.3	10.1	8.9
16 to 17 years.	485	619	424	328	334	312	260	7.3	9.2	6.4	4.9
18 to 21 years.	1,618	2,032	1,678	1,690	1,516	1,558	1,323	14.3	14.7	13.1	12.3
22 to 24 years.	1,356	1,416	1,372	1,236	1,235	1,287	1,075	16.3	14.0	14.0	12.1
Black [2]	1,047	934	748	648	611	631	642	22.2	16.0	10.9	11.3
16 to 17 years.	125	80	70	61	73	77	60	12.8	6.9	6.9	5.6
18 to 21 years.	500	486	376	363	345	354	340	30.5	23.0	16.0	16.9
22 to 24 years.	397	346	279	220	185	191	235	37.8	24.0	13.5	15.6
Hispanic [2][3]	(NA)	919	820	1,168	1,122	1,262	1,031	(NA)	29.5	26.8	24.2
16 to 17 years.	(NA)	92	97	80	89	102	86	(NA)	16.6	12.9	11.9
18 to 21 years.	(NA)	470	335	538	502	574	475	(NA)	40.3	32.9	30.7
22 to 24 years.	(NA)	323	365	524	523	565	461	(NA)	40.6	42.8	38.1

NA Not available.   [1] Includes other groups not shown separately.   [2] Includes persons 14 to 15 years, not shown separately.   [3] Persons of Hispanic origin may be of any race.

Source: U.S. Bureau of the Census, *Current Population Reports*, P20-474; and earlier reports.

No. 262. Enrollment Status, by Race, Hispanic Origin, and Sex: 1975 and 1992

[As of October. For persons 18 to 21 years old. For the civilian noninstitutional population. Based on the Current Population Survey; see text, section 1 and Appendix III]

CHARACTERISTIC	TOTAL PERSONS 18 TO 21 YEARS OLD (1,000)		PERCENT DISTRIBUTION							
			Enrolled in high school		High school graduates				Not high school graduates	
					Total		In college			
	1975	1992	1975	1992	1975	1992	1975	1992	1975	1992
Total [1]	**15,693**	**13,419**	**5.7**	**8.9**	**78.0**	**78.2**	**33.5**	**43.4**	**16.3**	**12.8**
White	13,448	10,784	4.7	7.8	80.6	79.8	34.6	45.3	14.7	12.3
Black . . [2]	1,997	2,014	12.5	14.5	60.4	68.5	24.9	30.1	27.0	16.9
Hispanic [2]	899	1,545	12.0	13.4	57.2	55.1	24.4	27.8	30.8	30.7
Male [1]	7,584	6,613	7.4	11.1	76.6	75.0	35.4	40.4	15.9	13.8
White	6,545	5,329	6.2	9.6	79.7	76.6	36.9	42.5	14.1	13.7
Black . . [2]	911	964	15.9	19.8	55.0	64.6	23.9	24.6	29.0	15.5
Hispanic [2]	416	762	17.3	15.9	54.6	48.4	25.2	22.7	27.9	35.7
Female [1]	8,109	6,806	4.2	6.8	79.2	81.2	31.8	46.4	16.6	11.9
White	6,903	5,456	3.2	5.4	81.4	82.8	32.4	48.0	15.3	10.9
Black . . [2]	1,085	1,050	9.7	9.8	65.0	72.2	25.8	35.2	25.4	18.1
Hispanic [2]	484	782	7.6	11.4	59.3	61.8	23.6	32.9	33.1	26.0

[1] Includes other races not shown separately.   [2] Persons of Hispanic origin may be of any race.

Source: U.S. Bureau of the Census, *Current Population Reports*, P20-474.

No. 263. Employment Status of High School Graduates and School Dropouts: 1980 to 1992

[In thousands, except percent. As of October. For civilian noninstitutional population 16 to 24 years old. Based on Current Population Survey; see text, section 1, and Appendix III]

EMPLOYMENT STATUS, SEX, AND RACE	GRADUATES [1]				DROPOUTS [2]			
	1980	1985	1990	1992	1980	1985	1990	1992
Civilian population	**11,622**	**10,381**	**8,370**	**6,887**	**5,254**	**4,323**	**3,800**	**3,420**
In labor force	9,795	8,825	7,107	5,653	3,549	2,920	2,506	2,154
Percent of population	84.3	85.0	84.9	82.1	67.5	67.5	66.0	63.0
Employed	8,567	7,707	6,279	4,889	2,651	2,165	1,993	1,631
Percent of labor force	87.5	87.3	88.3	86.5	74.7	74.1	79.5	75.7
Unemployed	1,228	1,118	828	763	898	755	513	522
Unemployment rate, total [3]	12.5	12.7	11.7	13.5	25.3	25.9	20.5	24.3
Male	13.5	12.5	11.1	13.7	23.5	23.9	18.8	18.8
Female.	11.5	12.9	12.3	13.3	28.7	29.8	23.5	34.6
White.	10.8	9.8	9.0	10.5	21.6	23.6	17.0	20.7
Black.	26.1	29.4	26.0	26.8	43.9	41.5	43.3	46.7
Not in labor force	1,827	1,556	1,262	1,234	1,705	1,403	1,294	1,266
Percent of population	15.7	15.0	15.1	17.9	32.5	32.5	34.1	37.0

[1] For persons not enrolled in college who have completed 4 years of high school only.   [2] For persons not in regular school and who have not completed the 12th grade nor received a general equivalency degree.   [3] Includes other races not shown separately.

Source: U.S. Bureau of Labor Statistics, Bulletin 2307, *News*, USDL 93-226, June 22, 1993; and unpublished data.

No. 264. Scholastic Aptitude Test (SAT) Scores and Characteristics of College-Bound Seniors: 1967 to 1993

[For school year ending in year shown]

TYPE OF TEST AND CHARACTERISTIC	Unit	1967	1970	1975	1980	1985	1989	1990	1991	1992	1993
TEST SCORES [1]											
Verbal, total [2]	Point ...	466	460	434	424	431	427	424	422	423	424
Male	Point ...	463	459	437	428	437	434	429	426	428	428
Female	Point ...	468	461	431	420	425	421	419	418	419	420
Math, total [2]	Point ...	492	488	472	466	475	476	476	474	476	478
Male	Point ...	514	509	495	491	499	500	499	497	499	502
Female	Point ...	467	465	449	443	452	454	455	453	456	457
PARTICIPANTS											
Total	1,000 ...	(NA)	(NA)	996	992	977	1,088	1,026	1,033	1,034	1,044
Male	Percent ...	(NA)	(NA)	49.9	48.2	48.3	47.9	47.8	47.7	47.6	47.4
White	Percent .	(NA)	(NA)	86.0	82.1	81.0	74.7	73.0	72.0	71.5	70.4
Black	Percent .	(NA)	(NA)	7.9	9.1	7.5	9.6	10.0	10.0	10.4	10.8
Obtaining scores [1] of—											
600 or above:											
Verbal	Percent .	(NA)	(NA)	7.9	7.2	7.9	7.8	7.4	7.2	7.3	7.8
Math	Percent .	(NA)	(NA)	15.6	15.1	17.1	18.0	18.4	17.8	18.1	18.8
Below 400:											
Verbal	Percent .	(NA)	(NA)	37.8	41.8	39.4	40.4	41.2	42.4	41.3	41.3
Math	Percent .	(NA)	(NA)	28.5	30.2	28.2	28.0	28.4	29.1	28.2	27.7
Selected intended area of study:											
Business and commerce	Percent .	(NA)	(NA)	11.5	18.6	21.0	22.3	21.0	19.0	16.8	15.0
Engineering	Percent .	(NA)	(NA)	6.7	11.1	11.7	10.1	10.0	10.0	10.5	10.2
Social science	Percent .	(NA)	(NA)	7.7	7.8	7.5	12.6	13.0	12.0	12.1	12.2
Education	Percent .	(NA)	(NA)	9.1	6.1	4.7	7.1	7.0	8.0	8.1	8.0
SAT average [1] by high school rank:											
Top tenth	Point ...	(NA)	(NA)	(NA)	539	547	550	549	548	549	550
Second tenth	Point ...	(NA)	(NA)	(NA)	470	482	483	481	480	480	481
Second fifth	Point ...	(NA)	(NA)	(NA)	431	442	440	438	437	438	439
Third fifth	Point ...	(NA)	(NA)	(NA)	386	396	394	392	391	392	393

NA Not available. [1] Minimum score 200; maximum score, 800. [2] 1967 and 1970 are estimates based on total number of persons taking SAT.

Source: College Entrance Examination Board, New York, NY, *National College-Bound Senior*, annual (copyright).

No. 265. American College Testing (ACT) Program Scores and Characteristics of College-Bound Students: 1967 to 1993

[For academic year ending in year shown. Except as indicated, test scores and characteristics of college-bound students. Through 1985, data based on 10 percent sample; thereafter, based on all ACT tested seniors]

TYPE OF TEST AND CHARACTERISTIC	Unit	1967	1970	1975	1980	1985	1989	1990 [1]	1991 [1]	1992 [1]	1993 [1]
TEST SCORES [2]											
Composite	Point ...	19.9	18.6	18.5	18.5	18.6	18.6	20.6	20.6	20.6	20.7
Male	Point ...	20.3	19.5	19.3	19.3	19.4	19.3	21.0	20.9	20.9	21.0
Female	Point ...	19.4	17.8	17.9	17.8	17.9	18.0	20.3	20.4	20.5	20.5
English	Point ...	18.5	17.7	17.9	17.8	18.1	18.4	20.5	20.3	20.2	20.3
Male	Point ...	17.6	17.1	17.3	17.3	17.6	17.8	20.1	19.8	19.8	19.8
Female	Point ...	19.4	18.3	18.3	18.2	18.6	18.9	20.9	20.7	20.6	20.6
Math	Point ...	20.0	17.6	17.4	17.3	17.2	17.1	19.9	20.0	20.0	20.1
Male	Point ...	21.1	19.3	18.9	18.9	18.6	18.3	20.7	20.6	20.7	20.8
Female	Point ...	18.8	16.2	16.2	16.0	16.0	16.1	19.3	19.4	19.5	19.6
Reading [3]	Point ...	19.7	17.4	17.2	17.2	17.4	17.2	(NA)	21.2	21.1	21.2
Male	Point ...	20.3	18.7	18.2	18.3	18.3	18.1	(NA)	21.3	21.1	21.2
Female	Point ...	19.0	16.4	16.4	16.4	16.6	16.4	(NA)	21.1	21.1	21.2
Science reasoning [4]	Point ...	20.8	21.1	21.1	21.0	21.2	21.2	(NA)	20.7	20.7	20.8
Male	Point ...	21.6	22.4	22.4	22.3	22.6	22.6	(NA)	21.3	21.4	21.5
Female	Point ...	20.0	20.0	20.0	20.0	20.0	20.0	(NA)	20.1	20.1	20.3
PARTICIPANTS [5]											
Total	1,000 ...	788	714	822	836	739	855	817	796	832	876
Male	Percent .	52	46	45	45	46	46	46	45	45	45
White	Percent .	(NA)	77	83	83	82	80	79	79	80	80
Black	Percent .	4	7	8	8	8	9	9	9	9	9
Obtaining composite scores [6] of—											
27 or above	Percent .	14	14	13	13	14	14	12	11	12	12
18 or below	Percent .	21	33	33	33	32	32	35	35	35	35
Planned educational major:											
Business [7]	Percent .	18	21	20	19	21	22	20	18	17	15
Engineering	Percent .	8	6	8	10	9	9	9	11	11	10
Social science [8]	Percent .	10	9	6	6	7	11	10	10	10	10
Education	Percent .	16	12	9	7	6	8	8	10	10	9

NA Not available. [1] Beginning 1990, not comparable with previous years because a new version of the ACT was introduced. Estimated average composite scores for prior years: 1989, 20.6; 1988, 1987, and 1986, 20.8. [2] Minimum score, 1; maximum score, 36. [3] Prior to 1990, social studies; data not comparable with previous years. [4] Prior to 1990, natural sciences; data not comparable with previous years. [5] Beginning 1985, data are for seniors who graduated in year shown and had taken the ACT in their junior or senior years. [6] Prior to 1990, 26 or above and 15 or below. [7] Includes political and persuasive (e.g. sales) fields through 1975; thereafter, business and commerce. [8] Includes religion through 1975.

Source: The American College Testing Program, Iowa City, IA, *High School Profile Report*, annual.

No. 266. Proficiency Test Scores for Selected Subjects, by Characteristic: 1977 to 1990

[Based on The National Assessment of Educational Progress Tests which are administered to a representative sample of students in public and private schools. Test scores can range from 0 to 500, except for writing, 0 to 400. For details, see source]

TEST AND YEAR	Total	SEX		RACE		His-panic origin	PARENTAL EDUCATION				
		Male	Fe-male	White [1]	Black [1]		Less than high school	High school	More than high school		
									Total	Some college	College graduate
READING											
9 year olds:											
1979-80	215	210	220	221	189	190	194	213	226	(NA)	(NA)
1983-84	211	208	214	218	186	187	195	209	223	(NA)	(NA)
1987-88	212	208	216	218	189	194	193	211	220	(NA)	(NA)
1989-90	209	204	215	217	182	189	193	209	218	(NA)	(NA)
13 year olds:											
1979-80	259	254	263	264	232	237	239	254	271	(NA)	(NA)
1983-84	257	253	262	263	236	240	240	253	268	(NA)	(NA)
1987-88	258	252	263	261	243	240	247	253	265	(NA)	(NA)
1989-90	257	251	263	262	242	238	241	251	267	(NA)	(NA)
17 year olds:											
1979-80	286	282	290	293	243	261	262	277	299	(NA)	(NA)
1983-84	289	284	294	296	264	268	269	281	301	(NA)	(NA)
1987-88	290	286	294	295	274	271	267	282	300	(NA)	(NA)
1989-90	290	284	297	297	267	275	270	283	300	(NA)	(NA)
WRITING											
4th graders:											
1983-84	179	176	184	186	154	163	157	171	187	(NA)	193
1987-88	186	176	195	193	154	169	158	183	179	(NA)	195
1989-90	183	174	193	191	155	168	169	183	195	(NA)	191
8th graders:											
1983-84	206	199	214	210	190	191	196	203	210	(NA)	215
1987-88	203	193	213	207	190	188	195	198	213	(NA)	208
1989-90	198	187	208	202	182	189	191	195	207	(NA)	203
11th graders:											
1983-84	212	201	223	218	195	188	200	207	218	(NA)	220
1987-88	214	204	223	219	200	199	202	211	217	(NA)	220
1989-90	212	200	224	217	194	198	190	204	215	(NA)	221
MATHEMATICS											
9 year olds:											
1977-78	219	217	220	224	192	203	200	219	(NA)	230	231
1981-82	219	217	221	224	195	204	199	218	(NA)	225	229
1985-86	222	222	222	227	202	205	201	218	(NA)	229	231
1989-90	230	229	230	235	208	214	210	226	(NA)	236	238
13 year olds:											
1977-78	264	264	265	272	230	238	245	263	(NA)	273	284
1981-82	269	269	268	274	240	252	251	263	(NA)	275	282
1985-86	269	270	268	274	249	254	252	263	(NA)	274	280
1989-90	270	271	270	276	249	255	253	263	(NA)	277	280
17 year olds:											
1977-78	300	304	297	306	268	276	280	294	(NA)	305	317
1981-82	299	302	296	304	272	277	279	293	(NA)	304	312
1985-86	302	305	299	308	279	283	279	293	(NA)	305	314
1989-90	305	306	303	310	289	284	285	294	(NA)	308	316
SCIENCE											
9 year olds:											
1976-77	220	222	218	230	192	175	199	223	(NA)	237	232
1981-82	221	221	221	229	189	187	198	218	(NA)	229	231
1985-86	224	227	221	232	199	196	204	220	(NA)	236	235
1989-90	229	230	227	238	196	206	210	226	(NA)	238	236
13 year olds:											
1976-77	247	251	244	256	208	213	224	245	(NA)	260	267
1981-82	250	256	245	257	217	226	225	243	(NA)	259	264
1985-86	251	256	247	259	222	226	229	245	(NA)	258	264
1989-90	255	259	252	264	226	232	233	247	(NA)	263	268
17 year olds:											
1976-77	290	297	282	298	262	240	265	284	(NA)	296	309
1981-82	283	292	275	293	249	235	259	275	(NA)	290	300
1985-86	289	295	282	298	259	253	258	277	(NA)	295	304
1989-90	290	296	285	301	253	262	261	276	(NA)	297	306

NA Not available. [1] Non-Hispanic.

Source: U.S. National Center for Education Statistics, *Digest of Education Statistics,* annual.

No. 267. Public High School Graduates With Projections, by State, 1980 to 1994

[In thousands. For school year ending in year shown. Projections will not agree with data in table 225 due to revised projections on the national level]

STATE	1980	1985	1987	1988	1989	1990	1991	1992, est.	1993, est.	1994, proj.
U.S.	2,747.7	2,414.0	2,428.8	2,500.2	2,458.8	2,320.3	2,237.5	2,246.2	2,276.8	2,209.1
AL.	45.2	40.0	42.5	43.8	43.4	40.5	39.0	38.6	39.2	38.3
AK.	5.2	5.2	5.7	5.9	5.6	5.4	5.5	5.5	5.7	5.5
AZ.	28.6	27.9	29.5	29.8	31.9	32.1	31.3	29.0	29.2	31.2
AR.	29.1	26.3	27.1	27.8	27.9	26.5	25.7	25.4	25.8	25.5
CA.	249.2	225.4	237.4	249.6	244.6	236.3	234.2	250.3	257.1	249.9
CO.	36.8	32.3	34.2	36.0	35.5	33.0	31.3	31.1	32.2	31.3
CT.	37.7	32.1	31.1	32.4	30.9	27.9	27.3	25.4	24.5	25.3
DE.	7.6	5.9	5.9	6.0	6.1	5.6	5.2	5.3	5.5	5.5
DC.	5.0	3.9	3.8	3.9	3.6	3.6	3.4	3.4	3.3	2.7
FL.	87.3	81.1	82.2	89.2	90.8	88.9	87.4	92.1	93.2	84.0
GA.	61.6	58.7	60.0	61.8	61.9	56.6	60.1	59.7	60.6	58.1
HI	11.5	10.1	10.4	10.6	10.4	10.3	9.0	9.2	8.9	9.9
ID	13.2	12.1	12.2	12.4	12.5	12.0	12.0	12.7	13.2	12.6
IL.	135.6	117.0	116.1	119.1	116.7	108.1	103.3	102.7	103.3	102.7
IN	73.1	63.3	60.4	64.0	63.6	60.0	58.6	57.7	58.9	55.4
IA	43.4	36.1	34.6	35.2	34.3	31.8	28.6	29.0	30.3	30.6
KS.	30.9	26.0	26.9	27.0	26.8	25.4	24.4	24.0	24.2	25.5
KY.	41.2	38.0	36.9	39.5	38.9	38.0	35.8	34.8	36.6	34.1
LA	46.3	39.7	39.1	39.1	37.2	36.1	33.5	32.2	31.7	32.3
ME.	15.4	13.9	13.7	13.8	13.9	13.8	13.2	14.2	13.9	11.9
MD.	54.3	48.3	46.1	47.2	45.8	41.6	39.0	39.0	39.0	38.4
MA.	73.8	63.4	61.0	59.5	57.3	55.9	52.1	50.8	46.6	45.7
MI	124.3	105.9	102.7	106.2	101.8	93.8	88.2	86.7	89.7	83.3
MN.	64.9	53.4	53.5	54.6	53.1	49.1	46.5	46.1	47.5	48.7
MS.	27.6	25.3	26.2	27.9	24.2	25.2	23.7	23.0	23.2	23.1
MO.	62.3	51.3	50.8	51.3	52.0	49.0	46.9	46.6	47.4	46.1
MT.	12.1	10.0	10.1	10.3	10.5	9.4	9.0	9.0	9.3	9.3
NE.	22.4	18.0	18.1	18.3	18.7	17.7	16.5	17.5	17.8	16.8
NV.	8.5	8.6	9.5	9.4	9.5	9.5	9.4	9.2	9.9	10.5
NH.	11.7	11.1	10.8	11.7	11.3	10.8	10.1	10.2	9.7	9.4
NJ	94.6	81.5	79.4	80.9	76.3	69.8	67.0	63.8	63.0	61.3
NM.	18.4	15.6	15.7	15.9	15.5	14.9	15.2	14.8	14.5	15.2
NY.	204.1	166.8	163.8	165.4	154.6	143.3	133.6	134.7	136.4	131.4
NC.	70.9	67.2	65.4	67.8	70.0	64.8	62.8	60.9	60.4	57.9
ND.	9.9	8.1	7.8	8.4	8.1	7.7	7.6	7.5	7.6	7.5
OH.	144.2	122.3	121.1	124.5	125.0	114.5	107.5	106.2	106.1	104.3
OK.	39.3	34.6	35.5	36.1	36.8	35.6	33.0	32.7	32.5	31.5
OR.	29.9	26.9	27.2	28.1	26.9	25.5	24.6	25.5	26.9	26.3
PA.	146.5	127.2	121.2	124.4	118.9	110.5	104.8	103.8	103.2	99.5
RI	10.9	9.2	8.8	8.9	8.6	7.8	7.7	7.7	7.8	7.3
SC.	38.7	34.5	36.0	36.1	37.0	32.5	33.1	32.8	32.5	31.9
SD.	10.7	8.2	8.1	8.4	8.2	7.7	7.1	7.4	8.0	7.9
TN.	49.8	43.3	44.7	47.9	48.6	46.1	44.8	45.2	45.8	41.8
TX.	171.4	159.2	168.4	171.4	177.0	172.5	174.3	176.2	178.5	172.9
UT.	20.0	19.9	20.9	22.2	22.9	21.2	22.2	24.9	26.0	27.0
VT.	6.7	5.8	6.0	6.2	6.0	6.1	5.2	5.2	5.3	5.2
VA.	66.6	61.0	65.0	65.7	65.0	60.6	58.4	58.6	58.4	55.6
WA	50.4	45.4	49.9	51.8	48.9	45.9	42.5	44.2	46.1	46.9
WV	23.4	22.3	22.4	22.4	22.9	21.9	21.1	20.8	21.0	19.9
WI	69.3	58.9	56.9	58.4	55.0	52.0	49.3	47.0	53.4	49.1
WY	6.1	5.7	5.9	6.1	6.1	5.8	5.7	5.8	6.1	5.5

Source: U.S. National Center for Education Statistics, *Digest of Education Statistics,* annual; and *Projections of Education Statistics,* annual.

No. 268. General Educational Development (GED) Credentials Issued: 1974 to 1992

YEAR	GED's issued (1,000)	PERCENT DISTRIBUTION BY AGE OF TEST TAKER				
		Under 19 years old	20 to 24 years old	25 to 29 years old	30 to 34 years old	35 years old or over
1974	294	35	27	13	9	17
1975	340	33	26	14	9	18
1980	479	37	27	13	8	15
1983	465	34	29	14	8	15
1984	427	32	28	15	9	16
1985	413	32	26	15	10	16
1986	428	32	26	15	10	17
1987	444	33	24	15	10	18
1988	410	35	22	14	10	18
1989	357	36	22	14	10	17
1990	410	35	25	14	10	17
1991	462	33	27	14	10	17
1992	457	32	28	13	11	16

Source: U.S. National Center for Education Statistics, *Digest of Education Statistics,* 1993.

No. 269. College Enrollment and High School Graduates Enrolled in or Completed at Least 1 Year of College: 1960 to 1992

[As of October, except as noted. Covers civilian noninstitutional population 14 to 24 years old, except as noted]

ITEM AND YEAR	ALL PERSONS				MALE			FEMALE		
	Total [1]	White	Black	Hispanic origin [2]	White	Black	Hispanic origin [2]	White	Black	Hispanic origin [2]
College enrollment (1,000): 1960 [3]...	2,279	2,138	[4]141	(NA)	1,297	[4]68	(NA)	841	[4]73	(NA)
1970	6,065	5,535	437	(NA)	3,213	202	(NA)	2,322	236	(NA)
1975	7,228	6,368	699	308	3,437	308	148	2,931	392	160
1980	7,475	6,546	718	325	3,303	292	156	3,243	426	168
1985	7,799	6,729	755	391	3,374	355	178	3,357	400	211
1988	7,973	6,796	785	463	3,310	303	237	3,486	482	228
1989	7,987	6,778	867	470	3,286	332	216	3,493	535	255
1990	8,142	6,767	929	448	3,355	442	226	3,413	486	222
1991	8,304	6,917	846	526	3,311	382	216	3,607	461	310
1992	8,547	7,075	914	603	3,373	364	256	3,701	552	346
Percent of high school graduates enrolled: 1960 [3]	23.8	24.3	[4]18.7	(NA)	31.1	[4]21.1	(NA)	18.1	[4]16.9	(NA)
1970	33.3	33.9	26.7	(NA)	42.9	29.5	(NA)		24.7	(NA)
1975	33.1	33.0	32.5	36.2	36.9	33.4	37.9	29.4	32.0	34.8
1980	32.3	32.5	28.3	30.3	34.3	27.0	31.2	30.9	29.2	29.4
1985	34.3	35.0	26.5	27.5	36.6	28.2	26.4	33.6	25.1	28.4
1988	37.6	38.4	28.6	31.3	39.6	25.1	32.2	37.3	31.3	30.5
1989	38.5	39.1	31.5	29.4	39.7	27.5	28.2	38.6	34.7	30.5
1990	39.6	39.8	33.7	29.4	40.7	35.1	29.4	38.9	32.4	29.5
1991	41.4	42.0	31.8	34.6	41.9	32.2	29.7	42.1	31.4	39.2
1992	42.3	42.7	34.3	37.6	42.1	29.7	34.8	43.2	38.2	39.9
Percent of high school graduates enrolled in college or completed 1 or more years of college: 1960 [3]	40.4	41.0	[4]32.5	(NA)	47.1	[4]33.5	(NA)	35.6	[4]31.8	(NA)
1970	52.3	53.4	39.4	(NA)	60.9	41.4	(NA)	47.2	39.3	(NA)
1975	52.5	52.7	48.1	50.8	56.6	50.5	55.4	49.1	46.4	46.7
1980	51.1	51.4	45.9	47.3	51.8	44.1	49.5	50.9	47.4	45.4
1985	54.3	55.3	43.8	46.7	55.5	43.6	44.9	55.2	44.0	48.0
1988 [5]	57.4	58.5	46.3	47.0	57.8	42.5	48.3	59.1	49.2	45.8
1989 [5]	57.9	58.9	49.1	43.6	58.5	45.8	42.7	59.2	51.8	44.5
1990 [5]	58.9	60.1	48.0	44.7	58.7	48.9	46.5	61.4	47.3	43.0
1991 [5]	60.7	62.3	46.1	47.6	59.9	46.1	42.2	64.5	47.0	52.5
1992 [5]	65.6	67.0	53.3	55.0	65.8	49.4	52.2	68.1	56.6	57.4

NA Not available.   [1] Includes other races, not shown separately.   [2] Persons of Hispanic origin may be of any race.   [3] As of April.   [4] Black and other races.   [5] Population 16 to 24 years old.

Source: U.S. Bureau of the Census, *U.S. Census of Population: 1960*, vol. I, *Characteristics of the Population*, part 1; *Current Population Reports*, P20-474, and earlier reports; and unpublished data.

No. 270. College Enrollment, by Sex and Attendance Status, With Projections: 1989 to 2004

[As of fall. In thousands]

SEX AND AGE	1989		1991, est.		1992, proj.		1999, proj.		2004, proj.	
	Total	Part-time	Total	Part-time	Total	Part-time	Total	Part-time	Total	Part-time
Total	13,539	5,878	14,359	6,244	14,558	6,419	15,304	6,793	15,892	6,805
Male	6,190	2,450	6,502	2,573	6,654	2,662	6,892	2,747	7,216	2,770
14 to 17 years old	71	12	46	6	62	10	71	12	74	12
18 to 19 years old	1,342	113	1,217	121	1,202	129	1,420	146	1,537	154
20 to 21 years old	1,189	198	1,306	230	1,289	228	1,318	249	1,503	301
22 to 24 years old	1,090	367	1,214	378	1,294	397	1,211	378	1,369	429
25 to 29 years old	1,038	639	1,082	587	1,093	586	1,042	573	971	534
30 to 34 years old	603	439	664	475	699	504	653	459	619	435
35 years old and over	857	682	972	775	1,013	807	1,176	930	1,143	904
Female	7,349	3,428	7,857	3,672	7,904	3,757	8,412	4,046	8,676	4,035
14 to 17 years old	101	12	76	1	89	9	108	10	113	11
18 to 19 years old	1,515	184	1,496	185	1,459	189	1,753	235	1,841	247
20 to 21 years old	1,253	213	1,462	239	1,428	238	1,432	251	1,601	285
22 to 24 years old	1,104	470	1,072	412	1,125	437	1,095	441	1,258	504
25 to 29 years old	1,052	732	1,053	679	1,029	667	1,013	675	947	631
30 to 34 years old	750	563	804	593	829	612	777	578	741	552
35 years old and over	1,574	1,253	1,895	1,564	1,942	1,603	2,233	1,854	2,175	1,805

Source: U.S. Department of Education, National Center for Education Statistics, *Projections of Education Statistics*, annual.

No. 271. College Enrollment, by Selected Characteristics: 1978 to 1992

[In thousands. As of fall. Totals may differ from other tables because of adjustments to underreported and nonreported racial/ethnic data. Nonresident alien students are not distributed among racial/ethnic groups]

CHARACTERISTIC	1978	1980	1984	1988	1990	1991, est.	1992, prel.
Total	11,231.2	12,086.8	12,233.0	13,043.1	13,819.5	14,359.0	14,491.2
Male	5,621.5	5,868.1	5,858.3	5,998.2	6,284.4	6,501.8	6,526.1
Female	5,609.6	6,218.7	6,374.7	7,044.9	7,535.1	7,857.1	7,965.1
Public	8,769.8	9,456.4	9,456.4	10,156.4	10,844.7	11,309.6	11,387.8
Private	2,461.4	2,630.4	2,776.6	2,886.7	2,974.8	3,049.4	3,103.5
2-year	4,028.8	4,521.4	4,526.9	4,868.1	5,240.1	5,651.9	5,723.2
4-year	7,202.4	7,565.4	7,706.1	8,175.0	8,579.4	8,707.1	8,768.0
Undergraduate	9,665.8	10,469.1	10,610.8	11,304.2	11,959.2	12,439.3	12,539.8
Graduate	1,310.4	1,340.9	1,343.7	1,471.9	1,586.2	1,639.1	1,670.0
First professional	255.0	276.8	278.5	267.1	274.1	280.5	281.4
White [1]	9,194.0	9,833.0	9,814.7	10,283.2	10,723.0	10,989.8	10,870.0
Male	4,613.1	4,772.9	4,689.9	4,711.6	4,861.3	4,962.2	4,882.5
Female	4,580.9	5,060.1	5,124.7	5,571.6	5,861.7	6,027.6	5,987.6
Public	7,136.1	7,656.1	7,542.4	7,963.8	8,385.4	8,622.2	8,486.9
Private	2,057.9	2,176.9	2,272.3	2,319.4	2,337.6	2,367.5	2,383.1
2-year	3,166.9	3,558.5	3,514.3	3,701.5	3,954.3	4,198.8	4,123.1
4-year	6,027.1	6,274.5	6,300.4	6,581.6	6,768.7	6,791.0	6,746.9
Undergraduate	7,870.6	8,480.7	8,484.0	8,906.7	9,272.6	9,507.7	9,380.6
Graduate	1,094.1	1,104.7	1,087.3	1,153.2	1,228.4	1,258.0	1,268.4
First professional	229.3	247.7	243.4	223.2	222.0	224.0	220.9
Black [1]	1,054.4	1,106.8	1,075.8	1,129.6	1,247.1	1,335.4	1,393.5
Male	453.3	463.7	436.8	442.7	484.7	517.0	537.1
Female	601.1	643.0	639.0	686.9	762.4	818.4	856.4
Public	839.5	876.1	844.0	881.1	976.5	1,053.4	1,101.1
Private	214.9	230.7	231.8	248.5	270.6	281.9	292.4
2-year	442.6	472.5	458.7	473.3	524.3	577.6	602.0
4-year	611.8	634.3	617.0	656.3	722.8	757.8	791.5
Undergraduate	966.5	1,018.8	994.9	1,038.8	1,147.2	1,229.3	1,281.2
Graduate	76.4	75.1	67.4	76.5	83.9	88.9	94.1
First professional	11.4	12.8	13.4	14.3	16.0	17.2	18.2
Hispanic	417.3	471.7	534.9	680.0	782.6	866.6	954.4
Male	212.5	231.6	253.8	310.3	354.0	390.5	427.4
Female	204.7	240.1	281.2	369.6	428.6	476.0	527.1
Public	362.5	406.2	456.1	586.9	671.4	742.1	821.7
Private	54.7	65.5	78.9	93.1	111.1	124.5	132.7
2-year	226.9	255.1	288.8	383.9	424.2	483.7	544.5
4-year	190.4	216.6	246.1	296.0	358.3	382.9	409.9
Undergraduate	384.0	433.1	495.2	631.2	724.6	804.2	887.2
Graduate	28.0	32.1	31.7	39.5	47.2	50.9	55.2
First professional	5.4	6.5	8.0	9.3	10.9	11.4	12.0
American Indian [1]	77.9	83.9	83.6	92.5	102.8	113.7	118.8
Male	36.8	37.8	37.4	39.1	43.1	47.6	50.1
Female	41.0	46.1	46.1	53.4	59.7	66.1	68.8
Public	68.5	74.2	72.1	81.1	90.4	100.2	103.0
Private	9.5	9.7	11.4	11.5	12.4	13.6	15.9
2-year	43.1	47.0	45.5	50.4	54.9	62.6	64.0
4-year	34.8	36.9	38.1	42.1	47.9	51.1	54.9
Undergraduate	71.9	77.9	77.8	85.9	95.5	105.8	110.4
Graduate	4.9	5.2	4.8	5.6	6.2	6.6	7.0
First professional	1.1	0.8	1.0	1.1	1.1	1.3	1.5
Asian [1]	235.1	286.4	389.5	496.7	572.5	637.2	696.8
Male	126.3	151.3	210.0	259.2	294.9	325.1	351.3
Female	108.7	135.2	179.5	237.5	277.6	312.0	345.5
Public	195.4	239.7	322.7	405.7	461.0	516.3	565.6
Private	39.6	46.7	66.8	91.0	111.6	120.9	131.1
2-year	97.2	124.3	167.1	199.3	215.2	255.7	289.2
4-year	137.8	162.1	222.4	297.4	357.3	381.5	407.6
Undergraduate	202.8	248.7	343.0	436.6	500.5	558.7	612.7
Graduate	27.5	31.6	37.1	45.7	53.2	57.6	61.6
First professional	4.8	6.1	9.3	14.4	18.8	20.8	22.5
Nonresident alien	252.6	305.0	334.6	361.2	391.5	416.4	457.6
Male	179.5	210.8	230.4	235.3	246.3	259.4	277.8
Female	73.1	94.2	104.1	125.9	145.2	157.0	179.8
Public	167.7	204.1	219.0	237.8	260.0	275.3	309.4
Private	84.8	100.8	115.5	123.3	131.5	141.0	148.2
2-year	52.0	64.1	52.5	59.6	67.1	73.5	100.4
4-year	200.5	240.9	282.1	301.5	324.4	342.8	357.2
Undergraduate	170.1	209.9	215.8	205.0	218.7	233.6	267.7
Graduate	79.5	92.2	115.3	151.4	167.3	177.0	183.7
First professional	3.0	2.9	3.4	4.7	5.4	5.8	6.3

[1] Non-Hispanic.
Source: U.S. National Center for Education Statistics, *Digest of Education Statistics*, annual.

No. 272. College Enrollment, by Sex, Age, Race, and Hispanic Origin: 1972 to 1992

[In thousands. As of October for the civilian noninstitutional population, 14 years old and over. Based on the Current Population Survey; see text, section 1, and Appendix III]

CHARACTERISTIC	1972	1975	1980	1985	1986 [1]	1987	1988	1989	1990	1991	1992
Total [2]	9,095	10,880	11,387	12,524	12,651	12,719	13,116	13,180	13,621	14,057	14,035
Male [3]	5,218	5,911	5,430	5,906	5,957	6,030	5,950	5,950	6,192	6,439	6,192
18 to 24 years	3,534	3,693	3,604	3,749	3,702	3,867	3,770	3,717	3,922	3,954	3,912
25 to 34 years	1,178	1,521	1,325	1,464	1,545	1,421	1,395	1,443	1,412	1,605	1,392
35 years old and over	365	569	405	561	628	625	727	716	772	832	789
Female [3]	3,877	4,969	5,957	6,618	6,694	6,689	7,166	7,231	7,427	7,618	7,844
18 to 24 years	2,724	3,243	3,625	3,788	3,775	3,826	4,021	4,085	4,042	4,218	4,429
25 to 34 years	581	947	1,378	1,599	1,559	1,564	1,568	1,637	1,749	1,680	1,732
35 years old and over	418	614	802	1,100	1,240	1,176	1,452	1,396	1,546	1,636	1,575
White	8,147	9,547	9,926	10,782	10,707	10,731	11,140	11,243	11,488	11,686	11,710
Male	4,723	5,263	4,804	5,101	5,074	5,104	5,078	5,136	5,235	5,304	5,210
Female	3,427	4,285	5,123	5,681	5,632	5,627	6,063	6,107	6,253	6,382	6,499
Black	727	1,099	1,163	1,208	1,359	1,351	1,321	1,287	1,393	1,477	1,424
Male	384	523	476	518	580	587	494	480	587	629	527
Female	343	577	686	689	779	764	827	807	807	848	897
Hispanic origin [4]	242	411	443	665	794	739	747	754	748	830	918
Male	126	218	222	301	377	390	355	353	364	347	388
Female	117	193	221	363	417	349	391	401	384	483	530

[1] Revised. Beginning 1986, based on a revised edit and tabulation package.   [2] Includes other races not shown separately.   [3] Includes persons 14 to 17 years old, not shown separately.   [4] Persons of Hispanic origin may be of any race.

Source: U.S. Bureau of the Census, *Current Population Reports*, P20-474; and earlier reports.

No. 273. College Population, by Selected Characteristics: 1987 and 1992

[In thousands, except percent. As of October. Based on the Current Population Survey. See text, section 1, and Appendix III]

CHARACTERISTIC	Total population	ENROLLED IN COLLEGE					PERCENT EMPLOYED		
		Total	Type of school			Percent enrolled full-time	Total	Full-time	Part-time
			2-year	4-year	Graduate school				
Total, 1987 [1]	190,058	12,719	3,648	6,656	2,415	62.6	60.4	31.7	28.7
Male	90,610	6,030	1,522	3,356	1,152	67.2	60.6	31.7	28.9
Female	99,449	6,689	2,127	3,299	1,264	58.4	60.1	31.6	28.5
White	162,757	10,731	3,039	5,617	2,075	61.6	62.2	32.6	29.6
Black	21,520	1,351	422	748	181	66.3	50.5	28.6	21.9
Hispanic origin [2]	13,687	739	307	342	90	57.3	65.5	37.0	28.6
14 to 19 years old	21,410	3,284	1,111	2,172	1	88.1	44.0	7.6	36.4
20 and 21 years old	7,078	2,642	624	1,961	58	84.4	53.3	14.5	38.8
22 to 24 years old	11,712	2,006	457	1,055	494	67.2	62.5	29.8	32.7
25 to 34 years old	42,374	2,985	851	996	1,137	36.4	74.0	55.8	18.2
35 years and older	107,484	1,802	605	471	725	22.3	83.1	62.8	20.3
Total, [1] 1992	195,586	14,035	4,239	7,404	2,392	65.5	60.4	31.3	29.1
Male	93,604	6,192	1,688	3,403	1,102	69.9	60.5	31.8	28.7
Female	101,982	7,844	2,551	4,002	1,291	61.9	60.4	31.0	29.4
White	165,757	11,710	3,527	6,152	2,030	64.4	62.7	32.2	30.5
Black	22,614	1,424	466	815	143	68.6	50.3	30.8	19.5
Hispanic origin [2]	15,763	918	448	409	62	56.2	59.6	32.4	27.2
15 to 19 years old	16,648	3,097	1,084	2,013	-	91.6	45.9	7.5	38.4
20 and 21 years old	6,884	2,938	789	2,113	36	86.4	54.2	12.7	41.5
22 to 24 years old	10,859	2,512	581	1,423	508	72.2	60.1	27.4	32.7
25 to 34 years old	41,661	3,125	988	1,102	1,035	42.0	70.6	54.6	16.0
35 years and older	119,532	2,364	797	753	814	29.0	74.0	59.2	14.8

- Represents or rounds to zero.   [1] Includes other races, not shown separately.   [2] Persons of Hispanic origin may be of any race.

Source: U.S. Bureau of the Census, *Current Population Reports*, P20-443 and P20-474.

No. 274. Higher Education—Summary: 1970 to 1992

[Institutions, staff, and enrollment as of fall. Finances for fiscal year ending in the following year. Covers universities, colleges, professional schools, junior and teachers colleges, both publicly and privately controlled, regular session. Includes estimates for institutions not reporting. See also Appendix III, and *Historical Statistics, Colonial Times to 1970*, series H 680, H 690-692, H 699-705, and H 710]

ITEM	Unit	1970	1980	1985	1987	1988	1989	1990	1991, est.	1992, prel.
ALL INSTITUTIONS										
Number of institutions [1]	Number.	2,556	3,231	3,340	3,587	3,565	3,535	3,559	3,601	3,638
4-year	Number .	1,665	1,957	2,029	2,135	2,129	2,127	2,141	2,157	2,169
2-year	Number .	891	1,274	1,311	1,452	1,436	1,408	1,418	1,444	1,469
Instructional staff [2]	1,000. . .	474	686	715	793	804	824	840	(NA)	(NA)
Percent full-time	Percent .	78	66	64	66	(NA)	64	61	(NA)	(NA)
Total enrollment [3]	1,000. . .	8,581	12,097	12,247	12,767	13,055	13,539	13,820	14,359	14,491
Male	1,000. . .	5,044	5,874	5,818	5,932	6,002	6,190	6,285	6,502	6,526
Female	1,000. . .	3,537	6,223	6,429	6,835	7,053	7,349	7,535	7,857	7,965
4-year institutions.	1,000. . .	6,262	7,571	7,716	7,990	8,180	8,388	8,579	8,707	8,768
2-year institutions.	1,000. . .	2,319	4,526	4,531	4,776	4,875	5,151	5,240	5,652	5,724
Full-time.	1,000. . .	5,816	7,098	7,075	7,231	7,437	7,661	7,821	8,115	8,165
Part-time	1,000. . .	2,765	4,999	5,172	5,536	5,619	5,878	5,998	6,244	6,326
Public	1,000. . .	6,428	9,457	9,479	9,973	10,161	10,578	10,844	11,310	11,388
Private	1,000. . .	2,153	2,640	2,768	2,793	2,894	2,961	2,975	3,049	3,104
Undergraduate [4]	1,000. . .	7,376	10,475	10,597	11,046	11,317	11,743	11,959	12,439	12,540
Men	1,000. . .	4,254	5,000	4,962	5,068	5,138	5,311	5,380	5,571	5,584
Women.	1,000. . .	3,122	5,475	5,635	5,978	6,179	6,432	6,579	6,868	6,956
First-time freshmen	1,000. . .	2,063	2,588	2,292	2,246	2,379	2,341	2,257	2,278	2,186
First professional	1,000. . .	173	278	274	268	267	274	274	281	281
Men	1,000. . .	159	199	180	170	167	168	167	170	169
Women	1,000. . .	15	78	94	98	100	105	107	111	112
Graduate [4]	1,000. . .	1,031	1,343	1,376	1,452	1,472	1,522	1,586	1,639	1,670
Men	1,000. . .	630	675	677	693	697	710	737	761	773
Women.	1,000. . .	400	670	700	759	774	811	849	878	897
Current funds revenues [5]	Mil. dol.	23,879	65,585	100,438	117,340	128,502	139,635	149,766	(NA)	(NA)
Tuition and fees	Mil. dol.	5,021	13,773	23,117	27,837	30,807	33,926	37,434	(NA)	(NA)
Federal government.	Mil. dol.	4,190	9,748	12,705	14,772	15,894	17,255	18,236	(NA)	(NA)
State government	Mil. dol.	6,503	20,106	29,912	33,517	36,031	38,349	39,481	(NA)	(NA)
Auxiliary enterprises	Mil. dol.	3,125	7,287	10,674	11,948	12,856	13,938	14,903	(NA)	(NA)
Plant funds [6]	Mil. dol.	(NA)	4,774	7,713	(NA)	(NA)	(NA)	(NA)	(NA)	(NA)
Increase in fund balance [7]	Mil. dol.	498	2,793	7,239	(NA)	(NA)	(NA)	(NA)	(NA)	(NA)
Current funds expenditures [5]	Mil. dol .	23,375	64,053	97,536	113,786	123,867	134,656	146,088	(NA)	(NA)
Educational and general [8]	Mil. dol .	17,616	50,074	76,128	89,157	96,803	105,585	114,140	(NA)	(NA)
Auxiliary enterprises [9]	Mil. dol .	2,988	7,288	10,528	11,400	12,280	13,204	14,272	(NA)	(NA)
Gross addition to plant value . .	Mil. dol .	4,165	6,471	10,149	11,589	13,638	17,107	19,672	(NA)	(NA)
Value of plant	Mil. dol .	46,054	88,761	122,261	139,456	158,693	182,609	190,355	(NA)	(NA)
Endowment (market value). . . .	Mil. dol .	13,714	23,465	50,281	57,392	64,155	67,979	72,049	(NA)	(NA)
TWO-YEAR INSTITUTIONS										
Number of institutions [1][10] . . .	Number.	891	1,274	1,311	1,452	1,436	1,408	1,418	1,444	1,469
Public	Number .	654	945	932	992	984	968	972	999	1,024
Private.	Number .	237	329	379	460	452	440	446	445	445
Instructional staff [2]	1,000. . .	92	192	211	246	(NA)	241	(NA)	(NA)	(NA)
Enrollment [3][4]	1,000. . .	2,319	4,526	4,531	4,776	4,875	5,151	5,240	5,652	5,723
Public	1,000. . .	2,195	4,329	4,270	4,541	4,615	4,884	4,996	5,405	5,486
Private.	1,000. . .	124	198	261	235	260	267	244	247	238
Male	1,000. . .	1,375	2,047	2,002	2,073	2,090	2,217	2,232	2,401	2,414
Female	1,000. . .	945	2,479	2,529	2,704	2,785	2,934	3,008	3,250	3,309
Current funds revenue [5]	Mil. dol .	2,504	8,505	12,293	14,060	15,387	16,777	18,021	(NA)	(NA)
Tuition and fees	Mil. dol .	413	1,618	2,618	3,057	3,376	3,623	4,029	(NA)	(NA)
State government	Mil. dol .	926	3,961	5,659	6,350	6,898	7,558	8,001	(NA)	(NA)
Local government	Mil. dol .	701	1,623	2,027	2,352	2,662	2,831	3,044	(NA)	(NA)
Current funds expenditures . .	Mil. dol .	2,327	8,212	11,976	13,644	14,726	16,077	17,494	(NA)	(NA)
Education and general [8]	Mil. dol .	2,073	7,608	11,118	12,701	13,676	14,936	16,270	(NA)	(NA)
Instruction.	Mil. dol .	1,205	3,764	5,398	6,082	6,617	7,236	7,903	(NA)	(NA)

NA Not available.   [1] Beginning 1974, number of institutions includes count of branch campuses. Due to revised survey procedures, data beginning 1987 are not comparable with previous years.   [2] Due to revised survey methods, data beginning 1987 not comparable with previous years.   [3] Beginning 1974, branch campuses counted according to actual status, e.g., 2-year branch in 2-year category; previously a 2-year branch included in university category.   [4] Includes unclassified students. (Students taking courses for credit, but are not candidates for degrees.)   [5] Includes items not shown separately.   [6] Annual net increase in plant funds.   [7] Includes endowment, and, beginning 1980, annuity and student loans.   [8] Data for 1970 are not strictly comparable with later years.   [9] Includes activities.   [10] Beginning 1980, includes schools accredited by the National Association of Trade and Technical Schools.

Source: U.S. National Center for Education, Statistics, *Digest of Education Statistics*, annual; *Projections of Education Statistics*, annual; and unpublished data.

No. 275. Colleges—Number and Enrollment, by State, 1992

[Number of institutions beginning in academic year. Opening fall enrollment of resident and extension students attending full-time or part-time. Excludes students taking courses for credit by mail, radio, or TV, and students in branches of U.S. institutions operated in foreign countries. See Appendix III]

STATE	Number of institutions [1]	Enrollment, prel. (1,000)										Nonresident alien
		Total	Male	Female	Public	Private	Full-time	White [2]	Minority enrollment			
									Total [3]	Black [2]	Hispanic	
United States..	3,638	14,491	6,526	7,965	11,388	3,104	8,165	10,870	3,164	1,393	954	458
Alabama.........	86	231	104	127	206	24	155	172	54	49	1	5
Alaska..........	8	31	13	18	29	2	12	25	6	1	1	1
Arizona..........	40	276	127	149	256	20	124	209	59	9	34	8
Arkansas	34	97	42	56	86	12	69	80	16	14	1	2
California	322	1,977	902	1,076	1,748	229	862	1,115	764	140	315	98
Colorado........	59	240	112	128	211	29	126	198	37	8	20	5
Connecticut......	47	166	73	93	108	58	83	138	23	11	6	5
Delaware	10	43	18	24	35	7	26	35	7	5	1	1
District of Columbia .	18	82	38	44	12	70	50	41	32	25	3	9
Florida	105	618	275	343	511	107	299	436	166	73	75	17
Georgia	115	293	130	163	233	61	194	211	76	65	4	6
Hawaii	17	61	28	33	50	12	34	17	39	1	1	5
Idaho..........	11	58	26	32	47	11	39	53	3	(Z)	1	2
Illinois..........	169	748	336	412	566	182	375	543	187	94	55	18
Indiana.........	78	297	138	159	235	62	194	260	28	17	5	8
Iowa	61	178	82	96	128	50	125	158	11	5	3	8
Kansas.........	49	169	76	93	153	16	97	146	17	8	4	6
Kentucky	62	188	78	110	158	30	121	170	15	12	1	3
Louisiana	33	204	88	116	177	27	144	140	59	50	4	5
Maine..........	31	58	24	34	41	17	32	55	3	1	(Z)	1
Maryland	56	268	115	153	228	40	124	189	71	52	5	9
Massachusetts.....	117	423	189	234	183	240	266	343	58	20	15	23
Michigan........	102	560	249	311	473	86	288	461	83	57	10	15
Minnesota.......	99	273	123	150	212	61	160	249	18	6	3	6
Mississippi	46	124	54	69	110	14	94	85	36	34	(Z)	2
Missouri........	96	297	134	162	199	98	169	253	36	25	4	8
Montana........	19	40	19	21	34	6	30	34	5	(Z)	(Z)	1
Nebraska.......	37	123	56	67	103	19	69	111	9	4	2	3
Nevada	9	64	28	35	63	1	21	51	12	3	4	1
New Hampshire....	29	64	28	36	35	29	40	60	3	1	1	1
New Jersey.......	62	342	152	191	278	65	173	247	82	38	26	13
New Mexico......	31	99	44	56	95	4	49	59	39	3	29	2
New York........	320	1,070	468	602	611	459	674	754	277	129	88	39
North Carolina	122	383	168	216	316	68	237	292	85	72	4	6
North Dakota.....	20	40	20	20	37	4	32	36	3	(Z)	(Z)	2
Ohio	165	573	263	310	437	136	353	490	67	50	7	16
Oklahoma........	46	182	83	99	159	23	116	144	31	13	3	7
Oregon.........	45	167	79	88	145	23	94	144	17	3	4	6
Pennsylvania......	220	630	288	342	363	267	395	537	77	46	11	17
Rhode Island.....	12	79	36	44	43	36	49	69	8	3	2	3
South Carolina.....	60	171	74	98	146	26	110	128	40	36	1	3
South Dakota	19	38	17	21	30	7	26	34	3	(Z)	(Z)	1
Tennessee	78	243	109	134	192	51	157	198	41	35	2	4
Texas..........	176	939	434	504	832	106	511	617	295	89	169	27
Utah	16	133	68	66	97	36	91	120	7	1	3	6
Vermont.........	22	37	16	21	21	16	25	35	1	(Z)	(Z)	1
Virginia.........	86	354	157	198	298	57	199	274	74	53	6	6
Washington.......	62	276	123	153	239	38	159	230	40	9	8	6
West Virginia.....	28	90	40	50	79	11	61	84	5	3	-	2
Wisconsin.......	64	308	138	170	257	51	186	275	26	12	6	7
Wyoming	9	32	14	18	31	1	17	29	2	(Z)	1	1
U.S. military [4] ..	10	53	30	22	53	-	31	40	11	5	4	1

- Represents zero.   Z Fewer than 500.   [1] Branch campuses counted as separate institutions.   [2] Non-Hispanic.   [3] Includes other races not shown separately.   [4] Service schools.

Source: U.S. National Center for Education Statistics, *Digest of Education Statistics*, annual.

No. 276. Higher Education Price Indexes: 1965 to 1992

[1983 = 100. For years ending June 30. Reflects prices paid by colleges and universities]

YEAR	Index, total	PERSONNEL COMPENSATION				CONTRACTED SERVICES, SUPPLIES, AND EQUIPMENT					
		Total	Professional salaries	Nonprofessional salaries	Fringe benefits	Total	Services	Supplies and materials	Equipment	Library acquisitions	Utilities
1965 ..	29.8	30.5	34.9	31.0	13.0	27.6	35.8	33.8	36.0	19.3	15.7
1970 ..	39.5	42.1	47.7	38.8	24.7	31.9	42.8	37.6	41.9	25.7	16.3
1975 ..	54.3	56.3	60.3	54.6	42.9	48.5	56.8	58.0	58.3	46.7	31.8
1977 ..	61.7	63.5	66.4	63.1	52.8	56.1	63.5	63.8	64.8	58.6	40.5
1978 ..	65.8	67.6	69.9	68.1	58.4	60.4	67.0	66.6	69.3	64.3	45.9
1979 ..	70.6	72.4	74.1	73.4	64.5	65.2	71.0	71.7	74.7	71.4	50.3
1980 ..	77.5	78.4	79.4	80.2	72.6	75.0	76.5	84.6	81.6	79.5	64.1
1981 ..	85.9	85.8	86.3	87.7	81.8	86.2	85.3	95.6	89.6	89.3	79.7
1982 ..	94.0	93.5	93.7	94.6	91.5	95.3	94.8	100.4	96.4	95.5	92.4
1983 ..	100.0	100.0	100.0	100.0	100.0	100.0	100.0	100.0	100.0	100.0	100.0
1984 ..	104.7	105.4	104.7	105.2	108.3	102.8	104.7	103.1	102.2	103.8	100.8
1985 ..	110.5	112.0	111.4	109.1	117.7	106.1	109.2	105.4	104.8	108.5	103.0
1986 ..	115.6	118.8	118.2	113.0	127.7	106.2	114.3	104.2	106.9	117.2	95.5
1987 ..	120.4	125.4	125.0	116.4	137.5	105.2	117.8	103.5	108.8	129.9	84.4
1988 ..	125.8	131.6	130.9	120.4	147.1	108.4	122.1	107.9	110.9	138.7	84.4
1989 ..	133.1	139.5	138.8	125.2	158.8	114.0	129.0	116.9	115.8	149.9	85.2
1990 ..	140.8	148.2	147.6	130.2	171.4	118.8	134.2	118.7	120.8	163.6	88.4
1991 ..	148.3	156.6	155.6	135.5	184.5	123.8	140.2	121.4	123.4	179.0	91.2
1992 ..	153.1	162.4	160.8	140.4	193.9	125.4	144.6	118.1	125.9	189.8	89.4

Source: Research Associates of Washington, Washington, DC, *Inflation Measures for Schools and Colleges*, annual (copyright).

No. 277. Institutions of Higher Education—Finances: 1980 to 1991

[In millions of dollars. For fiscal years ending in year shown. For coverage, see headnote, table 274. See also Appendix III and *Historical Statistics, Colonial Times to 1970* , series H 729-738 and H 747-749]

ITEM	1980	1985	1987	1988	1989	1990	1991		
							Total	Public	Private
Current funds revenues.........	58,520	92,473	108,810	117,340	128,502	139,635	149,766	94,905	54,861
Tuition and fees..............	11,930	21,283	25,706	27,837	30,807	33,926	37,434	15,258	22,176
Federal government...........	8,902	11,509	13,904	14,772	15,894	17,255	18,236	9,763	8,473
State government	18,378	27,583	31,309	33,517	36,031	38,349	39,481	38,240	1,241
Local government	1,588	2,387	2,799	3,006	3,364	3,640	3,931	3,532	400
Private gifts, grants, and contracts [1]	2,808	4,896	5,953	6,359	7,061	7,781	8,361	3,651	4,710
Endowment earnings	1,177	2,096	2,378	2,586	2,914	3,144	3,269	431	2,837
Educational activities [2]	1,239	2,127	2,642	2,918	3,316	3,632	4,055	2,700	1,355
Auxiliary enterprises..........	6,481	10,100	11,364	11,948	12,856	13,907	14,903	9,059	5,844
Hospitals	(3)	7,475	9,278	10,627	11,991	13,217	15,150	9,787	5,362
Other funds revenues [4]........	6,015	3,015	3,477	3,770	4,269	4,753	4,946	2,483	2,463
Current funds expenditures [5]	56,914	89,951	105,764	113,786	123,867	134,656	146,088	92,961	53,127
Educational and general	44,543	70,061	82,956	89,157	96,803	105,585	114,140	74,395	39,744
Instruction	18,497	28,777	33,711	35,834	38,813	42,146	45,496	31,371	14,125
Institutional support..........	5,054	8,587	10,085	10,774	11,529	12,674	13,726	8,031	5,696
Research	5,099	7,552	9,352	10,351	11,432	12,506	13,444	9,364	4,080
Plant operation [6]..........	4,700	7,345	7,819	8,231	8,740	9,458	10,063	6,656	3,407
Academic support..........	3,876	6,074	7,575	8,142	8,904	9,438	10,051	6,934	3,117
Libraries..............	1,624	2,362	2,441	2,836	3,010	3,254	3,344	2,167	1,177
Student services..........	2,567	4,178	4,976	5,397	5,781	6,388	7,025	4,398	2,627
Scholarships and fellowships ...	2,200	3,670	4,776	5,325	5,919	6,656	7,551	2,689	4,863
Unrestricted funds	905	1,962	2,645	2,941	3,283	3,854	4,445	1,270	3,175
Restricted funds	1,296	1,709	2,131	2,384	2,636	2,802	3,106	1,418	1,688
Public service..............	1,817	2,861	3,448	3,786	4,227	4,690	5,076	3,990	1,086
Mandatory transfers	732	1,016	1,212	1,318	1,458	1,630	1,707	962	744
Auxiliary enterprises [5]	6,486	10,012	11,037	11,400	12,280	13,204	14,272	9,050	5,222
Hospitals [5]	4,757	8,010	9,173	10,406	11,825	12,679	14,326	9,316	5,010
Independent operations [5]	1,128	1,868	2,598	2,823	2,959	3,187	3,350	200	3,150

[1] Private grants represent nongovernmental revenue for sponsored research and other sponsored programs; includes private contracts.   [2] Sales and service of educational departments only.   [3] Included in other.   [4] Includes sales and services of federally funded research and development centers, and others sources.   [5] Includes mandatory transfers which are primarily current expenditures for plant.   [6] Includes maintenance.

Source: U.S. National Center for Education Statistics, *Digest of Education Statistics*, annual.

No. 278. Major Federal Student Financial Assistance Programs: 1970 to 1993

[For award years July 1 of year shown to the following June 30, except as indicated. Funds utilized exclude operating costs, etc., and represent funds given to students]

PROGRAM	Unit	1970	1980	1985	1988	1989	1990	1991, est.	1992, est.	1993, est.
Pell Grants:										
Number of recipients...	1,000...	(X)	2,708	2,813	3,198	3,322	3,405	3,786	4,171	4,300
Funds utilized........	Mil. dol..	(X)	2,387	3,597	4,476	4,778	4,935	5,793	6,303	6,099
Average grant.......	Dollars..	(X)	882	1,279	1,399	1,438	1,449	1,530	1,511	1,418
Supplemental Educational Opportunity Grants: [1]										
Number of recipients...	1,000...	253.4	716.5	686.0	678.8	727.6	761.2	881.3	907.0	908.0
Funds utilized........	Mil. dol..	134	368	410	423	466	503	586	648	663
Average grant.......	Dollars..	527	513	598	621	641	661	665	715	730
Perkins Loans: [2]										
Number of recipients...	1,000...	452.0	813.4	700.9	692.1	695.9	660.2	654.2	699.0	571.0
Loan funds utilized [3]...	Mil. dol..	241	694	703	874	903	870	868	873	720
Average loan........	Dollars..	532	853	1,003	1,262	1,297	1,318	1,326	1,250	1,261
Loans in default [4].....	Mil. dol..	(NA)	612.0	690.0	749.8	741.1	727.5	(NA)	(NA)	(NA)
Default rate........	Percent .	(NA)	11.6	8.3	7.3	6.8	6.2	(NA)	(NA)	(NA)
College Work-Study:										
Number of recipients...	1,000...	425.0	819.1	728.4	672.7	676.7	687.4	697.3	812.0	813.0
Funds utilized [3]......	Mil. dol..	200	660	656	625	664	728	760	808	813
Average annual earnings	Dollars..	470	806	901	930	980	1,059	1,090	995	1,000
Stafford Loans: [5]										
Number of loans.. [6]...	1,000...	1,017	2,905	3,730	4,584	4,558	4,587	4,403	4,677	5,551
Loan funds utilized [6]...	Mil. dol..	1,015	6,200	8,839	11,965	12,166	12,669	12,336	13,427	16,425
Average loan.......	Dollars..	998	2,135	2,369	2,610	2,669	2,762	2,802	2,871	2,959
Loans in default [7]....	Mil. dol..	(NA)	1,440	4,256	8,417	10,454	13,134	16,373	19,452	(NA)
Default rate [8].......	Percent .	(NA)	10.1	8.9	9.2	9.6	10.4	11.6	12.9	(NA)

NA Not available. X Not applicable. [1] For 1970, data represents Educational Opportunity Grants Program. [2] Formerly National Direct Student Loans. [3] Includes institutional matching funds. [4] Loans in default represents all loans in institutions' portfolio. [5] Formerly Guaranteed Student Loans. Beginning with 1985, data include activity under the PLUS (Parent Loans for Undergraduate Students), FISL (Federally Insured Student Loans), and SLS (Supplemental Loans Students) programs. [6] Represents dollar amount of commitments. [7] As of September 30 of year shown. [8] Cumulative dollar amount of default claims to lenders, minus cumulative collections as a percent of all loans that have ever gone into repayment.

Source: U.S. Dept. of Education, Office of Postsecondary Education, unpublished data.

No. 279. Finances of Public Colleges, 1989 to 1991, and by State, 1992

[For academic years ending in year shown. Data provided by the State higher education finance officers]

STATE	FTE [1] enrollment (1,000)	Appropriations for current operations [2] (mil. dol.)	Net tuition revenues [3]	STATE	FTE [1] enrollment (1,000)	Appropriations for current operations [2] (mil. dol.)	Net tuition revenues [3]
Total, 1989	7,593.9	31,206.6	10,158.4	Minnesota	176.9	795.1	315.6
Total, 1990	7,898.2	33,791.7	11,327.7	Mississippi	96.5	279.5	169.5
Total, 1991	8,082.0	35,142.0	12,462.6	Missouri	153.6	529.1	313.6
Total, 1992	**8,293.5**	**35,304.0**	**13,724.8**	Montana	28.7	116.1	35.1
				Nebraska	65.2	266.7	87.7
Alabama	176.1	536.6	313.9	Nevada	33.7	168.8	44.2
Alaska	15.7	157.1	27.2	New Hampshire	27.6	71.4	111.6
Arizona	160.8	632.5	237.8	New Jersey	176.6	992.4	365.1
Arkansas	71.2	280.7	108.8	New Mexico	66.5	335.2	71.2
California	1,285.4	5,937.2	884.9	New York	441.4	2,277.8	748.6
Colorado	134.4	396.4	327.1	North Carolina	232.9	1,100.1	266.0
Connecticut	62.9	386.1	162.2	North Dakota	29.1	121.5	59.4
Delaware	24.0	110.2	119.7	Ohio	354.6	1,216.0	924.0
District of Columbia....	8.2	73.5	7.8	Oklahoma	108.1	492.6	133.1
Florida	348.6	1,592.4	429.4	Oregon	102.3	435.1	179.7
Georgia	191.9	772.1	275.4	Pennsylvania	291.3	1,285.4	1,025.0
Hawaii	30.8	267.5	28.1	Rhode Island	28.8	102.6	91.2
Idaho	36.7	186.1	23.9	South Carolina	112.0	438.6	239.8
Illinois...........	387.0	1,577.9	392.6	South Dakota.......	21.0	71.6	42.3
Indiana	177.9	744.6	395.3	Tennessee	150.0	538.6	230.0
Iowa	103.0	460.8	222.0	Texas	618.9	2,477.8	666.8
Kansas	107.1	414.0	161.0	Utah............	71.5	292.2	95.2
Kentucky..........	129.1	437.7	185.3	Vermont	16.1	36.9	110.4
Louisiana	132.9	428.7	241.9	Virginia	220.9	728.8	481.2
Maine	36.2	155.4	75.6	Washington	156.8	782.9	210.9
Maryland..........	160.9	617.2	338.9	West Virginia	63.3	166.3	104.8
Massachusetts.......	119.6	522.0	225.0	Wisconsin	187.5	897.7	397.5
Michigan	339.0	1,463.1	998.0	Wyoming	22.6	137.4	23.5

[1] Full-time equivalent (FTE). Credit and noncredit program enrollment including summer session. Excludes medical enrollments. [2] State and local appropriations. Includes aid to students attending in-State public institutions. Excludes sums for research, agriculture stations and cooperative extension, and hospitals and medical schools. [3] Excludes appropriated aid to students attending in-State public institutions.

Source: Research Associates of Washington, Washington, DC, *State Profiles: Financing Public Higher Education*, annual (copyright).

Education

No. 280. Institutions of Higher Education—Charges: 1980 to 1993

[In dollars. Estimated. **For the entire academic year ending in year shown.** Figures are average charges per full-time equivalent student. Room and board are based on full-time students]

ACADEMIC CONTROL AND YEAR	TUITION AND REQUIRED FEES [1]				BOARD RATES [2]				DORMITORY CHARGES			
	All institutions	2-yr. colleges	4-yr. colleges	Other 4-yr. schools	All institutions	2-yr. colleges	4-yr. colleges	Other 4-yr. schools	All institutions	2-yr. colleges	4-yr. colleges	Other 4-yr. schools
Public:												
1980	583	355	840	662	867	893	898	.833	715	574	750	703
1985	971	584	1,386	1,117	1,241	1,302	1,276	1,201	1,196	921	1,237	1,200
1990	1,356	756	2,035	1,608	1,635	1,581	1,728	1,561	1,513	962	1,561	1,554
1991	1,454	824	2,159	1,707	1,691	1,594	1,767	1,641	1,612	1,050	1,658	1,655
1992	1,624	937	2,410	1,933	1,780	1,612	1,852	1,745	1,731	1,074	1,789	1,782
1993	1,787	1,018	2,610	2,190	1,843	1,660	1,981	1,763	1,764	1,115	1,858	1,792
Private:												
1980	3,130	2,062	3,811	3,020	955	923	1,078	912	827	766	1,001	768
1985	5,315	3,485	6,843	5,135	1,462	1,294	1,647	1,405	1,426	1,424	1,753	1,309
1990	8,174	5,196	10,348	7,778	1,948	1,811	2,339	1,823	1,923	1,663	2,411	1,774
1991	8,772	5,570	11,379	8,389	2,074	1,989	2,470	1,943	2,063	1,744	2,654	1,889
1992	9,434	5,752	12,192	9,053	2,252	2,090	2,727	2,098	2,221	1,789	2,860	2,038
1993	10,031	6,101	13,043	9,636	2,353	1,925	2,827	2,204	2,357	1,946	3,022	2,157

[1] For in-State students.   [2] Beginning 1990, rates reflect 20 meals per week, rather than meals served 7 days a week.

Source: U.S. National Center for Education Statistics, *Digest of Education Statistics,* annual.

No. 281. Average College Costs for Undergraduates: 1993 and 1994

[In dollars. Based on survey responses of colleges, representing 80% percent of all colleges. See source for details. Data are weighted by enrollment to reflect the charges incurred by the average undergraduate enrolled at each type of institution]

TYPE OF INSTITUTION AND ITEM	1992-93				1993-94			
	Public colleges [1]		Private colleges		Public colleges [1]		Private colleges	
	Resident	Commuter	Resident	Commuter	Resident	Commuter	Resident	Commuter
4-year colleges, total	8,071	6,473	17,027	14,621	8,562	6,809	17,846	15,200
Tuition and fees	2,315	2,315	10,498	10,498	2,527	2,527	11,025	11,025
Books and supplies	528	528	531	531	552	552	556	556
Room and board	3,526	1,549	4,575	1,762	3,680	1,601	4,793	1,722
Transportation	497	843	487	794	557	870	498	824
Other	1,205	1,238	936	1,036	1,246	1,259	974	1,073
2-year colleges, total	(B)	5,282	11,266	9,444	(B)	5,372	12,142	10,190
Tuition and fees	1,292	1,292	5,621	5,621	1,229	1,229	6,175	6,175
Books and supplies	502	502	512	512	533	533	566	566
Room and board	(B)	1,592	3,750	1,558	(B)	1,643	3,980	1,589
Transportation	(B)	926	517	812	(B)	923	487	890
Other	(B)	970	866	941	(B)	1,044	934	970

B Base too small to meet statistical standards for reliability of a derived figure.   [1] For in-State students.

Source: The College Board, New York, NY, Annual Survey of Colleges 1992 and 1993.

No. 282. Range of Undergraduate Tuitions at 4-Year Colleges: 1993 and 1994

[See headnote, table 281. Data presented here are unweighted by enrollment and reflect the average amounts charged by each type of institution]

TYPE OF CONTROL AND RANGE OF TUITION	1992-93		1993-94		TYPE OF CONTROL AND RANGE OF TUITION	1992-93		1993-94	
	Number of colleges	Percent of enrollment	Number of colleges	Percent of enrollment		Number of colleges	Percent of enrollment	Number of colleges	Percent of enrollment
Total, public [1] . .	554	100.0	526	100.0	$16,000 to $16,999.	(NA)	(NA)	28	3.5
$6,000 to $6,499 . .	(NA)	(NA)	1	0.2	$15,000 to $15,999.	[3]100	[3]15.6	32	3.5
$5,500 to $5,599 . .	(NA)	(NA)	1	0.1	$14,000 to $14,999.	29	3.1	23	2.7
$5,000 to $5,400 . .	(NA)	(NA)	6	1.3	$13,000 to $13,999.	34	3.3	59	5.5
$4,500 to $4,999 . .	(NA)	(NA)	11	1.9	$12,000 to $12,999.	61	6.0	70	7.6
$4,000 to $4,499 . .	(NA)	(NA)	20	2.9	$11,000 to $11,999.	82	8.0	90	7.9
$3,500 to $3,999 . .	(NA)	(NA)	38	7.6	$10,000 to $10,999.	104	10.6	106	12.2
$3,000 to $3,499 . .	[2]96	[2]17.8	49	11.3	$9,000 to $9,999 . .	110	10.5	118	8.8
$2,500 to $2,999 . .	107	20.9	93	18.1	$8,000 to $8,999 . .	138	10.0	112	8.0
$2,000 to $2,499 . .	84	15.6	88	16.0	$7,000 to $7,999 . .	118	7.7	96	7.5
$1,500 to $1,999 . .	150	25.5	155	30.1	$6,000 to $6,999 . .	97	6.7	81	5.6
$1,000 to $1,499 . .	100	18.8	52	9.2	$5,000 to $5,999 . .	84	4.7	65	3.6
Less than $1,000 . .	12	1.4	12	1.3	$4,000 to $4,999 . .	84	5.2	76	2.8
Total, private . . .	1,169	100.0	1,112	100.0	$3,000 to $3,999 . .	66	2.0	48	2.7
$19,000 or more. . .	(NA)	(NA)	7	1.0	$2,000 to $2,999 . .	45	5.5	28	5.2
$18,000 to $18,999.	(NA)	(NA)	31	4.3	$1,000 to $1,999 . .	7	0.1	5	0.1
$17,000 to $17,999.	(NA)	(NA)	29	6.4	Less than $1,000 . .	10	1.0	11	1.1

NA Not available.   [1] For in-State students.   [2] $3,000 or more.   [3] $15,000 or more.

Source: The College Board, New York, NY, Annual Survey of Colleges 1992 and 1993.

No. 283. Voluntary Financial Support of Higher Education: 1970 to 1992

[For school years ending in years shown; enrollment as of fall of preceding year. Voluntary support, as defined in Gift Reporting Standards, excludes income from endowment and other invested funds as well as all support received from Federal, State, and local governments and their agencies and contract research]

ITEM	Unit	1970	1980	1985	1988	1989	1990	1991	1992
Estimated support, total [1]	**Mil. dol.**	**1,780**	**3,800**	**6,320**	**8,200**	**8,925**	**9,800**	**10,200**	**10,700**
Individuals	Mil. dol .	822	1,757	2,876	3,969	4,369	4,770	4,990	5,340
Alumni	Mil. dol .	381	910	1,460	2,042	2,292	2,540	2,680	2,840
Business corporations	Mil. dol .	269	696	1,574	1,853	1,947	2,170	2,230	2,260
Foundations	Mil. dol .	434	903	1,175	1,607	1,742	1,920	2,030	2,090
Religious organizations	Mil. dol .	102	155	208	197	237	240	240	240
Current operations	Mil. dol .	960	2,250	3,800	4,666	5,045	5,440	5,830	6,100
Capital purposes	Mil. dol .	820	1,550	2,520	3,534	3,880	4,360	4,370	4,600
Enrollment, higher education	1,000 ..	8,094	11,570	12,242	12,767	13,055	13,539	13,820	14,359
Support per student	Dollars .	220	328	516	642	684	724	738	745
In 1991-92 dollars	Dollars .	804	585	675	766	779	788	762	745
Expenditures, higher education .	Bil. dol .	24.7	62.5	98.3	125.4	137.5	151.8	165.8	175.9
Expenditures per student	Dollars .	3,052	5,402	8,030	9,822	10,532	11,212	11,997	12,250
In 1991-92 dollars	Dollars .	11,160	9,616	10,498	11,720	12,008	12,200	12,384	12,250
Institutions reporting support	Number.	1,045	1,019	1,114	1,142	1,132	1,056	1,046	1,060
Total support reported	**Mil. dol.**	**1,472**	**3,055**	**5,295**	**7,041**	**7,546**	**8,214**	**8,559**	**9,033**
Private 4-year institutions	Mil. dol .	1,154	2,178	3,522	4,466	4,847	5,072	5,262	5,360
Public 4-year institutions	Mil. dol .	292	856	1,728	2,506	2,625	3,056	3,222	3,583
2-year colleges	Mil. dol .	26	20	45	69	74	85	75	89

[1] Includes other contributions not shown separately.
Source: Council for Aid to Education, New York, NY, *Voluntary Support of Education,* annual.

No. 284. Average Salaries for College Faculty Members: 1991 to 1993

[In thousands of dollars. For academic year ending in year shown. Figures are for 9 months teaching for full-time faculty members in 4-year institutions. Fringe benefits in 1993 averaged $11,500 in public institutions and $13,100 in private institutions]

TYPE OF CONTROL AND ACADEMIC RANK	1991	1992	1993	TYPE OF CONTROL AND ACADEMIC RANK	1991	1992	1993
Public: All ranks	44.0	45.3	46.0	Private: [1] All ranks	47.0	50.0	51.6
Professor	55.8	57.4	58.4	Professor	61.6	66.1	68.7
Associate professor	42.2	43.4	44.1	Associate professor	43.2	45.6	46.9
Assistant professor	35.2	36.3	37.0	Assistant professor	35.5	37.8	38.6
Instructor	26.3	27.2	27.8	Instructor	26.2	28.5	28.3

[1] Excludes church-related colleges and universities.
Source: Maryse Eymonerie Associates/American Association of University Professors, Washington, DC, *AAUP Annual Report on the Economic Status of the Profession.*

No. 285. Tenure Status of Full-Time College Faculty Members: 1992

[In percent. For academic year ending in year shown. Data are for those institutions of higher education reporting tenure status. Excludes schools with no tenure]

TYPE OF INSTITUTION AND CONTROL	Total faculty	ACADEMIC RANK						SEX	
		Professor	Associate professor	Assistant professor	Instructor	Lecturer	No academic rank	Male	Female
All institutions	63.7	95.7	81.0	17.7	20.2	6.7	72.5	70.1	49.1
4-year	61.7	95.8	80.6	14.9	4.2	5.7	18.1	68.8	43.9
University	65.4	97.3	85.8	8.5	3.4	2.2	1.6	72.0	43.8
Other 4-year ...	59.3	94.7	77.2	18.6	4.4	8.8	27.1	68.4	43.9
2-year	72.9	93.9	85.0	50.2	47.9	27.6	77.4	78.2	65.6
Public institutions ...	66.4	96.5	84.1	20.9	25.3	8.1	74.6	72.6	52.4
4-year	64.2	96.8	84.0	16.9	5.3	6.9	9.0	71.2	45.9
University	66.4	97.5	88.8	8.6	3.9	2.1	0.4	73.1	44.5
Other 4-year ...	62.5	96.2	80.2	22.5	5.9	10.3	17.2	69.5	46.7
2-year	73.5	94.0	85.2	51.5	49.1	27.9	77.8	78.6	66.5
Private institutions ..	56.6	93.8	74.0	11.5	1.9	1.9	38.7	63.7	40.1
4-year	56.8	93.8	73.9	11.4	1.9	1.9	28.6	63.8	40.1
University	62.7	96.6	77.5	8.1	1.5	2.4	5.1	69.1	42.1
Other 4-year ...	53.8	92.0	72.2	12.7	2.0	1.1	34.3	60.9	39.4
2-year	47.4	87.2	79.5	17.7	2.6	(NA)	58.2	56.5	38.4

NA Not available.
Source: U.S. National Center for Education Statistics, *Digest of Education Statistics,* 1993.

No. 286. Higher Education Registrations in Foreign Languages: 1960 to 1990

[As of fall]

ITEM	1960	1968	1970	1974	1977	1980	1983	1986	1990
Registrations [1] (1,000)	[2]647.1	1,127.4	1,111.5	946.6	933.5	924.8	966.0	1,003.2	1,184.1
Index (1960=100)	100.0	174.2	171.8	146.3	144.3	142.9	149.3	155.0	183.0
By selected language (1,000):									
Spanish	178.7	364.9	389.2	362.2	376.7	379.4	386.2	411.3	533.9
French	228.8	388.1	359.3	253.1	246.1	248.4	270.1	275.3	272.5
German	146.1	216.3	202.6	152.1	135.4	126.9	128.2	121.0	133.3
Italian	11.1	30.4	34.2	33.0	33.3	34.8	38.7	40.9	49.7
Japanese	1.7	4.3	6.6	9.6	10.7	11.5	16.1	23.5	45.7
Russian	30.6	40.7	36.1	32.5	27.8	24.0	30.4	34.0	44.6
Latin	[2]25.7	35.0	27.6	25.2	24.4	25.0	24.2	25.0	28.2
Chinese	1.8	5.1	6.2	10.6	9.8	11.4	13.2	16.9	19.5
Ancient Greek	[2]12.7	19.3	16.7	24.4	25.8	22.1	19.4	17.6	16.4
Hebrew	3.8	10.2	16.6	22.4	19.4	19.4	18.2	15.6	13.0
Portuguese	1.0	4.0	5.1	5.1	5.0	4.9	4.4	5.1	6.2
Arabic	0.5	1.1	1.3	2.0	3.1	3.5	3.4	3.4	3.5
12 languages as percent of total	99.3	99.3	99.1	98.5	98.3	98.5	98.6	98.6	98.5

[1] Includes other foreign languages, not shown separately.   [2] Estimated.

Source: Association of Departments of Foreign Languages, New York, NY, *ADFL Bulletin*, vol. 23, No. 3, and earlier issues (copyright).

No. 287. College Freshmen—Summary Characteristics: 1970 to 1993

[In percent. As of fall for first-time full-time freshmen. Based on sample survey and subject to sampling error; see source]

CHARACTERISTIC	1970	1980	1985	1988	1989	1990	1991	1992	1993
Sex: Male	55	49	48	46	46	46	47	46	45
Female	45	51	52	54	54	54	53	54	55
Applied to three or more colleges	[1]15	26	29	37	37	36	34	33	37
Average grade in high school:									
A- to A+	16	21	21	24	23	23	24	26	27
B- to B+	58	60	59	58	59	58	57	57	57
C to C+	27	19	20	19	17	19	19	17	16
D	1	1	1	1	-	-	-	-	-
Political orientation:									
Liberal	34	20	21	22	22	23	24	24	25
Middle of the road	45	60	57	54	54	55	54	53	50
Conservative	17	17	19	20	21	20	19	19	21
Probable field of study:									
Arts and humanities	16	9	8	10	9	9	8	8	8
Biological sciences	4	4	4	4	4	4	4	5	6
Business	16	24	27	26	25	21	18	16	16
Education	11	7	7	9	9	10	9	10	10
Engineering	9	12	11	10	10	8	10	9	9
Physical science	2	3	2	2	2	2	2	2	3
Social science	14	7	8	9	10	10	8	9	9
Professional	(NA)	15	13	12	13	15	18	20	20
Technical	4	6	5	2	3	4	4	3	3
Data processing/computer programming	(NA)	2	2	1	1	1	1	1	1
Other [2]	(NA)	(NA)	16	16	15	16	17	17	17
Communications	(NA)	2	2	3	3	2	2	2	2
Computer science	(NA)	1	2	2	2	2	2	1	2
Recipient of financial aid:									
Pell grant	(NA)	33	19	20	22	23	23	23	24
Supplemental educational opportunity grant	(NA)	8	5	6	6	7	7	6	6
State scholarship or grant	(NA)	16	14	14	15	16	13	14	14
College grant	(NA)	13	19	20	20	22	22	24	24
Federal guaranteed student loan	(NA)	21	23	22	23	23	22	23	28
Perkins loan [3]	(NA)	9	6	3	2	8	7	8	8
College loan	(NA)	4	4	6	8	6	5	6	6
College work-study grant	(NA)	15	10	10	10	10	11	12	12
Attitudes—agree or strongly agree:									
Activities of married women are best confined to home and family	48	27	22	26	26	25	26	26	24
Capital punishment should be abolished	56	34	27	23	21	22	21	21	22
Legalize marijuana	38	39	22	19	17	19	21	23	28
There is too much concern for the rights of criminals	52	66	(NA)	69	69	(NA)	65	67	68
Abortion should be legalized	(NA)	54	55	57	65	65	63	64	62
Aspires to an advanced degree	49	49	51	59	60	61	60	55	65

- Represents or rounds to zero.   NA Not available.   [1] 1969 data.   [2] Includes other fields, not shown separately. [3] National Direct Student Loan prior to 1990.

Source: The Higher Education Research Institute, University of California, Los Angeles, CA, *The American Freshman: National Norms*, annual.

No. 288. Foreign (Nonimmigrant) Student Enrollment in College: 1976 to 1993

[For fall of the previous year]

REGION OF ORIGIN	ENROLLMENT (1,000)									PERCENT ENROLLED IN—					
										Engineering		Science[1]		Business	
	1976	1980	1985	1988	1989	1990	1991	1992	1993	1980	1992	1980	1992	1980	1992
All regions	179	286	342	356	366	387	408	420	439	25	18	8	10	16	20
Africa	25	36	40	28	26	25	24	22	21	20	15	9	9	19	19
Nigeria	11	16	18	8	6	4	4	3	2	19	12	9	7	22	17
Asia [2]	97	165	200	224	232	245	263	277	291	32	22	8	10	16	20
China: Taiwan	11	18	23	27	29	31	34	36	37	17	22	15	9	17	21
Hong Kong	12	10	10	11	11	11	13	13	14	22	18	9	6	26	33
India	10	9	15	21	23	26	29	23	36	31	39	16	10	21	14
Indonesia	1	2	7	9	9	9	10	10	11	27	20	7	4	21	41
Iran	20	51	17	10	9	7	6	5	4	45	29	7	15	11	7
Japan	7	12	13	18	24	30	37	42	43	7	4	5	3	19	24
Malaysia	2	4	22	19	16	14	14	13	13	13	29	14	4	22	30
Saudi Arabia	3	10	8	5	5	4	4	4	4	30	24	4	5	14	15
South Korea	3	5	16	21	21	22	23	26	29	17	16	11	11	15	15
Thailand	7	7	7	6	7	7	7	8	9	17	12	6	3	26	40
Europe	14	23	33	39	43	46	50	54	58	15	10	9	9	14	22
Latin America [3]	30	42	49	45	45	48	48	43	43	20	15	8	7	14	21
Mexico	5	6	6	6	6	7	7	7	8	16	15	7	8	11	18
Venezuela	5	10	10	4	3	3	3	3	3	30	19	8	7	11	20
North America	10	16	16	16	17	19	19	20	22	8	7	6	7	13	14
Canada	10	15	15	16	16	18	18	19	21	8	7	6	7	12	14
Oceania	3	4	4	4	4	4	4	4	4	5	5	7	5	16	19

[1] Physical and life sciences. [2] Includes countries not shown separately. [3] Includes Central America, Caribbean, and South America.

Source: Institute of International Education, New York, NY, *Open Doors*, annual (copyright).

No. 289. Salary Offers to Candidates for Degrees: 1990 to 1993

[In dollars. Data are average beginning salaries based on offers made by business, industrial, government, and nonprofit and educational employers to graduating students. Data from representative colleges throughout the United States]

FIELD OF STUDY	BACHELOR'S			MASTER'S [1]			DOCTOR'S		
	1990	1992	1993	1990	1992	1993	1990	1992	1993
Accounting	26,391	27,179	27,493	29,647	31,259	30,284	(NA)	(NA)	(NA)
Business, general [2]	23,529	24,305	24,555	36,175	35,734	36,513	(NA)	(NA)	(NA)
Marketing	23,543	23,914	24,361	35,440	39,508	40,104	(NA)	(NA)	(NA)
Engineering:									
Civil	28,136	29,376	29,211	32,336	34,303	34,606	44,481	46,501	48,268
Chemical	35,122	39,203	39,482	37,862	40,611	40,874	50,524	54,451	55,078
Computer	31,490	32,848	33,963	35,748	40,207	39,161	50,526	55,325	53,912
Electrical	31,778	33,754	34,313	37,526	41,024	41,291	53,147	56,826	57,076
Mechanical	32,064	34,462	34,460	36,506	39,298	40,457	49,887	51,880	54,217
Nuclear [3]	31,750	34,447	34,755	36,728	38,607	(NA)	(NA)	(NA)	(NA)
Petroleum	35,202	40,679	38,387	38,412	43,600	(NA)	(NA)	(NA)	(NA)
Engineering technology	29,318	31,051	29,236	(NA)	(NA)	(NA)	(NA)	(NA)	(NA)
Chemistry	27,494	27,557	28,002	32,320	35,104	35,690	45,356	50,719	50,933
Mathematics	27,032	28,434	26,524	30,069	33,636	33,183	42,775	40,954	39,500
Physics	28,002	29,019	26,835	31,480	31,626	31,800	41,486	40,940	50,600
Humanities	23,213	22,941	24,373	(NA)	(NA)	(NA)	(NA)	(NA)	(NA)
Social sciences [4]	21,627	21,623	22,684	(NA)	(NA)	(NA)	(NA)	(NA)	(NA)
Computer science	29,804	30,523	31,329	36,849	39,120	40,115	54,788	61,555	56,513

NA Not available. [1] Candidates with 1 year or less of full-time nonmilitary employment. [2] For master's degree, offers are after nontechnical undergraduate degree. [3] Includes engineering physics. [4] Excludes economics.

Source: College Placement Council, Inc., Bethlehem, PA, *Salary Survey, A Study of Beginning Offers*, annual (copyright).

No. 290. Time Spent Earning Bachelor's Degree, by Selected Characteristic: 1990

[As of **spring**. Based on Survey of Income and Program Participation; for details, see source]

CHARACTERISTIC	Total with bachelor's degrees (1,000)	YEARS TO BA DEGREE FROM END OF HIGH SCHOOL						Mean duration [1]
		Number (1,000)			Percent			
		4 years or less	5 years or less	6 years or less	4 years or less	5 years or less	6 years or less	
All persons	33,553	14,509	21,905	24,822	43.2	65.3	74.0	6.21
Male	18,145	6,893	10,914	12,710	38.0	60.1	70.0	6.23
Female	15,409	7,616	10,991	12,111	49.4	71.3	78.6	6.19
White	30,048	13,267	19,845	22,347	44.2	66.0	74.4	6.18
Male	16,374	6,297	9,920	11,509	38.5	60.6	70.3	6.20
Female	13,675	6,970	9,926	10,838	51.0	72.6	79.3	6.16
Black	1,908	623	1,052	1,266	32.7	55.1	66.4	7.01
Male	846	242	428	536	28.6	50.6	63.4	7.12
Female	1,062	382	624	731	36.0	58.8	68.8	6.92
Hispanic origin [2]	1,065	395	610	733	37.1	57.3	68.8	6.58
Male	579	210	343	410	36.3	59.2	70.8	6.05
Female	487	184	267	323	37.8	54.8	66.3	7.21
Field of Bachelor's degree: [3]								
Agriculture/Forestry	273	79	162	189	28.9	59.3	69.2	6.30
Biology	670	281	449	514	41.9	67.0	76.7	5.75
Business/Management	4,871	1,872	2,959	3,499	38.4	60.7	71.8	6.47
Economics	587	246	371	454	41.9	63.2	77.3	5.47
Education	3,456	1,628	2,335	2,609	47.1	67.6	75.5	6.55
Engineering	2,449	738	1,333	1,553	30.1	54.4	63.4	6.80
English/Journalism	1,121	538	831	923	48.0	74.1	82.3	5.79
Home Economics	322	217	266	282	67.4	82.6	87.6	4.73
Law	73	11	23	28	(B)	(B)	(B)	(B)
Liberal Arts/Humanities	2,321	964	1,416	1,675	41.5	61.0	72.2	6.38
Mathematics/Statistics	485	192	294	364	39.6	60.6	75.1	5.81
Medicine/Dentistry	140	52	103	126	(B)	(B)	(B)	(B)
Nursing/Pharmacy/Technical Health	1,379	403	759	888	29.2	55.0	64.4	7.65
Physical/Earth Sciences	529	203	352	387	38.4	66.5	73.2	5.84
Police Science/Law Enforcement	196	69	76	98	(B)	(B)	(B)	(B)
Psychology	700	247	409	505	35.3	58.4	72.1	6.39
Religion/Theology	153	58	82	90	(B)	(B)	(B)	(B)
Social Sciences	1,441	666	942	1,037	46.2	65.4	72.0	6.54
Vo-tech Studies	141	46	86	102	(B)	(B)	(B)	(B)
Other	1,539	595	984	1,120	38.7	63.9	72.8	6.14
Advanced degree	10,708	5,405	7,673	8,377	50.5	71.7	78.2	5.71

B Base is less than 200,000 persons.　[1] For definition of mean, see Guide to Tabular Presentation.　[2] Persons of Hispanic origin may be of any race.　[3] For persons whose highest degree is the BA.

Source: U.S. Bureau of the Census, *Current Population Reports*, P70-32.

No. 291. Earned Degrees Conferred, by Level and Sex, With Projections: 1950 to 2004

[In thousands, except percent. Beginning 1960, includes Alaska and Hawaii. See *Historical Statistics, Colonial Times to 1970*, series H-751-763 for similar data. See also Appendix III]

YEAR ENDING	ALL DEGREES		ASSOCIATE'S		BACHELOR'S		MASTER'S		FIRST PROFESSIONAL		DOCTOR'S	
	Total	Percent male	Male	Female	Male	Female	Male	Female	Male	Female	Male	Female
1950 [1]	497	75.7	(NA)	(NA)	329	103	41	17	(NA)	(NA)	6	1
1960 [1]	477	65.8	(NA)	(NA)	254	138	51	24	(NA)	(NA)	9	1
1965	664	61.6	(NA)	(NA)	289	213	78	40	27	1	15	2
1970	1,271	59.2	117	89	451	341	126	83	33	2	26	4
1975	1,666	56.1	191	169	505	418	162	131	49	7	27	7
1980	1,731	51.1	184	217	474	456	151	147	53	17	23	10
1981	1,752	50.3	189	228	470	465	147	149	53	19	23	10
1982	1,788	49.8	197	238	473	480	146	150	52	20	22	10
1983	1,822	49.6	207	249	479	490	145	145	51	22	22	11
1984	1,819	49.6	203	250	482	492	144	141	51	23	22	11
1985	1,828	49.3	203	252	483	497	143	143	50	25	22	11
1986	1,830	49.0	196	250	486	502	144	145	49	25	22	12
1987	1,825	48.4	192	246	481	510	141	148	47	25	22	12
1988	1,835	48.0	190	245	477	518	145	154	45	25	23	12
1989	1,873	47.3	186	250	483	535	149	161	45	26	23	13
1990	1,940	46.6	191	264	492	560	154	171	44	27	24	14
1991	2,025	45.8	199	283	504	590	156	181	44	28	25	15
1995, proj.	2,189	46.4	216	302	548	630	182	195	44	31	25	17
2000, proj.	2,204	46.2	219	309	556	634	176	195	44	30	23	19
2003, proj.	2,286	46.0	230	324	587	667	170	193	44	30	22	20
2004, proj.	2,316	46.0	233	327	598	680	170	193	43	31	21	20

NA Not available.　[1] First-professional degrees are included with bachelor's degrees.

Source: U.S. National Center for Education Statistics, *Digest of Education Statistics*, annual and *Projections of Education Statistics to 2003*, annual.

No. 292. Degrees Earned Below Bachelor's, by Field: 1984 to 1991

[Covers associate degrees and other awards based on postsecondary curriculums of less than 4 years in institutions of higher education]

FIELD OF STUDY	1984	1985	1988	1989	1990	1991	PERCENT FEMALE 1984	1991
Total	610,332	614,749	601,713	601,280	640,089	662,252	54.3	58.4
Agriculture and natural resources	10,641	10,466	8,769	7,541	9,321	8,110	28.9	31.5
Architecture and environmental design	1,927	1,939	2,520	2,452	2,530	3,550	84.3	87.2
Area and ethnic studies	64	69	172	208	242	214	60.9	80.4
Business and management	166,238	170,170	158,844	153,072	153,320	148,013	66.5	73.0
Communications [1]	4,162	4,580	4,414	5,300	4,564	4,835	43.2	42.5
Computer and information sciences	16,111	15,896	11,936	10,321	13,343	12,933	49.1	54.2
Education	8,503	8,551	7,958	8,314	8,831	8,450	72.2	73.1
Engineering [1]	100,080	100,146	104,036	94,655	93,369	[2]83,909	7.9	8.7
Foreign languages	372	427	584	629	707	710	57.5	59.2
Health sciences	107,142	107,248	96,119	96,884	109,307	116,849	87.0	84.9
Home economics	14,344	14,966	15,142	15,286	18,538	20,905	75.0	73.7
Law	2,551	2,948	4,661	6,068	7,939	8,345	83.1	86.5
Letters	822	681	574	626	774	956	64.8	54.9
Liberal/general studies	109,451	107,814	114,882	119,577	130,126	139,293	54.9	59.4
Library and archival sciences	260	253	165	204	215	244	86.2	93.0
Life sciences	1,297	1,205	980	1,050	1,186	1,183	52.4	58.2
Mathematics	821	813	695	664	809	711	36.4	39.0
Military sciences	87	34	141	164	129	85	4.6	9.4
Multi/interdisciplinary studies	8,398	8,697	11,053	11,444	12,684	12,368	54.5	57.6
Parks and recreation	819	893	717	678	593	475	50.9	39.2
Philosophy, religion, and theology	1,740	1,830	1,427	1,502	1,593	1,404	44.3	46.7
Physical sciences	2,990	2,296	1,998	2,079	2,301	2,549	34.7	38.1
Psychology	1,147	1,032	1,105	1,143	1,147	1,036	67.0	74.0
Protective services	15,554	16,057	17,832	17,901	20,187	19,913	23.8	24.7
Public affairs	5,812	6,230	7,007	8,765	10,478	11,178	47.2	32.8
Social sciences [3]	2,755	2,613	2,915	2,962	3,133	2,652	57.1	59.6
Visual and performing arts	26,244	24,358	23,107	21,438	22,809	24,415	32.7	34.8
Undistributed	-	2,537	1,960	10,353	9,914	26,967	(X)	57.1

- Represents zero. X Not applicable. [1] includes technologies. [2] Decrease largely in less than 1-year awards in engineering technologies. [3] Includes history.

Source: U.S. National Center for Education Statistics, *Digest of Education Statistics*, annual.

No. 293. Bachelor's Degrees Earned, by Field: 1971 to 1991

FIELD OF STUDY	1971	1980	1985	1990	1991	PERCENT FEMALE 1971	1991
Total	839,730	929,417	979,477	1,051,344	1,094,538	43.4	53.9
Agriculture and natural resources	12,672	22,802	18,107	12,900	13,124	4.2	32.7
Architecture and environmental design	5,570	9,132	9,325	9,364	9,781	11.9	40.8
Area and ethnic studies	2,582	2,840	2,867	4,411	4,623	52.4	59.8
Business and management	114,865	185,361	233,351	249,365	249,960	9.1	47.2
Communications [1]	10,802	28,616	42,083	51,345	52,799	35.3	60.9
Computer and information sciences	2,388	11,154	38,878	27,257	25,083	13.6	29.3
Education	176,614	118,169	88,161	105,267	111,010	74.5	78.9
Engineering [1]	50,046	68,893	96,105	81,598	78,864	0.8	13.9
Foreign languages	19,945	11,133	9,954	11,415	12,095	74.6	72.3
Health sciences	25,190	63,607	64,513	58,454	59,268	77.1	83.6
Home economics	11,167	18,411	15,555	15,042	15,474	97.3	89.6
Law	545	683	1,157	1,592	1,758	5.0	67.4
Letters	64,933	33,497	34,091	48,493	52,880	65.5	66.8
Liberal/general studies	5,461	20,069	19,191	25,176	26,692	29.0	59.1
Library and archival sciences	1,013	398	202	80	93	92.0	93.5
Life sciences	35,743	46,370	38,445	37,204	39,530	29.1	50.9
Mathematics	24,801	11,378	15,146	14,509	14,661	38.0	47.2
Military sciences	357	251	299	417	418	0.3	11.2
Multi/interdisciplinary studies	8,306	14,404	15,727	19,276	21,653	28.4	56.8
Parks and recreation	1,621	5,753	4,593	4,384	4,062	34.7	56.6
Philosophy, religion, and theology	11,890	13,276	12,439	12,067	12,128	25.5	31.5
Physical sciences	21,412	23,410	23,732	16,066	16,344	13.8	31.6
Psychology	37,880	41,962	39,811	53,794	58,451	44.5	72.6
Protective services	2,045	15,015	12,510	15,354	16,806	9.2	38.1
Public affairs	6,252	18,422	13,838	16,328	16,976	60.2	68.1
Social sciences [2]	155,236	103,519	91,461	117,855	124,893	36.8	45.1
Visual and performing arts	30,394	40,892	37,936	39,618	41,854	59.7	62.1
Unclassified	-	-	-	2,713	13,258	(X)	42.5

- Represents zero. X Not applicable. [1] Includes technologies. [2] Includes history.

Source: U.S. National Center for Education Statistics, *Digest of Education Statistics*, annual.

No. 294. Masters and Doctorate's Degrees Earned, by Field: 1971 to 1991

LEVEL AND FIELD OF STUDY	1971	1980	1985	1990	1991	PERCENT FEMALE 1971	PERCENT FEMALE 1991
MASTER'S DEGREES							
Total	**230,509**	**298,081**	**286,251**	**324,301**	**337,168**	**40.1**	**53.6**
Agriculture and natural resources	2,457	3,976	3,928	3,382	3,295	5.9	34.4
Architecture and environmental design	1,705	3,139	3,275	3,499	3,490	13.8	35.7
Area and ethnic studies	1,032	852	879	1,196	1,250	38.3	49.0
Business and management	26,481	55,006	67,527	77,146	78,681	3.9	34.9
Communications [1]	1,856	3,082	3,669	4,362	4,336	34.6	60.5
Computer and information sciences	1,588	3,647	7,101	9,677	9,324	10.3	29.6
Education	88,952	103,951	76,137	86,399	88,904	56.2	76.6
Engineering [1]	16,443	16,243	21,557	24,773	24,959	1.1	14.1
Foreign languages	4,755	2,236	1,724	2,015	2,073	65.5	69.4
Health sciences	5,445	15,068	17,383	20,364	21,228	55.9	79.0
Home economics	1,452	2,690	2,383	2,102	2,021	93.9	85.2
Law	955	1,817	1,796	1,888	2,057	4.8	29.8
Letters	11,148	6,807	5,934	7,332	7,810	60.2	66.8
Liberal/general studies	549	1,373	1,180	1,596	1,736	44.3	65.8
Library and archival sciences	7,001	5,374	3,893	4,399	4,805	81.3	79.2
Life sciences	5,728	6,510	5,059	4,869	4,765	33.6	51.7
Mathematics	5,191	2,860	2,882	3,676	3,615	29.2	40.9
Military sciences	2	46	119	-	-	(X)	(X)
Multi/interdisciplinary studies	1,157	3,579	3,184	3,505	2,548	30.9	52.4
Parks and recreation	218	647	544	418	393	29.8	57.0
Philosophy, religion, and theology	4,036	5,126	5,519	5,959	5,949	27.1	36.9
Physical sciences	6,367	5,219	5,796	5,449	5,309	13.3	27.7
Psychology	4,431	7,806	8,408	9,192	9,731	37.2	69.4
Protective services	194	1,805	1,235	1,151	1,108	10.3	33.3
Public affairs	8,215	18,413	16,045	18,137	18,534	49.2	66.8
Social sciences [2]	16,476	12,101	10,380	11,497	12,069	28.5	42.6
Visual and performing arts	6,675	8,708	8,714	8,482	8,655	47.4	55.7
Unclassified	-	-	-	1,836	8,523	(X)	45.0
DOCTORATE'S DEGREES							
Total	**32,107**	**32,615**	**32,943**	**38,371**	**39,294**	**14.3**	**37.0**
Agriculture and natural resources	1,086	991	1,213	1,295	1,185	2.9	19.6
Architecture and environmental design	36	79	89	103	135	8.3	25.2
Area and ethnic studies	144	151	137	130	167	16.7	43.7
Business and management	807	792	866	1,142	1,243	2.9	25.7
Communications [1]	145	193	234	273	274	13.1	44.9
Computer and information sciences	128	240	248	627	676	2.3	13.6
Education	6,403	7,941	7,151	6,991	6,697	21.2	58.1
Engineering [1]	3,638	2,507	3,230	4,981	5,272	0.6	9.2
Foreign languages	781	549	437	517	526	38.0	56.3
Health sciences	459	771	1,199	1,536	1,614	16.3	57.0
Home economics	123	192	276	302	255	61.0	75.7
Law	20	40	105	111	90	(X)	27.8
Letters	1,857	1,500	1,239	1,285	1,416	28.0	55.4
Life sciences	3,645	3,636	3,432	3,844	4,093	16.3	37.0
Mathematics	1,199	724	699	917	978	7.8	19.2
Multi/interdisciplinary studies	80	295	285	312	258	13.8	41.9
Philosophy, religion, and theology	866	1,693	1,608	1,751	1,531	5.8	16.3
Physical sciences	4,390	3,089	3,403	4,164	4,290	5.6	19.7
Psychology	1,782	2,768	2,908	3,322	3,422	24.0	61.2
Public affairs	185	372	431	508	430	23.8	55.8
Social sciences [2]	3,659	3,219	2,851	3,010	3,012	13.9	35.1
Visual and performing arts	621	655	693	848	836	22.2	44.3
Other and unclassified	53	218	209	402	894	28.3	45.2

- Represents zero.   X Not applicable.   [1] Includes technologies.   [2] Includes history.

Source: U.S. National Center for Education Statistics, *Digest of Education Statistics*, annual.

No. 295. First Professional Degrees Earned in Selected Professions: 1960 to 1991

[See Appendix III]

TYPE OF DEGREE AND SEX OF RECIPIENT	1960	1970	1975	1980	1985	1987	1988	1989	1990	1991 [1]
Medicine (M.D.):										
Institutions conferring degrees.....	79	86	104	112	120	122	122	124	124	121
Degrees conferred, total.........	7,032	8,314	12,447	14,902	16,041	15,620	15,358	15,460	15,075	15,043
Percent to women	5.5	8.4	13.1	23.4	30.4	32.4	33.1	33.3	34.2	36.0
Dentistry (D.D.S. or D.M.D.):										
Institutions conferring degrees.....	45	48	52	58	59	58	57	58	57	55
Degrees conferred, total.........	3,247	3,718	4,773	5,258	5,339	4,741	4,477	4,265	4,100	3,699
Percent to women	0.8	0.9	3.1	13.3	20.7	24.0	26.3	26.8	30.9	32.1
Law (LL.B. or J.D.):										
Institutions conferring degrees.....	134	145	154	179	181	180	180	182	182	179
Degrees conferred, total.........	9,240	14,916	29,296	35,647	37,491	36,172	35,397	35,634	36,485	37,945
Percent to women	2.5	5.4	15.1	30.2	38.5	40.2	40.5	40.9	42.2	43.0
Theological (B.D., M.Div., M.H.L.):										
Institutions conferring degrees.....	(NA)	(NA)	(NA)	(NA)	(NA)	(NA)	(NA)	(NA)	(NA)	(NA)
Degrees conferred, total.........	(NA)	5,298	5,095	7,115	7,221	7,181	6,466	6,012	5,851	5,695
Percent to women	(NA)	2.3	6.8	13.8	18.5	19.3	21.4	22.8	24.8	23.4

NA Not available.   [1] Preliminary.

Source: U.S. National Center for Education Statistics, *Digest of Education Statistics*, annual.

No. 296. Degrees Earned, by Level and Race/Ethnicity: 1981 to 1991

[For **school year ending in year shown.** Data exclude some institutions not reporting field of study and are slight undercounts of degrees awarded]

LEVEL OF DEGREE AND RACE/ETHNICITY	TOTAL					PERCENT DISTRIBUTION		
	1981	1985	1989	1990	1991 [1]	1981	1985	1991 [1]
All degrees, total [2]	1,743,336	1,781,911	1,864,779	1,930,216	1,982,017	100.0	100.0	100.0
White, non-Hispanic.........	1,478,161	1,492,230	1,543,364	1,591,727	1,621,071	84.8	83.7	81.8
Black, non-Hispanic.........	117,332	111,386	111,096	116,414	123,920	6.7	6.3	6.3
Hispanic	48,090	54,706	60,470	66,231	72,508	2.8	3.1	3.7
Asian or Pacific Islander......	36,059	46,013	64,853	67,900	71,744	2.1	2.6	3.6
American Indian/Alaskan Native	7,533	8,822	8,724	9,378	9,687	0.4	0.5	0.5
Nonresident alien	56,161	68,754	76,272	78,566	83,087	3.2	3.9	4.2
Bachelor's degrees, total	934,800	968,311	1,016,350	1,048,631	1,081,280	100.0	100.0	100.0
White, non-Hispanic.........	807,319	826,106	859,699	884,372	904,061	86.4	85.3	83.6
Black, non-Hispanic.........	60,673	57,473	58,065	61,065	65,338	6.5	5.9	6.0
Hispanic	21,832	25,874	29,910	32,846	36,612	2.3	2.7	3.4
Asian or Pacific Islander......	18,794	25,395	37,686	39,247	41,622	2.0	2.6	3.8
American Indian/Alaskan Native	3,593	4,246	3,954	4,393	4,513	0.4	0.4	0.4
Nonresident alien	22,589	29,217	27,036	26,708	29,134	2.4	3.0	2.7
Master's degrees, total	294,183	280,421	309,770	322,465	328,645	100.0	100.0	100.0
White, non-Hispanic.........	241,216	223,628	242,756	251,689	255,286	82.0	79.7	77.7
Black, non-Hispanic.........	17,133	13,939	14,096	15,446	16,136	5.8	5.0	4.9
Hispanic	6,461	6,864	7,282	7,954	8,382	2.2	2.4	2.6
Asian or Pacific Islander......	6,282	7,782	10,336	10,578	11,180	2.1	2.8	3.4
American Indian/Alaskan Native	1,034	1,256	1,086	1,099	1,136	0.4	0.4	0.3
Nonresident alien	22,057	26,952	34,214	35,699	36,525	7.5	9.6	11.1
Doctor's degrees, total	32,839	32,307	35,659	38,113	38,547	100.0	100.0	100.0
White, non-Hispanic.........	25,908	23,934	24,882	25,880	25,328	78.9	74.1	65.7
Black, non-Hispanic.........	1,265	1,154	1,065	1,152	1,212	3.9	3.6	3.1
Hispanic	456	677	628	788	732	1.4	2.1	1.9
Asian or Pacific Islander......	877	1,106	1,324	1,235	1,458	2.7	3.4	3.8
American Indian/Alaskan Native	130	119	85	99	102	0.4	0.4	0.3
Nonresident alien	4,203	5,317	7,675	8,959	9,715	12.8	16.5	25.2
First-professional degrees, total	71,340	71,057	70,856	70,744	71,515	100.0	100.0	100.0
White, non-Hispanic.........	64,551	63,219	61,214	60,240	60,327	90.5	89.0	84.4
Black, non-Hispanic.........	2,931	3,029	3,148	3,410	3,575	4.1	4.3	5.0
Hispanic	1,541	1,884	2,269	2,427	2,527	2.2	2.7	3.5
Asian or Pacific Islander......	1,456	1,816	2,976	3,362	3,755	2.0	2.6	5.3
American Indian/Alaskan Native	192	248	264	257	261	0.3	0.3	0.4
Nonresident alien	669	861	985	1,048	1,070	0.9	1.2	1.5

[1] Preliminary data.   [2] Includes associates degrees, not shown separately.

Source: U.S. National Center for Education Statistics, *Digest of Education Statistics*, annual.

No. 297. Libraries—Number, by Type: 1980 to 1992

TYPE	1980	1985	1990	1992	TYPE	1980	1985	1990	1992
Total [1]	31,564	32,323	34,613	35,825	Junior college . . .	1,191	1,188	1,233	1,256
United States . . .	28,638	29,843	30,761	31,850	Colleges, universities	3,400	3,846	3,360	3,364
Public	8,717	8,849	9,060	9,076	Departmental. .	1,489	1,824	1,454	1,459
Public branches . . .	5,936	6,330	5,833	6,093	Law,				
Special [2]	7,649	7,530	9,051	9,811	medicine,				
Medicine	1,674	1,667	1,861	1,893	religious . . .	269	531	501	496
Religious	913	839	946	981	Government.	1,260	1,574	1,735	1,776
Law [3]	417	435	647	1,124	Armed Forces	485	526	489	474
Academic	4,591	5,034	4,593	4,620	Outlying areas. . .	113	114	110	(NA)

NA Not available.   [1] Includes Canadian libraries, and libraries in regions administered by the United States, not shown separately. Data are exclusive of elementary and secondary school libraries. Law libraries with fewer than 10,000 volumes are included only if they specialize in a particular field.   [2] Includes other types of special libraries, not shown separately. Increase between 1985 and 1990 is due mainly to revised criteria for identifying special libraries and improved methods of counting. [3] Increase beginning 1992 due to increased effort in identifying special libraries.

Source: R.R. Bowker Co., New York, NY, *The Bowker Annual: Library and Book Trade Almanac* and *American Library Directory*, annual. (Copyright by Reed Publishing (USA) Inc.)

No. 298. Public Libraries, Selected Characteristics: 1992

[Based on survey of public libraries. Data are for public libraries in the 50 States and the District of Columbia. The response rates for these items are between 97 and 100 percent, except for library visits (82 percent). See source for details]

POPULATION OF SERVICE AREA	NUMBER OF—		OPERATING INCOME				PAID STAFF [3]		Books and serial volumes (per capita)
	Public libraries	Stationary outlets [1]	Total (mil. dol.) [2]	Source (percent)			Total	Librarians with ALA-MLS [4]	
				State government	Local government				
Total	8,946	15,870	4,997	12.0	78.6		109,926	24,461	2.7
1,000,000 or more	22	866	848	10.1	79.1		13,669	3,855	2.3
500,000 to 999,000	49	1,034	765	18.3	74.4		15,072	3,917	2.5
250,000 to 499,999	98	1,058	605	11.7	81.5		12,711	3,156	2.3
100,000 to 249,999	293	1,820	735	9.9	81.9		16,870	3,786	2.2
50,000 to 99,999	505	1,631	633	12.6	78.8		14,756	3,284	2.4
25,000 to 49,999	861	1,652	575	11.6	79.4		14,028	3,010	2.8
10,000 to 24,999	1,654	2,130	513	10.1	78.8		12,801	2,488	3.3
5,000 to 9,999	1,481	1,647	192	11.1	74.5		5,360	679	4.1
2,500 to 4,999	1,327	1,371	77	7.0	73.4		2,467	199	5.2
1,000 to 2,499	1,661	1,672	44	5.3	67.0		1,628	72	7.4
Fewer than 1,000	995	989	11	9.0	63.9		565	14	13.0

[1] The sum of central and branches libraries. The total number of central libraries was 8,835; the total of branch libraries was 7,035.   [2] Includes income from the Federal Government (1.0%) and other sources (8.4%), not shown separately.   [3] Full-time equivalents.   [4] Librarians with master's degrees from a graduate library education program accredited by the American Library Association (ALA). Total librarians, including those without ALA-MLS, were 35,999.

Source: U.S. National Center for Education Statistics, *Public Libraries in the United States: 1992*.

No. 299. College and University Libraries—Summary 1975 to 1990

[For school year ending in year shown, except enrollment as of fall of the prior year. Prior to 1982, includes outlying areas]

ITEM	1975	1977	1979	1982	1985	1988	1990
Number of libraries	2,972	3,058	3,122	3,104	3,322	3,438	3,274
Total enrollment (1,000)	10,322	11,121	11,392	12,372	12,242	12,767	13,539
COLLECTIONS (1,000)							
Number of volumes	447,059	481,442	519,895	567,826	631,727	706,504	717,042
Volumes added during year.	23,242	22,367	21,608	19,507	20,658	21,907	19,003
Number of serial subscriptions	4,434	4,670	4,775	4,890	6,317	6,416	5,748
STAFF							
Total	56,836	57,087	58,416	58,476	58,476	67,251	69,359
Librarians and professional	23,530	23,308	23,676	23,816	21,822	25,115	26,101
OPERATING EXPENDITURES ($1,000)							
Total [1]	1,091,784	1,259,637	1,502,158	1,943,769	2,404,524	2,770,075	3,257,813
Salaries.	592,568	698,090	824,438	1,081,894	1,156,138	1,451,551	1,693,813
Collection	327,904	373,699	450,180	561,199	750,282	891,281	1,040,928

[1] Includes other expenditures, not shown separately.

Source: U.S. National Center for Education Statistics, *Digest of Education Statistics*, 1991; and *Academic Libraries: 1990*, 1992.

No. 300. Participation in Adult Education: 1990-91

[For the civilian noninstitutional population 17 years old and over not enrolled full-time in elementary or secondary school at the time of the survey. Adult education is considered any part-time enrollment in any educational activity at any time in the prior 12 months. Based on a telephone survey and subject to sampling error; source for details]

CHARACTERISTIC	Adult population (1,000)	PARTICIPANTS IN ADULT EDUCATION						
		Number taking adult ed. courses (1,000)	Percent of total	Reason for taking course (percent) [1]				
				Personal/ social	Advance on the job	Train for a new job	Complete degree or diploma	
Total	181,800	57,391	32	30	60	9	13	
Age: 17 to 24 years old	21,688	7,125	33	30	38	18	29	
25 to 34 years old	47,244	17,530	37	25	63	12	14	
35 to 44 years old	38,565	17,083	44	27	66	8	12	
45 to 54 years old	25,375	8,107	32	29	70	6	7	
55 to 64 years old	19,967	4,516	23	35	61	5	5	
65 years old and over.	28,960	3,031	10	73	22	4	3	
Sex: Male	82,154	25,923	32	24	67	8	11	
Female	99,646	31,469	32	35	54	10	14	
Race/ethnicity:								
White [2]	143,144	47,401	33	30	62	8	13	
Black [2]	20,141	4,586	23	30	53	14	13	
Hispanic	13,804	4,032	29	31	48	16	12	
Other races [2]	4,711	1,371	29	32	51	8	17	
Marital status:								
Never married.	36,652	11,539	31	30	48	14	24	
Currently married.	118,397	39,323	33	30	63	8	10	
Other	26,752	6,529	24	34	59	11	11	
Children under 16 in household:								
Yes.	68,868	25,349	37	26	65	10	12	
No	112,932	32,042	28	33	56	9	14	
Educational attainment:								
Up to 8th grade	10,163	735	7	56	16	5	14	
9th to 11th grade	17,581	2,520	14	30	43	13	16	
Twelfth grade	67,129	15,077	22	31	55	13	9	
Vocational school after high school .	6,994	2,219	32	28	68	6	10	
Some college	36,823	14,488	39	33	53	10	19	
Associate's degree	5,034	2,461	49	22	71	7	15	
Bachelor's or higher	38,076	19,891	52	28	70	6	11	
Labor force status:								
Employed	115,620	47,143	41	24	68	9	13	
Unemployed.	9,820	2,099	21	27	29	27	25	
Not in the labor force.	56,361	8,149	14	64	17	10	11	
Occupation: [3]								
Professional	19,898	12,693	64	22	79	5	15	
Executive, administrative, and managerial	10,574	6,255	59	22	78	6	13	
Technical, sales, and related support	3,082	1,947	63	18	75	12	13	
Sales workers.	12,234	5,154	42	34	56	12	11	
Administrative support [4]	18,971	7,044	37	28	66	10	15	
Service	15,904	4,426	28	27	61	11	15	
Agriculture, forestry, and fishing. . . .	2,783	303	11	31	62	6	10	
Precision production, craft and repair.	11,393	3,918	34	27	61	13	10	
Machine operators, assemblers [5] . . .	7,768	2,201	28	20	73	10	10	
Transportation and materials moving.	3,962	1,030	26	23	68	7	9	
Handlers, equipment cleaners, helpers and laborers	3,297	767	23	17	60	18	10	
Nonclassifiable, undetermined	5,753	1,403	24	8	19	8	6	
Income: Under $10,000.	27,504	3,843	14	37	34	16	14	
$10,001 to $15,000	15,465	3,178	21	31	48	16	15	
$15,001 to $20,000	16,117	3,308	21	32	50	13	16	
$20,001 to $25,000	16,092	4,063	25	32	56	11	14	
$25,001 to $30,000	17,973	5,445	30	33	53	14	15	
$30,001 to $40,000	26,110	9,043	35	30	64	10	13	
$40,001 to $50,000	21,303	9,313	44	29	64	6	12	
$50,001 to $75,000	24,540	11,235	46	28	67	6	12	
More than $75,000	16,695	7,963	48	27	66	6	10	

[1] Reason for taking at least one course. Includes duplication. Excludes "to improve basic skills," cited by no more than 4 percent of participants.   [2] Non-Hispanic.   [3] For the currently employed.   [4] Includes clerical.   [5] Includes inspectors.

Source: U.S. National Center for Education Statistics, *Adult Education Profile for 1990-91;* and unpublished data.

Figure 5.1
Violent and Property Crime Rates: 1980 to 1992

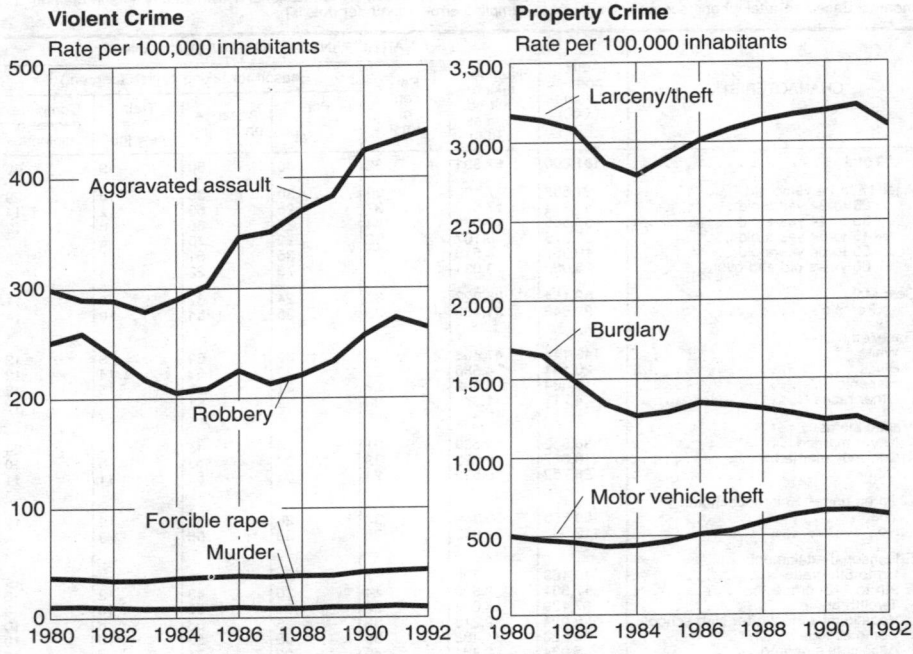

Violent Crime
Rate per 100,000 inhabitants

Property Crime
Rate per 100,000 inhabitants

Source: Chart prepared by U.S. Bureau of the Census. For data, see table 301.

Figure 5.2
Child Abuse and Neglect Cases: 1992

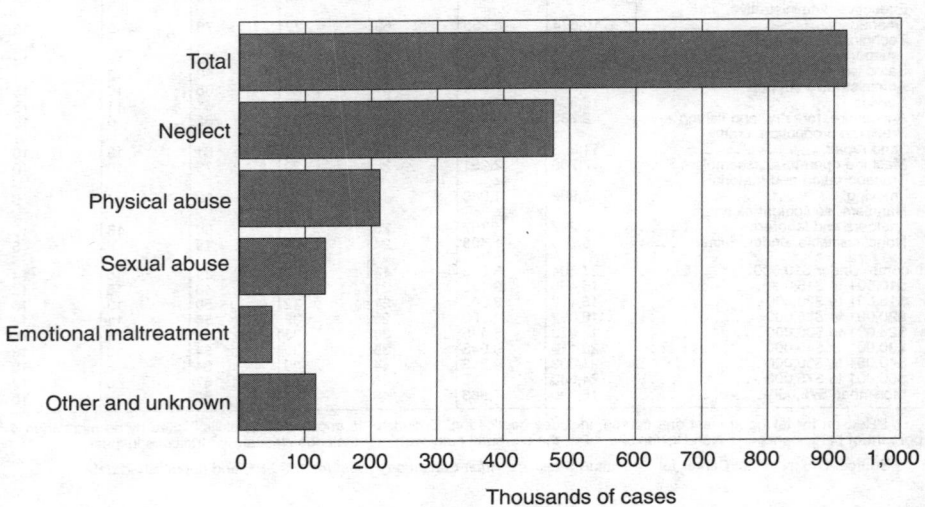

Thousands of cases

Note: More than one type of maltreatment may be substantiated per child. Therefore, items add up to more than the total shown.
Source: Chart prepared by U.S. Bureau of the Census. For data, see table 336.

Law Enforcement, Courts, and Prisons

This section presents data on crimes committed, victims of crimes, arrests, and data related to criminal violations, and the criminal justice system. The major sources of these data are the Bureau of Justice Statistics (BJS) and the Federal Bureau of Investigation (FBI). BJS issues several reports, including *Sourcebook of Criminal Justice Statistics, Criminal Victimization in the United States, Prisoners in State and Federal Institutions, Children in Custody, National Survey of Courts, Census of State Correctional Facilities* and *Survey of Prison Inmates, Census of Jails* and *Survey of Jail Inmates, Parole in the United States, Capital Punishment,* and the annual *Expenditure and Employment Data for the Criminal Justice System.* The Federal Bureau of Investigation's major annual report is *Crime in the United States,* which presents data on reported crimes as gathered from State and local law enforcement agencies.

Other major sources of these data include: *Annual Report of the Director, Federal Court Management Statistics, Federal Offenders,* and *Sentences Imposed Chart* issued by the Administrative Office of the U.S. Courts; *Governmental Finances and Public Employment,* issued annually by the Bureau of the Census; and the *Statistical Report,* issued annually by the Federal Bureau of Prisons.

Legal jurisdiction and law enforcement.—Law enforcement is, for the most part, a function of State and local officers and agencies. The U.S. Constitution reserves general police powers to the States. By act of Congress, Federal offenses include only offenses against the U.S. Government and against or by its employees while engaged in their official duties, and offenses which involve the crossing of State lines or an interference with interstate commerce. Excluding the military, there are 52 separate criminal law jurisdictions in the United States: 1 in each of the 50 States, 1 in the District of Columbia, and the Federal jurisdiction. Each of these has its own criminal law and procedure and its own

In Brief

Crime rate, as reported by the FBI, fell in 1992 for the first time since 1984 from 5,898 per 100,000 population in 1991 to 5,660 in 1992

Handguns were used in 55 percent of the murders in 1992

918,263 child victims in cases of substantiated maltreatment and neglect in 1992

law enforcement agencies. While the systems of law enforcement are quite similar among the States, there are often substantial differences in the penalties for like offenses.

Law enforcement can be divided into three parts: Investigation of crimes and arrests of persons suspected of committing them; prosecution of those charged with crime; and the punishment or treatment of persons convicted of crime.

Crime.—There are two major approaches taken in determining the extent of crime. One perspective is provided by the FBI through its Uniform Crime Reporting Program (UCR). The FBI receives monthly and annual reports from law enforcement agencies throughout the country, currently representing 98 percent of the national population. Each month, city police, sheriffs, and State police file reports on the number of index offenses that become known to them. The FBI Crime Index offenses are as follows: *Murder and nonnegligent manslaughter,* is based on police investigations, as opposed to the determination of a medical examiner or judicial body, includes willful felonious homicides, and excludes attempts and assaults to kill, suicides, accidental deaths, justifiable homicides, and deaths caused by negligence; *forcible rape* includes forcible rapes and attempts; *robbery* includes stealing or taking anything of value by force or violence or threat of force or violence and includes attempted robbery; *aggravated assault* includes assault with intent to kill; *burglary* includes any unlawful entry to commit a felony or a theft and includes attempted burglary and burglary followed by larceny; *larceny* includes theft of property or articles of value without use of force and violence or fraud and excludes embezzlement, "con games," forgery, etc.; *motor vehicle theft* includes all cases where vehicles are driven away and abandoned, but excludes vehicles taken for temporary use and returned by the taker. Arson was added as the eighth Index offense in April 1979 following a Congressional mandate. *Arson* includes any willful or malicious burning or attempt to burn with or without intent to defraud, a dwelling house, public building, motor vehicle or aircraft, personal property of another, etc. The monthly Uniform Crime Reports also contain data on crimes cleared by arrest and on characteristics of persons arrested for all criminal offenses. In summarizing and publishing crime data, the FBI depends primarily on the adherence to the established standards of reporting for statistical accuracy, presenting the data as information useful to persons concerned with the problem of crime and criminal-law enforcement.

National Crime Victimization Survey (NCVS).—A second perspective on crime is provided by this survey (formerly the National Crime Survey until August 1991) of the Bureau of Justice Statistics. Details about the crimes come directly from the victims. No attempt is made to validate the information against police records or any other source. The NCVS measures rape, robbery, assault, household and personal larceny, burglary, and motor vehicle theft. The NCVS includes offenses reported to the police, as well as those not reported. Police reporting rates (percent of victimizations) varied by type of crime. In 1991, for instance, 59 percent of the rapes were reported; 55 percent of the robberies; 47 percent of assaults; 28 percent of personal larcenies without contact; 50 percent of the household burglaries; and 74 percent of motor vehicle thefts.

Murder and kidnaping are not covered. Commercial burglary and robbery were dropped from the program during 1977. The so-called victimless crimes, such as drunkenness, drug abuse, and prostitution, also are excluded, as are crimes for which it is difficult to identify knowledgeable respondents or to locate data records.

Crimes of which the victim may not be aware also cannot be measured effectively. Buying stolen property may fall into this category, as may some instances of embezzlement. Attempted crimes of many types probably are under recorded for this reason. Events in which the victim has shown a willingness to participate in illegal activity also are excluded.

In any encounter involving a personal crime, more than one criminal act can be committed against an individual. For example; a rape may be associated with a robbery; or a household offense, such as a burglary, can escalate into something more serious in the event of a personal confrontation. In classifying the survey-measured crimes, each criminal incident has been counted only once—by the most serious act that took place during the incident and ranked in accordance with the seriousness classification system used by the Federal Bureau of Investigation. The order of seriousness for crimes against persons is as follows: Rape, robbery, assault, and larceny. Consequently, if a person were both robbed and assaulted, the event would be classified as robbery; if the victim suffered physical harm, the crime would be categorized as robbery with injury. Personal crimes take precedence over household offenses.

A *victimization,* basic measure of the occurrence of a crime, is a specific criminal act as it affects a single victim. The number of victimizations is determined by the number of victims of such acts. Victimization counts serve as key elements in computing rates of victimization. For crimes against persons, the rates are based on the total number of individuals age 12 and over or on a portion of that population sharing a particular characteristic or set of traits. As general indicators of the danger of having been victimized during the reference period, the rates are not sufficiently refined to represent true measures of risk for specific individuals or households.

An *incident* is a specific criminal act involving one or more victims; therefore, the number of incidents of personal crimes lower than that of victimizations.

Courts.—Statistics on criminal offenses and the outcome of prosecutions are incomplete for the country as a whole, although data are available for many States individually. The only national compilations of such statistics were made by the Bureau of the Census for 1932 to 1945 covering a maximum of 32 States, and by the Bureau of Justice Statistics for 1986 based on a nationally representative sample survey.

The bulk of civil and criminal litigation in the country is commenced and determined in the various State courts. Only when the U.S. Constitution and acts of Congress specifically confer jurisdiction upon the Federal courts may civil litigation be heard and decided by them. Generally, the Federal courts have jurisdiction over the following types of cases: Suits or proceedings by or against the United States; civil actions between private parties arising under the Constitution, laws, or treaties of the United States; civil actions between private litigants who are citizens of different States; civil cases involving admiralty, maritime, or prize jurisdiction; and all matters in bankruptcy.

There are several types of courts with varying degrees of legal jurisdiction. These jurisdictions include original, appellate, general, and limited or special. A *court of original jurisdiction* is one having the authority initially to try a case and pass judgment on the law and the facts; a *court of appellate jurisdiction* is one with the legal authority to review cases and hear appeals; a *court of general jurisdiction* is a trial court of unlimited original jurisdiction in civil and/or criminal cases, also called a "major trial court"; a *court of limited or special jurisdiction* is a trial court with legal authority over only a particular class of cases, such as probate, juvenile, or traffic cases.

The 94 Federal courts of original jurisdiction are known as the U.S. district courts. One or more of these courts is established in every State and one each in the District of Columbia, Puerto Rico, the Virgin Islands, the Northern Mariana Islands, and Guam. Appeals from the district courts are taken to intermediate appellate courts of which there are 13, known as U.S. courts of appeals and the United States Court of Appeals for the Federal Circuit. The Supreme Court of the United States is the final and highest appellate court in the Federal system of courts.

Juvenile offenders.—For statistical purposes, the FBI and most States classify as juvenile offenders persons under the age of 18 years who have committed a crime or crimes.

Delinquency cases are all cases of youths referred to a juvenile court for violation of a law or ordinance or for seriously "antisocial" conduct. Several types of facilities are available for those adjudicated delinquent, ranging from the short-term physically unrestricted environment to the long-term very restrictive atmosphere.

Prisoners.—Data on prisoners in Federal and State prisons and reformatories were collected annually by the Bureau of the Census until 1950, by the Federal Bureau of Prisons until 1971, transferred then to the Law Enforcement Assistance Administration, and, in 1979, to the Bureau of Justice Statistics. Adults convicted of criminal activity may be given a prison or jail sentence. A *prison* is a confinement facility having custodial authority over adults sentenced to confinement of more than one year. A *jail* is a facility, usually operated by a local law enforcement agency, holding persons detained pending adjudication and/or persons committed after adjudication to one year or less. Nearly every State publishes annual data either for its whole prison system or for each separate State institution.

Statistical reliability.—For discussion of statistical collection, estimation, and sampling procedures and measures of statistical reliability pertaining to the National Crime Victimization Survey and Uniform Crime Reporting Program, see Appendix III.

Historical statistics.—Tabular headnotes provide cross-references, where applicable, to *Historical Statistics of the United States, Colonial Times to 1970.* See Appendix IV.

No. 301. Crimes and Crime Rates, by Type: 1983 to 1992

[Data refer to offenses known to the police. Rates are based on Bureau of the Census estimated resident population as of July 1, except 1990 enumerated as of April 1. Annual totals for years prior to 1984 were adjusted in 1984 and may not be consistent with those in prior editions. See source for details. Minus sign (-) indicates decrease. For definitions of crimes, see text, section 5. See *Historical Statistics, Colonial Times to 1970*, series H 952-961 for related data]

ITEM AND YEAR	Total	VIOLENT CRIME					PROPERTY CRIME			
		Total	Murder [1]	Forcible rape	Robbery	Aggravated assault	Total	Burglary	Larceny—theft	Motor vehicle theft
Number of offenses (1,000):										
1983	12,109	1,258	19.3	78.9	507	653	10,851	3,130	6,713	1,008
1984	11,882	1,273	18.7	84.2	485	685	10,609	2,984	6,592	1,032
1985	12,431	1,329	19.0	88.7	498	723	11,103	3,073	6,926	1,103
1986	13,212	1,489	20.6	91.5	543	834	11,723	3,241	7,257	1,224
1987	13,509	1,484	20.1	91.1	518	855	12,025	3,236	7,500	1,289
1988	13,923	1,566	20.7	92.5	543	910	12,357	3,218	7,706	1,433
1989	14,251	1,646	21.5	94.5	578	952	12,605	3,168	7,872	1,565
1990	14,476	1,820	23.4	102.6	639	1,055	12,656	3,074	7,946	1,636
1991	14,873	1,912	24.7	106.6	688	1,093	12,961	3,157	8,142	1,662
1992	14,438	1,932	23.8	109.1	672	1,127	12,506	2,980	7,915	1,611
Percent change, number of offenses:										
1983 to 1992	19.2	53.6	23.0	38.2	32.8	72.5	15.3	-4.8	17.9	59.8
1988 to 1992	3.7	23.4	14.9	17.9	23.9	23.8	1.2	-7.4	2.7	12.4
1991 to 1992	-2.9	1.0	-3.6	2.3	-2.3	3.1	-3.5	-5.6	-2.8	-3.1
Rate per 100,000 population:										
1983	5,175	538	8.3	33.7	217	279	4,637	1,338	2,869	431
1984	5,031	539	7.9	35.7	205	290	4,492	1,264	2,791	437
1985	5,207	557	7.9	37.1	209	303	4,651	1,287	2,901	462
1986	5,480	618	8.6	37.9	225	346	4,863	1,345	3,010	508
1987	5,550	610	8.3	37.4	213	351	4,940	1,330	3,081	529
1988	5,664	637	8.4	37.6	221	370	5,027	1,309	3,135	583
1989	5,741	663	8.7	38.1	233	383	5,078	1,276	3,171	630
1990	5,820	732	9.4	41.2	257	424	5,089	1,236	3,195	658
1991	5,898	758	9.8	42.3	273	433	5,140	1,252	3,229	659
1992	5,660	758	9.3	42.8	264	442	4,903	1,168	3,103	631
Percent change, rate per 100,000 population:										
1983 to 1992	9.4	40.9	12.0	27.0	21.8	58.2	5.7	-12.7	8.2	46.6
1988 to 1992	-0.1	18.9	10.7	13.8	19.3	19.3	-2.5	-10.8	-1.0	8.3
1991 to 1992	-4.0	-0.1	-0.1	-5.1	1.2	2.0	-4.6	-6.7	-3.9	-4.2

[1] Includes nonnegligent manslaughter.

Source: U.S. Federal Bureau of Investigation, *Crime in the United States*, annual.

No. 302. Crimes and Crime Rates, by Type and Area: 1992

[In thousands, except rate. Rate per 100,000 population; see headnote, table 301. Estimated totals based on reports from city and rural law enforcement agencies representing 96 percent of the national population. For definitions of crimes, see text, section 5]

TYPE OF CRIME	UNITED STATES		METROPOLITAN AREAS [1]		OTHER CITIES		RURAL AREAS	
	Total	Rate	Total	Rate	Total	Rate	Total	Rate
Total	14,438	5,660	12,660	6,272	1,130	5,317	648	2,026
Violent crime	1,932	758	1,759	871	103	486	70	220
Murder and nonnegligent manslaughter	24	9	21	10	1	5	2	5
Forcible rape	109	43	93	46	8	37	8	25
Robbery	672	264	652	323	15	70	5	16
Aggravated assault	1,127	442	992	492	79	373	56	174
Property crime	12,506	4,903	10,902	5,401	1,027	4,830	577	1,805
Burglary	2,980	1,168	2,554	1,265	215	1,012	211	661
Larceny-theft	7,914	3,103	6,818	3,378	765	3,601	331	1,036
Motor vehicle theft	1,611	632	1,530	758	46	217	35	109

[1] For definition, see Appendix II.

Source: U.S. Federal Bureau of Investigation, *Crime in the United States*, annual.

No. 303. Crime Rates, by State, 1990 to 1992, and by Type, 1992

[Offenses known to the police per 100,000 population. Based on Bureau of the Census estimated resident population as of July 1, except 1990, enumerated as of April. For definitions of crimes, see text, section 5]

REGION, DIVISION, AND STATE	1990, total	1991, total	1992 Total	Violent crime Total	Murder[1]	Forcible rape	Robbery	Aggravated assault	Property crime Total	Burglary	Larceny-theft	Motor vehicle theft
United States.....	5,820	5,898	5,660	758	9.3	43	264	442	4,903	1,168	3,103	631
Northeast............	5,193	5,155	4,837	731	7.8	30	336	358	4,105	935	2,443	727
New England........	4,996	4,950	4,614	535	3.5	32	149	350	4,079	1,008	2,442	630
Maine.............	3,698	3,768	3,524	131	1.7	24	23	82	3,393	822	2,426	144
New Hampshire.....	3,645	3,448	3,081	126	1.6	38	33	53	2,955	622	2,138	195
Vermont..........	4,341	3,955	3,410	109	2.1	25	9	74	3,301	826	2,370	105
Massachusetts......	5,298	5,322	5,003	779	3.6	36	184	555	4,224	1,072	2,361	791
Rhode Island.......	5,353	5,039	4,578	395	3.6	31	95	265	4,183	1,048	2,393	743
Connecticut........	5,387	5,364	5,053	495	5.1	27	211	252	4,558	1,109	2,727	722
Middle Atlantic.......	5,263	5,227	4,914	800	9.3	29	401	361	4,114	910	2,444	761
New York..........	6,364	6,245	5,858	1,122	13.2	28	597	484	4,736	1,068	2,736	932
New Jersey........	5,447	5,431	5,064	626	5.1	31	285	305	4,439	969	2,654	816
Pennsylvania.......	3,476	3,559	3,393	427	6.2	28	181	212	2,966	631	1,867	468
Midwest............	5,102	5,257	4,975	607	7.6	46	207	347	4,368	964	2,928	477
East North Central....	5,322	5,482	5,136	671	8.6	50	243	370	4,465	974	2,952	538
Ohio.............	4,843	5,033	4,666	526	6.6	52	199	268	4,140	947	2,721	471
Indiana...........	4,683	4,818	4,687	508	8.2	42	122	336	4,178	952	2,776	450
Illinois [2]...........	5,935	6,132	5,765	977	11.4	37	412	516	4,788	1,077	3,092	619
Michigan..........	5,995	6,138	5,611	770	9.9	80	221	459	4,841	1,041	3,174	626
Wisconsin.........	4,395	4,466	4,319	276	4.4	26	120	125	4,043	692	2,920	431
West North Central ...	4,579	4,722	4,594	455	5.4	35	123	291	4,139	939	2,870	330
Minnesota.........	4,539	4,496	4,591	338	3.3	41	110	184	4,253	890	3,008	355
Iowa [3]...........	4,101	4,134	3,957	278	1.6	19	40	218	3,679	754	2,766	159
Missouri..........	5,121	5,416	5,097	740	10.5	36	227	466	4,357	1,100	2,759	497
North Dakota.......	2,922	2,794	2,903	83	1.9	23	8	50	2,820	391	2,280	149
South Dakota.......	2,909	3,079	2,999	195	0.6	52	17	125	2,804	541	2,162	101
Nebraska..........	4,213	4,354	4,324	349	4.2	31	57	256	3,975	715	3,060	201
Kansas...........	5,193	5,534	5,320	511	6.0	41	130	334	4,809	1,294	3,192	324
South..............	6,334	6,417	6,155	810	11.1	46	241	511	5,345	1,379	3,388	578
South Atlantic......	6,546	6,585	6,428	867	10.6	45	276	535	5,561	1,430	3,572	559
Delaware.........	5,360	5,869	4,848	621	4.6	86	151	380	4,227	958	2,964	306
Maryland..........	5,830	6,209	6,225	1,000	12.1	46	429	513	5,224	1,131	3,367	726
District of Columbia [4]..	10,774	10,768	11,407	2,833	75.2	37	1,266	1,455	8,574	1,820	5,206	1,548
Virginia..........	4,441	4,607	4,299	375	8.8	31	138	197	3,924	709	2,909	306
West Virginia.......	2,503	2,663	2,610	212	6.3	22	43	140	2,398	623	1,611	164
North Carolina.....	5,486	5,889	5,802	681	10.6	36	187	448	5,121	1,653	3,182	287
South Carolina.....	6,045	6,179	5,893	944	10.4	58	171	706	4,949	1,379	3,225	345
Georgia..........	6,764	6,493	6,405	733	11.0	45	250	427	5,672	1,443	3,653	576
Florida...........	8,811	8,547	8,358	1,207	9.0	54	367	777	7,151	1,889	4,434	828
East South Central....	4,389	4,687	4,589	672	9.7	42	157	464	3,917	1,118	2,407	392
Kentucky..........	3,299	3,358	3,324	535	5.8	32	87	410	2,788	729	1,843	216
Tennessee	5,051	5,367	5,136	746	10.4	47	218	470	4,390	1,267	2,546	576
Alabama..........	4,915	5,366	5,268	872	11.0	41	165	655	4,396	1,186	2,848	362
Mississippi........	3,869	4,221	4,282	412	12.2	45	124	230	3,871	1,283	2,251	337
West South Central ...	7,092	7,118	6,589	793	12.5	50	231	499	5,796	1,442	3,641	713
Arkansas.........	4,867	5,175	4,762	577	10.8	41	126	399	4,185	1,093	2,763	329
Louisiana.........	6,487	6,425	6,546	985	17.4	42	271	653	5,562	1,366	3,567	628
Oklahoma.........	5,599	5,669	5,432	623	6.5	48	136	432	4,809	1,360	2,932	517
Texas............	7,827	7,819	7,058	806	12.7	53	253	488	6,252	1,523	3,907	822
West	6,405	6,478	6,388	864	9.7	47	295	513	5,524	1,273	3,452	799
Mountain...........	6,268	6,125	6,012	563	6.6	46	127	384	5,449	1,150	3,791	508
Montana..........	4,502	3,648	4,596	170	2.9	25	27	115	4,426	644	3,549	233
Idaho............	4,057	4,196	3,996	281	3.5	32	21	225	3,715	744	2,814	157
Wyoming..........	4,211	4,389	4,575	320	3.6	35	18	263	4,256	671	3,434	150
Colorado..........	6,054	6,074	5,959	579	6.2	47	120	405	5,380	1,091	3,780	509
New Mexico.......	6,684	6,679	6,434	935	8.9	63	139	724	5,499	1,511	3,610	378
Arizona..........	7,889	7,406	7,029	671	8.1	43	153	467	6,358	1,412	4,125	822
Utah.............	5,660	5,608	5,659	291	3.0	45	56	186	5,368	885	4,245	238
Nevada...........	6,064	6,299	6,204	697	10.9	63	331	292	5,507	1,289	3,520	697
Pacific.............	6,452	6,602	6,521	970	10.8	47	354	558	5,551	1,317	3,332	902
Washington........	6,223	6,304	6,173	535	5.0	72	140	318	5,638	1,122	4,045	471
Oregon...........	5,646	5,755	5,821	510	4.7	53	151	301	5,311	1,107	3,671	533
California.........	6,604	6,773	6,679	1,120	12.7	41	424	642	5,560	1,385	3,138	1,037
Alaska...........	5,153	5,702	5,570	660	7.5	99	109	445	4,909	881	3,531	497
Hawaii...........	6,107	5,970	6,112	258	3.6	38	99	118	5,854	1,121	4,357	375

[1] Includes nonnegligent manslaughter. [2] Forcible rape figures for 1990 to 1992 were estimated using the national rate of forcible rapes when grouped by like agencies as figures submitted were not in accordance with national Uniform Crime Reporting program guidelines. [3] Data for 1991 were not available; therefore, data presented are estimates. [4] Includes offenses reported by the police at the National Zoo.

Source: U.S. Federal Bureau of Investigation, Crime in the United States, annual.

No. 304. Crime Rates, by Type—Selected Large Cities: 1992

[Offenses known to the police per 100,000 population. Based on Bureau of the Census estimated resident population as of July 1. For definitions of crimes, see text, section 5]

CITY RANKED BY POPULATION SIZE, 1992 [1]	Crime index, total	VIOLENT CRIME					PROPERTY CRIME			
		Total	Murder	Forcible rape	Robbery	Aggravated assault	Total	Burglary	Larceny—theft	Motor vehicle theft
New York, NY	8,491	2,164	27.1	38.2	1,237	861	6,327	1,403	3,202	1,722
Los Angeles, CA	9,364	2,460	30.3	51.8	1,093	1,285	6,904	1,598	3,426	1,880
Chicago, IL	(²)	(²)	33.1	(²)	1,357	1,450	7,545	1,731	4,225	1,588
Houston, TX	8,747	1,465	27.4	69.0	657	712	7,282	1,782	3,675	1,825
Philadelphia, PA	6,071	1,189	26.5	48.7	728	385	4,882	1,010	2,474	1,398
San Diego, CA	8,010	1,284	12.7	42.1	462	768	6,725	1,427	3,542	1,756
Dallas, TX	12,430	2,072	37.0	104.7	911	1,019	10,358	2,370	6,027	1,960
Phoenix, AZ	9,222	1,091	13.6	47.6	314	716	8,131	2,032	4,601	1,498
Detroit, MI	11,229	2,533	57.0	117.3	1,168	1,191	8,696	2,112	3,966	2,619
San Antonio, TX	11,218	733	22.5	63.3	358	289	10,485	2,258	6,714	1,513
San Jose, CA	4,906	669	5.3	55.2	152	457	4,237	835	2,934	468
Indianapolis, IN	7,260	1,380	17.8	109.5	437	816	5,880	1,640	3,185	1,055
San Francisco, CA	10,195	1,821	15.6	52.6	1,102	651	8,374	1,576	5,111	1,687
Baltimore, MD	11,928	2,885	44.3	99.1	1,623	1,119	9,042	2,157	5,389	1,496
Jacksonville, FL	10,510	1,739	18.5	107.4	544	1,069	8,771	2,456	4,991	1,324
Columbus, OH	9,054	1,093	17.6	106.4	558	412	7,961	2,336	4,543	1,083
Milwaukee, WI	8,670	985	22.7	81.3	674	207	7,686	1,360	4,111	2,215
Memphis, TN	9,849	1,553	28.0	109.4	849	566	8,296	2,589	3,605	2,101
Washington, DC	11,398	2,832	75.2	36.5	1,266	1,454	8,566	1,820	5,198	1,548
Boston, MA	9,846	2,038	12.7	93.7	832	1,099	7,808	1,522	4,294	1,992
El Paso, TX	9,044	1,088	8.2	50.8	301	728	7,956	1,429	5,513	1,014
Seattle, WA	12,001	1,345	11.0	64.8	473	796	10,657	1,697	7,547	1,413
Cleveland, OH	8,284	1,662	30.6	166.3	861	603	6,622	1,753	2,773	2,096
Nashville-Davidson, TN	9,687	1,628	17.5	96.7	518	996	8,058	1,989	5,071	998
Austin, TX	10,944	589	7.6	60.7	300	221	10,355	2,109	7,301	944
New Orleans, LA	9,988	1,982	55.2	56.8	1,058	812	8,007	2,172	4,028	1,807
Denver, CO	8,155	1,076	19.3	88.7	366	602	7,078	1,806	3,632	1,641
Fort Worth, TX	14,135	2,019	32.9	112.8	750	1,123	12,116	3,074	6,905	2,136
Oklahoma City, OK	11,177	1,400	13.4	104.0	404	878	9,777	2,476	5,991	1,310
Portland, OR	11,266	1,831	10.0	107.0	586	1,128	9,435	1,912	5,798	1,725
Long Beach, CA	7,934	1,555	23.3	48.9	804	678	6,379	1,696	3,264	1,419
Kansas City, MO	12,475	2,855	34.0	127.8	1,019	1,674	9,620	2,845	4,952	1,823
Virginia Beach, VA	5,216	285	5.7	37.8	151	91	4,931	916	3,729	286
Charlotte, NC	12,591	2,312	24.2	88.3	748	1,452	10,278	3,073	6,606	600
Tucson, AZ	10,413	1,021	9.9	91.1	229	691	9,392	1,608	6,755	1,029
Albuquerque, NM	9,467	1,536	10.5	73.2	364	1,089	7,931	2,168	5,040	724
Atlanta, GA	17,347	3,859	48.2	152.6	1,418	2,241	13,488	3,180	8,251	2,057
St. Louis, MO	14,800	3,291	57.4	86.7	1,226	1,920	11,509	3,056	6,359	2,094
Sacramento, CA	10,017	1,220	11.7	61.9	606	540	8,797	1,907	4,755	2,135
Fresno, CA	12,112	1,460	22.0	55.3	842	540	10,653	2,562	4,549	3,542
Tulsa, OK	8,208	1,335	8.8	98.1	358	870	6,872	2,147	3,449	1,277
Oakland, CA	12,455	2,626	42.7	108.3	1,194	1,281	9,828	2,297	5,520	2,012
Honolulu, HI	6,119	272	3.5	37.2	116	116	5,847	1,040	4,406	401
Miami, FL	17,488	3,731	34.2	72.8	1,890	1,734	13,757	3,232	8,195	2,330
Pittsburgh, PA	8,210	1,202	11.8	59.1	800	332	7,008	1,391	3,444	2,173
Cincinnati, OH	8,840	1,567	13.3	131.5	621	802	7,273	1,914	4,786	573
Minneapolis, MN	11,103	1,643	15.9	159.0	815	653	9,461	2,466	5,624	1,370
Toledo, OH	8,714	934	12.7	108.8	448	364	7,780	1,809	4,750	1,221
Buffalo, NY	10,030	1,927	23.0	104.7	907	892	8,104	2,484	3,960	1,660
Wichita, KS	9,123	889	9.4	82.3	432	365	8,234	2,102	5,217	916
Mesa, AZ	7,026	682	3.0	39.5	98	542	6,344	1,481	4,030	833
Colorado Springs, CO	6,819	521	5.7	76.3	151	287	6,299	1,278	4,657	364
Las Vegas, NV	7,353	888	14.6	57.9	532	284	6,464	1,524	3,850	1,091
Santa Ana, CA	6,918	1,060	19.0	23.6	652	366	5,858	1,244	3,234	1,379
Tampa, FL	15,803	3,379	16.8	103.8	1,027	2,231	12,424	3,427	6,482	2,514
Arlington, TX	8,489	756	5.9	53.7	267	430	7,733	1,577	5,073	1,083
Anaheim, CA	6,779	633	12.7	32.6	323	265	6,146	1,434	3,455	1,258
Louisville, KY	6,796	1,082	14.2	43.7	452	571	5,714	1,524	3,207	984
St. Paul, MN	7,676	940	11.8	85.0	300	543	6,737	1,672	4,209	856
Newark, NJ	14,624	3,500	31.3	112.8	1,942	1,415	11,124	2,205	3,899	5,019
Corpus Christi, TX	10,317	957	11.2	53.8	190	702	9,360	1,960	6,746	654
Birmingham, AL	11,950	2,255	48.8	132.9	681	1,393	9,695	2,734	5,591	1,370
Norfolk, VA	8,407	1,005	29.3	96.5	451	428	7,402	1,406	5,186	810
Anchorage, AK	7,056	816	7.0	104.7	200	504	6,240	1,097	4,476	667
Aurora, CO	8,556	1,737	6.8	77.8	287	1,365	6,819	1,272	4,830	717
Riverside, CA	8,553	1,487	9.8	55.3	497	925	7,066	1,872	3,703	1,491
St. Petersburg, FL	10,363	2,316	12.5	78.4	720	1,505	8,047	2,333	4,988	726
Rochester, NY	11,782	1,081	21.0	72.9	653	334	10,701	2,964	6,553	1,184
Lexington-Fayette, KY	6,437	861	7.8	65.8	229	559	5,576	1,233	4,058	285
Jersey City, NJ	8,906	1,985	10.9	40.4	1,122	812	6,921	1,976	2,859	2,087
Baton Rouge, LA	14,261	2,597	24.4	71.2	698	1,804	11,663	2,858	7,074	1,731
Akron, OH	7,611	1,168	10.6	90.1	427	641	6,443	1,480	4,004	958
Raleigh, NC	7,564	1,011	8.9	55.9	413	533	6,552	1,759	4,352	442
Stockton, CA	10,860	1,531	24.2	77.7	700	730	9,329	2,110	5,563	1,656

[1] Crime data are not available for Omaha, NE, in 1992.   ² The rates for forcible rape, violent crime, and crime index are not shown because the forcible rape figures were not in accordance with national Uniform Crime Reporting guidelines.

Source: U.S. Federal Bureau of Investigation, *Crime in the United States,* annual.

No. 305. Murder—Circumstances and Weapons Used or Cause of Death: 1980 to 1992

[Based solely on police investigation. For definition of murder, see text, section 5]

CHARACTERISTIC	1980	1990	1991	1992	CHARACTERISTIC	1980	1990	1991	1992
Murders, total	**21,860**	**20,273**	**21,676**	**22,540**	Other motives.	20.6	19.4	19.7	19.1
Percent distribution . . .	100.0	100.0	100.0	100.0	Unknown	15.1	24.8	25.9	27.6
CIRCUMSTANCES					TYPE OF WEAPON OR CAUSE OF DEATH				
Felonies, total.	17.7	20.8	21.4	21.7					
Robbery	10.8	9.2	10.3	10.0	Guns.	62.4	64.3	66.3	68.2
Narcotics	1.7	6.7	6.2	5.7	Handguns.	45.8	49.8	53.0	55.4
Sex offenses	1.5	1.1	0.9	0.9	Cutting or stabbing . . .	19.3	17.4	15.8	14.5
Other felonies	3.7	3.7	4.0	5.1	Blunt objects [1]	5.0	5.4	5.1	4.6
Suspected felonies . . .	6.7	0.7	1.0	1.2	Personal weapons [2] . . .	5.9	5.5	5.5	5.0
Argument, total	39.9	34.4	32.0	30.4	Strangulations,				
Property or money . .	2.6	2.5	2.4	2.1	asphyxiations	2.3	2.0	2.0	1.9
Romantic triangle . . .	2.3	2.0	1.4	1.5	Fire.	1.3	1.4	0.9	0.9
Other arguments . . .	35.0	29.8	28.2	26.7	All other [3]	3.8	4.0	4.3	5.0

[1] Refers to club, hammer, etc. [2] Hands, fists, feet, etc. [3] Includes poison, drowning, explosives, narcotics, and unknown.
Source: U.S. Federal Bureau of Investigation, *Crime in the United States*, annual.

No. 306. Murder Victims, by Age, Sex, and Race: 1992

AGE	Total	Sex			Race			
		Male	Female	Unknown	White	Black	Other	Unknown
Total	**22,540**	**17,576**	**4,936**	**28**	**10,647**	**11,175**	**548**	**170**
Percent distribution	100.0	78.0	21.9	0.1	47.2	49.6	2.4	0.8
Under 18 yrs. old	2,428	1,748	679	1	1,103	1,240	72	13
18 yrs. old and over.	19,803	15,608	4,193	2	9,409	9,820	469	105
Infant (under 1 yr. old)	254	137	116	1	147	99	3	5
1 to 4 yrs. old.	408	237	171	-	204	192	12	-
5 to 9 yrs. old.	126	64	62	-	60	56	10	-
10 to 14 yrs. old	351	230	121	-	163	171	14	3
15 to 19 yrs. old	2,851	2,444	407	-	1,114	1,664	60	13
20 to 24 yrs. old	4,181	3,551	630	-	1,614	2,451	97	19
25 to 29 yrs. old	3,455	2,749	706	-	1,479	1,891	69	16
30 to 34 yrs. old	3,045	2,382	662	1	1,420	1,530	76	19
35 to 39 yrs. old	2,231	1,706	525	-	1,145	1,027	51	8
40 to 44 yrs. old	1,650	1,262	388	-	858	731	47	14
45 to 49 yrs. old	1,072	819	253	-	634	396	35	7
50 to 54 yrs. old	695	519	175	1	406	265	21	3
55 to 59 yrs. old	449	356	93	-	281	146	18	4
60 to 64 yrs. old	412	307	105	-	283	120	6	3
65 to 69 yrs. old	315	205	110	-	187	120	7	1
70 to 74 yrs. old	262	159	103	-	177	80	4	1
75 yrs. old and over.	474	229	245	-	340	121	11	2
Age unknown	309	220	64	25	135	115	7	52

- Represents zero.

Source: U.S. Federal Bureau of Investigation, *Crime in the United States*, annual.

No. 307. Homicide Victims, by Race and Sex: 1970 to 1991

[**Rates per 100,000 resident population in specified group.** Excludes deaths to nonresidents of United States. Beginning 1980, deaths classified according to the ninth revision of the *International Classification of Diseases*; for earlier years, classified according to revision in use at the time; see text, section 2. See also *Historical Statistics, Colonial Times to 1970*, series H 971-978]

YEAR	HOMICIDE VICTIMS					HOMICIDE RATE [2]				
	Total [1]	White		Black		Total [1]	White		Black	
		Male	Female	Male	Female		Male	Female	Male	Female
1970	16,848	5,865	1,938	7,265	1,569	8.3	6.8	2.1	67.6	13.3
1975	21,310	8,222	2,751	8,092	1,929	9.9	9.0	2.9	69.0	14.9
1980	24,278	10,381	3,177	8,385	1,898	10.7	10.9	3.2	66.6	13.5
1981	23,646	9,941	3,125	8,312	1,825	10.3	10.4	3.1	64.8	12.7
1982	22,358	9,260	3,179	7,730	1,743	9.6	9.6	3.1	59.1	12.0
1983	20,191	8,355	2,880	6,822	1,672	8.6	8.6	2.8	51.4	11.3
1984	19,796	8,171	2,956	6,563	1,677	8.4	8.3	2.9	48.7	11.2
1985	19,893	8,122	3,041	6,616	1,666	8.3	8.2	2.9	48.4	11.0
1986	21,731	8,567	3,123	7,634	1,861	9.0	8.6	3.0	55.0	12.1
1987	21,103	7,979	3,149	7,518	1,969	8.7	7.9	3.0	53.3	12.6
1988	22,032	7,994	3,072	8,314	2,089	9.0	7.9	2.9	58.0	13.2
1989	22,909	8,337	2,971	8,888	2,074	9.2	8.2	2.8	61.1	12.9
1990	24,932	9,147	3,006	9,981	2,163	10.0	9.0	2.8	69.2	13.5
1991	26,513	9,581	3,201	10,628	2,330	10.5	9.3	3.0	72.0	14.2

[1] Includes races not shown separately. [2] Rate based on enumerated population figures as of April 1 for 1970, 1980, and 1990; July 1 estimates for other years.
Source: U.S. National Center for Health Statistics, *Vital Statistics of the United States*, annual, and unpublished data.

No. 308. Forcible Rape—Number and Rate: 1970 to 1992

[For definition of rape, see text, section 5]

ITEM	1970	1980	1985	1986	1987	1988	1989	1990	1991	1992
NUMBER										
Total.................	37,990	82,990	88,670	91,460	91,110	92,490	94,500	102,560	106,590	109,060
By force	26,888	63,599	71,060	73,453	73,456	75,441	78,411	86,541	91,522	93,825
Attempt................	11,102	19,391	17,610	18,007	17,654	17,049	16,089	16,019	15,068	15,235
RATE										
Per 100,000 population	18.7	36.8	37.1	37.9	37.4	37.6	38.1	41.2	42.3	42.8
Per 100,000 females	30.4	71.6	72.3	73.9	73.0	73.4	74.3	80.5	82.5	83.5
Per 100,000 females 12 years years old and over..........	46.3	86.3	86.6	88.6	87.5	88.1	89.3	96.6	100.9	100.5
AVERAGE ANNUAL PERCENT CHANGE IN RATE [1]										
Per 100,000 population	(NA)	6.1	3.9	2.2	-1.3	0.5	1.3	8.1	2.7	1.2
Per 100,000 females 12 years old and over..............	(NA)	6.0	4.3	2.3	-1.2	0.7	1.4	8.2	4.5	-0.4

NA Not available. [1] Represents annual average from prior year shown except for 1980, from 1979; and for 1985, from 1984.

Source: U.S. Federal Bureau of Investigation, *Population-at-Risk Rates and Selected Crime Indicators*, annual.

No. 309. Robbery and Property Crimes, by Type and Selected Characteristic: 1980 to 1992

[For definition of crime, see text, section 5]

ITEM	NUMBER OF OFFENSES (1,000)				RATE PER 100,000 INHABITANTS				AVERAGE VALUE LOST (dol.)	
	1980	1990	1991	1992	1980	1990	1991	1992	1991	1992
Robbery, total [1]	**566**	**639**	**688**	**672**	**251.1**	**257.0**	**272.7**	**263.6**	**817**	**840**
Type of crime:										
Street or highway	293	359	387	374	130.1	144.2	153.3	146.7	627	672
Commercial house..........	78	73	80	80	34.6	29.5	31.9	31.3	1,456	1,380
Gas station	23	18	18	17	10.4	7.1	7.1	6.6	474	513
Convenience store	38	39	39	35	17.0	15.6	15.6	13.8	387	402
Residence	60	62	68	68	26.8	25.1	26.8	26.5	1,126	1,123
Bank..................	8	9	11	11	3.8	3.8	4.4	4.4	3,177	3,325
Weapon used:										
Firearm................	228	234	274	271	101.3	94.1	108.8	106.2	(NA)	(NA)
Knife or cutting instrument	73	76	76	71	32.3	30.7	30.1	27.8	(NA)	(NA)
Other dangerous weapon	51	61	64	64	22.8	24.5	25.4	25.2	(NA)	(NA)
Strongarm	214	268	274	267	94.8	107.7	108.5	104.5	(NA)	(NA)
Burglary, total	**3,795**	**3,074**	**3,157**	**2,980**	**1,684.1**	**1,235.9**	**1,252.0**	**1,168.2**	**1,246**	**1,278**
Forcible entry	2,789	2,150	2,200	2,049	1,237.5	864.5	872.4	803.3	(NA)	(NA)
Unlawful entry	711	678	713	692	315.6	272.8	282.8	271.2	(NA)	(NA)
Attempted forcible entry	295	245	244	239	131.0	98.7	96.7	93.7	(NA)	(NA)
Residence	2,525	2,033	2,088	1,973	1,120.6	817.4	828.1	773.4	1,281	1,215
Nonresidence	1,270	1,041	1,069	1,007	563.5	418.5	423.8	394.8	1,180	1,400
Occurred during the night	1,508	1,135	1,165	1,099	669.0	456.4	462.1	431.0	(NA)	(NA)
Occurred during the day	1,263	1,151	1,156	1,123	560.3	462.8	458.4	440.1	(NA)	(NA)
Larceny-theft, total.......	**7,137**	**7,946**	**8,142**	**7,915**	**3,167.0**	**3,194.8**	**3,228.8**	**3,103.0**	**478**	**483**
Pocket picking	85	81	83	78	37.9	32.4	33.0	30.7	366	430
Purse snatching...........	107	82	83	75	47.5	32.8	33.0	29.3	280	292
Shoplifting...............	773	1,291	1,343	1,254	343.0	519.1	532.6	491.5	104	106
From motor vehicles..........	1,231	1,744	1,828	1,792	546.4	701.3	724.7	702.7	544	555
Motor vehicle accessories	1,366	1,185	1,150	1,107	606.2	476.3	456.2	434.0	305	297
Bicycles	715	443	475	469	317.5	178.2	188.4	183.7	233	231
From buildings............	1,187	1,118	1,150	1,107	526.9	449.4	456.2	433.9	788	802
From coin-operated machines ...	58	63	79	72	25.8	25.4	31.5	28.3	139	141
Other..................	1,613	1,940	1,950	1,961	715.7	780.0	773.2	768.9	681	665
Motor vehicles, total [2].....	**1,132**	**1,636**	**1,662**	**1,611**	**502.2**	**657.8**	**658.9**	**631.5**	**4,983**	**4,713**
Automobiles	845	1,304	1,325	1,282	374.8	524.3	525.2	502.5	(NA)	(NA)
Trucks and buses...........	149	238	244	243	66.1	95.5	96.8	95.1	(NA)	(NA)

NA Not available. [1] Includes other crimes not shown separately. [2] Includes other types of motor vehicles not shown separately.

Source: U.S. Federal Bureau of Investigation, *Population-at-Risk Rates and Selected Crime Indicators*, annual.

No. 310. Number and Rate of Victimizations for Crimes Against Persons and Households, by Type: 1973 to 1992

[Data based on National Criminal Victimization Survey; see text, section 5, and Appendix III]

YEAR	PERSONAL SECTOR								HOUSEHOLD SECTOR			
	Total	Violent crimes						Larce-ny—theft	Total	Bur-glary	Lar-ceny	Motor vehi-cle theft
		Total	Rape	Rob-bery	Assault							
					Total	Aggra-vated	Simple					
NUMBER (1,000)												
1973.........	20,322	5,351	156	1,108	4,087	1,655	2,432	14,971	15,340	6,459	7,537	1,344
1975.........	21,867	5,573	154	1,147	4,272	1,631	2,641	16,294	17,400	6,744	9,223	1,433
1980.........	21,430	6,130	174	1,209	4,747	1,707	3,041	15,300	18,821	6,973	10,468	1,381
1985.........	19,296	5,823	138	985	4,699	1,605	3,094	13,474	15,568	5,594	8,703	1,270
1986.........	18,751	5,515	130	1,009	4,376	1,543	2,833	13,235	15,368	5,557	8,455	1,356
1987.........	19,371	5,796	148	1,046	4,602	1,587	3,014	13,575	15,966	5,705	8,788	1,473
1988.........	19,966	5,910	127	1,048	4,734	1,741	2,993	14,056	15,830	5,777	8,419	1,634
1989.........	19,691	5,861	135	1,092	4,634	1,665	2,969	13,829	16,128	5,352	8,955	1,820
1990.........	18,984	6,009	130	1,150	4,729	1,601	3,128	12,975	15,419	5,148	8,304	1,968
1991.........	19,472	6,587	174	1,203	5,210	1,634	3,575	12,885	16,025	5,187	8,702	2,136
1992......	18,832	6,621	141	1,226	5,255	1,849	3,406	12,211	14,817	4,757	8,101	1,959
RATE [1]												
1973.........	123.6	32.6	1.0	6.7	24.9	10.1	14.8	91.1	217.8	91.7	107.0	19.1
1975.........	128.9	32.8	0.9	6.8	25.2	9.6	15.6	96.0	236.5	91.7	125.4	19.5
1980.........	116.3	33.3	0.9	6.6	25.8	9.3	16.5	83.0	227.4	84.3	126.5	16.7
1985.........	99.4	30.0	0.7	5.1	24.2	8.3	15.9	69.4	174.4	62.7	97.5	14.2
1986.........	95.6	28.1	0.7	5.1	22.3	7.9	14.4	67.5	170.0	61.5	93.5	15.0
1987.........	98.0	29.3	0.8	5.3	23.3	8.0	15.2	68.7	173.9	62.1	95.7	16.0
1988.........	100.1	29.6	0.6	5.3	23.7	8.7	15.0	70.5	169.6	61.9	90.2	17.5
1989.........	97.8	29.1	0.7	5.4	23.0	8.3	14.7	68.7	169.9	56.4	94.4	19.2
1990.........	93.4	29.6	0.6	5.7	23.3	7.9	15.4	63.8	161.0	53.8	86.7	20.5
1991.........	95.3	32.2	0.9	5.9	25.5	8.0	17.5	63.1	166.4	53.9	90.4	22.2
1992.........	91.2	32.1	0.7	5.9	25.5	9.0	16.5	59.2	152.2	48.9	83.2	20.1

[1] Rate per 1,000 persons, 12 years old and over; and per 1,000 households.
Source: U.S. Bureau of Justice Statistics, *Criminal Victimization in the United States*, annual.

No. 311. Personal Crimes—Victimization Rate, by Type of Crime and Characteristic: 1992

[Rate per 1,000 persons age 12 years or older. Based on the National Criminal Victimization Survey; see text, section 5, and Appendix III]

ITEM	Total	Rape	Robbery	Assault			Larce-ny—Theft
				Total	Aggra-vated	Simple	
Total	**91.2**	**0.7**	**5.9**	**25.5**	**9.0**	**16.5**	**59.2**
Male	101.4	0.6	8.1	30.1	12.0	18.1	62.6
Female	81.8	0.8	3.9	21.1	6.1	15.0	55.9
12 to 15 yrs. old	171.0	1.1	9.8	64.8	20.1	44.7	95.3
16 to 19 yrs. old	172.7	1.6	15.4	60.9	26.3	34.5	94.8
20 to 24 yrs. old	177.0	2.6	11.4	56.0	18.1	38.0	106.9
25 to 34 yrs. old	111.1	0.5	7.7	29.4	9.3	20.1	73.4
35 to 49 yrs. old	75.1	0.4	3.8	17.1	6.8	10.2	53.9
50 to 64 yrs. old	43.3	0.1	2.8	7.1	2.3	4.8	33.3
65 yrs. old and over	21.1	0.2	1.5	3.1	1.3	1.8	16.3
White	88.7	0.6	4.7	24.6	7.8	16.8	58.8
Black	110.8	1.3	15.6	33.5	18.3	15.2	60.4
Other	88.3	0.0	5.1	18.6	5.3	13.3	64.6
Hispanic	100.1	0.6	10.6	26.9	10.0	16.8	61.9
Non-Hispanic..................	90.3	0.7	5.4	25.3	8.9	16.4	58.9

Source: U.S. Bureau of Justice Statistics, *Criminal Victimization in the United States*, annual.

No. 312. Crime Incidents, by Place and Time of Occurrence and Injury: 1992

INCIDENT CHARACTERISTICS	Rape	ROBBERY			ASSAULT			Personal larceny with contact
		Total	Completed	Attempted	Total	Aggravated	Simple assault	
Incidents, total	**131,530**	**1,113,300**	**741,590**	**371,710**	**4,719,250**	**1,594,210**	**3,125,030**	**478,170**
PERCENT DISTRIBUTION								
Place of occurrence	[1]100.0	100.0	100.0	100.0	100.0	100.0	100.0	100.0
Inside own home.	[1]16.3	10.1	9.4	11.6	12.4	9.8	13.7	[1]1.4
Near own home, on the street near home	[1]12.4	11.0	10.9	11.3	11.7	14.0	10.5	[1]5.2
Friend's, relative's, or neighbor's home . .	[1]14.1	[1]3.1	[1]3.1	[1]3.0	8.3	9.2	7.9	[1]4.3
Inside commercial property	[1]1.5	4.2	[1]3.8	[1]5.0	12.2	9.1	13.7	23.2
In parking lot or garage	[1]6.5	13.6	12.2	[1]6.3	7.3	8.0	7.0	[1]3.0
Inside school, on school property.	[1]7.9	3.9	[1]3.6	[1]4.4	14.1	8.1	17.1	8.6
In park, field, or playground.	[1]8.5	6.4	6.6	[1]5.8	4.4	5.1	4.1	[1]1.5
On street not near own or friend's home .	[1]25.9	39.7	44.8	29.5	20.6	27.6	17.1	31.9
Other	[1]6.9	8.0	5.5	13.0	9.0	9.1	9.0	20.9
Time of occurrence:								
Daytime (6 a.m. to 6 p.m.)	40.3	39.5	41.3	35.8	50.2	42.6	54.0	62.9
Nighttime	59.7	58.9	56.7	63.5	49.5	57.4	45.4	35.3
Percent of incidents:								
Involving the presence of a weapon	27.6	54.0	55.4	51.2	31.8	94.1	(X)	(X)
Resulting in victim injury.	(NA)	35.7	41.4	24.7	29.7	35.6	26.6	(X)

NA Not available.   X Not applicable.   [1] Estimate based on about 10 or fewer sample cases.
Source: U.S. Bureau of Justice Statistics, *Criminal Victimization in the United States*, annual.

No. 313. Handgun Crime Victimization Rate, by Sex, Race, and Age: 1987-1992 Period

[Number of victimizations rates per 1,000 population. Rates do not include murder or nonnegligent manslaughter committed with handguns. Based on National Crime Victimization Survey; see Appendix III]

AGE OF VICTIM	MALE VICTIMS			FEMALE VICTIMS		
	Total[1]	White	Black	Total[1]	White	Black
All ages	**4.9**	**3.7**	**14.2**	**2.1**	**1.6**	**5.8**
12 to 15 yrs. old.	5.0	3.1	14.1	2.5	2.1	4.7
16 to 19 yrs. old.	14.2	9.5	39.7	5.1	3.6	13.4
20 to 24 yrs. old.	11.8	9.2	29.4	4.3	3.5	9.1
25 to 34 yrs. old.	5.7	4.9	12.3	3.1	2.1	9.0
35 to 49 yrs. old.	3.3	2.7	8.7	1.7	1.4	3.3
50 to 64 yrs. old.	1.5	1.2	3.5	0.8	0.7	1.6
65 yrs. old and older.	0.8	0.6	3.7	0.3	0.2	2.3

[1] Includes persons of other races not shown separately.
Source: U.S. Bureau of Justice Statistics, *Guns and Crime*, Crime Data Brief, NCJ-147003.

No. 314. Households Touched by Crime, 1990 and 1992, and by Characteristic, 1992

[A household is considered "touched by crime" if during the year it experienced a burglary, auto theft or household theft, or if a household member was raped, robbed, or assaulted, or a victim of personal theft, no matter where the crime occurred. Data based on the National Crime Survey; see text, section 5, and Appendix III]

TYPE OF CRIME	1990		1992						
	Number (1,000)	Percent touched	Number (1,000)	Percent touched					
				Total[1]	White	Black	Urban	Suburban	Rural
Total[2]	**22,652**	**23.7**	**22,093**	**22.6**	**21.9**	**27.2**	**28.1**	**21.4**	**16.9**
Violent crime	4,478	4.7	4,888	5.0	4.8	7.1	6.4	4.6	3.8
Rape	104	0.1	149	0.2	0.2	0.1	0.2	0.1	0.1
Robbery	967	1.0	998	1.0	0.9	2.2	1.8	0.7	0.4
Assault	3,591	3.8	3,975	4.1	4.0	5.1	4.7	3.9	3.5
Theft	15,905	16.7	15,343	15.7	15.5	17.1	19.5	15.0	11.4
Burglary	4,557	4.8	4,116	4.2	4.0	5.8	5.0	3.8	3.7
Motor vehicle theft	1,825	1.9	1,947	2.0	1.8	3.3	3.2	1.8	0.6

[1] Includes other races not shown separately.   [2] Types of crime will not add to "total" since each household may report as many crime categories as experienced.
Source: U.S. Bureau of Justice Statistics, *Crime and the Nation's Households, 1992.*

No. 315. Persons Arrested, by Charge and Race: 1992

[Represents arrests (not charges) reported by 10,950 agencies with a total 1992 population 213,130,000 as estimated by FBI]

OFFENSE CHARGED	TOTAL ARRESTS (1,000)					PERCENT DISTRIBUTION				
	Total	White	Black	American Indian or Alaskan Native	Asian or Pacific Islander	Total	White	Black	American Indian or Alaskan Native	Asian or Pacific Islander
Total	11,876	8,030	3,598	131	117	100.0	67.6	30.3	1.1	1.0
Serious crimes [1]	2,478	1,553	872	23	29	100.0	62.7	35.2	0.9	1.2
Murder and nonnegligent										
manslaughter...........	19	8	11	(Z)	(Z)	100.0	43.5	55.1	0.5	0.8
Forcible rape............	33	18	14	(Z)	(Z)	100.0	55.5	42.8	0.9	0.9
Robbery...............	153	58	93	1	1	100.0	37.7	60.9	0.4	0.9
Aggravated assault	434	259	169	4	4	100.0	59.5	38.8	0.8	0.8
Burglary..............	359	244	109	3	4	100.0	67.8	30.4	0.8	1.0
Larceny/theft	1,290	854	405	14	18	100.0	66.2	31.4	1.1	1.4
Motor vehicle theft........	171	100	67	1	2	100.0	58.4	39.4	0.8	1.4
Arson	16	12	4	(Z)	(Z)	100.0	76.4	21.9	0.8	0.8
All other nonserious crimes:										
Other assaults...........	911	585	308	11	8	100.0	64.2	33.8	1.2	0.9
Forgery and counterfeiting....	89	57	30	(Z)	1	100.0	64.8	33.6	0.6	1.0
Fraud	346	223	119	2	2	100.0	64.6	34.4	0.4	0.5
Embezzlement	12	8	3	(Z)	(Z)	100.0	68.6	29.7	0.4	1.3
Stolen property—buying, receiving, possessing	136	78	57	1	1	100.0	56.9	41.7	0.6	0.9
Vandalism	262	200	57	3	2	100.0	76.2	21.9	1.0	0.9
Weapons; carrying, possessing, etc...........	204	115	85	1	2	100.0	56.6	41.8	0.5	1.1
Prostitution and commercialized vice	87	54	32	(Z)	1	100.0	62.0	36.3	0.6	1.1
Sex offenses (except forcible rape and prostitution)	91	72	17	1	1	100.0	79.1	18.9	0.9	1.0
Drug abuse violations.......	920	546	365	4	5	100.0	59.4	39.6	0.4	0.6
Gambling	15	7	7	(Z)	1	100.0	47.9	45.0	0.4	6.7
Offenses against family and children	84	56	24	1	2	100.0	67.0	29.2	1.2	2.6
Driving under the influence ...	1,318	1,156	133	18	11	100.0	87.7	10.1	1.4	0.9
Liquor laws.............	442	378	47	12	4	100.0	85.6	10.7	2.7	0.9
Drunkenness............	664	535	113	14	4	100.0	80.6	17.1	2.1	0.3
Disorderly conduct.........	605	394	199	8	4	100.0	65.2	32.9	1.3	0.6
Vagrancy	29	15	14	(Z)	(Z)	100.0	50.9	47.5	1.3	0.4
All other offenses (except traffic)	2,950	1,819	1,067	30	34	100.0	61.7	36.2	1.0	1.1
Suspicion	15	8	8	(Z)	(Z)	100.0	49.4	49.8	0.2	0.7
Curfew and loitering law violations...........	74	57	16	1	1	100.0	76.3	21.0	0.9	1.8
Runaways	146	114	25	2	5	100.0	78.5	17.3	1.1	3.1

Z Less than 500.   [1] Includes arson.
Source: U.S. Federal Bureau of Investigation, *Crime in the United States*, annual.

No. 316. Juvenile Arrests for Selected Offenses: 1970 to 1992

[Juveniles are persons between the ages 10-17]

OFFENSE	1970	1975	1980	1985	1987	1988	1989	1990	1991	1992
Number of contributing agencies ..	5,073	7,528	8,178	11,263	10,616	10,077	10,502	10,765	10,148	11,052
Population covered (1,000)......	145,014	156,854	169,439	206,269	202,337	192,275	199,098	204,543	189,962	217,677
NUMBER										
Violent crime, total	54,860	76,131	77,220	75,077	72,829	71,251	84,551	97,103	95,677	118,334
Murder................	1,350	1,373	1,475	1,384	1,592	1,827	2,204	2,661	2,626	3,026
Forcible rape............	3,233	3,457	3,668	5,073	4,909	4,278	4,691	4,971	4,766	5,446
Robbery...............	29,363	39,388	38,529	31,833	27,682	25,459	30,728	34,944	35,632	42,637
Aggravated assault........	20,914	31,913	33,548	36,787	38,646	39,687	46,928	54,527	52,653	67,225
Weapon law violations........	17,111	19,341	21,203	27,035	25,653	27,473	31,480	33,123	37,575	49,907
Drug abuse, total	71,517	136,996	86,685	78,660	71,716	72,303	86,757	66,300	58,603	73,220
Sale and manufacturing.......	(¹)	(¹)	13,004	14,846	18,718	23,174	33,652	24,575	22,929	25,331
Heroin/cocaine...........	10,041	4,902	1,318	2,851	9,315	14,914	19,760	17,511	16,915	17,881
Marijuana..............	35,818	95,027	8,876	8,646	5,922	4,811	6,781	4,372	3,579	4,853
Synthetic narcotics	8,971	3,010	465	414	1,189	846	701	346	570	663
Dangerous nonnarcotic drugs .	16,687	34,057	2,345	2,935	2,292	2,603	6,410	2,346	1,865	1,934
Possession	(¹)	(¹)	73,681	63,814	52,998	49,129	53,105	41,725	35,674	47,889
Heroin/cocaine...........			2,614	7,809	13,428	15,754	19,745	15,194	13,747	16,855
Marijuana..............			64,465	50,582	34,981	28,885	27,253	20,940	16,490	24,992
Synthetic narcotics			1,524	1,085	1,051	1,096	1,115	1,155	885	897
Dangerous nonnarcotic drugs .			5,078	4,338	3,538	3,394	4,992	4,436	4,552	5,145

[1] Prior to 1976, drug abuse arrests were collected with no distinctions between the present day classifications of sales/ manufacturing and possession.
Source: U.S. Federal Bureau of Investigation, *Crime in the United States*, annual.

No. 317. Persons Arrested, by Charge, Sex, and Age: 1992

[Represents arrests (not charges) reported by 10,962 agencies (reporting 12 months) with a total 1992 population of 213 million as estimated by FBI]

CHARGE	Total (1,000)	PERCENT DISTRIBUTION							
		Male	Under 15 years	Under 18 years	18-24 years	25-44 years	45-54 years	55-64 years	65 yr. and over
Total arrests	**11,893**	**81.0**	**5.8**	**16.3**	**28.2**	**47.8**	**5.2**	**1.7**	**0.7**
Serious crimes [1]	2,481	77.9	11.9	29.1	26.9	38.2	3.7	1.3	0.8
Murder and nonnegligent manslaughter.	19	90.3	1.6	14.5	40.5	37.2	4.9	1.7	1.1
Forcible rape	33	98.7	6.1	16.1	27.7	48.5	5.0	1.8	0.9
Robbery	153	91.5	7.5	26.3	35.3	36.5	1.4	0.3	0.1
Aggravated assault	435	85.2	4.7	14.7	27.7	49.8	5.3	1.7	0.8
Burglary [2]	360	90.8	13.9	34.1	29.8	33.7	1.9	0.3	0.1
Larceny—theft	1,292	67.9	14.1	31.1	24.2	37.6	4.3	1.7	1.1
Motor vehicle theft	171	89.2	12.9	44.3	29.8	24.1	1.4	0.3	0.1
Arson	16	86.6	31.9	48.8	18.1	27.3	3.9	1.3	0.5
All other nonserious crimes	9,413	81.8	4.2	13.0	28.6	50.3	5.6	1.8	0.7
Other assaults	913	82.8	6.6	15.8	25.7	51.6	4.9	1.4	0.6
Forgery and counterfeiting	89	65.3	1.4	7.9	33.5	53.3	4.0	0.9	0.3
Fraud	346	57.9	1.2	4.3	27.1	59.5	6.5	1.7	0.8
Embezzlement	12	61.0	0.9	5.7	33.1	52.3	6.6	1.7	0.5
Stolen property [3]	137	87.5	7.8	26.6	35.1	34.8	2.7	0.7	0.2
Vandalism	262	88.7	22.4	45.0	25.2	26.9	2.0	0.6	0.3
Weapons (carrying, etc.).	204	92.5	6.8	22.7	35.6	35.6	4.1	1.4	0.7
Prostitution and commercialized vice	87	34.7	0.2	1.3	26.2	67.1	3.9	1.1	0.5
Sex offenses [4]	92	92.3	9.3	18.2	19.4	47.8	8.2	4.2	2.2
Drug abuse violations.	920	83.6	1.2	8.0	32.1	55.4	3.6	0.7	0.2
Gambling.	15	86.1	1.3	7.2	19.8	42.6	15.4	9.8	5.2
Offenses against family and children.	84	82.0	1.6	4.7	22.9	64.1	6.2	1.6	0.6
Driving under the influence	1,320	86.2	(Z)	0.9	23.3	61.9	9.2	3.4	1.3
Liquor laws	443	80.7	2.2	22.0	22.0	53.1	20.1	3.1	1.2	0.5
Drunkenness	664	89.2	0.3	2.3	21.9	60.2	10.1	4.0	1.5
Disorderly conduct.	605	79.4	6.2	18.1	32.0	43.4	4.4	1.4	0.7
Vagrancy.	29	90.2	4.0	11.8	19.3	55.9	9.2	3.1	0.7
Suspicion.	15	82.6	12.2	32.4	23.0	40.2	3.4	0.7	0.2
Curfew, loitering (juveniles)	75	73.2	30.2	100.0	(X)	(X)	(X)	(X)	(X)
Runaways (juveniles)	146	43.2	44.6	100.0	(X)	(X)	(X)	(X)	(X)
All other offenses, except traffic.	2,954	82.9	2.9	10.0	30.3	52.4	5.2	1.5	0.6

X Not applicable.   Z Less than .05 percent.   [1] Includes arson arrests, a newly established index offense in 1979. [2] Breaking or entering.   [3] Buying, receiving, possessing.   [4] Excludes forcible rape and prostitution, shown separately.

Source: U.S. Federal Bureau of Investigation, *Crime in the United States*, annual.

No. 318. Drug Use Among Persons Arrested—Percent Testing Positive, by Sex and Selected City: 1992 and 1993

[Based on the Drug Use Forecasting System, which measures drug use among persons arrested for primarily serious nondrug crimes. The program obtains voluntary, confidential urinalysis specimens from a new sample of arrestees each quarter]

CITY	MALES					FEMALES				
	April-June 1992	July-Sept. 1992	Oct.-Dec. 1992	Jan.-Mar. 1993	Apr.-June 1993	April-June 1992	July-Sept. 1992	Oct.-Dec. 1992	Jan.-Mar. 1993	Apr.-June 1993
Birmingham, AL	65	67	55	67	60	52	50	64	48	59
Chicago, IL	75	65	72	79	73	(NA)	(NA)	(NA)	(NA)	(NA)
Cleveland, OH	64	65	65	62	65	76	65	76	83	68
Dallas, TX.	60	60	56	58	64	64	71	70	70	56
Denver, CO.	56	59	59	64	67	55	69	63	71	64
Detroit, MI.	52	55	57	65	61	68	74	72	72	81
Ft. Lauderdale, FL . .	62	63	62	62	68	62	55	55	56	58
Houston, TX	60	50	67	68	60	58	58	44	38	61
Indianapolis, IN	46	52	58	53	58	51	47	52	51	56
Kansas City, MO . . .	62	56	67	(NA)	(NA)	76	70	73	(NA)	(NA)
Los Angeles, CA . . .	69	62	67	65	66	77	67	72	77	78
New Orleans, LA . . .	61	65	56	64	60	58	48	46	46	44
New York, NY	77	77	(NA)	76	82	82	83	(NA)	80	86
Omaha, NE.	50	48	48	51	59	(NA)	(NA)	(NA)	(NA)	(NA)
Philadelphia, PA. . . .	75	80	79	79	78	80	79	74	84	79
Phoenix, AZ	48	54	52	60	68	63	66	58	54	75
Portland, OR	57	63	63	66	62	68	81	80	88	67
St. Louis, MO	65	61	66	58	70	65	70	71	62	68
San Antonio, TX. . . .	57	48	58	56	55	61	50	31	44	43
San Diego, CA	79	77	74	79	80	66	78	70	85	72
San Jose, CA	50	50	52	54	59	54	67	58	43	46
Washington, DC. . . .	59	62	64	62	58	73	71	67	69	65

NA Not available.
Source: U.S. National Institute of Justice, *Drug Use Forecasting*, quarterly.

No. 319. Drug Arrest Rates for Drug Abuse Violations, 1980 to 1992, and by Region, 1992

[Rate per 100,000 inhabitants. Based on Bureau of the Census estimated resident population as of **July 1,** except 1980 and 1990, enumerated as of **April 1.** For composition of regions, see table 26]

OFFENSE	1980	1985	1990	1991	1992 Total	North-east	Mid-west	South	West
Drug arrest rate, total	256.0	346.2	435.3	400.6	430.9	481.7	253.8	407.7	559.2
Sale and/or manufacture	57.9	82.0	139.0	133.8	136.5	208.2	76.7	116.6	150.4
Heroin or cocaine [1]	10.8	27.8	93.7	90.1	88.7	170.1	28.8	72.9	88.0
Marijuana	28.4	36.4	26.4	24.6	28.2	27.3	20.0	28.0	35.7
Synthetic or manufactured drugs	2.8	2.6	2.7	3.1	3.0	5.3	1.6	3.2	1.7
Other dangerous nonnarcotic drugs	15.9	15.2	16.2	16.0	16.7	5.6	26.3	12.4	25.0
Possession	198.1	264.1	296.3	266.8	294.3	273.5	177.2	291.1	408.7
Heroin or cocaine [1]	22.2	74.4	144.4	131.3	139.8	157.4	59.7	126.5	206.6
Marijuana	146.2	156.1	104.9	89.6	109.9	99.8	92.6	136.5	93.0
Synthetic or manufactured drugs	6.7	5.6	6.6	5.6	5.1	5.7	2.6	7.2	3.5
Other dangerous nonnarcotic drugs	23.0	28.1	40.4	40.3	39.6	10.6	22.2	20.9	105.6

[1] Includes other derivatives such as morphine, heroin, and codeine.

Source: U.S. Federal Bureau of Investigation, *Crime in the United States,* annual.

No. 320. Drug Removals, Laboratory Seizures, and Persons Indicted, by DEA: 1985 to 1993

[Represents domestic drug removals. 1 kg=.454 lbs; du=dosage unit]

ITEM	Unit	1985	1988	1989	1990	1991	1992	1993
Domestic drug removals:								
Heroin	kg	447	829	629	637	1,124	696	555
Cocaine	kg	18,129	57,113	82,438	73,635	57,080	78,211	56,171
Cannabis (Marijuana)	1,000 kg	745	602	336	149	108	202	162
Dangerous drugs	mil. du	26	114	109	148	532	49	82
Clandestine laboratory seizures	Number	338	810	852	549	408	335	268
Narcotic Title III intercepts	Number	136	129	192	235	256	291	308
Asset removals:								
Total seizures	$1,000	246,344	671,290	975,884	1,106,827	956,960	879,058	668,800
DEA seizures	$1,000	171,888	483,355	659,802	886,184	705,003	669,581	547,800
Seizures through inter-agency cooperation	$1,000	74,456	187,936	316,082	220,643	251,957	209,478	120,999
Arrests	Number	15,727	23,994	25,718	23,082	23,025	24,386	22,500
Convictions	Number	10,519	13,091	15,917	15,662	15,962	17,476	17,000

Source: Drug Enforcement Administration (DEA), *Annual Report.*

No. 321. Authorized Intercepts of Communication—Summary: 1980 to 1992

[Data for jurisdictions with statutes authorizing or approving interception of wire or oral communication]

ITEM	1980	1982	1983	1984	1985	1986	1987	1988	1989	1990	1991	1992
Jurisdictions: [1]												
With wiretap statutes	28	29	31	31	32	32	33	34	37	40	41	41
Reporting interceptions	22	22	20	24	22	24	22	23	25	25	23	23
Intercept applications authorized	564	578	648	801	784	754	673	738	763	872	856	919
Intercept installations	524	518	602	773	722	676	634	678	720	812	802	846
Federal	79	129	205	277	235	247	233	286	305	321	349	332
State	445	389	397	496	487	429	401	392	415	491	453	514
Intercepted communications, average [2]	1,058	1,082	1,107	1,209	1,320	1,328	1,299	1,251	1,656	1,487	1,584	1,861
Incriminating	315	209	229	298	275	253	230	316	337	321	290	347
Persons arrested [3]	1,871	1,725	1,716	2,393	2,469	2,410	2,226	2,486	2,804	2,057	2,364	2,685
Convictions [3]	259	453	521	649	660	761	506	543	706	420	605	607
Major offense specified:												
Gambling	199	150	157	186	206	189	135	126	111	116	98	66
Drugs	282	333	360	483	434	348	379	435	471	520	536	634
Homicide and assault	13	31	31	30	25	34	18	14	20	21	21	35
Other	70	64	100	102	119	183	141	163	161	204	201	184

[1] Jurisdictions include Federal Government, States, and District of Columbia.   [2] Average per authorized installation.
[3] Based on information received from intercepts installed in year shown; additional arrests/convictions will occur in subsequent years but are not shown here.

Source: Administrative Office of the U.S. Courts, *Report on Applications for Orders Authorizing or Approving the Interception of Wire, Oral or Electronic Communications,* (Wiretap Report), annual.

No. 322. Aliens Expelled and Immigration Violations: 1980 to 1993

[For fiscal years ending in year shown. See text, section 9. See also *Historical Statistics, Colonial Times to 1970,* series C 144, C 149, and C 158-160]

ITEM	Unit	1980	1985	1987	1988	1989	1990	1991	1992	1993
Aliens expelled.	1,000	737	1,062	1,113	934	860	1,045	1,091	1,142	(NA)
Deported	1,000	17	21	22	23	30	26	28	38	(NA)
Required to depart	1,000	719	1,041	1,091	911	830	1,019	1,063	1,105	(NA)
Prosecutions disposed of	Number ..	14,863	17,688	18,894	18,360	18,580	20,079	18,882	14,655	14,730
Immigration violations	Number...	14,498	16,976	18,200	17,590	17,992	19,351	18,297	14,138	14,164
Nationality violations	Number...	365	712	694	770	588	728	585	517	566
Convictions	Number ..	12,935	9,833	11,996	12,208	12,561	12,719	11,509	9,865	9,570
Immigration violations	Number...	12,678	9,635	11,786	11,929	12,379	12,515	11,392	9,766	9,344
Nationality violations	Number...	257	198	210	279	182	204	117	99	226

NA Not available.

No. 323. Immigration Border Patrol and Investigation Activities: 1980 to 1993

[In thousands, except where indicated. For fiscal years ending in year shown. See text, section 9]

ITEM	Unit	1980	1985	1987	1988	1989	1990	1991	1992	1993
BORDER PATROL										
Border patrol agents:										
Authorized number	Number...	2,484	3,228	4,812	4,812	4,804	4,852	4,968	4,948	4,853
On duty	Number...	2,329	3,023	3,180	4,074	3,857	4,360	4,312	4,759	4,713
Border patrol obligations	Mil. dol....	82.5	141.9	194.6	205.3	246.4	261.1	295.5	325.8	357.6
Persons apprehended [1]	1,000	766.6	1,272.4	1,168.9	980.5	906.5	1,123.2	1,152.7	1,221.9	1,221.9
Deportable aliens located [2]	1,000	759.4	1,262.4	1,159.0	971.1	893.0	1,103.4	1,132.9	1,199.6	1,199.6
Mexican	1,000	734.2	1,218.7	1,124.6	929.8	832.2	1,054.8	1,095.1	1,168.9	1,168.9
Canadian	1,000	5.3	5.9	4.8	4.3	5.3	5.7	6.7	6.2	6.2
Other	1,000	19.9	37.8	29.6	37.0	55.5	42.8	31.1	24.4	24.4
Number of seizures	Number...	1,920	7,827	7,512	6,643	10,789	17,275	14,693	17,113	17,113
Value of seizures	Mil. dol....	116.1	122.0	590.6	721.2	1,212.7	843.6	950.2	1,247.9	1,247.9
Narcotics	Mil. dol....	110.3	119.8	582.4	700.5	1,191.5	797.8	910.1	1,216.8	1,216.8
INVESTIGATIONS										
Deportable aliens located	1,000	150.9	83.9	31.5	37.0	61.1	64.1	63.6	57.4	60.4
Mexican	1,000	83.3	48.3	15.0	19.9	33.1	35.8	35.5	36.2	38.8
Canadian	1,000	1.5	1.1	0.4	0.4	0.5	0.4	0.5	0.4	0.4
Other	1,000	66.1	34.5	16.1	16.7	28.5	30.0	29.7	20.8	21.1

[1] Covers deportable aliens located and U.S. citizens engaged in smuggling or other immigration violations. [2] Beginning 1988, includes apprehension by the antismuggling unit.

Source of tables 322 and 323: U.S. Immigration and Naturalization Service, *Statistical Yearbook,* annual; and unpublished data.

No. 324. Law Enforcement Officers Killed and Assaulted: 1980 to 1992

[Covers officers killed feloniously and accidentally in line of duty; includes Federal officers. 1988 excludes Florida and Kentucky. For composition of regions, see table 26. See also *Historical Statistics, Colonial Times to 1970,* series H 987-998]

ITEM	1980	1985	1986	1987	1988	1989	1990	1991	1992
OFFICERS KILLED									
Total killed	165	148	133	148	155	145	132	123	128
Northeast	31	19	15	24	17	23	13	16	16
Midwest	23	23	20	31	18	22	20	26	15
South	72	64	63	51	77	68	68	55	68
West	32	29	29	40	39	23	23	17	23
Puerto Rico	6	10	6	2	-	8	8	8	6
Outlying areas, foreign countries	1	3	-	-	4	1	-	1	-
ASSAULTS									
Population (1,000) [1]	182,288	198,935	196,030	190,025	186,418	189,641	199,065	191,397	217,997
Number of—									
Agencies represented	9,235	9,906	9,755	8,957	8,866	9,213	9,483	9,263	10,682
Police officers	345,554	389,808	380,249	378,977	369,743	380,232	412,314	405,069	460,430
Total assaulted	57,847	61,724	64,259	63,842	58,752	62,172	71,794	62,852	81,252
Firearm	3,295	2,793	2,852	2,789	2,759	3,154	3,662	3,532	4,455
Knife or cutting instrument	1,653	1,715	1,614	1,561	1,367	1,379	1,641	1,493	2,095
Other dangerous weapon	5,415	5,263	5,721	5,685	5,573	5,778	7,390	7,014	8,604
Hands, fists, feet, etc	47,484	51,953	54,072	53,807	49,053	51,861	59,101	50,813	66,098

- Represents zero. [1] Represents the number of persons covered by agencies shown.

Source: U.S. Federal Bureau of Investigation, *Law Enforcement Officers Killed and Assaulted,* annual.

No. 325. Criminal Justice System—Public Expenditures and Employment, by Activity and Level of Government: 1990

[Based on a sample survey of local governments. Data for State governments were compiled from State financial records and for the Federal Government from the *Budget of the United States Government*]

TYPE OF GOVERNMENT	Total	ACTIVITY					
		Police protection	Judicial	Legal services	Public defense	Corrections	Other justice
TOTAL EXPENDITURES [1] (mil. dol.)							
All governments [2]	74,249	31,805	9,307	5,500	1,742	24,961	934
Federal government	10,059	4,020	1,553	1,518	406	1,597	964
State and local government [2]	64,918	27,784	7,754	3,982	1,336	23,504	557
State government	28,005	5,197	3,478	1,451	604	16,693	582
Local government	39,667	23,081	4,635	2,686	788	8,244	233
FULL-TIME EQUIVALENT EMPLOYMENT (1,000)							
All governments	1,722	800	225	118	16	556	7
Federal government	136	65	22	24	(Z)	22	(Z)
State and local government	1,586	735	203	93	15	534	7
State government	576	121	70	30	7	345	5
Local government	1,007	614	133	63	8	188	2

Z Fewer than 500. [1] Covers direct and intergovernmental expenditures. [2] Totals are adjusted to exclude duplication from intergovernmental expenditures.

Source: U.S. Bureau of Justice Statistics, *Justice Expenditure and Employment in the U.S., 1990.*

No. 326. State and Local Government Police Protection and Correction—Employment and Expenditures: 1991

[Employment as of **October**. Expenditures for fiscal years. Local government data are estimates subject to sampling variation; see Appendix III and source]

REGION, DIVISION, AND STATE	FULL-TIME EQUIVALENT EMPLOYMENT			EXPENDI-TURES		REGION, DIVISION, AND STATE	FULL-TIME EQUIVALENT EMPLOYMENT			EXPENDI-TURES	
	Total	Per 10,000 population [1]		Total [2] (mil. dol.)	Per capita[1] (dol.)		Total	Per 10,000 population [1]		Total [2] (mil. dol.)	Per capita[1] (dol.)
		Police protection	Correction					Police protection	Correction		
U.S.	1,228,464	28.0	20.7	75,506	299	DC.	9,963	89.0	77.6	754	1,261
						VA.	29,324	24.2	22.4	1,636	260
Northeast. . . .	274,921	32.0	21.9	18,367	361	WV	4,286	16.3	7.5	212	118
N.E.	55,825	27.8	14.6	3,904	296	NC	32,265	25.7	22.2	1,559	231
ME.	4,696	23.8	14.2	233	189	SC	17,570	25.0	24.4	797	224
NH.	4,360	26.6	12.9	257	233	GA.	35,852	27.6	26.5	1,763	266
VT	1,907	21.7	11.9	105	185	FL	85,083	33.9	30.2	4,697	354
MA.	25,476	28.9	13.8	1,882	315	**E.S.C.**	63,114	23.6	17.5	2,902	189
RI	4,762	29.7	17.7	288	287	KY	14,648	21.0	18.5	704	190
CT	14,624	28.1	16.3	1,139	346	TN	22,439	25.0	20.3	1,094	221
M.A.	219,096	33.5	24.5	14,463	383	AL	16,662	25.5	15.3	756	185
NY	124,608	37.1	31.9	9,013	499	MS	9,365	22.0	14.2	348	134
NJ	47,759	39.4	22.2	2,712	349	**W.S.C**	129,892	26.5	21.3	6,094	224
PA	46,729	24.4	14.6	2,738	229	AR	8,786	21.5	15.6	337	142
						LA	21,495	27.9	22.6	1,024	241
Midwest.	252,255	26.2	15.7	14,539	241	OK	14,311	27.6	17.5	619	195
E.N.C	184,071	27.1	16.3	10,931	258	TX	85,300	26.6	22.5	4,114	237
OH.	43,256	25.0	14.5	2,728	249						
IN	22,299	23.3	16.4	970	173	**West**	263,893	27.3	21.5	20,217	374
IL	59,233	34.6	16.8	3,068	266	**Mountain.** . .	68,041	28.0	20.5	4,239	302
MI	40,153	23.1	19.8	2,838	303	MT	3,095	24.2	14.1	158	196
WI	19,130	25.8	12.8	1,327	268	ID	4,172	25.8	14.4	205	197
W.N.C	68,184	24.2	14.1	3,608	203	WY	2,377	33.2	18.5	138	300
MN.	14,216	20.5	11.6	1,009	228	CO	15,185	27.3	17.6	978	290
IA	8,868	21.6	10.1	532	190	NM.	8,130	29.3	23.2	440	284
MO	23,314	28.3	16.9	975	189	AZ	20,707	29.6	25.6	1,394	372
ND.	1,911	21.5	8.6	91	143	UT	6,596	22.4	14.9	390	220
SD.	2,342	22.0	11.4	113	161	NV.	7,779	32.9	27.7	536	417
NE	6,364	24.1	15.9	292	183	**Pacific**	195,852	27.1	21.8	15,978	399
KS	11,169	26.5	18.3	596	239	WA	19,904	21.7	18.0	1,310	261
						OR	11,898	22.2	18.5	842	288
South.	437,395	27.4	23.0	22,378	257	CA	155,996	28.4	23.0	13,121	432
S.A.	244,389	29.2	25.8	13,382	301	AK	2,913	27.6	23.5	342	600
DE	3,543	28.1	24.0	223	328	HI	5,141	28.7	16.6	363	320
MD.	26,503	30.4	24.2	1,741	358						

[1] Based on resident population as of July 1. [2] Includes judicial and legal, not shown separately.

Source: U.S. Bureau of the Census, *Public Employment*, series GE, No. 1, annual, and *Government Finances*, series GF, No. 5, annual.

No. 327. Lawyers—Selected Characteristics: 1960 to 1991

[Data based on editions of Martindale-Hubbell Law Directory. Represents all persons who are members of the bar, including those in industries, educational institutions, etc., and those inactive or retired. See also *Historical Statistics, Colonial Times to 1970*, series H 1028-1062]

CHARACTERISTIC	1960	1970	1980	1985	1988	1991
All lawyers [1]	**285,933**	**355,242**	**542,205**	**655,191**	**723,189**	**805,872**
Lawyers reporting [2]	252,385	324,818	(X)	(X)	(X)	(X)
Male	245,897	315,715	498,019	569,649	606,768	646,495
Female	6,488	9,103	44,185	85,542	116,421	159,377
Status in practice: [3]						
Government	25,621	35,803	50,490	53,035	57,742	66,227
Federal	13,045	18,710	20,132	19,989	23,042	27,985
State	4,316	9,293	30,358	33,046	34,700	38,242
City or county	8,260	7,800	(4)	(4)	(4)	(4)
Judicial [5]	8,180	10,349	19,160	21,677	19,547	21,536
Federal	599	878	2,611	3,003	2,846	3,119
State and county	5,301	7,548	16,549	18,674	16,701	18,417
City	2,280	1,923	(4)	(4)	(4)	(4)
Private practice	192,353	236,085	370,111	460,206	519,941	587,289
Individual	116,911	118,963	179,923	216,336	240,141	262,622
Partner	60,709	92,442	144,279	177,392	194,976	213,016
Associate [5]	14,733	24,680	45,908	66,478	84,824	111,651
Salaried	25,198	40,486	73,862	83,843	85,671	93,849
Private industry	22,533	33,593	54,626	63,622	66,627	71,022
Educational institutions	1,798	3,732	6,606	7,254	7,575	8,177
Other private employment	867	3,161	12,630	12,967	11,469	14,650
Inactive or retired	10,887	16,812	28,582	36,430	40,288	36,971

X Not applicable. [1] 1960 to 1970 includes lawyers not reporting and an adjustment (subtraction) for duplications; 1980 to 1991, weighted to account for nonreporters and duplicate listings. [2] 1960 and 1970 includes duplications; 1980, 1985, and figures are weighted to adjust for duplication of entries. [3] 1960 and 1970, in cases where more than one subentry was applicable, the individual was tabulated in each. In 1980 and 1985 lawyers who were in both private practice and government service are coded in private practice. [4] Data no longer available separately; included with category above. [5] Associates are lawyers designated as such by their employers.

Source: American Bar Foundation, Chicago, IL, 1960 to 1970, *The 1971 Lawyer Statistical Report*, 1971 (copyright); 1980, *The Lawyer Statistical Report: A Statistical Profile of the U.S. Legal Profession in the 1980's*, 1985 (copyright); 1985 and 1988, *Supplement to The Lawyer Statistical Report: The U.S. Legal Profession in 1988*, 1991 and similar report for 1985; 1991 Lawyer Statistical Report: The U.S. Legal Profession in the 1990's, 1994 (copyright).

No. 328. U.S. Supreme Court—Cases Filed and Disposition: 1980 to 1992

[Statutory term of court begins first Monday in October. See *Historical Statistics, Colonial Times to 1970*, series H 1063-1078, for related but not comparable data]

ACTION	1980	1985	1986	1987	1988	1989	1990	1991	1992
Total cases on docket	**5,144**	**5,158**	**5,123**	**5,268**	**5,657**	**5,746**	**6,316**	**6,770**	**7,245**
Appellate cases on docket	2,749	2,571	2,547	2,577	2,587	2,416	2,351	2,451	2,441
From prior term	527	400	476	440	446	384	365	365	379
Docketed during present term	2,222	2,171	2,071	2,137	2,141	2,032	1,986	2,086	2,062
Cases acted upon [1]	2,324	2,185	2,189	2,224	2,271	2,096	2,042	2,125	2,140
Granted review	167	166	152	157	130	103	114	103	83
Denied, dismissed, or withdrawn	1,999	1,863	1,876	1,919	1,973	1,881	1,802	1,914	1,920
Summarily decided	90	78	71	66	75	44	81	52	84
Cases not acted upon	425	386	358	353	316	320	309	326	301
Pauper cases on docket	2,371	2,577	2,564	2,675	3,056	3,316	3,951	4,307	4,792
Cases acted upon	2,027	2,189	2,250	2,263	2,638	2,891	3,436	3,768	4,261
Granted review	17	20	15	23	17	18	27	17	14
Denied, dismissed, or withdrawn	1,968	2,136	2,186	2,210	2,577	2,824	3,369	3,716	4,209
Summarily decided	32	24	38	21	32	35	28	22	25
Cases not acted upon	344	388	314	412	418	425	515	539	531
Original cases on docket	24	10	12	16	14	14	14	12	12
Cases disposed of during term	7	2	1	5	2	2	3	1	1
Total cases available for argument	**264**	**276**	**270**	**280**	**254**	**204**	**201**	**196**	**166**
Cases disposed of	162	175	179	175	173	147	131	130	120
Cases argued	154	171	175	167	170	146	125	127	116
Cases dismissed or remanded without argument	8	4	4	8	3	1	6	3	4
Cases remaining	102	101	91	105	81	57	70	66	46
Cases decided by signed opinion	144	161	164	151	156	143	121	120	111
Cases decided by per curiam opinion	8	10	10	9	12	3	4	3	4
Number of signed opinions	123	146	145	139	133	129	112	107	107

[1] Includes cases granted review and carried over to next term, not shown separately.

Source: Office of the Clerk, Supreme Court of the United States, unpublished data.

No. 329. U.S. Courts of Appeals—Cases Commenced and Disposition: 1980 to 1993
[For years ending June 30. See also *Historical Statistics, Colonial Times to 1970*, series H 1079-1096]

ITEM	1980	1985	1987	1988	1989	1990	1991	1992	1993
Cases commenced [1]	23,200	33,360	35,176	37,524	39,734	40,898	42,033	46,032	49,770
Criminal	4,405	4,989	5,260	6,012	8,020	9,493	9,949	10,956	11,885
U.S. civil	4,654	6,744	6,292	6,210	6,349	6,626	6,663	7,113	7,758
Private civil	10,200	16,827	19,246	20,464	20,626	20,490	20,798	22,862	24,030
Administrative appeals	2,950	3,179	2,723	3,043	2,965	2,578	2,764	3,052	3,824
Cases terminated [1]	20,887	31,387	34,444	35,888	37,372	38,520	41,414	42,933	47,466
Criminal	3,993	4,892	5,039	5,284	6,297	7,509	9,198	9,830	11,043
U.S. civil	4,346	6,363	6,227	6,386	6,127	6,379	6,579	6,797	7,462
Private civil	8,942	15,743	18,338	19,798	20,313	20,369	20,698	21,628	23,437
Administrative appeals	2,643	2,760	3,237	2,625	2,914	2,582	3,148	2,801	3,464
Cases disposed of [2]	10,607	16,369	18,502	19,178	19,322	21,006	22,707	23,162	25,567
Affirmed or granted	8,017	12,286	13,681	14,953	15,240	16,629	17,988	18,463	20,604
Reversed or denied	1,845	2,770	2,924	2,664	2,617	2,565	2,503	2,681	2,514
Other	745	1,313	1,897	1,561	1,465	1,812	2,216	2,018	2,449
Median months [3]	8.9	10.3	10.3	10.1	10.1	10.1	10.1	10.2	10.4

[1] Includes original proceedings and bankruptcy appeals not shown separately. [2] Terminated on the merits after hearing or submission. [3] Prior to 1985, the figure is from filing of complete record to final disposition; beginning 1985, figure is from filing notice of appeal to final disposition. For definition of median, see Guide to Tabular Presentation.

No. 330. U.S. District Courts—Civil and Criminal Cases: 1980 to 1993
[In thousands, except percent. For years ending June 30. See also *Historical Statistics, Colonial Times to 1970*, series H 1097-1111]

ITEM	1980	1985	1987	1988	1989	1990	1991	1992	1993
Civil cases: Commenced	168.8	273.7	239.0	239.6	233.5	217.9	207.7	226.9	228.6
Cases terminated [1]	155.0	268.6	237.5	238.1	234.6	213.4	211.7	239.6	225.2
No court action	68.7	129.4	97.8	79.6	64.3	51.6	44.6	51.4	44.0
Court action, total	86.2	139.2	139.7	158.6	170.4	161.8	166.5	187.6	181.2
Before pretrial	53.8	95.5	95.3	114.7	129.7	127.0	136.9	153.4	152.3
Pretrial	22.4	31.1	32.5	32.2	29.5	25.5	21.1	26.2	21.1
Trials	10.1	12.6	11.9	11.6	11.2	9.2	8.4	8.0	7.9
Percent reaching trial	6.5	4.7	5.0	4.9	4.8	4.3	4.0	3.4	3.5
Criminal cases: Commenced [2]	28.0	38.5	42.2	43.5	44.9	46.5	45.1	47.5	45.7
Defendants disposed of [3]	36.6	47.4	54.2	52.8	54.6	56.5	56.7	58.4	59.5
Not convicted	8.0	8.8	10.2	9.9	10.1	9.8	10.0	10.0	9.2
Convicted	28.6	38.5	43.9	42.9	44.5	46.7	46.8	48.4	50.4
Imprisonment	13.2	18.7	23.3	22.5	24.9	27.8	29.2	31.1	34.2
Probation	11.1	14.4	16.0	16.1	15.0	14.2	13.8	13.1	12.6
Fine and other	4.4	5.4	4.6	4.4	4.7	4.7	3.8	4.3	3.7

[1] Excludes land condemnation cases. [2] Excludes transfers. [3] Includes Guam, Virgin Islands, and Northern Mariana Islands; 1980 includes Canal Zone.

No. 331. U.S. District Courts—Civil Cases Commenced and Pending: 1990 to 1993
[For years ending June 30]

TYPE OF CASE	CASES COMMENCED				CASES PENDING			
	1990	1991	1992	1993	1990	1991	1992	1993
Cases total	217,879	207,690	226,895	228,562	244,570	237,040	215,574	218,396
Contract actions [1]	46,039	42,396	51,246	38,240	42,497	41,588	40,525	34,036
Recovery of overpayments [2]	10,878	7,932	17,475	7,255	4,686	4,663	5,995	2,585
Real property actions	9,505	9,795	10,143	8,436	8,743	7,657	7,743	6,810
Tort actions	43,759	37,287	36,469	40,939	77,998	69,734	45,148	46,785
Personal injury	40,593	34,007	33,147	37,409	74,141	65,792	41,324	43,105
Personal injury product liability [1]	18,679	12,399	10,769	16,545	47,288	39,264	15,208	14,721
Asbestos	13,687	7,142	4,673	4,900	38,849	31,218	7,154	7,053
Other personal injury	21,914	21,608	22,378	20,864	26,853	26,528	26,116	24,635
Personal property damage	3,166	3,280	3,322	3,530	3,857	3,942	3,824	3,680
Actions under statutes [1]	118,465	118,085	128,921	140,811	114,853	117,538	121,964	130,504
Civil rights [1]	18,793	19,337	23,419	26,483	23,791	24,009	26,477	29,179
Employment	8,413	8,144	10,275	12,221	11,490	11,156	12,530	14,386
Bankruptcy suits	5,056	5,013	5,243	6,192	3,941	4,083	4,203	4,922
Commerce (ICC rates, etc.)	2,401	1,556	2,475	1,475	1,441	1,189	1,238	1,149
Environmental matters	958	1,075	1,252	1,077	1,538	1,719	1,943	1,949
Prisoner petitions	42,630	42,476	46,452	52,454	35,793	37,259	39,512	42,956
Forfeiture and penalty	6,193	5,581	5,492	4,832	4,886	4,967	4,850	4,323
Labor laws	13,841	14,684	15,800	16,174	12,112	12,778	13,026	12,859
Protected property rights [3]	5,700	5,231	5,670	6,202	5,448	5,296	5,281	5,559
Securities commodities and exchanges	2,629	2,245	1,998	1,875	4,636	4,555	3,983	3,642
Social Security laws	7,439	7,695	8,415	11,602	8,068	8,154	8,304	11,473
Tax suits	2,604	2,639	2,305	2,267	2,850	2,713	2,255	2,087
Freedom of information	407	363	439	425	451	465	498	478

[1] Includes other types not shown separately. [2] Includes enforcement of judgments in student loan cases and overpayments of veterans benefits. [3] Includes copyright, patent, and trademark rights.

Source of tables 329-331: Administrative Office of the U.S. Courts, *Annual Report of the Director*.

No. 332. U.S. District Courts—Offenders Convicted and Sentenced to Prison, and Length of Sentence: 1992

MOST SERIOUS OFFENSE OF CONVICTION	Offenders convicted	Convicted offenders sentenced to prison	Length of sentence (mo.)	MOST SERIOUS OFFENSE OF CONVICTION	Offenders convicted	Convicted offenders sentenced to prison	Length of sentence (mo.)
Total [1]	51,936	33,622	62.2	Drug offenses [2]	18,698	16,401	82.2
				Possession	1,120	414	21.8
Violent offenses	2,919	2,618	88.5	Trafficking and			
Property offenses	14,217	6,557	19.9	manufacturing	17,578	15,987	83.8
Fraudulent offenses [2]	10,253	5,039	19.4	Public-order offenses	16,101	8,045	47.6
Embezzlement	1,743	718	15.2	Regulatory offenses	2,179	856	35.5
Fraud [3]	7,215	3,669	20.3	Other offenses	13,922	7,189	49.1
Forgery	726	336	18.2	Weapons	3,985	3,426	76.9
Other offenses [2]	3,964	1,518	21.8	Immigration	2,364	1,741	15.1
Larceny	3,086	901	17.0	Tax law violations [4]	1,062	436	19.0

[1] Total may include offenders for whom offense category could not be determined.   [2] Includes offenses not shown separately.   [3] Excludes tax fraud.   [4] Includes tax fraud.
Source: U.S. Bureau of Justice Statistics, *Federal Criminal Case Processing*, annual.

No. 333. U.S. District Courts—Defendants Charged With Violations of Drug Abuse Prevention and Control Act: 1990 to 1993

[For years ending June 30]

ITEM	MARIJUANA				DRUGS				CONTROLLED SUBSTANCES (prescribed drugs)			
	1990	1991	1992	1993	1990	1991	1992	1993	1990	1991	1992	1993
Defendants disposed of	5,139	5,272	5,438	5,615	12,649	12,288	12,776	12,713	1,483	1,667	2,011	3,215
Not convicted	1,011	895	946	870	1,850	1,712	1,807	1,675	222	274	272	422
Dismissed	915	809	850	780	1,506	1,399	1,474	1,415	189	236	233	339
Convicted	4,128	4,377	4,492	4,745	10,799	10,576	10,969	11,038	1,261	1,393	1,739	2,793
By guilty plea and nolo contendere	3,624	3,948	4,056	4,310	8,423	8,479	8,806	9,278	1,020	1,127	1,512	2,430
Imprisonment, total [2]	3,004	3,566	3,585	3,906	9,804	9,669	10,050	10,230	1,030	1,147	1,397	2,412
Regular sentence	2,931	3,552	3,538	3,886	9,551	9,592	9,936	10,005	980	1,142	1,355	2,356
Avg. sentence (mo.)	48.9	68.0	51.4	45.7	86.2	104.0	98.1	96.8	79.3	95.7	105.0	93.3
Other sentences to prison [2]	73	14	47	20	253	77	114.0	225	50	5	42	56
Probation, total	1,054	779	838	754	874	888	831	724	207	229	285	345
Avg. sentence (mo.)	25.1	54.5	32.7	31.1	40.0	55.7	42.4	41.0	32.3	53.4	48.5	36.0
Fine only	39	30	69	84	17	14	88.0	85	8	16	57	36
Other [3]	31	2	1	4	104	5	3.0	2	16	1	-	5

- Represents zero.   [1] Includes defendants committed under 28 USC 2902, Narcotic Addict Rehabilitation Act of 1966.
[2] Split or mixed sentences of prison and probation in the same case as well as indeterminate and Youth Corrections Act sentences are included under total imprisonment and other sentences to prison.   [3] Includes deportation, suspended sentences, imprisonment for four days or less or for time already served, remitted and suspended fines and life sentences.
Source: Administrative Office of the U.S. Courts, *Annual Report of the Director*.

No. 334. Federal Prosecutions of Public Corruption: 1980 to 1991

[As of Dec. 31. Prosecution of persons who have corrupted public office in violation of Federal Criminal Statutes]

PROSECUTION STATUS	1980	1981	1982	1983	1984	1985	1986	1987	1988	1989	1990	1991
Total: [1] Indicted	721	878	729	1,073	936	1,182	1,193	1,340	1,274	1,349	1,176	1,452
Convicted	552	730	671	972	934	997	1,026	1,081	1,067	1,149	1,084	1194
Awaiting trial	213	231	186	222	269	256	246	368	288	375	300	346
Federal officials: Indicted	123	198	158	[2]460	408	563	596	651	629	695	615	803
Convicted	131	159	147	[2]424	429	470	523	545	529	610	583	665
Awaiting trial	16	23	38	58	77	90	83	118	86	126	103	149
State officials: Indicted	72	87	49	81	58	79	88	102	66	71	96	115
Convicted	51	66	43	65	52	66	71	76	69	54	79	77
Awaiting trial	28	36	18	26	21	20	24	26	14	18	28	42
Local officials: Indicted	247	244	257	270	203	248	232	246	276	269	257	242
Convicted	168	211	232	226	196	221	207	204	229	201	225	180
Awaiting trial	82	102	58	61	74	49	55	89	79	122	98	88

[1] Includes individuals who are neither public officials nor employees but who were involved with public officials or employees in violating the law, not shown separately.   [2] Increases in the number indicted and convicted between 1982 and 1983 resulted from a greater focus on federal corruption nationwide and more consistent reporting of cases involving lower-level employees.
Source: U.S. Department of Justice, *Federal Prosecutions of Corrupt Public Officials, 1970-1980* and *Report to Congress on the Activities and Operations of the Public Integrity Section*, annual.

No. 335. Delinquency Cases Disposed by Juvenile Courts, by Reason for Referral: 1983 to 1991

[In thousands. A delinquency offense is an act committed by a juvenile for which an adult could be prosecuted in a criminal court. Disposition of a case involves taking a definite action such as transferring the case to criminal court, dismissing the case, placing the youth on probation, placing the youth in a facility for delinquents, or such actions as fines, restitution, and community service]

REASON FOR REFERRAL	1983	1984	1985	1986	1987	1988	1989	1990	1991
All delinquency offense......	1,030	1,034	1,112	1,151	1,154	1,164	1,207	1,274	1,338
Case rate [1]	38.3	38.7	42.2	43.9	44.5	45.4	47.6	50.0	51.3
Violent offenses.............	55	61	67	73	67	70	77	94	103
Criminal homicide	1	1	1	2	1	2	2	3	3
Forcible rape...............	3	3	4	5	4	4	4	4	5
Robbery...................	24	22	26	26	22	22	23	28	30
Aggravated assault	27	35	36	40	39	43	49	59	66
Property offenses.............	451	442	489	496	498	498	524	538	577
Burglary...................	145	129	139	140	131	128	131	141	149
Larceny	270	276	307	308	314	309	318	321	351
Motor vehicle theft..........	31	31	36	42	47	54	68	69	70
Arson	5	6	7	6	6	7	7	7	7
Delinquency offenses	524	530	555	583	590	596	606	642	658
Simple assault..............	81	73	92	95	100	103	108	121	130
Vandalism	64	69	84	84	83	81	83	93	103
Drug law violations..........	57	65	76	73	73	82	78	69	59
Obstruction of justice	55	63	68	76	79	79	82	85	79
Other [2].................	268	260	235	255	256	251	257	275	286

[1] Number of cases disposed per 1,000 youth (ages 10 to 17) at risk.   [2] Includes such offenses as stolen property offenses, trespassing, weapons offenses, other sex offenses, liquor law violations, disorderly conduct, and miscellaneous offenses.
Source: National Center for Juvenile Justice, Pittsburgh, PA, *Juvenile Court Statistics,* annual.

No. 336. Child Abuse and Neglect Cases Substantiated and Indicated—Victim Characteristics: 1990 to 1992

[Based on reports alleging child abuse and neglect that were referred for investigation by the respective child protective services agency in each State. The reporting period may be either calendar or fiscal year. The majority of States were unable to provide unduplicated counts. Also, varying number of States reported the various characteristics presented below. Excludes the Armed Forces. A substantiated case represents a type of investigation disposition that determines that there is sufficient evidence under State law to conclude that maltreatment occurred or that the child is at risk of maltreatment]

ITEM	1990		1991		1992	
	Number	Percent	Number	Percent	Number	Percent
TYPES OF SUBSTANTIATED MALTREATMENT						
Victims, total [1].....................	801,143	(X)	819,922	(X)	918,263	(X)
Neglect..........................	358,846	44.8	366,462	44.7	474,945	51.7
Physical abuse.....................	205,057	25.6	206,235	25.2	212,281	23.1
Sexual abuse......................	127,853	16.0	129,425	15.8	129,982	14.2
Emotional maltreatment..............	47,673	6.0	46,334	5.7	48,928	5.3
Other and unknown.................	61,714	7.7	71,466	8.7	115,848	12.6
SEX OF VICTIM						
Victims, total	775,596	100.0	816,223	100.0	951,312	100.0
Male............................	360,531	46.5	376,617	46.1	440,493	46.3
Female..........................	409,286	52.8	434,729	53.3	498,952	52.4
Unknown.........................	5,779	0.7	4,877	0.6	11,867	1.2
AGE OF VICTIM						
Victims, total	788,338	100.0	813,057	100.0	950,333	100.0
1 year and younger.................	107,217	13.6	112,227	13.8	127,487	13.4
2 to 5 years old	194,485	24.7	208,183	25.6	250,780	26.4
6 to 9 years old	177,396	22.5	189,124	23.3	221,625	23.3
10 to 13 years old	151,971	19.3	162,049	19.9	187,202	19.7
14 to 17 years old	117,312	14.9	122,603	15.1	141,169	14.9
18 and over......................	7,184	0.9	6,327	0.8	8,009	0.8
Unknown.........................	32,773	4.2	12,544	1.5	14,061	1.5
RACE/ETHNIC GROUP OF VICTIM [2]						
Victims, total	775,409	100.0	818,527	99.9	952,620	100.0
White...........................	424,470	54.7	454,059	55.5	525,399	55.2
Black	197,400	25.5	218,044	26.6	245,777	25.8
Asian and Pacific Islander	6,408	0.8	6,585	0.8	8,007	0.8
American Indian, Eskimo, and Aleut..........	10,283	1.3	10,873	1.3	13,087	1.4
Other races......................	11,749	1.5	12,982	1.6	15,969	1.7
Hispanic origin....................	73,132	9.4	77,985	9.5	90,840	9.5
Unknown.........................	51,967	6.7	37,999	4.6	53,541	5.6

X Not applicable.   [1] More than one type of maltreatment may be substantiated per child.   [2] Some States were unable to report on the number of Hispanic victims, thus it is probable that nationwide the percentage of Hispanic victims is higher.

Source: U.S. Department of Health and Human Services, National Center on Child Abuse and Neglect, National Child Abuse and Neglect Data System, *Working Paper 2, 1991 Summary Data Component,* May 1993; *Child Maltreatment - 1992,* May 1994.

No. 337. Child Abuse and Neglect Cases Reported and Investigated, by State: 1991 and 1992

[Based on reports alleging child abuse and neglect that were referred for investigation by the respective child protective services agency in each State. The reporting period may be either calendar or fiscal year. The majority of States were unable to provide unduplicated counts. Only nine jurisdictions (Alaska, Hawaii, Michigan, Montana, Ohio, Oregon, South Carolina, Vermont, and Washington) provided unduplicated counts of children subject of report. Excludes the Armed Forces]

STATE	1991				1992			
		Reports		Investigation		Reports		Investigation
	Population under 18 years old	Number of reports [1]	Number of children subject of a report	gation disposition, number of children substantiated [2]	Population under 18 years old	Number of reports [1]	Number of children subject of a report	gation disposition, number of children substantiated [2]
United States ...	65,142,000	1,767,674	2,689,193	860,261	66,166,000	1,898,911	2,855,691	991,758
Alabama	1,071,000	28,462	43,969	21,334	1,076,000	28,311	43,246	23,265
Alaska	180,000	[3]8,983	8,983	6,252	185,000	[3]9,892	9,892	8,544
Arizona	1,010,000	26,531	44,844	28,091	1,047,000	29,339	51,216	30,556
Arkansas	626,000	15,860	33,520	8,118	629,000	17,250	36,089	7,538
California	8,163,000	302,834	416,757	71,226	8,423,000	326,120	463,090	73,675
Colorado	883,000	31,796	50,874	8,688	909,000	34,409	55,740	9,237
Connecticut	764,000	14,369	22,080	15,957	771,000	14,369	22,080	15,957
Delaware	168,000	4,367	7,941	2,209	172,000	4,586	8,292	2,157
District of Columbia ...	121,000	5,119	9,444	4,046	117,000	5,596	12,093	3,718
Florida	2,998,000	117,887	184,720	82,386	3,106,000	116,403	180,285	88,563
Georgia	1,775,000	40,142	68,057	43,460	1,800,000	51,225	46,192	46,192
Hawaii	288,000	[3]5,017	5,017	2,191	293,000	[3]5,310	5,310	2,277
Idaho	318,000	9,477	19,507	7,103	324,000	12,230	24,020	6,395
Illinois	2,998,000	67,751	117,912	39,572	3,029,000	74,220	131,592	43,433
Indiana	1,465,000	41,954	63,192	33,329	1,461,000	39,233	58,970	30,283
Iowa	725,000	19,025	27,553	8,154	735,000	19,432	28,094	7,834
Kansas	672,000 [4]	9,133	[4]19,280	(NA)	678,000	[3]22,079	22,079	11,585
Kentucky	959,000	33,505	52,912	24,469	964,000	35,997	56,438	24,437
Louisiana	1,233,000	25,579	44,612	14,997	1,238,000	26,087	47,893	16,050
Maine	310,000	4,080	9,503	4,373	306,000	4,826	10,177	4,927
Maryland	1,201,000	29,254	46,806	(NA)	1,226,000	30,062	48,699	(NA)
Massachusetts	1,374,000	35,614	58,218	28,048	1,384,000	32,286	52,581	24,601
Michigan	2,484,000	49,074	113,932	26,366	2,509,000	51,601	117,316	25,931
Minnesota	1,189,000	17,480	26,663	9,948	1,206,000	17,988	27,462	11,217
Mississippi	751,000	14,377	20,138	7,207	748,000	17,528	32,076	10,712
Missouri	1,340,000	46,343	76,249	22,235	1,350,000	49,286	79,493	24,339
Montana	224,000	7,236	[4]11,029	(NA)	226,000	9,691	14,760	5,328
Nebraska	435,000	7,993	17,087	5,841	439,000	7,961	17,029	5,262
Nevada	321,000	12,858	20,573	7,413	338,000	13,914	22,540	7,699
New Hampshire	280,000	6,550	10,480	2,872	280,000	6,755	10,943	917
New Jersey	1,842,000	[3]53,750	53,750	19,489	1,863,000	[3]50,443	50,443	17,499
New Mexico	458,000	[3]18,234	18,234	5,117	469,000	[3]26,969	26,969	6,716
New York	4,366,000	131,476	212,420	55,586	4,422,000	137,779	228,457	92,238
North Carolina	1,643,000	45,315	71,427	24,636	1,662,000	55,411	88,472	29,546
North Dakota	173,000	3,925	6,435	3,262	172,000	4,515	7,565	3,669
Ohio	2,819,000	88,255	144,218	57,934	2,820,000	95,376	148,101	61,327
Oklahoma	845,000	[3]21,328	21,328	8,287	858,000	[3]24,092	24,092	8,063
Oregon	748,000	23,530	37,648	7,961	766,000	[3]25,622	41,506	8,705
Pennsylvania	2,830,000	[3]23,861	23,861	7,986	2,844,000	[3]25,891	25,891	8,419
Rhode Island	230,000	8,844	13,820	5,919	233,000	8,395	12,886	4,931
South Carolina	938,000	18,956	30,978	10,735	945,000	19,712	33,854	11,348
South Dakota	200,000	[3]11,205	11,205	3,826	204,000	[3]10,486	10,486	2,903
Tennessee	1,230,000	[3]29,715	29,715	10,367	1,246,000	[3]31,231	31,231	11,469
Texas	4,969,000	97,676	153,753	58,199	5,072,000	110,937	174,255	62,342
Utah	642,000	14,534	23,254	10,179	654,000	15,910	27,047	10,875
Vermont	145,000	3,175	2,689	1,437	144,000	2,750	3,205	1,498
Virginia	1,539,000	34,067	50,732	13,702	1,562,000	35,880	55,680	14,472
Washington	1,315,000	39,067	59,311	(NA)	1,355,000	39,704	55,836	41,879
West Virginia	437,000	13,888	22,221	(NA)	438,000	12,932	20,949	(NA)
Wisconsin	1,311,000	[3]44,963	44,963	17,657	1,330,000	[3]47,622	47,622	19,213
Wyoming	136,000	3,260	5,379	2,097	138,000	3,268	5,458	2,017

NA Not available.   [1] Except as noted, reports are on incident/family based basis or based on number of reported incidents regardless of the number of children involved in the incidents.   [2] Type of investigation disposition that determines that there is sufficient evidence under State law to conclude that maltreatment occurred or that the child is at risk of maltreatment.   [3] Child-based report that enumerates each child who is a subject of a report.   [4] 1990 data.

Source: U.S. Department of Health and Human Services, National Center on Child Abuse and Neglect, National Child Abuse and Neglect Data System, Working Paper 2, 1991 Summary Data Component, May 1993; Child Maltreatment - 1992, May 1994.

No. 338. Jail Inmates, by Race and Detention Status: 1978 to 1992

[Excludes Federal and State prisons or other correctional institutions; institutions exclusively for juveniles; State-operated jails in Alaska, Connecticut, Delaware, Hawaii, Rhode Island, and Vermont; and other facilities which retain persons for less than 48 hours. As of June 30. For 1978, 1983, and 1988, data based on National Jail Census; for other years, based on sample survey and subject to sampling variability]

CHARACTERISTIC	1978	1983	1985	1987	1988	1989	1990	1991	1992
Total inmates [1]...........	158,394	223,552	256,615	295,873	343,569	395,553	405,320	426,479	444,584
Percent of rated capacity....	65	85	94	98	101	108	104	101	99
Male.......................	148,839	207,783	235,909	270,172	313,158	356,050	368,002	386,865	403,768
Female.....................	9,555	15,769	19,077	23,920	30,411	37,253	37,318	39,614	40,816
White......................	89,418	130,118	151,403	168,647	166,302	201,732	186,989	190,333	191,362
Black......................	65,104	87,508	102,646	124,267	141,979	185,910	174,335	187,618	195,156
Other races................	3,872	5,926	2,566	2,959	3,932	7,911	5,321	5,391	5,831
Hispanic [2]................	16,349	31,297	35,926	41,422	51,455	55,377	57,449	60,129	62,961
Non-Hispanic...............	142,045	192,254	220,689	254,451	292,114	340,176	347,871	366,350	381,623
Adult [3]...................	156,783	221,815	254,986	294,092	341,893	393,303	403,019	424,129	441,781
Awaiting arraignment or trial......	77,453	113,984	127,059	150,101	175,669	204,291	207,358	217,671	223,840
Convicted	75,438	107,660	123,409	139,394	166,224	189,012	195,661	206,458	217,940
Juvenile [4]................	1,611	1,736	1,629	1,781	1,676	2,250	2,301	2,350	2,804

[1] For 1985, 1987, 1989-1992, includes juveniles not shown separately by sex, and for 1988 and 1990-1992 includes 31,356, 38,675, 43,138, and 52,235 persons, respectively, of unknown race not shown separately. [2] Hispanic persons may be of any race. [3] Includes inmates not classified by conviction status. [4] Juveniles are persons whose age makes them initially subject to juvenile court authority although they are sometimes tried as adults in criminal court.
Source: U.S. Bureau of Justice Statistics, *Profile of Jail Inmates, 1978 and 1989; Jail Inmates*, annual; and *1988 Census of Local Jails*.

No. 339. Federal and State Prisoners: 1970 to 1992

[Based on Bureau of the Census estimated resident population, as of July 1. Prior to 1970, excludes State institutions in Alaska. Beginning 1980, includes all persons under jurisdiction of Federal and State authorities rather than those in the custody of such authorities. Represents inmates sentenced to maximum term of more than a year. See also *Historical Statistics, Colonial Times to 1970*, series H 1135-1140]

YEAR	PRESENT AT END OF YEAR						RECEIVED FROM COURTS					
	All institutions		Federal		State		All institutions		Federal		State	
	Number	Rate [1]	Number	Rate [1]	Number	Rate [1]	Number	Rate [1]	Number	Rate [1]	Number	Rate [1]
1970....	196,429	96.7	20,038	9.8	176,391	86.8	79,351	39.1	12,047	5.9	67,304	33.1
1975....	240,593	113.3	24,131	11.4	216,462	102.0	129,573	61.0	16,770	7.9	112,803	53.1
1980....	315,974	139.2	20,611	9.1	295,363	130.1	142,122	62.7	10,907	4.8	131,215	57.9
1985....	480,568	216.5	32,695	13.6	447,873	187.6	198,499	82.7	15,368	6.4	183,131	76.3
1986....	522,084	230.4	36,531	15.0	485,553	201.4	219,382	91.0	16,067	7.0	203,315	84.0
1987....	560,812	229.0	39,523	16.0	521,289	214.2	241,887	99.0	16,260	7.0	225,627	92.0
1988....	603,732	244.0	42,738	17.0	560,994	227.0	261,242	106.0	15,932	6.4	245,310	99.3
1989....	680,907	274.3	47,168	19.0	633,739	255.3	316,215	127.4	18,388	7.4	297,827	120.0
1990....	739,980	295.0	50,403	20.1	689,577	274.9	(NA)	(NA)	(NA)	(NA)	323,169	128.8
1991....	789,610	309.6	56,696	22.2	732,914	287.3	(NA)	(NA)	(NA)	(NA)	317,237	124.4
1992....	847,271	330.2	65,706	25.6	781,565	304.6	(NA)	(NA)	(NA)	(NA)	334,301	130.3

NA Not available. [1] Rate per 100,000 estimated population.
Source: U.S. Bureau of Justice Statistics, *Prisoners in State and Federal Institutions on December 31*, annual, and *Correctional Populations in the United States*, annual.

No. 340. State Prison Inmates—Selected Characteristics: 1986 and 1991

[Based on a sample survey of about 13,986 inmates in 1991 and 13,711 inmates in 1986; subject to sampling variability]

CHARACTERISTIC	NUMBER		PERCENT OF PRISON INMATES		CHARACTERISTIC	NUMBER		PERCENT OF PRISON INMATES	
	1986	1991	1986	1991		1986	1991	1986	1991
Total [1]..........	450,416	711,643	100.0	100.0	Never married........	241,707	389,302	53.7	55.3
					Married.............	91,492	127,389	20.3	18.1
Under 18 years old.....	2,057	4,552	0.5	0.6	Widowed............	8,343	13,036	1.9	1.9
18 to 24 years old	120,384	151,328	26.7	21.3	Divorced............	81,264	129,913	18.1	18.5
25 to 34 years old	205,817	325,429	45.7	45.7	Separated...........	26,985	44,095	6.0	6.3
35 to 44 years old	87,502	161,651	19.4	22.7	Years of school:				
45 to 54 years old	23,524	46,475	5.2	6.5	Less than 12 years ...	276,309	[2]290,722	61.6	[2]41.2
55 to 64 years old	8,267	16,997	1.8	2.4	12 years or more....	172,386	415,451	38.4	58.8
65 years old and over...	2,808	5,210	0.6	0.7	Pre-arrest employment status:				
Male	430,604	672,847	95.6	94.5	Employed	309,364	476,068	69.0	67.3
Female.............	19,812	38,796	4.4	5.5	Not employed.......	139,097	230,876	31.0	32.7
White..............	223,648	349,628	49.7	49.1	Looking for work ...	80,750	115,590	18.0	16.4
Black..............	211,021	336,920	46.9	47.3	Not looking for work .	58,347	115,286	13.0	16.3
Other races.........	15,412	25,094	3.4	3.5					

[1] For 1986, includes data not reported for all characteristics except sex. For 1991, includes data not reported for marital status, re-arrest, employment status, and years of school. [2] In 1991 the survey question was revised; therefore, the response may not be entirely comparable with 1986 and before.
Source: U.S. Bureau of Justice Statistics, *Profile of State Prison Inmates, 1986*; and *Survey of State Prison Inmates, 1991*.

No. 341. State Prison Inmates, by Criminal History and Selected Characteristics of the Inmate: 1991

[Violent/nonviolent refers to the current or past criminal offense for which the inmate is or was incarcerated; see table 301 for types of violent crimes. Data based on a sample survey of 13,986 inmates; subject to sampling variability]

CHARACTERISTIC	Total	CRIMINAL HISTORY OF PRISON INMATES							
		First-timers			Recidivists [1]				
		Total	Non-violent	Violent	Total	Non-violent	Prior violent	Current violent only	Current and prior violent
Prison inmates, total	697,853	134,131	45,559	88,572	563,722	223,117	88,689	131,289	120,626
Percent of total	100.0	19.2	6.5	12.7	80.8	32.0	12.7	18.8	17.3
Percent distribution	100.0	100.0	100.0	100.0	100.0	100.0	100.0	100.0	100.0
Male	94.5	92.0	89.7	93.2	95.1	92.1	96.5	96.9	97.8
Female	5.5	8.0	10.3	6.8	4.9	7.9	3.5	3.1	2.2
White	49.0	52.6	50.9	53.4	48.2	52.9	40.1	50.4	42.9
Black	47.5	43.6	45.7	42.6	48.4	43.7	56.5	45.6	54.0
Other races	3.5	3.8	3.4	4.0	3.5	3.4	3.4	4.0	3.1
Median age (years)	30	31	30	31	30	29	30	30	32
Median age at first arrest (years)	18	24	25	23	17	18	16	17	16

[1] An individual who has been previously sentenced to probation or incarceration as a juvenile or adult.

Source: U.S. Bureau of Justice Statistics, *Survey of State Prison Inmates, 1991.*

No. 342. Prisoners Under Jurisdiction of State and Federal Correctional Authorities—Summary, by State: 1980 to 1992

[For years ending December 31]

SEX, REGION, DIVISION, AND STATE	1980	1990	1991	1992 Total	1992 Percent change, 1991-1992	SEX, REGION, DIVISION, AND STATE	1980	1990	1991	1992 Total	1992 Percent change, 1991-1992
U.S. . . .	329,821	773,919	825,619	883,656	7.0	DE [2][3] .	1,474	3,471	3,717	4,051	9.0
Male.	316,401	729,840	777,968	833,163	7.1	MD . . .	7,731	17,848	19,291	19,977	3.6
Female . . .	13,420	44,079	47,651	50,493	6.0	DC [2][3] .	3,145	9,947	10,455	10,875	4.0
Federal [1] . .	24,363	65,526	71,608	80,259	12.1	VA . . .	8,920	17,593	19,829	21,199	6.9
State . . .	305,458	708,393	754,011	803,397	6.5	WV . . .	1,257	1,565	1,502	1,674	11.5
						NC [3] . . .	15,513	18,411	18,903	20,454	8.2
Northeast .	45,796	123,464	132,126	138,144	4.6	SC [3] . . .	7,862	17,319	18,269	18,643	2.0
N.E.	9,926	25,151	27,393	28,781	5.1	GA [3] . . .	12,178	22,411	23,743	25,290	6.5
ME. . . .	814	1,523	1,579	1,519	-3.8	FL [3] . . .	20,735	44,387	46,533	48,302	3.8
NH . . .	326	1,342	1,533	1,777	15.9	E.S.C. . . .	21,055	43,451	46,937	48,446	3.2
VT [2] . .	480	1,049	1,118	1,254	12.2	KY . . .	3,588	9,023	9,799	10,364	5.8
MA [3] . .	3,185	8,345	9,415	10,053	6.8	TN . . .	7,022	[4]10,388	[4]11,474	[4]11,849	3.3
RI [2] . .	813	2,392	2,771	2,775	0.1	AL . . .	6,543	15,665	16,760	17,453	4.1
CT [2] . .	4,308	10,500	10,977	11,403	3.9	MS . . .	3,902	8,375	8,904	8,780	-1.4
M.A. . . .	35,870	98,313	104,733	109,363	4.4	W.S.C. . . .	46,488	88,248	92,786	105,180	13.4
NY . . .	21,815	54,895	57,862	61,736	6.7	AR . . .	2,911	7,322	7,766	8,285	6.7
NJ . . .	[4]5,884	21,128	23,483	22,653	-3.5	LA . . .	8,889	18,599	20,003	20,896	4.5
PA . . .	8,171	22,290	23,388	24,974	6.8	OK [3] . . .	4,796	12,285	13,340	14,821	11.1
Midwest . .	66,211	145,894	156,724	167,023	6.6	TX [3] . . .	29,892	50,042	51,677	61,178	18.4
E.N.C. . .	51,175	113,806	122,915	131,988	7.4	West	47,093	154,384	163,196	174,139	6.7
OH . . .	13,489	31,822	35,744	38,378	7.4	Mt.	13,141	37,433	40,094	42,310	5.5
IN [3] . .	6,683	12,736	13,779	13,945	1.2	MT. . . .	739	1,425	1,478	1,498	1.4
IL [3] . .	11,899	27,516	29,115	31,640	8.7	ID . . .	817	1,961	2,143	2,256	5.3
MI [3] . .	15,124	34,267	36,423	39,113	7.4	WY . . .	534	1,110	1,099	1,063	-3.3
WI . . .	3,980	7,465	7,854	8,912	13.5	CO . . .	2,629	7,671	8,392	8,997	7.2
W.N.C. . .	15,036	32,088	33,809	35,035	3.6	NM [3] . .	1,279	3,187	3,119	3,271	4.9
MN . . .	2,001	3,176	3,472	3,822	10.1	AZ [3] . .	4,372	14,261	15,415	16,477	6.9
IA [3] . .	2,481	3,967	4,145	4,518	9.0	UT . . .	932	2,496	2,625	2,699	2.8
MO . . .	5,726	14,943	15,897	16,189	1.8	NV . . .	1,839	5,322	5,823	6,049	3.9
ND . . .	253	483	492	477	-3.0	Pac.	33,952	116,951	123,102	131,829	7.1
SD . . .	635	1,341	1,374	1,487	8.2	WA . . .	[4]4,399	7,995	9,156	9,959	8.8
NE . . .	1,446	2,403	2,526	2,514	-0.5	OR [3] . .	3,177	6,492	6,732	6,583	-2.2
KS . . .	2,494	5,775	5,903	6,028	2.1	CA [3] . .	24,569	97,309	101,808	109,496	7.6
South. . . .	146,358	284,651	301,965	324,091	7.3	AK [2] . .	822	2,622	2,706	2,865	5.9
S.A.	78,815	152,952	162,242	170,465	5.1	HI [2] . .	985	2,533	2,700	2,926	8.4

[1] Includes persons held under other jurisdiction, not shown separately. [2] Includes both jail and prison inmates (State has combined jail and prison system). [3] Numbers are custodial, not jurisdictional counts. [4] Jurisdiction counts exclude prisoners held in jail because of crowding.

Source: U.S. Bureau of Justice Statistics, *Prisoners in 1991,* and earlier reports.

No. 343. Adults Under Correctional Supervision: 1990

[In thousands except rate. As of Dec. 31. Excludes juveniles, persons incarcerated in mental health institutions in lieu of prison, persons held by the armed services, persons held on Indian reservations, parolees under county jurisdiction, parolees whose sentences were for 1 year or less, and court probationers (those not placed under the supervisory authority of a probation agency)]

REGION, DIVISION, AND STATE	Total [1]	Rate [2]	Prison [3]	Parole [4]	Proba-tion [5]	REGION, DIVISION, AND STATE	Total [1]	Rate [2]	Prison [3]	Parole [4]	Proba-tion [5]
U.S.. . . .	4,349.8	235.0	745.2	531.4	2,670.2	DC	25.4	517.4	8.6	5.3	9.7
						VA	55.4	118.3	14.6	9.0	21.3
Northeast . .	783.5	201.4	119.2	128.9	466.0	WV	9.4	69.9	1.6	1.0	5.1
N.E	190.7	188.0	24.6	6.2	151.1	NC	114.6	228.3	18.6	9.9	77.8
ME	11.1	121.2	1.5	0.0	7.5	SC	57.0	222.2	15.6	3.5	32.3
NH	6.0	72.8	1.4	0.5	3.1	GA	201.0	423.0	22.3	22.6	134.8
VT	7.2	171.5	1.0	0.3	5.9	FL.	288.6	286.6	44.0	2.1	210.8
MA	91.2	195.7	8.3	4.7	72.5	E.S.C	167.1	149.2	39.8	24.0	76.1
RI	18.1	232.2	2.4	0.3	15.4	KY	24.7	90.4	8.3	3.2	7.5
CT	57.0	224.7	10.1	0.3	46.6	TN	63.8	174.2	8.5	11.3	32.7
M.A	592.8	206.2	94.5	122.8	314.9	AL.	55.4	185.7	15.4	6.0	27.7
NY	272.5	198.5	54.9	42.8	145.3	MS	23.3	127.7	7.6	3.5	8.2
NJ.	127.2	214.4	17.7	23.3	72.3	W.S.C.	639.8	333.5	81.2	125.8	378.9
PA	193.1	212.5	21.9	56.7	97.3	AR	28.9	166.8	6.6	4.0	16.0
Midwest . . .	838.8	190.4	145.5	65.7	567.8	LA. . . .	66.6	222.4	14.1	8.9	30.2
E.N.C	614.6	197.9	113.3	45.4	410.6	OK	41.1	178.2	10.5	3.2	24.4
OH	132.0	164.0	31.5	7.9	83.4	TX	503.2	414.2	50.0	109.7	308.4
IN	92.3	225.8	12.7	3.8	68.7	West.	891.9	230.4	152.6	99.3	536.2
IL	152.7	180.0	27.5	17.7	95.7	Mountain .	164.1	167.8	37.0	12.1	92.7
MI. . . .	190.7	278.9	34.3	11.9	133.4	MT	7.3	126.1	1.4	0.8	4.1
WI. . . .	47.0	130.3	7.2	4.1	29.4	ID	8.3	119.2	1.8	0.2	4.4
W.N.C	224.3	172.6	32.3	20.3	157.3	WY	4.8	151.4	1.1	0.3	3.0
MN	68.1	212.4	3.2	1.9	59.3	CO	45.7	187.7	6.8	2.4	31.1
IA	22.2	107.7	4.0	2.1	13.9	NM	13.2	123.7	3.4	1.2	6.3
MO	70.9	186.6	14.9	9.2	42.3	AZ	54.2	201.9	14.3	2.7	30.4
ND	2.8	59.6	0.5	0.1	1.7	UT	11.3	103.3	2.5	1.6	5.8
SD	5.7	113.5	1.4	0.6	3.2	NV	19.2	212.7	5.6	2.9	7.7
NE	19.3	168.2	2.4	0.6	14.7	Pacific . . .	727.8	251.5	115.7	87.2	443.4
KS	35.3	194.2	5.8	5.8	22.2	WA	109.2	303.0	7.4	9.6	84.8
South	1,694.9	267.2	267.0	215.8	1,042.0	OR	55.1	260.2	6.2	8.0	37.6
S.A	888.0	268.6	146.0	66.0	587.0	CA	541.3	246.0	97.3	67.6	305.7
DE	16.6	329.3	3.1	1.3	12.2	AK	6.7	176.5	2.4	0.6	3.6
MD	119.9	331.4	17.6	11.2	82.9	HI [6]	15.5	187.0	2.4	1.4	11.7

[1] Includes persons in jail not shown separately.   [2] Rate per 10,000 persons 18 years old and over.   [3] Includes all inmates of Federal and State institutions.   [4] Includes all adults under State parole supervision whether released from prison via parole board decision or mandatory release, who were sentenced to more than 1 year in prison.   [5] Includes all adults who, as part of a State, or local court order, have been placed under the supervisory authority of a probation agency.   [6] Jail population for Hawaii included with prison population.

Source: U.S. Bureau of Justice Statistics, *Correctional Populations in the United States,* annual.

No. 344. Prisoners Under Sentence of Death: 1980 to 1992

[As of December 31. Excludes prisoners under sentence of death who remained within local correctional systems pending exhaustion of appellate process or who had not been committed to prison]

CHARACTERISTIC	1980	1989	1990	1991	1992	CHARACTERISTIC	1980	1989	1990	1991	1992
Total [1]	688	2,243	2,346	2,466	2,594	Unknown	163	263	279	313	315
						Marital status:					
White	418	1,308	1,368	1,450	1,519	Never married.	268	956	998	1,071	1,141
Black and other	270	935	978	1,016	1,075	Married	229	610	632	663	665
						Divorced [2]	217	684	726	746	788
Under 20 years	11	6	8	14	12						
20 to 24 years	173	191	168	179	189	Time elapsed since					
25 to 34 years	334	1,080	1,110	1,087	1,088	sentencing:					
35 to 54 years	186	917	1,006	1,129	1,220	Less than 12 months .	185	231	231	252	265
55 years and over.	10	56	64	73	85	12 to 47 months	389	809	753	718	731
Years of school						48 to 71 months	102	408	438	441	450
completed:						72 months and over. .	38	802	934	1,071	1,148
7 years or less	68	183	178	173	182						
8 years	74	178	186	181	182	Legal status at arrest:					
9 to 11 years	204	739	775	810	841	Not under sentence [3] .	384	1,301	1,345	1,415	1,493
12 years.	162	695	729	783	840	Parole or probation [3] .	115	585	578	615	704
More than 12						Prison or escaped . . .	45	94	128	102	101
years	43	192	209	222	234	Unknown	170	270	305	321	296

[1] For 1980 to 1991, revisions to the total number of prisoners were not carried to the characteristics except for race.   [2] Includes persons married but separated, widows, widowers, and unknown.   [3] Includes prisoners on mandatory conditional release, work release, leave, AWOL, or bail. Covers 24 prisoners in 1989, 28 in 1990, and 29 in 1991 and 1992.

Source: U.S. Bureau of Justice Statistics, *Capital Punishment,* annual.

No. 345. Movement of Prisoners Under Sentence of Death: 1980 to 1992

[Prisoners reported under sentence of death by civil authorities. The term "under sentence of death" begins when the court pronounces the first sentence of death for a capital offense]

STATUS	1980	1983	1984	1985	1986	1987	1988	1989	1990	1991	1992
Under sentence of death, Jan. 1 . .	595	1,063	1,209	1,420	1,575	1,800	1,967	2,117	2,243	2,346	2,466
Received death sentence [1][2]	203	263	296	281	297	299	296	251	244	266	265
White	125	156	173	165	164	190	196	133	147	163	147
Black	77	105	119	114	123	106	91	114	94	101	114
Dispositions other than executions [2]	101	117	69	108	73	90	128	102	108	116	106
Executions	-	5	21	18	18	25	11	16	23	14	31
Under sentence of death, Dec. 31 [1]	688	1,209	1,420	1,575	1,800	1,967	2,117	2,243	2,346	2,466	2,594
White	425	694	809	896	1,006	1,128	1,238	1,308	1,368	1,450	1,519
Black	268	508	595	664	750	813	853	898	940	1,016	1,037

- Represents zero.   [1] Includes races other than White or Black.   [2] Revisions to total number of prisoners under death sentence not carried to this category.
Source: U.S. Bureau of Justice Statistics, *Capital Punishment*, annual.

No. 346. Prisoners Executed Under Civil Authority: 1930 to 1992

[Excludes executions by military authorities. The Army (including the Air Force) carried out 160 (148 between 1942 and 1950; 3 each in 1954, 1955, and 1957; and 1 each in 1958, 1959, and 1961). Of the total, 106 were executed for murder (including 21 involving rape), 53 for rape, and 1 for desertion. The Navy carried out no executions during the period. See also *Historical Statistics, Colonial Times to 1970*, series H 1155-1167]

YEAR OR PERIOD	Total [1]	White	Black	EXECUTED FOR MURDER			EXECUTED FOR RAPE			EXECUTED, OTHER OFFENSES [2]		
				Total [1]	White	Black	Total [1]	White	Black	Total [1]	White	Black
All years	4,047	1,863	2,140	3,522	1,776	1,704	455	48	405	70	39	31
1930 to 1939.	1,667	827	816	1,514	803	687	125	10	115	28	14	14
1940 to 1949.	1,284	490	781	1,064	458	595	200	19	179	20	13	7
1950 to 1959.	717	336	376	601	316	280	102	13	89	14	7	7
1960 to 1967.	191	98	93	155	87	68	28	6	22	8	5	3
1968 to 1976.	-	-	-	-	-	-	-	-	-	-	-	-
1977 to 1980.	3	3	-	3	3	-	-	-	-	-	-	-
1981	1	1	-	1	1	-	-	-	-	-	-	-
1982	2	1	1	2	1	1	-	-	-	-	-	-
1983	5	4	1	5	4	1	-	-	-	-	-	-
1984	21	13	8	21	13	8	-	-	-	-	-	-
1985	18	11	7	18	11	7	-	-	-	-	-	-
1986	18	11	7	18	11	7	-	-	-	-	-	-
1987	25	13	12	25	13	12	-	-	-	-	-	-
1988	11	6	5	11	6	5	-	-	-	-	-	-
1989	16	8	8	16	8	8	-	-	-	-	-	-
1990	23	16	7	23	16	7	-	-	-	-	-	-
1991	14	7	7	14	7	7	-	-	-	-	-	-
1992	31	18	11	31	18	11	-	-	-	-	-	-

- Represents zero.   [1] Includes races other than White or Black.   [2] Includes 25 armed robbery, 20 kidnapping, 11 burglary, 8 espionage (6 in 1942 and 2 in 1953), and 6 aggravated assault.
Source: Through 1978, U.S. Law Enforcement Assistance Administration; thereafter, U.S. Bureau of Justice Statistics, *Correctional Populations in the United States*, annual.

No. 347. Prisoners Under Sentence of Death and Executed Under Civil Authority, by States: 1950 to 1992

[No executions took place in Delaware, Maine, Massachusetts, Michigan, Minnesota, Montana, New Hampshire, North Dakota, Rhode Island, South Dakota, and Wisconsin from 1950 to 1991. Maine, Minnesota, and Wisconsin never authorized the death penalty during the period. New Hampshire and Rhode Island authorized it for most of the 4 decades but did not apply it. Michigan abolished the penalty in 1963, and North Dakota allowed the these data after receiving statehood in 1959, but neither has authorized the death penalty]

STATE	1950 to 1969	1977 to 1989[1]	1990	1991	1992	STATE	1950 to 1969	1977 to 1989[1]	1990	1991	1992	STATE	1950 to 1969	1977 to 1989[1]	1990	1991	1992
U.S.[2]	**908**	**120**	**23**	**14**	**31**	IA	3	-	-	-	-	OH . . .	39	-	-	-	-
AL . . .	25	7	1	-	2	KS	10	-	-	-	-	OK . . .	13	-	1	-	2
AZ . . .	12	-	-	-	1	KY . . .	17	-	-	-	-	OR . . .	5	-	-	-	-
AR . . .	27	-	2	-	2	LA . . .	28	18	1	1	-	PA . . .	34	-	-	-	-
CA . . .	104	-	-	-	1	MD . . .	7	-	-	-	-	SC . . .	34	2	1	1	-
CO . . .	9	-	-	-	-	MS . . .	46	4	-	-	-	TN . . .	9	-	-	-	-
CT . . .	6	-	-	-	-	MO . . .	11	1	4	1	1	TX . . .	103	33	4	5	13
DC . . .	4	-	-	-	-	NE . . .	2	-	-	-	-	UT . . .	7	3	-	-	1
FL . . .	61	21	4	2	2	NV . . .	11	4	1	-	-	VT . . .	2	-	-	-	-
GA . . .	99	14	-	1	-	NJ . . .	20	-	-	-	-	VA . . .	29	-	3	2	4
ID . . .	3	-	-	-	-	NM . . .	4	-	-	-	-	WA . . .	8	-	-	-	-
IL . . .	11	-	1	-	-	NY . . .	62	-	-	-	-	WV . . .	9	-	-	-	-
IN . . .	3	2	-	-	-	NC . . .	20	3	-	1	-	WY . . .	1	-	-	-	1

- Represents zero.   [1] No executions occurred during the period 1970 to 1976.   [2] Includes 10 Federal executions not shown by State (1950 to 1959, 9; and 1960 to 1969, 1).
Source: Through 1978, U.S. Law Enforcement Assistance Administration; thereafter, U.S. Bureau of Justice Statistics, *Capital Punishment*, annual.

No. 348. Fire Losses—Total and Per Capita: 1970 to 1992

[Includes allowance for uninsured and unreported losses but excludes losses to government property and forests. Represents incurred losses]

YEAR	Total (mil. dol.)	Per capita [1]	YEAR	Total (mil. dol.)	Per capita [1]	YEAR	Total (mil. dol.)	Per capita [1]
1970.	2,328	11.41	1978.	4,008	18.05	1986.	8,488	35.21
1971.	2,316	11.20	1979.	4,851	21.60	1987.	8,634	35.44
1972.	2,304	11.01	1980.	5,579	24.55	1988.	9,626	39.11
1973.	2,639	12.49	1981.	5,625	24.50	1989.	9,514	38.33
1974.	3,190	14.95	1982.	5,894	25.41	1990.	9,495	38.18
1975.	3,190	14.81	1983.	6,320	26.98	1991.	11,302	44.82
1976.	3,558	16.35	1984.	7,602	32.15	1992.	12,305	48.24
1977.	3,764	17.13	1985.	7,753	32.47			

[1] Based on Bureau of the Census estimated resident population as of July 1.

Source: 1960, National Board of Fire Underwriters, New York, NY, *Report of the Committee on Statistics and Origin of Losses;* thereafter, Insurance Information Institute, New York, NY, *Insurance Facts,* annual.

No. 349. Fires—Number and Loss, by Type and Property Use: 1989 to 1992

[Based on annual sample survey of fire departments. No adjustments were made for unreported fires and losses. Property loss includes direct property loss only]

TYPE AND PROPERTY USE	NUMBER (1,000)				PROPERTY LOSS (mil. dol.)			
	1989	1990	1991	1992	1989	1990	1991	1992
Fires, total	2,115	2,019	2,041	1,965	8,655	7,818	9,467	8,295
Structure.	688	624	640	638	7,518	6,713	8,320	6,957
Outside of structure [1]	55	52	54	50	132	90	55	318
Brush and rubbish	819	787	806	743	-	-	-	-
Vehicle.	435	436	428	405	963	967	1,049	965
Other	118	120	113	129	42	48	43	55
Structure by property use:								
Public assembly	18	17	16	17	286	317	362	361
Educational	9	9	9	10	116	136	58	68
Institutional	12	11	12	12	43	33	28	35
Stores and offices	35	31	33	33	703	603	[2]931	[3]1,105
Residential.	513	467	478	472	3,998	4,253	[4]5,552	3,880
1-2 family units [5]	402	359	363	358	3,335	3,534	3,354	3,178
Apartments	96	95	102	101	541	623	609	597
Hotels and motels	7	6	6	6	87	66	52	56
Other residential	8	7	7	7	35	30	37	49
Storage [6]	44	40	44	42	673	534	594	734
Industry, utility, defense [6]	25	22	19	19	[7]1,406	623	605	597
Special structures	32	27	29	33	293	214	190	177

- Represents zero.   [1] Includes outside storage, crops, timber, etc.   [2] Includes one large store and office fire totaling $325 million.   [3] Includes estimated loss of $567 involving 862 structures from the April 1992 civil disturbance in Los Angeles, CA.   [4] Includes the Oakland, CA fire which resulted in $1.5 billion in residential property damage.   [5] Includes mobile homes.   [6] Data underreported as some incidents were handled by private fire brigades or fixed suppression systems which do not report.   [7] Includes one large industrial fire totaling $750 million.

Source: National Fire Protection Association, Quincy, MA, "NFPA Reports on U.S. Fire Loss — 1992," *NFPA Journal,* September 1993, and prior issues (copyright 1993).

No. 350. Fires and Property Loss for Incendiary and Suspicious Fires and Civilian Fire Deaths and Injuries, by Selected Property Type: 1989 to 1992

[Based on sample survey of fire departments]

ITEM	1989	1990	1991	1992	ITEM	1989	1990	1991	1992
NUMBER (1,000)					**CIVILIAN FIRE DEATHS**				
Structure fires, total	688	624	640	638	Deaths, total [2]	5,410	5,195	4,465	4,730
Structure fires of incendiary or suspicious origin	97	97	98	94	Residential property	4,435	4,115	3,575	3,765
					One- and two-family dwellings	3,545	3,370	2,905	3,160
Fires of incendiary origin	59	58	62	58	Apartments	790	680	595	545
Fires of suspicious origin	38	39	36	36	Vehicles	685	695	605	730
PROPERTY LOSS [1] (mil. dol.)					**CIVILIAN FIRE INJURIES**				
Structure fires, total	7,518	6,713	8,320	6,957	Injuries, total [2]	28,250	28,600	29,375	28,700
Structure fires of incendiary or suspicious origin	1,558	1,394	1,531	1,999	Residential property	20,750	20,650	21,850	21,600
					One- and two-family dwellings	15,225	15,250	15,600	15,275
Fires of incendiary origin	1,057	875	1,072	[3]1,493	Apartments	5,050	4,975	5,675	5,825
Fires of suspicious origin	501	519	459	506	Vehicles	3,025	3,350	3,050	3,000

[1] Direct property loss only.   [2] Includes other not shown separately.   [3] Includes estimated loss of $567 from the April 1992 civil disturbance in Los Angeles, CA.

Source: National Fire Protection Association, Quincy, MA, "NFPA Reports on Fire Loss — 1992," *NFPA Journal,* September 1993, and prior issues (copyright 1993).

Figure 6.1
National Air Pollutant Emissions: 1970 to 1992

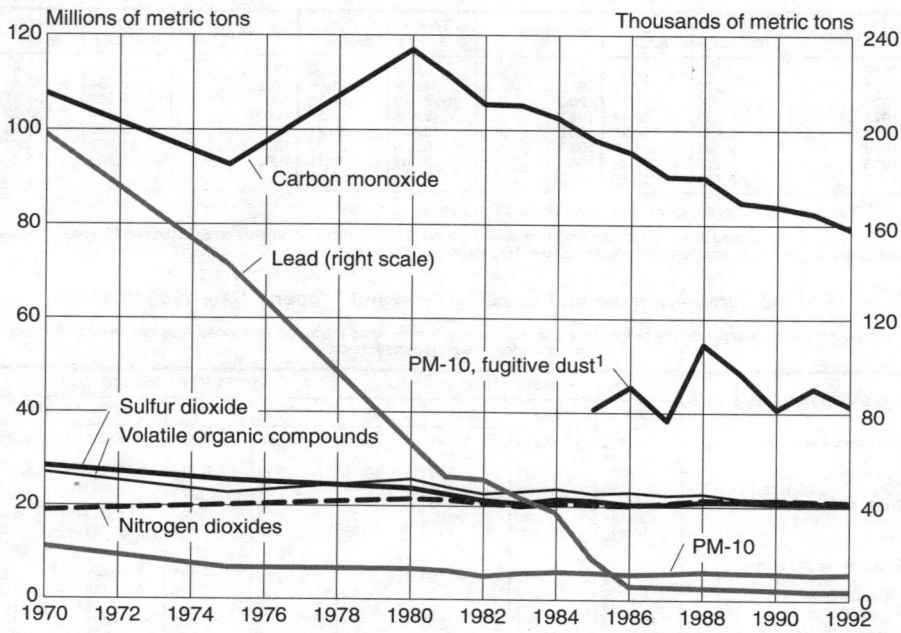

¹ PM-10=Particulate matter of less than ten microns. From sources such as agricultural tilling, construction, mining and quarrying, paved and unpaved roads, and wind erosion.
Source: Chart prepared by U.S. Bureau of the Census. For data, see table 364.

Figure 6.2
Toxic Releases—Top 10 Industries: 1992

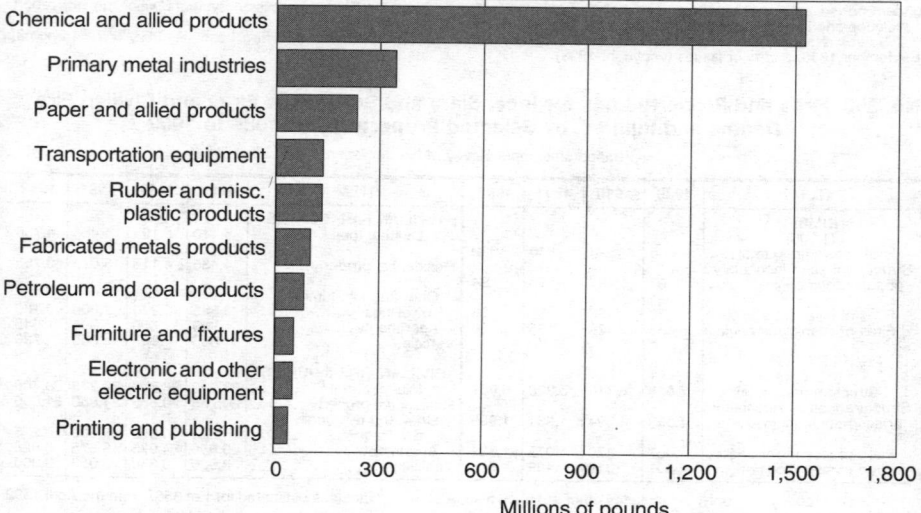

Source: Chart prepared by U.S. Bureau of the Census. For data, see table 369.

Geography and Environment

This section presents a variety of information on the physical environment of the United States, starting with basic area measurement data and ending with climatic data for selected weather stations around the country. The subjects covered between those points are mostly concerned with environmental trends, but include such related subjects as land use, water consumption, air pollutant emissions, toxic releases, oil spills, hazardous waste sites, threatened and endangered wildlife, and expenditures for pollution abatement and control. New water area figures appear in table 357 for the first time since the 1940 census.

The information in this section is selected from a wide range of Federal agencies that compile the data for various administrative or regulatory purposes, such as the Environmental Protection Agency, Geological Survey, National Oceanic and Atmospheric Administration, Soil Conservation Service, and General Services Administration. Other agencies include the Bureau of the Census, which presents nationwide area measurement information and the Bureau of Economic Analysis, which compiles data on pollution abatement and control expenditures.

Area.—For the 1990 census, area measurements were calculated by computer based on the information contained in a single, consistent geographic data base, the TIGER File (described below), rather than relying on historical, local, and manually calculated information. This especially affects water area figures reported in 1990; these had only included those bodies of water of least 40 acres and those streams with a width of at least one- eighth of a statute mile from 1940 to 1980. Water area figures for 1990 increased because the data reflected all water recorded in the Census Bureau's geographic data base including coastal, Great Lakes and territorial waters.

Geography.—The Geological Survey conducts investigations, surveys, and research in the fields of geography, geology, topography, geographic information

In Brief

Revenues for the environmental industry amount to $133.5 billion in 1993, while employing 1,078,000 people

Release of toxic chemicals amount to 3.2 billion pounds in 1992, down 6.4 percent from 1991

Emissions of lead in the air down 93% between 1980 and 1992

systems, mineralogy, hydrology, and geothermal energy resources as well as natural hazards. In cooperation with State and local agencies, the Geological Survey prepares and publishes topographic, land use/land cover, geologic, and hydrologic maps and data compilations. The Geological Survey provides United States cartographic data through the Earth Sciences Information Center, water resources data through the National Water Data Exchange (NAWDEX) and a variety of research and Open-File reports which are announced monthly in New Publications of the Geological Survey. In a joint project with the Census Bureau, the Geological Survey provided the basic information on geographic features for input into a national geographic and cartographic data base prepared by the Census Bureau, called the TIGER (Topologically Integrated Geographic Encoding and Referencing) System.

Maps prepared by the Bureau of the Census show the names and boundaries of various types of legal and statistical entities, such as places, county subdivisions, and larger areas, and are available as of the specific decennial census. An inventory is available for the 1990 census, both on computer tape and CD-ROM as the 1990 TIGER/GICS (Geographic Identification Code Scheme) and for the 1992 economic censuses in the Geographic Reference Manual (EC92-R-1). The Census Bureau maintains a current inventory of governmental units and their legal boundaries through its Boundary and Annexation Survey.

The TIGER System contains information on the legal and statistical entities used by the Census Bureau, as well as on both manmade and natural features, such as streets, roads, railroads, rivers, and lakes; information is available to the public in the form of machine-readable TIGER extract files.

An inventory of the Nation's land resources by type of use/cover was conducted by the Soil Conservation Service in 1982 and 1987. The results, published in the 1987 National Inventory of Land Resources, cover all non-Federal land in Puerto Rico, the Virgin Islands, and the U.S. except Alaska. 1992 results are expected in late 1994.

Environment.— The principal Federal agency responsible for pollution abatement and control activities is the Environmental Protection Agency (EPA). It is responsible for establishing and monitoring national air quality standards, water quality activities, solid and hazardous waste disposal, and control of toxic substances.

National Ambient Air Quality Standards (NAAQS) for suspended particulate matter, sulfur dioxide, photochemical oxidants, carbon monoxide, and nitrogen dioxide were originally set by the EPA in April 1971. Every 5 years each of the NAAQS is reviewed and revised if new health or welfare data indicates that a change is necessary. The standard for photochemical oxidants, now called ozone, was revised in February 1979. Also, a new NAAQS for lead was promulgated in October 1978 and for suspended particulate matter in 1987. Table 363 gives some of the health-related standards for the six air pollutants having NAAQS. Responsibility for demonstrating compliance with or progress toward achieving these standards lies with the State agencies. In 1992, there were 1,471 non-Federal sampling stations for particulates, 722 for sulfur dioxide, 507 for carbon monoxide, 853 for ozone, 332 for nitrogen dioxide, and 437 for lead. Data from these State networks are periodically submitted to EPA's National Aerometric Information Retrieval System (AIRS) for summarization in annual reports on the nationwide status and trends in air quality; for details, see National Air Quality and Emissions Trends Report, 1992.

Pollution abatement and control expenditures.—Data on expenditures for pollution abatement and control are compiled and published by the Bureau of Economic Analysis (BEA) and the U.S. Bureau of the Census. The BEA conducts surveys on national expenditures for pollution abatement and control and presents the data in its Survey of Current Business. The Bureau of the Census collects data on expenditures for pollution control activities for State and local governments and industry. Data on government expenditures are reported in an annual series of publications, Government Finances, which covers expenditures on sewage and sanitation outlays. Industry data are reported annually in Current Industrial Reports. The Council on Environmental Quality published some expenditure data in Environmental Quality along with other environmental indicator.

Climate.—NOAA, through the National Weather Service and the National Environmental Satellite, Data and Information Service, is responsible for data on climate. NOAA maintains about 11,600 weather stations, of which over 3,000 produce autographic precipitation records, about 600 take hourly readings of a series of weather elements, and the remainder record data once a day. These data are reported monthly in the Climatological Data (published by State), and monthly and annually in the Local Climatological Data (published by location for major cities).

The normal climatological temperatures, precipitation, and degree days listed in this publication are derived for comparative purposes and are averages for the 30-year period, 1961-90. For stations that did not have continuous records for the entire 30 years from the same instrument site, the normals have been adjusted to provide representative values for the current location. The information in all other tables is based on data from the beginning of the record at that location through 1992, except as noted.

Historical statistics.—Tabular headnotes provide cross-references, where applicable, to Historical Statistics of the United States, Colonial Times to 1970. See Appendix IV.

No. 351. Land and Water Area of States and Other Entities: 1990

[One square mile=2.59 square kilometers. Excludes territorial water, which was included in the 1993 edition of the *Statistical Abstract*. See *Historical Statistics of the United States, Colonial Times to 1970*, series A 210-263, for land area]

REGION, DIVISION, STATE, AND OTHER AREA	TOTAL AREA Sq. mi.	TOTAL AREA Sq. km.	LAND AREA Sq. mi.	LAND AREA Sq. km.	WATER AREA Total Sq. mi.	WATER AREA Total Sq. km.	WATER AREA Inland Sq. mi.	WATER AREA Coastal Sq. mi.	WATER AREA Great Lakes Sq. mi.
United States	3,732,396	9,666,906	3,536,338	9,159,115	196,058	507,790	78,641	42,491	74,926
Northeast	176,618	457,441	162,274	420,290	14,344	37,151	6,145	3,549	4,650
New England	68,655	177,816	62,811	162,680	5,844	15,136	3,696	2,148	-
Maine	33,741	87,389	30,865	79,940	2,876	7,449	2,263	613	-
New Hampshire	9,283	24,043	8,969	23,230	314	813	314	-	-
Vermont	9,615	24,903	9,249	23,955	366	948	366	-	-
Massachusetts	9,241	23,934	7,838	20,300	1,403	3,634	424	979	-
Rhode Island	1,231	3,188	1,045	2,707	186	482	168	18	-
Connecticut	5,544	14,359	4,845	12,549	699	1,810	161	538	-
Middle Atlantic	107,963	279,624	99,463	257,609	8,500	22,015	2,449	1,401	4,650
New York	53,989	139,832	47,224	122,310	6,765	17,521	1,888	976	3,901
New Jersey	8,215	21,277	7,419	19,215	796	2,062	371	425	-
Pennsylvania	45,759	118,516	44,820	116,084	939	2,432	190	-	749
Midwest	836,639	2,166,895	751,520	1,946,437	85,119	220,458	14,843	-	70,276
East North Central	316,245	819,075	243,539	630,766	72,706	188,309	4,976	-	67,730
Ohio	44,828	116,105	40,953	106,068	3,875	10,036	376	-	3,499
Indiana	36,420	94,328	35,870	92,903	550	1,425	315	-	235
Illinois	57,918	150,008	55,593	143,986	2,325	6,022	750	-	1,575
Michigan	96,705	250,466	56,809	147,135	39,896	103,331	1,704	-	38,192
Wisconsin	80,374	208,169	54,314	140,673	26,060	67,495	1,831	-	24,229
West North Central	520,394	1,347,820	507,981	1,315,671	12,413	32,150	9,867	-	2,546
Minnesota	86,943	225,182	79,617	206,208	7,326	18,974	4,780	-	2,546
Iowa	56,276	145,755	55,875	144,716	401	1,039	401	-	-
Missouri.	69,709	180,546	68,898	178,446	811	2,100	811	-	-
North Dakota	70,704	183,123	68,994	178,694	1,710	4,429	1,710	-	-
South Dakota	77,121	199,743	75,896	196,571	1,225	3,173	1,225	-	-
Nebraska.	77,359	200,360	76,878	199,114	481	1,246	481	-	-
Kansas	82,282	213,110	81,823	211,922	459	1,189	459	-	-
South	907,237	2,349,744	871,070	2,256,071	36,167	93,673	27,354	8,813	-
South Atlantic	284,146	735,938	266,221	689,512	17,925	46,426	12,557	5,368	-
Delaware.	2,397	6,208	1,955	5,063	442	1,145	71	371	-
Maryland.	12,297	31,849	9,775	25,317	2,522	6,532	680	1,842	-
District of Columbia . . .	68	176	61	158	7	18	7	-	-
Virginia	42,326	109,624	39,598	102,559	2,728	7,066	1,000	1,728	-
West Virginia	24,232	62,761	24,087	62,385	145	376	145	-	-
North Carolina	52,672	136,420	48,718	126,180	3,954	10,241	3,954	-	-
South Carolina	31,189	80,780	30,111	77,987	1,078	2,792	1,006	72	-
Georgia	58,977	152,750	57,919	150,010	1,058	2,740	1,011	47	-
Florida.	59,988	155,369	53,997	139,852	5,991	15,517	4,683	1,308	-
East South Central	183,079	474,175	178,615	462,613	4,464	11,562	3,354	1,110	-
Kentucky	40,411	104,664	39,732	102,906	679	1,759	679	-	-
Tennessee.	42,145	109,156	41,219	106,757	926	2,398	926	-	-
Alabama	52,237	135,294	50,750	131,443	1,487	3,851	968	519	-
Mississippi	48,286	125,061	46,914	121,507	1,372	3,553	781	591	-
West South Central. . . .	440,012	1,139,631	426,234	1,103,946	13,778	35,685	11,443	2,335	-
Arkansas	53,182	137,741	52,075	134,874	1,107	2,867	1,107	-	-
Louisiana.	49,650	128,594	43,566	112,836	6,084	15,758	4,153	1,931	-
Oklahoma	69,903	181,049	68,679	177,879	1,224	3,170	1,224	-	-
Texas	267,277	692,247	261,914	678,357	5,363	13,890	4,959	404	-
West	1,811,902	4,692,826	1,751,474	4,536,318	60,428	156,509	30,299	30,129	-
Mountain	863,614	2,236,760	856,121	2,217,353	7,493	19,407	7,493	-	-
Montana	147,046	380,849	145,556	376,990	1,490	3,859	1,490	-	-
Idaho	83,574	216,457	82,751	214,325	823	2,132	823	-	-
Wyoming	97,819	253,351	97,105	251,502	714	1,849	714	-	-
Colorado	104,100	269,619	103,729	268,658	371	961	371	-	-
New Mexico	121,598	314,939	121,364	314,333	234	606	234	-	-
Arizona	114,006	295,276	113,642	294,333	364	943	364	-	-
Utah	84,904	219,901	82,168	212,815	2,736	7,086	2,736	-	-
Nevada	110,567	286,369	109,806	284,398	761	1,971	761	-	-
Pacific	948,288	2,456,066	895,353	2,318,964	52,935	137,102	22,806	30,129	-
Washington	70,637	182,950	66,581	172,445	4,056	10,505	1,545	2,511	-
Oregon	97,093	251,471	96,002	248,645	1,091	2,826	1,050	41	-
California	158,869	411,471	155,973	403,970	2,896	7,501	2,674	222	-
Alaska.	615,230	1,593,446	570,374	1,477,269	44,856	116,177	17,501	27,355	-
Hawaii.	6,459	16,729	6,423	16,636	36	93	36	-	-
Other areas:									
Puerto Rico	3,508	9,085	3,427	8,875	81	210	65	16	-
American Samoa	90	233	77	200	13	34	7	6	-
Guam.	217	561	210	543	7	18	7	-	-
No. Mariana Islands	189	490	179	464	10	26	10	-	-
Palau	241	624	177	458	64	166	40	24	-
Virgin Islands of the U.S .	171	443	134	346	37	96	17	20	-

- Represents or rounds to zero.
Source: U.S. Bureau of the Census, *1990 Census of Population and Housing*, series CPH-1; and unpublished data.

No. 352. Territorial Expansion of the United States and Acquisitions of Other Areas

[One square mile=2.59 square kilometers. Boundaries of all acquisitions listed under "United States" were indefinite, at least in part at time of acquisition. Because different sources are used for land area, the sums of the acquisitions will not equal the United States or the total. See also Historical Statistics, Colonial Times to 1970, series J 1–2]

ACCESSION	Acquisition date	LAND AREA		ACCESSION	Acquisition date	LAND AREA	
		Sq. ml.	Sq. km.			Sq. ml.	Sq. km.
Total[1]	(X)	3,540,558	9,170,043	Alaska[1]	1867	570,374	1,477,267
				Hawaii[1]	1898	6,423	16,636
United States[1]	(X)	3,536,288	9,158,960	Other areas:[1]			
Territory in 1790[2]	(X)	895,415	2,319,125	Puerto Rico	[4]1898	3,427	8,875
Louisiana Purchase	1803	909,380	2,355,294	Guam	[5]1898	210	543
Purchase of Florida[3]	1819	58,666	151,945	American Samoa	[6]1899	77	200
Texas	1845	388,687	1,006,699	Virgin Islands of the U.S.	1917	134	346
Oregon Territory	1846	286,541	742,141	Palau[7]	1947	179	464
Mexican Cession	1848	529,189	1,370,600	No. Mariana Islands	[8]1947	177	458
Gadsden Purchase	1853	29,670	76,845	All other	(X)	16	41

X Not applicable. [1]Source: U.S. Bureau of the Census, 1990 Census of Population and Housing, series CPH–2. Reflects correction made after publication of results. [2]Includes that part of drainage basin of Red River of the North, south of 49th parallel, sometimes considered part of Louisiana Purchase. [3]Also acquired areas west of the Mississippi River amounting to 22,834 square miles, but relinquished to Spain 97,150 square miles, or a net loss of 15,650 square miles. [4]Ceded by Spain in 1898, ratified in 1899, and became Commonwealth of Puerto Rico by Act of Congress on July 25, 1952. [5]Acquired 1898; ratified 1899. [6]Acquired 1899; ratified 1900. [7]Remaining portion of the Trust Territory of the Pacific Islands, under U.N. trusteeship since 1947. The Federated States of Micronesia and the Marshall Islands, also formerly part of the TTPI, became freely associated States in 1986 and are not included in this table. [8]Attained Commonwealth status in 1986, separate from the TTPI, of which it had been a part since 1947.

Source: Except as noted, U.S. Geological Survey, *Boundaries of the United States and the Several States*, Paper 909, 1976.

No. 353. Area and Acquisition of the Federal Public Domain: 1781 to 1991

[In millions of acres. Areas of acquisitions are as computed in 1912, and do not agree with figures in square miles shown in table 351 which include later adjustments and reflect subsequent remeasurement. Excludes outlying areas of the United States amounting to 645,949 acres in 1978. See also *Historical Statistics, Colonial Times to 1970*, series J 3-6]

YEAR	Land area total [1]	YEAR	LAND AREA [1]			YEAR AND ACQUISITION	ACREAGE		
			Total	Public domain	Acquired		Total	Land	Inland water
1802....	200.0	1978 ...	775.2	712.0	63.3	Aggregate	1,837.8	1,804.7	33.1
1850....	1,200.0	1979 ...	744.1	684.3	59.8				
1880....	900.0	1980 ...	719.5	648.0	71.5	1781-1802 (State Cessions)......	236.8	233.4	3.4
1912....	600.0	1981 ...	730.8	668.7	62.2	1803, Louisiana Purchase [2]......	529.9	523.4	6.5
1946....	413.0	1982 ...	729.8	670.0	59.8	1819, Cession from Spain.......	46.1	43.3	2.8
1950....	412.0	1983 ...	732.0	672.4	59.6	Red River Basin [3]........	29.6	29.1	0.5
1955....	407.9	1984 ...	726.6	658.9	67.7				
1959....	768.6	1985 ...	726.7	656.2	70.5	1846, Oregon Compromise	183.4	180.6	2.7
1960....	771.5	1986 ...	727.1	662.7	64.4	1848, Mexican Cession [2]........	338.7	334.5	4.2
1965....	765.8	1987 ...	724.3	661.0	63.3	1850, Purchase from Texas......	78.9	78.8	0.1
1970....	761.3	1988 ...	688.2	623.2	65.0	1853, Gadsden Purchase	19.0	19.0	(Z)
1975....	760.4	1989 ...	662.2	597.9	64.3	1867, Alaska Purchase	375.3	362.5	12.8
1976....	762.2	1990 ...	649.8	587.4	62.4				
1977....	741.5	1991 ...	649.3	587.6	61.8				

Z Less than 50,000.   [1] Owned by Federal Government. Comprises original public domain plus acquired lands. Estimated from imperfect data available for indicated years. Prior to 1959, excludes Alaska, and 1960, Hawaii. Source: Beginning 1955, U.S. General Services Administration, *Inventory Report on Real Property Owned by the United States Throughout the World*, annual.   [2] Data for Louisiana Purchase exclude areas eliminated by Treaty of 1819 with Spain. Such areas are included in figures for Mexican Cession.   [3] Represents drainage basin of Red River of the North, south of 49th parallel. Authorities differ as to method and date of its acquisition. Some hold it as part of the Louisiana Purchase; others, as acquired from Great Britain.

Source: Except as noted, U.S. Dept. of the Interior. Estimated area, Bureau of Land Management; all other data, Office of the Secretary, *Areas of Acquisitions to the Territory of the U.S.*, 1922.

No. 354. Total and Federally Owned Land, 1960 to 1991, and by State, 1991

[As of end of fiscal year; see text, section 9. Total land area figures are not comparable with those in table 351]

REGION, DIVISION, AND STATE	Total (1,000 acres)	Not owned by Federal Government (1,000 acres)	OWNED BY FEDERAL GOVERNMENT [1]		REGION, DIVISION, AND STATE	Total (1,000 acres)	Not owned by Federal Government (1,000 acres)	OWNED BY FEDERAL GOVERNMENT [1]	
			Acres (1,000)	Percent				Acres (1,000)	Percent
1960.......	2,273,407	1,501,894	771,512	33.9	South........	561,238	540,183	21,055	3.8
1965.......	2,271,343	1,505,546	765,797	33.7	S.A.......	171,325	161,181	10,144	5.9
1970.......	2,271,343	1,510,042	761,301	33.5	DE......	1,266	1,239	27	2.2
1975.......	2,271,343	1,510,929	760,414	33.5	MD......	6,319	6,133	187	3.0
1980.......	2,271,343	1,551,822	719,522	31.7	DC......	39	29	10	26.1
1985.......	2,271,343	1,544,658	726,686	32.0	VA......	25,496	23,900	1,597	6.3
1988.......	2,271,343	1,583,090	688,253	30.3	WV......	15,411	14,382	1,028	6.7
1989.......	2,271,343	1,609,185	662,158	29.2	NC......	31,403	29,432	1,970	6.3
1990.......	2,271,343	1,621,541	649,802	28.6	SC......	19,374	18,652	722	3.7
1991, total.	2,271,343	1,621,998	649,346	28.6	GA......	37,295	35,807	1,488	4.0
Northeast....	104,700	102,411	2,288	2.2	FL......	34,721	31,607	3,114	9.0
N.E......	40,401	39,079	1,322	3.3	E.S.C.....	115,141	110,686	4,455	3.9
ME.....	19,848	19,692	155	0.8	KY......	25,512	24,433	1,080	4.2
NH.....	5,769	5,035	734	12.7	TN......	26,728	25,734	994	3.7
VT.....	5,937	5,579	358	6.0	AL......	32,678	31,603	1,075	3.3
MA.....	5,035	4,969	66	1.3	MS......	30,223	28,916	1,306	4.3
RI.....	677	675	2	0.3	W.S.C	274,772	268,316	6,456	2.3
CT.....	3,135	3,129	6	0.2	AR......	33,599	30,837	2,762	8.2
M.A.....	64,299	63,332	966	1.5	LA......	28,868	28,123	745	2.6
NY.....	30,681	30,472	209	0.7	OK......	44,088	43,383	705	1.6
NJ.....	4,813	4,664	149	3.1	TX......	168,218	165,973	2,245	1.3
PA.....	28,804	28,196	608	2.1	West	1,122,535	519,978	602,557	53.7
Midwest....	482,870	459,425	23,446	4.9	Mountain...	548,449	283,625	264,823	48.3
E.N.C	156,679	146,849	9,830	6.3	MT......	93,271	67,129	26,142	28.0
OH.....	26,222	25,880	342	1.3	ID......	52,933	20,319	32,614	61.6
IN.....	23,158	22,757	401	1.7	WY......	62,343	31,866	30,477	48.9
IL.....	35,795	34,834	961	2.7	CO......	66,486	42,332	24,154	36.3
MI.....	36,492	31,903	4,589	12.6	NM......	77,766	52,564	25,203	32.4
WI.....	35,011	31,474	3,537	10.1	AZ......	72,688	38,380	34,308	47.2
W.N.C	326,191	312,576	13,616	4.2	UT......	52,697	19,036	33,661	63.9
MN.....	51,206	45,839	5,367	10.5	NV......	70,264	12,000	58,265	82.9
IA.....	35,860	35,524	336	0.9	Pacific	574,086	236,353	337,733	58.8
MO.....	44,248	42,152	2,096	4.7	WA......	42,694	30,614	12,080	28.3
ND.....	44,452	42,574	1,879	4.2	OR......	61,599	29,308	32,291	52.4
SD.....	48,882	46,076	2,806	5.7	CA......	100,207	55,500	44,707	44.6
NE.....	49,032	48,322	710	1.4	AK......	365,482	117,461	248,021	67.9
KS.....	52,511	52,089	422	0.8	HI	4,106	3,471	634	15.5

[1] Excludes trust properties.

Source: U.S. General Services Administration, *Inventory Report on Real Property Owned by the United States Throughout the World*, annual.

No. 355. Land Cover/Use, by State: 1987

[In thousands of acres. Excludes Alaska and District of Columbia]

REGION, DIVISION, AND STATE	Total surface area [1]	Federal land	NONFEDERAL LAND							
			Total	Developed [2]	Rural					
					Total	Cropland	Pasture land	Range-land	Forest land	Minor cover/use
United States . .	1,937,726	404,069	1,484,156	77,305	1,406,851	422,416	129,021	401,685	393,904	59,826
Northeast	108,080	2,392	100,778	9,611	91,166	14,532	7,669	-	64,246	4,720
New England	42,670	1,332	38,609	3,005	35,604	2,311	1,248	-	30,307	1,739
Maine	21,290	161	19,517	508	19,009	943	419	-	16,933	714
New Hampshire . .	5,938	729	4,971	372	4,599	163	115	-	4,052	269
Vermont	6,153	335	5,556	208	5,348	653	388	-	4,184	122
Massachusetts . .	5,302	89	4,849	1,063	3,786	291	179	-	2,937	379
Rhode Island . . .	776	4	661	161	500	22	37	-	404	37
Connecticut	3,212	14	3,056	693	2,362	239	110	-	1,797	218
Middle Atlantic	65,410	1,060	62,168	6,606	55,562	12,221	6,422	-	33,939	2,981
New York	31,429	234	29,782	2,485	27,297	5,774	3,686	-	16,650	1,187
New Jersey	4,984	148	4,563	1,325	3,239	673	229	-	1,890	447
Pennsylvania	28,997	677	27,823	2,796	25,027	5,774	2,507	-	15,398	1,348
Midwest	490,474	17,883	460,128	23,789	436,339	233,455	40,718	71,859	71,637	18,670
East North Central .	159,066	6,269	148,602	12,368	136,233	72,743	12,982	-	42,482	8,027
Ohio	26,451	347	25,686	2,925	22,762	12,537	2,444	-	6,426	1,354
Indiana	23,159	487	22,302	1,780	20,522	13,930	2,073	-	3,698	821
Illinois	36,061	492	34,792	2,792	32,000	25,121	2,689	-	3,447	744
Michigan	37,457	3,130	33,051	2,921	30,130	9,484	2,735	-	15,483	2,429
Wisconsin	35,938	1,813	32,770	1,951	30,820	11,671	3,041	-	13,428	2,680
West North Central.	331,408	11,615	311,527	11,421	300,105	160,713	27,736	71,859	29,155	10,643
Minnesota	54,017	3,390	47,077	2,136	44,941	22,990	3,425	157	13,952	4,417
Iowa	36,016	172	35,387	1,688	33,699	27,031	3,866	-	1,841	961
Missouri.	44,606	2,060	41,655	2,165	39,491	15,090	12,606	56	10,959	781
North Dakota	45,250	1,882	42,255	1,242	41,013	28,064	1,206	9,933	428	1,382
South Dakota	49,354	2,873	45,467	1,064	44,403	17,819	2,354	22,152	565	1,513
Nebraska.	49,507	652	48,218	1,250	46,967	20,601	1,957	22,900	728	782
Kansas	52,658	587	51,467	1,876	49,592	29,119	2,324	16,660	681	808
South	575,044	26,391	527,041	30,657	496,384	107,532	67,937	113,837	189,507	17,571
South Atlantic	178,469	12,757	156,196	13,346	142,849	26,495	16,165	3,592	88,408	8,190
Delaware.	1,309	33	1,213	165	1,048	521	30	-	357	141
Maryland.	6,695	159	6,048	936	5,111	1,795	514	-	2,415	388
Virginia	26,091	2,368	22,812	1,663	21,150	3,309	3,315	-	13,622	904
West Virginia	15,508	1,116	14,227	532	13,695	1,053	1,892	-	10,466	284
North Carolina . . .	33,708	2,309	28,622	2,487	26,135	6,548	1,992	-	16,528	1,067
South Carolina . . .	19,912	1,340	17,785	1,422	16,363	3,371	1,177	-	11,073	742
Georgia	37,702	2,062	34,664	2,375	32,289	6,307	3,040	-	21,860	1,083
Florida.	37,545	3,369	30,825	3,766	27,059	3,592	4,205	3,592	12,088	3,583
East South Central .	116,446	5,116	108,068	5,705	102,363	22,870	18,493	96	58,115	2,789
Kentucky.	25,862	1,169	24,023	1,224	22,799	5,818	5,955	-	10,054	972
Tennessee.	26,972	1,369	24,759	1,669	23,090	5,765	5,019	-	11,601	706
Alabama	33,091	904	31,230	1,640	29,591	4,210	3,595	96	21,017	673
Mississippi	30,521	1,674	28,056	1,172	26,884	7,078	3,924	-	15,443	439
West South Central.	280,129	8,518	262,778	11,606	251,172	58,167	33,279	110,149	42,984	6,593
Arkansas	34,040	3,129	29,904	1,232	28,672	8,182	5,678	164	14,268	380
Louisiana.	30,561	1,174	26,472	1,455	25,016	6,484	2,276	234	12,736	3,286
Oklahoma	44,772	1,176	42,431	1,716	40,715	11,557	7,590	14,546	6,505	517
Texas	170,756	3,040	163,971	7,203	156,768	31,944	17,735	95,204	9,476	2,410
West	764,128	357,403	396,209	13,247	382,962	66,896	12,697	215,989	68,514	18,865
Mountain	552,680	266,171	280,033	5,964	274,069	44,235	7,828	182,653	27,532	11,822
Montana	94,109	27,074	65,682	999	64,682	17,881	3,169	36,769	5,253	1,611
Idaho	53,481	33,190	19,628	477	19,152	6,532	1,354	6,596	4,071	600
Wyoming	62,598	29,457	32,576	501	32,075	2,362	928	26,784	984	1,017
Colorado	66,618	23,833	42,320	1,375	40,945	10,967	1,266	23,427	4,079	1,207
New Mexico	77,819	26,423	51,144	698	50,445	2,297	186	40,782	4,685	2,496
Arizona	72,960	30,647	41,994	1,116	40,878	1,306	81	31,867	4,912	2,712
Utah	54,336	35,476	16,440	465	15,975	2,002	563	8,507	3,194	1,711
Nevada	70,759	60,071	10,250	333	9,916	489	282	7,921	356	469
Pacific	211,448	91,232	116,176	7,283	108,893	22,662	4,869	33,337	40,982	7,043
Washington	43,608	12,471	29,947	1,564	28,383	7,758	1,421	5,574	12,634	997
Oregon	62,127	32,305	28,918	941	27,977	4,348	1,916	9,152	11,857	705
California	101,572	46,014	53,654	4,621	49,033	10,209	1,501	17,719	15,073	4,531
Hawaii.	4,141	443	3,657	157	3,500	348	31	891	1,419	811

- Represents zero. [1] Includes water area not shown separately. [2] Includes urban and built-up areas in units of 10 acres or greater, and rural transportation.

Source: U.S. Dept. of Agriculture, Soil Conservation Service, and Iowa State University, Statistical Laboratory; Statistical Bulletin No. 790, *Summary Report, 1987 National Resources Inventory*, December 1989. 1992 data forthcoming in late 1994.

No. 356. Extreme and Mean Elevations States and Other Areas

[One foot=.305 meter]

STATE OR OTHER AREA	HIGHEST POINT Name	Elevation Feet	Meters	LOWEST POINT Name	Elevation Feet	Meters	APPROXIMATE MEAN ELEVATION Feet	Meters
U.S.	Mt. McKinley (AK)	20,320	6,198	Death Valley (CA)	-282	-86	2,500	763
AL	Cheaha Mountain	2,405	733	Gulf of Mexico	(1)	(1)	500	153
AK	Mount McKinley	20,320	6,198	Pacific Ocean	(1)	(1)	1,900	580
AZ	Humphreys Peak	12,633	3,853	Colorado River	70	21	4,100	1,251
AR	Magazine Mountain	2,753	840	Ouachita River	55	17	650	198
CA	Mount Whitney	14,494	4,419	Death Valley	-282	-86	2,900	885
CO	Mt. Elbert	14,433	4,402	Arkansas River	3,350	1,022	6,800	2,074
CT	Mt. Frissell on South slope	2,380	726	Long Island Sound	(1)	(1)	500	153
DE	Ebright Road,² New Castle County	442	135	Atlantic Ocean	(1)	(1)	60	18
DC	Tenleytown at Reno Reservoir	410	125	Potomac River	1	(Z)	150	46
FL	Sec. 30, T6N, R20W, Walton County	345	105	Atlantic Ocean	(1)	(1)	100	31
GA	Brasstown Bald	4,784	1,459	Atlantic Ocean	(1)	(1)	600	183
HI	Puu Wekiu	13,796	4,208	Pacific Ocean	(1)	(1)	3,030	924
ID	Borah Peak	12,662	3,862	Snake River	710	217	5,000	1,525
IL	Charles Mound	1,235	377	Mississippi River	279	85	600	183
IN	Franklin Twp., Wayne Co Sec. 29, T100N, R41W,	1,257	383	Ohio River	320	98	700	214
IA	Osceola County³	1,670	509	Mississippi River	480	146	1,100	336
KS	Mount Sunflower	4,039	1,232	Verdigris River	679	207	2,000	610
KY	Black Mountain	4,139	2,162	Mississippi River	257	78	750	229
LA	Driskill Mountain	535	163	New Orleans	-8	-2	100	31
ME	Mount Katahdin	5,267	1,606	Atlantic Ocean	(1)	(1)	600	183
MD	Backbone Mountain	3,360	1,025	Atlantic Ocean	(1)	(1)	350	107
MA	Mount Greylock	3,487	1,064	Atlantic Ocean	(1)	(1)	500	153
MI	Mount Arvon	1,979	604	Lake Erie	571	174	900	275
MN	Eagle Mountain, Cook Co	2,301	702	Lake Superior	600	183	1,200	366
MS	Woodall Mountain	806	246	Gulf of Mexico	(1)	(1)	300	92
MO	Taum Sauk Mountain	1,772	540	St. Francis River	230	70	800	244
MT	Granite Peak	12,799	3,904	Kootenai River	1,800	549	3,400	1,037
NE	Johnson Twp., Kimball Co.	5,426	1,654	Missouri River	840	256	2,600	793
NV	Boundary Peak	13,140	4,007	Colorado River	479	146	5,500	1,678
NH	Mount Washington	6,288	1,918	Atlantic Ocean	(1)	(1)	1,000	305
NJ	High Point	1,803	550	Atlantic Ocean	(1)	(1)	250	76
NM	Wheeler Peak	13,161	4,014	Red Bluff Reservoir	2,842	867	5,700	1,739
NY	Mount Marcy	5,344	1,630	Atlantic Ocean	(1)	(1)	1,000	305
NC	Mount Mitchell	6,684	2,039	Atlantic Ocean	(1)	(1)	700	214
ND	White Butte, Slope Co	3,506	1,069	Red River	750	229	1,900	580
OH	Campbell Hill	1,549	472	Ohio River	455	139	850	259
OK	Black Mesa	4,973	1,517	Little River	289	88	1,300	397
OR	Mount Hood	11,239	3,428	Pacific Ocean	(1)	(1)	3,300	1,007
PA	Mount Davis	3,213	980	Delaware River	(1)	(1)	1,100	336
RI	Jerimoth Hill	812	248	Atlantic Ocean	(1)	(1)	200	61
SC	Sassafras Mountain	3,560	1,086	Atlantic Ocean	(1)	(1)	350	107
SD	Harney Peak	7,242	2,209	Big Stone Lake	966	295	2,200	671
TN	Clingmans Dome	6,643	2,026	Mississippi River	178	54	900	275
TX	Guadalupe Peak	8,749	2,668	Gulf of Mexico	(1)	(1)	1,700	519
UT	Kings Peak	13,528	4,126	Beaverdam Wash	2,000	610	6,100	1,861
VT	Mount Mansfield	4,393	1,340	Lake Champlain	95	29	1,000	305
VA	Mount Rogers	5,729	1,747	Atlantic Ocean	(1)	(1)	950	290
WA	Mount Rainier	14,410	4,395	Pacific Ocean	(1)	(1)	1,700	519
WV	Spruce Knob	4,861	1,483	Potomac River	240	73	1,500	458
WI	Timms Hill	1,951	595	Lake Michigan	579	177	1,050	320
WY	Gannett Peak	13,804	4,210	Belle Fourche River	3,099	945	6,700	2,044
Other areas:								
Puerto Rico	Cerro de Punta	4,390	1,339	Atlantic Ocean	(1)	(1)	1,800	549
American Samoa	Lata Mountain	3,160	964	Pacific Ocean	(1)	(1)	1,300	397
Guam	Mount Lamlam	1,332	406	Pacific Ocean	(1)	(1)	330	101
Virgin Is.	Crown Mountain	1,556	475	Atlantic Ocean	(1)	(1)	750	229

Z Less than 0.5 meter.   ¹ Sea level.   ² At DE-PA State line.   ³ "Sec." denotes section; "T," township; "R," range; "N," north; "W," west.

Source: U.S. Geological Survey, for highest and lowest points, *Elevations and Distances in the United States, 1990*; for mean elevations, 1983 edition.

No. 357. Water Areas for Selected Major Bodies of Water: 1990

[Includes only that portion of body of water under the jurisdiction of the United States, excluding Hawaii. One square mile=2.59 square kilometers]

BODY OF WATER AND STATE	Sq. mi.	Sq. km.	BODY OF WATER AND STATE	Sq. mi.	Sq. km.
Atlantic Coast water bodies:			Pyramid Lake (NV)	170	440
Chesapeake Bay (MD-VA)	2,747	7,115	Leech Lake (MN)	162	419
Pamlico Sound (NC)	1,622	4,200	Lake St Clair (MI) [1]	161	416
Long Island Sound (CT-NY)	914	2,368	Eufaula Lake (OK)	157	407
Delaware Bay (DE-NJ)	614	1,591	Sam Rayburn Resevoir (TX)	150	389
Cape Cod Bay (MA)	598	1,548	Goose Lake (CA-OR)	147	381
Albemarle Sound (NC)	492	1,274	Utah Lake (UT)	139	361
Biscayne Bay (FL)	218	565	Lake Marion (SC)	139	360
Buzzards Bay (MA)	215	558	Lake Francis Case (SD)	134	346
Tangier Sound (MD-VA)	172	445	Lake Pend Oreille (ID)	133	343
Currituck Sound (NC)	116	301	Lake Texoma (OK-TX)	132	342
Pocomoke Sound (MD-VA)	111	286	Yellowstone Lake (WY)	131	339
Chincoteague Bay (MD-VA)	105	272	Livingston Reservoir (TX)	127	330
Great South Bay (NY)	94	243	Franklin D Roosevelt Lake (WA)	124	322
Core Sound (NC)	88	229	Moosehead Lake (ME)	116	301
			Clark Hill Lake (GA-SC)	105	272
Gulf Coast water bodies:			Lake Maurepas (LA)	91	235
Mississippi Sound (AL-LA-MS)	813	2,105	Lake Moultrie (SC)	89	230
Laguna Madre (TX)	733	1,897	Lake Winnibigoshish (MN)	87	225
Lake Pontchartrain (LA)	631	1,635	Hartwell Lake (GA-SC)	86	224
Florida Bay (FL)	616	1,596	Upper Klamath Lake (OR)	85	221
Breton Sound (LA)	511	1,323	Harry S. Truman Reservoir (MO)	84	217
Mobile Bay (AL)	310	802	Oneida Lake (NY)	80	207
Lake Borgne (LA-MS)	271	702	Malheur Lake (OR)	75	195
Matagorda Bay (TX)	253	656			
Atchafalaya Bay (LA)	245	635	**Alaska water bodies:**		
Galveston Bay (TX)	236	611	Chatham Strait	1,559	4,039
Tampa Bay (FL)	212	549	Prince William Sound	1,382	3,579
Vermilion Bay (LA)	189	489	Clarence Strait	1,199	3,107
Corpus Christi Bay (TX)	151	392	Iliamna Lake	1,022	2,646
West Cote Blanche Bay (LA)	146	378	Frederick Sound	792	2,051
Trinity Bay (TX)	129	335	Sumner Strait	791	2,048
Choctawhatchee Bay (FL)	122	315	Stephens Passage	702	1,819
San Antonio Bay (TX)	118	306	Kvichak Bay	640	1,659
Timbalier Bay (LA)	112	291	Montague Strait	463	1,198
Charlotte Harbor (FL)	112	291	Becharof Lake	447	1,158
Aransas Bay (TX)	104	268	Icy Strait	436	1,130
Apalachicola Bay (FL)	101	262	Hotham Inlet	433	1,120
Terrebonne Bay (LA)	99	256	Selawik Lake	403	1,044
East Cote Blanche Bay (LA)	94	243	Nushagak Bay	393	1,018
St George Sound (FL)	93	240	Baird Inlet	348	902
Sabine Lake (LA-TX)	89	229	Yakutat Bay	345	894
White Lake (LA)	85	221	Teshekpuk Lake	324	839
Old Tampa Bay (FL)	83	214	Behm Canal	324	839
Bon Secour Bay (AL)	79	204	Turnagain Arm	322	834
Pine Island Sound (FL)	75	194	Kachemak Bay	310	803
			Glacier Bay	310	803
Pacific Coast water bodies:			Stefansson Sound	301	780
Puget Sound (WA)	808	2,092	Revillagigedo Channel	295	764
San Francisco Bay (CA)	264	684	Kasegaluk Lagoon	293	759
Willapa Bay (WA)	125	325	Cordova Bay	241	623
Hood Canal (WA)	117	303	Sitka Sound	229	593
			Naknek Lake	225	582
Interior water bodies:			Eschscholtz Bay	210	543
Lake Michigan (IL-IN-MI-WI) [1]	22,342	57,866	Stepovak Bay	206	534
Lake Superior (MI-MN-WI) [1]	20,557	53,243	Keku Strait	206	534
Lake Huron (MI) [1]	8,800	22,792	Port Clarence	187	486
Lake Erie (MI-NY-OH-PA) [1]	5,033	13,036	Orca Bay	184	476
Lake Ontario (NY) [1]	3,446	8,926	Knik Arm	169	437
Great Salt Lake (UT)	1,836	4,756	Dall Lake	167	433
Green Bay (MI-WI)	1,396	3,617	Knight Island Passage	167	432
Lake Okeechobee (FL)	663	1,717	Scammon Bay	163	423
Lake Sakakawea (ND)	563	1,459	Port Moller	159	412
Lake Oahe (ND-SD)	538	1,394	Ernest Sound	158	410
Lake of the Woods (MN) [1]	462	1,196	Spafarief Bay	157	405
Lake Champlain (NY-VT) [1]	414	1,072	Pavlov Bay	153	396
Fort Peck Lake (MT)	379	981	Shishmaref Inlet	153	395
Salton Sea (CA)	364	944	Smith Bay	140	363
Toledo Bend Reservoir (LA-TX)	268	694	Seymour Canal	140	361
Lower Red Lake (MN)	257	666	Sitkalidak Strait	135	349
Lake Powell (AZ-UT)	250	649	Tlevak Strait	135	349
Kentucky Lake (KY-TN)	234	605	Lake Clark	130	336
Lake Mead (AZ-NV)	233	603	Lynn Canal	130	336
Lake Winnebago (WI)	206	535	Chignik Bay	119	309
Mille Lacs Lake (MN)	200	518	Elson Lagoon	119	309
Flathead Lake (MT)	191	495	Bucareli Bay	119	307
Lake Tahoe (CA-NV)	187	486	Hinchinbrook Entrance	118	306
Upper Red Lake (MN)	186	483			

[1] Area measurements for Lake Champlain, Lake Erie, Lake Huron, Lake Ontario, Lake St. Clair, Lake Superior, and Lake of the Woods include only those portions under the jurisdiction of the United States.

Source: U. S. Bureau of the Census, unpublished data from the Census TIGER ™ data base.

No. 358. Flows of Largest U.S. Rivers—Length, Discharge, and Drainage Area

RIVER	Location of mouth	Source stream (name and location)	Length (miles) [1]	Average discharge at mouth (1,000 cubic ft. per second)	Drainage area (1,000 sq. mi.)
Mississippi	Louisiana	Mississippi River, MN	[2]2,340	[3]593	[4][5]1,150
St. Lawrence	Canada	North River, MN	1,900	348	[5]396
Ohio	Illinois-Kentucky	Allegheny River, PA	1,310	281	203
Columbia	Oregon-Washington	Columbia River, Canada	1,240	265	[5]258
Yukon	Alaska	McNeil River, Canada	1,980	225	[5]328
Missouri	Missouri	Red Rock Creek, MT	2,540	76.2	[5]529
Tennessee	Kentucky	Courthouse Creek, NC	886	68	40.9
Mobile	Alabama	Tickanetley Creek, GA	774	67.2	44.6
Kuskokwim	Alaska	South Fork Kuskokwim River, AK	724	67	48
Copper	Alaska	Copper River, AK	286	59	24.4
Atchafalaya [6]	Louisiana	Tierra Blanca Creek, NM	1,420	58	95.1
Snake	Washington	Snake River, WY	1,040	56.9	108
Red	Louisiana	Tierra Blanca Creek, NM	1,290	56	93.2
Stikine	Alaska	Stikine River, Canada	379	56	[5]20
Susitna	Alaska	Susitna River, AK	313	51	20
Tanana	Alaska	Nabesna River, AK	659	41	44.5
Arkansas	Arkansas	East Fork Arkansas River, CO	1,460	41	161
Susquehanna	Maryland	Hayden Creek, NY	447	38.2	27.2
Willamette	Oregon	Middle Fork Willamette River, OR	309	37.4	11.4
Nushagak	Alaska	Nushagak River, AK	285	36	13.4
Alabama	Alabama	Tickanetley Creek, GA	729	34.6	22.8
Wabash	Indiana-Illinois	Wabash River, OH	512	31	32.9
White	Arkansas	White River, AR	722	30.5	27.8
Pend Oreille	Canada	Blacktail Creek, MT	531	30.4	[5]26.3
Alsek	Alaska	Aishihik River, Canada	290	30	[5]10.7

[1] From source to mouth. [2] The length from the source of the Missouri River to the Mississippi River and thence to the Gulf of Mexico is about 3,710 miles. [3] Includes about 167,000 cubic ft. per second diverted from the Mississippi into the Atchafalaya River but excludes the flow of the Red River. [4] Excludes the drainage areas of the Red and Atchafalaya Rivers. [5] Drainage area includes both the United States and Canada. [6] In east-central Louisiana, the Red River flows into the Atchafalaya River, a distributary of the Mississippi River. Data on average discharge, length, and drainage area include the Red River, but exclude all water diverted into the Atchafalaya from the Mississippi River.
Source: U.S. Geological Survey, *Largest Rivers in the United States, Open File Report 87-242*, August 1987.

No. 359. Water Withdrawals and Consumptive Use—States and Other Areas: 1990

[In millions of gallons per day, except as noted. Figures may not add due to rounding. Withdrawal signifies water physically withdrawn from a source. Includes fresh and saline water]

STATE OR OTHER AREA	WATER WITHDRAWN Total	Per capita (gal. per day) fresh	Source Ground water	Surface water	Consumptive use[1] fresh water
U.S. [2]	407,900	1,340	80,640	327,260	93,980
Alabama	8,090	2,000	403	7,680	454
Alaska	641	517	112	529	26
Arizona	6,570	1,790	2,740	3,830	4,350
Arkansas	7,840	3,330	4,710	3,130	4,140
California	46,800	1,180	14,900	31,900	20,900
Colorado	12,700	3,850	2,800	9,910	5,250
Connecticut	4,840	325	165	4,680	103
Delaware	1,370	1,540	89	1,280	59
Dist. of Columbia	9	15	1	8	16
Florida	17,900	582	4,660	13,200	3,130
Georgia	5,350	816	996	4,360	822
Hawaii	2,740	1,070	590	2,150	627
Idaho	19,700	19,600	7,590	12,100	6,090
Illinois	18,000	1,570	945	17,100	750
Indiana	9,430	1,700	621	8,810	451
Iowa	2,860	1,030	495	2,370	271
Kansas	6,080	2,460	4,360	1,720	4,410
Kentucky	4,320	1,170	247	4,070	309
Louisiana	9,350	2,200	1,340	8,010	1,590
Maine	1,140	433	85	1,060	51
Maryland	6,420	307	239	6,180	126
Massachusetts	5,520	338	338	5,180	195
Michigan	11,600	1,250	707	10,900	738
Minnesota	3,270	748	797	2,480	872
Mississippi	3,640	1,290	2,670	963	1,800
Missouri	6,930	1,150	728	6,200	529
Montana	9,320	11,600	218	9,100	2,090
Nebraska	8,940	5,660	4,800	4,150	4,230
Nevada	3,350	2,780	1,070	2,280	1,690
New Hampshire	1,310	378	64	1,250	26
New Jersey	12,800	287	566	12,200	211
New Mexico	3,480	2,300	1,760	1,720	2,060
New York	19,000	583	840	18,100	562
North Carolina	8,940	1,350	435	8,510	390
North Dakota	2,680	4,190	141	2,540	228
Ohio	11,700	1,080	904	10,800	901
Oklahoma	1,670	452	905	760	659
Oregon	8,430	2,970	767	7,660	3,160
Pennsylvania	9,830	827	1,020	8,810	581
Rhode Island	526	132	25	501	18
South Carolina	6,000	1,720	282	5,720	293
South Dakota	592	851	251	341	345
Tennessee	9,190	1,880	503	8,690	252
Texas	25,200	1,180	7,880	17,300	9,020
Utah	4,480	2,540	971	3,510	2,230
Vermont	632	1,120	45	587	29
Virginia	6,860	762	443	6,420	224
Washington	7,940	1,630	1,450	6,490	2,830
West Virginia	4,580	2,560	728	3,860	509
Wisconsin	6,510	1,330	681	5,830	461
Wyoming	7,600	16,700	403	7,200	2,730
Puerto Rico	3,040	163	157	2,880	199
Virgin Islands	164	91	3	160	2

[1] Water that has been evaporated, transpired, or incorporated into products, plant or animal tissue; and therefore, is not available for immediate reuse. [2] Includes Puerto Rico and Virgin Islands.
Source: U.S. Geological Survey, *Estimated Use of Water in the United States in 1990*, circular 1081.

No. 360. U.S. Water Withdrawals and Consumptive Use Per Day, by End Use: 1940 to 1990

[Includes Puerto Rico. Withdrawal signifies water physically withdrawn from a source. Includes fresh and saline water; excludes water used for hydroelectric power. See also *Historical Statistics, Colonial Times to 1970*, series J 92-103]

YEAR	Total (bil. gal.)	Per capita [1] (gal.)	Irrigation (bil. gal.)	PUBLIC SUPPLY [2] Total (bil. gal.)	PUBLIC SUPPLY [2] Per capita[3] (gal.)	Rural [4] (bil. gal.)	Industrial and misc. [5] (bil. gal.)	Steam electric utilities (bil. gal.)
WITHDRAWALS								
1940	140	1,027	71	10	75	3.1	29	23
1950	180	1,185	89	14	145	3.6	37	40
1955	240	1,454	110	17	148	3.6	39	72
1960	270	1,500	110	21	151	3.6	38	100
1965	310	1,602	120	24	155	4.0	46	130
1970	370	1,815	130	27	166	4.5	47	170
1975	420	1,972	140	29	168	4.9	45	200
1980	440	1,953	150	34	183	5.6	45	210
1985	399	1,650	137	38	189	7.8	31	187
1990	408	1,620	137	41	195	7.9	30	195
CONSUMPTIVE USE								
1960	61	339	52	3.5	25	2.8	3.0	0.2
1965	77	403	66	5.2	34	3.2	3.4	0.4
1970	87	427	73	5.9	36	3.4	4.1	0.8
1975	96	451	80	6.7	38	3.4	4.2	1.9
1980	100	440	83	7.1	38	3.9	5.0	3.2
1985	95	380	74	(6)	(6)	9.2	6.1	6.2
1990	96	370	76	(6)	(6)	8.9	6.7	4.0

[1] Based on Bureau of the Census resident population as of July 1. [2] Includes commercial water withdrawals. [3] Based on population served. [4] Rural farm and nonfarm household and garden use, and water for farm stock and dairies. [5] For 1940 to 1960, includes manufacturing and mineral industries, rural commercial industries, air-conditioning, resorts, hotels, motels, military and other State and Federal agencies, and miscellaneous; thereafter, includes manufacturing, mining and mineral processing, ordnance, construction, and miscellaneous. [6] Public supply consumptive use included in end-use categories.

Source: 1940-1960, U.S. Bureau of Domestic Business Development, based principally on committc·) prints, *Water Resources Activities in the United States*, for the Senate Committee on National Water Resources, U.S. Senate, thereafter, U.S. Geological Survey, *Estimated Use of Water in the United States in 1990*, circular 1081, and previous quinquennial issues.

No. 361. National Ambient Water Quality in Rivers and Streams—Violation Rate: 1980 to 1993

[In percent. Violation level based on U.S. Environmental Protection Agency water quality criteria. Violation rate represents the proportion of all measurements of a specific water quality pollutant which exceeds the "violation level" for that pollutant. "Violation" does not necessarily imply a legal violation. Data based on U.S. Geological Survey's National Stream Quality Accounting Network (NASQAN) data system; for details, see source. Years refer to water years. A water year begins in Oct. and ends in Sept. μg=micrograms; mg=milligrams. For metric conversion, see page ix]

POLLUTANT	VIOLATION LEVEL	1980	1985	1987	1988	1989	1990	1991	1992	1993
Fecal coliform bacteria ...	Above 200 cells per 100 ml .	31	28	23	22	30	26	15	28	31
Dissolved oxygen	Below 5 mg per liter	5	3	2	2	3	2	2	2	1
Phosphorus, total, as phosporous	Above 1.0 mg per liter	4	3	3	4	3	3	2	2	2
Lead, dissolved	Above 50 μg per liter......	(Z)	(Z)	(Z)	(Z)	(Z)	(Z)	(Z)	(Z)	(NA)
Cadmium, dissolved	Above 10 μg per liter......	1	(Z)	(Z)	(Z)	(Z)	(Z)	(Z)	(Z)	(NA)

Z Less than 1. NA Not available.

Source: U.S. Geological Survey, national-level data, unpublished; State-level data, *Water-Data Report*, annual series prepared in cooperation with the State governments.

No. 362. Oil Polluting Incidents Reported in and Around U.S. Waters: 1973 to 1992

YEAR	Incidents	Gallons	YEAR	Incidents	Gallons
1973	11,054	15,289,188	1986	6,330	4,427,544
1974	12,083	15,739,792	1987	6,083	3,759,983
1975	10,998	21,528,444	1988	6,155	6,617,278
1976	11,066	18,517,384	1989	7,923	13,506,643
1977	10,979	8,188,398	1990	9,600	11,375,576
1978	12,174	11,035,890	1991	9,850	1,452,103
1979	11,556	10,051,271			
1980	9,886	12,638,848	1992	8,790	1,503,862
1981	9,589	8,919,789	Tankships	198	117,899
1982	9,416	10,404,646	Tank barges	328	73,559
1983	10,530	8,378,719	Other vessels	4,893	400,296
1984	10,089	19,007,332	Nonvessels	3,371	912,108
1985	7,740	8,465,055			

Source: U.S. Coast Guard. Based on unpublished data from the *Marine Safety Information System*.

No. 363. National Ambient Air Pollutant Concentrations: 1985 to 1992

[Data represent annual composite averages of pollutant based on daily 24-hour averages of monitoring stations, except carbon monoxide is based on the second-highest, non-overlapping, 8-hour average; ozone, average of the second-highest daily maximum one hour value; and lead, quarterly average of ambient lead levels. Based on data from the Aerometric Information Retrieval System. $\mu g/m^3$=micrograms of pollutant per cubic meter of air; ppm=parts per million]

POLLUTANT	Unit	Monitoring stations, number	Air quality standard	1985	1986	1987	1988	1989	1990	1991	1992
Carbon monoxide	ppm	308	[2]9	6.98	7.13	6.69	6.35	6.32	5.85	5.54	5.19
Ozone	ppm	509	[3].12	0.124	0.119	0.126	0.137	0.116	0.114	0.116	0.107
Sulfur dioxide	ppm	476	.03	0.009	0.009	0.009	0.009	0.009	0.008	0.008	0.007
Particulates (PM-10) [4]	$\mu g/m^3$	652	50	(X)	(X)	(X)	33.6	33.6	30.7	30.4	27.8
Nitrogen dioxide	ppm	183	.053	0.023	0.023	0.023	0.023	0.023	0.022	0.022	0.021
Lead	$\mu g/m^3$	203	[5]1.5	0.266	0.153	0.105	0.087	0.071	0.058	0.049	0.043

X Not applicable. [1] Refers to the primary National Ambient Air Quality Standard that protects the public health. [2] Based on 8-hour standard of 9 ppm. [3] Based on 1-hour standard of .12 ppm. [4] The particulates (PM-10) standard replaced the previous standard for total suspended particulates in 1987. [5] Based on 3-month standard of 1.5 $\mu g/m^3$
Source: U.S. Environmental Protection Agency, *National Air Quality and Emissions Trends Report*, annual.

No. 364. National Air Pollutant Emissions: 1940 to 1992

[In millions of metric tons, except lead in thousands of metric tons. PM-10=Particulate matter of less than 10 microns. Metric ton=1.1023 short tons]

YEAR	PM-10	PM-10, fugitive dust[1]	Sulfur dioxide	Nitrogen dioxides	Volatile organic compounds	Carbon monoxide	Lead
1940	14.0	(NA)	18.1	6.9	15.5	82.4	(NA)
1950	14.7	(NA)	20.3	9.4	18.9	89.6	(NA)
1960	12.6	(NA)	20.2	13.2	22.1	94.2	(NA)
1970	11.0	(NA)	28.4	18.9	27.0	107.7	199.1
1980	6.4	(NA)	23.8	21.5	25.7	117.0	68.0
1981	6.0	(NA)	22.5	21.3	24.0	111.6	53.4
1982	4.9	(NA)	21.2	20.6	22.6	105.4	52.3
1983	5.5	(NA)	20.6	20.0	23.1	105.2	44.7
1984	5.8	(NA)	21.5	20.5	23.7	102.5	38.3
1985	5.6	40.7	21.2	20.3	22.7	97.9	18.3
1986	5.3	45.4	20.4	20.2	23.0	95.2	6.6
1987	5.5	38.3	20.5	20.7	22.4	90.1	6.2
1988	5.9	54.5	21.0	21.4	22.7	89.9	5.9
1989	5.7	48.4	21.0	21.3	21.7	84.7	5.5
1990, prel.	5.5	40.7	20.7	21.4	21.5	83.8	5.1
1991, prel.	5.3	45.1	20.7	21.2	21.2	82.3	4.6
1992, prel.	5.4	41.4	20.6	21.0	20.6	79.1	4.7

NA Not available. [1] Sources such as agricultural tilling, construction, mining and quarrying, paved roads, unpaved roads, and wind erosion.

No. 365. Air Pollutant Emissions, by Pollutant and Source: 1990 to 1992

[In millions of metric tons, except lead in thousands of metric tons. Metric ton=1.1023 short tons]

YEAR AND POLLUTANT	Total emissions	CONTROLLABLE EMISSIONS								PERCENT OF TOTAL		
		Transportation		Fuel combustion [1]		Industrial processes	Solid waste disposal	Misc. uncontrollable	Transportation	Fuel combustion [1]	Industrial
		Total	Road vehicles	Total	Electric utilities						
1990: Carbon monoxide	83.8	67.5	54.3	6.1	0.3	4.7	1.5	3.9	80.5	7.3	5.6
Sulfur oxides	20.7	0.9	0.7	17.8	14.4	2.0	-	-	4.3	86.0	9.7
Volatile organic compounds	21.5	8.3	6.3	0.7	-	10.0	2.1	0.5	38.6	3.3	46.5
Particulates [2]	46.1	1.6	1.3	1.1	0.2	1.8	0.2	41.5	3.5	2.4	3.9
Nitrogen oxides	21.4	9.7	7.1	10.7	6.8	0.8	0.1	0.1	45.3	50.0	3.7
Lead	5.1	1.7	1.5	0.5	0.1	2.2	0.7	-	33.3	9.8	43.1
1991: Carbon monoxide	82.3	66.3	53.4	6.0	0.3	4.7	1.5	3.8	80.6	7.3	5.7
Sulfur oxides	20.7	0.9	0.7	17.7	14.3	2.0	-	-	4.3	85.5	9.7
Volatile organic compounds	21.2	8.0	6.2	0.7	-	10.0	2.0	0.5	37.7	3.3	47.2
Particulates [2]	50.2	1.6	1.4	1.0	0.1	1.7	0.2	45.6	3.2	2.0	3.4
Nitrogen oxides	21.2	9.5	7.0	10.7	6.8	0.8	0.1	0.1	44.8	50.5	3.8
Lead	4.5	1.5	1.4	0.4	0.1	2.0	0.5	-	33.3	8.9	44.4
1992: Carbon monoxide	79.1	63.5	50.2	5.6	0.3	4.6	1.5	3.9	80.3	7.1	5.8
Sulfur oxides	20.6	1.0	0.7	17.7	14.4	1.9	-	-	4.9	85.9	9.2
Volatile organic compounds	20.6	7.5	5.5	0.6	-	9.9	2.1	0.5	36.4	2.9	48.1
Particulates [2]	46.7	1.7	1.4	1.0	0.1	1.8	0.2	42.0	3.6	2.1	3.9
Nitrogen oxides	21.0	9.4	6.8	10.6	6.8	0.8	0.1	0.1	44.8	50.5	3.8
Lead	4.7	1.4	1.3	0.4	0.1	2.1	0.7	-	29.8	8.5	44.7

- Represents zero. [1] Stationary sources. [2] Represents both PM-10 and PM-10 fugitive dust; see table 364.
Source of tables 364 and 365: U.S. Environmental Protection Agency, *National Air Pollutant Emission Trends, 1900-1992*.

No. 366. Metropolitan Areas Failing to Meet National Ambient Air Quality Standards for Carbon Monoxide—Number of Days Exceeding Standards: 1991 and 1992

[Areas generally represent the officially defined metropolitan area, but may, in some cases, not have all the counties identified as part of the area; see *Federal Register*, 40 CFR, part 81, *Air Quality Designations: Revised*, June 23, 1992. Nonattainment status was as of November 2, 1993]

METROPOLITAN AREA	1991	1992	METROPOLITAN AREA	1991	1992	METROPOLITAN AREA	1991	1992
Albuquerque, NM	2	-	Hartford, CT CMSA	1	1	Philadelphia, PA-NJ-DE-		
Anchorage, AK	3	2	Klamath County, OR [1]	1	-	MD CMSA	-	-
Baltimore, MD.	-	-	Lake Tahoe S. Shore,			Phoenix, AZ.	3	5
Boston, MA-NH CMSA....	-	-	CA [1]	-	1	Portland, OR-WA CMSA.	2	-
Chico, CA	-	-	Las Vegas, NV ...	6	2	Provo-Orem, UT	6	3
Cleveland, OH CMSA.	-	-	Longmont, CO [1]	-	-	Raleigh-Durham, NC	-	-
Colorado Springs, CO	-	-	Los Angeles, CA CMSA ...	41	35	Reno, NV.	2	-
Denver-Boulder, CO CMSA.	4	7	Medford, OR	3	-	Sacramento, CA	5	-
Duluth, MN.	-	-	Memphis, TN-AR-MS	-	1	San Diego, CA	-	-
El Paso, TX	3	3	Minneapolis-St. Paul,			San Francisco, CA CMSA..	4	-
Fairbanks, AK [1]	3	2	MN-WI	2	-	Seattle-Tacoma, WA		
Fort Collins, CO	2	-	Missoula County, MT [1]	5	-	CMSA	1	1
Fresno, CA	1	-	Modesto, CA	1	-	Spokane, WA.	13	6
Grant Pass, OR [1]	-	-	New York, NY-NJ-CT			Stockton, CA	1	-
Greensboro-Winston-			CMSA	2	2	Washington, DC-MD-VA ...	-	-
Salem, NC	-	-	Ogden, UT	-	-			

- Represents zero.   [1] Not a metropolitan area.

No. 367. Metropolitan Areas Failing to Meet National Ambient Air Quality Standards for Ozone—Average Number of Days Exceeding Standards: 1990 to 1992

[See headnote, table 366. Nonattainment status was as of November 2, 1993]

METROPOLITAN AREA	1990-92, avg.	1992[1]	METROPOLITAN AREA	1990-92, avg.	1992[1]
Albany-Schenectady-Troy, NY	0.6	-	Manchester, NH	1.0	-
Allentown-Bethlehem-Easton, PA-NJ	0.3	-	Manitowoc Co, WI	2.8	-
Altoona, PA	-	-	Memphis, TN-AR-MS	-	-
Atlanta, GA	4.4	2.2	Miami-Fort Lauderdale, FL CMSA	0.3	-
Atlantic City, NJ	2.8	1.0	Milwaukee-Racine, WI CMSA	4.7	2.4
Baltimore, MD.	4.9	2.0	Monterey Bay, CA [7].	0.4	-
Baton Rouge, LA	5.1	2.0	Muskegon, MI.	3.0	1.0
Beaumont-Port Arthur, TX............	3.6	2.1	Nashville, TN	2.3	-
Birmingham, AL	2.1	-	New York, NY-NJ-CT CMSA [8]	3.4	2.0
Boston-Lawrence-Salem, MA-NH CMSA [2]..	2.9	2.2	Norfolk-Virginia Beach-Newport News, VA..	0.7	2.0
Buffalo-Niagara Falls, NY CMSA	-	-	Owensboro, KY.	1.0	-
Canton, OH	0.3	-	Paducah, KY [4]	-	-
Charleston, WV.	0.3	-	Parkersburg-Marietta, WV-OH	-	-
Charlotte-Gastonia-Rock Hill, NC-SC [3] ..	0.3	-	Philadelphia, PA-NJ-DE-MD CMSA	8.4	4.1
Chicago-Gary-Lake County, IL-IN-WI CMSA.	4.7	2.4	Phoenix, AZ.	9.4	9.6
Cincinnati-Hamilton, OH-KY-IN CMSA.....	2.3	-	Pittsburgh-Beaver Valley, PA CMSA	0.6	-
Cleveland-Akron-Lorain, OH CMSA	2.0	2.0	Portland-Vancouver, OR-WA CMSA	2.4	1.5
Columbus, OH	0.7	-	Portland, ME.	4.5	2.3
Dallas-Fort Worth, TX CMSA.	3.1	2.7	Portsmouth-Dover-Rochester, NH-ME....	2.1	-
Dayton-Springfield, OH...............	-	-	Poughkeepsie, NY.	1.1	-
Detroit-Ann Arbor, MI CMSA	1.0	-	Providence, RI [9].	5.5	1.0
Door County, WI [4].	2.7	-	Raleigh-Durham, NC	-	-
Edmonton County, KY [4].	-	-	Reading, PA.	0.3	-
El Paso, TX	3.7	5.1	Reno, NV.	1.4	-
Erie, PA.	-	-	Richmond-Petersburg, VA...........	0.7	1.1
Essex County, NY [4].	2.1	-	Sacramento, CA	6.1	7.1
Evansville, IN-KY.	-	-	St. Louis, MO-IL.	1.4	2.0
Grand Rapids, MI .... [5]	3.4	-	Salt Lake City-Ogden, UT.	0.3	-
Greater Connecticut, CT [5].	8.3	4.0	San Diego, CA	7.3	6.1
Greenbrier County, WV [4]	0.4	-	San Joaquin Valley, CA	22.6	17.5
Hancock and Waldo counties, ME [4]	1.3	-	San Francisco-Bay area, CA	2.8	-
Harrisburg-Lebanon-Carlisle, PA......	0.3	-	Santa Barbara-Santa Maria-Lompoc, CA ..	1.3	2.0
Houston-Galveston-Brazoria, TX CMSA....	13.0	6.9	Scranton-Wilkes-Barre, PA	0.6	-
Huntington-Ashland, WV-KY-OH	1.5	-	Seattle-Tacoma, WA	1.1	-
Indianapolis, IN.	0.3	-	Sheboygan, WI.	3.2	-
Jefferson County, NY [4].	-	-	Smyth County, VA [4].	(NA)	(NA)
Jersey Co., IL [4].	0.7	-	South Bend-Mishawaka, IN	-	-
Johnstown, PA.	-	-	Southeast Desert Modified AQMD, CA [10].	52.9	57.8
Kent County and Queen Anne's Co., MD [4].	2.4	-	Springfield, MA	3.6	2.0
Kewaunee County, WI [4]	0.8	-	Sussex County, DE [4]	1.4	-
Knox and Lincoln counties, ME [4]	2.8	-	Tampa-St. Petersburg-Clearwater, FL	0.5	-
Lake Charles, LA	1.5	1.3	Toledo, OH	-	-
Lancaster, PA.	-	-	Ventura County, CA.	17.6	6.2
Lewiston-Auburn, ME.	0.5	-	Walworth County, WI.	0.3	-
Lexington-Fayette, KY.	0.3	-	Washington, DC-MD-VA	2.4	1.1
Louisville, KY-IN.	1.8	-	York, PA.	0.3	-
Los Angeles South Coast Air, CA [6]	106.1	124.4	Youngstown-Warren, OH [11].	0.3	-

- Represents zero.   NA Not available.   [1] May represent a different monitoring location than one used to calculate average. [2] Includes also both the Worcester, MA, and New Bedford, MA MSA's.   [3] Excludes York Co., SC.   [4] Not a metropolitan area. [5] Primarily represents Hartford-New Haven area.   [6] Primarily represents Los Angeles and Orange counties.   [7] Primarily represents Monterey, Santa Cruz, and San Benito counties.   [8] Excludes the Connecticut portion.   [9] Covers entire State of Rhode Island.   [10] Represents primarily San Joaquin, Turlock, Merced, Madera, Fresno, Kings, Tulare, and Kern counties. [11] Includes Sharon, PA.

Source of tables 366 and 367: U.S. Environmental Protection Agency, Published in *1992 Air Quality Update*, November 2, 1993.

No. 368. Emissions of Greenhouse Gases, by Type and Source: 1985 to 1991

[Emission estimates were mandated by Congress through Section 1605(a) of the Energy Policy Act of 1992 (title XVI). Gases that contain carbon can be measured either in terms of the full molecular weight of the gas or just in terms of their carbon content]

TYPE AND SOURCE	Unit	1985	1986	1987	1988	1989	1990	1991
Carbon dioxide:								
Gas	Mil. metric tons	4,667.1	4,662.1	4,806.3	5,031.6	5,067.5	5,012.4	(NA)
Carbon content	Mil. metric tons	1,272.9	1,271.5	1,310.8	1,372.3	1,382.1	1,367.0	1,351.7
Energy sources	Mil. metric tons	1,240.6	1,239.0	1,277.6	1,339.8	1,352.0	1,338.0	1,317.2
Cement production.	Mil. metric tons	9.6	9.7	9.6	9.5	9.5	9.5	8.8
Gas flaring	Mil. metric tons	1.3	1.3	1.7	1.9	1.9	2.0	2.3
Other industrial	Mil. metric tons	6.1	5.7	6.2	6.8	6.9	6.9	6.8
Other, adjustments.	Mil. metric tons	15.3	15.8	15.7	14.3	11.8	10.6	16.6
Methane:								
Gas	1,000 metric tons	29,486	29,179	29,134	29,263	28,891	29,109	(NA)
Energy sources	1,000 metric tons	7,442	7,436	7,665	7,865	8,039	8,446	8,190
Landfills	1,000 metric tons	11,310	11,360	11,240	11,220	10,980	10,720	(NA)
Agricultural sources	1,000 metric tons	10,734	10,383	10,229	10,178	9,852	9,933	10,046
Carbon content	Mil. metric tons	22.1	21.9	21.8	22.0	21.7	21.8	(NA)
Nitrous oxide	1,000 metric tons	303	304	316	334	334	343	354
Fertilizer	1,000 metric tons	124	108	106	107	108	109	117
Adipic acid production [1]	1,000 metric tons	[2]51	54	56	57	53	55	57
Transportation	1,000 metric tons	81	93	106	121	127	133	136
Stationary combustion . . . . . . [3] .	1,000 metric tons	47	49	48	49	46	46	44
Chlorofluorocarbons (CFC) gases [3] . .	1,000 metric tons	(NA)	(NA)	(NA)	(NA)	(NA)	222	(NA)
Carbon monoxide:								
Gas	Mil. metric tons	83.12	76.03	75.05	75.53	68.32	67.74	62.10
Energy related.	Mil. metric tons	69.81	64.93	62.38	59.72	55.70	52.78	48.17
Industrial processes	Mil. metric tons	4.38	4.20	4.33	4.60	4.58	4.64	4.69
Solid waste disposal.	Mil. metric tons	1.85	1.70	1.70	1.70	1.70	1.70	2.06
Other.	Mil. metric tons	7.09	5.15	6.44	9.51	6.34	8.62	7.18
Carbon content	Mil. metric tons	35.62	32.58	32.16	32.37	29.28	29.03	26.61
Nitrogen oxide.	Mil. metric tons	19.39	18.83	19.03	19.65	19.29	19.38	18.76
Energy related	Mil. metric tons	18.53	18.04	18.19	18.71	18.44	18.46	17.85
Industrial processes	Mil. metric tons	0.56	0.56	0.56	0.58	0.59	0.59	0.60
Solid waste disposal	Mil. metric tons	0.08	0.08	0.08	0.08	0.08	0.08	0.10
Other	Mil. metric tons	0.21	0.16	0.19	0.28	0.19	0.26	0.21
Nonmethane volatile organic								
compounds (VOC's)	Mil. metric tons	19.80	18.45	18.64	18.61	17.35	17.58	16.88
Energy related	Mil. metric tons	8.37	7.77	7.49	7.15	6.36	6.16	5.75
Industrial processes	Mil. metric tons	8.35	7.92	8.17	8.00	7.97	8.02	7.86
Solid waste disposal	Mil. metric tons	0.60	0.58	0.58	0.58	0.58	0.58	0.69
Other	Mil. metric tons	2.49	2.19	2.40	2.88	2.44	2.82	2.59

NA Not available.   [1] A common industrial chemical which is an intermediate product in the production of nylon.   [2] 1985 data not available; EIA estimate is an average of 1984 and 1986 data.   [3] Covers only CFC-11, CFC-12, and CFC-113.

Source: U.S. Energy Information Administration, *Emissions of Greenhouse Gases in the United States, 1985-1990*, September 1993.

No. 369. Toxic Release Inventory, by Industry and Source: 1988 to 1992

[In millions of pounds. Based on reports from almost 23,000 manufacturing facilities which have 10 or more full-time employees and meet established thresholds for manufacturing, processing, or otherwise using the list of more than 300 chemicals covered. Only chemicals that were reportable in all years shown are compared so that data do not reflect any chemicals added or deleted from the list covered. The inventory was established under the Emergency Planning and Community Right-to-Know Act of 1986 (EPCRA)]

INDUSTRY	1987 SIC [1] code	1988	1989	1990	1991	1992 Total [2]	Air [3], point	Air [4], non-point	Water
Total.	(X)	4,852.9	4,377.4	3,693.2	3,373.2	3,157.3	1,284.3	536.7	272.9
Food and kindred prod.	20	28.2	37.0	38.9	39.5	38.6	16.5	11.7	2.0
Tobacco products	21	1.8	1.8	2.5	2.3	2.0	1.9	0.1	(Z)
Textile mill products.	22	38.2	32.2	27.1	25.0	21.5	15.3	5.8	0.3
Apparel and other textile prod. . .	23	1.1	1.4	1.3	1.4	1.6	1.1	0.5	(Z)
Lumber and wood products. . . .	24	32.9	37.8	35.6	32.6	32.4	25.2	7.0	0.1
Furniture and fixtures	25	66.8	65.3	61.7	55.9	55.1	47.0	7.7	(Z)
Paper and allied products	26	271.8	257.1	253.3	245.8	233.0	176.6	23.2	27.6
Printing and publishing	27	61.0	58.2	51.4	46.6	40.5	17.2	23.3	(Z)
Chemical and allied products. . .	28	2,324.4	2,083.4	1,619.5	1,541.5	1,527.3	398.0	151.0	224.3
Petroleum and coal products. . .	29	92.8	94.7	85.8	78.2	82.7	22.6	38.5	3.5
Rubber and misc. plastic prod. .	30	170.4	184.0	177.5	149.8	134.4	93.3	40.1	0.5
Leather and leather products. . .	31	15.8	13.5	12.7	9.9	10.5	6.7	3.5	0.3
Stone, clay, glass products . . .	32	39.2	37.1	31.2	29.4	25.7	15.4	2.6	0.1
Primary metal industries	33	565.9	522.3	476.3	424.1	345.2	100.3	35.3	6.5
Fabricated metals products. . . .	34	136.9	137.3	128.2	111.0	101.2	61.8	38.3	0.2
Industrial machinery and equip. .	35	60.6	57.8	48.8	38.6	33.7	19.8	13.5	0.1
Electronic, electric equip.	36	125.7	100.4	82.3	66.0	52.2	35.7	15.7	0.2
Transportation equipment	37	216.6	205.3	175.3	149.5	136.0	92.0	42.1	0.1
Instruments and related prod. . .	38	57.1	52.5	44.3	39.6	33.0	22.6	9.6	0.8
Misc. manufacturing industries . .	39	31.3	29.0	25.8	20.3	18.2	12.4	5.8	(Z)
Multiple codes	20-39	498.4	358.9	299.7	239.8	217.8	96.7	57.1	6.0
No codes.	20-39	16.2	10.8	13.8	26.6	14.7	6.1	4.4	0.4

X Not applicable.   Z Less than 50,000 pounds.   [1] Standard Industrial Classification, see text, section 13.   [2] Includes other releases not shown separately.   [3] Stack.   [4] Fugitive.

Source: U.S. Environmental Protection Agency, *1992 Toxics Release Inventory Public Data Release.*

No. 370. Municipal Solid Waste Generation, Recovery, and Disposal: 1960 to 1990

[In millions of tons, except as indicated. Covers post-consumer residential and commercial solid wastes which comprise the major portion of typical municipal collections. Excludes mining, agricultural and industrial processing, demolition and construction wastes, sewage sludge, and junked autos and obsolete equipment wastes. Based on material-flows estimating procedure and wet weight as generated]

ITEM AND MATERIAL	1960	1970	1980	1985	1986	1987	1988	1989	1990
Waste generated	87.8	121.9	151.5	164.4	170.7	178.1	184.2	191.4	195.7
Per person per day (lb.)	2.66	3.27	3.65	3.77	3.88	4.01	4.12	4.2	4.3
Materials recovered............	5.9	8.6	14.5	16.4	18.3	20.1	23.5	29.9	33.4
Per person per day (lb.)	0.18	0.23	0.35	0.38	0.42	0.45	0.52	0.7	0.7
Combustion for energy recovery	(NA)	0.4	2.7	7.6	9.6	16.0	24.5	27.1	29.7
Per person per day (lb.)	(NA)	0.02	0.06	0.17	0.22	0.36	0.59	0.6	0.7
Combustion without energy recovery .	27.0	24.7	11.0	4.1	3.0	2.0	1.0	2.0	2.2
Per person per day (lb.)	0.82	0.66	0.27	0.10	0.07	0.05	0.02	0.4	0.5
Landfill, other disposal...........	54.9	88.2	123.3	136.4	139.8	140.0	135.1	132.4	130.4
Per person per day (lb.)	1.67	2.37	2.97	3.13	3.18	3.15	3.02	2.9	2.9
Percent distribution of generation:									
Paper and paperboard	34.1	36.3	36.1	37.4	38.4	39.1	38.9	37.6	37.5
Glass......................	7.6	10.4	9.9	8.0	7.6	6.9	6.8	6.7	6.7
Metals.....................	12.0	11.6	9.6	8.6	8.5	8.3	8.3	8.2	8.3
Plastics	0.5	2.5	5.2	7.1	7.2	7.5	7.8	8.0	8.3
Rubber and leather	2.3	2.6	2.8	2.3	2.5	2.5	2.5	2.4	2.4
Textiles	1.9	1.6	1.7	1.7	1.6	2.1	2.1	2.9	2.9
Wood	3.4	3.3	4.4	5.0	5.3	5.5	6.1	6.1	6.3
Food wastes................	13.9	10.5	8.7	8.0	7.7	7.4	7.2	6.9	6.7
Yard wastes................	22.8	19.0	18.2	18.2	17.7	17.4	17.2	18.1	17.9
Other wastes	1.6	2.2	3.4	3.6	3.4	3.3	3.1	3.1	3.1

NA Not available.

Source: Franklin Associates, Ltd., Prairie Village, KS, *Characterization of Municipal Solid Waste in the United States: 1992 Update.* Prepared for the U.S. Environmental Protection Agency.

No. 371. Generation and Recovery of Selected Materials in Municipal Solid Waste: 1960 to 1990

[In millions of tons, except as indicated. Covers post-consumer residential and commercial solid wastes which comprise the major portion of typical municipal collections. Excludes mining, agricultural and industrial processing, demolition and construction wastes, sewage sludge, and junked autos and obsolete equipment wastes. Based on material-flows estimating procedure and wet weight as generated]

ITEM AND MATERIAL	1960	1970	1980	1985	1986	1987	1988	1989	1990
Waste generated, total	**87.8**	**121.9**	**151.5**	**164.4**	**170.7**	**178.1**	**184.2**	**191.4**	**195.7**
Paper and paperboard	29.9	44.2	54.7	61.5	65.6	69.6	71.7	71.9	73.3
Ferrous metals	9.9	12.6	11.6	10.9	11.1	11.3	11.6	12.0	12.3
Aluminum..................	0.4	0.8	1.8	2.3	2.4	2.4	2.5	2.5	2.7
Other nonferrous metals	0.2	0.7	1.1	1.0	1.0	1.1	1.1	1.2	1.2
Glass.....................	6.7	12.7	15.0	13.2	13.0	12.3	12.5	12.9	13.2
Plastics	0.4	3.1	7.9	11.6	12.2	13.4	14.4	15.4	16.2
Yard waste.................	20.0	23.2	27.5	30.0	30.2	31.0	31.6	34.7	35.0
Other wastes	20.3	24.6	31.9	33.9	35.2	37.0	38.8	40.8	41.8
Materials recovered, total	**5.9**	**8.6**	**14.5**	**16.4**	**18.3**	**20.1**	**23.5**	**29.9**	**33.4**
Paper and paperboard	5.4	7.4	11.9	13.1	14.8	16.3	18.4	19.1	20.9
Ferrous metals	0.1	0.1	0.4	0.4	0.4	0.4	0.7	1.5	1.9
Aluminum..................	-	-	0.3	0.6	0.6	0.7	0.8	0.9	1.0
Other nonferrous metals	0.0	0.3	0.5	0.5	0.6	0.6	0.7	0.8	0.8
Glass.'....................	0.1	0.2	0.8	1.0	1.1	1.3	1.5	2.5	2.6
Plastics	-	-	-	0.1	0.1	0.1	0.2	0.3	0.4
Yard waste.................	-	-	-	-	-	-	0.5	3.5	4.2
Other wastes	0.3	0.6	0.6	0.7	0.7	0.7	0.7	1.3	1.6
Percent of generation recovered, total	**6.7**	**7.1**	**9.6**	**10.0**	**10.7**	**11.2**	**12.8**	**15.6**	**17.1**
Paper and paperboard	18.1	16.7	21.8	21.3	22.6	23.4	25.6	26.6	28.6
Ferrous metals	1.0	0.8	3.4	3.7	3.6	3.5	5.8	12.6	15.4
Aluminum..................	-	-	16.7	26.1	25.0	29.2	31.7	35.5	38.1
Other nonferrous metals	-	42.9	45.5	50.0	60.0	54.5	65.1	68.3	67.7
Glass.....................	1.5	1.6	5.3	7.6	8.5	10.6	12.0	19.5	19.9
Plastics	-	-	-	0.9	0.8	0.7	1.1	1.7	2.2
Yard waste.................	-	-	-	-	-	-	1.6	10.0	12.0
Other wastes	1.5	2.4	1.9	2.1	2.0	1.9	1.8	3.2	3.8

- Represents zero.

Source: Franklin Associates, Ltd., Prairie Village, KS, *Characterization of Municipal Solid Waste in the United States: 1992 Update.* Prepared for the U.S. Environmental Protection Agency.

No. 372. Hazardous Waste Sites on the National Priority List, by State: 1993

[Includes both proposed and final sites listed on the National Priorities List for the Superfund program as authorized by the Comprehensive Environmental Response, Compensation, and Liability Act of 1980 and the Superfund Amendments and Reauthorization Act of 1986]

STATE	Total sites	Rank	Percent distribution	Federal	Non-Federal	STATE	Total sites	Rank	Percent distribution	Federal	Non-Federal
Total	1,270	(X)	(X)	143	1,127	Montana.........	8	41	0.6	-	8
						Nebraska	10	36	0.8	1	9
United States ..	**1,258**	**(X)**	**100.0**	**141**	**1,117**	Nevada	1	50	0.1	-	1
Alabama.........	14	26	1.1	3	11	New Hampshire....	17	23	1.4	1	16
Alaska.........	8	41	0.6	6	2	New Jersey.......	109	1	8.7	6	103
Arizona.........	10	36	0.8	3	7	New Mexico	11	34	0.9	2	9
Arkansas	12	29	1.0	-	12	New York	85	4	6.8	4	81
California	95	3	7.6	22	73	North Carolina.....	22	18	1.7	1	21
Colorado.........	18	22	1.4	3	15	North Dakota......	2	49	0.2	-	2
Connecticut......	15	24	1.2	1	14	Ohio	36	11	2.9	3	33
Delaware	19	21	1.5	1	18	Oklahoma........	11	34	0.9	1	10
District of Columbia .	-	(X)	-	-	-	Oregon..........	12	29	1.0	2	10
Florida	55	7	4.4	4	51	Pennsylvania......	99	2	7.9	4	95
Georgia	13	27	1.0	2	11	Rhode Island......	12	29	1.0	2	10
Hawaii	3	47	0.2	2	1	South Carolina.....	24	15	1.9	1	23
Idaho	10	36	0.8	2	8	South Dakota	4	45	0.3	1	3
Illinois	37	10	2.9	4	33	Tennessee	15	24	1.2	3	12
Indiana.........	33	12	2.6	-	33	Texas...........	30	14	2.4	4	26
Iowa	20	19	1.6	1	19	Utah	13	27	1.0	4	9
Kansas.........	10	36	0.8	1	9	Vermont.........	8	41	0.6	-	8
Kentucky	20	19	1.6	1	19	Virginia.........	24	15	1.9	5	19
Louisiana	12	29	1.0	1	11	Washington.......	55	6	4.4	18	37
Maine..........	10	36	0.8	3	7	West Virginia......	6	44	0.5	1	5
Maryland	12	29	1.0	3	9	Wisconsin........	40	9	3.2	-	40
Massachusetts....	31	13	2.5	8	23	Wyoming	3	47	0.2	1	2
Michigan.........	76	5	6.0	-	76						
Minnesota........	41	8	3.3	2	39	Guam	2	(X)	(X)	1	1
Mississippi	4	45	0.3	-	4	Puerto Rico.......	9	(X)	(X)	1	8
Missouri	23	17	1.8	3	20	Virgin Islands......	1	(X)	(X)	-	1

- Represents zero.   X Not applicable.

Source: U.S. Environmental Protection Agency, *Supplementary Materials: National Priorities List, Proposed Rule*, Vol. 3, No. 2, June 1993.

No. 373. Environmental Industry—Revenues and Employment, by Industry Segment: 1989 to 1993

[Covers approximately 59,000 private and public companies engaged in environmental activities]

INDUSTRY SEGMENT	REVENUE (bil. dol.)					EMPLOYMENT (1,000)				
	1989	1990	1991	1992	1993	1989	1990	1991	1992	1993
Industry total	**111.5**	**122.0**	**124.7**	**129.6**	**133.5**	**895**	**983**	**1,008**	**1,049**	**1,078**
Analytical services [1]	1.5	1.5	1.6	1.6	1.6	16	17	17	18	18
Solid waste management [2]	23.5	26.1	27.0	28.2	29.4	196	218	225	235	245
Hazardous waste management ...	7.5	8.3	8.5	8.8	8.6	65	72	74	77	75
Remediation/Industrial services...	8.2	8.5	7.9	8.2	8.4	78	81	75	78	80
Consulting & engineering	10.2	12.2	13.4	14.2	14.4	113	135	149	158	160
Water equipment and chemicals ..	11.7	12.1	12.5	13.0	13.2	90	93	96	100	102
Instrument manufacturing.......	1.5	1.6	1.7	1.8	1.8	13	14	14	15	15
Air pollution control equipment ...	3.6	3.7	3.7	3.8	3.8	26	27	27	27	27
Waste management equipment ...	9.8	10.4	11.0	11.4	11.2	75	80	85	88	86
Process and prevention technology..............	0.3	0.4	0.5	0.6	0.7	3	3	4	5	6
Water utilities..............	18.8	20.2	21.1	21.7	23.1	118	126	132	136	144
Resource recovery	13.3	15.2	14.0	14.3	15.2	89	101	93	95	101
Environmental energy sources....	1.6	1.8	1.9	2.0	2.1	14	16	17	18	19

[1] Covers environmental laboratory testing and services.   [2] Covers such activities as collection, transportation, transfer stations, disposal, landfill ownership and management for solid waste.

Source: Environmental Business International, Inc., San Diego, CA, *Environmental Business Journal*, monthly, (copyright).

No. 374. Pollution Abatement and Control Expenditures, in Current and Constant (1987) Dollars, 1972 to 1991, and by Media, 1991

[In millions of dollars]

YEAR	Total expenditures	POLLUTION ABATEMENT								Regulation and monitoring	Research and development
		Total	Personal consumption	Business	Government						
					Total	Federal	State and local	Govt. enterprise [1]			
CURRENT DOLLARS											
1972	17,037	15,848	1,349	11,090	3,409	139	1,311	1,959	367	823
1975	28,424	26,668	3,231	16,531	6,906	432	1,752	4,722	653	1,104
1980	51,478	48,432	6,568	30,618	11,246	494	2,778	7,973	1,296	1,751
1981	56,472	53,346	8,140	34,453	10,752	506	3,053	7,194	1,378	1,749
1982	56,576	53,395	8,309	34,151	10,935	550	3,274	7,111	1,397	1,783
1983	60,002	56,283	9,758	35,357	11,167	795	3,547	6,825	1,385	2,335
1984	66,445	62,746	10,771	39,467	12,508	944	3,886	7,679	1,362	2,337
1985	70,941	67,250	11,839	41,559	13,852	1,225	4,324	8,304	1,279	2,412
1986	74,178	70,074	12,244	42,636	15,195	1,346	4,793	9,056	1,532	2,573
1987	76,672	72,506	12,506	44,501	17,130	1,237	5,356	10,538	1,519	2,648
1988	81,081	76,605	12,044	46,928	17,633	1,402	6,149	10,082	1,695	2,781
1989	85,407	80,630	10,636	50,817	19,177	1,381	7,076	10,720	1,803	2,974
1990	89,996	85,116	9,088	55,059	20,969	1,391	8,089	11,489	1,784	3,097
1991 [2]	91,456	86,419	7,285	57,135	21,998	1,417	8,980	11,601	1,818	3,220
Air	28,060	25,423	7,285	17,881	258	73	16	168	483	2,153
Water	37,310	36,205	-	23,486	12,719	753	533	11,433	677	427
Solid Waste	26,640	26,026	-	17,338	8,688	341	8,348	-	427	187
CONSTANT (1987) DOLLARS											
1972	46,298	43,080	3,449	30,533	9,098	402	3,669	5,028	959.00	2,259
1975	57,333	53,673	6,165	33,113	14,395	937	3,737	9,720	1,346	2,313
1980	67,291	63,005	7,311	40,148	15,546	679	4,051	10,816	1,873	2,414
1981	66,536	62,556	8,494	40,470	13,592	627	3,984	8,981	1,810	2,170
1982	63,219	59,457	8,518	37,790	13,150	649	4,068	8,434	1,709	2,053
1983	65,052	60,870	10,016	38,042	12,813	911	4,203	7,698	1,608	2,574
1984	69,981	65,996	10,967	41,178	13,851	1,048	4,381	8,422	1,507	2,478
1985	72,656	68,802	11,780	42,408	14,615	1,300	4,646	8,668	1,361	2,493
1986	76,384	72,163	12,685	43,797	15,681	1,402	4,990	9,289	1,589	2,633
1987	76,672	72,506	10,875	44,501	17,130	1,237	5,356	10,538	1,519	2,648
1988	79,086	74,785	11,831	45,963	16,991	1,340	5,875	9,777	1,643	2,658
1989	80,106	75,720	10,147	47,755	17,818	1,273	6,502	10,043	1,657	2,730
1990	81,703	77,337	8,512	49,949	18,875	1,228	7,074	10,573	1,636	2,370
1991 [2]	80,597	76,270	6,654	50,728	18,888	1,220	7,621	10,047	1,611	2,716
Air	25,264	22,995	6,654	16,115	226	63	14	150	446	1,824
Water	33,554	32,589	-	21,481	11,108	652	558	9,897	607	359
Solid Waste	22,329	21,810	-	14,535	7,276	296	6,980	-	363	156

- Represents or rounds to zero. [1] Fixed capital. [2] Includes "other and unallocated" expenditures (such as for noise, radiation, and pesticide pollution and business expenditures not assigned to media) which may be either positive or negative; therefore, data may not add.

No. 375. Air and Water Pollution Abatement Expenditures in Constant (1987) Dollars: 1980 to 1991

[In millions of dollars. Excludes agricultural production of crops and livestock except feedlots]

YEAR	AIR							WATER				
	Total	Mobile sources [1]			Stationary sources			Total [5]	Industrial		Public sewer systems	
		Total	Cars [2]	Trucks [2]	Total [3]	Industrial			Facilities	Operations [4]	Facilities	Operations [4]
						Facilities	Operations [4]					
1980	25,661	12,367	9,103	2,840	13,294	6,011	6,443	26,482	3,696	3,988	10,148	5,148
1981	27,012	13,932	11,092	2,700	13,080	5,951	6,295	24,251	3,405	4,025	8,270	5,297
1982	25,719	13,754	10,914	2,777	11,965	5,501	5,601	23,337	3,284	3,844	7,679	5,616
1983	26,085	15,456	12,756	3,177	10,629	3,893	5,911	23,751	2,666	4,264	7,063	5,959
1984	27,659	16,896	14,119	4,090	10,763	3,820	6,151	25,382	2,865	4,482	7,791	6,149
1985	29,041	18,073	14,896	4,463	10,968	3,539	6,320	26,542	2,879	4,658	8,124	6,550
1986	30,270	19,513	15,424	4,670	10,757	3,573	6,732	27,765	2,392	4,866	8,807	7,285
1987	28,548	17,629	13,166	4,433	10,919	3,728	6,575	29,695	2,354	5,383	10,053	7,792
1988	29,531	19,190	14,727	4,607	10,341	3,342	6,436	29,107	2,381	5,310	9,376	8,269
1989	26,010	16,222	(NA)	(NA)	9,788	3,270	6,069	30,057	2,802	5,462	9,383	8,803
1990	24,728	13,994	(NA)	(NA)	10,734	3,969	6,371	33,066	4,226	5,935	10,334	9,488
1991	22,995	11,902	(NA)	(NA)	11,093	4,932	5,784	32,589	3,730	5,575	9,839	10,300

NA Not available. [1] Excludes expenditures to reduce emissions from sources other than cars and trucks. [2] Includes expenditures for devices such as catalytic convertors, and expenditures for devices. [3] Includes other expenditures not shown separately for fixed capital of government enterprises such as Tennessee Valley Authority. [4] Operation of facilities. [5] Includes expenditures for private connectors to sewer systems, by owners of animal feedlots, and by government enterprises.

Source of tables 374 and 375: U.S. Bureau of Economic Analysis, *Survey of Current Business*, May 1993.

No. 376. Pollution Abatement Capital Expenditures and Operating Costs of Manufacturing Establishments, 1990 to 1992, and by Selected Industry Group, 1992

[In millions of dollars. Based on probability sample of about 20,000 manufacturing establishments. Excludes apparel and other textile establishments and establishments with less than 20 employees]

YEAR AND INDUSTRY GROUP	POLLUTION ABATEMENT CAPITAL EXPENDITURES					POLLUTION ABATEMENT GROSS OPERATING COSTS [1]				
	Total	Air	Water	Solid waste		Total	Air	Water	Solid waste	
				Hazard-ous	Non-hazard-ous				Hazard-ous	Non-hazard-ous
1990...............	6,030.8	2,562.0	2,651.4	326.8	490.7	17,070.7	5,010.9	6,416.4	2,285.0	3,358.5
1991...............	7,390.1	3,706.3	2,814.6	322.9	546.2	17,386.8	5,033.5	6,345.0	2,553.2	3,455.0
All industries,1992 [2] .	7,866.9	4,403.1	2,509.8	333.5	620.4	17,466.4	5,395.0	6,576.9	2,157.1	3,337.4
Food and kindred products.	316.8	85.1	202.6	1.5	27.6	1,312.0	162.7	835.7	25.8	287.8
Lumber, wood products ...	94.5	50.7	18.9	4.7	20.3	243.0	89.3	49.5	22.7	81.5
Paper and allied products..	1,004.6	396.7	373.4	12.9	221.7	1,860.7	535.6	822.7	50.0	452.3
Chemicals & allied prod. ..	2,120.9	774.5	1,017.3	174.0	155.1	4,425.1	1,026.9	1,946.8	715.3	736.1
Petroleum & coal prod.	2,685.0	2,079.8	492.6	60.2	52.3	2,585.4	1,428.9	742.8	239.8	173.9
Stone, clay, glass products.	138.8	93.4	20.2	2.6	22.7	491.2	248.5	94.6	25.4	122.7
Primary metal industries...	525.7	342.6	123.5	12.7	46.9	1,993.4	933.1	575.0	200.2	285.1
Fabricated metals prod....	103.3	42.4	42.4	7.4	11.0	761.2	130.4	284.3	161.7	184.9
Machinery, exc. electrical..	150.3	88.8	31.7	11.2	18.6	463.7	65.4	160.5	101.4	136.5
Electrical, electronic equipment	126.6	63.0	45.6	10.4	7.5	657.1	117.9	288.8	129.7	120.7
Transportation equipment..	281.0	179.4	69.2	19.9	12.6	1,171.7	298.5	347.0	271.3	254.9
Instruments, related prod..	89.1	52.7	18.8	9.5	8.1	331.9	48.0	89.4	81.9	112.6

[1] Includes payments to governmental units.   [2] Includes industries not shown separately; excludes Major Group 23, Apparel and Other Textile Products.
Source: U.S. Bureau of the Census, *Current Industrial Reports,* series MA-200, annual.

No. 377. Threatened and Endangered Wildlife and Plant Species—Number: 1994

[As of October 19. Endangered species: One in danger of becoming extinct throughout all or a significant part of its natural range. Threatened species: One likely to become endangered in the foreseeable future]

ITEM	Mammals	Birds	Reptiles	Amphibians	Fishes	Snails	Clams	Crustaceans	Insects	Arachnids	Plants
Endangered species, total...........	307	226	80	14	64	15	52	11	23	4	386
U.S. only............	36	57	9	6	60	14	50	11	16	4	375
U.S. and foreign.......	20	16	8	-	3	-	-	-	3	-	10
Foreign only [1]	251	153	63	8	1	1	2	-	4	-	1
Threatened species, total...........	31	17	32	5	38	7	6	2	9	-	85
U.S. only............	5	8	14	4	32	7	6	2	9	-	74
U.S. and foreign.......	4	9	4	1	6	-	-	-	-	-	9
Foreign only [1]	22	-	14	-	-	-	-	-	-	-	2

- Represents zero.   [1] Species outside United States and outlying areas as determined by Fish and Wildlife Service.
Source: U.S. Fish and Wildlife Service, *Endangered Species Technical Bulletin,* quarterly.

No. 378. Tornadoes, Floods, and Tropical Storms: 1983 to 1993

[See also *Historical Statistics, Colonial Times to 1970,* series J 268-278]

ITEM	1983	1984	1985	1986	1987	1988	1989	1990	1991	1992	1993, prel.
Tornadoes, number [1]	931	907	684	764	656	702	856	1,133	1,132	1,303	(NA)
Lives lost, total	34	122	94	15	59	32	50	53	39	39	(NA)
Most in a single tornado	3	16	18	3	30	5	21	29	13	10	(NA)
Property loss of $500,000 and over	95	125	69	75	38	48	60	91	64	(NA)	(NA)
Floods: Lives lost..........	200	126	304	80	82	29	81	147	63	87	(NA)
Property loss (mil. dol.).......	4,100	4,000	3,000	4,000	1,490	114	415	2,058	1,416	800	(NA)
North Atlantic tropical storms and hurricanes: [2]											
Number reaching U.S. coast ...	4	12	11	6	7	12	11	14	6	6	8
Hurricanes only	1	1	6	2	1	1	3	-	1	1	1
Lives lost in U.S	22	4	30	9	-	6	56	13	15	24	3
Property loss (mil. (1990) dol.)[3] .	2,392	77	4,457	18	8	9	7,840	57	1,500	25,000	35

- Represents zero.   NA Not available.   [1] A violent, rotating column of air descending from a cumulonimbus cloud in the form of a tubular- or funnel-shaped cloud, usually characterized by movements along a narrow path and wind speeds from 100 to over 300 miles per hour. Also known as a "twister" or "waterspout."   [2] Source: National Hurricane Center, Coral Gables, FL, unpublished data. Tropical storms have maximum winds of 39 to 73 miles per hour; hurricanes have maximum winds of 74 miles per hour or higher.   [3] Source: Hebert, Jarrell, & Mayfield, "The Deadliest, Costliest, and Most Intense U.S. Hurricanes of this Century," NOAA Technical Memo, NHC-31, February 1993.
Source: Except as noted, U.S. National Oceanic and Atmospheric Administration, *Storm Data,* monthly.

No. 379. Normal Daily Mean Temperature—Selected Cities

[In Fahrenheit degrees. Airport data except as noted. Based on standard 30-year period, 1961 through 1990. See *Historical Statistics, Colonial Times to 1970*, series J 110-136 and J 164-267, for related data]

STATE	STATION	Jan.	Feb.	Mar.	Apr.	May	June	July	Aug.	Sept.	Oct.	Nov.	Dec.	Annual avg.
AL	Mobile.........	49.9	53.2	60.5	67.8	74.5	80.4	82.3	81.8	77.9	68.4	59.8	53.0	67.5
AK	Juneau	24.2	28.4	32.7	39.7	47.0	53.0	56.0	55.0	49.4	42.2	32.0	27.1	40.6
AZ	Phoenix.........	53.6	57.7	62.2	69.9	78.8	88.2	93.5	91.5	85.6	74.5	61.9	54.1	72.6
AR	Little Rock.......	39.1	43.6	53.1	62.1	70.2	78.4	81.9	80.6	74.1	63.0	52.1	42.8	61.8
CA	Los Angeles......	56.8	57.6	58.0	60.1	62.7	65.7	69.1	70.5	69.9	66.8	61.6	56.9	63.0
	Sacramento	45.2	50.7	53.6	58.3	65.3	71.6	75.7	75.1	71.5	64.2	53.3	45.3	60.8
	San Diego	57.4	58.6	59.6	62.0	64.1	66.8	71.0	72.6	71.4	67.7	62.0	57.4	64.2
	San Francisco	48.7	52.2	53.3	55.6	58.1	61.5	62.7	63.7	64.5	61.0	54.8	49.4	57.1
CO	Denver	29.7	33.4	39.0	48.2	57.2	66.9	73.5	71.4	62.3	51.4	39.0	31.0	50.3
CT	Hartford.........	24.6	27.5	37.5	48.7	59.6	68.5	73.7	71.6	63.3	52.2	41.9	29.5	49.9
DE	Wilmington.......	30.6	33.4	42.7	52.2	62.5	71.5	76.4	75.0	68.0	56.2	46.3	35.8	54.2
DC	Washington	34.6	37.5	47.2	56.5	64.4	75.6	80.0	78.5	71.3	59.7	49.8	39.4	58.0
FL	Jacksonville......	52.4	55.2	61.1	67.0	73.4	79.1	81.6	81.2	78.1	69.8	61.9	55.1	68.0
	Miami..........	67.2	68.5	71.7	75.2	78.7	81.4	82.6	82.8	81.9	78.3	73.6	69.1	75.9
GA	Atlanta.........	41.0	44.8	53.5	61.5	69.2	76.0	78.8	78.1	72.7	62.3	53.1	44.5	61.3
HI	Honolulu	72.9	73.0	74.4	75.8	77.5	79.4	80.5	81.4	81.0	79.6	77.2	74.1	77.2
ID	Boise	29.0	35.9	42.4	49.1	57.5	66.5	74.0	72.5	62.6	51.8	39.9	30.1	50.9
IL	Chicago.........	21.0	25.4	37.2	48.6	58.9	68.6	73.2	71.7	64.4	52.8	40.0	26.6	49.0
	Peoria..........	21.6	26.3	39.0	51.4	61.9	71.5	75.5	73.1	66.1	54.0	41.2	27.0	50.7
IN	Indianapolis	25.5	29.6	41.4	52.4	62.8	71.9	75.4	73.2	66.6	54.7	43.0	30.9	52.3
IA	Des Moines	19.4	24.7	37.3	50.9	62.3	71.8	76.6	73.9	65.1	53.5	39.0	24.4	49.9
KS	Wichita	29.5	34.8	45.4	56.4	65.6	75.7	81.4	79.3	70.3	58.6	44.7	33.0	56.2
KY	Louisville	31.7	35.7	46.3	56.3	65.3	73.2	77.2	75.8	69.5	57.6	47.1	36.9	56.1
LA	New Orleans	51.3	54.3	61.6	68.5	74.8	80.0	81.9	81.5	78.1	69.1	61.1	54.5	68.1
ME	Portland.........	20.8	23.3	33.0	43.3	53.3	62.4	68.6	67.3	59.1	48.5	38.7	26.5	45.4
MD	Baltimore.......	31.8	34.8	44.1	53.4	63.4	72.5	77.0	75.6	68.5	56.6	46.8	36.7	55.1
MA	Boston	28.6	30.3	38.6	48.1	58.2	67.7	73.5	71.9	64.8	54.8	45.3	33.6	51.3
MI	Detroit..........	22.9	25.4	35.7	47.3	58.4	67.6	72.3	70.5	63.2	51.2	40.2	28.3	48.6
	Sault Ste. Marie ...	12.9	14.0	24.0	38.2	50.5	58.0	63.8	62.6	55.1	45.3	33.0	19.0	39.7
MN	Duluth	7.0	12.3	24.4	38.6	50.8	59.8	66.1	63.7	54.2	43.7	28.4	12.8	38.5
	Minneapolis-St. Paul	11.8	17.9	31.0	46.4	58.5	68.2	73.6	70.5	60.5	48.8	33.2	17.9	44.9
MS	Jackson.........	44.1	47.9	56.7	64.6	72.0	78.8	81.5	80.9	75.9	64.7	55.8	47.8	64.2
MO	Kansas City	25.7	31.2	42.7	54.5	64.1	73.2	78.5	76.1	67.5	56.6	43.1	30.4	53.6
	St. Louis	29.3	33.9	45.1	56.7	66.1	75.4	79.8	77.6	70.2	58.4	46.2	33.9	56.1
MT	Great Falls.......	21.2	27.4	33.3	43.6	53.1	61.6	68.2	66.9	56.6	47.5	33.9	23.9	44.8
NE	Omaha	21.1	26.9	38.6	51.9	62.4	72.1	76.9	74.1	65.1	53.4	39.0	25.1	50.6
NV	Reno	32.9	38.0	42.8	48.6	56.5	65.1	71.6	69.6	60.4	50.8	40.3	32.7	50.8
NH	Concord	18.6	21.8	32.4	43.9	55.2	64.2	69.5	67.3	58.8	47.8	37.1	24.3	45.1
NJ	Atlantic City	30.9	33.0	41.5	50.0	60.4	69.4	74.7	73.4	66.1	54.9	45.8	35.8	53.0
NM	Albuquerque......	34.2	40.0	46.9	55.2	64.2	74.2	78.5	75.9	68.6	57.0	44.3	35.3	56.2
NY	Albany..........	20.6	23.5	34.3	46.4	57.6	66.9	71.8	69.6	61.3	50.2	39.7	26.5	47.4
	Buffalo	23.6	24.5	33.8	45.2	56.6	65.9	71.1	69.0	61.9	51.1	40.5	29.1	47.7
	New York [1]	31.5	33.6	42.4	52.5	62.7	71.6	76.8	75.5	68.2	57.5	47.6	36.6	54.7
NC	Charlotte	39.3	42.5	50.9	59.4	67.4	75.7	79.3	78.3	72.4	61.3	52.1	42.6	60.1
	Raleigh	38.9	42.0	50.4	59.0	67.0	74.3	78.1	77.1	71.1	60.1	51.2	42.6	59.3
ND	Bismarck........	9.2	15.7	28.2	43.0	55.0	64.4	70.4	68.3	57.0	45.7	28.6	14.0	41.6
OH	Cincinnati........	28.1	31.8	43.0	53.2	62.9	71.0	75.1	73.5	67.3	55.1	44.3	33.5	53.2
	Cleveland	24.8	27.2	37.3	47.6	58.0	67.6	71.9	70.4	63.9	52.8	42.6	30.9	49.6
	Columbus	26.4	29.6	40.9	51.0	61.2	69.2	73.2	71.5	65.5	53.7	42.9	31.9	51.4
OK	Oklahoma City	35.9	40.9	50.3	60.4	68.4	76.7	82.0	81.1	73.0	62.0	49.6	39.3	60.0
OR	Portland.........	39.6	43.6	47.3	51.0	57.1	63.5	68.2	68.6	63.3	54.5	46.1	40.2	53.6
PA	Philadelphia	30.4	33.0	42.4	52.4	62.9	71.8	76.7	75.5	68.2	56.4	46.4	35.8	54.3
	Pittsburgh	26.1	28.7	39.4	49.6	59.5	67.9	72.1	70.5	63.9	52.4	42.3	31.5	50.3
RI	Providence......	27.9	29.7	37.4	47.4	57.3	66.9	72.7	71.3	64.1	53.6	44.0	32.8	50.4
SC	Columbia	43.8	46.8	55.2	63.0	70.9	77.4	80.8	79.7	74.2	63.3	54.6	46.9	63.1
SD	Sioux Falls......	13.8	19.7	32.5	46.9	58.4	68.3	74.3	71.4	60.9	48.6	33.0	18.3	45.5
TN	Memphis	39.7	44.2	53.1	62.9	71.2	79.1	82.6	81.0	74.2	63.1	52.5	43.7	62.3
	Nashville	36.2	40.4	50.2	59.2	67.7	75.6	79.3	78.1	71.8	60.4	50.0	40.5	59.1
TX	Dallas-Fort Worth ..	43.4	47.9	56.7	65.5	72.8	81.0	85.3	84.9	77.4	67.2	56.2	46.9	65.4
	El Paso	42.8	48.1	55.1	63.4	71.8	80.4	82.3	80.1	74.4	64.0	52.4	44.1	63.2
	Houston	50.4	53.9	60.6	68.3	74.5	80.4	82.6	82.3	78.2	69.6	61.0	53.5	67.9
UT	Salt Lake City.....	27.9	34.1	41.8	49.7	58.8	69.1	77.9	75.6	65.2	53.2	40.8	29.7	52.0
VT	Burlington	16.3	18.2	30.7	43.9	56.3	65.2	70.5	67.9	58.9	47.8	36.8	23.0	44.6
VA	Norfolk	39.1	41.0	48.6	57.0	66.1	74.1	78.2	77.2	71.9	61.2	52.5	43.8	59.2
	Richmond	35.7	38.7	48.0	57.3	66.0	73.9	78.0	76.8	70.0	58.6	49.6	40.1	57.7
WA	Seattle-Tacoma ...	40.1	43.5	45.6	49.2	55.1	60.9	65.2	65.5	60.6	52.8	45.3	40.5	52.0
	Spokane	27.1	33.3	38.7	45.9	53.9	62.0	68.8	68.4	58.9	47.3	35.1	27.8	47.3
WV	Charleston.......	32.1	35.5	45.9	54.8	63.5	71.4	75.1	73.9	67.7	56.2	46.8	37.0	55.0
WI	Milwaukee	18.9	23.0	33.3	44.4	54.6	65.0	70.9	69.3	61.7	50.3	37.7	24.4	46.1
WY	Cheyenne	26.5	29.3	33.6	42.5	52.0	61.3	68.4	66.4	57.4	47.0	35.2	27.8	45.6
PR	San Juan........	77.0	77.1	78.0	79.4	80.9	82.3	82.6	82.7	82.5	81.9	80.0	78.1	80.2

[1] City office data.

Source: U.S. National Oceanic and Atmospheric Administration, *Climatography of the United States*, No. 81.

No. 380. Normal Daily Maximum Temperature—Selected Cities

[In Fahrenheit degrees. Airport data except as noted. Based on standard 30-year period, 1961 through 1990]

STATE	STATION	Jan.	Feb.	Mar.	Apr.	May	June	July	Aug.	Sept.	Oct.	Nov.	Dec.	Annual avg.
AL	Mobile..........	59.7	63.6	70.9	78.5	84.6	90.0	91.3	90.5	86.9	79.5	70.3	62.9	77.4
AK	Juneau	29.4	34.1	38.7	47.2	55.1	60.9	63.9	62.7	55.9	47.1	36.7	31.6	46.9
AZ	Phoenix.........	65.9	70.7	75.5	84.5	93.6	103.5	105.9	103.7	98.3	88.1	74.9	66.2	85.9
AR	Little Rock......	49.0	53.9	64.0	73.4	81.3	89.3	92.4	91.4	84.6	75.1	62.7	52.5	72.5
CA	Los Angeles.....	65.7	65.9	65.5	67.4	69.0	71.9	75.3	76.6	76.6	74.4	70.3	65.9	70.4
	Sacramento	52.7	60.0	64.0	71.1	80.3	87.8	93.2	92.1	87.3	77.9	63.1	52.7	73.5
	San Diego	65.9	66.5	66.3	68.4	69.1	71.6	76.2	77.8	77.1	74.6	69.9	66.1	70.8
	San Francisco ...	55.6	59.4	60.8	63.9	66.5	70.3	71.6	72.3	73.6	70.1	62.4	56.1	65.2
CO	Denver	43.2	46.6	52.2	61.8	70.8	81.4	88.2	85.8	76.9	66.3	52.5	44.5	64.2
CT	Hartford.........	33.2	36.4	46.8	59.9	71.6	80.0	85.0	82.7	74.8	63.7	51.0	37.5	60.2
DE	Wilmington......	38.7	41.9	52.1	62.6	72.9	81.4	85.6	84.1	77.7	66.6	55.5	43.9	63.6
DC	Washington	42.3	45.9	56.5	66.7	76.2	84.7	88.5	86.9	80.1	69.1	58.3	47.0	66.9
FL	Jacksonville	64.2	67.0	73.0	79.1	84.7	89.3	91.4	90.7	87.2	80.2	73.6	66.8	78.9
	Miami	75.2	76.5	79.1	82.4	85.3	87.6	89.0	89.0	87.8	84.5	80.4	76.7	82.8
GA	Atlanta	50.4	55.0	64.3	72.7	79.6	85.8	88.0	87.1	81.8	72.7	63.4	54.0	71.2
HI	Honolulu	80.1	80.5	81.6	82.8	84.7	86.5	87.5	88.7	88.5	86.9	84.1	81.2	84.4
ID	Boise	36.4	44.2	52.9	61.4	71.0	80.9	90.2	88.1	77.0	64.6	48.7	37.7	62.8
IL	Chicago.........	29.0	33.5	45.8	58.6	70.1	79.6	83.7	81.8	74.8	63.3	48.4	34.0	58.6
	Peoria..........	29.9	34.9	48.1	62.0	72.8	82.2	85.7	83.1	76.9	64.8	49.8	34.6	60.4
IN	Indianapolis	33.7	38.3	50.9	63.3	73.8	82.7	85.5	83.6	77.6	65.8	51.9	38.5	62.1
IA	Des Moines	28.1	33.7	46.9	61.8	73.0	82.2	86.7	84.2	75.6	64.3	48.0	32.6	59.8
KS	Wichita	39.8	45.9	57.2	68.3	76.9	86.8	92.8	90.7	81.4	70.6	55.3	43.0	67.4
KY	Louisville.......	40.3	44.8	56.3	67.3	76.0	83.5	87.0	85.7	80.3	69.2	56.8	45.1	66.0
LA	New Orleans	60.8	64.1	71.6	78.5	84.4	89.2	90.6	90.2	86.6	79.4	71.1	64.3	77.6
ME	Portland.........	30.3	33.1	41.4	52.3	63.2	72.7	78.8	77.4	69.3	58.7	47.0	35.1	54.9
MD	Baltimore........	40.2	43.7	54.0	64.3	74.2	83.2	87.2	85.4	78.5	67.3	56.5	45.2	65.0
MA	Boston	35.7	37.5	45.8	55.9	66.6	76.3	81.8	79.8	72.8	62.7	52.2	40.4	59.0
MI	Detroit..........	30.3	33.3	44.4	57.7	69.6	78.9	83.3	81.3	73.9	61.5	48.1	35.2	58.1
	Sault Ste. Marie ...	21.1	23.2	32.8	48.0	62.6	70.5	76.3	73.8	65.9	54.3	40.0	26.2	49.6
MN	Duluth..........	16.2	21.7	32.9	48.2	61.9	71.0	77.1	73.9	63.8	52.3	35.2	20.7	47.9
	Minneapolis-St. Paul	20.7	26.6	39.2	56.5	69.4	78.8	84.0	80.7	70.7	58.8	41.0	25.5	54.3
MS	Jackson.........	55.6	60.1	69.3	77.4	84.0	90.6	92.4	92.0	88.0	79.1	69.2	59.5	76.4
MO	Kansas City	34.7	40.6	52.8	65.1	74.3	83.3	88.7	86.4	78.1	67.5	52.6	38.8	63.6
	St. Louis	37.7	42.6	54.6	66.9	76.1	85.2	89.3	87.3	79.9	68.5	54.7	41.7	65.4
MT	Great Falls......	30.6	37.5	43.7	55.3	65.2	74.6	83.3	81.6	69.6	59.3	43.5	33.1	56.4
NE	Omaha	31.3	37.1	49.4	63.8	74.0	83.7	87.9	85.2	76.5	65.6	49.3	34.6	61.5
NV	Reno	45.1	51.7	56.3	63.7	72.9	83.1	91.9	89.6	79.5	68.6	53.8	45.5	66.8
NH	Concord	29.8	33.0	42.8	56.3	68.9	77.3	82.4	79.8	71.6	60.7	47.1	34.2	57.0
NJ	Atlantic City	40.4	42.5	51.6	60.7	71.2	80.0	84.5	83.3	76.6	66.0	55.7	45.3	63.2
NM	Albuquerque.....	46.8	53.5	61.4	70.8	79.7	90.0	92.5	89.0	81.9	71.0	57.3	47.5	70.1
NY	Albany..........	30.2	33.2	44.0	57.5	69.7	79.0	84.0	81.4	73.2	61.8	48.7	34.9	58.1
	Buffalo	30.2	31.6	41.7	54.2	66.1	75.3	80.2	77.9	70.8	59.4	47.1	35.3	55.8
	New York [1]	37.6	40.3	50.0	61.2	71.7	80.1	85.2	83.7	76.2	65.3	54.0	42.5	62.3
NC	Charlotte	49.0	53.0	62.3	71.2	78.3	85.8	88.9	87.7	81.9	72.0	62.6	52.3	70.4
	Raleigh	48.9	52.6	62.1	71.7	78.6	85.0	88.0	86.8	81.1	71.6	62.6	52.7	70.1
ND	Bismarck........	20.2	26.4	38.5	54.9	67.8	77.1	84.4	82.7	70.8	58.7	39.3	24.5	53.8
OH	Cincinnati........	36.6	40.8	53.0	64.2	74.0	82.0	85.5	84.1	77.9	66.0	53.3	41.5	63.2
	Cleveland	31.9	35.0	46.3	57.9	68.6	78.3	82.4	80.5	73.6	62.1	50.0	37.4	58.7
	Columbus	34.1	38.0	50.5	62.0	72.3	80.4	83.7	82.1	76.2	64.5	51.4	39.2	61.2
OK	Oklahoma City	46.7	52.1	62.0	71.9	79.1	87.3	93.4	92.5	83.8	73.6	60.4	49.9	71.1
OR	Portland.........	45.4	51.0	56.0	60.6	67.1	74.0	79.9	80.3	74.6	64.0	52.6	45.6	62.6
PA	Philadelphia	37.9	41.0	51.6	62.6	73.1	81.7	86.1	84.6	77.6	66.3	55.1	43.4	63.4
	Pittsburgh	33.7	36.9	49.0	60.3	70.6	78.9	82.6	80.8	74.3	62.5	50.4	38.6	59.9
RI	Providence.......	36.6	38.3	46.1	57.0	67.3	76.9	82.1	80.7	74.3	64.1	53.0	41.2	59.8
SC	Columbia........	55.3	59.3	68.2	76.5	83.5	88.8	91.6	90.1	85.1	76.3	67.8	58.8	75.1
SD	Sioux Falls......	24.3	29.6	42.3	59.0	70.7	80.5	86.3	83.3	73.1	61.2	43.4	28.0	56.8
TN	Memphis	48.5	53.5	63.2	73.3	81.0	89.3	92.3	90.8	83.9	74.3	62.3	52.5	72.1
	Nashville	45.9	50.8	61.2	70.8	78.8	86.5	89.5	88.4	82.5	72.5	60.4	50.2	69.8
TX	Dallas-Fort Worth ..	54.1	58.9	67.8	76.3	82.9	91.9	96.5	96.2	87.8	78.5	66.8	57.5	76.3
	El Paso	56.1	62.2	69.9	78.7	87.1	96.5	96.1	93.5	87.1	78.4	66.4	57.5	77.5
	Houston	61.0	65.3	71.1	78.4	84.6	90.1	92.7	92.5	88.4	81.6	72.4	64.7	78.6
UT	Salt Lake City.....	36.4	43.6	52.2	61.3	71.9	82.8	92.2	89.4	79.2	66.1	50.8	37.8	63.6
VT	Burlington	25.1	27.5	39.3	53.6	67.2	75.8	81.2	77.9	69.0	57.0	44.0	30.4	54.0
VA	Norfolk.........	47.3	49.7	57.9	66.9	75.3	82.9	86.4	85.1	79.6	69.5	61.2	52.2	67.8
	Richmond	45.7	49.2	59.5	70.0	77.8	85.1	88.4	87.1	80.9	70.7	61.3	50.2	68.8
WA	Seattle-Tacoma ...	45.0	49.5	52.7	57.2	63.9	69.9	75.2	75.2	69.3	59.7	50.5	45.1	59.4
	Spokane	33.2	40.6	47.7	57.0	65.8	74.7	83.1	82.5	72.0	58.6	41.4	33.8	57.5
WV	Charleston.......	41.2	45.3	56.7	66.8	75.5	83.1	85.7	84.4	78.8	68.2	57.3	46.0	65.8
WI	Milwaukee	26.1	30.1	40.4	52.9	64.3	74.9	79.9	77.8	70.6	58.7	44.7	31.2	54.3
WY	Cheyenne	37.7	40.5	44.9	54.7	64.6	74.4	82.2	80.0	71.1	60.0	46.8	38.8	58.0
PR	San Juan........	83.2	83.6	84.4	85.8	87.2	88.6	88.5	88.7	88.8	88.3	85.9	83.8	86.4

[1] City office data.

Source: U.S. National Oceanic and Atmospheric Administration, *Climatography of the United States*, No. 81.

Geography and Environment

No. 381. Normal Daily Minimum Temperature—Selected Cities

[In Fahrenheit degrees. Airport data except as noted. Based on standard 30-year period, 1961 through 1990]

STATE	STATION	Jan.	Feb.	Mar.	Apr.	May	June	July	Aug.	Sept.	Oct.	Nov.	Dec.	Annual avg.
AL	Mobile.........	40.0	42.7	50.1	57.1	64.4	70.7	73.2	72.9	68.7	57.3	49.1	43.1	57.4
AK	Juneau.........	19.0	22.7	26.7	32.1	38.9	45.0	48.1	47.3	42.9	37.2	27.2	22.6	34.1
AZ	Phoenix........	41.2	44.7	48.8	55.3	63.9	72.9	81.0	79.2	72.8	60.8	48.9	41.8	59.3
AR	Little Rock......	29.1	33.2	42.2	50.7	59.0	67.4	71.5	69.8	63.5	50.9	41.5	33.1	51.0
CA	Los Angeles......	47.8	49.3	50.5	52.8	56.3	59.5	62.8	64.2	63.2	59.2	52.8	47.9	55.5
	Sacramento.....	37.7	41.4	43.2	45.5	50.3	55.3	58.1	58.0	55.7	50.4	43.4	37.8	48.1
	San Diego.......	48.9	50.7	52.8	55.6	59.1	61.9	65.7	67.3	65.6	60.9	53.9	48.8	57.6
	San Francisco	41.8	45.0	45.8	47.2	49.7	52.6	53.9	55.0	55.2	51.8	47.1	42.7	49.0
CO	Denver	16.1	20.2	25.8	34.5	43.6	52.4	58.6	56.9	47.6	36.4	25.4	17.4	36.2
CT	Hartford........	15.8	18.6	28.1	37.5	47.6	56.9	62.2	60.4	51.8	40.7	32.8	21.3	39.5
DE	Wilmington......	22.4	24.8	33.1	41.8	52.2	61.6	67.1	65.9	58.2	45.7	37.0	27.6	44.8
DC	Washington	26.8	29.1	37.7	46.4	56.6	66.5	71.4	70.0	62.5	50.3	41.1	31.7	49.2
FL	Jacksonville.....	40.5	43.3	49.2	54.9	62.1	69.1	71.9	71.8	69.0	59.3	50.2	43.4	57.1
	Miami..........	59.2	60.4	64.2	67.8	72.1	75.1	76.2	76.7	75.9	72.1	66.7	61.5	69.0
GA	Atlanta.........	31.5	34.5	42.5	50.2	58.7	66.2	69.5	69.0	63.5	51.9	42.8	35.0	51.3
HI	Honolulu	65.6	65.4	67.2	68.7	70.3	72.2	73.5	74.2	73.5	72.3	70.3	67.0	70.0
ID	Boise	21.6	27.5	31.9	36.7	43.9	52.1	57.7	56.8	48.2	39.0	31.1	22.5	39.1
IL	Chicago........	12.9	17.2	28.5	38.6	47.7	57.5	62.6	61.6	53.9	42.2	31.6	19.1	39.5
	Peoria.........	13.2	17.7	29.8	40.8	50.9	60.7	65.4	63.1	55.2	43.1	32.5	19.3	41.0
IN	Indianapolis	17.2	20.9	31.9	41.5	51.7	61.0	65.2	62.8	55.6	43.5	34.1	23.2	42.4
IA	Des Moines	10.7	15.6	27.6	40.0	51.5	61.2	66.5	63.6	54.5	42.7	29.9	16.1	40.0
KS	Wichita	19.2	23.7	33.6	44.5	54.3	64.6	69.9	67.9	59.2	46.6	33.9	23.0	45.0
KY	Louisville	23.2	26.5	36.2	45.4	54.7	62.9	67.3	65.8	58.7	45.8	37.3	28.6	46.0
LA	New Orleans	41.8	44.4	51.6	58.4	65.2	70.8	73.1	72.8	69.5	58.7	51.0	44.8	58.5
ME	Portland........	11.4	13.5	24.5	34.1	43.4	52.1	58.3	57.1	48.9	38.3	30.4	17.8	35.8
MD	Baltimore.......	23.4	25.9	34.1	42.5	52.6	61.8	66.8	65.7	58.4	45.9	37.1	28.2	45.2
MA	Boston	21.6	23.0	31.3	40.2	49.8	59.1	65.1	64.0	56.8	46.9	38.3	26.7	43.6
MI	Detroit.........	15.6	17.6	27.0	36.8	47.1	56.3	61.3	59.6	52.5	40.9	32.2	21.4	39.0
	Sault Ste. Marie . . .	4.6	4.8	15.3	28.4	38.4	45.5	51.3	51.3	44.3	36.2	25.9	11.8	29.8
MN	Duluth	-2.2	2.8	15.7	28.9	39.6	48.5	55.1	53.3	44.5	35.1	21.5	4.9	29.0
	Minneapolis-St. Paul	2.8	9.2	22.7	36.2	47.6	57.6	63.1	60.3	50.3	38.8	25.2	10.2	35.3
MS	Jackson.........	32.7	35.7	44.1	51.9	60.0	67.1	70.5	69.7	63.7	50.3	42.3	36.1	52.0
MO	Kansas City	16.7	21.8	32.6	43.8	53.9	63.1	68.2	65.7	56.9	45.7	33.6	21.9	43.7
	St. Louis	20.8	25.1	35.5	46.4	56.0	65.7	70.4	67.9	60.5	48.3	37.7	26.0	46.7
MT	Great Falls......	11.6	17.2	22.8	31.9	40.9	48.6	53.2	52.2	43.5	35.8	24.3	14.6	33.1
NE	Omaha	10.9	16.7	27.7	39.9	50.9	60.4	65.9	62.9	53.6	41.2	28.7	15.6	39.5
NV	Reno	20.7	24.2	29.2	33.3	40.1	46.9	51.3	49.6	41.3	32.9	26.7	19.9	34.7
NH	Concord........	7.4	10.4	22.1	31.5	41.4	51.2	56.5	54.7	46.0	34.9	27.0	14.4	33.1
NJ	Atlantic City	21.4	23.5	31.3	39.3	49.6	58.7	64.8	63.5	55.5	43.7	35.8	26.3	42.8
NM	Albuquerque.....	21.7	26.4	32.2	39.6	48.6	58.3	64.4	62.6	55.2	43.0	31.2	23.1	42.2
NY	Albany.........	11.0	13.8	24.5	35.1	45.4	54.6	59.6	57.8	49.4	38.6	30.7	18.2	36.6
	Buffalo.........	17.0	17.4	25.9	36.2	47.0	56.5	61.9	60.1	53.0	42.7	33.9	22.9	39.5
	New York [1]	25.3	26.9	34.8	43.8	53.7	63.0	68.4	67.3	60.1	49.7	41.1	30.7	47.1
NC	Charlotte.......	29.6	31.9	39.4	47.5	56.4	65.6	69.6	68.9	62.9	50.6	41.5	32.8	49.7
	Raleigh........	28.8	31.3	38.7	46.2	55.3	63.6	68.1	67.5	61.1	48.4	39.7	32.4	48.4
ND	Bismarck........	-1.7	5.1	17.8	31.0	42.2	51.6	56.4	53.9	43.1	32.5	17.8	3.3	29.4
OH	Cincinnati.......	19.5	22.7	33.1	42.2	51.8	60.0	64.8	62.9	56.6	44.2	35.3	25.3	43.2
	Cleveland	17.6	19.3	28.2	37.3	47.3	56.8	61.4	60.3	54.2	43.5	35.0	24.5	40.5
	Columbus	18.5	21.2	31.2	40.0	50.1	58.0	62.7	60.8	54.8	42.9	34.3	24.6	41.6
OK	Oklahoma City	25.2	29.6	38.5	48.8	57.7	66.1	70.6	69.6	62.2	50.4	38.6	28.6	48.8
OR	Portland........	33.7	36.1	38.6	41.3	47.0	52.9	56.5	56.9	52.0	44.9	39.5	34.8	44.5
PA	Philadelphia	22.8	24.8	33.2	42.1	52.7	61.8	67.2	66.3	58.7	46.4	37.6	28.1	45.1
	Pittsburgh	18.5	20.3	29.8	38.8	48.4	56.9	61.6	60.2	53.5	42.3	34.1	24.4	40.7
RI	Providence......	19.1	20.9	28.8	37.7	47.3	56.8	63.2	61.9	53.8	43.0	34.9	24.4	41.0
SC	Columbia	32.1	34.2	42.2	49.4	58.2	66.0	70.0	69.2	63.2	50.1	41.5	34.9	50.9
SD	Sioux Falls.......	3.3	9.7	22.6	34.8	45.9	56.1	62.3	59.4	48.7	36.0	22.6	8.6	34.2
TN	Memphis	30.9	34.6	43.0	52.4	61.2	68.9	72.9	71.1	64.5	51.9	42.7	34.8	52.4
	Nashville	26.5	29.9	39.1	47.5	56.6	64.7	68.9	67.7	61.1	48.3	39.6	30.9	48.4
TX	Dallas-Fort Worth . .	32.7	36.9	45.6	54.7	62.6	70.0	74.1	73.6	66.9	55.8	45.4	36.3	54.6
	El Paso	29.4	33.9	40.2	48.0	56.5	64.3	68.4	66.6	61.6	49.6	38.4	30.7	49.0
	Houston	39.7	42.6	50.0	58.1	64.4	70.6	72.4	72.0	67.9	57.6	49.6	42.2	57.3
UT	Salt Lake City.....	19.3	24.6	31.4	37.9	45.6	55.4	63.7	61.8	51.0	40.2	30.9	21.6	40.3
VT	Burlington	7.5	8.9	22.0	34.2	45.4	54.6	59.7	57.9	48.8	38.6	29.6	15.5	35.2
VA	Norfolk	30.9	32.3	39.3	47.1	56.8	65.2	70.0	69.4	64.2	52.9	43.8	35.4	50.6
	Richmond.......	25.7	28.1	36.3	44.6	54.2	62.7	67.5	66.4	59.0	46.5	37.9	29.9	46.6
WA	Seattle-Tacoma ...	35.2	37.4	38.5	41.2	46.3	51.9	55.2	55.7	51.9	45.8	40.1	35.8	44.6
	Spokane	20.8	25.9	29.6	34.7	41.9	49.2	54.4	54.3	45.8	36.0	28.8	21.7	36.9
WV	Charleston	23.0	25.7	35.0	42.8	51.5	59.8	64.4	63.4	56.5	44.2	36.3	28.0	44.2
WI	Milwaukee	11.6	15.9	26.2	35.8	44.8	55.0	62.0	60.8	52.8	41.8	30.7	17.5	37.9
WY	Cheyenne	15.2	18.1	22.1	30.1	39.4	48.3	54.6	52.8	43.7	33.9	23.7	16.7	33.2
PR	San Juan........	70.8	70.6	71.6	72.9	74.5	76.1	76.8	76.7	76.2	75.5	74.0	72.4	74.0

[1] City office data.

Source: U.S. National Oceanic and Atmospheric Administration, Climatography of the United States, No. 81.

No. 382. Highest Temperature of Record—Selected Cities

[In Fahrenheit degrees. Airport data, except as noted. For period of record through 1992]

STATE	STATION	Length of record (yr.)	Jan.	Feb.	Mar.	Apr.	May	June	July	Aug.	Sept.	Oct.	Nov.	Dec.	Annual
AL	Mobile..........	51	84	82	90	94	100	102	104	102	99	93	87	81	104
AK	Juneau.........	48	57	57	59	71	82	86	90	83	72	61	56	54	90
AZ	Phoenix.........	55	88	92	100	105	113	122	118	116	118	107	93	88	122
AR	Little Rock.......	51	83	85	91	95	98	105	112	108	106	97	86	80	112
CA	Los Angeles......	57	88	92	95	102	97	104	97	98	110	106	101	94	110
	Sacramento......	42	70	76	88	93	105	115	114	109	108	101	87	72	115
	San Diego.......	52	88	88	93	98	96	101	95	98	111	107	97	88	111
	San Francisco	65	72	78	85	92	97	106	105	98	103	99	85	75	106
CO	Denver.........	58	73	76	84	90	96	104	104	101	97	89	79	75	104
CT	Hartford.........	38	65	73	87	96	97	100	102	101	99	91	81	74	102
DE	Wilmington.......	45	75	78	86	94	95	99	102	101	100	91	85	74	102
DC	Washington......	51	79	82	89	95	99	101	104	103	101	94	86	75	104
FL	Jacksonville......	51	85	88	91	95	100	103	105	102	100	96	88	84	105
	Miami	50	88	89	92	96	95	98	98	98	97	95	89	87	98
GA	Atlanta	44	79	80	85	93	95	101	105	102	98	95	84	79	105
HI	Honolulu........	23	87	88	88	89	93	92	92	93	94	94	93	89	94
ID	Boise	53	63	71	81	92	98	109	111	110	102	94	74	65	111
IL	Chicago.........	34	65	71	88	91	93	104	102	101	99	91	78	71	104
	Peoria..........	53	70	72	86	92	93	105	103	103	100	90	81	71	105
IN	Indianapolis......	53	71	74	85	89	93	102	104	102	100	90	81	74	104
IA	Des Moines	53	65	73	91	93	98	103	105	108	101	95	76	69	108
KS	Wichita	40	75	84	89	96	100	110	113	110	107	95	85	83	113
KY	Louisville	45	77	77	86	91	95	102	105	101	104	92	84	76	105
LA	New Orleans	46	83	85	89	92	96	100	101	102	101	92	87	84	102
ME	Portland.........	52	64	64	86	85	94	98	99	103	95	88	74	69	103
MD	Baltimore........	42	75	79	87	94	98	100	104	105	100	92	83	77	105
MA	Boston	41	63	70	81	94	95	100	102	102	100	90	78	73	102
MI	Detroit..........	34	62	65	81	89	93	104	102	100	98	91	77	68	104
	Sault Ste. Marie ...	52	45	47	75	85	89	93	97	98	95	80	67	60	98
MN	Duluth..........	51	52	55	78	88	90	93	97	97	95	86	70	55	97
	Minneapolis-St. Paul	54	58	60	83	95	96	102	105	102	98	89	75	63	105
MS	Jackson.........	29	82	85	89	94	99	105	106	102	104	95	88	84	106
MO	Kansas City	20	69	76	86	93	92	105	107	109	102	92	82	70	109
	St. Louis	35	76	85	89	93	93	102	107	107	104	94	85	76	107
MT	Great Falls......	55	67	70	78	89	93	101	105	106	98	91	76	69	106
NE	Omaha.........	56	69	78	89	97	99	105	114	110	104	96	80	72	114
NV	Reno	51	70	75	83	89	96	103	104	105	101	91	77	70	105
NH	Concord........	51	68	66	85	95	97	98	102	101	98	90	80	68	102
NJ	Atlantic City	49	78	75	87	94	99	106	104	102	99	90	84	75	106
NM	Albuquerque.....	53	69	76	85	89	98	105	105	101	100	91	77	72	105
NY	Albany..........	46	62	67	86	92	94	99	100	99	100	89	82	71	100
	Buffalo	49	72	65	81	94	90	96	97	99	98	87	80	74	99
	New York [1]	124	72	75	86	96	99	101	106	104	102	94	84	72	106
NC	Charlotte........	53	78	81	90	93	100	103	103	103	104	98	85	77	104
	Raleigh.........	53	62	69	81	93	98	107	109	109	105	95	75	65	109
ND	Bismarck........	48	79	84	92	95	97	104	105	105	104	98	88	79	105
OH	Cincinnati........	31	69	73	84	89	93	102	103	102	98	88	81	75	103
	Cleveland	51	73	69	83	88	92	104	103	102	101	90	82	77	104
	Columbus	53	74	73	85	89	94	102	100	101	100	90	80	76	102
OK	Oklahoma City	39	80	84	93	100	104	105	109	110	102	96	87	86	110
OR	Portland.........	52	63	71	80	87	100	100	107	107	105	92	73	64	107
PA	Philadelphia......	51	74	74	87	94	97	100	104	101	100	96	81	72	104
	Pittsburgh	40	69	69	82	89	89	91	98	103	100	97	87	82	103
RI	Providence.......	39	66	72	80	98	94	97	102	104	100	86	78	70	104
SC	Columbia........	45	84	84	91	94	101	107	107	107	101	101	90	83	107
SD	Sioux Falls.......	47	66	70	87	94	100	110	108	108	104	94	76	61	110
TN	Memphis........	51	78	81	85	94	99	104	108	105	103	95	85	81	108
	Nashville........	53	78	84	86	91	97	106	107	104	105	94	84	79	107
TX	Dallas-Fort Worth ..	39	88	88	96	95	103	113	110	108	106	102	89	88	113
	El Paso.........	53	80	83	89	98	104	111	112	108	104	96	87	80	112
	Houston........	23	84	91	91	95	97	103	104	107	102	96	89	83	107
UT	Salt Lake City.....	64	62	69	78	86	93	104	107	104	100	89	75	67	107
VT	Burlington	49	63	62	84	91	93	97	99	101	94	85	75	65	101
VA	Norfolk	44	78	81	88	97	100	101	103	104	99	95	86	80	104
	Richmond.......	63	80	83	93	96	100	104	105	102	103	99	86	80	105
WA	Seattle-Tacoma ...	48	64	70	75	85	93	96	99	99	98	89	74	63	99
	Spokane........	45	59	61	71	90	96	101	103	108	98	86	67	56	108
WV	Charleston.......	45	79	78	89	94	93	98	104	101	102	92	85	80	104
WI	Milwaukee	52	62	65	82	91	93	101	101	103	98	89	77	63	103
WY	Cheyenne	57	66	71	74	83	90	100	100	96	93	83	73	69	100
PR	San Juan.......	38	92	96	96	97	96	97	95	97	97	98	96	94	98

[1] City office data.

Source: U.S. National Oceanic and Atmospheric Administration, *Comparative Climatic Data*, annual.

Geography and Environment

No. 383. Lowest Temperature of Record—Selected Cities

[In Fahrenheit degrees. Airport data, except as noted. For period of record through 1992]

STATE	STATION	Length of record (yr.)	Jan.	Feb.	Mar.	Apr.	May	June	July	Aug.	Sept.	Oct.	Nov.	Dec.	Annual
AL	Mobile	51	3	11	21	32	43	49	60	59	42	32	22	8	3
AK	Juneau	48	-22	-22	-15	6	25	31	36	27	23	11	-5	-21	-22
AZ	Phoenix	55	17	22	25	32	40	50	61	60	47	34	25	22	17
AR	Little Rock	51	-4	-5	11	28	40	46	54	52	37	29	17	-1	-5
CA	Los Angeles	57	23	32	34	39	43	48	49	51	47	41	34	32	23
	Sacramento	42	23	23	26	32	36	41	48	49	43	36	26	18	18
	San Diego	52	29	36	39	41	48	51	55	57	51	43	38	34	29
	San Francisco	65	24	25	30	31	36	41	43	42	38	34	25	20	20
CO	Denver	56	-25	-30	-11	-2	22	30	43	41	17	3	-8	-25	-30
CT	Hartford	38	-26	-21	-6	9	28	37	44	36	30	17	1	-14	-26
DE	Wilmington	45	-14	-6	2	18	30	41	48	43	36	24	14	-7	-14
DC	Washington	51	-5	4	11	24	34	47	54	49	39	29	16	1	-5
FL	Jacksonville	51	7	19	23	34	45	47	61	63	48	36	21	11	7
	Miami	50	30	32	32	46	53	60	69	68	68	51	39	30	30
GA	Atlanta	44	-8	5	10	26	37	46	53	55	36	28	3	-	-8
HI	Honolulu	23	53	53	55	57	60	65	66	67	66	64	57	54	53
ID	Boise	53	-17	-15	6	19	22	31	35	34	23	11	-3	-25	-25
IL	Chicago	34	-27	-17	-8	7	24	36	40	41	28	17	1	-25	-27
	Peoria	53	-25	-18	-10	14	25	39	47	41	26	19	-2	-23	-25
IN	Indianapolis	53	-22	-21	-7	16	28	37	44	41	28	17	-2	-23	-23
IA	Des Moines	53	-24	-20	-22	9	30	38	47	40	26	14	-4	-22	-24
KS	Wichita	40	-12	-21	-2	15	31	43	51	48	31	21	1	-16	-21
KY	Louisville	45	-20	-19	-1	22	31	42	50	46	33	23	-1	-15	-20
LA	New Orleans	46	14	19	25	32	41	50	60	60	42	35	24	11	11
ME	Portland	52	-26	-39	-21	8	23	33	40	33	23	15	3	-21	-39
MD	Baltimore	42	-7	-3	6	20	32	40	50	45	35	25	13	-	-7
MA	Boston	41	-12	-4	6	16	34	45	50	47	38	28	15	-7	-12
MI	Detroit	34	-21	-15	-4	10	25	36	41	38	29	17	9	-10	-21
	Sault Ste. Marie	52	-36	-35	-24	-2	18	26	36	29	25	16	-10	-25	-36
MN	Duluth	51	-39	-33	-29	-5	17	27	35	32	22	8	-23	-34	-39
	Minneapolis-St. Paul	54	-34	-28	-32	2	18	34	43	39	26	15	-17	-29	-34
MS	Jackson	29	2	11	15	27	38	47	51	55	35	29	17	4	2
MO	Kansas City	20	-17	-19	-10	12	30	42	52	43	33	21	1	-23	-23
	St. Louis	35	-18	-10	-5	22	31	43	51	47	36	23	1	-16	-18
MT	Great Falls	55	-37	-35	-29	-6	15	31	40	30	21	-11	-25	-43	-43
NE	Omaha	56	-23	-21	-16	5	27	38	44	43	25	13	-9	-23	-23
NV	Reno	51	-16	-16	-2	13	18	25	33	24	20	8	1	-16	-16
NH	Concord	51	-33	-37	-16	8	21	30	35	29	21	10	-5	-22	-37
NJ	Atlantic City	49	-10	-11	5	12	25	37	42	40	32	20	10	-7	-11
NM	Albuquerque	53	-17	-5	8	19	28	40	52	50	37	21	-7	-7	-17
NY	Albany	46	-28	-21	-21	10	26	36	40	34	24	16	5	-22	-28
	Buffalo	49	-16	-20	-7	12	26	35	43	38	32	20	9	-10	-20
	New York [1]	124	-6	-15	3	12	32	44	52	50	39	28	5	-13	-15
NC	Charlotte	53	-5	5	4	24	32	45	53	53	39	24	11	2	-5
	Raleigh	53	-44	-39	-31	-12	15	30	35	33	11	-10	-30	-43	-44
ND	Bismarck	48	-9	5	11	23	31	38	48	46	37	19	11	4	-9
OH	Cincinnati	31	-25	-11	-11	17	27	39	47	43	33	16	1	-20	-25
	Cleveland	51	-19	-15	-5	10	25	31	41	38	32	19	3	-15	-19
	Columbus	53	-19	-13	-6	14	25	35	43	39	31	20	5	-17	-19
OK	Oklahoma City	39	-4	-3	3	20	37	47	53	51	36	22	11	-8	-8
OR	Portland	52	-2	-3	19	29	29	39	43	44	34	26	13	6	-3
PA	Philadelphia	51	-7	-4	7	19	28	44	51	44	35	25	15	1	-7
	Pittsburgh	40	-18	-12	-1	14	26	34	42	39	31	16	-1	-12	-18
RI	Providence	39	-13	-7	1	14	29	41	48	40	33	20	6	-10	-13
SC	Columbia	45	-1	5	4	26	34	44	54	53	40	23	12	4	-1
SD	Sioux Falls	47	-36	-31	-23	5	17	33	38	34	22	9	-17	-28	-36
TN	Memphis	51	-4	-11	12	29	38	48	52	48	36	25	9	-13	-13
	Nashville	53	-17	-13	2	23	34	42	51	47	36	26	-1	-10	-17
TX	Dallas-Fort Worth	39	4	7	15	29	41	51	59	56	43	29	20	-1	-1
	El Paso	53	-8	8	14	23	31	46	57	56	41	25	1	5	-8
	Houston	23	12	20	22	31	44	52	62	60	48	32	19	7	7
UT	Salt Lake City	64	-22	-30	2	14	25	35	40	37	27	16	-14	-21	-30
VT	Burlington	49	-30	-30	-20	2	24	33	39	35	25	15	-2	-26	-30
VA	Norfolk	44	-3	8	18	28	36	45	54	49	45	27	20	7	-3
	Richmond	63	-12	-10	11	23	31	40	51	46	35	21	10	-1	-12
WA	Seattle-Tacoma	48	-	1	11	29	28	38	43	44	35	28	6	6	-
	Spokane	45	-22	-17	-7	17	24	33	37	35	24	10	-21	-25	-25
WV	Charleston	45	-15	-6	-	19	26	33	46	41	34	17	6	-12	-15
WI	Milwaukee	52	-26	-19	-10	12	21	33	40	44	28	18	-5	-20	-26
WY	Cheyenne	57	-29	-34	-21	-8	16	25	38	36	8	-1	-14	-28	-34
PR	San Juan	38	61	62	60	64	66	69	69	70	69	67	66	63	60

- Represents zero.   [1] City office data.

Source: U.S. National Oceanic and Atmospheric Administration, *Comparative Climatic Data*, annual.

No. 384. Normal Monthly and Annual Precipitation—Selected Cities

[In inches. Airport data, except as noted. Based on standard 30-year period, 1961 through 1990. See *Historical Statistics, Colonial Times to 1970*, series J 164-267, for related data]

STATE	STATION	Jan.	Feb.	Mar.	Apr.	May	June	July	Aug.	Sept.	Oct.	Nov.	Dec.	Annual
AL	Mobile.	4.76	5.46	6.41	4.48	5.74	5.04	6.85	6.96	5.91	2.94	4.10	5.31	63.96
AK	Juneau	4.54	3.75	3.28	2.77	3.42	3.15	4.16	5.32	6.73	7.84	4.91	4.44	54.31
AZ	Phoenix.	0.67	0.68	0.88	0.22	0.12	0.13	0.83	0.96	0.86	0.65	0.66	1.00	7.66
AR	Little Rock	3.42	3.61	4.91	5.49	5.17	3.57	3.60	3.26	4.05	3.75	5.20	4.83	50.86
CA	Los Angeles.	2.40	2.51	1.98	0.72	0.14	0.03	0.01	0.15	0.31	0.34	1.76	1.66	12.01
	Sacramento	3.73	2.87	2.57	1.16	0.27	0.12	0.05	0.07	0.37	1.08	2.72	2.51	17.52
	San Diego	1.80	1.53	1.77	0.79	0.19	0.07	0.02	0.10	0.24	0.37	1.45	1.57	9.90
	San Francisco . . .	4.35	3.17	3.06	1.37	0.19	0.11	0.03	0.05	0.20	1.22	2.86	3.09	19.70
CO	Denver	0.50	0.57	1.28	1.71	2.40	1.79	1.91	1.51	1.24	0.98	0.87	0.64	15.40
CT	Hartford.	3.41	3.23	3.63	3.85	4.12	3.75	3.19	3.65	3.79	3.57	4.04	3.91	44.14
DE	Wilmington	3.03	2.91	3.43	3.39	3.84	3.55	4.23	3.40	3.43	2.88	3.27	3.48	40.84
DC	Washington	2.72	2.71	3.17	2.71	3.66	3.38	3.80	3.91	3.31	3.02	3.12	3.12	38.63
FL	Jacksonville	3.31	3.93	3.68	2.77	3.55	5.69	5.60	7.93	7.05	2.90	2.19	2.72	51.32
	Miami	2.01	2.08	2.39	2.85	6.21	9.33	5.70	7.58	7.63	5.64	2.66	1.83	55.91
GA	Atlanta	4.75	4.81	5.77	4.26	4.29	3.56	5.01	3.66	3.42	3.05	3.86	4.33	50.77
HI	Honolulu	3.55	2.21	2.20	1.54	1.13	0.50	0.59	0.44	0.78	2.28	3.00	3.80	22.02
ID	Boise	1.45	1.07	1.29	1.24	1.08	0.81	0.35	0.43	0.80	0.75	1.48	1.36	12.11
IL	Chicago.	1.53	1.36	2.69	3.64	3.32	3.78	3.66	4.22	3.82	2.41	2.92	2.47	35.82
	Peoria.	1.51	1.42	2.91	3.77	3.70	3.99	4.20	3.10	3.87	2.65	2.69	2.44	36.25
IN	Indianapolis	2.32	2.46	3.79	3.70	4.00	3.49	4.47	3.64	2.87	2.63	3.23	3.34	39.94
IA	Des Moines	0.96	1.11	2.33	3.36	3.66	4.46	3.78	4.20	3.53	2.62	1.79	1.32	33.12
KS	Wichita	0.79	0.96	2.43	2.38	3.81	4.31	3.13	3.02	3.49	2.22	1.59	1.20	29.33
KY	Louisville	2.86	3.30	4.66	4.23	4.62	3.46	4.51	3.54	3.16	2.71	3.70	3.64	44.39
LA	New Orleans	5.05	6.01	4.90	4.50	4.56	5.84	6.12	6.17	5.51	3.05	4.42	5.75	61.88
ME	Portland.	3.53	3.33	3.67	4.08	3.62	3.44	3.09	2.87	3.09	3.90	5.17	4.55	44.34
MD	Baltimore.	3.05	3.12	3.38	3.09	3.72	3.67	3.69	3.92	3.41	2.98	3.32	3.41	40.76
MA	Boston	3.59	3.62	3.69	3.60	3.25	3.09	2.84	3.24	3.06	3.30	4.22	4.01	41.51
MI	Detroit.	1.76	1.74	2.55	2.95	2.92	3.61	3.18	3.43	2.89	2.10	2.67	2.82	32.62
	Sault Ste. Marie . . .	2.42	1.74	2.30	2.35	2.71	3.14	2.71	3.61	3.69	3.23	3.45	2.88	34.23
MN	Duluth	1.22	0.80	1.91	2.25	3.03	3.82	3.61	3.99	3.84	2.49	1.80	1.24	30.00
	Minneapolis-St. Paul	0.95	0.88	1.94	2.42	3.39	4.05	3.53	3.62	2.72	2.19	1.55	1.08	28.32
MS	Jackson.	5.24	4.70	5.82	5.57	5.05	3.18	4.51	3.77	3.55	3.26	4.81	5.91	55.37
MO	Kansas City	1.09	1.10	2.51	3.12	5.04	4.72	4.38	4.01	4.86	3.29	1.92	1.58	37.62
	St. Louis	1.81	2.12	3.58	3.50	3.97	3.72	3.85	2.85	3.12	2.68	3.28	3.03	37.51
MT	Great Falls.	0.91	0.57	1.10	1.41	2.52	2.39	1.24	1.54	1.24	0.78	0.66	0.85	15.21
NE	Omaha	0.74	0.77	2.04	2.66	4.52	3.87	3.51	3.24	3.72	2.28	1.49	1.02	29.86
NV	Reno	1.07	0.99	0.71	0.38	0.69	0.46	0.28	0.32	0.39	0.38	0.87	0.99	7.53
NH	Concord	2.51	2.53	2.72	2.91	3.14	3.15	3.23	3.32	2.81	3.23	3.66	3.16	36.37
NJ	Atlantic City	3.46	3.06	3.62	3.56	3.33	2.64	3.83	4.14	2.93	2.82	3.58	3.32	40.29
NM	Albuquerque.	0.44	0.46	0.54	0.52	0.50	0.59	1.37	1.64	1.00	0.89	0.43	0.50	8.88
NY	Albany.	2.36	2.27	2.93	2.99	3.41	3.62	3.18	3.47	2.95	2.83	3.23	2.93	36.17
	Buffalo	2.70	2.31	2.68	2.87	3.14	3.55	3.08	4.17	3.49	3.09	3.83	3.67	38.58
	New York [1]	3.42	3.27	4.08	4.20	4.42	3.67	4.35	4.01	3.89	3.56	4.47	3.91	47.25
NC	Charlotte	3.71	3.84	4.43	2.68	3.82	3.39	3.92	3.73	3.50	3.36	3.23	3.48	43.09
	Raleigh	3.48	3.69	3.77	2.59	3.92	3.68	4.01	4.02	3.19	2.86	2.98	3.24	41.43
ND	Bismarck	0.45	0.43	0.77	1.67	2.18	2.72	2.14	1.72	1.49	0.90	0.49	0.51	15.47
OH	Cincinnati.	2.59	2.69	4.24	3.75	4.28	3.84	4.24	3.35	2.88	2.86	3.46	3.15	41.33
	Cleveland	2.04	2.19	2.91	3.14	3.49	3.70	3.52	3.40	3.44	2.54	3.17	3.09	36.63
	Columbus	2.18	2.24	3.27	3.21	3.93	4.04	4.31	3.72	2.96	2.15	3.22	2.86	38.09
OK	Oklahoma City	1.13	1.56	2.71	2.77	5.22	4.31	2.61	2.60	3.84	3.23	1.98	1.40	33.36
OR	Portland.	5.35	3.85	3.56	2.39	2.06	1.48	0.63	1.09	1.75	2.67	5.34	6.13	36.30
PA	Philadelphia	3.21	2.79	3.46	3.62	3.75	3.74	4.28	3.80	3.42	2.62	3.34	3.38	41.41
	Pittsburgh	2.54	2.39	3.41	3.15	3.59	3.71	3.75	3.21	2.97	2.36	2.85	2.92	36.85
RI	Providence.	3.88	3.61	4.05	4.11	3.76	3.33	3.18	3.63	3.48	3.69	4.43	4.38	45.53
SC	Columbia	4.42	4.12	4.82	3.28	3.68	4.80	5.50	6.09	3.67	3.04	2.90	3.59	49.91
SD	Sioux Falls.	0.51	0.64	1.64	2.52	3.03	3.40	2.68	2.85	3.02	1.78	1.09	0.70	23.86
TN	Memphis	3.73	4.35	5.41	5.46	4.98	3.57	3.79	3.43	3.53	3.01	5.10	5.74	52.10
	Nashville	3.58	3.81	4.85	4.37	4.88	3.57	3.97	3.46	3.46	2.62	4.12	4.61	47.30
TX	Dallas-Fort Worth . .	1.83	2.18	2.77	3.50	4.88	2.98	2.31	2.21	3.39	3.52	2.29	1.84	33.70
	El Paso	0.40	0.41	0.29	0.20	0.25	0.67	1.54	1.58	1.70	0.76	0.44	0.57	8.81
	Houston	3.29	2.96	2.92	3.21	5.24	4.96	3.60	3.49	4.89	4.27	3.79	3.45	46.07
UT	Salt Lake City.	1.11	1.23	1.91	2.12	1.80	0.93	0.81	0.86	1.28	1.44	1.29	1.40	16.18
VT	Burlington	1.82	1.63	2.23	2.76	3.12	3.47	3.65	4.06	3.30	2.88	3.13	2.42	34.47
VA	Norfolk	3.78	3.47	3.70	3.06	3.81	3.82	5.06	5.03	3.90	3.15	2.85	3.23	44.64
	Richmond	3.24	3.16	3.61	2.96	3.84	3.62	5.03	4.40	3.34	3.53	3.17	3.26	43.16
WA	Seattle-Tacoma . . .	5.38	3.99	3.54	2.33	1.70	1.50	0.76	1.14	1.88	3.23	5.83	5.91	37.19
	Spokane	1.98	1.49	1.49	1.18	1.41	1.26	0.67	0.72	0.73	0.99	2.15	2.42	16.49
WV	Charleston	2.91	3.04	3.63	3.31	3.94	3.59	4.99	4.01	3.24	2.89	3.59	3.39	42.53
WI	Milwaukee	1.60	1.45	2.67	3.50	2.84	3.24	3.47	3.53	3.38	2.41	2.51	2.33	32.93
WY	Cheyenne	0.40	0.39	1.03	1.37	2.39	2.08	2.09	1.69	1.27	0.74	0.53	0.42	14.40
PR	San Juan.	2.81	2.15	2.35	3.76	5.93	4.00	4.37	5.32	5.28	5.71	5.94	4.72	52.34

[1] City office data.

Source: U.S. National Oceanic and Atmospheric Administration, *Climatography of the United States*, No. 81.

No. 385. Average Number of Days With Precipitation of .01 Inch or More—Selected Cities

[Airport data, except as noted. For period of record through 1992, except as noted]

STATE	STATION	Length of record (yr.)	Jan.	Feb.	Mar.	Apr.	May	June	July	Aug.	Sept.	Oct.	Nov.	Dec.	Annual
AL	Mobile	51	11	10	10	7	9	11	16	14	10	6	8	10	122
AK	Juneau [1]	48	18	17	18	17	17	15	17	18	20	23	20	21	222
AZ	Phoenix	53	4	4	4	2	1	1	4	5	3	3	3	4	36
AR	Little Rock	50	9	9	10	10	10	8	8	7	7	7	8	9	105
CA	Los Angeles	57	6	6	6	3	1	(Z)	1	(Z)	1	2	3	5	35
	Sacramento	53	10	9	9	5	3	1	(Z)	(Z)	1	3	7	9	57
	San Diego	52	7	6	7	4	2	1	(Z)	1	1	2	5	6	42
	San Francisco	65	11	10	10	6	3	1	(Z)	(Z)	1	4	7	10	62
CO	Denver	58	6	6	9	9	11	9	9	9	6	5	6	5	89
CT	Hartford	38	11	10	11	11	12	11	10	10	9	8	11	12	127
DE	Wilmington	45	11	9	11	11	11	10	9	9	8	8	9	10	116
DC	Washington	51	10	9	11	10	11	9	10	9	8	7	9	9	112
FL	Jacksonville	51	8	8	8	7	8	12	14	15	13	8	6	8	116
	Miami	50	7	6	6	6	10	15	16	17	17	14	9	6	130
GA	Atlanta	58	11	10	11	9	9	10	12	10	8	6	8	10	115
HI	Honolulu	43	10	9	9	9	7	6	7	6	7	9	9	10	99
ID	Boise	53	12	10	10	8	8	6	2	3	4	6	10	11	90
IL	Chicago	34	11	9	12	13	11	10	10	9	10	9	11	11	126
	Peoria	53	9	8	11	12	11	11	9	9	8	9	8	9	114
IN	Indianapolis	53	12	10	13	12	12	10	10	9	8	8	10	12	126
IA	Des Moines	53	7	7	10	11	11	11	9	9	9	8	7	8	107
KS	Wichita	39	5	5	8	8	11	9	7	8	8	6	5	6	86
KY	Louisville	45	11	11	13	12	12	10	11	8	8	8	10	11	125
LA	New Orleans	44	10	9	9	7	8	11	15	13	10	6	7	10	114
ME	Portland	52	11	10	11	12	12	11	10	10	8	9	12	11	128
MD	Baltimore	42	10	9	11	11	11	9	9	10	8	7	9	9	113
MA	Boston	41	11	10	12	11	12	11	9	10	9	9	11	12	126
MI	Detroit	34	13	11	13	13	11	10	9	9	10	10	12	14	136
	Sault Ste. Marie	51	19	15	13	11	11	11	10	11	13	13	17	19	166
MN	Duluth	51	12	10	11	10	12	13	11	11	12	9	11	12	134
	Minneapolis-St. Paul	54	9	7	10	10	11	12	10	10	10	8	9	9	114
MS	Jackson	29	11	9	10	8	10	8	10	10	8	6	8	10	110
MO	Kansas City	20	7	7	10	11	11	10	8	9	8	8	8	8	105
	St. Louis	35	8	8	11	11	11	9	9	8	8	6	10	9	111
MT	Great Falls	55	9	8	9	9	11	12	7	8	7	6	7	8	101
NE	Omaha	56	6	7	9	10	12	11	9	9	8	6	6	6	99
NV	Reno	50	6	6	6	4	4	3	2	2	2	3	5	6	50
NH	Concord	51	11	10	11	12	12	11	10	10	9	9	11	11	125
NJ	Atlantic City	49	11	10	11	11	10	9	9	9	8	7	9	10	112
NM	Albuquerque	53	4	4	5	3	5	4	9	9	6	5	3	4	61
NY	Albany	46	12	11	12	12	12	11	10	10	10	9	12	12	134
	Buffalo	49	20	17	16	14	12	10	10	11	11	12	16	20	169
	New York [2]	123	11	10	11	11	11	10	11	10	8	8	9	10	121
NC	Charlotte	53	10	10	11	9	10	10	11	10	7	7	8	10	111
	Raleigh	53	8	7	8	8	10	11	9	8	7	6	6	8	96
ND	Bismarck	48	10	10	10	9	10	9	11	10	8	7	8	9	112
OH	Cincinnati	45	12	11	13	13	12	10	10	9	8	8	11	12	130
	Cleveland	51	16	14	15	14	13	11	10	10	10	11	15	16	156
	Columbus	53	13	11	14	13	13	11	11	9	8	9	12	13	137
OK	Oklahoma City	53	5	6	7	8	10	9	6	7	7	6	5	6	83
OR	Portland	52	18	16	17	14	12	9	4	5	8	12	18	19	151
PA	Philadelphia	52	11	9	11	11	11	10	9	9	8	8	9	10	117
	Pittsburgh	40	16	14	16	14	13	11	11	10	9	10	13	16	153
RI	Providence	39	11	10	12	11	11	11	9	9	8	9	11	12	124
SC	Columbia	45	10	10	10	8	9	10	12	11	8	6	7	9	109
SD	Sioux Falls	47	6	6	9	9	11	11	10	9	8	6	6	6	97
TN	Memphis	42	10	10	11	10	9	8	9	8	7	6	9	10	106
	Nashville	51	11	11	12	11	11	9	10	9	8	7	9	11	118
TX	Dallas-Fort Worth	39	7	6	7	8	9	7	5	5	7	6	6	7	79
	El Paso	53	4	3	2	2	3	3	8	8	5	4	3	4	49
	Houston	23	11	9	9	7	8	9	10	9	9	7	9	9	106
UT	Salt Lake City	64	10	9	10	9	8	5	5	6	5	6	8	9	90
VT	Burlington	49	14	12	13	12	14	12	12	13	12	12	14	15	154
VA	Norfolk	44	11	10	11	10	10	9	11	11	8	8	8	9	115
	Richmond	55	10	9	11	9	11	9	11	10	8	7	8	9	113
WA	Seattle-Tacoma	48	19	16	17	14	10	9	5	6	9	13	18	19	155
	Spokane	45	14	11	11	9	9	8	4	5	6	8	13	15	113
WV	Charleston	45	15	14	15	14	13	11	13	11	10	9	12	14	151
WI	Milwaukee	52	11	10	12	12	12	11	10	9	9	9	11	11	125
WY	Cheyenne	57	6	6	9	10	12	11	11	10	7	6	6	6	100
PR	San Juan	37	17	13	12	13	16	15	19	18	17	17	18	19	196

Z Less than 1/2 day.   [1] For period of record through 1989.   [2] City office data.

Source: U.S. National Oceanic and Atmospheric Administration, Comparative Climatic Data, annual.

No. 386. Snow and Ice Pellets—Selected Cities

[In inches. Airport data, except as noted. For period of record through 1992. T denotes trace]

STATE	STATION	Length of record (yr)	Jan.	Feb.	Mar.	Apr.	May	June	July	Aug.	Sept.	Oct.	Nov.	Dec.	Annual
AL	Mobile	51	0.1	0.2	-	T	T	-	T	-	-	-	T	0.1	0.4
AK	Juneau	48	25.8	18.6	15.2	3.6	-	T	-	-	T	1.1	12.0	22.8	99.1
AZ	Phoenix	55	T	-	T	T	T	-	-	-	-	T	-	-	T
AR	Little Rock	50	2.4	1.4	0.5	T	-	-	-	-	-	T	0.2	0.7	5.2
CA	Los Angeles	57	T	T	T	-	-	-	-	-	-	-	-	T	T
	Sacramento	44	T	-	T	-	-	-	-	-	-	-	-	T	T
	San Diego	52	T	-	T	-	-	-	-	-	-	-	T	T	T
	San Francisco	65	0.0	T	T	-	-	-	-	-	-	-	-	-	T
CO	Denver	58	8.3	7.3	12.7	9.0	1.6	-	T	T	1.6	3.7	8.8	7.4	60.4
CT	Hartford	38	12.0	11.3	9.3	1.6	-	-	-	-	-	0.1	2.0	10.4	46.7
DE	Wilmington	45	6.7	5.9	3.1	0.2	T	T	T	-	-	0.1	0.9	3.3	20.2
DC	Washington	49	5.4	5.3	2.0	-	T	-	T	T	-	-	0.9	3.1	16.7
FL	Jacksonville	51	T	-	-	-	-	-	T	-	-	-	-	-	T
	Miami	50	-	-	-	-	-	-	-	-	-	-	-	-	-
GA	Atlanta	58	0.9	0.5	0.4	T	-	-	-	-	-	-	-	0.2	2.0
HI	Honolulu	46	-	-	-	-	-	-	-	-	-	-	-	-	-
ID	Boise	53	6.6	3.5	1.7	0.7	0.1	T	T	T	-	0.1	2.2	5.9	20.8
IL	Chicago	34	10.5	8.1	6.8	1.7	0.1	T	T	T	T	0.4	1.9	8.5	38.0
	Peoria	49	6.6	5.3	4.1	0.9	-	-	T	-	T	0.1	2.0	6.0	25.0
IN	Indianapolis	61	6.1	5.6	3.4	0.5	-	T	-	T	-	0.2	1.8	4.9	22.5
IA	Des Moines	53	8.1	7.1	6.2	1.9	-	-	T	-	T	0.2	3.1	6.7	33.3
KS	Wichita	39	4.5	4.2	2.5	0.3	T	T	-	-	-	-	1.3	3.3	16.1
KY	Louisville	45	5.2	4.3	3.2	0.2	T	-	-	-	-	-	1.1	2.1	16.1
LA	New Orleans	46	-	0.1	T	T	T	-	-	-	-	-	T	0.1	0.2
ME	Portland	52	19.0	17.1	12.3	2.9	0.2	-	-	-	T	0.2	3.0	14.6	69.3
MD	Baltimore	42	6.0	6.4	3.5	0.1	T	-	T	-	-	-	1.0	3.5	20.5
MA	Boston	57	12.0	11.2	7.4	0.9	-	-	-	-	-	-	1.3	7.4	40.2
MI	Detroit	34	10.2	8.9	6.7	1.6	T	-	-	-	T	0.2	3.0	10.4	41.0
	Sault Ste. Marie	51	28.7	19.0	15.1	5.5	0.5	T	-	T	0.1	2.4	15.4	30.0	116.7
MN	Duluth	49	16.6	11.2	13.4	6.5	0.8	T	T	T	0.1	1.4	12.2	15.4	77.6
	Minneapolis-St. Paul	54	9.7	8.5	10.8	2.9	0.1	T	-	T	-	0.5	7.9	9.4	49.8
MS	Jackson	29	0.5	0.2	0.2	-	-	-	-	-	-	-	-	-	0.9
MO	Kansas City	58	5.7	4.3	3.6	0.8	T	T	T	-	-	T	1.1	4.4	19.9
	St. Louis	56	5.3	4.4	4.3	0.4	T	T	-	-	-	-	1.4	3.9	19.7
MT	Great Falls	55	9.8	8.3	10.5	7.2	1.8	0.3	T	0.2	1.5	3.4	7.4	8.8	59.2
NE	Omaha	57	7.3	6.6	6.4	1.0	0.1	T	-	-	T	0.4	2.6	5.5	29.9
NV	Reno	50	5.6	5.1	4.5	1.3	0.9	-	-	-	-	0.3	2.2	4.5	24.4
NH	Concord	51	17.7	14.4	10.4	2.3	0.1	-	-	-	T	0.1	3.9	13.6	62.5
NJ	Atlantic City	48	5.3	5.4	2.6	0.3	T	-	T	-	-	T	0.4	2.2	16.2
NM	Albuquerque	53	2.6	2.2	1.9	0.6	-	T	T	T	T	0.1	1.2	2.7	11.3
NY	Albany	46	16.1	13.9	10.6	2.7	0.1	T	T	-	T	0.2	4.2	15.1	62.9
	Buffalo	49	23.5	18.2	11.3	3.2	0.3	T	-	T	T	0.2	11.6	22.6	90.9
	New York [1]	53	2.1	1.7	1.2	-	-	-	-	-	-	-	0.1	0.5	5.6
NC	Charlotte	124	7.6	8.4	4.9	0.9	T	-	T	-	-	-	0.9	5.4	28.1
	Raleigh	53	7.1	6.7	8.2	3.8	0.9	T	T	T	0.3	1.8	5.9	6.8	41.5
ND	Bismarck	48	2.3	2.6	1.3	-	-	-	-	-	-	-	0.1	0.7	7.0
OH	Cincinnati	45	6.8	5.2	4.2	0.5	-	-	-	T	-	0.2	2.1	3.9	22.9
	Cleveland	51	12.6	11.8	10.3	2.3	0.1	-	-	-	T	0.6	5.1	11.8	54.6
	Columbus	45	8.3	6.1	4.4	0.9	-	T	-	-	T	0.0	2.3	5.5	27.5
OK	Oklahoma City	53	3.1	2.5	1.4	-	T	-	-	-	T	T	0.5	1.8	9.3
OR	Portland	52	3.3	0.9	0.4	T	T	-	T	T	-	-	0.4	1.4	6.4
PA	Philadelphia	50	6.5	6.3	3.6	0.3	T	-	-	-	-	-	0.7	3.5	20.9
	Pittsburgh	40	11.5	9.1	8.0	1.7	0.1	T	T	-	T	0.2	3.3	8.2	42.1
RI	Providence	39	9.5	9.5	7.4	0.8	0.2	-	-	-	-	0.1	1.0	6.9	35.4
SC	Columbia	45	0.5	0.8	0.2	T	-	-	-	-	-	-	-	0.2	1.7
SD	Sioux Falls	47	6.4	8.0	9.5	2.2	-	T	-	-	-	0.7	5.3	7.3	39.4
TN	Memphis	42	2.4	1.4	0.9	T	T	-	-	-	-	T	0.1	0.7	5.5
	Nashville	51	3.9	3.0	1.4	-	-	-	-	T	-	-	0.5	1.5	10.3
TX	Dallas-Fort Worth	39	1.2	1.0	0.2	T	T	-	-	-	-	-	0.1	0.2	2.7
	El Paso	53	1.4	0.8	0.4	0.3	T	T	T	-	-	-	1.0	1.7	5.6
	Houston	58	0.2	0.2	-	-	T	-	-	-	-	-	-	0.0	0.4
UT	Salt Lake City	64	13.0	9.3	9.6	5.0	0.6	T	T	T	0.1	1.3	6.6	12.0	57.5
VT	Burlington	49	18.7	16.5	11.9	3.6	0.2	T	T	-	T	0.2	6.6	18.3	76.0
VA	Norfolk	44	2.7	2.9	1.0	-	-	T	-	T	-	-	-	0.9	7.5
	Richmond	55	4.9	4.1	2.4	0.1	T	-	-	-	-	T	0.4	2.0	13.9
WA	Seattle-Tacoma	48	5.0	1.7	1.4	0.1	T	-	-	-	-	T	1.2	2.6	12.0
	Spokane	45	16.1	7.5	4.1	0.7	0.1	T	-	-	T	0.4	6.3	15.3	50.5
WV	Charleston	45	10.3	8.6	4.7	0.9	-	T	T	T	-	0.1	2.3	4.9	31.8
WI	Milwaukee	52	12.8	9.6	8.6	1.7	0.1	T	T	T	T	0.3	2.9	10.6	46.6
WY	Cheyenne	57	6.4	5.8	12.2	8.9	3.4	0.2	T	T	T	0.7	3.7	7.2	54.7
PR	San Juan	37	-	-	-	-	-	-	-	-	-	-	-	-	-

- Represents zero or rounds to zero.   [1] City office data.

Source: U.S. National Oceanic and Atmospheric Administration, *Comparative Climatic Data*, annual.

No. 387. Sunshine, Average Wind Speed, Mean Number of Days Minimum Temperature Below 32 Degrees Fahrenheit, and Average Relative Humidity—Selected Cities

[Airport data, except as noted. For period of record through 1991, except as noted. M=morning. A=afternoon]

STATE	STATION	AVERAGE PERCENTAGE OF POSSIBLE SUNSHINE — Length of record (yr.)	Annual	AVERAGE WIND SPEED (m.p.h.) — Length of record (yr.)	Annual	Jan.	July	MINIMUM TEMPERATURE 32 DEGREES OR LESS — Length of record (yr.)	Mean number (days)	AVERAGE RELATIVE HUMIDITY (percent) — Length of record (yr.)	Annual M	Annual A	Jan. M	Jan. A	July M	July A
AL	Mobile	[1]41	[1]59	43	9.0	10.4	7.0	29	2.2	29	83	57	79	61	87	60
AK	Juneau	33	30	46	8.3	8.2	7.5	47	14.1	25	86	73	81	77	87	70
AZ	Phoenix	96	86	46	6.3	5.2	7.2	31	0.8	31	51	23	66	32	45	20
AR	Little Rock	32	62	49	7.8	8.5	6.7	31	6.0	31	79	57	76	61	83	56
CA	Los Angeles	[2]32	[2]73	43	7.5	6.7	7.8	32	(Z)	32	79	64	70	59	86	68
	Sacramento	43	78	42	7.9	7.2	9.0	41	1.7	31	82	45	90	70	76	28
	San Diego	51	68	51	6.9	5.9	7.4	31	(Z)	31	76	62	70	56	82	66
	San Francisco	(NA)	(NA)	64	10.6	7.2	13.6	32	0.2	32	84	62	86	66	86	59
CO	Denver	42	70	43	8.7	8.6	8.3	31	15.7	31	67	40	63	49	68	34
CT	Hartford	37	56	37	8.5	9.0	7.5	32	13.5	32	76	52	69	56	82	51
DE	Wilmington	(NA)	(NA)	43	9.1	9.8	7.8	44	10.0	44	78	55	73	60	83	54
DC	Washington	43	56	43	9.4	10.0	8.2	31	7.0	31	72	53	67	55	77	53
FL	Jacksonville	40	63	42	8.0	8.2	7.1	50	1.5	55	86	56	85	57	88	58
	Miami	15	72	42	9.3	9.5	7.9	27	(Z)	27	81	61	81	59	82	63
GA	Atlanta	56	61	53	9.1	10.4	7.6	31	5.3	31	77	56	74	59	85	60
HI	Honolulu	39	69	42	11.4	9.5	13.2	22	-	22	76	56	81	61	73	51
ID	Boise	49	64	52	8.7	8.0	8.4	52	12.4	52	69	43	81	70	54	21
IL	Chicago	11	54	33	10.4	11.7	8.2	33	13.3	33	77	60	75	67	79	56
	Peoria	48	57	48	10.0	11.1	7.8	32	12.9	32	79	62	78	68	82	59
IN	Indianapolis	47	55	43	9.6	10.9	7.4	32	11.8	32	80	62	78	70	84	59
IA	Des Moines	41	59	42	10.9	11.7	9.0	30	13.5	30	75	60	74	67	76	57
KS	Wichita	38	65	38	12.3	12.2	11.3	38	11.1	38	73	55	76	63	67	48
KY	Louisville	44	56	44	8.4	9.6	6.8	31	8.9	31	76	58	72	64	81	58
LA	New Orleans	18	59	43	8.2	9.4	6.1	45	1.3	43	85	63	82	66	89	66
ME	Portland	51	57	51	8.8	9.2	7.6	51	15.7	51	82	59	74	60	89	59
MD	Baltimore	40	57	41	9.2	9.7	8.0	41	9.7	38	75	54	69	57	81	53
MA	Boston	56	58	34	12.5	13.9	11.0	27	9.8	27	72	58	65	57	77	56
MI	Detroit	26	53	33	10.4	12.0	8.5	33	13.6	33	79	60	78	69	81	53
	Sault Ste. Marie	50	47	50	9.2	9.7	7.8	50	18.1	50	85	67	81	75	90	61
MN	Duluth	41	52	42	11.1	11.6	9.4	30	18.5	30	77	63	74	70	82	59
	Minneapolis-St. Paul	53	58	53	10.6	10.5	9.4	32	15.6	32	73	60	72	67	74	54
MS	Jackson	27	60	28	7.4	8.5	6.0	28	5.0	28	87	58	84	65	90	59
MO	Kansas City	19	62	19	10.8	11.5	9.4	19	11.0	19	74	59	72	63	75	56
	St. Louis	32	57	42	9.7	10.6	8.0	31	10.0	31	76	59	77	66	77	56
MT	Great Falls	46	61	50	12.8	15.3	10.1	30	15.7	30	67	45	66	60	66	29
NE	Omaha	[2]55	[2]60	55	10.6	10.9	8.9	27	14.1	27	76	59	75	65	78	57
NV	Reno	43	79	49	6.6	5.6	7.1	28	17.4	28	70	31	79	50	63	18
NH	Concord	50	54	49	6.7	7.2	5.7	26	17.3	25	82	54	74	58	90	51
NJ	Atlantic City	31	56	33	10.0	11.0	8.4	27	11.0	27	82	56	76	58	87	57
NM	Albuquerque	52	76	52	9.0	8.1	9.1	31	11.9	31	60	29	70	40	60	27
NY	Albany	53	52	53	8.9	9.8	7.4	26	14.9	26	79	57	76	63	84	55
	Buffalo	48	49	52	12.0	14.3	10.3	31	13.2	31	79	63	77	72	79	55
	New York [3]	105	58	58	9.4	10.7	7.6	78	7.9	49	70	56	60		74	55
NC	Charlotte	41	63	42	7.4	7.9	6.6	31	6.6	31	76	54	72	56	83	57
	Raleigh	37	59	42	7.7	8.5	6.6	27	7.8	27	80	54	73	55	88	58
ND	Bismarck	52	59	52	10.2	10.0	9.2	32	18.6	32	74	56	75	68	74	46
OH	Cincinnati	8	52	44	9.1	10.7	7.2	29	10.8	29	77	59	75	67	83	57
	Cleveland	48	49	50	10.6	12.3	8.6	31	12.3	31	77	62	75	69	81	57
	Columbus	40	49	42	8.4	10.0	6.6	32	11.9	32	77	59	74	67	82	56
OK	Oklahoma City	(NA)	(NA)	43	12.4	12.8	10.9	26	7.7	26	72	54	72	59	70	49
OR	Portland	42	48	43	7.9	9.9	7.6	51	4.3	51	86	60	86	75	82	45
PA	Philadelphia	49	56	51	9.5	10.3	8.1	32	9.7	32	76	55	71	59	81	54
	Pittsburgh	39	46	39	9.1	10.6	7.2	32	12.3	31	75	57	73	65	80	54
RI	Providence	38	58	38	10.6	11.2	9.5	28	11.8	28	76	55	66	63	83	56
SC	Columbia	38	64	43	6.9	7.2	6.3	25	6.0	25	83	51	78	54	87	54
SD	Sioux Falls	[4]49	[4]63	43	11.1	11.1	9.8	28	16.8	28	76	60	75	68	75	53
TN	Memphis	35	64	43	8.9	10.1	7.4	50	5.7	52	76	57	75	63	79	57
	Nashville	49	56	50	8.0	9.2	6.5	26	7.6	26	79	57	75	63	85	57
TX	Dallas-Fort Worth	13	63	38	10.8	11.1	9.6	28	4.0	28	72	56	73	60	67	49
	El Paso	49	84	49	8.9	8.3	8.3	31	6.5	31	57	28	66	35	63	30
	Houston	22	56	22	7.9	8.2	6.9	22	2.1	22	86	60	82	64	86	58
UT	Salt Lake City	53	66	62	8.8	7.6	9.6	32	12.5	32	67	43	79	69	52	22
VT	Burlington	48	49	48	9.0	9.7	7.9	27	15.5	26	77	59	70	63	82	53
VA	Norfolk	27	61	43	10.6	11.5	9.0	43	5.4	43	78	57	72	59	84	59
	Richmond	41	62	43	7.7	8.1	6.8	62	8.5	57	82	53	77	57	88	56
WA	Seattle-Tacoma	25	46	43	9.0	9.7	8.3	32	3.1	32	83	62	81	74	82	49
	Spokane	43	54	44	8.9	8.8	8.6	32	13.9	32	78	52	85	78	64	27
WV	Charleston	[5]8	[5]40	44	6.3	7.5	5.0	44	10.0	44	79	56	74	63	90	60
WI	Milwaukee	51	54	51	11.6	12.7	9.7	31	14.1	31	78	64	75	68	80	61
WY	Cheyenne	52	65	34	13.0	15.3	10.4	32	17.2	32	65	44	57	50	70	38
PR	San Juan	36	66	36	8.4	8.5	9.6	36	-	36	83	65	82	64	84	67

- Represents zero. NA Not available. Z Less than one-half a day. [1] Recording site is in Montgomery, AL. [2] Site is not at the airport. [3] City office data. [4] Recording site is in Rapid City, SD. [5] Recording site is Elkins, WV.

Source: U.S. National Oceanic and Atmospheric Administration, *Comparative Climatic Data*, annual.

Parks, Recreation, and Travel

This section presents data on national parks and forests, State parks, recreational activities, the arts and humanities, and domestic and foreign travel.

Parks and recreation.—The Department of the Interior has responsibility for administering the national parks. As part of this function, it issues reports relating to the usage of public parks for recreation purposes. The National Park Service publishes information on visits to national park areas in its annual report, *National Park Statistical Abstract.* The *National Parks: Index (year)* is a biannual report which has appeared under a variety of *Index* titles prior to 1985. Beginning with the 1985 edition, the report has appeared under the current title. The *Index* contains brief descriptions, with acreages, of each area administered by the Service, plus certain "related" areas. A statistical summary of Service-administered areas is also presented. The annual *Federal Recreation Fee Report* summarizes the prior year's recreation fee receipts and recreation visitation statistics for seven Federal land managing agencies.

Statistics for State parks are compiled by the National Association of State Park Directors which issues its annual *Information Exchange.* The Bureau of Land Management, in its *Public Land Statistics,* also issues data on recreational use of its lands. The Department of Agriculture's Forest Service, in its *Report of the Forest Service,* issues data on recreational uses of the national forests.

Visitation.—Data on visitation to reporting areas are collected by several different agencies and groups. The methodology used to collect these results may vary accordingly, from visual counts and estimates to the use of electromagnetic traffic counters. In using and comparing these data, one should also be aware of several different definitions that follow: Recreation visit, which is the entry of any person into an area for recreation purposes; nonrecreation visits, which include visits going to and from inholdings, through traffic, tradespeople and personnel with business in the area; and visitor hour, which constitutes the presence of a person in a recreation

In Brief

Percent of households with guns:

1974	46%
1993	42%

1992, percent of adults attending:

Opera	3%
Musical play	17%
Historic park	35%

area or site for recreational purposes for periods of time aggregating 60 minutes.

Recreation and leisure activities.—Statistics on the participation in various recreation and leisure time activities are based on several sample surveys. Data on participation in fishing, hunting, and other forms of wildlife-associated recreation are published periodically by the U.S. Department of Interior, Fish and Wildlife Service. The most recent data are from the 1991 survey. Data on participation in various sports recreation activities are published by the National Sporting Goods Association.

Travel.—Information on foreign travel and personal expenditures abroad, as well as expenditures by foreign citizens traveling in the United States, is compiled annually by the U.S. Bureau of Economic Analysis and published in selected issues of the monthly *Survey of Current Business.* Statistics on arrivals to the United States are reported by the U.S. Travel and Tourism Administration (USTTA), in cooperation with the U.S. Immigration and Naturalization Service, and are published in *Summary and Analysis of International Travel to the United States.* Sources of statistics on departures from the United States include USTTA's in-flight survey, the Department of Transportation's *International Air Travel Statistics,* and other sources. Data on domestic travel, business receipts and employment of the travel industry, and travel expenditures are published by the U.S. Travel Data Center, the national nonprofit center for travel and tourism research which is located in Washington, DC. Other data on household transportation characteristics may be found in section 21.

Figure 7.1
Participation in 10 Most Popular Sports Activities, by Sex: 1992

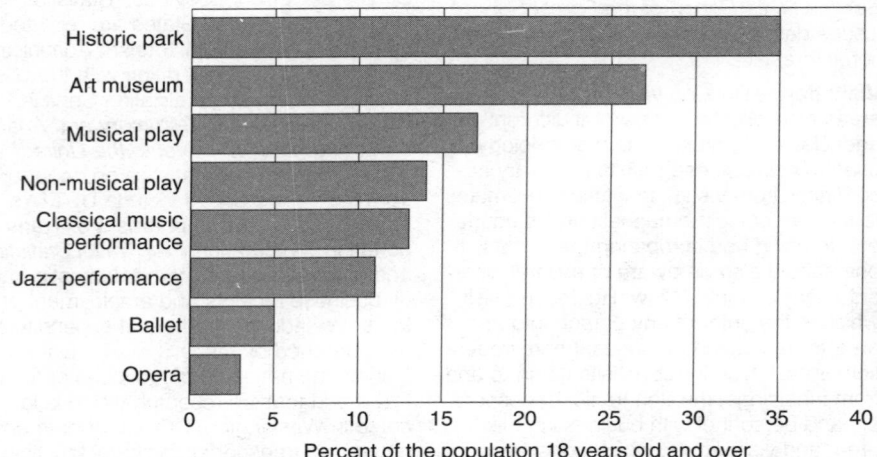

Exercise walking
Swimming
Bicycle riding
Camping
Bowling
Fishing (fresh water)
Exercising with equipment
Basketball
Aerobic exercising
Golf

Male
Female

0 5 10 15 20 25 30 35 40

Percent of the population 7 years old and over

Source: Chart prepared by U.S. Bureau of the Census. For data, see table 406.

Figure 7.2
Attendance for Various Arts Activities: 1992

Historic park
Art museum
Musical play
Non-musical play
Classical music performance
Jazz performance
Ballet
Opera

0 5 10 15 20 25 30 35 40

Percent of the population 18 years old and over

Source: Chart prepared by U.S. Bureau of the Census. For data, see table 411.

No. 388. Visitation to Federal Recreation Areas: 1980 to 1992

[In **millions of visitor hours.** For years ending **September 30.** Covers persons entering and using a recreation area over a specified period of time. For definition of visitor hour, see text, section 7]

ADMINISTERING FEDERAL AGENCY	1980	1985	1986	1987	1988	1989	1990	1991	1992
All areas.	6,367	6,403	6,858	7,332	7,419	7,475	7,567	7,829	7,995
Fish and Wildlife Service	17	65	67	72	81	45	(NA)	(NA)	(NA)
Forest Service	2,819	2,705	2,718	2,861	2,908	3,030	3,157	3,346	3,452
U.S. Army Corps of Engineers [1]	1,926	1,721	2,068	2,176	2,290	2,296	2,280	2,306	2,306
National Park Service	1,042	1,298	1,348	1,394	1,376	1,315	1,322	1,344	1,390
Bureau of Land Management [2]	68	246	284	515	461	493	518	540	563
Bureau of Reclamation	407	289	296	306	294	286	280	280	269
Tennessee Valley Authority [3]	87	79	77	8	9	10	10	13	14

NA Not available.   [1] Beginning 1986, not comparable with previous years.   [2] Data not comparable for all years.
[3] Beginning in 1989, the TVA discontinued reporting visitation to nonfee charging areas. Data for 1987 and 1988 have been adjusted to reflect this policy.

Source: 1980, U.S. Heritage Conservation and Recreation Service, *Federal Recreation Fee Report,* annual; thereafter, U.S. National Park Service.

No. 389. National Park System—Summary: 1985 to 1992

[For **fiscal years ending in year shown, except as noted;** see text, section 10. Includes data for five areas in Puerto Rico and Virgin Islands, one area in American Samoa, and one area in Guam. See also *Historical Statistics, Colonial Times to 1970,* series H 806-828]

ITEM	1985	1986	1987	1988	1989	1990	1991	1992
Finances (mil. dol.): [1]								
Expenditures reported	848.1	818.3	909.3	922.9	1,036.8	986.1	1,104.4	1,268.7
Salaries and wages	369.4	372.2	401.5	423.9	441.4	459.1	495.3	518.1
Improvements, maintenance.	127.4	119.6	144.1	154.7	197.5	160.0	179.6	212.1
Construction	84.7	125.9	102.6	86.3	85.2	108.5	134.1	193.3
Other.	266.6	200.6	261.1	258.0	312.7	258.5	295.4	345.2
Funds available.	1,248.2	1,271.5	1,276.0	1,338.4	1,440.0	1,505.5	1,988.4	2,274.8
Appropriations.	821.6	769.3	846.2	874.6	996.7	1,052.5	1,284.7	1,392.8
Other [2]	426.6	502.2	429.8	463.8	443.3	453.0	703.7	882.0
Revenue from operations	50.6	50.7	70.8	77.2	86.3	78.6	78.1	88.3
Recreation visits (millions): [3]								
All areas	263.4	281.1	287.2	282.5	269.4	258.7	267.8	274.7
National parks [4]	50.0	53.5	56.6	56.4	57.4	57.7	57.4	58.7
National monuments.	15.9	21.2	23.5	23.2	23.7	23.9	25.8	26.6
National historical, commemorative, archaeological [5]	61.9	65.5	68.6	61.2	63.9	57.5	61.0	63.3
National parkways	40.0	41.6	39.3	42.0	31.2	29.1	28.8	30.7
National recreation areas [4]	49.4	54.8	56.5	54.5	49.6	47.2	49.8	50.3
National seashores and lakeshores . . .	25.3	23.0	21.9	23.2	21.9	23.3	24.4	23.9
National Capital Parks.	8.3	6.9	8.1	9.0	8.9	7.5	7.5	8.1
Miscellaneous other areas . . . . [3] . .	12.6	14.5	12.7	12.9	12.8	12.5	13.1	13.1
Recreation overnight stays (millions) [3] . .	15.8	16.0	17.1	17.0	17.4	17.6	17.7	18.3
In commercial lodgings	3.5	3.5	3.7	3.8	3.9	3.9	4.0	4.1
In Park Service campgrounds.	7.3	7.2	8.0	7.9	7.8	7.9	7.8	8.1
In tents	3.6	3.5	4.0	3.9	3.9	4.1	4.2	4.4
In recreation vehicles.	3.8	3.8	4.0	3.9	3.9	3.8	3.6	3.7
In backcountry.	1.7	1.6	1.6	1.6	1.6	1.7	2.0	2.2
Other	3.2	3.6	3.8	3.7	4.1	4.2	3.9	3.9
Land (1,000 acres): [6]								
Total.	75,749	75,863	75,970	76,176	76,331	76,362	76,607	76,492
Parks.	45,739	45,791	45,875	45,955	46,081	46,089	46,135	46,208
Recreation areas	3,335	3,337	3,339	3,339	3,342	3,344	3,346	3,347
Other.	26,675	26,735	26,756	26,882	26,907	26,929	27,126	26,937
Acquisition, gross	34	177	134	38	73	21	66	23
By purchase	29	69	27	37	14	18	15	21
By gift	2	20	(Z)	(Z)	58	2	43	1
By transfer or exchange	3	88	107	1	1	1	8	1
Exclusion.	(Z)	4	(Z)	(Z)	1	1	(Z)	(Z)
Acquisition, net.	34	173	134	38	71	21	66	23

Z Less than 500 acres.   [1] Financial data are those associated with the National Park System. Certain other functions of the National Park Service (principally the activities absorbed from the former Heritage Conservation and Recreation Service in 1981) are excluded.   [2] Includes funds carried over from prior years.   [3] For calendar year.   [4] Combined data for North Cascades National Park and two adjacent National Recreation Areas are included in National Parks total.   [5] Includes military areas.   [6] Federal land only, as of Dec. 31. Federal land acreages, in addition to National Park Service administered lands, also include lands within national park system area boundaries but under the administration of other agencies. Year-to-year changes in the federal lands figures include changes in the acreages of these other lands and hence often differ from "net acquisition."

Source: U.S. National Park Service, Visits, *National Park Statistical Abstract,* annual; and unpublished data. Other data are unpublished.

No. 390. National Forest Recreation Use, Summary: 1980 to 1992

[For year ending September 30. Estimated. Represents recreational use of National Forest land and water in States which have a Forest Service recreation program. See also *Historical Statistics, Colonial Times to 1970*, series H 829-835]

YEAR AND ACTIVITY	Recreation visitor-days [1] (1,000)	Per-cent	STATE	Recreation visitor-days [1], 1992 (1,000)	STATE OR OTHER AREA	Recreation visitor-days [1], 1992 (1,000)
1980	233,549	100.0	U.S.	287,691	NV	3,360
1981	235,709	100.0			NH	3,037
1982	233,438	100.0	AL	701	NM	8,603
1983	227,708	100.0	AK	5,888	NY	31
1984	227,554	100.0	AZ	25,544	NC	5,767
1985	225,407	100.0	AR	2,153	ND	142
1986	226,533	100.0	CA	67,614	OH	672
1987	238,458	100.0	CO	29,053	OK	369
1988	242,316	100.0	FL	3,104	OR	19,898
1989	252,495	100.0	GA	2,993	PA	2,942
1990	263,051	100.0	ID	13,087	SC	950
1991	278,849	100.0	IL	900	SD	3,244
1992, total	**287,691**	**100.0**	IN	552	TN	2,978
			KS	76	TX	2,273
Mechanized travel and viewing scenery	100,916	35.1	KY	2,113	UT	18,413
Camping, picnicking and swimming	77,211	26.8	LA	507	VT	1,565
Hiking, horseback riding and water travel	24,239	8.4	MA	61	VA	4,269
Winter sports	18,045	6.3	MI	4,755	WA	18,740
Hunting	16,962	5.9	MN	5,739	WV	1,264
Resorts, cabins and organization camps	16,480	5.7	MS	1,298	WI	2,185
Fishing	16,268	5.7	MO	1,803	WY	7,516
Nature studies	2,497	0.9	MT	11,046		
Other [2]	15,073	5.2	NE	200	PR	289

[1] One recreation visitor-day is the recreation use of National Forest land or water that aggregates 12 visitor-hours. This may entail 1 person for 12 hours, 12 persons for 1 hour, or any equivalent combination of individual or group use, either continuous or intermittent.   [2] Includes team sports, gathering forest products, attending talks and programs, and other uses.

Source: U.S. Forest Service, unpublished data.

No. 391. Recreational Use of Public Lands Administered by Bureau of Land Management: 1982 to 1992

[In thousands. For year ending Sept. 30. Beginning 1987, increase due to an estimated longer length of stay per visit, especially in California. See text, section 7]

YEAR AND STATE	Number of visits	TYPE OF RECREATION USE (visitor hours)										
		Total	Off-highway vehicle travel	Other motorized travel	Non-motorized travel	Camping	Hunting	Misc. site based	Fishing	Boating	Misc. water based	Snow- and ice-based recreational activity, winter sports
1982	58,135	316,959	19,471	32,646	11,237	63,928	108,996	44,587	19,287	10,101	1,043	5,663
1983	56,270	334,010	24,397	35,534	12,237	84,066	92,974	39,734	20,290	16,869	4,992	2,917
1984	59,228	271,373	21,348	25,433	9,579	73,032	73,898	37,650	14,263	11,184	2,092	2,894
1985	51,739	244,612	36,995	24,053	10,047	65,397	51,842	23,098	14,254	11,710	2,193	5,023
1986	54,253	284,142	49,688	25,866	14,397	95,196	35,570	19,331	18,227	15,891	3,951	6,025
1987	56,427	514,716	123,325	34,325	19,172	195,315	57,624	38,412	22,932	15,140	5,212	3,259
1988	57,460	492,756	122,014	35,748	19,761	178,703	55,285	38,340	21,617	13,294	4,979	3,015
1989	60,957	493,214	65,808	74,075	36,676	173,597	46,760	45,871	23,392	18,491	5,425	3,119
1990	71,820	523,753	63,016	83,445	41,316	165,366	47,053	57,958	28,664	20,806	8,313	7,816
1991	72,541	539,779	50,849	85,835	44,398	196,310	49,593	59,928	20,939	19,676	8,353	3,898
1992, total	**69,418**	**519,429**	**46,411**	**93,477**	**43,845**	**181,536**	**44,557**	**59,857**	**19,768**	**18,735**	**7,586**	**3,657**
AK [1]	254	5,901	138	509	81	3,909	452	233	299	164	4	112
AZ [1]	10,888	60,239	715	522	2,728	33,818	2,392	10,352	952	6,313	2,443	4
CA	26,001	227,095	29,814	46,834	23,820	86,385	9,102	25,227	2,344	1,472	1,865	232
CO	3,860	24,223	1,436	6,311	945	5,902	5,058	1,627	761	1,774	65	344
ID	2,658	18,567	1,069	1,334	711	5,385	2,484	1,563	2,452	1,467	577	1,525
MT [2]	2,290	13,184	2,523	1,169	494	3,175	2,862	433	1,720	439	55	314
NV	3,693	26,544	1,470	11,235	2,775	4,396	2,200	2,622	1,332	227	162	125
NM	3,063	18,755	2,573	1,402	1,297	3,815	5,676	2,086	1,071	763	69	3
OR [3]	6,823	60,513	1,812	8,216	5,432	15,830	6,312	10,493	7,199	2,892	1,810	517
UT	9,054	54,593	4,527	15,429	5,248	16,917	4,802	3,769	435	2,872	484	110
WY	834	9,815	334	516	314	2,004	3,217	1,452	1,203	352	52	371

[1] Includes concession visitation data.   [2] Includes North Dakota and South Dakota.   [3] Includes Washington.

Source: U.S. Bureau of Land Management, *Public Land Statistics*, annual.

No. 392. State Parks and Recreation Areas—States: 1991

[For year ending June 30. Data are shown as reported by State park directors. In some States, park agency has under its control forests, fish and wildlife areas, and/or other areas. In other States, agency is responsible for State parks only]

STATE	Acreage (1,000)	Visitors (1,000) [1]	REVENUE		STATE	Acreage (1,000)	Visitors (1,000) [1]	REVENUE	
			Total ($1,000)	Percent of operating budget				Total ($1,000)	Percent of operating budget
United States ...	11,148	736,897	454,248	41.5	Missouri	117	14,998	3,780	21.0
					Montana	32	1,652	1,022	43.9
Alabama	50	6,084	22,505	80.7	Nebraska	142	9,215	7,550	92.2
Alaska	3,169	6,815	853	16.5	Nevada.	142	2,563	756	16.4
Arizona	42	2,236	2,073	35.1	New Hampshire ...	31	2,815	4,000	125.0
Arkansas	47	6,949	11,227	59.5	New Jersey	303	10,945	6,514	23.8
California.	1,314	70,444	70,211	43.9	New Mexico......	123	4,251	2,657	29.3
Colorado.	307	8,653	10,854	108.0	New York	260	60,744	32,914	30.1
Connecticut	172	6,743	3,327	32.2	North Carolina	134	9,463	1,700	16.0
Delaware.	13	3,212	3,889	48.1	North Dakota	19	954	813	50.7
Florida	444	13,087	16,248	41.3	Ohio............	208	67,222	12,082	26.9
Georgia.	57	16,262	14,811	39.7	Oklahoma	77	16,031	15,320	47.4
Hawaii	25	19,112	1,231	17.7	Oregon	90	39,479	7,682	30.5
Idaho	42	2,500	1,651	36.6	Pennsylvania	277	36,311	7,150	13.2
Illinois..........	405	34,594	3,058	9.7	Rhode Island	9	5,075	2,854	47.1
Indiana	57	10,536	9,011	74.2	South Carolina ...	80	7,970	10,587	61.4
Iowa...........	82	12,111	1,571	21.0	South Dakota.....	92	5,894	3,810	62.4
Kansas.........	30	4,117	2,426	32.3	Tennessee	133	26,974	19,737	53.9
Kentucky.	42	27,272	37,668	69.1	Texas..........	499	23,957	12,722	37.0
Louisiana	39	1,107	1,860	30.5	Utah...........	97	4,940	2,970	24.3
Maine..........	75	2,448	1,310	31.4	Vermont	90	982	4,402	95.0
Maryland........	226	7,828	6,320	27.4	Virginia	59	3,862	2,686	28.5
Massachusetts....	273	11,975	10,408	60.5	Washington	241	46,813	6,292	25.0
Michigan........	264	25,260	21,383	79.3	West Virginia	202	8,278	12,973	58.6
Minnesota.......	231	7,981	7,117	40.2	Wisconsin	139	12,252	5,221	40.8
Mississippi.......	23	3,912	4,796	44.3	Wyoming........	120	2,018	247	7.9

[1] Includes overnight visitors.

Source: National Association of State Park Directors, Tallahassee, FL, 1992 Annual Information Exchange.

No. 393. Personal Consumption Expenditures for Recreation in Constant (1987) Dollars: 1970 to 1992

[In billions of dollars, except percent. Represents market value of purchases of goods and services by individuals and nonprofit institutions]

TYPE OF PRODUCT OR SERVICE	1970	1980	1985	1988	1989	1990	1991	1992
Total recreation expenditures	91.3	149.1	195.5	240.0	250.9	261.9	269.1	283.7
Percent of total personal consumption [1].........	5.0	6.1	6.8	7.6	7.8	8.0	8.3	8.5
Books and maps...................	10.5	10.2	11.4	14.1	14.7	15.3	15.4	16.5
Magazines, newspapers, and sheet music	13.2	18.4	17.9	19.9	20.3	20.9	20.3	20.1
Nondurable toys and sport supplies.............	9.5	17.4	22.3	26.2	27.5	28.7	29.5	30.5
Wheel goods, sports and photographic equipment [2].......	10.3	20.2	24.4	28.9	29.0	28.3	27.5	29.2
Video and audio products, computer equipment, and musical instruments............	8.8	17.6	29.7	45.5	49.2	54.1	62.7	70.3
Radio and television repair....................	2.7	3.5	3.3	3.4	3.4	3.4	3.2	3.0
Flowers, seeds, and potted plants.................	4.0	5.9	7.0	9.2	9.7	9.7	9.1	9.2
Admissions to specified spectator amusements.........	8.2	9.9	10.2	10.5	10.6	11.5	11.6	12.2
Motion picture theaters..................	4.2	3.8	3.6	3.4	3.4	3.8	3.9	4.1
Legitimate theaters and opera, and entertainments of nonprofit institutions [3].....................	1.3	2.7	2.9	3.4	3.5	3.7	3.7	3.9
Spectator sports [4]....................	2.8	3.4	3.7	3.7	3.7	4.0	4.0	4.1
Clubs and fraternal organizations except insurance [5]	3.8	4.0	6.3	7.2	7.4	7.5	7.4	7.6
Commercial participant amusements [6]................	6.3	12.5	16.1	18.5	19.0	20.3	20.0	20.8
Pari-mutuel net receipts......................	2.8	3.6	3.2	3.2	3.1	3.2	3.2	3.2
Other [7].............................	11.3	25.8	43.5	53.4	57.1	58.9	59.1	61.1

[1] See table 694.　[2] Includes boats and pleasure aircraft.　[3] Except athletic.　[4] Consists of admissions to professional and amateur athletic events and to racetracks, including horse, dog, and auto.　[5] Consists of dues and fees excluding insurance premiums.　[6] Consists of billiard parlors; bowling alleys; dancing, riding, shooting, skating, and swimming places; amusement devices and parks; golf courses; sightseeing buses and guides; private flying operations; casino gambling; and other commercial participant amusements.　[7] Consists of net receipts of lotteries and expenditures for purchases of pets and pet care services, cable TV, film processing, photographic studios, sporting and recreation camps, video cassette rentals, and recreational services, not elsewhere classified.

Source: U.S. Bureau of Economic Analysis, The National Income and Product Accounts of the United States: Volume 2, 1959-88, and Survey of Current Business, August, 1993.

No. 394. Expenditures per Consumer Unit for Entertainment and Reading: 1985 to 1992

[Data are **annual averages. In dollars, except as indicated.** Based on Consumer Expenditure Survey; see text, section 14, for description of survey. See also headnote, table 703. For composition of regions, see table 26]

YEAR AND CHARACTERISTIC	ENTERTAINMENT AND READING		ENTERTAINMENT				Reading
	Total	Percent of total expenditures	Total	Fees and admissions	Television, radios, and sound equipment	Other equipment and services [1]	
1985....................	1,311	5.6	1,170	320	371	479	141
1990....................	1,575	5.6	1,422	371	454	597	153
1991....................	1,635	5.5	1,472	378	468	627	163
1992, total.............	**1,662**	**5.6**	**1,500**	**379**	**492**	**629**	**162**
Age of reference person:							
Under 25 years old..........	1,001	5.8	928	210	394	323	73
25 to 34 years old...........	1,711	5.8	1,569	320	528	720	142
35 to 44 years old...........	2,224	6.0	2,041	527	648	866	183
45 to 54 years old...........	2,100	5.6	1,896	488	603	805	204
55 to 64 years old...........	1,775	5.6	1,587	458	453	676	188
65 to 74 years old...........	1,106	4.8	953	280	326	346	153
75 years old and over.........	644	3.6	510	156	213	140	134
Race: White and other.........	1,781	5.7	1,608	414	507	686	173
Black...................	740	3.8	667	110	373	183	73
Region of residence: Northeast	1,701	5.5	1,516	429	528	559	185
Midwest.................	1,547	5.4	1,376	356	475	544	171
South...................	1,419	5.1	1,285	328	449	507	134
West...................	2,161	6.4	1,990	439	546	1,006	171
Size of consumer unit: One person..	920	5.2	799	225	320	253	121
Two persons...............	1,965	5.7	1,787	442	562	782	178
Two or more persons.........	1,647	5.4	1,461	403	469	590	186
Three persons............	1,854	5.3	1,687	380	550	757	167
Four persons.............	2,647	6.5	2,458	572	668	1,218	189
Five persons or more.......	2,108	5.5	1,953	475	713	765	155

[1] Other equipment and services includes pets, toys, and playground equipment, and sports, exercise, and photographic equipment.

Source: U.S. Bureau of Labor Statistics, *Consumer Expenditure Survey*, annual.

No. 395. Motion Pictures and Amusement and Recreation Services—Annual Receipts: 1986 to 1992

[**In billions of dollars.** For taxable employer and nonemployer firms]

KIND OF BUSINESS	1987 SIC code [1]	1986	1987	1988	1989	1990	1991	1992
Motion pictures...........................	78	23.8	27.8	31.2	35.0	38.1	41.1	43.8
Production, distribution, and allied services.......	781,782	17.0	20.8	22.6	24.7	26.1	28.5	30.6
Theaters	783	3.9	4.1	4.7	5.7	6.6	7.0	6.9
Video tape rental.......................	784	(NA)	(NA)	(NA)	(NA)	5.4	5.6	6.3
Amusement and recreation services............	79	34.0	36.6	40.2	42.2	46.5	46.7	51.1
Dance studios, schools, and halls.............	791	(NA)	(NA)	(NA)	(NA)	0.6	0.6	0.7
Theatrical producers (except motion picture), bands, orchestras, and entertainers...........	792	7.6	7.7	8.1	7.5	9.2	9.5	10.1
Bowling centers........................	793	2.6	2.6	2.7	2.8	2.8	2.7	2.9
Commercial sports......................	794	5.1	6.0	6.9	7.9	9.3	9.7	10.6
Professional sports clubs and promoters.......	7941	(NA)	(NA)	(NA)	(NA)	4.6	5.2	5.9
Racing, including track operation............	7948	(NA)	(NA)	(NA)	(NA)	4.7	4.5	4.7
Miscellaneous amusement and recreation services [2].	799	(NA)	(NA)	(NA)	(NA)	24.6	24.2	26.8
Physical fitness facilities..................	7991	(NA)	(NA)	(NA)	(NA)	3.2	2.9	3.3
Public golf courses	7992	(NA)	(NA)	(NA)	(NA)	2.3	2.4	2.6
Coin-operated amusement devices	7993	1.4	1.5	1.6	1.5	1.5	1.5	1.5
Amusement parks......................	7996	3.4	3.9	4.3	4.7	4.9	4.8	5.4
Membership sports and recreation clubs......	7997	3.9	4.1	4.1	4.1	4.3	4.4	4.4

NA Not available. [1] 1987 Standard Industrial Classification code; see text, section 13. [2] Includes kinds of businesses, not shown separately.

Source: U.S. Bureau of the Census, *Current Business Reports, Service Annual Survey*, BS/92; and earlier reports.

No. 396. Quantity of Books Sold and Value of U.S. Domestic Consumer Expenditures: 1982 to 1992

[Includes all titles released by publishers in the United States and imports which appear under the imprints of American publishers. Multi-volume sets, such as encyclopedias, are counted as one unit]

TYPE OF PUBLICATION AND MARKET AREA	UNITS SOLD (mil.)					CONSUMER EXPENDITURES (mil. dol.)				
	1982	1985	1990	1991	1992	1982	1985	1990	1991	1992
Total [1]	1,723	1,788	2,005	2,040	2,041	9,889	12,611	19,043	20,101	21,141
Hardbound, total	646	694	824	838	825	6,190	7,969	11,789	12,398	13,056
Softbound, total	1,077	1,094	1,181	1,202	1,216	3,699	4,642	7,254	7,703	8,085
Trade	459	553	705	738	762	2,484	3,660	6,498	7,110	7,806
Adult	315	360	403	412	442	2,028	2,871	4,777	5,147	5,809
Juvenile	144	193	301	326	320	456	789	1,721	1,963	1,997
Religious	144	134	130	135	139	706	926	1,362	1,476	1,557
Professional	106	110	131	130	134	1,630	2,043	2,957	3,060	3,314
Bookclubs	133	130	108	109	106	510	582	705	729	722
Elhi text	233	234	209	206	202	1,067	1,415	1,948	1,974	1,943
College text	115	110	137	133	138	1,388	1,575	2,319	2,329	2,442
Mail order publications	134	121	138	132	110	581	650	752	755	646
Mass market paperbacks-rack sized	382	382	433	443	433	1,102	1,244	1,775	1,923	1,927
General retailers	756	829	1,010	1,049	1,062	3,743	5,103	8,465	9,195	9,878
College stores	224	225	255	254	260	1,910	2,309	3,403	3,497	3,715
Libraries and institutions [2]	80	80	88	89	91	888	1,090	1,592	1,669	1,786
Schools [2]	262	260	244	241	238	1,313	1,685	2,365	2,416	2,409
Direct to consumers	319	300	304	299	282	1,889	2,214	2,901	2,979	2,992
Other	82	94	104	108	108	146	210	316	346	361

[1] Types of publications include university press publications and subscription reference works, not shown separately. [2] Elhi libraries included in schools.

Source: Book Industry Study Group, Inc., New York, NY, *Book Industry Trends*, annual, (copyright).

No. 397. Book Purchasing by Adults: 1991 and 1992

[In percent. Excludes books purchased for or by children under 13. Based on a survey of 16,000 households conducted over 12 months ending in March of year shown. For details, see source]

CHARACTERISTIC	TOTAL		MASS MARKET [1]		TRADE [2]		HARDCOVER	
	1991	1992	1991	1992	1991	1992	1991	1992
Total	100.0	100.0	100.0	100.0	100.0	100.0	100.0	100.0
Age of purchaser:								
Under 25 years old	6.0	4.1	4.7	3.6	8.2	4.8	5.7	4.1
25 to 34 years old	18.6	18.8	14.7	13.9	23.5	25.5	19.9	19.2
35 to 44 years old	27.4	23.9	26.3	22.4	29.9	26.3	26.4	23.7
45 to 54 years old	22.4	21.9	25.8	25.7	17.9	17.2	21.3	20.9
55 to 64 years old	12.8	15.9	13.2	15.9	11.1	14.5	14.4	17.4
65 years old and over	12.8	15.4	15.3	18.5	9.4	11.7	12.3	14.7
Household income:								
Under $30,000	35.4	37.1	39.5	42.3	30.8	32.4	33.3	33.8
$30,000 to 49,999	26.8	27.7	26.9	27.6	27.1	27.9	26.3	27.5
$50,000 to 59,999	12.4	10.8	11.7	9.2	13.7	12.8	12.1	11.0
$60,000 to 69,999	7.1	6.9	6.9	7.2	7.6	7.4	6.8	6.0
$70,000 and over	18.3	17.5	15.0	13.7	20.8	19.5	21.5	21.7
Household size:								
Singles	16.6	21.2	15.2	17.7	17.6	24.6	18.1	23.3
Families with no children	38.9	39.5	38.9	42.6	38.1	35.8	39.8	38.3
Families with children	44.5	39.3	45.9	39.7	44.3	39.6	42.1	38.4
Age of reader:								
Under 25 years old	9.0	7.2	6.4	5.0	13.1	10.1	8.8	7.2
25 to 34 years old	19.3	18.8	14.7	13.9	24.3	24.8	21.2	19.5
35 to 44 years old	25.7	22.9	25.4	22.0	27.6	24.5	24.5	22.6
45 to 54 years old	20.8	20.4	24.9	24.6	16.2	15.6	19.1	18.9
55 to 64 years old	12.1	15.1	13.0	15.8	9.4	13.2	13.4	16.3
65 years old and over	13.1	15.6	15.6	18.7	9.4	11.8	13.0	15.5
Category of book:								
Popular fiction	54.9	54.1	91.3	93.3	15.5	16.0	34.2	32.0
General nonfiction	10.2	10.4	5.0	3.5	15.7	15.4	13.5	16.4
Cooking/crafts	10.5	10.8	0.6	0.4	19.2	20.2	18.4	17.7
Other	24.4	24.7	3.1	2.8	49.6	48.4	33.9	33.9
Sales outlet:								
Independent	28.1	30.5	20.8	25.8	40.2	39.3	26.9	28.3
Chain book store	26.4	26.1	23.0	18.9	33.0	35.5	25.2	27.3
Book clubs	16.1	15.3	15.7	17.3	8.8	8.0	25.4	20.7
Other [3]	29.4	28.1	40.5	38.0	18.0	17.2	22.5	23.7

[1] "Pocket size" books sold primarily through magazine and news outlets, supermarkets, variety stores, etc. [2] All paperbound books, except mass market. [3] Includes mail order, price clubs, discount stores, food/drug stores, used book stores, and other outlets.

Source: Book Industry Study Group, Inc., New York, NY, *1991-1992 Consumer Research Study on Book Purchasing*, (copyright).

No. 398. Recording Media—Manufacturers' Shipments and Value: 1980 to 1991

[Domestic shipments based on reports of manufacturers representing more than 85 percent of the market. Domestic value data based on list prices of records and other media]

TYPE OF MEDIA	UNIT SHIPMENTS [1] (mil.)				MANUFACTUERS' VALUE (mil. dol.)			
	1980	1985	1990	1991	1980	1985	1990	1991
Total	**683.7**	**652.9**	**865.7**	**801.0**	**3,862.4**	**4,387.8**	**7,541.1**	**7,834.2**
Phonograph records	487.1	287.7	39.3	26.8	2,559.6	1,561.5	180.9	93.3
Long-playing albums [2]	322.8	167.0	11.7	4.8	2,290.3	1,280.5	86.5	29.4
Singles	164.3	120.7	27.6	22.0	269.3	281.0	94.4	63.9
Pre-recorded	196.6	342.6	529.6	429.1	1,302.8	2,436.8	3,730.3	3,250.0
8-track cartridges	86.4	3.5	-	-	526.4	25.3	(X)	(X)
Cassettes	110.2	339.1	442.2	360.1	776.4	2,411.5	3,472.4	3,019.6
Cassette singles	(X)	(X)	87.4	69.0	(X)	(X)	257.9	230.4
Compact disks (CD's)	(X)	22.6	286.5	333.3	(X)	389.5	3,451.6	4,337.7
CD singles	(X)	(X)	1.1	5.7	(X)	(X)	6.0	35.1
Music video	(X)	(X)	9.2	6.1	(X)	(X)	172.3	118.1

- Rounds to zero.   X Not applicable.   [1] Units net after returns.   [2] Includes extended play albums.

Source: Recording Industry Association of America, Inc., Washington, DC, *Inside the Recording Industry: A Statistical Overview: 1991*, and earlier issues.

No. 399. Household Participation in Lawn and Garden Activities: 1988 to 1992

[Based on national household sample survey conducted by the Gallup Organization. Subject to sampling variability; see source]

ACTIVITY	PERCENT HOUSEHOLDS ENGAGED IN—					RETAIL SALES (mil. dol.)				
	1988	1989	1990	1991	1992	1988	1989	1990	1991	1992
Total	**(X)**	**(X)**	**(X)**	**(X)**	**(X)**	**15,518**	**16,285**	**20,802**	**22,134**	**22,824**
Lawn care	58	57	66	62	54	5,342	5,660	6,412	6,890	7,460
Indoor houseplants	41	37	43	42	34	819	822	928	852	926
Flower gardening	42	41	48	41	39	1,679	1,857	2,275	2,302	2,167
Insect control	32	29	39	35	27	880	1,052	1,370	1,260	1,593
Shrub care	34	29	38	32	27	853	844	1,099	1,030	1,437
Vegetable gardening	34	32	37	31	31	982	1,026	1,384	1,652	1,440
Tree care	23	23	31	27	20	1,140	886	1,445	1,443	1,664
Landscaping	22	22	31	26	22	2,356	2,605	3,837	4,828	4,444
Flower bulbs	24	23	31	26	23	396	478	579	520	503
Fruit trees	16	14	19	15	13	416	287	502	371	350
Container gardening	11	11	15	13	9	235	240	359	330	239
Raising transplants [1]	11	11	15	12	8	122	139	181	141	169
Herb gardening	5	7	9	9	7	50	58	84	161	135
Growing berries	8	7	9	7	6	57	73	79	90	62
Ornamental gardening	6	5	7	7	5	191	266	268	264	235

X Not applicable.   [1] Starting plants in advance of planting in ground.

Source: The National Gardening Association, Burlington, VT, *National Gardening Survey*, annual, (copyright).

No. 400. Household Pet Ownership: 1991

[Based on a sample survey of 80,000 households in 1991; for details, see source]

ITEM	Unit	Dog	Cat	Pet bird	Horse
Households owning companion pets [1]	Million	34.6	29.2	5.4	1.9
Percent of all households	Percent	36.5	30.9	5.7	2.0
Average number owned	Number	1.5	2.0	2.2	2.5
Total companion pet population [1]	Million	52.5	57.0	11.7	4.9
Households obtaining veterinary care [2]	Percent	82	62	11	54
Average visits per year	Number	2.6	1.8	0.2	2.4
Average annual cost	Dollars	131.84	79.75	7.60	163.23
Total expenditures	Mil. dol.	4,557	2,330	185	314
PERCENT DISTRIBUTION OF HOUSEHOLDS OWNING PETS					
Annual household income: Under $12,500	Percent	14	15	16	9
$12,500 to $24,999	Percent	20	20	21	21
$25,000 to $39,999	Percent	24	23	24	25
$40,000 to $59,999	Percent	22	22	21	22
$60,000 and over	Percent	20	20	18	23
Family size: [1] One person	Percent	14	18	16	10
Two persons	Percent	32	33	27	34
Three persons	Percent	21	20	20	20
Four or more persons	Percent	33	29	37	36

[1] As of December.   [2] During 1991.

Source: American Veterinary Medical Association, Schaumburg, IL, *U.S. Pet Ownership and Demographics Sourcebook, 1993*, (copyright).

No. 401. Sport Fishing and Hunting Licenses—Number and Cost: 1970 to 1992

[In millions, except as indicated. For fiscal years ending in year shown; see text, section 9. See also *Historical Statistics, Colonial Times to 1970*, series H 875-876]

ITEM	1970	1975	1980	1985	1987	1988	1989	1990	1991	1992
Fishing licenses: Sales	31.1	34.7	35.2	35.7	36.5	36.8	36.6	37.0	37.0	37.4
Resident	26.8	30.0	30.1	30.5	31.0	31.3	31.0	31.0	31.1	31.4
Nonresident	4.3	4.7	5.1	5.2	5.6	5.5	5.6	6.0	5.9	6.0
Paid license holders [1]	24.4	27.5	28.0	29.7	30.3	31.4	30.3	30.7	30.7	30.6
Cost to anglers (mil. dol.)	91	142	196	282	315	330	341	363	375	398
Hunting licenses: Sales	22.2	25.9	27.0	27.7	28.8	30.0	29.3	30.0	30.7	31.3
Resident	21.0	24.7	25.6	26.1	27.1	27.7	27.3	27.4	28.5	29.1
Nonresident	1.2	1.3	1.4	1.6	1.7	2.0	2.0	2.3	2.2	2.2
Paid license holders [1]	15.4	16.6	16.3	15.9	15.8	15.9	15.9	15.8	15.7	15.7
Cost to hunters (mil. dol.)	102	155	222	301	345	381	400	422	439	481
Federal duck stamps sold (1,000)	2,072	2,222	2,090	1,914	1,794	1,663	1,395	1,401	1,420	1,330

[1] Resident and nonresident. Includes multiple counting of license holders who bought nonresident licenses as well as a home State license. "Licenses" includes licenses, tags, permits, and stamps.

Source: U.S. Fish and Wildlife Service, *Federal Aid in Fish and Wildlife Restoration*, annual.

No. 402. Anglers and Hunters: 1991

[For persons 16 years old and over. An angler or hunter is anyone who has fished or hunted in 1991. Based on the 1991 National Survey of Fishing, Hunting, and Wildlife-Associated Recreation conducted for the U.S. Fish and Wildlife Service by the U.S. Bureau of the Census]

TYPE OF FISHING	ANGLERS				TYPE OF HUNTING	HUNTERS			
	Number (1,000)	Percent of population	Days of fishing [1] (mil.)	Expenditures [2] (mil. dol.)		Number (1,000)	Percent of population	Days of fishing [1] (mil.)	Expenditures [2] (mil. dol.)
All fishing	[3]35,578	19	[3]511	23,990	All hunting	[3]14,063	7	[3]236	12,336
All freshwater fishing	[3]31,041	16	[3]440	15,149	Big game	10,745	6	128	5,090
Freshwater, except					Small game	7,642	4	77	1,550
Great Lakes	30,186	16	431	13,812	Migratory birds	3,009	2	22	686
Great Lakes	2,552	1	25	1,337	Other animals	1,411	1	19	255
Saltwater	8,885	5	75	4,992					

[1] Any part of a day constitutes a day. [2] Totals include expenditures for equipment, trips, magazines, membership dues, contributions, land leasing and ownership, licenses, stamps, tags, and other expenditures. Figures by type of fishing and hunting include only expenditures for trips and equipment. [3] Includes duplication for persons who participate in more than one category.

Source: U.S. Fish and Wildlife Service, *1991 National Survey of Fishing, Hunting, and Wildlife-Associated Recreation*.

No. 403. Wildlife-Associated Recreation Expenditures: 1991

[Sportsmen are any persons who fished or hunted in 1991. See headnote, table 402]

TYPE OF EXPENDITURE	EXPENDITURES (mil. dol.)				EXPENDITURE PER PARTICIPANT (dol.)			
	Total	Fishing	Hunting	Primary nonconsumptive [1]	Total	Fishing	Hunting	Primary nonconsumptive [1]
Total [2]	[3]59,027	23,990	12,336	18,104	[3]543	674	877	238
Food and lodging	11,202	4,953	1,824	4,425	103	139	130	58
Transportation	6,748	2,800	1,339	2,609	62	79	95	34
Other trip costs	4,820	4,094	278	448	44	115	20	6
Licenses, stamps, tags and permits	898	487	533	(NA)	22	14	38	(NA)
Equipment	12,727	3,740	3,283	5,704	123	105	233	75
Auxiliary equipment	[3]2,157	619	635	350	[3]20	17	45	5
Special equipment	[3]13,001	5,006	1,250	3,506	[3]120	141	89	46

NA Not available. [1] Observing, photographing, and feeding wildlife. [2] Includes expenditures for magazines, membership dues and contributions, and land leasing and ownership, not shown separately. [3] Includes expenditures not specified by type of activity.

Source: U.S. Fish and Wildlife Service, *1991 National Survey of Fishing, Hunting, and Wildlife-Associated Recreation*.

No. 404. Selected Spectator Sports: 1980 to 1992

[See also *Historical Statistics, Colonial Times to 1970,* series H 865-870 and H 872]

SPORT	Unit	1980	1985	1987	1988	1989	1990	1991	1992
Baseball, major leagues: [1]									
Attendance	1,000 ..	43,746	47,742	53,182	53,800	55,910	55,512	57,820	56,852
Regular season	1,000 ..	43,014	46,824	52,011	52,999	55,173	54,824	56,814	55,873
National League	1,000 ..	21,124	22,292	24,734	24,499	25,324	24,492	24,696	24,113
American League	1,000 ..	21,890	24,532	27,277	28,500	29,849	30,332	32,118	31,760
Playoffs	1,000 ..	407	591	784	541	514	479	633	668
World Series	1,000 ..	325	327	387	260	223	209	373	311
Players' salaries: [2]									
Average	$1,000 .	144	371	412	439	497	598	851	1,029
Basketball: [3][4]									
NCAA—Men's college:									
Teams	Number.	715	753	760	761	772	767	796	813
Attendance	1,000 ..	24,862	26,584	26,798	27,453	28,270	28,741	29,250	29,378
NCAA—Women's college:									
Teams	Number.	(NA)	746	756	754	765	782	806	815
Attendance	1,000 ..	(NA)	2,072	2,156	2,325	2,502	2,777	3,013	3,397
Pro: [5]									
Teams	Number.	22	23	23	23	25	27	27	27
Attendance, total [6]	1,000 ..	10,697	11,534	13,190	14,070	16,586	18,586	18,009	18,609
Regular season	1,000 ..	9,938	10,506	12,065	12,654	15,465	17,369	16,876	17,367
Average per game	Number.	11,017	11,141	12,765	13,419	15,088	15,690	15,245	15,689
Playoffs	1,000 ..	740	985	1,091	1,397	1,077	1,203	1,109	1,227
Players' salaries:									
Average	$1,000 .	170	325	440	510	603	817	989	1,042
Football:									
College: [4]									
Teams	Number.	642	661	667	673	673	673	681	674
Attendance	1,000 ..	35,541	36,312	36,463	35,581	36,406	36,627	36,566	36,199
National Football League: [7]									
Teams	Number.	28	28	28	28	28	28	28	28
Attendance, total [8]	1,000 ..	14,092	14,058	[9]15,180	17,024	17,400	17,666	17,752	17,784
Regular season	1,000 ..	13,392	13,345	[9]11,406	13,539	13,626	13,960	13,841	13,829
Average per game	Number.	59,787	59,567	[9]54,315	60,446	60,829	62,321	61,792	61,736
Postseason games [10]	1,000 ..	700	711	656	658	686	848	813	815
Players' salaries: [11]									
Average	$1,000 .	79	194	203	239	295	352	415	488
Median base salary	$1,000 .	70	140	175	180	200	236	250	275
National Hockey league: [12]									
Regular season attendance	1,000 ..	10,534	11,633	12,116	12,418	12,423	12,578	12,344	(NA)
Playoffs attendance	1,000 ..	977	1,109	1,336	1,323	1,322	1,356	1,442	(NA)
Horseracing: [13][14]									
Racing days	Number.	13,133	13,745	14,208	14,285	14,240	13,841	(NA)	(NA)
Attendance	1,000 ..	74,690	73,346	70,105	69,949	69,551	63,803	(NA)	(NA)
Pari-mutuel turnover	Mil. dol .	11,218	12,222	13,122	13,616	13,867	7,162	(NA)	(NA)
Revenue to government	Mil. dol .	713	625	608	596	585	611	(NA)	(NA)
Greyhound: [13]									
Total performances	Number.	5,855	9,590	11,156	12,904	13,393	14,915	(NA)	(NA)
Attendance	1,000 ..	20,874	23,853	26,215	26,477	33,818	28,660	(NA)	(NA)
Pari-mutuel turnover	Mil. dol .	2,064	2,702	3,193	3,291	3,278	3,388	(NA)	(NA)
Revenue to government	Mil. dol .	152	201	221	230	239	235	(NA)	(NA)
Jai alai: [13]									
Total performances	Number.	1,616	2,736	2,906	3,615	3,835	3,620	(NA)	(NA)
Games played	Number.	25,349	32,260	38,476	47,716	(NA)	(NA)	(NA)	(NA)
Attendance	1,000 ..	3,939	4,722	6,816	6,414	5,227	5,329	(NA)	(NA)
Pari-mutuel turnover	Mil. dol .	(NA)	664.0	707.5	663.6	553.0	545.5	(NA)	(NA)
Revenue to government	Mil. dol .	35	50	51	44	39	39	(NA)	(NA)
Professional rodeo: [15]									
Rodeos	Number.	631	617	637	707	741	754	798	770
Performances	Number.	1,921	1,887	1,832	2,037	2,128	2,159	2,241	2,203
Members	Number.	5,114	5,239	5,342	5,479	5,560	5,693	5,748	5,714
Permit-holders (rookies)	Number.	4,038	2,534	2,746	3,310	3,584	3,290	3,006	2,857

NA Not available.   [1] Source: The National League of Professional Baseball Clubs, New York, NY, *National League Green Book;* and The American League of Professional Baseball Clubs, New York, NY, *American League Red Book.*   [2] Source: Major League Baseball Players Association, New York, NY.   [3] Season ending in year shown.   [4] Source: National Collegiate Athletic Assn., Overland Park, KS. For women's attendance total, excludes double-headers with men's teams.   [5] Source: National Basketball Assn., New York, NY.   [6] Includes All-Star game, not shown separately.   [7] Source: National Football League, New York, NY.   [8] Beginning 1987, includes preseason attendance, not shown separately.   [9] Season was interrupted by a strike.   [10] Includes Pro Bowl, a nonchampionship game and Super Bowl.   [11] Source: National Football League Players Association, Washington, DC.   [12] Source: National Hockey League, Montreal, Quebec.   [13] Source: Association of Racing Commissioners International, Inc., Lexington, KY.   [14] Includes thoroughbred, harness, quarter horse, and fairs.   [15] Source: Professional Rodeo Cowboys Association, Colorado Springs, CO., *Official Professional Rodeo Media Guide,* annual, (copyright).

Source: Compiled from sources listed in footnotes.

No. 405. Selected Recreational Activities: 1975 to 1992

[See also *Historical Statistics, Colonial Times to 1970*, series H 862-864, H 871, H 874, and H 877]

ACTIVITY	Unit	1975	1980	1985	1988	1989	1990	1991	1992
Softball, amateur: [1]									
Total participants [2]	Million..	26	30	41	41	41	41	41	41
Youth participants	1,000 ..	450	650	712	722	900	1,100	1,205	1,206
Adult teams [3]	1,000 ..	66	110	152	182	188	188	200	198
Youth teams [3]	1,000 ..	9	18	31	40	46	46	51	57
Golfers (one round or more) [4] [5]	1,000 ..	13,036	15,112	17,520	23,000	24,200	27,800	24,800	24,800
Golf rounds played [5]	1,000 ..	308,562	357,701	414,777	484,000	469,000	502,000	479,000	505,400
Golf facilities	Number.	11,370	12,005	12,346	12,582	12,658	12,846	13,004	13,210
Classification:									
Private	Number.	4,770	4,839	4,861	4,897	4,862	4,810	4,686	4,568
Daily fee	Number.	5,014	5,372	5,573	5,748	5,833	6,024	6,272	6,552
Municipal	Number.	1,586	1,794	1,912	1,937	1,963	2,012	2,046	2,090
Tennis: [6]									
Players	1,000 ..	[7][8]29,201	(NA)	[9]18,951	[9]17,314	[9]18,844	[9]18,401	[9]16,702	[9]17,323
Courts	1,000 ..	130	(NA)	220	220	220	220	230	(NA)
Indoor	1,000 ..	8	(NA)	14	14	14	14	14	(NA)
Tenpin bowling:									
Participants, total [10]	Million..	62.5	72.0	67.0	68.0	71.0	71.0	82.0	82.0
Male	Million..	29.9	34.0	32.0	33.1	35.4	35.4	40.2	40.2
Female	Million..	32.6	38.0	35.0	34.9	35.6	35.6	41.8	41.8
Establishments [11]	Number.	8,577	8,591	8,275	7,923	7,671	7,544	7,395	7,250
Lanes [11]	1,000 ..	141	154	155	150	147	146	144	143
Membership, total [11] [12]	1,000 ..	8,751	9,595	8,064	7,167	6,570	6,357	5,881	5,591
American Bowling Congress	1,000 ..	4,300	4,688	3,657	3,313	3,036	2,922	2,712	2,577
Women's Bowling Congress	1,000 ..	3,692	4,118	3,714	3,189	2,859	2,742	2,523	2,403
Young American Bowling Alliance [13]	1,000 ..	759	789	693	665	675	693	646	611
Motion picture theaters [14] [15]	1,000 ..	15	18	21	23	23	24	25	26
Four-wall	1,000 ..	11	14	18	22	22	23	24	25
Drive-in	1,000 ..	4	4	3	2	1	1	1	1
Receipts, box office	Mil. dol..	2,115	2,749	3,749	4,458	5,033	5,022	4,803	4,871
Admission, average price	Dollars .	2.05	2.69	3.55	4.11	3.99	4.23	4.21	4.15
Attendance	Million..	1,033	1,022	1,056	1,085	1,263	1,187	1,141	1,173
Bicycles: [16]									
Domestic shipments	Million..	5.6	6.9	5.8	4.5	5.3	6.0	7.3	7.4
Imports	Million..	1.7	2.0	5.6	5.4	5.4	4.8	4.4	4.3
Boating: [17]									
Recreational boats owned	Million..	9.7	11.8	13.8	15.1	15.6	16.0	16.3	16.5
Outboard boats	Million..	5.7	6.8	7.4	7.7	7.9	7.9	7.9	8.0
Inboard boats	Million..	0.8	1.2	1.4	1.8	2.0	2.2	2.4	2.4
Sailboats	Million..	0.8	1.0	1.2	1.3	1.3	1.3	1.3	1.3
Canoes	Million..	2.4	1.3	1.8	2.1	2.2	2.3	2.4	2.4
Rowboats and other	Million..	([18])	1.5	1.8	2.2	2.1	2.3	2.3	2.4
Expenditures, total [19]	Bil. dol.	4.8	7.4	13.3	17.9	17.1	13.7	10.6	10.3
Outboard motors in use	1,000 ..	7,649	8,241	9,733	10,860	11,225	11,524	11,769	12,000
Motors sold	1,000 ..	435	315	392	460	430	352	289	272
Value, retail	Mil. dol..	411	554	1,319	1,828	1,764	1,546	1,311	1,268
Outboard boats sold	1,000 ..	328	290	305	355	291	227	195	192
Value, retail	Mil. dol..	263	408	759	1,225	1,134	978	871	839
Inboard/outdrive boats sold	1,000 ..	70	56	115	148	133	97	73	75
Value, retail	Mil. dol..	420	616	1,663	2,585	2,354	1,794	1,293	1,239
All terrain vehicles: [20]									
Vehicles in use or owned	1,000 ..	(NA)	(NA)	2,000	2,517	2,309	2,240	2,100	1,930
Imports	1,000 ..	(NA)	(NA)	683	209	121	100	80	65

NA Not available. [1] Source: Amateur Softball Association, Oklahoma City, OK. [2] Amateur Softball Association teams and other amateur softball teams. [3] Amateur Softball Association teams only. [4] Source: National Golf Foundation, Jupiter, FL. [5] Prior to 1986, for persons 5 years of age and over; thereafter for persons 12 years of age and over. [6] Source: U.S. Tennis Association, White Plains, NY. [7] Survey by A. C. Nielsen Co. [8] 1976 data. [9] Based on National Sporting Goods Association Sports Participation Survey. [10] For season ending in year shown. Persons 5 years old and over. Source: National Bowling Council, Arlington, VA. [11] Source: American Bowling Congress, Greendale, WI. Season ending in year shown. [12] Membership totals are for U.S., Canada and for U.S. military personnel worldwide. [13] Prior to 1985, represents American Jr. Bowling Congress and ABC/WIBC Collegiate Division. [14] Source: Motion Picture Association of America, Inc., New York, NY. [15] Prior to 1975, figures represent theaters; thereafter, screens. [16] Source: Bicycle Manufacturers Association of America, Inc., Washington, DC. [17] Source: National Marine Manufacturers Association, Chicago, IL. [18] Included in canoes. [19] Represents estimated expenditures for new and used boats, motors, accessories, safety equipment, fuel, insurance, docking, maintenance, storage, repairs, and other expenses. [20] Source: Motorcycle Industry Council, Inc., Irvine, CA.

Source: Compiled from sources listed in footnotes.

No. 406. Participation in Selected Sports Activities: 1992

[In thousands, except rank. For persons 7 years of age or older. Except as indicated, a participant plays a sport more than once in the year. Based on a sampling of 10,000 households]

ACTIVITY	ALL PERSONS Number	ALL PERSONS Rank	SEX Male	SEX Female	AGE 7-11 years	AGE 12-17 years	AGE 18-24 years	AGE 25-34 years	AGE 35-44 years	AGE 45-54 years	AGE 55-64 years	AGE 65 years and over	HOUSEHOLD INCOME Under 15,000	HOUSEHOLD INCOME 15,000-24,999	HOUSEHOLD INCOME 25,000-34,999	HOUSEHOLD INCOME 35,000-49,999	HOUSEHOLD INCOME 50,000-74,999	HOUSEHOLD INCOME 75,000 and over
Total	**229,906**	**(X)**	**111,522**	**118,385**	**18,539**	**21,025**	**26,157**	**42,739**	**40,203**	**27,633**	**21,098**	**32,512**	**45,695**	**37,164**	**35,611**	**43,310**	**46,273**	**21,853**
Number participated in [1]:																		
Aerobic exercising [1]	27,834	9	5,076	22,758	1,040	2,606	5,771	8,432	4,981	2,641	1,153	1,209	3,874	3,801	4,385	5,962	6,428	3,385
Backpacking [2]	9,698	24	6,021	3,676	884	1,223	1,547	2,996	1,999	768	166	116	1,763	1,487	1,507	2,085	1,918	938
Baseball	15,140	17	12,476	2,664	4,893	4,176	1,921	1,907	1,719	334	90	39	2,215	2,050	2,586	3,444	3,589	1,257
Basketball	28,181	8	20,566	7,615	5,479	8,176	4,896	5,548	3,193	710	119	61	3,806	3,604	4,306	6,455	7,157	2,852
Bicycle riding [1]	54,632	3	28,000	26,632	12,494	9,684	5,547	9,980	8,410	3,541	2,758	2,217	8,750	7,319	8,345	11,054	13,582	5,581
Bowling	42,494	5	21,768	20,726	4,982	5,757	7,024	10,932	7,533	3,138	1,521	1,607	6,679	6,081	6,983	8,853	10,447	3,451
Calisthenics [1]	11,475	21	5,046	6,428	1,190	1,761	1,583	2,766	1,710	1,038	498	929	1,966	1,582	1,986	2,012	2,788	1,141
Camping [1]	47,328	4	25,671	21,657	5,777	5,881	5,297	11,529	9,987	4,491	2,571	1,795	6,769	7,385	8,793	9,912	10,686	3,783
Exercise walking [1]	67,822	1	23,204	44,619	1,874	2,924	6,310	13,879	14,216	10,648	8,499	9,472	11,793	11,034	9,828	12,682	15,126	7,360
Exercising with equipment [1]	39,360	7	19,068	20,292	624	3,555	6,913	10,938	8,011	4,706	2,284	2,328	4,872	5,374	6,340	7,724	9,871	5,178
Fishing—fresh water	41,656	6	28,190	13,467	4,204	4,629	4,282	9,811	8,354	4,962	2,915	2,500	7,288	7,435	7,685	8,020	8,244	2,985
Fishing—salt water	12,607	19	8,757	3,851	998	1,104	1,709	2,817	2,457	1,629	1,058	837	1,942	1,793	1,735	2,634	3,293	1,209
Football	13,494	18	11,707	1,787	2,830	4,697	2,762	2,070	845	235	26	28	2,080	1,822	1,937	3,297	3,036	1,175
Golf	24,021	10	18,459	5,562	928	1,895	3,048	6,188	4,668	3,018	1,876	2,399	2,772	2,226	3,040	5,073	7,124	3,931
Hiking	21,619	13	11,588	10,031	1,625	2,621	2,644	5,272	4,791	2,295	1,298	1,071	3,376	3,220	3,516	3,730	5,310	2,468
Hunting with firearms	17,819	15	15,960	1,859	405	1,835	2,614	4,204	4,352	2,397	1,083	929	2,398	3,615	3,563	3,756	3,253	1,233
Racquetball	6,560	25	4,840	1,720	128	577	1,980	2,113	1,194	478	45	45	802	880	1,045	1,267	1,723	842
Running/jogging [1]	21,932	12	12,711	9,222	2,272	4,494	4,490	4,854	3,344	1,667	461	349	3,055	2,934	2,609	4,886	5,780	2,669
Skiing—alpine/downhill	10,782	22	6,484	4,298	740	1,920	2,601	2,721	1,751	714	263	72	701	1,008	1,400	2,267	2,705	2,701
Skiing—cross country	3,470	26	1,752	1,718	290	304	327	671	1,056	461	196	166	307	376	659	724	808	596
Soccer	10,619	23	7,179	3,439	4,246	3,751	1,296	683	572	71	-	-	1,275	1,377	1,309	2,457	2,976	1,225
Softball	19,187	14	11,837	7,350	3,078	4,315	2,906	5,117	2,766	739	194	73	2,491	3,245	3,046	4,521	4,464	1,420
Swimming [1]	63,146	2	29,837	33,309	10,976	10,609	7,690	12,572	11,068	4,627	2,807	2,800	8,424	9,378	10,419	12,236	15,065	7,625
Target shooting	12,309	20	9,812	2,496	686	1,544	1,888	3,286	2,627	1,496	459	323	1,432	2,067	2,304	2,681	2,604	1,221
Tennis	17,323	16	9,965	7,358	1,385	3,165	3,933	4,394	2,477	1,289	525	155	1,781	1,925	2,034	3,896	4,457	3,230
Volleyball	22,130	11	11,414	10,716	1,717	5,196	5,111	5,399	3,435	926	282	64	3,661	3,675	3,316	4,641	5,022	1,814

- Represents or rounds to zero.   X Not applicable.   [1] Participant engaged in activity at least six times in the year.   [2] Includes wilderness camping.   [3] Vacation/overnight.

Source: National Sporting Goods Association, Mt. Prospect, IL, *Sports Participation in 1992: Series I* (copyright).

No. 407. Sporting Goods Sales, by Product Category: 1980 to 1993

[In millions of dollars, except percent. Based on a sample survey of consumer purchases of 80,000 households, except recreational transport, which was provided by industry associations. Excludes Alaska and Hawaii]

SELECTED PRODUCT CATEGORY	1980	1985	1986	1987	1988	1989	1990	1991	1992	1993, proj.
Sales, all products	16,691	27,446	30,614	33,942	42,093	45,184	44,111	42,943	42,434	44,624
Annual percent change [1]	-1.4	4.0	11.5	10.9	24.0	7.3	-2.4	-2.6	-1.2	5.2
Percent of retail sales	1.7	2.0	2.1	2.2	2.5	2.6	2.4	2.3	2.2	2.1
Athletic and sport clothing [2]	3,127	3,376	3,931	4,645	10,736	11,557	11,382	12,057	10,101	10,801
Athletic and sport footwear [3]	1,731	2,610	3,199	3,524	3,772	5,763	6,263	6,300	6,242	6,339
Walking shoes	(NA)	263	368	512	752	1,237	1,509	1,375	1,375	1,388
Gym shoes, sneakers	465	656	642	693	783	1,125	1,177	1,181	1,113	1,124
Jogging and running shoes	397	572	476	475	460	515	519	555	574	586
Tennis shoes	359	470	448	367	353	508	582	597	589	601
Aerobic shoes	(NA)	178	333	401	327	425	389	381	376	368
Basketball shoes	86	185	187	169	226	293	428	449	456	465
Golf shoes	68	109	120	130	128	129	157	173	182	189
Athletic and sport equipment [3]	6,487	8,922	9,477	9,900	10,705	11,503	11,965	12,063	12,816	13,519
Firearms and hunting	1,351	1,699	1,675	1,804	1,894	2,139	2,202	2,091	2,533	2,913
Exercise equipment	(NA)	1,216	1,206	1,191	1,452	1,748	1,824	2,106	2,050	2,071
Golf	386	730	828	946	1,111	1,167	1,219	1,149	1,338	1,391
Camping	646	724	833	858	945	996	1,072	1,006	903	921
Bicycles (10-12-15-18+ speed)	(NA)	975	1,089	930	819	906	1,092	(NA)	(NA)	(NA)
Fishing tackle	539	681	773	830	766	769	776	711	678	685
Snow skiing	379	593	622	661	710	606	606	577	627	648
Tennis	237	273	260	238	264	315	287	295	296	301
Archery	149	212	214	224	235	261	265	270	334	400
Baseball and softball	158	176	180	173	174	206	217	214	245	250
Water skis	123	125	132	148	160	96	88	63	55	57
Bowling accessories	107	106	114	129	129	143	155	155	164	167
Recreational transport	5,345	12,547	14,007	15,873	16,880	16,360	14,502	12,524	13,275	13,965
Pleasure boats	2,718	6,753	7,372	8,906	9,637	9,319	7,644	5,862	5,765	5,938
Recreational vehicles	1,178	3,515	3,940	4,507	4,839	4,481	4,113	3,615	4,412	4,816
Bicycles and supplies	1,233	2,109	2,518	2,272	2,131	2,259	2,423	2,686	2,723	2,822
Snowmobiles	216	162	177	188	273	301	322	362	376	389

NA Not available. [1] Represents change from immediate prior year. [2] Category expanded in 1988; not comparable with earlier years. [3] Includes other products not shown separately.

Source: National Sporting Goods Association, Mt. Prospect, IL, The Sporting Goods Market in 1993; and prior issues, (copyright).

No. 408. Consumer Purchases of Sporting Goods, by Consumer Characteristics: 1992

[In percent. Based on sample survey of consumer purchases of 80,000 households. Excludes Alaska and Hawaii]

CHARACTERISTIC	Total households	FOOTWEAR				EQUIPMENT					
		Aerobic shoes	Gym shoes/ sneakers	Jogging/ running shoes	Walking shoes	Fishing tackle	Camping equipment	Exercise equipment	Hunting equipment guns	Team sports equipment	Golf equipment
Total	100.0	100.0	100.0	100.0	100.0	100.0	100.0	100.0	100.0	100.0	100.0
Age of user:											
Under 14 years old	21	6	42	9	3	8	12	1	3	44	2
14 to 17 years old	5	4	17	9	2	3	8	2	3	15	2
18 to 24 years old	10	8	5	11	3	4	8	3	7	5	5
25 to 34 years old	17	26	9	19	10	23	21	24	28	13	20
35 to 44 years old	15	25	11	21	18	27	23	27	30	9	22
45 to 64 years old	19	22	12	25	36	26	17	32	25	2	31
65 years old and over	13	9	4	6	28	7	4	7	1	1	13
Multiple ages	-	-	-	-	-	3	7	4	2	11	5
Sex of user:											
Male	49	16	52	59	36	87	64	43	92	77	82
Female	51	84	48	41	64	12	29	51	5	17	14
Both sexes	-	-	-	-	-	1	8	6	2	6	4
Education of household head:											
Less than high school	12	7	7	5	9	9	6	6	8	3	3
High school	30	26	30	21	28	27	23	24	28	22	15
Some college	28	30	31	29	28	33	34	23	35	32	27
College graduate	30	37	32	45	33	30	37	47	28	43	54
Annual household income:											
Under $15,000	22	12	13	9	17	10	10	7	8	7	2
$15,000 to $24,999	17	13	15	11	16	15	16	9	13	12	6
$25,000 to $34,999	16	15	16	16	16	16	16	14	12	17	10
$35,000 to $49,999	18	21	23	22	18	25	24	23	26	24	20
$50,000 to $74,999	17	24	20	21	18	19	20	28	23	25	26
$75,000 and over	10	15	14	21	15	14	14	18	19	15	35

- Represents or rounds to zero.

Source: National Sporting Goods Association, Mt. Prospect, IL, The Sporting Goods Market in 1993, (copyright).

No. 409. Gun Ownership: 1974 to 1993

[In percent. For the 50 States and DC, except prior to 1984 excludes Alaska and Hawaii. Represents respondents indicating there is a gun in the home or garage. Based on samples of noninstitutionalized English speaking persons 18 years old and older. For details, see source]

CHARACTERISTIC	1974	1976	1980	1984	1987	1990	1991	TYPE OF FIREARM, 1993			
								Total [1]	Pistol	Shotgun	Rifle
Total	46	47	48	44	46	43	40	42	24	27	23
Age:											
18 to 20 years old. . . .	34	38	48	39	43	40	22	48	21	34	21
21 to 29 years old. . . .	48	45	48	40	35	34	36	38	21	23	17
30 to 49 years old. . . .	49	52	50	48	51	46	40	44	27	27	24
50 years old and older .	44	44	46	44	47	42	42	42	22	28	25
Sex:											
Male	51	52	56	54	51	53	50	53	28	38	31
Female	42	43	41	36	43	34	32	34	20	19	17
Race:											
White	48	58	50	46	49	45	42	45	25	29	26
Black/other	32	37	29	29	33	29	29	26	17	14	9
Education:											
Grade school	49	42	51	38	44	47	39	47	18	30	27
High school	48	50	51	49	50	47	46	46	25	32	27
College	42	44	41	40	43	37	34	38	24	22	20
Religion:											
Protestant	52	53	56	50	52	48	46	47	27	31	26
Catholic.	37	36	36	35	36	36	30	36	17	23	20
Jewish.	7	26	6	9	25	6	10	9	-	4	4
None	40	43	39	44	39	34	31	37	24	17	20
Politics:											
Republican.	49	50	53	47	51	48	42	51	29	34	28
Democrat.	45	45	46	47	44	40	41	35	18	21	17
Independent.	47	48	47	39	44	42	37	42	26	28	25

- Represents or rounds to zero.   [1] Includes other types of firearms, not shown separately.

Source: U.S. Bureau of Justice Statistics, *Sourcebook of Criminal Justice Statistics*, annual.

No. 410. Arts and Humanities—Selected Federal Aid Programs: 1980 to 1992

[In millions of dollars, except as indicated. For fiscal years ending in year shown, see text, section 9]

TYPE OF FUND AND PROGRAM	1980	1985	1986	1987	1988	1989	1990	1991	1992
National Endowment for the Arts:									
Funds available [1]	188.1	171.7	167.1	170.9	171.1	166.7	170.8	166.5	163.0
Program appropriation.	97.0	118.7	115.7	120.8	122.2	123.5	124.3	124.6	123.0
Matching funds [2]	42.9	29.5	30.0	29.3	32.9	23.6	32.4	32.4	30.3
Grants awarded (number).	5,505	4,801	4,484	4,542	4,628	4,604	4,475	4,239	4,229
Funds obligated.	166.4	149.4	146.6	151.4	156.3	148.3	157.6	158.0	154.6
Music	13.6	15.3	14.6	15.1	15.3	15.3	16.5	14.1	14.9
State programs.	22.1	24.4	23.8	24.6	24.9	25.5	26.1	37.7	37.0
Museums.	11.2	11.9	11.5	11.5	12.6	12.7	12.1	11.3	11.1
Theater.	8.4	10.6	10.2	10.8	10.7	10.7	10.6	9.4	9.4
Dance.	8.0	9.0	9.0	9.1	9.2	9.5	9.6	8.5	8.2
Media arts	8.4	9.9	12.3	12.9	12.4	12.7	13.9	11.8	12.0
Challenge [3]	50.8	20.7	20.7	20.8	24.8	15.4	19.7	19.7	13.8
Visual arts	7.3	6.2	5.7	6.2	6.0	6.1	5.9	5.3	5.6
Other	36.6	41.3	38.8	40.4	40.4	40.2	43.1	40.2	42.7
National Endowment for the Humanities:									
Funds available [1]	186.2	125.6	121.1	128.4	125.2	137.1	140.6	152.1	156.5
Program appropriation.	100.3	95.2	[4]91.9	[4]95.8	96.7	108.3	114.2	125.1	131.2
Matching funds [2]	38.4	30.4	27.3	28.5	28.5	28.7	26.3	27.0	25.2
Grants awarded (number).	2,917	2,241	2,297	2,888	2,113	2,285	2,195	2,171	2,199
Funds obligated.	185.5	125.7	121.1	128.4	125.2	137.1	141.0	149.8	159.1
Education programs.	18.3	17.9	14.8	16.4	16.6	16.5	16.3	18.5	20.0
State programs.	26.0	24.4	24.1	25.0	25.3	29.0	29.6	30.8	31.8
Research grants	32.0	24.4	21.0	21.7	21.9	22.1	22.5	24.0	25.3
Fellowship program	18.0	15.3	14.4	15.3	15.3	15.3	15.3	16.2	17.4
Challenge [3]	53.5	19.6	16.2	16.5	16.5	16.7	14.6	15.1	12.4
Public programs . . . . ͘.	25.1	24.1	24.7	25.4	24.9	25.1	25.4	25.3	27.0
Preservation and access [5]	(X)	(X)	4.1	4.1	4.7	12.3	17.5	19.9	25.1
National Capital Arts and Cultural									
Affairs Program.	(X)	(X)	1.9	4.0	(X)	(X)	(X)	(X)	(X)
Other	12.6	(X)	(X)	(X)	(X)	(X)	(X)	(X)	(X)

X Not applicable.   [1] Includes other funds, shown separately. Excludes administrative funds. Gifts are included through 1980; excluded thereafter.   [2] Represents Federal funds appropriated only upon receipt or certification by Endowment of matching non-Federal gifts.   [3] Program designed to stimulate new sources and higher levels of giving to institutions for the purpose of guaranteeing long-term stability and financial independence. Program requires a match of at least 3 private dollars to each Federal dollar. Funds for challenge grants are not allocated by program area because they are awarded on a grant-by-grant basis. [4] Excludes National Capital Arts and Cultural Affairs Program.   [5] Program designed to support projects which preserve and guarantee access to print and nonprint media in danger of disintegration or deterioration.

Source: U.S. National Endowment for the Arts, *Annual Report*; and U.S. National Endowment for the Humanities, *Annual Report*.

No. 411. Attendance for Various Arts Activities: 1992

[In percent, except as indicated. For persons 18 years old and over. Excludes elementary and high school performances. Based on 1992 household survey Public Participation in the Arts conducted January through June 1992. Data are subject to sampling error; see source]

ITEM	Adult popu-lation (mil.)	ATTENDANCE AT LEAST ONCE IN THE PRIOR 12 MONTHS AT—							
		Jazz perfor-mance	Classical music perfor-mance	Opera	Musical play	Non-musical play	Ballet	Art museums	Historic park
Total	185.8	11	13	3	17	14	5	27	35
Sex: Male.	89.0	12	12	3	15	12	4	27	35
Female	96.8	9	13	4	20	15	6	27	34
Race: White	158.8	10	13	3	18	14	5	28	37
Black	21.1	16	7	2	14	12	3	19	18
Other	5.9	6	12	5	11	10	6	29	23
Age: 18 to 24 years old . .	24.1	11	10	3	16	13	5	29	33
25 to 34 years old.	42.4	14	10	3	16	12	5	29	36
35 to 44 years old.	39.8	13	12	3	19	14	5	30	40
45 to 54 years old.	27.7	11	17	4	22	17	5	29	41
55 to 64 years old.	21.2	8	15	4	19	15	5	25	33
65 to 74 years old.	18.3	7	14	4	17	13	4	20	29
75 to 96 years old.	12.3	2	8	2	9	7	2	10	12
Education: Grade school. .	14.3	1	2	1	3	2	1	4	8
Some high school. . . .	18.6	2	3	1	5	4	1	7	15
High school graduate . .	69.4	6	7	1	12	8	2	16	26
Some college.	39.2	14	14	3	21	16	6	35	43
College graduate	26.2	20	23	6	30	23	9	46	52
Graduate school.	18.1	25	36	12	37	35	12	59	64
Income: Under $5,000 . . .	8.6	6	5	2	8	8	2	12	17
$5,000 to $9,999	15.2	5	6	1	7	6	3	14	16
$10,000 to $14,999. . . .	19.2	5	6	2	8	7	2	13	20
$15,000 to $24,999. . . .	32.9	9	11	2	14	11	3	23	31
$25,000 to $49,999. . . .	62.2	11	13	3	18	14	5	29	40
$50,000 and over	32.1	18	23	8	33	24	10	44	51
Not reported	15.6	11	13	4	18	15	5	28	33

Source: U.S. National Endowment for the Arts, *Arts Participation in America: 1982 to 1992.*

No. 412. Participation in Various Leisure Activities: 1992

[In percent, except as indicated. Covers activities engaged in at least once in the prior 12 months. See headnote, table 411]

ITEM	Adult popu-lation (mil.)	ATTENDANCE AT—			PARTICIPATION IN—				
		Movies	Sports events	Amuse-ment park	Exercise program	Playing sports	Outdoor activ-ities [1]	Home improve-ment/ repair	Reading literature
Total.	185.8	59	37	50	60	39	34	48	54
Sex: Male	89.0	60	44	51	61	50	39	53	47
Female	96.8	59	30	50	59	29	29	42	60
Race: White	158.8	60	38	51	61	40	37	50	56
Black	21.1	54	32	45	51	32	10	32	45
Other	5.9	62	20	46	51	38	28	31	42
Age: 18 to 24 years old.	24.1	82	51	68	67	59	43	33	53
25 to 34 years old.	42.4	70	47	68	67	52	41	47	54
35 to 44 years old.	39.8	68	43	58	62	44	42	58	59
45 to 54 years old.	27.7	58	35	44	62	34	36	57	57
55 to 64 years old.	21.2	40	23	30	56	21	21	53	53
65 to 74 years old.	18.3	34	20	29	50	18	21	42	50
75 to 96 years old.	12.3	19	7	14	34	7	5	20	40
Education: Grade school	14.3	16	9	24	24	10	11	24	17
Some high school	18.6	35	19	35	39	18	21	34	32
High school graduate. . . .	69.4	54	33	51	55	34	31	47	49
Some college.	39.2	21	45	59	71	49	42	53	65
College graduate.	26.2	77	51	58	75	55	42	52	71
Graduate school.	18.1	81	51	54	79	57	51	65	79
Income: Under $5,000.	8.6	43	23	35	40	20	17	21	37
$5,000 to $9,999.	15.2	35	22	34	39	21	21	25	40
$10,000 to $14,999	19.2	44	22	39	45	25	22	35	43
$15,000 to $24,999	32.9	53	32	52	54	36	34	42	50
$25,000 to $49,999	62.2	67	42	57	66	45	40	57	58
$50,000 and over	32.1	76	52	57	77	54	44	64	71
Not reported.	15.6	58	34	46	60	36	30	41	50

[1] Camping, hiking, and canoeing.

Source: U.S. National Endowment for the Arts, *Arts Participation in America: 1982 to 1992.*

No. 413. Performing Arts—Selected Data: 1980 to 1992

[Receipts and expenditures in millions of dollars. For season ending in year shown, except as indicated]

ITEM	1980	1984	1985	1986	1987	1988	1989	1990	1991	1992
Legitimate theater: [1]										
Broadway shows:										
New productions[3]	67	36	31	33	40	31	29	35	28	36
Playing weeks [2][3]	1,541	1,119	1,062	1,049	1,031	1,114	1,097	1,062	970	901
Number of tickets sold (1,000)	9,380	7,898	7,156	6,527	6,968	8,142	7,968	8,039	7,314	7,365
Gross box office receipts	143.4	226.5	208.0	190.6	207.2	253.4	262.0	283.3	267.2	292.4
Road shows:										
Playing weeks [3]	1,351	1,057	993	983	901	893	869	944	1,152	1,171
Gross box office receipts	181.2	206.2	225.9	235.6	224.2	222.9	255.5	367.1	450.2	502.7
Nonprofit professional theatres: [4]										
Companies reporting	147	230	217	201	188	189	192	185	184	182
Gross income	113.6	226.6	234.7	263.8	271.2	276.4	349.0	307.6	333.9	359.1
Earned income	67.3	145.7	146.1	160.8	165.2	167.0	224.6	188.4	202.6	222.5
Contributed income	46.3	80.9	88.6	103.0	106.0	109.4	124.4	119.2	131.3	136.6
Gross expenses	113.6	230.3	239.3	263.3	272.8	277.9	349.2	306.3	336.7	365.6
Productions	1,852	3,434	2,710	2,944	2,427	2,369	2,469	2,265	2,277	2,310
Performances	42,109	56,735	52,341	57,727	46,768	46,149	53,263	46,131	48,695	46,184
Total attendance (mil.)	14.2	15.5	14.2	14.8	14.6	13.9	18.7	15.2	16.9	16.0
OPERA America professional member companies: [5]										
Number of companies [6]	79	90	97	100	100	99	101	98	98	100
Expenses [6]	122.4	204.5	216.4	252.6	260.1	294.4	311.7	321.2	346.7	371.8
Performances [7]	1,372	1,671	1,909	2,054	2,254	2,378	2,429	2,336	2,283	2,424
Total attendance (mil.) [7][8]	5.5	5.9	6.7	6.2	6.6	6.8	7.4	7.5	7.6	7.3
Main season attendance (mil.) [7][9]	(NA)	2.9	3.3	3.4	3.8	3.9	4.0	4.1	4.3	4.3
Symphony orchestras: [10]										
Concerts	(NA)	18,441	19,573	20,051	19,319	21,306	20,630	18,931	18,074	19,778
Attendance (mil.)	(NA)	22.3	24.0	25.4	24.5	27.4	25.8	24.7	26.7	26.3
Gross revenue	(NA)	222.8	252.4	281.2	306.9	325.3	353.2	377.5	394.5	414.0
Concert income	(NA)	150.9	168.6	184.5	200.4	218.0	231.0	253.3	273.8	284.1
Endowment income	(NA)	71.9	83.8	96.7	106.5	42.6	46.8	52.1	52.5	55.3
Other earned income	(NA)	379.4	426.1	469.7	64.7	75.4	72.1	68.2	74.6	
Operating expenses	(NA)	379.4	426.1	469.7	503.5	541.2	583.5	621.7	662.2	683.0
Artistic personnel	(NA)	209.6	231.9	253.4	270.0	288.0	310.2	327.3	355.8	398.9
Concert production	(NA)	60.1	69.2	71.4	79.5	85.8	89.0	104.3	110.3	117.2
Advertising and promotion	(NA)	27.8	32.5	36.6	40.4	42.0	47.5	51.3	57.3	58.3
General and administrative	(NA)	46.8	51.3	56.2	59.4	61.5	68.4	73.3	75.6	76.2
Other	(NA)	35.1	41.3	52.2	54.3	63.9	68.4	65.6	63.2	32.4
Support	(NA)	162.8	188.1	202.7	219.5	229.2	249.0	257.8	281.2	279.6
Tax supported grants	(NA)	38.1	42.2	49.0	49.3	52.1	54.5	55.6	58.3	49.1
Private sector support	(NA)	124.7	145.9	153.8	170.1	177.1	194.5	202.1	222.9	230.5

NA Not available.　[1] Source: Variety, New York, NY, various June issues, (copyright).　[2] All shows (new productions and holdovers from previous seasons).　[3] Eight performances constitute one playing week.　[4] Source: Theatre Communications Group, New York, NY. For years ending on or prior to Aug. 31.　[5] Source: OPERA America, Washington, DC.　[6] United States companies.　[7] United States and Canadian companies.　[8] Includes educational performances, outreach, etc.　[9] For paid performances.　[10] Source: American Symphony Orchestra League, Inc., Washington, DC. For years ending Aug. 31. Data represent all United States orchestras, excluding college/university and youth orchestras.

Source: Compiled from sources listed in footnotes.

No. 414. Boy Scouts and Girl Scouts—Membership and Units: 1970 to 1992

[In thousands. Boy Scouts as of Dec. 31; Girl Scouts as of Sept. 30. Includes Puerto Rico and outlying areas]

ITEM	1970	1975	1980	1985	1986	1987	1988	1989	1990	1991	1992
BOY SCOUTS OF AMERICA											
Membership	6,287	5,318	4,318	4,845	5,171	5,347	5,364	5,356	5,448	5,319	5,338
Boys	4,683	3,933	3,207	3,755	4,037	4,180	4,228	4,247	4,293	4,150	4,150
Adults	1,604	1,385	1,110	1,090	1,134	1,168	1,136	1,109	1,155	1,168	1,188
Total units (packs, troops, posts, group	157	150	129	134	132	131	131	130	130	128	128
GIRL SCOUTS OF THE U.S.A.											
Membership	3,922	3,234	2,784	2,802	2,917	2,947	3,052	3,166	3,269	3,383	3,510
Girls	3,248	2,723	2,250	2,172	2,248	2,274	2,345	2,415	2,480	2,561	2,647
Adults	674	511	534	630	669	673	707	751	788	822	863
Total units (troops, groups)	164	159	141	166	174	180	189	196	202	210	219

Source: Boy Scouts of America, National Council, Irving, TX, Annual Report; and Girl Scouts of the United States of America, New York, NY, Annual Report.

No. 415. Travel by U.S. Residents, by Selected Trip Characteristics: 1985 to 1991

[In millions. See headnote, table 416]

CHARACTERISTIC	TRIPS				PERSON TRIPS [1]			
	1985	1989	1990	1991	1985	1989	1990	1991
Total.................	558.4	664.3	661.1	664.5	1,077.6	1,260.1	1,274.5	1,306.6
Purpose:								
Visit friends and relatives	206.8	231.4	246.0	225.9	430.8	476.5	523.3	496.5
Other pleasure	177.6	225.9	214.5	239.3	376.0	469.3	447.5	496.5
Business or convention	133.3	169.7	155.6	152.8	185.2	232.0	209.5	209.1
Other	40.7	37.3	45.0	46.5	85.6	82.3	94.2	104.5
Mode of transport:								
Auto, truck, recreation vehicle	376.1	479.8	483.9	498.4	797.7	982.7	1,011.3	1,045.2
Airplane..................	140.5	154.6	144.9	132.9	217.3	234.3	214.5	209.1
Other	41.8	29.9	32.3	33.2	62.6	43.1	48.7	52.3
Vacation trip [2]...............	339.8	416.7	422.3	418.6	728.7	878.3	883.9	901.6
Weekend trip [2]................	224.0	282.4	280.0	392.1	470.1	582.1	580.2	770.9

[1] A count of times each person (child or adult) goes on a trip.   [2] A trip can be counted as both a weekend and a vacation trip.

Source: U.S. Travel Data Center, Washington, DC, *National Travel Survey*, annual, (copyright).

No. 416. Characteristics of Business Trips and Pleasure Trips: 1985 to 1991

[Represents trips to places 100 miles or more from home by one or more from home by one or more household members traveling together. Based on a monthly telephone survey of 1,500 U.S. adults. For details, see source]

CHARACTERISTIC	Unit	BUSINESS TRIPS				PLEASURE TRIPS			
		1985	1989	1990	1991	1985	1989	1990	1991
Total trips	Millions .	133.3	169.7	155.6	152.8	384.4	457.3	460.9	465.2
Average household members on trip . .	Number .	1.4	1.4	1.4	1.4	2.1	2.0	2.1	2.1
Average nights per trip.[1].........	Nights . .	3.6	3.2	3.7	3.8	5.6	4.4	4.4	4.0
Average miles per trip [2].........	Miles...	1,180	1,090	1,020	862	1,010	950	867	870
Traveled primarily by auto/truck/RV [3] rental car	Percent .	51	57	58	55	73	76	77	81
Traveled primarily by air	Percent .	44	39	37	38	21	19	18	15
Used a rental car while on trip	Percent .	20	16	14	12	6	7	7	9
Stayed in a hotel while on trip	Percent .	62	65	71	75	39	38	37	39
Used a travel agent	Percent .	28	20	21	16	13	12	12	13
Also a vacation trip.............	Percent .	13	17	17	26	80	81	82	79
Male travelers	Percent .	67	72	71	66	48	49	49	53
Female travelers	Percent .	33	28	29	34	52	51	51	47
Household income:									
Less than $40,000.............	Percent .	58	44	42	41	73	65	63	51
$40,000 or more..............	Percent .	42	56	56	59	27	35	38	49

[1] Includes no overnight stays.   [2] United States only.   [3] Recreational vehicle.

Source: U.S. Travel Data Center, Washington, DC, *National Travel Survey*, annual, (copyright).

No. 417. Domestic Travel Expenditures, by State: 1990

[Represents U.S. spending on domestic overnight trips and day trips of 100 miles or more away from home. Excludes spending by foreign visitors and by U.S. residents in U.S. territories and abroad]

STATE	Total (mil. dol.)	Share of total (percent)	Rank	STATE	Total (mil. dol.)	Share of total (percent)	Rank	STATE	Total (mil. dol.)	Share of total (percent)	Rank
U.S., total . .	290,446	100.0	(X)	KS	2,249	0.8	34	ND	743	0.3	49
				KY	3,092	1.1	30	OH	7,822	2.7	10
AL	3,380	1.2	27	LA	4,344	1.5	23	OK	2,482	0.9	33
AK	1,049	0.4	45	ME	1,402	0.5	40	OR	3,323	1.1	28
AZ	4,799	1.7	19	MD	4,463	1.5	22	PA	9,097	3.1	8
AR	2,181	0.8	37	MA	6,524	2.2	14	RI........	669	0.2	51
CA	40,489	13.9	1	MI	6,764	2.3	12	SC	4,497	1.5	21
CO	5,361	1.8	18	MN	3,849	1.3	25	SD	732	0.3	50
CT	3,208	1.1	29	MS	1,934	0.7	38	TN	5,780	2.0	15
DE	774	0.3	48	MO	5,590	1.9	17	TX	16,835	5.8	4
DC	2,809	1.0	31	MT	1,299	0.4	41	UT	2,229	0.8	35
FL	26,095	9.0	2	NE	1,596	0.5	39	VT	919	0.3	47
GA	7,772	2.7	11	NV	10,981	3.8	6	VA	8,086	2.8	9
HI........	5,726	2.0	16	NH	1,231	0.4	43	WA	4,791	1.6	20
ID........	1,299	0.4	42	NJ	9,759	3.4	7	WV	1,220	0.4	44
IL	11,641	4.0	5	NM	2,200	0.8	36	WI	3,974	1.4	24
IN........	3,827	1.3	26	NY	19,312	6.6	3	WY	1,000	0.3	46
IA........	2,555	0.9	32	NC	6,696	2.3	13				

X Not applicable.

Source: U.S. Travel Data Center, Washington, DC, *Impact of Travel on State Economies, 1990*, (copyright).

No. 418. Business Receipts and Employment of Selected Travel Industries: 1975 to 1990

YEAR	BUSINESS RECEIPTS (mil. dol.)							EMPLOYMENT (1,000)					
	Travel industry, total	Transportation [1]			Motel, hotel	Eating and drinking places	Amusement and recreation services	Travel industry, total	Transportation		Eating and drinking places	Hotels, motels, and tourist courts	Amusement and recreation services
		Air [2]	Bus	Rail [3]					Intercity highway passengers	Air			
1975 ..	94,549	10,301	1,172	247	13,002	51,067	18,760	5,229	40	363	3,380	850	597
1980 ..	163,015	23,405	1,709	382	26,832	90,058	20,629	6,918	38	453	4,626	1,038	764
1985 ..	235,437	33,343	1,989	563	41,837	127,949	29,756	8,396	35	522	5,709	1,290	840
1986 ..	251,213	33,846	1,890	592	43,300	139,415	32,170	8,718	33	567	5,916	1,338	864
1987 ..	276,157	37,555	1,826	639	48,200	153,461	34,476	9,059	30	603	6,106	1,427	893
1988 ..	301,817	41,963	2,036	738	52,400	166,860	37,820	9,377	29	644	6,282	1,503	918
1989 ..	320,348	45,320	2,185	842	58,138	173,894	39,969	9,760	31	684	6,439	1,561	1,045
1990 ..	334,881	45,324	2,000	888	60,490	182,044	44,135	10,027	26	751	6,565	1,595	1,089

[1] Passenger transport service. [2] U.S. certificated carriers in domestic service. [3] Covers fiscal years October 1 through September 30.

Source: U.S. Travel Data Center, Washington, DC, *The 1990-91 Economic Review of Travel in America*, (copyright).

No. 419. International Travelers and Expenditures, With Projections: 1970 to 1994

[For coverage, see tables 420 and 421. Beginning 1984, receipts, payments, and fares not comparable with previous years. See source for details. Minus sign (-) indicates deficit. See also *Historical Statistics, Colonial Times to 1970*, series H 921, 928, 941, and 945]

YEAR	TRAVEL AND PASSENGER FARE (mil. dol.)				U.S. net travel and passenger payments (mil. dol.)	U.S. travelers to foreign countries (1,000)	Foreign visitors to the U.S. (1,000)
	Payments by U.S. travelers		Receipts from foreign visitors				
	Total [1]	Expenditures abroad	Total [1]	Travel receipts			
1970	5,195	3,980	2,708	2,331	-2,487	(NA)	12,362
1980	14,004	10,397	12,650	10,588	-1,354	[2]22,365	22,326
1984	28,648	22,913	21,243	17,177	-7,405	33,977	26,934
1985	31,042	24,558	22,173	17,762	-8,869	34,715	25,399
1986	32,418	25,913	25,967	20,385	-6,451	37,158	26,008
1987	36,593	29,310	30,566	23,563	-6,027	39,410	29,500
1988	39,843	32,114	38,409	29,434	-1,434	40,669	34,095
1989	41,666	33,418	46,863	36,250	5,197	41,138	36,564
1990	47,879	37,349	58,305	43,007	10,426	44,623	39,539
1991	45,334	35,322	64,237	48,384	18,904	41,566	42,986
1992	50,815	39,872	71,214	53,861	20,399	43,895	44,647
1993, est. ..	52,585	41,260	74,560	56,470	21,975	45,490	45,650
1994, proj. .	55,375	43,450	80,950	61,310	25,575	47,335	47,945

NA Not available. [1] Includes passenger fares not shown separately. [2] Mexico visitation data are under-reported.

Source: Travelers and visitors: U.S. Travel and Tourism Administration (USTTA), and unpublished data. Fares and Payments: Through 1983, U.S. Bureau of Economic Analysis, (BEA) *Survey of Current Business;* beginning 1984, USTTA, based on data from BEA.

No. 420. U.S. Travel to Foreign Countries, With Projections: 1985 to 1994

[Travelers in thousands; expenditures in millions of dollars. Covers residents of the United States, its territories and possessions. See source for details. See also *Historical Statistics, Colonial Times to 1970*, series H 921-940]

ITEM AND AREA	1985	1988	1989	1990	1991	1992	1993, est.	1994, proj.
Total travelers	34,715	40,669	41,138	44,623	41,566	43,895	45,490	47,335
Canada	11,558	12,763	12,184	12,252	12,003	11,818	11,910	12,080
Mexico	10,461	13,463	14,163	16,381	15,042	16,112	16,710	17,375
Total overseas	12,696	14,443	14,791	15,990	14,521	15,965	16,870	17,880
Europe...............	6,780	7,438	7,233	8,043	6,316	7,136	(NA)	(NA)
Latin America [1]	3,592	4,203	4,392	4,749	5,155	5,285	(NA)	(NA)
Other................	2,324	2,802	3,166	3,198	3,050	3,544	(NA)	(NA)
Expenditures abroad........	24,558	32,114	33,418	37,349	35,322	39,872	41,260	43,450
Canada	2,506	3,232	3,396	3,541	3,705	3,507	(NA)	(NA)
Mexico	2,548	3,622	4,276	4,879	5,111	5,229	(NA)	(NA)
Total overseas	19,504	25,260	25,746	28,929	26,506	31,136	(NA)	(NA)
Europe...............	9,403	11,347	11,967	13,996	11,524	13,689	(NA)	(NA)
Latin America [1]	3,995	5,172	5,123	5,395	3,072	3,553	(NA)	(NA)
Other................	6,106	8,741	8,656	9,538	11,910	13,894	(NA)	(NA)
Fares to foreign carriers	6,444	7,729	8,248	10,530	10,012	10,943	11,325	11,925

NA Not available. [1] Includes Central and South America and the Caribbean.

Source: Travelers: U.S. Travel and Tourism Administration (USTTA), unpublished data. Expenditures: USTTA, based on data from the Bureau of Economic Analysis.

No. 421. Foreign Travel to the United States, With Projections: 1985 to 1994

[Travelers in thousands; receipts in millions of dollars. Includes travelers for business and pleasure, foreigners in transit through the United States, and students; excludes travel by foreign government personnel and foreign businessmen employed in the United States. See source for details. See also *Historical Statistics, Colonial Times to 1970*, series H 946-951]

AREA OF ORIGIN	1985	1988	1989	1990	1991	1992	1993, est.	1994, proj.
International travelers..............	25,399	34,095	36,564	39,539	42,986	44,647	45,650	47,945
Canada......................	10,721	13,700	15,325	17,263	19,113	18,598	17,520	17,095
Mexico.....................	7,141	7,883	7,240	7,217	7,718	8,258	9,250	10,410
Total overseas.................	7,537	12,512	13,999	15,059	16,155	17,791	18,880	20,440
Europe..... , ...	2,905	5,772	6,251	6,659	7,360	8,262	8,931	9,717
Latin America [1]...............	1,795	2,366	2,627	2,877	3,080	3,255	3,738	4,198
Other.....................	2,837	4,374	5,121	5,523	5,715	6,274	6,211	6,525
Total travel receipts..............	17,762	29,434	36,250	43,007	48,384	53,861	56,470	61,310
Canada......................	2,580	4,150	5,385	7,093	8,499	7,975	(NA)	(NA)
Mexico.....................	2,101	2,970	3,926	5,108	5,367	5,822	(NA)	(NA)
Total overseas.................	13,081	22,313	26,939	30,806	34,518	40,064	(NA)	(NA)
Europe..... , ...	4,774	9,778	11,004	12,602	14,332	17,532	(NA)	(NA)
Latin America [1]...............	3,122	3,726	4,418	5,126	5,927	6,822	(NA)	(NA)
Other.....................	5,185	8,809	11,517	13,078	14,259	15,710	(NA)	(NA)
Fares to U.S. carriers...........	4,411	8,976	10,613	15,298	15,854	17,353	18,090	19,640

NA Not available.   [1] Includes Central and South America and the Caribbean.

Source: Travelers: U.S. Travel and Tourism Administration (USTTA), unpublished data. Receipts: USTTA, based on data from the Bureau of Economic Analysis.

No. 422. Foreign Visitors for Pleasure Admitted, by Country of Last Residence: 1985 to 1992

[In thousands. For years ending September 30. See headnote, table 7, section 1]

COUNTRY	1985	1990	1991	1992	COUNTRY	1985	1990	1991	1992
Total [1].........	6,609	13,418	14,734	16,450	Africa [2]..............	101	105	106	112
					Egypt..............	16	16	16	16
Europe [2].............	2,048	5,383	6,119	6,979	Nigeria.............	25	11	13	11
Austria.............	34	87	101	131					
Belgium............	39	95	115	131	Oceania [2]...........	282	562	572	581
Denmark...........	36	75	77	80	Australia...........	195	380	404	416
Finland............	24	83	84	75	New Zealand........	74	153	135	127
France.............	226	566	632	667	North America	1,664	2,463	2,570	2,605
Greece............	34	43	40	44	Canada	79	119	146	166
Ireland............	55	81	91	99	Mexico... , ...	773	1,061	1,154	1,238
Italy..............	155	308	389	508	Caribbean [2].........	584	963	931	844
Netherlands	82	214	248	272	Bahamas, The	211	332	306	286
					Barbados.........	17	34	37	32
Norway............	41	80	71	80	Cayman Islands	18	31	33	30
Poland............	40	55	44	38	Dominican Republic...	57	137	129	135
Soviet Union........	2	53	57	45	Haiti.............	56	57	51	34
Spain.............	64	183	234	295	Jamaica..........	74	132	120	101
Sweden	71	230	219	222	Netherlands Antilles...	27	31	35	38
Switzerland.........	110	236	254	276	Trinidad and Tobago ..	71	81	72	65
United Kingdom.......	598	1,899	2,122	2,395	Central America [2].....	228	320	339	357
Germany [3].........	373	969	1,214	1,487	Costa Rica.........	41	62	63	75
					El Salvador	38	46	46	52
Asia [2]............	1,866	3,830	4,017	4,699	Guatemala.........	53	91	89	93
China (Mainland China					Panama...........	38	43	49	51
and Taiwan)........	83	187	209	249					
Hong Kong.........	64	111	127	142	South America [2]	606	1,016	1,272	1,423
India.............	52	75	71	68	Argentina..........	66	136	231	302
Israel..............	80	128	141	124	Brazil.............	148	300	390	380
Japan.............	1,277	2,846	2,932	3,486	Chile	28	54	65	79
Korea.............	26	120	184	230	Colombia	123	122	124	140
Philippines	59	76	83	94	Ecuador...........	42	57	64	72
Saudi Arabia........	31	33	33	40	Peru.............	44	97	96	92
Singapore..........	23	32	34	42	Venezuela..........	122	199	238	291

[1] Includes countries unknown or not reported.   [2] Includes countries not shown separately.   [3] Data prior to 1991 for former West Germany.

Source: U.S. Immigration and Naturalization Service, *Statistical Yearbook*, annual.

Figure 8.1
Political Party Identification of the Adult Population: 1960 to 1992

(Democrat and Republican parties include individuals identifying themselves as strong, weak, or independent.)

1992

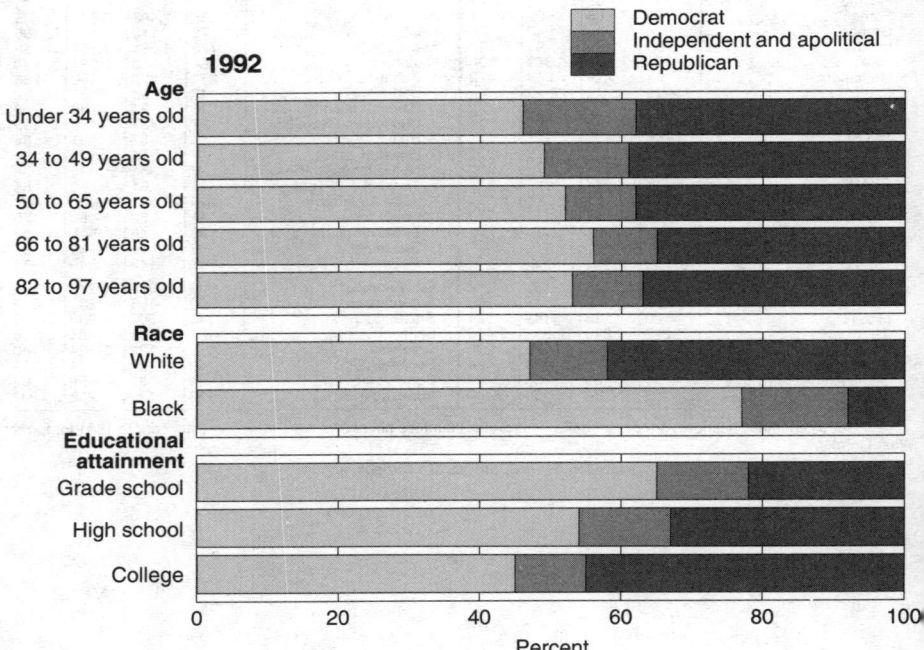

Source: Chart prepared by U.S. Bureau of the Census. For data, see table 446.

Elections

This section relates primarily to Presidential, congressional, and gubernatorial elections. Also presented are summary tables on congressional legislation; State legislatures; Black, Hispanic, and female officeholders; population of voting age; voter participation; and campaign finances.

Official statistics on Federal elections, collected by the Clerk of the House, are published biennially in *Statistics of the Presidential and Congressional Election* and *Statistics of the Congressional Election*. Federal and State elections data appear also in *America Votes*, a biennial volume of the Elections Research Center, Chevy Chase, MD. Federal elections data also appear in the U.S. Congress, *Congressional Directory*, and in official State documents. Data on reported registration and voting for social and economic groups are obtained by the U.S. Bureau of the Census as part of the Current Population Survey (CPS) and are published in *Current Population Reports*, P20 (see text, section 1).

Almost all Federal, State, and local governmental units in the United States conduct elections for political offices and other purposes. The conduct of elections is regulated by State laws or, in some cities and counties, by local charter. An exception is that the U.S. Constitution prescribes the basis of representation in Congress and the manner of electing the President, and grants to Congress the right to regulate the times, places, and manner of electing Federal officers. Amendments to the Constitution have prescribed national criteria for voting eligibility. The 15th Amendment, adopted in 1870, gave all citizens the right to vote regardless of race, color, or previous condition of servitude. The 19th Amendment, adopted in 1919, further extended the right to vote to all citizens regardless of sex. The payment of poll taxes as a prerequisite to voting in Federal elections was banned by the 24th Amendment in 1964. In 1971, as a result of the 26th Amendment, eligibility to vote in national elections was extended to all citizens, 18 years old and over.

In Brief

Percent of voting-age population voting for President:

1980	52.6%
1992	55.2%

Members of Congress:

	1981	1993
Black	17	39
Hispanic	6	17
Female	21	54

Presidential election.—The Constitution specifies how the President and Vice President are selected. Each State elects, by popular vote, a group of electors equal in number to its total of members of Congress. The 23d Amendment, adopted in 1961, grants the District of Columbia three presidential electors, a number equal to that of the least populous State. Subsequent to the election, the electors meet in their respective States to vote for President and Vice President. Usually, each elector votes for the candidate receiving the most popular votes in his or her State. A majority vote of all electors is necessary to elect the President and Vice President. If no candidate receives a majority, the House of Representatives, with each State having one vote, is empowered to elect the President and Vice President, again, with a majority of votes required.

The 22d Amendment to the Constitution, adopted in 1951, limits presidential tenure to two elective terms of 4 years each, or to one elective term for any person who, upon succession to the Presidency, has held the office or acted as President for more than 2 years.

Congressional election.—The Constitution provides that Representatives be apportioned among the States according to their population; that a census of population be taken every 10 years as a basis for apportionment; and that each State have at least one Representative. At the time of each apportionment, Congress decides what the total number of

Representatives will be. Since 1912, the total has been 435, except during 1960 to 1962 when it increased to 437, adding one Representative each for Alaska and Hawaii. The total reverted to 435 after reapportionment following the 1960 census. Members are elected for 2-year terms, all terms covering the same period. The District of Columbia, American Samoa, Guam, and the Virgin Islands each elect one nonvoting Delegate and Puerto Rico elects a nonvoting Resident Commissioner.

The Senate is composed of 100 members, two from each State, who are elected to serve for a term of 6 years. One-third of the Senate is elected every 2 years. Senators were originally chosen by the State legislatures. The 17th Amendment to the Constitution, adopted in 1913, prescribed that Senators be elected by popular vote.

Voter eligibility and participation.—The Census Bureau publishes estimates of the population of voting age and the percent casting votes in each State for Presidential and congressional election years. These voting-age estimates include a number of persons who meet the age requirement but are not eligible to vote, (e.g. aliens and some institutionalized persons). In addition, since 1964, voter participation and voter characteristics data have been collected during November of election years as part of the CPS. These survey data include noncitizens in the voting age population estimates, but exclude members of the Armed Forces and the institutional population.

Statistical reliability.—For a discussion of statistical collection and estimation, sampling procedures, and measures of statistical reliability applicable to Census Bureau data, see Appendix III.

Historical statistics.—Tabular headnotes provide cross-references, where applicable, to *Historical Statistics of the United States, Colonial Times to 1970.* See Appendix IV.

Figure 8.1
Popular Vote Cast for President, by Major Party: 1972 to 1992

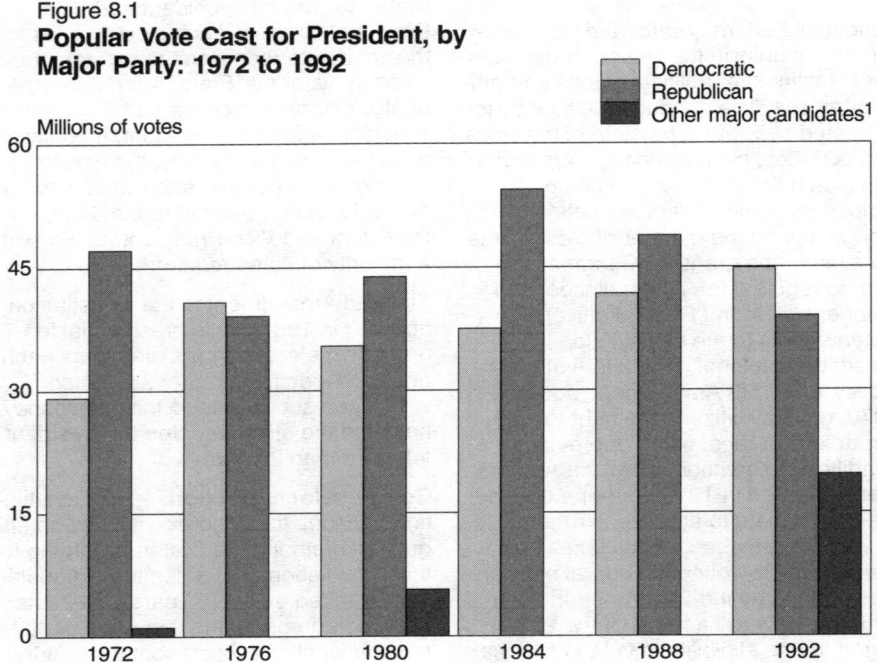

[1]1972–American, John Schmitz; 1980–Independent, John Anderson; 1992–Independent, H. Ross Perot.
Source: Chart prepared by U.S. Bureau of the Census. For data, see tables 423 and 424.

No. 423. Vote Cast for President, by Major Political Party: 1936 to 1992

[Prior to 1960, excludes Alaska and Hawaii; prior to 1964, excludes DC. Vote cast for major party candidates include the votes of minor parties cast for those candidates. See also *Historical Statistics, Colonial Times to 1970,* series Y 79-83 and Y 135]

YEAR	CANDIDATES FOR PRESIDENT		VOTE CAST FOR PRESIDENT						
			Total popular vote [1] (1,000)	Democratic			Republican		
	Democratic	Republican		Popular vote		Elec- toral vote	Popular vote		Elec- toral vote
				Number (1,000)	Per- cent		Number (1,000)	Per- cent	
1936	F. D. Roosevelt . .	Landon	45,655	27,757	60.8	523	16,684	36.5	8
1940	F. D. Roosevelt . .	Willkie	49,900	27,313	54.7	449	22,348	44.8	82
1944	F. D. Roosevelt . .	Dewey	47,977	25,613	53.4	432	22,018	45.9	99
1948	Truman	Dewey	48,794	24,179	49.6	303	21,991	45.1	189
1952	Stevenson	Eisenhower. . . .	61,551	27,315	44.4	89	33,936	55.1	442
1956	Stevenson	Eisenhower.	62,027	26,023	42.0	73	35,590	57.4	457
1960	Kennedy	Nixon.	68,838	34,227	49.7	303	34,108	49.5	219
1964	Johnson.	Goldwater	70,645	43,130	61.1	486	27,178	38.5	52
1968	Humphrey	Nixon.	73,212	31,275	42.7	191	31,785	43.4	301
1972	McGovern	Nixon.	77,719	29,170	37.5	17	47,170	60.7	520
1976	Carter	Ford	81,556	40,831	50.1	297	39,148	48.0	240
1980	Carter	Reagan	86,515	35,484	41.0	49	43,904	50.7	489
1984	Mondale.	Reagan	92,653	37,577	40.6	13	54,455	58.8	525
1988	Dukakis	Bush	91,595	41,809	45.6	111	48,886	53.4	426
1992	Clinton.	Bush	104,425	44,909	43.0	370	39,104	37.4	168

[1] Include votes for minor party candidates, independents, unpledged electors, and scattered write-in votes.

No. 424. Vote Cast for Leading Minority Party Candidates for President: 1936 to 1992

[See headnote, table 423]

YEAR	Candidate	Party	Popular vote (1,000)	Candidate	Party	Popular vote (1,000)
1936 . .	William Lemke	Union	892	Norman Thomas . . .	Socialist	188
1940 . .	Norman Thomas . . .	Socialist	116	Roger Babson	Prohibition.	59
1944 . .	Norman Thomas . . .	Socialist	79	Claude Watson	Prohibition.	75
1948 . .	Strom Thurmond . . .	States' Rights	1,176	Henry Wallace	Progressive	1,157
1952 . .	Vincent Hallinan . . .	Progressive	140	Stuart Hamblen	Prohibition	73
1956 . .	T. Coleman Andrews.	States' Rights	111	Eric Hass	Socialist Labor	44
1960 . .	Eric Hass	Socialist Labor	48	Rutherford Decker . .	Prohibition.	46
1964 . .	Eric Hass	Socialist Labor	45	Clifton DeBerry	Socialist Workers . . .	33
1968 . .	George Wallace	American Independent.	9,906	Henning Blomen . . .	Socialist Labor	53
1972 . .	John Schmitz.	American.	1,099	Benjamin Spock. . . .	People's	79
1976 . .	Eugene McCarthy. . .	Independent	757	Roger McBride	Libertarian.	173
1980 . .	John Anderson	Independent	5,720	Ed Clark	Libertarian	921
1984 . .	David Bergland	Libertarian.	228	Lyndon H. LaRouche.	Independent	79
1988 . .	Ron Paul	Libertarian	432	Lenora B. Fulani . . .	New Alliance	217
1992 . .	H. Ross Perot	Independent	19,742	Andre Marrou	Libertarian	292

Source of tables 423 and 424: Elections Research Center, Chevy Chase, MD, *America at the Polls 2,* 1965, and *America Votes,* biennial (copyright).

No. 425. Democratic and Republican Percentages of Two-Party Presidential Vote, by Selected Characteristics of Voters: 1988 and 1992

[In percent. Covers citizens of voting age living in private housing units in the contiguous United States. Percentages for Democratic Presidential vote are computed by subtracting the percentage Republican vote from 100 percent; third-party or independent votes are not included as valid data. Data are from the National Election Studies and are based on a sample and subject to sampling variability; for details, see source]

CHARACTERISTIC	1988		1992		CHARACTERISTIC	1988		1992	
	Demo- cratic	Repub- lican	Demo- cratic	Repub- lican		Demo- cratic	Repub- lican	Demo- cratic	Repub- lican
Total [1]	47	53	58	42	Race:				
Year of birth:					White	41	59	53	47
1959 or later	48	52	58	42	Black	92	8	94	6
1943 to 1958.	47	53	58	42					
1927 to 1942.	49	51	57	43	Education:				
1911 to 1926.	44	56	62	38	Grade school.	61	39	70	30
1895 to 1910.	47	53	55	45	High school.	51	49	63	37
					College.	42	58	55	45
Sex:									
Male	44	56	55	45	Union household	59	41	68	32
Female.	50	50	61	39	Non-union household. .	44	56	56	44

[1] Includes other characteristics, not shown separately.

Source: Center for Political Studies, University of Michigan, Ann Arbor, MI, unpublished data, (copyright).

No. 426. Electoral Vote Cast for President, by Major Political Party—States: 1952 to 1992

[D=Democratic, R=Republican. For composition of regions, see table 26. See also *Historical Statistics, Colonial Times to 1970*, series Y 84-134]

REGION, DIVISION, AND STATE	1952	1956 [1]	1960 [2]	1964	1968 [3]	1972 [4]	1976 [5]	1980	1984	1988 [6]	1992
Democratic......	89	73	303	486	191	17	297	49	13	111	370
Republican......	442	457	219	52	301	520	240	489	525	426	168
Northeast: Democratic .	-	-	121	126	102	14	86	4	-	53	106
Republican .	133	133	12	-	24	108	36	118	113	60	-
Midwest: Democratic ..	-	13	71	149	31	-	58	10	10	29	100
Republican ..	153	140	82	-	118	145	87	135	127	108	29
South: Democratic	89	60	101	121	45	3	149	31	3	8	68
Republican	77	105	50	47	77	165	20	138	174	168	116
West: Democratic.....	-	-	10	90	13	-	4	4	-	21	96
Republican.....	79	79	75	5	82	102	97	98	111	90	23
New England: ME	R-5	R-5	R-5	D-4	D-4	R-4	R-4	R-4	R-4	R-4	D-4
NH	R-4	R-4	R-4	D-4	R-4	R-4	R-4	R-4	R-4	R-4	D-4
VT	R-3	R-3	R-3	D-3	R-3	R-3	R-3	R-3	R-3	R-3	D-3
MA	R-16	R-16	D-16	D-14	D-14	D-14	D-14	R-14	R-13	D-13	D-12
RI	R-4	R-4	D-4	D-4	D-4	R-4	D-4	D-4	R-4	D-4	D-4
CT	R-8	R-8	D-8	D-8	D-8	R-8	R-8	R-8	R-8	R-8	D-8
Middle Atlantic: NY ...	R-45	R-45	D-45	D-43	D-43	R-41	D-41	R-41	R-36	D-36	D-33
NJ	R-16	R-16	D-16	D-17	R-17	R-17	R-17	R-17	R-16	R-16	D-15
PA	R-32	R-32	D-32	D-29	D-29	R-27	D-27	R-27	R-25	R-25	D-23
East North Central: OH	R-25	R-25	R-25	D-26	R-26	R-25	D-25	R-25	R-23	R-23	D-21
IN	R-13	R-13	R-13	D-13	R-13	R-13	R-13	R-13	R-13	R-12	R-12
IL	R-27	R-27	D-27	D-26	R-26	R-26	R-26	R-26	R-24	R-24	D-22
MI	R-20	R-20	D-20	D-21	D-21	R-21	R-21	R-21	R-20	R-20	D-18
WI	R-12	R-12	R-12	D-12	R-12	R-11	D-11	R-11	R-11	R-11	D-11
West North Central: MN	R-11	R-11	D-11	D-10	D-10	R-10	D-10	D-10	D-10	D-10	D-10
IA	R-10	R-10	R-10	D-9	R-9	R-8	R-8	R-8	R-8	D-8	D-7
MO	R-13	D-13	D-13	D-12	R-12	R-12	D-12	R-12	R-11	R-11	D-11
ND	R-4	R-4	R-4	D-4	R-4	R-3	R-3	R-3	R-3	R-3	R-3
SD	R-4	R-4	R-4	D-4	R-4	R-4	R-4	R-4	R-3	R-3	R-3
NE	R-6	R-6	R-6	D-5	R-5	R-5	R-5	R-5	R-5	R-5	R-5
KS	R-8	R-8	R-8	D-7	R-7	R-7	R-7	R-7	R-7	R-7	R-6
South Atlantic: DE....	R-3	R-3	D-3	D-3	R-3	R-3	D-3	R-3	R-3	R-3	D-3
MD	R-9	R-9	D-9	D-10	D-10	R-10	D-10	R-10	R-10	D-10	D-10
DC	(X)	(X)	(X)	D-3	D-3	D-3	D-3	D-3	D-3	D-3	D-3
VA	R-12	R-12	R-12	D-12	R-12	[4]R-11	R-12	R-12	R-12	R-12	R-13
WV	D-8	R-8	D-8	D-7	D-7	R-6	D-6	D-6	R-6	[6]D-5	D-5
NC	D-14	D-14	D-14	D-13	[3]R-12	R-13	D-13	R-13	R-13	R-13	R-14
SC	D-8	D-8	D-8	R-8	R-8	R-8	D-8	R-8	R-8	R-8	R-8
GA	D-12	D-12	D-12	R-12	([3])	R-12	D-12	D-12	R-12	R-12	D-13
FL	R-10	R-10	R-10	D-14	R-14	R-17	D-17	R-17	R-21	R-21	R-25
East South Central: KY	D-10	R-10	R-10	D-9	R-9	R-9	D-9	R-9	R-9	R-9	D-8
TN	R-11	R-11	R-11	D-11	R-11	R-10	D-10	R-10	R-11	R-11	D-11
AL	D-11	[1]D-10	[2]D-5	R-10	([3])	R-9	D-9	R-9	R-9	R-9	R-9
MS	D-8	D-8	([2])	R-7	([3])	R-7	D-7	R-7	R-7	R-7	R-7
West South Central: AR	D-8	D-8	D-8	D-6	([3])	R-6	D-6	R-6	R-6	R-6	D-6
LA	D-10	R-10	D-10	D-10	([3])	R-10	D-10	R-10	R-10	R-10	D-9
OK	R-8	R-8	[2]R-7	D-8	R-8	R-8	R-8	R-8	R-8	R-8	R-8
TX	R-24	R-24	D-24	D-25	D-25	R-26	D-26	R-26	R-29	R-29	R-32
Mountain: MT	R-4	R-4	R-4	D-4	R-4	R-4	R-4	R-4	R-4	R-4	D-3
ID	R-4	R-4	R-4	D-4	R-4	R-4	R-4	R-4	R-4	R-4	R-4
WY	R-3	R-3	R-3	D-3	R-3	R-3	R-3	R-3	R-3	R-3	R-3
CO	R-6	R-6	R-6	D-6	R-6	R-7	R-7	R-7	R-8	R-8	D-8
NM	R-4	R-4	D-4	D-4	R-4	R-4	R-4	R-4	R-5	R-5	D-5
AZ	R-4	R-4	R-4	R-5	R-5	R-6	R-6	R-6	R-7	R-7	R-8
UT	R-4	R-4	R-4	D-4	R-4	R-4	R-4	R-4	R-5	R-5	R-5
NV	R-3	R-3	D-3	D-3	R-3	R-3	R-3	R-3	R-4	R-4	D-4
Pacific: WA.........	R-9	R-9	R-9	D-9	D-9	R-9	[5]R-8	R-9	R-10	D-10	D-11
OR	R-6	R-6	R-6	D-6	R-6	R-6	R-6	R-6	R-7	D-7	D-7
CA	R-32	R-32	R-32	D-40	R-40	R-45	R-45	R-45	R-47	R-47	D-54
AK	(X)	(X)	R-3	D-3	R-3	R-3	R-3	R-3	R-3	R-3	R-3
HI	(X)	(X)	D-3	D-4	D-4	R-4	D-4	D-4	R-4	D-4	D-4

- Represents zero.   X Not applicable.   [1] Excludes one electoral vote cast for Walter B. Jones in Alabama.   [2] Excludes 15 electoral votes cast for Harry F. Byrd as follows: AL 6, MS 8, and OK 1.   [3] Excludes 46 electoral votes cast for American Independent George C. Wallace as follows: AL 10, AR 6, GA 12, LA 10, MS 7, and NC 1.   [4] Excludes one electoral vote cast for Libertarian John Hospers in Virginia.   [5] Excludes one electoral vote cast for Ronald Reagan in Washington.   [6] Excludes one electoral vote cast for Lloyd Bentsen for President in West Virginia.

Source: 1952-72, U.S. Congress, Clerk of the House, *Statistics of the Presidential and Congressional Election*, quadrennial; 1976-92, Elections Research Center, Chevy Chase, MD, *America Votes*, biennial, (copyright).

No. 427. Popular Vote Cast for President, by Political Party—States: 1988 and 1992

[In thousands, except percent. See also *Historical Statistics, Colonial Times to 1970*, series Y 135-186]

REGION, DIVISION, AND STATE	1988 Total [1]	1988 Democratic Party	1988 Republican Party	1988 Percent for leading party [2]	1992 Total [1]	1992 Democratic Party	1992 Republican Party	1992 Perot (Independent)	Percent of total vote — Democratic Party	Percent of total vote — Republican Party	Percent of total vote — Perot (Independent)
United States . .	91,595	41,809	48,886	R-53.4	104,425	44,909	39,104	19,742	43.0	37.4	18.9
Northeast	19,852	9,689	9,961	R-50.2	21,581	9,940	7,507	3,994	46.1	34.8	18.5
N.E.	5,730	2,826	2,836	R-49.5	6,351	2,820	2,012	1,479	44.4	31.7	23.3
ME	555	244	307	R-55.3	679	263	207	207	38.8	30.4	30.4
NH	451	164	282	R-62.4	538	209	202	121	38.9	37.6	22.6
VT.	243	116	124	R-51.1	290	134	88	66	46.1	30.4	22.8
MA	2,633	1,401	1,195	D-53.2	2,774	1,319	805	631	47.5	29.0	22.7
RI	405	225	178	D-55.6	453	213	132	105	47.0	29.0	23.2
CT	1,443	677	750	R-52.0	1,616	682	578	349	42.2	35.8	21.6
M.A	14,121	6,863	7,125	R-50.5	15,230	7,120	5,495	2,515	46.7	36.1	16.5
NY.	6,486	3,348	3,082	D-51.6	6,927	3,444	2,347	1,091	49.7	33.9	15.7
NJ.	3,100	1,320	1,743	R-56.2	3,344	1,436	1,357	522	43.0	40.6	15.6
PA.	4,536	2,195	2,300	R-50.7	4,960	2,239	1,792	903	45.1	36.1	18.2
Midwest.	24,663	11,556	12,915	R-52.4	27,735	11,692	10,234	5,668	42.2	36.9	20.4
E.N.C	16,982	7,819	9,038	R-53.2	19,102	8,199	7,104	3,702	42.9	37.2	19.4
OH	4,394	1,940	2,417	R-55.0	4,940	1,985	1,894	1,036	40.2	38.3	21.0
IN	2,169	861	1,298	R-59.8	2,306	848	989	456	36.8	42.9	19.8
IL	4,559	2,216	2,311	R-50.7	5,050	2,453	1,734	841	48.6	34.3	16.6
MI	3,669	1,676	1,965	R-53.6	4,275	1,871	1,555	825	43.8	36.4	19.3
WI	2,192	1,127	1,047	D-51.4	2,531	1,041	931	544	41.1	36.8	21.5
W.N.C	7,681	3,737	3,877	R-50.5	8,633	3,493	3,130	1,966	40.5	36.3	22.8
MN	2,097	1,109	962	D-52.9	2,348	1,021	748	563	43.5	31.9	24.0
IA	1,226	671	545	D-54.7	1,355	586	505	253	43.3	37.3	18.7
MO	2,094	1,002	1,085	R-51.8	2,392	1,054	811	519	44.1	33.9	21.7
ND	297	128	167	R-56.0	308	99	136	71	32.2	44.2	23.1
SD.	313	146	165	R-52.8	336	125	137	73	37.1	40.7	21.8
NE.	661	259	398	R-60.2	738	217	344	174	29.4	46.6	23.6
KS.	993	423	554	R-55.8	1,157	390	450	312	33.7	38.9	27.0
South	28,558	12,004	16,327	R-57.2	33,625	14,118	14,014	5,325	42.0	41.7	15.8
S.A.	14,234	5,927	8,207	R-57.7	17,195	7,352	7,103	2,667	42.8	41.3	15.5
DE.	250	109	140	R-55.9	290	126	102	59	43.5	35.3	20.4
MD	1,714	826	876	R-51.1	1,985	989	707	281	49.8	35.6	14.2
DC.	193	159	28	D-82.6	228	193	21	10	84.6	9.1	4.3
VA.	2,192	860	1,309	R-59.7	2,559	1,039	1,151	349	40.6	45.0	13.6
WV	653	341	310	D-52.2	684	331	242	109	48.4	35.4	15.9
NC	2,134	890	1,237	R-58.0	2,612	1,114	1,135	358	42.7	43.4	13.7
SC.	986	371	606	R-61.5	1,203	480	578	139	39.9	48.0	11.5
GA	1,810	715	1,081	R-59.8	2,321	1,009	995	310	43.5	42.9	13.3
FL	4,302	1,657	2,619	R-60.9	5,314	2,073	2,173	1,053	39.0	40.9	19.8
E.S.C	5,269	2,174	3,055	R-58.0	6,145	2,689	2,751	673	43.8	44.8	10.9
KY.	1,323	580	734	R-55.5	1,493	665	617	204	44.6	41.3	13.7
TN.	1,636	680	947	R-57.9	1,983	934	841	200	47.1	42.4	10.1
AL.	1,378	550	816	R-59.2	1,688	690	804	183	40.9	47.6	10.8
MS	932	364	558	R-59.9	982	400	488	86	40.8	49.7	8.7
W.S.C	9,054	3,903	5,065	R-55.9	10,285	4,077	4,160	1,985	39.6	40.4	19.3
AR.	828	349	467	R-56.4	951	506	337	99	53.2	35.5	10.4
LA.	1,628	717	884	R-54.3	1,790	816	733	211	45.6	41.0	11.8
OK	1,171	483	678	R-57.9	1,390	473	593	320	34.0	42.6	23.0
TX.	5,427	2,353	3,037	R-56.0	6,154	2,282	2,496	1,355	37.1	40.6	22.0
West	18,522	8,560	9,683	R-52.3	21,484	9,160	7,349	4,755	42.6	34.2	22.1
Mountain	5,014	2,043	2,887	R-57.6	5,970	2,167	2,272	1,437	36.3	38.1	24.1
MT	366	169	190	R-52.1	411	155	144	107	37.6	35.1	26.1
ID	409	147	254	R-62.1	482	137	203	130	28.4	42.0	27.0
WY	177	67	107	R-60.5	201	68	79	51	34.0	39.6	25.6
CO	1,372	621	728	R-53.1	1,569	630	563	366	40.1	35.9	23.3
NM	521	244	270	R-51.9	570	262	213	92	45.9	37.3	16.1
AZ.	1,172	454	703	R-60.0	1,487	543	572	354	36.5	38.5	23.8
UT.	647	207	428	R-66.2	744	183	323	203	24.7	43.4	27.3
NV.	350	133	206	R-58.9	506	189	176	133	37.4	34.7	26.2
Pacific	13,509	6,517	6,797	R-50.3	15,514	6,993	5,076	3,318	45.1	32.7	21.4
WA	1,865	934	904	D-50.0	2,288	993	731	542	43.4	32.0	23.7
OR	1,202	616	560	D-51.3	1,463	621	476	354	42.5	32.5	24.2
CA.	9,887	4,702	5,055	R-51.1	11,132	5,121	3,631	2,296	46.0	32.6	20.6
AK.	200	73	119	R-59.6	259	78	102	73	30.3	39.5	28.4
HI	354	192	159	D-54.3	373	179	137	53	48.1	36.7	14.2

[1] Includes other parties. [2] D=Democratic, R=Republican. Leading party vote refers to the party vote representing either a majority or a plurality for the victorious party in the area shown.

Source: Elections Research Center, Chevy Chase, MD, *America Votes*, biennial, (copyright).

272

Elections

No. 428. Vote Cast for United States Senators, 1990 and 1992, and Incumbent Senators, 1993—States

[D=Democrat; R=Republican]

DIVISION AND STATE	1990 Total (1,000)	1990 Percent for leading party	1992 Total (1,000)	1992 Percent for leading party	INCUMBENT SENATORS AND YEAR TERM EXPIRES Name, party, and year	Name, party, and year
N.E.:						
ME......	520	R-61.3	(X)	(X)	George J. Mitchell (D) 1995	William S. Cohen (R) 1997
NH......	291	R-65.1	518	R-48.1	Judd Gregg (R) 1999	Robert C. Smith (R) 1997
VT......	(X)	(X)	286	D-54.2	Patrick J. Leahy (D) 1999	James M. Jeffords (R) 1995
MA......	2,316	D-57.1	(X)	(X)	Edward M. Kennedy (D) 1995	John F. Kerry (D) 1997
RI	364	D-61.8	(X)	(X)	Claiborne Pell (D) 1997	John H. Chafee (R) 1995
CT......	(X)	(X)	1,501	D-58.8	Christopher J. Dodd (D) 1999	Joseph I. Lieberman (D) 1995
M.A.:						
NY......	(X)	(X)	6,459	R-49.0	Daniel P. Moynihan (D) 1995	Alfonse M. D'Amato (R) 1999
NJ	1,938	D-50.4	(X)	(X)	Bill Bradley (D) 1997	Frank R. Lautenberg (D) 1995
PA	[1]3,383	[1]D-55.0	4,802	R-49.1	Harris Wofford (D) 1995	Arlen Specter (R) 1999
E.N.C.:						
OH......	(X)	(X)	4,794	D-51.0	John Glenn (D) 1999	Howard Metzenbaum (D) 1995
IN	[2]1,504	[2]R-53.6	2,211	R-57.3	Dan Coats (R) 1999	Richard G. Lugar (R) 1995
IL........	3,251	D-65.1	4,940	D-53.3	Carol Moseley Braun (D) 1999	Paul Simon (D) 1997
MI	2,560	D-57.5	(X)	(X)	Carl Levin (D) 1997	Donald W. Riegle, Jr. (D) 1995
WI	(X)	(X)	2,455	D-52.6	Herb Kohl (D) 1995	Russell Feingold (D) 1999
W.N.C.:						
MN......	1,808	D-50.4	(X)	(X)	Paul David Wellstone (D) 1997	Dave Durenberger (R) 1995
IA	984	D-54.5	1,292	R-69.6	Tom Harkin (D) 1997	Charles E. Grassley (R) 1999
MO	(X)	(X)	2,355	R-51.9	Christopher S. Bond (R) 1999	John C. Danforth (R) 1995
ND......	(X)	(X)	304	D-59.0	Byron L. Dorgan (D) 1999	[3]Kent Conrad (D) 1995
SD......	259	R-52.4	334	D-64.9	Thomas A. Daschle (D) 1999	Larry Pressler (R) 1997
NE	594	D-58.9	(X)	(X)	J. James Exon (D) 1997	J. Robert Kerrey (D) 1995
KS......	786	R-73.6	1,126	R-62.7	Bob Dole (R) 1999	Nancy Kassebaum (R) 1997
S.A.:						
DE......	180	D-62.7	(X)	(X)	Joseph R. Biden Jr. (D) 1997	William V. Roth, Jr. (R) 1995
MD......	(X)	(X)	1,842	D-71.0	Barbara A. Mikulski (D) 1999	Paul S. Sarbanes (D) 1995
VA......	1,084	R-80.9	(X)	(X)	Charles S. Robb (D) 1995	John W. Warner (R) 1997
WV	404	D-68.3	(X)	(X)	Robert C. Byrd (D) 1995	John D. Rockefeller IV (D) 1997
NC......	2,070	R-52.5	2,578	R-50.3	Lauch Faircloth (R) 1999	Jesse Helms (R) 1997
SC......	751	R-64.2	1,180	D-50.1	Ernest F. Hollings (D) 1999	Strom Thurmond (R) 1997
GA......	1,034	D-100.0	[4]1,254	[4]R-50.6	Paul Coverdell (R) 1999	Sam Nunn (D) 1997
FL	(X)	(X)	4,962	D-65.4	Bob Graham (D) 1999	Connie Mack (R) 1995
E.S.C.:						
KY......	916	R-52.2	1,331	D-62.9	Wendell H. Ford (D) 1999	Mitch McConnell (R) 1997
TN......	784	D-67.7	(X)	(X)	[5]Harlan Mathews (D) 1997	Jim Sasser (D) 1995
AL......	1,186	D-60.5	1,578	D-64.8	Howell Heflin (D) 1997	Richard C. Shelby (D) 1999
MS......	274	R-100.0	(X)	(X)	Thad Cochran (R) 1997	Trent Lott (R) 1995
W.S.C.:						
AR......	495	D-99.8	920	D-60.2	Dale Bumpers (D) 1999	David Pryor (D) 1997
LA......	[6]1,396	[6]D-56.5	[6]843	[6]D-78.5	John B. Breaux (D) 1999	J. Bennett Johnston (D) 1997
OK......	884	D-83.2	1,294	R-58.5	David L. Boren (D) 1997	Don Nickles (R) 1999
TX......	3,822	R-60.2	[7]1,765	[7]R-67.3	Kay Bailey Hutchison (R) 1995	Phil Gramm (R) 1997
Mountain:						
MT......	319	D-68.1	(X)	(X)	Max Baucus (D) 1997	Conrad Burns (R) 1995
ID	316	R-61.3	479	R-56.5	Larry E. Craig (R) 1997	Dirk Kempthorne (R) 1999
WY	158	R-63.9	(X)	(X)	Alan K. Simpson (R) 1997	Malcolm Wallop (R) 1995
CO......	1,022	R-55.7	1,552	D-51.8	Ben N. Campbell (D) 1999	Hank Brown (R) 1997
NM......	407	R-72.9	(X)	(X)	Jeff Bingaman (D) 1995	Pete V. Domenici (R) 1997
AZ......	(X)	(X)	1,382	R-55.8	Dennis DeConcini (D) 1995	John McCain (R) 1999
UT......	(X)	(X)	758	R-55.4	Robert F. Bennett (R) 1999	Orrin G. Hatch (R) 1995
NV......	(X)	(X)	496	D-51.0	Harry Reid (D) 1999	Richard H. Bryan (D) 1995
Pacific:						
WA	(X)	(X)	2,219	D-54.0	Patty Murray (D) 1999	Slade Gorton (R) 1995
OR......	1,099	R-53.7	1,376	R-52.1	Mark O. Hatfield (R) 1997	Bob Packwood (R) 1999
CA......	(X)	(X)	10,800	D-47.9	Barbara Boxer (D) 1999	[8]Dianne Feinstein (D) 1995
AK......	190	R-66.2	240	R-53.0	Frank H. Murkowski (R) 1999	Ted Stevens (R) 1997
HI	[9]350	[9]D-54.0	364	D-57.3	Daniel K. Akaka (D) 1995	Daniel K. Inouye (D) 1999

X Not applicable.   [1] Special election in November 1991 to fill vacancy caused by death of Senator John Heinz.   [2] Special election to fill the unexpired term of Vice-President Quayle.   [3] In a special election in 1992 to fill an unexpired term, the Democratic candidate received 63.2 percent of 163,311 total votes cast.   [4] Results of run-off election. In the first election no candidate received more than 50 percent of the vote. First election: Total votes cast, 2,251,587; Democratic candidate, 1,108,416; Republican candidate, 1,073,282.   [5] Appointed to fill the unexpired term of Vice-President Gore.   [6] Louisiana holds an open-primary election with candidates from all parties running on the same ballot. Any candidate who receives a majority is elected. In 1990 and 1992 the indicated Senators received more than 50 percent of the vote in the October open-primary.   [7] Special election in June 1993 to fill the unexpired term of Senator Bentsen.   [8] In a special election in 1992 to fill an unexpired term, the Democratic candidate received 54.3 percent of 10,782,743 total votes cast.   [9] Special election to fill the unexpired term of Senator Matsunaga.

Source: Elections Research Center, Chevy Chase, MD, *America Votes*, biennial, (copyright).

No. 429. Representatives Elected, by Percent of Vote Cast for Winner and Major Party, 1980 to 1992, and by State, 1992

YEAR, REGION, DIVISION, AND STATE	TOTAL REPRESENTATIVES ELECTED				DEMOCRATS ELECTED				REPUBLICANS ELECTED				REPRESENTATIVES ELECTED WITH NO MAJOR PARTY OPPOSITION		
	Total	Under 55	55-59.9	60 and over	Total	Under 55	55-59.9	60 and over	Total	Under 55	55-59.9	60 and over	Total	Democrats	Republicans
1980	435	78	63	294	243	35	35	173	192	43	28	121	54	39	15
1982	435	76	73	286	269	40	33	196	166	36	40	90	56	46	10
1984	435	58	56	321	253	33	38	182	182	25	18	139	68	54	14
1986	435	46	41	348	258	22	18	218	177	24	23	130	75	57	18
1988	435	37	34	364	260	21	15	224	175	16	19	140	80	60	20
1990	[1]435	51	[1]72	312	267	29	40	198	167	22	31	114	85	49	36
1992, total	[1]435	109	[1]80	246	258	60	47	151	176	49	32	95	40	24	16
Northeast	[1]88	27	[1]10	51	50	15	6	29	37	12	3	22	9	6	3
N.E	[1]23	9	[1]1	13	14	4	-	10	8	5	-	3	1	1	-
ME	2	1	-	1	1	-	-	1	1	1	-	-	-	-	-
NH	2	1	-	1	1	-	-	1	1	1	-	-	-	-	-
VT	[1]1	-	[1]1	-	-	-	-	-	-	-	-	-	-	-	-
MA	10	5	-	5	8	3	-	5	2	2	-	-	1	1	-
RI	2	-	-	2	1	-	-	1	1	-	-	1	-	-	-
CT	6	2	-	4	3	1	-	2	3	1	-	2	-	-	-
M.A	65	18	9	38	36	11	6	19	29	7	3	19	8	5	3
NY	31	9	5	17	18	5	3	10	13	4	2	7	4	4	-
NJ	13	3	3	7	7	2	2	3	6	1	1	4	-	-	-
PA	21	6	1	14	11	4	1	6	10	2	-	8	4	1	3
Midwest	105	23	23	59	61	16	13	32	44	7	10	27	4	1	3
E.N.C	74	14	15	45	43	11	7	25	31	3	8	20	3	1	2
OH	19	5	2	12	10	4	1	5	9	1	1	7	2	1	1
IN	10	2	3	5	7	1	2	4	3	1	1	1	-	-	-
IL	20	-	7	13	12	-	3	9	8	-	4	4	-	-	-
MI	16	6	1	9	10	6	-	4	6	-	1	5	1	-	1
WI	9	1	2	6	4	-	1	3	5	1	1	3	-	-	-
W.N.C	31	9	8	14	18	5	6	7	13	4	2	7	1	-	1
MN	8	3	2	3	6	2	2	2	2	1	-	1	-	-	-
IA	5	2	-	3	1	-	-	1	4	2	-	2	1	-	1
MO	9	2	2	5	6	1	2	3	3	1	-	2	-	-	-
ND	1	-	1	-	1	-	1	-	-	-	-	-	-	-	-
SD	1	-	-	1	1	-	-	1	-	-	-	-	-	-	-
NE	3	1	1	1	1	1	-	-	2	-	1	1	-	-	-
KS	4	1	2	1	2	1	1	-	2	-	1	1	-	-	-
South	149	28	30	91	92	14	19	59	57	14	11	32	24	14	10
S.A	75	17	19	39	42	10	9	23	33	7	10	16	6	2	4
DE	1	-	1	-	-	-	-	-	1	-	1	-	-	-	-
MD	8	3	-	5	4	1	-	3	4	2	-	2	-	-	-
VA	11	1	3	7	7	1	2	4	4	-	1	3	1	-	1
WV	3	-	-	3	3	-	-	3	-	-	-	-	1	1	-
NC	12	4	2	6	8	3	2	3	4	1	-	3	-	-	-
SC	6	1	-	5	3	-	-	3	3	1	-	2	1	-	1
GA	11	2	6	3	7	1	3	3	4	1	3	-	-	-	-
FL	23	6	7	10	10	4	2	4	13	2	5	6	3	1	2
E.S.C	27	5	3	19	19	2	3	14	8	3	-	5	7	6	1
KY	6	2	-	4	4	1	-	3	2	1	-	1	4	4	-
TN	9	1	2	6	6	1	2	3	3	-	-	3	1	1	-
AL	7	2	-	5	4	-	-	4	3	2	-	1	2	1	1
MS	5	-	1	4	5	-	1	4	-	-	-	-	-	-	-
W.S.C	47	6	8	33	31	2	7	22	16	4	1	11	11	6	5
AR	4	2	-	2	2	-	-	2	2	2	-	-	-	-	-
LA	7	-	-	7	4	-	-	4	3	-	-	3	6	4	2
OK	6	2	1	3	4	1	1	2	2	-	-	2	-	-	-
TX	30	2	7	21	21	2	6	13	9	-	1	8	5	2	3
West	93	31	17	45	55	15	9	31	38	16	8	14	3	3	-
Mountain	24	6	7	11	11	4	3	4	13	2	4	7	-	-	-
MT	1	1	-	-	1	1	-	-	-	-	-	-	-	-	-
ID	2	-	1	1	1	-	1	-	1	-	-	1	-	-	-
WY	1	-	1	-	-	-	-	-	1	-	1	-	-	-	-
CO	6	1	1	4	2	1	-	1	4	1	1	2	-	-	-
NM	3	-	1	2	2	1	-	1	1	-	-	1	-	-	-
AZ	6	2	1	3	3	2	-	1	3	-	1	2	-	-	-
UT	3	1	1	1	2	1	1	-	1	-	-	1	-	-	-
NV	2	1	1	-	1	-	-	1	1	1	-	-	-	-	-
Pacific	69	25	10	34	44	11	6	27	25	14	4	7	3	3	-
WA	9	4	2	3	8	4	2	2	1	-	-	1	-	-	-
OR	5	1	-	4	4	1	-	3	1	-	-	1	-	-	-
CA	52	19	8	25	30	6	4	20	22	13	4	5	3	3	-
AK	1	1	-	-	-	-	-	-	1	1	-	-	-	-	-
HI	2	-	-	2	2	-	-	2	-	-	-	-	-	-	-

- Represents zero.   [1] Includes one Representative elected as an Independent.

Source: Compiled by U.S. Bureau of the Census from Elections Research Center, Chevy Chase, MD, *America Votes*, biennial, (copyright).

No. 430. Vote Cast for United States Representatives, by Major Political Party—States: 1988 to 1992

[In thousands, except percent. In each State, totals represent the sum of votes cast in each Congressional District or votes cast for Representative at Large in States where only one member is elected. In all years there are numerous districts within the State where either the Republican or Democratic party had no candidate. In some States the Republican and Democratic vote includes votes cast for the party candidate by endorsing parties. See also *Historical Statistics, Colonial Times to 1970*, series Y 211-214]

REGION, DIVISION, AND STATE	1988				1990				1992			
	Total[1]	Democratic	Republican	Percent for leading party	Total[1]	Democratic	Republican	Percent for leading party	Total[1]	Democratic	Republican	Percent for leading party
U.S. [2] ...	81,786	43,662	37,175	D-53.4	61,513	32,565	27,648	D-52.9	96,239	48,964	43,833	D-50.9
Northeast ...	17,806	9,490	7,989	D-53.3	12,792	6,483	5,868	D-50.7	19,417	9,567	8,871	D-49.3
N.E	5,327	3,086	2,066	D-57.4	4,453	2,523	1,742	D-56.7	5,910	3,007	2,334	D-50.9
ME	555	276	278	R-50.2	517	284	233	D-55.0	670	364	278	D-54.3
NH	429	176	252	R-58.6	291	141	149	R-51.2	511	266	227	D-52.0
VT	240	45	99	R-41.2	210	6	83	[3]I-56.0	282	22	87	[3]I-57.8
MA	2,371	1,787	509	D-75.4	2,051	1,420	567	D-69.2	2,614	1,518	857	D-58.1
RI	391	140	251	R-64.1	347	182	165	D-52.5	399	193	186	D-48.3
CT	1,341	660	677	R-50.5	1,037	489	546	R-52.6	1,435	644	699	R-48.7
M.A.	12,479	6,403	5,923	D-51.3	8,339	3,959	4,126	R-47.1	13,507	6,560	6,537	D-48.6
NY [4] . . .	5,506	2,950	2,441	D-53.6	3,662	1,830	1,662	D-50.0	5,925	3,051	2,687	D-51.5
NJ	2,776	1,336	1,412	R-50.9	1,827	837	911	R-49.9	2,992	1,355	1,503	R-50.2
PA	4,197	2,117	2,070	D-50.4	2,851	1,293	1,552	R-54.5	4,591	2,154	2,347	R-51.1
Midwest	23,539	12,270	11,205	D-52.1	17,484	9,370	7,970	D-53.6	26,232	13,260	12,238	D-50.5
E.N.C.	16,111	8,360	7,715	D-51.9	11,699	6,202	5,363	D-53.0	17,899	9,149	8,315	D-51.1
OH	4,155	2,087	2,068	D-50.2	3,418	1,807	1,590	D-52.9	4,577	2,198	2,154	D-48.0
IN	2,120	1,097	1,023	D-51.7	1,514	831	683	D-54.9	2,219	1,206	998	D-54.3
IL	4,344	2,317	2,023	D-53.3	3,077	1,646	1,349	D-53.5	4,831	2,678	2,097	D-55.4
MI	3,456	1,824	1,605	D-52.8	2,434	1,321	1,089	D-54.3	3,884	1,913	1,855	D-49.3
WI	2,035	1,035	997	D-50.9	1,256	597	652	R-51.9	2,388	1,154	1,211	R-50.7
W.N.C	7,429	3,910	3,490	D-52.6	5,785	3,168	2,607	D-54.8	8,333	4,111	3,923	D-49.3
MN	1,969	1,149	810	D-58.3	1,781	1,042	736	D-58.5	2,275	1,178	931	D-51.8
IA	1,189	580	607	R-51.0	792	401	385	D-50.6	1,242	493	729	R-58.7
MO	2,070	1,148	910	D-55.5	1,353	728	625	D-53.8	2,349	1,269	1,036	D-54.1
ND	300	213	84	D-70.9	234	153	81	D-65.2	298	169	117	D-56.8
SD	312	224	88	D-71.7	257	174	83	D-67.6	333	230	89	D-69.1
NE	656	230	426	R-64.9	587	277	309	R-52.7	711	283	427	R-60.1
KS	932	367	565	R-60.6	781	394	387	D-50.4	1,125	488	592	R-52.6
South [2] . . .	22,979	12,951	9,826	D-56.4	17,180	9,691	7,265	D-56.4	30,107	15,638	13,815	D-51.9
S.A. [2]	12,121	6,660	5,420	D-54.9	9,409	5,222	4,063	D-55.5	15,982	8,088	7,577	D-50.6
DE	235	158	76	D-67.5	177	116	58	D-65.5	276	117	153	R-55.4
MD	1,561	937	624	D-60.0	1,091	566	517	D-51.9	1,808	956	843	D-52.9
DC	171	122	23	D-71.3	160	98	42	D-61.7	197	167	20	D-84.8
VA	1,891	802	1,077	R-57.0	1,153	663	411	D-57.5	2,368	1,149	1,143	D-48.5
WV	569	437	132	D-76.8	375	251	123	D-67.1	562	439	123	D-78.1
NC	1,985	1,108	876	D-55.8	2,011	1,076	935	D-53.5	2,527	1,282	1,204	D-50.7
SC	991	550	439	D-55.4	670	383	275	D-57.2	1,115	506	581	R-52.1
GA	1,672	1,115	557	D-66.7	1,394	855	539	D-61.3	2,214	1,215	999	D-54.9
FL [5][6] . . .	3,047	1,431	1,616	R-53.0	2,378	1,213	1,163	D-51.0	4,915	2,257	2,511	R-51.1
E.S.C	4,611	2,707	1,841	D-58.7	2,866	1,712	1,070	D-59.7	5,655	3,170	2,292	D-56.1
KY	1,105	534	564	R-51.1	764	353	397	R-52.0	1,361	722	638	D-53.0
TN	1,409	844	536	D-59.9	717	369	289	D-51.5	1,726	883	738	D-51.2
AL	1,178	722	432	D-61.3	1,017	690	315	D-67.9	1,603	896	643	D-55.9
MS	918	607	308	D-66.1	369	299	69	D-81.2	965	670	273	D-69.4
W.S.C	6,248	3,583	2,565	D-57.3	4,906	2,758	2,132	D-56.2	8,470	4,380	3,946	D-51.7
AR [5][7] . . .	606	353	253	D-58.3	665	369	296	D-55.5	889	525	357	D-59.1
LA [8] . . .	205	89	116	R-56.8	106	106	-	D-100.0	684	285	399	R-58.3
OK [5][9] . . .	767	406	362	D-52.9	857	519	338	D-60.6	1,276	764	504	D-59.9
TX	4,670	2,736	1,834	D-58.6	3,278	1,763	1,498	D-53.8	5,622	2,806	2,686	D-49.9
West	17,461	8,952	8,155	D-51.3	14,057	7,022	6,545	D-50.0	20,483	10,499	8,910	D-51.3
Mountain . . .	4,793	2,062	2,664	R-55.6	3,872	1,783	2,043	R-52.8	5,736	2,627	2,886	R-50.3
MT	365	193	172	D-52.9	317	157	160	R-50.5	404	204	190	D-50.5
ID	407	198	203	R-49.9	315	183	131	D-58.2	473	222	231	R-48.8
WY	178	57	118	R-66.6	158	71	87	R-55.1	197	77	114	R-57.8
CO	1,315	645	667	R-50.7	1,001	504	487	D-50.3	1,479	691	758	R-51.2
NM	449	209	236	R-52.6	359	146	214	R-59.5	556	273	278	R-50.0
AZ	1,125	322	766	R-68.1	966	345	621	R-64.3	1,409	582	740	R-52.5
UT	609	260	341	R-56.0	442	234	191	D-52.9	727	331	362	R-49.8
NV	344	177	160	D-51.4	313	144	151	R-48.2	492	245	214	D-49.9
Pacific	12,669	6,891	5,492	D-54.4	10,185	5,239	4,502	D-51.4	14,747	7,872	6,024	D-53.4
WA	1,731	988	743	D-57.1	1,313	696	596	D-53.0	2,223	1,237	912	D-55.6
OR	1,024	665	358	D-64.9	1,053	667	342	D-63.4	1,391	825	553	D-59.3
CA	9,381	4,945	4,174	D-52.7	7,287	3,568	3,347	D-49.0	10,535	5,447	4,365	D-51.7
AK	193	72	121	R-62.5	192	92	99	R-51.7	239	102	112	R-46.8
HI	340	221	97	D-65.1	341	216	118	D-63.3	358	261	82	D-72.8

- Represents zero.   [1] Includes vote cast for minor parties.   [2] Includes vote cast for nonvoting Delegate at Large in District of Columbia.   [3] Leading party candidate was Independent.   [4] Includes votes cast by other endorsing parties for Democratic and Republican candidates.   [5] State law does not require tabulation of votes for unopposed candidates.   [6] In 1988 Districts 3, 5, 7, 12, 17, and 18 were unopposed; in 1990 Districts 8, 10, 12, 13, and 16 were unopposed; in 1992 District 21 was unopposed. [7] In 1988 District 1 was unopposed.   [8] 1988 data are for a general election runoff in one district. 1988 open primary totals-total, 550,370; Democratic 337,724; Republican, 212,646. 1990 data are for a general election runoff in one district. 1990 open primary totals-total, 1,186,253; Democratic, 706,004; Republican, 450,867. 1992 data are for general election runoffs in three districts. [9] In 1988 Districts 3 and 4 were unopposed.

Source: Elections Research Center, Chevy Chase, MD, *America Votes*, biennial, (copyright).

No. 431. Vote Cast for United States Representatives, by Major Political Party—Congressional Districts: 1992

[In some States the Democratic and Republican vote includes votes cast for the party candidate by endorsing parties]

STATE AND DIS-TRICT	Total vote cast (1,000)	DEMOCRATIC CANDIDATE Name	Per cent of total	REPUBLICAN CANDIDATE Name	Per cent of total
AL	**1,603**	(X)	56	(X)	40
1st...	214	Brewer ...	37	Callahan ...	60
2d ...	228	Wallace...	48	Everett	49
3d ...	198	Browder...	60	Sledge	37
4th...	231	Bevill.....	68	Strickland ..	29
5th...	244	Cramer ...	66	Smith	32
6th...	280	Erdreich...	45	Bachus	52
7th...	208	Hilliard....	69	Jones	17
AK	**239**	Devens ...	43	Young.....	47
AZ	**1,409**	(X)	41	(X)	53
1st...	255	Cooper-smith....	51	Rhodes....	45
2d ...	137	Pastor....	66	Shooter. ..	30
3d ...	259	Hartstone.	34	Stump.....	61
4th...	264	Mybeck ...	27	Kyl......	59
5th...	260	Toevs	30	Kolbe	67
6th...	234	English ...	53	Wead	41
AR	**889**	(X)	59	(X)	40
1st...	214	Lambert....	70	Hayes.....	30
2d ...	209	Thornton ..	74	Scott	26
3d ...	249	Van Winkle.	47	Hutchinson .	50
4th...	216	McCuen....	48	Dickey	52
CA	**10,535**	(X)	52	(X)	41
1st...	251	Hamburg ..	48	Riggs.....	45
2d ...	257	Freedman .	28	Herger	65
3d ...	239	Fazio	51	Richardson .	40
4th...	283	Malberg...	46	Doolittle ...	50
5th...	231	Matsui....	69	Dinsmore ..	25
6th...	292	Woolsey ..	65	Filante	34
7th...	218	Miller.....	70	Scholl.....	25
8th...	233	Pelosi....	82	Wolin	11
9th...	228	Dellums ...	72	Hunter	24
10th..	280	Williams...	48	Baker.....	52
11th..	198	Garamendi.	46	Pombo	48
12th..	228	Lantos....	69	Tomlin	23
13th..	206	Stark.....	60	Teyler.....	32
14th..	259	Eshoo	57	Huening ...	39
15th..	265	Mineta....	64	Wick......	31
16th..	156	Edwards ...	62	Bundesen ..	32
17th..	210	Panetta ...	72	McCamp-bell......	24
18th..	165	Condit....	85	(¹)	(¹)
19th..	217	Lehman ...	47	Cloud	46
20th..	112	Dooley ...	65	Hunt......	35
21st..	196	Vollmer ...	35	Thomas ...	65
22d ..	250	Ochoa....	35	Huffington .	53
23d ..	213	Ferguson..	41	Gallegly ...	54
24th..	255	Beilenson .	56	McClintock .	39
25th..	219	Gilmartin ..	33	McKeon ...	52
26th..	121	Berman....	61	Frosch	30
27th..	212	Kahn.....	39	Moorhead .	50
28th..	209	Wachtel....	37	Dreier.....	58
29th..	261	Waxman ..	61	Robbins ...	26
30th..	84	Becerra ...	58	Waksberg ..	24
31st..	109	Martinez ..	63	Franco	37
32d ..	173	Dixon	87	(¹)	(¹)
33d ..	51	Roybal-Allard....	63	Guzman ...	30
34th..	150	Torres.....	61	Hernandez. .	34
35th..	125	Waters ...	83	Truman....	14
36th..	260	Harman...	48	Flores.....	42
37th..	113	Tucker....	86	(¹)	(¹)
38th..	189	Braude ...	43	Horn......	49
39th..	214	McClana-han.....	38	Royce.....	57
40th..	205	Rusk.....	31	Lewis.....	63
41st..	171	Baker	34	Kim	60
42d ..	157	Brown....	51	Rutan.....	44
43d ..	191	Takano ...	46	Calvert	47
44th..	204	Smith	40	McCandless.	54
45th..	227	McCabe...	39	Rohra-bacher ...	55
46th..	111	Banuelos..	41	Dornan....	50
47th..	254	Anwiler ...	30	Cox	65
48th..	230	Farber....	29	Packard ...	61
49th..	249	Schenk ...	51	Jarvis.....	43
50th..	137	Filner	57	Valencia ...	29
51st..	253	Herbert ...	34	Cunning-ham.....	56
52d ..	214	Gastil	41	Hunter	53
CO	**1,479**	(X)	47	(X)	51
1st...	228	Schroeder .	69	Aragon	31
2d ...	271	Skaggs ...	61	Day	33
3d ...	262	Callihan...	44	McInnis....	55
4th...	242	Redder ...	42	Allard.....	58
5th...	243	Oriez.....	26	Hefley.....	71
6th...	233	Kolbe	39	Schaefer...	61
CT	**1,435**	(X)	45	(X)	49
1st...	245	Kennelly ..	67	Steele.....	31
2d ...	243	Gejdenson.	51	Munster ...	49
3d ...	248	DeLauro ..	66	Scott	34
4th...	220	Schropfer..	27	Shays.....	67
5th...	240	Lawlor.....	31	Franks	44
6th...	240	Slason....	25	Johnson ...	70
DE	**276**	Woo.....	43	Castle.....	55
FL.....	**4,915**	(X)	46	(X)	51
1st...	229	Hutto	52	Ketchel....	44
2d ...	152	Peterson..	60	Wagner....	40
3d ...	167	Brown....	62	Weidner ...	38
4th...	239	Hair	43	Fowler	57
5th...	264	Thurman ..	49	Hogan	43
6th...	221	Denton ...	35	Stearns....	65
7th...	223	Webster...	43	Mica......	56
8th...	207	Kovaleski..	31	McCollum ..	69
9th...	268	Knapp.....	41	Bilirakis....	59
10th..	264	Moffitt....	43	Young.....	57
11th..	191	Gibbons...	53	Sharpe	41
12th..	193	Mims.....	48	Canady....	52
13th..	275	Snell.....	42	Miller	58
14th..	269	(¹)	(¹)	Goss	82
15th..	261	Bacchus ..	51	Tolley.....	49
16th..	259	Comerford .	39	Lewis.....	61
17th..	103	Meek	100	(¹)	(¹)
18th..	157	Davis	33	Ros-Lehtinen ..	67
19th..	281	Johnston ..	63	Metz......	37
20th..	238	Deutsch...	55	Kennedy ...	39
21st..	(NA)	(¹)	(¹)	Diaz-Balart..	(NA)
22d ..	247	Margolis...	37	Shaw	52
23d ..	144	Hastings ..	59	Fielding....	31
GA	**2,214**	(X)	55	(X)	45
1st...	180	Christmas .	42	Kingston ...	58
2d ...	150	Bishop....	64	Dudley	36
3d ...	208	Ray	45	Collins	55
4th...	250	Steinberg..	49	Linder.....	51
5th...	204	Lewis	72	Stabler	28
6th...	275	Center....	42	Gingrich ...	58
7th...	194	Darden ...	57	Beverly....	43
8th...	195	Rowland ..	56	Cunning-ham.....	44
9th...	191	Deal.....	59	Becker	41
10th..	201	Johnson ..	54	Hudgens...	46
11th..	164	McKinney..	73	Lovett.....	27
HI....	**358**	(X)	73	(X)	23
1st...	177	Aber-crombie..	73	Sutton	23
2d ...	181	Mink.....	73	Price	22
ID....	**473**	(X)	47	(X)	49
1st...	243	Larocco...	58	Gilbert	37
2d ...	230	Williams...	35	Crapo.....	61

See footnotes at end of table.

No. 431. Vote Cast for United States Representatives, by Major Political Party—Congressional Districts: 1992—Continued

[See headnote, p. 275]

STATE AND DISTRICT	Total vote cast (1,000)	DEMOCRATIC CANDIDATE Name	Percent of total	REPUBLICAN CANDIDATE Name	Percent of total	STATE AND DISTRICT	Total vote cast (1,000)	DEMOCRATIC CANDIDATE Name	Percent of total	REPUBLICAN CANDIDATE Name	Percent of total
IL.....	4,831	(X)	55	(X)	43	1st...	234	McMillen	48	Gilchrest	51
1st...	253	Rush	83	Walker	17	2d...	254	Hickey	35	Bentley	65
2d...	234	Reynolds	78	Blackstone	14	3d...	222	Cardin	73	Bricker	26
3d...	255	Lipinski	64	Lepinske	36	4th...	182	Wynn	75	Dyson	25
4th...	117	Gutierrez	78	Rodriguez-Scheiman	22	5th...	223	Hoyer	53	Hogan	44
5th...	232	Rostenkowski	57	Zenkich	39	6th...	232	Hattery	46	Bartlett	54
6th...	252	Watkins	34	Hyde	66	7th...	179	Mfume	85	Kondner	15
7th...	225	Collins	81	Boccio	16	8th...	280	Heffernan	27	Morella	73
8th...	239	Smith	40	Crane	56	MA....	2,614	(X)	58	(X)	33
9th...	240	Yates	68	Sohn	27	1st...	262	Olver	52	Larkin	43
10th...	241	Kennedy	35	Porter	65	2d...	247	Neal	53	Ravosa	31
11th..	243	Sangmeister	56	Herbolsheimer	44	3d...	261	Early	44	Blute	50
12th..	237	Costello	71	Starr	29	4th...	270	Frank	68	McCormick	26
13th..	262	Temple	32	Fawell	68	5th...	257	Meehan	52	Cronin	37
14th..	231	Reich	33	Hastert	67	6th...	290	Mavroules	45	Torkildsen	55
15th..	240	Mattis	41	Ewing	59	7th...	282	Markey	62	Sohn	28
16th..	256	Cox	44	Manzullo	56	8th...	180	Kennedy	83	(¹)	(¹)
17th..	260	Evans	60	Schloemer	40	9th...	254	Moakley	69	Conboy	21
18th..	271	Hawkins	42	Michel	58	10th..	312	Studds	61	Daly	24
19th..	271	Poshard	69	Lee	31	MI....	3,884	(X)	49	(X)	48
20th..	274	Durbin	57	Shimkus	43	1st...	269	Stupak	54	Ruppe	44
IN....	2,219	(X)	54	(X)	45	2d...	247	Miltner	35	Hoekstra	63
1st...	212	Visclosky	69	Vucich	31	3d...	265	Kooistra	36	Henry	61
2d...	229	Sharp	57	Frazier	40	4th...	252	Donaldson	35	Camp	63
3d...	211	Roemer	57	Baxmeyer	43	5th...	245	Barcia	60	Muxlow	38
4th...	217	Long	62	Pierson	38	6th...	233	Davis	38	Upton	62
5th...	220	Jontz	49	Buyer	51	7th...	153	(¹)	(¹)	Smith	88
6th...	258	Bruner	28	Burton	72	8th...	285	Carr	48	Chrysler	46
7th...	217	Wedum	41	Myers	59	9th...	250	Kildee	54	O'Neill	45
8th...	238	McCloskey	53	Mourdock	45	10th..	260	Bonior	53	Carl	44
9th...	231	Hamilton	70	Bailey	30	11th..	293	Briggs	40	Knollenberg	58
10th..	184	Jacobs	64	Horvath	35	12th..	261	Levin	53	Pappageorge	46
IA....	1,242	(X)	40	(X)	59	13th..	246	Ford	52	Geake	43
1st...	261	Zonneveld	31	Leach	68	14th..	201	Conyers	82	Gordon	16
2d...	268	Nagle	49	Nussle	50	15th..	185	Collins	81	Vincent	17
3d...	257	Baxter	47	Lightfoot	49	16th..	241	Dingell	65	Beaumont	31
4th...	258	Smith	62	Lunde	37	MN....	2,275	(X)	52	(X)	41
5th...	198	(¹)	(¹)	Grandy	99	1st...	279	Penny[8]	74	Droogsma	26
KS....	1,125	(X)	43	(X)	53	2d...	276	Minge[6]	48	Ludeman	48
1st...	285	West	29	Roberts	68	3d...	315	Mandell	33	Ramstad	64
2d...	269	Slattery	56	Van Slyke	41	4th...	278	Vento	57	Maitland	37
3d...	293	Love	38	Meyers	58	5th...	277	Sabo	63	Moriarty	28
4th...	278	Glickman	52	Yost	42	6th...	301	Sikorski	33	Grams	44
KY....	1,361	(X)	53	(X)	47	7th...	266	Peterson	50	Omann	49
1st...	213	Barlow	60	Hamrick	39	8th...	283	Oberstar	59	Herwig	30
2d...	207	Natcher	61	Bartley	39	MS....	965	(X)	69	(X)	28
3d...	281	Mazzoli	53	Stokes	47	1st...	205	Whitten	59	Whitaker	41
4th...	227	Poore	38	Bunning	62	2d...	175	Espy	76	Benford	24
5th...	211	Hays	45	Rogers	55	3d...	201	Montgomery	81	Williams	19
6th...	223	Baesler	61	Ellinger	39	4th...	195	Parker	67	McMillan	22
LA[2] ...	(NA)	(X)	(X)	(X)	(X)	5th...	191	Taylor	63	Harvey	35
1st...	(X)	(X)	(X)	Livingston[3]	(X)	MO....	2,349	(X)	54	(X)	44
2d...	(X)	Jefferson[3]	(X)	(X)	(X)	1st...	233	Clay	68	Montgomery	32
3d...	(X)	Tauzin[3]	(X)	(X)	(X)	2d...	312	Horn	48	Talent	50
4th...	195	Fields[4]	100	(X)	(X)	3d...	272	Gephardt	64	Holekamp	33
5th...	244	Huckaby	37	McCrery	63	4th...	251	Skelton	70	Carley	30
6th...	245	(X)	(X)	Baker[5]	100	5th...	255	Wheat	59	Moody	37
7th...	(X)	Hayes[3]	(X)	(X)	(X)	6th...	269	Danner	55	Coleman	43
ME....	670	(X)	54	(X)	42	7th...	260	Deaton	38	Hancock	62
1st...	358	Andrews	65	Bean	35	8th...	234	Bullock	37	Emerson	63
2d...	311	McGowan	42	Snowe	49	9th...	261	Volkmer	48	Hardy	45
MD...	1,808	(X)	53	(X)	47	MT....	404	Williams	50	Marlenee	47

See footnotes at end of table.

No. 431. Vote Cast for United States Representatives, by Major Political Party—Congressional Districts: 1992—Continued

[See headnote, p. 275]

STATE AND DISTRICT	Total vote cast (1,000)	DEMOCRATIC CANDIDATE Name	Percent of total	REPUBLICAN CANDIDATE Name	Percent of total	STATE AND DISTRICT	Total vote cast (1,000)	DEMOCRATIC CANDIDATE Name	Percent of total	REPUBLICAN CANDIDATE Name	Percent of total
NE	711	(X)......	40	(X).....	60	5th...	224	Neal.....	53	Burr	46
1st...	239	Finnegan...	40	Bereuter..	60	6th...	230	Hood.....	29	Coble....	71
2d...	233	Hoagland..	51	Staskiewicz	49	7th...	163	Rose.....	57	Anderson..	41
3d...	238	Fisher.....	28	Barrett....	72	8th...	191	Hefner....	59	Privette...	38
NV....	492	(X)......	50	(X).....	43	9th...	228	Blake.....	33	McMillan..	67
1st...	221	Bilbray....	58	Pettyjohn..	38	10th..	235	Neill......	34	Ballenger..	63
2d...	270	Sferrazza...	43	Vucanovich	48	11th..	238	Stevens...	45	Taylor....	55
NH....	511	(X)......	52	(X).....	44	12th..	181	Watt.....	70	Washington	27
1st...	256	Preston....	42	Zeliff.....	53	ND....	298	Pomeroy...	57	Korsmo...	39
2d...	255	Swett.....	62	Hatch....	36	OH....	4,577	(X)......	48	(X).....	47
NJ....	2,992	(X)......	45	(X).....	50	1st...	234	Mann.....	51	(¹)......	(¹)
1st...	228	Andrews...	67	Solomon..	29	2d...	254	Chandler...	30	Gradison..	70
2d...	237	Hughes....	56	Lobiondo..	41	3d...	245	Hall......	60	Davis....	40
3d...	256	Ryan.....	37	Saxton....	59	4th...	240	Ball......	39	Oxley....	61
4th...	241	Hughes....	35	Smith.....	62	5th...	188	(¹)......	(¹)	Gillmor...	100
5th...	274	Lucas.....	25	Roukema..	72	6th...	242	Strickland..	51	McEwen..	49
6th...	226	Pallone....	52	Kyrillos...	45	7th...	230	Heskett....	29	Hobson...	71
7th...	248	Sendelsky..	43	Franks....	53	8th...	238	Stennet....	26	Boehner..	74
8th...	206	Klein......	47	Bubba....	41	9th...	243	Kaptur....	74	Brown....	22
9th...	239	Torricelli..	58	Roma....	37	10th..	240	Oakar.....	43	Hoke.....	57
10th..	150	Payne.....	78	Palermo...	20	11th..	224	Stokes....	69	Rothschild .	20
11th..	268	Spirdellis..	26	Gallo.....	70	12th..	239	Fitrakis...	29	Kasich....	71
12th..	273	Abate.....	30	Zimmer...	64	13th..	252	Brown.....	53	Mueller...	35
13th..	146	Menendez..	64	Theemling.	31	14th..	244	Sawyer....	68	Morgan...	32
NM....	556	(X)......	49	(X).....	50	15th..	250	Cordray....	38	Pryce....	44
1st...	205	Aragon....	37	Schiff.....	63	16th..	249	Mendenhall .	36	Regula...	64
2d...	168	Sosa.....	44	Skeen....	56	17th..	257	Traficant...	84	Pansino...	16
3d...	182	Richardson .	67	Bemis....	30	18th..	243	Applegate..	68	Ress.....	32
NY....	5,925	(X)......	51	(X).....	45	19th..	263	Fingerhut..	53	Gardner...	47
1st...	228	Hoch-brueckner	52	Romaine..	48	OK....	1,276	(X)......	60	(X).....	40
2d...	206	Downey...	47	Lazio.....	53	1st...	226	Selph.....	47	Inhofe....	53
3d...	252	Orlins....	46	King.....	50	2d...	214	Synar....	56	Hill.....	41
4th...	221	Schiliro....	45	Levy.....	50	3d...	208	Brewster...	75	Stokes...	25
5th...	211	Ackerman..	52	Binder....	45	4th...	199	McCurdy...	71	Bell.....	29
6th...	120	Flake.....	81	Bhag-wandin..	19	5th...	231	Williams...	47	Istook....	53
7th...	127	Manton....	57	Shea.....	43	6th...	199	English....	68	Anthony...	32
8th...	170	Nadler....	81	Askren...	15	OR....	1,391	(X)......	59	(X).....	40
9th...	132	Schumer...	89	(¹).....	(¹)	1st...	294	Furse.....	52	Meeker...	48
10th..	102	Towns....	96	(¹).....	(¹)	2d...	274	Ferguson...	33	Smith....	67
11th..	85	Owens....	94	(¹).....	(¹)	3d...	270	Wyden....	77	Ritter....	19
12th..	73	Velazquez..	77	Diaz.....	20	4th...	279	DeFazio...	71	Schulz....	29
13th..	192	Albanese...	38	Molinari...	56	5th...	273	Kopetski...	64	Seagraves .	36
14th..	202	Maloney...	50	Green....	48	PA....	4,591	(X)......	47	(X).....	51
15th..	111	Rangel....	95	(¹).....	(¹)	1st...	186	Foglietta...	81	Snyder...	19
16th..	93	Serrano....	91	Walters...	9	2d...	214	Blackwell...	77	Hollin...	22
17th..	122	Engel.....	80	Richman..	13	3d...	222	Borski.....	59	Dougherty .	39
18th..	209	Lowey.....	56	DioGuardi.	44	4th...	238	Klink.....	78	Johnston...	20
19th..	232	McCarthy..	40	Fish.....	60	5th...	189	(¹)......	(¹)	Clinger...	100
20th..	227	Levine....	29	Gilman...	66	6th...	208	Holden....	52	Jones....	48
21st..	265	McNulty...	63	Norman...	34	7th...	274	Daly......	33	Weldon....	66
22d..	251	Roberts....	35	Solomon..	65	8th...	250	Kostmayer..	46	Green-wood....	52
23d..	220	DiPerna....	28	Boehlert..	64	9th...	182	(¹)......	(¹)	Shuster...	100
24th..	201	Raven-scroft....	24	McHugh...	61	10th..	210	(¹)......	(¹)	McDade...	90
25th..	242	Jezer.....	44	Walsh....	56	11th..	207	Kanjorski...	67	Fescina...	33
26th..	237	Hinchey...	50	Moppert...	47	12th..	167	Murtha.. ₇	100	(¹)......	(¹)
27th..	247	Call.....	36	Paxon....	64	13th..	254	Mezvinsky [7]	50	Fox.....	50
28th..	255	Slaughter..	55	Polito....	44	14th..	229	Coyne.....	72	King.....	27
29th..	235	LaFalce...	54	Miller.....	42	15th..	213	McHale....	52	Ritter....	47
30th..	243	Gorski.....	46	Quinn....	52	16th..	213	Peters.....	35	Walker...	65
31st..	214	Leahey....	24	Houghton..	71	17th..	216	Sturges....	30	Gekas....	70
NC....	2,527	(X)......	51	(X).....	48	18th..	254	Pecora....	38	Santorum..	61
1st...	173	Clayton....	67	Tyler.....	31	19th..	218	Kilker.....	34	Goodling..	45
2d...	212	Valentine...	54	Davis....	44	20th..	226	Murphy....	51	Townsend .	49
3d...	187	Lancaster..	54	Pollard....	43	21st..	222	Harkins....	32	Ridge....	68
4th...	265	Price.....	65	Goudie...	34	RI....	399	(X)......	48	(X).....	47
						1st...	194	Carlin.....	25	Machtley..	70
						2d...	204	Reed.....	71	Bell......	24

See footnotes at end of table.

No. 431. Vote Cast for United States Representatives, by Major Political Party—Congressional Districts: 1992—Continued

[See headnote, p. 275]

STATE AND DIS-TRICT	Total vote cast (1,000)	DEMOCRATIC CANDIDATE Name	Percent of total	REPUBLICAN CANDIDATE Name	Percent of total	STATE AND DIS-TRICT	Total vote cast (1,000)	DEMOCRATIC CANDIDATE Name	Percent of total	REPUBLICAN CANDIDATE Name	Percent of total
SC	**1,115**	(X)	45	(X)	52	30th ..	151	Johnson ...	72	Cain	25
1st...	185	Oberst	32	Ravenel...	66	**UT**	**727**	(X)	46	(X)	50
2d ...	170	(¹)	(¹)	Spence ...	88	1st...	245	Holt	28	Hansen ...	65
3d ...	195	Derrick	61	Bland	39	2d ...	253	Shepherd ..	50	Greene ...	47
4th...	198	Patterson ..	47	Inglis.....	50	3d ...	229	Orton	59	Harrington .	37
5th...	183	Spratt.....	61	Horne	39	**VT** [8] ...	**282**	Young.....	8	Philbin....	31
6th...	185	Clyburn	65	Chase	35	**VA**	**2,368**	(X)	49	(X)	48
SD	**333**	Johnson ...	69	(X)	27	1st...	232	Fox	39	Bateman ..	58
TN	**1,726**	(X)	51	(X)	43	2d ...	177	Pickett	56	Chapman..	44
1st...	170	Christian ...	28	Quillen ...	67	3d ...	168	Scott	79	Jenkins ...	21
2d ...	205	Goodale ...	26	Duncan ...	72	4th...	216	Sisisky ...	68	Zevgolis ...	32
3d ...	217	Lloyd	49	Wamp....	47	5th...	193	Payne.....	69	Hurlburt...	31
4th...	155	Cooper	64	Johnson ..	33	6th...	212	Mussel-white.	40	Goodlatte	60
5th...	188	Clement ...	67	Stone	26						
6th...	212	Gordon	57	Blackburn .	41	7th...	255	(¹)	(¹)	Bliley.....	83
7th...	203	Davis	36	Sundquist .	62	8th...	247	Moran.....	56	McSlarrow .	42
8th...	163	Tanner	84	(¹)......	(¹)	9th...	211	Boucher ...	63	Weddle ...	37
9th...	213	Ford......	58	Black	28	10th..	227	Vickery	33	Wolf	64
TX	**5,622**	(X)	50	(X)	48	11th..	228	Byrne	50	Butler....	45
1st...	152	Chapman ..	100	(¹)......	(¹)	**WA**	**2,223**	(X)	56	(X)	41
2d ...	211	Wilson	56	Peterson ..	44	1st...	271	Cantwell ...	55	Nelson ...	42
3d ...	234	(¹)	(¹)	Johnson ...	86	2d ...	256	Swift	52	Metcalf ...	42
4th...	220	Hall	58	Bridges ...	38	3d ...	247	Unsoeld ...	56	Fiske....	44
5th...	167	Bryant.....	59	Stokley ...	37	4th...	210	Inslee....	51	Hastings ..	49
6th...	263	Dietrich....	28	Barton....	72	5th...	246	Foley	55	Sonneland .	45
7th...	169	(¹)	(¹)	Archer....	100	6th...	238	Dicks	64	Phillips ...	28
8th...	233	Robinson ...	23	Fields....	77	7th...	284	McDermott .	78	Hampson..	19
9th...	221	Brooks	54	Stockman .	43	8th...	258	Tamblyn ...	34	Dunn.....	60
10th..	262	Pickle	68	Spiro.....	26	9th...	213	Kreidler....	52	Von Reich-bauer.	43
11th..	178	Edwards ...	67	Broyles ...	33						
12th..	200	Geren.....	63	Hobbs....	37	**WV**	**562**	(X)	78	(X)	22
13th..	195	Sarpalius...	60	Boulter...	40	1st...	173	Mollohan...	100	(¹)......	(¹)
14th..	200	Laughlin...	68	Garza....	27	2d ...	203	Wise.....	71	Cravotta ..	29
15th..	143	De La Garza.	60	Haughey ..	40	3d ...	186	Rahall....	66	Waldman..	34
16th..	129	Coleman ...	52	Taberski..	48	**WI**	**2,388**	(X)	48	(X)	51
17th..	206	Stenholm ..	66	Sadowski..	34	1st...	256	Aspin.....	58	Neumann..	41
18th..	172	Washington .	65	Blum.....	33	2d ...	293	Deer......	37	Klug	63
19th..	209	Moser.....	23	Combest...	77	3d ...	260	Sacia.....	42	Gunderson.	56
20th..	104	Gonzalez...	100	(¹)......	(¹)	4th...	264	Kleczka...	66	Cook.....	32
21st..	265	Gaddy....	24	Smith....	72	5th...	234	Barrett	69	Hammer-smith....	30
22d ..	218	Konrad....	31	Delay	69						
23d ..	166	Bustamante .	38	Bonilla...	59	6th...	272	Lauten-schlager ..	47	Petri	53
24th..	174	Frost	60	Masterson .	40						
25th..	177	Andrews ...	56	McKenna..	41	7th...	258	Obey	64	Vannes ...	36
26th..	206	Caton	27	Armey....	73	8th...	274	Helms....	30	Roth	70
27th..	157	Ortiz......	55	Kimbrough .	43	9th...	277	Buxton....	28	Sensen-brenner .	70
28th..	141	Tejeda....	87	(¹)......	(¹)						
29th..	99	Green....	65	Ervin.....	35	**WY**	**197**	Herschler ..	39	Thomas...	58

NA Not available.   X Not applicable.   [1] No candidate.   [2] Louisiana holds an open-primary election with candidates from all parties running on the same ballot. Any candidate who receives a majority is elected; if no candidate receives 50 percent, there is a run-off election in November between the top two finishers.   [3] Candidate listed won seat in open-primary.   [4] Both candidates in run-off election were Democrats.   [5] Both candidates in run-off election were Republicans.   [6] The winning Democratic candidate received 132,156 votes; the Republican candidate, 131,587.   [7] The winning Democratic candidate received 127,685 votes; the Republican candidate, 126,312.   [8] The winning candidate was Sanders, an Independent, who received 58 percent of the vote.

Source: Elections Research Center, Chevy Chase, MD, *America Votes*, biennial, (copyright).

No. 432. Composition of Congress, by Political Party: 1961 to 1994

[D=Democratic, R=Republican. Data for beginning of first session of each Congress (as of January 3), except as noted. Excludes vacancies at beginning of session. See also *Historical Statistics, Colonial Times to 1970*, series Y 204-210]

YEAR	Party and President	Congress	HOUSE			SENATE		
			Majority party	Minority party	Other	Majority party	Minority party	Other
1961	D (Kennedy)	87th	D-263	R-174	-	D-65	R-35	-
1963	D (Kennedy)	88th	D-258	R-177	-	D-67	R-33	-
1965	D (Johnson)	89th	D-295	R-140	-	D-68	R-32	-
1967	D (Johnson)	90th	D-247	R-187	-	D-64	R-36	-
1969 [1]	R (Nixon)	91st	D-243	R-192	-	D-57	R-43	-
1971 [1] [2]	R (Nixon)	92d	D-254	R-180	-	D-54	R-44	2
1973 [1] [2]	R (Nixon)	93d	D-239	R-192	1	D-56	R-42	2
1975 [3]	R (Ford)	94th	D-291	R-144	-	D-60	R-37	2
1977 [4]	D (Carter)	95th	D-292	R-143	-	D-61	R-38	1
1979 [4]	D (Carter)	96th	D-276	R-157	-	D-58	R-41	1
1981 [4]	R (Reagan)	97th	D-243	R-192	-	R-53	D-46	1
1983	R (Reagan)	98th	D-269	R-165	-	R-54	D-46	-
1985	R (Reagan)	99th	D-252	R-182	-	R-53	D-47	-
1987	R (Reagan)	100th	D-258	R-177	-	D-55	R-45	-
1989 [5]	R (Bush)	101st	D-259	R-174	-	D-55	R-45	-
1991 [5]	R (Bush)	102d	D-267	R-167	1	D-56	R-44	-
1993 [5]	D (Clinton)	103d	D-258	R-176	1	D-57	R-43	-
1994 [5] [6]	D (Clinton)	103d	D-257	R-176	1	D-56	R-44	-

- Represents zero. [1] Senate had one Independent and one Conservative-Republican. [2] House had one Independent-Democrat. [3] Senate had one Independent, one Conservative-Republican, and one undecided (New Hampshire). [4] Senate had one Independent. [5] House had one Independent-Socialist. [6] As of beginning of second session (January 25th).

Source: U.S. Congress, Joint Committee on Printing, *Congressional Directory*, annual; beginning 1977, biennial.

No. 433. U.S. Congress—Measures Introduced and Enacted and Time in Session: 1977 to 1993

[Excludes simple and concurrent resolutions. See also *Historical Statistics, Colonial Times to 1970*, series Y 189-198]

ITEM	95th Cong., 1977-78	96th Cong., 1979-80	97th Cong., 1981-82	98th Cong., 1983-84	99th Cong., 1985-86	100th Cong., 1987-88	101st Cong., 1989-90	102d Cong., 1991-92	103d Cong., 1993
Measures introduced	19,387	12,583	11,490	11,156	9,885	9,588	6,664	6,775	5,968
Bills	18,045	11,722	10,582	10,134	8,697	8,515	5,977	6,212	5,505
Joint resolutions	1,342	861	908	1,022	1,188	1,073	687	563	463
Measures enacted	803	736	529	677	483	761	666	609	211
Public	633	613	473	623	466	713	650	589	210
Private	170	123	56	54	17	48	16	20	1
HOUSE OF REPRESENTATIVES									
Number of days	323	326	303	266	281	298	281	280	142
Number of hours	1,898	1,876	1,420	1,705	1,794	1,659	1,688	1,796	982
Number of hours per day	5.9	5.8	4.7	6.4	6.4	5.6	6.0	6.4	6.9
SENATE									
Number of days	337	333	312	281	313	307	274	287	153
Number of hours	2,510	2,324	2,158	1,951	2,531	2,341	2,254	2,292	1,269
Number of hours per day	7.4	7.0	6.9	6.9	8.1	7.6	8.2	8.0	8.3

Source: U.S. Congress, *Congressional Record* and *Daily Calendar*, selected issues.

No. 434. Congressional Bills Vetoed: 1961 to 1993

[See also *Historical Statistics, Colonial Times to 1970*, series Y 199-203]

PERIOD	President	Total vetoes	Regular vetoes	Pocket vetoes	Vetoes sus- tained	Bills passed over veto
1961-63	Kennedy	21	12	9	21	-
1963-69	Johnson	30	16	14	30	-
1969-74	Nixon	42	24	18	36	6
1974-77	Ford	72	53	19	60	12
1977-81	Carter	31	13	18	29	2
1981-89	Reagan	78	39	39	69	9
1989-93	Bush	45	29	16	44	1

- Represents zero.

Source: U.S. Congress, Senate Library, *Presidential Vetoes ... 1789-1968*; U.S. Congress, *Calendars of the U.S. House of Representatives and History of Legislation*, annual.

No. 435. Composition of Congress, by Political Party Affiliation—States: 1987 to 1994

[Figures are for the beginning of the first session (as of January 3), except as noted. Dem.=Democratic; Rep.=Republican]

REGION, DIVISION, AND STATE	REPRESENTATIVES								SENATORS							
	100th Cong., 1987		101st Cong., 1989 [1][2]		102d Cong., 1991 [3]		103rd Cong., 1994 [3][4][5]		100th Cong., 1987		101st Cong., 1989		102d Cong., 1991		103rd Cong., 1994 [4]	
	Dem.	Rep.	Dem.	Rep.	Dem.	Rep.	Dem.	Rep.	Dem.	Rep.	Dem.	Rep.	Dem.	Rep.	Dem.	Rep.
U.S.	258	177	259	174	267	167	257	176	55	45	55	45	56	44	56	44
Northeast	55	40	55	40	56	38	50	37	9	9	10	8	10	8	11	7
N.E.	15	9	14	10	16	7	14	8	6	6	7	5	7	5	7	5
ME	1	1	1	1	1	1	1	1	1	1	1	1	1	1	1	1
NH	-	2	-	2	1	1	1	1	-	2	-	2	-	2	-	2
VT	-	1	-	1	-	-	-	-	1	1	1	1	1	1	1	1
MA	10	1	10	1	10	1	8	2	2	-	2	-	2	-	2	-
RI	1	1	-	2	1	1	1	1	1	1	1	1	1	1	1	1
CT	3	3	3	3	3	3	3	3	1	1	2	-	2	-	2	-
M.A.	40	31	41	30	40	31	36	29	3	3	3	3	3	3	4	2
NY	20	14	21	13	21	13	18	13	1	1	1	1	1	1	1	1
NJ	8	6	8	6	8	6	7	6	2	-	2	-	2	-	2	-
PA	12	11	12	11	11	12	11	10	-	2	-	2	-	2	1	1
Midwest	62	51	64	48	68	45	61	44	13	11	13	11	14	10	15	9
E.N.C	46	34	47	32	49	31	43	31	7	3	7	3	7	3	8	2
OH	11	10	11	10	11	10	10	9	2	-	2	-	2	-	2	-
IN	6	4	6	3	8	2	7	3	-	2	-	2	-	2	-	2
IL	13	9	14	8	15	7	12	8	2	-	2	-	2	-	2	-
MI	11	7	11	7	11	7	10	6	2	-	2	-	2	-	2	-
WI	5	4	5	4	4	5	4	5	1	1	1	1	1	1	2	-
W.N.C	16	17	17	16	19	14	18	13	6	8	6	8	7	7	7	7
MN	5	3	5	3	6	2	6	2	-	2	2	-	1	1	1	1
IA	2	4	2	4	2	4	1	4	1	1	1	1	1	1	1	1
MO	5	4	5	4	6	3	6	3	-	2	-	2	-	2	-	2
ND	1	-	1	-	1	-	1	-	2	-	2	-	2	-	2	-
SD	1	-	1	-	1	-	1	-	1	1	1	1	1	1	1	1
NE	-	3	1	2	1	2	1	2	2	-	2	-	2	-	2	-
KS	2	3	2	3	2	3	2	2	-	2	-	2	-	2	-	2
South	96	46	95	46	95	47	91	57	23	9	22	10	22	10	19	13
S.A.	48	21	47	22	45	24	42	33	11	5	11	5	11	5	9	7
DE	1	-	1	-	1	-	-	1	1	1	1	1	1	1	1	1
MD	6	2	6	2	5	3	4	4	2	-	2	-	2	-	2	-
VA	5	5	5	5	6	4	7	4	-	2	1	1	1	1	1	1
WV	4	-	4	-	4	-	3	-	2	-	2	-	2	-	2	-
NC	8	3	8	3	7	4	8	4	1	1	1	1	1	1	-	2
SC	4	2	4	2	4	2	3	3	1	1	1	1	1	1	1	1
GA	8	2	9	1	9	1	7	4	2	-	2	-	2	-	1	1
FL	12	7	10	9	9	10	10	13	2	-	1	1	1	1	1	1
E.S.C	19	9	18	9	20	8	19	8	6	2	5	3	5	3	5	3
KY	4	3	4	3	4	3	4	2	1	1	1	1	1	1	1	1
TN	6	3	6	3	6	3	6	3	2	-	2	-	2	-	2	-
AL	5	2	4	2	5	2	4	3	2	-	2	-	2	-	2	-
MS	4	1	4	1	5	-	5	-	1	1	-	2	-	2	-	2
W.S.C	29	16	30	15	30	15	30	16	6	2	6	2	6	2	5	3
AR	3	1	3	1	3	1	2	2	2	-	2	-	2	-	2	-
LA	5	3	4	4	4	4	4	3	2	-	2	-	2	-	2	-
OK	4	2	4	2	4	2	3	3	1	1	1	1	1	1	1	1
TX	17	10	19	8	19	8	21	9	1	1	1	1	1	1	-	2
West	45	40	45	40	48	37	55	38	10	16	10	16	10	16	11	15
Mountain	9	15	9	15	11	13	11	13	6	10	6	10	6	10	6	10
MT	1	1	1	1	1	1	1	-	2	-	1	1	1	1	1	1
ID	1	1	1	1	2	-	1	1	-	2	-	2	-	2	-	2
WY	-	1	-	1	-	1	-	1	-	2	-	2	-	2	-	2
CO	3	3	3	3	3	3	2	4	1	1	1	1	1	1	1	1
NM	1	2	1	2	1	2	1	2	1	1	1	1	1	1	1	1
AZ	1	4	1	4	1	4	3	3	1	1	1	1	1	1	1	1
UT	1	2	1	2	2	1	2	1	-	2	-	2	-	2	-	2
NV	1	1	1	1	1	1	1	1	1	1	2	-	2	-	2	-
Pacific	36	25	36	25	37	24	44	25	4	6	4	6	4	6	5	5
WA	5	3	5	3	5	3	8	1	1	1	1	1	1	1	1	1
OR	3	2	3	2	4	1	4	1	-	2	-	2	-	2	-	2
CA	27	18	27	18	26	19	30	22	1	1	1	1	1	1	2	-
AK	-	1	-	1	-	1	-	1	-	2	-	2	-	2	-	2
HI	1	1	1	1	2	-	2	-	2	-	2	-	2	-	2	-

- Represents zero. [1] Indiana had one vacancy. [2] Alabama had one vacancy. [3] Vermont had one Independent-Socialist Representative. [4] As of beginning of second session (January 25th). [5] Oklahoma had one vacancy.

Source: U.S. Congress, Joint Committee on Printing, *Congressional Directory*, biennial; and unpublished data.

No. 436. Members of Congress—Incumbents Re-elected: 1970 to 1992

ITEM	PRESIDENTIAL-YEAR ELECTIONS						MIDTERM ELECTIONS					
	1972	1976	1980	1984	1988	1992	1970	1974	1978	1982	1986	1990
REPRESENTATIVES:												
Incumbent candidates......	390	384	398	412	409	368	401	391	382	393	394	407
Re-elected............	365	368	361	393	402	325	379	343	358	354	385	391
Percent of candidates...	93.6	95.8	90.7	95.4	98.3	88.3	94.5	87.7	93.7	90.1	97.7	96.1
Defeated: In primaries	12	3	6	3	1	[1]19	10	8	5	[1]10	3	1
In general elections	13	13	31	16	6	[2]24	12	40	19	29	6	15
SENATORS:												
Incumbent candidates......	27	25	29	29	27	28	31	27	25	30	28	32
Re-elected............	20	16	16	26	23	23	24	23	15	28	21	31
Percent of candidates...	74.1	64.0	55.2	89.7	85.2	82.1	77.4	85.2	60.0	93.3	75.0	96.9
Defeated: In primaries	2	-	4	-	-	1	1	2	3	-	-	-
In general elections	5	9	9	3	4	4	6	2	7	2	7	1

- Represents zero.   [1] Number of incumbents defeated in primaries by other incumbents due to redistricting: six in 1982 and four in 1992.   [2] Five incumbents defeated in general election by other incumbents due to redistricting.

Source: Ornstein, Norman J., Thomas E. Mann, and Michael J. Malbin, *Vital Statistics on Congress, 1993-1994*, Congressional Quarterly, Inc., Washington, DC, 1994 and Congressional Quarterly, Inc., Washington, DC, *Congressional Quarterly Weekly Report*, vol. 50, No. 44, Nov. 7, 1992, and selected prior issues, (copyright).

No. 437. Members of Congress—Selected Characteristics: 1981 to 1993

[As of beginning of first session of each Congress, (January 3). Figures for Representatives exclude vacancies]

MEMBERS OF CONGRESS AND YEAR	Male	Female	Black[1]	Hispanic[2]	AGE[3] (in years)						SENIORITY[4]				
					Under 40	40 to 49	50 to 59	60 to 69	70 to 79	80 and over	Less than 2 years	2 to 9 years	10 to 19 years	20 to 29 years	30 years or more
REPRESENTATIVES															
97th Cong., 1981 ...	416	19	17	6	94	142	132	54	12	1	77	231	96	23	8
98th Cong., 1983 ...	413	21	21	8	86	145	132	57	13	1	83	224	88	28	11
99th Cong., 1985 ...	412	22	20	10	71	154	131	59	17	2	49	237	104	34	10
100th Cong., 1987 ..	412	23	23	11	63	153	137	56	24	2	51	221	114	37	12
101st Cong., 1989 ..	408	25	24	10	41	163	133	74	20	2	39	207	139	35	13
102d Cong., 1991.. .	407	28	25	11	39	152	134	86	20	4	55	178	147	44	11
103d Cong., 1993 [5] .	388	47	38	17	47	151	128	89	12	3	118	141	132	32	12
SENATORS															
97th Cong., 1981 ...	98	2	-	-	9	35	36	14	6	-	19	51	17	11	2
98th Cong., 1983 ...	98	2	-	-	7	28	39	20	3	3	5	61	21	10	3
99th Cong., 1985 ...	98	2	-	-	4	27	38	25	4	2	8	56	27	7	2
100th Cong., 1987 ..	98	2	-	-	5	30	36	22	5	2	14	41	36	7	2
101st Cong., 1989 ..	98	2	-	-	-	30	40	22	6	2	23	22	43	10	2
102d Cong., 1991.. .	98	2	-	-	-	23	46	24	5	2	5	34	47	10	4
103d Cong., 1993 [5] .	93	7	1	1	1	16	48	22	11	1	15	30	39	11	5

- Represents zero.   [1] Source: Joint Center for Political and Economic Studies, Washington, DC, *Black Elected Officials: A National Roster*, annual (copyright).   [2] Source: National Association of Latino Elected and Appointed Officials, Washington, DC, *National Roster of Hispanic Elected Officials*, annual.   [3] Some members do not provide date of birth.   [4] Represents consecutive years of service.   [5] Includes members elected to fill vacant seats through June 14, 1993.

Source: Except as noted, compiled by U.S. Bureau of the Census from data published in *Congressional Directory*, biennial.

No. 438. Congressional Staff, by Location of Employment: 1970 to 1991

[Excludes those persons employed in Congressional support agencies such as the U.S. General Accounting Office, the Library of Congress, and the Congressional Budget Office]

YEAR	PERSONAL STAFF House	PERSONAL STAFF Senate	YEAR	STANDING COMMITTEE STAFF House	STANDING COMMITTEE STAFF Senate	LOCATION OF EMPLOYMENT	1981	1985	1989	1990	1991
1972 ..	5,280	2,426	1970..	702	635	Total	17,422	18,136	17,306	17,625	17,821
1978 ..	6,944	3,268	1978..	1,844	1,151						
1979 ..	7,067	3,593	1979..	1,909	1,269	House of Representatives...	11,217	11,636	11,184	11,064	11,041
1980 ..	7,371	3,746	1980..	1,917	1,191	Committee staff [2].......	1,917	2,146	2,267	2,173	2,321
1981 ..	7,487	3,945	1981..	1,843	1,022	Personal staff	7,487	7,528	7,569	7,496	7,278
1982 ..	7,511	4,041	1982..	1,839	1,047	Leadership staff........	127	144	133	156	149
1983 ..	7,606	4,059	1983..	1,970	1,075	Officers of House, staff ...	1,686	1,818	1,215	1,239	1,293
1984 ..	7,385	3,949	1984..	1,944	1,095						
1985 ..	7,528	4,097	1985..	2,009	1,080	Senate	6,079	6,369	5,984	6,425	6,635
1986 ..	[1]7,920	[1]3,774	1986..	1,954	1,075	Committee staff [2].......	1,150	1,178	1,116	1,207	1,154
1987 ..	7,584	4,075	1987..	2,024	1,074	Personal staff	3,945	4,097	3,837	4,162	4,294
			1988..	1,976	970	Leadership staff	106	118	105	94	95
1989 ..	7,569	3,837	1989..	1,986	1,013	Officers of Senate, staff ..	878	976	926	962	1,092
1990 ..	7,496	4,162	1990..	1,993	1,090						
1991 ..	7,278	4,294	1991..	2,201		Joint committee staff	126	131	138	136	145

[1] House figure is average for year, and Senate figure only covers period following implementation of Gramm-Rudman budget reductions.   [2] Covers standing, select, and special committees.

Source: Ornstein, Norman J., Thomas E. Mann, and Michael J. Malbin, *Vital Statistics on Congress, 1993-1994*, Congressional Quarterly, Inc., Washington, DC, 1994, (copyright).

No. 439. Number of Governors, by Political Party Affiliation: 1970 to 1994

[Reflects results of elections in previous year and holdover incumbents]

YEAR	Demo-cratic	Re-pub-lican	Inde-pen-dent	YEAR	Demo-cratic	Re-pub-lican	Inde-pen-dent	YEAR	Demo-cratic	Re-pub-lican	Inde-pen-dent
1970......	18	32	-	1985......	34	16	-	1990......	29	21	-
1975......	36	13	1	1986......	34	16	-	1991[1].....	28	20	2
1980......	31	19	-	1987......	26	24	-	1992......	27	21	2
1983......	34	16	-	1988......	27	23	-	1993......	30	18	2
1984......	35	15	-	1989......	28	22	-	1994......	28	20	2

- Represents zero.   [1] Reflects result of runoff election in Arizona in February 1991.
Source: National Governors' Association, Washington, DC, *Directory of Governors of the American States, Commonwealths & Territories*, annual, (copyright).

No. 440. Vote Cast for and Governor Elected, by State: 1986 to 1992

[In thousands, except percent. D=Democratic, R=Republican, I=Independent]

DIVISION AND STATE	1986		1988		1990		1992		Candidate elected at most recent election
	Total vote [1]	Percent leading party	Total vote [1]	Percent leading party	Total vote [1]	Percent leading party	Total vote [1]	Percent leading party	
N.E.:									
ME.........	427	R-39.9	(X)	(X)	522	R-46.7	(X)	(X)	John R. McKernan Jr.
NH........	251	R-53.7	442	R-60.4	295	R-60.3	516	R-56.0	Steve Merrill
VT........	197	D-47.0	243	D-55.4	211	R-51.8	286	D-74.7	Howard B. Dean
MA........	1,684	D-68.7	(X)	(X)	2,343	R-50.2	(X)	(X)	William F. Weld
RI.........	323	R-64.7	401	R-50.8	357	D-74.1	425	D-61.5	Bruce G. Sundlun
CT........	994	D-57.9	(X)	(X)	1,141	I-40.4	(X)	(X)	Lowell P. Weicker Jr.
M.A.:									
NY........	4,294	D-64.6	(X)	(X)	4,057	D-53.2	(X)	(X)	Mario M. Cuomo
NJ [2].....	1,973	R-69.6	(X)	(X)	2,254	D-61.2	2,506	R-49.3	Christine T. Whitman
PA........	3,388	D-50.7	(X)	(X)	3,053	D-67.7	(X)	(X)	Robert P. Casey
E.N.C.:									
OH........	3,067	D-60.6	(X)	(X)	3,478	R-55.7	(X)	(X)	George V. Voinovich
IN.........	(X)	(X)	2,141	D-53.2	(X)	(X)	2,229	D-62.0	Evan Bayh
IL.........	3,144	R-52.7	(X)	(X)	3,257	R-50.7	(X)	(X)	Jim Edgar
MI.........	2,397	D-68.1	(X)	(X)	2,565	R-49.8	(X)	(X)	John Engler
WI........	1,527	R-52.7	(X)	(X)	1,380	R-58.2	(X)	(X)	Tommy G. Thompson
W.N.C.:									
MN........	1,416	D-55.8	(X)	(X)	1,807	R-49.6	(X)	(X)	Arne Carlson
IA.........	911	R-51.9	(X)	(X)	976	R-60.6	(X)	(X)	Terry E. Branstad
MO........	(X)	(X)	2,086	R-64.2	(X)	(X)	2,344	D-58.7	Mel Carnahan
ND........	(X)	(X)	299	D-59.9	(X)	(X)	305	R-57.9	Edward T. Schafer
SD........	294	R-51.8	(X)	(X)	257	R-58.9	(X)	(X)	George S. Mickelson
NE........	564	R-52.9	(X)	(X)	587	D-49.9	(X)	(X)	Ben Nelson
KS........	841	R-51.9	(X)	(X)	783	D-48.6	(X)	(X)	Joan Finney
S.A.:									
DE........	(X)	(X)	240	R-70.7	(X)	(X)	277	D-64.7	Thomas R. Carper
MD........	1,101	D-82.4	(X)	(X)	1,111	D-59.8	(X)	(X)	William Donald Schaefer
VA [2].....	1,343	D-55.2	(X)	(X)	1,789	D-50.1	1,794	R-58.3	George F. Allen
WV........	(X)	(X)	650	D-58.9	(X)	(X)	657	D-56.0	Gaston Caperton
NC........	(X)	(X)	2,180	R-56.1	(X)	(X)	2,595	D-52.7	James B. Hunt
SC........	754	R-51.0	(X)	(X)	761	R-69.5	(X)	(X)	Carroll A. Campbell Jr.
GA........	1,175	D-70.5	(X)	(X)	1,450	D-52.9	(X)	(X)	Zell Miller
FL.........	3,386	R-54.6	(X)	(X)	3,531	D-56.5	(X)	(X)	Lawton Chiles
E.S.C.:									
KY [3].....	781	D-64.6	(X)	(X)	835	D-64.7	(X)	(X)	Brereton C. Jones
TN........	1,210	D-54.2	(X)	(X)	790	D-60.8	(X)	(X)	Ned McWherter
AL [3].....	1,236	R-56.3	(X)	(X)	1,216	R-52.1	(X)	(X)	Guy Hunt
MS [3].....	722	D-53.4	(X)	(X)	711	R-50.8	(X)	(X)	Kirk Fordice
W.S.C.:									
AR........	689	D-63.9	(X)	(X)	696	D-57.5	(X)	(X)	Jim Guy Tucker [4]
LA........	[5]1,559	[5]33.1	(X)	(X)	[6]1,728	[6]D-61.2	(X)	(X)	Edwin W. Edwards
OK........	910	R-47.5	(X)	(X)	911	D-57.4	(X)	(X)	David Walters
TX........	3,441	R-52.7	(X)	(X)	3,893	D-49.5	(X)	(X)	Ann W. Richards
Mountain:									
MT........	(X)	(X)	367	R-51.9	(X)	(X)	408	R-51.3	Marc Racicot
ID.........	387	D-49.9	(X)	(X)	321	D-68.2	(X)	(X)	Cecil D. Andrus
WY........	165	D-54.0	(X)	(X)	160	D-65.4	(X)	(X)	Mike Sullivan
CO........	1,059	D-58.2	(X)	(X)	1,011	D-61.9	(X)	(X)	Roy Romer
NM........	395	R-53.0	(X)	(X)	411	D-54.6	(X)	(X)	Bruce King
AZ........	867	R-39.7	(X)	(X)	[7]941	[7]R-52.4	(X)	(X)	Fife Symington
UT........	(X)	(X)	649	R-40.1	(X)	(X)	763	R-42.2	Mike Leavitt
NV........	260	D-71.9	(X)	(X)	321	D-64.8	(X)	(X)	Robert J. Miller
Pacific:									
WA........	(X)	(X)	1,875	D-62.2	(X)	(X)	2,271	D-52.2	Mike Lowry
OR........	1,060	D-51.9	(X)	(X)	1,113	D-45.7	(X)	(X)	Barbara Roberts
CA........	7,444	R-60.5	(X)	(X)	7,699	R-49.2	(X)	(X)	Pete Wilson
AK........	180	D-47.3	(X)	(X)	195	I-38.9	(X)	(X)	Walter J. Hickel
HI.........	334	D-52.0	(X)	(X)	340	D-59.8	(X)	(X)	John Waihee III

X Not applicable.   [1] Includes minor party and scattered votes.   [2] Voting years 1985, 1989, and 1993.   [3] Voting years 1987 and 1991.   [4] Jim Guy Tucker assumed the governorship upon the resignation of Bill Clinton following the 1992 presidential election.   [5] Primary election in Oct. 1987, held on a nonparty basis. Winner was Democratic. Runner-up withdrew from runoff.   [6] Result of runoff election in 1991.   [7] Result of runoff election in February 1991.
Source: Elections Research Center, Chevy Chase, MD, *America Votes*, biennial, and unpublished data, (copyright).

No. 441. Composition of State Legislatures, by Political Party Affiliation: 1986 to 1992

[Data reflect election results in year shown for most States; and except as noted, results in previous year for other States. Figures reflect immediate results of elections, including holdover members in State houses which do not have all of their members running for re-election. Dem.=Democrat, Rep.=Republican. In general, Lower House refers to body consisting of State Representatives; Upper House, of State Senators]

STATE	LOWER HOUSE								UPPER HOUSE							
	1986 [1][2]		1988 [3][4]		1990 [5][6]		1992 [7][8]		1986 [1][9]		1988 [3][10]		1990 [5][11]		1992 [7][12]	
	Dem.	Rep.	Dem.	Rep.	Dem.	Rep.	Dem.	Rep.	Dem.	Rep.	Dem.	Rep.	Dem.	Rep.	Dem.	Rep.
U.S.	3,294	2,164	3,277	2,176	3,242	2,202	3,186	2,223	1,177	762	1,192	751	1,186	757	1,132	799
AL [13]	89	16	85	17	82	23	82	23	30	5	28	6	28	7	27	8
AK [14]	24	16	23	17	23	17	20	18	8	12	8	12	10	10	10	10
AZ [15]	24	36	26	34	27	33	25	35	11	19	13	17	17	13	12	18
AR [14]	91	9	88	11	90	9	88	11	31	4	31	4	31	4	30	5
CA [14]	44	36	46	33	47	33	47	33	23	15	24	15	25	13	21	16
CO [14]	25	40	26	39	27	38	31	34	10	25	11	24	12	23	16	19
CT [15]	92	59	88	63	87	64	85	64	25	11	23	13	20	16	19	17
DE [14]	19	22	18	23	17	24	18	23	13	8	13	8	15	6	15	6
FL [14]	75	45	73	47	74	46	71	49	25	15	23	17	22	18	20	20
GA [15]	153	27	144	36	145	35	128	51	46	10	45	11	45	11	41	15
HI [14]	40	10	45	6	45	6	47	4	20	5	22	3	22	3	22	3
ID [15]	20	64	20	64	28	56	20	50	16	26	19	23	21	21	12	23
IL [14]	67	51	67	51	72	46	67	51	31	28	31	28	31	28	27	32
IN [14]	48	52	50	50	52	48	55	45	19	30	24	26	24	26	22	28
IA [14]	58	42	61	39	55	45	49	51	30	20	30	20	29	21	27	23
KS [14]	51	74	58	67	63	62	59	66	16	24	18	22	18	22	13	27
KY [14]	71	29	72	28	68	32	71	29	29	9	30	8	27	11	25	13
LA [13]	87	15	86	17	89	16	88	16	34	5	34	5	34	5	33	6
ME [15]	86	65	97	54	97	54	93	58	20	15	20	15	21	14	20	15
MD [13]	124	17	125	16	116	25	116	25	40	7	40	7	38	9	38	9
MA [15]	127	33	128	32	118	37	123	34	32	8	32	8	25	15	31	9
MI [14]	64	46	61	49	61	49	55	55	18	20	18	20	18	20	16	22
MN [14]	83	51	80	53	78	56	85	49	47	20	44	23	46	21	45	22
MS [13]	113	9	112	9	98	23	91	29	45	7	44	8	43	9	37	15
MO [14]	111	52	104	58	99	64	98	65	21	13	22	12	23	11	20	14
MT [14]	49	51	52	48	61	39	47	53	25	25	23	27	29	21	30	20
NE.	(16)	(16)	(16)	(16)	(16)	(16)	(16)	(16)	(16)	(16)	(16)	(16)	(16)	(16)	(16)	(16)
NV [14]	29	13	30	12	22	19	27	12	9	12	8	13	10	10	10	11
NH [15]	132	268	119	281	125	268	136	258	8	16	8	16	11	13	11	13
NJ [14]	39	41	44	36	22	58	27	53	24	16	22	17	13	27	16	24
NM [14]	47	23	45	25	49	21	53	17	21	21	26	16	26	16	27	15
NY [15]	92	56	92	58	95	55	100	50	25	36	27	34	26	35	26	35
NC [15]	84	36	74	46	81	39	78	42	40	10	37	13	36	14	39	11
ND [14]	45	61	45	61	48	58	33	65	27	26	32	21	27	26	25	24
OH [14]	60	39	59	40	61	38	53	46	15	18	14	19	12	21	13	20
OK [14]	70	31	68	32	68	33	70	31	30	17	33	15	37	11	37	11
OR [14]	31	29	32	28	28	32	28	32	17	13	19	11	20	10	16	14
PA [14]	103	100	104	99	107	94	105	98	23	26	23	27	24	26	24	25
RI [15]	80	20	83	17	89	11	85	15	38	12	41	9	45	5	39	11
SC [14]	92	32	87	37	79	43	71	52	36	10	35	11	33	13	30	16
SD [15]	22	48	24	46	25	45	28	42	11	24	15	20	17	18	20	15
TN [14]	61	38	59	40	57	42	63	36	23	10	22	11	20	13	19	14
TX [14]	94	56	93	57	93	57	91	58	25	6	23	8	22	9	18	13
UT [14]	27	48	28	47	31	44	26	49	8	21	7	22	10	19	11	18
VT [15]	74	75	74	76	73	75	87	57	19	11	16	14	15	15	14	16
VA [14]	64	35	59	39	58	41	52	47	30	10	30	10	22	18	22	18
WA [14]	61	37	63	35	58	40	65	33	25	24	24	25	24	25	28	21
WV [14]	78	22	81	19	74	26	79	21	27	7	29	5	33	1	32	2
WI [14]	54	45	56	43	58	41	51	47	20	11	20	13	19	14	16	17
WY [14]	20	44	23	41	22	42	19	41	11	19	11	19	10	20	10	20

[1] Status as of Jan. 1, 1987, except for KY, LA, MS, NJ, and VA which are as of Jan. 1988 and reflect elections held in 1987. [2] Excludes one Independent each for VT and VA; two Liberals for NY; one vacancy each for HI and KY; and three vacancies for LA. [3] Status as of Jan. 1989, except for NJ and VA which are as of Jan. 1990. [4] Excludes one Independent for AR; two Independents for VA; one Independent Democrat for MS; one vacancy each for CA, MN, MO, and OK; two vacancies for LA; and three vacancies for AL. [5] Status as of May 1992; reflects results of elections held in LA, KY, MS, and NJ in 1991. [6] Excludes one Independent each for MA, MS, NH, SC, and VA; one Independent Democrat for NH; two Independents for VT; one vacancy each for AR, NV, and SC; two vacancies for PA; four vacancies for MA; and five vacancies for NH. [7] Status as of November 11, 1993. [8] Excludes one Independent each for AR, LA, NH, SC, and VA; two Independents for VT; members of political parties other than Democratic, Republican, or Independent (one in MA, two in VT, and four in NH); one vacancy each for GA, NH, TX, and WI; two vacancies each for CT and MA; and three vacancies for NV. [9] Excludes one Independent for CA; one vacancy each for CA, IN, OK, and PA; and two vacancies for WI. [10] Excludes one Independent for CA and one vacancy each for AK and MS. [11] Excludes two Independents for CA; and one vacancy for NV. [12] Excludes two Independents for CA; and one vacancy each for CA and PA. [13] Members of both houses serve 4-year terms. [14] Upper House members serve 4-year terms and Lower House members serve 2-year terms. [15] Members of both houses serve 2-year terms. [16] Single chamber (unicameral body) of 49 members, elected without party designation.

Source: 1986-90, The Council of State Governments, Lexington, KY, *State Elective Officials and the Legislatures*, biennial (copyright); 1992, National Conference of State Legislatures, Denver, CO, unpublished data, (copyright).

No. 442. Political Party Control of State Legislatures, by Party: 1961 to 1994

[As of beginning of year. Until 1972 there were two nonpartisan legislatures in Minnesota and Nebraska. Since then only Nebraska has had a nonpartisan legislature]

YEAR	LEGISLATURES UNDER—			YEAR	LEGISLATURES UNDER—			YEAR	LEGISLATURES UNDER—		
	Democratic control	Split control or tie	Republican control		Democratic control	Split control or tie	Republican control		Democratic control	Split control or tie	Republican control
1961...	27	6	15	1973...	27	6	16	1985...	27	11	11
1963...	25	7	16	1975...	37	7	5	1987...	28	12	9
1965...	32	10	6	1977...	36	8	5	1989 [2] .	28	13	8
1967...	24	8	16	1979...	30	7	12	1990...	29	11	9
1969...	20	8	20	1981...	28	6	15	1992...	29	14	6
1971...	23	9	16	1983 [1] .	34	4	11	1994...	25	16	8

[1] Two 1984 midterm recall elections resulted in a change in control of the Michigan State Senate. At the time of the 1984 election, therefore, Democrats controlled 33 legislatures. [2] A party change during the year by a Democratic representative broke the tie in the Indiana House of Representatives, giving the Republicans control of both chambers.

Source: National Conference of State Legislatures, Denver, CO, *State Legislatures*, periodic.

No. 443. Black Elected Officials, by Office, 1970 to 1993, and by Region and State, 1993

[As of January 1993, no Black elected officials had been identified in Hawaii, Idaho, Montana, North Dakota, or Utah]

REGION, DIVISION, AND STATE	Total	U.S. and State legislatures [1]	City and county offices [2]	Law enforcement [3]	Education [4]	REGION, DIVISION, AND STATE	Total	U.S. and State legislatures [1]	City and county offices [2]	Law enforcement [3]	Education [4]
1970 (Feb.)..	1,469	179	715	213	362	IA.....	11	1	6	1	3
1975 (Apr.)..	3,503	299	1,878	387	939	MO....	185	18	134	14	19
1980 (July)..	4,890	326	2,832	526	1,206	SD....	3	1	2	-	-
1981 (July)..	5,014	343	2,863	549	1,259	NE....	6	1	2	-	3
1982 (July)..	5,115	342	2,951	563	1,259	KS....	21	6	7	3	5
1983 (July)..	5,559	386	3,197	607	1,369	**South**	**5,492**	**328**	**3,675**	**518**	**971**
1984 (Jan.)..	5,654	396	3,259	636	1,363	**S.A.**	**2,200**	**173**	**1,522**	**147**	**358**
1985 (Jan.)..	6,016	407	3,517	661	1,431	DE....	23	3	14	-	6
1986 (Jan.)..	6,384	410	3,800	676	1,498	MD....	140	32	79	23	6
1987 (Jan.)..	6,646	428	3,949	728	1,541	DC....	198	[5]4	185	-	9
1988 (Jan.)..	6,793	424	4,089	738	1,542	VA....	155	14	126	15	-
1989 (Jan.)..	7,191	437	4,392	760	1,602	WV....	21	1	17	3	-
1990 (Jan.)..	7,335	436	4,485	769	1,645	NC....	468	28	328	31	81
1991 (Jan.)..	7,445	473	4,496	847	1,629	SC....	450	26	269	15	140
1992 (Jan.)..	7,517	499	4,557	847	1,614	GA....	545	43	371	32	99
1993 (Jan.)..	7,984	561	4,819	922	1,682	FL....	200	22	133	28	17
						E.S.C. ...	**1,681**	**85**	**1,175**	**175**	**246**
Northeast ..	**777**	**96**	**291**	**126**	**264**	KY....	63	4	47	5	7
N.E.	**109**	**35**	**60**	**4**	**10**	TN....	168	16	104	24	24
ME....	1	-	1	-	-	AL....	699	23	529	58	89
NH....	2	2	-	-	-	MS....	751	42	495	88	126
VT....	2	2	-	-	-	**W.S.C.** ...	**1,611**	**70**	**978**	**196**	**367**
MA....	30	8	18	2	2	AR....	380	13	214	51	102
RI....	12	9	3	-	-	LA....	636	33	346	104	153
CT....	62	14	38	2	8	OK....	123	6	95	1	21
M.A.	**668**	**61**	**231**	**122**	**254**	TX....	472	18	323	40	91
NY....	299	30	63	70	136	**West**......	**354**	**31**	**96**	**107**	**120**
NJ....	211	13	113	-	85	**Mountain** .	**49**	**11**	**11**	**16**	**11**
PA....	158	18	55	52	33	WY....	1	-	-	-	1
Midwest ...	**1,361**	**106**	**757**	**171**	**327**	CO....	20	4	4	10	2
E.N.C	**1,119**	**78**	**604**	**143**	**294**	NM....	3	-	-	2	1
OH....	219	16	124	30	49	AZ....	15	4	3	3	5
IN....	72	12	50	4	6	NV....	10	3	4	1	2
IL....	465	25	282	37	121	**Pacific** ...	**305**	**20**	**85**	**91**	**109**
MI....	333	17	133	68	115	WA....	19	2	9	5	3
WI....	30	8	15	4	3	OR....	10	4	2	4	-
W.N.C ...	**242**	**28**	**153**	**28**	**33**	CA....	273	13	72	82	106
MN....	16	1	2	10	3	AK....	3	1	2	-	-

- Represents zero. [1] Includes elected State administrators. [2] County commissioners and councilmen, mayors, vice mayors, aldermen, regional officials, and other. [3] Judges, magistrates, constables, marshals, sheriffs, justices of the peace, and other. [4] Members of State education agencies, college boards, school boards, and other. [5] Includes two shadow senators and one shadow representative.

Source: Joint Center for Political and Economic Studies, Washington, DC, *Black Elected Officials: A National Roster*, annual, (copyright).

No. 444. Hispanic Public Officials, by Office, 1985 to 1993, and by State, 1993

[As of **September**. For States not shown, no Hispanic public officials had been identified]

REGION, DIVISION, AND STATE	Total	State executives and legislators [1]	County and municipal officials	Judicial and law enforcement	Education and school boards	REGION, DIVISION, AND STATE	Total	State executives and legislators [1]	County and municipal officials	Judicial and law enforcement	Education and school boards
1985	3,147	129	1,316	517	1,185	MO	1	-	1	-	-
1986	3,202	132	1,352	530	1,188	NE	3	-	2	-	1
1987	3,317	138	1,412	568	1,199	KS	6	4	1	-	1
1988	3,360	135	1,425	574	1,226	South	2,113	53	925	397	738
1989	3,783	143	1,724	575	1,341	S.A	72	15	42	12	3
1990	4,004	144	1,819	583	1,458	DE	1	-	1	-	-
1991	4,202	151	1,867	596	1,588	MD	2	-	1	-	1
1992	4,994	150	1,908	628	2,308	SC	1	-	1	-	-
1993	5,170	182	2,023	633	2,332	FL	68	15	39	12	2
						W.S.C	2,041	38	883	385	735
Northeast	168	21	43	12	92	AR	1	-	-	-	1
N.E	23	5	9	-	9	LA	9	-	1	8	-
MA	3	-	-	-	3	OK	1	-	1	-	-
RI	1	1	-	-	-	TX	2,030	38	881	377	734
CT	19	4	9	-	6	West	2,050	94	1,010	216	730
M.A	145	16	34	12	83	Mountain	1,233	75	650	164	344
NY	93	13	15	11	54	MT	2	-	-	1	1
NJ	44	2	16	-	26	ID	2	1	1	-	-
PA	8	1	3	1	3	WY	5	1	4	-	-
Midwest	839	14	45	8	772	CO	204	8	132	10	54
E.N.C	826	8	41	7	770	NM	661	52	359	102	148
OH	9	-	6	2	1	AZ	350	11	150	50	139
IN	8	1	5	1	1	UT	4	1	3	-	-
IL	797	7	22	3	[2]765	NV	5	1	1	1	2
MI	10	-	6	1	3	Pacific	817	19	360	52	386
WI	2	-	2	-	-	WA	15	3	4	1	7
W.N.C	13	6	4	1	2	OR	5	-	3	1	1
MN	3	2	1	-	1	CA	797	16	353	50	378

- Represents zero. [1] Includes U.S. Representatives. [2] Includes local school council members in the Chicago area. Source: National Association of Latino Elected and Appointed Officials, Washington, DC, *National Roster of Hispanic Elected Officials*, annual.

No. 445. Women Holding State and Local Public Offices, by Office and State: 1985 to 1993

[For data on women in U.S. Congress, see table 437]

STATE	State-wide elective executive office,[1][2] 1993	State legislature,[1] 1993	County governing boards, 1988	Mayors and municipal council members, 1985	STATE	State-wide elective executive office,[1][2] 1993	State legislature,[1] 1993	County governing boards, 1988	Mayors and municipal council members, 1985
United States	72	1,524	1,653	14,672	Missouri	2	37	17	-
Alabama	1	8	7	281	Montana	1	30	18	110
Alaska	-	13	17	233	Nebraska	[3]2	10	27	241
Arizona	2	30	8	87	Nevada	3	17	10	15
Arkansas	2	14	71	365	New Hampshire	-	142	8	113
California	2	27	56	465	New Jersey	-	15	15	451
Colorado	3	35	18	315	New Mexico	1	22	17	86
Connecticut	2	47	(X)	240	New York	-	35	131	797
Delaware	3	9	2	57	North Carolina	-	31	45	337
Dist. of Columbia	(X)	(X)	(X)	7	North Dakota	4	24	11	174
Florida	1	28	51	311	Ohio	1	28	25	1,129
Georgia	-	41	28	251	Oklahoma	[3]3	13	5	312
Hawaii	-	18	8	3	Oregon	3	25	20	344
Idaho	1	32	14	141	Pennsylvania	2	25	35	-
Illinois	1	41	152	-	Rhode Island	2	37	(X)	30
Indiana	4	29	10	-	South Carolina	1	22	36	184
Iowa	3	22	35	732	South Dakota	2	21	16	149
Kansas	2	48	24	445	Tennessee	-	16	117	144
Kentucky	1	7	17	-	Texas	[3]2	29	30	786
Louisiana	2	11	32	183	Utah	2	14	2	137
Maine	-	59	3	243	Vermont	1	61	(X)	87
Maryland	-	46	21	133	Virginia	-	17	49	211
Massachusetts	-	46	5	217	Washington	4	58	15	341
Michigan	1	30	123	2,779	West Virginia	-	22	11	202
Minnesota	2	55	37	542	Wisconsin	1	36	241	-
Mississippi	-	19	8	176	Wyoming	2	22	5	86

- Represents zero. X Not applicable. [1] As of January. [2] Excludes women elected to the judiciary, women appointed to State cabinet-level positions, women elected to executive posts by the legislature, and elected members of university Board of Trustees or board of education. [3] Includes one official who was appointed to an elective position.

Source: Center for the American Woman and Politics, Eagleton Institute of Politics, Rutgers University, New Brunswick, NJ, information releases, (copyright).

No. 446. Political Party Identification of the Adult Population, by Degree of Attachment, 1970 to 1992, and by Selected Characteristics, 1992

[In percent. Covers citizens of voting-age living in private housing units in the contiguous United States. Data are from the National Election Studies and are based on a sample and subject to sampling variability; for details, see source]

YEAR AND SELECTED CHARACTERISTIC	Total	Strong Democrat	Weak Democrat	Independent Democrat	Independent	Independent Republican	Weak Republican	Strong Republican	Apolitical
1970.	100	20	24	10	13	8	15	9	1
1972.	100	15	26	11	13	11	13	10	1
1976.	100	15	25	12	15	10	14	9	1
1980.	100	18	23	11	13	10	14	9	2
1984.	100	17	20	11	11	12	15	12	2
1986.	100	18	22	10	12	11	15	11	2
1988.	100	18	18	12	11	13	14	14	2
1990.	100	20	19	12	11	12	15	10	2
1992, total [1]	**100**	**18**	**18**	**14**	**12**	**12**	**14**	**11**	**1**
Year of birth:									
1959 or later (Under 34 years old) .	100	10	19	17	15	14	15	9	2
1943 to 1958 (34 to 49 years old)..	100	17	18	14	11	13	15	11	1
1927 to 1942 (50 to 65 years old)..	100	22	17	13	11	12	13	13	1
1911 to 1926 (66 to 81 years old)..	100	30	15	11	8	9	13	13	(Z)
1895 to 1910 (82 to 97 years old)..	100	30	14	9	10	7	11	19	(Z)
Sex:									
Male .	100	16	15	13	12	14	15	13	1
Female .	100	20	19	15	11	11	14	9	1
Race:									
White.	100	15	17	15	12	13	16	13	1
Black.	100	41	23	13	13	3	3	2	3
Education:									
Grade school .	100	35	16	14	11	4	9	9	3
High school .	100	20	19	15	13	12	12	9	2
College .	100	14	17	14	11	14	17	14	(Z)

Z Less than 0.5 percent.   [1] Includes other characteristics, not shown separately.

Source: Center for Political Studies, University of Michigan, Ann Arbor, MI, unpublished data. Data prior to 1988 published in Warren E. Miller and Santa A. Traugott, *American National Election Studies Data Sourcebook, 1952-1986*, Harvard University Press, Cambridge, MA, 1989, (copyright).

No. 447. Persons Reported Registered and Voted, by State: 1992

[See headnote, table 448]

STATE	Voting-age population (1,000)	PERCENT OF VOTING-AGE POPULATION		STATE	Voting-age population (1,000)	PERCENT OF VOTING-AGE POPULATION		STATE	Voting-age population (1,000)	PERCENT OF VOTING-AGE POPULATION	
		Registered	Voted			Registered	Voted			Registered	Voted
U.S. .	185,684	68.2	61.3	KS. ...	1,818	77.1	71.9	ND ...	444	90.8	71.1
				KY. ...	2,724	64.9	57.6	OH ...	8,060	69.6	64.3
AL. ...	3,007	77.1	63.6	LA. ...	2,972	77.0	68.6	OK ...	2,295	74.3	67.5
AK. ...	347	75.1	68.6	ME ...	938	85.4	74.1	OR ...	2,206	74.7	69.1
AZ. ...	2,671	70.5	64.7	MD ...	3,605	71.7	66.4	PA. ...	9,170	65.1	59.9
AR. ...	1,745	66.5	58.0	MA ...	4,501	72.5	65.8	RI	757	74.0	69.0
CA. ...	22,340	57.6	52.8	MI	6,811	74.6	65.9	SC. ...	2,580	67.0	58.0
CO ...	2,451	74.7	68.8	MN ...	3,237	86.1	74.2	SD. ...	500	80.1	70.2
CT. ...	2,428	76.8	71.7	MS ...	1,839	79.3	66.7	TN. ...	3,714	65.0	55.6
DE. ...	519	70.7	66.1	MO ...	3,803	74.2	66.2	TX. ...	12,267	64.9	55.6
DC. ...	398	73.9	66.1	MT ...	570	77.3	71.4	UT. ...	1,097	78.8	72.3
FL. ...	10,342	62.7	55.8	NE. ...	1,167	73.1	66.1	VT. ...	443	76.1	68.6
GA ...	4,723	62.0	54.1	NV. ...	955	63.4	58.1	VA. ...	4,585	65.4	61.2
HI ...	813	60.6	55.2	NH ...	853	69.9	64.6	WA ...	3,699	71.5	66.3
ID	726	71.8	66.9	NJ. ...	5,838	68.0	61.2	WV ...	1,367	64.9	57.3
IL	8,676	72.1	65.1	NM ...	1,079	67.1	62.0	WI ...	3,611	84.4	75.3
IN	4,183	68.0	63.0	NY. ...	13,401	62.0	56.8	WY ...	331	68.1	64.2
IA	2,100	77.9	70.8	NC ...	4,976	68.7	60.0				

Source: U.S. Bureau of the Census, *Current Population Reports*, P20-466.

No. 448. Voting-Age Population, Percent Reporting Registered, and Voted: 1978 to 1992

[As of **November**. Covers civilian noninstitutional population 18 years old and over. Includes aliens. Figures are based on Current Population Survey (see text, section 1, and Appendix III) and differ from those in table 449 based on population estimates and official vote counts]

CHARACTERISTIC	Pop 1978	Pop 1980	Pop 1982	Pop 1984	Pop 1986	Pop 1988	Pop 1990	Pop 1992	Reg-Pres 1980	Reg-Pres 1984	Reg-Pres 1988	Reg-Pres 1992	Reg-Cong 1978	Reg-Cong 1982	Reg-Cong 1986	Reg-Cong 1990	Vot-Pres 1980	Vot-Pres 1984	Vot-Pres 1988	Vot-Pres 1992	Vot-Cong 1978	Vot-Cong 1982	Vot-Cong 1986	Vot-Cong 1990
Total [1]	151.6	157.1	165.5	170.0	173.9	178.1	182.1	185.1	66.9	68.3	66.6	68.2	62.6	64.1	64.3	62.2	59.2	59.9	57.4	61.3	45.9	48.5	46.0	45.0
18 to 20 years old	12.2	12.3	12.1	11.2	10.7	10.7	10.8	9.7	44.7	47.0	44.9	48.3	34.7	35.0	35.4	35.4	35.7	36.7	33.2	38.5	20.1	19.8	18.6	18.4
21 to 24 years old	15.5	15.9	16.7	16.7	15.7	14.8	14.0	14.6	52.7	54.3	50.6	55.3	45.1	47.8	46.6	43.3	43.1	43.5	38.3	45.7	26.2	28.4	24.2	22.0
25 to 34 years old	33.4	35.7	38.8	40.3	41.9	42.7	42.7	41.6	62.0	63.3	57.8	60.6	55.5	57.1	55.8	52.0	54.6	54.5	48.0	53.2	38.0	40.4	35.1	33.8
35 to 44 years old	24.2	25.6	28.1	30.7	33.0	35.2	37.9	39.7	70.6	70.9	69.3	69.2	66.7	67.5	67.9	65.5	64.4	63.5	61.3	63.6	50.1	52.2	49.3	48.4
45 to 64 years old	43.4	43.6	44.2	44.3	44.8	45.9	46.9	49.1	75.8	76.6	75.5	75.3	74.3	75.6	74.8	71.4	69.3	69.8	67.9	70.0	58.5	62.2	58.7	55.8
65 years old and over	23.0	24.1	25.6	26.7	27.7	28.8	29.9	30.8	74.6	76.9	78.4	78.0	72.8	75.2	76.9	76.5	65.1	67.7	68.8	70.1	55.9	59.9	60.9	60.3
Male	71.5	74.1	78.0	80.3	82.4	84.5	86.6	88.6	66.6	67.3	65.2	66.9	62.6	63.7	63.4	61.2	59.1	59.0	56.4	60.2	46.6	48.7	45.8	44.6
Female	80.2	83.0	87.4	89.6	91.5	93.6	95.5	97.1	67.1	69.3	67.8	69.3	62.5	64.4	65.0	63.1	59.4	60.8	58.3	62.3	45.3	48.4	46.1	45.4
White	133.4	137.7	143.6	146.8	149.9	152.9	155.6	157.8	68.4	69.6	67.9	70.1	63.8	65.6	65.3	63.8	60.9	61.4	59.1	63.6	47.3	49.9	47.0	46.7
Black	15.6	16.4	17.6	18.4	19.0	19.7	20.4	21.0	60.0	66.3	64.5	63.9	57.1	59.1	64.0	58.8	50.5	55.8	51.5	54.0	37.2	43.0	43.2	39.2
Hispanic [2]	6.8	8.2	8.8	9.5	11.8	12.9	13.8	14.7	36.3	40.1	35.5	35.0	32.9	35.3	35.9	32.3	29.9	32.6	28.8	28.9	23.5	25.3	24.2	21.0
Region: [3]																								
Northeast	35.1	35.5	36.4	36.9	37.3	37.9	38.1	38.3	64.8	66.6	64.8	67.0	62.3	62.5	62.0	61.0	58.5	59.7	57.4	61.2	48.1	49.8	44.4	45.2
Midwest	40.3	41.5	41.9	42.7	42.8	43.3	43.9	44.4	73.8	74.6	72.5	74.6	68.2	71.1	70.7	68.0	65.8	65.7	62.9	67.2	50.5	54.7	49.5	48.6
South	48.8	50.6	55.4	57.6	59.2	60.7	62.4	63.7	64.8	66.9	65.6	67.2	60.1	61.7	63.0	61.3	55.6	56.8	54.5	59.0	39.6	41.8	43.0	42.4
West	27.5	29.5	31.9	33.4	34.6	36.2	37.7	39.3	63.3	64.7	63.0	63.6	59.1	60.6	60.8	57.7	57.2	58.5	55.6	58.5	47.5	50.7	48.4	45.0
School years completed:																								
8 years or less	23.6	22.7	22.4	20.6	19.6	19.1	17.7	15.4	53.0	53.4	47.5	43.9	53.2	52.3	50.5	44.0	42.6	42.9	36.7	35.1	34.6	35.7	32.7	27.7
High school:																								
1 to 3 years	22.3	22.5	22.3	22.1	21.4	21.1	21.0	21.0 [4]	54.6	54.9	52.8	50.4 [4]	52.9	53.3	52.4	47.9	45.6	44.4	41.3	41.2 [4]	35.1	37.7	33.8	30.9
4 years	58.4	61.2	65.2	67.8	68.6	70.0	71.5	65.3 [5]	66.4	67.3	64.6	64.9 [5]	62.0	62.9	62.9	60.0	58.9	58.7	54.7	57.5 [5]	45.3	47.1	44.1	42.2
College:																								
1 to 3 years	25.1	26.7	28.8	30.9	33.0	34.3	36.3	46.7 [6]	74.4	75.7	73.5	75.4 [6]	68.7	70.0	70.0	68.7	67.2	67.5	64.5	68.7 [6]	51.5	53.3	49.9	50.0
4 years or more	22.2	24.0	26.9	28.6	31.3	33.6	35.6	37.4 [7]	84.3	83.8	83.1	84.8 [7]	76.9	79.4	77.8	77.3	79.9	79.1	77.6	81.0 [7]	63.9	66.5	62.5	62.5
Employed	93.2	95.0	97.2	104.2	108.5	113.8	115.5	116.3	68.7	69.4	67.1	69.9	63.0	65.5	64.4	62.6	61.8	61.6	58.4	63.8	46.7	50.0	45.7	45.1
Unemployed	4.9	6.9	10.8	7.4	6.6	6.6	6.7	8.3	50.3	54.3	50.4	53.7	44.1	49.8	50.6	44.6	41.2	44.0	38.6	46.2	27.4	27.9	31.2	27.9
Not in labor force	53.5	55.2	57.5	58.4	58.8	58.5	59.9	61.1	65.8	68.1	67.2	66.8	63.4	64.3	65.4	63.4	57.0	58.9	57.3	58.7	46.2	48.7	48.2	46.7

[1] Includes other races not shown separately.   [2] Hispanic persons may be of any race.   [3] For composition of regions, see table 26.   [4] Represents those who completed 9th to 12th grade, but have no high school diploma.   [5] High school graduate.   [6] Some college or associate degree.   [7] Bachelor's or advanced degree.

Source: U.S. Bureau of the Census, *Current Population Reports*, P20-466, and earlier reports.

No. 449. Participation in Elections for President and U.S. Representatives: 1932 to 1992

[As of **November.** Estimated resident population 21 years old and over, 1932-70, except as noted, and 18 years old and over thereafter; includes Armed Forces. Prior to 1960, excludes Alaska and Hawaii. District of Columbia is included in votes cast for President beginning 1964 and in votes cast for Representative beginning 1972]

YEAR	Resident population (incl. aliens) of voting age [1] (1,000)	VOTES CAST				YEAR	Resident population (incl. aliens) of voting age [1] (1,000)	VOTES CAST			
		For President [2] (1,000)	Percent of voting-age population	For U.S. Representatives (1,000)	Percent of voting-age population			For President [2] (1,000)	Percent of voting-age population	For U.S. Representatives (1,000)	Percent of voting-age population
1932 . . .	75,768	39,758	52.5	37,657	49.7	1964 . . .	114,090	70,645	61.9	65,895	57.8
1934 . . .	77,997	(X)	(X)	32,256	41.4	1966 . . .	116,638	(X)	(X)	52,908	45.4
1936 . . .	80,174	45,654	56.9	42,886	53.5	1968 . . .	120,285	73,212	60.9	66,288	55.1
1938 . . .	82,354	(X)	(X)	36,236	44.0	1970 . . .	124,498	(X)	(X)	54,173	43.5
1940 . . .	84,728	49,900	58.9	46,951	55.4	1972 . . .	140,777	77,719	55.2	71,430	50.7
1942 . . .	86,465	(X)	(X)	28,074	32.5	1974 . . .	146,338	(X)	(X)	52,495	35.9
1944 . . .	85,654	47,977	56.0	45,103	52.7	1976 . . .	152,308	81,556	53.5	74,422	48.9
1946 . . .	92,659	(X)	(X)	34,398	37.1	1978 . . .	158,369	(X)	(X)	55,332	34.9
1948 . . .	95,573	48,794	51.1	45,933	48.1	1980 . . .	164,595	86,515	52.6	77,995	47.4
1950 . . .	98,134	(X)	(X)	40,342	41.1	1982 . . .	169,936	(X)	(X)	64,514	38.0
1952 . . .	99,929	61,551	61.6	57,571	57.6	1984 . . .	174,468	92,653	53.1	83,231	47.7
1954 . . .	102,075	(X)	(X)	42,580	41.7	1986 . . .	178,566	(X)	(X)	59,619	33.4
1956 . . .	104,515	62,027	59.3	58,426	55.9	1988 . . .	182,779	91,595	50.1	81,786	44.7
1958 . . .	106,447	(X)	(X)	45,818	43.0	1990 . . .	185,812	(X)	(X)	61,513	33.1
1960 . . .	109,672	68,838	62.8	64,133	58.5	1992 . . .	189,044	104,425	55.2	96,239	50.9
1962 . . .	112,952	(X)	(X)	51,267	45.4						

X Not applicable.   [1] Population 18 and over in Georgia, 1944-70, and in Kentucky, 1956-70; 19 and over in Alaska and 20 and over in Hawaii, 1960-70.   [2] Source: 1932-58, U.S. Congress, Clerk of the House, *Statistics of the Presidential and Congressional Election,* biennial.

Source: Except as noted, U.S. Bureau of the Census, *Current Population Reports,* P25-1085; and Elections Research Center, Chevy Chase, MD, *America Votes,* biennial, (copyright).

No. 450. Presidential Primaries—Votes Cast and Percent of Voting-Age Population Casting Votes, by Party: 1992

[For States not shown, no presidential primaries were held]

STATE	Voting age population (VAP) (1,000)	VOTES CAST IN DEMOCRATIC PRIMARY		VOTES CAST IN REPUBLICAN PRIMARY		STATE	Voting age population (VAP) (1,000)	VOTES CAST IN DEMOCRATIC PRIMARY		VOTES CAST IN REPUBLICAN PRIMARY	
		Total (1,000)	Percent of VAP	Total (1,000)	Percent of VAP			Total (1,000)	Percent of VAP	Total (1,000)	Percent of VAP
AL	3,056	451	14.8	165	5.4	NE	1,167	151	12.9	192	16.5
AR	1,768	503	28.4	52	2.9	NH	852	168	19.7	174	20.4
CA	22,668	2,864	12.6	2,156	9.5	NJ	5,943	393	6.6	310	5.2
CO	2,501	240	9.6	196	7.8	NM	1,104	181	16.4	87	7.9
CT	2,535	173	6.8	99	3.9	NY	13,609	1,008	7.4	([1])	([1])
DC	459	62	13.5	5	1.1	NC	5,217	692	13.3	284	5.4
FL	10,586	1,124	10.6	893	8.4	ND	458	33	7.2	48	10.4
GA	4,950	455	9.2	454	9.2	OH	8,146	1,042	12.8	860	10.6
ID	740	55	7.4	116	15.6	OK	2,328	416	17.9	218	9.4
IL	8,568	1,504	17.6	831	9.7	OR	2,226	354	15.9	304	13.7
IN	4,176	477	11.4	468	11.2	PA	9,129	1,265	13.9	1,009	11.1
KS	1,836	160	8.7	213	11.6	RI	776	51	6.5	16	2.0
KY	2,779	371	13.3	101	3.6	SC	2,672	116	4.4	149	5.6
LA	2,992	384	12.9	135	4.5	SD	502	60	11.9	45	8.9
MD	3,719	567	15.3	240	6.5	TN	3,783	318	8.4	246	6.5
MA	4,607	793	17.2	270	5.9	TX	12,524	1,483	11.8	797	6.4
MI	6,923	586	8.5	449	6.5	UT	1,142	32	2.8	([1])	([1])
MN	3,278	204	6.2	133	4.0	WA	3,818	148	3.9	130	3.4
MS	1,861	191	10.3	155	8.3	WV	1,350	307	22.7	124	9.2
MT	586	117	20.0	91	15.5	WI	3,669	773	21.1	482	13.1

[1] No primary held.

Source: Committee for the Study of the American Electorate, Washington, DC, unpublished data.

No. 451. Resident Population of Voting Age and Percent Casting Votes—States: 1988 to 1992, and Projections, 1994

[As of November. Estimated population, 18 years old and over. Includes Armed Forces stationed in each State, aliens, and institutional population]

REGION, DIVISION, AND STATE	VOTING-AGE POPULATION						PERCENT CASTING VOTES FOR—				
	1988 (1,000)	1990 (1,000)	1992 (1,000)	1994, proj. (1,000)			Presidential electors		U.S. Representatives		
				Total	Black	His-panic [1]	1988	1992	1988	1990	1992
U.S.	182,779	185,812	189,044	193,650	22,172	17,103	50.1	55.2	44.7	33.1	50.9
Northeast	38,590	38,838	38,824	38,849	4,303	2,826	51.4	55.6	46.1	32.9	50.0
N.E	9,950	10,137	10,143	10,017	456	420	57.6	62.6	53.5	43.9	58.3
ME	908	924	944	931	2	5	61.1	72.0	61.1	56.0	70.9
NH	817	835	852	843	3	8	55.2	63.1	52.5	34.8	60.0
VT	420	422	429	429	-	2	57.9	67.5	57.1	49.7	65.6
MA	4,565	4,646	4,607	4,564	226	208	57.7	60.2	51.9	44.1	56.7
RI	765	776	764	764	29	37	52.9	58.4	51.1	44.7	51.4
CT	2,476	2,534	2,535	2,486	196	160	58.3	63.8	54.2	40.9	56.6
M.A	28,640	28,701	28,681	28,832	3,847	2,406	49.3	53.1	43.6	29.1	47.1
NY	13,574	13,683	13,609	13,646	2,248	1,618	47.8	50.9	40.6	26.8	43.5
NJ	5,894	5,927	5,943	5,974	795	608	52.6	56.3	47.1	30.8	50.3
PA	9,171	9,091	9,129	9,212	804	180	49.5	54.3	45.8	31.4	50.3
Midwest	44,403	44,160	44,656	45,529	4,131	1,276	55.5	62.1	53.0	39.6	58.7
E.N.C	31,204	31,133	31,482	32,083	3,497	1,064	54.4	60.7	51.6	37.6	56.9
OH	8,059	8,066	8,146	8,313	845	104	54.5	60.6	51.6	42.4	56.2
IN	4,111	4,105	4,176	4,298	319	76	52.8	55.2	51.6	36.9	53.1
IL	8,636	8,495	8,568	8,712	1,219	674	52.8	58.9	50.3	36.2	56.4
MI	6,805	6,851	6,923	6,983	942	145	53.9	61.7	50.8	35.5	56.1
WI	3,593	3,616	3,669	3,777	172	65	61.0	69.0	56.6	34.7	65.1
W.N.C	13,199	13,027	13,174	13,446	634	212	58.2	65.5	56.3	44.4	63.3
MN	3,201	3,222	3,278	3,362	63	39	65.5	71.6	61.5	55.3	69.4
IA	2,125	2,061	2,075	2,112	37	25	57.7	65.3	56.0	38.4	59.9
MO	3,840	3,813	3,858	3,902	385	46	54.5	62.0	53.9	35.5	60.9
ND	484	462	458	467	2	2	61.4	67.3	62.0	50.6	65.0
SD	518	498	502	522	2	2	60.4	67.0	60.2	51.7	66.3
NE	1,183	1,152	1,167	1,192	40	29	55.9	63.2	55.5	50.9	60.9
KS	1,848	1,819	1,836	1,889	105	69	53.7	63.0	50.4	42.9	61.3
South	62,470	63,821	65,411	67,501	11,569	5,407	45.7	51.4	36.8	26.9	46.0
S.A	32,069	33,312	34,320	35,211	6,689	1,895	44.4	50.1	37.8	28.2	46.6
DE	498	507	525	534	88	11	50.2	55.2	47.2	35.0	52.6
MD	3,498	3,640	3,719	3,750	940	106	49.0	53.4	44.6	30.0	48.6
DC	472	481	459	452	281	26	40.9	49.6	36.2	33.2	42.9
VA	4,568	4,716	4,842	4,967	891	132	48.0	52.8	41.4	24.4	48.9
WV	1,398	1,349	1,350	1,389	38	9	46.7	50.6	40.7	27.8	41.7
NC	4,880	5,061	5,217	5,364	1,088	66	43.7	50.1	40.7	39.7	48.4
SC	2,531	2,587	2,672	2,740	753	26	39.0	45.0	39.2	25.9	41.7
GA	4,593	4,791	4,950	5,159	1,292	94	39.4	46.9	36.4	29.1	44.7
FL	9,632	10,180	10,586	10,856	1,318	1,425	44.7	50.2	[2]31.6	[2]23.4	[2]46.4
E.S.C	11,254	11,252	11,479	11,813	2,091	76	46.8	53.5	41.0	25.5	49.3
KY	2,752	2,740	2,779	2,857	194	16	48.1	53.7	40.2	27.9	49.0
TN	3,660	3,685	3,783	3,913	567	28	44.7	52.4	38.5	19.5	45.6
AL	2,997	2,995	3,056	3,138	721	19	46.0	55.2	39.3	34.0	52.4
MS	1,845	1,832	1,861	1,905	609	13	50.5	52.8	49.8	20.1	51.9
W.S.C	19,148	19,257	19,612	20,477	2,789	3,436	47.3	52.4	32.6	25.5	43.2
AR	1,750	1,737	1,768	1,817	247	18	47.3	53.8	[2]34.6	[3]8.3	50.3
LA	3,112	2,988	2,992	3,100	882	77	52.3	59.8	[3]6.6	[3]3.5	[3]22.8
OK	2,366	2,310	2,328	2,394	161	62	49.5	59.7	[2]32.4	37.1	54.8
TX	11,919	12,222	12,524	13,166	1,499	3,279	45.5	49.1	39.2	26.8	44.9
West	37,316	38,993	40,153	41,771	2,169	7,594	49.6	53.5	46.8	36.0	51.0
Mountain	9,548	9,856	10,157	10,906	287	1,519	52.5	58.8	50.2	39.3	56.5
MT	586	579	586	623	1	8	62.4	70.1	62.3	54.8	68.9
ID	703	707	740	803	2	41	58.2	65.2	57.9	44.5	63.9
WY	339	319	322	343	2	20	52.1	62.3	52.5	49.5	61.2
CO	2,440	2,447	2,501	2,713	106	321	56.2	62.7	53.9	40.9	59.1
NM	1,065	1,075	1,104	1,167	21	434	48.9	51.6	42.2	33.4	50.3
AZ	2,543	2,696	2,749	2,923	80	513	46.1	54.1	44.2	35.8	51.3
UT	1,067	1,104	1,142	1,246	9	60	60.6	65.1	57.1	40.1	63.7
NV	804	929	1,013	1,088	66	122	43.5	50.0	42.8	33.7	48.6
Pacific	27,768	29,137	29,996	30,865	1,882	6,075	48.6	51.7	45.6	35.0	49.2
WA	3,491	3,650	3,818	4,000	108	170	53.4	59.9	49.6	36.0	58.2
OR	2,096	2,140	2,226	2,311	35	88	57.3	65.7	48.9	49.2	62.5
CA	21,006	22,124	22,668	23,225	1,701	5,740	47.1	49.1	44.7	32.9	46.5
AK	359	382	395	429	16	13	55.7	65.4	53.8	50.2	60.5
HI	815	841	889	900	22	64	43.5	41.9	41.7	40.5	40.3

- Represents or rounds to zero.   [1] Persons of Hispanic origin may be of any race.   [2] State law does not require tabulation of votes for unopposed candidates.   [3] See footnote 8, table 430.

Source: Compiled by U.S. Bureau of the Census. Population data from U.S. Bureau of the Census, *Current Population Reports*, P25-1117; votes cast from Elections Research Center, Chevy Chase, MD, *America Votes*, biennial, (copyright).

No. 452. Political Party Financial Activity, by Major Political Party: 1981 to 1992

[In millions of dollars. Covers financial activity during 2-year calendar period indicated. Some political party financial activities, such as building funds and State and local election spending, are not reported to the source. Also excludes contributions earmarked to Federal candidates through the party organizations, since some of those funds never passed through the committees' accounts]

YEAR AND TYPE OF COMMITTEE	DEMOCRATIC				REPUBLICAN			
	Receipts, net [1]	Dis- burse- ments, net [1]	Contribu- tions to candi- dates	Monies spent on behalf of party's nomi- nees [2]	Receipts, net [1]	Dis- burse- ments, net [1]	Contribu- tions to candi- dates	Monies spent on behalf of party's nomi- nees [2]
1981-82...............	39.3	40.1	1.7	3.3	215.0	214.0	5.6	14.3
1983-84...............	98.5	97.4	2.6	9.0	297.9	300.8	4.9	20.1
1985-86...............	64.8	65.9	1.7	9.0	255.2	258.9	3.4	14.3
1987-88, total	135.2	129.1	1.8	17.9	267.1	261.0	3.4	22.7
National committee	52.3	47.0	0.1	8.1	91.0	89.9	0.3	8.3
Senatorial committee	16.3	16.3	0.4	6.2	65.9	63.3	0.8	10.2
Congressional committee	12.5	12.5	0.7	2.4	34.7	33.7	1.6	4.1
Conventions, other national..........	19.2	19.2	-	-	9.6	9.6	-	-
State and local	35.0	34.1	0.6	1.2	65.9	64.5	0.7	0.1
1989-90, total	85.8	90.9	1.5	8.7	206.3	213.5	2.9	10.7
National committee	14.5	18.5	0.1	0.1	68.7	70.4	0.3	0.1
Senatorial committee	17.5	17.6	0.4	4.5	65.1	67.6	0.7	7.7
Congressional committee	9.1	9.1	0.4	2.9	33.2	34.4	0.9	2.8
Conventions, other national..........	8.8	9.2	-	-	-	-	-	-
State and local	35.8	36.4	0.5	1.2	39.3	41.1	1.0	0.2
1991-92, total	183.5	177.2	1.9	28.0	267.0	258.5	3.0	33.8
National committee	65.8	65.0	0.3	11.3	85.4	81.9	0.8	11.3
Senatorial committee	25.4	25.5	0.6	11.2	72.1	71.8	0.7	16.5
Congressional committee	12.8	12.6	0.8	4.1	34.4	34.3	0.7	5.1
Conventions, other national..........	21.3	20.7	-	-	11.6	11.3	-	-
State and local	58.2	53.4	0.5	1.4	63.5	59.2	0.8	0.9

- Represents zero.   [1] Excludes monies transferred between affiliated committees.   [2] Monies spent in the general election.

Source: U.S. Federal Election Commission, *FEC Reports on Financial Activity, Final Report, Party and Non-Party Political Committees*, biennial.

No. 453. Independent Expenditures for Presidential and Congressional Campaigns: 1983 to 1992

[In thousands of dollars. Covers campaign finance activity during 2-year calendar period indicated. An "independent expenditure" is money spent to support or defeat a clearly identified candidate. According to Federal election law, such an expenditure must be made without cooperation or consultation with the candidate or his/her campaign. Independent expenditures are not limited, as are contributions]

TYPE OF OFFICE AND YEAR	ALL PARTIES			DEMOCRATS		REPUBLICANS		OTHERS	
	Total	For	Against	For	Against	For	Against	For	Against
TOTAL									
1983-84	23,420	19,951	3,468	1,693	1,016	18,257	2,453	1	-
1985-86	10,205	8,832	1,373	3,450	888	5,376	485	6	-
1987-88	21,341	16,654	4,687	2,865	4,248	13,784	439	6	-
1989-90	5,774	4,177	1,597	1,530	735	2,645	862	2	-
1991-92	11,018	8,698	2,320	3,056	1,460	5,528	848	114	12
PRESIDENTIAL									
1983-84	17,468	16,638	831	806	487	15,830	344	1	-
1985-86	841	795	45	76	28	719	17	-	-
1987-88	14,127	10,628	3,499	568	3,352	10,054	146	6	-
1989-90	497	322	174	5	169	318	5	-	-
1991-92	4,399	3,662	737	574	561	3,032	163	56	12
SENATE									
1983-84	4,627	2,134	2,493	326	410	1,808	2,082	-	-
1985-86	5,312	4,331	980	988	632	3,343	348	-	-
1987-88	4,401	3,641	761	831	617	2,810	143	(Z)	-
1989-90	3,506	2,362	1,144	756	428	1,604	716	2	-
1991-92	2,618	1,925	693	1,026	462	898	231	1	-
HOUSE OF REPRESENTATIVES									
1983-84	1,325	1,180	145	561	118	619	27	-	-
1985-86	4,053	3,706	347	2,386	227	1,314	120	6	-
1987-88	2,813	2,385	427	1,466	279	920	149	(Z)	-
1989-90	1,772	1,493	279	770	138	723	141	-	-
1991-92	4,000	3,110	890	1,456	436	1,597	454	57	-

- Represents zero.   Z Less than $500.

Source: U.S. Federal Election Commission, *FEC Index of Independent Expenditures, 1987-88*, May 1989; press release of May 19, 1989; and unpublished data.

No. 454. Political Action Committees—Number, by Committee Type: 1980 to 1993

[As of **December 31**, except **1993**, as of **June 30**]

COMMITTEE TYPE	1980	1985	1988	1989	1990	1991	1992	1993
Total	2,551	3,992	4,268	4,178	4,172	4,094	4,195	4,025
Corporate	1,206	1,710	1,816	1,796	1,795	1,738	1,735	1,715
Labor	297	388	354	349	346	338	347	338
Trade/membership/health	576	695	786	777	774	742	770	767
Nonconnected	374	1,003	1,115	1,060	1,062	1,083	1,145	1,011
Cooperative	42	54	59	59	59	57	56	55
Corporation without stock	56	142	138	137	136	136	142	139

Source: U.S. Federal Election Commission, press release of January 29, 1993, and unpublished data.

No. 455. Political Action Committees—Financial Activity Summary, by Committee Type: 1987 to 1992

[**In millions of dollars.** Covers financial activity during 2-year calendar period indicated. Data have not been adjusted for transfers between affiliated committees]

COMMITTEE TYPE	RECEIPTS			DISBURSEMENTS [1]			CONTRIBUTIONS TO CANDIDATES		
	1987-88	1989-90	1991-92	1987-88	1989-90	1991-92	1987-88	1989-90	1991-92
Total	384.6	372.1	392.8	364.2	357.6	402.3	159.2	159.1	188.9
Corporate	96.9	106.5	112.8	89.8	101.1	112.6	56.2	58.1	68.4
Labor	78.5	88.9	89.9	74.1	84.6	94.7	35.5	34.7	41.4
Trade/membership/health	89.5	92.5	96.7	83.7	88.1	98.5	41.2	44.8	53.9
Nonconnected	106.3	71.6	79.8	104.9	71.4	82.3	20.3	15.1	18.3
Cooperative	4.9	5.0	4.8	4.5	4.8	4.9	2.7	2.9	3.0
Corporation without stock	8.5	7.6	8.8	7.2	7.7	9.2	3.3	3.4	4.0

[1] Comprises contributions to candidates, independent expenditures, and other disbursements.

Source: U.S. Federal Election Commission, *FEC Reports on Financial Activity, Final Report, Party and Non-Party Political Committees,* biennial.

No. 456. Presidential Campaign Finances—Federal Funds for General Election: 1980 to 1992

[**In millions of dollars.** Based on FEC certifications, audit reports, and Dept. of Treasury reports]

1980		1984		1988		1992	
Candidate	Amount	Candidate	Amount	Candidate	Amount	Candidate	Amount
Total	62.7	Total	80.3	Total	92.2	Total	110.4
Anderson [1]	4.2	Mondale	40.2	Bush	46.1	Bush	55.2
Carter	29.4	Reagan	40.1	Dukakis	46.1	Clinton	55.2
Reagan	29.2					Perot	-

- Represents zero.   [1] John Anderson, as the candidate of a new party, was permitted to raise funds privately. Total receipts for the Anderson campaign, including Federal funds, were $17.6 million, and total expenditures were $15.6 million.

Source: U.S. Federal Election Commission, periodic press releases.

No. 457. Presidential Campaign Finances—Primary Campaign Receipts and Disbursements: 1983 to 1992

[**In millions of dollars.** Covers campaign finance activity during 2-year calendar period indicated. Covers candidates who received Federal matching funds or who had significant financial activity]

ITEM	TOTAL			DEMOCRATIC			REPUBLICAN		
	1983-84 [1]	1987-88 [2]	1991-92 [3]	1983-84	1987-88	1991-92	1983-84	1987-88	1991-92
Receipts, total [4]	105.0	213.8	124.3	77.5	91.9	70.0	27.1	116.0	49.7
Individual contributions	62.8	141.1	81.8	46.2	59.4	44.7	16.4	76.8	34.4
Federal matching funds	34.9	65.7	42.2	24.6	30.1	24.6	10.1	34.7	15.0
Disbursements	103.6	210.7	117.8	77.4	90.2	64.4	25.9	114.6	48.8

[1] Includes Citizens Party candidate, not shown separately.   [2] Includes a minor party candidate who sought several party nominations and a Democratic candidate who did not receive Federal matching funds, but who had significant financial activity. [3] Includes other parties, not shown separately.   [4] Includes other types of receipts, not shown separately.

Source: U.S. Federal Election Commission, *FEC Reports on Financial Activity, Final Report, Presidential Pre-Nomination Campaigns,* quadrennial.

No. 458. Congressional Campaign Finances—Receipts and Disbursements: 1987 to 1992

[Covers all campaign finance activity during 2-year calendar period indicated for primary, general, run-off, and special elections. For 1987-88 relates to 1,582 House of Representatives candidates and 210 Senate candidates; for 1989-90 to 1,580 House of Representatives candidates and 179 Senate candidates; for 1991-92 to 2,580 House of Representatives candidates and 365 Senate candidates. Data have been adjusted to eliminate transfers between all committees within a campaign. For further information on legal limits of contributions, see Federal Election Campaign Act of 1971, as amended]

ITEM	HOUSE OF REPRESENTATIVES						SENATE					
	Amount (mil. dol.)			Percent distribution			Amount (mil. dol.)			Percent distribution		
	1987-88	1989-90	1991-92	1987-88	1989-90	1991-92	1987-88	1989-90	1991-92	1987-88	1989-90	1991-92
Total receipts [1]	278.3	285.4	395.9	100	100	100	199.3	186.3	263.4	100	100	100
Individual contributions	129.9	129.9	192.4	47	46	49	128.1	119.6	162.8	64	64	62
Other committees	102.2	108.5	127.4	37	38	32	45.7	41.2	51.2	23	22	19
Candidate loans	23.2	20.9	43.0	8	7	11	8.2	10.0	28.7	4	5	11
Candidate contributions	4.9	4.8	11.4	2	2	3	6.8	2.4	6.5	3	1	2
Democrats	160.3	163.4	217.7	58	57	55	107.7	89.5	143.8	54	48	55
Republicans	117.0	120.9	174.3	42	42	44	91.3	96.8	118.4	46	52	45
Others	1.0	1.1	3.9	(Z)	(Z)	1	0.3	(Z)	1.2	(Z)	(Z)	(Z)
Incumbents	175.6	181.9	203.5	63	64	51	98.3	118.7	99.7	49	64	38
Challengers	52.5	47.7	91.3	19	17	23	56.3	54.8	95.6	28	29	36
Open seats [2]	50.2	55.9	101.1	18	20	26	44.7	12.8	68.2	22	7	26
Total disbursements	257.6	265.8	408.2	100	100	100	201.4	180.4	272.1	100	100	100
Democrats	145.6	151.0	228.3	57	57	56	107.9	87.6	147.6	54	49	54
Republicans	111.0	113.7	176.0	43	43	43	93.1	92.9	123.2	46	52	45
Others	1.0	1.1	3.9	(Z)	(Z)	1	0.3	(Z)	1.2	(Z)	(Z)	(Z)
Incumbents	156.6	163.4	218.5	61	62	53	101.2	113.5	107.2	50	63	39
Challengers	51.7	47.0	90.0	20	18	22	56.1	54.9	95.3	28	30	35
Open seats [2]	49.3	55.4	99.6	19	21	24	44.1	12.1	69.6	22	7	26

Z Less than $50,000 or 0.5 percent.   [1] Includes other types of receipts, not shown separately.   [2] Elections in which an incumbent did not seek re-election.

Source: U.S. Federal Election Commission, *FEC Reports on Financial Activity, Final Report, U.S. Senate and House Campaigns*, biennial.

No. 459. Contributions to Congressional Campaigns by Political Action Committees (PAC), by Type of Committee: 1981 to 1992

[In millions of dollars. Covers amounts given to candidates in primary, general, run-off, and special elections during the 2-year calendar period indicated. For number of political action committees, see table 454]

TYPE OF COMMITTEE	Total	Democrats	Republicans	Incumbents	Challengers	Open seats [1]
HOUSE OF REPRESENTATIVES						
1981-82	61.1	34.2	26.8	40.8	10.9	9.4
1983-84	75.7	46.3	29.3	57.2	11.3	7.2
1985-86	87.4	54.7	32.6	65.9	9.1	12.4
1987-88	102.2	67.4	34.7	82.2	10.0	10.0
1989-90	108.5	72.2	36.2	87.5	7.3	13.6
1991-92, total [2]	127.4	85.4	41.7	94.4	12.2	20.8
Corporate	42.9	23.4	19.5	35.1	2.8	5.0
Trade association [3]	38.8	23.2	15.5	29.2	2.9	6.6
Labor	30.7	29.0	1.5	20.0	4.5	6.2
Nonconnected [4]	10.4	6.7	3.7	6.3	1.7	2.4
SENATE						
1981-82	22.6	11.2	11.4	14.3	5.2	3.0
1983-84	29.7	14.0	15.6	17.9	6.3	5.4
1985-86	45.3	20.2	25.1	23.7	10.2	11.4
1987-88	45.7	24.2	21.5	28.7	8.0	9.0
1989-90	41.2	20.2	21.0	29.5	8.2	3.5
1991-92, total [2]	51.2	29.0	22.2	31.9	9.4	10.0
Corporate	21.2	8.7	12.5	14.6	2.9	3.8
Trade association [3]	12.5	6.6	5.9	8.2	1.8	2.4
Labor	8.6	8.3	0.4	3.8	2.9	1.9
Nonconnected [4]	7.0	4.2	2.8	4.0	1.5	1.5

[1] Elections in which an incumbent did not seek re-election.   [2] Includes other types of political action committees not shown separately.   [3] Includes membership organizations and health organizations.   [4] Represents "ideological" groups as well as other issue groups not necessarily ideological in nature.

Source: U.S. Federal Election Commission, *FEC Reports on Financial Activity, Final Report, U.S. Senate and House Campaigns*, biennial.

State and Local Government Finances and Employment

This section presents data on revenues, expenditures, debt, and employment of State and local governments. Nationwide statistics relating to State and local governments, their numbers, finances, and employment, are compiled primarily by the Bureau of the Census through a program of censuses and surveys. Every fifth year (for years ending in "2" and "7") the Bureau conducts a Census of Governments involving collection of data for all governmental units in the United States. In addition, the Bureau conducts annual surveys which cover all the State governments and a sample of local governments.

Publications issued annually by the Bureau of the Census include a report on finances which presents figures for the Federal Government, nationwide totals for State and local governments by type, and State-local data by States. Also issued annually is a series of publications on State, city, county, and school finances, and on city, county, and other public employment. Financial data are published in the GF publication series, employment data in the GE series. There is also a series of quarterly reports covering tax revenue and finances of major public employee retirement systems.

Basic information for Census Bureau statistics on governments is obtained by mail canvass from State and local officials; however, financial data for each of the State governments and for many of the large local governments are compiled from their official records and reports by Census Bureau personnel. In over half of the States, all or part of local government financial data are obtained through central collection arrangements with State governments. Financial data on the Federal Government is based on the *Budget* published by the Office of Management and Budget (see text, Section 10).

Governmental units.—The governmental structure of the United States includes, in addition to the Federal Government and the States, thousands of

---

In Brief

State government revenue
(from own sources) in 1992:
$574,330 million

Taxes	*57%*
Insurance trust funds	*23%*
Charges	*9%*
Interest earnings	*5%*
Utility and liquor stores	*1%*

State government
direct expenditures in 1992:
$498,640 million

Public welfare	*25%*
Education	*17%*
Insurance trust funds	*16%*
Health and hospitals	*8%*

---

local governments—counties, municipalities, townships, school districts, and numerous kinds of "special districts." In 1992, 86,743 local governments were identified by the Census of Governments. As defined by the census, governmental units include all agencies or bodies having an organized existence, governmental character, and substantial autonomy. While most of these governments can impose taxes, many of the special districts—such as independent public housing authorities, the New York Port Authority, and numerous local irrigation, power, and other types of districts—are financed from rentals, charges for services, benefit assessments, grants from other governments, toll charges, and other nontax sources. The count of governments excludes semi-autonomous agencies through which States, cities, and counties sometimes provide for certain functions—for example, "dependent" school systems, State institutions of higher education, and certain other "authorities" and special agencies which are under the administrative or fiscal control of an established governmental unit.

Finances.—The financial statistics relate to government fiscal years ending June 30, or at some date within the 12 previous months. The following governments are exceptions and are included as though they were part of the June 30 group; ending September 30, the State governments of Alabama and Michigan, The District of Columbia, and Alabama school districts; and ending August 31, the State government of Texas and Texas school districts. New York State ends its fiscal year on March 31. The Federal Government ended the fiscal year June 30 until 1976 when its fiscal year, by an act of Congress, was revised to extend from Oct. 1 to Sept. 30. A 3-month quarter (July 1 to Sept. 30, 1976) bridged the transition.

Nationwide government finance statistics have been classified and presented in terms of uniform concepts and categories, rather than according to the highly diverse terminology, organization, and fund structure utilized by individual governments. Accordingly, financial statistics which appear here for the Federal Government and for individual States or local governments have been standardized and may not agree directly with figures appearing in the original sources.

Statistics on governmental finances distinguish among general government, utilities, liquor stores, and insurance trusts. *General government* comprises all activities except utilities, liquor stores, and insurance trusts. Utilities include government water supply, electric light and power, gas supply, and transit systems. Liquor stores are operated by 17 States and by local governments in 6 States. Insurance trusts relate to employee retirement, unemployment compensation, and other social insurance systems administered by the Federal, State, and local governments.

Data for cities relate only to municipal corporations and their dependent agencies and do not include amounts for other local governments overlying city areas. Therefore, expenditure figures for "education" do not include spending by the separate school districts which administer public schools within most municipal areas. Variations in the assignment of governmental responsibility for public assistance, health, hospitals, public housing, and other functions to a lesser degree also have an important effect upon reported amounts of city expenditure, revenue, and debt. Therefore, any intercity comparisons based upon these figures should be made with caution and with due recognition of variations that exist among urban areas in the relative role of the municipal corporation.

Employment and payrolls.—These data are based mainly on mail canvassing of State and local governments. Payroll includes all salaries, wages, and individual fee payments for the month specified, and employment relates to all persons on governmental payrolls during a pay period of the month covered—including paid officials, temporary help, and (unless otherwise specified) part-time as well as full-time personnel. Beginning 1986, statistics for full-time equivalent employment have been computed with a formula using hours worked by part-time employees. A payroll based formula was used prior to 1985. Full-time equivalent employment statistics were not computed for 1985. Figures shown for individual governments cover major dependent agencies such as institutions of higher education, as well as the basic central departments and agencies of the government.

Statistical reliability.—For a discussion of statistical collection and estimation, sampling procedures, and measures of statistical reliability applicable to Census Bureau data, see Appendix III.

Historical statistics.—Tabular headnotes provide cross-references, where applicable, to *Historical Statistics of the United States, Colonial Times to 1970.* See Appendix IV.

No. 460. Number of Governmental Units, by Type: 1942 to 1992

TYPE OF GOVERNMENT	1942	1952 [1]	1957 [1]	1962	1967	1972	1977	1982	1987	1992
Total	155,116	116,807	102,392	91,237	81,299	78,269	79,913	81,831	83,237	86,743
U.S. Government	1	1	1	1	1	1	1	1	1	1
State government	48	50	50	50	50	50	50	50	50	50
Local governments	155,067	116,756	102,341	91,186	81,248	78,218	79,862	81,780	83,186	86,692
County	3,050	3,052	3,050	3,043	3,049	3,044	3,042	3,041	3,042	3,043
Municipal	16,220	16,807	17,215	18,000	18,048	18,517	18,862	19,076	19,200	19,296
Township and town	18,919	17,202	17,198	17,142	17,105	16,991	16,822	16,734	16,691	16,666
School district	108,579	67,355	50,454	34,678	21,782	15,781	15,174	14,851	14,721	14,556
Special district	8,299	12,340	14,424	18,323	21,264	23,885	25,962	28,078	29,532	33,131

[1] Adjusted to include units in Alaska and Hawaii which adopted statehood in 1959.

No. 461. Number of Local Governments, by Type—States: 1992

[Governments in existence in January. Limited to governments actually in existence. Excludes, therefore, a few counties and numerous townships and "incorporated places" existing as areas for which statistics can be presented as to population and other subjects, but lacking any separate organized county, township, or municipal government]

STATE	All governmental units [1]	County [2]	Municipal [2]	Township [2]	School district	Special district			
						Total [3]	Natural resources	Fire protection	Housing and community development
U.S	86,743	3,043	19,296	16,666	14,556	33,131	6,564	5,354	3,663
Alabama	1,134	67	440	-	129	497	68	4	153
Alaska	176	12	149	-	-	14	-	-	13
Arizona	598	15	86	-	228	268	71	130	-
Arkansas	1,473	75	489	-	324	584	230	48	130
California	4,495	57	460	-	1,080	2,897	489	395	92
Colorado	1,826	62	266	-	180	1,317	170	247	96
Connecticut	575	-	30	149	17	378	1	59	95
Delaware	281	3	57	-	19	201	192	-	4
Dist. of Columbia	2	-	1	-	-	1	-	-	-
Florida	1,041	66	390	-	95	489	136	60	107
Georgia	1,321	157	536	-	185	442	38	6	207
Hawaii	21	3	1	-	-	16	16	-	-
Idaho	1,105	44	199	-	116	745	170	130	13
Illinois	6,810	102	1,282	1,433	997	2,995	928	813	117
Indiana	2,976	91	566	1,008	310	1,000	132	1	62
Iowa	1,904	99	953	-	445	406	242	72	19
Kansas	3,918	105	627	1,355	324	1,506	261	-	207
Kentucky	1,345	119	438	-	177	610	128	93	24
Louisiana	461	61	301	-	66	32	2	-	1
Maine	799	16	22	468	88	204	13	-	27
Maryland	416	23	155	-	-	237	165	-	21
Massachusetts	851	12	39	312	86	401	14	15	255
Michigan	2,727	83	534	1,242	587	280	82	2	-
Minnesota	3,616	87	854	1,804	477	393	111	-	172
Mississippi	898	82	294	-	176	345	256	-	57
Missouri	3,368	114	933	324	553	1,443	175	208	159
Montana	1,305	54	128	-	544	578	129	150	18
Nebraska	2,997	93	534	452	842	1,075	96	422	137
Nevada	212	16	18	-	17	160	33	14	17
New Hampshire	531	10	13	221	168	118	10	16	23
New Jersey	1,625	21	320	247	550	486	17	171	83
New Mexico	494	33	99	-	94	267	220	-	5
New York	3,319	57	620	929	714	998	2	909	-
North Carolina	954	100	518	-	-	335	150	-	104
North Dakota	2,795	53	366	1,351	284	740	79	277	38
Ohio	3,534	88	942	1,317	665	521	98	41	59
Oklahoma	1,822	77	589	-	614	541	102	18	124
Oregon	1,487	36	240	-	340	870	202	268	22
Pennsylvania	5,397	66	1,022	1,548	516	2,244	10	1	88
Rhode Island	128	-	8	31	4	84	3	38	26
South Carolina	705	46	270	-	91	297	48	85	46
South Dakota	1,803	64	310	971	184	273	109	51	42
Tennessee	960	93	339	-	14	513	117	-	96
Texas	4,919	254	1,171	-	1,101	2,392	432	96	402
Utah	635	29	228	-	40	337	77	20	18
Vermont	690	14	50	237	278	110	14	22	9
Virginia	461	95	230	-	-	135	44	-	-
Washington	1,796	39	268	-	296	1,192	160	410	51
West Virginia	708	55	231	-	55	366	15	-	36
Wisconsin	2,752	72	583	1,267	430	399	179	-	188
Wyoming	576	23	97	-	56	399	128	62	-

- Represents zero. [1] Includes the Federal Government and the 50 State governments not shown separately. [2] Includes "town" governments in the six New England States and in Minnesota, New York, and Wisconsin. [3] Includes other special districts not shown separately.

Source of tables 460 and 461: U.S. Bureau of the Census, 1992 Census of Governments, *Government Organization*.

No. 462. County, Municipal, and Township Governments: 1992

[Number of governments as of **January 1992**. Population enumerated as of **April 1, 1990**. Consolidated city-county governments are classified as municipal rather than county governments. Township governments include "towns" in the six New England States, Minnesota, New York, and Wisconsin]

POPULATION-SIZE GROUP	COUNTY GOVERNMENTS			MUNICIPAL GOVERNMENTS			TOWNSHIP GOVERNMENTS		
	Number, 1992	Number (1,000)	Percent	Number, 1992	Number (1,000)	Percent	Number, 1992	Number (1,000)	Percent
Total	3,043	224,924	100	19,279	153,819	100	16,656	53,051	100
200,000 or more	[1]174	[1]120,551	[1]54	76	47,809	31	6	2,140	4
100,000 to 199,999	[2]244	[2]37,336	[2]17	119	16,390	11	27	3,554	7
50,000 to 99,999	377	26,555	12	310	21,282	14	77	5,214	10
25,000 to 49,999	612	21,510	10	566	19,877	13	249	8,461	16
10,000 to 24,999	908	14,851	7	1,290	20,324	13	728	11,225	21
5,000 to 9,999	[3]728	[3]4,121	[3]2	1,566	11,135	7	1,019	7,112	13
2,500 to 4,999	(NA)	(NA)	(NA)	2,036	7,238	5	1,800	6,301	12
1,000 to 2,499	(NA)	(NA)	(NA)	3,670	5,894	4	3,626	5,796	11
Less than 1,000	(NA)	(NA)	(NA)	9,646	3,874	3	9,124	3,251	6

NA Not available. [1] For population group of 250,000 or more. [2] 100,000 to 249,999. [3] Less than 10,000.

Source: U.S. Bureau of the Census, 1992 Census of Governments, vol. 1, No. 1, *Government Organization*.

Figure 9.1
State Lottery Proceeds: 1980 to 1993

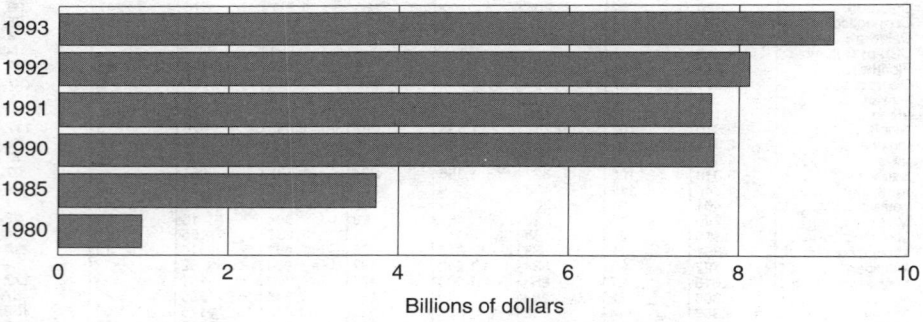

Billions of dollars

Percent distribution of
1993
State lottery proceeds
($9 billion)

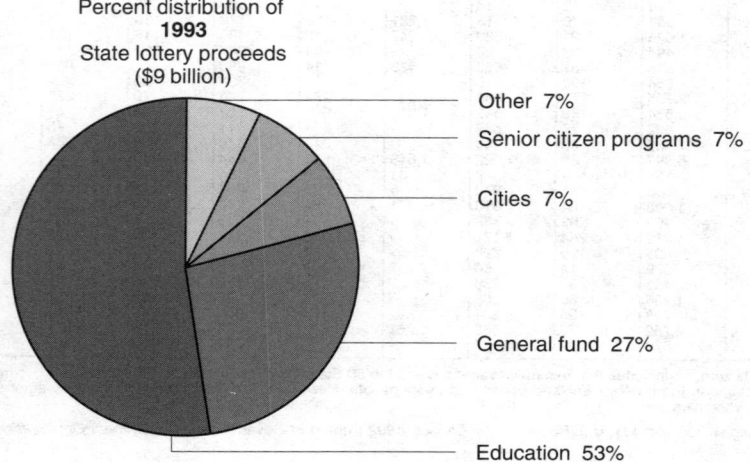

Other 7%

Senior citizen programs 7%

Cities 7%

General fund 27%

Education 53%

Source: Chart prepared by U.S. Bureau of the Census. For data, see table 483.

No. 463. All Governments—Revenue, Expenditure, and Debt: 1980 to 1992

[For fiscal year ending in year shown; see text, section 9. Local government amounts are estimates subject to sampling variation; see Appendix III and source. See also *Historical Statistics, Colonial Times to 1970*, series Y 505-637 and Y 652-848]

ITEM	All governments (bil. dol.)	FEDERAL [1]		STATE AND LOCAL (bil. dol.)			PER CAPITA [2] (dollars)		
		Total (bil. dol.)	Percent of total	Total	State	Local	Total	Federal	State and local
Revenue: [3] 1980	[4]932	565	60.7	[4]452	277	258	[4]4,115	2,496	1,993
1990.	[4]2,047	1,155	56.4	[4]1,032	632	580	[4]8,230	4,642	4,150
1991.	[4]2,124	1,201	56.5	[4]1,081	660	612	[4]8,423	4,762	4,286
1992.	[4]2,262	1,259	47.2	[4]1,185	744	648	[4]8,864	4,937	4,646
Intergovernmental: 1980 . . .	(X)	2	(X)	[4]83	64	102	(X)	8	367
1990	(X)	3	(X)	[4]137	126	191	(X)	12	550
1991	(X)	3	(X)	[4]154	170	216	(X)	13	611
1992	(X)	3	(X)	[4]179	170	216	(X)	13	702
General, own sources:									
1980	717	417	58.2	299	169	130	3,163	1,842	1,321
1990	1,493	780	52.2	713	391	322	6,004	3,138	2,866
1991	1,557	809	52.0	748	408	340	6,175	3,208	2,967
1992	1,645	851	51.8	793	436	357	6,445	3,338	3,110
Taxes: [3] 1980	574	351	61.1	223	137	86	2,535	1,548	986
1990.	1,134	632	55.7	502	300	201	4,559	2,542	2,017
1991	1,167	642	55.0	525	311	215	4,629	2,546	2,083
1992	1,215	659	54.3	556	328	227	4,762	2,584	2,178
Property: 1980	68	(X)	(X)	68	3	66	302	(X)	302
1990	156	(X)	(X)	156	6	150	626	(X)	626
1991	168	(X)	(X)	168	6	162	666	(X)	666
1992	179	(X)	(X)	179	7	172	700	(X)	700
Individual income:									
1980	286	244	85.3	42	37	5	1,263	1,077	186
1990	573	467	81.6	106	96	10	2,302	1,877	425
1991	577	468	81.1	109	99	10	2,290	1,855	434
1992	592	476	80.5	115	105	11	2,319	1,868	452
Corporate income:									
1980	78	65	82.9	13	13	-	344	285	59
1990	117	94	80.3	24	22	2	471	376	95
1991	120	98	81.5	22	20	2	477	389	88
1992	124	100	81.0	24	22	2	485	393	93
Sales or gross receipts:									
1980	112	[5]32	28.6	80	68	12	494	[5]141	353
1990	232	[5]54	23.3	178	147	31	932	[5]217	715
1991	244	[5]58	24.0	186	154	32	968	[5]232	736
1992	260	[5]64	24.7	196	163	33	1,021	[5]252	769
Current charges and									
miscellaneous: 1980	142	67	46.7	76	32	44	629	294	335
1990.	359	148	41.3	211	91	120	1,445	596	849
1991.	390	167	42.9	223	98	125	1,546	663	884
1992.	430	192	44.7	238	108	130	1,686	754	932
Expenditures: [3] 1980	[4]959	617	64.4	[4]434	258	261	[4]4,232	2,724	1,916
1990.	[4]2,219	1,393	62.8	[4]976	572	581	[4]8,921	5,601	3,924
1991.	[4]2,577	1,480	62.2	[4]1,261	629	632	[4]10,221	5,867	5,002
1992.	[4]2,488	1,527	61.4	[4]1,355	700	655	[4]10,599	5,988	5,353
Intergovernmental: 1980 . . .	(X)	91	(X)	[4]2	85	2	(X)	401	8
1990	(X)	147	(X)	[4]3	175	6	(X)	591	13
1991	(X)	160	(X)	[4]3	187	5	(X)	635	14
1992	(X)	186	(X)	[4]4	201	7	(X)	729	14
Direct: [3] 1980.	959	526	54.9	432	173	259	4,232	2,323	1,908
1990.	2,219	1,246	56.2	973	397	575	8,921	5,010	3,911
1991.	2,379	1,319	55.5	1,060	442	618	9,435	5,232	4,203
1992.	2,488	1,341	53.9	1,147	499	648	9,747	5,258	4,495
Current operation: 1980 . .	2,577	209	40.5	308	108	200	2,282	923	1,359
1990.	1,190	490	41.2	700	258	442	4,785	1,970	2,815
1991.	1,283	522	40.6	762	287	475	5,086	2,065	3,022
1992.	1,324	500	37.7	823	322	501	4,810	1,962	3,228
Capital outlay: 1980	99	36	36.7	63	23	40	439	161	278
1990.	221	98	44.3	123	46	78	888	394	495
1991.	227	96	42.1	132	48	84	901	379	522
1992.	228	93	40.9	135	50	84	892	365	527
Debt outstanding: [6] 1980	1,250	914	73.2	337	122	214	5,517	4,036	1,481
1990.	4,127	3,266	79.2	861	318	542	16,592	13,132	3,460
1991.	4,599	3,683	80.1	916	346	570	18,236	14,605	3,631
1992.	5,054	4,083	80.8	970	372	599	19,813	16,006	3,807

- Represents or rounds to zero.   X Not applicable.   [1] Data adjusted to system for reporting State and local data and therefore differ from figures in section 10 tables.   [2] 1980 and 1990 based on enumerated resident population as of April 1; all other years based on estimated resident population as of July 1.   [3] Includes amounts not shown separately.   [4] Excludes duplicative transactions between levels of government; see source.   [5] Includes customs.   [6] End of fiscal year.

Source: U.S. Bureau of the Census, *Government Finances*, series GF, No. 5, annual.

No. 464. All Governments—Detailed Finances: 1992

[For fiscal year ending in year shown, see text, section 9. Local government amounts are estimates subject to sampling variation; see Appendix III and source. See also *Historical Statistics, Colonial Times to 1970*, series Y 505-637 and Y 652-848]

ITEM	All governments (mil. dol.)	Federal (mil. dol.)	State (mil. dol.)	Local (mil. dol.)	PER CAPITA [1] (dol.) Federal	PER CAPITA [1] (dol.) State and local
Revenue	2,261,849	1,259,383	744,232	647,872	4,937	4,646
Intergovernmental revenue	([2])	3,431	169,902	216,305	13	702
Revenue from own sources	2,261,849	1,255,952	574,330	431,567	4,924	3,943
General revenue from own sources	1,644,789	851,390	435,980	357,419	3,338	3,110
Taxes [3]	1,214,651	659,041	328,370	227,240	2,584	2,178
Property	178,536	(X)	6,673	171,863	(X)	700
Individual income	591,636	476,465	104,609	10,562	1,868	452
Corporation income	123,865	100,270	21,566	2,029	393	93
Sales and gross receipts	260,394	64,282	162,721	33,391	252	769
Customs duties	17,480	17,480	(X)	(X)	69	(X)
General	130,830	(X)	107,757	23,073	(X)	513
Selective [3]	112,084	46,802	54,964	10,318	183	256
Motor fuel	42,809	19,865	22,250	694	78	90
Alcoholic beverages	11,787	7,907	3,599	281	31	15
Tobacco products	11,500	5,190	6,119	191	20	25
Public utilities	21,338	7,851	7,762	5,725	31	53
Motor vehicle and operators' licenses	12,601	(X)	11,771	830	(X)	49
Death and gift	15,629	11,143	4,456	30	44	18
Charges and miscellaneous [3]	430,138	192,349	107,610	130,179	754	932
Current charges [3]	226,382	89,482	52,941	83,959	351	537
National defense and international relations	8,677	8,677	(X)	(X)	34	(X)
Postal service	45,158	45,158	(X)	(X)	177	(X)
Education [3]	39,102	-	28,901	10,201	-	153
School lunch sales	3,737	-	-	3,737	-	15
Higher education	32,027	-	28,434	3,593	-	126
Natural resources	16,970	15,148	1,396	426	59	7
Hospitals	37,876	124	12,729	25,023	(Z)	148
Sewerage and sanitation	3,115	(X)	287	2,828	(X)	12
Parks and recreation	3,899	110	788	3,001	(Z)	15
Housing and community development	5,749	2,708	213	2,828	11	12
Airports	5,888	21	650	5,217	(Z)	23
Water transport and terminals	2,889	1,265	393	1,231	5	6
Special assessments	368	(X)	127	241	(X)	1
Sale of property	4,445	3,723	183	539	15	3
Interest earnings	65,746	10,397	26,603	28,746	41	217
Utility and liquor store revenue	62,431	(X)	6,579	55,852	(X)	245
Insurance trust revenue	554,629	404,562	131,771	18,296	1,586	588
Expenditure	2,487,885	1,527,311	699,954	655,325	5,988	5,353
Intergovernmental expenditure	([2])	186,036	201,314	7,355	729	14
Direct expenditure	2,487,885	1,341,275	498,640	647,970	5,258	4,495
General expenditure [3]	1,858,519	886,545	409,132	562,842	3,476	3,810
Education [3]	353,591	26,821	86,650	240,120	105	1,281
Elementary and secondary education	228,917	-	2,221	226,696	-	897
Higher education	84,328	-	70,904	13,424	-	331
Public welfare	201,956	47,722	125,500	28,734	187	605
Health and hospitals	118,791	30,679	41,643	46,469	120	345
Highways	67,290	813	40,266	26,211	3	261
Police protection	41,248	6,703	4,863	29,682	26	135
Fire protection	14,358	(X)	(X)	14,358	(X)	56
Corrections	31,017	2,411	18,306	10,300	9	112
Natural resources	63,650	51,501	9,022	3,127	202	48
Sewerage and sanitation	32,398	(X)	2,235	30,163	(X)	127
Housing and community development	32,549	15,482	1,606	15,461	61	67
Governmental administration	67,180	16,845	19,847	30,488	66	197
Parks and recreation	17,712	1,984	2,688	13,040	8	62
Interest on general debt	254,968	199,713	24,622	30,633	783	217
Utility and liquor store expenditure	84,361	(X)	9,613	74,748	(X)	331
Insurance trust expenditure	545,006	454,730	79,895	10,381	1,783	354
By character and object:						
Current operation	1,323,835	500,341	322,353	501,141	1,962	3,228
Capital outlay	227,807	93,095	50,126	84,586	365	528
Construction	99,797	10,920	39,001	49,876	43	348
Equip., land, and existing structures	112,433	82,175	11,125	19,133	322	119
Assistance and subsidies	129,852	96,622	20,784	12,446	379	130
Interest on debt (general and utility)	264,611	199,713	25,482	39,416	783	254
Insurance trust and repayments	545,006	454,730	79,895	10,381	1,783	354
Expenditure for salaries and wages [4]	*540,355*	*161,551*	*112,685*	*266,119*	*633*	*1,485*

- Represents or rounds to zero.   X Not applicable.   Z Less than 50 cents.   [1] Based on estimated resident population as of July 1.   [2] Aggregates exclude duplicative transactions between levels of government; see source.   [3] Includes amounts not shown separately.   [4] Included in items shown above.

Source: U.S. Bureau of the Census, *Government Finances*, series GF, No. 5, annual.

No. 465. All Governments—Capital Outlays: 1970 to 1992

[In millions of dollars, except percent. For fiscal year ending in year shown; see text, section 9. Except for 1987, local government amounts are subject to sampling variation; see Appendix III and source. See also *Historical Statistics, Colonial Times to 1970*, series Y 523-524, Y 673-674, Y 740-741, and Y 787-788]

LEVEL AND FUNCTION	1970	1980	1985	1986	1987	1988	1989	1990	1991	1992
Total.................	47,519	99,386	156,912	176,096	195,713	197,844	211,734	220,960	227,225	227,616
Federal Government:										
Total.................	17,869	36,492	77,014	85,647	96,871	93,531	99,790	97,891	95,575	93,095
Annual percent change [1]....	-6	11	6	11	13	-3	7	-2	-2	-3
Percent of direct expenditure.	10	7	8	9	9	8	9	8	6	7
By function:										
National defense [2]........	14,027	28,161	64,154	71,995	78,222	74,790	78,891	75,624	72,775	69,061
Education...............	9	97	39	5	13	7	9	41	97	90
Highways..............	9	132	121	204	173	173	165	181	143	310
Health and hospitals......	166	673	916	1,160	1,327	1,228	1,403	1,096	1,387	1,594
Natural resources........	1,691	4,046	4,092	3,651	4,058	3,581	3,786	4,698	4,721	5,466
Housing [3].............	853	317	1,935	2,515	3,642	5,180	5,032	4,343	4,147	4,017
Air transportation........	234	151	785	391	494	407	658	664	778	879
Water transportation [4].....	285	1,003	583	245	315	370	306	385	459	506
Other.................	595	1,912	4,389	5,481	8,627	7,792	9,540	10,859	10,068	11,172
State and local governments:										
Total.................	29,650	62,894	79,898	90,449	98,842	104,313	111,944	123,069	131,650	134,712
Annual percent change [1]....	5	7	13	13	9	6	7	10	7	2
Percent of direct expenditure.	20	15	12	13	13	13	13	13	12	9
By function:										
Education [5].............	7,621	10,737	13,477	15,490	17,803	18,529	21,854	25,997	27,251	30,854
Higher education........	2,705	2,972	4,629	5,217	6,141	6,397	6,851	7,441	7,064	9,180
Elementary and secondary..	4,658	7,362	8,358	10,009	11,355	11,789	14,584	18,057	19,852	21,328
Highways..............	10,762	19,133	23,900	26,807	28,352	31,635	32,754	33,867	36,409	37,031
Health and hospitals......	790	2,443	2,709	2,810	3,029	3,436	3,445	3,848	4,142	4,331
Natural resources........	789	1,052	1,736	1,803	2,157	1,894	2,019	2,545	2,474	2,266
Housing [3].............	1,319	2,248	3,217	3,516	3,394	3,619	3,765	3,997	4,389	4,182
Air transportation........	691	1,391	1,875	2,183	2,632	2,896	2,965	3,434	3,941	4,605
Water transportation [4].....	258	623	717	911	869	911	943	924	984	778
Sewerage.............	1,385	6,272	5,926	6,461	7,483	8,300	8,343	8,356	9,104	8,926
Parks and recreation......	684	2,023	2,196	2,554	2,838	3,142	3,350	3,877	4,702	3,934
Utilities...............	2,437	9,933	13,435	15,340	15,638	14,782	15,371	16,601	17,028	17,785
Water...............	1,201	3,335	4,160	5,134	6,135	6,052	6,372	6,873	7,499	7,567
Electric..............	820	4,572	5,247	6,127	5,086	4,473	4,291	3,976	3,579	3,950
Transit..............	366	1,921	3,830	3,830	4,165	3,998	4,430	5,443	5,636	5,836
Gas................	50	105	198	250	253	259	279	310	314	432
Other.................	2,915	7,039	10,711	12,573	14,645	15,172	15,172	17,135	21,226	20,020

[1] Change from prior year shown except 1970, change from 1969, and 1980, change from 1975. [2] Includes international relations and U.S. service schools. [3] Includes community development. [4] Includes terminals. [5] Includes other education.

Source: U.S. Bureau of the Census, *Historical Statistics on Governmental Finances and Employment*; and *Government Finances*, series GF, No. 5, annual.

No. 466. All Governments—Expenditure for Public Works: 1980 to 1992

[In millions of dollars. Public works include expenditures on highways, airports, water transport and terminals, sewerage, solid waste management, water supply, and mass transit systems. Represents direct expenditures excluding intergovernmental grants]

ITEM	Total	Highways	Airport transportation	Water transport and terminals	Sewerage	Solid waste management	Water supply	Mass transit
1980: Total	72,177	33,745	5,071	3,278	9,892	3,322	9,228	7,641
Federal	5,114	434	2,570	2,110	-	-	-	-
State	22,832	20,661	360	360	334	-	91	1,026
Local	44,231	12,650	2,141	808	9,558	3,322	9,137	6,615
Capital expenditures (percent) ...	48	57	30	50	63	11	36	25
1990: Total	146,762	61,913	10,983	4,524	18,309	10,144	22,101	18,788
Federal	7,911	856	4,499	2,556	-	-	-	-
State	43,787	36,464	635	504	636	891	136	4,521
Local	95,064	24,593	5,848	1,464	17,673	9,253	21,966	14,267
Capital expenditures (percent) ...	42	55	37	29	46	18	31	29
1992: Total	162,872	67,196	12,791	4,582	20,138	12,022	24,264	21,879
Federal	8,213	813	4,679	2,721	-	-	-	-
State	48,469	40,266	963	504	908	1,327	209	4,292
Local	106,190	26,117	7,149	1,357	19,230	10,695	24,055	17,587
Capital expenditures (percent) ...	42	56	43	28	44	13	31	27

- Represents or rounds to zero.

Source: U.S. Bureau of the Census, *Government Finances*, series GF, No. 5, annual.

No. 467. Federal Grants-in-Aid Summary: 1970 to 1994

[For fiscal year ending in year shown; see text, section 9. Minus sign (-) indicates decrease]

YEAR	CURRENT DOLLARS							CONSTANT (1982) DOLLARS	
	Total grants (bil. dol.)	Average annual percent change [1]	Grants to individuals		Grants as percent of—			Total grants (bil. dol.)	Average annual percent change [1]
			Total (bil. dol.)	Percent of total grants	State-local govt. outlays [2]	Federal outlays	Gross domestic product		
1970	24.0	17.2	8.6	35.8	19.0	12.3	2.4	61.2	11.6
1975	49.8	15.7	16.4	33.0	22.6	15.0	3.1	87.1	7.3
1980	91.5	10.4	31.9	34.9	25.8	15.5	3.3	105.9	-0.7
1985	105.9	8.5	48.1	45.4	20.9	11.2	2.6	94.0	4.2
1988	115.3	6.4	61.0	52.9	18.2	10.8	2.4	92.5	2.0
1989	121.8	5.6	65.9	54.1	17.3	10.7	2.3	93.4	1.1
1990	136.9	12.2	78.6	57.5	17.9	10.9	2.5	100.9	7.7
1991	152.0	12.1	89.9	59.2	20.5	11.5	2.7	112.9	11.9
1992, estimate	182.2	19.9	114.6	62.9	(NA)	12.3	3.1	(NA)	(NA)
1993, projection	199.1	9.3	128.8	64.7	(NA)	13.1	3.2	(NA)	(NA)
1994, projection	220.1	10.5	145.5	66.1	(NA)	14.9	3.3	(NA)	(NA)

NA Not available. [1] Average annual percent change from prior year shown. For explanation, see Guide to Tabular Presentation. 1970, change from 1965. [2] Outlays as defined in the national income and product accounts.

Source: Advisory Commission on Intergovernmental Relations, Washington, DC, *Significant Features of Fiscal Federalism,* 1992 Edition, vol. II, based on *Budget of the United States Government,* FY 93, table 12.1.

No. 468. Federal Aid to State and Local Governments: 1970 to 1994

[In millions of dollars. For fiscal year ending in year shown; see text, section 9. Includes trust funds. See *Historical Statistics, Colonial Times to 1970,* series Y 638-651, for related data]

PROGRAM	1970	1980	1985	1990	1991	1992	1993	1994
Grant-in-aid shared revenue [1]	[2]24,065	91,451	105,897	135,377	154,570	178,117	193,664	217,265
National defense	37	93	157	241	185	318	152	175
Natural resources and environment	411	5,363	4,069	3,745	4,040	3,929	3,796	4,192
Environmental Protection Agency	194	4,603	3,197	2,874	3,071	3,038	2,852	3,126
Energy	25	499	529	461	457	448	460	464
Agriculture	604	569	2,420	1,285	1,220	1,142	1,117	1,041
Transportation [1]	4,599	13,087	17,055	19,225	19,878	20,608	22,343	23,049
Airports	83	590	789	1,220	1,541	1,672	1,931	1,850
Highways	4,395	9,208	12,841	14,171	14,417	15,250	16,409	17,828
Urban mass transit	104	3,129	3,304	3,730	3,821	3,585	3,892	3,228
Community and regional development [1]	1,780	6,486	5,221	4,965	4,273	4,539	5,666	6,300
Appalachian development	184	335	198	124	157	125	138	143
Community development block grants	(X)	3,902	3,817	2,818	2,976	3,090	3,198	3,746
Education, employment, training, social services [1]	6,417	21,862	17,817	23,359	26,566	28,795	30,160	34,429
Compensatory education for the disadvantaged [3]	1,470	3,370	4,194	4,437	5,193	6,129	6,582	6,877
School improvement programs [3]	86	523	479	1,080	1,243	1,361	1,903	1,522
Bilingual and immigrant education [3]	-	166	111	152	148	160	101	209
Federally affected areas impact aid	622	622	629	799	747	785	468	979
Vocational and adult education	285	854	633	1,287	1,038	1,020	1,133	1,251
Libraries	105	158	79	127	132	190	159	147
Payments to States for Family Support Activities	81	383	274	265	546	594	736	860
Social services-block grants to States	574	2,763	2,743	2,749	2,822	2,708	2,785	2,877
Human development services	390	1,548	1,807	2,267	2,920	3,621	3,191	3,856
Training and employment assistance	954	6,191	2,775	3,042	2,985	3,388	3,245	3,467
Health [1]	3,849	15,758	24,451	43,890	55,783	71,416	79,665	91,524
Alcohol, drug abuse, and mental health [4]	146	679	501	1,241	1,744	1,778	1,994	2,089
Medicaid [4]	2,727	13,957	22,655	41,103	52,533	67,827	75,774	87,156
Income security [1]	5,795	18,495	27,153	35,189	38,864	43,486	46,991	52,234
Family support payments to States [4]	4,142	6,888	8,592	12,246	13,520	15,103	15,628	16,413
Food stamps-administration	559	412	886	1,199	1,406	1,611	1,586	1,539
Child nutrition and special milk programs [4]	380	3,388	3,479	4,871	5,418	5,993	6,589	7,228
Housing assistance	436	3,435	6,407	9,516	10,444	12,262	14,100	15,952
Veterans benefits and services	18	90	91	134	141	164	189	226
Administration of justice	42	529	95	574	940	987	987	1,253
General government [5]	479	8,616	6,838	2,309	2,224	2,274	2,131	2,370

- Represents or rounds to zero.   X Not applicable.   [1] Includes items not shown separately.   [2] Includes $5 million for international affairs subsequently provided to a private institution.   [3] The 1983 Budget proposed dismantlement of the Dept. of Education (DED). Budget data for elementary and secondary education previously performed by DED are included in the Foundation for Education Assistance under compensatory education for the disadvantaged, school improvement (formerly titled "Special programs and populations") programs and bilingual and immigrant education.   [4] Includes grants for payments to individuals.   [5] Includes general purpose fiscal assistance.

Source: U.S. Office of Management and Budget, *Historical Tables, Budget of the United States Government,* annual.

No. 469. Federal Aid to State and Local Governments—Selected Programs, by State: 1993

[In millions of dollars, except per capita. For fiscal year ending September 30]

STATE	FEDERAL AID [1]		OE [3] compensatory education [4]	EPA [5] waste treatment facilities construction	HHS [6]		HUD [8]		ETA [10] employment/ training	DOT [11] highway trust fund
	Total	Per capita [2] (dol.)			Administration for Children and Families [7]	Medicaid	Lower income housing assistance [9]	Community development		
United States [12]	195,201	746	6,582	2,126	28,347	75,774	12,457	3,198	6,811	16,152
Alabama	3,081	736	137	23	271	1,204	155	50	115	307
Alaska	948	1,583	22	6	117	168	53	4	44	223
Arizona	2,640	671	70	17	388	976	148	32	94	245
Arkansas	1,855	765	79	16	150	782	93	21	64	204
California	21,635	693	661	137	5,189	7,414	1,384	324	898	1,380
Colorado	2,109	592	52	14	265	728	141	26	70	246
Connecticut	2,691	821	68	29	341	1,103	251	33	105	329
Delaware	455	650	18	6	59	132	37	6	19	57
District of Columbia	1,961	3,392	30	11	207	345	71	14	36	52
Florida	7,579	554	296	77	1,004	2,857	405	126	234	630
Georgia	4,408	637	186	24	572	1,762	252	65	124	410
Hawaii	984	840	18	22	123	221	82	22	31	193
Idaho	712	648	23	4	76	221	36	9	36	104
Illinois	7,845	671	298	127	1,174	2,545	734	186	330	544
Indiana	3,732	653	98	33	378	1,797	183	71	139	383
Iowa	1,737	617	48	21	255	617	86	37	63	216
Kansas	1,608	635	46	20	234	667	66	25	44	162
Kentucky	3,041	802	117	33	386	1,298	188	48	96	215
Louisiana	4,817	1,122	154	23	368	2,820	160	62	99	292
Maine	1,166	941	37	19	152	525	85	15	39	87
Maryland	3,310	667	104	53	445	1,093	260	51	101	258
Massachusetts	5,520	918	150	166	757	2,017	542	94	172	773
Michigan	6,654	702	256	89	1,343	2,547	343	135	326	437
Minnesota	3,297	730	71	33	514	1,276	237	47	100	317
Mississippi	2,285	864	124	16	233	933	108	32	66	190
Missouri	3,566	681	106	52	454	1,404	202	73	122	339
Montana	831	990	18	11	101	232	39	10	27	161
Nebraska	1,108	690	30	8	149	362	64	21	34	137
Nevada	767	552	16	22	77	217	52	8	37	100
New Hampshire	652	579	16	20	83	210	58	9	23	98
New Jersey	6,189	786	208	60	775	2,820	513	117	214	440
New Mexico	1,534	949	47	9	177	438	70	15	40	218
New York	21,166	1,163	694	245	3,434	10,228	1,701	322	504	855
North Carolina	4,498	648	160	43	586	1,926	237	53	146	425
North Dakota	640	1,008	16	7	71	197	37	7	23	109
Ohio	7,716	696	232	124	1,257	3,230	521	154	288	529
Oklahoma	2,111	653	61	14	307	797	135	24	66	159
Oregon	2,099	692	59	29	303	642	115	27	94	170
Pennsylvania	8,517	707	316	71	1,258	3,321	545	205	347	659
Rhode Island	1,107	1,107	25	7	137	480	116	15	35	132
South Carolina	2,521	692	98	15	227	1,210	117	32	80	214
South Dakota	654	915	20	14	65	194	44	8	21	121
Tennessee	3,925	770	134	30	374	1,859	193	50	117	244
Texas	11,035	612	435	98	1,083	4,736	552	199	322	1,061
Utah	1,173	631	23	7	157	357	41	13	47	154
Vermont	557	967	16	8	86	167	29	5	19	116
Virginia	2,945	454	122	35	391	922	241	51	111	226
Washington	3,722	708	80	56	669	1,372	190	50	153	367
West Virginia	1,884	1,035	55	16	195	917	80	18	50	141
Wisconsin	3,397	674	90	86	579	1,304	179	55	128	348
Wyoming	645	1,372	9	4	51	103	15	3	19	119
Outlying areas	3,579	923	281	20	290	81	272	123	141	92

[1] Includes amounts not shown separately.   [2] Based on estimated resident population as of July 1.   [3] Office of Education.   [4] For the disadvantaged.   [5] Environmental Protection Agency.   [6] Department of Health and Human Services.   [7] Includes family support payments (Aid to Families with Dependent Children), social services block grants, children and family services, foster care and adoption assistance, low-income home energy assistance, community services block grants, refugee assistance, and assistance for legalized aliens.   [8] Department of Housing and Urban Development.   [9] Includes public housing, housing payments (section 8) to public agencies, and college housing.   [10] Employment and Training Administration, Job Training Partnership Act.   [11] Department of Transportation.   [12] Includes undistributed amounts not shown separately.

Source: U.S. Bureau of the Census, *Federal Expenditures by State for Fiscal Year 1993*.

No. 470. State and Local Governments—Summary of Finances: 1980 to 1992

[For fiscal year ending in year shown; see text, section 9. Local government amounts are estimates subject to sampling variation; see Appendix III and source. See also *Historical Statistics, Colonial Times to 1970*, series Y 652-709]

ITEM	TOTAL (mil. dol.)				PER CAPITA [1] (dol.)			
	1980	1990	1991	1992	1980	1990	1991	1992
Revenue [2]	451,537	1,032,115	1,080,862	1,185,191	1,993	4,150	4,286	4,646
From Federal Government	83,029	136,802	154,099	179,184	367	550	611	702
Public welfare	24,921	59,961	72,661	91,788	110	241	288	360
Highways	8,980	14,368	14,561	14,800	40	58	58	58
Education	14,435	23,233	25,197	27,821	64	93	100	109
Health and hospitals	2,513	5,904	6,504	7,293	11	24	26	29
Housing and community development	3,905	9,655	10,233	10,876	17	39	41	43
Other and unallocable	28,275	23,683	24,943	26,606	125	95	99	104
From State and local sources	368,509	895,313	926,763	1,006,007	1,627	3,600	3,687	3,944
General, net intergovernmental	299,293	712,700	748,108	793,399	1,321	2,866	2,967	3,110
Taxes	223,463	501,619	525,355	555,610	986	2,017	2,083	2,178
Property	68,499	155,613	167,999	178,536	302	626	666	700
Sales and gross receipts	79,927	177,885	185,570	196,112	353	715	736	769
Individual income	42,080	105,640	109,341	115,170	186	425	434	452
Corporation income	13,321	23,566	22,242	23,595	59	95	88	93
Other	19,636	38,915	40,202	42,197	87	156	159	165
Charges and miscellaneous	75,830	211,081	222,753	237,789	335	849	883	932
Utility and liquor stores	25,560	58,642	60,736	62,540	113	236	241	245
Water supply system	6,766	17,674	18,034	19,147	30	71	72	75
Electric power system	11,387	29,268	30,489	30,999	50	118	121	122
Transit system	2,397	5,216	5,629	5,742	11	21	22	23
Gas supply system	1,809	3,043	3,013	3,034	8	12	12	12
Liquor stores	3,201	3,441	3,571	3,618	14	14	14	14
Insurance trust revenue [3]	43,656	123,970	117,919	150,067	193	498	468	588
Employee retirement	25,441	94,268	87,206	108,310	112	379	346	425
Unemployment compensation	13,529	18,441	18,025	27,019	60	74	71	106
Direct expenditure	432,328	972,662	1,059,805	1,146,610	1,908	3,911	4,203	4,495
By function:								
Direct general expenditure [3]	367,340	834,786	908,108	971,973	1,621	3,343	3,601	3,805
Education [3]	133,211	288,148	309,302	326,769	588	1,159	1,227	1,281
Elementary and secondary	92,930	202,009	217,643	228,917	410	812	863	897
Higher education	33,919	73,418	78,749	84,329	150	295	312	331
Highways	33,311	61,057	64,937	66,477	147	245	258	261
Public welfare	45,552	110,518	130,402	154,235	201	431	517	605
Health	8,387	24,223	26,706	29,344	37	97	106	115
Hospitals	23,787	50,412	54,404	58,768	105	203	216	230
Police protection	13,494	30,577	32,772	34,545	60	123	130	135
Fire protection	5,718	13,186	13,796	14,358	25	53	55	56
Natural resources	5,509	12,330	12,575	13,049	24	50	50	51
Sanitation and sewerage	13,214	28,453	31,014	32,398	58	114	123	127
Housing and community development	6,062	15,479	16,648	17,067	27	62	66	67
Parks and recreation	6,520	14,326	15,930	15,728	29	58	63	62
Financial administration	6,719	16,217	16,995	18,090	30	65	67	71
Interest on general debt [4]	14,747	49,739	52,234	55,255	65	200	208	217
Utility and liquor stores [4]	36,191	77,801	81,004	84,361	160	313	321	331
Water supply system	9,228	22,101	23,561	24,378	41	89	93	96
Electric power system	15,016	30,997	31,090	31,983	66	125	123	125
Transit system	7,641	18,788	20,379	21,879	34	76	81	86
Gas supply system	1,715	2,989	2,970	3,058	8	12	12	12
Liquor stores	2,591	2,926	3,005	3,063	11	12	12	12
Insurance trust expenditure [3]	28,797	63,321	74,159	90,276	127	255	294	354
Employee retirement	14,008	38,355	42,121	46,419	62	154	167	182
Unemployment compensation	12,070	16,499	22,135	32,887	53	66	88	129
By character and object:								
Current operation	307,811	700,131	762,007	823,494	1,359	2,828	3,022	3,228
Capital outlay	62,894	123,069	131,650	134,521	278	495	522	527
Construction	51,492	89,114	96,654	100,533	227	358	383	394
Equipment, land, and existing structures	11,402	33,955	34,996	33,988	50	137	139	133
Assistance and subsidies	15,222	27,227	30,456	33,230	67	109	121	130
Interest on debt (general and utility)	17,604	58,914	61,533	64,789	78	237	244	354
Insurance benefits and repayments	28,797	63,321	74,159	90,276	127	255	294	354
Expenditure for salaries and wages	*163,896*	*341,158*	*366,406*	*378,804*	*723*	*1,372*	*1,453*	*1,485*
Debt outstanding, year end	335,603	860,584	915,711	970,043	1,481	3,460	3,631	3,719
Long-term	322,456	841,278	894,019	948,710	1,423	3,383	3,545	3,458
Short-term	13,147	19,306	21,692	21,333	58	78	86	85
Long-term debt:								
Issued	42,364	108,468	118,054	155,060	187	436	468	608
Retired	17,404	64,831	65,666	99,233	77	261	260	389

[1] 1980 and 1990 based on enumerated resident population as of April 1. Other years based on estimated resident population as of July 1. [2] Aggregates exclude duplicative transactions between State and local governments; see source. [3] Includes amounts not shown separately. [4] Interest on utility debt included in "utility expenditure." For total interest on debt, see "Interest on debt (general and utility)."

Source: U.S. Bureau of the Census, *Historical Statistics on Governmental Finances and Employment* and *Government Finances*, series GF, No. 5, annual.

No. 471. State and Local Government Receipts and Expenditures in the National Income and Product Accounts: 1980 to 1992

[In billions of dollars. For explanation of national income, see text, section 14]

ITEM	1980	1984	1985	1986	1987	1988	1989	1990	1991	1992
Receipts	361.4	492.2	528.7	571.2	594.3	631.3	681.5	730.0	780.5	837.8
Personal tax and nontax receipts [1].	56.2	87.1	94.0	101.6	111.8	117.6	131.4	138.9	145.5	154.0
Income taxes	42.6	67.5	72.1	77.4	86.0	89.9	101.4	106.3	110.4	116.7
Nontaxes	5.0	8.7	9.9	11.4	11.9	12.7	14.1	15.3	16.7	18.3
Corporate profits tax accruals	14.5	18.8	20.2	22.7	23.9	26.0	24.2	22.3	22.7	26.0
Indirect business tax and nontax accruals [1].	172.3	251.7	271.4	292.0	306.5	324.5	352.8	378.2	397.5	421.5
Sales taxes.	82.9	121.1	131.1	140.4	149.8	161.4	172.3	183.3	189.6	200.8
Property taxes	68.8	99.7	107.0	114.5	121.1	127.6	143.5	155.5	167.6	177.7
Contributions for social insurance. .	29.7	40.2	42.8	47.3	49.2	51.9	54.8	58.3	61.7	64.9
Federal grants-in-aid	88.7	94.4	100.3	107.6	102.8	111.3	118.2	132.3	153.0	171.4
Expenditures.	**336.6**	**434.1**	**472.6**	**517.0**	**554.2**	**593.0**	**636.7**	**704.9**	**773.2**	**830.6**
Purchases	298.0	389.9	428.1	465.3	496.6	531.7	573.6	620.9	653.4	683.0
Compensation of employees . . .	193.5	261.9	283.2	305.9	327.3	351.9	379.8	412.7	436.5	457.3
Transfer payments to persons. . . .	65.7	93.5	101.2	110.9	119.6	130.0	143.6	165.4	199.2	228.6
Net interest paid [2].	−19.3	−34.0	−38.7	−40.4	−41.2	−44.2	−52.3	−51.3	−47.1	−46.0
Less: Dividends received	1.9	3.9	4.5	5.1	5.9	6.9	8.1	9.0	9.5	10.2
Subsidies [3]	−5.8	−11.4	−13.5	−13.7	−14.9	−17.5	−20.1	−21.1	−22.9	−24.8
Surplus.	**24.8**	**58.1**	**56.1**	**54.3**	**40.1**	**38.4**	**44.8**	**25.1**	**7.3**	**7.2**
Social insurance funds.	26.9	42.8	46.9	52.7	54.8	56.8	62.3	60.7	58.5	59.4

[1] Includes other items not shown separately.   [2] Interest paid less interest received.   [3] Less current surplus of government.

Source: U.S. Bureau of Economic Analysis, *National Income and Product Accounts of the United States: volume 2, 1959-88,* and *Survey of Current Business,* August 1993.

No. 472. State and Local Government Detailed Expenditures in the National Income and Product Accounts: 1980 to 1992

[In billions of dollars. For explanation of national income, see text, section 14]

EXPENDITURE	1980	1984	1985	1986	1987	1988	1989	1990	1991	1992
Purchases	298.0	389.9	428.1	465.3	496.6	531.7	573.6	620.9	653.4	683.0
Durable goods.	12.8	19.6	22.3	24.6	26.0	28.1	31.9	34.9	36.1	37.6
Nondurable goods	28.8	35.9	38.7	39.1	42.3	45.5	50.7	56.2	58.3	60.2
Services	207.4	281.4	307.5	335.1	357.3	382.2	410.1	442.8	466.4	485.3
Compensation of employees. .	193.5	261.9	283.2	305.9	327.3	351.9	379.8	412.7	436.5	457.3
Other services	13.9	19.6	24.3	29.2	29.9	30.3	30.4	30.1	29.9	28.0
Structures.	49.0	53.0	59.5	66.4	71.0	75.9	80.9	87.1	92.6	99.8
Transfers.	65.7	93.5	101.2	110.9	119.6	130.0	143.6	165.4	199.2	228.6
Benefits from social insurance funds	17.8	27.9	30.4	33.9	37.4	40.9	44.6	49.6	55.2	61.1
State and local employee retirement	15.1	23.5	25.5	28.4	31.2	34.1	36.9	40.6	44.5	48.9
Temporary disability insurance.	0.8	1.1	1.4	1.5	1.6	1.8	1.9	2.2	2.8	3.0
Workers' compensation	2.0	3.3	3.5	3.9	4.6	5.1	5.8	6.9	8.0	9.3
Public assistance	42.8	60.5	65.1	70.7	75.6	82.0	91.3	107.0	134.4	156.8
Medical care	24.6	37.9	41.2	45.4	49.8	55.0	62.9	75.6	100.1	120.5
Aid to Families with Dependent Children.	12.4	14.8	15.4	16.4	16.7	17.3	18.0	19.8	22.0	23.3
Supplemental Security Income.	2.0	2.1	2.3	2.6	2.9	3.1	3.4	3.8	3.8	4.1
General assistance	1.4	2.4	2.4	2.5	2.6	2.7	2.8	3.0	2.9	3.3
Other	2.3	3.4	3.7	3.7	3.6	4.0	4.1	4.8	5.4	5.6
Other.	4.9	5.0	5.6	6.3	6.5	7.0	7.7	8.7	9.6	10.7

Source: U.S. Bureau of Economic Analysis, National Income and Product Accounts of the United States: volume 2, 1959-88, and *Survey of Current Business,* August 1993.

No. 473. New Issues of Long-Term State and Local Government Securities: 1980 to 1993

[In billions of dollars. Beginning 1985, includes outlying areas]

ITEM	1980	1985	1987	1988	1989	1990	1991	1992	1993
All issues, new capital and refunding	41.2	201.4	101.5	115.3	121.9	126.1	171.0	232.5	289.1
General obligations	11.4	39.8	30.2	30.9	37.7	40.1	57.9	80.3	91.1
Revenue	29.9	161.7	71.3	84.4	84.2	86.0	113.1	152.2	198.0
Type of issuer:									
City, town	6.7	36.5	17.2	20.9	23.9	22.8	31.3	44.6	51.3
College or university	0.2	2.9	1.0	1.7	2.0	1.5	3.6	3.7	5.1
County/parish	4.1	15.9	9.6	10.9	10.0	10.0	15.3	20.2	24.2
District	2.6	15.4	10.1	13.1	13.3	14.9	23.3	30.7	36.9
Local authority	8.6	51.2	22.4	22.2	23.5	20.7	28.4	42.4	57.8
State	5.1	12.1	10.1	9.5	11.9	15.5	19.5	25.3	28.2
State authority	14.0	67.5	30.8	37.1	37.3	40.7	49.6	65.5	85.6
Issues for new capital	37.5	124.4	55.1	77.6	84.2	98.3	116.3	108.3	96.2
Use of proceeds:									
Economic development	0.1	1.9	2.2	1.4	1.4	1.5	2.2	2.5	2.2
Education	2.6	10.3	8.4	11.1	14.0	16.4	18.0	17.3	14.9
General purpose/public improvement .	9.7	22.3	17.5	24.8	28.8	32.2	43.4	34.7	32.7
Health care	1.7	15.7	3.6	5.6	7.9	8.2	11.4	8.5	9.1
Single family housing	10.6	14.2	4.4	10.0	6.4	10.2	7.1	5.6	3.4
Transportation	0.9	5.8	2.5	3.4	5.0	7.0	6.3	9.4	7.3
Water, sewer, and gas facilities.	1.4	4.8	5.4	6.7	6.9	7.6	10.9	9.1	8.8

Source: Securities Data Company, Newark, NJ, Municipal New Issues Database.

No. 474. State and Local Governments—Indebtedness: 1980 to 1992

[In billions of dollars, except per capita. For fiscal year ending in year shown; see text, section 9. Local government amounts are estimates subject to sampling variation; see Appendix III and source. See *Historical Statistics, Colonial Times to 1970*, series Y 680, Y 747, and Y 794, for debt outstanding]

ITEM			DEBT OUTSTANDING				LONG-TERM		
	Total	Per capita [1] (dol.)	Long-term			Short-term	Net long-term	Debt issued	Debt retired
			Local schools [2]	Utilities	All other				
1980: Total	335.6	1,482	32.3	55.2	235.0	13.1	262.9	42.4	17.4
State.	122.0	540	3.8	4.6	111.5	2.1	79.8	16.4	5.7
Local	213.6	942	28.5	50.6	123.5	11.0	183.1	25.9	11.7
1985: Total	568.6	2,390	43.8	90.8	414.5	19.6	430.5	101.2	43.5
State.	211.9	891	6.7	8.6	193.8	2.8	110.4	41.7	16.4
Local	356.7	1,499	37.1	82.2	220.6	16.8	320.1	59.5	27.2
1986: Total	658.9	2,744	43.0	104.8	492.8	18.3	458.9	162.0	74.4
State.	247.7	1,032	4.1	10.0	232.0	1.6	129.1	64.0	26.4
Local	411.2	1,712	38.9	94.9	260.6	16.7	329.8	98.1	48.0
1987: Total	727.1	3,001	49.2	120.5	541.5	15.9	518.3	134.4	83.0
State.	265.7	1,097	7.9	11.9	244.1	1.6	143.4	50.2	33.3
Local	461.5	1,905	41.3	108.6	297.3	14.3	375.0	84.1	49.8
1988: Total	755.0	3,088	47.5	124.9	566.9	15.7	425.4	89.7	63.8
State.	276.8	1,132	3.3	12.2	260.0	1.3	108.8	36.4	26.1
Local	478.2	1,956	44.2	112.7	306.9	14.4	316.5	53.3	37.6
1989: Total	798.4	3,235	52.7	127.5	600.2	18.0	445.5	102.2	63.8
State.	295.5	1,197	3.7	12.2	277.4	2.3	118.2	42.0	26.9
Local	502.9	2,037	49.0	115.3	322.8	15.7	327.2	60.2	36.8
1990: Total	860.6	3,460	60.4	134.8	646.1	19.3	477.0	108.5	64.8
State.	318.3	1,280	4.4	12.3	298.8	2.8	125.5	43.5	22.9
Local	542.3	2,181	56.0	122.4	347.4	16.5	351.5	65.0	42.0
1991: Total	915.8	3,631	71.0	141.2	703.5	21.7	509.9	118.1	65.7
State.	345.6	1,370	5.9	12.5	327.1	3.4	139.9	50.5	25.4
Local	570.2	2,261	65.1	128.7	376.4	18.3	369.9	67.6	40.3
1992: Total	971.0	3,807	78.4	150.4	742.2	21.4	561.6	155.1	99.2
State.	371.9	1,458	7.6	13.7	350.7	2.9	125.4	70.2	45.0
Local	599.1	2,349	70.9	136.7	391.5	18.4	409.1	85.0	54.3

[1] 1980 and 1990 based on enumerated resident population as of April 1; other years based on estimated resident population as of July 1.   [2] Includes debt for education activities other than higher education.

Source: U.S. Bureau of the Census, *Government Finances*, series GF, No. 5, annual; and unpublished data.

No. 475. State Governments—Revenue, by State: 1992

[In millions of dollars, except as indicated. Data will not match other tables due to later revisions. For fiscal year ending in year shown; see text, section 9]

STATE	Total revenue [1]	GENERAL REVENUE							
		Total		Per capita [2]		Intergovernmental revenue		Taxes	Charges and miscella-neous
		Amount	Rank	Total (dol.)	Rank	From Federal Govern-ment	From local govern-ments		
United States.....	741,853	605,334	(X)	2,379	(X)	159,041	10,861	327,822	107,610
Alabama..........	10,536	8,910	24	2,154	35	2,707	30	4,218	1,955
Alaska...........	6,327	5,343	31	9,101	1	762	11	1,603	2,966
Arizona..........	9,551	7,975	25	2,081	38	1,852	258	4,827	1,038
Arkansas.........	5,864	5,190	33	2,164	33	1,630	6	2,748	806
California........	100,154	79,399	1	2,572	17	21,562	1,867	46,128	9,842
Colorado.........	9,079	7,016	28	2,022	43	1,843	75	3,533	1,564
Connecticut.......	11,784	10,137	20	3,090	6	2,270	5	6,059	1,803
Delaware.........	2,824	2,456	43	3,565	4	397	15	1,340	704
Florida..........	28,311	23,652	5	1,754	50	5,407	305	14,412	3,529
Georgia..........	14,761	12,379	14	1,833	48	3,724	47	7,267	1,340
Hawaii...........	5,299	4,568	36	3,938	2	845	3	2,710	1,010
Idaho...........	2,902	2,447	44	2,294	27	616	28	1,391	413
Illinois..........	27,865	23,103	7	1,986	44	5,559	181	13,463	3,899
Indiana..........	13,490	12,265	16	2,166	32	3,098	105	6,476	2,585
Iowa............	7,520	6,519	30	2,318	25	1,579	72	3,602	1,266
Kansas..........	5,794	4,968	34	1,969	45	1,341	18	2,802	807
Kentucky.........	10,640	9,222	23	2,456	20	2,594	16	5,081	1,532
Louisiana........	11,842	10,362	19	2,417	23	3,676	19	4,250	2,416
Maine...........	3,755	3,312	40	2,682	14	928	3	1,664	716
Maryland.........	13,730	11,320	18	2,306	26	2,588	74	6,502	2,155
Massachusetts.....	20,456	18,234	10	3,040	7	4,226	401	9,903	3,704
Michigan.........	26,298	22,079	9	2,340	24	5,903	231	11,279	4,666
Minnesota........	15,090	12,347	15	2,756	13	2,687	223	7,450	1,987
Mississippi.......	6,177	5,290	32	2,024	42	2,011	66	2,494	718
Missouri.........	11,619	9,872	21	1,901	47	2,945	11	5,131	1,785
Montana.........	2,661	2,121	46	2,574	16	670	15	951	485
Nebraska.........	3,751	3,526	39	2,195	29	877	20	1,890	739
Nevada..........	3,948	2,715	42	2,046	41	524	24	1,817	350
New Hampshire	2,727	2,303	45	2,073	39	733	67	856	647
New Jersey	28,922	23,400	6	3,004	8	5,130	208	12,803	5,260
New Mexico.......	5,582	4,743	35	3,000	9	1,116	87	2,238	1,303
New York	74,931	60,412	2	3,334	5	17,347	4,795	30,110	8,160
North Carolina	17,664	14,981	11	2,189	30	3,695	322	9,010	1,954
North Dakota	2,072	1,810	47	2,845	11	558	23	755	475
Ohio............	35,590	22,990	8	2,087	37	6,268	201	12,115	4,406
Oklahoma	8,379	6,941	29	2,161	34	1,736	43	3,874	1,287
Oregon	10,025	7,297	27	2,451	21	2,036	27	3,313	1,921
Pennsylvania......	36,699	29,859	4	2,486	19	7,725	292	16,270	5,573
Rhode Island	3,609	2,849	41	2,835	12	943	45	1,276	585
South Carolina	9,897	7,862	26	2,182	31	2,347	97	3,936	1,482
South Dakota	1,756	1,518	50	2,136	36	545	4	565	404
Tennessee........	11,126	9,624	22	1,916	46	3,385	42	4,526	1,671
Texas...........	36,763	31,346	3	1,775	49	8,505	73	17,031	5,737
Utah............	4,917	4,060	38	2,239	28	1,106	45	1,988	922
Vermont	1,898	1,701	49	2,985	10	504	5	763	428
Virginia	15,292	13,087	13	2,052	40	2,563	163	7,025	3,335
Washington	17,366	13,434	12	2,616	15	2,930	65	8,468	1,972
West Virginia	5,452	4,559	37	2,516	18	1,476	14	2,352	717
Wisconsin	17,131	12,107	17	2,418	22	2,921	94	6,911	2,180
Wyoming	2,026	1,723	48	3,697	3	646	20	646	410

X Not applicable.   [1] Includes items not shown separately.   [2] Based on estimated resident population as of July 1.

Source: U.S. Bureau of the Census, *State Government Finances*, series GF, No. 3, annual.

No. 476. State Governments—Expenditures and Debt, by State: 1992

[In millions of dollars, except as indicated. Data will not match other tables due to later revisions. For fiscal year ending in year shown; see text, section 9]

STATE	Total expendi- ture [1]	GENERAL EXPENDITURE							DEBT OUTSTANDING	
		Total		Selected functions					Total	Per capita [2] (dol.)
		Amount	Per capita [2] (dol.)	Educa- tion	Public welfare	High- ways	Health and hospi- tals	Correc- tions		
United States	700,894	611,922	2,405	211,570	156,364	48,747	48,123	20,120	371,901	1,461
Alabama	9,651	8,788	2,125	3,571	1,853	695	1,175	183	4,129	998
Alaska.	5,255	4,788	8,157	1,201	508	547	205	136	4,942	8,418
Arizona	9,096	8,236	2,149	2,930	1,812	954	431	344	2,849	743
Arkansas	5,478	5,062	2,110	2,123	1,177	577	360	106	1,942	810
California	97,079	83,360	2,701	28,285	25,248	4,375	5,259	3,226	37,824	1,225
Colorado	7,492	6,494	1,871	2,709	1,438	652	373	265	2,977	858
Connecticut	11,627	9,957	3,035	2,506	2,434	823	1,058	421	11,957	3,644
Delaware	2,475	2,241	3,253	789	292	234	164	109	3,542	5,141
Florida.	27,089	24,851	1,842	8,814	5,334	2,175	1,924	1,037	12,295	912
Georgia	14,054	12,781	1,893	5,184	3,313	875	1,025	601	4,471	662
Hawaii.	5,301	4,903	4,226	1,344	598	359	411	105	4,687	4,040
Idaho	2,604	2,316	2,170	987	352	291	94	58	1,292	1,211
Illinois	26,832	23,639	2,032	7,295	6,261	2,462	1,604	625	18,742	1,611
Indiana	12,341	11,691	2,065	4,653	2,621	1,078	853	321	5,172	913
Iowa	7,227	6,711	2,387	2,649	1,306	949	590	167	1,884	670
Kansas	5,484	5,052	2,002	2,198	891	649	439	189	486	193
Kentucky	10,154	9,235	2,459	3,572	2,383	934	494	210	6,618	1,763
Louisiana	11,750	10,683	2,492	3,687	2,545	880	1,072	276	9,994	2,331
Maine	3,722	3,232	2,617	1,010	1,003	273	167	67	2,637	2,135
Maryland	13,004	11,012	2,244	3,449	2,677	972	908	556	8,335	1,698
Massachusetts	20,368	17,812	2,970	3,271	5,303	1,021	1,574	645	24,008	2,003
Michigan	25,522	21,840	2,314	7,416	5,575	1,482	2,447	855	10,357	1,097
Minnesota	13,526	12,322	2,750	4,556	3,022	1,043	936	194	4,143	925
Mississippi	5,762	5,217	1,996	1,993	1,210	539	397	87	1,626	622
Missouri.	10,446	9,513	1,832	3,529	2,516	958	721	202	6,301	1,213
Montana	2,460	2,108	2,558	771	334	283	123	37	1,868	2,267
Nebraska.	3,624	3,535	2,201	1,259	706	443	379	73	1,754	1,092
Nevada.	3,826	2,953	2,225	1,113	449	295	106	128	1,934	1,458
New Hampshire	2,871	2,453	2,208	468	937	193	138	46	4,314	3,883
New Jersey	29,316	24,109	3,095	7,018	6,048	1,835	1,396	659	19,786	2,540
New Mexico.	4,972	4,594	2,905	1,919	710	384	415	128	1,605	1,015
New York	73,153	60,869	3,359	17,972	20,307	2,478	5,356	2,008	55,868	3,083
North Carolina	16,046	14,671	2,144	6,313	2,949	1,448	1,154	551	3,819	558
North Dakota	2,001	1,834	2,883	685	338	228	95	16	1,027	1,615
Ohio	30,425	24,106	2,188	8,489	6,494	2,287	1,881	691	12,192	1,107
Oklahoma	8,183	7,063	2,199	3,026	1,540	816	595	201	3,657	1,138
Oregon	7,979	6,842	2,298	1,935	1,327	672	673	209	6,295	2,115
Pennsylvania	35,095	30,338	2,526	9,973	9,600	2,191	2,400	588	12,962	1,079
Rhode Island	3,968	3,331	3,315	813	771	181	251	101	5,151	5,125
South Carolina	9,433	7,969	2,212	3,071	1,618	530	967	297	4,685	1,300
South Dakota	1,565	1,490	2,095	430	290	211	87	30	1,889	2,657
Tennessee.	10,406	9,633	1,917	3,101	2,817	1,134	736	380	2,806	559
Texas	33,894	30,744	1,741	13,283	7,410	2,473	2,476	1,336	8,001	453
Utah	4,481	4,057	2,238	1,951	668	324	342	97	2,153	1,188
Vermont	1,841	1,690	2,966	563	381	176	65	34	1,543	2,706
Virginia	13,921	12,694	1,991	4,931	2,094	1,521	1,424	580	7,403	1,161
Washington	17,316	14,724	2,867	6,224	2,809	1,154	1,262	545	7,192	1,400
West Virginia	5,262	4,396	2,426	1,753	1,094	510	197	36	2,594	1,432
Wisconsin	13,596	12,258	2,448	4,191	2,809	854	831	338	7,299	1,458
Wyoming	1,925	1,725	3,703	595	191	326	91	24	895	1,920

[1] Includes items not shown separately.   [2] Based on estimated resident population as of July 1.

Source: U.S. Bureau of the Census, *State Government Finances*, series GF, No. 3, annual.

No. 477. State Governments—Summary of Finances: 1980 to 1992

[For fiscal year ending in year shown; see text section 9. See also *Historical Statistics, Colonial Times to 1970,* series Y 710-782]

ITEM	TOTAL (mil. dol.)				PER CAPITA [1] (dollars)			
	1980	1990	1991	1992	1980	1990	1991	1992
Borrowing and revenue	293,356	672,994	707,846	802,030	1,291	2,698	2,807	3,144
Borrowing	16,394	40,532	46,654	60,177	72	163	185	236
Revenue	276,962	632,462	661,192	741,853	1,219	2,536	2,622	2,908
General revenue	233,592	517,720	551,722	605,334	1,028	2,076	2,188	2,373
Taxes	137,075	300,719	310,561	327,822	603	1,206	1,232	1,285
Sales and gross receipts	67,855	147,404	153,535	162,308	299	591	609	636
General	43,168	99,929	103,165	107,579	190	401	409	422
Motor fuels	9,722	19,379	20,639	22,198	43	78	82	87
Alcoholic beverages	2,478	3,191	3,400	3,509	11	13	13	14
Tobacco products	3,738	5,541	5,980	6,103	16	22	24	24
Other	8,750	19,365	20,349	22,919	39	78	81	90
Licenses	8,690	18,849	19,419	21,691	38	76	77	85
Motor vehicles	4,936	9,850	10,131	10,766	22	39	40	42
Corporations in general	1,388	3,096	3,114	4,104	6	12	12	16
Other	2,366	5,903	6,174	6,821	10	24	24	27
Individual income	37,089	96,076	99,279	104,401	163	385	394	409
Corporation net income	13,321	21,751	20,357	21,566	59	87	81	85
Property	2,892	5,775	6,228	6,594	13	23	25	26
Other	7,227	10,922	11,745	11,262	32	44	47	44
Charges and miscellaneous	32,190	90,612	97,627	107,610	142	363	387	422
Intergovernmental revenue	64,326	126,329	143,534	169,902	283	507	569	666
From Federal Government	61,892	118,353	134,926	159,041	272	475	535	623
Public welfare	24,680	59,397	71,961	91,091	109	238	285	357
Education	12,765	21,271	23,337	25,867	56	85	93	101
Highways	8,860	13,931	14,098	14,367	39	56	56	56
Other	15,587	23,755	25,530	27,716	69	95	101	109
From local governments	2,434	7,976	8,607	10,861	11	32	34	43
Utility revenue	1,304	3,305	3,460	3,512	6	13	14	14
Liquor store revenue	2,765	2,907	3,013	3,067	12	12	12	12
Insurance trust revenue [2]	39,301	108,530	102,996	129,940	173	435	408	509
Employee retirement	21,146	78,898	72,356	88,281	93	316	287	346
Unemployment compensation	13,468	18,370	17,952	26,921	59	74	71	106
Expenditure and debt redemption	263,494	592,213	650,460	736,095	1,160	2,375	2,580	2,886
Expenditure	257,812	572,318	628,804	700,894	1,135	2,295	2,494	2,748
General expenditure	228,223	508,284	554,901	611,922	1,004	2,038	2,201	2,399
Education	87,939	184,935	196,648	211,570	387	742	780	829
Public welfare	44,219	104,971	124,456	156,364	195	421	494	613
Highways	25,044	44,249	47,038	48,747	110	177	187	191
Health and hospitals	17,855	42,666	45,878	48,123	79	171	182	189
Corrections	4,449	17,266	19,240	20,120	20	69	76	79
Natural resources	4,346	9,909	10,256	10,521	19	40	41	41
General control	3,232	8,384	9,355	10,020	14	34	37	39
Financial administration	3,031	8,616	9,101	9,751	13	35	36	38
Police protection	2,263	5,166	5,506	5,489	10	21	22	22
Employment security	2,001	3,003	3,238	3,702	9	12	13	15
Housing and community development	601	2,856	2,827	2,668	3	11	11	10
Other and unallocable	33,242	76,264	81,358	84,847	146	306	322	333
Utility expenditure	2,401	7,131	7,217	7,036	11	29	29	28
Liquor store expenditure	2,206	2,452	2,504	2,577	10	10	10	10
Insurance trust expenditure [2]	24,981	54,452	64,182	79,359	110	218	255	311
Employee retirement	10,256	29,562	32,264	35,628	45	119	128	140
Unemployment compensation	12,006	16,423	22,017	32,761	53	66	87	128
By character and object:								
Intergovernmental expenditure	84,504	175,028	186,540	201,313	372	702	740	789
Direct expenditure	173,307	397,291	442,264	499,580	763	1,593	1,754	1,959
Current operation	108,131	258,046	287,079	323,830	476	1,035	1,139	1,270
Capital outlay	23,325	45,524	47,937	50,126	103	183	190	197
Construction	19,736	34,803	37,647	39,001	87	140	149	153
Land and existing structures	1,345	3,471	3,401	3,822	6	14	13	15
Equipment	2,243	7,250	6,889	7,303	10	29	27	29
Assistance and subsidies	9,818	16,902	18,876	20,784	43	68	75	81
Interest on debt	7,052	22,367	24,189	25,482	31	90	96	100
Insurance benefits [3]	24,981	54,452	64,182	79,359	110	218	255	311
Debt outstanding, year end	121,958	318,254	345,554	371,901	537	1,276	1,371	1,458
Long-term	119,821	315,490	342,164	368,951	527	1,265	1,357	1,446
Full-faith and credit	49,364	74,972	84,749	96,598	217	301	336	379
Nonguaranteed	70,457	240,518	257,415	272,353	310	964	1,021	1,068
Short-term	2,137	2,764	3,390	2,949	9	11	13	12
Net long-term	79,810	125,524	140,405	152,423	351	503	557	598
Full-faith and credit only	39,357	63,481	73,220	85,258	173	255	290	334
Debt redemption	5,682	19,895	21,656	35,201	25	80	86	138

[1] 1980 and 1990 based on enumerated resident population as of April 1; other years based on estimated resident population as of July 1. [2] Includes other items not shown separately. [3] Includes repayments.

Source: U.S. Bureau of the Census, *State Government Finances,* series GF, No. 3, annual.

No. 478. State Resources, Expenditures, and Balances: 1992 and 1993

[For fiscal year ending in year shown; see text; section 9. **General funds** exclude special funds earmarked for particular purposes, such as highway trust funds and federal funds; they support most on-going broad-based State services and are available for appropriation to support any governmental activity. Minus sign (-) indicates deficit]

| STATE | EXPENDITURES BY FUND SOURCE | | | | | STATE GENERAL FUND | | | | | |
| | Total, 1992 (mil. dol.) | 1993 [1] | | | | Resources [3][4] | | Expenditures [4] | | Balance [5] | |
		Total [2] (mil. dol.)	General fund (percent)	Federal funds (percent)	Other State funds (percent)	1992 (mil. dol.)	1993 [1] (mil. dol.)	1992 (mil. dol.)	1993 [1] (mil. dol.)	1992 (mil. dol.)	1993 [1] (mil. dol.)
United States ...	**592,779**	**631,078**	**48**	**27**	**23**	**305,443**	**318,962**	**302,425**	**312,299**	**2,993**	**6,654**
Alabama	9,489	10,170	35	58	7	3,433	3,643	3,407	3,562	13	-
Alaska.	4,492	4,708	59	19	22	2,886	3,355	2,886	2,759	19	[6]47
Arizona	7,737	8,368	49	30	19	3,606	3,804	3,601	3,737	-65	-46
Arkansas	5,819	6,343	32	28	39	1,935	2,077	1,935	2,077	[6]268	[6]129
California	83,003	86,540	47	34	14	41,107	38,874	43,327	41,107	-	7
Colorado	6,080	7,021	44	28	28	3,039	3,596	2,906	3,276	110	76
Connecticut	9,525	10,286	61	15	13	7,022	7,535	6,912	7,458	-	-
Delaware	2,618	2,828	45	18	31	1,383	1,470	1,230	1,260	761	848
Florida.	30,440	34,410	34	21	40	11,169	12,371	11,047	11,990	9	218
Georgia.	13,755	14,615	56	27	13	7,415	8,340	7,354	8,160	91	111
Hawaii.	5,390	6,239	49	13	24	3,016	3,326	2,642	3,063	139	10
Idaho	2,140	2,353	44	32	23	991	1,044	991	1,033	131	[6]172
Illinois	22,190	24,533	44	21	32	11,897	12,235	11,766	12,063	-	[6]21
Indiana	10,158	11,666	55	32	12	5,894	6,319	5,755	6,309	74	153
Iowa	7,601	8,199	42	22	36	3,181	3,482	3,179	3,444	449	657
Kansas	5,488	6,111	44	27	28	2,632	3,075	2,491	2,690	2	38
Kentucky	9,913	10,906	42	32	26	4,588	4,591	4,539	4,564	60	206
Louisiana.	11,415	12,329	36	33	30	4,438	4,226	4,521	4,214	85	20
Maine	3,656	3,746	42	29	27	1,577	1,607	1,563	1,607	6	-
Maryland	11,845	11,996	53	20	23	6,177	6,395	6,233	6,384	201	123
Massachusetts	14,670	16,101	73	21	6	13,543	14,707	13,104	14,332	141	385
Michigan	19,675	20,180	38	30	32	7,411	7,773	7,406	7,771	153	210
Minnesota	11,469	12,101	63	21	15	7,620	8,101	7,171	7,444	-56	11
Mississippi	5,117	5,869	34	41	25	1,972	2,160	1,945	1,985	68	169
Missouri.	8,980	9,729	44	27	28	4,347	4,524	4,287	4,318	57	71
Montana	2,088	2,248	23	29	48	548	573	523	527	165	579
Nebraska.	3,465	3,676	44	23	32	1,746	1,737	1,545	1,614	8	159
Nevada	(NA)	(NA)	(NA)	(NA)	(NA)	1,050	1,136	1,016	1,077	61	[6]105
New Hampshire	2,007	2,179	35	34	28	724	819	705	752	123	381
New Jersey	22,149	22,113	65	20	13	15,468	15,289	14,707	14,440	49	27
New Mexico.	(NA)	(NA)	(NA)	(NA)	(NA)	2,093	2,265	2,055	2,168	159	216
New York	52,329	54,795	53	28	16	29,842	30,896	29,842	30,896	26	81
North Carolina	13,799	14,376	56	25	19	7,975	8,458	7,810	7,879	27	175
North Dakota	1,563	1,674	36	33	31	627	673	542	653	-	-
Ohio	24,101	25,314	41	24	32	10,434	10,678	10,344	10,567	-83	12
Oklahoma	7,007	7,269	45	26	28	3,327	3,423	3,160	3,318	167	105
Oregon	8,729	8,984	32	16	52	3,088	3,271	2,688	2,912	379	1,330
Pennsylvania	27,053	28,548	50	27	22	13,766	14,178	13,757	13,960	24	46
Rhode Island	2,830	2,955	52	31	15	1,720	1,585	1,720	1,578	-	11
South Carolina	8,515	9,513	38	30	30	3,404	3,680	3,396	3,521	53	-12
South Dakota	1,409	1,532	37	39	25	574	585	568	585	133	320
Tennessee.	8,875	10,421	40	35	23	4,095	4,872	3,936	4,656	116	213
Texas	28,974	33,765	55	27	16	17,167	19,807	16,787	18,477	5	67
Utah	3,750	4,044	49	23	26	1,809	1,963	1,852	1,963	29	39
Vermont	1,429	1,493	42	33	21	592	597	657	643	33	59
Virginia	13,529	14,214	45	17	37	6,211	6,601	6,143	6,432	251	189
Washington	14,754	14,580	52	21	23	7,766	7,912	7,515	7,723	400	360
West Virginia	4,607	5,011	40	34	23	2,016	2,100	1,959	2,029	-2,220	-2,233
Wisconsin	15,301	13,499	52	23	25	6,692	7,043	6,618	6,891	-	[6]527
Wyoming	1,851	1,528	28	24	47	436	420	383	432	374	263

- Represents zero.   NA Not available.   [1] Estimated.   [2] Includes bonds not shown separately.   [3] Includes funds budgeted, adjustments, and balances from previous year.   [4] May or may not include budget stabilization fund transfers, depending on State accounting practices.   [5] Resources less expenditures.   [6] Ending balance is held in a budget stabilization fund.

Source: National Association of State Budget Officers, Washington, DC, *1993 State Expenditure Report,* and National Governors' Association and NASBO, *Fiscal Survey of the States,* semi-annual (copyright).

No. 479. State Government Tax Collections and Excise Taxes, by State: 1992

[Preliminary. Tax collections for **fiscal year ending in year shown; see text, section 9.** Excise tax rates as of **September 1.** Collections include local shares of State-imposed taxes]

STATE	STATE TAX COLLECTIONS (mil. dol.)								EXCISE TAX RATES		
		Sales and gross receipts							Motor vehicle and operators' licenses	General sales and gross receipts (percent) [2]	Cigarettes (cents per package)	Gasoline (cents per gallon)
	Total [1]	Total [1]	General sales and gross receipts	Motor fuels	Alcoholic beverages and tobacco products	Individual income	Corporation net income				
United States [3]	328,370	162,721	107,757	22,250	9,717	104,609	21,566	11,674	(X)	(X)	(X)
Alabama	4,218	2,219	1,116	331	178	1,234	165	160	[4]D	16.5	16
Alaska	1,590	101	(X)	43	29	(X)	200	25	(X)	29	8
Arizona	4,827	2,782	2,088	370	94	1,240	211	202	[5]5 F&D	18	18
Arkansas	2,746	1,518	1,033	304	93	850	126	131	[4]4.5D	22	18.5
California	46,128	19,549	14,925	2,248	1,014	17,030	4,518	1,456	[4]6.5F&D	35	16
Colorado	3,521	1,473	914	360	83	1,612	123	117	[4]3 F&D	20	22
Connecticut	6,060	3,074	2,090	362	162	1,866	594	197	6 F&D	45	26
Delaware [3]	1,341	195	(X)	73	31	498	129	20	(X)	24	19
Dist. of Columbia [3]	2,440	672	442	29	23	628	121	20	6 F&D	50	18
Florida	14,504	11,377	8,326	1,085	962	(X)	695	631	[4]6 F&D	33.9	4
Georgia	7,267	3,503	2,687	450	199	3,082	376	104	[4]D	12	[6]7.5
Hawaii	2,710	1,659	1,295	72	69	907	68	40	4D	([7])	[8]16
Idaho	1,402	658	439	132	36	535	68	53	5D	18	21
Illinois	13,463	6,739	4,242	1,030	370	4,582	971	657	[4][5] 6.25	30	19
Indiana	6,476	3,589	2,779	542	144	2,202	386	156	5 F&D	15.5	15
Iowa	3,602	1,571	1,010	333	110	1,411	193	243	5 F&D	36	20
Kansas	2,802	1,419	958	251	110	834	199	119	[4]4.9D	24	18
Kentucky	5,081	2,228	1,367	360	68	1,679	271	154	6 F&D	3	15
Louisiana	4,250	2,162	1,269	470	149	867	232	93	[9]4D	20	20
Maine	1,664	853	573	143	89	591	70	57	6 F&D	37	19
Maryland	6,502	2,740	1,580	463	117	2,907	217	169	5 F&D	36	23.5
Massachusetts	9,903	3,101	1,979	541	206	5,337	757	315	5 F&D	26	21
Michigan	11,279	4,989	3,666	745	368	3,242	1,730	552	4 F&D	25	15
Minnesota	7,450	3,359	2,191	465	218	2,999	423	413	[4]6 F&D	48	20
Mississippi	2,494	1,677	1,182	317	86	440	145	72	7D	18	18
Missouri	5,131	2,589	1,917	384	103	1,844	230	217	[4]4.225D	13	13
Montana	1,025	202	(X)	121	28	322	58	44	(X)	19.25	20
Nebraska	1,890	999	663	222	54	653	104	59	[4]5 F&D	27	23.7
Nevada	1,823	1,539	893	139	63	(X)	(X)	75	[4]6.5F&D	35	18.75
New Hampshire	829	530	(X)	93	49	35	96	59	(X)	25	18
New Jersey	12,803	7,008	4,049	410	350	4,102	846	341	6 F&D	40	10.5
New Mexico	2,243	1,307	983	183	36	445	78	111	[4]5	15	16
New York	30,113	10,659	6,006	495	829	14,913	2,519	616	[4]4 F&D	39	8
North Carolina	9,010	3,973	2,171	861	196	3,583	644	335	[4]D	5	22.3
North Dakota	755	441	257	75	19	119	39	38	5 F&D	29	17
Ohio	12,115	6,070	3,752	1,129	288	4,407	642	503	[4]5 F&D	18	21
Oklahoma	3,765	1,576	971	340	126	1,218	149	305	[4]4.5D	23	17
Oregon	3,313	439	(X)	272	98	2,221	152	260	(X)	28	22
Pennsylvania	16,270	7,266	4,500	694	481	4,689	1,624	503	6 F&D	31	12
Rhode Island	1,307	667	389	94	46	478	49	52	7 F&D	37	23
South Carolina	3,936	2,052	1,452	287	138	1,411	142	94	5D	7	16
South Dakota	565	449	289	83	23	(X)	35	27	[4]4 D	23	18
Tennessee	4,526	3,516	2,515	657	143	93	295	186	[4]6D	13	20
Texas	17,031	13,610	8,576	1,953	970	(X)	(X)	764	[4]6D	41	20
Utah	1,989	1,018	802	136	43	781	76	54	[4]5D	23	19
Vermont	763	368	157	56	28	271	31	40	5 F&D	18	15
Virginia	7,025	2,858	1,571	629	113	3,321	273	280	[4]3.5D	2.5	17.5
Washington	8,477	6,349	5,032	627	267	(X)	(X)	224	6.5F&D	34	23
West Virginia	2,352	1,222	797	208	41	613	182	84	6D	17	15.5
Wisconsin	7,389	3,244	2,127	569	193	3,142	438	229	[4]5 F&D	38	22.2
Wyoming	646	239	183	38	7	(X)	(X)	40	[4]3D	12	9

X Not applicable.   [1] Includes amounts not shown separately.   [2] F=food exempt from sales tax; D=prescription drugs exempt from sales tax.   [3] Washington, D.C., excluded from total.   [4] Local sales tax rates are additional.   [5] Food and prescription drugs are subject to a 1 percent State tax. In addition, these items may be subject to a 1 percent local tax.   [6] An additional tax is levied at the rate of 3 percent of the retail sales price, less than the current 7.5 cents per gallon tax.   [7] Tax is 40 percent of wholesale price.   [8] Combined State and county rates are Hawaii 24.8 cents, Honolulu 32.5 cents, Kauai 26 cents, and Maui 25 cents.   [9] Food products subject to a 2 percent State tax.

Source: U.S. Bureau of the Census, *State Government Tax Collections,* series GF, No. 1, annual.

No. 480. Estimated State and Local Taxes Paid by a Family of Four in Selected Cities: 1992

[Preliminary. Data based on average family of four (two wage earners and two school age children) owning their own home and living in a city where taxes apply. Comprises State and local sales, income, auto, and real estate taxes. For definition of median, see Guide to Tabular Presentation]

CITY	TOTAL TAXES PAID, BY GROSS FAMILY INCOME LEVEL (dollars)				TOTAL TAXES PAID AS PERCENT OF INCOME			
	$25,000	$50,000	$75,000	$100,000	$25,000	$50,000	$75,000	$100,000
Albuquerque, NM	1,478	3,434	5,943	8,461	5.9	6.9	7.9	8.5
Atlanta, GA	2,838	5,593	9,107	12,019	11.4	11.2	12.1	12.0
Baltimore, MD	4,068	8,246	12,791	16,659	16.3	16.5	17.1	16.7
Bridgeport, CT	4,519	9,416	16,270	21,185	18.1	18.8	21.7	21.2
Burlington, VT	1,909	4,132	7,197	10,134	7.6	8.3	9.6	10.1
Charleston, WV	1,691	3,542	6,373	8,836	6.8	7.1	8.5	8.8
Charlotte, NC	2,085	4,412	7,253	9,734	8.3	8.8	9.7	9.7
Chicago, IL	2,954	5,938	9,326	12,084	11.8	11.9	12.4	12.1
Columbus, OH	2,151	4,713	7,712	10,650	8.6	9.4	10.3	10.7
Columbia, SC	1,971	4,799	8,151	10,905	7.9	9.6	10.9	10.9
Des Moines, IA	1,844	4,120	6,770	9,109	7.4	8.2	9.0	9.1
Detroit, MI	4,723	9,680	14,773	19,290	18.9	19.4	19.7	19.3
Honolulu, HI	1,853	4,306	7,272	9,921	7.4	8.6	9.7	9.9
Indianapolis, IN	2,017	3,703	6,268	8,061	8.1	7.4	8.4	8.1
Jackson, MS	1,451	3,421	6,080	8,237	5.8	6.8	8.1	8.2
Kansas City, MO	1,965	4,358	7,024	9,224	7.9	8.7	9.4	9.2
Louisville, KY.	2,439	5,100	8,099	10,777	9.8	10.2	10.8	10.8
Memphis, TN.	1,718	2,896	4,506	5,702	6.9	5.8	6.0	5.7
Milwaukee, WI	3,274	7,288	11,425	15,071	13.1	14.6	15.2	15.1
Newark, NJ	5,853	11,445	17,696	23,420	23.4	22.9	23.6	23.4
New York City, NY	2,603	6,579	11,199	15,247	10.4	13.2	14.9	15.2
Omaha, NE.	2,159	4,529	7,872	10,668	8.6	9.1	10.5	10.7
Philadelphia, PA.	3,956	7,610	11,361	14,755	15.8	15.2	15.1	14.8
Portland, ME.	2,132	5,144	9,361	12,759	8.5	10.3	12.5	12.8
Portland, OR.	2,428	5,369	8,623	11,542	9.7	10.7	11.5	11.5
Providence, RI	4,271	8,393	13,542	17,945	17.1	16.8	18.1	17.9
Salt Lake City, UT	2,038	4,682	7,564	10,020	8.2	9.4	10.1	10.0
Sioux Falls, SD	1,837	3,180	5,312	6,701	7.3	6.4	7.1	6.7
Virginia Beach, VA	2,089	4,423	7,521	9,930	8.4	8.8	10.0	9.9
Washington, DC.	2,278	5,041	8,416	11,556	9.1	10.1	11.2	11.6
Median [1].	1,970	4,306	7,253	9,921	7.9	8.6	9.7	9.9

[1] Median of all 51 cities. For complete list of cities, see table 481.

Source: Government of the District of Columbia, Department of Finance and Revenue, *Tax Rates and Tax Burdens in the District of Columbia: A Nationwide Comparison,* annual.

No. 481. Residential Property Tax Rates in Selected Cities: 1992

CITY	EFFECTIVE TAX RATE PER $100		Assessment level (percent)	Nominal rate per $100	CITY	EFFECTIVE TAX RATE PER $100		Assessment level (percent)	Nominal rate per $100
	Rank	Rate				Rank	Rate		
Detroit, MI	1	4.53	49.4	9.17	Billings, MT.	27	1.47	3.9	38.21
Milwaukee, WI.	2	3.83	99.9	3.84	Jackson, MS.	28	1.47	10.0	14.73
Newark, NJ.	3	3.14	15.8	19.96	Salt Lake City, UT . . .	29	1.43	95.0	1.50
Manchester, NH	4	2.75	99.0	2.78	Minneapolis, MN	30	1.39	12.1	11.50
Des Moines, IA	5	2.66	65.8	4.04	Columbia, SC	31	1.25	4.0	31.36
Philadelphia, PA	6	2.64	32.0	8.26	Charlotte, NC	32	1.17	98.2	1.20
Providence, RI	7	2.55	100.0	2.55	Kansas City, MO	33	1.15	19.0	6.03
Bridgeport, CT.	8	2.49	39.4	6.33	Boston, MA	34	1.12	100.0	1.12
Baltimore, MD.	9	2.44	40.0	6.11	Virginia Beach, VA. . .	35	1.09	100.0	1.09
Sioux Falls, IA	10	2.36	84.9	2.78	Seattle, WA	36	1.05	95.5	1.10
Portland, OR.	11	2.32	100.0	2.32	Oklahoma City, OK . .	37	1.04	11.0	9.45
Omaha, NE.	12	2.29	88.3	2.60	Albuquerque, NM. . . .	38	1.04	33.3	3.11
Jacksonville, FL.	13	2.15	100.0	2.15	Las Vegas, NV	39	1.02	35.0	2.92
Houston, TX	14	2.00	100.0	2.00	Denver, CO	40	0.97	14.3	6.73
Boise City, ID	15	1.98	95.0	2.08	Little Rock, AR	41	0.95	18.7	5.08
Columbus, OH.	16	1.80	35.0	5.14	Louisville, KY	42	0.95	92.0	1.03
Fargo, ND	17	1.78	4.3	41.49	Wilmington, DE	43	0.94	57.7	1.63
Wichita, KS.	18	1.76	12.0	14.66	Washington, DC	44	0.91	94.7	0.96
Indianapolis, IN	19	1.75	15.0	11.65	New York City, NY . . .	45	0.87	8.0	10.89
Atlanta, GA.	20	1.74	30.0	5.81	Cheyenne, WY	46	0.74	9.5	7.83
Portland, ME.	21	1.74	46.4	3.75	Birmingham, AL.	47	0.70	10.0	6.95
Anchorage, AK	22	1.71	95.0	1.80	Charleston, WV.	48	0.68	39.8	1.70
New Orleans, LA	23	1.61	10.0	16.06	Memphis, TN	49	0.67	25.0	2.68
Phoenix, AZ	24	1.53	10.0	15.28	Los Angeles, CA	50	0.63	61.2	1.03
Burlington, VT	25	1.51	59.8	2.52	Honolulu, HI	51	0.30	84.3	0.35
Chicago, IL.	26	1.49	16.0	9.31					

Source: Government of the District of Columbia, Department of Finance and Revenue, *Tax Rates and Tax Burdens in the District of Columbia: A Nationwide Comparison,* annual.

No. 482. Gross Revenue From Parimutuel and Amusement Taxes and Lotteries—Selected States: 1992

[For fiscal years; see text, section 9]

STATE	Gross revenue (mil. dol.)	Parimutuel taxes (mil. dol.)	Amusement taxes [1] (mil. dol.)	LOTTERY REVENUE			
				Total [2] (mil. dol.)	Apportionment of funds (percent)		
					Prizes	Administration	Proceeds available from ticket sales
United States [3]	20,633	595	820	19,217	54	6	40
Alabama............	5	5	(Z)	(X)	(X)	(X)	(X)
Alaska.............	2	(X)	2	(X)	(X)	(X)	(X)
Arizona............	243	8	1	234	51	10	39
Arkansas	19	19	-	(X)	(X)	(X)	(X)
California	1,399	121	-	1,278	52	11	37
Colorado...........	235	9	1	225	55	11	34
Connecticut........	75	55	20	(X)	(X)	(X)	(X)
Delaware	75	(Z)	-	75	55	7	38
Florida	2,168	94	2	2,072	53	5	42
Idaho	53	1	-	52	54	19	27
Illinois	1,546	44	26	1,476	55	4	41
Indiana............	360	-	-	360	60	8	32
Iowa	171	5	15	151	62	12	26
Kansas............	74	-	1	73	51	22	27
Kentucky	409	7	(Z)	402	67	7	26
Louisiana	369	11	3	356	54	7	39
Maine.............	115	1	-	114	54	10	36
Maryland	776	3	2	771	51	4	45
Massachusetts......	1,646	26	9	1,611	66	4	30
Michigan...........	1,141	20	-	1,121	53	4	43
Minnesota..........	337	2	55	280	61	19	20
Missouri	208	-	-	208	56	12	32
Montana...........	26	(Z)	-	26	52	26	22
Nebraska	9	1	8	(X)	(X)	(X)	(X)
Nevada	366	-	366	(X)	(X)	(X)	(X)
New Hampshire......	109	8	2	99	59	5	36
New Jersey	1,551	7	257	1,287	52	3	45
New York	1,959	77	1	1,881	52	3	46
North Dakota.......	6	-	6	(X)	(X)	(X)	(X)
Ohio	1,715	14	-	1,701	52	5	43
Oklahoma..........	7	7	-	(X)	(X)	(X)	(X)
Oregon............	249	4	-	244	58	22	20
Pennsylvania.......	1,327	12	(Z)	1,315	47	4	49
Rhode Island.......	67	9	(Z)	58	55	5	40
South Carolina......	20	-	20	(X)	(X)	(X)	(X)
South Dakota.......	61	1	-	61	20	8	72
Texas.............	22	-	22	(X)	(X)	(X)	(X)
Vermont...........	49	(Z)	-	49	57	8	35
Virginia............	826	-	(Z)	826	55	10	35
Washington.........	308	6	-	302	50	14	36
West Virginia.......	95	9	-	86	53	13	34
Wisconsin..........	439	12	1	426	61	6	33

- Represents or rounds to zero.   X Not applicable.   Z Less than $500,000.   [1] Represents nonlicense taxes.   [2] Excludes commissions.   [3] Includes States whose gross revenues were less than $1 million not shown separately.

Source: U.S. Bureau of the Census, *State Government Finances*, series GF, No. 3, annual.

No. 483. Lottery Sales—Type of Game and Use of Proceeds: 1980 to 1993

[In millions of dollars. For fiscal years]

GAME	1980	1985	1990	1991	1992	1993	USE OF PROCEEDS	1993
Total ticket sales..........	2,393	9,035	20,017	21,200	22,069	25,170	Total [1]	9,106
Passive [2]	206	88	(NA)	(NA)	(NA)	(NA)	Education............	4,833
Instant [3]	527	1,296	5,204	5,218	6,104	7,948	General fund.........	2,439
3-digit [4]	1,554	3,376	4,572	4,889	4,767	4,861	Cities..............	651
4-digit [4]	55	693	1,302	1,357	1,637	1,739	Senior citizen programs ..	605
Lotto [5]	52	3,583	8,563	8,619	8,506	9,516	Taxes	231
Other [6]	(NA)	(NA)	409	1,118	1,055	1,106	Economic development...	180
							Infrastructure	124
State proceeds	978	3,735	7,703	7,672	8,118	9,106	Environment	23
							Compulsive gambling	1

NA Not available.   [1] Includes other uses not shown separately.   [2] Also known as draw game or ticket. Player must match his ticket to winning numbers drawn by lottery. Players cannot choose their numbers.   [3] Player scratches a latex section on ticket which reveals instantly whether ticket is a winner.   [4] Players choose and bet on three or four digits, depending on game, with various payoffs for different straight order or mixed combination bets.   [5] Players typically select six digits out of a large field of numbers. Varying prizes are offered for matching three through six numbers drawn by lottery.   [6] Includes breakopen tickets, spiel, keno, video lottery, etc.

Source: TLF Publications, Inc., Boyds, MD, *World Lottery Almanac*, annual; *LaFleur's Fiscal 1993 Lottery Special Report;* and *LaFleur's Lottery World*, May 1994, (copyright).

No. 484. State Government Intergovernmental Expenditures, by State: 1992

[For fiscal year ending in year shown; see text, section 9]

STATE	Total (mil. dol.)	Per capita [1] (dol.)	Rank	Percent of general expenditure	STATE	Total (mil. dol.)	Per capita [1] (dol.)	Rank	Percent of general expenditure
United States .	201,313	791	(X)	33	Missouri	2,773	534	41	29
					Montana	610	740	14	29
Alabama	2,143	518	45	24	Nebraska	1,048	653	22	30
Alaska	1,049	1,787	1	22	Nevada	1,108	835	10	38
Arizona	2,997	782	12	36	New Hampshire. .	294	265	49	12
Arkansas	1,465	611	31	29	New Jersey . . .	7,859	1,009	7	33
California	39,402	1,277	4	47	New Mexico	1,619	1,024	6	35
Colorado	1,969	567	35	30	New York	24,711	1,364	3	41
Connecticut	2,091	637	24	21	North Carolina. . .	5,523	807	11	38
Delaware	391	567	35	17	North Dakota . . .	403	634	26	22
Florida	8,406	623	29	34	Ohio	7,999	726	17	33
Georgia	3,724	552	38	29	Oklahoma.	2,166	674	21	31
Hawaii	128	110	50	3	Oregon	1,613	542	40	24
Idaho.	781	732	16	34	Pennsylvania. . . .	8,616	718	18	28
Illinois	6,707	577	32	28	Rhode Island . . .	501	499	46	15
Indiana	3,678	650	23	31	South Carolina . .	2,032	564	37	25
Iowa	2,161	768	13	32	South Dakota . . .	280	394	48	19
Kansas	1,441	571	34	29	Tennessee	2,289	456	47	24
Kentucky	2,392	637	24	26	Texas	9,365	530	43	30
Louisiana	2,635	615	30	25	Utah	1,140	629	28	28
Maine	712	577	32	22	Vermont.	303	532	42	18
Maryland	2,559	521	44	23	Virginia	3,490	547	39	27
Massachusetts . .	4,048	675	19	23	Washington	4,579	892	9	31
Michigan	6,971	739	15	32	West Virginia. . . .	1,149	634	26	26
Minnesota	4,733	1,056	5	38	Wisconsin.	4,845	968	8	40
Mississippi	1,765	675	19	34	Wyoming	650	1,395	2	38

X Not applicable.   [1] Based on estimated resident population as of July 1.

Source: U.S. Bureau of the Census, *State Government Finances*, series GF, No. 3, annual.

No. 485. Local Government General Revenue, by State: 1992

[In millions of dollars. For fiscal year ending in year shown; see text, section 9. Data are estimates subject to sampling variation; see Appendix III and source]

STATE	Total [1]	INTERGOVERNMENTAL FROM—		FROM OWN SOURCES		STATE	Total [1]	INTERGOVERNMENTAL FROM—		FROM OWN SOURCES	
		Federal	State	Total	Taxes			Federal	State	Total	Taxes
U.S.	572,274	20,047	195,539	356,687	226,696	MO.	8,133	261	2,543	5,329	3,515
AL	6,078	222	2,122	3,734	1,720	MT.	1,487	102	460	925	561
AK	2,201	87	799	1,315	665	NE	3,106	110	829	2,167	1,345
AZ	8,116	309	2,997	4,810	2,921	NV	3,298	191	1,252	1,855	889
AR	3,061	90	1,355	1,617	887	NH	2,049	51	256	1,742	1,510
CA	90,382	2,650	39,996	47,736	25,946	NJ	20,615	244	7,382	12,989	10,080
CO	8,061	242	2,226	5,593	3,493	NM.	2,806	122	1,451	1,233	586
CT	6,924	201	2,018	4,704	3,976	NY	70,750	1,804	23,169	45,778	33,880
DE	1,054	41	479	534	277	NC	11,857	417	4,866	6,575	3,387
DC	4,712	1,776	(X)	2,936	2,407	ND	1,056	46	393	617	363
FL	31,384	948	8,887	21,549	11,377	OH	21,808	815	7,278	13,714	9,222
GA	13,823	517	3,776	9,530	5,102	OK	4,985	155	1,869	2,960	1,475
HI.	1,239	94	137	1,008	683	OR	6,449	380	1,706	4,363	2,916
ID.	1,716	51	710	954	496	PA	23,993	1,074	7,920	14,999	9,998
IL.	24,779	1,176	6,884	16,719	12,146	RI.	1,550	70	400	1,080	938
IN.	9,887	228	3,606	6,052	3,631	SC	5,520	183	1,896	3,441	1,771
IA.	5,599	156	1,902	3,541	2,093	SD	1,019	54	236	729	543
KS	4,852	77	1,318	3,457	2,138	TN	7,744	305	2,149	5,290	2,868
KY	5,271	199	2,246	2,826	1,508	TX	35,085	864	9,635	24,586	15,808
LA	7,719	342	2,490	4,887	2,826	UT	3,037	82	1,102	1,853	1,093
ME	2,052	70	669	1,313	995	VT	927	13	276	638	540
MD	9,710	421	2,506	6,783	4,965	VA	11,902	392	3,563	7,947	5,659
MA	11,775	622	3,934	7,218	5,406	WA	11,361	402	4,545	6,414	3,467
MI	19,334	395	6,154	12,785	8,718	WV	2,601	63	1,198	1,341	651
MN	12,279	439	4,801	7,039	3,631	WI	11,584	291	4,951	6,342	4,220
MS	4,163	170	1,653	2,340	964	WY	1,379	31	548	800	440

X Not applicable.   [1] Excludes duplicative intergovernmental transactions.

Source: U.S. Bureau of the Census, *Government Finances*, series GF, No. 5, annual.

No. 486. County Governments—Summary of Finances, by Population-Size Group: 1980 to 1991

[For fiscal year ending in year shown; see text, section 9. Represents all counties and their dependent agencies (including dependent school systems where applicable). Size classifications based on 1986 populations; counties distributed according to their 1990 enumerated population]

ITEM	ALL COUNTIES [1] (mil. dol.)			PER CAPITA (dollars), 1991								
				All counties		Counties with 1990 population (1,000) of—						
	1980	1990	1991	Total (3,043) [2]	Per-cent distribution	Less than 100 [1] (2,631)	100 to 149.9 (133)	150 to 199.9 (66)	200 to 299.9 (74)	300 to 499.9 (62)	500 to 999.9 (52)	1,000 or more (24)
General revenue	54,573	135,775	137,223	610	100	539	527	544	551	551	733	704
Intergovernmental revenue [3]	24,746	53,953	49,863	222	36	194	195	184	179	184	228	305
From State governments	18,969	49,225	44,535	198	32	174	175	162	157	167	200	274
From Federal government	4,948	2,780	3,058	14	2	12	14	14	14	9	15	16
Tax revenue [3]	18,813	48,750	52,154	232	38	189	184	234	212	227	333	239
Property	14,300	35,723	38,610	172	28	136	135	163	156	169	232	195
Charges and miscellaneous	11,014	33,072	35,207	157	26	157	148	126	160	140	173	160
General expenditure	54,291	127,626	139,267	619	100	535	542	568	559	562	764	710
Capital outlay	6,505	13,467	15,332	68	11	53	60	62	63	61	104	71
Current expenditure	47,786	114,159	123,934	551	89	482	482	506	496	501	660	638
Education	8,412	18,395	19,821	88	14	111	103	120	86	80	126	22
Public welfare	8,591	18,114	20,171	90	14	50	74	71	70	97	97	151
Hospitals	5,975	13,018	14,164	63	10	65	47	22	56	32	60	95
Health	2,806	8,791	9,362	42	7	32	40	40	42	39	47	53
Highways	5,227	9,415	10,246	46	7	68	42	45	37	38	39	28
Police protection	2,661	6,693	7,382	33	5	27	28	36	29	28	39	44
Correction	1,759	6,590	7,447	33	5	17	21	25	31	31	35	53
Natural resources	687	1,314	1,371	6	1	5	4	3	5	4	10	11
Parks and recreation	1,094	2,487	2,830	13	2	5	6	10	10	13	27	15
Financial administration	1,521	3,363	3,613	16	3	17	14	17	17	15	16	16
General control [4]	3,374	9,149	9,948	42	7	51	23	22	24	28	35	58
General public buildings	1,072	2,182	2,317	10	2	10	10	11	12	10	14	7
Interest on general debt	1,542	7,976	8,223	37	6	27	30	29	32	30	52	47
Other and unallocable	9,570	20,139	22,372	102	16	49	101	116	109	117	167	111
Debt outstanding, year end	32,993	118,608	121,755	541	100	401	433	468	480	480	732	697
Long-term	31,543	115,392	117,041	520	96	395	426	459	449	458	715	643
Short-term	1,450	3,216	4,714	21	4	6	8	9	10	22	18	54

[1] Data for counties under 100,000 population are estimates subject to sampling variation; see Appendix III and source.
[2] Figures in parentheses represent number of counties in each size group.   [3] Includes other revenues not shown separately.
[4] Includes judicial and legal as well as other administrative expenditures.
Source: U.S. Bureau of the Census, County Government Finances, series GF, No. 8, annual.

No. 487. Gross Assessed Value of Property and Government Revenue From Property Taxes: 1975 to 1991

[In billions of dollars, except percent. Data are estimates subject to sampling variation; see Appendix III and source]

ITEM	1975	1979	1981	1984	1986	1987	1988	1989	1990	1991
Gross assessed value of property [1]	1,096	1,679	2,958	4,053	4,818	(NA)	(NA)	6,013	(NA)	(NA)
State assessed	75	114	159	200	243	(NA)	(NA)	257	(NA)	(NA)
Locally assessed	1,022	1,565	2,799	3,853	4,575	(NA)	(NA)	5,756	(NA)	(NA)
Real property	882	1,359	2,515	3,447	4,105	(NA)	(NA)	5,220	(NA)	(NA)
Percent of locally assessed	86	87	90	89	90	(NA)	(NA)	91	(NA)	(NA)
Net assessed value of locally taxable property [2]	1,063	1,607	2,838	3,869	4,620	(NA)	(NA)	5,791	(NA)	(NA)
Percent of gross assessed	97	96	96	96	96	(NA)	(NA)	96	(NA)	(NA)
REVENUE FROM PROPERTY TAXES										
State and local governments	52	65	75	97	112	121	132	143	156	168
Percent of general revenue	23	19	18	18	17	18	18	18	18	19
Percent of tax revenue	36	32	31	30	30	30	30	30	31	32
State governments	2	3	3	4	4	5	5	5	6	6
Percent of general revenue	1	1	1	1	1	1	1	1	1	1
Percent of tax revenue	2	2	2	2	2	2	2	2	1	1
Local governments	50	63	72	93	107	117	127	137	150	162
Annual percent change from prior year	[3]7	6	7	8	8	9	9	8	9	9
Percent of general revenue	32	27	25	25	25	25	29	29	29	30
Percent of tax revenue	82	78	76	75	74	74	74	74	75	75

NA Not available.   [1] Gross assessed value amounts may include prior year components for those States unable to report data for indicated year at time of publication. See sources for definitions of terms and limitations of data.   [2] Value subject to local general property taxation, including State-assessed property, after deduction of partial exemptions.   [3] Change from 1971.
Source: U.S. Bureau of the Census, 1982 and 1987 Census of Governments, vol. 2; Property Values Subject to Local General Property Taxation in the United States: 1975 and 1979, and Government Finances, series GF, No. 5, annual.

No. 488. City Governments—Summary of Finances: 1980 to 1992

[For fiscal year ending in year shown; see text, section 9. Represents all municipalities and their dependent agencies (including dependent school systems where applicable); excludes other local governments overlying city areas. Includes sample-based estimates for cities of less than 50,000; thus subject to sampling variation. See Appendix III and source]

ITEM	TOTAL (mil. dol.)				PER CAPITA [1] (dol.)			
	1980	1990	1991	1992	1980	1990	1991	1992
Revenue	94,862	202,393	210,498	220,048	672	1,323	1,368	1,430
General revenue	76,056	158,301	164,319	171,618	539	1,035	1,068	1,116
Intergovernmental revenue	28,270	45,306	46,260	48,152	200	296	301	313
From State governments only	15,939	34,243	34,901	36,222	113	224	227	235
Taxes	31,256	68,788	72,213	75,486	222	450	469	491
Property	16,859	35,024	37,654	39,706	119	229	245	258
Percent of total taxes	54	51	52	53	(X)	(X)	(X)	(X)
Sales and gross receipts	8,208	19,190	19,604	20,190	58	125	127	131
General	5,096	11,645	11,738	11,976	36	76	76	78
Selective	3,112	7,545	7,866	8,214	22	49	51	53
Income, licenses, and other	6,189	14,574	14,954	15,590	44	95	97	101
Charges and miscellaneous	16,530	44,207	45,846	47,980	117	289	298	312
Current charges only	9,875	25,265	27,221	29,449	70	165	177	191
Utility and liquor store revenue	15,719	33,266	34,486	35,460	111	217	224	231
Water system	4,989	11,578	12,067	12,724	35	76	78	83
Electric power system	8,007	17,312	17,926	18,232	57	113	117	119
Gas supply system	1,444	2,335	2,299	2,321	10	15	15	15
Transit system	1,032	1,766	1,924	1,892	7	12	13	13
Liquor stores	247	275	270	292	2	2	2	2
Insurance trust revenue	3,088	10,827	11,693	12,969	22	71	76	84
Expenditure	93,699	198,822	211,506	219,293	664	1,299	1,375	1,426
General expenditure	72,433	153,717	164,226	170,680	513	1,005	1,068	1,110
Police protection	8,200	18,183	19,388	20,420	58	119	126	133
Fire protection	4,535	9,487	10,045	10,412	32	62	65	68
Highways	5,977	12,106	12,627	12,961	42	79	82	84
Sewerage and sanitation	7,907	16,476	17,603	18,260	56	108	114	119
Public welfare	3,801	7,890	8,941	9,528	27	52	58	62
Education	9,284	17,368	18,793	19,382	66	114	122	126
Libraries	883	1,939	2,119	2,106	6	13	14	14
Health and hospitals	4,457	9,141	9,818	10,338	32	60	64	67
Parks and recreation	3,433	7,584	8,450	8,232	24	50	55	54
Housing and community develop	3,459	7,661	8,286	8,576	25	50	54	56
Airports	1,100	2,878	2,970	3,552	8	19	19	23
Financial administration	1,843	3,895	3,907	4,172	13	25	25	27
General control [2]	2,015	5,274	6,195	6,055	14	34	40	39
General public buildings	1,090	1,767	1,947	1,884	8	12	13	12
Interest on general debt	3,054	11,317	11,370	12,429	22	74	74	81
Other and unallocable	11,395	20,751	21,767	22,373	81	136	142	145
Utility and liquor store expenditure	18,274	38,436	39,728	40,740	130	251	257	265
Water system	5,933	13,579	14,229	14,661	42	89	93	95
Electric power system	8,596	17,490	17,656	18,023	61	114	115	117
Gas supply system	1,334	2,263	2,218	2,177	9	15	14	14
Transit system	2,189	4,855	5,375	5,613	16	32	35	36
Liquor stores	222	250	250	266	2	2	2	2
Insurance trust expenditure	2,993	6,669	7,552	7,973	21	44	49	51
By character and object:								
Direct expenditure	91,692	193,933	206,637	213,379	650	1,268	1,343	1,387
Current operation	66,687	138,818	147,644	153,501	473	907	960	998
Capital outlay	16,285	31,779	34,106	33,274	115	208	222	216
Construction	13,341	22,842	23,977	23,929	95	149	156	156
Land and existing structures [3]	2,944	8,937	10,129	9,345	21	58	66	61
Assistance payments	1,546	2,212	2,549	2,788	11	14	17	18
Interest on debt	4,182	14,455	14,786	15,944	30	94	96	104
Insurance benefits, repayments	2,992	6,669	7,552	7,873	21	44	49	52
Intergovernmental expenditure	2,007	4,890	4,869	5,913	14	32	32	34
Expenditure for salaries and wages [4]	34,709	66,973	72,108	74,192	246	438	469	482
Debt outstanding, year end	86,019	212,919	226,554	241,551	610	1,392	1,473	1,570
Long-term	82,346	207,487	220,591	236,144	584	1,356	1,434	1,535
Full faith and credit	39,570	68,510	75,147	81,748	280	448	489	531
Nonguaranteed	42,776	138,977	145,444	154,396	303	908	946	1,004
Short-term	3,673	5,432	5,963	5,407	26	36	39	34
Net long-term debt outstanding	72,528	139,109	152,880	167,329	514	909	994	1,088
Long-term debt issued	12,582	27,991	30,166	35,795	89	183	196	233
Long-term debt retired	5,541	17,980	16,245	22,227	39	118	106	144

X Not applicable.   [1] 1980 data based on April 1 enumerated resident population; 1990 data based on July 1, 1988, estimated resident population; 1991 and 1992 based on April 1, 1990, enumerated population.   [2] Includes judicial and legal as well as other governmental administration.   [3] Includes equipment.   [4] Included in items shown above.

Source: U.S. Bureau of the Census, *City Government Finances*, series GF, No. 4, annual.

City Government Finances 315

No. 489. City Governments—Total and Per Capita Finances for Largest Cities: 1992

[For fiscal year ending in year show; see text, section 9. Cities ranked by size of population enumerated as of April 1, 1990, except Honolulu and Baton Rouge ranked by county population. Data reflect inclusion of fiscal activity of dependent school systems where applicable. Intercity comparisons should be made with caution due to variations in responsibilities among urban areas; for details see text, section 9, and source]

CITIES RANKED BY 1990 POPULATION	GENERAL REVENUE Total (mil. dol.)	Per capita [1] (dol.)	INTERGOV REVENUE Total (mil. dol.)	Per capita [1] (dol.)	TAXES Total (mil. dol.)	Per capita [1] (dol.)	GENERAL EXPENDITURE Total (mil. dol.)	Per capita [1] (dol.)	DEBT OUTSTANDING Total (mil. dol.)	Per capita [1] (dol.)
New York City, NY [2]	36,782	5,023	14,480	1,977	17,141	2,341	34,331	4,688	34,984	4,778
Los Angeles, CA	3,889	1,116	522	150	1,933	554	3,534	1,014	8,003	2,296
Chicago, IL	3,298	1,185	822	295	1,592	572	3,281	1,179	6,012	2,160
Houston, TX	1,417	869	64	39	779	478	1,452	890	3,962	2,430
Philadelphia, PA [2]	2,818	1,777	874	551	1,483	935	2,823	1,780	3,835	2,418
San Diego, CA	1,174	1,057	233	210	383	345	1,084	976	1,646	1,482
Detroit, MI	1,567	1,524	706	686	551	536	1,577	1,534	1,685	1,640
Dallas, TX	1,083	1,076	58	58	505	502	1,373	1,363	3,586	3,562
Phoenix, AZ	988	1,005	312	317	334	339	924	940	2,310	2,349
San Antonio, TX	555	593	118	126	224	239	657	702	4,239	4,529
San Jose, CA	642	821	95	122	328	419	892	1,140	1,051	1,344
Baltimore, MD [2]	1,760	2,391	882	1,198	664	903	710	965	1,249	1,697
Indianapolis, IN [2]	933	1,276	284	388	419	574	1,550	2,120	1,308	1,789
San Francisco, CA [2]	2,640	3,647	900	1,243	977	1,349	895	1,236	1,232	1,702
Jacksonville, FL [2]	731	1,151	145	229	248	391	2,302	3,624	3,174	4,996
Columbus, OH	558	881	105	166	287	453	779	1,231	4,654	7,353
Milwaukee, WI	601	957	307	490	166	265	600	955	1,247	1,985
Memphis, TN	882	1,445	573	939	159	260	584	957	600	984
Washington, DC [2]	4,419	7,282	1,508	2,485	2,407	3,965	879	1,448	811	1,336
Boston, MA [2]	1,595	2,778	657	1,144	641	1,117	4,586	7,985	3,942	6,864
Seattle, WA	713	1,381	98	189	370	718	1,560	3,021	1,071	2,074
El Paso, TX	271	526	31	59	129	250	737	1,430	1,032	2,002
Cleveland, OH	535	1,058	132	262	273	539	268	530	448	887
New Orleans, LA [2]	658	1,323	123	247	301	605	552	1,110	761	1,532
Nashville-Davidson, TN [2]	989	2,026	258	529	479	980	684	1,400	1,126	2,305
Denver, CO [2]	1,046	2,236	249	532	391	836	857	1,833	2,216	4,739
Austin, TX	560	1,203	34	74	176	378	1,513	3,250	3,344	7,182
Fort Worth, TX	381	851	42	94	196	437	611	1,366	3,190	7,126
Oklahoma City, OK	355	798	19	42	194	436	436	981	935	2,102
Portland, OR	402	920	66	150	203	464	362	827	571	1,306
Kansas City, MO	541	1,244	57	130	330	758	495	1,137	759	1,744
Long Beach, CA	604	1,407	115	267	183	425	570	1,327	905	2,108
Tucson, AZ	361	891	120	295	132	326	598	1,476	791	1,950
St. Louis, MO [2]	494	1,247	74	186	277	698	343	864	825	2,079
Charlotte, NC	428	1,080	111	279	165	416	517	1,306	767	1,937
Atlanta, GA	695	1,763	138	350	223	566	500	1,269	999	2,536
Virginia Beach, VA [2]	736	1,872	271	689	374	950	624	1,587	1,433	3,646
Albuquerque, NM	470	1,222	151	392	132	344	682	1,772	566	1,470
Oakland, CA	540	1,451	102	274	222	596	395	1,062	754	2,026
Pittsburgh, PA	373	1,009	91	245	237	640	508	1,373	1,144	3,093
Sacramento, CA	331	895	31	83	154	417	379	1,025	661	1,789
Minneapolis, MN	620	1,682	170	461	192	522	352	957	452	1,227
Tulsa, OK	416	1,133	29	79	167	454	736	2,004	2,290	6,234
Honolulu, HI [2]	871	1,042	123	147	482	577	444	532	1,585	1,895
Cincinnati, OH	523	1,437	96	263	238	653	525	1,443	260	713
Miami, FL	306	854	48	135	171	476	324	903	565	1,575
Fresno, CA	242	682	47	132	109	306	236	666	248	701
Omaha, NE	228	678	36	107	144	429	209	621	195	580
Toledo, OH	235	705	45	134	128	384	234	703	194	582
Buffalo, NY	690	2,101	467	1,425	143	436	757	2,308	500	1,524
Wichita, KS	247	812	76	250	80	262	260	857	539	1,772
Santa Ana, CA	180	613	39	134	103	349	204	694	304	1,035
Mesa, AZ	183	636	59	204	45	158	197	685	484	1,681
Colorado Springs, CO	286	1,016	27	96	85	302	306	1,087	730	2,597
Tampa, FL	306	1,094	50	178	126	449	327	1,169	683	2,438
Newark, NJ	453	1,646	265	963	97	353	450	1,634	207	750
St. Paul, MN	414	1,522	142	521	93	343	409	1,504	865	3,177
Louisville, KY	255	946	57	211	147	547	255	947	442	1,642
Anaheim, CA	267	1,003	39	145	112	421	333	1,252	766	2,874
Birmingham, AL	277	1,042	30	111	158	595	309	1,162	807	3,035
Arlington, TX	180	686	11	42	96	367	154	589	378	1,446
Norfolk, VA [2]	566	2,167	211	807	216	827	586	2,244	1,023	3,914
Las Vegas, NV	235	912	101	393	64	250	246	951	134	518
Corpus Christi, TX	164	637	15	59	71	276	154	596	429	1,668
St. Petersburg, FL	237	993	33	138	91	381	212	889	574	2,405
Rochester, NY	615	2,656	362	1,563	140	602	628	2,712	284	1,228
Riverside, CA	216	955	32	140	74	325	219	966	727	3,208
Anchorage, AK [2]	696	3,074	270	1,191	179	792	699	3,088	1,055	4,662
Lexington-Fayette, KY [2]	197	873	16	73	101	450	190	842	414	1,837
Akron, OH	200	898	41	182	95	426	200	895	152	683
Aurora, CO	173	777	16	74	100	452	157	706	429	1,932
Baton Rouge, LA [2]	414	1,089	56	147	203	533	476	1,254	1,269	3,340
Stockton, CA	146	693	21	102	68	322	145	687	283	1,342

[1] Based on enumerated population as of April 1, 1990.   [2] Represents, in effect, city-county consolidated government.

Source: U.S. Bureau of the Census, *City Government Finances*, series GF, No. 4, annual.

No. 490. City Governments—Finances, by Population-Size Groups: 1992

[For fiscal year ending in year shown; see text, section 9. Represents all municipalities and their dependent agencies, including dependent school systems where applicable]

ITEM	All cities [1]	CITIES HAVING A 1990 POPULATION OF—						
		Less than 75,000 [1]	75,000 to 99,999	100,000 to 199,999	200,000 to 299,999	300,000 to 499,999	500,000 to 999,999	1,000,000 or more
Number of cities, 1992.	19,296	19,003	98	119	24	28	16	8
Population, 1990 (1,000)	153,827	81,012	8,455	16,390	5,975	11,088	10,954	19,953
FINANCES, 1992 (mil. dol.)								
General revenue [2].	171,618	55,827	7,963	15,995	7,228	13,884	18,694	52,027
Taxes [2]	75,486	23,630	3,704	7,047	2,691	5,940	8,108	24,366
Property	39,706	13,983	2,404	4,351	1,396	2,593	4,313	10,666
Sales and gross receipts	20,190	6,355	991	2,038	787	2,313	1,791	5,915
Intergovernmental [2]	48,152	12,655	1,824	4,338	2,189	3,118	6,269	17,759
From State governments	36,222	9,201	1,414	3,128	1,518	1,970	3,580	15,411
From Federal Government	8,033	1,638	316	775	420	732	2,147	2,005
Current charges.	29,449	11,900	1,479	2,632	1,370	2,875	2,611	6,582
Utility and liquor store revenue	35,460	17,321	1,703	3,597	1,445	2,095	3,698	5,601
General expenditure [2]	170,680	56,198	8,128	16,373	7,423	14,629	18,475	49,454
Police and fire protection	30,832	12,451	1,710	3,444	1,438	2,698	2,992	6,099
Education.	19,382	3,328	1,229	2,414	1,058	1,018	2,261	8,074
Sewerage and sanitation.	18,260	8,040	756	1,770	714	1,646	1,791	3,543
Highways	12,961	6,478	748	1,367	581	1,070	940	1,777
Health and hospitals.	10,338	2,872	335	284	267	622	1,693	4,265
Public welfare	9,528	367	68	282	146	183	1,320	7,162
Housing and community development .	8,576	1,934	466	828	597	701	956	3,094
Interest on general debt	12,429	3,838	557	1,207	681	1,735	1,326	3,085
Utility and liquor store expenditure.	40,740	17,791	1,978	3,804	1,596	2,340	4,456	8,775
Debt outstanding	241,551	73,666	10,772	22,488	12,701	29,081	29,129	63,714
Long-term	236,144	71,806	10,581	22,110	12,476	28,753	28,865	61,553
Short-term	5,407	1,857	192	379	226	328	264	2,161
PERCENT DISTRIBUTION								
General revenue [2].	100	33	5	9	4	8	11	30
Taxes [2]	100	31	5	9	4	8	11	32
Property	100	35	6	11	4	7	11	27
Sales and gross receipts	100	31	5	10	4	11	9	29
Intergovernmental	100	26	4	9	5	7	13	37
Current charges.	100	40	5	9	5	10	9	22
General expenditure [2]	100	33	5	10	4	9	11	29
Police and fire protection	100	40	6	11	5	9	10	20
Education.	100	17	6	13	6	5	12	42
Sewerage and sanitation.	100	44	4	10	4	9	10	19
Highways	100	50	6	11	5	8	7	14
Health and hospitals.	100	28	3	3	3	6	16	41
Public welfare	100	4	1	3	2	2	14	75
Housing and community development .	100	23	5	10	7	8	11	36
Interest on general debt	100	31	5	10	6	14	11	25
PER CAPITA [3] (dollars)								
General revenue [2].	1,116	689	942	976	1,210	1,252	1,707	2,607
Taxes [2]	491	292	438	430	450	536	740	1,221
Property	258	173	284	265	234	234	394	535
Sales and gross receipts	131	78	117	124	132	209	163	296
Intergovernmental [2]	313	156	216	265	366	281	572	890
From State governments	235	114	167	191	254	178	327	772
From Federal Government	52	20	37	47	70	66	196	100
Current charges.	191	147	175	161	229	259	238	330
Utility and liquor store revenue	231	214	201	219	242	189	338	281
General expenditure [2]	1,110	694	961	999	1,242	1,319	1,687	2,479
Police and fire protection	200	154	202	210	241	243	273	306
Education.	126	41	145	147	177	92	206	405
Sewerage and sanitation.	119	99	89	108	120	148	164	178
Highways	84	80	88	83	97	96	86	89
Health and hospitals.	67	35	40	17	45	56	155	214
Public welfare	62	5	8	17	24	17	121	359
Housing and community development .	56	24	55	50	100	63	87	155
Interest on general debt	81	47	66	74	114	156	121	155
Utility and liquor store expenditure.	265	220	234	232	267	211	407	440
Debt outstanding	1,570	909	1,274	1,372	2,126	2,623	2,659	3,193
Long-term	1,535	886	1,251	1,349	2,088	2,593	2,635	3,085
Short-term	35	23	23	23	38	30	24	108

[1] Data are estimates subject to sampling variation, see Appendix III and source.   [2] Includes items not shown separately.
[3] Based on 1990 enumerated resident population as of April 1.

Source: U.S. Bureau of the Census, *City Government Finances*, series GF, No. 4, annual.

No. 491. City Governments—Revenue and Debt for Largest Cities: 1992

[In millions of dollars. For fiscal year ending in year shown; see text, section 9. See headnote, table 489]

CITIES RANKED BY 1990 POPULATION	Total [1]	General revenue Total [1]	Intergovernmental From State and local govts.	Intergovernmental From Federal Government	Taxes Total [1]	Taxes Property	Taxes Sales and gross receipts	Utility and liquor store	Debt outstanding
New York City, NY [2]	44,888	36,782	13,330	1,150	17,141	7,899	3,432	1,993	34,984
Los Angeles, CA	6,993	3,889	385	137	1,933	774	758	2,141	8,003
Chicago, IL	4,514	3,298	565	256	1,592	596	855	228	6,012
Houston, TX	1,802	1,417	23	41	779	400	359	235	3,962
Philadelphia, PA [2]	3,471	2,818	717	157	1,483	330	73	587	3,835
San Diego, CA	1,427	1,174	142	92	383	156	194	125	1,646
Detroit, MI	2,043	1,567	576	130	551	215	44	169	1,685
Dallas, TX	1,371	1,083	16	42	505	295	201	122	3,586
Phoenix, AZ	1,152	988	230	82	334	117	197	103	2,310
San Antonio, TX	1,427	555	96	22	224	124	94	839	4,239
San Jose, CA	768	642	86	9	328	129	146	8	1,249
Baltimore, MD [2]	1,997	1,760	828	53	664	458	48	52	1,308
Indianapolis, IN [2]	965	933	248	35	419	322	20	7	1,232
San Francisco, CA [2]	3,417	2,640	778	122	977	536	233	225	3,174
Jacksonville, FL [2]	1,556	731	88	57	248	198	41	729	4,654
Columbus, OH	647	558	58	47	287	23	6	89	1,247
Milwaukee, WI	833	601	257	50	166	155	5	48	600
Memphis, TN [2]	1,891	882	546	27	159	118	30	844	811
Washington, DC [2]	4,754	4,419	58	1,451	2,407	903	672	54	3,942
Boston, MA [2]	1,830	1,595	634	23	641	599	25	69	1,071
Seattle, WA	1,104	713	76	21	370	128	154	332	1,032
El Paso, TX	359	271	8	22	129	66	59	42	448
Cleveland, OH	703	535	69	63	273	49	4	167	761
New Orleans, LA [2]	747	658	45	78	301	138	137	56	1,126
Nashville-Davidson, TN [2]	1,636	989	246	13	479	263	173	605	2,216
Denver, CO [2]	1,171	1,046	221	27	391	99	246	85	3,344
Austin, TX	1,130	560	26	8	176	98	74	500	3,190
Fort Worth, TX	501	381	23	19	196	130	61	65	935
Oklahoma City, OK	407	355	8	10	194	27	161	38	571
Portland, OR	455	402	54	12	203	138	31	52	759
Kansas City, MO	671	541	29	28	330	62	147	47	905
Long Beach, CA	725	604	73	42	183	72	91	120	791
Tucson, AZ	455	361	98	22	132	24	104	76	825
St. Louis, MO [2]	604	494	41	32	277	37	109	30	767
Charlotte, NC	473	428	89	22	165	140	12	34	999
Atlanta, GA	811	695	82	55	223	123	68	61	1,433
Virginia Beach, VA [2]	775	736	179	91	374	233	113	39	566
Albuquerque, NM	514	470	122	29	132	47	80	43	1,269
Baton Rouge, LA [2]	455	414	32	24	203	54	137	3	754
Oakland, CA	566	540	73	29	222	113	68	-	1,144
Pittsburgh, PA	407	373	70	21	237	122	29	-	661
Sacramento, CA	386	331	30	1	154	52	90	20	452
Minneapolis, MN	750	620	144	26	192	142	38	23	2,290
Tulsa, OK	473	416	14	15	167	19	144	44	1,585
Honolulu, HI [2]	962	871	62	61	482	389	59	91	1,051
Cincinnati, OH	675	523	69	27	238	43	4	64	260
Miami, FL	381	306	35	14	171	127	35	-	565
Fresno, CA	320	242	34	13	109	39	50	23	248
Omaha, NE	259	228	32	4	144	66	70	-	195
Toledo, OH	255	235	31	13	128	10	-	21	194
Buffalo, NY	709	690	422	45	143	122	15	20	500
Wichita, KS	313	247	66	10	80	52	25	25	539
Santa Ana, CA	197	180	22	17	103	48	47	17	304
Mesa, AZ	255	183	52	6	45	5	37	71	484
Colorado Springs, CO	546	286	15	12	85	18	66	260	730
Tampa, FL	383	306	38	12	126	58	59	30	683
Newark, NJ	491	453	203	62	97	62	8	37	207
St. Paul, MN	448	414	102	40	93	72	17	22	865
Louisville, KY	317	255	36	21	147	38	1	62	442
Anaheim, CA	510	267	17	21	112	38	65	243	766
Birmingham, AL	326	277	16	13	158	28	56	-	807
Arlington, TX	212	180	2	9	96	57	37	33	378
Norfolk, VA [2]	633	566	163	48	216	127	69	33	1,023
Las Vegas, NV	235	235	98	3	64	30	14	-	134
Corpus Christi, TX	214	164	5	10	71	36	34	50	429
St. Petersburg, FL	296	237	30	3	91	58	29	49	574
Rochester, NY	641	615	308	54	140	126	11	26	284
Riverside, CA	414	216	28	4	74	25	42	197	727
Anchorage, AK [2]	815	696	264	6	179	165	7	94	1,055
Lexington-Fayette, KY [2]	221	197	6	11	101	24	6	1	414
Akron, OH	226	200	18	22	95	18	-	25	152
Aurora, CO	205	173	14	2	100	16	80	25	429
Stockton, CA	152	146	17	5	68	18	40	6	283

- Represents or rounds to zero.   [1] Includes items not shown separately.   [2] Represents, in effect, city-county consolidated government.

Source: U.S. Bureau of the Census, *City Government Finances*, series GF, No. 4, annual.

No. 492. City Governments—Expenditures for Largest Cities: 1992

[In millions of dollars. For fiscal year ending in year shown; see text, section 9. See headnote, table 489]

CITIES RANKED BY 1990 POPULATION	Total expenditure [1]	General expenditure								Utility and liquor store
		Total [1]	Education	Housing and community development	Public welfare	Health and hospitals	Police protection	Fire protection	Highways	
New York City, NY [2]	42,499	34,331	8,008	2,445	6,840	3,646	1,872	699	795	4,690
Los Angeles, CA.......	6,577	3,534	9	256	-	11	650	265	153	2,411
Chicago, IL..........	3,887	3,281	35	128	110	97	627	231	365	198
Houston, TX. .,......	1,758	1,452	-	21	-	59	269	147	128	238
Philadelphia, PA [2].....	3,723	2,823	17	89	213	335	345	123	95	607
San Diego, CA........	1,311	1,084	-	90	(Z)	2	168	75	76	181
Detroit, MI..........	2,131	1,577	6	51	-	98	290	93	100	305
Dallas, TX..........	1,620	1,373	-	14	-	19	168	75	63	146
Phoenix, AZ..........	1,091	924	1	57	-	1	155	83	68	143
San Antonio, TX......	1,501	657	9	13	12	18	99	66	53	829
San Jose, CA.,.......	760	710	-	110	-	-	110	55	64	17
Baltimore, MD [2].......	1,687	1,550	537	63	2	58	154	84	144	46
Indianapolis, IN [2].,....	954	895	-	30	77	176	88	38	49	24
San Francisco, CA [2]....	3,024	2,302	58	75	313	549	164	101	42	490
Jacksonville, FL [2]......	1,686	779	-	50	17	21	78	56	45	867
Columbus, OH........	729	600	-	4	-	23	127	67	53	129
Milwaukee, WI........	684	584	-	46	-	12	118	54	46	37
Memphis, TN .,.......	1,762	879	435	20	-	16	74	59	37	819
Washington, DC [2]......	5,036	4,586	743	219	872	535	273	97	122	78
Boston, MA [2]	1,781	1,560	479	45	26	237	137	86	51	57
Seattle, WA	1,173	737	-	49	-	14	95	62	51	384
El Paso, TX...........	359	268	-	5	1	15	43	23	24	74
Cleveland, OH .,......	803	552	-	68	(Z)	10	123	67	48	252
New Orleans, LA [2] .,...	773	684	-	82	6	14	77	37	39	54
Nashville-Davidson, TN [2] .	1,525	857	271	5	11	80	64	39	35	629
Denver, CO [2]	1,649	1,513	-	11	133	134	92	53	65	113
Austin, TX	1,113	611	-	5	1	142	52	35	22	478
Fort Worth, TX	523	436	-	6	-	11	53	32	52	65
Oklahoma City, OK	417	362	-	6	-	1	68	48	41	49
Portland, OR	581	495	-	20	-	-	71	48	64	50
Kansas City, MO.......	662	570	24	8	(Z)	41	78	41	51	62
Long Beach, CA	737	598	-	70	-	25	95	56	26	137
Tucson, AZ .,........	463	343	-	33	2	1	51	24	47	110
St. Louis, MO [2]	603	517	3	27	4	31	88	26	21	28
Charlotte, NC	566	500	-	12	1	3	43	33	53	61
Atlanta, GA .....,....	767	624	19	15	(Z)	-	74	39	25	82
Virginia Beach, VA [2]	716	682	334	5	15	17	41	19	56	34
Albuquerque, NM	546	476	-	17	5	7	55	29	38	70
Baton Rouge, LA [2]	423	395	-	11	1	31	39	20	41	6
Oakland, CA..........	554	508	4	46	1	-	75	40	17	-
Pittsburgh, PA........	429	379	-	9	(Z)	7	58	43	22	16
Sacramento, CA	399	352	(Z)	-	-	2	73	40	49	28
Minneapolis, MN	795	736	-	131	-	10	56	29	49	29
Tulsa, OK .,.........	491	444	-	5	-	19	46	34	28	42
Honolulu, HI [2]	1,101	892	-	102	-	9	114	44	44	209
Cincinnati, OH	659	525	-	54	-	32	65	50	44	81
Miami, FL............	359	324	-	17	1	(Z)	88	46	9	-
Fresno, CA	303	236	-	9	-	°	41	21	30	43
Omaha, NE	222	209	(Z)	10	-	1	33	25	30	-
Toledo, OH	258	234	-	10	-	5	46	31	28	24
Buffalo, NY	774	757	362	68	-	2	55	41	21	17
Wichita, KS..........	309	260	-	10	2	7	27	17	69	32
Santa Ana, CA	221	204	-	47	-	3	52	22	18	17
Mesa, AZ............	265	197	-	4	(Z)	-	40	19	22	68
Colorado Springs, CO ...	590	306	-	4	-	109	34	19	54	284
Tampa, FL...........	408	327	-	5	-	4	54	22	26	54
Newark, NJ	491	450	(Z)	66	45	13	66	44	6	34
St. Paul, MN..........	451	409	-	59	-	8	34	25	55	27
Louisville, KY	291	255	-	23	11	7	33	22	18	37
Anaheim, CA	600	333	-	97	-	1	47	25	22	266
Birmingham, AL	329	309	3	1	-	3	36	28	25	-
Arlington, TX	189	154	-	13	-	1	24	16	21	34
Norfolk, VA [2]	646	586	196	66	32	30	34	21	20	44
Las Vegas, NV	246	246	-	4	(Z)	2	39	26	54	(Z)
Corpus Christi, TX......	195	154	-	1	-	5	25	13	14	42
St. Petersburg, FL......	285	212	-	3	-	5	40	16	33	58
Rochester, NY	645	628	320	54	-	-	38	27	18	17
Riverside, CA.,........	398	219	-	18	-	1	37	17	28	180
Anchorage, AK [2].,.....	868	699	284	2	6	27	40	22	43	162
Lexington-Fayette, KY [2] ..	203	190	-	21	5	13	22	19	8	5
Akron, OH	232	200	-	10	-	7	27	20	22	32
Aurora, CO.	188	157	-	2	-	(Z)	30	17	22	29
Stockton, CA	152	145	-	4	-	1	35	21	9	7

- Represents or rounds to zero.   Z Less than $500,000.   [1] Includes items not shown separately.   [2] Represents, in effect, city-county consolidated government.

Source: U.S. Bureau of the Census, *City Government Finances*, series GF, No. 4, annual.

No. 493. Governmental Employment and Payrolls: 1980 to 1992

[For October. Covers both full-time and part-time employees. Except for 1987, local government data are estimates subject to sampling variation; see Appendix III and source. See also *Historical Statistics, Colonial Times to 1970*, series Y 272-307]

TYPE OF GOVERNMENT	1980	1983	1984	1985	1986	1987	1988	1989	1990	1991	1992
EMPLOYEES (1,000)											
Total	16,213	16,034	16,436	16,690	16,933	17,212	17,588	17,879	18,369	18,554	18,745
Federal (civilian)[1]	2,898	2,875	2,942	3,021	3,019	3,091	3,112	3,114	3,105	3,103	3,047
State and local	13,315	13,159	13,494	13,669	13,913	14,121	14,476	14,765	15,263	15,452	15,698
Percent of total	82	82	82	82	82	82	82	83	83	83	84
State	3,753	3,816	3,898	3,984	4,068	4,116	4,236	4,365	4,503	4,521	4,595
Local	9,562	9,344	9,595	9,685	9,846	10,005	10,240	10,400	10,760	10,930	11,103
Counties	1,853	1,811	1,872	1,891	1,926	1,963	2,024	2,085	2,167	2,196	2,253
Municipalities	2,561	2,424	2,434	2,467	2,494	2,493	2,570	2,569	2,642	2,662	2,665
School districts	4,270	4,211	4,387	4,416	4,502	4,627	4,679	4,774	4,950	5,045	5,134
Townships	394	379	386	392	400	393	415	405	418	415	424
Special districts	484	519	516	519	524	529	552	568	585	612	627
OCTOBER PAYROLLS (mil. dol.)											
Total	19,935	24,525	26,904	28,945	30,670	32,669	34,203	36,763	39,228	41,237	43,120
Federal (civilian)[1]	5,205	6,301	7,137	7,580	7,561	7,924	7,976	8,636	8,999	9,687	9,937
State and local	14,730	18,224	19,767	21,365	23,109	24,745	26,227	28,127	30,229	31,551	33,183
Percent of total	74	74	74	74	75	76	77	77	77	77	77
State	4,285	5,346	5,815	6,329	6,810	7,263	7,842	8,443	9,083	9,437	9,828
Local	10,445	12,878	13,952	15,036	16,298	17,482	18,385	19,684	21,146	22,113	23,355
Counties	1,936	2,387	2,596	2,819	3,009	3,270	3,532	3,855	4,192	4,404	4,698
Municipalities	2,951	3,640	3,872	4,191	4,407	4,770	4,979	5,274	5,564	5,784	6,207
School districts	4,683	5,729	6,283	6,746	7,517	7,961	8,298	8,852	9,551	9,975	10,394
Townships	330	398	421	446	474	522	556	599	642	664	685
Special districts	546	724	780	834	892	959	1,020	1,104	1,197	1,287	1,370

[1] Includes employees outside the United States.

Source: U.S. Bureau of the Census, *Historical Statistics on Governmental Finances and Employment*, and *Public Employment*, series GE, No. 1, annual.

No. 494. All Governments—Employment and Payroll, by Function: 1992

[For October. Covers both full-time and part-time employees. Local government amounts are estimates subject to sampling variation; see Appendix III and source]

FUNCTION	EMPLOYEES (1,000)					OCTOBER PAYROLLS (mil. dol.)				
	Total	Federal (civilian)[1]	State and local			Total	Federal (civilian)[1]	State and local		
			Total	State	Local			Total	State	Local
Total	18,745	3,047	15,698	4,595	11,103	43,120	9,937	33,183	9,828	23,355
National defense[2]	984	984	(X)	(X)	(X)	2,913	2,913	(X)	(X)	(X)
Postal Service	774	774	(X)	(X)	(X)	2,654	2,654	(X)	(X)	(X)
Space research and technology	25	25	(X)	(X)	(X)	112	112	(X)	(X)	(X)
Education	8,239	14	8,225	2,050	6,174	16,565	45	16,521	3,774	12,747
Highways	565	4	561	261	300	1,271	19	1,252	626	626
Health and hospitals	1,854	310	1,544	721	823	4,292	952	3,340	1,613	1,727
Public welfare	506	10	496	215	281	1,051	36	1,015	471	544
Police protection	858	88	770	87	683	2,396	335	2,061	247	1,814
Fire protection	344	(X)	344	(X)	344	825	(X)	825	(X)	825
Sanitation and sewerage	244	(X)	244	3	241	554	(X)	554	7	547
Parks and recreation	345	27	318	42	276	514	72	441	70	371
Natural resources	436	232	204	164	40	1,249	818	431	355	76
Financial administration	493	138	355	151	205	1,176	425	751	351	400
Other government administration	399	29	370	52	318	668	100	568	125	443
Judicial and legal	374	51	323	114	209	1,013	181	832	350	482
Other	2,303	360	1,943	734	1,209	5,865	1,273	4,592	1,839	2,753

X Not applicable.   [1] Includes employees outside the United States.   [2] Includes international relations.

Source: U.S. Bureau of the Census, *Public Employment*, series GE, No. 1.

No. 495. State and Local Government—Full-Time Employment and Salary, by Sex and Race/Ethnic Group: 1973 to 1991

[As of June 30. Excludes school systems and educational institutions. Based on reports from State governments (44 in 1973, 48 in 1975, 1976, and 1979, 47 in 1977 and 1983, 45 in 1978, 42 in 1980, 49 in 1981 and 1984 through 1987, and 50 in 1989 through 1991) and a sample of county, municipal, township, and special district jurisdictions employing 15 or more nonelected, nonappointed full-time employees. Data for 1982 and 1988 not available. For definition of median, see Guide to Tabular Presentation]

YEAR AND OCCUPATION	EMPLOYMENT (1,000)							MEDIAN ANNUAL SALARY ($1,000)					
					Minority							Minority	
	Total	Male	Fe-male	White [1]	Total [2]	Black [1]	His-panic [3]	Male	Fe-male	White [1]	Total [1]	Black [2]	His-panic [3]
1973	3,809	2,486	1,322	3,115	693	523	125	9.6	7.0	8.8	7.5	7.4	7.4
1975	3,899	2,436	1,464	3,102	797	602	147	11.3	8.2	10.2	8.8	8.6	8.9
1976	4,369	2,724	1,645	3,490	880	664	165	11.8	8.6	10.7	9.2	9.1	9.4
1977	4,415	2,737	1,678	3,480	935	705	175	12.4	9.1	11.3	9.7	9.5	9.9
1978	4,447	2,711	1,736	3,481	966	723	181	13.3	9.7	12.0	10.4	10.1	10.7
1979	4,576	2,761	1,816	3,568	1,008	751	192	14.1	10.4	12.8	10.9	10.6	11.4
1980	3,987	2,350	1,637	3,146	842	619	163	15.2	11.4	13.8	11.8	11.5	12.3
1981	4,665	2,740	1,925	3,591	1,074	780	205	17.7	13.1	16.1	13.5	13.3	14.7
1983	4,492	2,674	1,818	3,423	1,069	768	219	20.1	15.3	18.5	15.9	15.6	17.3
1984	4,580	2,700	1,880	3,458	1,121	799	233	21.4	16.2	19.6	17.4	16.5	18.4
1985	4,742	2,789	1,952	3,563	1,179	835	248	22.3	17.3	20.6	18.4	17.5	19.2
1986	4,779	2,797	1,982	3,549	1,230	865	259	23.4	18.1	21.5	19.6	18.7	20.2
1987	4,849	2,818	2,031	3,600	1,249	872	268	24.2	18.9	22.4	20.9	19.3	21.1
1989	5,257	3,030	2,227	3,863	1,394	961	308	26.1	20.6	24.1	22.1	20.7	22.7
1990	5,374	3,071	2,302	3,918	1,456	994	327	27.3	21.8	25.2	23.3	22.0	23.8
1991, total	**5,459**	**3,110**	**2,349**	**3,965**	**1,494**	**1,011**	**340**	**28.4**	**22.7**	**26.4**	**23.8**	**22.7**	**24.5**
Officials/admin-istrators	304	212	93	262	43	28	10	43.7	37.0	41.9	41.2	41.6	41.8
Professionals	1,227	609	619	957	270	164	53	35.9	30.8	33.1	30.9	30.4	32.5
Technicians	501	294	207	381	120	74	30	28.9	23.0	26.6	23.6	23.3	25.8
Protective serv-ice	913	792	121	697	216	148	56	29.5	24.9	29.1	28.3	27.1	31.9
Paraprofes-sionals	403	110	292	245	158	126	23	21.3	19.3	20.0	19.6	19.1	20.0
Admin. support	976	121	856	683	293	190	75	21.2	19.6	19.6	19.8	19.9	20.1
Skilled craft	455	436	19	349	106	67	30	26.0	20.7	25.7	25.6	25.0	26.5
Service/mainte-nance	679	537	141	390	288	213	62	21.1	16.6	20.4	20.5	18.9	20.7

[1] Non-Hispanic.   [2] Includes other minority groups not shown separately.   [3] Persons of Hispanic origin may be of any race.

Source: U.S. Equal Employment Opportunity Commission, *State and Local Government Information Report*, annual.

No. 496. State and Local Government—Employer Costs per Hour Worked: 1993

[As of March. Based on a sample; see source for details. For additional data, see table 661]

ITEM	Total com-pensa-tion	Wages and salaries	Benefits						
			Total	Paid leave	Supple-mental pay	Insur-ance	Retire-ment and savings	Legally required benefits	Other [1]
All State & local government workers	$24.44	$17.00	$7.44	$1.86	$0.21	$2.02	$1.87	$1.44	$0.03
Occupational group:									
White-collar occupations	27.67	19.72	7.95	1.98	0.14	2.17	2.08	1.55	0.03
Professional specialty and technical	32.91	24.07	8.83	1.95	0.16	2.37	2.54	1.77	0.04
Teachers	36.02	26.87	9.15	1.72	0.09	2.55	2.91	1.84	0.04
Executive, admin., & managerial	30.66	21.26	9.39	3.07	0.15	2.02	2.35	1.80	0.02
Admin. support including clerical	15.59	10.18	5.41	1.44	0.09	1.85	1.01	0.99	0.02
Blue-collar occupations	18.78	12.13	6.65	1.71	0.35	1.84	1.32	1.42	(Z)
Service occupations	17.04	10.83	6.21	1.58	0.37	1.65	1.50	1.09	0.02
Industry group:									
Services	26.02	18.58	7.44	1.74	0.16	2.12	1.95	1.45	0.03
Health services	19.31	12.91	6.41	1.97	0.50	1.56	1.02	1.33	0.02
Hospitals	19.60	13.20	6.40	2.01	0.49	1.53	1.02	1.34	0.02
Educational services	27.68	20.00	7.68	1.69	0.09	2.24	2.15	1.49	0.03
Elementary and secondary education	27.88	20.18	7.70	1.59	0.08	2.32	2.21	1.46	0.04
Higher education	28.13	20.29	7.84	1.97	0.12	2.07	2.06	1.61	(Z)
Public administration	21.35	14.02	7.33	2.10	0.28	1.79	1.80	1.32	0.03

Z Cost per hour is less than one cent.   [1] Includes severance pay and supplemental unemployment benefits.

Source: U.S. Bureau of Labor Statistics, News, *Employer Costs for Employee Compensation*, USDL 93-220.

No. 497. State and Local Government—Employee Benefits: 1992

[In percent. For January through July. Covers full-time employees in State and local governments. Covers only benefits for which the employer pays part or all of the premium or expenses involved, except unpaid maternity and paternity leave, and long-term care insurance. Based on sample. For data on employee benefits in businesses, see table 673]

BENEFIT	All employees	White collar employees [1]	Teachers [2]	Blue collar employees [3]	BENEFIT	All employees	White collar employees [1]	Teachers [2]	Blue collar employees [3]
Paid: Vacations	67	87	10	91	Life	89	89	87	89
Holidays	75	88	38	91	Noncontributory	75	76	73	77
Jury duty leave	97	97	98	97	Accident/sickness	22	25	15	23
Funeral leave	65	64	61	70	Noncontributory	16	18	13	17
Rest time	53	68	20	64	Long-term disability	28	30	33	22
Military leave	83	87	76	85	Noncontributory	22	23	27	18
Sick leave	95	94	97	94	Retirement and savings plans:				
Personal leave	38	31	55	33	Defined benefit pension	87	86	89	87
Lunch time	10	6	14	13	Noncontributory	24	25	22	24
Unpaid: Maternity leave	59	59	63	54	Defined contribution	9	10	8	9
Paternity leave	44	46	44	40	Money purchase pension [4]	7	7	7	8
Insurance plans:					Additional benefits:				
Medical	90	91	90	89	Child care	8	10	6	7
Dental	65	65	65	64	Educational assistance:				
Extended care facility	76	76	75	75	Job related	66	73	57	64
Home health care	78	79	77	77	Not job related	18	20	14	18
Hospital/room & board	90	91	90	89	Eldercare	13	14	15	11
In HMO's	27	25	25	30	Employee assistance				
Inpatient surgery	90	91	90	89	program	63	70	47	68
Mental health care:					Flexible benefits plans	5	5	7	4
Inpatient	89	90	88	88	In-house infirmary	17	18	16	14
Outpatient	83	85	83	84	Long-term care insurance	5	6	5	3
Vision	35	34	33	38	Nonproduction bonuses,				
Alcohol abuse treatment:					cash	38	43	26	44
Inpatient detox	89	90	89	89	Prepaid legal services	7	8	7	7
Inpatient rehab	65	66	64	65	Recreation facilities	15	15	19	12
Outpatient	67	67	65	67	Reimbursement accounts [5]	50	55	44	48
Drug abuse treatment:					Severance pay	32	30	31	35
Inpatient detox	89	90	88	88	Travel accident insurance	15	17	13	13
Inpatient rehab	64	65	62	64	Wellness programs	30	34	23	30
Outpatient	66	66	63	66					

[1] Includes all professional, administrative, technical, and clerical employees except teachers. [2] Includes all personnel in primary and secondary schools, junior colleges, and universities whose primary duty is teaching or closely related activities. [3] Includes police, firefighters, and all production and service employees. [4] Fixed contributions are periodically placed in an employee's account and benefits are based on how much money has accumulated at retirement. [5] Account which is used throughout the year to pay for plan premiums or to reimburse the employee for benefit related expenses. Account may be financed by employer, employee, or both.
Source: U.S. Bureau of Labor Statistics, *Employee Benefits in State and Local Governments, 1992.*

No. 498. State and Local Government Major Collective Bargaining Agreements— Average Percent Changes in Wage and Compensation Rates Negotiated: 1986 to 1993

[In percent, except as indicated. Averages presented are means; for definition, see Guide to Tabular Presentation]

ITEM	1986	1987	1988	1989	1990	1991	1992	1993
Compensation rate changes, [1] all settlements:								
First year	6.2	4.9	5.4	5.1	5.1	1.8	0.6	0.9
Over life of contract [2]	6.0	4.8	5.3	4.9	5.1	2.9	1.9	1.9
State government: First year	6.8	4.3	5.3	4.9	4.4	1.9	0.2	1.2
Over life of contract [2]	6.0	4.3	4.9	4.6	3.9	2.8	2.0	2.2
Local government: First year	5.6	5.4	5.5	5.6	5.4	1.6	1.2	0.7
Over life of contract [2]	6.0	5.1	5.8	5.5	5.8	2.9	1.5	1.7
Wage rate changes, [3] all settlements:								
First year	5.7	4.9	5.1	5.1	4.9	2.3	1.1	1.1
Over life of contract [2]	5.7	5.1	5.3	5.1	5.0	2.8	2.1	2.1
State government: First year	6.3	4.1	5.3	5.0	4.7	2.0	0.5	1.3
Over life of contract [2]	6.0	4.2	5.0	4.7	4.2	3.0	2.0	2.5
Local government: First year	5.3	5.3	5.0	5.2	5.0	2.5	1.7	1.0
Over life of contract [2]	5.6	5.5	5.5	5.4	5.2	2.7	2.1	1.9
Number of workers affected (mil.) [4]	0.9	1.3	1.1	1.1	0.9	0.8	1.2	1.6
State government	0.3	0.5	0.4	0.5	0.2	0.4	0.6	0.5
Local government	0.6	0.8	0.7	0.6	0.7	0.4	0.6	1.1
Wage rate changes, all agreements [5]	5.5	4.9	4.7	5.1	4.6	2.6	1.9	2.7
Source: Current settlements	2.4	2.7	2.3	2.5	2.0	0.6	0.8	1.5
Prior settlements	3.0	2.2	2.4	2.6	2.6	1.8	1.1	1.1
Cost-of-living adjustments	(Z)	(Z)	(Z)	(Z)	(Z)	0.1	(Z)	(Z)
State government	5.6	4.3	4.1	4.0	4.7	2.5	1.6	3.4
Local government	5.4	5.3	5.1	5.9	4.6	2.6	2.1	2.2

Z Less than .05 percent. [1] Data relate to settlements of 5,000 workers or more in each calendar year, whether wages and benefits were changed or not. [2] Average annual rate of change. [3] Data relate to settlements covering 1,000 workers or more in each calendar year but exclude possible changes in wages under cost-of-living adjustment (COLA) clauses, except increases guaranteed by the contract. Includes all settlements, whether wages were changed or not. [4] Number of workers covered by settlements reached in each calendar year. [5] Data relate to all wage changes implemented in the year stemming from settlements reached in the year, deferred from prior-year agreements, and cost-of-living clauses.
Source: U.S. Bureau of Labor Statistics, *Current Wage Developments,* monthly.

No. 499. State and Local Government Full-Time Eqivalent Employment, by Selected Function and State: 1992

[In thousands, for October. Local government amounts are estimates subject to sampling variation; see Appendix III and source]

STATE	EDUCATION				HEALTH AND HOSPITALS		HIGHWAYS		POLICE AND FIRE PROTECTION		PUBLIC WELFARE	
	Total		Higher education									
	State	Local	State	Local	State	Local	State	Local	State[1]	Local	State	Local
United States ...	1,412.4	5,243.1	1,285.7	261.3	685.8	736.3	257.3	286.5	86.2	887.7	211.7	261.0
Alabama	34.1	81.7	30.1	-	18.9	21.8	4.3	7.1	1.1	13.8	4.5	1.3
Alaska	9.3	11.8	5.9	-	0.8	0.1	3.0	0.6	0.4	1.7	1.7	0.2
Arizona	21.5	81.0	18.8	7.4	3.4	7.3	3.2	3.7	1.7	13.0	5.0	3.4
Arkansas	17.5	53.7	14.9	-	8.8	4.4	4.0	3.3	0.9	6.4	3.6	0.4
California	111.1	528.8	106.6	63.5	44.7	107.1	19.3	21.1	11.1	108.2	3.1	47.0
Colorado	28.8	68.9	27.3	1.2	6.0	9.5	3.1	4.7	1.0	11.8	1.3	4.1
Connecticut	15.1	61.4	12.4	-	12.7	1.8	3.7	3.6	1.5	11.8	4.2	2.0
Delaware	6.7	12.1	6.4	-	3.6	0.2	1.4	0.6	0.7	1.5	1.6	0.1
District of Columbia ...	(X)	12.8	(X)	1.5	(X)	7.6	(X)	0.9	(X)	7.0	(X)	1.9
Florida	39.3	252.0	36.7	20.3	28.7	42.2	10.9	13.9	3.8	57.7	9.7	5.3
Georgia	37.5	152.9	32.8	0.6	29.4	44.8	6.2	7.0	2.1	24.7	7.5	0.8
Hawaii	28.9	-	7.1	-	6.2	0.1	0.9	1.1	-	5.1	1.2	0.1
Idaho	7.8	23.9	7.1	0.9	2.0	4.4	1.8	1.5	0.4	3.0	1.6	0.1
Illinois	49.4	228.8	46.5	19.4	23.8	22.6	8.9	11.0	3.8	51.6	12.6	7.4
Indiana	50.1	113.8	45.2	0.0	13.4	23.5	4.8	5.8	1.8	17.0	5.4	2.9
Iowa	19.7	66.7	18.5	5.7	8.8	10.2	2.8	5.7	0.8	7.0	3.3	1.7
Kansas	20.6	67.6	19.9	5.7	8.4	8.3	3.7	5.1	1.0	8.3	1.7	0.7
Kentucky	32.3	80.7	28.1	-	7.7	8.5	5.8	3.0	1.7	8.7	4.9	0.6
Louisiana	31.0	96.1	27.4	0.2	23.9	12.1	5.6	5.0	1.1	15.0	5.9	0.6
Maine	7.1	30.0	5.7	-	2.9	1.2	2.8	1.7	0.6	3.6	1.9	0.2
Maryland	22.1	92.9	20.2	7.3	13.0	3.1	5.1	5.2	2.3	18.4	7.1	1.8
Massachusetts	21.5	105.6	20.7	0.1	20.5	8.9	4.7	5.6	2.0	27.5	7.3	1.8
Michigan	67.2	202.9	65.2	12.4	14.9	21.3	3.9	8.9	3.1	25.0	12.8	2.8
Minnesota	34.8	90.6	33.2	2.6	9.4	17.8	5.1	7.4	0.8	10.7	1.7	10.2
Mississippi	15.9	67.0	14.5	5.0	10.9	15.2	3.5	4.4	0.9	7.3	3.2	0.3
Missouri	22.5	103.0	20.5	4.6	15.3	11.4	6.3	6.0	1.9	17.8	6.8	2.4
Montana	6.3	26.0	5.6	0.2	1.8	0.8	1.9	1.3	0.4	2.1	1.2	0.9
Nebraska	10.7	38.4	9.9	2.5	4.9	4.6	2.4	3.1	0.7	4.4	2.6	1.3
Nevada	6.3	23.6	6.0	-	1.5	3.9	1.4	1.0	0.5	5.6	1.0	0.3
New Hampshire	5.5	22.3	5.2	-	1.8	0.2	1.9	1.4	0.4	3.9	1.1	2.3
New Jersey	33.9	170.6	27.3	8.6	22.4	10.6	8.3	10.4	3.7	34.4	5.9	11.1
New Mexico	17.6	38.2	16.7	1.8	7.5	2.6	2.7	1.5	0.6	5.3	2.0	0.4
New York	48.3	409.0	42.7	18.9	71.8	85.1	14.9	35.6	5.5	83.2	7.4	57.0
North Carolina	41.8	151.6	38.8	13.4	17.8	28.6	12.1	3.1	3.1	19.8	1.2	11.8
North Dakota	7.1	13.3	6.8	-	3.2	0.2	1.1	1.1	0.2	1.4	0.2	0.9
Ohio	68.3	205.7	66.0	4.3	22.2	30.8	8.9	13.0	2.3	37.3	2.1	23.0
Oklahoma	25.6	75.6	23.6	-	11.6	8.1	3.5	5.4	1.7	10.8	7.9	0.3
Oregon	15.3	64.1	14.1	6.8	7.6	5.1	3.9	3.8	1.1	8.5	4.4	0.7
Pennsylvania	50.8	213.8	48.1	8.1	25.6	5.1	12.7	10.5	5.3	29.3	9.8	21.9
Rhode Island	6.7	17.4	5.8	-	2.8	0.1	1.0	0.9	0.3	4.8	1.6	0.1
South Carolina	29.0	74.6	26.1	-	16.7	14.5	5.2	2.0	1.8	10.0	5.0	0.1
South Dakota	4.7	17.0	4.3	-	2.1	0.7	1.3	1.5	0.3	1.6	1.1	0.3
Tennessee	30.6	87.9	28.6	-	14.2	20.9	4.8	6.7	1.5	16.8	4.7	3.6
Texas	86.7	459.7	81.9	27.2	51.1	58.9	14.3	17.2	3.0	63.1	15.5	2.6
Utah	20.0	33.6	19.2	-	5.5	2.0	1.8	1.4	0.6	4.4	2.6	0.5
Vermont	4.8	13.5	4.5	-	1.0	-	1.1	1.0	0.5	1.0	1.1	0.0
Virginia	45.7	137.3	42.5	-	25.0	8.5	11.3	3.9	2.4	19.7	2.4	8.1
Washington	41.0	89.5	39.3	-	14.2	11.6	6.2	6.4	1.9	15.3	7.5	1.0
West Virginia	13.0	50.8	11.5	-	3.2	4.4	5.8	0.9	0.8	3.1	2.3	-
Wisconsin	37.6	107.4	36.3	9.4	10.1	10.3	2.1	8.7	0.9	16.6	1.2	13.1
Wyoming	3.3	15.5	3.2	1.7	2.1	3.3	1.9	0.8	0.2	1.7	0.3	0.1

- Represents or rounds to zero.   X Not applicable.   [1] For State government, represents police protection only.

Source: U.S. Bureau of the Census, *Public Employment*, series GE, No. 1, annual.

No. 500. State and Local Government Employment and Average Earnings, by State: 1986 and 1992

[For October]

STATE	FULL-TIME EQUIVALENT EMPLOYMENT (1,000)				FULL-TIME EQUIVALENT EMPLOYMENT PER 10,000 POPULATION [2]				AVERAGE OCTOBER EARNINGS [3] (dol.)			
	State		Local [1]		State		Local [1]		State		Local [1]	
	1986	1992	1986	1992	1986	1992	1986	1992	1986	1992	1986	1992
United States	3,437	3,856	8,415	9,513	143	151	349	373	2,052	2,621	1,992	2,539
Alabama	70	81	131	154	174	196	324	373	1,884	2,243	1,532	1,830
Alaska	21	24	20	22	393	413	377	371	3,228	3,258	3,324	3,590
Arizona	43	54	119	145	128	141	358	379	2,126	2,361	2,185	2,557
Arkansas	39	47	71	82	163	194	299	342	1,724	2,195	1,388	1,724
California	279	323	965	1,108	104	104	358	359	2,751	3,420	2,535	3,281
Colorado	50	53	122	132	155	153	375	381	2,368	3,016	2,017	2,450
Connecticut	56	54	95	97	175	165	297	296	2,336	3,286	2,089	3,160
Delaware	17	20	16	18	272	293	252	254	1,795	2,463	1,991	2,669
District of Columbia	(X)	(X)	51	55	(X)	(X)	817	928	(X)	(X)	2,594	3,175
Florida	124	164	407	500	106	122	348	370	1,748	2,202	1,872	2,294
Georgia	91	114	239	283	149	170	391	419	1,811	2,075	1,589	1,968
Hawaii	41	51	12	14	389	437	113	120	1,844	2,554	2,010	3,031
Idaho	18	20	33	40	175	190	332	373	1,766	2,265	1,535	1,943
Illinois	130	137	385	431	113	117	333	370	2,165	2,642	2,166	2,672
Indiana	75	95	182	202	136	168	330	358	2,056	2,506	1,686	2,199
Iowa	57	47	101	108	199	168	355	386	2,049	2,895	1,735	2,179
Kansas	43	48	96	109	174	190	390	433	1,687	2,191	1,700	2,133
Kentucky	63	76	102	121	170	203	275	322	1,651	2,349	1,596	1,980
Louisiana	86	89	151	161	191	207	337	375	1,673	2,227	1,494	1,800
Maine	20	22	36	43	168	178	307	349	1,714	2,437	1,590	2,101
Maryland	80	82	143	158	178	167	321	321	2,046	2,720	2,233	2,892
Massachusetts	88	85	192	192	151	142	329	321	2,034	2,645	2,082	2,775
Michigan	128	138	315	323	140	146	344	342	2,541	3,134	2,329	2,906
Minnesota	61	67	137	173	145	150	326	385	2,428	3,101	2,318	2,673
Mississippi	42	47	95	108	161	181	364	412	1,430	2,000	1,324	1,608
Missouri	66	74	157	174	130	143	310	334	1,621	2,075	1,826	2,133
Montana	16	17	29	37	192	207	349	451	1,864	2,300	1,727	1,995
Nebraska	29	29	65	71	184	179	407	441	1,509	2,185	1,785	2,198
Nevada	15	19	33	47	154	144	343	353	1,990	2,738	2,140	2,772
New Hampshire	18	16	29	36	172	147	285	320	1,759	2,416	1,701	2,456
New Jersey	96	116	283	302	126	149	372	387	2,278	3,100	2,146	3,062
New Mexico	34	42	49	60	231	267	332	381	1,792	2,253	1,680	1,858
New York	272	267	810	884	153	148	456	488	2,355	3,143	2,266	3,147
North Carolina	93	109	216	260	147	159	341	380	1,935	2,413	1,662	2,092
North Dakota	15	16	22	21	222	259	318	331	1,805	2,231	2,017	2,269
Ohio	122	140	365	399	113	127	340	363	1,984	2,691	1,911	2,417
Oklahoma	64	67	109	121	195	209	329	376	1,733	2,044	1,595	1,903
Oregon	44	50	91	106	163	167	338	354	1,975	2,607	2,018	2,599
Pennsylvania	124	143	340	367	104	119	286	305	1,915	2,696	1,976	2,622
Rhode Island	19	20	24	28	195	198	245	276	2,041	2,817	2,215	2,832
South Carolina	69	78	109	124	204	216	322	344	1,705	2,098	1,558	1,970
South Dakota	13	14	23	26	177	190	330	361	1,684	2,166	1,441	1,833
Tennessee	71	76	157	178	147	151	327	354	1,746	2,153	1,554	2,004
Texas	193	240	633	748	115	136	379	424	1,927	2,351	1,748	2,107
Utah	33	40	47	53	197	219	283	294	1,654	2,100	1,900	2,204
Vermont	11	13	15	18	211	227	270	309	1,842	2,514	1,653	2,240
Virginia	102	116	195	229	177	182	336	359	1,895	2,270	1,787	2,322
Washington	79	98	143	177	177	191	320	345	2,231	2,760	2,134	2,738
West Virginia	34	34	61	59	180	185	317	324	1,574	1,969	1,625	2,002
Wisconsin	74	73	168	189	154	145	351	377	2,128	3,216	2,035	2,594
Wyoming	11	12	25	25	213	242	494	543	1,924	2,055	1,967	2,202

X Not applicable.   [1] Estimates subject to sampling variation; see Appendix III and source.   [2] Based on estimated resident population as of July 1.   [3] For full-time employees.

Source: U.S. Bureau of the Census, *Public Employment*, series GE, No. 1, annual.

No. 501. City Government Employment and Payroll: 1980 to 1992

[For **October**. Includes only those school systems operated as part of the city government. 1982 and 1987 based on complete census of all cities; other years based on sample and subject to sampling variation]

YEAR	ALL EMPLOYEES, FULL-TIME AND PART-TIME (1,000)		OCTOBER PAYROLLS (mil. dol.)		ANNUAL PERCENT CHANGE		FULL-TIME EQUIVALENT EMPLOYMENT [1] (1,000)			AVERAGE EARNINGS IN OCTOBER, FULL-TIME EMPLOYEES (dollars)	
	Total	Excl. education	Total	Excl. education	All employees	October payroll	Total	Education	Other	Education	Other
1980	2,561	2,130	2,942	2,403	0.3	7.8	2,166	360	1,806	1,501	1,338
1981	2,469	2,056	3,222	2,640	-3.6	9.5	2,111	346	1,765	1,686	1,500
1982	2,396	2,015	3,428	2,861	-2.9	6.4	2,088	317	1,770	1,791	1,625
1983	2,423	2,051	3,640	3,059	1.1	6.2	2,060	300	1,760	1,962	1,739
1984	2,434	2,070	3,872	3,268	0.4	6.4	2,090	300	1,790	2,033	1,831
1985	2,467	2,102	4,191	3,536	1.4	8.2	(NA)	(NA)	(NA)	2,117	1,953
1986	2,494	2,126	4,407	3,724	1.1	5.1	2,181	320	1,860	2,186	2,044
1987	2,493	2,110	4,770	3,977	(Z)	8.2	2,223	337	1,885	2,406	2,163
1988	2,570	2,188	4,979	4,136	3.1	4.4	2,251	342	1,910	2,566	2,220
1989	2,569	2,190	5,274	4,405	(Z)	5.9	2,268	341	1,927	2,669	2,343
1990	2,642	2,237	5,564	4,675	2.8	5.5	2,295	338	1,957	2,683	2,449
1991	2,662	2,324	5,784	4,878	0.7	4.0	2,303	338	1,965	2,739	2,547
1992	2,665	2,312	6,207	5,146	0.1	7.3	2,340	371	1,969	2,931	2,683

NA Not available.   Z Less than .05 percent.   [1] Beginning 1986, data not comparable to previous years due to a change in how full-time equivalent is calculated; see text, section 9.

Source: U.S. Bureau of the Census, *Compendium of Public Employment*, and *City Employment*, series GE, No. 2, annual.

No. 502. City Government Employment and Payroll, by Function: 1980 to 1992

[For October]

ITEM	EMPLOYEES (1,000)					OCTOBER PAYROLLS (mil. dol.)				
	All cities [1]				Cities with 75,000 population or more, [2] 1992	All cities [1]				Cities with 75,000 population or more, [2] 1992
	1980	1990	1991	1992		1980	1990	1991	1992	
Total	2,561	2,642	2,662	2,665	1,568	2,942	5,564	5,784	6,207	4,281
Full-time	2,071	2,149	2,153	2,197	1,418	2,826	5,334	5,543	5,980	4,178
Part-time	489	493	509	468	150	116	229	241	227	103
Full-time equivalent [3]	2,166	2,295	2,303	2,340	1,480	(X)	(X)	(X)	(X)	(X)
Education [4]	360	338	338	371	301	539	889	906	1,061	880
Percent of total	17	15	15	16	20	18	16	16	17	21
Instructional staff	266	264	262	261	209	436	754	765	848	698
Others	94	74	76	110	92	102	134	141	212	182
Libraries	34	45	45	45	27	38	80	84	86	57
Public welfare	41	57	58	55	49	47	118	116	132	121
Hospitals	131	124	124	125	82	143	282	297	301	217
Health	35	42	41	43	35	47	93	94	104	89
Highways	121	133	132	130	56	141	274	283	301	152
Police protection	365	412	418	423	234	550	1,093	1,162	1,249	783
Fire protection	190	199	201	200	117	300	579	603	642	416
Correction	18	35	36	36	34	27	90	94	108	103
Parks and recreation	103	121	123	123	71	116	211	222	232	141
Housing and community development	44	46	46	45	38	57	104	108	115	97
Sewerage	60	74	75	76	38	74	155	164	172	95
Solid waste management	104	86	85	83	49	118	174	177	193	135
Financial administration	69	74	75	74	35	85	164	169	179	96
Judicial, legal, other governmental administration	112	129	129	132	73	147	314	326	345	209
Local utilities [5]	209	226	226	226	144	306	594	619	615	439
Water supply	93	101	103	103	53	116	219	230	240	137
Electric power	44	51	51	51	28	67	142	149	159	101
Transit	66	66	65	64	60	115	217	224	198	191
Other	171	154	152	152	97	208	350	360	372	252

X Not applicable.   [1] Data are estimates subject to sampling variation; see Appendix III and source.   [2] Based on enumerated resident population as of April 1, 1990.   [3] 1980 data not directly comparable to later years due to a change in 1986 in how full-time equivalent was calculated; see text, section 9.   [4] City-operated schools and colleges only.   [5] Includes gas supply not shown separately.

Source: U.S. Bureau of the Census, *City Employment*, series GE, No. 2, annual.

No. 503. City Government Employment and Payroll—Largest Cities: 1980 and 1992

[For October. See footnote 3, table 491, for those areas representing city-county consolidated governments]

CITIES RANKED BY 1990 POPULATION	TOTAL EMPLOYMENT (1,000)		FULL-TIME EQUIVALENT EMPLOYMENT [1]				OCTOBER PAYROLL (mil. dol.)		AVERAGE EARNINGS IN OCTOBER, FULL-TIME EMPLOYEES (dol.)	
			Total (1,000)		Per 10,000 population [2]					
	1980	1992	1980	1992	1980	1992	1980	1992	1980	1992
New York, NY [3][4]	364	442	319	415	451	557	504	1,307	1,587	3,154
Los Angeles, CA [2]	42	50	41	50	138	140	73	188	1,806	3,815
Chicago, IL	47	41	45	41	150	148	71	135	1,569	3,269
Houston, TX	18	21	18	21	111	129	26	51	1,499	2,404
Philadelphia, PA	33	31	32	30	189	189	51	92	1,611	3,092
San Diego, CA	8	11	7	9	81	93	12	29	1,773	2,894
Detroit, MI	22	19	22	19	179	180	40	49	1,852	2,700
Dallas, TX	14	14	14	14	153	137	20	36	1,465	2,642
Phoenix, AZ	9	11	9	11	114	110	14	32	1,517	3,104
San Antonio, TX	10	14	10	13	128	140	13	32	1,282	2,472
San Jose, CA [2][6]	[5]4	7	[5]4	6	[5]60	76	[5]7	24	[5]1,714	4,206
Baltimore, MD [3][6]	44	28	40	27	514	372	47	70	1,172	2,613
Indianapolis, IN	13	13	12	13	174	172	13	26	1,098	2,164
San Francisco, CA	21	26	21	26	310	354	37	99	1,761	3,881
Jacksonville, FL	[7]11	11	[7]11	10	[7]202	156	[7]11	27	[7]1,031	2,888
Columbus, OH	8	8	7	8	122	125	10	20	1,498	2,607
Milwaukee, WI	10	9	9	8	145	133	15	23	1,631	2,782
Memphis, TN [3]	25	24	22	22	342	366	29	53	1,335	2,361
Washington, DC [3][4]	45	48	42	46	651	763	73	138	1,761	3,022
Boston, MA [3]	[5]28	21	[5]25	21	[5]444	361	[5]35	61	1,398	2,949
Seattle, WA	10	11	9	10	188	197	17	35	1,830	3,494
El Paso, TX	5	5	4	5	104	99	3	11	942	2,220
Cleveland, OH	[8]13	10	[8]13	10	[8]225	149	[8]11	12	[8]919	1,623
New Orleans, LA	[9]18	18	[9]17	17	[9]374	340	[9]22	40	[9]1,295	2,430
Nashville-Davidson, TN [3]	13	14	12	12	244	266	18	35	1,540	2,859
Denver, CO	8	12	7	11	199	246	10	27	1,515	2,496
Austin, TX	[7]5	5	[7]5	5	[7]120	114	[7]5	11	[7]1,198	2,277
Fort Worth, TX	5	5	4	5	104	104	6	12	1,323	2,567
Oklahoma City, OK	5	[10]5	4	[10]5	115	[10]104	8	[10]15	1,916	[10]3,363
Portland, OR	5	[10]6	4	[10]6	145	[10]146	9	[10]16	1,368	[10]2,485
Kansas City, MO	[7]5	5	[5]4	5	[5]122	123	[5]7	18	[5]1,678	3,627
Long Beach, CA	[5]5	6	[5]4	5	[5]124	118	6	12	1,474	2,645
Tucson, AZ	4	5	4	5	124	118	6	12	1,279	2,405
St. Louis, MO	13	8	13	7	280	188	15	18	1,290	2,436
Charlotte, NC	4	5	4	5	125	115	5	11	1,230	2,373
Atlanta, GA	8	8	8	8	187	197	10	18	1,204	2,275
Virginia Beach, VA [3]	10	15	9	14	346	356	11	30	[7]1,135	2,100
Albuquerque, NM	4	6	4	5	109	130	7	17	2,011	3,985
Oakland, CA	[8]6	7	[8]6	5	[8]135	145	[8]6	14	[8]1,116	3,092
Pittsburgh, PA	3	4	3	4	119	107	6	13	1,762	3,384
Sacramento, CA	6	7	5	6	136	161	9	18	1,821	3,097
Minneapolis, MN	[5]4	4	[5]4	4	[5]115	120	[5]5	11	[5]1,184	2,463
Tulsa, OK	9	11	9	9	117	111	12	29	1,401	3,139
Honolulu, HI	7	8	7	7	174	191	10	20	1,527	3,092
Cincinnati, OH	4	4	4	4	118	101	6	14	1,408	3,994
Miami, FL	3	3	3	3	115	73	4	8	1,607	3,043
Fresno, CA	3	3	3	3	92	81	5	8	1,684	3,138
Omaha, NE	4	3	3	3	96	86	6	9	1,758	2,955
Toledo, OH [3]	14	14	13	13	348	390	18	36	1,475	2,986
Buffalo, NY [3]	3	3	3	3	111	97	4	7	1,327	2,429
Wichita, KS	2	2	1	2	68	64	2	9	1,819	5,162
Santa Ana, CA	1	2	1	2	89	82	2	7	1,592	2,908
Mesa, AZ	4	5	3	5	158	181	5	11	1,445	2,594
Colorado Springs, CO	5	4	5	4	165	140	5	12	1,178	2,861
Tampa, FL	12	3	12	3	374	139	17	12	1,387	3,220
Newark, NJ [11]	5	4	3	4	125	119	6	11	1,734	3,429
St. Paul, MN	6	4	6	4	186	160	7	8	1,358	1,965
Louisville, KY	6	4	6	4	186	160	7	8	1,616	4,235
Anaheim, CA	4	4	4	4	128	145	5	9	1,333	2,293
Birmingham, AL	[7]1	2	[7]1	2	[7]63	73	[7]1	5	[7]1,180	2,721
Arlington, TX [11]	2	2	2	2	71	68	3	7	1,222	2,349
Norfolk, VA [3]	11	11	10	10	380	394	12	24	1,222	2,349

[1] 1992 data not comparable with 1980 due to a change in 1986 in how full-time equivalent was calculated; see text, section 9. [2] 1980 based on enumerated resident population as of April 1, 1980. 1992 based on enumerated resident population as of April 1, 1990. [3] Includes city-operated elementary and secondary schools. [4] Includes city-operated university or college. [5] 1979 data. [6] Prior to 1990, includes data for city operated colleges. [7] 1978 data. [8] 1977 data. [9] Noneducation data are for 1979. [10] 1991 data. [11] Prior to 1983, city-operated elementary and secondary schools.

Source: U.S. Bureau of the Census, City Employment, series GE, No. 2, annual; and unpublished data.

Figure 10.1
The Government of the United States
(As of July 1, 1993)

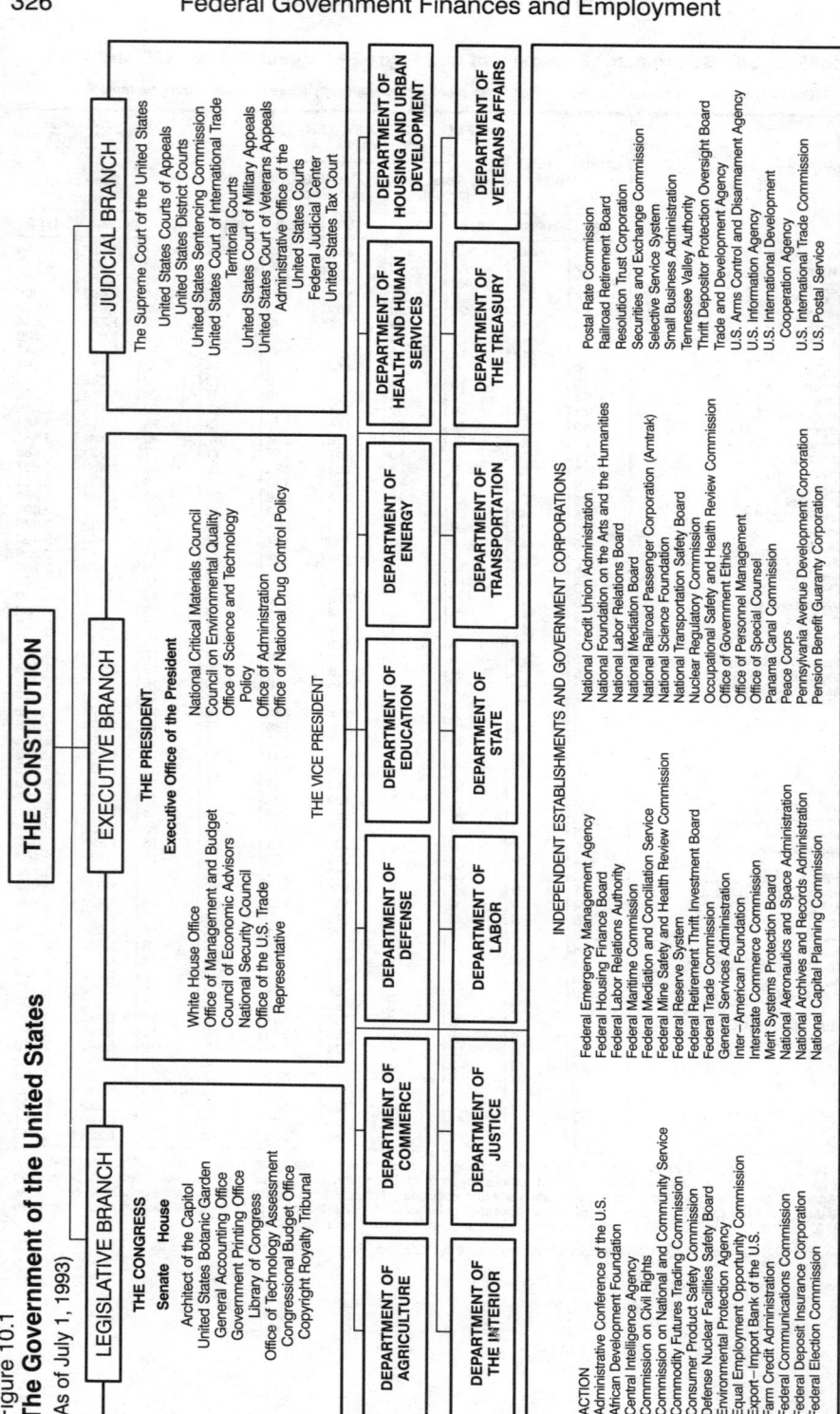

Source: Chart prepared by U.S. Bureau of the Census.

Federal Government Finances and Employment

This section presents statistics relating to the financial structure and the civilian employment of the Federal Government. The fiscal data cover taxes, other receipts, outlays, and debt. The principal sources of fiscal data are *The Budget of the United States Government* and related documents, published annually by the Office of Management and Budget (OMB), and the Department of the Treasury's *United States Government Annual Report* and its *Appendix.* Detailed data on tax returns and collections are published annually by the Internal Revenue Service. Personnel data relating to staffing and payrolls for the various public functions and agencies, to employee characteristics, and to civil service status; are published by the Office of Personnel Management and the Bureau of Labor Statistics. The primary source for data on public lands is *Public Land Statistics,* published annually by the Bureau of Land Management, Department of the Interior. Data on federally owned land and real property are collected by the General Services Administration and presented in its annual *Inventory Report on Real Property Owned by the United States Throughout the World.*

Budget concept.—Under the unified budget concept, all Federal monies are included in one comprehensive budget. These monies comprise both Federal funds and trust funds. Federal funds are derived mainly from taxes and borrowing and are not restricted by law to any specific government purpose. Trust funds, such as the Unemployment Trust Fund, collect certain taxes and other receipts for use in carrying out specific purposes or programs in accordance with the terms of the trust agreement or statute. Fund balances include both cash balances with Treasury and investments in U.S. securities. Part of the balance is obligated, part unobligated. Prior to 1985, the budget totals, under provisions of law, excluded some Federal activities—including the Federal Financing Bank, the Postal Service, the Synthetic Fuels Corporation, and the lending activities of

In Brief	
	1994
Gross Federal debt	$4,676 bil.
Net interest on the public debt	$299 bil.

the Rural Electrification Administration. The Balanced Budget and Emergency Deficit Control Act of 1985 (P.L.99-177) repealed the off-budget status of these entities and placed social security (Federal old-age and survivors insurance and the Federal disability insurance trust funds) off-budget. Though social security is now off-budget and, by law, excluded from coverage of the congressional budget resolutions, it continues to be a Federal program.

Receipts arising from the Government's sovereign powers are reported as governmental receipts; all other receipts, i.e., from business-type or market-oriented activities, are offset against outlays. Outlays are reported on a checks-issued (net) basis (i.e., outlays are recorded at the time the checks to pay bills are issued).

Debt concept.—For most of U.S. history, the total debt consisted of debt borrowed by the Treasury (i.e., public debt). The present debt series includes both public debt and agency debt. The *gross Federal debt* includes money borrowed by the Treasury and by various Federal agencies; it is the broadest generally used measure of the Federal debt. *Total public debt* is covered by a statutory debt limitation and includes only borrowing by the Treasury.

Treasury receipts and outlays.—All receipts of the Government, with a few exceptions, are deposited to the credit of the U.S. Treasury regardless of ultimate disposition. Under the Constitution, no money may be withdrawn from the Treasury unless appropriated by the Congress.

The day-to-day cash operations of the Federal Government clearing through the accounts of the U.S. Treasury are reported in the *Daily Treasury Statement*. Extensive detail on the public debt is published in the *Monthly Statement of the Public Debt of the United States*.

Budget receipts such as taxes, customs duties, and outlays represented by checks issued and cash payments made by disbursing officers as well as government agencies are reported in the *Daily Treasury Statement of Receipts and Outlays of the United States Government* and in the Treasury's *United States Government Annual Report* and its *Appendix*. These deposits in and payments from accounts maintained by Government agencies are on the same basis as the unified budget.

The quarterly *Treasury Bulletin* contains data on fiscal operations and related Treasury activities, including financial statements of Government corporations and other business-type activities.

Income tax returns and tax collections.—Tax data are compiled by the Internal Revenue Service of the Treasury Department. The *Annual Report of the Commissioner and Chief Counsel of the Internal Revenue Service* gives a detailed account of tax collections by kind of tax and by regions, districts, and States. The agency's annual *Statistics of Income* reports present detailed data from individual income tax returns and corporation income tax returns. The quarterly *Statistics of Income Bulletin* has, in general, replaced the supplemental *Statistics of Income* publications which presented data on such diverse subjects as tax-exempt organizations, unincorporated businesses, fiduciary income tax and estate tax returns, sales of capital assets by individuals, international income and taxes reported by corporations and individuals, and estate tax wealth.

Employment and payrolls.—The Office of Personnel Management collects employment and payroll data from all departments and agencies of the Federal Government, except the Central Intelligence Agency, the National Security Agency, and the Defense Intelligence Agency. Employment figures represent the number of persons who occupied civilian positions at the end of the report month shown and who are paid for personal services rendered for the Federal Government, regardless of the nature of appointment or method of payment.

Federal payrolls include all payments for personal services rendered during the report month and payments for accumulated annual leave of employees who separate from the service. Since most Federal employees are paid on a biweekly basis, the calendar month earnings are partially estimated on the basis of the number of work days in each month where payroll periods overlap.

Federal employment and payroll figures are published by the Office of Personnel Management in its *Federal Civilian Workforce Statistics—Employment and Trends*. It also publishes biennial employment data for minority groups, data on occupations of white- and blue-collar workers, and data on employment by geographic area; reports on salary and wage distribution of Federal employees are published annually. General schedule is primarily white-collar; wage system primarily blue-collar. Data on Federal employment are also issued by the Bureau of Labor Statistics in its *Monthly Labor Review* and in *Employment and Earnings* and by the Bureau of the Census in its annual *Public Employment*.

Public lands.—These data refer to transactions which involve the disposal, under public land laws, of Federal public lands to non-Federal owners. In general, original entries and selections are applications to secure title to public lands which have been accepted as properly filed (i.e., allowed). Some types of applications, however, are not reported until issuance of the final certificate, which passes equitable title to the land to the applicant. Applications are approved when full compliance with the requirements of the laws is shown and become final entries (perfected entries) upon issuance of a final certificate. Patents are Government deeds which pass legal title to the land to the applicant. Certifications are issued in lieu of patents in connection with certain State selections.

Historical statistics.—Tabular headnotes provide cross-references, where applicable, to *Historical Statistics of the United States, Colonial Times to 1970*. See Appendix IV.

Figure 10.2
Federal Budget—Receipts, Outlays, and Deficit: 1970 to 1994

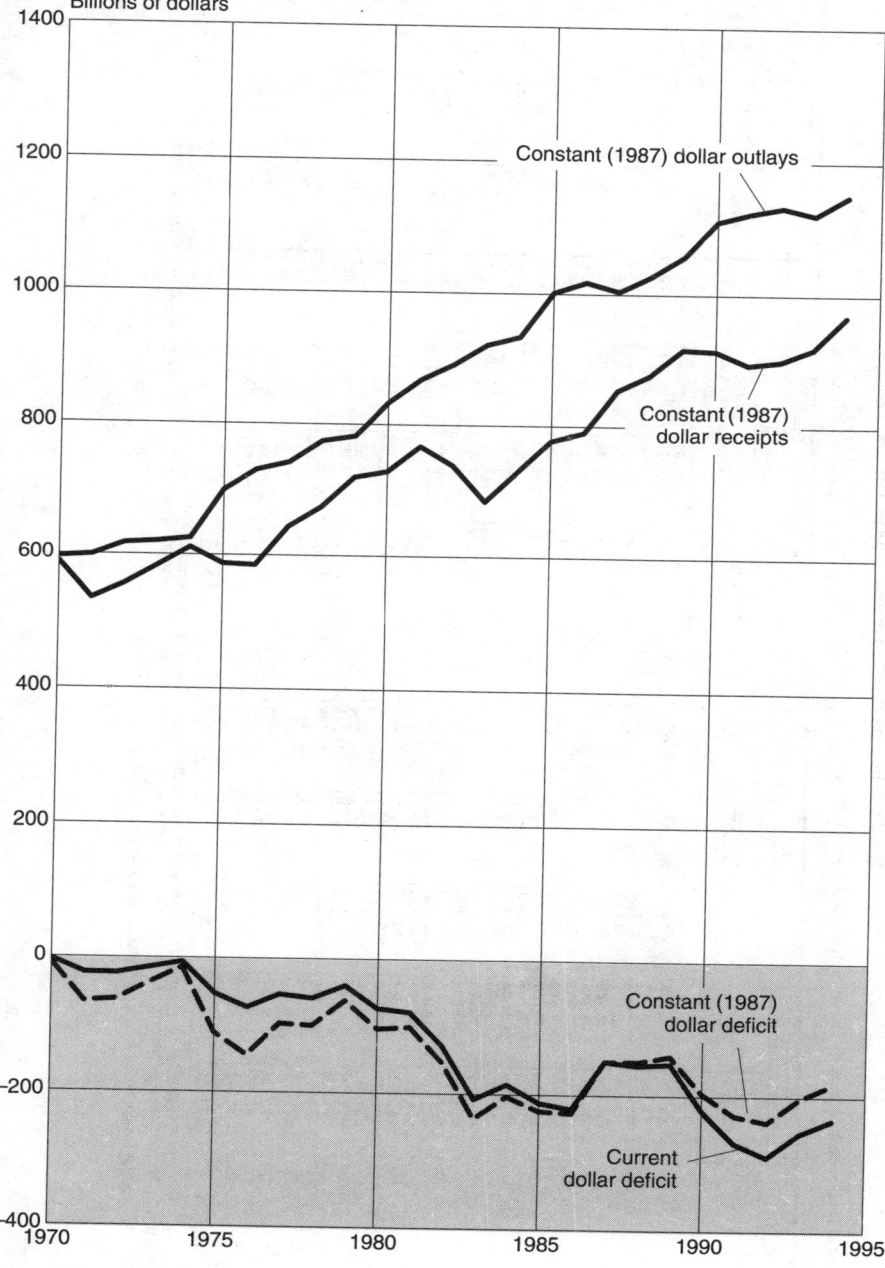

Billions of dollars

Note: Data for 1994 is projected.
Source: Chart prepared by U.S. Bureau of the Census. For data, see tables 504 and 508.

No. 504. Federal Budget—Summary: 1945 to 1994

[In millions of dollars, except percent. For fiscal years ending in year shown; see text, section 9. The Balanced Budget and Emergency Deficit Control Act of 1985 put all the previously off-budget Federal entities into the budget and moved Social Security off-budget. Minus sign (-) indicates deficit or decrease]

YEAR	Receipts [1]	OUTLAYS [1] Total	OUTLAYS [1] Human resources	OUTLAYS [1] National defense	OUTLAYS [1] Percent of GDP [2]	Surplus or deficit (-)	GROSS FEDERAL DEBT [3] Total	Held by— Federal Gov't Account	Held by— The public	Held by— Federal Reserve System	As percent of GDP [2]	ANNUAL PERCENT CHANGE [4] Receipts	ANNUAL PERCENT CHANGE [4] Outlays	ANNUAL PERCENT CHANGE [4] Gross Federal debt [3]	Outlays, off-budget
1945	45,159	92,712	1,859	82,965	43.7	-47,553	260,123	24,941	235,182	21,792	122.7	3.2	1.5	27.5	143
1950	39,443	42,562	14,221	13,724	16.0	-3,119	256,853	37,830	219,023	18,331	96.6	0.1	9.6	1.7	524
1955	65,451	68,444	14,908	42,729	17.8	-2,993	274,366	47,751	226,616	23,607	71.3	-6.0	-3.4	1.3	3,983
1960	92,492	92,191	26,184	48,130	18.3	301	290,525	53,686	236,840	26,523	57.6	16.7	0.1	1.1	10,850
1965	116,817	118,228	36,576	50,620	17.6	-1,411	322,318	61,540	260,778	39,100	48.0	3.7	-0.3	2.0	16,529
1970	192,807	195,649	75,349	81,692	19.9	-2,842	380,921	97,723	283,198	57,714	38.7	3.2	6.5	4.1	27,607
1972	207,309	230,681	107,211	79,174	20.1	-23,373	435,936	113,559	322,377	71,426	38.0	10.8	9.8	6.8	36,857
1973	230,799	245,707	119,522	76,681	19.3	-14,908	466,291	125,381	340,910	75,181	36.6	11.3	6.5	7.0	45,589
1974	263,224	269,359	135,783	79,347	19.2	-6,135	483,893	140,194	343,699	80,648	34.5	14.0	9.6	3.8	52,089
1975	279,090	332,332	173,245	86,509	22.0	-53,242	541,925	147,225	394,700	84,993	35.9	6.0	23.4	12.0	60,440
1976	298,060	371,792	203,594	89,619	22.1	-73,732	628,970	151,566	477,404	94,714	37.3	6.8	11.9	16.1	69,609
1976 [5]	81,232	95,975	52,065	22,269	21.6	-14,744	643,561	148,052	495,509	96,702	36.2	(X)	(X)	(X)	19,421
1977	355,559	409,218	221,895	97,241	21.3	-53,659	706,398	157,295	549,103	105,004	36.8	19.3	10.1	12.3	80,716
1978	399,561	458,746	242,329	104,495	21.3	-59,186	776,602	169,477	607,125	115,480	36.0	12.4	12.1	9.9	89,657
1979	463,302	503,485	267,574	116,342	20.7	-40,183	828,923	189,162	639,761	115,594	34.1	16.0	9.8	6.7	99,978
1980	517,112	590,947	313,374	133,995	22.3	-73,835	908,503	199,212	709,291	120,846	34.4	11.6	17.4	9.6	114,329
1981	599,272	678,249	362,022	157,513	22.9	-78,976	994,298	209,507	784,791	124,466	33.5	15.9	14.8	9.4	135,196
1982	617,766	745,755	388,681	185,309	23.9	-127,989	1,136,798	217,560	919,238	134,497	36.4	3.1	10.0	14.3	131,404
1983	600,562	808,380	426,003	209,903	24.4	-207,818	1,371,164	240,114	1,131,049	155,527	41.3	-2.8	8.4	20.6	147,108
1984	666,457	851,846	432,042	227,413	23.1	-185,388	1,564,110	264,159	1,299,931	155,122	42.3	11.0	5.4	14.1	165,813
1985	734,057	946,391	471,822	252,748	23.9	-212,334	1,816,974	317,612	1,499,362	169,806	45.8	10.1	11.1	16.2	176,807
1986	769,091	990,336	481,594	273,375	23.5	-221,245	2,120,082	383,919	1,736,163	190,855	50.3	4.8	4.6	16.7	183,498
1987	854,143	1,003,911	502,196	281,999	22.5	-149,769	2,345,578	457,444	1,888,134	212,040	52.7	11.1	1.4	10.6	193,832
1988	908,954	1,064,140	533,404	290,361	22.1	-155,187	2,600,760	550,507	2,050,252	229,218	54.1	6.4	6.0	10.9	202,691
1989	990,691	1,143,172	568,668	303,559	22.1	-152,481	2,867,538	678,157	2,189,336	220,088	55.4	9.0	7.4	10.3	210,911
1990	1,031,321	1,252,705	619,327	299,331	22.9	-221,384	3,206,207	795,841	2,410,366	234,410	58.5	4.1	9.6	11.8	225,065
1991	1,054,272	1,323,793	689,691	273,292	23.3	-269,521	3,598,303	910,362	2,687,942	258,591	63.4	2.2	5.7	12.2	241,687
1992	1,090,453	1,380,856	772,450	298,350	23.3	-290,403	4,001,941	1,003,302	2,998,639	296,397	67.4	3.4	4.3	11.2	252,339
1993	1,153,535	1,408,205	827,541	281,086	22.4	-254,670	4,351,223	1,104,045	3,247,178	325,653	69.1	5.8	2.0	8.7	266,587
1994, est.	1,249,071	1,483,829	879,911	279,824	22.3	-234,758	4,676,029	1,203,617	3,472,412	(NA)	70.4	8.3	5.4	7.5	280,876

NA Not available.   X Not applicable.   [1] Includes off-budget receipts and outlays.   [2] Gross domestic product; for calendar year GDP, see section 14.   [3] See text, section 10, for discussion of debt concept.   [4] Change from previous year. For explanation of average annual percent see Guide to Tabular Presentation.   [5] Represents transition quarter, July-Sept.

Source: U.S. Office of Management and Budget, Budget of the United States Government, annual.

No. 505. Federal Receipts, by Source: 1980 to 1994

[In millions of dollars. For fiscal years ending in year shown; see text, section 9. Receipts reflect collections. Covers both Federal funds and trust funds; see text, section 10. Excludes government-sponsored but privately-owned corporations, Federal Reserve System, District of Columbia government, and money held in suspense as deposit funds. See *Historical Statistics, Colonial Times to 1970*, series Y 343-351, and Y 472-487 for related data]

SOURCE	1980	1985	1990	1991	1992	1993	1994, est.
Total receipts [1]	**517,112**	**734,057**	**1,031,321**	**1,054,272**	**1,090,453**	**1,153,535**	**1,249,071**
Individual income taxes	244,069	334,531	466,884	467,827	475,964	509,680	549,901
Corporation income taxes	64,600	61,331	93,507	98,086	100,270	117,520	130,719
Social insurance	157,803	265,163	380,047	396,016	413,689	428,300	461,923
Employment taxes and contributions	138,748	234,646	353,891	370,526	385,491	396,939	430,153
Old-age and survivors insurance	96,581	169,822	255,031	265,503	273,137	281,735	291,708
Disability insurance	16,628	16,348	26,625	28,382	29,289	30,199	44,471
Hospital insurance	23,217	44,871	68,556	72,842	79,108	81,224	90,115
Railroad retirement/ pension fund	2,323	2,213	2,292	2,371	2,449	2,367	2,387
Railroad social security equivalent account		1,391	1,387	1,428	1,508	1,414	1,472
Unemployment insurance	15,336	25,758	21,635	20,922	23,410	26,556	27,041
Other retirement contributions	3,719	4,759	4,522	4,568	4,788	4,805	4,729
Excise taxes [1]	24,329	35,992	35,345	42,402	45,569	48,057	54,550
Federal funds	15,563	19,097	15,591	18,275	21,836	24,522	28,672
Alcohol	5,601	5,562	5,695	7,364	8,011	7,583	7,592
Tobacco	2,443	4,779	4,081	4,706	5,049	5,875	5,652
Ozone depletion	-	-	360	562	637	854	943
Trust funds [1]	8,766	16,894	19,754	24,127	23,733	23,535	25,878
Highways	6,620	13,015	13,867	16,979	16,733	18,039	18,290
Airport and airway	1,874	2,851	3,700	4,910	4,645	3,262	5,407
Black lung disability	272	581	665	652	626	634	654
Hazardous substance response	-	273	818	810	818	826	838
Aquatic resources	-	126	218	260	271	276	296
Leaking underground storage	-	-	122	123	157	153	153
Vaccine injury compensations	-	-	159	81	118	38	148
Oil spill liability	-	-	143	254	295	229	-
Estate and gift taxes	6,389	6,422	11,500	11,138	11,143	12,577	12,749
Customs duties	7,174	12,079	16,707	15,949	17,359	18,802	19,198
Federal Reserve deposits	11,767	17,059	24,319	19,158	22,920	14,908	15,847

- Represents or rounds to zero.   [1] Totals reflect interfund and intragovernmental transactions and/or other functions, not shown separately.

Source: U.S. Office of Management and Budget, *Budget of the United States Government*, annual.

No. 506. Federal Trust Fund Receipts, Outlays, and Balances: 1992 to 1994

[In billions of dollars. For fiscal years ending in year shown; see text section 9. Receipts deposited. Outlays on a checks-issued basis less refunds collected. Balances: That which have not been spent. See text, section 10, for discussion of the budget concept and trust funds]

DESCRIPTION	INCOME			OUTLAYS			BALANCES [1]		
	1992	1993	1994, est.	1992	1993	1994, est.	1992	1993	1994, est.
Total [2]	**663**	**702**	**730**	**567**	**602**	**630**	**973**	**1,080**	**1,180**
Airport and airway trust fund	6	4	6	6	7	7	15	13	13
Federal employees retirement funds	61	63	65	34	35	37	291	319	347
Federal old-age, survivors and disability insurance trust funds	338	351	378	288	305	321	319	374	431
Foreign military sales trust fund	12	13	13	12	13	13	7	7	7
Health insurance trust funds	146	156	163	132	146	161	139	149	152
Highway trust funds	18	20	20	17	19	21	22	23	21
Military retirement trust funds	37	35	35	25	26	27	88	98	106
Railroad retirement trust funds	11	11	11	10	11	11	13	12	12
Unemployment trust funds	29	41	33	41	40	31	36	37	39
Veterans life insurance trust funds	2	2	1	1	1	1	13	13	14
Other trust funds [3]	7	8	7	4	4	4	32	36	39

[1] Balances available on a cash basis (rather than an authorization basis) at the end of the year. Balances are primarily invested in Federal debt securities.   [2] Includes funds not shown separately.   [3] Effective August 9, 1989, the permanent insurance fund of the FDIC was classified under law as a Federal fund.

Source: U.S. Office of Management and Budget, *Budget of the United States Government*, annual.

No. 507. Federal Budget Outlays—Defense, Human and Physical Resources, and Net Interest Payments: 1940 to 1994

[In millions of dollars. For fiscal year ending in year shown. Minus sign (-) indicates offsets]

YEAR	Outlays, total	National defense	HUMAN RESOURCES Total	Social Security	Income security	Medicare	Health	Education	Veterans benefits	PHYSICAL RESOURCES Total [2]	Transportation	Commerce and housing	Net interest	Other	Undistributed offsets
1940	9,468	1,660	4,139	28	1,514	(NA)	55	1,972	570	2,312	392	550	899	775	-317
1945	92,712	82,965	1,859	267	1,137	(NA)	211	134	110	1,747	3,654	-2,630	3,112	4,418	-1,389
1950	42,562	13,724	14,221	781	4,097	(NA)	268	241	8,834	3,667	967	1,035	4,812	7,955	-1,817
1955	68,444	42,729	14,908	4,427	5,071	(NA)	291	445	4,675	2,732	1,246	92	4,850	6,718	-3,493
1960	92,191	48,130	26,184	11,602	7,378	(NA)	795	968	5,441	7,991	4,126	1,618	6,947	7,760	-4,820
1964	118,528	54,757	35,294	16,620	9,641	(NA)	1,788	1,563	5,682	9,528	5,242	1,157	8,199	16,458	-5,708
1965	118,228	50,620	36,576	17,460	9,455	(NA)	1,791	2,146	5,723	11,264	5,730	3,245	8,591	17,086	-5,908
1966	134,532	58,111	43,257	20,694	9,662	64	2,543	4,372	5,923	13,410	5,898	3,979	9,386	16,911	-6,542
1967	157,464	71,417	51,272	21,725	10,248	2,748	3,351	6,458	6,743	14,674	6,316	4,280	10,268	17,126	-7,294
1968	178,134	81,926	59,375	23,854	11,798	4,649	4,390	6,743	7,042	16,002	6,526	-119	11,090	17,786	-8,045
1969	183,640	82,497	66,410	27,298	13,066	5,695	5,162	7,042	7,642	11,869	7,008	2,112	12,699	18,151	-7,986
1970	195,649	81,692	75,349	30,270	15,645	6,213	5,907	7,642	8,679	15,574	8,052	2,366	14,380	17,286	-8,632
1971	210,172	78,872	91,901	35,872	22,936	6,622	6,843	7,548	9,778	18,286	8,392	2,222	14,841	16,379	-10,107
1972	230,681	79,174	107,211		27,638	7,479	8,674	8,634	10,732	19,574	9,066	931	15,478	18,828	-9,583
1973	245,707	76,681	119,522	49,090	28,264	8,052	9,356	9,849	12,015	20,614	9,172	4,705	17,349	24,950	-13,409
1974	269,359	79,347	135,783	55,867	33,699	9,639	10,733	12,529	13,388	25,106	10,918	9,947	21,449	24,423	-16,749
1975	332,332	86,509	173,245	64,658	50,160	12,875	12,930	12,457	16,599	35,449	13,739	7,619	23,244	27,487	-13,602
1976	371,792	89,619	203,594	73,899	60,784	15,834	15,734	16,022	18,433	39,188			26,727	27,050	-14,386
1976 [3]	95,975	22,269	52,065	19,763	14,981	4,264	3,924	5,169	3,963	9,512	3,358	931	6,949	9,388	-4,206
1977	409,218	97,241	221,895	85,061	61,044	19,345	17,302	21,104	18,038	40,746	15,521		29,901	34,315	-14,879
1978	458,746	104,495	242,329	93,861	61,488	22,768	18,524	26,710	18,978	52,591	17,532		35,458	39,594	-15,720
1979	503,485	116,342	267,574	104,073	66,359	26,495	20,494	30,223	19,931	54,013		3,093	42,636	40,396	-17,476
1980	590,947	133,995	313,374	118,547	86,540	32,090	23,169	31,843	21,185	65,985		6,254	52,538	44,996	-19,942
1981	678,249	157,513	362,022	139,584	99,723	39,149	26,866	33,709	22,991	70,886		9,390	68,774	47,095	-28,041
1982	745,755	185,309	388,681	155,964	107,717	46,567	27,445	27,029	23,958	61,752		8,206	85,044	51,069	-26,099
1983	808,380	209,903	426,003	170,724	122,598	52,588	28,641	26,606	24,846	57,600	23,379	6,256	89,828	59,023	-33,976
1984	851,846	227,413	432,042	178,223	112,668	57,540	30,417	27,579	25,614	57,938	21,334	6,681	111,123	55,287	-31,957
1985	946,391	252,748	471,822	188,623	128,200	65,822	33,542	29,342	26,292	56,789	23,669	6,917	129,504	68,227	-32,698
1986	990,336	273,375	481,594	198,757	119,796	70,164	35,936	30,585	26,356	58,614	25,838	4,229	136,047	73,713	-33,007
1987	1,003,911	281,999	502,196	207,353	123,250	75,120	39,967	29,724	26,782	54,932	28,117	6,182	138,652	62,588	-36,455
1988	1,064,140	290,361	533,404	219,341	129,332	78,878	44,487	31,938	29,428	68,283	26,222	18,815	151,838	57,822	-36,967
1989	1,143,172	303,559	568,668	232,542	136,031	84,964	48,390	36,674	30,066	81,068	27,272	29,211	169,266	60,896	-37,212
1990	1,252,705	299,331	619,327	248,623	147,019	98,102	57,716	38,755	29,112	125,546	29,485	67,142	184,221	71,081	-36,615
1991	1,323,793	273,292	689,691	269,015	170,301	104,489	71,183	43,354	31,349	134,544	31,099	75,639	194,541	75,136	-39,356
1992	1,380,856	298,350	772,450	287,585	196,958	119,024	89,497	45,248	34,138	74,779	33,333	10,083	199,421	82,263	-39,280
1993	1,408,205	291,086	827,541	304,585	207,257	130,552	99,415	50,012	35,720	45,890	35,004	-22,725	198,811	83,892	-37,386
1994, est.	1,483,829	279,824	879,911	320,460	214,626	143,651	112,252	50,793	38,129	74,642	37,582	504	203,448		-37,887

NA Not available. [1] Also includes training, employment, and social services. [2] Includes outlays not shown separately. [3] Transition quarter, July to September.

Source: U. S. Office of Management and Budget, *Budget of the United States Government*, annual.

No. 508. Federal Budget Outlays in Constant (1987) Dollars: 1980 to 1994

[Dollar amounts in billions of dollars. For fiscal years ending in year shown; see text, section 9. Given the inherent imprecision in deflating outlays, the data shown in constant dollars present a reasonable perspective—not precision. The deflators and the categories that are deflated are as comparable over time as feasible. See headnote, table 504. Minus sign (-) indicates offset]

OUTLAYS	1980	1983	1984	1985	1986	1987	1988	1989	1990	1991	1992	1993	1994, est.
Outlays, total	**832**	**921**	**934**	**1,001**	**1,017**	**1,004**	**1,027**	**1,057**	**1,110**	**1,123**	**1,132**	**1,121**	**1,149**
National defense	187	230	242	261	276	282	283	286	273	240	250	236	220
Nondefense outlays	645	691	692	740	741	722	744	771	838	882	882	885	929
Payments for individuals	395	460	447	459	468	471	480	490	510	541	586	612	632
Direct payments	-349	-411	-396	-406	-411	-414	-420	-429	-442	-464	-495	-515	-524
Grants to State and local gov't's	-46	-49	-51	-53	-56	-58	-60	-62	-67	-77	-91	-97	-107
Other grants	81	58	58	60	60	51	51	50	52	54	56	58	62
Net interest	74	103	122	137	140	139	147	156	163	165	164	160	159
All other	123	109	100	119	108	98	102	109	146	156	108	85	105
Undistributed offsetting receipts	-29	-38	-35	-34	-34	-37	-36	-34	-32	-33	-32	-29	-29
PERCENT OF GDP													
Outlays, total	22.3	24.4	23.1	23.9	23.5	22.5	22.1	22.1	22.9	23.3	23.3	22.4	22.3
National defense	5.1	6.3	6.2	6.4	6.5	6.3	6.0	5.9	5.5	4.8	5.0	4.6	4.2
Nondefense outlays	17.3	18.0	16.9	17.5	17.0	16.2	16.1	16.2	17.4	18.5	18.2	17.7	18.1
Payments for individuals	10.5	12.0	10.9	10.8	10.7	10.6	10.4	10.4	10.7	11.5	12.3	12.4	12.5
Direct payments	-9.3	-10.7	-9.6	-9.5	-9.4	-9.3	-9.1	-9.1	-9.2	-9.8	-10.4	-10.5	-10.4
Grants to State and local gov't's	-1.2	-1.3	-1.2	-1.2	-1.3	-1.3	-1.3	-1.3	-1.4	-1.6	-1.9	-2.0	-2.1
Other grants	2.2	1.5	1.4	1.4	1.4	1.1	1.1	1.1	1.1	1.1	1.1	1.1	1.1
Net interest	2.0	2.7	3.0	3.3	3.2	3.1	3.2	3.3	3.4	3.4	3.4	3.2	3.1
All other	3.3	2.9	2.5	2.9	2.5	2.2	2.2	2.3	3.0	3.2	2.2	1.7	2.0
Undistributed offsetting receipts	-0.8	-1.0	-0.9	-0.8	-0.8	-0.8	-0.8	-0.7	-0.7	-0.7	-0.7	-0.6	-0.6
PERCENT OF OUTLAYS													
Outlays, total	100.0	100.0	100.0	100.0	100.0	100.0	100.0	100.0	100.0	100.0	100.0	100.0	100.0
National defense	22.7	26.0	26.7	26.7	27.6	28.1	27.3	26.6	23.9	20.6	21.6	20.7	18.9
Nondefense outlays	77.3	74.0	73.3	73.3	72.4	71.9	72.7	73.4	76.1	79.4	78.4	79.3	81.1
Payments for individuals	47.1	49.1	47.1	45.2	45.6	46.9	47.0	46.9	46.6	49.1	52.7	55.5	55.9
Direct payments	-41.6	-43.8	-41.8	-39.9	-40.1	-41.2	-41.2	-41.0	-40.5	-42.1	-44.6	-46.7	-46.4
Grants to State and local gov't's	-5.5	-5.3	-5.3	-5.2	-5.5	-5.8	-5.9	-5.9	-6.2	-7.0	-8.1	-8.8	-9.5
Other grants	9.9	6.2	6.1	6.0	5.9	5.0	4.8	4.8	4.6	4.7	4.8	4.9	5.1
Net interest	8.9	11.1	13.0	13.7	13.7	13.8	14.3	14.8	14.7	14.7	14.4	14.1	13.7
All other	14.7	11.9	10.8	12.0	10.6	9.8	9.9	10.2	13.1	13.8	9.3	7.4	8.9
Undistributed offsetting receipts	-3.4	-4.2	-3.8	-3.5	-3.3	-3.6	-3.5	-3.3	-2.9	-3.0	-2.8	-2.7	-2.6

Source: U.S. Office of Management and Budget, *Budget of the United States Government*, annual.

No. 509. Federal Outlays, by Detailed Function: 1980 to 1994

[In millions of dollars. For fiscal years ending in year shown; outlays stated in terms of checks issued or cash payments. See headnote, table 505]

FUNCTION	1980	1985	1990	1991	1992	1993	1994, est.
Total outlays	**590,947**	**946,391**	**1,252,705**	**1,323,793**	**1,380,856**	**1,408,205**	**1,483,829**
Legislative branch.	1,224	1,610	2,241	2,296	2,677	2,406	2,755
The Judiciary . . . . ¹ . .	567	966	1,646	1,997	2,308	2,628	2,872
Funds appropriated to President ¹ . .	8,542	11,858	10,087	11,724	11,113	11,245	11,383
Departments:							
Agriculture	34,785	55,523	46,012	54,119	56,437	63,144	64,931
Commerce	3,129	2,140	3,734	2,585	2,567	2,798	3,234
Defense-Military.	130,912	245,154	289,755	261,925	286,632	278,574	267,484
Defense-Civil.	15,161	18,770	24,975	26,543	28,270	29,266	30,980
Education.	14,770	16,682	23,109	25,339	26,047	30,290	28,738
Energy.	6,467	10,587	12,084	12,479	15,523	16,942	17,206
Health and Human Services	76,374	132,104	193,678	217,969	257,332	282,779	316,615
Housing and Urban Development .	12,735	28,720	20,167	22,751	24,470	25,181	25,535
Interior.	4,477	4,825	5,796	6,097	6,549	6,796	7,240
Justice.	2,641	3,586	6,507	8,244	9,802	10,170	10,817
Labor ²	29,731	23,699	25,215	33,954	47,078	44,651	37,111
State.	1,940	2,645	3,979	4,252	5,007	5,244	5,785
Transportation.	19,802	25,020	28,650	30,511	32,491	34,457	36,687
Treasury.	76,568	164,967	255,172	276,339	292,987	298,804	309,268
Veterans Affairs.	21,137	26,333	28,998	31,214	33,897	35,487	37,919
Independent agencies:							
Environmental Protection Agency .	5,603	4,490	5,108	5,769	5,950	5,930	6,539
General Services Administration. .	249	-2	-123	487	469	743	1,048
NASA ³	4,959	7,251	12,429	13,878	13,961	14,305	14,183
Office of Personnel Management .	15,056	23,727	31,949	34,808	35,596	36,794	38,101
Small Business Administration . . .	2,026	680	692	613	546	785	604
Other independent agencies	16,333	10,169	74,617	81,319	18,656	-10,047	15,672
Undistributed offsetting receipts . . .	-31,988	-58,656	-98,930	-110,005	-117,111	-119,711	-123,733
Outlays, by function	**590,947**	**946,391**	**1,252,705**	**1,323,793**	**1,380,856**	**1,408,205**	**1,483,829**
National defense	133,995	252,748	299,331	273,292	298,350	291,086	279,824
Dept. of Defense—Military.	130,912	245,154	289,755	262,389	286,892	278,561	267,360
Military personnel	40,897	67,842	75,622	83,439	81,171	75,904	70,980
Operation and maintenance . . .	44,788	72,371	88,340	101,769	91,984	94,094	88,695
Procurement	29,021	70,381	80,972	82,028	74,881	69,936	60,814
R and D, test, and evaluation . .	13,127	27,103	37,458	34,589	34,632	36,968	35,546
Military construction	2,450	4,260	5,080	3,497	4,262	4,831	5,143
Family housing.	1,680	2,642	3,501	3,296	3,271	3,255	3,484
Other	-1,050	553	-1,218	-46,229	-3,308	-6,428	2,699
Atomic energy defense activities .	2,878	7,098	8,988	10,004	10,619	11,017	11,184
Defense related activities	206	495	587	899	839	1,508	1,280
International affairs	12,714	16,176	13,764	15,851	16,107	16,826	18,968
International development and							
humanitarian assistance	3,626	5,409	5,498	5,141	6,133	5,413	7,325
Conduct of foreign affairs	1,366	2,043	3,050	3,282	3,894	4,325	4,742
Other.	7,722	8,725	5,216	7,428	6,081	8,312	6,901
Income security	86,540	128,200	147,019	170,301	196,958	207,257	214,626
General retirement and disability							
insurance	5,083	5,617	5,148	4,945	5,483	4,347	5,203
Federal employee retirement and							
disability	26,594	38,591	51,981	56,106	57,572	60,047	62,257
Housing assistance	5,632	25,263	15,891	17,200	18,914	21,548	23,840
Food and nutrition assistance . . .	14,016	18,540	23,964	28,481	32,622	35,148	38,183
Other income security.	17,163	22,715	31,146	36,485	42,901	48,366	55,933
Unemployment compensation . . .	18,051	17,475	18,889	27,084	39,466	37,802	29,210
Health	23,169	33,542	57,716	71,183	89,497	99,415	112,252
Health care services.	18,003	26,984	47,642	60,723	77,719	86,860	98,969
Health research.	4,161	5,376	8,611	8,899	10,021	10,794	11,336
Consumer and occupational							
health and safety	1,006	1,182	1,462	1,560	1,757	1,762	1,947
Medicare.	32,090	65,822	98,102	104,489	119,024	130,552	143,651
Social Security	118,547	188,623	248,623	269,015	287,585	304,585	320,460
Veterans benefits and services	21,185	26,292	29,112	31,349	34,138	35,720	38,129
Income security for veterans	11,688	14,714	15,241	16,961	17,296	17,758	19,801
Educ., training, and rehab	2,342	1,059	278	427	783	826	1,170
Hospital and medical care.	6,515	9,547	12,134	12,889	14,091	14,812	15,842
Housing for veterans	(Z)	214	517	85	901	1,299	212
Other.	665	758	943	987	1,067	1,025	1,104

See footnotes at end of table.

No. 509. Federal Outlays, by Detailed Function: 1980 to 1994—Continued

[In millions of dollars. See headnote, table 505]

FUNCTION	1980	1985	1990	1991	1992	1993	1994, est.
Education, training, employment, and social services............	31,843	29,342	38,755	43,354	45,248	50,012	50,793
Elementary, secondary, and vocational education............	6,893	7,598	9,918	11,372	12,402	13,481	15,252
Higher education...............	6,723	8,156	11,107	11,961	11,268	14,483	10,575
Research and general educ. aids	1,212	1,229	1,577	1,773	1,996	2,040	2,219
Training and employment	10,345	4,972	5,619	5,934	6,479	6,700	7,136
Other labor services.............	551	678	810	788	884	948	952
Social services	6,119	6,710	9,723	11,526	12,219	12,360	14,660
Commerce and housing credit........	9,390	4,229	67,142	75,639	10,083	-22,725	504
Mortgage credit................	5,887	3,054	3,845	5,362	4,320	1,554	-388
Postal Service.................	1,246	1,351	2,116	1,828	1,169	1,602	1,879
Deposit insurance	-285	-2,198	58,081	66,394	2,518	-27,957	-3,285
Other commerce	2,542	2,022	3,100	2,054	2,076	2,077	2,298
Transportation	21,329	25,838	29,485	31,099	33,333	35,004	37,582
Ground transportation............	15,274	17,606	18,954	19,545	20,347	21,251	23,380
Air transportation..............	3,723	4,895	7,234	8,184	9,313	10,049	10,103
Water transportation............	2,229	3,201	3,151	3,148	3,430	3,423	3,783
Other transportation.............	104	137	146	223	244	281	315
Natural resources and environment	13,858	13,357	17,080	18,559	20,025	20,239	22,285
Water resources	4,223	4,122	4,401	4,366	4,559	4,258	5,596
Conservation and land management ..	1,043	1,481	3,553	4,047	4,581	4,777	4,772
Recreational resources..........	1,677	1,621	1,876	2,137	2,378	2,620	2,655
Pollution control and abatement.....	5,510	4,465	5,170	5,861	6,075	6,061	6,667
Other natural resources	1,405	1,668	2,080	2,148	2,432	2,522	2,595
Energy	10,156	5,685	3,341	2,436	4,500	4,319	4,988
Supply......................	8,367	2,615	1,976	1,945	3,226	3,286	3,743
Conservation.................	569	491	365	386	468	521	586
Emergency preparedness	342	1,838	442	-235	319	336	279
Information, policy, and regs	878	740	559	340	486	176	380
Community/regional develop	11,252	7,680	8,498	6,811	6,838	9,051	9,282
Community development..........	4,907	4,598	3,530	3,543	3,643	3,681	4,311
Area and regional development	4,303	3,117	2,868	2,743	2,315	2,443	2,538
Disaster relief and insurance	2,043	(Z)	2,100	525	881	2,927	2,434
Agriculture.....................	8,839	25,565	11,958	15,183	15,205	20,443	16,868
Farm income stabilization	7,441	23,751	9,761	12,924	12,666	17,799	14,162
Research and services	1,398	1,813	2,197	2,259	2,539	2,643	2,705
Net interest	52,538	129,504	184,221	194,541	199,421	198,811	203,448
On-budget	*54,877*	*133,622*	*200,212*	*214,763*	*223,059*	*225,599*	*232,521*
Off-budget	*-2,339*	*-4,118*	*-15,991*	*-20,222*	*-23,637*	*-26,788*	*-29,073*
Interest on the public debt........	74,808	178,898	264,724	285,455	292,323	292,502	298,505
Interest received by on-budget trust funds	-9,707	-21,838	-46,321	-50,426	-54,193	-55,537	-56,772
Interest received by off-budget trust funds	-2,339	-4,118	-15,991	-20,222	-23,637	-26,788	-29,073
Other interest	-10,224	-23,438	-18,191	-20,266	-15,071	-11,367	-9,212
General science, space, and technology.....................	5,832	8,627	14,444	16,111	16,409	17,030	17,279
Gen. science and basic research	1,381	2,019	2,835	3,154	3,571	3,938	4,445
General government	13,028	11,588	10,734	11,661	12,990	13,009	14,299
Legislative functions.............	1,038	1,355	1,763	1,916	2,124	2,124	2,169
Exec. direction and management	97	113	160	190	188	197	254
Central fiscal operations	2,612	3,492	6,004	6,097	6,612	6,976	7,578
General property and records management.................	327	96	31	657	692	1,005	1,324
General purpose fiscal assistance....	8,582	6,353	2,161	2,100	1,865	1,935	2,158
Other general government.........	569	521	800	1,280	1,782	1,329	1,346
Deductions, offsetting receipts......	-351	-506	-361	-718	-480	-739	-691
Administration of justice...........	4,584	6,270	9,995	12,276	14,426	14,955	16,479
Federal law enforcement.........	2,239	3,520	4,648	5,661	6,462	6,674	6,843
Federal litigative and judicial	1,347	2,064	3,579	4,352	5,054	5,336	6,151
Federal correctional activities.......	342	537	1,291	1,600	2,114	2,124	2,482
Criminal justice assistance........	656	150	477	663	795	822	1,002
Undistributed offsetting receipts	*-19,942*	*-32,698*	*-36,615*	*-39,356*	*-39,280*	*-37,386*	*-37,887*

Z Less than $500,000.   [1] Represents international affairs funds mainly.   [2] Includes Pension Benefit Guaranty Corporation.   [3] National Aeronautics and Space Administration.

Source: U.S. Office of Management and Budget, *Budget of the United States Government,* annual.

No. 510. Tax Expenditures, by Function: 1993 to 1996

[In millions of dollars. For years ending, **Sept. 30, except as noted.** Tax expenditures are defined as *revenue losses* attributable to provisions of the Federal tax laws which allow a special exclusion, exemption, or deduction from gross income or which provide a special credit, a preferential rate of tax, or a deferral of liability. Represents tax expenditures of **$1 billion or more in 1996**]

DESCRIPTION	1993	1994	1995	1996
National defense:				
Excl. benefits/allowances to Armed Forces personnel	2,115	2,060	2,030	2,020
International affairs: [1]				
Exclusion of income of foreign sales corporations	1,200	1,300	1,400	1,500
Deferral of income from controlled foreign corps. [2]	1,600	1,600	1,700	1,800
Inventory property sales source rules exception	1,100	1,200	1,300	1,400
General science, space, and technology: [1]				
Expensing of R and D expenditures [2]	2,060	2,230	2,390	2,560
Energy:				
Excess of percent over cost depletion: Oil and gas	995	1,010	1,035	1,055
Alternative fuel production credit	760	900	970	1,000
Commerce and housing credit: [1]				
Exclusion of interest on—				
Life insurance savings.	7,520	8,115	8,730	9,385
Owner-occupied mortgage subsidy bonds.	1,715	1,760	1,785	1,775
Capital gains (excl. agric., timber, iron ore and coal) [2]	5,510	6,565	6,920	7,045
Deferral of capital gains on home sales.	13,265	13,925	14,620	15,195
Exclusion of capital gains on home sales for persons				
age 55 and over	4,625	4,770	4,960	5,155
Deductibility of—				
Mortgage interest on owner-occupied homes	48,705	51,835	54,800	57,985
Property tax on owner-occupied homes	13,055	13,865	14,655	15,545
Accelerated depreciation on rental housing [2]	1,190	1,085	1,100	1,145
Accelerated deprec. of bldgs. excl. rental housing [2]	2,895	2,995	3,185	3,430
Step-up basis of capital gains at death	25,340	26,850	28,305	29,480
Accelerated depreciation of machinery and equipment [3]	19,625	22,775	23,210	22,550
Expensing of certain small investments [2]	1,540	2,095	1,560	1,235
Graduated corporation income tax rate [2]	3,325	3,655	3,890	4,140
Exception from passive loss rules for $25,000 rental loss	6,070	5,945	5,775	5,680
Transportation:				
Exclusion of reimbursed employee parking expenses.	1,790	1,845	1,930	2,015
Community and regional development: [1]				
Credit for low income housing investments	1,545	1,925	2,265	2,600
Education, training, employment, and social services: [1]				
Deductibility of—				
Charitable contributions (education).	1,960	2,120	2,230	2,340
Charitable contributions other than education	1,770	1,910	2,020	2,130
Charitable contributions other than education and health.	13,130	14,290	15,080	15,830
Credit for child and dependent care expenses.	2,540	2,675	2,820	2,975
Health: [1]				
Excl. of employer contrib. for medical insurance				
premiums and medical care.	46,895	51,445	56,265	61,675
Deductibility of medical expenses.	3,010	3,270	3,560	3,870
Excl. of interest on State and local debt for private				
nonprofit health facilities	1,405	1,455	1,495	1,535
Deductibility of charitable contributions (health)	1,770	1,910	2,020	2,130
Social Security: [1]				
Exclusion of Social Security benefits:				
Disability insurance benefits	1,725	1,765	1,905	2,105
OASI benefits for retired workers	18,310	16,695	16,525	17,370
Benefits for dependents and survivors	3,620	3,610	3,730	3,940
Income security: [1]				
Exclusion of workmen's compensation benefits	3,815	4,240	4,455	4,740
Net exclusion of pension contributions and earnings:				
Employer plans	49,430	48,750	55,540	59,010
Individual Retirement Accounts.	5,720	5,415	5,290	5,275
Keoghs	3,245	3,670	3,875	4,130
Exclusion of other employee benefits:				
Premiums on group term life insurance	2,620	2,750	2,880	3,020
Special ESOP rules (other than investment credit)	2,070	2,035	1,760	1,635
Additional deduction for the elderly [4]	1,510	1,535	1,555	1,570
Earned income credit.	3,605	3,940	5,100	5,795
Veterans benefits and services: [1]				
Exclusion of veterans disability compensation	1,755	1,860	1,920	1,855
Deferral of interest on savings bonds.	1,130	1,190	1,250	1,310
General purpose fiscal assistance: [1]				
Excl. of interest on public State & local debt	11,575	11,970	12,350	12,690
Deductibility of nonbusiness State & local taxes other				
than on owner-occupied homes	22,555	24,255	25,640	27,130
Tax credit for corporations receiving income from doing				
business in United States possessions	3,075	2,890	2,630	2,680

[1] Total (after interactions).   [2] Normal tax method.   [3] Pre-1983 budget method.   [4] Data on calendar year basis.

Source: U.S. Office of Management and Budget, *Budget of the United States Government,* annual.

No. 511. Government—Human and Capital Investment—Summary: 1993 to 1995

[Discretionary budget authority, in millions of dollars, except as indicated]

INVESTMENT	1993, actual	1994, enacted	1995, proposed	PERCENT CHANGE	
				1993-94	1994-95
HUMAN INVESTMENTS					
Young children	5,977	7,064	8,054	18.2	14.0
Immunization funds [1]	341	528	888	54.8	68.2
Head Start funds	2,776	3,326	4,026	19.8	21.0
WIC (women, infants, and children) funds	2,860	3,210	3,564	12.2	11.0
Family preservation and support funds	-	60	150	(X)	150.0
Children receiving immunization (1,000) [2]	(NA)	(NA)	13,186	(NA)	(NA)
Head Start slots (1,000)	714	750	840	5.0	12.0
Percent of targeted population reached [3]	51.0	54.0	60.0	5.9	11.1
WIC Recipients (1,000)	5,920	6,510	7,220	10.0	10.9
Percent of target population reached [4]	79.0	85.0	95.0	7.6	11.8
Education	7,278	7,539	9,089	3.6	20.6
Workforce Investments	5,010	5,474	6,480	9.3	18.4
Grants for training the disadvantaged	1,692	1,647	1,729	-2.7	5.0
Dislocated worker assistance	651	1,118	1,465	71.7	31.0
Job Corps	966	1,040	1,157	7.7	11.3
Summer youth employment	1,025	888	1,056	-13.4	18.9
School-to-work	-	50	150	(X)	200.0
One-stop career shopping	-	50	250	(X)	400.0
Other employment and training	676	681	673	0.7	-1.2
National Service	279	575	850	106.1	47.8
INFRASTRUCTURE INVESTMENT (bil. dol.)					
Transportation (DOT):					
Highways:					
Core categorical highway grants	16.5	19.1	19.8	15.8	3.7
Emergency repair [5]	0.5	0.7	0.1	40.0	-85.7
Highway demonstrations and other projects	1.0	0.5	0.4	-50.0	-20.0
Mass transit:					
Formula capital grants	0.9	1.6	2.3	77.8	43.7
Discretionary grants	1.7	1.7	1.5	-	-11.8
Railroads:					
Northeast corridor	0.2	0.2	0.2	-	-
Penn Station redevelopment	-	(Z)	0.1	(X)	(X)
Amtrak capital	0.2	0.2	0.3	-	50.0
Air transportation:					
Air traffic control facilities and equip	2.3	2.1	2.3	-8.7	9.5
Grants for airports	1.8	1.7	1.7	-5.6	-
Water treatment and supply (EPA):					
Clean water State revolving funds	1.9	1.2	1.6	-36.8	33.3
Drinking water State revolving funds	-	0.6	0.7	(X)	16.7
Targeted whitewater assistance	0.6	0.6	0.3	-	-50.0
Rural water and wastewater programs (Dept. of Agri.):					
Grants and loans	0.5	0.6	0.7	20.0	16.7
Loan level	-0.8	-0.8	-1.0	0.0	25.0
Water resources development:					
Army Corps of engineers	1.7	1.6	1.2	-5.9	-25.0
Bureau of Reclamation (Dept. of Interior)	0.5	0.4	0.4	-20.0	-
Community development block grants	0.8	0.9	0.9	12.5	-

- Represents or rounds to zero. NA Not available. X Not applicable. [1] 1995 funding shows a combined $464 million (current discretionary immunization program) and $424 million (new entitlement program). [2] Represents children through age 18. [3] Target population is 1.4 million Head Start eligible children. [4] Based on a 1993 CBO study estimating that 84 percent of all WIC eligibles will apply for WIC. [5] Does not include estimates associated with the recent San Fernando earthquake.

Source: U.S. Office of Management and Budget, *Budget of the United States Government,* annual.

No. 512. Federal Debt Held by the Public: 1980 to 1994

[In billions of dollars, except percents. Based on end of fiscal year]

ITEM	1980	1985	1990	1991	1992	1993	1994, est.
Current dollars.......,..............	709	1,499	2,410	2,688	2,999	3,247	3,472
Constant (1987) dollars [1].............	1,005	1,590	2,134	2,284	2,472	2,607	2,743
Percent of GDP.................,........	26.8	37.8	44.0	47.4	50.5	51.6	52.3
Percent of credit market debt [2]....[3].......	18.6	22.7	22.9	24.4	25.9	26.8	(NA)
Interest as percent of total outlays [3]......	10.6	16.2	16.2	16.2	15.5	14.9	14.3

NA Not available.   [1] Debt in current dollars deflated by the gross domestic product (GDP) deflator with FY 1987=100.
[2] Unpublished and preliminary estimates from the Federal Reserve Board flow of funds accounts. Total credit market debt owed by domestic nonfinancial sectors, modified to be consistent with budget concepts for the measurement of Federal debt. [3] Represents *interest on the public debt* less *interest received by trust funds* subfunction 901 less subfunction 902 and 903. Excludes the comparatively small amount of interest on agency debt or the offsets for other interest received by Government accounts.

Source: U.S. Office of Management and Budget, *Budget of the United States Government*, annual.

No. 513. Summary of Federal Debt: 1985 to 1993

[In millions of dollars. Based on end of fiscal year]

ITEM	1985	1990	1991	1992	1993
Debt outstanding, total	**1,827,470**	**3,266,073**	**3,683,054**	**4,082,871**	**4,436,171**
Public debt securities	1,823,103	3,233,313	3,665,303	4,064,621	4,411,489
Agency securities.........................	4,366	32,758	17,751	18,250	24,682
Securities held by—					
Government accounts, total	317,612	795,907	919,713	1,016,453	1,116,713
Public debt securities	316,545	795,762	919,573	1,016,330	1,116,693
Agency securities......................	1,067	145	139	123	21
The public, total	1,509,857	2,470,166	2,763,341	3,066,418	3,319,458
Public debt securities	1,506,558	2,437,551	2,745,729	3,048,291	3,294,796
Agency securities......................	3,299	32,613	17,612	18,127	24,661
Interest-bearing public debt, total	**1,821,010**	**3,210,943**	**3,662,759**	**4,061,801**	**4,408,567**
Marketable, total	1,360,179	2,092,759	2,390,660	2,677,476	2,904,910
Treasury bills	384,220	482,454	564,589	634,287	658,381
Treasury notes.........................	776,449	1,218,081	1,387,717	1,566,349	1,734,161
Treasury bonds.........................	199,510	377,224	423,354	461,840	497,367
Nonmarketable, total.....................	460,831	1,118,184	1,272,099	1,384,325	1,503,657
U.S. savings bonds	77,011	122,152	133,512	148,266	167,024
Foreign series: Government	6,638	36,041	41,639	37,039	42,459
Government account series, total............	313,928	779,412	908,406	1,011,020	1,114,289
Airport and airway trust fund	7,410	14,312	15,194	15,090	12,672
Bank insurance fund....................	16,130	8,438	6,108	4,664	4,325
Employees life insurance fund	6,312	9,561	11,140	12,411	13,575
Exchange stabilization trust fund	2,073	1,863	2,378	3,314	5,637
Federal disability insurance trust fund	5,443	11,254	12,854	12,774	10,162
Federal employees retirement funds	127,253	223,229	246,631	273,732	301,711
Federal hospital insurance trust fund........	20,721	96,249	109,327	120,647	126,078
Federal Housing Administration.............	3,485	6,678	6,839	6,077	5,380
Fed. old-age & survivors insurance trust fund	30,968	203,717	255,557	306,524	355,510
Fed. S&L Corp., resolution fund	4,953	929	966	1,346	828
Fed. supplementary medical insur. trust fund.....	10,736	14,286	16,241	18,534	23,269
Government life insurance fund	269	184	148	134	125
Highway trust fund	9,422	9,530	10,146	11,167	11,475
National service life insurance fund	9,296	10,917	11,150	11,310	11,666
Postal Service fund....................	2,362	3,063	3,339	4,679	3,826
Railroad retirement account...............	4,232	8,356	9,097	10,081	10,457
Treasury deposit funds	681	304	151	212	147
Unemployment trust fund.................	16,454	50,186	47,228	34,898	36,563
Other......................	35,728	106,376	143,912	163,426	180,883
State and local government series............	62,778	161,248	158,117	157,570	149,449
Domestic series.........................	(X)	18,886	29,995	29,995	29,995
Other	477	447	439	435	442
MATURITY DISTRIBUTION					
Amount outstanding, privately held	**1,185,675**	**1,841,903**	**2,113,799**	**2,363,802**	**2,562,336**
Maturity class:					
Within 1 year	472,661	626,297	713,778	808,705	858,135
1-5 years................................	402,766	630,144	761,243	866,329	978,714
5-10 years	159,383	267,573	280,574	295,921	306,663
10-20 years	62,853	82,713	84,900	84,706	94,346
20 years and over......................	88,012	235,176	273,304	308,141	324,479

X Not applicable.

Source: U.S. Department of the Treasury, *Treasury Bulletin*, quarterly.

No. 514. Federal Participation in Domestic Credit Markets: 1965 to 1993

[In billions of dollars, except percent. See headnote, table 515. Federal credit programs are primarily in three forms: direct loans from the Federal Government, Federal guarantees of private lending, and lending by privately-owned government-sponsored enterprises]

TYPE OF PARTICIPATION	1965	1970	1975	1980	1985	1990	1991	1992	1993
Total net borrowing in credit market [1]	67	88	170	325	804	690	504	553	544
Federal borrowing from the public	4	4	51	70	199	221	278	311	247
Guaranteed borrowing	5	8	9	32	22	41	22	20	-2
Government-sponsored enterprise borrowing [2]	1	5	5	21	58	115	125	151	170
Total, Federal and federally assisted borrowing . .	10	16	65	123	279	377	424	481	416
Federal borrowing participation rate (percent)	15.1	18.4	38.3	37.7	34.7	54.6	84.2	87.0	76.3
Total net lending in credit market [1]	67	88	170	325	804	690	504	553	544
Direct loans	2	3	13	24	28	3	-8	7	-2
Guaranteed loans	5	8	9	32	22	41	22	20	-2
Government-sponsored enterprise loans	1	5	6	24	61	90	91	145	163
Total, Federal and federally assisted lending	8	16	27	80	110	134	105	172	160
Federal lending participation rate (percent)	12.4	18.1	15.9	24.6	13.7	19.3	20.9	31.1	29.3

[1] Total net borrowing (or lending) in credit market by domestic nonfinancial sectors, excluding equities. Financial sectors are omitted to avoid double counting. [2] Most Government-sponsored enterprises (GSE's) are financial intermediaries. In order to avoid double counting, GSE borrowing and lending are calculated net of transactions with Federal agencies, transactions between GSE's, and transactions in guaranteed loans.

Source: U.S. Office of Management and Budget, *Analytical Perspectives, Budget of the United States Government,* annual.

No. 515. Federal Direct and Guaranteed Loans: 1970 to 1989

[In billions of dollars. As of end of fiscal year; see text, section 9. Government guaranteed loans are not included in Federal budget outlays. They constitute contingent liabilities not resulting in outlays, except in event of default]

ITEM	1970	1975	1980	1982	1983	1984	1985	1986	1987	1988	1989
Direct loans, amount: [1]											
Gross (new) loans dispersed	12.4	28.8	49.3	37.1	43.8	41.4	64.4	42.2	35.2	33.7	26.0
Net loan outlays	3.0	12.8	24.2	23.4	15.3	6.3	28.0	11.2	-19.0	-13.4	-14.6
Direct loans outstanding	51.1	74.1	163.9	207.8	223.0	229.3	257.4	251.6	234.2	222.0	207.0
Guaranteed loans: [2]											
Primary [3]	27.5	31.2	66.2	59.6	78.0	73.3	55.5	89.6	151.7	96.4	96.3
Net loans	8.4	8.7	31.6	20.9	34.1	20.1	21.6	34.6	60.4	40.3	41.7
Outstanding loans	125.1	198.3	298.5	331.2	363.8	386.7	410.4	449.8	507.0	550.0	588.6

[1] Includes loans from "off-budget" government accounts. [2] Includes capital subscriptions to international financial institutions. To avoid double counting, secondary guaranteed loans and guaranteed loans held as direct loans are excluded. [3] Gross loan guarantees minus both secondary guaranteed loans, and guaranteed loans held as direct loans by the Government—by either on- or off-budget accounts.

Source: U.S. Office of Management and Budget, *Budget of the United States Government,* annual.

No. 516. U.S. Savings Bonds: 1970 to 1993

[In billions of dollars, except percent. As of end of fiscal year, see text, section 9. See *Historical Statistics, Colonial Times to 1970,* series Y 500, for similar but not exactly comparable data]

ITEM	1970	1980	1985	1986	1987	1988	1989	1990	1991	1992	1993
Amounts outstanding, total [1]	52	73	77	86	97	107	114	123	134	149	167
Funds from sales	5	5	5	8	10	7	8	8	9	14	17
Accrued discounts	1	4	5	6	6	8	8	8	10	9	9
Redemptions [2]	6	17	6	5	5	6	7	8	8	7	8
Percent of total outstanding . . .	12.2	23.0	7.4	6.0	5.1	5.6	6.3	6.1	5.6	5.0	4.7

[1] Interest-bearing debt only for amounts end of year. [2] Matured and unmatured bonds.

Source: U.S. Dept. of the Treasury, *Treasury Bulletin,* quarterly.

No. 517. Government-Sponsored Enterprise Securities and Guarantees Outstanding: 1970 to 1991

[As of December 31. In billions of dollars]

ENTERPRISE	1970	1980	1990	1991	ENTERPRISE	1970	1980	1990	1991
Total	39	177	981	1,082	Mortgage-backed securities . .	(X)	(X)	300	372
Farm credit system:					Freddie Mac: [2]				
Farm credit banks	11	52	42	40	Debt	(X)	5	28	28
Banks for cooperatives	2	9	13	13	Mortgage-backed securities . .	(X)	17	316	359
Fannie Mae: [1]					Fed. home loan bank system . .	11	37	118	108
Debt	15	55	123	134	Sallie Mae [3]	(X)	3	39	43

X Not applicable. [1] Federal National Mortgage Association. [2] Federal Home Loan Mortgage Corporation. [3] Student Loan Mortgage Association.

Source: Congressional Budget Office, *Controlling the Risks of Government-Sponsored Enterprises,* April 1991.

No. 518. Federal Funds—Summary Distribution, by State: 1993

[In millions of dollars. For year ending Sept. 30. Data for grants, salaries and wages and direct payments to individuals are on an expenditures basis; procurement is on obligation basis]

REGION, DIVISION, AND STATE	FEDERAL FUNDS		Defense	Non-defense	Direct payments to individuals	Procure-ment	Grants to State and local govern-ments	Salaries and wages
	Total [1]	Per capita [2] (dol.)						
U.S. [3]	1,260,213	4,814	231,245	1,028,968	650,953	201,369	195,201	166,189
Northeast	250,215	(NA)	30,185	220,030	143,606	28,531	47,565	23,111
New England	69,146	(NA)	13,889	55,257	35,822	12,615	11,693	6,458
Maine	6,664	5,379	1,728	4,936	3,349	1,222	1,166	810
New Hampshire	4,128	3,669	626	3,502	2,478	465	652	404
Vermont	2,320	4,029	146	2,174	1,338	122	557	246
Massachusetts	34,300	5,705	7,067	27,233	17,014	7,062	5,520	3,020
Rhode Island	5,287	5,287	819	4,468	2,972	467	1,107	610
Connecticut	16,447	5,017	3,503	12,944	8,671	3,277	2,691	1,368
Middle Atlantic	181,069	(NA)	16,296	164,773	107,784	15,916	35,872	16,653
New York	87,442	4,802	6,506	80,936	49,121	7,438	21,166	7,241
New Jersey	35,885	4,555	4,198	31,687	21,631	3,740	6,189	3,671
Pennsylvania	57,742	4,792	5,592	52,150	37,032	4,738	8,517	5,741
Midwest	257,590	(NA)	28,464	229,126	150,531	25,382	41,954	25,383
East North Central	171,396	(NA)	15,395	156,001	106,180	14,029	29,344	15,833
Ohio	45,985	4,146	5,664	40,321	27,825	5,114	7,716	4,353
Indiana	22,111	3,870	2,867	19,244	12,908	2,116	3,732	2,066
Illinois	47,559	4,066	3,214	44,345	29,368	3,189	7,845	5,306
Michigan	36,830	3,886	2,373	34,457	24,177	2,243	6,654	2,725
Wisconsin	18,911	3,754	1,277	17,634	11,902	1,367	3,397	1,383
West North Central	86,194	(NA)	13,069	73,125	44,351	11,353	12,610	9,550
Minnesota	18,017	3,989	1,921	16,096	9,549	2,034	3,297	1,525
Iowa	12,131	4,311	594	11,537	7,163	658	1,737	864
Missouri	29,278	5,594	6,923	22,355	13,967	6,641	3,566	3,293
North Dakota	3,642	5,735	513	3,129	1,586	235	640	559
South Dakota	3,627	5,073	357	3,270	1,730	240	654	553
Nebraska	7,613	4,737	929	6,684	3,918	559	1,108	966
Kansas	11,886	4,696	1,832	10,054	6,438	986	1,608	1,790
South	448,269	(NA)	92,809	355,460	223,901	70,096	61,711	76,703
South Atlantic	252,320	(NA)	58,869	193,451	120,135	42,092	29,561	51,450
Delaware	2,833	4,047	413	2,420	1,687	186	455	438
Maryland	33,775	6,803	7,157	26,618	12,743	7,745	3,310	7,227
District of Columbia	20,250	35,034	2,828	17,422	2,435	4,012	1,961	10,236
Virginia	44,295	6,824	18,622	25,673	16,086	11,432	2,945	12,346
West Virginia	8,928	4,906	361	8,567	5,663	463	1,884	756
North Carolina	27,210	3,918	5,254	21,956	15,350	1,868	4,498	4,727
South Carolina	16,367	4,493	3,263	13,104	8,275	2,734	2,521	2,537
Georgia	30,139	4,357	8,201	21,938	14,505	4,670	4,408	5,832
Florida	68,523	5,009	12,770	55,753	43,391	8,982	7,579	7,351
East South Central	74,835	(NA)	11,334	63,501	39,880	11,093	12,332	9,689
Kentucky	16,797	4,433	2,630	14,167	9,376	1,461	3,041	2,535
Tennessee	23,778	4,663	1,951	21,827	12,544	4,285	3,925	2,600
Alabama	21,180	5,058	4,030	17,150	11,135	3,333	3,081	3,085
Mississippi	13,080	4,949	2,723	10,357	6,825	2,014	2,285	1,469
West South Central	121,114	(NA)	22,606	98,508	63,886	16,911	19,818	15,564
Arkansas	10,843	4,473	1,016	9,827	6,848	533	1,855	969
Louisiana	20,204	4,685	2,891	17,313	9,965	2,601	4,817	2,099
Oklahoma	14,799	4,580	2,618	12,181	8,420	1,022	2,111	2,609
Texas	75,268	4,174	16,081	59,187	38,653	12,755	11,035	9,887
West	268,615	(NA)	61,664	206,951	127,942	52,332	39,799	39,842
Mountain	72,377	(NA)	14,264	58,113	32,860	15,111	10,411	11,100
Montana	4,376	5,216	333	4,043	2,074	254	831	612
Idaho	4,825	4,391	401	4,424	2,365	924	712	615
Wyoming	2,217	4,717	244	1,973	996	143	645	357
Colorado	18,159	5,092	4,824	13,335	7,461	4,253	2,109	3,452
New Mexico	11,197	6,929	1,888	9,309	3,750	4,046	1,534	1,572
Arizona	18,376	4,669	4,211	14,165	9,804	3,181	2,640	2,250
Utah	7,461	4,011	1,540	5,921	3,263	1,279	1,173	1,504
Nevada	5,766	4,151	823	4,943	3,147	1,031	767	738
Pacific	196,238	(NA)	47,400	148,838	95,082	37,221	29,388	28,742
Washington	24,832	4,726	5,205	19,627	12,584	3,461	3,722	4,105
Oregon	12,379	4,083	633	11,746	7,928	562	2,099	1,389
California	147,364	4,720	36,910	110,454	70,952	31,483	21,635	19,239
Alaska	4,611	7,697	1,724	2,887	886	972	948	1,624
Hawaii	7,052	6,017	2,928	4,124	2,732	743	984	2,385
Undistributed	25,239	(X)	16,923	8,316	206	24,408	592	20

NA Not available.   X Not applicable.   [1] Includes other programs not shown separately.   [2] Based on 1993 population estimates. All computations were based on dollar amounts in thousands.   [3] Includes territories not shown separately.

Source: U.S. Bureau of the Census, *Federal Expenditures by State for Fiscal Year,* annual.

No. 519. Tax Returns Filed—Examination Coverage: 1970 to 1992

[In thousands, except as indicated. Identification of returns with either schedule C (nonfarm sole proprietorships) or schedule F (farm proprietorships) for audit examination purposes was based on the largest source of income on the return and certain other characteristics. Therefore, the number with schedule C is not comparable to the number of nonfarm sole proprietorships returns in table 835]

YEAR AND ITEM	Returns filed [1]	RETURNS EXAMINED					AVERAGE TAX AND PENALTY—DOLLARS PER RETURN		
		Total	Percent of returns filed	By—			Revenue agents	Tax auditors	Service centers
				Revenue agents	Tax auditors	Service centers			
INDIVIDUAL RETURNS									
1970	76,431	1,672	2.2	(NA)	(NA)	-	(NA)	(NA)	-
1975	81,272	1,839	2.3	355.2	1,483.4	-	2,609	219	-
1980	90,727	1,834	2.0	292.5	1,346.3	195.1	1,335	602	39
1981	93,052	1,644	1.8	289.5	1,193.1	161.5	6,374	579	223
1982	94,013	1,455	1.6	285.5	1,066.6	103.2	7,505	751	364
1983	95,419	1,428	1.5	277.9	1,001.9	147.9	10,248	990	316
1984	95,541	1,216	1.3	276.2	859.4	80.4	11,584	1,314	692
1985	96,497	1,266	1.3	332.6	810.9	122.1	10,854	1,539	496
1986	99,529	1,091	1.1	298.9	732.5	59.6	14,052	1,945	862
1987	101,751	1,109	1.1	317.5	610.4	181.3	12,235	2,107	4,084
1988	103,251	1,061	1.0	352.8	532.3	175.7	9,750	2,190	4,195
1989	107,029	985	0.9	243.0	542.7	199.0	11,347	1,827	2,393
1990	109,868	883	0.8	202.8	517.2	163.2	16,248	1,965	3,817
1991	112,305	1,124	1.0	200.7	499.9	422.9	19,981	2,403	3,436
1992, total	113,829	1,039	0.9	210.2	536.6	292.6	18,648	2,280	3,072
1040A, income under $25,000	43,431	300	0.7	12.4	154.4	133.7	15,839	1,489	2,647
Non 1040A, income: [2]									
Under $25,000	18,656	120	0.6	16.0	83.4	20.3	8,276	1,502	3,129
$25,000 - $49,999, simple	27,492	162	0.6	25.5	106.9	29.2	7,685	1,948	2,307
$50,000 - $99,999, complex	13,657	138	1.0	27.5	81.2	29.3	8,386	2,323	2,073
$100,000 and over	3,173	156	4.9	47.1	45.8	63.2	40,785	3,920	4,761
Schedule C-TGR: [3]									
Under $25,000	2,185	33	1.5	9.8	21.3	1.5	6,703	2,721	1,110
$25,000 - $99,999	2,805	56	2.0	24.3	26.5	5.1	9,749	5,080	1,528
$100,000 and over	1,582	63	4.0	41.7	11.5	9.3	19,881	7,881	4,182
Schedule F-TGR: [3]									
Under $100,000	572	7	1.1	1.8	4.0	0.4	6,015	1,214	829
$100,000 and over	278	6	2.2	4.0	1.7	0.6	25,234	2,496	6,031
1992—OTHER RETURNS									
Fiduciary	2,779	3	0.1	1.9	-	1.5	15,064	-	807
Partnerships	1,631	12	0.7	8.2	-	3.7	-	-	-
Corporations, total	2,622	78	3.0	75.8	-	2.6	238,289	-	8,536
Estate, total	65	12	18.6	11.9	-	0.1	101,791	-	4,571
Gift	157	2	1.3	2.1	-	-	93,737	-	-
Excise	821	46	5.6	42.8	2.8	0.2	8,400	1,226	332
Employment	28,465	73	0.3	65.1	7.7	-	8,528	2,169	4,549
Windfall profit	-	2	-	0.3	-	1.6	540,380	-	365
Miscellaneous	-	1	-	0.6	-	0.1	41,382	-	9,348
Service center corrections	-	169	-	-	-	168.7	-	-	1,608

- Represents zero.   NA Not available.   [1] Returns filed in previous calendar year.   [2] Income from positive sources only.   [3] Total gross receipts.

Source: U.S. Internal Revenue Service, *Annual Report of the Commissioner and Chief Counsel of the Internal Revenue Service.*

No. 520. Internal Revenue Gross Collections, by Source: 1980 to 1992

[For fiscal year ending in year shown; see text section 9. See also *Historical Statistics, Colonial Times to 1970,* series Y 358-373]

SOURCE OF REVENUE	COLLECTIONS (bil. dol.)					PERCENT OF TOTAL				
	1980	1985	1990	1991	1992	1980	1985	1990	1991	1992
All taxes	519	743	1,056	1,087	1,121	100.0	100.0	100.0	100.0	100.0
Individual income taxes	288	397	540	547	558	54.9	53.4	51.1	50.3	50.0
Withheld by employers	224	299	388	404	408	43.1	40.2	36.8	37.2	36.4
Employment taxes [1]	128	225	367	385	400	24.7	30.2	34.8	35.4	35.7
Old-age and disability insurance	123	216	358	375	390	23.6	29.0	33.8	34.5	34.8
Unemployment insurance	3	6	6	6	6	0.6	0.8	0.5	0.5	0.5
Corporation income taxes	72	77	110	114	118	13.9	10.4	10.4	10.5	10.5
Estate and gift taxes	7	7	12	12	12	1.3	0.9	1.1	1.1	1.0
Excise taxes	25	37	27	31	34	4.7	5.0	2.6	2.8	3.0
Alcohol and tobacco	8	10	10	12	13	1.6	1.3	1.0	1.1	1.2
Manufactures	7	10	11	14	17	1.3	1.3	1.0	1.3	1.5
Windfall profits tax	3	5	(Z)	(Z)	(Z)	0.6	0.7	(Z)	(Z)	(Z)
Other	10	17	6	4	4	1.9	2.3	0.6	0.4	0.3

Z Less than $50 million or .05 percent.   [1] Includes railroad retirement, not shown separately.

Source: U.S. Internal Revenue Service, *Annual Report of the Commissioner and Chief Counsel of the Internal Revenue Service.*

No. 521. Federal Individual Income Tax Returns With Adjusted Gross Income (AGI)—Summary: 1980 to 1991

[Includes Puerto Rico and Virgin Islands. Includes returns of resident aliens, based on a sample of unaudited returns as filed. Data are not comparable for all years because of tax changes and other changes, as indicated. See Statistics of Income, Individual Income Tax Returns publications for a detailed explanation. See Appendix III. See Historical Statistics, Colonial Times to 1970, series Y 393-411, for related data]

ITEM	NUMBER OF RETURNS (1,000)				AMOUNT (mil. dol.)				AVERAGE AMOUNT (dollars)			
	1980	1985	1990	1991	1980	1985	1990	1991	1980	1985	1990	1991
Total returns	93,902	101,660	113,717	114,730	1,613,731	2,305,951	3,405,427	3,464,534	17,185	22,683	29,947	30,197
Form 1040	57,123	67,006	69,270	68,993	1,310,088	1,938,263	2,772,625	2,795,559	22,935	28,927	40,026	40,519
Salaries and wages	83,802	87,198	96,730	97,066	1,349,843	1,928,201	2,599,401	2,674,261	16,108	22,113	26,873	27,551
Interest received	49,020	64,526	70,370	70,162	102,009	182,109	227,084	209,412	2,081	2,822	3,227	2,985
Dividends in AGI	10,739	15,528	22,905	23,229	38,761	55,046	80,169	77,284	3,609	3,545	3,500	3,327
Business or profession profit less loss	8,881	11,900	11,222	11,549	55,129	78,773	141,430	162,870	6,207	6,620	12,603	14,103
Sales of capital assets, net gain less loss, in AGI	9,971	11,126	14,288	15,009	30,029	67,694	114,231	102,775	3,012	6,084	7,995	6,848
Pensions and annuities in AGI	7,374	13,133	17,041	17,907	43,340	95,096	159,294	176,502	5,878	7,241	9,348	9,857
Rents and royalties, net income less loss	8,208	9,964	10,314	10,426	4,105	-10,946	-3,156	-1,053	500	-1,099	-306	-101
Partnerships and S Corporations, profit less loss	3,910	5,488	5,978	5,499	10,099	-2,527	67,022	63,190	2,583	-460	11,213	11,491
Farm profit less loss	2,608	2,621	2,321	2,291	-1,792	-12,005	-434	-2,853	-687	-4,580	-187	-1,245
Statutory adjustments, total	13,149	37,763	16,648	16,990	28,614	95,082	33,974	34,716	2,176	2,518	2,041	2,043
Individual Retirement Arrangements	2,564	16,206	5,224	4,666	3,431	38,212	9,858	9,030	1,338	2,358	1,887	1,935
Self-employed retirement (Keogh) plan	569	676	824	840	2,008	5,182	6,778	6,913	3,529	7,666	8,226	8,230
Married couples who both work	(NA)	24,835	(NA)	(NA)	(NA)	24,615	(NA)	(NA)	(NA)	991	(NA)	(NA)
Exemptions, total [2]	227,925	244,180	227,549	231,297	227,569	253,720	485,985	491,084	998	1,039	2,135	2,123
Age 65 or older	11,847	16,749	(NA)	(NA)	(NA)	(NA)	(NA)	(NA)	(NA)	(NA)	(NA)	(NA)
Blind	185	327	(NA)	(NA)	(NA)	(NA)	(NA)	(NA)	(NA)	(NA)	(NA)	(NA)
Standard and itemized deductions, total [3]	88,105	96,849	112,796	113,795	362,776	554,734	789,942	818,762	4,118	5,728	7,003	7,195
Itemized deductions, total [3]	28,950	39,848	32,175	32,490	218,028	405,024	458,485	467,698	7,531	10,164	14,250	14,395
Medical and dental expenses	19,458	10,777	5,091	5,339	14,972	22,926	21,457	23,726	769	2,127	4,215	4,444
Taxes paid	28,749	39,548	31,594	31,969	69,404	128,085	140,011	147,858	2,414	3,239	4,432	4,625
Interest paid	26,677	36,287	29,395	27,418	91,187	180,095	208,354	213,724	3,418	4,963	7,088	7,795
Contributions	26,601	36,162	29,230	29,551	25,810	47,963	57,243	60,574	970	1,326	1,958	2,050
Taxable income [4]	88,105	96,124	93,148	92,718	1,279,985	1,820,741	2,263,661	2,284,088	14,528	18,942	24,302	24,635
Income tax before credits	76,136	85,994	93,089	92,636	256,294	332,165	453,128	454,503	3,366	3,863	4,868	4,906
Tax credits, total [4][5]	19,674	20,995	12,484	12,737	7,216	10,246	6,831	7,286	367	488	547	572
Child care	4,231	8,418	6,144	5,896	956	3,128	2,549	2,524	226	372	415	428
Elderly and disabled	562	463	339	285	135	109	61	57	240	235	180	200
Residential energy	4,670	2,979	(NA)	(NA)	560	812	(NA)	(NA)	120	273	(NA)	(NA)
Foreign tax	393	454	772	875	1,342	783	1,682	1,824	3,415	1,725	2,179	2,085
General business credit [6]	(NA)	4,614	263	260	(NA)	4,791	616	523	(NA)	1,038	2,342	2,012
Income tax, total [7]	73,906	82,846	89,862	88,734	250,341	325,710	447,127	448,430	3,387	3,932	4,976	5,054

NA Not available.　[1] S Corporations are certain small corporations with up to 35 shareholders (25 for 1982; 15 for 1980-81; 10 for 1970-75), mostly individuals, electing to be taxed at the shareholder level.　[2] Includes items not shown separately.　[3] For 1985, includes charitable deduction for nonitemizers. Starting 1989, includes additional standard deductions for age 65 or older for blindness.　[4] For 1980 and 1985, includes amounts "taxed" at zero percent.　[5] For 1981, includes tax reduction credit.　[6] Investment credit was included in the more-inclusive general business tax credit starting with 1984. With exceptions, investment credit was repealed effective 1986.　[7] Includes minimum tax or alternative minimum tax.

Source: U.S. Internal Revenue Service, Statistics of Income Bulletin, and Statistics of Income, Individual Income Tax Returns, annual.

No. 522. Individual Income Tax Returns—Number, Income Tax, and Average Tax, by Size of Adjusted Gross Income: 1980 and 1991

[Number in thousands; money amounts in billions of dollars, except as indicated]

SIZE OF ADJUSTED GROSS INCOME	NUMBER OF RETURNS		ADJUSTED GROSS INCOME (AGI)		TAXABLE INCOME		INCOME TAX TOTAL [1]		TAX AS PERCENT OF AGI		AVERAGE TAX ($1,000)	
	1990	1991, prel.	1990	1991, prel.	1990	1991, prel.	1990	1991, prel.	1990	1991, prel.	1990	1991, prel.
Total	113,717	114,730	3,405.4	3,464.2	2,263.6	2,284.1	447.2	448.4	13.6	13.4	5.0	5.0
Less than $1,000 [2] .	3,688	3,775	−44.0	−49.9	0.1	0.1	0.2	0.2	(X)	(X)	0.1	0.1
$1,000-$2,999	7,379	7,084	14.6	13.9	1.1	1.0	0.2	0.2	4.7	4.7	0.1	0.1
$3,000-$4,999	6,317	6,136	25.2	24.5	2.1	1.7	0.4	0.3	4.0	3.6	0.2	0.1
$5,000-$6,999	6,004	6,103	36.1	36.7	4.9	4.1	0.8	0.6	3.6	3.3	0.2	0.2
$7,000-$8,999	6,026	6,100	48.2	48.8	10.2	9.7	1.6	1.5	5.3	4.9	0.4	0.4
$9,000-$10,999 . . .	5,891	5,871	58.9	58.6	16.2	15.0	2.3	2.2	6.3	6.1	0.6	0.6
$11,000-$12,999. . .	5,573	5,573	66.9	66.8	25.3	20.5	3.1	2.8	6.8	6.4	0.8	0.8
$13,000-$14,999. . .	5,382	5,364	75.3	75.2	31.1	29.2	4.1	3.8	7.2	7.1	1.0	1.0
$15,000-$16,999. . .	4,686	5,104	74.9	81.6	35.8	36.3	4.9	4.7	7.3	7.3	1.2	1.2
$17,000-$18,999. . .	4,656	4,478	83.9	80.6	42.9	39.1	6.1	5.3	7.6	7.4	1.4	1.3
$19,000-$21,999. . .	6,308	6,106	129.2	125.1	71.8	66.6	10.6	9.6	8.4	7.9	1.7	1.6
$22,000-$24,999. . .	5,465	5,592	128.1	131.2	75.9	75.0	11.3	11.1	8.9	8.7	2.1	2.0
$25,000-$29,999. . .	7,838	7,874	215.3	216.1	133.5	131.5	20.5	20.0	9.7	9.4	2.7	2.6
$30,000-$39,999. . .	12,283	12,347	426.4	429.1	280.6	279.5	45.3	45.1	10.7	10.6	3.7	3.7
$40,000-$49,999. . .	8,837	8,817	394.8	393.5	270.5	266.3	44.9	43.5	11.4	11.1	5.1	4.9
$50,000-$74,999. . .	10,944	11,390	657.2	685.6	466.6	481.2	87.2	87.8	13.3	12.8	8.0	7.7
$75,000-$99,999. . .	3,276	3,572	279.6	305.0	205.3	222.0	44.3	47.0	15.9	15.4	13.6	13.2
$100,000-$199,999. .	2,330	2,598	305.6	339.1	230.4	258.3	57.9	62.8	19.0	18.6	24.9	24.2
$200,000-$499,999. .	644	676	188.1	196.3	152.6	165.2	43.5	46.3	23.1	23.6	67.5	68.5
$500,000-$999,999. .	130	118	87.1	79.6	74.4	69.7	20.9	20.5	24.1	25.8	161.0	173.4
$1,000,000 or more. .	61	52	154.7	127.1	134.6	112.1	37.4	33.3	24.2	26.3	616.5	641.3

X Not applicable.　[1] Consists of income after credits, and alternative minimum tax.　[2] In addition to low income taxpayers, this size class (and others) includes taxpayers with "tax preferences," not reflected in adjusted gross income or taxable income which are subject to the "alternative minimum tax" (included in total income tax).

Source: U.S. Internal Revenue Service, *Statistics of Income Bulletin*, quarterly and *Statistics of Income, Individual Income Tax Returns*, annual.

No. 523. Individual Income Tax Returns—Itemized Deductions and Statutory Adjustments, by Size of Adjusted Gross Income: 1991

[Preliminary]

ITEM	Unit	ADJUSTED GROSS INCOME CLASS						
		Total	Under $10,000	$10,000 to $19,999	$20,000 to $29,999	$30,000 to $39,999	$40,000 to $49,999	$50,000 to $99,999	$100,000 and over
Returns with itemized deductions:									
Number.	1,000 . .	32,490	805	2,455	3,963	4,895	5,071	12,056	3,245
Amount.	Mil. dol .	467,686	7,785	23,277	36,134	48,774	55,341	176,499	119,877
Medical and dental expenses:									
Returns	1,000 . .	5,339	512	1,223	1,258	924	610	734	78
Amount	Mil. dol .	23,726	2,769	6,905	4,177	3,047	2,040	3,458	1,331
Taxes paid: Returns, total	1,000 . .	31,969	687	2,274	3,879	4,845	5,038	12,020	3,226
State, local income taxes . .	1,000 . .	27,026	330	1,587	3,138	4,228	4,375	10,524	2,846
Real estate taxes	1,000 . .	28,629	588	1,893	3,294	4,210	4,460	11,144	3,039
Amount, total.	Mil. dol .	147,858	1,157	3,733	7,842	12,328	15,830	56,036	50,932
State, local income taxes . .	Mil. dol .	88,032	195	953	3,045	6,077	8,375	32,296	37,092
Real estate taxes	Mil. dol .	54,119	887	2,538	4,319	5,659	6,711	21,466	12,539
Interest paid: Returns.	1,000 . .	27,418	509	1,669	3,187	4,123	4,365	10,772	2,793
Amount	Mil. dol .	213,725	2,960	8,784	16,763	23,674	26,923	84,498	50,122
Home mortgages interest:									
Returns.	1,000 . .	27,001	490	1,639	3,141	4,079	4,327	10,653	2,674
Amount	Mil. dol .	200,995	2,853	8,505	16,438	23,074	26,327	82,343	41,454
Contributions: Returns	1,000 . .	29,551	550	1,922	3,393	4,378	4,710	11,470	3,129
Amount	Mil. dol .	60,574	488	2,167	4,096	5,771	6,571	21,065	20,416
Employee business expense:									
Returns	1,000 . .	8,463	67	426	916	1,341	1,450	3,467	796
Amount	Mil. dol .	23,680	159	1,094	2,258	3,034	3,183	9,358	4,594
Returns with statutory adjus'mts: [1]									
Returns	1,000 . .	16,990	2,851	3,039	2,876	2,201	1,744	2,994	1,286
Amount of adjustments	Mil. dol .	34,716	1,870	3,395	4,246	3,799	3,004	8,241	10,161
Payments to IRA's: [2] Returns . .	1,000 . .	6,124	337	854	1,414	1,205	903	934	477
Amount	Mil. dol .	9,030	511	1,308	2,037	1,704	1,036	1,593	842
Payments to Keogh plans:									
Returns	1,000 . .	840	9	31	58	59	68	305	311
Amount	Mil. dol .	6,913	17	43	150	174	236	1,663	4,629
Alimony paid: Returns	1,000 . .	673	49	93	59	97	84	181	110
Amount	Mil. dol .	5,302	267	358	400	508	482	1,372	1,999

[1] Includes disability income exclusion, employee business expenses, moving expenses, forfeited interest penalty, alimony paid, deduction for expense of living abroad, and other data not shown separately.　[2] Individual Retirement Account.

Source: U.S. Internal Revenue Service, *Statistics of Income, Individual Income Tax Returns*, annual.

No. 524. Federal Individual Income Tax Returns—Adjusted Gross Income (AGI), by Source of Income and Income Class for Taxable Returns: 1991

[In millions of dollars, except as indicated. Minus sign (-) indicates net loss was greater than net income. See headnote, table 521]

ITEM	Total [1]	Under $10,000	$10,000 to $19,999	$20,000 to $29,999	$30,000 to $39,999	$40,000 to $49,999	$50,000 to $99,999	$100,000 and over
Number of returns(1,000)	88,734	12,916	19,186	17,223	12,250	8,791	14,929	3,438
Adjusted gross income (AGI)								
by source.	3,336,673	74,041	289,756	425,240	425,797	392,443	988,649	740,749
Salaries and wages.	2,531,690	57,799	213,183	344,271	351,977	326,497	816,045	421,918
Percent of AGI for taxable returns . . .	75.9	78.1	73.6	81.0	82.7	83.2	82.5	57.0
Interest received.	190,507	8,222	24,981	21,890	20,421	16,661	41,297	57,035
Dividends in AGI.	73,151	1,864	4,955	5,540	5,569	4,806	16,958	33,459
Business; profession, net profit less loss.	134,424	2,276	9,527	12,927	11,998	10,852	36,118	50,725
Pensions and annuities in AGI.	165,334	4,776	29,376	30,454	23,489	20,489	41,811	14,940
Sales of property, net [2]	96,339	1,558	1,559	2,668	2,656	3,076	14,878	69,944
Rents, royalties, net [3]	96,709	-416	1,317	1,178	956	1,019	7,727	84,928
Other sources, net	19,005	593	989	1,247	1,192	1,061	3,904	10,019
Percent of all returns:								
Number of returns.	77.3	11.3	16.8	15.1	10.7	7.7	13.1	3.0
Adjusted gross income	96.3	2.2	8.4	12.3	12.3	11.3	28.5	21.4
Salaries and wages.	94.7	2.1	8.0	12.9	13.2	12.2	30.5	15.8
Interest received.	90.8	3.7	11.9	10.5	9.8	8.0	19.7	27.2
Dividends in AGI.	94.7	2.3	6.4	7.2	7.2	6.2	21.9	43.3
Business; profession, net profit less loss.	94.8	1.7	6.5	9.1	8.5	7.6	25.5	35.8
Pensions and annuities in AGI.	93.7	2.9	17.8	18.4	14.2	11.6	23.7	8.0
Sales of property [2]	95.8	1.6	1.6	2.8	2.8	3.2	15.4	68.4

[1] Includes a small number of taxable returns with no adjusted gross income.   [2] Includes sales of capital assets and other property; net gain less loss.   [3] Excludes rental passive losses disallowed in the compilation of AGI; net income less loss.

Source: U.S. Internal Revenue Service, Statistics of Income, Individual Income Tax Returns, 1991.

No. 525. Federal Individual Income Tax Returns, by State, 1991

YEAR, DIVISION, STATE	Number of returns [1] (1,000)	Adjusted gross income (AGI) [2]	INCOME TAX		YEAR, DIVISION, STATE	Number of returns [1] (1,000)	Adjusted gross income (AGI) [2]	INCOME TAX	
			Total [3] (mil. dol.)	Per capita [4] (dol.)				Total [3] (mil. dol.)	Per capita [4] (dol.)
U.S. . . .	115,767	3,453,028	473,533	1,878	VA	2,908	93,151	12,516	1,991
Northeast . .	23,708	792,547	113,621	2,229	WV. . . .	700	17,540	2,166	1,203
N.E	6,260	210,914	30,570	2,317	NC	3,094	82,315	10,191	1,513
ME. . . .	556	14,428	1,766	1,430	SC	1,567	39,605	4,703	1,321
NH . . .	534	16,883	2,345	2,123	GA	2,947	84,162	10,933	1,651
VT	266	7,095	903	1,593	FL	6,250	177,889	25,504	1,921
MA	2,836	95,333	13,698	2,285	E.S.C.	6,529	165,199	21,044	1,372
RI.	458	13,676	1,821	1,814	KY	1,538	39,331	4,933	1,329
CT	1,610	63,499	10,037	3,050	TN	2,208	57,976	7,784	1,572
M.A.	17,448	581,633	83,051	2,199	AL	1,747	45,109	5,682	1,390
NY	8,119	279,687	40,339	2,234	MS	1,036	22,783	2,645	1,020
NJ	3,827	140,841	20,650	2,661	W.S.C	11,661	312,338	43,655	1,608
PA	5,502	161,105	22,062	1,845	AR	984	22,981	2,791	1,177
Midwest . . .	27,632	802,729	108,329	1,799	LA	1,723	43,423	5,743	1,351
E.N.C. . . .	19,532	578,193	78,523	1,852	OK	1,347	34,025	4,382	1,381
OH	5,129	142,204	18,692	1,709	TX	7,607	211,909	30,739	1,772
IN.	2,544	71,240	9,384	1,673	West	24,752	762,104	104,189	1,928
IL.	5,391	172,970	25,118	2,176	Mt.	6,339	174,125	22,997	1,639
MI	4,181	126,862	16,974	1,812	MT	368	8,489	1,073	1,328
WI	2,287	64,917	8,355	1,687	ID. . . .	445	11,225	1,402	1,350
W.N.C	8,100	224,536	29,806	1,674	WY	211	5,858	835	1,816
MN	2,048	62,289	8,255	1,863	CO	1,627	48,145	6,657	1,972
IA. . . .	1,281	33,209	4,294	1,537	NM	680	16,303	1,994	1,289
MO. . . .	2,295	63,471	8,473	1,643	AZ	1,654	44,520	5,680	1,515
ND	284	6,860	911	1,435	UT	711	19,447	2,340	1,322
SD	319	7,469	1,016	1,446	NV	643	20,138	3,016	2,349
NE	745	19,315	2,536	1,592	Pac	18,413	587,979	81,192	2,029
KS	1,128	31,923	4,321	1,732	WA	2,378	75,255	10,898	2,172
South	38,619	1,073,999	144,707	1,665	OR	1,339	37,305	4,801	1,643
S.A	20,429	596,462	80,008	1,801	CA	13,790	448,325	61,650	2,029
DE	331	10,748	1,451	2,134	AK	339	9,315	1,427	2,504
MD	2,321	81,110	11,044	2,273	HI	567	17,779	2,416	2,129
DC	311	9,942	1,500	2,509	Other [5]	1,059	21,650	2,688	(NA)

[1] Includes returns filled by nonresident aliens and certain self-employment tax returns.   [2] Less deficit.   [3] Includes additional tax for tax preferences, self-employment tax, tax from investment credit recapture, and other income-related taxes. Total is before earned income credit.   [4] Based on resident population as of July 1.   [5] Includes returns filed from Army Post Office and Fleet Post Office addresses by members of the armed forces stationed overseas; returns by other U.S. citizens abroad; and returns filed by residents of Puerto Rico with income from sources outside of Puerto Rico or with income earned as U.S. Government employees.

Source: U.S. Internal Revenue Service, Statistics of Income Bulletin. Quarterly.

No. 526. Federal Individual Income Tax—Effective (Average) and Marginal Tax Rates, for Selected Income Groups: 1990 to 1993

[Refers to income after exclusions. Effective rate represents tax liability divided by stated income. The marginal tax rate is the percentage of the first additional dollar of income which would be paid in income tax. Computations assume the low income allowance, standard deduction, zero bracket amount, or itemized deductions equal to 10 percent of adjusted gross income, whichever is greatest. Excludes self employment tax. See Historical Statistics, Colonial Times to 1970, series Y 412-439, for similar data on net income]

CURRENT DOLLARS

ADJUSTED GROSS INCOME [1]	TAX LIABILITY (dol.)				EFFECTIVE RATE (percent)				MARGINAL TAX RATE (percent)			
	1990	1991	1992	1993	1990	1991	1992	1993	1990	1991	1992	1993
Single person, no dependents:												
$5,000	-	-	-	-	-	-	-	0.0	-	-	-	-
$10,000	705	668	615	593	7.1	6.7	6.2	5.9	15.0	15.0	15.0	15.0
$20,000	2,205	2,168	2,115	2,093	11.0	10.8	10.6	10.5	15.0	15.0	15.0	15.0
$25,000	2,988	2,918	2,865	2,843	12.0	11.7	11.5	11.4	28.0	28.0	28.0	28.0
$35,000	5,718	5,573	5,360	5,233	16.3	15.9	15.3	15.0	28.0	28.0	28.0	28.0
$50,000	9,498	9,353	9,168	9,069	19.0	18.7	18.3	18.1	28.0	28.0	28.0	28.0
$75,000	16,718	16,134	15,867	15,719	22.3	21.5	21.2	21.0	33.0	31.0	31.0	31.0
Married couple, 2 dependents: [2]												
$5,000 [3]	-700	-865	-920	-975	-14.0	-17.3	-18.4	-19.5	-14.0	-17.3	-18.4	-19.5
$10,000 [3]	-953	-1,235	-1,384	-1,511	-9.5	-12.4	-13.8	-15.1	25.0	27.4	28.1	28.9
$20,000 [3]	926	701	409	235	4.6	3.5	2.0	1.2	15.0	15.0	15.0	15.0
$25,000	1,703	1,605	1,470	1,410	6.8	6.4	5.9	5.6	15.0	15.0	15.0	15.0
$35,000	3,203	3,105	2,970	2,910	9.2	8.9	8.5	8.3	28.0	28.0	28.0	28.0
$50,000	5,960	5,576	5,220	5,160	11.9	11.2	10.4	10.3	28.0	28.0	28.0	28.0
$75,000	12,386	12,072	11,670	11,471	16.5	16.1	15.6	15.3	28.0	28.0	28.0	28.0

CONSTANT (1990) DOLLARS

ADJUSTED GROSS INCOME [1]	CURRENT INCOME EQUIVALENT TO CONSTANT INCOME (dol.)				EFFECTIVE RATE (percent)				MARGINAL TAX RATE (percent)			
	1990	1991	1992	1993	1990	1991	1992	1993	1990	1991	1992	1993
Single person, no dependents:												
$5,000	5,000	5,220	5,390	5,540	7.1	7.0	6.8	6.8	15.0	15.0	15.0	15.0
$10,000	10,000	10,440	10,780	11,070	11.0	11.0	10.9	10.9	15.0	15.0	15.0	15.0
$20,000	20,000	20,870	21,570	22,140	12.0	11.9	11.7	11.7	28.0	28.0	28.0	28.0
$25,000	25,000	26,090	26,960	27,680	16.3	16.3	16.1	16.1	28.0	28.0	28.0	28.0
$35,000	35,000	36,520	37,740	38,750	19.0	19.0	18.8	18.8	28.0	28.0	28.0	28.0
$50,000	50,000	52,180	53,920	55,350	22.3	21.8	21.6	21.6	33.0	31.0	31.0	31.0
$75,000	75,000	78,260	80,870	83,030								
Married couple, 2 dependents: [3]												
$5,000	5,000	5,220	5,390	5,540	-14.0	-17.3	-18.4	-19.5	14.0	-17.3	-18.4	-19.5
$10,000	10,000	10,440	10,780	11,070	-9.5	-11.8	-12.9	-13.7	25.0	27.4	28.1	28.9
$20,000	20,000	20,870	21,570	22,140	4.6	4.5	3.9	3.9	15.0	15.0	15.0	15.0
$25,000	25,000	26,090	26,960	27,680	6.8	6.8	6.5	6.5	15.0	15.0	15.0	15.0
$35,000	35,000	36,520	37,740	38,750	9.2	9.1	9.0	9.0	28.0	28.0	28.0	28.0
$50,000	50,000	52,180	53,920	55,350	11.9	11.9	11.5	11.4	28.0	28.0	28.0	28.0
$75,000	75,000	78,260	80,870	83,030	16.5	16.5	16.3	16.3	28.0	28.0	28.0	28.0

- Represents zero.   [1] See headnote, table 521.   [2] Only one spouse is assumed to work.   [3] Refundable earned income credit.

Source: U.S. Dept. of the Treasury, Office of Tax Analysis,

No. 527. Federal Civilian Employment, by Branch and Agency: 1980 to 1992

[As of September 30]

AGENCY	1980	1985	1989	1990	1991	1992
Total, all agencies	**2,875,866**	**3,020,531**	**3,123,731**	**3,128,267**	**3,111,912**	**3,085,323**
Legislative Branch, total [1]	39,710	38,764	37,690	37,495	38,504	38,509
Congress [1]	19,096	19,656	19,504	19,474	20,178	20,084
U.S. Senate	7,195	7,294	7,401	7,369	7,571	7,620
House of Representatives	11,888	12,351	12,090	12,089	12,587	12,446
Architect of the Capitol.	2,168	2,145	2,161	2,235	2,316	2,346
Judicial Branch	15,178	18,225	21,915	23,605	25,805	27,987
Supreme Court	331	337	327	332	343	353
U.S. Courts	14,847	17,888	21,588	23,221	25,392	27,551
Executive Branch, total [1]	2,820,978	2,963,542	3,064,126	3,067,167	3,047,603	3,018,827
Executive Office of the President [1]	1,886	1,526	1,577	1,731	1,758	1,866
White House Office	406	367	371	396	347	392
Office of the Vice-President.	16	20	20	21	16	20
Office of Management and Budget	616	566	527	574	609	586
Office of Administration.	166	194	202	205	228	247
Council of Economic Advisors	35	30	32	34	34	34
Executive Departments	1,716,970	1,789,270	2,065,038	2,065,542	2,054,094	2,038,675
State.	23,497	25,254	25,327	25,288	25,699	25,734
Treasury.	124,663	130,084	152,548	158,655	166,433	161,951
Defense.	960,116	1,084,549	1,075,437	1,034,152	1,012,716	982,774
Justice.	56,327	64,433	79,667	83,932	90,821	96,927
Interior.	77,357	77,485	77,545	77,679	81,683	85,260
Agriculture	129,139	117,750	122,062	122,594	125,640	128,324
Commerce	48,563	35,150	45,091	69,920	38,087	38,086
Labor.	23,400	18,260	18,125	17,727	17,938	17,889
Health & Human Services	155,662	140,151	122,259	123,959	129,483	131,191
Housing & Urban Development	16,964	12,289	13,544	13,596	14,998	13,701
Transportation.	72,361	62,227	65,615	67,364	69,831	70,558
Energy.	21,557	16,749	17,130	17,731	19,539	20,962
Education.	7,364	4,889	4,696	4,771	5,081	5,113
Veterans Affairs [2]	228,285	247,156	245,992	248,174	256,145	260,205
Independent agencies [1]	1,102,122	1,172,746	997,511	999,894	991,751	978,286
Environmental Protection Agency	14,715	13,788	15,590	17,123	18,218	18,196
Equal Employment Opportunity Comm. .	3,515	3,222	2,743	2,880	2,889	2,899
Federal Deposit Insurance Corporation .	3,520	6,723	9,031	17,641	22,007	22,467
Fed. Emergency Management Agency. .	3,427	3,133	3,048	3,137	3,130	5,632
General Services Administration [3]	37,654	25,782	20,063	20,277	21,122	20,770
National Aeronautics & Space Admin . .	23,714	22,562	24,165	24,872	25,737	25,425
Nuclear Regulatory Commission	3,283	3,605	3,288	3,353	3,534	3,528
Office of Personnel Management	8,280	6,353	6,859	6,636	6,757	6,941
Small Business Administration	5,804	4,960	4,653	5,128	4,867	5,897
Smithsonian Institution, Summary	4,403	4,757	5,158	5,092	5,360	5,514
Tennessee Valley Authority	51,714	32,035	26,676	28,392	24,870	19,493
U.S. Information Agency	8,138	8,851	8,723	8,555	8,213	8,342
U.S. International Development Cooperation Agency	6,152	5,054	4,816	4,698	4,575	4,542
U.S. Postal Service	660,014	750,021	826,310	816,886	804,338	791,992

[1] Includes branches, or agencies, not shown separately.   [2] Formerly Veterans Administration.   [3] 1980 figure includes the National Archives and Records Administration which became an independent agency in 1985.

Source: U.S. Office of Personnel Management, *Federal Civilian Workforce Statistics— Employment and Trends*, bimonthly.

No. 528. Federal Government Employment, by Race and National Origin and Pay System: 1982 and 1992

[As of Sept. 30. Covers total employment for only Executive Branch agencies participating in OPM's Central Personnel Data File (CPDF)]

PAY SYSTEM	1982					1992				
		Race/national origin					Race/national origin			
	Total employ-ees (1,000)	Race and origin [1] (1,000)	Per-cent of total	Black non-His-panic (1,000)	His-panic (1,000)	Total employ-ees (1,000)	Race and origin [1] (1,000)	Per-cent of total	Black non-His-panic (1,000)	Hispanic (1,000)
All pay systems, total	**2,008.6**	**484.0**	**24.1**	**311.1**	**90.0**	**2,175.7**	**604.9**	**27.8**	**360.7**	**120.3**
General Schedule and equivalent [2] . .	1,507.4	336.1	22.3	222.0	59.0	1,680.5	451.9	26.9	277.3	87.9
Grades 1-4 ($10,581-$18,947) . . .	303.6	101.9	33.6	71.0	16.1	198.9	86.0	43.2	56.7	14.2
Grades 5-8 ($16,305-$29,081) . . .	464.9	126.5	27.2	90.2	20.2	517.0	178.8	34.6	120.3	31.7
Grades 9-12 ($24,705-$46,571) . .	530.0	87.6	16.5	50.1	18.7	654.7	144.7	22.1	79.0	33.1
Grades 13-15 ($42,601-$76,982). .	208.9	20.1	9.6	10.7	4.0	309.9	42.4	13.7	21.4	8.9
Executive, total	9.7	0.6	6.2	0.4	0.1	14.9	1.2	8.1	0.7	0.3
Wage pay system	414.0	134.6	32.5	83.5	28.0	354.0	121.2	34.3	70.0	26.2
Other pay systems [3]	77.5	12.6	16.3	5.2	2.9	126.3	30.6	24.2	12.8	5.9

[1] Includes American Indians, Alaska Natives, Asians, and Pacific total.   [2] Pay rates as of January 1990 for general schedule. Each grade (except Executive) includes several salary steps. Range is from lowest to highest step of grades shown.
[3] Includes white-collar employment in other than General Schedule and Equivalent.

Source: U.S. Office of Personnel Management, Central Personnel Data File.

No. 529. Federal Civilian Employment and Annual Payroll, by Branch: 1970 to 1992

[Average Annual employment: **For fiscal year ending in year shown;** see text, section 9. Includes employees in U.S. territories and foreign countries. Data represent employees in active-duty status, including intermittent employees. Annual employment figures are averages of monthly figures. Excludes Central Intelligence Agency, National Security Agency, and, as of November 1984, the Defense Intelligence Agency. See also *Historical Statistics, Colonial Times to 1970*, series Y 308-317]

YEAR		EMPLOYMENT					PAYROLL (mil. dol.)				
	Total (1,000)	Percent of U.S. employed [1]	Executive		Legisla-tive (1,000)	Judicial (1,000)	Total	Executive		Legisla-tive	Judi-cial
			Total (1,000)	Defense (1,000)				Total	Defense		
1970 [2]	2,997	3.8	2,961	1,263	29	7	27,322	26,894	11,264	338	89
1975 [3]	2,877	3.4	2,830	1,044	37	10	39,126	38,423	13,418	549	154
1980 [3]	2,987	3.0	2,933	971	40	14	58,012	56,841	18,795	883	288
1981	2,909	2.9	2,855	986	40	15	63,793	62,510	21,227	922	360
1982	2,871	2.9	2,816	1,019	39	16	65,503	64,125	22,226	980	398
1983	2,878	2.9	2,823	1,033	39	16	69,878	68,420	23,406	1,013	445
1984	2,935	2.8	2,879	1,052	40	17	74,616	73,084	25,253	1,081	451
1985	3,001	2.8	2,944	1,080	39	18	80,599	78,992	28,330	1,098	509
1986	3,047	2.8	2,991	1,089	38	19	82,598	80,941	29,272	1,112	545
1987	3,075	2.7	3,018	1,084	38	19	85,543	83,797	29,786	1,153	593
1988	3,113	2.7	3,054	1,073	38	21	88,841	86,960	29,609	1,226	656
1989	3,133	2.7	3,074	1,067	38	22	92,847	90,870	30,301	1,266	711
1990 [4]	3,233	2.7	3,173	1,060	38	23	99,138	97,022	31,990	1,329	787
1991	3,101	2.7	3,038	1,015	38	25	104,273	101,965	32,956	1,434	874
1992	3,106	2.6	3,040	1,004	39	27	108,054	105,402	31,486	1,569	1,083

[1] Civilian only. See table 616.   [2] Includes 33,000 temporary census workers.   [3] Includes 81,116 temporary census workers.   [4] Includes 111,020 temporary census workers.

Source: U.S. Office of Personnel Management, *Federal Civilian Workforce Statistics—Employment and Trends*, bimonthly; and unpublished data.

No. 530. Federal Civilian Employment—Summary: 1980 to 1992

[**In thousands.** As of **Dec. 31.** Excludes U.S. Territories and foreign countries, Central Intelligence Agency, National Security Agency, and the Defense Intelligence Agency. Partially estimated]

CHARACTERISTICS	UNITED STATES					WASHINGTON, DC [1]			
	1980	1985	1990	1991	1992	1980	1985	1990	1992
Paid employment	2,782	2,902	2,940	2,977	2,983	366	353	358	375
Male, est	1,806	1,769	1,685	1,688	1,697	202	191	183	189
Female, est.	976	1,133	1,255	1,289	1,286	164	162	175	186
Full-time	2,504	2,589	2,632	2,678	2,642	342	335	342	359
Other	278	313	308	299	341	24	18	16	16
Competitive service	1,692	1,710	1,694	1,732	1,717	258	246	248	260
Permanent appointment	1,622	1,628	1,637	1,671	1,658	247	234	241	253
Temp. and indef. appointment	70	82	57	61	59	11	12	7	7
Excepted and Senior Executive Services (SES) [2]	1,091	1,191	1,246	1,245	1,266	107	108	109	115
Permanent appointment	917	1,015	1,029	1,037	1,005	70	73	76	80
Temp. and indef. appointm't	174	176	217	208	261	37	35	33	35
White-collar	[3]2,324	2,478	2,576	2,621	2,638	335	327	336	354
Blue-collar	[3]458	424	364	356	345	31	26	22	21

[1] Represents MSA.   [2] Excepted from competitive requirements of Civil Service Act.   [3] Based on total workforce.

No. 531. Federal General Schedule Employee Pay Increases: 1965 to 1994

[Percent change from prior year shown, except 1965, change from 1964. Represents legislated pay increases. For some years data based on range; for details see source]

EFFECTIVE DATE	Average increase	EFFECTIVE DATE	Average increase	EFFECTIVE DATE	Average increase
Oct. 1, 1965	3.6	Oct. 1, 1974	5.5	Jan. 1, 1985	3.5
July 1, 1966	2.9	Oct. 1, 1975	5.0	Jan. 1, 1986	-
Oct. 1, 1967	4.5	Oct. 1, 1976	5.2	Jan. 1, 1987	3.0
July 1, 1968	4.9	Oct. 1, 1977	7.0	Jan. 1, 1988	2.0
July 1, 1969	9.1	Oct. 1, 1978	5.5	Jan. 1, 1989	4.1
Dec. 27, 1969	6.0	Oct. 1, 1979	7.0	Jan. 1, 1990	3.6
Jan. 1, 1971	6.0	Oct. 1, 1980	9.1	Jan. 1, 1991	4.1
Jan. 1, 1972	5.5	Oct. 1, 1981	4.8	Jan. 1, 1992	4.2
Oct. 1, 1972	5.1	Oct. 1, 1982	4.0	Jan. 1, 1993	3.7
Oct. 1, 1973	4.8	Jan. 1, 1984	4.0	Jan. 1, 1994, est	-

- Represents zero.

Source of tables 530 and 531: U.S. Office of Personnel Management, *Pay Structure of the Federal Civil Service*, annual.

No. 532. Paid Civilian Employment in the Federal Government: 1992

[As of December 31. Excludes members and employees of Congress, Central Intelligence Agency, Defense Intelligence Agency employees overseas, temporary census enumerators, seasonal and on-call employees, temporary Christmas help of the U.S. Postal Service, and National Security Agency]

DIVISION AND STATE	Total (1,000)	Percent defense	DIVISION AND STATE	Total (1,000)	Percent defense
United States............	2,988	30.1	District of Columbia..........	223	7.6
			Virginia.................	168	63.7
Northeast.................	481	25.2	West Virginia...............	17	11.8
New England	126	24.6	North Carolina..............	51	33.3
Maine.................	16	56.3	South Carolina.............	33	51.5
New Hampshire..........	8	12.5	Georgia.................	93	39.8
Vermont................	6	16.7	Florida.................	114	28.1
Massachusetts..........	62	17.7	East South Central	176	33.0
Rhode Island...........	10	40.0	Kentucky...............	38	36.8
Connecticut	24	20.8	Tennessee..............	54	13.0
Middle Atlantic.............	355	25.4	Alabama...............	58	44.8
New York..............	149	12.1	Mississippi.............	26	42.3
New Jersey	74	32.4	West South Central...........	281	33.8
Pennsylvania...........	132	36.4	Arkansas...............	21	23.8
North Central	512	23.6	Louisiana..............	35	25.7
East North Central	332	25.3	Oklahoma..............	46	47.8
Ohio.................	94	37.2	Texas.................	179	33.0
Indiana...............	43	34.9	West	655	35.3
Illinois...............	106	17.9	Mountain	202	28.7
Michigan..............	59	20.3	Montana...............	12	8.3
Wisconsin.............	30	10.0	Idaho.................	11	9.1
West North Central...........	180	20.6	Wyoming..............	7	14.3
Minnesota.............	34	8.8	Colorado..............	57	24.6
Iowa.................	20	10.0	New Mexico............	28	32.1
Missouri..............	66	27.3	Arizona...............	40	25.0
North Dakota..........	8	25.0	Utah.................	35	57.1
South Dakota..........	10	10.0	Nevada...............	12	16.7
Nebraska..............	16	25.0	Pacific	453	38.2
Kansas...............	26	26.9	Washington	69	42.0
South.................	1,297	32.8	Oregon...............	31	9.7
South Atlantic.............	840	32.4	California	312	37.8
Delaware..............	5	40.0	Alaska................	16	31.3
Maryland	136	30.1	Hawaii................	25	76.0

Source: U.S. Office of Personnel Management, Biennial Report of Employment by Geographic Area.

No. 533. Paid Full-Time Federal Civilian Employment, all Areas: 1990 to 1993

[As of March 31. Excludes employees of Congress and Federal courts, maritime seamen of Dept. of Commerce, and small number for whom rates were not reported. See text, section 10, for explanation of general schedule and wage system. See also Historical Statistics, Colonial Times to 1970, series Y 318-331]

COMPENSATION AUTHORITY	EMPLOYEES (1,000)				AVERAGE PAY			
	1990	1991	1992	1993	1990	1991	1992	1993
Total............	2,697	2,665	2,051	2,017	31,174	33,340	35,357	37,327
General Schedule......	1,506	1,499	1,537	1,520	31,239	33,288	35,254	37,332
Wage System	369	328	328	315	26,565	27,543	28,852	30,136
Postal pay system [1]....	661	651	(NA)	(NA)	31,992	33,186	(NA)	(NA)
Other..............	161	187	186	182	41,149	43,926	42,689	49,743

NA Not available.   [1] Source: U.S. Postal Service, National Payroll Hours, annual.

Source: Except as noted, U.S. Office of Personnel Management, Pay Structure of the Federal Civil Service, annual.

No. 534. Accessions to and Separations From Paid Civilian Employment in the Federal Government: 1980 to 1993

[In thousands, except rate. For fiscal year ending in year shown; see text, section 9. Includes accessions and separations of full-time, part-time, and intermittent employees]

ITEM	UNITED STATES						WASHINGTON, DC [2]					
	1980 [1]	1985	1990 [1]	1991	1992	Oct. 1992- Aug. 1993	1980 [1]	1985	1990 [1]	1991	1992	Oct. 1992- Aug. 1993
Accessions, total.......	995	630	898	573	505	513	94	63	59	63	52	43
Monthly rate [3].......	2.9	1.9	2.5	1.6	1.4	1.5	2.3	1.6	1.5	1.5	1.2	1
Separations, total......	1,004	530	889	598	518	554	89	58	52	48	45	42
Monthly rate [3].......	3.0	1.6	2.4	1.7	1.5	1.6	2.2	1.5	1.3	1.2	1.1	1
Quit [4]	228	218	191	153	136	125	33	25	23	19	18	15

[1] Includes temporary census enumerators.   [2] Represents MSA.   [3] Per 100 employees.   [4] Represents voluntary resignations by employees or separations by agency if employee declines new assignment, abandons position, joins military, or fails to return from military furlough.

Source: U.S. Office of Personnel Management, Federal Civilian Workforce Statistics—Employment and Trends, bimonthly; and unpublished data.

No. 535. Accessions to and Separations From Employment in the Federal Government: 1992 and 1993

[As of September 30]

AGENCY	ACCESSIONS 1992 Number	1992 Rate	1993 Number	1993 Rate	SEPARATIONS 1992 Number	1992 Rate	1993 Number	1993 Rate
Total, all agencies.	555,801	18.2	599,530	20.0	579,422	18.9	659,487	22.0
Legislative Branch, total [1]	1,726	9.3	1,147	6.3	2,247	12.1	2,037	11.2
General Accounting Office	407	7.6	181	3.5	625	11.6	483	9.4
Government Printing Office	404	8.3	92	1.9	381	7.8	245	5.1
Library of Congress	524	10.4	511	10.3	630	12.5	663	13.3
Judicial Branch	31	39.2	14	16.3	17	21.5	9	10.5
Executive Branch, total	554,044	18.2	598,369	20.1	577,158	19.0	657,441	22.1
Executive Office of the President [1]	432	23.5	860	45.3	305	16.6	934	49.2
Executive Departments	401,213	19.6	358,106	17.9	416,999	20.3	397,609	19.8
State	4,129	15.9	4,166	16.0	3,664	14.1	4,060	15.6
Treasury	54,752	32.2	53,484	32.5	63,717	37.5	59,243	36.1
Defense	175,985	17.5	152,473	16.0	209,177	20.8	197,838	20.8
Justice	15,316	16.2	9,149	9.3	5,824	6.1	4,481	4.6
Interior	23,188	28.8	20,898	25.6	16,890	21.0	17,393	21.3
Agriculture	41,004	33.5	34,258	28.3	38,117	31.2	39,365	32.6
Commerce	6,547	17.3	8,013	20.9	9,098	24.1	6,312	16.5
Labor	1,595	8.9	1,083	6.1	1,625	9.1	1,593	9.0
Health & Human Services	17,601	13.4	15,702	11.9	12,436	9.4	13,441	10.2
Housing & Urban Development	547	3.9	971	7.3	1,877	13.3	1,235	9.3
Transportation	5,795	8.2	3,208	4.6	6,248	8.9	5,469	7.8
Energy	3,677	17.9	1,570	7.6	2,251	11.0	2,083	10.1
Education	546	10.8	583	11.6	323	6.4	353	7.0
Veterans Affairs [2]	50,531	19.6	52,548	19.9	45,752	17.7	44,743	17.0
Independent agencies [1]	152,399	15.5	239,403	24.7	159,854	16.2	258,898	26.7
Board of Governors, Fed RSRV System . . .	189	12.1	249	15.2	157	10.1	167	10.2
Environmental Protection Agency	2,190	12.0	2,196	11.9	2,089	11.4	1,961	10.6
Equal Employment Opportunity Comm.	219	7.6	179	6.1	160	5.6	168	5.7
Federal Deposit Insurance Corporation . . .	4,207	18.6	3,280	14.9	3,819	16.9	4,168	18.9
Fed. Emergency Management Agency	3,228	87.8	2,759	60.3	982	26.7	2,621	57.3
General Services Administration	2,003	9.5	1,926	9.3	1,816	8.6	1,705	8.2
National Aeronautics & Space Admin	2,685	10.5	2,130	8.5	3,012	11.7	2,669	10.6
National Archives & Records Admin	757	24.5	644	20.4	377	12.2	316	10.0
Nuclear Regulatory Commission	240	6.8	150	4.2	215	6.0	195	5.5
Office of Personnel Management	1,071	15.5	707	10.3	934	13.5	864	12.6
Panama Canal Comm.	1,420	16.4	1,388	16.2	1,561	18.0	1,289	15.1
Railroad Retirement Board	137	7.6	92	5.1	106	5.8	131	7.2
Securities and Exchange Commission	603	23.9	349	12.9	296	11.7	278	10.3
Small Business Administration	2,118	41.6	2,057	36.4	1,088	21.4	2,452	43.4
Smithsonian Institution	1,076	19.7	849	15.4	923	16.9	892	16.2
Tennessee Valley Authority	1,998	9.8	951	5.0	7,450	36.6	1,402	7.3
U.S. Information Agency	658	8.0	529	6.4	547	6.6	556	6.7
U.S. International Dev. Coop. Agency	499	10.9	463	10.5	579	12.7	733	16.6
U.S. Postal Service	124,018	15.5	215,964	27.5	131,026	16.4	233,602	29.7

[1] Includes other branches, or other agencies, not shown separately.   [2] Formerly Veterans Administration.

Source: U.S. Office of Personnel Management, *Federal Civilian Workforce Statistics— Employment and Trends,* bimonthly.

No. 536. Federal Land and Buildings Owned and Leased, and Predominant Land Usage: 1980 to 1991

[For fiscal years ending in years shown; see text, section 9. Covers Federal real property throughout the world, except as noted. Cost of land figures represent total cost of property owned in year shown. For further details see source. For data on Federal land by State, see table 354]

ITEM AND AGENCY	Unit	1980	1985	1986	1987	1988	1989	1990	1991
Federally owned: Land	Mil. acres.	720	727	727	724	688	662	650	650
Buildings, number [1]	1,000 . . .	403	454	429	412	442	451	446	441
Cost of land, buildings, etc.[2]	Bil. dol. . .	107	148	158	165	164	164	180	181
Federally leased: Land	Mil. acres.	1.4	1.3	1.3	1.6	1.6	1.5	0.9	(NA)
Buildings, floor area [1]	Mil. sq/ft .	214	237	246	246	248	254	234	242
Rental property, cost	Mil. dol . .	1,054	1,681	1,774	1,893	2,001	2,127	2,125	(NA)
Predominant usage (U.S. only)	Mil. acres.	720	727	727	724	688	662	650	650
Forest and wildlife	Mil. acres.	422	431	431	431	400	375	368	(NA)
Grazing	Mil. acres.	162	155	155	154	151	151	154	(NA)
Parks and historic sites	Mil. acres.	93	94	96	96	99	98	96	(NA)
Other	Mil. acres.	43	48	46	43	38	39	33	(NA)

NA Not available.   [1] Excludes data for Dept. of Defense military functions outside United States.   [2] Includes other uses not shown separately.

Source: U.S. General Services Administration, *Inventory Report on Real Property Owned by the United States Throughout the World,* annual.

Figure 11.1
Military and Civilian Personnel: 1985 to 1993

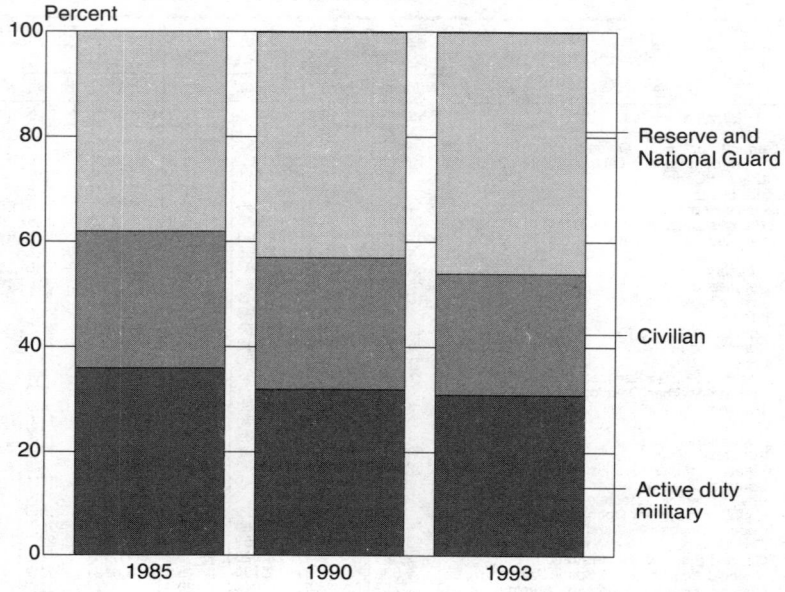

Source: Chart prepared by U.S. Bureau of the Census. For data, see table 541.

Figure 11.2
DOD Military Expenditures, by Major Location: 1993

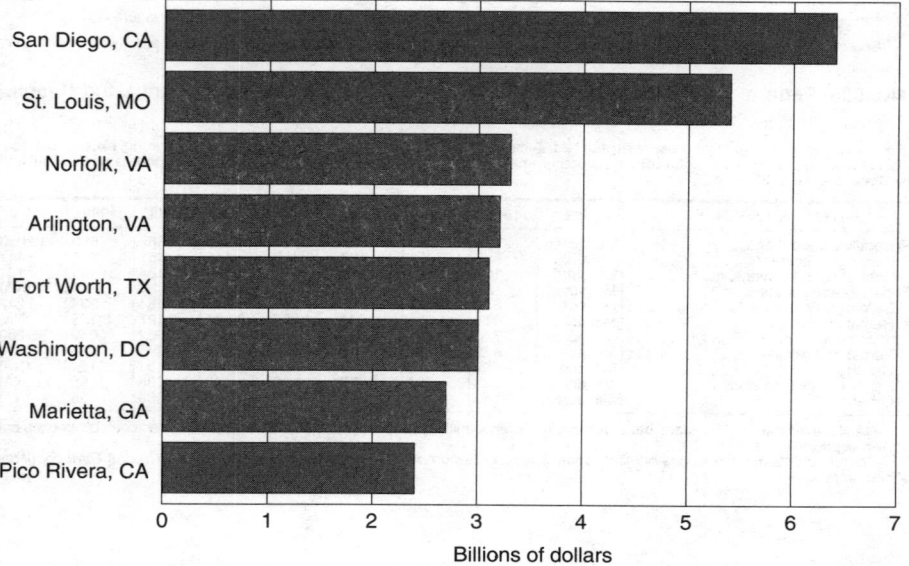

Source: Chart prepared by U.S. Bureau of the Census. For data, see table 541.

National Defense and Veterans Affairs

This section presents data on national defense and its human and financial costs; active and reserve military personnel; ships, equipment and aircraft; and federally sponsored programs and benefits for veterans. The principal sources of these data are the annual *Selected Manpower Statistics* and the *Atlas/Data Abstract for the United States and Selected Areas* issued by the Office of the Secretary of Defense; *Annual Report of Secretary of Veterans Affairs, Department of Veterans Affairs,* and *The Budget of the United States Government,* Office of Management and Budget. For more data on expenditures, personnel, and ships, see section 31.

Department of Defense (DOD).—DOD is responsible for providing military forces of the United States. The President serves as Commander in Chief of the Armed Forces; from him, the authority flows to the Secretary of Defense and through the Joint Chiefs of Staff to the commanders of unified and specified commands (e.g., United States European Command).

Reserve components.—Reserve personnel of the Armed Forces consist of the Army National Guard, Army Reserve, Naval Reserve, Marine Corps Reserve, Air National Guard, Air Force Reserve, and Coast Guard Reserve. They provide trained personnel available for active duty in the Armed Forces in time of war or national emergency and at such other times as authorized by law. The National Guard has dual Federal-State responsibilities and uses jointly provided equipment, facilities, and budget support. The President is empowered to mobilize the National Guard and to use such of the Armed Forces as he considers necessary to enforce Federal authority in any State.

The ready reserve includes selected reservists who are intended to assist active forces in a war and the individual ready reserve who, in a major war, would be used to fill out active and reserve units and later would be a source of combat replacements; a portion of the ready reserve serves in an active status. The

In Brief

1993 National defense outlays	$280 bil.

standby reserve cannot be called to active duty unless the Congress gives explicit approval. The retired reserve represents a low potential for mobilization.

Department of Veterans Affairs.—The Department of Veterans Affairs administers laws authorizing benefits for eligible former and present members of the Armed Forces and for the beneficiaries of deceased members. Veterans benefits available under various acts of Congress include compensation for service-connected disability or death; pensions for nonservice-connected disability or death; vocational rehabilitation, education, and training; home loan insurance; life insurance; health care; special housing and automobiles or other conveyances for certain disabled veterans; burial and plot allowances; and educational assistance to families of deceased or totally disabled veterans, servicemen missing in action, or prisoners of war. Since these benefits are legislated by Congress, the dates they were enacted and the dates they apply to veterans may be different from the actual dates the conflicts occurred.

VA estimates of veterans cover all persons with active duty service during periods of war or armed conflict and until 1982 include those living outside the United States. Veteran population estimates for September 1982 are for the 50 States, the District of Columbia and Puerto Rico. Veterans whose active duty service was entirely during periods of peacetime are eligible for some veterans benefits and, where appropriate, are included in VA estimates.

Historical statistics.—Tabular headnotes provide cross-references, where applicable, to *Historical Statistics of the United States, Colonial Times to 1970.* See Appendix IV.

No. 537. National Defense Outlays and Veterans Benefits: 1960 to 1994

For fiscal year ending in year shown; see text, section 9. Includes outlays of Department of Defense, Department of Veterans Affairs, and other agencies for activities primarily related to national defense and veterans programs. For explanation of average annual percent change, see Guide to Tabular Presentation. Minus sign (-) indicates decline. See *Historical Statistics, Colonial Times to 1970*, series Y 472, 473, and Y 476, for related data]

YEAR	NATIONAL DEFENSE AND VETERANS OUTLAYS				ANNUAL PERCENT CHANGE [1]			DEFENSE OUTLAYS, PERCENT OF—	
	Total outlays (bil. dol.)	Defense outlays		Veterans outlays (bil. dol.)	Total outlays	Defense outlays	Veterans outlays	Federal outlays	Gross domestic product [2]
		Current dollars (bil. dol.)	Constant (1987) dollars (bil. dol.)						
1960	53.5	48.1	220.1	5.4	2.5	2.4	3.1	52.2	9.5
1965	56.3	50.6	203.9	5.7	-6.8	-7.6	0.7	42.8	7.5
1966	64.0	58.1	225.9	5.9	13.7	14.8	3.5	43.2	7.9
1967	78.1	71.4	269.1	6.7	22.1	22.9	13.8	45.4	9.0
1968	88.9	81.9	295.5	7.0	13.8	14.7	4.4	46.0	9.7
1969	90.1	82.5	282.5	7.6	1.3	0.7	8.5	44.9	8.9
1970	90.4	81.7	262.9	8.7	0.3	-1.0	13.6	41.8	8.3
1971	88.7	78.9	236.9	9.8	-1.9	-3.5	12.7	37.5	7.5
1972	89.9	79.2	219.7	10.7	1.4	0.4	9.8	34.3	6.9
1973	88.7	76.7	197.2	12.0	1.3	-3.1	12.0	31.2	6.0
1974	92.7	79.3	185.3	13.4	4.6	3.5	11.4	29.5	5.7
1975	103.1	86.5	183.9	16.6	11.2	9.0	24.0	26.0	5.7
1976	108.1	89.6	177.8	18.4	4.8	3.6	11.0	24.1	5.3
1976, TQ [3]	26.2	22.3	42.4	4.0	(X)	(X)	(X)	23.2	5.0
1977	115.2	97.2	176.8	18.0	6.7	8.5	-2.1	23.8	5.1
1978	123.5	104.5	177.2	19.0	7.1	7.5	5.2	22.8	4.8
1979	136.2	116.3	180.4	19.9	10.4	11.3	5.0	23.1	4.8
1980	155.2	134.0	187.1	21.2	13.9	15.2	6.3	22.7	5.1
1981	180.5	157.5	198.2	23.0	16.3	17.6	8.5	23.2	5.3
1982	209.3	185.3	214.3	24.0	15.9	17.6	4.2	24.9	5.9
1983	234.7	209.9	230.4	24.8	12.1	13.3	3.3	26.0	6.3
1984	253.0	227.4	241.7	25.6	7.8	8.3	3.2	26.7	6.2
1985	279.0	252.7	261.2	26.3	10.3	11.1	2.7	26.7	6.4
1986	299.8	273.4	276.4	26.4	7.4	8.2	0.4	27.6	6.5
1987	308.8	282.0	282.0	26.8	3.0	3.1	1.5	28.1	6.3
1988	319.8	290.4	283.3	29.4	3.6	3.0	9.7	27.3	6.0
1989	333.7	303.6	285.9	30.1	4.3	4.5	2.4	26.6	5.9
1990	328.4	299.3	272.5	29.1	-1.6	-1.4	-3.3	23.9	5.5
1991	304.6	273.3	240.4	31.3	-7.2	-8.7	7.6	20.6	4.8
1992	332.5	298.4	250.2	34.1	12.0	12.4	8.0	21.6	5.0
1993	326.1	291.1	265.7	35.7	-1.9	-2.4	4.6	20.7	4.6
1994, est.	279.8	279.8	220.1	38.1	-14.2	-3.9	6.7	18.9	4.2

X Not applicable.   [1] Change from prior year shown; for 1960, change from 1955.   [2] Represents fiscal year GDP; for definition, see text, section 14.   [3] Transition quarter, July-Sept.

Source: U.S. Office of Management and Budget, *Budget of the United States Government,* annual.

No. 538. Federal Budget Outlays for National Defense Functions: 1970 to 1994

[In billions of dollars, except percent. For fiscal year ending in year shown; see text, section 9. Minus sign (-) indicates decline. See *Historical Statistics, Colonial Times to 1970*, series Y 473, for total]

DEFENSE FUNCTION	1970	1980	1985	1986	1987	1988	1989	1990	1991	1992	1993	1994, est.
Total................	81.7	134.0	252.7	273.4	282.0	290.4	303.6	299.3	273.3	298.4	291.1	279.8
Percent change [1]	10.1	15.2	11.1	8.2	3.1	3.0	4.5	-1.4	-8.7	9.2	-2.4	-3.9
Defense Dept., military	80.1	130.9	245.2	265.5	274.0	281.9	294.9	289.8	262.4	286.9	278.6	267.4
Military personnel	29.0	40.9	67.8	71.5	72.0	76.3	80.7	75.6	83.4	81.2	75.9	71.0
Percent of military	36.2	31.2	27.7	26.9	26.3	27.1	27.0	26.1	31.8	28.3	27.2	26.5
Operation, maintenance	21.6	44.8	72.4	75.3	76.2	84.5	87.0	88.3	101.8	92.0	94.1	88.7
Procurement	21.6	29.0	70.4	76.5	80.7	77.2	81.6	81.0	82.0	74.9	69.9	60.8
Research and development ..	7.2	13.1	27.1	32.3	33.6	34.8	37.0	37.5	34.6	34.6	37.0	35.5
Military construction	1.2	2.5	4.3	5.1	5.9	5.9	5.3	5.1	3.5	4.3	4.8	5.1
Family housing...........	0.6	1.7	2.6	2.8	2.9	3.1	3.3	3.5	3.3	3.3	3.3	3.5
Other [2]	-1.1	-1.1	0.6	2.0	2.6	0.2	0.1	-1.2	-46.2	-3.3	-6.4	2.7
Atomic energy activities [3]	1.4	2.9	7.1	7.4	7.5	7.9	8.1	9.0	10.0	10.6	11.0	11.2
Defense-related activities [4]	0.2	0.2	0.5	0.5	0.5	0.6	0.6	0.6	0.9	0.8	1.5	1.3

[1] Change from immediate prior year; for 1970, change from 1965.   [2] Revolving and management funds, trust funds, special foreign currency program, allowances, and offsetting receipts.   [3] Defense activities only.   [4] Includes civil defense activities.

Source: U.S. Office of Management and Budget, *Budget of the United States Government,* annual.

No. 539. National Defense—Budget Authority and Outlays: 1980 to 1994

[In billions of dollars, except percent. For fiscal year ending in year shown, except as noted; see text, section 9. See Historical Statistics, Colonial Times to 1970, series Y 458-460 for outlays]

ITEM	1980	1985	1986	1987	1988	1989	1990	1991	1992	1993	1994, est.
Budget authority [1]	143.9	294.7	289.1	287.4	292.0	299.6	303.3	288.9	295.1	281.1	260.9
Department of Defense-Military [2]	140.6	286.8	281.4	279.5	283.8	290.8	293.0	276.2	282.1	267.2	249.0
Atomic energy [1] [3]	3.2	7.8	7.7	8.0	8.3	8.7	10.3	12.7	12.9	13.9	12.0
Outlays (Defense) [1]	134.0	252.7	273.4	282.0	290.4	303.6	299.3	273.3	298.4	291.1	279.8
Department of Defense-Military	130.9	245.2	265.5	274.0	281.9	294.9	289.8	262.4	286.9	278.6	267.4
Atomic energy [1] [3]	3.1	7.6	7.9	8.0	8.4	8.7	8.7	9.6	10.9	11.5	12.5

[1] Includes defense budget authority, balances, and outlays by other departments.   [2] Excluding accruals.   [3] Includes other defense related activities.

Source: U.S. Office of Management and Budget, Budget of the United States Government, annual.

No. 540. Defense-Related Agencies: 1970 to 1991

[In thousands, except percent. Annual averages]

EMPLOYMENT	1970	1980	1985	1986	1987	1988	1989	1990	1991
Total U.S. employment [1]	80,796	100,907	108,856	111,303	114,177	116,677	119,030	119,550	118,440
Federal	4,763	4,386	4,608	4,601	4,709	4,690	4,662	4,577	4,541
Resident Armed Forces	2,118	1,604	1,706	1,706	1,737	1,709	1,688	1,637	1,564
Civilian personnel [2]	2,645	2,782	2,902	2,895	2,972	2,981	2,974	2,940	2,977
DOD-Civilian employment [3]	1,211	948	1,073	1,059	1,079	1,041	1,067	1,024	1,083
Percent of Federal civilian personnel	44.3	33.1	37.3	36.5	36.3	34.9	35.8	34.8	36.4
DOD-Military and civilian employment	3,329	2,552	2,779	2,765	2,816	2,750	2,755	2,661	2,647
Percent of total Federal	68.7	57.1	60.7	60.0	59.8	58.6	59.1	58.1	58.3
Percent of total U.S.	4.1	2.5	2.6	2.5	2.5	2.4	2.3	2.2	2.2

[1] Includes resident Armed Forces.   [2] See table 530.   [3] Source: Beginning 1980, U.S. Dept. of Defense, Civilian Manpower Statistics, annual (Sept. issues).

Source: Except as noted, U.S. Bureau of Labor Statistics, Employment and Earnings, monthly.

No. 541. Military and Civilian Personnel and Expenditures: 1985 to 1993

ITEM	1985	1989	1990	1991	1992	1993
Personnel, total [1] (1,000)	3,808	3,885	3,693	3,872	3,889	3,762
Active duty military	1,354	1,342	1,185	1,263	1,214	1,171
Civilian	976	965	931	911	899	847
Reserve and National Guard	1,478	1,578	1,577	1,697	1,777	1,744
Expenditures, total (mil. dol.)	216,045	212,509	209,904	221,089	211,534	214,655
Payroll outlays	75,949	92,593	88,650	96,970	99,250	100,510
Active duty military pay	29,818	38,221	33,705	39,118	39,447	38,782
Civilian pay	24,815	27,960	28,230	29,901	31,205	31,619
Retired military pay	17,029	20,591	21,159	22,584	23,936	25,658
Reserve and National Guard pay	4,287	5,821	5,556	5,366	4,661	4,451
Prime contract awards [2] (mil. dol.)	140,096	119,917	121,254	124,119	112,285	114,145
Supply contracts	92,375	67,540	66,895	66,981	54,880	54,856
Service contracts	24,224	24,347	28,540	31,222	30,503	32,163
R and D contracts	18,752	22,996	21,955	20,469	21,508	22,076
Construction contracts	3,245	3,668	2,088	3,469	2,894	2,829
Civil function contracts	1,500	1,365	1,775	1,979	2,500	2,222
Major area of work (mil. dol.):						
Aircraft, fixed wing	11,683	5,335	6,329	6,543	8,197	6,926
Research, development, testing, and evaluation	2,848	1,630	1,856	1,236	1,266	1,422
Gas turbines and jet engines	(NA)	(NA)	(NA)	(NA)	974	(NA)
Guided missiles	(NA)	886	928	921	(NA)	793
Guided missile handling and servicing equip.	(NA)	875	446	921	(NA)	757
Major location of expenditures (mil. dol.):						
San Diego, CA	4,027	4,534	4,820	4,628	5,289	6,405
Pico Rivera, CA	(NA)	(NA)	(NA)	2,600	4,284	2,428
St. Louis, MO	7,412	5,965	5,616	5,869	3,462	5,442
Norfolk, VA	2,200	2,597	2,741	2,928	3,257	3,265
Arlington, VA	(NA)	2,314	2,527	2,836	2,974	3,246
Fort Worth, TX	3,912	4,122	3,594	3,973	2,948	3,136
Washington, DC	(NA)	2,352	2,771	2,706	2,828	3,045
Marietta, GA	(NA)	(NA)	(NA)	(NA)	2,573	2,734
Los Angeles, CA	7,125	2,339	2,459	(NA)	2,319	(NA)
San Antonio, TX	(NA)	(NA)	(NA)	(NA)	2,117	(NA)

NA Not available.   [1] Includes those based ashore and excludes those temporarily shore-based, in a transient status, or afloat.   [2] Represents contract awards over $25,000.

Source: U.S. Dept. of Defense, Atlas/Data Abstract for the United States and Selected Areas, annual.

No. 542. Military Prime Contract Awards to All Businesses, by Program: 1980 to 1993

[In billions of dollars. Net values for fiscal year ending in year shown; see text, section 9. Includes all new prime contracts; debit or credit changes in contracts are also included. Actions cover official awards, amendments, or other changes in prime contracts to obtain military supplies, services, or construction. Excludes term contracts and contracts which do not obligate a firm total dollar amount or fixed quantity, but includes job orders, task orders, and delivery orders against such contracts]

DOD PROCUREMENT PROGRAM	1980	1985	1987	1988	1989	1990	1991	1992	1993
Total	83.7	163.7	156.5	151.4	139.3	144.7	150.9	136.3	138.3
Intragovernmental [1]	10.2	12.4	8.8	8.9	9.6	10.0	11.9	9.6	12.9
For work outside the U.S.	5.4	8.6	8.9	8.2	6.4	7.1	9.2	5.9	5.8
Educ. and nonprofit institutions	1.5	3.1	3.5	3.5	3.3	3.5	3.6	3.4	3.4
With business firms for work in the U.S. [2]	66.7	139.6	135.3	130.8	120.0	123.8	125.9	117.2	116.0
Major hard goods	41.0	98.1	93.0	85.9	79.9	79.1	74.1	67.1	64.5
Aircraft	12.5	34.6	27.7	25.0	24.2	24.0	23.6	24.1	23.0
Electronics and communication equip.	9.6	22.0	22.6	17.8	18.1	18.5	15.2	14.2	14.2
Missiles and space systems	7.9	18.7	19.8	19.7	18.7	17.1	16.4	13.1	12.1
Ships	6.0	10.4	11.5	13.7	9.6	10.3	9.3	8.3	9.0
Tanks, ammo. and weapons	5.1	12.5	11.6	9.7	9.2	9.2	9.6	7.4	6.2
Services	5.9	9.1	11.0	12.0	11.7	14.6	16.9	17.3	17.5

[1] Covers only purchases from other Federal agencies and reimbursable purchases on behalf of foreign governments.
[2] Includes Department of Defense. Includes other business not shown separately. Contracts awarded for work in U.S. possessions, and other areas subject to complete sovereignty of United States; contracts in a classified location; and any intragovernmental contracts entered into overseas.

Source: U.S. Dept. of Defense, Prime Contract Awards, semiannual.

No. 543. Department of Defense Contract Awards, Payroll, and Civilian and Military Personnel—States: 1992

[For years ending Sept. 30. Contracts refer to awards made in year specified; expenditures relating to awards may extend over several years. Civilian employees include United States citizen and foreign national direct hire civilians subject to Office of Management and Budget (OMB) ceiling controls and civilian personnel involved in civil functions in the United States. Excludes indirect hire civilians and those direct hire civilian not subject to OMB ceiling controls. Military personnel include active duty personnel based ashore. Excludes personnel temporarily shore-based in a transient status, or afloat. Payroll outlays include the gross earnings of civilian and active duty military personnel for services rendered to the government and for cash allowances for benefits. Excludes employer's share of employee benefits, accrued military retirement benefits and most permanent change of station costs]

REGION, DIVISION, AND STATE	Contract awards [1] (mil. dol.)	Payroll (mil. dol.)	PERSONNEL (1,000) Civilian	Military	REGION, DIVISION, AND STATE	Contract awards [1] (mil. dol.)	Payroll (mil. dol.)	PERSONNEL (1,000) Civilian	Military
U.S.	112,285	99,250	899.0	1,213.7	DC	1,546	1,282	16.8	14.1
					VA	6,571	11,157	106.3	92.3
Northeast	22,846	9,004	121.6	61.1	WV	83	205	1.7	0.5
N.E.	11,033	2,989	30.5	22.5	NC	1,540	4,041	17.1	95.0
ME	1,305	644	8.3	4.7	SC	756	2,699	17.6	39.1
NH	424	219	1.4	0.4	GA	3,796	4,234	37.3	60.8
VT	63	76	0.6	0.1	FL	4,995	6,277	32.3	74.8
MA	5,686	993	11.1	7.2	E.S.C.	6,215	6,045	58.7	73.1
RI	455	437	4.2	3.7	KY	437	1,843	14.2	34.8
CT	3,099	620	4.8	6.5	TN	1,262	984	7.6	8.4
M.A.	11,813	6,015	91.0	38.5	AL	1,949	2,139	26.0	17.6
NY	5,430	1,810	17.8	23.7	MS	2,567	1,079	11.0	12.3
NJ	3,319	1,601	24.7	9.6	W.S.C.	10,923	11,112	93.5	165.3
PA	3,065	2,605	48.5	5.2	AR	288	703	4.5	6.6
Midwest	15,398	11,021	120.6	117.6	LA	1,204	1,358	9.0	21.6
E.N.C.	8,365	6,397	84.1	53.4	OK	759	2,035	21.9	28.3
OH	3,033	2,182	34.7	10.9	TX	8,672	7,016	58.2	108.8
IN	1,517	1,095	15.7	5.3	West	33,463	28,683	233.2	383.2
IL	1,354	1,775	19.3	29.8	Mt.	6,188	7,213	58.8	101.2
MI	1,568	904	11.1	6.5	MT	56	232	1.2	4.4
WI	893	441	3.4	0.9	ID	66	290	1.5	4.7
W.N.C.	7,032	4,624	36.4	64.2	WY	61	171	1.1	3.5
MN	1,496	358	2.9	0.9	CO	2,471	2,190	14.0	37.7
IA	442	202	1.5	0.4	NM	728	1,019	9.2	15.4
MO	3,714	1,622	18.3	15.3	AZ	1,946	1,658	9.8	22.0
ND	146	328	1.9	9.7	UT	616	1,050	19.9	5.6
SD	83	254	1.3	6.1	NV	243	603	2.1	7.7
NE	297	674	3.8	10.5	Pac.	27,274	21,470	174.4	281.9
KS	855	1,186	6.8	21.3	WA	2,217	3,305	29.0	35.7
South	40,578	50,542	423.7	651.8	OR	206	432	2.9	1.0
S.A.	23,440	33,384	271.4	413.4	CA	23,843	14,202	119.9	178.2
DE	103	267	1.8	4.4	AK	385	1,189	4.7	22.2
MD	4,050	3,222	40.5	32.3	HI	623	2,342	17.9	44.9

[1] Military awards for supplies, services, and construction. Net value of contracts of over $25,000 for work in each State and DC. Figures reflect impact of prime contracting on State distribution of defense work. Often the State in which a prime contractor is located in is not the State where the subcontracted work is done. See also headnote, table 542. Undistributed civilians and military personnel, their payrolls, and prime contract awards for performance in classified locations are excluded.
Source: U.S. Dept. of Defense, Atlas/Data Abstract for the United States and Selected Areas, annual.

No. 544. Worldwide Military Expenditures: 1982 to 1991

[In billions of dollars. For military expenditures and Armed Forces by country, see section 31. GNP=Gross national product]

COUNTRY GROUP	1982	1983	1984	1985	1986	1987	1988	1989	1990	1991
Current dollars, total [1] ...	792	852	903	959	996	1,032	1,058	1,070	1,086	1,038
United States............	196	218	237	266	281	288	293	304	306	280
Percent of total.........	24.8	25.6	26.3	27.7	28.2	27.9	27.7	28.4	28.2	27.0
Developed countries [2]......	627	676	719	773	807	843	871	877	861	797
Developing countries [2]......	165	176	183	186	188	188	188	192	226	242
NATO countries [3]...........	330	361	388	425	444	461	469	489	501	480
Constant (1988) dollars, total	1,113	1,150	1,167	1,196	1,210	1,215	1,200	1,161	1,130	1,038
United States............	276	294	307	332	341	339	332	330	318	280
Percent of total.........	24.8	25.6	26.3	27.7	28.2	27.9	27.7	28.4	28.2	27.0
Developed countries [2]......	881	913	930	965	981	993	987	952	895	797
Developing countries [2]......	232	238	237	231	229	222	213	209	235	242
NATO countries [3]...........	464	488	502	530	540	543	532	531	521	480
Percent of GNP...........	**5.7**	**5.7**	**5.6**	**5.5**	**5.4**	**5.3**	**5.0**	**4.7**	**4.5**	**4.2**
United States.............	6.2	6.3	6.2	6.6	6.6	6.3	6.0	5.8	5.5	4.9
Developed countries [2]......	5.5	5.6	5.5	5.5	5.5	5.4	5.2	4.8	4.5	4.1
Developing countries [2]......	6.2	6.2	5.9	5.5	5.2	4.8	4.4	4.1	4.5	4.5
NATO countries [3]..........	4.7	4.8	4.7	4.8	4.8	4.8	4.7	4.4	4.3	3.8

[1] Includes countries not shown separately.   [2] Twenty-eight developed countries; see table 545 for selected countries; for complete list, see source.   [3] North Atlantic Treaty Organization.

No. 545. Arms Trade in Constant (1991) Dollars—Selected Countries: 1989 to 1991

[In millions of dollars, except percent. Because some countries exclude arms imports or exports from their trade statistics and their "total" imports and exports are therefore understated, and because arms transfers may be estimated independently of trade data, the ratio of arms to total imports or exports may be overstated and may even exceed 100 percent]

COUNTRY	1989	1990	1991 Total	1991 Arms imports as percent of total imports	COUNTRY	1989	1990	1991 Total	1991 Arms imports as percent of total imports
World total [1]....	54,320	39,780	25,530	(NA)	RECIPIENTS				
					Developing [1]	41,320	31,920	19,390	2.2
EXPORTERS					Afghanistan.......	4,123	3,640	1,900	217.4
					Algeria	651	302	100	1.1
					Angola	814	510	30	(NA)
Canada..........	488	499	420	0.2	Argentina........	54	94	10	0.1
China: Mainland	2,495	1,456	925	0.4	Cuba...........	1,302	1,456	525	14.4
Czechoslovakia.....	949	198	270	0.5	Egypt..........	759	572	525	6.7
France	2,061	3,952	1,100	0.1	El Salvador	76	62	50	3.6
Poland	434	52	90	-	Ethiopia.........	1,058	333	80	16.9
Soviet Union.......	21,480	14,770	6,600	-	Greece	2,170	125	130	0.6
United Kingdom	5,099	4,472	3,700	0.3	India...........	4,231	1,768	800	3.9
United States	14,650	10,300	9,600	0.4	Iran...........	1,410	1,456	1,600	8.3
West Germany	1,302	1,040	1,300	0.1	Iraq...........	2,495	2,912	-	-
					Israel	1,193	478	460	2.7
IMPORTERS					Jordan..........	217	83	60	2.4
					Kuwait..........	532	291	50	1.1
Developed [1].....	13,060	8,414	6,325	0.2	Libya..........	1,058	374	370	5.5
Australia	841	322	210	0.5	Morocco	65	166	30	0.4
Canada	217	125	200	0.2	Nicaragua	467	62	-	-
Czechoslovakia.....	499	291	50	0.5	North Korea......	651	208	90	(NA)
East Germany	1,134	895	83	(NA)	Oman	65	10	40	1.3
Hungary.........	33	-	-	-	Pakistan	542	624	120	1.4
Italy	423	187	180	0.1	Peru	152	73	10	0.2
Japan	1,844	1,040	775	0.3	Saudi Arabia......	5,642	6,136	6,900	(NA)
Poland	678	156	-	-	South Korea......	570	572	775	1.0
Romania	22	447	170	3.0	Spain	841	416	150	0.2
Soviet Union......	976	104	-	-	Syria...........	1,085	1,014	650	24.1
United Kingdom	841	884	525	0.3	Turkey..........	1,302	936	800	3.8
United States	1,736	1,768	1,900	0.4	Venezuela	184	208	140	1.3
West Germany	1,302	624	440	0.1	Vietnam.........	1,410	1,144	200	10.5
					Yemen (Sanaa).....	456	675	200	(NA)

- Represents or rounds to zero.   NA Not available.   [1] Includes countries not shown separately.

Source of tables 544 and 545: U.S. Arms Control and Disarmament Agency, *World Military Expenditures and Arms Transfers*, annual.

No. 546. Arms Transfers—Cumulative Value for Period 1987-91, by Major Supplier and Recipient Country

[In millions of dollars]

RECIPIENT	Total [1]	SUPPLIER					
		Soviet Union [2]	United States	France	United Kingdom	China: Mainland	West Germany [3]
World, total............	227,260	84,350	58,855	11,350	22,275	9,515	6,365
Africa [1]..................	17,810	12,795	690	320	125	420	51
Algeria..................	2,490	2,000	20	-	-	10	-
Angola..................	4,630	4,100	-	40	-	-	-
Ethiopia.................	3,130	2,900	-	-	-	90	-
Libya...................	3,010	2,400	-	-	-	20	-
Morocco.................	790	-	210	50	-	20	-
Mozambique.............	560	525	-	-	-	20	-
Nigeria.................	215	20	20	20	-	5	-
Sudan..................	460	-	40	-	-	70	-
East Asia [1]...............	28,890	10,470	14,235	220	460	720	190
China: Mainland...........	1,610	550	130	150	140	(X)	-
Taiwan..............	3,880	-	3,000	-	-	-	-
North Korea.............	2,375	2,300	-	-	-	40	-
Malaysia................	230	-	130	20	10	-	-
South Korea.............	3,045	-	3,000	10	20	-	-
Thailand................	1,820	-	1,300	-	10	280	110
Vietnam................	5,930	5,900	-	-	-	-	-
South Asia [1]..............	28,795	23,450	1,025	480	340	880	390
Afghanistan.............	13,210	13,200	-	-	-	-	-
India...................	13,250	10,200	180	450	310	-	370
Pakistan................	1,895	-	825	30	30	600	20
Europe [1]................	44,525	10,010	22,445	1,505	1,035	-	3,065
Belgium................	1,160	-	1,100	60	-	-	-
Bulgaria................	1,990	1,800	-	-	-	-	-
Czechoslovakia..........	1,930	1,900	-	-	-	-	-
Denmark................	490	-	450	-	10	-	-
East Germany [3].........	2,210	1,900	-	-	-	-	-
France.................	1,005	-	975	(X)	-	-	-
Greece.................	3,045	-	1,800	1,000	-	-	180
Hungary................	550	420	-	-	-	-	-
Italy...................	1,225	-	1,200	-	-	-	-
Netherlands.............	2,300	-	2,200	-	-	-	50
Norway.................	1,600	-	725	-	30	-	270
Poland.................	2,570	2,400	-	-	-	-	-
Soviet Union [2].........	3,610	(X)	-	-	-	-	10
Spain..................	3,400	-	2,900	70	200	-	10
Sweden................	580	-	330	20	20	-	30
Switzerland.............	1,680	-	480	30	200	-	950
Turkey.................	4,835	-	3,700	-	250	-	825
United Kingdom..........	3,200	-	3,200	-	(X)	-	-
West Germany [3].........	3,930	-	2,800	290	310	-	(X)
Yugoslavia..............	785	675	100	-	-	-	-
Latin America [1]..........	13,310	8,060	1,870	775	225	-	485
Argentina...............	580	-	50	30	-	-	230
Chile..................	590	-	5	170	20	-	20
Colombia...............	470	-	130	-	30	-	-
Cuba..................	6,550	6,500	-	-	-	-	-
Ecuador................	180	-	60	20	60	-	-
Peru..................	705	160	40	240	-	-	30
Venezuela..............	740	-	310	110	90	-	-
Middle East [1]..............	78,750	19,565	14,225	7,275	16,875	7,465	1,100
Egypt..................	4,235	625	2,600	360	20	120	20
Iran...................	8,815	2,100	-	100	260	2,600	70
Iraq...................	16,265	7,400	5	2,700	20	1,700	70
Israel..................	5,040	-	5,000	-	-	-	40
Jordan.................	1,100	390	300	80	70	20	10
Kuwait.................	1,180	240	150	60	90	-	-
Saudi Arabia............	29,740	390	5,100	2,400	16,300	3,000	525
Syria..................	5,955	5,500	-	-	-	5	-
Yemen (Sanaa)...........	1,595	1,500	20	-	-	-	5
North America............	11,165	-	775	775	3,200	30	1,100
Canada................	855	-	775	-	-	-	-
United States...........	10,310	-	(X)	775	3,200	30	1,100

- Nil or negligible ($2.5 million or less).   X Not applicable.   [1] Includes countries not shown separately.   [2] Estimates of the Soviet Union's arms exports in value terms in this and the previous three editions are revised and substantially larger than in earlier editions.   [3] Unified Germany as of 1991 is shown under West Germany; data for East Germany are for the period 1987-1990.

Source: U.S. Arms Control and Disarmament Agency, *World Military Expenditures and Arms Transfers*, annual.

No. 547. Arms Delivered, by Selected Supplier and Major Weapon Type: 1987-91

[The suppliers included are the five largest single exporters of major weapons in terms of magnitude of deliveries as well as other countries of the two major alliances; excluded are Albania, Bulgaria, Greece, Malta, Spain, Turkey, and Yugoslavia]

TYPE OF WEAPON	Total [1]	United States [2]	France	United Kingdom	China: Mainland
Land armaments: Tanks	6,626	586	80	-	440
Anti-air artillery [3]	2,092	2	-	-	570
Field artillery [4]	7,707	652	185	35	1,995
Armored personnel carriers	10,762	922	240	95	520
Naval craft: Major surface combatants [5]	61	-	3	6	3
Other surface combatants [6]	313	13	28	14	33
Submarines	20	-	-	-	-
Missile attack boats	8	-	-	-	4
Aircraft: Combat aircraft (supersonic)	1,453	408	95	65	180
Combat aircraft (subsonic)	240	55	-	75	15
Other aircraft [7]	1,116	196	30	45	65
Helicopters	1,240	145	165	15	-
Missiles (surface-to-air)	15,746	2,026	300	570	395

- Represents $2.5 million or less.   [1] Includes other countries not shown separately.   [2] United States data are by fiscal years, while other suppliers' data are by calendar years.   [3] Includes weapons over 23 millimeters.   [4] Includes mobile rocket launchers mortars, and recoilless rifles over 100 millimeters.   [5] Includes aircraft carriers, cruisers, destroyers, destroyer and frigates.   [6] Includes motor torpedo boats, subchasers, and minesweepers.   [7] Includes reconnaissance aircraft, trainers, transports, and utility aircraft.

Source: U.S. Arms Control and Disarmament Agency, *World Military Expenditures and Arms Transfers*, annual.

No. 548. Estimates of Total Dollar Costs of American Wars

[In millions of dollars, except percent. Service-connected veterans' benefits estimated at 40 percent of total veterans benefits, except as noted]

ITEM	World War II	Vietnam Conflict	Korean Conflict	World War I	Civil War: Union	Civil War: Con-fed-eracy	Spanish Amer-ican War	Amer-ican Revolu-tion	War of 1812	Mexi-can War
Original incremental, direct costs: [1]										
Current dollars	360,000	140,600	50,000	32,700	2,300	1,000	270	100-140	89	82
Constant (1967) dollars	816,300	148,800	69,300	100,000	8,500	3,700	1,100	400-680	170	300
Percent 1 year's GNP	188	14	15	43	74	123	2	104	14	4
Service-connected benefits to 1992 [2]	107,500	35,400	22,700	19,630	3,290	-	2,111	28	20	26
Interest, pmts. on war loans [3]	(4)	(4)	(4)	11,000	1,200	(4)	60	20	14	10
Current cost to 1992 [5]	468,000	176,000	73,000	63,000	6,790	(4)	2,441	170	120	120

- Represents zero.   [1] Figures are rounded and taken from Claudia D. Goldin, *Encyclopedia of American Economic History*, p. 938.   [2] Total cost to Oct. 1, 1992. For World War I and later wars, benefits are actual service-connected figures from *Annual Report of Veterans Administration*. For earlier wars, service-connected benefits are estimated at 40 percent of total, the approximate ratio of service-connected to total benefits since World War I.   [3] Total cost to 1992. Interest payments are a very rough approximation based on the percentage of the original costs of each war financed by money creation and debt, the difference between the level of public debt at the beginning of the war and at its end, and the approximate time required to pay off the war debts.   [4] Unknown.   [5] Figures are rounded estimates.

Source: Originally presented in U.S. Congress, Joint Economic Committee, *The Military Budget and National Economic Priorities*, part 1, 91st Congress, 1st session (statement of James L. Clayton); subsequently revised and updated by James L. Clayton, University of Utah, Salt Lake City, Utah.

No. 549. U.S. Military Sales and Assistance to Foreign Governments: 1950 to 1992

[In millions of dollars, except as indicated. For fiscal year ending in year shown; see text, section 9. Department of Defense (DOD) sales deliveries cover deliveries against DOD sales orders sales orders authorized under Arms Export Control Act, as well as earlier and applicable legislation. For details regarding individual programs, see source]

ITEM	1950-84 [1]	1985	1986	1987	1988	1989	1990	1991	1992
Military sales agreements	133,306	10,403	6,302	6,254	11,395	10,486	13,735	22,726	14,984
Weapons and ammunition	58,469	3,384	2,121	1,780	4,971	4,353	5,407	6,273	7,525
Support equipment [2]	18,792	1,703	631	752	973	904	1,625	5,092	1,066
Spare parts and mods	28,431	2,312	1,499	1,569	2,970	2,333	2,617	5,187	2,650
Support services	27,614	3,004	2,051	2,153	2,481	2,896	4,086	6,174	3,743
Military constr. sales agrmts	15,154	958	69	130	210	79	551	743	188
Military sales deliveries [3]	97,591	8,431	7,810	11,142	9,202	7,333	7,787	9,176	10,017
Military sales financing	39,553	4,921	4,916	4,053	4,049	4,273	4,813	4,707	4,275
Military assistance programs [4]	55,685	812	834	958	697	535	137	177	116
Military assist. program delivery [5]	54,497	76	75	78	55	51	26	142	130
IMET program/deliveries [5]	2,142	54	51	54	45	46	44	46	45
Students trained (1,000)	525	7	6	6	6	5	5	5	4

[1] Includes transition quarter, July-September 1976.   [2] Includes aircraft, ships, support vehicles, communications equipment, and other supplies.   [3] Includes military construction sales deliveries.   [4] Also includes Military Assistance Service Funded (MASF) program data, section 506(a) drawdown authority, and MAP Merger Funds.   [5] Includes Military Assistance Service Funded (MASF) program data and section 506(a) drawdown authority.

Source: U.S. Defense Security Assistance Agency, *Foreign Military Sales, Foreign Military Construction Sales, and Military Assistance Facts*, annual; and unpublished data.

No. 550. U.S. Military Sales Deliveries to Foreign Governments, by Country: 1950 to 1992

[In millions of dollars. For fiscal years ending in year shown; see text, section 9. Represents Department of Defense military sales]

COUNTRY	1950-1984 [1]	1985	1986	1987	1988	1989	1990	1991	1992 Total	1992 Percent distribution
Total [2]	97,591	8,431	7,810	11,142	9,202	7,333	7,787	9,176	10,017	100.0
Australia	2,806	514	399	599	850	384	267	206	160	1.6
Belgium	1,658	119	28	27	222	153	178	184	45	0.5
Canada	1,837	73	113	127	212	148	103	112	110	1.1
China: Taiwan	2,628	339	244	370	485	348	529	557	827	8.3
Denmark	994	47	24	62	149	93	38	55	46	0.5
Egypt	2,910	594	617	962	498	322	447	579	1,129	11.3
El Salvador	129	114	108	79	93	92	87	58	65	0.7
France	464	45	143	99	37	36	109	32	35	0.4
Germany	7,800	222	206	315	382	633	359	480	503	5.0
Greece	1,844	93	73	79	129	138	114	127	175	1.8
Indonesia	265	18	13	23	32	35	192	18	21	0.2
Israel	8,295	475	164	1,294	751	230	151	239	697	7.0
Italy	882	54	66	71	62	64	61	69	56	0.6
Japan	1,894	387	151	237	212	169	221	324	447	4.5
Jordan	1,292	122	63	50	55	60	44	23	20	0.2
Kuwait	790	34	69	58	41	60	52	112	253	2.5
Morocco	636	49	37	43	74	33	41	20	39	0.4
Netherlands	2,380	339	256	417	327	391	381	371	301	3.0
Norway	1,459	30	43	83	117	96	122	82	60	0.6
Pakistan	1,232	317	128	134	139	175	431	-	-	-
Philippines	202	16	37	32	69	72	62	98	96	1.0
Portugal	67	97	27	26	15	32	83	46	51	0.5
Saudi Arabia	27,245	2,265	2,773	3,398	1,330	976	1,154	3,109	2,697	26.9
Singapore	335	22	135	143	191	38	47	64	25	0.3
South Korea	2,580	258	343	343	328	320	294	217	298	3.0
Spain	1,025	92	262	822	637	687	423	156	135	1.4
Sudan	192	25	27	26	24	30	-	-	-	-
Thailand	1,181	117	116	95	291	212	176	180	105	1.1
Tunisia	205	155	26	44	20	25	33	27	20	0.2
Turkey	1,437	390	282	279	702	619	720	707	771	7.7
United Kingdom	4,025	386	363	205	180	131	205	245	157	1.6
Venezuela	427	194	65	50	27	13	20	23	16	0.2

- Represents or rounds to zero.   [1] Includes transactions for the transition quarter, July-September 1976.   [2] Includes countries not shown.

Source: U.S. Defense Security Assistance Agency, Foreign Military Sales, Foreign Military Construction Sales, and Military Assistance Facts, annual.

No. 551. Summary of Active and Reserve Military Personnel and Forces: 1989 to 1995

ITEM	1989	1994	1995, est.	ITEM	1989	1994	1995, est.
Military personnel (1,000):				Navy aircraft carrier	-	-	1
Active	2,130	1,611	1,526	Navy ships	26	16	17
Guard and Reserve	1,171	1,025	979	Marine divisions	1	1	1
Active Forces:				Marine air wings	1	1	1
Army divisions	18	12	12	Air Force tactical wings	12	9	8
Navy aircraft carriers	16	12	11	Nuclear Deterrent:			
Navy air wings	13	11	10	Intercontinental Ballistic Missiles	1,000	642	550
Navy combatants & attack subs.	287	196	198	Ballistic missile submarines	34	15	15
Marine divisions and air wings	3	3	3	Missiles	608	352	360
Air Force tactical wings	25	13	13	Bombers	268	152	107
Reserve Forces:				Mobility Forces:			
Army combat brigades	56	48	46	Strategic airlift aircraft	367	356	365
Navy air wings	2	1	1	Sealift ships [1]	163	174	178

- Represents or rounds to zero.   [1] Includes ships in the Ready Reserve Force funded.

Source: U.S. Office of Management and Budget, Budget of the United States Government, annual.

No. 552. Military Installations in the United States: 1993
[Represents bases with active-duty populations of 300 or more. Excludes the Coast Guard]

STATE AND BRANCH	Active duty personnel	Family members	Civilians	STATE AND BRANCH	Active duty personnel	Family members	Civilians
United States	1,430,820	1,686,328	724,657	Michigan	4,566	8,109	2,491
Alabama	18,377	33,235	28,034	Air Force	4,566	8,109	2,491
Army	11,750	25,735	22,788	Minnesota	-	-	-
Navy	1,105	NA	125	Mississippi	13,849	23,113	8,760
Air Force	5,522	7,500	5,121	Navy	6,900	5,700	3,100
Alaska	20,802	28,631	7,005	Air Force	6,949	17,413	5,660
Army	9,900	12,575	2,810	Missouri	12,903	12,141	2,260
Navy	1,266	650	257	Army	9,603	8,241	1,856
Air Force	9,636	15,406	3,938	Air Force	3,300	3,900	404
Arizona	23,751	39,911	9,850	Montana	4,611	7,158	527
Army	5,682	4,760	5,597	Air Force	4,611	7,158	527
Marine Corps	5,293	4,706	1,160	Nebraska	11,000	18,500	1,400
Air Force	12,776	30,445	3,093	Air Force	11,000	18,500	1,400
Arkansas	5,920	7,664	1,549	Nevada	7,605	19,800	2,031
Air Force	5,920	7,664	1,549	Navy	1,000	1,800	1,000
California	233,137	144,597	118,201	Air Force	6,605	18,000	1,031
Army	11,136	9,615	6,760	New Hampshire.....	1,104	1,350	5,600
Navy	127,858	43,238	51,926	Navy	1,104	1,350	5,600
Marine Corps	61,900	43,486	22,141	New Jersey	8,998	12,414	16,104
Air Force	32,243	48,258	37,374	Army	3,501	6,414	10,504
Colorado	34,681	49,243	14,243	Navy	997	-	3,400
Army	17,433	37,232	4,887	Air Force	4,500	6,000	2,200
Air Force	17,248	12,011	9,356	New Mexico	16,186	21,307	23,579
Connecticut	11,000	22,500	1,800	Army	993	1,724	7,808
Navy	11,000	22,500	1,800	Air Force	15,193	19,583	15,771
Delaware	4,348	6,001	2,362	New York	28,075	28,508	5,705
Air Force	4,348	6,001	2,362	Army	17,136	14,000	2,200
District of Columbia ..	11,561	3,555	11,182	Navy	4,200	5,000	340
Army	5,200	50	5,200	Air Force	6,739	9,508	3,165
Navy	2,000	-	4,550	North Carolina.....	104,529	170,588	20,944
Marine Corps	1,200	5	40	Army	40,000	76,000	9,000
Air Force	3,161	3,500	1,392	Marine Corps	54,833	81,576	10,407
Florida	91,164	113,626	35,878	Air Force	9,696	13,012	1,537
Navy	61,897	60,659	25,308	North Dakota	9,389	6,744	1,042
Air Force	29,267	52,967	10,570	Air Force	9,389	6,744	1,042
Georgia	81,391	101,017	43,109	Ohio	9,578	18,308	18,000
Army	65,739	80,416	21,814	Air Force	9,578	18,308	18,000
Navy	6,000	8,350	5,150	Oklahoma	29,290	37,642	7,046
Marine Corps	1,000	2,000	3,000	Army	16,485	31,997	6,250
Air Force	8,652	10,251	13,145	Air Force	12,805	5,645	796
Hawaii	57,030	52,996	26,623	Oregon	-	-	-
Army	18,277	17,600	4,653	Pennsylvania	5,233	6,963	9,380
Navy	22,078	21,065	15,243	Army	1,133	1,663	1,180
Marine Corps	11,870	6,724	2,713	Navy	4,100	5,300	8,200
Air Force	4,805	7,607	4,014	Rhode Island	4,866	4,000	4,085
Idaho	4,563	5,669	483	Navy	4,866	4,000	4,085
Navy	1,200	1,000	NA	South Carolina	43,770	85,820	18,640
Air Force	3,363	4,669	483	Army	5,388	11,691	2,226
Illinois	23,114	27,366	15,924	Navy	22,551	45,526	11,720
Army	2,120	3,560	8,390	Marine Corps	5,651	9,286	1,646
Navy	14,361	14,200	3,987	Air Force	10,180	19,317	3,048
Air Force	6,633	9,606	3,547	South Dakota	5,711	10,000	714
Indiana	3,700	4,909	6,068	Air Force	5,711	10,000	714
Army	2,700	3,000	5,790	Tennessee	8,441	2,536	3,021
Air Force	1,000	1,909	278	Navy	8,441	2,536	3,021
Iowa	-	-	-	Texas	107,505	171,386	63,947
Kansas	21,208	29,241	6,596	Army	72,564	124,014	27,085
Army	18,200	22,200	6,200	Navy	6,569	12,800	6,285
Air Force	3,008	7,041	396	Air Force	28,372	34,572	30,577
Kentucky	34,600	41,194	8,462	Utah	5,000	9,200	11,000
Army	34,600	41,194	8,462	Air Force	5,000	9,200	11,000
Louisiana	21,594	27,369	9,125	Vermont	-	-	-
Army	11,408	18,474	4,952	Virginia	182,945	187,801	84,672
Navy	4,286	1,295	2,973	Army	23,555	26,039	22,519
Air Force	5,900	7,600	1,200	Navy	148,690	152,512	61,026
Maine	6,169	7,517	2,120	Marine Corps	10,700	9,250	1,127
Navy	3,142	3,350	921	Air Force	9,000	12,000	3,000
Air Force	3,027	4,167	1,199	Washington	51,063	24,600	5,500
Maryland	36,207	40,027	52,295	Army	15,500	24,600	5,500
Army	16,290	21,639	42,275	Navy	26,252	16,270	24,210
Navy	9,908	8,400	6,820	Air Force	9,311	13,175	3,237
Air Force	10,009	9,988	3,200	West Virginia	-	-	-
Massachusetts	6,486	6,348	4,750	Wisconsin	300	724	1,900
Army	3,328	4,388	2,271	Army	300	724	1,900
Navy	600	NA	250	Wyoming	3,500	5,000	650
Air Force	2,558	1,960	2,229	Air Force	3,500	5,000	650

- Represents zero.

Source: Army Times Publishing Co. Springfield, VA 22159, Guide to Military Installations in the U.S. November 1, 1993 (copyright).

National Defense and Veterans Affairs

No. 553. Department of Defense Manpower: 1950 to 1993

[In thousands. As of end of fiscal year; see text, section 9. Includes National Guard, Reserve, and retired regular personnel on extended or continuous active duty. Excludes Coast Guard. Other officer candidates are included under enlisted personnel. See also *Historical Statistics, Colonial Times to 1970*, series Y 904-916]

YEAR	Total [1][2]	ARMY			NAVY [3]			MARINE CORPS			AIR FORCE		
		Total [2]	Offi-cers	Enlist-ed	Total [2]	Offi-cers	Enlist-ed	Total [2]	Offi-cers	Enlist-ed	Total [2]	Offi-cers	Enlist-ed
1950	1,459	593	73	519	381	45	333	74	7	67	411	57	354
1955	2,935	1,109	122	986	661	75	583	205	18	187	960	137	823
1960	2,475	873	101	770	617	70	545	171	16	154	815	130	683
1961	2,483	859	100	757	626	70	552	177	16	161	821	129	690
1962	2,806	1,066	116	949	664	75	585	191	17	174	884	135	746
1963	2,699	976	108	866	664	76	584	190	17	173	869	134	733
1964	2,686	973	111	861	666	76	585	190	17	173	857	133	721
1965	2,654	969	112	855	670	78	588	190	17	173	825	132	690
1966	3,092	1,200	118	1,080	743	80	659	262	21	241	887	131	753
1967	3,375	1,442	144	1,297	750	82	664	285	24	262	897	135	759
1968	3,546	1,570	166	1,402	764	85	674	307	25	283	905	140	762
1969	3,458	1,512	173	1,337	774	85	684	310	26	284	862	135	723
1970	3,065	1,323	167	1,153	691	81	606	260	25	235	791	130	657
1971	2,713	1,124	149	972	622	75	542	212	22	191	755	126	625
1972	2,322	811	121	687	587	73	511	198	20	178	726	122	600
1973	2,252	801	116	682	564	71	490	196	19	177	691	115	572
1974	2,162	783	106	674	546	67	475	189	19	170	644	110	529
1975	2,128	784	103	678	535	66	466	196	19	177	613	105	503
1976	2,082	779	99	678	525	64	458	192	19	174	585	100	481
1977	2,075	782	98	680	530	63	462	192	19	173	571	96	470
1978	2,062	772	98	670	530	63	463	191	18	172	570	95	470
1979	2,027	759	97	657	523	62	457	185	18	167	559	96	459
1980	2,051	777	99	674	527	63	460	188	18	170	558	98	456
1981	2,083	781	102	675	540	65	470	191	18	172	570	99	467
1982	2,109	780	103	673	553	67	481	192	19	173	583	102	476
1983	2,123	780	106	669	558	68	485	194	20	174	592	105	483
1984	2,138	780	108	668	565	69	491	196	20	176	597	106	486
1985	2,151	781	110	667	571	71	495	198	20	178	602	108	489
1986	2,169	781	110	667	581	72	504	199	20	179	608	109	495
1987	2,174	781	108	668	587	72	510	200	20	179	607	107	495
1988	2,138	772	107	660	593	72	516	197	20	177	576	105	467
1989	2,130	770	107	658	593	72	516	197	20	177	571	104	463
1990	2,044	732	104	624	579	72	503	197	20	177	535	100	431
1991	1,986	711	104	603	570	71	495	194	20	174	510	97	409
1992	1,807	610	95	511	542	69	468	185	19	165	470	90	376
1993	1,705	572	88	480	510	66	439	178	18	160	444	84	356

[1] Beginning 1980, excludes Navy Reserve personnel on active duty for Training and Administration of Reserves (TARS). From 1969, the full-time Guard and Reserve. [2] Includes Cadets. [3] Prior to 1980, includes Navy Reserve personnel on active duty for Training and Administration of Reserves (TARS).

Source: U.S. Dept. of Defense, *Selected Manpower Statistics*, annual.

No. 554. Military Personnel on Active Duty, by Location: 1970 to 1993

[In thousands. 1970 as of Dec. 31; thereafter, as of end of fiscal year; see text, section 9

ITEM	1970	1980	1985	1986	1987	1988	1989	1990	1991	1992	1993, prel.
Total	3,065	2,051	2,151	2,169	2,174	2,138	2,130	2,044	1,986	1,807	1,705
Shore-based [1]	2,798	1,840	1,920	1,929	1,928	1,891	1,884	1,794	1,743	1,589	1,505
Afloat [2]	268	211	231	240	246	248	246	252	243	218	200
United States [3]	2,033	1,562	1,636	1,644	1,650	1,598	1,620	1,437	1,539	1,463	1,397
Foreign countries	1,033	488	516	526	524	541	510	609	448	344	308

[1] Includes Navy personnel temporarily on shore. [2] Includes Marine Corps. [3] Includes outlying areas.

Source: U.S. Dept. of Defense, *Selected Manpower Statistics*, annual.

No. 555. Military Personnel on Active Duty in Foreign Countries: 1991

[As of end of fiscal year]

COUNTRY	1991	COUNTRY	1991	COUNTRY	1991
Total	447,572	E. Asia and Pacific [1]	104,781	Saudi Arabia	14,617
Ashore	396,014	Australia	707	United Arab Emirates	39
Afloat	51,558	China	33	Afloat	17,266
Western Europe [1]	284,939	Hong Kong	31	Western Hemisphere [1]	19,456
Austria	32	Indonesia	40	Antigua	74
Denmark	64	Japan	44,566	Bahamas, The	44
France	81	New Zealand	58	Bermuda	1,178
Germany	203,423	Philippines	7,761	Brazil	46
Greece	1,375	Rep. of Korea	40,062	Canada	513
Greenland	163	Singapore	68	Colombia	43
Iceland	3,209	Thailand	111	Costa Rica	12
Italy	13,389	Afloat	11,300	Cuba (Guantanamo)	2,323
Netherlands	2,635	Africa, Near East,		El Salvador	96
Norway	225	and South Asia [1]	35,335	Honduras	1,005
Portugal	2,031	Bahrain	255	Mexico	28
Spain	6,166	Egypt	1,135	Panama	10,568
Switzerland	29	India	29	Peru	31
Turkey	6,343	Israel	438	Venezuela	34
U.S.S.R.	56	Kenya	28	Afloat	3,234
United Kingdom	23,442	Morocco	40	Antarctica	61
Afloat	19,758	Pakistan	31		

[1] Includes areas not shown separately.

Source: U.S. Department of Defense, *Selected Manpower Statistics,* annual.

No. 556. Coast Guard Personnel on Active Duty: 1970 to 1993

[As of end of fiscal year; see text, section 9]

YEAR	Total	Officers	Cadets	Enlisted	YEAR	Total	Officers	Cadets	Enlisted
1970	37,689	5,512	653	31,524	1986	37,284	6,577	754	29,953
1975	36,788	5,630	1,177	29,981	1987	38,576	6,644	859	31,073
1979	38,559	6,340	806	31,413	1988	37,723	6,530	887	30,306
1980	39,381	6,463	877	32,041	1989	37,474	6,611	869	29,994
1981	39,760	6,519	981	32,260	1990	36,939	6,876	927	29,136
1982	38,248	6,431	902	30,915	1991	38,377	7,192	900	30,285
1983	39,708	6,535	811	32,362	1992	39,388	7,507	919	30,962
1984	38,705	6,790	759	31,156	1993	39,234	7,628	907	30,699
1985	38,595	6,775	733	31,087					

Source: U.S. Dept. of Transportation, *Annual Report of the Secretary of Transportation.*

No. 557. Vietnam Conflict—U.S. Military Forces in Vietnam and Combat Area Casualties: 1957 to 1992

[Military forces as of Dec. 31. All U.S. forces withdrawn by Jan. 27, 1973]

ITEM	Unit	1957-1992 total [1]	1957-1964	1965	1966	1967	1968	1969	1970	1971	1972	1973-1989
Military forces [2]	1,000	(X)	[3]23.3	184.3	385.3	485.6	536.1	475.2	234.6	156.8	24.2	-
Battle deaths [4]	Number	47,366	279	1,432	5,047	9,463	14,623	9,426	4,230	1,376	361	1,118
Killed	Number	38,506	197	1,124	4,142	7,525	12,624	8,117	3,486	1,082	205	-
Died of wounds	Number	5,224	10	111	579	1,598	979	1,168	555	160	28	22
Died while missing [5]	Number	3,636	72	197	326	401	959	141	189	134	128	1,068

- Represents zero.   X Not applicable.   [1] Number in this column indicates 11 more deaths than a tally of the number by time period, due to revisions. The Cambodia area includes North and South Vietnam, Cambodia, Thailand, Laos, and China. [2] Source: U.S. Dept. of Defense, *Selected Manpower Statistics,* annual.   [3] For 1964 only.   [4] Casualties from enemy action. Deaths exclude 10,799 servicemen who died in accidents, from disease, or other causes.   [5] Includes servicemen who died while captured.

Source: Except as indicated, National Archives and Records Administration, unpublished data from Combat Area Casualties database, as of November 1992.

No. 558. Armed Forces Personnel—Summary of Major Conflicts

[For Revolutionary War, number of personnel serving not known, but estimates range from 184,000 to 250,000; for War of 1812, 286,730 served; for Mexican War, 78,718 served. Dates of the major conflicts may differ from those specified in various laws providing benefits for veterans. See table 557 for data on Vietnam conflict. See also *Historical Statistics, Colonial Times to 1970*, series Y 856-903]

ITEM	Unit	Civil War [1]	Spanish-American War	World War I	World War II	Korean conflict	Vietnam conflict
Personnel serving [2].	1,000 . . .	2,213	307	4,735	[3]16,113	[4]5,720	[5]8,744
Average duration of service	Months. .	20	8	12	33	19	23
Service abroad: Personnel serving.	Percent. .	(NA)	[6]29	53	73	[7]56	(NA)
Average duration [8]	Months. .	(NA)	1.5	6	16	13	(NA)
Casualties: [9] Battle deaths [2].	1,000 . . .	140	(Z)	53	292	34	[10]47
Wounds not mortal [2]	1,000 . . .	282	2	204	671	103	[10]153
Draftees: Classified.	1,000 . . .	777	(X)	24,234	36,677	9,123	[5]75,717
Examined.	1,000 . . .	522	(X)	3,764	17,955	3,685	[5]8,611
Rejected	1,000 . . .	160	(X)	803	6,420	1,189	[5]3,880
Inducted	1,000 . . .	46	(X)	2,820	10,022	1,560	[5]1,759

NA Not available. X Not applicable. Z Fewer than 500. [1] Union forces only. Estimates of the number serving in Confederate forces range from 600,000 to 1.5 million. [2] Source: U.S. Department of Defense, *Selected Manpower Statistics*, annual. [3] Covers Dec. 1, 1941, to Dec. 31, 1946. [4] Covers June 25, 1950, to July 27, 1953. [5] Covers Aug. 4, 1964, to Jan. 27, 1973. [6] Army and Marines only. [7] Excludes Navy. Covers July 1950 through Jan. 1955. Far East area only. [8] During hostilities only. [9] For periods covered, see footnotes 3, 4, and 5. [10] Covers Jan. 1, 1961, to Jan. 27, 1973. Includes known military service personnel who have died from combat related wounds.

Source: Except as noted, the President's Commission on Veterans' Pensions, Veterans' *Benefits in the United States*, vol. I, 1956; and U.S. Dept. of Defense, unpublished data.

No. 559. Enlisted Military Personnel Accessions: 1980 to 1990

[In thousands. For years ending Sept. 30]

BRANCH OF SERVICE	1980	1985	1989	1990	BRANCH OF SERVICE	1980	1985	1989	1990
Total	582	529	530	461	**Marine Corps**	58	57	49	48
Army	265	201	224	182	First enlistments	42	36	33	33
First enlistments	163	117	112	85	Reenlistments	15	19	16	14
Reenlistments	97	84	111	97					
Navy	127	139	155	135	**Air Force**	132	133	102	104
First enlistments	75	67	74	62	First enlistments	76	68	44	37
Reenlistments	36	50	62	59	Reenlistments	56	64	58	68

Source: U.S. Dept. of Defense, *Selected Manpower Statistics*, annual.

No. 560. Military Personnel on Active Duty and Monthly Basic Pay: 1990 to 1993

[Personnel as of Sept. 30; basic pay as of January, except as noted]

RANK/GRADE	PERSONNEL (1,000)				MONTHLY BASIC PAY (dollars)			
	1990	1991	1992	1993	1990	1991	1992	1993
Total [1]	2,043.7	1,985.6	1,807.2	1,705.1	(X)	(X)	(X)	(X)
Recruit—E-1.	97.6	74.6	83.2	75.4	684	710	752	769
Private—E-2.	140.3	125.8	110.9	114.1	803	838	873	909
Pvt. 1st class—E-3	280.1	275.6	233.5	214.6	871	900	937	976
Corporal—E-4.	427.8	426.1	383.5	352.2	1,014	1,066	1,107	1,154
Sergeant—E-5	361.5	355.5	305.1	295.6	1,245	1,297	1,356	1,409
Staff Sgt.—E-6	239.1	238.9	227.4	214.6	1,480	1,563	1,634	1,711
Sgt. 1st class—E-7	134.1	134.2	130.5	124.7	1,784	1,866	1,946	2,028
Master Sgt.—E-8.	38.0	36.1	33.2	31.6	2,117	2,210	2,302	2,406
Sgt. Major—E-9	15.3	14.8	13.5	12.8	2,583	2,682	2,794	2,933
Warrant Officer—W-1.	3.2	2.8	2.2	2.4	1,686	1,747	1,809	1,849
Chief Warrant—W-4.	3.0	3.0	2.7	2.4	2,943	3,085	3,214	3,383
2d Lt.—0-1.	31.9	27.3	25.8	25.0	1,485	1,562	1,627	1,697
1st Lt.—0-2	37.9	37.6	33.5	29.7	2,056	2,135	2,220	2,311
Captain—0-3	106.6	106.1	100.2	93.0	2,618	2,727	2,829	2,924
Major—0-4.	53.2	53.1	50.4	48.0	3,196	3,321	3,453	3,588
Lt. Colonel—0-5	32.3	32.2	30.9	29.5	3,894	4,041	4,197	4,359
Colonel—0-6	14.0	13.7	13.2	12.5	4,758	4,942	5,137	5,371
Brig. General—0-7.	0.5	0.5	0.5	0.4	5,751	5,987	6,238	6,469
Major General—0-8.	0.4	0.3	0.3	0.3	[2]6,516	6,783	7,068	7,330
Lt. General—0-9	0.1	0.1	0.1	0.1	[2]6,516	7,482	7,788	8,075
General—0-10	(Z)	(Z)	(Z)	(Z)	[2]6,516	8,441	8,733	9,017

X Not applicable. Z Fewer than 50. [1] Includes cadets and midshipmen and warrant officers, W-2 and W-3. [2] Statutory limitation.

Source: U.S. Dept. of Defense, *Selected Manpower Statistics*, annual, and Office of the Comptroller, unpublished data.

No. 561. Military Reserve Personnel: 1970 to 1993

[In thousands. As of end of fiscal year; see text, section 9. Excludes U.S. Coast Guard Reserve. The ready reserve includes selected reservists who are intended to assist active forces in a war and the individual ready reserve who, in a major war, would be used to fill out active and reserve units and later would be a source of combat replacements; a portion of the ready reserve serves in an active status. The standby reserve cannot be called to active duty unless the Congress gives its explicit approval. The retired reserve represents a low potential for mobilization]

RESERVE STATUS AND BRANCH OF SERVICE	1970	1975	1980	1984	1985	1986	1987	1988	1989	1990	1991	1992	1993
Total reserves	3,639	1,836	1,349	1,534	1,610	1,653	1,657	1,677	1,661	1,670	1,786	1,883	1,867
Ready reserve	2,574	1,471	1,263	1,491	1,566	1,612	1,620	1,642	1,631	1,641	1,758	1,857	1,841
Standby reserve	492	365	86	44	44	41	38	344	29	29	28	26	26
Retired reserve	573	(NA)	338	379	760	390	377	1,792	1,823	1,845	1,879	1,772	1,821
Army	2,221	1,168	804	996	1,045	1,067	1,064	1,070	1,062	1,050	1,124	607	569
Navy	808	273	207	201	214	228	238	244	248	252	271	537	506
Marine Corp	(NA)	124	94	92	92	93	88	87	82	83	96	185	179
Air Force	610	271	243	246	259	266	268	275	270	286	295	467	441

NA Not available.

Source: U.S. Dept. of Defense, *Official Guard and Reserve Manpower Strengths and Statistics*, quarterly.

No. 562. Ready Reserve Personnel Profile—Race, and Sex: 1989 to 1993

ITEM	RACE					PERCENT DISTRIBUTION			
	Total	White	Black	Asian	American Indian	White	Black	Asian	American Indian
1989, total	1,676,105	1,282,456	372,765	13,237	7,647	76.5	22.2	0.8	0.5
1990, total	1,558,867	1,269,278	271,470	14,608	3,511	81.4	17.4	0.9	0.2
1991, total	1,154,515	906,748	190,214	12,711	5,652	78.5	16.5	1.1	0.5
1992, total [1]	1,114,905	725,963	172,770	11,479	4,842	65.1	15.5	1.0	0.4
1993, total [1]	1,057,676	829,797	173,444	13,350	4,785	78.5	16.4	1.3	0.5
Male	915,151	735,197	133,289	11,631	4,014	80.3	14.6	1.3	0.4
Officers	138,988	126,245	7,823	1,506	274	90.8	5.6	1.1	0.2
Enlisted	776,163	608,952	125,466	10,125	3,740	78.5	16.2	1.3	0.5
Female	142,493	94,593	40,154	1,719	771	66.4	28.2	1.2	(Z)
Officers	24,811	19,689	3,784	277	56	79.4	15.3	1.1	0.2
Enlisted	117,682	74,904	36,370	1,442	715	63.6	30.9	1.2	0.6

Z Represents or rounds to zero. [1] Includes unknown sex.

Source: U.S. Dept. of Defense, *Official Guard and Reserve Manpower Strengths and Statistics*, annual.

No. 563. Military Reserve Costs: 1980 to 1992

[In millions of dollars. As of end of fiscal year; see text, section 9. Army and Air Force data include National Guard]

TYPE OF COST	1980	1985	1986	1987	1988	1989	1990	1991	1992
Total	7,969	19,414	19,640	18,947	19,234	20,630	22,081	22,373	22,251
Operations and maintenance	3,526	5,734	5,770	6,168	6,670	6,765	6,757	9,034	9,656
Personnel	2,456	7,703	8,500	8,382	8,837	9,129	9,106	7,469	7,714
Procurement	1,459	5,009	4,383	3,316	2,533	3,520	4,914	4,480	3,533
Active-duty support	408	566	616	601	610	611	638	700	731
Construction	120	402	371	480	584	605	666	690	617

Source: U.S. Dept. of Defense, unpublished data.

No. 564. National Guard—Summary: 1980 to 1992

[As of end of fiscal year; see text, section 9. Includes Puerto Rico]

ITEM	Unit	1980	1985	1986	1987	1988	1989	1990	1991	1992
Army National Guard: Units	Number	3,379	4,353	5,712	6,125	5,982	5,715	4,055	6,470	6,727
Personnel [1]	1,000	368	438	446	452	455	457	444	446	427
Funds obligated [2]	Bil. dol.	1.8	4.4	4.8	5.0	5.3	5.4	5.2	5.4	6.3
Value of equipment	Bil. dol.	7.6	18.8	19.7	22.3	27.4	30.1	29.0	29.0	29.0
Air National Guard: Units	Number	1,054	1,184	1,229	1,281	1,272	1,339	1,339	1,450	1,425
Personnel [1]	1,000	96	109	113	115	115	116	118	115	119
Funds obligated [2]	Bil. dol.	1.7	2.8	2.8	2.9	3.1	3.2	3.2	1.2	1.9
Value of equipment (est.) [3]	Bil. dol.	5.2	21.4	26.1	23.7	25.7	27.5	26.4	27.1	38.3

[1] Officers and enlisted personnel. [2] Federal funds; includes personnel, operations, maintenance, and military construction. [3] Beginning 1985, increase due to repricing of aircraft to current year dollars to reflect true replacement value.

Source: National Guard Bureau, *Annual Review of the Chief, National Guard Bureau*; and unpublished data.

No. 565. Wartime Veterans—States: 1993

[As of end of fiscal year; see text, section 9. Data were estimated starting with veteran's place of residence as of April 1, 1980, based on 1980 Census of Population data, extended to later years on the basis of estimates of veteran interstate migration, separations from the Armed Forces, and mortality; not directly comparable with earlier estimates previously published by the VA. Excludes 423,000 veterans whose only active-duty military service occurred since September 8, 1980, and who failed to satisfy the minimum service requirement. Also excludes a small indeterminate number of National Guard personnel or reservists who incurred service-connected disabilities while on an initial tour of active duty for training only]

STATE	All veterans [1]	War veterans [1]	World War I	World War II	Korean conflict	Vietnam era [2]	Persian Gulf War
U.S......	26,654,700	20,575,800	25,100	8,124,600	4,656,100	8,251,700	1,021,300
AL.........	432,400	337,900	300	128,600	83,000	135,300	26,000
AK.........	65,900	46,000	(Z)	8,600	8,200	30,500	1,800
AZ.........	461,800	357,100	500	149,600	83,700	145,700	15,600
AR.........	262,300	207,800	200	86,200	47,100	79,300	15,100
CA.........	2,886,300	2,182,800	2,700	832,200	518,700	947,000	84,000
CO.........	394,300	301,800	300	97,600	68,800	149,200	15,200
CT.........	352,600	271,400	400	115,200	61,800	98,800	8,500
DE.........	79,900	60,500	(Z)	23,700	13,400	24,300	3,800
DC.........	52,900	41,300	100	17,300	11,000	14,800	3,100
FL.........	1,719,000	1,357,300	2,300	660,800	316,900	477,000	55,600
GA	689,400	510,800	400	163,700	113,100	246,200	34,400
HI	117,000	86,500	100	29,300	21,000	42,100	4,000
ID	114,200	88,400	100	34,100	19,000	36,600	5,300
IL	1,108,900	868,600	1,100	348,700	190,600	322,300	40,100
IN	605,600	463,500	600	175,600	102,000	181,200	23,800
IA	299,800	240,900	500	94,800	54,200	87,400	13,300
KS.........	270,000	213,500	400	83,900	47,100	86,600	10,000
KY.........	373,800	293,700	300	112,800	64,200	116,900	17,700
LA	389,700	308,200	400	118,800	66,100	120,300	26,100
ME	156,100	118,800	200	44,500	26,300	50,300	6,500
MD	541,800	399,000	300	145,200	91,400	174,900	19,100
MA	617,600	479,500	700	211,500	110,400	166,700	15,100
MI	972,700	748,400	700	284,700	156,200	293,500	39,100
MN	473,700	364,800	600	131,600	80,100	150,900	15,600
MS	236,700	186,800	200	75,300	44,400	67,600	17,400
MO	598,200	467,300	600	182,700	107,800	182,600	23,800
MT	98,200	77,800	100	29,400	17,100	31,700	4,700
NE.........	172,100	135,700	300	51,100	32,800	52,400	7,500
NV.........	184,800	138,900	100	50,900	36,600	62,500	4,200
NH	137,800	103,400	100	36,900	23,600	45,900	4,400
NJ.........	770,600	603,300	700	268,100	141,300	201,400	19,200
NM	174,300	134,100	200	49,800	30,400	60,600	7,300
NY.........	1,602,100	1,243,300	1,600	536,200	277,000	416,200	56,300
NC	716,600	544,400	400	202,700	123,000	231,200	31,700
ND	61,400	48,400	100	17,000	10,900	19,200	3,100
OH	1,218,800	948,300	1,100	378,300	201,900	357,300	48,900
OK	360,000	286,500	400	111,500	67,000	119,600	14,700
OR	376,600	293,600	500	115,200	61,000	124,100	13,000
PA.........	1,402,300	1,104,200	1,300	490,400	240,000	374,500	47,900
RI	112,900	88,700	100	40,300	20,200	31,000	3,400
SC.........	381,800	289,700	200	105,100	66,200	129,600	20,700
SD.........	75,600	59,600	100	22,100	15,000	21,600	4,400
TN.........	524,100	404,800	500	150,300	90,200	169,700	24,000
TX.........	1,676,300	1,287,700	1,200	464,400	289,500	586,800	74,000
UT.........	142,300	113,600	200	44,000	25,400	44,900	7,100
VT.........	63,300	47,300	100	17,200	10,500	19,800	2,400
VA	715,300	531,300	500	182,400	128,100	261,800	27,700
WA	640,200	483,700	700	168,000	109,400	232,400	22,100
WV	204,800	165,300	200	68,700	37,400	59,500	9,500
WI	519,800	399,600	700	154,100	86,800	152,400	21,000
WY	50,300	39,800	(Z)	13,600	8,500	17,900	2,300

Z Less than 50.   [1] Veterans who served in more than one wartime period are counted only once. "All Veterans" includes Vietnam era (no prior wartime service), Korean conflict (no prior wartime service), World War II, post Vietnam era, Persian Gulf War era, and other.   [2] Excludes reservists.

Source: U.S. Dept. of Veterans Affairs, Management Sciences Service (008B2), *Annual Report of the Secretary of Veterans Affairs*, Fiscal Year 1993.

No. 566. Veterans Living in the United States and Puerto Rico, by Age and by Service: 1993

[In thousands, except as indicated. As of Sept. 30. Estimated. Excludes 453,000 veterans whose only active duty military service occurred since Sept. 30, 1980. See headnote, table 565. See *Historical Statistics, Colonial Times to 1970*, series Y 943-956, for all veterans]

AGE	Total veterans	WARTIME VETERANS						Peace-time veterans
		Total [1]	Persian Gulf	Vietnam era	Korean conflict	World War II	World War I	
All ages	26,789	20,675	1,027	8,287	4,692	8,150	25	6,114
Under 30 years old . . .	1,334	588	588	-	-	-	-	746
30-34 years old	1,367	184	157	27	-	-	-	1,183
35-39 years old	1,644	789	89	723	-	-	-	855
40-44 years old	2,503	2,320	104	2,296	-	-	-	183
45-49 years old	3,431	3,211	60	3,194	-	-	-	220
50-54 years old	2,465	1,230	21	1,205	18	-	-	1,236
55-59 years old	2,557	1,234	6	349	994	-	-	1,323
60-64 years old	3,104	2,851	2	252	2,601	297	-	253
65 years old and over .	8,384	8,269	(Z)	239	1,079	7,853	25	115

- Represents zero. Z Less than 500. [1] Veterans who served in more than one wartime period are counted only once.

Source: U.S. Dept. of Veterans Affairs, Office of Information Management and Statistics, *Veteran Population*, annual.

No. 567. Disabled Veterans Receiving Compensation: 1970 to 1993

[In thousands, except as indicated. As of end of fiscal year; see text, section 9. Represents veterans receiving compensation for service-connected disabilities. Totally disabled refers to veterans with any disability, mental or physical, deemed to be total and permanent which prevents the individual from maintaining a livelihood and are rated for disability at 100 percent]

MILITARY SERVICE	1970	1980	1985	1987	1988	1989	1990	1991	1992	1993
Disabled, all periods [1]	2,092	2,274	2,240	2,212	2,199	2,192	2,184	2,179	2,181	2,198
Peace-time	185	262	352	382	398	421	444	468	500	471
World War I [1]	85	30	12	8	6	5	3	3	2	1
World War II.	1,416	1,193	1,049	982	947	912	876	841	805	769
Korea	239	236	223	218	215	212	209	205	202	198
Vietnam.	167	553	604	623	633	643	652	662	671	682
Persian Gulf.	(X)	(X)	(X)	(X)	(X)	(X)	(X)	(X)	(X)	76
Totally disabled, all periods [1].	124	121	136	132	131	131	131	131	132	135
Peace-time	16	20	26	26	26	26	27	27	28	28
World War I [1]	11	3	1	1	1	(Z)	(Z)	(Z)	(Z)	(Z)
World War II.	63	51	54	49	47	45	43	41	39	37
Korea	16	16	17	16	16	16	16	16	15	15
Vietnam.	18	31	38	40	41	43	44	46	49	52
Persian Gulf.	(X)	(X)	(X)	(X)	(X)	(X)	(X)	(X)	(X)	2
Compensation (mil. dol.) . . .	2,393	6,104	8,270	8,424	8,722	8,937	9,284	9,612	10,031	10,389

X Not applicable. Z Less than 500. [1] Includes Spanish-American War and Mexican Border service, not shown separately.

Source: U.S. Dept. of Veterans Affairs, *Annual Report of the Secretary of Veterans Affairs*; and unpublished data.

No. 568. Veterans Benefits—Expenditures, by Program: 1970 to 1992

[In millions of dollars. For fiscal years ending in year shown; see text, section 9. Beginning with fiscal year 1988, data are for outlays]

PROGRAM	1970	1980	1985	1987	1988	1989	1990	1991	1992
Total	10,201	23,187	29,359	31,812	29,271	30,041	28,998	31,214	33,894
Medical programs	1,765	6,042	9,227	9,876	10,283	10,745	11,582	12,472	13,815
Construction	75	300	557	589	649	703	661	608	639
General operating expenses	243	605	765	765	781	766	811	884	914
Compensation and pension	5,252	11,044	14,037	14,241	14,710	15,009	14,674	16,080	16,282
Vocational rehabilitation and education	1,032	2,350	1,164	847	717	589	452	541	695
All other [1]	1,835	2,846	3,609	5,494	2,130	2,228	818	629	1,549

[1] Includes insurance and indemnities, and miscellaneous funds and expenditures. (Excludes expenditures from personal funds of patients.)

Source: U.S. Dept. of Veterans Affairs, *Trend Data, Fiscal Years 1968-1992*.

No. 569. Veterans Compensation and Pension Benefits—Number on Rolls and Average Payment, by Period of Service and Status: 1980 to 1993

[As of Sept. 30. Living refers to veterans receiving compensation for disability incurred or aggravated while on active duty and war veterans receiving pension and benefits for nonservice connected disabilities. Deceased refers to deceased veterans whose dependents were receiving pensions and compensation benefits. See also *Historical Statistics, Colonial Times to 1970*, series Y 998-999]

PERIOD OF SERVICE AND VETERAN STATUS	VETERANS ON ROLLS (1,000)					AVERAGE PAYMENT (annual basis) [1] (dol.)				
	1980	1990	1991	1992	1993	1980	1985	1990	1991	1992
Total	4,646	3,584	3,509	3,428	3,374	2,370	3,505	4,335	4,552	4,712
Living veterans..............	3,195	2,746	2,709	2,674	2,660	2,600	3,666	4,320	4,491	4,611
Service connected	2,273	2,184	2,179	2,181	2,198	2,669	3,692	4,250	4,406	4,593
Nonservice connected	922	562	530	493	462	2,428	3,581	4,591	4,837	4,689
Deceased veterans...........	1,451	838	800	754	714	1,863	3,066	4,382	4,761	5,071
Service connected	358	320	318	314	310	3,801	5,836	7,349	7,815	8,244
Nonservice connected	1,093	518	482	440	404	1,228	1,809	2,548	2,748	2,810
Prior to World War I..........	14	4	4	3	3	1,432	1,855	2,616	2,921	3,073
Living..................	(Z)	(Z)	(Z)	(Z)	(Z)	2,634	4,436	10,502	10,441	8,176
World War I...............	692	198	172	146	124	1,683	2,461	3,435	3,674	3,754
Living..................	198	18	13	9	6	2,669	4,439	6,922	7,239	6,476
World War II...............	2,5(X)	1,723	1,638	1,543	1,453	2,307	3,317	4,052	4,238	4,334
Living..................	1,849	1,294	1,226	1,153	1,083	2,462	3,460	4,123	4,278	4,333
Korean conflict [2]...........	446	390	388	387	377	2,691	4,114	5,105	5,330	5,462
Living..................	317	305	304	300	296	2,977	4,260	5,103	5,288	5,390
Peacetime................	312	495	518	550	518	3,080	3,973	4,132	4,216	4,292
Living..................	262	444	468	500	471	2,828	3,589	3,709	3,789	3,866
Vietnam era [3].............	662	774	789	804	821	2,795	4,021	4,945	5,242	5,551
Living..................	569	685	698	711	727	2,709	3,849	4,671	4,936	5,234
Persian Gulf War [4]........	(X)	(X)	(X)	(Z)	78	(X)	(X)	(X)	(X)	1,673
Living..................	(X)	(X)	(X)	(Z)	76	(X)	(X)	(X)	(X)	1,386

X Not applicable.   Z Fewer than 500.   [1] Averages calculated by multiplying average monthly payment by 12.   [2] Service during period June 27, 1950, to Jan. 31, 1955.   [3] Service from Aug. 5, 1964, to May 7, 1975.   [4] Service from August 2, 1990 to the present.

Source: U.S. Dept. of Veterans Affairs, *Annual Report of the Secretary of Veterans Affairs;* and unpublished data.

No. 570. Veterans Administration Health Care Summary: 1980 to 1993

[For years ending Sept. 30]

ITEM	Unit	1980	1990	1993	ITEM	Unit	1980	1990	1993
Facilities operating:					Obligations [2]	Mil. dol.	6,215	11,827	15,079
Hospitals	Number	172	172	171	Prescriptions dispensed .	Millions	36.7	58.6	59.1
Domiciliaries	Number	16	32	37	Laboratory..........	Millions	215	188	(NA)
Outpatient clinics.....	Number	226	339	353	Inpatients treated [3] ...	1,000..	1,359	1,113	1,043
Nursing home units ..	Number	92	126	128	Average daily	1,000..	105	88	84
Employment [1]	1,000..	194	199	210	Outpatient visits	Millions	18.0	22.6	24.2

NA Not available.   [1] Net full-time equivalent.   [2] 1980, cost basis; thereafter, obligation basis.   [3] Based on the number of discharges and deaths during the fiscal year, plus the number on the rolls (bed occupants and patients on authorized leave of absence) at the end of the fiscal year. Excludes interhospital transfers.

Source: U.S. Dept. of Veterans Affairs, *Annual Report of the Secretary of Veterans Affairs; Directory of VA Facilities,* biennial; and unpublished data.

No. 571. Veterans Assistance: Education and Training—1980 to 1993

[In thousands, except where indicated. For fiscal years ending in year shown; see text, section 9. Represents persons in training during year]

PROGRAM	1980	1985	1988	1989	1990	1991	1992	1993
Veteran Education Assistance [1]	1,107	402	203	164	102	143	195	246
Institutions of higher education	842	326	176	144	94	132	177	223
Resident schools other than college....	149	54	19	13	6	9	14	18
Correspondence schools	42	7	4	3	1	1	3	3
On-the-job training................	74	15	4	3	1	1	1	2
Children's Educational Assistance.......	82.6	55.3	40.9	38.7	37.5	37.3	37.2	36.4
Institutions of higher education	75.5	50.0	37.8	36.2	35.3	35.2	35.1	34.3
Schools other than college..........	6.5	5.2	3.0	2.4	2.1	2.1	2.1	2.0
Special restorative training	0.1	(Z)	(Z)	(Z)	(Z)	(Z)	(Z)	(Z)
On-the-job training................	0.5	0.2	0.1	0.1	0.1	(Z)	(Z)	(Z)
Spouses, Widows/Widowers Educational Assistance Program	13.0	6.6	5.0	4.6	4.5	4.4	4.5	4.4
Institutions of higher education	10.8	5.7	4.3	4.1	4.1	4.0	4.0	4.0
Schools other than college..........	2.2	1.0	0.6	0.5	0.4	0.4	0.4	0.4
Disabled Veterans Vocational Rehab.	25.5	26.9	24.7	27.0	27.8	35.9	36.8	40.7
Guaranteed and insured loans, (1,000)....	297.4	178.9	234.7	189.7	196.6	181.2	266.0	383.3
Guaranteed and insured loans, (mil. dol.) . .	14,815	11,452	17,302	14,416	15,779	15,454	22,960	34,635
Guaranty and insurance (mil. dol.).......	6,370	4,363	6,172	5,211	5,561	5,299	7,819	11,601

Z Fewer than 50.   [1] Data for 1980-89 are for Post-Korean Conflict GI Bill (Title 38 USC Chapter 34). Data for 1990-93 are for the Active Duty Montgomery GI Bill (Title 38 USC Chapter 30).

Source: U.S. Dept. of Veterans Affairs, *Annual Report of the Secretary of Veterans Affairs;* and unpublished data.

Social Insurance and Human Services

This section presents data related to governmental expenditures for social welfare; governmental programs for old-age, survivors, disability, and health insurance (OASDHI); governmental employee retirement; private pension plans; government unemployment and temporary disability insurance; Federal supplemental security income payments and aid to the needy; child and other welfare services; and Federal food programs. Also included here are selected data on workers' compensation, vocational rehabilitation; child support; child care; charity contributions; and philanthropic trusts and foundations.

The principal sources for these data are the Department of Health and Human Services' (HHS) quarterly *Social Security Bulletin* and the *Annual Statistical Supplement to the Social Security Bulletin* which present current data on many of the programs. Current data on employment security are published annually in the Department of Labor's *Unemployment Insurance, Financial Data.* Statistics on aid to families with dependent children (AFDC) are presented in the U.S. Administration for Children and Families' annual publication, *Quarterly Public Assistance Statistics.*

Social insurance under the Social Security Act.—Programs established by the Social Security Act provide protection against wage loss resulting from retirement, prolonged disability, death, or unemployment, and protection against the cost of medical care during old age and disability. The Federal OASDHI program provides monthly benefits to retired or disabled insured workers and their dependents and to survivors of insured workers. To be eligible, a worker must have had a specified period of employment in which OASDHI taxes were paid. A worker becomes eligible for full benefits at age 65, although reduced benefits may be obtained up to 3 years earlier; the worker's spouse is under the same limitations. Survivor benefits are payable to dependents of deceased insured

In Brief

In 1992, households below poverty level receiving:

Medicaid	*48%*
Food stamps	*44%*

Social Security beneficiaries, 1992:

Total	*42 million*
Retired workers	*26 million*

workers. Disability benefits are payable to an insured worker under age 65 with a prolonged disability and to the disabled worker's dependents on the same basis as dependents of retired workers. Disability benefits are provided at age 50 to the disabled widow or widower of a deceased worker who was fully insured at the time of death. Disabled children, aged 18 or older, of retired, disabled, or deceased workers are also eligible for benefits. A lump-sum benefit is generally payable on the death of an insured worker to a spouse or minor children. For information on the Medicare program, see section 3.

Retirement, survivors, disability, and hospital insurance benefits are funded by a payroll tax on annual earnings (up to a maximum of earnings set by law) of workers, employers, and the self-employed. The maximum taxable earnings are adjusted annually to reflect increasing wage levels (see table 580). Effective January 1994, there is no dollar limit on wages and self-employment income subject to hospital insurance tax. Tax receipts and benefit payments are administered through Federal trust funds. Special benefits for uninsured persons; hospital benefits for persons 65 and over with specified amounts of Social Security coverage less than that required for cash benefit eligibility; and that part of the cost of supplementary medical insurance not financed by contributions from participants are financed from Federal general revenues.

Unemployment insurance is presently administered by the U.S. Employment and Training Administration and each State's employment security agency. By agreement with the U.S. Secretary of Labor, State agencies also administer unemployment compensation for eligible ex-service members and Federal employees, unemployment assistance under the Disaster Relief Act of 1970, and workers assistance and relocation allowances under the Trade Act. Under State unemployment insurance laws, benefits related to the individual's past earnings are paid to unemployed eligible workers. State laws vary concerning the length of time benefits are paid and their amount. In most States, benefits are payable for 26 weeks and, during periods of high unemployment, extended benefits are payable under a Federal-State program to those who have exhausted their regular State benefits. The basic benefit can vary among States by over 100 percent. Some States also supplement the basic benefit with allowances for dependents.

Unemployment insurance is funded by a Federal unemployment tax levied on the taxable payrolls of most employers. Taxable payroll under the Federal Act and 14 State laws is the first $7,000 in wages paid each worker during a year. Thirty-nine States have taxable payrolls above $7,000. Employers are allowed a percentage credit of taxable payroll for contributions paid to States under State unemployment insurance laws. The remaining percent of the Federal tax finances administrative costs, the Federal share of extended benefits, and advances to States. About 97 percent of wage and salary workers are covered by unemployment insurance.

Retirement Programs for Government Employees.—The Civil Service Retirement System (CSRS) and the Federal Employees' Retirement System (FERS) are the two major programs providing age and service, disability, and survivor annuities for Federal civilian employees. In general, employees hired after December 31, 1983, are covered under FERS and the social security program (OASDHI), and employees on staff prior to that date are members of CSRS and are covered under Medicare. CSRS employees were offered the option of

transferring to FERS during 1987. There are separate retirement systems for the uniformed services (supplementing OASDHI) and for certain special groups of Federal employees. State and local government employees are covered for the most part by State and local retirement systems similar to the Federal civil service retirement system. In many jurisdictions these benefits supplement OASDHI coverage.

Workers' compensation.—All States provide protection against work-connected injuries and deaths, although some States exclude certain workers (e.g., domestic help). Federal laws cover Federal employees, private employees in the District of Columbia, and longshoremen and harbor workers. In addition, the Social Security Administration and the Department of Labor administer "black lung" benefits programs for coal miners disabled by pneumoconiosis and for specified dependents and survivors. Specified occupational diseases are compensable to some extent. In most States, benefits are related to the worker's salary. The benefits may or may not be augmented by dependents' allowances or automatically adjusted to prevailing wage levels.

Public aid.—State-administered public assistance programs (Aid to Families with Dependent Children (AFDC), emergency assistance and general assistance) and the Federal Supplemental Security Income (SSI) program administered by the Social Security Administration provide benefits to persons who qualify. AFDC and emergency assistance are in part federally funded while the costs of general assistance are met entirely with State and local funds. The SSI program replaced Federal grants for aid to the aged, blind, and disabled in the 50 States and the District of Columbia in 1974. Residents of the Northern Mariana Islands became eligible in 1978. Federal grants continue for aid to the aged, blind, and disabled in Guam, Puerto Rico, and the Virgin Islands. The SSI program provides a minimum income for the aged, blind, and disabled and establishes uniform national basic eligibility requirements and payment standards. Most States supplement the basic SSI payment.

Federal Food Stamp program.—Under the Food Stamp program, single persons and those living in households meeting nationwide standards for income and assets may receive coupons redeemable for food at most retail food stores. The monthly amount of coupons a unit receives is determined by household size and income. Households without income receive the determined monthly cost of a nutritionally adequate diet for their household size. This amount is updated to account for food price increases. Households with income receive the difference between the amount of a nutritionally adequate diet and 30 percent of their income, after certain allowable deductions.

To qualify for the program, a household must have less than $2,000 in disposable assets ($3,000 if one member is aged 60 or older), gross income below 130 percent of the official poverty guidelines, and net income below 100 percent of the poverty guidelines. Households with a person aged 60 or older or a disabled person receiving SSI, Social Security, or veterans' disability benefits may have gross income exceeding 130 percent of the poverty guidelines. All households must meet these requirements, even those receiving other Federal assistance payments. Households are certified for varying lengths of time, depending on their income sources and individual circumstances.

Health and welfare services.—Programs providing health and welfare services are aided through Federal grants to States for child welfare services, vocational rehabilitation, activities for the aged, maternal and child health services, maternity and infant care projects, comprehensive health services, and a variety of public health activities. For information about the Medicaid program, see section 3.

Noncash benefits.—The Bureau of the Census annually collects data on the characteristics of recipients of noncash (in-kind) benefits to supplement the collection of annual money income data in the Current Population Survey (see text, section 1 and section 15). Noncash benefits are those benefits received in a form other than money which serve to enhance or improve the economic well-being of the recipient. As for money income, the data for noncash benefits are for the calendar year prior to the date of the interview. The major categories of noncash benefits covered are public transfers (e.g. food stamps, school lunch, public housing, and Medicaid) and employer or union-provided benefits to employees.

Statistical reliability.—For discussion of statistical collection, estimation, and sampling procedures and measures of statistical reliability applicable to HHS and Census Bureau data, see Appendix III.

Historical statistics.—Tabular headnotes provide cross-references, where applicable, to *Historical Statistics of the United States, Colonial Times to 1970.* See Appendix IV.

No. 572. Social Welfare Expenditures Under Public Programs: 1970 to 1991

[In billions of dollars, except percent. For fiscal years ending in year shown; see text, section 9. Represents outlays from trust funds (mostly social insurance funds built up by earmarked contributions from insured persons, their employers, or both) and budgetary outlays from general revenues. Includes administrative expenditures, capital outlay, and some expenditures and payments outside the United States. See table 573 for program detail. See *Historical Statistics, Colonial Times to 1970*, series H 1-47, for related but not comparable data]

YEAR	Total	Social insur-ance	Public aid	Health and medical programs [1]	Vet-erans pro-grams	Educa-tion	Housing	Other social welfare	All health and medical care [2]
Total:									
1970	146	55	16	10	9	51	1	4	25
1975	289	123	41	17	17	81	3	7	51
1980	493	230	73	27	21	121	7	14	100
1985	732	370	98	39	27	172	13	14	171
1988	887	434	120	53	29	219	17	15	218
1989	957	468	129	57	30	239	18	17	240
1990	1,050	513	146	64	31	258	19	18	275
1991	1,165	564	180	69	33	277	22	20	315
Federal:									
1970	77	45	10	5	9	6	1	2	16
1975	167	100	27	8	17	9	3	4	33
1980	303	191	49	13	21	13	6	9	69
1985	451	310	63	18	27	14	11	8	122
1988	527	360	76	23	29	17	14	8	149
1989	565	387	82	24	30	19	15	8	165
1990	617	422	93	27	30	18	17	9	190
1991	676	454	113	30	32	19	19	10	213
State and local:									
1970	68	9	7	5	(Z)	45	(Z)	2	9
1975	122	23	14	9	(Z)	72	1	3	18
1980	190	39	23	14	(Z)	108	1	5	31
1985	281	59	35	21	(Z)	158	2	6	49
1988	360	74	44	30	(Z)	202	3	7	68
1989	392	81	47	33	(Z)	220	3	8	75
1990	434	92	53	37	(Z)	240	3	9	85
1991	489	111	67	40	1	258	3	10	103
Percent of total expenditures, by type:									
1970	100	38	11	7	6	35	1	3	17
1980	100	47	15	6	4	25	1	3	20
1985	100	51	13	5	4	24	2	2	24
1989	100	49	13	6	3	25	2	2	25
1990	100	49	14	6	3	25	2	2	26
1991	100	48	15	6	3	24	2	2	27
Percent Federal:									
1970	53	83	59	48	99	12	83	55	65
1980	62	83	68	47	99	11	91	65	69
1985	62	84	64	46	99	8	88	56	71
1989	59	83	63	43	99	8	84	51	69
1990	59	82	64	44	98	7	85	50	69
1991	58	80	63	43	98	7	87	50	67
Per capita (current dollars): [3]									
1970	698	262	79	46	43	244	3	20	120
1980	2,126	990	314	118	92	523	30	59	434
1985	3,009	1,516	405	161	111	708	52	56	705
1989	3,804	1,857	512	228	118	951	72	66	958
1990	4,129	2,017	575	251	120	1,018	77	71	1,084
1991	4,542	2,196	705	271	126	1,083	84	77	1,234
Per capita (constant (1991) dollars): [3] [4]									
1970	2,352	882	267	156	145	823	10	67	406
1980	3,571	1,662	528	198	155	879	50	99	728
1985	3,874	1,952	522	207	142	912	67	72	908
1989	4,173	2,037	562	250	129	1,043	79	73	1,050
1990	4,308	2,105	600	262	125	1,062	80	74	1,131
1991	4,542	2,196	705	271	126	1,083	84	77	1,234

Z Less than $500 million.   [1] Excludes program parts of social insurance, public aid, veterans, and other social welfare. [2] Combines "Health and medical programs" with medical services included in social insurance, public aid, veterans, vocational rehabilitation, and antipoverty programs.   [3] Excludes payments within foreign countries for education, veterans, OASDHI, and civil service retirement.   [4] Constant dollar figures are based on implicit price deflators for personal consumption expenditures published by U.S. Bureau of Economic Analysis in *Survey of Current Business*, August 1993.

Source: U.S. Social Security Administration, *Social Security Bulletin*, summer 1993; and unpublished data.

No. 573. Social Welfare Expenditures, by Source of Funds and Public Program: 1980 to 1991

[In millions of dollars. See headnote, table 572, and *Historical Statistics, Colonial Times to 1970*, series H 1-47, for related but not comparable data]

PROGRAM	FEDERAL				STATE AND LOCAL			
	1980	1985	1990	1991	1980	1985	1990	1991
Total.	303,167	450,791	616,535	676,406	189,547	281,460	433,621	488,740
Social insurance.	191,162	310,175	422,236	453,538	38,592	59,421	91,565	110,548
Old-age, survivors, disability, health. . . .	152,110	257,535	355,264	382,290	(X)	(X)	(X)	(X)
Health insurance (Medicare).	34,992	71,384	109,709	116,651	(X)	(X)	(X)	(X)
Public employee retirement [1].	26,983	40,504	53,519	56,884	12,507	22,540	36,851	40,391
Railroad employee retirement	4,769	6,276	7,230	7,532	(X)	(X)	(X)	(X)
Unemployment insurance and employment services [2]	4,408	2,604	3,096	3,613	13,919	15,740	16,878	27,700
Other railroad employee insurance [3] . . .	224	189	105	94	(X)	(X)	(X)	(X)
State temporary disability insurance [4] . .	(X)	(X)	(X)	(X)	1,377	1,944	3,224	3,879
Workers' compensation [5]	2,668	3,067	3,021	3,125	10,789	19,197	34,613	38,578
Hospital and medical benefits.	130	280	460	506	3,596	6,800	13,849	15,503
Public aid	49,394	63,480	92,858	113,235	23,309	34,882	53,019	67,176
Public assistance [6].	23,542	33,523	54,747	69,315	21,522	32,647	49,414	63,426
Medical assistance payments [7].	14,550	22,677	40,690	53,393	13,020	21,182	34,700	47,740
Social services.	1,757	2,057	2,065	2,117	586	686	688	706
Supplemental security income	6,440	9,605	13,625	15,896	1,787	2,235	3,605	3,751
Food stamps.	9,083	12,513	16,254	19,471	(X)	(X)	(X)	(X)
Other [8]	10,329	7,839	8,232	8,553	(X)	(X)	(X)	(X)
Health and medical programs	12,840	18,029	27,121	29,713	14,423	21,024	36,669	39,652
Hospital and medical care.	6,636	9,877	14,733	16,790	5,667	6,688	12,281	12,636
Civilian programs	2,438	2,455	3,447	4,139	5,667	6,688	12,281	12,636
Defense Department [9]	4,198	7,422	11,286	12,651	(X)	(X)	(X)	(X)
Maternal and child health programs	351	422	492	522	519	800	1,374	1,454
Medical research	4,428	5,992	9,172	9,793	496	899	1,390	1,494
Medical facilities construction.	210	339	410	-	1,450	1,336	1,485	1,625
Other.	1,215	1,399	2,314	2,608	6,291	11,301	20,139	22,443
Veterans programs	21,255	26,704	30,428	32,331	212	338	488	526
Pensions and compensation	11,306	14,333	15,793	16,284	(X)	(X)	(X)	(X)
Health and medical programs	6,204	9,493	12,004	13,222	(X)	(X)	(X)	(X)
Hospital and medical care	5,750	8,809	11,321	12,190	(X)	(X)	(X)	(X)
Hospital construction.	323	458	445	776	(X)	(X)	(X)	(X)
Medical and prosthetic research	131	227	238	256	(X)	(X)	(X)	(X)
Education.	2,401	1,171	523	570	(X)	(X)	(X)	(X)
Life insurance [10]	665	796	1,038	1,039	(X)	(X)	(X)	(X)
Welfare and other	679	912	1,070	1,217	212	338	488	526
Education [11]	13,452	13,796	18,374	19,062	107,597	158,251	240,011	258,063
Elementary and secondary [12].	7,430	7,278	9,944	12,018	79,720	113,419	189,333	203,819
Construction [13].	41	23	23	39	6,483	8,335	10,613	12,324
Higher	4,468	5,102	6,747	5,339	21,708	36,028	50,678	54,243
Construction [13]	42	32		31	1,486	2,314	3,953	3,950
Vocational and adult [13].	1,207	1,087	1,293	1,314	6,169	8,804	([12])	([12])
Housing	6,278	11,059	16,612	18,696	601	1,540	2,856	2,826
Other social welfare	8,786	7,549	8,905	9,831	4,813	6,004	9,012	9,949
Vocational rehabilitation	1,006	1,187	1,661	1,751	245	350	466	485
Medical services and research	237	275	415	439	56	85	116	121
Institutional care [14]	74	121	143	142	408	259	486	523
Child nutrition [15]	4,209	4,349	5,470	6,098	643	960	1,696	1,869
Child welfare [16]	57	200	253	274	743	(NA)	(NA)	(NA)
Special CSA and ACTION programs [17] . .	2,303	504	169	192	(X)	(X)	(X)	(X)
Welfare, not elsewhere classified [18] . . .	1,137	1,188	1,209	1,375	2,774	4,435	6,365	7,071

- Represents zero. NA Not available. X Not applicable. [1] Excludes refunds to those leaving service. Federal data include military retirement. [2] Includes compensation for Federal employees and ex-servicemen, trade readjustment and cash training allowance, and payments under extended, emergency, disaster, and special unemployment insurance programs. [3] Unemployment and temporary disability insurance. [4] Cash and medical benefits in five areas. Includes private plans where applicable. [5] Benefits paid by private insurance carriers, State funds, and self-insurers. Federal includes black lung benefit programs. [6] Includes payments under State general assistance programs and work incentive activities, not shown separately. [7] Medicaid payments and State and local general assistance medical payments. [8] Refugee assistance, surplus food for the needy, and work-experience training programs under the Comprehensive Employment and Training Act. Beginning 1985, includes low-income energy assistance program. [9] Includes medical care for military dependent families. [10] Excludes servicemen's group life insurance. [11] Federal expenditures include administrative costs (Department of Education) and research, not shown separately. [12] Beginning 1990, all State and local vocational education costs included with elementary-secondary. [13] Construction costs of vocational and adult education programs included under elementary-secondary expenditures. [14] Federal expenditures represent primarily surplus foods for nonprofit institutions. [15] Surplus food for schools and programs under National School Lunch and Child Nutrition Acts. [16] Represents primarily child welfare services under Title V of the Social Security Act. [17] Includes domestic volunteer programs under ACTION and community action and migrant workers programs under Community Services Administration. Beginning 1990, represents ACTION funds only. [18] Federal expenditures include administrative expenses of the Secretary of Health and Human Services; Indian welfare and guidance; and aging and juvenile delinquency activities. State and local include antipoverty and manpower programs, child care and adoption services, legal assistance, and other unspecified welfare services.

Source: U.S. Social Security Administration, *Social Security Bulletin*, summer 1993; and unpublished data.

No. 574. Social Welfare Expenditures Under Public Programs as Percent of GDP and Total Government Outlays: 1970 to 1991

[See headnote, table 572]

YEAR	TOTAL EXPENDITURES				FEDERAL				STATE AND LOCAL GOVERNMENT			
	Total (bil. dol.)	Percent change [1]	Percent of—		Total (bil. dol.)	Percent change [1]	Percent of—		Total (bil. dol.)	Percent change [1]	Percent of—	
			Total GDP [2]	Total govt. outlays			Total GDP [2]	Total Federal outlays			Total GDP [2]	Total State and local outlays
1970....	146	14.6	14.8	46.5	77	13.2	7.8	40.0	68	16.3	6.9	57.9
1975....	289	21.2	19.1	56.6	167	21.9	11.0	53.7	122	19.6	8.1	61.6
1980....	493	14.7	18.6	57.2	303	15.2	11.4	54.4	190	13.8	7.2	62.9
1985....	732	8.0	18.4	52.2	451	7.1	11.3	48.7	281	9.3	7.1	59.9
1989....	957	7.9	18.5	55.2	565	7.2	10.9	49.5	392	8.8	7.6	68.0
1990....	1,050	9.7	19.2	56.7	617	9.0	11.2	51.4	434	10.7	7.9	67.9
1991....	1,165	10.9	20.5	57.4	676	9.7	11.9	51.4	489	12.7	8.6	70.2

[1] Percent change from immediate prior year.   [2] Gross domestic product.

Source: U.S. Social Security Administration, *Social Security Bulletin*, summer 1993; and unpublished data.

No. 575. Private Expenditures for Social Welfare, by Type: 1980 to 1991

[In millions of dollars, except percent]

TYPE	1980	1985	1986	1987	1988	1989	1990	1991
Total expenditures	251,612	456,288	506,653	538,385	588,501	652,849	702,179	756,365
Percent of gross domestic product.	9.3	11.3	11.9	11.9	12.0	12.4	12.9	13.4
Health	145,000	248,000	265,200	286,100	318,900	351,000	390,000	421,800
Income maintenance.........	51,169	116,207	140,793	140,433	145,380	163,138	160,876	171,016
Private pension plan payments [1] [2] ...	37,560	98,450	122,209	120,442	124,546	140,911	137,739	146,737
Short-term sickness and disability [2] ...	6,280	8,026	8,046	8,896	9,636	9,869	10,362	10,615
Long-term disability [2] ...,.........	1,282	1,937	2,253	2,293	2,295	2,892	2,926	3,172
Life insurance and death [3] .,......	5,075	7,489	7,797	8,166	8,418	9,063	9,278	9,472
Supplemental unemployment [2]......	972	305	488	636	485	403	571	1,020
Education	32,667	53,167	57,574	64,423	71,003	79,245	85,974	92,095
Welfare and other services.........	22,776	38,914	43,086	47,429	53,218	59,466	65,329	71,454

[1] Covers benefits paid for solely by employers and all benefits of employment-related pension plans to which employee contributions are made. Excludes individual savings plans such as IRA's and Keogh plans. Pension plan benefits include monthly benefits and lump-sum distributions to retired and disabled employees and their dependents and to survivors of deceased employees. Also includes preretirement lump-sum distributions.   [2] Covers wage and salary workers in private industry.
[3] Covers all wage and salary workers.

Source: U.S. Social Security Administration, *Annual Statistical Supplement* to the *Social Security Bulletin*, annual.

No. 576. Public Income-Maintenance Programs—Cash Benefit Payments: 1980 to 1992

[Includes payments outside the United States and benefits to dependents, where applicable]

PROGRAM	PAYMENTS (bil. dol.)										PERCENT		
	1980	1984	1985	1986	1987	1988	1989	1990	1991	1992	1980	1990	1991
Total [1]	228.1	309.1	335.2	356.6	372.0	393.8	421.9	455.8	504.4	(NA)	100	100	100
Percent of personal income [2]	10.1	9.9	9.9	10.1	9.8	9.7	9.6	9.8	10.4	(NA)	(X)	(X)	(X)
OASDI [3] ....,......	120.3	175.5	186.1	196.1	204.7	216.4	229.6	245.6	265.6	281.7	53	54	53
Public employee retirement [4]	40.6	59.0	63.0	66.9	72.1	78.0	83.8	90.4	97.3	(NA)	18	20	19
Railroad retirement...........	4.9	6.1	6.3	6.4	6.5	6.7	6.9	7.2	7.5	7.3	2	2	1
Veterans' pensions, compensation....,........	11.4	13.8	14.1	14.3	14.3	14.7	15.3	15.8	16.3	16.5	5	3	3
Unemployment benefits [5].......	18.9	13.6	14.4	16.0	14.4	13.2	16.4	20.0	31.3	37.3	8	4	6
Temporary disability benefits	1.4	1.8	1.8	2.1	2.5	2.8	2.9	3.2	3.9	(NA)	1	1	1
Workers' compensation [6].......	9.7	13.3	22.3	24.7	27.1	30.3	33.8	37.6	41.7	(NA)	4	8	8
Public assistance	12.1	14.6	15.3	16.1	16.5	17.0	17.4	18.8	21.2	23.7	5	4	4
Supplemental Security Income ...	7.9	10.4	11.1	12.9	13.6	14.7	15.8	17.2	19.6	19.4	3	4	4

NA Not available.   X Not applicable.   [1] Includes lump sum death benefits, not shown separately. Lump sum death benefits for State and local government employee retirement systems are not available beginning 1987.   [2] For base data, see table 695.   [3] Old-age, survivors, and disability insurance under Federal Social Security Act; see text, section 12.   [4] Excludes refunds of contributions to employees who leave service.   [5] Beginning 1984, covers State unemployment insurance, Ex-Servicemen's Compensation Act and railroad unemployment insurance only.   [6] Includes black lung benefits.

Source: U.S. Social Security Administration, *Social Security Bulletin*, quarterly; and unpublished data.

No. 577. Cash and Noncash Benefits for Persons With Limited Income: 1990 and 1992

[For years ending September 30, except as noted. Programs covered provide cash, goods, or services to persons who make no payment and render no service in return. In case of job and training programs and some educational benefits, recipients must work or study for wages, training allowances, stipends, grants, or loans. Most of the programs base eligibility on individual, household, or family income, but some use group or area income tests; and a few offer help on the basis of presumed need]

| PROGRAM | AVERAGE MONTHLY RECIPIENTS (1,000) | | EXPENDITURES (mil. dol.) | | | | | |
| | | | Total | | Federal | | State and local | |
	1990	1992	1990	1992	1990	1992	1990	1992
Total [1]	(X)	(X)	210,176	289,880	151,478	207,566	58,698	82,314
Medical care [2]	(X)	(X)	86,144	134,032	50,190	78,529	35,954	55,503
Medicaid [3] [4]	25,253	30,776	72,492	118,067	41,103	67,827	31,389	50,240
Veterans [5] [6] [7]	585	580	6,624	7,838	6,624	7,838	-	-
General assistance [7]	(NA)	(NA)	4,212	4,850	-	-	4,212	4,850
Indian Health Services [8]	1,100	1,160	1,176	1,431	1,176	1,431	-	-
Maternal and child health services	(NA)	(NA)	907	1,059	554	646	353	413
Cash aid [2]	(X)	(X)	54,255	69,350	36,445	48,374	17,810	20,976
A.F.D.C. [4] [9]	11,465	13,754	21,200	24,923	11,507	13,569	9,693	11,354
Supplemental Security Income [4]	4,938	5,559	17,233	22,774	[10]13,607	[10]18,744	3,626	4,030
Earned income tax credit (refunded portion) [11]	37,836	39,909	5,303	9,553	5,303	9,553	-	-
Foster care	168	222	2,741	4,170	1,473	2,233	1,268	1,937
Pensions for needy veterans [12] [13]	1,106	969	3,954	3,667	3,954	3,667	-	-
General assistance [11]	1,205	1,205	2,924	3,340	-	-	2,924	3,340
Food benefits [2]	(X)	(X)	25,106	34,107	23,871	32,661	1,235	1,446
Food stamps [4] [14]	21,500	26,900	17,686	24,918	16,512	23,540	1,174	1,378
School lunch program [15] [16]	11,600	13,000	3,154	3,895	3,154	3,895	(NA)	(NA)
Women, infants and children [17]	4,500	5,400	2,126	2,600	2,126	2,600	-	-
School breakfast [15]	3,600	4,500	548	782	548	782	-	-
Nutrition program for elderly [6] [18]	3,540	3,349	575	659	514	591	61	68
Child and adult care food program [19]	842	1,019	447	624	447	624	-	-
Housing benefits [2]	(X)	(X)	17,548	20,535	17,548	20,535	-	-
Lower-income housing asst. (Sec. 8) [20]	2,500	2,797	10,577	12,307	10,577	12,307	-	-
Low-rent public housing [20]	1,405	1,409	3,918	5,008	3,918	5,008	(NA)	(NA)
Rural housing loans [21] [22]	26	26	1,311	1,468	1,311	1,468	-	-
Interest reduction payments [21]	531	510	630	652	630	652	-	-
Education aid [2]	(X)	(X)	14,390	16,037	13,761	15,423	629	614
Stafford loans [23]	4,496	5,135	5,648	5,683	5,648	5,683	-	-
Pell grants [23] [24]	3,214	4,259	4,484	5,374	4,484	5,374	-	-
Head Start	541	621	1,940	2,753	1,552	2,202	388	551
Services [2]	(X)	(X)	6,460	8,551	3,781	5,346	2,679	3,205
Social services (Title 20) [25]	(NA)	(NA)	5,346	5,419	2,762	2,800	2,584	2,619
Child care and development block grant [26]	(X)	570	(X)	825	(X)	825	(X)	-
Child care for AFDC recipients and ex-recipients [26]	(NA)	265	211	755	116	438	95	317
"At risk" child care (to avert AFDC eligibility)	(X)	(NA)	(X)	604	(X)	335	(X)	269
Jobs and training [2]	(X)	(X)	4,242	5,500	3,975	5,024	267	476
Training for disadvantaged adults and youth [27] [28] [29]	630	602	1,745	1,774	1,745	1,774	-	-
Summer youth employment program [28] [29] [30]	585	783	709	1,183	709	1,183	-	-
JOBS and WIN (for AFDC recipients) [31]	444	510	452	1,010	265	623	187	387
Job Corps [28] [29]	61	65	803	955	803	955	-	-
Energy assistance [2]	(X)	(X)	1,728	1,768	1,604	1,674	124	94
Low-income energy assistance [4] [32] [33]	5,800	6,200	1,567	1,594	1,443	1,500	124	94

- Represents zero. NA Not available. X Not applicable. [1] Includes State Legalization Impact Assistance Grants to offset State and local costs of welfare, health care, and education provided to legalized aliens. [2] Includes other programs not shown separately. [3] Recipient data represent unduplicated annual number. [4] Expenditures include administrative expenses. [5] Medical care for veterans with a non-service-connected disability. [6] Recipients are estimated number of inpatients. [7] Estimated expenditures. [8] Recipients data represent annual numbers. [9] Aid to Families with Dependent Children program. Excludes data for foster care and child support operations (cost and collections). [10] Excludes Federal sums spent for SSI (State supplements) to Indochinese refugees. [11] Estimated recipients. [12] Estimated recipients as of September. [13] Includes dependents and survivors. [14] Includes Puerto Rico's nutritional assistance program. [15] Free and reduced-price segments. [16] Includes estimate of commodity assistance. [17] Special supplemental food program for women, infants and children. [18] No income test required but preference given to those with greatest need. [19] Recipient data are numbers of children receiving free or reduced price meals and snacks in child care centers and estimates of children in family day care homes with incomes below 185 percent of poverty. Adult participants and funding are not included. [20] Recipient data represent units eligible for payment at end of year. [21] Recipient data represent total families or dwelling units during year. [22] Expenditure data represent amount of loans obligated. [23] Recipient data are total numbers for the school year ending in year shown. [24] Expenditure data are appropriations available for school year ending the fiscal year named. [25] Non-Federal expenditure data are rough estimates. [26] Recipient data are estimated number of children served. [27] Recipient data are average monthly enrollment for program year. [28] Programs represent specific titles under the Job Training and Partnership Act (JTPA). [29] Federal funds are appropriations. [30] Total participants (June-August). [31] Job opportunities and basic skills training program (JOBS) and work incentive (WIN) program. [32] Households served during the year with heating and winter crisis aid. [33] Federal funds include amounts transferred to other programs serving the needy. State spending includes funds received as "oil overcharge" settlements.

Source: Library of Congress, Congressional Research Service, "Cash and Noncash Benefits for Persons With Limited Income: Eligibility Rules, Recipient and Expenditure Data, FY 1990-92," Report 93-832 EPW and earlier reports.

No. 578. Households Receiving Means-Tested Noncash Benefits: 1980 to 1992

[In thousands, except percent. Households as of **March** of following year. Covers civilian noninstitutional population, including persons in the Armed Forces living off post or with their families on post. A means-tested benefit program requires that the household's income and/or assets fall below specified guidelines in order to qualify for benefits. The means-tested noncash benefits covered are food stamps, free or reduced-price school lunches, public or subsidized housing, and Medicaid. There are general trends toward under-estimation of noncash beneficiaries. Households are classified according to poverty status of family or nonfamily householder; for explanation of poverty level, see text, section 14. Based on Current Population Survey; see text, section 1, and Appendix III]

TYPE OF BENEFIT RECEIVED	1980	1985	1990	1991	1992			
					Total	Below poverty level		Above poverty level
						Number	Percent distribution	
Total households	82,368	88,458	94,312	95,669	96,391	13,376	100	83,015
Receiving at least one noncash benefit..	14,266	14,466	16,098	17,387	18,380	8,453	63	9,927
Not receiving cash public assistance ..	7,860	7,860	8,819	9,539	10,273	3,515	26	6,758
Receiving cash public assistance [1] ...	6,407	6,607	7,279	7,849	8,107	4,938	37	3,169
Total households receiving—								
Food stamps.................	6,769	6,779	7,163	7,839	8,518	5,877	44	2,641
School lunch.................	5,532	5,752	6,252	6,922	7,102	3,602	27	3,500
Public housing...............	2,777	3,799	4,339	4,511	4,478	2,616	20	1,862
Medicaid...................	8,287	8,178	10,321	11,458	12,300	6,455	48	5,845

[1] Households receiving money from Aid to Families with Dependent Children program, Supplemental Security Income program or other public assistance programs.

Source: U.S. Bureau of the Census, *Current Population Reports*, P60-155, and earlier reports; and unpublished data.

No. 579. Selected Social Insurance Programs—Estimated Payrolls of Covered Employment in Relation to Wages and Salaries: 1980 to 1991

[In billions of dollars, except percent. Data for Federal civilian and military personnel cover all areas. Gross amount before deduction of social insurance contributions. OASDHI: Old-age, survivors, disability, and health insurance programs under Social Security Act; see text, section 12. See also *Historical Statistics, Colonial Times to 1970*, series H 57-69]

PROGRAM	1980	1983	1984	1985	1986	1987	1988	1989	1990	1991
Total earnings [1]	1,553	1,867	2,073	2,232	2,377	2,573	2,767	2,934	3,110	3,180
All wages and salaries [1]...........	1,372	1,676	1,839	1,975	2,094	2,250	2,443	2,586	2,743	2,812
Civilian...................	1,342	1,634	1,794	1,928	2,044	2,198	2,390	2,531	2,685	2,751
Payrolls covered by—										
Retirement programs [2]	1,318	1,614	1,775	1,896	2,011	2,149	2,360	2,469	2,641	2,716
OASDHI [3][4]............	1,229	1,502	1,665	1,782	1,896	2,042	2,225	2,368	2,507	2,579
Railroad retirement [3]..........	13	12	13	13	12	12	12	12	12	12
Federal civil service...........	52	62	65	70	72	74	80	83	88	92
State and local government	123	153	162	175	190	195	210	225	239	254
Unemployment insurance [3] ...[5]...	1,303	1,583	1,739	1,870	1,983	2,046	2,205	2,336	2,479	2,537
Workers' compensation program [5] ..	1,136	1,382	1,516	1,618	1,725	1,845	1,997	2,115	2,250	2,300
Net earnings in self-employment covered by OASDHI.............	98	109	117	130	139	156	208	221	213	213
Percent of civilian payrolls covered by—										
OASDHI [3][6]................	92.6	92.6	92.9	92.4	92.8	92.9	93.1	93.6	93.4	93.7
Railroad retirement [3].........	1.0	0.7	0.7	0.7	0.6	0.5	0.5	0.5	0.4	0.4
Federal civil service retirement.....	3.9	3.8	3.7	3.6	3.5	3.4	3.3	3.3	3.3	3.3
State and local government retirement	9.2	9.4	9.0	9.1	9.3	9.2	8.8	8.9	8.9	9.2
Unemployment insurance [3] .....[6]..	97.1	96.9	97.0	97.0	97.0	97.0	93.1	92.3	92.3	92.2
Workers' compensation programs [5]..	84.6	84.6	84.5	83.9	84.4	84.0	83.6	83.6	83.9	83.6

[1] Data from U.S. Bureau of Economic Analysis. Earnings include self-employed; wages and salaries represent civilian and military pay in cash and in kind. [2] Adjusted for duplication in coverage by both OASDHI and State and local government retirement systems. [3] Taxable plus estimated nontaxable wages and salaries. [4] Includes Armed Forces in all areas. [5] Payrolls of employers insured with private carriers, State funds, or self-insured, and pay covered by Federal programs in all areas. [6] Percent computed after excluding Armed Forces payroll covered by OASDHI.

Source: U.S. Social Security Administration, *Annual Statistical Supplement to the Social Security Bulletin*; and unpublished data.

No. 580. Social Security—Covered Employment, Earnings, and Contribution Rates: 1970 to 1992

[Includes Puerto Rico, Virgin Islands, American Samoa, and Guam. Represents all reported employment. Data are estimated. OASDHI=Old-age, survivors, disability, and health insurance; SMI=Supplementary medical insurance. See also *Historical Statistics, Colonial Times to 1970*, series H 172-185]

ITEM	Unit	1970	1980	1985	1986	1987	1988	1989	1990	1991	1992
Workers with insured status [1]	Million	105.7	137.4	148.7	150.6	152.7	155.4	158.2	161.2	163.6	166.0
Male	Million	61.9	75.4	79.7	80.7	81.5	82.6	83.7	85.1	86.1	87.2
Female	Million	43.8	62.0	69.0	69.9	71.2	72.8	74.5	76.1	77.5	78.8
Under 25 years old	Million	17.7	25.5	22.3	21.9	21.3	21.3	21.3	21.3	21.2	21.0
25 to 34 years old	Million	22.3	34.9	39.9	40.0	40.6	41.0	41.4	41.5	41.5	41.2
35 to 44 years old	Million	19.0	22.4	28.5	29.8	31.2	32.3	33.5	34.9	36.2	37.2
45 to 54 years old	Million	19.0	18.6	19.0	19.3	19.8	20.5	21.4	22.1	22.8	23.9
55 to 59 years old	Million	7.8	9.2	9.1	9.0	8.9	8.8	8.7	8.7	8.7	8.8
60 to 64 years old	Million	6.3	7.9	8.7	8.8	8.7	8.7	8.6	8.7	8.7	8.7
65 to 69 years old	Million	5.1	6.7	7.3	7.5	7.6	7.7	7.8	8.1	8.2	8.2
70 years old and over	Million	8.5	12.1	13.9	14.3	14.7	15.0	15.5	15.8	16.3	16.8
Workers reported with—											
Taxable earnings [2]	Million	93	113	120	123	126	130	132	133	132	132
Maximum earnings [2]	Million	24	10	8	8	8	8	8	8	8	8
Earnings in covered employment [2]	Bil. dol.	532	1,329	1,937	2,082	2,237	2,433	2,583	2,703	2,780	2,960
Reported taxable [2]	Bil. dol.	416	1,181	1,723	1,844	1,960	2,089	2,239	2,363	2,423	2,541
Percent of total	Percent	78.2	88.9	88.9	88.9	87.6	85.9	86.7	87.4	87.2	85.8
Annual maximum taxable earnings [3]	Dollars	7,800	25,900	39,600	42,000	43,800	45,000	48,000	51,300	53,400	55,500
Maximum tax	Dollars	374	1,588	2,792	3,003	3,132	3,380	3,605	3,924	5,123	5,329
Contribution rates for OASDHI: [4]											
Each employer and employee	Percent	4.80	6.13	7.05	7.15	7.15	7.51	7.51	7.65	7.65	7.65
Self-employed [5]	Percent	6.90	8.10	14.10	14.30	14.30	15.02	15.02	15.30	15.30	15.30
SMI, monthly premium [6]	Dollars	5.30	9.60	15.50	15.50	17.90	24.80	31.90	28.60	29.90	31.80

[1] Fully insured for retirement and/or survivor benefits as of beginning of year. [2] Includes self-employment. [3] The maximum taxable earnings for HI was $125,000 in 1991 and $130,200 in 1992. [4] As of January 1, 1993 and 1994, each employee and employer pays 7.65 percent and the self-employed pay 15.3 percent. [5] Self-employed pays 11.8 percent in 1985, 12.3 percent in 1986 and 1987, and 13.02 percent in 1988 and 1989. The additional amount is supplied from general revenues. Beginning 1990, self-employed pays 15.3 percent, and half of the tax is deductible for income tax purposes and for computing self-employment income subject to social security tax. [6] 1970 and 1980, as of July 1; beginning 1985, as of January 1. As of January 1, 1993, the monthly premium is $36.60 and as of January 1, 1994, the monthly premium is $41.10.

Source: U.S. Social Security Administration, *Annual Statistical Supplement* to the *Social Security Bulletin;* and unpublished data.

No. 581. Social Security Trust Funds: 1980 to 1992

[In billions of dollars. See also *Historical Statistics, Colonial Times to 1970*, series H 238-242]

TYPE OF TRUST FUND	1980	1985	1986	1987	1988	1989	1990	1991	1992
Old-age and survivors insurance (OASI):									
Net contribution income [1]	103.5	180.2	194.2	206.0	233.2	252.6	272.4	278.4	286.8
Interest received [2]	1.8	1.9	3.1	4.7	7.6	12.0	16.4	20.8	24.3
Benefit payments [3]	105.1	167.2	176.8	[4]183.6	[4]195.5	208.0	223.0	240.5	254.9
Assets, end of year	22.8	[5]35.8	39.1	62.1	102.9	155.1	214.2	267.8	319.2
Disability insurance (DI):									
Net contribution income [1]	13.3	17.4	18.6	19.7	22.1	24.1	28.7	29.3	30.4
Interest received [2]	0.5	0.9	0.8	0.6	0.6	0.7	0.9	1.1	1.1
Benefit payments [3]	15.5	18.8	19.9	[4]20.5	[4]21.7	22.9	24.8	27.7	31.1
Assets, end of year	3.6	[6]6.3	7.8	6.7	6.9	7.9	11.1	12.9	12.3
Hospital insurance (HI):									
Net contribution income [1] [7]	23.9	47.7	54.7	58.8	62.6	68.5	71.1	78.4	82.4
Interest received [2]	1.1	3.4	3.6	4.5	5.8	7.3	8.5	9.5	10.5
Benefit payments	25.1	47.5	49.8	49.5	52.5	60.0	66.2	71.5	83.9
Assets, end of year	13.7	[8]20.5	40.0	53.7	69.6	85.6	98.9	115.2	124.0
Supplementary medical insurance (SMI):									
Net premium income	3.0	5.6	5.7	7.4	8.8	10.8	11.3	11.9	14.1
Transfers from general revenue	7.5	18.3	17.8	23.6	26.2	30.9	33.0	37.6	41.4
Interest received	0.4	1.2	1.1	0.9	0.9	1.1	1.6	1.7	1.8
Benefit payments	10.6	22.9	26.2	30.8	34.0	38.4	42.5	47.3	49.3
Assets, end of year	4.5	10.9	8.3	8.4	9.0	12.2	15.5	17.8	24.2

[1] Includes deposits by States and deductions for refund of estimated employee-tax overpayment. Beginning in 1985, includes government contributions on deemed wage credits for military service in 1957 and later. Beginning in 1985 includes tax credits on net earnings from self-employment in 1985-89; and taxation of benefits (OASI and DI, only). [2] Beginning in 1985, includes interest on advance tax transfers and interest on reimbursement for unnegotiated checks. [3] Includes payments for vocational rehabilitation services furnished to disabled persons receiving benefits because of their disabilities. Beginning in 1985, amounts reflect deductions for unnegotiated benefit checks. [4] Data adjusted to reflect 12 months of benefit payments. [5] Includes $13.2 billion borrowed from the DI and HI Trust Funds. [6] Excludes $2.5 billion lent to the OASI Trust Fund. [7] Includes premiums from aged ineligibles enrolled in HI. [8] Excludes $10.6 billion lent to the OASI Trust Fund.

Source: U.S. Social Security Administration, *Annual Report of Board of Trustees, OASI, DI, HI, and SMI Trust Funds.* Also published in *Social Security Bulletin,* quarterly.

No. 582. Social Security (OASDI)—Benefits, by Type of Beneficiary: 1970 to 1992

[A person eligible to receive more than one type of benefit is generally classified or counted only once as a retired-worker beneficiary. OASDI=Old-age, survivors, and disability insurance. See also headnote, table 580; Appendix III; and *Historical Statistics, Colonial Times to 1970*, series H 197-229]

TYPE OF BENEFICIARY	1970	1980	1985	1986	1987	1988	1989	1990	1991	1992
	BENEFITS IN CURRENT-PAYMENT STATUS[1] (end of year)									
Number of benefits (1,000)...	26,229	35,585	37,058	37,703	38,190	38,627	39,151	39,832	40,592	41,507
Retired workers [2] (1,000).....	13,349	19,562	22,432	22,980	23,440	23,858	24,327	24,838	25,289	25,758
Disabled workers [3] (1,000)..	1,493	2,859	2,657	2,728	2,786	2,830	2,895	3,011	3,195	3,468
Wives and husbands [2 4] (1,000)..	2,952	3,477	3,375	3,387	3,381	3,367	3,365	3,367	3,370	3,382
Children (1,000).................	4,122	4,607	3,319	3,295	3,244	3,204	3,165	3,187	3,268	3,391
Under age 18.............	3,315	3,423	2,699	2,665	2,604	2,534	2,488	2,497	2,558	2,664
Disabled children [5].......	271	450	526	545	561	574	586	600	616	637
Students [6].............	537	733	94	84	79	96	91	89	95	90
Of retired workers.......	546	639	457	450	439	432	423	422	426	432
Of deceased workers.....	2,688	2,610	1,917	1,878	1,837	1,809	1,780	1,776	1,791	1,808
Of disabled workers......	889	1,358	945	966	968	963	962	989	1,052	1,151
Widowed mothers [7] (1,000)..	523	562	372	351	329	318	312	304	301	294
Widows and widowers [2 8] (1,000)..	3,227	4,411	4,863	4,928	4,984	5,029	5,071	5,111	5,158	5,205
Parents [2] (1,000)............	29	15	10	9	8	7	6	6	5	5
Special benefits [9] (1,000)	534	93	32	25	19	14	10	7	5	4
Average monthly benefit, current dollars										
Retired workers [2].............	118	341	479	489	513	537	567	603	629	653
Retired worker and wife [2].....	199	567	814	831	873	914	966	1,027	1,072	1,111
Disabled workers [3]...........	131	371	484	488	508	530	556	587	609	626
Wives and husbands [2 4].......	59	164	236	241	253	265	281	298	311	322
Children of retired workers.....	45	140	198	204	216	228	242	259	273	285
Children of deceased workers....	82	240	330	337	352	368	385	406	420	432
Children of disabled workers.....	39	110	142	141	146	151	157	164	168	170
Widowed mothers [7]...........	87	246	332	338	353	368	388	409	424	438
Widows and widowers, nondisabled [2]...........	102	311	433	444	468	493	522	557	584	608
Parents [2]..................	103	276	378	386	407	428	454	482	506	526
Special benefits [9]...........	45	105	138	140	145	151	158	167	173	178
Average monthly benefit, constant (1992) dollars [10]										
Retired workers [2].............	421	561	622	627	631	632	638	640	647	653
Retired worker and wife [2].....	710	932	1,057	1,067	1,073	1,076	1,087	1,089	1,103	1,111
Disabled workers [3]...........	467	610	628	627	625	624	626	623	627	626
Wives and husbands [2 4].......	210	270	306	309	311	312	316	316	320	322
Children of deceased workers....	292	395	430	433	433	433	433	431	432	432
Widowed mothers [7]...........	310	404	431	434	434	433	437	434	436	438
Widows and widowers, nondisabled [2]...........	364	511	562	570	575	581	587	590	600	608
	BENEFITS AWARDED DURING YEAR (1,000)									
Number of benefits.......	3,722	4,215	3,796	3,853	3,734	3,681	3,646	3,717	3,865	4,051
Retired workers [2]...........	1,338	1,620	1,690	1,734	1,682	1,654	1,657	1,665	1,695	1,708
Disabled workers [3].........	350	389	377	417	416	409	426	468	536	637
Wives and husbands [2 4].....	436	469	440	441	411	391	380	379	380	383
Children [7]................	1,091	1,174	714	701	685	706	675	695	727	795
Widowed mothers [7 2 8]......	112	108	72	69	65	63	60	58	58	56
Widows and widowers [2 8]....	363	452	502	491	475	458	449	452	469	472
Parents [2].................	2	1	(Z)	(Z)	(Z)	(Z)	(Z)	(Z)	(Z)	(Z)
Special benefits [9]...........	30	1	1	(Z)	(Z)	(Z)	(Z)	(Z)	(Z)	(Z)
	BENEFIT PAYMENTS DURING YEAR (bil. dol.)									
Total amount [11]...........	31.9	120.5	186.2	196.7	204.2	217.2	230.9	247.8	268.1	286.0
Monthly benefits [12].........	31.6	120.1	186.0	196.5	204.0	217.0	230.6	247.6	267.9	285.8
Retired workers [2]..........	18.4	70.4	116.8	123.6	128.5	137.0	146.0	156.8	169.1	179.4
Disabled workers [3]........	2.4	12.8	16.5	17.4	18.1	19.2	20.3	22.1	24.7	27.9
Wives and husbands [2 4]....	2.2	7.0	11.1	11.7	12.1	12.8	13.6	14.5	15.5	16.4
Children................	3.5	10.5	10.7	10.9	11.0	11.3	11.5	12.0	12.8	13.6
Under age 18...........	2.7	7.4	8.5	8.7	8.5	8.7	8.7	9.0	9.5	10.1
Disabled children [5].....	0.3	1.0	1.8	2.0	2.0	2.2	2.3	2.5	2.8	3.0
Students [6]............	0.6	2.1	0.4	0.3	0.4	0.5	0.5	0.5	0.5	0.5
Of retired workers.......	0.3	1.1	1.1	1.2	1.2	1.2	1.2	1.3	1.4	1.5
Of deceased workers.....	2.8	7.4	7.8	7.8	7.8	8.1	8.3	8.6	9.0	9.4
Of disabled workers......	0.5	2.0	1.8	1.9	1.9	2.0	2.0	2.2	2.4	2.7
Widowed mothers [7 2 8].....	0.6	1.6	1.5	1.5	1.4	1.4	1.4	1.4	1.5	1.5
Widows and widowers [2 8]..	4.1	17.6	29.3	31.3	32.8	35.2	37.7	40.7	44.1	47.1
Parents [2]...............	(Z)	0.1	0.1	(Z)	(Z)	(Z)	(Z)	(Z)	(Z)	(Z)
Special benefits [9].........	0.3	0.1	0.1	0.1	(Z)	(Z)	(Z)	(Z)	(Z)	(Z)
Lump sum.............	0.3	0.4	0.2	0.2	0.2	0.2	0.2	0.2	0.2	0.2

Z Fewer than 500 or less than $50 million. [1] Benefit payment actually being made at a specified time with no deductions or with deductions amounting to less than a month's benefits; i.e., the benefits actually being received. [2] 62 years and over. [3] Disabled workers under age 65. [4] Includes wife beneficiaries with entitled children in their care and entitled divorced wives. [5] 18 years old and over. Disability began before age 18 and, beginning 1973, before age 22. [6] Full-time students aged 18-21 through 1984 and aged 18 and 19 beginning 1985. [7] Includes surviving divorced mothers with entitled children in their care and, beginning 1980, widowed fathers with entitled children in their care. [8] Includes widows aged 60-61, surviving divorced wives aged 60 and over, disabled widows and widowers aged 50 and over; and beginning 1980, widowers aged 60-61. [9] Benefits for persons aged 72 and over not insured under regular or transitional provisions of Social Security Act. [10] Constant dollar figures are based on the consumer price index for December as published by the U.S. Bureau of Labor Statistics. [11] Represents total disbursements of benefit checks by the U.S. Dept. of the Treasury during the years specified. [12] Distribution by type estimated.

Source: U.S. Social Security Administration, *Annual Statistical Supplement* to the *Social Security Bulletin;* and unpublished data.

No. 583. Social Security—Beneficiaries, Annual Payments, and Average Monthly Benefit, 1980 to 1992, and by State and Other Areas, 1992

[Number of beneficiaries in current-payment status and average monthly benefit as of **December**. See also headnote, table 582, and Appendix III]

YEAR, DIVISION, STATE, AND OTHER AREA	NUMBER OF BENEFICIARIES [1] (1,000)				ANNUAL PAYMENTS (mil. dol.)				AVERAGE MONTHLY BENEFIT (dol.)		
	Total	Retired workers and dependents [2]	Survivors	Disabled workers and dependents	Total	Retired workers and dependents [2]	Survivors [3]	Disabled workers and dependents	Retired workers [4]	Disabled workers [4]	Widows and widowers [5]
1980	35,585	23,309	7,598	4,678	120,472	78,025	27,010	15,437	341	371	311
1985	37,058	25,989	7,162	3,907	186,195	128,536	38,824	18,836	479	484	433
1990	39,832	28,369	7,197	4,266	247,796	172,042	50,951	24,803	603	587	557
1991	40,592	28,824	7,255	4,513	268,098	185,545	54,891	27,662	629	609	584
1992, total [6]	**41,497**	**29,296**	**7,297**	**4,903**	**285,980**	**196,688**	**58,203**	**31,089**	**653**	**626**	**608**
United States	**40,524**	**28,711**	**7,077**	**4,735**	**281,673**	**194,301**	**57,052**	**30,320**	**(NA)**	**(NA)**	**(NA)**
New England	**2,231**	**1,656**	**336**	**239**	**15,913**	**11,544**	**2,852**	**1,517**	**(NA)**	**(NA)**	**(NA)**
Maine	224	159	36	28	1,436	991	281	164	601	567	574
New Hampshire	172	129	25	18	1,210	885	211	114	655	627	630
Vermont	92	65	15	12	624	432	121	71	640	601	608
Massachusetts	1,011	743	155	114	7,144	5,103	1,314	727	655	612	638
Rhode Island	186	140	27	20	1,314	969	222	123	652	596	633
Connecticut	546	420	78	47	4,185	3,164	703	318	718	636	679
Middle Atlantic	**6,470**	**4,735**	**1,088**	**648**	**48,001**	**34,175**	**9,361**	**4,465**	**(NA)**	**(NA)**	**(NA)**
New York	2,910	2,111	475	324	21,642	15,377	4,030	2,235	698	658	653
New Jersey	1,267	946	201	120	9,720	7,100	1,778	842	716	654	670
Pennsylvania	2,293	1,678	412	204	16,639	11,698	3,553	1,388	672	648	640
East North Central	**7,006**	**4,953**	**1,261**	**794**	**50,976**	**34,900**	**10,773**	**5,303**	**(NA)**	**(NA)**	**(NA)**
Ohio	1,859	1,289	357	213	13,259	8,813	3,032	1,414	669	652	637
Indiana	938	661	164	113	6,799	4,661	1,405	733	679	644	644
Illinois	1,800	1,293	320	188	13,267	9,299	2,706	1,262	692	651	656
Michigan	1,546	1,079	280	188	11,478	7,748	2,430	1,300	697	685	654
Wisconsin	863	631	140	92	6,173	4,379	1,200	594	669	632	639
West North Central	**3,105**	**2,251**	**541**	**313**	**21,263**	**14,893**	**4,411**	**1,959**	**(NA)**	**(NA)**	**(NA)**
Minnesota	689	510	117	62	4,706	3,346	964	396	637	610	608
Iowa	532	391	92	49	3,706	2,622	772	312	653	617	620
Missouri	941	661	165	115	6,402	4,360	1,316	726	638	615	600
North Dakota	114	82	22	10	736	508	168	60	615	590	575
South Dakota	132	94	24	13	836	576	185	75	602	567	573
Nebraska	276	203	48	26	1,891	1,338	399	154	643	605	624
Kansas	421	310	73	38	2,986	2,143	607	236	669	601	632
South Atlantic	**7,548**	**5,332**	**1,295**	**923**	**50,714**	**34,934**	**9,933**	**5,847**	**(NA)**	**(NA)**	**(NA)**
Delaware	112	82	18	12	813	581	152	80	680	642	638
Maryland	641	462	118	61	4,501	3,124	958	419	652	643	619
District of Columbia	79	55	15	8	477	325	101	51	556	562	510
Virginia	883	608	162	114	5,810	3,875	1,225	710	619	614	564
West Virginia	376	231	82	63	2,542	1,488	648	406	644	672	578
North Carolina	1,143	775	202	167	7,394	4,929	1,447	1,018	612	590	535
South Carolina	575	380	106	90	3,686	2,407	727	552	611	604	528
Georgia	937	599	184	154	6,010	3,777	1,309	924	610	602	542
Florida	2,802	2,140	408	254	19,481	14,428	3,366	1,687	651	638	627
East South Central	**2,752**	**1,732**	**559**	**461**	**17,253**	**10,590**	**3,971**	**2,692**	**(NA)**	**(NA)**	**(NA)**
Kentucky	674	412	139	123	4,238	2,501	1,010	727	602	623	543
Tennessee	870	567	167	135	5,581	3,556	1,220	805	611	592	548
Alabama	739	468	156	116	4,674	2,874	1,114	686	604	601	536
Mississippi	469	285	97	87	2,760	1,659	627	474	569	577	491
West South Central	**4,032**	**2,679**	**831**	**525**	**26,151**	**16,826**	**6,229**	**3,096**	**(NA)**	**(NA)**	**(NA)**
Arkansas	482	313	90	79	2,975	1,881	637	457	588	594	524
Louisiana	679	405	159	116	4,263	2,447	1,150	666	607	631	555
Oklahoma	552	386	104	63	3,636	2,451	800	385	622	609	578
Texas	2,319	1,575	478	267	15,277	10,047	3,642	1,588	633	616	588
Mountain	**2,098**	**1,506**	**336**	**257**	**14,207**	**9,911**	**2,673**	**1,623**	**(NA)**	**(NA)**	**(NA)**
Montana	146	101	25	20	974	654	195	125	633	640	610
Idaho	166	121	27	18	1,113	785	217	111	634	626	612
Wyoming	66	47	11	9	455	316	90	49	651	633	620
Colorado	453	318	76	59	3,045	2,059	613	373	635	622	610
New Mexico	235	158	44	33	1,468	966	313	189	612	609	572
Arizona	635	468	93	74	4,416	3,168	757	491	660	655	634
Utah	205	149	33	23	1,392	992	267	133	658	611	638
Nevada	192	144	27	22	1,344	971	221	152	658	659	634
Pacific	**5,279**	**3,871**	**830**	**579**	**37,195**	**26,528**	**6,849**	**3,818**	**(NA)**	**(NA)**	**(NA)**
Washington	747	553	113	81	5,377	3,866	970	541	677	639	646
Oregon	521	392	78	52	3,675	2,684	653	338	663	632	637
California	3,819	2,779	611	429	26,852	19,008	5,010	2,834	667	627	635
Alaska	37	24	7	5	250	163	56	31	653	620	575
Hawaii	155	123	21	12	1,041	807	160	74	643	625	583
Puerto Rico	581	321	117	144	2,504	1,276	563	665	418	519	377
Guam	6	3	2	1	25	13	9	3	459	542	442
American Samoa	4	2	2	1	14	5	6	3	388	441	344
Virgin Islands	11	7	2	1	59	37	14	8	548	584	489
Abroad	350	243	91	16	1,705	1,056	559	90	452	544	456

NA Not available. [1] Data for 1992 based on 10-percent sample. [2] Includes special benefits; see footnote 9, table 582. [3] Includes lump-sum payments to survivors of deceased workers. [4] Excludes persons with special benefits. [5] Nondisabled only. [6] Number of beneficiaries includes those with State or area unknown.

Source: U.S. Social Security Administration, *Social Security Bulletin*, quarterly.

No. 584. Public Employee Retirement Systems—Participants and Finances: 1980 to 1992

[For fiscal year of retirement system, except data for the Thrift Savings Plan are for calendar year]

RETIREMENT PLAN	Unit	1980	1985	1986	1987	1988	1989	1990	1991	1992
TOTAL PARTICIPANTS [1]										
Federal retirement systems:										
Defined benefit:										
Civil Service Retirement System	1,000 .	4,629	4,919	4,970	4,295	4,261	4,332	4,167	4,086	4,014
Federal Employees Retirement System [2]	1,000 .	(X)	(X)	(X)	800	924	1,068	1,180	1,325	1,367
Military Service Retirement System [3] . .	1,000 .	3,380	3,672	3,725	3,765	3,762	3,790	3,763	3,732	3,579
Thrift Savings Plan [4]	1,000 .	(X)	(X)	(X)	1,022	1,317	1,446	1,625	1,700	1,900
State and local retirement systems [5][6]	1,000 .	(NA)	15,234	15,426	15,093	15,777	16,684	16,858	17,502	(NA)
ACTIVE PARTICIPANTS										
Federal retirement systems:										
Defined benefit:										
Civil Service Retirement System	1,000 .	2,700	2,800	2,800	2,080	2,011	1,918	1,826	1,726	1,654
Federal Employees Retirement System [2]	1,000 .	(X)	(X)	(X)	800	919	1,052	1,136	1,260	1,276
Military Service Retirement System [3] . .	1,000 .	2,050	2,192	2,219	2,229	2,196	2,188	2,130	2,064	1,868
Thrift Savings Plan [4]	1,000 .	(X)	(X)	(X)	960	1,099	1,269	1,419	1,200	1,300
State and local retirement systems [5][6]	1,000 .	(NA)	10,364	10,529	10,744	10,732	11,357	11,345	11,696	(NA)
ASSETS										
Total.	Bil. dol.	258	529	622	732	825	922	1,047	1,150	(NA)
Federal retirement systems	Bil. dol.	73	154	186	219	262	289	326	367	411
Defined benefit	Bil. dol.	73	154	186	218	260	284	318	355	394
Civil Service Retirement System	Bil. dol.	73	142	161	175	198	204	220	237	256
Federal Employees Retirement System [2]	Bil. dol.	(X)	(X)	(X)	4	8	12	18	24	32
Military Service Retirement System [3] . .	Bil. dol.	(⁷)	12	25	39	53	68	80	94	106
Thrift Savings Plan [4]	Bil. dol.	(X)	(X)	(X)	1	3	5	8	12	16
State and local retirement systems [5]	Bil. dol.	185	374	437	513	563	633	721	783	(NA)
CONTRIBUTIONS										
Total.	Bil. dol.	43	90	95	97	100	104	108	115	(NA)
Federal retirement systems	Bil. dol.	19	54	56	56	58	60	61	65	68
Defined benefit	Bil. dol.	19	54	56	55	56	58	59	62	64
Civil Service Retirement System	Bil. dol.	19	27	28	24	25	26	28	29	30
Federal Employees Retirement System [2]	Bil. dol.	(X)	(X)	(X)	2	3	4	4	5	6
Military Service Retirement System [3] . .	Bil. dol.	(⁷)	27	28	29	29	28	27	28	28
Thrift Savings Plan [4]	Bil. dol.	(X)	(X)	(X)	1	2	2	2	3	4
State and local retirement systems [5]	Bil. dol.	24	37	39	42	43	44	46	49	(NA)
BENEFITS										
Total.	Bil. dol.	39	62	67	71	77	83	89	96	(NA)
Federal retirement systems	Bil. dol.	27	40	42	44	47	50	53	57	58
Defined benefit	Bil. dol.	27	40	42	44	47	50	53	56	58
Civil Service Retirement System	Bil. dol.	15	23	25	26	28	30	31	33	33
Federal Employees Retirement System [2]	Bil. dol.	(X)	(X)	(X)	(Z)	(Z)	(Z)	(Z)	(Z)	(Z)
Military Service Retirement System [3] . .	Bil. dol.	12	17	18	18	19	20	22	23	25
Thrift Savings Plan [4]	Bil. dol.	(X)	(X)	(X)	(Z)	(Z)	(Z)	(Z)	(Z)	(Z)
State and local retirement systems [5]	Bil. dol.	12	22	24	27	30	33	36	39	(NA)

NA Not available.   X Not applicable.   Z Less than $500 million.   [1] Includes active, separated vested, retired employees, and survivors.   [2] The Federal Employees Retirement system was established June 6, 1986.   [3] Includes nondisability and disability retirees, surviving families, and all active personnel with the exception of active reserves.   [4] The Thrift Savings Plan (a defined contribution plan) was established April 1, 1987.   [5] Excludes state and local plans that are fully supported by employee contributions.   [6] Not adjusted for double counting of individuals participating in more than one plan.   [7] The Military Retirement System was unfunded until October 1, 1984.

Source: Employee Benefit Research Institute, Washington, DC, *EBRI Databook on Employee Benefits, Third Edition*, (copyright).

No. 585. Federal Civil Service Retirement: 1980 to 1992

[As of **Sept. 30** or for **year ending Sept. 30**. Covers both Civil Service Retirement System and Federal Employees Retirement System. See also *Historical Statistics, Colonial Times to 1970*, series H 262-270]

ITEM	Unit	1980	1985	1986	1987	1988	1989	1990	1991	1992
Employees covered [1]	1,000 . .	2,720	2,750	2,800	2,810	2,800	2,880	2,945	2,885	2,902
Annuitants, total	1,000 . .	1,675	1,955	2,008	2,032	2,089	2,120	2,143	2,184	2,185
Age and service	1,000 . .	905	1,122	1,166	1,186	1,237	1,267	1,288	1,325	1,322
Disability	1,000 . .	343	332	326	318	311	305	297	289	282
Survivors	1,000 . .	427	501	516	528	541	548	558	570	581
Receipts, total [2]	Mil. dol .	24,389	40,790	43,216	43,640	46,696	49,249	52,689	56,815	60,003
Employee contributions.	Mil. dol .	3,686	4,679	4,714	4,641	4,544	4,491	4,501	4,563	4,713
Federal government contributions. . .	Mil. dol .	15,562	22,301	22,980	23,144	24,258	25,367	27,368	29,509	31,050
Disbursements, total [3]	Mil. dol .	14,977	23,203	24,694	25,772	28,306	29,713	31,416	33,209	33,187
Age and service annuitants [4]	Mil. dol .	12,639	19,414	20,702	21,678	23,889	25,095	26,495	27,997	27,693
Survivors	Mil. dol .	1,912	3,158	3,304	3,485	3,749	4,033	4,366	4,716	5,065
Average monthly benefit:										
Age and service	Dollars .	992	1,189	1,197	1,267	1,263	1,310	1,369	1,439	1,493
Disability	Dollars .	723	881	881	893	930	966	1,008	1,059	1,094
Survivors	Dollars .	392	528	536	552	583	616	653	698	731
Cash and security holdings.	Bil. dol . .	73.7	142.3	160.8	178.7	197.1	216.7	238.0	261.6	288.4

[1] Excludes employees in Leave Without Pay status.   [2] Includes interest on investments.   [3] Includes refunds, death claims, and administration.   [4] Includes disability annuitants.

Source: U.S. Office of Personnel Management, *Compensation Report*, annual.

No. 586. State and Local Government Retirement Systems— Beneficiaries and Finances: 1980 to 1991

[In millions of dollars, except as indicated. For fiscal years closed during the 12 months ending June 30]

YEAR AND LEVEL OF GOVERNMENT	Number of benefi-ciaries (1,000)	RECEIPTS					BENEFITS AND WITHDRAWALS			Cash and security holdings
		Total	Em-ployee contri-butions	Government contributions		Earn-ings on invest-ments	Total	Ben-efits	With-drawals	
				State	Local					
1980: All systems	(NA)	37,313	6,466	7,581	9,951	13,315	14,008	12,207	1,801	185,226
State-administered	(NA)	28,603	5,285	7,399	5,611	10,308	10,257	8,809	1,448	144,682
Locally administered . .	(NA)	8,710	1,180	181	4,340	3,008	3,752	3,399	353	40,544
1985: All systems	3,378	71,411	9,468	12,227	15,170	34,546	24,413	21,999	2,414	374,433
State-administered	2,661	55,960	7,901	11,976	8,944	27,139	18,230	16,183	2,047	296,951
Locally administered . .	716	15,451	1,567	251	6,226	7,407	6,183	5,816	367	77,481
1990: All systems	4,026	111,339	13,853	13,994	18,583	64,907	38,396	35,966	2,430	703,772
State-administered	3,232	89,162	11,648	13,964	11,538	52,012	29,603	27,562	2,041	565,641
Locally administered . .	794	22,177	2,205	32	7,045	12,895	8,793	8,404	389	138,131
1991: All systems	4,179	108,240	16,268	14,473	18,691	58,808	42,028	39,421	2,607	783,405
State-administered	3,357	85,576	12,563	14,455	11,553	47,006	32,323	30,167	2,156	630,551
Locally administered . .	822	22,664	3,705	18	7,138	11,803	9,706	9,255	451	152,854

NA Not available.

Source: U.S. Bureau of the Census, *Finances of Employee-Retirement Systems of State and Local Governments*, series GF, No. 2, annual.

No. 587. Private Pension Plans—Summary, by Type of Plan: 1975 to 1990

["Pension plan" is defined by the Employee Retirement Income Security Act (ERISA) as "any plan, fund, or program which was heretofore or is hereafter established or maintained by an employer or an employee organization, or by both, to the extent that such plan (a) provides retirement income to employees, or (b) results in a deferral of income by employees for periods extending to the termination of covered employment or beyond, regardless of the method of calculating the contributions made to the plan, the method of calculating the benefits under the plan, or the method of distributing benefits from the plan." A defined benefit plan provides a definite benefit formula for calculating benefit amounts - such as a flat amount per year of service or a percentage of salary times years of service. A defined contribution plan is a pension plan in which the contributions are made to an individual account for each employee. The retirement benefit is dependent upon the account balance at retirement. The balance depends upon amounts contributed, investment experience, and, in the case of profit sharing plans, amounts which may be allocated to the account due to forfeitures by terminating employees. Employee Stock Ownership Plans (ESOP) (see table 852) and 401(k) plans (see table 589) are included among defined contribution plans. Data are based on Form 5500 series reports filed with the Internal Revenue Service]

ITEM	Unit	TOTAL				DEFINED CONTRIBUTION PLAN				DEFINED BENEFIT PLAN			
		1975	1980	1985	1990	1975	1980	1985	1990	1975	1980	1985	1990
Number of plans [1] [2] [3]	1,000 . . .	311.1	488.9	632.1	712.3	207.7	340.8	462.0	599.2	103.3	148.1	170.2	113.1
Total participants [2] [3] . .	Million . .	44.5	57.9	74.7	76.9	11.5	19.9	35.0	38.1	33.0	38.0	39.7	38.8
Active participants [2] [4] .	Million . .	38.4	49.0	62.3	61.8	11.2	18.9	33.2	35.5	27.2	30.1	29.0	26.3
Contributions [5]	Bil. dol. . .	37.1	66.2	95.1	98.8	12.8	23.5	53.1	75.8	24.2	42.6	42.0	23.0
Benefits [6]	Bil. dol. . .	19.1	35.3	101.9	129.4	6.2	13.1	47.4	63.0	12.9	22.1	54.5	66.4

[1] Excludes all plans covering only one participant.   [2] Includes double counting of workers in more than one plan.   [3] Total participants include active participants, vested separated workers, and retirees.   [4] Any workers currently in employment covered by a plan and who are earning or retaining credited service under a plan. Includes any nonvested former employees who have not yet incurred breaks in service.   [5] Includes both employer and employee contributions.   [6] Benefits paid directly from trust and premium payments made from plan to insurance carriers. Excludes benefits paid directly by insurance carriers.

Source: U.S. Dept. of Labor, Pension and Welfare Benefits Administration, *Private Pension Plan Bulletin*, summer 1993.

No. 588. Pension Plan Coverage of Workers, by Selected Characteristics: 1992

[Covers workers as of **March** of following year who had earnings in year shown. Based on Current Population Survey; see text, section 1, and Appendix III]

SEX AND AGE	NUMBER WITH COVERAGE (1,000)				PERCENT OF TOTAL WORKERS			
	Total [1]	White	Black	Hispanic [2]	Total [1]	White	Black	Hispanic [2]
Total	53,899	46,628	5,519	2,586	40	40	39	25
Male	30,197	26,607	2,624	1,499	42	43	37	24
Under 65 years old	29,617	26,097	2,572	1,486	43	43	38	24
15 to 24 years old	1,411	1,223	140	91	12	12	10	7
25 to 44 years old	17,428	15,186	1,628	952	46	47	42	27
45 to 64 years old	10,777	9,688	804	443	54	55	50	36
65 years old and over	579	509	52	14	22	21	31	16
Female	23,703	20,021	2,896	1,087	38	38	41	26
Under 65 years old	23,287	19,657	2,850	1,074	39	39	41	26
15 to 24 years old	1,206	1,044	129	67	11	11	11	8
25 to 44 years old	13,857	11,561	1,796	701	43	43	45	29
45 to 64 years old	8,224	7,052	925	306	48	48	54	34
65 years old and over	416	364	46	12	21	21	26	20

[1] Includes other races, not shown separately.   [2] Hispanic persons may be of any race.

Source: U.S. Bureau of the Census, unpublished data.

No. 589. 401(k) Plans—Summary: 1984 to 1990

[A 401(k) plan is a qualified retirement plan that allows participants to have a portion of their compensation (otherwise payable in cash) contributed pretax to a retirement account on their behalf]

ITEM	1984	1985	1986	1987	1988	1989	1990
Number of plans [1]	17,303	29,869	37,420	45,054	68,121	83,301	97,614
Active participants [2] (1,000)	7,540	10,339	11,559	13,131	15,451	17,337	19,548
Assets (mil. dol.)	91,754	143,939	182,784	215,477	276,995	357,015	384,859
Contributions (mil. dol.)	16,291	24,322	29,226	33,185	39,412	46,081	48,998
Benefits (mil. dol.)	10,617	16,399	22,898	22,215	25,235	30,875	32,028
Percentage of all private defined contribution plans:							
Assets	27	34	37	41	46	52	54
Contributions	38	46	50	53	60	57	64
Benefits	33	35	37	40	42	43	51

[1] Excludes single-participant plans. [2] May include some employees who are eligible to participate in the plan but have not elected to join. 401(k) participants may participate in one or more additional plans.

Source: Employee Benefit Research Institute, Washington, DC, *EBRI Databook on Employee Benefits, Third Edition,* (copyright).

No. 590. State Unemployment Insurance—Summary: 1980 to 1992

[Includes unemployment compensation for State and local government employees where covered by State law. See also *Historical Statistics, Colonial Times to 1970,* series H 305-317]

ITEM	Unit	1980	1984	1985	1986	1987	1988	1989	1990	1991	1992
Insured unemployment, avg. weekly	1,000	3,350	2,476	2,611	2,641	2,330	2,081	2,158	2,522	3,342	3,245
Percent of covered employment [1]	Percent	3.9	2.8	2.9	2.8	2.3	2.0	2.1	2.4	3.3	3.1
Percent of civilian unemployed	Percent	43.9	29.0	31.4	32.1	31.4	31.0	33.0	36.0	40.0	34.0
Unemployment benefits, avg. weekly	Dollars	99	123	127	135	140	145	152	162	170	174
Percent of weekly wage	Percent	37.5	35.8	35.3	35.8	35.3	34.9	35.4	36.2	36.4	35.4
Weeks compensated	Million	149.0	111.6	119.3	121.4	105.2	94.2	97.6	116.0	155.1	150.2
Beneficiaries, first payments	1,000	10,001	7,765	8,350	8,361	7,205	6,861	7,369	8,629	10,075	9,243
Average duration of benefits [2]	Weeks	14.9	14.4	14.3	14.5	14.6	13.7	13.2	13.4	15.4	16.2
Claimants exhausting benefits	1,000	3,072	2,600	2,575	2,688	2,409	1,979	1,940	2,323	3,472	3,821
Percent of first payment [3]	Percent	33.2	34.1	31.3	32.1	30.6	28.5	28.0	29.4	34.8	39.7
Contributions collected [4]	Bil. dol.	11.4	18.8	19.3	18.1	17.6	17.7	16.5	15.2	14.5	16.9
Benefits paid	Bil. dol.	13.8	12.6	14.0	15.4	14.2	13.2	14.3	18.1	25.4	25.2
Funds available for benefits [5]	Bil. dol.	11.4	11.6	16.0	19.6	23.2	31.1	37.5	38.4	31.9	27.9
Average employer contribution rate [6]	Percent	2.5	3.2	3.1	2.7	2.6	2.5	2.2	2.0	2.1	2.3

[1] Insured unemployment as percent of average covered employment in preceding year. [2] Weeks compensated divided by first payment. [3] Based on first payments for 12-month period ending June 30. [4] Contributions from employers; also employees in States which tax workers. [5] End of year. Sum of balances in State clearing accounts, benefit-payment accounts, and State accounts in Federal unemployment trust funds. [6] As percent of taxable wages.

No. 591. State Unemployment Insurance, by State and Other Areas: 1992

[See headnote, table 590. For State data on insured unemployment, see table 652]

STATE OR OTHER AREA	Benefi-ciaries, first pay-ments (1,000)	Benefits paid (mil. dol.)	Avg. weekly unemploy-ment benefits (dol.)	STATE OR OTHER AREA	Benefi-ciaries, first pay-ments (1,000)	Benefits paid (mil. dol.)	Avg. weekly unemploy-ment benefits (dol.)	STATE OR OTHER AREA	Benefi-ciaries, first pay-ments (1,000)	Benefits paid (mil. dol.)	Avg. weekly unemploy-ment benefits (dol.)
Total	9,243	25,153	174	KY	127	228	144	OH	357	972	180
AL	157	209	121	LA	110	210	118	OK	66	148	159
AK	44	117	170	ME	59	146	167	OR	142	382	172
AZ	90	211	147	MD	145	461	180	PA	518	1,751	201
AR	100	185	151	MA	249	1,036	226	RI	61	196	206
CA	1,444	3,852	152	MI	487	1,288	211	SC	125	215	143
CO	79	179	178	MN	134	409	198	SD	9	12	128
CT	157	587	211	MS	79	129	123	TN	190	289	124
DE	29	72	181	MO	184	380	146	TX	430	1,181	176
DC	27	128	228	MT	25	45	135	UT	38	82	174
FL	339	861	158	NE	33	50	133	VT	26	66	155
GA	232	381	148	NV	60	155	168	VA	138	288	164
HI	39	138	240	NH	40	61	136	WA	219	661	176
ID	46	84	156	NJ	340	1,429	225	WV	61	148	163
IL	391	1,339	183	NM	32	73	138	WI	216	463	175
IN	150	217	126	NY	673	2,635	197	WY	12	29	163
IA	89	195	170	NC	244	378	158	PR	113	179	84
KS	71	189	179	ND	15	30	146	VI	3	6	161

Source of tables 590 and 591: U.S. Employment and Training Administration, *Unemployment Insurance Data Summary,* annual.

No. 592. Workers' Compensation Payments: 1980 to 1991

[In billions of dollars, except as indicated. See headnote, table 593. See also *Historical Statistics, Colonial Times to 1970*, series H 332-345]

ITEM	1980	1982	1983	1984	1985	1986	1987	1988	1989	1990	1991
Workers covered [1] (mil.)	79	77	78	82	84	86	88	91	94	95	94
Premium amounts paid	**22.3**	**22.8**	**23.0**	**25.1**	**29.2**	**34.0**	**38.1**	**43.3**	**48.0**	**53.1**	**55.2**
Private carriers	15.7	15.4	15.4	16.6	19.5	22.8	25.4	28.5	31.9	35.1	35.7
State funds	3.0	2.6	2.7	3.0	3.5	4.5	5.3	6.7	7.2	8.0	8.7
Federal programs [2]	1.1	1.5	1.5	1.6	1.7	1.8	1.8	1.9	2.0	2.2	2.1
Self-insurers	2.4	3.2	3.5	3.9	4.5	4.9	5.5	6.2	6.9	7.9	8.7
Annual benefits paid	**13.6**	**16.4**	**17.6**	**19.7**	**22.2**	**24.6**	**27.3**	**30.7**	**34.3**	**38.2**	**42.2**
By private carriers [3]	7.0	8.6	9.3	10.6	12.3	13.8	15.5	17.5	19.9	22.2	24.5
From State funds [4]	4.3	4.8	5.1	5.4	5.7	6.2	6.8	7.5	8.0	8.7	9.7
Employers' self-insurance [5]	2.3	3.0	3.2	3.7	4.1	4 5	5.1	5.7	6.4	7.4	7.9
Type of benefit:											
Medical/hospitalization	3.9	5.1	5.7	6.4	7.5	8.6	9.9	11.5	13.4	15.2	16.8
Compensation payments	9.7	11.3	11.9	13.3	14.7	16.0	17.4	19.2	20.9	23.1	25.3
Disability	8.4	9.9	10.4	11.7	13.1	14.3	15.8	17.6	19.2	21.2	23.3
Survivor	1.3	1.5	1.5	1.6	1.7	1.6	1.6	1.6	1.7	1.8	2.0
Percent of covered payroll:											
Workers' compensation costs [6][7]	1.96	1.75	1.67	1.66	1.82	1.99	2.07	2.16	2.27	2.36	2.40
Benefits [7]	1.07	1.16	1.17	1.21	1.30	1.37	1.43	1.49	1.58	1.66	1.79

[1] Estimated per month. [2] Includes Federal employer compensation program and that portion of Federal black lung benefits program financed from employer contributions. [3] Net cash and medical benefits paid under standard workers' compensation policies. [4] Net cash and medical benefits paid by competitive and exclusive State funds and by Federal workers' compensation programs, including black lung benefit program. [5] Cash and medical benefits paid by self-insurers, plus value of medical benefits paid by employers carrying workers' compensation policies that exclude standard medical coverage. [6] Premiums written by private carriers and State funds, and benefits paid by self-insurers increased by 5-10 percent to allow for administrative costs. Also includes benefits paid and administrative costs of Federal system for government employees. [7] Excludes programs financed from general revenue—black lung benefits and supplemental pensions in some States.

Source: U.S. Social Security Administration, *Annual Statistical Supplement* to the *Social Security Bulletin*.

No. 593. Workers' Compensation Payments, by State: 1980 to 1991

[In millions of dollars. Calendar-year data, except fiscal-year data for Federal civilian and other programs and for a few States with State funds. Payments represent cash and medical benefits and include insurance losses paid by private insurance carriers (compiled from the *Spectator (Insurance by States . . . of Casualty Lines)*, from reports of State insurance commissions, and from A. M. Best Co.); net disbursements of State funds (from the *Spectator*, from *Argus Casualty and Surety Chart*, and from State reports), estimated for some States; and self-insurance payments, estimated from available State data. Includes benefit payments under Longshoremen's and Harbor Workers' Compensation Act and Defense Bases Compensation Act for States in which such payments are made]

STATE	1980	1985	1989	1990	1991	STATE	1980	1985	1989	1990	1991
Total	**13,618**	**22,224**	**34,316**	**38,238**	**42,169**	Nebraska	42	68	112	137	146
						Nevada	69	123	250	339	392
Alabama	112	203	380	444	472	New Hampshire	48	91	154	169	203
Alaska	60	109	113	113	124	New Jersey	316	501	761	844	916
Arizona	120	198	324	371	368	New Mexico	54	140	226	228	232
Arkansas	83	129	196	229	251	New York	637	985	1,528	1,752	2,014
California	1,628	3,243	5,242	6,065	7,248	North Carolina	131	236	386	480	545
Colorado	114	284	532	595	657	North Dakota	17	33	50	60	73
Connecticut	147	305	587	694	773	Ohio	776	1,387	1,816	1,960	2,195
Delaware	21	41	68	75	80	Oklahoma	127	289	313	369	434
District of Columbia	69	74	84	86	91	Oregon	275	396	576	573	587
Florida	362	815	1,732	1,976	1,961	Pennsylvania	572	998	1,820	2,019	2,329
Georgia	185	360	661	735	791	Rhode Island	55	97	200	219	214
Hawaii	60	133	180	216	250	South Carolina	79	152	240	277	292
Idaho	37	66	93	105	115	South Dakota	13	26	44	56	64
Illinois	699	912	1,432	1,607	1,745	Tennessee	129	204	390	463	515
Indiana	110	152	297	350	380	Texas	701	1,564	2,843	2,896	3,264
Iowa	99	121	190	231	241	Utah	39	80	142	187	183
Kansas	84	142	220	266	295	Vermont	15	30	-55	61	67
Kentucky	161	225	326	383	432	Virginia	182	276	465	507	545
						Washington	324	619	811	883	949
Louisiana	301	466	586	575	560	West Virginia	176	285	375	389	417
Maine	81	194	342	380	419	Wisconsin	170	287	487	561	627
Maryland	187	306	437	505	523	Wyoming	22	47	47	49	59
Massachusetts	296	510	1,078	1,235	1,276						
Michigan	626	769	1,120	1,205	1,286	Federal programs:					
Minnesota	260	453	497	582	646	Civilian employees	776	1,055	1,274	1,448	1,595
Mississippi	60	98	171	198	203	Black lung					
Missouri	124	237	423	496	557	benefits [1]	1,739	1,603	1,479	1,435	1,391
Montana	41	102	153	150	168	Other [2]	8	7	8	11	11

[1] Includes payments by Social Security Administration and by Department of Labor. [2] Primarily payments made to dependents of reservists who died while on active duty in the Armed Forces.

Source: U.S. Social Security Administration, *Social Security Bulletin*, fall 1993, and selected prior issues; and unpublished data.

No. 594. Persons With Work Disability, by Selected Characteristics: 1992

[In thousands, except percent. As of March. Covers civilian noninstitutional population and members of Armed Forces living off post or with their families on post. Persons are classified as having a work disability if they (1) have a health problem or disability which prevents them from working or which limits the kind or amount of work they can do; (2) have a service-connected disability or ever retired or left a job for health reasons; (3) did not work in survey reference week or previous year because of long-term illness or disability; or (4) are under age 65, and are covered by Medicare or receive Supplemental Security Income. Based on Current Population Survey; see text, section 1, and Appendix III]

AGE AND PARTICIPATION STATUS IN ASSISTANCE PROGRAMS	Total [1]	Male	Female	White	Black	Hispanic [2]
Persons with work disability	**14,959**	**7,573**	**7,386**	**11,819**	**2,670**	**1,192**
16 to 24 years old	1,196	553	643	916	237	123
25 to 34 years old	2,727	1,412	1,315	2,057	562	208
35 to 44 years old	3,226	1,748	1,478	2,568	560	288
45 to 54 years old	3,154	1,547	1,607	2,508	560	254
55 to 64 years old	4,656	2,313	2,343	3,769	751	318
Percent work disabled of total population . . .	9.3	9.6	9.0	8.7	13.8	8.5
16 to 24 years old	3.9	3.6	4.1	3.6	5.2	3.5
25 to 34 years old	6.4	6.7	6.2	5.8	10.4	4.9
35 to 44 years old	8.2	9.0	7.4	7.7	12.6	9.1
45 to 54 years old	11.7	11.8	11.6	10.8	20.1	14.0
55 to 64 years old	22.0	23.1	21.1	20.6	34.7	25.4
Percent of work disabled—						
Receiving Social Security income	28.2	29.3	27.1	28.3	28.2	24.2
Receiving food stamps	22.8	18.4	27.4	19.1	39.1	31.7
Covered by Medicaid..................	29.7	23.8	35.8	25.6	47.2	44.1
Residing in public housing	4.8	3.1	6.5	3.2	12.1	7.0
Residing in subsidized housing	3.9	2.6	5.2	3.2	7.1	5.5

[1] Includes other races not shown separately.   [2] Hispanic persons may be of any race.
Source: U.S. Bureau of the Census, unpublished data.

No. 595. Vocational Rehabilitation—Summary: 1980 to 1992

[For fiscal years ending in year shown; see text, section 9. Includes Puerto Rico, Guam, Virgin Islands, American Samoa, Northern Mariana Islands, and Trust Territory of the Pacific Islands. Vocational rehabilitation of the disabled defined as restoration, preservation, or development of the ability to function in productive activity. Rehabilitation services provided by State vocational rehabilitation agencies with matching State and Federal funds include medical restoration, training, counseling, guidance, and placement services. See also *Historical Statistics, Colonial Times to 1970*, series H 392-397]

ITEM	Unit	1980	1985	1986	1987	1988	1989	1990	1991	1992
Federal and State expenditures [1]	Mil. dol. .	[2]1,076	1,452	1,506	1,649	1,776	1,867	1,910	2,092	2,240
Federal expenditures..............	Mil. dol. .	[2]817	1,100	1,144	1,275	1,373	1,446	1,525	1,622	1,731
Applicants processed for program eligibility.	1,000 . . .	717	594	594	597	606	623	625	619	713
Percent accepted into program.......	Percent .	58	60	58	58	58	58	57	57	57
Total persons rehabilitated [3]..........	1,000 .	277	228	223	220	218	220	216	203	192
Rehabilitation rate [4]...............	Percent .	64	64	64	63	63	63	62	60	58
Severely disabled persons rehabilitated [3][5].	1,000 . .	143	135	135	136	141	147	146	140	134
Rehabilitation rate [4]...............	Percent .	61	62	62	62	62	62	62	59	57
Percent of total persons rehabilitated . . .	Percent .	51	59	61	62	65	67	68	69	70
Persons served, total [6] ....,,	1,000 . . .	1,095	932	924	917	919	929	938	942	950
Persons served, severely disabled [5][6]	1,000 . . .	606	581	580	584	604	625	640	654	667
Percent of total persons served......	Percent .	55	62	63	64	66	67	68	69	70

[1] Includes expenditures only under the basic support provisions of the Rehabilitation Act.   [2] Estimates based on amounts appropriated.   [3] Persons successfully placed into gainful employment.   [4] Persons rehabilitated as a percent of all active case closures (whether rehabilitated or not).   [5] Severely disabled individuals fall into any of the following three categories: (a) clients with specified major disabling conditions such as blindness and deafness; (b) clients who at any time in the vocational rehabilitation process had been Social Security disability beneficiaries or recipients of Supplemental Security Income; and (c) other individuals with substantial loss in conducting certain specified activities.   [6] Includes active cases accepted for rehabilitation services during year plus active cases on hand at beginning of year.
Source: U.S. Dept. of Education, Rehabilitation Services Administration, *Caseload Statistics of State Vocational Rehabilitation Agencies in Fiscal Years*, and *State Vocational Rehabilitation Agency Program Data in Fiscal Years*, both annual.

No. 596. Protection Against Short-Term Sickness Income Loss: 1980 to 1992

[In millions of dollars, except percent. "Short-term sickness" refers to short-term or temporary nonwork-connected disability (lasting not more than 6 months) and the first 6 months of long-term disability. See also *Historical Statistics, Colonial Times to 1970*, series H 115-124]

ITEM	1980	1985	1986	1987	1988	1989	1990	1991	1992
Short-term sickness: Income loss	38,529	59,145	62,981	68,166	73,481	77,917	82,601	84,722	89,417
Total protection provided [1]	**14,426**	**19,587**	**20,285**	**22,466**	**23,964**	**25,417**	**27,276**	**28,332**	**30,141**
Protection as percent of loss	37.4	33.1	32.2	33.0	32.6	32.6	33.0	34.4	33.7
Benefits provided by protection:									
Individual insurance..................	1,280	1,796	1,774	2,062	2,057	2,451	2,701	2,588	2,479
Group benefits to workers in private employment	7,634	9,896	10,018	11,357	12,239	12,680	13,426	14,001	15,056
Private cash insurance [2]	3,271	2,601	2,275	2,692	2,903	2,732	2,711	2,590	2,475
Publicly operated cash sickness funds [3] . . .	770	1,179	1,255	1,696	1,779	1,907	2,269	2,810	3,482
Sick leave.....................	3,593	6,116	6,488	6,969	7,557	8,041	8,446	8,601	9,099
Sick leave for government employees......	5,338	7,700	8,299	8,827	9,462	10,062	10,875	11,432	11,901

[1] Provided by individual insurance, group benefits to workers in private employment, and sick leave for government employees. Includes benefits for the sixth month of disability payable under old-age, survivors, disability, and health insurance program, not shown separately.   [2] Group accident and sickness insurance and individual insurance privately written either on a voluntary basis or in compliance with State temporary disability insurance laws in CA, HI, NJ, and NY. Includes a small but undetermined amount of group disability insurance benefits paid to government workers and to self-employed persons through farm, trade, or professional associations.   [3] Includes State-operated plans in RI, CA, and NJ; State Insurance Fund and special fund for disabled unemployed in New York; and provisions of Railroad Unemployment Insurance Act.
Source: U.S. Social Security Administration, *Social Security Bulletin*, fall 1992; and unpublished data.

No. 597. Public Aid—Recipients and Average Monthly Cash Payments Under Supplemental Security Income (SSI) and Public Assistance: 1980 to 1992

[As of **December**, except as noted. Public assistance data for all years include Puerto Rico, Guam, and Virgin Islands; SSI data are for federally administered payments only. See text, section 12. Excludes payments made directly to suppliers of medical care. See also Appendix III and *Historical Statistics, Colonial Times to 1970*, series H 355-367]

PROGRAM	RECIPIENTS (1,000)					AVG. MONTHLY PAYMENTS (dol.)				
	1980	1985	1990	1991	1992	1980	1985	1990	1991	1992
SSI, total	4,142	4,138	4,817	5,118	5,566	168	226	299	321	358
Aged	1,808	1,504	1,454	1,465	1,471	128	164	213	221	227
Blind	78	82	84	85	85	213	274	342	351	362
Disabled	2,256	2,551	3,279	3,569	4,010	198	261	337	361	407
Old-age assistance [1]	19	18	17	17	17	39	36	45	55	40
Aid to the blind [1]	(Z)	(Z)	(Z)	(Z)	(Z)	36	39	42	56	36
Aid to permanently, totally disabled [1]	21	23	26	27	28	35	38	40	58	40
AFDC: [2] Families	3,843	3,721	4,218	4,708	4,936	288	341	392	388	381
Recipients [3]	11,101	10,924	12,159	13,489	14,035	100	118	136	135	134
Children	7,599	7,247	8,208	9,104	9,471	(NA)	(NA)	(NA)	(NA)	(NA)
General assistance cases	796	1,051	1,060	1,078	979	161	(NA)	(NA)	(NA)	(NA)

NA Not available.   Z Fewer than 500.   [1] Average monthly recipients and payments for the year.   [2] Aid to Families with Dependent Children program.   [3] Includes the children and one or both parents, or one caretaker relative other than a parent, in families where the needs of such adults were considered in determining the amount of assistance.

No. 598. Public Aid Payments: 1980 to 1992

[**In millions of dollars**. See headnote, table 597. Supplemental Security Income data cover federally- and State-administered payments. See also Appendix III and *Historical Statistics, Colonial Times to 1970*, series H 346-354]

PROGRAM	1980	1984	1985	1986	1987	1988	1989	1990	1991	1992
Payments, total	[1]21,994	25,035	26,431	28,311	29,556	30,910	32,762	36,047	39,788	44,646
Supplemental Security Income [2]	7,941	10,371	11,060	12,081	12,951	13,786	14,980	16,599	18,524	22,233
Aged	2,734	2,973	3,035	3,096	3,194	3,299	3,476	3,736	3,890	4,140
Blind	190	249	264	277	291	302	316	334	347	371
Disabled	5,014	7,143	7,755	8,700	9,458	10,177	11,180	12,521	14,268	17,711
Public assistance	[1]14,048	14,664	15,371	16,230	16,605	17,124	17,782	19,448	21,264	22,413
Old-age assistance	9	8	8	8	7	7	7	7	11	8
Blind	(Z)	(Z)	(Z)	(Z)	(Z)	(Z)	(Z)	(Z)	(Z)	(Z)
Permanently, totally disabled	9	10	10	11	11	11	12	12	19	13
Families with dependent children	12,475	14,505	15,196	16,033	16,373	16,827	17,466	19,078	20,931	22,106
Emergency assistance	113	141	157	178	214	279	297	349	303	286

Z Less than $500,000.   [1] Includes general assistance payments.   [2] Includes data not available by reason for eligibility.

Source of tables 597 and 598: U.S. Social Security Administration, *Social Security Bulletin*, quarterly and *Annual Statistical Supplement* to the *Social Security Bulletin*, and U.S. Administration for Children and Families, *Quarterly Public Assistance Statistics*, annual.

No. 599. Public Aid Recipients as Percent of Population, by State: 1990 and 1992

[Total recipients as of **June** of Aid to Families with Dependent Children and of Federal Supplemental Security Income as percent of resident population. Based on resident population as of April 1 for 1990 and as of July 1 for 1992]

DIVISION AND STATE	1990	1992	DIVISION AND STATE	1990	1992	DIVISION AND STATE	1990	1992	DIVISION AND STATE	1990	1992
U.S	6.5	7.6	IL	7.1	7.9	WV	8.8	9.7	Mt	4.2	5.3
			MI	8.6	9.0	NC	5.7	7.2	MT	4.9	5.4
N.E	5.6	6.8	WI	6.6	6.9	SC	5.8	6.7	ID	2.7	3.2
ME	6.6	7.6	**W.N.C**	4.8	5.5	GA	7.1	8.5	WY	3.8	5.2
NH	2.2	3.4	MN	4.9	5.7	FL	4.6	6.8	CO	4.3	5.0
VT	5.7	7.2	IA	4.7	5.0	**E.S.C**	7.9	9.0	NM	5.8	8.0
MA	6.4	7.5	MO	5.8	6.8	KY	7.9	9.8	AZ	4.7	6.4
RI	6.4	8.0	ND	3.6	4.3	TN	7.2	8.6	UT	3.3	3.8
CT	4.7	6.0	SD	4.2	4.6	AL	6.5	7.1	NV	2.9	3.6
M.A	6.7	7.8	NE	3.7	4.2	MS	11.4	11.8	**Pac**	8.4	9.7
NY	7.7	9.0	KS	4.1	4.6				WA	6.0	6.9
NJ	5.3	6.1	**S.A**	5.4	6.9	**W.S.C**	6.2	7.0	OR	4.3	5.2
PA	6.0	6.9	DE	4.4	5.2	AR	6.3	6.8	CA	9.4	10.7
E.N.C	7.0	7.8	MD	5.1	6.0	LA	9.8	10.2	AK	4.6	6.7
OH	7.3	8.7	DC	10.9	13.3	OK	5.6	6.4	HI	5.2	5.9
IN	3.9	5.0	VA	3.9	4.8	TX	5.4	6.3			

Source: Compiled by U.S. Bureau of the Census. Data from U.S. Social Security Administration, *Social Security Bulletin*, quarterly, and U.S. Administration for Children and Families, *Quarterly Public Assistance Statistics*, annual.

No. 600. Aid to Families With Dependent Children (AFDC) and Supplemental Security Income (SSI)—Recipients and Payments, by State and Other Areas: 1990 to 1992

[Recipients as of December. Data for SSI cover Federal SSI payments and/or federally-administered State supplementation except as noted. For explanation of methodology, see Appendix III]

DIVISION AND STATE OR OTHER AREA	AFDC Recipients [1] (1,000)			AFDC Payments for year (mil. dol.)			AFDC Average monthly payment per family		SSI Recipients (1,000)		SSI Payments for year (mil. dol.)	
	1990	1991	1992	1990	1991	1992	1990	1992	1990	1992	1990	1992
Total	12,159	13,489	14,035	19,078	20,931	22,106	$392	$381	[2]4,817	[2]5,566	16,133	[2]21,682
U.S.	11,958	13,285	13,834	18,995	20,843	22,017	396	385	4,817	5,566	16,133	21,680
New England	577	653	680	1,250	1,384	1,502	535	535	209	241	652	879
ME	62	69	67	104	116	118	422	414	24	26	56	73
NH	21	28	29	35	49	55	431	428	[3]7	[3]8	[3]19	[3]27
VT	25	29	29	51	59	70	527	583	10	12	31	42
MA	282	311	335	647	682	750	556	558	119	138	397	534
RI	52	59	61	104	122	130	499	506	17	20	53	70
CT	135	157	159	309	355	379	571	565	[3]32	[3]37	[3]96	[3]132
Middle Atlantic	1,903	2,061	2,120	3,623	3,872	4,073	472	464	711	835	2,533	3,463
NY	1,031	1,108	1,171	2,337	2,496	2,633	556	544	415	491	1,557	2,109
NJ	323	364	347	459	496	518	352	341	105	124	340	470
PA	549	590	601	827	881	922	382	380	191	220	635	884
East North Central	2,397	2,561	2,519	3,611	3,701	3,708	379	356	622	754	2,021	2,940
OH	657	746	721	896	955	979	328	310	156	190	483	715
IN	164	195	199	174	202	221	263	263	[3]60	[3]75	[3]174	[3]271
IL	656	698	682	868	929	891	342	325	[3]177	[3]220	[3]593	[3]880
MI	684	680	684	1,232	1,163	1,167	464	431	143	171	483	667
WI	236	241	233	441	452	450	464	462	86	98	288	406
West North Central	647	704	719	955	1,030	1,077	366	363	216	253	584	835
MN	177	183	186	355	379	388	512	502	[3]40	[3]49	[3]110	[3]163
IA	96	103	101	154	162	164	371	369	33	37	86	119
MO	218	249	260	237	265	286	274	275	[3]85	[3]98	[3]237	[3]332
ND	16	18	19	24	26	28	359	357	[3]7	[3]8	[3]18	[4]24
SD	19	20	20	22	24	25	272	290	10	12	26	37
NE	44	48	48	60	63	66	336	329	[3]16	[3]18	[3]42	[3]60
KS	77	84	86	103	111	121	332	346	25	30	65	99
South Atlantic	1,654	1,986	2,212	1,844	2,171	2,499	272	268	847	969	2,370	3,205
DE	22	26	28	30	34	38	292	292	8	9	22	29
MD	198	220	222	304	337	335	370	348	60	69	185	249
DC	54	61	63	87	100	101	380	371	16	18	54	68
VA	158	185	194	181	208	228	265	264	[3]95	[3]110	[3]257	[3]353
WV	109	119	119	112	116	121	249	247	[4]47	[4]55	[4]146	[4]209
NC	255	308	335	257	312	343	237	230	[3]149	[3]166	[3]403	[3]519
SC	118	137	147	97	111	119	203	196	[3]90	[3]99	[3]234	[3]313
GA	320	383	400	333	392	427	265	257	159	177	415	555
FL	420	546	704	443	560	787	263	278	222	267	653	911
East South Central	742	816	858	510	570	600	168	171	501	566	1,371	1,912
KY	204	230	229	185	208	214	224	214	[3]115	[3]134	[3]337	[3]481
TN	230	266	316	176	200	210	186	179	140	159	384	523
AL	132	142	141	63	73	88	115	144	[3]133	[3]147	[3]351	[3]479
MS	176	178	172	86	88	89	120	122	114	126	300	429
West South Central	1,154	1,238	1,268	811	896	941	180	180	564	655	1,478	2,201
AR	73	76	73	57	60	60	190	188	76	86	187	275
LA	279	276	269	188	189	184	167	167	[3]133	[3]157	[3]378	[3]622
OK	129	133	142	135	157	173	279	302	[3]60	[3]67	[3]158	[3]210
TX	673	753	784	431	489	524	165	162	[4]295	[4]345	[4]755	[4]1,095
Mountain	454	543	575	523	642	739	297	320	162	201	476	699
MT	29	32	34	40	43	46	344	349	10	12	29	39
ID	17	19	21	20	23	24	266	272	[3]10	[3]13	[3]29	[3]47
WY	16	19	18	20	26	27	313	337	[3]3	[3]5	[3]9	[3]14
CO	109	127	125	138	154	163	320	323	[3]38	[3]47	[3]110	[3]160
NM	67	86	94	66	92	109	273	307	[3]32	[3]37	[3]90	[3]126
AZ	144	178	194	146	197	252	268	320	[3]45	[3]57	[3]139	[3]204
UT	47	51	53	65	73	76	347	348	13	16	38	59
NV	25	32	35	28	35	41	278	284	11	15	33	50
Pacific	2,427	2,723	2,883	5,866	6,578	6,878	606	581	984	1,091	4,646	5,545
WA	237	269	283	447	533	572	452	488	62	75	208	290
OR	99	117	116	150	187	200	374	401	[3]32	[3]39	[3]95	[3]135
CA	2,023	2,258	2,395	5,107	5,664	5,875	637	598	873	957	4,278	5,037
AK	24	30	35	62	81	100	651	750	[3]5	[3]5	[3]14	[3]19
HI	44	49	54	100	112	130	581	639	14	16	51	63
PR	193	195	191	74	77	77	103	105	(X)	(X)	(X)	(X)
GU	4	5	6	6	7	8	418	506	(X)	(X)	(X)	(X)
VI	3	4	4	3	3	3	279	275	(X)	(X)	(X)	(X)
N. Mariana	(X)	(X)	(X)	(X)	(X)	(X)	(X)	(X)	[4]1	[4]1	[4]2	[4]2

X Not applicable.   [1] See footnote 3, table 597.   [2] Includes data for those recipients whose residence was "unknown."   [3] Data for persons with Federal SSI payments only; State has State-administered supplementation.   [4] Data for persons with Federal SSI payments only; State supplementary payments not made.

Source: U.S. Social Security Administration, *Social Security Bulletin*, quarterly, and *Annual Statistical Supplement* to the *Social Security Bulletin*; and U.S. Administration for Children and Families, *Quarterly Public Assistance Statistics*, annual.

No. 601. Federal Food Stamp and National School Lunch Programs, by State: 1990 to 1993

[Cost data for years ending Sept. 30. Data on food stamp households and persons are average monthly number participating in year ending Sept. 30. Data on pupils participating in National School Lunch Program are for month in which the highest number of children participated nationwide. For National School Lunch Program, covers public and private elementary and secondary schools and residential child care institutions. Food Stamp costs are for benefits only and exclude administrative expenditures. National School Lunch Program costs include Federal cash reimbursements at rates set by law for each meal served but do not include the value of USDA donated commodities utilized in this program]

REGION, DIVISION, AND STATE	Households participating, 1993 Number (1,000)	Households participating, 1993 Percent of all households	Persons (1,000) 1990	Persons (1,000) 1992	Persons (1,000) 1993	Cost (mil. dol.) 1990	Cost (mil. dol.) 1992	Cost (mil. dol.) 1993	Persons (1,000) 1990	Persons (1,000) 1992	Persons (1,000) 1993	Cost (mil. dol.) 1990	Cost (mil. dol.) 1992	Cost (mil. dol.) 1993
			FOOD STAMP PROGRAM						NATIONAL SCHOOL LUNCH PROGRAM					
Total [1]	10,791	(NA)	20,067	25,406	26,983	14,187	20,906	22,009	24,589	25,114	25,334	3,214	3,856	4,075
U.S.	10,782	11.3	20,036	25,369	26,953	14,153	20,859	21,972	24,019	24,546	24,770	3,098	3,739	3,960
Northeast	2,113	11.1	3,589	4,479	4,769	2,462	3,642	3,964	4,033	4,029	4,070	489	592	635
N.E	434	8.7	707	962	1,007	426	707	738	991	949	964	95	120	127
ME	61	12.9	94	133	138	63	109	112	108	106	106	11	14	15
NH	26	6.2	31	58	60	20	45	46	91	90	87	6	8	9
VT	25	11.5	38	54	58	22	37	38	47	48	49	4	6	6
MA	189	8.4	347	429	443	207	315	326	454	429	441	44	53	57
RI	40	10.6	64	87	92	42	69	73	60	55	56	7	10	10
CT	93	7.6	133	202	215	72	131	143	231	220	226	23	29	31
M.A.	1,679	11.9	2,882	3,517	3,762	2,036	2,935	3,226	3,042	3,080	3,106	393	472	508
NY	943	14.1	1,548	1,885	2,045	1,086	1,586	1,796	1,546	1,588	1,617	232	274	290
NJ	218	7.7	382	494	531	289	433	469	507	513	505	60	76	88
PA	518	11.4	952	1,137	1,186	661	916	961	990	979	985	102	122	130
Midwest	2,360	10.3	4,806	5,616	5,813	3,566	4,739	4,780	5,806	5,920	5,912	619	724	764
E.N.C.	1,757	11.0	3,616	4,183	4,304	2,765	3,627	3,626	3,687	3,743	3,739	421	494	519
OH	535	12.8	1,089	1,251	1,269	861	1,102	1,101	919	953	943	109	125	130
IN	184	8.6	311	448	497	226	373	406	635	610	602	54	65	67
IL	[2]493	[2]11.5	1,013	1,156	[2]1,178	835	1,070	[2]1,060	932	955	959	131	155	161
MI	419	12.0	917	994	1,022	663	846	837	733	746	747	82	96	105
WI	125	6.7	286	334	337	180	236	221	468	480	487	45	53	56
W.N.C	603	8.8	1,190	1,433	1,510	801	1,112	1,154	2,119	2,177	2,173	197	231	245
MN	131	7.7	263	309	317	165	234	229	489	506	510	42	49	53
IA	[2]78	[2]7.3	170	192	[2]196	109	143	[2]147	392	396	383	31	36	38
MO	[2]236	[2]11.8	431	549	[2]591	312	447	[2]478	547	557	562	58	68	72
ND	19	7.9	39	46	48	25	35	36	94	94	92	8	9	10
SD	20	7.6	50	55	56	35	42	43	102	106	108	12	13	14
NE	45	7.4	95	107	113	59	78	81	191	206	203	18	21	22
KS	73	7.6	142	175	188	96	133	141	302	313	316	29	34	36
South	4,332	13.0	8,040	10,576	11,199	5,928	8,908	9,234	9,890	10,079	10,177	1,334	1,604	1,692
S.A	1,890	10.9	2,993	4,404	4,705	2,223	3,781	3,933	4,454	4,515	4,579	558	686	736
DE	21	8.0	33	51	58	25	42	46	59	59	61	6	7	8
MD	159	8.7	255	342	375	203	316	336	347	352	352	40	48	52
DC	41	17.1	62	82	87	43	70	81	47	47	47	10	11	12
VA	225	9.3	346	495	535	247	406	432	586	589	586	60	72	78
WV	124	17.7	262	310	322	192	255	261	198	184	199	29	31	31
NC	253	9.6	419	597	627	282	461	480	749	750	751	91	108	113
SC	146	11.1	299	369	394	240	297	306	451	458	459	60	72	76
GA	315	12.4	536	754	807	382	627	657	908	927	948	106	131	140
FL	606	11.3	781	[2]1,404	1,500	609	[2]1,306	1,334	1,110	1,149	1,174	158	205	227
E.S.C.	932	15.9	1,938	2,316	2,401	1,386	1,864	1,907	2,085	2,102	2,110	281	324	333
KY	200	14.1	458	529	530	334	430	422	498	523	521	61	73	75
TN	317	16.4	527	702	774	372	562	611	590	592	601	68	80	83
AL	216	13.8	454	550	560	328	451	457	570	567	565	77	87	89
MS	200	21.4	499	536	537	352	421	416	428	420	423	76	84	86
W.S.C	1,510	15.0	3,109	3,856	4,093	2,319	3,263	3,395	3,351	3,462	3,489	495	595	623
AR	106	11.6	235	277	285	155	207	209	292	310	310	41	46	51
LA	282	18.4	727	[2]779	779	549	[2]677	653	694	691	691	104	116	121
OK	146	11.9	267	346	370	186	275	294	362	370	370	46	55	58
TX	975	15.2	1,880	2,454	2,659	1,429	2,103	2,239	2,003	2,091	2,119	304	377	393
West	1,977	9.9	3,601	4,699	5,172	2,197	3,570	3,993	4,289	4,518	4,611	657	818	869
Mountain	529	9.7	988	1,313	1,415	726	1,079	1,134	1,362	1,415	1,467	170	210	225
MT	27	8.4	57	66	70	41	52	54	84	88	87	10	11	12
ID	29	7.4	59	72	79	40	53	57	131	135	140	14	17	18
WY	13	7.5	28	33	34	21	26	26	57	59	58	5	6	7
CO	108	7.8	221	260	273	156	219	226	282	290	295	31	38	40
NM	85	14.7	157	221	244	117	182	194	179	183	183	30	36	37
AZ	178	12.1	317	457	489	239	377	393	331	356	365	47	61	67
UT	47	8.1	99	123	133	71	96	97	233	221	249	24	30	31
NV	42	7.8	50	80	93	41	74	86	67	83	89	8	11	13
Pacific	1,448	10.0	2,613	3,386	3,757	1,471	2,491	2,859	2,927	3,103	3,144	487	608	644
WA	191	9.5	340	431	462	229	344	369	361	396	406	43	55	61
OR	123	10.5	216	265	283	168	226	235	234	246	250	26	33	35
CA	1,075	10.0	1,955	2,558	2,866	968	1,760	2,079	2,147	2,270	2,292	396	494	522
AK	14	6.8	25	38	43	25	[2]41	45	39	43	45	8	11	11
HI	44	11.6	77	[2]94	103	81	[2]121	132	145	148	150	14	16	15

NA Not available.   [1] Includes Puerto Rico (for NSLP), other outlying areas and Dept. of Defense overseas.   [2] Includes disaster relief.

Source: U.S. Dept. of Agriculture, Food and Nutrition Service. In "Annual Historical Review of FNS Programs" and unpublished data.

No. 602. Federal Food Programs: 1980 to 1993

[For fiscal years ending in year shown; see text, section 9. Program data include Puerto Rico, Virgin Islands, Guam, American Samoa, Northern Marianas, and the former Trust Territory when a Federal food program was operated in these areas. Participation data are average monthly figures except as noted. Participants are not reported for the nutrition program for the elderly and the commodity distribution programs. Cost data are direct Federal benefits to recipients; they exclude Federal administrative payments and applicable State and local contributions. Federal costs for commodities and cash-in-lieu of commodities are shown separately from direct cash benefits for those programs receiving both]

PROGRAM	Unit	1980	1985	1988	1989	1990	1991	1992	1993, prel.
Food Stamp:									
Participants	Million . .	21.1	19.9	18.6	18.8	20.1	22.6	25.4	27.0
Federal cost	Mil. dol. .	8,721	10,744	11,149	11,676	14,187	17,339	20,906	22,009
Monthly average coupon value per recipient .	Dollars . .	34.47	44.99	49.83	51.85	58.93	63.86	68.57	67.97
Nutrition assistance program for Puerto Rico: [1]									
Federal cost	Mil. dol. .	(X)	825	879	908	937	963	1,002	1,040
National school lunch program (NSLP): [2]									
Free lunches served	Million . .	1,671	1,657	1,651	1,627	1,662	1,749	1,891	1,978
Reduced-price lunches served	Million . .	308	255	262	263	273	293	285	288
Children participating [3]	Million . .	26.6	23.6	24.2	24.3	24.1	24.2	24.6	24.8
Federal cost	Mil. dol. .	2,279	2,578	2,908	3,006	3,214	3,525	3,856	4,075
School breakfast (SB):									
Children participating [3]	Million . .	3.6	3.4	3.7	3.8	4.1	4.4	4.9	5.3
Federal cost	Mil. dol. .	288	379	482	513	596	685	787	866
Special supplemental food program (WIC): [4]									
Participants	Million . .	1.9	3.1	3.6	4.1	4.5	4.9	5.4	5.9
Federal cost	Mil. dol. .	584	1,193	1,435	1,489	1,637	1,752	1,958	2,118
Commodity supplemental food program: [5]									
Participants	Million . .	0.1	0.2	0.2	0.2	0.3	0.3	0.3	0.4
Federal cost	Mil. dol. .	19	42	52	62	71	76	87	94
Child and adult care (CC): [6]									
Participants	Million . .	0.7	1.0	1.3	1.4	1.5	1.6	1.8	1.9
Federal cost	Mil. dol. .	207	390	538	612	720	834	966	1,076
Summer feeding (SF): [8]									
Children participating [9]	Million . .	1.9	1.5	1.6	1.7	1.7	1.8	1.9	2.1
Federal cost	Mil. dol. .	104	103	113	132	145	160	182	190
Nutrition program for the elderly:									
Meals served	Million . .	166	225	240	243	246	245	245	243
Federal cost	Mil. dol. .	75	134	146	146	142	140	145	139
Federal cost of commodities donated to— [10]									
Child nutrition (NSLP, CC, SF and SB)	Mil. dol. .	930	840	853	793	646	701	736	715
Charitable institutions, summer camps	Mil. dol. .	71	170	158	136	104	93	115	89
Emergency feeding [11]	Mil. dol. .	(X)	973	593	266	286	252	229	229

X Not applicable. [1] Puerto Rico was included in the food stamp program until June 30, 1982. [2] See headnote, table 601. [3] Nine month (September through May) average daily meals (lunches or breakfasts) served divided by the ratio of average daily attendance to enrollment. [4] WIC serves women, infants, and children. [5] Program provides commodities to women, infants, children, and the elderly. [6] Program provides year-round subsidies to feed preschool children in child care centers and family day care homes. Certain care centers serving disabled or elderly adults also receive meal subsidies. [7] Quarterly average daily attendance at participating institutions. [8] Program provides free meals to children in poor areas during summer months. [9] Peak month (July) average daily attendance at participating institutions. [10] Includes the Federal cost of commodity entitlements, cash-in-lieu of commodities, and bonus foods. [11] Provides free commodities to needy persons for home consumption through food banks, hunger centers, soup kitchens, and similar nonprofit agencies. Includes the Emergency Food Assistance Program, the commodity purchases for soup kitchens/food banks program, and commodity disaster relief.

Source: U.S. Dept. of Agriculture, Food and Nutrition Service. In "Annual Historical Review of FNS Programs" and unpublished data.

No. 603. Primary Child Care Arrangements Used by Employed Mothers for Children Under 5 Years Old: 1991

[As of fall. Data were obtained for the three youngest children in the household. Based on the Survey of Income and Program Participation; see text, section 14]

TYPE OF ARRANGEMENT	Total	AGE			MONTHLY FAMILY INCOME			
		Under 1 year	1 to 2 years	3 to 4 years	Less than $1,500	$1,500 to $2,999	$3,000 to $4,499	$4,500 or more
Children under 5 years old, total (1,000) . .	9,854	1,650	4,021	4,183	1,618	3,173	2,594	2,403
PERCENT DISTRIBUTION								
Care in child's home	35.7	40.5	38.7	31.1	37.4	39.6	36.2	29.5
By father	20.0	21.6	21.2	18.3	21.2	25.3	20.3	12.2
By grandparent	7.2	8.7	8.0	5.8	5.6	7.6	8.2	6.6
By other relative	3.2	2.7	3.9	2.7	7.0	3.2	2.2	1.7
By nonrelative	5.4	7.5	5.5	4.3	3.6	3.5	5.5	9.0
Care in another home	31.0	40.5	33.8	24.5	32.8	31.2	32.6	27.2
By grandparent	8.6	14.3	8.6	6.3	10.8	9.5	9.9	3.9
By other relative	4.5	5.6	4.7	3.8	5.7	6.0	3.8	2.5
By nonrelative	17.9	20.5	20.4	14.4	16.3	15.7	18.9	20.8
Organized child care facilities	23.0	11.5	17.5	32.9	20.4	17.5	21.9	33.7
Day/group care center	15.8	9.8	15.2	18.6	14.8	10.9	17.0	21.9
Nursery school/preschool	7.3	1.7	2.3	14.2	5.6	6.6	4.9	11.8
School-based activity	0.5	-	0.1	1.1	0.4	1.1	-	0.5
Mother cares for child at work [1]	8.7	7.6	9.9	7.9	7.2	10.3	7.8	7.9
Other arrangements [2]	1.1	-	-	2.5	1.8	0.4	1.3	1.2

- Represents or rounds to zero. [1] Includes mothers working at home or away from home. [2] Includes children in kindergarten/grade school.

Source: U.S. Bureau of the Census, Current Population Reports, P70-36.

No. 604. Child Support—Award and Recipiency Status of Women: 1981 to 1989

[Women with own children under 21 years of age present from absent fathers. For 1989, women 15 years old and over as of April 1990; for previous years, women 18 years old and over as of April of following year. Covers civilian noninstitutional population. Based on Current Population Survey; see text, section 1, and Appendix III]

AWARD AND RECIPIENCY STATUS	ALL WOMEN						WOMEN BELOW THE POVERTY LEVEL					
	Number (1,000)			Percent distribution			Number (1,000)			Percent distribution		
	1981	1985	1989	1981	1985	1989	1981	1985	1989	1981	1985	1989
Total	8,387	8,808	9,955	100	100	100	2,566	2,797	3,206	100	100	100
Payments awarded	4,969	5,396	5,748	59	61	58	1,018	1,130	1,387	40	40	43
Supposed to receive payments .	4,043	4,381	4,953	48	50	50	806	905	1,190	31	32	37
Not supposed to receive payments	926	1,015	795	11	12	8	212	225	197	8	8	6
Payments not awarded	3,417	3,411	4,207	41	39	42	1,547	1,668	1,819	60	60	57
Supposed to receive payments .	4,043	4,381	4,953	100	100	100	806	905	1,190	100	100	100
Actually received payments	2,902	3,243	3,725	72	74	75	495	595	813	61	66	68
Received full amount	1,888	2,112	2,546	47	48	51	(NA)	(NA)	(NA)	(NA)	(NA)	(NA)
Received partial amount	1,014	1,131	1,179	25	26	24	(NA)	(NA)	(NA)	(NA)	(NA)	(NA)
Did not receive payments	1,140	1,138	1,228	28	26	25	311	310	377	39	34	32

NA Not available.

Source: U.S. Bureau of the Census, *Current Population Reports*, P60-173.

No. 605. Child Support and Alimony—Selected Characteristics of Women: 1989

[See headnote, table 604. Alimony data are for ever-divorced and currently separated women. For definition of mean, see Guide to Tabular Presentation]

RECIPIENCY STATUS OF WOMEN	Unit	Total [1]	AGE				RACE		His-panic [2]	CURRENT MARITAL STATUS			
			18 to 29 years	30 to 39 years	40 years and over	White	Black		Divorced	Married [3]	Never married	Separated
CHILD SUPPORT													
All women, total	1,000 . .	9,955	3,086	4,175	2,566	6,905	2,770	1,112	3,056	2,531	2,950	1,352
Payments awarded	1,000 . .	5,748	1,408	2,685	1,632	4,661	955	452	2,347	1,999	704	648
Percent of total	Percent.	58	46	64	64	68	35	41	77	79	24	48
Supposed to receive child support in 1989	1,000 . .	4,953	1,208	2,413	1,309	4,048	791	364	2,123	1,685	583	527
Percent received payment.	Percent.	75	76	74	76	77	70	70	77	72	73	80
Mean child support	Dollars .	2,995	1,981	3,032	3,903	3,132	2,263	2,965	3,322	2,931	1,888	3,060
Percent of total income .	Percent.	19	20	18	19	19	16	20	17	20	20	21
Women with incomes below the poverty level in 1989	1,000 . .	3,206	1,531	1,189	434	1,763	1,314	536	820	176	1,590	612
Payments awarded	1,000 . .	1,387	608	568	195	962	384	177	577	127	389	288
Percent of total	Percent.	43	40	48	45	55	29	33	70	72	25	47
Supposed to receive child support in 1989	1,000 . .	1,190	507	500	168	827	325	148	525	106	334	221
Percent received payment.	Percent.	68	68	67	72	68	70	64	66	67	69	74
Mean child support	Dollars .	1,889	1,515	2,167	2,316	1,972	1,674	1,824	2,112	2,275	1,553	1,717
Percent of total income .	Percent.	37	33	36	56	39	32	37	38	52	34	35
ALIMONY													
All women, total	1,000 . .	20,610	2,464	6,093	12,051	17,245	2,863	1,499	8,888	7,738	(X)	2,790
Number awarded payments . . .	1,000 . .	3,189	184	610	2,394	2,801	305	171	1,472	1,170	(X)	316
Percent of total	Percent.	16	8	10	20	16	11	11	17	15	(X)	11
Supposed to receive payments	1,000 . .	922	85	267	569	787	98	63	567	170	(X)	164
Women with incomes below the poverty level in 1989	1,000 . .	3,692	726	1,206	1,758	2,640	931	477	1,860	420	(X)	1,147
Number awarded payments . . .	1,000 . .	429	60	96	273	340	76	31	223	55	(X)	110
Percent of total	Percent.	12	8	8	16	13	8	6	12	13	(X)	10
Supposed to receive payments	1,000 . .	178	43	56	79	149	26	21	112	11	(X)	54

X Not applicable.   [1] Includes other items, not shown separately.   [2] Hispanic women may be of any race.   [3] Remarried women whose previous marriage ended in divorce.

Source: U.S. Bureau of the Census, *Current Population Reports*, P60-173.

No. 606. Child Support Enforcement Program—Caseload and Collections: 1980 to 1992

[For years ending Sept. 30. Includes Puerto Rico, Guam, and the Virgin Islands. The Child Support Enforcement program locates absent parents, establishes paternity of children born out-of-wedlock, and establishes and enforces support orders. By law, these services are available to all families that need them. The program is operated at the State and local government level but 68 percent of administrative costs are paid by the Federal government. Child support collected for families not receiving Aid to Families with Dependent Children (AFDC) goes to the family to help it remain self-sufficient. Most of the child support collected on behalf of AFDC families goes to Federal and State governments to offset AFDC payments. Based on data reported by State agencies. Minus sign (-) indicates net outlay]

ITEM	Unit	1980	1985	1987	1988	1989	1990	1991	1992
Total cases	1,000 . . .	5,432	8,401	10,635	11,078	11,876	12,796	13,423	15,172
AFDC and AFDC arrears only caseload	1,000 . . .	(NA)	(NA)	7,655	7,501	7,610	7,953	8,034	8,712
AFDC cases	1,000 . . .	4,583	6,242	5,776	5,703	5,709	5,872	6,166	6,755
AFDC arrears only cases [1]	1,000 . . .	(NA)	(NA)	1,879	1,798	1,901	2,082	1,868	1,957
Non-AFDC cases	1,000 . . .	849	2,159	2,981	3,577	4,266	4,843	5,389	6,461
Cases for which a collection was made:									
AFDC cases.	1,000 . . .	503	684	609	621	658	701	755	832
AFDC arrears only cases [1]	1,000 . . .	(NA)	(NA)	196	181	202	224	278	255
Non-AFDC cases	1,000 . . .	243	654	934	1,083	1,247	1,363	1,555	1,752
Percentage of cases with collections:									
AFDC cases.	Percent .	11.0	11.0	10.5	10.9	11.5	11.9	12.2	12.3
AFDC arrears only cases [1]	Percent .	(NA)	(NA)	10.5	10.1	10.6	10.8	14.9	13.1
Non-AFDC cases	Percent .	28.7	30.3	31.3	30.3	29.2	28.1	28.9	27.1
Absent parents located, total	1,000 . . .	643	878	1,145	1,388	1,628	2,062	2,577	3,704
Paternities established, total.	1,000 . . .	144	232	269	307	339	393	472	517
Support obligations established, total [2] .	1,000 . . .	374	669	812	870	938	1,022	821	895
FINANCES									
Collections, total	Mil. dol .	1,478	2,694	3,917	4,605	5,241	6,010	6,886	7,965
AFDC collections	Mil. dol . .	603	1,090	1,348	1,486	1,593	1,750	1,984	2,259
State share.	Mil. dol . .	274	415	473	525	563	620	700	787
Incentive payments to States	Mil. dol . .	72	145	185	222	266	264	278	299
Federal share	Mil. dol . .	246	341	413	449	458	533	626	738
Payments to AFDC families [3]	Mil. dol . .	10	189	278	289	307	334	381	435
Non-AFDC collections	Mil. dol . .	874	1,604	2,569	3,119	3,648	4,260	4,902	5,706
Administrative expenditures, total	Mil. dol . .	466	814	1,066	1,171	1,363	1,606	1,804	1,995
State share	Mil. dol . .	117	243	316	366	426	545	593	652
Federal share	Mil. dol . .	349	571	750	804	938	1,061	1,212	1,343
Program savings, total.	Mil. dol . .	127	86	5	26	-77	-190	-201	-171
State share	Mil. dol . .	230	317	342	381	403	338	385	434
Federal share.	Mil. dol . .	-103	-231	-337	-355	-480	-528	-586	-605
Total fees and costs recovered for									
non-AFDC cases	Mil. dol . .	5	3	7	7	7	22	34	29
Percentage of AFDC payments recovered	Percent .	5.2	7.3	9.1	9.8	10.0	10.3	10.7	11.4

NA Not available. [1] Reflects cases that are no longer receiving AFDC but still have outstanding child support due. [2] Through 1990 covers new support orders and modifications. Beginning 1991 covers only new support orders. [3] Beginning 1985, States were required to pass along to the family the first $50 of any current child support collected each month.
Source: U.S. Department of Health and Human Services, Office of Child Support Enforcement, *Annual Report to Congress*.

No. 607. Percent of Adult Population Doing Volunteer Work: 1991

[Covers persons 18 years and over. Volunteers are persons who worked in some way to help others for no monetary pay during the previous year. See headnote, table 608]

AGE, SEX, RACE AND HISPANIC ORIGIN	Percent of population volunteering	Average hours volunteered per week	EDUCATIONAL ATTAINMENT AND HOUSEHOLD INCOME	Percent of population volunteering	Average hours volunteered per week	TYPE OF ACTIVITY	Percent of volunteers involved in activity
Total	51.1	4.2	Elementary school	25.0	(NA)	Arts, culture, humanities. .	6.2
			Some high school	22.1	5.1	Education	15.4
18-24 years old	48.3	3.2	High school graduate	44.7	4.1	Environment	8.6
25-34 years old	52.9	4.2	Technical, trade, or			Health	12.9
35-44 years old	60.8	4.7	business school	51.5	3.9	Human services	12.1
45-54 years old	55.9	4.0	Some college	66.1	3.5		
55-64 years old	49.4	4.5	College graduate	76.6	4.6	Informal	23.4
65-74 years old	42.0	4.3				International, foreign	2.3
75 years old and over.	26.6	(NA)	Under $10,000.	31.6	4.0	Political organizations . . .	4.7
			$10,000-$19,999	37.9	3.9	Private, community	
Male	49.2	3.3	$20,000-$29,999	51.3	4.0	foundations	2.3
Female	52.9	5.0	$30,000-$39,999	56.4	4.7		
			$40,000-$49,999	67.4	4.2	Public and societal benefit.	6.4
White.	52.6	4.2	$50,000-$59,999	67.7	3.9	Recreation - adults	6.7
Black.	43.3	4.5	$60,000-$74,999	55.0	5.1	Religion	26.8
			$75,000-$99,999	62.8	3.7	Work-related organizations	7.1
Hispanic [1]	37.6	4.5	$100,000 or more.	73.7	3.7	Youth development	14.7

NA Not available. [1] Hispanic persons may be of any race.

Source: Hodgkinson, Virginia, Murray Weitzman, and the Gallup Organization, Inc., *Giving and Volunteering in the United States: 1992 Edition*. (Copyright and published by INDEPENDENT SECTOR, Washington, DC, fall 1992.)

No. 608. Charity Contributions—Average Dollar Amount and Percent of Household Income, 1987 to 1991, and by Age of Respondent and Household Income, 1991

[Estimates cover households' contribution activity for the year and are based on respondents' replies as to contribution and volunteer activity of household. Based on a sample survey conducted during the spring of the following year and subject to sampling variability; see source]

YEAR AND AGE	ALL CONTRIBUTING HOUSEHOLDS		CONTRIBUTORS AND VOLUNTEERS		HOUSEHOLD INCOME	ALL CONTRIBUTING HOUSEHOLDS		CONTRIBUTORS AND VOLUNTEERS	
	Average amount (dol.)	Percent of household income	Average amount (dol.)	Percent of household income		Average amount (dol.)	Percent of household income	Average amount (dol.)	Percent of household income
1987.	790	1.9	1,021	2.4	1991—				
1989.	978	2.5	1,192	2.9	Under $10,000 . . .	239	3.6	215	3.4
1991, total.	899	2.2	1,155	2.6	$10,000-$19,999 . .	507	3.4	601	3.9
18-24 years.	233	0.8	261	0.9	$20,000-$29,999 . .	617	2.5	778	3.1
25-34 years.	629	1.5	815	1.9	$30,000-$39,999 . .	640	1.8	762	2.2
35-44 years.	1,135	2.4	1,381	2.7	$40,000-$49,999 . .	1,038	2.3	1,286	2.9
45-54 years.	1,243	2.4	1,581	2.8	$50,000-$59,999 . .	1,293	2.4	1,461	2.7
55-64 years.	1,228	2.9	1,592	3.4	$60,000-$74,999 . .	1,180	1.7	1,397	2.1
65-74 years.	891	3.2	1,260	3.9	$75,000-$99,999 . .	1,666	1.9	2,131	2.4
75 years and over. .	710	3.2	(B)	(B)	$100,000 and over.	2,450	2.5	2,722	2.7

B Base too small to meet statistical standards for reliability.

No. 609. Charity Contributions—Percent of Households Contributing, by Dollar Amount, 1987 to 1991, and Type of Charity, 1991

[In percent, except as noted. See headnote, table 608]

ANNUAL AMOUNT OF HOUSEHOLD CONTRIBUTIONS	ALL HOUSEHOLDS			GIVERS			TYPE OF CHARITY	1991	
	1987	1989	1991	1987	1989	1991		Percentage of households	Average contribution [1] (dol.)
None	28.9	24.9	27.8	(X)	(X)	(X)	Arts, culture, humanities .	9.4	194
Givers	71.0	75.1	72.2	100.0	100.0	100.0	Education	21.1	225
$1 to $100. . . .	20.8	16.3	14.9	32.7	27.0	24.9	Environment.	16.3	99
$101 to $200 . .	7.4	8.1	8.1	11.6	13.4	13.5	Health.	32.9	154
$201 to $300 . .	6.6	4.8	7.3	10.5	8.0	12.2	Human services	27.5	260
$301 to $400 . .	3.5	4.6	3.3	5.6	7.6	5.6	International	3.5	198
$401 to $500 . .	3.2	3.1	3.2	5.0	5.1	5.4	Private, community		
$501 to $600 . .	2.3	2.6	2.6	3.7	4.3	4.4	foundations.	6.0	113
$601 to $700 . .	2.0	1.5	2.5	3.2	2.5	4.2	Public, societal benefit . .	11.2	132
$701 to $999 . .	3.7	4.8	3.4	5.8	7.9	5.7	Recreation - adults	6.3	164
$1,000 or more .	13.9	14.5	14.5	21.9	24.0	24.2	Religion.	51.3	800
Not reported. . .	7.6	14.7	12.4	(X)	(X)	(X)	Youth development	22.1	114

X Not applicable.   [1] Average contribution per contributing household.
Source of tables 608 and 609: Hodgkinson, Virginia, Murray Weitzman, and the Gallup Organization, Inc., *Giving and Volunteering in the United States: 1992 Edition.* (Copyright and published by INDEPENDENT SECTOR, Washington, DC, fall 1992.)

No. 610. Private Philanthropy Funds, by Source and Allocation: 1980 to 1992

[In billions of dollars. Estimates for sources of funds based on U.S. Internal Revenue Service reports of individual charitable deductions, household surveys of giving by Independent Sector, and, for years prior to 1986, an econometric model. For corporate giving, data are those prepared by the Council for Aid to Education. Data about foundation donations are based upon surveys of foundations and data provided by the Foundation Center. Estimates of the allocation of funds were derived from surveys of nonprofits conducted by source and other groups. See *Historical Statistics, Colonial Times to 1970*, series H 398-411, for similar but not comparable data]

SOURCE AND ALLOCATION	1980	1981	1982	1983	1984	1985	1986	1987	1988	1989	1990	1991	1992
Total funds.	48.6	55.3	59.2	63.2	68.8	73.2	83.9	90.3	98.4	107.0	111.7	116.8	124.3
Individuals.	40.7	46.0	47.6	52.1	56.5	58.7	67.6	72.3	80.1	87.8	91.0	95.3	101.8
Foundations.	2.8	3.1	3.2	3.6	4.0	4.9	5.4	5.9	6.2	6.6	7.2	7.7	8.3
Corporations	2.2	2.7	3.2	3.7	4.3	4.8	5.1	5.5	5.6	5.8	5.9	6.0	6.0
Charitable bequests	2.9	3.6	5.2	3.9	4.0	4.8	5.7	6.6	6.6	7.0	7.6	7.8	8.2
Allocation:													
Religion.	22.2	25.1	28.1	31.8	35.6	38.2	41.7	43.5	45.2	47.8	49.8	53.9	56.7
Health	5.3	5.8	6.2	6.7	6.8	7.7	8.4	9.2	9.6	9.9	9.9	9.7	10.2
Education.	5.0	5.8	6.0	6.7	7.3	8.2	9.4	9.8	10.2	11.0	12.4	13.5	14.0
Human service	4.9	5.6	6.3	7.2	7.9	8.5	9.1	9.8	10.5	11.4	11.8	11.1	11.6
Arts, culture and humanities. . .	3.2	3.7	5.0	4.2	4.5	5.1	5.8	6.3	6.8	7.5	7.9	8.8	9.3
Public/societal benefit	1.5	1.8	1.7	1.9	1.9	2.2	2.5	2.9	3.2	3.8	4.9	4.9	5.1
Environment/wildlife.	(1)	(1)	(1)	(1)	(1)	(1)	(1)	2.1	2.4	2.0	2.6	2.9	3.1
International	(1)	(1)	(1)	(1)	(1)	(1)	(1)	0.9	1.0	1.2	1.5	1.8	1.7
Undesignated	6.5	7.6	6.0	4.8	4.8	3.3	7.0	5.7	10.0	12.5	10.9	10.3	12.6

[1] Included in "Undesignated."
Source: AAFRC Trust for Philanthropy, New York, NY, *Giving USA*, annual, (copyright).

Social Insurance and Human Services

No. 611. Foundations—Number and Finances, by Asset Size

[Figures are for latest year reported by foundations, usually 1990 or 1991. Covers nongovernmental nonprofit organizations with funds and programs managed by their own trustees or directors, whose goals were to maintain or aid social, educational, religious, or other activities deemed to serve the common good. Excludes organizations that make general appeals to the public for funds, act as trade associations for industrial or other special groups, or do not currently award grants]

ASSET SIZE	Number	Assets (mil. dol.)	Gifts received (mil. dol.)	Expen-ditures (mil. dol.)	Grants (mil. dol.)	PERCENT DISTRIBUTION				
						Number	Assets	Gifts received	Expen-ditures	Grants
Total	33,348	162,859	5,460	11,134	9,208	100.0	100.0	100.0	100.0	100.0
Under $50,000	7,898	145	208	255	236	23.7	0.1	3.8	2.3	2.5
$50,000-$99,999	3,433	251	69	94	83	10.3	0.2	1.3	0.8	0.9
$100,000-$249,999	5,588	919	144	197	169	16.8	0.6	2.6	1.8	1.8
$250,000-$499,999	4,214	1,512	182	282	246	12.6	0.9	3.3	2.5	2.7
$500,000-$999,999	3,727	2,647	262	390	337	11.2	1.6	4.8	3.5	3.7
$1,000,000-$4,999,999	5,505	12,131	922	1,352	1,156	16.5	7.4	16.9	12.1	12.6
$5,000,000-$9,999,999	1,236	8,629	521	767	642	3.7	5.3	9.5	6.9	7.0
$10,000,000-$49,999,999	1,329	27,099	1,354	2,331	1,938	4.0	16.6	24.8	20.9	21.0
$50,000,000-$99,999,999	212	14,719	548	1,001	767	0.6	9.0	10.0	9.0	8.3
$100,000,000-$249,999,999	119	17,958	713	1,120	907	0.4	11.0	13.1	10.1	9.9
$250,000,000 or more	87	76,849	537	3,345	2,726	0.3	47.2	9.8	30.0	29.6

Source: The Foundation Center, New York, NY, Guide to U.S. Foundations, 1st Edition, 1993.

No. 612. Foundations—Grants Reported, by Subject Field and Recipient Organization: 1992

[Covers grants of $10,000 or more in size. Based on reports of 960 foundations. Grant sample totaling $5.31 billion represented about 57 percent of all grant dollars awarded by private, corporate, and community foundations. For definition of foundations, see headnote, table 611]

SUBJECT FIELD	NUMBER OF GRANTS		DOLLAR VALUE OF GRANTS		RECIPIENT ORGANIZATION [1]	NUMBER OF GRANTS		DOLLAR VALUE OF GRANTS	
	Num-ber	Per-cent distri-bution	Amount (mil. dol.)	Per-cent distri-bution		Num-ber	Per-cent distri-bution	Amount (mil. dol.)	Per-cent distri-bution
Total	65,049	100.0	5,312	100.0	Community improvement organizations	2,961	4.6	181	3.4
Arts and culture	9,537	14.7	675	12.7	Educational institutions	19,454	29.9	1,975	37.2
Education	15,003	23.1	1,347	25.4	Colleges & universities	11,356	17.5	1,290	24.3
Environment & animals	3,527	5.4	255	4.8	Educational support agencies	2,786	4.3	257	4.8
Health	8,631	13.3	944	17.8	Schools	3,451	5.3	220	4.1
Human services	13,836	21.3	847	16.0	Environmental agencies	2,513	3.9	156	2.9
International affairs, development & peace	2,073	3.2	179	3.4	Federated funds	2,375	3.7	227	4.3
Public/societal benefit	7,755	11.9	590	11.1	Hospitals/medical care facilities	3,522	5.4	401	7.5
Science and technology	1,968	3.0	215	4.0	Human service agencies	11,229	17.3	578	10.9
Social sciences	1,051	1.6	143	2.7	Museums/historical societies	3,048	4.7	302	5.7
Religion	1,588	2.4	115	2.2	Performing arts groups	3,688	5.7	206	3.9
Other	80	0.1	3	0.1	Professional societies & associations	3,539	5.4	243	4.6

[1] Grants may be awarded to multiple types of recipient organizations and would thereby be double-counted.

Source: The Foundation Center, New York, NY, The Foundation Grants Index, 1994, 22nd Edition, 1993.

No. 613. Corporate Philanthropy—Donations, by Type of Beneficiary: 1980 to 1992

[In millions of dollars. Based on a sample of corporations that gave at least $100,000; see source]

BENEFICIARY	1980	1984	1985	1986	1987	1988	1989	1990	1991	1992
Total [1]	994.6	1,444.3	1,694.7	1,673.7	1,658.4	1,645.7	1,820.1	2,051.5	2,245.5	2,061.4
Health and human services [1]	337.9	399.9	494.1	468.6	450.5	480.2	481.0	580.2	608.9	570.8
Federated drives	170.7	193.9	(NA)	225.9	203.6	235.0	218.3	262.6	285.0	271.4
Education [1]	375.8	561.7	650.0	718.0	610.1	614.1	699.8	789.2	783.6	764.7
Employee matching gifts [2]	45.4	72.2	(NA)	98.7	108.3	108.3	115.0	105.0	142.0	143.7
Culture and art	108.7	154.7	187.5	198.7	178.6	183.6	201.2	243.6	265.4	243.6
Civic, community activities [1]	116.8	271.6	279.5	220.5	236.1	212.1	253.5	254.5	253.5	214.3
Community improvement	47.0	30.5	(NA)	12.6	53.4	57.3	87.0	43.0	(NA)	(NA)
Environment; ecology	10.8	97.1	(NA)	35.9	44.0	17.3	11.7	18.7	22.0	(NA)

NA Not available.   [1] Includes other beneficiaries not shown separately.   [2] Higher education institutions.

Source: The Conference Board, New York, NY, Annual Survey of Corporate Contributions, (copyright).

Labor Force, Employment, and Earnings

This section presents statistics on the labor force; its distribution by occupation and industry affiliation; and the supply of, demand for, and conditions of labor. The chief source of these data is the Current Population Survey conducted by the U.S. Bureau of the Census. Comprehensive historical data are published by the Bureau of Labor Statistics (BLS) in *Labor Force Statistics Derived From the Current Population Survey, 1948-87, BLS Bulletin 2307.* These data are supplemented on a current basis by the BLS monthly publications *Employment and Earnings* and the *Monthly Labor Review.* Detailed data on the labor force are also available from the Census Bureau's decennial census of population.

Types of data.—Most statistics in this section are obtained by two methods: household interviews or questionnaires, and reports of establishment payroll records. Each method provides data which the other cannot suitably supply. Population characteristics, for example, are readily obtainable only from the household survey, while detailed industrial classifications can be readily derived only from establishment records.

Household data are obtained from a monthly sample survey of the population. The Current Population Survey (CPS) is used to gather data for the calendar week including the 12th of the month and provides current comprehensive data on the labor force (see text, section 1). The CPS provides information on the work status of the population without duplication since each person is classified as employed, unemployed, or not in the labor force. Employed persons holding more than one job are counted only once, according to the job at which they worked the most hours during the survey week.

Monthly data from the CPS are published by the Bureau of Labor Statistics in *Employment and Earnings* and the related reports mentioned above. Data presented include national totals of the number of persons in the civilian labor force by sex, race, Hispanic origin, and age; the number employed; hours of work; industry and

In Brief

Labor force participation rate of married women with children under 6 years old:

1960	18.6%
1970	30.3%
1980	45.1%
1993	59.6%

Fastest growing occupations, 1992–2005:

Home health aids	+138%
Human services workers	+136%
Personal and home care aides	+130%
Computer engineers and scientists	+112%

occupational groups; and the number unemployed, reasons for, and duration of unemployment. Monthly data from the CPS are also presented for regions and 11 large States. Annual data shown in this section are averages of monthly figures for each calendar year, unless otherwise specified.

In addition to monthly data, the CPS also produces annual estimates of employment and unemployment for each State, 50 large metropolitan statistical areas, and selected cities. These estimates are published by BLS in its annual *Geographic Profile of Employment and Unemployment.* More detailed geographic data (e.g., for counties and cities) are provided by the decennial population censuses.

Data based on establishment records are compiled by BLS and cooperating State agencies as part of an ongoing Current Employment Statistics Program. Data, gathered from a sample of employers who voluntarily complete mail questionnaires monthly, are supplemented by data from other government agencies and adjusted at intervals to data from government social insurance program reports. The estimates exclude proprietors of unincorporated firms, self-employed persons, private household workers, unpaid family workers, agricultural workers, and the Armed Forces. In March 1992, reporting establishments employed 9 million manufacturing workers (50 percent of the total manufacturing employment at the time), 18 million workers in nonmanufacturing industries (26 percent of the total in nonmanufacturing), and 14 million Federal, State, and local government employees (75 percent of total government).

The establishment survey counts workers each time they appear on a payroll during the reference week (as with the CPS, the week including the 12th of the month). Thus, unlike the CPS, a person with two jobs is counted twice. The establishment survey is designed to provide detailed industry information for the Nation, States, and metropolitan areas on nonfarm wage and salary employment, average weekly hours, and average hourly and weekly earnings. Establishment survey data are published in *Employment and Earnings* and the *Monthly Labor Review,* cited above. Historical national and geographic data are published in *BLS Bulletin 2370, Employment, Hours, and Earnings, United States, 1909-90; Bulletin 2429, Employment and Earnings, United States, 1981–93,* (updated annually); and *Bulletin 2320, Employment, Hours, and Earnings, States and Areas, 1972-87.*

Labor force.—According to the CPS definitions, the civilian labor force comprises all civilians in the noninstitutional population 16 years and over classified as "employed" or "unemployed" according to the following criteria: Employed civilians comprise (a) all civilians, who, during the reference week, did any work for pay or profit (minimum of an hour's work) or worked 15 hours or more as unpaid workers in a family enterprise, and (b) all civilians who were not working but who had jobs or businesses from which they were temporarily absent for noneconomic reasons (illness, weather conditions, vacation, labor-management dispute, etc.) whether they were paid for the time off or were seeking other jobs. Unemployed persons comprise all civilians who had no employment during the reference week, who made specific efforts to find a job within the previous 4 weeks (such as applying directly to an employer, or to a public employment service, or checking with friends), and who were available for work during that week, except for temporary illness. Persons on layoff from a job and expecting recall are also classified

as unemployed. All other civilian persons, 16 years old and over, are "not in the labor force." The total labor force includes, in addition to the civilian employed and unemployed, members of the Armed Forces stationed in the United States. They are also included in the employed totals.

Beginning in 1982, changes in the estimation procedures and the introduction of 1980 census data caused substantial increases in the population and estimates of persons in all labor force categories. Rates on labor force characteristics, however, were essentially unchanged. In order to avoid major breaks in series, some 30,000 labor force series were adjusted back to 1970. The effect of the 1982 revisions on various data series and an explanation of the adjustment procedure used are described in "Revisions in the Current Population Survey in January 1982," in the February 1982 issue of *Employment and Earnings.* The revisions did not, however, smooth out the breaks in series occurring between 1972 and 1979, and data users should make allowances for them in making certain data comparisons.

Beginning in January 1985, and again in January 1986, the CPS estimation procedures were revised due to the implementation of a new sample design (for the 1985 revision) and to reflect an explicit estimate of the number of undocumented immigrants (for the 1986 revision). The greatest impact of these revisions was on estimates of persons of Hispanic origin. Where possible, these estimates were revised back to January 1980. A description of the changes and an indication of their effect on the national estimates of labor force characteristics appear in "Changes in the Estimation Procedure in the Current Population Survey Beginning in January 1985" in the February 1985 issue of *Employment and Earnings* and "Changes in the Estimation Procedure in the Current Population Survey Beginning in January 1986" in the February 1986 issue of *Employment and Earnings.*

Hours and earnings.—Average hourly earnings, based on establishment data, are gross earnings (i.e., earnings before payroll deductions) and include overtime premiums; they exclude irregular bonuses and value of payments in kind. Hours are those for which pay was received. Wages and salaries from the CPS consist of total monies received for work performed by an employee during the income year. It includes wages, salaries, commissions, tips, piece-rate payments, and cash bonuses earned before deductions were made for taxes, bonds, union dues, etc. Persons who worked 35 hours or more are classified as working full time (see table 632).

Industrial and occupational groups.— Establishments responding to the establishment survey are classified into industries on the basis of their principal product or activity (determined by annual sales volume) in accordance with the *Standard Industrial Classification (SIC) Manual,* Office of Management and Budget. The SIC is a classification structure for the entire national economy. The structure provides data on a division and industry code basis, according to the level of industrial detail. For example, manufacturing is a major industrial division; food and kindred products (code 20) is one of its major groups. One of the ways this group is further divided is into meat products (code 201) and meat packing plants (code 2011). Periodically, the SIC is revised to reflect changes in the industrial composition of the economy. The *1987 SIC Manual* has been issued; the previous was the *1972 SIC Manual.* Tables shown in this *Abstract* indicate which *SIC Manual* the data shown are based on.

Industry data derived from the CPS for 1983-91 utilize the 1980 census industrial classification developed from the 1972 SIC. CPS data from 1971 to 1982 were based on the 1970 census classification system which was developed from the 1967 SIC. Most of the industry categories were not affected by the change in classification.

The occupational classification system used in the 1980 census and in the CPS for 1983-91 evolved from the 1980 Standard Occupational Classification (SOC) system, first introduced in 1977. Occupational categories used in the 1980 census classification system are so radically different from the 1970 census system used in the CPS through 1982, that their implementation represented a break in historical data series. In cases where data have not yet been converted to the 1980 classifications and still reflect the 1970 classifications (e.g., table 668), comparisons between the two systems should not be made. To help users bridge the

data gap, a limited set of estimates was developed for the 1972-82 period based on the new classifications. The estimates were developed by means of applying conversion factors created by double coding a 20-percent sample of CPS occupational records for 6 months during 1981-82. For further details, contact BLS.

Beginning in January 1992, the occupational and industrial classification system used in the 1990 census were introduced into the CPS. (These systems were largely based on the 1980 Standard Occupational Classification and the 1987 Standard Industrial Classification.) There were a few breaks in comparability between the 1980 and 1990 census–based systems, particularly within the "technical, sales, and administrative support" categories. The most notable changes in industry classification were the shift of several industries from "business services" to "professional services" and the splitting of some industries into smaller, more detailed categories. A number of industry titles were changed as well, with no change in content.

Productivity.—The Bureau of Labor Statistics (BLS) publishes data on productivity as measured by output per hour (labor productivity), output per combined unit of labor and capital input (multifactor productivity), and, for manufacturing industries, output per combined unit of capital, labor, energy, materials, and purchased service inputs. Labor productivity and related indexes are published for the business sector as a whole and its major subsectors: nonfarm business, manufacturing, nonfinancial corporations, 177 specific industries, and various functional areas of the Federal and State and local governments. Multifactor productivity and related measures are published for the private business sector and its major subsectors. Productivity indexes which take into account capital, labor, energy, materials, and service inputs are published for the 20 major two-digit industry groups which comprise the manufacturing sector and for the tire and inner tubes, footwear, steel, farm and garden machinery, motor vehicles, and railroad transportation industries. The major sector data are published in the BLS quarterly news release, *Productivity and Costs* and in the annual *Multifactor Productivity Measures* release. The specific industry productivity measures are published annually in the BLS Bulletin, *Productivity Measures for Selected Industries and Government Services,* and the *Handbook of Labor Statistics.* Detailed information on methods, limitations, and data sources appears in the *BLS Handbook of Methods,* BLS Bulletin 2414 (1992), chapters 10 and 11.

Unions.—As defined here, unions include traditional labor unions and employee associations similar to labor unions. Data on union membership status provided by BLS are for employed wage and salary workers and relate to their principal job. Earnings by union membership status are usual weekly earnings of full-time wage and salary workers. The information is collected through the Current Population Survey. For a full description of the method of collection and comparability with earlier data, see "New Data on Union Members and Their Earnings" in the January 1985 issue of *Employment and Earnings,* and "Changing Employment Patterns of Organized Workers" in the February 1985 issue of the *Monthly Labor Review.* Collective bargaining settlements data are available for bargaining situations involving 1,000 or more workers in private industry and State and local government.

Work stoppages.—Work stoppages include all strikes and lockouts known to BLS which last for at least one full day or shift and involve 1,000 or more workers. All stoppages, whether or not authorized by a union, legal or illegal, are counted.

Excluded are work slowdowns and instances where employees report to work late, or leave early, to attend mass meetings or mass rallies.

Seasonal adjustment.—Many economic statistics reflect a regularly recurring seasonal movement which can be estimated on the basis of past experience. By eliminating that part of the change which can be ascribed to usual seasonal variation (e.g., climate or school openings and closings), it is possible to observe the cyclical and other nonseasonal movements in the series. However, in evaluating deviations from the seasonal pattern—that is, changes in a seasonally adjusted series—it is important to note that seasonal adjustment is merely an approximation based on past experience. Seasonally adjusted estimates have a broader margin of possible error than the original data on which they are based, since they are subject not only to sampling and other errors, but also are affected by the uncertainties of the adjustment process itself.

Statistical reliability.—For discussion of statistical collection, estimation, sampling procedures, and measures of statistical reliability applicable to Census Bureau and BLS data, see Appendix III.

Historical statistics.—Tabular headnotes provide cross-references, where applicable, to *Historical Statistics of the United States, Colonial Times to 1970.* See Appendix IV.

Figure 13.1
Fastest Growing Occupations: 1992 to 2005

Source: Chart prepared by U.S. Bureau of the Census. For data, see table 639.

No. 614. Employment Status of the Population: 1950 to 1993

[In thousands, except as indicated. Annual averages of monthly figures. For the noninstitutional population 16 years of age and older. Based on Current Population Survey; see text, section 1, and Appendix III. See also *Historical Statistics, Colonial Times to 1970*, series D 11-19 and D 85-86]

YEAR	Noninsti-tutional popula-tion	LABOR FORCE								Not in labor force
		Number	Employed						Unemployed	
			Total	Resi-dent Armed Forces	Civilian				Number	Percent of labor force [1]
					Total	Agricul-ture	Non-agricul-ture indus-tries			
1950	106,164	63,377	60,087	1,169	58,918	7,160	51,758		3,288	5.2	42,787
1960	119,106	71,489	67,639	1,861	65,778	5,458	60,318		3,852	5.4	47,617
1970	139,203	84,889	80,796	2,118	78,678	3,463	75,215		4,093	4.8	54,315
1975	154,831	95,453	87,524	1,678	85,846	3,408	82,438		7,929	8.3	59,377
1980	169,349	108,544	100,907	1,604	99,303	3,364	95,938		7,637	7.0	60,806
1985	179,912	117,167	108,856	1,706	107,150	3,179	103,971		8,312	7.1	62,744
1990	189,686	126,424	119,550	1,637	117,914	3,186	114,728		6,874	5.4	63,262
1991	191,329	126,867	118,440	1,564	116,877	3,233	113,644		8,426	6.6	64,462
1992	193,142	128,548	119,164	1,566	117,598	3,207	114,391		9,384	7.3	64,593
1993	195,034	129,525	120,791	1,485	119,306	3,074	116,232		8,734	6.7	65,509
PERCENT DISTRIBUTION										
1950	100.0	59.7	56.6	1.1	55.5	6.7	48.8		3.1	(X)	40.3
1960	100.0	60.0	56.8	1.6	55.2	4.6	50.6		3.2	(X)	40.0
1970	100.0	61.0	58.0	1.5	56.5	2.5	54.0		2.9	(X)	39.0
1980	100.0	64.1	59.6	0.9	58.6	2.0	56.7		4.5	(X)	35.9
1990	100.0	66.6	63.0	0.9	62.2	1.7	60.5		3.6	(X)	33.4
1992	100.0	66.6	61.7	0.8	60.9	1.7	59.2		4.9	(X)	33.4
1993	100.0	66.4	61.9	0.8	61.2	1.6	59.6		4.5	(X)	33.6

X Not applicable.   [1] Unemployment as a percent of the labor force, including resident Armed Forces.

Source: U.S. Bureau of Labor Statistics, Bulletin 2307; and *Employment and Earnings*, monthly.

No. 615. Civilian Labor Force and Participation Rates, With Projections: 1970 to 2005

[For civilian noninstitutional population 16 years old and over. Annual averages of monthly figures. Rates are based on annual average civilian noninstitutional population of each specified group and represent proportion of each specified group in the civilian labor force. Based on Current Population Survey; see text, section 1, and Appendix III. See also *Historical Statistics, Colonial Times to 1970*, series D 42-48]

RACE, SEX, AND AGE	CIVILIAN LABOR FORCE (millions)						PARTICIPATION RATE (percent)					
	1970	1980	1990	1993	2000, proj.	2005, proj.	1970	1980	1990	1993	2000, proj.	2005, proj.
Total [1]	82.8	106.9	124.8	128.0	141.8	150.5	60.4	63.8	66.4	66.2	68.2	68.8
White	73.6	93.6	107.2	109.4	118.8	124.8	60.2	64.1	66.8	66.7	68.7	69.3
Male	46.0	54.5	59.3	60.2	63.8	66.0	80.0	78.2	76.9	76.1	76.0	75.3
Female	27.5	39.1	47.9	49.2	55.1	58.8	42.6	51.2	57.5	58.0	61.8	63.6
Black [2]	9.2	10.9	13.5	13.9	16.0	17.4	61.8	61.0	63.3	62.4	65.5	66.2
Male	5.2	5.6	6.7	6.9	7.8	8.3	76.5	70.3	70.1	68.6	70.8	70.5
Female	4.0	5.3	6.8	7.0	8.2	9.0	49.5	53.1	57.8	57.4	61.2	62.6
Hispanic [3]	(NA)	6.1	9.6	10.4	14.3	16.6	(NA)	64.0	67.0	65.9	68.0	68.4
Male	(NA)	3.8	5.8	6.3	8.7	9.6	(NA)	81.4	81.2	80.0	80.2	79.5
Female	(NA)	2.3	3.8	4.1	5.8	7.0	(NA)	47.4	53.0	52.0	55.8	57.3
Male	51.2	61.5	68.2	69.6	75.3	78.7	79.7	77.4	76.1	75.2	75.3	74.7
16 to 19 years	4.0	5.0	3.9	3.6	4.4	4.6	56.1	60.5	55.7	53.1	55.4	55.5
20 to 24 years	5.7	8.6	7.3	7.2	7.2	8.1	83.3	85.9	84.3	83.1	84.0	84.4
25 to 34 years	11.3	17.0	19.8	19.1	17.2	16.5	96.4	95.2	94.2	93.5	73.1	93.5
35 to 44 years	10.5	11.8	17.3	18.5	20.7	19.6	96.9	95.5	94.4	93.5	93.7	93.5
45 to 54 years	10.4	9.9	11.2	12.6	15.8	18.1	94.3	91.2	90.7	90.1	90.4	90.2
55 to 64 years	7.1	7.2	6.8	6.6	7.7	9.6	83.0	72.1	67.7	66.5	69.1	69.7
65 years and over	2.2	1.9	2.0	2.0	2.1	2.2	26.8	19.0	16.4	15.6	15.0	14.7
Female	31.5	45.5	56.6	58.4	66.6	71.8	43.3	51.5	57.5	57.9	61.6	63.2
16 to 19 years	3.2	4.4	3.5	3.3	4.0	4.2	44.0	52.9	51.8	49.9	52.0	52.4
20 to 24 years	4.9	7.3	6.6	6.4	6.4	7.2	57.7	68.9	71.6	71.3	72.5	73.6
25 to 34 years	5.7	12.3	16.0	15.4	14.9	14.8	45.0	65.5	73.6	73.6	78.1	80.7
35 to 44 years	6.0	8.6	14.6	15.7	18.8	18.6	51.1	65.5	76.5	76.7	83.0	86.2
45 to 54 years	6.5	7.0	9.3	10.9	14.7	17.4	54.4	59.9	71.2	73.5	79.7	82.8
55 to 64 years	4.2	4.7	5.1	5.2	6.2	7.8	43.0	41.3	45.3	47.3	50.3	52.4
65 years and over	1.1	1.2	1.5	1.5	1.6	1.7	9.7	8.1	8.7	8.2	8.5	8.8

NA Not available.   [1] Beginning 1980, includes other races not shown separately.   [2] For 1970, Black and other.   [3] Persons of Hispanic origin may be of any race.

Source: U.S. Bureau of Labor Statistics, Bulletin 2307; *Employment and Earnings*, monthly, January issues; *Monthly Labor Review*, November 1993; and unpublished data.

No. 616. Employment Status of the Civilian Population: 1960 to 1993

[In thousands, **except as indicated**. Annual averages of monthly figures. For the civilian noninstitutional population 16 years old and over. Based on Current Population Survey; see text, section 1, and Appendix III. See also *Historical Statistics, Colonial Times to 1970*, series D 11-19 and D 85-86]

YEAR, SEX, RACE, AND HISPANIC ORIGIN	Civilian noninstitutional population	CIVILIAN LABOR FORCE							NOT IN LABOR FORCE	
		Total	Percent of population	Employed	Employment/ population ratio [1]	Unemployed			Number	Percent of population
						Number	Percent of labor force			
Total: [2]										
1960	117,245	69,628	59.4	65,778	56.1	3,852	5.5		47,617	40.6
1970	137,085	82,771	60.4	78,678	57.4	4,093	4.9		54,315	39.6
1980	167,745	106,940	63.8	99,303	59.2	7,637	7.1		60,806	36.2
1985	178,206	115,461	64.8	107,150	60.1	8,312	7.2		62,744	35.2
1989	186,393	123,869	66.5	117,342	63.0	6,528	5.3		62,523	33.5
1990	188,049	124,787	66.4	117,914	62.7	6,874	5.5		63,262	33.6
1991	189,765	125,303	66.0	116,877	61.6	8,426	6.7		64,462	34.0
1992	191,576	126,982	66.3	117,598	61.4	9,384	7.4		64,593	33.7
1993	193,550	128,040	66.2	119,306	61.6	8,734	6.8		65,509	33.8
Male:										
1960	55,662	46,388	83.3	43,904	78.9	2,486	5.4		9,274	16.7
1970	64,304	51,228	79.7	48,990	76.2	2,238	4.4		13,076	20.3
1980	79,398	61,453	77.4	57,186	72.0	4,267	6.9		17,945	22.6
1985	84,469	64,411	76.3	59,891	70.9	4,521	7.0		20,058	23.7
1989	88,762	67,840	76.4	64,315	72.5	3,525	5.2		20,923	23.6
1990	89,650	68,234	76.1	64,435	71.9	3,799	5.6		21,417	23.9
1991	90,552	68,411	75.5	63,593	70.2	4,817	7.0		22,141	24.5
1992	91,541	69,184	75.6	63,805	69.7	5,380	7.8		22,356	24.4
1993	92,620	69,633	75.2	64,700	69.9	4,932	7.1		22,987	24.8
Female:										
1960	61,582	23,240	37.7	21,874	35.5	1,366	5.9		38,343	62.3
1970	72,782	31,543	43.3	29,688	40.8	1,855	5.9		41,239	56.7
1980	88,348	45,487	51.5	42,117	47.7	3,370	7.4		42,861	48.5
1985	93,736	51,050	54.5	47,259	50.4	3,791	7.4		42,686	45.5
1989	97,630	56,030	57.4	53,027	54.3	3,003	5.4		41,601	42.6
1990	98,399	56,554	57.5	53,479	54.3	3,075	5.4		41,845	42.5
1991	99,214	56,893	57.3	53,284	53.7	3,609	6.3		42,321	42.7
1992	100,035	57,798	57.8	53,793	53.8	4,005	6.9		42,237	42.2
1993	100,930	58,407	57.9	54,606	54.1	3,801	6.5		42,522	42.1
White:										
1960	105,282	61,915	58.8	58,850	55.9	3,065	5.0		43,367	41.2
1970	122,174	73,556	60.2	70,217	57.5	3,339	4.5		48,618	39.8
1980	146,122	93,600	64.1	87,715	60.0	5,884	6.3		52,523	35.9
1985	153,679	99,926	65.0	93,736	61.0	6,191	6.2		53,753	35.0
1989	159,338	106,355	66.7	101,584	63.8	4,770	4.5		52,983	33.3
1990	160,415	107,177	66.8	102,087	63.6	5,091	4.7		53,237	33.2
1991	161,511	107,486	66.6	101,039	62.6	6,447	6.0		54,025	33.4
1992	162,658	108,526	66.7	101,479	62.4	7,047	6.5		54,132	33.3
1993	163,921	109,359	66.7	102,812	62.7	6,547	6.0		54,562	33.3
Black:										
1973	14,917	8,976	60.2	8,128	54.5	846	9.4		5,941	39.8
1980	17,824	10,865	61.0	9,313	52.2	1,553	14.3		6,959	39.0
1985	19,664	12,364	62.9	10,501	53.4	1,864	15.1		7,299	37.1
1989	21,021	13,497	64.2	11,953	56.9	1,544	11.4		7,524	35.8
1990	21,300	13,493	63.3	11,966	56.2	1,527	11.3		7,808	36.7
1991	21,615	13,542	62.6	11,863	54.9	1,679	12.4		8,074	37.4
1992	21,958	13,891	63.3	11,933	54.3	1,958	14.1		8,067	36.7
1993	22,329	13,943	62.4	12,146	54.4	1,796	12.9		8,386	37.6
Hispanic: [3]										
1980	9,598	6,146	64.0	5,527	57.6	620	10.1		3,451	36.0
1985	11,915	7,698	64.6	6,888	57.8	811	10.5		4,217	35.4
1986	12,344	8,076	65.4	7,219	58.5	857	10.6		4,268	34.6
1990	14,297	9,576	67.0	8,808	61.6	769	8.0		4,721	33.0
1991	14,770	9,762	66.1	8,799	59.6	963	9.9		5,008	33.9
1992	15,244	10,131	66.5	8,971	58.9	1,160	11.4		5,113	33.5
1993	15,753	10,377	65.9	9,272	58.9	1,104	10.6		5,377	34.1
Mexican:										
1986	7,377	4,941	67.0	4,387	59.5	555	11.2		2,436	33.0
1990	8,742	5,970	68.3	5,478	62.7	492	8.2		2,773	31.7
1991	8,947	5,984	66.9	5,363	59.9	621	10.4		2,963	33.1
1992	9,368	6,319	67.5	5,581	59.6	739	11.7		3,049	32.5
1993	9,693	6,499	67.0	5,805	59.9	693	10.7		3,194	33.0
Puerto Rican:										
1986	1,494	804	53.8	691	46.3	113	14.0		690	46.2
1990	1,546	859	55.6	780	50.5	79	9.1		687	44.4
1991	1,629	930	57.1	822	50.5	108	11.6		699	42.9
1992	1,628	934	57.4	802	49.2	132	14.1		694	42.6
1993	1,676	950	56.7	828	49.4	122	12.8		725	43.3
Cuban:										
1986	842	570	67.7	533	63.3	36	6.4		272	32.3
1990	847	552	65.1	512	60.4	40	7.2		295	34.8
1991	849	543	63.9	499	58.8	44	8.1		306	36.0
1992	867	529	61.1	488	56.3	42	7.9		337	38.9
1993	927	554	59.8	511	55.1	43	7.8		373	40.2

[1] Civilian employed as a percent of the civilian noninstitutional population. [2] Includes other races, not shown separately. [3] Persons of Hispanic origin may be of any race. Includes persons of other Hispanic origin, not shown separately.

Source: U.S. Bureau of Labor Statistics, Bulletin 2307; and *Employment and Earnings*, monthly, January issues.

No. 617. Civilian Labor Force and Participation Rates, by Educational Attainment, Sex, and Race: 1970 to 1991

[As of **March**, except as noted. For civilian noninstitutional population 25 to 64 years of age. See headnote, table 615. Beginning 1992, the method of computing educational attainment data was changed. See table 618 for later data for persons 25 years old and over]

ITEM	CIVILIAN LABOR FORCE					PARTICIPATION RATE [1]				
	Total (1,000)	Percent distribution				Total	Less than high school	High school graduate	College	
		Less than high school	High school graduate	College						
				1-3 years	4 years or more				1-3 years	4 years or more
Total: [2] 1970	61,765	36.1	38.1	11.8	14.1	70.3	65.5	70.2	73.8	82.3
1980	78,010	20.6	39.8	17.6	22.0	73.9	60.7	74.2	79.5	86.1
1985	88,424	15.9	40.2	19.0	24.9	76.2	59.9	75.9	81.6	87.7
1990 [3]	99,981	13.3	39.4	20.8	26.5	78.9	61.4	78.4	83.5	88.6
1991 [3]	101,171	12.8	39.2	21.3	26.7	78.8	61.0	78.2	83.4	88.3
Male: 1970	39,303	37.5	34.5	12.2	15.7	93.5	89.3	96.3	95.8	96.1
1980	45,417	22.2	35.7	17.7	24.3	89.4	78.8	91.9	92.4	95.3
1985	49,647	17.7	36.9	18.3	27.1	88.6	72.2	90.0	91.2	94.6
1990 [3]	55,049	14.9	37.3	19.8	28.0	89.3	76.4	90.1	92.1	94.6
1991 [3]	55,554	14.5	37.1	20.3	28.2	88.9	75.9	89.4	91.9	94.3
Female: 1970	22,462	33.5	44.3	10.9	11.2	49.0	43.0	51.3	50.9	60.9
1980	32,593	18.4	45.4	17.4	18.7	59.5	43.7	61.2	66.4	73.4
1985	38,779	13.7	44.4	19.9	22.0	64.7	44.3	65.0	72.5	78.6
1990 [3]	44,932	11.2	42.1	22.1	24.6	69.1	46.5	68.8	75.7	81.3
1991 [3]	45,617	10.7	41.8	22.5	25.0	69.3	46.0	68.9	75.8	81.3
White: 1970	55,044	33.7	39.3	12.2	14.8	70.1	65.2	69.7	73.3	81.9
1980	68,509	19.1	40.2	17.7	22.9	74.2	61.4	73.7	79.2	86.0
1985	76,739	14.7	40.7	19.1	25.6	76.6	60.7	75.8	81.1	87.7
1990 [3]	85,882	12.5	39.4	20.8	27.3	79.5	63.0	78.6	83.4	88.6
1991 [3]	86,776	12.1	39.1	21.3	27.5	79.5	62.6	78.5	83.4	88.5
Black: 1970	6,721	55.5	28.2	8.0	8.3	72.0	67.1	76.8	81.0	87.4
1980	7,731	34.7	38.1	16.3	11.0	71.5	58.1	79.2	82.0	90.1
1985	9,157	26.2	39.5	19.2	15.0	73.4	57.0	77.2	85.6	89.9
1990 [3]	10,711	19.4	43.0	21.8	15.8	75.4	55.7	78.6	84.6	91.0
1991 [3]	10,863	18.4	43.0	22.5	16.0	75.0	55.1	77.4	84.6	90.4

[1] Percent of the civilian population in each group in the civilian labor force.   [2] Includes other races, not shown separately. For 1970, White and Black races only.   [3] Not strictly comparable with previous years. Annual averages of monthly figures.

Source: U.S. Bureau of Labor Statistics, Bulletin 2307; and unpublished data.

No. 618. Civilian Labor Force and Participation Rates, by Educational Attainment, Sex, Race, and Hispanic Origin: 1992 and 1993

[**Annual averages of monthly figures**, for civilian noninstitutional population 25 years old and over. See table 651 for unemployment data. Based on Current Population Survey; see text, section 1, and Appendix III]

YEAR, SEX, AND RACE	CIVILIAN LABOR FORCE (1,000)					PARTICIPATION RATE [1]				
	Total	Less than high school diploma	High school graduates, no degree	Less than a bachelor's degree	College graduate	Total	Less than high school diploma	High school graduate, no degree	Less than a bachelor's degree	College graduate
Total: [2]										
1992	106,530	13,191	37,993	27,089	28,257	66.3	40.7	66.2	75.1	81.2
1993	107,657	12,360	37,821	28,413	29,062	66.2	39.7	65.4	75.0	81.0
Male:										
1992	58,393	8,105	19,914	14,038	16,336	76.6	53.8	78.0	83.6	86.8
1993	58,904	7,669	19,916	14,668	16,652	76.2	52.8	77.0	83.4	86.3
Female:										
1992	48,138	5,086	18,080	13,051	11,920	57.0	29.4	56.7	67.7	74.7
1993	48,753	4,692	17,906	13,745	12,410	57.1	28.3	56.0	67.7	74.9
White:										
1992	91,242	10,543	32,488	23,273	24,938	66.3	40.8	65.4	74.5	80.9
1993	92,168	9,960	32,273	24,345	25,590	66.3	40.1	64.8	74.4	80.8
Black:										
1992	11,422	2,110	4,505	3,004	1,803	65.7	39.7	72.3	80.5	85.6
1993	11,477	1,873	4,492	3,216	1,896	64.7	37.1	69.9	79.7	84.8
Hispanic: [3]										
1992	7,993	3,124	2,358	1,592	919	67.9	55.9	75.2	82.1	83.0
1993	8,261	3,130	2,411	1,756	963	67.6	55.7	73.2	81.6	83.7

[1] See footnote 1, table 617.   [2] Includes other races, not shown separately.   [3] Persons of Hispanic origin may be of any race.

Source: U.S. Bureau of Labor Statistics, unpublished data.

No. 619. Civilian Labor Force—Percent Distribution, by Sex and Age: 1960 to 1993

[For civilian noninstitutional population 16 years old and over. Annual averages of monthly figures. Based on Current Population Survey; see text, section 1, and Appendix III. See *Historical Statistics, Colonial Times to 1970*, series D 29-41, for similar but not exactly comparable data]

YEAR AND SEX	Civilian labor force (1,000)	PERCENT DISTRIBUTION						
		16 to 19 years	20 to 24 years	25 to 34 years	35 to 44 years	45 to 54 years	55 to 64 years	65 yrs. and over
Total: 1960	69,628	7.0	9.6	20.7	23.4	21.3	13.5	4.6
1970	82,771	8.8	12.8	20.6	19.9	20.5	13.6	3.9
1980	106,940	8.8	14.9	27.3	19.1	15.8	11.2	2.9
1985	115,461	6.8	13.6	29.1	22.6	15.0	10.4	2.5
1989	123,869	6.4	11.4	29.0	24.7	16.1	9.6	2.8
1990	124,787	5.9	11.1	28.7	25.5	16.4	9.5	2.8
1991	125,303	5.5	10.9	28.2	26.3	16.9	9.4	2.8
1992	126,982	5.3	10.8	27.6	26.5	17.6	9.3	2.8
1993	128,040	5.3	10.6	26.9	26.8	18.4	9.3	2.7
Male: 1960	46,388	6.0	8.9	22.1	23.6	20.6	13.8	4.9
1970	51,228	7.8	11.2	22.1	20.4	20.3	13.9	4.2
1980	61,453	8.1	14.0	27.6	19.3	16.1	11.8	3.1
1985	64,411	6.4	12.9	29.2	22.5	15.3	11.0	2.7
1989	67,840	6.1	11.0	29.3	24.5	16.1	10.0	3.0
1990	68,234	5.7	10.7	29.0	25.3	16.4	9.9	3.0
1991	68,411	5.2	10.6	28.6	26.1	16.8	9.8	2.9
1992	69,184	5.1	10.5	28.0	26.3	17.5	9.7	3.0
1993	69,633	5.1	10.3	27.4	26.6	18.1	9.5	2.9
Female: 1960	23,240	8.8	11.1	17.8	22.8	22.7	12.8	3.9
1970	31,543	10.3	15.5	18.1	18.9	20.7	13.2	3.3
1980	45,487	9.6	16.1	26.9	19.0	15.4	10.4	2.6
1985	51,050	7.4	14.6	28.9	22.7	14.6	9.7	2.3
1989	56,030	6.8	12.0	28.5	25.0	16.1	9.1	2.6
1990	56,554	6.3	11.6	28.3	25.8	16.5	9.0	2.7
1991	56,893	5.9	11.3	27.7	26.6	17.0	8.9	2.7
1992	57,798	5.5	11.2	27.2	26.7	17.8	8.9	2.6
1993	58,407	5.6	10.9	26.4	26.9	18.7	9.0	2.5

Source: U.S. Bureau of Labor Statistics, Bulletin 2307, and *Employment Earnings*, monthly, January issues.

No. 620. Civilian Labor Force, by Selected Metropolitan Area: 1993

[For the civilian noninstitutional population 16 years old and over. Annual averages of monthly figures. Except as noted, data are derived from the Local Area Unemployment Statistics Program. For composition of metropolitan areas, see Appendix II]

METROPOLITAN AREAS RANKED BY LABOR FORCE SIZE, 1993	Civilian labor force (1,000)	Unemployment rate [1]	METROPOLITAN AREAS RANKED BY LABOR FORCE SIZE, 1993	Civilian labor force (1,000)	Unemployment rate [1]
U.S. total	128,040	6.8	San Jose, CA	838.8	6.8
Los Angeles-Long Beach, CA [2]	4,411.0	9.7	Cincinnati, OH-KY-IN	797.6	5.6
Chicago, IL	3,951.9	7.1	Fort Worth-Arlington, TX	789.3	6.4
New York, NY	3,901.6	9.4	Indianapolis, IN	757.4	4.4
Washington, DC-MD-VA-WV	2,550.3	4.5	Columbus, OH	756.7	4.9
Philadelphia, PA-NJ	2,452.4	6.8	Milwaukee-Waukesha, WI	755.5	4.4
Detroit, MI	2,114.8	7.1	Orlando, FL	719.7	6.2
Houston, TX	1,923.4	7.2	Fort Lauderdale, FL	693.9	6.8
Atlanta, GA	1,773.1	5.2	Norfolk-Virginia Beach-Newport News,		
Boston, MA-NH	1,745.4	6.0	VA-NC	692.0	5.4
Dallas, TX	1,617.4	6.0	Sacramento, CA	684.6	8.3
Minneapolis-St. Paul, MI-WI	1,509.9	4.3	San Antonio, TX	681.6	5.6
Nassau-Suffolk, NY	1,359.1	6.4	Charlotte-Gastonia-Rock Hill, NC-SC	673.2	4.6
Orange County, CA	1,315.5	6.7	Bergen-Passaic-NJ	655.0	7.7
St. Louis, MO-IL [3]	1,270.3	6.5	Hartford, CT	627.6	6.6
Riverside-San Bernardino, CA	1,245.2	10.5	Greensboro-Winston-Salem-High Point,		
Baltimore, MD	1,215.0	7.3	NC	599.6	4.1
San Diego, CA	1,208.8	7.8	Providence-Fall River-Warwick, RI-MA	588.1	8.4
Seattle-Bellevue-Everett, WA	1,194.7	6.4	Salt Lake City-Ogden, UT	587.8	3.6
Phoenix-Mesa, AZ	1,165.6	5.1	New Orleans, LA	585.6	6.8
Pittsburgh, PA	1,153.8	6.8	Middlesex-Somerset-Hunterdon, NJ	581.1	6.0
Oakland, CA	1,109.9	6.6	Buffalo-Niagara Falls, NY	577.2	6.6
Cleveland-Lorain-Elyria, OH	1,082.1	6.7	Rochester, NY	568.2	4.9
Tampa-St. Petersburg-Clearwater, FL	1,031.9	6.5	Nashville, TN	555.3	4.2
Miami, FL	1,019.8	7.7	Raleigh-Durham-Chapel Hill, NC	551.4	3.2
Newark, NJ	994.3	7.6	Austin-San Marcos, TX	547.7	4.0
Denver, CO	974.3	4.7	Las Vegas, NV-AZ	533.8	7.3
Portland-Vancouver, OR-WA	915.8	6.1	Grand Rapids-Muskegon-Holland, MI	515.3	5.7
San Francisco, CA	899.5	6.1	Louisville, KY-IN	506.0	4.9
Kansas City, MO-KS	873.9	5.4			

[1] Percent unemployed of the civilian labor force. [2] Derived from the Current Population Survey. [3] Excludes the part of Sullivan City in Crawford County, Missouri.

Source: U.S. Bureau of Labor Statistics, *Employment and Earnings*, May 1994.

No. 621. Characteristics of the Civilian Labor Force, by State: 1993

[In thousands, except ratio and rate. For civilian noninstitutional population, 16 years old and over. Annual averages of monthly figures. Because of separate processing and weighting procedures, the totals for the United States may differ from results obtained by aggregating totals for States]

STATE	TOTAL		EMPLOYED		Employed/population ratio [1]	UNEMPLOYED					PARTICIPATION RATE [3]	
						Total		Rate [2]				
	Number	Female	Total	Female		Number	Female	Total	Male	Female	Male	Female
United States . .	128,040	58,407	119,306	54,606	61.6	8,734	3,801	6.8	7.1	6.5	75.2	57.9
Alabama..........	1,990	901	1,840	830	57.7	149	71	7.5	7.1	7.9	72.2	53.6
Alaska...........	298	135	276	126	68.1	23	8	7.6	8.8	6.1	81.2	66.2
Arizona..........	1,837	829	1,723	779	58.3	114	50	6.2	6.3	6.0	71.8	53.4
Arkansas	1,163	533	1,091	499	59.3	72	34	6.2	5.9	6.4	72.0	55.2
California	15,259	6,670	13,853	6,092	59.5	1,407	577	9.2	9.7	8.7	75.8	55.8
Colorado.........	1,904	879	1,805	841	67.2	99	39	5.2	5.9	4.4	78.5	63.7
Connecticut......	1,788	822	1,678	783	66.0	111	38	6.2	7.5	4.7	78.7	62.6
Delaware	373	168	354	159	66.4	20	9	5.3	5.5	5.2	77.5	62.7
District of Columbia .	306	152	280	139	61.1	26	13	8.5	8.6	8.4	73.1	61.5
Florida..........	6,628	3,061	6,166	2,851	57.7	462	209	7.0	7.1	6.8	70.5	54.4
Georgia..........	3,467	1,655	3,267	1,558	63.1	200	96	5.8	5.7	5.8	75.4	59.6
Hawaii	583	277	558	266	65.3	25	11	4.2	4.5	3.9	75.4	61.8
Idaho...........	545	242	512	227	64.1	34	15	6.1	6.2	6.0	77.6	59.2
Illinois	5,983	2,734	5,538	2,547	62.7	444	187	7.4	7.9	6.8	76.9	59.4
Indiana..........	2,937	1,375	2,780	1,297	64.4	157	77	5.3	5.1	5.6	77.7	59.6
Iowa............	1,550	702	1,488	676	70.4	62	26	4.0	4.2	3.8	81.8	65.1
Kansas..........	1,318	601	1,253	570	67.4	66	31	5.0	4.8	5.2	78.6	63.6
Kentucky	1,794	810	1,684	761	58.4	110	49	6.2	6.2	6.1	71.2	54.0
Louisiana	1,879	833	1,740	770	55.4	139	63	7.4	7.2	7.5	70.8	50.2
Maine...........	631	296	581	275	61.2	50	21	7.9	8.7	7.0	72.3	60.8
Maryland	2,672	1,287	2,507	1,218	66.0	165	69	6.2	6.9	5.4	76.8	64.6
Massachusetts.....	3,170	1,468	2,953	1,383	63.3	217	85	6.9	7.8	5.8	76.4	60.3
Michigan.........	4,702	2,111	4,374	1,967	61.3	328	145	7.0	7.1	6.9	75.2	57.3
Minnesota........	2,466	1,155	2,341	1,110	69.9	125	45	5.1	6.1	3.9	81.0	66.7
Mississippi	1,212	532	1,135	490	58.3	77	42	6.3	5.2	7.8	72.1	52.9
Missouri	2,650	1,241	2,481	1,148	63.2	169	94	6.4	5.4	7.5	75.5	60.3
Montana.........	427	193	401	182	63.8	26	11	6.0	6.4	5.6	74.5	61.3
Nebraska	853	410	830	396	70.1	22	13	2.6	2.0	3.2	78.8	65.8
Nevada	745	334	692	309	65.0	54	25	7.2	6.9	7.5	77.3	62.8
New Hampshire....	620	282	579	265	67.4	41	17	6.6	7.0	6.1	80.0	64.5
New Jersey.......	4,001	1,803	3,706	1,685	60.7	295	118	7.4	8.1	6.5	75.6	56.4
New Mexico	756	333	700	310	59.0	57	23	7.5	7.9	6.9	73.5	54.6
New York........	8,649	3,986	7,985	3,714	56.9	664	272	7.7	8.4	6.8	70.8	53.5
North Carolina.....	3,555	1,682	3,383	1,591	64.0	173	91	4.9	4.3	5.4	74.8	60.4
North Dakota......	318	149	305	143	65.9	14	6	4.3	4.7	3.8	76.3	61.8
Ohio	5,488	2,514	5,132	2,360	61.1	357	153	6.5	6.8	6.1	74.7	56.9
Oklahoma........	1,524	683	1,432	640	59.6	92	43	6.0	5.8	6.3	74.0	53.9
Oregon..........	1,587	718	1,473	672	63.3	114	45	7.2	7.9	6.3	75.4	61.1
Pennsylvania......	5,893	2,664	5,479	2,494	59.0	414	170	7.0	7.5	6.4	73.2	54.7
Rhode Island.....	512	244	472	227	62.0	40	17	7.7	8.5	6.9	74.7	60.6
South Carolina.....	1,823	845	1,685	778	61.7	138	68	7.5	7.2	8.0	76.8	57.9
South Dakota	360	163	347	156	67.6	12	7	3.5	3.0	4.0	78.1	62.4
Tennessee	2,500	1,185	2,358	1,110	60.1	142	74	5.7	5.1	6.3	72.3	56.2
Texas...........	9,149	4,054	8,508	3,758	64.0	642	296	7.0	6.8	7.3	79.0	59.2
Utah	910	408	875	391	69.4	35	17	3.9	3.6	4.2	81.2	63.5
Vermont.........	316	152	299	146	68.0	17	5	5.4	7.3	3.5	77.7	66.4
Virginia..........	3,376	1,583	3,208	1,502	66.0	168	82	5.0	4.8	5.2	76.9	62.5
Washington.......	2,693	1,228	2,490	1,146	63.2	203	82	7.5	8.3	6.7	76.2	60.9
West Virginia.....	786	338	702	311	49.1	85	27	10.8	12.8	8.1	66.0	45.0
Wisconsin........	2,715	1,276	2,589	1,223	68.6	127	53	4.7	5.1	4.2	78.4	65.9
Wyoming	239	108	226	103	65.9	13	5	5.4	5.9	4.8	77.6	62.2

[1] Civilian employment as a percent of civilian noninstitutional population. [2] Percent unemployed of the civilian labor force. [3] Percent of civilian noninstitutional population of each specified group in the civilian labor force.

Source: U.S. Bureau of Labor Statistics, *Geographic Profile of Employment and Unemployment, 1993.*

No. 622. Hispanic Persons—Civilian Labor Force Participation: 1992 and 1993

[For civilian noninstitutional population, 16 years old and over. Annual averages of monthly figures. Based on Current Population Survey; see text, section 1, and Appendix III]

ITEM	1992					1993				
	Total	Mexi-can	Puerto Rican	Cuban	Other His-panic origin [1]	Total	Mexi-can	Puerto Rican	Cuban	Other His-panic origin [1]
Total (1,000)..............	15,244	9,368	1,628	867	3,381	15,753	9,693	1,676	927	3,457
Percent in labor force:										
Male.....................	80.5	82.0	69.9	73.2	82.5	80.0	81.5	70.6	73.3	81.2
Female	52.6	52.1	47.1	50.3	57.4	52.0	51.9	45.3	47.9	56.7
Employed (1,000).............	8,971	5,581	802	488	2,100	9,272	5,805	828	511	2,128
Percent by occupation	100.0	100.0	100.0	100.0	100.0	100.0	100.0	100.0	100.0	100.0
Managerial and professional.....	13.4	10.8	18.2	25.1	16.0	14.1	11.5	19.1	25.0	16.6
Tech., sales, and admin. support..	24.8	23.2	31.8	32.5	24.8	24.9	23.3	32.1	32.9	24.3
Services..................	20.3	19.2	19.7	12.1	25.2	19.9	19.1	19.9	12.9	23.8
Precision production, craft, and repair	13.4	14.2	11.0	13.0	12.4	13.2	14.4	9.8	10.2	12.0
Operators, fabricators and laborers	22.2	24.4	18.1	15.4	19.6	22.2	23.7	17.9	17.0	20.9
Farming, forestry, and fishing	5.8	8.3	1.1	1.9	1.9	5.8	8.0	1.2	2.2	2.3
Percent of labor force unemployed:										
Male......................	11.5	11.7	15.6	7.1	10.5	10.4	10.2	14.4	7.8	10.1
Female	11.3	11.7	12.3	8.9	10.5	10.9	11.4	10.8	7.7	10.8

[1] Includes Central or South American and other Hispanic origin.

Source: U.S. Bureau of Labor Statistics, *Employment and Earnings*, monthly, January issues.

No. 623. School Enrollment and Labor Force Status: 1980 and 1992

[In thousands, except percent. As of October. For the civilian noninstitutional population 16 to 24 years old. Based on Current Population Survey; see text, section 1, and Appendix III]

CHARACTERISTIC	POPULATION		CIVILIAN LABOR FORCE			EMPLOYED		UNEMPLOYED		
	1980	1992	1980, total	1992		1980	1992	1980, total	1992	
				Total	Per-cent [1]				Total	Rate [2]
Total, 16 to 24 years [3]	37,103	30,969	24,918	19,950	64.4	21,454	17,335	3,464	2,615	13.1
Enrolled in school [3]	15,713	15,868	7,454	7,737	48.8	6,433	6,718	1,021	1,019	13.2
16 to 19 years	11,126	10,276	4,836	4,318	42.0	4,029	3,574	807	744	17.2
20 to 24 years	4,587	5,592	2,618	3,419	61.1	2,404	3,144	214	275	8.0
Sex:										
Male	7,997	7,917	3,825	3,871	48.9	3,259	3,322	566	549	14.2
Female.................	7,716	7,951	3,629	3,866	48.6	3,174	3,396	455	469	12.1
College level	7,664	8,524	3,996	4,931	57.9	3,632	4,534	364	397	8.1
Full-time.................	6,396	7,165	2,854	3,710	51.8	2,554	3,400	300	309	8.3
Race:										
White..................	13,242	12,777	6,687	6,631	51.9	5,889	5,900	798	731	11.0
Below college..........	6,566	5,720	3,095	2,399	41.9	2,579	1,950	516	449	18.7
College level	6,678	7,057	3,592	4,232	60.0	3,310	3,950	282	282	6.7
Black..................	2,028	2,199	595	751	34.2	406	522	189	229	30.5
Below college..........	1,282	1,288	294	323	25.0	174	172	120	151	46.8
College level	747	911	300	428	47.0	230	350	70	78	18.3
Not enrolled [3]	21,390	15,101	17,464	12,213	80.9	15,021	10,617	2,443	1,597	13.1
White	18,103	12,207	15,121	10,149	83.1	13,318	9,092	1,803	1,057	10.4
Black	2,864	2,393	2,055	1,677	70.1	1,451	1,204	604	474	28.2

[1] Percent of civilian noninstitutional population.   [2] Percent of civilian labor force in each category.   [3] Includes other races, not shown separately.

Source: U.S. Bureau of Labor Statistics, Bulletin 2307; *News*, USDL 93-226, June 22, 1993; and unpublished data.

No. 624. Labor Force Participation Rates, by Marital Status, Sex, and Age: 1960 to 1993

[Annual averages of monthly figures. See table 621 for definition of participation rate. Based on Current Population Survey; see text, section 1, and Appendix III]

MARITAL STATUS AND YEAR	MALE PARTICIPATION RATE							FEMALE PARTICIPATION RATE						
	Total	16-19 years	20-24 years	25-34 years	35-44 years	45-64 years	65 and over	Total	16-19 years	20-24 years	25-34 years	35-44 years	45-64 years	65 and over
Single:														
1960...	69.8	42.6	80.3	91.5	88.6	80.1	31.2	58.6	30.2	77.2	83.4	82.9	79.8	24.3
1970...	65.5	54.6	73.8	87.9	86.2	75.7	25.2	56.8	44.7	73.0	81.4	78.6	73.0	19.7
1975...	68.7	57.9	77.9	86.7	83.2	69.9	21.0	59.8	49.6	72.5	80.8	78.6	68.3	15.8
1980...	72.6	59.9	81.3	89.2	82.2	66.9	16.8	64.4	53.6	75.2	83.3	76.9	65.6	13.9
1985...	73.8	56.3	81.5	89.4	84.6	65.5	15.6	66.6	52.3	76.3	82.4	80.8	67.9	9.8
1989...	75.5	57.4	82.5	90.0	84.6	64.6	18.2	68.0	54.1	76.4	82.2	81.6	66.3	11.4
1990...	74.9	55.1	81.5	89.9	84.6	67.1	15.7	66.9	51.8	74.7	81.2	81.0	66.1	12.2
1991...	74.2	52.6	80.6	89.6	84.8	66.8	14.0	66.5	50.3	73.5	80.3	81.2	68.4	12.7
1992...	74.6	52.9	80.7	89.8	84.9	67.6	16.3	66.4	49.2	73.7	80.5	80.6	68.2	11.3
1993...	74.2	52.5	80.5	89.2	84.5	68.2	15.0	66.4	49.8	74.2	79.1	79.1	68.8	12.5
Married:[1]														
1960...	89.2	91.5	97.1	98.8	98.6	93.7	36.6	31.9	27.2	31.7	28.8	37.2	36.0	6.7
1970...	86.1	92.3	94.7	98.0	98.1	91.2	29.9	40.5	37.8	47.9	38.8	46.8	44.0	7.3
1975...	83.0	92.9	95.3	97.4	97.1	86.8	23.3	44.3	46.2	57.0	48.4	52.0	43.8	7.0
1980...	80.9	91.3	96.9	97.5	97.2	84.3	20.5	49.8	49.3	61.4	58.8	61.8	46.9	7.3
1985...	78.7	91.0	95.6	97.4	96.8	81.7	16.8	53.8	49.6	65.7	65.8	68.1	49.4	6.6
1989...	78.5	93.7	95.9	97.2	96.8	82.4	17.8	57.8	51.9	65.7	69.0	73.5	55.5	8.1
1990...	78.2	92.3	95.6	96.9	96.8	82.5	17.6	58.4	50.0	66.5	69.8	74.0	56.5	8.5
1991...	77.8	93.2	95.4	96.6	96.6	82.3	16.8	58.5	48.7	65.0	70.1	74.3	57.1	8.3
1992...	77.6	90.2	94.8	96.6	96.2	82.7	17.2	59.2	49.0	66.3	70.9	74.8	58.6	7.9
1993...	77.3	91.2	95.0	96.6	96.1	82.5	16.6	59.4	50.1	65.6	70.8	74.7	60.0	7.6
Other:[2]														
1960...	63.1	(B)	96.9	95.2	94.4	83.2	22.7	41.6	43.5	58.0	63.1	70.0	60.0	11.4
1970...	60.7	(B)	90.4	93.7	91.1	78.5	19.3	40.3	48.6	60.3	64.6	68.8	61.9	10.0
1975...	63.4	(B)	88.8	92.4	89.4	73.4	15.4	40.1	47.6	65.3	68.6	69.2	59.0	8.3
1980...	67.5	(B)	92.6	94.1	91.9	73.3	13.7	43.6	50.0	68.4	76.5	77.1	60.2	8.2
1985...	68.7	(B)	95.1	93.7	91.8	72.8	11.4	45.1	51.9	66.2	76.9	81.6	61.0	7.5
1989...	67.9	(B)	91.1	93.6	90.9	74.2	11.7	47.0	48.2	65.8	78.3	82.2	64.7	8.3
1990...	68.3	(B)	93.1	93.0	90.8	74.6	12.0	47.2	54.4	65.6	77.3	82.3	65.0	8.5
1991...	67.7	(B)	93.9	92.1	90.5	73.5	12.3	46.8	45.8	63.3	74.8	82.1	65.2	8.4
1992...	68.0	(B)	91.8	93.5	90.3	74.7	12.2	47.0	47.8	66.9	75.7	81.6	66.4	8.4
1993...	67.4	(B)	91.7	91.9	89.6	74.2	12.0	47.1	53.3	65.2	75.2	81.6	66.9	8.2

B For 1960, percentage not shown where base is less than 50,000; beginning 1970, 35,000. [1] Spouse present. [2] Widowed, divorced, and married (spouse absent).

Source: U.S. Bureau of Labor Statistics, Bulletins 2217 and 2340; and unpublished data.

No. 625. Marital Status of Women in the Civilian Labor Force: 1960 to 1993

[Annual averages of monthly figures. For civilian noninstitutional population 16 years old and over. Based on Current Population Survey; see text, section 1, and Appendix III. See also *Historical Statistics, Colonial Times to 1970*, series D 49-62]

YEAR	FEMALE LABOR FORCE (1,000)				FEMALE PARTICIPATION RATE [3]			
	Total	Single	Married[1]	Other[2]	Total	Single	Married[1]	Other[2]
1960	23,240	5,410	12,893	4,937	37.7	58.6	31.9	41.6
1965	26,200	5,976	14,829	5,396	39.3	54.5	34.9	40.7
1970	31,543	7,265	18,475	5,804	43.3	56.8	40.5	40.3
1975	37,475	9,125	21,484	6,866	46.3	59.8	44.3	40.1
1978	42,631	11,067	23,539	8,025	50.0	63.7	47.8	42.8
1979	44,235	11,597	24,378	8,260	50.9	64.6	49.0	43.1
1980	45,487	11,865	24,980	8,643	51.5	64.4	49.9	43.6
1981	46,696	12,124	25,428	9,144	52.1	64.5	50.5	44.6
1982	47,755	12,460	25,971	9,324	52.6	65.1	51.1	44.8
1983	48,503	12,659	26,468	9,376	52.9	65.0	51.8	44.4
1984	49,709	12,867	27,199	9,644	53.6	65.6	52.8	44.7
1985	51,050	13,163	27,894	9,993	54.5	66.6	53.8	45.1
1986	52,413	13,512	28,623	10,277	55.3	67.2	54.9	45.6
1987	53,658	13,885	29,381	10,393	56.0	67.4	55.9	45.7
1988	54,742	14,194	29,921	10,627	56.6	67.7	56.7	46.2
1989	56,030	14,377	30,548	11,104	57.4	68.0	57.8	47.0
1990	56,554	14,229	30,970	11,354	57.5	66.9	58.4	47.2
1991	56,893	14,295	31,175	11,423	57.3	66.5	58.5	46.8
1992	57,798	14,477	31,720	11,601	57.8	66.4	59.2	47.0
1993	58,407	14,624	31,978	11,805	57.9	66.4	59.4	47.1

[1] Husband present. [2] Widowed, divorced, or separated. [3] See table 621 for definition of participation rate.

Source: U.S. Bureau of Labor Statistics, Bulletin 2307; and unpublished data.

No. 626. Employment Status of Women, by Marital Status and Presence and Age of Children: 1960 to 1993

[As of **March**. For 1960, civilian noninstitutional persons 14 years and over, thereafter 16 years old and over. Based on Current Population Survey; see text, section 1, and Appendix III]

ITEM	TOTAL			WITH ANY CHILDREN								
				Total			Children 6 to 17 only			Children under 6		
	Single	Mar-ried [1]	Other [2]	Single	Mar-ried [1]	Other [2]	Single	Mar-ried[1]	Other [2]	Single	Mar-ried [1]	Other [2]
IN LABOR FORCE (mil.)												
1960	5.4	12.3	4.9	(NA)	6.6	1.5	(NA)	4.1	1.0	(NA)	2.5	0.4
1970	7.0	18.4	5.9	(NA)	10.2	1.9	(NA)	6.3	1.3	(NA)	3.9	0.6
1980	11.2	24.9	8.8	0.6	13.7	3.6	0.2	8.4	2.6	0.3	5.2	1.0
1985	12.9	27.7	10.3	1.1	14.9	4.0	0.4	8.5	2.9	0.7	6.4	1.1
1989	14.0	30.5	10.7	1.5	16.4	4.0	0.6	9.4	2.8	1.0	7.0	1.1
1990	14.0	31.0	11.2	1.5	16.5	4.2	0.6	9.3	3.0	0.9	7.2	1.2
1991	14.1	31.1	11.1	1.7	16.6	4.1	0.6	9.1	3.0	1.1	7.4	1.2
1992	14.1	31.7	11.5	1.7	16.8	4.2	0.7	9.5	3.0	1.0	7.3	1.2
1993	14.1	32.2	11.3	1.9	16.9	4.2	0.7	9.7	3.0	1.1	7.3	1.2
PARTICIPATION RATE [3]												
1960	44.1	30.5	40.0	(NA)	27.6	56.0	(NA)	39.0	65.9	(NA)	18.6	40.5
1970	53.0	40.8	39.1	(NA)	39.7	60.7	(NA)	49.2	66.9	(NA)	30.3	52.2
1980	61.5	50.1	44.0	52.0	54.1	69.4	67.6	61.7	74.6	44.1	45.1	60.3
1985	65.2	54.2	45.6	51.6	60.8	71.9	64.1	67.8	77.8	46.5	53.4	59.7
1989	66.0	57.6	46.0	54.7	65.6	72.0	69.0	73.4	78.2	48.9	57.4	60.1
1990	66.4	58.2	46.8	55.2	66.3	74.2	69.7	73.6	79.7	48.7	58.9	63.6
1991	65.1	58.5	46.2	53.6	66.8	72.7	64.8	73.6	79.5	48.8	59.9	59.8
1992	64.7	59.3	46.7	52.5	67.8	73.2	67.2	75.4	80.0	45.8	59.9	60.5
1993	64.5	59.4	45.9	54.4	67.5	72.1	70.2	74.9	78.3	47.4	59.6	60.0
EMPLOYMENT (mil.)												
1960	5.1	11.6	4.6	(NA)	6.2	1.3	(NA)	3.9	0.9	(NA)	2.3	0.4
1970	6.5	17.5	5.6	(NA)	9.6	1.8	(NA)	6.0	1.2	(NA)	3.6	0.6
1980	10.1	23.6	8.2	0.4	12.8	3.3	0.2	8.1	2.4	0.2	4.8	0.9
1985	11.6	26.1	9.4	0.9	13.9	3.5	0.3	8.1	2.6	0.5	5.9	0.9
1989	12.8	29.4	10.1	1.2	15.8	3.6	0.5	9.1	2.6	0.7	6.7	1.0
1990	12.9	29.9	10.5	1.2	15.8	3.8	0.5	8.9	2.7	0.7	6.9	1.1
1991	12.9	29.7	10.4	1.4	15.7	3.7	0.5	8.8	2.7	0.8	6.9	1.0
1992	12.8	30.1	10.6	1.4	15.9	3.7	0.6	9.1	2.7	0.8	6.8	1.0
1993	12.7	30.8	10.5	1.5	16.1	3.9	0.6	9.3	2.8	0.9	6.8	1.1
UNEMPLOY-MENT RATE [4]												
1960	6.0	5.4	6.2	(NA)	6.0	8.4	(NA)	4.9	6.8	(NA)	7.8	12.5
1970	7.1	4.8	4.8	(NA)	6.0	7.2	(NA)	4.8	5.9	(NA)	7.9	9.8
1980	10.3	5.3	6.4	23.2	5.9	9.2	15.6	4.4	7.9	29.2	8.3	12.8
1985	10.2	5.7	8.5	23.8	6.6	12.1	15.4	5.5	10.6	28.5	8.0	16.1
1989	8.1	3.4	5.7	21.3	3.8	8.4	14.3	3.7	7.2	25.3	4.1	11.3
1990	8.2	3.5	5.7	18.4	4.2	8.5	14.5	3.8	7.7	20.8	4.8	10.2
1991	8.8	4.6	6.8	17.9	5.3	9.1	10.7	4.2	7.7	22.0	6.7	12.7
1992	9.1	4.9	7.6	17.3	5.7	10.8	14.1	4.6	8.6	19.4	7.0	16.3
1993	9.8	4.4	6.9	19.2	4.8	8.5	13.7	3.8	7.0	22.8	6.2	12.5

NA Not available.   [1] Husband present.   [2] Widowed, divorced, or separated.   [3] Percent of women in each specific category in the labor force.   [4] Unemployed as a percent of civilian labor force in specified group.

Source: U.S. Bureau of Labor Statistics, Bulletin 2307; and unpublished data.

No. 627. Labor Force Participation Rates for Wives, Husband Present, by Age of Own Youngest Child: 1975 to 1993

[As of **March**. For civilian noninstitutional population, 16 years old and over. For definition of participation rate, see table 626. Based on Current Population Survey; see text, section 1, and Appendix III]

PRESENCE AND AGE OF CHILD	TOTAL			WHITE			BLACK		
	1975	1985	1993	1975	1985	1993	1975	1985	1993
Wives, total	44.4	54.2	59.4	43.6	53.3	58.9	54.1	63.8	64.8
No children under 18	43.8	48.2	52.4	43.6	47.5	52.2	47.6	55.2	53.8
With children under 18	44.9	60.8	67.5	43.6	59.9	66.9	58.4	71.7	75.3
Under 6, total	36.7	53.4	59.6	34.7	52.1	58.6	54.9	69.6	70.9
Under 3	32.7	50.5	57.3	30.7	49.4	56.7	50.1	66.2	65.6
1 year or under	30.8	49.4	57.5	29.2	48.6	56.8	50.0	63.7	64.8
2 years	37.1	54.0	58.1	35.1	52.7	56.5	56.4	69.9	74.5
3 to 5 years	42.2	58.4	63.1	40.1	56.6	61.6	61.2	73.8	78.1
3 years	41.2	55.1	61.6	39.0	52.7	60.2	62.7	72.3	79.4
4 years	41.2	59.7	65.7	38.7	58.4	64.3	64.9	70.6	79.3
5 years	44.4	62.1	63.1	43.8	59.9	61.4	56.3	79.1	77.5
6 to 13 years	51.8	68.2	74.7	50.7	67.7	74.5	65.7	73.3	80.6
14 to 17 years	53.5	67.0	75.6	53.4	66.6	75.6	52.3	74.4	75.7

Source: U.S. Bureau of Labor Statistics, Bulletin 2340; and unpublished data.

No. 628. Civilian Labor Force—Employment Status, by Sex, Race, and Age: 1993

[For civilian noninstitutional population 16 years old and over. Annual averages of monthly figures. Based on Current Population Survey; see text, section 1, and Appendix III]

AGE AND RACE	TOTAL (1,000)	MALE (1,000)			FEMALE (1,000)			PERCENT OF LABOR FORCE			
		Total	Employed	Unemployed	Total	Employed	Unemployed	Employed Male	Employed Female	Unemployed Male	Unemployed Female
All workers [1] ..	128,040	69,633	64,700	4,932	58,407	54,606	3,801	92.9	93.5	7.1	6.5
16 to 19 years.....	6,826	3,564	2,836	728	3,261	2,694	568	79.6	82.6	20.4	17.4
20 to 24 years.....	13,558	7,164	6,356	808	6,393	5,780	613	88.7	90.4	11.3	9.6
25 to 34 years.....	34,465	19,053	17,734	1,319	15,412	14,373	1,038	93.1	93.3	6.9	6.7
35 to 44 years.....	34,264	18,537	17,508	1,029	15,727	14,894	833	94.4	94.7	5.6	5.3
45 to 54 years.....	23,542	12,634	11,997	638	10,907	10,415	492	95.0	95.5	5.0	4.5
55 to 64 years.....	11,867	6,639	6,294	345	5,228	5,017	211	94.8	96.0	5.2	4.0
65 years and over ..	3,520	2,041	1,976	65	1,479	1,433	46	96.8	96.9	3.2	3.1
White	109,359	60,150	56,397	3,753	49,208	46,415	2,793	93.8	94.3	6.2	5.7
16 to 19 years.....	5,831	3,035	2,500	535	2,795	2,387	408	82.4	85.4	17.6	14.6
20 to 24 years.....	11,360	6,021	5,448	573	5,339	4,921	418	90.5	92.2	9.5	7.8
25 to 34 years.....	28,996	16,217	15,211	1,006	12,779	12,045	734	93.8	94.3	6.2	5.7
35 to 44 years.....	29,190	16,043	15,248	795	13,148	12,529	619	95.0	95.3	5.0	4.7
45 to 54 years.....	20,407	11,099	10,584	516	9,308	8,907	400	95.4	95.7	4.6	4.3
55 to 64 years.....	10,385	5,861	5,588	274	4,524	4,349	175	95.3	96.1	4.7	3.9
65 years and over ..	3,189	1,873	1,818	55	1,316	1,277	39	97.1	97.0	2.9	3.0
Black........	13,943	6,911	5,957	954	7,031	6,189	842	86.2	88.0	13.8	12.0
16 to 19 years.....	776	413	247	166	363	227	136	59.8	62.5	40.2	37.5
20 to 24 years.....	1,689	854	658	196	835	661	174	77.0	79.2	23.0	20.8
25 to 34 years.....	4,168	2,115	1,854	261	2,053	1,789	264	87.7	87.1	12.3	12.9
35 to 44 years.....	3,738	1,788	1,600	188	1,950	1,783	167	89.5	91.4	10.5	8.6
45 to 54 years.....	2,213	1,050	964	85	1,163	1,096	67	91.9	94.2	8.1	5.8
55 to 64 years.....	1,102	566	515	51	536	508	28	91.0	94.8	9.0	5.2
65 years and over ..	257	126	119	7	131	126	5	94.4	96.2	5.6	3.8
Hispanic [2]	10,377	6,256	5,603	653	4,120	3,669	451	89.6	89.1	10.4	10.9
16 to 19 years.....	660	385	285	101	274	202	72	73.8	73.7	26.2	26.3
20 to 24 years.....	1,456	895	782	113	561	482	79	87.4	85.9	12.6	14.1
25 to 34 years.....	3,365	2,119	1,930	189	1,246	1,123	123	91.1	90.1	8.9	9.9
35 to 44 years.....	2,671	1,562	1,424	138	1,109	1,003	106	91.2	90.4	8.8	9.6
45 to 54 years.....	1,442	842	768	74	600	550	50	91.2	91.7	8.8	8.3
55 to 64 years.....	646	369	338	31	277	257	20	91.6	92.8	8.4	7.2
65 years and over ..	137	84	76	8	53	52	1	90.5	98.1	9.5	1.9

[1] Includes other races not shown separately.   [2] Persons of Hispanic origin may be of any race.

Source: U.S. Bureau of Labor Statistics, *Employment and Earnings*, monthly, January 1994.

No. 629. Employed Civilians and Weekly Hours: 1970 to 1993

[In thousands, except as indicated. For civilian noninstitutional population 16 years old and over. Annual averages of monthly figures. Based on Current Population Survey; see text, section 1, and Appendix III]

ITEM	1970	1980	1985	1989	1990	1991	1992	1993
Total employed	78,678	99,303	107,150	117,342	117,914	116,877	117,598	119,306
Age:								
16 to 19 years old	6,144	7,710	6,434	6,759	6,261	5,628	5,398	5,530
20 to 24 years old	9,731	14,087	13,980	12,962	12,622	12,233	12,157	12,137
25 to 34 years old	16,318	27,204	31,208	34,045	33,831	32,914	32,441	32,107
35 to 44 years old	15,922	19,523	24,732	29,443	30,543	31,286	31,662	32,402
45 to 54 years old	16,473	16,234	16,509	19,279	19,765	20,164	21,246	22,412
55 to 64 years old	10,974	11,586	11,474	11,499	11,464	11,268	11,267	11,311
65 years old and over	3,118	2,960	2,813	3,355	3,428	3,384	3,427	3,409
Class of worker:								
Nonagriculture.................	75,215	95,938	103,971	114,142	114,728	113,644	114,391	116,232
Wage and salary worker	69,491	88,525	95,871	105,259	105,715	104,520	105,540	107,011
Self-employed................	5,221	7,000	7,811	8,605	8,760	8,899	8,619	9,003
Unpaid family workers	502	413	289	279	252	225	232	218
Agriculture	3,463	3,364	3,179	3,199	3,186	3,233	3,207	3,074
Wage and salary worker	1,154	1,425	1,535	1,665	1,679	1,673	1,696	1,637
Self-employed................	1,810	1,642	1,458	1,403	1,400	1,442	1,398	1,332
Unpaid family workers	499	297	185	131	107	118	113	105
Weekly hours:								
Nonagriculture:								
Wage and salary workers	38.3	38.1	38.7	39.3	39.2	39.0	38.8	39.3
Self-employed................	45.0	41.2	41.1	41.1	40.8	40.4	40.1	40.5
Unpaid family workers	37.9	34.7	35.1	35.1	33.9	35.4	34.5	34.2
Agriculture:								
Wage and salary workers	40.0	41.6	40.8	41.8	41.3	41.0	40.6	40.8
Self-employed................	51.0	49.3	48.2	47.9	46.9	46.8	47.1	46.5
Unpaid family workers	40.0	38.6	38.5	39.4	38.5	40.3	40.5	36.9

Source: U.S. Bureau of Labor Statistics, *Employment and Earnings*, monthly, January issues; and unpublished data.

No. 630. Self-Employed Workers, by Industry and Occupation: 1970 to 1993

[In thousands. For civilian noninstitutional population 16 years old and over. Annual averages of monthly figures. Data from 1992 forward are not fully comparable with data for prior years because of the introduction of the occupational and industrial classification used in the 1990 census. Based on the Current Population Survey; see text, section 1, and Appendix III]

ITEM	1970	1975	1980	1985	1990	1991	1992	1993
Total self-employed..............	7,031	7,427	8,642	9,269	10,160	10,341	10,017	10,335
Industry: Agriculture.................	1,810	1,722	1,642	1,458	1,400	1,442	1,398	1,332
Nonagriculture..................	5,221	5,705	7,000	7,811	8,760	8,899	8,619	9,003
Mining......................	14	16	28	20	24	23	23	17
Construction..................	687	839	1,173	1,301	1,463	1,447	1,466	1,555
Manufacturing.................	264	273	358	347	429	420	392	442
Transportation and public utilities.......	196	223	282	315	302	318	337	372
Trade.......................	1,667	1,709	1,899	1,792	1,859	1,879	1,776	1,890
Finance, insurance, and real estate......	254	335	458	558	635	619	630	664
Services.....................	2,140	2,310	2,804	3,477	4,048	4,193	3,995	4,062
Occupation:								
Managerial and professional specialty......	(NA)	(NA)	(NA)	2,585	3,067	3,117	2,919	3,102
Technical, sales, and administrative support..	(NA)	(NA)	(NA)	2,059	2,252	2,245	2,192	2,336
Service occupations...............	(NA)	(NA)	(NA)	980	1,213	1,273	1,079	1,043
Precision production, craft, and repair......	(NA)	(NA)	(NA)	1,611	1,680	1,697	1,803	1,891
Operators, fabricators, and laborers.......	(NA)	(NA)	(NA)	568	568	584	626	632
Farming, forestry, and fishing..........	(NA)	(NA)	(NA)	1,465	1,380	1,427	1,390	1,331

NA Not available.

Source: U.S. Bureau of Labor Statistics, Bulletin 2307; *Employment and Earnings*, monthly, January issues; and unpublished data.

No. 631. Persons With a Job But Not at Work: 1970 to 1993

[In thousands, except percent. For civilian noninstitutional population 16 years old and over. Annual averages of monthly figures. Based on Current Population Survey; see text, section 1, and Appendix III. See *Historical Statistics, Colonial Times to 1970*, series D 116-126, for related but not comparable data]

REASON FOR NOT WORKING	1970	1975	1980	1985	1987	1988	1989	1990	1991	1992	1993
All industries, number.......	4,645	5,221	5,881	5,789	5,910	5,831	6,170	6,157	5,909	6,082	6,028
Percent of employed	5.9	6.1	5.9	5.4	5.3	5.1	5.3	5.2	5.1	5.2	5.1
Reason for not working:											
Vacation.................	2,341	2,815	3,320	3,338	3,421	3,236	3,437	3,531	3,297	3,414	3,330
Illness..................	1,324	1,343	1,426	1,308	1,320	1,364	1,405	1,341	1,302	1,258	1,290
Bad weather	128	139	155	141	92	122	133	89	118	126	151
Industrial dispute	156	95	105	42	34	30	63	24	17	19	24
All other	696	829	876	960	1,043	1,080	1,132	1,172	1,175	1,265	1,233

Source: U.S. Bureau of Labor Statistics, *Employment and Earnings*, monthly, January issues; and unpublished data.

No. 632. Employed and Unemployed Workers, by Work Schedules: 1980 to 1993

[In thousands. See headnote, table 631]

CHARACTERISTIC	EMPLOYED			CHARACTERISTIC	UNEMPLOYED		
	1980	1990	1993		1980	1990	1993
Total	99,303	117,914	119,306	Total.............	7,637	6,874	8,734
Full-time [1]...........	82,562	97,994	98,439	Looking for full-time work ...	6,269	5,541	7,146
Male	51,717	57,982	57,643	Male	3,703	3,264	4,277
16 to 19 years old ..	2,017	1,343	1,042	16 to 19 years old.....	537	328	343
20 to 24 years old ..	6,533	5,452	4,968	20 to 24 years old.....	994	582	704
25 to 54 years old ..	35,644	44,229	44,946	25 to 54 years old.....	1,923	2,098	2,884
55 years and over ..	7,521	6,959	6,688	55 years and over.....	250	255	346
Female	30,845	40,011	40,796	Female.............	2,564	2,277	2,869
16 to 19 years old ..	1,456	975	744	16 to 19 years old.....	430	233	246
20 to 24 years old ..	5,098	4,386	3,955	20 to 24 years old.....	636	439	476
25 to 54 years old ..	20,395	30,485	31,889	25 to 54 years old.....	1,363	1,491	1,968
55 years and over ..	3,897	4,166	4,208	55 years and over.....	135	115	179
Part-time [1]	16,740	19,920	20,868	Looking for part-time			
Male	5,471	6,452	7,057	work	1,369	1,332	1,588
16 to 19 years old ..	2,068	1,894	1,794	Male	563	535	655
20 to 24 years old ..	999	1,174	1,388	16 to 19 years old.....	377	301	385
25 to 54 years old ..	1,092	1,842	2,293	20 to 24 years old.....	81	84	103
55 years and over ..	1,314	1,543	1,582	25 to 54 years old.....	54	89	102
Female	11,270	13,468	13,810	55 years and over.....	52	61	64
16 to 19 years old ..	2,169	2,049	1,950	Female.............	806	797	933
20 to 24 years old ..	1,456	1,611	1,825	16 to 19 years old.....	326	286	322
25 to 54 years old ..	5,827	7,584	7,793	20 to 24 years old.....	124	116	137
55 years and over ..	1,815	2,224	2,243	25 to 54 years old.....	299	323	396
				55 years and over.....	57	72	78

[1] Full-time workers include employed persons on full-time (35 hours or more per week) schedules and those working part-time (between 1 and 34 hours) for economic reasons who usually work full-time. Part-time workers include employed persons working part-time voluntarily and those working part-time for economic reasons, who usually work part-time. Employed persons with a job but not at work are distributed according to whether they usually work full- or part-time.

Source: U.S. Bureau of Labor Statistics, Bulletin 2307; and *Employment and Earnings*, monthly, January issues.

No. 633. Multiple Jobholders, by Industry and Occupation: 1991

[As of **May**. Multiple jobholders are employed persons who, either 1) had jobs as wage or salary workers with two employers or more; 2) were self-employed and also held a wage and salary job; or 3) were unpaid family workers on their primary jobs but also held wage and salary job. Based on the Current Population Survey; see text, section 1, and Appendix III]

CHARACTERISTIC	TOTAL			MALE			FEMALE		
	Employed (1,000)	Multiple jobholders		Employed (1,000)	Multiple jobholders		Employed (1,000)	Multiple jobholders	
		Number (1,000)	Rate [1]		Number (1,000)	Rate [1]		Number (1,000)	Rate [1]
Total, 16 years and over	116,626	7,183	6.2	63,499	4,054	6.4	53,127	3,129	5.9
Industry and class of worker of primary job:									
Agriculture	3,466	179	5.2	2,737	139	5.1	728	41	5.6
Nonagricultural industries	113,160	7,003	6.2	60,762	3,915	6.4	52,399	3,088	5.9
Wage and salary workers	104,193	6,691	6.4	55,063	3,733	6.8	49,129	2,958	6.0
Mining	737	25	3.4	592	17	2.8	145	8	5.8
Construction	5,745	271	4.7	5,231	239	4.6	514	33	6.4
Manufacturing	19,993	1,044	5.2	13,497	798	5.9	6,496	245	3.8
Transportation and public utilities	7,848	487	6.2	5,526	356	6.4	2,321	131	5.6
Wholesale trade	4,255	261	6.1	3,010	190	6.3	1,245	70	5.7
Retail trade	17,250	914	5.3	8,354	444	5.3	8,896	470	5.3
Finance, insurance, and real estate	7,066	414	5.9	2,860	187	6.5	4,206	227	5.4
Services	35,592	2,747	7.7	12,719	1,125	8.8	22,873	1,622	7.1
Public administration	5,709	528	9.3	3,274	376	11.5	2,434	152	6.2
Self-employed workers	8,733	306	3.5	5,663	182	3.2	3,070	123	4.0
Unpaid family workers	235	7	2.9	36	-	-	199	7	3.4
Occupation of primary job:									
Managerial and professional specialty	31,154	2,259	7.3	16,678	1,269	7.6	14,476	990	6.8
Technical, sales, and admin. support	36,002	2,154	6.0	12,584	803	6.4	23,418	1,351	5.8
Service occupations	15,534	1,063	6.8	6,252	527	8.4	9,282	536	5.8
Precision production, craft, and repair	13,115	652	5.0	12,019	608	5.1	1,096	44	4.0
Operators, fabricators, and laborers	17,065	851	5.0	12,804	682	5.3	4,261	169	4.0
Farming, forestry, and fishing	3,756	203	5.4	3,162	164	5.2	594	39	6.6

- Represents or rounds to zero.   [1] Multiple jobholders as a percent of all employed persons in specified group.

Source: U.S. Bureau of Labor Statistics, *News,* USDL 91-547, October 28, 1991.

No. 634. Workers on Flexible Schedules: 1985 and 1991

[In **thousands, except percent**. As of **May**. For employed persons 16 years old and over who usually work full-time and who were at work during the survey reference week. A flexible schedule allows workers to vary the time they begin and end their work day. Based on Current Population Survey; see text, section 1, and Appendix III]

CHARACTERISTIC	ALL WORKERS			WORKERS WITH FLEXIBLE SCHEDULES					
				Number			Percent		
	Total	Male	Female	Total	Male	Female	Total	Male	Female
Total, 1985	73,395	43,779	29,616	9,061	5,760	3,300	12.3	13.2	11.1
Total, 1991	80,452	46,308	34,145	12,118	7,168	4,950	15.1	15.5	14.5
Age:									
16 to 19 years	1,413	855	558	150	82	67	10.6	9.6	12.0
20 to 24 years	8,332	4,694	3,638	999	542	456	12.0	11.5	12.5
25 to 34 years	25,523	14,917	10,606	4,008	2,358	1,650	15.7	15.8	15.6
35 to 44 years	22,749	13,001	9,749	3,744	2,213	1,531	16.5	17.0	15.7
45 to 54 years	14,306	8,003	6,302	2,184	1,299	885	15.3	16.2	14.0
55 to 64 years	7,197	4,286	2,910	880	574	306	12.2	13.4	10.5
65 years and over	933	552	382	153	99	54	16.4	17.9	14.1
Race:									
White	68,795	40,267	28,528	10,630	6,416	4,214	15.5	15.9	14.8
Black	8,943	4,522	4,421	1,083	525	558	12.1	11.6	12.6
Hispanic [1]	6,598	4,172	2,425	702	427	275	10.6	10.2	11.3
Marital Status:									
Single	18,420	10,621	7,799	2,887	1,606	1,281	15.7	15.1	16.4
Married, spouse present	49,101	30,510	18,591	7,195	4,794	2,401	14.7	15.7	12.9
Other	12,932	5,177	7,755	2,035	768	1,267	15.7	14.8	16.3
Occupation:									
Managerial and professional	22,630	12,037	10,593	4,991	3,053	1,937	22.1	25.4	18.3
Technical, sales, administrative	24,116	8,910	15,206	4,258	1,984	2,274	17.7	22.3	15.0
Service occupations	8,389	4,329	4,060	883	432	450	10.5	10.0	11.1
Precision production, craft, and repair	10,270	9,464	807	833	764	69	8.1	8.1	8.6
Operators, fabricators, and laborers	13,514	10,211	3,303	980	783	197	7.3	7.7	6.0
Farming, forestry, and fisheries	1,533	1,355	177	173	151	22	11.3	11.1	12.4
Industry:									
Private sector	65,556	38,909	26,647	10,010	6,018	3,992	15.3	15.5	15.0
Goods producing [2]	24,057	17,776	6,281	2,815	2,060	755	11.7	11.6	12.0
Service producing	41,499	21,132	20,367	7,196	3,959	3,237	17.3	18.7	15.9
Public sector	14,896	7,399	7,497	2,108	1,150	958	14.2	15.5	12.8
Federal government	3,007	1,868	1,140	812	481	331	27.0	25.7	29.0
State government	3,616	1,801	1,814	655	351	304	18.1	19.5	16.8
Local government	8,274	3,730	4,543	640	319	322	7.7	8.6	7.1

[1] Persons of Hispanic origin may be of any race.   [2] Includes agriculture, mining, construction, and manufacturing.

Source: U.S. Bureau of Labor Statistics, *News,* USDL 92-491, August 4, 1992; and unpublished data.

No. 635. Workers on Shift Schedules: 1985 and 1991

[See headnote, table 634]

CHARACTERISTIC	Total employ-ed [1]	WORK SCHEDULES—PERCENT DISTRIBUTION						
		Regular daytime sched-ules	Shift workers					
			Total	Evening	Night	Rotating	Irregu-lar [2]	Other
Total, 1985 [3]	73,395	84.1	15.9	6.3	2.7	4.3	(NA)	2.6
Total, 1991 [3]	**80,452**	**81.8**	**17.8**	**5.1**	**3.7**	**3.4**	**3.7**	**2.0**
Age: 16 to 19 years old	1,413	70.6	28.6	12.0	5.5	3.2	6.4	1.5
20 to 24 years old	8,332	74.8	25.0	8.5	4.7	4.6	5.5	1.7
25 to 34 years old	25,523	81.3	18.3	5.0	3.9	3.8	3.7	1.9
35 to 44 years old	22,749	83.7	16.0	4.1	3.5	3.2	3.2	2.0
45 to 54 years old	14,306	83.6	16.2	4.6	2.9	2.9	3.4	2.3
55 to 64 years old	7,197	84.1	15.3	4.2	3.4	2.4	3.0	2.3
65 years old and over	933	88.1	11.7	2.3	2.7	1.1	2.4	3.3
Sex:								
Male	46,308	79.5	20.2	5.4	4.2	4.0	4.2	2.3
Female	34,145	85.0	14.6	4.6	2.9	2.6	2.9	1.7
Race and Hispanic origin:								
White	68,795	82.6	17.1	4.6	3.4	3.3	3.8	2.1
Black	8,943	76.0	23.3	8.4	5.6	4.7	2.9	1.8
Hispanic [4]	6,598	80.3	19.1	6.4	4.6	2.7	3.1	2.4
Marital status: Single	18,420	77.6	22.0	7.0	4.0	4.0	4.7	2.2
Married, spouse present	49,101	83.9	15.8	4.2	3.3	3.2	3.3	1.9
Other	12,932	80.1	19.4	5.8	4.4	3.4	3.5	2.4
Occupation:								
Managerial and professional	22,630	89.6	10.0	1.6	1.4	1.8	2.8	2.3
Technical, sales, administrative	24,116	85.9	13.8	3.5	2.4	2.7	3.6	1.7
Service occupations	8,389	57.1	42.5	14.7	8.7	7.9	6.6	4.6
Precision production, craft, and repair	10,270	85.3	14.4	4.3	3.7	3.4	2.5	0.5
Operators, fabricators, and laborers	13,514	73.4	26.2	8.6	6.8	4.8	4.2	1.7
Farming, forestry, and fisheries	1,533	89.2	10.4	1.1	1.2	0.7	4.4	3.0

NA Not available.　[1] Includes a small number of workers who did not report data on shift worked.　[2] Employer arranged.　[3] Data for 1985 are not strictly comparable to those for 1991 because of the addition of the "irregular" category in the May 1991 survey. Includes other races, not shown separately.　[4] Persons of Hispanic origin may be of any race.

Source: U.S. Bureau of Labor Statistics, *News,* USDL 92-491, August 4, 1992; and unpublished data.

No. 636. Workers Doing Job-Related Work at Home: 1991

[As of **May.** For persons 16 years old and over doing job-related work at home as part of their primary job in nonagriculture industries]

CHARACTERISTIC	Total at work (1,000)	PERSONS DOING JOB RELATED WORK AT HOME					
		Total [1] (1,000)	Worked at home for pay				Mean hours worked (number) [3]
			Total (1,000)	Worked 8 hours or more			
				Total (1,000)	Rate [2]	35 hours or more (1,000)	
Total [4]	**109,126**	**19,967**	**7,432**	**3,651**	**3.3**	**1,069**	**14.1**
Age: 16 to 24 years old	16,268	862	329	122	0.7	40	12.3
25 to 34 years old	31,248	5,290	1,798	839	2.7	259	13.7
35 to 44 years old	29,500	6,755	2,430	1,144	3.9	297	13.0
45 to 54 years old	18,842	4,368	1,567	876	4.6	264	15.4
55 to 64 years old	10,291	1,995	865	462	4.5	161	16.8
65 years old and over	2,977	697	445	207	7.0	47	13.3
Sex: Male	58,794	10,731	4,210	1,894	3.2	438	12.0
Female	50,332	9,236	3,222	1,757	3.5	632	16.8
Race and Hispanic origin:							
White	94,387	18,520	7,022	3,403	3.6	966	13.8
Black	11,020	970	239	147	1.3	76	22.8
Hispanic [5]	7,977	667	255	137	1.7	36	13.7
Occupation:							
Managerial and professional	29,971	11,517	3,151	1,511	5.0	360	12.8
Executive, administrative, managerial	14,384	4,729	1,636	749	5.2	191	12.8
Professional	15,587	6,789	1,515	763	4.9	169	12.9
Technical, sales, administrative	34,554	5,611	2,458	1,123	3.2	201	11.2
Sales	13,177	3,528	1,623	813	6.2	133	11.9
Administrative support	17,786	1,617	690	253	1.4	63	10.0
Service occupations	14,955	1,144	733	553	3.7	381	31.7
Precision production, craft, repair	12,608	1,070	731	306	2.4	68	11.6
Operators, fabricators, and laborers	16,271	546	312	139	0.9	58	14.9

[1] Includes those that did not report pay status and unpaid family members.　[2] Persons working at home for pay as a percent of the total at work.　[3] For definition of mean, see Guide to Tabular Presentation.　[4] Includes other industries and occupations, not shown separately.　[5] Persons of Hispanic origin may be of any race.

Source: U.S. Bureau of Labor Statistics, *Monthly Labor Review,* February 1994; and unpublished data.

No. 637. Employed Civilians, by Occupation, Sex, Race, and Hispanic Origin: 1983 and 1993

[For civilian noninstitutional population 16 years old and over. Annual average of monthly figures. Based on Current Population Survey; see text, section 1, and Appendix III. Persons of Hispanic origin may be of any race. See headnote, table 630]

OCCUPATION	1983 Total employed (1,000)	1983 Female	1983 Black	1983 Hispanic	1993 Total employed (1,000)	1993 Female	1993 Black	1993 Hispanic
Total	100,834	43.7	9.3	5.3	119,306	45.8	10.2	7.8
Managerial and professional specialty	23,592	40.9	5.6	2.6	32,280	47.8	6.6	4.0
Executive, administrative, and managerial [1]	10,772	32.4	4.7	2.8	15,376	42.0	6.2	4.5
Officials and administrators, public	417	38.5	8.3	3.8	581	45.2	11.3	4.5
Financial managers	357	38.6	3.5	3.1	529	46.2	4.4	4.2
Personnel and labor relations managers	106	43.9	4.9	2.6	96	60.7	7.9	4.6
Purchasing managers	82	23.6	5.1	1.4	109	34.9	8.0	5.3
Managers, marketing, advertising and public relations	396	21.8	2.7	1.7	496	31.2	3.1	3.5
Administrators, education and related fields	415	41.4	11.3	2.4	635	59.9	13.0	3.8
Managers, medicine and health	91	57.0	5.0	2.0	450	70.5	6.5	4.2
Managers, properties and real estate	305	42.8	5.5	5.2	481	45.7	6.6	6.3
Management-related occupations [1]	2,966	40.3	5.8	3.5	4,155	52.7	7.5	4.6
Accountants and auditors	1,105	38.7	5.5	3.3	1,387	49.2	7.0	4.2
Professional specialty [1]	12,820	48.1	6.4	2.5	16,904	53.2	7.0	3.6
Architects	103	12.7	1.6	1.5	123	18.6	3.1	2.3
Engineers [1]	1,572	5.8	2.7	2.2	1,716	8.6	3.7	3.6
Aerospace engineers	80	6.9	1.5	2.1	83	7.5	2.1	3.9
Chemical engineers	67	6.1	3.0	1.4	58	10.0	2.5	4.9
Civil engineers	211	4.0	1.9	3.2	221	9.4	4.7	3.8
Electrical and electronic	450	6.1	3.4	3.1	533	7.6	4.5	3.4
Industrial engineers	210	11.0	3.3	2.4	201	16.4	3.4	4.4
Mechanical	259	2.8	3.2	1.1	296	5.2	4.4	3.3
Mathematical and computer scientists [1]	463	29.6	5.4	2.6	1,051	32.4	6.0	2.5
Computer systems analysts, scientists	276	27.8	6.2	2.7	769	29.9	5.8	2.4
Operations and systems researchers and analysts	142	31.3	4.9	2.2	236	39.7	6.3	3.0
Natural scientists [1]	357	20.5	2.6	2.1	531	30.1	3.6	1.9
Chemists, except biochemists	98	23.3	4.3	1.2	133	28.8	4.3	3.0
Geologists and geodesists	65	18.0	1.1	2.6	54	14.0	1.0	2.1
Biological and life scientists	55	40.8	2.4	1.8	114	40.4	3.9	1.4
Health diagnosing occupations [1]	735	13.3	2.7	3.3	909	20.5	3.0	3.9
Physicians	519	15.8	3.2	4.5	605	21.8	3.7	4.6
Dentists	126	6.7	2.4	1.0	152	10.5	1.9	3.0
Health assessment and treating occupations	1,900	85.8	7.1	2.2	2,602	86.4	8.3	3.5
Registered nurses	1,372	95.8	6.7	1.8	1,859	94.4	8.4	3.2
Pharmacists	158	26.7	3.8	2.6	187	38.1	6.1	2.7
Dietitians	71	90.8	21.0	3.7	94	92.8	17.5	6.0
Therapists [1]	247	76.3	7.6	2.7	416	74.9	6.9	4.1
Inhalation therapists	69	69.4	6.5	3.7	92	58.4	10.0	6.9
Physical therapists	55	77.0	9.7	1.5	115	72.5	3.0	5.0
Speech therapists	51	90.5	1.5	-	83	91.8	6.7	1.2
Physicians' assistants	51	36.3	7.7	4.4	(2)	(2)	(2)	(2)
Teachers, college and university	606	36.3	4.4	1.8	772	42.5	4.8	3.1
Teachers, except college and university [1]	3,365	70.9	9.1	2.7	4,397	75.1	8.6	3.6
Prekindergarten and kindergarten	299	98.2	11.8	3.4	501	97.7	11.7	5.0
Elementary school	1,350	83.3	11.1	3.1	1,668	85.9	9.3	3.9
Secondary school	1,209	51.8	7.2	2.3	1,237	57.5	6.9	3.1
Special education	81	82.2	10.2	2.3	286	84.0	10.1	2.3
Counselors, educational and vocational	184	53.1	13.9	3.2	224	67.6	14.3	6.9
Librarians, archivists, and curators	213	84.4	7.8	1.6	223	83.5	6.2	3.8
Librarians	193	87.3	7.9	1.8	195	88.3	7.0	3.5
Social scientists and urban planners [1]	261	46.8	7.1	2.1	399	57.0	5.9	3.0
Economists	98	37.9	6.3	2.7	117	47.6	4.8	3.5
Psychologists	135	57.1	8.6	1.1	241	64.1	7.1	3.1
Social, recreation, and religious workers [1]	831	41.1	12.1	3.8	1,096	50.5	15.6	5.0
Social workers	407	64.3	18.2	6.3	586	68.9	21.4	6.0
Recreation workers	65	71.9	15.7	2.0	89	75.1	14.8	4.7
Clergy	293	5.6	4.9	1.4	350	11.4	8.7	3.1
Lawyers and judges	651	15.8	2.7	1.0	815	22.8	2.8	2.1
Lawyers	612	15.3	2.6	0.9	777	22.9	2.7	2.1
Writers, artists, entertainers, and athletes [1]	1,544	42.7	4.8	2.9	2,026	46.6	5.3	4.7
Authors	62	46.7	2.1	0.9	139	57.2	2.4	1.9
Technical writers	(2)	(2)	(2)	(2)	63	52.8	2.7	2.3
Designers	393	52.7	3.1	2.7	541	52.6	3.7	4.4
Musicians and composers	155	28.0	7.9	4.4	174	32.8	8.8	5.8
Actors and directors	60	30.8	6.6	3.4	96	38.3	10.4	4.7
Painters, sculptors, craft-artists, and artist printmakers	186	47.4	2.1	2.3	222	48.0	3.5	4.1
Photographers	113	20.7	4.0	3.4	135	26.2	6.5	7.1
Editors and reporters	204	48.4	2.9	2.1	266	48.5	5.0	3.4
Public relations specialists	157	50.1	6.2	1.9	155	59.6	7.0	3.5
Athletes	58	17.6	9.4	1.7	80	23.9	10.1	3.9

See footnotes at end of table.

No. 637. Employed Civilians, by Occupation, Sex, Race, and Hispanic Origin: 1983 and 1993—Continued

[See headnote, page 407]

OCCUPATION	1983 Total em- ployed (1,000)	1983 Percent of total Fe- male	Black	His- panic	1993 Total em- ployed (1,000)	1993 Percent of total Fe- male	Black	His- panic
Technical, sales, and administrative support	**31,265**	**64.6**	**7.6**	**4.3**	**36,814**	**63.8**	**9.3**	**6.3**
Technicians and related support	3,053	48.2	8.2	3.1	4,014	50.5	9.6	5.0
Health technologists and technicians [1]	1,111	84.3	12.7	3.1	1,522	81.0	12.4	5.8
Clinical laboratory technologists and technicians	255	76.2	10.5	2.9	315	76.1	12.1	6.1
Dental hygienists	66	98.6	1.6	-	76	99.3	0.4	2.0
Health record technologists and technicians	(2)	(2)	(2)	(2)	63	88.8	20.4	5.7
Radiologic technicians	101	71.7	8.6	4.5	146	70.2	8.3	7.0
Licensed practical nurses	443	97.0	17.7	3.1	425	94.6	17.2	3.4
Engineering and related technologists and technicians [1]	822	18.4	6.1	3.5	870	17.8	7.4	4.9
Electrical and electronic technicians	260	12.5	8.2	4.6	297	15.5	7.4	5.6
Drafting occupations	273	17.5	5.5	2.3	244	18.1	6.9	5.9
Surveying and mapping technicians	(2)	(2)	(2)	(2)	73	5.0	4.8	2.8
Science technicians [1]	202	29.1	6.6	2.8	261	37.5	7.2	5.2
Biological technicians	52	37.7	2.9	2.0	85	59.7	6.1	3.8
Chemical technicians	82	26.9	9.5	3.5	74	26.0	7.1	3.9
Technicians, except health, engineering, and science [1]	917	35.3	5.0	2.7	1,361	39.9	8.4	4.0
Airplane pilots and navigators	69	2.1	-	1.6	101	3.9	5.5	2.4
Computer programmers	443	32.5	4.4	2.1	578	31.5	6.7	3.5
Legal assistants	128	74.0	4.3	3.6	254	79.6	8.6	4.9
Sales occupations	11,818	47.5	4.7	3.7	14,245	48.1	6.7	5.9
Supervisors and proprietors	2,958	28.4	3.6	3.4	4,016	36.4	4.4	5.3
Sales representatives, finance and business services [1]	1,853	37.2	2.7	2.2	2,317	40.5	4.7	3.7
Insurance sales	551	25.1	3.8	2.5	583	33.3	5.1	3.8
Real estate sales	570	48.9	1.3	1.5	710	51.4	2.5	4.1
Securities and financial services sales	212	23.6	3.1	1.1	355	28.1	4.1	2.2
Advertising and related sales	124	47.9	4.5	3.3	161	50.8	4.5	3.1
Sales representatives, commodities, except retail	1,442	15.1	2.1	2.2	1,538	21.0	2.9	3.9
Sales workers, retail and personal services	5,511	69.7	6.7	4.8	6,281	64.9	9.7	7.5
Cashiers	2,009	84.4	10.1	5.4	2,581	78.4	13.2	8.7
Sales-related occupations	54	58.7	2.8	1.3	93	60.5	5.3	6.1
Administrative support, including clerical	16,395	79.9	9.6	5.0	18,555	78.8	11.2	6.8
Supervisors	676	53.4	9.3	5.0	778	58.4	11.9	6.8
Computer equipment operators	605	63.9	12.5	6.0	603	61.9	13.8	6.2
Computer operators	597	63.7	12.1	6.0	597	61.9	13.7	6.1
Secretaries, stenographers, and typists [1]	4,861	98.2	7.3	4.5	4,174	96.2	8.9	5.9
Secretaries	3,891	99.0	5.8	4.0	3,586	98.9	7.7	5.8
Typists	906	95.6	13.8	6.4	494	94.3	18.8	7.4
Information clerks	1,174	88.9	8.5	5.5	1,678	88.8	9.3	7.9
Receptionists	602	96.8	7.5	6.6	899	97.2	8.6	7.6
Records processing occupations, except financial [1]	866	82.4	13.9	4.8	908	79.1	14.9	6.6
Order clerks	188	78.1	10.6	4.4	212	78.1	17.1	6.5
Personnel clerks, except payroll and time keeping	64	91.1	14.9	4.6	63	89.2	15.2	3.9
Library clerks	147	81.9	15.4	2.5	146	75.9	11.6	3.4
File clerks	287	83.5	16.7	6.1	288	79.6	15.0	10.4
Records clerks	157	82.8	11.6	5.6	184	77.9	14.3	4.8
Financial records processing [1]	2,457	89.4	4.6	3.7	2,272	89.9	5.4	5.3
Bookkeepers, accounting, and auditing clerks	1,970	91.0	4.3	3.3	1,806	90.9	4.5	4.9
Payroll and time keeping clerks	192	82.2	5.9	5.0	173	88.3	6.6	5.2
Billing clerks	146	88.4	6.2	3.9	160	88.5	8.4	6.6
Cost and rate clerks	96	75.6	5.9	5.3	60	72.9	10.9	9.7
Billing, posting, and calculating machine operators	(2)	(2)	(2)	(2)	72	86.1	12.0	8.2
Duplicating, mail and other office machine operators	68	62.6	16.0	6.1	63	47.8	19.2	9.2
Communications equipment operators	256	89.1	17.0	4.4	208	86.1	20.9	8.0
Telephone operators	244	90.4	17.0	4.3	197	86.9	21.0	7.9
Mail and message distributing occupations	799	31.6	18.1	4.5	953	37.6	19.0	7.4
Postal clerks, except mail carriers	248	36.7	26.2	5.2	297	44.8	26.8	6.8
Mail carrier, postal service	259	17.1	12.5	2.7	333	28.4	12.6	7.0
Mail clerks, except postal service	170	50.0	15.8	5.9	166	51.5	22.5	8.8
Messengers	122	26.2	16.7	5.2	157	29.1	14.2	7.9
Material recording, scheduling, and distributing [1][3]	1,562	37.5	10.9	6.6	1,852	44.0	14.0	8.3
Dispatchers	157	45.7	11.4	4.3	221	52.7	11.8	5.7
Production coordinators	182	44.0	6.1	2.2	196	50.2	7.8	4.7
Traffic, shipping, and receiving clerks	421	22.6	9.1	11.1	570	30.9	15.1	11.9
Stock and inventory clerks	532	38.7	13.3	5.5	489	43.4	14.5	6.8
Weighers, measurers, and checkers	79	47.2	16.9	5.8	67	45.6	15.9	10.4
Expediters	112	57.5	8.4	4.3	227	67.0	13.9	7.1
Adjusters and investigators	675	69.9	11.1	5.1	1,372	74.0	12.2	6.1
Insurance adjusters, examiners, and investigators	199	65.0	11.5	3.3	372	71.5	12.1	4.0
Investigators and adjusters, except insurance	301	70.1	11.3	4.8	748	76.2	11.2	6.3
Eligibility clerks, social welfare	69	88.7	12.9	9.4	86	84.7	16.2	6.0
Bill and account collectors	106	66.4	8.5	6.5	166	64.3	14.8	9.5
Miscellaneous administrative support [1]	2,397	85.2	12.5	5.9	3,694	82.3	12.4	7.8
General office clerks	648	80.6	12.7	5.2	731	82.0	11.4	9.6
Bank tellers	480	91.0	7.5	4.3	446	88.4	6.9	6.2
Data entry keyers	311	93.6	18.6	5.6	623	82.4	16.4	8.3
Statistical clerks	96	75.7	7.5	3.4	50	78.4	15.4	3.3
Teachers' aides	348	93.7	17.8	12.6	508	92.2	15.7	12.3

See footnotes at end of table.

No. 637. **Employed Civilians, by Occupation, Sex, Race, and Hispanic Origin: 1983 and 1993—Continued**
[See headnote, page 407]

OCCUPATION	1983 Total employed (1,000)	1983 Percent of total Female	1983 Black	1983 Hispanic	1993 Total employed (1,000)	1993 Percent of total Female	1993 Black	1993 Hispanic
Service occupations.	13,857	60.1	16.6	6.8	16,522	59.5	17.3	11.2
Private household [1]	980	96.1	27.8	8.5	912	95.1	17.1	21.6
Child care workers	408	96.9	7.9	3.6	345	97.2	9.0	15.0
Cleaners and servants	512	95.8	42.4	11.8	534	94.0	21.6	25.7
Protective service	1,672	12.8	13.6	4.6	2,152	17.2	17.4	6.6
Supervisors, protective service	127	4.7	7.7	3.1	185	7.8	12.2	4.8
Supervisors, police and detectives	58	4.2	9.3	1.2	96	10.3	6.6	6.1
Firefighting and fire prevention	189	1.0	6.7	4.1	208	3.7	7.6	4.5
Firefighting occupations	170	1.0	7.3	3.8	188	3.3	7.5	5.0
Police and detectives	645	9.4	13.1	4.0	923	16.0	18.0	5.4
Police and detectives, public service	412	5.7	9.5	4.4	511	12.0	14.5	5.9
Sheriffs, bailiffs, and other law enforcement officers	87	13.2	11.5	4.0	117	19.5	13.4	4.6
Correctional institution officers	146	17.8	24.0	2.8	295	21.6	25.8	5.0
Guards	711	20.6	17.0	5.6	836	23.9	20.4	8.8
Guards and police, except public service	602	13.0	18.9	6.2	711	17.2	22.6	9.5
Service except private household and protective	11,205	64.0	16.0	6.9	13,457	63.9	17.3	11.2
Food preparation and service occupations [1]	4,860	63.3	10.5	6.8	5,691	58.4	12.8	11.7
Bartenders	338	48.4	2.7	4.4	321	53.3	3.8	3.1
Waiters and waitresses	1,357	87.8	4.1	3.6	1,414	80.0	4.6	7.5
Cooks	1,452	50.0	15.8	6.5	1,992	44.2	19.0	13.9
Food counter, fountain, and related occupations	326	76.0	9.1	6.7	367	69.2	12.6	8.1
Kitchen workers, food preparation	138	77.0	13.7	8.1	260	75.3	15.0	10.8
Waiters' and waitresses' assistants	364	38.8	12.6	14.2	368	43.7	11.4	18.1
Health service occupations	1,739	89.2	23.5	4.8	2,213	87.4	27.3	7.7
Dental assistants	154	98.1	6.1	5.7	181	97.8	3.4	10.4
Health aides, except nursing	316	86.8	16.5	4.8	312	78.9	22.2	4.7
Nursing aides, orderlies, and attendants	1,269	88.7	27.3	4.7	1,719	87.9	30.7	7.9
Cleaning and building service occupations [1]	2,736	38.8	24.4	9.2	2,959	42.2	22.4	16.2
Maids and housemen	531	81.2	32.3	10.1	661	81.7	27.3	18.6
Janitors and cleaners	2,031	28.6	22.6	8.9	2,086	30.7	21.5	16.1
Personal service occupations [1]	1,870	79.2	11.1	6.0	2,594	80.7	12.9	7.6
Barbers	92	12.9	8.4	12.1	86	22.3	27.5	8.5
Hairdressers and cosmetologists	622	88.7	7.0	5.7	758	90.1	9.4	6.3
Attendants, amusement and recreation facilities	131	40.2	7.1	4.3	161	39.4	7.4	5.8
Public transportation attendants	63	74.3	11.3	5.9	104	80.4	8.8	7.4
Welfare service aides	77	92.5	24.2	10.5	73	82.1	21.2	16.6
Family child care providers	(NA)	(NA)	(NA)	(NA)	302	99.0	9.4	10.2
Early childhood teachers' assistants	(NA)	(NA)	(NA)	(NA)	418	96.6	15.7	6.4
Precision production, craft, and repair	12,328	8.1	6.8	6.2	13,326	8.6	7.4	9.2
Mechanics and repairers	4,158	3.0	6.8	5.3	4,416	3.5	7.3	7.9
Mechanics and repairers, except supervisors [1]	3,906	2.8	7.0	5.5	4,196	3.3	7.3	8.1
Vehicle and mobile equipment mechanics/repairers [1]	1,683	0.8	6.9	6.0	1,800	1.0	6.1	9.9
Automobile mechanics	800	0.5	7.8	6.0	854	0.6	6.4	10.8
Aircraft engine mechanics	95	2.5	4.0	7.6	139	4.1	5.1	11.5
Electrical and electronic equipment repairers [1]	674	7.4	7.3	4.5	655	9.5	9.0	5.8
Data processing equipment repairers	98	9.3	6.1	4.5	152	10.7	10.2	5.0
Telephone installers and repairers	247	9.9	7.8	3.7	188	12.5	9.9	3.4
Construction trades	4,289	1.8	6.6	6.0	5,004	1.9	6.5	9.5
Construction trades, except supervisors	3,784	1.9	7.1	6.1	4,269	1.9	7.0	10.2
Carpenters	1,160	1.4	5.0	5.0	1,276	0.9	4.5	7.7
Extractive occupations	196	2.3	3.3	6.0	148	1.8	4.6	7.9
Precision production occupations	3,685	21.5	7.3	7.4	3,758	23.6	8.8	10.5
Operators, fabricators, and laborers	16,091	26.6	14.0	8.3	17,038	24.5	14.9	12.1
Machine operators, assemblers, and inspectors [1]	7,744	42.1	14.0	9.4	7,415	38.7	14.7	13.8
Textile, apparel, and furnishings machine operators [1]	1,414	82.1	18.7	12.5	1,159	74.4	20.8	19.9
Textile sewing machine operators	806	94.0	15.5	14.5	616	85.8	18.5	24.1
Pressing machine operators	141	66.4	27.1	14.2	147	62.7	24.0	20.4
Fabricators, assemblers, and hand working occupations	1,715	33.7	11.3	8.7	1,882	32.7	12.7	12.0
Production inspectors, testers, samplers, and weighers	794	53.8	13.0	7.7	777	52.4	15.0	13.7
Transportation and material moving occupations	4,201	7.8	13.0	5.9	5,004	9.3	14.0	8.6
Motor vehicle operators	2,978	9.2	13.5	6.0	3,825	10.8	14.2	8.9
Trucks, heavy and light	2,195	3.1	12.3	5.7	2,786	4.5	12.3	8.8
Transportation occupations, except motor vehicles	212	2.4	6.7	3.0	170	4.1	10.2	3.1
Material moving equipment operators	1,011	4.8	12.9	6.3	1,009	4.5	13.9	8.5
Industrial truck and tractor operators	369	5.6	19.6	8.2	432	7.3	20.9	12.0
Handlers, equipment cleaners, helpers, and laborers [1]	4,147	16.8	15.1	8.6	4,619	18.3	16.1	12.9
Freight, stock, and material handlers	1,488	15.4	15.3	7.1	1,850	20.7	16.7	9.9
Laborers, except construction	1,024	19.4	16.0	8.6	1,127	17.0	16.7	13.7
Farming, forestry, and fishing	3,700	16.0	7.5	8.2	3,326	15.4	6.3	16.0
Farm operators and managers	1,450	12.1	1.3	0.7	1,170	14.3	0.9	2.4
Other agricultural and related occupations	2,072	19.9	11.7	14.0	1,963	17.0	9.5	24.8
Farm workers	1,149	24.8	11.6	15.9	801	20.0	7.0	28.5
Forestry and logging occupations	126	1.4	12.8	2.1	132	5.9	10.4	11.8
Fishers, hunters, and trappers	53	4.5	1.8	2.5	61	4.4	1.7	4.8

- Represents or rounds to zero.   NA Not available.   [1] Includes other occupations, not shown separately.   [2] Level of total employment below 50,000.   [3] Includes clerks.

Source: U.S. Bureau of Labor Statistics, *Employment and Earnings*, monthly, January issues.

No. 638. Civilian Employment in Occupations With the Largest Job Growth: 1992 to 2005

[Occupations are in descending order of absolute employment change 1992-2005 (moderate growth). Includes wage and salary jobs, self-employed, and unpaid family members. Estimates based on the Current Employment Statistics estimates and the Occupational Employment Statistics estimates. See source for methodological assumptions. Minus sign (-) indicates decrease]

OCCUPATION	EMPLOYMENT (1,000)				PERCENT CHANGE 1992-2005		
	1992	2005 [1]			Low	Moderate	High
		Low	Moderate	High			
Total, all occupations [2]	121,099	139,007	147,482	154,430	14.8	21.8	27.5
Salespersons, retail	3,660	4,137	4,446	4,611	13.1	21.5	26.0
Registered nurses	1,835	2,479	2,601	2,637	35.1	41.7	43.7
Cashiers	2,747	3,201	3,417	3,520	16.5	24.4	28.1
General office clerks	2,688	3,143	3,342	3,489	16.9	24.3	29.8
Truck drivers light and heavy	2,391	2,836	3,039	3,235	18.6	27.1	35.3
Waiters and waitresses	1,756	2,280	2,394	2,415	29.8	36.3	37.5
Nursing aides, orderlies, and attendants	1,308	1,824	1,903	1,937	39.4	45.4	48.0
Janitors and cleaners [3]	2,862	3,246	3,410	3,519	13.4	19.1	23.0
Food preparation workers	1,223	1,661	1,748	1,775	35.8	42.9	45.1
Systems analysts	455	891	956	1,001	95.7	110.1	120.0
Home health aides	347	794	827	835	128.7	138.1	140.6
Teachers, secondary school	1,263	1,640	1,724	1,789	29.9	36.6	41.7
Child care workers	684	1,100	1,135	1,183	60.6	65.8	72.8
Guards	803	1,138	1,211	1,255	41.7	50.8	56.2
Marketing and sales worker supervisors	2,036	2,303	2,443	2,565	13.1	20.0	26.0
Teacher aides and educational assistants	885	1,209	1,266	1,308	36.6	43.1	47.8
General managers and top executives	2,871	3,050	3,251	3,418	6.2	13.2	19.0
Maintenance repairers, general utility	1,145	1,388	1,464	1,542	21.2	27.8	34.7
Gardeners and groundskeepers, except farm	884	1,152	1,195	1,261	30.3	35.2	42.7
Teachers, elementary	1,456	1,683	1,767	1,830	15.6	21.3	25.6
Food counter, fountain, and related workers	1,564	1,776	1,872	1,895	13.6	19.7	21.2
Receptionists and information clerks	904	1,149	1,210	1,245	27.1	33.8	37.7
Accountants and auditors	939	1,167	1,243	1,301	24.3	32.3	38.6
Clerical supervisors and managers	1,267	1,473	1,568	1,622	16.3	23.8	28.0
Cooks, restaurant	602	837	879	889	39.0	45.8	47.5
Teachers, special education	358	594	625	648	65.9	74.4	81.0
Licensed practical nurses	659	879	920	933	33.4	39.7	41.6
Cooks, short order and fast food	714	921	971	978	29.0	36.0	37.0
Human services workers	189	429	445	451	127.6	135.9	139.2
Computer engineers and scientists	211	409	447	484	93.9	111.9	129.2
Teachers, preschool and kindergarten	434	646	669	682	48.9	54.3	57.2
Food service and lodging managers	532	732	764	787	37.6	43.5	48.0
Hairdressers, hairstylists, and cosmetologists	628	824	846	876	31.2	34.7	39.4
Blue collar worker supervisors	1,757	1,844	1,974	2,131	5.0	12.4	21.3
College and university faculty	812	976	1,026	1,064	20.2	26.4	31.1
Carpenters	978	1,131	1,176	1,317	15.7	20.2	34.6
Correction officers	282	452	479	503	60.0	69.9	78.1
Physicians	556	720	751	769	29.5	35.0	38.3
Lawyers	626	781	821	850	24.7	31.1	35.8
Social workers	484	645	676	693	33.3	39.5	43.0
Financial managers	701	828	875	917	18.1	24.8	30.7
Computer programmers	555	673	723	759	21.3	30.4	36.8
Automotive mechanics	739	857	907	960	15.9	22.7	29.8
Personal and home care aides	127	283	293	296	122.0	129.8	132.0
Legal secretaries	280	415	439	447	48.3	57.1	59.9
Stock clerks	1,782	1,801	1,940	2,024	1.0	8.8	13.6
Marketing, advertising, and public relations managers	432	548	588	616	26.8	36.1	42.6
Traffic, shipping, and receiving clerks	824	889	971	1,034	7.9	17.8	25.4
Dining room and cafeteria attendants and bar helpers	441	546	572	580	23.8	29.8	31.5
Painters and paperhangers, construction and maintenance	440	547	569	624	24.3	29.2	41.8
Medical assistants	181	296	308	313	63.5	70.5	73.0
Secretaries, except legal and medical	2,810	2,766	2,930	3,067	-1.5	4.3	9.2
Teachers and instructors, vocational ed. and training	305	396	416	430	29.7	36.5	41.1
Freight, stock, and material movers, hand	845	885	955	1,011	4.8	13.1	19.7
Bus drivers, school	395	471	504	519	19.3	27.6	31.5
Engineering, mathematical, and natural science managers	337	410	444	476	21.5	31.5	41.1
Medical secretaries	235	326	341	345	39.0	45.2	47.0
Radiologic technologists and technicians	162	252	264	267	55.4	62.7	64.6
Personnel, training, and labor relations specialists	281	360	383	398	28.1	36.1	41.7
Electricians	518	588	618	698	13.6	19.3	34.7
Amusement and recreation attendants	207	294	303	309	41.9	46.1	49.2
Instructors and coaches, sports and physical training	260	343	355	363	31.6	36.2	39.3
Bill and account collectors	235	309	328	339	31.9	40.0	44.5
Adjustment clerks	352	412	445	462	17.2	26.5	31.2
Electrical and electronics engineers	370	422	459	501	14.0	24.2	35.4
Management analysts	208	283	297	313	35.8	42.7	50.2
Counter and rental clerks	242	314	331	341	29.5	36.3	40.6

[1] Based on low, moderate, or high trend assumptions.   [2] Includes other occupations, not shown separately.   [3] Includes maids and housekeepers.

Source: U.S. Bureau of Labor Statistics, *Monthly Labor Review*, November 1993.

No. 639. Civilian Employment in the Fastest Growing and Fastest Declining Occupations: 1992 to 2005

[Occupations are in order of employment percent change 1992-2005 (moderate growth). Includes wage and salary jobs, self-employed, and unpaid family members. Estimates based on the Current Employment Statistics estimates and the Occupational Employment Statistics estimates. See source for methodological assumptions. Minus sign (-) indicates decrease]

OCCUPATION	EMPLOYMENT (1,000)				PERCENT CHANGE 1992-2005		
	1992	2005 [1]			Low	Moderate	High
		Low	Moderate	High			
Total, all occupations [2]	121,099	139,007	147,482	154,430	14.8	21.8	27.5
FASTEST GROWING							
Home health aides	347	794	827	835	128.7	138.1	140.6
Human services workers	189	429	445	451	127.6	135.9	139.2
Personal and home care aides	127	283	293	296	122.0	129.8	132.0
Computer engineers and scientists	211	409	447	484	93.9	111.9	129.2
Systems analysts	455	891	956	1,001	95.7	110.1	120.0
Physical and corrective therapy assistants and aides	61	113	118	119	84.6	92.7	95.1
Physical therapists	90	163	170	173	80.2	88.0	91.4
Paralegals	95	166	176	180	75.8	86.1	89.8
Occupational therapy assistants and aides	12	20	21	21	70.5	78.1	80.1
Electronic pagination systems workers	18	29	32	33	65.1	77.9	84.0
Teachers, special education	358	594	625	648	65.9	74.4	81.0
Medical assistants	181	296	308	313	63.5	70.5	73.0
Detectives, except public	59	94	100	104	60.1	70.2	76.8
Correction officers	282	452	479	503	60.0	69.9	78.1
Child care workers	684	1,100	1,135	1,183	60.6	65.8	72.8
Travel agents	115	167	191	196	45.2	65.7	69.9
Radiologic technologists and technicians	162	252	264	267	55.4	62.7	64.6
Nursery (farm) workers	72	110	116	123	53.1	62.0	71.3
Medical records technicians	76	118	123	125	54.4	61.5	63.6
Operations research analysts	45	67	72	75	50.1	61.4	68.0
Occupational therapists	40	61	64	65	52.9	59.6	62.5
Subway and streetcar operators	22	33	35	37	48.1	57.2	64.9
Legal secretaries	280	415	439	447	48.3	57.1	59.9
Teachers, preschool and kindergarten	434	646	669	682	48.9	54.3	57.2
Manicurists	35	54	55	56	51.2	54.1	58.3
EEG technologists	6	9	10	10	46.6	53.8	55.4
Producers, directors, actors, and entertainers	129	190	198	205	47.0	53.5	58.7
Speech-language pathologists and audiologists	73	105	110	113	44.6	51.3	55.7
Flight attendants	93	121	140	144	30.3	51.0	55.5
Guards	803	1,138	1,211	1,255	41.7	50.8	56.2
Nuclear medicine technologists	12	17	18	18	43.1	50.1	51.6
Insurance adjusters, examiners, and investigators	147	205	220	220	39.3	49.1	49.5
Respiratory therapists	74	104	109	110	41.4	48.3	49.9
Psychologists	143	204	212	222	42.1	48.0	54.7
FASTEST DECLINING							
Frame wirers, central office	11	2	3	3	-77.4	-75.3	-74.7
Signal or track switch maintainers	3	1	1	1	-76.6	-74.6	-72.9
Peripheral EDP equipment operators	30	11	12	12	-62.6	-60.2	-59.0
Directory assistance operators	27	12	13	14	-54.9	-50.6	-49.4
Central office operators	48	22	24	24	-54.7	-50.3	-49.1
Station installers and repairers, telephone	40	18	20	20	-54.7	-50.3	-49.1
Portable machine cutters	11	5	6	6	-48.3	-40.1	-39.4
Computer operators, except peripheral equipment	266	151	161	168	-43.2	-39.3	-36.6
Shoe sewing machine operators and tenders	16	9	10	10	-46.3	-38.4	-35.8
Central office and PBX installers and repairers	70	41	45	46	-41.3	-35.6	-34.1
Child care workers, private household	350	220	227	242	-37.1	-35.1	-31.0
Job printers	15	9	10	10	-39.4	-35.0	-33.2
Roustabouts	33	20	22	32	-38.4	-33.2	-2.0
Separating and still machine operators and tenders	21	13	14	15	-37.0	-32.8	-29.8
Cleaners and servants, private household	483	316	326	347	-34.6	-32.5	-28.2
Coil winders, tapers, and finishers	20	12	14	16	-41.2	-32.4	-22.1
Billing, posting, and calculating machine operators	93	62	66	68	-33.6	-29.5	-27.0
Sewing machine operators, garment	556	338	393	396	-39.1	-29.2	-28.7
Compositors and typesetters, precision	11	7	8	8	-30.7	-26.5	-23.3
Data entry keyers, composing	16	11	12	12	-31.7	-26.4	-23.8
Motion picture projectionists	9	7	7	7	-29.3	-25.8	-24.0
Telephone and cable TV line installers and repairers	165	117	125	134	-29.4	-24.4	-18.7
Cutting and slicing machine setters [3]	94	68	73	76	-28.1	-22.6	-19.5
Watchmakers	9	7	7	8	-26.5	-22.6	-18.4
Tire building machine operators	14	10	11	12	-29.4	-22.3	-19.0
Packaging and filling machine operators and tenders	319	232	248	257	-27.1	-22.3	-19.4
Head sawyers and sawing machine operators and tenders [4]	59	44	46	53	-25.7	-22.3	-10.3
Switchboard operators	239	177	188	194	-25.9	-21.3	-18.8
Farmers	1,088	831	857	914	-23.7	-21.2	-16.0
Machine forming operators and tenders, metal and plastic	155	112	123	133	-27.8	-20.8	-14.3
Cement and gluing machine operators and tenders	35	26	28	30	-25.7	-20.2	-12.7

[1] Based on low, moderate, or high trend assumptions.   [2] Includes other occupations, not shown separately.   [3] Includes operators and tenders.   [4] Includes setters and set-up operators.

Source: U.S. Bureau of Labor Statistics, *Monthly Labor Review*, November 1993.

No. 640. Occupations of the Employed, by Selected Characteristics: 1993

[In thousands. Annual averages of monthly figures. For civilian noninstitutional population 25 years and over. Based on Current Population Survey; see text, section 1, and Appendix III]

SEX, RACE, AND EDUCATIONAL ATTAINMENT	Total employed	Mana-gerial/ profes-sional	Tech./ sales/ adminis-trative	Service [1]	Precision produc-tion [2]	Operators/ fabrica-tors [3]	Farming, forestry, fishing
Male, total [4]	**55,508**	**16,020**	**11,250**	**4,720**	**10,943**	**10,297**	**2,278**
Less than a high school diploma.....	6,851	352	518	903	1,870	2,460	749
High school graduates, no college....	18,596	2,001	3,153	1,853	5,324	5,352	912
Less than a bachelor's degree......	13,894	3,145	3,877	1,429	3,024	2,009	409
College graduates	16,167	10,522	3,702	534	725	476	208
White	48,449	14,541	9,947	3,582	9,885	8,430	2,063
Less than a high school diploma..	5,709	314	449	658	1,666	1,978	643
High school graduates, no college.	16,115	1,828	2,808	1,357	4,858	4,429	835
Less than a bachelor's degree ...	12,174	2,860	3,422	1,146	2,723	1,641	382
College graduates	14,451	9,540	3,268	421	638	382	203
Black	5,052	816	869	888	766	1,553	160
Less than a high school diploma..	884	27	52	181	149	396	80
High school graduates, no college.	1,983	118	259	398	349	799	60
Less than a bachelor's degree ...	1,324	207	346	229	222	301	19
College graduates	860	464	212	79	46	58	2
Female, total [4]	**46,132**	**14,349**	**19,198**	**7,486**	**1,040**	**3,626**	**433**
Less than a high school diploma.....	4,181	210	896	1,734	198	1,030	114
High school graduates, no college....	16,871	2,233	8,351	3,626	535	1,943	183
Less than a bachelor's degree......	13,040	3,555	6,962	1,681	219	536	89
College graduates	12,040	8,352	2,990	445	90	116	48
White	39,107	12,624	16,689	5,733	837	2,814	410
Less than a high school diploma..	3,276	181	779	1,241	159	815	102
High school graduates, no college.	14,367	2,020	7,458	2,788	427	1,497	176
Less than a bachelor's degree ...	11,035	3,104	5,930	1,329	177	408	86
College graduates	10,428	7,319	2,522	373	73	94	47
Black	5,301	1,181	1,875	1,453	142	635	16
Less than a high school diploma..	703	22	81	420	25	146	9
High school graduates, no college.	2,024	162	706	702	80	371	3
Less than a bachelor's degree ...	1,611	344	834	291	30	111	-
College graduates	963	652	255	40	7	8	-

- Represents or rounds to zero.   [1] Includes private household workers.   [2] Includes craft and repair.   [3] Includes laborers. [4] Includes other races, not shown separately.

Source: U.S. Bureau of Labor Statistics, unpublished data.

No. 641. Employment, by Industry: 1970 to 1993

[In thousands, except percent. See headnote, table 622. Data from 1985 to 1990, and also beginning 1993, not strictly comparable with other years due to changes in industrial classification]

INDUSTRY	1970	1980	1985	1990	1993 Total	Percent Female	Percent Black	Percent Hispanic[1]
Total employed	**78,678**	**99,303**	**107,150**	**117,914**	**119,306**	**45.8**	**10.2**	**7.8**
Agriculture	3,463	3,364	3,179	3,186	3,074	20.7	4.6	15.2
Mining	516	979	939	730	669	16.2	3.7	5.0
Construction....................	4,818	6,215	6,987	7,696	7,220	8.6	6.4	8.7
Manufacturing	20,746	21,942	20,879	21,184	19,557	32.3	10.1	9.0
Transportation, communication, and other public utilities..............	5,320	6,525	7,548	8,136	8,481	28.5	13.8	7.1
Wholesale and retail trade.........	15,008	20,191	22,296	24,269	24,769	46.7	8.4	8.4
Wholesale trade...............	2,672	3,920	4,341	4,651	4,606	28.9	6.0	7.9
Retail trade..................	12,336	16,270	17,955	19,618	20,163	50.8	8.9	8.5
Finance, insurance, real estate......	3,945	5,993	7,005	8,021	7,962	58.6	8.4	6.0
Services [2]	20,385	28,752	33,322	39,084	41,817	61.7	11.4	6.9
Business and repair services [2]	1,403	3,848	5,969	7,409	6,838	35.1	10.4	9.0
Advertising	147	191	263	277	284	52.3	5.3	7.0
Services to dwellings and buildings.	(NA)	370	571	813	749	43.5	18.1	17.4
Personnel supply services......	(NA)	235	590	704	698	61.0	18.7	7.4
Computer and data processing. ...	(NA)	221	549	799	957	36.3	5.2	3.7
Detective/protective services.....	(NA)	213	318	373	475	17.8	20.8	7.7
Automobile services..........	600	952	1,322	1,429	1,477	13.5	8.3	12.4
Personal services [2]	4,276	3,839	4,352	4,667	4,443	70.0	14.1	13.0
Private households...........	1,782	1,257	1,254	1,023	1,114	86.9	17.8	20.3
Hotels and lodging places	979	1,149	1,451	1,780	1,435	56.7	15.3	14.1
Entertainment and recreation	717	1,047	1,278	1,503	2,060	41.8	9.4	6.8
Professional and related services [2] ..	12,904	19,853	21,563	25,335	28,293	68.6	11.5	5.5
Hospitals	2,843	4,036	4,269	4,690	5,032	76.2	15.6	5.6
Health services, except hospitals ..	1,628	3,345	3,641	4,757	5,521	78.2	12.7	6.3
Elementary, secondary schools ...	6,126	5,550	5,431	6,028	6,372	74.5	11.6	5.9
Colleges and universities.......	(³)	2,108	2,281	2,609	2,633	52.6	9.1	5.1
Social services.............	828	1,590	1,682	2,234	2,770	81.6	16.6	6.8
Legal services..............	429	776	995	1,217	1,253	55.1	5.2	4.1
Public administration [4]..........	4,476	5,342	4,995	5,608	5,756	42.9	15.0	5.3

NA Not available.   [1] Persons of Hispanic origin may be of any race.   [2] Includes industries not shown separately. [3] Included with elementary/secondary schools.   [4] Includes workers involved in uniquely governmental activities, e.g., judicial and legislative.

Source: U.S. Bureau of Labor Statistics, *Employment and Earnings*, monthly, January issues.

No. 642. Employment by Selected Industry, With Projections: 1979 to 2005

[Figures may differ from those in other tables since these data exclude establishments not elsewhere classified (SIC 99); in addition, agriculture services (SIC 074, 5, 8) are included in agriculture, not services. See source for details. Minus sign (-) indicates decrease]

INDUSTRY	1987 SIC [1] code	EMPLOYMENT (1,000)			ANNUAL GROWTH RATE	
		1979	1992	2005, proj. [2]	1979-1992	1992-2005, proj. [2]
Total	(X)	101,363	121,093	147,484	1.4	1.5
Nonfarm wage and salary	(X)	89,491	107,888	132,960	1.4	1.6
Goods-producing (excluding agriculture)	(X)	26,461	23,142	23,717	-1.0	0.2
Mining	10-14	958	631	562	-3.2	-0.9
Construction	15,16,17	4,463	4,471	5,632	-	1.8
Manufacturing	20-39	21,040	18,040	17,523	-1.2	-0.2
Durable manufacturing	24,25,32-39	12,730	10,237	9,673	-1.7	-0.4
Lumber and wood products	24	782	674	690	-1.1	0.2
Furniture and fixtures	25	498	476	523	-0.3	0.7
Stone, clay and glass products	32	674	512	437	-2.1	-1.2
Primary metal industries	33	1,254	693	618	-4.5	-0.9
Blast furnaces/basic steel products	331	571	250	224	-6.1	-0.9
Fabricated metal products	34	1,713	1,322	1,196	-2.0	-0.8
Industrial machinery and equipment	35	2,508	1,922	1,868	-2.0	-0.2
Computer equipment [3]	3571,2,5,7	318	353	237	0.8	-3.0
Electronic and other electric equipment [3]	36	1,793	1,526	1,354	-1.2	-0.9
Telephone and telegraph apparatus	3661	171	108	81	-3.4	-2.3
Semiconductors and related devices	3674	201	218	224	0.6	0.2
Transportation equipment	37	2,059	1,822	1,765	-0.9	-0.2
Motor vehicles and equipment [3]	371	990	809	759	-1.5	-0.5
Instruments and related products [3]	38	1,006	925	887	-0.6	-0.3
Measuring/controlling devices, watches	382	431	300	255	-2.8	-1.2
Medical instruments and supplies	3841-3	144	216	295	3.2	2.4
Miscellaneous manufacturing industries	39	445	363	334	-1.5	-0.6
Nondurable manufacturing	20-23,26-31	8,310	7,804	7,851	-0.5	-
Food and kindred products	20	1,733	1,655	1,648	-0.4	-
Tobacco manufactures	21	70	49	37	-2.7	-2.1
Textile mill products	22	885	671	571	-2.1	-1.2
Apparel and other textile products	23	1,304	1,005	760	-2.0	-2.1
Paper and allied products	26	697	687	729	-0.1	0.4
Printing and publishing	27	1,235	1,504	1,751	1.5	1.2
Chemicals and allied products	28	1,109	1,083	1,090	-0.2	0.1
Petroleum and coal products	29	210	159	128	-2.1	-1.6
Rubber/misc. plastics products	30	821	872	1,066	0.5	1.6
Leather and leather products	31	246	119	71	-5.4	-3.9
Service producing	(X)	63,030	84,746	109,243	2.3	2.0
Transportation, communications, utilities	40-42,44-49	5,136	5,709	6,497	0.8	1.0
Transportation	40-42,44-47	3,019	3,486	4,310	1.1	1.6
Communications	48	1,309	1,268	1,116	-0.2	-1.0
Electric, gas, and sanitary services	49	807	955	1,072	1.3	0.9
Wholesale trade	50,51	5,221	6,045	7,191	1.1	1.3
Retail trade	52-59	14,972	19,346	23,777	2.0	1.6
Eating and drinking places	58	4,513	6,602	8,778	3.0	2.2
Finance, insurance, and real estate	60-67	4,975	6,571	7,969	2.2	1.5
Services	70-87,89	16,779	28,422	41,788	4.1	3.0
Hotels and other lodging places	70	1,060	1,572	2,209	3.1	2.6
Personal services	72	821	1,111	1,382	2.4	1.7
Business services [3]	73	2,410	5,313	8,370	6.3	3.6
Advertising	731	146	226	288	3.4	1.9
Services to buildings	734	487	805	1,000	3.9	1.7
Personnel supply services	736	508	1,649	2,581	9.5	3.5
Computer and data processing services	737	271	831	1,626	9.0	5.3
Auto repair, services, and garages	75	575	878	1,293	3.3	3.0
Miscellaneous repair shops	76	282	345	449	1.6	2.0
Motion pictures	78	228	404	499	4.5	1.6
Video tape rental	784	(NA)	125	107	(NA)	-1.2
Amusement and recreation services	79	751	1,169	1,626	3.5	2.6
Health services	80	4,993	8,523	12,539	4.2	3.0
Offices of health practitioners	801,2,3,4	1,200	2,387	3,617	5.4	3.2
Nursing and personal care facilities	805	951	1,543	2,306	3.8	3.1
Hospitals, private	806	2,608	3,760	5,040	2.9	2.3
Health services, n.e.c. [4]	807,8,9	234	833	1,577	10.3	5.0
Legal services	81	460	915	1,355	5.4	3.1
Educational services	82	1,090	1,700	2,162	3.5	1.9
Social services	83	1,081	1,958	3,691	4.7	5.0
Museums, zoos, and membership organizations	84,86,8733	1,652	2,164	2,674	2.1	1.6
Engineering, management, and services, n.e.c. [4][5]	87,89	1,341	2,370	3,538	4.5	3.1
Government	(X)	15,947	18,653	22,021	1.2	1.3
Federal government	(X)	2,773	2,969	2,815	0.5	-0.4
State and local government	(X)	13,174	15,683	19,206	1.4	1.6
Agriculture	01,02,07,08,09	3,398	3,295	3,325	-0.2	0.1
Private households	88	1,264	1,116	802	-1.0	-2.5
Nonagriculture self-employed and unpaid family	(X)	7,210	8,794	10,397	1.5	1.3

- Rounds to zero.   NA Not available.   X Not applicable.   [1] 1987 Standard Industrial Classification; see text, section 13.
[2] Based on assumptions of moderate growth; see source.   [3] Includes other industries, not shown separately.   [4] N.e.c. means not elsewhere classified.   [5] Excludes SIC 8733.

Source: U.S. Bureau of Labor Statistics, *Monthly Labor Review*, November 1993.

Labor Force, Employment, and Earnings

No. 643. High Technology Industries—Summary: 1992

[For workers on private industry payrolls and excludes the self-employed. Based on surveys of the Occupational Employment Statistics Program and subject to sampling error; for details see source]

INDUSTRY	1987 SIC [1] code	Establishments (1,000)	Employment Total (1,000)	Employment Percent distribution	Average annual pay (dol.)
All high technology industries	(X)	348.0	9,620	100.0	40,748
Level I industries [3]	(X)	312.5	8,358	86.9	41,953
Crude petroleum and natural gas operations	131	9.7	183	1.9	54,439
Cigarettes	211	-	35	0.4	51,105
Industrial inorganic chemicals	281	1.5	136	1.4	45,432
Plastics materials and synthetics	282	1.0	172	1.8	43,370
Drugs	283	1.8	257	2.7	48,327
Soap, cleaners, and toilet goods	284	2.5	154	1.6	40,506
Paints and allied products.	285	1.5	58	0.6	35,824
Industrial organic chemicals	286	1.0	153	1.6	49,735
Agricultural chemicals	287	1.2	58	0.6	40,868
Miscellaneous chemical products	289	2.7	93	1.0	39,646
Petroleum refining	291	0.7	120	1.2	52,023
Miscellaneous petroleum and coal products.	299	0.5	12	0.1	35,289
Nonferrous rolling and drawing	335	1.2	162	1.7	35,360
Special industry machinery	355	4.1	148	1.5	35,586
Computer and office equipment	357	2.6	387	4.0	48,917
Electrical industrial apparatus	362	1.9	157	1.6	30,784
Communications equipment	366	2.2	238	2.5	40,688
Electronic components and accessories	367	6.4	524	5.4	35,272
Motor vehicles and equipment.	371	5.7	819	8.5	40,425
Aircraft and parts	372	2.9	614	6.4	43,743
Guided missiles, space vehicles, parts	376	0.3	144	1.5	48,440
Search and navigation equipment	381	0.9	230	2.4	45,573
Measuring and controlling devices	382	5.1	291	3.0	36,670
Medical instruments and supplies.	384	4.1	265	2.8	35,428
Photographic equipment and supplies	386	0.9	95	1.0	45,623
Computer and data-processing services	737	60.5	839	8.7	44,100
Engineering and architectural services	871	65.2	749	7.8	41,209
Research and testing services.	873	23.5	562	5.8	38,176
Management and public relations	874	92.4	664	6.9	42,495
Services, n.e.c. [4]	899	8.6	41	0.4	49,211
Level II industries [5]	(X)	35.5	1,262	13.1	32,764
Miscellaneous textile goods	229	0.9	51	0.5	27,113
Pulp mills.	261	0.1	14	0.1	45,238
Miscellaneous converted paper products	267	3.1	240	2.5	32,234
Ordinance and accessories, n.e.c. [4]	348	0.4	65	0.7	34,940
Engines and turbines	351	0.5	87	0.9	41,533
General industry machinery.	356	4.6	236	2.4	33,429
Industrial machines, n.e.c. [4]	359	21.9	292	3.0	29,654
Household audio and video equipment	365	1.2	81	0.8	35,252
Miscellaneous electrical equipment and supplies.	369	1.8	150	1.6	32,767
Miscellaneous transportation equipment	379	1.1	45	0.5	30,173

- Rounds to zero.   X Not applicable.   [1] 1987 Standard Industrial Classification; see text, section 13.   [2] Those industries whose proportion of R&D employment is at least equal to the average proportion of all industries surveyed.   [3] Industries whose proportion of R&D employment is at least 50 percent higher than the average of all industries surveyed.   [4] N.e.c. means not elsewhere classified.   [5] Industries whose proportion of R&D employment is at least equal to the average of all industries surveyed, but less than 50 percent higher than the average.

Source: U.S. Bureau of Labor Statistics, *Employment and Wages, Annual Averages 1992*, BLS Bulletin 2433.

No. 644. Occupational and Employer Tenure, by Occupation: 1991

[As of January. For the 35 occupations with the longest occupational tenure. Covers occupations with 50,000 or more workers. Based on Current Population Survey; see text section 1, and Appendix III]

CURRENT OCCUPATION	Number (1,000)	OCCUPATIONAL TENURE [1]		EMPLOYER TENURE [2]		Median age [3]
		Total (years)	Rank	Total (years)	Rank	
Total employed, 16 years old and over [4]	114,979	6.5	(X)	4.5	(X)	37.2
Airplane pilots and navigators................	116	12.2	30	4.5	32	36.2
Automobile body and related repairers	202	12.1	31	3.1	34	34.1
Barbers........................	111	27.2	1	11.0	12	51.7
Brickmasons and stonemasons...............	160	12.6	21	5.1	30	38.2
Chemical engineers.....................	72	12.6	21	6.4	22	38.0
Civil engineers.......................	284	13.2	15	7.4	18	42.0
Crane and tower operators.................	77	13.7	13	6.1	24	41.9
Dental laboratory & medical appliance technicians ...	59	12.9	17	5.5	27	39.9
Dentists..........................	136	15.1	7	13.7	7	40.5
Electrical power installers and repairers	128	12.6	21	12.5	9	39.2
Electricians........................	718	12.3	27	4.9	31	38.3
Farmers, except horticultural................	1,037	21.8	2	20.2	2	48.0
Geologists and geodesists	60	12.3	27	7.3	19	40.8
Health specialties teachers.................	50	15.1	7	11.4	11	45.7
Heavy equipment mechanics	158	13.7	13	6.7	20	38.1
Locomotive operators	58	19.8	3	19.7	3	46.5
Machinists.........................	526	12.3	27	6.6	21	39.3
Managers, farms, except horticultural	145	11.6	34	8.9	15	36.9
Millwrights.........................	79	12.5	24	6.2	23	43.1
Musicians and composers	143	15.2	5	5.4	29	36.8
Operating engineers	247	12.0	32	5.7	26	37.8
Pharmacists........................	182	12.7	20	5.8	25	39.1
Plumbers, pipefitters, and steamfitters	427	13.1	16	5.5	27	38.4
Public transportation attendants	60	12.5	24	8.2	17	39.2
Railroad conductors and yardmasters...........	56	15.2	5	18.8	4	43.1
Stationary engineers	120	15.4	4	11.8	10	42.2
Structural metal workers	52	12.4	26	1.1	35	36.5
Supervisors, firefighting & fire prevention	65	15.0	10	20.3	1	44.5
Supervisors, police and detectives............	69	12.9	17	15.1	6	41.5
Teachers, elementary school	1,592	12.0	32	8.4	16	41.3
Teachers, secondary school................	1,392	14.1	11	9.5	14	42.0
Telephone installers and repairers.............	193	12.9	17	16.5	5	40.3
Timber cutting and logging.................	68	11.5	35	3.5	33	33.3
Tool and die makers....................	125	15.1	7	12.6	8	39.5
Veterinarians	66	14.0	12	10.2	13	39.5

X Not applicable.　[1] Cumulative tenure in current occupation.　[2] Continuous tenure with current employer.　[3] For definition of median, see Guide to Tabular Presentation.　[4] Includes other occupations, not shown separately.

Source: U.S. Bureau of Labor Statistics, *News,* USDL 92-386; and unpublished data.

No. 645. Displaced Workers, by Selected Characteristics: 1992

[As of January. In percent, except total. For persons 20 years old and over with tenure of 3 years or more who lost or left a job between January 1987 and January 1992 because of plant closings or moves, slack work, or the abolishment of their positions. Based on Current Population Survey and subject to sampling error; see source and Appendix III]

SEX, AGE, RACE, AND HISPANIC ORIGIN	Total (1,000)	EMPLOYMENT STATUS			REASON FOR JOB LOSS		
		Employed	Unemployed	Not in the labor force	Plant or company closed down or moved	Slack work	Position or shift abolished
Total [1].....................	5,584	64.9	22.2	12.9	52.1	31.6	16.3
Males	3,447	66.6	24.5	8.9	49.4	34.7	15.9
20 to 24 years old	127	55.6	32.5	11.8	45.0	49.4	5.6
25 to 54 years old	2,728	71.6	24.5	3.9	49.5	34.0	16.5
55 to 64 years old	488	52.3	24.2	23.5	49.0	34.6	16.4
65 years old and over.............	103	15.8	15.3	68.9	53.3	35.7	11.0
Females	2,137	62.2	18.6	19.2	56.6	26.4	17.0
20 to 24 years old	76	72.7	7.3	20.1	43.8	46.1	10.0
25 to 54 years old	1,688	65.8	19.9	14.3	54.4	26.7	18.9
55 to 64 years old	262	51.4	17.4	31.2	70.5	19.4	10.1
65 years old and over.............	111	26.5	8.7	64.8	66.3	25.1	8.6
White	4,828	65.7	21.2	13.0	52.5	30.6	16.9
Male	3,003	67.6	23.3	9.1	49.4	34.1	16.5
Female...................	1,825	62.7	17.8	19.5	57.6	24.8	17.6
Black	626	58.7	28.6	12.7	51.3	36.3	12.4
Male	356	58.9	33.4	7.7	52.3	36.6	11.1
Female...................	270	58.5	22.2	19.3	50.0	35.9	14.1
Hispanic origin [2]	511	60.4	27.4	12.3	57.0	34.5	8.5
Male	323	64.6	27.2	8.2	57.6	35.7	6.7
Female...................	188	53.0	27.7	19.3	56.0	32.5	11.6

[1] Includes other races, not shown separately.　[2] Persons of Hispanic origin may be of any race.

Source: U.S. Bureau of Labor Statistics, *News,* USDL 92-530.

No. 646. Unemployed Workers—Summary: 1980 to 1993

[In thousands, except as indicated. For civilian noninstitutional population 16 years old and over. Annual averages of monthly figures. For data on unemployment insurance, see table 590. See also *Historical Statistics, Colonial Times to 1970*, series D 87-101]

AGE, SEX, RACE, HISPANIC ORIGIN	1980	1985	1988	1989	1990	1991	1992	1993
UNEMPLOYED								
Total [1]	7,637	8,312	6,701	6,528	6,874	8,426	9,384	8,734
16 to 19 years old	1,669	1,468	1,226	1,194	1,149	1,290	1,352	1,296
20 to 24 years old	1,835	1,738	1,261	1,218	1,221	1,477	1,546	1,421
25 to 44 years old	2,964	3,681	3,095	3,010	3,273	4,106	4,603	4,220
45 to 64 years old	1,075	1,331	1,032	1,016	1,124	1,437	1,748	1,686
65 years and over	94	93	87	91	107	116	135	111
Male	4,267	4,521	3,655	3,525	3,799	4,817	5,380	4,932
16 to 19 years old	913	806	667	658	629	709	761	728
20 to 24 years old	1,076	944	676	660	666	849	884	808
25 to 44 years old	1,619	1,950	1,657	1,572	1,774	2,331	2,603	2,348
45 to 64 years old	600	766	606	585	668	862	1,062	983
65 years and over	58	55	49	49	61	66	69	65
Female	3,370	3,791	3,046	3,003	3,075	3,609	4,005	3,801
16 to 19 years old	755	661	558	536	519	581	591	568
20 to 24 years old	760	794	585	558	555	628	662	613
25 to 44 years old	1,345	1,732	1,439	1,437	1,498	1,775	1,999	1,871
45 to 64 years old	473	566	427	430	456	575	686	703
65 years and over	36	39	38	41	46	50	66	46
White [2]	5,884	6,191	4,944	4,770	5,091	6,447	7,047	6,547
16 to 19 years old	1,291	1,074	910	863	856	977	983	943
20 to 24 years old	1,364	1,235	874	856	844	1,063	1,084	991
Black [2]	1,553	1,864	1,547	1,544	1,527	1,679	1,958	1,796
16 to 19 years old	343	357	288	300	258	270	313	302
20 to 24 years old	426	455	349	322	335	362	401	371
Hispanic [2][3]	620	811	732	750	769	963	1,160	1,104
16 to 19 years old	145	141	148	132	131	149	185	173
20 to 24 years old	138	171	145	158	135	172	193	191
Full-time workers	6,269	6,793	5,357	5,211	5,541	6,932	7,746	7,146
Part-time workers	1,369	1,519	1,343	1,317	1,332	1,494	1,638	1,588
UNEMPLOYMENT RATE (percent) [4]								
Total [1]	7.1	7.2	5.5	5.3	5.5	6.7	7.4	6.8
16 to 19 years old	17.8	18.6	15.3	15.0	15.5	18.6	20.0	19.0
20 to 24 years old	11.5	11.1	8.7	8.6	8.8	10.8	11.3	10.5
25 to 44 years old	6.0	6.2	4.8	4.5	4.8	6.0	6.7	6.1
45 to 64 years old	3.7	4.5	3.3	3.2	3.5	4.4	5.1	4.8
65 years and over	3.1	3.2	2.7	2.6	3.0	3.3	3.8	3.2
Male	6.9	7.0	5.5	5.2	5.6	7.0	7.8	7.1
16 to 19 years old	18.3	19.5	16.0	15.9	16.3	19.8	21.5	20.4
20 to 24 years old	12.5	11.4	8.9	8.8	9.1	11.7	12.2	11.3
25 to 44 years old	5.6	5.9	4.6	4.3	4.8	6.2	6.9	6.2
45 to 64 years old	3.5	4.5	3.5	3.3	3.7	4.7	5.6	5.1
65 years and over	3.1	3.1	2.5	2.4	3.0	3.3	3.3	3.2
Female	7.4	7.4	5.6	5.4	5.4	6.3	6.9	6.5
16 to 19 years old	17.2	17.6	14.4	14.0	14.7	17.4	18.5	17.4
20 to 24 years old	10.4	10.7	8.5	8.3	8.5	9.8	10.2	9.6
25 to 44 years old	6.4	6.6	4.9	4.8	4.9	5.7	6.4	6.0
45 to 64 years old	4.0	4.6	3.2	3.1	3.2	3.9	4.4	4.4
65 years and over	3.1	3.3	2.9	2.9	3.1	3.3	4.5	3.1
White [2]	6.3	6.2	4.7	4.5	4.7	6.0	6.5	6.0
16 to 19 years old	15.5	15.7	13.1	12.7	13.4	16.4	17.1	16.2
20 to 24 years old	9.9	9.2	7.1	7.2	7.2	9.2	9.4	8.7
Black [2]	14.3	15.1	11.7	11.4	11.3	12.4	14.1	12.9
16 to 19 years old	38.5	40.2	32.4	32.4	31.1	36.3	39.8	38.9
20 to 24 years old	23.6	24.5	19.6	18.0	19.9	21.6	23.9	22.0
Hispanic [2][3]	10.1	10.5	8.2	8.0	8.0	9.9	11.4	10.6
16 to 19 years old	22.5	24.3	22.0	19.4	19.5	22.9	27.5	26.2
20 to 24 years old	12.1	12.6	9.8	10.7	9.1	11.6	13.2	13.1
Experienced workers [5]	6.9	6.8	5.2	5.0	5.3	6.5	7.1	6.5
Women maintaining families [1]	9.2	10.5	8.2	8.1	8.2	9.1	9.9	9.5
White	7.3	8.1	6.0	6.1	6.3	7.2	7.8	7.7
Black	14.0	16.4	13.7	13.0	13.1	13.9	14.7	13.7
Married men, wife present [1]	4.2	4.3	3.3	3.0	3.4	4.4	5.0	4.4
White	3.9	4.0	3.0	2.8	3.1	4.2	4.7	4.1
Black	7.4	8.0	5.8	5.8	6.2	6.5	8.3	7.2
Percent without work for—								
Fewer than 5 weeks	43.1	42.1	46.0	48.6	46.1	40.1	34.8	36.2
5 to 10 weeks	23.4	22.2	22.2	22.2	23.5	22.9	20.9	20.6
11 to 14 weeks	9.0	8.0	7.8	8.1	8.6	9.5	8.5	8.3
15 to 26 weeks	13.8	12.3	12.0	11.2	11.8	14.5	15.2	14.6
27 weeks and over	10.7	15.4	12.1	9.9	10.1	13.0	20.6	20.4
Unemployment duration, average (weeks)	11.9	15.6	13.5	11.9	12.1	13.8	17.9	18.1

[1] Includes other races, not shown separately.　[2] Includes other ages, not shown separately.　[3] Persons of Hispanic origin may be of any race.　[4] Unemployed as percent of civilian labor force in specified group.　[5] Wage and salary workers.

Source: U.S. Bureau of Labor Statistics, *Employment and Earnings*, monthly, January issues; and unpublished data.

No. 647. Unemployed Persons, by Sex and Reason: 1970 to 1993

[In thousands. For civilian noninstitutional population 16 years old and over. Annual averages of monthly figures. Based on Current Population Survey; see text, section 1, and Appendix III]

SEX AND REASON	1970	1980	1984	1985	1986	1987	1988	1989	1990	1991	1992	1993
Male, total	**2,238**	**4,267**	**4,744**	**4,521**	**4,530**	**4,101**	**3,655**	**3,525**	**3,799**	**4,817**	**5,380**	**4,932**
Job losers	1,199	2,649	2,976	2,749	2,725	2,432	2,078	1,975	2,208	3,105	3,518	3,091
Job leavers	282	438	375	409	520	494	503	495	511	492	479	490
Reentrants	533	776	867	876	805	761	697	726	782	865	950	914
New entrants	224	405	526	487	480	413	376	328	298	356	433	437
Female, total	**1,855**	**3,370**	**3,794**	**3,791**	**3,707**	**3,324**	**3,046**	**3,003**	**3,075**	**3,609**	**4,005**	**3,801**
Job losers	614	1,297	1,445	1,390	1,308	1,134	1,014	1,008	1,114	1,503	1,773	1,677
Job leavers	267	453	449	468	494	471	480	529	503	487	496	456
Reentrants	696	1,152	1,317	1,380	1,355	1,213	1,112	1,117	1,101	1,222	1,278	1,230
New entrants	279	468	584	552	549	506	440	349	357	398	457	438

Source: U.S. Bureau of Labor Statistics, *Employment and Earnings,* monthly, January issues; Bulletin 2307; and unpublished data.

No. 648. Unemployment Rates, by Industry, 1975 to 1993, and by Sex, 1980 and 1993

[In percent. For civilian noninstitutional population 16 years old and over. Annual averages of monthly figures. Rate represents unemployment as a percent of labor force in each specified group. Data for 1985-90, and also beginning 1992, not strictly comparable with other years due to changes in industrial classification]

INDUSTRY	1975	1980	1985	1990	1992	1993	MALE		FEMALE	
							1980	1993	1980	1993
All unemployed [1]	**8.5**	**7.1**	**7.2**	**5.5**	**7.4**	**6.8**	**6.9**	**7.1**	**7.4**	**6.5**
Industry: [2]										
Agriculture	10.4	11.0	13.2	9.7	12.3	11.6	9.7	11.2	15.1	12.8
Mining	4.1	6.4	9.5	4.8	7.9	7.3	6.7	7.6	4.5	5.6
Construction	18.0	14.1	13.1	11.1	16.7	14.3	14.6	14.8	8.9	9.9
Manufacturing	10.9	8.5	7.7	5.8	7.8	7.2	7.4	6.5	10.8	8.4
Transportation and public utilities	5.6	4.9	5.1	3.8	5.5	5.1	5.1	5.4	4.4	4.3
Wholesale and retail trade	8.7	7.4	7.6	6.4	8.4	7.8	6.6	7.3	8.3	8.3
Finance, insurance, and real estate	4.9	3.4	3.5	3.0	4.5	4.1	3.2	3.8	3.5	4.2
Services	7.1	5.9	6.2	5.0	6.5	6.1	6.3	6.6	5.8	5.7
Government	4.1	4.1	3.9	2.6	3.5	3.3	3.9	3.6	4.3	3.0

[1] Includes the self-employed, unpaid family workers, and persons with no previous work experience, not shown separately.
[2] Covers unemployed wage and salary workers.

Source: U.S. Bureau of Labor Statistics, *Employment and Earnings,* monthly, January issues.

No. 649. Unemployment by Occupation, 1983 to 1993, and by Sex, 1993

[For civilian noninstitutional population 16 years old and over. Beginning 1985, annual averages of monthly data; 1983 data estimated, see text, section 13. Rate represents unemployment as a percent of the labor force for each specified group. Based on Current Population Survey; see text, section 1, and Appendix III. See also headnote, table 630 concerning 1993 data]

OCCUPATION	NUMBER (1,000)			UNEMPLOYMENT RATE				
	1983	1985	1993	1983	1985	1993		
						Total	Male	Female
Total [1]	**10,717**	**8,312**	**8,734**	**9.6**	**7.2**	**6.8**	**7.1**	**6.5**
Managerial and professional specialty	795	645	983	3.3	2.4	3.0	2.8	3.1
Executive, administrative, and managerial	396	329	527	3.5	2.6	3.3	2.9	3.8
Professional specialty	399	316	456	3.0	2.3	2.6	2.7	2.5
Technical sales, and administrative support	2,116	1,694	2,075	6.3	4.9	5.3	4.8	5.6
Technicians and related support	152	110	163	4.7	3.3	3.9	3.9	3.9
Sales occupations	850	702	908	6.7	5.3	6.0	4.8	7.3
Administrative support, including clerical	1,114	882	1,003	6.4	4.9	5.1	5.5	5.0
Service occupations	1,697	1,386	1,359	10.9	8.8	7.6	7.9	7.4
Private household	79	69	63	7.4	6.4	6.5	9.6	6.3
Protective service	120	85	105	6.7	4.7	4.7	4.3	6.5
Service except private household and protective	1,498	1,233	1,190	11.8	9.5	8.1	9.2	7.5
Precision production, craft, and repair	1,466	1,038	1,141	10.6	7.2	7.9	7.9	7.7
Mechanics and repairers	344	225	256	7.6	4.8	5.5	5.5	5.3
Construction trades	709	531	624	14.2	10.1	11.1	11.1	10.1
Other precision production, craft, and repair	412	281	262	9.6	6.4	6.3	5.8	7.9
Operators, fabricators, and laborers	2,955	2,140	1,877	15.5	11.3	9.9	9.7	10.6
Machine operators, assemblers, inspectors	1,411	980	795	15.4	11.1	9.7	8.9	10.9
Transportation and material moving occupations	596	422	399	12.4	8.5	7.4	7.4	7.0
Handlers, equipment cleaners, helpers, laborers	948	739	682	18.6	14.3	12.9	13.2	11.5
Construction laborers	207	186	167	25.8	21.3	20.2	20.2	(B)
Farming, forestry, and fishing	407	315	296	9.9	8.3	8.2	7.8	10.1

B Base is less than 35,000. [1] Includes persons with no previous work experience and those whose last job was in the Armed Forces.

Source: U.S. Bureau of Labor Statistics, *Employment and Earnings,* monthly, January issues.

No. 650. Unemployment Rates, by Educational Attainment, Sex, and Race: 1970 to 1991

[In percent. As of March, except as indicated. Civilian noninstitutional population 25 to 64 years of age. Due to a change in the method of reporting educational attainment, 1992 are not comparable with data for earlier years. See table 651 for data beginning 1992 data for persons 25 years old and over. Based on the Current Population Survey; see text, section 1, and Appendix III]

ITEM	1970	1975	1980	1984	1985	1986	1987	1988	1989	1990 [1]	1991 [1]
Total	3.3	6.9	5.0	6.6	6.1	6.1	5.7	4.7	4.4	4.4	5.5
Less than 4 years of high school [2]..	4.6	10.7	8.4	12.1	11.4	11.6	11.1	9.6	9.1	8.5	11.0
4 years of high school, only	2.9	6.9	5.1	7.2	6.9	6.9	6.3	5.4	4.8	4.9	5.9
College: 1-3 years	2.9	5.5	4.3	5.3	4.7	4.7	4.5	3.7	3.4	3.7	4.8
4 years or more	1.3	2.5	1.9	2.7	2.4	2.3	2.3	1.7	2.2	2.2	2.8
Male: Total	2.9	6.7	4.9	6.9	6.1	6.2	6.0	5.1	4.7	4.4	5.8
Less than 4 years of high school [2]..	4.0	10.5	8.2	12.3	11.2	11.7	11.2	10.1	9.7	8.2	11.0
4 years of high school, only	2.4	6.7	5.3	8.1	7.2	7.4	6.7	6.2	5.4	5.1	6.4
College: 1-3 years	2.7	5.1	4.4	5.2	4.5	4.7	5.0	3.9	3.2	3.7	4.9
4 years or more	1.1	2.2	1.7	2.7	2.4	2.3	2.5	1.6	2.3	2.1	2.8
Female: Total	4.0	7.4	5.0	6.1	6.0	5.8	5.2	4.2	4.0	4.4	5.2
Less than 4 years of high school [2]..	5.7	10.5	8.9	11.7	11.7	11.4	10.9	8.9	8.4	9.0	10.9
4 years of high school, only	3.6	7.1	5.0	6.3	6.5	6.3	5.8	4.6	4.2	4.6	5.4
College: 1-3 years	3.1	6.3	4.1	5.3	4.8	4.8	4.0	3.4	3.7	3.7	4.7
4 years or more	1.9	3.4	2.2	2.7	2.5	2.4	2.1	1.9	2.0	2.3	2.8
White: Total	3.1	6.5	4.4	5.7	5.3	5.5	5.0	4.0	3.8	3.8	5.0
Less than 4 years of high school [2]..	4.5	10.1	7.8	10.9	10.6	10.9	10.2	8.3	7.4	7.6	10.3
4 years of high school, only	2.7	6.5	4.6	6.4	6.1	6.2	5.5	4.6	4.2	4.2	5.4
College: 1-3 years	2.8	5.1	3.9	4.6	3.9	4.2	4.1	3.2	3.0	3.2	4.2
4 years or more	1.3	2.4	1.8	2.4	2.1	2.2	2.2	1.5	2.0	2.1	2.7
Black: Total [3]	4.7	10.9	9.6	13.3	12.0	10.7	10.6	10.0	9.2	8.6	9.6
Less than 4 years of high school [2]..	5.2	13.5	11.7	17.4	15.3	15.3	14.8	15.7	15.9	13.3	14.7
4 years of high school, only	5.2	10.7	9.5	14.5	13.0	11.7	11.7	11.2	9.2	9.5	9.9
College: 1-3 years	3.5	9.8	9.0	9.7	10.6	8.7	7.6	7.4	6.9	6.8	8.8
4 years or more	0.9	3.9	4.0	6.2	5.4	3.2	4.2	3.3	4.7	3.0	4.1

[1] Not strictly comparable with data for earlier years. Annual averages of monthly figures.   [2] Includes persons reporting no school years completed.   [3] For 1970 and 1975, data refer to Black and other workers.

Source: U.S. Bureau of Labor Statistics, Bulletin 2307; and unpublished data.

No. 651. Unemployed and Unemployment Rates, by Educational Attainment, Sex, Race, and Hispanic Origin: 1992 and 1993

[Annual averages of monthly figures, for civilian noninstitutional population 25 years old and over. See table 618 for civilian labor force and participation rate data. Based on Current Population Survey; see text, section 1, and Appendix III]

YEAR, SEX, AND RACE	UNEMPLOYED (1,000)					UNEMPLOYMENT RATE [1]				
	Total	Less than high school diploma	High school graduates, no degree	Less than a bachelor's degree	College graduate	Total	Less than high school diploma	High school graduate, no degree	Less than a bachelor's degree	College graduate
Total: [2]										
1992	6,491	1,502	2,577	1,519	893	6.1	11.4	6.8	5.6	3.2
1993	6,017	1,328	2,354	1,480	855	5.6	10.7	6.2	5.2	2.9
Male:										
1992....	3,735	922	1,454	825	533	6.4	11.4	7.3	5.9	3.3
1993....	3,396	817	1,320	773	485	5.8	10.7	6.6	5.3	2.9
Female:										
1992....	2,756	580	1,123	694	360	5.7	11.4	6.2	5.3	3.0
1993....	2,621	510	1,035	707	370	5.4	10.9	5.8	5.1	3.0
White:										
1992....	4,982	1,126	1,936	1,168	751	5.5	10.7	6.0	5.0	3.0
1993....	4,612	975	1,791	1,136	711	5.0	9.8	5.5	4.7	2.8
Black:										
1992....	1,246	318	555	294	79	10.9	15.1	12.3	9.8	4.4
1993....	1,124	285	485	281	73	9.8	15.2	10.8	8.7	3.8
Hispanic: [3]										
1992....	781	400	213	122	46	9.8	12.8	9.0	7.7	5.0
1993....	740	377	202	123	38	9.0	12.1	8.4	7.0	3.9

[1] Percent unemployed of the civilian labor force.   [2] Includes other races, not shown separately.   [3] Persons of Hispanic origin may be of any race.

Source: U.S. Bureau of Labor Statistics, unpublished data.

No. 652. Total Unemployed and Insured Unemployed—States: 1980 to 1992

[For civilian noninstitutional population 16 years old and over. Annual averages of monthly figures. Total unemployment estimates based on the Current Population Survey (CPS); see text, section 1, and Appendix III. U.S. totals derived by independent population controls; therefore State data may not add to U.S. totals. See table 621 for 1993 unemployment data]

STATE	TOTAL UNEMPLOYED								INSURED UNEMPLOYED [2]			
	Number (1,000)				Percent [1]				Number (1,000)		Percent [3]	
	1980	1985	1990	1992	1980	1985	1990	1992	1991	1992	1991	1992
United States	7,637	8,312	6,874	9,384	7.1	7.2	5.5	7.4	[4]3,342	[4]3,245	[4]3.1	[4]3.2
Alabama............	147	160	127	143	8.8	8.9	6.8	7.3	41.7	38.8	2.5	2.5
Alaska.............	18	24	19	26	9.7	9.7	6.9	9.1	13.2	13.9	6.4	6.4
Arizona............	83	96	96	135	6.7	6.5	5.3	7.4	34.1	34.2	2.3	2.3
Arkansas	76	91	77	83	7.6	8.7	6.9	7.2	31.7	31.5	3.6	3.6
California	790	931	850	1,393	6.8	7.2	5.6	9.1	528.4	552.5	4.5	4.5
Colorado...........	88	101	87	108	5.9	5.9	4.9	5.9	26.2	26.4	1.8	1.8
Connecticut........	94	83	93	137	5.9	4.9	5.1	7.5	61.0	57.3	3.8	3.8
Delaware	22	17	18	19	7.7	5.3	5.1	5.3	7.8	7.9	2.3	2.3
District of Columbia	24	27	21	26	7.3	8.4	6.6	8.4	12.0	11.0	2.5	3.2
Florida	251	319	384	533	5.9	6.0	5.9	8.2	120.8	127.0	2.4	2.4
Georgia	163	187	179	232	6.4	6.5	5.4	6.9	66.3	56.4	2.0	2.0
Hawaii	21	27	15	26	4.9	5.6	2.8	4.5	7.9	11.6	2.3	2.3
Idaho	34	37	29	34	7.9	7.9	5.8	6.5	14.0	14.3	3.7	3.7
Illinois	458	513	363	451	8.3	9.0	6.2	7.5	156.5	156.0	3.1	3.1
Indiana............	252	215	147	185	9.6	7.9	5.3	6.5	46.9	42.3	1.9	1.8
Iowa	82	113	61	70	5.8	8.0	4.2	4.6	24.9	24.8	2.1	2.1
Kansas............	53	62	56	55	4.5	5.0	4.4	4.2	22.9	22.7	2.2	2.2
Kentucky	133	161	102	122	8.0	9.5	5.8	6.9	40.6	33.9	2.5	2.5
Louisiana	121	229	114	156	6.7	11.5	6.2	8.1	35.2	40.9	2.7	2.7
Maine.............	39	30	32	46	7.8	5.4	5.1	7.1	25.7	19.3	5.0	4.0
Maryland	140	103	121	176	6.5	4.6	4.6	6.6	63.5	59.9	3.1	3.1
Massachusetts.......	162	121	193	267	5.6	3.9	6.0	8.5	127.3	100.8	4.4	3.7
Michigan...........	534	433	345	408	12.4	9.9	7.1	8.8	154.9	133.7	4.0	3.6
Minnesota..........	125	133	115	124	5.9	6.0	4.8	5.1	48.0	44.2	2.2	2.2
Mississippi	79	115	88	97	7.5	10.3	7.5	8.1	28.2	27.3	3.1	3.1
Missouri	167	159	149	151	7.2	6.4	5.7	5.7	66.1	61.7	2.8	2.8
Montana...........	23	31	23	28	6.1	7.7	5.8	6.7	8.7	8.8	3.1	3.1
Nebraska	31	44	18	25	4.1	5.5	2.2	3.0	9.1	9.3	1.3	1.3
Nevada	27	41	33	47	6.2	8.0	4.9	6.6	20.2	20.2	3.3	3.3
New Hampshire......	22	21	35	46	4.7	3.9	5.6	7.5	14.7	10.7	3.0	2.3
New Jersey.........	259	218	202	337	7.2	5.7	5.0	8.4	135.6	131.7	3.9	3.9
New Mexico	42	57	44	51	7.5	8.8	6.3	6.8	12.9	13.5	2.5	2.5
New York	597	544	458	734	7.5	6.5	5.2	8.5	292.6	281.2	3.7	3.7
North Carolina	187	167	141	210	6.6	5.4	4.1	5.9	80.3	60.8	2.0	2.0
North Dakota........	15	20	12	15	5.0	5.9	3.9	4.9	4.6	4.7	2.0	2.0
Ohio	426	455	305	397	8.4	8.9	5.7	7.2	132.1	127.5	2.8	2.8
Oklahoma..........	66	112	84	86	4.8	7.1	5.6	5.7	20.8	22.8	2.0	2.0
Oregon............	108	117	82	116	8.3	8.8	5.5	7.5	50.5	51.1	4.3	4.3
Pennsylvania.......	425	442	311	442	7.8	8.0	5.4	7.5	199.2	195.5	4.1	4.1
Rhode Island........	34	25	35	46	7.2	4.9	6.7	8.9	23.9	20.5	5.5	5.0
South Carolina.......	96	107	82	112	6.9	6.8	4.7	6.2	41.0	37.6	2.6	2.6
South Dakota	16	18	13	11	4.9	5.1	3.7	3.1	2.4	2.6	0.9	0.9
Tennessee	152	180	124	156	7.3	8.0	5.2	6.4	63.0	55.4	2.7	2.7
Texas..............	352	564	531	675	5.2	7.0	6.2	7.5	135.8	152.3	2.2	2.2
Utah	40	43	35	42	6.3	5.9	4.3	4.9	10.3	10.7	1.6	1.6
Vermont	16	13	15	21	6.4	4.8	5.0	6.6	10.6	9.5	4.3	4.0
Virginia............	128	161	138	216	5.0	5.6	4.3	6.4	45.3	41.8	1.6	1.6
Washington.........	157	171	124	198	7.9	8.1	4.9	7.5	80.3	83.9	4.0	4.0
West Virginia........	74	100	63	87	9.4	13.0	8.3	11.3	22.9	21.4	3.7	3.7
Wisconsin..........	167	171	113	135	7.2	7.2	4.4	5.1	65.2	62.0	2.8	2.8
Wyoming	9	18	13	13	4.0	7.1	5.4	5.6	3.7	4.2	2.3	2.3

[1] Total unemployment as percent of civilian labor force.   [2] Source: U.S. Employment and Training Administration, Unemployment Insurance, Financial Data, annual updates.   [3] Insured unemployment as percent of average covered employment in the previous year.   [4] Includes 50,400 in Puerto Rico and the Virgin Islands in 1991 and 55,100 in 1992.

Source: Except as noted, U.S. Bureau of Labor Statistics, Geographic Profile of Employment and Unemployment, annual.

No. 653. Job Openings and Placements and Help-Wanted Advertising: 1970 to 1992

[Openings 1970 and 1980, for years ending Sept. 30; beginning 1985, for years ending June 30]

ITEM	1970	1980	1985	1987	1988	1989	1990	1991	1992
Job openings: [1] Received (1,000) ...	6,130	8,122	7,529	6,968	7,240	6,998	5,651	5,635	5,752
Average per month	511	677	627	581	603	583	471	470	479
Nonagricultural placements [1] (1,000) .	4,604	5,610	3,270	4,516	4,503	4,284	3,714	3,507	3,396
Index of help-wanted advertising in newspapers [2] (1967=100)		93	128	138	153	157	150	129	92	100

[1] As reported by State employment agencies. Beginning 1985, all placements. Placements include duplication for individuals placed more than once.   [2] Source: The Conference Board, New York, NY, The Statistical Bulletin. Further reproduction prohibited without permission. Index based on number of advertisements in classified sections of 51 newspapers, each in a major employment area.

Source: Except as noted, U.S. Employment and Training Administration, unpublished data.

No. 654. Nonfarm Establishments, Employees, Hours, and Earnings, by Industry: 1960 to 1993

[Based on data from establishment reports. Includes all full- and part-time employees who worked during, or received pay for, any part of the pay period reported. Excludes proprietors, the self-employed, farm workers, unpaid family workers, private household workers, and Armed Forces. Establishment data shown here conform to industry definitions in the 1987 Standard Industrial Classification and are adjusted to March 1992 employment benchmarks, and reflect historical corrections to previously published data. Based on the Current Employment Statistics Program; see Appendix III. See also *Historical Statistics, Colonial Times to 1970*, series D 127-141 and D 803, 878, 881, 884, and 890]

ITEM AND YEAR	Total	GOODS-PRODUCING				SERVICE-PRODUCING						
		Total	Mining	Construction	Manufacturing	Total	Transportation and public utilities	Wholesale trade	Retail trade	Finance, insurance, and real estate	Services	Government
EMPLOYEES (1,000)												
1960	54,189	20,434	712	2,926	16,796	33,755	4,004	3,153	8,238	2,628	7,378	8,353
1965	60,765	21,926	632	3,232	18,062	38,839	4,036	3,477	9,239	2,977	9,036	10,074
1970	70,880	23,578	623	3,588	19,367	47,302	4,515	4,006	11,034	3,645	11,548	12,554
1975	76,945	22,600	752	3,525	18,323	54,345	4,542	4,430	12,630	4,165	13,892	14,686
1980	90,406	25,658	1,027	4,346	20,285	64,748	5,146	5,292	15,018	5,160	17,890	16,241
1985	97,387	24,842	927	4,668	19,248	72,544	5,233	5,727	17,315	5,948	21,927	16,394
1989	107,895	25,254	692	5,171	19,391	82,642	5,625	6,187	19,475	6,668	26,907	17,779
1990	109,419	24,905	709	5,120	19,076	84,514	5,793	6,173	19,601	6,709	27,934	18,304
1991	108,256	23,745	689	4,650	18,406	84,511	5,762	6,081	19,284	6,646	28,336	18,402
1992	108,519	23,142	631	4,471	18,040	85,377	5,709	6,045	19,346	6,571	29,053	18,653
1993	110,178	22,975	599	4,574	17,802	87,203	5,708	6,113	19,743	6,604	30,192	18,842
PERCENT DISTRIBUTION												
1960	100.0	37.7	1.3	5.4	31.0	62.3	7.4	5.8	15.2	4.9	13.6	15.4
1965	100.0	36.1	1.0	5.3	29.7	63.9	6.6	5.7	15.2	4.9	14.9	16.6
1970	100.0	33.3	0.9	5.1	27.3	66.7	6.4	5.7	15.6	5.1	16.3	17.8
1975	100.0	29.4	1.0	4.6	23.8	70.6	5.9	5.8	16.4	5.4	18.1	19.1
1980	100.0	28.4	1.1	4.8	22.4	71.6	5.7	5.9	16.6	5.7	19.8	18.0
1985	100.0	25.5	1.0	4.8	19.8	74.5	5.4	5.9	17.8	6.1	22.5	16.8
1989	100.0	23.4	0.6	4.8	18.0	76.6	5.2	5.7	18.1	6.2	24.9	16.5
1990	100.0	22.8	0.7	4.7	17.4	77.2	5.3	5.6	17.9	6.1	25.5	16.7
1991	100.0	22.0	0.6	4.3	17.0	78.1	5.3	5.6	17.8	6.1	26.2	17.0
1992	100.0	21.3	0.6	4.1	16.7	78.7	5.3	5.6	17.8	6.1	26.8	17.2
1993	100.0	20.9	0.5	4.2	16.2	79.1	5.2	5.5	17.9	6.0	27.4	17.1
WEEKLY HOURS [1]												
1960	38.6	(NA)	40.4	36.7	39.7	(NA)	(NA)	40.5	38.0	37.2	(NA)	(NA)
1965	38.8	(NA)	42.3	37.4	41.2	(NA)	41.3	40.8	36.6	37.2	35.9	(NA)
1970	37.1	(NA)	42.7	37.3	39.8	(NA)	40.5	39.9	33.8	36.7	34.4	(NA)
1975	36.1	(NA)	41.9	36.4	39.5	(NA)	39.7	38.6	32.4	36.5	33.5	(NA)
1980	35.3	(NA)	43.3	37.0	39.7	(NA)	39.6	38.4	30.2	36.2	32.6	(NA)
1985	34.9	(NA)	43.4	37.7	40.5	(NA)	39.5	38.4	29.4	36.4	32.5	(NA)
1989	34.6	(NA)	43.0	37.9	41.0	(NA)	38.9	38.0	28.9	35.8	32.6	(NA)
1990	34.5	(NA)	44.1	38.2	40.8	(NA)	38.9	38.1	28.8	35.8	32.5	(NA)
1991	34.3	(NA)	44.4	38.1	40.7	(NA)	38.7	38.1	28.6	35.7	32.4	(NA)
1992	34.4	(NA)	43.9	38.0	41.0	(NA)	38.9	38.2	28.8	35.8	32.5	(NA)
1993	34.5	(NA)	44.2	38.4	41.4	(NA)	39.7	38.2	28.8	35.7	32.5	(NA)
HOURLY EARNINGS [1]												
1960	$2.09	(NA)	$2.60	$3.07	$2.26	(NA)	(NA)	$2.24	$1.52	$2.02	(NA)	(NA)
1965	2.46	(NA)	2.92	3.70	2.61	(NA)	$3.03	2.60	1.82	2.39	$2.05	(NA)
1970	3.23	(NA)	3.85	5.24	3.35	(NA)	3.85	3.43	2.44	3.07	2.81	(NA)
1975	4.53	(NA)	5.95	7.31	4.83	(NA)	5.88	4.72	3.36	4.06	4.02	(NA)
1980	6.66	(NA)	9.17	9.94	7.27	(NA)	8.87	6.95	4.88	5.79	5.85	(NA)
1985	8.57	(NA)	11.98	12.32	9.54	(NA)	11.40	9.15	5.94	7.94	7.90	(NA)
1989	9.66	(NA)	13.26	13.54	10.48	(NA)	12.60	10.39	6.53	9.53	9.38	(NA)
1990	10.01	(NA)	13.68	13.77	10.83	(NA)	12.97	10.79	6.75	9.97	9.83	(NA)
1991	10.32	(NA)	14.19	14.00	11.18	(NA)	13.22	11.15	6.94	10.39	10.23	(NA)
1992	10.58	(NA)	14.54	14.15	11.46	(NA)	13.46	11.39	7.13	10.82	10.55	(NA)
1993	10.83	(NA)	14.60	14.35	11.76	(NA)	13.64	11.71	7.29	11.32	10.81	(NA)
WEEKLY EARNINGS [1]												
1960	$81	(NA)	$105	$113	$90	(NA)	(NA)	$91	$58	$75	(NA)	(NA)
1965	95	(NA)	124	138	108	(NA)	$125	106	67	89	$74	(NA)
1970	120	(NA)	164	195	133	(NA)	156	137	82	113	97	(NA)
1975	164	(NA)	249	266	191	(NA)	233	182	109	148	135	(NA)
1980	235	(NA)	397	368	289	(NA)	351	267	147	210	191	(NA)
1985	299	(NA)	520	464	386	(NA)	450	351	175	289	257	(NA)
1989	334	(NA)	570	513	430	(NA)	490	395	189	341	306	(NA)
1990	345	(NA)	603	526	442	(NA)	505	411	194	357	319	(NA)
1991	354	(NA)	630	533	455	(NA)	512	425	199	371	331	(NA)
1992	364	(NA)	638	538	470	(NA)	524	435	205	387	343	(NA)
1993	374	(NA)	645	551	487	(NA)	542	447	210	404	351	(NA)

NA Not available.   [1] Average hours and earnings. Private production and related workers in mining, manufacturing, and construction; nonsupervisory employees in other industries.

Source: U.S. Bureau of Labor Statistics, Bulletins 2370 and 2429, and *Employment and Earnings*, monthly, March issues.

No. 655. Employees in Nonfarm Establishments—States: 1980 to 1993

[In thousands. For coverage, see headnote, table 654. National totals differ from the sum of the State figures because of differing benchmarks among States and differing industrial and geographic stratification. Based on 1987 *Standard Industrial Classification Manual*, see text, section 13]

STATE	1980	1992	1993							
			Total[1]	Construction	Manufacturing	Transportation and public utilities	Wholesale and retail trade	Finance, insurance, and real estate	Services	Government
United States	90,406	108,519	110,178	4,574	17,802	5,708	25,857	6,604	30,192	18,842
Alabama	1,356	1,675	1,712	78	383	85	376	76	363	341
Alaska	169	247	253	11	17	23	49	11	57	74
Arizona	1,014	1,517	1,571	89	174	78	385	100	448	286
Arkansas	742	963	990	37	243	57	220	40	220	169
California	9,849	12,154	12,000	446	1,804	602	2,787	786	3,463	2,078
Colorado	1,251	1,597	1,666	84	188	104	403	106	468	297
Connecticut	1,427	1,526	1,529	47	294	69	329	139	443	207
Delaware	259	341	348	18	65	15	76	35	89	50
District of Columbia	616	674	670	8	14	21	53	31	255	287
Florida	3,576	5,359	5,567	287	484	286	1,452	357	1,814	882
Georgia	2,159	2,987	3,106	128	555	202	773	166	729	547
Hawaii	405	543	539	232	19	41	133	39	164	112
Idaho	330	416	437	25	69	21	110	23	98	90
Illinois	4,850	5,235	5,316	198	933	310	1,245	382	1,465	768
Indiana	2,130	2,554	2,589	119	639	134	608	128	562	393
Iowa	1,110	1,253	1,277	48	236	57	320	74	317	223
Kansas	945	1,115	1,135	47	182	66	274	58	269	230
Kentucky	1,210	1,509	1,534	69	292	82	360	63	363	276
Louisiana	1,579	1,627	1,643	97	186	105	382	78	409	341
Maine	418	512	519	21	91	22	130	26	134	95
Maryland	1,712	2,081	2,100	120	180	98	499	129	655	417
Massachusetts	2,652	2,795	2,842	81	454	124	644	199	952	387
Michigan	3,443	3,927	3,982	133	902	156	935	192	1,016	640
Minnesota	1,770	2,185	2,242	79	405	109	537	136	615	354
Mississippi	829	960	998	39	255	46	209	39	196	210
Missouri	1,970	2,334	2,395	95	411	153	569	141	644	377
Montana	280	317	326	14	23	20	87	15	88	74
Nebraska	628	750	763	31	103	47	193	50	188	150
Nevada	400	639	670	46	30	35	133	31	294	89
New Hampshire	385	487	500	17	97	18	128	30	136	74
New Jersey	3,060	3,455	3,493	115	516	235	815	229	1,015	566
New Mexico	465	602	624	36	43	29	147	28	167	159
New York	7,207	7,730	7,736	239	982	401	1,553	728	2,408	1,420
North Carolina	2,380	3,126	3,245	153	846	156	730	138	688	529
North Dakota	245	277	285	12	19	18	75	14	77	67
Ohio	4,367	4,848	4,905	184	1,049	214	1,173	259	1,277	737
Oklahoma	1,138	1,222	1,240	42	168	72	288	61	304	270
Oregon	1,045	1,274	1,310	54	211	66	327	91	327	233
Pennsylvania	4,753	5,076	5,110	197	940	267	1,147	303	1,527	708
Rhode Island	398	425	429	12	88	14	93	25	135	61
South Carolina	1,189	1,528	1,570	82	374	66	351	66	332	297
South Dakota	238	309	318	13	39	15	81	18	83	67
Tennessee	1,747	2,245	2,328	94	528	126	534	104	574	362
Texas	5,851	7,269	7,479	351	987	437	1,808	428	1,926	1,377
Utah	551	769	810	40	111	47	192	41	212	160
Vermont	200	251	256	11	43	11	60	12	74	44
Virginia	2,157	2,848	2,920	153	405	149	648	157	797	598
Washington	1,608	2,222	2,250	118	340	114	545	121	579	429
West Virginia	646	640	652	31	83	39	149	25	167	133
Wisconsin	1,938	2,358	2,407	93	559	113	553	131	595	360
Wyoming	210	206	210	12	10	15	48	8	43	57

[1] Includes mining, not shown separately.　　[2] Hawaii includes mining with construction.

Source: U.S. Bureau of Labor Statistics, *Employment and Earnings*, monthly, May issues. Compiled from data supplied by cooperating State agencies.

No. 656. Nonfarm Industries—Employees and Earnings: 1980 to 1993

[Annual averages of monthly figures. Covers all full- and part-time employees who worked during, or received pay for, any part of the pay period including the 12th of the month. For mining and manufacturing, data refer to production and related workers; for construction, to employees engaged in actual construction work; and for other industries, to nonsupervisory employees and working supervisors. See also headnote table 654. See *Historical Statistics, Colonial Times to 1970*, series D 127-151, D 802-810, and D 877-892, for related data]

INDUSTRY	1987 SIC [1] code	ALL EMPLOYEES TOTAL (1,000)			PRODUCTION WORKERS					
					Total (1,000)			Average hourly earnings (dollars)		
		1980	1990	1993	1980	1990	1993	1980	1990	1993
Total	(X)	90,406	109,419	110,178	(NA)	(NA)	(NA)	(NA)	(NA)	(NA)
Private sector [2]	(X)	74,166	91,115	91,336	60,331	73,800	74,353	6.66	10.01	10.83
Mining.	(B)	1,027	709	599	762	509	423	9.17	13.68	14.60
Metal mining	10	98	58	51	74	46	41	10.26	14.05	15.31
Coal mining	12	246	147	105	204	119	84	10.86	16.71	17.25
Oil and gas extraction.	13	560	395	343	389	261	224	8.59	12.94	14.13
Nonmetallic minerals, except fuels	14	123	110	100	96	83	75	7.52	11.58	12.70
Construction	(C)	4,346	5,120	4,574	3,421	3,974	3,524	9.94	13.77	14.35
General building contractors	15	1,173	1,298	1,061	900	938	749	9.22	13.01	13.60
Heavy construction, except building . . .	16	895	770	709	720	643	590	9.20	13.34	14.09
Special trade contractors	17	2,278	3,051	2,804	1,802	2,393	2,185	10.63	14.20	14.68
Manufacturing	(D)	20,285	19,076	17,802	14,214	12,947	12,143	7.27	10.83	11.76
Durable goods	(X)	12,159	11,109	10,047	8,416	7,363	6,726	7.75	11.35	12.34
Lumber and wood products [3]	24	704	733	686	587	603	564	6.57	9.08	9.61
Logging.	241	88	85	76	71	70	62	8.64	11.22	11.43
Sawmills and planing mills	242	215	198	176	190	172	153	6.70	9.22	9.78
Millwork, plywood, and structural members.	243	206	262	246	170	210	197	6.44	9.04	9.64
Wood containers	244	43	45	44	37	38	37	4.95	6.64	7.02
Mobile homes	2451	46	41	46	36	33	38	6.08	8.67	9.39
Furniture and fixtures [3]	25	466	506	481	376	400	380	5.49	8.52	9.27
Household furniture.	251	301	289	273	253	241	228	5.12	7.87	8.71
Office furniture	252	51	68	62	40	51	45	5.91	9.64	10.04
Partitions and fixtures	254	63	78	76	47	57	56	6.68	9.77	10.54
Stone, clay, and glass products [3] . . .	32	629	556	512	486	432	395	7.50	11.12	11.85
Flat glass	321	18	17	14	14	13	11	9.65	15.15	17.54
Glass and glassware, pressed and blown	322	124	83	78	105	72	66	7.97	12.40	13.32
Products of purchased glass.	323	45	60	59	32	46	44	6.50	9.75	10.28
Cement, hydraulic.	324	31	18	17	25	14	13	10.55	13.90	15.12
Structural clay products	325	46	36	31	34	28	24	6.14	9.55	10.37
Pottery and related products.	326	47	39	38	39	31	30	6.25	9.62	10.23
Concrete, gypsum, and plaster	327	204	206	189	157	157	143	7.45	10.76	11.33
Primary metal industries [3]	33	1,142	756	676	878	574	515	9.77	12.92	14.00
Blast furnaces and basic steel products	331	512	276	238	396	212	182	11.39	14.82	16.39
Iron and steel foundries	332	209	132	118	167	105	94	8.20	11.55	12.46
Primary nonferrous metals	333	71	46	43	53	34	32	10.63	14.36	15.19
Nonferrous rolling and drawing	335	211	172	160	151	124	117	8.81	12.29	13.21
Nonferrous foundries (castings). . . .	336	90	84	76	72	66	61	7.30	10.21	11.17
Fabricated metal products [3].	34	1,609	1,419	1,311	1,194	1,045	968	7.45	10.83	11.69
Metal cans and shipping containers .	341	75	50	43	63	43	37	9.84	14.27	15.14
Cutlery, handtools, and hardware. . .	342	164	131	123	125	96	91	7.02	10.78	11.59
Plumbing and heating, exc. electric . .	343	71	60	57	52	43	41	6.59	9.75	10.49
Fabricated structural metal products	344	506	427	386	351	303	274	7.27	10.16	10.88
Screw machine products	345	109	96	90	84	73	69	6.96	10.70	11.54
Metal forgings and stampings	346	260	225	217	205	178	173	8.56	12.70	14.00
Industrial machinery and equipment [3] . .	35	2,517	2,095	1,900	1,614	1,260	1,150	8.00	11.77	12.73
Engines and turbines.	351	135	89	88	87	58	55	9.73	14.55	16.11
Farm and garden machinery	352	169	106	97	116	78	70	8.78	10.99	12.08
Construction and related machinery . .	353	389	229	207	255	141	127	8.60	11.92	12.92
Metalworking machinery.	354	398	330	305	290	236	214	8.13	12.27	13.33
Special industry machinery.	355	194	159	146	125	94	84	7.53	11.90	13.14
General industrial machinery.	356	300	247	233	196	158	148	7.95	11.32	12.45
Computer and office equipment. . . .	357	420	438	361	181	137	121	6.75	11.51	12.52
Refrigeration and service machinery	358	175	177	175	120	125	123	7.23	10.93	11.48
Electronic and other elec. equip. [3] . . .	36	1,771	1,673	1,513	([4])	1,055	967	([4])	10.30	11.24
Electric distribution equipment. . . .	361	117	97	81	82	67	56	6.96	10.15	10.94
Electrical industrial apparatus	362	232	169	158	163	119	111	([4])	10.00	10.64
Household appliances	363	162	124	121	128	99	97	6.95	10.26	10.48
Electric lighting and wiring equip	364	211	189	173	157	136	125	6.43	10.12	10.98
Household audio and video equip . . .	365	109	85	83	79	59	55	6.42	9.68	10.96
Communications equipment	366	([4])	264	231	([4])	133	118	([4])	11.03	11.72
Electronic components and accessories	367	539	582	518	325	329	302	6.05	10.00	11.24
Transportation equipment [3]	37	1,881	1,989	1,727	1,220	1,224	1,099	9.35	14.08	15.84
Motor vehicles and equipment	371	789	812	820	575	617	629	9.85	14.56	16.14
Aircraft and parts	372	633	712	540	344	345	251	9.28	14.79	17.30
Ship and boat building and repairing	373	221	188	157	176	141	122	8.22	10.94	12.34
Railroad equipment.	374	71	33	27	53	25	20	9.93	13.41	14.89
Guided missiles, space vehicles, and parts.	376	111	185	120	35	57	34	9.22	14.39	16.81

See footnotes at end of table.

No. 656. Nonfarm Industries—Employees and Earnings: 1980 to 1993—Continued

[See headnote, p. 422]

INDUSTRY	1987 SIC [1] code	ALL EMPLOYEES TOTAL (1,000)			PRODUCTION WORKERS Total (1,000)			PRODUCTION WORKERS Average hourly earnings (dollars)		
		1980	1990	1993	1980	1990	1993	1980	1990	1993
Durable goods—Continued	(X)									
Instruments and related products	38	1,022	1,006	881	(4)	499	430	(4)	11.29	12.25
Search and navigation equipment	381	(4)	284	201	(4)	94	63	(4)	14.62	16.25
Measuring and controlling devices	382	(4)	323	277	(4)	180	142	(4)	10.68	12.09
Medical instruments and supplies	384	(4)	246	265	(4)	144	153	(4)	9.85	10.86
Ophthalmic goods	385	44	43	38	31	30	26	5.30	8.18	8.77
Photographic equipment and supplies	386	135	100	92	67	43	40	8.83	14.08	14.65
Watches, clocks, watchcases, and parts	387	22	11	8	17	8	7	5.24	7.70	8.22
Misc. manufacturing industries [3]	39	418	375	362	313	272	259	5.46	8.61	9.37
Jewelry, silverware, and plated ware	391	56	52	50	40	37	35	5.76	9.23	9.68
Toys and sporting goods	394	117	104	106	88	76	76	5.01	7.94	8.79
Pens, pencils, office and art supplies	395	37	34	31	27	24	21	5.58	8.89	10.27
Costume jewelry and notions	396	(4)	34	29	(4)	25	22	(4)	7.40	8.10
Nondurable goods [3]	(X)	8,127	7,968	7,755	5,798	5,584	5,417	6.56	10.12	11.00
Food and kindred products [3]	20	1,708	1,661	1,650	1,175	1,194	1,205	6.85	9.62	10.43
Meat products	201	358	422	443	298	359	377	6.99	7.94	8.49
Dairy products	202	175	155	151	96	95	95	6.86	10.56	11.66
Preserved fruits and vegetables	203	246	247	242	202	206	202	5.94	8.95	10.05
Grain mill products	204	144	128	123	99	89	88	7.67	11.52	12.61
Bakery products	205	230	213	207	139	133	133	7.14	10.85	11.73
Sugar and confectionery products	206	108	99	101	81	78	78	6.56	10.26	11.26
Fats and oils	207	44	31	31	32	22	21	7.03	10.10	10.90
Beverages	208	234	184	176	105	78	80	8.12	13.51	14.53
Tobacco products	21	69	49	47	54	36	35	7.74	16.23	17.04
Cigarettes	211	46	35	33	35	26	25	9.23	19.57	21.03
Textile mill products [3]	22	848	691	666	737	593	567	5.07	8.02	8.89
Broadwoven fabric mills, cotton	221	150	91	85	135	82	76	5.25	8.31	9.25
Broadwoven fabric mills, synthetics	222	116	77	69	104	68	58	5.30	8.63	9.69
Broadwoven fabric mills, wool	223	19	17	18	16	14	15	5.21	8.61	9.40
Narrow fabric mills	224	23	24	22	20	20	18	4.63	7.39	8.20
Knitting mills	225	224	205	196	194	179	170	4.77	7.37	8.11
Textile finishing, except wool	226	74	62	69	62	50	56	5.39	8.45	9.18
Carpets and rugs	227	54	61	60	44	50	49	5.20	8.25	8.91
Yarn and thread mills	228	125	103	97	113	92	87	4.76	7.68	8.61
Apparel and other textile products [3]	23	1,264	1,036	977	1,079	869	819	4.56	6.57	7.10
Men's and boys' suits and coats	231	77	50	43	67	42	36	5.34	7.34	7.78
Men's and boys' furnishings	232	362	274	273	310	235	236	4.23	6.06	6.70
Women's and misses outerwear	233	417	328	297	360	274	249	4.61	6.26	6.68
Women's and children's undergarments	234	90	62	55	76	51	46	4.15	6.18	6.84
Girls' and children's outerwear	236	64	56	45	55	47	38	4.20	5.95	6.39
Paper and allied products [3]	26	685	697	680	519	522	513	7.84	12.31	13.42
Papermills	262	178	180	169	133	136	128	9.05	15.10	16.58
Paperboard mills	263	65	52	52	51	40	40	9.28	15.26	16.77
Paperboard containers and boxes	265	205	209	211	157	162	165	6.94	10.39	11.31
Misc. converted paper products	267	220	241	236	163	174	171	6.89	10.79	11.79
Printing and publishing [3]	27	1,252	1,569	1,504	699	871	830	7.53	11.24	11.94
Newspapers	271	420	474	452	164	166	157	7.72	11.17	11.86
Periodicals	272	90	129	125	16	47	43	7.16	11.95	13.24
Books	273	101	121	119	52	66	65	6.76	10.10	10.99
Commercial printing	275	410	552	531	304	401	385	7.85	11.52	12.10
Blankbooks and bookbinding	278	62	72	67	51	56	51	5.78	8.83	9.33
Chemicals and allied products [3]	28	1,107	1,086	1,074	626	600	568	8.30	13.54	14.84
Industrial inorganic chemicals	281	161	138	136	88	70	59	9.07	14.66	16.42
Plastics materials and synthetics	282	205	180	168	137	116	106	8.21	13.97	15.26
Drugs	283	196	237	261	97	105	115	7.69	12.90	14.70
Soap, cleaners, and toilet goods	284	141	159	154	86	98	95	7.67	11.71	12.31
Paints and allied products	285	65	61	58	33	31	31	7.39	11.99	12.69
Industrial organic chemicals	286	174	155	150	88	86	78	9.67	15.97	17.67
Agricultural chemicals	287	72	56	57	45	34	33	8.12	13.73	15.11
Petroleum and coal products [3]	29	198	157	155	125	103	102	10.10	16.24	18.55
Petroleum refining	291	155	118	116	93	75	74	10.94	17.58	20.36
Asphalt paving and roofing materials	295	31	27	28	24	21	21	7.69	12.87	13.77
Rubber and misc. plastics products [3]	30	764	888	886	588	687	685	6.58	9.76	10.60
Tires and inner tubes	301	115	84	84	81	62	62	9.74	15.42	17.57
Rubber and plastics footwear	302	22	11	11	20	9	9	4.43	6.66	7.59
Leather and leather products [3]	31	233	133	116	197	109	93	4.58	6.91	7.62
Leather tanning and finishing	311	19	15	15	16	12	13	6.10	9.04	9.92
Footwear, except rubber	314	144	74	62	123	63	51	4.42	6.61	7.18
Luggage	316	16	11	10	12	8	7	4.90	6.91	7.82
Handbags and personal leather goods	317	30	15	12	25	12	8	4.33	6.08	6.84

See footnotes at end of table.

No. 656. Nonfarm Industries—Employees and Earnings: 1980 to 1993—Continued

[See headnote, p. 422]

INDUSTRY	1987 SIC [1] code	ALL EMPLOYEES TOTAL (1,000)			PRODUCTION WORKERS					
					Total (1,000)			Average hourly earnings (dollars)		
		1980	1990	1993	1980	1990	1993	1980	1990	1993
Transp. and public utilities [3]	(E)	5,146	5,793	5,708	4,293	4,807	4,780	8.87	12.97	13.64
Railroad transportation	40	532	279	250	(4)	(4)	(4)	(4)	(4)	(4)
Class I railroads [5]	4011	482	241	218	(4)	(4)	(4)	[6] 9.92	[6] 16.08	[6] 16.93
Local and interurban passenger transit	41	265	338	367	244	308	336	6.34	9.23	9.99
Trucking and warehousing	42	1,280	1,625	1,629	1,121	1,416	1,419	9.13	11.71	12.34
Water transportation	44	211	177	167	(4)	(4)	(4)	(4)	(4)	(4)
Transportation by air	45	453	745	733	(4)	(4)	(4)	(4)	(4)	(4)
Pipelines, except natural gas	46	21	19	18	15	14	14	10.50		19.51
Transportation services	47	198	345	347	159	278	273	6.94	10.43	11.05
Communication [3]	48	1,357	1,309	1,252	1,014	978	970	8.50	13.51	14.95
Telephone communication	481	1,072	913	872	779	658	656	8.72	14.13	15.67
Radio and television broadcasting	483	192	234	225	154	193	188	7.44	12.71	14.29
Cable and other pay television services	484	(4)	126	130	(4)	105	110	(4)	10.50	11.44
Electric, gas, and sanitary services [3] ...	49	829	957	945	678	759	744	8.90	15.23	16.74
Electric services	491	391	454	433	316	351	338	9.12	15.80	17.36
Gas production and distribution	492	168	165	162	138	129	126	8.27	14.25	16.30
Combination utility services	493	197	193	189	162	156	143	9.64	17.58	19.86
Sanitary services	495	50	115	132	44	99	113	7.16	11.55	12.10
Wholesale trade	(F)	5,292	6,173	6,113	4,328	4,959	4,930	6.95	10.79	11.71
Retail trade [3]	(G)	15,018	19,601	19,743	13,484	17,358	17,386	4.88	6.75	7.29
General merchandise stores	53	2,245	2,540	2,371	2,090	2,380	2,216	4.77	6.83	7.29
Food stores	54	2,384	3,215	3,210	2,202	2,953	2,927	6.24	7.31	7.81
Automotive dealers and service stations	55	1,689	2,063	2,035	1,430	1,718	1,690	5.66	8.92	9.62
Apparel and accessory stores	56	957	1,183	1,141	820	991	939	4.30	6.25	7.03
Furniture and home furnishings stores	57	606	820	843	502	670	684	5.53	8.53	9.44
Eating and drinking places	58	4,626	6,509	6,863	4,256	5,905	6,206	3.69	4.97	5.35
Finance, insurance, real estate	(H)	5,160	6,709	6,604	3,907	4,860	4,798	5.79	9.97	11.32
Depository institutions	60	(4)	2,251	2,115	(4)	1,632	1,531	(4)	8.43	9.12
Nondepository institutions	61	(4)	373	410	(4)	270	309	(4)	10.40	12.30
Security and commodity brokers	62	227	424	463	(4)	(4)	(4)	(4)	(4)	(4)
Insurance carriers	63	1,224	1,462	1,465	854	982	1,011	6.29	11.18	13.16
Insurance, agents, brokers, service	64	464	663	647	(4)	(4)	(4)	(4)	(4)	(4)
Real estate	65	989	1,315	1,280	(4)	(4)	(4)	(4)	(4)	(4)
Holding and other investment offices	67	115	221	225	(4)	(4)	(4)	(4)	(4)	(4)
Services [3]	(I)	17,890	27,934	30,192	15,921	24,387	26,368	5.85	9.83	10.81
Hotels and other lodging places	70	1,076	1,631	1,577	(4)	(4)	(4)	(4)	(4)	(4)
Hotels and motels	701	1,038	1,578	1,524	954	1,398	1,343	4.45	6.98	7.57
Personal services [3]	72	818	1,104	1,109	(4)	(4)	(4)	(4)	(4)	(4)
Laundry, cleaning, garment services	721	356	426	420	318	379	371	4.47	6.82	7.28
Beauty shops	723	284	372	382	264	333	341	4.26	7.10	7.83
Business services [3]	73	2,564	5,139	5,749	(4)	4,522	5,106	(4)	9.48	10.11
Advertising	731	153	235	226	116	169	164	8.07	13.51	14.99
Personnel supply services	736	543	1,535	1,977	(4)	(4)	(4)	(4)	(4)	(4)
Employment agencies	7361	(4)	246	266	(4)	(4)	(4)	(4)	(4)	(4)
Help supply services	7363	(4)	1,288	1,711	(4)	1,245	1,658	(4)	8.09	8.31
Computer and data processing services	737	304	772	882	254	603	716	7.16	15.11	16.35
Prepackaged software	7372	(4)	113	143	(4)	(4)	(4)	(4)	(4)	(4)
Data processing and preparation	7374	(4)	197	214	(4)	(4)	(4)	(4)	(4)	(4)
Auto repair, services, and parking	75	571	914	927	488	756	762	6.10	8.77	9.31
Automotive repair shops	753	350	524	523	297	429	423	6.52	9.67	10.27
Motion pictures	78	(4)	408	421	(4)	344	348	(4)	10.95	12.95
Motion picture theaters	783	124	112	107	(4)	(4)	(4)	(4)	(4)	(4)
Amusement and recreation services	79	(4)	1,076	1,182	(4)	944	1,032	(4)	8.11	8.39
Health services [3]	80	5,278	7,814	8,871	4,712	6,948	7,869	5.68	10.41	11.77
Offices and clinics of medical doctors	801	802	1,338	1,545	(4)	1,105	1,262	(4)	10.58	11.88
Nursing and personal care facilities	805	997	1,415	1,615	898	1,279	1,458	4.17	7.24	8.15
Hospitals	806	2,750	3,549	3,816	2,522	3,248	3,498	6.06	11.79	13.47
Home health care services	808	(4)	291	474	(4)	269	439	(4)	8.72	10.42
Legal services	81	498	908	930	427	748	749	7.35	14.16	15.28
Educational services	82	1,138	1,661	1,747	(4)	(4)	(4)	(4)	(4)	(4)
Social services	83	1,134	1,734	2,068	(4)	1,494	1,790	(4)	7.11	7.86
Membership organizations	86	1,539	1,946	1,960	(4)	(4)	(4)	(4)	(4)	(4)
Engineering and management services	87	(4)	2,478	2,522	(4)	1,886	1,926	(4)	13.56	15.04
Government	(J)	16,241	18,304	18,842	(NA)	(NA)	(NA)	(NA)	(NA)	(4)
Federal government	(X)	2,866	3,085	2,915	(NA)	(NA)	(NA)	(NA)	(NA)	(4)
State government	(X)	3,610	4,305	4,467	(NA)	(NA)	(NA)	(NA)	(NA)	(4)
Local government	(X)	9,765	10,914	11,459	(NA)	(NA)	(NA)	(NA)	(NA)	(4)

NA Not available. X Not applicable. [1] 1987 Standard Industrial Classification, see text, section 13. [2] Excludes government. [3] Includes industries not shown separately. [4] Included in totals; not available separately. [5] For changes in "Class I" classification, see text, section 21. [6] Includes all employees except executives, officials, and staff assistants who received pay during the month.

Source: U.S. Bureau of Labor Statistics, Bulletins 2370 and 2429, and *Employment and Earnings*, March and June issues.

No. 657. Indexes of Output per Hour—Selected Industries: 1975 to 1992

[See text, section 13. Minus sign (-) indicates decrease. See also *Historical Statistics, Colonial Times to 1970*, series W 14, 17, and 19, W 30-54, and 62-65]

INDUSTRY	1987 SIC code [1]	INDEXES (1987=100)						AVERAGE ANNUAL PERCENT CHANGE [2]	
		1975	1980	1985	1990	1991	1992, prel.	1975 -91	1991 -92
Mining:	(B)								
Coal mining	12	57.9	61.9	85.2	118.6	122.2	134.1	4.8	9.7
Crude petroleum and natural gas	1311	142.9	97.5	83.4	96.9	98.0	102.5	-2.3	4.6
Nonmetallic minerals, except fuels	14	79.4	84.6	93.9	108.3	103.4	110.9	1.7	7.3
Manufacturing:	(D)								
Red meat products	2011,13	69.1	87.6	99.7	92.3	93.5	(NA)	1.9	(NA)
Poultry dressing and processing.	2015	64.6	77.8	98.2	106.1	112.5	(NA)	3.5	(NA)
Dairy products	202	66.3	77.4	93.3	104.5	106.8	112.1	3.0	5.0
Preserved fruits and vegetables	203	77.8	83.7	94.6	97.7	99.9	(NA)	1.6	(NA)
Grain mill products	204	58.4	70.4	93.8	104.1	104.6	(NA)	3.7	(NA)
Bakery products	2051,52	81.2	81.5	95.5	93.8	90.5	89.9	0.7	-0.7
Bottled and canned soft drinks	2086	55.7	66.6	85.1	126.6	135.1	143.5	5.7	6.2
Cotton and synthetic broadwoven fabrics	2211,21	65.2	79.0	94.1	106.1	114.0	120.8	3.6	6.0
Hosiery	2251,52	81.5	92.9	101.3	105.7	111.4	117.6	2.0	5.6
Yarn spinning mills	2281	65.3	64.3	87.5	107.1	106.9	114.8	3.1	7.4
Sawmills and planing mills, general	2421	67.4	70.9	92.3	100.3	102.9	110.5	2.7	7.4
Millwork	2431	103.8	97.0	95.5	98.3	96.2	96.2	-0.5	0.0
Wood kitchen cabinets	2434	83.6	95.0	85.2	94.3	92.5	(NA)	0.6	(NA)
Household furniture	251	82.4	84.5	94.6	100.8	104.3	106.2	1.5	1.8
Office furniture	252	71.8	94.1	98.6	95.6	95.0	97.6	1.8	2.7
Pulp, paper, and paperboard mills	2611,21,31	62.8	76.1	89.1	103.2	105.2	112.9	3.3	7.3
Corrugated and solid fiber boxes	2653	78.1	90.1	99.3	100.3	100.0	101.1	1.6	1.1
Industrial inorganic chemicals	281	69.6	75.9	86.1	90.3	85.4	(NA)	1.3	(NA)
Industrial inorganic chemicals, n.e.c. [3] . . .	2819 (pt.)	74.3	79.9	87.4	86.5	81.3	(NA)	0.6	(NA)
Synthetic fibers	2823,24	53.7	73.4	86.2	99.1	101.9	108.3	4.1	6.3
Cosmetics and other toiletries	2844	94.7	84.2	88.9	100.3	102.5	(NA)	0.5	(NA)
Industrial organic chemicals, n.e.c. [3] . . .	2869	64.9	75.4	85.7	98.0	91.8	90.4	2.2	-1.5
Petroleum refining	2911	77.0	81.6	84.3	109.9	107.4	111.6	2.1	3.9
Tires and inner tubes	3011	53.1	59.2	88.1	108.3	109.8	116.7	4.6	6.3
Miscellaneous plastics products, n.e.c. [3]	308	67.0	74.3	88.0	100.1	100.8	100.5	2.6	-0.3
Footwear	314	94.6	92.5	100.3	92.6	92.8	93.6	-0.1	0.9
Concrete products	3271,72	88.7	87.2	97.3	105.8	107.5	109.9	1.2	2.2
Ready-mixed concrete	3273	93.3	89.0	93.2	99.7	96.1	97.9	0.2	1.9
Steel	331	61.3	67.5	91.4	110.4	106.3	116.2	3.5	9.3
Gray and ductile iron foundries	3321	90.3	84.5	96.1	103.7	99.0	104.5	0.6	5.6
Fabricated structural metal	3441	82.4	86.4	99.6	97.2	99.5	(NA)	1.2	(NA)
Metal doors, sash, and trim	3442	86.2	87.3	102.5	98.3	96.0	(NA)	0.7	(NA)
Metal stampings	3465,66,69	80.8	86.7	90.6	98.3	100.5	(NA)	1.4	(NA)
Valves and pipe fittings	3491,92,94	83.0	92.5	94.4	102.1	102.1	(NA)	1.3	(NA)
Farm and garden machinery	352	90.4	86.3	93.3	117.7	112.6	118.8	1.4	5.5
Construction machinery	3531	85.8	89.1	96.7	114.5	99.8	(NA)	0.9	(NA)
Pumps and compressors	3561,63,94	75.1	82.4	89.6	105.9	106.1	(NA)	2.2	(NA)
Refrigeration and heating equipment. . . .	3585	85.0	88.7	98.2	106.0	103.1	(NA)	1.2	(NA)
Motors and generators	3621	82.7	85.7	95.9	102.6	105.3	104.6	1.5	-0.7
Major household appliances	3631,32,33,39	70.0	79.0	93.0	102.6	104.5	112.9	2.5	8.0
Lighting fixtures and equipment	3645,46,47,48	79.9	83.5	96.4	94.4	92.4	93.0	0.9	0.6
Motor vehicles and equipment.	371	69.6	71.9	95.0	102.0	96.3	104.1	2.1	8.1
Aircraft	3721	84.0	101.0	92.4	106.2	124.5	125.2	2.5	0.6
Instruments to measure electricity	3825	72.0	81.6	98.3	108.0	111.6	(NA)	2.8	(NA)
Photographic equipment and supplies . .	3861	71.2	84.4	90.3	109.5	110.6	(NA)	2.8	(NA)
Service producing:	(E,G,H,I)								
Railroad transportation, revenue traffic . .	4011	43.4	52.0	78.4	122.4	132.7	140.2	7.2	5.7
Air transportation [4]	4512,13,22 (pts)	59.9	72.8	93.6	89.6	90.9	94.1	2.6	3.5
Telephone communications.	481	50.0	68.6	90.4	110.7	116.2	122.0	5.4	5.0
Gas and electric utilities	491,2,3	101.6	103.2	97.4	106.3	108.4	109.9	0.4	1.4
Hardware stores	5251	84.0	95.9	96.0	110.5	102.4	109.9	1.2	7.3
Department stores	5311	64.3	74.5	93.1	95.0	98.9	103.2	2.7	4.3
Variety stores	5331	143.3	126.1	129.1	131.8	130.0	117.8	-0.6	-9.4
Food stores	54	106.0	107.5	102.4	94.6	93.8	94.5	-0.8	0.7
New and used car dealers	5511	83.9	87.9	99.8	107.1	105.5	106.2	1.4	0.7
Auto and home supply stores	5531	70.8	84.0	95.0	114.2	114.6	114.0	3.1	-0.5
Gasoline service stations	5541	58.8	72.3	93.8	101.1	102.1	106.6	3.5	4.4
Apparel and accessory stores	56	72.6	81.4	102.0	101.6	102.3	109.4	2.2	6.9
Home furniture, furnishings, & equipment stores	57	64.6	75.3	92.4	113.5	118.1	128.7	3.8	9.0
Eating and drinking places	581	107.5	106.5	96.2	104.6	106.1	104.6	-0.1	-1.4
Drug stores and proprietary stores	5912	89.5	101.5	101.4	106.6	109.6	108.0	1.3	-1.5
Liquor stores	5921	89.9	95.2	101.6	110.6	112.3	126.6	1.4	12.7
Commercial banks.	602	76.3	78.6	94.3	108.5	112.3	117.3	2.4	4.5
Hotels and motels	7011	100.2	103.8	101.1	90.6	91.3	97.8	-0.6	7.1
Laundry, cleaning, and garment services.	721	112.5	105.9	103.2	99.0	96.6	97.1	-0.9	0.5
Beauty and barber shops	7231,41	83.2	86.8	94.7	92.2	88.4	92.8	0.4	5.0
Automotive repair shops.	753	107.0	100.7	99.4	106.4	99.9	103.2	-0.4	3.3

NA Not available.   [1] 1987 Standard Industrial Classification; see text, section 13.   [2] Average annual percent change based on compound rate formula.   [3] N.e.c. means not elsewhere classified.   [4] Refers to output per employee.

Source: U.S. Bureau of Labor Statistics, Bulletin 2440, *Productivity Measures for Selected Industries and Government Services*, March 1994.

No. 658. Productivity and Related Measures: 1970 to 1993

[See text, section 13. Minus sign (-) indicates decrease. See also *Historical Statistics, Colonial Times to 1970,* series D 689-704 and W 22-25]

ITEM	1970	1975	1980	1985	1989	1990	1991	1992	1993
INDEXES (1982=100)									
Output per hour, business sector	87.0	95.5	98.6	106.3	109.9	110.7	111.8	115.5	117.6
Nonfarm business	88.5	96.7	99.0	105.6	108.6	109.1	110.3	113.7	115.7
Manufacturing	(NA)	(NA)	92.9	106.8	120.0	122.2	124.5	129.8	136.4
Output,[1] business sector	75.8	85.0	100.5	116.7	132.3	133.3	131.6	135.4	140.3
Nonfarm business	75.7	84.9	100.8	116.8	132.7	133.5	131.8	135.4	140.6
Manufacturing	(NA)	(NA)	102.0	114.0	131.2	130.6	127.8	131.7	138.0
Hours,[2] business sector	87.2	89.0	101.9	109.8	120.4	120.5	117.7	117.3	119.4
Nonfarm business	85.6	87.9	101.8	110.7	122.2	122.4	119.5	119.1	121.5
Manufacturing	(NA)	(NA)	109.8	106.7	109.3	106.9	102.6	101.5	101.1
Compensation per hour,[3] business sector	36.7	54.5	85.0	113.2	133.0	140.6	147.4	154.9	160.8
Nonfarm business	37.0	54.9	84.9	112.8	131.9	139.2	146.2	153.7	159.2
Manufacturing	(NA)	(NA)	83.3	111.2	127.9	134.7	141.9	148.2	152.3
Real hourly compensation,[3] business sector	91.3	97.8	99.5	101.5	103.5	103.8	104.5	106.5	107.4
Nonfarm business	92.0	98.4	99.4	101.2	102.7	102.8	103.6	105.7	106.3
Manufacturing	(NA)	(NA)	97.5	99.8	99.5	99.4	100.5	101.9	101.7
Unit labor costs,[4] business sector	42.2	57.1	86.2	106.5	121.0	127.1	131.9	134.1	136.8
Nonfarm business	41.8	56.8	85.7	106.8	121.5	127.6	132.6	135.1	137.6
Manufacturing	(NA)	(NA)	89.6	104.2	106.6	110.3	114.0	114.1	111.6
ANNUAL PERCENT CHANGE [5]									
Output per hour, business sector	1.4	2.4	-0.8	1.4	-0.7	0.7	1.0	3.3	1.8
Nonfarm business	1.0	2.3	-0.9	0.8	-0.9	0.4	1.1	3.1	1.7
Manufacturing	(NA)	(NA)	-2.2	3.2	0.6	1.8	1.9	4.2	5.1
Output,[1] business sector	-0.5	-1.9	-1.6	3.6	1.7	0.7	-1.3	2.9	3.6
Nonfarm business	-0.6	-2.0	-1.7	3.4	1.7	0.6	-1.3	2.7	3.8
Manufacturing	(NA)	(NA)	-6.7	2.4	0.9	-0.4	-2.2	3.1	4.7
Hours,[2] business sector	-1.8	-4.2	-0.9	2.1	2.5	0.1	-2.3	-0.4	1.8
Nonfarm business	-1.5	-4.2	-0.8	2.5	2.6	0.2	-2.4	-0.4	2.1
Manufacturing	(NA)	(NA)	-4.6	-0.7	0.3	-2.2	-4.1	-1.1	-0.3
Compensation per hour,[3] business sector	7.5	10.0	10.7	4.5	3.5	5.7	4.9	5.0	3.8
Nonfarm business	7.2	10.0	10.7	4.1	3.3	5.5	5.0	5.1	3.6
Manufacturing	(NA)	(NA)	11.9	5.0	3.9	5.3	5.4	4.4	2.8
Real hourly compensation,[3] business sector	1.7	0.8	-2.5	0.9	-1.3	0.3	0.6	2.0	0.8
Nonfarm business	1.4	0.8	-2.5	0.6	-1.4	0.1	0.8	2.0	0.6
Manufacturing	(NA)	(NA)	-1.4	1.4	-0.9	-0.1	1.1	1.3	-0.2
Unit labor costs,[4] business sector	6.1	7.5	11.5	3.0	4.3	5.0	3.8	1.7	2.0
Nonfarm business	6.2	7.5	11.7	3.3	4.3	5.1	3.9	2.0	1.8
Manufacturing	(NA)	(NA)	14.4	1.8	3.3	3.5	3.4	0.2	-2.2

NA Not available. [1] Refers to gross domestic product originating in the sector, in 1987 prices. [2] Hours at work of all persons engaged in the business and nonfarm business sectors (employees, proprietors, and unpaid family workers); employees' and proprietors' hours in manufacturing. [3] Wages and salaries of employees plus employers' contributions for social insurance and private benefit plans. Also includes an estimate of same for self-employed. Real compensation deflated by the consumer price index for all urban consumers, see text, section 15. [4] Hourly compensation divided by output per hour. [5] All changes are from the immediate prior year.

Source: U.S. Bureau of Labor Statistics, *Employment and Earnings,* monthly; and unpublished data.

No. 659. Persons Receiving Work-Related Training, by Selected Characteristics: 1990

[In thousands, except as indicated. As of spring. For persons 18 to 64 years old. Based on Survey of Income and Program Participation; for details, see source]

CHARACTERISTIC	Total	SEX		RACE		His-panic origin[1]	EDUCATION		
		Male	Female	White	Black		Less than 9 years	9 to 12 years	More than 12 years
All persons	152,815	74,828	77,987	129,575	17,891	12,463	9,714	77,599	65,502
Persons ever receiving work training	39,238	19,950	19,288	33,984	4,241	2,218	1,050	20,447	17,742
Uses training on current or most recent job	26,563	14,073	12,489	23,595	2,316	1,486	580	12,671	13,311
Location: Apprenticeship	1,749	1,411	338	1,616	76	114	70	999	680
Business/vo-tech school	10,213	4,388	5,825	8,659	1,301	537	192	6,562	3,460
Community college	4,077	1,664	2,413	3,722	275	220	92	1,838	2,147
Four-year college	2,738	1,396	1,341	2,488	198	89	22	355	2,360
High school vo-tech program	2,158	1,068	1,090	1,875	250	183	36	1,798	324
Training program at work	13,330	7,393	5,936	11,774	1,164	598	270	5,903	7,156
Military	2,229	1,990	238	1,968	180	139	12	1,151	1,065
Previous job	1,821	968	853	1,636	134	134	87	705	1,029
Other	9,720	4,874	4,845	8,304	1,169	497	413	4,524	4,783
Program paid for by—									
Self or family	11,540	4,708	6,832	10,348	914	588	215	6,014	5,311
Employer	17,834	10,019	7,815	16,059	1,379	880	426	7,885	9,524
Federal, State, or local government	10,429	5,543	4,886	8,079	2,010	748	387	6,675	3,366
Someone else	1,000	553	447	859	99	84	41	586	373
Length of training program (average number of weeks)	22	25	20	23	21	22	20	25	19

[1] Persons of Hispanic origin may be of any race.

Source: U.S. Bureau of the Census, *Current Population Reports,* P70-32.

No. 660. Annual Total Compensation and Wages and Salaries Per Full-Time Equivalent Employee, by Industry: 1985 to 1992

[In dollars. Wage and salary payments include executives' compensation, bonuses, tips, and payments-in-kind; total compensation includes in addition to wages and salaries, employer contributions for social insurance, employer contributions to private and welfare funds, director's fees, jury and witness fees, etc. 1985 based on 1972 Standard Industrial Classification Code (SIC); beginning 1990, based on the 1987 SIC. See text, section 13]

INDUSTRY	ANNUAL TOTAL COMPENSATION				ANNUAL WAGES AND SALARIES			
	1985	1990	1991	1992	1985	1990	1991	1992
Domestic industries	25,263	31,398	32,649	34,536	21,059	26,138	27,178	28,665
Agriculture, forestry, and fisheries	13,084	17,672	16,578	18,976	11,773	15,299	15,646	15,925
Mining	38,883	46,216	48,655	51,811	32,054	37,903	39,756	42,032
Construction	26,721	32,826	34,105	35,005	22,775	27,679	28,487	29,222
Manufacturing	30,145	36,572	38,324	30,342	24,600	29,746	30,942	32,370
Transportation	30,638	35,430	37,107	38,775	25,240	28,916	30,144	31,397
Communication	39,635	47,926	50,063	53,567	31,342	38,382	39,567	42,076
Electric, gas, and sanitary services	39,179	47,936	50,559	53,657	31,653	38,930	40,779	42,998
Wholesale trade.	29,195	37,147	38,540	40,408	25,016	31,772	32,760	34,225
Retail trade.	15,694	16,588	19,543	20,352	13,603	16,036	16,769	17,406
Finance, insurance, and real estate	27,873	37,049	36,875	42,492	23,724	31,682	33,116	36,159
Services	21,441	28,381	29,376	31,031	18,698	24,801	25,516	26,869
Government and government enterprises . .	27,839	35,616	37,686	39,668	21,988	27,772	29,284	30,652

Source: U.S. Bureau of Economic Analysis, *The National Income and Product Accounts of the United States, Volume 2, 1958-88;* and *Survey of Current Business,* August 1993; and unpublished data.

No. 661. Average Hourly and Weekly Earnings, by Private Industry Group: 1980 to 1993

[Average earnings include overtime. Data are for production and related workers in mining, manufacturing, and construction and nonsupervisory employees in other industries. Excludes agriculture. See headnote, table 654. See also *Historical Statistics, Colonial Times to 1970,* series D 877-892]

PRIVATE INDUSTRY GROUP	CURRENT DOLLARS					CONSTANT (1982) DOLLARS [1]				
	1980	1985	1990	1992	1993	1980	1985	1990	1992	1993
Average hourly earnings	6.66	8.57	10.01	10.58	10.83	7.78	7.77	7.52	7.42	7.39
Mining	9.17	11.98	13.68	14.54	14.60	10.71	10.86	10.28	10.20	9.96
Construction	9.94	12.32	13.77	14.15	14.35	11.61	11.17	10.35	9.92	9.79
Manufacturing	7.27	9.54	10.83	11.46	11.76	8.49	8.65	8.14	8.04	8.02
Transportation, public utilities	8.87	11.40	12.97	13.46	13.64	10.36	10.34	9.74	9.44	9.30
Wholesale trade.	6.95	9.15	10.79	11.39	11.71	8.12	8.30	8.11	7.99	7.99
Retail trade	4.88	5.94	6.75	7.13	7.29	5.70	5.39	5.07	5.00	4.97
Finance, insurance, real estate	5.79	7.94	9.97	10.82	11.32	6.76	7.20	7.49	7.59	7.72
Services	5.85	7.90	9.83	10.55	10.81	6.83	7.16	7.39	7.40	7.37
Average weekly earnings.	235	299	345	364	374	275	271	259	255	255
Mining	397	520	603	638	645	464	471	453	448	440
Construction	368	464	526	538	551	430	421	395	377	376
Manufacturing	289	386	442	470	487	337	350	332	330	332
Transportation, public utilities	351	450	505	524	542	410	408	379	367	369
Wholesale trade.	267	351	411	435	447	312	318	309	305	305
Retail trade	147	175	194	205	210	172	158	146	144	143
Finance, insurance, real estate	210	289	357	387	404	245	262	268	272	276
Services	191	257	319	343	351	223	233	240	240	240

[1] Earnings in current dollars divided by the Consumer Price Index (CPI-W) on a 1982 base; see text, section 15.

Source: U.S. Bureau of Labor Statistics, Bulletins 2370 and 2429, and *Employment and Earnings,* monthly.

No. 662. Annual Percent Changes in Earnings and Compensation: 1980 to 1993

[Annual percent change from immediate prior year. Minus sign (-) indicates decrease]

ITEM	1980	1985	1987	1988	1989	1990	1991	1992	1993
Current dollars:									
Hourly earnings, total [1]	8.1	3.0	2.5	3.3	4.1	3.6	3.1	2.5	2.4
Hourly earnings, manufacturing . . , ...	8.5	3.8	1.8	2.8	2.8	3.3	3.2	2.5	2.6
Compensation per employee-hour [1]	10.7	4.1	3.5	4.2	3.3	5.5	5.0	5.1	3.6
Constant (1982) dollars:									
Hourly earnings, total [1]	-4.8	-0.4	-1.0	-0.5	-0.7	-1.6	-0.9	-0.4	-0.4
Hourly earnings, manufacturing . . , ...	-4.5	0.3	-1.6	-1.2	-1.9	-1.7	-0.9	-0.4	-0.2
Compensation per employee-hour [1]	-2.5	0.6	-0.2	0.1	-1.4	0.1	0.8	2.0	0.6
Consumer Price Index [2].	13.5	3.6	3.6	4.1	4.8	5.4	4.2	3.0	3.0

[1] Nonfarm business sector. [2] See text, section 15.

Source: U.S. Bureau of Labor Statistics, *Monthly Labor Review;* and unpublished data.

No. 663. Average Annual Pay, by State: 1991 and 1992

[In dollars, except percent change. For workers covered by State unemployment insurance laws and for Federal civilian workers covered by unemployment compensation for Federal employees, approximately 90 percent of total civilian employment. Excludes most agricultural workers on small farms, all Armed Forces, elected officials in most States, railroad employees, most domestic workers, employees of certain nonprofit organizations and most self-employed individuals. Pay includes bonuses, cash value of meals and lodging, and tips and other gratuities]

STATE	AVERAGE ANNUAL PAY		Percent change, 1991-92 [1]	STATE	AVERAGE ANNUAL PAY		Percent change, 1991-92 [1]
	1991	1992 [1]			1991	1992 [1]	
United States......	24,578	25,903	5.4	Missouri	22,574	23,550	4.3
Alabama............	21,287	22,340	4.9	Montana...........	18,648	19,378	3.9
Alaska	30,830	31,825	3.2	Nebraska	19,372	20,355	5.1
Arizona............	22,207	23,161	4.3	Nevada............	23,083	24,743	7.2
Arkansas..........	19,008	20,108	5.8	New Hampshire	23,600	24,925	5.6
California..........	27,513	28,934	5.2	New Jersey	29,991	32,125	7.1
Colorado..........	23,981	25,040	4.4	New Mexico........	20,272	21,051	3.8
Connecticut	30,689	32,587	6.2	New York	30,011	32,399	8.0
Delaware..........	25,647	26,596	3.7	North Carolina	21,095	22,248	5.5
District of Columbia....	35,570	37,971	6.8	North Dakota........	18,132	18,945	4.5
Florida............	21,992	23,144	5.2	Ohio..............	23,602	24,846	5.3
Georgia...........	23,165	24,373	5.2	Oklahoma	20,968	21,699	3.5
Hawaii	24,104	25,613	6.3	Oregon	22,338	23,514	5.3
Idaho	19,688	20,649	4.9	Pennsylvania	24,393	25,785	5.7
Illinois.............	26,317	27,910	6.1	Rhode Island	23,082	24,315	5.3
Indiana	22,522	23,570	4.7	South Carolina	20,439	21,423	4.8
Iowa..............	19,810	20,937	5.7	South Dakota	17,143	18,016	5.1
Kansas	21,002	21,982	4.7	Tennessee	21,541	22,807	5.9
Kentucky..........	20,730	21,858	5.4	Texas.............	23,760	25,080	5.6
Louisiana	21,503	22,340	3.9	Utah..............	20,874	21,976	5.3
Maine.............	20,870	21,808	4.5	Vermont	21,355	22,347	4.6
Maryland...........	25,962	27,145	4.6	Virginia	23,805	24,937	4.8
Massachusetts.......	28,041	29,664	5.8	Washington	23,942	25,553	6.7
Michigan	26,125	27,463	5.1	West Virginia	21,356	22,169	3.8
Minnesota..........	23,962	25,315	5.6	Wisconsin	21,838	23,022	5.4
Mississippi.........	18,411	19,237	4.5	Wyoming...........	20,591	21,215	3.0

[1] Preliminary.

Source: U.S. Bureau of Labor Statistics, *Employment and Wages Annual Averages 1992;* and USDL News Release 93-371, *Average Annual Pay by State and Industry, 1992.*

No. 664. Average Annual Pay, by Selected Metropolitan Areas: 1991 and 1992

[In dollars. Metropolitan areas ranked by average pay 1992. Data are for MSA's and PMSA's, except New England data are for NECMA's. See headnote table 663]

METROPOLITAN AREA	1991	1992 [1]	METROPOLITAN AREA	1991	1992 [1]
Metropolitan areas..............	25,729	27,173	Kokomo, IN.................	27,918	28,676
Bridgeport-Stamford-Norwalk-Danbury, CT .	35,998	39,006	Huntsville, AL	26,625	28,432
New York, NY...................	35,073	38,802	Manchester-Nashua, NH	26,448	28,372
San Jose, CA...................	34,462	37,068	Atlanta, GA....................	26,636	28,159
Middlesex-Somerset-Hunterdon, NJ......	32,523	34,826	Minneapolis-St. Paul, MN-WI	26,423	28,035
Newark, NJ....................	32,231	34,712	Brazoria, TX...................	27,027	27,979
San Francisco, CA...............	32,031	34,358	New London-Norwich, CT	26,821	27,926
Trenton, NJ....................	31,888	33,960	Denver, CO....................	26,526	27,734
Bergen-Passaic, NJ	31,292	33,592	Rochester, NY.................	26,572	27,562
Anchorage, AK	31,828	33,007	Monmouth-Ocean, NJ.............	25,784	27,468
Washington, DC-MD-VA	31,057	32,899	Rochester, MN.................	26,189	27,416
Hartford-New Britain-Middletown-Bristol, CT.............	30,375	31,967	Sacramento, CA................	25,658	26,999
			Cleveland, OH.................	25,462	26,857
Boston-Lawrence-Salem-Lowell-Brockton, MA....................	29,968	31,872	Baltimore, MD	25,708	26,795
			Saginaw-Bay City-Midland, MI..........	25,706	26,650
Jersey City, NJ	29,045	31,628	Honolulu, HI	25,014	26,638
Los Angeles-Long Beach, CA..........	29,697	31,267	Lansing-East Lansing, MI...........	25,681	26,548
Chicago, IL....................	28,711	30,692	Midland, TX...................	25,726	26,321
Oakland, CA...................	29,111	30,622	Worcester-Fitchburg-Leominster, MA	25,077	26,309
Lake County, IL.................	28,521	30,461	St Louis, MO-IL................	25,209	26,285
Detroit, MI....................	28,664	30,408	Oxnard-Ventura, CA..............	25,124	26,267
Houston, TX...................	28,026	29,802	Cincinnati, OH-KY-IN.............	24,763	26,187
Nassau-Suffolk, NY	28,167	29,708	Pittsburgh, PA.................	24,733	26,163
Flint, MI.....................	29,318	29,672	San Diego, CA.................	25,002	26,153
Seattle, WA...................	27,327	29,586	Kalamazoo, MI.................	25,170	26,143
Philadelphia, PA-NJ	27,607	29,355	Raleigh-Durham, NC.............	24,789	26,140
Anaheim-Santa Ana, CA	27,852	29,353	West Palm Beach-Boca Raton-Delray Beach, FL...................	24,564	26,050
New Haven-Waterbury-Meriden, CT.....	27,729	29,347			
Poughkeepsie, NY	28,382	29,262	Melbourne-Titusville-Palm Bay, FL.......	24,473	26,023
Wilmington, DE-NJ-MD	27,766	29,047	Albany-Schenectady-Troy, NY	24,817	26,020
Dallas, TX....................	27,364	28,988	Portland, OR..................	24,555	26,007
Ann Arbor, MI..................	27,503	28,714	Battle Creek, MI................	24,743	25,969

[1] Preliminary.

Source: U.S. Bureau of Labor Statistics, USDL News Release 93-428, *Average Annual Pay Levels in Metropolitan Areas 1992.*

No. 665. Full-Time Wage and Salary Workers—Number and Earnings: 1983 to 1993

[In current dollars of usual weekly earnings. Data represent annual averages of quarterly data. See text, section 13, and headnote table 630, for a discussion of occupational data. Based on Current Population Survey; see text, section 1, and Appendix III. For definition of median, see Guide to Tabular Presentation]

CHARACTERISTIC	NUMBER OF WORKERS (1,000)				MEDIAN WEEKLY EARNINGS (dol.)			
	1983	1985	1990	1993	1983	1985	1990	1993
All workers [1]	70,976	77,002	85,082	85,211	313	343	415	463
Male	42,309	45,589	49,015	48,384	378	406	485	514
16 to 24 years old	6,702	6,956	6,313	5,556	223	240	283	289
25 years old and over	35,607	38,632	42,702	42,828	406	442	514	559
Female	28,667	31,414	36,068	36,827	252	277	348	395
16 to 24 years old	5,345	5,621	5,001	4,324	197	210	254	274
25 years old and over	23,322	25,793	31,066	32,503	267	296	370	416
White	61,739	66,481	72,637	72,395	319	355	427	478
Male	37,378	40,030	42,563	41,825	387	417	497	531
Female	24,361	26,452	30,075	30,571	254	281	355	403
Black	7,373	8,393	9,642	9,729	261	277	329	370
Male	3,883	4,367	4,909	4,855	293	304	360	392
Female	3,490	4,026	4,733	4,873	231	252	308	349
Hispanic origin [2]	(NA)	(NA)	6,993	7,106	(NA)	(NA)	307	335
Male	(NA)	(NA)	4,410	4,495	(NA)	(NA)	322	352
Female	(NA)	(NA)	2,583	2,611	(NA)	(NA)	280	314
Family relationship:								
Husbands	28,720	30,260	31,326	31,061	410	455	532	587
Wives	14,884	16,270	18,666	19,570	257	285	363	412
Women who maintain families	3,948	4,333	5,007	5,279	256	278	339	379
Men who maintain families	1,331	1,313	1,786	1,827	377	396	444	482
Other persons in families:								
Men	5,518	6,173	6,434	5,908	219	238	296	307
Women	4,032	4,309	4,475	4,003	201	213	271	295
All other men [3]	6,740	7,841	9,468	9,587	350	380	442	479
All other women [3]	5,803	6,503	7,920	7,975	274	305	376	419
Occupation, male:								
Managerial and professional	10,312	11,078	12,263	12,454	516	583	731	791
Exec., admin., managerial	5,344	5,835	6,401	6,611	530	593	742	791
Professional specialty	4,967	5,243	5,863	5,843	506	571	720	791
Technical, sales, and administrative support	8,125	8,803	9,596	9,774	385	420	496	534
Tech. and related support	1,428	1,563	1,747	1,773	424	472	570	615
Sales	3,853	4,227	4,666	4,664	389	431	505	544
Admin. support, incl. clerical	2,844	3,013	3,183	3,337	362	391	440	492
Service	3,723	3,947	4,476	4,680	255	272	320	350
Private household	11	13	12	25	(B)	(B)	(B)	(B)
Protective	1,314	1,327	1,523	1,646	355	391	477	524
Other service	2,398	2,607	2,942	3,009	217	230	273	290
Precision production [4]	9,180	10,026	10,169	9,609	387	408	488	511
Mechanics and repairers	3,418	3,752	3,669	3,578	377	400	477	509
Construction trades	2,966	3,308	3,603	3,275	375	394	480	495
Other	2,796	2,966	2,897	2,756	408	433	510	539
Operators, fabricators and laborers	9,833	10,585	11,257	10,685	308	325	378	399
Machine operators, assemblers, and inspectors	4,138	4,403	4,510	4,242	319	341	391	407
Transportation and material moving	3,199	3,459	3,721	3,681	335	369	418	456
Handlers, equipment cleaners, helpers, and laborers	2,496	2,724	3,027	2,762	251	261	308	319
Farming, forestry, and fishing	1,137	1,150	1,253	1,182	200	216	263	274
Occupation, female:								
Managerial and professional	7,139	8,302	10,595	11,636	357	399	511	580
Exec., admin., managerial	2,772	3,492	4,764	5,131	339	383	485	528
Professional specialty	4,367	4,810	5,831	6,505	367	408	534	605
Technical, sales, and administrative support	13,517	14,622	16,202	16,120	247	269	332	376
Tech. and related support	1,146	1,200	1,470	1,587	299	331	417	468
Sales	2,460	2,929	3,531	3,398	204	226	292	329
Admin. support, incl. clerical	9,911	10,494	11,202	11,135	248	270	332	375
Service	3,598	3,963	4,531	4,699	173	185	230	259
Private household	267	330	298	313	116	130	171	183
Protective	139	156	216	286	250	278	405	417
Other service	3,193	3,477	4,017	4,099	176	188	231	259
Precision production [4]	784	906	893	880	256	268	316	344
Mechanics and repairers	120	144	139	140	337	392	459	543
Construction trades	45	53	50	38	(B)	265	394	(B)
Other	619	709	704	702	244	253	300	319
Operators, fabricators, and laborers	3,486	3,482	3,675	3,335	204	216	262	288
Machine operators, assemblers, and inspectors	2,853	2,778	2,840	2,539	202	216	260	284
Transportation and material moving	159	189	227	244	253	252	314	358
Handlers, equipment cleaners, helpers and laborers	474	514	608	551	211	209	250	286
Farming, forestry, and fishing	143	138	171	158	169	185	216	242

B Data not shown where base is less than 50,000. NA Not available. [1] Includes other races, not shown separately. [2] Persons of Hispanic origin may be of any race. [3] The majority of these persons are living alone or with nonrelatives. Also included are persons in families where the husband, wife or other person maintaining the family is in the Armed Forces, and persons in unrelated subfamilies. [4] Includes craft and repair.

Source: U.S. Bureau of Labor Statistics, Bulletin 2307, and *Employment and Earnings*, monthly, January issues.

No. 666. Families With Earners—Number and Earnings: 1980 to 1993

[In current dollars of usual weekly earnings. Annual averages of quarterly figures based on Current Population Survey; see text, section 1, and Appendix III. For families with wage and salary earners]

CHARACTERISTIC	NUMBER OF FAMILIES (1,000)				MEDIAN WEEKLY EARNINGS (dollars)			
	1980	1985	1990	1993	1980	1985	1990	1993
TOTAL								
Total families with earners [1]	41,162	41,616	43,759	44,383	400	522	653	707
Married-couple families	33,825	33,459	34,219	34,257	433	582	732	804
One earner	14,797	13,347	12,166	12,185	303	385	455	481
Husband.	12,127	10,346	8,994	8,643	336	440	520	565
Wife.	2,059	2,243	2,407	2,773	159	217	267	314
Other family member	611	758	764	769	163	204	280	282
Two or more earners [2]	19,028	20,112	22,053	22,071	535	715	880	973
Husband and wife only	12,990	14,019	15,934	16,349	507	684	844	944
Husband and other family member(s). .	2,369	2,159	1,751	1,509	557	689	825	875
Wife and other family member(s).	426	514	527	574	350	454	557	613
Other family members only	139	176	176	150	356	468	554	605
Families maintained by women	5,690	6,470	7,323	7,792	222	297	363	393
One earner	4,022	4,397	4,983	5,452	184	234	288	307
Householder	3,104	3,432	3,937	4,402	188	243	296	315
Other family member	918	965	1,045	1,050	168	200	254	263
Two or more earners	1,668	2,073	2,340	2,340	370	487	607	655
Families maintained by men	1,647	1,688	2,218	2,334	360	450	514	523
One earner	1,016	1,031	1,352	1,523	283	346	396	429
Two or more earners	631	656	866	811	502	625	778	763
WHITE								
Total families with earners [1]	35,786	35,848	37,239	37,458	411	543	681	739
Married-couple families	30,316	29,899	30,361	30,288	438	589	745	816
One earner [2]	13,437	12,097	10,856	10,790	311	395	473	492
Husband.	11,152	9,496	8,162	7,755	343	452	535	583
Wife.	1,740	1,925	2,044	2,383	160	218	270	313
Two or more earners	16,878	17,802	19,505	19,497	542	723	892	984
Husband and wife only	11,448	12,394	14,148	14,546	511	691	855	954
Families maintained by women	4,140	4,616	5,127	5,355	233	311	382	415
Families maintained by men	1,331	1,333	1,751	1,816	374	475	539	547
BLACK								
Total families with earners [1]	4,503	4,668	5,082	5,268	299	378	459	490
Married-couple families	2,802	2,671	2,724	2,698	366	487	601	674
One earner [2]	1,103	902	893	909	210	257	304	344
Husband.	769	580	527	539	244	292	345	381
Wife.	279	257	290	287	151	206	243	321
Two or more earners	1,700	1,769	1,831	1,789	472	622	748	846
Husband and wife only	1,238	1,258	1,297	1,285	461	603	713	819
Families maintained by women	1,438	1,703	1,986	2,168	192	259	314	334
Families maintained by men	263	294	372	403	307	360	397	413
HISPANIC ORIGIN [3]								
Total families with earners [1]	(NA)	(NA)	3,624	3,879	(NA)	(NA)	496	505
Married-couple families	(NA)	(NA)	2,599	2,800	(NA)	(NA)	555	566
One earner [2]	(NA)	(NA)	1,050	1,177	(NA)	(NA)	322	334
Husband.	(NA)	(NA)	814	912	(NA)	(NA)	356	365
Wife.	(NA)	(NA)	164	183	(NA)	(NA)	236	262
Two or more earners	(NA)	(NA)	1,549	1,622	(NA)	(NA)	716	744
Husband and wife only	(NA)	(NA)	924	1,032	(NA)	(NA)	672	733
Families maintained by women	(NA)	(NA)	691	749	(NA)	(NA)	326	353
Families maintained by men	(NA)	(NA)	334	330	(NA)	(NA)	468	432

NA Not available.   [1] Excludes families in which there is no wage or salary earner or in which the husband, wife, or other person maintaining the family is either self-employed or in the Armed Forces.   [2] Includes other earners, not shown separately. [3] Persons of Hispanic origin may be of any race.

Source: U.S. Bureau of Labor Statistics, Bulletin 2307; and *Employment and Earnings*, monthly, January issues.

No. 667. Workers With Earnings, by Occupation of Longest Job Held and Sex: 1992

[Covers persons 15 years old and over as of **March 1993**. Based on Current Population Survey; see text, section 1, and Appendix III. For definition of median, see Guide to Tabular Presentation]

MAJOR OCCUPATION OF LONGEST JOB HELD	ALL WORKERS				YEAR ROUND FULL-TIME			
	Women		Men		Women		Men	
	Number (1,000)	Median earnings	Number (1,000)	Median earnings	Number (1,000)	Median earnings	Number (1,000)	Median earnings
Total [1]	62,050	$13,677	72,318	$22,173	33,180	$21,440	48,308	$30,358
Executive, administrators, and managerial.	7,097	24,338	9,400	40,100	5,334	27,495	7,826	42,509
Professional specialty	9,579	25,759	8,214	40,059	5,749	31,261	6,347	44,015
Technical and related support	2,235	20,601	2,095	29,711	1,396	24,797	1,614	32,720
Sales	8,258	8,565	8,012	23,485	3,408	17,924	5,675	31,346
Admin. support, incl. clerical.	15,906	15,746	4,367	20,708	9,589	20,321	2,949	27,186
Precision production, craft and repair	1,202	14,794	12,980	23,219	728	19,045	8,786	28,923
Machine operators, assemblers, and inspectors.	3,391	11,834	5,004	19,498	1,952	15,714	3,412	23,884
Transportation and material moving	559	10,874	4,893	21,167	204	20,131	3,136	25,787
Handlers, equipment cleaners, helpers, and laborers	1,107	7,461	4,755	10,043	397	14,522	2,004	18,793
Service workers	11,972	6,506	8,110	10,739	4,174	12,931	4,060	20,606
Private household	1,090	2,350	73	(B)	202	9,668	25	(B)
Service, except private household	10,882	6,917	8,037	10,785	3,972	13,195	4,035	20,656
Farming, forestry, and fishing	678	3,686	3,630	7,858	208	10,079	1,769	14,897

B Base less than 75,000.   X Not applicable.   [1] Includes persons whose longest job was in the Armed Forces.

Source: U.S. Bureau of the Census, *Current Population Reports*, P60-184

No. 668. Employment Cost Index (ECI), by Industry and Occupation: 1982 to 1993

[As of **December**. The ECI is a measure of the rate of change in employee compensation (wages, salaries, and employer costs for employee benefits). Data are not seasonally adjusted: 1982-1985 based on fixed employment counts from 1970 Census of Population; thereafter, based on fixed employment counts from the 1980 Census of Population]

ITEM	INDEXES (June 1989=100)						PERCENT CHANGE FOR 12 MONTHS ENDING—				
	1982	1985	1990	1991	1992	1993	1985	1990	1991	1992	1993
Civilian workers [1]	74.8	86.8	107.6	112.2	116.1	120.2	4.3	4.9	4.3	3.5	3.5
Workers, by occupational group:											
White-collar workers	72.9	85.8	108.3	112.8	116.6	120.6	4.9	5.2	4.2	3.4	3.4
Blue-collar workers	78.2	88.4	106.5	111.1	115.2	119.4	3.3	4.4	4.3	3.7	3.6
Service workers	74.3	87.2	108.0	113.1	116.7	120.5	3.9	5.1	4.7	3.2	3.3
Workers, by industry division:											
Manufacturing	76.9	87.8	107.2	112.2	116.5	121.3	3.3	5.1	4.7	3.8	4.1
Nonmanufacturing	73.9	86.4	107.8	112.3	116.0	119.8	4.7	4.9	4.2	3.3	3.3
Services	70.5	84.1	110.2	114.6	119.2	122.9	4.7	6.3	4.0	4.0	3.1
Public administration [2]	71.9	85.4	108.7	112.6	116.3	120.0	4.9	5.3	3.6	3.3	3.2
Private industry workers [3]	75.8	87.3	107.0	111.7	115.6	119.8	3.9	4.6	4.4	3.5	3.6
Workers, by occupational group:											
White-collar workers	73.7	86.4	107.4	112.2	115.9	120.2	4.9	4.9	4.5	3.3	3.7
Blue-collar workers	78.4	88.5	106.4	111.0	115.0	119.3	3.1	4.4	4.3	3.6	3.7
Service workers	76.3	88.4	107.3	112.4	115.9	119.5	3.0	4.7	4.8	3.1	3.1
Workers, by industry division:											
Manufacturing	76.9	87.8	107.2	112.2	116.5	121.3	3.3	5.1	4.7	3.8	4.1
Nonmanufacturing	75.1	87.0	106.9	111.5	115.1	119.0	4.3	4.5	4.3	3.2	3.4
Services	(NA)	84.1	109.3	114.0	118.9	123.1	(NA)	6.2	4.3	4.3	3.5
Business services	(NA)	(NA)	107.4	111.1	115.9	118.6	(NA)	6.0	3.4	4.3	2.3
Health services	(NA)	83.7	110.8	116.5	121.8	126.0	(NA)	6.8	5.1	4.5	3.4
Hospitals	(NA)	(NA)	110.7	116.1	121.6	125.6	(NA)	7.0	4.9	4.7	3.3
Workers by bargaining status:											
Union	79.6	90.1	106.2	111.1	115.9	120.9	2.6	4.3	4.6	4.3	4.3
Nonunion	74.3	86.3	107.3	111.9	115.5	119.5	4.6	4.8	4.3	3.2	3.5
State and local government	70.8	84.6	110.4	114.4	118.6	121.9	5.6	5.8	3.6	3.7	2.8
Workers, by occupational group:											
White-collar workers	70.4	84.2	110.9	114.6	118.9	121.9	5.8	6.0	3.3	3.8	2.5
Blue-collar workers	73.9	86.7	108.7	112.9	117.8	121.4	5.3	4.8	3.9	4.3	3.1
Workers, by industry division:											
Services	70.0	84.0	111.3	115.3	119.6	122.6	5.9	6.3	3.6	3.7	2.5
Schools	69.0	83.6	111.6	115.6	119.9	122.9	6.2	6.0	3.6	3.7	2.5
Elementary and secondary	68.6	83.6	112.1	116.2	120.7	123.6	6.4	6.3	3.7	3.9	2.4
Colleges and universities	(NA)	(NA)	110.2	113.5	117.2	120.7	(NA)	5.3	3.0	3.3	3.0
Services, excluding schools [4]	73.1	85.2	110.2	114.4	118.6	121.9	4.7	6.8	3.8	3.7	2.8
Public administration [2]	71.9	85.4	108.7	112.6	116.3	120.0	4.9	5.3	3.6	3.3	3.2

NA Not available.   [1] Includes private industry and State and local government workers and excludes farm, household, and Federal government workers.   [2] Consists of legislative, judicial, administrative, and regulatory activities.   [3] Excludes farm and household workers.   [4] Includes library, social, and health services. Formerly called hospitals and other services.

Source: U.S. Bureau of Labor Statistics, *News, Employment Cost Index*, quarterly.

No. 669. Effective Federal Minimum Hourly Wage Rates: 1950 to 1993

[Employee estimates as of **September 1991**, except as indicated. The Fair Labor Standards Act of 1938 and subsequent amendments provide for minimum wage coverage applicable to specified nonsupervisory employment categories. Exempt from coverage are executives and administrators or professionals]

IN EFFECT	MINIMUM RATES FOR NONFARM			Minimum rates for farm workers [4]	SEX, RACE, AND INDUSTRY	NONSUPERVISORY EMPLOYEES, 1991		
	Laws prior to 1966 [1]	Percent, avg. earnings [2]	1966 and later [3]			Total (1,000)	Subject to minimum wage rates	
							Total (1,000)	Percent of total
Jan. 25, 1950....	$0.75	54	(X)	(X)	Total	91,373	80,540	88.1
Mar. 1, 1956	1.00	52	(X)	(X)				
Sept. 3, 1961....	1.15	50	(X)	(X)	Male.......................	45,909	40,276	87.7
Sept. 3, 1963....	1.25	51	(X)	(X)	Female	45,464	40,264	88.6
Feb. 1, 1967	1.40	50	$1.00	$1.00	White	80,222	70,494	87.9
Feb. 1, 1968	1.60	54	1.15	1.15	Black and other	11,151	10,046	90.1
Feb. 1, 1969	(5)	51	1.30	1.30	Black only.................	10,150	9,148	90.1
Feb. 1, 1970	(5)	49	1.45	(5)				
Feb. 1, 1971	(5)	46	1.60	(5)	**Private industry**	**80,149**	**69,316**	**86.5**
					Agriculture [6]...................	1,702	653	38.4
May 1, 1974	2.00	46	1.90	1.60	Mining.....................	606	603	99.5
Jan. 1, 1975	2.10	45	2.00	1.80	Construction.................	4,452	4,294	96.5
Jan. 1, 1976	2.30	46	2.20	2.00	Manufacturing...............	16,400	15,947	97.2
Jan. 1, 1977	(5)	42	2.30	2.20	Transp., public utilities	5,208	5,175	99.4
Jan. 1, 1978	2.65	44	2.65	2.65	Wholesale trade	5,204	4,158	79.9
Jan. 1, 1979	2.90	45	2.90	2.90	Retail trade	17,439	15,800	90.6
Jan. 1, 1980	3.10	44	3.10	3.10	Finance, insurance, and real estate ..	5,736	4,349	75.8
Jan. 1, 1981	3.35	43	3.35	3.35	Service [7]	22,111	17,466	79.0
Apr. 1, 1990.....	3.80	35	3.80	3.80	Private households	1,291	871	67.5
Apr. 1, 1991.....	4.25	38	4.25	4.25	**Government** [7][8]	**11,224**	**11,224**	**100.0**
Apr. 1, 1992.....	(5)	37	(5)	(5)				
Apr. 1, 1993.....	(5)	36	(5)	(5)				

X Not applicable.   [1] Applies to workers covered prior to 1961 amendments and, after Sept. 1965, to workers covered by 1961 amendments. Rates set by 1961 amendments were: Sept. 1961, $1.00; Sept. 1964, $1.15; and Sept. 1965, $1.25.   [2] Percent of gross average hourly earnings of production workers in manufacturing.   [3] Applies to workers newly covered by amendments of 1966, 1974, and 1977, and Title IX of Education amendments of 1972.   [4] Included in coverage as of 1966, 1974, and 1977 amendments.   [5] No change in rate.   [6] Estimates based on average employment for the 10-month active season.   [7] Estimates for educational services in private industry and government relate to October.   [8] Federal, State, and local employees.

Source: U.S. Department of Labor, Employment Standards Administration, *Minimum Wage and Maximum Hours Standards Under the Fair Labor Standards Act*, 1981, annual; and unpublished data.

No. 670. Workers Paid Hourly Rates, by Selected Characteristics: 1993

[Annual average of monthly figures; for employed wage and salary workers. Based on Current Population Survey; see text, section 1, and Appendix III]

CHARACTERISTIC	NUMBER OF WORKERS [1] (1,000)				PERCENT OF ALL WORKERS PAID HOURLY RATES			Median hourly earnings of workers paid hourly rates [2]
	Total paid hourly rates	At or below $4.25			At or below $4.25			
		Total	At $4.25	Below $4.25	Total	At $4.25	Below $4.25	
Total, 16 years and over [3]	**63,316**	**4,186**	**2,518**	**1,668**	**6.6**	**4.0**	**2.6**	**7.92**
16 to 24 years............	14,331	2,241	1,434	807	15.6	10.0	5.6	5.50
16 to 19 years	5,021	1,308	928	380	26.1	18.5	7.6	4.79
25 years and over	48,984	1,946	1,085	861	4.0	2.2	1.8	8.97
Male, 16 years and over......	**31,699**	**1,583**	**1,032**	**551**	**5.0**	**3.3**	**1.7**	**8.96**
16 to 24 years...........	7,385	966	678	288	13.1	9.2	3.9	5.75
16 to 19 years	2,532	599	462	137	23.7	18.2	5.4	4.86
25 years and over	24,314	618	355	263	2.5	1.5	1.1	10.21
Women, 16 years and over....	**31,617**	**2,603**	**1,486**	**1,117**	**8.2**	**4.7**	**3.5**	**7.15**
16 to 24 years...........	6,946	1,275	756	519	18.4	10.9	7.5	5.27
16 to 19 years	2,489	709	465	244	28.5	18.7	9.8	4.73
25 years and over	24,671	1,328	730	598	5.4	3.0	2.4	7.88
White......................	52,971	3,467	2,036	1,431	6.5	3.8	2.7	8.03
Black.....................	8,078	572	392	180	7.1	4.9	2.2	7.19
Hispanic origin [4].............	6,047	544	427	117	9.0	7.1	1.9	6.87
Full-time workers [5]..........	47,125	1,448	835	613	3.1	1.8	1.3	8.89
Part-time workers [5]..........	16,191	2,739	1,684	1,055	16.9	10.4	6.5	5.55
Private sector .... [5] ..	54,862	3,874	2,294	1,580	7.1	4.2	2.9	7.66
Goods-producing industries [6]..	17,596	422	300	122	2.4	1.7	0.7	9.22
Service-producing industries [7]..	37,266	3,452	1,994	1,458	9.3	5.4	3.9	6.92
Public sector...............	8,454	313	225	88	3.7	2.7	1.0	9.96

[1] Excludes the incorporated self-employed.   [2] For definition of median, see Guide to Tabular Presentation.   [3] Includes races not shown separately.   [4] Persons of Hispanic origin may be of any race.   [5] Working fewer than 35 hours per week.   [6] Includes agriculture, mining, construction, and manufacturing.   [7] Includes transportation and public utilities; wholesale trade; finance, insurance, and real estate; private households; and other service industries, not shown separately.

Source: U.S. Bureau of Labor Statistics, unpublished data.

No. 671. Employer Costs for Employee Compensation per Hour Worked: 1989 to 1993

[As of **March**, for private industry workers. Based on a sample of establishments; see source for details]

COMPENSATION COMPONENT	1989	1990	1991	1992	1993				
					Total	Goods producing [1]	Service producing [2]	Manufacturing	Nonmanufacturing
Total compensation	14.28	14.96	15.40	16.14	16.70	20.22	15.51	20.09	15.85
Wages and salaries	10.38	10.84	11.14	11.58	11.90	13.54	11.34	13.35	11.54
Total benefits	3.90	4.13	4.27	4.55	4.80	6.67	4.17	6.74	4.31
Paid leave	1.00	1.03	1.05	1.09	1.11	1.38	1.01	1.52	1.00
Vacation.	0.50	0.51	0.52	0.54	0.54	0.72	0.48	0.78	0.48
Holiday.	0.34	0.34	0.35	0.37	0.38	0.50	0.34	0.56	0.33
Sick.	0.12	0.13	0.13	0.14	0.14	0.11	0.15	0.13	0.14
Other.	0.04	0.04	0.05	0.05	0.05	0.05	0.05	0.06	0.05
Supplemental pay	0.34	0.37	0.36	0.39	0.42	0.67	0.34	0.71	0.35
Premium pay.	0.17	0.17	0.17	0.18	0.19	0.39	0.12	0.39	0.14
Nonproduction bonuses.	0.12	0.16	0.13	0.15	0.19	0.21	0.18	0.23	0.18
Shift pay.	0.05	0.05	0.05	0.05	0.05	0.08	0.04	0.10	0.04
Insurance.	0.85	0.92	1.01	1.12	1.19	1.74	1.01	1.86	1.03
Health insurance	(NA)	(NA)	(NA)	1.02	1.10	1.59	0.93	1.69	0.95
Retirement and savings	0.42	0.45	0.44	0.46	0.48	0.77	0.39	0.72	0.43
Pensions	0.34	0.36	0.35	0.36	0.38	0.60	0.31	0.55	0.34
Savings and thrift.	0.08	0.09	0.10	0.10	0.10	0.17	0.08	0.17	0.09
Legally required [3]	1.27	1.35	1.40	1.47	1.55	1.99	1.40	1.79	1.49
Social Security.	0.84	0.89	0.92	0.96	0.99	1.17	0.93	1.16	0.95
Federal unemployment	0.03	0.03	0.03	0.03	0.03	0.03	0.03	0.03	0.03
State unemployment.	0.11	0.09	0.09	0.10	0.11	0.15	0.10	0.14	0.11
Workers compensation	0.27	0.31	0.33	0.36	0.39	0.63	0.31	0.44	0.38
Other benefits [4]	0.02	(Z)	(Z)	0.02	0.04	0.12	(NA)	0.14	0.02

NA Not available.　Z Represents or rounds to zero.　[1] Mining, construction, and manufacturing.　[2] Transportation, communications, public utilities, wholesale trade, retail trade, finance, insurance, real estate, and services.　[3] Includes railroad retirement, railroad unemployment, railroad supplemental unemployment, and other legally required benefits, not shown separately.　[4] Includes severance pay, and supplemental unemployment benefits.

Source: U.S. Bureau of Labor Statistics, *News, Employer Costs for Employee Compensation*, USDL 89-295, 90-317, 91-292, 92-391, and 93-220.

No. 672. Employees With Employer- or Union-Provided Pension Plans or Group Health Plans: 1992

[For wage and salary workers 15 years old and over as of **March 1993**. Based on Current Population Survey; see text, section 1, and Appendix III]

OCCUPATION	Total	PERCENT WITH—		CHARACTERISTIC	Total	PERCENT WITH—	
		Pension plan	Group health plan			Pension plan	Group health plan
Total	134,516	40.1	50.8	AGE			
Executive, admin., managerial. . . .	16,501	52.6	65.9	Total.	134,516	40.1	50.8
Professional specialty	17,793	59.1	66.0	15 to 24 years	22,797	11.5	21.7
				25 to 44 years	70,336	44.5	56.3
Technical/related support	4,330	55.7	68.4	45 to 64 years	36,818	51.6	60.0
Sales workers	16,286	27.6	41.1	65 years and over	4,564	21.8	36.2
Admin. support, inc. clerical	20,341	46.9	56.5	WORK EXPERIENCE			
				Worked	134,516	40.1	50.8
Precision prod., craft/repair	14,185	41.6	55.1	Full-time	104,919	48.2	60.6
				50 weeks or more	81,545	55.1	68.2
Mach. operators, assemblers [1] . .	8,395	42.1	59.2	27 to 49 weeks	13,589	30.2	43.5
Transportation/material moving [2] . .	5,457	39.4	55.3	26 weeks or fewer	9,784	15.4	20.9
Handlers, equipment cleaners [2] . .	5,868	24.4	36.8	Part-time	29,597	11.2	16.0
				50 weeks or more	12,393	17.0	23.1
Service workers	20,091	20.8	28.7	27 to 49 weeks	6,887	11.6	14.9
Private households	1,163	2.2	3.2	26 weeks or fewer	10,317	4.0	8.2
Other	18,928	22.0	30.3	EMPLOYER SIZE			
				Under 25	40,489	12.0	24.6
Farming, forestry and fishing	4,344	8.5	16.8	25 to 99	18,110	30.4	50.2
				100 to 499.	19,100	47.2	61.2
Armed Forces	924	72.3	6.5	500 to 999.	7,422	54.9	64.9
				Over 1,000.	49,396	61.6	66.2

[1] Includes inspectors.　[2] Includes helpers and laborers.

Source: U.S. Bureau of the Census, unpublished data.

No. 673. Employee Benefits in Private Establishments: 1991 and 1992

[Covers full-time employees in private industry. Medium and large establishments exclude establishments with fewer than 100 workers, executive and traveling operating employees, and Alaska and Hawaii. Small establishments include those with fewer than 100 employees. Covers only benefits for which the employer pays part or all of the premium or expenses involved, except unpaid parental leave and long-term care insurance. Based on a sample survey of establishments; for details, see sources. For data on employee benefits in State and local governments, see table 497]

MEDIUM AND LARGE PRIVATE ESTABLISHMENTS, 1991	All employees	Professional, technical and related	Clerical and sales	Production and service	SMALL PRIVATE ESTABLISHMENTS, 1992	All employees	Professional, technical and related	Clerical and sales	Blue collar and service
Percent of employees participating in—					**Percent of employees participating in—**				
Paid: Vacations	96	97	98	95	Paid: Vacations	88	94	94	81
Holidays	92	93	94	90	Holidays	82	94	90	74
Jury duty leave	86	92	88	82	Jury duty leave	58	76	65	47
Funeral leave	80	84	82	77	Funeral leave	50	60	56	43
Rest time	67	58	67	71	Rest time	49	40	43	56
Military leave	54	63	56	48	Military leave	21	33	27	13
Sick leave	67	87	82	48	Sick leave	53	74	70	35
Personal leave	21	29	26	13	Personal leave	12	19	16	7
Lunch time	8	5	4	11	Lunch time	9	12	8	8
Maternity leave	2	3	2	1	Maternity leave	2	3	2	1
Paternity leave	1	1	1	(Z)	Paternity leave	1	1	(Z)	(Z)
Unpaid: Maternity leave	37	43	38	33	Unpaid: Maternity leave	18	27	20	13
Paternity leave	26	31	26	23	Paternity leave	8	13	9	6
Insurance plans:					**Insurance plans:**				
Medical care	83	85	81	84	Medical care	71	83	78	61
Noncontributory	41	38	35	46	Noncontributory	37	43	40	34
Hospital/room and board	83	85	81	84	Hospital/room and board	71	83	78	61
Inpatient surgery	83	85	81	84	Inpatient surgery	71	83	78	61
Mental health care	81	83	79	82	Mental health care:				
Inpatient	81	83	79	82	Inpatient	68	80	76	57
Outpatient	80	82	78	81	Outpatient	67	80	74	57
Dental	60	67	60	57	Dental	33	43	37	27
Extended care facility	66	70	66	66	Extended care facility	60	72	66	49
Home health care	67	71	66	66	Home health care	57	69	66	46
Hospice care	46	48	45	45	Hospice care	40	50	44	34
Vision	23	21	21	25	Vision	10	9	10	10
In HMO's	14	15	15	12	In HMO's	14	14	13	16
Alcohol abuse treatment	82	83	80	82	Alcohol abuse treatment:				
Inpatient detoxification	81	82	79	81	Inpatient detoxification	67	79	74	59
Inpatient rehabilitation	64	63	63	66	Inpatient rehabilitation	50	58	52	43
Outpatient	64	66	63	64	Outpatient	50	61	55	43
Drug abuse treatment	81	83	79	80	Drug abuse treatment:				
Inpatient detoxification	80	82	79	80	Inpatient detoxification	66	78	71	58
Inpatient rehabilitation	63	62	62	65	Inpatient rehabilitation	48	57	50	41
Outpatient	62	65	62	61	Outpatient	49	60	53	41
Life	94	98	95	92	Life	64	77	73	53
Noncontributory	80	83	82	77	Noncontributory	53	66	62	42
Accident/sickness	45	32	35	57	Accident/sickness	26	24	27	27
Noncontributory	33	19	23	46	Noncontributory	17	17	16	18
Long-term disability	40	61	49	24	Long-term disability	23	43	31	10
Noncontributory	31	46	38	20	Noncontributory	18	38	26	6
Retirement and savings plans:					**Retirement and savings plans:**				
Defined benefit pension	59	60	56	59	Defined benefit pension	22	21	25	20
Earnings-based formula [1]	41	52	46	32	Earnings-based formula [1]	15	19	20	9
Defined contribution	48	57	53	39	Defined contribution	33	43	38	26
Savings and thrift	29	38	35	20	Savings and thrift	14	20	17	9
Employee stock ownership	3	4	4	2	Employee stock ownership	1	1	1	1
Deferred profit sharing	16	13	16	18	Deferred profit sharing	16	18	19	14
Money purchase pension	7	11	7	5	Money purchase pension	5	9	5	4
Additional benefits:					**Additional benefits:**				
Parking	88	86	85	92	Parking [3]	86	84	85	88
Educational assistance	72	87	73	64	Educational assistance	36	51	43	26
Travel accident insurance	42	55	47	32	Travel accident insurance	16	24	19	11
Severance pay	41	55	48	30	Severance pay	15	26	21	8
Relocation allowance	31	50	30	21	Relocation allowance [3]	12	22	15	6
Recreation facilities	26	34	25	23	Recreation facilities	7	13	7	4
Nonproduction bonuses, cash	35	33	36	35	Nonproduction bonuses, cash	47	52	50	43
Child care	8	11	9	5	Child care	2	3	3	(Z)
Flexible benefits plans	10	16	10	6	Flexible benefits plans	2	4	4	(Z)
Reimbursement accounts [2]	36	48	40	26	Reimbursement accounts [2]	14	24	20	7
Eldercare	9	11	12	6	Eldercare	3	4	5	2
Long-term care insurance	4	6	5	2	Long-term care insurance	1	2	1	2
Wellness programs	35	47	34	28	Wellness programs	17	24	21	12
Employee assistance programs	56	64	56	51	Employee assistance programs	17	24	21	12

Z Represents or rounds to zero.   [1] Earnings-based formulas pay a percent of employee's annual earnings (usually earnings in the final years of employment) per year of service.   [2] Account which is used throughout the year to pay for plan premiums or to reimburse the employee for benefit related expenses. Account may be financed by employer, employee, or both.   [3] 1990 data.

Source: U.S. Bureau of Labor Statistics, *Employee Benefits in Medium and Large Private Establishments, 1991*, Bulletin 2422; and *Employee Benefits in Small Private Establishments, 1992*, forthcoming bulletin.

No. 674. Major Collective Bargaining Agreements—Average Percent Wage Rate Changes Under All Agreements: 1970 to 1993

[In percent, except as indicated. Data represent all wage rate changes implemented under the terms of private nonfarm industry agreements affecting 1,000 workers or more. Series covers production and related workers in manufacturing and nonsupervisory workers in nonmanufacturing industries. Data measure all wage rate changes effective in the year stemming from settlements reached in the year, deferred from prior year settlements, and cost-of-living adjustment (COLA) clauses]

CHANGES	1970	1975	1980	1985	1988	1989	1990	1991	1992	1993
Average wage rate change (prorated over all workers)	8.8	8.7	9.9	3.3	2.6	3.2	3.5	3.6	3.1	3.0
Source:										
Current settlements	5.1	2.8	3.6	0.7	0.7	1.2	1.3	1.1	0.8	0.9
Prior settlements	3.1	3.7	3.5	1.8	1.3	1.3	1.5	1.9	1.9	1.9
COLA provisions	0.6	2.2	2.8	0.7	0.6	0.7	0.7	0.5	0.4	0.2
Industry:										
Manufacturing	7.1	8.5	10.2	2.8	2.8	3.5	4.4	3.7	3.1	3.3
Nonmanufacturing	10.5	8.9	9.7	3.6	2.5	3.0	3.0	3.5	3.1	2.8
Construction	(NA)	8.1	9.9	3.0	2.9	3.1	3.4	3.4	3.4	2.7
Transportation and public utilities	(NA)	9.7	10.8	3.6	2.1	2.3	2.2	3.3	2.7	3.0
Wholesale and retail trade	(NA)	9.2	7.6	3.3	2.3	3.2	3.6	3.5	3.5	2.3
Services	(NA)	6.4	8.1	5.1	3.5	5.3	4.3	4.9	3.7	3.4
Nonmanufacturing, excluding construction	(NA)	9.3	9.6	3.7	2.4	3.0	2.9	3.6	3.0	2.8
Average wage rate increase for workers receiving an increase	9.4	9.0	10.1	4.2	3.4	4.0	4.2	4.0	3.7	3.5
Source:										
Current settlements	11.9	10.2	9.4	4.1	3.3	4.2	4.1	4.2	3.6	3.2
Prior settlements	5.8	5.2	5.6	3.7	3.1	3.4	3.3	3.7	3.8	3.4
COLA provisions	3.7	4.8	7.7	2.2	2.7	3.3	2.7	2.0	2.0	1.3
Total number of workers receiving a wage rate increase (mil.)	10.2	9.7	8.9	5.5	4.7	4.8	4.9	5.1	4.7	4.8
Source (mil.):										
Current settlements	4.7	2.7	3.5	1.4	1.4	1.7	1.9	1.5	1.3	1.7
Prior settlements	5.7	7.3	5.6	3.4	2.6	2.3	2.7	3.0	2.8	3.0
COLA provisions	1.8	4.7	3.4	2.3	1.3	1.3	1.4	1.3	1.0	0.9
Number of workers not receiving a wage rate increase (mil.)	0.6	0.4	0.2	1.5	1.3	1.2	1.0	0.5	0.9	0.7

NA Not available.

Source: U.S. Bureau of Labor Statistics, *Compensation and Working Conditions*, monthly.

No. 675. Major Collective Bargaining Settlements—Average Percent Changes in Wage and Compensation Rates Negotiated: 1970 to 1993

In percent, except as indicated. Data represent private nonfarm industry settlements affecting production and related workers in manufacturing and nonsupervisory workers in nonmanufacturing industries. Wage data cover units with 1,000 workers or more. Compensation data relate to units of 5,000 or more. Data relate to contracts negotiated in each calendar year but exclude possible changes in wage rates under cost-of-living adjustment (COLA) clauses, except increases guaranteed by the contract. Includes all settlements, whether wage and benefit rates were changed or not. Minus sign (-) indicates decrease]

CHANGES	1970	1975	1980	1985	1987	1988	1989	1990	1991	1992	1993
Compensation rates:											
First year	13.1	11.4	10.4	2.6	3.0	3.1	4.5	4.6	4.1	3.0	3.0
Over life of contract [1]	9.1	8.1	7.1	2.7	2.6	2.5	3.4	3.2	3.4	3.1	2.4
Wage rates:											
All industries:											
First year	11.9	10.2	9.5	2.3	2.2	2.5	4.0	4.0	3.6	2.7	2.3
Contracts with COLA	(NA)	12.2	8.0	1.6	2.3	2.4	3.9	3.4	3.4	2.7	2.8
Contracts without COLA	(NA)	9.1	11.7	2.7	2.1	2.7	4.0	4.4	3.7	2.7	2.1
Over life of contract [1]	8.9	7.8	7.1	2.7	2.1	2.4	3.4	3.2	3.2	3.0	2.1
Contracts with COLA	(NA)	7.1	5.0	2.5	1.5	1.8	2.8	1.9	3.0	2.5	1.4
Contracts without COLA	(NA)	8.3	10.3	2.8	2.5	2.8	3.5	4.0	3.3	3.1	2.5
Manufacturing:											
First year	8.1	9.8	7.4	0.8	2.1	2.2	3.9	3.7	3.9	2.6	2.7
Over life of contract [1]	6.0	8.0	5.4	1.8	1.3	2.1	3.2	2.1	3.1	2.6	1.5
Nonmanufacturing:											
First year	15.2	10.4	10.9	3.3	2.3	2.8	4.0	4.3	3.4	2.7	2.1
Over life of contract [1]	11.5	7.8	8.3	3.3	2.7	2.5	3.4	4.0	3.3	3.0	2.5
Number of workers affected (mil.)	4.7	2.9	3.8	2.2	2.0	1.8	1.9	2.0	1.8	1.6	2.1
Manufacturing (mil.)	2.2	0.8	1.6	0.9	0.9	0.7	0.4	0.9	0.6	0.3	0.8
Nonmanufacturing (mil.)	2.5	2.1	2.2	1.3	1.1	1.1	1.5	1.1	1.2	1.3	1.3

NA Not available.   [1] Average annual rate of change.

Source: U.S. Bureau of Labor Statistics, *Compensation and Working Conditions*, monthly.

No. 676. Workers Killed or Disabled on the Job: 1960 to 1992

[Data for 1992 are preliminary estimates. Estimates based on data from the U.S. National Center for Health Statistics, State Departments of Health, and State industrial commissions. Numbers of workers based on data from the U.S. Bureau of Labor Statistics]

YEAR	DEATHS						Disabling injuries [2] (mil.)	YEAR AND INDUSTRY GROUP	DEATHS		Disabling injuries [2] (1,000)
	Total		Manufacturing		Nonmanufacturing				Number (1,000)	Rate [1]	
	Number (1,000)	Rate [1]	Number (1,000)	Rate [1]	Number (1,000)	Rate [1]					
1960. . . .	13.8	21	1.7	10	12.1	25	2.0	1992, total.	8.5	7	3,300
1965. . . .	14.1	20	1.8	10	12.3	24	2.1	Agriculture [3].	1.2	37	140
1970. . . .	13.8	18	1.7	9	12.1	21	2.2	Mining and quarrying [4]. .	0.2	29	30
1975. . . .	13.0	15	1.6	9	11.4	17	2.2	Construction.	1.3	22	300
1980. . . .	13.2	13	1.7	8	11.5	15	2.2	Manufacturing.	0.6	3	600
1984. . . .	11.5	11	1.1	6	10.4	12	1.9	Transportation and			
1985. . . .	11.5	11	1.2	6	10.3	12	2.0	utilities.	1.2	20	250
1986. . . .	11.1	10	1.0	5	10.1	11	1.8	Trade [5]	1.0	4	720
1987. . . .	11.3	10	1.0	5	10.3	11	1.8	Services [6]	1.3	3	740
1988. . . .	11.0	10	1.1	6	9.9	10	1.8	Government.	1.7	9	520
1989. . . .	10.9	9	1.1	6	9.8	10	1.7				
1990. . . .	10.1	9	1.0	5	9.1	9	3.9				
1991. . . .	9.3	8	0.8	4	8.5	9	3.6				
1992. . . .	8.5	7	0.6	3	7.9	8	3.3				

[1] Per 100,000 workers.   [2] Disabling injury defined as one which results in death, some degree of physical impairment, or renders the person unable to perform regular activities for a full day beyond the day of the injury. Due to change in methodology, data beginning 1990 not comparable with prior years.   [3] Includes forestry and fishing.   [4] Includes oil and gas extraction.   [5] Includes wholesale and retail trade.   [6] Includes finance, insurance, and real estate.

Source: National Safety Council, Itasca, IL, *Accident Facts*, annual (copyright).

No. 677. Worker Deaths and Injuries and Production Time Lost: 1990 to 1992

ITEM	DEATHS (1,000)			DISABLING INJURIES [1] (mil.)			PRODUCTION TIME LOST (mil. days)					
							In the current year			In future years [2]		
	1990	1991	1992	1990	1991	1992	1990	1991	1992	1990	1991	1992
All accidents	46.9	42.6	40.0	4.6	8.5	8.1	95.0	170.0	165.0	380.0	435.0	410.0
On the job	10.6	9.3	8.5	1.8	3.6	3.3	35.0	70.0	65.0	100.0	115.0	110.0
Off the job	36.3	33.3	31.5	2.8	4.9	4.8	60.0	100.0	100.0	280.0	320.0	300.0
Motor vehicle	23.4	21.4	19.8	0.9	1.2	1.1	(NA)	(NA)	(NA)	(NA)	(NA)	(NA)
Public nonmotor vehicle . . .	6.5	5.9	6.1	0.9	1.9	2.0	(NA)	(NA)	(NA)	(NA)	(NA)	(NA)
Home	6.4	6.0	5.6	1.0	1.8	1.7	(NA)	(NA)	(NA)	(NA)	(NA)	(NA)

NA Not available.   [1] See footnote 2, table 676 for a definition of disabling injuries. Data revised beginning 1991.   [2] Based on an average of 5,850 days lost in future years per fatality and 565 days lost in future years per permanent injury.

Source: National Safety Council, Itasca, IL, *Accident Facts*, 1993 (copyright).

No. 678. Fatal Work Injuries, by Cause: 1992

[For the 50 States and DC. Based on the 1992 Census of Fatal Occupational Injuries. Due to methodological differences, data differ from those in table 676. For details, see source]

CAUSE	Number of fatalities	Percent distribution	CAUSE	Number of fatalities	Percent distribution
Total	6,083	100	Struck by object [1]	558	9
			Struck by falling objects	360	6
Transportation accidents [1]	2,441	40	Struck by flying object	79	1
Highway accidents [1]	1,121	18	Caught in or compressed by—		
Collision between vehicles, mobile			equipment or objects	312	5
equipment.	553	9	collapsing materials	110	2
Noncollision accidents	292	5			
Nonhighway accident (farm, industrial			Falls [1]	590	10
premises).	436	7	Fall to lower level	500	8
Aircraft accidents	350	6	Fall on same level	60	1
Workers struck by a vehicle	342	6			
Water vehicle accidents.	110	2	Exposure to harmful substances or		
Railway accidents.	66	1	environments [1]	593	10
			Contact with electric current	334	5
Assaults and violent acts [1]	1,216	20	Exposure to caustic, noxious		
Homicides [1]	1,004	17	or allergenic substances.	118	2
Shooting	822	14	Oxygen deficiency.	109	2
Stabbing	82	1	Drowning, submersion	76	1
Self-inflicted injury.	183	3			
			Fires and explosions	167	3
Contacts with objects and equipment [1] .	1,001	16	Other events and exposures	75	1

[1] Includes other causes, not shown separately.

Source: U.S. Bureau of Labor Statistics, *Monthly Labor Report*, October, 1993.

No. 679. Industries With the Highest Total Case Incidence Rates for Injuries and Illnesses: 1991 and 1992

[Rates per full-time employees. Industries shown are those with highest rates in 1992. See headnote, table 680]

INDUSTRY	1987 SIC [1] code	1991	1992 [2]	INDUSTRY	1987 SIC [1] code	1991	1992 [2]
Private sector, total.	(X)	8.4	8.9	Truck and bus bodies	3713	23.4	22.3
				Prefabricated wood buildings	2452	23.5	21.3
Meat packing plants	2011	45.5	44.4	Metal barrels, drums, and pails	3412	22.1	21.3
Ship building and repairing	3731	44.1	37.8	Iron and steel forgings.	3462	20.7	21.1
Metal sanitary ware.	3431	42.0	35.0	Flat glass	3211	21.7	21.1
Motor vehicles and car bodies	3711	28.3	32.3	Sausages and other prepared meats . .	2013	20.8	21.0
Gray and ductile iron foundries	3321	31.3	31.6	Creamery butter	2021	19.8	21.0
Automotive stampings . . . . ,3	3465	27.5	29.2	Leather tanning and finishing	3111	20.4	20.5
Household appliances, n.e.c. 3	3639	30.7	27.2	Aluminum die-castings.	3363	20.9	20.5
Malt.	2083	21.7	26.6	Travel trailers and campers	3792	20.7	20.5
Truck trailers . . . . . , 3	3715	25.5	25.0	Malleable iron foundries.	3322	17.4	20.3
Steel foundries, n.e.c. 3	3325	24.1	24.4	Fresh or frozen prepared fish	2092	21.0	20.3
Poultry slaughtering and processing. .	2015	23.1	23.2	Aluminum foundries.	3365	21.3	20.1
Mobile homes	2451	22.9	23.0	Primary aluminum	3334	23.5	20.0
Household laundry equipment.	3633	17.7	22.6	Railroad equipment.	3743	21.1	20.0
Motorcycles, bicycles, and parts . . .	3751	22.0	22.5	Canned and cured fish and seafoods .	2091	(NA)	20.0
Structural wood members, n.e.c. 3 . . .	2439	22.9	22.4	Prepared flour mixes and doughs . . .	2045	19.0	20.0

X Not applicable. [1] 1987 Standard Industrial Classification; see text, section 13. [2] See footnote 2, table 680. [3] N.e.c. means not elsewhere classified.

Source: U.S. Bureau of Labor Statistics, *Occupational Injuries and Illnesses in the United States by Industry,* annual.

No. 680. Occupational Injury and Illness Incidence Rates, by Industry: 1991 and 1992

[Rates per 100 full-time employees. For nonfarm employment data, see table 656. Rates refer to any occupational injury or illness resulting in (1) fatalities (except 1992), (2) lost workday cases, or (3) nonfatal cases without lost workdays. Incidence rates were calculated as: Number of injuries and illnesses divided by total hours worked by all employees during year multiplied by 200,000 as base for 100 full-time equivalent workers (working 40 hours per week, 50 weeks a year)]

INDUSTRY	1987 SIC [1] code	1991	1992 [2]	INDUSTRY	1987 SIC [1] code	1991	1992 [2]
Private sector 3 . . . . ; . .	(X)	8.4	8.9	Local passenger transit	41	9.5	11.0
Agriculture, forestry, fishing 3	A	10.8	11.6	Trucking and warehousing	42	14.5	13.4
Mining.	B	7.4	7.3	Water transportation	44	11.6	11.5
Metal mining	10	6.5	6.1	Transportation by air	45	14.0	13.8
Coal mining	12	11.1	12.5	Pipelines, except natural gas	46	4.0	3.1
Oil and gas extraction	13	6.4	6.0	Transportation services	47	3.8	3.9
Nonmetallic minerals, exc. fuels . .	14	7.0	6.5	Communications.	48	3.2	3.4
Construction	C	13.0	13.1	Electric, gas, sanitary services . . .	49	7.7	7.6
General building contractors	15	12.0	12.2	Wholesale and retail trade	F, G	7.6	8.4
Heavy construction, except				Wholesale trade	F	7.2	7.6
building	16	12.8	12.1	Retail trade	G	7.7	8.7
Special trade contractors	17	13.5	13.8	Finance, insurance, real estate . . .	H	2.4	2.9
Manufacturing	D	12.7	12.5	Depository institutions	60	1.8	2.1
Durable goods.	(X)	13.6	13.4	Nondepository institutions	61	1.1	1.0
Lumber and wood products	24	16.8	16.3	Security and commodity brokers . .	62	(NA)	0.7
Furniture and fixtures.	25	15.9	14.8	Insurance carriers.	63	2.4	(NA)
Stone, clay, and glass products. . .	32	14.8	13.6	Insurance agents, brokers, and			
Primary metal industries.	33	17.7	17.5	service	64	1.4	1.4
Fabricated metal products	34	17.4	16.8	Real estate	65	5.4	6.8
Industrial machinery and equip . . .	35	11.2	11.1	Holding and other investment			
Electronic/other electric equip . . .	36	8.6	8.4	offices.	67	2.6	2.7 A
Transportation equipment.	37	18.3	18.7	Services 4	I	6.2	7.1
Instruments/related products	38	6.0	5.9	Hotels and other lodging places . .	70	10.3	11.2
Miscellaneous manufacturing				Personal services	72	4.0	5.1
industries.	39	11.3	10.7	Business services	73	5.2	5.4
Nondurable goods	(X)	11.5	11.3	Auto repair, services, and			
Food and kindred products.	20	19.5	18.8	parking	75	6.5	7.8
Tobacco products.	21	6.4	6.0	Miscellaneous repair services	76	7.7	8.7
Textile mill products	22	10.0	9.9	Motion pictures.	78	3.6	(NA)
Apparel and other textile				Amusement and recreation			
products	23	9.2	9.5	services.	79	8.8	10.1
Paper and allied products.	26	11.2	11.0	Health services	80	8.9	10.2
Printing and publishing.	27	6.7	7.3	Legal services	81	0.7	1.2
Chemicals and allied products. . . .	28	6.4	6.0	Educational services	82	3.8	5.6
Petroleum and coal products	29	6.2	5.9	Social services	83	6.6	8.0
Rubber and misc. plastics				Museums, botanical, zoological			
products	30	15.1	14.5	gardens.	84	6.5	7.8
Leather and leather products	31	12.5	12.1	Engineering and management			
Transportation/public utilities . . .	E	9.3	9.1	services.	87	2.3	2.4
Railroad transportation.	40	7.6	6.6	Services, n.e.c. 5	89	(NA)	2.7

NA Not available. X Not applicable. [1] 1987 Standard Industrial Classification; see text, section 13. [2] Data for 1992 exclude fatal work-related injuries and illnesses. Because fatalities account for about 4,200 of the 6.8 million cases, the inclusion of fatalities in the survey estimates would marginally impact the reported rates. [3] Excludes farms with fewer than 11 employees. [4] Includes categories not shown separately. [5] N.e.c means not elsewhere classified.

Source: U.S. Bureau of Labor Statistics, *Occupational Injuries and Illnesses in the United States by Industry,* annual.

No. 681. Work Stoppages: 1960 to 1993

[Excludes work stoppages involving fewer than 1,000 workers and lasting less than 1 day. Information is based on reports of labor disputes appearing in daily newspapers, trade journals, and other public sources. The parties to the disputes are contacted by telephone, when necessary, to clarify details of the stoppages]

YEAR	Number of work stoppages [1]	Workers involved [2] (1,000)	DAYS IDLE		YEAR	Number of work stoppages [1]	Workers involved [2] (1,000)	DAYS IDLE	
			Number [3] (1,000)	Percent estimated working time [4]				Number [3] (1,000)	Percent estimated working time [4]
1960	222	896	13,260	0.09	1981	145	729	16,908	0.07
1965	268	999	15,140	0.10	1982	96	656	9,061	0.04
1969	412	1,576	29,397	0.16	1983	81	909	17,461	0.08
1970	381	2,468	52,761	0.29	1984	62	376	8,499	0.04
1971	298	2,516	35,538	0.19	1985	54	324	7,079	0.03
1972	250	975	16,764	0.09	1986	69	533	11,861	0.05
1973	317	1,400	16,260	0.08	1987	46	174	[5]4,481	0.02
1974	424	1,796	31,809	0.16	1988	40	118	[5]4,381	0.02
1975	235	965	17,563	0.09	1989	51	452	16,996	0.07
1976	231	1,519	23,962	0.12	1990	44	185	5,926	0.02
1977	298	1,212	21,258	0.10	1991	40	392	4,584	0.02
1978	219	1,006	23,774	0.11	1992	35	364	3,989	0.01
1979	235	1,021	20,409	0.09	1993	35	182	3,981	0.01
1980	187	795	20,844	0.09					

[1] Beginning in year indicated. [2] Workers counted more than once if involved in more than one stoppage during the year. [3] Resulting from all stoppages in effect in a year, including those that began in an earlier year. [4] Agricultural and government employees are included in the total working time; private household and forestry and fishery employees are excluded. [5] Revised since originally published.

Source: U.S. Bureau of Labor Statistics, *Compensation and Conditions*, monthly.

No. 682. U.S. Membership in AFL-CIO Affiliated Unions, by Selected Union: 1979 to 1993

[In thousands. Figures represent the labor organizations as constituted in 1989 and reflect past merger activity. Membership figures based on average per capita paid membership to the AFL-CIO for the 2-year period ending in June of the year shown and reflect only actively-employed members. Labor unions shown had a membership of 50,000 or more in 1993]

LABOR ORGANIZATION	1979	1989	1993	LABOR ORGANIZATION	1979	1989	1993
Total [1]	13,621	14,100	13,299	Longshoreman's Association	63	62	58
Actors and Artists	75	97	93	Machinists and Aerospace			
Automobile, Aerospace and				(IAM) [2]	688	517	474
Agriculture (UAW)	(X)	917	771	Marine Engineers			
Bakery, Confectionery and				Beneficial Assn.	23	48	52
Tobacco	131	103	99	Mine Workers	(X)	(X)	75
Boiler Makers, Iron Ship-				Office and Professional			
builders [2][3]	129	75	58	Employees	83	84	89
Bricklayers [2]	106	84	84	Oil, Chemical, Atomic			
Carpenters [2]	626	613	408	Workers (OCAW)	146	71	86
Clothing and Textile Workers				Painters	160	128	106
(ACTWU) [2]	308	180	143	Paperworkers Int'l	262	210	188
Communication Workers				Plumbing and Pipefitting	228	220	220
(CWA)	485	492	472	Postal Workers	245	213	249
Electrical Workers (IBEW)	825	744	710	Retail, Wholesale Depart-			
Electronic, Electrical and				ment Store	122	137	80
Salaried [2][4]	243	171	143	Rubber, Cork, Linoleum,			
Operating Engineers	313	330	305	Plastic	158	92	81
Fire Fighters	150	142	151	Seafarers	84	80	80
Food and Commercial				Service Employees			
Workers (UFCW) [2]	1,123	999	997	(SEIU) [2][5]	537	762	919
Garment Workers (ILGWU)	314	153	133	Sheet Metal Workers	120	108	108
Glass, Molders, Pottery, and				Stage Employees, Moving			
Plastics [2]	50	86	73	Picture Machine Operators	50	50	51
Government, American				State, County, Municipal			
Federation (AFGE) [2]	236	156	149	(AFSCME) [5]	889	1,090	1,167
Graphic Communications [2]	171	124	95	Steelworkers	964	481	421
Hotel Employees and				Teachers (AFT)	423	544	574
Restaurant Employees	373	278	258	Teamsters [6]	(X)	1,161	1,316
Ironworkers	146	111	91	Transit Union	94	96	94
Laborers	475	406	408	Transport Workers	85	85	78
Letter Carriers (NALC)	151	201	210	Transportation Union, United	121	(X)	60

X Not applicable. [1] Includes other AFL-CIO affiliated unions, not shown separately. [2] Figures reflect mergers with one or more unions since 1979. For details see source. [3] Includes Blacksmiths, Forgers, and Helpers. [4] Includes Machine and Furniture Workers. [5] Excludes Hospital and Health Care Employees which merged into both unions on June 1, 1989, (membership of 23,000 in 1985; 60,000 in 1987; and 58,000 in 1989). [6] Includes Chauffeurs, Warehousemen, and Helpers.

Source: American Federation of Labor and Congress of Industrial Organizations, Washington, DC, *Report of the AFL-CIO Executive Council*, biannual.

No. 683. Union Members, by Selected Characteristics: 1983 and 1993

[Annual averages of monthly data. Covers employed wage and salary workers 16 years old and over. Excludes self-employed workers whose businesses are incorporated although they technically qualify as wage and salary workers. See headnote table 630 regarding data by occupation and industry. Based on Current Population Survey, see text, section 1, and Appendix III]

CHARACTERISTIC	EMPLOYED WAGE AND SALARY WORKERS						MEDIAN USUAL WEEKLY EARNINGS [3] (dol.)							
	Total (1,000)		Percent union members [1]		Percent represented by unions [2]		Total		Union members [1]		Represented by unions [2]		Not represented by unions	
	1983	1993	1983	1993	1983	1993	1983	1993	1983	1993	1983	1993	1983	1993
Total	**88,290**	**105,067**	**20.1**	**15.8**	**23.3**	**17.7**	**313**	**463**	**388**	**575**	**383**	**569**	**288**	**426**
16 to 24 years old	19,305	17,193	9.1	5.9	11.1	6.8	210	283	281	377	275	366	203	277
25 to 34 years old	25,978	29,479	19.6	13.0	23.1	14.9	321	439	382	520	376	514	304	420
35 to 44 years old	18,722	28,144	24.8	18.8	28.6	21.1	369	519	411	595	407	593	339	499
45 to 54 years old	13,150	18,885	27.0	23.1	30.5	25.7	366	543	404	622	402	620	335	507
55 to 64 years old	9,201	9,064	26.9	20.8	30.3	23.0	346	492	392	576	390	573	316	462
65 years and over	1,934	2,303	10.1	8.6	12.1	10.0	260	394	338	467	330	462	238	381
Men	47,856	54,776	24.7	18.4	27.7	20.2	378	514	416	608	414	606	349	490
Women	40,433	50,292	14.6	13.0	18.0	15.1	252	395	309	504	307	500	237	374
White	**77,046**	**89,643**	**19.3**	**15.2**	**22.3**	**17.0**	**319**	**478**	**396**	**589**	**391**	**585**	**295**	**444**
Men	42,168	47,186	24.0	18.0	26.9	19.7	387	531	423	619	421	618	362	505
Women	34,877	42,458	13.5	12.1	16.7	14.1	254	403	314	514	313	510	240	382
Black	**8,979**	**11,612**	**27.2**	**21.0**	**31.7**	**23.9**	**261**	**370**	**331**	**490**	**324**	**485**	**222**	**330**
Men	4,477	5,588	31.7	23.2	36.1	25.8	293	392	366	514	360	510	244	345
Women	4,502	6,024	22.7	18.9	27.4	22.0	231	349	292	454	287	447	209	320
Hispanic [4]	**(NA)**	**8,575**	**(NA)**	**15.1**	**(NA)**	**16.6**	**(NA)**	**335**	**(NA)**	**481**	**(NA)**	**478**	**(NA)**	**311**
Men	(NA)	5,085	(NA)	16.3	(NA)	17.5	(NA)	352	(NA)	511	(NA)	509	(NA)	318
Women	(NA)	3,490	(NA)	13.3	(NA)	15.4	(NA)	314	(NA)	413	(NA)	415	(NA)	297
Full-time workers	70,976	85,211	22.9	17.8	26.4	19.9	313	463	388	575	383	569	288	426
Part-time workers	17,314	19,856	8.4	7.2	10.3	8.3	(X)	(X)	(X)	(X)	(X)	(X)	(X)	(X)
Managerial and professional specialty	19,657	27,168	17.1	14.9	21.9	18.0	437	675	423	696	421	688	446	670
Technical sales, and admin. support	28,024	33,429	12.1	10.4	15.0	12.1	281	419	350	509	341	501	270	408
Service occupations	12,875	15,371	15.3	13.8	17.9	15.3	205	293	305	478	299	467	182	265
Precision, production, craft, and repair	10,542	11,024	32.9	25.6	35.7	27.2	377	501	456	642	450	637	322	453
Operators, fabricators, and laborers	15,416	16,316	35.4	24.7	37.9	26.0	275	365	366	501	361	497	226	321
Farming, forestry, and fishing	1,775	1,759	5.5	5.1	6.9	5.7	196	269	292	436	287	413	189	264
Agricultural wage and salary workers	1,446	1,472	3.4	1.6	3.8	2.1	198	277	(B)	(B)	(B)	(B)	195	277
Private nonagr. wage and salary workers	71,225	84,978	16.8	11.2	18.8	12.3	307	441	389	544	385	538	286	420
Mining	869	643	20.7	16.0	23.1	17.6	481	645	470	631	470	631	488	657
Construction	4,109	4,638	27.5	20.0	29.4	21.0	348	482	518	692	510	689	296	425
Manufacturing	19,066	18,710	27.8	19.2	30.5	20.3	335	466	370	505	368	505	315	448
Transportation and public utilities	5,142	6,313	42.4	30.5	46.2	32.5	417	570	449	640	445	631	386	516
Wholesale and retail trade, total	18,081	21,655	8.7	6.3	9.8	6.9	252	356	353	465	348	459	242	347
Finance, insurance, and real estate	5,559	6,783	2.9	1.9	4.1	2.6	296	490	284	484	285	481	297	490
Services	18,400	26,235	7.7	5.8	9.6	7.0	272	420	303	482	303	478	268	416
Government	15,618	18,618	36.7	37.7	45.5	43.8	351	547	386	602	381	596	316	498

B Data not shown where base is less than 50,000. NA Not applicable. X Not applicable. [1] Members of a labor union or an employee association similar to a labor union. [2] Members of a labor union or an employee association similar to a union as well as workers who report no union affiliation but whose jobs are covered by a union or an employee association contract. [3] For full-time employed wage and salary workers; 1983 revised since originally published. [4] Persons of Hispanic origin may be of any race.

Source: U.S. Bureau of Labor Statistics, Employment and Earnings, January issues.

Figure 14.1
Disposable Personal Income Per Person: 1993
(Percent of national average)

United States
$18,177

Less than 95%
95% to 105%
Greater than 105%

Source: Chart prepared by U.S. Bureau of the Census. For data, see table 697.

Income, Expenditures, and Wealth

This section presents data on gross domestic product (GDP), gross national product (GNP), national and personal income, saving and investment, money income, poverty, and national and personal wealth. The data on income and expenditures measure two aspects of the U.S. economy. One aspect relates to the national income and product accounts (NIPA's), a summation reflecting the entire complex of the Nation's economic income and output and the interaction of its major components; the other relates to the distribution of money income to families and individuals, or consumer income.

The primary source for data on GDP, GNP, national and personal income, gross saving and investment, and fixed reproducible tangible wealth is the *Survey of Current Business,* published monthly by the Bureau of Economic Analysis (BEA). A comprehensive revision to the NIPA's was completed in December 1991. A discussion of the revision appears in the August through October, 1991 and the December 1991 issues of *Survey of Current Business.* Detailed historical data appear in *The National Income and Product Accounts of the United States, volume 1, 1929-58* and *volume 2, 1959-88* and the July 1992 and August 1993 issues of *Survey of Current Business*; detailed data for the most recent years are normally published each July in the *Survey.*

Sources of income distribution data are the decennial censuses of population and the Current Population Survey (CPS), both products of the Bureau of the Census (see text, section 1). Annual data on income of families, individuals, and households are presented in *Current Population Reports-Consumer Income,* P60 series.

Data on individuals' saving and assets are published by the Board of Governors of the Federal Reserve System in the quarterly *Flow of Funds Accounts;* and detailed information on personal wealth

In Brief

Gross domestic product, constant (1987) dollars
annual percent change:

1990-91	–0.7
1991-92	2.6
1992-93	3.0

Median household income in 1992: $30,786

Poverty status of persons in 1992:
Number below poverty level:
36.9 million
Percent below poverty level: 14.5

is published periodically by the Internal Revenue Service (IRS) in *SOI Bulletin.*

National income and product.— *Gross domestic product* is the total output of goods and services produced by labor and property located in the United States, valued at market prices. GDP can be viewed in terms of expenditure categories that comprise purchases of goods and services by consumers and government, gross private domestic investment, and net exports of goods and services. The goods and services included are largely those bought for final use (excluding illegal transactions) in the market economy. A number of inclusions, however, represent imputed values, the most important of which is rental value of owner-occupied housing. GDP, in this broad context, measures the output attributable to the factors of production located in the United States. *Gross State product* (GSP) is the gross market value of the goods and services attributable to labor and property located in a State. It is the State counterpart of the Nation's gross domestic product.

Gross national product measures the output attributable to all labor and property supplied by United States residents. GNP differs from "national income" mainly in that GNP includes allowances for depreciation and for indirect business taxes (sales and property taxes); see table 690.

In December 1991, the Bureau of Economic Analysis began featuring gross domestic product rather than gross national product as the primary measure of U.S. production. GDP is now the standard measure of growth because it is the appropriate measure for much of the short-term monitoring and analysis of the economy. In addition, the use of GDP facilitates comparisons of economic activity in the United States with that in other countries. GDP is the primary measure of production in the United Nation's System of National Accounts, the set of international guidelines for economic accounting that the U.S. economic accounts will be moving toward in the mid-1990's. Virtually all other countries already use GDP as their primary measure of production. The dollar levels of GDP and GNP differ little, but percentage changes often differ. The annual rates of growth of real GNP have been slightly less than the annual rates of growth of real GDP in most years of the 1980's. The quarterly differences are larger and they fluctuate more.

National income is the aggregate of labor and property earnings which arises in the current production of goods and services. It is the sum of employee compensation, proprietors' income, rental income of persons, corporate profits, and net interest. It measures the total factor costs of the goods and services produced by the economy. Income is measured before deduction of taxes.

Capital consumption adjustment for corporations, and for nonfarm sole proprietorships and partnerships is the difference between capital consumption based on income tax returns and capital consumption measured at straight-line depreciation, consistent service lives, and replacement cost. The tax return data are valued at historical costs and reflect changes over time in service lives and depreciation patterns as permitted by tax regulations. *Inventory valuation adjustment* represents the difference between the book value of inventories used up in production and the cost of replacing them.

Personal income is the current income received by persons from all sources minus their personal contributions for social insurance. Classified as "persons" are individuals (including owners of unincorporated firms), nonprofit institutions that primarily serve individuals, private trust funds, and private noninsured welfare funds. Personal income includes transfers (payments not resulting from current production) from government and business such as Social Security benefits, public assistance, etc., but excludes transfers among persons. Also included are certain nonmonetary types of income—chiefly estimated net rental value to owner-occupants of their homes and the value of services furnished without payment by financial intermediaries.

Disposable personal income is personal income less personal tax and nontax payments. It is the income available to persons for spending or saving. Personal tax and nontax payments are tax payments (net of refunds) by persons (except personal contributions for social insurance) that are not chargeable to business expense, and certain personal payments to general government that are treated like taxes. Personal taxes include income, estate and gift, and personal property taxes and motor vehicle licenses. Nontax payments include passport fees, fines and forfeitures, and donations.

Consumer Expenditure Survey.—The Consumer Expenditure Survey program was begun in late 1979. The principal objective of the survey is to collect current consumer expenditure data which provide a continuous flow of data on the buying habits of American consumers. The data are necessary for future revisions of the Consumer Price Index.

The survey conducted by the Bureau of the Census for the Bureau of Labor Statistics, consists of two components: (1) An interview panel survey in which the expenditures of consumer units are obtained in five interviews conducted every 3 months; and (2) a diary or record-keeping survey completed by participating households for two consecutive 1-week periods.

Each component of the survey queries an independent sample of consumer units representative of the U.S. total population. Over 52 weeks of the year, 5,000 consumer units are sampled for the diary survey. Each consumer unit keeps a diary for two 1-week periods yielding approximately 10,000 diaries a year. The interview sample is selected on a rotating panel basis, targeted at 5,000 consumer units per quarter. Data are collected in 88 urban and 16 rural areas of the country that are representative of the U.S. total population. The survey includes students in student housing. Data from the two surveys are combined; integration is necessary to permit analysis of total family expenditures because neither the diary nor quarterly interview survey was designed to collect a complete account of consumer spending.

The Diary survey is designed to obtain expenditures on small, frequently purchased items which are normally difficult for respondents to recall. Detailed records of expenses are kept for food and beverages, both at home and in eating places, tobacco, housekeeping supplies, nonprescription drugs, and personal care products and services.

The Interview survey is designed to obtain data on the types of expenditures which respondents can be expected to recall for a period of 3 months or longer. In general, these include relatively large expenditures, such as those for property, automobiles, and major appliances, or expenditures which occur on a fairly regular basis, such as rent, utilities, or insurance premiums. Including "global estimates" for food, it is estimated that about 95 percent of expenditures are covered in the interview. Excluded are nonprescription drugs, household supplies, and personal care items. The interview survey also provides data on expenditures incurred while on trips. Both surveys exclude all business related expenditures for which the family is reimbursed.

Distribution of money income to families and individuals.—Money income statistics are based on data collected in various field surveys of income conducted since 1936. Since 1947, the Bureau of the Census has collected the data on an annual basis and published them in *Current Population Reports,* P60 series. In each of the surveys, field representatives interview samples of the population with respect to income received during the previous year. Money income as defined by the Bureau of the

Census differs from the BEA concept of "personal income."

Data on consumer income collected in the CPS by the Bureau of the Census cover money income received (exclusive of certain money receipts such as capital gains) before payments for personal income taxes, Social Security, union dues, Medicare deductions, etc. Therefore, money income does not reflect the fact that some families receive part of their income in the form of noncash benefits (see section 12) such as food stamps, health benefits, and subsidized housing; that some farm families receive noncash benefits in the form of rent-free housing and goods produced and consumed on the farm; or that noncash benefits are also received by some nonfarm residents which often take the form of the use of business transportation and facilities, full or partial payments by business for retirement programs, medical and educational expenses, etc. These elements should be considered when comparing income levels. For data on noncash benefits, see section 12. None of the aggregate income concepts (GDP, national income, or personal income) is exactly comparable with money income, although personal income is the closest.

Several changes were made in the collection and presentation of data from the March 1980 CPS. The changes include (1) the use of a more detailed income questionnaire for all sample households, (2) the use of an expanded sample, (3) the implementation of the "householder" concept rather than the traditional "head" concept, (4) the exclusion of a small number of "secondary families" from the count of all families, (5) the use of more detailed income intervals in the upper range of the income distribution, (6) the introduction of the new farm definition, and (7) the restriction of the population with income to persons 15 years old and over. For more information on the impact and comparability, see the source.

Beginning in the March 1981 Current Population Survey, 1980 census population controls were used; for income years 1971 through 1979, 1970 census population controls had been used. This change had little impact on income summary measures (means and medians)

and proportional measures (percent distributions and poverty rates); however, use of the controls may have significant impact on the absolute numbers.

Income and poverty data for 1986 are the first estimates based entirely on households selected from the 1980 census-based sample design. Estimates by type of residence categories such as metropolitan, nonmetropolitan, farm, and nonfarm reflect metropolitan areas defined as of June 1984. In addition, the March 1987 CPS income supplement was revised to allow for the coding of larger earnings amounts on the questionnaire. A description of this change and its effect on estimates in this report can be found in *Current Population Reports,* series P60-157.

A new computer processing system was introduced to the March 1989 CPS income supplement. The system in use before this year was first introduced in 1976 but was never fully updated to reflect questionnaire changes. In addition, the programs used to process the CPS file were written in a language which was phased out of Census. The March 1988 file was reprocessed based on the new procedures to better evaluate the new processing procedures and allow year to year comparisons to be made using a consistent processing system. A description of this change and its effect on estimates in this report can be found in *Current Population Reports,* P60-166.

In October 1983, the Census Bureau began to collect data under the new Survey of Income and Program Participation (SIPP). The information supplied by this survey is expected to provide better measures of the status and changes in income distribution and poverty of households and persons in the United States. The data collected in SIPP will be used to study Federal and State aid programs (such as food stamps, welfare, Medicaid, and subsidized housing), to estimate program costs and coverage, and to assess the effects of proposed changes in program eligibility rules or benefit levels. The core questions are repeated at each interview and cover labor force activity, the types and amounts of income received, and participation status in various programs. The core also

contains questions covering attendance in postsecondary schools and private health insurance coverage. Various supplements or topical modules covering areas such as educational attainment, assets and liabilities, and pension plan coverage are periodically included.

Poverty.—Families and unrelated individuals are classified as being above or below the poverty level using the poverty index originated at the Social Security Administration in 1964 and revised by Federal Interagency Committees in 1969 and 1980. The poverty index is based solely on money income and does not reflect the fact that many low-income persons receive noncash benefits such as food stamps, Medicaid, and public housing. The index is based on the Department of Agriculture's 1961 Economy Food Plan and reflects the different consumption requirements of families based on their size and composition. The poverty thresholds are updated every year to reflect changes in the Consumer Price Index. The following technical changes to the thresholds were made in 1981: (1) distinctions based on sex of householder have been eliminated; (2) separate thresholds for farm families have been dropped; and (3) the matrix has been expanded to families of nine or more persons from the old cutoff of seven or more persons. These changes have been incorporated in the calculation of poverty data beginning with 1981.

In the recent past, the Bureau of the Census has published a number of technical papers that presented experimental poverty estimates based on income definitions that counted the value of selected government noncash benefits. The Census Bureau has also published annual reports on after-tax income. The *Current Population Reports,* series P60-186RD brings together the benefit and tax data that previously appeared in the separate reports. This report shows the distribution of income among households and the prevalence of poverty under the official definition of money income and under definitions that add or subtract income components. The types of income that are included in one or more of the definitions: (1) money income excluding capital gains or lump-sum payments before taxes, (2) capital gains,

(3) government cash transfers, (4) Earned Income Tax Credit, (5) the value of employer contributions to health insurance plans, (6) the value of food stamps, (7) the subsidy value of school lunches, (8) the subsidy value of housing assistance, (9) the fungible values of Medicare and Medicaid coverage (that is, the benefits are counted as income to the extent that they free up resources that could have been spent on medical care), and (10) the imputed net return on equity in own home. The types of taxes accounted for are Federal and State income taxes and payroll taxes.

The poverty statistics presented by the Bureau of the Census and Congressional Budget Office reflect alternative adjustments for inflation. The study used a variation of the Consumer Price Index to adjust poverty thresholds for the effects of changing prices since 1967. The alternative measure of inflation uses estimates of the cost of renting equivalent housing to assess homeownership costs; this methodology has been used in the official Consumer Price Index since 1983. See text, section 15, and source for more details.

Personal wealth.—Personal wealth estimates, issued by the IRS, are based on a sample of Federal estate tax returns which must be filed for deceased persons. Estimates are weighted to adjust for age, sex, and "social class" (as determined by the IRS through insurance holdings). Gross estate is the gross value of all assets, including the full face value of life insurance (reduced by policy loans), before reduction by the amount of debts. The level of gross estate or gross assets required for filing estate tax returns was $600,000 in 1989. Net worth is one's level of worth after all debts have been removed.

Statistical reliability.—For a discussion of statistical collection and estimation, sampling procedures, and measures of statistical reliability pertaining to Census Bureau data, see Appendix III.

Historical statistics.—Tabular headnotes provide cross-references, where applicable, to *Historical Statistics of the United States, Colonial Times to 1970.* See Appendix IV.

No. 684. GDP in Current and Constant (1987) Dollars: 1929 to 1993

[In billions of dollars. For explanation of gross domestic product, see text, section 14]

ITEM	1929	1940	1950	1960	1970	1980	1982	1983	1984
CURRENT DOLLARS									
Gross domestic product (GDP)	103.1	100.0	287.0	513.4	1,010.7	2,708.0	3,149.6	3,405.0	3,777.2
Personal consumption expenditures	77.5	71.2	192.7	332.4	646.5	1,748.1	2,059.2	2,257.5	2,460.3
Durable goods	9.2	7.8	30.8	43.5	85.3	212.5	236.5	275.0	317.9
Nondurable goods	37.7	37.0	98.2	153.1	270.4	682.9	772.3	817.8	873.0
Services	30.5	26.4	63.7	135.9	290.8	852.7	1,050.4	1,164.7	1,269.4
Gross private domestic investment	16.7	13.6	54.2	78.7	150.3	467.6	503.4	546.7	718.9
Fixed investment	14.9	11.2	48.3	75.5	148.1	477.1	519.3	552.2	647.8
Nonresidential	11.0	7.7	27.8	49.2	106.7	353.8	413.7	400.2	468.9
Residential	4.0	3.5	20.5	26.3	41.4	123.3	105.7	152.0	178.9
Change in business inventories	1.7	2.4	5.9	3.2	2.3	-9.5	-15.9	-5.5	71.1
Net exports of goods and services	0.4	1.4	0.7	2.4	1.2	-14.7	-20.6	-51.4	-102.7
Exports	5.9	4.8	12.3	25.3	57.0	279.2	282.6	276.7	302.4
Imports	5.6	3.4	11.6	22.8	55.8	293.9	303.2	328.1	405.1
Government purchases	8.6	13.8	39.5	99.8	212.7	507.1	607.6	652.3	700.8
Federal	1.5	6.0	20.2	55.3	100.1	209.1	266.6	292.0	310.9
National defense	-	2.3	14.3	45.3	76.8	142.7	193.8	214.4	233.1
State and local	7.1	7.8	19.3	44.5	112.6	298.0	341.1	360.3	389.9
CONSTANT (1987) DOLLARS									
Gross domestic product (GDP)	821.8	906.0	1,418.5	1,970.8	2,873.9	3,776.3	3,760.3	3,906.6	4,148.5
Personal consumption expenditures	554.5	595.2	874.3	1,210.8	1,813.5	2,447.1	2,503.7	2,619.4	2,746.1
Durable goods	48.1	48.3	95.0	115.4	183.7	262.7	262.5	297.7	338.5
Nondurable goods	238.5	293.0	400.4	526.9	717.2	860.5	872.2	900.3	934.6
Services	267.9	253.9	378.9	568.5	912.5	1,323.9	1,368.9	1,421.4	1,473.0
Gross private domestic investment	152.8	121.8	256.4	290.8	429.7	594.4	540.5	599.5	757.5
Fixed investment	142.1	107.1	233.9	282.7	423.8	602.7	558.0	595.1	689.6
Nonresidential	100.6	69.0	132.5	173.3	292.0	437.8	433.9	420.8	490.2
Residential	41.6	38.1	101.4	109.4	131.8	164.8	124.1	174.2	199.3
Change in business inventories	10.6	14.7	22.5	8.1	5.9	-8.3	-17.5	4.4	67.9
Net exports of goods and services	1.9	8.2	3.2	-7.6	-35.2	30.7	-7.4	-56.1	-122.0
Exports	36.0	37.5	53.0	88.4	161.3	320.5	296.7	285.9	305.7
Imports	34.1	29.2	49.7	96.1	196.4	289.9	304.1	342.1	427.7
Government purchases	112.6	180.7	284.5	476.9	665.8	704.2	723.6	743.8	766.9
Federal	21.9	76.2	145.6	259.0	315.0	284.8	306.0	320.8	331.0
National defense	-	-	-	-	-	194.2	221.4	234.2	245.8
State and local	90.7	104.5	138.9	217.9	350.9	419.4	417.6	423.0	436.0

	1985	1986	1987	1988	1989	1990	1991	1992	1993
CURRENT DOLLARS									
Gross domestic product (GDP)	4,038.7	4,268.6	4,539.9	4,900.4	5,250.8	5,546.1	5,722.9	6,038.5	6,377.9
Personal consumption expenditures	2,667.4	2,850.6	3,052.2	3,296.1	3,523.1	3,761.2	3,906.4	4,139.9	4,391.8
Durable goods	352.9	389.6	403.7	437.1	459.4	468.2	457.8	497.3	537.9
Nondurable goods	919.4	952.2	1,011.1	1,073.8	1,149.5	1,229.2	1,257.9	1,300.9	1,350.0
Services	1,395.1	1,508.8	1,637.4	1,785.2	1,914.2	2,063.8	2,190.7	2,341.6	2,503.9
Gross private domestic investment	714.5	717.6	749.3	793.6	832.3	808.9	736.9	796.5	891.7
Fixed investment	689.9	709.0	723.0	777.4	789.9	802.0	745.5	789.1	876.1
Nonresidential	504.0	492.4	497.8	545.4	568.1	586.7	555.9	565.5	623.7
Residential	185.9	216.6	225.2	232.0	230.9	215.3	189.6	223.6	252.4
Change in business inventories	24.6	8.6	26.3	16.2	33.3	6.9	-8.6	7.3	15.6
Net exports of goods and services	-115.6	-132.5	-143.1	-108.0	-79.7	-71.4	-19.6	-29.6	-63.6
Exports	302.1	319.2	364.0	444.2	508.0	557.1	601.5	640.5	661.7
Imports	417.6	451.7	507.1	552.2	587.7	628.5	621.1	670.1	725.3
Government purchases	772.3	833.0	881.5	918.7	975.2	1,047.4	1,099.3	1,131.8	1,158.1
Federal	344.3	367.8	384.9	387.0	401.6	426.5	445.9	448.8	443.4
National defense	258.6	276.7	292.1	295.6	299.9	314.0	322.5	313.8	303.4
State and local	428.1	465.3	496.6	531.7	573.6	620.9	653.4	683.0	714.6
CONSTANT (1987) DOLLARS									
Gross domestic product (GDP)	4,279.8	4,404.5	4,540.0	4,718.6	4,838.0	4,897.3	4,861.4	4,986.3	5,136.0
Personal consumption expenditures	2,865.8	2,969.1	3,052.2	3,162.4	3,223.3	3,272.6	3,258.6	3,341.8	3,453.2
Durable goods	370.1	402.0	403.7	428.7	440.7	443.1	426.6	456.6	490.0
Nondurable goods	958.7	991.0	1,011.1	1,035.1	1,051.6	1,060.7	1,048.2	1,062.9	1,088.1
Services	1,537.0	1,576.1	1,637.4	1,698.5	1,731.0	1,768.8	1,783.8	1,822.3	1,875.2
Gross private domestic investment	745.9	735.1	749.3	773.4	784.0	746.8	675.7	732.9	820.3
Fixed investment	723.8	726.5	723.0	753.4	754.2	741.1	684.1	726.4	806.0
Nonresidential	521.8	500.3	497.8	530.8	540.0	546.5	514.5	529.2	591.8
Residential	202.0	226.2	225.2	222.7	214.2	194.5	169.5	197.1	214.2
Change in business inventories	22.1	8.5	26.3	19.9	29.8	5.7	-8.4	6.5	14.3
Net exports of goods and services	-145.3	-155.1	-143.0	-104.0	-73.7	-54.7	-19.1	-33.6	-76.5
Exports	309.2	329.6	364.0	421.6	471.8	510.5	543.4	578.0	598.3
Imports	454.6	484.7	507.1	525.7	545.4	565.1	562.5	611.6	674.8
Government purchases	813.4	855.4	881.5	886.8	904.4	932.6	946.3	945.2	938.9
Federal	355.2	373.0	384.9	377.3	376.1	384.1	386.5	373.0	354.9
National defense	265.6	280.6	292.1	287.0	281.4	283.6	281.3	261.2	242.4
State and local	458.2	482.4	496.6	509.6	528.3	548.5	559.7	572.2	584.0

- Represents or rounds to zero.

Source: U.S. Bureau of Economic Analysis, *National Income and Product Accounts of the United States: volume 1, 1929-58*, and *volume 2, 1959-88*, and *Survey of Current Business*, August 1993 and March 1994.

No. 685. Gross Domestic Product, by Industry: 1980 to 1991

[In billions of dollars. 1980 and 1985 data are based on the 1972 Standard Industrial Classification (SIC), and 1990-91 are based on the 1987 SIC. Data include nonfactor charges (capital consumption allowances, indirect business taxes, etc.) as well as factor charges against gross product; corporate profits and capital consumption allowances have been shifted from a company to an establishment basis]

INDUSTRY	CURRENT DOLLARS				CONSTANT (1987) DOLLARS			
	1980	1985	1990	1991	1980	1985	1990	1991
Gross domestic product................	2,708	4,039	5,546	5,723	3,776	4,280	4,897	4,861
Private industries........................	2,370	3,571	4,862	4,993	3,203	3,759	4,324	4,315
Agriculture, forestry, and fishing.............	67	84	112	109	63	82	96	97
Farms	56	67	85	79	51	64	72	70
Agricultural services....................	11	17	27	30	12	18	24	27
Mining [1].............................	113	131	103	92	80	83	92	92
Construction..............................	129	179	240	223	185	209	210	195
Manufacturing............................	588	798	1,025	1,026	725	811	929	908
Durable goods.........................	349	472	564	551	424	468	537	526
Lumber and wood products.............	19	24	31	30	22	25	28	26
Furniture and fixtures.................	8	14	16	16	12	14	14	14
Stone, clay, and glass products..........	18	24	25	23	24	25	26	23
Primary metal industries...............	44	36	44	42	49	35	35	37
Fabricated metal products	45	57	67	65	55	58	60	57
Machinery, except electrical	77	87	(X)	(X)	81	78	(X)	(X)
Industrial machinery..................	(X)	(X)	109	102	(X)	(X)	102	101
Electric and electronic equipment........	55	84	(X)	(X)	70	83	(X)	(X)
Electronic & other electric equipment	(X)	(X)	86	88	(X)	(X)	91	94
Motor vehicles and equipment...........	27	58	46	41	40	63	49	41
Other transportation equipment..........	26	48	65	65	38	47	64	61
Instruments and related products........	20	27	56	59	24	27	50	54
Misc. manufacturing industries.........	10	14	19	19	10	14	17	17
Nondurable goods	239	327	461	475	301	342	392	383
Food and kindred products.............	52	72	97	102	64	75	84	84
Tobacco manufactures.................	7	11	16	17	20	14	9	8
Textile mill products..................	15	17	22	22	17	18	21	21
Apparel and other textile products	17	21	25	26	20	21	24	24
Paper and allied products..............	23	33	46	45	31	36	42	42
Printing and publishing................	33	52	72	73	53	59	62	58
Chemicals and allied products..........	48	67	104	106	58	67	88	86
Petroleum and coal products...........	24	24	40	43	15	23	26	23
Rubber and misc. plastic products	17	26	35	36	19	26	32	32
Leather and leather products...........	4	4	4	4	5	4	4	4
Transportation and public utilities............	242	378	481	506	336	382	463	478
Transportation......................	103	136	177	181	120	137	169	173
Railroad transportation...............	21	22	22	22	19	20	24	25
Local & interurban passenger transit.......	5	7	10	11	9	8	9	9
Trucking and warehousing	40	54	73	73	51	58	69	71
Water transportation	7	8	10	11	9	8	8	8
Transportation by air	18	27	40	42	19	26	40	40
Pipelines, except natural gas...........	5	6	4	5	5	5	5	5
Transportation services	6	11	17	18	9	12	15	15
Communications	69	113	147	155	94	116	141	149
Telephone and telegraph	62	100	123	128	81	103	121	126
Radio and television broadcasting	7	12	24	27	14	13	20	23
Electric, gas, and sanitary services	70	129	158	170	122	129	153	156
Wholesale trade	192	277	363	375	191	273	320	326
Retail trade	245	391	516	532	320	421	478	474
Finance, insurance, and real estate [2]	418	682	982	1,040	693	776	868	878
Services [3]	377	651	1,040	1,090	609	722	869	867
Private households....................	6	7	9	9	7	8	9	8
Government	324	482	676	721	509	528	582	587
Federal	115	171	221	240	179	183	193	194
General government..................	96	140	180	193	139	149	156	157
Government enterprise	19	31	41	47	39	34	37	37
State and local	209	311	455	481	330	345	388	392
General government..................	194	283	413	436	301	313	353	357
Government enterprise	15	28	42	44	29	32	35	35
Statistical discrepancy....................	14	-14	8	10	19	-15	7	8
Residual...............................	(X)	(X)	(X)	(X)	46	8	-15	-48

X Not applicable. [1] For additional mining industries, see table 1163. [2] For additional finance, real estate, and insurance industries, see table 768. [3] For additional service industries, see table 1276.

Source: U.S. Bureau of Economic Analysis, *Survey of Current Business*, May and November 1993.

No. 686. Gross Domestic Product, by Type of Product and Sector: 1980 to 1993

[In billions of dollars]

ITEM	1980	1985	1986	1987	1988	1989	1990	1991	1992	1993
Gross domestic product...	2,708.0	4,038.7	4,268.6	4,539.9	4,900.4	5,250.8	5,546.1	5,722.9	6,038.5	6,377.9
PRODUCT										
Goods..................	1,176.2	1,652.6	1,705.3	1,794.5	1,942.0	2,097.0	2,185.2	2,218.4	2,312.8	2,421.9
Services	1,215.4	1,939.0	2,097.3	2,267.2	2,460.9	2,642.1	2,849.4	3,032.7	3,221.1	3,410.5
Structures	316.4	447.1	466.0	478.2	497.5	511.7	511.5	471.9	504.6	545.5
SECTOR										
Business	2,328.9	3,473.5	3,665.7	3,890.8	4,201.0	4,495.9	4,725.9	4,848.5	5,114.4	5,404.5
Households and institutions	89.3	141.7	153.3	170.5	187.6	206.1	227.5	245.3	267.0	286.3
General government	289.8	423.6	449.6	478.7	511.7	548.8	592.8	629.1	657.1	687.1

Source: U.S. Bureau of Economic Analysis, *National Income and Product Accounts of the United States: volume 2, 1959-88,* and *Survey of Current Business,* August 1993 and March 1994.

No. 687. GDP Components—Annual Percent Change: 1969 to 1993

[Minus sign (-) indicates decrease]

ITEM	1969-1970	1979-1980	1985-1986	1986-1987	1987-1988	1988-1989	1989-1990	1990-1991	1991-1992	1992-1993
CURRENT DOLLARS										
Gross domestic product	5.3	8.8	5.7	6.4	7.9	7.2	5.6	3.2	5.5	5.6
Personal consumption expenditures	7.1	10.4	6.9	7.1	8.0	6.9	6.8	3.9	6.0	6.1
Durable goods............	-1.0	-0.8	10.4	3.6	8.3	5.1	1.9	-2.2	8.6	8.2
Nondurable goods	7.2	11.3	3.6	6.2	6.2	7.0	6.9	2.3	3.4	3.8
Services.................	9.6	12.8	8.1	8.5	9.0	7.2	7.8	6.1	6.9	6.9
Gross private domestic investment.	-3.2	-2.6	0.4	4.4	5.9	4.9	-2.8	-8.9	8.1	12.0
Fixed investment	1.8	2.1	2.8	2.0	7.5	2.8	-0.4	-7.0	5.8	11.0
Nonresidential	3.7	8.4	-2.3	1.1	9.6	4.2	3.3	-5.2	1.7	10.3
Residential.............	-2.8	-12.6	16.5	4.0	3.0	-0.5	-6.8	-11.9	17.9	12.9
Exports of goods and services ...	15.6	22.0	5.7	14.0	22.0	14.4	9.7	8.0	6.5	3.3
Imports of goods and services....	10.5	16.3	8.2	12.3	8.9	6.4	6.9	-1.2	7.9	8.2
Government purchases	5.4	13.1	7.9	5.8	4.2	6.1	7.4	5.0	3.0	2.3
Federal	-0.4	16.6	6.8	4.6	0.5	3.8	6.2	4.5	0.7	-1.2
State and local	11.2	10.7	8.7	6.7	7.1	7.9	8.2	5.2	4.5	4.6
CONSTANT (1987) DOLLARS										
Gross domestic product	-	-0.5	2.9	3.1	3.9	2.5	1.2	-0.7	2.6	3.0
Personal consumption expenditures	2.4	-0.1	3.6	2.8	3.6	1.9	1.5	-0.4	2.6	3.3
Durable goods............	-3.7	-9.1	8.6	0.4	6.2	2.8	0.5	-3.7	7.0	7.3
Nondurable goods	2.0	-0.3	3.4	2.0	2.4	1.6	0.9	-1.2	1.4	2.4
Services.................	4.0	2.1	2.5	3.9	3.7	1.9	2.2	0.8	2.2	2.9
Gross private domestic investment.	-6.9	-11.2	-1.4	1.9	3.2	1.4	-4.7	-9.5	8.5	11.9
Fixed investment	-2.9	-8.1	0.4	-0.5	4.2	0.1	-1.7	-7.7	6.2	11.0
Nonresidential	-1.5	-2.5	-4.1	-0.5	6.6	1.7	1.2	-5.9	2.9	11.8
Residential.............	-5.9	-20.5	12.0	-0.4	-1.1	-3.8	-9.2	-12.9	16.3	8.7
Exports of goods and services ...	9.1	9.2	6.6	10.4	15.8	11.9	8.2	6.4	6.4	3.5
Imports of goods and services....	3.8	-4.7	6.6	4.6	3.7	3.7	3.6	-0.5	8.7	10.3
Government purchases	-2.4	2.2	5.2	3.1	0.6	2.0	3.1	1.5	-0.1	-0.7
Federal	-7.4	4.8	5.0	3.2	-2.0	-0.3	2.1	0.6	-3.5	-4.9
State and local	2.6	0.4	5.3	2.9	2.6	3.7	3.8	2.0	2.2	2.1

- Represents or rounds to zero.

Source: U.S. Bureau of Economic Analysis, *National Income and Product Accounts of the United States: volume 2, 1959-88,* and *Survey of Current Business,* August 1993 and March 1994.

No. 688. Gross State Product in Current and Constant (1987) Dollars: 1980 to 1990

[In billions of dollars. For definition of gross State product, see text, section 14]

DIVISION AND STATE	CURRENT DOLLARS					CONSTANT (1987) DOLLARS				
	1980	1985	1988	1989	1990	1980	1985	1988	1989	1990
United States	2,685	4,038	4,913	5,234	5,499	3,687	4,261	4,730	4,842	4,877
New England	141	229	303	320	327	200	246	292	297	291
Maine	10	16	21	23	23	14	17	20	21	21
New Hampshire	9	16	22	23	24	13	18	22	21	21
Vermont	5	7	10	11	11	7	8	10	10	10
Massachusetts	67	110	145	152	154	95	118	139	141	137
Rhode Island	10	15	19	20	21	13	16	18	19	19
Connecticut	41	65	86	91	94	58	70	83	85	84
Middle Atlantic	440	663	839	883	920	625	711	808	820	817
New York	221	340	428	448	467	321	366	415	419	416
New Jersey	89	144	191	201	208	125	154	182	185	184
Pennsylvania	129	179	221	234	245	179	191	211	216	217
East North Central	483	683	813	865	895	666	726	783	802	798
Ohio	123	170	202	214	222	167	180	193	198	198
Indiana	59	83	100	109	112	81	88	96	100	100
Illinois	145	203	245	261	272	200	216	236	242	242
Michigan	103	153	177	186	188	145	163	172	174	169
Wisconsin	53	74	89	95	101	73	79	86	88	89
West North Central	196	281	327	352	369	265	298	314	325	328
Minnesota	49	73	88	96	100	66	77	84	88	89
Iowa	34	42	48	53	56	45	45	46	49	50
Missouri	53	79	94	100	104	73	85	91	93	93
North Dakota	8	11	10	11	12	10	11	10	10	11
South Dakota	7	10	11	12	13	9	11	11	11	12
Nebraska	18	26	29	31	33	24	27	28	29	30
Kansas	28	40	46	48	51	37	42	45	45	45
South Atlantic	385	627	815	874	921	550	674	782	806	815
Delaware	7	12	16	18	20	10	13	15	17	17
Maryland	45	73	96	103	109	65	79	92	95	96
District of Columbia	18	26	32	35	36	28	28	31	32	32
Virginia	58	95	125	135	142	85	103	120	124	125
West Virginia	19	23	26	27	28	24	24	25	25	26
North Carolina	59	96	125	134	141	86	103	119	123	124
South Carolina	27	43	56	60	64	38	46	54	55	57
Georgia	56	96	124	131	137	77	103	119	121	122
Florida	96	163	215	231	245	136	176	206	213	217
East South Central	139	201	247	261	273	190	213	237	241	243
Kentucky	37	50	60	64	67	50	53	58	60	60
Tennessee	45	68	87	92	95	62	73	83	85	85
Alabama	35	52	63	67	70	48	55	61	62	63
Mississippi	22	31	36	38	40	29	32	35	35	35
West South Central	332	481	497	523	558	411	473	481	483	489
Arkansas	20	29	35	37	39	27	31	33	34	34
Louisiana	65	85	83	85	91	75	79	80	78	78
Oklahoma	38	51	51	54	56	48	51	50	50	50
Texas	210	315	328	348	372	262	312	317	322	327
Mountain	140	209	241	256	271	187	218	232	238	242
Montana	9	11	12	13	13	12	11	12	12	12
Idaho	10	14	16	18	19	14	15	15	16	16
Wyoming	11	13	12	12	13	12	12	12	11	11
Colorado	37	58	64	68	71	51	61	62	63	63
New Mexico	16	23	23	25	27	20	23	23	23	24
Arizona	29	49	62	65	67	41	52	60	60	60
Utah	15	24	27	28	31	21	25	26	26	27
Nevada	12	18	25	28	31	17	19	24	26	27
Pacific	428	663	832	899	964	594	702	801	832	854
Washington	51	72	91	100	109	71	78	87	92	97
Oregon	30	39	48	52	55	42	42	46	48	49
California	320	508	647	698	745	446	541	623	645	660
Alaska	16	26	22	23	26	17	22	22	22	23
Hawaii	12	18	24	26	29	18	20	23	24	25

Source: U.S. Bureau of Economic Analysis, *Survey of Current Business*, December 1993; and unpublished data.

No. 689. Gross State Product, by Industry: 1990

[In billions of dollars. For definition of gross state product, see text, section 14. Industries based on 1987 Standard Industrial Classification]

DIVISION AND STATE	Total [1]	Farms, forestry, fisher- ies [2]	Con- struction	Manu- facturing	Trans- portation, public utilities	Whole- sale trade	Retail trade	Finance, insur- ance, real estate	Services	Govern- ment [3]
United States ...	5,499	111	241	1,018	482	360	516	975	1,041	656
New England	327	3	14	64	22	22	31	68	71	32
Maine.........	23	1	1	4	2	1	3	4	4	3
New Hampshire....	24	(Z)	1	5	1	1	3	5	5	2
Vermont.........	11	(Z)	1	2	1	1	1	2	2	1
Massachusetts.....	154	1	6	28	10	11	13	31	38	15
Rhode Island......	21	(Z)	1	4	1	1	2	4	4	2
Connecticut.......	94	1	4	19	7	7	9	21	18	8
Middle Atlantic	920	7	39	154	82	66	76	197	198	98
New York........	467	3	18	67	40	33	36	112	105	53
New Jersey.......	208	1	10	37	19	18	17	42	43	21
Pennsylvania......	245	3	11	50	23	15	22	44	50	24
East North Central....	895	16	37	227	76	61	83	146	156	89
Ohio...........	222	3	9	61	19	14	21	34	38	22
Indiana..........	112	3	5	33	10	6	11	16	16	11
Illinois	272	4	12	53	25	22	24	50	53	26
Michigan.........	188	3	7	51	14	12	18	30	33	20
Wisconsin........	101	4	4	28	8	6	9	16	15	10
West North Central ...	369	20	14	73	35	26	34	59	61	43
Minnesota........	100	4	4	22	8	7	9	17	17	11
Iowa...........	56	5	2	13	5	4	5	9	8	6
Missouri.........	104	2	4	22	11	7	10	16	19	11
North Dakota......	12	1	(Z)	1	1	1	1	2	2	2
South Dakota......	13	2	(Z)	1	1	1	1	3	2	2
Nebraska	33	3	1	5	3	3	3	5	5	5
Kansas.........	51	2	2	10	6	4	5	8	8	7
South Atlantic.......	921	16	47	154	81	58	92	152	175	139
Delaware	20	(Z)	1	5	1	1	1	6	3	2
Maryland	109	1	8	11	9	6	11	20	23	18
District of Columbia .	36	(Z)	1	1	2	1	2	5	12	13
Virginia..........	142	2	8	23	12	8	13	23	26	27
West Virginia......	28	(Z)	1	5	4	1	3	4	4	3
North Carolina....	141	3	6	44	11	9	14	19	19	17
South Carolina....	64	1	4	16	6	3	7	8	9	10
Georgia	137	2	6	26	14	13	13	21	23	17
Florida..........	245	6	13	23	22	17	29	47	56	32
East South Central ...	273	7	10	65	25	16	28	38	42	37
Kentucky	67	2	3	17	6	3	6	9	10	8
Tennessee	95	2	4	22	7	7	11	14	17	12
Alabama........	70	2	3	16	7	4	6	9	11	11
Mississippi	40	1	1	10	5	2	4	6	5	5
West South Central ...	558	12	20	101	57	35	52	83	89	62
Arkansas........	39	2	1	10	4	2	4	5	5	4
Louisiana	91	1	3	17	9	4	7	13	13	9
Oklahoma........	56	2	2	9	6	3	6	8	9	8
Texas..........	372	7	14	65	38	25	35	57	62	41
Mountain..........	271	8	12	31	27	15	27	44	55	38
Montana.........	13	1	(Z)	1	2	1	2	2	2	2
Idaho..........	19	2	1	3	2	1	2	3	3	2
Wyoming........	13	(Z)	(Z)	1	2	(Z)	1	2	1	2
Colorado........	71	2	3	10	7	5	7	12	15	10
New Mexico	27	1	1	2	3	1	3	4	5	5
Arizona.........	67	1	3	9	6	4	8	12	13	10
Utah	31	(Z)	1	5	3	2	3	5	6	5
Nevada	31	(Z)	2	1	3	1	3	5	10	3
Pacific...........	964	23	46	150	75	62	93	188	194	118
Washington.......	109	4	5	21	9	8	11	18	18	16
Oregon.........	55	2	2	11	5	4	5	9	10	7
California	745	16	36	116	55	48	72	152	157	86
Alaska..........	26	1	1	1	3	(Z)	1	4	2	4
Hawaii..........	29	(Z)	2	1	3	1	3	6	6	6

Z Less than $500 million.   [1] Includes mining not shown separately.   [2] Includes agricultural services.   [3] Includes Federal civilian and military and State and local government.

Source: U.S. Bureau of Economic Analysis, *Survey of Current Business*, December 1993.

No. 690. Relation of GDP, GNP, Net National Product, National Income, Personal Income, Disposable Personal Income, and Personal Saving: 1980 to 1993

[In billions of dollars. For definitions, see text, section 14]

ITEM	1980	1985	1987	1988	1989	1990	1991	1992	1993
Gross domestic product	2,708.0	4,038.7	4,539.9	4,900.4	5,250.8	5,546.1	5,722.9	6,038.5	6,377.9
Plus: Receipts of factor income from the rest of the world [1]	80.6	97.3	105.1	128.7	157.5	168.6	146.1	129.2	131.7
Less: Payments of factor income to the rest of the world [2]	46.5	82.4	100.5	120.8	141.5	146.9	131.9	121.9	131.6
Equals: Gross national product	2,742.1	4,053.6	4,544.5	4,908.2	5,266.8	5,567.8	5,737.1	6,045.8	6,378.1
Less: Consumption of fixed capital	311.9	454.5	502.2	534.0	580.4	602.7	626.1	657.9	671.3
Equals: Net national product [3]	2,430.2	3,599.1	4,042.4	4,374.2	4,686.4	4,965.1	5,111.0	5,387.9	5,706.8
Less: Indirect business tax and nontax liability	212.0	329.9	365.0	385.3	414.7	444.0	476.6	502.8	530.5
Plus: Subsidies [4]	4.8	6.4	14.1	10.9	5.4	5.4	-0.3		7.0
Equals: National income	2,198.2	3,268.4	3,692.3	4,002.6	4,249.5	4,491.0	4,598.3	4,836.6	5,140.9
Less: Corporate profits [5]	177.7	280.8	319.8	365.0	362.8	380.6	369.5	407.2	467.3
Net interest	191.2	326.2	360.4	387.7	452.7	463.7	462.8	442.0	445.6
Contributions for social insurance	216.6	353.8	400.7	442.3	473.2	503.1	528.4	555.6	585.3
Plus: Personal interest income	274.0	498.1	548.1	583.2	668.2	698.2	715.6	694.3	695.2
Personal dividend income	57.1	87.9	100.4	108.4	126.5	144.4	127.9	140.4	158.3
Government transfer payments to persons	312.6	468.1	521.3	555.9	603.8	666.3	749.2	836.8	890.2
Business transfer payments to persons	8.8	17.8	20.8	20.8	21.1	21.3	20.7	21.6	21.9
Wage accruals less disbursements	-	-0.2	-	-	-	0.1	-0.1	-20.0	20.0
Equals: Personal income	2,265.4	3,379.8	3,802.0	4,075.9	4,380.3	4,673.8	4,850.9	5,144.9	5,388.3
Less: Personal tax and nontax payments	312.4	436.8	512.5	527.7	593.3	623.3	620.4	644.8	681.6
Equals: Disposable personal income	1,952.9	2,943.0	3,289.5	3,548.2	3,787.0	4,050.5	4,230.5	4,500.2	4,706.7
Less: Personal outlays	1,799.1	2,753.7	3,147.5	3,392.5	3,634.9	3,880.6	4,029.0	4,261.5	4,516.8
Equals: Personal saving	153.8	189.3	142.0	155.7	152.1	170.0	201.5	238.7	189.9

- Represents or rounds to zero.   [1] Consists largely of receipts by U.S. residents of interest and dividends and reinvested earnings of foreign affiliates of U.S. corporations.   [2] Consists largely of payments to foreign residents of interest and dividends and reinvested earnings of U.S. affiliates of foreign corporations.   [3] Includes items not shown separately.   [4] Less current surplus of government enterprises.   [5] With inventory valuation and capital consumption adjustments.

Source: U.S. Bureau of Economic Analysis, National Income and Product Accounts of the United States: volume 2, 1959-88, and Survey of Current Business, August 1993 and March 1994.

No. 691. Selected Per Capita Income and Product Items: 1929 to 1993

[Based on Bureau of the Census estimated population including Armed Forces abroad; based on quarterly averages. Prior to 1960, excludes Alaska and Hawaii]

YEAR	CURRENT DOLLARS					CONSTANT (1987) DOLLARS			
	Gross domestic product	Gross national product	Personal income	Disposable personal income	Personal consumption expenditures	Gross domestic product	Gross national product	Disposable personal income	Personal consumption expenditures
1929	846	852	691	672	636	6,743	6,789	4,807	4,550
1930	734	739	611	594	570	6,079	6,122	4,402	4,221
1940	757	760	586	568	539	6,857	6,878	4,747	4,505
1945	1,523	1,526	1,215	1,068	857	11,453	11,470	6,367	5,107
1950	1,892	1,902	1,502	1,369	1,270	9,352	9,398	6,214	5,764
1955	2,446	2,461	1,903	1,693	1,568	10,699	10,764	6,842	6,335
1960	2,840	2,858	2,264	1,994	1,839	10,903	10,969	7,264	6,698
1965	3,616	3,643	2,845	2,527	2,287	12,712	12,807	8,508	7,703
1970	4,928	4,959	4,052	3,521	3,152	14,013	14,099	9,875	8,842
1971	5,283	5,320	4,302	3,779	3,372	14,232	14,329	10,111	9,022
1972	5,750	5,791	4,671	4,042	3,658	14,801	14,904	10,414	9,425
1973	6,368	6,428	5,184	4,521	4,002	15,422	15,564	11,013	9,752
1974	6,819	6,893	5,637	4,893	4,337	15,185	15,346	10,832	9,602
1975	7,343	7,404	6,053	5,329	4,745	14,917	15,036	10,906	9,711
1976	8,109	8,187	6,632	5,796	5,241	15,502	15,646	11,192	10,121
1977	8,961	9,055	7,269	6,316	5,772	16,039	16,201	11,406	10,425
1978	10,029	10,127	8,121	7,042	6,384	16,635	16,795	11,851	10,744
1979	11,055	11,198	9,032	7,787	7,035	16,867	17,082	12,039	10,876
1980	11,892	12,042	9,948	8,576	7,677	16,584	16,790	12,005	10,746
1981	13,177	13,321	11,021	9,455	8,375	16,710	16,890	12,156	10,770
1982	13,564	13,694	11,589	9,989	8,868	16,194	16,348	12,146	10,782
1983	14,531	14,657	12,216	10,642	9,634	16,672	16,813	12,349	11,179
1984	15,978	16,081	13,345	11,673	10,408	17,549	17,659	13,029	11,617
1985	16,933	16,995	14,170	12,339	11,184	17,944	18,007	13,258	12,015
1986	17,735	17,773	14,917	13,010	11,843	18,299	18,337	13,552	12,336
1987	18,694	18,712	15,655	13,545	12,568	18,694	18,712	13,545	12,568
1988	19,994	20,026	16,630	14,477	13,448	19,252	19,284	13,890	12,903
1989	21,224	21,289	17,706	15,307	14,241	19,556	19,615	14,005	13,029
1990	22,189	22,276	18,699	16,205	15,048	19,593	19,670	14,101	13,093
1991	22,647	22,703	19,196	16,741	15,459	19,238	19,290	13,965	12,895
1992	23,637	23,665	20,139	17,615	16,205	19,518	19,548	14,219	13,081
1993	24,696	24,697	20,864	18,225	17,006	19,888	19,897	14,330	13,372

Source: U.S. Bureau of Economic Analysis, National Income and Product Accounts of the United States: volume 1, 1929-58, and volume 2, 1959-88, and Survey of Current Business, August 1993 and March 1994.

No. 692. National Income, by Type of Income: 1980 to 1993

[In billions of dollars]

INCOME	1980	1985	1987	1988	1989	1990	1991	1992	1993
National income	2,198.2	3,268.4	3,692.3	4,002.6	4,249.5	4,491.0	4,598.3	4,836.6	5,140.3
Compensation of employees	1,644.4	2,382.8	2,698.7	2,921.3	3,100.2	3,297.6	3,402.4	3,582.0	3,772.2
Wages and salaries	1,376.6	1,986.3	2,261.2	2,443.0	2,586.4	2,745.0	2,814.9	2,953.1	3,100.5
Government	261.4	373.7	421.8	449.0	478.5	516.0	545.3	567.5	589.7
Other	1,115.2	1,612.6	1,839.4	1,994.0	2,107.9	2,229.0	2,269.6	2,385.6	2,510.8
Supplements to wages and salaries	267.8	396.5	437.4	478.3	513.8	552.5	587.5	629.0	671.7
Employer contributions for social insurance	127.9	204.7	227.1	247.8	261.9	278.3	290.6	306.3	321.0
Other labor income	139.8	191.8	210.4	230.5	251.9	274.3	296.9	322.7	350.7
Proprietors' income [1][2]	171.8	259.9	310.2	324.3	347.3	363.3	376.4	414.3	443.2
Farm	11.5	21.5	31.3	30.9	40.2	41.9	36.8	43.7	46.0
Nonfarm	160.3	238.4	279.0	293.4	307.0	321.4	339.5	370.6	397.3
Rental income of persons [1]	13.2	18.7	3.2	4.3	-13.5	-14.2	-12.8	-8.9	12.6
Corporate profits [1][2]	177.7	280.8	319.8	365.0	362.8	380.6	369.5	407.2	466.6
Corporate profits [2]	197.8	225.3	273.4	320.3	325.4	354.7	367.3	390.1	442.3
Profits before tax	240.9	225.0	287.9	347.5	342.9	365.7	362.3	395.4	449.4
Profits tax liability	84.8	96.5	127.1	137.0	141.3	138.7	129.8	146.3	174.0
Profits after tax	156.1	128.5	160.8	210.5	201.6	227.1	232.5	249.1	275.4
Dividends	59.0	92.4	106.2	115.3	134.6	153.5	137.4	150.5	169.0
Undistributed profits	97.1	36.1	54.6	95.2	67.1	73.6	95.2	98.6	106.4
Inventory valuation adjustment	-43.0	0.2	-14.5	-27.3	-17.5	-11.0	4.9	-5.3	-7.1
Capital consumption adjustment	-20.2	55.5	46.4	44.7	37.4	25.9	2.2	17.1	24.3
Net interest	191.2	326.2	360.4	387.7	452.7	463.7	462.8	442.0	445.6
Addenda:									
Corporate profits after tax [1][2]	92.9	184.2	192.8	228.0	221.5	241.9	239.7	260.9	292.6
Net cash flow [1][2]	218.9	369.7	394.2	440.3	439.3	456.7	485.6	507.0	532.4
Undistributed profits [1][2]	33.9	91.9	86.5	112.6	86.9	88.5	102.3	110.4	123.6
Consumption of fixed capital	185.1	277.8	307.7	327.6	352.4	368.2	383.2	396.6	408.8
Less: Inventory valuation adjustment	-43.0	0.2	-14.5	-27.3	-17.5	-11.0	4.9	-5.3	-7.1
Equals: Net cash flow	262.0	369.5	408.7	467.5	456.9	467.7	480.6	512.3	539.5

[1] With capital consumption adjustment. [2] With inventory valuation adjustment.

Source: U.S. Bureau of Economic Analysis, *National Income and Product Accounts of the United States, volume 2, 1959-88,* and *Survey of Current Business,* August 1992 and April 1994.

No. 693. National Income, by Sector: 1980 to 1992

[In billions of dollars]

SECTOR	1980	1985	1986	1987	1988	1989	1990	1991	1992
National income	2,198.2	3,268.4	3,437.9	3,692.3	4,002.6	4,249.5	4,491.0	4,598.3	4,836.6
Domestic business	1,785.0	2,688.3	2,825.9	3,038.5	3,295.4	3,478.6	3,649.1	3,709.7	3,905.3
Corporate business	1,318.8	1,957.9	2,050.7	2,208.7	2,399.1	2,524.6	2,643.1	2,676.8	2,815.5
Compensation of employees	1,119.4	1,615.3	1,710.5	1,816.1	1,965.2	2,075.8	2,185.0	2,225.8	2,337.4
Corporate profits [1]	142.7	250.0	238.7	280.3	315.9	303.4	312.6	302.6	344.9
Net interest	56.7	92.6	101.5	112.2	118.0	145.5	145.6	148.4	133.2
Sole proprietorships and partnerships	310.9	470.6	504.5	541.5	584.9	631.0	658.5	671.6	721.9
Compensation of employees	104.9	139.1	142.9	160.7	177.8	185.9	202.0	207.6	220.0
Proprietors' income [1]	170.5	258.2	282.2	308.6	322.5	345.4	361.4	374.4	415.2
Net interest	35.4	73.3	79.4	72.1	84.6	99.7	95.1	89.6	86.7
Other private business [2]	122.1	210.3	218.8	232.9	251.0	259.3	278.5	288.6	290.6
Compensation of employees	7.8	13.8	15.7	17.2	18.7	20.1	21.7	22.1	23.3
Proprietors' income [1]	1.3	1.7	1.6	1.6	1.8	1.9	2.0	1.9	-0.9
Rental income of persons [3]	13.2	18.7	8.7	3.2	4.3	-13.5	-14.2	-12.8	-8.9
Net interest	99.8	176.0	192.8	210.8	226.2	250.9	269.1	277.4	277.0
Government enterprises [4]	33.2	49.6	52.0	55.6	60.4	63.7	68.9	72.7	77.3
Households and institutions [5]	89.3	141.7	153.3	170.5	187.6	206.1	227.5	245.3	267.0
General government [4]	289.8	423.6	449.6	478.7	511.7	548.8	592.8	629.1	657.1
Rest of the world	34.1	14.8	9.1	4.6	7.9	16.0	21.7	14.2	7.3

[1] With inventory valuation and capital consumption adjustments. [2] Consists of all business activities reported on the individual income tax return in Schedule E—Supplemental Income Schedule; tax-exempt cooperatives; and owner-occupied nonfarm housing and buildings and equipment owned and used by nonprofit institutions servicing individuals, which are considered to be business activities selling their current services to their owners. [3] With capital consumption adjustment. [4] Compensation of employees. [5] Compensation of employees in private households; nonprofit social and athletic clubs; labor organizations; nonprofit schools and hospitals; religious, charitable, and welfare organizations; and all other nonprofit organizations serving individuals.

Source: U.S. Bureau of Economic Analysis, *National Income and Product Accounts of the United States, volume 2, 1959-88,* and *Survey of Current Business,* September 1993.

No. 694. Personal Consumption Expenditures, by Type of Expenditure: 1980 to 1992

[In billions of dollars]

EXPENDITURE	CURRENT DOLLARS				CONSTANT (1987) DOLLARS			
	1980	1990	1991	1992	1980	1990	1991	1992
Personal consumption expenditures [1]	1,748.1	3,761.2	3,906.4	4,139.9	2,447.1	3,272.6	3,258.6	3,341.8
Food and tobacco [1]	362.6	648.2	666.8	684.5	487.5	555.8	548.7	551.5
Food purchased for off-premise consumption	241.7	400.2	411.1	418.0	307.5	345.0	341.9	343.0
Purchased meals and beverages [2]	93.4	193.1	198.5	203.5	132.3	168.8	166.7	167.3
Tobacco products	20.9	43.4	45.4	50.9	38.7	32.0	30.0	30.9
Clothing, accessories, and jewelry [1]	131.8	259.3	264.3	282.4	157.1	229.6	225.6	235.4
Shoes	17.4	31.4	31.3	32.3	19.9	28.1	27.2	27.2
Clothing	89.8	175.7	181.6	195.7	106.0	157.9	157.4	166.3
Jewelry and watches	15.0	31.3	31.6	34.0	16.8	25.4	24.5	25.3
Personal care	26.9	59.2	60.9	63.2	38.0	52.3	51.9	52.6
Housing [1]	255.2	547.5	574.4	600.0	399.4	474.6	478.6	484.2
Owner-occupied nonfarm dwellings-space rent	178.4	379.5	399.1	417.8	278.7	326.6	330.7	334.8
Tenant-occupied nonfarm dwellings-space rent	61.8	141.1	147.7	153.8	98.2	125.5	126.9	128.8
Household operation [1]	233.6	437.3	452.7	475.2	315.3	408.4	412.5	427.2
Furniture [3]	20.7	36.7	36.8	40.0	25.8	34.8	34.7	36.4
Semidurable house furnishings [4]	10.6	21.2	21.9	23.6	14.9	19.8	20.2	21.3
Cleaning and polishing preparations	22.9	51.8	53.0	54.2	31.2	45.5	45.2	46.2
Household utilities	81.1	136.7	145.3	149.9	111.7	124.3	128.0	128.8
Electricity	37.2	70.8	76.2	76.4	54.0	66.2	68.7	67.5
Gas	19.1	26.7	28.1	29.4	27.6	26.1	27.1	27.8
Water and other sanitary services	9.4	26.1	28.0	30.3	16.2	21.5	21.4	21.6
Fuel oil and coal	15.4	13.2	13.0	13.8	14.0	10.5	10.7	11.9
Telephone and telegraph	27.6	53.8	56.2	58.7	41.1	54.9	56.9	59.1
Medical care [1]	207.2	597.8	651.7	704.6	346.5	483.5	495.1	504.9
Drug preparations and sundries [5]	21.8	60.6	64.4	65.9	38.8	49.3	48.8	47.2
Physicians	42.8	133.8	144.0	153.1	72.9	108.5	110.2	110.2
Dentists	13.7	31.6	32.9	36.4	22.4	26.1	25.3	26.2
Hospitals and nursing homes [6]	98.7	268.4	295.9	323.9	164.0	217.1	224.6	233.4
Health insurance	12.8	36.6	40.0	45.9	23.0	25.2	25.5	25.5
Medical care [7]	7.6	30.8	35.0	39.6	17.7	19.9	20.0	20.4
Personal business [1]	101.6	296.0	323.4	356.0	175.5	249.7	254.8	259.6
Expense of handling life insurance [8]	23.4	57.5	66.1	69.6	37.8	49.8	55.3	55.0
Legal services	13.6	49.2	49.9	54.0	26.6	41.5	39.8	41.0
Funeral and burial expenses	4.6	8.5	9.0	9.6	8.8	7.4	7.3	7.5
Transportation [1]	235.7	453.9	434.6	463.1	274.8	401.8	373.6	389.0
User-operated transportation [1]	214.9	414.0	395.5	423.9	247.4	369.1	340.2	356.2
New autos	46.4	96.6	79.5	87.3	60.2	91.5	72.7	77.9
Net purchases of used autos	10.8	33.1	36.7	39.5	20.8	33.0	35.1	36.0
Tires, tubes, accessories, etc.	14.9	22.9	23.3	23.7	15.3	21.8	22.0	22.1
Repair, greasing, washing, parking, storage, rental, and leasing	33.7	82.6	82.4	89.5	48.3	72.6	69.7	73.1
Gasoline and oil	86.7	108.4	102.9	103.4	72.0	86.4	83.1	83.9
Purchased local transportation	4.8	8.9	9.1	9.2	7.8	7.9	7.6	7.3
Mass transit systems	2.9	5.7	5.7	5.9	5.3	5.1	4.9	4.8
Taxicab	1.9	3.2	3.4	3.3	2.5	2.8	2.7	2.6
Purchased intercity transportation [1]	16.1	30.9	30.0	30.0	19.7	26.2	25.8	25.4
Railway (commutation)	0.3	0.7	0.7	0.7	0.5	0.6	0.6	0.5
Bus	1.4	1.4	1.5	1.5	2.4	1.3	1.3	1.3
Airline	13.5	26.4	25.6	25.7	15.2	22.4	22.2	21.9
Recreation [1] [9]	117.6	285.7	299.4	318.8	149.1	261.9	269.1	283.7
Magazines, newspapers, and sheet music	12.0	23.8	24.7	25.4	18.4	20.9	20.3	20.1
Nondurable toys and sport supplies	14.6	32.1	33.5	35.2	17.4	28.7	29.5	30.5
Radio and television receivers, records, and musical instruments	19.9	50.4	55.4	59.1	17.6	54.1	62.7	70.3
Education and research	33.6	86.2	91.8	98.2	51.7	73.6	74.3	75.8
Religious and welfare activities	38.6	101.6	105.7	116.2	51.3	90.1	90.7	97.2

[1] Includes other expenditures not shown separately.   [2] Consists of purchases (including tips) of meals and beverages from retail, service, and amusement establishments; hotels; dining and buffet cars; schools; school fraternities; institutions; clubs; and industrial lunch rooms. Includes meals and beverages consumed both on and off-premise.   [3] Includes mattresses and bedsprings.   [4] Consists largely of textile house furnishings including piece goods allocated to house furnishing use. Also includes lamp shades, brooms, and brushes.   [5] Excludes drug preparations and related products dispensed by physicians, hospitals, and other medical services.   [6] Consists of (1) current expenditures (including consumption of fixed capital) of nonprofit hospitals and nursing homes and (2) payments by patients to proprietary and government hospitals and nursing homes.   [7] Consists of (1) premiums, less benefits and dividends, for health, hospitalization and accidental death and dismemberment insurance provided by commercial insurance carriers and (2) administrative expenses (including consumption of fixed capital) of Blue Cross and Blue Shield plans and of other independent prepaid and self-insured health plans.   [8] Consists of (1) operating expenses of life insurance carriers and private noninsured pension plans and (2) premiums, less benefits and dividends of fraternal benefit societies. Excludes expenses allocated by commercial carriers to accident and health insurance.   [9] For additional details, see table 393.

Source: U.S. Bureau of Economic Analysis, National Income and Product Accounts, volume 2, 1959-88, and Survey of Current Business, August 1993.

No. 695. Personal Income and Its Disposition: 1980 to 1993

[In billions of dollars, except percent. For definition of personal income, see text, section 14]

ITEM	1980	1985	1989	1990	1991	1992	1993
Personal income	2,265.4	3,379.8	4,380.3	4,673.8	4,850.9	5,144.9	5,388.3
Wage and salary disbursements	1,376.6	1,986.5	2,586.4	2,745.0	2,815.0	2,973.1	3,080.5
Commodity-producing industries [1]	471.9	612.2	724.2	745.7	738.1	756.5	763.6
Manufacturing	355.7	461.3	542.2	555.6	557.2	577.6	577.3
Distributive industries [2]	336.4	475.9	607.0	635.1	648.0	682.0	706.6
Service industries [3]	306.9	524.5	776.8	848.3	883.5	967.0	1,020.6
Government	261.4	373.9	478.5	515.9	545.4	567.5	589.7
Other labor income	139.8	191.8	251.9	274.3	296.9	322.7	350.7
Proprietors' income [4]	171.8	259.9	347.3	363.3	376.4	414.3	443.2
Rental income of persons [5]	13.2	18.7	-13.5	-14.2	-12.8	-8.9	12.6
Personal dividend income	57.1	87.9	126.5	144.4	127.9	140.4	158.3
Personal interest income	274.0	498.1	668.2	698.2	715.6	694.3	695.2
Transfer payments to persons	321.5	485.9	625.0	687.6	769.9	858.4	912.1
Old-age, survivors, disability, and health insurance benefits	154.2	253.4	325.1	352.0	382.3	413.9	438.4
Gov't unemployment insurance benefits	16.1	15.7	14.4	19.0	26.7	39.2	34.1
Veterans benefits	15.0	16.7	17.3	17.8	18.3	19.3	20.0
Gov't employees retirement benefits	43.0	66.6	87.5	94.5	102.0	108.3	115.5
Other transfer payments	93.2	133.5	180.6	204.3	240.5	277.7	304.1
Less: Personal contributions for social insurance	*88.6*	*149.1*	*211.4*	*224.9*	*237.8*	*249.3*	*264.3*
Less: Personal tax and nontax payments	*312.4*	*436.8*	*593.3*	*623.3*	*620.4*	*644.8*	*681.6*
Equals: Disposable personal income	**1,952.9**	**2,943.0**	**3,787.0**	**4,050.5**	**4,230.5**	**4,500.2**	**4,706.7**
Less: Personal outlays	*1,799.1*	*2,753.7*	*3,634.9*	*3,880.6*	*4,029.0*	*4,261.5*	*4,516.8*
Personal consumption expenditures	1,748.1	2,667.4	3,523.1	3,761.2	3,906.4	4,139.9	4,391.8
Interest paid by persons	49.4	83.6	103.0	109.3	112.2	111.1	114.0
Personal transfer payments to foreigners (net)	1.6	2.7	8.9	10.1	10.5	10.4	11.0
Equals: Personal saving	**153.8**	**189.3**	**152.1**	**170.0**	**201.5**	**238.7**	**189.9**
Percent of disposable personal income	7.9	6.4	4.0	4.2	4.8	5.3	4.0
Disposable personal income, 1987 dollars	2,733.6	3,162.1	3,464.9	3,524.5	3,529.0	3,632.5	3,700.9
PERCENT DISTRIBUTION							
Personal income	100	100	100	100	100	100	100
Wage and salary disbursements	61	59	59	59	58	58	57
Other labor income	6	6	6	6	6	6	7
Proprietors' income [4]	8	8	8	8	8	8	8
Rental income of persons [5]	1	1	(-Z)	(-Z)	(-Z)	(-Z)	(-Z)
Personal dividend income	3	3	3	3	3	3	3
Personal interest income	12	15	15	15	15	13	13
Transfer payments	14	14	14	15	16	17	17
Less: Personal contributions for social insurance	*-4*	*-4*	*-5*	*-5*	*-5*	*-5*	*-5*

Z Less than 0.5 percent. [1] Comprises agriculture, forestry, fishing, mining, construction, and manufacturing. [2] Comprises transportation, communication, public utilities, and trade. [3] Comprises finance, insurance, real estate, services, and rest of world. [4] With capital consumption and inventory valuation adjustments. [5] With capital consumption adjustment.

Source: U.S. Bureau of Economic Analysis, *National Income and Product Accounts of the United States, volume 2, 1959-88,* and *Survey of Current Business,* July 1992, August 1993, and March 1994.

No. 696. Gross Saving and Investment: 1980 to 1993

[In billions of dollars]

ITEM	1980	1985	1986	1987	1988	1989	1990	1991	1992	1993
Gross saving	**465.4**	**610.4**	**574.6**	**619.0**	**704.0**	**741.8**	**722.7**	**733.7**	**717.8**	**780.9**
Gross private saving	499.6	735.7	721.4	730.7	802.3	819.4	861.1	929.9	986.9	1,005.2
Personal saving	153.8	189.3	187.5	142.0	155.7	152.1	170.0	201.5	238.7	189.9
Undistributed corporate profits [1]	33.9	91.9	55.4	86.5	112.6	86.9	88.5	102.3	110.4	124.0
Undistributed profits	97.1	36.1	1.6	54.6	95.2	67.1	73.6	95.2	98.6	106.7
Inventory valuation adjustment	-43.0	0.2	9.7	-14.5	-27.3	-17.5	-11.0	4.9	-5.3	-7.1
Capital consumption adjustment	-20.2	55.5	44.1	46.4	44.7	37.4	25.9	2.2	17.1	24.3
Corporate consumption of fixed capital	185.1	277.8	294.2	307.7	327.6	352.4	368.2	383.2	396.6	408.8
Noncorporate consumption of fixed capital	126.8	176.7	184.4	194.4	206.4	228.0	234.5	242.8	261.3	262.5
Government surplus or deficit (-) [2]	-35.3	-125.3	-146.8	-111.7	-98.3	-77.5	-138.4	-196.2	-269.1	-224.3
Federal	-60.1	-181.4	-201.0	-151.8	-136.6	-122.3	-163.5	-203.4	-276.3	-226.2
State and local	24.8	56.1	54.3	40.1	38.4	44.8	25.1	7.3	7.2	1.9
Capital grants received by the U.S. (net)	1.2	-	-	-	-	-	-	-	-	-
Gross investment	**479.1**	**596.5**	**575.9**	**594.2**	**675.6**	**742.9**	**730.4**	**743.3**	**741.4**	**795.4**
Gross private domestic investment	467.6	714.5	717.6	749.3	793.6	832.3	808.9	736.9	796.5	891.7
Net foreign investment	11.5	-118.1	-141.7	-155.1	-118.0	-89.3	-78.5	6.4	-55.1	-96.2
Statistical discrepancy	**13.6**	**-13.9**	**1.2**	**-24.8**	**-28.4**	**1.1**	**7.8**	**9.6**	**23.6**	**14.6**

- Represents or rounds to zero. [1] With inventory valuation and capital consumption adjustments. [2] National income and product accounts basis.

Source: U.S. Bureau of Economic Analysis, *National Income and Product Accounts of the United States: volume 2, 1959-88,* and *Survey of Current Business,* August 1993 and March 1994.

No. 697. Disposable Personal Income Per Capita, by State: 1980 to 1993

[1993 data preliminary]

REGION, DIVISION, AND STATE	CURRENT DOLLARS				Income rank		CONSTANT (1987) DOLLARS			
	1980	1985	1990	1993	1980	1993	1980	1985	1990	1993
United States	8,569	12,324	16,173	18,177	(X)	(X)	12,001	13,237	14,076	14,290
Northeast	9,140	13,502	18,539	20,753	(X)	(X)	12,801	14,503	16,135	16,315
New England	9,055	13,789	18,828	20,867	(X)	(X)	12,682	14,811	16,386	16,405
Maine	7,283	10,779	15,064	16,898	38	29	10,200	11,578	13,111	13,285
New Hampshire	8,611	13,946	18,120	20,278	15	7	12,060	14,980	15,770	15,942
Vermont	7,485	11,026	15,225	17,076	35	28	10,483	11,843	13,251	13,425
Massachusetts	9,052	13,897	18,926	20,985	13	3	12,678	14,927	16,472	16,498
Rhode Island	8,306	12,437	16,570	18,384	26	17	11,633	13,359	14,421	14,453
Connecticut	10,321	15,500	21,604	23,776	2	1	14,455	16,649	18,802	18,692
Middle Atlantic	9,169	13,404	18,437	20,713	(X)	(X)	12,842	14,397	16,046	16,284
New York	9,249	13,388	18,733	20,948	10	4	12,954	14,380	16,304	16,469
New Jersey	9,974	15,465	20,852	23,354	5	2	13,969	16,611	18,148	18,360
Pennsylvania	8,549	12,103	16,417	18,632	17	14	11,973	13,000	14,288	14,648
Midwest	8,494	12,069	15,676	17,713	(X)	(X)	11,897	12,964	13,643	13,926
East North Central	8,672	12,176	15,863	17,961	(X)	(X)	12,146	13,078	13,806	14,120
Ohio	8,405	11,707	15,247	17,180	24	25	11,772	12,575	13,270	13,506
Indiana	7,988	11,095	14,636	16,824	30	31	11,188	11,917	12,738	13,226
Illinois	9,276	13,173	17,412	19,648	9	10	12,992	14,149	15,154	15,447
Michigan	8,779	12,356	15,837	17,886	14	20	12,296	13,272	13,783	14,061
Wisconsin	8,401	11,743	15,047	17,196	25	24	11,766	12,613	13,096	13,519
West North Central	8,065	11,815	15,231	17,122	(X)	(X)	11,296	12,691	13,256	13,461
Minnesota	8,505	12,352	15,990	17,907	18	19	11,912	13,267	13,916	14,078
Iowa	7,987	11,292	14,516	15,782	31	38	11,186	12,129	12,634	12,407
Missouri	8,030	11,930	15,246	17,158	28	26	11,246	12,814	13,269	13,489
North Dakota	6,600	10,984	13,837	15,688	48	39	9,244	11,798	12,043	12,333
South Dakota	6,890	10,357	14,120	15,981	45	35	9,650	11,125	12,289	12,564
Nebraska	7,769	11,742	15,340	17,416	32	23	10,881	12,612	13,351	13,692
Kansas	8,419	11,959	15,258	17,635	23	21	11,791	12,845	13,279	13,864
South	7,768	11,274	14,826	16,939	(X)	(X)	10,879	12,109	12,904	13,317
South Atlantic	7,956	11,716	15,859	17,847	(X)	(X)	11,143	12,584	13,802	14,031
Delaware	8,502	12,641	16,545	18,374	19	18	11,908	13,578	14,399	14,445
Maryland	9,097	13,753	18,700	20,552	12	5	12,741	14,772	16,275	16,157
District of Columbia	10,542	14,714	20,312	24,595	(X)	(X)	14,765	15,805	17,678	19,336
Virginia	8,443	12,628	16,886	18,762	21	13	11,825	13,564	14,696	14,750
West Virginia	6,944	9,281	12,479	14,552	43	47	9,725	9,969	10,861	11,440
North Carolina	6,939	10,321	14,243	16,421	44	34	9,718	11,086	12,396	12,910
South Carolina	6,627	9,696	13,327	15,071	47	42	9,282	10,415	11,599	11,848
Georgia	7,309	11,092	14,891	16,871	37	30	10,237	11,914	12,960	13,263
Florida	8,595	12,340	16,535	18,513	16	16	12,038	13,255	14,391	14,554
East South Central	6,834	9,706	13,204	15,414	(X)	(X)	9,571	10,425	11,492	12,118
Kentucky	7,066	9,732	12,901	15,010	41	44	9,896	10,453	11,228	11,800
Tennessee	7,117	10,360	14,315	16,705	40	33	9,968	11,128	12,459	13,133
Alabama	6,741	9,656	13,227	15,332	46	40	9,441	10,372	11,512	12,053
Mississippi	6,122	8,552	11,491	13,631	50	50	8,574	9,186	10,001	10,716
West South Central	8,050	11,490	14,061	16,313	(X)	(X)	11,275	12,342	12,238	12,825
Arkansas	6,502	9,499	12,236	14,424	49	48	9,106	10,203	10,649	11,340
Louisiana	7,523	10,421	12,728	14,947	34	45	10,536	11,193	11,077	11,751
Oklahoma	8,017	10,877	13,291	15,060	29	43	11,228	11,683	11,567	11,840
Texas	8,459	12,188	14,785	17,116	20	27	11,847	13,091	12,868	13,456
West	9,422	13,199	16,643	18,297	(X)	(X)	13,196	14,177	14,485	14,384
Mountain	8,247	11,482	14,522	16,567	(X)	(X)	11,550	12,333	12,639	13,024
Montana	7,565	10,068	12,834	15,128	33	41	10,595	10,814	11,170	11,893
Idaho	7,452	10,014	13,836	15,974	36	36	10,437	10,756	12,042	12,558
Wyoming	9,705	11,686	15,114	17,504	6	22	13,592	12,552	13,154	13,761
Colorado	9,130	13,198	16,231	18,628	11	15	12,787	14,176	14,126	14,645
New Mexico	7,246	10,162	12,658	14,587	39	46	10,148	10,915	11,017	11,468
Arizona	8,147	11,629	14,338	15,921	27	37	11,410	12,491	12,479	12,517
Utah	6,897	9,664	12,153	14,066	42	49	9,786	10,380	10,581	11,058
Nevada	10,058	12,991	17,584	19,781	4	9	14,087	13,954	15,304	15,551
Pacific	9,843	13,822	17,818	18,916	(X)	(X)	13,786	14,846	15,129	14,871
Washington	9,317	12,864	16,890	19,290	7	11	13,049	13,817	14,700	15,165
Oregon	8,425	11,268	14,711	16,731	22	32	11,800	12,103	12,803	13,153
California	10,084	14,232	17,690	18,997	3	12	14,123	15,287	15,396	14,935
Alaska	11,639	16,628	18,354	20,306	1	6	16,301	17,860	15,974	15,964
Hawaii	9,286	12,588	17,693	20,038	8	8	13,006	13,521	15,399	15,753

X Not applicable.

Source: U.S. Bureau of Economic Analysis, *Survey of Current Business,* August issues; and unpublished data.

No. 698. Personal Income, by State: 1980 to 1993

[In billions of dollars, except percent. 1993 preliminary. Represents a measure of income received from all sources during the calendar year by residents of each State. Data exclude Federal employees overseas and U.S. residents employed by private U.S. firms on temporary foreign assignment. Totals may differ from those in tables 690, 691, and 695. For definition of average annual percent change, see Guide to Tabular Presentation. Minus sign (-) indicates decrease]

REGION, DIVISION, AND STATE	CURRENT DOLLARS				CONSTANT (1987) DOLLARS				Average annual percent change		Percent distribution	
	1980	1985	1990	1993	1980	1985	1990	1993	1980-1993	1992-1993	1980	1993
United States...	2,259.0	3,368.2	4,655.4	5,369.0	3,163.9	3,617.9	4,051.7	4,220.9	2.2	2.0	100.0	100.0
Northeast	526.2	789.0	1,103.6	1,238.8	736.9	847.4	960.5	973.9	2.2	0.8	23.3	23.1
New England	130.9	204.9	290.0	321.0	183.3	220.1	252.4	252.4	2.5	1.2	5.8	6.0
Maine...........	9.3	14.1	21.0	23.4	13.0	15.2	18.3	18.4	2.7	1.6	0.4	0.4
New Hampshire ...	9.1	15.7	22.5	25.5	12.7	16.9	19.6	20.0	3.6	1.6	0.4	0.5
Vermont......	4.4	6.7	9.8	11.2	6.1	7.2	8.6	8.8	2.8	1.7	0.2	0.2
Massachusetts....	61.2	96.3	133.9	147.7	85.7	103.4	116.5	116.1	2.4	1.4	2.7	2.8
Rhode Island.....	9.1	13.6	19.1	21.1	12.7	14.6	16.6	16.6	2.1	1.2	0.4	0.4
Connecticut......	37.9	58.5	83.6	92.1	53.0	62.9	72.8	72.4	2.4	0.8	1.7	1.7
Middle Atlantic	395.3	584.0	813.6	917.8	553.6	627.3	708.1	721.5	2.1	0.7	17.5	17.1
New York	191.6	284.5	401.8	448.1	268.3	305.6	349.7	352.3	2.1	0.0	8.5	8.3
New Jersey	85.9	135.9	187.2	212.5	120.3	145.9	162.9	167.0	2.6	1.4	3.8	4.0
Pennsylvania	117.8	163.6	224.6	257.2	165.0	175.8	195.5	202.2	1.6	1.2	5.2	4.8
Midwest	581.6	812.0	1,079.8	1,240.8	814.6	872.2	939.8	975.5	1.4	1.6	25.7	23.1
East North Central...	420.3	577.7	769.9	885.9	588.6	620.5	670.1	696.4	1.3	1.9	18.6	16.5
Ohio...........	105.2	143.7	190.6	218.4	147.3	154.4	165.9	171.7	1.2	1.4	4.7	4.1
Indiana..........	50.6	69.1	93.4	109.7	70.9	74.2	81.3	86.2	1.5	2.8	2.2	2.0
Illinois..........	124.4	172.3	230.8	264.2	174.3	185.1	200.9	207.7	1.4	1.8	5.5	4.9
Michigan........	94.0	129.2	169.8	193.8	131.6	138.8	147.8	152.4	1.1	2.2	4.2	3.6
Wisconsin	46.1	63.3	85.3	99.8	64.5	68.0	74.2	78.5	1.5	2.3	2.0	1.9
West North Central ..	161.4	234.3	309.9	355.0	226.0	251.7	269.7	279.1	1.6	0.7	7.1	6.6
Minnesota	40.8	60.0	82.4	95.2	57.1	64.4	71.7	74.8	2.1	1.2	1.8	1.8
Iowa...........	27.3	36.1	46.4	51.5	38.2	38.7	40.4	40.5	0.5	-2.0	1.2	1.0
Missouri	45.6	67.8	89.2	101.9	63.8	72.8	77.7	80.1	1.8	0.8	2.0	1.9
North Dakota.....	5.0	8.2	9.8	11.1	7.0	8.8	8.5	8.7	1.7	0.1	0.2	0.2
South Dakota.....	5.3	7.9	10.9	12.6	7.5	8.4	9.5	9.9	2.2	1.0	0.2	0.2
Nebraska	14.1	20.7	27.5	31.7	19.8	22.3	23.9	24.9	1.8	1.7	0.6	0.6
Kansas.........	23.3	33.7	43.8	51.0	32.6	36.2	38.1	40.1	1.6	1.8	1.0	0.9
South	678.4	1,047.4	1,448.4	1,713.9	950.2	1,125.1	1,260.6	1,347.4	2.7	3.1	30.0	31.9
South Atlantic	341.9	542.3	797.7	931.6	478.8	582.5	694.2	732.4	3.3	3.3	15.1	17.4
Delaware.......	6.2	9.3	13.2	15.0	8.6	10.0	11.5	11.8	2.5	2.3	0.3	0.3
Maryland........	45.7	71.3	106.0	119.4	64.1	76.6	92.2	93.8	3.0	1.6	2.0	2.2
District of Columbia.	8.0	11.2	14.9	17.0	11.2	12.1	12.9	13.4	1.4	1.6	0.4	0.3
Virginia........	52.9	83.7	121.4	140.4	74.1	89.9	105.7	110.4	3.1	2.4	2.3	2.6
West Virginia	15.6	19.8	25.0	29.5	21.8	21.3	21.8	23.2	0.5	1.9	0.7	0.5
North Carolina ...	47.2	74.4	108.3	129.9	66.1	79.9	94.3	102.1	3.4	3.6	2.1	2.4
South Carolina ...	23.7	36.2	52.9	61.6	33.2	38.9	46.0	48.5	3.0	2.8	1.0	1.1
Georgia.........	45.8	76.3	111.4	133.3	64.2	82.0	97.0	104.8	3.8	3.4	2.0	2.5
Florida	96.8	160.0	244.6	285.3	135.5	171.9	212.9	224.3	4.0	4.6	4.3	5.3
East South Central...	113.6	163.1	225.0	270.6	159.1	175.2	195.8	212.7	2.3	2.9	5.0	5.0
Kentucky........	29.5	40.9	54.5	65.1	41.3	43.9	47.4	51.2	1.7	2.1	1.3	1.2
Tennessee......	36.9	54.6	77.8	94.0	51.6	58.6	67.7	73.9	2.8	3.1	1.6	1.8
Alabama........	29.9	43.3	60.3	72.2	41.8	46.5	52.5	56.7	2.4	2.8	1.3	1.3
Mississippi......	17.4	24.3	32.4	39.4	24.3	26.2	28.2	30.9	1.9	4.1	0.8	0.7
West South Central ..	223.0	342.0	425.8	511.7	312.3	367.4	370.5	402.3	2.0	2.9	9.9	9.5
Arkansas........	16.9	24.8	32.5	39.1	23.6	26.7	28.2	30.8	2.0	1.8	0.7	0.7
Louisiana	36.7	51.4	60.2	71.6	51.3	55.2	52.4	56.3	0.7	2.3	1.6	1.3
Oklahoma	28.3	40.5	47.6	55.0	39.7	43.5	41.4	43.2	0.7	1.8	1.3	1.0
Texas..........	141.1	225.3	285.5	346.0	197.6	242.0	248.5	272.0	2.5	3.4	6.2	6.4
West	472.8	719.8	1,023.6	1,175.4	662.2	773.2	890.9	924.1	2.6	2.0	20.9	21.9
Mountain	108.3	166.1	227.5	279.3	151.6	178.4	198.0	219.6	2.9	4.8	4.8	5.2
Montana........	6.9	9.3	11.8	14.5	9.6	10.0	10.3	11.4	1.3	6.1	0.3	0.3
Idaho..........	8.0	11.1	15.5	19.4	11.2	11.9	13.5	15.2	2.4	6.5	0.4	0.4
Wyoming.......	5.4	6.7	7.7	9.2	7.5	7.2	6.7	7.2	-0.3	3.4	0.2	0.2
Colorado........	30.9	48.4	62.2	76.9	43.3	52.0	54.1	60.5	2.6	4.6	1.4	1.4
New Mexico.....	10.7	16.4	21.6	26.3	15.0	17.6	18.8	20.7	2.5	4.9	0.5	0.5
Arizona.........	25.4	42.0	59.8	71.3	35.5	45.1	52.1	56.1	3.6	4.2	1.1	1.3
Utah...........	11.7	18.0	24.3	30.1	16.4	19.4	21.2	23.7	2.9	3.9	0.5	0.6
Nevada.........	9.4	14.2	24.7	31.6	13.1	15.2	21.5	24.8	5.0	6.3	0.4	0.6
Pacific	364.5	553.8	796.1	896.1	510.5	594.8	692.8	704.5	2.5	1.1	16.1	16.7
Washington......	44.5	62.8	94.4	115.0	62.4	67.5	82.2	90.4	2.9	2.3	2.0	2.1
Oregon........	26.1	34.6	49.2	58.9	36.5	37.1	42.8	46.3	1.9	3.9	1.2	1.1
California.......	278.0	431.4	617.7	681.1	389.3	463.4	537.6	535.4	2.5	0.6	12.3	12.7
Alaska	5.5	10.0	11.5	13.7	7.8	10.7	10.1	10.8	2.5	2.8	0.2	0.3
Hawaii	10.4	15.0	23.3	27.4	14.6	16.1	20.2	21.5	3.0	3.9	0.5	0.5

Source: U.S. Bureau of Economic Analysis, *Survey of Current Business*, August issues; and unpublished data.

No. 699. Personal Income Per Capita, by State: 1980 to 1993

[1993 data preliminary. See headnote, table 698]

REGION, DIVISION, AND STATE	CURRENT DOLLARS					CONSTANT (1987) DOLLARS					Income rank	
	1980	1990	1991	1992	1993	1980	1990	1991	1992	1993	1980	1993
United States . . .	9,940	18,667	19,163	20,105	20,817	13,922	16,246	15,982	16,227	16,366	(X)	(X)
Northeast	10,699	21,700	22,225	23,412	24,123	14,984	18,886	18,536	18,896	18,965	(X)	(X)
New England	10,582	21,935	22,338	23,406	24,265	14,821	19,091	18,631	18,891	19,076	(X)	(X)
Maine.	8,218	17,041	17,294	18,163	18,895	11,510	14,831	14,424	14,659	14,855	38	32
New Hampshire	9,803	20,231	20,973	21,933	22,659	13,730	17,607	17,492	17,702	17,814	23	9
Vermont	8,546	17,444	17,750	18,792	19,467	11,969	15,182	14,804	15,167	15,304	35	26
Massachusetts.	10,659	22,248	22,719	23,676	24,563	14,929	19,363	18,948	19,109	19,311	12	4
Rhode Island.	9,576	19,035	19,340	20,276	21,096	13,412	16,567	16,130	16,365	16,585	26	17
Connecticut.	12,170	25,426	25,705	27,150	28,110	17,045	22,129	21,439	21,913	22,099	2	1
Middle Atlantic	10,738	21,618	22,185	23,415	24,074	15,039	18,815	18,503	18,898	18,926	(X)	(X)
New York	10,906	22,322	22,866	24,095	24,623	15,275	19,427	19,071	19,447	19,358	7	3
New Jersey.	11,648	24,182	24,644	26,091	26,967	16,314	21,046	20,554	21,058	21,200	4	2
Pennsylvania.	9,923	18,884	19,557	20,642	21,351	13,898	16,435	16,311	16,660	16,785	17	16
Midwest	9,872	18,067	18,568	19,622	20,318	13,826	15,724	15,486	15,837	15,974	(X)	(X)
East North Central. . . .	10,077	18,297	18,762	19,814	20,594	14,113	15,924	15,648	15,992	16,190	(X)	(X)
Ohio.	9,738	17,547	18,047	19,040	19,688	13,639	15,272	15,052	15,367	15,478	25	24
Indiana.	9,215	16,815	17,251	18,366	19,203	12,906	14,634	14,388	14,823	15,097	31	30
Illinois	10,875	20,159	20,602	21,774	22,657	15,231	17,545	17,183	17,574	17,753	8	10
Michigan.	10,154	18,239	18,667	19,586	20,453	14,221	15,874	15,569	15,808	16,079	15	20
Wisconsin.	9,772	17,399	17,954	19,038	19,811	13,686	15,143	14,974	15,366	15,575	24	22
West North Central . . .	9,374	17,519	18,104	19,164	19,662	13,129	15,247	15,099	15,467	15,458	(X)	(X)
Minnesota.	9,982	18,784	19,276	20,503	21,063	13,980	16,348	16,077	16,548	16,559	16	18
Iowa	9,346	16,683	17,096	18,275	18,315	13,090	14,520	14,259	14,750	14,399	27	35
Missouri	9,256	17,407	18,121	18,970	19,463	12,964	15,150	15,113	15,311	15,301	30	27
North Dakota.	7,641	15,320	15,617	17,048	17,488	10,702	13,333	13,025	13,759	13,748	47	39
South Dakota	7,701	15,628	16,286	17,198	17,666	10,786	13,601	13,583	13,881	13,888	45	37
Nebraska.	8,988	17,379	18,059	18,974	19,726	12,588	15,125	15,062	15,314	15,508	32	23
Kansas.	9,829	17,639	18,290	19,387	20,139	13,766	15,352	15,254	15,647	15,833	22	21
South.	8,958	16,894	17,482	18,360	19,162	12,546	14,704	14,581	14,818	15,065	(X)	(X)
South Atlantic.	9,204	18,230	18,712	19,488	20,367	12,891	15,866	15,606	15,729	16,012	(X)	(X)
Delaware	10,356	19,719	20,195	20,724	21,481	14,504	17,162	16,843	16,726	16,888	14	15
Maryland	10,824	22,088	22,494	23,268	24,044	15,160	19,224	18,761	18,780	18,903	9	5
District of Columbia .	12,508	24,643	26,069	27,909	29,438	17,518	21,447	21,742	22,525	23,143	(X)	(X)
Virginia.	9,857	19,543	20,071	20,883	21,634	13,805	17,009	16,740	16,855	17,008	19	13
West Virginia.	7,972	13,964	14,695	15,598	16,209	11,165	12,153	12,256	12,589	12,743	43	47
North Carolina. . . .	8,000	16,284	16,802	17,863	18,702	11,204	14,172	14,013	14,417	14,703	42	33
South Carolina.	7,558	15,101	15,484	16,212	16,923	10,585	13,143	12,914	13,085	13,304	48	44
Georgia	8,353	17,121	17,666	18,549	19,278	11,699	14,901	14,734	14,971	15,156	37	29
Florida	9,835	18,785	19,180	19,711	20,857	13,775	16,349	15,997	15,909	16,397	21	19
East South Central . . .	7,730	14,793	15,471	16,485	17,215	10,826	12,875	12,903	13,305	13,534	(X)	(X)
Kentucky	8,051	14,751	15,483	16,528	17,173	11,276	12,838	12,913	13,340	13,501	40	42
Tennessee	8,010	15,903	16,524	17,674	18,434	11,218	13,841	13,781	14,265	14,492	41	34
Alabama.	7,656	14,899	15,614	16,522	17,234	10,723	12,967	13,023	13,335	13,549	46	41
Mississippi	6,868	12,578	13,218	14,082	14,894	9,619	10,947	11,024	11,366	11,709	50	50
West South Central . . .	9,329	15,905	16,606	17,570	18,287	13,066	13,842	13,850	14,181	14,377	(X)	(X)
Arkansas	7,371	13,779	14,485	15,635	16,143	10,324	11,992	12,081	12,619	12,691	49	49
Louisiana	8,672	14,279	15,100	15,931	16,667	12,146	12,427	12,594	12,858	13,103	34	45
Oklahoma.	9,308	15,117	15,636	16,420	17,020	13,036	13,157	13,041	13,253	13,381	28	43
Texas.	9,840	16,747	17,440	18,437	19,189	13,782	14,575	14,545	14,881	15,086	20	31
West	10,889	19,298	19,641	20,362	20,973	15,251	16,795	16,381	16,434	16,488	(X)	(X)
Mountain	9,455	16,590	17,250	18,055	18,906	13,242	14,439	14,387	14,572	14,863	(X)	(X)
Montana	8,728	14,743	15,632	16,227	17,322	12,224	12,831	13,038	13,097	13,618	33	40
Idaho	8,433	15,304	15,773	16,649	17,646	11,811	13,319	13,155	13,437	13,873	36	38
Wyoming	11,356	16,905	18,076	18,631	19,539	15,905	14,713	15,076	15,037	15,361	6	25
Colorado.	10,616	18,818	19,740	20,666	21,564	14,868	16,378	16,464	16,680	16,953	13	14
New Mexico	8,147	14,213	14,781	15,458	16,297	11,410	12,370	12,328	12,476	12,812	39	46
Arizona.	9,272	16,262	16,697	17,401	18,121	12,986	14,153	13,926	14,044	14,246	29	36
Utah	7,942	14,063	14,759	15,573	16,187	11,123	12,239	12,309	12,569	12,720	44	48
Nevada	11,559	20,248	20,639	21,648	22,729	16,189	17,622	17,214	17,472	17,869	5	8
Pacific.	11,403	20,242	20,478	21,175	21,713	15,971	17,617	17,079	17,090	17,070	(X)	(X)
Washington.	10,716	19,268	20,087	21,289	21,887	15,008	16,769	16,753	17,182	17,207	11	11
Oregon.	9,863	17,201	17,714	18,605	19,443	13,814	14,970	14,774	15,016	15,285	18	28
California	11,681	20,656	20,748	21,348	21,821	16,360	17,977	17,304	17,230	17,155	3	12
Alaska	13,692	20,887	21,498	22,067	22,846	19,176	18,178	17,930	17,810	17,961	1	7
Hawaii	10,774	20,905	21,576	22,200	23,354	15,090	18,194	17,995	17,918	18,360	10	6

X Not applicable.

Source: U.S. Bureau of Economic Analysis, *Survey of Current Business*, August issues; and unpublished data.

No. 700. Personal Income, by Metropolitan Area: 1990 to 1992

[As defined **June 30, 1993**. CMSA=Consolidated Metropolitan Statistical Area; NECMA=New England County Metropolitan Area; MSA=Metropolitan Statistical Area. See Appendix II]

METROPOLITAN AREA RANKED BY 1990 POPULATION	PERSONAL INCOME				PER CAPITA PERSONAL INCOME			
	1990 (mil. dol.)	1991 (mil. dol.)	1992 (mil. dol.)	Annual percent change, 1991-92	1990 (dol.)	1991 (dol.)	1992 (dol.)	Percent of national average, 1992
United States [1]	4,655,420	4,831,697	5,128,373	6.1	18,667	19,163	20,105	(X)
New York-Northern New Jersey-Long Island, NY-NJ-CT-PA CMSA	491,234	502,459	533,759	6.2	25,229	25,760	27,259	135.6
Los Angeles-Riverside-Orange County, CA CMSA	301,614	306,300	318,442	4.0	20,663	20,679	21,162	105.3
Chicago-Gary-Kenosha, IL-IN-WI CMSA	178,641	184,540	196,063	6.2	21,635	22,154	23,312	116.0
Washington-Baltimore, DC-MD-VA-WV CMSA	159,226	165,232	173,591	5.1	23,593	24,173	25,087	124.8
San Francisco-Oakland-San Jose, CA CMSA	155,119	158,704	166,781	5.1	24,755	25,057	26,019	129.4
Philadelphia-Wilmington-Atlantic City, PA-NJ-DE-MD CMSA	126,512	130,654	137,832	5.5	21,443	22,056	23,210	115.4
Boston-Brockton-Nashua, MA-NH NECMA	128,494	130,808	136,695	4.5	22,589	23,094	24,109	119.9
Detroit-Ann Arbor-Flint, MI CMSA	104,758	106,805	112,702	5.5	20,175	20,460	21,484	106.9
Dallas-Fort Worth, TX CMSA	80,619	85,095	91,422	7.4	19,868	20,543	21,692	107.9
Houston-Galveston-Brazoria, TX CMSA	73,025	78,812	84,663	7.4	19,452	20,419	21,367	106.3
Miami-Fort Lauderdale, FL CMSA	62,388	63,975	64,453	0.7	19,458	19,611	19,477	96.9
Seattle-Tacoma-Bremerton, WA CMSA	63,334	67,616	73,562	8.8	21,161	22,123	23,492	116.8
Atlanta, GA MSA	60,882	63,623	68,668	7.9	20,439	20,806	21,849	108.7
Cleveland-Akron, OH CMSA	55,519	57,388	60,580	5.6	19,397	19,955	20,959	104.2
Minneapolis-St. Paul, MN-WI MSA	54,579	56,693	60,958	7.5	21,421	21,955	23,284	115.8
San Diego, CA MSA	49,587	50,820	53,019	4.3	19,731	19,875	20,384	101.4
St. Louis, MO-IL MSA	50,212	52,158	54,652	4.8	20,112	20,793	21,700	107.9
Pittsburgh, PA MSA	45,437	47,864	50,956	6.5	18,969	19,946	21,175	105.3
Phoenix-Mesa, AZ MSA	40,237	41,676	44,319	6.3	17,916	18,244	19,018	94.6
Tampa-St. Petersburg-Clearwater, FL MSA	37,291	38,570	40,882	6.0	17,964	18,405	19,400	96.5
Denver-Boulder-Greeley, CO CMSA	40,913	43,822	47,203	7.7	20,600	21,591	22,592	112.4
Cincinnati-Hamilton, OH-KY-IN CMSA	33,873	35,189	37,562	6.7	18,588	19,080	20,140	100.2
Portland-Salem, OR-WA CMSA	33,612	35,527	38,081	7.2	18,614	19,148	20,076	99.9
Milwaukee-Racine, WI CMSA	31,851	33,058	35,218	6.5	19,787	20,398	21,614	107.5
Kansas City, MO-KS MSA	30,369	31,854	33,871	6.3	19,133	19,876	20,948	104.2
Sacramento-Yolo, CA CMSA	28,820	30,107	31,777	5.5	19,271	19,550	20,326	101.1
Norfolk-Virginia Beach-Newport News, VA-NC MSA	24,258	25,475	27,056	6.2	16,735	17,412	18,077	89.9
Indianapolis, IN MSA	26,638	27,853	29,893	7.3	19,242	19,816	20,992	104.4
Columbus, OH MSA	24,664	25,870	27,845	7.6	18,264	18,859	19,974	99.3
San Antonio, TX MSA	20,691	21,940	23,825	8.6	15,583	16,264	17,282	86.0
New Orleans, LA MSA	21,038	22,256	23,562	5.9	16,382	17,227	18,087	90.0
Orlando, FL MSA	21,645	22,628	24,262	7.2	17,465	17,734	18,596	92.5
Buffalo-Niagara Falls, NY MSA	21,277	22,194	23,242	4.7	17,881	18,614	19,467	96.8
Charlotte-Gastonia-Rock Hill, NC-SC MSA	21,727	22,517	24,107	7.1	18,592	18,876	19,884	98.9
Hartford, CT NECMA	27,085	27,400	28,554	4.2	24,090	24,357	25,461	126.6
Salt Lake City-Ogden, UT MSA	16,429	17,598	19,025	8.1	15,262	15,992	16,865	83.9
Rochester, NY MSA	21,245	21,982	22,941	4.4	19,960	20,504	21,217	105.5
Greensboro-Winston-Salem-High Point, NC MSA	19,457	20,111	21,503	6.9	18,467	18,865	19,940	99.2
Memphis, TN-AR-MS MSA	18,001	18,800	20,177	7.3	17,821	18,405	19,517	97.1
Nashville, TN MSA	18,127	19,219	21,049	9.5	18,333	19,144	20,569	102.3
Oklahoma City, OK MSA	15,701	16,333	17,356	6.3	16,355	16,834	17,645	87.8
Dayton-Springfield, OH MSA	16,900	17,719	18,665	5.3	17,749	18,512	19,411	96.5
Louisville, KY-IN MSA	17,294	18,178	19,556	7.6	18,197	18,859	20,211	100.5
Grand Rapids-Muskegon-Holland, MI MSA	16,308	17,166	18,249	6.3	17,320	17,987	18,924	94.1
Providence-Warwick, RI NECMA	17,372	17,656	18,488	4.7	18,942	19,273	20,214	100.5
Jacksonville, FL MSA	16,443	17,164	18,238	6.3	18,010	18,409	19,146	95.2
West Palm Beach-Boca Raton, FL MSA	25,319	26,866	27,831	3.6	29,103	30,347	30,901	153.7
Richmond-Petersburg, VA MSA	18,535	18,952	19,985	5.5	21,314	21,517	22,303	110.9

X Not applicable.   [1] Includes other areas not listed separately.

Source: U.S. Bureau of Economic Analysis, *Survey of Current Business,* August issues; and unpublished data.

No. 701. Percent Distribution of Shares of National Income: 1980 to 1993

INCOME	1980	1985	1986	1987	1988	1989	1990	1991	1992	1993
National Income...........	100.0	100.0	100.0	100.0	100.0	100.0	100.0	100.0	100.0	100.0
Compensation of employees......	74.8	72.9	73.4	73.1	73.0	73.0	73.4	74.0	74.1	73.4
Wages and salaries...........	62.6	60.8	61.2	61.2	61.0	60.9	61.1	61.2	61.1	60.3
Supplements to wages, salaries ..	12.2	12.1	12.2	11.8	11.9	12.1	12.3	12.8	13.0	13.1
Proprietors' income [1]...........	7.8	8.0	8.3	8.4	8.1	8.2	8.1	8.2	8.6	8.6
Farm....................	0.5	0.7	0.6	0.8	0.8	0.9	0.9	0.8	0.9	0.9
Nonfarm [2]..............	7.3	7.3	7.6	7.6	7.3	7.2	7.2	7.4	7.7	7.7
Rental income of persons [2].......	0.6	0.6	0.3	0.1	0.1	-0.3	-0.3	-0.3	-0.2	0.2
Corporate profits [1]............	8.1	8.6	7.9	8.7	9.1	8.5	8.5	8.0	8.4	9.1
Profits before tax..........	11.0	6.9	6.3	7.8	8.7	8.1	8.1	7.9	8.2	8.7
Profits after tax...........	7.1	3.9	3.2	4.4	5.3	4.7	5.1	5.1	5.2	5.4
Inventory valuation adjustment ...	-2.0	-	0.3	-0.4	-0.7	-0.4	-0.2	0.1	-0.1	-0.1
Capital consumption adjustment ..	-0.9	1.7	1.3	1.3	1.1	0.9	0.6	(Z)	0.4	0.5
Net interest	8.7	10.0	10.2	9.8	9.7	10.7	10.3	10.1	9.1	8.7

- Represents or rounds to zero.   Z Less than .05 percent.   [1] With inventory valuation and capital consumption adjustments.
[2] With capital consumption adjustment.

Source: U.S. Bureau of Economic Analysis, *National Income and Product Accounts of the United States: volume 2, 1959-88*, and *Survey of Current Business*, August 1993 and April 1994.

No. 702. Flow of Funds Accounts—Composition of Individuals' Savings: 1980 to 1993

[In billions of dollars. Combined statement for households, farm business, and nonfarm noncorporate business. Minus sign (-) indicates decrease. See *Historical Statistics, Colonial Times to 1970*, series F 566-594, for similar but not exactly comparable data]

COMPOSITION OF SAVINGS	1980	1985	1987	1988	1989	1990	1991	1992	1993
Increase in financial assets.............	328.6	625.1	502.4	489.9	556.2	483.3	452.0	514.7	498.8
Checkable deposits and currency.........	9.2	28.6	-1.9	27.7	-0.5	12.3	51.8	141.1	84.6
Time and savings deposits.............	120.8	116.6	92.8	134.8	78.2	34.0	-103.9	-123.3	-99.6
Money market fund shares............	23.7	3.7	24.3	20.2	85.1	44.7	24.5	-3.8	6.7
Securities......................	19.6	93.4	116.0	76.2	-17.8	182.6	41.7	233.5	131.5
U.S. savings bonds...............	-7.3	5.3	7.8	8.5	8.2	8.5	11.9	19.1	14.7
Other U.S. Treasury securities.........	25.4	-12.2	-20.6	23.3	-17.1	56.2	-85.9	-45.0	-17.7
U.S. Government agency securities......	8.6	15.8	35.1	79.9	59.8	43.7	-6.5	39.8	4.2
Tax-exempt securities.............	2.8	69.0	89.9	46.1	50.4	26.7	35.0	5.1	-25.7
Corporate and foreign bonds..........	-13.4	-10.8	25.1	-29.4	-24.0	18.3	22.8	-19.6	-44.3
Open-market paper.............	2.9	63.9	6.3	35.0	-0.6	7.9	-17.5	31.7	-24.4
Mutual fund shares..............	2.2	76.0	59.4	12.5	37.0	43.1	107.5	171.1	268.1
Other corporate equities............	-1.5	-113.5	-87.0	-99.5	-131.4	-21.8	-25.6	31.2	-43.5
Private life insurance reserves..........	9.7	10.4	25.7	24.9	28.4	25.3	25.6	27.7	56.0
Private insured pension reserves........	22.3	63.4	62.7	85.0	77.8	84.4	81.1	75.2	103.0
Private noninsured pension reserves......	59.0	136.2	60.0	-28.4	142.4	-11.9	197.5	63.8	50.7
Government insurance and pension reserves.	35.8	71.9	72.5	83.9	89.8	86.0	80.2	88.3	87.7
Inv. in bank pers. trusts..............	-7.3	19.8	-5.6	7.2	23.1	21.5	29.8	-7.5	10.9
Miscellaneous financial assets.........	35.8	81.2	55.8	58.4	49.7	4.5	23.6	19.7	67.1
Gross investment in tangible assets......	406.1	651.8	735.4	778.9	821.8	807.3	754.4	833.3	905.3
Owner-occupied homes..............	101.6	161.4	198.3	206.6	206.6	191.7	173.2	205.5	232.1
Other fixed assets [1]...............	98.4	130.8	138.2	145.2	152.8	144.2	123.9	125.3	139.8
Consumer durables...............	212.5	353.0	403.7	437.1	459.4	468.2	457.8	497.3	537.8
Inventories [1]....................	-6.3	6.7	-4.8	-10.0	3.1	3.3	-0.5	5.1	-4.4
Capital consumption allowances.........	314.3	435.5	496.9	532.4	580.0	614.2	649.1	692.6	716.5
Owner-occupied homes..............	50.3	67.7	75.0	80.0	92.1	93.2	97.6	111.5	111.2
Other fixed assets [1]...............	77.8	110.6	121.1	127.9	137.5	142.9	146.9	151.5	152.9
Consumer durables...............	186.2	257.1	300.8	324.5	350.4	378.1	404.7	429.7	452.3
Net investment in tangible assets........	91.8	216.3	238.5	246.5	241.8	193.1	105.3	140.6	188.8
Owner-occupied homes..............	51.3	93.6	123.3	126.5	114.4	98.5	75.7	94.0	120.9
Other fixed assets [1]...............	20.6	20.2	17.1	17.3	15.3	1.3	-23.0	-26.2	-13.2
Consumer durables...............	26.3	95.8	102.9	112.6	109.0	90.0	53.1	67.7	85.5
Inventories [1]....................	-6.3	6.7	-4.8	-10.0	3.1	3.3	-0.5	5.1	-4.4
Net increase in liabilities..............	202.8	451.1	377.1	375.1	348.4	241.2	173.0	195.3	277.7
Mortgage debt on nonfarm homes........	94.1	171.7	240.9	219.0	211.8	176.7	165.5	175.5	192.1
Other mortgage debt [1]..............	50.9	98.3	69.4	49.1	38.9	14.7	-0.6	-29.0	-11.6
Consumer credit................	4.8	82.3	32.9	50.1	49.5	13.4	-13.1	9.3	49.0
Security credit..................	7.3	18.9	-16.3	1.7	-1.0	-3.7	16.3	-1.8	21.8
Policy loans..................	6.7	-0.1	(Z)	-0.1	3.2	4.1	4.8	5.7	5.4
Other liabilities [1]................	39.0	80.2	50.4	55.4	46.0	36.1	-	35.7	21.0
Personal saving...................	217.6	390.3	363.8	361.3	449.6	435.3	384.4	460.0	409.8
Less: Government insurance and pension reserve	35.8	71.9	72.5	83.9	89.8	86.0	80.2	88.3	87.7
Net investment in consumer durables	26.3	95.8	102.9	112.6	109.0	90.0	53.1	67.7	85.5
Net saving by farm corporations........	0.5	0.9	0.9	1.4	1.8	2.2	1.6	0.8	0.4
Equals: Personal saving, flow of funds basis.	155.1	221.7	187.5	163.5	249.0	257.1	249.4	303.3	236.2
Personal saving, NIPA basis.............	153.9	189.3	142.0	155.7	152.1	170.0	201.6	238.7	190.3
Difference [2].....................	1.2	32.5	45.5	7.8	96.9	87.0	47.9	64.7	45.9

- Represents or rounds to zero.   Z Less than $50 million.   [1] Includes corporate farms.   [2] Personal saving on national income account basis measures personal saving as income less taxes and consumption; flow-of-funds basis measures the same concept from acquisition of assets less borrowing.

Source: Board of Governors of the Federal Reserve System, *Flow of Funds Accounts*, quarterly.

No. 703. Average Annual Expenditures of All Consumer Units: 1992

[In dollars. Based on Consumer Expenditure Survey. Data are averages for the noninstitutional population. Expenditures reported here are out-of-pocket]

ITEM	All con- sumer units	White and other	Black	AGE					
				Under 25 yrs.	25 to 34 yrs.	35 to 44 yrs.	45 to 54 yrs.	55 to 64 yrs.	65 yrs. and over
Total	29,846	31,158	19,695	17,258	29,554	37,196	37,427	31,704	20,616
Food	4,273	4,416	3,156	2,621	4,218	5,218	5,233	4,354	3,198
Food at home	2,643	2,699	2,203	1,440	2,486	3,201	3,102	2,833	2,211
Cereals and bakery products	411	420	336	211	388	490	483	440	354
Cereals and cereal products	141	142	134	82	144	175	159	138	113
Bakery products	270	279	202	129	245	315	324	301	242
Meats, poultry, fish, and eggs	687	681	736	350	631	832	822	753	579
Beef	210	213	195	107	203	262	255	219	164
Pork	156	152	188	73	140	177	188	179	142
Other meats	94	94	90	43	86	120	110	102	77
Poultry	123	122	133	73	114	149	142	132	104
Fish and seafood	77	74	100	40	64	95	92	89	66
Eggs	28	28	29	14	24	30	35	32	27
Dairy products	302	316	192	167	287	380	350	303	247
Fresh milk and cream	134	140	86	84	132	165	148	128	115
Other dairy products	168	176	106	83	156	215	202	175	132
Fruits and vegetables	428	436	367	226	370	494	485	490	416
Fresh fruits	127	130	108	63	103	148	139	154	130
Fresh vegetables	127	130	100	67	114	142	149	143	119
Processed fruits	100	102	87	49	88	116	107	111	103
Processed vegetables	74	75	72	48	65	87	90	81	64
Other food at home	814	845	573	486	810	1,005	961	847	615
Food away from home	1,631	1,717	953	1,181	1,732	2,017	2,131	1,521	987
Alcoholic beverages	301	315	191	356	365	352	299	321	159
Housing	9,477	9,833	6,718	5,135	10,018	12,120	11,036	9,436	6,733
Shelter	5,411	5,628	3,735	3,148	6,132	7,215	6,299	5,105	3,241
Owned dwellings	3,310	3,571	1,299	363	3,146	4,926	4,406	3,514	1,978
Mortgage interest and charges	1,968	2,124	760	227	2,264	3,405	2,745	1,656	469
Property taxes	782	842	318	81	531	909	1,027	1,070	803
Maintenance, repair, insurance	560	604	220	54	351	613	633	788	706
Rented dwellings	1,761	1,684	2,355	2,656	2,817	1,901	1,313	1,016	1,039
Other lodging	340	373	82	129	169	387	580	575	223
Utilities, fuels, and public services	1,984	2,000	1,859	1,024	1,797	2,232	2,375	2,255	1,816
Natural gas	252	244	315	101	212	281	295	305	255
Electricity	787	801	678	384	688	899	959	892	725
Fuel oil and other fuels	92	99	43	19	65	94	86	119	132
Telephone	623	619	647	469	648	698	753	652	465
Water and other public services	230	237	177	51	185	260	281	286	238
Household operations	487	518	245	141	579	664	393	374	474
Personal services	242	252	166	94	445	394	69	58	178
Other household expenses	245	266	79	47	134	270	324	316	296
Housekeeping supplies	433	455	257	170	365	507	560	450	413
Laundry and cleaning supplies	118	121	101	65	111	137	162	116	94
Other household products	195	208	99	57	158	228	247	210	201
Postage and stationery	119	127	57	48	96	142	151	123	118
Household furnishings, equipment	1,162	1,232	621	652	1,145	1,502	1,409	1,252	789
Household textiles	92	99	42	48	86	109	116	101	75
Furniture	316	329	219	238	352	450	381	317	127
Floor coverings	71	78	16	2	45	82	57	61	125
Major appliances	141	145	108	67	127	163	160	150	138
Small appliances, misc. housewares	84	91	33	45	70	87	120	136	55
Misc. household equipment	458	491	202	253	465	612	575	487	268
Apparel and services	1,710	1,741	1,468	1,267	1,842	2,210	2,245	1,631	882
Men and boys	450	466	328	273	504	588	672	395	185
Women and girls	680	695	560	483	606	894	902	708	425
Children under 2 years old	78	79	69	121	138	91	53	53	22
Footwear	231	226	267	165	272	275	283	223	136
Other	272	275	244	224	322	363	335	252	114
Transportation	5,228	5,465	3,404	3,622	5,376	6,228	6,755	5,684	3,290
Vehicle purchases (net outlay)	2,189	2,299	1,334	1,743	2,355	2,584	2,772	2,329	1,289
Cars and trucks, new	1,131	1,193	654	744	1,189	1,350	1,200	1,483	744
Cars and trucks, used	1,022	1,066	679	947	1,139	1,192	1,476	841	541
Other vehicles	36	40	1	52	27	42	96	5	5
Gasoline and motor oil	973	1,013	666	649	994	1,165	1,269	1,046	621
Other vehicle expenses	1,776	1,855	1,162	1,086	1,772	2,155	2,364	1,945	1,122
Vehicle finance charges	256	268	169	172	328	337	359	226	79
Maintenance and repairs	612	633	446	435	592	728	738	715	429
Vehicle insurance	629	656	423	351	589	694	873	738	463
Rent, lease, licenses, other	279	299	124	128	263	396	393	267	152
Public transportation	290	297	242	144	255	324	350	364	257
Health care [1]	1,634	1,743	795	416	1,053	1,570	1,646	1,993	2,474
Entertainment [2]	1,500	1,608	667	928	1,569	2,041	1,896	1,587	754
Personal care products and services	387	391	355	253	361	461	481	408	306
Reading	162	173	73	73	142	183	204	188	144
Education	426	460	163	833	305	533	809	282	93
Tobacco products, smoking supplies	275	282	219	220	278	326	376	310	147
Miscellaneous	765	799	500	408	780	985	982	788	484
Cash contributions	958	1,028	417	124	428	938	1,208	1,620	1,227
Personal insurance and pensions	2,750	2,902	1,569	1,003	2,821	4,030	4,256	3,103	724
Life and other personal insurance	353	363	273	50	238	456	531	491	259
Pensions and Social Security	2,397	2,539	1,297	953	2,583	3,574	3,725	2,612	465
Personal taxes	3,068	3,275	1,408	786	3,010	4,405	4,527	3,709	1,284

See footnotes at end of table.

No. 703. Average Annual Expenditures of All Consumer Units: 1992—Continued

[See headnote, page 460]

ITEM	REGION				SIZE OF CONSUMER UNIT				
	North-east	Mid-west	South	West	One person	Two persons	Three persons	Four persons	Five or more
Total	31,177	28,445	27,750	33,647	17,797	30,773	34,982	40,658	38,019
Food	4,524	4,165	4,028	4,549	2,277	4,298	5,085	5,950	6,229
Food at home	2,838	2,555	2,478	2,819	1,273	2,525	3,173	3,825	4,397
Cereals and bakery products	452	405	382	423	196	385	472	626	701
Cereals and cereal products	149	139	133	147	61	124	161	224	271
Bakery products	302	266	249	276	135	261	311	402	430
Meats, poultry, fish, and eggs	785	640	670	674	305	656	867	984	1,169
Beef	221	202	209	212	88	195	279	292	385
Pork	154	160	162	142	67	158	182	231	256
Other meats	103	96	87	92	42	85	111	143	169
Poultry	170	104	115	112	59	118	155	176	196
Fish and seafood	107	56	68	84	34	76	108	100	116
Eggs	28	22	30	31	15	25	32	41	46
Dairy products	332	302	270	321	150	274	347	450	537
Fresh milk and cream	141	135	125	140	65	116	149	203	264
Other dairy products	191	167	145	182	85	158	198	247	274
Fruits and vegetables	489	386	394	475	233	441	500	556	657
Fresh fruits	144	115	112	151	71	135	145	154	198
Fresh vegetables	153	105	115	145	66	134	147	163	192
Processed fruits	115	96	91	105	57	101	114	136	148
Processed vegetables	77	70	76	73	39	70	94	102	118
Other food at home	781	821	763	926	389	770	987	1,208	1,332
Food away from home	1,686	1,610	1,550	1,730	1,004	1,773	1,912	2,125	1,832
Alcoholic beverages	343	290	250	355	273	366	287	297	213
Housing	10,701	8,504	8,422	11,150	6,461	9,246	10,963	12,808	11,707
Shelter	6,588	4,488	4,423	6,961	4,012	5,042	6,200	7,220	6,709
Owned dwellings	4,007	2,957	2,654	4,110	1,626	3,218	4,067	5,320	4,341
Mortgage interest and charges	2,172	1,581	1,621	2,804	808	1,653	2,499	3,635	3,020
Property taxes	1,274	802	494	728	441	904	900	1,050	821
Maintenance, repair, insurance	562	574	539	578	378	661	668	636	499
Rented dwellings	2,135	1,249	1,500	2,435	2,217	1,365	1,755	1,459	2,112
Other lodging	446	282	270	416	169	460	378	440	257
Utilities, fuels, and public services	2,094	1,951	2,032	1,832	1,303	2,053	2,231	2,493	2,627
Natural gas	295	382	156	209	163	252	282	320	366
Electricity	745	695	954	667	466	832	892	1,042	1,040
Fuel oil and other fuels	230	77	51	37	67	110	96	108	81
Telephone	636	589	624	646	470	616	700	722	821
Water and other public services	187	208	248	273	137	241	261	301	317
Household operations	420	443	475	629	273	355	651	914	621
Personal services	203	244	238	288	87	86	395	604	397
Other household expenses	217	200	237	341	186	269	256	310	224
Housekeeping supplies	443	428	438	421	248	466	482	630	501
Laundry and cleaning supplies	122	124	119	107	61	115	141	176	176
Other household products	197	178	217	179	103	216	211	305	213
Postage and stationery	124	126	102	134	84	135	130	149	111
Household furnishings, equipment	1,157	1,193	1,054	1,307	625	1,331	1,399	1,552	1,250
Household textiles	96	99	82	97	40	102	119	128	118
Furniture	319	328	277	364	167	331	368	486	372
Floor coverings	44	64	96	65	33	112	88	60	42
Major appliances	135	139	129	169	88	157	154	183	163
Small appliances, misc. housewares	94	78	77	94	42	108	91	111	81
Misc. household equipment	470	485	393	519	255	522	580	584	474
Apparel and services	2,077	1,637	1,540	1,702	948	1,703	1,927	2,410	2,578
Men and boys	586	461	395	385	231	431	507	719	658
Women and girls	808	676	595	693	384	726	755	897	964
Children under 2 years old	90	69	69	91	14	41	150	138	173
Footwear	304	207	214	213	119	213	224	361	431
Other	290	223	267	320	201	292	292	295	352
Transportation	4,514	5,352	5,087	6,044	2,549	5,670	6,241	7,251	7,118
Vehicle purchases (net outlay)	1,534	2,466	2,193	2,515	844	2,434	2,585	3,247	3,180
Cars and trucks, new	876	1,227	1,099	1,327	425	1,400	1,255	1,749	1,253
Cars and trucks, used	626	1,217	1,064	1,120	390	1,007	1,264	1,456	1,908
Other vehicles	32	22	29	67	30	27	66	42	19
Gasoline and motor oil	842	961	1,021	1,044	497	1,015	1,175	1,330	1,396
Other vehicle expenses	1,740	1,673	1,693	2,077	988	1,867	2,171	2,393	2,257
Vehicle finance charges	177	280	288	257	105	243	376	380	364
Maintenance and repairs	590	567	595	718	366	659	680	801	800
Vehicle insurance	684	545	612	705	345	674	814	827	734
Rent, lease, licenses, other	288	282	198	397	172	291	301	385	359
Public transportation	399	252	180	408	220	354	310	281	285
Health care [1]	1,653	1,535	1,711	1,610	1,049	2,047	1,760	1,840	1,570
Entertainment [2]	1,516	1,376	1,285	1,990	799	1,461	1,687	2,458	1,953
Personal care products and services	379	366	396	409	216	407	477	509	502
Reading	185	171	134	171	121	186	167	189	155
Education	509	432	369	427	309	285	550	681	624
Tobacco products, smoking supplies	268	298	295	220	178	275	340	335	367
Miscellaneous	715	672	724	997	549	768	899	965	875
Cash contributions	924	1,081	945	864	761	1,249	1,032	816	731
Personal insurance and pensions	2,869	2,566	2,564	3,158	1,307	2,811	3,567	4,150	3,398
Life and other personal insurance	367	333	395	293	122	407	436	546	441
Pensions and Social Security	2,502	2,233	2,169	2,865	1,185	2,404	3,130	3,604	2,957
Personal taxes	3,525	2,512	2,557	4,049	1,703	3,408	3,681	4,593	2,838

See footnotes at end of table.

No. 703. Average Annual Expenditures of All Consumer Units: 1992—Continued
[See headnote, page 460]

ITEM	Husband and wife only	Husband and wife with children				One parent, at least one child under 18	Single person and other consumer units
		Total	Oldest child under 6	Oldest child 6 to 17	Oldest child 18 and over		
Total	33,361	41,918	37,175	42,895	44,198	20,826	20,380
Food	4,616	6,020	4,747	6,324	6,592	3,483	2,802
Food at home	2,694	3,850	3,196	4,016	4,137	2,353	1,668
Cereals and bakery products	408	619	471	675	648	381	253
Cereals and cereal products	130	220	172	247	214	148	84
Bakery products	278	399	299	428	434	233	169
Meats, poultry, fish, and eggs	693	988	762	1,012	1,154	632	433
Beef	204	307	221	327	348	185	131
Pork	164	216	167	215	265	152	98
Other meats	89	142	114	150	154	81	58
Poultry	122	179	137	182	212	119	81
Fish and seafood	87	107	94	99	136	66	45
Eggs	27	38	30	41	39	29	19
Dairy products	293	448	380	482	446	291	188
Fresh milk and cream	120	201	184	211	197	134	84
Other dairy products	173	248	195	271	249	157	104
Fruits and vegetables	484	576	485	588	637	352	284
Fresh fruits	152	168	134	173	188	97	85
Fresh vegetables	146	167	132	169	194	102	83
Processed fruits	112	137	128	141	137	86	67
Processed vegetables	75	105	91	106	117	66	50
Other food at home	816	1,219	1,098	1,258	1,253	696	510
Food away from home	1,921	2,170	1,552	2,308	2,456	1,131	1,134
Alcoholic beverages	399	295	291	271	348	113	282
Housing	9,852	12,971	13,536	13,459	11,535	7,618	7,001
Shelter	5,260	7,413	7,658	7,861	6,330	4,459	4,204
Owned dwellings	3,723	5,590	5,431	5,990	4,947	1,621	1,752
Mortgage interest and charges	1,891	3,774	3,901	4,159	2,915	1,086	868
Property taxes	1,059	1,110	945	1,106	1,261	306	481
Maintenance, repair, insurance	773	706	586	725	771	230	402
Rented dwellings	972	1,371	1,965	1,426	755	2,709	2,280
Other lodging	565	452	261	445	629	129	173
Utilities, fuels, and public services	2,139	2,472	2,107	2,486	2,759	1,731	1,530
Natural gas	260	317	264	318	362	266	191
Electricity	881	1,027	834	1,043	1,162	684	564
Fuel oil and other fuels	120	105	89	115	99	41	77
Telephone	607	714	666	697	790	588	541
Water and other public services	272	308	254	313	346	153	156
Household operations	387	890	1,573	886	309	441	281
Personal services	65	565	1,314	508	31	321	108
Other household expenses	322	325	259	378	278	119	173
Housekeeping supplies	525	585	512	608	606	335	270
Laundry and cleaning supplies	124	168	140	171	189	113	72
Other household products	247	269	248	287	252	149	114
Postage and stationery	155	147	123	149	165	74	84
Household furnishings, equipment	1,541	1,611	1,686	1,617	1,530	652	717
Household textiles	113	134	107	134	162	57	52
Furniture	365	463	459	518	357	202	207
Floor coverings	150	82	186	54	40	13	29
Major appliances	173	179	166	182	184	83	103
Small appliances, misc. housewares	128	112	99	104	138	38	49
Misc. household equipment	611	641	669	624	649	258	277
Apparel and services	1,789	2,392	1,965	2,573	2,423	1,377	1,191
Men and boys	470	689	427	829	649	260	293
Women and girls	767	885	600	955	1,010	674	468
Children under 2 years old	48	156	451	77	41	69	33
Footwear	205	331	221	387	322	206	164
Other	300	331	265	325	400	168	231
Transportation	6,156	7,601	6,363	7,294	9,263	3,175	3,256
Vehicle purchases (net outlay)	2,673	3,319	2,842	3,181	3,997	1,414	1,197
Cars and trucks, new	1,515	1,666	1,670	1,484	2,018	751	592
Cars and trucks, used	1,149	1,588	1,156	1,651	1,837	625	571
Other vehicles	10	64	15	45	143	38	33
Gasoline and motor oil	1,090	1,405	1,139	1,351	1,739	614	630
Other vehicle expenses	2,004	2,568	2,095	2,479	3,149	985	1,189
Vehicle finance charges	252	434	386	431	482	159	142
Maintenance and repairs	705	819	665	828	935	349	441
Vehicle insurance	721	891	685	814	1,218	363	422
Rent, lease, licenses, other	326	424	359	406	514	113	184
Public transportation	388	309	286	283	377	162	240
Health care [1]	2,376	1,944	1,570	1,876	2,400	814	1,126
Entertainment [2]	1,607	2,406	1,886	2,608	2,463	928	897
Personal care products and services	447	522	408	540	589	307	256
Reading	206	200	166	208	215	81	159
Education	262	740	186	795	1,110	319	324
Tobacco products, smoking supplies	253	322	266	311	393	245	242
Miscellaneous	771	959	833	1,040	909	756	600
Cash contributions	1,532	1,070	947	996	1,320	310	707
Personal insurance and pensions	3,094	4,477	4,010	4,600	4,638	1,299	1,569
Life and other personal insurance	501	567	381	626	611	149	151
Pensions and Social Security	2,593	3,910	3,630	3,974	4,027	1,150	1,418
Personal taxes	3,997	4,888	4,176	5,214	4,887	724	1,807

[1] For additional health care expenditures, see table 164.　[2] For additional recreation expenditures, see table 394.
Source: U.S. Bureau of Labor Statistics, *Consumer Expenditures in 1992;* and unpublished data.

No. 704. Average Annual Expenditures of All Consumer Units: 1986 to 1992

[In dollars. See headnote, table 703]

ITEM	1986	1987	1988	1989	1990	1991	1992
Number of consumer units (1,000)	94,044	94,150	94,862	95,818	96,968	97,918	100,019
Total expenditures	23,866	24,414	25,892	27,810	28,381	29,614	29,846
Food	3,448	3,664	3,748	4,152	4,296	4,271	4,273
Food at home	1,993	2,099	2,136	2,390	2,485	2,651	2,643
Cereal and bakery products	275	299	312	359	368	404	411
Meats, poultry, fish, and eggs	562	572	551	611	668	709	687
Dairy products	251	274	274	304	295	294	302
Fruits and vegetables	320	356	373	408	408	429	428
Other food at home	585	598	625	708	746	815	814
Food away from home	1,455	1,565	1,612	1,762	1,811	1,620	1,631
Alcoholic beverages	271	289	269	284	293	297	301
Tobacco products, smoking supplies	230	232	242	261	274	276	275
Housing	7,292	7,569	7,918	8,434	8,703	9,252	9,477
Shelter	3,979	4,154	4,332	4,660	4,836	5,191	5,411
Fuels, utilities, public services	1,645	1,671	1,747	1,835	1,890	1,990	1,984
Household operations, furnishings	1,352	1,403	1,477	1,546	1,571	1,648	1,649
Housekeeping supplies	316	341	361	394	406	424	433
Apparel and services	1,346	1,446	1,489	1,582	1,618	1,735	1,710
Transportation	4,842	4,600	5,093	5,187	5,120	5,151	5,228
Vehicle purchase	2,338	2,022	2,361	2,291	2,129	2,111	2,189
Gasoline and motor oil	915	888	932	985	1,047	995	973
Other transportation	1,590	1,690	1,800	1,911	1,944	2,045	2,066
Health care	1,135	1,135	1,298	1,407	1,480	1,554	1,634
Life insurance	292	294	314	346	345	356	353
Pensions and Social Security	1,834	1,881	1,935	2,125	2,248	2,431	2,397
Other expenditures	3,174	3,305	3,586	4,030	4,003	4,291	4,198

No. 705. Average Annual Expenditures of All Consumer Units, by Metropolitan Area: 1992

[In dollars. Metropolitan areas defined June 30, 1983, CMSA=Consolidated Metropolitan Statistical Area; MSA=Metropolitan Statistical Area; PMSA=Primary Metropolitan Statistical Area. See text, section 1, and Appendix II. See headnote, table 703]

METROPOLITAN AREA	Total expenditures [1]	Food	HOUSING Total [1]	Shelter	Apparel and services	TRANSPORTATION Total [1]	Vehicle purchases	Gasoline and motor oil	Health care
Anchorage, AK MSA	42,331	5,213	13,800	8,675	2,211	6,684	2,485	1,019	2,014
Atlanta, GA MSA	36,774	4,236	12,409	6,913	2,227	6,167	2,417	1,152	1,903
Baltimore, MD MSA	32,746	4,655	11,362	7,193	1,925	5,050	2,014	1,035	1,536
Boston-Lawrence-Salem, MA-NH CMSA	31,824	4,371	11,296	7,356	2,067	5,147	2,153	918	1,708
Buffalo-Niagara Falls, NY CMSA	24,709	4,537	8,062	4,766	1,345	4,373	1,908	748	1,394
Chicago-Gary-Lake County, IL-IN-WI CMSA	34,105	4,867	11,160	6,649	2,466	5,751	2,296	1,011	1,650
Cincinnati-Hamilton, OH-KY-IN CMSA	29,769	4,662	9,137	5,081	1,818	5,307	2,089	1,023	1,515
Cleveland-Akron-Lorain, OH CMSA	27,751	4,353	8,364	4,234	1,990	4,754	1,933	930	1,564
Dallas-Fort Worth, TX CMSA	35,190	4,869	10,825	6,094	2,017	6,962	3,076	1,220	1,658
Detroit-Ann Arbor, MI CMSA	30,442	4,331	10,156	5,859	1,836	5,838	2,472	1,034	1,363
Honolulu, HI MSA	37,273	6,333	11,863	8,080	2,166	5,628	2,061	759	1,557
Houston-Galveston-Brazoria, TX CMSA	32,823	4,887	9,377	4,911	2,170	6,455	2,978	1,141	1,638
Kansas City, MO-Kansas City, KS CMSA	31,218	4,482	9,013	4,958	1,943	5,816	2,406	998	2,004
Los Angeles-Long Beach, CA PMSA	35,034	4,808	12,932	8,403	2,025	5,453	1,996	1,034	1,457
Miami-Fort Lauderdale, FL CMSA	30,002	4,941	9,862	6,107	1,594	5,047	1,711	920	1,550
Milwaukee, WI PMSA	30,296	4,268	9,535	5,734	1,672	5,702	2,796	964	1,433
Minneapolis-St. Paul, MN-WI MSA	38,887	4,837	12,047	6,967	2,248	6,153	2,507	1,085	1,619
New York-Northern New Jersey-Long Island, NY-NJ-CT CMSA	35,807	5,011	13,193	8,724	2,471	4,672	1,166	817	1,667
Philadelphia-Wilmington-Trenton, PA-NJ-DE-MD CMSA	31,985	4,596	10,705	6,285	2,099	4,252	1,268	862	1,475
Pittsburgh-Beaver Valley, PA CMSA	28,177	4,374	8,412	4,392	2,019	4,808	2,001	800	1,801
Portland-Vancouver, OR-WA CMSA	30,649	4,497	9,368	5,705	1,619	5,667	2,626	958	1,428
San Diego, CA MSA	35,670	4,587	12,518	8,536	1,657	7,164	3,369	1,086	1,324
San Francisco-Oakland-San Jose, CA CMSA	39,584	5,212	14,019	9,402	2,279	6,680	2,606	1,025	1,416
Seattle-Tacoma, WA CMSA	35,785	4,490	11,911	7,745	1,857	6,328	2,296	1,114	1,573
St. Louis-East St. Louis-Alton, MO-IL CMSA	28,341	3,993	8,347	4,403	1,240	5,086	2,130	952	1,595
Washington, DC-MD-VA MSA	39,745	4,713	13,609	8,682	2,328	5,868	1,960	997	1,643

[1] Includes items not shown separately.

Sources of tables 704 and 705: U.S. Bureau of Labor Statistics, *Consumer Expenditures in 1992,* (BLS Report 861, December 1993); and unpublished data.

No. 706. Money Income of Households—Percent Distribution, by Income Level, Race, and Hispanic Origin, in Constant (1992) Dollars: 1970 to 1992

[Constant dollars based on CPI-U-X1 deflator. Households as of **March** of **following year.** Based on Current Population Survey; see text, sections 1 and 14, and Appendix III. For definition of median, see Guide to Tabular Presentation]

YEAR	Number of households (1,000)	PERCENT DISTRIBUTION							Median income (dollars)
		Under $10,000	$10,000- $14,999	$15,000- $24,999	$25,000- $34,999	$35,000- $49,999	$50,000- $74,999	$75,000 and over	
ALL HOUSEHOLDS [1]									
1970	64,778	15.5	8.7	17.5	18.5	20.0	14.0	5.9	29,670
1975	72,867	15.5	9.9	17.9	16.4	19.7	14.6	6.3	29,458
1980 [2]	82,368	14.7	9.3	17.7	16.1	18.7	15.6	8.0	30,191
1985 [2]	88,458	14.9	8.9	17.3	15.2	17.9	16.0	9.8	30,796
1990 [3]	94,312	13.8	8.7	16.9	15.1	17.6	16.1	11.7	32,142
1991	95,669	14.5	9.2	17.1	14.8	17.5	15.7	11.2	31,033
1992	96,391	14.6	9.5	16.8	14.8	17.1	16.1	11.0	30,786
WHITE									
1970	57,575	14.2	8.2	16.9	18.8	20.9	14.7	6.3	30,903
1975	64,392	13.6	9.4	17.6	16.7	20.4	15.4	6.8	30,806
1980 [2]	71,872	12.9	8.8	17.4	16.3	19.5	16.5	8.6	31,851
1985 [2]	76,576	13.2	8.5	17.0	15.5	18.5	16.8	10.6	32,478
1990 [3]	80,968	11.8	8.4	16.8	15.4	18.2	16.9	12.4	33,525
1991	81,675	12.4	8.9	17.0	15.1	18.1	16.6	12.0	32,519
1992	82,083	12.5	9.1	16.7	15.1	17.7	17.0	11.9	32,368
BLACK									
1970	6,180	27.9	13.4	22.4	15.5	12.2	7.2	1.5	18,810
1975	7,489	29.0	14.1	20.1	14.6	13.5	7.1	1.6	18,494
1980 [2]	8,847	29.0	13.5	20.4	13.8	12.4	8.3	2.5	18,350
1985 [2]	9,797	29.0	12.5	20.3	12.8	13.0	9.2	3.1	19,323
1990 [3]	10,671	28.9	11.5	18.5	13.4	13.5	9.3	4.9	20,048
1991	11,083	30.3	11.4	18.2	13.4	13.7	9.0	4.0	19,373
1992	11,190	30.5	12.2	18.3	13.2	12.8	8.8	4.2	18,660
HISPANIC [4]									
1975	2,948	19.6	13.4	23.8	17.4	16.0	7.5	2.3	22,131
1980 [2]	3,906	18.8	12.5	22.5	16.7	15.3	10.6	3.5	23,271
1985 [2]	5,213	21.0	13.2	19.9	15.8	15.0	10.6	4.4	22,773
1990 [3]	6,220	19.3	12.6	20.0	16.3	16.2	10.0	5.5	23,970
1991	6,379	20.1	11.8	21.3	15.5	15.6	10.3	5.5	23,374
1992	6,626	20.4	12.6	20.8	16.3	14.5	10.5	5.0	22,848

[1] Includes other races not shown separately.   [2] Beginning 1983, data based on revised Hispanic population controls and not directly comparable with prior years.   [3] Beginning 1987, data based on revised processing procedures and not directly comparable with prior years.   [4] Persons of Hispanic origin may be of any race. Income data for Hispanic origin households are not available prior to 1972.

No. 707. Money Income of Households—Median Income, by Race and Hispanic Origin, in Current and Constant (1992) Dollars: 1970 to 1992

[See headnote, table 706]

YEAR	MEDIAN INCOME IN CURRENT DOLLARS					MEDIAN INCOME IN CONSTANT (1992) DOLLARS				
	All households [1]	White	Black	Asian, Pacific Islander	Hispanic [2]	All households [1]	White	Black	Asian, Pacific Islanders	Hispanic [2]
1970	8,734	9,097	5,537	(NA)	(NA)	29,670	30,903	18,810	(NA)	(NA)
1975	11,800	12,340	7,408	(NA)	8,865	29,458	30,806	18,494	(NA)	22,131
1980	17,710	18,684	10,764	(NA)	13,651	30,191	31,851	18,350	(NA)	23,271
1981	19,074	20,153	11,309	(NA)	15,300	29,701	31,381	17,610	(NA)	23,825
1982	20,171	21,117	11,968	(NA)	15,178	29,602	30,991	17,564	(NA)	22,275
1983 [3]	21,018	22,035	12,473	(NA)	15,794	29,607	31,039	17,570	(NA)	22,248
1984	22,415	23,647	13,471	(NA)	16,992	30,268	31,931	18,190	(NA)	22,945
1985	23,618	24,908	14,819	(NA)	17,465	30,796	32,478	19,323	(NA)	22,773
1986	24,897	26,175	15,080	(NA)	18,352	31,871	33,507	19,304	(NA)	23,493
1987 [4]	26,061	27,458	15,672	(NA)	19,336	32,186	33,912	19,355	(NA)	23,881
1988	27,225	28,781	16,407	32,267	20,359	32,288	34,133	19,458	38,268	24,125
1989	28,906	30,406	18,083	36,102	21,921	32,706	34,403	20,460	40,848	24,803
1990	29,943	31,231	18,676	38,450	22,330	32,142	33,525	20,048	41,274	23,970
1991	30,126	31,569	18,807	36,449	22,691	31,033	32,519	19,373	37,546	23,374
1992	30,786	32,368	18,660	38,153	22,848	30,786	32,368	18,660	38,153	22,848

NA Not available.   [1] Includes other races not shown separately.   [2] Hispanic persons may be of any race.   [3] Beginning 1983, data based on revised Hispanic population controls and not directly comparable with prior years.   [4] Beginning 1987, based on revised processing procedures and not directly comparable with prior years.

Source of tables 706 and 707: U.S. Bureau of the Census, *Current Population Reports,* P60-184; and unpublished data.

No. 708. Money Income of Households—Percent Distribution, by Income Level and Selected Characteristics: 1992

[See headnote, table 706. For composition of regions, see table 26]

CHARACTERISTIC	Number of households (1,000)	PERCENT DISTRIBUTION								Median income (dollars)
		Under $5,000	$5,000-$9,999	$10,000-$14,999	$15,000-$24,999	$25,000-$34,999	$35,000-$49,999	$50,000-$74,999	$75,000 and over	
Total [1]	96,391	4.6	10.0	9.5	16.8	14.8	17.1	16.1	11.0	30,786
Age of householder:										
15 to 24 years	5,022	12.5	15.0	14.8	24.5	15.0	12.2	4.6	1.4	17,778
25 to 34 years	19,741	4.8	7.4	7.6	17.9	18.4	20.6	16.4	7.0	31,434
35 to 44 years	21,717	3.6	4.8	6.1	13.3	14.6	21.0	22.0	14.7	40,090
45 to 54 years	16,576	3.0	4.9	5.6	11.8	12.7	18.4	23.2	20.4	44,540
55 to 64 years	12,438	4.4	8.6	8.1	15.5	14.5	17.0	17.6	14.2	34,062
65 years and over	20,896	5.0	21.7	17.4	22.5	13.6	9.9	5.7	4.2	17,160
White	82,083	3.6	8.9	9.1	16.7	15.1	17.7	17.0	11.9	32,368
Black	11,190	11.8	18.7	12.2	18.3	13.2	12.8	8.8	4.2	18,660
Hispanic [2]	6,626	6.6	13.8	12.6	20.8	16.3	14.5	10.5	5.0	22,848
Northeast	19,437	4.3	10.1	8.5	15.3	13.9	16.9	17.2	13.8	33,194
Midwest	23,307	4.3	9.6	9.4	17.3	15.2	18.4	16.3	9.5	30,911
South	33,392	5.6	11.1	10.4	18.1	15.2	15.9	14.6	9.0	27,741
West	20,255	3.5	8.7	8.9	15.8	14.7	17.7	17.1	13.5	33,621
Size of household:										
One person	23,642	8.4	24.0	16.5	20.9	13.5	9.6	4.8	2.3	15,423
Two persons	31,175	3.5	6.4	9.0	19.0	16.7	18.3	16.3	10.9	31,951
Three persons	16,895	4.2	5.2	6.3	13.8	14.9	20.1	20.9	14.6	38,937
Four persons	14,926	2.7	3.8	4.8	11.4	13.8	21.2	24.6	17.7	44,392
Five persons	6,357	2.5	5.1	5.9	12.8	13.1	20.3	24.1	16.3	42,471
Six persons	2,180	3.0	5.0	7.3	16.1	14.6	19.4	17.2	17.3	37,455
Seven or more persons	1,215	3.0	10.4	8.9	14.2	15.1	19.3	14.3	14.8	33,635
Family households	68,144	3.4	5.5	7.2	15.5	15.0	19.4	19.8	14.1	37,222
Married-couple	53,171	1.4	3.0	5.7	14.0	15.0	21.0	22.9	16.9	42,140
Male householder, wife absent	3,026	3.6	7.0	8.6	20.6	17.7	19.6	14.7	8.3	30,492
Female householder, husband absent	11,947	12.6	16.2	13.1	20.9	14.7	12.2	7.4	2.9	18,587
Nonfamily households	28,247	7.4	20.9	15.0	20.1	14.3	11.5	7.1	3.7	17,711
Male householder	12,254	5.8	13.9	12.9	20.2	16.4	14.9	10.3	5.7	23,168
Female householder	15,993	8.7	26.3	16.6	19.9	12.8	8.9	4.6	2.1	14,438
Educational attainment of householder: [3]										
Total	91,369	4.2	9.8	9.2	16.4	14.8	17.4	16.7	11.6	31,706
Less than 9th grade	9,060	9.4	27.7	18.2	21.8	10.9	7.5	3.2	1.3	13,383
9th to 12th grade (no diploma)	9,933	8.7	20.1	15.6	22.0	13.5	11.6	6.4	2.1	17,375
High school graduate	30,103	4.0	9.3	10.1	19.0	17.5	19.0	15.5	5.6	29,006
Some college, no degree	15,387	3.1	6.4	7.4	16.0	16.7	20.5	20.1	9.9	35,327
Associate degree	5,502	2.1	4.1	5.9	16.1	16.3	21.9	21.5	11.9	38,382
Bachelor's degree or more	21,382	1.4	1.9	3.1	8.3	11.7	18.4	25.2	29.9	54,117
Bachelor's degree	13,379	1.7	2.3	3.7	9.8	13.3	19.7	25.4	24.0	49,539
Master's degree	5,283	0.9	1.6	2.3	6.9	10.3	18.5	26.4	33.1	57,930
Professional degree	1,665	0.8	0.7	1.4	4.3	5.9	10.3	19.1	57.5	84,990
Doctorate degree	1,055	0.8	0.9	2.4	3.0	7.6	14.7	26.0	44.7	70,174
Tenure:										
Owner occupied	62,220	2.7	6.4	7.3	14.7	14.3	19.0	20.3	15.2	38,088
Renter occupied	32,499	7.8	16.5	13.2	20.7	15.9	13.8	8.5	3.6	20,731
Occupier paid no cash rent	1,672	13.6	18.3	15.3	20.5	13.6	10.1	5.9	2.6	15,919

[1] Includes other races not shown separately. [2] Persons of Hispanic origin may be of any race. [3] 25 years old and over.

Source: U.S. Bureau of the Census, *Current Population Reports*, P60-184; and unpublished data.

No. 709. Money Income of Households—Aggregate and Average Income, by Race and Hispanic Origin: 1992

[See headnote, table 706]

CHARACTERISTIC	ALL RACES [1]		WHITE		BLACK		HISPANIC [2]	
	Aggregate income (bil. dol.)	Mean income (dollars)	Aggregate income (bil. dol.)	Mean income (dollars)	Aggregate income (bil. dol.)	Mean income (dollars)	Aggregate income (bil. dol.)	Mean income (dollars)
Total	3,761	39,020	3,347	40,780	284	25,409	193	29,102
Age of householder:								
15 to 24 years old	109	21,606	94	23,023	10	13,675	11	18,490
25 to 34 years old	717	36,328	628	38,616	61	22,460	51	27,584
35 to 44 years old	1,012	46,584	891	48,998	80	30,232	54	32,140
45 to 54 years old	870	52,479	776	54,476	64	35,756	41	36,249
55 to 64 years old	535	42,988	480	44,980	38	26,944	23	32,568
65 years old and over	519	24,849	479	25,678	32	16,528	14	19,529
Region:								
Northeast	820	42,189	745	43,691	52	27,904	30	25,818
Midwest	885	37,972	814	39,465	58	24,935	15	30,392
South	1,193	35,740	1,025	38,377	146	24,135	58	28,014
West	863	42,592	764	43,134	29	29,733	89	30,987
Size of household:								
One person	505	21,374	446	22,077	47	16,108	18	17,154
Two persons	1,252	40,146	1,152	41,926	71	24,401	41	27,592
Three persons	777	46,013	687	48,712	62	28,577	39	30,080
Four persons	759	50,821	671	53,243	58	33,888	44	33,881
Five persons	312	49,021	268	51,513	27	31,307	27	33,547
Six persons	104	47,573	83	51,054	14	32,562	13	31,750
Seven or more persons	53	43,606	41	46,763	7	26,727	12	34,864

[1] Includes other races not shown separately.   [2] Persons of Hispanic origin may be of any race.

Source: U.S. Bureau of the Census, *Current Population Reports*, P60-184; and unpublished data.

No. 710. Money Income of Households—Median Income and Income Level, by Household Type: 1992

[See headnote, table 706]

ITEM	All households	FAMILY HOUSEHOLDS				NONFAMILY HOUSEHOLDS		
		Total	Married couple	Male householder, wife absent	Female householder, husband absent	Total [1]	Single-person household	
							Male householder	Female householder
MEDIAN INCOME (dollars)								
All households	30,786	37,222	42,140	30,492	18,587	17,711	20,011	12,944
White	32,368	39,320	42,820	32,412	21,970	18,479	21,171	13,413
Black	18,660	21,761	34,290	23,439	12,606	12,062	13,369	9,092
Hispanic [2]	22,848	24,926	29,007	21,994	13,994	14,862	16,360	9,136
NUMBER (1,000)								
All households	96,391	68,144	53,171	3,026	11,947	28,247	9,436	14,206
Under $5,000	4,437	2,340	729	108	1,503	2,097	628	1,356
$5,000 to $9,999	9,675	3,761	1,615	212	1,933	5,914	1,554	4,119
$10,000 to $14,999	9,120	4,880	3,054	259	1,567	4,240	1,397	2,500
$15,000 to $19,999	8,473	5,316	3,683	318	1,315	3,157	1,136	1,664
$20,000 to $24,999	7,763	5,254	3,769	305	1,181	2,509	883	1,257
$25,000 to $34,999	14,305	10,253	7,957	535	1,761	4,052	1,477	1,721
$35,000 to $49,999	16,480	13,233	11,186	592	1,454	3,248	1,248	1,023
$50,000 to $74,999	15,490	13,492	12,167	444	881	1,997	719	411
$75,000 and over	10,648	9,614	9,009	254	351	1,034	394	156

[1] Includes other nonfamily households not shown separately.   [2] Persons of Hispanic origin may be of any race.

Source: U.S. Bureau of the Census, *Current Population Reports*, P60-184.

No. 711. Money Income of Households—Percent Distribution, by Income Quintile and Top 5 Percent: 1992

[See headnote, table 706. For composition of regions, see table 26]

CHARACTERISTIC	Number (1,000)	PERCENT DISTRIBUTION						
		Total	Lowest fifth	Second fifth	Third fifth	Fourth fifth	Highest fifth	Top 5 percent
Total	96,391	100.0	20.0	20.0	20.0	20.0	20.0	5.0
15 to 24 years old...............	5,022	100.0	36.3	29.3	20.0	10.9	3.5	0.4
25 to 34 years old...............	19,741	100.0	16.4	20.3	24.4	23.3	15.6	2.7
35 to 44 years old...............	21,717	100.0	11.7	15.2	20.5	25.7	27.1	6.3
45 to 54 years old...............	16,576	100.0	11.2	13.3	17.5	24.0	34.0	9.7
55 to 64 years old...............	12,438	100.0	17.6	18.3	19.5	20.3	24.3	6.6
65 years old and over	20,896	100.0	36.5	28.9	17.7	9.8	7.1	2.2
White	82,083	100.0	17.6	19.7	20.4	20.9	21.4	5.4
Black	11,190	100.0	37.8	22.3	17.6	13.7	8.6	1.5
Hispanic [1]	6,626	100.0	27.6	25.4	20.9	15.7	10.5	1.9
Northeast.....................	19,437	100.0	19.3	18.0	18.6	20.4	23.7	6.6
Midwest......................	23,307	100.0	19.3	20.3	20.6	21.3	18.5	4.1
South	33,392	100.0	22.5	21.7	20.2	18.6	16.9	3.9
West	20,255	100.0	17.3	18.8	20.3	20.3	23.3	6.4
Family households.............	68,144	100.0	12.9	17.8	20.6	23.5	25.3	6.4
Married-couple families	53,171	100.0	7.5	15.8	20.7	26.0	30.0	7.7
Male householder............	3,026	100.0	15.8	23.0	23.5	21.8	15.9	3.7
Female householder...........	11,947	100.0	36.4	25.1	19.1	12.9	6.5	1.1
Nonfamily households	28,247	100.0	37.1	25.4	18.7	11.5	7.3	1.6
Male householder............	12,254	100.0	26.9	24.9	21.9	15.1	11.1	2.8
Living alone	9,436	100.0	31.6	26.8	21.2	12.4	8.0	2.2
Female householder...........	15,993	100.0	44.9	25.8	16.2	8.7	4.4	0.7
Living alone	14,206	100.0	49.2	26.6	15.2	6.7	2.3	0.4
Worked	69,000	100.0	10.0	17.6	21.9	24.6	25.9	6.5
Worked at full-time jobs..........	60,801	100.0	7.1	16.5	22.2	26.2	27.9	7.0
Worked at part-time jobs..........	8,199	100.0	31.0	26.0	19.2	12.9	10.9	2.8
Did not work..................	27,391	100.0	45.3	26.0	15.3	8.4	5.1	1.2

[1] Persons of Hispanic origin may be of any race.

Source: U.S. Bureau of the Census, *Current Population Reports*, P60-184.

No. 712. Money Income of Households—Percent Distribution, by Income Level, Race, and Hispanic Origin: 1992

[See headnote, table 706]

TYPE OF HOUSEHOLD	Number of house-holds (1,000)	PERCENT DISTRIBUTION									Median income (dollars)
		Under $5,000	$5,000-$9,999	$10,000-$14,999	$15,000-$24,999	$25,000-$34,999	$35,000-$49,999	$50,000-$74,999	$75,000-$99,999	$100,000 and over	
HOUSEHOLDS											
Total [1]	96,391	4.6	10.0	9.5	16.8	14.8	17.1	16.1	6.1	4.9	30,786
White........	82,083	3.6	8.9	9.1	16.7	15.1	17.7	17.0	6.6	5.3	32,368
Black........	11,190	11.8	18.7	12.2	18.3	13.2	12.8	8.8	2.7	1.5	18,660
Asian, Pacific Islander,.....	2,118	4.7	7.1	7.6	13.8	12.7	19.1	18.4	8.9	8.3	38,153
Hispanic [2].....	6,626	6.6	13.8	12.6	20.8	16.3	14.5	10.5	3.2	1.8	22,848
FAMILIES											
Total [1]	68,144	3.4	5.5	7.2	15.5	15.0	19.4	19.8	7.8	6.3	37,222
White........	57,858	2.4	4.2	6.5	15.1	15.3	20.1	21.0	8.4	6.8	39,320
Black........	7,888	10.7	14.5	11.7	18.9	13.3	14.6	10.9	3.5	1.9	21,761
Asian, Pacific Islander,.....	1,662	3.4	5.7	5.8	11.3	12.2	19.9	21.3	10.6	9.7	43,418
Hispanic [2].....	5,318	5.4	10.9	12.4	21.4	17.0	15.5	11.8	3.6	2.0	24,926
NONFAMILIES											
Total [1]	28,247	7.4	20.9	15.0	20.1	14.3	11.5	7.1	2.1	1.6	17,711
White........	24,225	6.4	20.0	15.2	20.5	14.6	11.8	7.5	2.2	1.7	18,479
Black........	3,302	14.4	28.6	13.4	16.9	12.9	8.7	3.9	0.8	0.4	12,062
Asian, Pacific Islander,.....	456	9.4	12.1	14.3	20.8	14.3	15.8	7.9	2.2	3.2	21,052
Hispanic [2].....	1,308	11.2	25.6	13.4	18.3	13.3	10.6	4.8	1.8	1.0	14,862

[1] Includes other races not shown separately.   [2] Persons of Hispanic origin may be of any race.

Source: U.S. Bureau of the Census, *Current Population Reports*, P60-184; and unpublished data.

No. 713. Money Income of Households—Median Income, by State, in Constant (1992) Dollars: 1984 to 1992

[Constant dollars based on the CPI-U-X1 deflator. Data based on the Current Population Survey; see text, sections 1 and 14, and Appendix III. The CPS is designed to collect reliable data on income primarily at the national level and secondarily at the regional level. When the income data are tabulated by State, the estimates are considered less reliable and, therefore, particular caution should be used when trying to interpret the results]

STATE	1984	1985	1986	1987 [1]	1988	1989	1990	1991	1992
United States	30,268	30,796	31,871	32,094	32,288	32,706	32,142	31,033	30,786
Alabama............	23,374	23,904	24,491	24,372	23,658	24,082	25,073	25,079	25,891
Alaska.............	43,692	45,352	40,139	41,044	39,259	40,739	42,184	41,835	41,969
Arizona............	28,931	31,133	32,643	33,036	31,351	32,305	31,371	31,662	29,593
Arkansas...........	21,165	22,754	23,976	23,252	23,923	24,250	24,460	24,140	23,893
California	34,146	35,181	37,136	37,231	35,919	37,348	35,735	34,677	35,173
Colorado...........	34,840	36,747	34,809	32,699	31,089	30,330	32,990	32,447	32,716
Connecticut........	40,444	40,538	41,886	40,586	42,947	47,884	41,725	43,423	41,059
Delaware	34,864	29,964	32,804	36,117	36,178	36,283	33,067	33,566	35,739
District of Columbia	27,558	27,481	31,135	33,908	31,714	30,269	29,404	30,785	30,357
Florida.............	26,716	27,829	29,249	30,245	30,131	29,514	28,645	28,072	27,456
Georgia	26,985	27,446	31,196	32,993	31,506	31,162	29,585	28,031	28,889
Hawaii	38,994	37,762	37,127	43,253	39,165	39,640	41,780	38,367	42,171
Idaho	28,481	27,070	26,561	25,633	27,811	27,895	27,164	26,902	27,784
Illinois	32,073	32,428	33,937	33,450	35,015	35,414	34,932	32,844	31,707
Indiana............	30,747	29,566	29,094	27,812	31,183	29,302	28,906	27,904	28,663
Iowa	26,822	27,287	28,750	27,405	28,825	29,718	29,292	29,413	28,880
Kansas............	33,257	29,713	30,628	31,596	30,320	30,393	32,114	30,177	30,447
Kentucky	23,874	22,637	25,441	25,532	23,609	26,344	26,600	24,479	23,567
Louisiana..........	25,588	27,615	26,741	26,367	24,309	25,866	24,051	26,061	25,479
Maine..............	27,882	26,755	29,985	29,147	31,312	31,931	29,481	28,707	29,705
Maryland	40,116	39,294	39,176	43,189	43,350	40,750	41,711	38,064	37,287
Massachusetts......	36,404	36,779	38,837	39,819	39,390	40,830	38,909	36,789	36,558
Michigan...........	31,010	31,609	34,057	34,213	34,953	34,820	32,136	33,084	32,347
Minnesota..........	32,997	31,106	33,850	34,682	34,496	34,153	33,776	30,366	31,077
Mississippi.........	20,836	21,401	21,138	22,864	21,544	22,535	21,660	20,061	20,585
Missouri	28,053	28,606	28,066	29,295	27,803	29,980	29,340	28,767	27,490
Montana...........	26,380	26,386	26,022	25,286	26,365	26,806	25,092	25,574	26,602
Nebraska	28,893	28,424	27,871	28,737	29,838	29,779	29,501	30,439	30,177
Nevada	34,806	30,347	33,561	33,195	33,187	33,197	34,375	33,929	32,026
New Hampshire......	34,993	34,427	39,105	39,939	41,064	42,466	43,802	37,117	39,644
New Jersey.........	37,507	40,395	40,599	42,289	43,035	44,262	41,579	41,255	39,227
New Mexico	27,857	26,630	25,404	25,637	22,884	25,573	26,878	27,339	26,158
New York	29,744	30,823	32,035	32,585	34,292	35,636	33,911	32,751	31,254
North Carolina......	27,775	27,970	27,984	28,109	28,955	29,877	28,263	27,661	27,835
North Dakota.......	28,048	27,649	27,533	27,882	28,572	28,545	27,120	26,671	27,105
Ohio	31,224	32,824	32,150	31,831	32,899	32,836	32,217	30,687	31,479
Oklahoma..........	28,557	27,649	26,816	26,789	28,068	26,778	26,175	26,228	25,363
Oregon............	28,896	28,548	31,712	30,923	32,908	32,279	31,432	31,099	32,114
Pennsylvania.......	27,474	29,829	30,476	31,400	31,715	32,461	31,135	31,281	29,985
Rhode Island.......	29,183	32,109	33,974	34,942	35,392	34,084	34,316	31,764	30,636
South Carolina......	27,424	26,125	28,121	30,936	30,281	26,926	30,846	28,290	27,667
South Dakota	26,209	23,655	25,472	26,122	26,440	27,277	26,376	25,381	26,351
Tennessee	22,661	23,181	23,370	26,157	24,735	25,583	24,251	25,189	24,339
Texas.............	31,090	30,959	30,930	30,531	29,605	29,289	30,301	28,568	28,282
Utah	31,135	32,908	33,643	32,764	31,206	34,755	32,356	28,859	34,433
Vermont	30,488	33,901	31,489	31,388	34,379	35,409	33,382	30,033	32,829
Virginia............	35,818	37,069	38,038	37,046	38,719	38,603	37,649	37,225	38,223
Washington.........	33,781	31,294	34,411	33,740	38,339	36,162	34,471	34,993	34,064
West Virginia.......	22,744	20,840	21,076	21,251	22,952	24,526	23,763	23,844	20,301
Wisconsin..........	28,010	30,311	33,833	32,567	35,075	32,951	32,967	32,070	33,415
Wyoming	32,160	28,791	30,158	34,075	31,332	33,402	31,624	29,924	30,379

[1] Beginning 1987, data based on revised processing procedures and not directly comparable with prior years.

Source: U.S. Bureau of the Census, *Current Population Reports*, P60-184.

No. 714. Money Income of Families—Percent Distribution, by Income Level, Race, and Hispanic Origin, in Constant (1992) Dollars: 1970 to 1992

[Constant dollars based on CPI-U-X1 deflator. Families as of **March** of following year. Beginning with 1980, based on householder concept and restricted to primary families. Based on Current Population Survey; see text, sections 1 and 14, and Appendix III. For definition of median, see Guide to Tabular Presentation. See also *Historical Statistics, Colonial Times to 1970*, series G 1-8, G 16-23, G 190-192, and G 197-199]

YEAR	Number of families (1,000)	PERCENT DISTRIBUTION							Median income (dollars)
		Under $10,000	$10,000-$14,999	$15,000-$24,999	$25,000-$34,999	$35,000-$49,999	$50,000-$74,999	$75,000 and over	
ALL FAMILIES [1]									
1970	52,227	8.6	7.5	17.4	20.2	23.1	16.3	6.8	33,519
1975	56,245	8.2	8.3	17.4	17.8	23.1	17.5	7.6	34,249
1980 [2]	60,309	8.3	7.4	16.5	16.8	21.8	19.2	10.0	35,839
1985 [2]	63,558	9.3	7.2	16.1	15.7	20.1	19.3	12.2	36,164
1989 [3]	66,090	8.3	7.1	14.8	14.6	19.7	20.1	15.4	38,710
1990	66,322	8.6	6.7	15.4	15.2	20.0	19.4	14.8	37,950
1991	67,173	9.4	7.0	15.6	15.2	19.6	19.2	14.0	37,021
1992	68,144	9.5	7.3	15.5	15.0	19.2	19.6	13.9	36,812
WHITE									
1970	46,535	7.3	6.9	16.7	20.5	24.1	17.2	7.3	34,773
1975	49,873	6.8	7.6	16.9	18.1	23.9	18.5	8.2	35,619
1980 [2]	52,710	6.7	6.6	16.0	17.1	22.7	20.2	10.7	37,341
1985 [2]	54,991	7.5	6.5	15.6	16.0	20.8	20.3	13.3	38,011
1989 [3]	56,590	6.4	6.3	14.4	14.8	20.5	21.1	16.5	40,704
1990	56,803	6.5	6.2	14.9	15.4	20.7	20.5	15.7	39,626
1991	57,224	7.1	6.4	15.3	15.4	20.4	20.3	15.1	38,920
1992	57,858	7.2	6.6	15.2	15.3	20.0	20.8	14.9	38,909
BLACK									
1970	4,928	20.8	13.5	24.1	17.4	14.0	8.5	1.7	21,330
1975	5,586	20.6	14.7	21.3	16.5	16.0	8.8	1.9	21,916
1980 [2]	6,317	21.5	13.7	21.3	14.8	14.8	10.5	3.2	21,606
1985 [2]	6,921	23.7	11.9	21.2	13.6	14.8	10.9	3.9	21,887
1989 [3]	7,470	22.3	13.0	18.5	13.7	14.9	11.9	5.9	22,866
1990	7,471	23.8	11.2	18.9	13.6	15.3	11.2	6.1	22,997
1991	7,716	25.9	11.0	18.2	14.2	14.9	11.0	5.0	22,197
1992	7,888	26.3	11.8	18.8	13.0	14.0	10.8	5.2	21,161
HISPANIC [4]									
1975	2,499	16.0	13.1	24.2	18.7	17.5	8.1	2.4	23,844
1980 [2]	3,235	15.1	12.5	22.7	17.8	16.6	11.6	3.8	25,087
1985 [2]	4,206	17.4	13.4	19.9	16.7	15.8	11.9	5.0	24,809
1989 [3]	4,840	16.3	11.0	20.6	15.9	16.6	13.4	6.3	26,528
1990	4,981	16.8	12.3	20.7	16.2	17.0	10.9	6.1	25,152
1991	5,177	18.2	11.6	21.2	16.3	15.7	11.1	5.9	24,614
1992	5,318	17.7	12.6	21.7	16.2	15.1	11.3	5.4	23,901

[1] Includes other races not shown separately.   [2] Beginning 1983, data based on revised Hispanic population controls and not directly comparable with prior years.   [3] Beginning 1987, data based on revised processing procedures and not directly comparable with prior years. See text, section 14, and source.   [4] Persons of Hispanic origin may be of any race.

No. 715. Money Income of Families—Median Income, by Race and Hispanic Origin, in Current and Constant (1991) Dollars: 1970 to 1992

[See headnote, table 714]

YEAR	MEDIAN INCOME IN CURRENT DOLLARS					MEDIAN INCOME IN CONSTANT (1992) DOLLARS				
	All families [1]	White	Black	Asian, Pacific Islander	Hispanic [2]	All families [1]	White	Black	Asian, Pacific Islander	Hispanic [2]
1970	9,867	10,236	6,279	(NA)	(NA)	33,519	34,773	21,330	(NA)	(NA)
1975	13,719	14,268	8,779	(NA)	9,551	34,249	35,619	21,916	(NA)	23,844
1980	21,023	21,904	12,674	(NA)	14,716	35,839	37,341	21,606	(NA)	25,087
1981	22,388	23,517	13,266	(NA)	16,401	34,862	36,620	20,657	(NA)	25,539
1982	23,433	24,603	13,598	(NA)	16,227	34,390	36,107	19,956	(NA)	23,814
1983 [3]	24,580	25,757	14,506	(NA)	16,956	34,757	36,395	20,511	(NA)	23,848
1984	26,433	27,686	15,432	(NA)	18,833	35,693	37,385	20,837	(NA)	25,430
1985	27,735	29,152	16,786	(NA)	19,027	36,164	38,011	21,887	(NA)	24,809
1986 [4]	29,458	30,809	17,604	(NA)	19,995	37,709	39,439	22,535	(NA)	25,596
1987 [4]	30,970	32,385	18,406	(NA)	20,300	38,249	39,997	22,732	(NA)	25,071
1988	32,191	33,915	19,329	36,560	21,769	38,177	40,222	22,924	43,359	25,817
1989	34,213	35,975	20,209	40,351	23,446	38,710	40,704	22,866	45,655	26,528
1990	35,353	36,915	21,423	42,246	23,431	37,950	39,626	22,997	45,349	25,152
1991	35,939	37,783	21,548	40,974	23,895	37,021	38,920	22,197	42,207	24,614
1992	36,812	38,909	21,161	42,556	23,901	36,812	38,909	21,161	42,556	23,901

NA Not available.   [1] Includes other races not shown separately.   [2] Persons of Hispanic origin may be of any race. [3] Beginning 1983, data based on revised Hispanic population controls and not directly comparable with prior years.   [4] Beginning 1987, data based on revised processing procedures and not directly comparable with prior years.

Source of tables 714 and 715: U.S. Bureau of the Census, *Current Population Reports*, P60-184; and unpublished data.

No. 716. Money Income of Families—Percent Distribution of Aggregate Income Received by Quintile and Income at Selected Positions, in Constant (1992) Dollars: 1980 and 1992

[See headnote, table 714. For composition of regions, see table 26. See also *Historical Statistics, Colonial Times to 1970*, series G 31-138]

ITEM	All families, 1980	1992						
		All families	RACE		REGION			
			White	Black	North-east	Midwest	South	West
Number (1,000).................	60,309	68,144	57,858	7,888	13,478	16,326	24,040	14,299
INCOME AT SELECTED POSITIONS (dollars) Upper limit of each fifth:								
Lowest......................	17,535	16,960	19,000	7,531	19,001	18,081	14,800	18,000
Second	29,645	30,000	32,000	15,609	33,070	30,700	26,600	31,540
Third	41,988	44,200	46,250	26,800	49,000	44,000	40,200	46,756
Fourth	58,871	64,300	66,252	44,200	71,185	62,115	59,888	68,653
Lower limit of top 5 percent	92,158	106,509	109,900	75,619	119,000	100,986	98,430	116,400
PERCENT DISTRIBUTION OF AGGREGATE INCOME								
Lowest fifth.....................	5.2	4.4	4.9	3.0	4.4	4.8	4.2	4.4
Second fifth....................	11.5	10.5	10.9	8.2	10.6	11.2	10.2	10.4
Third fifth.....................	17.5	16.5	16.7	15.0	16.7	17.0	16.4	16.3
Fourth fifth....................	24.3	24.0	23.7	25.0	24.0	23.9	24.3	23.7
Highest fifth...................	41.5	44.6	43.8	48.8	44.3	43.1	45.0	45.2
Top 5 percent..................	15.3	17.6	17.3	18.5	17.2	16.8	17.6	18.1

Source: U.S. Bureau of the Census, *Current Population Reports*, P60-184; and unpublished data.

No. 717. Money Income of Families—Percent Distribution, by Income Quintile and Top 5 Percent: 1992

[See headnote, table 714]

CHARACTERISTIC	Number (1,000)	PERCENT DISTRIBUTION						
		Total	Lowest fifth	Second fifth	Third fifth	Fourth fifth	Highest fifth	Top 5 percent
All families	68,144	100.0	20.0	20.0	20.0	20.0	20.0	5.0
White	57,858	100.0	16.8	19.9	20.6	21.2	21.5	5.5
Black	7,888	100.0	42.6	21.4	16.1	11.9	8.1	1.3
Hispanic [1]	5,318	100.0	35.4	26.0	17.4	12.7	8.6	1.6
Married-couple families............	53,171	100.0	12.9	18.9	21.1	22.9	24.2	6.1
Male householder, wife absent	3,026	100.0	27.7	25.7	21.1	14.8	10.7	2.4
Female householder, husband absent .	11,947	100.0	49.6	23.5	14.9	8.3	3.7	0.6
15 to 24 years old................	2,751	100.0	53.3	24.1	15.3	5.3	2.0	0.3
25 to 34 years old................	14,376	100.0	24.3	20.9	22.4	20.0	12.4	1.9
35 to 44 years old................	17,569	100.0	15.2	16.0	20.8	24.3	23.7	5.4
45 to 54 years old................	13,069	100.0	11.3	13.8	17.4	24.2	33.3	9.4
55 to 64 years old................	9,117	100.0	14.8	18.5	20.2	21.9	24.7	6.9
65 years old and over	11,261	100.0	28.2	32.4	19.7	10.5	9.2	2.9
Presence of related children under 18 years old:								
No related children.............	32,651	100.0	16.5	21.6	20.6	19.7	21.7	5.9
One or more related children	35,492	100.0	23.3	18.5	19.5	20.3	18.4	4.2
One child	14,727	100.0	23.7	19.3	19.2	19.1	18.7	4.5
Two children or more...........	20,766	100.0	23.0	18.0	19.7	21.1	18.2	4.0
Education attainment of householder: [2]								
Total	65,393	100.0	18.6	19.8	20.2	20.6	20.8	5.2
Less than 9th grade..............	5,888	100.0	46.2	30.4	14.5	5.9	3.0	0.8
9th to 12th grade (no diploma)	6,722	100.0	37.1	29.4	17.4	11.2	4.8	0.5
High school graduate (includes equiva-lency)	22,205	100.0	19.1	23.3	24.2	21.2	12.2	1.6
Some college, no degree	11,262	100.0	14.3	18.2	23.1	25.0	19.4	3.4
Associate degree	3,995	100.0	11.1	17.1	24.1	24.6	23.1	4.0
Bachelor's degree or more	15,321	100.0	4.2	8.4	14.7	25.3	47.4	15.7
Bachelor's degree	9,458	100.0	5.4	9.8	16.6	27.3	40.9	11.0
Master's degree...............	3,725	100.0	2.1	6.7	14.0	24.8	52.4	16.9
Professional degree	1,335	100.0	2.9	5.0	6.6	15.2	70.4	40.5
Doctorate degree	804	100.0	2.9	6.0	9.3	20.2	61.6	25.4

[1] Persons of Hispanic origin may be of any race.   [2] 25 years old and over.

Source: U.S. Bureau of the Census, *Current Population Reports*, P60-184.

No. 718. Money Income of Families—Median Income, by Race and Hispanic Origin: 1992

[See headnote, table 714. For composition of regions, see table 26]

CHARACTERISTIC	NUMBER (1,000)				MEDIAN INCOME (dollars)			
	All families [1]	White	Black	His-panic [2]	All families [1]	White	Black	His-panic [2]
All families	**68,144**	**57,858**	**7,888**	**5,318**	**36,812**	**38,909**	**21,161**	**23,901**
Region:								
Northeast	13,478	11,839	1,242	884	40,884	42,302	23,364	20,238
Midwest	16,326	14,454	1,621	400	37,195	38,995	20,181	24,007
South	24,040	19,184	4,361	1,676	33,028	36,279	20,429	22,983
West	14,299	12,381	663	2,358	38,929	39,502	24,827	25,682
Type of family:								
Married-couple families	53,171	47,601	3,748	3,674	42,064	42,738	34,196	28,515
Wife in paid labor force	31,425	27,914	2,425	1,964	49,984	50,653	41,799	37,335
Wife not in paid labor force	21,746	19,687	1,323	1,710	30,326	31,013	21,035	20,673
Male householder, wife absent	3,026	2,409	460	407	27,821	29,671	20,678	19,468
Female householder, husband absent	11,947	7,848	3,680	1,238	17,221	20,130	11,956	12,894
With related children, under 18	35,492	28,709	5,316	3,655	35,872	38,855	18,556	22,668
Married couple	25,714	22,406	2,175	2,497	44,483	45,290	36,357	28,379
Male householder, wife absent	1,549	1,243	244	213	22,366	24,420	17,936	15,808
Female householder, husband absent	8,230	5,060	2,898	945	13,445	15,700	10,393	11,274
Number of earners:								
No earners	10,339	8,411	1,630	706	15,536	17,880	6,532	8,166
One earner	19,228	15,691	2,828	1,832	26,292	28,666	16,131	17,134
Two earners	29,988	26,417	2,569	2,024	45,779	46,895	34,950	32,402
Three earners	6,404	5,433	694	544	56,550	57,440	50,770	39,393
Four or more earners	2,185	1,906	167	211	69,923	70,224	67,700	50,291

[1] Includes other races not shown separately. [2] Persons of Hispanic origin may be of any race.

No. 719. Money Income of Families—Percent Distribution, by Income Level and Selected Characteristics: 1992

[See headnote, table 714. See *Historical Statistics, Colonial Times to 1970,* series G 1-8 for U.S. data on total, White, Black, and other races. For composition of regions, see table 26]

ITEM	Number of fami-lies (1,000)	PERCENT DISTRIBUTION								Median income (dollars)
		Under $5,000	$5,000 to $9,999	$10,000 to $14,999	$15,000 to $24,999	$25,000 to $34,999	$35,000 to $49,999	$50,000 to $74,999	$75,000 and over	
All families [1]	**68,144**	**3.7**	**5.8**	**7.3**	**15.5**	**15.0**	**19.2**	**19.6**	**13.9**	**36,812**
White, total	57,858	2.7	4.5	6.6	15.2	15.3	20.0	20.8	15.0	38,909
Northeast	11,839	2.7	4.4	5.2	13.6	13.9	19.6	21.8	18.8	42,302
Midwest	14,454	2.3	3.7	6.3	15.3	16.0	21.9	21.5	13.1	38,995
South	19,184	3.1	5.1	7.7	16.2	16.0	19.3	19.8	12.9	36,279
West	12,381	2.5	4.7	6.7	14.9	14.5	19.2	20.6	16.8	39,502
Black, total	7,888	11.3	15.0	11.8	18.8	13.0	14.0	10.8	5.3	21,161
Northeast	1,242	7.9	14.7	10.9	18.7	12.3	14.3	12.8	8.5	23,364
Midwest	1,621	13.4	16.5	10.1	17.8	13.0	14.2	10.6	4.6	20,181
South	4,361	11.6	15.0	12.7	19.6	13.6	13.4	10.0	4.2	20,429
West	663	10.0	11.8	12.2	16.3	10.9	16.9	13.7	8.6	24,827
Hispanic, [2] total	5,318	6.0	11.7	12.6	21.7	16.3	15.1	11.3	5.4	23,901
Northeast	884	8.5	18.4	11.9	20.8	12.9	12.8	9.3	5.4	20,238
Midwest	400	7.0	10.3	11.3	23.0	15.0	14.8	13.3	6.0	24,007
South	1,676	6.1	10.6	14.4	22.1	18.0	13.0	10.5	5.5	22,983
West	2,358	4.9	10.2	11.9	21.5	16.6	17.5	12.3	5.1	25,682
Presence of related children under 18 years old:										
All families	68,144	3.7	5.8	7.3	15.5	15.0	19.2	19.6	13.9	36,812
No children	32,651	1.7	4.4	7.3	16.7	15.7	19.1	19.8	15.4	37,819
One or more children	35,492	5.6	7.2	7.3	14.5	14.3	19.4	19.4	12.5	35,872
Married-couple families	53,171	1.4	3.1	5.8	14.1	15.0	21.0	22.9	16.9	42,064
No children	27,457	1.5	3.6	6.8	15.9	15.3	19.1	20.7	17.2	39,768
One or more children	25,714	1.3	2.5	4.7	12.1	14.6	23.1	25.2	16.6	44,483
Female householder, no husband present	11,947	13.8	17.2	13.7	20.6	14.4	11.5	6.6	2.3	17,221
No children	3,717	3.3	9.3	11.2	21.5	18.2	18.0	13.6	4.8	27,495
One or more children	8,230	18.5	20.8	14.8	20.3	12.6	8.5	3.4	1.1	13,445

[1] Includes other races not shown separately. [2] Persons of Hispanic origin may be of any race.

Source of tables 718 and 719: U.S. Bureau of the Census, *Current Population Reports,* P60-184; and unpublished data.

No. 720. Money Income of Families—Distribution, by Type of Family and Income Level: 1992

[See headnote, table 714]

TYPE OF FAMILY	Number of families (1,000)	DISTRIBUTION (1,000)								Median income (dollars)
		Under $9,999	$10,000-$14,999	$15,000-$19,999	$20,000-$24,999	$25,000-$34,999	$35,000-$49,999	$50,000-$74,999	$75,000 and over	
All families	68,144	6,512	4,954	5,360	5,234	10,189	13,115	13,335	9,444	36,812
Married-couple families. . .	53,171	2,369	3,060	3,702	3,782	7,959	11,166	12,164	8,970	42,064
Wife in paid labor force .	34,096	627	906	1,439	1,776	4,703	7,852	9,680	7,113	49,984
Wife not in paid labor force	19,074	1,742	2,153	2,263	2,006	3,256	3,314	2,483	1,855	30,326
Male householder [1]	3,026	437	263	324	320	514	579	385	204	27,821
Female householder [1] . . .	11,947	3,705	1,631	1,335	1,132	1,717	1,370	788	269	17,221
With related children [2] . . .	35,492	4,517	2,581	2,629	2,510	5,060	6,889	6,886	4,421	35,872
Married-couple.	25,714	977	1,197	1,536	1,569	3,761	5,931	6,485	4,257	44,483
Female householder [1] . .	8,230	3,238	1,213	907	760	1,041	701	281	89	13,445

[1] No spouse present.   [2] Children under 18 years old. Includes male householders not shown separately.

No. 721. Median Income of Families and Unrelated Individuals in Current and Constant (1992) Dollars: 1970 to 1992

[Unrelated individuals are persons not living with any relatives. See headnote, table 714. See also *Historical Statistics, Colonial Times to 1970,* series G 179-188]

ITEM	1970	1980	1985 [1]	1986	1987 [2]	1988	1989	1990	1991	1992
CURRENT DOLLARS										
Families: [3]										
Married-couple families	10,516	23,141	31,100	32,805	34,879	36,389	38,547	39,895	40,995	42,064
Wife in paid labor force	12,276	26,879	36,431	38,346	40,751	42,709	45,266	46,777	48,169	49,984
Wife not in paid labor force. . .	9,304	18,972	24,556	25,803	26,640	27,220	28,747	30,265	30,075	30,326
Male householder, wife absent . .	9,012	17,519	22,622	24,962	25,208	26,827	27,847	29,046	28,351	27,821
Female householder, husband absent	5,093	10,408	13,660	13,647	14,683	15,346	16,442	16,932	16,692	17,221
Unrelated individuals:										
Male	4,540	10,939	14,921	15,281	16,082	16,976	17,860	17,927	18,069	17,817
Female.	2,483	6,668	9,865	10,142	11,029	11,881	12,390	12,450	12,731	12,949
CONSTANT (1992) DOLLARS										
Families: [3]										
Married-couple families	35,724	39,449	40,551	41,994	43,077	43,156	43,614	42,825	42,229	42,064
Wife in paid labor force	41,703	45,822	47,502	49,087	50,329	50,652	51,216	50,213	49,619	49,984
Wife not in paid labor force. . .	31,607	32,342	32,019	33,031	32,901	32,282	32,526	32,488	30,980	30,326
Male householder, wife absent . .	30,615	29,865	29,497	31,954	31,133	31,816	31,508	31,179	29,204	27,821
Female householder, husband absent	17,301	17,743	17,811	17,470	18,134	18,200	18,603	18,176	17,194	17,221
Unrelated individuals:										
Male	15,423	18,648	19,456	19,561	19,862	20,133	20,208	19,244	18,613	17,817
Female.	8,435	11,367	12,863	12,983	13,621	14,090	14,019	13,364	13,114	12,949

[1] Beginning 1983, data based on revised Hispanic population controls and not directly comparable with prior years.   [2] Beginning 1987, data based on revised processing procedures and not directly comparable with prior years.   [3] Beginning 1980, based on householder concept. Restricted to primary families, see source.

No. 722. Median Income of Year-Round Full-Time Workers With Income: 1980 to 1992

[Age as of **March of following year.** Prior to 1989, earnings are for civilian workers only. For definition of median, see Guide to Tabular Presentation]

ITEM	FEMALE					MALE				
	1980	1985 [1]	1990 [2]	1991	1992	1980	1985 [1]	1990 [2]	1991	1992
Total with income. .	$11,591	$16,252	$20,591	$21,245	22,167	$19,173	$24,999	$28,979	$30,332	31,012
15 to 19 years old	6,779	8,372	[3]13,944	[3]14,242	[3]14,698	7,753	9,050	[3]15,462	[3]15,307	[3]15,769
20 to 24 years old	9,407	11,757	(NA)	(NA)	(NA)	12,109	13,827	(NA)	(NA)	(NA)
25 to 34 years old	12,190	16,740	20,184	21,022	21,990	17,724	22,321	25,355	26,100	26,533
35 to 44 years old	12,239	18,032	22,505	23,385	24,189	21,777	28,966	32,607	33,588	34,945
45 to 54 years old	12,116	17,009	21,938	22,630	24,531	22,323	29,880	35,732	37,198	38,219
55 to 64 years old	11,931	16,761	20,755	21,325	22,623	21,053	28,387	33,169	35,720	35,351
65 years old and over. . . .	12,342	18,336	22,957	21,780	21,548	17,307	26,146	35,520	34,473	35,256
White.	11,703	16,482	20,839	21,555	22,423	19,720	25,693	30,081	30,953	31,737
Black.	10,915	14,590	18,544	19,134	20,299	13,875	17,971	21,481	22,628	22,942
Hispanic [4]	9,887	13,522	16,181	16,548	17,743	13,790	17,344	19,358	20,027	20,312

NA Not available.   [1] Beginning 1983, data based on revised Hispanic population controls and not directly comparable with prior years.   [2] Beginning 1987, data based on revised processing procedures and not directly comparable with prior years.   [3] 15 to 24 years old.   [4] Persons of Hispanic origin may be of any race.

Source of tables 720-722: U.S. Bureau of the Census, *Current Population Reports,* P60-184; and unpublished data.

No. 723. Money Income of Persons—Percent Distribution, by Income Level, in Constant (1992) Dollars: 1970 to 1992

[Constant dollars based on CPI-U-X1 deflator. As of **March of following year.** For 1970, persons 14 years old and over; thereafter, 15 years old and over. For definition of median, see Guide to Tabular Presentation. See also *Historical Statistics, Colonial Times to 1970*, series G 257-268. For composition of regions, see table 26]

ITEM	All persons (mil.)	PERSONS WITH INCOME									
		Total (mil.)	Percent distribution								Median income (dollars)
			$1 to $2,499 or loss [1]	$2,500 to $4,999	$5,000 to $9,999	$10,000 to $14,999	$15,000 to $24,999	$25,000 to $49,999	$50,000 to $74,999	$75,000 and over	
MALE											
1970	70.6	65.0	8.4	6.1	10.9	10.0	20.3	34.9	6.6	2.9	22,659
1980	82.9	78.7	7.3	5.4	12.1	11.2	20.3	32.8	7.4	3.3	21,360
1981	84.0	79.7	7.9	6.0	12.3	11.3	20.9	31.3	7.1	3.3	20,980
1982 [2]	85.0	79.7	8.3	5.8	12.5	12.1	20.5	30.0	7.4	3.5	20,473
1983 [2]	86.0	80.8	8.4	5.9	12.6	11.6	20.0	30.3	7.6	3.5	20,652
1984	87.3	82.2	7.8	5.8	12.8	11.8	19.6	30.3	8.1	3.7	21,065
1985	88.5	83.6	7.4	5.7	12.4	11.7	20.3	30.2	8.4	4.0	21,268
1986 [3]	89.4	84.5	7.2	5.3	12.1	11.2	20.0	30.8	9.0	4.5	21,908
1987 [3]	90.3	85.7	7.2	5.2	11.9	11.9	20.0	30.4	8.9	4.4	21,966
1988	91.0	86.6	6.8	5.1	11.9	11.2	20.8	30.7	8.8	4.7	22,424
1989	92.0	87.5	6.4	4.9	11.8	12.0	20.6	30.2	8.9	5.1	22,508
1990	92.8	88.2	6.5	4.9	12.4	11.7	21.5	30.0	8.3	4.7	21,784
1991	93.8	88.7	6.5	5.3	12.8	12.4	21.0	29.6	7.9	4.5	21,055
1992	**94.9**	**89.6**	**6.9**	**5.1**	**13.0**	**12.4**	**20.7**	**29.1**	**8.2**	**4.6**	**20,654**
15 to 24 years old	17.2	13.5	28.8	15.1	21.4	14.5	14.1	5.5	0.3	0.2	6,250
25 to 34 years old	20.9	20.3	3.4	3.7	10.8	12.9	27.0	34.6	5.6	2.0	21,605
35 to 44 years old	20.0	19.5	2.9	2.7	7.3	8.6	18.7	40.3	12.9	6.6	29,827
45 to 54 years old	13.8	13.6	2.9	2.4	7.5	7.6	16.0	38.5	15.5	9.6	32,379
55 to 64 years old	10.2	10.0	3.8	3.4	11.3	10.8	20.2	32.2	10.8	7.5	25,271
65 yr. old and over	12.8	12.7	2.1	4.7	23.6	21.4	25.9	16.0	3.3	2.9	14,548
White	80.8	77.2	6.4	4.5	12.1	12.1	20.8	30.3	8.8	5.0	21,645
Black	10.4	9.1	10.8	9.7	20.3	13.9	20.7	20.7	2.7	1.1	12,754
Hispanic [4]	8.0	7.2	7.6	7.1	20.9	17.8	23.1	19.1	3.0	1.3	13,810
Northeast	19.1	18.0	11.4	11.5	11.3	20.3	15.4	15.2	9.2	5.6	22,258
Midwest	22.6	21.6	12.4	11.7	12.1	21.2	16.4	14.7	7.4	4.1	21,086
South	32.5	30.5	12.8	14.6	13.4	21.2	14.6	12.2	7.4	3.9	18,793
West	20.7	19.5	10.6	13.3	12.2	19.7	14.6	14.8	9.3	5.6	21,345
FEMALE											
1970	77.6	51.6	21.3	16.5	20.4	15.2	17.7	8.2	0.5	0.2	7,599
1980	91.1	80.8	20.5	13.3	22.3	14.4	18.2	10.2	0.8	0.3	8,387
1981	92.2	82.1	20.3	13.1	22.7	14.2	18.5	10.2	0.7	0.2	8,499
1982 [2]	93.1	82.5	20.1	12.7	22.4	14.9	17.7	11.0	0.9	0.3	8,640
1983 [2]	94.3	83.8	19.2	12.6	22.3	14.1	18.2	12.1	1.1	0.4	9,022
1984	95.3	85.6	18.5	12.3	22.2	14.5	18.0	12.8	1.2	0.4	9,274
1985	96.4	86.5	18.0	12.5	21.9	14.0	18.2	13.6	1.4	0.5	9,410
1986 [3]	97.3	87.8	17.4	12.0	21.8	13.7	18.6	14.5	1.5	0.5	9,742
1987 [3]	98.2	89.7	16.7	11.9	21.5	14.1	18.9	14.6	1.7	0.6	10,245
1988	99.0	90.6	16.2	11.6	21.3	14.1	19.0	15.3	1.8	0.6	10,536
1989	99.8	91.4	15.4	11.5	20.6	14.7	19.1	15.8	2.0	0.7	10,889
1990	100.7	92.2	15.1	11.6	21.0	14.1	19.6	15.7	2.1	0.7	10,810
1991	101.5	92.6	14.7	11.2	21.8	14.9	19.2	15.4	2.0	0.8	10,791
1992	**102.4**	**93.2**	**14.6**	**11.2**	**21.4**	**14.7**	**18.7**	**16.5**	**2.1**	**0.8**	**10,774**
15 to 24 years old	17.2	13.0	30.4	18.7	22.9	13.9	10.8	3.1	0.2	0.1	5,174
25 to 34 years old	21.0	19.4	13.8	8.8	15.8	14.7	23.5	21.3	1.6	0.6	13,713
35 to 44 years old	20.4	19.2	13.6	6.7	14.5	13.9	22.4	24.5	3.3	1.1	15,468
45 to 54 years old	14.7	13.6	13.4	6.9	13.6	13.6	21.8	25.0	4.1	1.6	15,875
55 to 64 years old	11.0	10.2	17.0	11.0	21.5	13.3	18.1	15.7	2.6	0.9	10,168
65 yr. old and over	18.0	17.8	4.8	16.8	39.8	17.6	13.4	6.4	0.8	0.4	8,189
White	86.0	79.0	14.7	10.7	21.0	14.4	19.0	16.9	2.1	0.9	11,036
Black	12.5	10.9	13.0	15.1	25.9	14.1	16.5	13.9	1.3	0.2	8,857
Hispanic [4]	8.0	6.2	16.9	14.1	26.3	15.8	14.8	10.8	0.8	0.4	8,357
Northeast	21.2	19.5	24.1	21.4	14.0	18.5	11.2	6.8	2.8	1.0	11,354
Midwest	24.4	22.8	26.4	21.5	15.7	19.4	9.7	5.4	1.3	0.6	10,582
South	35.5	31.7	27.4	21.9	14.6	18.3	10.0	5.3	1.8	0.6	10,194
West	21.4	19.2	24.5	20.6	14.0	18.6	11.3	7.2	2.7	1.1	11,449

[1] Includes persons with income deficit. [2] Beginning 1983, data based on revised Hispanic population controls and not directly comparable with prior years. [3] Beginning 1987, data based on revised processing procedures and not directly comparable with prior years. [4] Persons of Hispanic origin may be of any race.

Source: U.S. Bureau of the Census, *Current Population Reports*, P60-184; and unpublished data.

No. 724. Median Income of Married-Couple Families, by Work Experience of Husbands and Wives: 1992

[As of **March 1993**. Based on Current Population Survey; see text, sections 1 and 14, and Appendix III]

WORK EXPERIENCE OF HUSBAND	NUMBER (1,000)				MEDIAN INCOME (dollars)			
	Total	Wife worked		Wife did not work	Total	Wife worked		Wife did not work
		Total	Worked year-round, full-time			Total	Worked year-round, full-time	
All families [1]	53,171	34,096	18,783	19,075	42,064	49,472	54,936	28,661
Husband worked	42,247	31,327	17,375	10,920	47,674	51,258	56,283	37,045
Worked year-round, full-time	33,024	24,962	14,316	8,062	51,652	54,681	59,286	41,435
Husband did not work	10,924	2,769	1,407	8,154	23,058	30,020	35,070	21,105
White	47,601	30,367	16,463	17,234	42,738	50,172	55,565	29,431
Husband worked	37,896	28,015	15,289	9,881	48,391	51,756	56,717	37,755
Worked year-round, full-time	29,711	22,388	12,617	7,324	52,093	55,188	59,863	42,172
Husband did not work	9,704	2,351	1,175	7,353	23,744	30,930	36,710	21,734
Black	3,748	2,569	1,614	1,179	34,196	41,431	47,123	19,056
Husband worked	2,860	2,253	1,444	607	40,511	44,611	50,369	25,973
Worked year-round, full-time	2,177	1,769	1,185	408	44,429	47,773	53,053	30,295
Husband did not work	888	316	171	572	17,030	22,926	25,712	13,440
Hispanic [2]	3,674	2,028	1,080	1,646	28,515	37,170	43,194	19,959
Husband worked	3,108	1,857	989	1,251	31,231	38,621	44,898	22,199
Worked year-round, full-time	2,252	1,347	757	905	35,747	43,344	49,053	25,697
Husband did not work	565	170	91	395	16,217	24,564	28,924	14,078

[1] Includes other races not shown separately.   [2] Persons of Hispanic origin may be of any race.

No. 725. Average Earnings of Year-Round, Full-Time Workers: 1992

[In dollars. For persons 25 years old and over as of March 1993]

AGE AND SEX	Total	Less than 9th grade	HIGH SCHOOL		COLLEGE		
			9th to 12th grade (no diploma)	High school graduate (includes equivalency)	Some college, no degree	Associate degree	Bachelor's degree or more
Male, total	$37,180	$19,853	$23,529	$28,944	$34,456	$35,315	$52,920
25 to 34 years old	29,361	15,564	19,185	24,441	28,188	29,671	40,035
35 to 44 years old	39,738	18,247	23,230	30,339	35,320	36,635	56,387
45 to 54 years old	43,401	22,240	26,128	33,336	39,917	40,870	61,249
55 to 64 years old	38,843	22,067	28,612	30,739	38,709	38,990	56,416
65 years old and over	38,719	21,258	(B)	26,809	37,749	(B)	56,955
Female, total	24,798	13,647	15,300	19,965	23,437	26,083	34,552
25 to 34 years old	23,222	13,203	14,836	18,918	21,538	24,173	30,542
35 to 44 years old	25,946	14,279	14,183	20,411	23,425	27,555	36,333
45 to 54 years old	26,126	14,486	16,750	20,741	25,431	27,421	37,236
55 to 64 years old	23,751	12,759	15,203	19,701	25,945	25,456	37,599
65 years old and over	19,932	(B)	(B)	20,211	(B)	(B)	26,508

B Base figure too small to meet statistical standards for reliability of derived figure.

No. 726. Per Capita Money Income, by Race and Hispanic Origin: 1970 to 1992

[In dollars. Constant dollars based on CPI-U-X1 deflator. As of March of following year]

YEAR	CURRENT DOLLARS				CONSTANT (1992) DOLLARS			
	All races [1]	White	Black	Hispanic [2]	All races [1]	White	Black	Hispanic [2]
1970	3,177	3,354	1,869	(NA)	10,793	11,394	6,349	(NA)
1975	4,818	5,072	2,972	2,847	12,028	12,662	7,419	7,107
1980 [3]	7,787	8,233	4,804	4,865	13,275	14,035	8,190	8,294
1985 [3]	11,013	11,671	6,840	6,613	14,360	15,218	8,919	8,623
1986	11,670	12,352	7,207	7,000	14,939	15,812	9,226	8,961
1987 [4]	12,391	13,143	7,645	7,653	15,303	16,232	9,442	9,452
1988	13,123	13,896	8,271	7,956	15,563	16,480	9,809	9,436
1989	14,056	14,896	8,747	8,390	15,904	16,854	9,897	9,493
1990	14,387	15,265	9,017	8,424	15,444	16,386	9,679	9,043
1991	14,617	15,510	9,170	8,662	15,057	15,977	9,446	8,923
1992	15,033	15,981	9,296	8,874	15,033	15,981	9,296	8,874

NA Not available.   [1] Includes other races not shown separately.   [2] Persons of Hispanic origin may be of any race. [3] Beginning 1983, data based on revised Hispanic population controls and not directly comparable with prior years.   [4] Beginning 1987, data based on revised processing procedures and not directly comparable with prior years.

Source of tables 724-726: U.S. Bureau of the Census, *Current Population Reports*, P60-184.

No. 727. Persons Below Poverty Level and Below 125 Percent of Poverty Level: 1960 to 1992

[Persons as of **March of the following year**. Based on Current Population Survey; see text, sections 1 and 14, and Appendix III]

YEAR	NUMBER BELOW POVERTY LEVEL (mil.)				PERCENT BELOW POVERTY LEVEL				BELOW 125 PERCENT OF POVERTY LEVEL		AVERAGE INCOME CUTOFFS FOR NONFARM FAMILY OF FOUR[3]	
	All races[1]	White	Black	His-panic[2]	All races[1]	White	Black	His-panic[2]	Number (mil.)	Percent of total population	At poverty level	At 125 percent of poverty level
1960	39.9	28.3	(NA)	(NA)	22.2	17.8	(NA)	(NA)	54.6	30.4	3,022	3,778
1966	28.5	20.8	8.9	(NA)	14.7	11.3	41.8	(NA)	41.3	21.3	3,317	4,146
1969	24.1	16.7	7.1	(NA)	12.1	9.5	32.2	(NA)	34.7	17.4	3,743	4,679
1970	25.4	17.5	7.5	(NA)	12.6	9.9	33.5	(NA)	35.6	17.6	3,968	4,960
1975	25.9	17.8	7.5	3.0	12.3	9.7	31.3	26.9	37.2	17.6	5,500	6,875
1976	25.0	16.7	7.6	2.8	11.8	9.1	31.1	24.7	35.5	16.7	5,815	7,269
1977	24.7	16.4	7.7	2.7	11.6	8.9	31.3	22.4	35.7	16.7	6,191	7,739
1978	24.5	16.3	7.6	2.6	11.4	8.7	30.6	21.6	34.2	15.8	6,662	8,328
1979[4]	26.1	17.2	8.1	2.9	11.7	9.0	31.0	21.8	36.6	16.4	7,412	9,265
1980	29.3	19.7	8.6	3.5	13.0	10.2	32.5	25.7	40.7	18.1	8,414	10,518
1981	31.8	21.6	9.2	3.7	14.0	11.1	34.2	26.5	43.7	19.3	9,287	11,609
1982[5]	34.4	23.5	9.7	4.3	15.0	12.0	35.6	29.9	46.5	20.3	9,862	12,328
1983[5]	35.3	24.0	9.9	4.6	15.2	12.1	35.7	28.0	47.2	20.3	10,178	12,723
1984	33.7	23.0	9.5	4.8	14.4	11.5	33.8	28.4	45.3	19.4	10,609	13,261
1985	33.1	22.9	8.9	5.2	14.0	11.4	31.3	29.0	44.2	18.7	10,989	13,736
1986[6]	32.4	22.2	9.0	5.1	13.6	11.0	31.1	27.3	43.5	18.2	11,203	14,004
1987[6]	32.2	21.2	9.5	5.4	13.4	10.4	32.4	28.0	43.0	17.8	11,611	14,514
1988	31.7	20.7	9.4	5.4	13.0	10.1	31.3	26.7	42.6	17.5	12,092	15,115
1989	31.5	20.8	9.3	5.4	12.8	10.0	30.7	26.2	42.7	17.3	12,674	15,843
1990	33.6	22.3	9.8	6.0	13.5	10.7	31.9	28.1	44.8	18.0	13,359	16,699
1991	35.7	23.7	10.2	6.3	14.2	11.3	32.7	28.7	47.5	18.9	13,924	17,405
1992	36.9	24.5	10.6	6.7	14.5	11.6	33.3	29.3	49.2	19.4	14,335	17,919

NA Not available.   [1] Includes other races not shown separately.   [2] Persons of Hispanic origin may be of any race. [3] Beginning 1981, income cutoffs for nonfarm families are applied to all families, both farm and nonfarm.   [4] Population controls based on 1980 census; see text, sections 1 and 14.   [5] Beginning 1983, data based on revised Hispanic population controls and not directly comparable with prior years.   [6] Beginning 1987, data based on revised processing procedures and not directly comparable with prior years.

Source: U.S. Bureau of the Census, *Current Population Reports*, P60-185.

No. 728. Children Below Poverty Level, by Race and Hispanic Origin: 1970 to 1992

[Persons as of **March of the following year**. Covers only related children in families under 18 years old. Based on Current Population Survey; see text, sections 1 and 14, and Appendix III]

YEAR	NUMBER BELOW POVERTY LEVEL (1,000)				PERCENT BELOW POVERTY LEVEL			
	All races[1]	White	Black	Hispanic[2]	All races[1]	White	Black	Hispanic[2]
1970	10,235	6,138	3,922	(NA)	14.9	10.5	41.5	(NA)
1975	10,882	6,748	3,884	1,619	16.8	12.5	41.4	33.1
1980	11,114	6,817	3,906	1,718	17.9	13.4	42.1	33.0
1981	12,068	7,429	4,170	1,874	19.5	14.7	44.9	35.4
1982	13,139	8,282	4,388	2,117	21.3	16.5	47.3	38.9
1983[3]	13,427	8,534	4,273	2,251	21.8	17.0	46.2	37.7
1984	12,929	8,086	4,320	2,317	21.0	16.1	46.2	38.7
1985	12,483	7,838	4,057	2,512	20.1	15.6	43.1	39.6
1986	12,257	7,714	4,037	2,413	19.8	15.3	42.7	37.1
1987[4]	12,275	7,398	4,234	2,606	19.7	14.7	44.4	38.9
1988	11,935	7,095	4,148	2,576	19.0	14.0	42.8	37.3
1989	12,001	7,164	4,257	2,496	19.0	14.1	43.2	35.5
1990	12,715	7,696	4,412	2,750	19.9	15.1	44.2	37.7
1991	13,658	8,316	4,637	2,977	21.1	16.1	45.6	39.8
1992	13,876	8,333	4,850	2,946	21.1	16.0	46.3	38.8

NA Not available.   [1] Includes other races not shown separately.   [2] Persons of Hispanic origin may be of any race. [3] Beginning 1983, data based on revised Hispanic population controls and not directly comparable with prior years.   [4] Beginning 1987, data based on revised processing procedures and not directly comparable with prior years.

Source: U.S. Bureau of the Census, *Current Population Reports*, P60-185.

No. 729. Children Under 6 Years Old Below Poverty Level, by Family Type and Race: 1992

[Excludes unrelated individuals and foster children. Based on Current Population Survey; see text, sections 1 and 14, and Appendix III. Numbers and percentages may not add due to rounding]

RACE AND FAMILY TYPE	ALL CHILDREN Number (mil.)	ALL CHILDREN Percent distribution	CHILDREN BELOW POVERTY LEVEL Number (mil.)	CHILDREN BELOW POVERTY LEVEL Percent	CHILDREN BELOW POVERTY LEVEL Percent distribution	RACE AND FAMILY TYPE	ALL CHILDREN Number (mil.)	ALL CHILDREN Percent distribution	CHILDREN BELOW POVERTY LEVEL Number (mil.)	CHILDREN BELOW POVERTY LEVEL Percent	CHILDREN BELOW POVERTY LEVEL Percent distribution
All races:						Black, non-Hispanic:					
All family types . .	23.2	100.0	5.6	24.0	100.0	All family types . .	3.6	100.0	1.8	50.7	100.0
Married-couple .	17.0	73.4	2.2	12.7	38.7	Married-couple .	1.3	34.7	0.2	19.3	13.2
Single-parent [1] .	6.2	26.6	3.4	55.2	61.3	Single-parent . .	2.3	65.3	1.6	67.5	86.8
Mother-only .	5.4	23.3	3.2	58.9	57.1	Mother-only .	2.2	61.3	1.5	69.2	83.6
White, non-Hispanic:						Hispanic [2]:					
All family types . .	15.7	100.0	2.3	14.4	100.0	All family types . .	2.9	100.0	1.3	44.0	100.0
Married-couple .	12.9	82.3	1.1	8.4	48.3	Married-couple .	2.0	69.1	0.7	34.3	53.9
Single-parent . .	2.8	17.6	1.2	42.2	51.7	Single-parent . .	0.9	30.9	0.6	65.5	46.1
Mother-only .	2.3	14.6	1.1	46.2	47.0	Mother-only .	0.8	26.9	0.5	68.6	42.1

[1] Includes father-only, relative-only, and nonrelative-only families.   [2] Persons of Hispanic origin may be of any race.
Source: Susan Einbinder, National Center for Children in Poverty, Columbia University School of Public Health, New York, NY, unpublished data.

No. 730. Persons Below Poverty Level, by Selected Characteristics: 1992

[Persons as of **March 1993**. Based on Current Population Survey; see text, sections 1 and 14, and Appendix III. For composition of regions, see table 26]

AGE AND REGION	NUMBER BELOW POVERTY LEVEL (1,000) All races [1]	NUMBER BELOW POVERTY LEVEL (1,000) White	NUMBER BELOW POVERTY LEVEL (1,000) Black	NUMBER BELOW POVERTY LEVEL (1,000) Hispanic [2]	PERCENT BELOW POVERTY LEVEL All races [1]	PERCENT BELOW POVERTY LEVEL White	PERCENT BELOW POVERTY LEVEL Black	PERCENT BELOW POVERTY LEVEL Hispanic [2]
Total	36,880	24,523	10,613	6,655	14.5	11.6	33.3	29.3
Under 18 years old. . . .	14,617	8,955	4,938	3,116	21.9	16.9	46.6	39.9
18 to 24 years old	4,367	3,023	1,121	844	18.0	15.3	31.7	30.0
25 to 34 years old	5,540	3,749	1,521	1,076	13.2	10.8	28.2	25.2
35 to 44 years old	3,944	2,641	1,077	719	9.8	7.8	23.3	21.6
45 to 54 years old	2,245	1,591	544	349	7.9	6.5	18.7	17.1
55 to 59 years old	1,073	771	262	137	10.0	8.4	22.9	20.2
60 to 64 years old	1,112	800	263	145	10.6	8.7	25.2	26.2
65 years old and over. . .	3,983	2,992	887	269	12.9	10.9	33.3	22.0
Northeast	6,227	4,319	1,663	1,167	12.3	9.9	31.6	34.5
Midwest	7,983	5,389	2,340	452	13.1	10.1	35.7	27.3
South.	14,763	8,433	5,976	1,997	16.9	12.4	34.2	28.5
West	7,907	6,381	634	3,038	14.4	13.5	24.4	28.5

[1] Includes other races not shown separately.   [2] Persons of Hispanic origin may be of any race.

No. 731. Persons 65 Years Old and Over Below Poverty Level: 1970 to 1992

[Persons as of **March of following year**]

CHARACTERISTIC	NUMBER BELOW POVERTY LEVEL (1,000) 1970	1979 [1]	1990 [2]	1991	1992	PERCENT BELOW POVERTY LEVEL 1970	1979 [1]	1990 [2]	1991	1992
Total [3]	4,793	3,682	3,658	3,781	3,983	24.6	15.2	12.2	12.4	12.9
White	4,011	2,911	2,707	2,802	2,992	22.6	13.3	10.1	10.3	10.9
Black	683	740	860	880	887	48.0	36.2	33.8	33.8	33.3
Hispanic [4]	(NA)	154	245	237	269	(NA)	26.8	22.5	20.8	22.0
In families	2,013	1,380	1,172	1,228	1,484	14.8	8.4	5.8	6.0	7.1
Unrelated individuals	2,779	2,299	2,479	2,553	2,498	47.2	29.4	24.7	24.9	24.9

NA Not available.   [1] Population controls based on 1980 census; see text, section 14.   [2] Beginning 1987, data based on revised processing procedures and not directly comparable with prior years.   [3] Beginning 1979, includes members of unrelated subfamilies not shown separately. For earlier years, unrelated subfamily members are included in the "In families" category.   [4] Persons of Hispanic origin may be of any race.

Source of tables 730 and 731: U.S. Bureau of the Census, *Current Population Reports*, P60-185; and unpublished data.

No. 732. Persons Below Poverty Level, by State: 1980 to 1992

[Based on the Current Population Survey; see text, sections 1 and 14, and Appendix III. The CPS is designed to collect reliable data on income primarily at the national level and secondarily at the regional level. When the income data are tabulated by State, the estimates are considered less reliable and, therefore, particular caution should be used when trying to interpret the results; for additional detail, see source]

STATE	NUMBER BELOW POVERTY LEVEL (1,000)					PERCENT BELOW POVERTY LEVEL				
	1980	1985	1990 [1]	1991	1992	1980	1985	1990 [1]	1991	1992
United States.............	29,272	33,064	33,585	35,708	36,880	13.0	14.0	13.5	14.2	14.5
Alabama.................	810	821	779	786	715	21.2	20.6	19.2	18.8	17.1
Alaska..................	36	45	57	62	53	9.6	8.7	11.4	11.8	10.0
Arizona.................	354	345	484	532	554	12.8	10.7	13.7	14.8	15.1
Arkansas...............	484	541	472	425	424	21.5	22.9	19.6	17.3	17.4
California...............	2,619	3,596	4,128	4,825	4,925	11.0	13.6	13.9	15.7	15.8
Colorado...............	247	324	461	347	353	8.6	10.2	13.7	10.4	10.6
Connecticut.............	255	237	196	287	303	8.3	7.6	6.0	8.6	9.4
Delaware...............	68	71	48	53	55	11.8	11.4	6.9	7.5	7.6
District of Columbia.......	131	123	120	98	108	20.9	20.4	21.1	18.6	20.3
Florida.................	1,692	1,551	1,896	2,069	2,097	16.7	13.4	14.4	15.4	15.3
Georgia................	727	1,037	1,001	1,077	1,151	13.9	17.7	15.8	17.2	17.8
Hawaii.................	81	109	121	90	129	8.5	10.7	11.0	7.7	11.0
Idaho..................	138	159	157	144	160	14.7	16.0	14.9	13.9	15.0
Illinois.................	1,386	1,830	1,606	1,598	1,836	12.3	15.6	13.7	13.5	15.3
Indiana................	645	639	714	866	660	11.8	12.0	13.0	15.7	11.7
Iowa..................	311	505	289	271	327	10.8	17.9	10.4	9.6	11.3
Kansas................	215	331	259	317	277	9.4	13.8	10.3	12.3	11.0
Kentucky...............	701	708	628	683	723	19.3	19.4	17.3	18.8	19.7
Louisiana...............	868	781	952	795	1,020	20.3	18.1	23.6	19.0	24.2
Maine.................	158	134	162	171	170	14.6	11.9	13.1	14.1	13.4
Maryland...............	389	364	468	432	568	9.5	8.7	9.9	9.1	11.6
Massachusetts...........	542	544	626	637	580	9.5	9.2	10.7	11.0	10.0
Michigan...............	1,194	1,308	1,315	1,308	1,254	12.9	14.5	14.3	14.1	13.5
Minnesota..............	342	523	524	564	554	8.7	12.6	12.0	12.9	12.8
Mississippi.............	591	644	684	635	660	24.3	25.1	25.7	23.7	24.5
Missouri...............	625	689	700	740	797	13.0	13.7	13.4	14.8	15.6
Montana...............	102	134	134	127	113	13.2	16.0	16.3	15.4	13.7
Nebraska..............	199	235	167	157	169	13.0	14.8	10.3	9.5	10.3
Nevada................	70	139	119	141	188	8.3	14.4	9.8	11.4	14.4
New Hampshire.........	63	59	68	81	99	7.0	6.0	6.3	7.3	8.6
New Jersey............	659	631	711	754	771	9.0	8.3	9.2	9.7	10.0
New Mexico............	268	267	319	349	327	20.6	18.5	20.9	22.4	21.0
New York..............	2,391	2,796	2,571	2,736	2,699	13.8	15.8	14.3	15.3	15.3
North Carolina..........	877	863	829	964	1,047	15.0	14.2	13.0	14.5	15.7
North Dakota...........	99	108	87	92	73	15.5	15.9	13.7	14.5	11.9
Ohio..................	1,046	1,359	1,256	1,488	1,381	9.8	12.8	11.5	13.4	12.4
Oklahoma..............	406	526	481	541	600	13.9	16.0	15.6	17.0	18.4
Oregon................	309	317	267	401	340	11.5	11.9	9.2	13.5	11.3
Pennsylvania...........	1,142	1,217	1,328	1,340	1,426	9.8	10.5	11.0	11.0	11.7
Rhode Island...........	97	84	71	99	116	10.7	9.0	7.5	10.4	12.0
South Carolina..........	534	489	548	582	687	16.8	15.2	16.2	16.4	18.9
South Dakota...........	127	119	93	96	105	18.8	17.3	13.3	14.0	14.8
Tennessee.............	884	837	833	744	849	19.6	18.1	16.9	15.5	17.0
Texas.................	2,247	2,582	2,684	2,965	3,079	15.7	15.9	15.9	17.5	17.8
Utah..................	148	180	143	222	162	10.0	10.9	8.2	12.9	9.3
Vermont...............	62	48	61	73	63	12.0	9.2	10.9	12.6	10.4
Virginia................	647	558	705	608	584	12.4	10.0	11.1	9.9	9.4
Washington............	538	526	434	474	555	12.7	12.0	8.9	9.5	11.0
West Virginia...........	297	423	328	327	396	15.2	22.3	18.1	17.9	22.3
Wisconsin..............	403	544	448	492	551	8.5	11.6	9.3	9.9	10.8
Wyoming...............	49	61	51	47	49	10.4	12.0	11.0	9.9	10.3

[1] Beginning 1987, data based on revised processing procedures and not directly comparable with prior years.

Source: U.S. Bureau of the Census, *Current Population Reports*, P60-185.

No. 733. Persons Below Poverty Level, by Race and Family Status: 1979 to 1992

[Persons as of March of following year. Based on Current Population Survey; see text, sections 1 and 14, and Appendix III]

RACE AND FAMILY STATUS	NUMBER BELOW POVERTY LEVEL (mil.)					PERCENT BELOW POVERTY LEVEL				
	1979 [1]	1985	1990 [2]	1991	1992	1979 [1]	1985	1990 [2]	1991	1992
All persons [3]	26.1	33.1	33.6	35.7	36.9	11.7	14.0	13.5	14.2	14.5
In families	20.0	25.7	25.2	27.1	27.9	10.2	12.6	12.0	12.8	13.0
Householder	5.5	7.2	7.1	7.7	8.0	9.2	11.4	10.7	11.5	11.7
Related children under 18 years.	10.0	12.5	12.7	13.7	13.9	16.0	20.1	19.9	21.1	21.1
Other family members.	4.5	6.0	5.4	5.8	6.1	6.1	7.7	6.7	7.2	7.5
Unrelated individuals	5.7	6.7	7.4	7.8	8.0	21.9	21.5	20.7	21.1	21.8
Male	2.0	2.5	2.9	3.0	3.1	16.9	17.4	16.9	17.3	18.0
Female.	3.8	4.2	4.6	4.7	4.9	26.0	24.8	24.0	24.5	25.1
White [3]	17.2	22.9	22.3	23.7	24.5	9.0	11.4	10.7	11.3	11.6
In families	12.5	17.1	15.9	17.3	17.6	7.4	9.9	9.0	9.7	9.8
Householder	3.6	5.0	4.6	5.0	5.2	6.9	9.1	8.1	8.8	8.9
Related children under 18 years.	5.9	7.8	7.7	8.3	8.3	11.4	15.6	15.1	16.1	16.0
Other family members.	3.0	4.3	3.6	3.9	4.2	4.7	6.4	5.2	5.7	6.0
Unrelated individuals	4.5	5.3	5.7	5.9	6.1	19.7	19.6	18.6	18.8	19.5
Black [3]	8.1	8.9	9.8	10.2	10.6	31.0	31.3	31.9	32.7	33.3
In families	6.8	7.5	8.2	8.5	8.9	30.0	30.5	31.0	32.0	32.7
Householder	1.7	2.0	2.2	2.3	2.4	27.8	28.7	29.3	30.4	30.9
Related children under 18 years.	3.7	4.1	4.4	4.6	4.9	40.8	43.1	44.2	45.6	46.3
Other family members.	1.3	1.5	1.6	1.5	1.6	18.2	17.7	17.6	17.6	18.2
Unrelated individuals	1.2	1.3	1.5	1.6	1.6	37.3	34.7	35.1	35.3	35.8
In families with female householder, no spouse present	9.4	11.6	12.6	13.8	13.7	34.9	37.6	37.2	39.7	38.5
Householder	2.6	3.5	3.8	4.2	4.2	30.4	34.0	33.4	35.6	34.9
Related children under 18 years.	5.6	6.7	7.4	8.1	8.0	48.6	53.6	53.4	55.5	54.3
Other family members.	1.1	1.4	1.4	1.6	1.5	16.9	17.3	17.6	18.7	17.0

[1] Population controls based on 1980 census; see text, section 14.   [2] Beginning 1987, data based on revised processing procedures and not directly comparable with prior years.   [3] Includes other races and members of unrelated subfamilies not shown separately.

Source: U.S. Bureau of the Census, *Current Population Reports*, P60-185; and unpublished data.

No. 734. Families Below Poverty Level, by Selected Characteristics: 1992

[Families as of March 1993. Based on Current Population Survey; see text, sections 1 and 14, and Appendix III. For composition of regions, see table 26]

CHARACTERISTIC	NUMBER BELOW POVERTY LEVEL (1,000)				PERCENT BELOW POVERTY LEVEL			
	All races [1]	White	Black	His-panic [2]	All races [1]	White	Black	His-panic [2]
Total	7,960	5,160	2,435	1,395	11.7	8.9	30.9	26.2
Age of householder:								
15 to 24 years old	1,051	665	345	194	38.2	31.1	67.4	45.6
25 to 34 years old	2,567	1,605	855	481	17.9	13.6	41.9	31.9
35 to 44 years old	1,904	1,237	567	367	10.8	8.4	26.5	25.3
45 to 54 years old	901	633	225	168	6.9	5.6	17.4	18.0
55 to 64 years old	659	423	196	113	7.2	5.3	21.5	20.2
65 years old and over	878	597	246	72	7.8	5.9	24.9	16.3
Northeast	1,369	968	353	289	10.2	8.2	28.4	32.7
Midwest	1,670	1,064	561	103	10.2	7.4	34.6	25.6
South	3,319	1,870	1,367	404	13.8	9.7	31.3	24.1
West	1,602	1,257	153	600	11.2	10.2	23.1	25.4
Size of family:								
Two persons	2,674	1,845	709	300	9.4	7.3	26.0	21.6
Three persons	1,882	1,173	620	310	11.7	8.8	30.0	24.8
Four persons	1,566	1,002	494	303	11.0	8.3	29.8	24.6
Five persons	1,004	656	300	225	16.6	13.3	37.0	29.2
Six persons	460	271	168	120	22.6	18.1	42.2	33.2
Seven persons or more	374	211	144	138	34.7	27.2	63.7	44.0
Average size	3.51	3.44	3.64	4.07	(X)	(X)	(X)	(X)
Avg. number of children per family with children . .	2.21	2.15	2.31	2.51	(X)	(X)	(X)	(X)
Education of householder: [3]								
No high school diploma	3,035	1,932	965	809	24.1	19.3	44.2	35.5
High school diploma, no college	2,446	1,590	769	251	11.0	8.4	28.4	19.4
Some college, less than Bachelor's degree	1,092	730	316	111	7.2	5.5	19.2	12.9
Bachelor's degree or more	336	242	40	30	2.2	1.8	4.7	6.6

X Not applicable.   [1] Includes other races not shown separately.   [2] Hispanic persons may be of any race.   [3] Householder 25 years old and over.

Source: U.S. Bureau of the Census, *Current Population Reports*, P60-185; and unpublished data.

No. 735. Families Below Poverty Level and Below 125 Percent of Poverty Level: 1960 to 1992

[Families as of **March of the following year.** Based on Current Population Survey, see text, sections 1 and 14, and Appendix III]

YEAR	NUMBER BELOW POVERTY LEVEL (1,000)				PERCENT BELOW POVERTY LEVEL				BELOW 125 PERCENT OF POVERTY LEVEL	
	All races [1]	White	Black	His- panic [2]	All races [1]	White	Black	His- panic [2]	Number (1,000)	Percent
1960	8,243	6,115	(NA)	(NA)	18.1	14.9	(NA)	(NA)	11,525	25.4
1970	5,260	3,708	1,481	(NA)	10.1	8.0	29.5	(NA)	7,516	14.4
1972	5,075	3,441	1,529	477	9.3	7.1	29.0	20.6	7,347	13.5
1973	4,828	3,219	1,527	468	8.8	6.6	28.1	19.8	7,044	12.8
1974	4,922	3,352	1,479	526	8.8	6.8	26.9	21.2	7,195	12.9
1975	5,450	3,838	1,513	627	9.7	7.7	27.1	25.1	7,974	14.2
1976	5,311	3,560	1,617	598	9.4	7.1	27.9	23.1	7,647	13.5
1977	5,311	3,540	1,637	591	9.3	7.0	28.2	21.4	7,713	13.5
1978 [3]	5,280	3,523	1,622	559	9.1	6.9	27.5	20.4	7,417	12.8
1979 [3]	5,461	3,581	1,722	614	9.2	6.9	27.8	20.3	7,784	13.1
1980	6,217	4,195	1,826	751	10.3	8.0	28.9	23.2	8,764	14.5
1981	6,851	4,670	1,972	792	11.2	8.8	30.8	24.0	9,568	15.7
1982 [4]	7,512	5,118	2,158	916	12.2	9.6	33.0	27.2	10,279	16.7
1983 [4]	7,647	5,220	2,161	981	12.3	9.7	32.3	25.9	10,358	16.7
1984	7,277	4,925	2,094	991	11.6	9.1	30.9	25.2	9,901	15.8
1985	7,223	4,983	1,983	1,074	11.4	9.1	28.7	25.5	9,753	15.3
1986 [5]	7,023	4,811	1,987	1,085	10.9	8.6	28.0	24.7	9,476	14.7
1987 [5]	7,005	4,567	2,117	1,168	10.7	8.1	29.4	25.5	9,338	14.3
1988	6,874	4,471	2,089	1,141	10.4	7.9	28.2	23.7	9,284	14.1
1989	6,784	4,409	2,077	1,133	10.3	7.8	27.8	23.4	9,267	14.0
1990	7,098	4,622	2,193	1,244	10.7	8.1	29.3	25.0	9,564	14.4
1991	7,712	5,022	2,343	1,372	11.5	8.8	30.4	26.5	10,244	15.3
1992	7,960	5,160	2,435	1,395	11.7	8.9	30.9	26.2	10,736	15.8

NA Not available.   [1] Includes other races not shown separately.   [2] Persons of Hispanic origin may be of any race.
[3] Population controls based on 1980 census; see text, section 14.   [4] Beginning 1983, data based on revised Hispanic population controls and not directly comparable with prior years.   [5] Beginning 1987, data based on revised processing procedures and not directly comparable with prior years.

Source: U.S. Bureau of the Census, *Current Population Reports*, P60-185.

No. 736. Families Below Poverty Level, by Type, Based on Alternative Inflation Adjustment: 1970 to 1992

[Families as of **March of following year.** Families include unrelated individuals and are therefore not directly comparable to Census Bureau definitions; see text, section 1. Annual adjustment for inflation is based on the CPI-U-X1; see text, section 14. Based on Current Population Survey]

ITEM	1970	1980	1985	1986	1987	1988	1989	1990	1991	1992
NUMBER BELOW POVERTY LEVEL (1,000)										
All families [1]	9,775	10,869	12,203	12,269	12,468	12,515	12,141	13,158	13,956	14,501
Families with children [1]	3,330	4,432	5,177	5,199	5,231	5,179	5,054	5,441	5,917	6,107
Married couples	1,558	1,555	1,803	1,644	1,638	1,515	1,498	1,610	1,711	1,770
Single mothers	1,509	2,498	2,957	3,121	3,142	3,195	3,072	3,302	3,597	3,682
Nonelderly units:										
Childless families	662	587	898	826	795	796	767	755	830	851
Unrelated individuals	2,146	3,307	3,990	4,016	4,100	4,214	4,077	4,532	4,660	4,913
Elderly units:										
Childless families	965	574	420	413	466	492	455	474	448	586
Unrelated individuals	2,672	1,969	1,718	1,815	1,876	1,834	1,787	1,956	2,102	2,044
PERCENT BELOW POVERTY LEVEL										
All families [1]	15	12	13	13	13	12	12	13	13	14
Families with children [1]	11	13	15	15	15	15	15	16	17	17
Married couples	6	6	7	7	7	6	6	7	7	7
Single mothers	45	42	44	46	45	45	43	44	46	46
Nonelderly units:										
Childless families	4	3	4	4	4	4	4	4	4	4
Unrelated individuals	23	17	18	18	17	17	16	18	18	18
Elderly units:										
Childless families	14	6	4	4	4	5	4	4	4	5
Unrelated individuals	46	25	19	20	20	19	18	19	21	20

[1] Includes other types of families not shown separately.

Source: Congressional Budget Office, *Trends in Family Income: 1970-1986*, February 1988; and unpublished data.

Income, Expenditures, and Wealth

No. 737. Persons Below Poverty Level, by Race, Based on Alternative Inflation Adjustment: 1974 to 1992

[Based on Current Population Survey; see text, sections 1 and 14, and Appendix III. Annual adjustment for inflation is based on the CPI-U-X1; see text, section 14]

YEAR	NUMBER BELOW POVERTY LEVEL (1,000)				PERCENT BELOW POVERTY LEVEL			
	All races [1]	White	Black	Hispanic [2]	All races [1]	White	Black	Hispanic [2]
1974	22,076	14,870	6,773	2,448	10.5	8.2	28.6	21.9
1975	24,232	16,547	7,170	2,787	11.5	9.0	29.8	25.1
1976	23,347	15,513	7,202	2,570	11.0	8.4	29.5	22.8
1977	22,933	15,190	7,230	2,480	10.7	8.2	29.3	20.6
1978	22,472	14,829	7,085	2,416	10.4	8.0	28.4	20.0
1979	23,504	15,382	7,388	2,614	10.5	8.0	28.5	19.5
1980	25,869	17,283	7,671	3,134	11.5	9.0	29.0	23.0
1981	27,731	18,456	8,311	3,302	12.2	9.5	31.0	23.6
1982	30,288	20,385	8,824	3,842	13.2	10.4	32.4	26.7
1983	31,649	21,180	9,130	4,215	13.7	10.7	33.0	25.5
1984	29,971	20,043	8,765	4,367	12.8	10.1	31.2	25.8
1985	29,558	20,157	8,284	4,712	12.5	10.0	29.1	26.1
1986	29,101	19,629	8,391	4,570	12.2	9.7	29.1	24.4
1987	28,890	18,777	8,744	4,899	12.0	9.2	29.8	25.3
1988	28,544	18,326	8,707	4,914	11.7	8.9	29.2	24.5
1989	27,967	18,152	8,504	4,827	11.4	8.8	28.0	23.3
1990	30,097	19,677	9,145	5,401	12.1	9.4	29.7	25.2
1991	32,009	21,027	9,421	5,695	12.7	10.0	30.1	25.8
1992	33,289	21,788	9,910	6,075	13.1	10.3	31.0	26.7

[1] Includes other races not shown separately.   [2] Persons of Hispanic origin may be of any race.

Source: U.S. Bureau of the Census, *Current Population Reports*, P60-185; and unpublished data.

No. 738. Weighted Average Poverty Thresholds Based on Alternative Inflation Adjustment: 1980 to 1992

[Annual adjustment for inflation is based on the CPI-U-X1; see text, section 14]

SIZE OF UNIT	1980 [1]	1985	1986	1987	1988	1989	1990	1991	1992
One person (unrelated individual)	$3,851	$5,032	$5,127	$5,316	$5,541	$5,807	$6,121	$6,379	$6,572
Under 65 years	3,942	5,146	5,246	5,437	5,663	5,936	6,257	6,520	6,716
65 years and over	3,629	4,744	4,835	5,012	5,221	5,472	5,767	6,010	6,191
Two persons	4,929	6,439	6,568	6,806	7,089	7,431	7,829	8,157	8,407
Householder under 65 years	5,088	6,653	6,783	7,031	7,322	7,676	8,091	8,433	8,689
Householder 65 years and over	4,579	5,983	6,100	6,323	6,585	6,902	7,273	7,583	7,809
Three persons	6,033	7,888	8,039	8,333	8,681	9,095	9,587	9,992	10,292
Four persons	7,732	10,111	10,308	10,683	11,124	11,662	12,292	12,812	13,190
Five persons	9,159	11,968	12,200	12,640	13,161	13,792	14,530	15,141	15,598
Six persons	10,356	13,522	13,789	14,270	14,856	15,569	16,414	17,101	17,608
Seven persons	11,727	15,325	15,687	16,239	16,775	17,631	18,624	19,376	19,869
Eight persons	13,049	17,033	17,290	17,956	18,635	19,624	20,778	21,719	22,131
Nine or more persons	15,527	20,319	20,700	21,259	22,201	23,444	24,703	25,710	26,449

[1] Poverty levels for nonfarm families.

Source: U.S. Bureau of the Census, *Current Population Reports*, P60-185; and unpublished data.

No. 739. Weighted Average Poverty Thresholds: 1980 to 1992

[Official poverty thresholds; see text, section 14]

SIZE OF UNIT	1980[1]	1985	1986	1987	1988	1989	1990	1991	1992
One person (unrelated individual)	$4,190	$5,469	$5,572	$5,778	$6,022	$6,310	$6,652	$6,932	$7,143
Under 65 years	4,290	5,593	5,701	5,909	6,155	6,451	6,800	7,086	7,299
65 years and over	3,949	5,156	5,255	5,447	5,674	5,947	6,268	6,532	6,729
Two persons	5,363	6,998	7,138	7,397	7,704	8,076	8,509	8,865	9,137
Householder under 65 years	5,537	7,231	7,372	7,641	7,958	8,343	8,794	9,165	9,443
Householder 65 years and over	4,983	6,503	6,630	6,872	7,157	7,501	7,905	8,241	8,487
Three persons	6,565	8,573	8,737	9,056	9,435	9,885	10,419	10,860	11,186
Four persons	8,414	10,989	11,203	11,611	12,092	12,674	13,359	13,924	14,335
Five persons	9,966	13,007	13,259	13,737	14,304	14,990	15,792	16,456	16,952
Six persons	11,269	14,696	14,986	15,509	16,146	16,921	17,839	18,587	19,137
Seven persons	12,761	16,656	17,049	17,649	18,232	19,162	20,241	21,058	21,594
Eight persons	14,199	18,512	18,791	19,515	20,253	21,328	22,582	23,605	24,053
Nine or more persons	16,896	22,083	22,497	23,105	24,129	25,480	26,848	27,942	28,745

[1] Poverty levels for nonfarm families.

Source: U.S. Bureau of the Census, *Current Population Reports*, P60-185; and earlier reports.

No. 740. Persons Below Poverty Level, by Definition of Income: 1992

[Persons as of **March 1993**. For explanation of income definitions, see text, section 14]

Definition number	DEFINITION	NUMBER BELOW POVERTY LEVEL (1,000)				PERCENT BELOW POVERTY LEVEL			
		All races [1]	White	Black	His-panic [2]	All races [1]	White	Black	His-panic [2]
	All persons......................	253,969	211,820	31,916	22,720	(X)	(X)	(X)	(X)
	INCOME BEFORE TAXES								
1	Money income excluding capital gains [3]....	36,880	24,523	10,613	6,655	14.5	11.6	33.3	29.3
2	Definition 1 less government money transfers.	57,287	41,630	13,357	8,320	22.6	19.7	41.9	36.6
3	Definition 2 plus capital gains...........	57,220	41,553	13,373	8,306	22.5	19.6	41.9	36.6
4	Definition 3 plus health insurance supplements to wage or salary income [4] ...	55,660	40,426	13,024	7,999	21.9	19.1	40.8	35.2
	INCOME AFTER TAXES								
5	Definition 4 less Social Security payroll taxes .	58,256	42,447	13,481	8,396	22.9	20.0	42.2	37.0
6	Definition 5 less Federal income taxes (excluding EITC) [5]	58,862	42,877	13,643	8,498	23.2	20.2	42.7	37.4
7	Definition 6 plus EITC [5]...............	56,940	41,432	13,264	8,137	22.4	19.6	41.6	35.8
8	Definition 7 less State income taxes	57,530	41,688	13,402	8,172	22.6	19.7	42.0	36.0
9	Definition 8 plus nonmeans-tested government cash transfers [6]	39,481	26,124	11,458	7,045	15.5	12.3	35.9	31.0
10	Definition 9 plus value of Medicare	38,331	25,316	11,164	6,827	15.1	12.0	35.0	30.1
11	Definition 10 plus value of regular-price school lunches..................	38,316	25,310	11,156	6,819	15.1	11.9	35.0	30.0
12	Definition 11 plus means-tested government cash transfers [7]...................	35,513	23,489	10,346	6,335	14.0	11.1	32.4	27.9
13	Definition 12 plus value of Medicaid	33,081	21,895	9,634	5,844	13.0	10.3	30.2	25.7
14	Definition 13 plus means-tested government noncash transfers [8]	29,719	19,865	8,487	5,185	11.7	9.4	26.6	22.8
15	Definition 14 plus net imputed return on equity in own home [9]	26,533	17,375	7,896	4,883	10.4	8.2	24.7	21.5

X Not applicable. [1] Includes other races not shown separately. [2] Persons of Hispanic origin may be of any race. [3] Official definition based on income before taxes and includes government cash transfers. [4] Employer contributions to the health insurance plans of employees. [5] Earned Income Tax Credit. [6] Includes Social Security and Railroad Retirement, veterans payments, unemployment and workers' compensation, Black Lung payments, Pell Grants, and other government educational assistance. [7] Includes AFDC and other public assistance or welfare payments, Supplemental Security Income, and veterans payments. Households must meet certain eligibility requirements in order to qualify for these benefits. [8] Includes Medicaid, food stamps, subsidies from free or reduced-price school lunches, and rent subsidies. [9] Estimated amount of income a household would receive if it chose to shift amount held as home equity into an interest bearing account.

No. 741. Money Income of Households—Percent Distribution and Index of Income Concentration, by Definition of Income: 1992

[Households as of **March 1993**. For income definitions, see table 740]

Definition number	DEFINITION	Total income (bil. dol.)	SHARE OF AGGREGATE INCOME					Index of income con-centra-tion [1]	Median income (dol.)
			Lowest quintile	Second quintile	Third quintile	Fourth quintile	Highest quintile		
	INCOME BEFORE TAXES								
1	Money income excluding capital gains......	3,761	3.8	9.4	15.9	24.1	46.8	0.430	30,786
2	Definition 1 less government money transfers.	3,435	1.0	7.8	15.6	25.3	50.4	0.490	27,655
3	Definition 2 plus capital gains...........	3,517	0.9	7.6	15.4	24.8	51.3	0.497	27,879
4	Definition 3 plus health insurance supplements to wage or salary income.....	3,677	0.9	7.4	15.4	25.3	51.0	0.497	29,350
	INCOME AFTER TAXES								
5	Definition 4 less Social Security payroll taxes .	3,467	0.9	7.4	15.4	25.0	51.3	0.499	27,472
6	Definition 5 less Federal income taxes (excluding the EITC) [2]...............	3,047	1.1	8.1	16.0	25.6	49.1	0.478	25,301
7	Definition 6 plus EITC [2].	3,055	1.1	8.3	16.0	25.6	49.0	0.476	25,376
8	Definition 7 less State income taxes	2,940	1.1	8.4	16.3	25.5	48.6	0.471	24,684
9	Definition 8 plus nonmeans-tested government cash transfers.............	3,232	3.6	10.2	16.5	24.5	45.1	0.415	27,651
10	Definition 9 plus value of Medicare	3,320	3.8	10.7	16.9	24.4	44.3	0.404	28,964
11	Definition 10 plus value of regular-price lunches	3,321	3.8	10.7	16.9	24.4	44.3	0.404	28,977
12	Definition 11 plus means-tested government cash transfers	3,356	4.4	10.8	16.8	24.2	43.9	0.395	29,139
13	Definition 12 plus value of Medicaid	3,375	4.5	10.9	16.8	24.2	43.7	0.392	29,395
14	Definition 13 plus means-tested government noncash transfers	3,401	4.9	11.0	16.7	24.0	43.3	0.385	29,522
15	Definition 14 plus net imputed return on equity in own home	3,620	5.1	11.0	16.7	23.9	43.3	0.381	31,321

[1] A statistical measure of income equality ranging from 0 to 1. A measure of 1 indicates perfect inequality (i.e. one person having all the wealth and the rest having none.) A measure of 0 indicates perfect equality (i.e. all persons having equal shares of wealth.) [2] Earned Income Tax Credit.

Source of tables 740 and 741: U.S. Bureau of the Census, *Current Population Reports*, P60-185RD.

No. 742. Household Wealth—Ownership and Median Value of Selected Nonfinancial Assets: 1991

[Net worth is the sum of the market value of assets owned by household members minus liabilities (secured or unsecured). Assets not covered: cash value of life insurance policies, equities in pension plans, and value of home furnishings and jewelry. Asset values are an average of balances at the end of February, March, April, and May of 1991. Based on Survey of Income and Program Participation. For definition of median, see Guide to Tabular Presentation. For data on financial assets, see table 774, section 16]

CHARACTERISTICS OF HOUSEHOLDER	Net worth	Business, profession	Motor vehicles	Own home	Rental property	Other real estate
OWNERSHIP (percent)						
All households [1]	(X)	12	86	65	9	11
White	(X)	13	90	68	10	12
Black	(X)	4	63	45	4	4
Hispanic [2]	(X)	7	76	41	7	5
Northeast	(X)	11	78	63	10	9
Midwest	(X)	13	88	68	10	10
South	(X)	11	88	67	8	12
West	(X)	13	89	59	10	12
Under 35 years old	(X)	9	86	39	4	4
35 to 44 years old	(X)	16	91	67	9	11
45 to 54 years old	(X)	17	92	76	13	15
55 to 64 years old	(X)	14	89	78	13	17
65 years old and over	(X)	5	76	77	10	11
Married-couple	(X)	16	96	79	11	14
Male householder	(X)	9	84	46	8	8
Female householder	(X)	4	69	49	6	5
Householder under 65 years old:						
With labor force activity	(X)	15	92	63	9	11
With job entire period	(X)	16	93	64	9	11
With job part of period	(X)	8	89	49	5	9
No job: spent time looking or on layoff	(X)	2	71	36	4	3
No labor force activity	(X)	3	70	53	8	9
MEDIAN VALUE (dollars)						
All households [1]	36,623	10,260	5,249	43,078	33,201	23,328
White	44,408	10,352	5,447	44,477	32,934	24,115
Black	4,604	3,444	3,207	26,992	30,838	10,975
Hispanic [2]	5,345	4,962	3,436	32,328	21,986	30,091
Northeast	57,294	5,462	6,165	74,347	24,202	36,406
Midwest	38,677	14,863	5,448	36,320	25,249	19,419
South	26,775	7,819	4,755	31,595	33,801	19,511
West	39,735	10,528	4,992	59,004	56,932	30,523
Under 35 years old	5,565	6,091	4,137	15,283	20,388	17,692
35 to 44 years old	31,148	9,703	5,466	31,082	30,114	18,284
45 to 54 years old	58,250	12,978	6,634	45,869	43,287	26,373
55 to 64 years old	83,041	17,094	6,352	59,128	47,780	28,607
65 years and over	88,192	8,493	4,753	63,284	30,100	30,607
Married-couple	60,065	10,936	6,642	44,588	44,245	24,073
Male householder	11,986	12,949	3,630	33,580	12,743	24,220
Female householder	14,762	1,202	3,194	43,098	6,307	20,573
Householder under 65 years old:						
With labor force activity	27,589	10,286	5,463	33,912	34,685	22,343
With job entire period	30,619	10,585	5,630	34,640	35,116	22,578
With job part of period	7,733	1	3,590	23,616	(B)	21,055
No job: spent time looking or on layoff	3,048	(B)	3,123	23,723	(B)	(B)
No labor force activity	14,310	10,693	4,036	46,360	33,395	24,210

B Base figure too small to meet statistical standards for reliability of a derived figure.   X Not applicable.   [1] Includes other races not shown separately.   [2] Persons of Hispanic origin may be of any race.
Source: U.S. Bureau of the Census, Current Population Reports, P70-34.

No. 743. Top Wealthholders With Gross Assets of $600,000 or More: 1989

[Figures are estimates based on samples of estate tax returns. Net worth equals assets minus debts and mortgages]

SIZE OF NET WORTH	ALL WEALTHHOLDERS			MALE WEALTHHOLDERS			FEMALE WEALTHHOLDERS		
	Number (1,000)	Assets (bil. dol.)	Net worth (bil. dol.)	Number (1,000)	Assets (bil. dol.)	Net worth (bil. dol.)	Number (1,000)	Assets (bil. dol.)	Net worth (bil. dol.)
Total	3,417	5,390	4,804	1,989	3,150	2,733	1,428	2,241	2,071
Under $600,000 [1]	812	483	299	610	356	212	202	127	87
$600,000 to $999,999	1,344	1,118	1,024	673	575	514	672	542	510
$1,000,000 to $2,499,999	945	1,539	1,404	523	869	778	422	670	626
$2,500,000 to $4,999,999	206	770	696	119	456	403	86	314	293
$5,000,000 to $9,999,999	73	530	492	43	311	287	31	218	205
$10,000,000 or more	36	951	890	22	582	539	15	369	351

[1] Includes top wealthholders with negative net worth.
Source: U.S. Internal Revenue Service, Statistics of Income Bulletin, spring 1993.

No. 744. Top Wealthholders With Gross Assets of $600,000 or More and Net Worth Under $10 Million, by State: 1989

[Figures are estimates based on samples of estate tax returns. Net worth equals assets minus debts and mortgages]

STATE	Number (1,000)	Rate per 10,000 people 18 years and over	Assets (bil. dol.)	Net worth (bil. dol.)	STATE	Number (1,000)	Rate per 10,000 people 18 years and over	Assets (bil. dol.)	Net worth (bil. dol.)
United States...	3,380	184	4,440	3,914	Missouri	55	146	64	60
Alabama........	30	101	45	40	Montana........	10	172	10	8
Alaska.........	7	180	8	6	Nebraska.......	20	178	24	21
Arizona........	42	160	67	59	Nevada.........	21	245	35	30
Arkansas.......	17	99	22	20	New Hampshire ...	15	181	18	16
California.......	662	306	944	810	New Jersey.....	162	274	212	191
Colorado.......	42	176	51	45	New Mexico......	15	139	15	13
Connecticut.....	99	390	124	110	New York	325	237	427	384
Delaware.......	13	264	16	14	North Carolina ...	71	142	96	88
District of Columbia.	13	262	16	15	North Dakota.....	10	206	8	7
Florida	241	245	349	308	Ohio..........	99	124	122	109
Georgia........	69	147	81	69	Oklahoma	30	129	36	33
Hawaii	22	274	28	26	Oregon.........	24	117	28	26
Idaho	8	112	9	8	Pennsylvania	127	140	148	133
Illinois.........	148	175	202	182	Rhode Island	17	214	18	16
Indiana........	37	91	46	43	South Carolina ...	42	164	41	37
Iowa..........	33	161	37	33	South Dakota.....	7	141	6	5
Kansas........	28	156	29	27	Tennessee	45	125	56	49
Kentucky.......	31	114	38	33	Texas..........	174	145	229	190
Louisiana	31	102	38	32	Utah..........	8	70	12	10
Maine.........	16	178	25	22	Vermont	7	168	8	7
Maryland.......	65	182	98	88	Virginia........	69	150	102	94
Massachusetts....	109	233	122	106	Washington	60	171	80	71
Michigan........	85	125	103	92	West Virginia	9	67	9	8
Minnesota......	44	139	51	46	Wisconsin	36	102	51	46
Mississippi......	17	92	17	15	Wyoming........	6	197	8	6

Source: U.S. Internal Revenue Service, *Statistics of Income Bulletin*, spring 1993; and unpublished data.

No. 745. Gross and Net Stock of Fixed Reproducible Tangible Wealth: 1980 to 1991

[In billions of dollars. As of December 31]

ITEM	1980	1981	1982	1983	1984	1985	1986	1987	1988	1989	1990	1991
CURRENT DOLLARS												
Gross stock......	14,306	15,670	16,527	17,277	18,259	19,330	20,503	21,774	22,966	24,361	25,652	26,699
Private..............	9,364	10,387	11,005	11,477	12,082	12,747	13,536	14,388	15,078	16,022	16,894	17,489
Nonresidential equipment	2,389	2,723	2,939	3,067	3,214	3,374	3,599	3,775	4,010	4,257	4,543	4,674
Nonresidential structures.	2,683	3,032	3,247	3,376	3,573	3,783	3,951	4,156	4,478	4,755	4,964	5,110
Residential..........	4,292	4,632	4,818	5,034	5,296	5,590	5,986	6,457	6,590	7,010	7,387	7,705
Government	2,979	3,141	3,237	3,368	3,568	3,772	3,916	4,083	4,306	4,516	4,713	4,904
Equipment..........	488	543	583	621	657	695	732	764	814	873	949	1,018
Structures..........	2,491	2,599	2,654	2,748	2,911	3,077	3,184	3,319	3,492	3,643	3,764	3,886
Federal............	885	968	1,018	1,067	1,119	1,176	1,227	1,269	1,325	1,394	1,469	1,543
Military............	493	535	566	601	638	678	715	738	776	818	873	927
State and local	2,094	2,173	2,219	2,301	2,449	2,596	2,690	2,814	2,981	3,122	3,244	3,361
Consumer durable goods. .	1,963	2,142	2,285	2,433	2,608	2,811	3,051	3,303	3,582	3,823	4,045	4,306
Net stock.........	8,619	9,374	9,792	10,172	10,734	11,367	12,063	12,803	13,458	14,245	14,936	15,412
Private............	5,814	6,413	6,737	6,987	7,348	7,752	8,224	8,729	9,108	9,650	10,130	10,412
Government	1,790	1,875	1,921	1,991	2,105	2,224	2,311	2,414	2,542	2,665	2,775	2,877
Consumer durable goods. .	1,014	1,086	1,134	1,194	1,281	1,391	1,527	1,660	1,808	1,930	2,031	2,123
CONSTANT (1987) DOLLARS												
Gross stock.......	17,469	17,963	18,370	18,845	19,441	20,091	20,753	21,400	22,062	22,717	23,339	23,849
Private..............	11,585	11,936	12,217	12,523	12,909	13,322	13,728	14,112	14,504	14,886	15,245	15,522
Nonresidential equipment	3,009	3,126	3,206	3,285	3,396	3,518	3,633	3,737	3,855	3,979	4,093	4,179
Nonresidential structures.	3,255	3,384	3,506	3,606	3,729	3,870	3,983	4,088	4,191	4,293	4,398	4,477
Residential..........	5,321	5,427	5,505	5,632	5,783	5,934	6,112	6,286	6,458	6,614	6,754	6,866
Government	3,544	3,603	3,648	3,705	3,770	3,849	3,934	4,026	4,115	4,204	4,307	4,403
Equipment..........	625	630	634	647	670	698	730	768	802	837	879	917
Structures..........	2,918	2,972	3,014	3,058	3,100	3,152	3,204	3,259	3,313	3,367	3,428	3,487
Federal............	1,122	1,138	1,142	1,156	1,177	1,204	1,233	1,266	1,293	1,319	1,351	1,379
Military............	641	643	644	652	668	691	716	743	767	786	813	831
State and local	2,421	2,465	2,506	2,549	2,593	2,645	2,701	2,760	2,822	2,885	2,956	3,025
Consumer durable goods. .	2,340	2,424	2,505	2,617	2,762	2,920	3,091	3,262	3,444	3,627	3,787	3,924
Net stock.........	10,524	10,755	10,902	11,112	11,441	11,823	12,214	12,577	12,942	13,293	13,598	13,785
Private............	7,198	7,384	7,499	7,642	7,866	8,112	8,346	8,558	8,774	8,980	9,157	9,258
Government	2,123	2,148	2,166	2,191	2,223	2,269	2,320	2,380	2,430	2,482	2,537	2,587
Consumer durable goods. .	1,203	1,223	1,236	1,278	1,352	1,442	1,547	1,639	1,738	1,831	1,903	1,940

Source: U.S. Bureau of Economic Analysis, *Survey of Current Business*, January 1992 and September 1993.

Figure 15.1
**Annual Percent Change in Consumer
Price Indexes: 1970 to 1993**

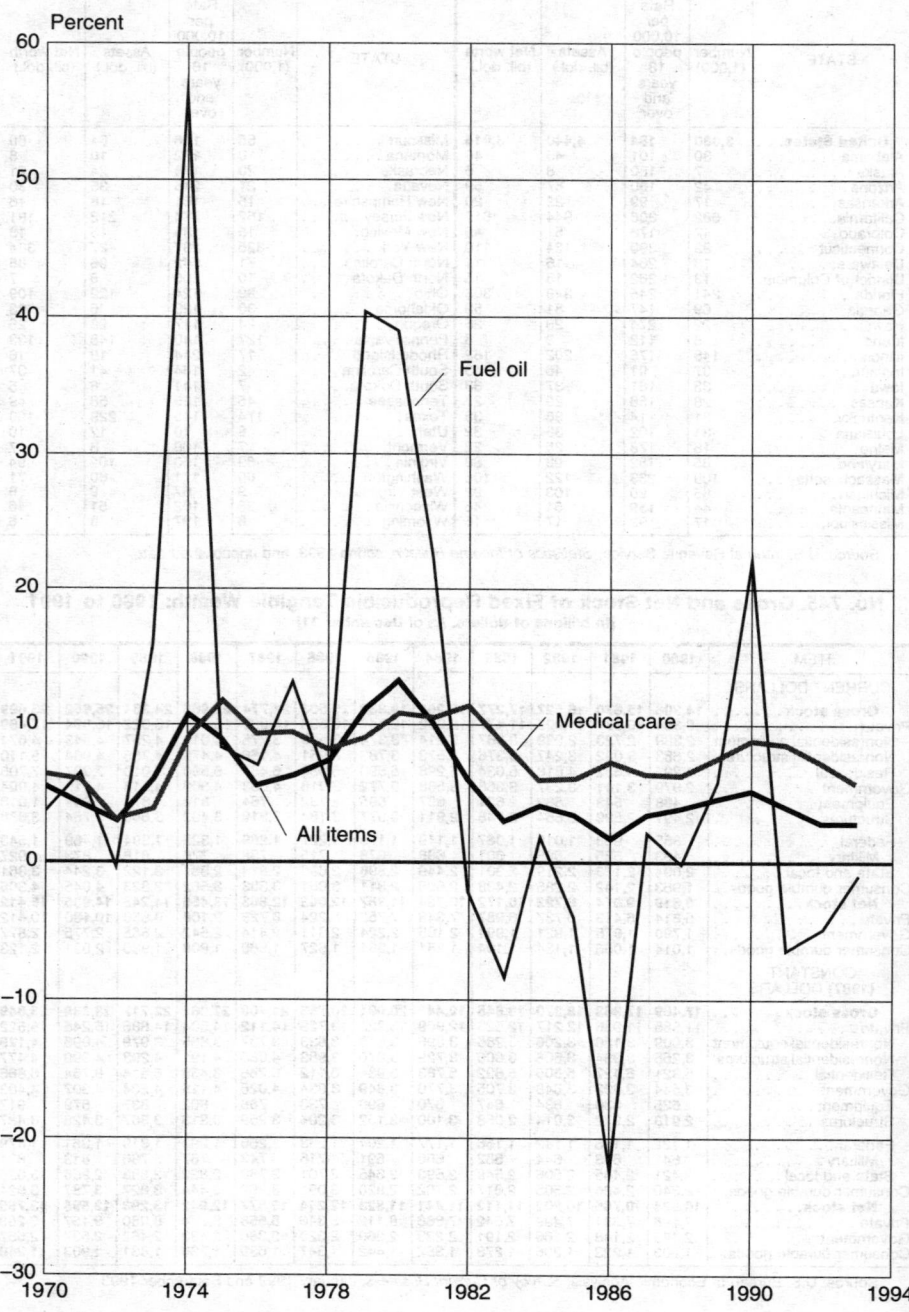

Source: Chart prepared by U.S. Bureau of the Census. For data, see table 747.

Prices

This section presents indexes of producer and consumer prices, actual prices for selected commodities, and energy prices. The primary sources of these data are monthly publications of the Department of Labor, Bureau of Labor Statistics (BLS), which include *Monthly Labor Review, Consumer Price Index, Detailed Report; Producer Price Indexes;* and *U.S. Import and Export Price Indexes.* The Department of Commerce, Bureau of Economic Analysis is the source for gross domestic product measures.

Producer price index (PPI).—This index, dating from 1890, is the oldest continuous statistical series published by BLS. It is designed to measure average changes in prices received by producers of all commodities, at all stages of processing, produced in the United States.

The index has undergone several revisions (see *Monthly Labor Review,* February 1962, April 1978, and August 1988). It is now based on approximately 3,200 commodity price series and 80,000 quotations per month. Indexes for the net output of manufacturing and mining industries have been added in recent years. Prices used in constructing the index are collected from sellers, and generally apply to the first significant large volume commercial transaction for each commodity—i.e., the manufacturer's or other producer's selling price or the selling price on an organized exchange or at a central market.

The weights used in the index represent the total net selling value of commodities produced or processed in this country. Values are f.o.b. (free-on-board) production point and are exclusive of excise taxes. Effective with the release of data for January 1988, many important producer price indexes were changed to a new reference base year, 1982=100, from 1967=100. The reference year of the PPI shipment weights has been taken primarily from the 1987 Census of Manufactures. For further detail regarding the PPI, see the *BLS Handbook of Methods, Bulletin 2414,* Chapter 16.

Consumer price indexes (CPI).—The CPI is a measure of the average change in prices over time in a fixed "market

In Brief

Consumer price changes: 1992-93:

All items index up 3.0 percent
Medical care index up 5.9 percent
Fuel oil index down -0.9 percent

basket" of goods and services purchased either by urban wage earners and clerical workers or by all urban consumers.

In 1919, BLS began to publish complete indexes at semiannual intervals, using a weighting structure based on data collected in the expenditure survey of wage-earner and clerical-worker families in 1917-19 (BLS Bulletin 357, 1924). The first major revision of the CPI occurred in 1940, with subsequent revisions in 1953, 1964, 1978, and 1987.

Beginning with the release of data for January 1988 in February 1988, most Consumer Price Indexes shifted to a new reference base year. All indexes previously expressed on a base of 1967=100, or any other base through December 1981, have been rebased to 1982-84=100. Selection of the 1982-84 period was made to coincide with the updated expenditure weights, which are based upon data tabulated from the Consumer Expenditure Surveys for 1982, 1983, and 1984.

BLS publishes CPI's for two population groups: (1) a CPI for All Urban Consumers (CPI-U) which covers approximately 80 percent of the total population; and (2) a CPI for Urban Wage Earners and Clerical Workers (CPI-W) which covers 32 percent of the total population. The CPI-U includes, in addition to wage earners and clerical workers, groups which historically have been excluded from CPI coverage, such as professional, managerial, and technical workers, the self-employed, short-term workers, the unemployed, and retirees and others not in the labor force.

The current CPI is based on prices of food, clothing, shelter, fuels, transportation fares, charges for doctors' and dentists' services, drugs, etc., purchased for day-to-day living. Prices are collected in 85 areas across the country from over

57,000 housing units and 19,000 establishments. Area selection was based on the 1980 census. All taxes directly associated with the purchase and use of items are included in the index. Prices of food, fuels, and a few other items are obtained every month in all 85 locations. Prices of most other commodities and services are collected monthly in the five largest geographic areas and every other month in other areas.

In calculating the index, each item is assigned a weight to account for its relative importance in consumers' budgets. Price changes for the various items in each location are then averaged. Local data are then combined to obtain a U.S. city average. Separate indexes are also published for regions, area size-classes, cross-classifications of regions and size-classes, and for 29 local areas, usually consisting of the Metropolitan Statistical Area (MSA); see Appendix II. Area definitions are those established by the Office of Management and Budget in 1983. Definitions do not include revisions made since 1983. Area indexes do not measure differences in the level of prices among cities; they only measure the average change in prices for each area since the base period. For further detail regarding the CPI, see the BLS *Handbook of Methods,* Bulletin 2414, Chapter 19; the Consumer Price Index, and Report 736, the CPI: 1987 Revision. In January 1983, the method of measuring homeownership costs in the CPI-U was changed to a rental equivalence approach. This treatment calculates homeowner costs of shelter based on the implicit rent owners would pay to rent the homes they own. The rental equivalence approach was introduced into the CPI-W in 1985. The CPI-U was used to prepare the consumer prices tables in this section.

International price indexes—The BLS International Price Program produces export and import price indexes for nonmilitary goods traded between the United States and the rest of the world. The export price index provides a measure of price change for all products sold by U.S. residents to foreign buyers. The import price index provides a measure of price change for goods purchased from other countries by U.S. residents. The reference period for the indexes is 1990=100, unless otherwise indicated.

The product universe for both the import and export indexes includes raw materials, agricultural products, semifinished manufactures, and finished manufactures, including both capital and consumer goods. Price data for these items are collected primarily by mail questionnaire. In nearly all cases, the data are collected directly from the exporter or importer, although in a few cases, prices are obtained from other sources.

To the extent possible, the data gathered refer to prices at the U.S. border for exports and at either the foreign border or the U.S. border for imports. For nearly all products, the prices refer to transactions completed during the first week of the month. Survey respondents are asked to indicate all discounts, allowances, and rebates applicable to the reported prices, so that the price used in the calculation of the indexes is the actual price for which the product was bought or sold.

In addition to general indexes for U.S. exports and imports, indexes are also published for detailed product categories of exports and imports. These categories are defined according to the five-digit level of detail for the Bureau of Economic Analysis End-use Classification, the three-digit level of detail for the Standard International Trade Classification (SITC), and the four-digit level of detail for the Harmonized System. Aggregate import indexes by country or region of origin are also available.

Other price indexes.—The *fixed-weighted price index* is a weighted average of the detailed price indexes used in the deflation of goods and services that make up the gross domestic product (GDP). These price indexes are combined using weights that reflect the composition of GDP in 1987. Because the same weights are used for each period, changes in this index measure changes in prices over any period.

Measures of inflation.—Inflation is defined as a time of generally rising prices for goods and factors of production. The Bureau of Labor Statistics samples prices of items in a representative market basket and publishes the results as the CPI. The media invariably announce the inflation rate as the percent change in the CPI from month to month. A much more meaningful indicator of inflation is the percent change from the same month of the prior year.

The Producer Price Index (PPI) measures prices at the producer/manufacturing level only. The PPI shows the same general pattern of inflation as does the CPI, but is more volatile. The PPI can be roughly viewed as a leading indicator. It often tends to foreshadow trends that later occur in the CPI.

Other measures of inflation include the index of industrial materials prices; the Dow Jones Commodity Spot Price Index; Futures Price Index, the Employment Cost Index, the Hourly Compensation Index, or the Unit Labor Cost Index as a measure of

the change in cost of the labor factor of production, and changes in long-term interest rates that are often used to measure changes in the cost of the capital factor of production.

Statistical reliability.—For a discussion of statistical collection and estimation, sampling procedures, and measures of statistical reliability pertaining to the producer price index and the CPI, see Appendix III.

Historical statistics.—Tabular headnotes provide cross-references, where applicable, to Historical Statistics of the United States, Colonial Times to 1970. See Appendix IV.

No. 746. Purchasing Power of the Dollar: 1950 to 1993

[Indexes: PPI, 1982=$1.00; CPI, 1982–84=$1.00. Producer prices prior to 1961, and consumer prices prior to 1964, exclude Alaska and Hawaii. Producer prices based on finished goods index. Obtained by dividing the average price index for the 1982=100, PPI; 1982–84=100, CPI base periods (100.0) by the price index for a given period and expressing the result in dollars and cents. Annual figures are based on average of monthly data]

YEAR	ANNUAL AVERAGE AS MEASURED BY—		YEAR	ANNUAL AVERAGE AS MEASURED BY—		YEAR	ANNUAL AVERAGE AS MEASURED BY—	
	Producer prices	Consumer prices		Producer prices	Consumer prices		Producer prices	Consumer prices
1950	$3.546	$4.151	1965	2.933	3.166	1980	1.136	1.215
1951	3.247	3.846	1966	2.841	3.080	1981	1.041	1.098
1952	3.268	3.765	1967	2.809	2.993	1982	1.000	1.035
1953	3.300	3.735	1968	2.732	2.873	1983	0.984	1.003
1954	3.289	3.717	1969	2.632	2.726	1984	0.964	0.961
1955	3.279	3.732	1970	2.545	2.574	1985	0.955	0.928
1956	3.195	3.678	1971	2.469	2.466	1986	0.969	0.913
1957	3.077	3.549	1972	2.392	2.391	1987	0.949	0.880
1958	3.012	3.457	1973	2.193	2.251	1988	0.926	0.846
1959	3.021	3.427	1974	1.901	2.029	1989	0.880	0.807
1960	2.994	3.373	1975	1.718	1.859	1990	0.839	0.766
1961	2.994	3.340	1976	1.645	1.757	1991	0.822	0.734
1962	2.985	3.304	1977	1.546	1.649	1992	0.812	0.713
1963	2.994	3.265	1978	1.433	1.532	1993	0.802	0.692
1964	2.985	3.220	1979	1.289	1.380			

Source: U.S. Bureau of Labor Statistics. Monthly data in U.S. Bureau of Economic Analysis, Survey of Current Business.

No. 747. Consumer Price Indexes (CPI-U), by Major Groups: 1960 to 1993

[1982-84 = 100. Represents annual averages of monthly figures. Reflects buying patterns of all urban consumers. Minus sign (-) indicates decrease. See text, section 15. See *Historical Statistics, Colonial Times to 1970*, series E 135-173 for similar data]

YEAR	All items	Energy	Food	Shelter	Apparel and upkeep	Trans-portation	Med-ical care	Fuel oil	Elec-tricity	Utility (piped) gas	Tele-phone serv-ices	All com-modities
1960	29.6	22.4	30.0	25.2	45.7	29.8	22.3	13.5	29.9	17.6	58.3	33.6
1961	29.9	22.5	30.4	25.4	46.1	30.1	22.9	14.0	29.9	17.9	58.5	33.8
1962	30.2	22.6	30.6	25.8	46.3	30.8	23.5	14.0	29.9	17.9	58.5	34.1
1963	30.6	22.6	31.1	26.1	46.9	30.9	24.1	14.3	29.9	17.9	58.6	34.4
1964	31.0	22.5	31.5	26.5	47.3	31.4	24.6	14.0	29.8	17.9	58.6	34.8
1965	31.5	22.9	32.2	27.0	47.8	31.9	25.2	14.3	29.7	18.0	57.7	35.2
1966	32.4	23.3	33.8	27.8	49.0	32.3	26.3	14.7	29.7	18.1	56.5	36.1
1967	33.4	23.8	34.1	28.8	51.0	33.3	28.2	15.1	29.9	18.1	57.3	36.8
1968	34.8	24.2	35.3	30.1	53.7	34.3	29.9	15.6	30.2	18.2	57.3	38.1
1969	36.7	24.8	37.1	32.6	56.8	35.7	31.9	15.9	30.8	18.6	58.0	39.9
1970	38.8	25.5	39.2	35.5	59.2	37.5	34.0	16.5	31.8	19.6	58.7	41.7
1971	40.5	26.5	40.4	37.0	61.1	39.5	36.1	17.6	33.9	21.0	61.6	43.2
1972	41.8	27.2	42.1	38.7	62.3	39.9	37.3	17.6	35.6	22.1	65.0	44.5
1973	44.4	29.4	48.2	40.5	64.6	41.2	38.8	20.4	37.4	23.1	66.7	47.8
1974	49.3	38.1	55.1	44.4	69.4	45.8	42.4	32.2	44.1	26.0	69.5	53.5
1975	53.8	42.1	59.8	48.8	72.5	50.1	47.5	34.9	50.0	31.1	71.7	58.2
1976	56.9	45.1	61.6	51.5	75.2	55.1	52.0	37.4	53.1	36.3	74.3	60.7
1977	60.6	49.4	65.5	54.9	78.6	59.0	57.0	42.4	56.6	43.2	75.2	64.2
1978	65.2	52.5	72.0	60.5	81.4	61.7	61.8	44.9	60.9	47.5	76.0	68.8
1979	72.6	65.7	79.9	68.9	84.9	70.5	67.5	63.1	65.6	55.1	75.8	76.6
1980	82.4	86.0	86.8	81.0	90.9	83.1	74.9	87.7	75.8	65.7	77.7	86.0
1981	90.9	97.7	93.6	90.5	95.3	93.2	82.9	107.3	87.2	74.9	84.6	93.2
1982	96.5	99.2	97.4	96.9	97.8	97.0	92.5	105.0	95.8	89.8	93.2	97.0
1983	99.6	99.9	99.4	99.1	100.2	99.3	100.6	96.5	98.9	104.7	99.2	99.8
1984	103.9	100.9	103.2	104.0	102.1	103.7	106.8	98.5	105.3	105.5	107.5	103.2
1985	107.6	101.6	105.6	109.8	105.0	106.4	113.5	94.6	108.9	104.8	111.7	105.4
1986	109.6	88.2	109.0	115.8	105.9	102.3	122.0	74.1	110.4	99.7	117.2	104.4
1987	113.6	88.6	113.5	121.3	110.6	105.4	130.1	75.8	110.0	95.1	116.5	107.7
1988	118.3	89.3	118.2	127.1	115.4	108.7	138.6	75.8	111.5	94.5	116.0	111.5
1989	124.0	94.3	125.1	132.8	118.6	114.1	149.3	80.3	114.7	97.1	117.2	116.7
1990	130.7	102.1	132.4	140.0	124.1	120.5	162.8	98.6	117.4	97.3	117.7	122.8
1991	136.2	102.5	136.3	146.3	128.7	123.8	177.0	92.4	121.8	98.5	119.7	126.6
1992	140.3	103.0	137.9	151.2	131.9	126.5	190.1	88.0	124.2	100.3	120.4	129.1
1993	144.5	104.2	140.9	155.7	133.7	130.4	201.4	87.2	126.7	106.5	121.2	131.5
PERCENT CHANGE [1]												
1960	1.7	2.3	1.0	2.0	1.6	-	3.7	-1.5	1.4	6.7	1.6	0.9
1961	1.0	0.4	1.3	0.8	0.9	1.0	2.7	3.7	-	1.7	0.3	0.6
1962	1.0	0.4	0.7	1.6	0.4	2.3	2.6	-	-	-	-	0.9
1963	1.3	-	1.6	1.2	1.3	0.3	2.6	2.1	-	-	0.2	0.9
1964	1.3	-0.4	1.3	1.5	0.9	1.6	2.1	-2.1	-0.3	-	-	1.2
1965	1.6	1.8	2.2	1.9	1.1	1.6	2.4	2.1	-0.3	0.6	-1.5	1.1
1966	2.9	1.7	5.0	3.0	2.5	1.3	4.4	2.8	-	0.6	-2.1	2.6
1967	3.1	2.1	0.9	3.6	4.1	3.1	7.2	2.7	0.7	-	1.4	1.9
1968	4.2	1.7	3.5	4.5	5.3	3.0	6.0	3.3	1.0	0.6	-	3.5
1969	5.5	2.5	5.1	8.3	5.8	4.1	6.7	1.9	2.0	2.2	1.2	4.7
1970	5.7	2.8	5.7	8.9	4.2	5.0	6.6	3.8	3.2	5.4	1.2	4.5
1971	4.4	3.9	3.1	4.2	3.2	5.3	6.2	6.7	6.6	7.1	4.9	3.6
1972	3.2	2.6	4.2	4.6	2.0	1.0	3.3	-	5.0	5.2	5.5	3.0
1973	6.2	8.1	14.5	4.7	3.7	3.3	4.0	15.9	5.1	4.5	2.6	7.4
1974	11.0	29.6	14.3	9.6	7.4	11.2	9.3	57.8	17.9	12.6	4.2	11.9
1975	9.1	10.5	8.5	9.9	4.5	9.4	12.0	8.4	13.4	19.6	3.2	8.8
1976	5.8	7.1	3.0	5.5	3.7	10.0	9.5	7.2	6.2	16.7	3.6	4.3
1977	6.5	9.5	6.3	6.6	4.5	7.1	9.6	13.4	6.6	19.0	1.2	5.8
1978	7.6	6.3	9.9	10.2	3.6	4.6	8.4	5.9	7.6	10.0	1.1	7.2
1979	11.3	25.1	11.0	13.9	4.3	14.3	9.2	40.5	7.7	16.0	-0.3	11.3
1980	13.5	30.9	8.6	17.6	7.1	17.9	11.0	39.0	15.5	19.2	2.5	12.3
1981	10.3	13.6	7.8	11.7	4.8	12.2	10.7	22.3	15.0	14.0	8.9	8.4
1982	6.2	1.5	4.1	7.1	2.6	4.1	11.6	-2.1	9.9	19.9	10.2	4.1
1983	3.2	0.7	2.1	2.3	2.5	2.4	8.8	-8.1	3.2	16.6	6.4	2.9
1984	4.3	1.0	3.8	4.9	1.9	4.4	6.2	2.1	6.5	0.8	8.4	3.4
1985	3.6	0.7	2.3	5.6	2.8	2.6	6.3	-4.0	3.4	-0.7	3.9	2.1
1986	1.9	-13.2	3.2	5.5	0.9	-3.9	7.5	-21.7	1.4	-4.9	4.9	-0.9
1987	3.6	0.5	4.1	4.7	4.4	3.0	6.6	2.3	-0.4	-4.6	-0.6	3.2
1988	4.1	0.8	4.1	4.8	4.3	3.1	6.5	-	1.4	-0.6	-0.4	3.5
1989	4.8	5.6	5.8	4.5	2.8	5.0	7.7	5.9	2.9	2.8	1.0	4.7
1990	5.4	8.3	5.8	5.4	4.6	5.6	9.0	22.8	2.4	0.2	0.4	5.2
1991	4.2	0.4	2.9	4.5	3.7	2.7	8.7	-6.3	3.7	1.2	1.7	3.1
1992	3.0	0.5	1.2	3.3	2.5	2.2	7.4	-4.8	2.0	1.8	0.6	2.0
1993	3.0	1.2	2.2	3.0	1.4	3.1	5.9	-0.9	2.0	6.2	0.7	1.9

- Represents zero.   [1] Change from immediate prior year.

Source: Bureau of Labor Statistics, *Monthly Labor Review* and *Handbook of Labor Statistics*, periodic.

No. 748. Consumer Price Indexes for All Urban Consumers (CPI-U) for Selected Items and Groups: 1980 to 1993

[1982-84 = 100. Annual averages of monthly figures. See headnote, table 747]

ITEM	1980	1985	1987	1988	1989	1990	1991	1992	1993
All items.	**82.4**	**107.6**	**113.6**	**118.3**	**124.0**	**130.7**	**136.2**	**140.3**	**144.5**
Food and beverages	86.7	105.6	113.5	118.2	124.9	132.1	136.8	138.7	141.6
Food	86.8	105.6	113.5	118.2	125.1	132.4	136.3	137.9	140.9
Food at home	88.4	104.3	111.9	116.6	124.2	132.3	135.8	136.8	140.1
Cereals and bakery products	83.9	107.9	114.8	122.1	132.4	140.0	145.8	151.5	156.6
Cereals and cereal products	84.2	107.2	113.9	122.5	133.8	141.1	147.5	153.3	157.9
Cereals	76.3	111.3	124.1	132.9	147.9	158.6	168.1	175.4	183.3
Rice, pasta, and cornmeal	90.9	102.1	101.7	114.4	120.0	122.0	126.5	128.3	129.7
Bakery products	83.8	108.2	115.0	121.8	131.5	139.2	144.7	150.4	155.7
White bread	85.9	105.8	110.7	118.6	129.4	136.4	139.3	146.2	152.2
Cookies, cakes, and cupcakes.	81.5	110.2	118.3	125.0	134.5	142.7	151.1	155.6	159.3
Meats, poultry, fish and eggs	92.0	100.1	110.5	114.3	121.3	130.0	132.6	130.9	135.5
Meats	92.7	98.9	109.6	112.2	116.7	128.5	132.5	130.7	134.6
Beef and veal	98.4	98.2	106.3	112.1	119.3	128.8	132.4	132.3	137.1
Ground beef excl. canned	104.6	95.9	100.2	103.4	108.6	118.1	119.9	118.9	121.7
Chuck roast	99.8	95.6	103.8	108.1	116.8	130.3	135.8	137.1	141.9
Round steak	98.9	97.0	105.3	110.6	116.6	125.1	129.5	129.9	134.4
Sirloin steak	96.2	99.7	111.2	120.0	126.0	130.6	133.5	132.4	138.5
Pork	81.9	99.1	116.0	112.5	113.2	129.8	134.1	127.8	131.7
Bacon	73.5	101.3	114.6	100.9	95.8	113.4	119.8	104.6	110.8
Chops	82.9	98.7	120.5	118.8	122.7	140.2	141.7	138.9	144.6
Ham	85.5	99.8	115.8	116.5	117.3	132.4	139.9	135.6	137.9
Poultry	93.7	106.2	112.6	120.7	132.7	132.5	131.5	131.4	136.9
Fresh whole chicken	94.4	104.5	113.3	125.1	137.1	134.9	131.7	131.9	138.0
Fresh, frozen chicken parts	91.7	104.6	114.4	123.3	135.7	135.9	134.7	134.4	140.1
Fish and seafood	87.5	107.5	129.9	137.4	143.6	146.7	148.3	151.7	156.6
Canned fish and seafood	93.7	97.8	103.9	117.0	124.3	119.5	119.0	118.7	121.5
Fresh and frozen fish and seafood	84.1	112.9	143.6	144.2	155.2	161.4	163.8	168.7	174.5
Eggs	88.6	91.0	91.5	93.6	118.5	124.1	121.2	108.3	117.1
Dairy products	90.9	103.2	105.9	108.4	115.6	126.5	125.1	128.5	129.4
Fruits and vegetables	82.1	108.4	119.1	128.1	138.0	149.0	155.8	155.4	159.0
Fresh fruits	84.8	116.3	132.0	143.0	152.4	170.9	193.9	184.2	188.8
Apples	92.1	113.1	131.0	134.2	140.5	147.5	172.8	179.5	169.0
Bananas	91.5	99.9	104.2	119.2	131.3	138.2	145.0	139.9	135.5
Oranges, tangerines	72.6	119.7	135.9	144.6	147.0	160.6	249.4	176.2	190.1
Fresh vegetables	79.0	103.5	121.6	129.3	143.1	151.1	154.4	157.9	168.7
Potatoes	81.0	101.6	116.0	119.1	153.5	162.6	144.6	141.5	154.6
Lettuce	77.8	106.1	136.4	148.6	151.5	150.3	159.8	155.7	178.2
Tomatoes	81.9	103.6	116.8	123.1	136.2	160.8	153.1	171.8	168.0
Processed fruits	82.1	109.5	110.6	122.0	125.9	136.9	131.8	137.7	132.3
Processed vegetables	83.1	104.4	107.1	112.2	124.2	127.5	128.5	128.8	130.8
Coffee	111.6	105.5	116.2	115.0	120.4	117.5	115.3	110.7	109.8
Lunch away from home	83.8	107.8	116.6	121.5	127.6	133.9	138.4	141.3	144.0
Dinner away from home	84.2	108.8	117.0	121.6	126.9	132.3	136.3	138.9	141.3
Alcoholic beverages	86.4	106.4	114.1	118.6	123.5	129.3	142.8	147.3	149.6
Alcoholic beverages at home	87.3	105.2	111.5	114.2	117.9	123.0	137.8	141.6	142.2
Beer and ale	84.8	106.7	110.9	114.4	118.2	123.6	138.4	143.5	143.2
Distilled spirits	89.8	105.3	114.4	116.1	119.9	125.7	139.2	141.5	143.2
Wine	89.5	100.2	105.7	107.8	110.9	114.4	129.9	132.6	134.0
Alcoholic beverages away from home	82.9	111.1	123.4	130.6	137.4	144.4	156.9	162.5	167.4
Housing	81.1	107.7	114.2	118.5	123.0	128.5	133.6	137.5	141.2
Shelter	81.0	109.8	121.3	127.1	132.8	140.0	146.3	151.2	155.7
Renters' cost	(NA)	115.4	128.1	133.6	138.9	146.7	155.6	160.9	165.0
Rent, residential	80.9	111.8	123.1	127.8	132.8	138.4	143.3	146.9	150.3
Tenants' insurance	78.9	109.4	120.4	124.9	128.3	130.6	133.2	136.5	140.8
Homeowners' costs	(NA)	113.1	124.8	131.1	137.3	144.6	150.2	155.3	160.2
Owners' equivalent rent.	(NA)	113.2	124.8	131.1	137.4	144.8	150.4	155.5	160.5
Household insurance	(NA)	112.4	124.0	129.0	132.6	135.3	138.4	142.2	146.9
Maintenance and repair	82.4	106.5	111.8	114.7	118.0	122.2	126.3	128.6	130.6
Fuels and other utilities	75.4	106.5	103.0	104.4	107.8	111.6	115.3	117.8	121.3
Fuels	74.8	104.5	97.3	98.0	100.9	104.5	106.7	108.1	111.2
Fuel oil and other	86.1	95.9	77.9	78.1	81.7	99.3	94.6	90.7	90.3
Fuel oil	87.7	94.6	75.8	75.8	80.3	98.6	92.4	88.0	87.2
Gas (piped) and electricity	71.4	107.1	103.8	104.6	107.5	109.3	112.6	114.8	118.5
Electricity	75.8	108.9	110.0	111.5	114.7	117.4	121.8	124.2	126.7
Utility (piped) gas	65.7	104.8	95.1	94.5	97.1	97.3	98.5	100.3	106.5
Telephone services	77.7	111.7	116.5	116.0	117.2	117.7	119.7	120.4	121.2
Local charges	72.8	120.4	139.3	141.3	146.5	149.3	153.9	155.7	156.4
Interstate toll charges	83.3	94.9	75.3	72.3	70.0	68.2	67.6	68.0	69.6
Intrastate toll charges	85.2	106.8	104.7	101.5	97.0	95.1	93.1	91.4	90.7
Water and sewerage maintenance	74.0	113.4	125.8	132.7	140.8	150.2	161.1	172.1	181.4
Cable television	(NA)	110.6	123.1	132.9	144.0	158.4	175.7	186.2	198.9
Refuse collection	(NA)	109.9	130.3	142.5	155.6	171.2	189.2	207.3	220.5

See footnotes at end of table.

No. 748. Consumer Price Indexes for All Urban Consumers (CPI-U) for Selected Items and Groups: 1980 to 1993—Continued

[1982-84 = 100. Annual averages of monthly figures. See headnote, table 747]

ITEM	1980	1985	1987	1988	1989	1990	1991	1992	1993
Household furnishings and operations	86.3	103.8	107.1	109.4	111.2	113.3	116.0	118.0	119.3
Housefurnishings	88.5	101.7	103.6	105.1	105.5	106.7	107.5	109.0	109.5
Furniture and bedding	88.0	104.9	109.7	113.2	113.9	115.7	116.6	120.6	123.5
Bedroom furniture	83.5	107.4	114.1	117.7	117.6	118.5	120.1	126.8	132.5
Sofas	(NA)	103.0	110.9	114.3	117.0	118.4	118.3	119.4	120.1
Living room chairs and tables	(NA)	103.2	107.2	111.0	112.5	116.7	118.4	121.9	125.0
Appliances and electronic equip.	93.5	95.2	91.4	90.2	89.1	87.8	86.0	84.6	83.4
Video and audio equipment	100.7	91.9	86.0	83.6	82.2	80.8	79.4	78.4	77.1
Television	104.6	88.7	79.7	77.6	76.1	74.6	72.9	72.4	70.7
Video products other than TV	(NA)	(NA)	(NA)	(NA)	96.8	91.5	84.6	81.0	78.5
Audio products	97.7	94.4	93.0	92.7	92.8	93.2	94.6	94.4	93.9
Housekeeping supplies	83.2	106.2	111.5	114.7	120.9	125.2	128.9	129.6	130.7
Housekeeping services	84.3	106.1	110.6	114.3	117.3	120.1	127.5	132.1	135.8
Postage	76.2	108.8	110.2	121.4	125.1	125.1	143.6	145.3	145.3
Apparel and upkeep	90.9	105.0	110.6	115.4	118.6	124.1	128.7	131.9	133.7
Apparel commodities	92.9	104.0	108.9	113.7	116.7	122.0	126.4	129.4	131.0
Apparel commodities less footwear	93.0	104.3	109.6	114.4	117.1	122.8	127.4	130.2	131.9
Men's and boy's apparel	89.4	105.0	109.1	113.4	117.0	120.4	124.2	126.5	127.5
Women's and girl's apparel	96.0	104.9	110.4	114.9	116.4	122.6	127.6	130.4	132.6
Infants' and toddlers'	85.5	107.2	112.1	116.4	119.1	125.8	128.9	129.3	127.1
Footwear	91.8	102.3	105.1	109.9	114.4	117.4	120.9	125.0	125.9
Transportation	83.1	106.4	105.4	108.7	114.1	120.5	123.8	126.5	130.4
Private transportation	84.2	106.2	104.2	107.6	112.9	118.8	121.9	124.6	127.5
New vehicles	88.5	106.1	114.4	116.5	119.2	121.4	126.0	129.2	132.7
New cars	88.4	106.1	114.6	116.9	119.2	121.0	125.3	128.4	131.5
New trucks	(NA)	105.5	112.2	113.5	117.0	121.6	127.0	130.9	135.7
Used cars	62.3	113.7	113.1	118.0	120.4	117.6	118.1	123.2	133.9
Motor fuel	97.4	98.7	80.2	80.9	88.5	101.2	99.4	99.0	98.0
Automobile maintenance and repair	81.5	106.8	114.8	119.7	124.9	130.1	136.0	141.3	145.9
Automobile insurance	82.0	119.2	146.2	156.6	166.6	177.9	191.5	205.5	216.7
Automobile finance charges	86.4	94.5	84.9	91.3	100.5	99.6	98.0	86.1	78.6
Vehicle rental, registration, other	78.3	111.7	123.0	128.1	135.0	148.1	154.8	162.3	169.8
Public transportation	69.0	110.5	121.1	123.3	129.5	142.6	148.9	151.4	167.0
Airline fares	68.0	112.5	122.8	124.2	131.6	148.4	155.2	155.2	178.7
Other intercity transportation	73.1	114.7	126.7	132.6	138.5	143.3	149.0	152.5	150.9
Intracity transportation	69.7	107.7	118.8	121.7	125.2	133.5	138.9	146.9	150.7
Medical care	74.9	113.5	130.1	138.6	149.3	162.8	177.0	190.1	201.4
Medical care commodities	75.4	115.2	131.0	139.9	150.8	163.4	176.8	188.1	195.0
Prescription drugs	72.5	120.1	140.8	152.0	165.2	181.7	199.7	214.7	223.0
Nonprescription drugs, medical sup	(NA)	(NA)	103.1	108.1	114.6	120.6	126.3	131.2	135.5
Medical care services	74.8	113.2	130.0	138.3	148.9	162.7	177.1	190.5	202.9
Professional medical services	77.9	113.5	128.8	137.5	146.4	156.1	165.7	175.8	184.7
Physicians' services	76.5	113.3	130.4	139.8	150.1	160.8	170.5	181.2	191.3
Dental services	78.9	114.2	128.8	137.5	146.1	155.8	167.4	178.7	188.1
Eye care	(NA)	(NA)	103.5	108.7	112.4	117.3	121.9	127.0	130.4
Hospital and related services	69.2	116.1	131.6	143.9	160.5	178.0	196.1	214.0	231.9
Hospital rooms	68.0	115.4	131.1	143.3	158.1	175.4	191.9	208.7	226.4
Entertainment	83.6	107.9	115.3	120.3	126.5	132.4	138.4	142.3	145.8
Entertainment commodities	84.5	105.8	110.5	115.0	119.8	124.0	128.6	131.3	133.4
Reading materials	77.7	110.7	119.5	124.3	129.5	136.2	144.7	150.9	156.2
Newspapers	79.4	109.3	118.4	123.7	129.2	134.6	146.5	154.8	161.1
Magazines, periodicals, and books	75.9	112.1	120.7	125.0	130.0	137.9	143.3	147.4	151.8
Sporting goods, equipment	88.5	104.6	104.3	108.1	111.1	114.9	118.5	120.2	120.1
Sport vehicles, including bicycles	87.9	106.3	105.5	108.9	112.3	115.3	117.5	119.7	120.6
Toys, hobbies; other entertainment	86.5	103.3	108.4	113.2	118.5	121.5	123.9	124.7	126.0
Pet supplies and expenses	83.3	106.4	111.0	114.5	120.7	124.6	129.1	128.1	128.8
Entertainment services	82.3	110.9	122.0	127.7	135.4	143.2	150.6	155.9	160.8
Club membership	(NA)	(NA)	101.0	107.2	112.6	117.0	122.5	125.2	128.4
Admissions	83.8	112.8	124.4	131.1	141.4	151.2	156.3	159.3	167.3
Tobacco and smoking products	72.0	116.7	133.6	145.8	164.4	181.5	202.7	219.8	228.4
Personal care	81.9	108.3	115.1	119.4	125.0	130.4	134.9	138.3	141.5
Personal care services	83.7	108.9	116.2	120.7	126.8	132.8	137.0	140.0	144.0
Beauty parlor services for women	83.4	108.8	116.0	120.3	126.5	133.0	137.2	139.8	143.6
Haircuts, etc. for men	84.4	109.0	116.5	121.7	127.3	131.5	135.9	140.3	144.6
Personal and educational expenses	70.9	119.1	138.5	147.9	158.1	170.2	183.7	197.4	210.7
School books and supplies	71.4	118.2	138.1	148.1	158.0	171.3	180.3	190.3	197.6
Personal and educational services	70.8	119.2	138.7	148.0	158.3	170.4	184.2	198.1	211.9
Tuition and other school fees	71.2	119.7	140.0	151.0	162.7	175.7	191.4	208.5	225.3
College tuition	70.8	119.9	139.4	150.0	161.9	175.0	192.8	213.5	233.5
Elementary and high school tuition	72.3	119.0	141.3	154.6	168.0	182.8	198.0	213.7	228.9
Day care and nursery school	(NA)	(NA)	(NA)	(NA)	(NA)	(NA)	103.2	108.3	113.6
All commodities	86.0	105.4	107.7	111.5	116.7	122.8	126.6	129.1	131.5
All commodities less food	85.7	105.2	104.3	107.7	112.0	117.4	121.3	124.2	126.3
Energy	86.0	101.6	88.6	89.3	94.3	102.1	102.5	103.0	104.2

NA Not available.

Source: U.S. Bureau of Labor Statistics, *Monthly Labor Review* and *CPI Detailed Report*, January issues.

No. 749. Consumer Price Indexes (CPI-U)—Selected Areas: 1980 to 1993

[1982–84=100, except as indicated. Represents annual averages of monthly figures. Local area CPI indexes are byproducts of the national CPI program. Each local index has a smaller sample size than the national index and is therefore, subject to substantially more sampling and other measurement error. As a result, local area indexes show greater volatility than the national index, although their long-term trends are similar. Area definitions are those established by the Office of Management and Budget in 1983. For further detail see the U.S. Bureau of Labor Statistics Handbook of Methods, Bulletin 2285, Chapter 19, the Consumer Price Index, and Report 736, the CPI: 1987 Revision. See also text, section 15]

AREA	1980	1985	1989	1990	1991	1992	1993 All items	1993 Food and beverages	1993 Food	1993 Housing	1993 Apparel and upkeep	1993 Transportation	1993 Medical care	1993 Entertainment	1993 Fuel and other utilities
U.S. city average	82.4	107.6	124.0	130.7	136.2	140.3	144.5	141.6	140.9	141.2	133.7	130.4	201.4	145.8	121.3
Anchorage, AK MSA	85.5	105.8	111.7	118.6	124.0	128.2	132.2	131.2	129.8	121.1	131.2	128.7	189.6	157.9	144.8
Atlanta, GA MSA	80.3	106.9	126.1	131.7	135.9	138.5	143.4	139.6	141.2	136.6	158.0	124.2	213.0	172.1	131.2
Baltimore, MD MSA	83.7	108.2	124.5	130.8	136.4	140.1	143.1	144.3	144.7	135.6	135.9	129.7	198.7	152.6	112.0
Boston-Lawrence-Salem, MA-NH CMSA	82.6	109.4	131.3	138.9	145.0	148.6	152.9	146.3	146.2	146.4	157.6	132.5	239.0	160.1	117.2
Buffalo-Niagara Falls, NY CMSA	83.5	108.6	121.6	127.7	133.4	137.9	142.7	139.3	138.7	152.1	112.6	117.5	172.4	167.4	122.4
Chicago-Gary-Lake County, IL-IN-WI CMSA	82.2	107.7	125.0	131.7	137.0	141.1	145.4	143.1	141.8	143.3	131.1	126.2	203.1	153.9	119.7
Cincinnati-Hamilton, OH-KY-IN CMSA	82.1	106.6	120.9	126.5	131.4	134.1	141.1	132.1	130.9	132.0	138.6	121.2	200.7	144.9	113.2
Cleveland-Akron-Lorain, OH CMSA	78.9	107.8	122.7	129.0	134.2	136.8	140.3	139.7	139.7	139.0	125.1	125.0	187.2	143.2	119.1
Dallas-Fort Worth, TX CMSA	81.5	108.2	119.5	120.9	125.6	133.9	137.3	139.0	139.5	125.3	147.8	128.9	196.8	144.0	122.0
Denver-Boulder, CO CMSA	78.4	107.1	115.8	120.9	125.6	130.3	135.9	131.5	131.5	124.1	95.1	141.1	217.9	141.9	117.0
Detroit-Ann Arbor, MI CMSA	85.3	106.8	122.3	128.6	133.1	135.9	139.6	135.2	134.5	134.4	137.9	132.5	190.9	137.7	116.8
Honolulu, HI MSA	83.0	106.8	128.7	138.1	148.0	155.1	160.1	152.9	152.7	166.5	116.5	150.5	197.4	138.3	117.5
Houston-Galveston-Brazoria, TX CMSA	82.7	104.9	114.1	120.6	125.1	127.1	133.4	132.4	131.4	116.8	142.1	128.2	200.8	153.2	106.9
Kansas City, MO-KS CMSA	83.6	107.7	121.6	126.0	131.2	134.3	138.1	137.7	137.6	130.4	125.3	124.7	195.6	152.5	121.8
Los Angeles-Anaheim-Riverside, CA CMSA	83.7	108.4	128.3	135.9	141.4	146.5	150.3	145.1	143.1	150.4	131.6	137.5	206.6	135.8	140.9
Miami-Fort Lauderdale, FL CMSA	81.1	106.5	121.5	128.0	132.3	134.5	139.1	146.9	147.5	130.4	140.1	131.9	181.9	129.5	113.4
Milwaukee, WI PMSA	81.4	107.0	120.8	126.2	132.2	137.1	142.1	138.1	138.6	142.8	123.2	128.5	185.5	133.1	108.6
Minneapolis-St. Paul, MN-WI MSA [1]	78.9	107.0	122.0	127.0	130.4	135.0	139.2	147.2	145.5	128.1	141.5	126.9	193.8	149.0	113.5
New Orleans, LA MSA [1]	(NA)	(NA)	107.2	111.5	116.0	120.2	124.7	120.2	121.2	114.2	165.1	118.5	157.8	130.1	128.7
New York-Northern New Jersey-Long Island, NY-NJ-CT CMSA	82.1	108.7	130.6	138.5	144.8	150.0	154.5	149.0	148.7	155.5	129.3	137.7	209.1	149.8	111.2
Philadelphia-Wilmington-Trenton, PA-NJ-DE-MD CMSA	83.6	108.8	128.3	135.8	142.2	146.6	150.2	139.7	138.1	131.9	106.0	139.5	211.6	147.5	118.2
Pittsburgh-Beaver Valley, PA CMSA	81.0	106.9	120.1	128.2	131.3	136.0	139.9	137.2	135.6	139.1	134.5	118.1	196.8	149.8	132.4
Portland-Vancouver, OR-WA CMSA	87.2	106.7	120.4	127.4	133.9	139.8	144.7	134.0	133.0	143.7	122.2	136.2	186.6	148.7	118.8
San Diego, CA MSA	79.4	110.4	130.6	138.4	143.4	147.4	150.6	145.3	143.9	149.5	135.6	138.0	213.7	155.2	110.6
San Francisco-Oakland-San Jose, CA CMSA	80.4	108.4	126.4	132.1	137.9	142.5	146.3	146.2	145.9	149.2	118.2	123.7	199.1	162.3	142.0
Seattle-Tacoma, WA CMSA	82.7	105.6	118.1	126.8	134.1	139.0	142.9	142.4	142.0	143.5	115.5	128.4	193.1	144.2	106.2
St. Louis-East St. Louis, MO-IL CMSA	82.5	107.1	121.8	128.1	132.1	134.7	137.5	140.1	139.1	133.0	122.8	125.1	191.5	137.3	118.8
Tampa-St. Petersburg-Clearwater, FL MSA [1]	(NA)	(NA)	107.2	111.7	116.4	119.2	124.0	118.2	117.4	116.7	157.7	116.6	165.8	108.6	113.0
Washington, DC-MD-VA MSA	82.9	109.0	128.0	135.6	141.2	144.7	149.3	142.8	141.5	148.0	144.4	134.9	195.3	151.0	121.7

NA Not available. [1] 1987 = 100.

Source: U.S. Bureau of Labor Statistics, *Monthly Labor Review* and *CPI Detailed Report*, January issues.

No. 750. Consumer Price Index for All Urban Consumers (CPI-U), by Region: 1980 to 1993

[1982-84 = 100. For composition of regions, see table 26]

ITEM	1980	1983	1984	1985	1986	1987	1988	1989	1990	1991	1992	1993
U.S. city average, all items . . .	82.4	99.6	103.9	107.6	109.6	113.6	118.3	124.0	130.7	136.2	140.3	144.5
Food	86.8	99.4	103.2	105.6	109.0	113.5	118.2	125.1	132.4	136.3	137.9	140.9
Housing	81.1	99.5	103.6	107.7	110.9	114.2	118.5	123.0	128.5	133.6	137.5	141.2
Gas (piped) and electricity . .	71.4	101.5	105.4	107.1	105.7	103.8	104.6	107.5	109.3	112.6	114.8	118.5
Northeast:												
All items	82.2	99.8	104.5	108.4	111.1	116.0	121.8	128.6	136.3	142.5	147.3	151.4
Food	86.5	99.4	103.3	106.2	110.1	115.8	121.1	128.7	135.9	139.8	141.9	145.1
Housing	80.7	99.7	104.6	109.0	112.7	117.3	124.0	130.8	138.0	144.4	149.0	152.6
Gas (piped) and electricity . .	73.8	100.9	104.7	105.9	104.6	101.2	100.2	105.4	109.6	113.4	117.2	121.4
North Central:												
All items	82.4	99.9	103.6	106.8	108.0	111.9	116.1	121.5	127.4	132.4	136.1	140.0
Food	88.5	99.3	102.7	104.4	107.5	111.8	116.0	122.2	129.6	133.5	135.0	137.8
Housing	80.0	100.3	103.5	107.0	109.4	112.4	115.9	119.9	124.1	128.5	132.1	135.8
Gas (piped) and electricity . .	70.1	103.3	106.1	108.6	107.1	104.6	104.3	105.5	104.0	105.6	107.6	111.6
South:												
All items	81.9	99.7	103.8	107.1	108.9	112.4	116.4	121.5	127.9	132.9	136.5	140.8
Food	86.6	99.3	103.6	105.7	108.8	113.1	117.6	124.2	131.6	135.0	136.1	138.6
Housing	80.8	99.6	103.0	106.3	109.0	111.0	113.9	117.2	121.8	125.6	128.8	132.8
Gas (piped) and electricity . .	70.2	100.9	105.0	106.0	105.1	104.3	106.1	108.2	110.4	112.9	114.9	118.3
West:												
All items	83.3	99.0	103.6	108.0	110.5	114.3	119.0	124.6	131.5	137.3	142.0	146.0
Food	85.2	99.7	103.6	106.1	109.0	112.9	117.6	124.9	132.0	136.4	138.5	141.9
Housing	83.3	98.2	103.3	108.8	113.0	116.5	120.7	124.8	130.9	136.9	141.2	144.6
Gas (piped) and electricity . .	72.1	99.9	105.6	108.1	105.8	105.5	108.8	112.9	115.8	122.9	123.6	126.6

Source: U.S. Bureau of Labor Statistics, Monthly Labor Review and CPI Detailed Report, January issues.

No. 751. Annual Percent Changes in Consumer Prices, United States and OECD Countries: 1975 to 1992

[Covers member countries of Organization for Economic Cooperation (OECD). For consumer price indexes for OECD countries, see section 30]

COUNTRY	1975	1980	1981	1982	1983	1984	1985	1986	1987	1988	1989	1990	1991	1992
United States	9.1	13.5	10.3	6.1	3.2	4.3	3.5	1.9	3.7	4.1	4.8	5.4	4.2	3.0
OECD	11.7	13.5	10.8	8.0	5.6	5.6	4.9	3.0	3.6	4.3	5.4	5.8	5.2	4.0
Australia	15.1	9.8	10.1	11.2	10.1	3.9	6.7	9.1	8.5	7.3	7.5	7.3	3.2	1.0
Canada	10.7	10.2	12.4	10.8	5.8	4.3	4.0	4.2	4.4	4.0	5.0	4.8	5.6	1.5
Japan.	11.8	7.8	4.9	2.7	1.9	2.2	2.0	0.6	0.1	0.7	2.3	3.1	3.3	1.7
New Zealand.	14.7	17.2	15.4	16.2	7.3	6.2	15.4	13.2	15.8	6.4	5.7	6.1	2.6	1.0
Austria	8.4	6.3	6.8	5.4	3.3	5.7	3.2	1.7	1.4	1.9	2.6	3.3	3.3	4.0
Belgium	12.8	6.7	7.1	8.7	7.7	6.3	4.9	1.3	1.6	1.2	3.1	3.4	3.2	2.4
Denmark	9.6	12.3	11.7	10.1	6.9	6.3	4.7	3.6	4.0	4.6	4.8	2.7	2.4	2.1
Finland.	17.9	11.6	12.0	9.6	8.3	7.1	5.9	2.9	4.1	5.1	6.6	6.1	4.3	2.9
France	11.8	13.6	13.4	11.8	9.6	7.4	5.8	2.7	3.1	2.7	3.6	3.4	3.2	2.4
Greece	13.6	24.7	24.5	21.0	20.2	18.5	19.3	23.0	16.4	13.5	13.7	20.4	19.5	15.9
Ireland	20.9	18.3	20.4	17.1	10.5	8.6	5.5	3.8	3.1	2.1	4.1	3.3	3.2	3.1
Italy [1]	17.2	21.1	18.7	16.3	15.0	10.6	8.6	6.1	4.6	5.0	6.6	6.1	6.5	5.3
Luxembourg	10.7	6.3	8.1	9.4	8.7	5.6	4.1	0.3	-0.1	1.4	3.4	3.7	3.1	3.2
Netherlands	10.2	6.5	6.7	5.9	2.7	3.3	2.3	0.1	-0.7	0.7	1.1	2.5	3.9	3.7
Norway.	11.7	10.9	13.7	11.3	8.4	6.3	5.7	7.2	8.7	6.7	4.6	4.1	3.4	2.3
Portugal [2]	20.4	16.6	20.0	22.4	25.5	28.8	19.6	11.8	9.4	9.7	12.6	13.4	11.4	8.9
Spain.	17.0	15.6	14.5	14.4	12.2	11.3	8.8	8.8	5.2	4.8	6.8	6.7	5.9	5.9
Sweden	9.8	13.7	12.1	8.6	8.9	8.0	7.4	4.2	4.2	5.8	6.4	10.5	9.3	2.3
Switzerland	6.7	4.0	6.5	5.6	3.0	2.9	3.4	0.8	1.4	1.9	3.2	5.4	5.8	4.0
Turkey [2]	19.5	110.2	36.6	29.7	31.4	48.4	45.0	34.6	38.9	75.4	63.3	60.3	66.0	70.1
United Kingdom	24.2	18.0	11.9	8.6	4.6	5.0	6.1	3.4	4.1	4.9	7.8	9.5	5.9	3.7
Germany	5.9	5.5	6.3	5.3	3.3	2.4	2.2	-0.1	0.2	1.3	2.8	2.7	3.5	4.0

[1] Households of wage and salary earners.   [2] Excludes rent.

Source: Organization for Economic Cooperation and Development, Paris, France, Main Economic Indicators, monthly.

No. 752. Cost of Living Index—Selected Metropolitan Areas: Second Quarter 1993

[Measures relative price levels for consumer goods and services in participating areas for a midmanagement standard of living. The national average equals 100, and each index is read as a percent of the national average. The index does not measure inflation, but compares prices at a single point in time. Excludes taxes. Metropolitan areas as defined by the Office of Management and Budget. For definitions and components of MSA's, see source for details. Selection based on 1990 MSA population]

METROPOLITAN AREAS	Composite index	Grocery items	Housing	Utilities	Transportation	Misc. goods and services
Birmingham AL MSA	100.6	94.2	100.7	117.9	100.6	98.4
Decatur AL MSA: Decatur-Hartselle	89.6	93.5	79.7	89.1	99.6	93.6
Dothan AL MSA: Dothan	89.5	96.9	84.4	96.5	98.9	87.1
Florence AL MSA	95.1	96.2	93.9	103.3	93.4	94.6
Gadsden AL MSA: Gadsden	90.5	93.2	73.2	117.3	98.1	94.7
Huntsville AL MSA: Huntsville	100.4	94.0	96.7	94.1	101.2	107.0
Mobile AL MSA: Mobile	95.1	99.4	78.5	110.4	113.6	98.3
Montgomery AL MSA: Montgomery	98.2	96.8	83.0	122.3	103.9	103.6
Tuscaloosa AL MSA: Tuscaloosa	97.9	95.8	89.6	116.3	101.2	100.3
Anchorage AK MSA: Anchorage	130.1	136.1	137.4	106.1	115.4	124.3
Las Vegas NV-AZ MSA: Lake Havasu City AZ	97.9	100.6	99.1	85.6	94.4	97.6
Phoenix-Mesa AZ MSA:						
Phoenix	101.2	101.6	92.9	89.6	116.8	103.8
Scottsdale	101.8	105.9	110.0	89.2	107.8	94.0
Tucson AZ MSA: Tucson	108.8	107.2	102.7	98.5	114.5	114.6
Yuma AZ	97.9	99.2	82.2	118.9	115.5	99.2
Fayetteville-Springdale-Rogers AR MSA:						
Fayetteville	91.4	98.8	77.6	86.4	98.2	100.2
Fort Smith AR-OK MSA: Fort Smith AR	92.6	99.5	79.5	103.2	90.5	97.1
Little Rock-North Little Rock AR MSA:						
Little Rock-North Little Rock	90.7	91.3	81.6	115.5	98.4	89.7
Bakersfield CA MSA: Bakersfield	111.0	109.6	112.6	123.7	110.7	105.2
Los Angeles-Long Beach CA PMSA	130.5	110.5	169.6	83.2	122.1	118.1
Riverside-San Bernardino CA PMSA:						
Indio	109.9	105.3	117.8	76.3	125.2	109.5
Palm Springs	119.2	108.5	129.2	105.5	124.6	116.4
Riverside City	114.2	105.7	128.7	71.9	122.7	113.4
San Diego CA MSA: San Diego	130.9	112.7	188.1	74.5	133.5	105.7
Boulder-Longmont CO PMSA: Boulder	120.3	102.3	166.8	91.7	105.9	103.8
Colorado Springs CO MSA: Colorado Springs	97.7	106.1	94.9	74.7	103.7	100.4
Denver CO PMSA	107.1	95.5	118.4	91.4	108.8	103.3
Fort Collins-Loveland CO MSA:						
Fort Collins	99.7	103.1	105.4	75.4	101.4	97.6
Loveland	90.3	98.2	86.0	76.5	97.5	90.6
Pueblo CO MSA: Pueblo	87.2	107.1	70.7	78.9	94.3	91.5
Dover DE MSA: Dover	106.4	107.4	107.0	113.7	99.2	106.2
Wilmington-Newark DE-MD PMSA: Wilmington DE	110.9	111.7	118.7	114.8	94.7	106.4
Washington DC-MD-VA-WV PMSA	134.2	124.0	166.8	114.8	134.2	115.0
Gainesville FL MSA: Gainesville	103.0	99.9	98.7	102.0	104.2	106.8
Jacksonville FL MSA: Jacksonville	96.1	97.5	85.7	101.0	96.2	100.7
Orlando FL MSA: Orlando	98.9	97.8	94.0	100.5	102.0	100.4
Sarasota-Bradenton FL MSA: Sarasota	101.1	95.9	96.5	118.2	112.6	99.4
Tallahassee FL MSA: Tallahassee	103.0	99.4	101.4	106.6	99.1	106.1
Tampa-St. Petersburg-Clearwater FL MSA: Tampa	98.6	99.9	98.4	100.5	104.7	96.7
West Palm Beach-Boca Raton FL MSA:						
Boca Raton	115.6	98.9	126.2	122.8	114.4	113.7
West Palm Beach	111.9	98.5	128.4	122.7	104.1	105.1
Atlanta GA MSA:						
Atlanta	99.6	101.2	97.4	110.3	102.5	92.9
Carrollton	93.0	92.8	83.6	109.3	91.2	97.5
Cartersville/Bartow County	92.4	97.5	88.3	94.9	84.9	95.9
Augusta-Aiken GA-SC MSA: Augusta GA MSA	100.7	97.6	97.9	104.9	99.5	104.2
Macon GA MSA: Macon	99.1	99.0	93.6	105.0	100.8	103.1
Boise City ID MSA: Boise	103.2	100.9	111.6	74.7	96.0	105.2
Bloomington-Normal IL MSA: Bloomington-Normal	104.2	100.4	100.2	113.1	102.6	108.3
Champaign-Urbana IL MSA: Champaign-Urbana	101.7	102.8	96.5	113.9	100.8	101.7
Chicago IL PMSA: Joliet/Will County	112.4	100.9	122.5	121.8	118.9	104.5
Davenport-Moline-Rock Island IA-IL MSA:						
Quad Cities IL-IA	98.3	98.8	99.4	92.8	98.8	100.1
Decatur IL MSA: Decatur	94.3	96.2	84.4	111.6	100.5	95.3
Peoria-Pekin IL MSA: Peoria	106.1	102.2	112.7	93.7	108.8	106.4
Rockford IL MSA: Rockford	108.6	98.7	110.9	130.9	107.4	104.9
Springfield IL MSA: Springfield	92.5	99.9	87.1	91.6	94.7	93.7
Bloomington IN MSA: Bloomington	100.9	104.6	98.5	97.3	96.1	103.7
Evansville-Henderson IN-KY MSA: Evansville IN	90.5	98.8	85.9	87.3	88.7	92.8
Fort Wayne IN MSA: Fort Wayne	90.3	97.5	88.1	103.5	89.7	86.7
Indianapolis IN MSA:						
Anderson	96.5	102.5	96.8	95.4	101.9	93.4
Indianapolis	96.7	97.0	95.3	90.4	100.1	98.8
Lafayette IN MSA: Lafayette	101.8	106.8	103.3	103.3	91.2	101.9
Muncie IN MSA: Muncie	102.9	105.1	110.1	96.5	103.4	99.5
South Bend IN MSA: South Bend-Mishawaka	93.8	91.6	91.2	101.7	89.7	96.2

See footnotes at end of table.

No. 752. Cost of Living Index—Selected Metropolitan Areas: Second Quarter 1993—Continued

[See headnote, page 493]

METROPOLITAN AREAS	Composite index	Grocery items	Housing	Utilities	Transportation	Misc. goods and services
Cedar Rapids IA MSA: Cedar Rapids	100.3	95.7	103.3	102.9	99.3	100.3
Waterloo-Cedar Falls IA MSA: Waterloo-Cedar Falls	96.8	98.7	92.7	87.5	104.7	100.7
Wichita KS MSA: Wichita	96.7	90.6	96.6	93.9	100.6	97.3
Lexington KY MSA	100.1	99.1	101.0	85.0	93.5	104.6
Louisville KY-IN MSA: Louisville KY	91.5	94.1	86.4	80.2	94.3	96.3
Owensboro KY MSA: Owensboro	95.1	99.2	88.3	87.5	88.8	101.6
Alexandria LA MSA: Alexandria	91.6	97.1	84.3	86.9	100.3	95.9
Baton Rouge LA MSA: Baton Rouge	101.4	99.8	93.6	128.7	102.0	101.7
Lake Charles LA MSA: Lake Charles	94.7	98.2	79.4	101.4	97.0	103.6
Monroe LA MSA: Monroe	102.0	97.4	84.3	156.9	100.6	105.4
New Orleans LA MSA: New Orleans	96.0	101.7	84.6	118.1	103.9	95.2
Cumberland MD-WV MSA: Cumberland MD	98.1	102.2	101.6	114.0	81.4	95.2
Hagerstown MD PMSA: Hagerstown	104.3	93.7	117.8	109.6	95.5	98.8
Boston MA-NH PMSA:						
Boston PMSA (MA Part)	136.8	116.0	178.8	147.8	114.5	113.2
Framingham-Natick MA	137.9	115.7	174.2	176.7	119.5	110.8
Benton Harbor MI MSA: Benton Harbor-St. Joseph	106.1	109.2	118.0	91.0	95.6	103.6
Grand Rapids-Muskegon-Holland MI MSA:						
Grand Rapids	104.1	103.3	121.1	92.2	94.7	98.1
Holland	101.1	103.0	111.4	83.0	104.0	97.7
Lansing-East Lansing MI MSA: Lansing	105.4	108.1	118.5	91.5	99.5	98.1
Fargo-Moorhead ND-MN MSA: Moorhead MN	94.3	102.8	89.4	80.0	101.7	95.8
Minneapolis-St. Paul MN-WI MSA:						
Minneapolis MN	106.6	99.2	113.8	89.2	112.9	104.2
St. Paul MN	102.8	101.5	100.9	91.4	112.3	102.8
Rochester MN MSA: Rochester	104.0	101.1	103.6	107.4	111.4	102.1
St. Cloud MN MSA	97.3	104.0	84.6	102.7	107.9	100.7
Columbia MO MSA: Columbia	93.4	96.8	87.7	72.8	94.6	100.1
Joplin MO MSA: Joplin	88.4	92.9	84.5	78.8	87.3	91.9
Kansas City MO-KS MSA	98.9	96.7	97.6	100.5	98.4	101.0
St Joseph MO MSA: St Joseph	92.4	96.9	101.7	88.2	90.3	84.9
St. Louis MO-IL MSA:						
St. Charles MO	94.5	108.3	94.0	105.6	89.6	87.7
St. Louis MO-IL	95.2	98.8	95.4	105.7	97.5	89.8
Springfield MO MSA: Springfield	95.5	95.7	86.7	86.7	103.7	101.6
Billings MT MSA: Billings	103.5	103.9	110.0	79.3	101.8	104.6
Lincoln NE MSA: Lincoln	90.8	96.2	84.1	83.7	104.3	93.5
Omaha NE-IA MSA: Omaha NE	92.4	94.4	86.4	98.6	105.3	91.3
Las Vegas NV-AZ MSA: Las Vegas NV	105.0	95.5	114.2	83.4	115.9	102.8
Reno NV MSA: Reno-Sparks	109.0	103.6	126.6	80.4	98.1	104.6
Manchester NH PMSA: Manchester	118.0	103.7	125.5	153.0	105.0	111.7
Albuquerque NM MSA: Albuquerque	101.2	97.2	107.9	95.0	103.1	96.9
Las Cruces NM MSA	99.9	95.0	103.0	88.8	111.5	99.8
Santa Fe NM MSA: Santa Fe	111.3	97.0	143.4	86.2	102.0	101.7
Albany-Schenectady-Troy NY MSA: Albany	111.4	112.7	105.6	142.4	105.6	108.8
Binghamton NY MSA: Binghamton/Broome County	99.6	100.9	89.5	116.0	101.6	103.5
Glens Falls NY MSA: Glens Falls	109.5	109.1	110.4	128.9	106.5	107.0
Jamestown NY MSA: Jamestown	98.9	109.8	91.5	108.2	106.7	97.7
Rochester NY MSA	112.2	116.9	119.8	116.0	109.4	103.5
Syracuse NY MSA: Syracuse	103.4	106.8	93.4	136.1	110.9	99.8
Utica-Rome NY MSA	106.6	104.0	99.6	137.0	107.7	104.6
Asheville NC MSA: Asheville	104.6	100.8	106.9	112.7	99.3	105.7
Charlotte-Gastonia-Rock Hill NC-SC MSA:						
Charlotte NC	101.6	99.0	103.2	106.6	98.0	99.2
Gastonia NC	89.2	93.8	86.6	106.1	86.8	87.1
Fayetteville NC MSA: Fayetteville	98.5	98.0	85.4	112.7	98.0	105.2
Goldsboro NC MSA: Goldsboro	99.7	100.3	98.2	113.9	97.8	99.1
Greensboro-Winston-Salem-High Point NC MSA:						
Burlington	95.1	91.8	99.1	105.8	86.0	93.7
Greensboro	98.6	93.2	92.6	107.3	89.1	108.2
Winston-Salem	96.0	94.5	93.6	105.9	97.5	96.4
Greenville NC MSA: Greenville	97.4	93.4	97.6	111.0	90.7	96.9
Hickory-Morganton NC MSA: Hickory	100.0	94.6	108.2	106.2	82.7	100.3
Raleigh-Durham-Chapel Hill NC MSA:						
Chapel Hill	103.5	96.1	107.9	95.2	93.2	107.6
Raleigh-Durham	97.4	94.2	95.1	109.9	96.1	96.8
Fargo-Moorhead ND-MN MSA: Fargo ND	99.1	106.6	98.2	89.0	99.1	99.2
Akron OH PMSA: Akron	95.9	93.9	90.9	119.1	100.4	93.0
Canton-Massillon OH MSA: Canton	95.0	91.5	89.4	105.8	95.8	98.0
Cincinnati OH-KY-IN PMSA: Cincinnati	105.1	93.7	106.5	101.1	106.4	109.7
Cleveland-Lorain-Elyria OH PMSA: Cleveland	111.5	103.2	116.5	126.6	117.6	105.1
Dayton-Springfield OH MSA: Dayton-Springfield	101.2	91.0	104.4	98.0	101.1	104.5
Mansfield OH MSA: Mansfield	99.0	96.6	95.9	126.7	94.7	97.3
Parkersburg-Marietta WV-OH MSA: Marietta OH	95.0	98.5	95.5	88.7	92.7	96.9
Toledo OH MSA: Toledo	103.6	104.8	102.3	121.5	109.7	98.6
Youngstown-Warren OH MSA: Youngstown	97.7	95.6	96.6	111.1	106.2	95.5
Lawton OK MSA: Lawton	97.1	95.4	92.6	105.9	103.0	97.9
Oklahoma City OK MSA: Oklahoma City	92.6	93.3	80.4	110.3	97.3	95.0
Tulsa OK MSA: Tulsa	90.4	97.3	78.6	91.2	87.9	97.7

See footnotes at end of table.

No. 752. Cost of Living Index—Selected Metropolitan Areas: Second Quarter 1993—Continued

[See headnote, page 493]

METROPOLITAN AREAS	Com-posite index	Gro-cery items	Hous-ing	Util-ities	Trans-port-ation	Misc. goods and services
Portland-Vancouver OR-WA PMSA: Portland OR	109.4	103.3	125.6	76.6	108.2	105.0
Salem OR PMSA: Salem	102.5	94.6	100.4	80.1	110.5	108.3
Allentown-Bethlehem-Easton PA MSA:						
Allentown-Bethlehem-Easton	106.7	108.5	108.0	107.0	96.2	107.9
Erie PA MSA: Erie	113.2	96.7	130.9	106.4	102.1	111.0
Harrisburg-Lebanon-Carlisle PA MSA: Harrisburg	106.6	98.6	108.0	129.9	105.3	103.0
Lancaster PA MSA: Lancaster	109.6	103.6	114.2	136.4	104.7	105.6
Philadelphia PA-NJ PMSA: Philadelphia PA	128.6	114.2	149.2	178.2	112.1	111.4
Scranton-Wilkes Barre-Hazleton PA MSA:						
Wilkes Barre	98.7	109.2	109.7	92.2	85.5	93.0
Sharon PA MSA: Mercer County	104.3	101.9	112.0	108.5	93.4	102.1
Williamsport PA MSA: Williamsport/Lycoming Co.	108.4	103.4	113.8	136.0	102.2	102.0
York PA MSA:						
Hanover	102.6	102.5	111.2	87.4	96.0	103.4
York County	98.0	94.5	100.2	98.7	106.9	94.4
Charleston-North Charleston SC MSA	102.9	95.0	100.3	98.6	96.1	110.7
Columbia SC MSA: Columbia	97.6	95.1	99.2	96.2	83.7	101.4
Greenville-Spartanburg-Anderson SC MSA:						
Greenville	100.6	97.1	102.4	108.9	93.5	102.4
Spartanburg	94.5	99.3	85.9	107.0	84.8	99.8
Myrtle Beach SC MSA: Myrtle Beach	95.3	96.6	90.3	88.2	97.7	100.0
Sumter SC MSA: Sumter	95.3	96.7	80.0	108.0	99.8	104.6
Sioux Falls SD MSA: Sioux Falls	95.4	100.3	97.0	89.2	96.4	93.5
Clarksville-Hopkinsville TN-KY MSA: Clarksville TN	90.7	95.9	81.2	92.8	97.3	95.9
Johnson City-Kingsport-Bristol TN-VA MSA:						
Johnson City TN	98.4	95.7	104.5	85.8	94.4	100.7
Kingsport TN	98.2	94.7	96.0	77.3	111.4	104.8
Knoxville TN MSA: Knoxville	94.7	94.1	89.3	97.5	92.8	99.3
Memphis TN-AR-MS MSA: Memphis TN.	97.9	102.8	95.3	88.2	106.1	98.2
Nashville TN MSA:						
Murfreesboro-Smyrna	94.4	97.2	87.5	92.5	98.4	99.4
Nashville-Franklin	90.4	94.9	84.9	90.2	92.2	94.4
Abilene TX MSA: Abilene	95.5	90.4	85.1	115.7	104.8	98.7
Amarillo TX MSA: Amarillo	90.1	100.4	82.3	78.3	97.4	95.0
Austin-San Marcos TX MSA: Georgetown	99.1	97.0	92.1	100.3	106.0	102.1
Beaumont-Port Arthur TX MSA: Beaumont	95.9	102.0	75.6	102.7	107.5	105.9
Brownsville-Harlingen-San Benito TX MSA: Harlingen	91.8	93.8	75.5	119.1	99.7	94.3
Corpus Christi TX MSA	92.1	92.5	81.2	109.7	80.4	99.8
Dallas TX PMSA	102.8	95.9	96.0	114.8	108.3	104.7
El Paso TX MSA: El Paso	98.8	95.4	89.6	94.5	116.2	104.3
Fort Worth-Arlington TX PMSA:						
Fort Worth	95.4	93.3	84.1	107.0	104.3	100.2
Weatherford	89.5	90.5	76.7	100.1	97.6	94.7
Houston TX PMSA	97.6	95.1	92.5	101.6	111.1	95.8
Killeen-Temple TX MSA: Killeen	92.8	96.6	85.0	107.8	91.3	93.5
Longview-Marshall TX MSA: Longview	88.7	90.7	75.3	84.7	96.5	97.8
Lubbock TX MSA: Lubbock	93.6	98.4	84.1	86.3	107.4	98.0
McAllen-Edinburg-Mission TX MSA: McAllen	92.4	91.2	77.7	119.6	95.3	98.6
San Antonio TX MSA: San Antonio	95.7	97.1	88.7	80.7	110.3	99.5
Texarkana TX-AR MSA: Texarkana TX-AR	94.3	97.5	82.9	96.2	98.4	100.3
Tyler TX MSA: Tyler	95.6	89.5	93.8	112.2	93.6	97.2
Waco TX MSA	94.2	91.9	81.7	111.3	100.8	98.7
Wichita Falls TX MSA: Wichita Falls	90.5	97.8	77.3	104.9	95.6	93.6
Provo-Orem UT MSA: Provo-Orem	100.2	97.7	104.4	86.4	110.6	97.7
Johnson City-Kingsport-Bristol TN-VA MSA:						
Bristol VA	94.4	95.8	88.6	96.6	90.0	100.4
Lynchburg VA MSA: Lynchburg	93.4	93.3	89.4	85.0	87.6	100.9
Norfolk-Virginia Beach-Newport News VA-NC MSA:						
Hampton Roads/SE Virginia	103.9	102.6	99.7	122.3	116.2	100.5
Richmond-Petersburg VA MSA: Richmond	108.9	103.4	101.9	117.4	111.5	113.8
Roanoke VA MSA: Roanoke	93.5	94.2	88.4	86.0	100.6	97.6
Washington DC-MD-VA-WV PMSA: Prince William VA	116.2	102.1	145.3	117.8	112.5	100.3
Bellingham WA MSA: Bellingham	105.9	98.3	119.8	59.6	94.6	107.7
Olympia WA PMSA: Olympia	104.9	101.2	113.1	70.4	101.0	104.7
Richland-Kennewick-Pasco WA MSA:						
Richland-Kennewick-Pasco	106.7	101.7	115.4	76.2	95.3	108.4
Spokane WA MSA	103.7	105.8	118.8	56.6	95.5	102.7
Tacoma WA PMSA: Tacoma	103.6	109.8	104.1	61.7	100.0	105.6
Yakima WA MSA: Yakima	103.2	109.3	103.9	106.8	87.8	101.8
Charleston WV MSA: Charleston	104.3	97.7	112.6	106.1	111.4	98.7
Washington DC-MD-VA-WV PMSA:						
Martinsburg/Berkeley County WV	90.6	90.3	94.9	87.9	85.6	89.8
Appleton-Oshkosh-Neenah WI MSA:						
Appleton-Neenah-Menasha	97.0	93.7	100.2	92.9	95.1	96.7
Oshkosh	99.8	103.7	102.2	89.6	95.0	100.3
Eau Claire WI MSA: Eau Claire	102.0	98.9	114.9	97.0	92.7	96.7
Green Bay WI MSA: Green Bay	97.7	95.2	103.4	93.8	98.1	94.9
Janesville-Beloit WI MSA: Janesville	99.3	101.8	115.9	85.8	92.4	90.7
La Crosse WI-MN MSA: La Crosse WI	101.1	98.6	100.9	95.8	102.8	99.2
Wausau WI MSA: Wausau	106.3	97.3	128.2	99.2	90.7	98.5

Source: ACCRA, Louisville KY 40206-6749, *ACCRA Cost of Living Index*, Third Quarter 1992 (copyright).

No. 753. Producer Price Indexes, by Stage of Processing: 1960 to 1993

[1982=100. Minus sign (-) indicates decline. See text, section 15. See *Historical Statistics, Colonial Times to 1970*, series E 73-86 for similar data]

YEAR	CRUDE MATERIALS				Inter-mediate mate-rials, sup-plies, and com-pon-ents	FINISHED GOODS		CONSUMER FOODS		Fin-ished con-sumer goods excl. food
	Total	Food-stuffs and feed-stuffs	Fuel	Crude non-food mate-rials except fuel		Con-sumer goods	Capital equip-ment	Crude	Proc-essed	
1960	30.4	38.4	10.5	26.9	30.8	35.5	30.2	35.2	28.4	33.5
1961	30.2	37.9	10.5	27.2	30.6	35.4	30.3	35.3	28.4	33.4
1962	30.5	38.6	10.4	27.1	30.6	35.7	30.5	35.6	28.4	33.4
1963	29.9	37.5	10.5	26.7	30.7	35.3	30.6	35.2	28.5	33.4
1964	29.6	36.6	10.5	27.2	30.8	35.4	31.0	35.2	28.4	33.3
1965	31.1	39.2	10.6	27.7	31.2	36.8	31.5	36.8	28.8	33.6
1966	33.1	42.7	10.9	28.3	32.0	39.2	32.5	39.2	29.3	34.1
1967	31.3	40.3	11.3	26.5	32.2	38.5	33.8	38.8	30.0	34.7
1968	31.8	40.9	11.5	27.1	33.0	40.0	35.0	40.0	30.6	35.5
1969	33.9	44.1	12.0	28.4	34.1	42.4	36.2	42.3	31.5	36.3
1970	35.2	45.2	13.8	29.1	35.4	43.8	38.1	43.9	32.5	37.4
1971	36.0	46.1	15.7	29.4	36.8	44.5	39.6	44.7	33.5	38.7
1972	39.9	51.5	16.8	32.3	38.2	41.5	42.8	48.0	47.2	39.4
1973	54.5	72.6	18.6	42.9	42.4	46.0	44.2	63.6	55.8	41.2
1974	61.4	76.4	24.8	54.5	52.5	53.1	50.5	71.6	63.9	48.2
1975	61.6	77.4	30.6	50.0	58.0	58.2	58.2	71.7	70.3	53.2
1976	63.4	76.8	34.5	54.9	60.9	60.4	62.1	76.7	69.0	56.5
1977	65.5	77.5	42.0	56.3	64.9	64.3	66.1	79.5	72.7	60.6
1978	73.4	87.3	48.2	61.9	69.5	69.4	71.3	85.8	79.4	64.9
1979	85.9	100.0	57.3	75.5	78.4	77.5	77.5	92.3	86.8	73.5
1980	95.3	104.6	69.4	91.8	90.3	88.6	85.8	93.9	92.3	87.1
1981	103.0	103.9	84.8	109.8	98.6	96.6	94.6	104.4	97.2	96.1
1982	100.0	100.0	100.0	100.0	100.0	100.0	100.0	100.0	100.0	100.0
1983	101.3	101.8	105.1	98.8	100.6	101.3	102.8	102.4	100.9	101.2
1984	103.5	104.7	105.1	101.0	103.1	103.3	105.2	111.4	104.9	102.2
1985	95.8	94.8	102.7	94.3	102.7	103.8	107.5	102.9	104.8	103.3
1986	87.7	93.2	92.2	76.0	99.1	101.4	109.7	105.6	107.4	98.5
1987	93.7	96.2	84.1	88.5	101.5	103.6	111.7	107.1	109.6	100.7
1988	96.0	106.1	82.1	85.9	107.1	106.2	114.3	109.8	112.7	103.1
1989	103.1	111.2	85.3	95.8	112.0	112.1	118.0	119.6	118.6	108.9
1990	108.9	113.1	84.8	107.3	114.5	118.2	122.9	123.0	124.4	115.3
1991	101.2	105.5	82.9	97.5	114.4	120.5	126.7	119.3	124.4	118.7
1992	100.4	105.1	84.0	94.2	114.7	121.7	129.1	107.6	124.4	120.8
1993	102.4	108.4	116.2	131.4	116.2	123.0	131.4	114.4	126.5	121.7
PERCENT CHANGE										
1960	-2.3	-1.0	1.0	-4.3	-	2.0	1.3	1.4	0.7	0.6
1961	-0.7	-1.3	-	1.1	-0.6	-0.3	0.3	0.3	-	-0.3
1962	1.0	1.8	-1.0	-0.4	-	0.8	0.7	0.8	-	-
1963	-2.0	-2.8	1.0	-1.5	0.3	-1.1	0.3	-1.1	0.4	-
1964	-1.0	-2.4	-	1.9	0.3	0.3	1.3	-	-0.4	-0.3
1965	5.1	7.1	1.0	1.8	1.3	4.0	1.6	4.5	1.4	0.9
1966	6.4	8.9	2.8	2.2	2.6	6.5	3.2	6.5	1.7	1.5
1967	-5.4	-5.6	3.7	-6.4	0.6	-1.8	4.0	-1.0	2.4	1.8
1968	1.6	1.5	1.8	2.3	2.5	3.9	3.6	3.1	2.0	2.3
1969	6.6	7.8	4.3	4.8	3.3	6.0	3.4	5.7	2.9	2.3
1970	3.8	2.5	15.0	2.5	3.8	3.3	5.2	3.8	3.2	3.0
1971	2.3	2.0	13.8	1.0	4.0	1.6	3.9	1.8	3.1	3.5
1972	10.8	11.7	7.0	9.9	3.8	-6.7	8.1	7.4	40.9	1.8
1973	36.6	41.0	10.7	32.8	11.0	10.8	3.3	32.5	18.2	4.6
1974	12.7	5.2	33.3	27.0	23.8	15.4	14.3	12.6	14.5	17.0
1975	0.3	1.3	23.4	-8.3	10.5	9.6	15.2	0.1	10.0	10.4
1976	2.9	-0.8	12.7	9.8	5.0	3.8	6.7	7.0	-1.8	6.2
1977	3.3	0.9	21.7	2.6	6.6	6.5	6.4	3.7	5.4	7.3
1978	12.1	12.6	14.8	9.9	7.1	7.9	7.9	7.9	9.2	7.1
1979	17.0	14.5	18.9	22.0	12.8	11.7	8.7	7.6	9.3	13.3
1980	10.9	4.6	21.1	21.6	15.2	14.3	10.7	1.7	6.3	18.5
1981	8.1	-0.7	22.2	19.6	9.2	9.0	10.3	11.2	5.3	10.3
1982	-2.9	-3.8	17.9	-8.9	1.4	3.5	5.7	-4.2	2.9	4.1
1983	1.3	1.8	5.1	-1.2	0.6	1.3	2.8	2.4	0.9	1.2
1984	2.2	2.8	-	2.2	2.5	2.0	2.3	8.8	4.0	1.0
1985	-7.4	-9.5	-2.3	-6.6	-0.4	0.5	2.2	-7.6	-0.1	1.1
1986	-8.5	-1.7	-10.2	-19.4	-3.5	-2.3	2.0	2.6	2.5	-4.6
1987	6.8	3.2	-8.8	16.4	2.4	2.2	1.8	1.4	2.0	2.2
1988	2.5	10.3	-2.4	-2.9	5.5	2.5	2.3	2.5	2.8	2.4
1989	7.4	4.8	3.9	11.5	4.6	5.6	3.2	8.9	5.2	5.6
1990	5.6	1.7	-0.6	12.0	2.2	5.4	4.2	2.8	4.9	5.9
1991	-7.1	-6.7	-2.2	-9.1	-0.1	1.9	3.1	-3.0	-	2.9
1992	-0.9	-0.4	1.3	-3.4	0.3	1.0	1.9	-9.8	-	1.8
1993	2.0	3.1	38.3	39.5	1.3	1.1	1.8	6.3	1.7	0.7

- Represents or rounds to zero.

Source: U.S. Bureau of Labor Statistics, *Producer Price Indexes*, monthly and annual.

No. 754. Producer Price Indexes for Selected Commodity Groupings, by Stage of Processing: 1970 to 1993

[1982=100, except as indicated]

COMMODITY	1970	1980	1985	1989	1990	1991	1992	1993
Finished goods	**39.3**	**88.0**	**104.7**	**113.6**	**119.2**	**121.7**	**123.2**	**124.7**
Finished consumer goods	39.1	88.6	103.8	112.1	118.2	120.5	121.7	123.0
Finished consumer foods	43.8	92.4	104.6	118.7	124.4	124.1	123.3	125.7
Fresh fruits	42.3	100.3	108.1	113.2	118.1	129.9	84.0	84.2
Fresh and dried vegetables	47.5	88.9	99.5	116.7	118.1	103.8	115.0	133.5
Eggs	71.0	95.7	95.7	119.6	117.6	110.7	94.1	105.9
Bakery products	40.0	90.0	113.9	135.4	141.0	146.6	152.5	156.6
Milled rice	52.4	131.5	105.0	104.9	102.5	109.9	108.8	102.7
Beef and veal	46.7	106.2	90.3	108.9	116.0	112.2	109.5	112.9
Pork	44.6	78.4	89.1	97.7	119.8	113.4	98.9	105.4
Processed young chickens	61.2	106.8	106.5	120.3	111.0	105.1	104.9	109.4
Processed turkeys	69.1	109.2	121.3	110.6	107.6	107.3	102.3	100.5
Fish	29.7	87.8	114.6	142.9	147.2	149.5	156.1	156.7
Dairy products	44.7	92.7	100.2	110.6	117.2	114.6	117.9	118.1
Processed fruits and vegetables	40.3	83.3	108.0	119.9	124.7	119.6	120.8	118.3
Soft drinks	37.8	81.8	107.7	117.7	122.3	125.5	125.6	126.3
Roasted coffee	37.7	110.4	107.2	115.9	113.0	107.8	100.5	100.5
Shortening and cooking oils	47.7	99.5	124.0	116.6	123.2	116.5	115.1	123.0
Finished consumer goods excl. foods	37.4	87.1	103.3	108.9	115.3	118.7	120.8	121.7
Alcoholic beverages	53.3	88.9	107.7	115.2	117.2	123.7	126.1	126.0
Women's apparel	62.8	86.9	105.4	113.5	116.1	117.9	119.9	120.2
Men's and boys' apparel	51.2	91.3	105.0	116.8	120.2	122.7	126.0	127.7
Girls', children's, and infants' apparel	58.8	87.1	103.1	110.5	115.3	117.8	119.0	119.9
Textile housefurnishings	43.4	86.8	100.6	106.6	109.5	111.8	113.7	115.8
Footwear	46.2	95.2	104.8	120.8	125.6	128.6	132.0	134.4
Residential natural gas (December 1990=100).	(NA)	(NA)	(NA)	(NA)	(NA)	99.2	100.9	107.4
Gasoline	14.4	93.3	83.3	65.1	78.7	69.9	68.1	64.0
Fuel oil No. 2	(NA)	82.8	81.6	58.0	73.3	65.2	61.7	59.2
Pharmaceutical preps, ethical (Prescription)	52.0	80.6	132.0	184.4	200.8	217.5	231.7	242.2
Pharmaceutical preps, propri.; Over-counter	42.3	81.3	121.6	152.1	156.8	165.4	173.6	180.0
Soaps and synthetic detergents	41.5	85.8	107.9	119.4	117.7	117.5	120.6	122.2
Cosmetics and other toilet preparations	47.8	83.8	109.0	119.3	121.6	124.6	126.7	129.1
Tires, tubes, tread, etc	42.7	92.8	93.0	97.2	96.8	98.2	98.9	99.0
Sanitary papers and health products	32.5	91.9	106.6	126.0	135.3	136.2	136.9	134.4
Household furniture	48.6	89.1	108.5	121.8	125.1	128.0	130.0	132.9
Floor coverings	54.9	90.0	105.6	117.6	119.0	120.4	120.3	120.0
Household appliances	52.9	87.5	106.7	108.7	110.8	111.3	111.4	113.0
Home electronic equipment	106.0	103.8	90.8	86.9	82.7	83.2	82.0	80.2
Household glassware	33.1	84.7	121.8	134.7	132.5	136.0	141.6	143.0
Household flatware	32.7	148.0	98.6	125.7	122.1	119.5	125.2	130.6
Lawn and garden equip., excl. tractors	46.8	87.5	110.3	119.8	123.0	124.7	125.3	126.0
Passenger cars	50.0	88.9	106.9	115.5	118.3	124.1	126.9	129.9
Toys, games, and children's vehicles	48.5	89.2	103.8	115.6	118.1	120.2	121.4	121.6
Sporting and athletic goods	52.7	90.6	99.7	109.8	112.6	115.3	118.2	118.4
Tobacco products	35.2	76.0	132.5	194.8	221.4	249.7	275.3	260.1
Mobile homes	(NA)	(NA)	101.7	114.0	117.5	120.4	121.7	128.6
Capital equipment	**40.1**	**85.8**	**107.5**	**118.8**	**122.9**	**126.7**	**129.1**	**131.4**
Agricultural machinery and equipment	36.4	83.3	108.7	117.7	121.7	125.7	129.5	133.5
Construction machinery and equipment	33.7	84.2	105.4	117.2	121.6	125.2	128.7	132.1
Metal cutting machine tools	30.8	85.1	107.3	123.4	129.8	134.6	138.9	141.1
Metal forming machine tools	28.6	85.7	107.0	118.1	128.7	133.5	135.9	138.3
Tools, dies, jigs, fixtures, and ind. molds	(NA)	(NA)	106.3	113.8	117.2	122.7	125.1	128.2
Pumps, compressors, and equipment	33.0	82.8	102.6	115.0	119.2	124.6	129.1	132.7
Industrial material handling equipment	39.8	88.4	102.7	111.7	115.0	117.4	118.4	120.2
Textile machinery	45.4	87.2	107.6	123.9	128.8	135.0	138.9	143.8
Paper industries machinery (June 1982=100).	(NA)	(NA)	109.8	128.5	134.8	140.1	142.7	144.9
Printing trades machinery	42.5	89.7	109.0	123.0	124.9	126.5	126.8	129.6
Transformers and power regulators	44.7	82.4	105.0	117.3	120.9	123.9	123.5	123.2
Oil field and gas field machinery	27.0	76.3	96.8	99.1	102.4	108.6	107.6	107.9
Mining machinery and equipment	30.9	85.2	105.4	116.3	121.0	125.2	127.4	129.4
Office and store machines and equipment	68.3	93.1	101.6	109.5	109.5	109.8	111.0	111.0
Commercial furniture	41.6	85.7	111.9	129.0	133.4	136.2	138.1	140.6
Light motor trucks	42.0	83.3	112.2	129.5	130.0	135.5	142.4	150.3
Heavy motor trucks	36.3	82.3	108.8	117.2	120.3	123.6	128.6	134.6
Truck trailers	(NA)	(NA)	106.2	110.4	110.8	112.1	115.1	118.1
Railroad equipment	33.2	90.4	104.9	114.0	118.6	122.2	123.7	125.2
Photographic and photocopy equipment	72.0	94.9	89.5	94.1	97.2	99.3	101.1	103.4
Intermed. materials, supplies, components	**35.4**	**90.3**	**102.7**	**112.0**	**114.5**	**114.4**	**114.7**	**116.2**
Intermediate foods and feeds	45.6	105.5	97.3	113.8	113.3	111.1	110.7	112.7
Flour	55.3	102.3	99.8	114.6	103.6	96.8	109.5	109.3
Crude vegetable oils	75.8	127.1	137.6	103.1	115.8	103.0	97.1	110.3
Prepared animal feeds	49.1	107.3	90.1	116.6	107.4	106.8	108.3	111.0

See footnotes at end of table.

No. 754. Producer Price Indexes for Selected Commodity Groupings by Stage of Processing: 1970 to 1993—Continued

[1982 = 100, except as indicated]

COMMODITY	1970	1980	1985	1989	1990	1991	1992	1993
Intermediate materials less foods and feeds. . . .	34.8	89.4	103.0	111.9	114.5	114.6	114.9	116.4
Leather	34.6	99.8	113.4	170.4	177.5	168.4	163.7	168.6
Liquefied petroleum gas	(NA)	102.3	86.3	52.7	77.4	75.4	65.8	63.7
Electric power	26.1	79.1	111.6	114.8	117.6	124.3	126.3	128.5
Jet fuels.	(NA)	87.5	81.0	58.1	76.0	66.4	61.9	59.1
No. 2 diesel fuel	(NA)	85.8	81.2	58.9	74.1	65.6	61.9	60.7
Residual fuel.	10.6	81.3	83.2	47.6	57.7	49.1	45.9	49.6
Industrial chemicals	28.6	91.9	96.0	114.8	113.2	111.8	109.3	110.5
Prepared paint	42.8	89.5	105.3	119.5	124.8	129.9	131.6	133.2
Paint materials	33.3	89.9	109.5	129.1	136.3	135.8	131.1	131.5
Medicinal and botanical chemicals	44.4	91.0	91.8	100.3	102.2	109.0	111.3	120.6
Fats and oils, inedible.	49.7	111.6	110.6	95.5	88.1	86.8	93.0	95.7
Mixed fertilizers	35.2	90.0	96.1	105.9	103.3	105.2	102.6	98.9
Nitrogenates.	32.7	90.0	96.3	94.9	92.3	98.5	95.4	99.5
Phosphates	27.5	93.0	91.6	105.6	96.5	98.1	92.5	83.0
Other agricultural chemicals.	23.2	80.1	98.7	115.1	119.9	125.6	129.2	134.5
Plastic resins and materials	32.0	98.5	107.5	133.4	124.1	120.0	116.4	117.2
Synthetic rubber	34.0	85.3	96.8	108.5	111.9	106.1	103.8	105.7
Plastic construction products	65.5	103.9	108.6	120.1	117.2	115.1	112.7	116.8
Softwood lumber	35.2	107.3	107.4	127.1	123.8	125.7	148.6	193.5
Hardwood lumber	43.7	96.0	117.1	128.2	131.0	128.5	140.7	163.3
Millwork	41.5	93.2	111.7	127.3	130.4	135.5	143.3	156.5
Plywood.	46.7	106.2	99.6	115.9	114.2	114.3	133.3	152.7
Woodpulp.	28.9	100.3	91.4	157.4	151.3	119.2	118.9	104.3
Paper	38.8	89.7	106.0	129.6	128.8	126.9	123.2	123.8
Paperboard.	39.7	92.0	107.7	140.1	135.7	130.2	134.3	130.0
Paper boxes and containers	43.3	89.4	108.8	129.8	129.9	128.6	130.6	130.0
Building paper and board	42.2	86.1	107.4	115.6	112.2	111.8	119.6	132.9
Commercial printing (June 1982 = 100)	(NA)	(NA)	111.6	124.9	128.0	130.0	131.1	134.8
Foundry and forge shop products	32.4	89.7	105.2	114.6	117.2	119.0	120.1	121.3
Steel mill products	32.7	86.6	104.7	114.5	112.1	109.5	106.4	108.2
Primary nonferrous metals.	44.9	132.7	93.6	149.2	133.4	114.0	108.1	98.1
Aluminum mill shapes.	36.7	89.3	107.8	135.4	127.9	123.2	121.9	120.3
Copper and brass mill shapes	63.4	112.6	106.9	182.0	174.6	160.5	166.0	150.8
Nonferrous wire and cable.	62.6	107.5	100.9	146.1	142.6	139.2	136.7	133.2
Metal containers	34.3	90.9	109.0	111.5	114.0	115.5	113.9	109.5
Hardware	39.8	85.8	109.1	120.4	125.9	130.2	132.7	135.2
Plumbing fixtures and brass fittings	39.9	88.5	111.9	137.7	144.3	149.7	153.1	155.8
Heating equipment.	46.6	87.0	109.5	125.1	131.6	134.1	137.3	140.3
Fabricated structural metal products	36.7	88.8	103.2	120.3	121.8	122.4	122.1	123.2
Mechanical power transmission equipment. . . .	36.9	84.5	108.2	121.1	125.3	129.1	132.1	136.2
Ball and roller bearings.	33.1	80.0	105.9	124.1	130.6	136.7	139.0	141.8
Wiring devices.	35.9	81.9	111.7	129.7	132.2	133.9	134.8	138.6
Motors, generators, motor generator sets.	37.7	86.0	113.3	129.0	132.9	134.9	136.6	138.6
Switchgear, switchboard, etc., equipment.	40.5	88.4	106.7	119.0	124.4	128.5	131.5	134.6
Electronic components and accessories	57.4	88.8	112.4	119.4	118.4	118.6	117.5	117.8
Internal combustion engines	34.5	81.7	104.9	114.7	120.2	126.0	128.4	130.2
Machine shop products.	31.1	81.0	112.8	121.3	124.3	125.9	126.8	128.0
Flat glass	52.2	88.7	101.7	109.7	107.5	105.9	106.5	107.5
Concrete products	37.7	92.0	107.5	111.2	113.5	116.6	117.2	120.1
Asphalt felts and coatings	25.8	99.6	102.6	95.8	97.1	98.2	96.2	96.9
Gypsum products.	38.9	100.1	132.3	110.0	105.2	99.3	99.9	108.4
Glass containers	33.9	82.3	106.8	115.2	120.4	125.4	125.1	125.9
Motor vehicle parts	32.9	72.9	102.5	109.7	111.2	112.5	113.1	113.7
Photographic supplies.	41.0	97.2	107.4	123.0	127.6	125.8	125.6	124.3
Crude materials for further processing.	35.2	95.3	95.8	103.1	108.9	101.2	100.4	102.4
Crude foodstuffs and feedstuffs.	45.2	104.6	94.8	111.2	113.1	105.5	105.1	108.3
Wheat	39.7	108.3	87.6	109.5	87.6	79.4	98.5	98.4
Corn	54.5	119.2	105.9	102.4	100.9	97.0	96.0	92.9
Cattle	46.9	104.9	91.2	113.8	122.5	115.8	115.4	116.7
Hogs.	45.5	74.5	80.7	80.5	94.1	82.7	70.7	76.1
Live chickens (broilers and fryers).	48.5	103.4	110.5	131.7	119.5	111.9	114.6	124.9
Live turkeys	59.9	112.2	144.6	119.1	116.9	109.5	106.6	113.1
Fluid milk	40.8	96.0	93.7	98.8	100.8	89.5	96.1	93.8
Soybeans	45.3	117.0	94.2	114.3	100.8	95.1	97.3	104.8
Cane sugar, raw	39.9	148.3	104.6	115.5	119.2	113.7	112.1	113.2
Crude nonfood materials.	23.8	84.6	96.9	93.4	101.5	94.6	93.5	94.7
Raw cotton.	43.6	135.7	97.7	105.6	118.2	116.2	89.8	91.9
Leaf tobacco.	40.3	82.1	101.2	93.8	95.8	101.1	101.0	99.6
Cattle hides	30.4	104.6	126.1	213.1	217.8	173.4	171.4	180.2
Coal	28.1	87.4	102.2	95.5	97.5	97.2	95.0	96.1
Natural gas.	7.9	63.3	102.9	82.0	80.4	79.1	80.6	84.6
Crude petroleum	14.5	75.9	84.5	56.3	71.0	61.9	58.0	51.4
Logs, timber, etc..	(NA)	(NA)	96.0	131.9	142.8	144.1	164.8	211.9
Wastepaper	103.2	172.2	122.9	157.1	138.9	121.4	117.5	118.0
Iron ore	35.9	87.8	97.5	82.8	83.3	83.6	83.7	82.7
Iron and steel scrap	59.6	140.9	112.6	173.7	166.0	147.6	139.2	172.6
Nonferrous metal ores (Dec. 1983 = 100)	(NA)	(NA)	73.2	109.6	98.3	82.6	75.4	67.3
Copper base scrap.	100.9	138.9	95.4	179.8	181.3	170.0	162.9	135.7
Aluminum base scrap.	34.4	183.9	123.4	204.4	172.6	143.1	137.6	129.1
Construction sand, gravel, and crushed stone. . .	40.9	85.3	110.7	122.8	125.4	128.6	130.6	133.9

NA Not available.

Source: U.S. Bureau of Labor Statistics, *Producer Price Indexes*, monthly and annual.

No. 755. Producer Price Indexes for the Net Output of Selected Industries: 1985 to 1993

[Indexes are based on selling prices reported by establishments of all sizes by probability sampling. Industries selected by value added. N.e.c.= not elsewhere classified. See text, section 26]

SIC code [1]	ITEM	Index base	1985	1989	1990	1991	1992	1993
2011	Meat packing plants	12/80	90.9	108.2	119.8	115.1	108.9	113.6
2013	Sausages and other prepared meats	12/82	95.7	102.4	112.7	113.0	108.7	110.4
2026	Fluid milk	12/82	102.6	112.8	121.4	119.0	121.6	121.3
2033	Canned fruits and vegetables	06/81	112.7	128.8	129.9	129.4	129.8	127.3
2038	Frozen specialties	12/82	110.8	123.5	127.3	130.4	131.0	130.6
2051	Bread, cake, and related products	06/80	127.1	153.6	159.4	165.0	173.3	179.1
2052	Cookies and crackers	06/83	112.0	134.6	141.9	148.5	151.2	152.2
2082	Malt beverages	06/82	110.0	115.4	115.2	121.3	123.6	122.2
2086	Bottled and canned soft drinks	06/81	112.5	122.5	127.2	130.3	131.0	132.5
2095	Coffee	06/81	111.5	120.4	120.0	116.5	110.0	109.8
2099	Food preparations, n.e.c	12/85	(NA)	110.4	114.3	117.3	117.2	118.6
2111	Cigarettes	12/82	110.7	173.1	197.6	225.0	250.5	235.0
2221	Synthetic fiber and silk broadwoven fabric	06/81	101.2	112.3	115.6	115.2	115.9	114.5
2335	Women's, misses', and juniors' dresses	12/80	108.0	122.0	125.6	129.0	129.7	130.1
2411	Logging camps and logging contractors	12/81	94.8	128.0	135.6	135.0	151.3	186.1
2421	Sawmills and planing mills	12/80	97.3	111.6	109.9	111.5	127.9	159.3
2431	Millwork	06/83	103.2	118.9	120.4	125.8	134.5	148.6
2511	Wood household furniture, except upholstered	12/79	133.3	153.7	158.9	163.3	166.9	173.4
2621	Paper mill products except building paper	06/81	109.5	134.6	134.0	131.0	126.6	126.6
2631	Paperboard mills	12/82	112.0	149.9	146.0	140.7	142.6	138.3
2653	Corrugated and solid fiber boxes	03/80	119.7	143.6	139.6	134.5	137.3	135.8
2711	Newspaper publishing	12/79	164.0	206.9	220.4	235.7	248.7	259.3
2721	Periodical publishing	12/79	157.9	194.0	205.7	217.8	227.9	233.1
2731	Book publishing	12/80	134.1	165.4	175.2	183.4	189.7	194.9
2752	Commercial printing, lithographic	06/82	111.0	124.1	127.9	129.7	130.8	135.0
2759	Commercial printing, n.e.c	06/82	112.9	133.7	136.1	140.8	143.6	145.6
2761	Manifold business forms	12/83	106.2	124.9	124.6	123.9	121.0	128.6
2819	Industrial inorganic chemicals, n.e.c	12/82	100.4	116.2	117.9	119.4	118.9	117.2
2821	Plastic materials and resins	12/80	113.6	147.3	139.5	137.9	131.8	132.4
2824	Noncellulosic manmade fibers	06/81	97.6	101.5	102.7	101.9	101.6	101.8
2834	Pharmaceutical preparations	06/81	141.3	190.2	203.5	217.3	231.2	240.8
2841	Soap and other detergents	06/83	104.2	115.5	115.2	116.0	118.5	120.0
2842	Specialty cleaning, polish. and sanitation preps.	06/83	103.9	115.6	118.6	121.5	123.1	124.7
2844	Toilet preparations	03/80	135.4	149.8	153.2	158.0	162.6	166.7
2851	Paints and allied products	06/83	104.9	119.5	125.0	130.3	132.3	133.6
2865	Cyclic (coal tar) crudes and intermediates	12/82	96.9	112.7	114.1	113.3	113.3	116.3
2869	Industrial organic chemicals, n.e.c	12/82	101.3	128.7	125.6	129.1	127.8	123.8
2899	Chemicals and chemical preparations, n.e.c	06/85	(NA)	111.3	112.5	115.7	117.1	120.0
2911	Petroleum refining	06/85	98.3	73.6	90.1	80.9	78.3	75.3
3011	Tires and inner tubes	06/81	96.8	102.9	103.0	105.0	106.0	106.3
3273	Ready-mixed concrete	06/81	108.6	111.5	114.3	116.9	117.4	121.0
3312	Blast furnaces and steel mills	06/82	104.9	113.0	110.8	108.4	105.8	107.5
3321	Gray iron foundries	12/80	115.6	120.9	123.4	125.6	127.0	128.2
3357	Nonferrous wire drawing and insulating	12/82	100.5	153.5	148.7	145.0	141.8	138.2
3411	Metal cans	06/81	110.4	113.7	116.6	118.1	117.0	113.1
3429	Hardware, n.e.c	06/85	(NA)	106.5	110.6	113.3	114.9	116.9
3441	Fabricated structural metal	06/82	103.0	118.0	118.6	117.3	116.6	118.2
3443	Fabricated plate work	03/80	120.8	137.1	142.3	145.8	147.0	146.5
3444	Sheet metal work	12/82	107.2	128.4	129.4	128.2	126.6	127.1
3465	Automotive stampings	12/82	110.4	109.9	112.6	111.7	111.5	111.3
3469	Metal stampings, n.e.c	06/84	101.4	118.8	121.1	122.5	123.2	123.1
3499	Fabricated metal products, n.e.c	06/85	(NA)	114.6	117.6	119.0	119.2	120.4
3519	Internal combustion engines, n.e.c	12/82	103.4	110.6	115.7	120.7	123.3	125.5
3523	Farm machinery and equipment	12/82	105.3	113.0	116.8	120.5	124.1	126.6
3531	Construction machinery	12/80	119.5	132.4	137.6	142.0	146.9	151.3
3544	Spec. tools, dies, jigs, fixtures and indus. molds	06/81	113.5	121.1	124.5	129.3	131.2	134.3
3559	Special industry machinery, n.e.c	12/81	116.4	132.9	137.5	142.4	146.2	151.0
3585	Refrigeration and heating equipment	12/82	104.7	115.5	119.0	119.7	121.1	122.2
3599	Machinery, except electrical, n.e.c	06/84	102.0	110.8	113.9	114.4	114.3	116.1
3621	Electric motors and generators	06/83	108.2	123.3	127.5	129.7	131.5	133.5
3661	Telephone and telegraph apparatus	12/85	(NA)	110.2	112.0	112.8	112.3	115.0
3674	Semiconductors and related devices	06/81	106.6	107.5	105.0	102.8	98.4	98.2
3679	Electronic components, n.e.c	06/82	108.6	113.9	115.1	115.2	117.8	119.7
3711	Motor vehicles and passenger car bodies	06/82	107.2	117.4	119.9	125.3	129.1	133.2
3714	Motor vehicle parts and accessories	12/82	100.6	107.4	108.9	110.3	111.0	111.6
3721	Aircraft	12/85	(NA)	110.2	116.0	120.4	124.3	128.5
3724	Aircraft engines and engine parts	12/85	(NA)	106.6	112.6	117.9	123.6	125.7
3728	Aircraft parts and auxiliary equipment, n.e.c	06/85	(NA)	113.1	116.3	120.3	124.9	128.0
3731	Ship building and repairing	12/85	(NA)	110.2	114.0	116.2	118.3	123.7
3861	Photographic equipment and supplies	12/83	101.5	109.3	112.2	111.9	112.1	112.7

NA Not available. [1] Standard Industrial Classification code.
Source: U.S. Bureau of Labor Statistics, *Producer Price Indexes*, monthly.

No. 756. Fixed-Weighted Price Indexes for Personal Consumption Expenditures: 1960 to 1993
[1987 = 100]

YEAR	Personal consump- tion expendi- tures [1]	Motor vehicles and parts	Furni- ture [2]	Food	Cloth- ing and shoes	Gas- oline and oil	Housing	House- hold oper- ation	Elec- tricity and gas	Trans- port- ation	Medical care
1960	30.8	40.6	79.2	27.4	46.1	30.5	28.8	32.0	24.6	25.5	17.8
1961	31.1	40.6	78.2	27.7	46.4	30.2	29.2	32.2	24.7	26.5	18.3
1962	31.3	40.8	76.5	28.0	46.5	30.4	29.5	32.3	24.8	26.8	18.8
1963	31.6	40.8	75.5	28.4	46.9	30.3	29.9	32.5	24.7	26.4	19.2
1964	31.9	41.0	74.9	29.0	47.3	30.1	30.2	32.6	24.7	26.4	19.9
1965	32.2	40.5	73.1	29.5	47.7	31.2	30.5	32.6	24.6	27.1	20.5
1966	32.8	40.1	71.5	30.7	49.0	32.0	30.9	32.5	24.6	27.9	21.5
1967	33.7	40.6	71.8	31.2	51.1	33.0	31.5	33.0	24.8	28.4	22.9
1968	35.0	41.9	73.0	32.3	54.0	33.5	32.3	33.6	25.0	29.2	24.6
1969	36.3	42.6	74.1	33.7	57.1	34.6	33.4	34.5	25.5	30.8	26.1
1970	37.9	43.8	74.9	35.9	59.4	34.9	34.8	35.6	26.4	33.8	27.9
1971	39.5	45.9	75.6	36.9	61.3	35.2	36.4	38.0	28.2	37.3	29.3
1972	40.8	45.9	76.2	38.6	62.7	35.7	37.7	39.9	29.7	38.6	30.7
1973	42.7	46.2	76.9	42.6	64.9	39.1	39.4	41.6	31.3	39.4	32.1
1974	46.7	49.1	80.6	48.7	69.5	52.7	40.9	45.8	36.6	42.1	34.7
1975	50.5	53.9	85.9	52.7	72.2	56.2	43.6	49.8	41.9	44.5	38.3
1976	53.3	57.8	88.3	54.4	74.5	58.6	46.5	53.6	45.6	49.3	41.7
1977	56.7	61.2	89.9	57.9	77.6	62.0	50.4	57.0	50.0	54.7	45.7
1978	60.7	65.3	92.9	63.1	79.5	64.7	54.0	60.2	53.8	57.9	50.0
1979	65.8	70.3	97.2	69.4	81.7	86.8	58.3	63.6	59.1	62.2	54.4
1980	72.6	75.6	98.2	75.9	85.2	120.7	63.8	69.7	69.0	71.9	60.4
1981	78.9	81.3	101.7	82.1	88.2	134.4	70.4	78.1	79.0	79.2	67.6
1982	83.2	85.1	103.6	85.4	90.0	127.5	75.9	86.7	89.1	83.0	74.7
1983	86.7	87.9	102.6	87.6	91.8	123.4	80.5	92.1	95.8	86.9	80.1
1984	89.9	90.5	101.7	91.1	93.1	121.5	84.9	96.3	100.0	89.6	85.0
1985	93.3	93.0	100.8	93.4	95.8	122.5	90.0	98.9	102.2	91.0	90.4
1986	96.1	95.7	99.5	96.5	95.8	96.2	95.4	100.4	101.7	94.0	94.6
1987	100.0	100.0	100.0	100.0	100.0	100.0	100.0	100.0	100.0	100.0	100.0
1988	104.3	101.5	101.0	104.0	104.2	100.9	104.9	101.4	100.8	104.9	107.1
1989	109.5	104.6	101.6	109.8	106.7	110.2	109.6	103.8	103.9	109.6	115.7
1990	115.2	105.3	102.4	115.7	111.4	125.5	115.4	105.8	105.6	114.9	124.3
1991	120.5	109.2	103.0	120.1	115.4	123.8	120.2	109.6	108.9	122.0	132.6
1992	124.9	112.2	104.0	122.0	117.9	123.3	124.1	112.5	111.0	128.3	140.9
1993	128.7	115.8	104.3	124.3	119.1	122.2	127.8	115.6	114.6	135.5	148.5
PERCENT CHANGE											
1960	1.3	-1.7	0.3	1.3	1.2	2.9	1.5	2.2	2.4	3.5	3.6
1961	0.8	-	-1.3	0.9	0.5	-0.9	1.3	0.7	0.5	3.7	2.7
1962	0.6	0.5	-2.2	1.2	0.2	0.6	1.2	0.4	-	1.3	2.8
1963	0.9	-	-1.3	1.4	1.0	-0.2	1.1	0.7	-0.1	-1.5	2.6
1964	1.1	0.4	-0.8	2.1	0.7	-0.6	1.0	0.3	-0.3	-0.1	3.2
1965	1.0	-1.2	-2.4	1.8	1.0	3.8	1.0	-0.2	-0.3	2.8	3.3
1966	1.8	-1.0	-2.2	3.9	2.6	2.3	1.4	-0.2	0.1	2.8	4.7
1967	2.6	1.3	0.4	1.7	4.2	3.3	1.9	1.5	0.7	2.0	6.6
1968	3.8	3.1	1.7	3.5	5.7	1.5	2.5	1.8	0.9	2.8	7.5
1969	3.8	1.9	1.5	4.6	5.7	3.3	3.4	2.6	2.0	5.3	5.9
1970	4.4	2.8	1.1	6.3	4.1	0.9	4.2	3.3	3.7	9.7	6.9
1971	4.4	4.8	0.9	2.9	3.2	0.8	4.6	6.6	6.8	10.3	5.1
1972	3.3	-	0.8	4.6	2.2	1.3	3.6	5.1	5.0	3.5	5.0
1973	4.6	0.6	0.9	10.4	3.6	9.5	4.4	4.2	5.6	2.1	4.4
1974	9.3	6.2	4.8	14.3	7.1	34.9	3.9	10.1	17.0	6.8	8.4
1975	8.1	9.9	6.6	8.2	3.8	6.7	6.6	8.6	14.5	5.7	10.1
1976	5.6	7.3	2.8	3.3	3.3	4.2	6.7	7.7	8.8	10.9	9.0
1977	6.4	5.7	1.8	6.5	4.1	5.8	8.5	6.3	9.6	10.9	9.6
1978	7.0	6.8	3.3	9.0	2.4	4.4	7.0	5.6	7.5	5.9	9.2
1979	8.5	7.6	4.6	10.0	2.9	34.2	8.0	5.7	9.9	7.3	9.0
1980	10.3	7.6	1.0	9.3	4.3	39.0	9.4	9.5	16.8	15.7	10.9
1981	8.7	7.5	3.6	8.2	3.5	11.3	10.3	12.1	14.4	10.2	11.8
1982	5.4	4.7	1.9	4.0	2.1	-5.1	7.8	11.1	12.8	4.7	10.6
1983	4.3	3.2	-1.0	2.6	2.0	-3.3	6.1	6.2	7.5	4.8	7.2
1984	3.7	3.0	-0.8	3.9	1.4	-1.5	5.4	4.6	4.5	3.1	6.1
1985	3.8	2.8	-1.0	2.6	3.0	0.8	6.1	2.7	2.2	1.5	6.4
1986	3.0	3.0	-1.2	3.3	-	-21.5	6.0	1.5	-0.5	3.3	4.6
1987	4.1	4.5	0.5	3.6	4.3	4.0	4.8	-0.4	-1.7	6.4	5.7
1988	4.3	1.5	1.0	4.0	4.2	0.9	4.9	1.4	0.8	4.9	7.1
1989	5.0	3.1	0.5	5.6	2.4	9.2	4.6	2.4	3.1	4.5	8.0
1990	5.3	0.7	0.8	5.4	4.4	13.9	5.3	1.9	1.6	4.8	7.4
1991	4.5	3.7	0.6	3.8	3.6	-1.4	4.2	3.6	3.1	6.2	6.7
1992	3.7	2.7	1.0	1.6	2.2	-0.4	3.2	2.6	1.9	5.2	6.3
1993	3.0	3.2	0.3	1.9	1.0	-0.9	3.0	2.8	3.2	5.6	5.4

- Represents or rounds to zero.   [1] Includes items not shown separately.   [2] Includes household equipment.

Source: U.S. Bureau of Economic Analysis, *The National Income and Product Accounts of the United States: Volume 2, 1959-88;* and *Survey of Current Business,* July issues.

No. 757. Fixed-Weighted Price Indexes: 1980 to 1993

[1987=100]

ITEM	1980	1984	1985	1986	1988	1989	1990	1991	1992	1993
Gross domestic product	(NA)	91.1	94.3	97.0	104.0	108.6	113.6	118.2	122.1	125.9
Personal consumption expenditures.	72.6	89.9	93.3	96.1	104.3	109.5	115.2	120.5	124.9	128.7
Durable goods	84.7	94.9	96.0	97.1	102.0	104.5	106.3	109.1	111.5	113.8
Nondurable goods.	79.6	93.7	96.2	96.1	103.8	109.5	116.2	120.5	123.0	124.9
Services	65.3	86.4	90.9	95.8	105.1	110.7	116.8	123.3	129.5	134.7
Gross private domestic investment:										
Fixed investment.	(NA)	94.7	95.7	97.9	103.3	106.3	109.1	110.8	112.0	114.7
Nonresidential	(NA)	96.8	97.3	98.8	102.8	105.6	108.4	110.2	111.4	113.3
Structures	78.5	94.1	96.9	98.5	104.6	109.0	112.4	113.9	114.6	117.8
Producers' durable equipment	(NA)	98.3	97.5	99.0	101.9	103.9	106.2	108.3	109.7	110.9
Residential	75.3	89.8	92.1	95.8	104.3	107.8	110.7	111.9	113.4	117.7
Exports of goods and services	(NA)	99.9	98.2	97.3	105.7	108.2	110.0	112.4	113.7	115.4
Imports of goods and services	(NA)	96.8	94.6	93.8	105.4	108.5	112.4	113.8	115.1	115.0
Government purchases	73.3	92.2	95.4	97.6	103.7	107.9	112.6	116.7	120.6	124.3
Federal	75.2	95.6	97.9	99.0	102.8	107.0	111.8	116.5	121.8	126.2
National defense	76.3	96.9	98.8	99.5	103.1	107.1	112.1	116.5	122.3	127.2
Nondefense	71.9	91.4	94.9	97.5	102.0	106.7	110.8	116.5	120.2	123.0
State and local	71.9	89.6	93.5	96.5	104.3	108.6	113.2	116.8	119.6	122.8

NA Not available.

Source: U.S. Bureau of Economic Analysis, *The National Income and Product Accounts of the United States: Volume 2 1959-1988*, and *Survey of Current Business*, July issues.

No. 758. Fixed-Weighted Price Indexes—Annual Percent Change: 1984 to 1993

[1987=100]

ITEM	1984-85	1985-86	1986-87	1987-88	1988-89	1989-90	1990-91	1991-92	1992-93
Gross domestic product	3.5	2.8	3.1	4.0	4.5	4.6	4.1	3.3	3.1
Personal consumption expend. . . .	3.8	3.0	4.1	4.3	5.0	5.3	4.5	3.7	3.0
Durable goods	1.1	1.2	3.0	2.0	2.4	1.7	2.6	2.2	2.0
Nondurable goods.	2.7	-	4.0	3.8	5.5	6.2	3.7	2.1	1.6
Services	5.2	5.4	4.4	5.1	5.3	5.6	5.5	5.0	4.0
Gross private domestic invest.:									
Fixed investment.	1.1	2.3	2.2	3.3	3.0	2.6	1.5	1.1	2.4
Nonresidential	0.5	1.6	1.2	2.8	2.7	2.6	1.7	1.1	1.7
Structures	3.1	1.6	1.5	4.6	4.2	3.1	1.4	0.6	2.8
Producers' durable equip. . . .	−0.8	1.6	1.0	1.9	2.0	2.3	1.9	1.3	1.1
Residential	2.5	4.0	4.4	4.3	3.4	2.7	1.1	1.3	3.8
Exports of goods and services . . .	−1.7	−0.9	2.8	5.7	2.4	1.7	2.2	1.2	1.5
Imports of goods and services . . .	−2.3	−0.8	6.6	5.4	3.0	3.5	1.3	1.2	−0.1
Government purchases	3.5	2.2	2.5	3.7	4.1	4.3	3.6	3.4	3.1
Federal	2.4	1.2	1.0	2.8	4.1	4.5	4.2	4.5	3.6
National defense	2.0	0.7	0.5	3.1	3.9	4.7	3.9	4.9	4.0
Nondefense	3.8	2.7	2.6	2.0	4.6	3.8	5.2	3.1	2.4
State and local	4.3	3.1	3.7	4.3	4.1	4.2	3.2	2.5	2.6

- Represents zero.

Source: U.S. Bureau of Economic Analysis, *The National Income and Product Accounts of the United States: Volume 2, 1959-1988*; and *Survey of Current Business*, July issues.

No. 759. Commodity Research Bureau Futures Price Index: 1975 to 1992

[1967=100. Index computed daily. Represents unweighted geometric average of commodity futures prices (through 9 months forward) of 21 major commodity futures markets. Represents end of year index]

ITEM	1975	1980	1982	1983	1984	1985	1986	1987	1988	1989	1990	1991	1992
All commodities	191.0	308.5	234.0	277.6	244.2	229.2	209.1	232.5	251.8	229.9	222.6	208.0	205.9
Imported	259.4	426.0	269.0	326.0	291.7	398.2	321.2	356.1	365.2	271.7	276.0	264.4	232.4
Industrial	154.8	324.6	249.9	249.0	217.0	211.7	210.4	252.5	248.2	249.6	245.5	217.2	224.7
Grains	195.6	312.1	215.1	249.6	224.9	198.5	164.6	186.1	261.9	205.7	171.2	196.1	196.9
Oilseeds	181.6	314.6	236.9	316.6	273.5	245.4	189.8	223.6	309.6	254.2	223.6	195.4	218.8
Livestock and meats	180.8	217.4	219.9	229.7	240.8	206.9	200.2	189.9	199.1	206.5	226.2	174.0	179.8
Metals (precious) [1]	141.0	531.4	366.0	328.5	243.3	256.6	296.6	346.4	318.7	296.9	257.8	226.0	228.5

[1] Prior to 1980, index for metals only.

Source: Commodity Research Bureau (CRB), New York City, NY, *CRB Commodity Index Report*, weekly (copyright).

No. 760. Indexes of Spot Primary Market Prices: 1980 to 1992

[1967 = 100. Computed weekly for 1980; daily thereafter. Represents unweighted geometric average of price quotations of 23 commodities; much more sensitive to changes in market conditions than is a monthly producer price index]

ITEMS AND NUMBER OF COMMODITIES	1980 (6-24)	1982 (5-25)	1983 (5-23)	1984 (5-22)	1985 (5-21)	1986 (5-20)	1987 (5-26)	1988 (5-27)	1989 (5-26)	1990 (5-25)	1991 (5-28)	1992 (5-26)
All commodities (23)........	265.1	247.6	249.8	293.9	251.4	218.0	250.0	270.3	281.3	279.2	235.3	242.3
Foodstuffs (10).............	260.9	252.8	246.1	299.9	248.1	205.5	215.2	230.1	222.5	231.5	197.7	201.3
Raw industrials (13)........	268.0	243.9	252.3	289.7	253.6	226.9	277.3	302.0	329.0	317.0	265.2	275.5
Livestock and products (5)....	250.5	312.1	278.1	364.5	284.5	231.2	303.3	316.1	285.2	306.9	286.6	276.4
Metals (5)................	257.9	218.2	225.9	253.4	220.2	191.2	239.5	276.7	347.1	313.9	348.8	262.7
Textiles and fibers (4).......	234.7	206.6	208.0	248.1	220.8	216.9	247.1	247.3	253.5	259.4	201.8	218.6
Fats and oils (4)..........	229.5	255.7	225.9	363.5	273.1	168.5	201.2	230.4	208.1	193.3	185.0	180.7

Source: Commodity Research Bureau, a Knight-Ridder Business Information Service, New York, NY, *CRB Commodity Index Report,* weekly (copyright).

No. 761. Average Prices of Selected Fuels and Electricity: 1980 to 1992

[In dollars per unit, except electricity, in cents per kWh. Represents price to end-users, except as noted]

ITEM	Unit [1]	1980	1983	1984	1985	1986	1987	1988	1989	1990	1991	1992
Crude oil, composite [2]...	Barrel.....	28.07	28.99	28.63	26.75	14.55	17.90	14.67	17.97	22.22	19.06	18.43
Motor gasoline: [3]												
Unleaded regular.....	Gallon	1.25	1.24	1.21	1.20	0.93	0.95	0.95	1.02	1.16	1.14	1.13
Unleaded premium ...	Gallon	(NA)	1.38	1.37	1.34	1.09	1.09	1.11	1.20	1.35	1.32	1.32
No. 2 heating oil	Gallon	0.79	0.92	0.92	0.85	0.56	0.58	0.54	0.59	0.73	0.67	0.63
No. 2 diesel fuel.......	Gallon	0.82	0.83	0.82	0.79	0.48	0.55	0.50	0.59	0.73	0.65	0.62
Residual fuel oil	Gallon	0.61	0.65	0.69	0.61	0.34	0.42	0.33	0.39	0.44	0.34	0.34
Natural gas, residential ..	1,000 cu/ft .	3.68	6.06	6.12	6.12	5.83	5.54	5.47	5.64	5.80	5.82	5.89
Electricity, residential ...	kWh......	5.4	7.2	7.5	7.8	7.4	7.4	7.5	7.6	7.8	8.1	8.2

NA Not available.　[1] See headnote.　[2] Refiner acquisition cost.　[3] Average, all service.

Source: U.S. Energy Information Administration, *Monthly Energy Review.*

No. 762. Weekly Food Cost: 1990 and 1993

[In dollars. Assumes that food for all meals and snacks is purchased at the store and prepared at home. See source for details on estimation procedures]

FAMILY TYPE	DECEMBER 1990				JANUARY 1993			
	Thrifty plan	Low-cost plan	Moderate-cost plan	Liberal plan	Thrifty plan	Low-cost plan	Moderate-cost plan	Liberal plan
FAMILIES								
Family of 2:								
20-50 years.................	48.10	60.60	74.70	92.70	50.20	63.60	78.30	97.60
51 years and over	45.60	58.30	71.80	85.80	47.50	61.10	75.30	90.10
Family of 4:								
Couple, 20-50 years and children—								
1-2 and 3-5 years	70.10	87.30	106.60	131.00	73.00	91.60	111.80	137.60
6-8 and 9-11 years	80.10	102.60	128.30	154.40	83.70	107.60	134.30	162.00
INDIVIDUALS [1]								
Child:								
1-2 years	12.70	15.40	18.00	21.80	13.20	16.20	18.90	22.90
3-5 years	13.70	16.80	20.70	24.90	14.20	17.60	21.70	26.00
6-8 years	16.60	22.20	27.90	32.50	17.40	23.30	29.10	34.00
9-11 years..................	19.80	25.30	32.50	37.60	20.70	26.50	34.00	39.30
Male:								
12-14 years.................	20.60	28.60	35.70	42.00	21.50	30.00	37.40	43.90
15-19 years.................	21.40	29.60	36.80	42.60	22.30	31.00	38.50	44.60
20-50 years.................	22.90	29.30	36.60	44.30	23.90	30.80	38.30	46.50
51 years and over	20.90	27.90	34.30	41.10	21.70	29.20	36.00	43.10
Female:								
12-19 years.................	20.80	24.80	30.10	36.30	21.70	26.00	31.50	38.10
20-54 years.................	20.80	25.80	31.30	40.00	21.70	27.00	32.90	42.20
55 years and over	20.60	25.10	31.00	36.90	21.50	26.30	32.50	38.80

[1] The costs given are for individuals in 4-person families. For individuals in other size families, the following adjustments are suggested: 1-person, add 20 percent; 2-person, add 10 percent; 3-person, add 5 percent; 5- or 6-person, subtract 5 percent; 7- (or more) person, subtract 10 percent.

Source: U.S. Dept. of Agriculture, *Human Information Service Admin. 329,* monthly.

No. 763. Food—Retail Prices of Selected Items: 1988 to 1993

[In dollars per pound, except as indicated. As of December]

FOOD	1988	1989	1990	1991	1992	1993
Cereals and bakery products:						
Flour, white, all purpose	0.22	0.24	0.24	0.22	0.23	0.22
Rice, white, lg. grain, raw	0.48	0.50	0.49	0.51	0.53	0.50
Spaghetti and macaroni	0.85	0.87	0.85	0.86	0.86	0.84
Bread, white, pan	0.66	0.69	0.70	0.72	0.74	0.76
Meats, poultry, fish and eggs:						
Ground chuck, 100% beef	1.79	1.88	2.02	1.93	1.91	1.91
Rib roast, USDA Choice	4.03	4.21	4.54	4.59	4.69	4.73
Round steak, USDA Choice	3.01	3.17	3.42	3.38	3.34	3.32
Sirloin steak, bone-in	3.23	3.46	3.65	3.78	3.75	3.69
T-bone steak	4.97	5.04	5.45	5.21	5.39	5.77
Pork:						
Bacon, sliced	1.79	1.96	2.28	1.99	1.86	2.02
Chops, center cut, bone-in	2.65	2.85	3.32	3.12	3.15	3.24
Shoulder picnic, bone-in, smoked	1.10	1.17	1.41	1.30	1.18	1.19
Sausage	1.92	2.12	2.42	2.24	2.14	1.99
Poultry:						
Chicken, fresh, whole	0.89	0.88	0.86	0.86	0.88	0.91
Chicken breast, bone-in	2.06	2.01	2.00	2.02	2.08	2.17
Chicken legs, bone-in	1.17	1.14	1.17	1.14	1.14	1.13
Turkey, frozen, whole	0.97	0.95	0.96	0.91	0.93	0.95
Eggs, Grade A, large, (dozen)	0.83	1.14	1.00	1.01	0.93	0.87
Dairy products:						
Milk, fresh, whole, fortified (1/2 gal.)	1.21	1.37	1.39	1.40	1.39	1.43
Butter, salted, grade AA, stick	2.15	2.11	1.92	1.94	1.64	1.61
Ice cream, prepack., bulk,reg.(1/2 gal.)	2.54	2.67	2.54	2.63	2.49	2.59
Fruits and vegetables:						
Fresh fruits and vegetables:						
Apples, red Delicious	0.71	0.57	0.77	0.86	0.76	0.78
Bananas	0.41	0.42	0.43	0.42	0.40	0.41
Oranges, navel	0.56	0.53	0.56	0.65	0.52	0.56
Grapefruit	0.45	0.47	0.56	0.53	0.52	0.50
Lemons	0.91	0.96	0.97	1.21	0.90	1.05
Pears, Anjou	0.64	0.76	0.79	0.88	0.80	0.89
Potatoes, white	0.30	0.31	0.32	0.28	0.31	0.36
Lettuce, iceberg	0.77	0.52	0.58	0.69	0.66	0.53
Tomatoes, field grown	0.81	0.90	0.86	0.79	1.23	1.31
Cabbage	0.33	0.34	0.39	0.46	0.38	0.37
Carrots, short trimmed and topped	0.39	0.35	0.44	0.51	0.44	0.41
Celery	0.44	0.46	0.49	0.45	0.48	0.49
Cucumbers	0.49	0.64	0.56	0.55	0.51	0.93
Processed fruits and vegetables:						
Orange juice, frozen concentrate, 12 oz. can, per 16 oz	1.82	1.80	2.02	1.74	1.70	1.67
Potatoes, frozen, french fried	0.70	0.80	0.85	0.92	0.86	0.88

No. 764. Average Price of Energy in Selected Metropolitan Areas: 1993

[In dollars per unit shown. As of January. One therm contains approximately 100 cubic feet of natural gas. See Appendix II]

CITY/MSA	Utility (piped) gas (100 therms)	Electricity (500 kWh)	Fuel oil No. 2 (gallon)	GASOLINE		
				All types [1]	Unleaded regular	Unleaded premium
U.S. city average	62.46	46.96	0.97	1.18	1.12	1.31
Baltimore, MD MSA	67.24	46.27	1.00	1.23	1.14	1.33
Boston-Lawrence-Salem, MA-NH CMSA	84.73	57.13	0.98	1.24	1.16	1.38
Chicago-Gary-Lake County, IL-IN-WI CMSA	66.22	57.91	1.08	1.20	1.12	1.34
Cleveland-Akron-Lorain, OH CMSA	46.36	57.79	(NA)	1.19	1.16	1.29
Dallas-Fort Worth, TX CMSA	58.82	43.22	(NA)	1.14	1.07	1.24
Detroit-Ann Arbor, MI CMSA	51.99	49.55	0.98	1.02	1.00	1.17
Houston-Galveston-Brazoria, TX CMSA	44.53	43.67	(NA)	1.11	1.05	1.25
Los Angeles-Anaheim-Riverside, CA CMSA	64.61	60.63	(NA)	1.39	1.30	1.49
Miami-Fort Lauderdale, FL CMSA	86.05	44.94	(NA)	1.21	1.13	1.31
New York-N. NJ-Long Island, NY-NJ-CT CMSA	85.84	67.75	1.08	1.32	1.21	1.45
Philadelphia-Wilmington-Trenton, PA-NJ-DE-MD CMSA	71.88	60.17	0.96	1.27	1.16	1.37
Pittsburgh-Beaver Valley, PA CMSA	57.83	54.23	0.86	1.16	1.09	1.30
St. Louis-East St. Louis, MO-IL CMSA	56.22	40.98	(NA)	1.02	0.95	1.16
San Francisco-Oakland-San Jose, CA CMSA	59.48	63.08	(NA)	1.35	1.30	1.49
Washington, DC-MD-VA MSA	79.98	41.81	1.10	1.25	1.18	1.35

NA Not available. [1] Includes types of gasoline not shown separately.

Source: U.S. Bureau of Labor Statistics, CPI Detailed Report, January issues.

No. 765. Import Price Indexes—Selected Commodities: 1985 to 1993

[1990 = 100. Indexes are weighted by the 1990 Tariff Schedule of the United States Annotated, a scheme for describing and reporting product composition and value of U.S. imports. Import prices are based on U.S. dollar prices paid by importer. F.o.b. = Free on board; c.i.f. = Cost, insurance, and freight; n.e.s. = Not elsewhere specified]

COMMODITY	1985	1987	1988	1989	1990 [1]	1991	1992	1993
All commodities	80.2	88.4	93.9	96.8	96.1	98.8	100.3	100.5
Food and live animals	87.2	95.5	100.5	98.2	98.6	102.4	97.9	101.1
Meat	68.8	79.1	78.4	80.3	100.0	105.6	94.9	99.3
Meat of bovine animals	77.1	86.1	91.2	95.2	98.5	100.8	91.1	100.8
Fish	75.5	96.5	99.1	94.1	96.7	107.6	107.9	107.9
Crustaceans; fresh, chilled, frozen, salted or dried	85.0	105.3	105.2	98.4	97.4	107.3	105.4	106.4
Cereals and cereal preparations	63.2	82.1	91.0	91.2	98.7	96.4	99.3	102.9
Sugar [2]	87.4	93.6	94.0	95.5	99.7	96.7	95.3	95.1
Coffee, tea and cocoa	145.1	130.4	140.0	128.0	99.4	93.2	77.3	81.2
Beverages and tobacco	77.1	87.7	90.3	91.1	99.2	110.8	113.4	112.6
Beverages	75.9	87.6	92.0	92.6	99.3	110.3	112.5	112.9
Crude materials	77.8	89.9	106.6	111.6	101.9	95.9	95.8	95.3
Crude rubber	98.3	101.0	147.1	100.6	101.2	98.4	100.8	102.9
Cork and wood	93.4	98.0	99.1	100.0	102.4	107.7	116.8	130.3
Pulp and waste paper	56.9	74.1	90.1	106.6	102.8	79.2	74.4	63.7
Crude fertilizers and minerals	102.8	101.7	103.1	106.9	99.6	100.9	89.0	82.5
Metalliferous ores and metal scrap	59.9	78.1	105.1	133.1	100.8	93.6	91.1	88.3
Crude animal and vegetable materials, n.e.s.	83.9	96.5	131.2	97.6	103.9	103.7	107.2	106.1
Mineral fuels and related products	114.5	85.1	72.8	84.2	73.1	83.2	86.7	79.9
Crude petroleum and petroleum products	112.1	83.9	71.7	83.8	72.0	82.8	86.7	79.2
Crude petroleum	123.8	84.7	70.9	82.7	66.8	81.4	87.8	76.6
Natural gas	(NA)	(NA)	(NA)	88.5	89.4	88.1	83.7	90.3
Animal and vegetable oils, fats and waxes	115.5	92.4	116.8	123.3	100.6	102.2	134.9	117.8
Chemicals and related products	83.7	87.3	97.0	100.4	98.5	100.7	101.7	102.8
Intermediate manufactured products	73.1	82.9	97.4	100.3	99.5	99.2	99.4	99.3
Rubber manufactures	85.9	90.3	93.0	96.9	99.8	100.6	102.0	103.8
Cork and wood manufactures	69.0	86.4	96.1	97.2	100.4	98.6	108.1	120.6
Paper and paperboard products	82.7	86.8	98.0	100.0	100.4	101.0	94.1	96.7
Textiles	77.6	87.8	94.6	95.8	98.7	103.0	106.0	108.1
Nonmetallic mineral manufactures	60.1	79.2	89.0	93.4	99.8	103.3	105.5	108.0
Iron and steel	79.3	84.4	100.7	105.8	99.7	99.3	97.6	98.2
Nonferrous metals	69.0	77.4	109.9	109.2	98.7	89.0	88.6	76.6
Silver, platinum and other platinum group metals	71.2	106.7	102.7	89.6	93.6	90.2	75.5	69.1
Copper	57.6	61.7	85.3	98.5	98.6	88.7	88.5	75.9
Nickel	62.4	49.3	154.9	152.2	95.5	97.6	87.5	72.9
Aluminum	(NA)	79.8	131.6	117.3	98.7	85.8	86.4	79.1
Zinc	56.7	52.5	76.2	108.9	113.4	77.2	89.3	67.7
Manufactures of metals, n.e.s.	72.9	82.8	93.2	97.4	98.9	101.2	103.0	104.5
Machinery and transport equipment	75.1	91.0	96.6	98.1	98.7	101.6	103.5	105.0
Machinery specialized for particular industries	59.1	83.4	91.8	89.3	97.3	101.7	105.4	107.5
Metalworking machinery	64.8	84.5	93.9	92.0	98.7	100.6	103.9	107.7
General industrial machinery, parts, n.e.s.	62.6	83.5	91.8	91.3	97.7	101.5	104.9	107.0
Computer equipment and office machines	85.0	98.4	103.1	103.0	99.8	97.3	95.7	91.9
Computer equipment	112.8	112.5	107.6	105.0	100.3	96.9	92.4	85.5
Telecommunications [3]	90.1	99.2	102.3	104.1	100.2	97.8	97.1	98.0
Electrical machinery and equipment	77.4	89.5	95.9	100.1	98.7	100.6	102.1	103.9
Electronic valves, diodes, transistors & integr. cir.	98.7	98.6	99.9	110.0	98.2	99.5	99.4	104.3
Road vehicles	75.1	91.5	97.0	98.5	98.4	103.5	105.6	108.4
Miscellaneous manufactured articles	74.3	88.3	94.2	94.9	98.9	100.6	103.7	105.2
Plumbing, heating & lighting fixtures	68.9	81.8	88.7	91.9	98.4	98.0	101.5	102.0
Furniture and parts	74.0	87.4	93.0	94.0	99.1	101.2	103.4	104.1
Articles of apparel and clothing	81.7	89.4	94.1	98.1	100.5	98.8	101.8	102.1
Footwear	70.6	86.2	93.3	92.0	99.0	100.9	102.6	101.2
Prof., scientific & contr'ing instr & appratus, n.e.s.	64.4	91.0	95.5	91.4	97.5	102.1	104.4	110.5
Photographic apparatus [4]	73.5	93.7	96.1	95.1	98.0	100.1	102.9	106.9
Miscellaneous manufactured articles, n.e.s.	71.1	86.4	94.3	93.8	97.9	101.8	106.0	108.3

NA Not available. [1] June 1990 may not equal 100 because indexes were reweighted to an "average" trade value in 1990. [2] Includes sugar preparations and honey. [3] Includes sound recording and reproducing equipment. [4] Includes photographic supplies, optical goods, watches, and clocks.

Source: U.S. Bureau of Labor Statistics, *News*, quarterly.

No. 766. Export Price Indexes—Selected Commodities: 1985 to 1993

[1990=100. Indexes are weighted by 1980 export values according to the Schedule B classification system of the U.S. Bureau of the Census. Prices used in these indexes were collected from a sample of U.S. manufacturers of exports and are factory transaction prices, except as noted. F.a.s. = free alongside ship. N.e.s. = not elsewhere specified. F.o.b. = free on board]

COMMODITY	1985	1987	1988	1989	1990 [1]	1991	1992	1993
All commodities	88.4	90.1	96.6	99.7	99.5	100.6	101.0	101.4
Food and live animals	96.3	86.1	99.1	110.6	104.3	100.7	102.8	97.8
Meat	78.6	96.4	104.3	102.0	98.5	101.9	106.1	111.6
Fish	78.5	97.5	112.5	123.2	98.4	94.7	98.1	96.5
Cereals and cereal preparations	109.3	75.7	93.0	113.5	108.6	96.8	104.8	90.9
Wheat	115.5	77.2	101.6	134.4	112.1	91.2	108.4	94.1
Rice	110.9	64.6	115.5	104.5	101.7	112.1	106.7	92.5
Maize	107.8	74.9	86.8	105.2	108.6	97.8	102.2	87.7
Other cereals	105.0	76.7	86.5	103.6	104.7	97.6	104.6	88.7
Fruits and vegetables	88.6	99.5	92.4	100.6	102.0	121.5	100.0	103.0
Feeding stuff for animals	74.9	102.0	130.3	118.8	97.6	100.0	102.2	100.7
Miscellaneous food products	90.6	91.2	93.2	97.9	99.9	100.5	100.2	100.3
Beverages and tobacco	79.9	83.8	88.3	93.8	99.3	105.7	109.8	113.1
Tobacco and tobacco manufactures	79.6	83.6	88.1	93.8	99.4	105.7	109.6	112.8
Crude materials	74.4	83.8	102.4	104.7	100.5	95.4	93.4	99.6
Raw hides and skins	63.3	97.1	108.3	97.4	105.2	81.5	80.8	79.2
Oil seeds and oleaginous fruits	92.8	89.5	125.8	114.3	97.1	99.4	98.4	97.9
Crude rubber, f.a.s.	85.6	86.7	91.0	98.3	99.1	103.2	101.0	99.2
Cork and wood	56.2	66.2	85.2	97.2	102.1	97.9	110.1	161.4
Pulp and waste paper	57.6	86.1	103.2	111.2	100.2	86.6	82.6	70.2
Textile fibers	85.3	92.7	90.6	95.3	102.6	107.0	86.0	83.5
Cotton textile fibers	87.4	96.7	92.0	93.8	103.7	107.9	79.7	77.5
Crude fertilizers and minerals	100.8	94.4	94.6	99.6	100.1	101.1	99.7	95.0
Metalliferous ores and metal scrap	70.7	75.0	102.3	110.1	99.9	89.1	85.1	83.9
Ferrous waste and scrap	73.0	69.8	107.6	112.4	99.8	93.4	82.2	99.0
Nonferrous base metal waste and scrap	56.5	72.5	106.1	112.5	99.4	84.2	86.0	72.2
Mineral fuels and related materials	104.6	85.0	84.4	88.4	91.1	89.9	86.5	88.0
Coal, coke and briquettes	103.1	90.5	94.5	96.8	100.1	98.6	96.9	93.9
Crude petroleum and petroleum products	(NA)	(NA)	75.1	81.4	83.9	80.1	77.2	80.7
Animal and vegetable oils, fats and waxes	123.5	85.8	105.9	95.1	103.0	93.8	94.9	98.4
Chemicals and related products	84.5	90.0	102.6	102.9	97.4	99.7	97.4	96.1
Organic chemicals	80.5	94.7	115.7	116.0	94.9	94.6	91.5	90.5
Hydrocarbons, n.e.s. and derivatives, f.a.s.	73.9	104.0	123.2	114.8	93.3	76.2	77.8	80.1
Alcohols, phenols, phenol-alcohols, & deriv., f.a.s.	78.6	80.9	113.2	147.1	96.3	101.8	93.1	93.2
Chemical materials and products, n.e.s.	86.7	84.8	88.3	95.0	98.7	103.4	102.9	105.7
Intermediate manufactured products	81.3	87.6	95.5	99.9	99.8	100.1	100.6	100.7
Rubber manufactures	86.6	88.6	94.0	97.6	98.9	105.0	105.6	108.5
Paper and paperboard products	76.7	89.4	98.6	102.1	99.5	99.5	98.4	93.9
Textiles	84.3	87.3	90.8	97.1	99.6	104.1	105.6	106.8
Nonmetallic mineral manufactures	(NA)	85.3	89.6	96.1	99.6	101.2	103.5	105.4
Nonferrous metals	77.1	85.4	108.4	110.2	100.2	88.1	87.9	81.3
Manufactures of metals, n.e.s.	84.9	86.3	91.7	97.1	99.8	102.7	103.6	105.1
Machinery and transport equipment [2]	90.7	92.3	94.3	97.2	99.8	102.9	104.4	104.5
Power generating machinery [3]	85.2	88.3	92.3	96.0	99.8	104.7	109.6	110.7
Rotating electric plant and parts thereof, n.e.s.	76.8	81.9	89.7	95.0	99.7	101.9	104.7	106.1
Machinery specialized for particular industries	87.7	87.7	90.8	95.4	99.3	103.3	105.5	108.0
Agricultural machinery and parts [4]	89.4	90.8	91.6	94.2	100.0	102.1	104.9	107.3
Civil engineering and contractors, plant and equip.	90.7	86.8	89.0	95.2	98.8	103.9	102.0	105.5
Metalworking machinery	82.1	87.8	91.2	96.5	99.6	106.5	109.1	111.0
General industrial machines, parts, n.e.s.	84.4	88.2	91.2	95.6	99.7	103.7	106.1	108.3
Computer equipment and office machines	105.9	101.9	101.5	100.6	100.3	98.4	94.7	87.7
Computer equipment	113.0	106.5	105.1	101.7	100.3	97.8	94.0	83.1
Telecommunications [5]	89.6	91.3	94.1	96.8	100.1	106.4	108.3	109.4
Electrical machinery and equipment	93.8	95.0	96.1	99.0	99.9	100.6	103.6	103.5
Electronic valves, diodes, transistors & integr. cir.	106.5	107.1	103.5	100.1	100.6	98.5	103.7	102.3
Road vehicles	89.8	92.9	94.1	96.8	99.6	102.4	104.0	105.2
Other transport equipment	81.7	86.9	90.2	94.4	99.8	112.4	113.0	117.4
Miscellaneous manufactured articles	85.4	89.6	92.0	96.1	99.1	104.2	106.2	106.9

NA Not available. [1] June 1990 may not equal 100 because indexes were reweighted to an "average" trade value in 1990. [2] Excludes military and commercial aircraft. [3] Includes equipment. [4] Excludes tractors. [5] Includes sound recording and reproducing equipment.

Source: U.S. Bureau of Labor Statistics, *News*, quarterly.

No. 767. Refiner/Reseller Sales Price of Gasoline, by State: 1991 to 1993

[In cents per gallon. As of **March.** Represents all refinery and gas plant operators' sales through company-operated retail outlets. Gasoline prices exclude excise taxes]

STATE	Gasoline excise taxes 1992 [1]	AVERAGE, ALL GRADES 1991	1992	1993	LEADED REGULAR 1991	1992	1993	UNLEADED REGULAR 1991	1992	1993	PREMIUM 1991	1992	1993
United States	14.1	76.5	72.2	75.5	71.6	70.7	75.2	73.6	68.3	71.6	87.3	84.3	87.8
Northeast:													
New England:													
Maine	19	90.0	80.8	80.9	(NA)	(2)	(2)	86.9	77.0	76.4	102.2	93.2	93.6
New Hampshire	19	85.2	79.6	80.3	(D)	(2)	(2)	82.0	75.3	75.2	95.7	92.3	94.6
Vermont	16	91.6	83.6	82.7	(D)	(2)	(2)	88.2	79.8	78.1	102.8	93.7	94.8
Massachusetts	21	83.1	76.5	79.0	86.4	(D)	(2)	78.8	71.0	73.3	94.4	88.4	92.6
Rhode Island	26	82.9	74.4	77.6	(NA)	(2)	(2)	78.9	69.4	72.2	91.7	83.6	87.3
Connecticut	26	83.0	78.3	81.6	(D)	(2)	(2)	78.5	72.7	75.3	93.7	89.8	96.2
Middle Atlantic:													
New York	23	87.0	74.8	75.8	87.1	74.9	(D)	83.2	70.1	70.5	99.5	88.6	91.1
New Jersey	15	83.4	77.8	85.4	(NA)	(2)	(2)	77.9	70.5	77.1	94.2	89.3	98.9
Pennsylvania	22	82.4	72.5	72.3	(D)	(2)	(2)	78.5	67.7	67.2	94.2	85.2	84.9
North Central:													
East North Central:													
Ohio	21	73.4	73.3	71.4	78.4	74.0	71.0	70.7	70.0	68.1	84.6	85.2	80.2
Indiana	20	77.3	68.9	71.6	84.8	80.3	79.3	75.0	66.1	69.2	87.6	78.1	76.7
Illinois	19	76.1	69.6	74.1	88.2	72.7	80.9	73.4	66.3	71.0	86.2	81.3	83.6
Michigan	16	74.0	67.2	70.8	79.2	76.4	81.6	71.7	64.4	68.2	84.9	79.1	80.0
Wisconsin	24	76.8	69.2	73.5	82.2	74.8	77.5	75.1	67.2	71.4	86.6	78.3	84.1
West North Central:													
Minnesota	21	77.6	73.0	81.1	79.3	73.3	80.2	76.1	71.4	79.3	85.0	80.3	90.2
Iowa	20	80.0	70.9	72.9	83.7	77.5	75.2	79.1	69.9	71.9	86.4	78.3	81.3
Missouri	11	75.6	68.4	69.8	78.7	70.3	73.6	73.1	65.4	66.9	85.5	79.3	78.3
North Dakota	17	82.8	79.1	85.1	85.5	81.6	89.8	82.2	78.4	84.0	85.6	85.1	93.2
South Dakota	19	80.8	75.9	78.2	80.2	77.1	85.1	79.9	75.1	76.9	90.4	86.2	89.1
Nebraska	24	80.9	73.5	76.8	78.6	75.3	79.2	79.0	72.4	75.7	87.9	80.7	85.2
Kansas	17	76.2	72.2	73.1	77.8	74.0	75.5	74.9	70.5	71.3	85.3	82.5	84.8
South:													
South Atlantic:													
Delaware	19	83.8	74.0	74.8	(NA)	(2)	(2)	78.8	68.6	69.7	98.4	87.7	88.3
Maryland	19	78.8	78.1	75.5	(NA)	(2)	(2)	73.0	72.2	70.0	93.3	91.1	87.9
District of Columbia	18	(D)	(D)	(D)	(D)	(2)	(2)	(D)	(D)	(D)	(D)	(D)	(D)
Virginia	18	77.2	73.3	75.4	72.4	(D)	(2)	72.7	67.7	69.2	89.1	86.6	89.6
West Virginia	20	81.1	76.8	78.4	(D)	(D)	(2)	76.9	72.3	73.6	95.8	89.4	90.7
North Carolina	23	76.2	69.9	71.2	(D)	(D)	(2)	72.3	64.5	65.9	88.3	83.3	84.5
South Carolina	17	75.6	69.3	69.8	(D)	(D)	(2)	71.3	64.5	64.7	91.0	84.7	85.5
Georgia	8	75.9	70.8	72.6	75.9	64.8	73.1	71.3	74.9	77.1	89.2	84.9	86.9
Florida	12	78.5	72.2	77.2	-	(D)	(2)	73.9	66.1	70.6	89.1	84.7	91.2
East South Central:													
Kentucky	15	78.6	72.3	72.9	83.8	70.3	(D)	75.5	68.8	68.4	90.2	82.9	84.9
Tennessee	21	74.4	70.3	72.5	(D)	(D)	(D)	70.0	64.9	66.4	87.5	82.9	85.9
Alabama	13	78.4	73.6	74.5	(D)	(D)	(D)	75.1	69.4	69.7	90.1	86.3	87.6
Mississippi	18	78.9	70.6	74.5	(D)	(D)	(D)	75.2	66.7	69.9	90.4	81.5	86.7
West South Central:													
Arkansas	19	77.5	70.1	72.8	79.5	67.3	67.8	74.8	66.9	69.3	90.6	81.9	86.0
Louisiana	20	77.2	73.6	75.3	(D)	(D)	(D)	73.2	68.5	69.8	88.4	85.2	88.3
Oklahoma	17	75.8	69.5	71.5	77.6	69.1	75.7	74.3	67.3	69.1	81.6	78.3	82.3
Texas	20	76.1	72.4	74.8	79.0	71.4	79.4	73.1	67.7	70.0	85.5	83.9	87.7
West:													
Mountain:													
Montana	20	81.3	73.1	77.1	80.4	73.3	76.5	90.6	71.9	76.4	86.6	78.1	81.9
Idaho	22	67.0	71.7	72.6	66.0	71.1	72.4	66.4	70.8	71.7	77.8	81.1	82.4
Wyoming	9	79.4	77.7	80.2	78.9	77.0	79.7	78.2	76.5	78.9	87.0	85.8	88.4
Colorado	22	73.4	74.7	80.4	73.3	75.3	83.3	71.3	71.8	77.0	83.0	84.4	93.3
New Mexico	17	77.8	73.7	85.9	75.6	72.3	85.0	76.9	72.2	84.4	88.1	85.7	97.7
Arizona	19	78.6	73.3	84.6	75.9	69.2	79.7	77.5	71.7	83.2	89.3	87.0	99.3
Utah	20	66.2	69.2	74.8	65.3	71.1	75.7	64.4	66.9	72.0	73.8	76.3	82.3
Nevada	21	79.2	77.8	83.1	74.5	73.4	81.2	77.6	76.1	80.6	90.4	90.1	97.1
Pacific:													
Washington	23	72.4	69.8	69.6	68.1	64.7	64.0	71.1	68.3	68.0	84.3	84.0	84.9
Oregon	22	75.8	78.3	79.9	71.5	73.7	74.5	75.1	77.5	78.9	89.8	92.3	96.1
California	17	65.3	73.7	71.4	61.4	(2)	(2)	63.2	69.9	80.6	75.2	85.4	98.6
Alaska	8	108.7	103.9	107.7	(NA)	100.0	104.7	108.6	104.4	(NA)	109.2	103.6	109.1
Hawaii	16	99.1	104.2	108.5	(NA)	(2)	(2)	93.0	97.5	103.0	110.3	115.3	119.2

- Represents zero.　D Withheld to avoid disclosure of individual company data.　NA Not available.　[1] Source: U.S. Advisory Commission on Intergovernmental Relations, *Significant Features of Fiscal Federalism*, annual, vol. I, based on CCH, *State Tax Reporter.*　[2] No data reported.

Source: Except as noted, U.S. Energy Information Administration, *Petroleum Marketing Monthly.*

Banking, Finance, and Insurance

This section presents data on the Nation's finances, various types of financial institutions, money and credit, securities, and insurance. The primary sources of these data are publications of several departments of the Federal Government, especially the Treasury Department, and independent agencies such as the Federal Deposit Insurance Corporation, the Federal Reserve System, and the Securities and Exchange Commission. National data on insurance are available primarily from private organizations, such as the American Council of Life Insurance.

In Brief

Conventional new-home mortgage rates:

1980	13.95%
1990	10.08%
1993	7.37%

Dow-Jones industrial average:

1980	891.4
1990	2,678.9
1993	3,754.1

Flow of funds.—The flow of funds accounts of the Federal Reserve System (see tables 770 to 773) bring together statistics on all of the major forms of financial transactions and financial claims to present an economy-wide view of asset and liability relationships. In flow form, the accounts relate borrowing and lending to one another and to the nonfinancial activities that generate income and production. Each claim outstanding is included simultaneously as an asset of the lender and as a liability of the debtor. The accounts also indicate the balance between asset totals and liability totals over the economy as a whole. Several publications of the Board of Governors of the Federal Reserve System contain information on the flow of funds accounts: Summary data on flows and outstandings, in the *Federal Reserve Bulletin, Flow of Funds Accounts* (quarterly), and *Annual Statistical Digest;* and concepts and organization of the accounts, in *Flow of Funds: A Guide to the Accounts* (April 1993).

Banking system.—Banks in this country are organized under the laws of both the States and the Federal Government and are regulated by several bank supervisory agencies. National banks are supervised by the Comptroller of the Currency. *Reports of Condition* have been collected from national banks since 1863. Summaries of these reports are published in the Comptroller's *Annual Report,* which also presents data on the structure of the national banking system.

The Federal Reserve System was established in 1913 to exercise central banking functions, some of which are shared with the U.S. Treasury. It includes national banks and such State banks that voluntarily join the System. Statements of State bank members are consolidated by the Board of Governors of the Federal Reserve System with data for national banks collected by the Comptroller of the Currency into totals for all member banks of the System. Balance sheet data for member banks and other commercial banks are published quarterly in the *Federal Reserve Bulletin.* The Federal Deposit Insurance Corporation (FDIC), established in 1933, insures each depositor up to $100,000. Major item balance sheet and income data for all commercial banks are published in the *FDIC Quarterly Banking Profile.*

The FDIC is the primary federal regulator of State-chartered banks that are not members of the Federal Reserve System and of most savings banks insured by the Bank Insurance Fund (BIF). The agency also has certain back–up supervisory authority, for safety and soundness purposes, over State-chartered banks that are members of the Federal Reserve System, national banks, and savings associations.

Savings institutions.—Savings institutions are primarily involved in credit extension in the form of mortgage loans. Statistics on savings institutions are collected by the U.S. Office of Thrift Supervision and the FDIC. The Financial Institutions Reform, Recovery, and Enforcement Act of 1989 (FIRREA) authorized the establishment of the Resolution Trust Corporation

(RTC). The RTC is responsible for the disposal of assets from failed savings institutions. FIRREA gave the FDIC the job of managing the federal deposit insurance fund for savings institutions (SAIF=Savings Association Insurance Fund). Major balance sheet and income data for all insured savings institutions are published in the *FDIC Quarterly Banking Profile.*

Other credit agencies.—Insurance companies, finance companies dealing primarily in installment sales financing, credit unions, and personal loan companies represent important sources of funds for the credit market. Statistics on loans, investments, cash, etc., of life insurance companies are published principally by the American Council of Life Insurance in its *Life Insurance Fact Book.* Consumer credit data are published currently in the *Federal Reserve Bulletin.*

Federally chartered credit unions are under the supervision of the National Credit Union Administration, established in 1970. State-chartered credit unions are supervised by the respective State supervisory authorities. The Administration publishes comprehensive program and statistical information on all Federal and federally insured State credit unions in the *Annual Report of the National Credit Union Administration.* Deposit insurance (up to $100,000 per account) is provided to members of all Federal and those State credit unions that are federally-insured by the National Credit Union Share Insurance Fund which was established in 1970. Deposit insurance for State chartered credit unions is also available in some States under private or State-administered insurance programs.

Government corporations and credit agencies make available credit of specified types or to specified groups of private borrowers, either by lending directly or by insuring or guaranteeing loans made by private lending institutions. Data on operations of Government credit agencies, along with other Government corporations, are available in reports of individual agencies; data on their debt outstanding are published in the *Federal Reserve Bulletin.*

Currency.—Currency, including coin and paper money, represents about 40 percent of all media of exchange in the United States, with most payments made by check. All currency is now issued by the Federal Reserve Banks.

Securities.—The Securities and Exchange Commission (SEC) was established in 1934 to protect the interests of the public and investors against malpractices in the securities and financial markets and to provide the fullest possible disclosure of information regarding securities to the investing public. Statistical data are published in the *SEC Annual Report.*

Insurance.—Insuring companies, which are regulated by the various States or the District of Columbia, are classified as either life or property. Companies that underwrite accident and health insurance only and those that underwrite accident and health insurance in addition to one or more property lines are included with property insurance. Insuring companies, other than those classified as life, are permitted to underwrite one or more property lines provided they are so licensed and have the necessary capital or surplus.

There are a number of published sources for statistics on the various classes of insurance—life, health, fire, marine, and casualty. Individual States collect data on all insurers operating within their respective jurisdictions, and many of the States publish an annual insurance report giving individual company data and aggregates of certain items for the companies operating within the State. Organizations representing certain classes of insurers publish reports for these classes. Among them are the annual commercial publishers, such as The National Underwriter Company whose *Argus Health Chart* (annual) contains financial and operating data for individual health and accident insurance companies, including Blue Cross and Blue Shield Plans. The American Council of Life Insurance publishes statistics on life insurance purchases, ownership, benefit payments, and assets in its biennial *Life Insurance Fact Book.*

Historical statistics.—Tabular headnotes provide cross-references, where applicable, to *Historical Statistics of the United States, Colonial Times to 1970.* See Appendix IV.

No. 768. Gross Domestic Product in Finance, Insurance, and Real Estate, in Current and Constant (1987) Dollars: 1987 to 1991

[In billions of dollars, except percent. For definition of gross domestic product, see text, section 14. Based on 1987 Standard Industrial Classification]

INDUSTRY	CURRENT DOLLARS				CONSTANT (1987) DOLLARS			
	1987	1989	1990	1991	1987	1989	1990	1991
Finance, insurance, real estate, total	809.7	926.5	982.4	1,039.7	809.7	865.5	868.3	878.4
Percent of gross domestic product	17.8	17.6	17.7	18.2	17.8	17.9	17.7	18.1
Depository institutions.................	134.7	145.4	158.7	171.8	134.7	135.4	135.1	129.4
Nondepository institutions	17.4	19.8	20.7	21.2	17.4	16.9	17.9	18.3
Security and commodity brokers	37.9	40.4	37.9	46.5	37.9	40.1	38.4	47.0
Insurance carriers....................	51.2	68.9	69.9	90.1	51.2	64.8	60.1	72.2
Insurance agents, brokers, and services......	30.2	34.0	37.7	37.9	30.2	30.4	32.1	30.6
Real estate.........................	521.5	609.5	641.7	661.5	521.5	560.2	566.7	562.5
Nonfarm housing services..............	375.6	432.4	458.7	482.7	375.6	393.1	398.3	403.2
Other real estate....................	145.9	177.1	183.0	178.8	145.9	167.1	168.5	159.3
Holding and other investment offices........	16.9	8.4	15.8	10.7	16.9	17.8	18.1	18.4

Source: U.S. Bureau of Economic Analysis, *Survey of Current Business*, November 1993.

No. 769. Finance, Insurance, and Real Estate—Establishments, Employees, and Payroll: 1990 and 1991

[Covers establishments with payroll. Excludes government employees, railroad employees, self-employed persons, etc. For statement on methodology, see Appendix III]

KIND OF BUSINESS	1987 SIC code [1]	ESTABLISHMENTS (1,000)		EMPLOYEES (1,000)		PAYROLL (bil. dol.)	
		1990	1991	1990	1991	1990	1991
Finance, insurance, real estate ...	(H)	544.7	577.1	6,957	6,860	197.4	200.3
Depository institutions [2]..............	60	81.2	100.5	2,033	2,215	48.4	54.4
Central reserve depositories	601	0.1	0.1	31	29	0.9	0.9
Commercial banks.................	602	52.3	61.4	1,472	1,606	35.6	39.7
Savings institutions	603	21.7	22.2	417	394	8.8	8.8
Credit unions	606	3.6	12.4	51	114	1.0	2.2
Functions closely related to banking....	609	2.8	3.8	44	48	1.4	1.6
Nondepository institutions [2]	61	42.0	38.4	506	446	14.0	13.6
Federal and fed.-sponsored credit	611	0.6	0.8	14	16	0.4	0.5
Personal credit institutions	614	25.0	20.0	236	176	5.5	4.6
Business credit institutions	615	3.7	4.1	88	101	3.1	3.4
Mortgage bankers and brokers	616	10.9	12.8	153	150	4.6	5.0
Security and commodity brokers [2].......	62	25.2	26.9	411	396	26.6	27.2
Security brokers and dealers........	621	15.9	17.0	308	295	20.8	21.1
Commodity contracts brokers, dealers ..	622	1.2	1.4	15	13	0.7	0.6
Security and commodity services.....	628	7.1	8.0	76	78	4.5	5.1
Insurance carriers [2]	63	43.3	53.9	1,407	1,519	41.5	46.6
Life insurance..................	631	14.1	14.5	572	617	16.3	18.0
Medical service and health insurance [2]..	632	2.1	2.6	188	212	5.1	5.9
Accident and health insurance	6321	1.1	1.4	48	55	1.3	1.5
Hospital and medical service plans ..	6324	1.0	1.2	139	156	3.8	4.4
Fire, marine, and casualty insurance....	633	18.3	21.7	533	570	17.0	19.1
Surety insurance................	635	0.6	0.8	15	19	0.5	0.6
Title insurance	636	3.2	3.5	57	49	1.6	1.5
Pension, health and welfare funds	637	3.8	10.3	25	47	0.6	1.3
Insurance agents, brokers, and service ...	64	110.8	112.6	712	678	20.3	19.6
Real estate [2].....................	65	217.0	217.3	1,374	1,304	28.5	27.2
Real estate operators and lessors	651	95.7	88.1	509	457	8.7	7.9
Real estate agents and managers	653	72.2	80.1	585	582	13.3	13.1
Title abstract offices	654	3.1	3.5	24	24	0.5	0.6
Subdividers and developers [2]	655	19.6	21.2	140	143	3.4	3.4
Subdividers and developers, n.e.c. [3] ..	6552	10.8	11.4	88	90	2.3	2.3
Cemetery subdividers and developers .	6553	4.4	5.8	35	38	0.6	0.7
Holding and other investment offices [2]....	67	22.6	26.2	263	248	10.0	9.6
Holding offices	671	6.2	7.0	124	126	5.4	5.6
Investment offices................	672	1.0	1.3	16	18	1.0	0.8
Trusts........................	673	7.8	10.8	65	62	1.4	1.5
Educational, religious, etc. trusts.....	6732	3.6	4.4	42	37	0.9	0.8
Miscellaneous investing	679	5.0	5.9	44	37	1.5	1.5
Patent owners and lessors.........	6794	0.9	0.9	15	13	0.4	0.5
Administrative and auxiliary	(X)	2.6	1.4	251	55	8.2	2.1

X Not applicable.   [1] Standard Industrial Classification; see text, section 13.   [2] Includes industries not shown separately.   [3] N.e.c.=Not elsewhere classified.

Source: U.S. Bureau of the Census, *County Business Patterns*, annual.

No. 770. Flow of Funds Accounts—Financial Assets of Financial and Nonfinancial Institutions, by Holder Sector: 1980 to 1993

[In billions of dollars. As of Dec. 31. See also Historical Statistics, Colonial Times to 1970, series X 192, X 229, X 821, and X 835]

SECTOR	1980	1985	1986	1987	1988	1989	1990	1991	1992	1993
All sectors	13,501	22,127	25,055	27,041	29,411	32,685	33,659	36,749	39,014	41,792
Households [1]	6,399	9,665	10,652	11,338	12,289	13,729	13,901	15,380	16,348	17,230
Nonfinancial business	1,348	1,984	2,193	2,372	2,582	2,733	2,872	2,944	3,060	3,148
Farm	24	33	38	40	43	45	48	51	52	51
Nonfarm noncorporate	148	318	357	372	412	440	450	445	446	451
Nonfinancial corporations	1,176	1,632	1,798	1,961	2,127	2,248	2,374	2,447	2,562	2,646
State and local government	249	525	597	678	722	757	769	785	790	793
U.S. Government	229	372	385	371	361	369	441	499	474	468
U.S. Government-sponsored credit agencies and mortgage pools	307	692	877	1,043	1,165	1,321	1,494	1,650	1,821	1,976
Monetary authorities [2]	173	243	274	285	304	315	343	365	381	423
Commercial banking [2]	1,482	2,375	2,615	2,771	2,950	3,229	3,334	3,440	3,639	3,869
Domestic commercial banks	1,266	1,990	2,166	2,257	2,385	2,545	2,644	2,677	2,775	2,934
Foreign banking offices in U.S.	98	143	182	232	263	357	363	436	493	517
Nonbank finance	2,856	5,464	6,444	7,007	7,670	8,605	8,761	9,828	10,463	11,583
Funding corporations	13	36	42	49	69	73	74	60	59	65
Savings institutions	792	1,275	1,378	1,510	1,647	1,521	1,365	1,176	1,083	1,033
Credit unions	68	135	163	178	192	202	217	240	264	281
Life insurance	464	796	906	1,005	1,133	1,260	1,367	1,505	1,614	1,792
Other insurance	182	299	354	405	454	503	533	577	597	637
Private pension funds	504	1,093	1,291	1,367	1,422	1,706	1,629	2,056	2,145	2,336
State and local govt. retirement funds	197	398	462	509	597	722	737	860	969	1,065
Finance companies	205	365	421	484	535	571	611	634	637	658
Mortgage companies	16	25	37	24	17	23	15	26	26	34
Real estate investment trusts	5	8	8	9	11	12	11	11	14	17
Investment companies	62	240	414	460	478	566	602	814	1,042	1,427
Closed-end funds	8	8	15	21	43	52	52	72	85	96
Money market funds	76	244	292	316	338	428	498	540	544	559
Security brokers, dealers	45	156	185	138	136	237	262	333	372	466
Asset-backed securities issuers	-	39	81	131	169	227	278	329	394	458
Bank personal trusts	219	348	397	401	431	503	510	597	619	659
Rest of the world	459	809	1,018	1,176	1,369	1,628	1,745	1,859	2,039	2,303

- Represents zero. [1] Includes nonprofit organizations. [2] Includes other sectors not shown separately.

Source: Board of Governors of the Federal Reserve System, Annual Statistical Digest.

No. 771. Flow of Funds Accounts—Credit Market Debt Outstanding: 1980 to 1993

[In billions of dollars. As of Dec. 31. N.e.c.=Not elsewhere classified]

ITEM	1980	1985	1986	1987	1988	1989	1990	1991	1992	1993
Credit market debt	4,700	8,448	9,628	10,685	11,673	12,678	13,537	14,169	15,003	15,901
Government	1,045	2,151	2,427	2,653	2,857	3,067	3,369	3,709	4,073	4,393
Federal	735	1,590	1,806	1,950	2,105	2,251	2,498	2,776	3,080	3,337
State and local	310	561	621	704	753	816	871	933	992	1,057
Nongovernment	3,654	6,297	7,202	8,032	8,815	9,611	10,168	10,460	10,930	11,508
Financial [1]	579	1,249	1,580	1,880	2,120	2,363	2,559	2,710	2,942	3,186
Funding corporations	13	36	54	73	112	125	138	124	135	130
Sponsored credit agencies [2]	163	264	279	308	353	378	399	408	448	529
Mortgage pools	114	369	532	670	745	870	1,020	1,157	1,272	1,349
Commercial banks	49	79	76	82	79	77	77	65	74	80
Bank affiliates	43	106	117	131	136	143	115	112	115	122
Savings institutions	55	110	134	163	184	169	139	95	88	99
Finance companies	127	224	276	299	323	350	374	393	389	384
Asset-backed securities issuers	-	39	81	131	169	227	278	329	394	458
Foreign	197	236	238	244	251	261	285	299	314	360
Private domestic nonfinancial	2,878	4,811	5,383	5,908	6,444	6,987	7,323	7,452	7,675	7,961
By sector:										
Individuals	2,002	3,306	3,654	4,007	4,354	4,705	4,949	5,090	5,269	5,502
Households [3]	1,391	2,224	2,484	2,772	3,069	3,371	3,595	3,763	3,978	4,229
Farm	162	173	156	144	134	134	135	135	136	138
Nonfarm noncorporate	449	909	1,015	1,091	1,150	1,200	1,219	1,192	1,155	1,135
Corporations	877	1,505	1,729	1,901	2,091	2,282	2,375	2,362	2,406	2,459
By type of instrument:										
Individuals	2,002	3,306	3,654	4,007	4,354	4,705	4,949	5,090	5,269	5,502
Mortgages	1,327	2,195	2,466	2,763	3,031	3,294	3,507	3,671	3,818	3,998
Tax-exempt debt	17	81	79	78	80	82	86	95	101	95
Consumer credit	355	602	659	692	742	800	813	800	809	858
Policy loan	43	56	55	55	55	58	63	67	73	78
Bank loans, n.e.c	135	168	174	177	185	197	193	171	177	183
Other loans	126	204	221	241	261	274	288	286	290	289
Corporations [1]	877	1,505	1,729	1,901	2,091	2,282	2,375	2,362	2,406	2,459
Bonds	412	705	823	900	1,004	1,077	1,123	1,201	1,268	1,340
Mortgages	131	114	147	198	196	219	209	209	184	175
Bank loans, n.e.c	230	424	474	482	519	554	555	531	519	517
Open-market paper	28	72	63	74	86	107	117	99	107	118
Nonbank finance loans	46	94	109	127	147	160	167	161	162	159
Foreign loans	5	53	71	75	96	121	166	131	138	125

- Represents zero. [1] Includes other types, not shown separately. [2] U.S. Government. [3] Includes nonprofit organizations.

Source: Board of Governors of the Federal Reserve System, Annual Statistical Digest.

No. 772. Flow of Funds Accounts—Financial Assets and Liabilities of Financial and Nonfinancial Institutions, by Sector and Type of Instrument: 1993

[In billions of dollars. As of Dec. 31. Preliminary. A=Assets; L=Liabilities, SDR=Special drawing rights, IMF=International Monetary Fund. RP's=Repurchase Agreements. "N.e.c."=Not elsewhere classified]

TYPE OF INSTRUMENT	ALL SECTORS, TOTAL A	L	PRIVATE DOMESTIC NONFINANCIAL INSTITUTIONS — Total A	L	Households[1] A	L	Business A	L	State and local govts. A	L	U.S. GOVERN- MENT A	L	FINANCIAL INSTITUTIONS — Total[2] A	L	Commercial banking A	L	Nonbank finance[3] A	L	Federally sponsored credit agencies and mortgage pools A	L	FOREIGN SECTOR A	L
Total	41,792	33,101	21,170	10,847	17,230	4,393	3,148	5,372	793	1,081	468	3,754	17,851	17,171	3,869	3,710	11,583	11,075	1,976	1,964	2,303	1,330
Gold stock and SDR's	20	-									9	-	11	-	11	-						
IMF position	12	12									12	-									-	12
Official foreign exchange	42	42									19	-	22	-	22	-					-	42
Treasury currency, SDR certificates	30	25										25	30	-								
Checkable deposits, currency	1,216	1,251	1,051	-	798		226		27		52		92	1,251	1	783	90	120	1		22	
Time and savings accounts	2,593	2,593	2,271	-	2,031		195		45		1		284	2,593		1,674	284	920	52		37	
Fed. funds and security RP's	368	458					48		98				195	458	65	314	130	143			27	
Money market fund shares	559	559	482	-	441		41						77	559			77	559				
Foreign deposits	119	119	109	-			109						10	-			10					119
Life insurance reserves	488	488	488	-	488							11		478								
Pension fund reserves	4,776	4,776	4,776	-	4,776							331		4,445								
Interbank claims[3]	142	137											69	137	64	69	3	68			73	
Mutual fund shares	1,427	1,427	1,101	-	1,084								326	1,427	4		322	1,427				
Other corporate equities[4]	6,121	-	3,009	-	3,009								2,791	-	7	-	2,784	-			321	
Credit market instruments[5]	15,901	15,901	2,226	9,018	1,370	4,229	273	3,732	583	1,057	215	3,337	12,304	3,186	3,095	201	6,972	1,108	1,901	1,877	1,155	360
U.S. Treasury securities[6]	3,310	3,310	682	-	190		97		395		-	3,310	2,007	-	320	-	1,287	-	68	-	621	-
Federal agency securities[7]	1,899	1,899	356	-	272		15		76		-	27	1,426	-	420	-	946		56	1,872	117	-
Tax-exempt securities	1,257	1,257	502	1,257	483	95	4	114	15	1,048	-	-	755	-	100	-	656	-				-
Corporate and foreign bonds	2,180	2,180	80	1,226	80			1,226					1,827	747	100	133	1,727	614			273	207
Mortgages	4,183	4,183	312	4,174	178	3,101	70	1,072			71	-	3,800	9	947	-	1,253	9	1,600	-		-
Consumer credit	858	858		858		858	70				11		788	-	394	-	342	-	15	-		
Bank loans, n.e.c.	781	781											781	-	781	-						69
Open-market paper	580	580	225	118	167		58						337	394	101	-	75	342		5	50	32
Security credit	276	276	101	75	101	75							176	201		52	64	201				24
Trade credit	1,150	1,021	1,008	912		69	1,008	819		24			64	34		1	5					
Taxes payable	51	75						24			28	43		7								
Proprietors' equity[8]	2,221	2,221	2,221	-	2,221			2,221														
Investment in bank personal trusts	659	659	659	-	659									659				659				
Miscellaneous claims	3,622	3,277	1,484	767	253	20	1,232	746			120	7	1,400	1,738	597	667	977	977	23	87	618	765

- Represents or rounds to zero.   [1] Includes nonprofit organizations.   [2] Includes monetary authority, not shown separately.   [3] Nonbank finance liability is redemption value of shares of open-end investment companies.   [4] Assets shown at market value. No specific liability attributed to issuers of stocks other than open-end investment companies for amounts outstanding.   [5] Includes "Other loans," not shown separately.   [6] Includes savings bonds and other nonmarketable debt held by public.   [7] Issues by agencies in the budget and by Government-sponsored enterprises in financial sectors, issues backed by federally-related mortgage pools, and loan participation certificates.   [8] Asset is corporate only; noncorporate credit deducted in liability total to conform to quarterly flow tables.

Source: Board of Governors of the Federal Reserve System, *Annual Statistical Digest*.

No. 773. Flow of Funds Accounts—Assets and Liabilities of Households: 1980 to 1993

[As of **December 31.** Includes nonprofit organizations. See also *Historical Statistics, Colonial Times to 1970,* series X 114-147]

TYPE OF INSTRUMENT	TOTAL (bil. dol.)							PERCENT DISTRIBUTION		
	1980	1985	1989	1990	1991	1992	1993	1980	1990	1993
Total financial assets	**6,399**	**9,665**	**13,729**	**13,901**	**15,380**	**16,348**	**17,230**	**100.0**	**100.0**	**100.0**
Deposit and market instrument [1]	2,040	3,358	4,483	4,703	4,603	4,710	4,640	31.9	33.8	26.9
Checkable deposits and currency	259	406	513	527	578	714	798	4.0	3.8	4.6
Small time and savings deposits	1,088	1,684	1,995	2,056	2,024	1,988	1,902	17.0	14.8	11.0
Large time deposits	153	217	281	252	184	139	130	2.4	1.8	0.8
Money market fund shares	63	200	368	413	437	434	441	1.0	3.0	2.6
Credit market instruments	477	851	1,327	1,455	1,380	1,434	1,370	7.5	10.5	8.0
U.S. Government securities	217	340	487	551	446	457	463	3.4	4.0	2.7
Treasury issues	182	292	284	298	212	189	190	2.8	2.1	1.1
Savings bonds	73	80	118	126	138	157	172	1.1	0.9	1.0
Other Treasury	110	213	167	172	74	32	19	1.7	1.2	0.1
Agency issues	34	48	203	253	234	268	272	0.5	1.8	1.6
Tax-exempt obligations	80	255	442	469	504	509	483	1.3	3.4	2.8
Corporate and foreign bonds	35	16	52	95	118	116	80	0.6	0.7	0.5
Mortgages	112	125	186	170	161	168	178	1.8	1.2	1.0
Open-market paper	33	114	159	170	152	185	167	0.5	1.2	1.0
Mutual fund shares	46	192	434	452	591	765	1,084	0.7	3.2	6.3
Other corporate equities	975	1,261	1,831	1,739	2,483	2,884	3,009	15.2	12.5	17.5
Life insurance reserves	216	257	354	380	406	433	489	3.4	2.7	2.8
Pension fund reserves [2]	949	2,032	3,356	3,400	4,057	4,358	4,776	14.8	24.5	27.7
Investment in bank personal trusts	219	348	503	510	597	619	659	3.4	3.7	3.8
Equity in noncorporate business	1,864	2,050	2,508	2,441	2,345	2,275	2,221	29.1	17.6	12.9
Security credit	16	35	53	62	87	76	101	0.3	0.4	0.6
Miscellaneous assets	74	133	206	215	213	228	253	1.1	1.5	1.5
Total liabilities	**1,451**	**2,326**	**3,482**	**3,706**	**3,897**	**4,116**	**4,393**	**100.0**	**100.0**	**100.0**
Credit market instruments	1,391	2,224	3,371	3,595	3,763	3,978	4,229	95.9	97.0	96.3
Home mortgages	905	1,379	2,226	2,419	2,580	2,751	2,938	62.4	65.3	66.9
Other mortgages	32	44	123	134	144	154	163	2.2	3.6	3.7
Installment consumer credit	302	526	736	753	749	757	807	20.8	20.3	18.4
Other consumer credit	53	75	63	60	51	52	51	3.7	1.6	1.2
Tax-exempt debt	17	81	82	86	95	101	95	1.2	2.3	2.2
Bank loans, not elsewhere classified	28	34	43	33	24	35	41	1.9	0.9	0.9
Other loans	55	84	99	110	120	128	134	3.8	3.0	3.0
Security credit	25	51	43	39	55	53	75	1.7	1.0	1.7
Trade credit	22	36	51	56	61	65	69	1.5	1.5	1.6
Unpaid life insurance premiums [3]	13	15	16	17	18	20	20	0.9	0.4	0.5

[1] Excludes corporate equities.   [2] See also table 825.   [3] Includes deferred premiums.

Source: Board of Governors of the Federal Reserve System, *Annual Statistical Digest.*

No. 774. Households Owning Selected Financial Assets: 1984 to 1991

[Assets not covered: cash value of life insurance policies and equities in pension plans. Asset values are an average of balances at the end of 4 consecutive months in year shown. Based on Survey of Income and Program Participation; see Appendix III. For definition of median, see Guide to Tabular Presentation. For data on other household assets, see table 742]

ASSET TYPE	PERCENT OF HOUSEHOLDS THAT OWN ASSET TYPE			MEDIAN VALUE OF HOLDINGS FOR ASSET OWNERS (constant (1991) dollars)		
	1984	1988	1991	1984	1988	1991
Interest-earning assets at financial institutions	71.8	72.9	73.2	$4,092	$4,053	$3,607
Savings accounts	62.9	61.6	62.4	(NA)	(NA)	(NA)
Money market deposit accounts	15.7	15.2	14.9	(NA)	(NA)	(NA)
Certificates of deposit	19.1	17.7	22.0	(NA)	(NA)	(NA)
Interest-earning checking	24.8	34.3	37.8	(NA)	(NA)	(NA)
Other interest-earning assets	8.5	9.4	9.0	12,857	12,657	16,369
Money market funds	3.8	3.6	4.2	(NA)	(NA)	(NA)
Government securities	1.4	2.2	2.2	(NA)	(NA)	(NA)
Corporate or municipal bonds	2.6	2.8	3.4	(NA)	(NA)	(NA)
Other	2.8	3.3	2.2	(NA)	(NA)	(NA)
Checking accounts	53.9	48.3	46.0	593	565	525
Stocks and mutual fund shares	20.0	21.8	20.7	5,133	5,232	5,469
U.S. savings bonds	15.0	17.5	18.1	397	633	722
IRA or Keogh accounts	19.5	24.2	22.9	6,357	10,459	11,638

NA Not available.

Source: U.S. Bureau of the Census, *Current Population Reports,* P70-34.

No. 775. Households Owning Selected Financial Assets, by Selected Householder Characteristics: 1991

[See headnote, table 774]

ASSET TYPE	Total	AGE					RACE		Hispanic origin [1]
		Under 35 years	35 to 44 years	45 to 54 years	55 to 64 years	65 years and over	White	Black	
Interest-earning assets at financial institutions	73.2	66.8	75.0	74.1	73.8	78.0	76.6	46.1	53.3
Savings accounts	62.4	58.7	67.3	66.1	62.1	59.2	64.9	42.4	48.3
Money market deposit accounts	14.9	7.4	13.5	16.7	18.9	21.8	16.3	4.1	4.4
Certificates of deposit	22.0	9.6	15.7	20.9	27.4	41.2	24.2	6.2	8.2
Interest-earning checking	37.8	32.0	37.6	37.9	40.4	43.6	40.9	13.8	19.8
Other interest-earning assets	9.0	3.7	7.4	11.2	11.2	14.1	10.0	1.7	1.7
Money market funds	4.2	2.0	4.1	5.7	4.7	5.4	4.7	0.5	0.8
Government securities	2.2	0.4	1.2	2.7	2.4	4.8	2.5	0.2	0.2
Corporate or municipal bonds	3.4	0.7	2.4	3.9	4.9	6.7	3.9	0.6	0.3
Other	2.2	1.0	1.6	2.9	2.8	3.2	2.4	0.7	0.6
Checking accounts	46.0	42.2	48.8	53.7	50.1	39.8	48.2	30.7	32.7
Stocks and mutual fund shares	20.7	12.9	21.3	25.4	25.1	23.7	22.9	5.6	5.7
U.S. savings bonds	18.1	15.9	23.2	21.0	19.3	12.4	19.4	8.9	7.4
IRA or Keogh accounts	22.9	10.8	25.8	32.8	38.8	17.7	25.2	5.7	7.4

[1] Persons of Hispanic origin may be of any race.

Source: U.S. Bureau of the Census, Current Population Reports, P70-34.

No. 776. Selected Financial Institutions—Number and Assets, by Asset Size: 1992

[As of December. FDIC=Federal Deposit Insurance Corporation]

ASSET SIZE	NUMBER OF INSTITUTIONS			ASSETS (bil. dol.)		
	F.D.I.C.-insured		Credit unions [2]	F.D.I.C.-insured		Credit unions [2]
	Commercial banks	Savings institutions [1]		Commercial banks [3]	Savings institutions [1]	
Total	11,461	2,391	12,594	3,506.0	1,035.2	258.4
Less than $5.0 million	(4)	(4)	7,008	(4)	(4)	11.9
$5.0 million to $9.9 million	(4)	(4)	1,809	(4)	(4)	13.0
$10.0 million to $24.9 million	[4]2,556	[4]199	1,848	[4]41.1	[4]3.1	29.7
$25.0 million to $49.9 million	2,949	382	898	107.4	14.4	32.0
$50.0 million to $99.9 million	2,785	528	519	197.4	38.4	36.1
$100.0 million to $499.9 million	2,539	940	467	502.9	208.8	90.4
$500.0 million to $999.9 million	252	153	34	177.4	106.4	22.8
$1.0 billion to $2.9 billion	202	133	9	350.4	227.1	12.4
$3.0 billion or more	178	56	2	2,129.4	436.9	10.1
	PERCENT DISTRIBUTION					
Total	100.0	100.0	100.0	100.0	100.0	100.0
Less than $5.0 million	(4)	(4)	55.6	(4)	(4)	4.6
$5.0 million to $9.9 million	(4)	(4)	14.4	(4)	(4)	5.0
$10.0 million to $24.9 million	[4]22.3	[4]8.3	14.7	[4]1.2	[4]0.3	11.5
$25.0 million to $49.9 million	25.7	16.0	7.1	3.1	1.4	12.4
$50.0 million to $99.9 million	24.3	22.1	4.1	5.6	3.7	14.0
$100.0 million to $499.9 million	22.2	39.3	3.7	14.3	20.2	35.0
$500.0 million to $999.9 million	2.2	6.4	0.3	5.1	10.3	8.8
$1.0 billion to $2.9 billion	1.8	5.6	0.1	10.0	21.9	4.8
$3.0 billion or more	1.6	2.3	(Z)	60.7	42.2	3.9

Z Less than 0.05 percent.   [1] Excludes institutions in Resolution Trust Corporation conservatorship.   [2] Source: National Credit Union Administration, National Credit Union Administration Yearend Statistics 1992. Excludes nonfederally insured State chartered credit unions and federally insured corporate credit unions.   [3] Includes foreign branches of U.S. banks.   [4] Data for institutions with assets less than $10 million included with those with assets of $10.0 million to $24.9 million.

Source: Except as noted, U.S. Federal Deposit Insurance Corporation, Statistics on Banking, 1992.

No. 777. Banking Offices, by Type of Bank: 1980 to 1992

[As of **December 31.** Includes Puerto Rico and outlying areas. Covers all FDIC-insured commercial banks and all Bank Insurance Fund-insured savings banks as well as those State-chartered Savings Association Insurance Fund-insured savings banks that are regulated by the FDIC. Data for 1980 include automatic teller machines which were reported by many banks as branches. See also *Historical Statistics, Colonial Times to 1970,* series X 716-724]

ITEM	1980	1985	1986	1987	1988	1989	1990	1991	1992
All banking offices	**57,232**	**60,890**	**61,897**	**62,914**	**63,960**	**64,570**	**66,945**	**67,783**	**67,777**
Number of banks	15,330	14,809	14,681	14,207	13,629	13,201	12,819	12,390	11,997
Number of branches	41,902	46,081	47,216	48,707	50,331	51,369	54,126	55,393	55,780
Commercial banks, total	53,649	57,764	58,565	59,423	60,200	60,796	63,160	64,006	63,903
Member, Federal Reserve System	29,985	33,854	34,542	35,196	35,763	36,755	38,201	39,449	39,271
National banks	24,217	27,844	28,218	28,744	29,270	30,019	31,279	31,771	31,064
State banks	5,768	6,010	6,324	6,452	6,493	6,736	6,922	7,678	8,207
Insured nonmember banks	[1]23,664	23,910	24,023	24,227	24,437	24,041	24,959	24,557	24,632
Savings banks, insured	[1]3,583	3,126	3,332	3,491	3,760	3,774	3,785	3,777	3,874

[1] Includes noninsured banks.

Source: U.S. Federal Deposit Insurance Corporation, 1980, *Annual Report* and, beginning 1985, *Statistics on Banking,* annual.

No. 778. BIF-Insured Commercial and Savings Banks Closed or Assisted Due to Financial Difficulties and Problem Banks: 1980 to 1993

[Banks are closed either permanently or temporarily by order of supervisory authorities or by directors of banks. B.I.F.=Bank Insurance Fund. See also *Historical Statistics, Colonial Times to 1970,* series X 741, 748, 756, and 761]

ITEM	Unit	1980	1985	1986	1987	1988	1989	1990	1991	1992	1993
Total banks closed or assisted	Number	11	120	145	203	221	207	169	127	122	41
Assets, closed and assisted banks	Bil. dol.	7.9	8.7	7.6	9.2	52.6	29.4	15.7	63.2	44.2	3.5
Deposits, closed and assisted banks	Bil. dol.	5.2	8.1	6.6	8.6	37.2	24.1	14.5	53.8	41.2	3.1
Problem banks [1]	Number	217	1,140	1,484	1,575	1,406	1,109	1,046	1,090	863	474
Assets, problem banks	Bil. dol.	(NA)	238	336	359	352	236	409	610	465	269

NA Not available.   [1] BIF-insured commercial and savings banks considered to be problem banks by the supervisory authorities, end-of-period.

Source: U.S. Federal Deposit Insurance Corporation, *Annual Report, The FDIC Quarterly Banking Profile,* and *Failed Bank Cost Analysis Report,* 1993.

No. 779. 500 Largest Banks in the World—Number and Deposits, by Location of Bank: 1980 to 1992

[**Deposits in billions of dollars, except percent.** Data cover U.S. commercial banks and foreign banks that conduct a commercial banking business; beginning 1984, includes U.S. and foreign savings banks. Beginning 1984, covers top 500 banks in assets available. Number of banks includes banks more than 50 percent owned by other banks. To avoid double-counting of deposits, banks more than 50 percent owned by other banks are excluded from deposit totals if their parent bank consolidates their deposits]

LOCATION OF BANK	1980	1984	1985	1986	1987	1988	1989	1990	1991	1992	PERCENT		
											1980	1990	1992
NUMBER													
U.S. banks	93	115	110	102	90	107	108	96	91	88	19	19	18
Foreign banks	407	385	390	398	410	393	392	404	409	412	81	81	82
Japan	78	95	96	108	111	111	108	106	110	118	16	21	24
United Kingdom	34	22	22	20	18	18	20	22	20	18	7	4	4
Germany	38	39	39	38	42	38	37	39	41	43	8	8	9
France	28	19	20	23	23	20	20	20	18	17	6	4	3
Italy	27	26	29	31	32	29	28	31	31	29	5	6	6
DEPOSITS													
Total	**4,994**	**5,854**	**7,022**	**9,220**	**12,090**	**12,837**	**13,565**	**15,854**	**16,479**	**17,001**	**100**	**100**	**100**
U.S. banks	754	961	1,014	1,084	1,108	1,347	1,352	1,329	1,311	1,313	15	8	8
Foreign banks	4,240	4,893	6,008	8,136	10,982	11,489	12,214	14,525	15,168	15,688	85	92	92
Japan	1,131	1,750	2,179	3,350	4,936	5,333	5,236	5,888	6,213	7,097	24	37	42
United Kingdom	349	343	403	458	588	646	673	822	880	800	7	5	5
Germany	603	500	684	912	1,208	1,151	1,309	1,692	1,909	1,907	12	11	11
France	483	440	502	650	836	822	970	1,175	1,101	1,032	10	7	6
Italy	290	296	395	527	647	606	708	870	1,008	873	6	5	5

Source: American Banker-Bond Buyer, New York, NY, *American Banker Ranking The Banks,* annual, (copyright).

No. 780. Insured Commercial Banks—Assets and Liabilities: 1980 to 1993

[In billions of dollars, except as indicated. As of Dec. 31. Includes outlying areas. Except as noted, includes foreign branches of U.S. banks. See *Historical Statistics, Colonial Times to 1970*, series X 588-609, for related data]

ITEM	1980	1985	1987	1988	1989	1990	1991	1992	1993 [1]
Number of banks	14,435	14,417	13,722	13,137	12,713	12,345	11,926	11,465	10,957
Assets, total.	**1,856**	**2,731**	**3,000**	**3,131**	**3,299**	**3,389**	**3,431**	**3,506**	**3,706**
Net loans and leases.	1,006	1,608	1,779	1,886	2,004	2,055	1,998	1,977	2,097
Real estate loans. . . . . ₂. . .	269	438	600	675	762	830	851	868	923
Home equity lines of credit [2]. . . .	(NA)	(NA)	29	40	51	61	70	73	(NA)
Commercial and industrial loans . . .	391	578	589	600	618	615	559	536	539
Loans to individuals	187	309	351	378	401	404	392	385	419
Farm loans.	32	36	29	30	31	33	35	35	37
Other loans and leases.	158	288	275	265	261	242	227	216	239
Less: Reserve for losses.	10	23	50	47	54	56	55	54	53
Less: Unearned income	21	18	15	16	15	14	11	9	7
Investment securities.	325	439	521	536	559	605	691	773	837
Other	524	684	700	709	736	730	742	755	772
Domestic office assets.	1,533	2,326	2,575	2,726	2,897	2,999	3,033	3,110	3,258
Foreign office assets.	323	406	425	405	402	390	398	396	448
Liabilities and capital, total	1,856	2,731	3,000	3,131	3,299	3,389	3,431	3,506	3,706
Noninterest-bearing deposits [3]	432	471	478	479	483	489	480	541	572
Interest-bearing deposits [4]	1,049	1,646	1,858	1,952	2,065	2,162	2,207	2,158	2,182
Subordinated debt.	7	15	18	17	19	24	25	34	37
Other liabilities	260	429	466	486	526	496	486	510	618
Equity capital	108	169	181	197	205	219	232	263	297
Domestic office deposits	1,187	1,796	1,994	2,117	2,237	2,357	2,383	2,412	2,424
Foreign office deposits.	294	322	342	315	312	293	305	287	330

NA Not available. [1] Preliminary. [2] For one- to four-family residential properties. [3] Prior to 1985, demand deposits. [4] Prior to 1985, time and savings deposits.

Source: U.S. Federal Deposit Insurance Corporation, *The FDIC Quarterly Banking Profile, Annual Report*, and *Statistics on Banking*, annual.

No. 781. Insured Commercial Banks—Income and Selected Measures of Financial Condition: 1980 to 1993

[In billions of dollars, except as indicated. Includes outlying areas. Includes foreign branches of U.S. banks. See *Historical Statistics, Colonial Times to 1970*, series X 588-609, for related data]

ITEM	1980	1985	1987	1988	1989	1990	1991	1992	1993 [1]
Interest income	177.4	248.2	244.8	272.3	317.3	320.4	289.2	255.2	245.2
Interest expense.	120.1	157.3	145.0	165.0	205.1	204.9	167.3	121.8	105.8
Net interest income	57.3	90.9	99.9	107.2	112.2	115.5	121.9	133.4	139.4
Provisions for loan losses.	4.5	17.8	37.5	17.2	31.0	32.1	34.3	26.0	16.6
Noninterest income.	13.3	31.1	41.5	45.0	50.9	54.9	59.7	65.6	75.0
Noninterest expense	46.7	82.4	97.2	101.3	108.1	115.7	124.8	130.9	139.6
Income taxes.	5.0	5.6	5.4	10.0	9.5	7.7	8.3	14.5	19.9
Securities gain/loss, net.	-0.5	1.6	1.4	0.3	0.8	0.5	3.0	4.0	3.1
Extraordinary gains, net	-	0.2	0.2	0.8	0.3	0.6	0.7	0.4	2.1
Net income.	14.0	18.0	2.8	24.8	15.6	16.0	17.9	32.0	43.4
RATIOS OF CONDITION									
Return on assets [2] (percent).	0.80	0.70	0.10	0.82	0.49	0.48	0.54	0.93	1.21
Return on equity [3] (percent).	13.66	11.31	2.00	13.30	7.78	7.55	8.05	12.99	15.48
Equity capital to assets (percent). . . .	5.80	6.20	6.02	6.28	6.21	6.45	6.75	7.51	8.01
Nonperforming assets	(NA)	51.0	73.8	67.1	75.4	98.1	102.2	91.5	69.2
Nonperforming assets to assets (percent)	(NA)	1.87	2.46	2.14	2.30	2.90	2.99	2.54	1.61
Net charge-offs [4]	3.6	13.6	16.4	18.6	22.9	29.7	32.9	25.6	17.5
Net charge-offs to loans and leases (percent)	0.36	0.84	0.92	1.00	1.14	1.44	1.61	1.27	0.84
Net interest margin [5] (percent)	3.66	4.09	3.89	4.06	3.31	3.41	4.18	4.51	4.40
Percentage of banks losing money . .	3.7	17.1	17.7	14.7	12.5	13.5	11.6	6.5	4.5

- Represents or rounds to zero. NA Not available. [1] Preliminary. [2] Net income (including securities transactions and nonrecurring items) as a percentage of average total assets. [3] Net income as a percentage of average total equity capital. [4] Total loans and leases charged off (removed from balance sheet because of uncollectibility), less amounts recovered on loans and leases previously charged off. [5] Interest income less interest expense as a percentage of average earning assets (i.e. the profit margin a bank earns on its loans and investments).

Source: U.S. Federal Deposit Insurance Corporation, *Annual Report; Statistics on Banking*, annual; and *FDIC Quarterly Banking Profile*.

No. 782. Insured Commercial Banks—Selected Measures of Financial Condition, by Asset Size and Region: 1993

[In percent, except as indicated. Preliminary. See headnote, table 781]

ASSET SIZE AND REGION	Number of banks	Return on assets	Return on equity	Equity capital to assets	Nonperforming assets to total assets	Net charge-offs to loans and leases	Percentage of banks losing money
Total	10,957	1.21	15.48	8.01	1.61	0.84	4.5
Less than $100 million ..	7,788	1.15	11.79	9.77	1.05	0.34	4.8
$100 million to $1 billion .	2,787	1.18	18.30	8.75	1.30	0.50	3.8
$1 billion to $10 billion ..	327	1.34	16.56	8.15	1.43	0.92	5.5
$10 billion or more	55	1.16	16.64	7.25	1.97	1.03	-
Northeast [1]	878	1.14	15.95	7.49	2.16	1.27	8.9
Southeast [2]	1,818	1.20	15.20	8.03	1.08	0.43	4.8
Central [3]	2,411	1.29	15.91	8.12	0.93	0.51	2.8
Midwest [4]	2,706	1.46	16.62	8.69	0.99	0.57	1.7
Southwest [5]	1,937	1.39	17.11	8.26	0.92	0.28	2.4
West [6]	1,207	1.12	12.99	8.74	2.19	0.96	13.9

- Represents zero.   [1] CT, DE, DC, ME, MD, MA, NH, NJ, NY, PA, PR, RI, and VT.   [2] AL, FL, GA, MS, NC, SC, TN, VA, and WV.   [3] IL, IN, KY, MI, OH, and WI.   [4] IA, KS, MN, MO, NE, ND, and SD.   [5] AR, LA, NM, OK, and TX.   [6] AK, AZ, CA, CO, HI, ID, MT, NV, OR, Pacific Islands, UT, WA, and WY.

Source: U.S. Federal Deposit Insurance Corporation, *The FDIC Quarterly Banking Profile*, Fourth Quarter 1993.

No. 783. Insured Commercial Banks and Banks Closed or Assisted, by State and Other Area: 1993

[In billions of dollars, except as indicated. Includes foreign branches of U.S. banks]

STATE	COMMERCIAL BANKS [1]			BANKS CLOSED OR ASSISTED [2]		STATE	COMMERCIAL BANKS [1]			BANKS CLOSED OR ASSISTED [2]	
	Number	Assets	Deposits	Number	Deposits		Number	Assets	Deposits	Number	Deposits
Total	10,957	3,705.9	2,753.9	41	3.1	WV	148	19.9	16.6	-	-
U.S....	10,941	3,683.7	2,737.5	41	3.1	NC	71	104.0	70.3	1	(Z)
Northeast ...	718	1,227.2	839.6	3	1.1	SC	78	27.7	20.6	-	-
N.E	183	166.1	121.2	2	0.9	GA	399	90.1	63.3	-	-
ME	20	8.7	6.8	-	-	FL	375	150.2	123.4	-	-
NH	26	7.4	5.8	-	-	E.S.C	891	173.9	139.6	-	-
VT	20	5.8	4.8	1	0.2	KY	309	45.5	35.1	-	-
MA	61	97.7	70.0	-	-	TN	250	57.0	46.6	-	-
RI	10	13.5	10.0	-	-	AL	214	46.9	37.4	-	-
CT	46	32.9	23.6	1	0.7	MS	118	24.4	20.5	-	-
M.A.	535	1,061.1	718.4	1	0.2	W.S.C	1,856	281.1	235.0	10	0.4
NY	175	770.5	493.9	1	0.2	AR	257	26.0	22.8	-	-
NJ	99	100.3	84.4	-	-	LA	217	40.1	34.0	-	-
PA	261	190.4	140.1	-	-	OK	371	31.0	27.0	-	-
Midwest	4,808	817.9	633.3	4	0.3	TX	1,011	184.0	151.2	10	0.4
E.N.C.	2,102	566.6	433.2	1	(Z)	West	1,284	566.3	453.0	21	1.3
OH	263	132.9	96.5	-	-	Mountain ..	702	141.7	112.0	1	0.1
IN	237	61.5	49.5	-	-	MT	117	7.9	6.8	-	-
IL	958	212.0	161.2	1	(Z)	ID	21	10.9	8.3	-	-
MI	208	106.0	81.6	-	-	WY	55	5.2	4.5	-	-
WI	436	54.2	44.4	-	-	CO	322	34.4	30.0	1	0.1
W.N.C	2,706	251.3	200.0	3	0.3	NM	81	12.8	11.2	-	-
MN	573	62.3	47.9	-	-	AZ	37	37.1	29.7	-	-
IA	530	38.7	32.0	1	(Z)	UT	48	15.4	11.2	-	-
MO	490	68.5	55.7	-	-	NV	21	18.0	10.2	-	-
ND	141	8.1	7.1	-	-	Pacific....	582	424.6	341.0	20	1.2
SD	121	19.2	11.0	-	-	WA	87	41.4	34.5	1	(Z)
NE	361	24.1	20.9	-	-	OR	45	27.4	21.4	-	-
KS	490	30.3	25.5	2	0.3	CA	425	328.5	267.0	19	1.2
South	4,131	1,072.3	811.6	13	0.5	AK	8	5.0	3.8	-	-
S.A.	1,384	617.3	437.1	3	0.1	HI.	17	22.3	14.3	-	-
DE	36	85.8	34.9	-	-	AM ...	1	0.1	(Z)	-	-
MD	94	52.0	40.7	-	-	PR ...	12	21.5	15.8	-	-
DC	18	13.3	9.8	1	(Z)	GU ...	2	0.6	0.6	-	-
VA	165	74.4	57.5	1	(Z)	Pac. Is	1	0.1	(Z)	-	-

- Represents zero.   Z Less than $50 million.   [1] As of December 31.   [2] Includes Bank Insurance Fund-insured savings banks.

Source: U.S. Federal Deposit Insurance Corporation, *Annual Report; Statistics on Banking*, annual; and *FDIC Quarterly Banking Profile.*

No. 784. U.S. Banking Offices of Foreign Banks—Summary: 1980 to 1993

[In billions of dollars, except as indicated. As of December, except as indicated. Covers agencies, branches, subsidiary commercial banks, and New York State investment companies]

| YEAR | Assets | LOANS | | Deposits | COUNTRY | NUMBER OF— | | Assets | Loans, commercial and industrial | Deposits |
		Total	Business			Banks with U.S. offices	U.S. offices			
1980	200.6	121.4	59.6	80.4	**1993** [2]					
1985	440.8	247.4	108.8	236.7	Japan	55	147	387.1	103.8	212.5
1988	650.6	338.8	167.3	335.1	Canada	6	39	59.0	17.0	31.2
1989	735.7	369.8	184.3	376.1	Netherlands . . .	3	22	42.9	12.5	25.7
1990	791.1	397.9	193.3	383.9	France	12	33	84.4	11.7	40.0
1991	860.7	412.3	206.4	444.5	United Kingdom	10	35	54.6	11.0	37.0
1992	869.0	407.5	208.7	464.3	Switzerland . . .	7	17	41.6	9.9	19.1
Share: [1] 1980 . .	11.9	13.4	18.2	6.6	Italy	12	25	38.5	6.8	16.3
1985 . .	16.1	15.4	22.5	12.1	Hong Kong . . .	10	32	21.8	4.3	15.5
1990 . .	21.4	18.0	30.8	14.5	Germany	12	21	31.9	3.6	22.9
1992 . .	22.2	18.9	35.6	16.6	South Korea. . .	8	30	11.0	3.5	2.4

[1] Percent of "domestically owned" commercial banks plus U.S. offices of foreign banks. [2] As of June 30. Source: American Banker-Bond Buyer, New York, NY, *American Banker Ranking The Banks*, annual, (copyright).
Source: Except as noted, Board of Governors of the Federal Reserve System, unpublished data.

No. 785. Foreign Lending by U.S. Banks, by Type of Borrower and Country: 1993

[In millions of dollars. As of December. Covers 137 U.S. banking organizations which do nearly all of the foreign lending in the country. Data represent claims on foreign residents and institutions held at all domestic and foreign offices of covered banks. Data cover only cross-border and nonlocal currency lending. These result from a U.S. bank's office in one country lending to residents of another country or lending in a currency other than that of the borrower's country. Excludes local currency loans and other claims and local currency liabilities held by banks' foreign offices on residents of the country in which the office was located (e.g. Deutsche mark loans to German residents booked at the German branch of the reporting U.S. bank). Criteria for country selection is $2.6 billion or more]

COUNTRY	Total	Bank	Public	Private non-bank	COUNTRY	Total	Bank	Public	Private non-bank
Total [1]	**218,568**	**74,947**	**63,317**	**80,303**	Italy.	6,385	2,016	3,791	577
Argentina	9,742	936	3,194	5,613	Japan	16,124	9,413	1,901	4,811
Australia.	2,634	719	637	1,278	Mexico.	19,556	3,194	12,513	3,851
Bahamas, The.	2,859	2,399	13	447	Netherlands	4,197	1,146	1,390	1,661
Belgium-Luxembourg .	5,204	2,485	835	1,883	Netherlands Antilles. .	2,688	216	10	2,462
Brazil.	9,532	1,774	3,636	4,122	Singapore.	5,127	3,033	389	1,705
Canada	7,552	2,127	1,445	3,981	South Korea	4,355	2,305	270	1,780
Cayman Islands.	6,727	5,119	22	1,586	Spain.	3,383	1,188	1,566	629
Chile	3,422	555	1,433	1,434	Sweden	3,068	898	1,317	853
France.	9,058	5,029	2,644	1,385	Switzerland.	3,859	856	122	2,881
Germany	7,152	2,003	3,646	1,502	United Kingdom.	28,375	12,764	669	14,942
Hong Kong.	5,623	2,328	196	3,098	Venezuela	6,295	130	4,370	1,792

[1] Includes other countries, not shown separately.
Source: Board of Governors of the Federal Reserve System, Federal Financial Institutions Examination Council, statistical release.

No. 786. Federal and State-Chartered Credit Unions—Summary: 1980 to 1992

[Except as noted, as of December 31. Federal data include District of Columbia, Puerto Rico, Canal Zone, Guam, and Virgin Islands. Excludes State-insured, privately-insured, and noninsured State-chartered credit unions and corporate central credit unions which have mainly other credit unions as members. See also *Historical Statistics, Colonial Times to 1970*, series X 684-878]

| YEAR | OPERATING CREDIT UNIONS | | Number of failed institutions [1] | MEMBERS (1,000) | | ASSETS (mil. dol.) | | LOANS OUTSTANDING (mil. dol.) | | SAVINGS (mil. dol.) | |
	Federal	State		Federal	State	Federal	State	Federal	State	Federal	State
1980. . . .	12,440	4,910	239	24,519	12,338	40,092	20,870	26,350	14,582	36,263	18,469
1985. . . .	10,125	4,920	94	29,579	15,689	78,188	41,525	48,241	26,168	71,616	37,917
1987. . . .	9,401	4,934	88	32,067	17,999	105,190	56,972	64,104	35,436	96,346	52,083
1988. . . .	9,118	4,760	85	34,438	18,519	114,565	60,740	73,766	39,977	104,431	55,217
1989. . . .	8,821	4,550	114	35,612	18,858	120,666	63,175	80,272	42,373	109,653	57,658
1990. . . .	8,511	4,349	164	36,241	19,454	130,073	68,133	83,029	44,102	117,892	62,082
1991. . . .	8,229	4,731	130	37,081	21,619	143,940	83,133	84,150	49,268	130,164	75,626
1992. . . .	7,908	4,686	114	38,124	23,238	162,066	96,312	87,350	52,192	145,637	87,371

[1] For year ending September 30. A failed institution is defined as a credit union which has ceased operation because it was involuntarily liquidated or merged with assistance from the National Credit Union Share Insurance Fund. Assisted mergers were not identified until 1981.

Source: National Credit Union Adminstration, *Annual Report of the National Credit Union Administration*, and unpublished data.

No. 787. Insured Savings Institutions—Financial Summary: 1988 to 1993

[In billions of dollars, except number of institutions. As of December 31. Includes Puerto Rico, Guam, and Virgin Islands. Covers SAIF (Savings Association Insurance Fund)- and BIF (Bank Insurance Fund)-insured savings institutions. Minus sign (-) indicates debt or loss]

ITEM	INSURED SAVINGS INSTITUTIONS [1]						RTC CONSERVATOR-SHIPS [4]	
	1988	1989	1990	1991	1992 [2]	1993 [2][3]	1991	1992
Number of institutions	3,438	3,088	2,816	2,560	2,390	2,264	91	81
Assets, total	1,629	1,437	1,267	1,119	1,030	1,001	44	37
Loans and leases, net	1,001	920	816	727	648	627	24	17
Liabilities, total	1,563	1,368	1,200	1,051	956	923	48	42
Deposits	1,195	1,082	987	907	828	774	37	31
Equity capital	66	69	68	69	74	79	-4	-4
Interest and fee income	127	135	117	98	78	66	3	1
Interest expense	101	111	91	70	46	35	3	1
Net interest income	26	24	26	28	32	32	(Z)	(Z)
Net income	-5	-6	-5	1	7	7	-2	-3

Z Less than $500 million.   [1] Excludes institutions in RTC conservatorship.   [2] Excludes one self-liquidating institution. [3] Preliminary.   [4] RTC=Resolution Trust Corporation. These savings institutions are members of the Savings Association Insurance Fund.

Source: U.S. Federal Deposit Insurance Corporation, *Statistics on Banking*, annual and *FDIC Quarterly Banking Profile*.

No. 788. Insured Savings Institutions—Finances, by Asset Size: 1992

[In billions of dollars, except as indicated. See headnote, table 787. Excludes institutions in Resolution Trust Corporation conservatorship]

ITEM	Total	Less than $100 million	$100 million to $1 billion	$1 billion or more	ITEM	Total	Less than $100 million	$100 million to $1 billion	$1 billion or more
Number of institutions	2,391	1,109	1,093	189	Equity capital	75	5	24	45
Assets, total	1,035	56	315	664					
Investment securities	268	11	84	173	Interest and fee income	78	4	25	49
Loans and leases, net [1]	651	37	197	417	Interest expense	46	3	14	30
Real estate loans	619	35	188	396	Net interest income	32	2	11	19
Commercial and					Provisions for loan losses	5	(Z)	1	4
industrial loans	12	(Z)	4	8	Noninterest income	9	(Z)	2	6
Loans to individuals	37	2	11	24	Noninterest expense	26	1	8	16
Less: Reserve for					Net operating income,				
losses	9	(Z)	2	7	pretax	9	(Z)	4	5
Liabilities, total	961	51	291	619	Securities gain/loss, net	1	(Z)	(Z)	1
Deposits	828	49	270	509	Income taxes	4	(Z)	2	2
Noninterest-bearing	27	1	8	18	Net income	7	(Z)	3	4
Interest-bearing	801	48	262	491	Net charge-offs [2]	4	(Z)	1	3

Z Less than $500 million.   [1] Includes other items, not shown separately.   [2] Total loans and leases charged off (removed from balance sheet because of uncollectibility), less amounts recovered on loans and leases previously charged off.

Source: U.S. Federal Deposit Insurance Corporation, *Statistics on Banking, 1992*.

No. 789. Savings Institutions (SAIF-Insured)—Deposit Accounts and Mortgage Activity: 1980 to 1992

[See headnote, table 790]

ITEM	Unit	1980	1985	1986	1987	1988	1989	1990	1991	1992
DEPOSIT ACCOUNTS										
Number of accounts	Millions	92.2	111.5	110.1	110.6	110.1	108.3	93.9	81.3	70.8
Average balance	Dollars	5,410	7,572	8,087	8,433	8,825	8,733	8,903	9,004	9,182
Net deposit gain [1]	Bil. dol.	41.0	53.0	55.1	46.4	44.0	-15.7	-28.1	-32.3	-36.6
Net new deposits received [2]	Bil. dol.	10.7	-4.6	-3.3	-1.8	-8.4	-72.8	-80.8	-75.4	-65.0
MORTGAGE LOANS										
Number of borrowers	Millions	15.7	15.0	14.1	13.6	13.7	12.5	12.8	9.4	8.8
Average balance	Dollars	31,311	43,168	46,359	49,967	52,999	56,556	48,205	57,398	54,208
Mortgage loans closed [3]	Bil. dol.	85.5	196.8	265.5	253.4	240.3	188.7	153.4	144.1	209.7
Refinancing loans	Bil. dol.	10.6	(NA)	(NA)	71.6	42.4	30.9	21.0	27.7	59.9
Delinquent mortgage loans: [4]										
Amount	Bil. dol.	7.3	21.7	32.6	37.7	33.3	36.1	36.0	30.6	22.1
Percent of mortgage holdings	Percent	1.48	3.36	4.97	5.56	4.58	4.96	5.63	5.50	4.62

NA Not available.   [1] Net new deposits received plus interest credited.   [2] New deposits received less deposits withdrawn. [3] Reported on a gross basis. Covers permanent loans and combination construction-purchase loans.   [4] Prior to 1987, covers all mortgage loans 60 or more days delinquent. Beginning 1987, covers construction and land loans past due, permanent loans secured by one- to four-dwelling unit properties 60 or more days delinquent, and all other permanent loans past due.

Source: U.S. Office of Thrift Supervision, 1980-89, *Savings and Home Financing Source Book*, annual; beginning 1990, *Surveillance and Analysis*.

No. 790. Savings Institutions (SAIF-Insured)—Selected Financial Items and Ratios of Condition: 1980 to 1992

[As of **Dec. 31** for assets, liabilities and net worth; calendar year for other items. Includes Puerto Rico, Guam, and Virgin Islands. SAIF=Savings Association Insurance Fund. Beginning 1985, includes SAIF-insured savings and loan associations which changed to SAIF-insured savings banks. Minus sign (-) indicates either loss or outflow]

ITEM	Unit	1980	1985	1986	1987	1988	1989	1990	1991	1992
Assets [1]	Bil. dol .	620.6	1,070.0	1,163.9	1,250.9	1,350.5	1,233.6	1,085.0	920.0	831.9
Mortgage assets [2]	Bil. dol .	494.9	645.5	655.7	679.2	726.6	708.9	615.7	537.7	477.6
Mortgage-backed securities	Bil. dol .	27.3	115.5	158.2	201.8	214.6	170.5	156.2	130.8	121.6
Cash and securities	Bil. dol .	57.0	143.5	164.8	169.7	187.0	166.0	146.7	120.1	132.7
Liabilities [1]	Bil. dol .	588.0	1,023.4	1,111.6	1,204.5	1,295.3	1,225.2	1,054.2	871.4	781.2
Deposit accounts	Bil. dol .	503.2	843.9	890.7	932.6	971.7	945.7	835.7	731.9	650.0
FHLB advances	Bil. dol .	47.0	84.4	100.0	116.4	134.2	124.6	100.4	65.8	64.6
Other borrowed money	Bil. dol .	17.2	73.3	96.9	133.5	165.2	131.4	97.0	56.1	50.4
Net worth	Bil. dol .	32.6	46.7	52.3	46.4	55.2	23.6	31.0	48.6	50.7
Net worth to total assets ratio	Ratio . .	5.2	4.4	4.5	3.7	4.1	1.9	2.8	5.3	6.1
Interest expense	Bil. dol .	47.5	87.7	83.5	80.5	89.3	97.5	86.2	63.8	38.4
Net income before taxes	Bil. dol .	1.2	5.8	3.3	-5.1	-11.6	-13.4	-11.8	4.5	2.6
Net income after taxes	Bil. dol .	0.8	3.7	0.1	-7.8	-13.4	-14.1	-13.2	-2.4	2.1
Average cost of funds	Percent.	8.94	9.19	8.06	7.20	7.49	8.26	8.60	7.36	5.31
Average effective dividend rate paid.	Percent.	8.78	9.02	7.84	6.92	7.20	7.91	7.44	6.53	4.83
Average interest return on mortgages	Percent.	9.34	11.52	10.65	9.70	9.62	10.32	10.22	9.71	8.66
Return on assets [3]	Percent.	0.14	0.39	0.02	-0.64	-1.08	-1.47	-1.12	-0.24	0.25

[1] Includes other items, not shown separately.   [2] Beginning 1985, reflects deductions from asset accounts.   [3] Net income after taxes as a percent of average assets.

Source: U.S. Office of Thrift Supervision, 1980-89, *Savings and Home Financing Source Book*, annual; beginning 1990, *Surveillance and Analysis.*

No. 791. Mortgage Debt Outstanding, by Type of Property and Holder: 1980 to 1992

[In billions of dollars. As of **Dec. 31.** Includes Puerto Rico and Guam. See also *Historical Statistics, Colonial Times to 1970*, series N 273 and N 276]

TYPE OF PROPERTY AND HOLDER	1980	1983	1984	1985	1986	1987	1988	1989	1990	1991	1992
Mortgage debt, total	1,460	1,825	2,051	2,303	2,634	2,990	3,288	3,549	3,761	3,923	4,042
Residential nonfarm	1,107	1,359	1,520	1,716	1,981	2,244	2,505	2,715	2,925	3,085	3,248
One- to four-family homes	965	1,198	1,334	1,501	1,724	1,964	2,208	2,408	2,615	2,779	2,953
Savings institutions	487	482	529	554	559	602	672	669	600	538	490
Mortgage pools or trusts [1]	125	271	322	407	553	702	790	887	1,044	1,214	1,380
Government National Mortgage Assoc.	92	156	176	207	257	309	331	358	392	416	411
Federal Home Loan Mortgage Corp . .	13	57	70	100	167	206	220	266	308	352	402
Commercial banks [2]	160	183	196	213	236	276	334	390	456	484	508
Individuals and others [2]	113	161	175	206	235	247	267	319	349	368	373
Federal and related agencies	61	87	98	110	127	124	134	131	153	163	192
Federal National Mortgage Assoc. . . .	52	73	82	92	91	90	96	91	94	100	124
Life insurance companies	18	15	14	12	13	13	11	12	13	12	11
Five or more units	142	161	185	214	257	280	297	306	309	306	295
Commercial	255	352	419	482	556	659	698	754	758	759	713
Farm	97	114	112	106	96	88	85	80	78	79	80
TYPE OF HOLDER											
Savings institutions	603	627	710	760	778	860	925	910	802	705	628
Commercial banks	263	331	379	429	503	592	674	767	845	876	895
Life insurance companies	131	151	157	172	194	212	233	254	268	265	247
Individuals and others	203	271	296	341	393	414	444	502	529	559	561
Mortgage pools or trusts [1]	146	297	351	439	565	718	812	918	1,079	1,251	1,426
Government National Mortgage Assoc . . .	94	160	180	212	263	318	341	368	. 404	425	420
Federal Home Loan Mortgage Corp	17	58	71	100	171	213	226	273	316	359	408
Federal National Mortgage Association [3]	-	25	36	55	97	140	178	228	300	372	445
Farmers Home Administration [3]	32	42	45	48	(Z)	(Z)	(Z)	(Z)	(Z)	(Z)	(Z)
Federal and related agencies	115	148	159	167	204	193	201	198	239	266	286
Federal National Mortgage Association [3]	57	78	88	98	98	97	103	99	105	112	138
Farmers Home Administration [3]	3	2	1	1	48	43	42	41	41	42	42
Federal Land Banks	38	52	52	47	40	34	32	30	29	29	28
Federal Home Loan Mortgage Corp	5	8	10	14	12	13	17	22	22	27	34
Federal Housing and Veterans Admin	6	5	5	5	5	6	6	6	9	11	13
Government National Mortgage Assoc . . .	5	3	2	1	1	(Z)	(Z)	(Z)	(Z)	(Z)	(Z)
Resolution Trust Corporation	(X)	(X)	(X)	(X)	(X)	(X)	(X)	(Z)	(Z)	33	32

- Represents zero.   X Not applicable.   Z Less than $500 million.   [1] Outstanding principal balances of mortgage pools backing securities insured or guaranteed by the agency indicated. Includes other pools not shown separately.   [2] Includes mortgage companies, real estate investment trusts, State and local retirement funds, noninsured pension funds, State and local credit agencies, credit unions, and finance companies.   [3] FmHA-guaranteed securities sold to the Federal Financing Bank were reallocated from FmHA mortgage pools to FmHA mortgage holdings in 1986 because of accounting changes by the Farmers Home Administration.

Source: Board of Governors of the Federal Reserve System, *Federal Reserve Bulletin*, monthly.

No. 792. Volume of Long-Term Mortgage Loans Originated, by Type of Property, 1980 to 1992, and by Lender, 1992

[In billions of dollars. Covers credit extended in primary mortgage markets for financing real estate acquisitions]

TYPE OF PROPERTY	1980	1985	1987	1988	1989	1990	1991	1992, BY LENDER				
								Total [1]	Com-mercial banks	Mort-gage com-panies	Savings and loan	Life insur-ance com-panies
Loans, total	197.2	430.0	729.4	673.6	642.3	710.5	793.3	1,123.7	409.9	440.8	196.0	24.0
1-4 unit family home . .	133.8	289.8	507.2	446.3	452.9	458.4	562.1	893.7	232.1	437.6	184.5	0.7
New units	49.1	59.0	79.0	85.2	90.4	110.7	120.0	132.4	66.5	45.5	14.8	0.2
Existing units	84.6	230.8	428.2	361.1	362.5	347.8	442.1	761.3	165.5	392.1	169.8	0.5
Multifamily residential .	12.5	31.9	45.1	38.2	31.1	32.6	25.5	25.7	11.7	2.1	7.3	1.4
New units	8.6	10.6	14.1	9.0	8.3	6.5	6.1	4.9	2.2	-	0.4	0.4
Existing units	3.9	21.3	31.0	29.2	22.8	26.0	19.4	20.9	9.5	2.1	7.0	1.0
Nonresidential	35.9	99.4	168.7	181.6	150.0	209.5	194.6	184.1	155.3	1.1	4.1	21.2
Farm properties	15.0	9.0	8.4	7.6	8.3	10.0	11.1	20.1	10.8	-	-	0.6

- Represents zero.   [1] Includes other lenders not shown separately.
Source: U.S. Dept. of Housing and Urban Development, monthly and quarterly press releases based on the Survey of Mortgage Lending Activity.

No. 793. Characteristics of Conventional First Mortgage Loans for Purchase of Single-Family Homes: 1980 to 1993

[In percent, except as indicated. Annual averages. Refers to loans originated directly by Savings Association Insurance Fund-insured savings institutions, mortgage bankers, commercial banks, and Federal Deposit Insurance Corporation-insured savings banks. Excludes interim construction loans, refinancing loans, junior liens, and federally underwritten loans]

LOAN CHARACTERISTICS	NEW HOMES						EXISTING HOMES					
	1980	1985	1990	1991	1992	1993	1980	1985	1990	1991	1992	1993
Contract interest rate, [1]												
all loans	12.3	11.1	9.7	9.0	8.0	7.0	12.5	11.2	9.8	9.1	7.8	6.9
Fixed-rate loans	(NA)	11.9	10.1	9.3	8.3	7.3	(NA)	11.9	10.1	9.4	8.2	7.3
Adjustable-rate loans [2]	(NA)	10.4	8.9	8.1	6.6	5.8	(NA)	10.5	8.9	8.0	6.3	5.5
Initial fees, charges [3]	2.09	2.52	1.98	1.72	1.59	1.29	1.91	2.50	1.74	1.54	1.58	1.19
Effective interest rate, [4]												
all loans	12.7	11.6	10.1	9.3	8.2	7.2	12.9	11.6	10.1	9.3	8.1	7.1
Fixed-rate loans	(NA)	12.4	10.4	9.6	8.5	7.5	(NA)	12.4	10.4	9.7	8.5	7.5
Adjustable-rate loans [2]	(NA)	10.8	9.2	8.4	6.9	5.9	(NA)	10.9	9.2	8.2	6.5	5.7
Term to maturity (years)	28.1	27.0	27.3	26.8	25.6	26.1	26.9	25.5	27.0	26.5	25.4	25.4
Purchase price ($1,000)	83.2	105.0	154.1	155.2	158.1	163.7	68.3	92.7	140.3	145.8	144.1	139.6
Loan to price ratio	73.2	77.1	74.9	75.0	76.6	78.0	73.5	75.7	74.9	74.4	76.5	77.1
Percent of number of loans with adjustable rates	(NA)	51	31	25	17	18	(NA)	50	27	22	21	20

NA Not available.   [1] Initial interest rate paid by the borrower as specified in the loan contract.   [2] Loans with a contractual provision for periodic adjustments in the contract interest rate.   [3] Includes all fees, commissions, discounts and "points" paid by the borrower, or seller, in order to obtain the loan. Excludes those charges for mortgage, credit, life or property insurance; for property transfer; and for title search and insurance.   [4] Contract interest rate plus fees and charges amortized over a 10-year period.

Source: U.S. Federal Housing Finance Board, annual and monthly press releases.

No. 794. Mortgage Delinquency and Foreclosure Rates: 1980 to 1993

[In percent, except as indicated. Covers one- to four-family residential nonfarm mortgage loans]

ITEM	1980	1985	1987	1988	1989	1990	1991	1992	1993
Number of mortgage loans outstanding (1,000)	30,033	35,353	39,031	41,802	43,571	45,187	45,812	46,888	(NA)
Delinquency rates: [1]									
Total.	5.0	5.8	5.0	4.8	4.8	4.7	5.0	4.6	4.2
Conventional loans.	3.1	4.0	3.2	2.9	3.1	3.0	3.3	3.0	2.7
VA loans.	5.3	6.6	6.2	6.2	6.4	6.4	6.8	6.5	6.3
FHA loans	6.6	7.5	6.6	6.6	6.7	6.7	7.3	7.1	7.1
Foreclosure rates: [2]									
Total.	0.5	1.0	1.3	1.2	1.0	0.9	1.0	1.0	1.0
Conventional loans.	0.2	0.7	0.8	0.7	0.6	0.7	0.8	0.8	0.8
VA loans.	0.6	1.1	1.6	1.6	1.3	1.2	1.3	1.3	1.3
FHA loans	0.7	1.3	1.8	1.8	1.4	1.3	1.4	1.4	1.5

NA Not available.   [1] Number of loans delinquent 30 days or more as percentage of mortgage loans serviced in survey. Annual average of quarterly figures.   [2] Percentage of loans in the foreclosure process at yearend, not seasonally adjusted.

Source: Mortgage Bankers Association of America, Washington, DC, *National Delinquency Survey*, quarterly.

No. 795. Mortgage Delinquency Rates, by Division: 1980 to 1993

[In percent. Annual average of quarterly figures. Covers one- to four-family residential nonfarm mortgage loans. Represents number of loans delinquent 30 days or more as percentage of loans serviced in survey. Excludes loans in foreclosure. For composition of divisions, see table 26]

YEAR	U.S., total	New England	Middle Atlantic	East North Central	West North Central	South Atlantic	East South Central	West South Central	Moun-tain	Pacific
1980	4.97	3.52	6.23	6.29	4.60	4.55	5.32	4.12	4.40	4.29
1990	4.67	3.53	4.54	5.06	3.82	4.80	6.32	6.45	5.10	3.21
1991	5.01	4.14	5.05	5.20	3.99	5.53	6.69	6.41	5.01	3.45
1992	4.56	4.02	4.86	4.56	3.34	5.05	5.93	5.50	4.12	3.45
1993	4.22	3.54	4.60	4.05	3.18	4.61	5.37	5.01	3.60	3.43

Source: Mortgage Bankers Association of America, Washington, DC, *National Delinquency Survey*, quarterly.

No. 796. Home Equity Loans—Insured Domestic Commercial Banks Offering Loans and Home Equity Balances, 1988 to 1992, and by Asset-Size of Bank, 1992

[As of December 31]

ITEM	1988	1989	1990	1991	1992 Total	1992 Less than $100 million	1992 $100 to $249 million	1992 $250 to $999 million	1992 $1 billion or more
Banks offering home equity loans	4,707	4,863	5,049	5,157	5,058	2,709	1,322	694	333
Percent of all commercial banks	36	38	41	43	44	33	68	83	89
Home equity debt outstanding (bil. dol.)	40	51	61	70	73	3	5	9	56
Home equity debt as percent of consumer loans plus home equity debt:									
All commercial banks	10	12	14	16	17	9	15	16	18
Banks offering home equity loans	12	15	17	19	20	19	20	20	21
Home equity debt as percent of consumer loans plus all loans secured by homes:									
All commercial banks	6	7	8	9	9	3	6	8	10
Banks offering home equity loans	8	9	9	10	11	7	8	9	11

Source: Board of Governors of the Federal Reserve System, *Domestic Offices, Commercial Bank Assets and Liabilities, Consolidated Report of Condition*, quarterly.

No. 797. Consumer Installment Credit Outstanding: 1980 to 1993

[In billions of dollars. Estimated amounts of seasonally adjusted credit outstanding as of end of year. See also *Historical Statistics, Colonial Times to 1970*, series X 551-560]

TYPE OF CREDIT	1980	1983	1984	1985	1986	1987	1988	1989	1990	1991	1992	1993
Installment credit outstanding	298.2	369.0	442.6	517.7	572.0	608.7	663.0	724.4	738.8	733.5	741.1	790.1
Automobile paper	112.0	143.6	173.6	210.2	247.8	266.3	285.5	292.5	284.7	260.9	259.6	278.3
Revolving [1]	55.1	79.1	100.3	121.8	135.8	153.1	174.3	198.5	222.6	243.6	254.3	281.5
Other	131.1	146.3	168.8	185.7	188.4	189.3	203.2	233.3	231.5	229.0	227.2	230.3

[1] Consists mainly of outstanding balances on credit card accounts, but also includes borrowing under check credit and overdraft plans, and unsecured personal lines of credit.

No. 798. Consumer Credit—Installment Credit Finance Rates: 1980 to 1993

[In percent. Annual averages]

TYPE OF CREDIT	1980	1983	1984	1985	1986	1987	1988	1989	1990	1991	1992	1993
Commercial banks:												
New automobiles (48 months) [1]	14.30	13.92	13.71	12.91	11.33	10.46	10.85	12.07	11.78	11.14	9.29	8.09
Mobile homes (120 months) [1]	14.99	16.08	15.58	14.96	14.00	13.38	13.54	14.11	14.02	13.70	12.67	11.87
Other consumer goods (24 months)	15.47	16.68	16.47	15.94	14.83	14.23	14.68	15.44	15.46	15.18	14.04	13.47
Credit-card plans	17.31	18.78	18.77	18.69	18.26	17.93	17.79	18.02	18.17	18.23	17.78	16.83
Finance companies:												
New automobiles	14.82	12.58	14.62	11.98	9.44	10.73	12.60	12.62	12.54	12.41	9.93	9.48
Used automobiles	19.10	18.74	17.85	17.59	15.95	14.61	15.11	16.18	15.99	15.60	13.80	12.79

[1] For 1980, maturities were 36 months for new car loans and 84 months for mobile home loans.

Source of tables 797 and 798: Board of Governors of the Federal Reserve System, *Federal Reserve Bulletin*, monthly; and *Annual Statistical Digest*.

No. 799. Credit Cards—Holders, Numbers, Spending, and Debt, 1990 and 1992, and Projections, 2000

TYPE OF CREDIT CARD	CARDHOLDERS (mil.)			NUMBER OF CARDS (mil.)			CREDIT CARD SPENDING (bil. dol.)			CREDIT CARD DEBT (bil. dol.)		
	1990	1992	2000, proj.	1990	1992	2000, proj.	1990	1992	2000, proj.	1990	1992	2000, proj.
Total [1]	110	113	125	1,019	1,075	1,339	467	539	1,004	233.1	273.4	436.8
Bank	79	83	95	217	235	318	243	296	586	154.1	184.9	284.5
Oil company	83	83	91	121	117	131	26	27	29	3.3	3.4	6.9
Phone	97	100	112	141	150	195	14	16	23	1.7	1.9	2.0
Retail store	96	98	109	467	500	610	74	77	135	49.2	51.4	78.7
Travel and entertainment	23	22	25	29	28	32	89	95	190	13.1	15.3	31.5
Other [2]	28	29	35	45	46	53	20	28	40	11.8	16.6	33.3

[1] Cardholders may hold more than one type of card.   [2] Includes airline, automobile rental, Discover, and hotel cards.

Source: HSN Consultants Inc., Oxnard, CA, The Nilson Report, bimonthly. (Copyright used by permission.)

No. 800. Delinquency Rates on Bank Installment Loans, by Type of Loan: 1980 to 1993

[In percent, except as indicated. As of end of year; seasonally adjusted, except as noted. Number of loans having an installment past due for 30 days or more as a percentage of total installment loans outstanding]

TYPE OF CREDIT	1980	1984	1985	1986	1987	1988	1989	1990	1991	1992	1993
DELINQUENCY RATES											
Closed-end installment loans, total	2.82	2.09	2.32	2.26	2.47	2.49	2.64	2.57	2.58	2.43	1.77
Personal loans [1]	3.53	3.16	3.63	3.11	3.66	3.34	3.52	3.37	2.95	3.18	2.30
Automobile, direct loans [2]	1.81	1.47	1.64	1.80	1.59	1.92	2.03	2.22	2.14	2.08	1.58
Automobile, indirect loans [3]	2.29	1.77	2.02	2.09	2.20	2.46	2.61	2.59	2.66	2.33	1.65
Property improvement [4]	1.93	2.00	1.91	1.77	1.88	2.06	2.25	2.30	2.38	2.18	1.61
Home equity and second mortgage loans [5]	(NA)	1.77	2.06	1.85	2.01	1.86	1.85	1.45	2.06	1.89	1.66
Mobile home loans	3.14	2.56	2.39	3.04	2.57	3.12	2.51	3.03	2.86	4.02	3.70
Recreational vehicle loans	1.94	1.87	1.84	1.92	1.99	2.07	2.24	2.63	2.25	2.27	1.26
Marine financing [5]	(NA)	(NA)	(NA)	(NA)	(NA)	(NA)	(NA)	(NA)	(NA)	2.52	1.72
Bank card loans	2.72	2.81	2.95	3.15	2.33	2.19	2.24	2.86	3.29	2.93	2.49
Revolving credit loans	2.70	1.50	1.96	1.53	2.33	2.87	2.92	3.00	2.75	2.63	2.90
Home equity lines of credit loans (open-end) [5]	(NA)	(NA)	(NA)	(NA)	0.74	0.68	0.78	0.85	0.88	0.85	0.70
REPOSSESSIONS PER 1,000 LOANS OUTSTANDING											
Mobile home	1.57	1.29	1.21	2.50	1.58	1.77	1.63	1.19	1.62	1.30	1.21
Automobile, direct loans [2]	1.10	0.72	1.11	1.15	0.86	1.03	1.75	1.17	0.92	0.83
Automobile, indirect loans [3]	2.75	1.58	2.08	1.95	2.04	1.86	1.70	1.61	2.07	1.47	0.97
Marine financing [5]	(NA)	(NA)	(NA)	(NA)	(NA)	(NA)	(NA)	(NA)	(NA)	1.21	1.03

NA Not available.   [1] Beginning 1984, includes home appliance loans.   [2] Made directly by bank's lending function.   [3] Made by automobile dealerships; loans in bank's portfolio.   [4] Beginning 1984, own plan and FHA Title I loans.   [5] Not seasonally adjusted.

Source: American Bankers Association, Washington, DC, Consumer Credit Delinquency Bulletin, quarterly.

No. 801. Electronic Funds Transfer Volume: 1980 to 1993

[As of September, except as noted. Electronic funds transfer cover automated teller machine (ATM) transactions and transactions at point-of-sale (POS) terminals. Point-of-sale terminals are electronic terminals in retail stores that allow a customer to pay for goods through a direct debit to a customer's account at the bank]

ITEM	Unit	1980	1985	1987	1988	1989	1990	1991	1992	1993
Total number of transactions	Million	(NA)	3,579	4,108	4,581	5,274	5,942	6,642	7,537	8,135
ATM transactions	Million	(NA)	3,565	4,048	4,480	5,116	5,751	6,418	7,206	7,705
POS transactions	Million	(NA)	14	60	92	157	191	223	289	430
ATM terminals, total	1,000	18.5	60.0	68.0	72.5	75.6	80.2	83.5	87.3	94.8
Monthly transactions per terminal	Number	5,405	4,951	4,962	5,151	5,638	5,980	6,403	6,876	6,772
Shared terminals	1,000	(NA)	35.5	55.0	65.1	70.1	75.3	79.6	84.7	92.6
Proprietary terminals	1,000	(NA)	24.5	13.0	7.4	5.5	4.9	4.0	2.6	2.3
POS terminals, total	1,000	(NA)	(NA)	(NA)	(NA)	(NA)	53.1	78.1	95.2	155.0
Grocery stores	1,000	(NA)	(NA)	(NA)	(NA)	(NA)	21.5	31.8	45.1	75.3
Gasoline service stations	1,000	(NA)	(NA)	(NA)	(NA)	(NA)	18.7	21.5	26.3	50.4
Specialty stores	1,000	(NA)	(NA)	(NA)	(NA)	(NA)	10.1	13.4	16.6	22.1
Convenience stores	1,000	(NA)	(NA)	(NA)	(NA)	(NA)	2.7	3.1	7.1	7.2

NA Not available.

Source: Faulkner & Gray, Chicago, IL, Bank Network News, vol. 12, No. 13, November 25, 1993, (copyright).

No. 802. Money Stock and Liquid Assets: 1970 to 1993

[In billions of dollars. As of December. Seasonally adjusted averages of daily figures. See Historical Statistics, Colonial Times to 1970, series X 410-417 for similar data]

ITEM	1970	1980	1981	1982	1983	1984	1985	1986	1987	1988	1989	1990	1991	1992	1993
M1, total [1]	214	409	436	474	521	552	620	725	750	787	795	826	898	1,025	1,128
Currency [2]	49	115	123	133	146	156	168	181	197	212	223	247	267	292	321
Travelers checks [3]	1	4	4	5	5	5	6	6	7	7	7	8	8	8	8
Demand deposits [3]	165	261	231	234	238	244	267	302	287	287	280	278	290	340	385
Other checkable deposits [4]	(Z)	28	78	104	132	147	180	236	260	281	285	294	333	385	414
M2, total	628	1,629	1,793	1,953	2,188	2,378	2,575	2,818	2,920	3,081	3,240	3,353	3,455	3,509	3,566
M1	214	409	436	474	521	552	620	725	750	787	795	826	898	1,025	1,128
Nontransaction components in M2 [5]	414	1,221	1,357	1,479	1,667	1,826	1,955	2,094	2,170	2,294	2,445	2,527	2,558	2,484	2,437
Overnight repurchase (RP) agreements and Eurodollars [6]	1	29	38	41	57	63	76	83	86	84	80	77	81	81	90
Money market funds, general purpose and broker/dealer	(Z)	62	151	186	139	168	177	210	223	244	320	355	370	352	350
Money market deposit accounts (MMDA) and savings deposits	261	401	344	400	685	705	815	941	938	927	891	920	1,041	1,184	1,215
Commercial banks	99	186	159	190	363	389	457	534	535	542	541	582	665	755	785
Thrift institutions [7]	162	215	185	210	322	316	359	407	403	384	350	338	376	429	430
Small time deposits [7]	151	728	823	851	784	889	886	859	923	1,039	1,154	1,174	1,067	871	785
Commercial banks	79	286	348	380	351	388	386	369	392	452	535	611	603	509	469
Thrift institutions	72	442	475	471	433	501	499	490	530	587	618	563	465	362	316
M3, total	677	1,989	2,236	2,443	2,696	2,995	3,212	3,497	3,681	3,920	4,067	4,126	4,180	4,183	4,228
M2	628	1,629	1,793	1,953	2,188	2,378	2,575	2,818	2,920	3,081	3,240	3,353	3,455	3,509	3,566
Nontransaction components in M3 [5]	49	359	443	490	509	617	637	679	761	839	827	773	725	674	662
Large time deposits [8]	45	260	303	327	328	417	434	431	475	526	549	489	426	360	339
Commercial banks [8]	44	215	249	264	231	270	282	281	313	351	388	369	342	293	278
Thrift institutions	1	45	54	64	97	147	152	150	163	175	161	121	83	67	62
Term RP's and term Eurodollars [6][10]	4	84	103	115	141	141	139	164	197	227	178	158	130	127	141
Money market funds, institution only	(Z)	15	38	50	41	63	65	85	92	92	109	135	181	201	197
L, total	816	2,326	2,599	2,853	3,158	3,536	3,839	4,138	4,340	4,675	4,897	4,975	4,993	5,057	5,131
M3	677	1,989	2,236	2,443	2,696	2,995	3,212	3,497	3,681	3,920	4,067	4,126	4,180	4,183	4,228
Savings bonds	52	72	68	68	71	74	79	92	101	109	118	126	138	157	172
Short-term Treasury securities [11]	49	134	150	184	212	261	298	280	253	269	325	332	316	333	328
Bankers acceptances	3	32	40	44	45	45	42	37	45	40	41	36	24	21	16
Commercial paper [12]	34	99	105	114	133	161	207	231	261	335	346	355	335	364	386

Z Less than $500 million. [1] Currency outside U.S. Treasury, Federal Reserve Banks and the vaults of depository institutions. [2] Outstanding amount of nonbank issuers. [3] At commercial banks and foreign-related institutions. [4] Consists of negotiable order of withdrawal (NOW) and automatic transfer service (ATS) accounts at all depository institutions, credit union share draft balances, and demand deposits at thrift institutions. [5] This sum is seasonally adjusted as a whole. [6] Not seasonally adjusted. [7] Issued in amounts of less than $100,000. Includes retail repurchase agreements. Excludes individual retirement accounts (IRA's) and Keogh accounts. [8] Issued in amounts of $100,000 or more. Excludes those booked at international banking facilities. [9] U.S. Treasury bills and coupons with remaining maturities of less than 12 months held by other than depository institutions, Federal Reserve banks, money market mutual funds, and foreign entities. [10] Excludes those held by depository institutions and money market mutual funds. [11] Excludes those held by depository institutions and official institutions. [12] Excludes commercial paper held by money market mutual funds.

Source: Board of Governors of the Federal Reserve System, Federal Reserve Bulletin, monthly, and Money Stock, Liquid Assets, and Debt Measures, Federal Reserve Statistical Release H.6, weekly.

No. 803. Bank Debits and Deposit Turnover: 1980 to 1992

[Debits in trillions of dollars; turnover as ratio of debits to deposits. Annual averages of monthly data]

ITEM	1980	1982	1983	1984	1985	1986	1987	1988	1989	1990	1991	1992
Debits to—												
Demand deposits, all banks [1]	63.1	96.5	112.3	131.6	156.3	188.8	214.9	219.2	256.2	277.6	278.0	316.0
Major New York City banks	25.3	39.8	47.6	57.3	70.7	91.6	110.4	115.5	129.7	131.9	137.4	165.7
Other banks.	37.9	56.7	64.7	74.2	85.6	97.1	104.5	103.7	126.5	145.7	140.5	150.3
Other checkable deposits [2] .	0.2	1.0	1.4	1.6	1.8	2.2	2.2	2.5	2.9	3.4	3.6	3.8
Money market deposit accounts	(NA)	(NA)	0.6	0.9	1.2	1.6	1.9	2.3	2.7	2.9	[3]3.3	[3]3.3
Savings deposits	(NA)	(NA)	0.5	0.4	0.4	0.4	0.5	0.5	0.6	0.6	(³)	(³)
Deposit turnover:												
Demand deposits, all banks [1]	203	343	386	441	501	557	608	620	734	799	804	833
Major New York City banks	816	1,354	1,522	1,840	2,200	2,500	2,670	2,904	3,435	3,831	4,279	4,805
Other banks.	135	225	249	278	306	322	335	331	406	466	448	436

NA Not available.   [1] Represents accounts of individuals, partnerships, and corporations and of States and political subdivisions at insured commercial banks.   [2] Accounts authorized for negotiable orders of withdrawal (NOW) and accounts authorized for automatic transfer to demand deposits (ATS).   [3] Beginning 1991, savings deposits included in money market deposit accounts.

Source: Board of Governors of the Federal Reserve System, *Federal Reserve Bulletin*, monthly, and *Annual Statistical Digest*.

No. 804. Selected Time Deposits and Other Accounts at Insured Commercial Banks— Deposits and Interest Rates: 1985 to 1993

[As of **December**. Estimates based on data collected from a sample of about 500 banks]

TYPE OF DEPOSIT	AMOUNT OUTSTANDING (bil. dol.)						ANNUAL EFFECTIVE YIELD (percent)					
	1985	1989	1990	1991	1992	1993	1985	1989	1990	1991	1992	1993
NOW accounts [1]	44.5	196.8	209.2	244.5	286.5	305.3	6.16	5.02	4.93	3.76	2.33	1.86
Savings deposits	(NA)	532.5	571.5	652.5	740.8	766.4	(NA)	6.10	5.83	4.30	2.88	2.46
Interest-bearing time deposits: [2]												
7-91 day	26.3	45.0	50.2	46.5	38.5	29.5	7.31	7.64	6.94	4.18	2.90	2.05
92-182 day	147.8	152.6	167.6	158.0	127.8	109.6	7.50	7.83	7.19	4.42	3.16	2.91
183 day-1 year	66.1	177.2	220.8	209.7	163.1	146.3	7.77	7.86	7.33	4.59	3.37	3.14
1-2½ year	81.2	125.3	150.0	172.3	153.0	140.1	8.23	7.88	7.42	4.95	3.88	3.55
2½ year or more	115.4	128.8	138.1	157.3	169.7	182.3	8.73	7.86	7.53	5.52	4.77	4.29
All IRA and Keogh Plan deposits.	59.4	109.1	131.2	147.9	147.4	144.0	(NA)	(NA)	(NA)	(NA)	(NA)	(NA)

NA Not available.   [1] Negotiable order of withdrawal accounts containing an agreement between depositor and depository such that some or all funds deposited are eligible to earn more than 5.25 percent. As of January 1, 1986, interest rate ceilings were removed from all NOW accounts. Beginning with the December 1989 data the NOW accounts category includes all NOW accounts, including those accounts which were subject to a 5.25 percent regulatory interest rate restriction prior to January 1, 1986. Estimates for NOW accounts beginning in December 1989 are based on reports of deposits.   [2] All interest-bearing time deposits and open account time deposits with balances of less than $100,000, including those held in IRA's and Keogh Plan deposits.

Source: Board of Governors of the Federal Reserve System, *Money Stock, Liquid Assets, and Debt Measures, Federal Reserve Statistical Release H.6*, Special Supplementary Table, Monthly Survey of Selected Deposits, monthly.

No. 805. Commercial Paper Outstanding, by Type of Company: 1980 to 1993

[In **billions of dollars**. As of **December 31**. Seasonally adjusted. Commercial paper is an unsecured promissory note having a fixed maturity of no more than 270 days]

TYPE OF COMPANY	1980	1984	1985	1986	1987	1988	1989	1990	1991	1992	1993
All issuers	124.4	237.6	298.8	330.0	359.0	458.5	525.8	562.7	531.7	549.4	555.1
Financial companies [1] [2]	87.7	167.0	213.8	252.9	277.1	354.7	394.6	414.7	397.2	401.1	399.3
Dealer-placed paper [2]	19.9	56.5	78.4	101.1	102.7	159.8	183.6	214.7	213.8	228.3	218.9
Directly-placed paper [3]	67.8	110.5	135.3	151.8	174.3	194.9	210.9	200.0	183.4	172.8	180.4
Nonfinancial companies [4]	36.7	70.6	85.0	77.1	81.9	103.8	131.3	147.9	134.5	148.4	155.7

[1] Institutions engaged primarily in activities such as, but not limited to, commercial, savings, and mortgage banking; sales, personal, and mortgage financing; factoring, finance leasing, and other business lending; insurance underwriting; and other investment activities.   [2] Includes all financial company paper sold by dealers in the open market.   [3] As reported by financial companies that place their paper directly with investors.   [4] Includes public utilities and firms engaged primarily in such activities as communications, construction, manufacturing, mining, wholesale and retail trade, transportation, and services.

No. 806. Federal Reserve Bank of New York—Discount Rates: 1980 to 1994

[**Percent per year**. Rates for short-term adjustment credit. For rates applicable to other types of discount window credit, see source. See also *Historical Statistics, Colonial Times to 1970*, series X 454-455]

EFFECTIVE DATE	Rate	EFFECTIVE DATE	Rate	EFFECTIVE DATE	Rate	EFFECTIVE DATE	Rate
1980: [1] Feb. 15	13	Dec. 4	12	Nov. 21	8½	**1989:** Feb. 24	7
May 30	12	**1982:** July 20	11½	Dec. 24	8	**1990:** Dec. 19	6½
June 13	11	Aug. 2	11	**1985:** May 20	7½	**1991:** Feb. 1	6
July 28	10	Aug. 16	10½	**1986:** March 7	7	April 30	5½
Sept. 26	11	Aug. 27	10	April 21	6½	Sept. 13	5
Nov. 17	12	Oct. 12	9½	July 11	6	Nov. 6	4½
Dec. 5	13	Nov. 22	9	Aug. 21	5½	Dec. 20	3½
1981: [1] May 5	14	Dec. 15	8½	**1987:** Sept. 4	6	**1992:** July 2	3
Nov. 2	13	**1984:** April 9	9	**1988:** Aug. 9	6½	In effect, **May 2, '94**. .	3

[1] The discount rates for 1980 and 1981 do not include the surcharge applied to frequent borrowings by large institutions. The surcharge reached 3 percent in 1980 and 4 percent in 1981. Surcharge was eliminated in Nov. 1981.

Source of tables 805 and 806: Board of Governors of the Federal Reserve System, *Federal Reserve Bulletin*, monthly, and *Annual Statistical Digest*.

No. 807. Money Market Interest Rates and Mortgage Rates: 1970 to 1993

[Percent per year. Annual averages of monthly data, except as indicated. See also *Historical Statistics, Colonial Times to 1970*, series X 444-453]

TYPE	1970	1975	1980	1981	1982	1983	1984	1985	1986	1987	1988	1989	1990	1991	1992	1993
Federal funds, effective rate [1,2]	7.17	5.82	13.35	16.39	12.24	9.09	10.23	8.10	6.80	6.66	7.57	9.21	8.10	5.69	3.52	3.02
Commercial paper, 3-month [1,2]	(NA)	6.25	12.61	15.34	11.90	8.88	10.12	7.95	6.49	6.82	7.66	8.99	8.06	5.87	3.75	3.22
Commercial paper, 6-month [1,2]	7.71	6.32	12.24	14.77	11.89	8.90	10.18	8.00	6.39	6.85	7.68	8.80	7.95	5.85	3.80	3.30
Prime rate charged by banks	7.91	7.86	15.26	18.87	14.85	10.79	12.04	9.93	8.33	8.21	9.32	10.87	10.01	8.46	6.25	6.00
Eurodollar deposits, 3-month	8.52	7.03	14.00	16.79	13.12	9.57	10.75	8.27	6.70	7.07	7.85	9.16	8.16	5.86	3.70	3.18
Finance paper, 3-month [2,3]	7.18	6.15	11.45	14.09	11.24	8.71	9.75	7.77	6.38	6.54	7.38	8.72	7.87	5.71	3.65	3.16
Finance paper, 6-month [2,3]	7.20	6.16	11.25	13.74	11.20	8.70	9.67	7.74	6.31	6.37	7.14	8.16	7.53	5.60	3.63	3.15
Bankers acceptances, 3-month [2,4]	7.23	6.29	12.67	15.34	11.89	8.91	10.17	7.91	6.38	6.75	7.56	8.87	7.93	5.70	3.62	3.13
Bankers acceptances, 6-month [2,4]	(NA)	(NA)	12.20	14.68	11.83	8.92	10.21	7.95	6.28	6.78	7.60	8.67	7.80	5.67	3.67	3.21
Large negotiable CD's, 3-month, secondary market [5]	7.56	6.44	13.07	15.91	12.27	9.07	10.37	8.05	6.52	6.86	7.73	9.09	8.15	5.83	3.68	3.17
Taxable money market funds [5]	(NA)	6.36	12.68	16.82	12.23	8.58	10.04	7.71	6.26	6.12	7.11	8.87	7.82	5.71	3.37	2.70
Certificates of deposit (CD's): [6]																
6-month	(NA)	(NA)	(NA)	(NA)	(NA)	(NA)	9.99	7.83	6.51	6.47	7.18	8.34	7.35	5.67	3.46	2.84
1-year	(NA)	(NA)	(NA)	(NA)	(NA)	(NA)	10.37	8.29	6.75	6.77	7.47	8.41	7.42	5.88	3.72	3.12
2½-year	(NA)	(NA)	(NA)	(NA)	(NA)	(NA)	10.82	9.00	7.13	7.16	7.77	8.33	7.52	6.29	4.47	3.73
5-year	(NA)	(NA)	(NA)	(NA)	(NA)	10.06	11.25	9.66	7.60	7.66	8.11	8.30	7.71	6.83	5.62	4.88
U.S. Government securities: Secondary market [7]																
3-month Treasury bill	6.39	5.78	11.39	14.04	10.60	8.62	9.54	7.47	5.97	5.78	6.67	8.11	7.50	5.38	3.43	3.00
6-month Treasury bill	6.48	6.09	11.32	13.81	11.06	8.74	9.78	7.65	6.02	6.03	6.91	8.03	7.46	5.44	3.54	3.12
1-year Treasury bill	6.48	6.28	10.85	13.16	11.07	8.80	9.94	7.81	6.07	6.33	7.13	7.92	7.35	5.52	3.71	3.29
Auction average: [8]																
3-month Treasury bill	6.46	5.84	11.51	14.03	10.69	8.63	9.35	7.47	5.98	5.82	6.68	8.12	7.51	5.42	3.45	3.02
6-month Treasury bill	6.56	6.12	11.37	13.78	11.08	8.75	9.77	7.64	6.03	6.05	6.92	8.04	7.47	5.49	3.57	3.14
1-year Treasury bill	6.39	6.37	10.75	13.16	11.10	8.86	9.91	7.76	6.07	6.33	7.17	7.91	7.36	5.54	3.75	3.33
Home mortgages: HUD series:																
FHA insured, secondary market [10]	9.02	9.19	13.44	16.31	15.30	13.11	13.81	12.24	9.91	10.16	10.49	10.24	10.17	9.25	8.46	7.46
Conventional, new-home [11,12]	8.52	9.10	13.95	16.52	15.79	13.43	13.80	12.28	10.07	10.17	10.30	10.21	10.08	9.20	8.43	7.37
Conventional, existing-home [11]	8.56	9.14	13.95	16.55	15.82	13.44	13.81	12.29	10.09	10.22	10.31	10.22	10.08	9.19	8.43	7.36
Conventional, 15 yr. fixed [6]	(NA)	(NA)	(NA)	(NA)	(NA)	(NA)	(NA)	(NA)	10.05	10.04	10.14	10.05	9.67	8.76	7.80	(NA)
Conventional, 30 yr. fixed [6]	(NA)	(NA)	(NA)	(NA)	(NA)	(NA)	(NA)	(NA)	10.39	10.40	10.38	10.26	10.01	9.09	8.27	(NA)

NA Not available. [1] Based on daily offering rates of dealers. [2] Yields are quoted on a bank-discount basis, rather than an investment yield basis (which would give a higher figure). [3] Placed directly; averages of daily offering rates quoted by finance companies. [4] Based on representative closing yields. From Jan. 1, 1981, rates of top-rated banks only. [5] 12 month return for period ending December 31. Source: IBC/Donoghue, Inc., Ashland, MA, *IBC's Money Market Insight*, monthly (copyright). [6] Annual averages. Source: Financial Rates, Inc., North Palm Beach, FL, *Bank Rate Monitor*, weekly (copyright). [7] Averages based on daily closing bid yields in secondary market; bank discount basis. [8] Averages computed on an issue-date basis; bank discount basis. [9] HUD=Housing and Urban Development. Averages based on quotations for 1 day each month as compiled by FHA. [11] Primary market. [12] Average contract rates on new commitments.

Source: Except as noted, Board of Governors of the Federal Reserve System, *Federal Reserve Bulletin*, monthly, and *Annual Statistical Digest*.

No. 808. Security Prices: 1970 to 1993

[Annual averages of daily figures, except as noted. See also *Historical Statistics, Colonial Times to 1970*, series X 492-498]

CLASS OR ITEM	1970	1980	1981	1982	1983	1984	1985	1986	1987	1988	1989	1990	1991	1992	1993
Bond prices (dollars per $100 bond):															
Standard & Poor's: Municipal [1][2]	72.3	57.4	43.2	41.8	51.4	47.9	53.0	65.1	62.7	62.0	66.1	66.0	68.8	73.7	80.9
Dow Jones and Co., Inc.:[3]															
Yearly high	69.7	76.6	65.8	71.5	77.8	72.9	83.7	93.7	95.5	91.3	94.2	93.0	98.9	103.9	109.8
Yearly low	64.4	61.0	55.0	55.7	69.4	64.8	72.3	83.7	81.3	86.9	87.4	88.4	91.3	98.4	103.5
Stock prices:															
Standard & Poor's common index (500 stocks) (1941-43=10)[4]	83.2	118.7	128.0	119.7	160.4	160.5	186.8	236.3	268.8	265.9	323.1	335.0	376.2	415.7	451.6
Industrial	91.3	134.5	144.2	133.6	180.5	181.3	207.8	262.2	330.5	306.5	392.9	391.4	445.8	489.8	517.4
N.Y. Stock Exchange common stock index (Dec. 31, 1965=50):															
Composite	45.7	68.1	74.0	68.9	92.6	92.5	108.1	136.0	161.8	150.0	180.1	183.7	206.4	229.0	249.2
Yearly high[6]	52.4	81.0	79.1	82.4	99.6	98.1	121.9	145.8	188.0	159.4	199.3	201.1	229.4	242.1	260.7
Yearly low[5]	37.7	55.3	65.0	58.8	79.8	85.1	94.6	117.8	125.9	136.7	155.0	162.2	171.0	217.9	236.2
Industrial	48.0	78.6	85.4	78.2	107.5	108.0	123.8	155.9	195.3	180.8	228.0	226.1	258.2	284.3	300.1
Transportation	32.1	60.5	72.6	60.4	89.4	85.6	104.1	119.9	140.5	134.1	174.9	158.8	174.0	201.0	242.7
Utility	37.2	37.3	38.9	39.8	47.0	46.4	56.8	71.4	74.3	72.2	94.3	90.7	92.6	99.5	114.6
Finance	54.6	64.3	73.5	72.0	95.3	89.3	114.2	147.2	146.5	127.4	162.0	133.2	150.8	179.3	216.6
American Stock Exchange Market Value Index (Aug. 31, 1973=50)	48.3	150.6	171.8	141.3	216.5	208.0	229.1	264.4	316.4	295.1	356.7	338.3	360.3	391.3	438.8
NASDAQ OTC composite[6]	(NA)	202.3	195.9	232.4	278.6	247.4	324.9	348.8	330.5	381.4	454.8	373.9	586.3	677.0	776.8
Industrial	(NA)	261.4	229.3	273.6	323.7	260.7	330.2	349.3	338.9	379.0	448.0	406.1	669.0	724.9	805.8
Insurance	(NA)	166.8	194.3	226.4	257.6	283.1	382.1	404.1	351.1	429.1	546.0	451.8	601.1	803.9	920.6
Banks	(NA)	118.4	143.1	156.4	203.8	229.8	349.4	412.5	390.7	435.3	391.0	254.9	350.6	532.9	689.4
Dow Jones and Co., Inc.:[1][7]															
Composite (65 stocks)	243.9	328.2	364.6	345.4	472.2	463.1	541.6	702.5	849.5	772.2	966.9	965.2	1,048.3	1,169.9	1,381.0
Industrial (30 stocks)	753.2	891.4	932.9	884.4	1,190.3	1,178.5	1,328.2	1,792.8	2,276.0	2,060.8	2,508.9	2,678.9	2,929.3	3,284.1	3,754.1
Transportation (20 stocks)	152.1	307.2	398.6	359.8	544.6	513.8	645.1	785.4	929.2	863.8	1,194.3	1,040.2	1,170.2	1,349.6	1,762.3
Utility (15 stocks)	108.8	110.4	108.6	112.0	130.0	131.8	157.6	195.2	202.2	179.7	205.7	211.5	210.3	214.4	229.3
Wilshire 5000 equity index (Dec. 31, 1980=1404.596)[8]	[9]830.3	1,220.7	1,343.7	1,233.7	1,691.5	1,644.6	1,923.8	2,418.8	2,843.7	2,636.9	3,172.6	3,187.3	3,604.6	4,041.1	4,468.0

NA Not available.   [1] Source: U.S. Bureau of Economic Analysis, *Survey of Current Business*, monthly.   [2] Derived from average yields on basis of assumed 4 percent, 20-year bond; Wednesday closing prices.   [3] Source: Dow Jones and Co. Inc., New York, NY. A 20-bond average consisting of 10 utility bonds and 10 industrial bonds.   [4] The index includes 400 industrial stocks, 20 transportation, 40 public utility, and 40 financial stocks.   [5] Source: New York Stock Exchange, Inc., New York, NY, *Fact Book*, annual.   [6] Source: National Association of Securities Dealers, Washington, DC, *Fact Book*, annual. OTC=over-the-counter. December monthly closing values.   [7] Based on stocks listed on the New York Stock Exchange and NASDAQ/NMS.   [8] Represents return on the market value of all common equity securities for which daily pricing is available. Source: Wilshire Associates, Santa Monica, CA, releases.   [9] Represents Dec. 31, 1970.

Source: Except as noted, Board of Governors of the Federal Reserve System, *Federal Reserve Bulletin*, monthly; *Annual Statistical Digest*; and unpublished data.

No. 809. Dow-Jones Equity Market Index, by Industry: 1992 and 1993

INDUSTRY	1992	1993	INDUSTRY	1992	1993
Equity Market Index, total.........	413.29	442.19	Energy.......................	264.73	290.55
			Financial services	410.85	436.98
Basic materials	401.09	443.38	Industrial	390.48	432.52
Consumer, cyclical...............	527.62	596.43	Technology....................	320.10	361.45
Consumer, noncyclical	734.03	684.89	Utilities......................	286.74	316.02

Source: Dow Jones & Company, Inc., New York, NY, *Wall Street Journal*, January 3, 1994, (copyright).

No. 810. Bond and Stock Dividend Yields: 1980 to 1993

[Percent per year. Annual averages of daily figures, except as indicated. See also *Historical Statistics, Colonial Times to 1970*, series X 474-491]

TYPE	1980	1984	1985	1986	1987	1988	1989	1990	1991	1992	1993
U.S. Treasury, constant maturities: [1] [2]											
3-year	11.51	11.92	9.64	7.06	7.68	8.26	8.55	8.26	6.82	5.30	4.44
5-year	11.45	12.26	10.12	7.30	7.94	8.47	8.50	8.37	7.37	6.19	5.14
7-year	11.40	12.42	10.50	7.54	8.23	8.71	8.52	8.52	7.68	6.63	5.54
10-year	11.43	12.46	10.62	7.67	8.39	8.85	8.49	8.55	7.86	7.01	5.87
30-year	11.27	12.41	10.79	7.78	8.59	8.96	8.45	8.61	8.14	7.67	6.59
U.S. Govt., long-term bonds [2] [3]	10.81	11.99	10.75	8.14	8.64	8.98	8.58	8.74	8.16	7.52	6.45
State and local govt. bonds, Aaa [4] ...	7.86	9.61	8.60	6.95	7.12	7.36	7.00	6.96	6.56	6.09	5.38
State and local govt. bonds, Baa [4] ...	9.02	10.38	9.58	7.75	8.17	7.84	7.40	7.14	6.99	6.48	5.82
High-graded municipal bonds (Standard & Poor's) [5]	8.51	10.15	9.18	7.38	7.73	7.74	7.24	7.25	6.89	6.41	5.63
Municipal (Bond Buyer, 20 bonds) ...	8.59	10.10	9.11	7.32	7.63	7.68	7.23	7.27	6.92	6.45	5.58
Corporate Aaa seasoned [4]	11.94	12.71	11.37	9.02	9.38	9.71	9.26	9.32	8.77	8.14	7.22
Corporate Baa seasoned [4]	13.67	14.19	12.72	10.39	10.58	10.83	10.18	10.36	9.80	8.98	7.93
Corporate (Moody's) [4] [6]	12.75	[7]13.49	12.05	9.71	9.91	10.18	9.66	9.77	9.23	8.55	7.54
Industrials (49 bonds) [8]	12.35	13.21	11.80	9.96	9.83	9.91	9.66	9.77	9.25	8.52	7.51
Public utilities (51 bonds) [9]	13.15	[7]14.03	12.29	9.46	9.98	10.45	9.66	9.76	9.21	8.57	7.56
Stocks (Standard & Poor's): [5]											
Preferred (10 stocks) [10]	10.60	11.62	10.44	8.76	8.37	9.24	9.04	8.96	8.17	7.46	6.91
Common: Composite (500 stocks) .	5.26	4.64	4.25	3.48	3.08	3.64	3.45	3.61	3.24	2.99	2.78
Industrials (400 stocks)	4.95	4.05	3.76	3.09	2.62	3.14	3.01	3.16	2.82	2.63	2.49

[1] Yields on the more actively traded issues adjusted to constant maturities by the U.S. Treasury. [2] Yields are based on closing bid prices quoted by at least five dealers. [3] Averages (to maturity or call) for all outstanding bonds neither due nor callable in less than 10 years, including several very low yielding "flower" bonds. [4] Source: Moody's Investors Service, New York, NY. [5] Source: U.S. Bureau of Economic Analysis, *Survey of Current Business*, monthly. Annual averages of weekly figures. [6] For 1980-88 includes railroad bonds which were discontinued as part of composite in 1989. [7] The Aaa public utility average was suspended on Jan. 17, 1984 because of a lack of appropriate issues. The average corporate does not include Aaa utilities from Jan. 17 to Oct. 12. The Aaa utility average was reinstated on Oct. 12. Thirty public utility bonds were used during the period Jan. 17-Oct. 12, 1984. [8] Covers 40 bonds for 1980, 38 bonds for 1984-86, and 37 bonds for 1987 and 1988. [9] Covers 40 bonds for period 1980-88. [10] Yields based on 10 stocks, 4 yields. Issues converted to a price equivalent to $100 par and a 7 percent annual dividend before averaging.

Source: Except as noted, Board of Governors of the Federal Reserve System, *Federal Reserve Bulletin*, monthly.

No. 811. New Security Issues of Corporations, by Type of Offering and Industry Group: 1985 to 1992

[In billions of dollars. Represents gross proceeds of issues maturing in more than one year. Figures are the principal amount or the number of units multiplied by the offering price. Excludes secondary offerings, employee stock plans, investment companies other than closed-end, intracorporate transactions, equities sold abroad, and Yankee bonds. Stock data include ownership securities issued by limited partnerships]

TYPE OF OFFERING AND INDUSTRY GROUP	1985	1989	1990	1991	1992	TYPE OF OFFERING AND INDUSTRY GROUP	1985	1989	1990	1991	1992
Total	239.2	377.8	339.1	465.2	559.4	Stocks, total	35.5	57.9	40.2	75.4	88.3
Bonds, total	203.7	320.0	298.9	389.8	471.1	Preferred.......	6.5	6.2	4.0	17.1	21.3
Public, domestic..	119.7	179.7	188.8	286.9	377.7	Common.......	29.0	26.0	19.4	48.2	57.1
Private placement,						Private place-					
domestic	46.2	117.4	87.0	74.9	65.9	ment........	(NA)	25.6	16.7	10.1	9.9
Sold abroad.....	37.8	22.9	23.1	28.0	27.6						
Manufacturing ...	63.6	74.7	51.8	86.6	82.0	Manufacturing ...	5.7	9.3	5.6	24.1	22.7
Commercial and						Commercial and					
miscellaneous...	17.2	50.3	40.7	36.7	42.9	miscellaneous...	9.1	7.4	10.2	19.4	20.2
Transportation ...	6.0	10.2	12.8	13.6	10.0	Transportation ...	1.5	1.9	0.4	2.4	2.6
Public utility.....	13.6	18.6	17.6	23.9	48.0	Public utility	2.0	3.1	0.4	3.5	6.5
Communication ..	10.9	9.3	6.7	9.4	15.4	Communication ..	1.0	1.9	3.8	0.5	2.4
Real estate and						Real estate and					
financial.......	92.3	156.9	169.3	219.6	272.8	financial.......	16.2	34.0	19.7	25.5	33.9

NA Not available.

Source: Board of Governors of the Federal Reserve System, *Federal Reserve Bulletin*, monthly, and *Annual Statistical Digest*.

No. 812. Sales of Stocks and Options on Registered Exchanges: 1980 to 1992

[Excludes over-the-counter trading. See also *Historical Statistics, Colonial Times to 1970*, series X 517-530]

EXCHANGE	Unit	1980	1984	1985	1986	1987	1988	1989	1990	1991	1992
Market value of all sales,											
all exchanges [1][2]	Bil. dol	522	1,004	1,260	1,868	2,492	1,702	2,010	1,752	1,908	2,156
New York	Bil. dol	398	815	1,024	1,453	1,987	1,380	1,581	1,394	1,534	1,759
American	Bil. dol	47	32	38	63	102	59	80	65	69	71
Midwest	Bil. dol	21	62	79	102	122	87	101	74	77	87
Chicago	Bil. dol	28	35	38	56	124	64	88	81	74	64
Pacific	Bil. dol	13	31	40	55	71	49	64	53	64	66
Philadelphia	Bil. dol	11	19	23	35	48	34	50	41	39	49
STOCKS [3]											
Shares sold, all exchanges [2] . . .	Million.	15,488	30,456	37,046	48,338	63,771	52,533	54,239	53,338	58,031	65,501
New York	Million.	12,390	25,150	30,222	39,258	53,038	44,018	44,140	43,829	47,674	53,344
American	Million.	1,659	1,584	2,115	2,999	3,496	2,576	3,248	3,125	3,103	3,631
Midwest	Million.	598	1,843	2,274	2,784	3,329	2,771	2,960	2,511	2,715	3,035
Pacific.	Million.	435	1,006	1,352	1,750	2,034	1,576	1,791	1,682	2,068	2,087
Market value, all exchanges [2] . .	Bil. dol	476	951	1,200	1,705	2,284	1,587	1,845	1,612	1,776	2,033
New York	Bil. dol	398	814	1,023	1,450	1,983	1,378	1,577	1,390	1,532	1,757
American	Bil. dol	35	21	26	43	53	31	43	36	40	42
Midwest	Bil. dol	21	62	79	102	122	87	101	74	77	87
Pacific.	Bil. dol	11	28	37	51	57	41	52	45	54	58
OPTIONS [4]											
Contracts traded, all exchanges [2]	Million.	97	197	233	289	305	196	227	210	199	202
Chicago	Million.	53	123	149	180	182	112	127	130	122	121
American.	Million.	29	40	49	65	71	45	50	41	39	42
Market value of contracts traded,											
all exchanges [2]	Bil. dol	45.8	53.0	59.1	87.9	118.9	62.6	76.8	79.0	76.1	72.2
Chicago	Bil. dol	27.9	34.9	38.4	55.9	76.9	39.7	47.3	55.4	50.7	44.5
American.	Bil. dol	12.5	10.5	11.6	19.0	25.7	12.4	15.1	12.8	14.0	14.1
Options exercised:											
Number of contracts	Million.	4.9	11.9	10.5	14.5	17.0	11.4	15.6	12.1	12.0	11.6
Value	Bil. dol	20.4	55.6	49.2	72.8	85.9	51.5	85.2	55.8	53.9	50.1

[1] Includes market value of rights and warrants. Excludes the value of options exercised.   [2] Includes other registered exchanges, not shown separately.   [3] Includes voting trust certificates, American Depository Receipts, and certificate of deposit for stocks.   [4] Data for 1980 exclude nonequity options.

Source: U.S. Securities and Exchange Commission, *SEC Monthly Statistical Review* (discontinued Feb. 1989); and unpublished data.

No. 813. Commodity Futures Trading on U.S. Exchanges—Volume of Trading: 1980 to 1993

[In millions. For year ending Sept. 30]

COMMODITY	1980	1984	1985	1986	1987	1988	1989	1990	1991	1992	1993
Number of contracts traded.	82.7	148.8	152.6	183.1	213.5	241.8	267.7	272.2	261.4	289.5	325.5
Grain	18.3	15.9	10.7	10.3	10.9	15.9	15.9	17.0	16.6	17.6	16.0
Oilseeds/products	15.7	23.5	14.9	13.8	14.2	22.5	21.1	20.4	19.8	18.6	20.7
Livestock/products	11.8	8.4	7.9	8.6	8.8	9.6	8.2	8.0	6.9	6.4	5.8
Other agriculturals	7.8	6.0	5.1	6.7	5.7	9.8	10.7	11.0	9.5	9.4	10.8
Energy products	1.1	4.9	7.0	11.5	20.3	26.3	31.3	35.2	31.8	38.4	42.8
Metals	14.1	22.4	18.4	16.2	19.4	18.9	17.9	17.8	13.9	12.2	15.2
Financial instruments	10.2	51.0	72.1	96.9	114.3	117.6	136.7	135.7	134.1	148.2	185.4
Currencies	3.7	16.7	16.4	19.1	19.9	21.2	25.7	27.2	28.8	38.7	28.8

Source: U.S. Commodity Futures Trading Commission, *Annual Report.*

No. 814. Volume of Trading on New York Stock Exchange: 1980 to 1992

[**Round lot:** A unit of trading or a multiple thereof. On the NYSE the unit of trading is generally 100 shares in stocks. For some inactive stocks, the unit of trading is 10 shares. **Odd lot:** An amount of stock less than the established 100-share unit or 10-share unit of trading]

ITEM	Unit	1980	1984	1985	1986	1987	1988	1989	1990	1991	1992
Shares traded	Million .	11,562	23,309	27,774	36,009	48,143	41,118	42,022	39,947	45,599	51,826
Round lots	Million . .	11,352	23,071	27,511	35,680	47,801	40,850	41,699	39,665	45,266	51,376
Average daily shares	Million . .	44.9	91.2	109.2	141.0	189.0	161.5	165.5	156.8	178.9	202.3
High day.	Million . .	84.3	236.6	181.0	244.3	608.1	343.9	416.4	292.4	317.4	389.0
Low day.	Million . .	16.1	46.4	62.1	48.9	86.7	72.1	68.9	56.9	69.6	95.1
Odd lots	Million . .	209	238	263	329	342	268	324	282	[1]333	450
Value of shares traded . .	Bil. dol .	382	773	981	1,389	1,889	1,366	1,556	1,336	1,533	1,764
Round lots	Bil. dol. .	375	765	971	1,374	1,874	1,356	1,543	1,325	1,520	1,745
Odd lots	Bil. dol. .	8	9	10	15	15	10	13	11	[1]13	19
Bond volume [2]	Mil. dol .	5,190	6,982	9,046	10,464	9,727	7,702	8,836	10,894	12,698	11,629
Daily average.	Mil. dol .	20.5	27.6	35.9	41.4	38.4	30.4	35.1	43.1	50.2	45.8

[1] Excludes odd lot statistics for February which were not available.   [2] Par value.

Source: New York Stock Exchange, Inc., New York, NY, *Fact Book,* annual.

No. 815. Securities Listed on New York Stock Exchange: 1980 to 1992
[As of December 31, except cash dividends are for calendar year]

ITEM	Unit	1980	1983	1984	1985	1986	1987	1988	1989	1990	1991	1992
Bonds:												
Number of issuers....	Number .	1,045	1,034	1,024	1,010	951	885	846	794	743	657	589
Number of issues	Number .	3,057	3,600	3,751	3,856	3,611	3,346	3,106	2,961	2,912	1,773	1,462
Face value.........	Bil. dol .	602	965	1,084	1,327	1,380	1,651	1,610	1,435	1,689	2,219	2,009
Market value	Bil. dol..	508	898	1,022	1,339	1,458	1,621	1,561	1,412	1,610	2,227	2,044
Average price.......	Percent .	84.41	93.04	94.29	100.90	105.66	98.20	96.94	98.42	95.31	100.34	101.77
Stocks:												
Companies.........	Number .	1,570	1,550	1,543	1,541	1,575	1,647	1,681	1,720	1,774	1,885	2,089
Number of issues	Number .	2,228	2,307	2,319	2,298	2,257	2,244	2,234	2,246	2,284	2,426	2,658
Shares listed	Billion..	33.7	45.1	49.1	52.4	59.6	72.0	76.1	83.0	90.7	99.6	115.8
Market value	Bil. dol .	1,243	1,584	1,586	1,950	2,199	2,216	2,457	3,030	2,820	3,713	4,035
Average price.......	Dollars ..	36.87	35.11	32.31	37.20	36.89	30.87	32.30	36.51	31.08	37.27	34.83
Cash dividends on common stock	Bil. dol .	53.1	67.1	68.2	74.2	76.2	84.4	102.2	101.8	103.2	123.4	109.7

Source: New York Stock Exchange, Inc., New York, NY, *Fact Book*, annual.

No. 816. NASDAQ—Securities Listed and Volume of Trading: 1980 to 1993

ITEM	Unit	1980	1985	1986	1987	1988	1989	1990	1991	1992	1993
Companies listed........	Number...	2,894	4,136	4,417	4,706	4,451	4,293	4,132	4,094	4,113	4,611
Issues...............	Number...	3,050	4,784	5,189	5,537	5,144	4,963	4,706	4,684	4,768	5,393
Shares traded.........	Million....	6,692	20,699	28,737	37,890	31,070	33,530	33,380	41,311	48,455	66,541
Average daily volume ...	Million....	26.5	82.1	113.6	149.8	122.8	133.1	131.9	163.3	190.8	263.0
Value of shares traded....	Bil. dol. ...	69	234	378	500	347	431	452	694	891	1,350

Source: National Association of Securities Dealers, Washington, DC, *Fact Book*, annual.

No. 817. Foreign Purchases and Sales of U.S. Securities, by Type of Security, 1980 to 1993, and by Selected Country, 1993

[In billions of dollars. Covers transactions in all types of long-term domestic securities by foreigners as reported by banks, brokers, and other entities in the United States (except nonmarketable U.S. Treasury notes, foreign series; and nonmarketable U.S. Treasury bonds and notes, foreign currency series). Data cover new issues of securities, transactions in outstanding issues, and redemptions of securities. Includes transactions executed in the United States for the account of foreigners, and transactions executed abroad for the account of reporting institutions and their domestic customers. Data by country show the country of domicile of the foreign buyers and sellers of the securities; in the case of outstanding issues, this may differ from the country of the original issuer. The term "foreigner" covers all institutions and individuals domiciled outside the United States, including U.S. citizens domiciled abroad, and the foreign branches, subsidiaries and other affiliates abroad of U.S. banks and businesses; the central governments, central banks, and other official institutions of foreign countries; and international and regional organizations. "Foreigner" also includes persons in the United States to the extent that they are known by reporting institutions to be acting on behalf of foreigners. Minus sign (-) indicates net sales by foreigners or a net outflow of capital from the United States]

	NET PURCHASES					TOTAL TRANSACTIONS [4]				
YEAR AND COUNTRY	Total	Treasury bonds and notes [1]	U.S. Govt. corporations [2] bonds	Corporate bonds [3]	Corporate stocks	Total	Treasury bonds and notes [1]	U.S. Govt. corporations [2] bonds	Corporate bonds [3]	Corporate stocks
1980	15.8	4.9	2.6	2.9	5.4	198	97	17	9	75
1985	78.3	29.2	4.3	39.8	4.9	1,256	968	46	84	159
1987	69.4	25.6	5.0	22.5	16.3	3,315	2,649	81	104	482
1988	74.8	48.8	6.7	21.2	-2.0	3,581	3,072	56	89	364
1989	96.5	54.2	15.1	17.3	9.9	4,767	4,140	88	121	418
1990	18.7	17.9	6.3	9.7	-15.1	4,204	3,620	104	117	362
1991	58.1	19.9	10.2	16.9	11.1	4,706	4,016	124	155	411
1992	73.2	39.3	18.3	20.8	-5.1	5,282	4,444	204	187	448
1993, total [5]	111.6	24.2	36.1	29.8	21.5	6,317	5,197	263	240	617
United Kingdom.......	29.7	6.3	7.1	11.8	4.5	2,278	1,924	80	107	166
Japan...............	32.5	17.1	6.8	4.8	3.8	1,075	972	43	19	41
Canada	9.7	11.3	0.4	1.3	-3.2	385	290	6	14	75
Netherlands Antilles	4.4	0.8	0.3	1.9	1.4	240	180	8	8	45
France	1.9	-0.3	0.4	1.9	-0.1	227	199	2	6	21
Bermuda............	-0.2	-5.1	2.8	2.0	0.1	176	126	13	11	26

[1] Marketable bonds and notes. [2] Includes federally-sponsored agencies. [3] Includes transactions in directly placed issues abroad by U.S. corporations and issues of States and municipalities. [4] Total purchases plus total sales. [5] Includes other countries, not shown separately.

Source: U.S. Dept. of Treasury, *Treasury Bulletin*, quarterly.

No. 818. United States Purchases and Sales of Foreign Stocks and Bonds, 1980 to 1993, and by Selected Country, 1993

[In billions of dollars. See headnote, table 817. Minus sign (-) indicates net sales by U.S. investors or a net inflow of capital into the United States]

YEAR AND COUNTRY	NET PURCHASES			TOTAL TRANSACTIONS [1]			PURCHASES		SALES	
	Total	Bonds	Stocks	Total	Bonds	Stocks	Bonds	Stocks	Bonds	Stocks
1980...................	3.1	1.0	2.1	53.1	35.2	17.9	18.1	10.0	17.1	7.9
1985...................	7.9	4.0	3.9	212.1	166.4	45.7	85.2	24.8	81.2	20.9
1990...................	31.2	21.9	9.2	906.7	652.2	254.5	337.1	131.9	315.1	122.6
1991...................	46.8	14.8	32.0	948.6	675.5	273.2	345.1	152.6	330.3	120.6
1992...................	47.9	15.6	32.3	1,375.1	1,042.8	332.4	529.2	182.3	513.6	150.1
1993, total [2]............	128.6	60.8	67.8	2,289.7	1,729.7	559.9	895.2	313.9	834.5	246.1
United Kingdom............	60.6	44.1	16.5	1,128.7	928.6	200.1	486.3	108.3	442.2	91.8
Canada.................	14.6	9.5	5.1	251.1	224.6	26.5	117.1	15.8	107.6	10.7
Japan..................	3.3	-2.9	6.2	181.3	102.9	78.5	50.0	42.3	52.9	36.1
France.................	2.4	0.3	2.0	96.7	76.8	19.9	38.6	11.0	38.2	8.9
Hong Kong..............	4.3	-2.0	6.3	56.8	19.5	37.3	8.8	21.8	10.7	15.5
Netherlands Antilles.........	-5.4	-4.9	-0.4	52.7	41.9	10.9	18.5	5.2	23.4	5.7

[1] Total purchases plus total sales.   [2] Includes other countries, not shown separately.

Source: U.S. Dept. of Treasury, *Treasury Bulletin*, quarterly.

No. 819. Foreign Stock Market Activity—Morgan Stanley Capital International Indexes: 1990 to 1993

[Index figures shown are as of **December 31. January 1, 1970 = 100, except as noted.** Based on share prices denominated in U.S. dollars. EMG = Emerging Markets Global. GDP = Gross Domestic Product]

INDEX AND COUNTRY	INDEX			PERCENT CHANGE [1]		INDEX AND COUNTRY	INDEX			PERCENT CHANGE [1]	
	1990	1992	1993	1992	1993		1990	1992	1993	1992	1993
All Country World index [2]...........	114.3	124.2	152.4	-6.8	22.6	United Kingdom......	514	532	641	-7.2	20.6
Combined Far East Free index [3]..........	88.9	79.1	108.3	18.7	36.8	Far East index.....	2,514	2,212	2,971	-19.7	34.4
						Hong Kong........	1,547	2,814	5,907	27.4	109.9
DEVELOPED MARKETS						Japan.............	2,638	2,225	2,773	-22.1	24.6
						Singapore.........	1,166	1,494	2,472	4.4	65.5
World index [4].......	462	497	598	-7.1	20.4						
EAFE index [5].......	789	749	977	-13.9	30.5	EMERGING MARKETS					
Pacific index........	1,735	1,544	2,075	-19.3	34.4	EMG index......	176.6	234.0	387.3	2.6	65.5
						EMG Far East index.	168.2	166.9	294.8	-1.8	76.7
GDP-weighted indexes:						China; Taiwan.......	177.7	149.7	272.9	-24.6	82.3
World index [5]......	540	581	711	-6.7	22.5	India [7]............	(NA)	100.0	133.0	(NA)	33.0
EAFE index [5].....	817	786	1,035	-11.4	31.6	Indonesia..........	610.8	320.3	647.6	-2.1	102.2
Europe..........	575	536	686	-11.1	28.2	Jordan............	55.3	85.2	100.3	34.7	17.8
						Malaysia.........	170.4	203.1	421.0	15.7	107.3
United States......	306.9	406.5	435.0	4.2	7.0	Pakistan [7].........	(NA)	100.0	161.4	(NA)	61.4
Canada..........	341.9	317.7	365.7	-14.2	15.1	Philippines........	94.1	226.5	521.5	36.1	130.2
Australia...........	184.6	206.8	273.0	-13.2	32.0	South Korea........	139.4	115.6	149.2	(Z)	29.1
New Zealand [6]......	53.0	56.6	92.0	-5.2	62.6	Sri Lanka [7]........	(NA)	100.0	163.2	(NA)	63.2
						Thailand..........	205.0	315.6	624.3	30.4	97.8
Europe index.....	479	488	616	-7.4	26.4						
Austria............	1,052	802	1,017	-12.0	26.7	EMG Latin America..	236.7	657.3	979.9	15.3	49.1
Belgium..........	568	588	702	-5.3	19.4	Argentina.........	318	975	1,520	-38.9	55.9
Denmark..........	867	708	933	-29.2	31.7	Brazil............	89.2	255.8	448.4	5.0	75.3
Finland [6].........	66.3	45.4	82.4	-14.4	81.3	Chile [7]...........	214	519	682	17.9	31.4
France...........	461	539	642	1.0	19.0	Colombia [7].......	(NA)	100.0	128.3	(NA)	28.3
Germany..........	551	516	690	-11.8	33.6	Mexico...........	424	1,209	1,742	29.8	44.0
Ireland [6].........	138.4	116.2	161.5	-13.8	38.9	Peru [7]...........	(NA)	100.0	125.4	(NA)	25.4
Italy.............	205.2	149.5	189.4	-24.0	26.7	Venezuela [7].......	(NA)	100.0	86.8	(NA)	-13.2
Netherlands........	594	670	881	-1.0	31.5						
Norway...........	896	571	801	-23.4	40.3	Greece [6].........	321.9	161.6	220.4	34.2	36.4
Spain............	132.0	110.7	139.1	-24.9	25.7	Jordan...........	55.3	85.2	100.3	34.7	17.8
Sweden..........	915	858	1,163	-16.4	35.6	Portugal [6]........	66.8	50.1	64.8	-19.3	29.5
Switzerland........	567	747	1,076	15.6	44.1	Turkey...........	195.2	75.1	231.0	-49.9	207.7

NA Not available.   Z Less than 0.05 percent.   [1] Percent change during calendar year (e.g. December 31, 1991, through December 31, 1992). Adjusted for foreign exchange fluctuations relative to U.S. dollar.   [2] Comprises World index, EMG index, and Luxembourg.   [3] Comprises Far East index and EMG Far East.   [4] Includes South African gold mines quoted in London. [5] Europe, Australia, Far East Index. Comprises countries listed under Europe and Far East plus Australia and New Zealand. [6] January 1, 1988 = 100.   [7] December 1992 = 100.

Source: Morgan Stanley Capital International, New York, NY, unpublished data, (copyright).

No. 820. United States and Foreign Stock Markets—Market Capitalization and Value of Shares Traded: 1985 to 1992

[In millions of U.S. dollars. Market capitalization is the total amount of the various securities (bonds, debentures, and stock) issued by corporations]

COUNTRY	MARKET CAPITALIZATION				VALUE OF SHARES TRADED			
	1985	1990	1991	1992	1985	1990	1991	1992
United States	2,324,646	3,089,651	4,180,210	4,757,879	997,189	1,815,476	2,254,983	2,678,523
Argentina	2,037	3,268	18,509	18,633	631	862	4,824	15,679
Australia	60,163	107,611	144,867	135,451	15,736	39,333	46,835	45,771
Austria	4,602	28,320	25,575	21,750	686	37,218	14,078	9,862
Belgium	20,871	65,449	71,319	64,072	1,876	6,755	6,240	8,082
Brazil	42,768	16,354	42,759	45,261	21,464	5,596	13,373	20,525
Canada	147,000	241,920	266,874	243,018	39,905	71,278	78,160	83,448
Chile	2,012	13,645	27,984	29,644	57	783	1,900	2,029
China: Taiwan	10,432	100,710	124,864	101,124	4,899	715,005	365,232	240,667
Colombia	416	1,416	4,036	5,681	30	71	203	554
Denmark	15,096	39,063	53,573	39,451	1,274	11,106	10,578	18,845
Finland	5,855	22,721	14,234	12,202	502	5,170	1,550	2,293
France	79,000	341,696	374,093	350,858	14,672	129,013	118,218	125,052
Germany	183,766	379,399	393,453	348,138	71,572	1,083,609	818,603	892,037
Greece	765	15,228	13,118	9,489	17	3,924	2,443	1,605
Hong Kong	34,504	83,397	121,986	172,106	9,732	34,633	42,993	90,611
India	14,364	38,567	47,730	65,119	4,959	21,918	24,296	20,597
Indonesia	117	8,080	6,823	12,038	3	3,992	2,922	3,903
Italy	58,502	149,776	154,126	115,258	13,782	42,566	43,307	28,129
Japan	978,663	2,917,679	3,130,863	2,399,004	329,970	1,602,388	995,939	635,261
Luxembourg	12,658	10,456	11,308	11,936	36	87	151	118
Malaysia	16,229	48,611	58,627	94,004	2,335	10,871	10,657	21,730
Mexico	3,815	32,725	98,178	139,061	2,360	12,212	31,723	44,582
Netherlands	59,363	148,521	169,314	171,435	16,864	80,398	76,974	89,849
New Zealand	8,761	8,835	14,336	15,348	935	1,969	3,126	3,277
Norway	10,063	26,130	22,043	17,821	1,877	14,100	11,667	10,163
Pakistan	1,370	2,850	7,326	8,028	236	231	620	980
Philippines	669	5,927	10,197	13,794	111	1,216	1,506	3,104
Portugal	192	9,201	9,613	9,213	5	1,687	2,818	3,455
South Korea	7,381	110,594	96,373	107,448	4,162	75,949	85,464	116,101
Spain	19,000	111,404	147,928	98,969	3,382	40,967	40,591	39,987
Sweden	37,296	92,102	97,495	76,622	9,644	15,797	20,561	28,411
Switzerland	90,000	165,913	179,540	195,285	(NA)	(NA)	68,836	76,407
Thailand	1,856	23,896	35,815	58,259	568	22,894	30,089	72,060
Turkey	(NA)	19,065	15,703	9,931	(NA)	5,841	8,571	8,191
United Kingdom	328,000	887,599	1,003,184	838,579	68,417	280,656	317,866	382,998

NA Not available.

Source: International Finance Corporation, Washington, DC, *Emerging Stock Markets Factbook, 1993*, (copyright).

No. 821. Securities Industry—Revenues and Expenses: 1980 to 1993

[In millions of dollars]

TYPE	ALL SECURITIES FIRMS								MEMBERS OF NY STOCK EXCHANGE [1]	
	1980	1985	1987	1988	1989	1990	1991	1992	1992	1993, proj.
Revenues, total	19,829	49,844	66,104	66,100	76,864	71,356	84,890	90,694	62,840	71,552
Commissions	6,777	10,955	16,574	11,932	13,452	12,032	14,210	16,289	11,584	13,382
Trading/investment gains	5,091	14,549	14,423	16,667	16,247	15,746	22,641	21,880	16,794	18,710
Underwriting profits	1,571	4,987	5,719	5,607	4,537	3,728	6,593	8,301	7,478	9,704
Margin interest	2,151	2,746	3,493	3,155	3,860	3,179	2,771	2,695	2,624	2,928
Mutual fund sales	278	2,754	4,069	2,644	3,038	3,242	4,176	5,949	2,787	3,422
Other	3,960	13,854	21,825	26,096	26,096	35,731	33,428	34,498	21,573	23,407
Expenses, total	16,668	43,342	62,894	62,623	74,041	70,566	76,234	81,570	56,654	62,752
Interest expense	3,876	11,470	16,473	19,502	29,822	28,093	27,512	24,592	15,983	16,663
Compensation	7,619	18,112	25,583	23,418	23,740	22,931	26,916	32,117	24,163	28,005
Commissions/clearance paid	1,055	2,314	3,563	2,804	3,057	2,959	3,200	3,731	1,867	2,207
Other	4,119	11,446	17,276	16,899	17,422	16,583	18,605	21,130	14,642	15,877
Net Income, pretax	3,160	6,502	3,210	3,477	2,823	790	8,656	9,124	6,186	8,800

[1] Covers all members of New York Stock Exchange doing public business. Source: Securities Industry Association, New York, NY, *Securities Industry Association Fact Book*, annual.

Source: Except as noted, U.S. Securities and Exchange Commission, *Annual Report*.

No. 822. Mutual Funds—Summary: 1980 to 1993

[See also *Historical Statistics, Colonial Times to 1970*, series X 536-539]

TYPE OF FUND	Unit	1980	1985	1987	1988	1989	1990	1991	1992	1993
Number of funds, total	Number. .	564	1,528	2,317	2,715	2,917	3,105	3,427	3,850	4,558
Equity funds	Number. .	267	579	846	1,016	1,080	1,127	1,217	1,356	1,615
Income and bond funds [1]	Number. .	191	492	930	1,094	1,173	1,235	1,389	1,629	2,023
Money market funds, tax-exempt [2]	Number. .	10	111	153	174	201	235	267	279	292
Money market funds, taxable [3]	Number. .	96	346	388	431	463	508	554	586	628
Shareholder accounts, total	Millions. .	12.1	34.7	54.5	54.7	58.2	62.6	68.6	80.3	95.5
Equity, bond, and income funds	Millions . .	7.3	19.8	36.9	36.2	36.9	39.6	45.0	56.6	71.9
Money market funds, total [2][3]	Millions . .	4.8	14.9	17.6	18.5	21.3	23.0	23.6	23.7	23.6
Assets, total	Bil. dol . .	135	496	770	810	982	1,067	1,396	1,646	2,075
Equity funds	Bil. dol. . .	44	117	181	195	249	246	412	523	749
Income and bond funds.	Bil. dol. . .	11	95	196	191	199	202	287	381	506
Municipal bond funds	Bil. dol. . .	3	39	77	87	106	120	154	196	255
Money market funds, tax-exempt [2]	Bil. dol. . .	2	36	61	66	69	84	90	95	103
Money market funds, taxable [3]	Bil. dol. . .	74	208	255	272	359	415	453	451	462
Sales, total	Bil. dol . .	248	954	1,252	1,177	1,445	1,565	2,038	2,751	3,189
Equity funds	Bil. dol. . .	6	30	72	31	55	71	99	145	229
Income and bond funds.	Bil. dol. . .	3	65	90	44	45	50	98	165	208
Municipal bond funds	Bil. dol. . .	2	19	29	21	27	28	40	55	74
Money market funds, tax-exempt [2]	Bil. dol. . .	5	109	192	178	185	197	231	286	342
Money market funds, taxable [3]	Bil. dol. . .	232	730	869	903	1,135	1,219	1,570	2,100	2,336
Redemptions, total	Bil. dol . .	217	865	1,179	1,167	1,327	1,471	1,879	2,548	2,905
Equity funds	Bil. dol. . .	6	18	40	35	38	45	54	62	93
Income and bond funds.	Bil. dol. . .	2	11	59	45	41	39	47	82	110
Municipal bond funds	Bil. dol. . .	1	4	17	13	12	14	15	21	28
Money market funds, tax-exempt [2]	Bil. dol. . .	4	99	197	175	181	190	227	282	337
Money market funds, taxable [3]	Bil. dol. . .	204	732	866	899	1,055	1,183	1,536	2,101	2,337

[1] Includes municipal bond funds. [2] Funds invest in municipal securities with relatively short maturities. [3] Funds invest in short-term, high-grade securities sold in the money market.

Source: Investment Company Institute, Washington, DC, *Mutual Fund Fact Book*, annual, (copyright).

No. 823. Individual Retirement Accounts (IRA) Plans—Value, by Type of Holder: 1985 to 1993

[As of **December 31**. Estimated]

TYPE OF HOLDER	AMOUNT (bil. dol.)									PERCENT DISTRIBUTION		
	1985	1986	1987	1988	1989	1990	1991	1992	1993	1985	1990	1993
Total.	200	277	334	390	455	529	657	746	857	100	100	100
Savings institutions	56	69	77	90	98	95	91	85	76	28	18	9
Commercial banks	52	67	77	88	99	119	134	137	134	26	22	15
Mutual funds	32	54	72	86	112	127	169	211	284	16	24	33
Self directed	29	45	59	68	82	117	181	225	271	15	22	32
Life insurance companies. . . .	17	22	26	33	38	42	50	56	60	9	8	7
Credit unions	14	21	23	25	26	29	32	32	32	7	6	4

Source: Investment Company Institute, Washington, DC, *Mutual Fund Fact Book*, annual, (copyright).

No. 824. 401(k) Plan Assets—Summary, 1984 to 1993, and Projections, 2000

YEAR	Total assets (bil. dol.)	TYPE OF ASSET	Percent of companies offering investment option	ASSETS, 1993		FINANCIAL INSTITUTION MANAGING ASSETS	ASSETS, 1993	
				Amount (bil. dol.)	Percent distribution		Amount (bil. dol.)	Percent distribution
1984	55	Total	(X)	475	100	All defined contribution		
1985	105	Guaranteed investment				plans [2]	885	100
1986	155	account [1]	56	130	27	Insurance companies. . .	320	36
1987	190	Equity	78	75	16	Banks	275	31
1988	230	Money market.	54	35	7	Mutual fund groups	175	20
1989	270	Balanced account . . .	51	60	13	Other	115	13
1990	300							
1991	350	Bond fund	46	35	7	401(k) plans	475	100
1992	410	Company stock	22	115	24	Insurance companies. . .	160	34
1993	475	Other.	20	25	6	Banks	130	27
						Mutual fund groups	125	26
2000, proj. .	1,250					Other	60	13

X Not applicable. [1] Covers bank certificate of deposits, guaranteed investment contracts (GIC's), GIC alternatives, and insurance company participating contracts. [2] Includes 401(k) plans.

Source: Access Research, Inc., Windsor, CT, *1993 Marketplace Update*, 1993, (copyright).

No. 825. Assets of Private and Public Pension Funds, by Type of Fund: 1980 to 1993

[In billions of dollars. As of end of year. Except for corporate equities, represents book value. Excludes Social Security trust funds, see table 581]

TYPE OF PENSION FUND	1980	1985	1986	1987	1988	1989	1990	1991	1992	1993
Total, all types	949	2,032	2,397	2,601	2,848	3,356	3,400	4,057	4,358	4,776
Private funds	676	1,485	1,765	1,904	2,044	2,405	2,413	2,921	3,085	3,380
Insured	172	392	474	537	622	700	784	865	941	1,044
Noninsured [1]	504	1,093	1,291	1,367	1,422	1,706	1,629	2,056	2,145	2,336
Corporate equities [2]	231	475	565	568	641	776	703	953	1,033	1,157
U.S. Government securities	51	190	221	241	250	311	322	363	383	400
Corporate bonds [3]	78	155	178	190	204	226	236	276	281	298
Time deposits	32	90	109	127	151	188	176	229	201	211
Public funds	273	547	632	697	805	951	987	1,136	1,273	1,396
State and local government	197	398	462	509	597	722	737	860	969	1,065
Corporate bonds [3]	92	117	125	103	126	158	147	150	181	197
Corporate equities [2]	44	120	150	170	220	300	296	387	449	507
U.S. Government securities	40	124	144	169	185	198	220	242	259	274
Other	20	37	43	67	67	65	74	81	80	88
U.S. Government	76	149	170	188	208	229	251	276	304	331
Civil service [4]	74	145	163	182	200	220	241	266	292	319
Railroad retirement	3	4	6	7	8	9	9	11	12	12

[1] Covers all pension funds of corporations, nonprofit organizations, unions, and multi-employer groups. Also includes deferred profit-sharing plans and Federal Employees Retirement System (FERS) Thrift Savings Fund. Excludes health, welfare, and bonus plans. Includes other types of assets not shown separately. [2] Includes mutual fund shares. [3] Includes foreign bonds. [4] Includes U.S. Foreign Service Retirement and Disability Trust Fund and the Federal Employees Retirement System.

Source: Board of Governors of the Federal Reserve System, *Annual Statistical Digest*, and unpublished data.

No. 826. U.S. Life Insurance Companies—Summary: 1980 to 1992

[As of December 31 or calendar year, as applicable. Covers domestic and foreign business of U.S. companies. See also *Historical Statistics, Colonial Times to 1970*, series X 879 and X 890-917]

ITEM	Unit	1980	1984	1985	1986	1987	1988	1989	1990	1991	1992
U.S. companies	Number	1,958	2,193	2,261	2,254	2,337	2,343	2,270	2,195	2,065	2,005
Sales	Bil. dol.	655	1,390	1,530	[1]1,578	1,656	1,716	1,788	2,024	[1]2,014	1,881
Ordinary	Bil. dol.	461	1,074	1,187	1,178	1,267	1,287	1,343	1,368	1,403	1,395
Group	Bil. dol.	190	315	342	[1]400	388	428	444	655	[1]611	485
Industrial	Bil. dol.	4	1	1	(Z)	(Z)	(Z)	(Z)	(Z)	(Z)	1
Income	Bil. dol.	130.9	206.1	234.0	282.3	314.3	338.1	367.3	402.2	411.0	426.9
Life insurance premiums	Bil. dol.	40.8	51.3	60.1	66.2	76.7	73.5	73.3	76.7	79.3	83.9
Percent of total	Percent	31.2	24.9	25.7	23.5	24.4	21.7	20.0	19.1	19.3	19.7
Annuity considerations	Bil. dol.	22.4	42.8	53.9	83.7	88.7	103.3	115.0	129.1	123.6	132.6
Health insurance premiums	Bil. dol.	29.4	40.7	41.8	44.2	47.6	52.3	56.1	58.2	60.9	65.5
Investment and other	Bil. dol.	38.3	71.3	78.2	88.2	101.3	109.0	122.9	138.2	147.2	144.9
Disbursements	Bil. dol.	88.2	138.5	151.8	186.5	202.3	221.4	246.8	277.1	299.2	305.0
Payments to policyholders [2][3]	Bil. dol.	59.0	89.8	95.7	131.4	144.4	156.8	178.3	200.9	218.6	222.1
Percent of total	Percent	66.9	64.8	63.0	70.5	71.4	70.8	72.2	72.5	73.1	72.8
Death payments	Bil. dol.	12.9	17.6	18.5	19.6	20.7	22.4	23.5	25.5	26.4	28.0
Matured endowments	Bil. dol.	0.8	0.7	0.8	0.8	0.8	0.8	0.8	0.8	0.7	0.7
Annuity payments	Bil. dol.	7.4	18.0	19.7	17.8	20.3	21.9	26.0	28.6	31.8	32.4
Policy dividends	Bil. dol.	8.1	11.4	12.4	12.4	13.0	13.8	14.9	15.7	15.8	15.3
Surrender values [3]	Bil. dol.	6.4	14.5	15.9	49.6	53.7	58.1	73.4	90.2	101.2	100.5
Disability benefits	Bil. dol.	0.5	0.4	0.5	0.5	0.5	0.4	0.5	0.5	0.5	0.6
Commissions, expenses, etc. [3]	Bil. dol.	27.8	46.0	53.1	51.4	54.7	61.3	63.5	70.2	75.1	77.8
Dividends to stockholders	Bil. dol.	1.4	2.7	3.0	3.7	3.3	3.4	5.0	6.0	5.5	5.1
BALANCE SHEET											
Assets	Bil. dol.	479	723	826	938	1,045	1,167	1,300	1,408	1,551	1,665
Government securities	Bil. dol.	33	100	125	145	151	160	178	211	269	320
Corporate securities	Bil. dol.	227	323	374	433	502	585	664	711	789	863
Percent of total assets	Percent	47.4	44.6	45.3	46.2	48.1	50.1	51.1	50.5	50.8	51.8
Bonds	Bil. dol.	180	259	297	342	406	480	538	583	624	670
Stocks	Bil. dol.	47	63	77	91	97	104	126	128	165	193
Mortgages	Bil. dol.	131	157	172	194	214	233	254	270	265	247
Real estate	Bil. dol.	15	26	29	32	34	37	40	43	47	51
Policy loans	Bil. dol.	41	55	54	54	54	54	57	63	66	72
Other	Bil. dol.	32	64	72	81	90	98	106	110	115	112
Interest earned on assets [4]	Percent	8.02	9.45	9.63	9.35	9.35	9.10	9.03	9.10	8.89	8.63	8.08
Liabilities [2][5]	Bil. dol.	445	673	769	873	977	1,092	1,216	1,317	1,445	1,549
Policy reserves [2]	Bil. dol.	390	584	665	762	862	969	1,084	1,197	1,305	1,407
Annuities	Bil. dol.	181	342	411	489	562	642	730	815	895	960
Group [6]	Bil. dol.	140	255	303	356	393	434	474	516	548	560
Individual [6]	Bil. dol.	41	87	108	133	169	208	256	299	347	400
Life insurance	Bil. dol.	198	226	236	252	276	300	324	349	372	402
Health insurance	Bil. dol.	11	17	19	21	24	27	30	33	38	45
Capital and surplus [2]	Bil. dol.	34	50	57	64	67	75	84	91	106	115

Z Less than $500 million. [1] Includes Servicemen's Group Life Insurance: $51 billion in 1986 and $167 billion in 1991; as well as Federal Employees' Group Life Insurance: $11 billion in 1986. [2] Includes operations of accident and health departments of life insurance companies. [3] Beginning in 1986, data not comparable to prior years due to change in accounting method. [4] Net rate. [5] Includes other obligations not shown separately. [6] Includes reserves for supplementary contracts with and without life contingencies.

Source: American Council of Life Insurance, Washington, DC, *Life Insurance Fact Book*, biennial; and unpublished data.

534 Banking, Finance, and Insurance

No. 827. Life Insurance Purchases in the United States—Number and Amount: 1980 to 1992

[Excludes revivals, increases, dividend additions, and reinsurance acquired. Includes long-term credit insurance (life insurance on loans of more than 10 years' duration). See also headnote, table 828]

YEAR	NUMBER OF POLICIES PURCHASED (1,000)						AMOUNT PURCHASED (bil. dol.)					
	Total	Ordinary			Group	Indus-trial	Total	Ordinary			Group	Indus-trial
		Total	Percent—					Total	Percent—			
			Whole life [1]	Term [2]					Whole life [1]	Term [2]		
1980	29,007	14,750	78	22	11,379	2,878	573	386	43	57	183	4
1985	33,880	17,104	78	22	16,243	533	1,231	911	57	43	320	1
1986	34,623	16,811	77	23	17,507	305	[3]1,309	934	55	45	[3]375	(Z)
1987	33,153	16,225	75	25	16,698	230	1,353	987	55	45	366	(Z)
1988	31,589	15,579	81	19	15,793	217	1,407	996	56	44	411	(Z)
1989	29,960	14,694	80	20	15,110	156	1,442	1,021	53	47	421	(Z)
1990	28,791	14,066	79	21	14,592	133	1,529	1,070	52	48	459	(Z)
1991	29,813	13,471	78	22	16,230	112	[3]1,616	1,042	50	50	[3]574	(Z)
1992	28,382	13,350	76	24	14,930	102	1,489	1,048	49	51	441	(Z)

Z Less than $500 million. [1] Life insurance payable to a beneficiary at the death of the insured whenever that occurs. Premiums may be payable for a specified number of years or for life. Includes a small number of endowment and retirement income policies. [2] Life insurance payable to a beneficiary only when an insured dies within a specified period. [3] Includes Servicemen's Group Life Insurance: $51 billion in 1986 and $167 billion in 1991.

No. 828. Life Insurance in Force in the United States—Summary: 1980 to 1992

[As of **December 31** or calendar year, as applicable. Covers life insurance with life insurance companies only. Represents all life insurance in force on lives of U.S. residents whether issued by U.S. or foreign companies. For definition of household, see text, section 1. See also *Historical Statistics, Colonial Times to 1970*, series X 879-889]

YEAR	LIFE INSURANCE IN FORCE						AVERAGE SIZE POLICY IN FORCE (dollars)				AVERAGE AMOUNT ($1,000)		Dispos-able per-sonal income per house-hold ($1,000)
	Number of poli-cies, total (mil.)	Value (bil. dol.)					Ordi-nary	Group	Indus-trial	Cred-it [1]	Per house-hold	Per in-sured house-hold	
		Total	Ordi-nary	Group	Indus-trial	Cred-it [1]							
1980	402	3,541	1,761	1,579	36	165	11,920	13,410	620	2,110	41.9	51.1	24.2
1985	386	6,053	3,247	2,562	28	216	22,780	19,720	640	3,100	66.6	82.2	33.9
1986	391	6,720	3,658	2,801	27	234	25,540	20,720	650	3,310	72.2	89.1	35.4
1987	395	7,452	4,139	3,043	27	243	28,510	22,380	650	3,330	78.7	98.4	36.5
1988	391	8,020	4,512	3,232	25	251	31,390	23,410	660	3,570	84.5	105.6	38.8
1989	394	8,694	4,940	3,470	24	260	34,410	24,510	670	3,600	89.9	112.4	40.8
1990	389	9,393	5,367	3,754	24	248	37,910	26,630	670	3,500	98.4	124.5	44.0
1991	375	9,986	5,678	4,058	22	228	41,450	28,760	680	3,580	102.7	130.0	44.6
1992	366	10,406	5,942	4,241	21	202	42,960	29,930	700	3,610	106.6	136.6	46.3

[1] Insures borrower to cover consumer loan in case of death.

Source of tables 827 and 828: American Council of Life Insurance, Washington, DC, *Life Insurance Fact Book*, biennial.

No. 829. Health Insurance—Premium Income and Benefit Payments of Insurance Companies: 1980 to 1991

[**In billions of dollars.** Includes Puerto Rico and other U.S. outlying areas. Represents premium income of and benefits paid by insurance companies only. Excludes Blue Cross-Blue Shield plans, medical-society sponsored plans, and all other independent plans]

ITEM	1980	1981	1982	1983	1984	1985	1986	1987	1988	1989	1990	1991
Premiums [1]	43.7	49.0	58.3	63.2	70.4	75.2	75.5	84.1	98.2	108.0	112.9	116.4
Group policies [2]	36.8	42.5	50.0	54.9	60.8	64.4	65.9	74.0	87.6	96.1	100.2	103.0
Individual and family policies..	6.9	6.5	8.3	8.3	9.6	10.8	9.6	10.1	10.6	11.8	12.7	13.3
Benefit payments	37.0	41.6	49.2	51.7	56.0	60.0	64.3	72.5	83.0	89.4	92.5	97.6
Group policies [2]	33.0	37.7	44.2	46.9	50.3	53.7	58.9	66.5	76.4	82.2	84.4	88.8
Individual and family policies..	4.0	3.9	5.0	4.8	5.7	6.3	5.4	5.9	6.6	7.2	8.2	8.8
Type of coverage:												
Loss of income	5.3	5.2	5.5	4.9	5.2	5.6	5.6	6.4	6.4	7.2	7.4	7.5
Medical expense	27.9	32.5	38.8	41.5	44.1	47.2	50.9	57.4	66.4	72.0	73.8	77.9
Dental	2.8	3.5	4.0	4.4	4.9	5.3	5.3	5.9	6.3	6.5	6.4	6.4
Medicare supplement	1.0	0.7	0.8	1.0	1.8	1.9	2.5	2.8	3.8	3.7	5.0	5.8

[1] Earned premiums. [2] Insurance company group premiums and benefit payments include administrative service agreements and minimum premium plans.

Source: Health Insurance Association of America, Washington, DC, *Source Book of Health Insurance Data*, annual.

No. 830. Property and Casualty Insurance—Summary: 1987 to 1993

[In billions of dollars. Minus sign (-) indicates loss]

ITEM	1987	1988	1989	1990	1991	1992	1993, est.
Premiums, net written	193.2	202.0	208.4	217.8	223.0	227.5	235.5
Automobile, private [1]	64.3	69.5	73.6	78.4	82.8	88.4	(NA)
Automobile, commercial [1]	16.9	16.9	17.3	17.0	16.6	16.1	(NA)
Liability other than auto	24.9	23.1	22.7	22.1	20.9	21.1	(NA)
Fire and allied lines	7.7	6.9	7.0	7.1	7.2	7.1	(NA)
Homeowners' multiple peril	16.7	17.1	17.7	18.6	19.3	20.5	(NA)
Commercial multiple peril	17.2	17.7	17.5	17.7	17.0	16.4	(NA)
Workers' compensation	23.4	26.1	28.5	31.0	31.3	29.7	(NA)
Marine, inland and ocean	5.5	5.5	5.6	5.7	5.5	5.5	(NA)
Accident and health	3.8	4.7	4.6	5.0	5.1	5.4	(NA)
Other lines	12.8	14.5	14.2	15.2	17.4	17.3	(NA)
Losses and expenses	196.4	208.6	223.6	234.7	239.3	259.6	(NA)
Underwriting gain/loss	-9.6	-11.2	-19.2	-20.9	-19.4	-35.5	(NA)
Net investment income	24.0	27.7	31.2	32.9	34.2	33.7	(NA)
Operating earnings after taxes	11.0	12.9	9.0	9.0	10.4	-3.3	(NA)
Assets	426.7	476.9	527.0	556.3	601.4	637.3	661.5
Policyholders' surplus	104.0	118.2	134.0	138.4	158.7	163.1	(NA)

NA Not available.   [1] Includes premiums for automobile liability and physical damage.

Source: U.S. Department of Commerce, International Trade Administration, *U.S. Industrial Outlook, 1994.*

No. 831. Automobile Insurance—Average Expenditures Per Insured Vehicle, by State: 1991 and 1992

[In dollars. The average expenditures for automobile insurance in a State are affected by a number of factors, including the underlying rate structure, the coverages purchased, the deductibles and limits selected, the types of vehicles insured, and the distribution of driver characteristics]

STATE	1991	1992	STATE	1991	1992
United States	596	617	Missouri	469	493
Alabama	475	510	Montana	370	393
Alaska	643	685	Nebraska	346	352
Arizona	647	667	Nevada	640	673
Arkansas	387	424	New Hampshire	646	638
California	783	800	New Jersey	984	957
Colorado	588	653	New Mexico	517	543
Connecticut	841	878	New York	681	799
Delaware	718	745	North Carolina	432	448
District of Columbia	863	880	North Dakota	329	319
Florida	669	684	Ohio	494	503
Georgia	541	514	Oklahoma	422	448
Hawaii	874	974	Oregon	529	535
Idaho	386	402	Pennsylvania	610	642
Illinois	552	534	Rhode Island	823	837
Indiana	474	497	South Carolina	491	528
Iowa	359	379	South Dakota	309	333
Kansas	368	392	Tennessee	466	478
Kentucky	435	473	Texas	612	646
Louisiana	679	724	Utah	436	463
Maine	484	468	Vermont	474	484
Maryland	689	702	Virginia	506	503
Massachusetts	814	860	Washington	549	588
Michigan	606	661	West Virginia	519	557
Minnesota	530	566	Wisconsin	463	492
Mississippi	482	519	Wyoming	330	366

Source: National Association of Insurance Commissioners, Kansas City, MO, *State Average Expenditures and Premiums for Personal Automobile Insurance,* annual, (copyright).

Figure 17.1
Mergers and Acquisitions: 1983 to 1992

Source: Chart prepared by U.S. Bureau of the Census. For data, see table 855.

Figure 17.2
Venture Capital: 1980 to 1993

Source: Chart prepared by U.S. Bureau of the Census. For data, see tables 853 and 854.

Business Enterprise

This section relates to the place and behavior of the business firm and to business initiative in the American economy. It includes data on the number, type, and size of businesses; financial data of domestic and multinational U.S. corporations; business investment, expenditures, and profits; sales and inventories; and business failures. Additional business data may be found in other sections, particularly 27 and 28.

The principal sources of these data are the *Survey of Current Business,* published by the Bureau of Economic Analysis (BEA), the *Federal Reserve Bulletin,* issued by the Board of Governors of the Federal Reserve System, the annual *Statistics of Income* reports of the Internal Revenue Service (IRS), *The Business Failure Record* issued by The Dun & Bradstreet Corporation, New York, and *Fortune* and *The Fortune Directory,* issued by Time, Inc., New York.

Business firms.—A firm is generally defined as a business organization under a single management and may include one or more establishments (i.e., a single physical location at which business is conducted). The terms firm, business, company, and enterprise are used interchangeably throughout this section. Examples of series where the industrial distribution is based on data collected from establishments are those on capital stock (table 864), those on gross national product by industry (table 685), and those on employment and earnings (section 13). Examples of company-based series are those on business expenditures for new plant and equipment (table 863), those from IRS *Statistics of Income* (tables 841 and 842), and those on corporation profits by industry (tables 874 and 875). A firm doing business in more than one industry is classified by industry according to the major activity of the firm as a whole. The industrial classification is based on the *Standard Industrial Classification (SIC) Manual* (see text, section 13). The IRS concept of a business firm relates primarily to the legal entity used for tax reporting purposes. The IRS *Statistics of Income* reports present data, based on a sample of tax returns before audit, separately for

In Brief

Patents issued in 1992: 107,400
*Percent issued to foreign country
residents:* 45%

Bankruptcies filed in 1993: 918,734
Business: 7%
Nonbusiness: 93%
Change from 1992 –6%

sole proprietorships, partnerships, and corporations. Data presented are for active enterprises only. A *sole proprietorship* is an unincorporated business owned by one person including large enterprises with many employees and hired managers and part-time operations in which the owner is the only person involved. A *partnership* is an unincorporated business owned by two or more persons, each of whom has a financial interest in the business. The "persons" could be individuals, estates, trusts, other partnerships, or corporations. A *corporation* is a business that is legally incorporated under State laws. The IRS recognizes many types of businesses as corporations, including joint-stock companies, insurance companies, and unincorporated associations such as business trusts, etc. While many corporations file consolidated tax returns, most corporate tax returns represent individual corporations, some of which are affiliated through common ownership or control with other corporations filing separate returns.

Assets and liabilities.—In its annual report, *Statistics of Income, Corporation Income Tax Returns,* the IRS presents balance sheet and income estimates for all active U.S. corporations. The Bureau of the Census issues the *Quarterly Financial Report for Manufacturing, Mining, and Trade Corporations* (QFR), which presents quarterly income account and balance sheet data for manufacturing, mining, and trade industries. This report was prepared by the Federal Trade Commission until responsibilities for QFR were transferred to Census beginning with the fourth quarter 1982 report.

One of the most comprehensive measures of the investment position of the business sector (and the only measure adjusted to current replacement cost) is the BEA capital stock series. See *Survey of Current Business,* January 1992.

Income, profits, dividends, and taxes.— Several agencies, among them IRS and BEA, compile corporate income account data. These data, however, are not comparable because of differing definitions and methods of compilation. A reconciliation of the two can be found in table 8.22 of *Survey of Current Business,* published by BEA. The IRS publishes financial data for all business enterprises. These data appear in *Statistics of Income, Corporation Income Tax Returns* and the *Statistics of Income Bulletin* (partnerships and sole proprietorships). Data on international income and taxes reported by U.S. corporations are also included in the *Statistics of Income Bulletin* and in the periodic *Compendium of Studies of International Income and Taxes.*

Corporate data issued by BEA are a part of its national income and product accounts (see text, section 14). The primary sources for BEA estimates of profits, taxes, dividends, and undistributed profits are the original corporate tax returns submitted to IRS. Various adjustments of IRS data are required by the national income treatment—particularly with respect to profits which would be disclosed if all tax returns were audited: depletion, capital gain or loss, treatment of bad debts, measurement of income received from abroad, and intercorporate dividends—to make the figures comparable with other entries in the national income accounts. For a discussion of two types of adjustments (inventory valuation and capital consumption), see text, section 14. The BEA's corporate profits data also include net earnings of Federal Reserve banks, credit unions, private noninsured pension funds, and several quasi-government credit agencies not included in IRS data.

Sources and uses of corporate funds.— These data (table 838, Federal Reserve Board) show capital requirements of corporations and the manner in which they are financed. Sources of funds should be equal to their uses. Certain discrepancies, however, interfere with this equality due to omission of (1) money accruing to corporations from an excess of sales over purchases of used plant and equipment,

(2) transactions in securities held as permanent investments except public offerings, and (3) net purchases of land. Also, the balance sheet data upon which many of the financial flow estimates are based are not fully comparable with the tax-return based estimates of internal sources or the establishment series underlying the figures on inventory change.

Fortune 500.—Sales include service and rental revenues but exclude dividends, interest, and other non-operating revenues. All companies must have derived more than 50 percent of their sales from manufacturing and/or mining. Sales of subsidiaries are included when they are consolidated. **Assets** are those shown at the company's year-end. **Net income** is shown after taxes and after extraordinary credits or charges when any are shown on the income statement. **Stockholder's equity** is the sum of capital stock, surplus, and retained earnings at the company's year-end. Redeemable preferred stock is excluded when its redemption is either mandatory or outside the control of the company, except in the case of cooperatives. **Total returns to investors** include both price appreciation and dividend yield. Returns are adjusted for stock splits, stock dividends, recapitalizations, and corporate reorganizations as they occur. For further discussion, see Time, Inc., New York, NY, *The Fortune Directories.*

Economic censuses.—The economic censuses constitute comprehensive and periodic canvasses of the Nation's industrial and business activities. The first economic census of the United States was conducted as part of the 1810 decennial census, when inquiries on manufacturing were included with the census of population. Minerals data were collected in 1840. The first censuses of construction and business were taken for 1929. An integrated economic census program was begun for 1954. In that year, the censuses covered the retail and wholesale trades, selected service industries, manufactures, and mineral industries. The economic censuses are taken at 5-year intervals covering years ending in "2" and "7." Special surveys are conducted every 5 years as part of the economic censuses to determine the extent of business ownership by specific minority groups and women.

No. 832. Number of Returns and Business Receipts, by Size of Receipts and Type of Business: 1970 to 1990

[Covers active enterprises only. Figures are estimates based on sample of unaudited tax returns; see Appendix III. The industrial distribution is based on data collected from companies; see text, section 17. See also *Historical Statistics, Colonial Times to 1970,* series V 1-12]

SIZE-CLASS OF RECEIPTS	RETURNS (1,000)					BUSINESS RECEIPTS [1] (bil. dol.)				
	1970	1980	1985	1989	1990	1970	1980	1985	1989	1990
Corporations	**1,665**	**3,277**	**3,563**	**3,628**	**3,717**	**1,706**	**6,172**	**8,050**	**10,440**	**10,914**
Under $25,000 [2]	452	711	818	865	879	3	4	5	5	5
$25,000 to $49,999	171	237	228	241	252	6	8	9	9	9
$50,000 to $99,999	220	330	350	332	359	16	22	24	24	26
$100,000 to $499,999	517	1,110	1,134	1,145	1,162	123	224	278	288	291
$500,000 to $999,999	141	352	409	415	416	99	197	249	292	294
$1,000,000 or more	165	538	623	630	649	1,459	5,717	7,484	9,821	10,289
Partnerships	**936**	**1,714**	**1,654**	**1,635**	**1,554**	**92**	**286**	**349**	**524**	**541**
Under $25,000 [2]	502	1,036	1,045	1,014	1,118	4	5	4	(NA)	4
$25,000 to $49,999	125	154	120	131	68	5	7	6	(NA)	5
$50,000 to $99,999	120	152	151	142	94	9	13	11	(NA)	10
$100,000 to $499,999	162	281	234	242	179	33	64	61	(NA)	57
$500,000 to $999,999	17	48	50	51	45	12	33	34	(NA)	36
$1,000,000 or more	10	42	54	56	49	30	164	234	(NA)	429
Nonfarm proprietorships [3]	**6,494**	**11,929**	**13,679**	**14,298**	**14,783**	**199**	**411**	**540**	**693**	**731**
Under $25,000 [2]	4,738	8,250	9,347	9,856	10,196	30	44	54	66	69
$25,000 to $49,999	746	1,394	1,601	1,660	1,660	27	39	50	60	58
$50,000 to $99,999	562	1,094	1,226	1,259	1,282	40	59	77	89	91
$100,000 to $499,999	420	1,060	1,337	1,334	1,444	76	159	213	276	296
$500,000 to $999,999	21	89	118	140	143	14	50	61	96	97
$1,000,000 or more	7	41	50	50	57	12	60	85	106	119

NA Not available. [1] Excludes investment income except for partnerships and corporations in finance, insurance, and real estate. Starting 1983, investment income no longer included for S corporations. S corporations are certain small companies with 35 shareholders (15 in 1980 and 10 in 1970), mostly individuals, electing to be taxed through shareholders. [2] Includes firms with no receipts. [3] Number of businesses for 1970 and 1980. Number of nonfarm sole proprietorship returns is not available by size prior to 1981. However, the number of returns and the number of businesses are very closely related. The ratio of number of returns to the number of businesses is approximately 1 to 1.3.

Source: U.S. Internal Revenue Service, *Statistics of Income; Statistics of Income Bulletin;* and unpublished data.

No. 833. Number of Returns, Receipts, and Net Income, by Type of Business and Industry: 1980 to 1990

[See headnote, table 832. Minus sign (-) indicates net loss]

ITEM	NUMBER OF RETURNS (1,000)			BUSINESS RECEIPTS [2] (bil. dol.)			NET INCOME (less loss) [3] (bil. dol.)		
	Nonfarm proprietorships [1]	Partnerships	Corporations	Nonfarm proprietorships [1]	Partnerships	Corporations	Nonfarm proprietorships [1]	Partnerships	Corporations
1980	8,932	1,380	2,711	411	286	6,172	55	8	239
1985	11,929	1,714	3,277	540	349	8,050	79	-9	240
1987	13,091	1,648	3,612	611	428	9,186	106	-5	328
1988	13,679	1,654	3,563	672	516	9,804	126	15	413
1989	14,298	1,635	3,628	693	524	10,440	133	14	389
1990 [4]	**14,783**	**1,554**	**3,717**	**731**	**541**	**10,914**	**141**	**17**	**371**
Agriculture, forestry, and fishing [5]	363	125	126	17	9	82	2	2	1
Mining	132	41	40	7	20	97	2	1	5
Construction	1,782	59	407	99	31	523	16	2	7
Manufacturing	380	28	302	22	65	3,434	2	1	171
Transportation, public utilities	615	25	160	31	33	874	4	-	35
Wholesale and retail trade [6]	2,650	176	1,023	250	96	3,217	14	3	30
Wholesale	400	21	329	47	37	1,590	5	1	14
Retail	2,250	154	690	203	61	1,622	9	2	16
Finance, insurance, real estate	1,331	822	609	49	122	1,955	16	-19	110
Services	7,335	267	1,029	252	162	726	84	27	11

[1] In 1980, represents individually owned businesses, including farms; thereafter, represents only nonfarm proprietors, i.e., business owners. [2] Excludes investment income except for partnerships and corporations in finance, insurance, and real estate. Starting 1985, investment income no longer included for S corporations. [3] Net income (less loss) is defined differently by form of organization, basically as follows: (a) Proprietorships: Total taxable receipts less total business deductions, including cost of sales and operations, depletion, and certain capital expensing, excluding charitable contributions and owners' salaries; (b) Partnerships: Total taxable receipts (including investment income except capital gains) less deductions, including cost of sales and operations and certain payments to partners, excluding charitable contributions, oil and gas depletion, and certain capital expensing; (c) Corporations: Total taxable receipts (including investment income, capital gains, and income from foreign subsidiaries deemed received for tax purposes, except for S corporations beginning 1983) less business deductions, including cost of sales and operations, depletion, certain capital expensing, and officers' compensation excluding S corporation charitable contributions and investment expenses starting 1983; net income is before income tax. [4] Includes businesses not allocable to individual industries. [5] Represents agricultural services only. [6] Includes trade business not identified as wholesale or retail.

Source: U.S. Internal Revenue Service, *Statistics of Income,* various publications.

No. 834. Number of Returns and Business Receipts, by Industry, Type of Business, and Size of Business Receipts: 1990

[Number of returns in thousands; receipts and net income in billions of dollars. Covers active enterprises only. Figures are estimates based on a sample of unaudited tax returns; see Appendix III. The industrial distribution is based on data collected from establishments; see text, section 17. See also Historical Statistics, Colonial Times to 1970, series V 42-53, for number of active corporations. Minus sign (-) indicates net loss]

INDUSTRY	Non-farm pro-prietor-ships	Partner-ships	CORPORATIONS				
			Under $1 mil. [1]	$1 mil.-$4.9 mil.	$5 mil.-$9.9 mil.	$10 mil.-$49.9 mil.	$50 mil. or more
Total: [2] Number	14,783	1,554	3,068	484	82	67	16
Business receipts [3]	731	541	625	1,035	574	1,349	7,331
Net income (less loss)	141	17	-10	11	10	36	323
Agriculture, forestry, fishing: [4] Number	363	125	114	11	1	1	(Z)
Business receipts [3]	17	10	18	22	8	13	22
Mining: Number	132	41	34	4	1	1	(Z)
Business receipts [3]	7	20	4	9	4	12	68
Construction: Number	1,782	59	323	67	10	6	1
Business receipts [3]	99	31	85	139	70	116	113
Manufacturing: Number	380	28	197	71	15	14	5
Business receipts [3]	22	65	53	156	107	297	2,820
Transportation, public utilities: Number	615	25	129	25	4	2	1
Business receipts [3]	31	33	26	57	26	50	715
Wholesale and retail trade: Number	2,650	176	754	196	36	31	5
Business receipts [3]	250	98	208	425	253	621	1,710
Finance, insurance, real estate: Number	1,331	822	561	33	6	7	3
Business receipts [3]	49	122	61	71	45	142	1,636
Services: Number	7,335	267	936	78	9	5	1
Business receipts [3]	252	162	168	156	61	98	243

Z Less than 500 returns.   [1] Includes businesses without receipts.   [2] Includes businesses not allocable to individual industries.   [3] Excludes investment income except for partnerships and corporations (other than S corporations) in finance, insurance, and real estate.   [4] Represents agricultural services only.

Source: U.S. Internal Revenue Service, Statistics of Income, various publications; and unpublished data.

No. 835. Sole Proprietorships—Selected Income and Deduction Items: 1970 to 1991

[In millions of dollars, except as indicated. Covers nonfarm sole proprietorships. All figures are estimates based on sample. Tax law changes have affected the comparability of the data over time; see Statistics of Income reports for a description. See also Historical Statistics, Colonial Times to 1970, series V 4-6]

ITEM	1970	1980	1985	1986	1987	1988	1989	1990	1991
Number of returns (1,000)	5,770	8,932	11,929	12,394	13,091	13,679	14,298	14,783	15,181
Businesses with net income (1,000).	(NA)	(NA)	8,641	9,248	9,884	10,492	11,018	11,223	11,551
Inventory, end of year	11,061	21,996	24,970	24,477	26,333	27,313	30,060	30,422	29,783
Business receipts	198,582	411,206	540,045	559,384	610,823	671,970	692,811	730,606	712,568
Income from sales and operations .	(NA)	407,169	528,675	548,273	598,315	658,687	678,616	719,008	700,681
Business deductions [1]	168,045	356,258	461,273	468,960	505,362	545,735	560,175	589,250	571,154
Cost of goods sold/operations [1] . . .	109,149	209,890	232,294	232,135	255,045	277,880	283,709	291,011	272,627
Purchases	88,586	168,302	(NA)	(NA)	173,400	197,220	204,681	210,225	200,861
Labor costs	7,704	10,922	14,504	17,318	19,631	21,143	22,540	22,680	21,918
Materials and supplies	6,216	12,909	(NA)	(NA)	23,842	27,800	29,870	30,195	28,072
Commissions	1,274	3,333	(NA)	5,461	6,262	6,540	6,843	8,816	7,628
Salaries and wages (net)	15,107	26,561	38,266	38,691	42,330	43,007	45,469	46,998	48,890
Car and truck expenses	(NA)	13,378	17,044	16,381	17,470	19,640	20,789	21,766	22,594
Rent paid	4,637	9,636	15,259	15,654	16,358	19,470	20,952	23,392	23,643
Repairs	2,445	5,032	(NA)	(NA)	7,438	8,104	8,149	8,941	9,159
Taxes paid	3,776	7,672	(NA)	(NA)	8,449	9,495	9,948	10,342	10,629
Utilities.	(NA)	4,790	(NA)	(NA)	13,362	14,618	13,601	13,539	13,260
Insurance	2,310	6,003	(NA)	10,783	11,719	12,528	12,879	13,358	13,065
Interest paid	1,784	7,190	11,914	11,500	11,616	12,071	13,280	13,312	12,077
Depreciation	5,452	13,953	26,291	26,418	25,557	26,078	24,479	23,735	23,076
Pension and profit sharing plans. . .	73	141	311	638	548	450	539	586	519
Net income (less loss)	30,537	54,947	78,773	90,423	105,461	126,323	132,738	141,430	141,516
Businesses with net income.	33,736	68,010	98,776	110,497	123,783	145,518	152,416	161,657	162,427

NA Not available.   [1] Includes other amounts not shown separately.

Source: U.S. Internal Revenue Service, Statistics of Income Bulletin.

No. 836. Partnerships—Selected Items, by Industry: 1980 to 1991

[In millions of dollars, except number of partners and partnerships in thousands. Covers active partnerships only. Includes partnerships not allocable by industry. Figures are estimates based on samples. See Appendix III]

YEAR	NUMBER OF PARTNERSHIPS			Number of partners	Total assets [1]	Business receipts [2][3]	Total deductions [3]	Net income less loss [3]	Net income [3]	Net loss [3]
	Total	With net income	With net loss							
All industries:										
1980	1,380	774	605	8,420	597,504	285,967	283,749	8,249	45,062	36,813
1985	1,714	876	838	13,245	1,269,434	349,169	376,001	-8,884	77,045	85,928
1988	1,654	901	753	17,291	1,580,194	515,475	464,991	14,493	111,384	96,892
1989	1,635	898	737	18,432	1,791,027	523,774	475,434	14,099	113,886	99,787
1990	1,554	854	700	17,095	1,735,285	540,647	549,603	16,610	116,318	99,708
1991	1,515	856	660	15,801	1,816,567	539,027	541,230	21,406	113,408	92,002
Agriculture, forestry, fishing:										
1980	126	72	54	381	24,595	21,611	22,859	472	2,539	2,067
1985	136	76	60	585	27,027	6,529	10,495	-1,049	2,797	3,846
1988	122	80	42	555	24,106	8,988	11,602	1,079	3,827	2,748
1989	131	83	48	591	25,219	7,708	10,133	1,380	3,679	2,299
1990	125	77	48	503	27,580	9,497	11,805	1,667	3,905	2,238
1991	127	78	49	552	32,391	8,422	10,892	1,740	3,992	2,252
Mining:										
1980	35	15	20	722	24,742	13,201	18,248	-4,208	3,920	8,128
1985	62	33	30	2,207	66,930	19,922	21,920	1,482	7,884	6,402
1988	48	31	17	2,467	65,652	15,977	18,759	934	6,641	5,707
1989	46	26	20	3,771	62,073	19,701	20,751	1,965	7,027	5,062
1990	41	29	14	2,149	58,246	19,967	20,869	2,183	7,009	4,825
1991	39	26	13	1,415	53,725	18,147	19,966	780	5,285	4,505
Construction:										
1980	67	51	16	160	9,811	18,407	17,202	1,560	2,119	559
1985	57	41	16	134	15,008	21,476	20,080	2,207	2,743	536
1988	74	60	14	179	20,070	30,978	28,712	3,284	3,929	645
1989	62	46	16	165	21,150	30,052	28,397	2,647	3,313	666
1990	59	45	15	162	17,989	30,716	29,672	1,908	3,020	1,112
1991	57	42	15	152	16,730	26,625	25,766	1,494	2,563	1,069
Transportation, public utilities:										
1980	20	11	10	73	9,291	5,868	5,821	248	1,092	844
1985	25	15	10	186	26,468	11,253	14,814	-3,066	1,360	4,426
1988	20	12	8	433	45,003	21,639	25,389	-2,292	2,951	5,244
1989	22	10	12	435	54,171	26,727	30,319	-1,977	3,695	5,671
1990	25	14	11	503	63,334	32,800	35,989	-117	5,887	6,004
1991	26	14	12	519	72,512	37,611	40,873	-1,431	4,710	6,142
Manufacturing:										
1980	30	20	10	92	11,252	15,327	16,142	-472	1,199	1,671
1985	30	12	18	105	24,838	22,588	24,225	-1,085	1,228	2,314
1988	26	12	14	173	41,714	43,724	43,345	1,540	3,598	2,058
1989	26	14	12	185	56,601	55,336	55,816	1,398	4,154	2,756
1990	28	15	13	246	59,789	65,354	65,833	1,166	4,791	3,626
1991	24	13	11	175	65,140	65,818	66,385	904	4,909	4,005
Wholesale and retail trade:										
1980	200	123	77	487	17,727	65,793	63,988	2,475	3,374	900
1985	201	113	88	493	20,568	69,079	68,119	1,977	3,467	1,490
1988	180	104	76	490	26,512	83,640	56,375	3,351	4,742	1,391
1989	173	98	75	496	27,294	90,306	89,418	2,529	4,550	2,021
1990	176	100	77	481	28,423	98,120	97,131	2,610	4,717	2,107
1991	171	97	74	448	29,786	99,749	98,940	2,628	4,718	2,090
Finance, insurance, and real estate:										
1980	637	313	325	5,566	454,531	87,133	91,382	-4,249	15,169	19,418
1985	844	369	475	7,755	979,787	92,309	118,237	-25,929	30,383	56,311
1988	869	398	471	10,880	1,200,673	115,415	127,356	-19,258	47,842	67,100
1989	853	419	434	11,327	1,394,319	71,243	91,965	-20,824	47,753	68,576
1990	822	401	422	10,846	1,329,452	64,313	87,011	-19,213	47,577	66,790
1991	804	410	394	10,317	1,386,914	57,398	126,042	-12,786	47,595	60,381
Services:										
1980	263	169	94	938	45,510	58,627	48,106	12,424	15,649	3,224
1985	341	207	134	1,713	106,597	104,197	96,202	16,541	26,942	10,400
1988	296	197	99	2,060	154,548	141,909	126,505	25,639	37,527	11,888
1989	299	189	110	2,370	148,688	162,325	147,280	26,652	39,296	12,643
1990	267	173	96	2,153	150,063	161,702	145,789	26,453	39,383	12,930
1991	260	170	91	2,207	159,117	169,073	152,011	28,036	39,588	11,552

[1] Total assets are understated because not all partnerships file complete balance sheets. [2] Includes investment income for partnerships in finance, insurance, and real estate. [3] Beginning 1981, only net (not gross) income from farming, rents, and royalties are included.

Source: U.S. Internal Revenue Service, *Statistics of Income Bulletin,* various publications.

No. 837. Partnerships—Selected Income and Balance Sheet Items: 1980 to 1991

[In billions of dollars, except as indicated. Covers active partnerships only. All figures are estimates based on samples. See Appendix III and *Historical Statistics, Colonial Times to 1970*, series V 7-9]

ITEM	1980	1984	1985	1986	1987	1988	1989	1990	1991
Number of returns (1,000)	1,380	1,644	1,714	1,703	1,648	1,654	1,635	1,554	1,515
Number with net income (1,000). . .	774	845	876	851	865	901	898	854	856
Number with balance sheets (1,000)	1,194	1,215	1,227	1,203	1,129	1,155	1,149	1,081	1,048
Number of partners (1,000).	8,420	12,427	13,245	15,229	16,963	17,291	18,432	17,095	15,801
Assets [1][2]	598	1,031	1,269	1,404	1,381	1,580	1,791	1,735	1,817
Depreciable assets (net)	239	582	696	780	567	621	670	1,033	1,075
Inventories, end of year	33	62	27	47	45	51	59	57	57
Land	70	122	152	179	178	200	214	215	213
Liabilities [1][2]	489	855	1,269	1,176	1,386	1,580	1,791	1,415	1,460
Accounts payable	34	33	47	44	41	49	52	67	63
Short-term debt [3]	48	69	103	92	82	87	87	88	117
Long-term debt [4]	178	322	382	429	430	474	512	498	491
Nonrecourse loans.	119	260	328	365	388	437	461	470	474
Partners' capital accounts [2]	109	175	200	228	247	267	356	320	357
Receipts [1]	292	375	367	397	443	541	551	565	563
Business receipts [5]	271	318	303	327	428	516	524	541	539
Interest received [6]	11	17	21	22	18	19	21	21	20
Deductions [1]	284	379	376	415	423	465	475	550	541
Cost of goods sold/operations. . . .	114	181	146	164	237	253	233	243	237
Salaries and wages	22	29	34	36	41	47	54	56	58
Taxes paid	10	7	8	8	7	8	9	9	10
Interest paid	28	25	29	29	20	23	33	30	28
Depreciation	22	20	23	23	19	20	20	19	19
Net income (less loss)	8	-4	-9	-17	-5	14	14	17	21
Net income	45	70	77	80	88	111	114	116	113

[1] Includes other amounts not shown separately. [2] Assets, liabilities, and partners' capital accounts are understated because not all partnerships file complete balance sheets. [3] Mortgages, notes, and bonds payable in less than 1 year. [4] Mortgages, notes, and bonds payable in 1 year or more. [5] Includes investment income for partnerships in finance, insurance, and real estate. [6] For 1984-86, also includes dividends.

Source: U.S. Internal Revenue Service, *Statistics of Income Bulletin*, various publications.

No. 838. Corporate Funds—Sources and Uses: 1980 to 1993

[In billions of dollars, except percent. Covers nonfarm nonfinancial corporate business. See text, section 17]

ITEM	1980	1985	1986	1987	1988	1989	1990	1991	1992	1993
Sources.	334.7	486.3	531.9	540.5	610.9	562.3	522.8	473.2	587.2	580.5
Internal	199.7	351.9	336.7	375.9	404.3	399.6	409.4	437.8	462.7	476.1
U.S. undistributed profits.	69.2	21.7	-2.1	41.3	73.6	32.2	20.5	38.2	52.2	46.4
IVA and CCA [1]	-61.4	54.4	53.4	30.6	15.7	19.8	21.8	17.5	21.9	27.8
Capital consumption allowances. .	173.2	256.0	269.2	279.2	295.1	314.8	326.6	338.6	349.5	358.6
Foreign earnings [2]	18.7	19.8	16.2	24.8	19.9	32.8	40.6	43.6	39.0	43.4
External [3]	135.0	134.4	195.2	164.6	206.6	162.6	113.4	35.4	124.5	104.5
Credit market funds	77.0	76.1	140.3	65.2	71.8	62.4	37.7	6.9	69.1	74.9
Securities and mortgages.	35.9	13.0	65.5	27.8	-14.6	-32.9	-18.9	95.9	68.8	85.9
Equity issues.	10.4	-84.5	-85.5	-75.5	-129.5	-124.2	-63.0	18.3	27.0	23.0
Bonds and mortgages [4] . . .	25.5	97.5	150.5	103.3	114.9	91.3	44.1	77.7	41.8	62.9
Loans and short-term paper . . .	41.1	63.1	74.7	37.4	86.4	95.2	56.6	-89.0	0.4	-11.0
Other.	58.0	58.3	54.9	99.4	134.9	100.2	75.7	28.4	55.4	29.6
Profit taxes payable.	2.9	-3.2	3.8	5.1	1.7	-3.1	-5.0	-9.4	6.8	2.3
Trade debt	38.0	34.0	13.7	39.9	59.2	30.5	29.3	4.7	35.2	19.6
Foreign direct investment in U.S.	17.1	27.4	37.4	54.5	74.0	72.8	51.4	33.2	13.3	7.7
Uses	337.8	465.8	503.3	489.9	558.2	523.6	502.0	451.2	537.8	546.3
Capital expenditures	255.8	374.9	351.9	365.0	394.4	403.8	407.3	381.6	397.2	454.6
Increase in financial assets.	82.1	91.0	151.5	124.9	163.8	119.8	94.7	69.6	140.6	91.7
Discrepancy (sources less uses) . . .	-3.1	20.4	28.5	50.7	52.7	38.7	20.8	22.0	49.4	34.2

[1] Inventory valuation and capital consumption adjustment. [2] Foreign earnings of subsidiaries retained abroad. [3] Net increases in liability. [4] Includes industrial pollution control revenue bonds issued by State and local governments.

Source: Board of Governors of the Federal Reserve System. Data derived from *Flow of Funds Accounts*, annual.

No. 839. Nonfinancial Corporate Business-Sector Balance Sheet: 1980 to 1992
[In billions of dollars. Represents yearend outstandings]

ITEM	1980	1982	1983	1984	1985	1986	1987	1988	1989	1990	1991	1992
Assets	4,455	5,197	5,413	5,746	6,032	6,345	6,711	7,183	7,579	7,699	7,509	7,377
Tangible assets (current cost)	3,279	3,860	3,980	4,216	4,399	4,546	4,750	5,056	5,331	5,326	5,062	4,816
Reproducible	2,771	3,240	3,320	3,514	3,659	3,772	3,938	4,182	4,393	4,573	4,629	4,699
Land	508	620	659	702	741	775	813	873	937	753	433	117
Financial assets [1]	1,176	1,337	1,433	1,530	1,632	1,798	1,961	2,127	2,248	2,374	2,447	2,562
Liquid assets [1]	197	269	321	360	403	472	507	531	550	565	592	587
Checkable deposits and currency . .	57	46	37	43	69	88	105	104	114	120	131	122
Time deposits	38	59	71	74	80	88	92	106	103	99	104	96
Consumer credit	25	26	30	33	37	41	48	54	57	58	54	57
Mutual fund shares	2	3	5	7	11	16	13	11	12	10	15	17
Trade credit	482	491	543	590	630	655	701	773	817	834	826	859
Miscellaneous assets	471	547	535	539	552	615	692	758	813	907	960	1,042
Liabilities	1,407	1,658	1,806	2,055	2,276	2,561	2,844	3,170	3,453	3,611	3,621	3,731
Credit market debt	877	1,050	1,149	1,340	1,505	1,729	1,901	2,091	2,282	2,375	2,362	2,405
Profit taxes payable.	44	36	39	42	39	43	48	50	47	42	32	39
Trade debt	348	381	418	452	486	500	540	599	629	659	663	699
Miscellaneous liabilities	138	191	200	221	246	290	356	432	496	536	564	588
Net worth	3,048	3,539	3,608	3,691	3,755	3,784	3,867	4,012	4,125	4,089	3,888	3,646

[1] Includes other assets not shown separately.
Source: Board of Governors of the Federal Reserve System, *Balance Sheets for the U.S. Economy.*

No. 840. Corporations—Selected Financial Items: 1980 to 1991
[In billions of dollars, except as noted. Covers active corporations only. All corporations are required to file returns except those specifically exempt. See source for changes in law affecting comparability of historical data. Based on samples; see Appendix III. See also *Historical Statistics, Colonial Times to 1970*, series Y 381-392]

ITEM	1980	1984	1985	1986	1987	1988	1989	1990	1991
Number of returns (1,000)	2,711	3,171	3,277	3,429	3,612	3,563	3,628	3,717	3,803
Number with net income (1,000)	1,597	1,778	1,820	1,908	1,995	1,909	1,922	1,911	1,942
S Corporation returns [1] (1,000)	545	701	725	826	1,128	1,257	1,423	1,575	1,698
Assets [2]	7,617	11,107	12,773	14,163	15,311	16,568	17,647	18,190	19,030
Cash	529	596	683	763	754	785	824	771	787
Notes and accounts receivable	1,985	2,897	3,318	3,594	3,763	4,099	4,196	4,198	4,191
Inventories	535	664	715	733	829	846	879	894	884
Investments in Govt. obligations	472	726	917	1,059	1,092	1,095	1,262	1,302	1,069
Mortgage and real estate	894	1,127	1,259	1,377	1,455	1,605	1,610	1,538	1,529
Other investments	1,214	1,973	2,414	2,848	3,227	3,614	3,971	4,137	4,750
Depreciable assets	2,107	2,913	3,174	3,383	3,603	3,821	4,070	4,318	4,549
Depletable assets	72	115	112	116	123	124	134	129	142
Land	93	128	141	150	159	177	191	210	215
Liabilities [2]	7,617	11,107	12,773	14,163	15,311	16,568	17,647	18,190	19,030
Accounts payable	542	741	892	909	998	1,023	1,090	1,094	1,681
Short-term debt [3]	505	867	1,001	1,084	1,247	1,431	1,602	1,803	1,500
Long-term debt [4]	987	1,494	1,699	1,958	2,141	2,352	2,490	2,665	2,698
Capital stock	417	839	920	1,191	1,292	1,429	1,477	1,585	1,741
Paid-in or capital surplus	532	1,066	1,421	1,726	1,988	2,154	2,595	2,814	3,257
Retained earnings [5]	1,070	1,308	1,366	1,394	1,417	1,493	1,522	1,410	1,441
Net worth	1,944	2,884	3,304	3,698	3,947	4,207	4,603	4,739	5,277
Receipts [3][6]	6,361	7,861	8,398	8,669	9,582	10,265	10,935	11,410	11,436
Business receipts [6][7]	5,732	6,948	7,370	7,535	8,415	8,950	9,427	9,860	9,966
Interest [8]	367	580	635	662	706	805	967	977	920
Rents and royalties	54	90	105	110	113	116	129	133	137
Deductions [3][6]	6,125	7,629	8,158	8,395	9,244	9,853	10,545	11,033	11,087
Cost of sales and operations [7]	4,205	4,693	4,894	4,923	5,596	5,945	6,317	6,611	6,654
Compensation of officers	109	157	171	185	200	203	198	205	201
Rent paid on business property	72	119	135	145	154	161	173	185	193
Taxes paid	163	192	201	203	211	222	236	251	258
Interest paid	345	536	569	573	590	672	832	825	733
Depreciation	157	265	304	313	317	328	337	333	334
Advertising	52	82	92	99	107	114	124	126	129
Net income (less loss) [6][9]	239	233	240	270	328	413	389	371	345
Net income	297	349	364	409	465	556	556	553	536
Deficit	58	116	124	139	137	143	167	182	191
Income subject to tax	247	257	266	276	312	383	371	366	350
Income tax before credits [10]	104	106	109	109	115	127	123	119	116
Tax credits [3]	42	44	48	37	31	35	32	32	29
Foreign tax credit	25	21	24	21	21	27	24	25	21
Income tax after credits [11]	62	62	61	72	84	92	96	96	93

[1] Represents certain small corporations with up to 35 shareholders (15 in 1980), mostly individuals, electing to be taxed at the shareholder level.   [2] Includes items not shown separately.   [3] Payable in less than 1 year.   [4] Payable in 1 year or more.   [5] Appropriated and unappropriated.   [6] Except for 1980, receipts, deductions and net income of S corporations are limited to those from trade or business. Those from investments are excluded.   [7] Beginning 1987, includes gross sales and cost of sales of securities, commodities, and real estate by exchanges, brokers, or dealers selling on their own accounts. Previously, net gain included in total receipts only. Excludes investment income.   [8] Includes tax-exempt interest in State and local government obligations.   [9] Excludes regulated investment companies.   [10] Consists of regular (and alternative tax) only.   [11] Includes minimum tax, alternative minimum tax, adjustments for prior year credits, and other income-related taxes.

Source: U.S. Internal Revenue Service, *Statistics of Income, Corporation Income Tax Returns*, annual.

No. 841. Corporations—Selected Financial Items, by Industry: 1980 to 1991

[In billions of dollars, except as indicated. Covers active corporations only. Industrial distribution based on data collected from companies; see text, section 17. Excludes corporations not allocable by industry]

INDUSTRY	1980	1985	1986	1987	1988	1989	1990	1991
Agriculture, forestry, and fishing:								
Returns (1,000)	81	103	107	117	120	123	126	130
Assets	40.7	52.7	53.5	55.4	60.5	63.4	68.3	67.8
Liabilities [1]	29.3	37.2	36.4	37.2	40.2	42.3	45.0	45.0
Receipts [2]	52.1	70.5	77.5	77.1	86.3	86.6	88.1	85.9
Deductions [2]	51.4	70.6	76.3	75.4	84.6	85.1	86.9	85.3
Net income (less loss) [2]	0.7	-0.1	1.1	1.6	1.6	1.6	1.2	0.6
Mining:								
Returns (1,000)	26	41	40	42	41	42	40	39
Assets	126.9	240.8	206.1	220.1	225.6	236.3	219.2	213.0
Liabilities [1]	72.9	136.0	107.5	110.6	113.8	109.9	108.9	106.4
Receipts [2]	176.7	142.0	98.6	96.8	100.4	102.4	111.4	103.3
Deductions [2]	169.1	145.4	102.1	96.7	96.8	99.5	106.5	99.5
Net income (less loss) [2]	7.8	-2.5	-3.1	0.3	4.1	3.1	5.3	4.0
Construction:								
Returns (1,000)	272	318	342	371	381	393	407	417
Assets	132.9	215.3	218.9	222.1	241.4	249.7	243.8	243.0
Liabilities [1]	100.1	160.6	166.1	168.1	178.9	183.0	180.0	172.4
Receipts [2]	267.2	387.2	412.5	454.8	499.7	517.5	534.7	515.1
Deductions [2]	262.1	382.8	406.7	446.1	488.4	508.8	527.8	509.2
Net income (less loss) [2]	5.3	4.4	5.8	8.7	11.3	8.7	6.8	6.1
Manufacturing:								
Returns (1,000)	243	277	285	294	300	301	302	300
Assets	1,709.5	2,644.4	2,931.6	3,111.7	3,390.4	3,721.2	3,921.3	4,028.4
Liabilities [1]	960.3	1,544.7	1,807.2	1,920.0	2,137.2	2,347.7	2,529.1	2,547.2
Receipts [2]	2,404.3	2,831.1	2,810.7	3,141.4	3,349.0	3,531.2	3,688.7	3,658.5
Deductions [2]	2,290.6	2,733.1	2,723.7	3,012.1	3,170.0	3,377.1	3,545.1	3,548.7
Net income (less loss) [2]	125.7	113.8	101.8	145.5	205.1	180.5	171.4	132.3
Transportation and public utilities:								
Returns (1,000)	111	138	138	148	149	156	160	165
Assets	758.4	1,246.4	1,310.2	1,352.5	1,411.2	1,474.4	1,522.0	1,573.8
Liabilities [1]	467.7	755.9	807.7	842.4	891.8	963.1	1,013.4	1,044.9
Receipts [2]	523.8	772.4	762.2	786.2	838.8	906.5	936.3	954.9
Deductions [2]	504.0	747.8	740.7	749.0	792.5	867.6	901.0	917.8
Net income (less loss) [2]	20.0	25.1	21.0	37.5	46.9	39.1	35.4	37.7
Wholesale and retail trade:								
Returns (1,000)	800	917	939	972	985	1,013	1,023	1,044
Assets	646.9	1,010.0	1,073.5	1,177.7	1,295.8	1,390.6	1,447.3	1,483.4
Liabilities [1]	424.6	723.7	773.4	861.2	963.9	1,047.8	1,092.5	1,108.6
Receipts [2]	1,955.5	2,473.9	2,547.4	2,766.7	2,978.0	3,184.9	3,309.0	3,380.6
Deductions [2]	1,919.5	2,440.4	2,512.1	2,728.5	2,935.5	3,148.8	3,279.1	3,350.9
Net income (less loss) [2]	35.8	33.1	34.0	38.0	42.8	36.2	30.1	30.0
Finance, insurance, and real estate:								
Returns (1,000)	493	518	537	521	572	593	609	618
Assets	4,022.2	7,029.5	7,985.6	8,732.3	9,411.5	9,957.5	10,193.3	10,780.7
Liabilities [1]	3,491.7	5,867.5	6,483.4	7,097.4	7,632.1	7,929.3	8,051.3	8,267.1
Receipts [2][3]	697.5	1,182.0	1,365.1	1,589.2	1,714.4	1,868.0	1,954.7	1,924.3
Deductions [2]	652.6	1,104.6	1,245.5	1,476.7	1,596.0	1,730.5	1,809.9	1,771.2
Net income (less loss) [2]	33.1	60.7	99.8	87.4	91.9	108.9	109.9	124.5
Services:								
Returns (1,000)	671	939	1,012	1,120	995	990	1,029	1,062
Assets	178.2	331.0	381.6	435.6	530.3	552.1	572.8	636.8
Liabilities [1]	125.3	241.1	281.4	323.1	402.2	419.8	429.7	459.1
Receipts [2]	279.9	534.6	591.9	663.1	695.3	735.5	779.3	809.7
Deductions [2]	271.8	528.7	584.3	654.0	686.3	724.9	769.0	800.2
Net income (less loss) [2]	8.2	5.9	7.0	9.3	9.3	11.0	10.6	9.8
ANNUAL PERCENT CHANGE RECEIPTS [4]								
Agriculture, forestry, and fishing	-2.4	5.9	9.9	-0.5	11.9	0.3	1.7	-0.5
Mining	33.3	15.0	-30.6	-1.8	3.7	1.9	8.8	-0.7
Construction	5.7	14.4	6.5	10.2	9.8	3.6	3.3	-0.3
Manufacturing	11.7	2.3	-0.7	11.7	6.6	5.4	4.5	-0.2
Transportation and public utilities	17.5	6.4	-1.3	3.1	6.6	8.1	3.3	2.0
Wholesale and retail trade	11.6	7.2	3.0	8.6	7.6	6.9	3.9	2.2
Finance, insurance, and real estate	24.3	14.4	15.5	16.4	7.8	9.0	4.6	-0.4
Services	14.2	9.0	10.7	12.0	4.8	5.8	6.0	3.9

[1] Liabilities does not include net worth.   [2] Beginning 1987, receipts, deductions, and net income of S corporations are limited to those from trade or business; those from investments are generally excluded. S corporations are certain small corporations with up to 35 shareholders (15 in 1980), mostly individuals, electing to be taxed at the shareholder level.   [3] Beginning 1987, includes gross sales (previously net sales) of securities, commodities, and real estate by exchanges, brokers, or dealers selling on their own account.   [4] Change from preceding year.

Source: U.S. Internal Revenue Service, Statistics of Income, Corporation Income Tax Returns, annual.

No. 842. Corporations, by Asset-Size Class and Industry: 1990

[In millions of dollars, except number of returns and percent distribution. Covers active corporations only. Excludes corporations not allocable by industry. The industrial distribution is based on data collected from companies; see text, section 17. Detail may not add to total because of rounding. See also *Historical Statistics, Colonial Times to 1970*, series V 167-183 and V 193-196]

INDUSTRY	Total	ASSET-SIZE CLASS					
		Under $10 mil. [1]	$10-$24.9 mil.	$25-$49.9 mil.	$50-$99.9 mil.	$100-$249.9 mil.	$250 mil. and over
Agriculture, forestry, and fishing:							
Returns	126,423	125,910	309	107	49	34	15
Assets	68,338	45,946	4,441	3,702	3,423	5,020	5,807
Receipts	88,101	60,306	6,549	5,063	4,159	5,294	6,729
Deductions	86,883	59,676	6,478	4,960	4,199	5,212	6,358
Net income (less loss)	1,156	568	75	104	-42	77	374
Mining:							
Returns	39,674	38,650	496	227	127	84	89
Assets	219,198	17,619	7,640	8,322	11,009	13,260	161,347
Receipts	111,444	21,940	6,600	5,809	7,183	7,541	62,371
Deductions	106,467	21,140	6,412	5,737	7,036	7,256	58,884
Net income (less loss)	5,302	791	182	96	155	291	3,787
Construction:							
Returns	406,874	404,608	1,636	332	176	75	45
Assets	243,829	138,331	23,852	11,226	13,510	11,405	45,504
Receipts	534,654	380,468	46,642	21,139	21,663	17,873	46,870
Deductions	527,801	375,593	45,513	20,729	21,362	17,784	46,819
Net income (less loss)	6,825	4,787	1,110	393	290	91	153
Manufacturing:							
Returns	301,669	290,411	5,851	2,169	1,199	970	1,070
Assets	3,921,324	197,125	90,962	75,336	84,729	175,716	3,297,456
Receipts	3,688,694	472,613	166,717	115,356	122,005	210,953	2,601,050
Deductions	3,545,122	466,909	162,250	112,133	118,116	202,409	2,483,305
Net income (less loss)	171,374	5,795	4,425	3,231	3,927	9,081	144,915
Transportation and public utilities:							
Returns	160,353	157,943	1,237	387	226	192	368
Assets	1,522,046	57,537	19,127	13,497	16,731	30,613	1,384,541
Receipts	936,277	142,446	22,891	15,658	15,163	24,000	716,118
Deductions	900,961	142,469	22,738	15,549	15,157	24,094	680,954
Net income (less loss)	35,414	-41	147	106	-2	-34	35,237
Wholesale and retail trade:							
Returns	1,023,057	1,013,841	5,856	1,705	744	494	415
Assets	1,447,297	417,728	87,843	59,122	52,626	79,845	750,133
Receipts	3,308,988	1,493,387	256,066	160,404	132,823	189,289	1,077,019
Deductions	3,279,067	1,487,020	253,255	159,040	131,304	187,499	1,060,950
Net income (less loss)	30,094	6,218	2,797	1,382	1,510	1,794	16,393
Finance, insurance, and real estate:							
Returns	609,138	584,746	7,605	5,265	4,465	3,692	3,364
Assets	10,193,295	242,129	123,855	188,459	316,675	576,278	8,745,899
Receipts [2]	1,954,710	221,650	28,834	45,445	55,876	99,732	1,503,174
Deductions	1,809,868	221,172	27,670	42,932	50,581	87,850	1,379,663
Net income (less loss)	109,902	-696	792	1,774	3,850	8,302	95,880
Services:							
Returns	1,029,447	1,025,503	2,178	827	419	297	223
Assets	572,842	177,045	34,485	29,032	29,504	46,746	256,031
Receipts	726,041	447,355	37,573	32,317	27,699	40,462	140,635
Deductions	769,036	462,605	40,320	33,801	30,250	44,532	157,528
Net income (less loss)	10,617	5,080	107	665	226	416	4,122
PERCENT DISTRIBUTION RECEIPTS							
Agriculture, forestry, and fishing	100	68	7	6	5	6	8
Mining	100	20	6	5	6	7	56
Construction	100	71	9	4	4	3	9
Manufacturing	100	13	5	3	3	6	71
Transportation and public utilities	100	15	2	2	2	3	76
Wholesale and retail trade	100	45	8	5	4	6	33
Finance, insurance, and real estate [2]	100	11	1	2	3	5	77
Services	100	62	5	4	4	6	19

[1] Includes returns with zero assets.   [2] Includes investment income.

Source: U.S. Internal Revenue Service, *Statistics of Income, Corporation Income Tax Returns*, annual.

No. 843. Employees and Payroll, by Employment-Size Class: 1980 to 1991

[Excludes government employees, railroad employees, self-employed persons, etc. See "General Explanation" in source for definitions and statement on reliability of data. An **establishment** is a single physical location where business is conducted or where services or industrial operations are performed]

EMPLOYMENT-SIZE CLASS	Unit	1980	1984	1985	1986	1987	1988	1989	1990	1991
Employees, total [1]	1,000 .	74,844	78,021	81,111	83,379	85,484	87,882	91,631	93,476	92,302
Under 20 employees	1,000 .	19,423	21,171	21,810	22,296	23,069	23,583	23,992	24,373	24,482
20 to 99 employees	1,000 .	21,168	22,449	23,539	24,311	25,221	25,930	26,829	27,414	26,906
100 to 499 employees	1,000 .	17,840	18,348	19,410	20,260	20,615	21,307	22,387	22,926	22,369
500 to 999 employees	1,000 .	5,689	5,614	5,716	5,780	5,922	6,078	6,442	6,551	6,325
1,000 or more employees	1,000 .	10,716	10,413	10,645	10,734	10,657	10,984	11,981	12,212	12,220
Annual payroll, total [1]	Bil. dol	1,035	1,339	1,514	1,608	1,724	1,860	1,990	2,104	2,145
Under 20 employees	Bil. dol.	231	326	352	375	414	440	461	485	502
20 to 99 employees	Bil. dol.	261	358	388	414	449	485	514	547	555
100 to 499 employees	Bil. dol.	249	334	362	391	417	452	488	518	523
500 to 999 employees	Bil. dol.	91	120	126	132	140	152	163	174	175
1,000 or more employees	Bil. dol.	208	269	286	298	305	331	364	381	390

[1] Prior to 1987, totals for employees and annual payroll have been revised. Detail may not add to totals because revisions for size class are not available.

Source: U.S. Bureau of the Census, *County Business Patterns*, annual.

No. 844. Establishments, Employees, and Payroll, by Industry: 1980 to 1991

[See headnote, table 843. Beginning 1990, data are based on the 1987 Standard Industrial Classification (SIC). Prior to 1990, data are based on the 1972 SIC]

INDUSTRY	ESTABLISHMENTS (1,000)				EMPLOYEES (1,000)				PAYROLL (bil. dol.)			
	1980	1985	1990	1991	1980	1985	1990	1991	1980	1985	1990	1991
All industries [1]	4,543	5,701	6,176	6,201	74,844	81,111	93,476	92,302	1,035	1,513	2,104	2,145
Agricultural services [2]	46	64	85	91	290	380	531	544	3	5	9	9
Mining	30	37	30	30	994	943	723	717	22	28	27	26
Construction	418	476	578	578	4,473	4,480	5,239	4,671	75	98	132	123
Manufacturing	319	358	378	374	21,165	19,429	19,173	18,383	355	458	544	545
Transportation [3]	168	203	235	245	4,623	4,809	5,592	5,584	88	123	166	169
Wholesale trade	385	438	476	478	5,211	5,624	6,328	6,219	89	130	181	183
Retail trade	1,223	1,407	1,530	1,547	15,047	16,851	19,815	19,600	124	178	242	247
Finance and insurance [4]	421	488	545	577	5,295	6,005	6,956	6,860	77	132	197	200
Services	1,278	1,712	2,059	2,142	17,186	21,549	28,800	29,575	197	346	599	639

[1] Includes nonclassifiable establishments not shown separately. [2] Includes forestry and fisheries. [3] Includes public utilities. [4] Includes real estate.

Source: U.S. Bureau of the Census, *County Business Patterns*, annual.

No. 845. Establishments, Employees, and Payroll, by Employment-Size Class and Industry: 1991

[See headnote, table 843. Data are based on the 1987 Standard Industrial Classification]

EMPLOYMENT SIZE-CLASS	Unit	All industries [1]	Agricultural services [2]	Mining	Construction	Manufacturing	Transportation [3]	Wholesale trade	Retail trade	Finance and insurance [4]	Services
Establishments, total	1,000 ..	6,201	91	30	578	374	245	478	1,547	577	2,142
Under 20 employees	1,000 ..	5,392	87	24	532	249	199	409	1,314	521	1,920
20 to 99 employees	1,000 ..	674	4	5	41	88	37	62	209	48	180
100 to 499 employees	1,000 ..	119	(Z)	1	4	31	8	7	24	7	37
500 to 999 employees	1,000 ..	9	(Z)	(Z)	(Z)	4	1	(Z)	1	1	3
1,000 or more employees	1,000 ..	6	(Z)	(Z)	(Z)	2	(Z)	(Z)	(Z)	(Z)	2
Employees, total	1,000 ..	92,302	544	717	4,671	18,383	5,584	6,219	19,600	6,860	29,575
Under 20 employees	1,000 ..	24,482	316	119	2,070	1,491	951	2,176	6,932	2,211	8,094
20 to 99 employees	1,000 ..	26,906	149	201	1,538	3,902	1,521	2,363	8,200	1,810	7,197
100 to 499 employees	1,000 ..	22,369	59	225	746	6,397	1,475	1,264	3,862	1,426	6,914
500 to 999 employees	1,000 ..	6,325	(D)	(D)	119	2,377	440	228	369	527	2,166
1,000 or more employees	1,000 ..	12,220	(D)	(D)	198	4,217	1,197	187	236	886	5,204
Annual payroll, total	Bil. dol .	2,145	9.1	26.2	122.7	544.8	168.9	182.8	247.0	200.3	639.4
Under 20 employees	Bil. dol .	502	5.2	3.5	46.4	34.7	22.2	59.2	84.2	56.6	185.9
20 to 99 employees	Bil. dol .	555	2.4	6.4	42.7	98.4	41.3	68.1	96.1	52.4	146.8
100 to 499 employees	Bil. dol .	523	1.1	8.9	23.6	172.4	46.2	40.6	53.4	43.6	133.5
500 to 999 employees	Bil. dol .	175	(D)	(D)	3.7	72.9	15.8	8.1	7.4	16.5	47.3
1,000 or more employees	Bil. dol .	390	(D)	(D)	6.3	166.6	43.4	6.8	5.8	31.2	125.8

D Withheld to avoid disclosing data for individual companies; data are included in higher-level totals.   Z Less than 500 establishments.   [1] Includes nonclassifiable establishments not shown separately.   [2] Includes forestry and fisheries. [3] Includes public utilities.   [4] Includes real estate.

Source: U.S. Bureau of the Census, *County Business Patterns*, annual.

No. 846. New Business Incorporations and Business Failures: 1970 to 1993

[1970 excludes Hawaii; 1970 and 1975 exclude Alaska. Total concerns and failure data prior to 1984 exclude agriculture, forestry, and fishing; finance, insurance, and real estate; and services; therefore, are not directly comparable with data for 1984 and later. See also *Historical Statistics, Colonial Times to 1970*, series V 20-30]

YEAR	Total concerns in business [1] (1,000)	Index of net business forma- tions [2] (1967 =100)	New incor- pora- tions (1,000)	FAILURES [3] Num- ber	Rate per 10,000 con- cerns	Cur- rent liabili- ties [4] (mil. dol.)	YEAR	Total concerns in busi- ness [1] (1,000)	Index of net busi- ness forma- tions [2] (1967 =100)	New incor- pora- tions (1,000)	FAILURES [3] Num- ber	Rate per 10,000 con- cerns	Cur- rent liabili- ties [4] (mil. dol.)
1970....	2,442	108.8	264	10,748	44	1,888	1986....	5,119	120.4	702	61,616	120	44,724
1975....	2,679	109.9	326	11,432	43	4,380	1987....	6,004	121.2	685	61,111	102	34,724
1980....	2,780	129.9	532	11,742	42	4,635	1988....	5,804	124.1	685	57,098	98	39,126
1981....	2,745	124.8	581	16,794	61	6,955	1989....	7,694	124.8	677	50,361	65	44,261
1982....	2,806	116.4	566	24,908	88	15,611	1990....	8,038	120.7	647	60,747	74	56,130
1983....	2,851	117.5	602	31,334	110	16,073	1991....	8,218	115.3	629	88,140	107	96,825
1984....	4,885	121.3	635	52,078	107	29,269	1992....	8,805	116.3	667	97,069	109	94,317
1985....	4,990	120.9	663	57,078	115	36,937	1993, prel.	8,966	120.8	(NA)	85,982	90	48,423

NA Not available. [1] Data through 1983 represent number of names listed in July issue of *Dun & Bradstreet Reference Book*. Data for 1984-93 represent the number of establishments listed in the Dun's Census of American Business. The base has been changed due to expanded business failure coverage. [2] Source: U.S. Bureau of Economic Analysis, *Survey of Current Business*. [3] Includes concerns discontinued following assignment, voluntary or involuntary petition in bankruptcy, attachment, execution, foreclosure, etc.; voluntary withdrawals from business with known loss to creditors; also enterprises involved in court action, such as receivership and reorganization or arrangement which may or may not lead to discontinuance; and businesses making voluntary compromise with creditors out of court. [4] Liabilities exclude long-term publicly held obligations; offsetting assets are not taken into account.

Source: Except as noted, Dun & Bradstreet Corporation, New York, NY, *New Business Incorporations*, monthly; and *Monthly Failure Report*.

No. 847. New Business Incorporations and Business Failures, by State: 1991 to 1993

[1993 preliminary]

DIVISION AND STATE	NEW BUSI- NESS INCOR- PORATIONS 1991	1992	NUMBER OF FAILURES 1992	1993	DIVISION AND STATE	NEW BUSI- NESS INCOR- PORATIONS 1991	1992	NUMBER OF FAILURES 1992	1993
United States ...	628,604	666,800	97,069	85,982	Virginia	16,883	16,936	2,174	1,738
					West Virginia......	2,219	2,236	403	315
New England	28,864	28,686	6,214	5,330	North Carolina......	11,944	12,580	1,502	1,194
Maine	2,326	2,431	463	383	South Carolina......	5,700	6,189	483	392
New Hampshire.....	2,387	2,577	721	617	Georgia	18,098	21,046	2,877	2,350
Vermont..........	1,486	1,589	261	173	Florida...........	81,083	86,037	5,375	5,088
Massachusetts	11,706	12,197	3,031	2,720	East South Central ...	24,806	26,514	4,148	3,213
Rhode Island	2,458	2,553	513	344	Kentucky	6,782	7,155	1,091	841
Connecticut	8,501	7,339	1,225	1,093	Tennessee	8,306	8,514	1,660	1,209
Middle Atlantic	109,142	114,433	14,807	12,883	Alabama	6,116	7,087	901	841
New York.........	63,808	67,503	7,882	6,916	Mississippi	3,602	3,758	496	322
New Jersey	27,994	29,983	2,828	2,843	West South Central...	55,943	58,135	10,327	9,386
Pennsylvania......	17,340	16,947	4,097	3,124	Arkansas	5,326	6,078	511	186
East North Central ...	84,261	92,792	10,937	9,082	Louisiana	8,973	10,839	858	664
Ohio	17,895	18,730	2,689	2,127	Oklahoma.........	7,073	7,207	1,419	1,440
Indiana	10,205	11,119	1,479	1,091	Texas	34,571	34,011	7,539	7,096
Illinois	29,068	30,928	3,101	2,094	Mountain	47,033	49,841	6,096	5,586
Michigan	20,099	24,726	2,438	2,546	Montana	1,572	1,948	211	173
Wisconsin........	6,994	7,289	1,230	1,224	Idaho............	1,944	2,127	361	350
West North Central ...	32,499	34,749	6,195	4,446	Wyoming	1,386	1,707	140	90
Minnesota	9,564	10,002	1,523	921	Colorado	13,583	14,876	1,729	1,542
Iowa	4,531	4,918	730	507	New Mexico	2,713	2,843	457	448
Missouri..........	9,521	10,020	1,833	1,230	Arizona	9,832	9,148	2,302	2,064
North Dakota	820	984	164	145	Utah	4,973	4,582	437	351
South Dakota	1,040	1,218	232	175	Nevada	11,030	12,610	459	568
Nebraska.........	3,093	3,302	633	399	Pacific	61,523	63,587	23,427	23,102
Kansas	3,930	4,305	1,080	1,069	Washington	11,521	12,500	1,974	2,025
South Atlantic.......	184,533	198,063	14,918	12,954	Oregon	8,375	8,861	1,265	969
Delaware	29,887	33,582	188	137	California.........	36,561	36,973	19,796	19,695
Maryland	16,463	17,201	1,708	1,540	Alaska...........	1,274	1,461	102	108
District of Columbia ..	2,256	2,256	208	200	Hawaii...........	3,792	3,792	290	305

Source: Dun & Bradstreet Corporation, New York, NY, *New Business Incorporations*, monthly; and *Business Failure Record*, annual, (copyright).

No. 848. Business Failures, by Industry: 1985 to 1993

INDUSTRY	NUMBER					RATE PER 10,000 FIRMS				
	1985	1990	1991	1992	1993, prel.	1985	1990	1991	1992	1993, prel.
Total................	57,253	60,747	88,140	97,069	85,982	115	74	107	109	90
Agriculture, forestry, fishing......	2,699	1,733	2,256	2,871	2,282	197	50	65	80	63
Mining..................	796	388	411	430	307	193	88	95	99	72
Construction................	7,005	8,162	11,963	12,452	10,496	109	91	128	129	109
Manufacturing...............	4,869	4,740	6,595	7,120	6,142	119	92	127	131	114
Food and kindred products	261	232	305	350	299	127	91	122	133	116
Textile mill products	110	102	143	171	148	129	97	135	158	139
Apparel, other textile products . .	338	318	505	566	566	128	114	177	191	191
Lumber and wood products	415	420	576	554	437	136	97	129	122	98
Furniture and fixtures	236	258	383	398	303	161	151	223	226	173
Paper and allied products	55	68	86	88	85	100	105	129	128	123
Printing and publishing	659	734	1,062	1,245	1,054	94	74	105	118	100
Chemicals and allied products . .	172	139	207	219	171	126	86	128	129	102
Petroleum refining	26	21	33	35	17	145	83	137	161	78
Rubber and misc. products	157	158	209	185	194	117	101	134	113	117
Leather and leather products . . .	47	40	40	35	43	130	113	114	95	120
Stone, clay, and glass products .	159	161	220	215	166	98	80	111	107	84
Primary metal products	122	115	145	141	97	169	123	157	152	106
Fabricated metal products	484	397	593	662	585	125	90	135	145	128
Machinery, exc. electric.......	721	656	823	951	861	110	84	105	117	107
Electric and electronic equipment...............	329	287	380	421	321	154	114	149	157	122
Transportation equipment	197	242	318	263	229	165	147	198	158	140
Instruments and related equipment...............	110	120	192	175	153	85	68	106	92	81
Miscellaneous	271	272	375	446	413	101	74	98	106	97
Transportation, public utilities	2,536	2,630	3,891	3,922	3,089	151	94	134	126	75
Wholesale trade	4,836	4,423	6,170	6,744	5,975	102	77	109	113	99
Retail trade	13,494	12,972	17,242	19,084	15,600	109	65	90	76	62
Finance, insurance, real estate	2,676	3,819	5,962	6,260	4,923	62	60	90	87	67
Services	16,649	16,119	22,852	26,871	24,311	115	49	87	93	71
Public administration	12	10	20	30	24	(NA)	(NA)	(NA)	(NA)	(NA)
Nonclassifiable establishments ...	1,681	5,751	10,778	11,285	12,833	(NA)	(NA)	(NA)	(NA)	(NA)

NA Not available.

Source: The Dun and Bradstreet Corporation, New York, NY, *Business Failure Record,* annual, (copyright).

No. 849. Bankruptcy Cases, by State: 1990 to 1993

[In thousands. For years ending June 30. Includes outlying areas, not shown separately. Covers only bankruptcy cases filed under the Bankruptcy Reform Act of 1978. **Bankruptcy:** legal recognition that a company or individual is insolvent and must restructure or liquidate. Petitions "filed" means the commencement of a proceeding through the presentation of a petition to the clerk of the court]

STATE	1990	1991	1992	1993	STATE	1990	1991	1992	1993
United States...	725.5	880.4	972.5	918.7	Missouri	13.4	17.3	19.2	16.6
Alabama	24.7	27.8	27.8	25.5	Montana	1.8	2.1	2.1	1.9
Alaska	1.2	1.1	1.1	1.0	Nebraska	3.8	4.5	4.4	3.9
Arizona	17.7	19.3	20.4	18.5	Nevada	6.2	6.9	7.7	7.9
Arkansas........	6.8	7.7	8.6	7.5	New Hampshire ...	1.8	3.4	4.0	3.7
California........	103.2	124.2	152.8	159.7	New Jersey	12.6	19.4	24.0	24.9
Colorado........	17.1	17.0	16.6	14.9	New Mexico......	4.0	4.5	4.5	4.3
Connecticut......	4.4	6.9	8.9	9.4	New York	29.0	40.3	49.6	51.3
Delaware........	0.9	1.3	1.4	1.6	North Carolina	10.7	15.5	16.3	13.8
District of Columbia.	1.0	1.2	1.4	1.4	North Dakota.....	1.1	1.2	1.2	1.1
Florida..........	31.9	43.4	52.4	46.6	Ohio............	36.8	42.8	44.0	37.9
Georgia.........	38.7	49.0	48.7	42.9	Oklahoma	14.3	16.2	15.3	13.9
Hawaii	0.9	1.0	1.3	1.5	Oregon.........	11.3	13.5	14.3	13.3
Idaho	4.1	4.2	4.1	3.9	Pennsylvania	15.8	20.8	24.3	23.0
Illinois..........	35.8	40.5	43.4	41.4	Rhode Island	1.7	3.1	3.6	3.5
Indiana	22.2	26.8	28.2	24.8	South Carolina ...	4.8	6.9	7.4	6.8
Iowa...........	5.5	5.8	6.4	5.9	South Dakota.....	1.4	1.6	1.4	1.4
Kansas.........	8.1	9.6	9.6	8.3	Tennessee	34.2	40.6	41.6	38.2
Kentucky........	13.6	15.6	15.5	12.8	Texas..........	41.7	46.6	49.5	47.3
Louisiana	12.9	13.3	14.2	13.2	Utah...........	8.0	8.0	8.3	7.5
Maine..........	1.5	2.2	2.3	2.0	Vermont	0.5	0.8	1.0	0.9
Maryland........	9.2	12.8	16.0	16.2	Virginia.........	19.3	25.3	29.1	26.8
Massachusetts....	7.6	12.9	15.9	16.4	Washington	17.0	17.2	18.7	17.9
Michigan........	18.8	23.3	26.7	25.1	West Virginia	3.5	4.0	4.5	4.0
Minnesota	14.0	16.7	17.8	15.5	Wisconsin	10.2	12.1	12.4	11.3
Mississippi	10.6	12.3	12.7	11.1	Wyoming........	1.5	1.5	1.4	1.3

Source: Administrative Office of the U.S. Courts, unpublished data.

No. 850. Bankruptcy Petitions Filed and Pending, by Type and Chapter: 1985 to 1993

[For years ending June 30. Covers only bankruptcy cases filed under the Bankruptcy Reform Act of 1978. **Bankruptcy:** legal recognition that a company or individual is insolvent and must restructure or liquidate. Petitions "filed" means the commencement of a proceeding through the presentation of a petition to the clerk of the court; "pending" is a proceeding in which the administration has not been completed]

ITEM	1985	1986	1987	1988	1989	1990	1991	1992	1993
Total, filed	364,536	477,856	561,278	594,567	642,993	725,484	880,399	972,490	918,734
Business [1]	66,651	76,281	88,278	68,501	62,534	64,688	67,714	72,650	66,428
Nonbusiness [2]	297,885	401,575	473,000	526,066	580,459	660,796	812,685	899,840	852,306
Voluntary	362,939	476,214	559,658	593,158	641,528	723,886	878,626	971,047	917,350
Involuntary	1,597	1,642	1,620	1,409	1,465	1,598	1,773	1,443	1,384
Chapter 7 [3]	244,650	332,679	397,551	423,796	457,240	505,337	612,330	679,662	638,916
Chapter 9 [4]	3	7	10	3	7	7	20	15	9
Chapter 11 [5]	21,425	24,443	22,566	18,891	17,465	19,591	22,495	24,029	20,579
Chapter 12 [6]	(X)	(X)	4,824	3,099	1,717	1,351	1,358	1,634	1,434
Chapter 13 [7]	98,452	120,726	136,300	148,771	166,539	199,186	244,192	267,121	257,777
Section 304 [8]	6	1	27	7	25	12	4	29	19
Total, pending . . .	608,945	728,577	808,504	814,195	869,340	961,919	1,123,433	1,237,357	1,191,128

X Not applicable.   [1] Business bankruptcies include those filed under chapters 7, 9, 11, or 12.   [2] Bankruptcies include those filed under chapters 7, 11, or 13.   [3] Chapter 7, liquidation of nonexempt assets of businesses or individuals.   [4] Chapter 9, adjustment of debts of a municipality.   [5] Chapter 11, individual or business reorganization.   [6] Chapter 12, adjustment of debts of a family farmer with regular income, effective November 26, 1986.   [7] Chapter 13, adjustment of debts of an individual with regular income.   [8] Chapter 11 U.S.C., Section 304, cases ancillary to foreign proceedings.

Source: Administrative Office of the U.S. Courts, *Annual Report of the Director.*

No. 851. Small Business Administration Loans to Small Businesses: 1980 to 1993

[For fiscal year ending in year shown; see text, section 9. A small business must be independently owned and operated, must not be dominant in its particular industry, and must meet standards set by the Small Business Administration as to its annual receipts or number of employees. Loans include both direct and guaranteed loans to small business establishments. Does not include Disaster Assistance Loans]

LOANS APPROVED	Unit	1980	1984	1985	1986	1987	1988	1989	1990	1991	1992	1993
Loans, all businesses	1,000. . .	31.7	21.3	19.3	16.8	17.1	17.1	17.0	18.8	19.4	25.1	28.1
Loans, minority-owned businesses . .	1,000. . .	6.0	3.1	2.8	2.0	2.1	2.2	2.4	2.4	2.9	3.6	4.3
Percent of all business loans	Percent .	19	15	15	12	12	13	14	13	15	14	15
Value of total loans [1]	Mil. dol. .	3,858	3,450	3,217	3,013	3,232	3,434	3,490	4,354	4,625	6,339	7,200
Value of loans to minority-operated businesses [2]	Mil. dol. .	470	383	324	265	299	343	385	473	601	808	932

[1] Includes both SBA and bank portions of loans.   [2] SBA direct loans and guaranteed portion of bank loans only.

Source: U.S. Small Business Administration, unpublished data.

No. 852. Employee Stock Ownership Plans: 1975 to 1992

[As of end of year]

YEAR	Number of plans	Number of employees (1,000)	YEAR	Number of plans	Number of employees (1,000)	YEAR	Number of plans	Number of employees (1,000)
1975.	1,601	248	1984.	6,904	6,576	1989.	9,385	10,631
1980.	5,009	4,048	1985.	7,402	7,353	1990.	9,870	11,271
1981.	5,680	4,537	1986.	8,046	7,860	1991.	9,888	11,329
1982.	6,082	4,745	1987.	8,514	8,860	1992.	9,764	11,153
1983.	6,456	5,397	1988.	8,862	9,076			

Source: National Center for Employee Ownership, Inc., Oakland, CA, unpublished data.

No. 853. Venture Capital Commitments, by Source: 1980 to 1993

[1993 data preliminary. **Venture capital commitment:** investment in venture capital partnerships]

SOURCE	1980	1985	1986	1987	1988	1989	1990	1991	1992	1993
Capital commitments (mil. dol.)..	661	2,327	3,332	4,184	2,947	2,399	1,847	1,271	2,548	2,545
PERCENT DISTRIBUTION										
Individuals/families	16	13	12	12	8	6	11	12	11	7
Endowments/foundations	14	8	6	10	12	12	13	24	18	11
Insurance companies/banks	13	11	10	15	9	13	9	5	15	11
Foreign investors	8	23	11	13	14	13	7	12	11	4
Corporations	19	12	11	11	11	20	7	5	3	8
Pension funds	30	33	50	39	46	36	53	42	42	59

Source: Venture Economics Investor Services, Boston, MA, *Venture Capital Journal,* monthly.

No. 854. Venture Capital Disbursements, by Stage and Industry: 1993

[Preliminary. **Venture capital disbursement:** investment by venture capital partnerships in young, high-growth companies that have the potential to contribute to technological development and to become strong competitors in regional, national or international markets]

ITEM	Compa-nies [1]	INVESTMENT			Number of invest-ments [1]
		Total ($1,000)	Percent	Average ($1,000)	
STAGE					
Total	1,057	3,098,395	100.0	1,081	2,867
Expansion.	504	1,689,536	54.5	1,188	1,422
LBO/acquisition	34	188,172	6.1	2,444	77
Bridge loans, public purchases	224	470,930	15.2	768	613
Other early-stage	93	319,670	10.3	1,269	252
Seed	104	212,518	6.9	767	277
Start-up	98	217,571	7.0	963	226
INDUSTRY					
Total	972	3,098,395	100.0	1,014	3,055
Biotechnology	92	284,097	9.2	950	299
Commercial communications	33	136,584	4.4	1,897	72
Computer hardware and systems	55	92,733	3.0	545	170
Consumer-related.	84	325,792	10.5	1,894	172
Energy-related.	4	6,767	0.2	1,353	5
Industrial automation.	7	29,775	1.0	1,985	15
Industry products and machinery.	43	54,590	1.8	501	109
Medical/healthcare-related	159	446,513	14.4	830	538
Other electronics	68	87,821	2.8	374	235
Other products and services	110	604,731	19.5	1,344	450
Software and services.	203	640,178	20.7	1,010	634
Telephone and data communications.	114	308,813	12.5	1,092	356

[1] Figures for total number of companies and financings differ with actual totals reported as a company may receive financings in more than one stage during the year.

Source: Venture Economics Investor Services, Boston, MA, *Venture Capital Journal,* monthly.

No. 855. Mergers and Acquisitions—Summary: 1984 to 1992

[Covers transactions valued at $5 million or more. Values based on transactions for which price data revealed. **All activity** includes mergers, acquisitions, acquisitions of partial interest that involve a 40% stake in the target or an investment of at least $100 million, divestitures, and leveraged transactions that result in a change in ownership. **Divestiture:** sale of a business, division, or subsidiary by corporate owner to another party. **Leveraged buyout:** acquisition of a business in which buyers use mostly borrowed money to finance purchase price and incorporate debt into capital structure of business after change in ownership]

ITEM	Unit	1984	1985	1986	1987	1988	1989	1990	1991	1992
All activity: Number	Number . .	2,243	1,719	2,497	2,479	2,970	3,752	4,239	3,446	3,502
Value	Bil. dol. . .	153.2	149.6	223.1	198.8	281.8	316.8	205.6	141.5	125.3
Divestitures: Number	Number . .	801	780	1,090	1,004	1,274	1,615	1,907	1,759	1,598
Value	Bil. dol. . .	44.8	51	84.7	77.8	115.8	94.9	90.8	61.4	57.2
Leveraged buyouts: Number	Number .	106	154	233	208	291	293	177	171	199
Value	Bil. dol. . .	15.3	16.3	46.5	40.5	55.2	75.5	17.6	7.3	7.2
Foreign acquisitions of U.S. companies:										
Number	Number . .	(NA)	259	345	365	536	693	773	504	361
Value	Bil. dol. . .	(NA)	27.9	31.4	55.3	66	69.2	56.4	29.1	17.6
U.S. acquisitions overseas:										
Number	Number . .	(NA)	91	111	162	223	347	392	402	455
Value	Bil. dol. . .	(NA)	3.7	3.4	6.9	11.1	27.1	20.5	14.8	13.7

NA Not available.

Source: Securities Data Company, Newark, NJ, Merger & Corporate Transactions Database, (copyright).

No. 856. Mergers and Acquisitions, by Industry: 1992

[See headnote table 855]

INDUSTRY	TOTAL		U.S. COMPANY ACQUIRING U.S. COMPANY		FOREIGN COMPANY ACQUIRING U.S. COMPANY		U.S. COMPANY ACQUIRING FOREIGN COMPANY	
	Number	Value (mil. dol.)	Number	Value (mil. dol.)	Number	Value (mil. dol.)	Number	Value (mil. dol.)
Total activity [1]	3,502	125,308	2,686	94,025	361	17,632	455	13,652
Agriculture, forestry, fishing	28	903	19	633	4	34	5	236
Mining	56	3,743	30	1,283	11	1,591	15	870
Construction	27	384	19	167	5	217	3	(NA)
Manufacturing:								
Food and kindred products	117	6,407	66	1,581	15	451	36	4,375
Textile and apparel	54	808	40	655	2	21	12	132
Lumber and wood products, and furniture and fixtures	26	363	20	274	-	-	6	89
Paper and allied products	36	1,826	27	1,220	3	(NA)	6	605
Printing and publishing	74	891	57	568	12	303	5	20
Chemicals and allied products	94	4,572	53	2,821	17	959	24	792
Drugs	68	1,271	37	484	7	444	24	342
Oil and gas and petroleum refining	127	5,418	95	5,044	15	198	17	175
Rubber and misc. plastic products	58	812	42	746	7	66	9	(NA)
Metal and metal products	96	3,272	60	1,760	18	870	18	642
Machinery	124	1,870	79	1,640	21	174	24	56
Computer and office equipment	56	1,484	39	1,223	7	36	10	226
Computer software	108	1,748	86	1,594	4	30	18	125
Electronic, other electric equipment	112	1,716	79	1,216	14	226	19	274
Communications equipment	38	1,093	30	537	4	88	4	468
Transportation equipment	33	1,392	22	1,378	6	(NA)	5	14
Instruments and related products	152	4,014	105	3,157	21	625	26	233
Transportation and public utilities:								
Transportation and shipping	53	1,905	38	1,366	8	95	7	444
Telecommunications	56	4,382	48	4,234	3	148	5	(NA)
Radio and television broadcasting	51	6,585	48	5,585	3	1,000	-	-
Electric, gas, water distribution	37	6,904	32	5,741	-	(NA)	5	1,162
Sanitary services	53	414	43	150	7	265	3	(NA)
Wholesale	205	4,595	145	3,113	25	883	35	599
Retail: General merchandise stores	32	411	30	311	2	100	-	-
Eating and drinking places	33	675	28	675	4	(NA)	1	(NA)
Finance, insurance, real estate:								
Commercial banks	166	16,390	158	16,027	6	175	2	189
Savings and loans	144	5,305	140	4,878	4	427	-	-
Security and commodity brokers	74	5,760	54	1,297	9	3,259	11	1,205
Insurance	106	5,169	87	4,766	11	126	8	277
Credit insurance	42	1,638	37	1,306	1	(NA)	4	332
Real estate, mortgage bankers and brokers	88	1,909	78	1,430	7	479	3	(NA)
Services: Hotels and casinos	22	749	13	645	6	56	3	48
Business	304	3,063	238	2,301	28	88	38	674
Advertising	34	(NA)	25	(NA)	1	(NA)	8	(NA)
Automobile repair	22	627	18	600	-	-	4	27
Motion pictures	22	1,548	19	894	2	519	2	135
Amusement and recreation	24	964	21	358	2	606	1	(NA)
Health	215	4,068	199	2,980	12	1,008	4	80

- Represents or rounds to zero.   NA Not available.   [1] Includes other items not shown separately.

Source: Securities Data Company, Newark, NJ, Merger & Corporate Transactions Database, (copyright).

No. 857. Patents and Trademarks: 1980 to 1992

[In thousands. Calendar year data. Covers patents issued to citizens of the United States and residents of foreign countries. For data on copyrights, see table 919. For data on foreign countries, see table 1386. See also *Historical Statistics, Colonial Times to 1970*, series W 96-108]

ITEM	1980	1985	1986	1987	1988	1989	1990	1991	1992
Patent applications filed	113.0	127.1	133.0	139.8	151.9	166.3	176.7	178.4	187.2
Inventions	104.3	117.0	122.4	127.9	139.8	152.8	164.6	164.3	173.1
Designs....................	7.8	9.6	9.9	11.2	11.3	12.6	11.3	13.1	13.1
Botanical plants	0.2	0.2	0.3	0.4	0.4	0.4	0.4	0.4	0.4
Reissues	0.6	0.3	0.3	0.4	0.4	0.5	0.5	0.6	0.6
Patents issued.................	66.2	77.3	77.0	89.6	84.4	102.7	99.2	106.8	107.4
Inventions	61.8	71.7	70.9	83.0	77.9	95.5	90.4	96.5	97.4
Individuals...............	13.8	12.9	13.3	15.3	14.3	18.0	17.3	18.1	17.3
Corporations: United States	27.7	31.2	29.5	33.8	31.5	38.7	36.1	39.2	40.3
Foreign [1]	19.1	26.4	27.0	32.9	31.4	38.0	36.0	38.1	38.7
U.S. Government	1.2	1.1	1.0	1.0	0.7	0.9	1.0	1.2	1.2
Designs...................	3.9	5.1	5.5	6.0	5.7	6.1	8.0	9.6	9.3
Botanical plants	0.1	0.2	0.2	0.2	0.4	0.6	0.3	0.4	0.3
Reissues	0.3	0.3	0.3	0.2	0.2	0.3	0.4	0.3	0.4
U.S. residents [2]..............	40.8	43.3	42.0	47.7	44.6	54.6	52.8	57.7	58.7
Foreign country residents [2]	25.4	33.9	34.9	41.7	39.7	47.9	46.2	49.0	48.7
Percent of total	38.4	43.9	45.4	46.6	47.1	46.7	46.7	46.0	45.3
Other published documents [3]......	(Z)	(Z)	0.2	0.2	0.2	0.2	0.1	0.1	0.1
Trademarks:									
Applications filed..............	46.8	65.1	69.1	71.3	78.3	94.4	127.3	123.3	127.8
Issued.....................	24.7	71.7	51.8	51.4	54.3	63.1	60.8	52.4	86.8
Trademarks.................	18.9	65.8	46.7	47.3	47.4	55.3	53.6	46.6	80.2
Trademark renewals	5.9	5.9	5.1	4.1	6.9	7.8	7.2	5.8	6.6

Z Less than 50.   [1] Includes patents to foreign governments.   [2] Includes patents for inventions, designs, botanical plants, and reissues.   [3] Includes Defensive Publications, a practice which began in November 1968 and ended in July 1986; and Statutory Invention Registrations, the current practice, which began May 1985. These documents are patent applications, which are published to provide the defensive properties of a patent, but do not have the enforceable rights of a patent.

Source: U.S. Patent and Trademark Office. Fiscal-year figures are published in the *Commissioner of Patents and Trademarks Annual Report*.

No. 858. Patents, by State: 1992

[Includes only U.S. patents granted to residents of the United States and territories]

STATE	Total	Inventions	Designs	Botanical plants	Reissues	STATE	Total	Inventions	Designs	Botanical plants	Reissues
U.S. [1]....	58,694	52,254	6,013	196	231	MO	821	700	118	2	1
AL..........	299	258	39	-	2	MT..........	103	87	14	-	1
AK..........	49	39	10	-	-	NE..........	159	144	14	-	1
AZ..........	900	836	61	-	3	NV..........	167	150	16	-	1
AR..........	175	140	35	-	-	NH..........	363	335	27	-	1
CA..........	9,099	7,887	1,051	128	33	NJ	3,128	2,867	252	1	8
CO..........	950	849	94	-	7	NM..........	252	237	15	-	-
CT..........	1,620	1,454	157	-	9	NY..........	4,966	4,482	467	4	13
DE..........	542	522	18	-	2	NC..........	944	851	89	2	2
DC..........	67	59	7	-	1	ND..........	68	58	10	-	-
FL	2,112	1,863	232	11	6	OH..........	2,950	2,574	339	21	16
GA..........	812	675	134	-	3	OK..........	651	576	73	-	2
HI	81	70	11	-	-	OR..........	696	512	174	7	3
ID	259	239	19	-	1	PA	2,902	2,680	214	-	8
IL...........	3,284	2,895	376	2	11	RI	242	195	47	-	-
IN	1,095	927	162	-	6	SC	498	446	50	1	1
IA	407	367	38	-	2	SD	43	33	10	-	-
KS..........	325	264	60	-	1	TN	594	534	55	1	4
KY..........	297	259	37	-	1	TX	3,672	3,358	296	1	17
LA	526	488	36	1	1	UT	433	376	53	-	4
ME..........	129	106	22	-	1	VT	133	116	15	-	2
MD..........	1,067	960	104	1	2	VA	983	891	90	-	2
MA..........	2,450	2,228	199	5	18	WA	1,024	929	84	3	8
MI	3,028	2,833	179	4	12	WV	188	181	6	-	1
MN..........	1,598	1,396	192	1	9	WI	1,338	1,153	182	-	3
MS..........	146	121	25	-	-	WY	34	34	-	-	-

- Represents zero.   [1] Includes U.S. territories not shown separately.

Source: U.S. Patent and Trademark Office, Technology Assessment and Forecast Data Base.

No. 859. Patents, by Industry: 1970 to 1992

[Based on the 1972 Standard Industrial Classification (SIC). Includes all patents for inventions granted to residents of the United States, its territories, and foreign citizens. Individual industries may not add to total since a patent may be recorded in more than one industry category. Except for total, data for all years have been revised to reflect the U.S. Patent Classification System as of 1993]

INDUSTRY	SIC code	1970	1980	1985	1990	1991	1992
Total	....	64,429	61,819	71,661	90,366	96,514	97,443
Durable goods:							
Stone, clay, and glass products	32	1,227	1,278	1,366	1,723	1,957	1,905
Primary metals	33, 3462-3 .	639	673	751	893	923	919
Fabricated metal products [1]	34	5,142	5,159	5,699	7,051	7,198	6,710
Machinery, except electrical	35	15,758	14,324	16,729	18,923	19,963	20,423
Electronic and other electric equipment.	36, 3825 ..	13,038	10,692	13,896	19,153	21,019	21,370
Transportation equipment.	37, 348 ...	3,053	2,935	3,585	4,418	4,752	4,547
Instruments and related products [2]	38	7,293	7,429	8,865	12,351	13,309	13,280
Nondurable goods:							
Food and kindred products	20	488	482	547	728	688	666
Textile mill products.	22	480	421	503	507	498	559
Chemicals and allied products	28	8,806	9,826	10,246	12,438	13,423	14,185
Oil and gas extraction, petroleum products ..	13, 29....	829	731	964	842	863	776
Rubber and miscellaneous plastics products .	30	2,478	2,610	3,072	3,847	4,056	4,273
Other industries	....	5,100	5,259	5,437	7,491	7,866	7,828

[1] Excludes SIC groups 3462, 3463, and 348.   [2] Excludes SIC group 3825.

Source: U.S. Patent and Trademark Office, *Patenting Trends in the United States, State Country Report, 1963-1992.*

No. 860. New Product Introductions of Consumer Packaged Goods: 1980 to 1993

[**Consumer packaged goods:** consumable products packaged by the manufacturer for retail sale primarily through grocery and drug stores. **New product:** a product not previously offered for sale by a particular manufacturer including new varieties, formats, sizes, and packaging for existing products]

ITEM	Food	Beverages	Health and beauty	Household products	Pet products	Miscella-neous products
Domestic and imports:						
1980	1,192	256	834	331	86	197
1981	1,356	262	868	315	74	237
1982	1,762	332	919	390	103	113
1983	3,013	587	1,355	473	138	105
1984	2,678	569	1,094	303	108	227
1985	2,327	585	1,222	463	139	294
1986	2,764	657	1,327	365	107	194
1987	2,895	634	1,526	362	152	292
1988	2,781	597	1,496	310	151	222
1989	2,866	524	1,492	313	204	206
1990	3,453	630	1,531	432	164	154
1991	3,130	589	1,614	422	175	113
1992	2,987	587	1,869	417	213	127
1993, total	3,107	767	2,068	376	173	161
Percent:						
New brands [1] . , ...	22.6	29.1	21.3	11.4	32.9	28.6
Brand extensions [2]	1.6	1.2	1.0	1.6	0.0	2.5
Line extensions [3]	75.8	69.7	77.7	87.0	67.1	68.9
Types of new product innovation (percent): [4]						
Formulation [5]	44.6	54.2	46.2	50.0	42.0	51.6
New market [6]	1.5	-	1.7	4.0	10.7	3.3
Packaging [7]	26.9	18.7	18.8	18.0	5.3	12.9
Positioning [8]	26.2	27.1	31.6	28.0	42.0	29.0
Technology [9]	0.8	-	1.7	-	-	3.2
CUMULATIVE						
Domestic, except imports, 1980-93.	32,596	6,401	18,048	5,043	1,920	2,468
Imports, 1980-93 [10]	3,715	1,175	1,167	229	67	174
International, 1985-93 [11].	12,739	3,646	11,161	2,329	516	793

- Represents or rounds to zero.   [1] Product introduced under completely or partly new brand name.   [2] Product introduced in a category with an existing brand name which has not been used in the category before.   [3] Introduction of a new variety, format, size, or package of an existing product/brand name.   [4] Product which offers consumers something significantly different from existing products.   [5] Added or new ingredient which offers a benefit not previously provided by existing products in its category.   [6] Special category for new products which do not compete with any existing category of products.   [7] New product packaged in a way that makes it easier to store, handle, prepare, or dispense than others in its category.   [8] New product presented for new users or uses compared to existing products in its category.   [9] New product with added consumer benefits resulting from use of a new technology.   [10] New products introduced in the United States by foreign companies.   [11] New products introduced by U.S. and foreign companies outside the United States.

Source: Marketing Intelligence Service Ltd., Naples, NY, *Product Alert Weekly.* Publication contains extract from data base, Productscan.

No. 861. Gross Stock of Fixed Private Capital, by Industry: 1980 to 1992

[In billions of dollars. Estimates as of Dec. 31. Based on the 1987 Standard Industrial Classification]

INDUSTRY	CURRENT DOLLARS				CONSTANT (1987) DOLLARS			
	1980	1990	1991	1992	1980	1990	1991	1992
Fixed private capital.	9,364.1	16,871.4	17,489.7	18,099.2	11,584.7	15,245.2	15,519.0	15,798.4
Nonresidential	5,072.1	9,484.8	9,786.1	10,031.2	6,263.6	8,491.0	8,654.1	8,808.3
Agriculture, forestry, and fishing	333.2	416.3	416.8	412.0	436.1	369.8	362.0	353.8
Farms	308.6	368.8	365.1	356.5	405.0	327.2	316.8	305.7
Agr. services, forestry, fishing	24.6	47.5	51.7	55.5	31.1	42.6	45.2	48.1
Mining.	403.3	536.4	526.8	505.8	383.7	448.8	432.5	412.2
Metal mining.	30.6	41.0	40.4	39.8	39.6	36.6	35.6	34.6
Coal mining	31.0	49.0	48.3	47.8	39.3	43.7	42.5	41.5
Oil and gas extraction.	323.2	418.4	408.8	388.8	280.8	343.6	329.0	310.8
Nonmetallic minerals, exc. fuels	18.4	28.1	29.4	29.4	24.0	24.9	25.5	25.2
Construction.	91.8	113.4	116.6	117.0	120.0	100.8	100.4	99.9
Manufacturing.	1,144.5	2,114.0	2,189.1	2,255.1	1,480.7	1,875.6	1,918.8	1,961.9
Durable goods.	622.6	1,137.6	1,167.6	1,190.0	797.9	1,016.7	1,030.8	1,045.6
Lumber and wood products	31.0	41.5	41.4	41.1	40.5	36.9	36.1	35.5
Furniture and fixtures.	9.6	19.2	19.7	20.1	12.6	17.2	17.4	17.7
Stone, clay, glass products.	47.8	64.5	64.3	63.8	61.4	58.0	57.1	56.7
Primary metal industries.	143.2	206.4	207.9	208.8	185.6	180.3	178.7	177.5
Fabricated metal products	70.0	126.1	129.1	130.0	90.2	111.7	112.2	112.1
Industrial machinery and equipment.	99.8	197.8	203.6	208.6	123.2	179.7	184.1	189.3
Electronic and electric equipment	65.4	168.2	175.7	181.8	84.8	152.0	157.0	161.7
Motor vehicles and equipment	73.3	120.0	123.0	124.8	93.6	106.3	107.3	108.0
Other transportation equipment.	41.2	96.4	100.5	104.6	53.1	86.1	88.7	91.5
Instruments, related products	29.5	78.2	82.9	86.2	37.6	71.5	75.0	78.1
Misc. manufacturing industries	11.8	19.2	19.6	20.2	15.3	17.0	17.2	17.5
Nondurable goods	521.9	976.5	1,021.6	1,065.2	682.8	858.9	888.0	916.3
Food and kindred products.	103.8	192.3	202.5	213.5	137.2	169.1	175.5	183.0
Tobacco products.	5.3	14.2	14.6	14.8	7.0	12.6	12.8	12.7
Textile mill products	34.7	52.2	52.7	53.0	47.1	45.8	45.4	45.2
Apparel, other textile products.	11.8	18.3	18.4	18.5	15.4	16.2	16.1	16.0
Paper and allied products.	69.8	145.3	151.7	156.6	91.9	126.0	129.9	132.7
Printing and publishing.	36.1	82.1	86.0	89.5	47.8	74.0	77.2	80.4
Chemicals, allied products	149.6	271.7	288.1	304.9	192.1	238.2	250.0	261.5
Petroleum and coal products	71.4	128.0	132.4	135.9	92.6	113.0	115.6	117.2
Rubber, misc. plastic products	36.7	68.4	71.2	74.3	48.0	60.4	62.0	64.1
Leather and leather products	2.8	4.0	4.0	4.0	3.7	3.6	3.5	3.5
Transportation, communication, and public utilities	1,498.3	2,400.0	2,455.7	2,493.7	1,810.2	2,141.4	2,154.8	2,167.6
Transportation.	492.4	616.0	616.8	607.2	603.1	552.5	540.3	528.4
Railroad transportation.	232.0	249.5	246.3	244.4	281.1	226.0	221.1	216.9
Local, interurban passenger transit	8.9	12.5	12.6	12.3	11.2	11.5	11.2	10.9
Trucking and warehousing	77.5	106.8	108.4	101.3	101.6	95.9	91.0	86.5
Water transportation	46.6	55.6	55.6	56.2	56.5	48.5	47.5	46.6
Transportation by air	64.0	106.7	107.7	107.1	78.9	95.4	94.3	92.3
Pipelines, exc. natural gas	33.3	41.2	41.4	41.3	40.1	35.8	35.6	35.5
Transportation services	30.0	43.8	44.8	44.6	33.8	39.3	39.6	39.6
Communications	360.2	608.6	625.2	643.6	426.7	563.2	569.2	575.5
Telephone and telegraph	336.4	526.7	537.0	548.6	395.3	487.4	488.7	489.0
Radio and television	23.8	81.9	88.2	95.0	31.4	75.8	80.5	86.6
Electric, gas, and sanitary services	645.7	1,175.3	1,213.7	1,242.8	780.4	1,025.8	1,045.3	1,063.7
Electric services.	492.6	908.5	934.5	953.8	596.3	790.3	801.2	810.1
Gas services	135.3	208.4	215.5	219.3	163.6	181.9	185.4	189.3
Sanitary services	17.8	58.4	63.8	69.7	20.4	53.6	58.7	64.3
Wholesale trade	160.5	401.8	420.0	435.5	199.6	374.2	389.2	404.5
Retail trade	259.6	604.6	634.5	665.7	334.8	548.9	569.2	593.6
Finance, insurance, real estate.	794.3	2,046.1	2,139.7	2,232.1	1,006.3	1,854.5	1,929.3	1,995.9
Depository institutions.	126.1	414.8	442.1	462.5	151.2	379.3	403.5	421.4
Nondepository institutions	39.1	106.6	113.6	121.9	44.8	96.7	102.5	110.1
Security and commodity brokers.	3.8	12.9	12.9	13.0	4.4	12.4	12.4	12.6
Insurance carriers	21.8	124.9	134.9	145.9	25.3	121.3	134.0	148.9
Insurance agents, brokers, and service	4.8	5.9	5.9	6.0	5.0	5.7	5.8	6.0
Real estate.	589.6	1,353.1	1,402.7	1,455.3	765.5	1,212.3	1,244.1	1,269.7
Holding, other investment offices	9.0	27.8	27.5	27.5	10.2	26.9	27.0	27.2
Services.	386.7	852.2	886.8	914.4	492.1	777.0	797.8	818.9
Hotels, other lodging places	63.2	129.1	131.1	131.3	82.4	115.9	116.4	114.9
Personal services	20.7	32.1	34.0	36.2	26.0	29.6	30.9	33.2
Business services	88.4	224.7	231.2	234.7	111.2	203.1	205.0	206.2
Auto repair, services, parking.	68.2	150.9	158.3	164.4	86.5	139.7	143.4	149.7
Misc. repair services.	9.4	15.1	15.3	15.6	12.0	13.5	13.6	13.9
Motion pictures	9.0	19.8	23.5	25.8	10.8	18.3	21.9	24.0
Amusement, recreation services.	28.5	41.3	42.0	42.9	36.4	37.5	37.7	37.9
Other services.	99.5	239.1	251.3	263.6	126.8	219.4	229.0	239.0
Health services	50.6	129.7	137.9	147.2	64.9	117.6	123.5	130.0
Legal services	7.9	25.5	26.9	27.7	9.9	24.1	25.4	26.7
Educational services	2.6	5.4	5.7	6.0	3.1	4.9	5.2	5.5
Other [1]	38.4	78.5	80.9	82.6	48.9	72.8	74.9	76.9
Residential	4,292.0	7,386.6	7,703.6	8,068.0	5,321.2	6,754.2	6,864.9	6,990.1
Farms.	129.1	159.8	163.1	165.3	160.8	146.4	144.7	142.6
Real estate	4,162.9	7,226.9	7,540.5	7,902.7	5,160.4	6,607.8	6,720.2	6,847.5

[1] Consists of social services, membership organizations, and miscellaneous professional services.

Source: U.S. Bureau of Economic Analysis, *Survey of Current Business*, January 1992 and September 1993.

No. 862. Fixed Nonresidential Private Capital: 1980 to 1992

[In billions of dollars. Stocks as of Dec. 31; depreciation over entire calendar year. Data refer to privately owned assets and are based on the fixed capital formation components of the gross domestic product. Excludes residential capital and government enterprises; includes nonprofit institutions. Gross stocks allow for retirement; net stocks allow for retirement and depreciation. Net stock and depreciation estimates are based on the straight-line depreciation formula. For manufacturing industry, see table 1242]

ITEM	CURRENT DOLLARS						CONSTANT (1987) DOLLARS					
	1980	1985	1989	1990	1991	1992	1980	1985	1989	1990	1991	1992
Gross stocks...	5,072	7,156	9,012	9,485	9,786	10,031	6,264	7,389	8,272	8,491	8,654	8,808
Equipment...	2,389	3,374	4,257	4,506	4,671	4,761	3,009	3,518	3,979	4,091	4,174	4,265
Structures...	2,683	3,783	4,756	4,979	5,115	5,270	3,255	3,870	4,293	4,400	4,480	4,543
Net stocks....	2,974	4,113	5,084	5,321	5,440	5,534	3,677	4,248	4,673	4,773	4,823	4,871
Equipment...	1,360	1,852	2,299	2,417	2,480	2,510	1,709	1,929	2,155	2,202	2,225	2,260
Structures...	1,615	2,261	2,786	2,904	2,960	3,025	1,968	2,319	2,518	2,571	2,598	2,611
Depreciation...	240	358	451	471	489	505	308	368	425	436	446	460
Equipment...	161	240	306	321	334	346	211	250	294	303	312	323
Structures...	78	118	145	150	155	159	97	118	132	132	134	137

Source: U.S. Bureau of Economic Analysis, *Survey of Current Business*, January 1992, September 1993; and unpublished data.

No. 863. Business Expenditures for New Plant and Equipment: 1980 to 1994

[In billions of dollars. Represents expenditures for new facilities and for expansion or replacement of existing facilities that are chargeable to fixed asset accounts and for which depreciation or amortization accounts are ordinarily maintained. Excludes expenditures for land and mineral rights; maintenance and repair; used plant and equipment, including that purchased or acquired through mergers or acquisitions; assets located in foreign countries; residential structures; etc. They also differ from the nonresidential fixed investment data in type of detail, data sources, coverage, and timing. For further information, see the February 1985 *Survey of Current Business*]

INDUSTRY	1980	1985	1986	1987	1988	1989	1990	1991	1992	1993	1994, plans
All industries [1]	286.4	410.1	399.4	410.5	455.5	507.4	532.6	528.4	546.6	584.6	616.5
Constant (1987) dollars [2]	354.6	424.5	405.9	410.6	443.2	482.3	496.2	489.2	511.6	554.8	593.9
Manufacturing	112.6	152.9	138.0	141.1	163.5	183.8	192.6	182.8	174.0	179.5	186.3
Durable goods................	54.8	70.9	65.7	68.0	77.0	82.6	82.6	77.6	73.3	81.5	84.9
Primary metals.............	6.7	7.5	6.7	8.6	11.0	12.0	12.2	10.7	9.8	9.8	11.1
Blast furnaces, steel works	3.7	4.7	3.8	5.3	7.0	7.9	7.8	6.5	5.6	5.7	7.1
Nonferrous metals...........	2.0	1.8	1.8	2.0	2.5	2.6	2.9	2.8	2.7	2.6	2.3
Fabricated metals............	3.3	3.3	3.6	3.6	3.9	4.2	4.4	4.0	3.7	3.9	3.8
Electrical machinery	10.2	17.1	15.6	16.8	20.8	20.5	22.0	21.0	20.4	23.9	25.4
Machinery, except electrical	10.7	13.8	11.4	11.9	13.7	14.6	13.7	12.7	10.6	10.1	9.8
Transportation equipment........	16.1	19.6	18.9	16.7	15.8	18.7	17.9	17.2	16.1	19.4	19.9
Motor vehicles	8.5	13.4	12.8	10.9	9.8	11.5	11.3	10.2	8.7	12.4	13.1
Aircraft...................	3.6	3.5	3.9	3.6	3.5	4.2	4.0	4.1	4.4	3.3	2.6
Stone, clay, and glass	3.7	3.6	3.1	3.3	3.6	4.0	3.3	2.9	3.4	4.3	5.0
Other durables	4.3	6.1	6.3	7.1	8.2	8.6	9.2	9.1	9.4	10.0	10.0
Nondurable goods.............	57.8	82.0	72.3	73.0	86.4	101.2	110.0	105.2	100.7	98.0	101.3
Food and beverage...........	8.5	11.4	11.6	12.1	14.2	15.9	16.4	17.4	19.0	19.2	21.1
Textiles...................	1.5	2.0	1.8	1.7	2.0	2.2	2.3	2.2	2.1	2.3	2.4
Paper....................	6.4	8.1	8.3	8.5	10.9	15.6	16.5	11.5	10.5	10.2	10.8
Chemicals	10.6	14.4	14.5	13.9	16.6	18.5	20.6	21.5	23.2	22.4	23.3
Petroleum	22.8	34.1	23.1	22.1	26.0	30.1	34.8	35.6	29.6	28.2	27.4
Rubber...................	1.7	3.3	3.3	2.9	3.3	3.8	3.5	3.4	3.9	3.2	3.3
Other nondurables...........	6.2	9.0	9.8	11.5	13.3	15.2	16.1	13.7	12.6	12.5	13.1
Nonmanufacturing.............	173.8	257.2	261.4	269.5	292.0	323.6	340.0	345.6	372.6	405.2	430.2
Mining....................	12.7	12.0	8.2	8.3	9.3	9.2	9.9	10.0	8.9	10.1	10.8
Transportation..............	13.6	14.6	15.1	15.1	16.6	18.8	21.5	22.7	22.6	22.4	20.9
Railroad	5.9	5.7	5.3	4.7	5.5	6.3	6.4	6.0	6.7	6.2	6.2
Air	3.7	4.1	5.2	5.3	5.6	6.7	8.9	10.2	8.9	6.8	4.5
Other	4.0	4.8	4.6	5.0	5.5	5.9	6.2	6.5	7.0	9.3	10.3
Public utilities	41.3	59.6	56.3	56.3	60.4	66.3	67.2	66.6	72.2	75.0	81.4
Electric..................	33.3	44.0	41.0	39.1	40.9	44.8	44.1	43.8	48.2	51.8	57.0
Gas and other	8.0	15.6	15.6	17.2	19.5	21.5	23.1	22.8	24.0	23.2	24.4
Commercial and other	106.2	171.1	181.6	189.8	205.8	229.3	241.4	246.3	268.8	297.7	317.1
Wholesale and retail trade	32.0	60.1	65.4	68.5	76.4	84.5	95.6	105.0	116.2	(NA)	(NA)
Finance and insurance........	22.6	45.2	49.6	54.1	59.2	70.3	69.0	64.0	72.8	(NA)	(NA)
Personal and business services [3] ...	24.9	28.8	28.4	30.1	32.9	34.6	33.7	34.7	38.3	(NA)	(NA)
Communication	26.8	37.1	38.2	37.2	37.2	39.8	43.1	42.7	41.5	(NA)	(NA)

NA Not available. [1] Surveyed quarterly. [2] For preparation of constant-dollar estimates, see source for detail. [3] Includes construction.

Source: U.S. Bureau of the Census, *Plant and Equipment Expenditures and Plans*, quarterly.

No. 864. Gross Private Domestic Investment: 1980 to 1992

[In billions of dollars]

YEAR	CURRENT DOLLARS						CONSTANT (1987) DOLLARS					
	Gross private domestic investment				Less: Consumption of fixed capital	Equals: Net private domestic investment	Gross private domestic investment				Less: Consumption of fixed capital	Equals: Net private domestic investment
	Total [1]	Fixed investment	Nonresidential	Residential			Total [1]	Fixed investment	Nonresidential	Residential		
1980	468	477	354	123	312	156	594	603	438	165	401	194
1981	558	533	410	123	362	196	631	607	455	152	418	213
1982	503	519	414	106	399	104	541	558	434	124	430	111
1983	547	552	400	152	418	128	600	595	421	174	447	152
1984	719	648	469	179	433	286	758	690	490	199	456	302
1985	715	690	504	186	455	260	746	724	522	202	472	274
1986	718	709	492	217	479	239	735	727	500	226	487	248
1987	749	723	498	225	502	247	749	723	498	225	502	247
1988	794	777	545	232	534	260	773	753	531	223	519	255
1989	832	799	568	231	580	252	784	754	540	214	545	239
1990	809	802	587	215	603	206	747	741	547	195	555	192
1991	737	746	556	190	626	111	676	684	515	170	569	106
1992	797	789	566	224	658	139	733	726	529	197	595	138

[1] Includes change in business inventories, not shown separately.

Source: U.S. Bureau of Economic Analysis, *National Income and Product Accounts, volume 2, 1959-88*, and *Survey of Current Business*, August 1993.

No. 865. Composite Indexes of Economic Cyclical Indicators: 1980 to 1992

[1992 figures are preliminary. See source for discussion of composite indexes. Minus sign (-) indicates decrease. **Leading indicators** are economic time series that tend to reach their cyclical high and low points earlier than the corresponding peaks and troughs in the overall economy. **Coincident indicators** are economic time series that tend to reach their cyclical high and low points about the same time as the corresponding peaks and troughs in the overall economy. **Lagging indicators** are economic time series that tend to reach their cyclical high and low points later than the corresponding peaks and troughs in the overall economy]

ITEM	Unit	1980	1984	1985	1986	1987	1988	1989	1990	1991	1992
LEADING INDICATORS											
Composite index	1987=100 . . .	88.6	95.3	95.3	97.7	100.0	100.1	99.7	98.4	97.1	98.1
Building permits [1]	1967=100 . . .	96.7	134.8	138.1	141.2	122.9	115.8	107.7	89.6	75.4	87.7
Common stock prices, index [2]	1941-43=10	118.8	160.5	186.8	236.4	286.8	265.8	322.8	334.6	376.2	415.7
Initial claims, unemployment insurance [3] . .	1,000	480	366	383	370	314	305	327	383	444	412
Change in sensitive materials prices [3][4] . .	Percent	4.8	3.2	-7.9	3.6	13.1	5.2	0.8	-2.9	-7.0	3.4
Vendor performance, slower deliveries . .	Percent	40.6	57.3	48.0	50.6	57.4	57.7	47.6	47.9	47.3	50.2
Average workweek, manufacturing [5]	Hours	39.7	40.7	40.5	40.7	41.0	41.1	41.0	40.8	40.7	41.0
Plant and equipment contracts and orders (1987 dol.)	Bil. dol.	358	334	350	341	373	422	437	420	380	394
Manufacturers new orders for consumer goods and materials (1987 dol.)	Bil. dol.	1,016	1,138	1,144	1,167	1,226	1,264	1,250	1,227	1,186	1,231
Money supply (M2) [6] (1987 dol.)	Bil. dol.	2,162	2,499	2,628	2,792	2,872	2,904	2,877	2,874	2,843	2,813
Change in manufacturers' unfilled orders, durable goods (1987 dol.) [4]	Bil. dol.	-13	33	3	2	20	18	22	13	-15	-37
COINCIDENT INDICATORS											
Composite index	1987=100 . . .	85.6	92.2	95.0	97.2	100.0	103.5	105.8	106.7	105.1	106.5
Industrial production index	1987=100 . . .	84.1	92.8	94.4	95.3	100.0	104.4	106.0	106.0	104.1	106.5
Employees, nonagricultural payrolls	Million	90.4	94.4	97.4	99.3	102.0	105.2	107.9	109.4	108.3	108.5
Personal income less transfer payments (1987 dol.)	Bil. dol.	2,722	3,015	3,110	3,200	3,260	3,357	3,436	3,469	3,405	3,460
Sales, mfg. and trade (1987 dol.)	Bil. dol.	4,522	4,955	5,109	5,307	5,505	5,736	5,825	5,839	5,735	5,905
LAGGING INDICATORS											
Composite index	1987=100 . . .	99.0	95.8	98.9	100.2	100.0	102.1	104.9	104.9	102.4	97.4
Change in labor cost per unit of output, manufacturing [4]	Percent	10.1	1.6	1.8	-0.2	-2.5	4.6	2.6	3.0	3.3	0.1
Ratio, consumer installment credit to personal income	Percent	13.2	13.0	14.3	15.3	15.5	15.7	16.1	15.7	15.2	14.3
Average prime rate charged by banks . . .	Percent	15.3	12.0	9.9	8.3	8.2	9.3	10.9	10.0	8.5	6.2
Average duration of unemployment	Weeks	11.9	18.2	15.6	15.0	14.5	13.5	11.9	12.1	13.8	17.9
Ratio, mfg. and trade inventories to sales (1987 dol.)	Ratio	1.61	1.57	1.59	1.58	1.55	1.54	1.59	1.62	1.65	1.61
Commercial and industrial loans outstanding (1987 dol.) [7]	Bil. dol.	231	304	338	359	364	374	401	413	396	372
Change in CPI for services [4][8]	Percent	15.2	5.6	5.0	4.8	4.2	4.7	5.0	5.9	4.6	3.8

[1] New private housing units authorized.　[2] Standard and Poor's 500 stocks.　[3] Producer prices of selected crude and intermediate materials and spot market prices of selected raw industrial materials.　[4] Smoothed by an autoregressive-moving-average filter developed by Statistics Canada.　[5] Production workers.　[6] See table 802.　[7] Includes commercial paper issued by nonfinancial companies.　[8] Consumer Price Index.

Source: U.S. Bureau of Economic Analysis, *Survey of Current Business*, monthly.

No. 866. Business Cycle Expansions and Contractions—Months of Duration: 1919 to 1993

[A trough is the low point of a business cycle; a peak is the high point. Contraction, or recession, is the period from peak to subsequent trough; expansion is the period from trough to subsequent peak. Business cycle reference dates are determined by the National Bureau of Economic Research, Inc.]

BUSINESS CYCLE REFERENCE DATE		Contraction (trough from previous peak)	Expansion (trough to peak)	LENGTH OF CYCLE	
Trough	Peak			Trough from previous trough	Peak from previous peak
March 1919.	January 1920	[1]7	10	[2]51	[1]17
July 1921	May 1923	18	22	28	40
July 1924	October 1926	14	27	36	41
November 1927	August 1929	13	21	40	34
March 1933	May 1937	43	50	64	93
June 1938.	February 1945	13	80	63	93
October 1945	November 1948	8	37	88	45
October 1949	July 1953	11	45	48	56
May 1954	August 1957	10	39	55	49
April 1958	April 1960	8	24	47	32
February 1961	December 1969	10	106	34	116
November 1970	November 1973	11	36	117	47
March 1975	January 1980	16	58	52	74
July 1980	July 1981	6	12	64	18
November 1982	July 1990	16	92	28	108
March 1991	(X)	8	(X)	100	(X)
Average, all cycles:					
1919 to 1945 (six cycles)		18	35	53	53
1945 to 1991 (nine cycles)		11	50	61	61

X Not applicable.   [1] Previous peak: August 1918.   [2] Previous trough: December 1914.

Source: U.S. Bureau of Economic Analysis, *Survey of Current Business*, November 1993.

No. 867. Manufacturing and Trade—Sales and Inventories in Current and Constant (1987) Dollars: 1980 to 1993

[In billions of dollars, except ratios]

ITEM	1980	1985	1986	1987	1988	1989	1990	1991	1992	1993
CURRENT DOLLARS										
Sales, average monthly	**328**	**424**	**432**	**459**	**496**	**523**	**542**	**538**	**559**	**592**
Manufacturing	154	195	195	206	224	233	239	236	245	259
Retail trade	80	115	121	128	138	147	154	155	163	173
Merchant wholesalers	94	115	116	124	135	144	149	147	152	160
Inventories [1]	**509**	**666**	**665**	**712**	**768**	**814**	**837**	**833**	**842**	**866**
Manufacturing	264	335	323	338	367	387	399	386	379	377
Retail trade	121	182	187	208	220	238	241	245	254	272
Merchant wholesalers	124	149	155	166	181	189	197	201	209	217
Inventory-sales ratios [2]	**1.55**	**1.57**	**1.53**	**1.55**	**1.54**	**1.55**	**1.54**	**1.54**	**1.50**	**1.46**
Manufacturing	1.71	1.71	1.65	1.64	1.63	1.66	1.66	1.63	1.54	1.45
Retail trade	1.51	1.58	1.54	1.62	1.59	1.61	1.56	1.58	1.55	1.57
Merchant wholesalers	1.31	1.29	1.33	1.33	1.34	1.31	1.32	1.36	1.37	1.35
CONSTANT (1987) DOLLARS										
Sales, average monthly [3]	**381**	**431**	**447**	**464**	**484**	**490**	**483**	**486**	**507**	**535**
Manufacturing	179	194	198	206	216	218	215	216	225	239
Retail trade	103	123	130	134	139	141	141	140	148	158
Merchant wholesalers	99	113	120	124	128	130	127	130	134	139
Inventories	**605**	**686**	**694**	**724**	**751**	**784**	**790**	**789**	**796**	**812**
Manufacturing	320	336	334	340	355	374	377	371	366	367
Retail trade	147	194	197	214	220	231	229	230	236	248
Merchant wholesalers	138	156	163	170	176	179	184	188	194	198
Inventory-sales ratios [4]	**1.59**	**1.59**	**1.55**	**1.56**	**1.55**	**1.60**	**1.64**	**1.63**	**1.57**	**1.52**
Manufacturing	1.79	1.73	1.69	1.65	1.64	1.71	1.75	1.71	1.62	1.54
Retail trade	1.42	1.57	1.51	1.60	1.58	1.63	1.63	1.65	1.59	1.57
Merchant wholesalers	1.40	1.38	1.36	1.37	1.37	1.37	1.45	1.45	1.45	1.43

[1] Seasonally adjusted end-of-year data. See text, section 17.   [2] End-of-year seasonally adjusted inventories to seasonally adjusted sales.   [3] Average monthly sales for fourth quarter.   [4] End of fourth quarter inventories to average monthly sales for fourth quarter.

Source: Current dollars from U.S. Bureau of the Census, Current Business Reports, *"Manufacturing and Trade Inventories and Sales"* February 1994, and unpublished data; constant dollars from U.S. Bureau of Economic Analysis, *Survey of Current Business*.

No. 868. Manufacturing Corporations—Number, Assets, and Profits, by Asset Size: 1980 to 1992

[Corporations and assets as of **end of 4th quarter;** profits for **entire year.** Based on complete canvass. The asset value for complete canvass was $25 million in 1980 and raised in 1988 to $50 million. Asset sizes less than these values are sampled, except as noted. For details regarding methodology, see source for first quarter, 1988]

YEAR	Unit	Total	ASSET-SIZE CLASS						
			Under[1] $10 mil.	$10-$25 mil.	$25-$50 mil.	$50-$100 mil.	$100-$250 mil.	$250 mil.-$1 bil.	$1 bil. and over
Corporations:									
1980	Number	(NA)	(NA)	1,777	941	590	491	369	244
1985	Number	(NA)	(NA)	(NA)	896	744	608	428	281
1986	Number	(NA)	(NA)	(NA)	962	741	628	445	291
1987	Number	(NA)	(NA)	(NA)	1,007	811	676	481	318
1988	Number	(NA)	(NA)	(NA)	(NA)	783	729	550	334
1989	Number	(NA)	(NA)	(NA)	(NA)	781	750	579	347
1990	Number	(NA)	(NA)	(NA)	(NA)	834	774	597	367
1991	Number	(NA)	(NA)	(NA)	(NA)	868	799	608	373
1992	Number	(NA)	(NA)	(NA)	(NA)	956	843	648	407
Assets:									
1980	Mil. dol	1,384,474	126,639	43,569	34,930	41,963	75,284	179,959	882,129
1985	Mil. dol	1,932,766	153,883	64,324	52,669	58,019	96,748	208,403	1,298,720
1986	Mil. dol	1,994,120	140,864	67,663	55,974	58,233	97,908	217,341	1,356,137
1987	Mil. dol	2,135,266	147,919	65,623	50,171	60,874	109,458	235,368	1,465,853
1988	Mil. dol	2,339,690	149,276	77,068	53,461	62,190	110,411	261,880	1,625,404
1989	Mil. dol	2,501,097	144,814	73,487	56,548	68,149	117,014	282,056	1,759,029
1990	Mil. dol	2,629,458	142,498	74,477	55,914	72,554	123,967	287,512	1,872,536
1991	Mil. dol	2,688,422	140,056	70,567	58,549	72,694	127,748	295,743	1,923,066
1992	Mil. dol	2,796,625	141,766	70,446	65,718	75,967	132,742	302,287	2,007,698
Net profit:[2]									
1980	Mil. dol	92,443	7,770	2,235	1,904	2,479	4,532	11,485	62,041
1985	Mil. dol	87,647	8,601	2,551	2,305	2,819	3,628	7,312	60,431
1986	Mil. dol	83,122	6,659	2,988	2,129	2,514	3,884	7,572	57,376
1987	Mil. dol	115,600	7,273	3,849	2,753	3,338	5,237	9,636	83,514
1988	Mil. dol	154,583	11,364	4,488	3,199	3,978	5,473	13,994	112,086
1989	Mil. dol	136,490	10,381	5,173	2,921	3,105	4,434	11,824	98,651
1990	Mil. dol	111,561	8,527	5,160	2,769	2,676	3,531	7,245	81,652
1991	Mil. dol	67,516	6,820	4,271	2,564	1,714	1,730	5,119	45,299
1992	Mil. dol	23,212	9,567	4,748	3,245	3,050	4,585	5,976	-7,956

NA Not available.   [1] Beginning 1986, excludes estimates for corporations with less than $250,000 in assets at time of sample selection. Prior periods include estimates for corporations in this size category.   [2] After taxes.
Source: U.S. Bureau of the Census, *Quarterly Financial Report for Manufacturing, Mining and Trade Corporations.*

No. 869. U.S. Largest Public Companies—Profitability and Growth: 1993

[In percent, except ranks. For fiscal years ending in the 12 month period ending September 30. Included in the Forbes Universe of 1,305 companies is every firm with revenue of over $400 million in 1993; electric and banking firms $800 million. Represents industry medians; calculated by listing companies in rank order and selecting the midpoint. Where there is an even number of companies, an arithmetic average of the two middle companies is substituted. Minus sign (-) indicates decrease]

INDUSTRY	PROFITABILITY					GROWTH					
	Return on equity[1]			Return on capital[2] latest 12 months	Debt/ capital	Sales[3]			Earnings per share		
	5-year rank	5-year average	Latest 12 months			5-year rank	5-year average	Latest 12 months	5-year rank	5-year average	Latest 12 months
All Industries, median	(X)	11.5	11.7	8.4	33.1	(X)	6.7	5.1	(X)	-19.8	8.6
Health	1	18.3	17.6	13.0	23.9	3	11.7	6.5	1	13.9	6.3
Food, drink, and tobacco	2	17.0	14.5	11.0	35.6	10	7.0	2.5	2	7.7	0.4
Consumer nondurables	3	14.5	13.6	11.2	26.3	5	8.1	4.1	6	-9.6	8.4
Retailing	4	13.6	11.6	9.4	31.5	2	11.8	9.1	12	-23.6	10.6
Chemicals	5	13.4	10.5	8.1	33.8	11	6.4	0.8	10	-19.5	-5.3
Insurance	6	13.2	13.4	11.8	17.2	13	6.0	4.6	3	5.5	6.5
Food distribution	7	12.9	10.9	8.7	43.4	7	7.6	5.0	4	-7.4	8.0
Financial services	8	12.8	16.0	12.6	30.4	8	7.4	-0.3	5	-8.6	21.6
Business services, supplies	9	12.5	10.9	9.0	31.7	6	8.1	6.0	8	-10.9	5.0
Computers, communications	10	11.9	11.1	8.8	20.0	1	12.3	9.1	11	-21.4	10.5
Electric utilities	11	11.9	11.8	6.9	37.9	18	3.6	6.4	7	-9.9	8.3
Entertainment, information	12	11.1	12.1	9.5	27.4	12	6.3	5.4	16	-30.4	11.0
Aerospace and defense	13	10.9	13.2	8.8	35.7	19	2.7	-6.1	13	-25.1	4.7
Capital goods	14	10.8	10.6	8.9	29.4	9	7.3	3.8	9	-12.2	4.4
Forest products, packaging	15	9.0	5.4	4.8	40.1	15	5.5	2.8	14	-25.9	-19.4
Transport	16	8.5	12.2	7.2	37.2	14	5.7	4.9	17	(NS)	37.7
Energy	17	8.4	10.2	7.0	39.4	16	5.3	6.6	17	(NS)	10.8
Consumer durables	18	7.5	11.2	9.3	33.5	17	4.3	7.8	17	(NS)	20.4
Metals	19	6.5	2.5	3.7	34.4	21	-2.0	5.8	17	(NS)	-32.3
Construction	20	5.8	6.2	6.0	40.0	20	2.2	5.6	15	-28.3	31.0
Travel	21	4.1	5.4	5.5	60.8	4	11.1	5.5	17	(NS)	-19.1

NS Not significant.   X Not applicable.   [1] Represents primary earnings per share before extraordinary item divided by common shareholders' equity per share. Common shareholders' equity is total shareholders' equity including the stated value of all preferred stock at the beginning of each year minus the involuntary liquidating value of nonconvertible preferred shares.   [2] After-tax profits, the amount remaining if the interest paid on long-term debt was taxed, and minority interest divided by a firm's total capitalization. Total capitalization is long-term debt, common and preferred equity, deferred taxes, investment tax credits, and minority interest in consolidated subsidiaries.   [3] Net sales plus other operating revenue.
Source: Forbes, Inc., New York, NY, *Forbes Annual Report on American Industry,* (copyright).

No. 870. 500 Largest Industrial Corporations—Sales, Assets, and Profits by Sales Group Rank: 1989 to 1992

[In billions of dollars. Excludes large privately owned companies that do not publish sales. Includes service and rental revenues, but companies must derive more than 50 percent of revenues from manufacturing or mining for years ending not later than Dec. 31 of year stated, sales exclude excise taxes collected by manufacturer and include discontinued operations. Minus sign (-) indicates decrease]

SALES RANK	SALES				ASSETS [1]				PROFITS [2]			
	1989	1990	1991	1992	1989	1990	1991	1992	1989	1990	1991	1992
Total	2,165	2,303	2,264	2,365	2,299	2,443	2,466	2,565	106	93	[3]55	[3](-Z)
Top 100	1,518	(NA)	1,619	1,681	1,709	(NA)	1,844	1,902	76	(NA)	38	-8
101-200	321	(NA)	323	341	300	(NA)	328	351	16	(NA)	9	3
201-300	163	(NA)	160	171	144	(NA)	151	160	7	(NA)	4	3
301-400	98	(NA)	96	104	86	(NA)	77	91	5	(NA)	3	2
401-500	64	(NA)	65	69	59	(NA)	57	60	2	(NA)	1	(Z)

NA Not available. Z Less than $500 million. [1] Total assets employed in business at end of fiscal year, less depreciation and depletion. [2] After taxes, special charges, and credits. [3] Total profits of $55 billion in 1991 and $200 million in 1992 include charge-offs for accounting rule change on retiree health benefits. Profits before charge-offs were $60 billion and $71 billion in 1991 and 1992 respectively.

No. 871. 500 Largest Industrial Corporations—Selected Financial Items: 1980 to 1992

ITEM	Unit	1980	1985	1986	1987	1988	1989	1990	1991	1992
Sales per employee	$1,000	78.1	106.0	110.7	124.4	137.9	146.0	153.9	159.2	169.3
Changes in profits	Percent	3.6	-19.1	-7.9	41.3	26.9	-8.1	-11.6	[1]-41.0	[1]-100.4
Sales per dollar of stockholder's equity	Dollar	3.00	2.80	2.79	2.77	2.93	2.96	2.97	2.81	2.91
Return on stockholder's equity	Percent	14.4	11.6	11.6	14.4	16.2	15.0	12.7	[2]10.2	[2]9.0
Return on sales	Percent	4.8	3.9	4.1	5.1	5.5	4.7	4.1	3.1	2.4
Total return to investors [3]	Percent	21.1	26.3	16.1	6.6	14.1	17.5	-10.2	29.5	9.1

[1] Changes in profits of -41% in 1991 and -100.4% in 1992 include charge-offs for accounting rule change on retiree health benefits. Changes before charge-offs were -35.8% and 18.3% in 1991 and 1992 respectively. [2] Beginning 1992, return on common equity. Prior years, return on total equity. [3] Includes both price appreciation and dividend yield, i.e., to an investor in the company's stock.

No. 872. 500 Largest Industrial Corporations—Selected Financial Items, by Industry: 1991 and 1992

[Data are medians and are ranked based on sales per employee for latest year shown. See headnote, table 870. Minus sign (-) indicates decrease. For definition of median, see Guide to Tabular Presentation]

INDUSTRY	SALES PER EMPLOYEE ($1,000)		CHANGES IN PROFITS FROM PREVIOUS YEAR [1] (percent)		SALES PER DOLLAR OF STOCK-HOLDER'S EQUITY (dol.)		RETURN ON COMMON EQUITY (percent)		RETURN ON SALES (percent)		TOTAL RETURN TO INVESTORS [2] (percent)	
	1991	1992	1991	1992	1991	1992	1991	1992	1991	1992	1991	1992
Total	159.2	169.3	-41.0	-6.9	2.81	2.91	10.2	9.0	3.1	2.4	29.5	9.1
Petroleum refining	567.0	609.2	-52.1	-76.5	3.44	4.30	8.5	2.0	1.5	0.2	0.7	-1.7
Mining, crude-oil production	414.5	306.2	-61.9	-16.5	1.64	1.61	7.7	7.0	4.8	5.1	-5.5	-0.7
Tobacco	267.7	274.7	27.2	17.5	2.00	2.06	5.2	21.9	2.1	2.6	137.3	0.4
Soaps, cosmetics	241.1	244.3	-12.9	6.6	3.11	2.69	14.7	14.4	5.1	5.8	19.4	8.3
Food	239.0	229.8	13.2	7.9	4.82	5.09	19.7	15.6	3.5	3.4	26.7	1.1
Beverages	201.1	229.6	5.9	-28.7	2.48	3.14	21.1	9.7	5.5	2.1	32.3	4.6
Chemicals	227.3	227.7	-17.8	-27.8	2.36	2.37	12.6	10.5	3.9	2.3	31.9	9.0
Metals	176.5	185.4	-51.8	-90.5	2.50	2.70	5.2	-13.9	1.5	-1.2	18.2	13.3
Forest and paper products	172.4	181.1	-39.6	-1.1	2.02	2.22	4.8	5.7	2.5	2.1	36.9	14.6
Pharmaceuticals	168.9	179.8	16.0	8.2	1.87	1.96	26.1	26.7	12.8	11.5	61.5	-10.2
Toys, sporting goods	(NA)	178.2	(NA)	73.5	(NA)	2.65	(NA)	17.0	(NA)	6.5	(NA)	18.7
Computers, office equipment	163.7	177.4	1.1	-36.6	2.38	2.50	10.2	4.6	4.9	1.0	12.3	25.9
Publishing, printing	133.0	163.1	-10.3	-7.4	2.14	2.18	10.7	11.3	5.2	5.7	19.4	14.7
Building materials, glass	157.9	151.0	-53.8	-104.0	1.95	2.16	-0.7	-26.0	-3.6	-3.0	39.8	-0.6
Industrial and farm equipment	137.7	144.5	-23.6	-97.1	3.31	3.66	6.0	0.4	1.7	0.4	14.8	6.5
Aerospace	135.7	143.0	0.7	-52.3	3.91	4.10	12.4	0.3	3.3	0.1	35.5	16.4
Motor vehicles and parts	128.7	138.7	-70.4	-72.5	3.44	4.82	0.7	-11.1	0.3	-1.3	16.3	43.2
Metal products	125.8	136.5	-1.0	14.5	3.43	3.18	11.7	12.1	3.4	4.3	40.8	13.1
Rubber and plastic products	152.7	135.5	13.3	3.0	3.23	3.13	11.6	10.6	3.4	3.0	90.3	23.3
Scientific, photo, control equip	130.0	132.8	16.3	8.0	2.50	2.68	14.3	15.4	5.3	5.6	50.2	7.1
Electronics, electrical equip	111.2	124.0	-9.3	5.1	2.78	2.75	10.7	9.1	2.7	2.9	37.6	16.5
Transportation equipment [3]	118.4	122.4	-11.7	-52.7	3.72	3.38	8.9	3.6	2.4	-0.3	54.3	20.7
Furniture	104.0	102.7	-23.8	17.5	3.25	2.75	10.2	12.0	2.1	4.0	45.2	24.3
Textiles	93.4	98.8	-7.3	65.7	2.97	3.19	4.6	7.6	1.4	2.2	47.5	30.3
Apparel	73.9	63.7	1.1	46.9	3.96	3.53	13.6	11.6	3.4	2.5	52.6	-11.0

NA Not available. [1] Changes in profits of -41% in 1991 and -100.4% in 1992 include charge-offs for accounting rule change on retiree health benefits. Changes before charge-offs were -35.8% and 18.3% in 1991 and 1992 respectively. [2] Includes both price appreciation and dividend yield, i.e., to an investor in the company's stock. [3] Excludes motor vehicles and aircraft.

Source of tables 870-872: Time Warner, New York, NY, The Fortune Directories, (copyright).

No. 873. Corporate Profits, Taxes, and Dividends: 1980 to 1993

[In billions of dollars. Covers corporations organized for profit and other entities treated as corporations. Represents profits to U.S. residents, without deduction of depletion charges and exclusive of capital gains and losses; intercorporate dividends from profits of domestic corporations are eliminated; net receipts of dividends, reinvested earnings of incorporated foreign affiliates, and earnings of unincorporated foreign affiliates are added]

ITEM	1980	1983	1984	1985	1986	1987	1988	1989	1990	1991	1992	1993
Profits before taxes	240.9	210.7	240.5	225.0	217.8	287.9	347.5	342.9	365.7	362.3	395.4	449.4
Less: Income tax liability [1]	84.8	77.2	94.0	96.5	106.5	127.1	137.0	141.3	138.7	129.8	146.3	174.0
Equals: Profits after taxes	156.1	133.5	146.4	128.5	111.3	160.8	210.5	201.6	227.1	232.5	249.1	275.4
Less: Net dividends [2]	59.0	81.2	82.7	92.4	109.8	106.2	115.3	134.6	153.5	137.4	150.5	169.0
Equals: Undistributed profits	97.1	52.3	63.8	36.1	1.6	54.6	95.2	67.1	73.6	95.2	98.6	106.4
Capital consumption allowances [3]	164.9	268.1	293.7	333.3	338.3	354.1	372.3	389.8	394.1	385.5	413.7	433.2
Profits after tax plus capital consumption allowances [3]	321.0	401.6	440.1	461.8	449.6	514.9	582.8	591.4	621.2	618.0	662.8	708.6

[1] Federal, State, and local.   [2] Disbursements to U.S. residents, measured after eliminations of intercorporate dividends. [3] Without capital consumption adjustment. Includes depreciation and accidental damages.

No. 874. Corporate Profits, by Industry: 1980 to 1992

[In billions of dollars. Profits are without inventory valuation and capital consumption adjustments. Minus sign (-) indicates loss. See headnote, table 873]

INDUSTRY	BEFORE TAXES				AFTER TAXES			
	1980	1990	1991	1992	1980	1990	1991	1992
Total	240.9	365.7	362.3	395.4	156.1	227.1	232.5	249.1
Domestic industries	205.9	297.8	295.5	333.2	121.1	159.1	165.6	186.9
Agriculture, forestry, fishing	0.6	1.6	1.7	1.8	0.2	1.0	1.1	1.0
Mining	6.2	2.2	-0.1	0.9	4.4	0.6	-1.3	-0.8
Construction	6.0	11.0	8.8	9.0	3.8	8.7	6.9	6.9
Manufacturing	93.8	112.7	86.9	113.9	54.6	66.2	50.1	67.6
Transportation	3.6	0.9	1.6	3.0	1.9	-2.1	-0.8	-0.1
Communications	8.0	19.3	22.4	26.2	6.0	11.2	14.4	16.7
Public utilities	10.8	24.4	27.5	24.0	8.2	15.4	17.4	15.0
Wholesale and retail trade	40.3	43.7	48.4	52.0	28.2	28.6	33.9	35.3
Finance, insurance, real estate	26.4	62.3	76.3	74.7	6.6	14.8	26.8	24.1
Services	10.3	19.8	22.0	27.7	7.2	14.6	17.2	21.2
Rest of world [1]	35.0	67.9	66.9	62.3	35.0	67.9	66.9	62.3

[1] Consists of receipts by all U.S. residents, including both corporations and persons, of earnings of unincorporated foreign affiliates, dividends from their incorporated foreign affiliates, and their share of their incorporated foreign affiliates, net of corresponding outflows.

No. 875. Corporate Profits With Inventory Valuation and Capital Consumption Adjustments—Financial and Nonfinancial Industries: 1980 to 1993

[In billions of dollars. Minus sign (-) indicates loss. See headnote, table 873]

ITEM	1980	1984	1985	1986	1987	1988	1989	1990	1991	1992	1993
Corporate profits with IVA [1] and CCA [2]	177.7	264.2	290.8	271.6	319.8	365.0	362.8	380.6	369.5	407.2	466.6
Domestic industries	142.7	233.0	250.0	238.7	280.3	315.9	303.4	312.6	302.6	344.9	407.9
Financial	22.0	18.7	28.6	34.9	36.1	41.5	48.2	56.2	68.7	66.7	87.4
Nonfinancial	120.7	214.3	221.4	203.8	244.2	274.4	255.2	256.4	233.9	278.3	320.5
Rest of the world	35.0	31.2	30.8	32.9	39.5	49.1	59.4	67.9	66.9	62.3	58.7
Corporate profits with IVA [1]	197.8	236.4	225.3	227.6	273.4	320.3	325.4	354.7	367.3	390.1	442.3
Domestic industries	162.9	205.2	194.5	194.6	233.9	271.2	266.0	286.7	300.4	327.8	383.6
Financial	24.3	20.3	28.7	35.8	36.4	41.8	50.6	65.7	80.7	78.1	99.0
Federal Reserve banks	11.8	16.4	16.3	15.5	15.7	17.6	20.1	21.4	20.2	17.8	16.2
Other	12.6	3.9	12.4	20.3	20.7	24.2	30.5	44.3	60.4	60.3	82.8
Nonfinancial	138.5	185.0	165.8	158.9	197.5	229.4	215.3	221.1	219.7	249.8	284.6
Manufacturing	75.8	86.7	80.1	59.0	87.0	117.5	108.0	109.1	89.8	115.5	131.7
Durable goods [3]	17.9	37.2	29.0	30.0	42.2	52.2	49.3	39.2	30.9	48.3	60.2
Primary metal industries	2.6	-0.4	-0.9	0.9	2.6	5.9	6.1	3.3	1.2	0.6	1.4
Fabricated metal products	4.3	4.5	4.7	5.3	5.2	6.4	6.6	6.1	5.6	7.4	6.5
Machinery, except electrical	7.5	6.3	5.3	3.2	7.3	10.5	10.3	9.6	5.2	6.6	7.2
Electric and electronic equipment	5.0	4.8	2.4	2.6	6.2	7.6	9.3	7.9	8.6	12.1	14.6
Motor vehicles and equipment	-4.3	8.9	7.3	4.4	3.7	5.7	2.3	-2.2	-5.6	3.5	9.0
Nondurable goods [3]	57.8	49.5	51.1	29.0	44.8	65.3	58.8	69.9	59.0	67.2	71.6
Food and kindred products	6.0	7.3	8.4	7.5	11.4	11.8	10.7	14.0	16.6	17.0	15.1
Chemicals and allied products	5.5	7.3	6.0	8.0	15.1	19.3	18.5	16.2	14.5	15.7	16.8
Petroleum and coal products	33.6	15.9	17.1	-8.5	-3.6	10.4	5.7	17.3	5.8	6.1	11.9
Transportation and public utilities	18.3	39.9	34.1	36.5	43.4	47.5	42.1	44.0	54.4	52.0	57.8
Wholesale and retail trade	22.8	44.9	43.1	46.3	39.3	39.7	39.7	37.2	47.4	46.3	54.4
Other	21.6	8.7	8.5	17.1	27.2	27.3	25.5	30.8	28.2	36.0	40.6

[1] Inventory valuation adjustment.   [2] Capital consumption adjustment.   [3] Includes other industries not shown separately.
Source of tables 873-875: U.S. Bureau of Economic Analysis, *National Income and Product Accounts of the United States, volume 2, 1959-88; Survey of Current Business*, July 1992, August 1993, and April 1994.

No. 876. Manufacturing, Mining, and Trade Corporations—Profits and Stockholders' Equity Ratios: 1980 to 1992

[Averages of quarterly figures at annual rates. Beginning 1990, manufacturing data exclude estimates for corporations with less than $250,000 in assets at time of sample selection. Data are not necessarily comparable from year to year due to changes in accounting procedures, industry classifications, sampling procedures, etc.; for detail, see source. Based on sample; see source for discussion of methodology. Minus sign (-) indicates loss]

INDUSTRY	RATIO OF PROFITS TO STOCKHOLDERS' EQUITY (percent)				PROFITS PER DOLLAR OF SALES (cents)				RATIO OF STOCKHOLDERS' EQUITY TO DEBT			
	1980	1990	1991	1992	1980	1990	1991	1992	1980	1990	1991	1992
Manufacturing corporations........	13.9	10.7	6.4	2.1	4.9	4.0	2.5	0.7	2.3	1.3	1.3	1.3
Durable goods....................	11.2	8.0	1.5	-5.3	4.0	3.0	0.6	-1.9	2.2	1.6	1.5	1.4
Lumber and wood products...........	(NA)	(NA)	(NA)	15.1	(NA)	(NA)	(NA)	3.8	(NA)	(NA)	(NA)	1.4
Furniture and fixtures..............	(NA)	(NA)	(NA)	8.9	(NA)	(NA)	(NA)	2.7	(NA)	(NA)	(NA)	1.3
Stone, clay, and glass products.......	10.8	5.4	-8.9	-2.6	4.2	1.8	-3.3	-1.3	1.9	0.8	0.7	0.7
Primary metal industries............	11.7	9.5	-1.5	-8.5	4.1	2.6	-0.4	3.0	1.7	1.1	1.0	0.9
Iron and steel.................	9.0	6.6	-13.3	-22.1	2.9	1.0	-2.9	-2.5	1.7	0.6	0.6	0.4
Nonferrous metals..............	15.6	10.4	3.8	10.3	5.8	4.0	1.5	-2.0	1.8	1.6	1.3	1.2
Fabricated metal products...........	13.9	11.7	8.8	10.2	4.2	3.4	2.6	3.0	2.1	1.3	1.3	1.3
Machinery, exc. electrical	15.0	8.1	-2.1	-7.8	6.5	4.4	-1.1	-3.5	2.2	2.2	1.9	1.8
Electrical and electronic equipment.....	15.1	7.5	5.1	8.5	5.0	3.0	2.1	3.6	2.6	1.6	1.6	1.7
Transportation equipment	-0.6	3.8	-4.3	-41.1	-0.3	1.3	-1.5	-9.3	2.7	1.9	1.6	1.2
Motor vehicles and equipment	-9.3	-1.0	-11.3	-71.0	-3.4	-0.5	-4.1	-15.1	3.4	2.2	1.7	1.1
Aircraft, guided missiles and parts	16.0	11.5	6.1	-5.2	4.3	3.4	1.9	-1.5	2.8	1.6	1.6	1.4
Instruments and related products	17.5	12.9	12.1	7.3	9.3	6.6	6.6	3.9	4.3	1.6	1.7	1.8
Miscellaneous manufacturing.........	(NA)	(NA)	(NA)	11.4	(NA)	(NA)	(NA)	3.8	(NA)	(NA)	(NA)	1.5
Nondurable goods	16.4	13.3	10.8	8.3	5.6	4.9	4.1	3.1	2.3	1.2	1.2	1.2
Food and kindred products [1]........	14.7	16.1	17.5	15.0	3.4	4.1	4.8	4.3	1.9	0.8	0.9	0.9
Tobacco products	19.8	(¹)	(¹)	(¹)	11.7	(¹)	(¹)	(¹)	1.8	(¹)	(¹)	(¹)
Textile mill products..............	8.5	3.4	6.0	12.4	2.2	0.8	1.5	3.5	2.0	0.7	0.7	1.1
Apparel (includes leather)...........	(NA)	(NA)	(NA)	28.5	(NA)	(NA)	(NA)	5.1	(NA)	(NA)	(NA)	1.0
Paper and allied products...........	12.1	10.6	4.4	2.5	5.1	4.2	1.8	0.9	2.0	1.1	0.9	0.9
Printing and publishing.............	16.4	8.3	6.1	7.2	5.5	3.6	2.7	3.2	2.1	1.2	1.2	1.2
Chemicals and allied products........	15.4	17.3	14.0	8.5	8.1	8.2	6.7	4.0	2.2	1.4	1.4	1.3
Industrial....................	11.9	13.8	8.0	-4.7	5.4	7.0	4.2	-2.3	1.9	1.4	1.3	1.1
Drugs......................	19.9	27.1	26.1	22.6	13.2	15.7	15.2	12.9	3.0	2.2	2.4	2.2
Residual of chemicals	(NA)	(NA)	(NA)	13.3	(NA)	(NA)	(NA)	5.1	(NA)	(NA)	(NA)	1.3
Petroleum and coal products.........	20.0	12.8	7.7	2.5	7.7	5.7	3.9	0.9	3.4	1.7	1.6	1.5
Rubber and misc. plastics products.....	6.7	6.9	3.5	7.0	2.0	1.8	0.8	1.7	1.6	1.0	0.9	1.5
Mining corporations [2]	19.2	8.1	2.6	-0.8	11.3	5.7	2.1	-0.8	1.3	1.3	1.3	1.4
Retail trade corporations [2]......	13.2	8.4	7.2	5.6	1.7	1.1	1.0	0.8	1.2	0.6	0.6	0.7
Wholesale trade corporations [2]	17.3	5.0	4.3	5.3	1.8	0.6	0.6	0.7	1.2	1.0	0.9	0.8

NA Not available.   [1] After 1980, tobacco included in food and kindred products.   [2] Asset cut-off raised to $50 million from $25 million in 1985.

No. 877. Manufacturing Corporations—Selected Finances: 1980 to 1992

[In billions of dollars. Data are not necessarily comparable from year to year due to changes in accounting procedures, industry classifications, sampling procedures, etc.; for detail, see source. See also *Historical Statistics, Colonial Times to 1970*, series P 93-106]

YEAR	ALL MANUFACTURING CORPS.					DURABLE GOODS INDUSTRIES					NONDURABLE GOODS INDUSTRIES				
	Sales	Profits		Stock holders' equity [1]	Debt [1]	Sales	Profits		Stock holders' equity [1]	Debt [1]	Sales	Profits		Stock holders' equity [1]	Debt [1]
		Before taxes	After taxes				Before taxes	After taxes				Before taxes	After taxes		
1980 ..	1,897	145	92	665	292	883	57	36	316	143	1,014	88	57	349	149
1981 ..	2,145	159	101	743	335	979	67	42	350	159	1,165	91	60	393	176
1982 ..	2,039	108	71	770	371	913	35	22	356	177	1,126	74	49	415	193
1983 ..	2,114	133	86	813	368	973	49	30	372	168	1,141	84	56	440	200
1984 ..	2,335	166	108	864	405	1,108	76	49	396	166	1,228	90	59	469	239
1985 ..	2,331	137	88	866	454	1,143	61	39	421	187	1,189	76	49	445	267
1986 [2] ..	2,221	129	83	875	501	1,126	52	33	436	203	1,096	77	51	438	298
1987 ..	2,378	173	116	901	553	1,178	78	53	444	229	1,200	95	63	457	324
1988 ..	2,596	216	155	958	622	1,285	92	67	469	265	1,312	124	88	489	357
1989 ..	2,745	189	136	999	733	1,357	75	56	501	308	1,388	114	81	498	425
1990 ..	2,812	160	112	1,044	782	1,357	58	41	515	328	1,454	102	71	529	453
1991 ..	2,761	100	68	1,064	814	1,304	14	7	507	338	1,457	86	60	557	476
1992 ..	2,890	32	23	1,035	819	1,390	-34	-24	474	335	1,500	66	47	561	485

[1] Annual data are average equity or debt for the year using four end-of-quarter figures.   [2] Beginning 1986, data exclude estimates for corporations with less than $250,000 in assets at time of sample selection.

Source of tables 876 and 877: Through 1981, U.S. Federal Trade Commission; thereafter, U.S. Bureau of Census, *Quarterly Financial Report for Manufacturing, Mining, and Trade Corporations*. In U.S. Council of Economic Advisers, *Economic Report of the President*, annual.

No. 878. Corporate Philanthropy: 1985 to 1992

[Percent of worldwide pretax net income. Data are based on a sample greater than 1,200 corporations. Medians by industry]

INDUSTRY	1985	1986	1987	1988	1989	1990	1991	1992
All firms, median.............	1.0	1.0	0.9	0.8	0.9	1.0	1.3	1.0
Manufacturing firms, median	1.1	1.2	1.0	0.8	0.9	1.0	1.3	1.1
Chemicals...................	1.1	1.1	0.8	0.7	0.8	0.9	1.0	0.9
Electrical machinery and equipment. . .	1.6	1.3	1.2	0.6	0.7	1.0	1.8	0.7
Food, beverage, tobacco..........	1.2	1.5	1.3	1.0	1.4	1.1	1.1	0.9
Machinery, nonelectrical	1.1	2.4	1.0	0.9	0.7	0.7	0.8	0.9
Paper and like products..........	1.2	0.7	0.7	0.6	0.7	1.4	1.9	1.2
Petroleum and gas [1].............	0.7	1.2	0.9	0.5	0.8	0.8	2.1	1.3
Pharmaceuticals...............	1.0	0.9	1.0	1.1	1.0	1.1	1.4	1.1
Primary metal industries	1.1	1.4	(NA)	(NA)	0.5	0.8	1.0	1.4
Printing and publishing	1.3	1.4	0.8	2.3	1.7	1.2	1.5	1.3
Transportation equipment [2]	1.0	1.6	0.9	1.1	1.2	2.0	1.1	1.8
Nonmanufacturing firms, median	0.9	0.9	0.7	0.9	1.0	0.9	1.2	0.9

NA Not available.   [1] Includes mining firms.   [2] Includes rubber and miscellaneous plastic firms.

Source: The Conference Board, New York, NY, *Annual Survey of Corporate Contributions*, (copyright).

No. 879. Foreign Corporate Activity in the United States: 1990

[In millions of dollars, except number of returns. Includes U.S. corporations controlled or owned by any foreign person (i.e., an individual, partnership, corporation, estate, or trust), directly or indirectly, based on 50 percent or more of a U.S. corporation's voting stock at the end of the tax year]

COUNTRY [1]	Number of returns	Assets	Receipts [2]	Net income (less deficit)	U.S. INCOME TAX	
					Before credits	After credits
All corporations in the U.S.	3,716,650	18,190,058	11,409,520	370,633	128,186	96,403
U.S. corporations controlled by a foreign person	44,124	1,652,786	1,060,435	4,023	8,720	7,440
Canada	7,866	180,125	102,666	−524	714	571
Latin America	6,362	83,431	47,252	−295	306	284
Other Western Hemisphere	386	11,148	7,124	−144	55	54
Europe.................	16,441	837,653	563,396	7,723	5,915	5,019
European Union [3]..........	13,897	725,054	483,603	6,914	5,232	4,515
Belgium	171	15,364	15,432	927	353	169
France...............	2,610	92,033	61,296	−3	265	211
West Germany	3,035	95,316	93,788	399	604	518
Netherlands	1,713	170,169	113,427	711	1,090	1,032
United Kingdom..........	4,513	314,511	183,998	5,070	2,836	2,506
Sweden	533	22,799	18,388	136	120	81
Switzerland	1,354	75,554	49,444	827	507	370
Africa	246	757	436	−45	2	2
Asia [3]	10,833	478,732	309,677	−2,931	1,484	1,402
Hong Kong	1,008	26,742	7,793	−284	17	16
Japan................	6,672	413,368	280,126	−1,936	1,391	1,313
South Korea	191	7,026	8,291	−289	9	9
Oceania.................	858	55,178	23,349	22	142	71
Puerto Rico and U.S. possessions	45	1,880	982	168	61	3
Country not stated..........	1,087	3,883	5,553	48	41	34

[1] Geographic location of the foreign owners' country of residence, incorporation, organization, creation, or administration.
[2] Includes business and investment receipts.   [3] Includes countries not shown separately.

Source: U.S. Internal Revenue Service, *Statistics of Income Bulletin*, fall 1993.

No. 880. U.S. Multinational Companies—Gross Product: 1982 and 1989

[In millions of dollars. Gross product measures valued added by a firm. Consists of nonbank U.S. parent companies and their nonbank foreign affiliates. A U.S. parent comprises the domestic operations of a multinational and is a U.S. person that owns or controls 10 percent or more of the voting securities, or the equivalent, of a foreign business enterprise. A U.S. person can be an incorporated business enterprise. A majority-owned foreign affiliate is a foreign business enterprise in which a U.S. parent company owns or controls 50% or more of the voting securities]

INDUSTRY	U.S. MULTINATIONALS		U.S. PARENTS		MAJORITY-OWNED FOREIGN AFFILIATES	
	1982	1989	1982	1989	1982	1989
All industries	1,019,734	1,364,878	796,017	1,044,884	223,717	319,994
Petroleum	211,937	165,680	134,096	93,128	77,841	72,552
Manufacturing	542,689	793,771	421,050	586,568	121,639	207,203
Food and kindred products	46,069	79,472	35,804	60,310	10,265	19,162
Chemical and allied products.	93,054	141,006	66,234	97,119	26,820	43,887
Primary and fabricated metals	43,592	45,775	37,215	37,556	6,377	8,219
Machinery, except electrical.	84,046	116,146	60,597	70,887	23,449	45,259
Electric and electronic equipment.	69,259	68,515	59,323	56,139	9,936	12,376
Transportation equipment	91,170	160,292	71,256	121,141	19,914	39,151
Other.	115,499	182,567	90,621	143,417	24,878	39,150
Wholesale trade.	17,427	28,766	13,604	22,587	3,823	6,179
Finance, insurance, real estate	31,823	62,715	22,801	50,535	9,022	12,180
Finance, except banking.	4,991	16,948	4,730	15,103	261	1,845
Insurance.	23,539	41,233	17,954	34,948	5,585	6,285
Real estate.	135	668	120	558	15	110
Holding companies	3,005	2,808	-2	-75	3,007	2,883
Services	29,362	66,999	25,997	57,090	3,365	9,909
Hotels and other lodging places.	2,838	6,676	2,693	5,780	145	896
Business services	10,026	24,067	8,501	18,756	1,525	5,311
Advertising	2,627	3,960	1,947	2,349	680	1,611
Equipment rental (exc. auto, computers). . . .	652	193	646	175	6	18
Computer and data processing	2,313	6,361	2,135	5,353	178	1,008
Other	4,434	13,551	3,773	10,878	661	2,673
Automotive rental and leasing	(¹)	4,998	(¹)	4,212	(¹)	786
Motion pictures, television tape and film	941	3,465	825	2,663	116	802
Health services	5,420	8,965	5,234	8,559	186	406
Engineering, architectural, surveying	3,350	3,498	2,422	2,998	928	500
Management and public relations	(¹)	1,702	(¹)	1,180	(¹)	522
Other.	6,787	13,629	6,322	12,943	465	686
Other industries	186,496	246,946	178,469	234,975	8,027	11,971

¹ Included in "other" services.

Source: U.S. Bureau of Economic Analysis, *Survey of Current Business*, February 1994.

No. 881. U.S. Multinational Companies—Selected Characteristics: 1991

[Preliminary. In billions of dollars, except as indicated. Consists of nonbank U.S. parent companies and their nonbank foreign affiliates. U.S. parent is a U.S. person that owns or controls directly or indirectly, 10 percent or more of the voting securities of an incorporated foreign business enterprise, or an equivalent interest in an unincorporated foreign business enterprise. A U.S. person can be an incorporated business enterprise. A foreign affiliate is a foreign business enterprise owned or controlled by a U.S. parent company]

INDUSTRY ¹	U.S. PARENTS				FOREIGN AFFILIATES				U.S. exports shipped to foreign affiliates	U.S. imports shipped from foreign affiliates
	Total assets	Sales	Employment (1,000)	Employee compensation	Total assets	Sales	Employment (1,000)	Employee compensation		
All industries	5,177	3,274	18,010	707	1,690	1,543	6,898	197	115	103
Petroleum	395	347	574	29	225	303	231	11	3	12
Manufacturing	1,973	1,574	9,538	411	606	760	4,270	123	78	81
Food and kindred products	182	199	1,145	31	62	82	464	10	2	1
Chemical and allied products. . . .	334	265	1,246	61	125	134	591	19	9	5
Primary and fabricated metals . . .	84	86	567	24	27	27	211	5	2	2
Machinery (except electrical)	206	170	1,120	57	94	121	533	21	13	14
Electric and electronic equipment .	251	152	996	41	68	79	743	17	10	11
Transportation equipment	456	342	1,903	98	117	193	841	27	32	39
Other.	459	359	2,559	98	114	125	887	24	10	9
Wholesale trade.	184	236	475	17	135	246	560	24	32	9
Finance (except banking), insurance, real estate.	1,719	411	1,015	50	567	73	155	7	(Z)	(Z)
Services	152	121	1,663	46	64	54	537	15	(Z)	(Z)
Other	754	584	4,745	153	93	108	1,145	17	2	2

Z Less than $500 million.   ¹ Represents industry of U.S. parent or industry of foreign affiliate.

Source: U.S. Bureau of Economic Analysis, *Survey of Current Business*, May 1994.

Figure 18.1
Media Usage: 1984 to 1997

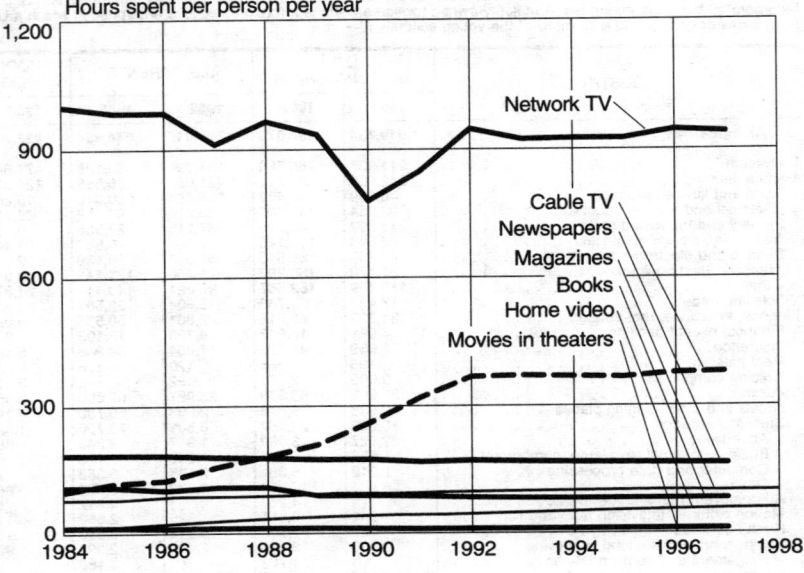

Hours spent per person per year

Note: Data for 1993 to 1997 are projected.
Source: Chart prepared by U.S. Bureau of the Census. For data, see table 884.

Figure 18.2
Microcomputer Software Sales: 1993

Billions of dollars

Percent change, 1992–93

Source: Chart prepared by U.S. Bureau of the Census. For data, see table 901.

Communications and Information Technology

This section presents statistics on the various communications media: telephone, telegraph, radio, television, newspapers and periodicals, and the usage, finances, and operations of the Postal Service. Expenditure data for advertising in the media are also included.

Consumer spending in 1992:

Basic cable	$92.82
Books	$71.12
Home video	$63.40
Daily newspapers	$54.44
Recorded music	$43.05
Magazines	$33.91
Movies in theaters	$23.24

Communication media.—The Bureau of the Census *Annual Survey of Communication Services* (ASCS) covers all employer firms with one or more establishments that are primarily engaged in providing point-to-point communication services, whether by wire or radio, and whether intended to be received aurally or visually. This includes telephone communications, including cellular and other radiotelephone services; telegraph and other message communications, such as electronic mail services, facsimile transmission services, telex services, and so on; radio and television broadcasting stations and networks; cable and other pay television services; and other communication services, such as radar station operations, satellite earth stations, satellite or missile tracking stations, and so on. The report presents statistics that are summarized by kind-of- business classification based on the 1987 edition of the *Standard Industrial Classification Manual.*

The Federal Communications Commission (FCC), established in 1934, regulates wire and radio communications. Only the largest carriers and holding companies file annual or monthly financial reports. The FCC has jurisdiction over interstate and foreign communication services, but not over intrastate or local services. The gross operating revenues of the telephone carriers reporting annually to the FCC, however, are estimated to cover about 90 percent of the revenues of all U.S. telephone companies. Data are not comparable with Bureau of the Census *Annual Survey of Communication Services* because of coverage (*ASCS* includes all domestic long-distance telephone companies, all local exchange carriers, and all cellular telephone companies) and different

accounting practices for those telephone companies which report to the FCC.

Reports filed by the broadcasting industry cover substantially all radio and television stations operating in the United States. The private radio services represent the largest and most diverse group of licensees regulated by the FCC. These services provide voice, data communications, point-to-point and point-to-multipoint radio communications for fixed and mobile communicators. Major users of these services are small businesses, the aviation industry, the maritime trades, the land transportation industry, manufacturing industries, State and local public safety and governmental authorities, emergency medical service providers, amateur radio operators, and personal radio operations (CB and the General Mobile Radio Service). The FCC also licenses entities as private and common carriers. Private and common carriers provide fixed and land mobile communications service on a for-profit basis. Principal sources of wire, radio, and television data are the FCC's *Annual Report* and its annual *Statistics of Communications Common Carriers.*

Statistics on the printed media are available from the U.S. Bureau of the Census, as well as from various private agencies. The censuses of manufactures (conducted by the Census Bureau every 5 years, for the years ending in "2" and "7") provide statistics on the number and circulation of newspapers and periodicals and on sales of books and pamphlets. Editor & Publisher Co. New York, NY, presents annual data on the number and circulation of daily and Sunday newspapers in its *International Year Book.* Monthly data on new books and new editions appear in *Publishers Weekly,* issued by R. R. Bowker Company, New York. (See table 899 for annual data.)

Advertising.—Data on advertising expenditures are compiled primarily by McCann-Erickson, Inc., (see table 912). Monthly index figures of advertising in certain media are also published periodically by McCann-Erickson in *Advertising Age.*

The Broadcast Advertisers Reports distinguishes between spot and local advertising primarily on the basis of the type of advertiser to whom the time is sold, rather than how and by whom it is sold. In general, time purchased on behalf of retail or service establishments in the market is considered local, even though the establishments may be part of a national or regional chain. That is, spot advertising promotes a product, while local advertising promotes a given establishment. Network advertising, mutually exclusive of spot and local, is broadcast through the network system.

Postal Service.—The Postal Service provides mail processing and delivery services within the United States. The Postal Reorganization Act of 1970 created the Postal Service, effective July 1971, as an independent establishment of the Federal Executive Branch.

Revenue and cost analysis describes the Postal Service's system of attributing revenues and costs to classes of mail and service. This system draws primarily upon probability sampling techniques to develop estimates of revenues, volumes, and weights, as well as costs by class of mail and special service. The costs attributed to classes of mail and special services are primarily incremental costs which vary in response to changes in volume; they account for roughly 60 percent of the total costs of the Postal Service. The balance represents "institutional costs." Statistics on revenues, volume of mail, and distribution of expenditures are presented in the Postal Service's annual report, *Cost and Revenue Analysis,* and its *Annual Report of the Postmaster General.*

Statistical reliability.—For a discussion of statistical collection and estimation, sampling procedures, and measures of statistical reliability applicable to Census Bureau data, see Appendix III.

Historical statistics.—Tabular headnotes provide cross-references, where applicable, to *Historical Statistics of the United States, Colonial Times to 1970.* See Appendix IV.

No. 882. Utilization of Selected Media: 1980 to 1993

ITEM	Unit	1980	1985	1986	1987	1988	1989	1990	1991	1992	1993
Households with—											
Telephone service [1]	Percent .	93.0	91.8	92.2	92.5	92.9	93.0	93.3	93.6	93.9	94.2
Radio [2]	Millions .	78.6	87.1	88.1	89.9	91.1	92.8	94.4	95.5	96.6	(NA)
Percent of total households . .	Percent .	99.0	99.0	99.0	99.0	99.0	99.0	99.0	99.0	99.0	(NA)
Average number of sets	Number .	5.5	5.5	5.4	5.4	5.6	5.6	5.6	5.6	5.6	(NA)
Television [3]	Millions .	76	85	86	87	89	90	92	93	92	93
Percent of total households . .	Percent .	97.9	98.1	98.1	98.1	98.1	98.2	98.2	98.2	98.3	98.3
Television sets in homes	Millions .	128	155	158	163	168	176	193	193	192	201
Average number of sets per home	Number .	1.7	1.8	1.8	1.9	1.9	1.9	2.1	2.1	2.1	2.2
Color set	Millions .	63	78	80	83	85	87	90	91	91	92
Cable television [4]	Millions .	15	36	39	42	44	48	52	55	55	57
Percent of TV households . . .	Percent .	19.9	42.8	45.6	47.7	49.4	52.8	56.4	58.9	60.2	61.4
VCR's [4]	Millions .	1	18	31	43	51	58	63	67	69	72
Percent of TV households . . .	Percent .	1.1	20.8	36.0	48.7	58.0	64.6	68.6	71.9	75.0	77.1
Commercial radio stations: [2]											
AM	Number .	4,589	[5]4,718	4,863	4,902	4,932	4,975	4,987	4,985	4,961	(NA)
FM	Number .	3,282	[5]3,875	3,944	4,041	4,155	4,269	4,392	4,570	4,785	(NA)
Television stations: [6] Total	Number .	1,011	1,182	1,235	1,290	1,362	1,403	1,442	1,459	1,481	1,505
Commercial [3]	Number .	734	883	919	968	1,028	1,061	1,092	1,099	1,118	1,137
VHF	Number .	516	520	522	524	539	545	547	547	551	552
UHF	Number .	218	363	397	444	489	516	545	552	567	585
Cable television:											
Systems [6]	Number .	4,225	6,844	7,600	7,900	8,500	9,050	9,575	10,704	11,075	11,461
Subscribers served [7]	Millions .	17.7	39.9	42.2	44.9	48.6	52.6	54.9	55.8	57.2	55.7
Daily newspaper circulation [8]	Millions .	62	63	63	63	63	(NA)	62	61	60	(NA)

NA Not available. [1] For occupied housing units. 1980 as of April 1; all other years as of March. Source: U.S. Bureau of the Census, *1980 Census of Housing*, vol. 1; and unpublished data. [2] As of December 31, except as noted. Source: Radio Advertising Bureau, New York, NY, *Radio Facts*, annual, (copyright). Number of stations on the air compiled from Federal Communications Commission reports. [3] As of January of year shown. Excludes Alaska and Hawaii. Source: Television Bureau of Advertising, Inc., *Trends in Television*, annual, (copyright). [4] As of February. Excludes Alaska and Hawaii. Source: See footnote 3. [5] As of February 1986. [6] As of January 1. Source: Warren Publishing, Washington DC, *Television and Cable Factbook*. [7] Source: AC Nielsen Company, *Nielsen Station Index*, November diary estimates. [8] As of September 30. Source: Editor & Publisher, Co., New York, NY, *Editor & Publisher International Year Book*, annual, (copyright).

Source: Compiled from sources mentioned in footnotes.

No. 883. Multimedia Audiences—Summary: 1993

[In percent, except as indicated. As of spring. For persons 18 years old and over. Represents the number of people viewing/listening during a specified time period. Based on sample and subject to sampling error; see source for details]

ITEM	Total population (1,000)	Television viewing	Television prime time viewing	Cable viewing	Radio listening	Newspaper reading
Total	186,909	93.3	80.2	60.1	85.6	84.0
18 to 24 years old	24,888	92.0	74.3	57.9	93.2	79.1
25 to 34 years old	43,782	92.5	80.1	60.6	92.4	83.4
35 to 44 years old	39,568	92.2	79.6	62.7	91.4	86.8
45 to 54 years old	26,024	92.7	79.3	65.5	86.5	86.9
55 to 64 years old	21,889	95.5	83.2	62.5	81.2	87.5
65 years old and over	30,758	96.0	84.7	51.7	64.5	80.0
Male	89,230	93.7	79.3	61.5	87.6	84.8
Female	97,679	93.0	81.0	58.9	83.7	83.2
White	159,629	93.1	80.1	61.9	85.8	84.9
Black	20,966	94.6	81.7	51.0	85.1	81.4
Other	6,314	94.3	77.6	46.2	80.6	68.8
Spanish speaking	13,768	95.5	82.4	47.7	87.6	72.5
Not high school graduate	39,918	94.5	81.7	48.9	75.7	68.4
High school graduate	73,377	94.1	81.9	62.1	85.7	84.9
Attended college	37,003	92.6	78.1	64.2	91.1	89.0
College graduate	36,612	91.4	77.3	64.3	90.5	93.8
Employed:						
Full-time	100,013	92.1	78.4	63.5	92.1	86.9
Part-time	16,874	92.1	76.0	58.8	88.9	86.9
Not employed	70,022	95.5	83.8	55.6	75.4	79.1
Household income:						
Less than $10,000	19,857	92.2	79.0	43.5	73.2	65.2
$10,000 to $19,999	29,241	95.3	84.2	47.3	77.8	76.9
$20,000 to $29,999	30,454	94.1	81.7	55.0	84.5	82.5
$30,000 to $34,999	13,911	95.3	81.8	61.5	85.9	84.8
$35,000 to $39,999	13,028	93.3	80.1	62.2	90.1	87.1
$40,000 to $49,999	22,522	93.6	80.9	68.2	90.3	89.1
$50,000 or more	57,896	91.8	77.2	71.1	91.3	91.8

Source: Mediamark Research Inc., New York, NY, *Multimedia Audiences*, fall 1993, (copyright).

No. 884. Media Usage and Consumer Spending: 1984 to 1997

[Estimates of time spent were derived using data for television and radio, survey research and consumer purchase data for recorded music, newspapers, magazines, books, home video, and admissions for movies. Adults 18 and older except for recorded music and movies in theaters, where estimates include persons 12 and older]

| YEAR | Total [1] | TELEVISION | | | | | Re-corded music | Daily news-papers | Con-sumer maga-zines | Con-sumer books | Home video [4] | Movies in theaters |
		Net-work sta-tions [2]	Inde-pen-dent sta-tions [2]	Basic cable [3]	Pay cable						
HOURS PER PERSON PER YEAR											
1984	3,297	1,000	335	100	85	191	185	110	80	9	12
1985	3,307	985	335	120	90	185	185	110	80	15	12
1986	3,313	985	339	126	72	173	184	103	88	22	10
1987	3,258	912	332	157	84	200	180	110	88	29	11
1988	3,294	965	349	182	94	215	178	110	90	35	11
1989	3,271	935	345	210	95	220	175	90	96	39	11
1990	3,252	780	340	260	90	235	175	90	95	42	10
1991	3,256	848	265	319	83	219	169	88	98	43	9
1992	3,350	947	159	367	82	233	172	85	100	46	9
1993 proj.	3,305	923	156	370	81	248	170	83	101	49	9
1994 proj.	3,292	925	153	368	81	257	168	82	102	52	9
1995 proj.	3,291	925	149	366	82	264	167	82	103	54	9
1996 proj.	3,323	945	146	376	85	269	166	82	101	56	9
1997 proj.	3,314	940	139	378	85	275	165	82	101	57	9
CONSUMER SPENDING PER PERSON PER YEAR (dollars)											
1984	201.51	-	-	40.36	(5)	22.51	40.52	24.32	40.17	12.87	20.76
1985	218.22	-	-	45.43	(5)	22.39	41.84	25.60	43.39	20.43	19.13
1986	235.77	-	-	49.71	(5)	23.52	43.28	26.89	44.81	28.45	19.11
1987	265.26	-	-	56.66	(5)	27.92	44.76	29.31	49.72	35.58	21.33
1988	293.48	-	-	65.40	(5)	31.01	46.80	29.88	54.29	43.99	22.10
1989	322.64	-	-	74.08	(5)	32.25	48.08	31.49	61.24	50.82	24.67
1990	346.98	-	-	82.58	(5)	36.64	49.81	33.14	63.90	56.50	24.40
1991	362.05	-	-	88.31	(5)	37.73	52.46	33.45	68.14	58.82	23.13
1992	381.97	-	-	92.82	(5)	43.05	54.44	33.91	71.12	63.40	23.24
1993 proj.	395.74	-	-	90.64	(5)	46.90	56.22	34.59	75.41	67.82	24.17
1994 proj.	412.85	-	-	88.94	(5)	50.11	58.20	35.47	80.63	73.86	25.64
1995 proj.	436.71	-	-	93.21	(5)	53.37	60.03	36.53	86.10	80.20	27.26
1996 proj.	457.85	-	-	97.48	(5)	55.92	62.05	37.26	91.63	84.88	28.64
1997 proj.	477.66	-	-	102.09	(5)	58.49	63.89	37.90	96.95	88.32	30.01

- Represents or rounds to zero. [1] Includes radio not shown separately. [2] Affiliates of the Fox network are counted as network affiliates for part of 1991 and all of 1992, but as independent stations in earlier years. [3] Includes TBS beginning in 1992. [4] Playback of prerecorded tapes only. [5] Included with basic cable.
Source: Veronis, Suhler & Associates, New York, NY, *Communications Industry Forecast Report*, annual, (copyright).

No. 885. Communications Industry—Finances: 1990 to 1992

[Covers 349 publicly reporting companies with revenues of over $1 million in 11 communication industries]

| INDUSTRY | REVENUE | | | | | OPERATING INCOME | | | | |
| | Total (mil. dol.) | | | Percent change | | Total (mil. dol.) | | | Percent change | |
	1990	1991	1992	1990-1991	1991-1992	1990	1991	1992	1990-1991	1991-1992
Total	121,778	128,784	137,064	6	6	16,163	15,395	18,088	-5	18
Television & radio broadcasting [1]	18,791	18,448	19,372	-2	5	2,792	2,042	2,454	-27	20
Television network companies	11,631	11,448	12,078	-2	6	1,608	1,108	1,202	-31	9
TV & radio station broadcasters	7,160	7,000	7,293	-2	4	1,184	934	1,252	-21	34
Cable television	14,803	16,357	17,951	11	10	2,315	3,053	3,723	32	22
Cable system operators	11,298	12,454	13,532	10	9	1,810	2,309	2,885	28	25
Cable network companies	3,505	3,903	4,420	11	13	504	744	838	48	13
Filmed entertainment	11,762	13,437	14,710	14	10	1,091	935	1,275	-14	36
Recorded music	6,043	6,668	6,885	10	3	611	684	707	12	4
Newspaper publishing	20,336	19,407	19,542	-5	1	3,148	2,380	2,697	-24	13
Book publishing	8,173	9,909	10,648	21	8	1,034	1,202	1,337	16	11
Magazine publishing	8,335	8,652	9,198	4	6	899	711	879	-21	24
Consumer magazine	6,418	6,823	7,349	6	8	698	596	730	-15	23
Business & professional	1,917	1,829	1,850	-5	1	201	116	149	-43	29
Business information services	18,021	18,962	20,451	5	8	2,711	2,782	3,206	3	15
Advertising agencies [2]	6,807	7,300	7,768	7	6	630	597	673	-5	13
Interactive digital media [3]	2,456	2,824	3,406	15	21	155	199	309	28	56
Miscellaneous communications	6,253	6,820	7,134	9	5	777	811	830	4	2

[1] Excludes agency commissions. [2] Net revenue including only commissions, fees, and other income, not gross billings. [3] Software for consumer data and transactions, consumer reference, education, games, home shopping, and infomercials.
Source: Veronis, Suhler & Associates, New York, NY, *Communications Industry Report*, annual, (copyright).

No. 886. Telephone and Telegraph Systems: 1980 to 1992

[Covers principal carriers filing annual reports with Federal Communications Commission. Minus sign (-) indicates loss. See Historical Statistics, Colonial Times to 1970, series R 46-70 and R 75-88, for data on telegraph systems]

ITEM	Unit	1980	1985	1986	1987	1988	1989	1990	1991	1992
DOMESTIC TELEPHONE [1]										
Carriers [2]	Number .	59	39	39	37	54	53	53	54	56
Access lines	Million . .	(NA)	103	106	111	122	126	130	137	140
Miles of wire	Million . .	1,131	1,313	1,338	1,371	1,483	1,502	1,528	(NA)	(NA)
Gross book cost of plant	Bil. dol. .	147	195	207	222	250	260	265	270	279
Depreciation reserves [3]	Bil. dol. .	27	50	59	70	85	94	98	102	108
Ratio to book cost	Percent .	18	26	28	31	34	36	37	38	39
Capital stock and premium	Bil. dol. .	31	48	42	43	45	46	46	47	48
Operating revenues	Bil. dol. .	56	89	94	95	100	102	104	106	122
Operating expenses [4]	Bil. dol. .	37	61	64	66	74	77	78	80	95
Net operating income [5]	Bil. dol. .	10	12	14	15	17	16	16	16	17
Net income	Bil. dol. .	7	10	10	11	13	12	13	12	12
Return on investment (domestic and overseas) [6]	Percent .	9	9	9	10	10	10	10	9	10
Employees	1,000. .	938	(NA)	(NA)	(NA)	688	663	648	616	608
Compensation of employees	Bil. dol. .	20	(NA)	(NA)	(NA)	25	24	26	25	26
OVERSEAS TELEPHONE										
Number of overseas calls . . . [7]	Million . .	200	412	478	580	706	1,008	1,201	2,279	2,724
Revenue from overseas calls [7]	Mil. dol. .	1,535	1,799	1,841	2,127	2,573	3,513	4,362	5,835	6,886
Ocean cable systems [8]	Number .	24	26	26	26	26	23	24	26	(NA)
Communications satellites [8]	Number .	5	6	11	11	14	15	16	16	(NA)
TELEGRAPH [9]										
Carriers	Number .	8	7	7	7	6	6	3	3	2
Revenue messages transmitted	Million . .	75	42	29	25	(NA)	(NA)	(NA)	(NA)	(NA)
Message revenues [10]	Mil. dol. .	676	708	678	594	483	521	259	219	(NA)
Total operating revenues	Mil. dol. .	1,232	1,367	1,206	1,076	882	1,019	408	383	317
Operating revenue deductions	Mil. dol. .	1,008	1,292	1,243	1,125	942	995	447	421	343
Operating income [11]	Mil. dol. .	147	102	-37	-48	-56	24	-28	-28	-77
Return on investment [6]	Percent .	16	7	-2	3	-6	4	1	-12	(NA)

NA Not available.   [1] Includes Virgin Islands, and prior to 1991, Puerto Rico. Excludes intercompany duplications. Gross operating revenues of carriers reporting estimated at 90 percent of all carriers. Beginning 1988, based on new accounting rules; prior years not directly comparable.   [2] Beginning 1985, number of carriers changed due to change in dollar requirement of reporting carriers from $1 million to $100 million.   [3] Includes amortization reserves.   [4] Excludes taxes.   [5] After tax deductions.   [6] Ratio of net operating income (after taxes) to average net book cost of communications plant.   [7] Beginning 1991, includes calls to and from Alaska, Hawaii, Puerto Rico, Canada, and Mexico.   [8] Excludes contingency and retired satellites.   [9] Domestic and overseas except for South American and most Caribbean operations of All America Cables and Radio, Inc.   [10] Includes telex service; for domestic telegraph, excludes TWX.   [11] After Federal income taxes.

Source: U.S. Federal Communications Commission, Statistics of Communications Common Carriers, annual; and unpublished data.

No. 887. Telephone Communications—Operating Revenue and Expenses: 1989 to 1992

[Covers taxable employer firms with one or more establishments that are primarily engaged in providing telephone, voice, and data communication services. Based on the 1987 Standard Industrial Classification]

ITEM	TOTAL (millions of dollars)				PERCENT DISTRIBUTION			
	1989	1990	1991	1992	1989	1990	1991	1992
OPERATING REVENUE								
Total	150,519	155,573	159,639	165,247	100	100	100	100
Local service	37,225	38,377	39,453	41,711	25	25	25	25
Long-distance service	64,228	65,991	67,266	67,459	43	42	42	41
Network access	29,122	29,278	29,180	29,337	19	19	18	18
Cellular and other radiotelephone	4,337	5,791	6,628	8,862	3	4	4	5
Directory advertising	7,683	8,169	8,469	8,677	5	5	5	5
Other	7,924	7,967	8,643	9,201	5	5	5	6
OPERATING EXPENSES								
Total	124,227	127,948	133,991	139,350	100	100	100	100
Annual payroll	29,117	30,685	31,050	31,557	23	24	23	23
Employer contributions to Social Security and other supplemental benefits	6,969	7,598	8,266	8,419	6	6	6	6
Access charges	23,488	23,680	24,520	25,032	19	19	18	18
Depreciation	23,102	23,348	24,032	24,053	19	18	18	17
Lease and rental	3,713	3,607	3,937	4,323	3	3	3	3
Purchased repairs	2,797	3,004	2,982	2,944	2	2	2	2
Insurance	193	194	220	225	(Z)	(Z)	(Z)	(Z)
Telephone and other purchased communication services	429	512	552	717	(Z)	(Z)	(Z)	1
Purchased utilities	1,117	1,124	1,169	1,199	1	1	1	1
Purchased advertising	1,923	2,371	2,594	2,686	2	2	2	2
Taxes	5,006	5,181	5,331	5,291	4	4	4	4
Other	26,373	26,644	29,338	32,904	21	21	22	24

Z Less than 0.5 percent.

Source: U.S. Bureau of the Census, Annual Survey of Communication Services.

No. 888. Telephone Companies—Summary: 1980 to 1991

[As of Dec. 31 or calendar year, as applicable. January 1, 1988, marked the beginning of significant rules changes in the way that local exchange carriers account for assets, liabilities, revenue, expenses, and income. Any comparisons with earlier data would not be meaningful. See also *Historical Statistics, Colonial Times to 1970*, series R 1-12 and 31-45]

ITEM	Unit	INDEPENDENT COMPANIES [1]				ALL TELEPHONE COMPANIES				
		1980	1985	1990	1991	1984	1985	1989	1990	1991
All companies	Number .	1,483	1,402	1,310	1,308	1,440	1,426	1,354	1,332	1,328
Access lines	Millions .	20.8	24.3	32.2	32.7	114.5	118.2	135.0	138.1	141.2
Total telephone plant	Bil. dol. .	35.3	49.1	64.7	68.7	193.8	207.3	249.0	256.0	264.1
Operating revenues. . . . ; . .	Bil. dol. .	10.5	17.2	22.1	25.1	73.9	78.4	89.1	90.1	93.0
Avg. daily conversations [2] . .	Millions .	192	226	(NA)	(NA)	1,199	1,264	9,569	9,515	9,773
Local calls	Millions .	177	203	(NA)	(NA)	1,111	1,162	(NA)	(NA)	(NA)
Toll calls	Millions .	15	20	(NA)	(NA)	88	102	(NA)	(NA)	(NA)
Reporting companies [3]	Number .	765	653	594	598	655	677	601	616	618
Access lines . . . . , .	Millions .	19.4	23.4	30.3	31.2	113.6	117.4	132.7	136.3	139.7
Telephone plant in service [4] .	Bil. dol. .	32.5	45.5	62.8	64.6	186.2	200.0	243.9	250.9	257.4
Depreciation reserves [5]	Bil. dol. .	7.8	14.3	23.7	24.7	45.7	52.9	89.6	95.0	100.0
Operating revenues.	Bil. dol. .	10.2	16.7	22.1	23.1	73.3	77.9	87.9	89.1	91.0
Operating expenses [6]	Bil. dol. .	7.3	11.9	15.6	16.2	59.8	63.7	63.9	65.2	67.1
Net income	Bil. dol. .	1.3	2.4	3.4	3.5	9.3	10.1	11.5	11.6	11.1
Stockholders' equity	Bil. dol. .	9.6	13.9	22.1	23.4	63.1	66.5	76.8	80.4	82.7
Net income to stockholders equity	Percent .	13.2	17.5	15.4	15.0	14.7	15.1	15.0	14.4	13.4
Employees	1,000 . .	189	170	161	158	724	695	626	606	574
Wages and salaries.	Bil. dol. .	3.4	4.6	(NA)	(NA)	22.1	21.4	(NA)	(NA)	(NA)

NA Not available.　[1] Companies independent of the Bell System, prior to divestiture of January 1984.　[2] Average business day minutes of use beginning in 1989.　[3] Comprises only companies submitting operating information to source cited below.　[4] Total property plant and equipment beginning 1988.　[5] Total accumulated depreciation and amortization beginning 1988.　[6] Excludes Federal income tax.

Source: United States Telephone Association, Washington, DC, *Statistics of the Local Exchange Carriers*, annual, (copyright).

No. 889. Percent of Households with Telephone Service: 1984 and 1993

[For March. Based on Current Population Survey, see text, section 1]

CHARACTERISTIC	1984				1993			
	All races	White	Black	Hispanic [1]	All races	White	Black	Hispanic [1]
Total.	92	93	80	81	94	95	85	87
Age of householder:								
15 to 24 years old [2]	78	80	58	59	83	85	68	69
25 to 54 years old	92	94	80	83	94	95	84	87
55 to 59 years old	95	96	88	89	96	97	88	90
60 to 64 years old	94	96	82	87	97	98	93	92
65 to 69 years old	96	97	88	86	97	98	92	93
70 years old and over	95	96	87	82	98	98	93	97
Household size:								
1 person.	89	91	74	72	93	94	83	83
2 to 3 persons.	93	95	82	81	95	96	86	88
4 to 5 persons	93	94	83	85	94	96	86	87
6 or more persons	86	89	79	79	90	91	83	85
Labor force status of persons, 15 years old and over: [2]								
Total civilian noninstitutional population	93	94	84	83	95	96	88	88
Employed	95	95	88	87	96	97	91	90
Unemployed.	82	84	76	73	88	90	80	85
Not in labor force	92	94	80	80	94	95	85	86
Income level:								
Under $5,000	71	75	63	54	73	77	65	71
$5,000 to $7,499	84	86	75	70	84	86	78	80
$7,500 to $9,999	86	88	76	72	87	89	82	75
$10,000 to $12,499	90	91	83	82	89	91	82	81
$12,500 to $14,999	93	94	85	89	92	93	85	84
$15,000 to $19,999	(NA)	(NA)	(NA)	(NA)	94	94	90	84
$15,000 to $17,499	94	94	88	89	(NA)	(NA)	(NA)	(NA)
$17,500 to $19,999	95	95	95	87	(NA)	(NA)	(NA)	(NA)
$20,000 to $24,999	97	97	95	90	96	97	93	92
$25,000 to $29,999	98	99	94	96	98	98	95	95
$30,000 to $34,999	99	99	98	99	98	98	95	93
$35,000 to $39,999	99	100	96	100	99	99	95	97
$40,000 to $49,999	99	100	98	100	99	99	98	97
$50,000 to $74,999	99	99	97	100	(NA)	(NA)	(NA)	(NA)
$50,000 to $59,999	(NA)	(NA)	(NA)	(NA)	99	99	97	99
$60,000 to $74,999	(NA)	(NA)	(NA)	(NA)	100	100	99	100
$75,000 and over.	99	99	94	95	100	100	99	100

NA Not available.　[1] Persons of Hispanic origin may be of any race.　[2] 16 to 24 years old in 1984.

Source: Federal Communications Commission, *Telephone Subscribership in the U.S.*, March 1994.

No. 890. Cellular Telephone Industry: 1986 to 1993
[Calendar year data. Based on a survey mailed to 1,529 cellular systems]

ITEM	Unit	1986	1987	1988	1989	1990	1991	1992	1993
Systems	Number .	166	312	517	584	751	1,252	1,506	1,529
Subscribers	1,000 . . .	682	1,231	2,069	3,509	5,283	7,557	11,033	16,009
Cell sites [1]	Number .	1,531	2,305	3,209	4,169	5,616	7,847	10,307	12,805
Employees	Number .	4,334	7,147	11,400	15,927	21,382	26,327	34,348	39,775
Service revenue	Mil. dol. .	462	672	1,073	1,934	2,422	3,055	4,189	6,073
Roamer revenue [2]	Mil. dol. .	(NA)	(NA)	89	173	264	401	537	773
Capital investment	Mil. dol. .	1,437	2,235	3,274	4,480	6,282	8,672	11,262	13,946
Average monthly bill [3]	Dollars. .	(NA)	96.83	98.02	89.30	80.90	72.74	68.68	61.48
Average length of call [3]	Minutes .	(NA)	2.33	2.26	2.48	2.20	2.38	2.58	2.41

NA Not available. [1] The basic geographic unit of a cellular system. A city or county is divided into smaller "cells," each of which is equipped with a lowpowered radio transmitter/receiver. The cells can vary in size depending upon terrain, capacity demands, etc. By controlling the transmission power, the radio frequencies assigned to one cell can be limited to the boundaries of that cell. When a cellular phone moves from one cell toward another, a computer at the Switching Office monitors the movement and at the proper time, transfers or hands off the phone call to the new cell and another radio frequency. [2] Service revenue generated by subscribers' calls outside of their system areas. [3] As of December 31.
Source: Cellular Telecommunications Industry Association, Washington, DC, State of the Cellular Industry, annual, (copyright).

No. 891. Private Radio Stations Authorized, by Class: 1989 to 1992
[In thousands. As of September 30. Includes Puerto Rico and Virgin Islands. See also Historical Statistics, Colonial Times to 1970, series R 140-148]

CLASS	1989	1990	1991	1992	CLASS	1989	1990	1991	1992
Private radio services [1]	2,828	2,880	2,935	2,956	Railroad	16	16	17	18
Personal [1]	502	528	566	611	Taxicab	6	6	6	6
General mobile	34	32	31	28	Interurban property	6	6	6	6
Amateur and disaster	467	496	535	583	Other	13	12	12	12
Aviation	251	251	241	210	Marine	620	623	641	634
Aircraft	210	210	200	193	Ship	605	607	626	619
Aeronautical and fixed	12	12	12	12	Alaskan	3	2	2	2
Civil air patrol	24	24	24	(Z)	Coastal and other	13	13	13	13
Other	5	5	5	5	Public safety	229	235	240	245
Industrial	874	865	854	840	Police	49	51	52	53
Power	44	46	47	48	Fire	43	44	45	46
Business	638	628	616	27	Forestry conservation	11	11	12	12
Petroleum	27	27	27	603	Highway maintenance	15	15	16	16
Forest products	12	12	12	12	Special emergency	41	41	41	41
Special industrial	115	114	112	110	Other	70	73	75	78
Other	38	39	40	41	Operational fixed				
Land transportation	40	40	41	41	services [2]	30	33	35	36

Z Less than 500. [1] Includes items not shown separately. Each license, construction permit, or combination construction permit and license is counted one as station; therefore, a station might include a transmitter and many mobile units. 1991 data exclude restricted permits. [2] Includes microwave operations.
Source: U.S. Federal Communications Commission, Annual Report; and unpublished data.

No. 892. Radio and Television Broadcasting Services—Operating Revenue and Expenses: 1990 to 1992
[In millions of dollars. Based on the 1987 Standard Industrial Classification. Based on a sample; see source]

ITEM	TOTAL BROADCASTING			RADIO			TELEVISION		
	1990	1991	1992	1990	1991	1992	1990	1991	1992
Operating revenue	29,006	27,793	28,843	7,220	6,927	7,056	21,786	20,866	21,787
Station time sales	19,693	18,662	19,238	6,637	6,334	6,511	13,056	12,328	12,727
Network compensation	571	531	477	110	103	99	461	428	378
National/regional advertising	7,478	6,899	6,967	1,580	1,488	1,363	5,898	5,411	5,604
Local advertising	11,644	11,232	11,794	4,947	4,743	5,049	6,697	6,489	6,745
Network time sales	8,182	7,914	8,509	321	329	291	7,861	7,585	8,218
Other	1,131	1,217	1,096	262	264	254	869	953	842
Operating expenses	24,986	24,781	24,990	6,558	6,396	6,376	18,428	18,385	18,614
Annual payroll	6,712	6,665	6,990	2,543	2,528	2,586	4,169	4,137	4,404
Employer contributions to Social Security and other supplemental benefits	1,060	1,063	1,157	341	341	359	719	722	798
Broadcast rights	7,797	8,085	7,895	272	283	216	7,525	7,802	7,679
Music license fees	383	371	380	164	156	154	219	215	226
Depreciation	1,389	1,328	1,304	491	477	462	898	851	842
Lease and rental	481	474	465	203	195	198	278	279	267
Purchased repairs	239	235	233	82	82	80	157	153	153
Insurance	148	152	163	66	66	68	82	86	95
Telephone and other purchased communication services	247	238	243	119	116	120	128	122	123
Purchased utilities	253	259	264	102	103	105	151	156	159
Purchased advertising	970	864	817	379	341	324	591	523	493
Taxes	180	176	191	61	59	66	119	117	125
Other	5,127	4,871	4,888	1,735	1,649	1,638	3,392	3,222	3,250

Source: U.S. Bureau of the Census, Annual Survey of Communication Services.

No. 893. Public Television Programming: 1980 to 1992

[1980 to 1990 are fiscal years; 1988 to 1992 surveys used October through September seasons. General programming is directed at the general community. Instructional programming is directed at students in the classroom or otherwise in the general context of formal education]

ITEM	1980	1982	1984	1986	1988	1990	1992
Stations broadcasting	281	291	303	305	322	341	349
Number of broadcasters [1]	160	164	169	178	186	193	198
Average annual hours per broadcaster.	5,128	5,421	5,542	5,650	6,135	6,392	6,303
BROADCAST HOURS, PERCENT DISTRIBUTION							
Program content [2]	100	100	100	100	100	100	100
General.	87	87	88	86	85	86	90
News and public affairs [2]	12	12	14	16	16	18	17
Information and skills	23	25	26	30	32	32	29
Cultural	22	23	20	21	18	19	18
General children's and youth's	9	8	8	7	6	6	15
Sesame Street.	16	15	15	11	12	11	11
Other	6	5	6	2	1	1	1
Instructional [3]	15	14	13	15	16	14	12
Children and youth	14	13	12	(NA)	(NA)	(NA)	9
Adult	1	1	1	(NA)	(NA)	(NA)	3
Producer.	100	100	100	100	100	100	100
Local	7	7	6	5	5	5	5
Any public TV source.	46	46	44	38	27	32	35
Consortium	3	3	3	3	10	10	1
Children's TV Workshop	17	16	16	[4]29	16	15	14
Independent producer	8	11	9	([4])	19	19	25
Foreign producer, international coproduction	13	10	13	15	14	12	11
Commercial producer.	3	4	3	6	4	4	5
Other	4	4	5	4	4	3	4
Distributor	100	100	100	100	100	100	100
Local distribution only	7	6	6	5	6	6	5
Public broadcasting service.	70	67	65	64	62	59	63
Regional public television network	8	11	13	14	18	24	23
Other	16	16	16	17	14	11	9

NA Not available. [1] Beginning 1990, only broadcasters in the 50 U.S. States were surveyed. [2] Beginning 1988, this category includes "Business or Consumer." [3] Some general audience programs with instructional applications were double counted if aired during school hours when school was in session. "The Electric Company" was one such program. [4] Independent producer included with Children's TV Workshop for 1986.
Source: Corporation for Public Broadcasting, Washington, DC, *PTV Programming Survey*, biennial.

No. 894. Public Broadcasting Systems—Income, by Source: 1980 to 1992

[In millions of dollars, except percent. Stations as of Dec. 31; fiscal year data for income. Includes nonbroadcast income]

NUMBER OF STATIONS AND INCOME SOURCE	1980	1985	1988	1989	1990	1991	1992	PERCENT DISTRIBUTION		
								1980	1990	1992
CPB-qualified public radio stations [1] . .	217	288	308	313	318	373	391	(X)	(X)	(X)
Public television stations	290	317	324	340	341	349	349	(X)	(X)	(X)
Total income.	705	1,096	1,368	1,549	1,581	1,721	1,790	100	100	100
Federal government	193	179	248	264	267	333	374	27	17	21
State and local government [2]	272	358	416	454	474	503	485	39	30	27
Subscribers and auction/marathon . . .	102	248	321	347	364	384	404	15	23	23
Business and industry	72	171	213	242	262	290	300	10	17	17
Foundation	24	43	51	69	71	70	80	3	5	5
Other	43	97	120	173	143	139	148	6	9	8

X Not applicable. [1] Includes CPB-supported developmental grantees/stations. [2] Includes income received from State and other public colleges and universities.
Source: Corporation for Public Broadcasting (CPB), Washington, DC, *Public Broadcasting Income, Fiscal Year, 1992*; and unpublished data.

No. 895. Cable Television—Systems and Subscribers: 1970 to 1994

[Subscribers in thousands, except percent. Estimated]

YEAR (As of Jan. 1)	Systems	Subscribers	YEAR (As of Jan. 1)	Systems	Subscribers	SUBSCRIBER SIZE-GROUP	NUMBER OF [1]—		PERCENT OF [1]—	
							Systems	Subscribers	Systems	Subscribers
1970	2,490	4,500	1985.	6,600	32,000	**1993, total [2]**	11,160	55,124	100	100
1975	3,506	9,800	1986.	7,600	37,500	50,000 and over	229	22,597	2	41
1976	3,681	10,800	1987.	7,900	41,100	20,000 to 49,999.	421	12,934	4	23
1977	3,832	11,900	1988.	8,500	44,000	10,000 to 19,999.	525	7,484	5	14
1978	3,875	13,000	1989.	9,050	47,500	5,000 to 9,999	673	4,762	6	9
1979	4,150	14,100	1990.	9,575	50,000	3,500 to 4,999	409	1,720	4	3
1980	4,225	16,000	1991.	10,704	51,000	1,000 to 3,499	1,922	3,658	17	7
1981	4,375	18,300	1992.	11,075	53,000	500 to 999.	1,432	1,023	13	2
1982	4,825	21,000	1993.	11,100	55,000	250 to 499	1,508	541	14	1
1983	5,600	25,000	1994.	11,200	57,000	Less than 250	3,235	405	29	1
1984	6,200	30,000								

[1] As of November. [2] Excludes 806 systems not available by subscriber size-group.
Source: Warren Publishing, Inc., Washington, DC, *Television & Cable Factbook*, annual, (copyright).

No. 896. Cable and Pay TV—Summary: 1970 to 1993
[Cable TV for calendar year. Pay TV as of **Dec. 31** of year shown]

YEAR	CABLE TV				PAY TV						
	Avg. basic sub-scribers (1,000)	Avg. monthly basic rate (dol.)	Revenue [1] (mil. dol.)		Units [2] (1,000)		Monthly rate (dol.)		Pay cable units		
			Total	Basic	Total [3]	Pay cable	Total pay [3]	Pay cable	Percent of homes passed	Percent basic
1970	5,100	5.50	345	339	(X)	(X)	(X)	(X)	(X)	(X)
1980	17,500	7.69	2,549	1,615	10,389	9,144	9.09	8.80	28	51
1985	35,500	9.73	8,938	4,145	31,063	30,596	10.46	10.42	47	84
1986	38,200	10.67	10,144	4,891	32,429	32,064	10.35	10.31	46	81
1987	41,200	12.18	11,765	6,014	35,089	34,793	10.17	10.15	48	82
1988	44,200	13.86	13,595	7,351	39,127	38,819	10.25	10.18	50	85
1989	47,500	15.21	15,678	8,670	41,234	41,095	10.26	10.21	50	83
1990	50,520	16.78	17,855	10,169	41,656	41,505	10.44	10.38	48	80
1991	52,600	18.10	19,463	11,414	40,114	39,900	10.36	10.27	45	75
1992	54,300	19.08	21,044	12,433	41,220	40,990	10.19	10.06	45	74
1993	56,300	19.39	22,863	13,552	41,500	(NA)	(NA)	9.11	45	72

NA Not available.   X Not applicable.   [1] Includes installation revenue, subscriber revenue, and nonsubscriber revenue.
[2] Individual program services sold to subscribers.   [3] Includes multipoint distribution service (MDS) and satellite TV (STV).

Source: Paul Kagan Associates Inc., Carmel, CA, *The Cable TV Financial Databook*, annual, (copyright); *The Kagan Census of Cable and Pay TV*, 1991, and *The Cable TV Investor*, March 1994.

No. 897. Cable and Pay TV Services—Operating Revenue and Expenses: 1989 to 1992
[Includes establishments primarily engaged in the dissemination of visual and textual television programs on a subscription or fee basis. Based on the 1987 Standard Industrial Classification]

ITEM	TOTAL (mil. dol.)				PERCENT DISTRIBUTION			
	1989	1990	1991	1992	Percent change, 1991-92	1990	1991	1992
Operating revenue [1]	(NA)	21,090	22,693	24,976	10	100	100	100
Advertising	1,338	1,711	1,909	2,265	19	8	8	9
Program revenue	2,693	3,458	3,726	4,008	8	16	16	16
Basic service.	8,693	9,942	10,898	12,306	13	46	47	49
Pay-per-view and other premium service	3,717	3,969	4,074	4,295	5	18	18	17
Installation fees	248	275	295	354	20	1	1	1
Other cable and pay TV revenue.	691	800	826	1,007	22	4	4	4
Operating expenses	(NA)	17,564	18,298	19,314	6	100	100	100
Annual payroll	(NA)	2,742	2,896	3,441	19	16	16	18
Employer contributions to Social Security and other supplemental benefits	(NA)	572	649	780	20	3	4	4
Program and production costs	(NA)	5,288	5,636	6,031	7	30	31	31
Depreciation	(NA)	3,229	3,249	3,312	2	18	18	17
Lease and rental payments	(NA)	456	459	525	14	3	3	3
Purchased repairs	(NA)	306	304	333	10	2	2	2
Insurance	(NA)	97	102	129	27	1	1	1
Telephone, other purchased communications . .	(NA)	119	124	141	14	1	1	1
Purchased utilities	(NA)	167	179	196	10	1	1	1
Purchased advertising	(NA)	417	421	479	14	2	2	3
Taxes.	(NA)	279	299	368	23	2	2	2
Other operating expenses	(NA)	3,892	3,980	3,579	-10	22	22	19

NA Not available.   [1] Includes other amounts not shown separately.
Source: U.S. Bureau of the Census, *Annual Survey of Communication Services*.

No. 898. Publishing Industry—Summary: 1982 to 1991
[**In millions of dollars**, except as noted. Number in parentheses represents Standard Industrial Classification code; see text, section 13. Based on the censuses of manufactures and the Annual Survey of Manufactures (ASM). For the 1990 ASM, a major change in the survey was introduced. This change resulted from a backlog of previously unclassified single-establishment companies now classified as manufacturing; for details, see text, section 27, and Appendix II]

ITEM	NEWSPAPERS (2711)				PERIODICALS (2721)				BOOKS (2731)			
	1982	1987	1990	1991	1982	1987	1990	1991	1982	1987	1990	1991
Establishments.	8,846	9,091	(NA)	(NA)	3,328	4,020	(NA)	(NA)	2,130	2,298	(NA)	(NA)
With 20 or more employees.	2,554	2,617	(NA)	(NA)	690	876	(NA)	(NA)	419	424	(NA)	(NA)
Employees [1] (1,000)	402	435	443	428	94	110	115	111	67	70	74	77
Payroll	6,555	9,025	10,407	10,309	1,986	2,983	3,659	3,661	1,327	1,860	2,300	2,514
Value of receipts	21,276	31,849	34,642	33,702	11,478	17,329	20,397	20,345	7,740	12,620	15,318	16,596
Cost of materials	6,006	7,533	8,087	7,606	4,568	5,873	6,580	6,459	2,420	3,663	4,466	5,001
Value added [2]	15,275	24,311	26,560	26,093	6,911	11,452	13,848	13,794	5,292	9,111	10,920	11,683
New capital expends.	1,029	1,523	1,886	1,538	195	246	275	223	174	240	329	331
Fixed assets, gross assets . .	8,701	14,028	(NA)	(NA)	1,370	2,528	(NA)	(NA)	1,109	1,680	(NA)	(NA)
Inventories, Dec. 31	755	857	975	915	724	902	1,118	1,012	1,380	2,091	2,769	2,818

NA Not available.   [1] Represents the average number of production workers plus the number of other employees in mid-March.   [2] By manufacture, derived by subtracting the cost of materials, supplies, containers, fuel, purchased electricity, and contract work from the value of shipments. This result is then adjusted by the addition of value added by merchandising operations, plus the net change in finished goods and work-in-process inventories between the beginning and the end of the year.

Source: U.S. Bureau of the Census, *1987 Census of Manufactures*, Industry Reports, series MC87-I-27A, and *Annual Survey of Manufactures*.

No. 899. New Books and Editions Published and Imports, by Subject: 1980 to 1992

[Covers listings in Bowker's Weekly Record in year shown, plus titles issued in that year which were listed in following 6 months. Comprises new books (published for first time) and new editions (with changes in text or format). Excludes government publications; books sold only by subscription; dissertations; periodicals and quarterlies; and pamphlets under 49 pages. See also *Historical Statistics, Colonial Times to 1970*, series R 191-216]

SUBJECT	NEW BOOKS AND NEW EDITIONS						IMPORTS					
	1980	1985	1989	1990	1991	1992	1980	1985	1989	1990	1991	1992
Total [1]	42,377	50,070	53,446	46,738	48,146	49,276	5,390	7,304	7,315	6,414	5,867	6,506
Agriculture	461	536	562	514	523	565	104	118	104	86	81	93
Art	1,691	1,545	1,569	1,262	1,283	1,392	157	166	128	94	101	156
Biography	1,891	1,953	2,193	1,957	2,120	2,007	126	216	144	115	124	124
Business	1,185	1,518	1,569	1,191	1,421	1,367	74	196	152	134	140	126
Education	1,011	1,085	1,054	1,039	1,129	1,184	133	211	233	234	176	232
Fiction	2,835	5,105	5,941	5,764	5,424	5,690	71	171	119	166	250	246
General works	1,643	2,905	2,332	1,760	1,886	2,153	132	329	322	266	252	313
History	2,220	2,327	2,563	2,243	2,331	2,322	296	395	376	329	314	348
Home economics	879	1,228	949	758	789	826	40	41	31	19	23	25
Juvenile	2,859	3,801	5,413	5,172	5,111	5,144	58	92	101	103	69	50
Language	529	632	586	649	566	617	134	216	182	202	171	164
Law	1,102	1,349	1,096	896	1,177	1,063	112	170	156	138	171	197
Literature	1,686	1,964	2,298	2,049	2,087	2,227	183	267	275	242	196	274
Medicine	3,292	3,579	3,447	3,014	3,027	3,234	671	598	712	588	447	514
Music	357	364	375	289	300	346	35	70	78	52	71	69
Philosophy, psychology	1,429	1,559	2,058	1,683	1,766	1,806	218	267	348	284	256	291
Poetry and drama	1,179	1,166	1,128	874	890	899	120	220	147	119	115	136
Religion	2,055	2,564	2,586	2,285	2,389	2,540	94	173	173	176	129	165
Science	3,109	3,304	3,288	2,742	2,710	2,729	1,069	1,242	1,187	1,030	795	840
Sociology, economics	7,152	7,441	7,971	7,042	7,241	7,432	1,050	1,559	1,575	1,368	1,278	1,521
Sports, recreation	971	1,154	1,077	973	1,063	1,113	85	107	94	75	93	112
Technology	2,337	2,526	2,690	2,092	2,421	2,152	373	419	638	546	558	458
Travel	504	465	701	495	492	468	55	61	39	48	57	52

[1] Increase in new books and editions after 1980 is due largely to a major improvement in the recording of paperbound books.

Source: R. R. Bowker Co., New York, NY, *Publishers Weekly*. (Copyright by Reed Publishing USA.)

No. 900. Books and Periodicals—Average Retail Prices: 1980 to 1993

[See headnote, table 899. For definition of mean, see Guide to Tabular Presentation]

SUBJECT	BOOKS (per volume)				SUBJECT	PERIODICALS [3]			
	1980	1990	1991	1992, prel.		1990	1991	1992	1993
Hardcover [1]	24.64	42.12	44.17	45.25	Agriculture	200.26	241.68	254.22	292.75
					Anthropology	121.16	136.60	146.61	148.49
Agriculture	27.55	54.24	57.73	54.74	Art and architecture	73.14	79.05	85.51	91.23
Art	27.70	42.18	44.99	43.35	Astronomy	494.29	606.25	655.25	810.84
Biography	19.77	29.58	27.52	29.80	Biology	372.62	443.14	474.94	548.21
Business	22.45	45.48	43.38	44.11	Botany	296.56	345.73	375.98	439.65
Education	17.01	38.72	41.26	49.12	Business and economics	131.08	159.79	175.55	196.86
Fiction	12.46	19.83	21.30	20.34	Chemistry	641.26	789.09	915.75	1,042.36
General works	29.84	54.77	51.74	56.11	Education	92.03	107.48	113.67	130.57
History	22.78	36.43	39.87	38.58	Engineering and technology	323.34	415.76	480.38	530.49
Home economics	13.31	23.80	24.23	25.08	Food science	256.59	339.03	367.88	422.85
Juvenile	8.16	13.01	16.64	14.51	General science	190.34	234.15	300.35	348.18
Language	22.16	42.98	51.71	50.89	General works	55.64	65.05	63.28	68.44
Law	33.25	60.78	64.89	75.85	Geography	155.85	193.25	218.88	236.79
Literature	18.70	35.80	36.76	39.18	Geology	297.66	366.22	380.53	443.72
Medicine	34.28	72.24	71.44	75.01	Health sciences	256.64	307.17	337.36	380.06
Music	21.79	41.86	41.04	46.78	History	57.20	63.49	69.10	74.16
Philosophy, psychology	21.70	40.58	42.74	45.97	Language and literature	51.36	59.02	62.08	67.57
Poetry and drama	17.85	32.19	33.29	36.88	Law	58.92	68.86	73.98	83.86
Religion	17.61	31.31	32.33	35.67	Library & information science	91.52	106.11	119.82	127.08
Science	37.45	74.39	80.14	80.63	Math & computer science	385.19	466.66	506.08	567.11
Sociology, economics	31.76	42.10	48.43	45.69	Music	43.18	47.97	53.53	56.61
Sports, recreation	15.92	30.52	30.68	34.73	Philosophy & religion	64.92	75.43	78.62	88.53
Technology	33.64	76.80	76.40	81.21	Physics	680.06	812.40	927.27	1,090.34
Travel	16.80	30.41	32.43	32.87	Political science	76.47	92.58	99.94	112.50
					Psychology	109.06	122.49	136.98	149.29
Paperbacks:					Recreation	47.95	56.86	60.75	65.81
Mass market [2]	(NA)	4.57	5.08	5.10	Sociology	98.54	113.13	123.95	138.00
Trade	8.60	17.45	18.40	18.60	Zoology	291.92	335.23	362.22	413.42

NA Not available. [1] Excludes publications of the United States and other governmental units, books sold only by subscription, and dissertations. [2] "Pocket-sized" books sold primarily through magazine and news outlets, supermarkets, variety stores, etc. [3] Average annual subscription prices. Includes foreign translations and non-U.S. journals.

Source: R. R. Bowker Co., New York, NY. Books, *Publishers Weekly*, March 1993 and *Bowker Annual: Library and Book Trade Almanac;* Periodicals, *Library Journal*, April 15, 1993, and earlier issues. (Copyright by Reed Publishing USA.)

No. 901. Microcomputer Software Sales: 1993

[Estimated North American retail sales. Figures do not add to totals because individual applications and totals derived independently]

APPLICATION	1993 (mil. dol.)					Percent change, 1992-93				
	Total	PC/ MS-DOS	Win- dows	Macin- tosh	Other	Total	PC/ MS-DOS	Win- dows	Macin- tosh	Other
Total	6,810	1,925	3,473	1,079	208	19	−26	80	9	−12
Entertainment	410	319	39	40	4	20	19	33	28	−72
Home education.......	243	110	89	41	2	66	5	614	83	−65
Finance	409	213	131	43	(B)	38	−3	191	38	(B)
Word processors	1,022	227	664	104	25	23	−9	59	−28	34
Spreadsheets	801	157	554	70	20	1	−53	61	−24	−25
Databases	476	157	239	66	1	37	−41	664	36	−37
Integrated...........	162	32	60	54	2	10	−52	108	14	−63
Utilities............	298	128	103	64	2	−8	−17	4	−6	(B)
Presentation graphic....	316	42	217	52	5	9	−56	52	6	35
Drawing and painting ...	325	(B)	173	148	3	24	(B)	20	34	−36
Desktop publishing.....	185	2	114	68	(B)	32	−83	50	26	(B)
Other graphics........	255	58	115	88	2	−4	−44	31	26	−38
Languages and tools ...	266	36	149	25	56	3	−54	71	37	−26
Other productivity......	1,770	570	977	266	88	36	−10	151	31	15

B Base figure too small to meet statistical standards for reliability of a derived figure.

Source: Software Publishers Association, Washington DC, *SPA Software Sales Report,* News Release, March 22, 1994.

No. 902. Recording Industry—U.S. Sales of Singles, Albums, Compact Discs, and Cassettes: 1975 to 1992

[In thousands. Returns from retailers]

YEAR	Singles	Albums- LP's/EP's	Compact discs	Cassettes
1975	164,000	257,000	(X)	16,200
1976	190,000	273,000	(X)	21,800
1977	190,000	344,000	(X)	36,900
1978	190,000	341,300	(X)	61,300
1979	195,500	318,300	(X)	82,800
1980	164,300	322,800	(X)	110,200
1981	154,700	295,200	(X)	137,000
1982	137,200	243,900	(X)	182,300
1983	124,800	209,600	800	236,800
1984	131,500	204,600	5,800	332,000
1985	120,700	167,000	22,600	339,100
1986	93,900	125,200	53,000	344,500
1987	82,000	107,000	102,100	410,000
1988	65,600	72,400	149,700	450,100
1989	36,600	34,600	207,200	446,200
1990	27,600	11,700	286,500	442,200
1991	22,000	4,800	333,300	360,100
1992	19,800	2,300	407,500	336,400

X Not applicable.

Source: Recording Industry Association of America, Washington DC, *Inside the Recording Industry: A Statistical Overview-1993 Update.*

No. 903. Newspapers and Periodicals—Number, by Type: 1980 to 1994

[Data refer to year of compilation of the Directory cited as the source, i.e., generally to year preceding year shown. See also *Historical Statistics, Colonial Times to 1970,* series R 232-243]

TYPE	1980	1985	1986	1987	1988	1989	1990	1991	1992	1993	1994
Newspapers [1] ..	9,620	9,134	9,144	9,031	10,088	10,457	11,471	11,689	11,339	12,597	12,513
Semiweekly.......	537	517	495	510	555	567	579	574	562	639	661
Weekly..........	7,159	6,811	6,857	6,750	7,438	7,622	8,420	8,546	8,293	9,177	9,067
Daily	1,744	1,701	1,651	1,646	1,745	1,773	1,788	1,781	1,755	1,850	1,831
Periodicals [1] ...	10,236	11,090	11,328	11,593	11,229	11,556	11,092	11,239	11,143	11,863	12,136
Weekly...,.....	1,716	1,367	1,383	1,400	880	828	553	511	466	485	487
Semimonthly [2].....	645	801	789	858	619	622	435	412	371	199	209
Monthly	3,985	4,088	4,066	4,031	4,192	4,445	4,239	4,340	4,326	4,545	4,494
Bimonthly	1,114	1,361	1,387	1,402	1,558	1,880	2,087	2,116	2,143	2,359	2,475
Quarterly	1,444	1,759	1,895	1,984	2,245	2,513	2,758	2,861	3,024	3,199	3,370

[1] Includes other items not shown separately.   [2] Includes fortnightly (every 2 weeks).

Source: Gale Research Inc., *1994 Gale Directory of Publications and Broadcast Media,* 126th edition; and earlier editions, (copyright).

No. 904. Daily and Sunday Newspapers—Number and Circulation: 1980 to 1992

[Number of newspapers as of **February 1** of the following year. Circulation figures as of **September 30** of year shown. For English language newspapers only. See also *Historical Statistics, Colonial Times to 1970,* series R 224-231]

TYPE	1980	1981	1982	1983	1984	1985	1986	1987	1988	1989	1990	1991	1992
NUMBER													
Daily: Total [1].............	1,745	1,730	1,711	1,701	1,688	1,676	1,657	1,645	1,642	1,626	1,611	1,586	1,570
Morning................	387	408	434	446	458	482	499	511	529	530	559	571	596
Evening................	1,388	1,352	1,310	1,284	1,257	1,220	1,188	1,166	1,141	1,125	1,084	1,042	996
Sunday.................	736	755	768	772	783	798	802	820	840	847	863	875	891
CIRCULATION (mil.)													
Daily: Total [1].............	62.2	61.4	62.5	62.6	63.1	62.8	62.5	62.8	62.7	62.6	62.3	60.7	60.1
Morning................	29.4	30.6	33.2	33.8	35.4	36.4	37.4	39.1	40.4	40.7	41.3	41.5	42.4
Evening................	32.8	30.9	29.3	28.8	27.7	26.4	25.1	23.7	22.2	21.8	21.0	19.2	17.8
Sunday.................	54.7	55.2	56.3	56.7	57.5	58.8	58.9	60.1	61.5	62.0	62.6	62.1	62.2

[1] All-day newspapers are counted in both morning and evening columns but only once in total. Circulation is divided equally between morning and evening.

Source: Editor & Publisher Co., New York, NY, *Editor & Publisher International Year Book,* annual, (copyright).

No. 905. Daily Newspapers—Number and Circulation, by Size of City: 1980 to 1992

[Number of newspapers as of **February 1** of the following year. Circulation as of **September 30** of year shown. For English language newspapers only. See table 43 for number of cities by population size. All-day newspapers are counted in both morning and evening columns; circulation is divided equally between morning and evening]

TYPE OF DAILY AND POPULATION-SIZE CLASS	NUMBER					NET PAID CIRCULATION (1,000)				
	1980	1985	1990	1991	1992	1980	1985	1990	1991	1992
Morning dailies, total ..	387	482	559	571	596	29,413	36,361	41,311	41,470	42,388
In cities of—										
1,000,001 or more.......	20	22	18	20	20	8,795	9,367	6,508	6,357	6,340
500,001 to 1,000,000.....	27	24	22	21	20	5,705	6,897	4,804	4,963	4,865
100,001 to 500,000......	99	121	138	143	142	8,996	12,197	20,051	19,752	20,099
50,001 to 100,000.......	75	87	100	118	123	2,973	3,653	4,373	4,914	5,238
25,001 to 50,000.......	64	83	102	97	104	1,701	2,145	3,209	3,204	3,369
Less than 25,000	102	145	179	172	187	1,243	2,099	2,365	2,280	2,477
Evening dailies, total. ...	1,388	1,220	1,084	1,042	996	32,788	26,407	21,017	19,217	17,777
In cities of—										
1,000,001 or more.......	11	8	7	7	7	2,984	2,169	1,423	1,263	1,289
500,001 to 1,000,000.....	23	14	12	11	10	4,101	1,626	1,350	1,201	1,105
100,001 to 500,000......	123	102	71	60	50	8,178	6,987	4,687	4,058	3,266
50,001 to 100,000.......	156	127	94	96	88	4,896	3,942	2,941	2,880	2,676
25,001 to 50,000.......	246	229	204	196	183	5,106	4,606	4,278	3,807	3,529
Less than 25,000	829	740	696	672	658	7,523	7,075	6,338	6,009	5,912

Source: Editor & Publisher Co., New York, NY, *Editor & Publisher International Year Book,* annual, (copyright).

No. 906. Daily and Sunday Newspapers—Number and Circulation, by State: 1991 and 1992

[Number of newspapers as of **February 1** of the following year. Circulation figures as of **September 30 of year shown.** For English language newspapers only. New York, Massachusetts, and Virginia Sunday newspapers include national circulation]

STATE	1991 DAILY			1991 SUNDAY		1992 DAILY			1992 SUNDAY	
		Circulation [1]			Net paid		Circulation [1]			Net paid
	Number	Net paid (1,000)	Per capita [2]	Number	circulation (1,000)	Number	Net paid (1,000)	Per capita [2]	Number	circulation (1,000)
United States ...	1,586	60,687	0.24	875	62,068	1,570	60,164	0.24	891	62,160
Alabama	27	749	0.18	20	756	27	761	0.18	20	768
Alaska	8	145	0.25	4	158	7	120	0.20	4	139
Arizona	20	734	0.20	12	825	22	761	0.20	4	845
Arkansas	31	421	0.18	16	481	31	476	0.20	14	530
California	114	6,535	0.21	71	6,775	108	6,428	0.21	16	6,710
Colorado	29	1,022	0.30	11	1,191	29	1,038	0.30	71	1,209
Connecticut	20	839	0.26	11	835	19	824	0.25	11	840
Delaware	2	144	0.21	2	173	3	154	0.22	11	176
District of Columbia	2	887	1.49	2	1,239	2	894	1.53	2	1,211
Florida	42	3,153	0.24	35	3,929	41	3,157	0.23	2	3,988
Georgia	36	1,175	0.18	19	1,333	35	1,102	0.16	35	1,293
Hawaii	6	240	0.21	5	261	6	244	0.21	18	262
Idaho	12	249	0.24	8	228	12	217	0.20	5	267
Illinois	70	2,618	0.23	27	2,744	69	2,601	0.22	10	2,760
Indiana	73	1,495	0.27	22	1,369	73	1,497	0.26	28	1,377
Iowa	37	712	0.26	10	728	37	703	0.25	22	723
Kansas	47	526	0.21	17	482	47	518	0.21	10	478
Kentucky	23	661	0.18	12	675	23	667	0.18	17	683
Louisiana	26	733	0.17	22	893	25	753	0.18	12	893
Maine	7	266	0.22	2	188	7	264	0.21	21	189
Maryland	15	708	0.15	7	669	15	656	0.13	7	672
Massachusetts	40	1,964	0.33	14	1,764	39	1,917	0.32	7	1,780
Michigan	52	2,262	0.24	24	2,405	52	2,195	0.23	14	2,422
Minnesota	25	954	0.22	14	1,212	25	957	0.21	27	1,184
Mississippi	22	402	0.15	15	381	22	404	0.15	14	381
Missouri	44	1,040	0.20	21	1,345	45	1,046	0.20	15	1,351
Montana	11	189	0.23	7	195	11	191	0.23	21	202
Nebraska	20	469	0.30	7	435	20	472	0.29	11	439
Nevada	8	260	0.20	4	303	8	264	0.20	20	308
New Hampshire	10	232	0.21	4	159	10	233	0.21	7	185
New Jersey	21	1,628	0.21	17	1,934	21	1,616	0.21	4	1,936
New Mexico	18	312	0.20	13	292	18	308	0.19	17	295
New York	71	7,019	0.39	41	5,601	73	6,985	0.39	13	5,700
North Carolina	50	1,416	0.21	36	1,467	49	1,411	0.21	44	1,496
North Dakota	10	186	0.29	7	187	10	187	0.29	36	190
Ohio	86	2,722	0.25	35	2,894	84	2,711	0.25	7	2,940
Oklahoma	48	744	0.23	42	888	47	665	0.21	37	875
Oregon	19	676	0.23	10	710	19	688	0.23	42	716
Pennsylvania	89	3,182	0.27	30	3,219	89	3,007	0.25	10	2,840
Rhode Island	6	285	0.28	3	307	6	282	0.28	32	309
South Carolina	16	638	0.18	14	739	16	667	0.19	3	750
South Dakota	11	169	0.24	4	138	11	169	0.24	14	139
Tennessee	27	891	0.18	17	1,090	27	910	0.18	4	1,107
Texas	96	3,254	0.19	88	4,229	93	3,181	0.18	18	4,199
Utah	6	290	0.16	6	329	6	298	0.16	87	339
Vermont	8	129	0.23	3	103	8	129	0.23	6	105
Virginia	31	2,540	0.40	15	970	30	2,607	0.41	3	981
Washington	25	1,187	0.24	16	1,230	24	1,202	0.23	16	1,285
West Virginia	23	425	0.24	11	406	23	426	0.24	16	414
Wisconsin	36	1,116	0.23	18	1,133	36	1,109	0.22	11	1,209
Wyoming	10	94	0.21	4	74	10	93	0.20	20	71

[1] Circulation figures based on the principal community served by a newspaper which is not necessarily the same location as the publisher's office. [2] Per capita based on estimated resident population as of July 1.

Source: Editor & Publisher Co., New York, NY, *Editor & Publisher International Year Book*, annual, (copyright).

No. 907. Copyright Registration, by Subject Matter: 1990 to 1993

[In thousands. For years ending **September 30.** Comprises claims to copyright registered for both U.S. and foreign works. See also *Historical Statistics, Colonial Times to 1970*, series W 82-95]

SUBJECT MATTER	1990	1991	1992	1993	SUBJECT MATTER	1990	1991	1992	1993
Total	643.5	663.7	606.2	564.7	Sound recordings	37.5	36.8	33.1	32.4
Monographs [1]	179.7	193.8	190.2	186.0	Renewals	51.8	52.3	49.1	37.7
Semiconductor chip products	1.0	1.2	0.9	1.0	Musical works [2]	185.3	191.2	162.1	152.3
Serials	111.5	109.2	92.9	81.9	Works of the visual arts [3]	76.7	79.2	78.0	73.5

[1] Includes computer software and machine readable works. [2] Includes dramatic works, accompanying music, choreography, pantomimes, motion pictures, and filmstrips. [3] Two-dimensional works of fine and graphic art, including prints and art reproductions; sculptural works; technical drawings and models; photographs; commercial prints and labels; works of applied arts, cartographic works, and multimedia works.

Source: The Library of Congress, Copyright Office, *Annual Report*.

No. 908. U.S. Postal Service—Summary: 1980 to 1991

[Employees in thousands; revenue and expenditures in millions of dollars, except as indicated. For fiscal years; see text, section 9. Includes Puerto Rico and all outlying areas except Canal Zone. See text, section 18. See also *Historical Statistics, Colonial Times to 1970*, series R 163-171]

ITEM	1980	1984	1985	1986	1987	1988	1989	1990	1991
Number of post offices	30,326	29,750	29,557	29,344	29,319	29,203	29,083	28,959	28,912
Pieces of mail handled (est.) (bil.)	106.3	131.5	140.1	147.4	153.9	161.0	161.6	166.3	165.9
First-class, number (bil.) [1]	60.3	68.4	72.4	76.2	78.9	84.7	85.9	89.3	90.3
Percent	56.7	52.0	51.7	51.7	51.3	52.6	53.2	53.7	54.4
Second class (bil.)	8.4	9.5	10.4	10.6	10.3	10.4	10.5	10.7	10.4
Employees, total	**667**	**702**	**744**	**785**	**791**	**824**	**817**	**819**	**808**
Regular	536	561	586	606	751	764	764	757	746
Postmasters	29	28	28	27	28	28	27	27	27
Office supervisors and tech. personnel	36	45	46	49	55	55	55	53	54
Office clerks and mail handlers [2]	229	235	249	260	345	347	345	333	324
City carriers and vehicle drivers	160	171	179	187	237	243	243	240	235
Rural carriers	33	35	35	36	37	39	40	42	42
Other	49	47	48	47	49	52	54	62	64
Substitute (part-time)	130	141	159	179	40	60	53	62	62
Compensation and employee benefits (mil. dol.)	16,541	22,157	24,349	25,576	27,229	30,749	32,368	34,214	36,076
Avg. salary per employee (dol.) [3]	24,799	31,562	32,727	32,581	34,424	36,989	39,619	41,775	44,649
Pieces of mail per employee, avg	159	187	188	188	195	195	198	203	205
Total revenue [4]	**19,106**	**26,474**	**28,956**	**31,021**	**32,297**	**35,939**	**38,920**	**40,074**	**44,202**
Operating postal revenue	17,143	25,314	27,736	30,102	31,528	35,036	37,979	39,201	43,323
Stamps, postal cards, etc	4,287	6,023	6,520	6,969	7,246	7,784	8,381	8,638	9,148
Second-class postage paid in money (pound rates) [5]	881	1,056	1,339	1,271	1,326	1,455	1,594	1,580	1,718
Other postage paid under permit and meter	10,828	16,067	17,747	19,294	20,280	22,676	24,534	25,311	28,019
Box rents	160	188	230	259	273	296	362	394	413
Miscellaneous	892	1,847	1,774	2,174	2,255	2,683	2,959	3,124	3,877
Money-order revenues	95	132	126	135	148	142	148	154	148
Government appropriations	1,610	879	970	716	650	517	436	453	562
Percent of total revenue	8.4	3.3	3.3	2.3	2.0	1.4	1.1	1.1	1.3
Investment income, net	353	282	250	203	119	386	504	420	317
Mail and service:								
First-class mail [1]	10,146	15,216	16,740	18,035	18,786	21,402	23,234	24,023	26,649
Priority mail [6]	612	928	960	1,011	1,086	1,329	1,416	1,555	1,765
Second-class publishers' mail [7]	864	1,025	1,093	1,222	1,280	1,400	1,519	1,509	1,668
Third-class mail [8]	2,412	4,241	4,887	5,606	6,148	7,311	7,924	8,082	8,956
Bulk rate	2,168	4,039	4,697	5,414	5,947	7,096	7,668	7,844	8,699
Single piece rate and fees	244	202	190	193	200	215	256	238	257
Fourth-class mail [9]	805	774	763	814	823	929	908	920	1,001
Zone rate mail (parcels, catalogs, etc.)	500	519	524	550	563	647	612	655	721
Special fourth-class rate	272	210	199	213	203	223	235	215	234
Library rate and fees	33	45	40	51	57	59	61	50	46
Government mail [10]	745	901	934	992	907	(NA)	(NA)	(NA)	(NA)
International mail [11]	596	859	882	934	957	992	1,081	1,163	1,206
Special services	518	868	918	979	1,030	1,136	1,314	1,310	1,403
Express mail	184	490	544	491	499	524	572	631	668
Mailgrams	15	13	15	17	13	12	10	8	7
Other [12]	2,205	1,159	1,220	919	769	903	938	873	879
Expenditures [13]	**19,412**	**26,357**	**29,207**	**30,716**	**32,520**	**36,119**	**38,370**	**40,490**	**43,291**

NA Not available.   [1] Items mailed at 1st-class rates and weighing 12 ounces or less.   [2] Includes mobile unit employees.   [3] Includes fringe benefits.   [4] Net revenues after refunds of postage. Includes operating reimbursements, embossed envelope purchases, indemnity claims, and miscellaneous revenue and expenditure offsets. Shown in year which gave rise to the earnings.   [5] Includes controlled circulation publications.   [6] Items otherwise qualified as 1st-class or airmail that exceeds 12 ounces and 8 ounces, respectively.   [7] Includes mail paid at other than bulk rates. Publishers' mail includes printed publications periodically issued and mailed at a known post office to paid subscribers, such as regular rate newspapers and magazines, and classroom and nonprofit rate publications. See source for further detail.   [8] Items less than 16 ounces in weight not mailed at either 1st- or 2d-class rates.   [9] Items not mailed at 1st-, 2d-, or 3d-class rates, except government and international mail. May include parcel post, catalogs weighing 16 ounces or more, books, films, and records.   [10] Penalty and franked. Beginning in 1988 penalty and franked mail are included in their appropriate classes of mail.   [11] Mail from United States to foreign countries paid at international mail rates.   [12] Consists of unassignable revenues.   [13] Shown in year in which obligation was incurred.

Source: U.S. Postal Service, *Annual Report of the Postmaster General*.

No. 909. U.S. Postal Service—Volume of Mail, by Class: 1980 to 1991

[In millions, except per capita. For fiscal years; see text, section 9. Includes Puerto Rico and all outlying areas except Canal Zone. For definition of classes of mail, see footnotes, table 896. See also *Historical Statistics, Colonial Times to 1970*, series R 172-186]

CLASS OF MAIL	PIECES OF MAIL					WEIGHT OF MAIL (lb.)				
	1980	1985	1989	1990	1991	1980	1985	1989	1990	1991
Total	106,311	140,098	161,603	166,301	165,851	12,958	16,783	18,412	18,826	18,340
Domestic	105,348	139,269	160,880	165,503	165,058	12,742	16,564	18,184	18,577	18,104
1st class and express [1]	60,332	72,517	85,926	89,343	90,356	2,213	2,807	3,315	3,452	3,505
Priority mail	248	308	471	518	530	591	672	939	1,007	1,017
2d class	10,221	10,380	10,523	10,680	10,399	3,478	3,966	4,170	4,233	4,015
3d class	30,381	52,170	62,779	63,725	62,430	3,240	6,453	7,479	7,648	7,386
4th class.	633	576	626	663	695	2,661	2,156	2,196	2,109	2,074
Penalty.	2,992	2,608	(NA)	(NA)	(NA)	503	470	(NA)	(NA)	(NA)
Franked and free for blind . . .	540	710	555	574	648	56	40	84	127	106
International	963	829	724	798	793	216	219	228	249	236
Per capita: [2]										
Total, all domestic mail [3] . .	463	584	650	662	653	56	69	74	74	72
1st class and express . . .	265	304	347	354	358	10	12	13	14	14
2d class	45	44	43	43	41	15	17	17	17	16
3d class	133	219	254	255	247	14	27	30	31	29
4th class.	3	2	3	3	3	12	9	9	8	8

NA Not available. [1] Includes mailgrams. [2] 1980 and 1990 based on April 1 population, including Armed Forces abroad; other years based on estimated total population as of Jan. 1, including Armed Forces abroad. [3] Includes types of mail not shown separately.

Source: U.S. Postal Service, *Annual Report of the Postmaster General;* and unpublished data.

No. 910. U.S. Postal Service Rates for Letters and Post Cards: 1958 to 1991

[Domestic airmail letters discontinued in 1973 at 13 cents per ounce; superseded by express mail. See also *Historical Statistics, Colonial Times to 1970*, series R 188-191]

DATE OF RATE CHANGE	SURFACE MAIL				Express mail [1]	DATE OF RATE CHANGE	SURFACE MAIL				Express mail [1]
	Letters		Each added oz.	Postal and post cards			Letters		Each added oz.	Postal and post cards	
	Each oz.	First oz.					Each oz.	First oz.			
1958 (Aug. 1) . .	$0.04	(X)	(X)	$0.03	(X)	1978 (May 29). .	(X)	$0.15	$0.13	$0.10	(X)
1963 (Jan. 7). . .	$0.05	(X)	(X)	$0.04	(X)	1981 (Mar. 22). .	(X)	$0.18	$0.17	$0.12	(X)
1968 (Jan. 7). . .	$0.06	(X)	(X)	$0.05	(X)	1981 (Nov. 1) . .	(X)	$0.20	$0.17	$0.13	$9.35
1971 (May 16). .	$0.08	(X)	(X)	$0.06	(X)	1985 (Feb.17) . .	(X)	$0.22	$0.17	$0.14	$10.75
1974 (Mar. 2) . .	$0.10	(X)	(X)	$0.08	(X)	1988 (Apr. 3). . .	(X)	$0.25	$0.20	$0.15	[3]$12.00
1975 (Sept. 14) .	(X)	$0.10	$0.09	$0.07	(X)	1991 (Feb. 3) . .	(X)	$0.29	$0.23	$0.19	[3]$13.95
1975 (Dec. 31). .	[2](X)	[2]$0.13	[2]$0.11	[2]$0.09	(X)						

X Not applicable. [1] Post Office to addressee rates. Rates shown are for weights up to 2 pounds, all zones. Beginning Feb. 17, 1985, for weights between 2 and 5 lbs, $12.85 is charged. Prior to Nov. 1, 1981, rate varied by weight and distances. Over 5 pounds still varies by distance. [2] As of October 11, 1975, surface mail service upgraded to level of airmail. [3] Over 8 ounces and up to 2 pounds.

No. 911. International Air Mail Rates From the United States: 1961 to 1991

[Excludes Canada and Mexico. Zones discontinued as of February 1991]

DATE OF RATE CHANGE	ZONE 1 [1]		ZONE 1 [2]		ZONE 1 [3]		Postal and post cards	Aero-grammes
	Each 1/2 oz. up to 2 ozs.	Each added 1/2 oz.	Each 1/2 oz. up to 2 ozs.	Each added 1/2 oz.	Each 1/2 oz. up to 2 ozs.	Each added 1/2 oz.		
1961 (July 1)	$0.13	$0.13	$0.15	$0.15	$0.25	$0.25	$0.11	$0.11
1967 (May 1)	$0.15	$0.15	$0.20	$0.20	$0.25	$0.25	$0.13	$0.13
1971 (July 1)	$0.17	$0.17	$0.21	$0.21	$0.21	$0.21	$0.13	$0.13
1974 (March 2)	$0.21	$0.17	$0.26	$0.21	$0.26	$0.21	$0.18	$0.18
1976 (January 3)	$0.25	$0.21	$0.31	$0.26	$0.31	$0.26	$0.21	$0.22
1981 (January 1)	$0.35	[4]$0.30	$0.40	$0.35	[5]$0.35	$0.40	$0.28	$0.30
1985 (February 17)	$0.39	[6]$0.33	$0.44	[7]$0.39	$0.44	[7]$0.39	$0.33	$0.36
1988 (April 17) [8]	$0.45	$0.42	$0.45	$0.42	$0.45	$0.42	$0.36	$0.39
1991 (February 3) [8]	[9]$0.50	(X)	(X)	(X)	(X)	(X)	$0.40	$0.45

X Not applicable. [1] Caribbean, Central and South America. The airmail letter rate to South America, 1961 to 1967, was the same as that to Europe. Beginning January 3, 1976, the airmail letter rate to all South American countries except Colombia and Venezuela is the same as Europe; Columbia and Venezuela are included in the first zone. [2] Europe and Mediterranean Africa. [3] Rest of world. [4] Up to 32 oz.; 30 cents per additional ounce over 32. [5] Up to 32 oz.; 35 cents per additional ounce over 32. [6] Up to 32 oz.; 33 cents per additional ounce over 32. [7] Up to 32 oz.; 39 cents per additional ounce over 32. [8] Air letters collapsed to a single schedule. [9] First 1/2 ounce = 50 cents; second 1/2 ounce = 40 cents, 39 cents for each additional 1/2 ounce up to the limit of 64 oz.

Sources of tables 910 and 911: U.S. Postal Service, *"United States Domestic Postage Rate: Recent History;"* and unpublished data.

No. 912. Advertising—Indexes of National Advertising Expenditures, by Medium: 1980 to 1992

[1982-84 = 100. Based on the average monthly expenditure for those major media which give national coverage. See also *Historical Statistics, Colonial Times to 1970*, series T 472-484]

MEDIUM	1980	1982	1983	1984	1985	1986	1987	1988	1989	1990	1991	1992
General index	71	87	98	114	118	124	128	136	141	146	138	145
Network television	72	86	97	116	113	117	119	128	128	131	125	134
Spot television	67	89	99	112	123	134	140	146	150	159	145	154
Magazines	73	86	99	115	120	124	131	142	156	159	152	163
Newspapers	71	89	99	112	122	123	127	130	135	140	134	131

No. 913. Advertising—Estimated Expenditures, by Medium: 1980 to 1993

[In millions of dollars. See text, section 18, for definitions of types of advertising. See also *Historical Statistics, Colonial Times to 1970*, series R 106-109, R 123-126, and T 444-471]

MEDIUM	1980	1985	1986	1987	1988	1989	1990	1991	1992	1993 [1]
Total	53,550	94,750	102,140	109,650	118,050	123,930	128,640	126,400	131,290	138,060
National	29,815	53,355	56,850	60,625	65,610	68,990	72,780	72,635	76,020	80,240
Local	23,735	41,395	45,290	49,025	52,440	54,940	55,860	53,765	55,270	57,820
Newspapers	14,794	25,170	26,990	29,412	31,197	32,368	32,281	30,409	30,737	(NA)
National	1,963	3,352	3,376	3,494	3,586	3,720	3,867	3,685	3,602	(NA)
Local	12,831	21,818	23,614	25,918	27,611	28,648	28,414	26,724	27,135	(NA)
Magazines	3,149	5,155	5,317	5,607	6,072	6,716	6,803	6,524	7,000	(NA)
Weeklies	1,418	2,297	2,327	2,445	2,646	2,813	2,864	2,670	2,739	(NA)
Women's	782	1,294	1,376	1,417	1,504	1,710	1,713	1,671	1,853	(NA)
Monthlies	949	1,564	1,614	1,745	1,922	2,193	2,226	2,183	2,408	(NA)
Farm publications	130	186	192	196	196	212	215	215	231	(NA)
Television	11,469	21,022	22,881	23,904	25,686	26,891	28,405	27,402	29,409	(NA)
Three networks	5,130	8,060	8,342	8,500	9,172	9,110	9,383	8,933	9,549	(NA)
Cable networks	45	594	676	760	942	1,197	1,393	1,521	1,685	(NA)
Syndication (nat'l)	50	520	600	762	901	1,288	1,589	1,853	2,070	(NA)
Spot (national)	3,269	6,004	6,570	6,846	7,147	7,354	7,788	7,110	7,551	(NA)
Spot (local)	2,967	5,714	6,514	6,833	7,270	7,612	7,856	7,565	8,079	(NA)
Cable (non-network)	8	130	179	203	254	330	396	420	475	(NA)
Radio	3,702	6,490	6,949	7,206	7,798	8,323	8,726	8,476	8,654	(NA)
Network	183	365	423	413	425	476	482	490	494	(NA)
Spot	779	1,335	1,348	1,330	1,418	1,547	1,635	1,575	1,505	(NA)
Local	2,740	4,790	5,178	5,463	5,955	6,300	6,609	6,411	6,725	(NA)
Yellow Pages	2,900	5,800	6,500	7,300	7,781	8,330	8,926	9,182	9,320	(NA)
National	330	695	759	830	944	1,011	1,132	1,162	1,188	(NA)
Local	2,570	5,105	5,741	6,470	6,837	7,319	7,794	8,020	8,132	(NA)
Direct mail	7,596	15,500	17,145	19,111	21,115	21,945	23,370	24,460	25,391	(NA)
Business papers	1,674	2,375	2,382	2,458	2,610	2,763	2,875	2,882	3,090	(NA)
Outdoor	578	945	985	1,025	1,064	1,111	1,084	1,077	1,031	(NA)
Miscellaneous	7,558	12,107	12,799	13,431	14,531	15,271	15,955	15,773	16,427	(NA)

NA Not available. [1] Projection.

Source of tables 912 and 913: McCann-Erickson, Inc., New York, NY. Compiled for Crain Communications, Inc., in *Advertising Age*, (copyright).

No. 914. Magazine Advertising—Expenditures, by Product: 1980 to 1992

[In millions of dollars. Space cost based on one-time rate; special rates used where applicable. Year-to-year data not strictly comparable, as a few minor publications are added or deleted]

PRODUCT	1980	1985	1986	1987	1988	1989	1990	1991	1992
Total	2,846	4,961	5,120	5,390	5,943	6,611	6,753	6,608	7,142
Apparel, footwear, accessories	112	251	291	323	363	396	428	419	483
Automotive, accessories, equipment	230	549	597	678	801	881	900	941	1,036
Beer, wine, and liquor	239	240	225	208	213	255	277	279	248
Computers, office equipment	79	250	219	247	252	284	283	291	351
Business and consumer services	190	463	484	491	466	522	516	453	507
Drugs and remedies	79	135	148	142	145	135	163	167	279
Food and food products	199	342	389	377	377	435	444	437	462
Household equipment and supplies	65	100	93	97	102	104	118	115	160
Household furnishings	73	87	103	111	116	126	116	123	127
Jewelry, cameras, optical goods	79	101	113	121	142	156	157	157	157
Mail orders/direct response	(NA)	328	363	407	467	513	531	574	628
Publishing and media	146	188	176	186	192	191	212	197	203
Retail	(NA)	121	143	138	176	211	255	201	187
Smoking materials	290	383	322	334	352	393	305	265	224
Toiletries and toilet goods	206	385	390	455	554	651	679	640	719
Travel, hotels, and resorts	123	245	249	273	311	374	380	346	338
Other	736	793	815	802	914	984	989	1,005	1,033

NA Not available.

Source: Publishers Information Bureau, Inc., New York, NY, as compiled by Leading National Advertisers.

No. 915. Television—Expenditures for Network Advertising: 1980 to 1992

[In millions of dollars. See text, section 18, for a definition of network advertising]

PRODUCT	1980	1990	1991	1992	PRODUCT	1980	1990	1991	1992
Total	5,147	10,132	9,330	9,973	Household equipment,				
Apparel, footwear, accessories.	131	276	275	305	supplies, and furnishings	225	297	301	307
Automotive	529	1,781	[1]1,469	1,541	Insurance	74	172	146	142
Beer and wine	242	293	337	313	Jewelry, cameras, optical				
Building material, equipment,					goods	119	127	123	118
fixtures	59	72	63	77	Laundry soaps, cleansers,				
Computers, office equipment,					polishes	306	317	277	285
and stationery	57	149	110	124	Movies	103	242	227	236
Confectionery, soft drinks	281	407	[1]470	531	Pet products	144	104	82	67
Consumer services	178	524	450	501	Proprietary medicines	430	817	876	882
Department, discount stores	94	248	232	318	Publishing and media	34	28	34	56
Financial planning services	20	51	62	95	Restaurants and drive-ins	132	624	541	601
Food and food products	844	1,704	[1]1,403	1,375	Tobacco products, supplies	8	-	-	-
Freight, industrial development.	7	55	65	91	Toiletries and toilet goods	765	944	867	937
Gas, lubricants, etc.	71	39	48	67	Toys and sporting goods	93	138	156	157
Home electronics equipment	50	85	107	121	Travel, hotels, and resorts	72	146	[1]105	122
Horticulture	15	36	29	26	Other	64	456	475	578

- Represents or rounds to zero.   [1] Beginning 1991, data not comparable with prior years due to reclassification of products.

Source: Television Bureau of Advertising, Inc., New York, NY. Data compiled by Competitive Media Reporting, New York, NY.

No. 916. Television—Estimated Time Charges for Spot Advertising: 1980 to 1992

[In millions of dollars. Data represent activity in the top 75 markets monitored by Competitive Media Reporting, currently covering approximately 356 stations. Beginning 1990, data exclude National Syndicated activity and therefore are not directly comparable to prior years. See text, section 18, for a definition of types of advertising]

PRODUCT	1980	1990	1991	1992	PRODUCT	1980	1990	1991	1992
Total	2,496	5,697	5,172	5,469	Home electronics equipment.	73	131	102	108
					Horticulture	35	41	35	40
Agriculture and farming	15	12	14	12	Household equipment,				
Apparel, footwear,					supplies, and furnishings	133	175	121	111
accessories	105	105	102	85	Insurance	34	120	100	115
Automotive	228	1,449	[1]1,339	1,635	Jewelry, cameras, optical				
Beer and wine	156	201	207	201	goods	55	48	32	25
Building material, equipment,					Laundry soaps, cleaners,				
fixtures	47	58	54	56	polishes	111	156	163	110
Computers, office equip-					Pet products	33	36	29	28
ment and stationery	15	21	17	14	Proprietary medicines	93	201	216	238
Confectionery, soft drinks	212	338	[1]340	316	Publishing and media	78	124	99	108
Consumer services	83	414	380	442	Tobacco products, supplies	8	4	-	-
Food and food products	507	1,069	[1]950	856	Toiletries and toilet goods	223	258	267	248
Freight, industrial					Toys and sporting goods	104	192	182	245
development	5	33	43	48	Travel, hotels, and resorts	76	276	[1]172	185
Gasoline, lubricants, etc.	50	169	152	134	Other	17	66	56	109

- Represents or rounds to zero.   [1] Beginning 1991, data not comparable with prior years due to reclassification of products.

Source: Television Bureau of Advertising, Inc., New York, NY. Data compiled by Competitive Media Reporting, New York, NY, in the top 75 markets.

No. 917. Television—Expenditures for Retail/Local Advertising: 1980 to 1992

[In millions of dollars. See headnote, table 916]

PRODUCT	1980	1990	1991	1992	PRODUCT	1980	1990	1991	1992
Total	1,983	5,200	4,960	5,271	Hotels, resorts, U.S.	18	76	57	69
Amusements, entertainment	68	146	147	144	Jewelry stores	19	23	20	21
Appliance stores, repair	38	178	198	203	Legal services	5	95	102	113
Auto repair, service stations	28	94	87	83	Leisure time stores and services	42	151	138	147
Auto supply, accessory stores.	12	34	32	40	Loan, mortgage companies	12	39	35	38
Auto, truck dealers	99	271	244	283	Mail order, catalog showrooms	13	10	7	8
Banks, S&L associations	141	179	172	183	Medical, dental services	13	150	143	141
Builders, home improvement	20	26	22	24	Movies	102	238	221	242
Carpet, floor covering stores.	24	47	53	52	Newspapers	15	29	25	30
Clothing stores	46	129	129	133	Optical services, supplies	14	84	62	56
Department stores	131	169	193	213	Political	70	203	37	170
Discount department stores	74	121	121	119	Radio, cable TV	69	168	174	186
Drug stores	26	101	109	118	Realtors, real estate developers	18	28	21	21
Education services	17	112	98	102	Rental services (nonauto)	15	30	34	30
Financial planning services	7	27	31	28	Restaurants, drive-ins	288	828	876	892
Food stores, supermarkets	149	344	335	316	Shoe stores	27	36	36	31
Furniture stores	111	273	270	268	Shopping centers	13	28	24	24
Gas, electric, water companies	16	46	46	41	Sport, hobby, toy stores	23	50	51	44
Health clubs, reducing salons	21	116	122	128	Other	137	413	381	399
Home centers and hardware.	42	108	107	131					

Source: Television Bureau of Advertising, Inc., New York, NY. Data compiled by Competitive Media Reporting, New York, NY, in the top 75 markets.

Figure 19.1
Energy Supply and Disposition: 1970 to 1993

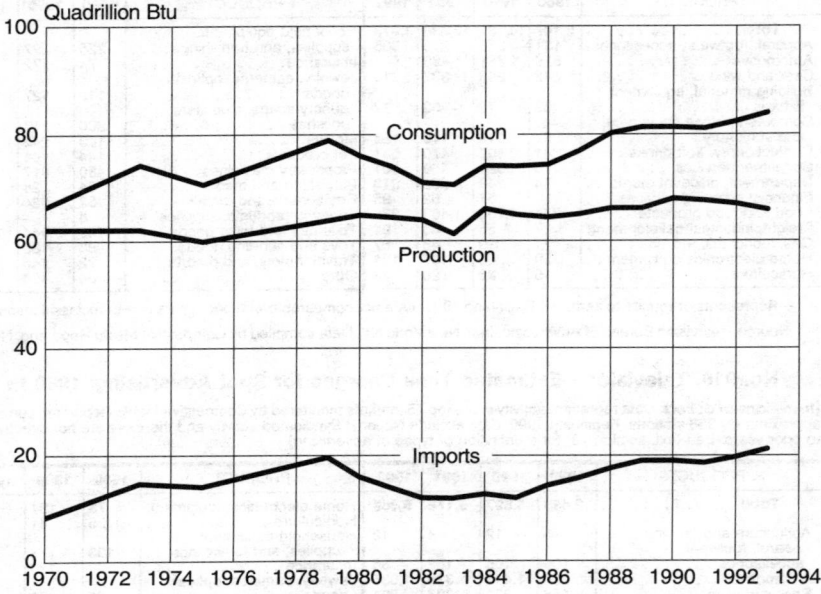

Source: Chart prepared by U.S. Bureau of the Census. For data, see table 920.

Figure 19.2
**Commercial Nuclear Power Generation—
Top 10 Countries: 1993**

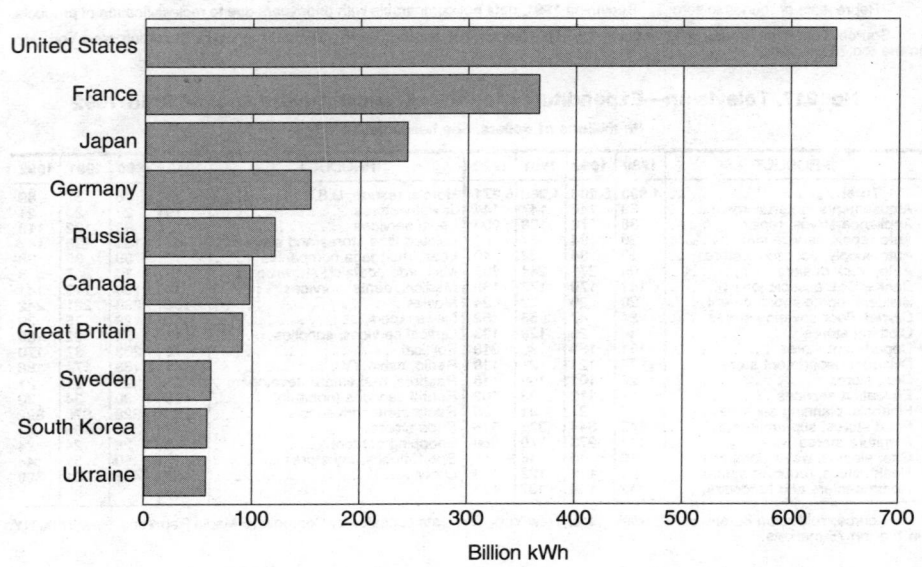

Source: Chart prepared by U.S. Bureau of the Census. For data, see table 952.

Energy

This section presents statistics on fuel resources, energy production and consumption, electric energy, hydroelectric power, nuclear power, solar energy, wood energy and the electric and gas utility industries. The principal sources are the U.S. Department of Energy's Energy Information Administration (EIA), the Edison Electric Institute, Washington, DC, and the American Gas Association, Arlington, VA. For additional data on transportation, see section 21; on fuels, see section 24; and on energy-related housing characteristics, see section 25.

In Brief

Energy expenditures amount to $467 billion in 1991

Crude oil imports almost equal domestic production in 1993 with 6.7 million barrels per day compared to 6.8 for production

Solar collector shipments up 8 percent between 1991 and 1992 to 7.1 million square feet

The EIA, in its *Annual Energy Review,* provides statistics and trend data on energy supply, demand, and prices. Information is included on petroleum and natural gas, coal, electricity, hydroelectric power, nuclear power, solar, wood, and geothermal energy. Among its annual reports are *Annual Energy Review, Electric Power Annual, Natural Gas Annual, Petroleum Supply Annual, State Energy Data Report, State Energy Price and Expenditure Report, Financial Statistics of Selected Electric Utilities, Performance Profiles of Major Energy Producers, Annual Energy Outlook,* and *International Energy Annual.* These various publications contain State, national, and international data on production of electricity, net summer capability of generating plants, fuels used in energy production, energy sales and consumption, and hydroelectric power. The EIA also issues the *Monthly Energy Review,* which presents current supply, disposition, and price data, and monthly publications on petroleum, coal, natural gas, and electric power. Data on residential energy consumption, expenditures, and conservation activities are available from EIA's Residential Energy Consumption Survey and are published triennially in *Residential Energy Consumption Survey: Consumption and Expenditures,* and *Residential Energy Consumption Survey: Housing Characteristics,* and several other reports.

The Edison Electric Institute's monthly bulletin and annual *Statistical Year Book of the Electric Utility Industry for the Year* contain data on the distribution of electric energy by public utilities; information on the electric power supply, expansion of electric generating facilities, and the manufacture of heavy electric power equipment is presented in the annual *Year End Summary of the Electric Power Situation in the United States.* The American Gas Association, in its monthly and quarterly bulletins and its yearbook, *Gas Facts,* presents data on gas utilities, including sales, revenues, customers, prices, and other financial and operating statistics.

Btu conversion factors.—Various energy sources are converted from original units (e.g., short tons, cubic feet, barrels, kilowatt-hours) to the thermal equivalent using British thermal units (Btu). A Btu is the amount of energy required to raise the temperature of 1 pound of water 1 degree Fahrenheit (F) at or near 39.2 degrees F. Factors are calculated annually from the latest final annual data available; some are revised as a result. The following list provides conversion factors used in 1992 for production and consumption, in that order, for various fuels: Petroleum, 5.800 and 5.376 mil. Btu per barrel; total coal, 21.675 and 21.164 mil. Btu per short ton; and natural gas (dry), 1,030 Btu per cubic foot for both. The factors for the production of nuclear power and geothermal power were 10,740 and 20,997 Btu per kilowatt-hour, respectively. The fossil fuel steam-electric power plant generation factor of 10,332 Btu per kilowatt-hour was used for hydroelectric power generation and for wood and waste, wind, photovoltaic, and solar thermal energy consumed at electric utilities.

No. 918. Total Horsepower of All Prime Movers: 1960 to 1992

[In millions, except percent. As of January, except as noted. Prime movers are mechanical engines and turbines, and work animals, which originally convert fuels or force (as wind or falling water) into work and power. Electric motors, which obtain their power from prime movers, are excluded to avoid duplication. See also Historical Statistics, Colonial Times to 1970, series S 1-14]

YEAR	Total horse-power	AUTOMOTIVE [1] [2]		NONAUTOMOTIVE							
		Total	Percent of total	Total	Facto-ries[3] [4]	Mines[3] [4]	Rail-roads[5]	Merchant ships and sailing vessels[4]	Farms	Electric central sta-tions[2]	Air-craft[5] [6]
1960.......	11,008	10,367	94.2	641	42	35	47	24	240	217	37
1965.......	15,096	14,306	94.8	790	48	40	44	24	272	307	55
1970.......	20,408	19,325	94.7	1,083	54	45	54	22	290	435	183
1975.......	25,100	23,752	94.6	1,348	60	47	62	22	318	654	185
1980.......	28,922	27,362	94.6	1,564	64	48	63	28	345	806	210
1981.......	29,507	27,909	94.6	1,598	64	48	65	29	345	835	212
1982.......	30,495	28,852	94.6	1,643	64	48	64	29	352	854	232
1983.......	31,337	29,662	94.7	1,675	64	47	62	29	356	877	240
1984.......	31,819	30,117	94.7	1,702	65	47	61	30	359	886	254
1985.......	32,529	30,792	94.7	1,737	65	47	58	29	358	912	268
1986.......	32,660	30,893	94.6	1,767	65	47	56	29	358	942	270
1987.......	33,266	31,488	94.7	1,778	65	47	53	29	357	958	269
1988.......	34,200	32,415	94.8	1,785	65	47	53	28	356	969	267
1989.......	34,579	32,790	94.8	1,789	65	47	50	28	356	976	267
1990.......	34,958	33,158	94.7	1,800	67	48	50	28	356	984	267
1991.......	34,962	33,158	94.8	1,804	67	48	50	27	355	991	266
1992.......	35,300	33,431	94.7	1,869	68	47	50	29	352	[7]1,057	266

[1] Includes passenger cars, trucks, buses, and motorcycles. [2] As of July 1, except beginning 1992, as of January 1. [3] Beginning 1965, data are estimates. [4] This is an extension of trends, since government agencies suspended compilation of these power capacity statistics. Beginning 1992, includes vessels on the Great Lakes. [5] Beginning 1965, not strictly comparable with earlier years. [6] Includes private planes and commercial airlines. [7] Includes 57 million horsepower in cogenerating and industrial electric power capacity.
Source: John A. Waring, Arlington, VA, unpublished estimates.

No. 919. Energy Production and Consumption, by Major Source: 1960 to 1993

[Btu=British thermal unit. For Btu conversion factors, see text, section 19. See also Historical Statistics, Colonial Times to 1970, series M 76-92]

YEAR	Total produc-tion (quad. Btu)	PERCENT OF PRODUCTION				Total con-sump-tion (quad. Btu)	PERCENT OF CONSUMPTION				Con-sump-tion/ pro-duc-tion ratio
		Coal	Petro-leum[1]	Natural gas[2]	Other[3]		Coal	Petro-leum[1]	Natural gas[2]	Other[3]	
1960........	41.5	26.1	36.0	34.0	3.9	43.8	22.5	45.5	28.3	3.8	1.06
1965........	49.3	26.5	33.5	35.8	4.3	52.7	22.0	44.1	29.9	4.0	1.07
1970........	62.1	23.5	32.9	38.9	4.7	66.4	18.5	44.4	32.8	4.3	1.07
1971........	61.3	21.5	32.7	40.5	5.3	67.9	17.1	45.0	33.1	4.8	1.11
1972........	62.4	22.6	32.1	39.7	5.6	71.3	16.9	46.2	31.9	5.0	1.14
1973........	62.1	22.5	31.4	39.9	6.2	74.3	17.5	46.9	30.3	5.3	1.20
1974........	60.8	23.1	30.5	38.9	7.4	72.5	17.5	46.1	30.0	6.5	1.19
1975........	59.9	25.0	29.6	36.8	8.6	70.5	17.9	46.4	28.3	7.4	1.18
1976........	59.9	26.1	28.8	36.4	8.6	74.4	18.3	47.3	27.4	7.1	1.24
1977........	60.2	26.2	29.0	36.4	8.5	76.3	18.2	48.7	26.1	7.0	1.27
1978........	61.1	24.4	30.2	35.6	9.9	78.1	17.6	48.6	25.6	8.1	1.28
1979........	63.8	27.4	28.4	35.1	9.1	78.9	19.0	47.0	26.2	7.7	1.24
1980........	64.8	28.7	28.2	34.2	8.9	76.0	20.3	45.0	26.9	7.8	1.17
1981........	64.4	28.5	28.2	34.2	9.1	74.0	21.5	43.2	26.9	8.4	1.15
1982........	63.9	29.1	28.6	32.1	10.2	70.9	21.6	42.6	26.1	9.7	1.11
1983........	61.3	28.1	30.0	30.6	11.2	70.5	22.5	42.6	24.6	10.2	1.15
1984........	66.0	29.9	28.6	30.7	10.8	74.1	23.0	41.9	25.0	10.1	1.12
1985........	64.9	29.8	29.3	29.6	11.3	74.0	23.6	41.8	24.1	10.5	1.14
1986........	64.4	30.3	28.6	29.0	12.1	74.3	23.2	43.3	22.5	10.9	1.15
1987........	65.0	31.0	27.2	29.8	12.0	76.9	23.4	42.7	23.1	10.8	1.18
1988........	66.1	31.4	26.1	30.0	12.4	80.2	23.5	42.7	23.1	10.7	1.21
1989........	66.1	32.3	24.4	30.3	13.1	81.3	23.3	42.1	23.8	10.8	1.23
1990........	[4]67.9	33.1	22.9	30.3	13.7	81.3	23.5	41.3	23.8	11.5	1.20
1991........	67.5	32.0	23.3	30.4	14.3	81.1	23.1	40.5	24.2	12.2	1.20
1992........	66.9	32.3	22.8	31.0	13.9	82.4	22.9	40.7	24.4	11.9	1.23
1993........	65.8	31.1	22.0	32.5	14.4	[5]84.0	23.4	40.2	24.8	11.6	1.28

[1] Production includes crude oil and lease condensate. Consumption includes domestically produced crude oil, natural gas liquids, and lease condensate, plus imported crude oil and products. [2] Production includes natural gas liquids; consumption excludes natural gas liquids. [3] Comprised of hydropower, nuclear power, geothermal energy, and other. [4] Represents peak year for U.S. energy production. [5] Represents peak year for U.S. energy consumption.
Source: U.S. Energy Information Administration, Annual Energy Review.

No. 920. Energy Supply and Disposition, by Type of Fuel: 1970 to 1993

[In quadrillion British thermal units (Btu). For Btu conversion factors, see text, section 19]

TYPE OF FUEL	1970	1973	1975	1980	1985	1986	1987	1988	1989	1990	1991	1992	1993
Production	62.1	62.1	59.9	64.8	64.9	64.4	65.0	66.1	66.1	[1]67.9	67.5	66.9	65.8
Crude oil [2]	20.4	19.5	17.7	18.3	19.0	18.4	17.7	17.3	16.1	15.6	15.7	15.2	14.5
Natural gas liquids	2.5	2.6	2.4	2.3	2.2	2.2	2.2	2.3	2.2	2.2	2.3	2.4	2.4
Natural gas [3]	21.7	22.2	19.6	19.9	17.0	16.5	17.1	17.6	17.9	18.4	18.3	18.3	19.0
Coal	14.6	14.0	15.0	18.6	19.3	19.5	20.1	20.7	21.4	22.5	21.6	21.6	20.5
Nuclear electric power	0.2	0.9	1.9	2.7	4.2	4.5	4.9	5.7	5.7	6.2	6.6	6.7	6.5
Hydroelectric power	2.6	2.9	3.2	2.9	3.0	3.1	2.6	2.3	2.8	2.9	2.9	2.5	2.8
Geothermal and other	(Z)	(Z)	0.1	0.1	0.2	0.2	0.2	0.2	0.2	0.2	0.2	0.2	0.2
Net trade [4]	-5.7	-12.7	-11.7	-12.3	-7.9	-10.3	-11.9	-13.2	-14.2	-14.1	-13.4	-14.6	-16.9
Exports	2.7	2.1	2.4	3.7	4.2	4.1	3.9	4.4	4.8	4.9	5.2	5.0	4.3
Coal	1.9	1.4	1.8	2.4	2.4	2.3	2.1	2.5	2.6	2.8	2.9	2.7	(NA)
Imports	8.4	14.7	14.1	16.0	12.1	14.4	15.8	17.6	19.0	19.0	18.6	19.7	21.2
Crude oil	2.8	6.9	8.7	11.2	6.8	9.0	10.1	11.0	12.6	12.8	12.6	(NA)	(NA)
Consumption	66.4	74.3	70.6	76.0	74.0	74.3	76.9	80.2	81.3	81.3	81.1	82.4	[5]84.0
Petroleum products	29.5	34.8	32.7	34.2	30.9	32.2	32.9	34.2	34.2	33.6	32.9	33.5	33.8
Natural gas [3]	21.8	22.5	20.0	20.4	17.8	16.7	17.7	18.6	19.4	19.3	19.6	20.3	20.8
Coal	12.3	13.0	12.7	15.4	17.5	17.3	18.0	18.9	18.9	19.1	18.8	18.9	19.6
Nuclear power [6]	0.2	0.9	1.9	2.7	4.2	4.5	4.9	5.7	5.7	6.2	6.6	6.7	6.5
Hydroelectric power [6]	2.7	3.0	3.2	3.1	3.4	3.5	3.1	2.7	2.9	3.0	3.1	2.8	3.1
Geothermal and other	(Z)	(Z)	0.1	0.1	0.2	0.2	0.2	0.3	0.3	0.2	0.2	0.2	0.2

Z Less than 50 trillion.   NA Not available.   [1] Represents peak year for U.S. energy production.   [2] Includes lease condensate.   [3] Dry marketed gas.   [4] Exports minus imports.   [5] Represents peak year for U.S. energy consumption.   [6] Includes industrial generation of hydropower and net electricity imports.

No. 921. Energy Imports and Exports, by Type of Fuel: 1970 to 1992

[In quadrillion of Btu. For definition of Btu, see text, section 19]

TYPE OF FUEL	1970	1973	1975	1980	1985	1986	1987	1988	1989	1990	1991	1992
Net imports: [1]												
Coal	-1.93	-1.42	-1.74	-2.39	-2.39	-2.19	-2.05	-2.45	-2.57	-2.70	-2.77	-2.59
Natural Gas (dry)	0.77	0.98	0.90	0.96	0.90	0.69	0.94	1.22	1.28	1.46	1.67	1.84
Petroleum	6.92	12.98	12.51	13.50	8.95	11.53	12.53	14.01	15.33	15.29	14.22	14.87
Other [2]	-0.04	0.14	0.08	0.18	0.41	0.36	0.49	0.37	0.14	0.03	0.24	0.30
Imports:												
Coal	(Z)	(Z)	0.02	0.03	0.05	0.06	0.04	0.05	0.07	0.07	0.08	0.10
Natural Gas (dry)	0.85	1.06	0.98	1.01	0.95	0.75	0.99	1.39	1.39	1.55	1.80	2.09
Petroleum	7.47	13.47	12.95	14.66	10.61	13.20	14.16	15.75	17.16	17.12	16.35	16.88
Other [2]	0.07	0.20	0.16	0.28	0.49	0.43	0.57	0.47	0.33	0.25	0.35	0.39
Exports:												
Coal	1.94	1.43	1.76	2.42	2.44	2.25	2.09	2.50	2.64	2.77	2.85	2.68
Natural Gas (dry)	0.07	0.08	0.07	0.05	0.06	0.06	0.05	0.07	0.11	0.09	0.13	0.25
Petroleum	0.55	0.49	0.44	1.16	1.66	1.67	1.63	1.74	1.84	1.82	2.13	2.01
Other [2]	0.11	0.06	0.08	0.09	0.08	0.08	0.08	0.10	0.18	0.23	0.11	0.09

Z Less than .005 quadrillion Btu.   [1] Net imports equals imports minus exports. Minus sign (-) denotes an excess of exports over imports.   [2] Coal coke and small amounts of electricity transmitted across U.S. borders with Canada and Mexico.

No. 922. Selected Energy Indicators—Summary: 1970 to 1993

[Btu=British thermal unit. For Btu conversion factors, see text, section 19. Minus sign (-) indicates decrease]

ITEM	1970	1973	1975	1980	1985	1986	1987	1988	1989	1990	1991	1992	1993
AVERAGE ANNUAL PERCENT CHANGE [1]													
Gross domestic product [2]	3.0	1.7	-0.7	-0.1	0.6	2.9	3.0	3.9	2.5	1.2	-0.7	2.5	3.0
Energy production, total [3]	4.6	-0.2	-1.8	0.3	-0.3	-0.8	0.9	1.8	0.0	2.6	-0.5	-0.9	-1.6
Crude oil [4]	4.2	-0.9	-4.7	0.2	0.2	-3.3	-3.9	-2.3	-6.9	-3.4	-3.1	-5.0	
Natural gas	6.4	0.0	-6.1	-0.2	-1.2	-2.6	3.5	2.7	1.4	2.8	-0.7	0.8	3.3
Coal	2.2	-0.2	3.4	1.2	0.4	1.0	3.2	2.9	2.9	5.1	-3.9	(-Z)	-5.2
Energy consumption, total [3]	4.6	1.4	-2.6	-0.8	-0.4	0.4	3.5	4.3	1.4	0.0	-0.3	1.6	1.9
Petroleum products	4.8	1.9	-3.1	-1.6	-0.1	4.2	2.1	4.0	0.0	-1.8	-2.1	1.3	2.2
Natural gas (dry)	6.5	-0.3	-6.0	-0.3	-0.7	-6.5	6.0	4.5	4.4	-0.5	1.6	2.1	0.7
Coal	1.1	2.4	-1.2	0.5	0.5	-1.2	4.2	4.6	0.4	0.9	-1.7	2.6	3.2
PER CAPITA [5] (mil. Btu)													
Energy production	304	294	278	285	273	268	268	270	268	272	268	262	255
Energy consumption	327	351	327	334	311	309	317	328	329	326	322	322	326
Energy consumption per dollar of GDP [2] (1,000 Btu)	23.1	22.7	21.9	20.1	17.3	16.9	16.9	17.0	16.8	16.6	16.7	16.5	16.3

Z Less than .05 percent.   [1] Represents percent change from immediate prior year; for example, 1970, change from 1965. Percent change derived from Btu values.   [2] Gross domestic product in constant (1987) dollars.   [3] Includes types of fuel or power, not shown separately.   [4] Includes lease condensate.   [5] Based on resident population estimated as of July 1.

Source of tables 929 to 931: U.S. Energy Information Administration, *Annual Energy Review*, and *Monthly Energy Review*, March 1994.

No. 923. Energy Consumption—End-Use Sector and Selected Source, by State: 1991

[In trillions of Btu, except as indicated. For Btu conversion factors, see text, section 19]

REGION, DIVISION, AND STATE	Total[1]	Per capita[2] (mil. Btu)	END-USE SECTOR				SOURCE				
			Residential	Commercial	Industrial	Transportation	Petroleum	Natural gas (dry)	Coal	Hydroelectric power	Nuclear electric power
United States	81,119	321.7	16,377	13,020	[3]29,601	22,121	32,846	19,625	18,754	3,116	6,579
Northeast	13,270	260.4	3,285	3,097	3,346	3,542	6,012	2,943	2,124	651	1,562
New England	3,920	296.9	1,030	1,071	812	1,007	1,898	905	353	349	373
Maine	362	292.9	79	58	119	106	229	5	9	52	67
New Hampshire	239	215.8	69	40	54	75	143	14	35	23	73
Vermont	132	232.5	39	25	26	42	75	7	(Z)	33	44
Massachusetts	1,313	219.0	376	342	213	382	759	261	117	23	47
Rhode Island	215	214.2	60	46	50	58	92	56	(Z)	2	-
Connecticut	732	222.5	221	172	135	204	419	105	23	6	132
Middle Atlantic	9,350	247.6	2,255	2,026	2,534	2,535	4,114	2,038	1,771	302	1,189
New York	3,558	197.2	951	1,013	693	901	1,669	900	344	297	306
New Jersey	2,300	295.9	485	481	539	795	1,202	476	62	[4]-2	266
Pennsylvania	3,492	292.3	819	532	1,302	839	1,243	662	1,365	7	617
Midwest	19,687	327.1	4,581	3,192	7,197	4,718	6,652	4,814	6,696	172	1,769
East North Central	13,787	325.2	3,216	2,195	5,253	3,124	4,397	3,447	4,679	45	1,339
Ohio	3,687	337.0	828	582	1,490	787	1,090	799	1,413	2	159
Indiana	2,421	431.8	440	272	1,147	562	806	464	1,340	4	-
Illinois	3,513	304.8	889	658	1,219	747	1,110	1,006	758	1	772
Michigan	2,754	293.8	697	442	927	689	911	844	760	6	290
Wisconsin	1,412	285.4	362	241	470	339	480	334	408	32	118
West North Central	5,900	331.7	1,365	997	1,944	1,594	2,255	1,367	2,017	127	430
Minnesota	1,364	308.2	324	197	485	357	511	318	301	32	130
Iowa	937	335.9	220	146	347	225	309	235	346	9	44
Missouri	1,513	293.4	399	295	346	473	622	259	534	11	107
North Dakota	320	505.3	54	40	159	67	114	42	379	23	-
South Dakota	205	292.2	53	33	53	67	101	27	36	41	-
Nebraska	522	328.2	127	116	132	147	204	114	152	11	86
Kansas	1,039	417.2	188	170	422	258	394	372	269	(Z)	63
South	33,578	386.3	5,893	4,443	14,508	8,737	13,772	8,592	7,834	499	2,586
South Atlantic	12,508	261.5	2,916	2,290	3,567	3,736	5,185	1,553	3,593	166	1,641
Delaware	237	348.1	47	35	90	64	136	43	57	-	-
Maryland	1,215	249.8	322	178	379	336	495	178	275	15	97
Dist. of Columbia	175	294.5	34	81	34	27	35	31	2	-	-
Virginia	1,848	293.9	421	384	466	578	744	182	357	(Z)	256
West Virginia	783	435.2	129	87	423	144	293	119	800	11	-
North Carolina	1,962	290.7	458	340	632	532	725	172	522	62	326
South Carolina	1,209	339.6	240	162	495	312	408	137	291	26	463
Georgia	2,057	310.3	441	323	630	663	791	332	646	49	279
Florida	3,022	227.7	824	700	418	1,080	1,558	359	643	3	220
East South Central	5,763	375.4	1,119	651	2,451	1,543	1,999	949	2,186	259	446
Kentucky	1,476	397.3	280	183	638	376	508	196	805	38	-
Tennessee	1,746	352.6	383	200	724	440	567	235	566	109	178
Alabama	1,591	389.0	287	164	731	409	526	261	720	112	170
Mississippi	950	366.5	169	104	358	318	398	257	95	-	98
West South Central	15,307	564.1	1,858	1,502	8,490	3,458	6,588	6,090	2,055	74	499
Arkansas	770	324.8	167	105	268	230	271	213	216	37	136
Louisiana	3,469	817.4	294	214	2,217	745	1,444	1,579	214	-	150
Oklahoma	1,283	405.0	241	183	515	344	432	582	292	19	-
Texas	9,785	563.9	1,156	1,000	5,490	2,139	4,441	3,716	1,333	18	213
West	15,503	286.7	2,803	2,677	4,757	5,265	6,590	3,735	2,271	2,004	670
Mountain	4,563	325.4	870	858	1,458	1,378	1,703	1,035	2,071	343	270
Montana	342	423.5	61	52	146	83	145	47	180	124	-
Idaho	388	373.9	81	71	146	90	127	53	12	87	-
Wyoming	391	853.8	36	40	236	78	116	103	450	8	-
Colorado	964	286.1	217	237	234	277	345	268	322	17	-
New Mexico	588	380.0	76	94	189	229	236	227	234	2	-
Arizona	924	246.7	205	204	184	331	353	128	348	75	270
Utah	566	320.4	108	89	217	153	207	142	345	6	-
Nevada	400	310.6	86	71	106	137	174	67	180	24	-
Pacific	10,940	273.2	1,933	1,819	3,299	3,887	4,887	2,700	200	1,661	400
Washington	1,965	391.7	390	294	700	581	776	178	89	908	45
Oregon	953	326.5	210	166	276	301	363	127	33	460	16
California	7,162	235.5	1,264	1,273	1,922	2,703	3,283	2,024	64	283	339
Alaska	588	1,033.9	46	58	334	149	198	368	13	9	-
Hawaii	272	239.7	23	28	67	153	267	3	1	1	-

- Represents zero. Z Less than 500 million Btu. [1] Sources of energy includes geothermal, wood and waste, and net interstate sales of electricity, including losses, not shown separately. [2] Based on estimated resident population as of July 1. [3] Includes 8.9 trillion Btu of net imports of coal coke not allocated by State. [4] A negative number occurs when more electricity is expended than is created to provide electricity during peak demand periods.

Source: U.S. Energy Information Administration, *State Energy Data Report, 1991*.

No. 924. Primary Energy Consumption, by End-Use Sector: 1960 to 1993

[Btu=British thermal unit. For residential and commercial, industrial, and transportation, represents consumption of fossil fuels only. For Btu conversion factors, see text, section 19]

YEAR	Total con- sumption (quad. Btu)	Residen- tial and commer- cial (quad. Btu)	Industrial and miscella- neous (quad. Btu)	Transpor- tation (quad. Btu)	Electricity genera- tion (quad. Btu)	PERCENT OF TOTAL			
						Residen- tial and commer- cial	Industrial and miscella- neous	Transpor- tation	Electricity genera- tion
1960	43.8	8.8	16.3	10.6	8.2	20.1	37.2	24.2	18.7
1970	66.4	12.1	21.9	16.1	16.3	18.2	33.0	24.2	24.5
1973	74.3	12.3	23.6	18.6	19.9	16.6	31.8	25.0	26.8
1975	70.6	11.6	20.4	18.2	20.4	16.4	28.9	25.8	28.9
1976	74.4	12.3	21.5	19.1	21.6	16.5	28.9	25.7	29.0
1977	76.3	11.9	21.9	19.8	22.7	15.6	28.7	26.0	29.8
1978	78.1	11.9	21.9	20.6	23.7	15.2	28.0	26.4	30.3
1979	78.9	11.5	22.8	20.4	24.1	14.6	28.9	25.9	30.5
1980	76.0	10.7	21.1	19.7	24.5	14.1	27.8	25.9	32.2
1981	74.0	10.0	19.7	19.5	24.8	13.5	26.6	26.4	33.5
1982	70.9	10.1	17.5	19.0	24.3	14.2	24.7	26.8	34.3
1983	70.5	9.7	16.8	19.1	25.0	13.8	23.8	27.1	35.5
1984	74.1	10.0	18.3	19.8	26.0	13.5	24.7	26.7	35.1
1985	74.0	9.8	17.7	20.0	26.5	13.2	23.9	27.0	35.8
1986	74.3	9.6	17.3	20.8	26.7	12.9	23.3	28.0	35.9
1987	76.9	9.7	18.2	21.4	27.6	12.6	23.7	27.8	35.9
1988	80.2	10.3	19.0	22.3	28.7	12.8	23.7	27.8	35.8
1989	81.3	10.4	19.1	22.5	29.3	12.8	23.5	27.7	36.0
1990	81.3	9.6	19.6	22.5	29.6	11.8	24.1	27.7	36.4
1991	81.1	9.8	19.3	22.1	29.9	12.1	23.8	27.3	36.9
1992	82.1	10.0	20.2	22.4	29.5	12.2	24.6	27.3	36.0
1993	84.0	10.4	20.3	22.8	30.4	12.4	24.2	27.1	36.3

Source: U.S. Energy Information Administration, *Annual Energy Review*, and *Monthly Energy Review*, March 1994.

No. 925. Energy Expenditures and Average Fuel Prices, by Source and Sector: 1970 to 1991

[For definition of Btu, see text, section 19. End-use sector and electric utilities exclude expenditures and prices on energy sources such as hydropower, solar, wind, and geothermal. Also excludes expenditures for reported amounts of energy consumed by the energy industry for production, transportation, and processing operations]

SOURCE AND SECTOR	1970	1973	1975	1980	1985	1986	1987	1988	1989	1990	1991
EXPENDITURES (mil. dol.)											
Total[1][2]	82,579	111,616	171,782	373,900	435,444	381,250	393,525	407,597	434,338	469,468	467,132
Natural gas	10,892	13,933	20,061	51,062	72,938	59,701	58,019	61,089	65,382	64,104	64,701
Petroleum products[2]	48,088	65,305	103,859	238,408	223,197	174,539	186,402	189,261	206,261	234,510	222,017
Motor gasoline	31,596	39,667	59,446	124,408	118,044	91,526	99,809	103,212	112,585	126,471	123,051
Coal	4,593	6,229	13,048	22,648	29,719	27,907	27,586	28,371	28,107	28,381	27,869
Electricity sales	23,351	33,780	50,680	98,098	149,242	151,806	154,692	162,070	169,340	176,742	184,822
Residential sector	20,083	27,078	36,844	68,825	98,307	96,203	97,552	102,773	108,423	109,265	114,740
Commercial sector	10,668	15,104	22,835	46,881	70,263	68,444	68,777	71,579	75,467	78,922	81,488
Industrial sector	16,458	23,531	41,169	94,520	105,723	90,496	89,975	91,315	93,812	100,951	99,701
Transportation sector[2]	35,370	45,904	70,934	163,674	161,150	126,107	137,220	141,930	156,637	180,330	171,203
Motor gasoline	30,525	38,598	57,992	121,809	115,201	89,404	97,527	100,988	110,168	123,775	120,555
Electric utilities	4,316	7,817	16,396	37,435	42,558	35,793	36,681	37,435	38,895	38,443	36,501
AVERAGE FUEL PRICES (dol. per mil. Btu)											
All sectors	1.65	2.02	3.33	6.91	8.42	7.36	7.37	7.30	7.69	8.37	8.33
Residential sector	2.12	2.73	3.83	7.55	11.14	10.99	10.95	10.90	11.26	12.14	12.34
Commercial sector	1.97	2.56	4.09	7.88	11.71	11.35	11.06	10.91	11.4	12.03	12.21
Industrial sector	0.83	1.08	2.20	4.71	6.09	5.40	5.19	5.03	5.11	5.40	5.34
Transportation sector	2.31	2.57	4.02	8.61	8.26	6.22	6.57	6.56	7.16	8.26	7.97
Electric utilities	0.32	0.46	0.96	1.75	1.85	1.55	1.55	1.51	1.45	1.46	1.37

[1] Includes electricity sales; excludes electricity generation. [2] Includes sources or fuel types not shown separately.

Source: U.S. Energy Information Administration, *State Energy Price and Expenditure Report*, annual.

No. 926. Energy Expenditures—End-Use Sector and Selected Source, by State: 1991

[In millions of dollars, except as indicated. End-use sector and electric utilities exclude expenditures on energy sources such as hydropower, solar, wind, and geothermal. Also excludes expenditures for reported amounts of energy consumed by the energy industry for production, transportation, and processing operations]

REGION, DIVISION, AND STATE	Total[1]	Per capita[2] (dol.)	END-USE SECTOR				SOURCE				
			Residential	Commercial	Industrial	Transportation	Petroleum products		Natural gas	Coal	Electricity sales
							Total	Gasoline			
U.S......	467,132	1,853	114,740	81,488	[3]99,701	171,203	222,016	123,051	64,700	27,869	184,822
Northeast	90,251	1,771	26,855	20,208	14,402	28,786	41,168	22,348	12,837	3,182	37,703
N.E.	24,093	1,826	7,477	5,130	3,395	8,092	12,431	6,665	2,625	343	9,714
ME	2,538	2,057	708	379	504	947	1,538	715	27	25	979
NH	1,906	1,727	597	301	318	691	1,045	609	87	63	800
VT	1,094	1,930	353	188	156	397	658	337	32	1	406
MA	10,598	1,767	3,264	2,498	1,301	3,535	5,284	2,864	1,471	205	4,271
RI	1,756	1,747	531	358	310	558	781	460	331	-	650
CT	6,201	1,885	2,024	1,405	806	1,965	3,126	1,681	678	50	2,608
M.A	66,159	1,752	19,378	15,079	11,007	20,695	28,737	15,683	10,212	2,839	27,988
NY	28,006	1,551	8,786	7,825	3,296	8,098	11,822	6,644	4,630	567	12,665
NJ	15,874	2,047	4,115	3,558	2,562	5,639	7,671	3,728	2,296	109	6,088
PA	22,279	1,863	6,478	3,695	5,149	6,957	9,244	5,311	3,286	2,163	9,235
Midwest.....	112,712	1,871	28,861	18,298	26,502	39,051	49,448	29,707	19,328	9,598	42,353
E.N.C	79,414	1,872	20,660	13,157	19,556	26,041	32,897	19,962	14,679	7,159	30,549
OH	21,089	1,928	5,421	3,559	5,285	6,823	8,421	5,326	3,509	2,110	8,827
IN	11,920	2,125	2,645	1,423	3,530	4,322	5,387	2,770	1,903	1,958	4,063
IL	21,500	1,863	6,018	4,140	4,880	6,463	8,155	5,005	4,308	1,286	8,857
MI	16,754	1,786	4,340	2,789	4,201	5,425	7,034	4,456	3,538	1,232	6,042
WI	8,152	1,645	2,237	1,247	1,660	3,008	3,900	2,406	1,421	574	2,761
W.N.C.....	33,298	1,869	8,201	5,140	6,946	13,011	16,551	9,745	4,648	2,439	11,805
MN	7,597	1,714	1,869	949	1,741	3,039	3,832	2,398	1,111	390	2,639
IA	5,212	1,865	1,356	750	1,161	1,946	2,476	1,553	833	398	1,829
MO	9,393	1,821	2,539	1,634	1,509	3,711	4,562	2,786	1,157	718	3,654
ND	1,589	2,502	303	202	505	579	831	415	110	442	416
SD	1,270	1,804	314	170	216	569	744	427	109	44	409
NE	3,093	1,942	681	562	556	1,295	1,634	882	438	118	1,019
KS	5,143	2,061	1,139	875	1,258	1,872	2,473	1,284	890	330	1,839
South	173,973	2,002	39,590	25,633	43,323	65,428	87,420	45,942	20,020	12,315	69,652
S.A.	77,618	1,748	20,804	13,594	13,415	29,806	36,834	22,822	6,073	6,073	35,361
DE	1,388	2,040	369	218	286	514	750	389	146	99	568
MD	8,049	1,657	2,310	1,093	1,658	2,988	3,809	2,433	822	445	3,483
DC	1,130	1,899	222	470	170	267	308	214	189	3	638
VA	11,038	1,758	2,921	2,042	1,508	4,567	5,501	3,340	818	558	4,558
WV	3,751	2,081	742	457	1,271	1,282	2,012	1,007	455	1,209	1,133
NC	12,601	1,871	3,391	1,988	2,579	4,643	5,849	3,735	676	926	5,973
SC	6,840	1,921	1,641	927	1,752	2,520	3,057	1,912	493	478	3,212
GA	12,479	1,884	3,063	2,133	2,457	4,826	5,605	3,494	1,471	1,161	5,317
FL	20,343	1,533	6,145	4,267	1,732	8,200	9,943	6,297	1,004	1,195	10,479
E.S.C	29,644	1,931	6,423	3,570	7,862	11,789	14,212	8,366	2,886	3,175	12,139
KY	7,188	1,936	1,474	852	1,924	2,938	3,592	2,054	659	998	2,800
TN	9,274	1,872	2,024	1,074	2,548	3,628	4,271	2,655	830	725	4,041
AL	8,301	2,029	1,858	1,001	2,309	3,133	3,832	2,260	872	1,292	3,357
MS	4,881	1,882	1,068	642	1,081	2,090	2,517	1,396	524	159	1,941
W.S.C	66,711	2,457	12,362	8,469	22,046	23,833	36,374	14,754	11,062	3,067	22,152
AR	4,687	1,975	1,169	621	1,032	1,866	2,223	1,342	636	347	1,860
LA	13,168	3,095	1,950	1,318	5,410	4,490	7,595	2,149	2,209	354	3,755
OK	5,996	1,888	1,442	945	1,089	2,520	2,944	1,778	1,263	384	2,267
TX	42,861	2,471	7,802	5,586	14,515	14,958	23,613	9,485	6,954	1,981	14,271
West	90,154	1,668	19,434	17,349	15,433	37,938	43,981	25,053	12,515	2,774	35,114
Mountain ...	25,204	1,796	5,476	4,728	4,628	10,372	12,604	7,347	2,957	2,408	9,594
MT	1,695	2,096	322	232	419	723	972	493	169	127	546
ID	1,910	1,837	392	298	470	750	1,019	556	174	23	694
WY	1,493	3,245	194	184	539	575	777	318	180	388	488
CO	5,415	1,603	1,215	1,173	739	2,289	2,693	1,730	854	355	1,858
NM	2,985	1,927	545	578	569	1,292	1,694	915	353	322	987
AZ	6,432	1,716	1,694	1,448	837	2,454	2,739	1,827	469	498	3,249
UT	2,868	1,621	621	438	596	1,214	1,420	795	513	441	857
NV	2,405	1,875	493	378	459	1,075	1,289	712	245	254	914
Pacific......	64,950	1,623	13,958	12,620	10,805	27,566	31,376	17,706	9,559	366	25,521
WA	8,591	1,714	1,680	1,122	1,433	4,356	4,914	2,604	590	147	3,069
OR	5,008	1,714	1,014	756	904	2,334	2,693	1,542	472	39	1,855
CA	47,460	1,562	10,643	10,114	7,941	18,762	21,023	12,830	8,243	127	19,413
AK	1,852	3,249	349	329	185	988	1,247	241	212	51	415
HI	2,039	1,793	273	298	341	1,127	1,499	490	41	2	769

- Represents zero.   [1] Includes sources not shown separately. Total expenditures are the sum of purchases for each source (including electricity sales) less electric utility purchases of fuel.   [2] Based on estimated resident population as of July 1. [3] Includes net imports of coal coke not shown separately by State.

Source: U.S. Energy Information Administration, *State Energy Price and Expenditure Report*, annual.

No. 927. Residential Energy Consumption, Expenditures, and Average Price, 1980 to 1990, and by Region, 1990

[For period April to March for 1980-1985; January to December for 1987 and 1990. Excludes Alaska and Hawaii in 1980. Covers occupied units only. Excludes household usage of gasoline for transportation and the use of wood or coal. Based on Residential Energy Consumption Survey; see Appendix III. For composition of regions, see table 26. Btu=British thermal unit; see text, section 19]

TYPE OF FUEL	Unit	1980	1982	1983	1985	1987	1990 Total	North-east	Mid-west	South	West
CONSUMPTION											
Total	Quad. Btu. .	9.74	9.51	8.62	9.04	9.13	9.22	2.30	2.81	2.60	1.51
Avg. per household	Mil. Btu	126	114	103	105	101	98	120	122	81	78
Natural gas	Quad. Btu. . .	5.31	5.39	4.77	4.98	4.83	4.86	1.03	1.88	1.03	0.92
Electricity	Quad. Btu. . .	2.42	2.48	2.42	2.48	2.76	3.03	0.47	0.66	1.36	0.54
Fuel oil, kerosene	Quad. Btu. . .	1.71	1.33	1.14	1.26	1.22	1.04	0.78	0.13	0.11	0.02
Liquid petroleum gas	Quad. Btu. . .	0.31	0.31	0.29	0.31	0.32	0.28	0.02	0.13	0.10	0.03
EXPENDITURES											
Total	Bil. dol.	63.2	85.0	87.8	97.0	97.7	110.2	28.3	26.9	37.2	17.9
Avg. per household	Dollars.	815	1,022	1,048	1,123	1,080	1,172	1,471	1,166	1,151	920
Natural gas	Bil. dol.	17.8	24.5	27.1	29.8	26.1	27.3	7.3	9.2	5.9	4.8
Electricity	Bil. dol.	32.6	45.9	48.4	54.5	61.6	71.5	14.6	15.4	29.1	12.5
Fuel oil, kerosene	Bil. dol.	10.7	11.8	9.6	9.6	7.2	8.3	6.1	1.0	1.0	0.2
Liquid petroleum gas	Bil. dol.	2.1	2.7	2.7	3.1	2.8	3.1	0.3	1.3	1.2	0.4
AVERAGE PRICE											
Total	Dol./mil. Btu .	6.49	8.93	10.18	10.73	10.71	12.0	12.3	9.6	14.3	11.8
Natural gas	Dol./mil. Btu .	3.36	4.55	5.67	5.97	5.41	5.6	7.1	4.9	5.7	5.2
Electricity	Dol./mil. Btu .	13.46	18.51	19.98	21.94	22.34	23.6	31.2	23.2	21.4	23.2
Fuel oil, kerosene	Dol./mil. Btu .	6.29	8.89	8.42	7.64	5.89	7.9	7.9	7.8	8.4	7.9
Liquid petroleum gas	Dol./mil. Btu .	6.71	8.74	9.42	9.91	8.91	11.2	14.3	9.7	12.2	12.2

Source: U.S. Energy Information Administration, *Household Energy Consumption and Expenditures, 1990* and prior reports. Survey not conducted in 1984, 1986, 1988 and 1989.

No. 928. Residential Energy Consumption and Expenditures, by Type of Fuel and Selected Household Characteristic: 1990

[For period January through December 1990. Quad.=quadrillion. See headnote, table 927]

CHARACTERISTIC	CONSUMPTION (Btu's)					EXPENDITURES				
	Total [1] (quad.)	Avg. per house-hold [1] (mil.)	Natural gas (quad.)	Elec-tricity (quad.)	Fuel oil [2] (quad.)	Total [1] (bil. dol.)	Avg. per house-hold [1] (dol.)	Natural gas (bil. dol.)	Elec-tricity (bil. dol.)	Fuel oil [2] (bil. dol.)
Total households	**9.22**	**98**	**4.86**	**3.03**	**1.05**	**110.2**	**1,172**	**27.3**	**71.5**	**8.3**
Single family detached.	6.61	113	3.45	2.20	0.74	78.2	1,340	18.8	51.0	5.9
Single family attached.	0.52	87	0.28	0.19	0.06	6.8	1,129	1.7	4.6	0.5
Two-to-four unit building.	0.94	95	0.62	0.20	0.11	10.2	1,015	3.8	5.3	0.9
Five-or-more unit building.	0.73	51	0.36	0.28	0.08	9.8	677	2.2	7.1	0.5
Mobile home	0.41	78	0.15	0.16	0.04	5.3	1,011	0.8	3.5	0.4
Year house built:										
1939 or earlier	2.57	120	1.57	0.51	0.42	26.1	1,216	9.0	13.0	3.3
1940 to 1949	0.74	105	0.45	0.19	0.07	7.9	1,130	2.5	4.5	0.6
1950 to 1959	1.47	110	0.81	0.41	0.22	16.8	1,254	4.6	10.2	1.7
1960 to 1969	1.41	95	0.77	0.48	0.13	17.1	1,155	4.4	11.4	1.0
1970 to 1979	1.82	85	0.78	0.82	0.17	24.5	1,143	4.2	18.3	1.3
1980 to 1984	0.58	72	0.21	0.32	0.01	9.0	1,120	1.2	7.4	0.1
1985 to 1990	0.63	80	0.28	0.30	(B)	8.8	1,117	1.4	6.8	(B)
Heating and cooling degree day zones: [3]										
Less than 2,000 CDD and —										
More than 7,000 HDD	1.12	111	0.53	0.29	0.21	11.5	1,132	2.7	6.3	1.6
5,500 to 7,000 HDD	3.29	123	2.04	0.75	0.43	33.4	1,251	10.8	18.4	3.5
4,000 to 5,499 HDD	2.12	102	1.06	0.67	0.34	25.6	1,222	6.6	15.6	2.7
Less than 4,000 HDD	1.41	73	0.72	0.59	0.04	19.4	1,008	4.2	14.3	0.3
More than 2,000 CDD and less than 4,000 HDD	1.28	75	0.50	0.74	(B)	20.4	1,197	3.0	16.9	(B)
1990 family income:										
Less than $10,000.	1.27	80	0.70	0.36	0.15	14.1	888	4.0	8.2	1.2
$10,000 to $19,999	1.66	84	0.88	0.53	0.17	19.4	978	5.0	12.3	1.4
$20,000 to $34,999	2.27	93	1.17	0.77	0.25	27.1	1,115	6.4	17.9	2.1
$35,000 to $49,999	1.75	105	0.90	0.62	0.19	21.7	1,296	5.1	14.6	1.5
$50,000 or more	2.27	132	1.21	0.75	0.27	27.9	1,618	6.8	18.6	2.2

B Base figure too small to meet statistical standards for reliability of derived figure. [1] Includes liquid petroleum gas not shown separately. [2] Includes kerosene. [3] CDD=Cooling degree day; HDD=Heating degree day.
Source: U.S. Energy Information Administration, *Household Energy Consumption and Expenditures, 1990.*

No. 929. Manufacturing Primary Energy Consumption for all Purposes, by Type of Fuel and Major Industry Group: 1991

[In trillions of Btu. Estimates represented in this table are for the primary consumption of energy for heat and power and as feedstocks or raw material inputs. Primary consumption is defined as the consumption of the energy that was originally produced offsite or was produced onsite from input materials not classified as energy. Examples of the latter are hydrogen produced from the electrolysis of brine; the output of captive (onsite) mines or wells; woodchips, bark, and woodwaste from wood purchased as a raw material input; and waste materials such as wastepaper and packing materials. Primary consumption excludes quantities of energy that are produced from other energy inputs and, therefore, avoids double counting. Based on the 1991 Manufacturing Energy Consumption Survey and subject to sampling variability]

INDUSTRY	SIC [1] code	Total	Net electricity [2]	Residual fuel oil	Distillate fuel oil [3]	Natural gas [4]	LPG	Coal	Coke and breeze	Other [5]
All industries............	(X)	20,257	2,370	454	146	6,095	1,574	2,006	308	7,304
Food and kindred products......	20	956	169	27	17	(D)	5	154	(D)	(D)
Tobacco products............	21	24	3	1	(Z)	4	(Z)	15	-	(Z)
Textile mill products.........	22	274	101	12	6	108	2	31	-	13
Apparel and other textile products .	23	44	19	(S)	1	19	1	2	-	1
Lumber and wood products.....	24	451	61	2	16	41	4	2	-	325
Furniture and fixtures.........	25	68	17	1	1	19	1	4	-	26
Paper and allied products.......	26	2,506	201	156	9	(D)	5	296	(D)	(D)
Printing and publishing........	27	108	53	(Z)	2	48	1	-	-	4
Chemicals and allied products....	28	5,051	440	(D)	14	2,227	(D)	(D)	10	526
Petroleum and coal products.....	29	5,967	105	65	21	838	(D)	(D)	(D)	4,864
Rubber and misc. plastic products .	30	238	116	8	3	96	3	7	-	6
Leather and leather products	31	12	3	1	1	5	(Z)	(S)	-	1
Stone, clay, and glass products...	32	880	105	9	20	381	(D)	293	(D)	(D)
Primary metal industries.......	33	2,467	499	(D)	11	708	(D)	853	278	72
Fabricated metal products	34	307	102	3	6	175	4	5	(D)	(D)
Industrial machinery & equipment..	35	237	101	3	4	109	2	11	1	5
Electric and electronic equipment..	36	212	102	4	2	79	1	(D)	(D)	(D)
Transportation equipment.......	37	323	118	12	7	133	2	(D)	(D)	17
Instruments and related products..	38	98	42	3	(D)	26	(S)	(D)	-	(D)
Misc. manufacturing industries....	39	32	12	1	(D)	15	(Z)	1	-	(S)

- Represents or rounds to zero. D Withheld to avoid disclosing data for individual establishments. S Withheld because Relative Standard Error is greater than 50 percent. X Not applicable. Z Less than 0.5 trillion Btu. [1] Standard Industrial Classification Code; see text, section 13. [2] Net electricity is obtained by aggregating purchases, transfers in, and generation from noncombustible renewable resources minus quantities sold and transferred out. Excludes electricity inputs from onsite cogeneration or generation from combustible fuels because that energy has already been included as generating fuel (for example, coal). [3] Includes Nos.1, 2, and 4 fuel oils and Nos. 1, 2, and 4 diesel fuels. [4] Includes natural gas obtained from utilities, transmission pipelines, and any other supplier such as brokers and producers. [5] Includes net steam, and other energy that respondents indicated was used to produce heat and power or as feedstock/raw material inputs.
Source: U.S. Energy Information Administration, *Manufacturing Energy Consumption 1991*, forthcoming.

No. 930. Manufacturing Energy Consumption for Fuel Purposes, by Type of Fuel and End-Use: 1991

[In trillions of Btu. See headnote, table 929]

END-USE CATEGORIES [1]	Total	Net electricity [2]	Residual fuel oil	Distillate fuel oil and diesel fuel [3]	Natural gas [4]	LPG	Coal (excluding coal coke and breeze)	Other [5]
Total inputs	15,027	2,370	414	139	5,506	105	1,184	5,309
Boiler fuel	(X)	(D)	296	40	2,098	18	859	(X)
Direct process uses...........	(X)	1,864	109	34	2,578	64	314	(X)
Process heating............	(X)	235	107	19	2,382	49	314	(X)
Process cooling and refrigeration .	(X)	124	(Z)	(Z)	13	(Z)	-	(X)
Machine drive	(X)	1,187	2	14	127	15	-	(X)
Electro-chemical processes	(X)	304	(X)	(X)	(X)	(X)	(X)	(X)
Other process use	(X)	15	(Z)	1	56	(Z)	(Z)	(X)
Direct nonprocess uses	(X)	396	7	53	702	19	(D)	(X)
Facility heating, ventilation, and air conditioning [6].......	(X)	192	4	8	283	3	(Z)	(X)
Facility lighting.............	(X)	161	(X)	(X)	(X)	(X)	(X)	(X)
Facility support	(X)	36	(D)	(Z)	23	(Z)	-	(X)
Onsite transportation	(X)	4	(X)	38	(Z)	16	(X)	(X)
Conventional electricity generation.	(X)	(X)	2	4	347	(Z)	(D)	(X)
Other nonprocess use.........	(X)	4	(D)	2	49	(Z)	-	(X)
End-use not reported	5,547	(D)	2	12	128	4	(D)	5,309

- Represents or rounds to zero. D Withheld to avoid disclosing data for individual establishments. X Not applicable. Z Less that 0.5 trillion. [1] Allocations to specific end-uses are made on the basis of reasonable approximations by respondents. [2] "Net electricity" is obtained by summing purchases, transfers in, and generation from noncombustible renewable resources, minus quantities sold and transferred out. It does not include electricity inputs from onsite cogeneration or generation from combustible fuels because that energy has already been included as generating fuel (for example, coal). [3] Includes Nos. 1, 2, and 4 fuel oils and Nos. 1, 2, and 4 diesel fuels. [4] Includes natural gas obtained from utilities, transmission pipelines, and any other supplier(s) such as brokers and producers. [5] Includes net steam (the sum of purchases, generation from renewables, and net transfers) and other energy that respondents indicated was used to produce heat and power. [6] Excludes steam and hot water.
Source: U.S. Energy Information Administration, *Manufacturing Energy Consumption 1991*, forthcoming.

No. 931. Commercial Buildings—Energy Consumption and Expenditures, by Major Fuel Type Used: 1989

[Covers buildings using one or more major fuel. Excludes industrial buildings predominantly residential buildings, and buildings of less than 1,000 sq. ft. Based on a sample survey of building representatives and energy suppliers; therefore, subject to sampling variability. For characteristics of commercial buildings, see tables in section 25. Tril.=trillion]

ITEM	Unit	All major fuels	Elec-tricity	Natural gas	Fuel oil	Pro-pane	District Heat
Number of buildings using the fuel	1,000	4,528	4,294	2,420	581	348	98
Square footage of floorspace	Million	63,184	61,563	41,143	12,600	4,695	6,578
Square footage per building	1,000	14.0	14.3	17.0	21.7	13.5	67.0
Energy consumed, total	Tril. Btu	5,788	2,773	2,073	357	-	585
Energy consumed per building	Mil. Btu	1,278	1,346	1,792	2,735	1,300	12,302
Energy consumed per square foot of floorspace	1,000 Btu	92	94	105	126	96	183
Energy consumed per employee	Mil. Btu	82	82	90	94	95	117
Expenditures, total	Mil. dol.	70,826	70,801	48,225	17,356	5,069	12,689
Expenditures per building	$1,000	15.6	16.5	19.9	29.9	14.6	129.3
Expenditures per square foot of floorspace	Dollars	1.12	1.15	1.17	1.38	1.08	2.03
Expenditures per million Btu of energy consumed	Dollars	12.24	12.25	11.12	10.93	11.20	10.51

- Represents zero.

Source: U.S. Energy Information Administration, *Commercial Buildings Energy Consumption and Expenditures, 1989.*

No. 932. Commercial Buildings—Energy Consumption and Expenditures: 1989

[Covers buildings using one or more major fuel. Excludes industrial buildings, predominantly residential buildings, and buildings of less than 1,000 sq. ft. Based on a sample survey of building representatives and energy suppliers; therefore, subject to sampling variability. For characteristics of commercial buildings, see tables in section 25. For composition of regions, see table 26]

BUILDING CHARACTERISTIC	ALL BUILDINGS USING ANY MAJOR FUEL		CONSUMPTION (tril. Btu)			EXPENDITURES (mil. dol.)		
	Number (1,000)	Square feet (mil.)	Major fuel, total [1]	Elec-tricity	Natural gas	Major fuel, total [1]	Elec-tricity	Natural gas
All buildings	**4,528**	**63,184**	**5,788**	**2,773**	**2,073**	**70,826**	**55,943**	**9,204**
Region:								
Northeast	783	13,569	1,354	586	353	17,505	13,188	1,807
Midwest	1,046	15,955	1,659	609	831	16,468	11,697	3,381
South	1,847	22,039	1,648	975	498	21,759	18,409	2,293
West	851	11,620	1,126	604	391	15,093	12,649	1,724
Year constructed:								
1900 or before	172	1,654	128	25	53	1,214	603	270
1901 to 1920	242	4,245	239	75	123	2,448	1,676	527
1921 to 1945	680	8,098	636	211	244	7,033	4,772	1,135
1946 to 1960	868	10,511	988	379	411	10,334	7,333	1,809
1961 to 1970	821	12,167	1,275	589	458	14,894	11,667	1,975
1974 to 1979	884	13,329	1,342	730	441	17,807	14,815	1,939
1980 to 1983	317	4,274	432	295	117	6,194	5,570	502
1984 to 1986	329	5,670	464	303	141	7,184	6,363	665
1987 to 1989	215	3,235	284	167	85	3,718	3,143	382
Principal activity within building:								
Assembly	617	6,909	441	186	174	5,986	4,648	809
Education	282	8,076	704	217	323	6,589	4,391	1,309
Food sales/services	343	1,959	394	218	155	5,445	4,512	812
Health care	80	2,054	449	154	186	4,052	2,670	712
Lodging	140	3,476	425	138	187	4,014	2,593	818
Mercantile/services	1,278	12,365	1,048	550	417	13,527	11,116	1,931
Office	679	11,802	1,230	781	238	18,323	15,757	1,128
Public order and safety	50	616	78	29	25	875	582	120
Warehouse	618	9,253	536	243	206	6,085	4,836	853
Other	62	1,529	344	201	102	4,224	3,558	420
Vacant	333	4,161	98	39	49	1,218	924	237
Square footage:								
1,001 to 5,000	2,529	6,790	692	326	302	9,601	7,592	1,620
5,001 to 10,000	890	6,532	567	246	265	7,870	6,232	1,304
10,001 to 25,000	644	10,393	791	381	278	9,869	7,809	1,348
25,001 to 50,000	247	8,801	756	331	309	8,950	6,919	1,318
50,001 to 100,000	127	9,130	855	433	249	10,124	8,042	1,094
100,001 to 200,000	61	8,277	777	387	238	9,265	7,410	1,016
200,000 to 500,000	23	7,022	698	366	228	7,853	6,326	836
500,000 and over	7	6,239	652	303	203	7,293	5,613	668

[1] Includes fuel oil, propane, and purchased steam not shown separately.

Source: U.S. Energy Information Administration, *Commercial Buildings Energy Consumption and Expenditures, 1989.*

No. 933. Fossil Fuel Prices in Current and Constant (1987) Dollars: 1970 to 1992

[In cents per million British thermal units (Btu), except as indicated. All fuel prices taken as close to the point of production as possible. See text, section 19, for explanation of Btu conversions from mineral fuels]

FUEL	1970	1973	1975	1980	1984	1985	1986	1987	1988	1989	1990	1991	1992
CURRENT DOLLARS													
Composite [1]	31.7	39.8	82.1	204.2	264.6	251.2	165.3	170.0	153.3	167.1	184.3	167.0	170.1
Crude oil	54.8	67.1	132.2	372.2	446.2	415.3	215.7	265.5	216.9	273.4	345.3	285.2	275.5
Natural gas	15.4	20.1	40.2	144.8	239.9	225.7	174.8	150.2	152.4	152.7	154.6	148.0	167.9
Bituminous coal [2]	26.2	36.5	83.9	109.4	115.9	114.8	108.2	104.9	100.8	100.0	99.5	98.9	97.7
Anthracite coal	48.8	61.7	149.5	185.9	208.7	204.2	191.1	188.9	189.8	183.6	174.5	161.0	175.2
CONSTANT (1987) DOLLARS													
Composite [1]	90.1	96.4	166.9	284.8	290.8	266.1	170.6	170.0	147.5	154.0	162.8	141.8	140.7
Crude oil	155.7	162.5	268.7	519.1	490.3	439.9	222.6	265.5	208.8	252.0	305.0	242.1	227.9
Natural gas	43.8	48.7	81.7	202.0	263.6	239.1	180.4	150.2	146.7	140.7	136.6	125.6	138.9
Bituminous coal [2]	74.4	88.4	170.5	152.6	127.4	121.6	111.7	104.9	97.0	92.2	88.1	84.0	80.8
Anthracite coal	138.6	149.4	303.9	259.3	229.3	216.3	197.2	188.9	182.7	169.2	154.2	136.7	144.9
GDP implicit price deflator[3] (1987=100)	35.2	41.3	49.2	71.7	91.0	94.4	96.9	100.0	103.9	108.5	113.2	117.8	120.9

[1] Weighted by relative importance of individual fuels in total fuels production. [2] Includes subbituminous and lignite. [3] GDP=Gross domestic product; see text, section 15.
Source: U.S. Energy Information Administration, *Annual Energy Review*.

No. 934. World Energy Consumption, by Region and Energy Source: 1970 to 1991

[In tons of coal equivalent. Metric ton=1.1023 short tons. Kilogram=2.205 pounds. See text, section 301, for general comment]

REGION AND ENERGY SOURCE	CONSUMPTION (mil. metric tons)				PER CAPITA (kilograms)				PERCENT DISTRIBUTION			
	1970	1980	1990	1991	1970	1980	1990	1991	1970	1980	1990	1991
World, total	6,412	8,783	10,825	10,950	1,208	1,626	2,003	2,026	100.0	100.0	100.0	100.0
North America [1]	2,486	2,825	3,201	3,242	5,949	6,667	7,447	7,543	38.9	32.7	29.6	29.6
United States	2,205	2,391	2,690	2,727	8,910	9,566	10,653	10,798	34.4	27.7	24.9	24.9
South America	142	247	310	323	490	841	1,037	1,080	2.2	2.9	2.9	3.0
Europe	1,709	2,230	2,347	2,337	2,963	3,854	4,670	4,650	26.7	25.1	21.7	21.3
Asia	904	1,592	2,636	2,761	292	506	826	865	14.0	18.5	24.4	25.2
Japan	333	455	571	590	3,246	3,684	4,608	4,754	5.2	5.1	5.3	5.4
Soviet Union	999	1,592	1,919	1,867	3,476	5,502	6,592	6,415	15.5	17.2	17.7	17.1
Oceania	72	107	149	150	2,753	3,993	5,511	5,549	1.1	1.2	1.4	1.4
Energy source:												
Solid fuels	2,143	2,650	3,246	3,216	586	595	613	597	33.5	30.8	30.0	29.4
Liquid fuels	2,802	3,806	4,002	4,036	770	855	756	750	44.0	44.2	37.0	36.9
Natural gas	1,289	1,838	2,527	2,605	351	413	477	484	20.1	21.5	23.3	23.8
Electricity	178	489	1,049	1,093	48	110	198	203	2.4	3.5	9.7	10.0

[1] Includes Central America.
Source: Statistical Office of the United Nations, New York, NY, *Energy Statistics Yearbook*, annual (copyright).

No. 935. World Primary Energy Production, by Region and Type: 1973 to 1992

[In quadrillion Btu. Btu=British thermal units. For Btu conversion factors, see source]

REGION AND TYPE	1973	1975	1980	1985	1986	1987	1988	1989	1990	1991	1992
World total	244.8	245.0	286.6	302.1	312.1	319.6	332.1	339.6	344.0	340.8	343.1
North America	73.3	71.1	80.5	84.1	82.7	84.1	86.2	86.2	88.2	89.1	88.8
United States	62.0	59.8	64.7	64.6	64.1	64.6	65.8	65.8	67.7	67.4	66.7
Central and South America	12.9	10.6	12.1	13.5	14.3	14.3	15.2	15.7	16.6	17.4	17.6
Western Europe	19.6	21.4	28.7	36.4	37.4	37.9	38.4	37.9	37.8	39.0	39.3
Eastern Europe and Soviet Union	51.4	55.9	69.3	74.5	77.4	79.4	81.8	81.5	79.1	70.8	67.0
Middle East	46.6	43.5	42.2	25.7	30.6	32.1	36.0	39.6	41.0	40.2	43.9
Africa	14.8	13.3	17.3	18.4	18.1	18.5	19.5	20.5	21.5	23.4	23.7
Far East and Oceania	26.2	29.3	36.5	49.5	51.6	53.2	54.9	58.3	59.9	60.9	62.8
Crude oil	117.8	111.6	127.6	115.4	120.2	121.0	125.8	127.8	129.3	128.6	129.2
Natural gas	43.2	43.9	52.8	60.6	61.9	64.9	68.1	70.6	72.0	74.0	74.3
Natural gas liquids	4.2	4.4	5.5	5.7	6.0	6.3	6.6	6.7	7.0	7.3	7.6
Coal	63.8	66.3	75.0	84.2	86.5	88.2	90.3	92.9	92.8	86.7	87.6
Hydroelectric power	13.5	15.0	18.2	20.7	21.1	21.3	22.0	21.8	22.5	22.9	22.9
Nuclear electric power	2.2	3.9	7.6	15.4	16.3	17.8	19.3	19.8	20.3	21.3	21.5

Source: U.S. Energy Information Administration, *International Energy Annual*.

No. 936. U.S. Foreign Trade in Selected Mineral Fuels: 1970 to 1991

[Btu=British thermal units. For Btu conversion factors, see text, section 19. Minus sign (-) indicates an excess of imports over exports. See also *Historical Statistics, Colonial Times to 1970*, series M 100, 101, 127, 128, 140, 141, 178, and 181]

MINERAL FUEL	1970	1973	1975	1980	1984	1985	1986	1987	1988	1989	1990	1991
NATURAL GAS												
Imports:												
Billion cubic feet . . .	821	1,033	953	985	843	950	750	993	1,294	1,382	1,532	1,693
Trillion Btu	846	1,060	978	1,006	847	952	748	992	1,296	1,387	1,550	1,713
Exports:												
Billion cubic feet . . .	70	77	73	49	55	55	61	54	74	107	86	122
Trillion Btu	72	79	74	49	55	56	62	55	75	109	88	124
Net trade:												
Billion cubic feet . . .	-751	-956	-880	-936	-788	-894	-689	-939	-1,220	-1,275	-1,446	-1,571
Trillion Btu	-774	-981	-904	-957	-792	-896	-686	-937	-1,221	-1,278	-1,462	-1,589
CRUDE OIL												
Imports: [1]												
Million barrels	483	1,184	1,498	1,926	1,254	1,168	1,525	1,706	1,869	2,133	2,151	2,110
Trillion Btu	2,814	6,887	8,721	11,195	7,302	6,814	9,002	10,067	11,027	12,597	12,764	12,550
Exports:												
Million barrels	5	1	2	105	66	75	56	55	57	52	40	42
Trillion Btu	29	4	12	609	384	432	326	319	329	301	232	244
Net trade:												
Million barrels	-478	-1,183	-1,496	-1,821	-1,188	-1,094	-1,469	-1,651	-1,812	-2,081	-2,111	-2,068
Trillion Btu	-2,785	-6,883	-8,708	-10,586	-6,918	-6,381	-8,676	-9,748	-10,698	-12,296	-12,532	-12,306
PETROLEUM PRODUCTS												
Imports:												
Million barrels	765	1,099	712	603	736	681	747	731	840	809	775	655
Trillion Btu	4,656	6,578	4,227	3,463	4,131	3,796	4,199	4,095	4,720	4,564	4,351	3,702
Exports:												
Million barrels	89	84	74	94	198	211	230	224	242	262	273	323
Trillion Btu	520	482	427	551	1,161	1,225	1,344	1,311	1,412	1,538	1,594	1,882
Net trade:												
Million barrels	-675	-1,015	-638	-509	-538	-471	-516	-508	-598	-548	-502	-332
Trillion Btu	-4,136	-6,097	-3,800	-2,912	-2,970	-2,570	-2,855	-2,784	-3,308	-3,026	-2,757	-1,820
COAL												
Imports:												
Thousand short tons	36	127	940	1,194	1,286	1,952	2,212	1,747	2,134	2,851	2,699	3,390
Trillion Btu	1	3	24	30	32	49	55	44	53	71	67	85
Exports:												
Thousand short tons	71,733	53,587	66,309	91,742	81,482	92,680	85,518	79,607	95,023	100,815	105,804	108,969
Trillion Btu	1,936	1,425	1,761	2,421	2,151	2,438	2,248	2,093	2,499	2,637	2,772	2,854
Net trade:												
Thousand short tons	71,697	53,460	65,369	90,548	80,196	90,728	83,306	77,860	92,889	97,964	103,105	105,579
Trillion Btu	1,935	1,422	1,738	2,391	2,119	2,389	2,193	2,049	2,446	2,566	2,705	2,769

[1] Beginning 1980, includes strategic petroleum reserve imports.

Source: U.S. Energy Information Administration, *Annual Energy Review*.

No. 937. Daily International Flow of Crude Oil, by Area: 1990

[In thousands of barrels per day]

EXPORTING AREA	Total [1]	IMPORTING AREA							
		North America		Central and South America	Western Europe	Eastern Europe	Middle East and Africa	Japan	Other Far East and Oceania
		U.S.	Canada						
World total	28,077	5,894	546	1,709	9,702	1,662	1,175	3,828	3,560
United States	109	(X)	11	[2]97	-	-	-	-	1
North America, except U.S.	1,920	1,332	12	66	325	-	29	146	10
Central and South America	1,738	934	29	492	170	87	4	8	14
Western Europe	2,655	252	339	61	1,990	7	5	-	(Z)
Eastern Europe and U.S.S.R.	2,170	1	-	34	942	1,052	13	1	97
Middle East	12,521	1,858	80	751	3,411	414	761	2,712	2,533
Africa	4,857	1,235	75	192	2,858	102	333	17	45
Far East and Oceania	2,107	282	-	16	6	-	-	944	859

- Represents zero.   X Not applicable.   Z Less than 50,000 barrels.   [1] Includes stocks at sea, exchanges, transshipments, and other statistical discrepancies not shown separately.   [2] Includes shipments to Puerto Rico and Virgin Islands.

Source: U.S. Energy Information Administration, *International Energy Annual*.

No. 938. Crude Oil Imports Into the United States, by Country of Origin: 1970 to 1993

[In millions of barrels. Barrels contain 42 gallons]

COUNTRY OF ORIGIN	1970	1973	1975	1980	1985	1986	1987	1988	1989	1990	1991	1992	1993
Total	483	1,184	1,498	1,921	1,168	1,525	1,706	1,864	2,133	2,151	2,110	2,226	2,457
Canada	245	365	219	73	171	208	222	249	230	235	271	292	330
Mexico	-	(Z)	26	185	261	227	220	246	261	251	277	288	316
Norway	-	-	4	53	11	19	26	23	46	35	27	43	43
Trinidad-Tobago	(Z)	22	42	42	36	34	27	26	27	28	26	26	20
United Kingdom	-	-	(Z)	63	101	116	111	93	58	57	39	73	111
OPEC [1]	222	765	1,172	1,410	479	771	876	984	1,232	1,283	1,233	1,247	1,339
Algeria	2	44	96	166	31	28	42	21	22	23	16	9	9
Ecuador	-	17	21	6	20	23	8	12	29	14	19	23	28
Gabon	-	-	10	9	19	9	13	5	18	23	31	45	55
Indonesia	26	73	138	115	107	108	96	68	58	36	37	26	24
Iran	12	79	101	3	10	7	36	(Z)	-	-	12	-	-
Iraq	-	1	1	10	17	30	30	125	161	188	-	-	-
Kuwait	12	15	1	10	1	-	10	26	29	57	29	2	125
Libya	17	49	81	200	-	-	-	-	-	-	-	-	-
Nigeria	17	164	272	307	102	160	193	222	292	286	249	243	263
Qatar	-	3	7	8	-	4	-	-	-	1	-	-	-
Saudi Arabia	15	169	256	456	48	226	234	333	407	436	622	585	466
United Arab Emirates	23	26	43	63	13	14	20	8	8	3	1	-	4
Venezuela	98	126	144	57	112	152	178	160	181	243	244	302	365
Other	16	32	34	95	108	150	225	244	279	264	237	258	298

- Represents zero.   Z Less than 500,000 barrels.   [1] Organization of Petroleum Exporting Countries.

Source: 1970, U.S. Bureau of Mines, *Minerals Yearbooks, vol. I;* thereafter, U.S. Energy Information Administration, *Petroleum Supply Annual,* vol. I.

No. 939. Crude Oil and Refined Products—Summary: 1973 to 1993

[Barrels of 42 gallons. Data are averages]

YEAR	CRUDE OIL (1,000 bbl. per day)					REFINED OIL PRODUCTS (1,000 bbl. per day)			Total oil imports[2] (1,000 bbl. per day)	CRUDE OIL STOCKS[3] (mil. bbl.)	
	Input to refineries	Domestic production	Imports Total[1]	Imports Strategic reserve	Exports	Domestic demand	Imports	Exports		Total	Strategic reserve
1973	12,431	9,208	3,244	(X)	2	17,308	3,012	229	6,256	242	(X)
1974	12,133	8,774	3,477	(X)	3	16,653	2,635	218	6,112	265	(X)
1975	12,442	8,375	4,105	(X)	6	16,322	1,951	204	6,056	271	(X)
1976	13,416	8,132	5,287	(X)	8	17,461	2,026	215	7,313	285	(X)
1977	14,602	8,245	6,615	21	50	18,431	2,193	193	8,807	348	7
1978	14,739	8,707	6,356	162	158	18,847	2,008	204	8,363	376	67
1979	14,648	8,552	6,519	67	235	18,513	1,937	236	8,456	430	91
1980	13,481	8,597	5,263	44	287	17,056	1,646	258	6,909	466	108
1981	12,470	8,572	4,396	256	228	16,058	1,599	367	5,996	594	230
1982	11,774	8,649	3,488	165	236	15,296	1,625	579	5,113	644	294
1983	11,685	8,688	3,329	234	164	15,231	1,722	575	5,051	723	379
1984	12,044	8,879	3,426	197	181	15,726	2,011	541	5,437	796	451
1985	12,002	8,971	3,201	118	204	15,726	1,866	577	5,067	814	493
1986	12,716	8,680	4,178	48	154	16,281	2,045	631	6,224	843	512
1987	12,854	8,349	4,674	73	151	16,665	2,004	613	6,678	890	541
1988	13,246	8,140	5,107	51	155	17,283	2,295	661	7,402	890	560
1989	13,401	7,613	5,843	56	142	17,325	2,217	717	8,061	921	580
1990	13,409	7,355	5,894	27	109	16,988	2,123	748	8,018	908	586
1991	13,301	7,417	5,782	-	116	16,714	1,844	885	7,627	893	569
1992, prel.	13,411	7,171	6,083	10	89	17,033	1,805	861	7,888	893	575
1993, prel.	13,610	6,838	6,731	15	98	17,193	1,795	905	8,526	922	587

- Represents zero.   X Not applicable.   [1] Includes Strategic Petroleum Reserve.   [2] Crude oil (including Strategic Petroleum Reserve imports) plus refined products.   [3] End of year.

Source: U.S. Energy Information Administration, *Monthly Energy Review,* March 1994.

No. 940. Strategic Petroleum Reserve: 1977 to 1992

[Million barrels, except as noted. The Strategic Petroleum Reserve is a stock of petroleum maintained by the Federal Government for use during periods of major supply interruption]

YEAR	Crude oil imports	Domestic crude oil deliveries	STOCKS AT YEAR-END			Days of net petroleum imports [3]
			Quantity [1]	Percent of crude oil stocks [2]	Percent of total petroleum stocks	
1977	7.54	[4]0.37	7.46	2.1	0.7	1
1980	16.07	1.30	107.80	23.1	7.8	17
1985	43.12	0.17	493.32	60.6	32.5	115
1986	17.56	1.21	511.57	60.8	32.1	94
1987	26.52	2.69	540.65	60.9	33.6	91
1988	18.76	0.01	559.52	63.0	35.0	85
1989	20.35	-	579.86	63.0	36.8	81
1990	9.77	-	585.69	64.5	36.1	82
1991	-	-	568.51	63.8	35.2	86
1992	3.59	2.60	574.72	64.5	36.1	83

- Represents zero.   [1] Stocks do not include imported quantities in transit to Strategic Petroleum Reserve terminals, pipeline fill, and above ground storage.   [2] Including lease condensate stocks.   [3] Derived by dividing end-of-year strategic petroleum reserve stocks by annual average daily net imports of all petroleum. Calculated prior to rounding.   [4] The quantity of domestic fuel oil which was in storage prior to injection of foreign crude oil.
Source: U.S. Energy Information Administration, *Annual Energy Review.*

No. 941. World Petroleum Consumption, by Major Consuming Country: 1983 to 1992

[Million barrels per day]

REGION AND COUNTRY	1983	1984	1985	1986	1987	1988	1989	1990	1991	1992
World, total	58.74	59.84	60.10	61.76	63.01	64.83	66.03	66.16	66.71	66.74
North America, total	18.03	18.66	18.70	19.28	19.74	20.53	20.73	20.41	20.14	20.53
Canada	1.45	1.47	1.50	1.51	1.55	1.69	1.73	1.69	1.62	1.64
Mexico	1.35	1.45	1.47	1.49	1.52	1.55	1.66	1.73	1.80	1.85
United States	15.23	15.73	15.73	16.28	16.67	17.28	17.33	16.99	16.71	17.03
Central & South America, total	3.19	3.22	3.19	3.41	3.52	3.57	3.58	3.60	3.65	3.68
Brazil	0.98	1.03	1.08	1.24	1.26	1.30	1.32	1.34	1.35	1.41
Western Europe, total	12.38	12.41	12.39	12.79	12.93	13.08	13.16	13.25	13.66	13.78
France	1.84	1.75	1.78	1.77	1.79	1.80	1.86	1.82	1.94	1.93
Germany	2.66	2.66	2.70	2.86	2.77	2.74	2.58	2.66	2.83	2.84
Italy	1.75	1.65	1.72	1.74	1.86	1.84	1.93	1.87	1.86	1.94
United Kingdom	1.53	1.85	1.63	1.65	1.60	1.70	1.74	1.75	1.80	1.80
Eastern Europe and former U.S.S.R.	10.47	10.42	10.46	10.46	10.51	10.38	10.19	9.73	9.43	7.63
Middle East, total	2.61	2.67	2.85	2.98	3.06	3.15	3.36	3.47	3.40	3.71
Africa, total	1.70	1.76	1.83	1.83	1.84	1.91	1.99	2.10	2.15	2.24
Far East & Oceania, total	10.36	10.70	10.69	11.03	11.42	12.21	13.03	13.61	14.28	15.18
China	1.73	1.74	1.89	2.00	2.12	2.28	2.38	2.30	2.50	2.63
India	0.77	0.82	0.90	0.95	0.99	1.08	1.15	1.17	1.19	1.25
Japan	4.40	4.58	4.38	4.44	4.48	4.75	4.98	5.14	5.28	5.45

Source: U.S. Energy Information Administration, *Annual Energy Review* and *Monthly Energy Review*, monthly

No. 942. Energy Producing Companies—Selected Financial and Investment Indicators: 1980 to 1992

[Based on data from major publicly-owned domestic crude oil producing companies which either had at least 1 percent of domestic production or reserves of oil, natural gas, coal, or uranium, or at least 1 percent of refining capacity or petroleum product sales. There were 26 companies in 1980; 25 in 1983; 22 during 1984 through 1987; and 23 in 1988 to 1992]

ITEM	1980	1983	1984	1985	1986	1987	1988	1989	1990	1991	1992
INCOME STATEMENT (bil. dol.)											
Operating revenues	518.6	511.0	517.4	492.5	378.5	417.4	419.8	433.6	510.4	469.3	472.8
Operating expenses	455.9	462.8	467.3	444.2	354.4	383.7	381.6	397.7	470.1	443.3	449.5
Operating income	62.7	48.2	50.1	48.3	24.0	33.7	38.2	35.9	40.2	26.0	23.3
Pretax income	66.9	47.4	47.6	43.6	20.6	25.0	34.3	32.3	37.5	25.1	22.5
Net income	31.0	21.9	21.3	17.4	9.2	11.3	22.3	19.8	21.6	14.7	1.8
Funds from operations [1]	59.0	60.7	63.6	63.5	53.1	51.6	57.8	48.3	54.9	47.8	44.8
BALANCE SHEET (bil. dol.)											
Net property, plant, and equipment	188.9	278.4	292.4	297.7	291.1	297.6	293.6	293.2	302.5	305.5	309.7
Net investment in place [2]	202.6	296.3	309.1	315.4	310.0	316.4	309.6	309.9	319.7	325.6	331.5
Total assets	333.0	421.8	442.9	438.4	427.0	443.6	437.8	434.5	457.2	447.1	453.6
RATIOS (percent)											
Net income to operating revenues	6.0	4.3	4.1	3.5	2.4	2.7	5.3	4.6	4.2	3.1	[3]0.4
Net income to total assets	9.3	5.2	5.0	4.0	2.2	2.5	5.1	4.6	4.7	3.3	0.4
Net income to stockholders' equity	21.1	11.4	12.1	10.5	5.6	6.8	13.5	12.3	12.9	8.8	1.1
Long-term debt to stockholders' equity [4]	31.5	34.8	49.5	54.3	56.3	57.6	56.6	56.4	53.0	54.3	59.4
Long-term debt to total assets [4]	13.9	15.9	20.6	20.5	21.6	21.5	21.3	20.9	19.4	20.3	20.6

[1] The sum of net income, depreciation, depletion and amortization, deferred taxes, dry hole expenses, etc.   [2] Composed of net property, plant and equipment plus investment, and advances to unconsolidated subsidiaries.   [3] The implementation of the new "Financial Accounting Standard No. 106" greatly reduced the reported profitability of large publicly traded corporations. Net income without these accounting changes would have been $12.5 billion.   [4] Long-term debt includes amounts applicable to capitalized leases.
Source: U.S. Energy Information Administration, *Performance Profiles of Major Energy Producers*, annual.

No. 943. Petroleum and Coal Products Corporations—Sales, Net Profit, and Profit Per Dollar of Sales: 1980 to 1992

[Represents SIC group 29. Profit rates are averages of quarterly figures at annual rates. Beginning 1986, excludes estimates for corporations with less than $250,000 in assets]

ITEM	Unit	1980	1982	1983	1984	1985	1986	1987	1988	1989	1990	1991	1992
Sales	Bil. dol. .	333.2	357.1	312.7	338.4	320.9	226.5	248.3	252.2	265.3	318.5	282.2	278.0
Net profit:													
Before income taxes	Bil. dol. .	39.1	27.8	27.1	24.5	17.7	9.8	14.2	27.3	23.7	23.3	12.2	2.0
After income taxes	Bil. dol. .	25.5	19.7	19.3	17.2	12.7	8.8	10.9	21.2	19.5	18.0	10.9	3.2
Depreciation[1]	Bil. dol. .	11.6	16.3	17.5	20.7	22.1	21.9	20.3	20.0	18.5	18.7	18.0	18.3
Profits per dollar of sales:													
Before income taxes	Cents . .	11.7	7.8	8.7	7.2	5.5	4.1	5.8	10.8	9.0	7.4	4.3	0.4
After income taxes	Cents . .	7.7	5.5	6.2	5.1	4.0	3.8	4.5	8.5	7.4	5.7	3.9	0.9
Profits on stockholders' equity:													
Before income taxes	Percent .	30.7	18.7	17.8	14.3	11.7	6.8	10.1	19.2	17.8	16.6	8.6	1.5
After income taxes	Percent .	20.0	13.2	12.7	10.0	8.5	6.1	7.7	14.9	14.6	12.8	7.7	2.4

[1] Includes depletion and accelerated amortization of emergency facilities.
Source: 1980, U.S. Federal Trade Commission; thereafter, U.S. Bureau of the Census, *Quarterly Financial Report for Manufacturing, Mining and Trade Corporations.*

No. 944. Major Petroleum Companies—Financial Data Summary: 1973 to 1992

[Data represent a composite of approximately 42 major worldwide petroleum companies aggregated on a consolidated, total company basis]

ITEM	1973	1975	1980	1985	1986	1987	1988	1989	1990	1991	1992
FINANCIAL DATA (bil. dol.)											
Net income	11.8	11.6	32.9	19.4	10.8	15.0	24.6	24.7	26.8	18.7	12.3
Depreciation, depletion, etc	10.5	11.3	32.5	53.0	43.7	45.0	34.3	33.7	38.7	36.5	41.1
Cash flow[1]	22.3	22.8	65.4	72.4	54.5	60.0	58.9	58.4	65.5	55.2	53.4
Dividends paid	4.0	4.7	9.3	12.0	12.1	12.4	14.0	16.0	15.9	16.3	16.6
Net internal funds available for investment or debt repayment [2]	18.3	18.1	56.1	60.4	42.4	47.6	44.9	42.4	49.6	38.9	36.8
Capital and exploratory expenditures . . .	16.3	26.9	62.1	58.3	38.3	50.1	62.4	55.1	59.6	61.5	55.0
Long-term capitalization	102.9	121.1	211.4	272.1	279.9	282.2	287.8	290.0	300.0	307.4	292.6
Long-term debt	22.5	28.9	49.8	93.5	95.5	88.4	88.5	91.4	90.4	95.9	93.9
Preferred stock	0.4	0.4	2.0	3.3	3.7	4.1	4.5	6.4	5.2	4.1	5.2
Common stock and retained earnings [3] .	80.0	91.9	159.6	175.3	180.7	189.7	194.8	192.2	204.4	207.4	193.5
Excess of expenditures over cash income [4]	-2.0	8.9	6.0	-2.1	3.0	-2.5	17.5	12.7	10.0	22.6	18.2
RATIOS [5] (percent)											
Long-term debt to long-term capitalization	22.0	23.8	23.6	34.4	34.1	31.3	30.8	31.5	30.1	31.2	32.1
Net income to total average capital	12.0	10.0	17.0	7.0	4.0	4.6	8.6	8.3	9.1	6.2	4.1
Net income to average common equity. .	15.6	13.1	22.5	10.8	6.2	7.3	12.8	12.4	13.5	9.1	6.1

[1] Generally represents internally-generated funds from operations. Sum of net income and noncash charges such as depreciation, depletion, and amortization.   [2] Cash flow minus dividends paid.   [3] Includes common stock, capital surplus, and earned surplus accounts after adjustments.   [4] Capital and exploratory expenditures plus dividends paid minus cash flow.   [5] Represents approximate year-to-year comparisons because of changes in the makeup of the group due to mergers and other corporate changes.
Source: Carl H. Pforzheimer & Co., New York, NY, *Comparative Oil Company Statements, 1992-1991,* and earlier reports.

No. 945. Electric Utility Sales and Average Prices, by End-Use Sector: 1970 to 1992

[Prior to 1980, covers Class A and B privately-owned electric utilities; thereafter, Class A utilities whose electric operating revenues were $100 million or more during the previous year]

YEAR	SALES (bil. kWh)				AVERAGE PRICE OF ELECTRICITY SOLD (cents per kWh)							
					Current dollars				Constant (1987) dollars [2]			
	Total [1]	Resi-dential	Com-mer-cial	Indus-trial	Total [1]	Resi-dential	Com-mer-cial	Indus-trial	Total [1]	Resi-dential	Com-mer-cial	Indus-trial
1970	1,392	466	307	571	1.7	2.2	2.1	1.0	4.8	6.3	6.0	2.8
1973	1,713	579	388	686	2.0	2.5	2.4	1.3	4.8	6.1	5.8	3.1
1975	1,747	588	403	688	2.9	3.5	3.5	2.1	5.9	7.1	7.1	4.3
1980	2,094	717	488	815	4.7	5.4	5.5	3.7	6.6	7.5	7.7	5.2
1981	2,147	722	514	826	5.5	6.2	6.3	4.3	7.0	7.9	8.0	5.4
1982	2,086	730	526	745	6.1	6.9	6.9	5.0	7.3	8.2	8.2	6.0
1983	2,151	751	544	776	6.3	7.2	7.0	5.0	7.2	8.3	8.0	5.7
1984	2,286	780	583	838	6.3	7.2	7.1	4.8	6.9	7.9	7.8	5.3
1985	2,324	794	606	837	6.4	7.4	7.3	5.0	6.8	7.8	7.7	5.3
1986	2,369	819	631	831	6.4	7.4	7.2	4.9	6.6	7.6	7.4	5.1
1987	2,457	850	660	858	6.4	7.4	7.1	4.8	6.4	7.4	7.1	4.8
1988	2,578	893	699	896	6.4	7.5	7.0	4.7	6.2	7.2	6.7	4.5
1989	2,647	906	726	926	6.5	7.6	7.2	4.7	6.0	7.0	6.6	4.3
1990	2,713	924	751	946	6.6	7.8	7.3	4.7	5.8	6.9	6.4	4.2
1991	2,762	955	766	947	6.7	8.0	7.5	4.8	5.7	6.8	6.4	4.1
1992	2,756	934	763	965	6.8	8.2	7.6	4.8	5.6	6.8	6.3	4.0

[1] Includes other sectors not shown separately.   [2] Based on the GNP implicit price deflator.
Source: U.S. Energy Information Administration, *Annual Energy Review.*

No. 946. Electric Utility Industry—Net Generation, Net Summer Capability, Generating Units, and Consumption of Fuels: 1970 to 1992

[Net Generation for **calendar years**; other data as of **December 31**. See also *Historical Statistics, Colonial Times to 1970*, series S 32-52, S 78-82, and S 86-107]

ITEM	Unit	1970	1975	1980	1985	1987	1988	1989	1990	1991	1992
NET GENERATION											
Total	Bil. kWh	1,532	1,918	2,286	2,470	2,572	2,704	2,784	2,808	2,825	2,797
Average annual change [1]	Percent	7.3	4.5	3.5	0.4	2.0	5.0	2.9	0.9	0.6	-1.0
Net generation, kWh per kW of net summer capability [2]	Rate	4,560	3,904	3,951	3,770	3,815	3,990	4,064	4,064	4,076	4,024
Investor owned	Bil. kWh	1,183	1,487	1,783	1,918	2,022	2,146	2,192	2,203	2,213	2,214
Percent of total utilities	Percent	77.2	77.5	78.0	77.7	78.6	79.4	78.7	78.4	78.4	79.2
Publicly owned	Bil. kWh	349	431	503	552	550	559	592	606	610	582
Municipal	Bil. kWh	71	82	87	74	86	97	100	98	97	94
Federal	Bil. kWh	186	221	235	233	205	201	224	235	241	225
Cooperatives and other	Bil. kWh	91	128	182	245	258	261	269	273	272	263
Source of energy:											
Coal [3]	Percent	46.0	44.6	51.0	57.2	57.4	57.4	56.2	55.5	54.9	56.3
Nuclear	Percent	1.4	9.0	11.0	15.5	17.7	19.5	19.0	20.5	21.7	22.1
Oil	Percent	12.0	15.1	10.8	4.1	4.6	5.5	5.7	4.2	3.9	3.2
Gas	Percent	24.3	15.6	15.1	11.8	10.6	9.3	9.6	9.4	9.4	9.4
Hydro	Percent	16.2	15.6	12.1	11.4	9.7	8.2	9.5	10.0	9.8	8.6
Type of prime mover: [4]											
Hydro	Bil. kWh	248	300	276	281	250	223	265	280	276	239
Steam conventional [5]	Bil. kWh	1,240	1,414	1,726	1,778	1,837	1,921	1,950	1,919	1,905	1,906
Gas turbine and internal combustion	Bil. kWh	22	28	28	16	18	22	29	22	22	21
Steam nuclear	Bil. kWh	22	173	251	384	455	527	529	577	613	619
Other	Bil. kWh	1	3	6	11	12	12	11	11	10	10
NET SUMMER CAPABILITY											
Total [6]	Mil. kW	336	491	579	655	674	678	685	691	693	695
Average annual change [1]	Percent	7.2	7.6	3.3	0.6	1.4	0.5	1.1	0.9	0.3	0.3
Hydro	Mil. kW	64	78	82	89	90	90	91	91	92	93
Steam conventional [7]	Mil. kW	248	333	397	437	440	442	444	448	447	447
Gas turbine	Mil. kW	13	37	43	44	44	44	45	46	48	50
Steam nuclear	Mil. kW	7	37	52	79	94	95	98	100	100	99
Internal combustion	Mil. kW	4	5	5	5	5	5	5	5	5	5
Geothermal and other	Mil. kW	(Z)	1	1	2	2	2	2	2	2	2
NUMBER OF GENERATING UNITS											
Total [8]	Number	9,717	(NA)	11,084	(NA)	10,406	10,305	10,325	10,296	10,260	10,221
Hydro	Number	3,108	(NA)	3,275	(NA)	3,488	3,496	3,479	3,479	3,476	3,497
Steam conventional	Number	2,813	(NA)	2,862	(NA)	2,437	2,383	2,363	2,354	2,284	2,307
Gas turbine	Number	658	(NA)	1,447	(NA)	1,408	1,397	1,438	1,460	1,485	1,501
Steam nuclear	Number	16	(NA)	74	(NA)	108	108	110	111	111	109
Internal combustion	Number	3,118	(NA)	3,410	(NA)	2,917	2,872	2,889	2,847	2,803	2,807
CONSUMPTION OF FUELS											
Net generation by fuel [9]	Bil. kWh	1,284	1,618	2,010	2,189	2,322	2,481	2,519	2,525	(NA)	(NA)
Average annual change [1]	Percent	(NA)	3.2	2.1	4.3	5.4	6.4	1.4	0.2	(NA)	(NA)
Coal	Bil. kWh	704	853	1,162	1,402	1,464	1,541	1,554	1,560	1,551	1,576
Percent of total	Percent	54.8	52.7	57.8	64.0	63.0	62.1	61.7	61.7	(NA)	(NA)
Petroleum	Bil. kWh	184	289	246	100	118	149	158	117	111	89
Gas	Bil. kWh	373	300	346	292	273	253	267	264	264	264
Nuclear	Bil. kWh	22	173	251	384	455	527	529	577	613	619
Fuel consumed:											
Total energy equivalent	Quad. Btu	13.40	15.19	18.57	18.79	19.37	20.12	20.54	20.32	20.06	19.96
Coal	Mil. sh. tons	320	406	569	694	718	758	767	774	772	780
Oil	Mil. bbl.	339	507	421	175	201	250	270	200	189	152
Gas	Bil cu. ft.	3,932	3,158	3,682	3,044	2,844	2,636	2,787	2,787	2,789	2,765

NA Not available.   Z Less than 0.5 million kW.   [1] Change from immediate prior year except for 1970, change from 1960. For explanation of average annual percent change, see Guide to Tabular Presentation.   [2] Net summer capability is the steady hourly output that generating equipment is expected to supply to system load, exclusive of auxiliary power as demonstrated by test at the time of summer peak demand.   [3] Includes small percentage (.5 percent) from wood and waste, geothermal, and petroleum coke.   [4] A prime mover is the engine, turbine, water wheel, or similar machine which drives an electric generator.   [5] Fossil fuels only.   [6] Includes wind, solar thermal, and photovoltaic, not shown separately.   [7] Includes fossil steam, wood, and waste.   [8] Each prime mover type in combination plants counted separately. Includes geothermal, wind, and solar, not shown separately.   [9] Includes small amounts of wood, waste, wind, geothermal, solar thermal, and photovoltaic.

Source: 1970, U.S. Federal Power Commission, *Electric Power Statistics*, and press releases; thereafter, U.S. Energy Information Administration, 1975 and 1980, *Power Production, Fuel Consumption, and Installed Capacity Data-Annual*, and unpublished data; thereafter, *Electric Power Annual, Annual Energy Review*, and unpublished data.

Energy

No. 947. Electric Utility Industry—Capability, Peak Load, and Capacity Margin: 1970 to 1992

[Excludes Alaska and Hawaii. Capability represents the maximum kilowatt output with all power sources available and with hydraulic equipment under actual water conditions, allowing for maintenance, emergency outages, and system operating requirements. Capacity margin is the difference between capability and peak load]

YEAR	CAPABILITY AT THE TIME OF—				NON-COINCIDENT PEAK LOAD		CAPACITY MARGIN			
	Summer peak load (1,000 kW)		Winter peak load[1] (1,000 kW)		Summer	Winter[1]	Summer		Winter[1]	
	Amount	Change from prior year[2]	Amount	Change from prior year[2]			Amount (1,000 kW)	Percent of capability	Amount (1,000 kW)	Percent of capability
1970	326,900	26,600	339,050	27,600	274,650	248,550	52,250	16.0	90,500	26.7
1975	479,300	34,900	492,450	25,050	356,800	331,100	122,500	25.6	161,350	32.8
1978	545,700	29,700	561,550	23,950	408,050	383,100	137,650	25.2	178,450	31.8
1979 [3]	544,506	(X)	554,525	(X)	398,424	368,876	146,082	26.8	185,649	33.5
1980	558,237	13,731	572,195	17,670	427,058	384,567	131,179	23.5	187,628	32.8
1981	572,219	13,982	586,569	14,374	429,349	397,800	142,870	25.0	188,769	32.2
1982	586,142	13,923	598,066	11,497	415,618	373,985	170,524	29.1	224,081	37.5
1983	596,449	10,307	612,453	14,387	447,526	410,779	148,923	25.0	201,674	32.9
1984	604,240	7,791	622,125	9,672	451,150	436,374	153,090	25.3	185,751	29.9
1985	621,597	17,357	636,475	14,350	460,503	423,660	161,094	25.9	212,815	33.4
1986	633,291	11,694	646,721	10,246	476,320	422,857	156,971	24.8	223,864	34.6
1987	648,118	14,827	662,977	16,256	496,185	448,277	151,933	23.4	214,700	32.4
1988	661,580	13,462	676,940	13,963	529,460	466,533	132,120	20.0	210,407	31.1
1989	673,316	11,736	685,249	8,309	523,432	496,378	149,884	22.3	188,871	27.6
1990	685,091	11,775	696,757	11,508	545,537	484,014	139,554	20.4	212,743	30.5
1991	690,915	5,824	703,212	6,455	551,320	485,435	139,595	20.2	217,777	31.0
1992	695,436	4,521	707,752	4,540	548,707	492,983	146,729	21.1	214,769	30.3

X Not applicable.   [1] 1970 is for the month of December.   [2] For 1970 and 1975, change from 1969 and 1974, respectively.
[3] Beginning 1979, data are not entirely comparable with prior years due to change in data source.

Source: Edison Electric Institute, Washington, DC, *Statistical Yearbook of the Electric Utility Industry,* annual.

No. 948. Electric Energy Sales, by Class of Service, 1970 to 1992, and by State, 1992

[In billions of kilowatt-hours]

REGION, DIVISION, AND STATE	Total[1]	Resi-dential	Com-mercial	Indus-trial	REGION, DIVISION, AND STATE	Total[1]	Resi-dential	Com-mercial	Indus-trial
					Kansas	27.1	8.9	9.4	8.5
1970	1,392.3	466.3	306.7	570.9	South	1,165.0	428.0	284.8	414.0
1973	1,712.9	579.2	388.3	686.1	South Atlantic	552.8	219.4	159.1	156.6
1975	1,747.1	588.1	403.0	687.7	Delaware	8.5	2.8	2.4	3.2
1980	2,094.4	717.5	488.2	815.1	Maryland	51.0	19.8	10.8	19.8
1985	2,309.5	790.0	609.0	824.5	Dist. of Columbia	10.0	1.5	5.2	3.0
1987	2,457.3	850.4	660.4	858.2	Virginia	76.4	29.8	21.6	16.7
1988	2,578.1	892.9	699.1	896.5	West Virginia	23.8	8.1	5.2	10.4
1989	2,646.8	905.5	725.9	925.7	North Carolina	94.2	34.8	25.1	32.5
1990	2,712.6	924.0	751.0	945.5	South Carolina	58.4	18.9	12.4	26.3
1991	2,762.0	955.4	765.7	946.6	Georgia	83.4	30.5	23.7	28.2
					Florida	147.0	73.2	52.6	16.5
1992, total [2]	2,763.3	935.9	761.3	972.7	East South Central	241.0	80.8	33.7	121.7
Northeast	411.8	136.1	142.7	116.9	Kentucky	67.1	17.8	9.6	37.1
New England	103.9	37.6	37.9	26.3	Tennessee	78.6	29.5	6.5	41.7
Maine	11.5	3.8	2.7	4.8	Alabama	62.2	21.1	10.9	29.5
New Hampshire	9.0	3.4	2.1	3.3	Mississippi	33.2	12.4	6.7	13.5
Vermont	4.9	1.9	1.5	1.4	West South Central	371.2	127.8	92.0	135.7
Massachusetts	45.0	15.6	18.6	9.7	Arkansas	28.5	10.4	6.2	11.3
Rhode Island	6.4	2.4	2.5	1.4	Louisiana	65.1	21.2	13.8	27.5
Connecticut	27.1	10.5	10.5	5.8	Oklahoma	38.3	14.3	10.3	11.6
Middle Atlantic	307.9	98.5	104.8	90.6	Texas	239.4	81.9	61.7	85.4
New York	128.5	38.7	46.6	31.0	West	513.7	163.4	163.5	167.4
New Jersey	63.1	20.5	27.4	14.7	Mountain	168.0	51.6	52.7	56.9
Pennsylvania	116.3	39.2	30.8	44.9	Montana	13.1	3.3	2.8	6.4
Midwest	659.8	204.3	165.8	269.9	Idaho	19.0	5.7	5.3	7.6
East North Central	469.3	136.6	113.8	204.0	Wyoming	11.7	1.8	2.4	7.4
Ohio	145.0	39.1	31.8	69.7	Colorado	31.8	10.2	13.9	6.8
Indiana	77.0	22.8	16.1	37.4	New Mexico	14.4	3.8	4.6	4.6
Illinois	112.5	32.4	31.5	40.9	Arizona	43.7	16.2	14.5	11.0
Michigan	83.8	25.7	21.2	35.7	Utah	16.6	4.5	5.0	6.2
Wisconsin	50.9	16.6	13.2	20.4	Nevada	17.7	6.1	4.2	6.7
West North Central	190.5	67.7	52.0	65.9	Pacific	345.7	111.8	110.8	110.5
Minnesota	47.4	14.8	8.3	23.6	Washington	89.3	28.4	18.7	38.3
Iowa	30.2	10.3	7.0	12.1	Oregon	42.9	15.2	11.8	15.1
Missouri	54.4	21.3	18.8	13.4	California	213.4	68.1	80.2	57.1
North Dakota	7.1	3.0	1.8	1.8	Alaska	4.3	1.6	2.0	0.5
South Dakota	6.5	2.8	1.5	1.8	Hawaii	8.7	2.4	2.4	3.8
Nebraska	17.8	6.6	5.3	4.8					

[1] Includes other service not shown separately.   [2] Preliminary.

Source: U.S. Energy Information Administration, *Electric Power Annual.*

No. 949. Electric Energy—Net Generation and Net Summer Capability, by State: 1990 to 1992

[Capacity as of Dec. 31. Covers utilities for public use]

DIVISION AND STATE	NET GENERATION (bil. kWh) 1990	1991	1992 Total	1992 Percent from coal	NET SUMMER CAPABILITY (mil. kW) 1990	1992	DIVISION AND STATE	NET GENERATION (bil. kWh) 1990	1991	1992 Total	1992 Percent from coal	NET SUMMER CAPABILITY (mil. kW) 1990	1992
U.S	2,808.2	2,825.0	2,797.2	56.3	690.5	695.1	VA	47.2	48.9	49.0	46.3	13.7	13.8
							WV	77.4	71.3	72.3	99.1	14.4	14.4
N.E	94.1	87.0	84.6	19.3	23.4	22.6	NC	79.8	83.5	83.0	65.1	20.2	20.1
ME	9.1	9.5	8.3	-	2.4	2.4	SC	69.3	69.8	71.5	32.2	14.9	16.3
NH	10.8	12.7	13.5	23.7	2.6	2.5	GA	97.6	90.8	91.8	63.5	20.7	21.4
VT	5.0	5.3	4.7	-	1.1	1.1	FL	123.6	130.7	134.0	46.0	32.7	33.4
MA	36.5	35.8	32.8	33.3	9.9	9.5	E.S.C	246.9	257.8	264.0	72.7	59.5	58.6
RI.....	0.6	0.2	0.1	-	0.3	0.2	KY	73.8	75.5	77.4	95.0	15.5	15.3
CT	32.2	23.6	25.2	8.5	7.1	7.0	TN	73.9	73.9	75.4	66.3	17.0	16.3
M.A	330.8	325.5	309.4	42.8	78.4	78.4	AL....	76.2	85.1	90.8	66.8	20.0	19.9
NY	128.7	126.1	112.2	22.2	31.2	31.1	MS	22.9	23.3	20.5	38.1	7.0	7.0
NJ....	36.5	37.0	31.2	17.4	13.7	13.8	W.S.C ...	374.3	378.7	378.5	49.2	101.2	101.9
PA	165.7	162.4	166.0	61.6	33.4	33.4	AR	37.1	38.4	37.4	53.6	9.6	9.6
E.N.C	485.8	500.5	487.6	73.9	113.1	113.5	LA....	58.2	57.2	55.2	35.9	16.8	16.7
OH	126.5	132.7	136.3	88.4	27.0	27.1	OK	45.1	44.9	45.9	60.2	12.8	12.9
IN	97.7	98.2	97.3	98.4	20.6	20.8	TX	234.0	238.3	240.0	49.5	62.0	62.7
IL	127.0	127.9	124.8	39.9	32.6	32.6	Mountain .	247.4	249.1	257.2	76.3	49.3	49.7
MI.....	89.1	94.6	82.7	74.3	22.3	22.4	MT	25.7	28.2	25.5	67.2	4.9	4.9
WI.....	45.6	47.1	46.5	70.5	10.6	10.5	ID.....	8.6	8.3	6.3	-	2.3	2.4
W.N.C ...	218.4	221.2	212.8	75.3	54.2	54.7	WY	39.4	38.7	41.9	98.3	5.8	5.8
MN	41.6	40.4	37.8	64.7	8.8	8.9	CO	31.3	31.0	31.9	94.1	6.6	6.6
IA	29.0	31.2	29.4	84.4	8.0	8.1	NM	28.5	25.1	27.7	91.5	5.0	5.1
MO	59.0	60.1	56.6	82.7	15.2	15.4	AZ	62.3	66.8	70.1	49.4	14.9	15.0
ND	26.8	27.5	28.6	94.0	4.5	4.5	UT	32.3	30.2	32.9	95.8	4.8	4.8
SD	6.4	6.6	6.2	42.0	2.7	2.7	NV	19.3	20.9	21.0	78.4	4.9	5.1
NE	21.6	23.0	22.4	55.4	5.5	5.5	Pacific ...	276.7	264.2	255.7	5.3	82.1	82.5
KS	33.9	32.3	31.8	69.7	9.6	9.7	WA	100.5	101.4	84.1	11.4	24.2	24.2
S.A	533.8	541.1	547.5	58.2	129.2	133.2	OR	49.2	46.3	41.2	8.9	11.2	11.2
DE	7.1	7.6	6.3	60.9	2.0	2.1	CA	114.5	105.0	119.3	-	43.7	43.8
MD	31.5	38.2	39.6	59.7	9.8	10.9	AK	4.5	4.3	4.2	7.0	1.5	1.7
DC	0.4	0.2	0.1	-	0.8	0.8	HI	8.0	7.3	6.9	-	1.5	1.6

- Represents zero.

Source: U.S. Energy Information Administration, 1980, *Power Production, Fuel Consumption, and Installed Capacity Data,* annual; thereafter, *Electric Power Annual, Electric Power Monthly,* December issues, and *Inventory of Power Plants in the United States,* annual.

No. 950. Nuclear Power Plants—Number of Units, Net Generation, and Net Summer Capability, by State: 1992

REGION, DIVISION, AND STATE	Number of units	NET GENERATION Total (mil. kWh)	Percent of total[1]	NET SUMMER CAPABILITY Total (mil. kW)	Percent of total[1]	REGION, DIVISION, AND STATE	Number of units	NET GENERATION Total (mil. kWh)	Percent of total[1]	NET SUMMER CAPABILITY Total (mil. kW)	Percent of total[1]
U.S..	109	618,776	22.1	99.0	14.2	KS	1	8,491	26.7	1.2	12.0
						South	42	244,804	20.6	39.2	13.3
Northeast ..	27	144,357	36.6	23.8	23.6	S.A	27	155,401	28.4	23.5	17.7
N.E	8	38,474	45.5	6.4	28.2	MD	2	10,664	26.9	1.7	15.2
ME	1	5,358	64.3	0.9	36.2	VA	4	23,334	47.7	3.3	24.1
NH	1	7,869	58.5	1.2	45.9	NC	5	22,754	27.4	4.6	23.0
VT	1	3,735	79.5	0.5	45.3	SC	7	45,537	63.7	6.4	39.0
MA	1	4,742	14.4	0.7	7.0	GA	4	27,996	30.5	3.7	17.5
CT	4	16,771	66.7	3.2	46.0	FL.....	5	25,116	18.7	3.8	11.5
M.A	19	105,883	34.2	17.4	22.2	E.S.C	8	43,225	16.4	8.3	14.1
NY.....	6	24,155	21.5	4.8	15.5	TN	2	15,654	20.8	2.3	14.1
NJ.....	4	21,595	69.3	3.9	27.9	AL....	5	19,397	21.4	4.8	24.3
PA	9	60,133	36.2	8.7	26.1	MS	1	8,174	39.9	1.1	16.3
Midwest ...	31	158,499	22.6	25.7	15.3	W.S.C....	7	46,178	12.2	7.3	7.2
E.N.C....	23	118,604	24.3	20.1	17.7	AR	2	11,326	30.3	1.7	17.6
OH	2	14,805	10.9	2.0	7.5	LA....	2	10,356	18.8	2.0	12.0
IL.....	13	73,742	59.1	12.6	38.6	TX	3	24,496	10.2	3.6	5.8
MI.....	5	18,849	22.8	3.9	17.6	West	9	71,118	13.9	10.3	7.8
WI.....	3	11,207	24.1	1.5	14.3	Mt	3	25,609	10.0	3.8	7.7
W.N.C ...	8	39,895	18.7	5.6	10.2	AZ	3	25,609	36.5	3.8	25.4
MN ...	3	11,166	29.6	1.5	17.4	Pac	6	45,509	17.8	6.5	7.9
IA	1	3,405	11.6	0.5	6.4	WA	1	5,692	6.8	1.1	4.5
MO	1	8,084	14.3	1.1	7.3	OR	1	4,573	11.1	1.1	9.8
NE	2	8,748	39.1	1.3	23.0	CA	4	35,244	29.5	4.3	9.8

[1] For total capability and generation, see table 949.

Source: U.S. Energy Information Administration, *Electric Power Annual* and *Electric Power Monthly*, December issues.

No. 951. Nuclear Power Plants—Number, Capacity, and Generation: 1965 to 1992

ITEM	1965	1970	1975	1980	1985	1986	1987	1988	1989	1990	1991	1992
Operable generating units[1]	6	18	54	70	95	100	107	108	110	111	111	109
Net summer capability[1 2] (mil. kW). .	0.8	7.0	37.3	51.8	79.4	85.2	93.6	94.7	98.2	99.6	99.6	99.0
Net generation (bil. kWh)	3.7	21.8	172.5	251.1	383.7	414.0	455.3	527.0	529.4	576.9	612.6	618.8
Percent of total electric utility generation	0.3	1.4	9.0	11.0	15.5	16.6	17.7	19.5	19.0	20.5	21.7	22.1
Capacity factor [3]	(NA)	(NA)	55.9	56.3	58.0	56.9	57.4	63.5	62.2	66.0	70.2	70.9

NA Not available. [1] As of year-end. [2] Net summer capability is the peak steady hourly output that generating equipment is expected to supply to system load, exclusive of auxiliary and other powerplant, as demonstrated by test at the time of summer peak demand. [3] Weighted average of monthly capacity factors. Monthly factors are derived by dividing actual monthly generation by the maximum possible generation for the month (hours in month times net maximum dependable capacity).
Source: U.S. Energy Information Administration, *Annual Energy Review.*

No. 952. Commercial Nuclear Power Generation, by Country: 1970 to 1993

[Generation for **calendar years**; other data as of **December**]

COUNTRY	REACTORS				GROSS ELECTRICITY GENERATED (bil. kWh)				GROSS CAPACITY (1,000 kW)			
	1970	1980	1990	1993	1970	1980	1990	1993	1970	1980	1990	1993
Total.	64	208	368	421	73.9	617.8	1,743.9	2,134.6	15,186	128,847	301,745	349,171
United States . .	15	74	112	110	23.2	265.2	606.4	641.2	5,211	56,529	105,998	105,276
Argentina	-	1	2	2	-	2.3	7.0	7.7	-	357	1,005	1,005
Belgium	1	3	7	7	0.3	12.5	42.7	41.9	11	1,744	5,740	5,843
Brazil.	-	-	1	1	-	-	2.0	4.4	-	-	657	657
Bulgaria	(NA)	(NA)	(NA)	6	(NA)	(NA)	(NA)	14.0	(NA)	(NA)	(NA)	3,760
Canada	1	9	19	22	0.9	40.4	74.0	97.5	220	5,588	13,855	16,709
China: Taiwan . .	-	2	6	6	-	8.2	32.9	34.3	-	1,272	5,146	5,146
Czech Republic .	(NA)	(NA)	(NA)	4	(NA)	(NA)	(NA)	3.6	(NA)	(NA)	(NA)	1,782
Finland.	-	4	4	4	-	7.0	18.9	19.6	-	2,296	2,400	2,400
France	4	22	58	56	5.7	61.2	314.1	365.8	1,606	15,412	58,862	59,751
Germany	4	11	22	22	5.3	43.7	147.2	153.5	907	8,996	23,973	24,143
Great Britain . . .	27	33	42	37	26.5	37.2	68.8	90.5	4,783	9,012	15,274	14,832
Hungary	-	-	4	4	-	-	13.6	13.8	-	-	1,760	1,840
India	2	4	6	9	2.2	2.9	6.0	6.2	400	860	1,330	2,020
Italy	3	4	2	-	3.3	2.2	-	-	631	1,490	1,132	-
Japan.	3	22	40	46	3.3	81.0	191.9	243.5	828	15,117	31,645	37,351
Mexico	-	-	1	1	-	-	2.1	4.9	-	-	675	675
Netherlands . . .	1	2	2	2	0.4	4.2	3.4	3.9	55	529	540	540
Pakistan	-	1	1	1	-	0.1	0.4	0.4	-	137	137	137
Russia	(NA)	(NA)	(NA)	29	(NA)	(NA)	(NA)	120.4	(NA)	(NA)	(NA)	21,316
Slovenia [1].	-	-	1	1	-	-	4.6	4.0	-	-	664	664
South Africa . . .	-	-	2	2	-	-	8.9	7.7	-	-	1,930	1,930
South Korea . . .	-	1	9	9	-	3.5	52.8	58.1	-	587	7,616	7,616
Spain.	1	3	10	9	0.9	5.2	54.3	56.0	160	1,117	7,984	7,405
Sweden	1	8	12	12	(Z)	26.7	68.2	61.4	12	5,770	10,344	10,394
Switzerland	1	4	5	5	1.9	14.3	23.6	23.3	364	2,034	3,079	3,099
Ukraine	(NA)	(NA)	(NA)	14	(NA)	(NA)	(NA)	57.0	(NA)	(NA)	(NA)	12,880

- Represents zero. NA Not available. Z Less than 50 million kWh. [1] Formerly Yugoslavia.
Source: McGraw-Hill, Inc., New York, NY, *Nucleonics Week,* March issues (copyright).

No. 953. Uranium Supply, Enrichment, and Discharged Commercial Reactor Fuel: 1970 to 1992

[Years ending **Dec. 31**, except as noted. For additional data on uranium, see section 25 on mining. For explanation of kilogram, see weights and measures]

ITEM	Unit	1970	1975	1980	1985	1987	1988	1989	1990	1991	1992
URANIUM CONCENTRATE											
Production	Mil. lb	25.81	23.20	43.70	11.31	12.99	13.13	13.84	8.89	7.95	5.69
Exports.	Mil. lb	4.20	1.00	5.80	5.30	1.00	3.30	2.10	2.00	3.50	3.00
Imports.	Mil. lb	-	1.40	3.60	11.70	15.10	15.80	13.10	23.70	16.30	16.10
Delivered price.	Dol./lb. . . .	(NA)	10.50	26.00	31.43	27.37	26.15	19.56	15.70	13.66	13.45
ENRICHMENT [1]											
Enriched product [2]	Mil. Swu[3] . .	5.10	9.92	10.69	10.2	8.1	9.9	11.9	10.2	10.3	(NA)
For domestic customers . . .	Mil. Swu[3] . .	3.74	4.36	6.89	6.0	3.4	6.3	7.6	6.8	6.7	(NA)
For foreign customers	Mil. Swu[3] . .	1.36	5.56	3.80	4.2	4.7	3.6	4.3	3.4	3.6	(NA)
Sales	Mil. dol . . .	(NA)	376	1,379	1,403	921	1,094	1,320	1,148	1,156	(NA)
DISCHARGED COMMERCIAL REACTOR FUEL [4]											
Annual discharge	Metric tons.	82	499	1,193	1,330	1,625	1,672	1,914	2,028	1,794	2,255
Inventory, year-end [5].	Metric tons.	118	1,538	6,434	12,481	15,506	17,178	19,092	21,120	22,914	25,169

- Represents zero. NA Not available. [1] Beginning 1985, numbers are fiscal years. [2] Based on sales. [3] Separative work units. The standard measure of enrichment services is based on operating tails assay in effect at the time the enriched product was placed in inventory. [4] Uranium content. Source: Nuclear Assurance Corporation, Atlanta, GA. [5] Reprocessed fuel not included as inventory.
Source: Except as noted, U.S. Energy Information Administration, *Annual Energy Review, Uranium Industry Annual* and unpublished data.

No. 954. Electric Utilities—Generation, Sales, Revenue, and Customers: 1970 to 1992

[Sales and revenue are to and from ultimate customers]

CLASS	Unit....	1970	1975	1980	1985	1987	1988	1989	1990	1991	1992, prel.
Generation [1]	Bil. kWh.	1,532	1,918	2,286	2,470	2,572	2,704	2,784	2,808	2,825	2,797
Sales [2]	Bil. kWh	1,391	1,733	2,126	2,306	2,435	2,554	2,621	2,684	2,737	2,730
Residential or domestic....	Bil. kWh.	448	586	734	793	846	886	899	916	949	927
Percent of total	Percent.	32.2	33.8	34.5	34.4	34.8	34.7	34.3	34.1	34.7	34.0
Commercial [3]	Bil. kWh.	313	418	524	606	658	698	716	739	753	756
Industrial [4]	Bil. kWh.	573	662	794	820	844	882	913	932	935	946
Revenue [2]	Bil. dol	22.1	46.9	95.5	149.2	155.7	162.4	169.6	176.5	185.1	186.7
Residential or domestic....	Bil. dol.	9.4	18.8	37.6	58.6	63.0	66.4	68.8	71.7	76.4	76.1
Percent of total	Percent.	42.7	40.1	39.4	39.3	40.5	40.9	40.5	40.6	41.2	40.7
Commercial [3]	Bil. dol.	6.3	13.5	27.4	44.1	46.7	49.1	51.6	54.2	56.8	58.0
Industrial [4]	Bil. dol.	5.4	12.7	27.3	41.4	40.6	41.6	43.7	44.9	45.9	46.5
Ultimate customers, Dec. 31 [2]	Million..	72.5	81.8	92.7	101.6	104.6	106.4	108.5	110.1	111.4	112.8
Residential or domestic....	Million..	64.0	72.6	82.2	89.8	92.4	93.9	95.6	97.0	98.2	99.4
Commercial [3]	Million..	7.9	8.6	9.7	10.9	11.4	11.6	12.0	12.1	12.3	12.4
Industrial [4]	Million..	0.4	0.4	0.5	0.5	0.5	0.5	0.5	0.5	0.5	0.5
Avg. kWh used per customer.	1,000..	19.4	21.4	23.2	22.9	23.5	24.2	24.4	24.6	24.7	24.3
Residential	1,000...	7.1	8.2	9.0	8.9	9.2	9.5	9.5	9.5	9.7	9.4
Commercial [3]	1,000...	40.0	49.0	54.5	56.1	58.4	60.4	60.6	61.3	61.6	61.1
Avg. annual bill per customer	Dollar..	307	579	1,040	1,482	1,501	1,536	1,576	1,614	1,670	1,664
Residential	Dollar.	149	262	462	658	688	712	725	744	782	770
Commercial [3]	Dollar.	804	1,580	2,848	4,080	4,147	4,256	4,363	4,494	4,646	4,682
Avg. revenue per kWh sold.	Cents ..	1.59	2.70	4.49	6.47	6.39	6.36	6.47	6.57	6.76	6.84
Residential	Cents ..	2.10	3.21	5.12	7.39	7.45	7.49	7.65	7.83	8.05	8.20
Commercial [3]	Cents ..	2.01	3.23	5.22	7.27	7.10	7.04	7.20	7.33	7.55	7.67
Industrial [4]	Cents ..	0.95	1.92	3.44	5.04	4.82	4.71	4.79	4.81	4.91	4.92

[1] Source: 1970 and 1975, U.S. Federal Power Commission; thereafter, U.S. Energy Information Administration, *Monthly Energy Review*, monthly. [2] Includes other types not shown separately. [3] Small light and power. [4] Large light and power.
Source: Except as noted, Edison Electric Institute, Washington, DC, *Statistical Yearbook of the Electric Utility Industry*, annual.

No. 955. Major Investor-Owned Electric Utilities—Balance Sheet and Income Account of Privately Owned Companies: 1982 to 1992

[In billions of dollars. As of Dec. 31. As of 1990, covers approximately 180 investor-owned electric utilities that during each of the last 3 years met any one or more of the following conditions — 1 mil. megawatthours of total sales; 100 megawatthours of sales for resale, 500 megawatthours of gross interchange out, and 500 megawatthours of wheeling for other. See also *Historical Statistics, Colonial Times to 1970*, series S 133-146 and V 197-212]

ITEM	1982	1984	1985	1986	1987	1988	1989	1990	1991	1992
COMPOSITE BALANCE SHEET										
Assets and other debits....	315.0	375.6	404.7	426.1	446.3	454.3	465.7	477.9	487.5	506.4
Electric utility plant [1]	321.2	364.7	396.9	419.5	434.6	449.4	462.4	480.6	497.9	518.8
Depreciation and amortization....	*67.6*	*77.1*	*85.1*	*93.9*	*103.2*	*113.5*	*125.0*	*135.7*	*148.3*	*160.5*
Net electric utility plant........	253.6	287.5	311.8	325.6	331.4	335.9	337.5	344.9	349.6	358.3
Other utility plant............	16.7	17.6	19.9	21.2	23.1	24.6	26.3	28.5	31.0	33.4
Depreciation and amortization....	*5.3*	*6.1*	*6.5*	*7.2*	*7.8*	*8.5*	*9.2*	*9.9*	*10.8*	*11.7*
Net other utility plant	11.4	12.1	13.4	14.0	15.2	16.1	17.1	18.6	20.2	21.7
Total utility plant............	337.9	395.3	431.1	455.9	475.7	493.0	507.9	528.7	548.4	571.9
Depreciation and amortization....	*72.9*	*88.0*	*97.4*	*107.7*	*118.7*	*131.3*	*144.6*	*157.4*	*171.7*	*185.1*
Net total utility plant.	265.0	307.3	333.8	348.2	357.0	361.6	363.2	371.3	376.8	386.9
Other property and investments...	9.1	10.8	12.1	13.5	15.6	15.2	16.1	17.7	17.4	18.0
Current and accrued assets	31.7	37.9	39.4	38.4	40.9	39.1	41.5	41.5	43.4	43.4
Deferred debits.............	9.3	19.3	19.4	26.1	32.9	38.3	44.8	47.3	50.0	58.0
Liabilities and other credits [2].	315.0	375.3	404.7	426.1	446.3	454.3	465.7	477.9	487.5	506.4
Capital stock	70.3	79.0	82.8	81.6	79.9	80.7	82.9	83.2	83.6	86.1
Other paid-in capital	27.7	34.0	36.3	38.4	40.3	40.4	39.1	40.5	42.9	44.7
Retained earnings	27.9	37.1	41.1	46.0	48.0	47.1	47.7	48.1	49.0	49.7
Subsidiary earnings [3]	1.6	1.9	2.2	2.3	2.6	2.5	2.8	2.9	3.0	2.7
Long-term debt.............	124.0	140.6	152.7	157.2	158.4	160.7	162.9	167.9	171.9	174.1
Current and accrued liabilities ...	28.6	32.0	32.0	34.0	39.3	38.4	42.0	44.3	43.4	45.6
Deferred credits and operating reserves	15.1	19.0	20.9	22.4	25.6	28.1	28.5	28.8	29.2	31.1
Deferred income taxes [4]	19.4	28.1	32.7	39.6	45.9	50.2	53.3	56.5	59.2	65.0
COMPOSITE INCOME ACCOUNTS										
Electric operating revenues......	109.3	128.3	135.3	136.3	138.5	143.9	150.9	157.3	166.8	169.5
Electric operating expenses	*91.1*	*105.5*	*111.1*	*110.2*	*111.6*	*115.3*	*121.6*	*127.9*	*135.9*	*139.0*
Net electric operating revenues....	18.1	22.8	24.1	26.1	27.0	28.6	29.4	29.4	30.9	30.5
Other utility operating income	0.9	1.1	1.2	1.1	1.1	1.2	1.2	1.2	1.2	1.3
Total utility operating income.....	19.1	24.0	25.3	27.2	28.1	29.8	30.6	30.5	32.1	31.8
Other income..............	5.3	6.8	7.4	7.2	6.6	5.0	5.2	4.1	3.9	2.9
Total income	24.4	30.8	32.7	34.4	34.6	34.8	35.8	34.6	36.0	34.7
Income deductions	*9.4*	*11.1*	*14.0*	*14.0*	*15.6*	*18.8*	*18.5*	*17.7*	*18.1*	*16.3*
Net income [5]	15.0	19.7	18.7	20.4	19.0	16.0	17.3	16.9	16.9	18.4

[1] Includes construction work in progress. [2] Includes contributions in aid of construction through 1970. [3] Unappropriated undistributed. [4] Cumulative. [5] Includes net extraordinary income.

Source: U.S. Energy Information Administration, 1981-84, *Financial Statistics of Selected Electric Utilities*, annual; thereafter, *Financial Statistics of Major U.S. Investor-Owned Electric Utilities*, annual.

No. 956. Water Power—Developed and Undeveloped Capacity, by Division: 1950 to 1992

[In millions of kilowatts. As of Dec. 31. Excludes Alaska and Hawaii for 1950 and all capacity of reversible equipment at pumped storage projects. Also excludes capacity precluded from development due to wild and scenic river legislation. For composition of division, see table 26. See also *Historical Statistics, Colonial Times to 1970*, series S 160-175]

DIVISION	DEVELOPED INSTALLED CAPACITY							ESTIMATED UNDEVELOPED CAPACITY						
	1950	1960	1970	1980	1990	1991	1992	1950	1960	1970	1980	1990	1991	1992
United States	18.7	33.2	52.0	64.4	73.0	73.6	74.1	87.6	114.2	128.0	129.9	73.9	73.3	73.6
New England	1.2	1.5	1.5	1.5	1.9	1.9	1.9	3.3	2.9	3.3	4.7	4.4	4.4	4.4
Middle Atlantic	1.7	2.5	4.3	4.3	4.9	4.9	4.9	6.6	7.6	4.5	5.1	5.1	4.9	4.9
East North Central	0.9	0.9	0.9	0.9	1.1	1.2	1.2	2.3	3.0	1.6	2.0	1.7	1.7	1.7
West North Central	0.6	1.6	2.7	2.8	3.1	3.1	3.1	5.8	6.4	4.4	3.4	3.1	3.1	3.1
South Atlantic	2.8	3.8	5.3	5.9	6.7	6.7	6.7	8.2	8.4	9.6	9.6	7.0	7.1	7.2
East South Central	2.7	3.8	5.2	5.6	5.9	5.9	5.9	4.7	4.6	3.8	3.3	2.4	2.4	2.4
West South Central	0.5	0.9	1.9	2.3	2.7	2.7	2.7	3.6	3.9	3.3	4.7	4.6	4.6	4.6
Mountain	2.3	4.6	6.2	7.4	9.2	9.4	9.5	23.4	23.6	26.7	34.2	19.4	19.1	19.1
Pacific	6.0	13.6	23.9	33.7	37.5	37.8	38.2	29.8	53.8	70.9	62.9	26.2	26.0	26.2

Source: U.S. Federal Energy Regulatory Commission (formerly U.S. Federal Power Commission), *Hydroelectric Power Resources of the United States, Developed and Undeveloped*, January 1, 1988; and unpublished data.

No. 957. Solar Collector Shipments, by Type, End Use, and Market Sector: 1975 to 1992

[In thousands of square feet, except number of manufacturers. Solar collector is a device for intercepting sunlight, converting the light to heat, and carrying the heat to where it will be either used or stored. 1985 data are not available]

YEAR	Number of manufac- turers	Total ship- ments [1]	COLLECTOR TYPE		END USE			MARKET SECTOR		
			Low tem- perature	Medium tempera- ture, spe- cial, other	Pool heating	Hot water	Space heating	Resi- dential	Com- mercial	Indus- trial
1975	131	3,743	3,026	717	(NA)	(NA)	(NA)	(NA)	(NA)	(NA)
1980	233	19,398	12,233	7,165	12,029	4,790	1,688	16,077	2,417	488
1981	203	20,133	8,677	11,456	9,781	7,204	2,017	15,773	2,561	1,518
1982	265	18,621	7,476	11,145	7,035	7,444	2,367	13,729	3,789	560
1983 [2]	203	16,828	4,853	11,975	4,839	9,323	2,082	11,780	3,039	1,665
1984 [2]	225	17,191	4,479	11,939	4,427	8,930	2,370	13,980	2,091	289
1986 [2]	98	9,360	3,751	1,111	3,494	1,181	127	4,131	703	13
1987 [2]	59	7,269	3,157	957	3,111	964	23	3,775	305	11
1988 [2]	51	8,174	3,326	732	3,304	726	7	3,796	255	7
1989 [2]	44	11,482	4,283	1,989	4,688	1,374	205	5,804	424	42
1990	51	11,409	3,645	2,527	5,016	1,091	2	5,835	294	22
1991	48	6,574	5,585	989	5,535	989	24	6,322	225	13
1992	45	7,086	6,187	897	6,210	801	35	6,832	204	27

NA Not available.   [1] Includes other end uses and market sectors not shown separately.   [2] Declines between 1984 and 1989 are primarily due to the expiration of the Federal energy tax credit and industry consolidation.

Source: U.S. Energy Information Administration, *Solar Collector Manufacturing Activity*, annual.

No. 958. Wood Energy Consumption, by Region and Sector: 1980 to 1990

[In trillions of Btu, except percent. For composition of regions, see table 26]

YEAR	Total	Percent of total energy consump- tion	REGION				SECTOR			
			Northeast	Midwest	South	West	Resi- dential	Industrial	Commer- cial	Electric utilities
1980	2,483	3.3	386	329	1,380	388	859	1,600	21	4
1981	2,412	3.3	389	331	1,291	402	869	1,519	21	3
1982	2,395	3.4	351	339	1,334	372	937	1,434	22	2
1983	2,556	3.6	369	318	1,471	396	925	1,606	22	3
1984	2,633	3.6	349	341	1,482	461	923	1,679	22	9
1987	2,437	3.2	350	474	1,147	467	852	1,576	(1)	9
1989	2,604	3.2	432	552	1,161	459	918	1,673	(1)	13
1990	2,267	2.8	256	330	1,176	505	581	1,674	(1)	12

[1] Commercial wood energy is not included because there are no accurate data sources to provide reliable estimates.

No. 959. Households That Burn Wood: 1980 to 1990

[Based on Residential Energy Consumption Survey; see Appendix III]

ITEM	Unit	HOUSEHOLDS THAT BURN WOOD					HOUSEHOLDS THAT BURN WOOD AS MAIN HEATING FUEL				
		1980	1982	1984	1987	1990	1980	1982	1984	1987	1990
Number of households	Millions	21.6	21.4	22.9	22.5	22.9	4.7	5.6	6.4	5.0	3.9
Percent of all households	Percent	26.4	25.6	26.6	24.8	24.3	5.8	6.7	7.5	5.6	4.1
Number of cords burned	Millions	42.7	48.6	49.0	42.6	29.1	22.4	28.7	29.4	23.5	15.0
Average number per household	Number	2.0	2.3	2.1	1.9	1.3	4.7	5.1	4.6	4.7	3.9
Median number per household	Number	0.7	1.0	1.0	0.7	0.5	3.3	4.0	4.0	4.0	3.3
Wood energy consumption	Tril. Btu	854	971	981	853	582	448	574	589	470	300

Source of tables 958 and 959: U.S. Energy Information Administration, *Annual Energy Review*.

No. 960. Renewable Energy Consumption Estimates, by Type: 1990 to 1992

[Renewable energy is obtained from sources that are essentially inexhaustible unlike fossil fuels of which there is a finite supply]

SOURCE AND SECTOR	QUANTITY (quadrillion Btu)			PERCENT CHANGE	
	1990	1991	1992	1990-1991	1991-1992
SOURCES					
Total	6.01	6.20	6.04	3.2	-2.6
Consumption for electricity	3.77	4.01	3.77	6.4	-6.0
Electric utilities	3.13	3.09	2.70	-1.3	-12.6
Hydroelectric power	2.93	2.90	2.51	-1.0	-13.4
Geothermal energy	0.18	0.17	0.17	-5.6	0.0
Biofuels [1]	0.02	0.02	0.02	0.0	0.0
Wind energy [2]	(Z)	(Z)	(Z)	(X)	(X)
Nonutility power generators	0.62	0.69	0.78	11.3	13.0
Hydroelectric power	0.08	0.08	0.10	1.2	19.0
Geothermal, solar, and wind energy	0.10	0.11	0.13	10.0	18.2
Biofuels [1]	0.44	0.49	0.55	13.0	11.3
Net imported electricity	0.02	0.23	0.29	1,050.0	26.1
Consumption for other uses [3]	2.23	2.19	2.27	-1.8	3.7
Biofuels [1]	2.17	2.13	2.21	-1.8	3.8
Solar and photovoltaic energy	0.06	0.06	0.06	0.0	0.0
SECTORS					
Total	6.01	6.20	6.04	3.2	-2.6
Residential and commercial	0.64	0.67	0.71	4.7	6.0
Industrial	2.13	2.14	2.26	0.5	5.6
Transportation	0.08	0.07	0.08	-12.5	14.3
Electric utilities	3.15	3.32	3.00	5.4	-9.6

Z Less than 0.005 quadrillion Btu.   X Not applicable.   [1] Biofuels are fuelwood, wood byproducts, waste wood, municipal solid waste, manufacturing process waste, and alcohol fuels.   [2] Also includes photovoltaic and solar thermal energy.   [3] Included are nonutility thermal energy uses, such as space heating and industrial process heat production. Excluded are estimates for mechanical energy, such as shaft power from dams, wind machines, and solar-powered motors and activators.
Source: U.S. Energy Information Administration, *Annual Energy Review*.

No. 961. Privately Owned Gas Utility Industry—Balance Sheet and Income Account: 1980 to 1992

[In millions of dollars. The gas utility industry consists of pipeline and distribution companies. Excludes operations of companies distributing gas in bottles or tanks. See also *Historical Statistics, Colonial Times to 1970*, series S 205-218]

ITEM	1980	1985	1986	1987	1988	1989	1990	1991	1992
COMPOSITE BALANCE SHEET									
Assets, total [1]	75,851	104,478	104,008	109,390	121,667	123,820	121,686	124,120	129,400
Total utility plant	67,071	88,121	91,606	93,540	99,933	106,017	112,863	119,772	129,272
Depreciation and amortization	26,162	36,377	36,776	41,162	44,423	47,054	49,483	52,400	57,005
Utility plant (net)	40,909	51,744	54,830	52,378	55,510	58,963	63,380	67,372	72,267
Investment and fund accounts [1]	15,530	23,871	21,850	25,660	31,552	28,111	23,872	22,883	21,883
Current and accrued assets	17,243	24,771	21,477	21,025	23,402	24,836	23,268	23,023	23,783
Deferred debits [2]	2,169	4,092	5,851	8,633	9,658	10,364	9,576	9,277	9,776
Liabilities, total [1]	75,851	104,478	104,008	109,390	121,667	123,820	121,686	124,120	129,400
Capitalization, total [1]	51,382	65,799	66,660	66,312	69,875	74,753	74,958	75,463	81,183
Capital stock [1]	29,315	39,517	39,902	38,212	39,898	43,889	43,810	43,435	46,318
Long-term debts	22,067	26,282	26,758	28,100	29,977	30,864	31,148	32,028	34,865
Current and accrued liabilities	18,119	26,125	23,855	26,664	33,735	31,005	29,550	28,128	26,438
Deferred income taxes [3]	4,149	7,769	8,363	9,901	10,685	11,292	11,360	10,527	10,952
Other liabilities and credits	2,201	4,785	5,130	6,513	7,372	6,770	5,818	10,002	10,827
COMPOSITE INCOME ACCOUNT									
Operating revenues, total	85,918	103,945	80,978	69,566	69,754	70,363	66,027	63,922	66,289
Operating expenses [4]	81,789	98,320	75,470	64,409	64,696	64,262	60,137	59,165	59,936
Operation and maintenance	74,508	88,572	66,032	56,054	57,032	55,990	51,627	50,867	50,028
Federal, State, and local taxes	4,847	6,590	6,133	5,179	4,241	4,843	4,957	4,446	6,020
Operating income	4,129	5,625	5,508	5,157	5,058	6,101	5,890	4,756	6,352
Utility operating income	4,471	6,030	5,943	5,452	5,202	6,274	6,077	4,962	6,562
Income before interest charges [1]	6,929	7,636	7,085	6,845	7,472	8,764	8,081	5,530	7,197
Net income [1]	4,194	3,785	3,390	2,971	3,352	4,641	4,410	1,894	3,677
Dividends	2,564	4,060	3,882	3,453	3,151	3,113	3,191	4,341	3,894

[1] Beginning 1980, not comparable with earlier years due to Federal Power Commission ruling requiring adoption of the equity method in reporting earnings of subsidiaries.   [2] Includes capital stock discount and expense and reacquired securities.   [3] Includes reserves for deferred income taxes.   [4] Includes expenses not shown separately.
Source: American Gas Association, Arlington, VA, *Gas Facts*, annual, (copyright).

No. 962. Gas Utility Industry—Summary: 1970 to 1992

[Covers natural, manufactured, mixed, and liquid petroleum gas. Based on questionnaire mailed to all privately and municipally owned gas utilities in United States, except those with annual revenues less than $25,000. See also *Historical Statistics, Colonial Times to 1970*, series S 190-204]

ITEM	Unit	1970	1975	1980	1985	1987	1988	1989	1990	1991	1992
Customers [1]	1,000	41,482	44,555	47,223	49,971	51,576	52,422	53,356	54,261	55,174	56,132
Residential	1,000	38,097	40,950	43,489	45,929	47,362	48,133	48,980	49,802	50,634	51,525
Commercial	1,000	3,131	3,367	3,498	3,816	3,980	4,069	4,161	4,246	4,322	4,397
Industrial and other	1,000	199	184	187	179	180	168	168	168	168	210
Sales [2]	Tril. Btu	16,044	14,863	15,413	12,616	10,543	10,705	10,551	9,842	9,605	9,906
Residential	Tril. Btu	4,923	4,991	4,826	4,513	4,385	4,695	4,798	4,468	4,550	4,694
Percent of total	Percent	30.7	33.6	31.3	35.8	41.6	43.9	45.5	45.4	47.4	47.4
Commercial	Tril. Btu	2,007	2,387	2,453	2,338	2,156	2,306	2,322	2,192	2,198	2,209
Industrial	Tril. Btu	8,439	6,837	7,957	5,635	3,848	3,544	3,243	3,010	2,631	2,772
Other	Tril. Btu	674	648	177	130	155	160	188	171	226	231
Revenues [2]	Mil. dol	10,283	19,101	48,303	63,293	45,492	46,162	47,493	45,153	44,647	46,178
Residential	Mil. dol	5,207	8,445	17,432	26,864	23,622	24,828	26,172	25,000	25,729	26,702
Percent of total	Percent	50.6	44.2	36.1	42.4	51.9	53.8	55.1	55.4	57.6	57.8
Commercial	Mil. dol	1,620	3,303	8,183	12,722	10,271	10,681	11,074	10,604	10,669	10,865
Industrial	Mil. dol	3,181	6,745	22,215	23,086	11,069	10,113	9,666	8,996	7,576	7,913
Other	Mil. dol	274	608	473	621	530	538	581	553	674	698
Prices per mil. Btu [3]	Dollars	0.64	1.29	3.13	5.02	4.32	4.31	4.50	4.59	4.65	4.66
Residential	Dollars	1.06	1.69	3.61	5.95	5.39	5.29	5.45	5.60	5.66	5.69
Commercial	Dollars	0.81	1.38	3.34	5.44	4.77	4.63	4.77	4.84	4.85	4.92
Industrial	Dollars	0.38	0.99	2.79	4.10	2.88	2.85	2.98	2.99	2.88	2.85
Gas mains mileage	1,000	913	980	1,052	1,119	1,151	1,169	1,185	1,207	1,225	1,254
Field and gathering	1,000	66	69	84	94	94	92	91	90	86	86
Transmission	1,000	252	263	266	271	274	276	276	280	282	285
Distribution	1,000	595	648	702	754	784	801	818	837	857	883
Construction expenditures [4]	Mil. dol	2,507	2,466	5,350	5,671	5,328	6,166	7,341	7,899	9,036	11,068
Transmission	Mil. dol	1,019	590	1,583	1,562	1,295	1,568	2,081	2,886	3,656	5,739
Distribution	Mil. dol	913	910	1,869	2,577	3,055	3,389	3,980	3,714	3,842	3,867
Production and storage	Mil. dol	203	555	1,150	790	251	268	276	309	430	349

[1] Annual average.   [2] Excludes sales for resale.   [3] For definition, see text, section 19.   [4] Includes general.

Source: American Gas Association, Arlington, VA, *Gas Facts*, annual (copyright).

No. 963. Gas Utility Industry—Customers, Sales, and Revenues, by State: 1992

[See headnote, table 962. For definition of Btu, see text, section 19]

REGION, DIVISION, AND STATE	CUSTOMERS [1] (1,000) Total [2]	Residential	SALES [3] (tril. Btu) Total [2]	Residential	REVENUES [3] (mil. dol.) Total [2]	Residential
U.S.	56,132	51,525	9,906	4,694	46,178	26,702
Northeast	11,132	10,196	1,885	1,035	11,528	7,326
N.E.	2,069	1,869	403	185	2,626	1,479
ME.	18	13	5	1	28	6
NH.	80	68	17	6	103	46
VT.	27	24	8	3	41	19
MA.	1,248	1,136	239	113	1,515	879
RI.	216	197	37	20	240	150
CT.	480	431	96	42	699	379
M.A.	9,063	8,327	1,482	850	8,902	5,847
NY.	4,272	3,952	594	378	3,916	2,762
NJ.	2,248	2,025	448	200	2,419	1,348
PA.	2,543	2,350	440	272	2,567	1,737
Midwest	17,195	15,685	3,001	1,883	13,891	9,319
E.N.C	12,342	11,330	2,187	1,438	10,292	7,136
OH.	3,060	2,818	532	354	2,560	1,773
IN.	1,506	1,372	284	155	1,328	823
IL.	3,625	3,321	616	441	2,853	2,123
MI.	2,852	2,640	510	362	2,332	1,695
WI.	1,299	1,179	245	125	1,217	722
W.N.C.	4,853	4,355	814	445	3,599	2,183
MN.	1,118	1,013	237	115	1,007	557
IA.	812	726	139	76	641	388
MO.	1,349	1,221	186	118	883	595
ND.	102	90	18	10	83	48
SD.	125	110	22	11	97	54
NE.	494	431	86	42	362	201
KS.	853	764	125	73	526	340
South	14,043	12,793	3,272	941	12,661	5,479
S.A.	5,332	4,850	970	378	4,810	2,429
DE.	102	94	22	9	105	51
MD.	857	789	135	70	729	436
DC.	148	133	32	13	195	89
VA.	727	653	127	57	692	379
WV.	385	352	65	39	330	223
NC.	651	575	157	44	688	274
SC.	408	364	110	23	466	161
GA.	1,489	1,376	215	107	1,119	673
FL.	565	516	106	18	486	143
E.S.C.	2,645	2,382	491	195	2,122	1,044
KY.	712	643	124	65	533	308
TN.	754	661	161	53	702	279
AL.	757	698	115	50	577	329
MS.	422	380	91	27	310	128
W.S.C.	6,066	5,561	1,811	368	5,729	2,006
AR.	569	505	82	40	357	203
LA.	990	928	438	56	1,124	307
OK.	922	833	153	67	564	327
TX.	3,585	3,296	1,139	205	3,684	1,169
West	13,761	12,852	1,749	836	8,096	4,576
Mt.	3,525	3,203	484	267	2,144	1,322
MT.	207	183	35	20	143	83
ID.	155	134	18	10	85	49
WY.	128	114	22	11	92	52
CO.	1,138	1,022	165	97	703	435
NM.	424	385	73	33	257	155
AZ.	649	601	65	29	359	201
UT.	505	468	71	48	337	244
NV.	319	296	35	19	168	103
Pac.	10,236	9,649	1,265	569	5,952	3,254
WA.	590	523	132	43	452	208
OR.	403	352	56	24	274	143
CA.	9,122	8,668	1,043	487	5,076	2,839
AK.	86	74	31	14	105	54
HI.	35	32	3	1	45	10

[1] Averages for the year.   [2] Includes other service, not shown separately.   [3] Excludes sales for resale.

Source: American Gas Association, Arlington, VA, *Gas Facts*, annual (copyright).

Science and Technology

This section presents statistics on scientific, engineering, and technological resources, with emphasis on patterns of research and development (R&D) funding and on scientific, engineering, and technical personnel, education, and employment. Also included are statistics on space program outlays and accomplishments. Principal sources of these data are the National Science Foundation (NSF) and the National Aeronautics and Space Administration (NASA).

NSF gathers data chiefly through recurring surveys. Current NSF publications containing data on funds for research and development and on scientific and engineering personnel include the *Science Resources Studies Highlights* summaries series; Detailed Statistical Tables; and annual, biennial, triennial, and special reports. Titles or the areas of coverage of these reports include the following: *Science and Engineering Indicators; National Patterns of R&D Resources; Science and Engineering Personnel-A National Overview; Women and Minorities in Science and Engineering;* science and technology data presented in chart and tabular form in a pocket-size publication; *International Science and Technology Data Update;* profiles on human resources and funding in individual fields of science and engineering; *Federal Funds for Research and Development; Federal R&D Funding by Budget Function; Federal Support to Universities, Colleges, and Selected Nonprofit Institutions; Scientific and Engineering Facilities at Universities and Colleges; Geographic Distribution of Industrial R&D Expenditures; Research and Development in Industry;* R&D funds and graduate enrollment and support in academic science and engineering; characteristics of doctoral scientists and engineers and of recent graduates in the United States; *U.S. Scientists and Engineers;* and scientists, engineers, and technicians in manufacturing, nonmanufacturing, and trade and regulated industries. Statistical surveys in these areas pose problems of concept and definition and the data should, therefore, be regarded as broad estimates

In Brief

R&D expenditures in constant (1987) dollars:

1970	74.6 bil.
1980	87.7 bil.
1993	130.1 bil.

Nondefense R&D spending as percent of GNP: 1991

Japan	3.0
Former West Germany	2.7
United States	1.9
France	1.9
Italy	1.3

rather than precise quantitative statements. See sources for details.

The National Science Board's biennial *Science and Engineering Indicators* contains data and analyses of international and domestic science and technology, including measures of inputs and outputs. *The Budget of the United States Government,* published by the U.S. Office of Management and Budget, contains summary financial data on Federal R&D programs.

Research and development outlays.—NSF defines research as a "systematic and intensive study directed toward a fuller knowledge of the subject studied" and development as "the systematic use of scientific knowledge directed toward the production of useful materials, devices, systems, methods, or processes." National coverage of R&D expenditures is developed primarily from periodic surveys in four principal economic sectors: (1) *Government,* made up primarily of Federal executive agencies; (2) *industry,* consisting of manufacturing and nonmanufacturing firms and the federally funded research and development centers (FFRDC's) they administer; (3) *universities and colleges,* composed of universities, colleges, and their affiliated institutions, agricultural experiment stations, and associated schools of agriculture, and FFRDC's administered by educational institutions; and (4) *other nonprofit institutions,* consisting of such organizations as private philanthropic foundations, nonprofit research institutes, voluntary health agencies, and FFRDC's administered by nonprofit organizations. The R&D funds reported consist of current operating costs, including planning and administration costs, except as otherwise noted. They exclude funds for routine testing, mapping and surveying, collection of general-purpose data, dissemination of scientific information, and training of scientific personnel.

Scientists, engineers, and technicians.—Scientists and engineers are defined as persons engaged in scientific and engineering work at a level requiring a knowledge of sciences equivalent at least to that acquired through completion of a 4-year college course. Technicians are defined as persons engaged in technical work at a level requiring knowledge acquired through a technical institute, junior college, or other type of training less extensive than 4-year college training. Craftsmen and skilled workers are excluded.

Historical statistics.—Tabular headnotes provide cross-references, where applicable, to *Historical Statistics of the United States, Colonial Times to 1970.* See Appendix IV.

Figure 20.1
Top 15 Universities—Federal Research and Development Obligations: 1991

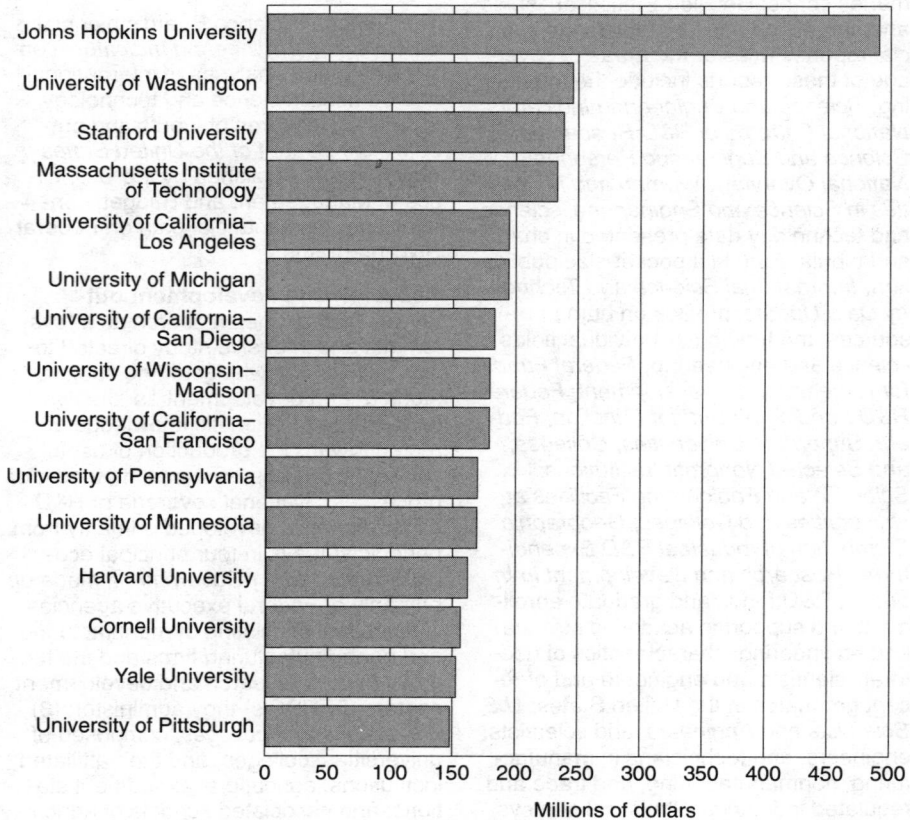

Millions of dollars

Source: Chart prepared by U.S. Bureau of the Census. For data, see table 973.

No. 964. R&D Expenditures: 1960 to 1993

[Includes basic research, applied research, and development. Defense-related outlays comprise all research and development spending by Dept. of Defense, including space activities, and a portion of Department of Energy funds. Space-related outlays are those of the National Aeronautics and Space Administration; they exclude space activities of other Federal agencies, estimated at less than 5 percent of all space research and development spending. Minus sign (-) indicates decrease]

YEAR	CURRENT DOLLARS (bil. dol.)			CONSTANT (1987) DOLLARS[1]		ANNUAL PERCENT CHANGE[3]		PERCENT OF TOTAL R&D OUTLAYS				
	Total	Defense space related	Other	Total (bil. dol.)	Percent of GDP[2]	Current dollars	Constant dollars	Federally funded defense/space-related			Other outlays	
								Total	Defense	Space	Non-Federal	Federal
1960	13.5	7.5	6.0	52.0	2.6	9.4	7.5	55	52	3	35	9
1965	20.0	10.8	9.3	70.6	2.9	6.3	3.7	54	33	21	35	11
1970	26.1	11.4	14.7	74.6	2.6	2.0	-3.2	44	33	10	43	13
1971	26.7	11.2	15.5	72.3	2.4	2.1	-3.0	42	33	10	44	14
1972	28.5	11.6	16.9	73.7	2.4	6.7	1.9	41	33	8	44	15
1973	30.7	11.9	18.9	74.9	2.3	7.9	1.7	39	32	7	47	15
1974	32.9	11.8	21.1	73.9	2.3	7.0	-1.4	36	29	7	49	15
1975	35.2	12.3	23.0	72.2	2.2	7.2	-2.3	35	27	7	49	17
1976	39.0	13.4	25.6	75.0	2.2	10.8	3.9	34	27	8	49	17
1977	42.8	14.3	28.5	76.7	2.2	9.6	2.2	33	27	7	50	17
1978	48.1	15.3	32.8	80.1	2.2	12.5	4.4	32	26	6	50	18
1979	55.0	16.6	38.4	84.1	2.2	14.2	5.0	30	25	6	51	19
1980	62.6	18.4	44.2	87.7	2.3	13.9	4.3	29	24	5	53	18
1981	71.9	21.2	50.6	91.4	2.4	14.8	4.3	30	24	5	54	17
1982	80.0	24.6	55.4	95.5	2.5	11.3	4.5	31	26	5	54	15
1983	89.1	28.3	60.9	102.3	2.6	11.4	7.1	32	27	4	54	14
1984	101.1	31.8	69.3	111.2	2.7	13.5	8.7	31	28	3	55	14
1985	113.8	37.5	76.3	120.6	2.8	12.5	8.5	33	30	3	54	13
1986	119.5	40.6	78.9	123.3	2.8	5.0	2.2	34	31	3	55	11
1987	125.4	43.2	82.2	125.4	2.8	4.9	1.7	34	31	3	54	12
1988	133.7	45.1	88.6	128.8	2.7	6.7	2.8	34	30	3	54	12
1989	140.8	45.6	95.2	129.8	2.7	5.3	0.8	32	28	4	56	12
1990	146.4	46.6	99.9	129.5	2.7	4.0	-0.3	32	27	4	56	12
1991	145.4	42.7	102.6	123.7	2.6	-0.7	-4.5	29	24	5	59	11
1992	154.5	46.2	108.3	128.0	2.6	6.3	3.5	30	25	5	58	12
1993	160.8	48.2	112.6	130.1	2.6	4.0	1.6	30	25	5	58	12

[1] Based on GDP implicit price deflator.   [2] GDP = Gross Domestic Product.   [3] Change from immediate prior year.

Source: U.S. National Science Foundation, *National Patterns of R&D Resources*, annual.

No. 965. R&D, Source of Funds and Performance Sector: 1970 to 1993

[In millions of dollars. See headnote, table 966]

YEAR	Total	SOURCE OF FUNDS				PERFORMANCE SECTOR				
		Federal Govt.	Industry	Univ., colleges	Other[1]	Federal Govt.	Industry	Univ., colleges	Associated FFRDC's[2]	Other[1]
Current dollars:										
1970	26,134	14,891	10,444	462	337	4,079	18,067	2,335	737	916
1975	35,213	18,109	15,820	749	535	5,354	24,187	3,409	987	1,276
1980	62,610	29,461	30,912	1,334	903	7,632	44,505	6,077	2,246	2,150
1985	113,818	52,127	57,978	2,369	1,344	12,945	84,239	9,686	3,523	3,425
1986	119,531	54,281	61,057	2,784	1,409	13,535	87,823	10,928	3,895	3,350
1987	125,353	57,912	62,643	3,192	1,606	13,413	92,155	12,154	4,206	3,425
1988	133,742	61,320	67,144	3,462	1,816	14,281	97,889	13,466	4,531	3,575
1989	140,771	62,634	72,110	3,947	2,080	15,121	101,854	15,016	4,730	4,050
1990	146,434	63,996	75,714	4,356	2,368	16,002	104,606	16,344	4,832	4,650
1991	145,383	59,146	78,804	4,850	2,583	15,238	102,246	17,620	5,079	5,200
1992	154,500	65,150	81,050	5,400	2,900	16,600	107,800	19,050	5,300	5,750
1993	160,750	68,000	83,550	6,000	3,200	16,600	112,300	20,550	5,300	6,000
Constant (1987) dollars:[3]										
1970	74,597	42,622	29,673	1,335	966	11,789	51,327	6,749	2,130	2,602
1975	72,237	37,396	32,162	1,574	1,105	11,248	49,161	7,162	2,074	2,593
1980	87,669	41,393	43,118	1,890	1,268	10,810	62,071	8,608	3,181	2,999
1985	120,599	55,245	61,418	2,512	1,425	13,727	89,236	10,271	3,736	3,628
1986	123,295	55,966	63,009	2,867	1,453	13,939	90,633	11,254	4,011	3,457
1987	125,353	57,912	62,643	3,192	1,606	13,413	92,155	12,154	4,206	3,425
1988	128,812	59,094	64,626	3,342	1,750	13,785	94,215	12,998	4,374	3,441
1989	129,832	57,801	66,463	3,648	1,920	13,975	93,875	13,878	4,372	3,733
1990	129,504	56,653	66,890	3,865	2,097	14,159	92,490	14,502	4,287	4,108
1991	123,691	50,431	66,905	4,152	2,202	13,046	86,796	15,086	4,348	4,414
1992	128,017	54,068	67,046	4,496	2,407	13,822	89,165	15,862	4,413	4,756
1993	130,070	55,102	67,496	4,878	2,593	13,496	90,711	16,707	4,309	4,847

[1] Nonprofit institutions.   [2] University associated federally-funded R&D centers.   [3] Based on gross domestic product implicit price deflator.

Source: U.S. National Science Foundation, *National Patterns of R&D Resources*, annual.

No. 966. R&D Funds, by Performance Sector: 1980 to 1993

[In millions of dollars, except percent. Data primarily on calendar year basis—calendar year data for industry and other non-profit institutions combined with Federal and university fiscal year data. Data refer, in general, to natural sciences including engineering, and to social sciences in all but industry sector. Excludes capital expenditures data. Expenditures at associated federally funded research and development centers administered by industry and other nonprofit institutions included in totals of respective sectors. See also *Historical Statistics, Colonial Times to 1970*, series W 109-125]

PERFORMANCE SECTOR	1980	1985	1988	1989	1990	1991	1992	1993
Total R&D [1]	**62,610**	**113,818**	**133,742**	**140,771**	**146,434**	**145,383**	**154,500**	**160,750**
In 1987 dollars [2]	87,669	120,599	128,812	129,832	129,504	123,691	128,017	130,070
Percent Federal as source	47.1	45.8	45.8	44.5	43.7	40.7	42.2	42.3
Percent of gross domestic product	2.3	2.8	2.7	2.7	2.7	2.6	2.6	2.6
Federal Government	7,632	12,945	14,281	15,121	16,002	15,238	16,600	16,600
Industry	44,505	84,239	97,889	101,854	104,606	102,246	107,800	112,300
Federal funds	14,029	27,196	32,117	31,292	30,626	25,308	28,800	31,000
Industry funds	30,476	57,043	65,772	70,562	73,980	76,938	79,000	81,300
Universities and colleges	6,077	9,686	13,466	15,016	16,344	17,620	19,050	20,550
Federal funds	4,104	6,063	8,191	8,991	9,636	10,221	10,800	11,400
Industry funds	236	560	872	998	1,134	1,216	1,350	1,500
University and college funds [3]	1,334	2,369	3,462	3,947	4,356	4,850	5,400	6,000
Other nonprofit institutions funds [3]	403	694	941	1,080	1,218	1,333	1,500	1,650
Universities and colleges, associated federally funded R&D centers	2,246	3,523	4,531	4,730	4,832	5,079	5,300	5,300
Other nonprofit institutions	2,150	3,425	3,575	4,050	4,650	5,200	5,750	6,000
Federal funds	1,450	2,400	2,200	2,500	2,900	3,300	3,650	3,700
Industry funds	200	375	500	550	600	650	700	750
Other [4]	500	650	875	1,000	1,150	1,250	1,400	1,550
Total research, basic and applied	**22,052**	**39,526**	**47,851**	**52,632**	**55,766**	**58,179**	**61,990**	**65,900**
In 1987 dollars [2]	30,990	41,889	46,112	48,567	49,357	49,578	51,429	53,391
Percent Federal as source	54.8	50.8	46.5	47.5	47.0	47.2	47.7	48.4
Federal Government	3,666	5,056	5,338	5,982	5,953	6,539	7,150	7,800
Industry	9,775	21,117	24,875	27,034	28,537	28,457	29,900	31,200
Federal funds	2,190	5,836	5,246	6,190	6,589	6,066	6,800	7,500
Industry funds	7,585	15,281	19,629	20,844	21,948	22,391	23,100	23,700
Universities and colleges	5,578	8,973	12,412	13,881	15,044	16,108	17,320	18,860
Federal funds	3,743	5,604	7,506	8,278	8,805	9,227	9,650	10,350
Industry funds	219	521	811	928	1,055	1,131	1,260	1,400
University and college funds [3]	1,241	2,203	3,220	3,671	4,051	4,510	5,020	5,580
Other nonprofit institutions funds [3]	375	645	875	1,004	1,133	1,240	1,390	1,530
Universities and colleges, associated federally funded R&D centers	1,548	2,340	2,756	2,935	3,032	3,505	3,700	3,850
Other nonprofit institutions	1,485	2,040	2,470	2,800	3,200	3,570	3,920	4,190
Federal funds	930	1,250	1,400	1,600	1,850	2,100	2,300	2,400
Industry funds	160	300	400	440	480	520	560	610
Other [4]	395	490	670	760	870	950	1,060	1,180
Total basic research	**8,433**	**14,192**	**18,775**	**20,648**	**22,099**	**22,829**	**24,380**	**26,220**
In 1987 dollars [2]	11,899	15,045	18,107	19,067	19,583	19,500	20,263	21,280
Percent of total R&D	13.5	12.5	14.0	14.7	15.1	15.7	15.8	16.3
Percent Federal as source	70.1	64.7	61.8	62.8	62.0	62.9	63.0	62.7
Federal Government	1,182	1,923	2,050	2,371	2,366	2,446	2,700	2,900
Industry	1,325	2,862	4,280	4,646	4,909	4,373	4,500	4,700
Federal funds	290	489	908	1,225	1,284	1,148	1,200	1,300
Industry funds	1,035	2,373	3,372	3,421	3,625	3,225	3,300	3,400
Universities and colleges	4,042	6,553	8,893	9,801	10,681	11,538	12,400	13,500
Federal funds	2,863	4,340	5,674	6,191	6,652	7,085	7,550	8,100
Industry funds	141	342	532	598	681	732	790	890
University and college funds [3]	797	1,447	2,113	2,365	2,616	2,919	3,180	3,540
Other nonprofit institutions funds [3]	241	424	574	647	732	802	880	970
Universities and colleges, associated federally funded R&D centers	1,124	1,749	2,222	2,330	2,403	2,572	2,700	2,850
Other nonprofit institutions	760	1,105	1,330	1,500	1,740	1,900	2,080	2,270
Federal funds	450	675	750	850	1,000	1,100	1,200	1,300
Industry funds	95	170	230	250	280	300	320	350
Other [4]	215	260	350	400	460	500	560	620
Total development	**40,558**	**74,292**	**85,891**	**88,139**	**90,668**	**87,204**	**92,510**	**94,850**
In 1987 dollars [2]	56,678	78,710	82,700	81,265	80,147	74,113	76,588	76,678
Percent of total R&D	64.8	65.3	64.2	62.6	61.9	60.0	59.9	59.0
Percent Federal as source	42.9	43.1	45.5	42.7	41.7	36.4	38.4	38.1

[1] Basic research, applied research, and development.   [2] Based on gross domestic product implicit price deflator.
[3] Includes State and local government funds received by these institutions and used for research and development.   [4] Includes estimates for independent nonprofit hospitals and voluntary health agencies.

Source: U.S. National Science Foundation, *National Patterns of R&D Resources*, annual.

No. 967. Funds for R&D—Performance Sector, by State: 1991

[In millions of dollars. See headnote, table 966]

STATE	Total	Federal government[1]	Industry	Universities and colleges[2]	Other nonprofit[3]	STATE	Total	Federal government[1]	Industry	Universities and colleges[2]	Other nonprofit[3]
U.S.	145,385	15,238	102,246	22,701	5,200	MO......	(NA)	71	(7)	306	22
						MT......	(NA)	26	(6)	38	1
AL......	1,503	701	521	245	36	NE......	211	22	59	124	6
AK......	146	59	18	67	2	NV......	261	109	83	67	3
AZ......	1,399	132	944	311	11	NH......	(NA)	88	(5)	79	-
AR......	198	35	106	55	2	NJ......	8,768	513	7,810	433	12
CA......	28,337	1,885	21,279	4,700	473	NM......	2,582	393	1,064	1,111	15
CO......	(NA)	275	(4)	340	106	NY......	10,363	174	8,268	1,751	170
CT......	1,913	47	1,535	317	15	NC......	1,965	151	1,285	502	27
DE......	(NA)	9	(5)	45	3	ND......	(NA)	24	(7)	31	1
DC......	1,737	1,433	40	118	145	OH......	5,975	689	4,726	504	57
FL......	3,700	658	2,599	438	5	OK......	604	41	392	153	18
GA......	1,479	121	868	484	6	OR......	600	47	349	179	24
HI......	145	45	11	78	11	PA......	7,621	315	6,262	906	138
ID......	(NA)	37	(6)	42	1	RI......	485	226	152	88	18
IL......	6,417	68	5,027	1,275	47	SC......	595	14	419	151	10
IN......	2,347	92	1,988	262	4	SD......	32	9	5	16	2
IA......	777	27	461	286	3	TN......	1,139	124	737	251	28
KS......	(NA)	12	(7)	124	5	TX......	6,635	405	4,755	1,218	257
KY......	317	62	154	98	2	UT......	665	103	356	202	4
LA......	457	43	172	240	2	VT......	(NA)	5	(9)	47	5
ME......	(NA)	14	(5)	27	16	VA......	2,771	1,107	1,115	366	182
MD......	5,864	3,432	1,203	1,078	151	WA......	3,890	133	3,215	350	193
MA......	8,561	278	6,335	1,338	610	WV......	(NA)	76	(10)	73	5
MI......	8,851	92	8,116	601	42	WI......	1,573	32	1,140	388	13
MN......	2,228	41	1,810	332	46	WY......	41	9	2	23	7
MS......	299	157	41	97	4	Other[11]....	3,835	577	675	349	2,234

- Represents or rounds to zero.   NA Not available.   [1] Total funds used by Federal government from Federal sources.
[2] Distribution by States includes R&D performed in only doctoral degree granting institutions; U.S. total includes R&D performed in all institutions.   [3] For other sector, funds distributed by State include only Federal obligations to organizations in the nonprofit sector. Nonprofit R&D performance using non-Federal funds are undistributed.   [4] Between $1,751 and $2,593 million.   [5] Between $863 and $995 million.   [6] Under $95 million.   [7] Under $1,963 million.   [8] Under $284 million.   [9] Between $102 and $120 million.   [10] Between $69 and $201 million.   [11] Includes unknown.

Source: U.S. National Science Foundation, *Science and Engineering Indicators*, 1993.

No. 968. Federal Obligations for R&D, by Agency: 1975 to 1993

[In millions of dollars. For fiscal years ending in year shown; see text, section 9. Includes those agencies with obligations of $1 billion or more in 1993. See *Historical Statistics, Colonial Times to 1970*, series W 142, for total R&D expenditures]

AGENCY	1975	1980	1985	1988	1989	1990	1991	1992	1993
CURRENT DOLLARS									
Obligations, total [1]...........	19,039	29,830	48,360	56,769	61,407	63,668	61,295	70,368	69,754
Dept. of Defense..............	9,013	13,981	29,792	35,249	37,577	37,268	32,135	38,309	36,155
Dept. of Health and Human Services..................	2,281	3,780	5,451	7,158	7,903	8,406	9,756	10,678	11,143
National Aeronautics and Space Administration...............	3,064	3,234	3,327	4,330	5,394	6,533	7,280	7,860	8,629
Dept. of Energy	2,047	4,754	4,966	5,036	5,193	5,631	5,983	6,766	6,731
National Science Foundation	595	882	1,346	1,533	1,670	1,690	1,785	1,937	2,247
Dept. of Agriculture	420	688	943	1,017	1,038	1,108	1,237	1,337	1,337
CONSTANT (1987) DOLLARS [2]									
Obligations, total [1]...........	39,998	42,253	51,283	54,796	56,753	56,493	52,479	58,591	56,711
Dept. of Defense..............	18,935	19,803	31,592	34,024	34,729	33,068	27,513	31,898	29,394
Dept. of Health and Human Services	4,792	5,354	5,780	6,909	7,304	7,459	8,353	8,891	9,059
National Aeronautics and Space Administration...............	6,437	4,581	3,528	4,180	4,985	5,797	6,233	6,545	7,015
Dept. of Energy	4,300	6,733	5,266	4,861	4,799	4,996	5,122	5,634	5,472
National Science Foundation	1,250	1,249	1,427	1,480	1,543	1,500	1,528	1,613	1,827
Dept. of Agriculture	882	974	1,000	981	959	983	1,059	1,113	1,087

[1] Includes other agencies, not shown separately.   [2] Based on gross domestic product implicit price deflator.

Source: U.S. National Science Foundation, *Federal Funds for Research and Development*, annual.

No. 969. Federal Funding for R&D, by Selected Budget Functions: 1970 to 1994

[In millions of dollars. For fiscal years ending in year shown; see text, section 9. Excludes R&D plant. Represents budget authority. Functions shown are those for which $1 billion or more was authorized for 1994. See *Historical Statistics, Colonial Times to 1970*, series W 126, for total obligations]

FUNCTION	1970	1980	1985	1989	1990	1991	1992	1993	1994, est.
CURRENT DOLLARS									
Total [1]	15,339	29,739	49,887	62,115	63,781	65,898	68,398	70,175	71,648
Eight functions, percent of total . .	96.6	96.5	98.3	98.2	98.0	97.9	98.0	97.9	97.9
National defense	7,981	14,946	33,698	40,665	39,925	39,328	40,083	41,539	41,978
Health	1,084	3,694	5,418	7,773	8,308	9,226	10,055	10,279	10,636
Space research and technology	3,606	2,738	2,725	4,555	5,765	6,511	6,744	6,880	6,724
Energy	574	3,603	2,389	2,419	2,715	2,943	3,099	2,648	2,855
General science	452	1,233	1,862	2,373	2,410	2,635	2,659	2,715	2,990
Natural resources and environment . .	340	999	1,059	1,255	1,386	1,582	1,688	1,708	1,790
Transportation	535	887	1,030	1,064	1,045	1,231	1,523	1,784	1,970
Agriculture	238	585	836	907	950	1,052	1,155	1,153	1,170
CONSTANT (1987) DOLLARS [2]									
Total [1]	44,332	42,123	52,902	57,408	56,594	56,420	56,951	57,053	56,863
National defense	23,066	21,170	35,735	37,583	35,426	33,671	33,375	33,772	33,316
Health	3,133	5,232	5,745	7,184	7,372	7,899	8,372	8,357	8,441
Space research and technology	10,422	3,878	2,890	4,210	5,115	5,574	5,615	5,593	5,337
Energy	1,659	5,103	2,533	2,236	2,409	2,520	2,580	2,153	2,266
General science	1,306	1,746	1,975	2,193	2,138	2,256	2,214	2,207	2,373
Natural resources and environment . .	983	1,415	1,123	1,160	1,230	1,354	1,405	1,389	1,421
Transportation	1,546	1,256	1,092	983	927	1,054	1,268	1,450	1,563
Agriculture	688	829	887	838	843	901	962	937	929

[1] Includes other functions, not shown separately. [2] Based on gross domestic product implicit price deflator.

Source: U.S. National Science Foundation, *Federal R&D Funding by Budget Function*, annual.

No. 970. National R&D Expenditures as a Percent of Gross Domestic Product, by Country: 1975 to 1992

YEAR	TOTAL R&D						NON DEFENSE R&D [1]					
	United States	Japan	Germany [2]	France	United Kingdom	Italy	United States	Japan	Germany [2]	France	United Kingdom	Italy
1975 ..	2.2	2.1	2.2	1.8	2.0	0.8	1.6	2.1	2.1	1.4	1.4	0.8
1980 ..	2.3	2.2	2.4	1.8	(NA)	0.7	1.8	2.2	2.3	1.4	(NA)	0.7
1985 ..	2.8	2.7	2.7	2.3	2.3	1.1	2.0	2.8	2.6	1.8	1.7	1.1
1989 ..	2.7	3.0	2.9	2.3	2.2	1.2	1.9	3.0	2.7	1.8	1.8	1.2
1990 ..	2.7	3.1	2.7	2.4	2.2	1.3	1.9	3.0	2.6	1.9	1.8	1.3
1991 ..	2.7	3.0	2.8	2.4	2.1	1.4	1.9	3.0	2.7	1.9	1.7	1.3
1992 ..	2.6	(NA)	(NA)	(NA)	(NA)	(NA)	1.9	(NA)	(NA)	(NA)	(NA)	(NA)

NA Not available. [1] Estimated. [2] Former West Germany.

Source: National Science Foundation, *National Patterns of R&D Resources*, annual; and Organization for Economic Co-operation and Development.

No. 971. R&D Expenditures in Science and Engineering at Universities and Colleges: 1981 to 1992

[In millions of dollars]

CHARACTERISTIC	1981	1990	1992	CHARACTERISTIC	1981	1990	1992
CURRENT DOLLARS				**CONSTANT (1987) DOLLARS [1]**			
Total	6,846	16,334	18,880	Total	8,799	14,493	15,720
Basic research	4,593	10,680	12,468	Basic research	5,904	9,476	10,381
Applied R&D	2,253	5,654	6,412	Applied R&D	2,896	5,017	5,339
Source of funds:				Source of funds:			
All governments	5,115	10,976	12,593	All governments	6,575	9,739	10,485
Institutions' own funds . . .	1,004	3,033	3,576	Institutions' own funds . . .	1,290	2,691	2,978
Industry	292	1,130	1,302	Industry	375	1,003	1,084
Other	435	1,195	1,409	Other	559	1,060	1,173
Fields:				Fields:			
Physical sciences	765	1,809	2,058	Physical sciences	983	1,605	1,714
Environmental sciences	550	1,080	1,249	Environmental sciences . .	707	958	1,040
Mathematical sciences . . .	87	221	247	Mathematical sciences . . .	112	196	206
Computer sciences	144	514	556	Computer sciences	185	456	463
Life sciences	3,695	8,748	10,228	Life sciences	4,749	7,762	8,516
Psychology	127	258	336	Psychology	163	229	280
Social sciences	366	706	817	Social sciences	470	626	680
Other sciences	145	335	307	Other sciences	186	297	256
Engineering	967	2,663	3,082	Engineering	1,243	2,363	2,566

[1] Based on gross domestic product implicit price deflator.

Source: U.S. National Science Foundation, *Survey of Scientific and Engineering Expenditures at Universities and Colleges*, annual.

No. 972. Federal Obligations to Universities and Colleges: 1970 to 1991

[In millions of dollars, except percent. For fiscal years ending in year shown; see text, section 9. Minus sign (-) indicates decrease]

ITEM	1970	1980	1985	1987	1988	1989	1990	1991
CURRENT DOLLARS								
Federal obligations, total.	3,237	8,299	10,972	13,434	14,066	15,504	15,198	17,415
Annual percent change [1]	-6.5	9.1	9.3	15.6	4.7	10.2	-2.0	14.6
Academic science/engineering obligations	2,188	4,791	7,258	8,567	9,136	10,075	10,443	11,815
Percent of total	67.6	57.7	66.2	63.8	65.0	65.0	68.7	67.8
Research and development	1,447	4,161	6,246	7,241	7,719	8,523	9,006	10,014
Research and development plant.	45	38	114	230	203	237	125	152
Other science/engineering activities	696	593	898	1,096	1,214	1,315	1,312	1,649
Nonscience/engineering activities	1,049	3,508	3,714	4,866	4,930	5,429	4,754	5,600
CONSTANT (1987) DOLLARS [2]								
Federal obligations, total.	9,355	11,755	11,635	13,434	13,577	14,329	13,485	14,910
Annual percent change [1]	-11.4	0.0	5.4	12.3	1.1	5.5	-5.9	10.6
Academic science/engineering obligations	6,324	6,786	7,697	8,567	8,819	9,311	9,266	10,116
Percent of total	67.6	57.7	66.2	63.8	65.0	65.0	68.7	67.9
Research and development	4,182	5,894	6,624	7,241	7,451	7,877	7,991	8,574
Research and development plant.	130	54	121	230	196	219	111	130
Other science/engineering activities	2,012	840	952	1,096	1,172	1,215	1,164	1,412
Nonscience/engineering activities	3,032	4,969	3,938	4,866	4,759	5,018	4,218	4,795

[1] Percent change from immediate prior year.   [2] Based on gross domestic product implicit price deflator.

Source: U.S. National Science Foundation, *Survey of Federal Support to Universities, Colleges, and Nonprofit Institutions,* annual.

No. 973. Federal R&D Obligations to Selected Universities and Colleges: 1981 to 1991

[For fiscal years ending in year shown; see text, section 9. For the top 40 institutions receiving Federal R&D funds in 1991. Awards to the administrative offices of university systems are excluded from totals for individual institutions because that allocation of funds is unknown, but those awards are included in "total all institutions"]

MAJOR INSTITUTION RANKED BY TOTAL 1991 FEDERAL R&D OBLIGATIONS	OBLIGATIONS ($1,000)			RANK		
	1981	1985	1991	1981	1985	1991
Total, all institutions [1]	4,410,931	6,246,181	10,014,322	(X)	(X)	(X)
40 institutions, percent of total	59.1	57.9	56.0	(X)	(X)	(X)
Johns Hopkins University.	363,429	297,374	490,893	1	1	1
University of Washington.	99,965	146,179	245,288	4	4	2
Stanford University	106,073	174,961	237,842	3	3	3
Massachusetts Institute of Technology.	146,035	189,558	232,619	2	2	4
University of California—Los Angeles.	94,945	128,211	194,217	5	5	5
University of Michigan.	73,999	108,035	193,954	11	11	6
University of California—San Diego	91,403	103,633	182,815	6	13	7
University of Wisconsin—Madison	86,918	124,604	179,079	8	7	8
University of California—San Francisco	64,814	98,536	178,698	15	16	9
University of Pennsylvania	76,136	103,119	169,352	10	15	10
University of Minnesota.	72,001	103,272	168,962	14	14	11
Harvard University	87,830	109,414	161,719	7	9	12
Cornell University	72,671	119,966	156,151	13	8	13
Yale University.	73,526	109,227	152,513	12	10	14
University of Pittsburgh	38,512	58,620	147,757	29	28	15
Pennsylvania State University.	47,099	76,726	144,400	21	19	16
University of California—Berkeley	64,065	106,710	136,020	16	12	17
Columbia University—Main Division	83,659	127,331	134,329	9	6	18
University of Southern California	49,221	89,706	133,074	20	17	19
Duke University	44,287	69,169	128,098	23	26	20
University of Colorado.	46,146	71,424	126,090	22	23	21
Washington University.	54,170	71,978	125,282	17	22	22
University of North Carolina at Chapel Hill	38,447	63,105	111,501	30	27	23
University of Illinois—Urbana	53,583	83,122	110,509	19	18	24
University of Rochester.	42,983	70,379	103,510	25	25	25
University of Chicago	53,992	71,194	97,949	18	24	26
University of Arizona.	36,308	49,740	95,206	33	37	27
University of Texas at Austin	43,756	72,379	95,063	24	21	28
University of Alabama—Birmingham	29,970	44,093	90,355	44	46	29
Case Western Reserve University	33,744	47,994	87,747	38	40	30
New York University	40,636	74,577	86,150	28	20	31
University of Iowa.	35,300	55,111	85,113	34	31	32
Baylor College of Medicine	35,062	45,837	82,849	35	45	33
Ohio State University	42,899	56,065	82,106	26	30	34
California Institute of Technology	32,959	55,083	80,585	40	32	35
University of California—Davis	31,757	43,156	79,671	42	47	36
University of Massachusetts.	22,418	46,046	76,630	55	44	37
Vanderbilt University.	27,426	39,909	76,437	49	48	38
University of Maryland—College Park.	27,313	51,073	72,115	50	35	39
Yeshiva University	42,590	56,988	72,115	27	29	40

X Not applicable.   [1] Includes other institutions, not shown separately.

Source: U.S. National Science Foundation, *Federal Support to Universities and Colleges and Nonprofit Institutions,* annual.

No. 974. Funds for Performance of Industrial R&D, by Source of Funds and Selected Industries: 1970 to 1991

[In millions of dollars. For calendar years. Covers basic research, applied research, and development. See also *Historical Statistics, Colonial Times to 1970*, series W 144-160]

INDUSTRY	1972 SIC[1] code	1970	1975	1980	1985	1990	1991
CURRENT DOLLARS							
Total funds	(X)	18,067	24,187	44,505	84,239	104,606	102,246
Chemicals and allied products	28	1,773	2,727	4,636	8,540	12,344	13,183
Petroleum refining and extraction	13,29	515	693	1,552	(D)	2,129	2,245
Machinery	35	1,729	3,196	5,901	12,216	(D)	(D)
Electrical equipment	36	4,220	5,105	9,175	14,432	17,723	17,279
Motor vehicles and motor vehicles equipment	371	1,591	2,340	4,955	6,984	(D)	(D)
Aircraft and missiles	372,376	5,219	5,713	9,198	22,231	25,356	21,692
Professional and scientific instruments	38	744	1,173	3,029	5,013	6,194	6,621
All other [2]	(X)	2,276	3,240	6,059	(D)	(D)	(D)
Company funds	(X)	10,288	15,582	30,476	57,043	73,980	76,938
Chemicals and allied products	28	1,593	2,490	4,264	8,310	12,277	13,094
Petroleum refining and extraction	13,29	493	(D)	1,401	2,194	2,113	2,235
Machinery	35	1,469	2687	5,254	10,701	13,780	14,034
Electrical equipment	36	2,008	2,798	5,431	9,271	12,131	12,455
Motor vehicles and motor vehicles equipment	371	1,278	2,022	4,300	6,164	8,548	8,998
Aircraft and missiles	372,376	1,213	1,285	2,570	5,649	6,140	6,588
Professional and scientific instruments	38	550	1,001	2,456	4,622	6,095	6,521
All other [2]	(X)	1,684	(D)	4,800	10,132	12,896	13,013
CONSTANT (1987) DOLLARS [3]							
Total funds	(X)	51,327	49,161	62,071	89,236	92,408	86,796
Chemicals and allied products	28	5,037	5,543	6,466	9,047	10,905	11,191
Petroleum refining and extraction	13,29	1,463	1,409	2,165	(D)	1,881	1,906
Machinery	35	4,912	6,496	8,230	12,941	(D)	(D)
Electrical equipment	36	11,989	10,376	12,796	15,288	15,656	14,668
Motor vehicles and motor vehicles equipment	371	4,520	4,756	6,911	7,398	(D)	(D)
Aircraft and missiles	372,376	14,827	11,612	12,828	23,550	22,399	18,414
Professional and scientific instruments	38	2,114	2,384	4,225	5,310	5,472	5,621
All other [2]	(X)	6,466	6,585	8,450	(D)	(D)	(D)
Company funds	(X)	29,227	31,671	42,505	60,427	65,353	65,312
Chemicals and allied products	28	4,526	5,061	5,947	8,803	10,845	11,115
Petroleum refining and extraction	13,29	1,401	(D)	1,954	2,324	1,867	1,897
Machinery	35	4,173	5,461	7,328	11,336	12,173	11,913
Electrical equipment	36	5,705	5,687	7,575	9,821	10,716	10,573
Motor vehicles and motor vehicles equipment	371	3,631	4,110	5,997	6,530	7,551	7,638
Aircraft and missiles	372,376	3,446	2,612	3,584	5,984	5,424	5,593
Professional and scientific instruments	38	1,563	2,035	3,425	4,896	5,384	5,536
All other [2]	(X)	4,784	(D)	6,695	10,733	11,392	11,047

D Figure withheld to avoid disclosure of information pertaining to a specific organization or individual. X Not applicable. [1] 1972 Standard Industrial Classification; see text, section 13. [2] All other manufacturing and nonmanufacturing. [3] Based on gross domestic product implicit price deflator.

Source: U.S. National Science Foundation, *Research and Development in Industry*, annual.

No. 975. R&D Funds in R&D-Performing Manufacturing Companies, by Industry: 1970 to 1991

INDUSTRY	1972 SIC[1] code	TOTAL R&D FUNDS AS A PERCENT OF NET SALES					COMPANY R&D FUNDS AS A PERCENT OF NET SALES				
		1970	1980	1985	1990	1991	1970	1980	1985	1990	1991
Total [2]	(X)	3.7	3.0	4.4	4.7	4.7	2.2	2.1	3.0	3.3	3.5
Food and kindred products [3]	20	0.5	0.4	(D)	(D)	0.5	0.5	(D)	0.6	0.5	0.5
Paper and allied products	26	0.9	1.0	(D)	0.8	0.8	(D)	1.0	0.8	0.8	0.8
Chemicals and allied products	28	3.9	3.6	5.0	5.6	5.7	3.5	3.3	4.9	5.6	5.7
Petroleum refining and extraction	13,29	1.0	0.6	(D)	1.0	1.1	0.9	0.5	0.9	1.0	1.1
Rubber products	30	2.3	2.2	(D)	(D)	(D)	1.7	(D)	1.8	1.7	1.8
Stone, clay, and glass products	32	1.8	1.4	(D)	(D)	(D)	1.7	1.3	2.3	2.4	2.6
Primary metals	33	0.8	0.7	(D)	(D)	1.1	0.8	0.5	0.9	1.0	1.1
Fabricated metal products	34	1.2	1.4	1.5	1.2	1.2	1.1	1.2	1.4	1.0	1.0
Machinery	35	4.0	5.0	7.6	8.9	9.9	3.4	4.5	6.7	8.3	9.2
Electrical equipment	36	7.3	6.6	7.6	6.9	6.6	3.4	3.9	4.8	4.7	4.7
Motor vehicles and motor vehicle equipment	371	3.5	4.9	3.8	(D)	(D)	2.8	4.2	3.1	3.9	4.5
Aircraft and missiles	372,376	16.2	13.7	14.9	14.3	12.5	3.8	3.8	3.9	3.5	3.8
Professional and scientific instruments	38	5.7	7.5	8.9	7.8	7.9	4.2	6.1	8.3	7.6	7.8

D Figure withheld to avoid disclosure of information pertaining to a specific organization or individual. X Not applicable. [1] 1972 Standard Industrial Classification; see text, section 13. [2] Includes all manufacturing industries. [3] Includes tobacco products (SIC 21) beginning 1985.

Source: U.S. National Science Foundation, *Research and Development in Industry*, annual.

No. 976. Federal Obligations for Research, by Field of Science: 1980 to 1993

[In millions of dollars. For fiscal years ending in year shown; see text, section 9. Excludes R&D plant]

FIELD	1980	1985	1987	1988	1989	1990	1991	1992, est.	1993, est.
CURRENT DOLLARS									
Research, total	**11,597**	**16,133**	**17,941**	**18,650**	**20,766**	**21,731**	**23,968**	**26,196**	**27,899**
Basic	4,674	7,819	8,942	9,474	10,602	11,286	12,171	13,254	14,184
Applied	6,923	8,315	8,998	9,177	10,164	10,446	11,798	12,941	13,715
Life sciences	4,192	6,363	7,341	7,725	8,495	8,830	9,622	10,589	11,338
Psychology	199	327	370	390	422	449	482	521	571
Physical sciences	2,001	3,046	3,253	3,317	3,705	3,809	4,235	4,534	4,790
Environmental sciences	1,261	1,404	1,512	1,607	1,773	2,174	2,150	2,360	2,503
Mathematics and computer sciences . . .	241	575	641	643	735	841	904	1,154	1,212
Engineering	2,830	3,618	3,906	3,956	4,442	4,335	4,945	5,488	5,935
Social sciences	524	460	480	486	551	630	727	790	718
Other sciences, n.e.c. [1]	350	342	438	527	642	664	903	760	832
CONSTANT (1987) DOLLARS [2]									
Research, total	**16,427**	**17,109**	**17,941**	**18,002**	**19,192**	**19,282**	**20,521**	**21,812**	**22,682**
Basic	6,621	8,291	8,942	9,144	9,799	10,014	10,420	11,036	11,532
Applied	9,806	8,817	8,998	8,858	9,394	9,269	10,101	10,775	11,150
Life sciences	5,938	6,747	7,341	7,457	7,851	7,835	8,238	8,817	9,218
Psychology	282	347	370	376	390	398	413	434	464
Physical sciences	2,834	3,230	3,253	3,202	3,424	3,380	3,626	3,775	3,894
Environmental sciences	1,786	1,489	1,512	1,551	1,639	1,929	1,841	1,965	2,035
Mathematics and computer sciences . . .	341	610	641	621	679	746	774	961	985
Engineering	4,009	3,836	3,906	3,819	4,105	3,846	4,234	4,570	4,825
Social sciences	742	488	480	469	509	559	622	658	584
Other sciences, n.e.c. [1]	495	362	438	508	593	589	773	633	676

[1] N.e.c. = Not elsewhere classified.   [2] Based on gross domestic product implicit price deflator.

Source: U.S. National Science Foundation, *Federal Funds for Research and Development*, annual.

No. 977. R&D Scientists and Engineers— Employment and Cost, by Industry: 1975 to 1991

[Data are estimates; on average full-time-equivalent (FTE) basis. See *Historical Statistics, Colonial Times to 1970*, series W 167, for total cost per scientist or engineer]

INDUSTRY	1972 SIC[1] code	1975	1980	1985	1986	1987	1988	1989	1990	1991
EMPLOYED SCIENTISTS										
Average FTE of scientists and engineers (1,000) [2] [3]	(X)	363.9	469.2	646.8	684.2	702.2	714.4	726.0	717.5	693.9
Chemicals [4]	28	44.8	53.1	73.5	74.4	75.5	76.7	78.3	78.9	80.5
Machinery	35	54.3	65.7	85.7	93.1	97.1	99.1	106.1	109.8	101.3
Electrical equipment [5]	36	81.5	100.7	115.6	123.1	131.5	136.6	139.3	137.9	141.2
Motor vehicles	371	25.7	36.7	31.3	42.1	46.9	46.6	47.8	47.6	45.2
Aircraft and missiles	372,376	67.2	90.6	137.5	137.5	136.4	139.4	135.4	123.2	116.7
CONSTANT (1987) DOLLARS [6]										
Cost per scientist or engineer ($1,000) [3] [7]	(X)	135.2	132.3	138.0	132.6	131.2	131.9	129.7	128.8	125.1
Chemicals [4]	28	123.8	121.9	123.2	120.8	127.6	135.2	135.2	138.3	139.0
Machinery	35	119.7	125.4	151.0	(D)	(D)	(D)	127.7	118.4	126.5
Electrical equipment [5]	36	127.5	127.0	132.4	124.5	120.6	114.5	112.2	113.5	104.0
Motor vehicles	371	185.2	188.5	236.4	(D)	(D)	(D)	(D)	(D)	(D)
Aircraft and missiles	372,376	173.0	141.7	171.3	154.6	179.4	179.0	174.7	181.9	157.8

D Withheld to avoid disclosure.   X Not applicable.   [1] 1972 Standard Industrial Classification; see text, section 13.   [2] The mean number of FTE R&D scientists and engineers employed in January of the year shown and the following January.   [3] Includes industries not shown separately.   [4] Includes allied products.   [5] Includes communication.   [6] Based on gross domestic product implicit price deflator.   [7] Represents the arithmetic mean of the numbers of R&D scientists and engineers reported in each industry for January in 2 consecutive years divided into total R&D expenditures in each industry.

Source: U.S. National Science Foundation, *Research and Development in Industry*, annual.

No. 978. Scientists and Engineers Employed in R&D: 1970 to 1989

[For full-time equivalent employees. Data are estimates. Yearly averages for industry sector only. Excludes those employed by State and local government agencies]

SECTOR	1970	1980	1983	1984	1985	1986	1987	1988	1989
Total (1,000)	543.8	651.1	751.6	797.6	841.6	882.3	910.2	927.3	949.3
PERCENT DISTRIBUTION									
Industry (excl. social scientists)	69.1	72.1	74.8	75.6	76.9	77.5	77.1	77.0	76.5
Federal Government	12.4	9.0	8.2	7.8	6.5	6.2	6.3	6.2	6.3
Other [1]	18.5	18.9	17.0	16.6	16.6	16.4	16.5	16.7	17.2

[1] Includes professional R&D personnel employed at universities and colleges, other nonprofit institutions, and federally funded R&D centers administered by organizations in these sectors and graduate students engaged in R&D at universities and colleges.

Source: U.S. National Science Foundation, National Patterns of R&D Resources, annual.

No. 979. Civilian Employment of Scientists, Engineers, and Technicians, by Occupation and Industry: 1992

[In thousands. Based on sample and subject to sampling error. For details, see source]

OCCUPATION	Total [1]	WAGE AND SALARY WORKERS									Self employed
		Mining [2]	Construction	Manufacturing	Transportation [3]	Trade	FIRE [4]	Services	Government		
Scientists and engineers . .	2,673.7	41.6	27.1	913.5	108.4	86.8	99.3	761.1	461.6		163.0
Scientists	1,319.8	19.5	1.2	272.8	33.1	30.8	88.0	458.9	271.7		134.0
Physical scientists	197.5	14.8	0.1	59.4	3.2	2.5	0.6	65.3	45.2		6.0
Life scientists	182.1	0.1	-	27.6	0.9	1.7	(NA)	57.7	72.9		12.0
Mathematical scientists	16.3	-	-	1.5	-	0.7	-	1.6	7.4		5.1
Social scientists	257.8	0.3	-	-	-	1.3	-	7.7	99.0		84.0
Computer systems analysts, engineers and scientists	666.2	4.2	1.1	184.4	26.9	26.5	78.1	229.5	83.3		32.0
Engineers [5]	1,353.8	22.2	25.9	640.7	75.4	56.0	11.3	302.2	189.9		29.0
Civil engineers	172.8	1.1	10.9	8.3	6.2	0.5	0.9	66.2	73.7		5.0
Electrical/electronics	369.9	0.9	5.8	167.6	34.5	35.5	1.1	78.7	39.8		6.0
Mechanical engineers	227.0	1.7	4.0	136.6	5.1	7.1	1.3	52.3	13.8		5.0
Engineering and science technicians	1,253.1	19.2	25.5	449.5	74.0	84.4	5.1	400.3	160.8		26.0
Electrical/electronics technicians	322.8	1.6	5.1	128.0	26.0	62.1	1.8	67.3	26.7		4.0
Engineering technicians	372.1	5.4	4.5	132.0	26.6	11.4	0.3	94.7	90.4		6.0
Drafters	314.2	2.7	15.9	100.1	17.5	6.6	1.1	144.9	11.3		12.0
Science technicians	244.1	9.5	-	89.3	3.9	4.3	1.9	93.4	32.4		4.0
Surveyors	99.3	2.6	3.3	-	-	3.3	-	0.6	55.9	23.0	10.0
Computer programmers	554.7	3.4	1.3	80.8	24.1	57.0	75.4	246.1	50.1		16.0

- Represents or rounds to zero. NA Not available. [1] Includes agriculture, forestry, and fishing not shown separately.
[2] Includes oil and gas extraction. [3] Includes communications and public utilities. [4] Finance, insurance, and real estate.
[5] Includes kinds of engineers and technicians not shown separately.

Source: U.S. Bureau of Labor Statistics, Monthly Labor Review, November 1993. (Data collected biennially.)

No. 980. Graduate Science/Engineering Students in Doctorate-Granting Colleges: 1985 to 1992

[As of fall. Includes outlying areas]

FIELD OF SCIENCE OR ENGINEERING	TOTAL (1,000)			PERCENT—							
				Female			Foreign		Part-time		
	1985	1990	1992	1985	1990	1992	1990	1992	1985	1990	1992
Total, all surveyed fields	353.8	394.8	427.8	34.5	37.5	38.6	25.6	25.1	32.2	30.7	29.9
Science/engineering	314.8	347.4	374.8	29.4	32.2	33.2	27.9	27.5	30.4	28.5	27.7
Engineering, total	89.7	99.1	108.3	11.5	13.6	14.4	36.7	36.3	39.5	35.6	33.7
Sciences, total	225.1	248.2	266.5	36.6	39.6	40.8	24.3	23.9	26.8	25.6	25.3
Physical sciences	29.4	32.4	33.6	20.5	23.4	24.5	37.1	36.8	11.7	11.2	10.7
Environmental	14.3	13.0	14.0	25.4	29.2	31.0	20.1	21.0	23.9	23.6	24.3
Mathematical sciences . . .	15.2	17.2	17.9	29.1	30.4	31.2	36.1	33.9	26.9	23.4	22.4
Computer sciences	23.4	27.4	29.0	24.9	22.8	21.8	33.2	35.0	48.0	46.6	46.4
Agricultural sciences	10.7	10.4	10.9	25.6	29.2	31.5	29.1	27.8	18.2	17.7	18.2
Biological sciences	42.1	46.2	50.2	42.4	45.5	46.3	24.2	24.9	16.0	14.6	14.8
Psychology	30.4	34.7	37.7	59.7	65.5	67.3	4.6	4.7	30.1	24.4	27.9
Social sciences	59.6	66.8	73.2	39.7	42.9	44.1	21.9	20.4	34.1	32.4	31.3
Health fields, total	39.0	47.4	53.0	75.5	76.6	76.4	8.6	8.1	46.2	47.1	45.7

Source: U.S. National Science Foundation, Survey of Graduate Science Engineering Students and Postdoctorates, annual.

No. 981. Science and Engineering Degree Recipients in 1988 and 1989: 1990

[Based on survey and subject to sampling error; see source for details]

DEGREE AND FIELD	Graduates 1988 and 1989 (1,000)	1990—PERCENT DISTRIBUTION				Median salary ($1,000)
		In school [1]	Employed		Not employed	
			In S&E [2]	In other		
Bachelor's recipients	643.2	20	44	32	5	26.0
All science fields	494.5	22	35	38	5	23.8
Physical sciences	29.4	39	38	18	5	25.1
Math/statistics	35.2	18	50	26	6	23.6
Computer science	69.3	6	77	13	4	30.1
Environmental science	7.3	30	49	15	5	23.7
Life sciences	111.2	32	34	28	6	21.0
Psychology	85.7	21	20	54	5	18.6
Social sciences	156.4	20	19	55	5	21.9
All engineering fields [3]	148.7	11	73	12	3	33.0
Civil	15.2	10	78	9	3	30.1
Electrical/electronics	55.5	11	76	10	3	34.0
Industrial	12.3	5	72	18	5	31.1
Mechanical	30.0	11	76	10	4	34.0
Master's recipients	136.6	23	61	13	4	37.0
All science fields	93.7	25	55	16	4	33.8
Physical sciences	9.2	41	49	8	2	34.9
Math/statistics	10.6	18	67	13	2	32.8
Computer science	22.2	9	78	10	3	42.1
Environmental science	5.2	21	71	6	2	33.8
Life sciences	19.3	35	47	15	4	26.9
Psychology	7.3	34	36	26	4	32.0
Social sciences	19.9	26	37	30	7	31.0
All engineering fields [3]	42.9	17	73	6	3	41.4
Civil	4.7	11	85	4	-	35.2
Electrical/electronics	13.8	19	72	4	5	46.5
Industrial	2.6	8	62	23	8	40.3
Mechanical	8.0	15	79	5	1	42.1

[1] Full-time graduate students. [2] In science and engineering. [3] Includes other fields, not shown separately.

Source: National Science Foundation/SRS, *Characteristics of Recent Science and Engineering Graduates: 1990.* (Data are biennial.)

No. 982. Doctorates Conferred, by Recipients' Characteristics: 1980 and 1992

[In percent, except as indicated]

CHARACTERISTIC	1980, total	1992									
		All fields [1]	Engineering	Physical sciences [2]	Earth sciences	Mathematics	Computer sciences	Biological sciences [3]	Agricultural	Social sciences [4]	Psychology
Total conferred (number)	31,020	38,814	5,437	3,749	824	1,058	867	4,794	1,063	3,338	3,253
Male	69.7	63.0	90.7	79.6	76.7	80.6	86.2	61.9	78.1	64.6	41.1
Female	30.3	37.0	9.3	20.4	23.3	19.4	13.8	38.1	21.9	35.4	58.9
Median age [5]	32.2	34.1	31.5	29.9	32.7	31.4	32.0	31.5	34.1	35.3	34.1
CITIZENSHIP [6]											
Total conferred (number)	30,156	37,605	5,245	3,654	801	1,016	850	4,683	1,036	3,256	3,096
U.S. citizen	83.6	68.5	40.1	58.2	65.3	44.5	49.2	70.4	49.1	60.7	92.4
Foreign citizen	16.4	31.5	59.1	41.8	34.7	55.5	50.8	29.6	50.9	39.3	7.6
RACE/ETHNICITY [7]											
Total conferred (number)	26,512	27,717	2,510	2,325	558	505	486	3,535	570	2,192	2,939
White [8]	84.7	84.5	74.7	83.6	89.6	83.8	77.4	86.1	86.1	82.6	88.8
Black [8]	4.2	3.9	1.9	1.0	1.3	0.8	1.0	1.7	2.1	5.5	3.4
Asian/Pacific [8]	4.2	6.2	17.8	9.6	4.8	10.1	17.7	7.4	6.3	5.9	1.9
Indian/Alaskan [8]	0.3	0.5	0.4	0.5	0.2	0.4	0.4	0.4	0.0	0.6	0.5
Hispanic	1.8	3.1	2.9	3.1	2.9	2.4	1.6	2.8	3.3	3.4	4.0
Other/unknown	4.9	1.6	2.3	2.1	1.3	2.6	1.9	1.6	2.1	2.0	1.3

[1] Includes other fields, not shown separately. [2] Astronomy, physics, and chemistry. [3] Biochemistry, botany, microbiology, physiology, zoology, and related fields. [4] Anthropology, sociology, political science, economics, and international relations and related fields. [5] For definition of median, see Guide to Tabular Presentation. [6] For those with known citizenship. Includes those with temporary visas. [7] Excludes those with temporary visas. [8] Non-Hispanic.

Source: U.S. National Science Foundation, Division of Science Resources Studies, Survey of Earned Doctorates, *Selected Data on Science and Engineering Doctorate Awards: 1992,* annual.

No. 983. Space Vehicle Systems—Net Sales and Backlog Orders: 1965 to 1992

[In millions of dollars. Backlog orders as of Dec. 31. Based on data from major companies engaged in manufacture of aerospace products. Includes parts but excludes engines and propulsion units]

YEAR	NET SALES			BACKLOG ORDERS			YEAR	NET SALES			BACKLOG ORDERS		
	Total	Military	Non-military	Total	Military	Non-military		Total	Military	Non-military	Total	Military	Non-military
1965. .	2,449	602	1,847	2,203	503	1,700	1985. .	6,300	4,241	2,059	6,707	4,941	1,766
1970. .	1,956	1,025	931	1,184	786	398	1986. .	6,304	4,579	[1]1,725	8,063	6,028	[1]2,035
1975. .	2,119	1,096	1,023	1,304	1,019	285	1987. .	8,051	5,248	[1]2,803	12,393	9,460	[1]2,933
1980. .	3,483	1,461	2,022	1,814	951	863	1988. .	8,622	6,190	[1]2,432	10,838	7,880	[1]2,958
1981. .	3,856	1,736	2,120	3,174	2,164	1,010	1989. .	9,758	6,457	[1]3,301	13,356	9,192	[1]4,164
1982. .	4,749	2,606	2,143	4,337	2,403	1,934	1990. .	9,691	6,556	[1]3,135	12,462	8,130	[1]4,332
1983. .	4,940	2,420	2,520	4,865	2,733	2,132	1991. .	10,515	6,770	[1]3,745	11,664	6,221	[1]5,443
1984. .	5,225	3,019	2,206	4,624	3,099	1,525	1992. .	10,029	5,887	[1]4,142	13,483	7,726	[1]5,757

[1] Includes data for nonmilitary missile systems and parts.

Source: U.S. Bureau of the Census, Current Industrial Reports, MA-37D, Aerospace Industry (Orders, Sales, and Backlog).

No. 984. Federal Space Program—Budget Authority, by Agency: 1960 to 1991

[In millions of dollars, except percent. For fiscal years ending in year shown; see text, section 9. NASA=National Aeronautics and Space Administration]

YEAR	Total	NASA [1]		DEFENSE		Other	YEAR	Total	NASA [1]		DEFENSE		Other
		Total	Percent of total	Total	Percent of total				Total	Percent of total	Total	Percent of total	
1960 . . .	1,066	462	43.3	561	52.6	43	1980 . . .	8,689	4,680	53.9	3,848	44.3	160
1965 . . .	6,956	5,138	73.9	1,574	22.6	244	1981 . . .	9,978	4,992	50.0	4,828	48.4	158
1970 . . .	5,341	3,547	66.4	1,678	31.4	115	1982 . . .	12,441	5,528	44.4	6,679	53.7	234
1971 . . .	4,741	3,101	65.4	1,512	31.9	127	1983 . . .	15,589	6,328	40.6	9,019	57.9	242
1972 . . .	4,575	3,071	67.1	1,407	30.8	97	1984 . . .	17,136	6,648	38.8	10,195	59.5	293
1973 . . .	4,825	3,093	64.1	1,623	33.6	109	1985 . . .	20,167	6,925	34.3	12,768	63.3	474
1974 . . .	4,640	2,759	59.4	1,766	38.1	116	1986 . . .	21,659	[3]9,809	33.1	14,126	65.2	368
1975 . . .	4,914	2,915	59.3	1,892	38.5	107	1987 . . .	26,448	9,809	37.1	16,287	61.6	352
1976 [2] . . .	6,660	4,075	61.2	2,444	36.7	142	1988 . . .	26,607	8,302	31.2	17,679	66.4	626
1977 . . .	5,983	3,440	57.5	2,412	40.3	131	1989 . . .	28,443	10,098	35.5	17,906	63.0	440
1978 . . .	6,518	3,623	55.6	2,738	42.0	157	1990 . . .	28,089	12,142	43.2	15,616	55.6	330
1979 . . .	7,244	4,030	55.6	3,036	41.9	178	1991 . . .	27,592	13,036	47.2	14,181	51.4	375

[1] Includes budget authority for the space transportation system of $3.1 billion in 1982; $4.1 billion in 1983; and $4.0 billion in 1984.   [2] Includes transition quarter, July 1 to Sept. 30, 1976.   [3] Includes $2.1 billion for replacement of shuttle orbiter Challenger.

Source: U.S. National Aeronautics and Space Administration, Aeronautics and Space Report of the President, annual. Data from U.S. Office of Management and Budget.

No. 985. NASA Financial Summary: 1970 to 1994

[In millions of dollars. For fiscal year ending in year shown; see text, section 9]

YEAR	TOTAL		R&D		COMMUNICA-TIONS [1]		FACILITIES CONSTRUCTION		RESEARCH AND PROGRAM DEVELOPMENT	
	Appro-priations	Outlays	Appro-priations	Outlays	Appro-priations	Outlays	Appro-priations	Outlays	Appro-priations	Outlays
1970	3,749	3,753	3,006	2,992	-	-	53	54	690	707
1975	3,231	3,267	2,331	2,420	-	-	140	85	760	761
1980	5,243	4,852	4,091	3,701	-	-	156	140	996	1,010
1985	7,552	7,318	2,468	2,118	3,602	3,707	150	170	1,332	1,323
1986	7,764	7,404	2,638	2,615	3,689	3,267	133	189	1,303	1,332
1987	10,621	7,592	3,166	2,436	5,561	3,597	469	149	1,425	1,409
1988	9,002	9,092	3,414	2,916	3,908	4,362	178	166	1,501	1,648
1989	10,898	11,051	4,267	3,922	4,464	5,030	305	190	1,862	1,908
1990 [2]	12,296	12,428	5,221	5,094	4,555	5,117	588	218	1,923	1,991
1991 [2]	15,078	13,877	6,024	5,766	6,334	5,590	498	326	2,212	2,185
1992 [2]	14,302	13,818	6,396	6,261	5,124	5,311	525	448	2,242	1,784
1993, est. [2] .	14,330	(NA)	7,089	(NA)	5,086	(NA)	525	(NA)	1,615	(NA)
1994, est. [2] .	14,551	(NA)	7,529	(NA)	4,854	(NA)	518	(NA)	1,636	(NA)

- Represents zero.   NA Not available.   [1] Space flight, control, and data communications.   [2] Include appropriations and outlays for the Inspector General, not shown separately.

Source: U.S. National Aeronautics and Space Administration, 1995 Budget Summary.

No. 986. National Aeronautics and Space Administration—Budget Summary: 1993 to 1995

[In millions of dollars. Data represent budget authority for fiscal years]

ITEM	1993	1994	1995
Total	**14,322.5**	**14,551.4**	**14,300.0**
Human space flight	6,672.0	6,069.7	5,719.9
Space station	2,162.0	1,937.0	1,889.6
Russian cooperation	79.5	170.8	150.1
Space shuttle	3,988.2	3,549.3	3,324.0
Payload and utilization operations	442.3	412.6	356.2
Science, aeronautics and technology	4,908.7	5,847.3	5,901.2
Space science	1,510.4	1,721.9	1,766.0
Life and microgravity sciences and applications	407.5	515.3	470.9
Mission to planet earth	936.3	1,024.5	1,238.1
Aeronautical research and technology	769.4	1,102.2	898.5
Advanced concepts and technology	464.9	495.3	608.4
Launch services	180.8	313.5	340.9
Mission communication services	546.5	589.1	481.2
Academic programs	92.9	85.5	97.2
Mission support	2,727.2	2,619.0	2,662.9
Safety, reliability and quality assurance	32.7	34.3	38.7
Space communication services	333.7	214.4	268.9
Research and program management	2,171.4	2,148.2	2,220.3
Construction of facilities	189.4	222.1	135.0
Inspector General	14.6	15.4	16.0

Source: U.S. National Aeronautics and Space Administration, *1995 Budget Summary.*

No. 987. U.S. Commercial Space Revenues: 1990 to 1994

[In millions of dollars. For calendar years]

INDUSTRY	1990	1991	1992	1993	1994 [1]
Total	**3,385**	**4,370**	**4,860**	**5,295**	**6,490**
Commercial satellites delivered	1,000	1,300	1,300	1,100	1,400
Satellite services	800	1,200	1,500	1,850	2,300
Fixed	735	1,115	1,275	1,600	1,950
Mobile	65	85	225	250	350
Satellite ground equipment	860	1,300	1,400	1,600	1,850
Mobile-equipment	145	280	350	420	480
Commercial launches	570	380	450	465	580
Remote sensing data and services	155	190	210	250	300
Commercial R&D infrastructure	-	-	-	30	60

- Represents zero.   [1] Forecast.

Source: U.S. Department of Commerce, International Trade Administration, *U.S. Industrial Outlook, 1994.*

No. 988. NASA Space Shuttle Operations Expenditures: 1993 to 1995

[In millions of dollars. Data are funding requirements fiscal years shown]

OPERATION	1993	1994	1995
Total	**2,857.2**	**2,570.6**	**2,420.1**
Orbiter	477.0	364.1	292.8
System integration	200.6	211.2	190.5
External tank	300.2	305.3	379.6
Space shuttle main engine	239.9	191.8	144.4
Redesigned solid rocket	409.4	368.9	373.1
Solid rocket booster	172.0	156.4	144.9
Launch and landing operations	697.1	650.1	596.4
Mission and crew operations	361.0	322.8	298.4

Source: U.S. National Aeronautics and Space Administration, *1995 Budget Summary.*

No. 989. Space Shuttle Flights—Summary: 1981 to June 1994

FLIGHT NUMBER	Date	Mission/ Orbiter name	Days duration	FLIGHT NUMBER	Date	Mission/ Orbiter name	Days duration
1	4/12/81	Columbia	2	33	11/22/89	Discovery	5
4	6/27/81	Columbia	7	32	1/9/90	Columbia	10
2	11/12/81	Columbia	2	36	2/28/90	Atlantis	5
3	3/22/82	Columbia	8	31	4/24/90	Discovery	6
5	11/11/82	Columbia	5	41	10/6/90	Discovery	4
6	4/4/83	Challenger	5	38	11/15/90	Atlantis	4
7	6/18/83	Challenger	6	35	12/2/90	Columbia	9
8	8/30/83	Challenger	6	39	4/28/91	Discovery	8
9	11/28/83	Columbia	10	37	4/5/91	Atlantis	6
10	2/3/84	Challenger	8	40	6/5/91	Columbia	9
11	4/6/84	Challenger	7	43	8/2/91	Atlantis	9
12	8/30/84	Discovery	6	44	11/24/91	Atlantis	7
13	10/5/84	Challenger	8	42	1/22/92	Discovery	8
14	11/8/84	Discovery	8	45	3/24/92	Atlantis	8
15	1/24/85	Discovery	3	49	5/7/92	Endeavour	8
16	4/12/85	Discovery	7	50	6/25/92	Columbia	13
17	4/29/85	Challenger	7	46	7/31/92	Atlantis	7
18	6/17/85	Discovery	7	47	9/12/92	Endeavour	7
19	7/29/85	Challenger	8	52	10/22/92	Columbia	9
20	8/27/85	Discovery	7	53	12/2/92	Discovery	7
21	10/3/85	Atlantis	4	54	1/13/93	Endeavour	6
22	10/30/85	Challenger	7	56	4/8/93	Discovery	9
23	11/26/85	Atlantis	7	55	4/26/93	Columbia	10
24	1/12/86	Columbia	6	57	6/21/93	Endeavour	10
25	1/28/86	Challenger	-	51	9/12/93	Discovery	10
26	9/29/88	Discovery	4	58	10/18/93	Columbia	14
27	12/2/88	Atlantis	4	61	12/2/93	Endeavour	11
29	3/13/89	Discovery	5	60	2/3/94	Discovery	8
30	5/4/89	Atlantis	4	62	3/4/94	Columbia	14
28	8/8/89	Columbia	5	59	4/9/94	Endeavour	11
34	10/18/89	Atlantis	5				

- Represents zero.

Source: U.S. National Aeronautics and Space Administration, *Payload Flight Assignments NASA Mixed Fleets*, January 1992, and "Space Shuttle Flights as of June 1994".

No. 990. World-Wide Successful Space Launches: 1957 to 1993

[Criterion of success is attainment of Earth orbit or Earth escape]

COUNTRY	Total	1957-1964	1965-1969	1970-1974	1975-1979	1980-1984	1985-1989	1989	1990	1991	1992	1993
Total	3,569	289	586	555	607	605	550	101	116	88	94	79
Soviet Union/CIS [1]	2,415	82	302	405	461	483	447	74	75	59	54	47
United States	1,001	207	279	139	126	93	61	18	27	18	28	23
Japan	45	-	-	5	10	12	11	2	3	2	1	1
ESA [2]	57	-	-	-	1	8	21	7	5	8	7	7
China: Mainland	33	-	-	2	6	6	9	-	5	1	3	1
France	10	-	4	3	3	-	-	-	-	-	-	-
India	4	-	-	-	-	3	-	-	-	-	1	-
Israel	2	-	-	-	-	-	1	-	1	-	-	-
Australia	1	-	1	-	-	-	-	-	-	-	-	-
United Kingdom	1	-	-	1	-	-	-	-	-	-	-	-

- Represents zero.   [1] Commonwealth of Independent States.   [2] European Space Agency.

Source: Library of Congress, Congressional Research Service, Science Policy Research Division, *Space Activities of the United States, CIS, and Other Launching Countries/Organizations 1957-1993*, March 29, 1994.

No. 991. Nobel Prize Laureates in Chemistry, Physics, and Physiology/ Medicine—Selected Countries: 1901 to 1992

[Presented by location of award-winning research and by date of award]

COUNTRY	1901-1992 Total	Physics	Chemistry	Physiology/ Medicine	1901-1915	1916-1930	1931-1945	1946-1960	1961-1975	1976-1992
Total	414	142	117	155	52	41	49	74	92	106
United States	165	57	37	71	3	3	14	38	41	66
United Kingdom	69	21	24	24	7	8	11	14	20	9
Germany [1]	59	17	28	14	15	12	11	4	8	9
France	24	10	7	7	10	3	2	-	5	4
Soviet Union	10	7	1	2	2	-	-	4	3	1
Japan	4	3	1	-	-	-	-	1	2	1
Other countries	83	27	19	37	15	15	11	13	13	16

- Represents zero.   [1] Between 1946 and 1991, data are for the former West Germany only.

Source: U.S. National Science Foundation, unpublished data.

Transportation—Land

This section presents statistics on revenues, passenger and freight traffic volume, and employment in various revenue-producing modes of the transportation industry, including motor vehicles, trains, and pipelines. Data are also presented on commuting travel, highway mileage and finances, motor vehicle travel, accidents, sales, and registrations, automobile operating costs, and characteristics of public transit, railroads, and pipelines.

In Brief

Transportation outlays reached $996 billion in 1992

State gasoline tax rates for 1993—
Lowest rate, 7.5 percent in Georgia
Highest rate, 29 percent in Connecticut

The principal compiler of data on public roads and on operation of motor vehicles is the U.S. Department of Transportation's (DOT) Federal Highway Administration (FHWA). These data appear in FHWA's annual *Highway Statistics* and other publications. The U.S. Interstate Commerce Commission (ICC) presents data on interstate land transport in its publications, the *Annual Report to Congress* and the *Transport Statistics in the United States,* which contain data on railroads and motor carriers subject to ICC regulations.

The U.S. National Highway Traffic Safety Administration issues data on traffic accident deaths and death rates in two annual reports: the *Fact Book* and the *Fatal Accident Reporting System Annual Report.* DOT's Federal Railroad Administration presents data on accidents involving railroads in its annual *Accident/Incident Bulletin,* and the *Rail-Highway Crossing Accident/Incident and Inventory Bulletin.*

Various censuses and surveys conducted by the U.S. Bureau of the Census also provide data. Results of the censuses of transportation are presented in the *Truck Inventory and Use Survey.* The *Annual Survey of Manufactures* and reports of the censuses of manufactures, wholesale and retail trade, and service industries contain statistics on the motor vehicle and equipment industry and on retail, wholesale, and services aspects of this industry. Data on persons commuting to work were collected as part of the 1980 census and are in various census reports.

Data are also presented in many nongovernment publications. Among them are the weekly and annual *Cars of Revenue Freight Loaded* and the annual *Yearbook of Railroad Facts,* both published by the Association of American Railroads, Washington, DC; and the *Transit Fact Book,* containing electric railway and motorbus statistics, published annually by the American Public Transit Association, Washington, DC. Useful annual handbooks in the field of transportation are *Motor Vehicle Facts and Figures* and *World Motor Vehicle Data,* issued by the American Automobile Manufacturers Association (AAMA), Detroit, MI; *Accident Facts,* issued by the National Safety Council, Chicago, IL; and *Transportation in America,* issued by the ENO Foundation for Transportation, Westport, Connecticut.

Urban and rural highway mileage.— Beginning in 1980, mileage is classified in urban and rural categories, rather than municipal and rural. Urban denotes the Federal-aid legislation definition of an area. Such areas include, as a minimum, a census place with a population of 5,000 to 49,999 or a designated urbanized area with a population of 50,000 or more. These Federal-aid urban areas may extend beyond corporate and census boundaries, and thus are not necessarily coextensive with municipal boundaries. Rural in 1980 refers to non-Federal-aid urban area mileage. Prior to 1980, municipal referred to roads within incorporated places, densely populated New England towns, and certain of the more populous unincorporated areas and rural to non-municipal roads.

Federal-aid Highway Systems.—The Intermodal Surface Transportation Efficiency Act (ISTEA of 1991 eliminated the historical Federal-aid Systems and created the National Highway System (NHS) and other Federal-aid highway categories. The final NHS has not been approved by Congress. In the interim, a system consisting of the Interstate, Other Freeways and Expressways, and Other Principal Arterial functional systems, serves as the NHS.

Functional Systems.—Roads and streets are assigned to groups according to the character of service they are intended to provide. The functional systems are: (1) arterial highways that generally handle the long trips, (2) collector facilities that collect and disperse traffiC between the arterials and the lower systems, and (3) local roads and streets that primarily serve direct access to residential areas.

Regulatory bodies.—The ICC, created by the U.S. Congress to regulate transportation in interstate commerce, has jurisdiction over railroads, trucking companies, bus lines, freight forwarders, water carriers, coal slurry pipelines, and transportation brokers. The Federal Energy Regulatory Commission is responsible for setting rates and charges for transportation and sale of natural gas and for establishing rates or charges for transportation.

Motor carriers.—For 1960-73, class I for-hire motor carriers of freight were classified by the ICC as those with $1 million or more of gross annual operating revenue; 1974-79, the class I minimum was $3 million. Effective January 1, 1980, class I carriers are those with $5 million or more in revenue. For 1960-68, class I motor carriers of passengers were classified by the ICC as those with $200,000 or more of gross annual operating revenue; for 1969-76, as those with revenues of $1 million or more; and since 1977, as those with $3 million or more. Effective January 1, 1988, class I motor carriers of passengers are those with $5 million or more in operating revenues; class II less than $5 million in operating revenues.

Railroads.—Railroad companies reporting to the ICC are divided into specific groups as follows: (1) Regular line-haul (interstate) railroads (and their non-operating subsidiaries); (2) switching and terminal railroads; (3) private railroads prior to 1964 (identified by ICC as "circular" because they reported on brief circulars); and (4) unofficial railroads, so designated when their reports are received too late for tabulation. For the most part, the last three groups are not included in the statistics shown here.

For years prior to 1978, class I railroads were those with annual revenues of $1 million or more for 1950-55; $3 million or more for 1956-64; $5 million or more for 1965-75; and $10 million or more for 1976-77. In 1978, the classification became class I, those having more than $50 million gross annual operating revenue; class II, from $10 million to $50 million; and class III, less than $10 million. Effective January 1, 1982, the ICC adopted a procedure to adjust the threshold for inflation by restating current revenues in constant 1978 dollars. In 1990, the criteria for class I and class II railroads were $94.4 million and $18.9 million, respectively. Also effective January 1, 1982, the ICC adopted a *Carrier Classification Index Survey Form* for carriers not filing annual report form R-1 with the commission. Effective January 1, 1992, the ICC adopted new revenue classification levels as follows: Class I–$250 million or more; Class II–less than $250 million but in excess of $20 million; Class III–$20 million or less. The inflation adjustment index still applies. Class II and class III railroads are currently exempted from filing any financial report with the Commission. The form is used for reclassifying carriers.

Statistical reliability.—For a discussion of statistical collection and estimation, sampling procedures, and measures of statistical reliability, see Appendix III.

Historical statistics.—Tabular headnotes provide cross-references, where applicable, to *Historical Statistics of the United States, Colonial Times to 1970.* See Appendix IV.

No. 992. Passenger and Freight Transportation Outlays, by Type of Transport: 1975 to 1992

[In billions of dollars. Freight data include outlays for mail and express. ICC=Interstate Commerce Commission]

TYPE OF TRANSPORT	1975	1979	1980	1981	1982	1983	1984	1985	1986	1987	1988	1989	1990	1991	1992
Total outlays [1]	298	492	543	593	591	643	716	753	761	808	869	916	965	952	996
Passenger, total	187	308	338	374	379	411	460	492	493	528	572	604	630	613	638
Private transportation	161	264	285	317	321	348	387	418	415	445	481	508	528	509	532
Automobiles [2]	157	257	277	307	313	340	379	410	407	436	472	498	517	499	522
New and used cars	46	73	73	83	86	105	126	139	157	151	164	164	166	153	164
Tires, tubes, accessories	12	20	22	25	25	26	27	30	29	21	23	24	25	26	26
Gasoline and oil	54	78	100	111	105	106	106	107	82	94	97	107	121	114	115
Insurance less claims	5	10	12	11	11	12	12	12	14	17	19	19	20	25	27
Interest on debt	7	15	18	21	22	20	25	27	27	29	34	37	36	32	26
Registration and operator's permit fees	2	3	3	4	4	4	5	5	6	6	6	7	7	7	7
Repair, greasing, washing, parking, tolls [3]	22	37	39	42	45	47	52	60	60	75	84	90	94	94	102
Air	5	7	8	9	8	7	8	8	8	9	10	10	10	10	10
For-hire transportation	26	43	53	57	59	63	72	74	77	84	91	96	103	104	107
Local [4]	11	15	20	22	23	24	27	27	30	31	32	33	34	36	36
Bus and transit [5]	5	8	9	10	11	12	13	14	15	15	16	16	17	18	18
School bus	5	3	4	5	5	5	6	6	6	7	7	7	8	8	8
Taxi	2	3	5	5	6	5	6	6	6	6	7	8	8	8	8
Intercity	13	23	28	30	30	33	39	40	40	44	48	51	53	53	53
Air	11	20	25	27	27	30	34	36	36	40	44	47	50	49	49
Rail [6]	1	1	2	2	2	2	2	2	2	2	2	2	2	2	2
Bus	1	1	2	2	2	2	2	2	2	2	2	2	2	2	2
International	3	5	5	5	5	6	7	7	7	9	11	12	15	14	16
Freight, total [4]	116	193	214	228	222	243	268	274	281	294	313	329	352	355	375
Highway	85	143	155	165	163	182	200	206	213	225	239	254	271	274	293
Truck, intercity	47	90	95	97	100	111	121	123	158	135	143	151	162	165	177
Truck, local	37	52	61	68	63	71	79	82	85	90	96	103	108	110	116
Rail	17	25	28	31	27	27	31	28	28	29	30	30	30	30	31
Water	8	13	16	17	16	16	16	18	19	19	20	20	21	20	20
Oil pipeline	2	6	8	9	9	9	9	9	8	9	8	8	8	8	9
Air carrier	2	3	4	4	4	5	6	7	8	9	10	12	14	14	15
Percent change, total	5.4	8.6	10.3	9.1	-0.2	8.8	11.3	5.2	1.0	6.1	7.6	5.4	5.4	-1.4	4.7
Passenger, total	9.4	7.0	9.9	10.6	1.4	8.3	11.9	7.1	-0.7	7.2	8.3	5.6	4.4	-2.7	4.1
Private transportation	9.2	5.6	7.9	11.2	1.3	8.4	11.4	8.0	-0.8	7.0	8.2	5.6	4.0	-3.5	4.5
Automobiles [2]	9.3	5.2	7.7	11.1	1.7	8.8	11.4	8.3	-0.8	7.1	8.1	5.6	3.9	-3.5	4.5
Air	6.8	22.4	14.1	16.0	-12.8	-9.8	10.8	-3.7	3.8	3.7	11.8	0.0	9.5	-2.9	1.0
For-hire transportation	11.0	15.2	23.3	7.3	2.1	2.1	14.2	2.4	4.6	8.2	8.7	5.8	6.7	1.3	2.5
Freight	-0.4	11.6	10.8	6.9	-2.8	9.5	10.2	2.1	2.7	4.7	6.4	5.1	6.9	1.0	5.6

[1] Total outlays less than sum of passenger and freight totals, as estimated freight costs included in costs of new cars, gasoline, oil, tires, and tubes have been excluded to prevent duplication. [2] Includes business-owned vehicles. [3] Includes storage and rental. [4] Includes items not shown separately. [5] Includes Federal, State, and local government operating subsidies and capital grants. [6] Includes Federal operating subsidies and capital grants for Amtrak.

Source: Eno Transportation Foundation, Inc., Lansdowne, VA, *Transportation in America*, annual (copyright).

No. 993. Employment and Earnings in Transportation, by Industry: 1980 to 1993

[Annual averages of monthly figures. Based on Current Employment Statistics program; see Appendix III. See also *Historical Statistics, Colonial Times to 1970,* series Q36-42]

INDUSTRY	SIC [1] code	1980	1985	1987	1988	1989	1990	1991	1992	1993
NUMBER (1,000)										
Total transportation.......	(X)	2,960	2,997	3,156	3,303	3,415	3,527	3,502	3,486	3,511
Railroads.................	40	532	359	309	298	293	279	262	254	250
Class I railroads...........	4011	482	323	271	259	252	241	231	222	218
Local and interurban passengers..	41	265	277	294	309	326	338	354	359	367
Trucking and warehousing	42	1,280	1,361	1,465	1,548	1,595	1,625	1,606	1,606	1,629
Water transportation..........	44	211	185	172	171	172	177	184	173	167
Air transportation	45	453	522	603	646	683	745	733	729	733
Pipelines, exc. natural gas	46	21	19	19	19	19	19	19	19	18
Transportation services	47	198	275	294	311	329	345	344	346	347
AVERAGE WEEKLY EARNINGS (dol.)										
Class I railroads...........	4011	427	595	627	674	693	727	707	736	782
Local and interurban passengers..	41	217	261	281	293	305	310	323	333	337
Trucking and warehousing	42	358	405	414	419	437	451	455	468	479
Pipelines, exc. natural gas	46	441	629	644	662	671	711	733	772	817

X Not applicable.　　[1] 1987 Standard Industrial Classification, see text, section 13.

Source: U.S. Bureau of Labor Statistics, Bulletin 2370 and, 2429 *Employment and Earnings,* March and June issues.

No. 994. Volume of Domestic Intercity Freight and Passenger Traffic, by Type of Transport: 1970 to 1992

[Freight traffic in bil. ton-miles; passenger traffic in bil. passenger-miles. A ton-mile is the movement of 1 ton (2,000 pounds) of freight for the distance of 1 mile. A passenger-mile is the movement of 1 passenger for the distance of 1 mile. Comprises public and private traffic, both revenue and nonrevenue. See also *Historical Statistics, Colonial Times to 1970,* series Q1-22]

TYPE OF TRANSPORT	TRAFFIC VOLUME						PERCENT DISTRIBUTION					
	1970	1980	1985	1990	1991	1992	1970	1980	1985	1990	1991	1992
Freight traffic, total.........	1,936	2,487	2,458	2,860	2,866	2,958	100.0	100.0	100.0	100.0	100.0	100.0
Railroads..........	771	932	895	1,071	1,077	1,107	39.8	37.5	36.4	37.4	37.6	37.4
Truck:												
ICC truck	167	242	250	311	320	342	8.6	9.7	10.2	10.9	11.2	11.6
Non-ICC truck.....	245	313	360	424	438	473	12.7	12.6	14.6	14.8	15.3	16.0
Water:												
Rivers/canals	205	311	306	373	359	370	10.6	12.5	12.4	13.0	12.5	12.5
Great Lakes	114	96	76	87	84	84	5.9	3.9	3.1	3.0	2.9	2.8
Oil pipelines.........	431	588	564	584	578	571	22.3	23.6	23.0	20.4	20.2	19.3
Domestic airways [1] ...	3	5	7	10	10	11	0.2	0.2	0.3	0.4	0.3	0.4
Passenger traffic, total....	1,181	1,467	1,635	1,993	2,011	2,066	100.0	100.0	100.0	100.0	100.0	100.0
Private automobiles...	1,026	1,210	1,310	1,598	1,623	1,663	86.9	82.5	80.1	80.2	80.7	80.5
Domestic airways [2] ...	119	219	290	359	351	367	10.1	14.9	17.7	18.1	17.4	17.7
Bus [3].............	25	27	24	23	24	24	2.1	1.8	1.5	1.2	1.2	1.1
Railroads [4]	11	11	11	13	14	14	0.9	0.8	0.7	0.7	0.7	0.7

[1] Revenue service only for scheduled and nonscheduled carriers, with small section 418 all-cargo carriers included from 1980. Includes express mail, and excess baggage.　　[2] Includes general aviation (mostly private business) flying.　　[3] Excludes school and urban transit buses.　　[4] Includes intercity (Amtrak) and rail commuter service.

Source: Eno Transportation Foundation, Inc., Lansdowne VA, *Transportation in America,* annual (copyright).

No. 995. Passenger Transportation Arrangement: 1990 to 1992

[In millions of dollars, except percent. Represents SIC 4722]

SOURCE OF RECEIPTS	1990	1991	1992	OPERATING EXPENSES	1990	1991	1992
Receipts, total [1] ...	9,036	8,547	8,968	Expenses, total [1].....	8,262	8,039	8,278
Air carriers	5,106	4,909	5,234	Payroll, annual	3,696	3,580	3,747
Water carriers	362	384	396	Employer contributions [2].	487	489	500
Hotels and motels	627	577	595	Lease and rental payments	676	666	671
Motor coaches........	279	288	282	Advertising and promotion	516	467	487
Railroads	79	83	78	Taxes and licenses	125	107	106
Rental cars..........	151	152	167	Utilities	268	267	289
Package tours	1,872	1,623	1,720	Depreciation.........	293	282	262
Other...............	560	531	496	Office Supplies	254	236	234
				Repair Services	99	93	89

[1] Receipts for firms primarily engaged in arranging passenger transportation. These estimates exclude receipts of transportation companies (airlines, railroads, etc.).　　[2] Includes contributions to Social Security and other supplemental benefits.

Source: U.S. Bureau of the Census, *Service Annual Survey.*

No. 996. Transportation Accidents, Deaths, and Injuries: 1975 to 1992

[For related data, see also tables 1014 and 1036]

YEAR AND CASUALTY	Total (1,000)	Motor vehicle [1] (1,000)	Rail-road [2]	TYPE OF TRANSPORT					General aviation [6]	Recreational boating [7]	Gas pipelines [8]	Liquid pipelines [9]	Water-borne [10]	Hazardous materials [11]
				Air carriers										
				Total	Airlines [3]	Commuter air carriers [4]	On demand air carriers [5]							
Accidents:														
1975....	16,534	16,500	8,041	237	37	48	152		3,995	6,308	1,373	254	3,310	10,951
1980....	17,940	17,900	8,451	228	19	38	171		3,590	5,513	1,996	219	4,624	15,737
1985....	19,322	19,300	3,275	195	22	21	152		2,738	6,237	331	183	3,439	6,019
1990....	11,524	11,500	2,879	149	26	15	108		2,218	6,411	199	177	3,613	8,853
1991....	11,323	11,300	2,659	137	27	22	88		2,143	6,573	233	216	2,222	9,093
1992....	10,020	10,000	2,339	116	19	23	74		1,956	6,048	192	224	(NA)	9,294
Deaths:														
1975....	48.3	44.5	575	219	122	28	69		1,252	1,466	14	7	243	27
1980....	54.5	51.1	584	143	1	37	105		1,239	1,360	11	3	206	19
1985....	47.3	43.8	454	639	526	37	76		955	1,116	26	5	131	8
1990....	47.0	44.6	599	94	39	6	49		763	865	5	3	85	8
1991....	43.8	41.5	586	200	50	77	73		746	924	14	-	30	10
1992....	(NA)	39.2	592	120	33	21	66		812	816	15	5	(NA)	16
Injuries:														
1975....	1,855	1,800	50,138	109	71	6	32		728	2,136	819	17	97	648
1980....	2,063	2,000	58,356	74	17	14	43		675	2,650	45	3	176	626
1985....	1,736	1,700	31,617	89	30	16	43		517	2,757	106	18	172	253
1990....	1,728	1,700	22,736	86	39	11	36		391	3,822	67	7	175	423
1991....	1,626	1,600	20,707	83	26	30	27		420	3,967	89	8	110	438
1992....	16,232	1,600	18,388	37	13	5	19		418	3,683	87	38	(NA)	587

- Represents or rounds to zero. NA Not available. [1] Data on deaths are from U.S. National Highway Traffic Safety Administration and are based on 30 day definition; see table 1014. Other data are from National Safety Council. [2] Accidents which result in damages to railroad property. Grade crossing accidents are also included when classified as a train accident. Deaths exclude fatalities in railroad-highway grade crossing accidents. [3] Includes scheduled and nonscheduled (charter) air carriers. Represents serious injuries. [4] All scheduled service. Represents serious injuries. [5] All nonscheduled service. Represents serious injuries. [6] 1975 excludes commuter and on-demand air taxis. [7] Accidents resulting in death; injury or requiring medical treatment beyond first aid; damages exceeding $200; or a person's disappearance. [8] Pipeline accidents/incidents are credited to year of occurrence. Beginning 1985, prior data are credited to the year filed. Fatalities and injuries as reported in annual report. [9] Pipelines carrying hazardous materials, petroleum, and liquid petroleum products. [10] Covers accidents involving commercial vessels which must be reported to U.S. Coast Guard if there is property damage exceeding $1,500; material damage affecting the seaworthiness or efficiency of a vessel; stranding or grounding; loss of life; or injury causing a person's incapacity for more than 3 days. [11] Accidents, deaths, and injuries involving hazardous materials cover all types of transport.

Source: U.S. Dept. of Transportation, Bureau of Transportation Statistics, *National Transportation Statistics Annual, Historical Compendium Information Report, 1960-1992.*

No. 997. Highway Mileage—Urban and Rural, by Type and Control, and Federal-Aid Highway System: 1980 to 1992

[In thousands, except percent. As of Dec. 31. Data for urban and rural mileage are not comparable to years prior to 1980 because of classification changes; see text, section 21. See also *Historical Statistics, Colonial Times to 1970,* series Q 50, 51, and 55]

TYPE AND CONTROL	1980	1985	1986	1987	1988	1989	1990	1991	1992
Total mileage [1]	[2]3,955	3,862	3,880	3,874	3,871	3,877	3,380	3,889	3,902
Urban mileage...........	624	691	701	710	739	754	757	750	785
Under State control......	79	111	94	95	96	97	96	96	104
Under local control	543	578	606	614	642	656	661	653	680
Rural mileage	[2]3,331	3,171	3,178	3,164	3,132	3,123	3,123	3,139	3,117
Percent surfaced [3]	77.5	88.1	88.4	88.4	88.1	88.4	88.6	89.7	88.9
Under State control.....	702	773	704	704	704	706	703	703	697
Under local control	2,270	2,173	2,243	2,249	2,244	2,238	2,242	2,255	2,239
Under Federal control ...	262	225	231	212	183	178	178	182	181

[1] Beginning 1985, includes only public road mileage as defined 23 USC 402. [2] Includes 98,000 miles of nonpublic road mileage previously contained in other rural categories. [3] Covers soil-surfaced roads and roads with slag, gravel, stone, bituminous, or concrete surfaces.

Source: U.S. Federal Highway Administration, *Highway Statistics,* annual.

No. 998. Highway Mileage—Functional Systems and Urban/Rural: 1992

[As of Dec. 31. For definition of urban, rural, see text, section 21]

STATE	FUNCTIONAL SYSTEMS					Urban	Rural
	Total	Inter-state	Other arterial	Collector	Local		
U.S.	3,901,715	45,493	373,433	801,538	2,681,251	785,160	3,116,555
AL.	92,201	900	8,714	20,315	62,272	19,366	72,835
AK.	13,634	1,088	1,487	2,415	8,644	1,648	11,986
AZ.	55,969	1,169	5,334	8,084	41,382	15,123	40,846
AR.	77,162	542	6,838	20,051	49,731	7,691	69,471
CA.	168,378	2,402	27,827	31,483	106,666	79,986	88,392
CO	78,043	951	8,281	16,336	52,475	12,777	65,266
CT.	20,280	341	2,961	3,171	13,807	11,496	8,784
DE.	5,524	41	604	938	3,941	1,855	3,669
DC.	1,104	12	279	157	656	1,104	-
FL.	110,640	1,474	10,732	14,679	83,755	48,637	62,003
GA	110,790	1,243	13,031	23,069	73,447	26,147	84,643
HI	4,106	44	666	749	2,647	1,799	2,307
ID	58,588	612	3,537	9,608	44,831	3,314	55,274
IL	136,402	2,053	13,451	21,099	99,799	32,266	104,136
IN	92,054	1,140	8,028	22,592	60,294	19,109	72,945
IA	112,586	783	9,377	31,515	70,911	9,096	103,490
KS.	133,655	872	9,282	33,128	90,373	9,508	124,147
KY.	71,765	763	5,099	17,623	48,280	10,008	61,757
LA.	58,629	869	4,906	12,764	40,090	12,319	46,310
ME	22,481	366	2,359	5,923	13,833	2,479	20,002
MD	29,172	481	3,778	4,969	19,944	13,574	15,598
MA	34,323	567	5,548	6,684	21,524	21,017	13,306
MI	117,520	1,240	12,214	25,920	78,146	28,012	89,508
MN	129,622	913	12,379	28,971	87,359	14,523	115,099
MS	72,795	685	7,006	15,511	49,593	7,888	64,907
MO	121,424	1,178	9,472	24,998	85,776	15,398	106,026
MT	70,357	1,191	5,795	16,026	47,345	2,348	68,009
NE.	92,686	481	7,887	20,738	63,580	5,030	87,656
NV.	45,657	545	2,763	4,854	37,495	4,513	41,144
NH	14,913	224	1,565	2,809	10,315	2,440	12,473
NJ.	34,286	396	5,437	4,927	23,526	22,503	11,783
NM	61,195	998	4,492	6,857	48,848	5,828	55,367
NY.	111,686	1,497	14,085	20,814	75,290	39,063	72,623
NC	95,582	970	9,099	17,889	67,624	21,451	74,131
ND	86,648	570	5,868	18,778	61,432	1,825	84,823
OH	113,823	1,573	10,323	23,062	78,865	31,568	82,255
OK	112,432	929	7,931	25,633	77,939	12,281	100,151
OR	95,237	727	6,376	17,946	70,188	9,494	85,743
PA.	116,788	1,587	13,726	19,727	81,748	30,823	85,965
RI	6,120	70	869	855	4,326	4,597	1,523
SC.	64,129	810	6,850	13,411	43,058	10,517	53,612
SD.	83,299	678	6,084	19,288	57,249	1,858	81,441
TN.	85,144	1,062	8,035	18,567	57,480	16,314	68,830
TX.	293,317	3,230	25,302	63,816	200,969	76,143	217,174
UT.	43,270	937	3,309	7,704	31,320	6,084	37,186
VT.	14,145	320	1,312	3,113	9,400	1,314	12,831
VA.	68,429	1,106	7,895	14,008	45,420	15,581	52,848
WA	79,413	762	7,308	16,678	54,665	17,025	62,388
WV	34,919	550	2,829	8,929	22,611	3,090	31,829
WI	110,371	638	11,653	21,525	76,555	14,841	95,530
WY	39,022	913	3,450	10,832	23,827	2,489	36,533

- Represents zero.

Source: U.S. Federal Highway Administration, *Highway Statistics*, annual.

No. 999. Highway Pavement Condition, by Type of Road System: 1980 to 1992

[Highway pavement condition is classified by the Present Serviceability Rating (PSR) system (5.0 - 0.1). The reported ranges are defined as: PSR 5.0-3.5, pavements give a first class ride and exhibit few, if any, visible signs of surface wear. Of the quality of new or nearly new pavements. PSR 3.4-2.0, pavements have a riding quality somewhat inferior to that of new pavements or may even be barely tolerable at high speeds. Surfaces may show signs of cracking, substantial patching, and rutting. PSR 1.9-0.1, pavements show extensive wear to the point of needing resurfacing or may even need complete reconstruction]

PAVEMENT CONDITION	INTERSTATE ROAD				ARTERIAL ROAD				COLLECTOR ROAD			
	1980	1990	1991	1992	1980	1990	1991	1992	1980	1990	1991	1992
URBAN AREAS												
Percent of road mileage rated—												
PSR 0.1-1.9 (0.1-2.4) [1]	6	6	5	4	7	4	4	4	9	13	9	6
PSR 2.0-3.4 (2.5-3.4) [1]	26	35	35	33	42	52	53	50	50	55	54	56
PSR 3.5-5.0	68	59	60	63	51	44	43	46	41	32	37	38
RURAL AREAS												
Percent of road mileage rated—												
PSR 0.1-1.9 (0.1-2.4) [1]	5	6	6	4	6	2	2	2	16	8	7	6
PSR 2.0-3.4 (2.5-3.4) [1]	26	35	34	33	46	48	48	44	55	54	55	54
PSR 3.5-5.0	69	59	60	63	48	50	50	54	29	38	38	40

[1] PSR range shown in parentheses applies to Interstate roads only.

No. 1000. Receipts and Disbursements for Highways, by Type: 1980 to 1994

[In millions of dollars. Data compiled from reports of State and local authorities. For Federal highway trust fund receipts, disbursements, and balances, see table 506. State data include District of Columbia]

TYPE	1980	1985	1990	1991	1992	1993, prel.	1994, proj. Total [1]	1994, proj. Federal	1994, proj. State
Total receipts	39,715	61,506	75,294	82,379	87,523	89,542	91,803	18,349	48,744
Current income	37,604	54,957	69,730	75,452	78,116	79,578	82,677	18,349	43,442
Imposts on highway users [2]	22,559	35,599	44,264	50,349	51,896	52,668	54,343	16,146	36,611
Other taxes and fees	11,808	15,127	19,827	19,077	19,854	20,222	21,327	1,388	3,562
Investment income, other receipts.	3,237	4,231	5,639	6,026	6,366	6,688	7,007	815	3,269
Bond issue proceeds [3]	2,111	6,549	5,564	6,927	9,407	9,964	9,126	-	5,302
Intergovernmental payments [4]	(X)	(X)	(X)	(X)	(X)	(X)	(X)	-18,266	6,916
Funds from (+) or to (-) reserves [4]	2,080	-4,058	114	-3,768	-3,281	-2,043	123	780	-501
Total funds available	41,795	57,448	75,408	78,611	84,242	87,499	91,926	863	55,159
Total disbursements	41,795	57,448	75,408	78,611	84,242	87,499	91,926	863	55,159
Current disbursements	40,084	54,725	72,457	74,895	79,944	83,271	87,570	863	52,645
Capital outlay	20,337	27,138	35,151	36,638	38,700	40,200	42,325	268	31,356
Maintenance and traffic services.	11,445	16,032	20,365	21,222	22,755	23,804	24,885	67	9,520
Administration and research.	3,022	4,033	6,501	6,856	7,702	8,013	8,596	528	5,101
Law enforcement and safety	3,824	5,334	7,235	7,040	7,182	7,522	7,819	-	4,339
Interest on debt	1,456	2,188	3,205	3,139	3,605	3,732	3,945	-	2,329
Debt retirement [3]	1,711	2,723	2,951	3,716	4,298	4,228	4,356	-	2,514

- Represents zero.   X Not applicable.   [1] Includes other levels of government not shown separately.   [2] Excludes amounts later allocated for nonhighway purposes.   [3] Excludes issue and redemption of short-term notes or refunding bonds.   [4] Plus sign (+) indicates net receipt of funds from other levels of government; minus sign (-) indicates net disbursement of funds to other levels.

No. 1001. Disbursements of State Highway Funds, by State: 1980 to 1992

[In millions of dollars. Comprises disbursements from current revenues or loans for construction, maintenance, interest and principal payments on highway bonds, transfers to local units, and miscellaneous. Includes transactions by State toll authorities. Excludes amounts allocated for collection and nonhighway purposes, and bonds redeemed by refunding. See also Historical Statistics, Colonial Times to 1970, series Q 90-94]

STATE	1980	1990	1992	STATE	1980	1990	1992	STATE	1980	1990	1992
U.S.	30,049	53,580	59,458	KS	440	697	858	ND	143	189	212
				KY	913	1,008	1,411	OH	1,032	2,271	2,424
AL	517	866	820	LA	682	923	1,014	OK	461	827	858
AK	274	336	398	ME	164	332	341	OR	482	765	830
AZ	365	1,525	1,172	MD	663	1,464	1,212	PA	1,557	2,885	2,988
AR	425	456	616	MA	704	1,055	1,832	RI	72	214	211
CA	1,930	4,294	5,002	MI	997	1,526	1,718	SC	309	585	622
CO	411	714	745	MN	611	1,228	1,367	SD	151	232	259
CT	393	1,204	1,202	MS	468	529	650	TN	609	1,174	1,177
DE	152	315	401	MO	555	937	1,056	TX	1,882	3,001	2,926
DC	57	273	268	MT	224	302	312	UT	241	355	368
FL	1,261	1,677	2,627	NE	274	449	544	VT	87	165	194
GA	762	1,278	1,334	NV	169	309	321	VA	894	1,874	1,688
HI	134	297	426	NH	152	299	328	WA	787	1,251	1,377
ID	153	300	292	NJ	662	1,831	2,657	WV	672	650	627
IL	1,652	2,645	2,820	NM	197	409	428	WI	468	979	1,228
IN	688	1,218	1,318	NY	1,650	2,874	3,268	WY	192	297	246
IA	504	869	1,010	NC	807	1,428	1,457				

Source of tables 999-1001: U.S. Federal Highway Administration, Highway Statistics, annual.

No. 1002. Federal Grants to State and Local Governments for Highway Trust Fund and Federal Transit Administration (FTA), by State: 1993

[Year ending Sept. 30]

STATE	HIGHWAY TRUST FUND		FTA [2]		STATE	HIGHWAY TRUST FUND		FTA [2]		STATE	HIGHWAY TRUST FUND		FTA [2]	
	Total (mil. dol.)	Per cap- ita [1]	Total (mil. dol.)	Per cap- ita [1]		Total (mil. dol.)	Per cap- ita [1]	Total (mil. dol.)	Per cap- ita [1]		Total (mil. dol.)	Per cap- ita [1]	Total (mil. dol.)	Per cap- ita [1]
U.S .	16,060	62.3	3,494	13.5	KS . . .	162	64.1	8	3.2	ND . . .	109	171.1	3	4.6
					KY . . .	215	56.8	18	4.7	OH. . .	529	47.7	81	7.3
AL . . .	307	73.4	16	3.8	LA . . .	292	68.0	29	6.7	OK. . .	159	49.3	9	2.9
AK . . .	223	371.7	2	3.7	ME. . .	87	70.3	5	4.0	OR. . .	170	55.9	68	22.6
AZ . . .	245	62.1	18	4.5	MD. . .	258	51.9	80	16.1	PA . . .	659	54.7	243	20.2
AR . . .	204	84.1	9	3.6	MA. . .	773	128.6	125	20.8	RI . . .	132	131.5	18	18.2
CA. . .	1,380	44.2	488	15.6	MI . . .	437	46.1	80	8.5	SC. . .	214	58.6	9	2.6
CO. . .	246	68.9	31	8.7	MN. . .	317	70.2	19	4.3	SD. . .	121	168.5	3	3.5
CT. . .	329	100.3	58	17.6	MS. . .	190	71.9	9	3.3	TN . . .	244	47.9	30	5.9
DE. . .	57	81.9	3	3.9	MO. . .	339	64.8	124	23.6	TX . . .	1,061	58.8	120	6.6
DC. . .	52	89.5	251	434.4	MT. . .	161	191.9	2	2.7	UT. . .	154	82.8	28	15.1
FL. . .	630	46.1	125	9.1	NE. . .	137	85.3	9	5.8	VT. . .	116	201.6	4	6.7
GA. . .	410	59.2	58	8.4	NV. . .	100	72.0	4	3.1	VA. . .	226	34.8	28	4.3
HI . . .	193	164.5	23	19.6	NH. . .	98	86.8	3	2.9	WA . .	367	69.7	30	5.7
ID . . .	104	94.7	2	2.3	NJ . . .	440	55.9	158	20.1	WV . .	141	77.7	6	3.2
IL. . .	544	46.5	369	31.6	NM. . .	218	135.0	5	2.9	WI . . .	348	69.0	33	6.6
IN . . .	383	67.0	27	4.7	NY. . .	855	47.0	577	31.7	WY . .	119	252.2	2	3.7
IA . . .	216	76.8	14	4.9	NC. . .	425	61.2	24	3.5					

[1] Based on Bureau of the Census resident population as of July 1, 1993. [2] Federal Transit Administration.

Source: U.S. Bureau of the Census, *Federal Expenditures by State for Fiscal Year,* annual.

No. 1003. State Gasoline Tax Rates, 1992 and 1993, and Motor Fuel Tax Receipts, 1992

[See also *Historical Statistics, Colonial Times to 1970,* series Q 233-234]

STATE	RATE [1] (cents/gal.)		Re- ceipts, [2] 1992 (mil. dol.)	STATE	RATE [1] (cents/gal.)		Re- ceipts, [2] 1992 (mil. dol.)	STATE	RATE [1] (cents/gal.)		Re- ceipts, [2] 1992 (mil. dol.)
	1992	1993			1992	1993			1992	1993	
Federal .	14.1	18.4	(NA)	KS . . .	18	18	260	ND. . .	17	17	72
State. . .	(NA)	(NA)	(NA)	KY [3] . .	15.4	15.4	369	OH. . .	21	22	1,142
AL . . .	18	18	434	LA . . .	20	20	460	OK [4] . .	17	17	335
AK . . .	8	8	22	ME. . .	19	19	134	OR. . .	22	24	299
AZ . . .	18	18	377	MD. . .	23.5	23.5	506	PA . . .	22.35	22.35	1,275
AR . . .	18.7	18.7	302	MA. . .	21	21	540	RI . . .	26	28	106
CA. . .	16	17	2,167	MI . . .	15	15	674	SC. . .	16	16	333
CO. . .	22	22	371	MN. . .	20	20	451	SD. . .	18	18	81
CT. . .	26	29	366	MS. . .	18.2	18.4	296	TN [5] . .	20	20	607
DE. . .	19	22	75	MO. . .	13.03	13.03	405	TX . . .	20	20	2,039
DC. . .	20	20	32	MT. . .	21.4	24	113	UT. . .	19	19	175
FL. . .	11.6	11.8	1,042	NE. . .	24.6	24.4	217	VT. . .	16	16	61
GA. . .	7.5	7.5	338	NV. . .	24	24	177	VA [3] . .	17.5	17.5	634
HI . . .	16	16	64	NH. . .	18.6	18.7	101	WA . .	23	23	612
ID . . .	21	21	128	NJ . . .	10.5	10.5	400	WV . .	20.35	25.35	219
IL. . .	19	19	1,026	NM. . .	17	23	169	WI . . .	22.2	23.2	566
IN . . .	15	15	581	NY. . .	22.89	22.89	1,462	WY . .	9	9	42
IA . . .	20	20	322	NC. . .	21.9	22	849				

NA Not available. [1] In effect Dec. 31. [2] Represents net gallonage receipts. [3] Trucks or combinations with more than two axles pay tax of 2 cents per gallon more in Kentucky, and 3.5 cents per gallon more in Virginia. [4] .08 cents per gallon is for inspection fee. [5] Includes 1 cent per gallon inspection fee.

No. 1004. Public Highway Debt—State and Local Governments: 1970 to 1992

[In millions of dollars. Long-term obligations. Data are for varying calendar and fiscal years. Excludes duplicated and interunit obligations. See also *Historical Statistics, Colonial Times to 1970,* series Q 136-147]

ITEM	1970	1980	1985	1986	1987	1988	1989	1990	1991	1992 [1]
Total debt issued	1,892	2,357	8,194	9,803	6,898	4,594	5,900	5,838	9,517	13,028
State	1,306	1,135	5,397	5,873	4,395	2,702	3,775	3,277	6,252	9,460
Local	586	1,222	2,797	3,930	2,503	1,892	2,125	2,561	3,265	3,568
Total debt redeemed . .	1,270	1,982	4,606	5,313	4,924	2,774	3,729	5,158	4,858	7,218
State	800	1,109	3,835	3,755	3,211	1,547	2,813	2,041	3,071	5,389
Local	470	873	771	1,558	1,713	1,227	916	3,117	1,787	1,829
Total debt outstanding .	19,124	27,519	33,379	37,869	39,843	41,663	43,834	44,514	49,173	54,983
Local	5,104	7,427	12,100	14,472	15,262	15,927	17,136	16,580	18,058	19,797

[1] Local debt estimated.

Source of tables 1003 and 1004: U.S. Federal Highway Administration, *Highway Statistics,* annual.

No. 1005. Transportation to Work: 1990

[In thousands, except as indicated. Based on workers 16 years old or older]

REGION, DIVISION, AND STATE	MEANS OF TRANSPORTATION TO WORK				Average travel time to work [1] (minutes)	HOUSEHOLDS WITH VEHICLES AVAILABLE		
	Car, truck, van		Percent using public transport-ation	Worked at home		None	One vehicle	Two or more vehicles
	Drove alone	Car-pooled						
United States	84,215	15,378	5.3	3,406	22.4	10,602	31,039	50,306
Northeast	15,902	2,771	12.8	630	24.5	3,603	6,408	8,862
New England	4,892	749	5.1	191	21.5	568	1,699	2,676
Maine.............	424	80	0.9	24	19.0	40	159	266
New Hampshire.......	443	70	0.7	20	21.9	26	132	254
Vermont............	200	36	0.7	17	18.0	17	72	122
Massachusetts........	2,148	318	8.3	75	22.7	321	819	1,107
Rhode Island........	376	58	2.5	10	19.2	40	132	206
Connecticut.........	1,301	187	3.9	45	21.1	124	386	721
Middle Atlantic	11,010	2,023	15.7	438	25.7	3,035	4,709	6,186
New York	4,461	861	24.8	213	28.6	1,994	2,153	2,492
New Jersey.........	2,731	472	8.8	80	25.3	360	966	1,468
Pennsylvania........	3,818	690	6.4	145	21.6	681	1,589	2,226
Midwest	21,091	3,207	3.5	987	20.7	2,238	7,365	12,714
East North Central.......	14,749	2,206	4.3	551	21.7	1,693	5,230	8,674
Ohio	3,889	521	2.5	119	20.7	416	1,351	2,320
Indiana............	2,040	332	1.3	73	20.4	175	670	1,221
Illinois............	3,742	653	10.1	144	25.1	588	1,476	2,138
Michigan...........	3,328	429	1.6	100	21.2	344	1,133	1,943
Wisconsin..........	1,751	270	2.5	114	18.3	170	600	1,052
West North Central	6,342	1,002	1.9	436	18.4	545	2,135	4,040
Minnesota..........	1,593	247	3.6	116	19.1	142	517	988
Iowa	971	157	1.2	89	16.2	75	332	657
Missouri	1,816	312	2.0	84	21.6	191	652	1,118
North Dakota........	210	31	0.6	24	13.0	16	73	152
South Dakota	233	33	0.3	31	13.8	17	76	166
Nebraska	590	87	1.2	44	15.8	43	182	377
Kansas............	929	136	0.7	49	17.2	60	302	583
South................	29,495	5,886	2.6	936	22.0	3,208	10,987	17,627
South Atlantic.........	15,481	3,156	3.4	501	22.5	1,725	5,725	9,053
Delaware	258	43	2.4	8	20.0	20	80	147
Maryland	1,733	376	8.1	65	27.0	216	554	979
District of Columbia	107	37	36.6	9	27.1	93	103	53
Virginia............	2,281	500	4.0	103	24.0	205	717	1,370
West Virginia........	493	107	1.1	16	21.0	94	247	347
North Carolina.......	2,528	530	1.0	71	19.8	242	786	1,489
South Carolina.......	1,235	277	1.1	31	20.5	137	402	720
Georgia	2,379	468	2.8	65	22.7	244	730	1,393
Florida	4,468	819	2.0	132	21.8	474	2,106	2,555
East South Central	5,110	1,005	1.2	149	21.1	607	1,814	3,231
Kentucky	1,195	229	1.6	47	20.7	159	447	773
Tennessee	1,763	324	1.3	52	21.5	181	593	1,079
Alabama	1,374	267	0.8	31	21.2	156	466	885
Mississippi	777	184	0.8	19	20.6	111	307	494
West South Central	8,904	1,725	2.0	286	21.6	876	3,448	5,343
Arkansas	765	153	0.5	28	19.0	88	303	501
Louisiana	1,239	247	3.0	31	22.3	209	542	749
Oklahoma..........	1,079	191	0.6	41	19.3	91	414	701
Texas.............	5,821	1,134	2.2	185	22.2	489	2,190	3,392
West	17,727	3,513	4.1	854	22.7	1,553	6,279	11,103
Mountain	4,586	873	2.1	229	19.7	343	1,697	2,993
Montana...........	250	41	0.6	22	14.8	20	91	194
Idaho.............	330	53	1.9	21	17.3	17	101	243
Wyoming	154	28	1.4	9	15.4	8	48	113
Colorado...........	1,217	210	2.9	67	20.7	89	412	781
New Mexico	472	96	1.0	24	19.1	38	185	320
Arizona............	1,178	239	2.1	48	21.6	107	532	730
Utah	541	111	2.3	26	18.9	29	153	355
Nevada	444	94	2.7	12	19.8	36	174	256
Pacific..............	13,141	2,640	4.8	625	23.8	1,210	4,582	8,111
Washington.........	1,701	282	4.5	86	22.0	141	582	1,149
Oregon............	949	165	3.4	56	19.6	88	355	660
California	9,982	2,036	4.9	453	24.6	923	3,452	6,006
Alaska	165	40	2.4	11	16.7	23	64	102
Hawaii	344	116	7.4	19	23.8	35	129	193

[1] Excludes persons who worked at home.

Source: U.S. Bureau of the Census, *Census of Population and Housing, 1990.*

No. 1006. Motor Vehicle Registrations, 1980 to 1992, Vehicle Miles of Travel, 1992, and Drivers Licenses, 1992, by State

[In thousands, except as indicated. Motor vehicle registrations cover publicly, privately, and commercially owned vehicles. For uniformity, data have been adjusted to a calendar-year basis as registration years in States differ; figures represent net numbers where possible, excluding re-registrations and nonresident registrations]

STATE	AUTOMOBILES, TRUCKS, AND BUSES [1]			1992		1992				
	1980	1990	1991	Total	Auto mobiles (incl. taxis)	Motor-cycle [1] regis-tration (incl. official)	Public road and street mileage (1,000 mi.)	Vehicle miles of travel		Drivers licenses
								Total (bil. mi.)	Per mile of road (1,000)	
U.S.	155,796	188,798	188,136	190,362	144,213	4,065	3,902	2,240	574	173,125
AL.	2,938	3,744	3,484	3,304	2,196	41	92	45.8	498	2,977
AK.	262	477	471	486	308	11	14	3.8	271	405
AZ.	1,917	2,825	2,849	2,801	1,994	71	56	35.0	625	2,506
AR.	1,574	1,448	1,480	1,501	974	14	77	23.0	299	1,712
CA.	16,873	21,926	22,253	22,202	17,219	623	168	262.5	1,563	20,111
CO.	2,342	3,155	3,045	2,915	2,165	89	78	28.9	371	2,392
CT.	2,147	2,623	2,589	2,569	2,429	50	20	26.5	1,325	2,358
DE.	397	526	534	545	419	10	6	6.9	1,150	501
DC.	268	262	246	256	238	2	1	3.6	3,600	352
FL.	7,614	10,950	9,980	10,232	8,131	194	111	114.3	1,030	10,538
GA.	3,818	5,489	5,714	5,899	4,121	80	111	77.9	702	4,600
HI	570	771	785	774	668	23	4	8.0	2,000	717
ID	834	1,054	1,055	1,034	610	33	59	10.8	183	721
IL	7,477	7,873	8,193	7,982	6,622	201	136	87.6	644	7,411
IN	3,826	4,366	4,414	4,516	3,301	95	92	57.0	620	3,800
IA	2,329	2,632	2,668	2,706	1,931	157	113	23.9	212	1,859
KS.	2,007	2,012	1,879	1,921	1,258	56	134	24.2	181	1,692
KY.	2,593	2,909	2,942	2,983	1,939	35	72	38.1	529	2,457
LA.	2,779	2,995	3,046	3,094	2,006	35	59	33.9	575	2,617
ME	724	977	979	978	754	30	22	12.2	555	918
MD	2,803	3,607	3,630	3,689	3,075	52	29	41.9	1,445	3,234
MA	3,749	3,726	3,664	3,663	3,156	63	34	47.3	1,391	4,170
MI	6,488	7,209	7,245	7,311	5,680	154	118	84.2	714	6,481
MN	3,091	3,508	3,273	3,484	2,736	106	130	41.2	317	2,625
MS	1,577	1,875	1,887	1,954	1,496	27	73	26.2	359	1,628
MO	3,271	3,905	3,950	4,004	2,821	60	121	53.3	440	3,454
MT	680	783	766	907	541	23	70	8.5	121	597
NE	1,254	1,384	1,404	1,355	893	19	93	14.6	157	1,129
NV	655	853	881	921	621	20	46	10.9	237	957
NH	704	946	906	894	694	34	15	10.1	673	850
NJ	4,761	5,652	5,519	5,591	5,136	100	34	59.4	1,747	5,285
NM	1,068	1,301	1,320	1,352	838	31	61	18.5	303	1,126
NY	8,002	10,196	9,771	9,780	8,467	194	112	109.9	981	10,360
NC	4,532	5,162	5,216	5,307	3,778	59	96	67.5	703	4,655
ND	627	630	629	655	394	18	87	6.1	70	433
OH	7,771	8,410	8,685	9,030	7,304	230	114	95.2	835	9,169
OK	2,583	2,649	2,669	2,737	1,758	57	112	35.1	313	2,287
OR	2,081	2,445	2,507	2,583	1,955	62	95	27.9	294	2,426
PA	6,926	7,971	8,038	8,179	6,535	167	117	89.2	762	8,019
RI	623	672	628	622	517	21	6	7.7	1,283	685
SC	1,996	2,521	2,471	2,601	1,948	33	64	35.0	547	2,400
SD	601	704	702	720	427	23	83	7.2	87	498
TN	3,271	4,444	4,542	4,645	3,726	75	85	50.0	588	3,486
TX	10,475	12,800	12,697	12,767	8,689	164	293	163.3	557	11,438
UT	992	1,206	1,230	1,252	810	24	43	16.3	379	1,143
VT	347	462	447	465	346	17	14	6.0	429	423
VA	3,626	4,938	5,022	5,239	3,961	59	68	63.4	932	4,697
WA	3,225	4,257	4,404	4,466	3,140	112	79	49.4	625	3,627
WV	1,320	1,225	1,273	1,273	778	18	35	16.5	471	1,314
WI	2,941	3,815	3,685	3,735	2,463	176	110	47.6	433	3,543
WY	467	528	469	483	249	16	39	6.2	159	343

[1] Excludes vehicles owned by military services.

Source: U.S. Federal Highway Administration, *Highway Statistics*, annual; and *Selected Highway Statistics and Charts*, annual.

No. 1007. Motor Vehicle Production and Trade: 1980 to 1992

ITEM	Unit	1980	1985	1987	1988	1989	1990	1991	1992
Production:									
Passenger car production	1,000 . . .	6,376	8,185	7,100	7,137	6,825	6,078	5,439	5,663
Truck and bus production	1,000 . . .	1,634	3,468	3,826	4,101	4,051	3,706	3,372	4,038
Imports:									
Passenger cars (new) [1][2]	1,000 . . .	3,116	4,398	4,589	4,450	4,043	3,945	3,736	3,615
Canada	1,000 . . .	595	1,145	927	1,191	1,151	1,220	1,196	1,200
Germany, Federal Republic of . . .	1,000 . . .	339	473	378	264	217	245	172	206
Japan	1,000 . . .	1,992	2,527	2,418	2,123	2,052	1,868	1,789	1,678
Trucks and buses (new) [2]	1,000 . . .	747	1,253	1,177	938	953	766	716	777
Japan	1,000 . . .	483	800	772	542	420	302	283	197
All-terrain vehicles [3]	1,000 . . .	(NA)	683	320	210	121	100	(NA)	(NA)
Motorcycles, total [3]	1,000 . . .	1,120	733	318	287	253	169	(NA)	(NA)
Import value:									
Passenger cars (new) [1]	Mil. dol. .	16,675	36,474	47,858	47,005	44,417	45,716	45,564	46,729
Trucks and buses, (new) [1]	Mil. dol. .	1,985	7,734	8,729	8,089	8,591	8,155	8,221	10,000
Motorcycles [3][4]	Mil. dol. .	1,142	783	463	512	542	361	(NA)	(NA)
Exports:									
Passenger cars (new) [1]	1,000 . . .	617	704	633	781	778	794	755	851
Trucks and buses (new) exports . . .	1,000 . . .	186	183	222	230	189	159	208	161
Export value [1][5]	Mil. dol. .	16,015	22,820	24,812	29,519	31,574	38,086	(NA)	(NA)
Passenger cars (new) [5]	Mil. dol. .	3,932	6,027	6,695	8,318	8,895	9,708	9,886	11,893
Trucks and buses (new) [5]	Mil. dol. .	2,977	2,789	3,375	3,683	3,471	2,845	3,388	3,073
Parts and accessories [6]	Mil. dol. .	9,106	14,004	14,742	17,518	19,208	24,996	(NA)	(NA)
Factory sales:									
Passenger cars	1,000 . . .	6,400	8,002	7,085	7,105	6,807	6,050	5,407	5,684
Trucks and buses	1,000 . . .	1,667	3,357	3,821	4,121	4,062	3,719	3,375	4,042
Retail sales:									
Passenger cars (new) [1]	1,000 . . .	8,979	11,042	10,277	10,530	9,772	9,300	8,175	8,214
Domestics [7]	1,000 . . .	6,581	8,205	7,081	7,526	7,073	6,897	6,137	6,277
Imports [8]	1,000 . . .	2,398	2,838	3,196	3,004	2,699	2,403	2,038	1,938
Trucks and buses [9]	1,000 . . .	2,232	3,984	4,174	4,608	4,483	4,261	3,842	4,513
Light duty (up to 14,000 GVW) [10]	1,000 . . .	1,964	3,700	3,885	4,273	4,171	3,984	3,621	4,264
Med. duty (14,001-26,000 GVW) [10]	1,000 . . .	92	53	55	83	73	71	50	57
Heavy duty (over 26,000 GVW) [10]	1,000 . . .	176	231	234	251	239	207	171	192
Under 6,000 pounds	1,000 . . .	985	2,408	2,696	2,926	2,854	2,866	2,724	3,217
Utility	1,000 . . .	51	429	403	445	447	490	549	666
Van	1,000 . . .	79	115	89	47	43	31	17	21
Minivan (cargo)	1,000 . . .	(X)	103	101	105	97	83	66	63
Station wagon (truck chassis) . .	1,000 . . .	(X)	86	108	138	138	112	110	201
Minipassenger carrier	1,000 . . .	(X)	301	546	692	688	750	706	840
6,000 to 10,000 pounds [11]	1,000 . . .	975	1,280	1,175	1,333	1,297	1,097	876	1,021
Utility	1,000 . . .	108	108	91	90	93	68	37	51
Van	1,000 . . .	172	261	254	302	289	254	203	241
Pickup, conventional	1,000 . . .	546	628	569	666	663	568	476	524
Station wagon (truck chassis) . .	1,000 . . .	39	95	91	104	100	85	55	80
10,001 pounds and over	1,000 . . .	271	295	302	349	331	298	242	275

NA Not available. X Not applicable. [1] Based on data from U.S. Dept. of Commerce. [2] Includes other countries, not shown separately. [3] Source: Motorcycle Industry Council, Inc., Irvine, CA. Data from U.S. Dept. of Commerce. Excludes mopeds/motorized bicycles and all-terrain vehicles. Excludes moped imports (motorcycle imports less than 51 cc's) from all countries (except Japan). [4] Represents c.i.f. value. [5] Covers assembled and unassembled vehicles. [6] Includes rubber tires and tubes and used vehicles. [7] Includes domestic models produced in Canada and Mexico. [8] Excludes domestic models produced in Canada. [9] Excludes motorcoaches and light-duty imports from foreign manufactures. Includes imports sold by franchised dealers of U.S. manufacturers. Starting in 1987, includes sales of trucks over 10,000 lbs. GVW by foreign manufacturers. [10] Gross vehicle weight (fully loaded vehicle). [11] Includes vehicles, not shown separately.

No. 1008. Motor Vehicles in Use: 1980 to 1992

ITEM	Unit	1980	1985	1988	1989	1990	1991	1992
Cars in use, total	**Million** . .	104.6	114.7	121.5	122.8	123.3	123.3	120.3
Under 5 years	Million . .	52.3	48.7	55.5	57.6	56.5	54.6	50.4
6-8 years	Million . .	25.2	27.8	21.6	20.7	22.6	25.5	27.5
9-11 years	Million . .	14.6	17.2	22.4	21.1	19.1	16.7	16.0
12 years and over	Million . .	12.5	21.0	22.0	23.4	25.1	26.6	26.4
Average age	Years . .	6.6	7.6	7.6	7.6	7.8	7.9	8.1
Cars retired from use [1]	1,000 . . .	8,405	7,729	8,754	8,981	8,897	8,565	11,194
Trucks in use, total	**Million** . .	35.2	42.4	50.2	53.2	56.0	58.2	61.2
Under 3 years	Million . .	8.8	9.0	12.5	12.5	12.8	12.0	11.3
3-5 years	Million . .	8.1	6.3	10.3	12.6	13.2	14.0	14.0
6-8 years	Million . .	7.4	10.2	5.9	6.3	8.0	9.9	11.9
9-11 years	Million . .	4.4	6.2	8.9	7.9	6.6	5.3	5.6
12 years and over	Million . .	6.5	10.7	12.6	14.0	15.5	17.0	18.3
Average age	Years . .	7.1	8.1	7.9	7.9	8.0	8.1	8.4
Trucks retired from use [1]	1,000 . . .	1,732	2,100	2,251	2,189	2,177	2,284	1,587

[1] For years ending June 30. Represents vehicles failing to re-register.

Source of tables 1007 and 1008: Except as noted, American Automobile Manufacturers Association Inc., Detroit, MI, *Motor Vehicle Facts and Figures*, annual (copyright); and *World Motor Vehicle Data*, annual (copyright).

No. 1009. Motor Vehicle Registrations: 1980 to 1992
[In thousands]

ITEM	1980	1985	1987	1988	1989	1990	1991	1992
Total [1]	155,796	171,654	179,044	184,397	187,261	188,798	188,136	190,362
Automobiles	121,601	131,864	137,324	141,252	143,081	143,550	142,569	144,213
Buses	529	593	602	616	625	627	631	645
Private and commercial:								
Commercial	107	109	111	112	113	114	114	144
School and other	147	157	160	160	162	161	161	161
Publicly owned:								
Federal	4	4	5	5	4	5	5	5
School	271	323	327	339	346	347	352	365
Private and commercial trailers, total	14,372	15,008	15,322	15,707	16,115	16,098	16,269	16,715
Motorcycles	5,694	5,444	4,917	4,584	4,434	4,259	4,177	4,065
Truck tractors	1,402	1,150	1,135	1,183	1,237	1,240	1,236	1,279
Light trucks [2]	(NA)	32,146	34,286	35,320	36,530	37,380	37,728	38,257

NA Not available.　[1] Components may not add to total because of double counting.　[2] Excludes farm trucks.

Source: U.S. Federal Highway Administration, *Highway Statistics*, annual.

No. 1010. Motor Vehicle Tires and Batteries: 1980 to 1992
[In millions]

ITEM	1980	1985	1987	1988	1989	1990	1991	1992
Tires, passenger car, total [1]	145.9	200.9	210.8	218.8	214.8	213.6	214.5	228.6
Radials	83.5	164.7	187.3	200.2	200.4	202.1	205.7	221.4
Replacement	106.9	141.5	151.9	155.3	151.2	152.3	155.4	165.8
Tires, truck and bus, total [1]	31.1	41.1	44.4	46.0	46.9	46.9	42.4	45.0
Radials	3.8	19.7	26.0	29.4	30.6	32.5	32.4	36.1
Replacement	24.4	32.1	34.5	33.9	35.2	36.6	32.9	33.7
Batteries, total [2]	61.7	74.4	75.7	80.1	80.3	79.7	79.8	(NA)
Replacement automobile batteries	50.1	58.7	59.9	63.5	64.4	65.2	66.6	(NA)

NA Not available.　[1] Includes original equipment. Also includes exports, not shown separately.　[2] Source: Battery Council International, Chicago, IL, and U.S. Bureau of the Census.

Source: Except as noted, The Rubber Manufacturers Association, Inc., Washington, DC, *RMA Monthly Tire Report*.

No. 1011. Automobile Output and Trade in National Income Accounts: 1980 to 1993
[In billions of dollars. Vehicle output equals final dollar sales value of new vehicles, plus net dollar value of used vehicle sales adjusted for changes in inventories and net balance of vehicle exports and imports]

ITEM	CURRENT DOLLARS					CONSTANT (1982) DOLLARS				
	1980	1990	1991	1992	1993	1980	1990	1991	1992	1993
Auto output, total	59.2	129.2	121.1	133.2	142.5	79.1	121.4	109.5	117.4	121.1
Final sales	60.1	132.3	121.1	133.5	137.6	80.5	125.3	109.9	117.8	117.7
Personal consumption expenditures	57.2	129.8	116.2	126.7	134.3	80.9	124.5	107.7	113.9	115.5
Producers' durable equipment	14.3	35.6	37.1	37.6	39.1	16.8	33.4	32.8	32.8	34.7
Net exports	−12.8	−35.4	−33.9	−32.8	−37.7	−19.2	−34.7	−32.1	−30.5	−34.1
Government purchases	1.4	2.3	1.8	2.0	1.9	2.0	2.1	1.6	1.7	1.6
Change in business inventories	−0.9	−3.1	−0.1	−0.3	4.9	−1.5	−3.9	−0.4	−0.4	3.4
New	−0.1	−2.3	−0.1	0.3	3.4	−0.1	−3.2	−0.4	0.1	2.2
Used	−0.8	−0.8	-	−0.6	1.4	−1.3	−0.8	-	−0.6	1.2

- Represents or rounds to zero.

Source: U.S. Bureau of Economic Analysis, *The National Income and Product Accounts of the United States: Volume 2, 1959-88*, and *Survey of Current Business*, July 1992, August 1993, and March 1994.

No. 1012. Recreational Vehicles—Number and Retail Value of Shipments: 1970 to 1992

ITEM	1970	1975	1980	1984	1985	1986	1987	1988	1989	1990	1991	1992
NUMBER (1,000)												
Total	380.3	339.6	181.4	398.2	359.2	379.5	400.2	427.3	395.7	354.5	300.5	389.8
Motorized homes	30.3	96.6	99.9	257.3	233.5	249.6	255.7	277.1	261.6	226.5	172.6	226.3
Travel trailers	138.0	150.6	52.0	82.9	82.9	86.0	92.8	96.9	90.3	87.6	84.4	109.6
Folding camping trailers	116.1	48.1	24.5	40.9	35.9	36.5	41.6	42.3	33.9	30.7	33.9	43.3
Truck campers	95.9	44.3	5.0	7.6	6.9	7.4	10.1	11.0	9.9	9.7	9.6	10.6
RETAIL VALUE (mil. dol.)												
Total	1,122	2,320	1,952	7,610	7,029	7,564	8,400	9,188	9,027	8,223	6,739	8,903
Motorized homes	318	1,251	1,381	6,262	5,724	6,155	6,826	7,543	7,420	6,660	5,284	6,963
Travel trailers	445	856	485	1,157	1,122	1,213	1,331	1,381	1,378	1,342	1,250	1,653
Folding camping trailers	175	101	69	145	137	144	167	175	147	134	146	189
Truck campers	183	112	17	46	46	53	76	88	81	86	87	99

Source: Recreation Vehicle Industry Association, Reston, VA, *RV's ... A Year-End Report/1989*. Data also in American Automobile Manufacturers Association of the United States, Inc., Detroit, MI, *Motor Vehicle Facts and Figures*, annual.

No. 1013. Roadway Congestion: 1990

[Various Federal, State, and local information sources were used to develop the data base with the primary source being the Federal Highway Administration's Highway Performance Monitoring System]

URBANIZED AREAS	DAILY VEHICLE MILES OF TRAVEL		VEHICLE HOURS OF DELAY		CONGESTION COST		Delay and fuel cost (mil. dol.)
	Total miles (1,000)	Per lane-mile of freeway	Total hours	Per 1,000 persons	Per reg. vehicle (dol.)	Per capita (dol.)	
Total, Average............	15,780	12,520	200,120	80	480	340	860
Northeastern cities...........	25,490	12,660	421,600	90	710	380	1,820
Baltimore, MD.............	15,800	12,640	127,010	60	530	270	550
Boston, MA..............	21,610	14,220	337,070	110	880	490	1,460
Hartford, CT..............	6,230	10,730	30,470	50	250	220	130
New York, NY.............	82,920	14,050	1,508,760	90	1,090	390	6,560
Philadelphia, PA..........	18,330	12,140	275,870	70	420	270	1,160
Pittsburgh, PA...........	8,200	8,200	119,040	60	400	270	500
Washington, DC..........	25,340	16,610	552,990	180	1,420	770	2,370
Midwestern cities...........	14,370	11,720	115,850	40	290	190	500
Chicago, IL.............	38,030	15,680	528,770	70	570	300	2,280
Cincinnati, OH	11,380	12,570	42,060	40	200	160	190
Cleveland, OH	13,700	12,450	48,220	30	140	120	210
Columbus, OH	8,350	10,440	40,430	50	230	200	170
Detroit, MI..............	22,650	13,320	360,540	90	530	380	1,530
Indianapolis, IN..........	8,050	10,590	17,420	20	130	80	80
Kansas City, MO..........	12,560	9,230	28,160	20	160	100	120
Louisville, KY...........	6,200	10,500	20,610	30	190	110	90
Milwaukee, WI	7,690	12,920	46,410	40	370	160	200
Minneapolis-St. Paul, MN	17,790	12,020	102,620	50	270	220	440
Oklahoma City, OK	6,940	9,630	21,310	30	190	120	90
St. Louis, MO............	19,120	11,280	133,630	70	540	290	560
Southern cities.............	7,000	11,710	86,290	80	390	330	370
Atlanta, GA..............	24,260	14,190	233,830	120	640	530	1,000
Charlotte, NC.............	2,300	7,670	34,020	80	390	320	150
Ft. Lauderdale, FL..........	7,110	11,840	70,740	60	290	240	300
Jacksonville, FL..........	5,380	11,960	55,790	80	400	330	240
Memphis, TN.............	4,340	11,130	20,580	20	140	100	90
Miami, FL...............	8,570	14,170	230,700	120	680	520	970
Nashville, TN............	5,000	10,200	40,640	70	340	310	170
New Orleans, LA..........	4,970	13,810	68,860	60	340	270	300
Norfolk, VA.............	5,450	11,720	74,680	80	390	350	320
Orlando, FL.............	5,950	10,080	71,790	80	420	360	310
Tampa, FL..............	3,630	12,100	47,540	70	310	290	200
Southwestern cities	10,000	11,640	109,560	70	380	300	470
Albuquerque, NM	2,400	11,160	20,680	40	210	170	90
Austin, TX...............	5,440	12,090	47,410	90	410	410	210
Corpus Christi, TX..........	1,560	8,430	2,690	10	50	40	10
Dallas, TX...............	23,680	13,850	257,570	130	750	570	1,120
Denver, CO	11,270	12,730	135,400	90	420	370	580
El Paso, TX	3,330	9,510	9,320	20	120	80	40
Fort Worth, TX	11,840	11,610	97,240	80	420	350	420
Houston, TX..............	28,230	14,700	383,250	130	750	570	1,650
Phoenix, AZ..............	7,670	12,270	177,570	90	630	400	750
Salt Lake City, UT..........	5,330	10,450	15,070	20	90	80	70
San Antonio, TX...........	9,280	11,250	58,990	50	290	220	260
Western cities.............	27,920	15,540	390,040	130	760	550	1,690
Honolulu, HI..............	4,620	13,590	53,180	80	470	360	240
Los Angeles, CA...........	110,350	21,100	1,780,170	160	980	670	7,670
Portland, OR	7,470	13,460	77,700	80	500	330	340
Sacramento, CA	9,260	12,350	81,400	70	280	320	350
San Bernardino-River, CA.....	14,580	16,290	236,880	200	1,320	880	1,030
San Diego, CA	27,690	16,050	152,600	70	480	290	670
San Francisco-Oakland, CA ...	42,590	17,820	644,570	180	930	760	2,810
San Jose, CA	15,780	13,600	223,170	160	960	690	970
Seattle-Everett, WA.........	18,920	15,640	260,710	150	880	660	1,140

Source: Texas Transportation Institute, College Station, Texas; *Roadway Congestion in Major Urban Areas*, annual (copyright).

No. 1014. Motor Vehicle Accidents—Number and Deaths: 1972 to 1992

[See also *Historical Statistics, Colonial Times to 1970*, series Q 208 and Q 224-232]

ITEM	Unit	1972 [1]	1980	1985	1987	1988	1989	1990	1991	1992
Motor vehicle accidents [2]	Million .	17.0	17.9	19.3	20.8	20.6	12.8	11.5	11.3	10.0
Cars	Million .	24.5	22.8	25.6	25.9	28.2	15.3	14.3	13.7	14.2
Trucks	Million .	3.5	5.5	6.1	6.0	6.8	6.5	4.4	4.7	5.3
Motorcycles	1,000 .	343	560	480	380	370	211	180	239	208
Motor vehicle deaths within 1 yr. [3]	1,000 .	56.3	53.2	45.9	48.3	49.1	47.6	46.8	43.5	40.3
Noncollision accidents	1,000 .	15.8	14.7	12.6	5.2	5.3	4.9	4.9	4.6	4.2
Collision accidents:										
With other motor vehicles.	1,000 .	23.9	23.0	19.9	20.7	20.9	20.3	19.9	18.6	17.4
With pedestrians.	1,000 .	10.3	9.7	8.5	7.5	7.7	7.8	7.3	6.7	6.5
With fixed objects	1,000 .	3.9	3.7	3.2	13.2	13.4	12.9	13.1	12.0	10.9
Deaths within 30 days [4]	1,000 .	54.6	51.1	43.8	46.4	47.1	45.6	44.6	41.5	39.2
Vehicle occupants	1,000 .	41.4	36.8	31.5	34.5	35.5	34.9	33.9	31.9	30.5
Pedestrians . .	1,000 .	9.2	8.1	6.8	6.7	6.9	6.6	6.5	5.8	5.5
Motorcyclists [5]	1,000 .	3.0	5.1	4.6	4.0	3.7	3.1	3.2	2.8	2.4
Bicyclists	1,000 .	1.0	1.0	0.9	0.9	0.9	0.8	0.9	0.8	0.7
Traffic death rates: [4] [6]										
Per 100,000 resident population . .	Rate . .	26.2	22.6	18.4	19.1	19.2	18.4	17.9	16.5	15.4
Per 100,000 registered vehicles . .	Rate . .	44.5	31.6	24.8	25.2	24.9	23.6	23.1	21.6	20.2
Per 100 million vehicle miles	Rate . .	4.3	3.3	2.5	2.4	2.3	2.2	2.1	1.9	1.8
Per 100,000 licensed drivers	Rate . .	46.1	35.2	27.9	28.7	28.9	27.6	26.7	24.6	22.7
Motor vehicle accidents [7]	Million .	24.9	24.1	32.5	33.9	34.2	34.4	33.4	31.3	31.8
Injuries [7]	1,000 .	5,190	5,230	5,044	5,400	5,500	5,560	5,560	5,285	5,445
Economic loss [7] [8]	Bil. dol.	28.7	57.1	76.0	85.0	89.0	93.9	95.9	93.8	98.1

[1] Represents peak year for deaths from motor vehicle accidents. [2] Covers only accidents occurring on the road. [3] Deaths that occur within 1 year of accident. Includes collision categories not shown separately. [4] Within 30 days of accident. Source: U.S. National Highway Traffic Safety Administration, unpublished data from Fatal Accident Reporting System. [5] Includes motor scooters and motorized bicycles (mopeds). [6] Based on 30-day definition of traffic deaths. [7] Source: Insurance Information Institute, New York, NY, *Insurance Facts*. Estimates based on official reports from a representative cross-section of States. Includes all motor vehicle accidents on and off the road and all injuries regardless of length of disability. [8] Wage loss; legal, medical, hospital, and funeral expenses; insurance administrative costs; and property damage.

Source: Except as noted, National Safety Council, Chicago, IL, *Accident Facts*, annual (copyright).

No. 1015. Motor Vehicle Deaths, by State: 1985 to 1992

[Includes both traffic and nontraffic motor vehicle deaths. See source for definitions]

REGION DIVISION STATE	1985	1990	1991	1992	MILEAGE RATE [1] 1985	MILEAGE RATE [1] 1992	REGION DIVISION STATE	1985	1990	1991	1992	MILEAGE RATE [1] 1985	MILEAGE RATE [1] 1992
U.S. . . .	45,901	47,151	43,500	40,300	2.6	1.8	DC . . .	96	91	63	(NA)	3.0	(NA)
							VA . . .	1,021	1,091	937	839	2.1	1.3
Northeast.	6,797	6,610	5,819	5,403	(NA)	(NA)	WV . .	461	502	414	420	3.6	2.5
N.E	1,873	1,617	1,400	1,292	(NA)	(NA)	NC . . .	1,553	1,489	1,365	1,262	3.1	2.4
ME . . .	224	215	202	213	2.4	1.7	SC . . .	943	987	890	807	3.5	2.3
NH . . .	198	154	144	123	2.6	1.2	GA . . .	1,462	1,659	1,393	1,323	2.7	1.8
VT . . .	117	94	106	96	2.5	1.6	FL . . .	2,968	3,049	2,519	2,480	3.4	2.1
MA . . .	761	655	550	485	1.9	1.0	E.S.C. . .	3,664	4,259	3,749	3,579	(NA)	(NA)
RI . . .	124	104	88	79	2.1	1.1	KY . . .	749	850	828	819	2.6	2.3
CT . . .	449	395	310	296	2.0	1.1	TN . . .	1,219	1,312	1,112	1,155	3.4	2.4
M.A.	4,924	4,993	4,419	4,111	(NA)	(NA)	AL . . .	1,005	1,234	1,108	1,001	2.9	2.3
NY . . .	2,121	2,318	1,973	1,800	2.3	1.6	MS . . .	691	863	701	604	3.6	2.4
NJ . . .	986	908	785	766	1.9	1.3	W.S.C . .	6,197	5,713	5,154	5,134	(NA)	(NA)
PA . . .	1,817	1,767	1,661	1,545	2.4	1.7	AR . . .	580	625	608	587	3.4	2.6
Midwest . .	9,760	10,248	9,169	8,565	(NA)	(NA)	LA . . .	1,011	1,023	824	871	3.0	2.4
E.N.C	6,602	6,913	6,218	5,656	(NA)	(NA)	OK . . .	781	684	643	619	2.5	1.8
OH . . .	1,581	1,708	1,544	1,440	2.1	1.5	TX . . .	3,825	3,381	3,079	3,057	2.7	1.9
IN . . .	1,045	1,097	1,020	902	2.6	1.6	West . . .	10,352	10,561	9,031	8,026	(NA)	(NA)
IL	1,594	1,650	1,451	1,375	2.3	1.6	Mt.	3,409	3,379	2,982	2,861	(NA)	(NA)
MI . . .	1,605	1,633	1,409	1,295	2.4	1.5	MT. . . .	233	225	200	190	3.1	2.2
WI . . .	777	825	794	644	2.1	1.4	ID . . .	268	259	263	243	3.5	2.3
W.N.C . .	3,158	3,335	2,951	2,909	(NA)	(NA)	WY . . .	145	130	122	118	2.7	1.9
MN . . .	657	644	534	581	2.0	1.4	CO . . .	628	583	542	519	2.4	1.8
IA . . .	478	481	491	437	2.4	1.8	NM . . .	561	534	469	461	4.2	2.7
MO . .	1,005	1,174	1,010	985	2.6	1.9	AZ . . .	942	947	816	810	4.4	2.3
ND . . .	117	128	94	88	2.2	1.4	UT . . .	335	296	273	269	2.8	1.7
SD . . .	142	166	143	161	2.3	2.3	NV . . .	297	405	297	251	3.9	2.3
NE . . .	259	289	275	270	2.1	1.9	Pac. . . .	6,943	7,182	6,049	5,165	(NA)	(NA)
KS . . .	500	453	404	387	2.6	1.6	WA . . .	786	875	682	651	2.3	1.4
South. . . .	19,250	19,732	17,295	16,648	(NA)	(NA)	OR. . .	605	608	483	464	2.8	1.7
S.A . . .	9,389	9,760	8,392	7,935	(NA)	(NA)	CA . . .	5,294	5,411	4,649	3,816	2.6	1.4
DE . . .	119	151	103	140	2.2	2.1	AK . . .	124	102	100	106	3.2	2.6
MD. . .	766	741	708	664	2.3	1.6	HI . . .	134	186	135	128	2.0	1.5

NA Not available. [1] Deaths per 100 million vehicle miles.

Source: 1985: National Center for Health Statistics; thereafter, National Safety Council, Itasca, IL, *Accident Facts*, annual (copyright).

No. 1016. Fatal Motor Vehicle Accidents—National Summary: 1980 to 1992

[Based on data from the Fatal Accident Reporting System (FARS). FARS gathers data on accidents that result in loss of human life. FARS is operated and maintained by National Highway Traffic Safety Administration's (NHTSA) National Center for Statistics and Analysis (NCSA). FARS data are gathered on motor vehicle accidents that occurred on a roadway customarily open to the public, resulting in the death of a person within 30 days of the accident. Collection of these data depend on the use of police, hospital, medical examiner/coroner, and Emergency Medical Services reports; State vehicle registration, driver licensing, and highway department files; and vital statistics documents and death certificates. See source for further detail]

ITEM	1980	1985	1987	1988	1989	1990	1991	1992
Fatal accidents, total.	**45,284**	**39,196**	**41,438**	**42,130**	**40,741**	**39,836**	**36,937**	**34,928**
One vehicle involved.	28,306	22,875	24,154	24,716	23,742	23,445	21,910	20,378
Two or more vehicles involved	16,978	16,321	17,284	17,414	16,999	16,391	15,027	14,550
Persons killed in fatal accidents	**51,091**	**43,825**	**46,390**	**47,087**	**45,582**	**44,599**	**41,508**	**39,235**
Occupants	41,927	36,043	38,565	39,170	38,087	37,134	34,740	32,869
Drivers	28,816	25,337	26,833	27,253	26,389	25,750	23,930	22,583
Passengers	12,972	10,619	11,623	11,805	11,624	11,276	10,688	10,201
Other	139	87	109	112	74	108	122	85
Nonmotorists.	9,164	7,782	7,825	7,917	7,495	7,465	6,768	6,366
Pedestrians	8,070	6,808	6,745	6,870	6,556	6,482	5,801	5,546
Pedalcyclists	965	890	948	911	832	859	843	722
Other	129	84	132	136	107	124	124	98
Occupant fatalities by type of vehicle, total.	**41,927**	**36,043**	**38,565**	**39,170**	**38,087**	**37,134**	**34,740**	**32,869**
Passenger cars	27,449	23,212	25,132	25,808	25,063	24,092	22,385	21,366
Mini-compact	3,141	3,571	3,815	3,813	3,812	3,556	3,039	2,705
Subcompact.	4,158	4,422	5,007	4,975	4,928	4,753	4,655	4,323
Compact.	927	2,635	3,943	4,764	5,099	5,310	5,338	5,349
Intermediate.	3,878	4,391	4,917	5,016	5,055	4,849	4,681	4,416
Full size.	4,831	2,974	2,937	2,840	2,641	2,386	2,073	2,119
Largest size.	6,746	3,612	3,160	2,904	2,610	2,249	1,967	1,674
Unknown.	3,768	1,607	1,353	1,496	929	989	632	780
Motorcycles	4,961	4,417	3,834	3,492	3,036	3,129	2,703	2,293
Other motorized cycles	183	147	202	170	105	115	103	101
Multipurpose vehicles	895	855	1,050	1,040	1,135	1,214	1,476	1,331
Light trucks.	6,591	5,834	7,008	7,266	7,416	7,387	6,915	6,751
Pickup.	5,483	4,640	5,502	5,880	5,870	5,979	5,671	5,376
Van.	1,000	791	1,025	1,001	1,214	1,154	1,154	1,285
Medium trucks.	285	157	125	125	128	134	115	98
Heavy trucks.	977	820	727	786	730	571	546	486
Buses	46	57	51	54	50	32	31	28
Other vehicles.	257	333	293	310	277	296	328	415
Unknown	283	211	143	119	147	164	138	96
Persons involved in fatal accidents...	**113,289**	**104,045**	**111,457**	**112,958**	**109,866**	**107,777**	**99,369**	**95,628**
Occupants	103,049	95,482	102,644	104,086	101,401	99,297	91,707	88,308
Drivers	62,957	57,883	61,442	62,253	6,435	58,893	54,391	51,881
Passengers	39,892	37,477	41,013	41,656	40,816	40,229	37,108	36,290
Other	200	122	189	177	150	175	208	137
Nonoccupants	10,240	8,563	8,813	8,872	8,465	8,480	7,662	7,320
Vehicle miles traveled (VMT) (100 million)	15,273	17,742	19,212	20,256	21,070	21,444	21,721	22,398
Licensed drivers (1,000)	145,295	156,868	161,818	162,853	165,555	167,015	168,995	173,125
Registered vehicles (1,000)	161,490	177,098	183,872	188,981	191,694	192,915	192,314	194,427
Fatalities by road type	(NA)	(NA)	46,390	47,087	45,582	44,599	41,508	39,235
Interstate	4,427	4,148	4,634	5,142	4,971	4,993	4,574	4,324
Federal-aid primary.	(NA)	14,526	15,561	15,185	14,732	14,203	13,158	12,035
Federal-aid secondary.	(NA)	6,429	6,597	6,919	6,769	6,892	6,249	5,844
Federal-aid urban.	(NA)	8,116	8,432	8,534	8,398	8,432	7,511	6,573
Non-Federal-aid.	(NA)	10,408	11,004	10,844	10,579	10,039	9,924	8,808
Unknown	(NA)	198	162	463	133	40	92	1,651
Fatality rate by age group:								
Under 5 years old	6.9	5.2	5.4	5.4	5.4	4.9	4.6	4.3
5 years to 15 years old	8.7	7.4	7.8	7.4	7.0	6.4	6.1	5.8
16 years to 24 years old.	46.0	37.1	38.8	40.0	36.7	35.2	33.0	29.5
25 years to 44 years old.	24.6	19.6	20.6	20.3	20.0	19.7	17.7	16.6
45 years to 64 years old.	17.2	14.5	14.9	15.0	15.0	14.9	13.5	13.1
65 years to 79 years old.	19.6	18.0	18.8	19.5	19.1	18.8	18.0	17.9
80 years old and over	25.3	25.1	27.1	29.1	28.8	26.8	26.9	25.9
Fatal accidents by the highest blood alcohol concentration (BAC) in accident:								
0.00 percent.	(NA)	48.5	49.3	50.1	51.1	50.6	52.1	54.8
0.01 to 0.09 percent	(NA)	10.3	10.7	10.2	9.8	9.7	9.4	9.0
0.10 percent and over	(NA)	41.2	40	39.7	39.1	39.7	38.5	36.1
National rates:								
Fatalities per 100 million VMT	3.3	2.5	2.4	2.3	2.2	2.1	1.9	1.8
Fatalities per 100,000 licensed drivers	35.2	27.9	28.7	28.9	27.5	26.7	24.6	22.7
VMT per registered vehicle	9,458	10,018	10,445	10,718	10,936	11,107	11,294	11,520
Fatal accidents per 100 million VMT.	2.9	2.2	2.2	2.1	1.9	1.9	1.7	1.6
Involved vehicles per fatal crash	1.4	1.5	1.5	1.5	1.5	1.5	1.5	1.5

NA Not available.

Source: National Highway Traffic Safety Administration, *Fatal Accident Reporting System*, annual.

No. 1017. Highway Mileage, Vehicle Miles of Travel, Accidents, and Fatalities, 1975 to 1992, and by Type of Highway System, 1992

YEAR AND TYPE OF SYSTEM	Highway mileage (1,000)	Vehicle miles of travel (bil.)	Daily vehicle miles per mile	FATAL ACCIDENTS		NONFATAL INJURY ACCIDENTS		FATALITIES [2]	
				Number	Rate [1]	Number (1,000)	Rate [1]	Number	Rate [1]
1975	3,838	1,328	948	39,993	3.01	1,861	140	44,525	3.43
1980	3,857	1,527	1,082	45,284	2.96	2,008	131	51,091	3.35
1985	3,862	1,774	1,259	39,168	2.21	2,219	125	43,825	2.47
1986	3,880	1,835	1,298	41,062	2.23	2,254	123	46,087	2.51
1987	3,874	1,921	1,361	41,434	2.15	2,294	119	46,390	2.41
1988	3,871	2,026	1,430	42,119	2.08	2,302	114	47,087	2.32
1989	3,877	2,096	1,489	40,718	1.93	2,384	113	45,582	2.16
1990	3,880	2,148	1,516	39,779	1.85	2,501	116	44,529	2.07
1991	3,889	2,172	1,530	36,895	1.70	2,210	102	41,462	
1992, total......	**3,902**	**2,240**	**1,568**	**34,928**	**1.56**	**2,216**	**98.93**	**39,235**	**1.75**
Urban.............	785	1,359	4,730	15,202	1.12	1,586	116.70	16,486	1.21
Rural.............	3,117	881	772	19,726	2.24	630	71.51	22,749	2.58
Interstate	45	507	30,783	3,746	0.74	160	31.56	4,339	0.86
Urban.............	12	302	68,761	1,670	0.55	118	39.07	1,865	0.62
Rural.............	33	205	16,973	2,076	1.01	42	20.49	2,474	1.21
Noninterstate.......	3,857	1,733	1,228	31,182	1.80	2,056	118.64	34,896	2.01
Urban.............	772	1,057	3,741	13,532	1.28	1,468	138.88	14,621	1.38
Rural.............	3,084	676	599	17,650	2.61	588	86.98	20,275	3.00

[1] Rate per 100 million vehicle miles of travel. [2] Represents fatalities occurring within 30 days of accident. Excludes nontraffic accidents which, for example, occur outside the rights-of-way or other boundaries of roads that are open for public use.

Source: U.S. Federal Highway Administration, *Fatal and Injury Accident Rates on Public Roads in the United States,* annual.

No. 1018. Motor Vehicle Safety Defect Recalls, by Domestic and Foreign Manufacturers: 1980 to 1993

[Covers manufacturers reporting to U.S. National Highway Traffic Administration under section 151 of National Traffic and Motor Vehicle Safety Act of 1966, as amended]

MANUFACTURER	Unit	1980	1985	1986	1987	1988	1989	1990	1991	1992	1993
Motor vehicles:											
Total recall campaigns [1]	Number	167	173	173	199	197	237	208	220	187	221
Domestic	Number.	129	137	138	150	152	182	159	169	142	178
Foreign.............	Number.	38	36	35	49	45	55	49	51	45	43
Total vehicles recalled..........	1,000 ..	4,868	5,629	2,879	9,091	4,486	7,137	5,985	8,279	10,122	10,938
Domestic	1,000 ..	3,943	4,995	1,730	7,298	3,171	6,173	4,070	6,646	6,545	7,671
Vehicles recalled by four leading auto manufacturers......	1,000 ..	3,735	4,811	1,382	6,946	[2]2,900	5,855	3,926	6,303	5,880	7,345
Foreign.............	1,000 ..	925	634	1,149	1,793	1,315	964	1,915	1,633	3,577	3,267
Motor vehicle tires:											
Recall campaigns [1] ...	Number.	24	19	14	16	12	11	13	12	7	5
Tires recalled........	1,000 ..	7,070	28	164	42	215	115	172	153	8	6

[1] A recall campaign is the notification to the Secretary of the U.S. Dept. of Transportation and to owners, purchasers, and dealers of motor vehicles and motor vehicle equipment. [2] Three leading automobile manufacturers.

Source: U.S. National Highway Traffic Safety Administration, *Motor Vehicles Recall Campaigns,* annual.

No. 1019. Cost of Owning and Operating an Automobile: 1980 to 1992

ITEM	Unit	1980	1985	1987	1988	1989	1990	1991	1992
Cost per mile [1]	Cents	27.95	27.20	32.64	33.40	38.20	40.96	43.64	45.77
Cost per 10,000 miles [1] ...	Dollars....	2,795	2,720	3,264	3,341	3,820	4,096	4,364	4,577
Variable cost.............	Cents/mile .	7.62	8.04	7.20	7.60	7.90	8.40	9.80	9.10
Gas and oil.............	Cents/mile .	5.86	6.16	4.80	5.20	5.20	5.40	6.70	6.00
Maintenance.............	Cents/mile .	1.12	1.23	1.60	1.60	1.90	2.10	2.20	2.20
Tires.................	Cents/mile .	0.64	0.65	0.80	0.80	0.80	0.90	0.90	0.90
Fixed cost...............	Dollars....	2,033	2,441	2,782	3,061	3,534	3,877	4,217	4,538
Insurance.............	Dollars....	490	503	535	573	663	675	726	747
License and registration	Dollars....	82	115	140	139	151	165	169	179
Depreciation............	Dollars....	1,038	1,253	1,506	1,784	2,094	2,357	2,543	2,780
Finance charge..........	Dollars....	423	570	601	565	626	680	779	832

[1] Beginning 1985, not comparable to previous data.

Source: American Automobile Manufacturers Association Inc., Detroit, MI, *Motor Vehicle Facts and Figures,* annual (copyright).

No. 1020. State Legislation—Alcohol and Road Safety Laws: Various Years

REGION, DIVISION, AND STATE	ALCOHOL LEGISLATION			MANDATORY BELT USE LAW			Child safety seat law date [5]	Motor-cycle helmet law [6]	65 SPEED LIMIT	
	21 year drinking age since [1]	Open con-tainer law [2]	BAC limit [3]	Effec-tive date	Enforce-ment [4]	Seating posi-tions			Effec-tive date [7]	Applic-able vehicles
Northeast:										
N.E:										
ME	1985	no	0.08	none	(X)	(X)	9/83	[8][9]15	6/87	all
NH	1985	yes	0.10	none	(X)	(X)	7/89	18	4/87	all
VT	1986	no	0.08	none	(X)	(X)	7/84	yes	4/87	all
MA	1985	yes	0.10	repealed	(X)	(X)	1/82	yes	12/91	all
RI	1984	no	[10]0.10	7/91	2	all	7/87	([11])	none	(X)
CT	1985	no	0.10	1/86	1	front	1982	18	none	(X)
M.A:										
NY	1985	no	0.10	12/84	1	front	4/82	yes	none	(X)
NJ	1982	yes	0.10	3/85	2	front	4/83	yes	none	(X)
PA	1935	no	0.10	11/87	2	front	11/83	yes	none	(X)
Midwest:										
E.N.C:										
OH	1987	yes	[10]0.10	5/86	2	front	6/83	[9]18	7/87	some
IN	1935	no	0.10	7/87	2	front	1/84	18	6/87	some
IL	1980	yes	0.10	7/85	2	front	7/83	no	4/87	some
MI	1978	yes	0.10	7/85	2	all	3/82	yes	12/87	some
WI	1986	yes	[10]0.10	12/87	1	front	4/84	[8]18	6/87	all
W.N.C:										
MN	1986	yes	0.10	8/86	2	front	8/83	[8]18	6/87	all
IA	1986	yes	0.10	7/86	1	front	1/85	no	5/87	all
MO	1945	no	0.10	9/85	2	front	1/84	yes	4/87	some
ND	1936	yes	0.10	none	(X)	(X)	1/84	18	4/87	all
SD	1987	yes	0.10	none	(X)	(X)	7/84	18	4/87	all
NE	1985	no	0.10	1/93	2	front	8/83	yes	4/87	all
KS	1985	yes	0.10	7/86	2	front	7/81	18	5/87	some
South:										
S.A:										
DE	1983	yes	0.10	1/92	2	front	6/82	[8][12]19	none	(X)
MD	1982	no	0.10	7/86	2	[13]front	1/84	yes	none	(X)
DC	1986	no	0.10	12/85	2	[13]front	7/83	yes	none	(X)
VA	1986	no	0.10	1/88	2	front	1/83	yes	7/88	some
WV	1986	no	0.10	none	(X)	(X)	7/81	yes	5/87	all
NC	1986	yes	0.10	10/85	1	front	7/85	yes	4/87	all
SC	1986	yes	0.10	7/89	2	front	1/89	21	7/87	all
GA	1986	yes	0.10	9/88	2	front	7/84	yes	2/88	all
FL	1985	yes	0.10	7/86	2	front	7/83	yes	4/87	all
E.S.C:										
KY	1938	no	0.10	none	(X)	(X)	7/82	yes	6/87	all
TN	1984	no	0.10	4/86	2	front	1/78	yes	5/87	all
AL	1985	no	0.10	7/92	2	front	1982	yes	1987	all
MS	1986	no	0.10	3/90	1	front	7/83	yes	4/87	all
W.S.C:										
AR	1957	no	0.10	7/91	2	front	8/83	yes	4/87	all
LA	1987	no	0.10	7/86	2	front	1/85	yes	4/87	all
OK	1983	yes	0.10	2/87	2	front	11/83	18	4/87	all
TX	1985	no	0.10	9/85	1	front	1/85	yes	5/87	some
West:										
Mountain:										
MT	1987	no	0.10	10/87	2	all	10/83	18	4/87	all
ID	1987	[14]Yes	0.10	7/86	2	front	1/85	18	5/87	all
WY	1988	no	0.10	6/89	2	front	4/85	18	5/87	all
CO	1987	no	0.10	7/87	2	front	1/84	no	4/87	all
NM	1934	yes	0.10	1/86	1	front	5/83	18	4/87	all
AZ	1984	no	0.10	1/91	2	front	1984	18	4/87	all
UT	1935	yes	0.08	4/86	2	front	4/83	18	5/87	all
NV	1933	yes	0.10	7/87	2	all	7/83	yes	4/87	all
Pacfic:										
WA	1934	yes	0.10	6/86	2	all	1/84	yes	4/87	some
OR	1935	yes	[10]0.08	12/90	1	all	1/84	yes	10/87	some
CA	1933	yes	0.08	1/86	1	all	1/83	yes	5/87	some
AK	1983	yes	0.10	9/90	2	all	6/85	18	8/92	all
HI	1986	Yes	0.10	12/85	1	front	1983	18	none	(X)

X Not applicable. [1] Year in which original law became effective, not when grandfather clauses expired. [2] Law prohibiting open liquor containers in motor vehicles. [3] Percent blood alcohol concentration (BAC) which constitutes the threshold of legal intoxication. [4] "1" indicates primary enforcement (law can be enforced on its own), "2" indicates secondary enforcement. (Law enforced only if vehicle stopped for a separate offense.) [5] Effective data of original law, not of subsequent revisions. [6] Presence of law or age below which riders are required to wear helmet. [7] Includes administrative action as well as legislation. [8] Plus instruction permit holders. [9] Plus novice license holders. [10] Different legal limit for minors. [11] Passengers only. [12] Possession of helmet required by all. [13] Excluding front center seat. [14] Does not include beer.

Source: National Safety Council, Itasca, IL, *Accident Facts*, annual.

No. 1021. Estimated Arrests for Driving Under the Influence, by Age: 1980 and 1989

[Total drivers and arrests in thousands. Represents licensed drivers and arrests for those 16 years old and over]

AGE	1980			1989			Percent change in rate, 1980-89
	Drivers	Arrests	Arrests per 100,000 drivers	Drivers	Arrests	Arrests per 100,000 drivers	
Total	145,207	1,425	981	165,518	1,735	1,048	6.9
Percent distribution.	100.0	100.0	(X)	100.0	100.0	(X)	(X)
16 to 17 years old. . . .	3.2	2.2	668	2.3	1.1	503	−24.7
18 to 24 years old. . . .	7.2	12.9	1,757	5.4	8.3	1,607	−8.5
25 to 29 years old. . . .	13.0	17.9	1,347	12.4	22.2	1,869	38.8
30 to 34 years old. . . .	12.0	13.1	1,076	12.4	17.6	1,486	38.1
35 to 39 years old. . . .	9.4	9.6	996	11.2	12.0	1,123	12.8
40 to 44 years old. . . .	7.7	7.4	944	9.7	8.1	872	−7.6
45 to 49 years old. . . .	6.9	5.9	837	7.6	5.3	725	−13.4
50 to 54 years old. . . .	6.9	4.9	686	6.2	3.3	558	−18.7
55 to 59 years old. . . .	6.7	3.5	509	5.7	2.2	400	−21.4
60 to 64 years old. . . .	5.7	1.9	335	5.6	1.4	262	−21.8
65 years old and over .	10.7	1.5	140	13.0	1.2	100	−28.6

X Not applicable.

Source: U.S. Bureau of Justice Statistics, *Drunk Driving, Special Report.*

No. 1022. Licensed Drivers, Fatal Motor Vehicle Accidents, and Alcohol Involvement, by Age of Driver: 1991

ITEM	Unit	Total	AGE OF DRIVER							
			16-17 years	18-21 years	22-24 years	25-34 years	35-44 years	45-54 years	55-64 years	65 years and over
Licensed drivers (estimated) [1] . . .	1,000. . .	168,995	3,463	11,809	10,191	40,322	36,987	24,514	18,705	22,939
Percent distribution	Percent .	100.0	2.0	7.0	6.0	23.9	21.9	14.5	11.1	13.6
Licensed drivers involved in fatal accidents	Number .	58,893	2,651	8,112	5,253	15,764	10,177	5,867	4,068	5,501
Percent distribution	Percent .	100.0	4.5	13.8	8.9	26.8	17.3	10.0	6.9	9.3
Drinking drivers involved in fatal accidents	Number .	14,060	355	2,483	1,774	4,805	2,509	1,084	492	452
Percent distribution	Percent .	100.0	2.5	17.7	12.6	34.2	17.8	7.7	3.5	3.2

[1] Source: U.S. Federal Highway Administration, *Selected Highway Statistics and Charts,* annual.

No. 1023. Police-Reported Traffic Accidents, by Age Group: 1992

[Based on probability sample of police-reported accidents. See source for details]

ITEM	Total	15 yrs. and under	16 to 20 yrs.	21 to 24 yrs.	25 to 34 yrs.	35 to 44 yrs.	45 to 54 yrs.	55 to 64 yrs.	65 yrs. and older
Accident-involved	10,484,000	45,000	1,788,000	1,336,000	2,665,000	1,950,000	1,212,000	701,000	787,000
Percent male	62	63	63	62	61	60	63	64	63
Percent female	38	37	37	38	39	40	37	36	37
Percent alcohol-involved.	5	2	3	4	5	4	3	2	1
Passengers injured or killed	972,000	279,000	191,000	94,000	149,000	87,000	56,000	46,000	70,000
Percent male	42	47	51	46	41	37	29	26	23
Percent female	58	53	49	54	59	63	71	74	77
Pedestrians injured or killed	85,000	32,000	7,000	6,000	12,000	11,000	7,000	3,000	7,000
Percent during day	67	78	57	67	50	55	57	67	86
Percent at night	33	22	43	33	50	45	43	33	14
Pedalcyclists injured or killed	62,000	29,000	7,000	7,000	9,000	5,000	2,000	2,000	1,000

Source of tables 1022 and 1023: Except as noted, U.S. National Highway Traffic Safety Administration, *General Estimates System,* annual; and unpublished data.

No. 1024. Domestic Motor Fuel Consumption, by Type of Vehicle: 1970 to 1992

[Comprises all fuel types used for propulsion of vehicles under State motor fuels laws. Excludes Federal purchases for military use. Minus sign (-) indicates decrease. See also *Historical Statistics, Colonial Times to 1970*, series Q 156-162]

YEAR	FUEL CONSUMPTION					AVG. FUEL CONSUMPTION PER VEHICLE (gal.)			AVG. MILES PER GALLON		
	All vehicles (bil. gal.)	Avg. annual percent change [1]	Cars [2] (bil. gal.)	Buses [3] (bil. gal.)	Trucks [4] (bil. gal.)	Cars [2]	Buses [3]	Trucks [4]	Cars [2]	Buses [3]	Trucks [4]
1970 ..	92.3	5.4	67.8	0.8	23.6	760	2,172	1,257	13.52	5.54	7.85
1975 ..	109.0	2.5	76.4	1.1	31.4	716	2,279	1,217	13.52	5.75	8.99
1980 ..	115.0	-5.9	71.9	1.0	41.9	591	1,926	1,243	15.46	5.95	9.54
1981 ..	114.5	-0.4	71.0	1.1	42.2	576	1,938	1,219	15.94	5.92	9.59
1982 ..	113.4	-0.9	70.1	1.0	42.1	566	1,756	1,191	16.65	5.93	9.80
1983 ..	116.1	2.4	69.9	0.9	45.1	553	1,507	1,229	17.14	5.92	9.77
1984 ..	118.7	2.3	68.7	0.8	49.0	536	1,359	1,308	17.83	5.85	9.83
1985 ..	121.3	2.2	69.3	0.8	51.0	525	1,407	1,302	18.20	5.84	9.79
1986 ..	125.2	3.2	71.4	0.9	52.9	526	1,463	1,320	18.27	5.84	9.81
1987 ..	127.5	1.8	70.6	0.9	55.8	514	1,500	1,357	19.20	5.89	9.87
1988 ..	130.1	2.0	71.9	0.9	57.2	509	1,496	1,345	19.95	5.93	10.16
1989 ..	131.8	1.3	72.7	0.9	57.9	509	1,518	1,328	20.40	5.96	10.41
1990 ..	130.8	-0.8	72.0	0.9	57.7	502	1,428	1,290	21.02	6.39	10.67
1991 ..	128.6	-1.7	70.7	0.9	56.8	496	1,369	1,264	21.69	6.65	10.97
1992 ..	132.9	3.2	73.9	0.9	58.0	512	1,360	1,275	21.60	6.54	10.84

[1] From prior year, except 1970, change from 1965.   [2] Includes taxicabs.   [3] Includes school buses.   [4] Includes combinations.

Source: U.S. Federal Highway Administration, *Highway Statistics Summary to 1985*, and *Highway Statistics, annual.*

No. 1025. U.S. Vehicle, by Model Year and Vehicle Fuel Efficiency: 1991

[For composition of regions, see table 26]

1990 HOUSEHOLD CHARACTERISTICS	U.S. VEHICLES (mil.)					U.S. VEHICLE FUEL EFFICIENCY (mpg)				
	All model years	Model year				All model years	Model year			
		1991 to 1992	1990	1989	1986 to 1988		1991 to 1992	1990	1989	1986 to 1988
Total	151.2	5.5	10.5	12.5	39.0	19.3	21.8	21.5	21.8	22.0
Regions:										
Northeast..............	27.0	1.0	2.3	2.8	8.8	20.9	23.0	22.2	22.4	22.7
Midwest..............	38.4	1.3	2.7	3.0	9.6	19.0	21.0	21.2	21.0	22.2
South................	52.7	2.0	3.6	4.4	12.7	19.2	21.5	21.0	22.4	21.9
West	33.2	1.2	1.9	2.3	7.8	18.9	22.1	21.8	21.0	21.3
Urban................	114.3	4.5	8.5	10.2	30.8	19.8	21.8	21.9	22.1	22.2
Rural	36.9	1.0	2.0	2.4	8.2	18.0	21.6	19.6	20.6	21.5
Household size:										
1 person..............	22.1	0.7	1.4	1.5	4.9	19.1	(S)	21.0	21.7	23.4
2 persons.............	49.9	1.9	3.7	4.0	13.1	19.3	20.9	21.1	22.1	21.3
3 persons.............	30.3	1.1	2.0	2.8	8.5	20.1	22.5	22.3	21.8	22.9
4 persons.............	29.3	1.3	2.0	2.9	7.7	19.4	21.7	21.7	21.6	22.2
5 persons.............	13.6	0.4	0.9	0.9	3.5	18.9	(S)	21.4	21.8	21.4
6 persons or more	6.0	(S)	(S)	(S)	1.2	17.6	(S)	(S)	(S)	19.3
Households with children	65.1	2.5	4.5	5.5	16.8	19.4	21.9	21.8	22.0	22.0
Under 7 years old	19.0	0.6	1.4	1.7	5.0	20.0	(S)	22.8	21.2	23.7
7 to 15 years old	32.3	1.3	2.4	2.8	8.6	19.2	21.6	21.2	22.6	21.8
16 or 17 years old	13.8	0.6	0.8	1.1	3.2	19.1	(S)	(S)	21.6	20.2
Households without children	86.2	3.0	6.0	7.0	22.2	19.3	21.7	21.2	21.7	22.0
One adult..............	22.1	0.7	1.4	1.5	4.9	19.1	(S)	21.0	21.7	23.4
Under 35 years old	5.0	(S)	(S)	(S)	1.4	20.7	(S)	(S)	(S)	25.0
35 to 59 years old	7.6	(S)	0.6	(S)	1.9	19.4	(S)	(S)	(S)	23.0
60 years old or older	9.6	(S)	(S)	(S)	1.6	17.5	(S)	(S)	(S)	21.6
Two or more adults	64.0	2.3	4.5	5.5	17.2	19.4	21.3	21.2	21.7	21.7
Under 35 years old	13.2	0.7	0.7	1.4	3.3	21.1	(S)	23.9	24.3
35 to 59 years old	27.8	1.0	2.2	2.3	7.9	19.3	21.4	20.7	21.8	21.4
60 years old or older	23.1	0.6	1.6	1.7	6.0	18.3	(S)	21.4	19.8	20.4
White	135.3	5.1	9.4	11.1	35.8	19.3	21.8	21.4	21.6	21.9
Black	12.8	(S)	0.7	1.1	2.5	19.4	(S)	(S)	24.3	23.5
Other	3.1	(S)	(S)	(S)	0.6	19.3	(S)	(S)	(S)	(S)
Hispanic descent:										
Yes	9.4	(S)	(S)	(S)	2.3	18.3	(S)	(S)	(S)	20.1
No	141.8	5.3	10.0	12.0	36.6	19.4	21.8	21.4	21.8	22.1

S Figure does not meet publications standards.

Source: U.S. Energy Information Administration, *Household Vehicles Energy Consumption, 1991.*

No. 1026. Household Vehicles—Annual Mileage, Fuel Consumption, and Fuel Expenditures: 1991

1990 HOUSEHOLD CHARACTERISTICS	VEHICLES		VEHICLE MILES TRAVELED		CONSUMPTION			EXPENDITURES	
	Total (mil.)	Percent	Total (bil.)	Percent	Total (bil. gal.)	Gallon (per-cent	Btu. (quadril-lion)	Total (bil. dol.)	Percent
Total	151.2	100.0	1,602	100.0	82.8	100.0	10.3	98.2	100.0
Urban	114.3	75.6	1,219	76.1	61.5	74.3	7.6	73.3	74.6
Rural	36.9	24.4	383	23.9	21.3	25.7	2.6	25.0	25.4
Household size:									
1 person	22.1	14.6	198	12.4	10.4	12.5	1.3	12.3	12.5
2 persons	49.9	33.0	494	30.8	25.6	30.9	3.2	30.3	30.8
3 persons	30.3	20.0	339	21.2	16.9	20.4	2.1	20.1	20.5
4 persons	29.3	19.4	349	21.8	18.0	21.7	2.2	21.4	21.7
5 persons	13.6	9.0	152	9.5	8.0	9.7	1.0	9.5	9.7
6 persons or more	6.0	3.9	70	4.4	4.0	4.8	0.5	4.7	4.8
Households with children	65.1	43.0	753	47.0	38.9	46.9	4.8	46.1	46.9
Under 7 years old	19.0	12.6	214	13.4	10.7	12.9	1.3	12.7	13.0
7 to 15 years old	32.3	21.3	378	23.6	19.7	23.8	2.4	23.4	23.8
16 or 17 years old	13.8	9.1	161	10.1	8.4	10.2	1.0	10.0	10.2
Households without children	86.2	57.0	849	53.0	44.0	53.1	5.5	52.2	53.1
One adult	22.1	14.6	198	12.4	10.4	12.5	1.3	12.3	12.5
Under 35 years old	5.0	3.3	59	3.7	2.9	3.5	0.4	3.4	3.5
35 to 59 years old	7.6	5.0	81	5.1	4.2	5.0	0.5	5.0	5.0
60 years old or older	9.6	6.3	58	3.6	3.3	4.0	0.4	3.9	4.0
Two or more adults	64.0	42.3	651	40.6	33.6	40.6	4.2	39.9	40.6
Under 35 years old	13.2	8.7	156	9.8	7.4	8.9	0.9	8.8	8.9
35 to 59 years old	27.8	18.4	298	18.6	15.4	18.7	1.9	18.3	18.7
60 years old or older	23.1	15.2	197	12.3	10.7	13.0	1.3	12.8	13.0
White	135.3	89.5	1,429	89.2	73.9	89.2	9.1	87.5	89.1
Black	12.8	8.4	143	8.9	7.4	8.9	0.9	8.9	9.0
Other	3.1	2.1	30	1.9	1.6	1.9	0.2	1.8	1.9
Hispanic descent:									
Yes	9.4	6.2	95	5.9	5.2	6.3	0.6	6.1	6.3
No	141.8	93.8	1,507	94.1	77.6	93.7	9.6	92.1	93.7
1990 family income:									
Less than $10,000	12.7	8.4	110	6.8	6.1	7.3	0.7	7.2	7.2
$10,000 to $14,999	13.5	8.9	120	7.5	6.6	7.9	0.8	7.7	7.9
$15,000 to $19,999	10.9	7.2	106	6.6	5.7	6.9	0.7	6.7	6.8
$20,000 to $24,999	15.6	10.3	153	9.5	8.5	10.3	1.1	10.1	10.2
$25,000 to $34,999	27.5	18.2	284	17.7	14.9	18.0	1.8	17.7	18.0
$35,000 to $49,999	32.1	21.2	361	22.6	17.8	21.5	2.2	21.1	21.5
$50,000 to $74,999	22.9	15.1	273	17.0	13.5	16.4	1.7	16.1	16.4
$75,000 or more	16.0	10.6	196	12.3	9.7	11.7	1.2	11.7	11.9
Below poverty line:									
100 percent	11.5	7.6	110	6.9	6.1	7.4	0.8	7.2	7.3
125 percent	17.6	11.6	163	10.2	9.3	11.2	1.2	10.9	11.1
Eligible for Federal assistance	29.8	19.7	279	17.4	15.6	18.8	1.9	18.3	18.6
Number of drivers (fall 1990):									
1	34.6	22.9	321	20.0	16.8	20.3	2.1	20.0	20.3
2	86.7	57.3	934	58.3	48.5	58.6	6.0	57.5	58.6
3	22.0	14.5	258	16.1	13.0	15.7	1.6	15.5	15.8
4 or more	7.2	4.7	84	5.2	4.2	5.1	0.5	4.9	5.0
Age of primary driver:									
16 to 17 years old	0.7	0.5	8	0.5	0.4	0.4	(Z)	0.4	0.4
18 to 22 years old	4.5	3.0	50	3.1	2.3	2.8	0.3	2.7	2.7
23 to 29 years old	9.6	6.3	117	7.3	5.6	6.8	0.7	6.7	6.8
30 to 39 years old	23.5	15.5	284	17.7	13.8	16.6	1.7	16.3	16.6
40 to 49 years old	18.1	12.0	219	13.7	11.3	13.6	1.4	13.4	13.7
50 to 59 years old	14.0	9.2	151	9.4	8.1	9.7	1.0	9.6	9.8
60 to 69 years old	12.2	8.0	100	6.3	5.4	6.6	0.7	6.5	6.6
70 to 79 years old	8.0	5.3	58	3.6	3.3	4.0	0.4	3.9	4.0
80 years old and over	2.2	1.5	12	0.7	0.7	0.8	0.1	0.8	0.8
No answer	58.5	38.7	604	37.7	32.0	38.7	4.0	37.9	38.6
Sex of primary driver:									
Female	44.0	29.1	483	30.1	22.9	27.6	2.8	27.2	27.7
Male	49.6	32.8	526	32.8	28.5	34.4	3.5	33.7	34.3
No answer	57.6	38.1	594	37.1	31.5	38.0	3.9	37.3	38.0
Average number of vehicles per household during the year:									
Part-year vehicle	2.1	1.4	21	1.3	1.1	1.3	0.1	1.3	1.4
Only 1	27.5	18.2	269	16.8	13.4	16.2	1.7	16.0	16.3
Between 1 and 2	14.1	9.3	152	9.5	7.9	9.5	1.0	9.4	9.5
Only 2	49.4	32.6	534	33.3	27.1	32.7	3.4	32.3	32.9
Between 2 and 3	19.3	12.8	219	13.7	11.6	14.1	1.4	13.7	14.0
Only 3	17.6	11.6	187	11.7	9.8	11.8	1.2	11.6	11.8
Between 3 and 4	10.6	7.0	112	7.0	6.0	7.2	0.7	7.0	7.1
4 or more	10.8	7.2	108	6.8	5.9	7.1	0.7	7.0	7.1

Source: U.S. Energy Information Administration, *Household Vehicles Energy Consumption, 1991.*

No. 1027. Motor Vehicle Travel, by Type of Vehicle and by Speed: 1970 to 1992

[Travel in billions of vehicle-miles, except as indicated. Travel estimates based on automatic traffic recorder data. Speed trend data for 1970-1975 were collected by several State highway agencies, normally during summer months; beginning Oct. 1975 all States have monitored speeds at locations on several highway systems Monitoring Program. See also *Historical Statistics, Colonial Times to 1970*, series Q 199-207]

| YEAR | VEHICLE-MILES OF TRAVEL (bil.) | | | | AVG. MILES PER VEHICLE (1,000) | | | MOTOR VEHICLE SPEED ON RURAL INTERSTATE | | | | |
| | Total | Cars [1] | Buses | Trucks | Passenger vehicles | | Trucks | Citations recorded (1,000) [2] | Avg. speed (miles per hour) | Percent of vehicles exceeding— | | |
					Cars [1]	Buses				55 mph	60 mph	65 mph
1970	1,110	920	4.5	186	10.0	12.0	9.9	200	63.8	87	69	44
1980	1,527	1,122	6.1	399	8.8	11.5	11.9	667	57.5	66	25	7
1984	1,720	1,234	4.6	482	9.2	8.0	12.8	8,067	59.3	75	43	16
1985	1,774	1,270	4.9	500	9.2	8.2	12.7	8,449	59.5	75	44	17
1986	1,834	1,311	5.1	519	9.3	8.5	13.0	8,549	59.7	76	46	18
1987	1,921	1,365	5.3	551	9.6	8.8	13.4	7,992	59.7	74	46	19
1988	2,025	1,439	5.5	581	9.9	8.9	13.6	7,566	59.5	74	46	19
1989	2,096	1,488	5.7	603	10.1	9.0	13.8	7,488	60.1	77	49	22
1990	2,144	1,513	5.7	616	10.5	9.1	13.8	7,511	60.3	78	50	23
1991	2,172	1,534	5.7	624	10.8	9.1	13.9	7,594	59.6	75	48	22
1992	2,240	1,595	5.7	629	11.1	8.9	13.8	7,004	53.5	81	56	28

[1] Includes motorcycles.   [2] Citations issued for 55 mph violations.

Source: U.S. Federal Highway Administration, *Highway Statistics Summary*, annual.

No. 1028. Passenger Transit Industry—Summary: 1980 to 1992

[Includes Puerto Rico. Includes aggregate information for all transit systems in the United States. Except as noted, 1980 data exclude commuter railroad, automated guideway, urban ferry boat, and demand response, as well as most transit systems outside of urbanized areas. Excludes nontransit services such as taxicab, school bus, unregulated jitney, sightseeing bus, intercity bus, and special application mass transportation systems (e.g., amusement parks, airports, island, and urban park ferries) Includes active vehicles only]

ITEM	Unit	1980	1985	1988	1989	1990	1991	1992, prel.
Operating systems . . , ...	Number...	1,044	4,972	5,036	5,046	5,078	5,084	5,086
Motor bus systems [1] . . ; . .	Number...	1,040	2,631	2,671	2,665	2,688	2,689	2,691
Publicly owned systems [1] .	Number...	576	1,435	(NA)	(NA)	1,580	(NA)	(NA)
Passenger vehicles owned [2] .	Number...	75,388	94,368	97,209	92,293	92,961	96,399	100,274
Motor bus	Number...	59,411	64,258	62,572	58,919	58,714	60,377	61,959
Trolley bus	Number...	823	676	710	725	832	752	907
Heavy rail	Number...	9,641	9,326	10,539	10,506	10,419	10,331	10,245
Light rail	Number...	1,013	717	831	755	913	1,095	1,058
Commuter rail	Number...	4,500	4,035	4,649	4,472	4,415	4,370	4,413
Demand response	Number...	(NA)	14,490	16,812	15,856	16,471	17,879	19,566
Total revenue	Mil. dol . .	6,510	12,195	14,537	14,985	16,053	16,533	16,473
Passenger revenue	Mil. dol . .	2,557	4,575	5,225	5,420	5,891	6,037	6,179
Other operating revenue [3] .	Mil. dol . .	248	702	841	837	895	767	806
Operating assistance	Mil. dol . .	3,705	6,918	8,471	8,728	9,267	9,729	9,488
Federal	Mil. dol . .	1,094	940	901	937	970	956	964
Local [4]	Mil. dol . .	2,611	5,979	4,893	4,995	5,327	5,573	4,748
State [4]	Mil. dol . .	(NA)	(NA)	2,677	2,796	2,970	3,200	3,776
Total expense	Mil. dol . .	6,711	14,077	16,442	17,169	17,979	19,332	19,872
Operating expense	Mil. dol . .	6,247	12,381	14,287	14,972	15,742	16,541	16,646
Transportation	Mil. dol . .	3,248	5,655	6,052	6,275	6,654	6,727	7,547
Maintenance	Mil. dol . .	1,774	3,672	4,313	4,493	4,631	4,597	4,857
Administration	Mil. dol . .	1,224	2,505	3,078	3,251	3,450	3,585	2,767
Reconciling expense	Mil. dol . .	464	1,696	2,155	2,196	2,237	2,791	3,226
Capital expenditure, Federal. .	Mil. dol . .	2,787	2,510	2,521	2,590	2,380	2,396	2,613
Vehicle-miles operated [2]	Million. . . .	2,287	2,791	3,157	3,203	3,242	3,306	3,384
Motor bus	Million. . . .	1,677	1,863	2,097	2,109	2,130	2,167	2,185
Trolley bus.	Million. . . .	13	16	15	15	14	14	14
Heavy rail	Million. . . .	385	451	517	532	537	527	525
Light rail	Million. . . .	18	17	21	21	24	28	29
Commuter rail.	Million. . . .	179	183	202	210	213	215	219
Demand response.	Million. . . .	(NA)	247	289	300	306	335	382
Passengers carried [2].	Million. . . .	8,567	8,636	8,666	8,931	8,799	8,575	8,519
Motor bus	Million. . . .	5,837	5,675	5,590	5,620	5,677	5,624	5,525
Trolley bus.	Million. . . .	142	142	136	130	126	125	127
Heavy rail	Million. . . .	2,108	2,290	2,308	2,542	2,346	2,172	2,207
Light rail	Million. . . .	133	132	154	162	175	184	189
Commuter rail.	Million. . . .	280	275	325	330	328	318	314
Demand response.	Million. . . .	(NA)	59	73	70	68	71	79
Avg. revenue per passenger. .	Cents	29.8	53.0	60.3	60.7	66.9	70.4	72.5
Employees, number (avg.) . . .	1,000	187	270	276	272	273	276	276
Payroll, employee	Mil. dol . . .	3,281	5,843	6,675	6,898	7,226	7,395	7,778
Fringe benefits, employee . . .	Mil. dol . . .	1,353	2,868	3,529	3,737	3,986	3,998	4,405

NA Not available.   [1] Includes systems with combined services including motor buses, heavy rail cars, light rail cars, trolley coaches, cable cars, and inclined plane cars. Combined services also include commuter rail cars, urban ferry boats, vanpools, aerial tramways, automated guideways, and demand response vehicles.   [2] Includes other not shown separately.   [3] Includes other operating revenue, nonoperating revenue, and auxiliary income.   [4] Prior to 1986, State and local combined.

Source: American Public Transit Association, Washington, DC, *Transit Fact Book*, annual.

No. 1029. Class I Intercity Motor Carriers of Passengers: 1980 to 1991

[Carriers subject to ICC regulations. See text, section 21. Minus sign (-) indicates deficit. See also *Historical Statistics, Colonial Times to 1970,* series Q 69-75]

ITEM	Unit	1980	1982	1983	1984	1985	1986	1987	1988	1989	1990	1991
Carriers reporting [1]	Number.	48	50	45	43	43	29	32	21	20	21	21
Number of employees, average	1,000	31	30	25	25	24	20	(NA)	(NA)	(NA)	(NA)	(NA)
Compensation of employees	Mil. dol	599	646	570	551	518	443	(NA)	(NA)	(NA)	(NA)	(NA)
Operating revenue	Mil. dol	1,397	1,447	1,276	1,255	1,233	1,117	1,079	1,122	1,205	943	980
Passenger revenue [2]	Mil. dol	947	969	876	861	836	765	751	825	890	738	793
Special bus revenue and other	Mil. dol	215	229	180	180	184	155	165	155	165	90	187
Operating expenses	*Mil. dol*	*1,318*	*1,416*	*1,283*	*1,254*	*1,168*	*1,082*	*1,081*	*1,059*	*1,133*	*1,015*	*967*
Net operating revenue	Mil. dol	79	30	-7	1	65	35	-2	63	72	-72	13
Ordinary income:												
Before income taxes	Mil. dol	107	35	16	53	65	50	-11	(NA)	(NA)	(NA)	(NA)
After income taxes	Mil. dol	90	37	26	43	53	36	-21	12	-180	162
Passenger vehicles in service [2]	1,000	8.6	8.1	7.3	7.0	8.4	8.3	(NA)	(NA)	(NA)	(NA)	(NA)
Vehicle-miles, passenger	Million.	781	717	591	585	567	495	(NA)	(NA)	(NA)	(NA)	(NA)
Revenue passengers carried	Million.	134	112	94	89	88	74	82	55	54	43	42
Expense per vehicle-mile	Dollar.	1.69	1.98	2.17	2.14	2.06	2.18	(NA)	(NA)	(NA)	(NA)	(NA)

NA Not available. [1] Excludes carriers preponderantly in local or suburban service and carriers engaged in transportation of both property and passengers. [2] Regular route, intercity, and local.

Source: U.S. Interstate Commerce Commission, *Transport Statistics in the United States,* part 2, annual.

No. 1030. Intercity Bus Lines—Summary of Operations: 1970 to 1991

ITEM	Unit	1970	1975	1980	1985	1986	1987	1988	1989	1990	1991
Operating companies	Number.	1,000	950	1,330	(NA)	(NA)	3,550	(NA)	3,628	(NA)	(NA)
Buses	1,000	22.0	20.5	21.4	20.1	19.1	18.4	(NA)	(NA)	23.5	20.6
Miles of highway served (Dec. 31) [1]	1,000	267	274	279	263	257	249	(NA)	(NA)	(NA)	(NA)
Employees (Dec. 31) [2]	1,000	50	47	49	43	41	39	42	45	41	41
Operating revenue, all services	Mil. dol	901	1,172	1,943	1,898	1,838	1,717	(NA)	(NA)	(NA)	929
Operating expenses	Mil. dol	812	1,103	1,811	1,839	1,781	1,669	(NA)	(NA)	(NA)	885
Net operating revenue [3]	Mil. dol	89	69	132	59	57	48	(NA)	(NA)	(NA)	44

NA Not available. [1] Includes duplication between carriers. [2] Operating companies only. [3] Before income taxes.

Source: American Bus Association, Washington, DC, *Bus Facts,* annual; and *Annual Report.*

No. 1031. Warehousing Services—Revenues, Expenses, and Payroll: 1991 and 1992

[In millions of dollars]

KIND OF BUSINESS	SIC [1] code	OPERATING REVENUE		OPERATING EXPENSES		ANNUAL PAYROLL	
		1991	1992	1991	1992	1991	1992
Motor frgt. transport. and warehousing services [2]	42	123,724	132,231	114,934	123,230	38,969	41,019
Trucking and courier services, except by air [3]	421	117,048	124,742	109,220	116,887	37,179	39,009
Public warehousing and storage	422	6,516	7,256	5,559	6,121	1,757	1,963
Local trucking without storage	4212	27,297	29,318	24,000	26,363	7,328	7,837
Trucking, except local	4213	68,516	72,618	65,642	69,601	20,724	21,726
Local trucking with storage	4214	3,992	4,159	3,805	3,900	1,349	1,372
Courier services, except by air	4215	17,243	18,647	15,773	17,023	7,778	8,074
Farm product warehousing and storage	4211	500	567	440	490	131	142
Refrigerated warehousing	4222	1,490	1,657	1,264	1,412	441	484
General warehousing and storage	4225	3,248	3,567	2,750	2,951	816	906
Special warehousing and storage [4]	4226	1,278	1,465	1,105	1,268	369	431

[1] Standard Industrial Classification. [2] Includes terminal and joint terminal maintenance facilities for motor carrier transportation (SIC 4231) not shown separately. [3] Excludes private motor carriers that operate as auxiliary establishments to nontransportation companies and independent owner-operators with no paid employees. [4] Includes household goods warehousing.

Source: U.S. Bureau of the Census, *Current Business Reports, 1992 Motor Freight Transportation and Warehousing Survey.*

No. 1032. Trucking and Courier Services—Operating Revenue, Operating Expenses, and Equipment, by Type of Carrier: 1990 to 1992

[In millions of dollars, except as indicated. Data cover SIC group 421. Excludes private motor carriers that operate as auxiliary establishments to nontransportation companies and independent owner-operators with no paid employees. Some unpublished estimates can be derived from this table by subtracting published data from their respective totals. However, the figures obtained by such subtraction are subject to these same limitations. These unpublished data are for internal use only]

ITEM	ALL CARRIERS			SPECIALTY CARRIERS			GENERAL CARRIERS		
	1990	1991	1992	1990	1991	1992	1990	1991	1992
Operating revenues:									
Total [1]	117,511	117,048	124,742	32,835	31,918	33,324	84,676	85,130	91,418
Motor carrier	107,997	108,604	116,974	28,302	27,905	29,616	79,695	80,699	87,358
Local trucking	25,246	24,582	27,803	13,183	13,077	14,345	12,063	11,505	13,458
Long-distance trucking	82,751	84,022	89,171	15,119	14,828	15,271	67,632	69,194	73,900
Operating expenses:									
Total	109,074	109,202	116,887	28,977	28,507	29,991	80,097	80,713	86,896
Annual payroll	36,490	37,179	39,009	8,242	8,123	8,397	28,248	29,056	30,612
Employer contrib. to Soc. Sec. and other benefits	9,365	9,721	10,486	1,937	1,881	1,980	7,428	7,840	8,506
Purchased fuels	8,647	8,719	9,712	1,653	1,667	1,855	6,994	7,052	7,857
Purchased transportation	19,630	19,321	21,054	5,701	5,384	5,797	13,929	13,937	15,257
Lease and rental	2,168	2,161	2,168	631	631	623	1,537	1,530	1,545
Insurance	3,898	3,998	4,152	1,108	1,161	1,220	2,790	2,837	2,932
Maintenance and repair	6,133	6,133	6,861	1,867	1,843	2,006	4,266	4,290	4,855
Depreciation	5,603	5,632	5,987	1,623	1,596	1,648	3,980	4,036	4,339
Taxes and licenses	2,325	2,439	2,762	518	510	584	1,807	1,929	2,178
Drug and alcohol testing and rehabilitation programs	27	35	46	7	10	13	20	25	33
Other operating expenses	14,788	13,882	14,650	5,690	5,701	5,868	9,098	8,181	8,782
Equipment (1,000 units): [2]									
Trucks	226	231	242	100	100	109	126	131	133
Truck-tractors	525	524	562	111	108	110	414	416	452
Trailers (full and semi)	1,179	1,191	1,244	214	205	203	965	986	1,041

[1] Includes other revenue not shown separately.   [2] Represents revenue generating equipment as of December 31. Includes owned and leased equipment.

Source: U.S. Bureau of the Census, *Current Business Reports, 1992 Motor Freight Transportation and Warehousing Survey.*

No. 1033. Class I Intercity Motor Carriers of Property, by Carrier: 1980 to 1991

[See headnote, table 1029. Common carriers are carriers offering regular scheduled service. Contract carriers provide service at request of user. Minus sign (-) indicates loss]

ITEM	Unit	1980	1985	1990	1991	1980	1985	1990	1991
		COMMON CARRIER, GENERAL FREIGHT				COMMON CARRIER OTHER THAN GENERAL FREIGHT			
Carriers reporting	Number	298	237	191	201	441	397	322	295
Number of employees, average	1,000	413	376	465	474	101	76	87	74
Compensation of employees	Mil. dol.	9,803	10,217	13,556	14,032	1,931	1,783	2,236	1,920
Operating revenues	Mil. dol.	19,725	22,314	29,682	31,619	8,792	7,962	9,042	7,761
Intercity freight	Mil. dol.	19,480	22,080	29,517	19,698	8,339	7,664	8,762	7,480
Operating expenses	Mil. dol.	18,870	21,037	28,340	30,269	8,426	7,752	8,702	7,509
Ordinary income before taxes	Mil. dol.	701	1,198	1,146	1,180	230	123	198	122
Net income	Mil. dol.	-72	658	746	749	14	94	153	85
Total power units, intercity service	1,000	102	108	(NA)	(NA)	95	77	(NA)	(NA)
Trucks, tractors owned in operation, avg	1,000	73	82	(NA)	(NA)	33	29	(NA)	(NA)
Intercity vehicle-miles	Million	6,547	5,760	6,804	7,615	6,889	5,714	6,566	5,372
Tons of intercity revenue freight carried	Million	178	136	157	169	324	303	302	253
		CONTRACT CARRIER OTHER THAN GENERAL FREIGHT				CARRIERS OF HOUSEHOLD GOODS			
Carriers reporting	Number	69	64	87	83	28	40	36	36
Number of employees, average	1,000	14	22	34	34	10	11	13	12
Compensation of employees	Mil. dol.	336	630	1,082	989	157	240	296	298
Operating revenues	Mil. dol.	1,272	1,942	3,486	3,644	1,824	2,684	3,152	3,026
Intercity freight	Mil. dol.	1,172	1,792	3,209	3,449	1,676	2,388	2,702	2,318
Operating expenses	Mil. dol.	1,207	1,807	3,422	3,547	1,781	2,635	3,129	2,973
Ordinary income before taxes	Mil. dol.	48	103	3	53	74	79	12	27
Net income	Mil. dol.	28	69	-13	20	42	54	8	17
Total power units, intercity service	1,000	13	16	(NA)	(NA)	25	35	(NA)	(NA)
Trucks, tractors owned in operation, avg	1,000	7	11	(NA)	(NA)	5	1	(NA)	(NA)
Intercity vehicle-miles	Million	934	1,227	2,044	2,339	969	1,171	1,366	1,086
Tons of intercity revenue freight carried	Million	37	41	80	76	5	7	8	7

NA Not available.

Source: U.S. Interstate Commerce Commission, *Transport Statistics in the United States,* part 2, annual.

No. 1034. Trucks—Percent Distribution, Operational Characteristics: 1977 to 1987

[See headnote, table 1035]

CHARACTERISTIC	1977	1982	1987	CHARACTERISTIC	1977	1982	1987
Total	100.0	100.0	100.0	Purchased used	50.0	51.5	50.1
				Leased [5]	2.4	2.8	2.6
Major use:				Fleet size: [6] 1	71.6	77.8	65.1
Agriculture [1]	17.0	12.2	8.5	2 to 5	16.3	10.9	24.9
Construction	6.7	11.2	10.0	6 to 19.	6.6	5.3	5.4
Manufacturing	1.4	1.6	1.3	20 or more	5.5	6.0	4.6
Wholesale and retail trade. ...	7.6	6.8	5.6	Truck-type:			
Personal transportation.	54.4	56.7	65.7	Single-unit	96.8	95.7	96.3
All other	13.0	11.4	8.8	Combination	3.2	4.3	3.7
Body type:				Annual miles:			
Pickup and panel [2]	83.3	85.8	89.0	Less than 5,000	23.9	26.0	25.3
Platform and cattlerack......	6.8	5.1	3.7	5,000 to 9,999.	24.0	25.5	23.4
Van [3]	4.5	3.8	3.2	10,000 to 19,999	37.0	35.0	34.5
All other.	5.5	5.2	4.0	20,000 to 29,999	9.2	8.4	10.7
Vehicle size: [4] Light.	85.4	89.3	91.9	30,000 miles or more	5.9	5.0	6.1
Medium	6.0	3.5	2.3	Range of operation: [7]			
Light-heavy.	3.1	2.4	1.7	Local.................	84.8	76.6	75.6
Heavy-heavy.	5.5	4.8	4.1	Short-range	8.4	10.3	14.8
Year model:				Long-range.	2.1	3.1	4.5
1 to 2 years old...........	17.1	8.9	17.2	Off-the-road [5]	4.7	10.0	5.1
3 to 4 years old.	17.5	16.5	16.5	Fuel type:			
4 years or more.	65.4	74.6	66.3	Gasoline	96.0	94.3	93.7
Vehicle acquisition:				Diesel and LPG...........	3.9	5.5	6.2
Purchased new	47.6	45.7	47.3	Not reported	-	0.2	0.1

- Represents zero.   [1] Includes forestry and lumbering.   [2] Also includes walk-in, minivan, station wagon, and utility trucks.
[3] Includes multi-stop or walk-in.   [4] See footnote 6, table 1035.   [5] Includes not reported.   [6] See footnote 8, table 1035.   [7] See footnote 9, table 1035.

No. 1035. Trucks and Truck-Miles, by Vehicle and Operational Characteristics: 1987

[Data are based on a stratified probability sample of trucks drawn from current registrations on file with motor vehicle departments in the 50 States and DC]

ITEM	TRUCKS (1,000)		TRUCK-MILES (bil.)	ITEM	TRUCKS (1,000)		TRUCK-MILES (bil.)
	Total	Excl. pickups, panels [1]			Total	Excl. pickups, panels [1]	
Total	44,572	4,886	529.3	Range of operation: [9]			
Major use:				Local	33,685	3,027	350.9
Agriculture [2]	3,819	1,114	39.0	Short-range	6,612	920	108.3
Construction	4,479	997	63.7	Long-range............	1,997	490	56.0
Manufacturing	581	241	12.5	Off-the-road [7]	2,278	449	14.1
Wholesale and retail trade ..	2,507	830	43.3	Products carried:			
Personal transportation	29,292	250	287.0	Farm products	1,558	769	16.2
All other	3,894	1,455	83.8	Building materials	1,141	640	18.6
Body type:				Mixed cargoes	686	325	21.1
Pickup and panel [3]	39,686	(X)	427	Craftsman's equipment	2,476	319	34.5
Platform [4]	1,668	1,668	25.0	Personal transportation	29,290	251	286.9
Van [5]	1,424	1,424	48.8	All other	9,422	2,583	152.0
All other	1,794	1,794	28.5	Hazardous materials			
Vehicle size: [6] Light.......	40,947	1,356	439.3	carried:			
Medium.	1,030	939	10.8	Less than 10 percent of time.	114	107	7.2
Light-heavy.	766	764	7.6	10-25 percent of time	28	19	1.2
Heavy-heavy	1,829	1,828	71.6	26-49 percent of time	18	15	0.7
Year model:				50-74 percent of time	25	24	1.0
1 to 2 years old	7,678	473	123.6	75-100 percent of time	94	89	2.8
3 to 4 years old	7,338	549	120.5	Not reported	61	25	1.7
4 years or more	29,543	3,864	285.2				
Vehicle acquisition:				Types of hazardous			
Purchased new	21,087	2,138	292.3	material: [10]			
Purchased used	22,325	2,511	215.2	Flammable liquids........	198	175	9.3
Leased [7]	1,160	237	21.8	Combustible liquids.......	95	95	5.8
Fleet size: [7][8] 1	29,026	1,170	308.7	Corrosive liquids........	70	66	4.6
2 to 5	11,094	1,547	122.9	Flammable solids	29	28	2.3
6 to 19	2,397	1,007	40.1	Oxidizers.............	28	28	2.3
20 or more	2,054	1,163	57.5	Flammable gas.........	26	26	2.2
Truck type:				Nonflammable gas	26	26	2.2
Single-unit.	42,917	3,587	462.0	Corrosive solids	21	21	1.9
Combination	1,656	1,300	67.3	Not reported	139	101	5.1

X Not applicable.   [1] Also excludes minivans, utilities, and station wagons.   [2] Includes forestry and lumbering.   [3] Also includes multi-stop, minivans, station wagon, and utilities, and station wagon.   [4] Includes livestock truck.   [5] Includes multi-stop or walk-in.   [6] Average vehicle weight (empty-weight of the vehicle plus the average weight of load carried). Light=10,000 lbs. or less; medium=10,001-19,500 lbs.; light-heavy=19,501-26,000 lbs.; and heavy-heavy=26,001 lbs. or more.   [7] Includes not reported.   [8] A fleet size of one truck was assumed when no response was obtained.   [9] Area in which usually operated. Local=less than 50 miles; short-range=50 to 200 miles; long-range=more than 200 miles.   [10] Detail does not add to totals because items were not applicable or multiple responses were possible.

Source of tables 1034 and 1035: U.S. Bureau of the Census, 1987 Census of Transportation, TC87-T-52.

No. 1036. Railroads, Class I—Summary: 1980 to 1992

[As of **Dec. 31, or calendar year** data, except as noted. Compiled from annual reports of class I railroads only except where noted. Beginning 1985, financial data are not comparable with earlier years due to change in method of accounting for track and related structures. Minus sign (-) indicates deficit. See also *Historical Statistics, Colonial Times to 1970*, series Q 284-312, Q 319, Q 330, Q 356-378, and Q 400-401]

ITEM	Unit	1980	1985	1986	1987	1988	1989	1990	1991	1992
Class I line-hauling companies [1] . . .	Number.	40	23	22	18	17	15	14	14	13
Employees [2]	1,000 . .	458	302	276	249	236	228	216	206	197
Compensation	Mil. dol .	11,318	10,563	9,900	9,373	9,301	9,043	8,654	8,695	8,753
Average per hour.	Dollars .	10.2	14.3	14.8	15.1	15.6	15.8	15.8	16.8	17.8
Average per year.	Dollars .	24,695	34,991	35,894	37,716	39,431	39,742	39,987	42,131	44,336
Mileage:										
Railroad line owned [3]	1,000 . .	179	155	154	152	150	149	144	140	136
Railroad track owned [4]	1,000 . .	290	257	256	254	251	249	239	234	227
Equipment:										
Locomotives in service	Number.	28,094	22,548	20,790	19,647	19,364	19,015	18,835	18,344	18,004
Average horsepower	1,000 lb	2,302	2,469	2,531	2,549	2,579	2,624	2,665	2,714	2,750
Cars in service:										
Passenger train	Number.	4,347	2,502	2,307	2,350	2,332	(NA)	(NA)	(NA)	(NA)
Freight train [5]	1,000 . .	1,711	1,422	1,339	1,288	1,239	1,224	1,212	1,190	1,173
Freight cars [6]	1,000 . .	1,168	867	799	749	725	682	659	633	605
Income and expenses:										
Operating revenues.	Mil. dol .	28,258	27,586	26,204	26,622	27,934	27,956	28,370	27,845	28,349
Operating expenses	Mil. dol .	26,355	25,225	24,896	23,878	23,878	24,811	25,038	28,061	25,325
Net revenue from operations . . .	*Mil. dol*	*1,902*	*2,361*	*1,308*	*2,744*	*3,123*	*2,918*	*3,718*	*-216*	*3,024*
Income before fixed charges. . . .	Mil. dol .	2,897	3,393	2,480	3,932	4,460	4,162	4,627	928	4,127
Provision for taxes [7]	Mil. dol .	592	660	163	1,051	1,162	1,040	1,088	-156	1,092
Ordinary income.	Mil. dol .	1,129	1,788	747	1,965	2,286	2,009	1,961	-91	2,055
Net income	Mil. dol .	1,129	1,882	544	2,055	2,382	2,203	1,977	-281	1,800
Net railway operating income . . .	Mil. dol .	1,339	1,746	507	1,756	1,980	1,894	2,648	-37	1,955
Total taxes [8]	Mil. dol .	2,585	3,169	2,728	3,553	3,871	3,742	3,780	2,649	3,732
Indus. return on net investment. .	Percent.	4.2	4.6	1.3	4.8	6.7	6.3	8.1	1.3	6.3
Gross capital expenditures.	Mil. dol .	3,238	4,485	3,645	3,076	3,546	3,865	3,591	3,439	3,680
Equipment	Mil. dol .	2,280	965	693	657	1,027	1,171	996	1,068	874
Roadway and structures	Mil. dol .	953	3,458	2,908	2,314	2,654	2,538	2,644	2,369	2,736
Other.	Mil. dol .	5	62	44	105	-135	156	-49	2	69
Balance sheet:										
Total property investment.	Mil. dol .	43,923	64,241	64,781	66,760	68,550	67,661	70,348	71,622	72,677
Accrued depreciation and amortization	Mil. dol .	10,706	19,756	20,940	21,070	21,497	21,481	22,222	23,057	23,378
Net investment.	Mil. dol .	33,414	46,237	45,434	45,690	47,053	47,370	48,126	48,565	49,299
Shareholder's equity	Mil. dol .	19,860	27,605	25,442	25,616	26,467	25,753	23,662	22,603	23,115
Net working capital	Mil. dol .	922	1,084	743	34	-190	-2119	-3505	-3,988	-4,372
Cash dividends.	Mil. dol .	610	1,444	1,376	1,252	1,814	1,910	2,074	915	830
AMTRAK passenger traffic:										
Passenger revenue	Mil. dol .	(NA)	604.9	633.6	681.1	784.2	893.0	941.9	962.3	933.2
Revenue passengers carried. . . .	1,000 . .	21,303	20,945	20,165	20,727	21,490	21,394	22,382	21,693	21,678
Revenue passenger miles	Million. .	4,645	4,977	5,015	5,368	5,686	5,912	6,125	6,249	6,181
Averages:										
Revenue per passenger	Dollars .	(NA)	28.9	31.4	32.9	36.5	41.8	42.1	44.4	43.0
Revenue per passenger mile . . .	Cents . .	(NA)	12.2	12.6	12.7	13.8	15.1	15.4	15.4	15.1
Trip per passenger.	Miles . .	218.1	237.6	248.7	259.0	264.6	276.3	273.7	288.0	285.1
Freight service:										
Freight revenue	Mil. dol .	26,200	26,688	25,344	25,797	27,092	27,059	24,471	26,949	27,508
Per ton-mile	Cents . .	2.8	3.0	2.9	2.7	2.7	2.7	2.7	2.6	2.6
Per ton originated	Dollar .	17.7	20.2	19.4	18.8	19.0	19.3	19.3	19.5	19.7
Revenue-tons originated	Million. .	1,492	1,320	1,305	1,372	1,430	1,402	1,425	1,383	1,399
Revenue-tons carried	Million. .	2,434	1,985	1,938	1,984	2,045	1,988	2,024	1,987	2,022
Tons carried one mile	Billion . .	919	877	868	944	996	1,014	1,034	1,039	1,067
Average miles of road operated .	1,000 . .	179	161	155	147	141	138	133	130	126
Revenue ton-miles per mile of road	1,000 . .	5,133	5,446	5,587	6,395	7,052	7,373	7,763	8,001	8,451
Revenue per ton-mile	Cents . .	3	3	3	3	3	3	3	3	3
Train miles	Million. .	428	347	347	361	379	383	380	375	390
Net ton-miles per train-mile [9] . . .	Number.	2,175	2,574	2,552	2,644	2,662	2,683	2,755	2,796	2,759
Net ton-miles per loaded car-mile [9]	Number.	63.5	62.7	63.2	64.0	65.5	67.0	69.1	71.6	70.9
Train-miles per train-hour	Miles . .	18.2	21.9	22.5	22.2	21.5	23.0	23.7	23.7	23.7
Haul per ton, U.S. as a system . .	Miles . .	616	664	664	688	697	723	726	751	763
Accident: [10]										
Persons killed	Number.	1,417	1,036	1,091	1,165	1,199	1,324	1,297	1,194	1,170
Persons injured	Number.	62,246	34,304	26,923	26,033	27,054	26,715	25,143	23,468	21,383

NA Not available. [1] See text, section 21, for definition of Class I. [2] Average midmonth count. [3] Represents the aggregate length of roadway of all line-haul railroads. Excludes yard tracks, sidings, and parallel lines. (Includes estimate for class II and III railroads). [4] Includes multiple main tracks, yard tracks, and sidings owned by both line-haul and switching and terminal. (Includes estimate for class II and III railroads). [5] Includes cars owned by all railroads, private car companies, and shippers. [6] Class I railroads only. [7] Includes State income taxes. [8] Includes payroll, income, and other taxes. [9] Revenue and nonrevenue freight. [10] Includes highway grade crossing casualties.

Source: Association of American Railroads, Washington, DC, *Railroad Facts, Statistics of Class I*, annual, and *Analysis of Class I Railroads*, annual. Accident data: U.S. Federal Railroad Administration, *Accident Bulletin*, annual.

No. 1037. Railroads, Class I-Cars of Revenue Freight Loaded, 1970 to 1992, and by Commodity Group, 1991 and 1992

[In thousands. Figures are 52-week totals. N.e.c.= Not elsewhere classified]

YEAR	CARLOADS		COMMODITY GROUP	CARLOADS		COMMODITY GROUP	CARLOADS	
	Total	Piggy-back		1991	1992		1991	1992
1970 . .	27,160	1,450	Coal	6,138	5,959	Metals and products	442	457
1975 . .	23,217	1,308	Metallic ores.	490	491	Stone, clay, and glass products . .	446	454
1980 . .	22,598	1,661	Chemicals, allied products. . . .	1,390	1,431	Crushed stone, gravel, sand	616	573
1985 . .	19,574	2,863	Grain.	1,375	1,425	Nonmetalic minerals, n.e.c	441	428
1988 . .	16,422	(NA)	Motor vehicles and equipment .	798	912	Waste and scrap materials	394	417
1989 . .	16,030	(NA)	Pulp, paper, allied products . . .	472	481	Lumber and wood products, n.e.c. [1]. .	268	276
1990 . .	16,177	(NA)	Primary forest products.	373	380	Coke.	244	269
1991 . .	15,533	(NA)	Food and kindred prod., n.e.c. .	456	462	Petroleum product.	251	266
1992 . .	15,592	(NA)	Grain mill products.	513	515	All other carloads	424	396

NA Not available.   [1] Excludes furniture.

Source: Association of American Railroads, Washington, DC, *Weekly Railroad Traffic,* annual.

No. 1038. Railroads, Class I Line-Haul-Revenue Freight Originated, by Commodity Group: 1980 to 1992

[See *Historical Statistics, Colonial Times to 1970,* series Q 332, for total carloads originated]

COMMODITY GROUP	1980	1985	1986	1987	1988	1989	1990	1991	1992
Carloads (1,000) [1].	**22,223**	**19,501**	**19,587**	**20,602**	**21,600**	**21,226**	**21,401**	**20,868**	**21,205**
Coal.	5,789	5,684	5,433	5,430	5,621	5,672	5,912	5,683	5,572
Farm products	1,866	1,494	1,602	1,907	1,977	1,781	1,689	1,605	1,646
Chemicals, allied products	1,322	1,296	1,287	1,410	1,497	1,486	1,531	1,556	1,568
Food and kindred products	1,767	1,224	1,276	1,326	1,318	1,284	1,307	1,316	1,352
Nonmetallic minerals [2]	1,474	1,196	1,113	1,188	1,290	1,254	1,202	1,075	1,029
Transportation equipment	1,004	1,202	1,148	1,085	1,160	1,141	1,091	1,068	1,181
Lumber and wood products [3] . . .	1,384	948	965	986	910	843	780	716	726
Pulp, paper, allied products	954	703	672	561	646	615	611	616	618
Petroleum and coal products . . .	596	491	477	520	568	561	573	533	583
Stone, clay, and glass products . .	776	551	530	559	577	565	539	479	483
Metallic ores	1,258	511	508	494	582	523	508	499	489
Primary metal products	756	449	389	428	479	452	477	469	481
Waste and scrap materials.	632	429	402	440	471	444	439	433	487
Machinery, exc. electrical.	77	35	31	33	40	38	39	39	39
Fabricated metal products [4]	72	31	26	24	26	27	31	34	32
Tons (mil.) [1]	**1,492**	**1,320**	**1,306**	**1,372**	**1,429**	**1,403**	**1,425**	**1,383**	**1,399**
Coal.	522	538	518	523	543	551	579	560	554
Farm products	156	127	136	163	170	154	147	144	149
Chemicals, allied products	108	106	106	116	123	123	126	127	130
Nonmetallic minerals [2]	125	108	101	109	115	111	109	99	94
Food and kindred products	92	74	78	81	81	79	81	83	86
Lumber and wood products [3] . . .	86	63	65	67	62	57	53	48	50
Metallic ores	105	47	46	45	52	47	47	45	45
Stone, clay, and glass products . .	54	44	42	44	46	47	44	39	40
Petroleum and coal products	38	33	33	35	39	39	40	37	41
Primary metal products	53	34	30	33	38	36	38	37	39
Pulp, paper, allied products	42	36	36	36	35	34	33	33	34
Waste and scrap materials.	34	26	25	28	30	28	28	27	30
Transportation equipment	24	27	26	24	25	24	23	22	25
Machinery, exc. electrical.	2	1	1	1	1	1	1	1	1
Fabricated metal products [4]	2	1	1	1	1	1	1	1	1
Gross revenue (mil. dol.) [1] .	**26,938**	**28,225**	**27,186**	**27,657**	**29,529**	**29,328**	**29,775**	**29,319**	**29,777**
Coal.	4,956	6,556	6,089	6,097	6,430	6,581	6,954	6,903	6,717
Chemicals, allied products	2,946	3,342	3,342	3,477	3,795	3,788	3,933	4,043	4,123
Transportation equipment	1,917	3,110	2,997	2,866	3,218	3,269	3,100	2,633	2,753
Farm products	2,801	1,977	2,007	2,246	2,534	2,444	2,422	2,332	2,454
Food and kindred products	2,837	2,256	2,192	2,171	2,198	2,128	2,188	2,254	2,308
Pulp, paper, allied products	1,652	1,641	1,572	1,542	1,540	1,514	1,486	1,502	1,508
Lumber and wood products [3] . . .	1,543	1,525	1,563	1,660	1,626	1,500	1,390	1,282	1,342
Primary metal products	1,332	872	787	863	1,013	972	979	977	970
Stone, clay, and glass products . .	1,025	960	907	914	965	960	931	878	911
Petroleum and coal products	865	861	800	809	903	917	918	888	943
Nonmetallic minerals [2]	948	949	839	854	890	868	885	824	812
Waste and scrap materials.	513	446	425	474	526	492	504	515	558
Metallic ores	597	403	375	348	415	397	408	400	409
Machinery, exc. electrical.	176	72	58	57	63	66	67	62	61
Fabricated metal products [4]	110	48	40	37	38	38	42	48	45

[1] Includes commodity groups and small packaged freight shipments, not shown separately.   [2] Except fuels.   [3] Except furniture.   [4] Except ordnance, machinery, and transport.

Source: Association of American Railroads, Washington, DC, *Freight Commodity Statistics,* annual.

No. 1039. Railroad Freight—Producer Price Indexes: 1980 to 1993

[Dec. 1984=100. Reflects prices for shipping a fixed set of commodities under specified and unchanging conditions]

COMMODITY	1980	1985	1986	1987	1988	1989	1990	1991	1992	1993
Total railroad freight	75.9	99.9	100.7	100.1	104.8	106.4	107.5	109.3	109.9	110.8
Coal	75.8	100.0	100.7	100.1	104.3	105.3	104.2	105.2	105.9	106.6
Farm products	75.6	99.0	99.6	99.3	105.5	108.5	110.4	111.4	111.1	113.8
Food products	75.2	100.0	99.9	98.6	103.1	103.9	105.4	108.1	108.7	108.8
Metallic ores	74.5	100.2	100.5	99.0	103.9	105.8	106.5	106.7	106.6	106.7
Chemicals or allied products	75.6	100.1	101.2	100.8	106.9	110.0	111.7	113.5	115.6	116.2
Nonmetallic minerals	72.2	100.1	101.6	101.1	106.1	108.3	111.7	115.9	117.6	119.3
Wood or lumber products	72.7	100.0	100.9	100.4	105.3	105.9	107.5	108.6	108.8	109.7
Transportation equipment	81.7	100.0	100.8	99.3	103.4	106.4	107.5	109.7	110.8	112.8
Pulp, paper, or allied products	76.7	100.0	101.0	100.6	104.0	105.1	108.0	111.5	111.8	112.6
Primary metal products	77.8	99.7	100.2	99.7	108.8	112.3	113.1	116.1	117.5	116.3
Clay, concrete, glass, or stone products	74.2	100.0	102.2	102.2	107.5	110.5	114.1	117.1	116.5	117.8

Source: U.S. Bureau of Labor Statistics, Producer Price Indexes, monthly and annual.

No. 1040. Petroleum Pipeline Companies—Characteristics: 1980 to 1992

[Covers pipeline companies operating in interstate commerce and subject to jurisdiction of Federal Energy Regulatory Commission]

ITEM	Unit	1980	1985	1986	1987	1988	1989	1990	1991	1992
Miles of pipeline, total	1,000	173	171	170	168	171	169	168	172	162
Gathering lines	1,000	36	35	34	35	34	33	32	31	29
Trunk lines	1,000	136	136	136	133	136	135	136	141	136
Total deliveries	Mil. bbl.	10,600	10,745	11,002	11,194	11,484	11,281	11,378	11,496	11,447
Crude oil	Mil. bbl.	6,405	6,239	6,286	6,278	6,509	6,435	6,563	6,685	6,541
Products	Mil. bbl.	4,195	4,506	4,716	4,917	4,974	4,847	4,816	4,811	4,906
Total trunk line traffic	Bil. bbl-miles.	3,405	3,342	3,467	3,524	3,619	3,505	3,500	3,470	3,428
Crude oil	Bil. bbl-miles.	1,948	1,842	1,893	1,932	1,970	1,918	1,891	1,899	1,853
Products	Bil. bbl-miles.	1,458	1,500	1,573	1,592	1,649	1,587	1,609	1,571	1,575
Carrier property value	Mil. dol.	19,752	21,605	22,384	21,353	24,332	24,638	25,828	26,943	27,106
Operating revenues	Mil. dol.	6,356	7,461	7,287	7,057	6,861	6,512	7,149	6,798	7,154
Net income	Mil. dol.	1,912	2,431	2,051	2,475	2,505	2,227	2,340	1,788	2,061

Source: PennWell Publishing Co., Tulsa, OK, Oil & Gas Journal, November 22, 1993, and earlier issues (copyright).

No. 1041. Major Interstate Natural Gas Pipeline Companies—Summary: 1985 to 1991

[The classification of A and B interstate natural gas pipeline companies changed to major companies and nonmajor companies. Major natural gas pipeline companies are those whose combined sales for resale and natural gas transported or stored for a fee exceed 50 billion cubic feet. They account for more than 85 percent of all interstate natural gas]

ITEM	Unit	1985	1986	1987	1988	1989	1990	1991
Sales	Tril. cu. ft.	11.3	7.8	6.5	6.4	5.6	4.5	3.9
Residential	Tril. cu. ft.	0.3	0.2	0.2	0.3	0.1	0.2	0.2
Commercial, industrial	Tril. cu. ft.	1.1	0.5	0.4	0.5	0.5	0.4	0.3
For resale	Tril. cu. ft.	9.9	7.1	5.8	5.6	4.9	3.9	3.3
Operating revenues	Mil. dol	49,106	33,859	27,565	27,501	25,695	22,574	21,420
From sales [1]	Mil. dol	44,996	29,508	22,942	22,512	19,786	15,981	14,135
Residential	Mil. dol	1,879	1,122	1,094	1,553	819	912	1,081
Commercial, industrial	Mil. dol	4,466	1,909	1,464	1,544	1,452	1,272	1,086
For resale	Mil. dol	38,545	26,413	20,351	19,420	17,505	13,791	11,967
From transportation of gas of others	Mil. dol	2,272	3,027	3,622	4,059	4,959	5,505	6,117
Other	Mil. dol	1,838	1,325	1,002	929	950	1,088	1,167
Operation, maintenance expenses	Mil. dol	42,528	27,460	21,794	22,742	20,829	17,446	17,335
Production	Mil. dol	36,739	22,208	16,955	17,625	15,257	12,124	11,663
Storage	Mil. dol	418	420	409	436	458	417	460
Transmission	Mil. dol	3,409	2,984	2,598	2,589	2,589	2,720	2,880
Distribution	Mil. dol	132	80	80	127	94	112	133
Administrative, general, and other	Mil. dol	1,830	1,768	1,752	1,966	2,430	2,074	2,048
Pipeline mileage	1,000	230.2	217.3	249.5	246.9	253.2	230.2	249.5
Transmission lines	1,000	189.7	184.6	181.2	191.6	194.1	195.5	146.8
Field lines	1,000	69.6	64.5	62.9	55.5	55.1	54.0	50.7
Storage	1,000	4.8	4.6	4.3	4.8	4.8	5.0	4.7

[1] Includes other ultimate customers not shown separately.

Source: U.S. Energy Information Administration, Statistics of Interstate Natural Gas Pipeline Companies, annual.

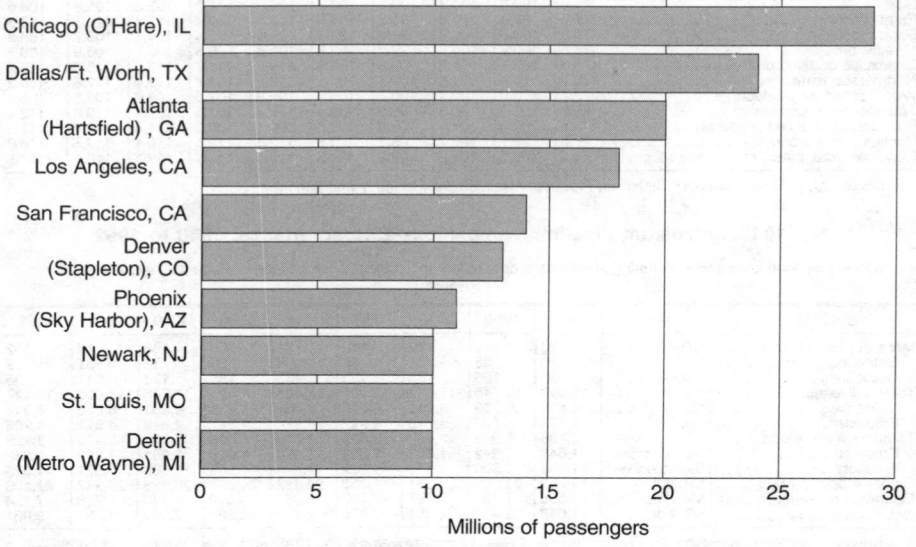

Figure 22.1
**Revenue Passengers Enplaned—
Top 10 Airports: 1992**

Source: Chart prepared by U.S. Bureau of the Census. For data, see table 1045.

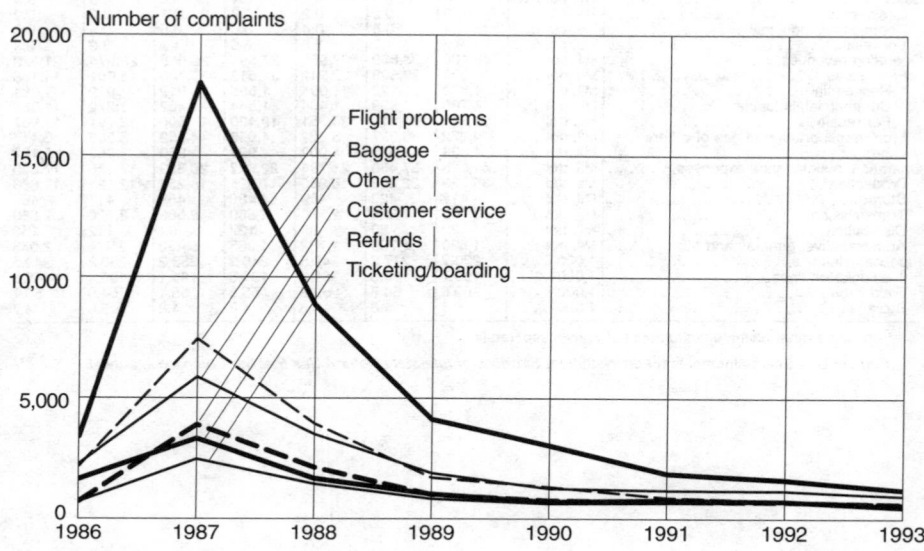

Figure 22.2
**Consumer Complaints Against
U.S. Airlines: 1986 to 1993**

Source: Chart prepared by U.S. Bureau of the Census. For data, see table 1051.

Transportation— Air and Water

This section presents data on civil air transportation, both passenger and cargo, and on water transportation, including inland waterways, oceanborne commerce, the merchant marine, cargo and vessel tonnages, and shipbuilding. Comparative data on various types of transportation carriers are presented in section 21.

Principal sources of these data are the annual *FAA Statistical Handbook of Aviation* issued by the Federal Aviation Administration (FAA); the annual *Waterborne Commerce of the United States* issued by the Corps of Engineers of the Department of the Army; the monthly and annual issues of *U.S. Waterborne Exports and General Imports,* and the annual *Vessel Entrances and Clearances,* and the monthly *Highlights of U.S. Export and Import Trade,* issued by the Bureau of the Census. In addition, the Bureau of the Census in its commodity transportation survey (part of the census of transportation, taken every 5 years, for years ending in "2" and "7") provides data on the type, weight, and value of commodities shipped by manufacturing establishments in the United States, by means of transportation, origin, and destination.

Air transportation data are also presented annually by the Air Transport Association of America, Washington, DC in *Air Transport Facts and Figures.* Additional sources of data on water transportation include *Merchant Fleets of the World* issued periodically by the U.S. Maritime Administration; *The Bulletin,* issued monthly by the American Bureau of Shipping, New York, NY; and the *Annual Summary of Merchant Ships Completed in the World* and the *Register Book,* published by Lloyd's Register of Shipping, London, England.

Civil aviation.—Federal promotion and regulation of civil aviation have been carried out by the FAA and the Civil Aeronautics Board (CAB). The CAB promoted and regulated the civil air transportation

In Brief

SCHEDULED AIR CARRIERS
Revenue passengers enplaned:

1985	382 million
1992	473 million

Net profit:

1985	+$863 million
1992	-$4,029 million

industry within the United States and between the United States and foreign countries. The Board granted licenses to provide air transportation service, approved or disapproved proposed rates and fares, and approved or disapproved proposed agreements and corporate relationships involving air carriers. In December 1984, the CAB ceased to exist as an agency. Some of its functions were transferred to the Department of Transportation (DOT), as outlined below. The responsibility for investigation of aviation accidents resides with the National Transportation Safety Board.

The Office of the Secretary, DOT aviation activities include the following: negotiation of international air transportation rights, selection of U.S. air carriers to serve capacity controlled international markets, oversight of international rates and fares, maintenance of essential air service to small communities, and consumer affairs. DOT's Research and Special Programs Administration (RSPA) handles aviation information functions formerly assigned to CAB.

The principal activities of the FAA include the promotion of air safety, controlling the use of navigable airspace, prescribing regulations dealing with the competency of airmen, airworthiness of aircraft, and air traffic control, operation of air route traffic control centers, airport traffic control towers, and flight service stations, the design, construction, maintenance, and inspection of navigation, traffic control, and communications equipment, and the development of general aviation.

The CAB published monthly and quarterly financial and traffic statistical data for the certificated route air carriers. RSPA continues these publications, including both certificated and noncertificated (commuter) air carriers. The FAA publishes data annually on the use of airway facilities; data related to the location of airmen, aircraft, and airports; the volume of activity in the field of nonair carrier (general aviation) flying; and aircraft production and registration.

General aviation comprises all civil flying (including such commercial operations as small demand air taxis, agriculture application, powerline patrol, etc.) but excludes certificated route air carriers, supplemental operators, large-aircraft commercial operators and commuter airlines.

Air carriers and service.—The CAB previously issued "certificates of public convenience and necessity" under Section 401 of the Federal Aviation Act of 1958 for scheduled and nonscheduled (charter) passenger services and cargo services. It also issued certificates under Section 418 of the Act to cargo air carriers for domestic all-cargo service only. The DOT Office of the Secretary now issues the certificates under a "fit, willing, and able" test of air carrier operations. Carriers operating only 60 seat or less aircraft are given exemption authority to carry passengers, cargo, and mail in scheduled and nonscheduled service under Part 298 of the DOT (formerly CAB) regulations. Exemption authority carriers who offer scheduled passenger service to an essential air service point must meet the "fit, willing, and able" test.

Vessel shipments, entrances, and clearances.—Shipments by dry cargo vessels comprise shipments on all types of watercraft, except tanker vessels; shipments by tanker vessels comprise all types of cargo, liquid and dry, carried by tanker vessels.

A vessel is reported as entered only at the first port which it enters in the United States, whether or not cargo is unloaded at that port. A vessel is reported as cleared only at the last port at which clearance is made to a foreign port, whether or not it takes on cargo. Army and Navy vessels entering or clearing without commercial cargo are not included in the figures.

Units of measurement.—Cargo (or freight) tonnage and shipping weight both represent the gross weight of the cargo including the weight of containers, wrappings, crates, etc. However, shipping weight excludes lift and cargo vans and similar substantial outer containers. Other tonnage figures generally refer to stowing capacity of vessels, 100 cubic feet being called 1 ton. Gross tonnage comprises the space within the frames and the ceiling of the hull, together with those closed-in spaces above deck available for cargo, stores, passengers, or crew, with certain minor exceptions. Net or registered tonnage is the gross tonnage less the spaces occupied by the propelling machinery, fuel, crew quarters, master's cabin, and navigation spaces. Substantially, it represents space available for cargo and passengers. The net tonnage capacity of a ship may bear little relation to weight of cargo. Deadweight tonnage is the weight in long tons required to depress a vessel from light water line (that is, with only the machinery and equipment on board) to load line. It is, therefore, the weight of the cargo, fuel, etc., which a vessel is designed to carry with safety.

Historical statistics.—Tabular headnotes provide cross-references, where applicable, to *Historical Statistics of the United States, Colonial Times to 1970.* See Appendix IV.

No. 1042. U. S. Scheduled Airline Industry—Summary: 1985 to 1992

[For calendar years or Dec. 31. For domestic and international operations. Covers carriers certificated under Section 401 of the Federal Aviation Act. Minus sign (-) indicates loss]

ITEM	Unit	1985	1986	1987	1988	1989	1990	1991	1992
SCHEDULED SERVICE									
Revenue passengers enplaned .	Mil.	382.0	418.9	447.7	454.6	453.7	465.6	452.3	473.3
Revenue passenger miles.	Bil.	336.4	366.5	404.5	423.3	432.7	457.9	448.0	478.1
Available seat miles.	Bil.	547.8	607.4	648.7	676.8	684.4	733.4	715.2	751.8
Revenue passenger load factor .	Percent .	61.4	60.3	62.3	62.5	63.2	62.4	62.6	63.6
Mean passenger trip length [1] . .	Miles . . .	881	875	903	931	954	984	990	1,010
Freight and express ton miles . .	Mil.	6,030.5	7,344.1	8,260.3	9,632.2	10,275.0	10,546.3	10,225.2	10,989.3
Aircraft departures.	1,000 . . .	5,835.5	6,427.0	6,581.3	6,699.6	6,622.1	6,923.6	6,782.8	6,866.3
FINANCES									
Total operating revenue [2] . . .	Mil. dol. .	46,664	50,525	56,986	63,749	69,316	76,142	75,159	77,950
Passenger revenue	Mil. dol. .	39,236	40,056	44,940	50,296	53,802	58,453	57,092	59,748
Freight and express revenue. . .	Mil. dol. .	2,681	5,628	6,398	7,478	6,893	5,432	5,509	5,891
Mail revenue	Mil. dol. .	890	838	923	972	955	970	957	1,174
Charter revenue	Mil. dol. .	1,280	1,269	1,612	1,698	2,052	2,877	3,717	2,736
Total operating expense.	Mil. dol. .	45,238	49,202	54,517	60,312	67,505	78,054	76,943	80,333
Operating profit.	Mil. dol. .	1,426	1,323	2,469	3,437	1,811	-1,912	-1,785	-2,384
Interest expense.	Mil. dol. .	1,588	1,693	1,695	1,846	1,944	1,978	1,177	1,726
Net profit.	Mil. dol. .	863	-235	593	1,686	128	-3,921	-1,940	-4,029
Revenue per passenger mile. . .	Cents. . .	11.7	10.9	11.1	11.9	12.4	12.8	12.7	12.5
Rate of return on investment. . .	Percent .	9.6	4.9	7.2	10.8	6.3	-6.0	-0.5	-6.4
Operating profit margin.	Percent .	3.1	2.6	4.3	5.4	2.6	-2.5	-2.3	-3.1
Net profit margin.	Percent .	1.8	-0.5	1.0	2.6	0.2	-5.1	-2.6	-5.2
EMPLOYEES									
Total	1,000 . . .	355	422	457	481	507	546	534	540
Pilots, copilots, and other flight personnel	1,000 . . .	40	46	51	52	52	56	56	58
Flight attendants.	1,000 . . .	63	68	73	76	78	83	82	84
Mechanics.	1,000 . . .	43	48	51	55	57	61	59	59
Aircraft and traffic servicing personnel	1,000 . . .	101	180	199	212	225	252	237	241
Other	1,000 . . .	108	80	84	86	95	94	98	99

[1] For definition of mean, see Guide to Tabular Presentation.   [2] Includes other types of revenues, not shown separately.

Source: Air Transport Association of America, Washington, DC, *Air Transport*, annual, and *Air Transport, Facts and Figures*, annual.

No. 1043. Airline Cost Indexes: 1980 to 1992

[Covers U.S. major and national service carriers. Major carriers have operating revenues of $1 billion or more; nationals have operating revenues from $75 million to $1 billion. Minus sign (-) indicates decrease]

ITEM	INDEX (1982=100)								PERCENT DISTRIBUTION OF CASH OPERATING EXPENSES [1]			
	1980	1985	1987	1988	1989	1990	1991	1992	1980	1985	1990	1992
INDEX												
Composite	86.3	103.1	98.4	102.4	109.0	117.0	119.8	121.9	100.0	100.0	100.0	100.0
Labor	84.8	111.1	110.2	115.0	118.4	121.1	127.6	134.1	35.1	34.9	32.6	34.2
Interest [2]	88.7	105.5	97.5	99.6	111.5	107.3	88.3	84.8	2.9	3.5	2.5	2.2
Fuel.	91.6	81.4	56.8	54.2	61.2	78.7	68.9	64.1	29.7	22.3	17.6	13.5
Passenger food	94.3	102.0	105.6	111.9	122.8	132.6	141.4	144.1	2.9	3.2	3.6	4.0
Advertising and promotion	69.5	99.8	90.9	96.9	105.0	107.6	97.9	89.8	1.7	2.3	2.1	1.8
Landing fees.	90.0	101.2	121.5	129.1	137.1	148.1	161.9	179.4	1.7	1.7	1.9	2.2
Passenger traffic commissions	77.3	117.6	128.9	148.3	163.4	176.8	193.5	192.2	4.8	7.4	9.8	10.9
All other	85.6	112.7	119.3	123.9	129.4	134.7	140.6	144.3	21.3	24.6	29.9	31.3
PERCENT CHANGE [3]												
Composite	23.3	0.3	1.9	4.1	6.4	7.3	2.4	1.8	(X)	(X)	(X)	(X)
Labor	10.0	2.9	1.3	4.4	3.0	2.3	5.4	5.1	(X)	(X)	(X)	(X)
Interest [2]	16.9	-3.2	-3.3	2.2	11.9	-3.8	-17.7	-4.0	(X)	(X)	(X)	(X)
Fuel.	55.8	-5.7	0.7	-4.6	12.9	28.6	-12.5	-7.0	(X)	(X)	(X)	(X)
Passenger food	11.9	-4.2	3.1	6.0	9.7	8.0	6.6	1.9	(X)	(X)	(X)	(X)
Advertising and promotion	24.3	-0.2	-12.1	6.6	8.4	2.5	-9.0	-8.3	(X)	(X)	(X)	(X)
Landing fees.	9.6	-0.2	7.9	6.3	6.2	8.0	9.3	10.8	(X)	(X)	(X)	(X)
Passenger traffic commissions	40.0	0.8	7.9	15.1	10.2	8.2	9.4	-0.7	(X)	(X)	(X)	(X)
All other	9.3	3.7	3.1	3.9	4.4	4.4	4.1	2.6	(X)	(X)	(X)	(X)

X Not applicable.   [1] Total operating expenses plus interest on long term debt, less depreciation and amortization. [2] Interest on debt.   [3] Change from immediate prior year.

Source: Air Transport Association of America, Washington, DC, *Air Transport*, annual; and unpublished data.

No. 1044. Net New Firm Orders Booked for U.S. Civil Jet Transport Aircraft: 1985 to 1992

[Value in millions of dollars. Minus sign (-) indicates net cancellations]

TYPE OF AIRCRAFT AND CUSTOMER	1985	1987	1988	1989	1990	1991	1992
Total number [1]	468	519	956	1,015	670	280	231
U.S. customers	242	217	404	507	259	36	82
Foreign customers	226	302	552	508	411	244	149
Boeing 737, total	253	234	311	397	189	75	91
U.S. customers	146	105	173	216	38	-8	43
Foreign customers	107	129	138	181	151	83	48
Boeing 747, total	37	61	57	57	153	48	41
U.S. customers	13	15	22	4	24	-5	-
Foreign customers	24	46	35	53	129	53	41
Boeing 757, total	51	44	186	190	66	80	7
U.S. customers	39	18	101	137	33	42	29
Foreign customers	12	26	85	53	33	38	-22
Boeing 767, total	10	42	87	138	60	58	20
U.S. customers	4	11	32	40	23	28	10
Foreign customers	6	31	55	98	37	30	10
Boeing 777, total	-	-	-	-	34	52	36
U.S. customers	-	-	-	-	34	-	-
Foreign customers	-	-	-	-	-	52	36
McDonnell Douglas MD-11, total	-	29	59	38	52	-31	1
U.S. customers	-	2	11	17	16	-26	4
Foreign customers	-	27	48	21	36	-5	-3
McDonnell Douglas MD-80/90, total	114	105	254	195	116	-2	35
U.S. customers	37	65	65	93	91	5	-4
Foreign customers	77	40	189	102	25	-7	39
Total value	14,811	18,737	39,806	47,470	45,485	23,351	16,640
U.S. customers	7,869	6,999	16,308	20,304	14,828	2,144	3,200
Foreign customers	6,942	11,738	23,498	27,166	30,657	21,207	13,440

- Represents zero. [1] Includes types of aircraft not shown separately.
Source: Aerospace Industries Association of America, Washington, DC, Research Center, Statistical Series 23.

No. 1045. Top 10 Airports—Traffic Summary: 1992

[In thousands, except percent change. For calendar year. Airports ranked by revenue passengers enplaned. For scheduled carriers only; excludes charter-only carriers]

AIRPORT	Rank	AIRCRAFT DEPARTURES		REVENUE PASSENGERS ENPLANED		ENPLANED REVENUE TONS		
		Total [1]	Completed scheduled	Total	Percent change, 1980-1992	Total	Freight	U.S. mail
All airports [2]	(X)	6,607	6,578	447,626	60.5	6,736	5,054	1,682
Atlanta, Hartsfield International	3	217	216	19,660	-1.7	260	158	102
Chicago, O'Hare	1	378	377	28,667	49.1	451	309	142
Dallas/Ft. Worth International	2	281	280	24,428	134.1	249	152	97
Denver, Stapleton International	6	161	161	13,426	39.6	121	79	42
Detroit, Metro Wayne	10	137	136	10,124	101.5	98	58	40
Los Angeles International	4	197	194	18,305	29.3	429	361	68
Newark International	8	134	133	10,442	148.3	218	177	41
Phoenix, Sky Harbor International	7	144	143	10,713	217.0	72	46	26
San Francisco International	5	169	169	14,193	51.0	238	205	33
St. Louis International	9	178	177	10,230	92.3	91	51	40

X Not applicable. [1] Includes completed scheduled and unscheduled. [2] Includes other airports, not shown separately.
Source: U.S. Federal Aviation Administration and Research and Special Programs Administration, *Airport Activity Statistics*, annual.

No. 1046. Domestic Airline Markets: 1992

[For calendar year. Data are for the 30 top markets and include all commercial airports in each metro area. Data do not include connecting passengers]

MARKET	Passengers	MARKET	Passengers
New York to—from Los Angeles	2,904,060	Honolulu to—from Lihue, Kauai	1,273,460
New York to—from Boston	2,350,240	Los Angeles to —from Las Vegas	1,217,420
New York to—from Chicago	2,330,750	Chicago to—from Los Angeles	1,188,980
New York to—from Washington	2,282,480	New York to—from West Palm Beach	1,187,110
Los Angeles to—from San Francisco	2,153,360	Los Angeles to—from Honolulu	1,165,470
New York to—from Miami	2,142,690	San Francisco to—from San Diego	1,058,870
Dallas/Ft. Worth to—from Houston	2,090,390	Honolulu to—from Kona, Hawaii	1,055,760
Honolulu to—from Kahului, Maui	2,035,100	Los Angeles to—from Oakland	1,042,880
New York to—from San Francisco	2,010,350	New York to—from Dallas/Ft. Worth	1,029,860
New York to—from Orlando	1,727,260	Honolulu to—from Hilo, Hawaii	1,019,250
New York to—from Ft. Lauderdale	1,547,970	Chicago to—from St. Louis	973,580
New York to—from San Juan	1,524,400	Boston to—from Washington	952,450
Los Angeles to—from Phoenix	1,402,160	Los Angeles to—from Washington	925,220
Chicago to—from Detroit	1,339,600	San Francisco to—from Honolulu	880,390
New York to—from Atlanta	1,330,730	Chicago to—from Washington	875,740

Source: Air Transport Association of America, Washington, DC, *Air Transport 1993*.

No. 1047. Worldwide Airline Fatalities: 1970 to 1992

[For scheduled air transport operations]

YEAR	Fatal accidents	Passenger deaths	Death rate [1]	YEAR	Fatal accidents	Passenger deaths	Death rate [1]
1970.	29	700	0.29	1985.	22	1,066	0.15
1975.	20	467	0.13	1986 [2]	22	546	0.06
1979.	31	877	0.16	1987 [2]	26	901	0.09
1980.	22	814	0.14	1988 [2]	28	729	0.07
1981.	21	362	0.06	1989 [2]	27	817	0.05
1982.	26	764	0.13	1990 [2]	25	495	0.03
1983.	20	809	0.13	1991 [2]	30	653	0.04
1984.	16	223	0.03	1992 [2][3]	29	1,097	0.06

[1] Rate per 100 million passenger miles flown.   [2] Includes former USSR which began reporting in 1986.   [3] Preliminary.

Source: International Civil Aviation Organization, Montreal, Canada, *Civil Aviation Statistics of the World*, annual.

No. 1048. Airline Passenger Screening Results: 1977 to 1991

[Calendar year data]

YEAR	Passengers screened (mil.)	WEAPONS DETECTED				Explosive/ incendiary devices	PERSONS ARRESTED	
			Firearms				Carrying firearms/ explosives	Giving false information
		Total	Handguns	Long guns	Other			
1977	509	2,034	1,730	64	240	5	810	44
1978	580	2,058	1,827	67	164	3	896	64
1979	593	2,161	1,962	55	144	3	1,060	47
1980	585	2,022	1,878	36	108	8	1,031	32
1981	599	2,255	2,124	44	87	11	1,187	49
1982	630	2,676	2,559	57	60	1	1,314	27
1983	709	2,784	2,634	67	83	4	1,282	34
1984	776	2,957	2,766	98	91	6	1,285	27
1985	993	2,987	2,823	90	74	12	1,310	42
1986	1,055	3,241	2,981	146	114	11	1,415	89
1987	1,096	3,252	3,012	99	141	14	1,581	81
1988	1,055	2,773	2,591	74	108	11	1,493	222
1989	1,113	2,879	2,397	92	390	26	1,436	83
1990	1,145	2,853	2,490	59	304	15	1,337	18
1991	1,015	1,919	1,597	47	275	94	893	28

Source: U.S. Federal Aviation Administration, *Annual Report to Congress on Civil Aviation Security*.

No. 1049. Aircraft Accidents and Hijackings: 1975 to 1992

[For years ending December 31]

ITEM	Unit	1975	1980	1985	1989	1990	1991	1992
Aircraft accidents: [1] General aviation [2]	Number...	3,995	3,590	2,738	2,233	2,218	2,143	1,956
Fatal	Number...	633	618	498	432	445	414	408
Rate per 100,000 aircraft hours flown	Rate.....	2.20	1.69	1.75	1.53	1.56	1.52	1.50
Fatalities	Number...	1,252	1,239	944	765	758	740	810
Air carrier, all services [3]	Number...	(NA)	19	22	28	26	27	19
Fatal	Number...	(NA)	1	7	11	6	4	4
Rate per 1,000,000 aircraft miles flown	Rate.....	(X)	-	0.002	0.002	0.001	0.001	0.001
Fatalities	Number...	(NA)	1	526	278	39	62	33
Air carrier, scheduled services	Number...	29	15	17	24	24	26	17
Fatal	Number...	2	-	4	8	6	4	4
Rate per 1,000,000 aircraft miles flown	Rate.....	0.001	0.000	0.001	0.002	0.001	0.001	0.001
Fatalities	Number...	122	-	197	131	39	62	33
Commuter air carriers [4]	Number...	48	38	21	18	15	22	23
Fatal	Number...	12	8	7	5	3	8	7
Rate per 1,000,000 aircraft miles flown	Rate.....	0.07	0.04	0.02	0.01	0.01	0.02	0.02
Fatalities	Number...	28	37	37	31	6	99	21
Air taxis [5]	Number...	152	171	154	111	108	88	74
Fatal	Number...	24	46	35	25	29	26	24
Rate per 100,000 aircraft hours flown	Rate.....	0.95	1.27	1.36	0.83	1.25	1.16	1.08
Fatalities	Number...	69	105	76	83	49	73	66
Hijacking incidents, worldwide	Number...	25	39	35	24	46	26	14
U.S. registered aircraft	Number...	12	21	4	6	4	3	2
Successful [6]	Number...	4	13	2	-	(NA)	(NA)	(NA)
Foreign-registered aircraft	Number...	13	18	31	18	42	23	12
Successful [6]	Number...	3	9	18	-	(NA)	(NA)	(NA)
Bomb threats:								
U.S. airports	Number...	449	268	256	487	448	498	188
Explosions	Number...	4	1	-	-	-	-	-
U.S. worldwide and foreign aircraft in U.S	Number...	1,853	1,179	372	479	338	388	215
Explosions	Number...	2	1	1	2	-	-	-

- Represents or rounds to zero.   NA Not available.   X Not applicable.   [1] Data from National Transportation Safety Board.   [2] See text, section 22.   [3] U.S. air carriers operating under 14 CFR 121.   [4] All scheduled service of U.S. air carriers operating under 14 CFR 135.   [5] All nonscheduled service of U.S. air carriers operating under 14 CFR 135.   [6] Hijacker controls flight and reaches destination or objective.

Source: U.S. Federal Aviation Administration, *FAA Statistical Handbook of Aviation*, annual; and unpublished data. Includes data from U.S. Department of Transportation, Research and Special Programs Administration.

No. 1050. On-Time Flight Arrivals and Departures at Major U.S. Airports: 1993

[In percent. Quarterly, based on gate arrival and departure times for domestic scheduled operations in the 48 contiguous States of major U.S. airlines, per DOT reporting rule effective September 1987. All U.S. airlines with 1 percent or more of total U.S. domestic scheduled airline passenger revenues are required to report on-time data. A flight is considered on time if it operated less than 15 minutes after the scheduled time shown in the carrier's computerized reservation system. Cancelled and diverted flights are considered late. Excludes flight operations delayed/cancelled due to aircraft mechanical problems reported on FAA maintenance records (4-5 percent of the reporting airlines' scheduled operations). See source for data on individual airlines]

AIRPORT	ON-TIME ARRIVALS				ON-TIME DEPARTURES			
	1st qtr.	2d qtr.	3d qtr.	4th qtr.	1st qtr.	2d qtr.	3d qtr.	4th qtr.
Total, all airports	76.0	84.4	84.9	80.9	81.5	89.9	90.1	86.1
Total 30 major airports.........	74.3	83.6	84.1	79.9	79.8	88.9	88.9	84.7
Atlanta, Hartsfield International........	65.7	79.2	80.8	79.9	76.9	86.6	86.4	85.9
Baltimore/Washington International......	75.9	86.5	85.5	84.9	78.7	90.0	90.2	86.0
Boston, Logan International...........	64.1	76.8	77.2	75.1	72.4	84.9	84.3	81.4
Charlotte, Douglas	82.8	91.2	90.5	86.7	81.4	89.2	89.4	86.1
Chicago, O'Hare	71.8	80.2	81.9	80.2	76.7	86.1	86.6	84.6
Cincinnati International	77.1	84.6	83.0	83.6	79.8	89.0	86.5	86.1
Dallas/Ft. Worth International.........	76.0	83.3	87.3	75.2	78.4	87.7	91.5	80.1
Denver, Stapleton International........	68.6	80.1	78.0	73.7	77.6	87.1	86.4	80.9
Detroit, Metro Wayne	78.9	88.9	88.2	88.3	81.2	91.1	90.1	88.6
Dulles International................	76.1	83.5	83.4	84.3	83.7	90.2	89.3	87.9
Houston Intercontinental	80.9	84.6	89.8	81.0	85.2	88.7	92.9	86.2
Las Vegas, McCarran International	80.1	87.9	88.8	83.2	83.8	91.5	90.8	86.7
Los Angeles International	71.9	83.9	83.9	77.5	80.9	91.2	91.0	86.4
Miami International.................	76.6	82.3	81.4	79.6	84.0	90.7	88.5	87.4
Minneapolis/St. Paul International......	79.6	85.5	86.3	85.6	83.8	90.7	90.2	88.7
Newark International................	64.6	74.4	73.6	66.4	74.6	83.0	83.2	77.8
New York, Kennedy International	70.9	82.0	80.5	75.1	79.8	87.4	85.1	80.6
New York, LaGuardia	74.5	83.2	83.7	81.1	80.1	89.5	90.2	86.8
Orlando International	76.5	85.5	84.2	80.9	82.3	90.8	90.2	89.2
Philadelphia International............	71.4	85.2	85.4	81.9	76.8	87.8	88.8	84.0
Phoenix, Sky Harbor International	80.6	88.8	90.1	82.9	81.5	90.2	90.2	85.0
Pittsburgh, Greater International	73.2	84.2	83.6	78.6	75.5	86.1	84.7	79.0
Raleigh/Durham.................	83.0	88.1	88.8	87.0	83.3	90.7	91.4	88.0
St. Louis, Lambert	78.4	87.1	86.2	83.7	81.1	90.0	89.0	85.6
Salt Lake City International	72.7	85.3	83.9	82.7	76.7	91.0	87.7	85.7
San Diego International, Lindbergh	72.4	86.1	87.4	80.7	81.8	92.8	92.9	87.8
San Francisco International	69.0	82.6	82.3	74.2	81.1	92.4	91.2	83.2
Seattle-Tacoma International	81.1	82.6	80.7	74.5	88.3	92.7	90.6	84.8
Tampa International	76.5	84.5	83.7	80.4	84.0	92.8	92.5	89.0
Washington National................	76.1	84.1	84.7	82.3	82.4	89.3	90.7	87.3

Source: U.S. Dept. of Transportation, Office of Consumer Affairs, *Air Travel Consumer Report,* monthly.

No. 1051. Consumer Complaints Against U.S. Airlines: 1986 to 1993

[Calendar year data. See source for data on individual airlines]

COMPLAINT CATEGORY	1986	1987	1988	1989	1990	1991	1992	1993
Total..............	10,802	40,985	21,493	10,553	7,703	6,106	5,639	4,438
Flight problems [1]	3,390	18,019	8,831	4,111	3,034	1,877	1,624	1,211
Baggage.................	2,149	7,438	3,938	1,702	1,329	883	752	627
Customer service [2]	702	3,888	2,120	1,002	758	714	695	599
Ticketing/boarding [3]	687	2,458	1,445	821	624	659	680	577
Refunds	1,627	3,313	1,667	1,023	701	783	721	482
Fares [4]...................	468	937	455	341	312	388	573	398
Oversales [5]................	849	2,122	1,353	607	399	301	265	257
Advertising	122	344	141	89	96	96	54	51
Smoking.................	311	888	546	232	74	30	25	30
Tours...................	33	90	37	22	29	23	12	16
Credit...................	40	101	35	19	5	10	10	4
Other...................	424	1,387	925	584	342	342	228	186

[1] Cancellations, delays, etc. from schedule.   [2] Unhelpful employees, inadequate meals or cabin service, treatment of delayed passengers.   [3] Errors in reservations and ticketing; problems in making reservations and obtaining tickets.   [4] Incorrect or incomplete information about fares, discount fare conditions, and availability, etc.   [5] All bumping problems, whether or not airline complied with DOT regulations.

Source: U.S. Dept. of Transportation, Office of Consumer Affairs, *Air Travel Consumer Report,* monthly.

No. 1052. Commuter/Regional Airline Operations—Summary: 1980 to 1992

[Calendar year data. Commuter/regional airlines operate primarily aircraft of predominately 75 passengers or less and 18,000 pounds of payload capacity serving short haul and small community markets. Represents operations within all North America by U.S. Regional Carriers. Averages are means. For definition of mean, see Guide to Tabular Presentation]

ITEM	Unit	1980	1985	1987	1988	1989	1990	1991	1992
Passenger carriers operating	Number.	214	179	169	163	151	150	144	127
Passengers enplaned	Millions .	14.8	[1]26.0	31.8	35.2	37.4	42.1	42.0	48.9
Average passengers enplaned per carrier.	1,000 .	69.2	152.4	187.7	213.9	247.4	277.5	291.4	385.0
Revenue passenger miles (RPM)	Billions .	1.92	[1]4.41	5.0	6.04	6.77	7.61	7.80	9.46
Average RPM's per carrier	Millions .	8.97	[1]24.64	29.60	37.05	44.84	50.75	54.18	74.50
Airports served	Number .	732	854	834	861	817	811	811	802
Average trip length	Miles...	129	173	158	173	181	183	186	194
Passenger aircraft operated	Number .	1,339	1,745	1,841	1,801	1,907	1,917	1,992	2,103
Average seating capacity (seats).	Number .	13.9	19.2	19.7	20.5	21.8	22.1	22.8	23.4
Fleet flying hours	1,000 .	1,740	2,854	2,942	3,078	3,266	3,447	3,671	4,259
Average annual utilization aircraft	Hours ..	1,299	1,635	1,598	1,709	1,712	1,798	1,843	2,025

[1] Adjusted to exclude a merger in 1986.

Source: Regional Airline Association, Washington, DC, Annual Report of the Regional Airline Industry (copyright).

No. 1053. Civil Flying—Summary: 1970 to 1992

[As of Dec. 31 or for years ending Dec. 31, except as noted. See also Historical Statistics, Colonial Times to 1970, series Q 604-623]

ITEM	Unit	1970	1980	1985	1989	1990	1991	1992
Airports in operation [1]	Number...	11,261	15,161	16,318	17,446	17,490	17,581	17,846
Heliports	Number...	790	2,336	3,120	4,016	4,085	4,199	4,323
Public	Number...	4,260	4,814	5,861	5,084	5,078	5,090	5,116
Private	Number...	7,001	10,347	10,457	12,362	12,412	12,491	12,730
Airports with runway lights	Number...	3,554	4,738	4,941	4,443	4,822	4,811	4,831
Airports with paved runways.	Number...	3,805	5,833	6,721	7,612	7,694	7,822	7,936
Airport Improvement Program [2]	Mil. dol ...	50.5	639.0	842.1	1,271.2	1,244.7	1,621.6	1,765.0
Total civil aircraft	1,000	154.5	259.4	274.9	274.8	275.9	275.5	277
Active aircraft [3]	1,000	134.5	214.8	215.4	225.4	218.9	204.6	191.7
Air carriers, total [4]	1,000	2.8	3.8	4.7	5.7	6.7	6.1	7.3
General aviation aircraft [5]	1,000	131.7	211.0	210.7	219.7	212.2	198.5	184.4
Fixed-wing aircraft: Multi-engine....	1,000	18.4	31.7	33.6	34.1	32.7	30.5	27.3
Single-engine	1,000	109.5	168.4	164.4	170.4	165.1	154.2	143.5
Rotorcraft [6]	1,000	2.2	6.0	6.4	7.5	7.4	6.3	5.8
Balloons, blimps, gliders, etc	1,000	1.6	5.0	6.3	7.7	7.0	7.6	7.8
Airman certificates held	1,000	1,002	1,195	1,105	1,168	1,195	1,210	1,224
Pilot [7]	1,000	733	827	710	700	703	692	683
Held by women	Percent...	4.0	6.4	6.1	6.1	5.8	5.9	5.9
Airline transport	1,000	34	70	83	102	108	112	116
Commercial	1,000	187	183	152	145	149	148	146
Private	1,000	304	357	311	293	299	293	288
Student	1,000	196	200	147	143	128	120	115
Nonpilot [8]	1,000	269	368	395	468	492	517	541
Ground technicians [9]	1,000	241	321	341	401	421	444	478
FAA employees: Total.	Number...	53,125	55,340	47,245	50,977	51,269	54,119	53,871
Air traffic control specialists [10].	Number...	(NA)	27,190	23,580	24,368	24,339	25,741	24,983
Full performance [11]	Number...	(NA)	16,317	11,672	12,640	12,985	13,480	14,377
Developmental [11]	Number...	(NA)	4,387	4,304	5,574	5,042	5,080	3,759
Assistants [11]	Number...	(X)	(X)	1,465	1,316	1,153	928	792
Traffic management coordinators [12] ..	Number...	(X)	(X)	(X)	350	370	448	471
Electronic technicians	Number...	(NA)	8,871	6,856	6,508	6,458	6,641	6,572
Aviation safety inspectors	Number...	(NA)	2,038	1,897	2,766	2,984	3,101	3,017
Engineers	Number...	(NA)	2,436	2,457	2,657	2,745	3,073	3,208
Other	Number...	(NA)	14,805	12,455	14,678	14,743	15,563	16,091
General aviation: [5]								
Hours flown	Million....	26.0	41.0	34.1	35.0	34.8	30.1	26.5
Fuel consumed: [13]								
Gasoline	Mil. gal ...	362	520	420	343	353	354	314
Jet fuel [14]	Mil. gal ...	415	766	691	688	663	577	494

NA Not available. X Not applicable. [1] Existing airports, heliports, seaplane bases, etc. recorded with FAA. Includes military airports with joint civil and military use. Includes U.S. outlying areas. Airport-type definitions: Public—publicly owned and under control of a public agency; private—owned by a private individual or corporation. May or may not be open for public use. [2] Fiscal year data. Does not include System Planning Grants. Includes U.S. outlying areas. 1970-1980 data are obligated Federal funds for the Airport Development Aid Program. Thereafter, data are appropriated Federal funds under the Airport and Airway Improvement Act of 1982. [3] Registered aircraft that flew 1 or more hours during the year. [4] Includes helicopters. [5] See text, section 22. [6] Includes autogyros; excludes air carrier helicopters. [7] Includes all active pilots. An active pilot is one with a pilot certificate and a valid medical certificate. Also includes pilots who hold only a helicopter, glider, or lighter than air certificate, not shown separately. [8] Includes dispatchers, flight navigators and engineers, and ground technicians—mechanics, parachute riggers, and ground instructors. [9] No medical examinations are required, therefore, data represent all certificates on record and include retired or otherwise inactive technicians. [10] Includes all air traffic control specialists (staff positions, managers, supervisors, and for 1970-1985 traffic management coordinators, not shown separately) and air traffic assistants. [11] Serving in-flight service stations, towers, and centers. [12] Prior to 1988, included in total air traffic control specialists. [13] Source: 1970, U.S. Bureau of Mines; thereafter, FAA General Aviation Activity and Avionics Survey. [14] Includes kerosene-type and naphtha-type jet fuels.

Source: Except as noted, U.S. Federal Aviation Administration, FAA Statistical Handbook of Aviation, annual; and unpublished data. Includes data from U.S. Department of Transportation, Research and Special Programs Administration.

No. 1054. U.S. Aircraft Shipments With Projections: 1970 to 1994

[Value in millions of dollars]

YEAR	TOTAL		CIVIL						MILITARY	
	Units	Value	Large transports		General Aviation [1]		Helicopters		Units	Value
			Units	Value	Units	Value	Units	Value		
1970	11,632	7,511	311	3,158	7,292	337	495	49	3,534	3,967
1975	16,958	9,355	285	4,006	14,056	1,033	838	266	1,779	4,050
1980	14,660	18,845	383	9,793	11,877	2,486	1,353	674	1,047	5,892
1985	3,597	29,312	273	9,375	2,029	1,431	376	505	919	18,001
1986	3,261	35,622	329	11,120	1,495	1,262	330	288	1,107	22,952
1987	2,995	37,317	255	11,900	1,160	1,320	270	320	1,210	23,777
1988	3,285	33,840	380	13,000	1,270	1,420	330	400	1,305	19,020
1989	3,675	34,228	398	15,074	1,535	1,803	515	251	1,227	17,100
1990	3,486	39,206	521	22,215	1,144	2,007	603	254	1,218	14,730
1991	2,934	40,776	589	26,856	1,021	1,968	571	211	753	11,741
1992 [2]	2,507	41,832	610	30,268	941	1,840	324	142	632	9,582
1993 [3]	2,282	37,108	408	26,456	964	2,144	260	122	650	8,386
1994 [3]	2,146	30,589	306	20,437	960	2,150	260	82	620	7,920

[1] Excludes off-the-shelf military aircraft.   [2] Estimated.   [3] Forecast.

Source: U.S. Department of Commerce, International Trade Administration, *U.S. Industrial Outlook, 1994;* and unpublished data.

No. 1055. Employment and Earnings in Aircraft Industries: 1980 to 1993

[Annual averages of monthly figures. See headnote, table 654]

ITEM	1987 SIC [1] code	Unit	1980	1985	1990	1992	1993
Employment: Total	(X)	1,000 . . .	744	794	898	756	661
Aircraft	3721	1,000 . . .	349	326	381	332	301
Aircraft engines and engine parts.	3724	1,000 . . .	163	148	152	127	111
Aircraft equipment, n.e.c. [2]	3728	1,000 . . .	121	143	180	152	129
Guided missiles, space vehicles, and parts . .	376	1,000 . . .	111	177	185	145	120
Average weekly earnings: [3]	(X)	. . . . . .					
Aircraft	3721	Dollars . .	404	(NA)	(NA)	(NA)	(NA)
Aircraft engines and parts..............	3724	Dollars . .	394	542	637	689	715
Guided missiles, space vehicles, and parts . .	376	Dollars . .	378	515	612	652	696
Average hourly earnings: [3]	(X)	. . . . . .					
Aircraft [4]	3721	Dollars . .	9.66	13.18	15.66	17.70	18.42
Aircraft engines and parts..............	3724	Dollars . .	9.42	12.85	14.84	16.28	16.70
Guided missiles, space vehicles, and parts . .	376	Dollars . .	9.22	12.14	14.39	15.99	16.81

NA Not available. X Not applicable. [1] 1987 Standard Industrial Classification; see text, section 13. [2] N.e.c.=Not elsewhere classified. [3] For production workers. [4] Excludes lump-sum payments. Earnings which include proration of lump-sum payments were: $13.40 in 1985; $16.32 in 1990; $17.16 in 1991; $18.18 in 1992; and $19.00 in 1993.

Source: U.S. Bureau of Labor Statistics, Bulletins 2370 and 2429; and *Employment and Earnings,* monthly, March and June issues.

No. 1056. Aerospace Industry—Summary With Projections: 1980 to 1994

[For calendar year, except employment and earnings annual averages of monthly figures. Includes Standard Industrial Classification Codes 372 and 376. Industry shipments refer to the total value of all products shipped by establishments classified in that industry. Product shipments refer to the total value of specific products shipped irrespective of how the establishments which made them are classified]

ITEM	Unit	1980	1985	1988	1989	1990	1991	1992 [1]	1993 [1]	1994 [2]
INDUSTRY DATA										
Value of shipments	Mil. dol.	58,483	90,795	107,746	113,477	125,194	131,345	133,613	120,742	101,962
In 1987 dollars	Mil. dol.	(NA)	(NA)	106,681	109,736	116,815	116,911	116,287	103,510	92,313
Employment, total.......	1,000 . .	721	746	820	823	816	746	674	587	542
Production workers	1,000 . .	387	372	399	400	396	362	323	279	267
Average hourly earnings . .	Dol . . .	9.90	13.88	15.35	15.84	16.36	16.73	17.56	18.37	(NA)
Capital expenditures	Mil. dol.	1,923	3,784	3,388	3,921	3,490	3,407	(NA)	(NA)	(NA)
PRODUCT DATA										
Value of shipments	Mil. dol.	53,296	80,625	102,242	106,320	118,141	124,109	126,800	112,244	93,921
In 1987 dollars	Mil. dol.	(NA)	(NA)	100,875	102,103	109,258	109,742	110,349	96,230	80,760

NA Not available. [1] Estimated. [2] Forecast.

Source: U.S. Department of Commerce, International Trade Administration, *U.S. Industrial Outlook, 1994.*

No. 1057. Aerospace—Sales, New Orders, and Backlog: 1980 to 1992

[In billions of dollars, except as indicated. Reported by establishments in which the principal business is the development and/or production of aerospace products]

ITEM	1980	1984	1985	1986	1987	1988	1989 [1]	1990 [1]	1991 [1]	1992 [1]
Net sales	58.4	88.9	100.5	105.6	110.3	113.5	122.1	136.6	123.9	121.9
Percent of U.S. Government	45.6	62.7	63.2	61.9	62.2	60.0	58.0	54.0	48.9	46.0
Complete aircraft and parts [2]	22.6	28.3	34.2	38.0	37.0	35.7	38.4	49.9	52.9	54.0
Aircraft engines and parts	6.9	9.1	9.7	9.8	12.0	15.0	15.4	16.4	15.6	13.9
Missiles and space vehicles, parts . . .	8.4	13.6	16.7	17.5	20.7	21.5	22.6	22.0	23.3	22.6
Other products, services	20.5	38.0	39.8	40.3	40.5	41.3	45.7	48.3	32.0	31.4
Net, new orders	70.4	104.9	111.0	110.8	121.2	147.1	173.6	146.0	122.5	103.5
Backlog, Dec. 31	90.5	132.5	143.0	148.2	158.7	191.5	252.4	250.1	245.2	225.7

[1] Data beginning 1989 are not comparable with earlier years. Data are being reported which were previously not available. The extent of this noncomparability is not known.   [2] Except engines sold separately.

Source: U.S. Bureau of the Census, *Current Industrial Reports*, series MA-37D.

No. 1058. Aerospace Industry Sales, by Product Group and Customer: 1985 to 1994

[In billions of dollars. Due to reporting practices and tabulating methods, figures may differ from those in table 1057]

ITEM	CURRENT DOLLARS					CONSTANT (1987) DOLLARS [3]				
	1985	1990	1992	1993 [1]	1994 [2]	1985	1990	1992	1993 [1]	1994 [2]
Total sales	96.6	134.4	137.9	123.7	115.6	97.8	121.6	117.5	102.3	92.8
PRODUCT GROUP										
Aircraft, total	50.5	71.4	73.6	65.3	59.3	51.1	64.6	62.7	54.0	47.6
Civil [4]	13.7	31.4	39.9	32.9	27.1	13.9	28.4	34.0	27.2	21.7
Military	36.8	40.1	33.7	32.4	32.2	37.2	36.3	28.7	26.8	25.9
Missiles	11.4	14.2	11.6	8.6	7.1	11.6	12.8	9.8	7.1	5.7
Space	18.6	26.4	29.8	29.2	29.9	18.8	23.9	25.3	24.1	24.0
Related products and services [5] . .	16.1	22.4	23.0	20.6	19.3	16.3	20.3	19.6	17.1	15.5
CUSTOMER GROUP										
Aerospace, total	80.5	112.0	115.0	103.1	96.3	81.5	101.3	97.9	85.3	77.3
DOD [6]	53.2	60.5	51.8	48.2	45.6	53.9	54.8	44.1	39.9	36.6
NASA [7] and other agencies . . .	6.3	11.1	12.3	12.1	12.5	6.3	10.0	10.5	10.0	10.0
Other customers [8]	21.0	40.4	50.9	42.8	38.2	21.3	36.5	43.3	35.4	30.7
Related products and services [5] . .	16.1	22.4	23.0	20.6	19.3	16.3	20.3	19.6	17.1	15.5

[1] Preliminary.   [2] Estimate.   [3] Based on AIA's aerospace composite price deflator.   [4] All civil sales of aircraft (domestic and export sales of jet transports, commuters, business, and personal aircraft and helicopters).   [5] Electronics, software, and ground support equipment, plus sales of non-aerospace products which are produced by aerospace-manufacturing use technology, processes, and materials derived from aerospace products.   [6] Department of Defense.   [7] National Aeronautics and Space Administration.   [8] Includes civil aircraft sales (see footnote 4), commercial space sales, all exports of military aircraft and missiles and related propulsion and parts.

Source: Aerospace Industries Association of America, Inc., Washington, DC, *1993 Year-end Review and Forecast*.

No. 1059. Aerospace Industry—Net Profits After Taxes: 1980 to 1993

[For calendar year. Minus sign (-) indicates loss]

YEAR	AEROSPACE INDUSTRY PROFITS				MANUFACTURING CORPORATIONS PROFITS			
	Total (mil. dol.)	As percent of—			Total (mil. dol.)	As percent of—		
		Sales	Assets	Equity		Sales	Assests	Equity
1980	2,588	4.3	5.2	16.0	93,149	4.8	6.9	13.9
1981	2,966	4.4	5.2	16.0	101,330	4.7	6.7	13.6
1982	2,193	3.3	3.7	12.0	70,966	3.5	4.5	9.2
1983	2,829	3.5	4.1	12.1	85,737	4.1	5.1	10.5
1984	3,639	4.1	4.7	14.1	107,657	4.6	6.0	12.5
1985	3,274	3.1	3.6	11.1	87,809	3.8	4.6	10.1
1986	3,093	2.8	3.1	9.4	82,762	3.7	4.2	9.5
1987	4,582	4.1	4.4	14.6	115,472	4.9	5.6	12.8
1988	4,883	4.3	4.4	14.9	154,647	6.0	6.9	16.2
1989	3,866	3.3	3.3	10.7	136,412	5.0	5.6	13.7
1990	4,487	3.4	3.4	11.5	110,737	4.0	4.3	10.7
1991	[1]2,484	1.8	1.9	6.1	66,379	2.5	2.6	6.4
1992	[1]-1,836	-1.4	-1.2	-5.2	25,206	0.9	0.9	2.3
1993, prel.	5,463	5.1	4.2	16.2	84,105	2.9	3.0	8.3

[1] Reflects unusually large nonoperating expenses totalling $3.4 billion in 1991 and $8.7 billion in 1992 due to the initial implementation of a change in accounting for future retirement benefit costs and defense-downsizing restructuring charges. Many large aerospace corporations chose to write off against first quarter earnings amounts required to comply with FASB 106.

Source: Aerospace Industries Association of America, Washington, DC, *1993 Year-end Review and Forecast*.

No. 1060. U.S. Exports of Aerospace Vehicles and Equipment: 1990 to 1993

ITEM	NUMBER OF UNITS				VALUE (mil. dol.)			
	1990	1991	1992	1993 [1]	1990	1991	1992	1993 [1]
Aerospace vehicles and equipment .	(NA)	(NA)	(NA)	(NA)	39,083	43,796	45,030	39,426
Civilian aircraft	3,779	3,329	2,086	1,758	18,148	22,388	24,337	19,845
Under 4,536 kg. unladen weight, new .	1,134	911	586	555	324	311	297	234
4,536-15,000 kg. unladen weight, new .	79	69	60	58	245	279	295	324
Over 15,000 kg. unladen weight, new .	306	385	387	276	16,691	20,881	22,379	18,146
Rotocraft, new	349	318	212	175	161	168	118	120
Nonpowered aircraft, new	(NA)	(NA)	(NA)	(NA)	15	15	7	9
Used or rebuilt	1,911	1,646	841	694	712	734	1,241	1,012
Military aircraft, new and used.	445	490	428	632	1,481	1,784	2,083	1,460
Aircraft engines and parts	(NA)	(NA)	(NA)	(NA)	6,883	7,049	6,699	6,278
Propellers, rotors, and parts	(NA)	(NA)	(NA)	(NA)	343	317	289	308
Landing gear and parts . . . . 2 . .	(NA)	(NA)	(NA)	(NA)	276	333	362	338
Aircraft parts and accessories, n.e.c. [2] . .	(NA)	(NA)	(NA)	(NA)	8,982	9,386	8,496	8,574
Guided missiles and parts	(NA)	(NA)	(NA)	(NA)	1,306	1,204	1,428	1,231
Flight simulators	(NA)	(NA)	(NA)	(NA)	255	245	205	197
Space launch equipment	(NA)	(NA)	(NA)	(NA)	660	308	336	548
Avionics	(NA)	(NA)	(NA)	(NA)	747	780	795	646

NA Not available. [1] Estimated. [2] N.e.c.=Not elsewhere classified.

Source: U.S. Dept. of Commerce, International Trade Administration, U.S. Industrial Outlook, 1994; and unpublished data.

No. 1061. International Transportation Transactions of the United States, by Type: 1980 to 1992

[In millions of dollars. Data are international transportation transactions recorded for balance of payment purposes (see table 1306). Receipts include freight on exports carried by U.S.-operated carriers and foreign carrier expenditures in U.S. ports. Payments include freight on imports carried by foreign carriers and U.S. carrier port expenditures abroad. Freight on exports carried by foreign carriers is excluded since such payments are directly or indirectly for foreign account. Similarly, freight on U.S. imports carried by U.S. carriers is a domestic rather than an international transaction. Minus sign (-) indicates excess of payments over receipts. See Historical Statistics, Colonial Times to 1970, series U 3 and U 10, for totals]

ITEM	1980	1985	1986	1987	1988	1989	1990	1991	1992
Total receipts	14,208	19,085	21,366	24,337	28,430	31,147	37,252	38,180	40,126
Ocean passenger fares	(Z)	60	90	102	128	132	154	156	173
Other ocean transportation.	7,757	8,846	9,169	10,060	11,218	11,704	12,141	12,260	12,431
Freight.	3,229	3,440	3,186	3,401	3,750	3,896	4,104	4,000	3,904
Port expenditures.	4,435	5,274	5,843	6,514	7,315	7,609	7,815	8,020	8,268
Charter hire	93	132	140	145	153	199	222	240	259
Air passenger fares [1]	2,591	4,351	5,492	6,901	8,847	10,482	15,144	15,698	17,180
Other air transportation	3,355	5,347	5,420	5,943	6,792	7,310	8,174	8,556	8,618
Freight.	742	706	783	982	1,385	1,719	2,432	2,722	2,589
Port expenditures	2,613	4,641	4,637	4,961	5,407	5,591	5,742	5,834	6,029
Miscellaneous receipts.	505	481	1,195	1,331	1,445	1,519	1,639	1,510	1,724
Total payments.	15,397	22,087	23,220	25,072	27,263	28,907	33,931	33,309	34,397
Ocean passenger fares	268	154	208	235	164	193	248	279	301
Other ocean transportation.	8,179	10,698	11,299	11,030	12,180	12,227	13,078	12,303	11,920
Import freight	5,809	8,114	8,636	8,365	9,372	9,391	10,290	9,593	9,269
Port expenditures	1,905	2,048	2,125	2,115	2,244	2,228	2,174	2,093	2,028
Charter hire	465	536	538	550	564	608	614	617	623
Air passenger fares [1]	3,339	6,290	6,297	7,048	7,565	8,055	10,282	9,733	10,642
Other air transportation	3,366	4,719	5,127	6,432	6,981	8,080	9,881	10,513	11,027
Import freight	562	1,666	2,051	2,242	2,226	2,197	2,207	2,257	2,370
Port expenditures	2,804	3,053	3,076	4,190	4,755	5,883	7,674	8,256	8,657
Miscellaneous payments	245	226	289	327	373	352	442	481	507
Balance	-1,189	-3,002	-1,854	-735	1,167	2,240	3,321	4,871	5,729

Z Less than $500,000. [1] Beginning 1990, includes interairline settlements.

Source: U.S. Bureau of Economic Analysis, Survey of Current Business, June issues; and unpublished data.

No. 1062. Exports and Imports, by Method of Transport: 1980 to 1993

[Exports are free alongside ship (f.a.s.) value (see text, section 29) for all years; imports are f.a.s. value for 1980 and customs value for other years. Export data include both domestic and foreign; import data for general imports only. For details, see source]

ITEM	Unit	EXPORTS					IMPORTS				
		1980	1985	1990	1992	1993	1980	1985	1990	1992	1993
All methods [1]	Bil. dol.	220.7	213.1	393.0	447.5	464.9	240.8	345.3	495.3	532.4	580.5
Vessel	Bil. dol.	120.9	91.7	150.8	169.8	166.6	165.1	208.4	283.4	293.1	310.4
Air.	Bil. dol.	46.1	52.3	110.5	121	135.1	28.0	51.3	90.9	105.3	119.7
Shipping weight: Vessel . . .	Bil. kg .	363.7	317.7	372.4	379.3	349.5	443.1	361.5	496.3	476.0	531.0
Air.	Bil. kg .	1.0	0.8	1.5	1.7	1.7	0.6	1.3	1.7	1.7	1.9

[1] Includes types other than vessel and air and revisions that are not distributed by method of transport.

Source: U.S. Bureau of the Census, Highlights of U.S. Export and Import Trade, through 1985, FT 990, monthly; thereafter, U.S. Merchandise Trade: Selected Highlights, FT-920, monthly.

No. 1063. Federal Expenditures for Civil Functions of the Corps of Engineers, United States Army: 1965 to 1991

[In millions of dollars. For fiscal years ending in year shown, see text, section 9. These expenditures represent the work of the Corps of Engineers to plan, design, construct, operate, and maintain civil works projects and activities, particularly in the management and improvement of rivers, harbors, and waterways for navigation, flood control, and multiple purposes. The amounts listed below do not include the expenditure of funds contributed, advanced, or reimbursed by other government agencies or local interests. Includes Puerto Rico and outlying areas]

FISCAL YEAR	Total program [1]	Navigation	Flood control	Multiple purpose	FISCAL YEAR	Total program [1]	Navigation	Flood control	Multiple purpose
1965.....	1,169	426	447	283	1985.....	2,956	1,234	1,187	419
1970.....	1,128	398	379	331	1986.....	3,163	1,345	1,300	402
1975.....	2,070	694	904	439	1987.....	2,937	1,135	1,272	411
1980.....	3,061	1,225	1,228	551	1988.....	3,086	1,271	1,271	423
1981.....	3,198	1,339	1,273	527	1989.....	3,252	1,395	1,253	462
1982.....	2,940	1,331	1,083	453	1990.....	3,297	1,391	1,397	375
1983.....	2,959	1,290	1,088	482	1991.....	3,511	1,473	1,447	443
1984.....	3,085	1,383	1,154	445					

[1] Includes expenditures which are not associated with a specific purpose (e.g., headquarters staff supervision, management, and administration activities, and some research and development activities).

Source: U.S. Army Corps of Engineers, *Report of Civil Works Expenditures by State and Fiscal Year*, annual.

No. 1064. Freight Carried on Inland Waterways, by System: 1960 to 1989

[In billions of ton-miles. Excludes Alaska and Hawaii, except as noted. Includes waterways, canals, and connecting channels]

ITEM	1960	1970	1980	1982	1983	1984	1985	1986	1987	1988	1989
Total	220.3	318.6	406.9	351.2	359.0	399.0	381.7	392.6	410.7	438.2	448.7
Atlantic coast waterways.......	28.6	28.6	30.4	25.4	22.5	24.7	24.8	25.7	25.9	28.1	28.2
Gulf coast waterways	16.9	28.6	36.6	31.8	32.4	36.7	36.5	39.0	37.9	44.6	42.5
Pacific coast waterways [1]	6.0	8.4	14.9	12.8	13.2	20.5	19.9	20.8	22.8	24.5	24.0
Mississippi River system [2]	69.3	138.5	228.9	218.0	223.0	234.6	224.7	239.3	251.6	257.8	268.1
Great Lakes System [3].........	99.5	114.5	96.0	63.2	67.9	82.5	75.8	67.9	72.5	83.1	85.8

[1] Includes Alaskan waterways. [2] Comprises main channels and all tributaries of the Mississippi, Illinois, Missouri, and Ohio Rivers. [3] Does not include traffic between foreign ports.

Source: U.S. Army Corps of Engineers, *Waterborne Commerce of the United States*, annual.

No. 1065. Waterborne Commerce, by Type of Commodity: 1980 to 1989

[In millions of short tons. Domestic trade includes all commercial movements between United States ports and on inland rivers, Great Lakes, canals, and connecting channels of the United States, Puerto Rico, and Virgin Islands. Figures may differ from those shown in table 1080 due to minor differences in basic concepts]

COMMODITY	1980		1985		1989			
	Total	Domestic	Total	Domestic	Total	Domestic	Foreign	
							Imports	Exports
Net total	1,998.9	1,077.5	1,788.4	1,014.1	2,140.4	1,102.5	589.5	448.4
Petroleum products [1] ...	423.2	339.2	368.8	259.0	441.9	289.2	108.8	43.9
Gasoline	87.3	81.0	94.0	78.0	107.9	86.2	19.8	1.9
Distillate fuel oil	74.6	72.1	70.0	55.0	75.2	58.1	12.9	4.2
Residual fuel oil	188.0	141.3	130.0	83.7	147.5	91.4	42.8	13.3
Crude petroleum	480.2	174.2	357.7	194.7	480.8	181.9	298.8	0.1
Coal and lignite	256.4	164.1	273.9	179.9	304.8	203.8	2.4	98.6
Nonmetallic minerals [1][2] .	157.1	111.6	150.7	108.5	158.7	111.6	25.7	21.4
Sand and gravel [3]....	65.1	60.8	66.4	62.0	58.8	54.9	2.1	1.8
Limestone	34.2	23.9	24.5	21.9	41.3	35.5	2.3	3.5
Phosphate rock......	23.7	9.5	19.4	8.4	15.8	6.1	0.8	8.9
Iron and concentrates...	98.4	64.9	72.7	50.0	86.5	59.6	21.4	5.5
Farm products [1].......	216.8	63.4	172.8	60.0	216.3	70.5	8.7	137.1
Corn	98.6	30.8	76.3	29.0	96.4	35.8	0.1	60.5
Wheat...........	53.4	14.3	38.0	10.6	55.8	16.5	0.2	39.1
Soybeans	39.6	16.1	32.9	14.9	28.8	12.8	(Z)	16.0
Chemicals and allied products	91.9	49.4	108.5	53.3	123.3	61.9	15.9	45.5
Food and kindred products	54.8	20.4	52.5	17.6	54.3	20.6	11.5	22.2
Lumber and wood products [4]	52.0	22.7	47.2	18.8	56.9	21.0	4.7	31.2
Primary metal products ..	28.9	9.0	33.4	8.5	31.5	8.7	17.9	4.9
Waste and scrap	31.1	18.8	37.4	23.9	54.6	37.3	0.9	16.4
Other............	108.1	39.8	112.8	40.0	130.8	36.4	72.8	21.6

Z Less than 50,000. [1] Includes categories not shown separately. [2] Excludes fuels. [3] Includes crushed rock. [4] Excludes furniture.

Source: U.S. Army Corps of Engineers, *Waterborne Commerce of the United States*, annual.

No. 1066. Waterborne Imports and Exports, by Coastal District: 1980 to 1992

[Exports are free alongside ship (f.a.s.) value for all years; imports are f.a.s. value for 1980 and customs value for other years, see text, section 28. Includes commodities classified for security reasons as "Special Category" (exports only) and exports by Dept. of Defense (grant-aid shipments), and merchandise shipped in transit through the United States. See Appendix III]

DISTRICT	CARGO TONNAGE (mil. sh. tons)						VALUE (bil. dol.)					
	1980	1985	1989	1990	1991	1992	1980	1985	1989	1990	1991	1992
Imports:												
Atlantic	183	190	211	207	176	185	71.5	94.4	109.3	110.8	101.1	108.2
Gulf.	243	141	217	225	217	232	56.4	32.8	36.1	41.0	36.4	36.3
Pacific	56	51	55	55	49	55	45.0	90.4	140.9	143.3	143.7	156.6
Great Lakes	16	17	16	16	13	14	1.9	2.8	3.7	7.6	8.4	9.2
Exports:												
Atlantic	117	93	94	101	107	102	51.0	35.2	56.3	62.4	70.1	78.2
Gulf.	163	144	152	148	167	165	41.5	31.8	40.9	41.2	44.2	45.0
Pacific	78	81	103	100	102	101	25.2	25.8	50.1	53.7	56.6	60.4
Great Lakes	45	34	34	26	18	24	4.6	2.4	3.6	1.7	1.2	1.6

Source: U.S. Bureau of the Census, *U.S. Waterborne Exports and General Imports*, through 1988, FT 985, annual; thereafter TM 985, monthly.

No. 1067. Vessels Entered and Cleared in Foreign Trade, Net Registered Tonnage: 1966 to 1992

[In millions of net registered tons, except as indicated. Includes Puerto Rico and Virgin Islands. Seaports comprise all ports except Great Lakes ports. See also *Historical Statistics, Colonial Times to 1970*, series Q 507-517]

YEARLY AVERAGE OR YEAR	Number of vessels	ALL PORTS			SEAPORTS					
		Tonnage, all vessels			Tonnage, all vessels			Tonnage, with cargo		
		Total	U.S.	Foreign	Total	U.S.	Foreign	Total	U.S.	Foreign
Entered:										
1966-70.	53,459	232	29	203	206	27	180	157	18	139
1971-75.	53,760	319	30	290	292	28	264	220	24	196
1976-80.	53,700	458	40	418	425	38	387	316	30	286
1981-85.	50,124	452	57	395	424	55	369	277	36	241
1986-90.	61,978	548	46	502	521	45	476	346	30	315
1970.	53,293	254	26	226	227	24	202	171	19	152
1975.	51,443	355	32	323	326	30	297	240	26	215
1980.	53,645	492	52	440	460	50	410	310	34	276
1985.	53,531	451	53	398	426	52	374	283	34	249
1988.	62,097	556	47	509	527	46	481	352	30	322
1989.	64,946	587	44	543	558	42	516	367	31	335
1990.	66,424	589	41	548	564	40	524	367	30	337
1991.	57,254	516	39	476	494	38	455	311	28	283
1992.	55,056	515	37	478	493	36	457	312	28	284
Cleared:										
1966-70.	52,415	232	30	202	206	27	179	122	23	99
1971-75.	53,039	324	31	293	296	29	267	149	21	127
1976-80.	52,931	453	41	412	420	38	382	203	26	177
1981-85.	50,291	460	57	403	432	55	377	251	34	217
1986-90.	60,249	551	47	504	524	46	478	284	31	253
1970.	52,195	253	27	226	226	25	201	132	20	112
1975.	51,017	363	34	329	334	31	303	168	23	144
1980.	52,928	487	54	433	456	51	405	246	33	213
1985.	53,095	461	55	406	435	53	382	253	36	217
1988.	60,540	561	49	512	531	47	484	295	31	264
1989.	63,042	590	45	545	561	44	517	304	30	274
1990.	63,648	592	43	550	566	41	525	304	29	275
1991.	55,100	521	40	480	498	39	459	282	28	253
1992.	54,127	519	38	481	496	37	460	276	28	248

Source: U.S. Bureau of the Census, *Vessel Entrances and Clearances*, through 1988, FT 975, annual; thereafter TA 987, annual.

No. 1068. Domestic Merchant Vessels Completed by U.S. Shipyards: 1970 to 1992

[Vessels of 1,000 gross tons and over. See also *Historical Statistics, Colonial Times to 1970*, series Q 438-48]

TYPE	Unit	1970	1975	1980	1983	1984	1985	1986	1987	1988	1992
Merchant vessels	Number	13	15	10	13	5	8	5	4	4	1
Gross tons	1,000	342	452	375	376	118	172	215	153	153	32
Cargo	Number	6	3	6	6	-	4	2	3	3	1
Gross tons	1,000	120	65	105	228	-	113	66	58	58	32
Deadweight tons	1,000	134	71	114	219	-	97	53	63	63	29
Tankers	Number	7	12	4	7	5	4	3	1	1	-
Gross tons	1,000	222	387	270	148	118	59	149	95	95	-
Deadweight tons	1,000	427	742	354	277	210	92	271	209	209	-

- Represents zero.

Source: U.S. Maritime Administration, *New Ship Construction*, annual.

No. 1069. United States Flag Merchant Vessels: 1993

[As of **January;**. Covers ocean-going vessels of 1,000 gross tons and over engaged in foreign and domestic trade, and inactive vessels. Excludes vessels operating exclusively on Great Lakes, inland waterways, and those owned by the United States Army and Navy, and special types such as cable ships, tugs, etc. See also *Historical Statistics, Colonial Times to 1970*, series Q 487-502]

VESSEL TYPE	NUMBER						DEADWEIGHT TONNAGE (1,000)					
	Total	Passenger [1]	Cargo [2]	Intermodal	Bulk carrier [3]	Tanker [4]	Total	Passenger [1]	Cargo [2]	Intermodal	Bulk carrier [3]	Tanker [4]
Total	**603**	**11**	**154**	**195**	**23**	**220**	**22,461**	**97**	**2,085**	**5,126**	**991**	**14,162**
Active vessels	365	7	21	145	16	176	16,765	56	353	4,112	756	11,488
Privately owned	351	2	17	141	16	175	16,606	14	304	4,061	756	11,471
U.S. foreign trade	131	-	10	80	12	29	5,487	-	149	2,547	651	2,140
Foreign-to-foreign	27	-	1	9	-	17	1,880	-	22	291	-	1,567
Domestic trade	143	2	-	24	4	113	7,965	14	-	497	105	7,349
Coastal	77	-	-	2	4	71	2,983	-	-	30	105	2,848
Noncontiguous	66	2	-	22	-	42	4,982	14	-	467	-	4,501
Military Sea Lift Command . .	50	-	6	28	-	16	1,274	-	133	726	-	415
Government owned	14	5	4	4	-	1	159	42	49	51	-	17
Ready reserve force	3	1	2	-	-	-	39	10	29	-	-	-
Inactive vessels	238	4	133	50	7	44	5,696	41	1,732	1,014	235	2,674
Privately owned	33	1	3	6	5	18	2,147	13	28	99	173	1,834
Temporarily inactive	5	-	-	1	2	2	273	-	-	26	84	163
Laid-up	23	1	3	5	1	13	1,695	13	28	73	16	1,565
Laid-up (MARAD Custody) [5]	5	-	-	-	2	3	179	-	-	-	73	106
Government owned (MARAD Custody) [5]	205	3	130	44	2	26	3,549	28	1,704	915	62	840
National defense reserve fleet	159	-	92	44	-	23	2,952	-	1,282	915	-	755
Ready reserve fleet	93	-	56	24	-	13	1,832	-	787	642	-	403
Other reserve	66	-	36	20	-	10	1,120	-	495	273	-	352
Nonretention [6]	44	3	38	-	-	3	535	28	422	-	-	85
Other Government owned . .	2	-	-	-	2	-	62	-	-	-	62	-

- Represents zero.   [1] Includes combination passenger and cargo vessels.   [2] General cargo.   [3] Includes tug barges.   [4] Includes tanker barges and liquified natural gas vessels.   [5] In the custody of the Maritime Administration.   [6] Vessels not actively maintained.

Source: U.S. Maritime Administration, *Employment Report of the United States Flag Merchant Fleet Ocean-Going Vessels 1,000 Gross Tons and Over*, annual.

No. 1070. Private Shipyards—Summary: 1980 to 1993

[For calendar year, unless noted. See also *Historical Statistics, Colonial Times to 1970*, series Q 449-458 and series Q 467-472]

ITEM	Unit	1980	1985	1987	1988	1989	1990	1991	1992	1993
Employment [1]	1,000. . .	177.3	130.3	120.4	121.0	123.4	121.8	127.2	123.5	111.0
Production workers	1,000. . .	141.8	99.0	90.8	90.9	88.6	86.4	95.5	93.3	84.3
Value of work done	Mil. dol. .	9,269	9,358	8,531	(NA)	(NA)	(NA)	(NA)	(NA)	(NA)
On ships only	Mil. dol. .	8,889	9,483	8,377	(NA)	(NA)	(NA)	(NA)	(NA)	(NA)
Value added	Mil. dol. .	5,338	5,740	5,227	(NA)	(NA)	(NA)	(NA)	(NA)	(NA)
Building activity: Merchant vessels: [2]										
Under construction [3]	Number .	69	10	6	-	-	-	3	3	1
Ordered	Number .	7	-	-	-	-	3	-	1	-
Delivered	Number .	23	3	4	-	-	-	-	3	-
Cancelled	Number .	4	-	2	-	-	-	-	-	-
Under contract [4]	Number .	49	7	-	-	-	3	3	1	1
Naval vessels: [2]										
Under construction [3]	Number .	99	100	79	83	105	98	91	90	82
Ordered	Number .	11	11	20	32	16	8	13	10	12
Delivered	Number .	19	26	16	10	23	15	14	18	19
Under contract [4] [5]	Number .	91	85	83	105	98	91	90	82	73
Repairs/conversions:										
Commercial ships	Mil. dol. .	1,335	852	806	202	279	373	380	226	292
Naval ships	Mil. dol. .	1,134	2,311	1,930	1,238	1,091	1,119	993	526	573
Unfinished work: [3]										
Commercial ships	Mil. dol. .	2,070	450	53	-	-	-	-	99	42
Naval ships	Mil. dol. .	7,107	12,091	8,265	10,500	16,010	15,450	14,151	12,286	(NA)

- Represents zero.   NA Not available.   [1] Annual average of monthly data.   [2] Vessels of 1,000 tons or larger.   [3] As of Jan. 1.   [4] As of Dec. 31.   [5] Two ships were cancelled in August 1993.

Source: Shipbuilders Council of America, Arlington, VA., *Annual Report*, through 1980; thereafter, unpublished data.

No. 1071. Employees in Government and Private Shipyards: 1960 to 1993

[In thousands. Annual average employment in establishments primarily engaged in building and repairing all types of ships, barges, canal boats, and lighters of 5 gross tons and over, whether propelled by sail or motor power or towed by other craft. Includes all full- and part-time employees]

YEAR	Total	Private yards	Navy yards	YEAR	Total	Private yards	Navy yards	YEAR	Total	Private yards	Navy yards
1960.	208	112	96	1984.	229	146	83	1989.	196	126	71
1970.	216	134	83	1985.	219	138	80	1990.	198	130	68
1975.	217	154	65	1986.	206	131	75	1991.	193	131	62
1980.	250	178	72	1987.	200	124	75	1992.	183	124	59
1983.	226	143	84	1988.	197	124	73	1993.	163	111	52

Source: U.S. Bureau of Labor Statistics, Bulletins 2370 and 2429; *Employment and Earnings*, monthly, March and June issues; and unpublished data.

No. 1072. Employment on U.S. Flag Merchant Vessels, 1970 to 1993, and Basic Monthly (January) Wage Scale for Able-Bodied Seamen, 1970 to 1994

[Employment in thousands. See also *Historical Statistics, Colonial Times to 1970*, series Q 414-416]

YEAR	Employ-ment [1]	YEAR	Employ-ment [1]	YEAR	East coast wage rate [2]	West coast wage rate [2]	YEAR	East coast wage rate [2]	West coast wage rate [2]
1970.	37.6	1988	10.7	1970	$470	$652	1989	$1,448	$2,218
1975.	20.5	1989	9.9	1975	612	900	1990	1,505	2,218
1980.	19.6	1990	11.1	1980	967	1,414	1991	1,581	2,329
1985.	13.1	1991	11.7	1985	1,419	2,069	1992	1,655	2,438
1986.	11.5	1992	9.2	1987	1,419	2,132	1993	1,721	2,438
1987.	10.4	1993	9.3	1988	1,419	2,175	1994	1,790	2,536

[1] As of June 30, except beginning 1980, as of Sept. 30. Estimates of personnel employed on merchant ships, 1,000 gross tons and over. Excludes vessels on inland waterways, Great Lakes, and those owned by, or operated for, U.S. Army and Navy, and special types such as cable ships, tugs, etc.　[2] Basic monthly wage, over and above subsistence (board and room); excludes overtime and fringe pay benefits. West coast incorporates extra pay for Saturdays and Sundays at sea into base wages but east coast does not.

Source: U.S. Maritime Administration, *U.S. Merchant Marine Data Sheet*, monthly; and unpublished data.

No. 1073. Worldwide Tanker Casualties: 1975 to 1993

[Data for 1975 and 1980 covers tankers, ore/oil carriers and bulk/oil vessels of 6,000 deadweight tons and over; beginning 1987, 10,000 deadweight tons and over; excludes liquid gas carriers. Incident is counted in the year it is reported. Based on data from "Lloyd's List" published by Lloyd's of London. "Casualties" include weather damage, strandings, collisions and other contact, fires and explosions, machinery damage, and other mishaps]

ITEM	Unit	1975	1980	1985	1987	1988	1989	1990	1991	1992	1993
Casualties.	Number	906	(NA)	340	408	456	528	541	507	396	314
Total losses [1]	Number	22	15	12	5	3	8	10	10	11	9
Deaths	Number	90	132	53	12	63	74	119	205	86	26
Oil spills	Number	45	32	9	12	13	31	31	26	17	24
Amount	1,000 tons	188	136	80	9	178	188	61	439	152	120
Amount	Mil. gallons	58	42	25	3	55	58	19	136	47	37

NA Not available.　[1] Excludes losses due to hostilities.

Source: Tanker Advisory Center, Inc., New York, NY, "Worldwide Tanker Casualty Returns," quarterly.

No. 1074. Merchant Vessels—World and United States: 1960 to 1992

[Vessels of 100 gross tonnage and above. Excludes sailing ships, nonpropelled craft, and all ships built of wood. See also *Historical Statistics, Colonial Times to 1970*, series Q 473-480]

YEAR	WORLD: COMPLETED		WORLD: OWNED		U.S.: COMPLETED		U.S.: REGISTERED	
	Number	Gross tonnage (1,000)	Number	Gross tonnage (1,000)	Number	Gross tonnage (1,000)	Number	Gross tonnage (1,000)
1960	2,005	8,382	36,311	129,770	49	379	4,059	24,837
1970	2,814	20,980	52,444	227,490	156	375	2,983	18,463
1980	2,412	13,101	73,832	419,911	205	555	5,579	18,464
1985	1,964	18,157	76,395	416,269	66	180	6,447	19,518
1987	1,528	12,259	75,240	403,498	29	164	6,427	20,178
1988	1,575	10,909	75,680	403,406	60	11	6,442	20,832
1989	1,593	13,236	76,100	410,481	10	4	6,375	20,588
1990	1,672	15,885	78,336	423,627	16	15	6,348	21,328
1991	1,574	16,095	80,030	436,027	17	9	6,222	20,291
1992	1,506	18,633	79,845	444,305	27	54	5,737	18,228

Source: Lloyd's Register of Shipping, London, England, *Statistical Tables*, annual; and *Annual Summary of Merchant Ships Completed in the World*.

No. 1075. Merchant Vessels—Ships and Tonnage Lost Worldwide: 1980 to 1992

[For merchant vessels of 100 gross tonnage and above. Excludes ships which have been declared constructive losses but have undergone repair during the year. Loss counted in the year the casualty occurred, providing that information was available at time of relevant publication]

TYPE OF SHIP	SHIPS LOST					GROSS TONNAGE LOST (1,000)				
	1980	1985	1990	1991	1992	1980	1985	1990	1991	1992
Total [1]	387	307	188	258	213	1,804	1,651	1,126	1,548	1,223
Tankers	24	19	8	13	7	707	776	138	571	332
Ore/bulk carriers [2]	21	22	15	20	13	458	405	687	574	576
General cargo	211	155	87	116	81	478	363	202	300	174
Container ships	2	5	-	1	4	6	41	-	2	40
Passenger [3]	9	-	-	2	1	112	-	-	14	13
Fishing	96	66	50	69	77	30	26	20	33	31

- Represents zero.　[1] Includes types not shown separately.　[2] Includes ore/bulk/oil carriers.　[3] Includes passenger cargo ships.

Source: Lloyd's Register of Shipping, London, England, *Casualty Return,* annual.

No. 1076. Merchant Fleets of the World: 1980 to 1992

[Vessels of 1,000 gross tons and over. As of Jan. 1 of the following year. Specified countries have 100 or more ships]

YEAR AND COUNTRY OF REGISTRY, 1992	TOTAL		PASSENGER/ CARGO COMB.		FREIGHTERS		BULK CARRIERS [1]		TANKERS	
	Number	Average age (yr.)	Number	Average age (yr.)	Number	Average age (yr.)	Number	Average age (yr.)	Number	Average age (yr.)
1980, world total	24,867	13	468	24	14,242	14	4,798	10	5,359	12
United States	864	23	65	34	471	23	20	22	308	20
Foreign	24,003	13	403	22	13,771	13	4,778	10	5,051	11
1985, world total	25,555	14	375	25	13,937	15	5,787	11	5,456	13
United States	737	23	37	38	417	25	25	9	258	19
Foreign	24,818	14	338	23	13,520	15	5,762	11	5,198	13
1992, world total	23,753	16	352	22	12,339	16	5,420	14	5,642	15
United States	603	25	11	44	349	26	23	17	220	22
Privately-owned	384	19	3	42	167	16	21	17	193	21
Government-owned	219	35	8	45	182	35	2	14	27	35
Foreign	23,150	16	341	21	11,990	16	5,397	14	5,422	15
Antigua and Barbuda	148	12	-	-	121	12	4	19	23	15
Bahamas	818	14	49	21	380	13	147	13	242	13
Brazil	220	15	1	31	59	18	77	13	83	16
Bulgaria	117	18	2	24	59	20	37	15	19	13
China: Mainland	1,231	17	24	21	752	18	285	17	170	16
Taiwan	215	12	-	-	134	13	60	10	21	10
Cyprus	1,251	16	7	33	616	15	488	17	140	15
Denmark (DIS) [2]	281	8	-	-	189	8	14	7	78	9
Egypt	128	19	3	32	100	19	14	9	11	23
France	106	15	7	14	45	13	6	12	48	16
Germany	419	9	7	11	351	9	22	12	39	9
Greece	904	18	22	34	193	20	458	16	231	18
Honduras	189	26	3	31	176	26	10	25	-	-
Hong Kong	200	12	1	31	64	13	104	11	31	15
India	296	14	3	16	97	15	119	14	77	12
Indonesia	365	18	7	18	247	19	19	13	92	18
Iran	124	17	-	-	38	19	50	13	36	19
Italy	468	17	19	16	172	16	60	14	217	18
Japan	913	9	15	12	351	9	251	11	296	9
Latvia	118	17	-	-	75	18	-	-	43	15
Liberia	1,568	13	22	18	367	12	540	13	639	12
Malaysia	185	16	-	-	107	20	24	12	54	11
Malta	752	19	7	41	343	19	255	18	147	20
Netherlands	367	10	5	18	285	10	19	13	58	10
Norway (NIS) [2]	737	13	14	12	193	14	219	13	311	13
Panama	3,171	14	31	30	1,719	15	717	14	704	13
Philippines	534	14	5	34	239	17	251	9	39	24
Poland	212	15	3	13	119	15	85	14	5	19
Romania	255	14	-	-	193	14	50	17	12	12
Russia	1,363	18	11	26	1,006	19	135	14	211	16
Saint Vincent	431	21	2	36	285	21	97	19	47	22
Singapore	411	13	-	-	227	15	-	-	184	13
South Korea	422	15	-	-	225	15	130	14	67	15
Spain	222	16	1	19	130	15	30	16	61	17
Sweden	172	15	5	7	90	15	10	19	67	15
Thailand	169	23	1	31	110	23	5	21	53	22
Turkey	339	17	3	35	189	15	93	17	54	19
United Kingdom	154	16	18	16	58	15	19	13	59	17
Vanuatu	119	13	1	40	55	13	52	13	11	14
All others	3,056	12	42	12	1,831	13	441	9	742	13

- Represents zero.　[1] Includes bulk/oil, ore/oil, and ore/bulk/oil carriers.　[2] International Shipping Registry which is an open registry under which the ship flies the flag of the specified nation but is exempt from certain taxation and other regulations.

Source: U.S. Maritime Administration, *Merchant Fleets of the World,* summary report, annual; and unpublished data.

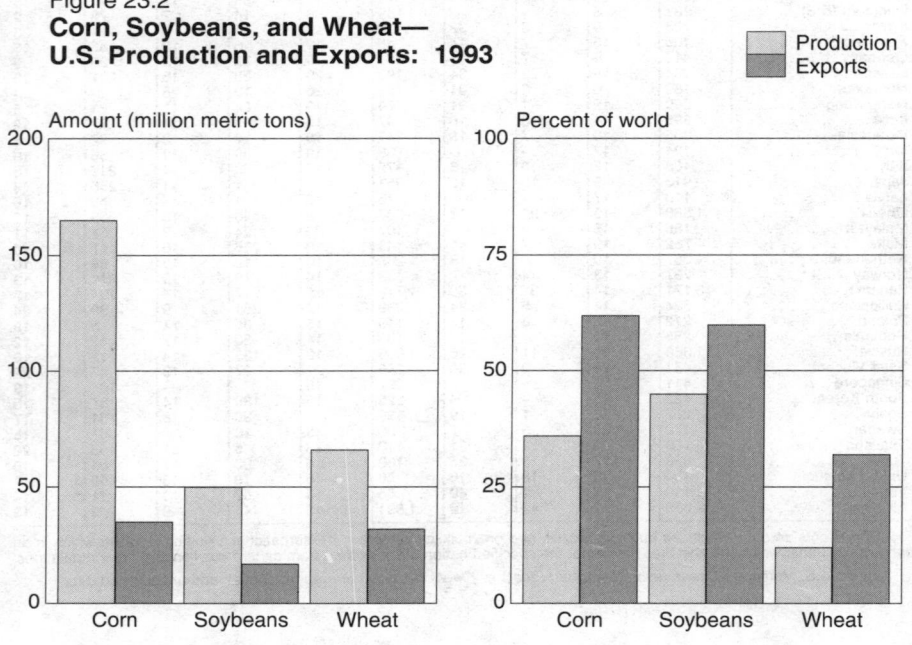

Figure 23.1
Consumer Expenditures for Farm Foods: 1970, 1980, and 1992

Marketing bill
Farm value

Total
Billions of dollars

At-home[1]

Away-from-home

[1]Food purchased from retail food stores for use at home.
Source: Chart prepared by U.S. Bureau of the Census. For data, see table 1099.

Figure 23.2
Corn, Soybeans, and Wheat— U.S. Production and Exports: 1993

Production
Exports

Amount (million metric tons)

Percent of world

Source: Chart prepared by U.S. Bureau of the Census. For data, see table 1104.

Agriculture

This section presents statistics on farms and farm acreage; land use and irrigation; farm income, expenditures, and debt; farm output, productivity, and marketings; foreign trade in agricultural products; specific crops; and livestock, poultry, and their products.

In Brief

Number of farms, 1993: 2.1 million
  Leading States—
  Texas   *185,000*
  Missouri   *106,000*
  Iowa   *100,000*

Farm marketings cash receipts, 1992: $171 billion
  Leading commodities—
  Cattle, calves   *$38 billion*
  Dairy products   *$20 billion*
  Corn   *$15 billion*

The principal sources are the reports issued by the U.S. Bureau of the Census and by the National Agricultural Statistics Service (NASS) and the Economic Research Service (ERS) of the U.S. Department of Agriculture. The Bureau of the Census has taken a census of agriculture every 10 years from 1840 to 1920 and every 5 years from 1925 through 1974. Two 4-year censuses, taken for 1978 and 1982, adjusted the data reference year to coincide with the economic censuses. A few State reports from the 1992 Census of Agriculture are presently available. The Department of Agriculture publishes annually *Agricultural Statistics,* a general reference book on agricultural production, supplies, consumption, facilities, costs, and returns. The Economic Research Service publishes a series of annual reports, *Economic Indicators of the Farm Sector.* This series comprises five reports: *National Financial Summary, State Financial Summary, Production and Efficiency Statistics, Costs of Production—Livestock and Dairy,* and *Costs of Production—Major Field Crops.* Sources of current data on agricultural exports and imports include *Foreign Agricultural Trade of the United States,* published by the ERS, and the reports of the Bureau of the Census, particularly *U.S. Imports for Consumption and General Imports—HTSUSA Commodity by Country of Origin* (FT247), *U.S. Exports, Harmonized Schedule B, Commodity by Country* (FT447), and *U.S. Merchandise Trade: Exports, General Imports, and Imports for Consumption* (FT925).

The 45 field offices of the NASS collect data on crops, livestock and products, agricultural prices, farm employment, and other related subjects mainly through sample surveys. Information is obtained on some 75 crops and 50 livestock items as well as scores of items pertaining to agricultural production and marketing. State estimates and supporting information are sent to the Agricultural Statistics Board of NASS which reviews the estimates and issues reports containing State and national data. Among these reports are annual summaries such as *Crop Production, Crop Values, Agricultural Prices,* and *Livestock Production, Disposition and Income.* For more information about concepts and methods underlying USDA's statistical series, see *Major Statistical Series of the U.S. Department of Agriculture* (Agricultural Handbook No. 671), a 12-volume set of publications.

Farms and farmland.—The Bureau of the Census has used varying definitions of a farm. Data from the census of agriculture reflect the definition of farm used for the census year. For the 1974 Census of Agriculture and each subsequent one, a farm was defined as any place from which $1,000 or more of agricultural products were produced and sold or normally would have been sold during the census year. Control may have been exercised through ownership or management, or through a lease, rental, or cropping arrangement. In the case of landowners who had one or more tenants or renters, the land operated by each was counted as a separate farm. The effect of the change in definition must be considered when comparing farms in the 1974 and subsequent censuses with those in previous censuses.

The definition of a farm applicable to data originated by the Department of Agriculture is the one used by the Bureau of the Census for the agriculture census immediately preceding the year or years for which the data are shown. Farmland refers to all land under the control of a farm operator, including land not actually under cultivation or not used for pasture or grazing. Land used for pasture or grazing on a per head basis that was neither owned nor leased by a farm operator is not included except for grazing lands controlled by grazing associations leased on a per acre basis. Coverage estimates for 1978, 1982, and 1987 indicate about 3.4, 9.1, and 7.2 percent of all farms, respectively, were not included in census totals. Farms undercounted in these censuses were usually small and accounted for approximately 1 percent of the total value of agricultural products sold and approximately 2 percent of the land in farms. For more explanation about mail list compilation and census coverage, see Appendixes A and C, *1987 Census of Agriculture,* volume 1 reports, and *Coverage Evaluation, Volume 2, Part 2.*

Farm income.—Gross farm income comprises cash receipts from farm marketings of crops and livestock, Federal government payments made directly to farmers for farm-related activities, rental value of farm homes, value of farm products consumed in farm homes, and other farm-related income such as machine hire and custom work. Farm marketings represent quantities of agricultural products sold by farmers multiplied by prices received per unit of production at the local market. Information on prices received for farm products is generally obtained by the NASS Agricultural Statistics Board from surveys of firms (such as grain elevators, packers, and processors) purchasing agricultural commodities directly from producers. In some cases, the price information is obtained directly from the producers.

Crops.—Estimates of crop acreage and production by the NASS are based on current sample survey data obtained from individual producers and objective yield counts, reports of carlot shipments, market records, personal field observations by field statisticians, and reports from other sources. Prices received by farmers are marketing year averages. These averages are based on U.S. monthly prices weighted by monthly marketings during specific periods. U.S. monthly prices are State average prices weighted by marketings during the month. Marketing year average prices do not include allowances for outstanding loans, government purchases, deficiency payments or disaster payments.

All State prices are based on individual State marketing years, while U.S. marketing year averages are based on standard marketing years for each crop. For a listing of the crop marketing years and the participating States in the monthly program, see *Crop Values,* January 1992. Value of production is computed by multiplying State prices by each State's production. The U.S. value of production is the sum of State values for all States. Value of production figures shown in tables 1113-1116, 1118, and 1119 should not be confused with cash receipts from farm marketings which relate to sales during a calendar year, irrespective of the year of production.

Livestock.—Annual inventory numbers of livestock and estimates of livestock, dairy, and poultry production prepared by the Department of Agriculture are based on information from farmers and ranchers obtained by probability survey sampling methods.

Statistical reliability.—For a discussion of statistical collection and estimation, sampling procedures, and measures of statistical reliability pertaining to Census Bureau and Department of Agriculture data, see Appendix III.

Historical statistics.—Tabular headnotes provide cross-references, where applicable, to *Historical Statistics of the United States, Colonial Times to 1970.* See Appendix IV.

No. 1077. Food and Fiber Sector of Domestic Economy—Employment and Value Added: 1980 to 1992

[Employment in millions; value added in billions of dollars, except as indicated]

SECTOR	1980	1984	1985	1986	1987	1988	1989	1990	1991	1992
EMPLOYMENT										
Food and fiber sector, total ...	23.4	22.6	22.3	22.4	22.4	22.7	23.4	23.5	23.2	22.8
Percent of domestic economy [1]	21.9	19.9	19.3	19.0	18.7	18.6	18.9	18.8	18.5	18.0
Farm sector.	2.7	2.3	2.1	2.0	2.0	2.0	2.0	2.1	2.0	2.0
Nonfarm sector	20.8	20.3	20.2	20.3	20.5	20.6	21.4	21.4	21.2	20.8
Food processing	1.7	1.6	1.6	1.6	1.6	1.5	1.5	1.5	1.5	1.5
Manufacturing.	3.8	3.4	3.3	3.2	3.1	3.0	3.2	3.1	3.1	3.0
Transportation, trade, and retailing .	7.2	7.3	7.4	7.5	7.5	7.6	7.9	8.0	7.9	7.8
Eating establishments.	4.6	4.7	4.7	4.8	5.0	5.2	5.3	5.4	5.3	5.2
Other.	3.4	3.2	3.2	3.2	3.2	3.3	3.5	3.5	3.5	3.4
VALUE ADDED [2]										
Food and fiber sector, total ...	560.6	672.1	697.8	716.6	744.7	784.5	850.3	889.8	913.8	950.2
Percent of domestic economy .	20.7	17.8	17.3	16.8	16.4	16.0	16.2	16.0	16.0	15.7
Farm sector.	49.3	55.5	58.5	52.6	53.0	49.7	65.2	68.1	63.4	67.0
Nonfarm sector	511.2	616.6	639.3	664.0	691.7	734.9	785.0	821.7	850.4	883.2
Food processing	63.8	80.5	82.3	87.4	86.2	91.8	96.1	99.8	103.4	106.2
Manufacturing.	94.7	109.9	109.8	113.2	111.5	115.2	124.5	125.6	130.8	135.7
Transportation, trade, and retailing .	179.1	201.2	208.9	212.0	222.5	235.7	247.2	257.4	265.6	277.5
Eating establishments.	54.6	62.9	64.5	66.0	73.0	78.5	80.7	85.6	88.3	90.9
Other.	119.0	162.1	173.8	185.3	198.4	213.8	236.6	253.2	262.3	272.9

[1] Based on civilian labor force.   [2] Value added equals profits, rent, interest, wages, indirect business taxes, and depreciation.

Source: U.S. Dept. of Agriculture, Economic Research Service, unpublished data.

No. 1078. Farms—Number, 1974 to 1987, and Acreage, 1978 to 1987, by Size of Farm

[See also *Historical Statistics, Colonial Times to 1970*, series K 162-173]

SIZE OF FARM	NUMBER OF FARMS (1,000)				LAND IN FARMS (mil. acres)			CROPLAND HARVESTED (mil. acres)			PERCENT DISTRIBUTION, 1987		
	1974	1978	1982	1987	1978	1982	1987	1978	1982	1987	Number of farms	All land in farms	Cropland harvested
Total	2,314	2,258	2,241	2,088	1,014.8	986.8	964.5	317.1	326.3	282.2	100.0	100.0	100.0
Under 10 acres.	128	151	188	183	0.6	0.7	0.7	0.2	0.3	0.2	8.8	0.1	0.1
10 to 49 acres	380	392	449	412	10.9	12.1	11.1	4.5	4.5	3.9	19.8	1.2	1.4
50 to 99 acres	385	356	344	311	25.9	24.8	22.5	10.2	9.5	7.9	14.9	2.3	2.8
100 to 179 acres.	443	403	368	334	55.0	49.9	45.3	23.3	21.2	17.1	16.0	4.7	6.1
180 to 259 acres.	253	234	211	192	50.6	45.7	41.5	23.7	21.7	17.2	9.2	4.3	6.1
260 to 499 acres.	363	348	315	286	124.6	113.0	103.0	64.5	60.5	47.3	13.7	10.7	16.8
500 to 999 acres.	207	213	204	200	146.7	140.5	138.5	75.2	77.6	67.4	9.6	14.4	23.9
1,000 to 1,999 acres .	93	98	97	102	133.0	132.4	138.8	58.2	64.5	61.1	4.9	14.4	21.7
2,000 acres and over. .	62	63	65	67	467.4	467.5	463.2	57.3	66.6	60.2	3.2	48.0	21.3

Source: U.S. Bureau of the Census, *Census of Agriculture: 1974*, vol. 1; and *1987*, vol. 1.

No. 1079. Farms—Number, Acreage, and Value, by Type of Organization: 1982 and 1987

[Data for 1982 exclude abnormal farms (institutional farms, experimental and research farms, Indian reservations, etc.)]

ITEM	Unit	Total [1]	Individual or family	Partnership	Corporation	PERCENT DISTRIBUTION			
						Total [1]	Individual or family	Partnership	Corporation
ALL FARMS									
Number of farms: 1982.	1,000 ...	2,239	1,946	223	60	100.0	86.9	10.0	2.7
1987.	1,000 ...	2,088	1,809	200	67	100.0	86.7	9.6	3.2
Land in farms: 1982	Mil. acres.	932	642	152	127	100.0	68.9	16.3	13.6
1987.	Mil. acres.	964	628	153	119	100.0	65.1	15.9	12.4
Value of land and buildings: [2] 1982. .	Bil. dol. ...	763	547	119	90	100.0	71.7	15.6	11.8
1987. .	Bil. dol. ...	604	424	95	69	100.0	70.1	15.7	11.4
Value of farm products sold: 1982 ..	Bil. dol. ...	132	78	22	31	100.0	59.2	16.4	23.9
1987 ..	Bil. dol. ...	136	77	23	35	100.0	56.3	17.1	25.6
FARMS WITH SALES OF $10,000 AND OVER									
Number of farms: 1982.	1,000 ...	1,143	934	152	52	100.0	81.7	13.3	4.6
1987.	1,000 ...	1,060	861	136	56	100.0	81.3	12.8	5.3
Land in farms: 1982	Mil. acres.	811	536	141	124	100.0	66.1	17.4	15.3
1987.	Mil. acres.	829	525	143	116	100.0	63.3	17.3	14.0

[1] Includes other types, not shown separately.   [2] Based on a sample of farms.

Source: U.S. Bureau of the Census, *1987 Census of Agriculture*, vol. 1.

No. 1080. Farms—Number and Acreage, by Tenure of Operator: 1974 to 1987

[*Full owners* own all the land they operate. *Part owners* own a part and rent from others the rest of the land they operate. See also *Historical Statistics, Colonial Times to 1970*, series K 109-113 and 142-146]

ITEM AND YEAR	Unit	Total	Full owner	Part owner	Tenant	PERCENT DISTRIBUTION			
						Total	Full owner	Part owner	Tenant
Number of farms:									
1974	1,000	2,314	1,424	628	262	100.0	61.5	27.2	11.3
1978	1,000	2,258	1,298	681	279	100.0	57.5	30.1	12.4
1982	1,000	2,241	1,326	656	259	100.0	59.2	29.3	11.5
1987	1,000	2,088	1,239	609	240	100.0	59.3	29.2	11.5
Under 50 acres	1,000	596	483	59	53	100.0	81.1	9.9	9.0
50 to 179 acres	1,000	645	449	130	66	100.0	69.6	20.1	10.3
180 to 499 acres	1,000	478	217	195	67	100.0	45.3	40.8	13.9
500 to 999 acres	1,000	200	53	117	31	100.0	26.3	58.3	15.4
1,000 acres or more	1,000	169	37	108	23	100.0	22.1	64.2	13.7
Land in farms:									
1974	Mil. acres	1,017	359	535	122	100.0	35.4	52.6	12.0
1978	Mil. acres	1,015	332	561	122	100.0	32.7	55.3	12.0
1982	Mil. acres	987	342	531	114	100.0	34.7	53.8	11.6
1987	Mil. acres	964	318	520	127	100.0	32.9	53.9	13.2

No. 1081. Farm Operators—Tenure and Characteristics: 1982 and 1987

[In thousands, except as indicated. See also *Historical Statistics, Colonial Times to 1970*, series K 82-113]

CHARACTERISTIC	ALL FARMS		FARMS WITH SALES OF $10,000 AND OVER		CHARACTERISTIC	ALL FARMS		FARMS WITH SALES OF $10,000 AND OVER	
	1982	1987	1982	1987		1982	1987	1982	1987
Total operators	**2,241**	**2,088**	**1,143**	**1,060**	Tenant	259	240	170	161
White	2,187	2,043	1,127	1,046					
Black	33	23	7	4	Principal occupation:				
American Indian, Eskimo, and Aleuts	7	7	2	2	Farming	1,235	1,138	901	811
					Other	1,006	950	242	248
Asian or Pacific Islander	8	8	5	5					
Other	6	7	2	2	Place of residence: [2]				
					On farm operated	1,581	1,488	833	776
Operators of Hispanic origin [1]	16	17	6	6	Not on farm operated	429	443	202	215
Female	122	132	37	42	Years on present farm: [2]				
					2 years or less	127	114	53	49
Under 25 years old	62	36	39	21	3 to 4 years	193	135	83	56
25 to 34 years old	294	243	173	147	5 to 9 years	360	304	167	138
35 to 44 years old	443	411	223	212	10 years or more	1,098	1,163	638	653
45 to 54 years old	505	455	264	228					
55 to 64 years old	536	496	288	263	Days worked off farm: [2]				
65 years old and over	400	447	156	188	None	862	844	591	561
Average age (years)	50.5	52.0	49.1	50.6	Less than 100 days	224	200	141	124
					100 to 199 days	189	178	77	80
Full owner	1,326	1,239	482	445	200 days or more	775	737	213	219
Part owner	656	609	491	454					

[1] Operators of Hispanic origin may be of any race. [2] Excludes not reported.

No. 1082. Irrigated Farms and Acreage, by State: 1982 and 1987

[See also *Historical Statistics, Colonial Times to 1970*, series J 85-91]

STATE	IRRIGATED FARMS				LAND IN IRRIGATED FARMS				IRRIGATED LAND			
	Number (1,000)		Percent of all farms		Acreage (1,000)		Percent of all land in farms		Acreage (1,000)		Percent of all land in farms	
	1982	1987	1982	1987	1982	1987	1982	1987	1982	1987	1982	1987
U.S. [1]	278.3	291.6	12.4	13.9	246,603	241,069	24.9	24.9	49,002	46,386	5.0	4.8
Arizona	4.4	4.2	60.4	55.3	18,871	17,167	49.9	47.3	1,098	914	2.9	2.5
California	58.4	58.9	70.8	70.7	18,402	17,567	57.2	57.4	8,461	7,596	26.3	24.8
Colorado	15.2	14.9	56.1	54.6	17,351	16,729	51.7	49.1	3,201	3,014	9.5	8.9
Florida	10.6	12.0	29.0	32.7	5,529	4,670	43.1	41.7	1,585	1,623	12.4	14.5
Idaho	17.4	16.6	70.2	68.8	9,168	9,053	65.8	64.9	3,450	3,219	24.8	23.1
Kansas	7.3	7.4	9.8	10.7	10,345	10,654	21.9	22.8	2,675	2,463	5.7	5.3
Montana	9.2	9.5	39.1	38.7	24,171	23,259	39.9	38.6	2,023	1,997	3.3	3.3
Nebraska	22.2	22.6	36.8	37.3	22,679	22,499	50.4	49.6	6,039	5,682	13.4	12.5
Oregon	15.3	14.4	44.9	45.0	11,382	11,340	64.1	63.6	1,808	1,648	10.2	9.3
Texas	19.8	19.8	10.6	10.4	22,161	20,270	16.8	15.5	5,576	4,271	4.2	3.3
Utah	11.2	11.1	79.9	79.2	7,598	7,594	77.7	76.0	1,082	1,161	11.1	11.6
Washington	16.3	15.4	45.0	45.9	6,003	5,468	36.4	33.9	1,638	1,519	9.9	9.4
Wyoming	5.3	5.2	59.6	56.7	18,132	18,207	54.1	54.1	1,565	1,518	4.7	4.5

[1] Includes other States not shown separately.

Source of tables 1080-82: U.S. Bureau of the Census, *Census of Agriculture: 1974*, vol. II; *1982*, vol. 1; and *1987*, vol. 1.

No. 1083. Farms—Number, Acreage, and Value, by State: 1987

[See also *Historical Statistics, Colonial Times to 1970,* series K 17-18]

REGION, DIVISION, AND STATE	ALL FARMS			FARMS WITH SALES OF $10,000 OR MORE			REGION, DIVISION, AND STATE	ALL FARMS			FARMS WITH SALES OF $10,000 OR MORE		
	Number of farms (1,000)	Land in farms (mil. acres)	Average size of farm (acres)	Number of farms (1,000)	Land in farms (mil. acres)	Average size of farm (acres)		Number of farms (1,000)	Land in farms (mil. acres)	Average size of farm (acres)	Number of farms (1,000)	Land in farms (mil. acres)	Average size of farm (acres)
U.S.	2,088	964.5	462	1,060	829.0	782	VA	45	8.7	194	16	5.9	377
Northeast..	123	21.4	174	61	16.0	261	WV	17	3.4	196	3	1.4	431
N.E	25	4.2	169	11	2.8	260	NC	59	9.4	159	26	7.1	276
ME	6	1.3	214	3	0.9	332	SC	20	4.8	232	7	3.3	491
NH	2	0.4	169	1	0.2	283	GA	44	10.7	247	18	7.9	439
VT	6	1.4	240	3	1.1	325	FL	37	11.2	306	15	9.4	638
MA	6	0.6	99	2	0.4	153	E.S.C	250	45.6	183	82	30.4	372
RI	1	0.1	84	(Z)	(Z)	116	KY	92	14.0	152	34	9.4	276
CT	4	0.4	111	1	0.3	179	TN	80	11.7	147	22	7.2	329
M.A.....	98	17.2	175	50	13.1	262	AL	43	9.1	211	14	5.9	424
NY	38	8.4	223	21	6.7	327	MS	34	10.7	315	12	7.9	662
NJ	9	0.9	99	3	0.7	191	W.S.C ...	335	184.4	551	129	153.3	1,184
PA	51	7.9	153	26	5.7	221	AR	48	14.4	298	21	11.2	522
Midwest ...	862	350.5	407	556	314.5	565	LA	27	8.0	293	11	6.4	607
E.N.C. ...	365	86.6	237	219	76.3	348	OK	70	31.5	449	29	25.1	878
OH	79	15.0	189	40	12.1	305	TX	189	130.5	691	69	110.5	1,606
IN	70	16.2	229	40	14.4	355	West	278	311.3	1,118	139	277.5	1,999
IL	89	28.5	321	63	27.0	431	Mt	124	244.1	1,965	67	218.3	3,271
MI	51	10.3	202	24	8.2	340	MT	25	60.2	2,451	16	54.4	3,427
WI	75	16.6	221	52	14.5	280	ID	24	13.9	577	14	12.0	881
W.N.C ...	497	263.8	531	337	238.3	707	WY	9	33.6	3,650	5	28.4	5,183
MN	85	26.6	312	58	23.8	407	CO	27	34.0	1,248	15	30.6	2,030
IA	105	31.6	301	83	30.2	365	NM	14	46.0	3,230	6	41.3	7,319
MO	106	29.2	275	50	22.7	457	AZ	8	36.3	4,732	4	33.7	9,411
ND	35	40.3	1,143	28	37.9	1,339	UT	14	10.0	710	6	8.6	1,452
SD	36	44.2	1,214	28	37.9	1,339	NV	3	10.0	3,300	1	9.3	6,288
NE	60	45.3	749	47	43.0	918	Pac	154	67.3	466	72	59.2	821
KS	69	46.6	680	43	42.8	1,002	WA	34	16.1	480	15	13.8	901
South	824	281.2	341	304	221.0	727	OR	32	17.8	556	12	15.4	1,319
S.A.	240	51.2	214	93	37.4	403	CA	83	30.6	368	43	27.7	647
DE	3	0.6	205	2	0.5	291	AK	1	1.0	1,789	(Z)	0.6	3,411
MD	15	2.4	162	7	1.9	278	HI	5	1.7	353	2	1.6	798

Z Less than 500 farms or 50,000 acres.

Source: U.S. Bureau of the Census, *Census of Agriculture: 1987,* vol. 1.

No. 1084. Farms—Number and Acreage, by State: 1990 and 1993

[As of **June 1.** Based on 1974 census definition of farms and farmland; see text, section 23. See also *Historical Statistics, Colonial Times to 1970,* series K 4-7]

STATE	FARMS (1,000)		ACREAGE (mil.)		ACREAGE PER FARM		STATE	FARMS (1,000)		ACREAGE (mil.)		ACREAGE PER FARM	
	1990	1993	1990	1993	1990	1993		1990	1993	1990	1993	1990	1993
U.S.	2,140	2,068	987	978	461	473	Missouri	108	106	30	30	281	285
							Montana	25	25	61	60	2,449	2,445
Alabama	47	47	10	10	215	213	Nebraska	57	55	47	47	826	856
Alaska	1	1	1	1	1,724	1,759	Nevada......	3	2	9	9	3,560	3,708
Arizona......	8	8	36	36	4,615	4,557	New Hampshire	3	3	(Z)	(Z)	169	174
Arkansas.....	47	46	16	15	330	335	New Jersey ...	8	8	1	1	107	104
California.....	85	76	31	30	362	391	New Mexico...	14	14	45	44	3,296	3,274
Colorado.....	27	26	33	33	1,249	1,286	New York	39	38	8	8	218	216
Connecticut ...	4	4	(Z)	(Z)	108	103	North Carolina..	62	59	10	9	156	159
Delaware.....	3	3	1	1	197	220	North Dakota..	34	33	41	40	1,191	1,224
Florida	41	39	11	10	266	264	Ohio........	84	76	16	15	187	200
Georgia......	48	45	13	12	260	269	Oklahoma	70	71	33	34	471	479
Hawaii	5	4	2	2	372	389	Oregon......	37	37	18	18	488	473
Idaho.......	22	21	14	14	628	659	Pennsylvania ..	53	51	8	8	153	155
Illinois.......	83	80	29	28	343	354	Rhode Island ..	1	1	(Z)	(Z)	95	90
Indiana	68	63	16	16	240	254	South Carolina.	25	24	5	5	208	212
Iowa.......	104	100	34	33	322	333	South Dakota..	35	35	44	44	1,266	1,281
Kansas......	69	65	48	48	694	735	Tennessee ...	89	86	12	12	139	144
Kentucky.....	93	91	14	14	152	155	Texas.......	186	185	132	130	710	703
Louisiana	32	29	9	9	278	297	Utah........	13	13	11	11	856	862
Maine.......	7	7	1	1	201	200	Vermont	7	7	2	2	216	219
Maryland	15	15	2	2	148	147	Virginia	46	43	9	9	193	200
Massachusetts.	7	7	1	1	99	98	Washington ...	37	36	16	16	432	444
Michigan.....	54	52	11	11	200	206	West Virginia ..	21	20	4	4	180	185
Minnesota....	89	87	30	30	337	341	Wisconsin	80	79	18	17	220	216
Mississippi....	40	39	13	13	325	333	Wyoming.....	9	9	35	35	3,910	3,742

Z Less than 500,000 acres.

Source: U.S. Dept. of Agriculture, National Agricultural Statistics Service, *Farm Numbers and Land in Farms* (July release).

No. 1085. Farms—Number and Acreage: 1975 to 1993

[Based on 1974 census definition; for definition of farms and farmland, see text, section 23. Data for census years (indicated by italics) have been adjusted for underenumeration and are used as reference points along with data from acreage and livestock surveys in estimating data for other years. Minus sign (-) indicates decrease. See also *Historical Statistics, Colonial Times to 1970*, series K 4-7]

YEAR	FARMS		LAND IN FARMS		YEAR	FARMS		LAND IN FARMS	
	Number (1,000)	Annual change [1] (1,000)	Total (mil. acres)	Average per farm (acres)		Number (1,000)	Annual change [1] (1,000)	Total (mil. acres)	Average per farm (acres)
1975.....	2,521	(X)	1,059	420	1985.....	2,293	-41	1,012	441
1976.....	2,497	-24	1,054	422	1986.....	2,250	-43	1,005	447
1977.....	2,456	-41	1,048	427	1987.....	2,213	-37	999	451
1978.....	2,436	-20	1,045	429	1988.....	2,197	-16	995	453
1979.....	2,437	1	1,042	428	1989.....	2,171	-26	991	457
1980.....	2,440	3	1,039	426					
1981.....	2,440	-	1,034	424	1990.....	2,140	-31	987	461
1982.....	2,407	-33	1,028	427	1991.....	2,105	-35	983	467
1983.....	2,379	-28	1,023	430	1992.....	2,094	-11	980	468
1984.....	2,334	-45	1,018	436	1993.....	2,068	-26	978	473

- Represents zero.   X Not applicable.   [1] Annual change from preceding year shown.

Source: U.S. Dept. of Agriculture, National Agricultural Statistics Service, *Farm Numbers, 1975-80; Farms and Land in Farms, Final Estimates by States, 1979-1987*; and *Farm Numbers and Land In Farms*, July release.

No. 1086. Farm Real Estate—Summary: 1980 to 1993

[1980 and 1986-89, value data as of Feb. 1; 1984 and 1985, as of April 1; 1990-93, as of January 1. Excludes Alaska and Hawaii. Total value of land and buildings is estimated by multiplying the number of acres of farmland by the average value per acre of land and buildings. Per acre values are based on data from the census of agriculture. For intercensal years, estimates are based on surveys conducted by the U.S. Dept. of Agriculture]

ITEM	Unit	1980	1984	1985	1986	1987	1988	1989	1990	1991	1992	1993
Total value	Bil. dol	763.3	812.9	719.4	641.1	597.1	626.9	653.5	658.2	667.7	668.1	684.6
Average value per acre.	Dollars	737	801	713	640	599	632	661	668	681	684	700
Average value, operating unit...	$1,000.....	313.5	349.1	314.5	285.6	270.5	286.0	301.8	308.2	318.0	319.6	327.4

Source: U.S. Dept. of Agriculture, Economic Research Service, 1980-84, *Farm Real Estate Market Developments*, annual; thereafter, *Agricultural Resources, Agricultural Land Values and Markets, Situation and Outlook Report*, annual.

No. 1087. Farm Real Estate—Value of Land and Buildings, by State: 1990 to 1993

[See headnote, table 1086. See also *Historical Statistics, Colonial Times to 1970*, series K 16]

STATE	VALUE OF LAND AND BUILDINGS (mil. dol.)			AVERAGE VALUE OF LAND AND BUILDINGS, PER ACRE			STATE	VALUE OF LAND AND BUILDINGS (mil. dol.)			AVERAGE VALUE OF LAND AND BUILDINGS, PER ACRE		
	1990	1992	1993	1990	1992	1993		1990	1992	1993	1990	1992	1993
U.S ..	658,187	668,145	684,554	$668	$684	$700	MT	14,399	15,127	16,216	238	252	270
							NE	25,905	26,790	27,326	550	569	580
AL	8,474	8,153	8,455	839	832	863	NV	1,727	2,057	1,917	194	231	215
AZ	9,468	10,879	10,966	263	302	305	NH	1,096	961	1,024	2,237	2,045	2,178
AR	11,625	11,219	11,769	750	724	759	NJ	4,032	4,201	3,991	4,634	4,774	4,536
CA	52,483	52,587	51,325	1,704	1,765	1,722	NM....	8,722	10,558	9,925	196	239	225
CO	11,850	12,043	12,548	358	367	383	NY	8,182	8,618	9,178	974	1,051	1,119
CT	1,855	1,655	1,763	4,417	4,036	4,299	NC	12,251	12,010	12,526	1,263	1,264	1,319
DE	1,288	1,191	1,323	2,259	2,126	2,362	ND	13,770	14,477	15,679	340	358	388
FL	22,727	21,648	21,778	2,085	2,062	2,074	OH	18,903	19,241	19,510	1,204	1,249	1,267
GA	12,650	10,917	11,660	1,012	902	964	OK	16,401	16,790	17,411	497	494	512
ID	9,056	9,272	9,328	661	687	691	OR	10,164	10,557	11,496	571	603	657
IL	39,587	42,760	42,846	1,389	1,500	1,503	PA	14,637	14,562	13,979	1,807	1,820	1,747
IN	20,277	20,843	21,864	1,244	1,303	1,366	RI	352	290	308	5,028	4,595	4,894
IA	36,917	39,355	41,598	1,102	1,178	1,245	SC	4,727	4,840	4,530	909	931	871
KS	22,130	23,131	23,616	462	484	494	SD	14,543	16,113	16,339	328	365	370
KY	13,832	13,998	15,286	981	993	1,084	TN	12,350	12,416	13,223	996	985	1,049
LA	8,144	7,870	8,225	915	905	945	TX	65,340	60,600	61,266	495	466	471
ME	1,478	1,322	1,408	1,019	931	992	UT	4,396	4,801	5,248	389	425	464
MD	5,445	4,960	5,545	2,420	2,255	2,521	VT	1,797	1,642	1,748	1,190	1,087	1,158
MA	2,559	2,338	2,490	3,763	3,439	3,662	VA	13,492	11,861	11,268	1,516	1,363	1,295
MI	10,854	11,937	12,200	1,005	1,105	1,130	WA	12,464	12,672	12,507	779	792	782
MN	24,150	26,028	26,705	805	873	896	WV	2,268	2,659	2,576	613	719	696
MS	9,464	9,441	9,686	728	738	757	WI	14,133	15,047	16,115	803	870	932
MO	20,642	20,889	21,662	679	689	715	WY	5,185	4,819	5,200	149	138	149

Source: U.S. Dept. of Agriculture, Economic Research Service, *Agricultural Resources, Agricultural Land Values and Markets, Situation and Outlook Report*, annual.

No. 1088. Balance Sheet of the Farming Sector: 1980 to 1992

[In billions of dollars, except as indicated. As of December 31. See *Historical Statistics, Colonial Times to 1970*, series K 204-219, for data before revisions]

ITEM	1980	1983	1984	1985	1986	1987	1988	1989	1990	1991	1992
CURRENT DOLLARS											
Assets	983.2	943.3	857.0	772.7	724.4	772.6	801.1	829.7	848.3	842.2	861.5
Physical assets:											
Real estate	782.8	753.4	661.8	586.2	542.3	578.9	595.5	615.7	628.2	623.2	633.1
Nonreal estate	173.6	158.9	162.6	153.3	147.7	158.7	170.2	177.3	181.9	178.5	184.9
Livestock and poultry [1]	60.6	49.5	49.5	46.3	47.8	58.0	62.2	66.2	70.9	68.1	71.3
Machinery, motor vehicles..	80.3	85.8	85.0	82.9	81.5	80.0	81.2	85.1	85.4	85.8	85.6
Crops stored..........	32.7	23.6	26.1	22.9	16.3	17.5	23.3	23.4	22.8	22.0	24.1
Purchased inputs........	(NA)	(NA)	2.0	1.2	2.1	3.2	3.5	2.6	2.8	2.6	3.9
Financial assets...........	26.7	30.9	32.6	33.3	34.4	35.2	35.4	36.8	38.4	40.5	43.3
Investment in cooperatives...	19.3	22.8	24.3	24.3	24.4	25.3	25.1	26.3	27.5	28.7	29.7
Other financial assets	7.4	8.1	8.3	9.0	10.0	9.9	10.3	10.5	10.9	11.8	13.6
Claims	983.2	943.3	857.0	772.7	724.4	772.6	801.1	829.7	848.3	842.2	861.5
Debt	166.8	191.1	193.8	177.6	157.0	144.4	139.4	137.2	137.4	138.8	138.6
Real estate debt.........	89.7	103.2	106.7	100.1	90.4	82.4	77.6	75.4	74.1	74.5	75.0
Nonreal estate debt	77.1	87.9	87.1	77.5	66.6	62.0	61.7	61.9	63.2	64.3	63.6
Equity	816.4	752.2	663.3	595.1	567.5	628.2	661.7	692.4	710.9	703.5	722.9
Farm debt/asset ratio (percent)	17.0	20.3	22.6	23.0	21.7	18.7	17.4	16.5	16.2	16.5	16.1
CONSTANT (1987) DOLLARS [2]											
Assets	1,371.2	1,081.7	941.8	818.6	747.6	772.6	771.0	764.7	748.7	715.6	711.4
Debt	232.7	219.1	213.0	188.1	162.0	144.4	134.1	126.5	121.2	117.9	114.5
Equity	1,138.6	862.6	728.9	630.4	585.6	628.2	636.9	638.2	627.5	597.7	596.9

NA Not available. [1] Excludes horses and mules. [2] Constant dollar figures are based on gross domestic product implicit price deflators for year.

Source: U.S. Dept. of Agriculture, Economic Research Service, *Economic Indicators of the Farm Sector: National Financial Summary, 1992.*

No. 1089. Gross Farm Product—Summary: 1980 to 1992

[In billions of dollars. For definition of gross product, see text, section 14. Minus sign (-) indicates decrease]

ITEM	1980	1983	1984	1985	1986	1987	1988	1989	1990	1991	1992
CURRENT DOLLARS											
Farm output, total [1]	142.9	135.1	160.0	152.7	144.0	152.1	158.2	178.7	186.4	182.0	187.2
Cash receipts from farm marketings	140.3	140.2	144.6	136.3	135.2	147.7	159.3	166.5	172.6	171.2	171.8
Farm housing	5.1	5.1	5.1	5.0	4.9	4.9	4.9	5.0	5.2	5.3	5.3
Other farm income	2.4	4.1	3.5	4.6	4.4	5.1	4.6	5.0	4.9	5.0	4.4
Change in farm inventories	-6.1	-15.4	5.7	5.8	-1.5	-6.4	-11.3	1.5	3.1	-	5.0
Less: Intermediate goods and services purchased [2]	86.8	85.9	91.4	85.6	81.1	86.1	90.6	97.6	101.3	103.1	102.7
Equals: Gross farm product	56.1	49.2	68.5	67.1	62.9	66.0	67.6	81.1	85.1	78.8	84.4
Less: Consumption of fixed capital	19.4	23.2	23.2	22.9	22.5	22.0	21.6	21.9	21.6	21.4	21.6
Indirect business tax [3]	3.0	3.2	3.1	3.3	3.3	3.6	3.6	3.8	4.2	4.2	4.4
Plus: Subsidies to operators	1.0	7.5	7.0	6.3	9.5	13.9	11.8	9.3	8.1	7.6	8.4
Equals: Farm national income.	34.7	30.3	49.2	47.2	46.6	54.3	54.2	64.7	67.4	60.8	66.8
CONSTANT (1987) DOLLARS											
Farm output, total [1]	137.1	133.2	139.0	146.0	146.4	152.1	146.5	151.1	158.7	158.7	168.3
Cash receipts from farm marketings	130.7	131.2	127.8	133.1	137.9	147.7	143.9	141.9	146.8	149.1	155.6
Farm housing	6.3	5.4	5.4	5.3	5.1	4.9	4.7	4.6	4.5	4.5	4.4
Other farm income	2.3	3.8	3.1	4.3	4.6	5.1	4.1	4.2	4.4	4.4	4.0
Change in farm inventories	-3.4	-8.3	1.7	2.4	-2.1	-6.4	-7.0	-0.1	2.5	0.2	3.8
Less: Intermediate goods and services purchased [2]	86.1	79.5	83.9	81.8	82.2	86.1	83.3	84.9	87.1	88.3	88.8
Equals: Gross farm product	51.0	53.7	55.1	64.2	64.3	66.0	63.2	66.2	71.6	70.4	79.6
Less: Consumption of fixed capital	26.7	25.8	25.1	24.3	23.1	22.0	21.1	20.5	19.5	18.8	18.6
Indirect business tax [3]	2.8	2.9	3.0	3.5	3.5	3.6	3.5	3.6	3.9	3.9	4.4
Plus: Subsidies to operators	11.9	11.6	10.7	11.4	12.3	13.9	12.9	12.7	13.5	13.6	14.5
Equals: Farm national income.	33.4	36.5	37.7	47.8	49.9	54.3	51.6	54.8	61.6	61.3	71.1

- Represents zero. [1] Includes farm products consumed in farm households where raised, not shown separately. [2] Includes rent paid to nonoperator landlords. [3] Includes nontax liability.

Source: U.S. Bureau of Economic Analysis, *Survey of Current Business,* July 1992 and August 1993; and *National Income and Product Accounts of the United States: Volume 2, 1959-88.*

No. 1090. Farms, Farm Income, Assets, and Debt, by Value of Sales: 1992

[In billions of dollars, except as indicated]

ITEM	Total	Less than $20,000	$20,000 to $39,999	$40,000 to $99,999	$100,000 to $249,999	$250,000 to $499,999	$500,000 to $999,999	$1 million and over
Number of farms [1] (1,000) . . .	2,094	1,132	254	338	247	76	32	15
Gross cash income [2]	187.9	9.4	9.4	29.1	46.0	29.9	24.5	39.5
Cash receipts	171.2	8.2	8.2	25.5	40.8	27.4	22.9	38.1
Government payments	9.2	0.4	0.7	2.0	3.2	1.6	0.8	0.5
Net cash income [2]	57.7	-2.6	1.9	9.0	14.7	10.1	9.1	15.5
Assets [3]	861.5	202.4	93.2	158.7	194.3	101.2	55.4	56.3
Debt [3]	138.6	24.6	10.4	24.5	33.0	17.7	14.3	14.2
Debt/asset ratio [3] (percent) . .	16.1	12.1	11.1	15.4	17.0	17.5	25.9	25.2
PERCENT DISTRIBUTION								
Number of farms [1]	100	54	12	16	12	4	2	1
Gross cash income [2]	100	5	5	16	25	16	13	21
Assets [3]	100	24	11	18	23	12	6	7

[1] Based on 1974 census definition. See text, section 23.　[2] For components of income, see table 1093. Minus sign (-) indicates loss.　[3] Data as of December 31.

Source: U.S. Dept. of Agriculture, Economic Research Service, *Economic Indicators of the Farm Sector: National Financial Summary*, annual.

No. 1091. Net Cash Income and Net Cash Flow From Farming: 1980 to 1992

[In billions of dollars. Net cash income measures the cash income from a farm operator's farm business and net cash flow measures the cash flow within the agricultural sector. Minus sign (-) indicates net loan redemption or decrease]

ITEM	1980	1982	1983	1984	1985	1986	1987	1988	1989	1990	1991	1992
Net cash income.	34.2	38.1	38.4	37.4	47.1	47.9	55.8	54.5	54.7	55.9	53.3	57.7
Gross cash income	143.3	151.3	151.1	156.1	157.9	152.9	165.2	172.9	179.8	186.8	184.7	187.9
Cash expenses	109.1	113.2	112.8	118.7	110.7	105.0	109.4	118.4	125.1	130.9	131.4	130.2
Change in loans outstanding. .	15.3	6.4	2.3	2.7	-16.2	-20.6	-12.6	-5.0	-2.1	0.1	1.4	-0.1
Real estate loans.	10.0	3.0	1.4	3.5	-6.6	-9.7	-8.0	-4.8	-2.3	-1.2	0.4	0.5
Nonreal estate loans [1]	5.3	3.4	0.9	-0.8	-9.6	-11.0	-4.6	-0.3	0.1	1.3	1.0	-0.6
Net change in other financial assets.	0.1	0.2	0.3	0.2	0.7	1.1	-0.2	0.5	0.1	0.4	1.0	1.8
Net rent received by nonoperator landlords	6.1	5.5	5.2	8.2	7.7	6.1	7.1	9.0	10.1	10.5	10.5	10.9
Capital expenditures	18.0	13.3	12.7	12.5	9.2	8.5	11.2	11.5	13.1	14.1	13.2	12.7
Net cash flow [2].	37.6	37.0	33.4	36.0	30.1	26.0	39.0	47.4	49.7	52.8	53.0	57.7

[1] Excludes Commodity Credit Corporation loans.　[2] Net cash income plus change in loans outstanding plus net change in other financial assets plus net rent received by nonoperator landlords minus capital expenditures.

Source: U.S. Dept. of Agriculture, Economic Research Service, *Economic Indicators of the Farm Sector: National Financial Summary*, annual.

No. 1092. Average Income to Farm Operator Households: 1988 to 1992

[In dollars per operator household. Data for 1988-90 are expanded to represent only the farm operator households surveyed in USDA's Farm Costs and Returns Survey; beginning 1991 data represent the total number of U.S. farms and ranches]

ITEM	1988	1989	1990	1991	1992
Farm income to household [1]	4,201	5,796	5,742	4,397	4,882
Self-employment farm income	3,837	4,723	4,973	2,283	2,874
Other farm income to household	364	1,073	768	2,114	2,008
Plus: Total off-farm income	28,829	26,223	33,265	31,638	35,731
Income from wages, salaries, and nonfarm businesses. .	22,220	19,467	24,778	23,551	27,022
Income from interest, dividends, transfer payments, etc. .	6,610	6,756	8,487	8,087	8,709
Equals: Farm operator household income	33,030	32,019	39,007	36,035	40,613

[1] Farm income to the household equals self-employment income plus amounts that operators pay themselves and family members to work on the farm, income from renting out acreage, and net income from a farm business other than the one being surveyed.

Source: U.S. Dept. of Agriculture, Economic Research Service, *Agricultural Income and Finance Situation and Outlook*, Sept. 1993.

No. 1093. Farm Income and Expenses: 1980 to 1992

[In billions of dollars. See also *Historical Statistics, Colonial Times to 1970*, series K 192, K 259-260, K 264-285, and K 326]

ITEM	1980	1982	1983	1984	1985	1986	1987	1988	1989	1990	1991	1992
Gross farm income	149.3	164.1	153.9	168.0	161.2	156.1	168.5	175.8	190.9	196.4	190.3	197.7
Cash income	143.3	151.3	151.1	156.1	157.9	152.9	165.2	172.9	179.8	186.8	184.7	187.9
Farm marketings	139.7	142.6	136.8	142.8	144.1	135.4	141.8	151.2	161.2	170.0	168.7	171.2
Crops	71.7	72.3	67.2	69.9	74.3	63.8	65.9	71.7	77.0	80.1	81.9	84.8
Livestock and products	68.0	70.3	69.6	72.9	69.8	71.6	76.0	79.4	84.1	89.8	86.8	86.4
Government payments	1.3	3.5	9.3	8.4	7.7	11.8	16.7	14.5	10.9	9.3	8.2	9.2
Other farm income [1]	2.3	5.2	5.1	4.9	6.0	5.7	6.6	7.3	7.8	7.6	7.8	7.6
Value of home consumption	1.2	1.1	1.0	1.0	0.9	0.9	0.7	0.7	0.7	0.7	0.6	0.6
Rental value of dwellings [2]	11.0	13.1	12.6	4.9	4.7	4.6	4.9	5.6	5.7	5.5	5.3	5.5
Value of inventory adjustment [3]	-6.3	-1.4	-10.9	6.0	-2.3	-2.2	-2.3	-3.4	4.8	3.4	-0.3	3.8
Expenses of farm production	133.1	140.3	139.6	141.9	132.4	125.1	128.8	137.0	144.0	149.9	150.3	149.1
Intermediate products	76.1	75.4	75.8	78.0	72.3	70.6	74.8	81.8	86.4	90.2	91.9	90.4
Farm origin	34.9	31.4	32.1	32.3	29.3	30.4	32.6	37.1	38.3	39.7	38.7	38.5
Feed purchased	21.0	18.6	20.6	19.4	17.0	17.5	17.5	20.2	20.7	20.4	19.3	19.8
Livestock, poultry purchased	10.7	9.7	8.8	9.5	9.2	9.8	11.8	12.8	13.1	14.8	14.3	13.8
Seed purchased [4]	3.2	3.2	2.7	3.4	3.1	3.2	3.3	4.1	4.4	4.5	5.1	4.9
Manufactured inputs	22.4	22.1	20.1	22.4	20.2	18.2	18.1	19.0	20.6	22.0	23.2	22.7
Fertilizer and lime	9.5	8.0	7.1	8.4	7.5	6.8	6.5	7.7	8.2	8.2	8.7	8.3
Pesticides	3.5	4.3	3.9	4.7	4.3	4.3	4.5	4.1	5.0	5.4	6.3	6.5
Fuel and oil	7.9	7.7	7.2	7.3	6.4	5.3	5.0	4.8	4.8	5.8	5.6	5.3
Electricity	1.5	2.0	2.0	2.1	1.9	1.8	2.2	2.4	2.7	2.6	2.6	2.6
Repairs and maintenance [5]	7.1	6.4	6.5	6.4	6.4	6.4	6.8	7.7	8.4	8.6	8.6	8.5
Other [6]	11.8	15.5	17.1	16.9	16.5	15.5	17.4	18.0	19.1	19.9	21.3	20.7
Interest	16.3	21.8	21.4	21.1	18.6	16.5	15.0	14.3	13.9	13.3	12.1	11.4
Real estate	7.5	10.5	10.8	10.7	9.9	9.1	8.2	7.6	7.2	6.7	6.0	5.6
Nonreal estate	8.7	11.3	10.6	10.4	8.7	7.4	6.8	6.7	6.7	6.5	6.1	5.8
Contract, hired labor expenses [7]	9.3	9.4	8.9	9.4	10.0	9.5	10.0	11.0	11.9	14.0	13.9	14.1
Net rent to nonoperator landlords [8]	6.1	5.5	5.2	8.2	7.7	6.1	7.1	7.7	8.7	9.2	9.1	9.6
Capital consumption [9]	21.5	24.2	23.8	20.8	19.3	17.8	17.1	17.4	17.9	17.7	17.7	17.8
Property taxes	3.9	4.0	4.5	4.3	4.5	4.6	4.9	5.0	5.2	5.7	5.6	5.8
Net farm income	16.1	23.8	14.2	26.1	28.8	31.1	39.7	38.8	46.9	46.5	40.0	48.6

[1] Includes forest product sales. [2] Data for 1980 to 1983 are not comparable with later data. [3] Minus sign (-) indicates decrease in inventories. [4] Includes bulbs, plants, and trees. [5] Expenditures for repairs and maintenance of farm buildings, motor vehicles, and machinery. [6] Includes machine hire and customwork expenses; marketing, storage, and transportation expenses and miscellaneous expenses. [7] Includes Social Security payments and perquisites. [8] Data for years 1980-83, and 1984 and later are based on different sources, creating potential inconsistencies in estimates among these periods. [9] Depreciation and accidental damage.

Source: U.S. Dept. of Agriculture, Economic Research Service, *Economic Indicators of the Farm Sector: National Financial Summary*, annual.

No. 1094. Commodity Credit Corporation—Net Outlays, by Commodity and Function: 1990 to 1993

[In millions of dollars. For fiscal year ending in year shown; see text, section 9. Excludes value of commodity certificates which may also be issued to farmers in lieu of cash under certain programs. Minus sign (-) indicates a net receipt (excess of repayments or other receipts over gross outlays of funds)]

COMMODITY	1990	1991	1992	1993	FUNCTION	1990	1991	1992	1993
Total	6,471	10,110	9,738	16,047	**Total**	6,471	10,110	9,738	16,047
Feed grains	2,721	2,722	2,510	5,764	Price support loans [4]	-399	418	584	2,062
Wheat	806	2,958	1,719	2,185	Direct payments	4,370	6,341	5,847	9,143
Cotton, upland	-79	382	1,443	2,240	Deficiency payments	4,178	6,224	5,491	8,607
Dairy	505	839	232	262					
Rice	667	867	715	887					
Wool	104	172	191	179	1988/93 crop disaster	[3]5	6	960	872
Honey	47	19	17	22	Emergency livestock/forage				
Peanuts	1	48	41	-13	assistance	156	115	94	72
Sugar	15	-20	-19	-35	Purchases [6]	-48	646	321	534
Tobacco	-307	-143	29	235	Producer storage payments	185	1	14	9
Soybeans	5	40	-29	115	Processing, storage and				
Operating expense [1]	618	625	6	6	transportation	317	394	185	136
Interest expenditure	632	745	532	129	Operating expense [1]	618	625	6	6
Export programs [2]	-34	733	1,459	2,194	Interest expenditure	632	745	532	129
1988/93 disaster/livestock					Export programs [2]	-34	733	1,459	2,194
assistance	[3]161	121	1,054	944	Other	669	86	-264	890
Other	609	2	-162	933					

[1] Excludes CCC transfers to the general sales manager. [2] Covers the direct export credit sales program, the export guarantee program, transfers to the general sales manager, market promotion program (beginning 1991), and beginning 1992, the export guarantee program-credit reform, export enhancement program, dairy export incentive program, and technical assistance to emerging democracies. [3] Approximately $1.5 billion in benefits to farmers under the Disaster Assistance Act of 1989 were paid in generic certificates and were not recorded directly as disaster assistance outlays. [4] Price support loans made less loans repaid. [5] Includes dairy termination program and loan deficiency payments. Cash payments only. Excludes generic certificates. [6] Purchases less sales proceeds.

Source: U.S. Agricultural Stabilization and Conservation Service, *Commodity Credit Corporation Report of Financial Condition and Operations*, annual, and *Agricultural Outlook*, monthly.

No. 1095. Farm Income—Cash Receipts From Farm Marketings: 1980 to 1992

[Represents gross receipts from commercial market sales as well as net Commodity Credit Corporation loans. See also *Historical Statistics, Colonial Times to 1970*, series K 286-302]

COMMODITY	FARM MARKETINGS (mil. dol.)								PERCENT		
	1980	1985	1987	1988	1989	1990	1991	1992	1980	1990	1992
Total	139,737	144,114	141,844	151,154	161,164	169,973	168,721	171,168	100.0	100.0	100.0
All crops [1]	71,746	74,293	65,851	71,720	77,042	80,130	81,942	84,810	51.3	47.1	49.5
Barley	736	1,039	754	862	765	823	813	852	0.5	0.5	0.5
Corn	13,959	16,880	9,983	8,923	11,388	13,340	14,405	14,742	10.0	7.8	8.6
Cotton lint, seed	4,447	3,687	4,189	4,546	5,033	5,489	5,236	5,207	3.2	3.2	3.0
Hay	1,917	2,390	2,533	3,119	3,388	3,281	2,973	2,913	1.4	1.9	1.7
Oats	(NA)	298	260	305	268	221	142	165	(NA)	0.1	0.1
Peanuts	607	1,005	1,027	1,116	1,117	1,258	1,392	1,286	0.4	0.7	0.8
Rice	1,519	1,042	720	1,086	942	1,076	1,092	1,232	1.1	0.6	0.7
Sorghum	1,392	1,981	1,100	1,071	1,240	1,002	1,152	1,397	1.0	0.6	0.8
Soybean	14,241	11,161	10,017	12,138	10,524	10,756	10,975	11,343	10.2	6.3	6.6
Sunflower/safflower	(NA)	242	211	224	213	217	288	327	(NA)	0.1	0.2
Tobacco	2,672	2,699	1,816	2,083	2,415	2,741	2,886	2,961	1.9	1.6	1.7
Wheat	8,854	7,909	5,044	6,361	7,286	6,426	6,303	7,641	6.3	3.8	4.5
Vegetables [2]	7,307	8,572	9,898	9,818	11,598	11,449	11,552	11,436	5.2	6.7	6.7
Dry beans	(NA)	439	444	421	688	692	519	487	(NA)	0.4	0.3
Snap beans	(NA)	167	171	166	228	205	205	217	(NA)	0.1	0.1
Broccoli	(NA)	239	240	292	276	268	242	280	(NA)	0.2	0.2
Carrots	(NA)	206	248	268	297	273	309	338	(NA)	0.2	0.2
Celery	(NA)	190	199	231	268	215	206	229	(NA)	0.1	0.1
Sweet corn	(NA)	368	372	360	468	468	497	447	(NA)	0.3	0.3
Cucumbers	(NA)	181	188	196	203	231	231	275	(NA)	0.1	0.2
Lettuce	(NA)	675	1,003	1,040	950	844	818	1,108	(NA)	0.5	0.6
Onions	(NA)	372	536	500	538	535	602	665	(NA)	0.3	0.4
Green peppers	(NA)	(NA)	182	103	121	150	207	368	(NA)	0.1	0.2
Potatoes	(NA)	1,601	1,707	1,630	2,336	2,448	2,141	2,033	(NA)	1.4	1.2
Tomatoes	(NA)	1,198	1,466	1,415	1,841	1,626	1,801	1,819	(NA)	1.0	1.1
Cantaloups	(NA)	(NA)	187	203	209	195	100	291	(NA)	0.1	0.2
Fruits, tree nuts [2]	6,557	6,946	8,065	9,027	9,173	9,440	9,888	10,183	4.7	5.6	5.9
Apples	(NA)	892	1,060	926	994	1,086	1,651	1,684	(NA)	0.6	1.0
Avocados	(NA)	139	120	212	224	245	204	187	(NA)	0.1	0.1
Cherries	(NA)	(NA)	181	189	173	156	229	235	(NA)	0.1	0.1
Grapefruit	(NA)	319	408	471	436	365	417	403	(NA)	0.2	0.2
Grapes	(NA)	961	1,362	1,600	1,867	1,677	1,736	1,713	(NA)	1.0	1.0
Lemons	(NA)	237	226	188	223	306	271	235	(NA)	0.2	0.1
Oranges	(NA)	1,404	1,363	1,825	1,786	1,728	1,393	1,616	(NA)	1.0	0.9
Peaches	(NA)	295	311	382	359	372	394	373	(NA)	0.2	0.2
Pears	(NA)	193	196	218	259	261	272	276	(NA)	0.2	0.2
Plums and prunes	(NA)	196	207	255	252	295	256	245	(NA)	0.2	0.1
Strawberries	(NA)	451	554	544	538	590	634	685	(NA)	0.3	0.4
Almonds	(NA)	361	648	600	481	598	564	670	(NA)	0.4	0.4
Pecans	(NA)	163	140	167	179	248	307	241	(NA)	0.1	0.1
Walnuts	(NA)	175	243	194	245	236	280	268	(NA)	0.1	0.2
Sugar beets	(NA)	774	1,028	1,022	1,057	1,178	1,084	1,109	(NA)	0.7	0.6
Sugarcane	(NA)	717	803	854	870	820	868	922	(NA)	0.5	0.5
Mushrooms	(NA)	491	519	573	630	667	661	659	(NA)	0.4	0.4
Greenhouse, nursery	(NA)	5,407	6,767	7,302	7,838	8,510	8,828	8,999	(NA)	5.0	5.3
All livestock and products [1].	67,991	69,822	75,993	79,434	84,122	89,843	86,780	86,358	48.7	52.9	50.5
Cattle and calves	31,819	29,002	33,583	36,810	36,894	39,945	39,644	37,882	22.8	23.5	22.1
Dairy products	16,365	18,055	17,727	17,641	19,396	20,149	18,037	19,848	11.7	11.9	11.6
Hogs	8,942	9,033	10,337	9,207	9,475	11,552	11,045	10,088	6.4	6.8	5.9
Broilers	4,303	5,668	6,177	7,435	8,778	8,365	8,383	9,156	3.1	4.9	5.3
Eggs	3,247	3,262	3,208	3,067	3,862	4,010	3,909	3,389	2.3	2.4	2.0
Turkeys	1,273	1,820	1,703	1,951	2,234	2,379	2,345	2,387	0.9	1.4	1.4
Sheep and lambs	471	514	558	476	487	414	400	456	(NA)	0.2	0.3
Horses and mules	(NA)	560	540	540	524	490	466	433	(NA)	0.3	0.3
Aquaculture	(NA)	205	290	323	407	541	469	502	(NA)	0.3	0.3

NA Not available.   [1] Includes other commodities not shown separately.   [2] Melons included with vegetables.

Source: U.S. Dept. of Agriculture, Economic Research Service, *Economic Indicators of the Farm Sector: National Financial Summary*, annual.

No. 1096. Farm Assets, Debt, and Income, by State: 1991 and 1992

[Assets and debt, as of December 31. Farm income data are after inventory adjustment and include income and expenses related to the farm operator's dwelling]

DIVISION AND STATE	ASSETS (mil. dol.)		DEBT (mil. dol.)		DEBT/ASSET RATIO (percent)		GROSS FARM INCOME (mil. dol.)		NET FARM INCOME (mil. dol.)	
	1991	1992	1991	1992	1991	1992	1991	1992	1991	1992
United States	842,238	861,497	138,785	138,645	16.5	16.1	190,329	197,741	40,022	48,647
New England:										
Maine	1,776	1,904	273	287	15.4	15.1	535	550	122	138
New Hampshire	1,164	1,227	66	67	5.7	5.5	174	184	36	45
Vermont	2,185	2,342	341	317	15.6	13.5	472	529	75	133
Massachusetts	3,424	3,650	296	299	8.6	8.2	537	556	179	200
Rhode Island	380	389	36	38	9.3	9.7	77	80	32	36
Connecticut	2,822	2,947	203	199	7.2	6.7	503	527	171	190
Middle Atlantic:										
New York	11,844	12,455	2,003	2,085	16.9	16.7	3,087	3,174	543	622
New Jersey	7,589	7,297	435	455	5.7	6.2	751	770	187	213
Pennsylvania	17,864	17,459	2,358	2,378	13.2	13.6	3,689	4,009	477	832
East North Central:										
Ohio	23,876	24,056	3,149	3,138	13.2	13.0	4,654	5,096	804	1,214
Indiana	25,016	26,447	4,547	4,521	18.2	17.1	4,759	5,469	159	729
Illinois	50,243	50,818	7,291	7,363	14.5	14.5	8,100	9,268	708	1,699
Michigan	15,161	15,567	2,555	2,602	16.8	16.7	3,756	3,787	517	581
Wisconsin	23,394	23,972	4,687	4,688	20.0	19.6	5,989	5,971	787	811
West North Central:										
Minnesota	35,021	35,484	6,583	6,708	18.8	18.9	7,885	7,976	1,271	1,481
Iowa	51,300	54,087	9,835	9,949	19.2	18.4	11,172	12,111	1,685	2,465
Missouri	26,725	27,756	4,558	4,565	17.1	16.4	4,700	5,127	582	875
North Dakota	20,116	21,595	3,326	3,262	16.5	15.1	3,342	3,809	693	1,091
South Dakota	21,136	21,840	3,410	3,424	16.1	15.7	3,903	3,953	1,324	1,395
Nebraska	35,070	36,115	6,594	6,856	18.8	19.0	9,802	9,970	2,423	2,692
Kansas	29,847	30,693	5,501	5,566	18.4	18.1	7,953	8,384	1,281	1,723
South Atlantic:										
Delaware	1,369	1,472	300	327	21.9	22.2	698	696	134	135
Maryland	5,759	6,244	940	962	16.3	15.4	1,533	1,596	327	388
Virginia	13,733	13,126	1,921	1,910	14.0	14.5	2,449	2,495	617	627
West Virginia	3,011	2,950	395	404	13.1	13.7	434	440	69	79
North Carolina	14,238	14,809	2,699	2,623	19.0	17.7	5,975	6,088	2,461	2,453
South Carolina	6,038	5,804	905	876	15.0	15.1	1,421	1,362	362	338
Georgia	13,639	14,338	2,752	2,779	20.2	19.4	4,599	4,716	1,496	1,681
Florida	24,305	24,458	3,546	3,622	14.6	14.8	6,360	6,372	2,744	2,777
East South Central:										
Kentucky	17,156	18,041	2,733	2,676	15.9	14.8	3,597	3,821	1,070	1,307
Tennessee	14,696	15,648	1,988	1,977	13.5	12.6	2,393	2,606	423	608
Alabama	9,907	10,073	1,401	1,466	14.1	14.6	3,518	3,369	1,224	1,141
Mississippi	11,272	11,639	2,459	2,413	21.8	20.7	2,996	3,211	373	674
West South Central:										
Arkansas	14,058	14,691	3,104	3,106	22.1	21.1	5,118	5,398	874	1,405
Louisiana	8,325	8,343	1,707	1,704	20.5	20.4	2,139	2,259	295	491
Oklahoma	20,693	21,969	3,679	3,588	17.8	16.3	4,372	4,350	863	1,083
Texas	73,129	74,387	9,648	9,300	13.2	12.5	14,184	14,236	2,970	3,464
Mountain:										
Montana	18,505	19,355	2,469	2,448	13.3	12.6	2,208	2,085	577	463
Idaho	11,582	11,788	2,463	2,467	21.3	20.9	2,953	3,025	865	939
Wyoming	6,130	6,562	862	832	14.1	12.7	1,032	922	231	239
Colorado	15,276	15,824	2,830	2,785	18.5	17.6	4,336	4,426	845	947
New Mexico	11,806	11,184	1,063	1,048	9.0	9.4	1,642	1,674	427	491
Arizona	11,223	11,316	1,286	1,172	11.5	10.4	2,027	1,954	668	595
Utah	5,428	5,858	659	651	12.1	11.1	830	893	224	281
Nevada	2,951	2,783	245	238	8.3	8.5	299	268	81	56
Pacific:										
Washington	15,282	15,224	2,858	2,805	18.7	18.4	4,691	5,007	1,044	1,337
Oregon	12,462	13,328	2,471	2,298	19.8	17.2	2,952	3,019	627	696
California	70,232	68,110	13,047	13,063	18.6	19.2	19,120	19,539	4,052	4,756
Alaska	582	597	23	48	4.0	8.0	33	33	7	6
Hawaii	3,496	3,475	288	295	8.2	8.5	581	581	21	27

Source: U.S. Dept. of Agriculture, Economic Research Service, *Economic Indicators of the Farm Sector: State Financial Summary, 1992*; and unpublished data.

No. 1097. Farm Income—Farm Marketings, 1991 and 1992, Government Payments, 1992, and Principal Commodities, 1992, by State

[In millions of dollars. Cattle include calves; sheep include lambs; and greenhouse includes nursery]

DIVISION AND STATE	1991			1992				
	Farm marketings			Farm marketings			Government payments	State rank for total farm marketings and four principal commodities in order of marketing receipts
	Total	Crops	Livestock and products	Total	Crops	Livestock and products		
U.S. .	168,721	81,942	86,780	171,168	84,810	86,358	9,169	Cattle, dairy products, corn, soybeans
N.E.	2,087	1,013	1,074	2,161	1,020	1,141	25	(X)
ME . . .	484	192	292	513	213	301	10	42-Potatoes, dairy products, eggs, aquaculture
NH . . .	142	79	63	144	79	65	2	48-Dairy products, greenhouse, apples, hay
VT. . . .	434	64	370	452	63	389	6	45-Dairy products, cattle, greenhouse, hay
MA . . .	485	356	129	491	356	135	5	43-Greenhouse, cranberries, dairy products, eggs
RI	69	57	12	72	60	13	(Z)	49-Greenhouse, dairy products, eggs, potatoes
CT. . . .	472	264	208	489	249	240	2	44-Greenhouse, dairy products, eggs, tobacco
M.A. . . .	6,934	2,543	4,391	7,221	2,561	4,661	107	(X)
NY. . . .	2,874	1,081	1,793	2,946	1,032	1,914	48	24-Dairy products, greenhouse, cattle, apples
NJ. . . .	658	465	193	657	465	192	11	39-Greenhouse, dairy products, eggs, peaches
PA. . . .	3,402	997	2,405	3,618	1,064	2,554	49	19-Dairy products, cattle, greenhouse, mushrooms
E.N.C . .	24,826	13,396	11,430	25,092	13,850	11,242	1,188	(X)
OH . . .	4,165	2,484	1,681	4,167	2,587	1,580	166	14-Soybeans, corn, dairy products, greenhouse
IN	4,500	2,583	1,917	4,505	2,684	1,821	233	12-Corn, soybeans, hogs, cattle
IL	7,534	5,181	2,353	7,634	5,431	2,202	481	5-Corn, soybeans, hogs, cattle
MI	3,210	1,922	1,288	3,286	1,962	1,325	143	20-Dairy products, corn, greenhouse, cattle
WI	5,417	1,225	4,191	5,499	1,186	4,313	166	9-Dairy products, cattle, corn, hogs
W.N.C. . .	43,520	18,410	25,110	43,641	19,264	24,378	3,164	(X)
MN . . .	7,378	3,786	3,593	7,082	3,460	3,622	422	6-Dairy products, corn, soybeans, cattle
IA	10,250	4,529	5,720	10,330	4,716	5,614	662	3-Hogs, corn, cattle, soybeans
MO . . .	3,911	1,642	2,268	4,123	1,935	2,188	294	15-Cattle, soybeans, hogs, corn
ND . . .	2,547	1,877	670	3,094	2,339	755	443	23-Wheat, cattle, barley, sunflowers
SD. . . .	3,314	1,188	2,125	3,229	1,263	1,966	272	21-Cattle, wheat, hogs, corn
NE. . . .	9,044	3,111	5,933	8,783	3,109	5,674	479	4-Cattle, corn, hogs, soybeans
KS. . . .	7,076	2,276	4,800	7,000	2,442	4,558	592	7-Cattle, wheat, corn, sorghum grain
S.A.	20,654	11,312	9,342	21,079	11,395	9,684	438	(X)
DE. . . .	622	184	438	636	184	451	3	40-Broilers, soybeans, corn, greenhouse
MD . . .	1,352	564	788	1,391	587	804	16	35-Broilers, greenhouse, dairy products, soybeans
VA. . . .	2,116	753	1,363	2,134	781	1,353	29	22-Cattle, broilers, dairy products, tobacco
WV . . .	324	71	253	343	75	267	7	46-Cattle, broilers, dairy products, turkeys
NC . . .	4,956	2,339	2,617	5,181	2,386	2,795	75	10-Tobacco, broilers, hogs, turkeys
SC. . . .	1,226	677	549	1,177	632	545	73	36-Tobacco, broilers, cattle, soybeans
GA . . .	3,934	1,772	2,162	4,073	1,764	2,309	182	16-Broilers, peanuts, cattle, eggs
FL. . . .	6,125	4,953	1,172	6,145	4,985	1,160	53	8-Oranges, greenhouse, tomatoes, cane/sugar
E.S.C . .	10,523	4,261	6,262	10,757	4,637	6,120	587	(X)
KY. . . .	3,196	1,491	1,705	3,221	1,580	1,641	72	22-Tobacco, cattle, horses, dairy products
TN. . . .	1,936	893	1,044	2,103	1,042	1,061	116	30-Cattle, dairy products, cotton, tobacco
AL. . . .	3,007	770	2,237	2,830	768	2,063	119	25-Broilers, cattle, greenhouse, peanuts
MS . . .	2,383	1,108	1,276	2,602	1,247	1,355	280	27-Cotton, broilers, soybeans, cattle
W.S.C . .	22,043	8,074	13,969	21,703	8,393	13,310	2,091	(X)
AR. . . .	4,242	1,578	2,664	4,602	1,901	2,702	410	11-Broilers, soybeans, rice, cotton
LA. . . .	1,728	1,092	636	1,846	1,259	587	271	31-Cotton, cane/sugar, soybeans, rice
OK . . .	3,856	1,068	2,788	3,635	1,137	2,498	248	18-Cattle, wheat, greenhouse, broilers
TX. . . .	12,217	4,336	7,881	11,620	4,097	7,523	1,162	2-Cattle, cotton, dairy products, greenhouse
Mt	13,102	5,373	7,729	13,746	5,400	8,346	859	(X)
MT . . .	1,514	704	810	1,742	821	921	299	33-Cattle, wheat, barley, hay
ID	2,651	1,586	1,065	2,816	1,643	1,173	137	26-Cattle, potatoes, dairy products, wheat
WY . . .	837	169	668	773	167	606	37	37-Cattle, sugar beets, hay, sheep
CO . . .	3,762	1,099	2,663	4,038	1,083	2,955	203	17-Cattle, corn, wheat, dairy products
NM . . .	1,452	474	978	1,530	490	1,040	60	34-Cattle, dairy products, hay, chili peppers
AZ. . . .	1,867	1,081	786	1,835	943	892	76	32-Cattle, cotton, dairy products, hay
UT. . . .	721	171	550	738	182	556	36	38-Cattle, dairy products, hay, turkeys
NV. . . .	297	88	209	273	71	202	11	47-Cattle, dairy products, hay, potatoes
Pac	25,033	17,560	7,473	25,768	18,291	7,476	710	(X)
WA . . .	4,143	2,844	1,299	4,454	2,922	1,532	189	13-Apples, cattle, dairy products, wheat
OR . . .	2,525	1,699	826	2,490	1,695	795	87	28-Cattle, greenhouse, dairy products, wheat
CA. . . .	17,777	12,523	5,254	18,234	13,179	5,055	430	1-Dairy products, greenhouse, grapes, cattle
AK. . . .	27	20	6	25	20	6	2	50-Greenhouse, dairy products, potatoes, hay
HI	562	474	88	564	476	88	2	41-Cane/sugar, pineapples, greenhouse, nuts

X Not applicable.   Z Less than $500,000.

Source: U.S. Dept. of Agriculture, Economic Research Service, *Economic Indicators of the Farm Sector: State Financial Summary, 1992.*

No. 1098. Indexes of Prices Received and Paid by Farmers: 1990 to 1993

[1977 = 100, except as noted. See also *Historical Statistics, Colonial Times to 1970*, series K 344-353]

ITEM	1990	1991	1992	1993, prel.
Prices received, all products.	149	146	139	143
Crops [1]	127	129	121	123
Food grains	123	115	139	129
Feed grains and hay	123	117	116	115
Cotton	107	108	88	89
Tobacco	152	161	154	154
Oil-bearing crops	94	91	86	95
Fruits	186	265	175	174
Commercial vegetables [2]	142	135	156	159
Livestock and products	170	161	157	162
Meat animals	193	186	176	183
Dairy products	141	126	135	132
Poultry and eggs	131	124	117	127
Prices paid, total [3]	184	187	189	195
Production [1]	171	172	173	178
Feed	128	123	123	124
Feeder livestock	213	214	202	218
Seed	165	163	162	169
Fertilizer	131	134	131	128
Agricultural chemicals	139	151	159	165
Fuels and energy	204	203	199	201
Farm and motor supplies	154	157	160	160
Interest payable per acre	(NA)	137	129	123
Taxes payable per acre	158	164	171	180
Wage rates [4]	193	200	209	217
Parity ratio (1910-14 = 100) [5]	54	51	49	49

NA Not available.   [1] Includes other items not shown separately.   [2] Excludes potatoes and dry beans.   [3] Includes production items, interest, taxes, wage rates, and a family living component. The family living component is the Consumer Price Index for all urban consumers from the Bureau of Labor Statistics. See text, section 15, and table 747.   [4] Straight average of seasonally adjusted indexes.   [5] Ratio of prices received by farmers to prices paid.

Source: U.S. Dept. of Agriculture, National Agricultural Statistics Service, *Agricultural Prices: Annual Summary*.

No. 1099. Civilian Consumer Expenditures for Farm Foods—Farm Value and Marketing Bill: 1980 to 1992

[In billions of dollars, except percent. Excludes imported and nonfarm foods, such as coffee and seafood, as well as food consumed by the military, or exported. See *Historical Statistics, Colonial Times to 1970*, series K 358-360 for data before revisions]

ITEM	1980	1983	1984	1985	1986	1987	1988	1989	1990	1991	1992
Consumer expenditures, total	264.4	315.0	332.0	345.4	359.6	375.5	398.8	419.4	449.8	465.1	476.8
Farm value, total	81.7	85.3	89.8	86.4	88.8	90.4	96.8	103.8	106.2	101.6	105.3
Marketing bill, total [1]	182.7	229.7	242.2	259.0	270.8	285.1	301.9	315.6	343.6	363.5	371.5
Percent of total consumer expenditures	69.1	72.9	73.0	75.0	75.3	75.9	75.7	75.3	76.4	78.2	77.9
At-home expenditures [2]	180.1	204.6	213.1	220.8	226.0	230.2	242.1	255.5	276.2	286.1	291.5
Farm value	65.9	66.5	69.5	66.6	67.6	67.5	72.5	77.9	80.2	76.7	77.4
Marketing bill [1]	114.2	138.1	143.6	154.2	158.4	162.7	169.6	177.6	196.0	209.4	214.1
Percent of at-home expenditures	63.4	67.5	67.4	69.8	70.1	70.7	70.1	69.5	71.0	73.2	73.4
Away-from-home expenditures	84.3	110.4	118.9	124.6	133.6	145.3	156.7	163.9	173.6	179.0	185.3
Farm value	15.8	18.8	20.3	19.8	21.2	22.9	24.3	25.9	26.0	24.9	27.9
Marketing bill [1]	68.5	91.6	98.6	104.8	112.4	122.4	132.4	138.0	147.6	154.1	157.4
Percent of away-from-home expenditures.	81.3	83.0	82.9	84.1	84.1	84.2	84.5	84.2	85.0	86.1	84.9
Marketing bill cost components:											
Labor cost [3]	81.5	102.4	109.3	115.6	122.9	130.0	137.9	145.1	154.0	160.9	167.8
Packaging materials	21.0	24.7	26.2	26.9	27.7	29.9	32.6	35.2	36.5	38.1	39.2
Rail and truck transport [4]	13.0	15.4	15.9	16.5	16.8	17.2	17.8	18.6	19.8	20.4	20.6
Corporate profits before taxes	9.9	9.6	9.6	10.4	10.3	11.1	11.6	12.2	15.0	16.1	15.9
Fuels and electricity	9.0	11.7	12.5	13.1	13.2	13.6	14.1	14.8	15.2	16.3	16.8
Other [5]	48.3	65.9	68.7	76.5	79.9	83.3	87.9	89.7	103.1	111.7	111.2
Processing	66.3	77.8	80.8	88.4	91.0	93.9	99.7	103.8	113.4	120.1	123.3
Wholesaling	20.4	27.1	28.6	29.8	30.5	31.8	33.8	35.2	39.0	40.5	40.7
Transportation	13.0	15.4	16.0	16.6	16.8	17.6	17.7	18.6	19.6	20.4	20.6
Retailing and food service	83.0	109.4	116.8	124.2	132.5	141.8	150.8	158.0	171.6	182.5	186.9
SELECTED FOOD COMMODITY GROUPS											
Meat products:											
Total expenditures	83.3	97.9	101.7	103.2	106.3	110.0	117.6	121.5	128.4	133.4	137.1
Farm value	30.8	31.4	32.4	30.5	30.9	32.7	33.5	34.0	36.9	34.7	34.4
Percent of total	37.0	32.1	31.9	29.6	29.1	29.7	28.5	28.0	28.7	26.0	25.1
Marketing bill [1]	52.5	66.5	69.3	72.7	75.4	77.3	84.1	87.5	91.5	98.7	102.7
Poultry and eggs:											
Total expenditures	18.3	21.7	24.2	26.0	27.6	29.4	31.3	33.9	36.6	37.7	38.4
Farm value	8.4	9.3	11.0	10.2	11.5	10.3	12.1	14.2	13.9	13.9	14.3
Percent of total	45.9	42.9	45.5	39.2	41.7	35.0	38.7	41.9	38.0	36.9	37.2
Marketing bill [1]	9.9	12.4	13.2	15.8	16.1	19.1	19.2	19.7	22.7	23.8	24.1
Dairy products:											
Total expenditures	37.8	45.0	47.4	49.4	51.4	54.0	55.8	58.1	62.5	63.0	63.8
Farm value	16.0	18.0	18.1	17.7	17.8	18.2	17.9	19.6	20.5	18.4	20.1
Percent of total	42.3	40.0	38.2	35.8	34.6	33.7	32.1	33.7	32.8	29.2	31.5
Marketing bill [1]	21.8	27.0	29.3	31.7	33.6	35.8	37.9	38.5	42.0	44.6	43.7
Fruits and vegetables:											
Total expenditures	55.5	70.0	74.7	78.5	81.6	84.7	89.3	96.0	103.7	107.9	111.1
Farm value	11.7	12.9	13.5	13.3	14.6	14.3	16.2	17.8	16.5	17.0	17.7
Percent of total	21.1	18.4	18.1	16.9	17.9	16.9	18.1	18.5	15.9	15.8	15.9
Marketing bill [1]	43.8	57.1	61.2	65.2	67.0	70.4	73.1	78.2	87.2	90.9	93.4
Bakery, grain mill products:											
Total expenditures	35.2	40.6	43.3	45.5	48.3	49.9	54.7	57.7	63.3	66.0	67.4
Farm value	5.1	4.9	5.1	4.7	4.0	3.8	4.9	5.9	5.1	4.6	5.1
Percent of total	14.5	12.1	11.8	10.3	8.3	7.6	9.0	10.2	8.1	7.0	7.6
Marketing bill [1]	30.1	35.7	38.2	40.8	44.3	46.1	49.8	51.8	58.2	61.4	62.3

[1] The difference between expenditures for domestic farm-originated food products and the farm value or payment farmers received for the equivalent farm products.   [2] Food primarily purchased from retail food stores for use at home.   [3] Covers employee wages and salaries, and their health and welfare benefits. Also includes imputed earnings of proprietors, partners, and family workers not receiving stated remuneration.   [4] Excludes local hauling.   [5] Represents advertising, rent, depreciation, interest on borrowed capital, taxes other than income, and other costs.

Source: U.S. Dept. of Agriculture, Economic Research Service, *Food Cost Review, 1992*, AER No. 672, September 1993; *FoodReview*, periodic; and *Agricultural Statistics*, annual.

No. 1100. Selected Indexes of Farm Inputs: 1970 to 1991

[1982=100. Inputs based on physical quantities of resources used in production. See *Historical Statistics, Colonial Times to 1970*, series K 486-495 for data before revisions]

INPUT	1970	1980	1983	1984	1985	1986	1987	1988	1989	1990	1991, prel.
Total	93	106	96	98	95	92	89	87	87	89	89
Farm labor	119	108	95	97	89	87	84	86	82	87	88
Farm real estate	94	101	92	98	97	94	91	90	91	90	89
Durable equipment	78	102	95	91	86	80	74	70	66	64	63
Energy	92	110	97	100	90	84	93	93	91	90	89
Agricultural chemicals [1]	76	131	93	106	101	111	100	90	93	90	94
Feed, seed, and livestock purchases [2]	87	102	99	101	106	105	101	98	99	105	104
Other purchased inputs [3]	90	116	107	108	99	89	92	90	96	97	100

[1] Includes fertilizer, lime, and pesticides. [2] Includes nonfarm portion of feed, seed, and livestock purchases. [3] Includes purchased services and miscellaneous inputs.

Source: U.S. Dept. of Agriculture, Economic Research Service, *Agricultural Outlook*, monthly. Also published in the U.S. Council of Economic Advisers, *Economic Report of the President*, annual.

No. 1101. Farm Machinery and Equipment: 1980 to 1992

[See also *Historical Statistics, Colonial Times to 1970*, series K 184-191]

ITEM	Unit	1980	1982	1983	1984	1985	1986	1987	1988	1989	1990	1991	1992
Value of farm implements and machinery [1]	Bil. dol.	80.3	86.0	85.8	85.0	82.9	81.5	80.0	81.2	85.1	85.4	85.8	85.6
Farmers' expenditures:													
Motor vehicles [2]	Mil. dol.	5,813	4,436	4,724	4,583	3,699	3,227	4,275	4,912	5,484	5,750	4,993	5,126
Tractors	Mil. dol.	3,683	2,597	2,606	2,539	1,937	1,513	2,104	2,540	2,903	3,119	2,593	2,826
Machinery, equipment	Mil. dol.	6,956	5,068	4,735	4,682	3,232	3,094	4,297	4,222	5,087	5,589	5,410	5,132
Repair and maintenance	Mil. dol.	5,205	4,635	4,793	4,908	4,834	4,825	5,017	5,869	6,607	6,311	6,414	5,966
Tractors, machinery and equipment	Mil. dol.	3,746	3,557	3,616	3,592	3,442	3,428	3,540	4,022	4,506	4,366	4,485	4,196
Autos and trucks	Mil. dol.	1,459	1,079	1,178	1,316	1,392	1,397	1,477	1,847	2,101	1,945	1,929	1,770
Retail sales: [3]													
Tractors, total [4]	1,000.	119.3	77.2	71.3	66.7	58.5	47.1	48.3	52.0	59.7	66.3	59.1	52.8
Two-wheel drive	1,000.	108.4	70.4	66.2	62.7	55.5	45.1	46.6	49.3	55.5	61.2	54.0	50.1
Four-wheel drive	1,000.	10.9	6.8	5.1	4.0	3.0	2.0	1.7	2.7	4.2	5.1	4.1	2.7
Combines	1,000.	25.7	16.2	12.8	11.4	8.4	7.7	7.2	6.0	9.1	10.4	9.7	7.7
Field forage harvesters	1,000.	9.5	5.1	4.1	3.5	2.5	2.2	2.3	2.4	2.8	(NA)	(NA)	(NA)

NA Not available. [1] Farm inventory valuations as of December 31. [2] For farm business use. [3] Source: Equipment Manufacturers Institute, Chicago, IL, unpublished data. [4] Covers tractors over 40 hp. only.

Source: Except as noted, U.S. Dept. of Agriculture, Economic Research Service, *Economic Indicators of the Farm Sector: National Financial Summary*, annual. Also in *Agricultural Statistics*, annual.

No. 1102. Hired Farmworkers—Workers and Weekly Earnings: 1990 and 1992

[Represents average number of persons 15 years old and over in the civilian noninstitutional population who were employed at hired farmwork at any time during the year. Based on Current Population Survey; see text, section 1, and Appendix III. For definition of median, see Guide to Tabular Presentation]

CHARACTERISTIC	WORKERS (1,000)		MEDIAN WEEKLY EARNINGS [1]		CHARACTERISTIC	WORKERS (1,000)		MEDIAN WEEKLY EARNINGS [1]	
	1990	1992	1990	1992		1990	1992	1990	1992
All workers	886	848	$200	$200	White [2]	540	506	201	225
					Black and other races [2]	85	82	175	190
15 to 19 years old	144	122	100	100	Hispanic	260	260	213	200
20 to 24 years old	135	113	206	200					
25 to 34 years old	251	246	240	235	Educational attainment: [3]				
35 to 44 years old	170	175	250	250	Less than 5th grade	98	119	204	200
45 to 54 years old	90	96	200	250	5th to 8th grade	191	135	200	200
55 years old and over	95	96	200	200	9th to 12th grade (no diploma)	202	229	168	175
					High school diploma	278	228	240	240
Male	735	711	216	220	Beyond high school	116	136	260	275
Female	151	137	175	175					

[1] The weekly earnings the farmworker usually earns at his farmwork job before deductions and includes any overtime pay or commissions. [2] Excludes persons of Hispanic origin. [3] Prior to 1992, reflected years of school completed rather than degrees or diplomas received.

Source: U.S. Dept. of Agriculture, Economic Research Service, unpublished data.

No. 1103. Farm Output Indexes: 1970 to 1991

[1982=100. See also *Historical Statistics, Colonial Times to 1970*, series K 414-429]

ITEM	1970	1980	1981	1983	1984	1985	1986	1987	1988	1989	1990	1991, prel.
Farm output [1]............	71	87	98	82	98	104	100	102	95	105	112	110
Per unit of total input........	77	82	95	86	100	110	109	114	109	120	126	124
Gross production:												
Livestock and products [2]........	90	99	101	102	100	103	103	105	108	110	112	114
Meat animals...............	100	104	104	102	100	99	99	100	102	102	102	105
Dairy products.............	86	95	98	103	99	105	106	105	107	106	109	109
Poultry and eggs	76	96	100	100	103	108	112	122	125	130	138	144
Crops [3]	58	78	96	67	95	104	95	97	83	99	111	106
Feed crops	49	64	102	31	108	125	119	101	63	117	114	114
Food grains	50	86	102	84	93	87	77	77	70	77	99	76
Oil crops..................	53	80	89	75	87	96	88	88	71	87	87	92
Cotton and cottonseed	92	95	135	69	112	114	83	128	134	104	139	141
Tobacco	98	90	106	75	89	77	58	61	69	71	83	85
Vegetables and melons........	66	54	66	62	66	97	80	85	75	70	115	95
Fruits and nuts.............	71	103	101	100	100	99	95	109	117	111	113	105
Other crops...............	65	94	98	101	110	111	120	132	137	141	141	148

[1] Annual production available for eventual human use. [2] Includes livestock products not shown separately and excludes horses and mules. [3] Includes crops not shown separately.

Source: U.S. Dept. of Agriculture, Economic Research Service, *Agricultural Outlook*, monthly.

No. 1104. Selected Farm Products—United States and World Production and Exports: 1991 to 1993

[In metric tons, except as indicated. Metric ton=1.102 short tons or .984 long tons]

ITEM	Unit	AMOUNT						UNITED STATES AS PERCENT OF WORLD		
		United States			World			1991	1992	1993
		1991	1992	1993	1991	1992	1993			
PRODUCTION [1]										
Wheat	Million......	54	67	66	542	561	560	10.0	11.9	11.8
Corn for grain	Million......	190	241	165	487	529	454	39.0	45.6	36.3
Soybeans..................	Million......	54	60	50	107	117	112	50.6	51.2	44.8
Rice, milled.................	Million......	5.0	5.7	5.1	348	351	344	1.4	1.6	1.5
Tobacco, unmanufactured [2]......	1,000	755	781	734	7,608	8,349	8,630	9.9	9.4	8.5
Cotton [3]....................	Million bales [4].	15.5	17.6	16.2	87.0	96.0	82.5	17.8	18.3	19.6
EXPORTS [5]										
Wheat [6]	Million......	35.1	37.0	31.5	108.9	109.4	99.1	32.2	33.8	31.8
Corn	Million......	40.6	41.8	34.5	61.6	60.1	55.8	65.9	69.6	61.8
Soybeans..................	Million......	18.6	20.9	17.0	28.5	29.5	28.5	65.3	70.8	59.7
Rice, milled basis............	Million......	2.2	2.1	2.5	12.0	14.0	14.4	18.3	15.0	17.4
Tobacco, unmanufactured [7]........	1,000	226	261	230	1,831	1,752	1,812	12.3	14.9	12.7
Cotton [3]..................	Million bales [4].	7.8	6.7	5.2	29.7	28.3	24.8	26.3	23.7	21.2

[1] Production years vary by commodity. In most cases, includes harvests from July 1 of the year shown through June 30 of the following year. [2] Farm sales weight basis. [3] For production and trade years ending in year shown. [4] Bales of 480 lb. net weight. [5] Trade years may vary by commodity. [6] Includes wheat flour on a grain equivalent. [7] Dried weight basis.

Source: U.S. Department of Agriculture, Foreign Agricultural Service, *Foreign Agricultural Commodity Circular Series*, periodic.

No. 1105. Agricultural Exports and Imports—Volume, by Principal Commodities: 1980 to 1992

[In thousands of metric tons]

EXPORTS	1980	1990	1991	1992	IMPORTS	1980	1990	1991	1992
Animal products [1]........	2,575	2,737	3,006	3,627	Fruits, nuts, vegetables ...	2,325	4,573	4,731	4,502
Wheat and products [2]......	37,130	28,286	31,946	34,655	Bananas	2,352	3,094	3,229	3,531
Feed grains and products	72,970	61,397	52,370	52,958	Green coffee	1,089	1,174	1,131	1,300
Rice.....................	3,075	2,509	2,313	2,181	Cocoa and products.....	325	765	761	755
Feeds and fodders.........	6,888	10,979	10,864	11,336	Meat and products [5]	931	1,165	1,147	1,119
Protein meal	7,427	5,138	6,274	7,020					
Oilseeds and products [3]	23,631	15,778	18,163	20,511	Vegetable oils	704	1,183	1,207	1,420
Vegetable oils	1,837	1,204	1,154	1,722	Rubber, crude natural	931	840	798	931
Fruits, nuts, vegetables [4].....	4,147	5,552	5,442	6,147	Sugar	3,744	1,856	1,613	1,648
Cotton and linters.........	1,880	1,733	1,543	1,449	Spices	86	129	140	155
Tobacco, unmanufactured	272	223	226	261	Tobacco, unmanufactured .	392	187	227	398

[1] Includes meat and products, poultry meats, dairy products, and fats, oils and greases. Excludes live animals, hides, skins, and eggs. [2] Includes flour and bulgur. [3] Includes soybeans, sunflowerseeds, peanuts, cottonseed, safflowerseed, flaxseed, and nondefatted soybean flour. [4] Excludes fruit juices. [5] Excludes poultry.

Source: U.S. Dept. of Agriculture, Economic Research Service, *Foreign Agricultural Trade of the United States*, Jan./Feb. 1993, and calendar year supplements.

No. 1106. Agricultural Exports and Imports—Value: 1980 to 1992

[In billions of dollars, except percent. Includes Puerto Rico. Excludes forest products and distilled liquors; includes crude rubber and similar gums (now mainly plantation products). Includes shipments under foreign aid programs. See also *Historical Statistics, Colonial Times to 1970*, series K 251-255]

YEAR	Trade balance	Exports, domestic products	Percent of all exports	Imports for consumption	Percent of all imports	YEAR	Trade balance	Exports, domestic products	Percent of all exports	Imports for consumption	Percent of all imports
1980	23.9	41.2	18	17.4	7	1987	8.3	28.7	12	20.4	5
1982	21.2	36.6	17	15.4	6	1988	16.1	37.1	12	21.0	5
1983	19.5	36.1	18	16.6	7	1989	18.2	39.9	11	21.7	5
1984	18.5	37.8	17	19.3	6	1990	16.6	39.4	10	22.8	5
1985	9.1	29.0	13	20.0	6	1991	16.5	39.2	10	22.7	5
1986	4.8	26.2	13	21.5	6	1992	18.3	42.9	10	24.6	5

Source: U.S. Dept. of Agriculture, Economic Research Service, *Foreign Agricultural Trade of the United States*, Jan.-Feb. issues, and calendar year supplements. Also in *Agricultural Statistics*, annual.

No. 1107. Agricultural Exports and Imports—Leading Trading Partners: 1992

[In billions of dollars. For year ending Sept. 30. Minus sign (-) denotes an excess of imports over exports]

TRADING PARTNER	Exports	Imports	Trade balance	MAJOR COMMODITIES	
				Exported by United States	Imported by United States
Japan	8.4	0.3	8.1	Corn, beef, soybeans	Processed vegetables, noodles, beer
Soviet Union (former)	2.7	(Z)	2.7	Corn, wheat, soybean meal	Casein, fur skins
European Union	7.7	5.2	2.5	Soybeans, corn gluten, tobacco	Wine, beer, dairy prod., processed vegetables
South Korea	2.2	0.1	2.1	Cattle hides, cotton, soybeans	Processed vegetables, noodles
China: Taiwan	1.9	0.1	1.8	Corn, soybeans, wheat	Processed vegetables, confectionery prod., noodles
Mexico	3.7	2.3	1.4	Sorghum, soybeans, beef	Fresh vegetables, cattle, fresh fruit
Canada	4.8	3.9	0.9	Fresh fruits & vegetables, beef	Cattle, pork, beef, canola
Hong Kong	0.8	0.1	0.7	Poultry, fresh fruit, cotton	Canned mushrooms, soy sauce
Egypt	0.7	(Z)	0.7	Wheat, cotton, corn	Spices
China: Mainland	0.7	0.4	0.3	Wheat, cotton	Canned mushrooms & water chestnuts, feathers & down
Turkey	0.3	0.7	-0.3	Tobacco, rice, vegetable oils	Tobacco
Thailand	0.3	0.7	-0.3	Cotton, wheat, soybeans	Processed fruits & vegetables, rice
Chile	0.1	0.5	-0.4	Corn, sugar, soybean meal	Fresh fruit, fruit juices
Costa Rica	0.1	0.5	-0.4	Corn, soybeans, wheat	Fresh fruit, coffee, beef
Indonesia	0.4	0.8	-0.4	Cotton, soybeans, fresh fruit	Rubber, cocoa
Colombia	0.1	0.9	-0.7	Corn, wheat, tallow	Coffee, cut flowers, bananas
New Zealand	0.1	0.8	-0.8	Processed fruits & vegetables, soybean meal, wheat	Beef, dairy products, fresh fruit
Australia	0.3	1.1	-0.8	Processed fruits & vegetables, tobacco	Beef, wool, sugar
Brazil	0.1	1.4	-1.2	Hops	Coffee, orange juice, cocoa

Z Less than $100 million.

Source: U.S. Dept. of Agriculture, Economic Research Service, *Agricultural Outlook*, August 1993.

No. 1108. Agricultural Imports—Value, by Selected Commodity, 1980 to 1992, and by Leading Countries of Origin, 1992

[In millions of dollars]

COMMODITY	1980	1985	1988	1989	1990	1991	1992	Leading countries of origin, 1992
Total	17,366	19,968	20,951	21,749	22,770	22,719	24,624	Canada, Mexico, Brazil
Competitive products	10,374	13,067	14,688	15,610	17,202	17,139	18,946	Canada, Mexico, Australia
Cattle, live	237	307	598	662	978	952	1,245	Canada, Mexico, Germany
Beef and veal	1,780	1,276	1,679	1,662	1,872	1,964	1,891	Australia, New Zealand, Canada
Pork	486	861	933	754	938	795	620	Canada, Denmark, Poland
Dairy products	488	765	875	828	867	772	857	Ireland, New Zealand, Italy
Fruits and preparations	564	1,738	1,866	1,820	2,219	2,131	2,216	Chile, Mexico, Brazil
Vegetables and preparations	864	1,385	1,615	2,047	2,266	2,211	2,184	Mexico, Canada, Spain
Wine	692	998	939	930	917	915	1,087	France, Italy, Spain
Malt beverages	367	633	918	855	923	825	864	Netherlands, Mexico, Canada
Grains and feeds	371	623	909	1,219	1,189	1,321	1,586	Canada, Thailand, Italy
Sugar and related products	2,205	1,190	690	956	1,172	1,065	1,139	Canada, Dominican Republic, Guatemala
Oilseeds and products	599	756	919	916	949	974	1,219	Canada, Philippines, Italy
Noncompetitive products	6,992	6,902	6,263	6,139	5,568	5,580	5,678	Indonesia, Colombia, Brazil
Coffee and products	4,186	3,322	2,470	2,432	1,915	1,859	1,706	Colombia, Brazil, Mexico
Rubber, crude natural	817	654	1,023	958	707	663	770	Indonesia, Thailand, Malaysia
Cocoa and products	920	1,351	1,003	991	1,094	1,092	1,080	Brazil, Canada, Ivory Coast
Bananas and plantains	430	763	832	872	939	1,006	1,097	Costa Rica, Ecuador, Colombia

Source: U.S. Dept. of Agriculture, Economic Research Service, *Foreign Agricultural Trade of the United States*, calendar year supplement.

No. 1109. Spices—Imports, by Type of Spice: 1980 to 1992

[**In millions of pounds**. Data shown are **annual averages**. The United States produces only three major spices - capsicum (red pepper), paprika, and mustard - in any profitable degree. Unground or unprocessed spices enter duty-free. Most spices imported into the United States are unground or unprocessed, generally ensuring better quality]

SPICE	1980-84	1985-89	1990	1991	1992	SPICE	1980-84	1985-89	1990	1991	1992
Total [1]	351.3	398.9	459.3	465.5	498.0	Mace	0.6	0.6	0.7	0.4	0.5
						Mustard seed	79.5	94.5	122.6	121.9	122.8
Anise seed	1.4	2.2	2.2	2.4	2.3	Nutmeg	4.8	4.2	3.8	4.1	3.7
Capsicum	13.9	23.8	44.0	38.7	59.3	Paprika	10.5	13.1	9.1	8.6	6.8
Caraway seed	7.5	7.7	6.8	8.2	7.2	Pepper, black and white	72.5	79.4	86.9	98.0	102.8
Cassia and cinnamon	23.4	29.4	25.7	31.6	34.3	Pimento	1.7	1.9	2.2	2.3	1.9
Celery seed	4.7	5.4	4.9	5.9	7.2	Poppy seed	7.2	8.8	5.2	11.0	10.8
Cloves	2.1	2.5	4.1	2.5	2.5	Sage	3.7	4.4	3.7	5.0	5.3
Coriander seed	10.4	7.7	4.8	5.4	5.1	Sesame seed	80.4	81.1	94.5	80.4	77.1
Cumin seed	8.8	9.2	10.3	8.9	14.2	Turmeric	3.7	4.4	3.7	4.1	5.7
Fennel seed	3.4	4.8	6.4	5.5	7.0	Vanilla beans	1.6	2.4	2.2	2.9	2.8
Ginger root	9.5	11.4	15.8	18.0	18.5						

[1] The United States also imports limited amounts of other spices which are not included in the total.

Source: U.S. Dept. of Agriculture, Economic Research Service, *Foreign Agricultural Trade of the United States*, calendar year supplement, and U.S. Bureau of the Census, *U.S. Imports for Consumption*, series FT247, annual.

No. 1110. Agricultural Exports—Value, by Principal Commodities and Selected Countries of Destination: 1980 to 1992

[See headnote, table 1106. Data by country of destination for 1980 are not adjusted for transshipments]

COMMODITY AND COUNTRY	VALUE (mil. dol.)								PERCENT		
	1980	1985	1987	1988	1989	1990	1991	1992	1980	1990	1992
Total agricultural exports [1]	41,234	29,041	28,709	37,080	39,909	39,363	39,192	42,930	100.0	100.0	100.0
Grains and feeds [2]	19,126	11,882	9,423	13,994	17,187	14,403	12,733	14,174	46.4	36.6	33.0
Feed grains and products	9,852	6,112	3,917	5,973	7,870	7,151	5,862	5,881	23.9	18.2	13.7
Corn	8,492	5,206	3,209	5,043	6,580	6,027	4,916	4,708	20.6	15.4	11.0
Wheat and products	6,660	3,898	3,280	5,126	6,136	4,033	3,511	4,675	16.2	10.2	10.9
Rice	1,289	665	576	809	971	800	750	725	3.2	2.1	1.7
Oilseeds and products [2]	9,394	5,794	6,446	7,695	6,313	5,684	6,397	7,197	22.8	14.5	16.8
Soybeans	5,880	3,732	4,378	4,863	3,942	3,551	3,957	4,387	14.3	9.1	10.2
Soybean oilcake and meal	1,666	870	1,211	1,580	1,181	992	1,145	1,242	4.1	2.6	2.9
Vegetable oils and waxes	1,216	870	626	983	872	808	768	1,018	3.0	2.1	2.4
Animals and animal products [2]	3,768	4,150	5,156	6,422	6,378	6,712	7,006	7,925	9.2	17.1	18.5
Hides and skins, incl. furskins	1,046	1,295	1,731	1,829	1,717	1,747	1,373	1,346	2.6	4.4	3.1
Cattle hides	637	1,007	1,328	1,513	1,383	1,428	1,137	1,132	1.6	3.7	2.6
Meats and meat products	890	905	1,366	1,974	2,348	2,558	2,854	3,339	2.2	6.5	7.8
Beef and veal	249	467	771	1,109	1,420	1,579	1,757	2,043	0.6	4.1	4.8
Fats, oils, and greases	769	619	431	577	512	424	442	525	1.9	1.1	1.2
Poultry and poultry products	603	384	602	689	713	954	1,094	1,211	1.5	2.5	2.8
Cotton, excluding linters	2,864	1,633	1,631	1,975	2,250	2,783	2,480	1,999	7.0	7.1	4.7
Tobacco, unmanufactured	1,334	1,521	1,090	1,253	1,301	1,441	1,428	1,651	3.3	3.7	3.9
Fruits and preparations	1,335	1,186	1,484	1,762	1,836	2,359	2,498	2,732	3.3	6.0	6.4
Fresh fruits	739	743	939	1,093	1,133	1,486	1,561	1,683	1.8	3.8	3.9
Vegetables and preparations	1,188	930	1,158	1,361	1,601	2,302	2,615	2,872	2.9	5.9	6.7
Nuts and preparations	757	683	804	884	846	976	1,020	1,139	1.9	2.5	2.7
Other	1,468	1,262	1,517	1,734	2,197	2,703	3,014	3,241	3.6	6.9	7.6
Asia [1]	15,046	11,191	12,535	16,858	18,828	17,640	16,451	17,924	36.5	44.9	41.8
Japan	6,133	5,409	5,723	7,640	8,162	8,104	7,729	8,437	14.9	20.6	19.7
South Korea	1,797	1,413	1,833	2,274	2,593	2,644	2,104	2,222	4.4	6.8	5.2
China: Taiwan	1,095	1,231	1,285	1,661	1,754	1,661	1,899	1,900	2.7	4.3	4.4
Mainland	2,277	157	362	759	1,435	814	722	545	5.6	2.1	1.3
Hong Kong	437	389	466	489	611	701	771	862	1.1	1.8	2.0
Western Europe [1] [3]	12,917	7,002	7,344	7,911	6,995	7,353	7,468	7,805	31.4	18.7	18.2
European Union [4]	12,177	6,542	6,914	7,370	6,503	6,850	6,916	7,291	29.6	17.4	17.0
Netherlands	3,476	1,869	1,985	2,059	1,722	1,581	1,698	1,853	8.5	4.1	4.3
Germany	2,373	1,009	1,320	1,248	1,075	1,158	1,076	1,163	5.8	3.0	2.7
Spain [5]	1,488	837	666	883	820	937	928	936	3.6	2.4	2.2
United Kingdom	996	604	661	835	703	829	831	910	2.5	2.1	2.1
Italy	1,203	669	699	699	637	710	674	670	3.0	1.8	1.6
France	765	403	524	534	458	528	581	595	1.9	1.4	1.4
Latin America [1]	6,154	4,224	3,678	4,935	5,337	5,092	5,684	6,668	15.0	13.0	15.5
Mexico	2,469	1,439	1,202	2,234	2,724	2,553	2,998	3,791	6.0	6.5	8.8
Canada	1,908	1,622	1,808	2,019	2,221	4,197	4,554	4,902	4.7	10.7	11.4
Soviet Union (former)	1,138	1,923	938	2,252	3,597	2,271	2,495	2,346	2.8	5.8	5.5
Eastern Europe	1,644	414	401	464	401	537	234	317	4.0	1.4	0.7
Africa [1]	2,237	2,488	1,766	2,387	2,260	1,935	1,909	2,570	5.5	5.0	6.0
Algeria	195	227	310	596	504	513	483	437	0.5	1.3	1.0
Egypt	774	891	679	841	989	693	687	766	1.9	1.8	1.8

[1] Includes areas not shown separately. [2] Includes commodities not shown separately. [3] Includes Canary Islands and Madeira Islands for all years. [4] Includes Belgium, Luxembourg, Denmark, Greece, Ireland, and Portugal, not shown separately. As of Jan. 1, 1981, Greece became a member of the European Union. As of Jan. 1, 1986, Spain and Portugal became members of the European Union. For consistency, data for all years are shown on same basis. [5] As of Jan. 1, 1984, includes Canary Islands and Spanish Africa, not elsewhere classified.

Source: U.S. Dept. of Agriculture, Economic Research Service, *Foreign Agricultural Trade of the United States*, Jan./Feb. 1993, and calendar year supplements. Also in *Agricultural Statistics*, annual.

No. 1111. Cropland Used for Crops and Acreages of Crops Harvested: 1980 to 1993

[See also *Historical Statistics, Colonial Times to 1970*, series K 496-501]

YEAR	CROPLAND USED FOR CROPS					Acres of crops harvested [2] (mil.)
	Number (mil. acres)				Index (1977 = 100)	
	Total	Cropland harvested [1]	Crop failure	Cultivated summer fallow		
1980	382	342	10	30	101	352
1985	372	334	7	31	98	342
1986	357	316	9	32	94	325
1987	331	293	6	32	88	302
1988	327	287	10	30	87	298
1989	341	306	8	27	90	318
1990	341	310	6	25	90	322
1991 [3]	337	306	7	24	89	318
1992 [3]	340	308	9	23	90	320
1993 [3]	332	299	11	22	88	309

[1] Land supporting one or more harvested crops. [2] Area in principal crops harvested as reported by Crop Reporting Board plus acreages in fruits, vegetables for sale, tree nuts, and farm gardens. [3] Preliminary.

Source: U.S. Dept. of Agriculture, Economic Research Service, *Economic Indicators of the Farm Sector: Production and Efficiency Statistics*, annual. Also in *Agricultural Statistics*, annual. Beginning 1991 data from *Agricultural Resources: Cropland, Water, and Conservation Situation and Outlook Report*.

No. 1112. Crops—Acreage and Value, by State: 1990 to 1993

STATE	ACREAGE HARVESTED (1,000)				FARM VALUE (mil. dol.)				
	1990	1991	1992	1993, prel.	1990	1991	1992	1993, prel.	
								Value	Rank
U.S. [1]	308,318	[2]303,864	[2]307,171	[2]295,918	80,855	79,482	87,487	83,715	(X)
AL.	2,338	2,229	2,130	2,116	464	584	617	539	33
AZ.	802	770	736	695	894	892	829	944	31
AR.	8,080	7,863	8,110	8,165	1,648	1,762	1,945	1,809	18
CA.	4,789	4,396	4,459	4,403	10,642	9,938	11,338	12,010	1
CO.	5,862	5,591	5,395	5,625	1,194	1,127	1,126	1,380	21
CT.	129	125	128	125	111	92	86	80	47
DE.	496	556	515	499	139	142	135	121	46
FL.	1,076	1,048	1,071	1,046	2,768	3,348	3,895	3,360	7
GA.	3,788	3,777	3,693	3,523	1,273	1,593	1,614	1,370	23
HI.	79	74	68	64	411	367	341	308	39
ID.	4,175	4,079	4,006	4,322	1,735	1,665	1,815	1,871	16
IL.	22,759	22,906	23,237	21,934	5,812	5,357	6,431	6,548	2
IN.	11,485	11,527	11,709	11,767	3,023	2,564	3,303	3,649	5
IA.	23,276	23,356	23,666	21,916	5,818	5,634	6,350	4,224	3
KS.	20,978	20,712	20,266	20,454	2,610	2,485	2,955	2,968	9
KY.	5,505	5,495	5,419	5,419	1,721	1,670	2,058	1,948	15
LA.	4,346	3,665	4,029	3,729	1,184	1,126	1,181	1,096	26
ME.	361	351	375	373	180	152	190	200	42
MD.	1,551	1,562	1,619	1,569	386	374	422	362	36
MA.	135	136	135	134	147	170	175	163	43
MI.	6,510	6,733	6,817	6,751	1,839	1,938	1,914	2,220	13
MN.	18,765	18,692	19,301	16,940	4,177	4,007	4,058	2,836	10
MS.	4,719	4,478	4,855	4,708	1,149	1,194	1,274	1,020	28
MO.	12,685	12,900	12,904	11,542	2,083	2,122	2,574	2,061	14
MT.	8,926	8,687	8,369	8,891	881	1,052	1,022	1,300	24
NE.	18,044	18,366	18,330	17,917	3,621	3,667	3,732	3,586	6
NV.	520	495	403	527	154	102	103	146	45
NH.	91	92	103	106	29	25	36	28	48
NJ.	361	380	391	413	170	186	264	275	40
NM.	880	1,042	1,051	995	395	395	395	383	35
NY.	3,538	3,443	3,185	3,150	916	964	928	944	30
NC.	4,336	4,397	4,519	4,127	1,981	2,144	2,081	1,851	17
ND.	21,014	20,655	21,011	19,782	2,082	2,188	2,649	2,404	12
OH.	10,132	9,972	10,087	10,037	2,597	2,278	2,698	2,663	11
OK.	9,688	8,518	9,392	8,771	1,142	913	1,079	1,029	27
OR.	2,290	2,260	2,147	2,260	1,035	1,032	1,100	1,176	25
PA.	4,094	4,067	4,065	4,035	1,358	1,159	1,410	1,371	22
RI.	10	10	11	12	5	5	7	6	49
SC.	2,046	1,824	1,885	1,603	517	639	564	498	34
SD.	15,528	15,606	15,858	14,223	1,638	1,611	1,825	1,638	19
TN.	4,477	4,379	4,326	4,408	954	956	1,147	990	29
TX.	18,544	17,714	18,769	18,524	4,023	3,707	3,840	4,100	4
UT.	992	973	990	1,031	257	220	227	251	41
VT.	441	434	463	434	77	156	215	159	44
VA.	2,725	2,656	2,705	2,659	846	723	794	635	32
WA.	3,999	3,861	3,957	4,227	2,529	2,625	2,577	3,096	8
WV.	668	615	639	621	114	348	350	321	37
WI.	8,550	8,449	8,096	7,498	1,830	1,785	1,529	1,462	20
WY.	1,735	1,899	1,723	1,804	294	300	284	317	38

X Not applicable. [1] Excludes Alaska. [2] Includes sunflower and sugarbeet acreage unallocated by State.
Source: U.S. Dept. of Agriculture, National Agricultural Statistics Service, *Crop Production*, annual; and *Crop Values*, annual.

No. 1113. Principal Crops—Production, Supply, and Disappearance: 1989 to 1993

[Marketing year beginning May 1 for hay, June 1 for wheat, August 1 for cotton and rice, September 1 for soybeans, corn, and sorghum. Acreage, production, and yield of all crops periodically revised on basis of census data. See also *Historical Statistics, Colonial Times to 1970*, series K 506-563]

CROP AND YEAR	ACREAGE (mil.)—			Yield per acre	Production	Farm price[2]	Farm value (mil. dol.)	Total supply[3]	DISAPPEARANCE		Ending stocks
	Set aside[1]	Plant-ed	Har-vested						Total[4]	Ex-ports	
Corn for grain:				Bu.	Mil. bu.	$/bu.			Mil. bu.		
1989	10.8	72.2	64.7	116.3	7,525	2.36	17,897	9,458	8,113	2,368	1,344
1990	10.7	74.2	67.0	118.5	7,934	2.28	18,192	9,282	7,761	1,725	1,521
1991	7.4	76.0	68.8	108.6	7,475	2.37	17,864	9,016	7,916	1,584	1,100
1992	5.2	79.3	72.2	131.4	9,482	2.07	19,735	10,589	8,476	1,663	2,113
1993, prel	10.4	73.3	63.0	100.7	6,344	2.60	16,597	8,477	7,675	1,300	802
Soybeans:				Bu.	Mil. bu.	$/bu.			Mil. bu.		
1989	-	60.8	59.5	32.3	1,924	5.69	10,732	2,109	1,870	623	239
1990	-	57.8	56.5	34.1	1,926	5.74	11,042	2,168	1,839	557	329
1991	-	59.2	58.0	34.2	1,987	5.58	11,092	2,319	2,041	684	278
1992	-	59.1	58.2	37.6	2,188	5.56	12,154	2,468	2,176	770	292
1993, prel	-	59.4	56.4	32.0	1,809	6.50	11,735	2,106	1,956	615	150
Hay:				Sh. tons	Mil. sh. tons	$/ton			Mil. sh. tons		
1989	-	(NA)	63.3	2.30	146	[5][6]87.40	11,514	163	136	(NA)	27
1990	-	(NA)	61.4	2.39	147	[5][6]80.60	10,462	174	147	(NA)	27
1991	-	(NA)	62.5	2.45	153	[5][6]71.20	10,006	180	152	(NA)	29
1992	-	(NA)	59.6	2.50	149	[5][6]74.30	10,573	178	157	(NA)	21
1993, prel	-	(NA)	60.4	2.26	149	[5][6]81.00	10,909	175	(NA)	(NA)	(NA)
Wheat:				Bu.	Mil. bu.	$/bu.			Mil. bu.		
1989	9.6	76.6	62.2	32.7	2,037	3.72	7,542	2,762	2,225	1,232	536
1990	7.5	77.2	69.3	39.5	2,736	2.61	7,184	3,309	2,443	1,068	866
1991	15.6	69.9	57.7	34.3	1,981	3.00	5,957	2,888	2,416	1,280	472
1992	7.3	72.3	62.4	39.4	2,459	3.24	7,984	3,001	2,472	1,354	529
1993, prel	5.3	72.2	62.6	38.3	2,402	3.20	7,713	3,021	2,423	1,225	598
Cotton:				Lb.	Mil. bales[7]	cents/lb.			Mil. bales[7]		
1989	3.5	10.6	9.5	614	[8]12.2	66.2	3,877	19.3	16.5	7.7	[9]3.0
1990	2.0	12.3	11.7	634	[8]15.5	67.1	5,076	18.5	16.4	7.8	[9]2.3
1991	1.2	14.1	13.0	652	[8]17.6	58.1	4,913	20.0	16.3	6.7	[9]3.7
1992	1.7	13.2	11.1	699	[8]16.2	54.9	4,274	19.9	15.4	5.2	[9]4.7
1993, prel	1.4	13.4	12.8	699	[8]16.2	[10]54.3	4,220	20.8	16.4	6.2	[9]4.5
Tobacco:[11]				Lb.	Mil. lb.	$/lb.			Mil. lb.		
1989	(NA)	(NA)	0.7	2,016	1,367	[6]1.71	2,338	4,081	1,677	582	[12]2,401
1990	(NA)	(NA)	0.7	2,218	1,626	[6]1.74	2,827	4,026	1,794	631	[12]2,232
1991	(NA)	(NA)	0.8	2,179	1,664	[6]1.77	2,951	3,896	1,616	640	[12]2,280
1992	(NA)	(NA)	0.8	2,195	1,722	[6]1.78	3,059	4,001	1,565	629	[12]2,436
1993, prel	(NA)	(NA)	0.7	2,162	1,615	[6]1.76	2,837	4,041	(NA)	(NA)	(NA)
Potatoes:				Cwt.	Mil. cwt.	$/cwt.			Mil. cwt.		
1989	(NA)	1.3	1.3	289	370	7.36	2,717	555	[13]315	[14]17	(NA)
1990	(NA)	1.4	1.4	293	402	6.08	2,431	582	[13]319	[14]17	(NA)
1991	(NA)	1.4	1.4	304	418	4.96	2,043	618	[13]330	[14]19	(NA)
1992	(NA)	1.3	1.3	323	425	5.52	2,336	640	[13]339	[14]23	(NA)
1993, prel	(NA)	1.4	1.3	318	419	6.22	2,599	642	[13]345	[14]24	(NA)
Rice, rough:				Lb.	Mil. cwt.	$/cwt.			Mil. cwt.		
1989	1.2	2.7	2.7	5,749	155	7.35	1,134	186	159	77	26
1990	1.0	2.9	2.8	5,529	156	6.70	1,047	187	163	71	25
1991	0.7	2.9	2.8	5,674	157	7.58	1,201	187	160	66	27
1992	0.4	3.2	3.1	5,736	180	5.89	1,057	213	174	77	39
1993, prel	0.7	2.9	2.8	5,510	156	9.00	1,429	202	182	83	21
Sorghum for grain:				Bu.	Mil. bu.	$/bu.			Mil. bu.		
1989	3.3	12.6	11.1	55.4	615	2.10	1,288	1,055	835	303	220
1990	3.3	10.5	9.1	63.1	573	2.12	1,221	793	650	232	143
1991	2.4	11.1	9.9	59.3	585	2.25	1,331	727	674	292	53
1992	2.0	13.3	12.2	72.8	884	1.89	1,684	937	762	277	175
1993, prel	2.2	10.5	9.5	59.9	568	2.40	1,316	743	658	175	85

- Represents zero. NA Not available. [1] Acreage set aside under diversion, PIK (payment-in-kind) and acreage reduction programs. [2] Except as noted, marketing year average price. U.S. prices are computed by weighting U.S. monthly prices by estimated monthly marketings and do not include an allowance for outstanding loans and government purchases and payments. [3] Comprises production, imports, and beginning stocks. [4] Includes feed, residual, and other domestic uses not shown separately. [5] Prices are for hay sold baled. [6] Season average prices received by farmers. U.S. prices are computed by weighting State prices by estimated sales and include an allowance for outstanding loans and government purchases, if any, for crops under government programs. [7] Bales of 480 pounds, net weight. [8] State production figures, which conform with U.S. totals. [9] Stock estimates based on Census Bureau data which results in an unaccounted difference between supply and use estimates and changes in ending stocks. [10] Weighted average for August 1-December 1. [11] Flue-cured and cigar wrapper, crop years July-June; all other types October-September. Farm-sales-weight basis. [12] Includes tobacco carried over on farms. [13] Covers potatoes used for table use, frozen and canned products, chips, and dehydration. [14] Covers fresh potatoes, chips, frozen and dehydrated products.

Source: Production—U.S. Dept. of Agriculture, National Agricultural Statistics Service. In *Crop Production*, annual; and *Crop Values*, annual. Supply and disappearance—U.S. Dept. of Agriculture, Economic Research Service, *Feed Situation*, quarterly; *Fats and Oils Situation*, quarterly; *Wheat Situation*, quarterly; *Tobacco Situation*, quarterly; *Cotton and Wool Outlook Statistics*, periodic; and *Agricultural Supply and Demand Estimates*, periodic. All data are also in *Agricultural Statistics*, annual; and *Agricultural Outlook*, monthly.

No. 1114. Corn—Acreage, Production, and Value, by Leading States: 1991 to 1993

[One bushel of corn=56 pounds. See also *Historical Statistics, Colonial Times to 1970*, series K 502-508]

STATE	ACREAGE HARVESTED (1,000 acres)			YIELD PER ACRE (bu.)			PRODUCTION (mil. bu.)			PRICE ($/bu.)			FARM VALUE (mil. dol.)		
	1991	1992	1993	1991	1992	1993	1991	1992	1993	1991	1992	1993	1991	1992	1993
U.S. [1]	68,847	72,162	62,991	109	131	101	7,475	9,482	6,344	2.37	2.07	2.60	17,864	19,735	16,597
IL	11,000	11,050	10,000	107	149	130	1,177	1,646	1,300	2.46	2.11	2.60	2,895	3,474	3,380
IA	12,200	12,950	11,000	117	147	80	1,427	1,904	880	2.30	2.00	2.50	3,283	3,807	2,200
NE	7,800	7,900	7,550	127	135	104	991	1,067	785	2.34	2.09	2.70	2,318	2,229	2,120
IN	5,550	5,970	5,400	92	147	132	511	878	713	2.45	2.09	2.60	1,251	1,834	1,853
OH	3,400	3,550	3,280	96	143	110	326	508	361	2.48	2.06	2.65	809	1,046	956
MN	6,000	6,500	4,600	120	114	70	720	741	322	2.22	1.91	2.45	1,598	1,415	789
MI	2,300	2,300	2,150	110	105	110	253	242	237	2.34	1.95	2.65	592	471	627
WI	3,200	2,950	2,350	119	104	92	381	307	216	2.30	2.12	2.65	876	650	573
KS	1,650	1,730	1,800	125	150	120	206	260	216	2.42	2.15	2.70	499	558	543
TX	1,500	1,620	1,850	110	125	115	165	203	213	2.68	2.41	2.70	442	488	574
MO	2,200	2,400	1,850	97	135	90	213	324	167	2.45	2.11	2.60	523	684	433
SD	3,250	3,300	2,550	74	84	63	241	277	161	2.16	1.84	2.40	519	510	386
KY	1,250	1,300	1,220	89	132	104	111	172	127	2.58	2.23	2.60	287	383	330
CO	840	835	825	153	148	120	129	124	99	2.43	2.23	2.75	312	276	272
PA	860	990	970	75	120	96	65	119	93	2.87	2.42	3.15	185	287	293
NY	660	670	580	98	92	105	65	62	61	2.70	2.30	2.60	175	142	158

[1] Includes other States, not shown separately.

Source: U.S. Dept. of Agriculture, National Agricultural Statistics Service, *Crop Production*, annual; and *Crop Values*, annual.

No. 1115. Soybeans—Acreage, Production, and Value, by Leading States: 1991 to 1993

[One bushel of soybeans=60 pounds. See also *Historical Statistics, Colonial Times to 1970*, series K 520-522]

STATE	ACREAGE HARVESTED (1,000 acres)			YIELD PER ACRE (bu.)			PRODUCTION (mil. bu.)			PRICE ($/bu.)			FARM VALUE (mil. dol.)		
	1991	1992	1993	1991	1992	1993	1991	1992	1993	1991	1992	1993	1991	1992	1993
U.S. [1]	58,011	58,183	56,447	34	38	32	1,987	2,188	1,809	5.58	5.56	6.50	11,092	12,154	11,735
IL	9,100	9,430	8,700	38	43	43	341	405	374	5.70	5.69	6.60	1,945	2,307	2,469
IA	8,630	8,120	8,200	41	44	30	350	357	246	5.51	5.54	6.50	1,926	1,979	1,599
IN	4,400	4,520	4,850	39	43	44	172	194	213	5.68	5.61	6.40	975	1,090	1,366
OH	3,770	3,630	4,040	36	40	38	136	145	154	5.69	5.65	6.45	772	820	990
MO	4,430	4,250	3,550	31	38	33	135	162	117	5.59	5.45	6.40	755	880	750
MN	5,350	5,400	5,000	37	32	22	195	173	110	5.41	5.52	6.30	1,056	954	693
NE	2,460	2,460	2,500	34	42	35	82	103	88	5.47	5.37	6.35	451	555	556
AR	3,200	3,160	3,450	28	33	25	90	104	86	5.71	5.64	6.85	512	588	591
MI	1,390	1,440	1,440	38	33	38	53	48	55	5.52	5.53	6.50	292	263	356
KS	1,900	1,850	1,850	23	37	28	44	68	52	5.55	5.42	6.45	243	371	334
MS	1,800	1,750	1,950	26	34	22	47	60	43	5.74	5.69	6.75	269	339	290
KY	1,130	1,160	1,150	33	38	33	37	44	38	5.78	5.68	6.70	212	250	254
SD	2,160	2,250	1,700	27	28	21	58	63	36	5.33	5.18	6.05	311	326	216
TN	1,050	950	990	30	35	31	32	33	31	5.73	5.61	6.65	180	187	204

[1] Includes other States, not shown separately.

Source: U.S. Dept. of Agriculture, National Agricultural Statistics Service, *Crop Production*, annual; and *Crop Values*, annual.

No. 1116. Wheat—Acreage, Production, and Value, by Leading States: 1991 to 1993

[One bushel of wheat= 60 pounds. See also *Historical Statistics, Colonial Times to 1970*, series K 506-508]

STATE	ACREAGE HARVESTED (1,000 acres)			YIELD PER ACRE (bu.)			PRODUCTION (mil. bu.)			PRICE ($/bu.)			FARM VALUE (mil. dol.)		
	1991	1992	1993	1991	1992	1993	1991	1992	1993	1991	1992	1993	1991	1992	1993
U.S. [1]	57,703	62,411	62,647	34.3	39.4	38.3	1,981	2,459	2,402	3.00	3.24	3.20	5,957	7,984	7,713
KS	11,000	10,700	11,100	33.0	34.0	35.0	363	364	389	2.81	3.13	3.05	1,020	1,139	1,185
ND	9,790	11,420	10,800	31.0	41.1	31.0	304	470	335	3.04	3.14	4.05	926	1,481	1,342
MT	4,379	4,707	5,214	36.4	29.7	39.2	160	140	204	3.17	3.42	3.55	506	476	712
WA	2,150	2,420	2,790	45.9	49.4	63.6	99	120	178	3.73	3.80	3.35	367	453	591
OK	5,000	5,900	5,400	28.0	29.0	30.0	140	171	162	2.85	3.19	2.90	399	546	470
TX	2,800	3,800	3,700	30.0	34.0	32.0	84	129	118	2.69	3.18	2.85	226	411	337
SD	3,117	3,733	3,488	30.9	32.0	32.0	96	120	112	3.06	3.21	3.40	295	385	384
ID	1,160	1,440	1,390	70.4	69.4	79.4	82	100	110	3.56	3.48	3.00	290	347	327
CO	2,336	2,347	2,583	31.7	30.9	37.5	74	73	97	3.07	3.15	3.15	227	228	305
NE	2,100	1,850	2,100	32.0	30.0	35.0	67	56	74	3.01	3.16	3.05	202	175	224
MN	2,155	2,805	2,298	31.1	49.9	31.0	67	140	71	3.21	3.17	3.35	215	443	242
IL	1,400	1,150	1,550	32.0	54.0	44.0	45	62	68	2.56	3.28	2.70	115	204	184
OR	846	925	925	51.9	51.7	70.2	44	48	65	3.65	3.81	3.25	160	183	211

[1] Includes other States, not shown separately.

Source: U.S. Dept. of Agriculture, National Agricultural Statistics Service, *Crop Production*, annual; and *Crop Values*, annual.

No. 1117. Greenhouse and Nursery Crops—Summary, by Type of Product: 1989 to 1993

[In millions of dollars, except per capita. Based on a survey of 36 commercial floriculture States and estimates by source]

ITEM	Total	Cut flowers	Potted flowering plants	Foliage plants	Bedding plants	Cut cultivated greens	Other [1]
Domestic production: [2]							
1989.................	7,617	542	682	575	996	111	4,711
1990.................	8,228	572	872	609	1,003	131	5,041
1991.................	8,828	580	952	576	1,146	135	5,439
1992.................	9,200	558	1,034	544	1,338	153	5,573
1993.................	9,700	545	1,139	529	1,500	169	5,818
Imports:							
1989.................	498	315	20	22	(NA)	13	128
1990.................	529	326	18	25	(NA)	14	146
1991.................	533	322	22	27	(NA)	13	149
1992.................	579	352	27	30	(NA)	15	155
1993.................	644	400	30	33	(NA)	16	165
RETAIL CONSUMER EXPENDITURES [3]							
Total:							
1989.................	30,456	5,082	1,547	1,297	2,241	608	19,681
1990.................	32,493	5,214	1,975	1,347	2,257	710	20,990
1991.................	34,539	5,209	2,157	1,278	2,578	742	22,575
1992.................	35,752	5,266	2,345	1,212	3,011	827	23,091
1993.................	37,569	5,472	2,585	1,179	3,375	906	24,052
Per capita (dol.): [4]							
1989.................	123	21	6	5	9	2	79
1990.................	130	21	8	5	9	3	84
1991.................	137	21	9	5	10	3	89
1992.................	140	21	9	5	12	3	90
1993.................	146	21	10	5	13	4	93

NA Not available. [1] Includes turfgrass (sod), bulbs, nursery stock, groundcovers, and other greenhouse and nursery products except the following: seeds, cut Christmas trees, and food crops grown under cover. [2] Equivalent wholesale values. [3] Excludes services such as landscaping, installation, and maintenance. [4] Based on U.S. Bureau of the Census estimated resident population as of July 1.

Source: U.S. Dept. of Agriculture, Economic Research Service, unpublished data.

No. 1118. Fruits and Nuts—Utilized Production and Value, 1990 to 1992, and Leading Producing States, 1992

FRUIT OR NUT	UTILIZED PRODUCTION [1]				FARM VALUE (mil. dol.)			Leading States in order of production, 1992
	Unit	1990	1991	1992	1990	1991	1992	
Apples (35 States) [2]...........	Mil. lb	9,658	9,659	10,614	1,457	1,733	1,422	WA, NY, MI
Apricots..................	1,000 tons..	120	92	108	41	37	40	CA, WA, UT
Avocados.................	1,000 tons..	156	185	267	206	196	166	CA, FL, HI
Bananas..................	Mil. lb	6	6	6	4	5	5	HI
Cherries, sweet...........	1,000 tons..	132	142	195	118	137	178	WA, OR, CA
Cherries, tart.............	Mil. lb	203	190	314	37	88	55	MI, UT, NY
Cranberries...............	1,000 bbl. [3]	3,392	4,220	4,080	156	207	(NA)	MA, WI, NJ
Dates....................	1,000 tons.	24	22	21	20	21	22	CA
Figs (fresh)...............	1,000 tons.	50	45	42	17	17	17	CA
Grapefruit (4 States)........	Mil. boxes [4]	56	55	69	395	431	294	FL, CA, AZ
Grapes (13 States).........	1,000 tons.	5,660	5,555	6,032	1,670	1,736	1,825	CA, WA, NY
Kiwifruit.................	1,000 tons.	34	27	46	14	22	13	CA
Lemons (2 States)..........	Mil. boxes [5]	19	20	25	290	261	241	CA, AZ
Limes (FL)...............	Mil. boxes [6]	1	2	1	28	23	7	FL
Nectarines...............	1,000 tons.	232	215	236	110	86	74	CA
Olives..................	1,000 tons.	132	65	165	56	36	92	CA
Oranges and tangerines (4 States)..	Mil. boxes [7]	179	209	258	1,585	1,543	1,314	FL, CA, AZ
Papayas.................	Mil. lb	69	56	72	15	16	14	HI
Peaches (32 States)........	Mil. lb	2,140	2,506	2,479	372	394	373	CA, GA, SC
Pears...................	1,000 tons.	963	904	924	269	274	273	CA, WA, OR
Pineapples...............	1,000 tons.	575	555	550	106	108	102	HI
Plums and prunes (fresh)......	1,000 tons [8]	729	831	822	271	280	253	CA, WA, MI
Tangelos (FL).............	Mil. boxes [8]	3	3	3	21	24	15	FL
Temples (FL).............	Mil. boxes [8]	3	2	3	21	20	10	FL
Almonds (shelled basis)........	Mil. lb	660	490	545	598	564	670	CA
Hazelnuts (in the shell)........	1,000 tons..	22	26	28	17	19	15	OR, WA
Macadamia nuts............	Mil. lb	50	50	48	41	35	33	HI
Pecans (in the shell) (11 States)...	Mil. lb	205	299	166	248	310	240	TX, GA, NM
Pistachios................	Mil. lb	120	77	147	122	96	151	CA
Walnuts, English (in the shell).....	1,000 tons..	227	259	203	236	275	268	CA

NA Not available. [1] Excludes quantities not harvested or not marketed. [2] Production in commercial orchards with 100 or more bearing age trees. [3] Barrels of 100 pounds. [4] Approximate average, net weight, is 65 lb. in AZ and CA, 85 in FL, and 80 in TX. [5] About 76 lb. net. [6] Approximate net weight is 80 lb. [7] Net contents of box varies. In CA and AZ approximate average for oranges and tangerines is 75 lb.; FL oranges, 90 lb.; TX oranges, 85 lb.; and FL tangerines, 95 lb. [8] Approximate net weight is 90 lb.

Source: U.S. Dept. of Agriculture, National Agricultural Statistics Service, Noncitrus Fruits and Nuts, annual; and Citrus Fruits, annual.

No. 1119. Commercial Vegetable and Other Specified Crops—Area, Production, and Value, 1990 to 1992, and Leading Producing States, 1992

[Relates to commercial production for fresh market and processing combined. Includes market garden areas but excludes minor producing acreage in minor producing States. Excludes production for home use in farm and nonfarm gardens. Value is for season or crop year and should not be confused with calendar-year income]

CROP	AREA [1] (1,000 acres)			PRODUCTION [2] (1,000 short tons)			VALUE [3] (mil. dol.)			Leading States in order of production, 1992
	1990	1991	1992	1990	1991	1992	1990	1991	1992	
Asparagus	96	92	89	122	113	116	148	150	162	CA, WA, MI
Beans, snap [4]	246	232	192	796	768	646	146	135	112	WI, OR, MI
Beans, dry edible	2,084	1,913	1,497	1,619	1,688	1,102	599	528	467	ND, MI, NE
Broccoli	111	101	118	617	560	611	268	242	280	CA, AZ, TX
Carrots	94	98	105	1,462	1,394	1,582	272	309	338	CA, WA, MI
Cauliflower	66	56	56	393	352	359	190	188	204	CA, AZ, OR
Celery	38	33	33	991	955	945	215	206	229	CA, FL, MI
Corn, sweet	678	721	692	3,968	4,146	4,114	471	497	462	WI, MN, WA
Cucumbers [4]	115	104	155	653	623	1,045	136	131	277	MI, NC, WI
Honeydew melons	26	26	23	225	187	207	81	69	62	CA, TX, AZ
Lettuce	231	222	212	3,660	3,539	3,302	844	810	822	CA, AZ, FL
Peppermint	102	114	112	3.5	3.3	3.7	97	87	46	OR, WA, ID
Spearmint	34	42	41	1.3	1.6	1.8	38	43	46	WA, ID, IN
Mushrooms [5]	139	138	142	357	375	373	645	653	669	PA, CA, FL
Onions	138	134	139	2,639	2,535	2,711	489	583	614	OR, CA, CO
Peas, green [4]	341	333	333	528	491	569	131	128	136	MN, WI, WA
Potatoes	1,371	1,375	1,302	20,106	20,881	20,582	2,431	2,043	2,160	ID, WA, ND
Strawberries	46	47	49	627	684	656	590	634	684	CA, FL, OR
Sweet potatoes	90	78	78	630	560	588	122	149	155	NC, LA, CA
Tomatoes	489	488	404	12,041	12,567	10,583	1,626	1,780	1,819	CA, FL, OH

[1] Area of crops for harvest for fresh market, including any partially harvested or not harvested because of low prices or other factors, plus area harvested for processing. [2] Excludes some quantities not marketed. [3] Fresh market vegetables valued at f.o.b. shipping point. Processing vegetables are equivalent returns at packinghouse door. [4] Processing only. [5] Area is shown in million square feet. All data are for marketing year ending June 30.

Source: U.S. Dept. of Agriculture, National Agricultural Statistics Service, *Vegetables*, annual summary. Also in *Agricultural Statistics*, annual.

No. 1120. Fresh Fruits and Vegetables—Consumption and Imports: 1992

[Data for vegetables may include some vegetables for processing]

FRUIT	Total U.S. consumption (mil. lb.)	PERCENT OF CONSUMPTION		VEGETABLE	Total U.S. consumption (mil. lb.)	PERCENT OF CONSUMPTION	
		Imported	Imported from Mexico			Imported	Imported from Mexico
All fruits, total	**25,202**	**38.3**	**5.5**	**Fresh vegetables, all**	**49,519**	**6.7**	**4.2**
Excluding bananas	18,240	14.9	7.5				
				Asparagus	151	38.3	29.5
Citrus fruits	6,207	4.8	3.2	Beans, snap	325	7.2	6.8
Oranges	3,294	1.0	0.2	Beans, dry edible [1]	1,914	3.6	0.9
Grapefruit	1,511	1.6	(Z)	Broccoli	871	2.4	1.9
Tangerines, tangelos	494	8.5	3.7	Cabbage	1,807	2.2	0.8
Lemons	647	3.1	(Z)	Cantaloup	2,161	22.3	10.2
Limes	261	68.2	65.5	Carrots	2,065	6.5	1.5
				Cauliflower	513	3.4	1.7
Noncitrus fruits	18,995	49.3	6.2	Celery	1,667	2.0	1.2
Apples	4,948	4.7	-	Corn, sweet	1,637	0.7	0.6
Apricots	39	7.2	-	Cucumbers	1,261	34.3	30.0
Avocados	542	9.8	0.4	Eggplant	100	37.1	36.7
Bananas	6,962	99.8	12.5	Garlic, all uses	417	15.6	6.0
Cherries, sweet	128	3.6	-	Honeydew melons	415	30.3	26.5
Cherries, tart	9	5.2	-	Lettuce, head	6,149	0.3	0.2
Grapes	1,840	41.9	4.9	Lettuce, romaine & leaf	1,152	0.5	0.2
Kiwifruit	121	36.9	-	Mushrooms	496	0.8	-
Mangoes	173	97.1	87.3	Onions	4,129	10.1	8.1
Papayas	61	37.9	30.5	Peppers	1,349	14.5	12.5
Peaches, nectarines	1,517	7.0	(Z)	Potatoes	12,535	3.2	-
Pears	793	15.8	(Z)	Radishes	150	17.4	16.8
Pineapple	512	53.3	4.6	Sweet potatoes	1,091	5.7	-
Plums and prunes	449	12.4	-	Tomatoes	3,678	11.8	11.0
Strawberries	901	2.6	2.2	Watermelon	3,486	6.1	5.2

- Represents zero.   Z Less than 0.05 percent.   [1] Includes garbanzo beans.

Source: U.S. Dept. of Agriculture, Economic Research Service, unpublished data.

No. 1121. Red Meats—Slaughtering, Supply, and Use: 1980 to 1993

[Quantities in millions of pounds (carcass weight equivalent), except as noted. Carcass weight equivalent is the weight of the animal minus entrails, head, and hide; includes internal organs, fat, and bone. Covers inspected, noninspected, retail, and farm slaughter. See also Historical Statistics, Colonial Times to 1970, series K 583-594]

YEAR AND TYPE OF MEAT	Animals slaughtered (mil. head)	Produc-tion	Imports	Supply, [1] total	Con-sump-tion [2]	Exports	Ending stocks
All red meats:							
1980	139.7	38,978	2,668	42,480	41,170	429	881
1985	131.3	39,408	3,255	43,503	42,310	462	732
1990	126.3	38,787	3,313	42,760	40,806	1,247	707
1991	128.6	39,585	3,241	43,533	41,239	1,474	820
1992	135.3	40,978	3,135	44,933	42,436	1,739	758
1993 [3]	133.5	40,790	3,170	44,718	42,183	1,696	839
Beef:							
1980	34.1	21,643	2,064	24,166	23,561	173	432
1985	36.6	23,728	2,071	26,271	25,523	328	420
1990	33.4	22,743	2,356	25,434	24,031	1,006	397
1991	32.9	22,917	2,406	25,720	24,113	1,188	419
1992	33.1	23,086	2,440	25,945	24,261	1,324	360
1993 [3]	33.5	23,081	2,400	25,841	24,116	1,275	450
Pork:							
1980	97.2	16,617	550	17,521	16,838	252	431
1985	84.9	14,807	1,128	16,282	15,866	128	288
1990	85.4	15,354	898	16,565	16,031	238	296
1991	88.4	15,999	775	17,070	16,399	283	388
1992	95.2	17,234	645	18,267	17,475	407	385
1993 [3]	93.3	17,095	720	18,200	17,413	410	375
Veal:							
1980	2.7	400	21	431	420	2	9
1985	3.5	515	20	549	534	5	11
1990	1.8	327	(NA)	331	325	(NA)	6
1991	1.5	306	(NA)	312	305	(NA)	7
1992	1.4	310	(NA)	317	312	(NA)	5
1993 [3]	1.3	279	(NA)	284	280	(NA)	4
Lamb and mutton:							
1980	5.7	318	33	362	351	2	9
1985	6.3	358	36	401	387	1	13
1990	5.7	363	59	430	419	3	8
1991	5.8	363	60	431	422	3	6
1992	5.6	348	50	404	388	8	8
1993 [3]	5.4	335	50	393	374	9	10

NA Not available.   [1] Total supply equals production plus imports plus ending stocks of previous year.   [2] Includes shipments to territories.   [3] Forecast.

Source: U.S. Dept. of Agriculture, Economic Research Service, Livestock and Meat Statistics, quarterly. Also published in Agricultural Outlook, monthly.

No. 1122. Livestock Inventory and Production: 1980 to 1993

[Production in live weight; includes animals for slaughter market, younger animals shipped to other States for feeding or breeding purposes, farm slaughter and custom slaughter consumed on farms where produced, minus livestock shipped into States for feeding or breeding with an adjustment for changes in inventory. See also Historical Statistics, Colonial Times to 1970, series K 564-569 and 575-582]

TYPE OF LIVESTOCK	Unit	1980	1984	1985	1986	1987	1988	1989	1990	1991	1992	1993
ALL CATTLE [1]												
Inventory: [2] Number on farms	Mil	111.2	113.4	109.6	105.4	102.1	99.6	98.1	98.2	98.9	99.6	100.9
Total value	Bil. dol.	55.8	44.8	44.0	41.2	41.6	52.1	56.9	60.3	64.7	63.0	65.5
Value per head	Dol	502	396	402	391	407	523	580	614	654	629	649
Production: Quantity	Bil. lb	40.3	40.1	40.1	40.6	40.5	40.6	40.2	40.4	41.1	40.9	(NA)
Beef, price per 100 lb	Dol	62.40	57.30	53.70	52.60	61.10	66.60	69.50	74.60	72.70	71.30	(NA)
Calves, price per 100 lb	Dol	76.80	59.90	62.10	61.10	78.50	89.20	90.80	95.60	98.00	89.00	(NA)
Value of production	Bil. dol.	25.5	22.1	21.2	21.0	24.8	27.2	28.0	30.2	30.3	29.1	(NA)
HOGS AND PIGS												
Inventory: [3] Number on farms	Mil	67.3	56.7	54.1	52.3	51.0	54.4	55.5	53.8	54.5	57.7	59.0
Total value	Bil. dol.	3.8	3.3	4.1	3.6	4.7	4.1	4.7	4.3	4.7	4.0	4.3
Value per head	Dol	56.00	58.80	75.00	69.60	91.90	76.00	66.30	79.10	85.40	68.90	71.60
Production: Quantity	Bil. lb	23.4	20.2	20.2	19.5	20.4	21.7	21.9	21.3	22.8	24.3	(NA)
Price per 100 lb	Dol	38.00	47.10	44.00	49.30	51.20	42.30	42.50	53.70	49.10	41.60	(NA)
Value of production	Bil. dol.	8.9	9.5	8.9	9.6	10.4	9.1	9.3	11.4	11.1	10.0	(NA)
SHEEP AND LAMBS												
Inventory: [2] Number on farms	Mil	12.7	11.6	10.7	10.1	10.6	10.9	10.9	11.4	11.2	10.8	10.2
Total value	Mil. dol	993	603	654	684	799	985	895	902	735	658	716
Value per head	Dol	78.20	52.10	61.10	67.40	75.70	90.00	82.40	79.30	65.60	61.20	70.20
Production: Quantity	Mil. lb	746	700	704	726	733	707	776	758	763	711	(NA)
Sheep, price per 100 lb	Dol	21.30	16.40	23.90	25.60	29.50	25.60	24.40	23.20	19.70	25.80	(NA)
Lambs, price per 100 lb	Dol	63.60	60.10	67.70	67.00	77.60	69.10	66.10	55.50	52.20	59.50	(NA)
Value of production	Mil. dol	403	378	434	445	503	420	446	362	342	339	(NA)

NA Not available.   [1] Includes milk cows.   [2] As of Jan. 1.   [3] As of Dec. 1 of preceding year.

Source: U.S. Dept. of Agriculture, National Agricultural Statistics Service, Meat Animals—Production, Disposition, and Income, annual; and annual livestock summaries. Also in Agricultural Statistics, annual.

No. 1123. Cattle and Calves; and Hogs and Pigs—Number, Production, and Value, by State: 1990 to 1993

[See headnote, table 1122]

STATE	NUMBER ON FARMS [1] (1,000)			QUANTITY PRODUCED (mil. lb.)			VALUE OF PRODUCTION (mil. dol.)			COMMERCIAL SLAUGHTER [2] (mil. lb.)		
	1991	1992	1993	1990	1991	1992	1990	1991	1992	1990	1991	1992
CATTLE AND CALVES [3]												
U.S. [4]	98,896	99,559	100,892	40,386	41,090	40,914	30,229	30,332	29,104	37,758	38,029	38,417
CA	4,600	4,500	4,500	1,943	1,978	1,848	1,273	1,272	1,107	1,408	1,338	1,116
CO	2,750	2,900	2,850	1,905	1,944	2,043	1,498	1,468	1,520	2,363	2,634	2,938
IL	2,000	1,980	2,000	786	773	771	617	577	574	(5)	(5)	(5)
IA	4,700	4,400	4,400	1,899	1,975	2,070	1,446	1,416	1,444	2,134	1,952	1,952
KS	5,700	5,650	5,890	3,122	3,144	3,087	2,428	2,370	2,311	7,091	6,937	7,027
MN	2,760	2,800	2,850	1,115	1,155	1,206	798	789	805	1,264	1,344	1,262
MO	4,400	4,500	4,600	1,158	1,163	1,229	969	980	951	351	299	263
MT	2,330	2,500	2,450	974	999	988	719	728	686	30	21	22
NE	6,000	5,800	5,900	3,784	3,741	3,776	2,895	2,782	2,783	6,804	7,424	7,808
OK	5,550	5,400	5,400	1,928	1,904	1,816	1,437	1,490	1,346	62	44	46
SD	3,400	3,550	3,750	1,756	1,696	1,709	1,385	1,336	1,283	702	625	482
TX	13,300	13,600	14,300	5,900	6,591	6,387	4,544	4,964	4,719	6,100	6,158	6,264
WI	4,170	4,000	3,950	1,210	1,216	1,151	879	818	751	1,368	1,347	1,584
HOGS AND PIGS												
U.S. [4]	54,477	57,684	59,016	21,347	22,809	24,278	11,376	11,104	9,991	21,230	22,200	23,952
IL	5,700	5,900	5,900	2,225	2,435	2,493	1,192	1,174	1,028	2,250	2,221	2,239
IN	4,400	4,600	4,550	1,666	1,742	1,817	870	824	718	876	924	1,148
IA	13,800	15,000	15,800	5,394	5,863	6,481	2,913	2,942	2,731	6,571	7,121	7,635
MN	4,500	4,900	4,700	1,714	1,811	1,961	948	915	836	1,382	1,827	2,093
NE	4,300	4,500	4,600	1,624	1,763	1,831	882	863	762	1,299	1,355	1,443
NC	2,800	3,650	4,500	1,190	1,484	1,822	607	693	756	(5)	(5)	(5)

[1] Cattle and calves, as of January 1; hogs and pigs as of December 1 of preceding year. [2] Data for cattle and calves cover cattle only. Includes slaughter in federally inspected and other slaughter plants; excludes animals slaughtered on farms. [3] Includes milk cows. [4] Includes other States not shown separately. [5] Included in U.S. total. Not printed to avoid disclosing individual operation.

Source: U.S. Dept. of Agriculture, National Agricultural Statistics Service, *Meat Animals-Production, Disposition and Income,* annual.

No. 1124. Milk Production and Commercial Use: 1980 to 1993

[In billions of pounds milkfat basis]

YEAR	Production	Farm use	COMMERCIAL			Commercial supply, total	CCC net removals [1]	COMMERCIAL		Milk price per 100 lb. [2] (dol.)
			Farm marketings	Beginning stock	Imports			Ending stock	Disappearance	
1980	128.4	2.3	126.1	5.3	2.1	133.5	9.0	5.6	118.8	13.1
1985	143.0	2.5	140.6	4.8	2.8	148.2	13.4	4.5	130.3	12.8
1990	148.3	2.0	146.3	4.1	2.7	153.1	9.0	5.1	138.9	13.7
1991	148.5	2.0	146.5	5.1	2.6	154.2	10.4	4.5	139.3	12.2
1992	151.7	1.9	149.8	4.5	2.5	156.7	10.1	4.7	142.0	13.1
1993	153.3	1.9	151.4	4.7	2.6	158.7	6.2	4.6	147.9	12.8

[1] Removals from commercial supply by Commodity Credit Corporation. [2] Wholesale price received by farmers for all milk delivered to plants and dealers.

Source: U.S. Dept. of Agriculture, *Agricultural Outlook,* monthly.

No. 1125. Milk Cows—Number, Production, and Value, by State: 1990 to 1992

STATE	NUMBER ON FARMS [1] (1,000)			MILK PRODUCED ON FARMS (mil. lb.)			VALUE OF PRODUCTION [2] (mil. dol.)		
	1990	1991	1992	1990	1991	1992	1990	1991	1992
United States [3]	10,127	9,992	9,839	148,313	148,477	151,747	20,495	18,349	20,105
California	1,135	1,155	1,158	20,947	21,407	22,084	2,561	2,444	2,613
Iowa	305	303	305	4,233	4,151	4,276	563	494	556
Michigan	344	341	339	5,233	5,256	5,397	739	654	721
Minnesota	710	683	660	10,030	9,772	9,854	1,326	1,164	1,266
New York	768	756	749	11,067	11,179	11,582	1,621	1,425	1,557
Ohio	342	337	324	4,668	4,695	4,690	649	596	628
Pennsylvania	683	669	655	9,933	10,106	10,364	1,513	1,362	1,500
Texas	386	380	376	5,539	5,418	5,590	814	688	766
Washington	237	237	249	4,392	4,459	4,836	603	560	648
Wisconsin	1,753	1,714	1,646	24,400	24,065	24,103	3,287	2,891	3,175

[1] Average number during year. Represents cows and heifers that have calved, kept for milk; excluding heifers not yet fresh. [2] Valued at average returns per 100 pounds of milk in combined marketings of milk and cream. Includes value of milk fed to calves. [3] Includes other States not shown separately.

Source: U.S. Dept. of Agriculture, National Agricultural Statistics Service, *Dairy Products,* annual; and *Milk: Production, Disposition, and Income,* annual.

No. 1126. Milk Production and Manufactured Dairy Products: 1980 to 1992

[See also *Historical Statistics, Colonial Times to 1970*, series K 595-601]

ITEM	Unit	1980	1985	1986	1987	1988	1989	1990	1991	1992
Number of farms with milk cows	1,000	334	269	249	228	217	204	194	181	172
Cows and heifers that have calved, kept for milk	Mil. head ..	10.8	11.0	10.8	10.3	10.3	10.1	10.1	10.0	9.8
Milk produced on farms	Bil. lb	128	143	143	143	145	144	148	148	152
Production per cow	1,000 lb...	11.9	13.0	13.3	13.8	14.1	14.2	14.6	14.9	15.4
Whole milk sold from farms [1]	Bil. lb	126	141	141	140	143	142	146	146	150
Sales to plants and dealers	Bil. lb	125	139	140	139	142	141	145	145	149
Value of milk produced	Bil. dol...	16.9	18.4	18.0	18.0	17.9	19.7	20.5	18.3	20.1
Gross farm income, dairy products	Bil. dol...	16.7	18.1	17.8	17.8	17.7	19.5	20.3	18.2	19.9
Cash receipts from marketing of milk and cream [1]	Bil. dol...	16.6	18.1	17.7	17.7	17.6	19.4	20.2	18.1	19.8
Sales to plants and dealers	Bil. dol...	16.3	17.8	17.5	17.5	17.4	19.1	20.0	17.8	19.6
Number of dairy manufacturing plants	Number...	2,257	2,061	1,998	1,933	1,846	1,754	1,723	1,680	1,603
Manufactured dairy products:										
Butter (incl. whey butter)	Mil. lb	1,145	1,248	1,202	1,104	1,208	1,295	1,302	1,336	1,365
Cheese, total [2]	Mil. lb	3,984	5,081	5,209	5,344	5,572	5,615	6,059	6,055	6,488
American (excl. full-skim American)	Mil. lb	2,376	2,855	2,798	2,717	2,757	2,674	2,894	2,769	2,937
Cream and Neufchatel	Mil. lb	229	294	322	342	376	401	431	447	517
All Italian varieties	Mil. lb	983	1,491	1,633	1,800	1,937	2,043	2,207	2,329	2,509
Cottage cheese: Creamed [3]	Mil. lb	825	716	705	675	647	572	531	498	457
Curd, pot, and bakers	Mil. lb	667	599	600	574	557	527	493	491	502
Condensed bulk milk	Mil. lb	952	1,232	1,362	1,383	1,364	1,417	1,426	1,530	1,624
Evaporated and condensed canned milk	Mil. lb	740	656	602	597	612	545	615	543	853
Nonfat dry milk [4]	Mil. lb	1,168	1,398	1,294	1,077	998	893	902	885	882
Dry whey [5]	Mil. lb	690	987	1,031	1,097	1,137	1,069	1,143	1,167	1,237
Ice cream of all kinds	Mil. gal...	830	901	924	928	882	831	824	863	875
Ice milk	Mil. gal...	293	301	315	328	355	377	352	345	329

[1] Comprises sales to plants and dealers, and retail sales by farmers direct to consumers. [2] Includes varieties not shown separately. [3] Includes partially creamed (low fat). [4] Includes dry skim milk for animal feed. [5] Includes animal but excludes modified whey production.

Source: U.S. Dept. of Agriculture, National Agricultural Statistics Service, *Dairy Products*, annual; and *Milk: Production, Disposition, and Income*, annual.

No. 1127. Broiler, Turkey, and Egg Production: 1980 to 1992

[For year ending November 30. See also *Historical Statistics, Colonial Times to 1970*, series K 614-623]

ITEM	Unit	1980	1983	1984	1985	1986	1987	1988	1989	1990	1991	1992
Broilers:[1] Number	Million ..	3,963	4,184	4,283	4,470	4,649	5,004	5,238	5,517	5,864	6,137	6,389
Weight	Bil. lb. ..	15.5	17.0	17.9	18.9	19.7	21.5	22.5	24.0	25.6	27.2	28.8
Price per lb	Cents ..	27.7	28.6	33.7	30.1	34.5	28.7	33.1	36.6	32.6	30.8	31.8
Production value	Mil. dol. .	4,303	4,873	6,020	5,668	6,784	6,177	7,435	8,778	8,365	8,383	9,156
Turkeys: Number	Million ..	165	171	171	185	207	240	242	261	282	285	289
Weight	Bil. lb. ..	3.1	3.3	3.4	3.7	4.1	4.9	5.1	5.5	6.0	6.1	6.3
Price per lb	Cents ..	41.3	38.0	48.9	49.1	47.1	34.8	38.6	40.9	39.4	38.0	38.0
Gross income	Mil. dol. .	1,272	1,269	1,655	1,819	1,948	1,703	1,951	2,234	2,379	2,345	2,387
Eggs: Number	Billion ..	69.7	68.2	68.2	68.4	69.1	70.4	69.7	67.2	67.9	69.0	71.0
Price per dozen	Cents ..	56.3	61.1	72.3	57.2	61.5	54.7	52.8	68.9	70.9	67.8	57.7
Production value	Mil. dol. .	3,268	3,469	4,110	3,262	3,543	3,209	3,067	3,861	4,011	3,909	3,389

[1] Young chickens of the heavy breeds and other meat-type birds, to be marketed at 2-5 lbs. live weight and from which no pullets are kept for egg production.

Source: U.S. Dept. of Agriculture, National Agricultural Statistics Service, *Poultry—Production and Value*, annual; *Turkeys*, annual; and *Layers and Egg Production*, annual.

No. 1128. Poultry—Production, by State: 1990 to 1992

[In millions of pounds, liveweight production. See *Historical Statistics, Colonial Times to 1970*, series K 614 and 621 for U.S. totals]

STATE	BROILERS			TURKEYS			STATE	BROILERS			TURKEYS		
	1990	1991	1992	1990	1991	1992		1990	1991	1992	1990	1991	1992
U.S. [1] ..	25,631	27,203	28,772	6,030	6,111	6,333	MS.	1,694	1,963	2,145	(NA)	(NA)	(NA)
AL	3,642	3,764	3,855	(NA)	(NA)	(NA)	MO	362	479	542	360	452	431
AR	3,995	4,215	4,499	453	490	518	NC	2,593	2,679	2,852	1,160	1,166	1,321
CA	1,109	1,153	1,188	712	653	498	OH	96	129	117	135	126	145
DE	1,159	1,206	1,256	(NA)	(NA)	(NA)	OK	540	592	600	(NA)	(NA)	(NA)
FL	490	506	541	(NA)	(NA)	(NA)	PA	520	544	572	169	168	178
GA	3,760	3,816	4,026	61	56	61	SC	343	395	447	168	178	196
IN	(NA)	(NA)	(NA)	288	320	350	TN	436	476	509	(NA)	(NA)	(NA)
IA	63	92	92	228	226	232	TX	1,454	1,497	1,582	(NA)	(NA)	(NA)
KY	6	89	173	(NA)	(NA)	(NA)	VA	882	984	1,048	316	324	363
MD.	1,141	1,183	1,262	2	3	3	WA	157	167	169	(NA)	(NA)	(NA)
MN.	198	225	231	852	805	809	WV	156	177	177	72	77	77

NA Not available. [1] Includes other States not shown separately.

Source: U.S. Dept. of Agriculture, National Agricultural Statistics Service, *Poultry—Production and Value*, annual; and *Turkeys*, annual.

Figure 24.1
**Employment in Timber-Based
Industries: 1970 to 1993**

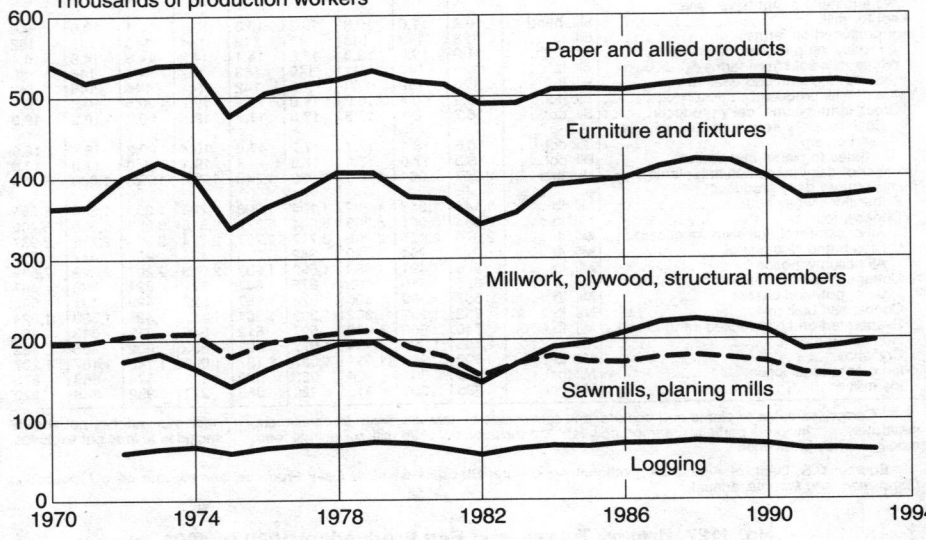

Thousands of production workers

Source: Chart prepared by U.S. Bureau of the Census. For data, see tables 656 and 1133.

Figure 24.2
**Fishery Products—
Domestic Catch and Imports: 1970 to 1992**

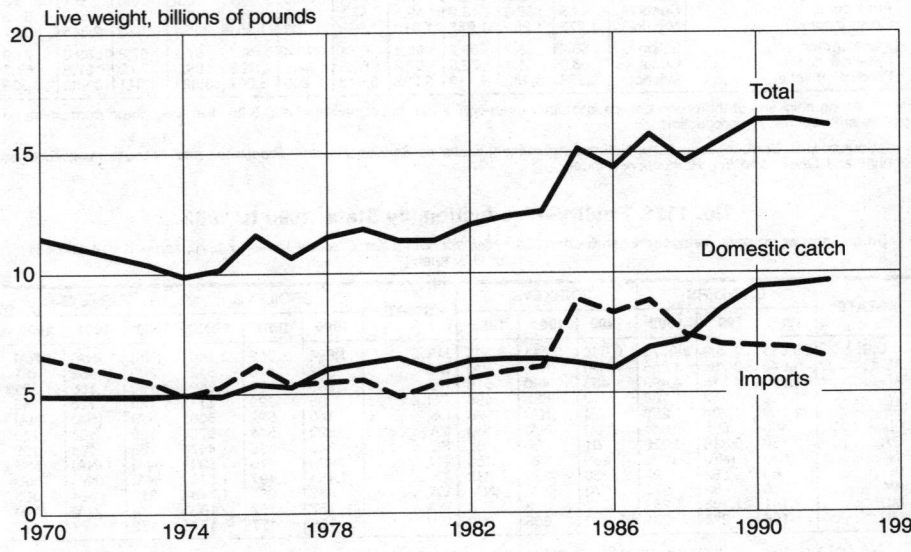

Live weight, billions of pounds

Source: Chart prepared by U.S. Bureau of the Census. For data, see table 1147.

Natural Resources

This section presents data on the area, ownership, production, trade, reserves and disposition of natural resources. Natural resources is defined here as including forestry, fisheries, and mining and mineral products.

Forestry.—Presents data on the area, ownership, and timber resource of commercial timberland; forestry statistics covering the National Forests and Forest Service cooperative programs; product data for lumber, pulpwood, woodpulp, paper and paperboard, and similar data.

The principal sources of data relating to forests and forest products are: An Analysis of the Timber Situation in the United States, 1989—2040, 1990; Forest Resources of the United States, 1992, 1993; U.S. Timber Production, Trade, Consumption, and Price Statistics; Land Areas of the National Forest System, issued annually by the Forest Service of the Department of Agriculture; Agricultural Statistics issued by the Department of Agriculture; and reports of the census of manufactures (taken every 5 years) and the annual Current Industrial Reports, issued by the Bureau of the Census. Additional information is published in the monthly Survey of Current Business of the Bureau of Economic Analysis; and the annual Wood Pulp and Fiber Statistics and The Statistics of Paper, Paperboard, and Wood Pulp of the American Forest and Paper Association, Washington, DC.

The Bureau of the Census also collects data on foreign trade of forest products. The Bureau of Labor Statistics publishes monthly and annual statistics of producer prices for lumber.

The completeness and reliability of statistics on forests and forest products vary considerably. The data for forest land area and stand volumes are much more reliable for areas which have been recently surveyed than for those for which only estimates are available. In general, more data are available for lumber and other manufactured products such as particle board and softwood panels, etc., than for the primary forest products such as poles and piling and fuelwood.

In Brief

	1993
Paper and board production	85.9 mil. sh. tns.
Recovered paper consumption	28.9 mil. sh. tns.
Petroleum balance, 1992:	
Products supplied	6.2 billion barrels
Net imports	2.2 billion barrels
Stocks	1.6 billion barrels

Fisheries.—The principal source of data relating to fisheries is Fisheries of the United States, issued annually by the National Marine Fisheries Service (NMFS), National Oceanic and Atmospheric Administration (NOAA).

The NMFS collects and disseminates data on commercial landings of fish and shellfish. Annual reports include quantity and value of commercial landings of fish and shellfish (by species, region, State, and type of fishing gear), disposition of landings, number of fishermen, and number and kinds of fishing vessels and fishing gear. Reports for the fish-processing industry include annual output of canned, packaged, and industrial products and, for the wholesaling and fish processing establishments, annual and seasonal employment, and number of firms, by product and State. The Magnuson Fishery Conservation and Management Act of 1976 (Magnuson Act), Public Law 94-265 as amended, provides for the conservation and management of all fishery resources within the U.S. Exclusive Economic Zone (EEZ), except highly migratory species of tuna, and gives the Federal Government exclusive authority over domestic and foreign fisheries within 200 nautical miles of U.S. shores and over certain living marine resources beyond the EEZ. Within the EEZ, the total allowable level of foreign fishing, if any, is that portion of the "optimum yield" not harvested by U.S. vessels. Adjustments in the "optimum yield" level may occur periodically. For details, see Fisheries of the United States, 1992.

The NMFS collects and disseminates data on catches by foreign fishing vessels in the EEZ.

Mining and mineral products.—Presents data relating to mineral industries and their products, general summary measures of production and employment, and more detailed data on production, prices, imports and exports, consumption, and distribution for specific industries and products. Data on mining and mineral products may also be found in sections 26 and 30 of this Abstract; data on mining employment may be found in section 13.

Mining comprises the extraction of minerals occurring naturally (coal, ores, crude petroleum, natural gas) and quarrying, well operation, milling, refining and processing and other preparation customarily done at the mine or well site or as a part of extraction activity. (Mineral preparation plants are usually operated together with mines or quarries.) Exploration for minerals is included as is the development of mineral properties.

The principal governmental sources of these data are the Minerals Yearbook, published by the Bureau of Mines, Department of the Interior, and various monthly and annual publications of the Energy Information Administration, Department of Energy. See text, section 19 for list of Department of Energy publications. In addition, the Bureau of the Census conducts a census of mineral industries every 5 years. Non-government sources include the Annual Statistical Report of the American Iron and Steel Institute, Washington, DC; Metals Week and the monthly Engineering and Mining Journal, issued by the McGraw-Hill Publishing Co., New York, NY; The Iron Age, issued weekly by the Chilton Co., Philadelphia, PA; and the Joint Association Survey of the U.S. Oil and Gas Industry, conducted jointly by the American Petroleum Institute, Independent Petroleum Association of America, and Mid-Continent Oil and Gas Association.

Mineral statistics, with principal emphasis on commodity detail, have been collected by the Geological Survey or by the Bureau of Mines since 1880. Current data in Bureau of Mines publications include quantity and value of nonfuel minerals produced, sold or used by producers, or shipped; quantity of minerals stocked; crude materials treated and prepared minerals recovered; and consumption of mineral raw materials. The U.S. Mine Safety and Health Administration also collects and publishes data on workhours, employment, accidents, and injuries in the mineral industries, except petroleum and natural gas. In October 1977, mineral fuel data collection activities of the Bureau of Mines were transferred to the Energy Information Administration.

Censuses of mineral industries have been conducted by the Bureau of the Census at various intervals since 1840. Beginning with the 1967 census, legislation provides for a census to be conducted every 5th year for years ending in "2" and "7." The censuses provide, for the various types of mineral establishments, information on operating costs, capital expenditures, labor, equipment, and energy requirements in relation to their value of shipments and other receipts. Commodity statistics on many manufactured mineral products are also collected by the Bureau at monthly, quarterly, or annual intervals and issued in its Current Industrial Reports series.

In general, figures shown in the individual commodity tables include data for outlying areas and may therefore not agree with summary table 1166. Except for crude petroleum and refined products, the export and import figures include foreign trade passing through the customs districts of United States and Puerto Rico, but exclude shipments between U.S. territories and the customs districts.

Historical statistics.—Tabular headnotes provide cross-references, where applicable, to *Historical Statistics of the United States, Colonial Times to 1970.* See Appendix IV.

No. 1129. National Forest System—Summary: 1970 to 1992

[For fiscal years ending in year shown; see text, section 9. Includes Alaska and Puerto Rico, except as noted. See *Historical Statistics, Colonial Times to 1970*, series J 33-34, for similar grazing data, and L 15-31]

ITEM	Unit	1970	1980	1985	1987	1988	1989	1990	1991	1992
Timber cut, total value	Mil. dol	309	737	725	1,019	1,243	1,313	1,191	1,012	938
Commercial and cost sales: [1]										
Volume	Mil. bd.	11,527	9,178	10,941	12,712	12,649	11,951	10,500	8,475	7,290
Value	Mil. dol	308	730	721	1,016	1,240	1,310	1,188	1,009	935
Free use:										
Volume	Mil. bd.	179	2,070	399	209	223	214	151	121	80
Value [2]	Mil. dol	0.3	5.7	2.2	1.1	1.2	1.2	1.0	1.0	0.8
Misc. forest products:										
Value	Mil. dol	0.7	1.1	1.7	1.9	2.0	2.2	2.6	2.7	2.7
Livestock grazing: [3]										
Cattle and horses [4]	1,000 .	1,607	1,521	1,565	1,410	1,313	1,526	1,236	1,265	(NA)
Sheep and goats	1,000 .	2,105	1,328	1,183	1,134	1,067	972	958	1,029	(NA)
Roads and trails:										
Road construction [5]	Miles. .	942	925	1,903	2,394	1,352	866	857	910	853
Trail construction [5] [6]	Miles. .	278	2,419	987	1,046	1,834	1,944	1,635	1,921	1,976
Receipts, total	Mil. dol	300	703	636	898	980	1,051	971	772	614
Timber use	Mil. dol	284	625	515	808	888	910	849	667	520
Grazing use	Mil. dol	4	16	9	8	9	11	10	11	11
Special land use, etc [7]	Mil. dol	11	62	112	82	83	130	112	93	84
Payments to local govt. [7]	Mil. dol	73	240	229	295	325	368	368	335	(NA)
25-percent fund [8]	Mil. dol	72	234	212	285	317	354	358	327	(NA)
Other [9]	Mil. dol	1	7	17	10	8	15	10	8	(NA)
Allotments to Forest Service [10] . . .	Mil. dol	30	73	60	88	104	111	106	88	(NA)
Roads and trails.	Mil. dol	29	65	55	84	92	96	91	73	(NA)
Other.	Mil. dol	1	8	5	4	12	15	14	16	(NA)

NA Not available. [1] Includes land exchanges. [2] Includes some free use timber not reducible to board feet. [3] For 1970, data for livestock permitted to graze; thereafter for number actually grazed. Calendar-year data, prior to 1980. Excludes Puerto Rico. [4] Excludes animals under 6 months of age. 1970 includes swine. Includes burros beginning in 1980. [5] Includes reconstruction. [6] Beginning 1980, includes work accomplished by Human Resource Programs and volunteers. [7] Payments made in following year. [8] Includes Tongass Alaska suspense account. [9] Includes Arizona and New Mexico School Fund (through 1980), State of Minnesota, and receipts paid to counties under Bankhead-Jones Farm Tenant Act. [10] For use in following year.

Source: U.S. Forest Service. In *Agricultural Statistics*, annual; and unpublished data.

No. 1130. Forest and Timberland Area, Sawtimber and Stock: 1970 to 1992

[As of **Jan. 1.** See table 26 for composition of regions]

YEAR AND REGION	Total forest land (mil. acres)	TIMBERLAND, OWNERSHIP [1]				SAWTIMBER, NET VOLUME [3]		GROWING STOCK, NET VOLUME [4]	
		All ownerships (mil. acres)	Federally owned or managed [2] (mil. acres)	State, county, and municipal (mil. acres)	Private (mil. acres)	Total (bil. bd. ft.)	Softwood (bil. bd. ft.)	Total (bil. cu. ft.)	Softwood (bil. cu. ft.)
United States, 1970 .	754	504	116	29	360	2,587	2,035	694	458
North	(NA)	154	11	18	126	295	81	146	39
South.	(NA)	203	15	3	185	569	302	191	87
Rocky Mountains	(NA)	65	42	2	20	398	384	101	95
Pacific Coast	(NA)	82	47	5	29	1,325	1,268	257	238
United States, 1987 .	731	485	97	34	354	2,853	2,040	766	453
North	165	154	11	19	124	459	126	190	48
South.	203	197	16	4	177	781	388	245	106
Rocky Mountains	142	61	39	3	20	411	394	108	100
Pacific Coast	220	72	31	8	32	1,202	1,132	223	199
United States, 1992 .	737	490	97	35	358	2,992	2,047	786	450
North	168	158	11	19	127	540	137	207	51
South.	212	199	16	4	179	842	389	251	103
Rocky Mountains	140	63	40	3	20	415	397	110	101
Pacific Coast	217	70	30	8	32	1,196	1,124	218	195

NA Not available. [1] Timberland is forest land that is producing or is capable of crops of industrial wood and not withdrawn from timber utilization by statute or administrative regulation. Areas qualifying as timberland have the capability of producing in excess of 20 cubic feet per acre per year of industrial wood in natural stands. Currently inaccessible and inoperable areas are included. [2] Includes Indian lands. [3] Sawtimber is timber suitable for sawing into lumber. Live trees of commercial species containing at least one 12-foot sawlog or two noncontiguous 8-foot logs, and meeting regional specifications for freedom from defect. Softwood trees must be at least 9.0-inches diameter, and hardwood trees must be at least 11.0-inches diameter at 4 1/2 feet above ground. International 1/4-inch rule. [4] Live trees of commercial species meeting specified standards of quality or vigor. Cull trees are excluded. Includes only trees 5.0-inches diameter or larger at 4 1/2 feet above ground.

Source: U.S. Forest Service, *Forest Resources of the United States, 1992.*

Natural Resources

No. 1131. National Forest System Land—States and Other Areas: 1990 and 1991

[In thousands of acres. As of Sept. 30. See also *Historical Statistics, Colonial Times to 1970*, series L 10-11]

STATE	GROSS AREA WITHIN UNIT BOUNDARIES [1]		NATIONAL FOREST SYSTEM LAND [2]		OTHER LANDS WITHIN UNIT BOUNDARIES	
	1990	1991	1990	1991	1990	1991
United States...........	231,443	231,502	191,324	191,453	40,119	40,049
Alabama................	1,280	1,288	658	659	622	629
Alaska.................	24,345	24,345	22,220	22,193	2,126	2,152
Arizona................	11,880	11,887	11,239	11,247	642	641
Arkansas	3,490	3,490	2,509	2,529	981	961
California	24,401	24,401	20,619	20,616	3,782	3,785
Colorado...............	16,039	16,037	14,462	14,467	1,577	1,570
Connecticut............	-	(Z)	-	(Z)	-	-
Delaware	-	-	-	-	-	-
Florida	1,246	1,254	1,128	1,135	118	119
Georgia	1,846	1,846	859	860	987	986
Hawaii	-	(Z)	-	(Z)	-	-
Idaho.................	21,674	21,674	20,438	20,441	1,236	1,233
Illinois	840	840	266	268	573	572
Indiana................	644	644	188	189	456	455
Iowa	-	-	-	-	-	-
Kansas................	116	116	108	108	8	8
Kentucky	2,102	2,102	670	673	1,431	1,428
Louisiana	1,022	1,022	601	601	422	421
Maine................	93	93	53	53	40	40
Maryland	-	-	-	-	-	-
Massachusetts..........	-	-	-	-	-	-
Michigan...............	4,885	4,895	2,816	2,849	2,069	2,046
Minnesota..............	5,467	5,467	2,810	2,815	2,657	2,652
Mississippi	2,310	2,310	1,150	1,153	1,160	1,157
Missouri	3,082	3,082	1,475	1,478	1,606	1,603
Montana...............	19,101	19,102	16,806	16,806	2,295	2,296
Nebraska	442	442	352	352	90	90
Nevada	6,275	6,275	5,797	5,801	478	474
New Hampshire..........	825	825	720	721	105	104
New Jersey.............	-	-	-	-	-	-
New Mexico	10,367	10,367	9,321	9,321	1,046	1,045
New York..............	13	13	13	13	-	-
North Carolina..........	3,165	3,165	1,232	1,234	1,934	1,932
North Dakota...........	1,106	1,106	1,106	1,106	-	(Z)
Ohio	833	833	203	212	630	622
Oklahoma..............	461	465	297	301	165	164
Oregon................	17,502	17,504	15,651	15,655	1,851	1,849
Pennsylvania...........	744	744	513	513	231	231
Rhode Island...........	-	-	-	-	-	-
South Carolina..........	1,376	1,376	607	609	768	767
South Dakota	2,344	2,352	1,996	2,013	349	339
Tennessee	1,212	1,212	628	628	585	585
Texas.................	1,994	1,994	753	755	1,241	1,240
Utah	9,186	9,186	8,099	8,099	1,087	1,087
Vermont	815	816	340	345	475	471
Virginia...............	3,223	3,223	1,645	1,648	1,578	1,575
Washington.............	10,050	10,061	9,151	9,160	899	901
West Virginia...........	1,863	1,863	1,025	1,025	838	838
Wisconsin.............	2,023	2,023	1,517	1,518	506	505
Wyoming	9,704	9,704	9,255	9,255	449	449

- Represents zero.   Z Less than half the unit of measure.   [1] Comprises all publicly and privately owned land within authorized boundaries of national forests, purchase units, national grasslands, Land utilization projects, research and experimental areas, and other areas.   [2] Federally owned land within the "gross area within unit boundaries."

Source: U.S. Forest Service, *Land Areas of the National Forest System*, annual.

No. 1132. Timber-Based Industries—Summary of Manufactures: 1990 and 1991

[Data based on *1987 Standard Industrial Classification Manual*, published by the Office of Management and Budget, see text, section 26. N.e.c. = Not elsewhere classified]

INDUSTRY	SIC [1] code	1990			1991		
		All employees		Value of ship- ments (bil. dol.)	All employees		Value of ship- ments (bil. dol.)
		Num- ber (1,000)	Payroll (mil. dol.)		Num- ber (1,000)	Payroll (mil. dol.)	
Logging and sawmills	241/242	254.2	5,076	32.2	207.6	4,307	28.9
Logging	2411	83.4	1,647	12.2	78.1	1,561	11.4
Sawmills and planing mills, general	2421	138.9	2,913	17.9	129.5	2,747	17.5
Hardwood dimension and flooring mills	2426	29.3	475	1.8	26.1	462	1.7
Special product sawmills, n.e.c.	2429	2.5	41	0.2	2.0	36	0.2
Millwork and veneer [2]	243	229.4	4,823	23.2	209.9	4,487	21.4
Millwork	2431	90.5	1,961	9.5	84.9	1,836	9.0
Wood kitchen cabinets	2434	62.8	1,217	4.6	57.1	1,139	4.2
Hardwood veneer and plywood	2435	18.7	335	2.1	17.3	320	1.9
Softwood veneer and plywood	2436	35.6	881	5.0	31.7	810	4.6
Structural wood members, n.e.c.	2439	21.8	429	2.0	18.9	382	1.8
Wood containers	244	41.5	636	2.9	39.8	634	2.9
Nailed and lock corner wood boxes	2441	6.0	98	0.4	6.2	100	0.4
Wood pallets and skids	2448	28.3	417	1.9	27.1	413	2.0
Wood containers, n.e.c	2449	7.2	122	0.5	6.5	120	0.4
Wood buildings, mobile homes	245	61.4	1,217	6.5	54.1	1,106	6.0
Mobile homes	2451	38.8	769	4.2	35.1	714	3.9
Prefabricated wood buildings and components	2452	22.6	448	2.3	19.0	392	2.0
Miscellaneous wood products	249	96.4	1,745	9.6	90.9	1,706	9.5
Wood preserving	2491	13.0	246	2.6	11.7	233	2.6
Reconstituted wood products	2493	22.3	554	3.0	21.0	537	3.0
Wood products, n.e.c	2499	61.1	945	3.9	58.1	936	3.8
Pulp mills	261	16.1	668	6.2	16.8	697	5.3
Paper mills	262	130.1	5,062	35.3	130.3	5,224	33.3
Paperboard mills	263	53.1	2,049	15.9	50.6	2,027	15.0
Paperboard containers and boxes	265	200.3	5,245	30.5	198.6	5,392	30.6
Setup paperboard boxes	2652	8.8	146	0.6	8.7	150	0.6
Corrugated and solid fiber boxes	2653	110.1	2,984	18.6	108.7	3,047	18.0
Fiber cans, tubes, drums, & similar prods	2655	13.3	341	1.9	12.9	341	1.9
Sanitary food containers, except folding	2656	17.5	392	2.5	17.6	411	2.7
Folding paperboard boxes, incl. sanitary	2657	50.7	1,382	7.0	50.7	1,443	7.4
Converted paper and paperboard products [3]	267	228.5	5,923	43.5	224.3	6,043	44.6
Packaging paper & plastics film, coated & laminated	2671	16.4	489	3.0	15.4	492	3.1
Coated and laminated paper, n.e.c	2672	35.0	985	7.1	34.2	992	7.4
Plastics, foil, and coated paper bags	2673	37.4	870	5.5	35.4	875	5.1
Uncoated paper and multiwall bags	2674	16.9	374	2.8	17.9	398	2.7
Die-cut paper and paperboard and cardboard	2675	16.8	395	2.1	17.0	408	2.3
Sanitary paper products	2676	39.0	1,299	14.7	38.8	1,343	15.6
Envelopes	2677	26.1	648	2.8	24.5	616	2.7
Stationery, tablets, and related products	2678	10.1	203	1.3	10.1	209	1.4
Converted paper and paperboard products, n.e.c	2679	30.7	659	4.1	30.9	711	4.3

[1] Standard Industrial Classification code; see text, section 13. [2] Includes plywood and structural members. [3] Except containers and boxes.

Source: U.S. Bureau of the Census, *Census of Manufactures, 1987 Final Industry Series*, MC87-I-24A-D and MC87-I-26A-C, and *Annual Survey of Manufactures*.

No. 1133. Timber-Based Industries—Employment and Average Hourly Earnings: 1980 to 1992

[Data for production workers]

SIC [1] code	ITEM	EMPLOYEES (1,000)						EARNINGS (dollars)					
		1980	1985	1989	1990	1991	1992	1980	1985	1989	1990	1991	1992
24	Lumber and wood products [2]..	587	593	628	605	556	563	6.57	8.25	8.84	9.08	9.24	9.43
241	Logging...............	71	67	72	70	64	76	8.64	10.92	11.13	11.22	11.08	11.24
242	Sawmills and planing mills ..	190	172	177	173	160	182	6.70	8.52	9.03	9.22	9.37	9.60
243	Millwork, plywood, and structural members	170	195	220	211	189	245	6.44	8.09	8.73	9.04	9.27	9.47
26	Paper and allied products	519	509	522	524	518	688	7.84	10.83	11.96	12.31	12.73	13.09
25	Furniture and fixtures	376	394	419	401	371	465	5.49	7.17	8.25	8.52	8.76	9.00

[1] 1987 Standard Industrial Classification; see text, section 27.   [2] Includes other industries, not shown separately.

Source: U.S. Bureau of Labor Statistics, Bulletin 2370 Supplement to Employment and Earnings, July 1991, and *Employment and Earnings*, monthly.

No. 1134. Timber Products—Production, Foreign Trade, and Consumption, by Type of Product: 1970 to 1988

[In millions of cubic feet, roundwood equivalent. See also *Historical Statistics, Colonial Times to 1970*, series L 72-86]

ITEM	1970	1975	1980	1982	1983	1984	1985	1986	1987	1988, prel.
Industrial roundwood:										
Domestic production [1]	11,105	10,575	12,120	10,910	12,065	12,725	12,515	13,845	14,670	14,985
Softwoods	8,635	8,380	9,290	8,450	9,285	9,790	9,690	10,595	11,390	11,430
Hardwoods	2,470	2,195	2,825	2,465	2,780	2,935	2,825	3,250	3,280	3,555
Imports	2,430	2,215	3,250	3,015	3,710	4,165	4,340	4,375	4,575	4,445
Exports	1,540	1,685	2,350	1,995	2,110	2,060	2,070	2,300	2,650	3,200
Consumption [2]	11,995	11,105	13,020	11,930	13,665	14,830	14,785	15,920	16,595	16,230
Softwoods	9,425	8,875	10,345	9,575	10,975	11,965	11,960	12,735	13,430	12,970
Hardwoods	2,565	2,230	2,675	2,355	2,690	2,865	2,825	3,180	3,165	3,260
Lumber:										
Domestic production	5,215	4,890	5,300	4,635	5,370	5,770	5,665	6,545	6,990	6,920
Imports	955	930	1,540	1,460	1,915	2,130	2,345	2,285	2,380	2,225
Exports	195	255	395	320	360	340	305	385	510	720
Consumption	5,970	5,565	6,450	5,780	6,925	7,560	7,700	8,445	8,860	8,425
Plywood and veneer:										
Domestic production	1,020	1,165	1,175	1,135	1,365	1,400	1,420	1,505	1,650	1,630
Imports	170	170	120	115	160	145	165	185	190	165
Exports	15	70	45	50	65	45	40	65	80	100
Consumption	1,170	1,265	1,250	1,200	1,460	1,500	1,550	1,625	1,760	1,695
Pulp products:										
Domestic production	3,835	3,485	4,390	3,980	4,165	4,355	4,165	4,545	4,670	4,885
Imports	1,280	1,105	1,565	1,415	1,605	1,860	1,810	1,895	1,985	2,045
Exports	720	715	1,070	900	965	930	920	1,080	1,195	1,345
Consumption	4,400	3,875	4,885	4,495	4,805	5,290	5,055	5,360	5,465	5,585
Logs:										
Imports	25	15	25	20	30	30	20	15	15	15
Exports	465	455	560	550	565	600	655	620	705	825
Pulpwood chips, exports......	145	195	275	175	155	145	145	150	160	215
Other [3]	425	385	415	435	445	455	465	475	495	510
Fuelwood consumption	540	570	3,105	3,355	3,235	3,620	3,450	3,115	3,150	3,360

[1] Includes log exports.   [2] Includes log imports.   [3] Includes cooperage logs, poles and piling, fence posts, hewn ties, round mine timbers, box bolts, etc.

No. 1135. Timber Products—Per Capita Consumption: 1970 to 1988

[Based on total population estimated as of **July 1**. See also *Historical Statistics, Colonial Times to 1970*, series L 87-97]

PRODUCT	Unit	1970	1975	1980	1982	1983	1984	1985	1986	1987	1988, prel.
All products	Cu. ft	61.1	54.0	70.8	65.7	72.0	77.9	76.2	78.8	81.0	79.5
Industrial roundwood	Cu. ft.	58.5	51.4	57.2	51.3	58.2	62.6	61.8	65.9	68.0	65.9
Lumber	Cu. ft.	29.1	25.8	28.3	24.9	29.5	31.9	32.2	35.0	36.3	34.2
Plywood and veneer.....	Cu. ft.	5.7	5.9	5.5	5.2	6.2	6.3	6.5	6.7	7.2	6.9
Pulp products	Cu. ft.	21.4	17.9	21.4	19.3	20.5	22.3	21.1	22.2	22.4	22.7
Other products	Cu. ft.	2.1	1.8	1.8	1.9	1.9	1.9	1.9	2.0	2.0	2.1
Fuelwood	Cu. ft.	2.6	2.6	13.6	14.4	14.4	15.3	14.4	12.9	12.9	13.6
Lumber	Bd. ft.	193.0	171.0	188.0	161.0	190.0	205.0	207.0	224.0	233.0	221.0
Plywood and veneer	Bd. ft.	34.0	32.0	30.0	28.0	34.0	34.0	35.0	37.0	39.0	37.0
Pulp products.........	Cords (128 cu. ft.)....	0.3	0.2	0.3	0.2	0.3	0.3	0.3	0.3	0.3	0.3

Source of tables 1134 and 1135: U.S. Forest Service, *U.S. Timber Production, Trade, Consumption, and Price Statistics, 1960-88*, annual.

No. 1136. Lumber Consumption, by Species Group and End Use: 1970 to 1991

[In million board feet, except per capita in board feet. Per capita consumption based on estimated resident population as of July 1]

ITEM	1970	1976	1986	1991	END-USE	1970	1976	1986	1991
Total	39.9	44.7	57.0	54.8	New housing	13.3	17.0	19.3	15.0
Per capita..........	194	205	237	217	Residential upkeep and improvements	4.7	5.7	10.1	11.6
Species group:					New nonresidential construction [1]	4.7	4.5	5.3	5.4
Softwoods........	32.0	36.6	48.0	44.0	Manufacturing........	4.7	4.9	4.8	5.6
Hardwoods	7.9	8.0	9.0	10.8	Shipping	5.7	5.9	6.8	8.2
					Other [2]	6.8	6.7	10.9	8.8

[1] In addition to new construction, includes railroad ties laid as replacements in existing track and lumber used by railroads for railcar repair. [2] Includes upkeep and improvement of nonresidential buildings and structures; made-at-home projects, such as furniture, boats, and picnic tables; made-on-the-job items such as advertising and display structures; and miscellaneous products and uses.

Source: U.S. Forest Service. *The 1993 RPA Timber Assessment Update*, forthcoming.

No. 1137. Selected Timber Products—Producer Price Indexes: 1980 to 1992

[See also *Historical Statistics, Colonial Times to 1970*, series L 206-210]

PRODUCT	Unit	1980	1985	1989	1990	1991	1992
Lumber and wood products, except furniture. . .	Dec. 1984=100 .	(NA)	100.3	115.3	117.0	119.4	129.6
Logging camps and logging contractors	Dec. 1981=100 .	(NA)	94.8	128.0	135.6	135.0	151.3
Sawmills and planing mills	Dec. 1984=100 .	(NA)	99.7	114.6	113.7	115.3	131.1
Millwork, veneer, and plywood [1]	Dec. 1984=100 .	(NA)	99.9	114.1	115.4	118.3	128.3
Softwood plywood	Dec. 1980=100 .	91.4	90.0	104.8	102.5	103.5	124.2
Wood containers	June 1985=100 .	(NA)	(NA)	109.7	113.9	115.8	123.4
Wood buildings and mobile homes	Dec. 1984=100 .	(NA)	100.6	112.1	115.5	118.9	121.4
Particleboard........................	Dec. 1982=100 .	92.1	110.0	127.8	117.1	117.0	121.0
Paper and allied products	Dec. 1984=100 .	(NA)	98.8	120.8	121.9	121.1	121.2
Pulp mills........................	Dec. 1982=100 .	105.5	100.9	161.3	153.8	121.8	119.3
Paper mill products; except building paper...	June 1981=100 .	93.5	109.5	134.6	134.0	131.0	126.6
Paperboard mills...................	Dec. 1982=100 .	97.3	112.0	149.9	146.0	140.7	142.8
Converted paper and paperboard products [2] .	June 1985=100 .	(NA)	(NA)	110.5	111.3	112.9	114.1
Paperboard containers and boxes	Dec. 1984=100 .	(NA)	98.4	117.2	117.7	116.6	118.6
Building paper and building board mills	Dec. 1985=100 .	(NA)	(NA)	114.4	(NA)	(NA)	(NA)

NA Not available. [1] Includes structural wood members. [2] Excludes containers and boxes.

Source: U.S. Bureau of Labor Statistics, *Producer Price Indexes*, monthly.

No. 1138. Selected Species—Stumpage Prices In Current and Constant (1982) Dollars: 1980 to 1992

[In dollars per 1,000 board feet. Stumpage prices are based on sales of sawtimber from National Forests. See also *Historical Statistics, Colonial Times to 1970*, series L 199-205]

SPECIES	1980	1982	1983	1984	1985	1986	1987	1988	1989	1990	1991	1992
CURRENT DOLLARS												
Softwoods:												
Douglas fir [1]	432	118	162	133	126	161	190	256	390	466	395	477
Southern pine [2]	155	127	141	139	91	104	136	142	131	127	166	198
Sugar pine [3]	667	72	138	84	110	170	288	260	289	285	241	492
Ponderosa pine [3][4]	206	67	104	123	101	157	209	182	292	252	238	292
Western hemlock [5]....	213	45	62	62	51	75	105	163	223	203	164	165
Hardwoods:												
All eastern hardwoods [6].	52	56	60	90	65	70	88	151	136	146	160	167
Oak, white, red, and black [6]...........	66	71	88	145	95	108	147	146	179	188	164	211
Maple, sugar [7]	70	71	55	81	70	66	81	108	129	135	121	145
CONSTANT (1982) DOLLARS [8]												
Softwoods:												
Douglas fir [1]	481	118	160	128	122	160	185	240	347	401	339	407
Southern pine [2]	173	127	139	134	88	103	132	133	117	109	143	169
Sugar pine [3]	742	72	136	81	106	169	280	244	258	245	207	419
Ponderosa pine [3][4]	230	67	103	118	98	156	204	170	260	217	204	249
Western hemlock [5]....	237	45	61	60	49	75	103	152	199	175	141	140
Hardwoods:												
All eastern hardwoods [6].	58	56	59	87	63	70	86	142	121	126	137	142
Oak, white, red, and black [6]...........	73	71	87	140	92	108	143	137	159	162	140	180
Maple, sugar [7]	78	71	54	78	68	66	78	101	115	116	104	123

[1] Western Washington and western Oregon. [2] Southern region. [3] Pacific Southwest region (formerly California region). [4] Includes Jeffrey pine. [5] Pacific Northwest region. [6] Eastern and Southern regions. [7] Eastern region. [8] Deflated by the producer price index, all commodities.

Source: U.S. Forest Service, *U.S. Timber Production, Trade, Consumption, and Price Statistics*, annual.

No. 1139. Lumber Production and Consumption, by Kind of Wood: 1980 to 1991

[In millions of board feet, except as indicated. Based on sample survey; see source for sampling variability. See also *Historical Statistics, Colonial Times to 1970*, series L 98-112 and L 122-137]

ITEM	1980	1983	1984	1985	1986	1987	1988	1989	1990 [1]	1991 [1]
Total production	35,354	34,572	37,065	36,445	41,999	44,886	44,576	43,576	43,466	40,031
Softwoods [2]	28,239	28,927	30,801	30,479	34,815	37,410	36,845	36,040	36,224	33,250
Cedar	722	744	752	759	860	924	863	828	959	863
Douglas fir	6,853	6,434	7,809	7,751	9,600	10,422	9,986	10,045	8,831	7,816
Hemlock	1,855	1,316	(NA)	(NA)	(NA)	(NA)	(NA)	(NA)	(NA)	(NA)
Ponderosa pine	3,269	2,869	3,679	3,773	3,967	4,125	3,940	3,914	3,645	3,304
Redwood.	770	852	999	1,155	984	1,157	1,157	1,048	1,077	887
Southern yellow pine	8,217	10,181	10,648	10,230	11,443	12,043	12,474	12,031	12,989	12,436
White fir [3]	1,643	1,316	2,017	2,272	2,659	2,899	2,919	3,296	3,272	2,900
Hardwoods [2]	7,115	5,644	6,264	5,966	7,184	7,476	7,731	7,536	7,242	6,781
Ash	(S)	224	219	218	257	265	293	278	210	184
Beech.	183	112	111	89	125	116	120	105	82	72
Cottonwood and aspen	303	197	133	216	247	235	234	217	167	154
Maple [4]	225	524	538	532	587	636	619	589	543	517
Oak . . . . . . [5]	3,356	2,163	2,786	2,793	3,410	3,804	3,790	3,546	2,615	2,434
Sweet gum [5]	371	278	300	293	375	330	356	306	219	167
Yellow poplar	661	475	569	544	724	805	828	802	666	629
Domestic consumption	44,536	48,674	52,661	53,468	57,448	61,754	58,834	58,847	54,482	51,134
Percent net imports [6]	16.8	20.6	21.9	24.4	21.3	19.4	16.5	16.7	15.7	15.5
Softwoods	33,812	39,611	42,832	44,240	47,492	50,558	48,513	47,975	45,003	41,998
Mill stocks, year-end	4,228	4,606	4,594	4,765	4,905	4,840	4,999	4,888	4,854	4,669
Exports	1,956	1,745	1,599	1,515	1,877	2,423	3,264	3,319	2,970	3,090
Imports	9,540	11,977	13,270	14,608	14,238	14,680	13,806	13,638	12,148	11,742
Hardwoods	10,724	9,063	9,829	9,228	9,956	11,196	10,321	10,872	9,480	9,136
Mill stocks, year-end	1,572	1,334	1,561	1,719	1,636	(NA)	(NA)	(NA)	(NA)	(NA)
Exports	379	478	467	397	498	775	1,232	856	878	934
Imports	293	261	328	364	347	511	390	375	255	226

NA Not available.　S Figure does not meet publication standards.　[1] New sample, based on the new MA-24T sample.
[2] Includes types not shown separately.　[3] Beginning 1988, also includes hemfir, and other western truefirs.　[4] Includes both hard and soft maple, except data for 1980 excludes hard maple.　[5] Includes black, tupelo, and sweet gum.　[6] Imports minus exports.

Source: U.S. Bureau of the Census, *Current Industrial Reports*, series MA-24T, annual.

No. 1140. Lumber Production, by Geographic Area: 1970 to 1992

[In billion board feet. Data based in part on a sample of sawmills and are subject to sampling variability; see source. See *Historical Statistics, Colonial Times to 1970*, series L 113-121, for data by regions]

SECTION AND DIVISION	1970	1975	1980	1984	1985	1986	1987	1988	1989	1990	1991	1992
United States	34.7	32.6	[1]35.4	[1]37.1	36.4	42.0	44.9	44.7	43.6	43.5	39.9	40.8
North [2][3]	4.4	4.1	(NA)	4.5	4.2	4.9	5.3	5.2	5.0	5.4	5.3	5.4
Hardwood.	3.4	3.0	(NA)	3.3	3.0	3.6	3.8	3.9	3.8	3.7	3.6	3.6
Softwood	1.0	1.1	(NA)	1.2	1.2	1.4	1.5	1.4	1.3	1.7	1.7	1.8
South [2]	10.8	9.7	(NA)	13.4	13.0	15.1	15.7	16.3	15.8	16.5	15.5	16.8
Hardwood.	3.6	2.7	(NA)	2.8	2.7	3.4	3.4	3.6	3.4	3.2	2.8	3.0
Softwood	7.2	7.0	(NA)	10.7	10.2	11.7	12.3	12.7	12.4	13.3	12.7	13.8
West [2]	19.4	18.8	17.2	19.1	19.3	22.0	23.9	23.2	22.7	21.6	19.1	18.7
Hardwood.	0.1	0.1	0.3	0.2	0.2	0.2	0.3	0.3	0.3	0.4	0.4	0.4
Softwood	19.3	18.6	16.9	19.0	19.1	21.7	23.6	22.9	22.4	21.2	18.7	18.3

NA Not available.　[1] Includes amounts not specified by division.　[2] Source: U.S. Forest Service. Sections are as defined by the Forest Service.　[3] Includes Kentucky.

Source: Except as noted, U.S. Bureau of the Census, *Current Industrial Reports*, series MA-24T, annual.

No. 1141. Wood Products—Production: 1980 to 1990

ITEM	Unit	1980	1981	1982	1983	1984	1985	1986	1987	1988	1989	1990, prel.
Hardwood flooring . .	Mil. bd. ft	78	83	75	98	110	122	145	174	193	206	205
Softwood plywood . .	Bil. sq. ft., 3/8" . .	15.5	15.5	15.1	18.3	18.9	19.3	20.4	21.1	22.9	21.4	20.7
Insulation boards [1] . .	1,000 short tons . .	1,051	845	593	713	785	735	732	605	529	460	474
Hardboard [1]	Mil. sq. ft., 1/8" . .	6,140	6,104	5,587	7,303	6,837	6,300	5,822	5,458	5,118	5,196	5,025
Particleboard.	Mil. sq. ft., 3/4" . .	2,950	2,869	2,393	3,009	3,196	3,331	3,603	3,706	3,829	3,858	3,806

[1] Beginning 1983, data are for shipments.

Source: U.S. Dept. of Commerce, International Trade Administration, *Forest Products Review*, monthly (discontinued April 1983); and unpublished data. Based on reports of U.S. Bureau of the Census, National Oak Flooring Manufacturers Association and National Particleboard Association.

No. 1142. Paper and Paperboard—Production and Consumption: 1980 to 1993

[In millions of short tons. See also *Historical Statistics, Colonial Times to 1970*, series L 172, L 174, and L 178-191]

ITEM	PRODUCTION						CONSUMPTION [1]					
	1980	1985	1990	1991	1992	1993	1980	1985	1990	1991	1992	1993
Total paper and paperboard. .	63.6	68.7	80.3	81.1	84.5	85.9	67.2	76.1	86.7	84.9	88.1	90.9
Paper: Newsprint	4.7	5.4	6.6	6.8	7.1	7.1	11.4	12.8	13.3	12.5	12.6	12.8
Coated printing, converting	4.6	5.9	7.5	7.4	8.1	8.2	4.6	6.3	8.3	7.8	8.6	9.0
Uncoated free sheet	8.0	9.7	11.5	11.5	12.2	12.4	8.0	10.0	12.0	11.8	12.5	12.9
Other printing, writing, etc.	2.9	2.9	3.3	3.2	3.1	3.3	3.5	4.4	5.2	5.0	4.9	5.5
Packaging and industrial con- verting	5.5	5.2	4.6	4.5	4.7	4.5	5.2	5.2	4.7	4.6	4.8	4.5
Tissue and other machine creped	4.4	4.9	5.8	5.7	5.8	6.0	4.4	5.0	5.9	5.7	5.8	6.0
Paperboard: Unbleached kraft . . .	15.3	16.4	20.4	21.0	21.7	21.4	13.0	14.6	17.8	17.8	18.5	18.5
Bleached kraft	3.8	3.9	4.4	4.6	4.5	4.6	3.3	3.4	3.7	3.8	3.7	3.9
Semichemical	4.7	5.1	5.7	5.7	5.9	5.9	4.4	5.0	5.7	5.6	5.9	6.0
Recycled finish	7.1	7.6	8.9	9.2	9.9	10.9	7.0	7.6	9.3	9.6	10.5	11.4
Construction paper and board [2].	2.6	1.7	1.6	1.6	1.6	1.6	3.0	2.0	1.7	1.6	1.7	1.7

[1] Total consumption of paper and paperboard includes net imports of paper and paperboard converted products; not available by grade.   [2] Beginning 1985, estimated. Source: 1980, U.S. Bureau of the Census, *Current Industrial Reports*. Includes wet machine board, approximately 100,000-160,000 tons per year.

Source: Except as noted, American Forest and Paper Association, Inc., New York, NY, *Statistics of Paper, Paperboard, and Woodpulp*, annual.

No. 1143. Newsprint—Production, Stocks, Consumption, Imports, and Price Index: 1970 to 1992

[In thousands of metric tons, except price index and imports (imports in short tons). See also *Historical Statistics, Colonial Times to 1970*, series L 192-198]

COUNTRY AND ITEM	1970	1975	1980	1985	1987	1988	1989	1990	1991	1992
Canada: Production	7,808	6,966	8,625	8,890	9,630	9,840	9,640	9,068	8,977	8,931
Shipments from mills	7,795	7,010	8,622	8,899	9,718	9,740	9,606	9,074	8,728	9,143
Stocks at mills, end of year. . . .	236	86	165	288	189	288	321	315	564	351
United States:										
Consumption, estimate	6,468	8,395	10,088	11,507	12,303	12,245	12,241	12,125	11,381	11,634
Production	3,142	3,348	4,239	4,924	5,300	5,427	5,523	5,997	6,206	6,424
Shipments from mills	3,136	3,347	4,234	4,927	5,310	5,415	5,515	6,007	6,152	6,464
Stocks, end of year: At mills . . .	33	19	21	57	36	48	56	46	98	59
At and in transit to publishers .	749	666	732	910	900	932	749	801	932	938
Producer price index (1982=100)	34.1	58.3	[1]88.5	105.3	112.3	127.6	122.5	119.5	120.9	109.9

[1] Average for 11 months.

Source: Except as noted, U.S. Bureau of Economic Analysis, *Survey of Current Business*, monthly. Data from American Forest and Paper Association, Inc., New York, NY, and Canadian Pulp & Paper Association.

No. 1144. Recovered Paper Utilization and Recovery Rates: 1970 to 1993

[In millions of short tons, except percent. Recovery rate is ratio of total recovered paper to new supply. Recovered paper utilization is the ratio of recovered paper consumption at paper and board mills to paper and board production. See also *Historical Statistics, Colonial Times to 1970*, series L 175, for U.S. wastepaper consumption]

ITEM	1970	1980	1985	1987	1988	1989	1990	1991	1992	1993
Paper and board, production [1]	51.7	63.6	68.7	75.9	78.1	78.4	80.3	81.1	84.5	85.9
Recovered paper consumption	11.8	14.9	16.4	18.7	19.7	20.2	21.7	23.7	26.2	28.9
Recovered paper utilization rate (percent). .	22.8	23.5	23.8	24.6	25.2	25.8	27.1	29.2	29.7	31.8
Other recovered paper uses [2]	0.42	0.47	0.53	0.66	0.70	0.72	1.00	1.08	1.10	1.15
Recovered paper exports	0.41	2.64	3.56	4.81	5.95	6.31	6.51	6.60	6.40	5.90
Total paper recovered.	12.6	17.9	20.4	24.0	26.2	27.1	29.1	31.2	33.6	35.7
Paper and board, new supply [3]	56.0	67.2	76.1	83.5	85.5	85.2	86.7	84.9	88.1	90.9
Recovery rate (percent).	22.4	26.7	26.8	28.8	30.6	31.8	33.6	36.8	38.1	39.3

[1] Excludes hard pressed board; includes construction paper and board, and wet machine board.   [2] Estimated.   [3] Excludes production of hard pressed board.

Source: American Forest and Paper Association, Inc., New York, NY, *Statistics of Paper, Paperboard, and Woodpulp*, annual; and unpublished data.

No. 1145. Selected Wood Products—Production and Consumption: 1970 to 1989

[See also *Historical Statistics, Colonial Times to 1970*, series L 151-170]

ITEM	Unit	1970	1975	1980	1984	1985	1986	1987	1988	1989
PULPWOOD										
Receipts, total	Mil. cords [1]	68.9	65.4	81.0	88.0	85.4	90.6	93.9	95.1	97.0
Softwood	Mil. cords [1]	52.4	49.3	60.2	62.9	60.2	63.3	65.3	65.8	67.1
Hardwood	Mil. cords [1]	16.5	16.2	20.8	25.2	25.1	27.3	28.6	29.3	29.9
Consumption, total	Mil. cords [1]	67.6	65.4	79.7	87.0	84.8	91.1	92.4	95.3	96.1
Softwood	Mil. cords [1]	51.3	48.9	58.8	62.0	59.7	63.1	64.2	65.9	66.3
Hardwood	Mil. cords [1]	16.3	16.5	20.9	24.9	25.1	28.1	28.2	29.4	29.7
Inventories [2]	Mil. cords [1]	6.6	6.6	6.7	5.2	5.1	4.7	5.6	5.3	5.8
WOODPULP										
Production	Mil. short tons	43.9	43.1	53.0	57.8	57.7	60.6	62.4	64.1	64.6
Consumption, [3] total	Mil. short tons	43.2	42.4	52.4	57.5	56.6	60.0	61.2	62.8	62.7
Own pulp	Mil. short tons	38.9	38.5	46.6	50.3	49.7	52.6	53.8	54.9	54.9
Purchased pulp	Mil. short tons	4.3	3.9	5.9	7.2	7.0	7.5	7.4	7.9	7.8
PLYWOOD										
Softwood:										
Production	Mil. sq. ft. [4]	14,149	15,706	15,483	18,865	19,341	20,363	22,312	22,233	20,919
Consumption, total	Mil. sq. ft. [4]	(NA)	(NA)	15,145	18,526	19,122	19,880	21,503	22,277	20,904
Value	Mil. dol.	949	(NA)	2,582	2,995	3,080	3,237	3,483	3,513	3,734
Hardwood:										
Production	Mil. sq. ft. [5]	1,904	1,280	1,311	1,185	1,016	1,088	1,256	1,217	1,213
Consumption, total	Mil. sq. ft. [5]	5,772	4,970	3,416	3,831	4,311	4,884	4,918	4,193	(NA)
Value	Mil. dol.	516	586	977	1,199	1,192	1,320	1,471	1,405	1,392

NA Not available.   [1] Standard cords. 128 cubic feet roughwood bases.   [2] As of Dec. 31.   [3] In the manufacture of paper and board.   [4] 3/8" basis.   [5] Surface measure.

Source: U.S. Bureau of the Census, *Current Industrial Reports*, series MA26-A, MA24-H, and MA24-F.

No. 1146. Selected Timber Products—Imports and Exports: 1970 to 1992

ITEM	Unit	1970	1980	1985	1987	1988	1989	1990	1991	1992, prel.
IMPORTS [1]										
Lumber, total [2]	Mil. bd. ft.	6,114	9,866	14,996	15,234	14,226	15,277	12,159	11,756	13,474
From Canada	Percent	96.0	97.5	97.6	96.9	97.5	91.3	98.5	98.3	98.3
Softwoods	Mil. bd. ft.	5,778	9,573	14,632	14,723	13,841	14,928	11,927	11,545	13,214
Value	Mil. dol	434	1,826	2,898	3,060	2,939	2,875	2,534	2,507	3,310
Hardwoods	Mil. bd. ft.	337	293	364	511	386	349	232	210	260
Value	Mil. dol	62	152	180	273	238	152	141	142	176
Logs, total	Mil. bd. ft. [3]	144	128	99	83	68	42	28	15	46
From Canada	Percent	79.6	97.4	81.8	91.6	91.9	61.5	67.5	74.5	88.9
Softwoods	Mil. bd. ft. [3]	107	114	71	69	56	24	18	9	40
Value	Mil. dol. [3]	9	17	17	19	15	12	7	6	20
Hardwoods	Mil. bd. ft. [3]	38	13	28	14	12	18	10	6	7
Value	Mil. dol	5	3	4	3	3	17	10	6	6
Paper and board [4]	1,000 tons	7,115	8,780	11,522	12,837	13,110	13,100	13,148	12,167	12,543
Value	Mil. dol	1,039	3,418	5,698	6,928	8,002	8,330	8,427	7,929	7,899
Woodpulp	1,000 tons	3,518	4,051	4,466	4,848	4,938	5,105	4,893	4,997	5,029
Value	Mil. dol	483	1,684	1,521	2,069	2,608	3,037	2,831	2,132	2,094
Plywood	Mil. sq. ft. [5]	2,049	1,235	1,817	2,083	1,698	1,955	1,687	1,457	1,776
Value	Mil. dol	208	409	463	638	577	516	537	457	574
EXPORTS										
Lumber, total [2]	Mil. bd. ft.	1,243	2,494	1,945	3,217	4,527	4,243	3,802	3,997	3,603
To: Canada	Percent	21.7	25.3	23.7	20.9	17.6	15.6	18.1	15.1	17.3
Japan	Percent	30.8	26.0	32.1	36.8	34.5	38.1	33.5	30.5	30.9
Europe	Percent	24.1	23.8	15.1	16.9	20.5	16.6	19.1	19.6	21.2
Softwoods	Mil. bd. ft.	1,115	2,007	1,518	2,424	3,266	3,379	2,941	3,055	2,613
Value	Mil. dol	163	789	497	856	1,143	1,404	1,336	1,358	1,363
Hardwoods	Mil. bd. ft.	128	487	427	793	1,261	863	861	942	990
Value	Mil. dol	31	272	263	493	683	659	818	879	988
Logs, total	Mil. bd. ft. [3]	2,741	3,261	3,843	4,110	4,798	4,745	4,262	3,816	3,316
To: Canada	Percent	10.6	9.7	11.6	10.3	7.9	5.8	9.3	11.2	12.6
Japan	Percent	86.3	78.0	49.4	58.3	50.3	63.5	62.5	56.7	62.1
China: Mainland	Percent	(NA)	2.7	27.8	14.1	23.4	9.6	8.5	9.7	7.1
Softwoods	Mil. bd. ft. [3]	2,672	3,109	3,732	3,960	4,594	4,532	4,044	3,532	3,092
Value	Mil. dol	320	1,452	1,169	1,526	2,090	2,176	2,170	1,870	1,925
Hardwoods	Mil. bd. ft. [3]	69	152	111	149	204	214	218	283	224
Value	Mil. dol	36	129	91	118	160	223	251	234	238
Paper and board [4]	1,000 tons	2,817	5,214	4,071	5,304	5,691	6,300	6,796	8,331	8,971
Value	Mil. dol	602	2,773	2,266	3,104	3,753	4,261	5,035	6,006	6,392
Woodpulp	1,000 tons	3,095	3,806	3,796	4,869	5,528	6,231	5,906	6,337	7,222
Value	Mil. dol	464	1,652	1,354	2,251	2,915	3,513	3,156	2,800	3,114
Plywood	Mil. sq. ft. [5]	172	413	358	846	1,093	1,562	1,767	1,552	1,759
Value	Mil. dol	16	108	86	194	247	292	338	295	366

NA Not available.   [1] Customs value of imports; see text, section 29.   [2] Includes railroad ties.   [3] Log scale.   [4] Includes paper and board products. Excludes hardboard.   [5] 3/8 inch basis.

Source: U.S. Forest Service, *U.S. Timber Production, Trade, Consumption, and Price Statistics: 1960-89*, forthcoming.

No. 1147. Fishery Products—Domestic Catch and Imports, Summary: 1970 to 1992

[Live weight, in millions of pounds, except percent. 1979-1992 preliminary. For data on commercial catch for selected countries, see table 1398, section 30. See Historical Statistics, Colonial Times to 1970, series L 224-226, for domestic catch]

ITEM	1970	1980	1983	1984	1985	1986	1987	1988	1989	1990	1991	1992
Total	11,474	11,357	12,352	12,552	15,150	14,368	15,744	14,628	15,485	16,349	16,364	16,106
For human food	6,213	8,006	8,413	8,498	9,337	9,620	10,561	10,505	12,268	12,662	13,020	13,242
Finfish	(NA)	6,139	6,358	6,303	6,991	7,087	7,919	7,786	9,735	10,120	10,186	10,297
Shellfish [1]	(NA)	1,867	2,055	2,195	2,346	2,533	2,642	2,719	2,533	2,542	2,834	2,945
For industrial use	5,261	3,351	3,939	4,054	5,813	4,748	5,183	4,123	3,217	3,687	3,344	2,864
Domestic catch	4,917	6,482	6,439	6,438	6,258	6,031	6,896	7,192	8,463	9,404	9,484	9,637
Percent of total	42.8	57.1	52.1	51.3	41.3	42.0	43.8	49.2	54.7	57.5	58.0	60.0
For human food	2,537	3,654	3,238	3,320	3,294	3,393	3,946	4,588	6,204	7,041	7,031	7,618
Finfish	(NA)	2,516	2,351	2,348	2,273	2,240	2,769	3,306	4,897	5,747	5,564	6,182
Shellfish [1]	(NA)	1,138	887	972	1,021	1,153	1,177	1,282	1,307	1,294	1,467	1,436
For industrial use	2,380	2,828	3,201	3,118	2,964	2,638	2,950	2,604	2,259	2,363	2,453	2,019
Imports [2]	6,557	4,875	5,913	6,114	8,892	8,337	8,848	7,436	7,022	6,945	6,879	6,469
Percent of total	57.2	42.9	47.9	48.7	58.7	58.0	56.2	50.8	45.3	42.5	42.0	40.0
For human food	3,676	4,352	5,175	5,178	6,043	6,227	6,615	5,917	6,064	5,621	5,989	5,624
Finfish	(NA)	3,623	4,007	3,955	4,718	4,847	5,150	4,480	4,838	4,373	4,622	4,115
Shellfish [1]	(NA)	729	1,168	1,223	1,325	1,380	1,465	1,437	1,226	1,248	1,367	1,509
For industrial use [3]	2,881	523	738	936	2,849	2,110	2,233	1,519	958	1,324	890	845

NA Not available. [1] For univalve and bivalve mollusks (conchs, clams, oysters, scallops, etc.), the weight of meats, excluding the shell, is reported. [2] Excludes imports of edible fishery products consumed in Puerto Rico; includes landings of tuna caught by foreign vessels in American Samoa. [3] Fish meal and sea herring.

Source: U.S. National Oceanic and Atmospheric Administration, National Marine Fisheries Service, Fishery Statistics of the United States, annual; and Fisheries of the United States, annual.

No. 1148. Fisheries—Employment, Fishing Craft, and Establishments: 1970 to 1991

[In thousands. As of Dec. 31. 1979-91 preliminary. Data for employment and establishments exclude Alaska. See also Historical Statistics, Colonial Times to 1970, series L 254-261]

ITEM	1970	1980	1982	1983	1984	1985	1986	1987	1988	1989 [1]	1990 [1]	1991 [1]
Persons employed in U.S.	227	296	314	333	340	351	347	359	364	(NA)	(NA)	(NA)
Fishermen	140	193	216	223	230	239	247	256	274	(NA)	(NA)	(NA)
Shore workers [2]	87	103	98	110	110	112	100	103	90	73	72	73
Craft used	88	113	123	127	127	130	128	[3]93	[3]110	111	95	(NA)
Vessels, 5 net tons and over	14	19	20	21	24	24	38	[3]23	[3]32	36	32	(NA)
Motorboats	72	93	102	105	102	104	88	[3]68	[3]78	75	63	(NA)
Other boats	2	1	1	1	1	2	2	[3]2	(NA)	(NA)	(NA)	(NA)
Fishery shore establishments	3.7	3.6	3.6	3.9	4.0	4.0	4.0	4.2	4.6	4.5	4.6	4.6

NA Not available. [1] Estimated and excludes Mississippi River, Maryland and Virginia represent only Federal collected data. [2] Seasonal average for processors and wholesaling plants. [3] Excludes Maryland and Virginia.

Source: U.S. National Oceanic and Atmospheric Administration, National Marine Fisheries Service, Fishery Statistics of the United States, annual; and Fisheries of the United States, annual.

No. 1149. Fisheries—Quantity and Value of Domestic Catch: 1970 to 1992

[1979-1992 preliminary. See also Historical Statistics, Colonial Times to 1970, series L 224-226, L 229, and L 310]

YEAR	QUANTITY (mil. lb. [1])			Value (mil. dol.)	Average price per lb. (cents)	YEAR	QUANTITY (mil. lb. [1])			Value (mil. dol.)	Average price per lb. (cents)
	Total	For human food	For industrial products [2]				Total	For human food	For industrial products [2]		
1970	4,917	2,537	2,380	613	12.5	1982	6,367	3,285	3,082	2,390	37.5
1971	5,018	2,441	2,577	651	13.0	1983	6,439	3,238	3,201	2,355	36.6
1972	4,806	2,435	2,371	748	15.6	1984	6,438	3,320	3,118	2,350	36.5
1973	4,858	2,398	2,460	937	19.3	1985	6,258	3,294	2,964	2,326	37.2
1974	4,967	2,496	2,471	932	18.7	1986	6,031	3,393	2,638	2,763	45.8
1975	4,877	2,465	2,412	977	20.0	1987	6,896	3,946	2,950	3,115	45.2
1976	5,388	2,775	2,613	1,349	25.0	1988	7,192	4,588	2,604	3,520	48.9
1977	5,271	2,952	2,319	1,554	29.5	1989	8,463	6,204	2,259	3,238	38.30
1978	6,028	3,177	2,851	1,854	30.7	1990	9,404	7,041	2,363	3,522	37.50
1979	6,267	3,318	2,949	2,234	35.6	1991	9,484	7,031	2,453	3,308	34.90
1980	6,482	3,654	2,828	2,237	34.5	1992	9,637	7,618	2,019	3,678	38.19
1981	5,977	3,547	2,430	2,388	40.0						

[1] Live weight. [2] Meal, oil, fish solubles, homogenized condensed fish, shell products, bait, and animal food.

Source: U.S. National Oceanic and Atmospheric Administration, National Marine Fisheries Service, Fishery Statistics of the United States, annual; and Fisheries of the United States, annual.

No. 1150. Fisheries—Quantity and Value of Catch, by State, and Catch of Principal Species, by Area: 1980 to 1992

[Catch in millions of pounds, live weight, value in millions of dollars. Preliminary. See also *Historical Statistics, Colonial Times to 1970*, series L 262-293]

AREA, STATE, CATCH, AND VALUE	1980	1990	1991	1992	AREA, STATE, CATCH, AND VALUE	1980	1990	1991	1992
Total:					Florida (east coast):				
Catch	6,482	9,403	9,484	9,637	Catch	77	58	45	47
Value	2,237	3,522	3,308	3,678	Value	39	54	50	46
New England:					Catch for certain species:				
Catch	788	649	646	647	Menhaden	218	74	113	60
Value	327	543	594	604	Shrimp	33	28	37	25
Maine:					Crabs	55	54	57	64
Catch	245	169	192	201	Scallops	1	2	1	(Z)
Value	93	130	155	163	Gulf States:				
New Hampshire:					Catch	1,979	1,625	1,679	1,426
Catch	19	11	11	10	Value	463	640	641	652
Value	5	10	13	12	Florida (west coast):				
Massachusetts:					Catch	115	122	117	105
Catch	438	328	289	274	Value	86	116	112	109
Value	178	303	296	280	Alabama:				
Rhode Island:					Catch	25	23	22	24
Catch	81	132	139	142	Value	25	36	37	36
Value	46	73	85	86	Mississippi:				
Connecticut:					Catch	334	320	239	188
Catch	5	9	15	20	Value	25	42	34	31
Value	5	27	45	63	Louisiana:				
Catch for certain species:					Catch	1,412	1,061	1,193	1,013
Clams	15	15	12	15	Value	174	263	244	295
Cod	118	95	92	61	Texas:				
Crabs	7	9	9	7	Catch	94	99	108	96
Flounder	118	60	50	53	Value	153	182	214	181
Haddock	55	5	4	5	Catch for certain species:				
Herring, sea	184	113	106	115	Crabs	45	51	65	71
Lobster, American	36	55	56	52	Mullet	31	24	25	19
Ocean perch, Atlantic	24	1	1	2	Oysters (meats)	17	11	13	18
Pollock	40	21	17	16	Shrimp	208	247	229	222
Scallops, sea	17	25	24	21	Great Lakes: [1]				
Squid	6	36	42	46	Catch	44	45	39	31
Whiting	18	28	26	28	Value	14	20	21	22
Middle Atlantic:					Mississippi River and				
Catch	244	207	234	261	tributaries:				
Value	97	150	154	155	Catch	85	(NA)	(NA)	(NA)
New York:					Value	21	(NA)	(NA)	(NA)
Catch	39	49	51	50	Pacific Coast:				
Value	45	56	53	54	Catch	2,140	5,722	5,795	6,319
New Jersey:					Value	1,025	1,775	1,529	1,895
Catch	201	149	175	204	Washington:				
Value	50	89	97	97	Catch	156	137	152	122
Delaware:					Value	86	118	110	105
Catch	4	9	8	7	Oregon:				
Value	2	4	4	4	Catch	126	139	150	257
Catch for certain species:					Value	56	70	63	76
Clams (meats)	40	93	97	110	California:				
Scup or porgy	8	4	7	6	Catch	804	347	348	302
Squid	3	6	26	35	Value	323	127	140	136
Chesapeake Bay:					Alaska:				
Catch	717	867	770	688	Catch	1,054	5,099	5,145	5,638
Value	130	160	142	127	Value	560	1,459	1,216	1,578
Maryland:					Catch for certain species:				
Catch	80	81	89	57	Anchovies	107	13	19	14
Value	45	54	47	36	Bonito	14	8	1	2
Virginia:					Cod	20	526	554	551
Catch	637	787	681	631	Crabs	347	281	409	418
Value	85	107	95	91	Flounder	60	182	330	574
Catch for certain species:					Hake	12	21	56	124
Crabs	65	91	98	54	Halibut	19	70	66	69
Clams	36	27	21	13	Herring, sea	107	108	123	159
Scallops, sea	6	9	9	7	Jack mackerel	44	9	4	3
Flounder	10	2	4	6	Mackerel	65	84	63	42
Oysters	21	4	3	2	Oysters	7	11	10	7
South Atlantic:					Pollock	3	3,108	2,855	2,952
Catch	473	262	293	238	Rockfish	106	132	97	125
Value	148	170	169	152	Sablefish	22	90	84	75
North Carolina:					Salmon	614	733	783	716
Catch	356	176	213	154	Shrimp	98	59	47	84
Value	69	72	67	57	Tuna	387	34	13	35
South Carolina:					Hawaii:				
Catch	21	14	19	19	Catch	11	26	28	28
Value	20	24	28	26	Tuna catch	7	14	9	(NA)
Georgia:					Value	12	65	58	70
Catch	19	13	16	18					
Value	20	20	24	23					

NA Not available.   Z Less than 500,000.   [1] Collected largely by State fishery agencies and compiled by State fishery agencies and National Marine Fisheries Service. Includes, in addition to the Great Lakes, small amounts for Lake St. Clair, Lake of the Woods, Namakan Lake, and Rainy Lake.

Source: U.S. National Oceanic and Atmospheric Administration, National Marine Fisheries Service, *Fishery Statistics of the United States*, annual; and *Fisheries of the United States*, annual.

No. 1151. Domestic Fisheries—Catch, by Selected Ports: 1985 to 1992

[See *Historical Statistics, Colonial Times to 1970*, series L 236-253, for data on quantity and value of catch]

PORT	CATCH (mil. lb.) 1985	1989	1990	1991	1992	VALUE (mil. dol.) 1985	1989	1990	1991	1992
New Bedford, MA.	90.6	90.4	114.8	106.4	103.3	103.2	141.0	160.4	157.7	151.8
Dutch Harbor-Unalaska, AK	106.3	504.3	509.9	731.7	736.0	21.3	107.0	126.2	130.6	194.0
Kodiak, AK	96.1	213.2	272.5	287.3	274.0	65.8	100.2	101.7	96.9	90.0
Dulac-Chauvin, LA	398.6	210.9	164.4	166.8	65.0	59.9	50.0	52.7	50.1	52.1
Empire-Venice, LA	224.5	272.7	244.2	309.4	269.1	34.3	49.2	46.3	50.2	50.1
Gloucester, MA	116.5	98.5	126.2	107.2	101.7	37.1	30.0	40.5	40.0	34.1
Petersburg, AK	(NA)	113.5	67.5	90.3	81.0	(NA)	61.4	39.4	34.6	33.0
Cordova, AK	(NA)	55.3	70.8	47.5	30.0	(NA)	35.3	36.8	19.5	17.0
Cape May-Wildwood, NJ	30.3	54.0	69.2	93.1	93.9	18.1	30.8	34.4	40.1	34.9
Point Judith, RI	56.8	48.3	58.7	64.7	66.7	28.0	23.6	32.2	37.5	36.6
Portland, ME	36.1	49.0	48.9	63.4	59.2	17.2	34.4	31.7	44.1	43.6
Ketchikan, AK	(NA)	91.6	52.6	68.5	70.0	(NA)	45.6	28.3	21.9	27.0
Beaufort-Morehead City, NC.	133.2	95.0	102.0	137.0	78.7	22.7	25.0	23.0	23.0	16.2
Cameron, LA.	673.6	352.7	232.6	288.4	246.0	29.9	20.5	20.6	26.3	26.5
Morgan City-Berwick, LA	7.7	68.1	146.5	112.3	130.8	(NA)	17.8	19.7	9.4	14.3
Pascagoula-Moss Point, MS.	423.2	282.1	303.9	227.3	177.0	18.4	16.9	18.8	15.1	12.4
Los Angeles, CA	150.3	177.6	158.5	141.5	94.9	32.5	20.3	21.3	17.4	14.6
Astoria, OR.	25.5	51.0	41.2	53.0	67.0	9.5	20.0	16.2	17.0	19.0
Port Hueneme-Oxnard-Ventura, CA.	19.9	65.3	39.4	52.0	18.7	5.4	12.0	12.5	14.0	10.7
Intercoastal City, LA	(NA)	207.2	173.0	211.4	175.9	(NA)	9.5	7.6	12.0	10.4

NA Not available.

Source: U.S. National Oceanic and Atmospheric Administration, National Marine Fisheries Service, *Fisheries of the United States*, annual.

No. 1152. Domestic Fish and Shellfish Catch and Value, by Species: 1985 to 1992

SPECIES	QUANTITY (1,000 lb.) 1986-90 5-year average	1985	1990	1992	VALUE ($1,000) 1985	1990	1992
Total	(X)	6,257,642	9,403,571	9,637,303	2326237	3,521,995	3,677,935
Fish, total [1]	(X)	5,214,363	8,091,068	8,174,183	1193427	1,900,097	2,012,605
Anchovies.	14,221	14,566	13,189	13,679	2704	2,723	5,228
Bluefish	13,908	13,743	13,802	11,595	2363	3,239	2,694
Butterfish	7,109	10,338	6,532	7,608	3537	3,334	3,701
Cod: Atlantic	80,423	82,823	95,881	61,283	35140	61,329	52,013
Pacific.	378,013	120,275	526,396	550,528	18556	91,384	132,480
Croaker	8,283	11,088	6,720	5,077	3658	3,390	1,893
Flounder.	258,060	195,718	254,519	645,829	129121	112,921	143,511
Haddock.	5,281	14,416	5,440	5,111	13545	5,967	5,582
Halibut.	73,935	61,032	70,454	68,579	38376	96,700	53,773
Herring, sea; Atlantic.	96,950	57,133	113,095	122,993	2968	5,746	6,821
Herring, sea; Pacific.	120,927	142,074	108,120	159,054	47025	32,178	35,907
Jack mackerel.	18,043	20,852	8,959	2,624	1770	535	245
Mackerel, Pacific.	85,964	75,453	83,721	41,879	6324	5,081	4,118
Menhaden	2,145,260	2,739,401	1,962,160	1,644,342	100680	93,896	82,973
Mullet.	30,326	21,205	28,554	22,479	5720	12,738	9,730
Ocean perch, Atlantic	2,088	9,666	1,322	1,867	3179	703	790
Ocean perch, Pacific.	29,040	9,034	60,972	45,484	1757	8,494	13,561
Pollock, Atlantic	28,066	43,477	21,042	15,843	6978	10,516	10,543
Pollock, Alaska	2,026,927	92,833	3,108,031	2,952,130	5409	268,344	324,735
Rockfish	120,908	82,109	131,545	125,069	23107	38,504	47,280
Sablefish	96,242	63,380	89,802	75,451	28692	58,865	79,634
Salmon.	694,093	726,946	733,146	715,828	439795	612,367	582,850
Scup or porgy.	13,166	15,996	11,452	14,014	9338	8,677	8,669
Sea trout, gray.	14,239	16,400	9,880	7,467	7330	5,777	4,479
Shark, Dogfish.	21,442	11,563	35,793	42,327	842	3,801	4,675
Snapper, red.	3,462	5,181	3,101	3,471	10661	8,411	7,354
Swordfish.	18,632	12,258	13,797	19,713	33191	40,851	60,320
Tuna	79,782	83,054	62,393	56,803	52515	105,040	90,822
Whiting. [1]	38,126	44,545	44,500	35,893	8274	11,281	10,990
Shellfish, total [1]	(X)	1,043,279	1,312,503	1,463,120	1132810	1,621,898	1,665,330
Clams	135,541	150,551	139,198	142,449	128349	130,194	127,329
Crabs.	489,957	337,632	499,416	624,322	203044	483,837	471,323
Lobsters: American.	54,296	46,152	61,017	55,841	114895	154,677	160,951
Oysters	32,535	44,173	29,193	36,156	70053	93,718	114,536
Scallops: Calico	5,605	12,513	1,135	25	12524	1,281	78
Sea	35,114	15,829	39,917	33,528	74562	153,696	162,229
Shrimp.	342,422	333,691	346,494	337,765	472850	491,433	479,954
Squid: Atlantic.	56,638	7,157	59,809	81,944	7256	21,178	33,925
Pacific.	57,765	22,276	36,082	30,436	4047	2,636	2,698

X Not applicable.   [1] Includes other types of fish and shellfish, not shown separately.

Source: U.S. National Oceanic and Atmospheric Administration, National Marine Fisheries Service, *Fisheries of the United States*, annual.

No. 1153. Disposition of U.S. Domestic Catch: 1970 to 1992

[**Live weight catch in millions of pounds.** 1980-90 preliminary. In addition to whole fish, a large portion of waste (400-500 million lb.) derived from canning, filleting, and dressing fish and shellfish utilized in production of fish meal and oil in each year shown. See *Historical Statistics, Colonial Times to 1970*, series L 305-310, for similar but not entirely comparable data]

DISPOSITION	1970	1975	1980	1984	1985	1986	1987	1988	1989	1990	1991	1992
Total	4,917	4,877	6,482	6,438	6,258	6,031	6,896	7,192	8,463	9,404	9,484	9,637
Fresh and frozen	1,595	1,744	2,621	2,336	2,242	2,487	3,157	3,813	5,585	6,501	6,541	7,288
Canned	1,150	907	1,161	1,128	1,232	1,134	1,009	1,017	798	751	674	543
Cured	71	55	96	82	70	60	89	86	128	126	119	100
Reduced to meal, oil, etc.	2,101	2,171	2,604	2,892	2,714	2,350	2,641	2,276	1,952	2,026	2,150	1,696

Source: U.S. National Oceanic and Atmospheric Administration, National Marine Fisheries Service, *Fishery Statistics of the United States*, annual; and *Fisheries of the United States*, annual.

No. 1154. U.S. Catch and Value of Fish and Shellfish, by Distance Caught Off U.S. Shores—Selected Species: 1992

[Preliminary. **Catch is shown in live weight**, except as indicated. Includes landings by U.S. flag vessels at Puerto Rico and other ports outside the 50 States and joint venture catches, therefore will not agree with other tables]

SPECIES	Total U.S. catch (mil. lb.)	BY DISTANCE FROM U.S. SHORES						Value of U.S. catch [1] (mil. dol.)
		Catch (mil. lb.)			Percent of U.S. catch			
		3 miles or less [1]	3 to 200 miles	International waters [2]	3 miles or less [1]	3 to 200 miles	International waters [2]	
Total	10,235	3,505	6,176	554	34	60	6	3,883
Fish [3]	1,105	267	825	13	24	75	1	483
Cod	612	34	578	-	6	94	-	184
Flounder	646	46	600	-	7	93	-	144
Halibut	70	4	66	-	6	94	-	55
Herring, sea.	291	203	88	-	70	30	-	43
Mackerel.	78	41	37	-	53	47	-	15
Menhaden.	1,705	1,370	335	-	80	20	-	84
Pollock	2,968	177	2,791	-	6	94	-	335
Salmon, Pacific	716	710	6	-	99	1	-	582
Tuna	577	1	35	541	(Z)	6	94	280
Shellfish [3]	153	145	8	(Z)	95	5	-	205
Clams (meats)	142	43	99	-	30	70	-	127
Crabs	624	242	382	-	39	61	-	471
Lobsters	61	48	13	(Z)	79	21	-	181
Scallops (meats).	34	3	31	-	9	91	-	164
Shrimp	341	140	201	-	41	59	-	493
Squid	112	31	81	-	28	72	-	37

- Represents or rounds to zero.   Z Less than 500,000 pounds or .05 percent.   [1] Includes all landings in Great Lakes and other inland waters.   [2] Greater than 200 nautical miles seaward from the U.S. shores except for two States. The boundaries for the Gulf Coast of Florida and Texas are 9 nautical miles.   [3] Includes other species, not shown separately.

Source: U.S. National Oceanic and Atmospheric Administration, National Marine Fisheries Service, *Fishery Statistics of the United States*, annual; and *Fisheries of the United States*, annual.

No. 1155. U.S. Private Aquaculture—Catfish Production and Value: 1980 to 1992

ITEM	Unit	1980	1985	1986	1987	1988	1989	1990	1991	1992
Fish sold to processors	Mil. lb	46.5	191.6	213.8	280.5	295.1	341.9	360.4	390.9	457.4
Avg. price paid by processors	Cents/lb.	67.6	72.5	66.8	61.8	76.4	71.7	75.8	63.1	59.8
Value	Mil. dol.	31.4	138.9	142.8	173.3	225.5	245.1	273.2	246.7	273.5
Processor sales	Mil. lb	27.8	99.3	113.9	146.5	149.6	176.3	183.1	199.8	231.3
Avg. price received by processors.	Cents/lb.	166.1	165.4	195.7	193.3	220.8	211.2	224.0	208.6	200.2
Value	Mil. dol.	46.2	164.2	222.9	283.2	330.3	372.3	410.1	416.8	463.1
Inventory (Jan. 1)	Mil. lb	1.0	4.7	5.0	4.2	5.3	8.8	8.1	9.4	9.6

Source: U.S. Dept. of Agriculture, National Agricultural Statistics Service, USDA.

No. 1156. U.S. Private Aquaculture—Trout Production and Value: 1988 to 1993

[Periods are from Sept. 1 of the previous year to Aug. 31 of stated year. Data are for foodsize fish, those over 12 inches long]

ITEM	Unit	1988	1989	1990	1991	1992	1993
Number sold	Mil	70.5	67.4	67.8	67.7	64.5	60.9
Total weight	Mil. lb	56.0	55.5	56.8	58.9	55.2	54.6
Total value of sales	Mil. dol	57.9	60.0	64.6	58.3	51.0	54.3
Average price received	$/lb	1.03	1.08	1.14	0.99	0.92	0.99
Average weight	Lb	0.79	0.82	0.84	0.87	0.86	0.90

Source: U.S. Dept. of Agriculture, National Agricultural Statistics Service, USDA.

No. 1157. Supply of Selected Fishery Items: 1980 to 1992

[In millions of pounds. Totals available for U.S. consumption are supply minus exports plus imports. Round weight is the complete or full weight as caught. Data are preliminary]

ITEM	Unit	1980	1984	1985	1986	1987	1988	1989	1990	1991	1992
Tuna, canned	Canned weight	666	777	759	873	866	843	1,028	856	933	923
Shrimp	Heads-off weight	425	584	633	706	773	767	743	734	744	820
Clams	Meat weight	102	144	164	162	151	145	150	152	144	155
Salmon, canned	Canned weight	126	150	113	87	76	59	159	148	131	75
American lobster	Round weight	69	100	108	113	116	121	85	95	107	95
Spiny lobster	Round weight	127	153	154	152	151	139	89	89	85	81
Scallops	Meat weight	51	87	72	70	79	74	79	74	62	69
Sardines, canned	Canned weight	69	58	76	68	77	63	61	61	52	41
Oysters	Meat weight	71	84	90	91	92	78	66	56	47	50
Crab meat, canned	Canned weight	9	7	8	9	8	8	8	9	11	9
Snow crab	Round weight	54	23	45	49	29	30	58	37	60	88
King crab	Round weight	133	13	11	19	14	10	18	19	20	15

Source: U.S. National Oceanic and Atmospheric Administration, National Marine Fisheries Service, *Fisheries of the United States*, annual.

No. 1158. Canned, Fresh, and Frozen Fishery Products: 1980 to 1992

[Fresh fishery products exclude Alaska and Hawaii. Canned fishery products data are for natural pack only. See also *Historical Statistics, Colonial Times to 1970*, series L 338-357 (production data in cases) and L 358]

PRODUCT	PRODUCTION (mil. lb.)						VALUE (mil. dol.)					
	1980	1985	1989	1990	1991	1992	1980	1985	1989	1990	1991	1992
Canned, [1]	1,516	1,161	1,455	1,178	1,386	1,343	1,928	1,360	1,992	1,562	1,644	1569
Tuna	602	545	686	581	593	609	1,144	821	1,058	902	877	888
Salmon	200	159	197	196	196	152	376	228	514	366	413	289
Clam products	77	117	135	110	129	126	66	109	91	76	84	84
Mackerel [2]	38	15	18	23	9	5	12	7	7	11	3	2
Sardines, Maine	20	20	13	13	14	17	32	38	17	17	19	25
Shrimp	16	4	3	1	1	1	80	19	9	3	4	4
Crabs [3]	5	1	1	(Z)	(Z)	(Z)	19	2	3	4	(Z)	1
Oysters [3]	(Z)	2	4	1	1	1	(NA)	2	1	1	2	(NA)
Fish fillets and steaks [4]	202	246	371	441	473	404	261	440	724	843	1,021	918
Cod	31	57	73	65	71	62	43	89	136	132	180	157
Flounder	49	69	44	54	48	43	87	157	142	154	147	124
Haddock	17	8	7	7	8	5	29	19	26	24	30	19
Ocean perch, Atlantic	7	2	2	1	1	1	9	3	3	1	1	3
Rockfish	14	18	25	33	22	18	13	25	40	53	36	28
Pollock, Atlantic	9	15	11	12	8	9	9	17	18	21	18	19
Pollock, Alaska	(NA)	11	106	164	152	125	(NA)	24	98	174	206	161
Other	74	66	103	105	163	141	71	106	279	284	403	407

NA Not available.   Z Less than 500,000 pounds or $500,000.   [1] Includes other products, not shown separately.   [2] Includes Jack and a small amount of Pacific mackerel.   [3] Includes oyster specialties.   [4] Fresh and frozen.

Source: U.S. National Oceanic and Atmospheric Administration, National Marine Fisheries Service, *Fisheries of the United States*, annual.

No. 1159. Processed Fishery Products—Production and Value: 1980 to 1992

[Includes Puerto Rico and American Samoa. See *Historical Statistics, Colonial Times to 1970*, series L 362-365, for meal, scrap, and oil]

PRODUCT	PRODUCTION (mil. lb.)						VALUE (mil. dol.)					
	1980	1988	1989	1990	1991	1992	1980	1988	1989	1990	1991	1992
Total ¹	(X)	(X)	(X)	(X)	(X)	(X)	4,456	5,369	(X)	(X)	(X)	(X)
Fresh and frozen ² . .	(X)	(X)	(X)	(X)	(X)	(X)	2,110	3,562	(X)	(X)	(X)	(X)
Fillets	197	362	345	414	420	348	247	707	656	764	907	774
Steaks.	5	22	26	26	53	56	14	70	86	80	114	144
Fish sticks	88	80	89	65	63	58	89	114	116	75	78	56
Fish portions	344	301	280	243	205	194	388	439	400	353	313	296
Breaded shrimp . .	83	99	121	111	116	122	254	293	404	353	335	349
Canned products ³ . .	1,516	1,130	1,455	1,178	1,386	1343	1,928	1,481	1,992	1,562	1,644	1,569
Fish and shellfish .	1,009	907	1,110	957	981	936	1,782	1,388	1,754	1,415	1,439	1,322
Animal food	507	223	345	221	405	407	146	93	238	147	205	247
Industrial products . .	(X)	(X)	(X)	(X)	(X)	(X)	270	236	206	207	208	192
Meal and scrap. . .	724	644	618	577	613	538	134	131	115	121	128	120
Oil (body & liver). .	312	225	225	282	267	181	58	44	24	29	30	27
Solubles	267	223	233	186	170	93	14	15	18	14	12	8
Other	(X)	(X)	(X)	(X)	(X)	(X)	64	47	50	43	38	37

X Not applicable.   ¹ Includes cured fish.   ² Includes items not shown (dressed fish, shellfish not breaded, specialties).
³ Includes salmon eggs for bait.
Source: U.S. National Oceanic and Atmospheric Administration, National Marine Fisheries Service, *Fisheries of the United States*, annual.

No. 1160. Imports and Exports: 1970 to 1991

[Imports include landings of tuna by foreign vessels at American Samoa. See also *Historical Statistics, Colonial Times to 1970*, series L 227-235]

YEAR	IMPORTS					EXPORTS				
	Total U.S. value (mil. dol.)	Fishery products				Total U.S. value (mil. dol.)	Fishery products			
		Total value (mil. dol.)	Edible products		Noned-ible, value (mil. dol.)		Total value (mil. dol.)	Edible products		Noned-ible, value (mil. dol.)
			Quantity (mil. lb.)	Value (mil. dol.)				Quantity (mil. lb.)	Value (mil. dol.)	
1970.	39,756	1,037	1,873	813	225	43,224	118	140	94	24
1980.	244,007	3,648	2,145	2,687	962	220,783	1,006	574	904	102
1985.	343,553	6,679	2,754	4,064	2,614	213,146	1,084	648	1,010	73
1986.	368,657	7,626	2,979	4,813	2,813	217,304	1,356	735	1,290	66
1987.	402,066	8,818	3,201	¹5,711	3,106	252,866	1,660	783	1,577	83
1988.	437,140	8,872	2,968	5,442	3,430	320,385	2,275	1,060	2,156	119
1989.	472,977	9,604	3,243	5,498	4,107	(NA)	4,707	1,374	2,283	2,424
1990.	490,554	9,048	2,885	5,233	3,815	(NA)	5,639	1,910	2,777	2,862
1991.	483,028	9,435	3,015	5,672	3,763	(NA)	¹6,162	¹2,020	¹3,037	3,125

NA Not available.   ¹ Record.

No. 1161. Selected Fishery Products—Imports and Exports: 1985 to 1992

[See *Historical Statistics, Colonial Times to 1970*, series L 312-318, for selected imports]

PRODUCT	QUANTITY (mil. lb.)					VALUE (mil. dol.)				
	1985	1989	1990	1991	1992	1985	1989	1990	1991	1992
Imports, edible ¹	2,754	3,243	2,885	3,015	2,894	4,064	5,498	5,233	5,672	5,706
Fresh or frozen ¹	2,229	2,612	2,336	2,419	2,345	3,462	4,695	4,521	4,859	4,946
Salmon ²	27	99	104	107	103	76	229	253	243	234
Tuna ³	479	650	454	496	437	266	402	339	341	353
Groundfish fillets, blocks ⁴ .	640	484	442	420	361	655	702	693	770	581
Other fillets and steaks . . .	231	253	257	310	276	334	490	458	533	523
Scallops (meats)	42	41	40	30	39	147	139	131	111	160
Lobster, American, spiny . .	77	72	74	27	26	465	453	440	274	276
Shrimp and prawn	343	492	492	530	586	1,121	1,685	1,639	1,836	2,000
Canned ¹	414	533	458	513	469	466	642	543	642	580
Sardines and herring ⁵	40	41	42	35	31	30	34	31	28	26
Tuna.	214	348	285	352	323	209	376	294	359	309
Oysters	29	20	14	12	13	30	37	27	32	37
Pickled or salted	57	51	45	45	42	53	55	49	56	60
Cod, haddock, hake, pollock, cusk.	35	17	11	11	10	41	25	18	22	23
Nonedible scrap and meal . . .	511	171	239	159	151	62	32	39	32	35
Exports: Canned salmon.	48	40	49	66	78	83	90	104	134	154
Fish oil, nonedible	279	195	222	254	177	37	20	24	35	29

¹ Includes products not shown separately.   ² Excludes fillets.   ³ Includes landings of tuna by foreign vessels at American Samoa.   ⁴ Includes cod, cusk, haddock, hake, pollock, Atlantic ocean perch, and whiting.   ⁵ Not in oil.
Source of tables 1160 and 1161: U.S. National Oceanic and Atmospheric Administration, National Marine Fisheries Service, *Fisheries of the United States*, annual. Compiled from U.S. Bureau of the Census data.

Figure 24.3
U.S. Mineral Production as a Percentage of World

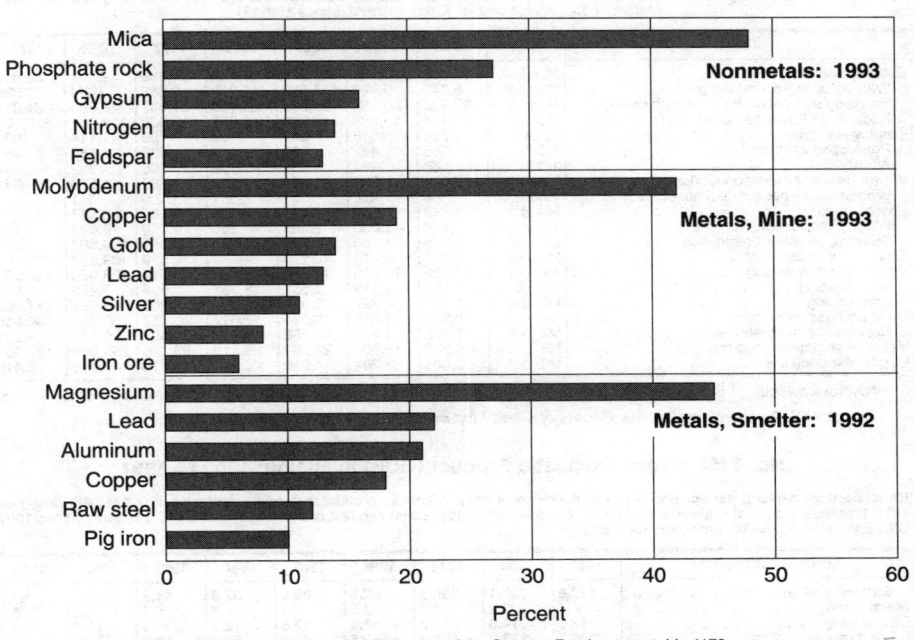

Source: Chart prepared by U.S. Bureau of the Census. For data, see table 1172.

Figure 24.4
Wells Drilled and Drilling Costs for Crude Petroleum and Natural Gas: 1980 to 1992

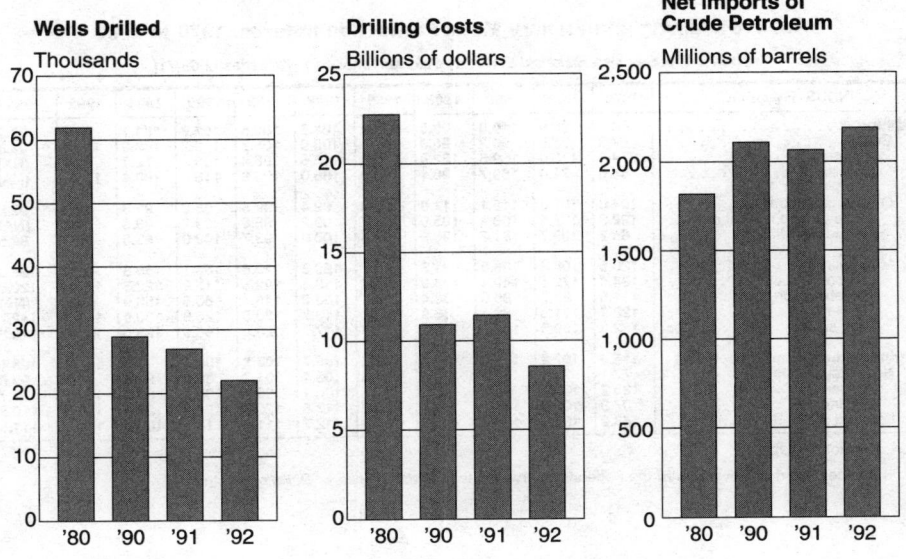

Source: Chart prepared by U.S. Bureau of the Census. For data, see tables 1180 and 1185.

No. 1162. Summary of Mineral Operations: 1958 to 1987

[Represents mineral operations only. Beginning 1967, excludes single unit establishments without paid employees. See also *Historical Statistics, Colonial Times to 1970*, series M 1-11]

ITEM	Unit	1958	1963	1967	1972	1977	1982	1987
Establishments	Number .	36,392	38,651	28,579	25,269	31,359	42,241	33,617
With 20 or more employees	Number .	6,045	5,499	5,682	5,312	6,632	(NA)	6,299
Including all operations in manufactures	Number .	37,966	40,532	29,688	26,178	31,967	42,585	34,041
Excluding oil and gas extraction	Number .	19,444	19,290	13,330	11,680	13,520	12,267	10,707
Employees, total	1,000 .	734	616	567	595	799	1,114	698
Production workers [1]	1,000 .	565	482	433	443	593	762	451
All other	1,000 .	169	134	134	152	206	352	247
Worker-hours, production workers [1]	Million .	1,081	973	892	909	1,183	1,578	942
Worker-hours per production workers	1,000 .	1.9	2.0	2.1	2.1	2.0	2.1	2.1
Payroll, total	Mil. dol. .	3,749	3,743	4,187	6,226	13,167	28,637	21,739
Wages, production workers [1]	Mil. dol. .	2,623	2,680	2,888	4,250	9,082	18,030	12,443
Salaries, all other employees	Mil. dol. .	1,126	1,063	1,299	1,976	4,085	10,607	9,296
Cost of supplies, etc. [2]	Mil. dol. .	7,521	8,974	10,576	14,884	46,079	109,697	62,423
Value added in mining	Mil. dol. .	13,385	15,910	19,330	26,471	68,013	188,056	110,959
Metal mining	Mil. dol. .	1,180	1,418	1,557	2,382	3,504	3,215	4,610
Coal mining	Mil. dol. .	1,780	1,727	2,091	3,754	11,266	18,631	17,068
Oil and gas extraction	Mil. dol. .	9,033	11,020	13,394	17,612	48,587	159,937	80,049
Nonmetallic minerals mining	Mil. dol. .	1,392	1,745	2,288	2,723	4,656	6,273	9,233
Value of shipments and receipts [3]	Mil. dol. .	16,373	18,804	22,784	36,319	96,375	250,000	157,964
Capital expenditures	Mil. dol. .	2,804	3,264	4,058	5,036	17,718	47,753	15,418

NA Not available.   [1] See footnote 4, table 1165.   [2] Includes purchased machinery installed.   [3] See footnote 6, table 1165.

Source: U.S. Bureau of the Census, *Census of Mineral Industries, 1972, 1977, 1982,* and *1987.*

No. 1163. Gross Domestic Product (GDP) in Mining: 1980 to 1991

[In millions of dollars, except percent. For definition of gross domestic product, see text, section 14. For 1947-86, based on 1972 Standard Industrial Classification (SIC); For 1987, estimates are shown first based on the 1972 SIC and then on the 1987 SIC. Estimates thereafter based on 1987 SIC]

MINING INDUSTRY	1980	1984	1985	1986	1987	1988	1989	1990	1991
Current dollars, total	112.6	137.1	130.6	82.7	83.0	87.9	84.2	103.1	91.8
Metal mining	4.4	3.2	2.5	2.5	2.6	4.8	5.2	6.2	5.7
Coal mining	13.6	14.6	13.8	14.0	12.5	12.5	12.9	12.7	12.2
Oil and gas extraction	89.1	113.0	108.4	59.5	60.8	63.2	58.8	76.9	66.7
Nonmetallic minerals, exc. fuels	5.5	6.2	5.9	6.7	7.2	7.3	7.4	7.2	7.2
Constant (1987) dollars, total	79.9	82.0	83.3	83.0	83.0	94.2	83.3	91.8	91.5
Metal mining	1.6	2.8	2.5	2.9	2.6	4.3	5.0	6.6	7.2
Coal mining	10.1	11.5	11.3	13.0	12.5	13.8	14.8	15.3	15.3
Oil and gas extraction	61.8	60.9	63.2	60.2	60.8	69.0	56.2	62.9	62.0
Nonmetallic minerals, exc. fuels	6.4	6.8	6.3	6.9	7.2	7.1	7.3	7.0	7.1

Source: U.S. Bureau of Economic Analysis, *Survey of Current Business,* May and November 1993.

No. 1164. Mining and Primary Metal Production Indexes: 1970 to 1993

[1987 = 100. See also *Historical Statistics, Colonial Times to 1970*, series M 68-71]

INDUSTRY GROUP	1970	1975	1980	1985	1986	1988	1989	1990	1991	1992	1993
Mining	100.4	98.0	110.0	109.0	101.0	101.8	100.5	102.6	101.1	98.7	97.2
Coal	67.2	71.5	90.2	96.3	97.1	105.0	105.7	113.2	109.2	105.5	103.8
Anthracite	274.1	175.0	169.6	132.8	120.8	115.6	96.3	103.2	72.7	66.1	(NA)
Bituminous	66.0	71.0	89.7	96.1	96.9	105.0	105.8	113.3	109.4	105.8	(NA)
Oil and gas extraction	104.8	101.8	112.1	111.9	102.0	99.4	99.5	95.5	95.8	93.2	92.2
Crude oil and natural gas	122.3	107.5	108.4	105.0	101.7	99.2	95.6	93.7	95.5	94.0	(NA)
Oil and gas drilling	65.2	109.7	181.2	198.9	109.8	100.0	93.7	109.0	93.3	78.3	82.5
Metal mining	129.5	106.4	108.8	91.3	95.2	120.3	140.5	153 1	155.8	161.2	166.3
Iron ore	194.4	172.1	149.4	104.9	84.4	119.4	122.5	117.9	122.3	120.5	120.8
Nonferrous ores	111.5	88.7	95.0	86.4	99.1	123.3	145.1	160.5	156.9	(NA)	(NA)
Copper ore	123.2	101.5	93.1	86.9	91.2	113.7	120.0	126.8	130.9	146.3	142.7
Lead and zinc ores	192.2	189.9	166.7	120.1	103.3	117.7	129.4	196.6	199.0	187.5	176.2
Primary metals, manufacturing	115.2	107.2	110.8	101.8	93.7	108.7	107.2	106.5	98.3	101.1	106.4
Nonferrous metals	77.1	75.3	92.5	98.5	97.3	103.1	101.7	99.5	95.3	96.1	99.5
Copper	135.2	103.0	94.7	99.8	99.1	100.1	98.9	102.2	109.7	109.9	117.7
Aluminum	107.8	105.2	138.7	104.7	90.9	117.6	120.5	121.0	123.2	120.5	110.5
Iron and steel	148.2	133.5	126.0	104.5	90.8	112.7	111.2	111.5	100.5	104.7	111.5

NA Not available.

Source: Board of Governors of the Federal Reserve System, *Federal Reserve Bulletin,* monthly.

No. 1165. Mineral Industries—Summary: 1977 to 1987

["N.e.c." means not elsewhere classified. See also Historical Statistics, Colonial Times to 1970, series M1-12]

Mineral industry	1977 Establishments	1977 All employees payroll[1] (mil. dol.)	1977 Value added in mining[2] (mil. dol.)	1982 Establishments Total	1982 Establishments With 20 or more employees	1982 All employees Number[3] (1,000)	1982 All employees Payroll[1] (mil. dol.)	1982 Value added in mining[2] (mil. dol.)	1987 Establishments Total	1987 Establishments With 20 or more employees	1987 All employees Number[3] (1,000)	1987 All employees Payroll[1] (mil. dol.)	1987 Production workers[4] Number[3] (1,000)	1987 Production workers[4] Hours[5] (millions)	1987 Production workers[4] Wages (mil. dol.)	1987 Value added in mining[2] (mil. dol.)	1987 Value of shipments and receipts[6] (mil. dol.)	1987 Capital expenditures (mil. dol.)
All Industries	31,359	13,167	68,013	42,241[7]	(NA)	1,114	28,637	188,056	33,617	6,299	698	21,739	451	942	12,443	110,959	157,964	15,418
Metal mining	1,206	1,485	3,504	1,434	(NA)	68	1,860	3,215	1,027	260	44	1,354	34	68	952	4,610	6,852	899
Iron ores	97	372	1,046	78	40	12	340	770	51	16	7	224	6	11	166	768	1,362	24
Copper ores	133	544	1,067	81	51	22	604	672	61	33	14	405	11	21	283	1,301	2,150	205
Lead and zinc ores	88	105	329	71	8	4	112	201	39	19	2	58	1	3	40	176	268	12
Gold and silver ores	175	71	161	371	80	10	263	650	372	101	13	423	10	21	305	1,814	2,261	555
Ferroalloy ores, except vanadium	56	107	256	69	16	5	150	146	58	10	1	46	1	2	24	61	110	8
Metal mining services	270	52	112	313	(NA)	3	61	90	268	42	3	81	2	5	60	176	251	26
Miscellaneous metal ores	387	234	533	451	91	12	332	686	178	42	4	116	3	5	75	313	449	70
Coal mining	5,451	4,171	11,266	5,087	1,787	251	6,805	18,631	3,905	1,418	163	5,567	129	259	4,251	17,068	25,955	1,665
Bituminous coal and lignite mining	4,944	4,005	10,837	4,513	1,787	241	6,570	18,041	3,507	1,335	158	5,410	124	249	4,125	16,679	25,347	1,614
Anthracite mining	156	48	116	152	40	3	67	172	107	26	2	41	2	3	32	109	206	12
Coal mining services	351	119	313	422	(NA)	7	168	418	291	57	4	116	3	7	94	280	402	39
Oil and gas extraction	18,447	5,902	48,587	29,974	(NA)	685	17,693	159,937	22,910	3,167	378	11,961	206	437	5,283	80,049	112,363	11,717
Crude petroleum and natural gas	8,573	2,738	38,337	12,087[7]	(NA)	264	8,084	126,035	10,203	1,171	199	7,510	69	142	2,154	67,955	76,518	10,549
Natural gas liquids	682	227	3,286	793	236	14	402	8,865	714	210	13	433	10	20	320	4,025	24,750	383
Oil and gas field services	9,182	2,936	6,974	17,094[7]	(NA)	406	9,207	25,037	11,993	1,786	167	4,018	127	275	2,809	8,069	11,095	786
Drilling oil and gas wells	2,625	1,317	3,307	4,385	(NA)	166	4,007	11,316	2,591	620	55	1,318	46	93	1,012	2,549	3,626	321
Oil, gas exploration services	1,252	220	545	2,934	(NA)	42	810	2,307	1,917	143	17	452	13	27	311	771	1,096	69
Oil, gas field services, n.e.c.	5,305	1,399	3,122	9,775	(NA)	199	4,391	11,415	7,485	1,023	95	2,248	69	154	1,486	4,748	6,373	395
Nonmetallic mining	6,255	1,609	4,656	5,746	(NA)	110	2,278	6,273	5,775	1,454	113	2,858	83	178	1,956	9,233	12,795	1,136
Dimension stone[8]	209	19	39	154	22	2	21	50	149	19	1	25	1	2	18	65	86	4
Crushed and broken stone[9]	2,055	543	1,501	1,932	567	37	701	1,787	2,002	711	44	1,082	33	72	754	3,465	4,768	521
Sand and gravel[9]	2,807	418	1,017	2,758	343	28	520	1,336	2,750	436	33	772	24	51	551	2,320	3,139	238
Clay and related minerals[9]	255	136	358	224	97	11	212	510	197	100	10	272	7	15	165	510	827	111
Chemical and fertilizer minerals	205	372	1,433	196	114	26	681	2,237	148	79	16	501	12	24	336	1,999	2,772	192
Nonmetallic minerals, services[9]	176	36	70	167	(NA)	2	35	70	177	23	2	45	1	3	32	119	165	25
Miscellaneous	548	87	238	315	72	6	109	283	352	86	7	162	5	10	101	438	616	46

NA Not available. [1] Gross earnings paid to all employees on payroll. [2] Computed by subtracting cost of supplies, minerals received for preparation, purchased fuel and electric energy, contract work, and purchased machinery from the value of shipments and capital expenditures. [3] Excludes proprietors and firm members of unincorporated concerns. [4] Represents employees up through the working foreman level engaged in manual work. Includes development and exploration workers. [5] Excludes paid vacations, holidays, and sick leave; includes actual overtime hours (not straight-time equivalent). [6] Represents value of shipments of primary and secondary products of the industry and amount received for services performed for other establishments on a contract, fee, or other basis. [7] Redefined to conform to 1987 and pre-1982 definition of establishment; for detail, see source. [8] Excludes data for dimension stone quarries operated in conjunction with dressing plants. [9] Excludes data for mining included in establishments classified in manufacturing industries.

Source: U.S. Bureau of the Census, Census of Mineral Industries: 1977, 1982, and 1987, final industry series reports.

No. 1166. Mineral Production and Value, 1990 to 1993,

[Data represent production as measured by mine shipments, mine sales, or marketable production

	MINERAL	Unit	PRODUCTION QUANTITY			
			1990	1991	1992	1993
1	Total mineral production	(X)	(X)	(X)	(X)	(X)
2	**Mineral fuels**	**(X)**	**(X)**	**(X)**	**(X)**	**(X)**
3	Coal: Bituminous and lignite	Mil. sh. tons	1,026	993	998	(NA)
4	Pennsylvania anthracite	Mil. sh. tons	4	3	3	(NA)
5	Natural gas (wet)	Tril. cu. ft.	1,859	1,871	1,871	(NA)
6	Petroleum (crude).	Mil. bbl. [1]	2,685	2,707	2,625	(NA)
7	Uranium [2]	Mil. lb.	8.9	8.0	5.6	(NA)
8	**Industrial minerals**	**(X)**	**(X)**	**(X)**	**(X)**	**(X)**
9	Abrasive stone [3]	Metric tons.	3,709	2,205	1,732	(NA)
10	Asbestos (sales)	1,000 metric tons . .	(D)	(D)	15.6	15.4
11	Asphalt and related bitumens (native) [4] .	Mil. metric tons. . . .	25	26	25	(NA)
12	Barite, primary, sold/used by producers . .	1,000 metric tons . .	430	448	326	303
13	Boron minerals, (producers)	1,000 metric tons . .	1,094	1,240	1,009	526
14	Bromine (sold or used by producers) . . .	1,000 metric tons . .	177	170	171	168
15	Calcium chloride	1,000 sh. tons	(D)	(D)	(D)	-
16	Carbon dioxide, natural (estimate)	Mil. cu. ft.	-	-	-	-
17	Cement: Portland	Mil. sh. tons	75.6	68.7	72.8	76.6
18	Masonry	Mil. sh. tons	3.3	2.6	2.9	3.0
19	Clays	1,000 metric tons . .	42,904	44,092	40,712	44,183
20	Diatomite	1,000 metric tons . .	631	610	595	622
21	Feldspar [6]	1,000 metric tons . .	630	580	726	760
22	Fluorspar, finished shipments	1,000 metric tons . .	64	58	51	50
23	Garnet (abrasive)	1,000 metric tons . .	47.0	50.9	54.1	46.1
24	Gem stones (estimate)	(X)	(NA)	(NA)	(NA)	(NA)
25	Gypsum, crude	Mil. sh. tons	16.4	15.5	16.3	17.0
26	Helium	Mil. cu. meters . . .	87	88	94	93
27	Lime, (sold or used by producers)	Mil. sh. tons	17.5	17.3	17.9	18.3
28	Mica, scrap & flake, (producers)	1,000 metric tons . .	109	103	85	89
29	Peat (sales by producers)	1,000 sh. tons	795	777	719	700
30	Perlite, processed (sold or used).	1,000 metric tons . .	576	514	541	548
31	Phosphate rock (marketable)	Mil. metric tons . . .	46.3	48.1	47.0	35.0
32	Potassium salts sales, K₂O equivalent . .	1,000 metric tons . .	1,716	1,709	1,767	1,500
33	Pumice & pumicite, producer sales	1,000 metric tons . .	443	401	481	492
34	Pyrites	1,000 metric tons . .	(D)	(D)	(D)	(D)
35	Salt, common, sold/used by producers . .	Mil. metric tons . . .	36.9	35.9	34.8	41.6
36	Sand & gravel, sold/used by producer . .	Mil. metric tons . . .	852	852	858	884
37	Construction	Mil. metric tons . . .	826	829	834	859
38	Industrial.	Mil. metric tons . . .	26	23	24	25
39	Sodium carbonate (natural) (soda ash). .	1,000 metric tons . .	9,156	9,005	9,379	9,200
40	Sodium sulfate (natural).	1,000 metric tons . .	349	354	337	315
41	Stone [8]	Mil. metric tons . . .	1,110	1,002	1,055	1,110
42	Crushed and broken	Mil. metric tons . . .	826	829	834	859
43	Dimension.	1,000 metric tons . .	26	23	24	25
44	Sulfur: Frasch mines (shipments)	1,000 metric tons . .	3,676	3,119	2,600	2,200
45	Talc, and pyrophyllite, crude [9]	1,000 metric tons . .	1,267	1,037	997	1,008
46	Tripoli.	1,000 metric tons . .	94	89	85	(NA)
47	Vermiculite concentrate.	1,000 metric tons . .	208	168	190	185
48	Industrial minerals, undistributed [10]	(X)	(X)	(X)	(X)	(X)
49	**Metals.**	**(X)**	**(X)**	**(X)**	**(X)**	**(X)**
50	Antimony ore and concentrate [11]	Metric tons.	(D)	(D)	(D)	(D)
51	Bauxite (dried) [13]	1,000 metric tons . .	(D)	(D)	(D)	(D)
52	Copper [2]	1,000 metric tons . .	1,588	1,631	1,765	1,773
53	Gold [2]	Metric tons.	295	296	329	332
54	Iron ore, [14] [15]	Mil. metric tons . . .	57.0	56.8	55.6	55.2
55	Lead [2]	1,000 metric tons . .	484	466	398	379
56	Magnesium metal.	1,000 metric tons . .	139	131	137	145
57	Manganiferous ore [15] [16]	1,000 metric ton . . .	(D)	(D)	(D)	(D)
58	Mercury [17]	Metric tons.	562	58	64	70
59	Molybdenum [18]	1,000 metric tons . .	62	54	50	39
60	Nickel [19]	1,000 metric tons . .	0.3	5.5	6.7	2.5
61	Palladium metal	Kilograms	5,930	6,050	6,470	6,500
62	Platinum metal.	Kilograms	1,810	1,730	1,840	1,800
63	Silver [2]	Metric tons.	2,125	1,855	1,804	1,750
64	Titanium concentrate: Ilmenite [15] . . .	1,000 metric tons . .	(D)	(D)	(D)	(D)
65	Tungsten ore and concentrate [19]	Metric tons.	(D)	(D)	(D)	(D)
66	Vanadium [2]	Metric tons.	(D)	(D)	(D)	(D)
67	Zinc mine production [2]	1,000 metric tons . .	515	518	523	505
68	Metals, undistributed.	(X)	(X)	(X)	(X)	(X)

- Represents zero. D Withheld to avoid disclosing individual company data. NA Not available. X Not applicable. [1] 42 gal. bbl. [2] Recoverable content of ores, etc. [3] Includes grindstones, oilstones, whetstones, and deburring media. Excludes grinding pebbles, and tubemill liners. [4] Contains bituminous limestone and sandstone, and Gilsonite. Includes road oil, 1989-92. Value excluded from industrial minerals, 1989-92. [5] Value included in "Industrial minerals, undistributed." [6] Includes aplite, 1992-93. [7] Refined only. [8] Excludes abrasive stone, bituminous limestone and sandstone, and ground soapstone, all included elsewhere in table; 1993 excludes dimension stone. State ranks based on publishable data. Includes calcareous marl and slate.

and Principal Producing States, 1993

(including consumption by producers). See *Historical Statistics, Colonial Times to 1970,* series M 13-37 for selected values]

PRODUCTION VALUE (mil. dol.)				Principal producing States ranked by quantity, 1993	
1990	1991	1992	1993		
141,741	(NA)	(NA)	(NA)	(X)	1
108,422	(NA)	(NA)	(NA)	(X)	2
22,274	21,598	(NA)	(NA)		3
133	(NA)	(NA)	(NA)		4
31,658	30,327	32,571	(NA)		5
53,772	44,666	(NA)	(NA)		6
140	(NA)	(NA)	(NA)		7
21,022	20,047	20,496	20,631		8
(Z)	(Z)	(Z)	(NA)	(NA)	9
(5)	(5)	6	6	CA, VT	10
3,480	2,979	2,794	(NA)	(NA)	11
16	21	20	18	NV, GA, MO	12
436	443	339	324	CA	13
173	167	170	110	AR	14
(5)	(5)	(5)	(X)	(X)	15
-	-	-	(X)	(X)	16
3,683	3,343	3,500	3,666	IN, FL, AL	17
225	188	195	200	TX, CA, MI	18
1620	1,505	1,482	1,773	GA, CA, AL	19
138	140	120	115	CA, NV, OR	20
28	26	29	30	NC, VA, OK	21
(5)	(5)	(5)	(5)	IL	22
7	8	5	5	ID, NY	23
53	84	66	52	(X)	24
100	94	101	105	OK, IA, TX	25
113	175	187	185	KS, WY, TX	26
902	890	950	971	OH, AL, PA	27
6	6	5	5	NC, NM, GA	28
19	18	17	17	FL, MI, WI	29
17	15	16	17	NM, AZ, CA	30
1,075	1,031	1,058	753	FL, NC, ID	31
303	305	334	275	NM, UT, CA	32
11	9	15	15	OR, NM, ID	33
(5)	(5)	(5)	(5)	AZ	34
827	802	803	854	LA, TX, NY	35
3,686	3,658	3,766	3,897	CA, OH, MI	36
3,249	3,268	3,341	3,495	CA, OH, MI	37
436	390	425	402	IL, NJ, CA	38
836	836	836	718	WY, CA	39
34	31	26	26	CA, TX, UT	40
5,822	5,396	5,775	6,021	TX, IL, PA	41
5,591	5,187	5,594	6,021	TX, IL, PA	42
231	210	181	(5)	IN, GA, VT	43
335	272	159	70	TX, LA	44
31	32	31	27	MT, TX, NY	45
3	3	3	(NA)	(NA)	46
19	13	15	(D)	SC, VA	47
504	538	478	374	(NA)	48
12,442	11,022	11,537	11,876	(NA)	49
(12)	(12)	(12)	(12)	ID	50
(12)	(12)	(12)	(12)	AL	51
4,311	3,931	4,180	3,595	AZ, UT, NM	52
3,650	3,457	3,650	3,793	NV, CA, UT	53
1,741	1,674	1,732	1,700	MN, MI	54
491	344	308	267	MO, AK, ID	55
433	337	360	406	TX, WA, UT	56
(12)	(12)	(12)	(12)	SC	57
(12)	0.2	0.4	0.4	NV	58
348	250	209	165	AZ, CO, UT	59
(NA)	(NA)	(12)	(12)	OR	60
22	17	18	26	MT	61
27	21	21	21	MT	62
329	241	229	236	NV, AK, ID	63
(12)	(12)	(12)	(12)	FL, CA	64
(12)	(12)	(12)	(12)	CA	65
(12)	(12)	(12)	(12)	ID	66
847	602	674	512	AK, TN, NY	67
242	148	156	179	(NA)	68

[9] For 1991-92, production quantity, talc only; 1989-92 dollar value is for talc only. [10] Comprises value of items that cannot be disclosed. [11] Antimony content. [12] Included with "Metals, undistributed." [13] Dried equivalent. [14] Represents shipments; includes byproduct ores. [15] Gross weight. [16] 5 to 35 percent manganiferous ore. [17] 1990, both primary product and byproduct of gold production; thereafter, produced as a byproduct of gold ores only. [18] Content of concentrate. [19] Content of ore and concentrate.

Source: U.S. Bureau of Mines, *Minerals Yearbook* thru 1991; *Annual Reports* and *Mineral Commodities Summaries*, annual U. S. Energy Information Administration, *Annual Energy Review, Uranium Industry Annual; Petroleum Supply Annual,* vol. 1; *Natural Gas Annual;* and *Quarterly Coal Report.*

No. 1167. Nonfuel Mineral Commodities—Summary: 1993

[Preliminary estimates. Average price in dollars per metric tons except as noted]

MINERAL	Unit	MINERAL DISPOSITION				Average price per unit (dollars)	Employment (number)
		Production	Exports	Net import reliance[1] (percent)	Consumption, apparent		
Aluminum	1,000 metric tons	5,300	1,200	16	6,300	[3]53	22,400
Antimony (contained)	Metric tons	[2]37,000	5,000	57	44,600	[3]80	110
Arsenic	Metric tons		[4]230	100	23,900	[3][4]54	
Asbestos	1,000 metric tons	15	32	95	33	(D)	70
Barite	1,000 metric tons	300	20	58	720	59.8	330
Bauxite and alumina	1,000 metric tons	(D)	1,305	100	4,500	15-18	35
Beryllium (contained)	Metric tons	159	16	4	165	[5][6]295	425
Bismuth (contained)	Metric tons	(D)	70	(D)	[7]1,450	2.5	30
Boron (B_2O_3 content)	1,000 metric tons	526	[8]580	[9]	244	[10]276	900
Bromine (contained)	1,000 metric tons	168	25	[9]	157	656	1,600
Cadmium (contained)	Metric tons	[2]1,050	16	66	3,110	[6][11]45	190
Cement	1,000 short tons	79,600	710	7	84,708	[12]49	18,000
Chromium	1,000 metric tons	[13]88	18	82	488	[14]110	(NA)
Clays	1,000 metric tons	44,183	4,045	[9]	40,184	(NA)	11,000
Cobalt (contained)	Metric tons	[13]1,600	900	75	6,320	[15]13.8	(NA)
Columbium (contained)	Metric tons	-	100	100	3,400	[15]67	(NA)
Copper (Mine, contained)	1,000 metric tons	1,770	200	6	2,450	[3][16]92	14,000
Diamond (industrial)	Million carats	116	100	15	136	[17]2.12	(NA)
Diatomite	1,000 metric tons	622	167	[9]	457	185	1,000
Feldspar	1,000 metric tons	760	19	[9]	749	39.08	400
Fluorspar	1,000 metric tons	152	13	89	438	(NA)	180
Gallium (contained)	Kilograms	-	(NA)	(NA)	[8]11,000	[18]425	20
Garnet (industrial)	Metric tons	52,400	12,100	[9]	52,100	100-2,000	150
Gemstones	Million dollars	72	1,612	98	3,644	[19]	1,000
Germanium (contained)	Kilograms	[2]10,000	(NA)	(NA)	25,000	[18][20]1,060	100
Gold (contained)	Metric tons	[2]390	(NA)	(NA)	(NA)	355	14,500
Graphite (crude)	1,000 metric tons	-	18	100	34	[22]767	(NA)
Gypsum (crude)	1,000 short tons	17,000	50	29	25,000	[23]6	6,700
Indium	Metric tons	(NA)	(NA)	(NA)	[8]35	[18][24]180	(NA)
Iodine	Metric tons	1,900	1,700	51	3,900	[18][25]8	35
Iron ore (usable)	Million metric tons	55	4	12	63	[26]73-74	7,800
Iron and steel scrap (metal)	Million metric tons	75	11	[9]	67	[27]106	106,200
Iron and steel slag (metal)	1,000 metric tons	21,000	4	0.5	[8]20,961	6	3,000
Lead (contained)	1,000 metric tons	1,170	130	11	1,280	[3]32	3,900
Lime	1,000 short tons	18,300	66	(NA)	18,431	[12]53	5,500
Magnesium compounds	1,000 metric tons	420	50	26	570	(NA)	650
Magnesium metal	1,000 metric tons	202	42	[9]	153	[6][28]1	1,400
Manganese (gross weight)	1,000 metric tons	-	34	100	[29]650	[30]3	(NA)
Mercury	Metric tons	270	90	(NA)	(NA)	[31]190	(NA)
Mica, scrap and flake	1,000 metric tons	89	5	11	98	54	80
Molybdenum (contained)	Metric tons	45,400	34,000	[9]	16,300	[18]5	550
Nickel (contained)	Metric tons	4,878	33,210	64	152,000	[32][33]130	40
Nitrogen (fixed)-ammonia	1,000 metric tons	12,700	400	15	15,010	[12][33]110	2,500
Nonrenewable organics	Million metric tons	117	8	4	122	107	(NA)
Peat	1,000 short tons	600	10	56	1,370	[12][23]24	650
Perlite	1,000 metric tons	548	30	3	563	[23]30	110
Phosphate rock	1,000 metric tons	35,000	3,000	[9]	36,000	[23]22	5,000
Platinum-group metals	Kilograms	64,400	86,000	88	112,300	[21][34]370	400
Potash (K_2O equivalent)	1,000 metric tons	1,500	360	71	5,120	[23]124	1,705
Pumice and pumicite	1,000 metric tons	492	20	25	652	[23]30	55
Salt	1,000 metric tons	37,700	700	12	43,000	[35]111	4,150
Silicon (contained)	1,000 metric tons	370	31	34	560	[3][36]42	(NA)
Silver (contained)	Metric tons	2,200	1,700	(NA)	4,000	5	1,500
Sodium carbonate (soda ash)	1,000 metric tons	9,200	2,900	[9]	6,496	[12][37]98	2,800
Sodium sulfate	1,000 metric tons	615	100	9	677	[12][38]114	240
Stone (crushed)	Million short tons	1,223	4	-	1,227	[12]5	76,000
Sulfur (all forms)	1,000 metric tons	10,600	570	15	12,600	[39]32	3,100
Talc	1,000 metric tons	928	168	[9]	839	13-400	800
Thallium (contained)	Kilograms	-	(NA)	100	800	[18]230	(NA)
Tin (contained)	Metric tons	[13]8,500	2,300	81	45,914	[3]244	5
Titanium dioxide	1,000 metric tons	1,158	258	[9]	1,071	[6][40]1	4,600
Tungsten (contained)	Metric tons	(D)	20	84	[41]6,800	[42]44	33
Vermiculite	1,000 metric tons	185	5	16	220	(D)	230
Zinc (contained)	1,000 metric tons	380	510	26	1,360	[3][43]46	1,360
Zirconium (ZrO2) content	Metric tons	(D)	25,950	(D)	(D)	[44]200	(NA)

- Represents or rounds to zero. D Withheld to avoid disclosure. NA Not available. [1] Calculated as a percent of apparent consumption. [2] Refinery production. [3] Cents per pound. [4] Metal price. [5] Metal, vacuum-cast ingot. [6] Dollars per pound. [7] Reported consumption. [8] Gross weight. [9] Net exporter. [10] Granulated pentahydrate borax in bulk, f.o.b. mine. [11] 1- to 5-short ton lots. [12] Dollars per short ton. [13] Secondary production. [14] Turkish. [15] Columbite price. [16] Domestic producer cathode. [17] Value of imports, dollars per carat. [18] Dollars per kilogram. [19] Variable, depending on size, type, and quality. [20] Zone refined, first reduction quality. [21] Dollars per troy ounce. [22] Price of flake imports. [23] F.o.b. mine (or mill). [24] 99.97% indium. [25] C.i.f. value, crude. [26] Lake Superior pellets. Cents per long ton unit of iron, delivered rail of vessel at lower lake ports. [27] Delivered, No. 1 Heavy Melting composite price. [28] Year-end price. [29] Estimated manganese content. [30] 46%-48% Mn metallurgical ore, per unit contained Mn, c.i.f. U.S. ports. [31] Price per 76-pound flask. [32] London Metal Exchange cash price. [33] F.o.b. gulf coast. [34] Dealer price of platinum. Per troy ounce, palladium price was $87 for 1992 and $120 for 1993; rhodium price was $2,365 for 1992 and $1,200 for 1993. [35] Vacuum and open pan, bulk, pellets and packaged, f.o.b. mine and plant. [36] Ferrosilicon, 50% Si. [37] Quoted year-end price, dense, bulk, f.o.b. Green River, WY. [38] Quoted price, bulk, f.o.b. works, East. [39] Elemental sulfur, f.o.b. mine and/or plant. [40] Rutile, list, year-end. [41] All forms. [42] Concentrate, unit WO3 (7.93 kilos of contained tungsten per unit). [43] Domestic producers price. [44] Price for imported zircon, f.o.b. U.S. east coast.

Source: U.S. Bureau of Mines, *Mineral Commodity Summaries*, annual.

No. 1168. Value of Domestic Nonfuel Mineral Production: 1980 to 1993

[In millions of dollars]

AREA	1980	1990	1991	1992	1993	Principal minerals in order of value
U.S. [1]	25,140	33,452	30,579	32,012	31,556	(X)
Northeast	1,581	2,479	2,095	2,308	2,411	(X)
N.E.	268	446	347	423	421	(X)
ME	37	55	41	56	61	Cement (portland), sand and gravel, and stone.
NH	25	36	30	42	36	Sand and gravel, stone, and gypsum.
VT.	43	87	60	[2]60	45	Stone, sand and gravel, and talc.
MA	91	128	112	147	166	Stone, sand and gravel, and lime.
RI	6	18	13	21	[2]27	Sand and gravel (construction), stone, and sand and gravel (industrial).
CT.	66	122	91	97	86	Stone, sand and gravel (construction), and sand and gravel (industrial).
M.A	1,313	2,033	1,748	1,885	1,990	(X)
NY.	496	773	699	766	845	Stone, salt, and sand and gravel.
NJ.	149	229	205	240	252	Stone, sand and gravel (construction), and sand and gravel (industrial).
PA.	668	1,031	844	879	893	Stone, cement (portland), and lime.
Midwest.	6,610	7,163	6,755	7,261	6,958	(X)
E.N.C	2,930	3,483	3,479	3,762	3,655	(X)
OH	562	733	684	742	814	Stone, sand and gravel, and salt.
IN	288	428	403	477	501	Stone, cement (portland), and sand and gravel.
IL	443	667	673	734	732	Stone, sand and gravel, and cement (portland).
MI	1,485	1,440	1,503	1,587	1,408	Iron ore, cement (portland), and sand and gravel.
WI	152	215	216	222	200	Stone, sand and gravel, and lime.
W.N.C	3,680	3,680	3,276	3,499	3,303	(X)
MN	1,782	1,482	1,289	1,364	1,323	Iron ore, sand and gravel, and stone.
IA	252	310	344	391	344	Stone, cement (portland), and sand and gravel.
MO	1,054	1,105	880	897	785	Lead, cement (portland), and stone.
ND	22	25	[2]17	26	[2]25	Sand and gravel (construction), lime, and sand and gravel (industrial).
SD.	228	319	290	301	324	Gold, cement (portland), and sand and gravel.
NE.	80	90	89	115	118	Sand and gravel (construction), cement (portland), and stone.
KS.	262	349	367	405	384	Salt, helium, and stone.
South	7,320	9,291	8,285	8,560	8,901	(X)
S.A. [2]	3,454	5,132	4,497	4,651	4,941	(X)
DE [2]	2	10	5	9	[2]11	Sand and gravel (construction).
MD.	186	368	348	339	361	Stone, cement (portland), and sand and gravel.
VA.	305	507	428	462	515	Stone, cement (portland), and sand and gravel.
WV	106	133	117	112	111	Stone, cement (portland), and sand and gravel.
NC	380	586	557	596	594	Stone, phosphate rock, and lithium minerals.
SC.	195	450	340	247	361	Cement (portland), stone, and gold.
GA	771	1,504	1,306	1,346	1,691	Clays, stone, and cement (portland).
FL.	1,509	1,574	1,396	1,440	1,297	Phosphate rock, stone, and cement (portland).
E.S.C	1,030	1,692	1,533	1,640	1,663	(X)
KY.	204	359	343	401	416	Stone, lime, and cement (portland).
TN.	394	663	548	576	538	Stone, zinc, and cement (portland).
AL.	328	559	540	543	570	Stone, cement (portland), and lime.
MS	104	111	102	120	139	Sand and gravel, cement (portland), and clays (Fuller's earth).
W.S.C	2,836	2,467	2,255	2,269	2,297	(X)
AR.	293	381	361	404	365	Stone, bromine, and cement (portland).
LA.	584	368	352	309	256	Salt, sand and gravel, and sulphur.
OK	224	259	276	253	282	Stone, cement (portland), and sand and gravel.
TX.	1,735	1,459	1,266	1,303	1,394	Cement (portland), stone, and magnesium metal.
West	9,629	14,512	13,435	13,858	13,235	(X)
Mountain	7,223	10,380	9,581	10,154	9,683	(X)
MT	280	573	534	539	496	Gold, copper, and cement (portland).
ID	522	375	298	306	283	Phosphate rock, gold, and sand and gravel.
WY	761	911	929	951	858	Soda ash, clays, and helium.
CO	1,265	406	338	385	432	Sand and gravel, cement (portland), and stone.
NM	766	1,103	986	871	788	Copper, potash, and sand and gravel.
AZ.	2,471	3,085	2,877	3,166	2,742	Copper, sand and gravel, and cement (portland).
UT.	764	1,335	1,190	1,348	1,350	Copper, gold, and magnesium.
NV.	394	2,621	2,429	2,588	2,734	Gold, sand and gravel, and silver.
Pacfic	2,406	4,132	3,854	3,704	3,552	(X)
WA	207	483	483	469	480	Sand and gravel, magnesium metal, and gold.
OR	152	205	198	214	234	Stone, sand and gravel, and cement (portland).
CA.	1,872	2,771	2,538	2,346	2,282	Sand and gravel, cement (portland), and gold.
AK.	115	577	494	526	421	Zinc, gold, and sand and gravel.
HI	60	106	141	149	[2]135	Stone, cement (portland) & (masonry), & gemstones.

X Not applicable. [1] Includes undistributed not shown separately. [2] Partial data only.

Source: U.S. Bureau of Mines, *Annual Reports, and Mineral Commodities Summary,* annual.

No. 1169. Mineral Industries—Gross Assets and Capital Expenditures: 1972 to 1987

[In millions of dollars]

INDUSTRY AND YEAR	END OF YEAR GROSS VALUE OF DEPRECIABLE ASSETS					CAPITAL EXPENDITURES					
	Total [1]	Buildings and other structures	Machinery and equipment	Mineral exploration and development [1]	Mineral land and rights [1]	Total [1]	New buildings and other structures	New machinery and equipment	Used buildings and other structures	Used machinery and equipment	Mineral exploration and development [1]
Mineral industries: [2]											
1972	21,690	4,244	15,038	([3])	[3]2,409	2,802	317	1,407	([3])	[3]128	230
1977	44,664	6,099	33,068	2,625	2,871	6,802	785	5,068	30	399	520
1982	94,613	10,228	73,419	5,036	5,930	13,472	1,229	10,551	78	937	677
1987	84,286	9,314	64,143	5,034	5,795	4,869	349	3,234	88	797	401
Crude oil, nat. gas:											
1972	47,500	(NA)	(NA)	(NA)	(NA)	2,954	403	842	([3])	[3]44	1,666
1977	94,414	(NA)	(NA)	(NA)	(NA)	10,916	571	2,269	14	93	7,969
1982	233,052	(NA)	(NA)	(NA)	(NA)	34,281	1,967	5,550	20	215	26,529
1987	(NA)	(NA)	(NA)	(NA)	(NA)	10,549	590	3,176	18	218	6,548

NA Not available.　[1] Excludes data for mineral exploration and development, and mineral land and rights portions for mining service industries and natural gas liquids industry.　[2] Excludes crude petroleum and natural gas.　[3] Not collected separately. Data for mineral exploration and development are combined with mineral land and rights. Data for used buildings and other structures are combined with used machinery and equipment.

Source: U.S. Bureau of the Census, *Census of Mineral Industries, 1987.*

No. 1170. Mineral Industries—Employment, Hours, and Earnings: 1991 to 1993

ITEM	Unit	1991	1992	1993	ITEM	Unit	1991	1992	1993
All mining:					Avg. weekly hours	No	44.5	43.8	43.8
All employees	1,000	689	631	599	Avg. weekly earnings	Dol	602	614	619
Production workers	1,000	489	445	423	Metal mining:				
Avg. weekly hours	No	44.4	43.9	44.2	All employees	1,000	56	53	51
Avg. weekly earnings	Dol	630	638	645	Production workers	1,000	44	42	41
Coal mining:					Avg. weekly hours	No	43.0	42.9	43.1
All employees	1,000	136	126	105	Avg. weekly earnings	Dol	639	655	660
Production workers	1,000	110	102	84	Nonmetallic minerals,				
Avg. weekly hours	No	44.6	44.0	44.4	except fuels:				
Avg. weekly earnings	Dol	761	755	766	All employees	1,000	105	102	100
Oil and gas extraction:					Production workers	1,000	78	76	75
All employees	1,000	393	350	343	Avg. weekly hours	No	44.5	44.9	46.1
Production workers	1,000	258	226	224	Avg. weekly earnings	Dol	531	551	585

Source: U.S. Bureau of Labor Statistics, *Bulletin 2370* and *Employment and Earnings,* March and June issues.

No. 1171. Selected Mineral Products—Average Prices: 1970 to 1993

[Excludes Alaska and Hawaii, except as noted. See *Historical Statistics, Colonial Times to 1970,* series M 96, M 139, M 209, M 248, and M 262, for bituminous coal, crude petroleum, iron ore, lead, and aluminum, respectively]

YEAR	Tantalum (dol. per lb.) [1]	Copper, electrolytic [2] (cents per lb.)	Platinum [3] (dol./ troy oz.)	Gold (dol./ fine oz.)	Silver (dol./ fine oz.)	Lead [4] (cents per lb.)	Tin (New York) [5] (cents per lb.)	Zinc [6] (cents per lb.)	Sulfur, crude [7] (dol./ metric ton)	Bituminous coal [8] (dol./ short ton)	Crude petroleum (dol./ bbl.)	Natural gas [8] (dol./ 1,000 cu. ft.)
1970	9.15	58	133	36	1.77	15.7	174.1	15.3	[9]22.41	6.26	3.18	0.17
1975	18.32	64	164	161	4.42	21.5	339.8	39.0	[9]44.20	19.23	7.67	0.44
1979	80.00	92	445	308	11.09	52.6	753.9	37.3	55.75	23.65	12.64	1.18
1980	126.37	101	677	613	20.63	42.5	846.0	37.4	89.06	24.52	21.59	1.59
1981	99.51	84	446	460	10.52	36.5	733.1	44.6	111.48	26.29	31.77	1.98
1982	49.95	73	327	376	7.95	25.5	653.9	38.5	108.27	27.14	28.52	2.46
1983	30.60	77	424	424	11.44	21.7	654.8	41.4	87.24	25.85	26.19	2.59
1984	37.44	67	357	361	8.14	25.6	623.8	48.6	94.31	25.51	25.88	2.66
1985	33.68	67	291	318	6.14	19.1	596.0	40.4	106.46	25.10	24.09	2.51
1986	23.74	66	461	368	5.47	22.1	383.2	38.0	105.22	23.70	12.51	1.94
1987	27.08	83	553	478	7.01	35.9	418.8	41.9	89.78	23.00	15.40	1.67
1988	47.37	121	523	438	6.53	37.1	441.4	60.2	85.95	22.00	12.58	1.69
1989	44.93	131	507	383	5.50	39.4	520.2	82.0	86.62	21.76	15.86	1.69
1990	38.06	123	467	385	4.82	46.0	386.3	74.6	80.14	21.71	20.03	1.71
1991	36.70	109	371	363	4.04	33.5	362.9	52.8	71.45	21.45	16.54	1.64
1992	34.42	107	356	345	3.94	35.1	402.4	58.4	48.14	21.17	15.99	1.74
1993, prel.	(NA)	92	370	355	4.20	32.0	385.0	46.0	32.00	(NA)	14.23	2.01

NA Not available.　[1] Dollars per pound of tantalum content.　[2] Domestic market prices for wirebar, 1970, 1975-77; prices for cathode thereafter.　[3] Average annual dealer prices.　[4] 1970, New York prices; beginning 1975, nationwide delivered basis.　[5] Straits tin through 1975; thereafter, composite price.　[6] Prime western. Beginning 1975, delivered price.　[7] F.o.b. works.　[8] Average value at the point of production. Source: U.S. Energy Information Administration, *Annual Energy Review.*

Source: Except as noted, U.S. Bureau of Mines, *Mineral Facts and Problems,* 1980 edition; and *Mineral Commodity Summaries,* annual.

No. 1172. Principal Fuels, Nonmetals, and Metals—U.S. Production, as Percent of World Production: 1980 to 1993

MINERAL	Unit	WORLD PRODUCTION				PERCENT U.S. OF WORLD			
		1980	1985	1990	1993, est.	1980	1985	1990	1993, est.
Fuels: [1]									
Coal	Bil. sh. ton	4.2	4.8	5.2	(NA)	20	18	20	(NA)
Petroleum (crude)	Bil. bbl	21.7	19.6	22	(NA)	14	17	12	(NA)
Natural gas (dry, marketable)	Tril. cu. ft	53.1	62	74.3	(NA)	37	26	24	(NA)
Natural gas plant liquids	Bil. bbl	1.4	1.5	1.8	(NA)	43	38	32	(NA)
Nonmetals:									
Asbestos	1,000 metric tons	4,699	4,249	4,003	3,110	2	1	(D)	(Z)
Barite	1,000 metric tons	7,495	6,067	5,633	5,200	27	11	8	8
Feldspar	1,000 metric tons	3,202	4,039	5,456	5,900	20	16	12	13
Fluorspar	1,000 metric tons	5,006	4,979	5,131	3,660	2	1	1	1
Gypsum	Mil. metric tons	78	87	100	98	14	15	15	16
Mica (incl. scrap)	1,000 metric tons	228	255	215	185	46	49	51	48
Nitrogen, (fixed) - ammonia	Mil. metric tons	74	91	97	93	20	14	13	14
Phosphate rock, gross wt.	Mil. metric tons	144	149	162	131	38	34	29	27
Potash (k₂O equivalent)	Mil. metric tons	28	29	28	22	8	4	6	6
Sulfur, elemental	Mil. metric tons	55	54	58	53	22	22	20	20
Metals, mine basis:									
Bauxite	Mil. metric tons	89	84	109	101	2	1	(D)	(D)
Columbian concentrates (Nb content)	1,000 metric tons	15	15	15	15	(NA)	-	(NA)	-
Copper	1,000 metric tons	7,405	7,988	9,017	9,300	16	14	18	19
Gold	Metric tons	1,219	1,532	2,133	2,290	2	5	14	14
Iron ore	Mil. metric tons	891	861	982	940	8	6	6	6
Lead [2]	1,000 metric tons	3,470	3,431	3,353	3,200	17	12	15	13
Mercury	Metric tons	6,806	6,136	4,523	2,900	16	9	12	2
Molybdenum	1,000 metric tons	111	98	128	108	62	50	48	42
Nickel [2]	1,000 metric tons	779	813	965	826	2	1	(Z)	(Z)
Silver	1,000 metric tons	11	13	16	15	9	9	13	11
Tantalum concentrates (ta content)	Metric tons	544	315	400	290	(NA)	-	(NA)	-
Titanium concentrates:									
Ilmenite	1,000 metric tons	3,726	3,457	4,072	3,300	14	(D)	(D)	(D)
Rutile	1,000 metric tons	436	373	481	430	(D)	(D)	(D)	(D)
Tungsten [2]	1,000 metric tons	52	47	43	26	5	2	14	(D)
Vanadium [2]	1,000 metric tons	37	30	31	28	12	(D)	(D)	(D)
Zinc [2]	1,000 metric tons	5,954	6,758	7,184	7,000	6	4	8	8
Metals, smelter basis:									
Aluminum	1,000 metric tons	15,383	15,398	19,292	(NA)	30	23	21	(NA)
Cadmium	1,000 metric tons	18	19	20	(NA)	9	8	8	(NA)
Copper	1,000 metric tons	7,649	8,630	9,472	(NA)	14	14	15	(NA)
Iron, pig	Mil. metric tons	514	499	532	(NA)	12	9	9	(NA)
Lead [3]	1,000 metric tons	5,430	5,641	5,763	(NA)	23	20	23	(NA)
Magnesium [4]	1,000 metric tons	316	325	354	(NA)	49	42	39	(NA)
Raw Steel	Mil. metric tons	717	718	771	(NA)	14	11	12	(NA)
Tin [5]	1,000 metric tons	251	193	223	(NA)	1	2	(NA)	(NA)
Zinc	1,000 metric tons	6,049	6,786	7,060	(NA)	6	5	5	(NA)

- Represents or rounds to zero.   D Withheld to avoid disclosing company data.   NA Not available.   Z Less than half the unit of measure.   [1] Source: Energy Information Administration, *International Energy Annual.*   [2] Content of ore and concentrate.   [3] Refinery production.   [4] Primary production; no smelter processing necessary.   [5] Production from primary sources only.

Source: Except as noted, U.S. Bureau of Mines, *Annual Reports,* and *Mineral Commodity Summaries,* annual.

No. 1173. Federal Strategic and Critical Materials Inventory: 1980 to 1992

[As of **Dec.** 31. Covers strategic and critical materials essential to military and industrial requirements in time of national emergency. Market values are estimated current trade values of similar materials and not necessarily amounts that would be realized at time of sale]

MINERAL	Unit	QUANTITY [1]				VALUE (mil. dol.)			
		1980	1985	1990	1992	1980	1985	1990	1992
Tin	1,000 metric ton	200	185	169	156	3,158	2,324	962	1,034
Silver	1,000 troy oz.	139,500	136,006	92,151	72,502	2,288	801	374	321
Cobalt	Mil. lb.	41	53	53	53	1,020	590	443	798
Bauxite [2]	1,000 lg. ton	14,333	17,957	18,033	17,373	583	871	888	318
Manganese [3]	1,000 sh. ton	5,130	4,470	4,017	3,647	599	520	962	753
Tungsten [4]	Mil. lb.	97	87	82	82	817	369	253	225
Zinc	1,000 sh. ton	380	378	379	379	317	268	483	388
Titanium	1,000 sh. ton	43	48	37	37	432	405	402	236
Platinum	1,000 troy oz.	466	466	453	453	215	154	186	131
Chromium [5]	1,000 sh. ton	804	854	1,074	1,281	773	836	917	943
Diamonds: Stones	Carat 1,000	19,224	12,549	7,777	7,777	349	336	267	62
Industrial, bort.	Carat 1,000	23,693	22,001	17,353	5,077	73	39	16	11

[1] Consists of stockpile and nonstockpile grades and reflects uncommitted balances.   [2] Consists of abrasive grade, metallic grade Jamaica, metallic grade Suriname, and refractory.   [3] Consists of chemical grade, dioxide battery natural, dioxide battery synthetic, electrolytic, ferro-high carbon, ferro-med. carbon, ferro-silicon, and metal.   [4] Consists of carbide powder, ferro, metal powder, and ores and concentrates.   [5] Consists of ferro-high carbon, ferro-low carbon, ferro-silicon, and metal.

Source: U.S. Defense Logistics Agency, *Statistical Supplement, Stockpile Report to the Congress* (AP-3).

No. 1174. Federal Strategic and Critical Materials—Summary: 1990 to 1993

ITEM	Unit	Tin	Silver	Cobalt	Bauxite	Manganese	Tungsten	Zinc	Titanium	Platinum	Chromium	DIAMONDS Stones	DIAMONDS Industrial bort
Production:													
1990	1,000 metric tons.	[1]13.2	2.1	[1]1.2	(D)	-	(D)	263	24.7	[2]7,740	[2]94	-	[3]90.0
1991	1,000 metric tons.	[1]13.1	1.9	1.6	(D)	-	(D)	253	13.4	[2]7,780	90	-	[3]90.0
1992	1,000 metric tons.	18.8	1.8	1.6	(D)	-	(D)	272	(D)	[2]8,310	95	-	[3]95.0
1993	1,000 metric tons.	18.5	1.7	1.6	(D)	-	(D)	255	(D)	[2]8,300	88	-	[3]100.3
Imports:													
1990	1,000 metric tons.	33.8	3.4	6.4	12,987	307	6.4	723	1.1	[2]125,354	346	[4]11.0	[4]85.4
1991	1,000 metric tons.	29.1	4.2	6.9	12,305	234	7.8	637	0.6	[2]125,661	309	7.6	[4]70.0
1992	1,000 metric tons.	27.3	5.0	5.8	11,372	247	2.5	740	0.7	[2]132,006	324	9.8	[4]97.3
1993	1,000 metric tons.	33.0	4.5	5.7	11,860	185	2.0	682	1.0	[2]143,000	342	5.5	[4]115.0
Export:													
1990	1,000 metric tons.	0.7	1.8	1.3	64	70	0.1	128	[5]15.8	[2]5,044	14	[4]1.7	[4]71.0
1991	1,000 metric tons.	1.0	1.7	1.5	58	66	(6)	112	[5]12.1	[2]39,624	31	2.9	[4]78.8
1992	1,000 metric tons.	1.9	1.8	1.4	68	13	(6)	120	[5]8.0	[2]57,829	16	5.6	[4]83.6
1993	1,000 metric tons.	2.3	1.7	0.9	90	14	(6)	130	[5]7.3	[2]86,000	18	3.7	[4]96.1
Consumption:													
1990	1,000 metric tons.	45.5	[7]4.4	7.6	[8]4,570	497	8.4	992	[9]23.2	[2]117,043	439	[4]9.8	[4]112.7
1991	1,000 metric tons.	48.7	[7]3.8	7.8	[8]4,609	472	11.8	933	[9]13.6	[2]111,798	377	5.0	[4]89.1
1992	1,000 metric tons.	43.6	[7]4.1	6.5	[8]4,863	438	7.5	1,035	[9]14.2	[2]109,469	416	4.3	[4]121.9
1993	1,000 metric tons.	45.9	[7]4.0	6.3	[8]4,500	450	6.8	1,120	[9]15.8	[2]112,300	488	1.8	[4]134.4
Net Import reliance:													
1990	Percent	71.0	(10)	84.0	98	100	81.0	41	(11)	88	79	95.0	13.0
1991	Percent	74.0	(10)	80.0	100	100	91.0	24	4.0	90	76	94.0	(1)
1992	Percent	80.0	(10)	75.0	100	100	86.0	30	(D)	87	77	98.0	19.0
1993	Percent	81.0	(10)	75.0	100	100	84.0	26	(D)	88	82	95.0	14.0
Stocks, end of year:													
1990	1,000 metric tons.	17.3	9.2	3.2	2,300	379	1.1	87	3.3	[2]30,324	125	NA	NA
1991	1,000 metric tons.	13.8	9.4	2.4	2,600	275	1.8	79	2.9	[2]24,313	118	NA	NA
1992	1,000 metric tons.	10.7	10.1	1.8	2,300	276	0.7	75	1.9	[2]26,946	118	NA	NA
1993	1,000 metric tons.	10.0	9.0	2.2	2,600	260	0.7	77	2.9	[2]24,000	117	NA	NA
World production:													
1990	1,000 metric tons.	221.7	16.2	35.9	108,609	25,252	51.8	7,184	100.8	[2]291,015	12,968	(12)	[4]58.8
1991	1,000 metric tons.	202.7	15.7	26.8	108,157	21,213	41.9	7,170	56.3	[2]288,338	13,445	(12)	[4]55.2
1992	1,000 metric tons.	179.5	15.3	21.9	103,625	19,929	31.6	7,137	38.6	[2]280,889	10,896	(12)	[4]55.7
1993	1,000 metric tons.	175.0	14.9	17.4	101,000	20,400	25.5	7,000	37.2	[2]273,000	10,000	(12)	[4]55.7

- Represents or rounds to zero. D Withheld to avoid disclosure of individual company data. NA Not available. [1] Production from scrap or secondary production. [2] Kilograms. [3] Manufactured diamond bort, grit, and powder and dust. [4] Million carats. [5] All metal forms. [6] Less than 50 metric tons. [7] Apparent demand. [8] Includes alumina. [9] Included with bort production; data not separable. [10] Net importer; however, changes in unreported investor stocks preclude calculation of a meaningful net import reliance. [11] Net exporter. [12] Included with bort production; data not separable.

Source: U.S. Bureau of Mines, *Annual Reports*, and *Mineral Commodity Summaries*, annual.

No. 1175. Selected Mineral and Metal Products—Quantity and Value of Imports and Exports: 1989 to 1992

[Imports represent imports for consumption. Exports include shipments under foreign aid programs. Beginning 1989, import and export data are not necessarily comparable to prior data due to change in tariff schedule to Harmonized System]

PRODUCT	Unit	QUANTITY				VALUE (mil. dol.)			
		1989	1990	1991	1992	1989	1990	1991	1992
IMPORTS									
Petroleum (crude) [1]	Mil. bbls.	2,128	2,222	2,124	(NA)	35,041	43,833	37,123	(NA)
Gem stones: Diamonds	Mil. carats	10.1	7.5	8.5	9.4	4,358	3,955	3,992	4,144
Ores and concentrates:									
Chromium (Cr_2O_3 content) .	1,000 metric tons	237	134	94	99	44	22	15	15
Copper	1,000 metric tons	46.5	91.5	60.8	102.1	51	131	69	125
Iron.	Mil. metric tons.	19.6	18.1	13.3	12.5	522	560	437	396
Tungsten	1,000 metric tons	7.9	6.4	7.8	2.5	45	31	43	16
Metals:									
Aluminum	1,000 metric tons	923	960	1,025	1156	1,898	1,597	1,428	1,501
Cobalt [2]	1,000 metric tons	5.4	6.0	6.4	5.3	92	107	158	246
Copper refined ingots, etc. .	1,000 metric tons	300	262	289	289	854	675	685	660
Gold (refined bullion)	Metric tons. . . .	97	65	147	141	1,199	795	1,722	1,568
Iron and steel products									
(major).	Mil. metric tons.	18.1	17.8	16.2	17.4	10,649	11,612	11,962	10,977
Platinum group [3]	Metric tons. . . .	113	125	126	132	1,382	1,906	1,743	1,484
Silver (refined bullion)	Metric tons. . . .	3,062	2,698	2,525	2,662	579	437	339	341
Zinc: Blocks, pigs, slabs . . .	1,000 metric tons	712	632	549	(NA)	1,184	992	620	(NA)
EXPORTS									
Fuels: [1]									
Bituminous coal	Mil. sh. tons . . .	90.8	95.3	98.4	(NA)	4,243	4,464	4,588	(NA)
Petroleum (crude)	Mil. bbls.	3.8	8.0	2.7	(NA)	62.1	198.6	54.1	(NA)
Nonmetallic minerals:									
Gem stones: Diamonds . . .	Mil. carats	1.1	1.2	1.8	4	1,244	1,433	1,383	1,450
Nitrogen compounds (maj.) .	Mil. metric tons.	12.5	11.9	13.9	12.8	(NA)	(NA)	(NA)	(NA)
Phosphatic fertilizers [4]	Mil. metric tons.	9.6	9.2	11.5	10.3	1,760	1,515	1,974	(NA)
Metals:									
Aluminum: Ingots, slabs,									
crude.	1,000 metric tons	593	684	793	604	1,260	1,169	1,274	843
Plates, sheets, bars, etc .	1,000 metric tons	416	419	489	534	1,196	1,278	1,384	1,416
Gold (refined bullion)	Metric tons. . . .	124	141	174	257	1,490	1,719	2,039	2,877
Iron and steel products									
(major).	Mil. metric tons.	4.7	4.7	6.6	4.7	2,582	4,665	5,753	5,374
Magnesium [5]	1,000 metric tons	56.6	51.8	55.2	52	170	164	150	132
Molybdenum [6]	Metric tons. . . .	253	180	88	74	3	2	1	1
Silver (refined bullion)	Metric tons. . . .	430	736	787	911	78	120	115	126
Scrap exports:									
Aluminum	1,000 metric tons	575	537	461	295	769	719	542	300
Iron and steel	Mil. metric tons.	11.3	11.7	9.5	9.4	1,785	1,653	1,253	1,113

NA Not available.   [1] Source: U.S. Bureau of the Census, *U.S. Imports for Consumption* and *General Imports, TSUSA Commodity and Country*, FT 246, annual; and *U.S. Exports, Schedule B Commodity and Country*, FT 446, annual; 1989 and 1990, *U.S. Exports of Merchandise* and *U.S. Imports of Merchandise* compact discs, December issues.   [2] Includes unwrought metal, waste and scrap.   [3] Unwrought and semimanufactured.   [4] Superphosphates and ammonium phosphates.   [5] Metal and alloys, scrap, semimanufactured forms.   [6] Metals and alloys, crude and scrap.

Source: Except as noted, U.S. Bureau of Mines, *Minerals Yearbook, 1984* and *1988-91*; and *Annual Reports, 1992*.

No. 1176. Mineral Industries—Lost Workday Injuries and Fatalities: 1985 to 1992

[Excludes office workers. Lost workday injuries are nonfatal occurrences that result in days away from work, days of restricted work activity or a permanent disability. Data for all years includes injuries to independent contractors at mine sites. Rates for the noncoal industries are based only on employment and hours worked by mine employees. See also *Historical Statistics, Colonial Times to 1970*, series M 271-286]

ITEM	COAL MINING			QUARRYING; RELATED INDUSTRY [1]			METAL; NONMETAL MINING [2]		
	1985	1990	1992	1985	1990	1992	1985	1990	1992
Injuries, total	9,073	12,226	9,256	2,545	3,794	2,964	2,212	3,778	2,847
Fatal.	68	66	54	26	18	18	22	26	16
Rate per million work-hours:									
Fatal	0.20	0.22	0.21	0.19	0.13	0.14	0.17	0.17	0.11
Nonfatal	26.6	41.4	35.8	18.5	28.1	23.7	16.8	24.5	19.8
Fatalities per 1,000 employed [3]	0.36	0.41	0.38	0.37	0.27	0.28	0.31	0.34	0.22

[1] Includes cement.   [2] Nonmetal mines exclude extraction of Frasch process sulfur.   [3] Average number of persons at work each day mines were active.

Source: U.S. Mine Safety and Health Administration, Denver, CO, unpublished data.

No. 1177. Net U.S. Imports of Selected Minerals and Metals as Percent of Apparent Consumption, 1980 to 1993, and by Major Foreign Sources

[Percent, based on net imports which equal the difference between imports and exports plus or minus Government stockpile and industry stock changes]

MINERAL	1980	1990	1991	1992	1993, est.	Rank of major foreign sources, 1989-92
Columbium	100	100	100	100	100	Brazil, 68%; Canada, 24%; Germany 4%
Manganese....	98	100	100	100	100	So. Africa, 25%; France, 14%; Brazil, 12%
Mica (sheet) ...	100	100	100	100	100	India, 63%; Belgium, 21%; Brazil, 3%
Strontium	100	100	100	100	100	Mexico, 91%; Germany, 7%
Bauxite [1]	94	98	100	100	100	Australia, 40%; Jamaica, 19%; Guinea, 18%
Asbestos	78	90	95	95	95	Canada, 98%; South Africa, 1%
Platinum group..	87	88	90	87	88	So. Africa, 50%; U. K., 15%; Russia, 13%.
Tantalum	90	86	86	85	86	Germany, 37%; Australia, 14%; Canada, 8%
Cobalt	93	84	80	75	75	Zambia, 26%; Zaire, 21%; Canada, 18%
Chromium.....	91	79	76	77	82	So. Africa, 47%; Turkey, 14%; Zimbabwe, 10%
Tungsten	53	81	91	86	84	China, 49%; Bolivia, 8%; Peru, 7%
Nickel	76	69	67	61	64	Canada, 54%; Norway, 16%; Australia, 8%
Tin..........	79	71	74	80	81	Brazil, 24%; Bolivia, 22%; China, 16%
Barite........	44	69	70	52	58	China, 76%; India, 19%; Mexico, 1%.
Potash.......	65	68	67	67	71	Canada, 92%; Israel, 3%; former U.S.S.R., 2%
Antimony	47	51	53	60	57	China, 60%; Mexico, 10%; So. Africa, 10%
Cadmium	55	62	48	49	66	Canada, 34%; Mexico, 17%; Australia, 8%
Selenium	59	46	50	48	46	Canada, 37%; Japan, 16%; Belgium, 14%
Petroleum [2][3]..	37	42	40	(NA)	(NA)	(NA)
Zinc.........	60	[4]41	[4]24	[4]30	[4]26	Canada, 61%; Mexico, 11%; Peru, 6%
Gypsum	35	36	31	31	29	Canada, 70%; Mexico, 23%; Spain, 6%.
Iron ore	25	21	11	12	12	Canada, 52%; Brazil, 24%; Venezuela, 19%
Iron and steel ..	13	13	12	13	12	EEC [5], 30%; Canada, 19%; Japan, 18%
Sulfur........	14	15	19	20	15	Canada, 60%; Mexico, 36%.
Natural gas [3]..	5	8	8	(NA)	(NA)	(NA)
Copper.......	16	[6]	[6]	2	6	Canada, 49%; Chile, 18%; Mexico, 15%
Aluminum	[6]	[6]	[6]	1	16	Canada, 79%; Venezuela, 6%; Mexico, 2%
Silver........	7	(NA)	(NA)	(NA)	(NA)	Mexico, 35%; Canada, 27%; United Kingdom, 9%
Mercury	27	(NA)	(NA)	(NA)	(NA)	Spain, 44%; Canada, 42%; Germany, 12%
Titanium	32	(D)	(D)	(D)	(D)	South Africa, 40%; Australia, 39%
Vanadium	35	(D)	(D)	(D)	(D)	So. Africa, 35%; EC, 11%; So. Amer.& Mexico, 21%

D Withheld to avoid disclosure.   NA Not available.   [1] Includes alumina.   [2] Includes crude and products.   [3] Source: Energy Information Administration, Annual Energy Review, and and Monthly Energy Review.   [4] Effect of sharp rise in exports of concentrates. If calculated on a refined zinc-only basis, reliance would be about the same as pre-1990 level; 1990, 64%; 1991, 61%; and 1992, 64%.   [5] European Economic Community.   [6] Net exports.

Source: Except as noted, U.S. Bureau of Mines, Mineral Commodity Summaries; import and export data from U.S. Bureau of the Census.

No. 1178. Federal Offshore Leasing, Exploration, Production, and Revenue: 1980 to 1992

[See source for explanation of terms and for reliability statement]

ITEM	Unit	1980	1985	1986	1987	1988	1989	1990	1991	1992
Tracts offered	Number..	483	15,754	10,724	10,926	33,376	11,013	10,459	16,800	9,618
Tracts leased	Number..	218	667	142	640	1,856	1,049	825	676	204
Acres offered	1,000 ...	2,563	87,029	58,670	59,762	85,366	60,096	56,788	80,288	52,380
Acres leased	1,000 ...	1,134	3,512	734	45,075	10,040	5,580	4,263	3,416	1,021
Bonus paid for leased tracts	Bil. dol. ..	4.2	1.5	0.2	0.5	1.2	0.6	0.6	0.4	0.1
New wells being drilled:										
Active	Number..	191	195	95	142	116	123	120	64	104
Suspended...........	Number..	739	348	279	265	289	361	266	249	180
Wells completed	Number..	9,638	12,285	12,536	12,734	12,827	12,938	13,167	13,184	13,209
Wells plugged and abandoned.	Number..	8,057	10,487	11,909	12,373	13,164	13,846	14,677	15,430	16,348
Revenue, total [1]	Bil. dol. ..	6.4	5.2	2.8	2.9	3.4	13.0	3.3	2.8	2.5
Bonuses	Bil. dol. ..	4.2	1.5	0.2	0.5	1.2	0.6	0.6	0.4	0.1
Oil and gas royalties [1]	Bil. dol. ..	2.1	3.6	2.6	2.3	2.1	2.1	2.6	2.3	2.3
Rentals	Bil. dol. ..	(Z)	0.1	0.1	0.1	0.1	0.1	0.1	0.1	0.1
Production, value [2]	Bil. dol. ..	13.1	22.2	15.7	14.6	12.9	13.0	16.5	14.2	14.5
Crude oil	Bil. dol. ..	4.8	9.6	5.8	5.6	4.2	4.4	5.9	5.2	5.3
Condensate	Bil. dol. ..	0.4	1.0	0.7	0.7	0.7	0.8	1.1	1.1	1.0
Natural gas	Bil. dol. ..	7.9	11.5	9.3	8.1	7.9	7.8	9.5	7.9	8.2
Production: [2]										
Crude oil	Mil. bbls. .	259	352	350	325	279	260	274	263	301
Condensate	Mil. bbls. .	19	37	39	41	41	45	51	52	52
Natural gas	Bil. cu. ft .	4,641	4,000	3,949	4,425	4,310	4,200	5,093	4,516	4,685

Z Less than $50 million.   [1] Includes condensate royalties.   [2] Production value is value at time of production, not current value.

Source: U.S. Dept. of the Interior, Minerals Management Service, Federal Offshore Statistics, annual.

No. 1179. Petroleum Industry—Summary: 1980 to 1992

ITEM	Unit	1980	1985	1986	1987	1988	1989	1990	1991	1992, est.
Crude oil producing wells (Dec. 31).	1,000...	548	647	623	620	612	603	602	614	594
Daily output per well	Bbl....	15.9	13.9	13.9	13.5	13.5	12.6	12.2	12.1	12.0
Completed wells drilled, total	1,000...	70	70	40	36	32	28	30	25	19
Crude oil	1,000...	32	35	19	16	13	10	12	11	8
Gas	1,000...	17	14	8	8	8	9	10	9	7
Dry	1,000...	20	21	13	12	10	8	8	5	4
Crude oil production, total	Mil. bbl.	3,146	3,275	3,168	3,047	2,979	2,785	2,685	2,707	2,625
Value at wells	Bil. dol..	67.9	78.9	39.6	46.9	37.5	44.1	53.7	44.7	41.8
Average price per barrel	Dollars..	21.59	24.09	12.51	15.40	12.58	15.86	20.03	16.54	15.98
Refinery input of crude oil	Mil. bbl.	4,934	4,381	4,641	4,692	4,848	4,891	4,895	4,855	4,909
Imports: Crude oil	Mil. bbl.	1,926	1,168	1,525	1,706	1,869	2,133	2,151	2,111	2,223
Refined petroleum products	Mil. bbl.	603	681	747	731	840	809	775	500	471
Import value	Mil. dol..	74,440	50,370	34,790	41,500	39,980	49,030	60,680	50,070	50,530
Export value	Mil. dol..	2,870	5,130	3,890	3,930	2,800	2,860	4,370	4,680	4,280
Operable refineries	Number .	319	223	216	219	213	204	205	202	199
Capacity (Jan. 1)	Mil. bbl.	6,584	5,716	5,643	5,681	5,825	5,714	5,683	5,723	5,731
Output	Mil. bbl.	5,352	5,019	5,301	5,339	5,498	5,539	5,570	5,933	6,050
Utilization rate	Percent .	75.4	77.6	82.9	83.1	84.7	86.6	87.1	86.0	86.6
Proved reserves	Bil. bbl..	29.8	28.4	26.9	27.3	26.8	26.5	26.3	24.7	23.7

Source: U.S. Energy Information Administration, *Annual Energy Review, Petroleum Supply Annual; U.S. Crude Oil, Natural Gas,* and *Natural Gas Liquids Reserves.*

No. 1180. Crude Petroleum and Natural Gas Wells Drilled—Summary: 1980 to 1992

[Includes all costs incurred for drilling and equipping wells to point of completion as productive wells or abandonment after drilling becomes unproductive. Based on sample of operators of different size drilling establishments]

ITEM	Unit	1980	1985	1986	1987	1988	1989	1990	1991	1992
Wells drilled	Number...	62,011	67,821	37,173	33,041	29,741	26,693	28,513	27,194	22,388
Offshore	Number...	1,272	1,247	898	709	866	746	704	718	440
Footage drilled	Mil. ft...	296.0	314.5	176.3	157.4	150.2	131.5	143.8	138.7	121.9
Drilling cost	Mil. dol....	22,800	23,697	13,552	9,239	10,550	9,669	10,937	11,461	8,566
Average depth per well ..	Feet	4,773	4,637	4,742	4,762	5,051	4,925	5,043	5,100	5,445
Average cost per well ...	$1,000....	368	349	365	280	355	362	384	421	383
Offshore	$1,000....	3,024	4,073	4,004	2,896	3,112	3,197	3,112	3,550	3,223
Average cost per foot ...	Dollars ...	77.02	75.35	76.88	58.71	70.23	73.55	76.07	82.64	70.27

Source: American Petroleum Institute, *Joint Association Survey of Drilling Costs,* annual.

No. 1181. Domestic Motor Gasoline Supply: 1980 to 1993

[In 1,000 barrels per day, except as noted]

ITEM	1980	1984	1985	1986	1987	1988	1989	1990	1991	1992	1993
Supply [1]	6,579	6,693	6,831	7,034	7,206	7,336	7,328	7,235	7,188	7,268	7,483
Production	6,506	6,453	6,419	6,752	6,841	6,956	6,963	6,959	6,975	7,058	7,351
Net imports	140	299	381	326	384	405	369	342	297	294	249
Stocks (mil. bbl.) [2]	261	243	223	233	226	228	213	220	219	216	226

[1] Production plus net imports less net increase in primary stocks.   [2] End of year, includes motor gasoline blending components.

Source: U.S. Energy Information Administration, *Monthly Energy Review.*

No. 1182. Natural Gas Plant Liquids—Production and Value: 1970 to 1992

[Barrels of 42 gallons. See also *Historical Statistics, Colonial Times to 1970,* series M 143-146]

ITEM	Unit	1970	1975	1980	1985	1987	1988	1989	1990	1991	1992
Field production [1]	Mil. bbl ...	606	596	576	587	582	595	564	566	606	621
Pentanes plus	Mil. bbl ...	197	149	126	103	106	111	113	112	118	121
Liquefied petroleum gases .	Mil. bbl ...	400	444	441	479	474	483	451	454	488	500
Natural gas processed	Tril. cu. ft. .	19	18	15	13	13	13	13	15	16	16

[1] Includes other finished petroleum products, not shown separately.

Source: Through 1975, U.S. Bureau of Mines, *Minerals Yearbook;* thereafter, U.S. Energy Information Administration, *Energy Data Reports, Petroleum Statement Annual, Petroleum Supply Annual,* and *Natural Gas Annual.*

No. 1183. World Crude Oil Production: 1980 to 1992

[In thousands of barrels]

COUNTRY	1980	1985	1986	1987	1988	1989	1990	1991
Total	59,599	53,981	56,601	58,662	59,773	60,471	60,105	60,255
Algeria	1,106	1,037	1,048	1,040	1,095	1,175	1,230	1,217
Iraq	2,514	1,433	2,079	2,685	2,897	2,040	305	450
Kuwait	1,656	1,023	1,585	1,492	1,783	1,175	190	1,029
Libya	1,787	1,059	972	1,175	1,150	1,375	1,483	1,483
Qatar	472	301	293	346	380	406	395	396
Saudi Arabia	9,900	3,388	4,265	5,086	5,064	6,410	8,115	8,438
United Arab Emirates	1,709	1,193	1,541	1,565	1,860	2,117	2,386	2,325
Indonesia	1,577	1,325	1,343	1,342	1,409	1,462	1,592	1,566
Iran	1,662	2,250	2,298	2,240	2,810	3,088	3,312	3,429
Nigeria	2,055	1,495	1,341	1,450	1,716	1,810	1,892	1,982
Venezuela	2,168	1,677	1,752	1,903	1,907	2,137	2,375	2,334
Canada	1,435	1,471	1,535	1,616	1,560	1,553	1,548	1,598
Mexico	1,936	2,745	2,548	2,512	2,520	2,553	2,680	2,668
United Kingdom	1,622	2,530	2,406	2,232	1,802	1,820	1,797	1,825
United States	8,597	8,971	8,349	8,140	7,613	7,355	7,417	7,171
China	2,114	2,505	2,690	2,730	2,757	2,774	2,835	2,838
U.S.S.R. (former)	11,706	11,585	11,985	11,978	11,625	10,880	9,887	8,388
Other	5,408	7,821	8,416	8,971	9,617	10,070	10,373	10,820
Arab OPEC	19,144	9,434	11,783	13,389	14,229	14,698	14,104	15,338
Total OPEC	26,781	16,353	18,692	20,483	22,279	23,465	23,569	24,947

Source: U. S. Energy Information Administration, *Monthly Energy Review*.

No. 1184. World Natural Gas Production: 1984 to 1992

[In quadrillion Btu's]

REGION AND COUNTRY	1984	1985	1986	1987	1988	1989	1990	1991	1992 [1]
World total	58.33	60.62	61.89	64.93	68.07	70.56	72.00	73.96	74.27
North America	21.54	20.80	20.13	20.88	21.87	22.34	22.99	23.37	23.76
Canada	2.61	2.98	2.77	3.00	3.47	3.67	3.72	4.18	4.56
Mexico	1.00	0.92	0.89	0.83	0.89	0.89	0.91	0.90	0.89
United States	17.93	16.91	16.47	17.05	17.52	17.78	18.36	18.28	18.31
Central and South America [2]	1.78	1.84	1.86	1.82	2.04	2.21	2.22	2.22	2.21
Argentina	0.46	0.47	0.51	0.49	0.62	0.67	0.59	0.60	0.57
Columbia	0.16	0.16	0.16	0.16	0.17	0.17	0.17	0.18	0.17
Trinidad and Tobago	0.20	0.23	0.16	0.15	0.16	0.17	0.19	0.21	0.20
Venezuela	0.69	0.70	0.77	0.75	0.79	0.88	0.98	0.94	0.96
Western Europe [2]	6.03	6.25	6.26	6.59	6.28	6.47	6.47	7.56	7.60
France	0.20	0.17	0.13	0.13	0.10	0.10	0.09	0.12	0.13
Germany	(NA)	(NA)	(NA)	(NA)	(NA)	(NA)	(NA)	0.60	0.60
Italy	0.50	0.52	0.58	0.59	0.60	0.62	0.62	0.62	0.65
Netherlands	2.52	2.59	2.44	2.53	2.33	2.41	2.41	2.72	2.73
Norway	1.06	1.07	1.09	1.22	1.10	1.23	1.09	1.05	1.07
United Kingdom	1.51	1.61	1.70	1.79	1.72	1.68	1.86	2.01	1.98
Yugoslavia (former)	0.08	0.09	0.10	0.09	0.12	0.11	0.10	0.10	0.10
Eastern Europe [2]	21.31	23.11	24.54	25.61	27.08	27.96	28.34	28.04	26.85
Hungary	0.27	0.29	0.28	0.25	0.25	0.24	0.18	0.20	0.19
Poland	0.22	0.23	0.21	0.20	0.21	0.19	0.14	0.15	0.15
Romania	1.50	1.43	1.50	1.48	1.22	1.27	1.16	0.98	0.88
U.S.S.R. (former)	19.27	21.12	22.50	23.63	25.34	26.20	26.82	26.68	(X)
Russia	(X)	(X)	(X)	(X)	(X)	(X)	(X)	(X)	21.08
Turkmenistan	(X)	(X)	(X)	(X)	(X)	(X)	(X)	(X)	1.98
Ukraine	(X)	(X)	(X)	(X)	(X)	(X)	(X)	(X)	0.69
Uzbekistan	(X)	(X)	(X)	(X)	(X)	(X)	(X)	(X)	1.32
Middle East [2]	2.10	2.50	2.76	3.18	3.53	3.87	3.89	3.89	4.31
Bahrain	0.14	0.17	0.19	0.23	0.17	0.19	0.21	0.24	0.26
Iran	0.50	0.63	0.57	0.60	0.75	0.83	0.88	0.97	0.93
Kuwait	0.15	0.15	0.18	0.20	0.25	0.30	0.19	0.02	0.23
Qatar	0.22	0.20	0.20	0.21	0.24	0.23	0.29	0.22	0.22
Saudi Arabia	0.65	0.75	0.93	0.99	1.08	1.10	1.13	1.18	1.26
United Arab Emirates	0.36	0.51	0.56	0.71	0.72	0.85	0.82	0.96	1.03
Africa [2]	1.91	1.97	1.99	2.23	2.32	2.53	2.60	2.82	2.92
Algeria	1.44	1.44	1.41	1.62	1.68	1.81	1.90	2.05	2.09
Egypt	0.15	0.18	0.21	0.23	0.26	0.29	0.30	0.34	0.36
Libya	0.17	0.19	0.21	0.20	0.20	0.22	0.23	0.25	0.26
Nigeria	0.10	0.11	0.12	0.14	0.14	0.17	0.14	0.18	0.20
Far East and Oceania [2]	3.66	4.16	4.35	4.63	4.96	5.18	5.48	6.06	6.62
Australia	0.42	0.47	0.50	0.51	0.52	0.59	0.68	0.80	0.88
Bangladesh	0.09	0.10	0.11	0.13	0.16	0.16	0.16	0.17	0.19
Brunei	0.34	0.33	0.33	0.34	0.34	0.34	0.35	0.31	0.31
China	0.46	0.48	0.51	0.52	0.53	0.53	0.53	0.55	0.52
India	0.12	0.14	0.19	0.23	0.31	0.33	0.41	0.46	0.48
Indonesia	1.11	1.29	1.24	1.35	1.42	1.49	1.60	1.81	2.00
Japan	0.09	0.10	0.08	0.08	0.08	0.08	0.08	0.08	0.08
Malaysia	0.34	0.45	0.55	0.57	0.60	0.63	0.68	0.77	0.95
New Zealand	0.11	0.13	0.16	0.15	0.19	0.18	0.14	0.19	0.20
Pakistan	0.34	0.36	0.38	0.41	0.43	0.46	0.40	0.52	0.56
Thailand	0.07	0.13	0.12	0.14	0.20	0.19	0.22	0.25	0.27

NA Not available. X Not applicable. [1] Preliminary. [2] Includes countries not shown separately.
Source: U. S. Energy Information Administration, *International Energy Annual*.

No. 1185. U.S. Petroleum Balance: 1980 to 1992
[In millions of barrels]

ITEM	1980	1985	1987	1988	1989	1990	1991	1992
Petroleum products supplied	**6,242**	**5,740**	**6,083**	**6,308**	**6,324**	**6,201**	**6,101**	**6,234**
New supply of products	6,249	5,676	6,053	6,290	6,270	6,259	6,110	6,206
Production of products	5,765	5,363	5,680	5,849	5,874	5,934	5,933	6,050
Crude input to refineries	4,934	4,381	4,692	4,835	4,891	4,894	4,855	4,909
Oil, field production.	3,146	3,275	3,047	2,979	2,779	2,685	2,707	2,624
Alaska.	592	666	716	738	684	647	656	627
Lower 48 States	2,555	2,608	2,331	2,241	2,095	2,037	2,050	1,997
Net imports	1,821	1,094	1,651	1,807	2,081	2,112	2,068	2,194
Imports (gross excluding SPR) [1] . . .	1,910	1,125	1,679	1,845	2,112	2,142	2,111	2,223
SPR [1] imports.	16	43	27	19	20	10	-	4
Exports	-105	75	55	57	52	40	42	32
Other sources	33	12	7	57	32	98	80	90
Natural gas plant liquids (NGPL), supply .	577	604	585	593	563	574	613	628
Other liquids.	253	378	403	418	420	465	466	513
Net imports of refined products.	484	313	373	441	396	326	177	156
Imports	578	523	596	681	656	598	500	471
Exports	94	210	223	240	260	272	323	315
Stock withdrawal, refined products	-7	64	30	17	53	-59	-10	28
Ending stocks, all oils	1,392	1,519	1,607	1,597	1,581	1,621	1,617	1,592
Crude oil and lease condensate.	358	321	349	330	341	323	325	318
Strategic Petroleum Reserve (SPR) [1]	108	493	541	560	580	586	569	575
Unfinished oils	124	107	93	100	(NA)	(NA)	(NA)	(NA)
Gasoline blending components	17	33	38	39	(NA)	(NA)	(NA)	(NA)
Pentanes plus.	(NA)	8	7	7	(NA)	(NA)	(NA)	(NA)
Finished refined products	785	557	580	562	580	712	724	(NA)
PRODUCT TYPE SUPPLIED								
Total products	**6,242**	**5,740**	**6,083**	**6,326**	**6,324**	**6,201**	**6,101**	**6,234**
Finished motor gasoline	2,407	2,493	2,630	2,678	2,675	2,641	2,623	2,660
Distillate fuel oil	1,049	1,047	1,086	1,140	1,152	1,103	1,066	1,090
Residual fuel oil	918	439	462	5,030	500	449	423	401
Liquified petroleum gases [2]	414	584	588	604	609	568	616	642
Pentanes plus, other liquids, etc	1,454	1,155	1,304	1,369	1,378	1,431	1,365	70
Crude oil	(NA)	22	12	15	10	9	7	5

-Represents zero.   NA Not available.   [1] SPR=Strategic petroleum reserve. (See table 940.)   [2] Includes ethane.

Source: U.S. Energy Information Administration, *Petroleum Supply Annual.*

No. 1186. Crude Petroleum and Natural Gas—Production, by State: 1985 to 1992

[See also *Historical Statistics, Colonial Times to 1970,* series M 138, M 142, and M 147-161]

STATE	CRUDE PETROLEUM						NATURAL GAS MARKETED PRODUCTION [1]					
	Quantity (mil. bbl.)			Value (mil. dol.)			Quantity (bil. cu. ft.)			Value (mil. dol.)		
	1985	1990	1992	1985	1990	1992	1985	1990	1992	1985	1990	1992
Total [2] . . .	**3,274**	**2,685**	**2,625**	**78,884**	**53,772**	**41,968**	**17,270**	**18,594**	**18,712**	**43,343**	**31,658**	**32,571**
AL.	22	18	19	579	387	347	107	135	355	398	373	814
AK.	666	658	627	10,655	10,086	7,180	321	403	444	236	554	625
AR.	19	10	10	443	222	178	155	175	202	393	360	435
CA.	424	322	305	8,386	5,732	4,139	491	363	366	1,653	857	856
CO	30	31	30	758	722	567	178	243	323	517	377	443
FL.	11	6	5	(NA)	(NA)	NA	11	6	7	26	15	17
IL.	30	20	19	795	467	372	1	1	(Z)	4	1	1
IN	5	3	3	134	73	58	(Z)	(Z)	(Z)	1	1	(Z)
KS.	75	59	54	1,939	1,359	992	528	574	658	671	893	1,013
KY.	8	5	5	201	124	103	73	75	80	174	169	153
LA.	508	148	143	5,387	3,409	2,718	5,014	5,242	4,914	13,355	9,587	8,502
MI	27	20	16	726	458	296	132	140	195	475	420	528
MS	31	30	25	796	630	421	144	95	92	456	167	150
MT	30	20	18	734	429	316	52	50	54	125	90	87
NE.	7	5	5	163	119	96	2	1	1	6	2	2
NM	79	66	70	2,028	1,472	1,298	905	965	1,269	2,370	1,629	2,030
NY.	1	(Z)	(Z)	25	9	8	32	25	24	106	55	53
ND	51	39	33	1,307	849	593	73	52	55	138	93	108
OH	15	8	9	361	196	174	182	155	145	560	393	340
OK	163	117	102	4,256	2,690	1,908	1,936	2,258	2,017	4,930	3,548	3,430
PA	5	2	2	114	54	41	150	178	139	474	417	270
TX.	889	674	651	23	15,060	11,919	6,053	6,343	6,146	14,097	9,939	10,878
UT.	41	23	23	773	524	441	83	146	171	293	249	279
WV	4	2	2	86	43	37	145	178	182	558	568	548
WY	129	103	97	3,061	2,169	1,586	417	736	843	1,252	856	952

NA Not available.   Z Less than 500 million cubic feet or less than $500,000.   [1] Excludes nonhydrocarbon gases.
[2] Includes other States not shown separately. State production does not include State offshore production.

Source: U.S. Energy Information Administration, *Energy Data Reports, Petroleum Supply Annual, Natural Gas Annual,* and *Natural Gas Monthly.*

No. 1187. Natural Gas—Supply, Consumption, Reserves, and Marketed Production: 1970 to 1992

[See also *Historical Statistics, Colonial Times to 1970*, series M 147-161]

ITEM	Unit	1970	1975	1980	1985	1986	1987	1988	1989	1990	1991	1992
Producing wells (year-end)	1,000 . .	117	130	182	243	242	249	257	262	270	277	276
Production value at wells.	Bil. dol . . .	3.7	8.9	32.1	43.2	32.6	29.0	30.3	30.6	31.8	30.3	32.6
Avg. per 1,000 cu. ft	Dollars	0.17	0.44	1.59	2.51	1.94	1.67	1.69	1.69	1.71	1.64	1.74
Proved reserves [1]	Tril. cu. ft . .	291	228	199	193	192	187	168	167	169	167	165
Marketed production [2] . . .	Tril. cu. ft . .	21.9	20.1	20.2	17.3	16.9	17.4	17.9	18.1	18.6	18.6	(NA)
Drawn from storage	Tril. cu. ft . .	1.5	1.8	2.0	2.4	1.8	1.9	2.3	2.9	2.0	2.8	2.7
Imports [3]	Tril. cu. ft . .	0.8	1.0	1.0	1.0	0.8	1.0	1.3	1.4	1.5	1.8	2.1
Consumption, total	Tril. cu. ft . .	21.1	19.5	19.9	17.3	16.2	17.2	18.0	18.8	18.7	19.1	19.7
Residential.	Tril. cu. ft . .	4.8	4.9	4.8	4.4	4.3	4.3	4.6	4.8	4.4	4.6	4.7
Commercial [4]	Tril. cu. ft . .	2.4	2.5	2.6	2.4	2.3	2.4	2.7	2.7	2.6	2.7	2.8
Industrial	Tril. cu. ft . .	9.3	8.4	8.2	6.9	6.5	7.1	7.5	7.9	8.3	8.4	8.8
Lease and plant fuel.	Tril. cu. ft . .	1.4	1.4	1.0	1.0	0.9	1.2	1.1	1.1	1.2	1.2	1.2
Other industrial	Tril. cu. ft . .	7.9	7.0	7.2	5.9	5.6	6.0	6.4	6.8	7.0	7.2	7.6
Electric utilities [5]	Tril. cu. ft . .	3.9	3.2	3.7	3.0	2.6	2.8	2.6	2.8	2.8	2.8	2.8
Transportation	Tril. cu. ft . .	0.7	0.6	0.6	0.5	0.5	0.5	0.6	0.6	0.7	0.6	0.7
Extraction losses [6]	Tril. cu. ft . .	0.9	0.9	0.8	0.8	0.8	0.8	0.8	0.8	0.8	0.8	(NA)
Exports. . . . . [7] . . .	Tril. cu. ft . .	0.1	0.1	0.1	0.1	0.1	0.1	0.1	0.1	0.1	0.1	0.2
Additions to storage [7] . . .	Tril. cu. ft . .	1.9	2.1	2.0	2.2	2.0	1.9	2.2	2.5	2.5	2.7	2.5
World production (dry). . .	Tril. cu. ft . .	(NA)	44.1	53.1	62.0	63.3	66.2	69.8	71.9	74.3	74.8	(NA)
U.S. production (dry) . .	Tril. cu. ft . .	21.0	19.2	19.4	16.4	16.0	16.5	17.0	17.3	17.8	17.8	17.7
Percent U.S. of world	Percent . . .	56.0	43.6	36.5	26.4	25.3	25.0	24.4	24.0	24.0	23.7	(NA)

NA Not available.　[1] Estimated, end of year. Source: 1970-1976; American Gas Association, Arlington, VA, (copyright); thereafter, U.S. Energy Information Administration, *U.S. Crude Oil, Natural Gas, and Natural Gas Liquids Reserves*, annual. [2] Marketed production includes gross withdrawals from reservoirs less quantities used for reservoir repressuring and quantities vented or flared. For 1980 and thereafter, it excludes the nonhydrocarbon gases subsequently removed. [3] Includes imports of liquefied natural gas. [4] Includes deliveries to municipalities and public authorities for institutional heating and other purposes. [5] Pipeline fuel and vehicle fuel. [6] Volumetric reduction in natural gas resulting from the extraction of natural gas constituents at natural gas processing plants. [7] Beginning with 1980, includes liquefied natural gas (LNG) storage in above ground tanks.

Source: Except as noted, U.S. Energy Information Administration, *Annual Energy Review, International Energy Annual, Natural Gas Annual*, Volume I and II and *Monthly Energy Review*.

No. 1188. Liquefied Petroleum Gases—Summary: 1980 to 1992

[In millions of 42-gallon barrels. Includes ethane]

ITEM	1980	1990	1991	1992	ITEM	1980	1990	1991	1992
Production	561	638	683	720	**Consumption**.	538	568	616	629
At natural gas plants.	441	456	488	500	Ethane [1]	164	186	208	209
At refineries.	121	182	196	222	Propane [1][2]	298	335	358	378
Imports	79	68	54	57	Butane (incl. isobutane) [2] . .	76	47	50	42
Refinery input	85	107	111	172	Stocks, Dec. 31.	116	98	92	98
Exports	9	14	15	18					

[1] Reported consumption of ethane-propane mixtures have been allocated 70 percent ethane and 30 percent propane. [2] Reported consumption of butane-propane mixtures have been allocated 60 percent butane and 40 percent propane.

Source: U.S. Energy Information Administration, *Petroleum Supply Annual*.

No. 1189. World Coal Trade: 1980 to 1990

[In millions of short tons]

COUNTRIES	1980	1981	1982	1983	1984	1985	1986	1987	1988	1989	1990
Exporting countries, total [1]	277.2	288.4	292.0	284.5	332.9	370.2	376.3	383.0	415.0	423.5	440.2
United States	88.7	106.5	106.5	78.2	82.0	93.2	85.5	79.6	94.9	100.8	105.8
Australia.	46.6	54.3	48.8	62.3	82.2	96.6	101.3	111.9	109.8	108.5	116.9
South Africa	30.7	33.3	30.5	32.7	40.9	49.8	50.1	46.9	47.4	51.6	54.5
Soviet Union	26.2	22.5	23.0	22.8	22.8	26.5	36.9	39.1	46.0	43.9	42.7
Germany [2]	13.8	13.1	11.2	11.5	12.4	10.5	7.9	6.9	5.5	5.9	6.0
Canada	16.1	17.9	16.6	18.6	26.8	30.3	28.6	29.5	35.0	36.1	34.2
Poland	34.6	16.6	30.6	38.7	47.2	39.7	37.9	34.2	35.5	31.8	61.8
China: Mainland	4.2	4.1	5.1	6.8	7.7	8.6	10.9	14.4	16.2	16.9	19.1
Importing countries, total [1]	277.2	288.4	292.0	284.5	332.9	370.2	376.3	383.0	415.0	423.5	440.2
Western Europe/Mediterranean	126.9	129.4	126.5	112.9	132.4	152.3	149.0	145.6	146.2	154.7	172.1
Japan.	75.6	86.0	86.5	82.8	96.2	103.0	99.6	100.2	111.6	111.7	113.9
Eastern Europe	34.8	30.1	37.0	39.7	39.9	39.1	45.4	44.9	45.1	39.6	30.6
Canada	17.4	16.3	17.3	16.7	20.3	16.1	14.7	15.8	19.3	15.1	15.7

[1] Includes areas not shown separately.　[2] Represents United Germany beginning, 1990.

Source: U.S. Energy Information Administration, 1975-84, *Outlook for U.S. Coal Imports*; thereafter, *Annual Prospects for World Coal Trade*.

No. 1190. Coal and Coke—Summary: 1970 to 1992

[Includes coal consumed at mines. Demonstrated coal reserve base for United States on Jan. 1, 1992, was an estimated 476 billion tons. Recoverability varies between 40 and 90 percent for individual deposits; 50 percent or more of overall U.S. coal reserve base is believed to be recoverable. See also *Historical Statistics, Colonial Times to 1970*, series M 93-126]

ITEM	Unit	1970	1980	1985	1988	1989	1990	1991	1992
Coal production, total [1].	**Mil. sh. tons** ..	**613**	**830**	**884**	**950**	**981**	**1,029**	**996**	**998**
Value	Mil. dol.	3,882	20,453	22,277	20,890	21,330	(NA)	(NA)	(NA)
Anthracite production . . . . ₂	Mil. sh. tons . . .	9.7	6.1	4.7	3.6	3.3	3.5	3.4	(NA)
Bituminous coal and lignite: [2]									
Number of mines	Number.	5,601	5,598	4,547	3,462	3,429	3,243	2,846	2,746
Production	Mil. sh. tons . . .	603	824	879	947	977	1,026	993	995
Value, total	Mil. dol.	3,774	20,196	22,061	20,828	21,260	22,274	21,598	(NA)
Average per ton	Dollars	6.26	24.52	25.10	22.00	21.76	21.71	21.75	21.03
Exports	Mil. sh. tons . .	71	90	93	95	101	106	109	103
Value	Mil. dol.	961	4,627	4,465	4,013	4,287	4,510	4,619	(NA)
Imports	1,000 sh. tons .	36	1,194	1,952	2,134	2,851	2,699	3,390	3,803
Method of mining:									
Underground	Mil. sh. tons . .	339	337	350	382	394	425	407	407
Surface	Mil. sh. tons . . .	264	487	529	568	587	605	589	590
Percent of total prod . .	Percent.	43.8	59.1	60.2	59.8	59.8	58.7	59.1	59.1
Value . . ₃	Mil. dol.	(Z)	30	70	(NA)	(NA)	(NA)	(NA)	(NA)
Consumption [3]	Mil. sh. tons . .	523	703	818	884	890	895	888	893
Electric power utilities . . .	Mil. sh. tons . .	320	569	694	758	767	774	772	780
Industrial.	Mil. sh. tons . .	184	126	116	118	118	116	109	107
Productivity average: [4]									
Daily employment	1,000	140	225	169	135	131	131	121	110
Days worked	Number	228	210	204	211	214	216	224	228
Tons per worker:									
Per day	Sh. tons.	18.84	16.32	23.13	30.30	31.75	32.90	35.18	37.71
Per year	Sh. tons.	4,296	3,427	4,719	6,393	6,795	7,106	7,880	(NA)
Production, by State:									
Alabama	Mil. sh. tons . . .	21	26	28	27	28	29	27	26
Illinois	Mil. sh. tons . .	65	63	59	59	59	60	60	60
Indiana	Mil. sh. tons . .	22	31	33	31	34	36	32	31
Kentucky	Mil. sh. tons . .	125	150	152	158	167	173	159	161
Montana	Mil. sh. tons . .	3	30	33	39	38	38	38	39
Ohio	Mil. sh. tons . .	55	39	36	34	34	35	31	30
Pennsylvania	Mil. sh. tons . .	90	93	71	67	71	71	65	68
Virginia	Mil. sh. tons . .	35	41	41	46	43	47	42	43
West Virginia	Mil. sh. tons . .	144	122	128	145	154	169	167	162
Wyoming	Mil. sh. tons . .	7	95	141	164	172	184	194	190
Other States.	Mil. sh. tons . .	44	140	161	178	182	187	181	189
World production	Mil. sh. tons . .	3,295	4,103	4,779	5,105	5,252	5,214	4,952	4,975
Coke production [5]	**Mil. sh. tons** ..	**66.5**	**46.1**	**28.7**	**32.4**	**33.0**	**27.6**	**24.0**	**23.0**
Oven coke [6].	Mil. sh. tons . .	65.7	46.1	28.7	32.4	33.0	27.6	24.0	23.0
Value of product at plant	Mil. dol.	2,193	6,029	(NA)	(NA)	(NA)	(NA)	(NA)	(NA)
Coke and breeze.	Mil. dol.	1,899	4,784	(NA)	(NA)	(NA)	(NA)	(NA)	(NA)
Avg. market value per ton . .	Dollars	28	103	103	(NA)	(NA)	(NA)	(NA)	(NA)
Coal carbonized.	Mil. sh. tons . .	96.5	66.7	41.1	41.9	41.4	38.9	33.9	32.4
Average value per ton	Dollars	12.47	56.26	54.30	47.70	47.50	47.73	48.88	47.9
Yield of coke from coal	Percent	69.1	69.2	69.8	77.3	79.8	71.0	71.0	(NA)

NA Not available.   Z Less than $500,000.   [1] Includes bituminous coal, lignite, and anthracite.   [2] All domestic production data for 1970 are for mines producing 1,000 short tons or more per year; thereafter, data are for all mines.   [3] Includes some categories not shown separately.   [4] Data for 1970 are for mines producing 1,000 short tons or more per year; thereafter, for mines producing 10,000 short tons more. Beginning 1985, includes anthracite.   [5] Includes beehive coke.   [6] Prior to 1980, excludes screenings or breeze; thereafter, includes beehive and other nonrecoverable coke-oven operations.

Source: 1970, U.S. Bureau of Mines, *Minerals Yearbook;* thereafter, U.S. Energy Information Administration, *Coal Production,* annual; *Annual Energy Review,* and *Quarterly Coal Report,* and unpublished data.

No. 1191. Uranium Concentrate (U_3O_8) Industry—Summary: 1980 to 1992

[Middle demand case. See table 953. See also *Historical Statistics, Colonial Times to 1970*, series M 266-267]

ITEM	Unit	1980	1984	1985	1986	1987	1988	1989	1990	1991	1992
Production	1,000 sh. tons .	21.9	7.4	5.6	6.8	6.5	6.50	6.90	4.4	4.0	2.8
Net imports (U_3O_8)	1,000 sh. tons .	-1.1	5.2	3.2	6.4	7.5	6.40	5.60	12.1	9.80	12.3
Utility and Suppliers inventories (U_3O_8 equivalent).	1,000 sh. tons .	54.4	[1]74.7	[1]68.3	[1]66.2	[1]64.5	[1]59.1	[1]54.9	45.6	36.70	(NA)
Price (1988 dol./lb. U_3O_8):											
Long-term contract price	Dollars	41.4	26.4	24.7	19.3	18.5	(NA)	(NA)	(NA)	(NA)	(NA)
Spot market price.	Dollars	45.0	19.4	17.0	18.1	17.3	14.5	14.2	(NA)	(NA)	(NA)
Delivered price.	Dollars	39.9	[2]36.5	[2]33.6	[2]31.9	[2]19.6	[2]25.7	[2]27.8	(NA)	(NA)	(NA)
Capital expenditures (1988 dollars)	Mil. dol.	1,107	43	37	29	63	36	35	(NA)	(NA)	(NA)
Employment.	1,000	19.9	3.6	2.4	2.1	2.0	2.10	1.6	1.3	1.0	0.7

NA Not available.   [1] Includes natural U_3O_8 (uranium oxide), natural UF_6 (uranium hexafluoride), natural UF_6 under usage agreement, UF_6 at enrichment suppliers, enriched UF_6 and fabricated fuel.   [2] Average U.S. contract prices and market price settlements.

Source: U.S. Department of Energy, *Domestic Uranium Mining and Milling Industry,* annual, and *Uranium Industry,* annual.

Figure 25.1
Single-Family Houses Sold and Sales Price: 1970 to 1993

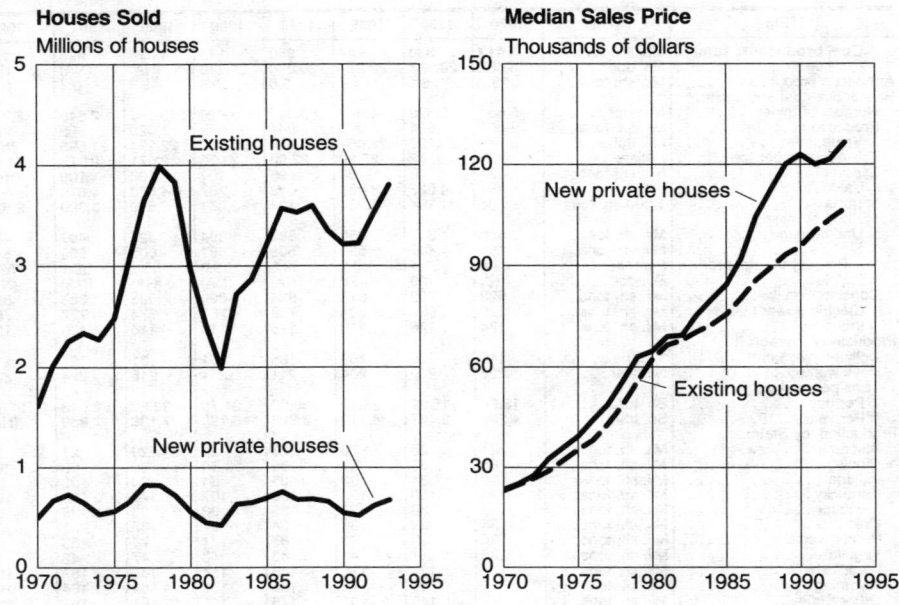

Source: Chart prepared by U.S. Bureau of the Census. For data, see tables 1205, 1206, and 1208.

Figure 25.2
**Commercial Office Space—Vacancy Rates for
Largest Metro Areas: 1992**

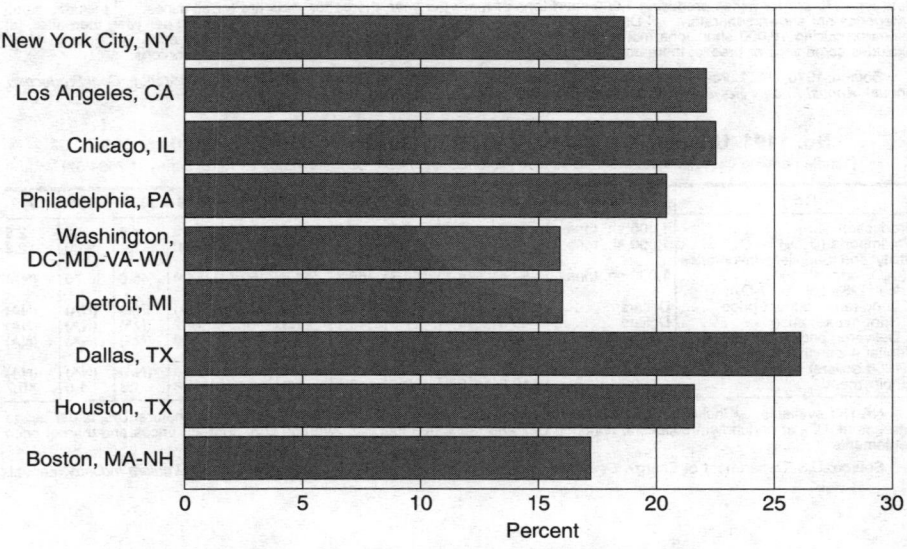

Source: Chart prepared by U.S. Bureau of the Census. For data, see table 1229.

Construction and Housing

This section presents data on the construction industry and on various indicators of its activity and costs; on housing units and their characteristics and occupants; and on the characteristics and vacancy rates for commercial buildings. Considerable data from the 1990 census are featured in tables 1214 to 1222. Also, there are new data on commercial building from the Energy Information Administration for the first time in three years.

The principal source of these data is the U.S. Bureau of the Census, which issues a variety of current publications. Construction statistics compiled by the Bureau appear in its monthly *Current Construction Reports* series with various quarterly or annual supplements; *Housing Starts* and *Housing Completions* present data by type of structure and by 4 major census regions; *New One-Family Houses Sold and For Sale* also provides statistics annually on physical and financial characteristics for all new housing by the 4 major census regions; *Price Index of New One-Family Houses Sold* presents quarterly figures and annual regional data; and *Housing Units Authorized by Building Permits* covers approximately 17,000 permit-issuing jurisdictions in the United States. Statistics on expenditures by owners of residential properties are issued quarterly and annually in *Expenditures for Residential Upkeep and Improvements. Value of New Construction Put in Place* presents data on all types of construction and includes monthly composite cost indexes. Reports of the censuses of construction industries (see below) are also issued on various topics.

Other Census Bureau publications include the *Current Housing Reports* series, which comprises the quarterly *Housing Vacancies,* the quarterly *Market Absorption of Apartments,* the American Housing Survey (formerly Annual Housing Survey) and reports of the censuses of housing and of construction industries. *Construction Review,* published quarterly by the International Trade Administration, U.S. Department of Commerce, contains many of the census series and other construction statistics series from the Federal Government and private agencies.

In Brief

New single-family homes sold in 1993 up 31 percent since 1991 with the South leading the rise with a 37 percent increase

U.S. home ownership rate in 1993 of 64.5 percent unchanged from rate in 1983

Commercial buildings total 4.8 million in number and occupy 67.9 billion square feet of floorspace in 1992

Other sources include the monthly *Dodge Construction Potentials* of F. W. Dodge Division, McGraw-Hill Information Systems Company, New York, NY, which presents national and State data on construction contracts; the National Association of Home Builders with State-level data on housing starts; the NATIONAL ASSOCIATION OF REALTORS, which presents data on existing home sales; the Society of Industrial and Office Realtors and Oncor International on commercial office space; the Bureau of Economic Analysis, which presents data on residential capital and gross housing product; and the U.S. Energy Information Administration, which provides data on commercial buildings through its periodic sample surveys.

Censuses and surveys.—Censuses of the construction industry were first conducted by the Bureau of the Census for 1929, 1935, and 1939; beginning in 1967, a census has been taken every five years (for years ending in "2" and "7"). The latest reports are for 1987. Reports from the 1992 Census are due out beginning late summer of 1994.

The 1987 Census of Construction Industries, in accordance with the 1987 *Standard Industrial Classification Manual* (see text, section 13), covers all employer establishments primarily engaged in (1) building construction by general contractors or operative builders; (2) heavy (non-building) construction by general contractors; and (3) construction by special trade contractors.

From 1850 through 1930, the Bureau of the Census collected some housing data as part of its censuses of population and agriculture. Beginning in 1940, separate censuses of housing have been taken at 10-year intervals. For the 1970 and 1980 censuses, data on year-round housing units were collected and issued on occupancy and structural characteristics, plumbing facilities, value, and rent; for 1990 such characteristics were presented for all housing units.

Evaluation studies of the 1950, 1960, 1970, and 1980 censuses estimated the underenumeration of occupied housing units at 2.9 percent, 2.4 percent, 1.7 percent, and 1.5 percent respectively. The missed rate in 1980 for all housing units was 2.6 percent or approximately 2.3 million units, 1 million of which were vacant housing units. Estimates for underenumeration from the 1990 census are not available at this time.

The American Housing Survey (*Current Housing Reports* series H-150 and H-170), which began in 1973, provided an annual and ongoing series of data on selected housing and demographic characteristics until 1983. In 1984 the name of the survey was changed from the Annual Housing Survey. It is currently based on a biennial national sample and on 11 annual MSA samples. All samples represent a cross section of the housing stock in their respective areas. Estimates are subject to both sampling and non-sampling errors; caution should therefore, be used in making comparisons with 1970 and 1980 census data.

Data on residential mortgages were collected continuously from 1890 to 1970, except 1930, as part of the decennial census by the Bureau of the Census. Since 1973, mortgage status data, limited to single family homes on less than ten acres with no business on the property, have been presented in the American Housing Survey. Data on mortgage activity are covered in section 16.

Housing units.—In general, a housing unit is a group of rooms or a single room occupied or intended for occupancy as separate living quarters; that is, the occupants do not live and eat with any other persons in the structure and there is direct access from the outside or through a common hall. Transient accommodations, barracks for workers, and institutional-type quarters are not counted as housing units.

Statistical reliability.—For a discussion of statistical collection and estimation, sampling procedures, and measures of statistical reliability applicable to Census Bureau data, see Appendix III.

Historical statistics.—Tabular headnotes provide cross-references, where applicable, to *Historical Statistics of the United States, Colonial Times to 1970.* See Appendix IV.

No. 1192. Construction Industries—Summary, by Industry: 1987

[Based on a probability sample of about 160,000 construction establishments with payroll in 1987; see Appendix III. N.e.c.= Not elsewhere classified]

INDUSTRY	SIC [1] code	Estab-lish-ments with payroll (1,000)	EMPLOYEES (1,000)		PAYROLL (mil. dol.)		VALUE OF CONSTRUCTION WORK (mil. dol.)		Value added [3] (mil. dol.)
			Total	Con-struction workers	Total	Con-struction workers	Total	Net [2]	
All industries, total	(X)	544.2	5,054	3,989	111,067	79,742	499,982	367,746	230,174
Contract construction		536.3	5,015	3,979	110,200	79,589	495,346	365,241	227,934
General building contractors	15	157.6	1,278	926	27,870	17,204	212,629	111,019	65,514
Single-family houses	1521	90.4	396	307	6,272	4,343	39,098	27,319	14,970
Other residential buildings	1522	8.1	82	61	1,752	1,130	13,316	6,257	3,659
Operative builders	1531	20.8	169	80	4,385	1,478	48,960	26,837	15,173
Industrial buildings and warehouses	1541	7.0	143	111	3,619	2,497	21,462	11,095	6,882
Nonresidential buildings, n.e.c	1542	31.3	488	367	11,843	7,756	89,793	39,510	24,831
Heavy construction contractors	16	36.6	827	683	20,408	15,461	82,285	68,435	44,940
Highway and street construction	1611	11.0	284	239	7,041	5,397	34,161	27,984	17,120
Bridge, tunnel, and elevated highway	1622	1.2	47	40	1,192	910	5,481	4,187	2,430
Water, sewer, and utility lines	1623	10.0	198	166	4,513	3,428	17,010	15,055	10,090
Heavy construction, n.e.c	1629	14.5	298	238	7,662	5,726	25,633	21,209	15,301
Special trade contractors	17	342.0	2,909	2,370	61,921	46,923	200,434	185,786	117,480
Plumbing, heating, air-conditioning	1711	69.6	617	471	14,330	10,311	49,503	44,518	25,912
Painting and paperhanging	1721	29.9	170	145	2,979	2,386	7,953	7,446	5,716
Electrical work	1731	49.4	509	406	12,664	9,622	35,838	34,658	21,817
Masonry and other stonework	1741	23.3	169	150	2,947	2,462	8,714	8,269	5,476
Plastering, drywall, insulation	1742	17.8	254	217	5,485	4,348	16,427	15,137	9,748
Terrazzo, tile, marble, and mosaic work.	1743	5.1	34	28	734	554	2,272	2,182	1,318
Carpentry	1751	36.0	190	164	3,272	2,610	11,244	10,039	6,078
Floorlaying and other floor work	1752	8.2	45	35	906	645	3,651	3,371	1,880
Roofing, siding, and sheet metal work.	1761	25.7	231	187	4,314	3,111	15,028	14,183	8,524
Concrete work	1771	23.4	218	187	4,175	3,278	15,056	13,854	8,443
Water well drilling	1781	3.4	18	14	335	249	1,330	1,299	780
Structural steel erection	1791	4.0	65	55	1,594	1,232	4,863	4,510	3,253
Glass and glazing work	1793	4.6	41	29	919	607	3,222	3,142	1,701
Excavation work	1794	13.4	95	79	2,060	1,598	8,244	7,491	5,708
Wrecking and demolition work	1795	1.2	14	12	261	195	912	845	782
Installing building equipment, n.e.c.	1796	3.8	62	50	1,858	1,447	5,360	5,010	3,723
Special trade contractors, n.e.c	1799	23.2	176	142	3,089	2,269	10,814	9,833	6,622
Land subdividers and developers, n.e.c.	6552	8.0	40	9	867	153	4,636	2,505	2,240

X Not applicable. [1] Standard Industrial Classification; see, text, section 13. [2] Value of construction work less payments for construction work subcontracted to others, not shown separately. [3] Dollar value of business done less (a) payments for materials, components, and supplies, and (b) payments for construction work subcontracted to others, not shown separately.
Source: U.S. Bureau of the Census, *Census of Construction Industries, 1987*, series CC87-I-28.

No. 1193. Construction Materials—Producer Price Indexes: 1980 to 1993

[1982=100, except as noted. For discussion of producer price index, see text, section 15. This index, more formally known as the special commodity grouping index for construction materials, covers materials incorporated as integral part of a building or normally installed during construction and not readily removable. Excludes consumer durables such as kitchen ranges, refrigerators, etc. This index is not the same as the stage-of-processing index of intermediate materials and components for construction. See *Historical Statistics, Colonial Times to 1970*, series N 140-155 for similar data]

COMMODITY	1980	1985	1986	1987	1988	1989	1990	1991	1992	1993
Construction materials	92.5	107.6	107.3	109.5	115.7	119.5	119.6	120.4	122.5	128.6
Interior solvent based paint	91.3	107.3	109.9	111.6	120.3	128.8	133.0	140.2	141.7	143.0
Plastic construction products	103.9	108.6	106.4	108.4	121.1	120.1	117.2	115.1	112.7	116.8
Douglas fir, dressed	132.6	126.5	124.5	125.1	135.7	151.6	138.4	139.6	169.5	237.4
Southern pine, dressed	104.0	105.2	104.9	114.1	112.4	108.0	111.2	111.0	130.6	168.9
Millwork	93.2	111.7	113.7	117.7	121.9	127.3	130.4	135.5	143.3	156.5
Softwood plywood	109.5	107.4	109.4	109.8	109.1	124.2	119.6	120.8	147.2	169.6
Hardwood plywood and related products	97.5	89.9	91.0	92.9	94.2	99.8	102.7	102.8	106.9	115.4
Softwood plywood veneer, ex. reinforced/backed	126.0	100.1	105.9	108.4	117.3	142.1	142.3	138.5	168.3	216.0
Building paper and building board mill products	86.1	107.4	108.8	111.2	113.3	115.6	112.2	111.8	119.6	132.9
Tube, drawn, 6000 alloy series	85.6	109.7	109.8	111.2	128.9	131.0	127.1	124.1	123.4	(NA)
Builders hardware	84.9	113.5	115.8	117.4	122.5	127.8	133.0	138.1	141.4	144.9
Plumbing fixtures and brass fittings	88.5	111.9	115.5	119.7	128.7	137.7	144.3	149.7	153.1	155.8
Heating equipment	87.0	109.5	113.0	115.5	119.2	125.1	131.6	134.1	137.3	140.3
Metal doors, sash, and trim	87.8	107.3	108.9	112.0	122.4	130.0	131.4	134.6	135.0	136.6
Incandescent outdoor lighting fixtures	82.7	109.2	112.0	117.2	122.4	128.0	137.3	136.5	139.1	136.6
Bright nails	90.9	100.2	99.8	101.2	104.7	110.4	(NA)	(NA)	115.1	115.9
Welded steel wire fabric for concrete reinforcing.	98.9	101.3	98.8	98.3	109.2	108.6	109.7	100.0	100.3	105.1
Elevators, escalators, and other lifts	87.3	97.7	99.2	100.4	103.6	107.1	110.1	108.7	109.4	110.7
Stamped metal outlet box	82.7	119.7	152.6	160.1	168.7	171.7	179.4	179.7	187.2	195.7
Concrete ingredients and related products	88.4	108.5	109.4	110.4	112.0	113.2	115.3	118.4	119.4	123.5
Concrete products	92.0	107.5	109.2	109.4	110.0	111.2	113.5	116.6	117.2	120.1
Clay construction products exc. refractories	88.8	113.5	118.0	121.4	124.9	127.0	129.9	130.2	132.0	135.1
Prep. asphalt and tar roofing and siding products.	105.5	100.5	96.8	91.9	94.4	95.6	97.1	96.2	94.3	95.0
Gypsum products	100.1	132.3	137.0	125.2	112.9	110.0	105.2	99.3	99.9	108.4
Insulation materials	80.7	105.2	105.7	105.0	105.8	106.7	108.4	110.8	102.3	106.0
Paving mixtures and blocks	83.7	111.6	104.9	100.8	102.7	101.0	101.2	103.2	100.2	101.8

NA Not available.
Source: U.S. Bureau of Labor Statistics, *Producer Price Indexes*, monthly and annual.

No. 1194. Price and Cost Indexes for Construction: 1980 to 1993

[1987=100. Excludes Alaska and Hawaii. Indexes of certain sources are published on bases different from those shown here. See *Historical Statistics, Colonial Times to 1970*, series N 118-137, for construction cost indexes on a 1947-49 base]

NAME OF INDEX	1980	1985	1986	1988	1989	1990	1991	1992	1993
Bureau of the Census:									
Composite fixed-weighted [1]	77.6	93.1	96.5	103.8	107.4	110.3	111.2	112.2	115.9
Implicit price deflator [2]	79.1	93.9	96.8	104.1	108.3	111.2	111.8	112.7	116.9
Bureau of the Census houses under construction: [3]									
Fixed-weighted	75.6	91.0	95.6	103.6	107.0	110.2	110.6	112.5	116.7
Price deflator	77.9	92.0	95.8	104.1	108.4	111.5	111.7	113.4	118.4
Federal Highway Administration, composite [4]	97.2	102.0	101.1	106.6	107.7	108.5	107.5	105.1	108.3
Bureau of Reclamation composite [5]	81	98	99	103	107	111	114	116	119
Turner Construction Co.: Building construction [6]	69	94	97	104	107	111	113	113	116
E. H. Boeckh, building cost index: [7]									
Residences	(NA)	96.2	98.0	102.5	106.3	109.9	113.0	116.7	121.3
Apartments, hotels, and office buildings	(NA)	96.3	98.0	102.7	106.2	109.0	112.0	114.9	118.1
Commercial and factory buildings	(NA)	96.7	98.3	103.0	107.2	110.8	114.2	117.4	120.5
Engineering News-Record: [8]									
Buildings	76.5	95.5	97.7	102.2	103.6	106.3	108.3	111.5	117.9
Construction	73.5	95.2	97.5	102.6	104.7	107.4	109.7	113.1	118.2
Handy-Whitman public utility: [9]									
Buildings	83	96	98	104	107	108	105	107	113
Electric [10]	80	98	99	107	111	115	116	118	122
Gas [11]	79	100	97	106	111	114	116	118	121
Water [11]	81	97	98	103	106	108	108	110	115
C. A. Turner Telephone Plant [12]	102	101	100	101	110	113	114	114	114

NA Not available. [1] Weighted average of the various indexes used to deflate the Construction Put in Place series. In calculating the index, the weights (i.e., the composition of current dollar estimates in 1987 by category) are held constant. [2] Derived ratio of total current to constant dollar Construction Put in Place (multiplied by 100). [3] Excludes value of site. [4] Based on average contract unit bid prices for composite mile (involving specific average amounts of excavation, paving, reinforcing steel, structural steel, and structural concrete). [5] Derived from the four quarterly indexes which are weighted averages of costs of labor, materials, and equipment for the construction of dams and reclamation projects. [6] Based on firm's cost experience with respect to labor rates, materials prices, competitive conditions, efficiency of plant and management, and productivity. [7] Average of 20 cities for types shown. Weights based on surveys of building costs. [8] Building index computed on the basis of a hypothetical unit of construction requiring 6 bbl. of portland cement, 1,088 M bd. ft. of 2" x 4" lumber, 2,500 lb. of structural steel, and 68.38 hours of skilled labor. Construction index based on same materials components combined with 200 hours of common labor. [9] Based on data covering public utility construction costs in six geographic regions. Covers skilled and common labor. [10] As derived by U.S. Bureau of the Census. Covers steam generation plants only. [11] As derived by U.S. Bureau of the Census. Reflects costs for structures and improvements at water pumping and treatment plants. [12] Computed by the Census Bureau by averaging the weighted component indexes published for six geographic regions.

Source: U.S. Bureau of the Census. In U.S. Department of Commerce, International Trade Administration, *Construction Review*, bimonthly.

No. 1195. Value of New Construction Put in Place: 1964 to 1993

[In millions of dollars. Represents value of construction put in place during year; differs from building permit and construction contract data in timing and coverage. Includes installed cost of normal building service equipment and selected types of industrial production equipment (largely site fabricated). Excludes cost of shipbuilding, land, and most types of machinery and equipment. For methodology, see Appendix III. See also *Historical Statistics, Colonial Times to 1970*, series N 1-29 and N 66-69]

YEAR	CURRENT DOLLARS					CONSTANT (1987) DOLLARS				
		Private					Private			
	Total	Total	Residential buildings	Nonresidential buildings	Public	Total	Total	Residential buildings	Nonresidential buildings	Public
1964	72,124	51,921	30,526	14,412	20,203	294,569	211,627	124,768	60,892	82,942
1970	100,727	72,819	35,863	23,008	27,908	309,244	225,168	114,138	71,796	84,077
1971	117,311	87,612	48,514	24,204	29,699	337,451	254,502	145,554	69,621	82,949
1972	133,318	103,288	60,693	26,568	30,030	360,780	281,593	170,190	71,490	79,187
1973	146,826	114,477	65,085	30,683	32,348	364,938	285,937	166,249	76,259	79,001
1974	147,476	109,344	55,967	32,195	38,132	319,362	242,274	130,126	70,029	77,089
1975	145,623	102,330	51,581	28,397	43,293	290,137	208,991	109,920	58,990	81,147
1976	165,441	121,462	68,273	27,936	43,979	315,865	235,338	136,685	55,617	80,527
1977	193,126	150,044	92,004	30,871	43,083	340,833	266,393	165,926	57,134	74,440
1978	230,178	180,032	109,838	39,135	50,146	362,862	285,880	174,695	65,343	76,982
1979	259,839	203,194	116,444	51,732	56,646	364,554	288,789	165,116	77,359	75,766
1980	259,746	196,100	100,381	58,290	63,646	328,435	252,645	128,926	78,972	75,790
1981	271,950	207,259	99,241	68,450	64,691	320,950	247,427	118,343	85,091	73,523
1982	260,594	197,531	84,676	73,953	63,064	297,759	226,510	97,595	87,505	71,249
1983	294,945	231,494	125,521	70,438	63,450	332,625	261,398	143,108	80,888	71,227
1984	348,817	278,600	153,849	87,493	70,217	382,435	306,152	170,732	96,664	76,284
1985	377,366	299,543	158,474	103,455	77,823	401,967	321,706	172,338	111,262	80,260
1986	407,693	323,100	187,148	98,674	84,593	421,367	335,709	195,377	102,596	85,658
1987	419,366	328,738	194,656	100,933	90,628	419,352	328,637	194,622	100,877	90,715
1988	432,304	337,516	198,101	106,994	94,788	415,084	324,404	190,292	103,037	90,680
1989	443,605	345,477	196,551	113,988	98,128	409,679	318,717	181,321	105,711	90,962
1990	442,143	334,682	182,856	117,971	107,460	397,627	300,101	163,980	106,067	97,526
1991	403,440	293,536	157,835	97,841	109,904	360,715	262,022	141,300	87,608	98,694
1992	436,043	317,258	187,819	87,241	118,785	386,928	279,300	165,418	77,182	107,628
1993	470,118	342,953	208,092	91,471	127,166	402,260	290,808	175,657	78,247	111,452

Source: U.S. Bureau of the Census, *Current Construction Reports*, series C30, and press release, CB-92-14.

No. 1196. Value of New Construction Put in Place in Current and Constant (1987) Dollars: 1989 to 1993

[In millions of dollars. Represents value of construction put in place during year; differs from building permit and construction contract data in timing and coverage. Includes installed cost of normal building service equipment and selected types of industrial production equipment (largely site fabricated). Excludes cost of shipbuilding, land, and most types of machinery and equipment. For details on derivation of constant values and description of revised series, see source. For description of nature of revisions and deflators used, see *Construction Reports*, series C30-9005. For methodology, see Appendix III. See also *Historical Statistics, Colonial Times to 1970*, series N 1-29 and N 66-69]

TYPE OF CONSTRUCTION	CURRENT DOLLARS					CONSTANT (1987) DOLLARS				
	1989	1990	1991	1992	1993	1989	1990	1991	1992	1993
Total new construction .	443,605	442,143	403,440	436,043	470,118	409,679	397,627	360,715	386,928	402,260
Private construction	345,477	334,682	293,536	317,258	¹342,953	318,717	300,101	262,022	279,300	¹290,808
Residential buildings	196,551	182,856	157,835	187,819	208,092	181,321	163,980	141,300	165,418	175,657
New housing units	139,202	127,987	110,592	129,600	144,503	128,435	114,784	99,002	114,165	121,978
1 unit	116,898	108,737	95,444	116,505	133,742	107,849	97,518	85,435	102,612	112,889
2 or more units	22,304	19,250	15,148	13,094	10,761	20,586	17,266	13,567	11,553	9,089
Improvements	57,349	54,869	47,243	58,219	(NA)	52,886	49,196	42,297	51,253	(NA)
Nonresidential buildings . . .	113,988	117,971	97,841	87,241	91,471	105,711	106,067	87,608	77,182	78,247
Industrial.	20,410	23,848	22,280	20,719	20,654	18,919	21,441	19,951	18,336	17,669
Office.	31,538	28,722	23,010	17,241	15,392	29,263	25,829	20,604	15,265	13,175
Hotels, motels	8,401	9,673	6,286	3,507	4,267	7,791	8,699	5,630	3,101	3,651
Other commercial.	33,958	34,140	25,470	24,283	27,754	31,482	30,693	22,805	21,469	23,733
Religious	3,278	3,390	3,415	3,382	3,515	3,040	3,046	3,058	2,990	3,008
Educational	3,648	4,219	3,929	4,254	4,093	3,382	3,792	3,518	3,765	3,501
Hospital and institutional .	8,312	9,450	9,189	10,110	11,045	7,711	8,494	8,228	8,943	9,451
Miscellaneous ²	4,443	4,528	4,260	3,746	4,750	4,122	4,072	3,814	3,313	4,060
Farm nonresidential	2,449	2,670	2,563	2,211	(NA)	2,271	2,400	2,295	1,955	(NA)
Public utilities	30,030	28,228	32,354	36,418	(NA)	27,138	24,967	28,193	31,505	(NA)
Telecommunications	9,614	9,803	9,203	9,272	9,800	8,660	8,709	8,100	8,171	8,647
Other public utilities	20,416	18,425	23,151	27,146	(NA)	18,478	16,258	20,093	23,335	(NA)
Railroads	2,650	2,600	2,406	3,165	(NA)	2,452	2,362	2,145	2,868	(NA)
Electric light and power .	13,038	10,594	14,440	16,605	(NA)	11,778	9,290	12,523	14,226	(NA)
Gas	4,386	4,820	5,555	6,527	(NA)	3,941	4,243	4,780	5,522	(NA)
Petroleum pipelines. . . .	342	411	750	849	(NA)	307	362	645	719	(NA)
All other private ³	2,460	2,957	2,943	3,570	3,281	2,276	2,688	2,626	3,238	2,892
Public construction.	98,128	107,460	109,904	118,785	127,166	90,962	97,526	98,694	107,628	111,452
Buildings	39,871	45,588	49,246	51,875	55,122	36,949	406,968	44,089	45,882	47,088
Housing and development	3,441	3,778	3,837	4,151	5,141	3,175	3,387	3,437	3,662	4,338
Industrial.	1,300	1,433	1,823	1,793	1,771	1,205	1,289	1,633	1,585	1,516
Educational	17,310	20,470	22,865	23,454	25,898	16,044	18,394	20,468	20,774	22,143
Hospital	2,542	2,605	2,598	3,099	3,588	2,358	2,343	2,326	2,741	3,070
Other ⁴	15,278	17,301	18,122	19,378	18,724	14,167	15,555	16,226	17,148	16,021
Highways and streets.	28,747	32,108	32,026	34,931	37,299	26,671	29,608	29,127	33,377	34,455
Military facilities.	3,520	2,665	1,837	2,502	2,447	3,261	2,427	1,660	2,299	2,178
Conservation and development	5,013	4,558	4,861	5,919	5,938	4,631	4,092	4,252	5,107	4,987
Sewer systems	8,913	9,490	9,328	9,446	9,634	8,235	8,509	8,161	8,151	8,089
Water supply facilities	3,797	4,536	4,629	4,798	5,545	3,566	4,185	4,289	4,363	4,821
Miscellaneous public ⁵	8,266	8,515	7,978	9,314	11,180	7,648	7,739	7,116	8,450	9,834

NA Not available. ¹ Includes estimates for types of construction indicated as (NA). ² Includes amusement and recreational buildings, bus and airline terminals, animal hospitals and shelters, etc. ³ Includes privately owned streets and bridges, parking areas, sewer and water facilities, parks and playgrounds, golf courses, airfields, etc. ⁴ Includes federal administrative buildings, prisons, police and fire stations, courthouses, civic centers, passenger terminals, space facilities, postal facilities, etc. ⁵ Includes open amusement and recreational facilities, power generating facilities, transit systems, airfields, open parking facilities, etc.

Source: U.S. Bureau of the Census, *Current Construction Reports*, series C30, monthly.

No. 1197. Value of Privately Owned Nonresidential Building Projects, by Construction Status, 1985 to 1993, and by Type of Project, 1993

[In billions of dollars]

CONSTRUCTION STATUS	1985	1986	1987	1988	1989	1990	1991	1992	1993				
									Total	Industrial	Office building	Other commercial	Other¹
Value of projects—													
Started	98.5	97.1	95.7	107.7	109.9	89.5	72.9	81.3	79.5	13.2	14.1	28.6	23.6
Completed	89.9	107.5	91.4	101.6	107.7	114.0	109.5	100.1	93.7	18.0	21.0	29.5	25.2

¹ Privately owned hotels and motels, religious, educational, hospital and institutional, and miscellaneous nonresidential building projects.

Source: U.S. Bureau of the Census, *Current Construction Reports*, series C30.

No. 1198. Construction Contracts—Value of Construction and Floor Space of Buildings, by Class of Construction: 1980 to 1993

[Includes new structures and additions, and major alterations to existing structures which affect only valuation, since no additional floor area is created by "alteration." See also *Historical Statistics, Colonial Times to 1970*, series N 7888-100]

YEAR	Total	Residential buildings	NONRESIDENTIAL BUILDINGS									Nonbuilding construction
			Total	Commercial [1]	Manufacturing	Educational [2]	Hospital	Public buildings	Religious	Social and recreational	Miscellaneous	
VALUE (bil. dol.)												
1980	151.8	60.4	56.9	27.7	9.2	7.4	5.4	1.6	1.2	2.7	1.7	34.5
1981	157.3	56.3	65.5	35.2	9.3	6.6	6.4	1.4	1.2	3.4	2.0	35.4
1982	157.1	55.0	64.6	32.3	9.6	6.8	8.0	1.9	1.2	2.8	2.0	37.5
1983	194.1	88.4	67.9	38.3	5.4	7.1	8.5	2.1	1.5	2.9	2.1	37.8
1984	214.3	95.3	82.1	48.2	7.9	8.5	7.4	2.7	1.7	3.3	2.4	36.9
1985	235.6	102.1	92.1	54.6	8.1	10.0	7.8	3.1	2.0	4.0	2.5	41.4
1986	249.3	115.6	91.6	52.4	7.3	11.7	7.9	3.2	2.1	4.2	2.8	42.1
1987	259.0	114.1	98.8	53.7	8.6	13.2	9.0	4.7	2.1	4.3	3.2	46.1
1988	262.2	116.2	97.9	51.6	9.5	14.1	8.2	4.4	2.2	4.7	3.2	48.1
1989	271.3	116.2	106.1	53.6	12.7	15.9	8.8	5.2	2.0	5.0	2.9	49.0
1990	245.9	100.9	95.3	44.8	8.4	16.6	9.2	5.7	2.2	5.3	3.1	49.7
1991	231.0	94.5	86.3	32.7	8.3	19.0	9.6	6.2	2.4	5.1	3.0	50.2
1992	252.3	110.6	87.1	32.8	8.9	17.7	10.8	5.8	2.5	5.5	3.1	54.6
1993	267.2	121.9	88.3	34.2	8.7	19.4	10.4	3.9	2.4	6.7	2.6	57.0
FLOOR SPACE (mil. sq. ft.)												
1980	3,102	1,839	1,263	738	220	103	55	18	28	49	52	(X)
1981	2,805	1,562	1,243	787	188	83	60	14	25	46	41	(X)
1982	2,455	1,440	1,015	631	119	82	71	19	25	38	30	(X)
1983	3,387	2,276	1,111	716	112	84	84	20	29	36	31	(X)
1984	3,661	2,311	1,350	901	157	100	70	23	29	37	34	(X)
1985	3,854	2,324	1,530	1,039	165	111	73	28	32	44	38	(X)
1986	3,936	2,481	1,455	960	148	129	73	30	32	44	39	(X)
1987	3,756	2,288	1,468	933	160	139	78	42	32	46	38	(X)
1988	3,595	2,181	1,414	883	162	142	71	38	32	49	37	(X)
1989	3,514	2,115	1,399	867	158	151	72	41	27	48	35	(X)
1990	3,019	1,817	1,202	694	128	152	69	47	29	51	32	(X)
1991	2,637	1,654	983	477	100	177	72	50	29	45	33	(X)
1992	2,800	1,864	936	462	95	157	77	41	30	42	32	(X)
1993	3,016	2,054	962	479	108	165	74	30	30	51	25	(X)

X Not applicable.   [1] Includes nonindustrial warehouses.   [2] Includes science.

No. 1199. Construction Contracts—Value, by State: 1990 to 1993

[In millions of dollars. See headnote, table 1198. Represents value of construction in States in which work was actually done]

STATE	1990	1991	1992	1993 Total (incl. non-bldg.)	1993 Residential	1993 Nonresidential	STATE	1990	1991	1992	1993 Total (incl. non-bldg.)	1993 Residential	1993 Nonresidential
U.S .	246,022	230,923	252,211	267,262	121,942	88,330	MO . . .	3,833	3,994	4,398	5,102	2,353	1,955
							MT . . .	332	522	603	737	341	125
AL. . . .	2,939	2,777	3,245	3,749	1,857	1,127	NE . . .	1,318	1,298	1,535	1,594	671	507
AK . . .	1,919	768	1,905	922	231	363	NV . . .	3,334	2,642	4,002	3,796	1,932	1,174
AZ . . .	4,553	4,690	5,312	6,256	3,980	1,348	NH . . .	1,021	863	1,013	926	454	293
AR . . .	1,438	1,772	2,021	2,150	1,103	571	NJ . . .	6,141	6,121	5,492	6,102	2,381	2,215
CA . . .	37,318	30,280	27,293	27,217	10,524	10,528	NM . . .	1,124	1,405	1,355	1,630	725	423
CO . . .	3,235	4,599	5,782	5,972	3,190	1,675	NY . . .	14,137	12,568	14,173	12,844	3,578	5,404
CT . . .	3,058	2,860	2,903	3,038	1,158	1,089	NC . . .	6,614	6,955	8,029	8,844	4,783	2,460
DE . . .	787	791	786	699	328	240	ND . . .	506	467	587	650	263	183
DC . . .	795	624	752	1,126	31	908	OH . . .	9,885	9,442	10,770	11,037	5,025	3,898
FL. . . .	16,975	15,401	16,750	18,503	10,380	5,039	OK . . .	2,164	2,046	2,488	2,401	1,192	703
GA . . .	7,120	7,243	8,159	9,340	5,392	2,525	OR . . .	3,101	2,590	2,837	3,567	1,982	921
HI . . .	2,831	2,790	2,878	2,288	926	875	PA . . .	10,117	9,461	9,958	10,243	3,840	3,468
ID . . .	986	1,051	1,277	1,686	947	470	RI . . .	594	763	651	1,228	277	171
IL . . .	10,796	9,039	10,414	11,173	4,943	4,162	SC . . .	3,664	3,761	3,439	4,307	1,945	1,299
IN . . .	6,350	5,391	6,522	7,162	3,434	2,462	SD . . .	468	356	586	773	260	263
IA . . .	2,034	2,229	2,177	2,358	984	747	TN . . .	4,388	4,358	5,221	5,481	3,046	1,520
KS . . .	2,193	2,307	2,539	2,674	1,302	714	TX . . .	13,197	14,740	16,657	18,985	8,545	6,576
KY . . .	3,174	3,858	3,863	4,250	1,962	1,368	UT . . .	1,884	1,662	2,113	3,015	1,382	1,262
LA . . .	3,191	2,930	3,015	3,585	1,192	1,440	VT . . .	515	581	580	538	279	169
ME . . .	897	862	1,163	959	467	300	VA . . .	7,180	6,455	7,366	7,541	3,941	2,025
MD . . .	6,056	5,068	5,243	5,170	2,567	1,437	WA . . .	6,185	6,426	7,582	6,878	3,522	2,102
MA . . .	5,135	5,135	5,719	6,276	2,236	2,241	WV . . .	1,253	856	1,091	1,160	216	417
MI . . .	7,646	7,140	7,470	7,952	3,656	2,778	WI . . .	4,654	4,198	5,074	5,061	2,439	1,784
MN . . .	4,953	4,409	5,237	5,274	2,789	1,564	WY . . .	462	473	468	672	165	101
MS . . .	1,569	1,906	1,719	2,366	825	944							

Source of tables 1198 and 1199: F. W. Dodge, McGraw-Hill, Inc., New York, NY. Figures reported currently in *Dodge Construction Potentials*.

No. 1200. New Privately-Owned Housing Units Authorized, by State: 1992 and 1993

[Based on about 17,000 places in United States having building permit systems]

STATE	HOUSING UNITS (1,000)			VALUATION (mil. dol.)			STATE	HOUSING UNITS (1,000)			VALUATION (mil. dol.)		
	1992	1993 Total	1993 1 unit	1992	1993 Total	1993 1 unit		1992	1993 Total	1993 1 unit	1992	1993 Total	1993 1 unit
U.S .	1,094.9	1,199.1	986.5	95,539	106,801	97,119	MO ...	20.1	21.7	18.3	1,526	1,750	1,626
							MT ...	2.1	2.9	1.9	169	212	171
AL. ...	13.9	16.1	12.8	940	1,147	1,046	NE ...	6.7	7.8	5.5	462	551	481
AK. ...	1.1	1.7	1.4	139	228	196	NV ...	17.3	23.3	19.5	1,187	1,637	1,471
AZ ...	31.8	38.7	34.7	3,112	3,778	3,592	NH ...	4.0	4.2	3.7	358	381	359
AR ...	7.9	10.0	7.0	517	644	554	NJ ...	19.1	25.2	21.3	1,648	2,087	1,926
CA ...	97.8	84.3	69.6	11,353	10,195	9,088	NM ...	7.2	8.9	8.1	613	775	750
CO ...	23.5	29.9	25.9	2,439	3,096	2,883	NY ...	29.9	28.6	21.1	2,598	2,621	2,243
CT ...	8.0	9.2	7.8	820	930	873	NC ...	48.2	53.3	45.9	3,740	4,431	4,169
DE ...	4.6	4.9	4.6	284	313	302	ND ...	2.6	2.9	1.6	159	190	147
DC ...	0.1	0.3	0.1	16	21	16	OH ...	42.6	44.2	34.1	3,927	4,319	3,938
FL. ...	102.0	115.1	91.3	8,558	9,658	8,291	OK ...	7.7	8.7	8.3	670	809	798
GA ...	44.6	53.9	47.6	3,497	4,302	4,058	OR ...	17.0	20.5	15.2	1,543	1,956	1,709
HI. ...	7.8	6.6	4.6	847	679	567	PA ...	38.3	40.1	35.9	3,308	3,547	3,363
ID ...	9.6	11.6	8.8	751	929	816	RI ...	2.6	2.6	2.4	212	235	227
IL. ...	40.4	44.7	36.2	3,962	4,487	4,048	SC ...	20.2	21.1	18.7	1,573	1,694	1,590
IN ...	28.7	30.8	25.9	2,595	2,896	2,715	SD ...	3.2	3.7	2.3	201	242	185
IA. ...	10.5	10.6	7.4	812	882	752	TN ...	23.3	27.0	24.1	1,780	2,171	2,086
KS ...	9.8	11.0	8.9	885	1,028	933	TX ...	64.2	77.8	62.7	5,599	6,896	6,414
KY ...	14.7	15.9	12.4	1,024	1,173	1,060	UT ...	12.8	17.3	13.9	1,123	1,508	1,361
LA. ...	9.8	11.2	10.4	710	859	831	VT ...	2.3	2.3	2.0	190	202	186
ME ...	4.3	3.8	3.6	334	309	295	VA ...	40.2	45.0	39.4	3,155	3,700	3,494
MD ...	32.4	30.0	25.4	2,511	2,309	2,140	WA ...	39.7	41.3	30.4	3,460	3,629	3,046
MA ...	16.4	17.5	15.8	1,747	1,891	1,788	WV ..	2.3	2.6	2.2	152	185	173
MI. ...	37.0	39.8	33.7	3,000	3,390	3,123	WI. ...	31.0	32.1	21.7	2,377	2,624	2,178
MN ...	26.4	27.3	23.0	2,482	2,672	2,469	WY ...	1.0	1.2	1.1	103	136	130
MS ...	6.3	8.1	6.9	370	495	464							

Source: U.S. Bureau of the Census, *Construction Reports,* series C40, annual.

No. 1201. Valuation of Construction Authorized by Permit, by Type of Construction and State: 1993

[In millions of dollars]

STATE	Total 1	Residential	NONRESIDENTIAL Total 2	Industrial	Office	Stores	STATE	Total 1	Residential	NONRESIDENTIAL Total 2	Industrial	Office	Stores
U.S..	186,117	106,801	35,601	4,926	6,123	11,612	MO ..	3,171	1,750	660	69	148	185
							MT...	369	212	69	6	9	40
AL ...	2,315	1,147	672	65	261	154	NE ...	1,046	551	229	55	35	71
AK...	451	228	129	6	20	95	NV ...	2,607	1,637	382	55	70	118
AZ ...	4,870	3,778	559	48	77	242	NH ...	722	381	136	28	10	54
AR...	1,174	644	317	37	61	127	NJ ...	4,177	2,087	498	39	107	127
CA...	20,183	10,195	3,563	422	612	1,324	NM ...	1,320	775	315	109	108	63
CO...	4,457	3,096	550	85	69	210	NY ...	7,021	2,621	2,220	75	171	639
CT...	1,890	930	254	32	46	80	NC...	7,014	4,431	1,381	222	300	377
DE...	649	313	146	8	85	29	ND...	346	190	65	10	18	16
DC...	255	21	130	-	76	3	OH...	7,636	4,319	1,552	239	309	465
FL...	14,752	9,658	2,391	107	335	708	OK...	1,372	809	294	29	37	122
GA...	6,754	4,302	1,303	223	302	453	OR...	3,065	1,956	438	98	46	152
HI ...	1,419	679	306	8	48	135	PA...	6,550	3,547	1,297	181	231	426
ID ...	1,401	929	258	62	45	62	RI ...	430	235	61	2	2	30
IL...	8,023	4,487	1,464	224	279	523	SC...	3,002	1,694	751	202	104	231
IN ...	5,106	2,896	1,091	193	171	421	SD...	512	242	95	13	20	26
IA ...	1,635	882	391	107	64	102	TN...	3,911	2,171	751	109	158	241
KS...	1,602	1,028	295	69	52	76	TX...	11,688	6,896	2,522	407	452	964
KY...	2,055	1,173	495	121	62	170	UT...	2,191	1,508	393	83	50	95
LA...	1,675	859	423	19	63	181	VT...	372	202	76	14	11	22
ME...	644	309	142	7	23	55	VA...	5,673	3,700	803	94	111	237
MD...	3,595	2,309	453	31	88	128	WA...	5,852	3,629	1,132	175	262	362
MA...	3,829	1,891	623	35	68	194	WV ..	529	185	185	87	19	43
MI ...	6,174	3,390	1,133	244	161	419	WI ...	4,552	2,624	924	208	173	256
MN...	4,488	2,672	635	111	54	177	WY...	262	136	62	6	4	23
MS...	1,327	495	586	49	36	159							

- Represents zero. [1] Includes residential and nonresidential additions and alterations, residential nonhousekeeping buildings, and residential garages and carports, not shown separately. [2] Includes other types of construction not shown separately.

Source: U.S. Bureau of the Census, unpublished data.

No. 1202. New Privately-Owned Housing Units Started—Selected Characteristics: 1970 to 1993

[In thousands. For composition of regions, see table 26. See also *Historical Statistics, Colonial Times to 1970,* series N 156-163 and 170]

YEAR	Total units	STRUCTURES WITH—			REGION				CONDOMINIUM UNITS [1]		
		One unit	2 to 4 units	5 or more units	North-east	Mid-west	South	West	Total	Single-family	Multi-family
1970	1,434	813	85	536	218	294	612	311	(NA)	(NA)	(NA)
1971	2,052	1,151	120	781	264	434	869	486	(NA)	(NA)	(NA)
1972	2,357	1,309	141	906	330	443	1,057	527	(NA)	(NA)	(NA)
1973	2,045	1,132	118	795	277	440	899	429	241	69	172
1974	1,338	888	68	382	183	317	553	285	175	46	130
1975	1,160	892	64	204	149	294	442	275	65	20	45
1976	1,538	1,162	86	289	169	400	569	400	95	30	64
1977	1,987	1,451	122	414	202	465	783	538	118	41	77
1978	2,020	1,433	125	462	200	451	824	545	156	42	114
1979	1,745	1,194	122	429	178	349	748	470	198	43	156
1980	1,292	852	110	331	125	218	643	306	186	35	150
1981	1,084	705	91	288	117	165	562	240	181	36	145
1982	1,062	663	80	320	117	149	591	205	170	40	130
1983	1,703	1,068	113	522	168	218	935	382	276	77	199
1984	1,750	1,084	121	544	204	243	866	436	291	96	194
1985	1,742	1,072	93	576	252	240	782	468	225	79	146
1986	1,805	1,179	84	542	294	296	733	483	214	80	134
1987	1,620	1,146	65	409	269	298	634	420	196	73	123
1988	1,488	1,081	59	348	235	274	575	404	148	53	95
1989	1,376	1,003	55	318	179	266	536	396	118	37	82
1990	1,193	895	37	260	131	253	479	329	75	22	53
1991	1,014	840	36	138	113	233	414	254	60	21	39
1992	1,200	1,030	31	139	127	288	497	288	74	35	40
1993	1,288	1,126	29	133	126	298	562	302	86	45	41

NA Not available.   [1] Type of ownership under which the owners of the individual housing units are also joint owners of the common areas of the building or community. Includes a small number of cooperatively-owned units.

Source: U.S. Bureau of the Census, *Current Construction Reports,* series C20, monthly.

No. 1203. New Privately-Owned Housing Units Started, by State: 1990 to 1993

[In thousands of units]

REGION, DIVISION, AND STATE	1990	1991	1992	1993 Total units	1993 Single-family units	REGION, DIVISION, AND STATE	1990	1991	1992	1993 Total units	1993 Single-family units
U.S. . . .	1,193.0	1,014.0	1,200.0	1,241.0	1,087.0	DC . . .	0.4	0.3	0.1	0.1	0.1
						VA . . .	43.2	34.8	41.6	44.6	40.7
Northeast .	131.0	113.0	127.0	124.0	110.0	WV . . .	3.1	3.4	3.9	4.3	3.9
N.E. . .	39.2	33.8	41.8	40.4	37.4	NC . . .	46.3	41.3	52.8	59.8	53.4
ME . . .	5.1	4.3	4.5	4.1	3.9	SC . . .	22.5	20.1	23.3	23.5	22.1
NH . . .	4.6	3.9	4.4	5.2	4.1	GA . . .	44.9	39.4	48.0	51.6	48.8
VT . . .	2.6	2.4	2.4	2.4	2.1	FL . . .	136.7	99.9	111.1	128.4	108.6
MA . . .	15.1	13.2	17.5	17.3	16.3	E.S.C. . . .	64.7	59.3	73.0	80.6	72.0
RI . . .	3.2	2.5	3.1	3.0	2.8	KY . . .	15.2	14.5	18.4	19.4	16.6
CT . . .	8.5	7.5	10.4	9.3	8.2	TN . . .	24.9	23.1	28.3	31.2	28.8
M.A.	91.9	79.1	85.0	83.2	72.8	AL . . .	16.8	14.9	17.8	20.1	17.3
NY . . .	33.5	27.7	29.2	26.9	21.4	MS . . .	7.8	6.8	8.5	10.0	9.3
NJ . . .	20.0	15.6	17.5	17.3	15.2	W.S.C. . . .	79.8	84.8	106.9	123.4	110.4
PA . . .	38.5	35.7	38.3	39.0	36.2	AR . . .	9.0	9.2	10.6	12.2	10.4
Midwest . .	252.0	233.0	289.0	285.0	244.0	LA . . .	7.8	8.7	11.7	12.7	12.3
E.N.C . .	181.4	163.9	203.7	200.2	170.6	OK . . .	7.9	8.3	11.3	13.5	13.1
OH . . .	42.7	39.5	51.9	48.1	40.9	TX . . .	55.1	58.6	73.3	85.1	74.5
IN . . .	28.5	27.4	35.3	35.4	31.7	West	330.0	254.0	288.0	279.0	240.0
IL . . .	41.9	36.0	44.8	47.5	40.5	Mt.	83.4	82.1	113.2	121.8	109.3
MI . . .	40.5	34.3	40.5	38.6	34.6	MT . . .	1.6	2.2	3.4	3.5	3.1
WI . . .	27.8	26.7	31.2	30.6	23.0	ID . . .	6.2	7.5	11.6	10.9	9.4
W.N.C . .	70.8	69.4	85.5	85.2	73.4	WY . . .	1.0	1.1	1.8	1.8	1.7
MN . . .	22.3	20.8	25.4	24.4	22.7	CO . . .	12.4	14.7	24.5	29.5	26.0
IA . . .	9.0	9.5	12.3	12.1	9.3	NM . . .	4.5	4.8	6.3	6.2	5.9
MO . .	17.2	17.6	21.4	22.1	19.8	AZ . . .	23.2	24.0	32.4	36.0	33.6
ND . . .	1.8	2.5	2.9	3.1	2.0	UT . . .	7.5	9.5	13.5	15.6	13.7
SD . . .	3.2	2.7	3.7	3.9	2.9	NV . . .	26.9	18.4	19.8	18.3	15.8
NE . . .	7.6	7.2	8.6	8.5	7.0	Pac	246.4	171.5	175.2	156.9	130.3
KS . . .	9.7	9.0	11.1	11.0	9.8	WA . . .	46.0	35.0	40.4	38.7	30.7
South	479.0	414.0	496.0	554.0	494.0	OR . . .	22.7	16.8	20.3	19.7	16.7
S.A.	334.8	270.0	316.0	350.4	311.3	CA . . .	170.5	110.6	106.0	90.0	76.0
DE . . .	5.9	4.9	5.8	6.3	5.9	AK . . .	1.0	1.3	1.6	1.8	1.7
MD . . .	31.8	26.0	29.3	31.8	27.7	HI . . .	6.3	7.7	6.8	6.7	5.1

Source: National Association of Home Builders, Economics, Mortgage Finance and Housing Policy Division, *Forecast of Housing Activity.*

No. 1204. Characteristics of New Privately Owned One-Family Houses Completed: 1970 to 1993

[Percent distribution, except as indicated. Data beginning 1980 show percent distribution of characteristics for all houses completed (includes new houses completed, houses built for sale completed, contractor-built and owner-built houses completed, and houses completed for rent). Data for 1970 cover contractor-built, owner-built, and houses for rent for year construction started and houses sold for year of sale. Percents exclude houses for which characteristics specified were not reported]

CHARACTERISTIC	1970	1980	1990	1992	1993	CHARACTERISTIC	1970	1980	1990	1992	1993
Total houses (1,000) ...	793	957	966	964	1,039	Bedrooms..........	100	100	100	100	100
						2 or less..........	13	17	15	12	12
Financing	100	100	100	100	100	3................	63	63	57	59	58
Mortgage	84	81	82	86	87	4 or more..........	24	20	29	29	30
FHA-insured.......	30	16	14	10	9	Bathrooms	100	100	100	100	100
VA-guaranteed.....	7	8	4	5	6	1 1/2 or less.......	20	10	5	13	12
Conventional	47	55	62	69	71	2................	32	48	42	40	40
Farmers Home						2 1/2 or more......	16	25	45	47	48
Administration.....	(¹)	3	2	1	1	Heating fuel	100	100	100	100	100
Cash or equivalent	16	18	18	14	13	Electricity	28	50	33	29	29
						Gas.............	62	41	59	65	66
Floor area..........	100	100	100	100	100	Oil..............	8	3	5	4	3
Under 1,200 sq. ft	36	21	11	10	9	Other............	1	5	3	2	2
1,200 to 1,599 sq. ft ...	28	29	22	22	21	Heating system	100	100	100	100	100
1,600 to 1,999 sq. ft ...	16	22	22	23	23	Warm air furnace	71	57	65	66	67
2,000 to 2,399 sq. ft ...	21	13	17	17	18	Electric heat pump	(NA)	24	23	24	24
2,400 sq. ft. and over ..	(²)	15	29	29	29	Other............	29	19	12	11	10
Average (sq. ft.)......	1,500	1,740	2,080	2,095	2,095	Central air-conditioning .	100	100	100	100	100
Median (sq. ft.)......	1,385	1,595	1,905	1,920	1,945	With.............	34	63	76	77	78
						Without...........	66	37	24	23	22
Number of stories	100	100	100	100	100	Fireplaces..........	100	100	100	100	100
1................	74	60	46	48	48	No fireplace	65	43	34	36	37
2 or more	17	31	49	47	48	1 or more	35	56	66	64	63
Split level	10	8	4	5	4	Parking facilities	100	100	100	100	100
Foundation..........	100	100	100	100	100	Garage...........	58	69	82	83	84
Full or partial basement.	37	36	38	42	40	Carport...........	17	7	2	2	2
Slab..............	36	45	40	38	40	No garage or carport ..	25	24	16	15	14
Crawl space	27	19	21	20	20						

NA Not available. ¹ Included with "Conventional" financing. ² Included with floor area of 2,000 to 2,399 square feet.
Source: U.S. Bureau of the Census and U.S. Dept. of Housing and Urban Development, *Current Construction Reports*, series C25, *Characteristics of New Housing*, annual.

No. 1205. New Privately Owned One-Family Houses Sold, by Region and Type of Financing, 1970 to 1993, and by Sales-Price Group, 1993

[In thousands. Based on a national probability sample of monthly interviews with builders or owners of one-family houses for which building permits have been issued or, for nonpermit areas, on which construction has started. For details, see source. For composition of regions, see table 26]

YEAR AND SALES-PRICE GROUP	Total sales	REGION				FINANCING TYPE			
		Northeast	Midwest	South	West	Conventional	FHA and VA	Farmers Home Admin.	Cash
1970	485	61	100	203	121	¹213	244	(¹)	27
1971	656	82	127	270	176	¹314	314	(¹)	28
1972	718	96	130	305	187	¹447	242	(¹)	30
1973	634	95	120	257	161	¹465	134	(¹)	34
1974	519	69	103	207	139	¹378	112	(¹)	28
1975	549	71	106	222	150	363	122	43	22
1976	646	72	128	247	199	458	134	23	31
1977	819	86	162	317	255	592	166	24	38
1978	817	78	145	331	262	575	174	26	43
1979	709	67	112	304	225	469	186	18	36
1980	545	50	81	267	145	302	196	14	32
1981	436	46	60	219	112	244	142	14	36
1982	412	47	48	219	99	193	173	11	34
1983	623	76	71	323	152	350	217	8	49
1984	639	94	76	309	160	423	149	9	58
1985	688	112	82	323	170	403	208	11	64
1986	750	136	96	322	196	411	268	12	59
1987	671	117	97	271	186	408	190	8	64
1988	676	101	97	276	202	437	171	6	62
1989	650	86	102	260	202	416	162	14	58
1990	534	71	89	225	149	337	138	10	50
1991	509	57	93	215	144	329	128	9	43
1992	610	65	116	259	170	428	134	7	41
1993	667	60	124	295	189	476	146	5	37
Under $80,000.	87	2	15	58	12	37	38	5	6
$80,000 to $119,999.	210	12	40	100	58	123	74	(B)	12
$120,000 to $149,999.	133	12	27	51	44	102	24	(B)	7
$150,000 to $199,999.	122	15	22	47	38	106	10	(B)	6
$200,000 and over	115	19	20	39	37	108	(B)	(B)	6

B Withheld because estimate did not meet publication standards on the basis of sample size. ¹ Houses financed by Farmers Home Administration included under conventional financing.
Source: U.S. Bureau of the Census and U.S. Dept. of Housing and Urban Development, *Current Construction Reports*, series C25, *Characteristics of New Housing*, annual; and *New One-Family Houses Sold*, monthly.

No. 1206. Median Sales Price of New Privately Owned One-Family Houses Sold, by Region: 1970 to 1993

[In dollars. For definition of median, see Guide to Tabular Presentation. For composition of regions, see table 26]

YEAR	U.S.	North-east	Midwest	South	West	YEAR	U.S.	North-east	Midwest	South	West
1970.....	23,400	30,300	24,400	20,300	24,000	1982.....	69,300	78,200	68,900	66,100	75,000
1971.....	25,200	30,600	27,200	22,500	25,500	1983.....	75,300	82,200	79,500	70,900	80,100
1972.....	27,600	31,400	29,300	25,800	27,500	1984.....	79,900	88,600	85,400	72,000	87,300
1973.....	32,500	37,100	32,900	30,900	32,400	1985.....	84,300	103,300	80,300	75,000	92,600
1974.....	35,900	40,100	36,100	34,500	35,800	1986.....	92,000	125,000	88,300	80,200	95,700
1975.....	39,300	44,000	39,600	37,300	40,600	1987.....	104,500	140,000	95,000	88,000	111,000
1976.....	44,200	47,300	44,800	40,500	47,200	1988.....	112,500	149,000	101,600	92,000	126,500
1977.....	48,800	51,600	51,500	44,100	53,500	1989.....	120,000	159,600	108,800	96,400	139,000
1978.....	55,700	58,100	59,200	50,300	61,300	1990.....	122,900	159,000	107,900	99,400	147,500
1979.....	62,900	65,500	63,900	57,300	69,600	1991.....	120,000	155,900	110,000	100,000	141,100
1980.....	64,600	69,500	63,400	59,600	72,300	1992.....	121,500	169,000	115,600	105,500	130,400
1981.....	68,900	76,000	65,900	64,400	77,800	1993.....	126,500	162,600	125,000	115,000	135,000

Source: U.S. Bureau of the Census and U.S. Dept. of Housing and Urban Development, *Current Construction Reports*, series C25, *Characteristics of New Housing*, annual; and *New One-Family Houses Sold*, monthly.

No. 1207. New Mobile Homes Placed for Residential Use and Average Sales Price, by Region: 1980 to 1993

[A mobile home is a moveable dwelling, 10 feet or more wide and 35 feet or more long, designed to be towed on its own chassis and without need of a permanent foundation. Excluded are travel trailers, motor homes, and modular housing. Data are based on a probability sample and subject to sampling variability; see source. For composition of regions, see table 26]

YEAR	UNITS PLACED (1,000)					AVERAGE SALES PRICE (dol.)				
	Total	North-east	Mid-west	South	West	U.S.	North-east	Mid-west	South	West
1980	233.7	12.3	32.3	140.3	48.7	19,800	18,500	18,600	18,200	25,400
1981	229.2	12.0	30.1	143.5	43.6	19,900	19,000	18,900	18,400	25,600
1982	234.1	12.4	25.6	161.1	35.0	19,700	19,800	20,000	18,500	24,700
1983	278.1	16.3	34.3	186.0	41.4	21,000	21,400	20,400	19,700	27,000
1984	287.9	19.8	35.2	193.4	39.4	21,500	22,200	21,100	20,200	27,400
1985	283.4	20.2	38.6	187.6	36.9	21,800	22,700	21,500	20,400	28,700
1986	256.1	21.2	37.2	162.3	35.4	22,400	24,400	21,800	20,700	29,900
1987	239.2	23.6	40.0	145.5	30.1	23,700	25,600	23,700	21,900	31,000
1988	224.3	22.7	39.1	130.7	31.8	25,100	27,000	24,600	22,700	33,900
1989	202.8	20.2	39.1	112.8	30.6	27,200	30,200	26,700	24,100	37,800
1990	195.4	18.8	37.7	108.4	30.6	27,800	30,000	27,000	24,500	39,300
1991	174.3	14.3	35.4	97.6	27.0	27,700	30,400	27,600	24,500	38,600
1992	212.0	15.0	42.2	124.4	30.4	28,400	30,900	28,800	25,400	39,000
1993	242.5	15.4	44.5	146.7	35.9	30,500	32,000	31,400	27,700	40,500

Source: U.S. Bureau of the Census, *Current Construction Reports*, series C20.

No. 1208. Existing One-Family Houses Sold and Price, by Region: 1970 to 1993

[Based on data (adjusted and aggregated to regional and national totals) reported by participating real estate multiple listing services. For definition of median, see Guide to Tabular Presentation. For composition of regions, see table 26]

YEAR	HOUSES SOLD (1,000)					MEDIAN SALES PRICE (dol.)				
	Total	North-east	Mid-west	South	West	Total	North-east	Mid-west	South	West
1970	1,612	251	501	568	292	23,000	25,200	20,100	22,200	24,300
1971	2,018	311	583	735	389	24,800	27,100	22,100	24,300	26,500
1972	2,252	361	630	788	473	26,700	29,800	23,900	26,400	28,400
1973	2,334	367	674	847	446	28,900	32,800	25,300	29,000	31,000
1974	2,272	354	645	839	434	32,000	35,800	27,700	32,300	34,800
1975	2,476	370	701	862	543	35,300	39,300	30,100	34,800	39,600
1976	3,064	439	881	1,033	712	38,100	41,800	32,900	36,500	46,100
1977	3,650	515	1,101	1,231	803	42,900	44,400	36,700	39,800	57,300
1978	3,986	516	1,144	1,416	911	48,700	47,900	42,200	45,100	66,700
1979	3,827	526	1,061	1,353	887	55,700	53,600	47,800	51,300	77,400
1980	2,973	403	806	1,092	672	62,200	60,800	51,900	58,300	89,300
1981	2,419	353	632	917	516	66,400	63,700	54,300	64,400	96,200
1982	1,990	354	490	780	366	67,800	63,500	55,100	67,100	98,900
1983	2,719	493	709	1,035	481	70,300	72,200	56,600	69,200	94,900
1984	2,868	511	755	1,073	529	72,400	78,700	57,100	71,300	95,800
1985	3,214	622	866	1,172	554	75,500	88,900	58,900	75,200	95,400
1986	3,565	703	991	1,261	610	80,300	104,800	63,500	78,200	100,900
1987	3,526	685	959	1,282	600	85,600	133,300	66,000	80,400	113,200
1988	3,594	673	929	1,350	642	89,300	143,000	68,400	82,200	124,900
1989	3,346	531	855	1,185	775	93,100	145,200	71,300	84,500	139,900
1990	3,211	469	831	1,202	709	95,500	141,200	74,000	85,900	139,600
1991	3,220	479	840	1,199	702	100,300	141,900	77,800	88,900	147,200
1992	3,520	534	939	1,292	755	103,700	140,000	81,700	92,100	143,800
1993	3,802	571	1,007	1,416	808	106,800	139,500	85,200	95,000	142,600

Source: National Association of REALTORS, Washington, DC, *Real Estate Outlook: Market Trends & Insights* (copyright).

No. 1209. Median Sales Price of Existing One-Family Homes, by Selected Metropolitan Area: 1990 to 1993

[In thousands of dollars. Areas are metropolitan statistical areas (MSA's) except as indicated; for definitions and components, see Appendix II]

METROPOLITAN AREA	1990	1991	1992	1993	METROPOLITAN AREA	1990	1991	1992	1993
U.S., all areas	**95.5**	**100.3**	**103.7**	**106.7**	Memphis, TN-AR-MS.	78.1	82.5	85.3	87.0
					Miami-Hialeah, FL PMSA	89.3	93.7	97.1	98.8
Albany-Schenectady-Troy, NY.	106.9	110.3	111.4	112.3	Milwaukee, WI PMSA	84.4	90.0	97.0	104.1
Anaheim-Santa Ana, CA MSA.	242.4	239.7	234.8	220.7	Minneapolis-St. Paul, MN-WI.	88.7	91.1	94.2	98.2
Baltimore, MD	105.9	110.1	113.4	115.7	Nashville, TN	81.8	86.9	88.8	90.4
Birmingham, AL	80.8	86.0	90.9	96.5	New Orleans, LA	67.8	71.8	73.6	76.8
Boston, MA PMSA	174.1	170.1	171.1	173.2	New York-Northern New Jersey-				
Buffalo-Niagara Falls, NY CMSA.	77.2	79.7	81.7	83.5	Long Island, NY-NJ-CT CMSA.	174.9	173.5	172.7	173.2
Charlotte-Gastonia-Rock Hill,					Oklahoma City, OK	53.2	57.0	61.6	64.9
NC-SC	93.1	101.4	102.2	106.1	Orlando, FL.	82.8	86.3	87.6	90.1
Chicago, IL PMSA.	116.8	131.1	136.8	142.0	Philadelphia, PA-NJ PMSA	108.7	118.4	117.0	118.0
Cincinnati, OH-KY-IN PMSA	79.8	84.9	88.6	91.4	Phoenix, AZ.	84.0	85.5	86.8	89.1
Cleveland, OH PMSA	80.6	86.2	90.7	95.0	Pittsburgh, PA PMSA.	70.1	74.2	78.6	82.2
Columbus, OH	81.6	85.2	91.0	91.8	Portland, OR PMSA	79.5	88.5	97.7	106.0
Dallas, TX PMSA	89.5	88.3	91.3	94.5	Richmond-Petersburg VA	87.5	92.5	93.9	94.1
Denver, CO PMSA	86.4	89.1	96.2	104.7	Riverside/San Bernardino, CA				
Detroit, MI PMSA	76.7	80.6	81.3	86.0	PMSA	132.1	137.6	136.2	134.5
Ft. Lauderdale-Hollywood-					Rochester, NY	79.8	81.5	84.7	84.8
Pompano Beach, FL PMSA.	92.6	96.2	99.1	103.1	St. Louis, MO-IL.	76.7	79.4	83.2	84.8
Ft. Worth-Arlington TX PMSA	76.7	77.6	80.2	82.9	Sacramento, CA.	137.5	137.7	134.0	129.4
Hartford, CT PMSA	157.3	148.2	141.1	135.3	Salt Lake City-Ogden, UT.	69.4	72.8	76.5	84.9
Honolulu, HI.	352.0	340.0	349.0	358.5	San Antonio, TX.	63.6	64.9	70.4	77.0
Houston, TX PMSA.	70.7	74.0	80.3	80.9	San Diego, CA.	183.2	187.5	183.1	177.4
Indianapolis, IN	74.8	79.1	83.7	86.6	San Francisco Bay Area-				
Jacksonville, FL	72.4	73.7	76.8	77.1	Seattle-Tacoma, WA CMSA	259.3	258.5	254.7	250.2
Kansas City, MO-KS	74.1	76.6	79.5	83.6	Tampa-St. Petersburg-	142.0	143.1	145.7	150.2
Las Vegas, NV.	93.0	101.4	104.3	108.2	Clearwater, FL	71.4	71.3	72.6	75.0
Los Angeles-Long Beach, CA					Washington, DC-MD-VA.	150.5	156.7	157.8	158.3
PMSA	212.1	218.9	213.1	197.9	West Palm Beach-Boca Raton-				
Louisville, KY-IN	60.8	65.4	69.5	74.5	Delray Beach, FL	108.0	116.3	114.1	114.6

Source: National Association of REALTORS, Washington, DC, *Real Estate Outlook: Market Trends & Insights* (copyright).

No. 1210. Existing Home Sales, by State: 1990 to 1993

[In thousands]

STATE	1990	1991	1992	1993	STATE	1990	1991	1992	1993
United States [1]	**3,211**	**3,220**	**3,520**	**3,802**	Missouri.	84.1	82.7	98.8	106.4
Alabama	61.1	64.0	72.5	77.9	Montana.	12.7	13.9	16.6	16.2
Alaska.	(NA)	(NA)	(NA)	(NA)	Nebraska.	19.3	19.9	22.4	23.2
Arizona	86.3	79.7	89.8	107.9	Nevada.	26.2	25.6	25.6	30.5
Arkansas [2]	44.8	43.4	47.8	52.8	New Hampshire	7.9	9.3	12.0	13.6
California [2]	452.1	425.4	428.2	437.7	New Jersey	114.8	118.8	132.1	139.0
Colorado	54.2	59.6	71.4	82.1	New Mexico	23.6	24.4	29.2	31.0
Connecticut	34.3	37.6	40.0	45.9	New York.	125.5	127.2	136.3	143.0
Delaware	9.7	10.4	10.0	9.4	North Carolina	135.9	139.9	160.2	185.0
District of Columbia	13.1	12.5	12.4	12.3	North Dakota	10.4	10.3	11.9	11.8
Florida.	183.3	176.0	179.2	208.9	Ohio	151.6	149.8	167.4	179.1
Georgia	73.2	70.7	(NA)	(NA)	Oklahoma	53.4	52.5	57.6	61.5
Hawaii	19.2	12.2	11.6	12.5	Oregon	56.6	48.1	52.5	58.8
Idaho	18.1	19.0	21.6	23.4	Pennsylvania	182.7	179.2	204.4	216.1
Illinois	160.9	168.1	186.2	193.9	Rhode Island	7.8	7.8	10.0	11.0
Indiana	80.1	76.0	84.8	100.8	South Carolina	57.8	53.9	58.9	62.2
Iowa	51.9	54.1	53.1	53.5	South Dakota	11.6	11.3	12.7	13.7
Kansas	38.8	37.1	46.2	53.7	Tennessee	92.7	92.0	102.2	120.5
Kentucky	66.4	67.8	78.7	83.3	Texas	240.0	242.0	242.7	258.8
Louisiana	41.6	47.1	47.0	49.3	Utah	22.1	26.3	31.5	31.2
Maine	(NA)	(NA)	10.3	11.6	Vermont.	6.1	8.1	9.5	11.0
Maryland	67.1	66.8	69.0	73.4	Virginia	96.9	90.3	101.3	104.2
Massachusetts	44.0	49.6	57.6	66.0	Washington	87.7	86.9	91.3	97.0
Michigan	145.0	145.0	157.3	170.6	West Virginia	42.0	43.3	46.8	45.7
Minnesota	64.8	66.3	75.7	81.8	Wisconsin	71.7	82.8	91.5	94.6
Mississippi	34.7	35.2	39.2	43.6	Wyoming	7.4	8.2	9.9	10.9

NA Not available. [1] U.S. totals are derived independently and therefore are not equal to the sum of the States. [2] Provided by the California Association of Realtors.

Source: National Association of REALTORS, Washington, DC, *Real Estate Outlook: Market Trends & Insights* (copyright).

No. 1211. New Apartments Completed and Rented in 3 Months, by Region: 1980 to 1992

[Structures with five or more units, privately financed, nonsubsidized, unfurnished apartments. Based on sample and subject to sampling variability. For composition of regions, see table 26]

YEAR AND RENT	NUMBER (1,000)					PERCENT RENTED IN 3 MONTHS				
	U.S.	North-east	Mid-west	South	West	U.S.	North-east	Mid-west	South	West
1980	196.1	14.2	43.8	91.5	46.6	75	77	77	74	75
1981	135.3	4.9	36.9	68.4	25.1	80	85	86	78	75
1982	117.0	4.6	21.9	66.8	23.7	72	74	79	70	72
1983	191.5	3.5	41.1	115.1	31.8	69	73	86	63	69
1984	313.2	3.8	41.2	194.4	73.9	67	64	79	63	70
1985	365.2	8.1	54.0	166.1	137.0	65	69	72	59	68
1986	407.6	16.9	64.5	171.7	154.5	66	70	70	62	67
1987	345.6	11.3	66.0	124.5	143.9	63	73	65	59	64
1988	284.5	8.7	60.4	91.7	123.8	66	52	73	58	69
1989	247.8	13.4	45.8	86.3	102.3	70	74	74	68	69
1990	214.3	12.7	44.3	77.2	80.0	67	66	75	64	65
1991	165.3	6.8	37.9	63.6	57.0	70	83	78	65	68
1992	110.5	11.0	33.8	37.5	28.3	74	75	80	72	70
Less than $350	9.5	2.9	1.0	4.1	1.5	83	85	88	75	99
$350-$449	13.2	2.0	6.0	3.7	1.5	70	67	71	70	71
$450-$549	24.3	0.3	11.7	7.2	5.1	83	30	90	77	75
$550-$649	21.6	0.2	8.9	6.9	5.6	71	92	74	70	68
$650-$749	12.4	0.3	3.0	4.9	4.1	69	62	75	66	68
$750 or more	29.5	5.3	3.0	10.7	10.5	71	74	78	74	65
Median asking rent	588	685	533	603	662	(X)	(X)	(X)	(X)	(X)

X Not applicable.
Source: U.S. Bureau of the Census, *Current Housing Reports*, series H130 and H131, and unpublished data.

No. 1212. Gross Housing Product—Summary: 1980 to 1992

[In billions of dollars. For definition of current and constant dollars, see Guide to Tabular Presentation]

ITEM	CURRENT DOLLARS					CONSTANT (1987) DOLLARS				
	1980	1985	1990	1991	1992	1980	1985	1990	1991	1992
Housing output [1]	245.3	377.0	525.7	552.1	576.9	383.1	418.7	456.6	462.0	468.0
Nonfarm housing	240.2	372.0	520.6	546.8	571.6	376.9	413.5	452.1	457.6	463.7
Owner-occupied	178.4	271.0	379.5	399.1	417.8	278.7	301.3	326.6	330.7	334.8
Tenant-occupied	61.8	101.0	141.1	147.7	153.8	98.2	112.2	125.5	126.9	128.8
Farm housing	5.1	5.0	5.2	5.3	5.3	6.3	5.3	4.5	4.5	4.4
Less: Intermediate goods and services consumed	35.8	49.9	71.6	74.5	71.4	55.9	55.4	62.3	63.2	65.2
Equals: Gross housing product	209.5	327.1	454.1	477.6	505.5	327.2	363.3	394.4	398.8	402.8

[1] Equals personal consumption expenditures (see text, section 14) for housing, less expenditures for transient hotels, motels, clubs, schools, and other group housing.
Source: U.S. Bureau of Economic Analysis, *Survey of Current Business*, July 1992 and August 1993 issues, and *National Income and Product Accounts of the United States: Volume 2, 1959-88*.

No. 1213. Residential Capital—Year-end Stocks and Average Age: 1970 to 1991

[As of **Dec. 31.** Data based on fixed residential capital formation components of the gross national product. For definition of current and constant dollars, see Guide to Tabular Presentation]

ITEM	CURRENT DOLLARS (bil. dol.)				CONSTANT (1987) DOLLARS (bil. dol.)				AVERAGE AGE [1] (years)			
	1970	1980	1990	1991	1970	1980	1990	1991	1970	1980	1990	1991
Gross stocks [2]	1,244	4,391	7,563	7,889	3,961	5,443	6,917	7,032	24.8	23.2	23.6	23.8
Private nonfarm:												
1 to 4 units	1,001	3,502	6,074	6,344	3,208	4,356	5,556	5,657	25.3	23.9	24.2	24.4
5 or more units	131	522	933	973	421	647	853	864	17.7	17.8	19.8	20.3
Farm (1 to 4 units)	55	136	163	166	176	170	150	147	43.9	42.8	43.2	43.2
Private nonhouse-keeping	10	24	32	32	32	29	29	29	14.6	19.3	23.7	23.9
Mobile homes	15	79	124	129	31	88	112	110	5.1	7.7	10.7	11.0
Public: Federal, State and local	25	99	176	184	80	122	162	166	14.9	17.2	19.5	19.8
Net stocks [2] [3]	813	2,910	4,913	5,095	2,590	3,607	4,491	4,542	16.2	15.8	16.8	17.1
Private nonfarm:												
1 to 4 units	656	2,334	3,991	4,147	2,102	2,902	3,649	3,698	16.8	16.3	17.2	17.4
5 or more units	93	371	629	648	301	459	575	576	11.0	12.8	15.2	15.7
Farm (1 to 4 units)	24	58	68	69	76	73	62	61	28.7	26.4	26.6	26.6
Private nonhouse-keeping	6	12	14	14	21	15	12	12	9.0	16.0	18.4	18.3
Mobile homes	11	48	62	63	23	54	55	53	3.8	6.0	7.5	7.7
Public: Federal, State and local	18	70	119	121	60	87	107	109	12.7	13.5	14.6	14.7

[1] Constant-dollar stocks.   [2] Includes equipment, not shown separately.   [3] Based on straight-line depreciation.
Source: U.S. Bureau of Economic Analysis, *Fixed Reproducible Tangible Wealth in the United States, 1925-89*, and *Survey of Current Business*, January 1992 and September 1993 issues.

No. 1214. Housing Units—Historical Trends for Selected Characteristics: 1940 to 1990

[As of **April 1.** Based on the Census of Population and Housing; see Appendix III]

CHARACTERISTIC	NUMBER OF UNITS						PERCENT DISTRIBUTION					
	1940	1950	1960	1970	1980	1990	1940	1950	1960	1970	1980	1990
UNITS IN STRUCTURE												
All housing units [1]	**37,325**	**45,983**	**58,315**	**67,699**	**86,759**	**102,264**	**100.0**	**100.0**	**100.0**	**100.0**	**100.0**	**100.0**
1 detached	23,731	29,116	40,103	44,801	53,596	60,383	63.6	63.3	68.8	66.2	61.8	59.0
1 attached.	[2]2,835	[3]2,799	3,655	1,990	3,587	5,378	[2]7.6	[3]6.1	6.3	2.9	4.1	5.3
2	3,464	5,302	4,464	5,444	5,309	4,948	9.3	11.5	7.7	8.0	6.1	4.8
3 or 4	2,259	3,374	3,088	3,563	4,373	4,928	6.1	7.3	5.3	5.3	5.0	4.8
5 or more	3,928	5,078	6,238	9,829	15,478	18,105	10.5	11.0	10.7	14.5	17.8	17.7
Mobile home or trailer	(NA)	315	767	2,073	4,416	7,400	(NA)	0.7	1.3	3.1	5.1	7.2
Other	[4]1,108	(NA)	(NA)	(NA)	(NA)	1,121	[4]3.0	(NA)	(NA)	(NA)	(NA)	1.1
PLUMBING FACILITIES												
All housing units [1]	**35,026**	**44,502**	**58,315**	**67,657**	**86,693**	**102,264**	**100.0**	**100.0**	**100.0**	**100.0**	**100.0**	**100.0**
Complete plumbing facilities .	19,174	28,729	48,537	62,984	84,359	101,162	54.7	64.6	83.2	93.1	97.3	98.9
Lacking complete plumbing facilities	15,852	15,773	9,778	4,672	2,334	1,102	45.3	35.4	16.8	6.9	2.7	1.1
Not reported	2,299	1,481	(NA)	(NA)	(NA)	(NA)	(X)	(X)	(NA)	(NA)	(NA)	(NA)
TELEPHONE IN HOUSING UNIT [5]												
Occupied housing units .	**33,884**	**41,829**	**53,024**	**63,450**	**80,390**	**91,947**	**(NA)**	**(NA)**	**100.0**	**100.0**	**100.0**	**100.0**
With telephone.	(NA)	(NA)	41,618	55,177	74,720	87,130	(NA)	(NA)	78.5	87.0	92.9	94.8
No telephone.	(NA)	(NA)	11,406	8,273	5,670	4,817	(NA)	(NA)	21.5	13.0	7.1	5.2

NA Not available. X Not applicable. [1] Data for 1970 and 1980 are "Year-round housing units," which exclude seasonal and migratory vacant units. [2] Includes 1,656,858 units classified as "2-family side-by-side." [3] Includes 1,588,902 units classified as "1 and 2 dwelling unit." [4] Covers 166,975 units classified as "Other dwelling place" and 940,726 units classified as "1- to 4-family with business." [5] Beginning 1980, data are not completely comparable with earlier years due to change in question asked.
Source: U.S. Bureau of the Census, *1990 Census of Housing,* series CH-1, and earlier census reports.

No. 1215. Occupied Housing Units—Tenure, by Race of Householder: 1920 to 1991

[In thousands, except as indicated. As of April 1, except 1991, as of fall. Prior to 1960, excludes Alaska and Hawaii. Statistics on the number of occupied units are essentially comparable although identified by various terms. See also *Historical Statistics, Colonial Times to 1970,* series N 238-245]

RACE AND TENURE	1920	1930	1940	1950	1960	1970	1980	1991
ALL RACES								
Occupied units, total.	**24,352**	**29,905**	**34,855**	**42,826**	**53,024**	**63,445**	**80,390**	**93,147**
Owner occupied.	11,114	14,280	15,196	23,560	32,797	39,886	51,795	59,796
Percent of occupied.	45.6	47.8	43.6	55.0	61.9	62.9	64.4	64.2
Renter occupied.	13,238	15,624	19,659	19,266	20,227	23,560	28,595	33,351
WHITE								
Occupied units, total.	**21,826**	**26,983**	**31,561**	**39,044**	**47,880**	**56,606**	**68,810**	**79,140**
Owner occupied.	10,511	13,544	14,418	22,241	30,823	37,005	46,671	53,749
Percent of occupied.	48.2	50.2	45.7	57.0	64.4	65.4	67.8	67.9
Renter occupied.	11,315	13,439	17,143	16,803	17,057	19,601	22,139	25,391
BLACK AND OTHER								
Occupied units, total.	**2,526**	**2,922**	**3,293**	**3,783**	**5,144**	**6,839**	**11,580**	**14,007**
Owner occupied.	603	737	778	1,319	1,974	2,881	5,124	6,047
Percent of occupied.	23.9	25.2	23.6	34.9	38.4	42.1	44.2	43.2
Renter occupied.	1,923	2,185	2,516	2,464	3,170	3,959	6,456	7,960

Source: U.S. Bureau of the Census, *Census of Housing: 1960,* vol. 1; *1970,* vol. 1; *1980 Census of Housing,* vol. 1, chapter A (HC80-1-A); and *1990 Census of Housing, General Housing Characteristics,* series CH-90-1; 1991 data, *Current Housing Reports,* series H150/91.

No. 1216. Occupied Housing Units—Tenure, by Race and Hispanic Origin of Householder: 1980 and 1990

[As of **April 1.** Based on the Census of Population and Housing; see Appendix III]

RACE AND HISPANIC ORIGIN OF HOUSEHOLDER	ALL HOUSEHOLDS			OWNER OCCUPIED		PERCENT OWNER OCCUPIED		RENTER OCCUPIED	
	1980	1990	Percent change, 1980-1990	1980	1990	1980	1990	1980	1990
Total units	**80,389,673**	**91,947,410**	**14.4**	**51,794,545**	**59,024,811**	**64.4**	**64.2**	**28,595,128**	**32,922,599**
White	68,810,123	76,880,105	11.7	46,670,775	52,432,648	67.8	68.2	22,139,348	24,447,457
Black	8,381,668	9,976,161	19.0	3,724,251	4,327,265	44.4	43.4	4,657,417	5,648,896
American Indian, Eskimo, or Aleut	397,252	591,372	48.9	212,209	318,001	53.4	53.8	185,043	273,371
Asian or Pacific Islander .	993,458	2,013,735	102.7	521,230	1,050,182	52.5	52.2	472,228	963,553
Other race	1,807,172	2,486,037	37.6	666,080	896,715	36.9	36.1	1,141,092	1,589,322
Hispanic origin [1]	4,007,896	6,001,718	49.7	1,738,920	2,545,584	43.4	42.4	2,268,976	3,456,134

[1] Persons of Hispanic origin may be of any race.
U.S. Bureau of the Census, *1980 Census of Housing,* vol. 1, chapter A (HC80-1-A); and *1990 Census of Housing, General Housing Characteristics,* series CH-90-1.

No. 1217. Occupied Housing Units—

[In thousands of units, except as indicated. As of April.

STATE	Total housing units	SPECIFIED OWNER OCCUPIED UNITS								
		Value categories						Lower quartile value[1] (dol.)	Median (dol.)	Upper quartile value[1] (dol.)
		Less than $50,000	$50,000 to $99,999	$100,000 to $149,000	$150,000 to $199,000	$200,000 to $299,000	$300,000 or more			
United States ..	44,918.0	11,402.5	16,957.5	6,773.3	4,017.2	3,376.9	2,390.7	49,500	79,100	137,800
Alabama	753.8	343.9	310.7	62.5	20.1	11.3	5.4	35,500	53,700	78,800
Alaska..........	77.5	11.0	31.9	23.0	7.5	3.2	0.9	66,400	94,400	128,500
Arizona	668.7	98.7	372.7	118.8	40.6	23.9	14.0	59,800	80,100	109,900
Arkansas	427.7	235.6	156.9	23.3	6.8	3.5	1.6	31,100	46,300	68,700
California	4,690.3	119.0	636.6	812.1	851.5	1,151.0	1,120.0	127,100	195,500	294,800
Colorado	637.6	84.1	363.1	122.8	37.4	19.9	10.3	62,500	82,700	109,700
Connecticut	643.5	4.6	36.7	165.3	188.0	150.3	98.5	139,000	177,800	246,000
Delaware	137.5	11.8	56.8	38.5	15.6	10.5	4.3	74,800	100,100	143,900
District of Columbia .	71.5	1.7	25.2	15.0	6.9	8.4	14.4	86,700	123,900	258,700
Florida..........	2,378.2	433.1	1,239.1	381.9	151.5	100.6	72.0	56,100	77,100	112,200
Georgia	1,138.8	314.5	531.2	163.2	66.9	39.9	23.1	47,300	71,300	102,100
Hawaii..........	144.4	3.3	13.1	16.7	21.1	39.7	50.5	156,800	245,300	358,800
Idaho	177.3	66.8	89.4	14.2	3.7	2.0	1.2	42,100	58,200	79,700
Illinois	2,084.7	525.1	786.6	403.2	183.7	114.5	71.6	49,800	80,900	128,300
Indiana	1,137.8	514.3	484.0	92.8	27.0	13.7	6.0	36,500	53,900	78,200
Iowa	566.6	317.8	209.7	27.7	7.0	3.3	1.1	30,200	45,900	65,900
Kansas	500.6	238.0	199.6	41.1	12.3	6.4	3.1	32,400	52,200	78,000
Kentucky	662.2	326.9	260.5	47.5	15.9	8.0	3.4	33,400	50,500	73,400
Louisiana	733.9	289.1	344.5	63.0	19.8	11.5	6.1	38,200	58,500	83,000
Maine	214.7	37.5	95.2	49.3	18.0	10.0	4.7	60,100	87,400	123,300
Maryland	970.9	87.3	300.9	274.2	139.6	103.3	65.6	79,000	116,500	169,300
Massachusetts ...	1,004.6	9.5	93.5	310.8	298.3	196.4	96.1	126,800	162,800	216,000
Michigan	1,916.1	737.2	814.5	219.2	79.3	46.0	20.0	38,500	60,600	90,600
Minnesota	894.3	204.9	482.3	138.2	38.6	21.1	9.2	52,200	74,000	98,200
Mississippi	441.8	249.3	156.1	24.2	7.0	3.6	1.6	31,400	45,600	67,800
Missouri.........	1,005.4	385.1	452.6	102.0	33.6	20.3	11.9	38,800	59,800	87,100
Montana	132.4	52.3	68.3	8.4	2.1	1.0	0.3	40,000	56,600	74,200
Nebraska........	314.4	155.3	132.4	18.5	4.7	2.4	1.0	32,800	50,400	70,400
Nevada	183.8	8.4	93.3	51.3	16.0	9.1	5.6	75,400	95,700	129,400
New Hampshire ...	199.4	6.3	45.6	79.9	39.9	21.1	6.6	98,400	129,400	167,600
New Jersey	1,466.3	45.5	241.4	348.8	367.3	301.5	161.9	112,300	162,300	225,000
New Mexico	262.3	73.5	128.2	37.3	12.8	7.2	3.3	46,700	70,100	97,800
New York........	2,387.6	243.8	674.4	431.6	439.0	381.0	217.8	76,200	131,600	200,400
North Carolina ...	1,218.0	382.8	575.7	155.2	56.3	33.1	15.0	44,700	65,800	94,900
North Dakota	103.7	50.6	46.3	5.1	1.1	0.5	0.1	30,800	50,800	70,000
Ohio	2,241.3	734.0	1,102.8	260.5	80.8	42.9	20.3	43,900	63,500	90,200
Oklahoma	616.3	323.7	235.6	36.8	10.9	6.1	3.3	30,800	48,100	71,000
Oregon	511.8	133.3	281.2	62.7	19.5	10.5	4.7	49,200	67,100	92,600
Pennsylvania	2,581.3	829.2	1,017.8	395.9	180.6	109.1	48.7	42,500	69,700	109,500
Rhode Island	176.5	3.0	31.0	78.4	35.6	19.4	9.0	106,000	133,500	171,800
South Carolina ...	615.4	225.7	280.1	63.5	23.7	14.8	7.6	41,100	61,100	89,100
South Dakota	113.1	64.2	42.4	4.6	1.0	0.5	0.2	27,300	45,200	64,500
Tennessee.......	938.4	371.8	416.4	91.5	32.2	17.8	8.7	39,600	58,400	85,300
Texas	2,949.1	1,151.2	1,261.1	314.8	111.3	66.5	44.2	38,300	59,600	89,200
Utah	303.7	61.1	188.6	35.2	10.6	5.7	2.5	53,100	68,900	92,000
Vermont.........	89.2	7.9	41.3	25.5	8.4	4.4	1.7	73,100	95,500	130,000
Virginia	1,192.1	206.7	466.2	203.9	132.8	116.5	66.0	60,100	91,000	155,800
Washington	896.4	124.0	371.3	192.7	101.0	67.8	39.6	63,700	93,400	145,400
West Virginia	350.1	185.3	136.8	18.9	5.4	2.8	0.9	31,200	47,900	69,400
Wisconsin	916.7	287.2	492.2	95.3	24.7	12.3	5.1	45,600	62,500	86,100
Wyoming	78.4	25.9	43.8	6.2	1.5	0.7	0.4	43,900	61,600	82,100

[1] This measure divides the distribution of value and rent categories into four equal parts. The lower quartile value is the value that defines the upper limit of the lowest one-quarter of the cases. The upper quartile value defines the lower limit of the upper one-quarter of the cases in the distribution.

Housing Value and Gross Rent, by State: 1990

Based on the Census of Population and Housing; see Appendix III]

Total housing units	SPECIFIED RENTER OCCUPIED UNITS							Median (dol.)	STATE
	Rent categories								
	Less than $200	$200 to $299	$300 to $399	$400 to $499	$500 to $599	$600 to $749	$750 or more		
32,170.0	2,815.1	3,736.2	5,879.2	5,935.0	4,407.0	4,064.4	3,913.8	447	United States
428.0	81.6	87.3	102.1	67.2	29.1	15.7	6.8	325	Alabama
81.9	1.4	4.4	9.8	12.9	11.3	13.1	17.9	559	Alaska
485.8	25.5	46.1	111.5	113.1	71.2	53.0	39.8	438	Arizona
258.1	38.6	57.8	64.8	39.3	17.2	8.5	4.3	328	Arkansas
4,553.4	136.2	198.5	379.5	621.9	736.4	1,004.1	1,361.9	620	California
472.6	36.5	63.3	110.0	96.4	62.2	51.9	36.0	418	Colorado
418.5	31.2	21.4	31.1	51.2	68.2	94.1	106.3	598	Connecticut
72.2	6.0	4.4	8.7	16.0	16.0	10.9	6.7	495	Delaware
152.1	14.7	11.0	25.5	29.5	21.7	20.3	26.6	479	District of Columbia
1,669.6	103.2	130.9	271.1	368.9	308.6	253.3	168.5	481	Florida
808.4	97.8	99.6	134.3	155.9	128.1	98.0	53.2	433	Georgia
162.8	9.1	7.5	12.6	15.6	17.5	26.2	52.3	650	Hawaii
102.4	14.0	24.5	26.3	16.3	6.5	4.0	2.2	330	Idaho
1,470.4	128.7	159.0	281.6	306.8	229.8	185.8	134.3	445	Illinois
589.9	61.5	104.8	156.4	128.6	65.9	29.3	14.1	374	Indiana
285.7	40.5	66.1	76.7	50.7	22.1	10.8	4.6	336	Iowa
289.8	32.3	54.8	69.0	57.7	30.4	19.3	10.3	372	Kansas
392.3	69.2	87.8	100.6	56.9	24.1	11.9	5.4	319	Kentucky
501.3	70.7	93.1	123.5	88.5	43.6	24.3	14.4	352	Louisiana
133.3	15.5	14.2	26.6	26.6	19.2	14.1	7.5	419	Maine
598.3	41.2	36.0	65.4	94.0	106.0	128.8	108.2	548	Maryland
910.0	98.4	58.2	74.9	106.8	130.2	184.5	231.1	580	Massachusetts
966.2	82.1	123.4	209.0	223.3	149.7	92.0	54.6	423	Michigan
445.9	54.6	54.7	85.1	94.3	66.0	50.2	28.4	422	Minnesota
247.5	49.8	54.0	54.0	32.7	15.7	7.9	3.4	309	Mississippi
585.0	74.0	108.7	138.7	115.2	62.5	37.6	18.1	368	Missouri
93.9	16.1	24.4	24.8	12.9	5.5	2.1	0.9	311	Montana
186.6	24.6	39.8	48.6	34.8	16.2	7.7	4.6	348	Nebraska
209.2	8.4	11.5	29.0	48.5	44.4	38.9	22.9	509	Nevada
127.8	7.7	7.1	12.3	21.6	24.9	27.3	21.5	549	New Hampshire
973.7	60.8	45.3	81.1	133.1	166.0	228.3	232.7	592	New Jersey
173.1	18.3	28.6	44.9	31.0	16.4	11.9	7.4	372	New Mexico
3,150.6	242.8	281.8	490.1	605.9	463.7	454.7	532.9	486	New York
777.9	83.5	121.5	187.4	162.2	90.6	49.8	22.3	382	North Carolina
78.5	13.8	18.7	19.8	11.4	4.0	1.8	0.7	313	North Dakota
1,293.4	149.2	206.4	341.2	280.5	146.7	79.0	40.8	379	Ohio
370.7	44.2	85.0	98.7	60.5	30.1	17.8	9.0	340	Oklahoma
394.9	30.2	52.5	99.2	96.1	52.1	33.7	18.1	408	Oregon
1,287.7	141.0	189.7	272.2	245.0	169.6	125.3	85.4	404	Pennsylvania
152.0	17.9	12.1	18.0	29.1	29.2	25.3	15.7	489	Rhode Island
368.9	45.3	59.5	83.9	77.1	38.5	21.2	10.4	376	South Carolina
81.2	16.2	19.4	18.7	11.6	4.5	2.3	0.9	306	South Dakota
568.9	86.8	101.6	134.5	110.3	55.1	27.6	13.9	357	Tennessee
2,332.9	179.0	345.2	614.2	480.6	263.7	193.8	139.7	395	Texas
169.8	12.4	31.3	53.8	33.9	15.7	9.6	6.3	369	Utah
61.8	5.1	5.8	11.3	14.2	9.9	7.5	4.5	446	Vermont
746.2	59.6	65.7	109.8	124.0	103.8	114.3	128.9	495	Virginia
687.0	49.0	73.5	135.2	152.7	109.0	85.1	56.2	445	Washington
168.3	30.7	41.7	40.8	21.4	8.1	3.8	1.4	303	West Virginia
582.4	51.6	83.9	147.8	142.2	76.6	43.7	18.8	399	Wisconsin
51.5	6.7	12.5	13.2	8.1	3.5	2.1	0.9	333	Wyoming

Source: U.S. Bureau of the Census, *1990 Census of Housing, General Housing Characteristics*, series CH-1, and *Detailed Housing Characteristics*, series CH-2; and *Census of Population and Housing, 1990: Summary Tape File 1C and 3C on CD-ROM.*

No. 1218. Housing Units—

[In thousands of units, except as indicated. As of April.

STATE	Total housing units (1,000)	YEAR STRUCTURE BUILT Percent			Median year built	LACKING COMPLETE PLUMBING		PERCENT OF UNITS WITH—	
		1939 or earlier	1970 to 1979	1980 to March 1990		Total units (1,000)	Percent of total housing units	Public water system or private company	Public sewer
United States ..	**102,263.7**	**18.4**	**21.8**	**20.7**	**1965**	**1,101.7**	**1.1**	**84.2**	**74.8**
Alabama	1,670.4	9.3	25.5	23.5	1970	27.5	1.6	87.1	54.5
Alaska.	232.6	3.0	32.7	38.0	1976	29.0	12.5	65.6	62.3
Arizona	1,659.4	3.2	30.7	37.8	1976	31.5	1.9	94.5	81.3
Arkansas	1,000.7	9.4	27.8	24.2	1971	18.4	1.8	81.5	60.1
California	11,182.9	10.7	21.7	22.9	1967	69.4	0.6	95.4	89.6
Colorado	1,477.3	13.0	28.9	24.7	1971	11.8	0.8	91.0	86.9
Connecticut	1,320.9	25.5	15.7	15.7	1959	5.7	0.4	77.7	70.8
Delaware	289.9	14.3	20.2	24.3	1967	1.7	0.6	76.2	73.4
District of Columbia .	278.5	37.7	8.4	5.5	1947	2.3	0.8	99.9	99.3
Florida	6,100.3	3.7	29.3	35.0	1975	28.0	0.5	86.9	73.8
Georgia	2,638.4	8.1	24.5	32.1	1973	28.5	1.1	81.3	62.1
Hawaii	389.8	6.7	30.5	20.8	1970	4.3	1.1	97.6	80.2
Idaho	413.3	15.9	32.4	18.0	1970	6.0	1.5	70.0	64.0
Illinois	4,506.3	27.1	18.4	11.7	1958	29.3	0.7	89.8	86.2
Indiana	2,246.0	24.2	20.2	14.5	1961	16.2	0.7	74.1	67.9
Iowa	1,143.7	35.0	20.2	10.0	1956	9.8	0.9	81.1	76.0
Kansas	1,044.1	24.5	20.3	16.9	1961	7.9	0.8	89.5	81.2
Kentucky	1,506.8	15.9	25.0	20.0	1967	44.2	2.9	80.6	56.4
Louisiana	1,716.2	10.6	25.3	22.1	1969	21.9	1.3	89.0	72.6
Maine	587.0	34.9	19.8	20.7	1960	20.8	3.5	53.2	45.4
Maryland	1,891.9	15.5	19.6	21.6	1965	12.7	0.7	82.8	81.1
Massachusetts	2,472.7	38.9	14.1	13.8	1953	12.4	0.5	91.6	72.9
Michigan	3,847.9	20.8	20.4	13.6	1960	32.5	0.8	70.5	70.8
Minnesota	1,848.4	24.5	22.1	18.5	1963	24.4	1.3	73.0	73.4
Mississippi	1,010.4	8.6	27.5	24.1	1971	21.9	2.2	87.3	57.9
Missouri.	2,199.1	20.4	21.5	18.3	1964	26.8	1.2	83.6	73.6
Montana	361.2	21.8	26.6	17.5	1966	7.0	1.9	65.5	60.5
Nebraska	660.6	30.7	22.1	12.9	1960	5.2	0.8	83.0	80.9
Nevada	518.9	2.9	30.5	40.1	1977	2.7	0.5	92.5	87.9
New Hampshire . . .	503.9	27.1	20.5	27.7	1968	5.9	1.2	60.3	49.6
New Jersey	3,075.3	24.6	14.9	14.8	1959	15.6	0.5	89.6	87.9
New Mexico	632.1	8.1	26.5	27.5	1972	20.0	3.2	83.1	71.7
New York.	7,226.9	35.7	11.9	9.4	1952	67.3	0.9	87.6	79.1
North Carolina	2,818.2	9.9	24.3	28.6	1971	43.0	1.5	65.4	49.8
North Dakota	276.3	24.7	26.6	16.6	1965	5.6	2.0	79.0	73.9
Ohio	4,371.9	25.8	18.6	12.2	1959	32.9	0.8	82.4	77.6
Oklahoma	1,406.5	12.4	25.4	22.1	1969	13.8	1.0	87.0	73.1
Oregon	1,193.6	16.8	28.7	16.6	1967	10.4	0.9	80.7	70.0
Pennsylvania	4,938.1	35.1	15.8	12.4	1954	47.1	1.0	78.1	74.3
Rhode Island	414.6	34.0	14.7	15.1	1955	2.3	0.5	88.8	70.9
South Carolina	1,424.2	8.5	26.3	29.0	1972	20.2	1.4	77.2	58.0
South Dakota	292.4	30.4	24.6	14.8	1961	5.9	2.0	81.4	71.1
Tennessee.	2,026.1	10.2	24.8	24.2	1970	32.4	1.6	85.7	59.9
Texas	7,009.0	7.1	25.9	29.7	1972	85.1	1.2	91.6	81.2
Utah	598.4	13.5	28.1	24.4	1971	5.9	1.0	95.8	88.4
Vermont.	271.2	36.5	19.6	22.4	1963	6.1	2.3	50.9	42.5
Virginia	2,496.3	11.0	23.6	26.3	1970	46.1	1.8	76.1	69.7
Washington	2,032.4	15.7	24.6	23.1	1969	18.6	0.9	85.7	68.3
West Virginia	781.3	23.7	22.8	17.7	1962	25.1	3.2	72.1	54.8
Wisconsin	2,055.8	28.5	21.1	14.5	1960	29.8	1.4	66.5	70.0
Wyoming	203.4	15.6	31.1	21.4	1971	3.2	1.6	77.6	74.2

Selected Characteristics: 1990

Based on the Census of Population and Housing; see Appendix III]

			PERCENT WITH—								
			Vehicles available		No tele-phone in unit	House heating fuel					
Occupied housing units (1,000)	Percent owner occu-pied	Percent condo-minium	None	2 or more		Utility gas	Bottled, tank, or LP gas	Electri-city	Fuel oil, kero-sene	Wood	STATE
91,947.4	64.2	4.4	11.5	54.7	5.2	51.0	5.7	25.8	12.2	3.9	**United States**
1,506.8	70.5	1.1	10.3	58.7	8.7	42.8	15.6	34.6	1.2	5.3	Alabama
188.9	56.1	5.3	11.9	54.0	8.3	42.8	1.9	11.8	32.3	7.7	Alaska
1,368.8	64.2	6.0	7.8	53.3	8.5	39.5	4.4	51.4	0.2	3.6	Arizona
891.2	69.6	0.7	9.8	56.2	10.9	52.8	11.6	22.7	0.2	12.5	Arkansas
10,381.2	55.6	7.4	8.9	57.9	3.0	73.2	3.1	19.2	0.3	3.1	California
1,282.5	62.3	7.3	6.9	60.9	4.2	77.0	4.8	12.9	0.3	3.3	Colorado
1,230.5	65.6	8.7	10.0	58.6	2.6	26.3	1.9	15.1	54.4	1.6	Connecticut
247.5	70.3	2.6	8.2	59.3	3.1	30.5	6.8	21.8	38.5	1.7	Delaware
249.6	38.9	10.4	37.4	21.2	4.2	63.5	2.0	20.5	12.5	0.0	District of Columbia
5,134.9	67.2	12.9	9.2	49.8	5.3	7.5	7.2	78.8	4.1	0.8	Florida
2,366.6	64.9	2.6	10.3	58.8	8.3	53.3	13.8	27.2	1.5	3.8	Georgia
356.3	53.9	18.4	9.9	54.1	2.6	3.3	2.0	37.9	0.2	0.5	Hawaii
360.7	70.1	1.2	4.6	67.3	5.8	28.2	3.1	39.8	9.0	18.0	Idaho
4,202.2	64.2	5.4	14.0	50.9	4.6	80.3	4.3	11.2	1.8	1.0	Illinois
2,065.4	70.2	1.4	8.5	59.1	5.9	63.1	6.4	19.3	6.2	4.2	Indiana
1,064.3	70.0	1.1	7.1	61.7	3.4	65.6	14.8	10.5	5.5	2.9	Iowa
944.7	67.9	1.7	6.4	61.7	4.4	75.9	8.8	11.8	0.3	2.9	Kansas
1,379.8	69.6	1.3	11.5	56.0	10.2	45.6	7.7	30.0	4.8	8.2	Kentucky
1,499.3	65.9	1.6	13.9	49.9	8.3	55.1	5.8	36.2	0.3	2.3	Louisiana
465.3	70.5	1.6	8.7	57.1	3.7	1.8	1.9	11.7	69.5	14.1	Maine
1,749.0	65.0	5.5	12.3	56.0	3.2	43.2	2.3	29.6	22.1	1.9	Maryland
2,247.1	59.3	6.1	14.3	49.3	2.1	38.0	2.1	13.5	44.0	1.5	Massachusetts
3,419.3	71.0	2.7	10.1	56.8	4.1	76.9	6.1	5.4	6.9	3.9	Michigan
1,647.9	71.8	3.1	8.6	60.0	2.4	62.9	8.2	10.5	11.9	4.9	Minnesota
911.4	71.5	0.6	12.1	54.2	12.6	40.8	20.1	30.6	0.5	7.8	Mississippi
1,961.2	68.8	2.0	9.8	57.0	5.2	60.4	12.0	18.1	1.5	7.6	Missouri
306.2	67.3	1.2	6.7	63.5	6.9	54.2	7.5	17.9	4.1	14.7	Montana
602.4	66.5	1.2	7.2	62.5	3.6	70.2	10.9	13.6	2.5	2.1	Nebraska
466.3	54.8	6.7	7.8	54.8	5.4	47.7	6.0	39.3	3.7	2.6	Nevada
411.2	68.2	5.8	6.3	61.7	3.4	15.2	6.1	12.4	55.8	9.0	New Hampshire
2,794.7	64.9	6.7	12.9	52.5	3.1	57.5	1.9	10.0	29.2	0.5	New Jersey
542.7	67.4	1.5	6.9	59.0	12.4	70.1	11.9	9.1	0.3	7.6	New Mexico
6,639.3	52.2	4.6	30.0	37.5	5.0	45.7	2.4	8.5	39.6	2.0	New York
2,517.0	68.0	2.5	9.6	59.2	7.1	18.6	8.5	42.0	22.5	7.8	North Carolina
240.9	65.6	2.3	6.5	63.2	3.5	39.7	14.0	26.2	15.7	1.2	North Dakota
4,087.5	67.5	2.5	10.2	56.8	4.7	68.2	3.8	16.8	7.5	2.5	Ohio
1,206.1	68.1	1.5	7.5	58.1	8.8	64.4	10.0	20.5	0.1	4.7	Oklahoma
1,103.3	63.1	1.7	8.0	59.9	4.5	24.7	1.5	44.6	11.4	16.9	Oregon
4496.0	70.7	2.0	15.2	49.5	2.6	49.5	1.7	14.8	27.9	2.6	Pennsylvania
378.0	59.5	2.8	10.6	54.5	3.1	40.7	2.4	7.9	47.0	1.4	Rhode Island
1,258.0	69.9	2.3	10.9	57.2	9.1	24.6	9.2	46.9	13.2	5.7	South Carolina
259.0	66.1	0.8	6.5	64.1	6.0	43.0	19.9	17.8	13.6	4.2	South Dakota
1,853.7	68.0	2.0	9.8	58.2	7.1	30.0	5.5	50.5	3.8	9.0	Tennessee
6,070.9	60.9	2.7	8.1	55.9	8.6	50.4	7.8	40.2	0.1	1.2	Texas
537.3	68.1	4.6	5.4	66.1	4.0	81.9	2.3	9.5	1.3	3.2	Utah
210.7	69.0	3.1	8.0	58.0	4.5	8.0	10.5	9.1	54.3	17.0	Vermont
2,291.8	66.3	4.8	9.0	59.8	5.4	28.9	2.6	40.1	20.2	6.7	Virginia
1,872.4	62.6	3.0	7.5	61.4	3.5	22.4	1.1	55.1	9.9	10.6	Washington
688.6	74.1	0.6	13.7	50.4	10.3	50.7	2.8	25.3	7.8	9.0	West Virginia
1,822.1	66.7	1.6	9.3	57.8	2.8	61.0	8.4	9.3	14.6	5.9	Wisconsin
168.8	67.8	1.2	4.7	66.9	5.6	62.9	9.0	16.5	0.7	7.9	Wyoming

Source: U.S. Bureau of the Census, *1990 Census of Housing, Detailed Housing Characteristics*, series CH-2, forthcoming, and *Census of Population and Housing, 1990: Summary Tape File 3C on CD-ROM.*

No. 1219. Occupied Housing Units—Housing Value and Gross Rent, by Region: 1991

[Specified owner-occupied units are limited to one-unit structures on less than 10 acres and no business on property. Specified renter-occupied units exclude one-unit on 10 acres or more. Based on the American Housing Survey; see Appendix III. For composition of regions, see table 26]

CATEGORY	NUMBER (1,000)					PERCENT DISTRIBUTION				
	Total units	North-east	Midwest	South	West	Total units	North-east	Mid-west	South	West
VALUE										
Specified owner occupied units.....	59,796	11,869	15,238	21,272	11,417	100.0	100.0	100.0	100.0	100.0
Less than $10,000.	2,227	221	586	1,164	257	3.7	1.9	3.8	5.5	2.3
$10,000 to $19,999	2,691	318	723	1,329	321	4.5	2.7	4.7	6.2	2.8
$20,000 to $29,999	2,898	367	919	1,350	262	4.8	3.1	6.0	6.3	2.3
$30,000 to $39,999	3,588	373	1,284	1,579	352	6.0	3.1	8.4	7.4	3.1
$40,000 to $49,999	4,574	470	1,691	1,964	449	7.6	4.0	11.1	9.2	3.9
$50,000 to $59,999	4,457	482	1,522	1,974	478	7.5	4.1	10.0	9.3	4.2
$60,000 to $69,999	4,963	607	1,569	2,180	607	8.3	5.1	10.3	10.2	5.3
$70,000 to $79,999	4,495	652	1,353	1,897	592	7.5	5.5	8.9	8.9	5.2
$80,000 to $99,999	7,471	1,469	2,124	2,666	1,212	12.5	12.4	13.9	12.5	10.6
$100,000 to $119,999	4,376	1,176	1,068	1,311	821	7.3	9.9	7.0	6.2	7.2
$120,000 to $149,999	4,906	1,467	989	1,317	1,133	8.2	12.4	6.5	6.2	9.9
$150,000 to $199,999	5,574	2,039	737	1,254	1,545	9.3	17.2	4.8	5.9	13.5
$200,000 to $249,999	2,863	933	310	520	1,100	4.8	7.9	2.0	2.4	9.6
$250,000 to $299,999	1,640	526	140	279	695	2.7	4.4	0.9	1.3	6.1
$300,000 or more	3,074	768	224	489	1,592	5.1	6.5	1.5	2.3	13.9
Median value (dol.)	80,015	116,577	65,699	65,859	129,439	(X)	(X)	(X)	(X)	(X)
GROSS RENT										
Specified renter occupied units.....	33,351	7,093	7,355	10,918	7,985	100.0	100.0	100.0	100.0	100.0
Less than $100.	615	79	182	300	53	1.8	1.1	2.5	2.7	0.7
$100 to $199	2,252	541	626	807	278	6.8	7.6	8.5	7.4	3.5
$200 to $249	1,420	248	411	523	238	4.3	3.5	5.6	4.8	3.0
$250 to $299	2,003	304	633	775	291	6.0	4.3	8.6	7.1	3.6
$300 to $349	2,591	389	803	915	485	7.8	5.5	10.9	8.4	6.1
$350 to $399	2,843	511	738	1,090	504	8.5	7.2	10.0	10.0	6.3
$400 to $449	3,019	568	826	1,061	563	9.1	8.0	11.2	9.7	7.1
$450 to $499	2,861	597	670	956	639	8.6	8.4	9.1	8.8	8.0
$500 to $599	4,641	1,063	929	1,412	1,238	13.9	15.0	12.6	12.9	15.5
$600 to $699	3,252	802	551	900	999	9.8	11.3	7.5	8.2	12.5
$700 to $799	2,078	563	265	479	771	6.2	7.9	3.6	4.4	9.7
$800 to $999	1,945	585	123	438	799	5.8	8.2	1.7	4.0	10.0
$1,000 to $1,249.	765	220	61	112	373	2.3	3.1	0.8	1.0	4.7
$1,250 to $1,499.	296	76	16	38	166	0.9	1.1	0.2	0.3	2.1
$1,500 or more.	244	79	19	33	113	0.7	1.1	0.3	0.3	1.4
No cash rent	2,526	468	502	1,082	474	7.6	6.6	6.8	9.9	5.9
Median gross rent (dol.) . . .	462	507	402	424	557	(X)	(X)	(X)	(X)	(X)

X Not applicable.

Source: U.S. Bureau of the Census, *Current Housing Reports,* series H-150/91, American Housing Survey.

No. 1220. Homeownership Rates, by Age of Householder: 1983 to 1993

[In percent. Represents the proportion of households that are owners or the number of owner occupied households divided by the total number of households]

AGE	1983	1984	1985	1986	1987	1988	1989	1990	1991	1992	1993
United States.	**64.6**	**64.5**	**63.9**	**63.8**	**64.0**	**63.8**	**63.9**	**63.9**	**64.1**	**64.1**	**64.5**
Less than 25 yrs. old	18.8	17.9	17.2	17.2	16.0	15.8	16.6	15.7	15.3	14.9	15.0
25 to 29 yrs. old	38.3	38.6	37.7	36.7	36.4	35.9	35.3	35.2	33.8	33.6	34.0
30 to 34 yrs. old	55.4	54.8	54.0	53.6	53.5	53.2	53.2	51.8	51.2	50.5	51.0
35 to 39 yrs. old	66.5	66.1	65.4	64.8	64.1	63.6	63.4	63.0	62.2	61.4	62.1
40 to 44 yrs. old	72.8	72.3	71.4	70.5	70.8	70.7	70.2	69.8	69.5	69.1	69.0
45 to 49 yrs. old	75.3	74.6	74.3	74.1	74.6	74.4	74.1	73.9	73.7	74.2	73.9
50 to 54 yrs. old	78.8	78.4	77.5	78.1	77.8	77.1	77.2	76.8	76.1	76.2	77.1
55 to 59 yrs. old	80.1	80.1	79.2	80.0	80.0	79.3	79.1	78.8	79.5	79.3	78.8
60 to 64 yrs. old	79.8	79.9	79.9	79.8	80.4	79.8	80.1	79.8	80.5	81.2	80.9
65 to 69 yrs. old	78.7	79.3	79.5	79.4	79.5	80.0	80.0	80.0	81.4	80.8	80.6
70 to 74 yrs. old	75.4	75.5	76.8	77.2	77.7	77.7	77.8	78.4	78.8	79.0	79.9
75 yrs. old and over	71.9	71.5	69.8	70.0	70.8	70.8	71.2	72.3	73.1	73.3	73.3

Source: Bureau of the Census, *Current Housing Reports,* series H111/93.

No. 1221. Housing Units—Summary of Characteristics and Equipment, by Tenure and Region: 1991

[In thousands of units, except as indicated. Based on the American Housing Survey; see Appendix III. For composition of regions, see table 26]

ITEM	Total housing units	Sea-sonal	YEAR-ROUND UNITS							Vacant
			Occupied							
			Total	Owner	Renter	North-east	Mid-west	South	West	
Total units	**104,592**	**2,728**	**93,147**	**59,796**	**33,351**	**18,962**	**22,593**	**32,190**	**19,402**	**8,717**
Percent distribution	100.0	2.6	89.1	57.2	31.9	18.1	21.6	30.8	18.6	8.3
Units in structure:										
Single family detached	62,646	1,637	57,485	49,084	8,401	9,761	15,092	20,954	11,678	3,524
Single family attached	6,156	74	5,442	2,722	2,720	1,544	923	1,814	1,161	640
2 to 4 units	10,890	90	9,490	1,909	7,581	3,211	2,409	2,119	1,751	1,309
5 to 9 units	5,368	56	4,639	398	4,240	975	969	1,520	1,175	674
10 to 19 units	4,764	69	3,993	317	3,676	714	765	1,479	1,036	701
20 to 49 units	3,713	58	3,118	328	2,790	882	615	741	880	536
50 or more units	4,073	98	3,350	505	2,845	1,373	726	682	569	625
Mobile home or trailer	6,983	645	5,630	4,532	1,098	502	1,095	2,882	1,151	708
Stories in structure: [1]										
One story	3,015	25	2,606	290	2,316	145	418	1,216	827	384
2 stories	10,398	118	8,920	929	7,992	947	1,347	3,434	3,193	1,360
3 stories	8,110	116	6,938	1,254	5,684	2,475	2,414	1,205	844	1,056
4 to 6 stories	4,724	58	4,024	628	3,396	2,265	954	386	419	642
7 or more stories	2,585	56	2,123	373	1,750	1,329	351	305	139	406
Foundation: [2]										
Full or partial basement	30,995	309	29,401	25,785	3,616	9,713	12,239	4,720	2,729	1,286
Crawlspace	18,152	603	16,067	12,520	3,547	621	2,165	8,520	4,761	1,481
Concrete slab	17,710	390	16,134	12,581	3,554	853	1,373	8,804	5,105	1,185
Other	1,945	410	1,324	921	403	119	238	723	245	211
Year structure built: [3]										
1939 and earlier	22,759	494	20,065	11,484	8,581	7,388	6,528	3,754	2,395	2,199
1940 to 1949	8,607	226	7,668	4,742	2,926	1,700	1,818	2,550	1,599	713
1950 to 1959	13,836	420	12,512	8,982	3,530	2,621	3,236	3,964	2,691	904
1960 to 1969	16,161	468	14,523	9,570	4,953	2,445	3,389	5,353	3,337	1,170
1970 to 1979	23,598	689	21,005	13,377	7,629	2,717	4,662	8,524	5,101	1,902
1980 or later	19,632	429	17,374	11,643	5,730	2,090	2,959	8,045	4,279	1,828
Median year	1964	1965	1964	1965	1963	1952	1959	1971	1969	1965
Main heating equipment:										
Warm-air furnace	54,015	774	49,423	34,860	14,563	6,418	16,446	16,256	10,303	3,818
Electric heat pump	8,755	237	7,638	5,497	2,141	405	587	5,579	1,068	880
Steam or hot water system	15,145	86	13,929	7,520	6,409	9,651	2,737	831	710	1,130
Floor, wall, or pipeless furnace	4,819	75	4,291	1,948	2,343	138	339	1,373	2,441	453
Built-in electric units	7,934	283	6,755	2,992	3,763	1,366	1,257	2,050	2,082	897
Room heaters with flue	3,182	238	2,549	1,349	1,200	256	389	1,325	578	396
Room heaters without flue	2,484	48	2,111	1,197	915	38	63	1,837	174	325
Stoves	3,552	390	2,887	2,219	668	453	459	1,238	738	275
Fireplaces	1,280	123	1,098	899	199	54	136	483	426	58
None	1,500	352	861	378	484	50	39	278	494	287
Portable elec. heaters	860	68	695	362	333	11	22	442	220	97
Other	1,067	56	910	577	333	122	120	498	170	101
Air conditioning:										
Central	43,274	664	39,330	28,217	11,113	3,159	9,639	20,465	6,067	3,280
Percent of total units	41.4	24.3	42.2	47.2	33.3	16.7	42.7	63.6	31.3	37.6
One or more room units	28,569	347	26,786	16,438	10,347	8,204	7,134	8,545	2,901	1,436
Source of water:										
Public system or private company	88,666	1,412	79,814	48,785	31,029	16,077	18,820	27,264	17,652	7,440
Percent of total units	84.8	51.8	85.7	81.6	93.0	84.8	83.3	84.7	91.0	85.4
Well serving 1 to 5 units	13,739	828	11,809	10,042	1,767	2,642	3,598	4,396	1,173	1,102
Other	2,187	488	1,525	969	556	242	176	530	577	174
Means of sewage disposal:										
Public sewer	78,943	1,003	71,302	41,427	29,876	14,632	17,775	22,446	16,450	6,638
Percent of total units	75.5	36.8	76.6	69.3	89.6	77.2	78.7	69.7	84.8	76.2
Septic tank, cesspool, chemical toilet	25,058	1,407	21,672	18,284	3,388	4,308	4,801	9,622	2,940	1,979
Other	591	318	173	86	87	21	17	123	12	100

[1] Limited to multiunit structures.　　[2] Limited to single-family units.　　[3] For mobile home, oldest category is 1939 or earlier.

Source: U.S. Bureau of the Census, *Current Housing Reports*, series H-150/91, American Housing Survey.

No. 1222. Heating Equipment and Fuels for Occupied Units: 1950 to 1991

[Based on the Census of Population and Housing and American Housing Survey; see Appendix III]

ITEM	NUMBER (1,000)					PERCENT DISTRIBUTION				
	1950	1960	1970	1980	1991	1950	1960	1970	1980	1991
Occupied units, total	42,826	53,024	63,445	80,390	93,147	100.0	100.0	100.0	100.0	100.0
Heating equipment:										
Warm air furnace	[1]11,508	17,378	27,515	39,279	49,423	[1]26.9	32.8	43.4	48.9	53.1
Heat pumps	(NA)	(NA)	(NA)	2,835	7,638	(NA)	(NA)	(NA)	3.5	8.2
Steam or hot water	10,071	11,990	13,211	13,859	13,929	23.5	22.6	20.8	17.2	15.0
Floor, wall, or pipeless furnace	([1])	6,088	5,552	4,693	6,755	([1])	11.5	8.8	5.8	7.3
Built-in electric units	-	664	3,236	6,370	4,291	-	1.3	5.1	7.9	4.6
Room heaters with flue	[2]15,399	[2]11,183	7,209	6,098	2,549	[2]36.0	[2]21.1	11.4	7.6	2.7
Room heaters without flue	5,268	5,218	3,558	2,736	2,111	12.3	9.8	5.6	3.4	2.3
Fireplaces, stoves, portable heaters or other	([2])	([2])	2,766	3,977	5,590	([2])	([2])	4.4	4.9	6.0
None	581	503	398	541	861	1.4	0.9	0.6	0.7	0.9
House heating fuel:										
Utility gas	11,387	22,851	35,014	42,658	47,010	26.6	43.1	55.2	53.1	50.5
Fuel oil, kerosene, etc.	9,686	17,158	16,473	14,655	12,462	22.6	32.4	26.0	18.2	13.4
Electricity	283	933	4,876	14,768	23,714	0.7	1.8	7.7	18.3	25.5
Bottled, tank, or LP gas.	787	2,686	3,807	4,535	3,882	1.8	5.1	6.0	5.6	4.2
Wood and other fuel	4,855	2,460	1,060	2,729	4,890	11.3	4.6	1.7	3.4	5.2
Coal or coke	14,828	6,456	1,821	504	319	34.6	12.2	2.9	0.6	0.3
None	999	478	395	541	862	2.3	0.9	0.6	0.7	0.9
Cooking fuel:										
Electricity	6,403	16,351	25,768	41,906	54,232	15.0	30.8	40.6	52.1	58.2
Gas [3]	25,501	33,787	36,558	37,944	38,119	59.6	63.7	57.6	47.2	40.9
Other fuel	10,796	2,603	908	398	424	25.2	4.9	1.4	0.5	0.5
None	124	280	213	142	372	0.3	0.5	0.3	0.2	0.4

- Represents zero.   NA Not available.   [1] "Floor, wall, or pipeless furnace" included in "Warm air furnace."   [2] "Fireplaces, stoves, or portable heaters" included in "Room heaters with flue."   [3] Includes utility, bottled, tank, and LP gas.

Source: U.S. Bureau of the Census, Census of Housing, 1960, vol. 1; 1970 and 1980, vol. 1; and 1990 Census of Housing, Detailed Housing Characteristics, series CH-2, and Current Housing Reports, series H-150/91.

No. 1223. Appliances Used by Households, by Region and Family Income: 1990

[In millions, except percent. As of November. Represents appliances possessed and generally used by the household. Based on Residential Energy Consumption Survey; see Appendix III. For composition of regions, see table 26]

TYPE OF APPLIANCE	HOUSEHOLDS USING APPLIANCE		REGION				FAMILY INCOME IN 1990			
	Number	Percent of total	North- east	Midwest	South	West	Under $15,000	$15,000 -$24,999	$25,000 -$34,999	$35,000 and over
Total households . .	94.0	100.0	19.2	23.1	32.3	19.4	27.3	17.4	15.3	34.0
Air conditioners: Room . .	29.1	31.0	8.1	8.0	10.3	2.8	9.7	5.5	4.9	9.0
Central system [1]	36.6	38.9	3.2	9.2	19.0	5.2	6.0	6.0	6.0	18.7
Clothes washer	71.7	76.3	14.4	17.7	25.6	14.0	16.3	12.3	12.3	30.7
Clothes dryer	64.7	68.8	12.4	16.9	22.7	12.8	12.7	10.6	11.4	29.9
Dehumidifier	11.3	12.0	3.5	5.3	2.0	0.5	1.5	1.7	1.7	6.4
Dishwasher	42.7	45.4	8.0	9.3	15.3	10.0	5.2	5.9	7.5	23.9
Evaporative cooler [2]	3.8	4.0	(B)	(B)	(B)	2.9	1.3	0.8	0.9	0.8
Freezer	32.4	34.5	5.0	9.1	12.3	5.9	7.9	5.7	5.4	13.4
Microwave oven [3]	74.1	78.8	13.6	19.4	25.7	15.3	16.9	13.4	12.8	31.0
Motor vehicles: [4] One . . .	33.1	35.3	35.3	35.3	35.6	34.7	13.4	8.3	5.0	6.4
Two or more	50.8	54.0	46.7	55.8	55.2	57.2	6.2	7.7	9.8	27.1
Outdoor gas grill	24.9	26.4	6.8	7.1	7.0	4.0	2.4	3.2	4.1	15.1
Outdoor gas light	1.0	1.1	0.3	0.3	0.3	(B)	0.2	0.2	0.1	0.5
Oven: Electric	55.3	58.9	9.3	12.7	22.1	11.2	13.7	9.7	9.8	22.2
Gas	39.6	40.8	9.8	10.5	10.1	8.0	13.3	7.7	5.5	11.9
Personal computer	14.8	15.7	15.6	14.0	15.0	19.1	5.1	7.5	13.1	29.7
Portable electric heater . .	13.5	14.4	2.2	2.8	5.4	3.1	3.9	2.8	2.0	4.8
Portable kerosene heater .	4.6	4.9	0.9	1.3	2.2	0.2	1.3	0.9	1.1	1.3
Range: Electric	54.3	57.8	9.1	12.6	21.8	10.8	16.4	9.7	9.8	21.3
Gas	39.6	42.1	10.0	10.6	10.5	8.6	13.6	7.8	5.5	12.6
Refrigerator: Frost-free . .	75.0	79.8	15.0	18.2	27.0	14.8	18.3	13.2	12.5	31.0
Nonfrost-free [5]	24.8	26.4	5.5	7.1	6.6	5.6	9.8	5.3	3.7	5.9
Television set: Color	90.3	96.1	18.6	22.3	30.8	18.6	25.0	16.9	14.8	33.5
Black and white	28.7	30.6	5.9	8.2	10.4	4.2	8.4	5.3	4.6	10.3
Water heater: [6] Gas	44.6	47.4	7.2	13.3	12.6	11.4	11.5	7.7	6.9	18.5
Electric	33.5	35.6	4.2	6.9	17.2	5.3	9.9	6.9	5.8	10.9
Other fuel	2.0	2.1	1.9	(B)	0.1	(B)	0.4	0.2	0.3	1.1
Whole house cooling fan .	9.4	10.1	2.1	2.1	4.0	1.2	1.5	1.4	1.5	5.1
Window or ceiling fan . . .	47.9	51.0	9.0	12.0	20.3	6.6	11.0	8.7	8.1	20.2

B Base figure too small to meet statistical standards for reliability.   [1] Includes the .9 million households with both central air conditioning and window or wall air conditioning units.   [2] An air-cooling unit used in dry climates that turns air into moist, cool air by saturating the air with water vapor.   [3] Microwave is first or second most used oven.   [4] All motorized vehicles used by U.S. households for personal transportation excluding motorcycles, mopeds, large trucks, and buses.   [5] Includes refrigerators without freezer compartments.   [6] Excludes water heaters that serve more than one household.

Source: U.S. Energy Information Administration, Housing Characteristics: 1990.

No. 1224. Expenditures by Residential Property Owners for Improvements and Maintenance and Repairs, by Type of Property and Activity: 1970 to 1993

[In millions of dollars]

YEAR AND TYPE OF EXPENDITURE	Total	1-unit properties with owner occupant	Other properties	ADDITIONS AND ALTERATIONS					Major replacements	Maintenance and repairs
				Total	To structures			To property outside of structures		
					Additions	Alterations				
1970	14,770	9,469	5,301	6,246	1,411	3,539		1,296	2,629	5,895
1975	25,239	15,684	9,556	10,997	1,971	6,844		2,182	4,484	9,758
1980	46,338	31,481	14,857	21,336	4,183	11,193		5,960	9,816	15,187
1981	46,351	30,201	16,150	20,414	3,164	11,947		5,303	9,915	16,022
1982	45,291	29,779	15,512	18,774	2,641	10,711		5,423	9,707	16,810
1983	49,295	32,524	16,771	20,271	4,739	11,673		3,859	10,895	18,128
1984	69,784	43,781	26,003	27,822	6,007	14,486		7,329	13,067	28,894
1985	80,267	47,742	32,525	28,775	3,966	17,599		7,211	16,134	35,358
1986	91,274	54,298	36,976	38,608	7,377	21,192		10,040	16,695	35,971
1987	94,082	54,791	39,291	39,978	9,557	21,641		8,779	15,875	38,229
1988	101,117	60,822	40,295	43,339	11,333	22,703		9,303	16,893	40,885
1989	100,891	59,858	41,033	39,786	6,828	23,129		9,828	18,415	42,689
1990	106,773	59,683	47,090	37,253	8,561	21,920		6,771	18,215	51,305
1991, total [1] .... [2]	97,528	58,083	39,445	30,944	7,914	16,076		6,954	16,744	49,840
Heating and air conditioning [2]	7,336	4,353	2,983	985	(NA)	985		(NA)	3,688	2,618
Plumbing	9,714	4,896	4,818	1,366	(NA)	1,366		(NA)	3,383	4,966
Roofing	8,867	5,275	3,592	(NA)	(NA)	(NA)		(NA)	5,237	3,630
Painting	12,918	6,522	6,396	(NA)	(NA)	(NA)		(NA)	(NA)	12,918
1992, total [1] .... [2]	103,734	67,316	36,418	40,186	6,783	22,700		10,704	18,393	45,154
Heating and air conditioning [2]	6,952	5,302	1,650	1,103	(NA)	1,103		(NA)	3,546	2,303
Plumbing	9,549	5,653	3,896	1,540	(NA)	1,540		(NA)	3,104	4,905
Roofing	10,714	5,327	5,387	(NA)	(NA)	(NA)		(NA)	6,257	4,457
Painting	11,147	5,867	5,280	(NA)	(NA)	(NA)		(NA)	(NA)	11,147
1993, total [1] .... [2]	108,305	70,746	37,559	45,797	12,757	24,781		8,259	20,809	41,699
Heating and air conditioning [2]	7,918	5,814	2,103	1,259	(NA)	1,259		(NA)	4,040	2,618
Plumbing	8,700	4,488	4,212	1,597	(NA)	1,597		(NA)	2,990	4,114
Roofing	8,943	5,559	3,385	(NA)	(NA)	(NA)		(NA)	4,821	4,122
Painting	12,566	6,567	5,998	(NA)	(NA)	(NA)		(NA)	(NA)	12,566

NA Not available.   [1] Includes types of expenditures not separately specified.   [2] Central air-conditioning.

Source: U.S. Bureau of the Census, *Current Construction Reports*, series C50.

No. 1225. Vacancy Rates for Housing Units—Characteristics: 1989 to 1993

[In percent. Annual averages. Based on Current Population Survey and Quarterly Household Survey. Rate is relationship between vacant housing for rent or for sale and the total rental and homowner supply, which comprises occupied units, units rented or sold and awaiting occupancy, and vacant units available for rent or sale. For composition of regions, see table 26. See also *Historical Statistics, Colonial Times to 1970*, series N 249-258]

CHARACTERISTIC	RENTAL UNITS					HOMEOWNER UNITS				
	1989	1990	1991	1992	1993	1989	1990	1991	1992	1993
Total units	**7.4**	**7.2**	**7.4**	**7.4**	**7.4**	**1.8**	**1.7**	**1.7**	**1.5**	**1.4**
Inside MSA's.	7.4	7.1	7.5	7.4	7.6	1.7	1.7	1.7	1.6	1.4
Outside MSA's.	7.7	7.6	7.3	7.0	6.4	1.9	1.8	1.8	1.5	1.4
Northeast	4.7	6.1	6.9	6.9	7.1	1.5	1.6	1.5	1.3	1.3
Midwest	6.8	6.4	6.7	6.7	6.6	1.4	1.3	1.3	1.2	1.1
South	9.7	8.8	8.9	8.2	8.0	2.2	2.1	2.2	1.7	1.6
West	7.1	6.6	6.5	7.1	7.5	1.6	1.8	1.7	1.9	1.4
Units in structure:										
1 unit	4.2	4.0	3.9	3.8	3.8	1.4	1.4	1.4	1.3	1.1
2 units or more . . .	9.2	9.0	9.4	9.4	9.4	7.1	7.1	6.8	5.8	5.2
5 units or more . . .	10.1	9.6	10.4	10.0	10.3	9.6	8.4	7.9	7.4	6.7
Units with—										
3 rooms or less. . .	10.3	10.3	10.8	11.4	10.8	10.8	10.2	10.5	8.6	6.8
4 rooms.	8.2	8.0	8.1	7.9	8.2	3.1	3.2	3.0	2.6	2.5
5 rooms	5.6	5.7	5.9	5.3	5.6	2.0	2.0	1.9	1.9	1.6
6 rooms or more . .	3.4	3.0	3.1	3.1	3.2	1.2	1.1	1.2	1.1	1.0

Source: U.S. Bureau of the Census, *Current Housing Reports*, series H/111.

No. 1226. Recent Home Buyers—General Characteristics: 1976 to 1992

[As of **October**. Based on a sample survey; subject to sampling variability]

ITEM	Unit	1976	1980	1985	1987	1988	1989	1990	1991	1992
Median purchase price . .	Dollars . .	43,340	68,714	90,400	99,260	121,910	129,800	131,200	134,300	141,000
First-time buyers	Dollars . .	37,670	61,450	75,100	84,730	97,100	105,200	106,000	118,700	122,400
Repeat buyers [1]	Dollars . .	50,090	75,750	106,200	115,430	141,400	144,700	149,400	152,500	158,000
Average monthly mortgage										
payment	Dollars . .	329	599	896	939	1,008	1,054	1,127	1,144	1,064
Percent of income	Percent. .	24.0	32.4	30.0	29.3	32.8	31.8	33.8	34.0	33.2
Percent buying—										
New houses.	Percent. .	15.1	22.4	23.8	23.8	26.2	21.8	21.2	19.7	20.5
Existing houses.	Percent. .	84.9	77.6	76.2	76.2	73.8	78.2	78.8	80.3	79.5
Single-family houses . .	Percent. .	88.8	82.4	87.0	87.3	83.3	84.8	83.8	85.3	85.0
Condominiums [2]	Percent. .	11.2	17.6	10.6	12.5	12.4	13.5	13.1	11.5	13.1
For the first time	Percent. .	44.8	32.9	36.6	36.8	37.8	40.2	41.9	45.1	47.7
Average age:										
First-time buyers [1] . . .	Years . . .	28.1	28.3	28.4	29.6	30.3	29.6	30.5	30.7	31.0
Repeat buyers [1]	Years . . .	35.9	36.4	38.4	39.1	38.9	39.4	39.1	39.8	40.8
Downpayment/sales price	Percent. .	25.2	28.0	24.8	27.2	24.0	24.4	23.3	22.6	21.4
First-time buyers	Percent. .	18.0	20.5	11.4	20.4	14.6	15.8	15.7	14.7	14.3
Repeat buyers [1]	Percent. .	30.8	32.7	32.7	31.3	29.7	30.3	28.9	29.1	28.0

[1] Buyers who previously owned a home. [2] Includes multiple-family houses.
Source: Chicago Title Insurance Company, Chicago, IL, *The Guarantor,* bimonthly (copyright).

No. 1227. Low-Income Public Housing Units, by Progress Stage: 1970 to 1992

[**In thousands.** As of **Dec. 31.** Housing for the elderly intended for persons 62 years old or over, disabled, or handicapped. Includes Puerto Rico and Virgin Islands. Covers units subsidized by HUD under annual contributions contracts. See also *Historical Statistics, Colonial Times to 1970,* series N 186-191]

YEAR	Total[1]	Occupied units [2]	Under construction	YEAR	Total[1]	Occupied units [2]	Under construction
1970.	1,155.3	893.5	126.8	1990.	1,305.3	1,028.1	7.6
Elderly.	249.4	143.4	65.7	Elderly.	(NA)	342.2	(NA)
1980.	1,321.1	1,195.6	20.9	1991.	1,320.0	1,197.7	7.7
Elderly.	358.3	317.7	11.5	Elderly.	(NA)	513.3	(NA)
1985.	1,378.0	1,344.6	9.6	1992.	1,323.3	1,199.4	7.2
Elderly.	373.5	361.1	2.1	Elderly	(NA)	513.5	(NA)

NA Not available. [1] Includes units to be constructed or to go directly "under management" because no rehabilitation needed not shown separately. [2] Under management or available for occupancy.
Source: U.S. Dept. of Housing and Urban Development, unpublished data based on the Field Office Report Monitoring System.

No. 1228. Office Buildings—Vacancy Rates for Major Cities, 1980 to 1993, and Status of Supply, 1993

[**As of December;** except 1993, as of June. Excludes government owned and occupied, owner-occupied, and medical office buildings]

CITY	VACANCY RATE FOR EXISTING SPACE (percent)									SUPPLY STATUS, June 1993 (mil. sq. ft.)		
										Existing space		Space under construction
	1980	1985	1987	1988	1989	1990	1991	1992	1993, June	Total	Available for lease	
Total [1]	4.6	16.9	19.0	18.6	19.5	20.0	20.2	20.5	19.9	2,423.1	481.2	4.7
Atlanta, GA	10.0	21.0	19.6	18.3	19.9	19.1	19.5	19.4	18.4	87.4	16.1	-
Baltimore, MD	7.2	11.5	15.8	13.4	16.4	20.0	21.0	20.6	18.4	38.9	7.1	-
Boston, MA	3.8	13.1	12.6	14.1	15.3	19.6	19.1	17.5	17.3	134.8	23.3	0.1
Charlotte, NC.	(NA)	16.7	15.1	16.5	14.3	16.5	19.4	(NA)	(NA)	(NA)	(NA)	(NA)
Chicago, IL	7.0	16.5	17.0	15.9	17.0	18.6	20.0	22.1	22.1	196.2	43.3	0.2
Dallas, TX	8.6	23.0	29.1	29.7	26.9	25.8	26.0	31.3	30.2	114.5	34.6	-
Denver, CO	6.6	24.7	27.9	27.6	26.1	24.8	23.0	21.5	19.1	67.8	13.0	-
Houston, TX	4.0	27.6	31.8	29.2	27.5	24.9	27.3	27.0	26.0	140.9	36.6	0.1
Indianapolis, IN . . .	(NA)	(NA)	(NA)	21.3	20.0	21.2	21.4	22.4	20.1	21.6	4.3	-
Kansas City, MO. . .	4.2	16.2	18.2	19.9	15.8	14.1	16.9	15.2	14.3	32.4	4.6	0.2
Los Angeles, CA. . .	0.9	15.3	19.0	15.8	19.7	16.8	20.2	21.2	20.0	190.8	38.2	0.1
Miami, FL	2.4	20.9	26.1	24.0	22.0	23.4	22.6	18.5	18.2	29.5	5.4	0.2
Milwaukee, WI	(NA)	(NA)	16.8	19.3	20.4	22.9	19.5	18.4	17.3	24.0	4.1	-
New Orleans, LA . . .	(NA)	21.8	24.3	25.6	25.7	29.0	25.0	(NA)	(NA)	(NA)	(NA)	(NA)
New York, NY [2] . . .	3.1	7.9	9.7	11.5	15.1	16.0	18.8	18.3	18.1	318.5	57.6	-
Philadelphia, PA . . .	6.3	14.5	16.5	15.8	16.3	18.2	17.3	19.0	18.9	70.2	13.3	0.2
Pittsburgh, PA	1.2	(NA)	12.3	17.6	16.3	16.3	14.2	(NA)	16.0	34.7	5.6	-
San Diego, CA	(NA)	24.7	22.8	20.1	17.6	19.5	23.7	23.8	22.7	38.1	8.6	-
San Francisco, CA . .	0.4	13.7	15.0	15.5	15.7	14.7	13.3	12.5	14.5	53.9	7.8	-
Seattle, WA	(NA)	(NA)	(NA)	13.2	12.4	12.3	12.8	15.9	15.0	30.6	4.6	-
St. Louis, MO.	(NA)	(NA)	15.6	18.4	22.6	21.0	20.5	21.8	19.2	33.2	6.4	-
Washington, DC . . .	2.5	9.0	13.4	13.2	14.4	19.0	17.6	15.4	14.6	186.5	27.2	1.4

- Represents zero. NA Not available. [1] Includes other cities not shown separately. In 1993, 51 cities were covered.
[2] Refers to Manhattan.
Source: ONCOR International, Houston, TX, 1980-1985, *National Office Market Report,* semi-annual; 1986-1990, *International Office Market Report,* semi-annual; thereafter, *Office Market Data Book* (copyright).

No. 1229. Commercial Office Space—Inventory and Vacancy Rates for the Largest Metropolitan Areas: 1992

[As of **December 31, except population as July 1**. Data based on responses from individuals knowledgeable in the local markets. Represents primarily the metropolitan as indicated, but in many cases may exclude outlying countries beyond the central portion]

METROPOLITAN AREAS	Resident population, 1992 (1,000)	Inventory (1,000 sq. ft.)	Vacant space (1,000 sq. ft.)	Vacancy rate (percent)	Construction (1,000 sq. ft.)	Absorption (1,000 sq. ft.)
Albany-Schenectady-Troy, NY MSA	872	11,016	1,077	9.8	70	-
Atlanta, GA MSA	3,143	97,144	14,481	14.9	335	2,871
Austin-San Marcos, TX MSA	901	19,517	3,164	16.2	-	651
Baltimore, MD PMSA	2,433	36,283	7,116	19.6	463	-55
Bergen-Passaic, NJ & Jersey City, NJ PMSA [1]	1,846	96,482	20,002	20.7	1,215	1,035
Birmingham, AL MSA	859	13,485	2,091	15.5	-	473
Boston, MA-NH PMSA	3,211	84,810	14,606	17.2	750	2,265
Buffalo-Niagara Falls, NY MSA	1,194	6,925	1,155	16.7	160	187
Charlotte, NC MSA	1,212	18,770	3,388	18.0	202	545
Chicago, IL PMSA	7,561	152,736	34,395	22.5	70	-2,873
Cincinnati, OH PMSA	1,560	21,887	3,751	17.1	-	425
Cleveland-Lorain-Elyria, OH PMSA	2,221	35,878	8,559	23.9	-	433
Columbus, OH MSA	1,394	25,010	2,202	8.8	100	154
Dallas, TX PMSA	4,215	117,161	30,609	26.1	-	-904
Dayton, OH MSA	962	6,717	1,173	17.5	-	171
Denver, CO PMSA	1,715	55,480	10,135	18.3	-	564
Detroit, MI PMSA [2]	4,308	55,651	8,900	16.0	150	750
El Paso, TX MSA	628	3,046	221	7.2	-	23
Fort Lauderdale, FL PMSA	1,301	15,933	3,721	23.4	-	366
Fort Worth, TX PMSA	1,419	17,905	3,138	17.5	-	341
Fresno, CA MSA	805	11,333	1,475	13.0	174	261
Grand Rapids-Muskegon-Holland, MI MSA	964	8,330	1,102	13.2	100	408
Greensboro-Winston Salem-High Point, NC MSA	1,078	23,625	2,949	12.5	-	749
Greenville-Spartanburg-Anderson, SC MSA	853	5,870	752	12.8	-	70
Hartford, CT MSA	1,156	20,877	3,276	15.7	-	506
Honolulu, HI MSA	863	13,365	1,217	9.1	637	331
Houston TX PMSA	3,530	135,171	29,151	21.6	1,533	2,240
Indianapolis, IN MSA	1,424	20,171	4,436	22.0	500	3
Jacksonville, FL MSA	953	13,227	2,548	19.3	230	466
Kansas City, MO-KS MSA	1,617	36,523	4,967	13.6	285	441
Las Vegas, NV MSA	971	7,190	914	12.7	30	247
Los-Angeles, CA PMSA	9,054	145,270	32,143	22.1	607	2,285
Louisville, KY MSA	968	12,265	2,120	17.3	160	719
Memphis, TN MSA	1,034	18,328	3,414	18.6	355	53
Miami, FL PMSA	2,008	30,260	7,400	24.5	163	660
Middlesex-Somerset-Hunterdon, NJ and Monmouth-Ocean, NJ PMSA [3]	2,051	68,962	9,482	13.7	-	558
Milwaukee-Waukesha, WI PMSA	1,450	24,145	3,702	15.3	-	778
Minneapolis-St. Paul, MN-WI MSA	2,618	45,958	9,317	20.3	-	1,327
Nashville, TN MSA	1,023	16,206	2,918	18.0	-	223
Nassau-Suffolk, NY PMSA	2,640	33,784	7,740	21.6	-	-453
New Orleans, LA MSA	1,303	20,373	4,801	23.6	-	384
New York City, NY PMSA [4]	9,705	384,044	71,252	18.6	324	-847
Norfolk-Virginia Beach-Newport News, VA MSA	1,497	15,515	2,009	12.9	664	1,085
Oakland, CA PMSA	2,148	19,391	3,171	16.4	44	188
Oklahoma City, OK MSA	984	14,960	3,700	24.7	-	490
Omaha, NE MSA	656	13,273	2,442	18.4	-	482
Orange County, CA PMSA	2,485	54,497	11,525	21.1	-	1,156
Orlando, FL MSA	1,305	22,936	3,818	16.6	-	82
Phoenix, AZ MSA	2,330	22,907	4,945	21.6	-	1,034
Philadelphia, PA PMSA	4,944	109,363	22,284	20.4	444	335
Pittsburgh, PA PMSA	2,406	28,290	3,498	12.4	-	916
Portland-Vancouver, OR PMSA	1,897	16,050	2,180	13.6	75	254
Providence, RI MSA	1,131	5,972	1,224	20.5	-	205
Raleigh-Durham-Chapel Hill, NC MSA	909	15,764	1,732	11.0	106	1,163
Richmond-Petersburg, VA MSA	896	17,671	3,345	18.9	-	167
Riverside-San Bernardino, CA PMSA	2,823	8,926	2,066	23.1	71	655
Sacramento-Yolo, CA MSA	1,563	33,016	5,170	15.7	1,256	2,246
Salt Lake City-Ogden, UT MSA	1,128	11,029	1,989	18.0	130	493
San Antonio, TX MSA [5]	1379	17,641	4,057	23.0	-	180
San Diego, CA MSA	2601	43,076	7,333	17.0	350	1,217
San Francisco, CA PMSA	2,523	80,672	12,172	15.1	-	-15
San Jose, CA PMSA	1,528	34,500	(NA)	(NA)	(NA)	(NA)
Seattle, WA PMSA	2,124	43,275	5,922	13.7	-	881
St. Louis, MO MSA	2,519	34,203	9,778	28.6	-	-1,376
Syracuse, NY MSA	752	8,625	1,275	14.8	-	104
Tampa-St. Petersburg-Clearwater, FL MSA [6]	2,107	20,210	3,834	19.0	-	369
Tucson, AZ MSA	690	6,394	1,333	20.9	-	82
Tulsa OK MSA	732	13,949	2,145	15.4	-	227
Washington, DC-MD-VA-WV PMSA [7]	4,630	260,767	41,461	15.9	5,806	5,613
West Palm Beach-Boca Raton, FL MSA	901	6,572	1,369	20.8	-	226

- Represents zero.   NA Not available.   [1] Data are for area identified by source as New Jersey-Northern with a market area of Bergen, Essex, Hudson, Morris, and Passaic counties.   [2] Represents only the suburban portion of the metropolitan area.   [3] Data are for area identified by source as New Jersey-Central with a market area of Hunterdon, Mercer, Middlesex, Monmouth, Somerset, and Union counties.   [4] Represents primarily Manhattan and Rockland and Westchester counties.   [5] Represents only Bexar County.   [6] Represents only Pinnellas and Hillsborough counties.   [7] Represents only the District of Columbia, Alexandria city, and Arlington, Fairfax, Loudoun, and Prince William counties in Virginia and Montgomery and Prince George's counties in Maryland.

Source: Resident population, U.S. Bureau of the Census. Office data, Society of Industrial and Office REALTORS, Washington, DC, *Comparative Statistics of Industrial and Office Real Estate Markets*, (copyright).

No. 1230. Commercial Buildings—Selected Characteristics, by Square Footage of Floorspace: 1992

[Excludes buildings 1,000 square feet or smaller. Building type based on predominant activity in which the occupants were engaged. Based on a sample survey of building representatives conducted between August and December 1992; therefore, subject to sampling variability. For composition of regions, see table 26]

| CHARACTERISTIC | Number of buildings (1,000) | FLOORSPACE (mil. sq. ft.) | | | | | | | Mean sq. ft. per building (1,000) | Median sq. ft. per building (1,000) |
| | | Total | Within all buildings having square footage of— | | | | | | | |
			5,000 or less	5,001 to 10,000	10,001 to 25,000	25,001 to 50,000	50,001 to 100,000	100,001 and over		
All buildings	**4,806**	**67,876**	**7,327**	**7,199**	**10,375**	**10,069**	**8,062**	**24,845**	**14.1**	**4.5**
Region:										
Northeast	771	13,400	1,074	1,337	1,663	1,976	1,752	5,597	17.4	5.2
Midwest	1,202	17,280	1,889	1,763	2,689	2,353	2,097	6,488	14.4	4.5
South	1,963	24,577	3,155	2,723	3,782	3,696	2,842	8,379	12.5	4.0
West	870	12,619	1,208	1,376	2,241	2,043	1,371	4,380	14.5	5.0
Year constructed:										
1899 or before	169	1,721	251	397	297	431	(S)	(S)	10.2	5.5
1900 to 1919	255	3,608	336	523	503	522	319	(S)	14.1	5.0
1920 to 1945	724	8,712	1,150	1,106	1,507	1,267	927	1,934	12.0	4.2
1946 to 1959	880	10,421	1,352	1,255	1,775	1,792	1,236	2,531	11.8	4.2
1960 to 1969	783	12,612	1,167	986	1,892	1,856	1,625	5,085	16.1	4.5
1970 to 1979	982	14,014	1,536	1,505	1,902	2,216	1,776	5,079	14.3	4.5
1980 to 1989	884	14,287	1,339	1,251	2,189	1,658	1,717	6,132	16.2	4.8
1990 to 1992	128	2,502	197	176	309	327	268	1,224	19.6	4.8
Principal activity within building:										
Public assembly [1]	644	8,303	1,002	1,056	1,742	1,278	378	418	12.9	(NA)
Education	301	8,470	292	307	997	1,551	2,045	3,262	28.2	9.0
Food sales	130	757	286	(S)	(S)	(S)	(S)	(S)	5.8	2.6
Food service	260	1,491	485	343	325	(S)	(S)	(S)	5.7	3.4
Health care	63	1,763	108	(S)	(S)	(S)	(S)	1,286	27.9	4.3
Lodging	154	2,891	159	294	412	711	420	758	18.8	8.0
Mercantile/services	1,272	12,402	2,203	1,987	2,003	1,369	1,268	3,570	9.7	4.0
Office	749	12,319	1,018	1,248	1,656	1,823	1,355	5,218	16.4	5.0
Parking garage	24	1,652	(S)	(S)	(S)	(S)	(S)	694	69.9	6.0
Public order and safety	60	820	91	(S)	(S)	(S)	(S)	(S)	13.7	5.0
Warehouse	761	11,484	1,089	1,106	2,066	1,631	1,250	4,343	15.1	5.0
Other	69	1,130	99	(S)	110	(S)	(S)	(S)	16.4	4.0
Vacant	319	4,396	473	459	635	768	503	821	13.8	4.2
Government owned	599	15,124	689	848	1,735	1,953	2,241	7,659	25.2	6.7
Nongovernment owned	4,206	52,752	6,638	6,351	8,640	8,116	5,821	17,186	12.5	4.3
Fuels used alone or in combination:										
Electricity	4,616	66,549	6,996	7,057	10,097	9,856	7,936	24,607	14.4	4.7
Natural gas	2,665	45,097	3,761	4,266	6,865	6,510	5,735	17,959	16.9	5.1
Fuel oil	559	13,218	829	925	978	1,377	1,539	7,570	23.7	5.0
Propane	337	3,393	573	466	456	501	411	500	10.1	3.5
District heat	95	5,339	56	73	450	545	653	3,562	56.0	17.0
District chilled water	28	2,066	(S)	(S)	115	311	(S)	1,504	72.6	26.5
Any other	163	1,551	250	311	(S)	(S)	(S)	(S)	9.5	3.6
Workers:										
Fewer than 5	2,718	17,944	5,095	3,329	3,053	2,107	910	(S)	6.6	3.0
5 to 9	895	7,524	1,554	1,612	1,801	1,348	595	(S)	8.4	4.8
10 to 19	561	8,077	537	1,446	2,323	1,538	643	(S)	14.4	8.0
20 to 49	405	10,556	120	757	2,608	3,049	1,899	(S)	26.1	16.3
50 to 99	130	7,763	(S)	(S)	450	1,445	2,151	(S)	59.7	38.5
100 to 249	64	7,378	(S)	(S)	(S)	517	1,303	5,433	114.6	79.0
250 or more	31	8,633	(S)	(S)	(S)	(S)	561	7,992	274.4	150.0
Weekly operating hours:										
39 or less	1,039	8,246	1,797	1,341	1,592	1,309	1,007	(S)	7.9	3.5
40 to 48	1,278	14,998	1,904	2,186	2,994	2,553	1,698	3,662	11.7	4.9
49 to 60	1,004	14,046	1,430	1,610	2,549	2,536	1,440	4,482	14.0	5.0
61 to 84	645	12,062	926	1,098	1,408	1,443	1,769	5,418	18.7	5.0
85 to 167	478	8,467	772	492	1,022	1,151	1,132	3,897	17.7	4.0
168 (open continuously)	362	10,057	498	472	810	1,077	1,015	6,185	27.8	5.0

NA Not available.   S Figure does not meet publication standards.   [1] Includes religious worship.

Source: U.S. Energy Information Administration, *Commercial Buildings Characteristics, 1992.*

No. 1231. Commercial Buildings—Number and Square Footage of Floorspace, by Type of Building and Characteristic: 1992

[For composition of regions, see table 26]

BUILDING CHARACTERISTICS	All buildings[1]	Public assembly[2]	Education	Food sales	Food service	Health care	Lodging	Mercantile/services	Offices	Public order and safety	Warehouse
NUMBER (1,000)											
All buildings	4,806	644	301	130	260	63	154	1,272	749	60	761
Region:											
Northeast	771	70	38	(S)	54	12	31	246	126	16	109
Midwest	1,202	162	46	29	73	14	26	329	170	(S)	233
South	1,963	314	112	57	83	15	56	510	299	(S)	316
West	870	99	104	32	50	23	41	187	154	(S)	103
Year constructed:											
1899 or before	169	29	(S)	(S)	(S)	(S)	(S)	34	31	(S)	(S)
1900 to 1919	255	48	12	(S)	(S)	(S)	(S)	59	38	(S)	27
1920 to 1945	724	98	28	(S)	43	7	14	210	108	(S)	112
1946 to 1959	880	131	76	(S)	51	10	24	235	136	(S)	117
1960 to 1969	783	111	72	(S)	33	15	38	208	102	(S)	107
1970 to 1979	982	107	46	28	73	14	27	247	163	16	185
1980 to 1986	671	69	37	(S)	23	9	22	200	113	(S)	125
1987 to 1989	212	-	12	(S)	(S)	(S)	(S)	47	42	(S)	50
1990 to 1992	128	12	17	(S)	(S)	(S)	4	32	15	(S)	21
Government owned	599	65	201	(NA)	10	13	15	63	69	49	59
Nongovernment owned	4,206	578	99	130	250	51	139	1,210	680	(S)	702
FLOORSPACE (mil. sq. ft.)											
All buildings	67,876	8,303	8,470	757	1,491	1,763	2,891	12,402	12,319	820	11,484
Region:											
Northeast	13,400	1,229	1,968	(S)	445	386	616	2,798	2,525	269	1,763
Midwest	17,280	1,998	2,386	182	432	487	577	3,156	2,804	(S)	3,108
South	24,577	3,635	2,620	245	407	597	1,043	4,233	4,152	238	4,964
West	12,619	1,441	1,496	209	208	292	654	2,214	2,838	(S)	1,649
Year constructed:											
1899 or before	1,721	267	(S)	(S)	(S)	(S)	(S)	239	435	(S)	(S)
1900 to 1919	3,608	575	441	(S)	(S)	(S)	(S)	422	716	(S)	269
1920 to 1945	8,712	850	1,077	(S)	246	227	410	1,381	1,389	(S)	1,853
1946 to 1959	10,421	1,434	1,903	(S)	283	152	328	1,883	1,400	(S)	1,805
1960 to 1969	12,612	1,180	2,405	(S)	187	492	482	2,680	2,187	(S)	1,815
1970 to 1979	14,014	1,601	1,728	155	365	544	579	2,607	2,283	168	2,397
1980 to 1986	10,149	819	480	(S)	103	240	550	2,109	2,419	(S)	2,233
1987 to 1989	4,138	(S)	173	(S)	(S)	(S)	(S)	535	899	(S)	610
1990 to 1992	2,502	197	253	(S)	(S)	(S)	97	545	590	(S)	377
Government owned	15,124	1,353	6,961	(NA)	157	521	370	1,082	1,654	767	599
Nongovernment owned	52,752	6,945	1,508	757	1,334	1,242	2,520	11,319	10,665	(S)	10,885

- Represents zero. S Figure does not meet publication standards. [1] Includes parking garages, vacant, and other commercial buildings, not shown separately. [2] Includes religious worship.
Source: U.S. Energy Information Administration, *Commercial Building Characteristics, 1992.*

No. 1232. Commercial Buildings and Workers—Selected Building Characteristics, by Floorspace: 1989

[See headnote, table 1230]

BUILDING CHARACTERISTICS	NUMBER OF BUILDINGS (1,000)							WORKERS		
	Total	Square footage of—						Number (1,000)	Average sq. ft. per worker	Median sq. ft. per worker
		5,000 or less	5,001 to 10,000	10,001 to 25,000	25,001 to 50,000	50,001 to 100,000	100,001 and over			
All buildings	4,806	2,681	975	647	280	116	106	71,236	953	1,013
Region:										
Northeast	771	383	180	109	54	25	19	18,570	722	1,050
Midwest	1,202	676	241	163	66	29	27	14,872	1,162	1,225
South	1,963	1,171	370	239	106	41	36	23,220	1,058	1,013
West	870	451	184	136	56	20	24	14,574	866	800
Principal activity within building:										
Public assembly[1]	644	339	143	111	34	6	1	5,050	1,644	(NA)
Education	301	112	43	57	40	30	18	6,872	1,232	960
Food sales	130	103	(S)	(S)	(S)	(S)	(S)	842	899	1,000
Food service	260	179	51	21	(S)	(S)	(S)	2,244	665	613
Health care	63	39	(S)	(S)	(S)	(S)	5	3,385	521	500
Lodging	154	56	39	26	21	7	4	2,022	1,429	1,700
Mercantile/services	1,272	807	265	127	40	18	14	15,979	776	1,077
Office	749	387	168	102	51	20	21	27,161	454	500
Public order and safety	60	30	(S)	(S)	(S)	(S)	(S)	801	1,023	1,050
Warehouse and storage	761	402	149	129	43	17	20	4,451	2,580	1,925
Other	93	(S)	(S)	(S)	(S)	(S)	(S)	1,232	918	1,273
Vacant	319	177	64	42	23	7	5	981	4,481	2,000
Nongovernment owned	4,206	2,423	861	540	228	82	73	52,310	1,008	1,025
Government owned	599	258	114	108	53	34	33	18,926	799	1,000

NA Not available. S Figure does not meet publication standards. [1] Includes religious worship.
Source: U.S. Energy Information Administration, *Commercial Building Characteristics, 1992.*

Figure 26.1
Hourly Earnings of Production Workers in Manufacturing: 1993
(Percent of national average)

United States
$11.76

Less than 95%
95% to 105%
Greater than 105%

Note: 1992 data for Maine.
Source: Chart prepared by U.S. Bureau of the Census. For data, see table 1238.

Manufactures

This section presents summary data for manufacturing as a whole and more detailed information for major industry groups and selected products. The types of measures shown at the different levels include data for establishments; employment and wages; raw materials, fuels, and electricity consumed; plant and equipment expenditures; value and quantity of production and shipments; value added by manufacture; inventories; and various indicators of financial status.

The principal sources of these data are Bureau of the Census reports of the censuses of manufactures conducted every 5 years; the *Annual Survey of Manufactures;* and the *Current Industrial Reports* series, which presents monthly, quarterly, or annual data on production, shipments, and stocks for particular commodities. Indexes of industrial production are presented monthly in the Federal Reserve Board's *Federal Reserve Bulletin.* Reports on current activities of industries, or current movements of individual commodities, are compiled by such government agencies as the Bureau of Labor Statistics; the Economic Research Service of the Department of Agriculture; the International Trade Administration; and by private research or trade associations such as The Conference Board, Inc., New York, NY and the American Iron and Steel Institute, Washington, DC.

Data on financial aspects of manufacturing industries are collected by the Bureau of Economic Analysis (BEA) and the Bureau of the Census. Industry aggregates in the form of balance sheets, profit and loss statements, analyses of sales and expenses, lists of subsidiaries, and types and amounts of security issues are published for leading manufacturing corporations registered with the Securities and Exchange Commission. The BEA issues data on capital in manufacturing industries and capacity utilization rates in manufacturing. See also section 17, Business Enterprise.

Censuses and annual surveys.—The first census of manufactures covered the year 1809. Between 1809 and 1963, a census was conducted at periodic intervals. Since 1967 it has been taken every

In Brief

Personal computer shipments topped 12.5 million units in 1992.

1-megabit DRAM chips:

	1965	1992
Revenue (millions)	$5	$2,919
Price	$162	$4

5 years (for years ending in "2" and "7"). Census data, either direct reports or estimates from administrative records, are obtained for every manufacturing plant with one paid employee or more.

The *Annual Survey of Manufactures (ASM),* conducted for the first time in 1949, collects data for the years between censuses for the more general measures of manufacturing activity covered in detail by the censuses. The annual survey data are estimates derived from a scientifically selected sample of establishments. The 1991 annual survey is based on a sample of about 55,000 establishments of an approximate total of 200,000. These establishments represent all manufacturing establishments of multiunit companies and all single-establishment manufacturing companies mailed schedules in the 1987 Census of Manufactures. The 1989 through 1993 ASM sample is similar to the previous sample. For the current panel, all establishments of companies with 1987 shipments in manufacturing in excess of $500 million were included in the survey with certainty. For the remaining portion of the mail survey, the establishment was defined as the sampling unit. For this portion, all establishments with 250 employees or more and establishments with a very large value of shipments also were included. Therefore, of the 55,000 establishments included in the ASM panel, approximately 28,000 are selected with certainty. These establishments account for approximately 80 percent of total value of shipments in the 1987 census. Smaller establishments in the remaining portion of the mail survey were selected by sample.

The basic statistical measures of manufacturing activity, such as employment, payrolls, value added, etc., are defined in essentially the same way for both the annual surveys and the census of manufactures. However, the bases for computing average employment vary for different years. For example, beginning with 1949, average employment was calculated from the figures reported for the pay periods ending nearest the 15th of March, May, August, and November; whereas, for 1947 such averages were based on 12 monthly employment figures. In 1967, the average employment calculation was revised to the pay periods which include the 12th of March, May, August, and November to provide data more comparable with other statistical series.

Establishments and classification.— The censuses of manufactures for 1947 through 1987 cover operating manufacturing establishments as defined in the *Standard Industrial Classification Manual (SIC),* issued by the U.S. Office of Management and Budget (see text, section 13). The *Manual* is also used for classifying establishments in the annual surveys. The comparability of manufactures data over time is affected by changes in the official definitions of industries as presented in the *Manual.* It is important to note, therefore, that the 1987 edition of the *Manual* was used for the 1987 census; and the 1972 edition of the *Manual* and the *1977 Supplement* were used for the 1972 through 1982 censuses. For the censuses from 1947 to 1963, reports were required from all establishments employing one or more persons at any time during the census year. Beginning with the 1967 census, an effort was made to relieve the very small establishments from the necessity of filing a census report. Approximately 150,000 small single-unit manufacturing firms identified as having less than 20 employees (cutoff varied by industry) benefited from this procedure. Data for these single-unit companies were estimated on the basis of government administrative records and industry averages. Each of the establishments tabulated was classified in one of the approximately 459

manufacturing industries as defined by the *SIC Manual* in 1987. The *Manual* defines an industry as a number of establishments producing a single product or a closely related group of products. In the main, an establishment is classified in a particular industry if its production of a product or product group exceeds in value added its production of any other product group. While some establishments produce only the products of the industry in which they are classified, few within an industry specialize to that extent. The statistics on employment, payrolls, value added, inventories, and expenditures, therefore, reflect both the primary and secondary activities of the establishments in that industry. For this reason, care should be exercised in relating such statistics to the total shipments figures of products primary to the industry.

The censuses for 1947 through 1987 were conducted on an establishment basis. The term "establishment" signifies a single physical plant site or factory. It is not necessarily identical to the business unit or company, which may consist of one or more establishments. A company operating establishments at more than one location is required to submit a separate report for each location. An establishment engaged in distinctly different lines of activity and maintaining separate payroll and inventory records is also required to submit separate reports.

Durable goods.—Items with a normal life expectancy of 3 years or more. Automobiles, furniture, household appliances, and mobile homes are common examples.

Nondurable goods.—Items which generally last for only a short time (3 years or less). Food, beverages, clothing, shoes, and gasoline are common examples.

Statistical reliability.—For a discussion of statistical collection and estimation, sampling procedures and measures of statistical reliability applicable to Census Bureau data, see Appendix III.

Historical statistics.—Tabular headnotes provide cross-references, where applicable, to *Historical Statistics of the United States, Colonial Times to 1970.* See Appendix IV.

No. 1233. Gross Domestic Product in Manufacturing: 1980 to 1991

[In billions of dollars. 1980 through 1986 data are shown on the basis of the 1972 Standard Industrial Classification (SIC). 1987 through 1991 data are based on the 1987 SIC. Data include nonfactor charges (capital consumption allowances, indirect business taxes, etc.) as well as factor charges against gross product; corporate profits and capital consumption allowances have been shifted from a company to an establishment basis]

ITEM	1980	1985	1986	1987	1988	1989	1990	1991
CURRENT DOLLARS								
Gross domestic product	2,708	4,039	4,269	4,540	4,900	5,251	5,546	5,723
Manufacturing	588	798	829	878	961	1,005	1,025	1,026
Durable goods	349	472	480	502	541	563	564	551
Lumber and wood products	19	24	27	31	32	33	31	30
Furniture and fixtures	8	14	14	15	16	16	16	16
Stone, clay, and glass products	18	24	26	24	24	25	25	23
Primary metal industries	44	36	37	36	43	46	44	42
Fabricated metal products	45	57	58	59	63	67	67	65
Machinery, exc. electrical	77	87	80	(X)	(X)	(X)	(X)	(X)
Industrial machinery and equipment	(X)	(X)	(X)	88	100	106	109	102
Electric and electronic equipment	55	84	85	(X)	(X)	(X)	(X)	(X)
Electronic and other electric equipment	(X)	(X)	(X)	77	81	87	86	88
Motor vehicles and equipment	27	58	58	59	59	53	46	41
Other transportation equipment	26	48	54	57	56	60	65	65
Instruments and related products	20	27	28	40	50	52	56	59
Misc. manufacturing industries	10	14	14	15	17	18	19	19
Nondurable goods	239	327	349	376	420	442	461	475
Food and kindred products	52	72	74	79	83	88	97	102
Tobacco manufactures	7	11	13	13	14	14	16	17
Textile mill products	15	17	19	20	20	21	22	22
Apparel and other textile products	17	21	22	23	24	25	25	26
Paper and allied products	23	33	35	39	44	47	46	45
Printing and publishing	33	52	57	61	65	71	72	73
Chemicals and allied products	48	67	73	82	94	100	104	106
Petroleum and coal products	24	24	26	26	41	38	40	43
Rubber and misc. plastics products	17	26	27	30	31	34	35	36
Leather and leather products	4	4	3	3	4	4	4	4
CONSTANT (1987) DOLLARS								
Gross domestic product	3,776	4,280	4,405	4,540	4,719	4,838	4,897	4,861
Manufacturing	725	811	819	878	924	932	929	908
Durable goods	424	468	472	502	536	543	537	526
Lumber and wood products	22	25	28	31	30	29	28	26
Furniture and fixtures	12	14	14	15	15	15	14	14
Stone, clay, and glass products	24	25	26	24	25	26	26	23
Primary metal industries	49	35	39	36	34	33	35	37
Fabricated metal products	55	58	56	59	62	61	60	57
Machinery, exc. electrical	81	78	75	(X)	(X)	(X)	(X)	(X)
Industrial machinery and equipment	(X)	(X)	(X)	88	97	102	102	101
Electric and electronic equipment	70	83	84	(X)	(X)	(X)	(X)	(X)
Electronic and other electric equipment	(X)	(X)	(X)	77	85	91	91	94
Motor vehicles and equipment	40	63	58	59	63	57	49	41
Other transportation equipment	38	47	51	57	58	61	64	61
Instruments and related products	24	27	27	40	50	50	50	54
Misc. manufacturing industries	10	14	14	15	17	17	17	17
Nondurable goods	301	342	348	376	387	389	392	383
Food and kindred products	64	75	73	79	82	79	84	84
Tobacco manufactures	20	14	15	13	12	10	9	8
Textile mill products	17	18	19	20	20	21	21	21
Apparel and other textile products	20	21	22	23	24	25	24	24
Paper and allied products	31	36	37	39	40	39	42	42
Printing and publishing	53	59	59	61	63	64	62	58
Chemicals and allied products	58	67	75	82	83	84	88	86
Petroleum and coal products	15	23	19	26	30	31	26	23
Rubber and misc. plastic products	19	26	26	30	30	32	32	32
Leather and leather products	5	4	3	4	4	4	4	4

X Not applicable.

Source: U.S. Bureau of Economic Analysis, *Survey of Current Business,* May and November 1993.

No. 1234. Manufactures—Summary: 1963 to 1991

[For establishment coverage, see text, section 27. For compostion of regions, see table 26. See also, *Historical Statistics, Colonial Times to 1970*, series P 1-12]

ITEM	Unit	1963	1967	1972	1977	1982	1987	1990 [1]	1991 [1]
ALL ESTABLISHMENTS									
Number of establishments [2]	1,000	312	311	321	360	358	369	(NA)	(NA)
With 20 or more employees	1,000	102	110	114	119	123	126	(NA)	(NA)
Employee size-class:									
Establishments [3]	1,000	305	306	313	351	348	359	(NA)	(NA)
Under 20	1,000	207	199	203	237	230	238	(NA)	(NA)
20 to 99	1,000	70	74	76	78	84	86	(NA)	(NA)
100 to 249	1,000	18	20	21	22	21	22	(NA)	(NA)
250 to 999	1,000	10	11	11	12	11	11	(NA)	(NA)
1,000 and over	1,000	3	3	3	2	2	2	(NA)	(NA)
Form of organization:									
Corporate	1,000	176.2	153.9	233.2	284.2	283.2	287.4	(NA)	(NA)
Noncorporate [4]	1,000	130.4	33.2	87.5	75.7	74.0	81.5	(NA)	(NA)
Individual proprietorship	1,000	99.2	24.9	42.5	52.3	45.6	35.4	(NA)	(NA)
Partnership	1,000	27.7	6.7	17.7	18.3	15.0	13.2	(NA)	(NA)
All employees: [5]									
Annual average [6]	Million	17.0	19.3	19.0	19.6	19.1	18.9	18.8	18.1
Payroll	Bil. dol.	100	132	174	264	380	476	532	529
Payroll per employee	$1,000.	5.9	6.8	9.2	13.5	19.9	25.2	28.3	29.3
Production workers:									
Annual average	Million	12.2	14.0	13.5	13.7	12.4	12.2	12.1	11.5
Percent of all employees	Percent ...	71.8	72.5	71.1	69.9	64.9	64.6	64.4	63.7
Hours	Billion	24.5	27.8	26.7	26.7	23.5	24.3	24.3	23.2
Hours per worker	1,000	2.0	2.0	2.0	1.9	1.9	2.0	2.0	2.0
Wages	Bil. dol.	62	81	106	157	205	251	272	266
Percent of payroll for all employees	Percent ...	62.0	61.4	60.9	59.5	53.9	52.8	51.1	50.0
Wages per worker	$1,000.	5.1	5.8	7.9	11.5	16.5	20.6	22.5	23.1
Wages per worker hour	Dollar	2.53	2.91	3.97	5.89	8.72	10.35	11.19	11.49
Value added by manufacture [7]	Bil. dol.	192	262	354	585	824	1,166	1,326	1,314
Per production worker	$1,000.	15.7	18.7	26.2	42.7	66.5	95.5	109.6	114.1
Per production worker hour	Dollar	7.84	9.42	13.26	21.91	35.06	47.97	54.57	56.70
Per dollar of workers' wages	Dollar	3.10	3.23	3.34	3.73	4.02	4.64	4.88	4.93
Value added, percent distribution									
Northeast	Percent	29.8	29.1	26.3	23.7	23.7	23.7	20.6	20.5
North Central	Percent ...	35.4	35.0	34.9	34.4	29.8	29.8	29.9	29.9
South	Percent ...	21.5	22.7	25.5	27.4	29.5	29.5	32.0	32.2
West	Percent ...	13.3	13.0	13.4	14.5	17.0	17.0	17.5	17.4
Cost of materials	Bil. dol.	230	299	407	782	1,130	1,320	1,554	1,504
Value of shipments [8]	Bil. dol.	421	557	757	1,359	1,960	2,476	2,874	2,826
Per production worker	$1,000.	34.5	39.8	56.1	99.2	158.1	203.0	237.5	245.5
End-of-year inventories	Bil. dol.	60	84	108	188	307	333	393	380
New capital expenditures [9]	Bil. dol.	11.4	21.5	24.1	47.5	75.0	78.6	102.0	99.0
Gross book value of depreciable assets	Bil. dol.	158	218	301	439	692	868	(NA)	(NA)
Machinery and equipment	Bil. dol.	(NA)	157	218	328	527	671	(NA)	(NA)
Assets per employee	$1,000.	9.3	11.3	16.4	22.4	36.2	48.6	(NA)	(NA)
Ratios:									
Value added to shipments	Ratio.	45.6	47.0	46.7	42.9	42.0	47.1	(NA)	(NA)
Inventories to shipments	Ratio.	14.2	15.0	14.2	13.8	15.7	13.4	(NA)	(NA)
Payroll to value added	Ratio.	52.0	50.3	49.1	45.2	46.1	40.8	(NA)	(NA)
MULTIUNIT COMPANIES									
Establishments	1,000	45.9	51.7	70.2	81.2	81.7	80.9	(NA)	(NA)
Employees	Million	11.0	13.3	14.3	15.0	14.3	13.8	(NA)	(NA)
Production workers	Million	8.1	9.8	9.8	10.1	8.8	8.5	(NA)	(NA)
Payroll	Bil. dol.	68.2	93.8	138.8	214.2	307.5	377.3	(NA)	(NA)
Wages, production workers	Bil. dol.	44.7	60.9	81.9	124.9	159.1	191.8	(NA)	(NA)
Value added by manufacture	Bil. dol.	146.6	206.4	286.1	485.0	678.4	953.6	(NA)	(NA)
New capital expenditures	Bil. dol.	8.9	18.6	20.0	41.0	65.2	66.5	(NA)	(NA)
SINGLE UNIT COMPANIES [10]									
Establishments	1,000	260.8	254.0	250.5	278.7	276.3	288.0	(NA)	(NA)
Employees	Million	5.2	5.2	4.8	4.6	4.8	5.1	(NA)	(NA)
Payroll	Bil. dol.	25.1	28.5	35.4	49.8	72.1	98.3	(NA)	(NA)
Value added by manufacture	Bil. dol.	45.5	55.5	67.9	100.1	145.7	212.1	(NA)	(NA)

NA Not available.   [1] Estimated data based on *Annual Survey of Manufactures;* see text, section 27.   [2] Includes administrative and auxiliary units.   [3] Excludes administrative offices and auxiliary units.   [4] Includes forms of organization not shown separately.   [5] Includes data for employees of manufacturing establishments engaged in distribution and construction work.   [6] Data are based on pay periods ending nearest 15th of March, May, August, and November.   [7] Adjusted value added; takes into account (a) value added by merchandising operations (that is, difference between the sales value and cost of merchandise sold without further manufacture, processing, or assembly), plus (b) net change in finished goods and work-in-process inventories between beginning and end of year.   [8] Includes extensive and unmeasurable duplication from shipments between establishments in the same industry classification.   [9] Includes plants under construction and not yet in operation.   [10] Beginning 1967, includes data obtained from Federal administrative records.

Source: Except as noted, U.S. Bureau of the Census, *Census of Manufactures, 1963, 1967, 1972, 1977, 1982,* and *1987.*

No. 1235. Manufactures—Summary, by Industry: 1982, 1987, and 1991

[Data based on various editions of the Standard Industrial Classification (SIC) Manual, published by the Office of Management and Budget; see text, section 27. N.e.c. = Not elsewhere classified. See also Historical Statistics, Colonial Times to 1970, series P 58-67]

SIC code	INDUSTRY	1982 Establishments	1982 All employees, Number [1] (1,000)	1982 Payroll (mil. dol.)	1982 Value of shipments (mil. dol.)	1987 Establishments	1987 All employees, Number [1] (1,000)	1987 Payroll (mil. dol.)	1987 Value of shipments (mil. dol.)	1991 All employees, Number [1] (1,000)	1991 Payroll (mil. dol.)	1991 Production workers	1991 Value added by manufacture (mil. dol.)	1991 Value of shipments (mil. dol.)
(X)	**All manufacturing establishments**	**358,061**	**19,094**	**379,627**	**1,960,206**	**368,897**	**18,950**	**475,651**	**2,475,901**	**18,062**	**529,019**	**11,513**	**1,313,829**	**2,826,207**
20	**Food and kindred products**	**22,130**	**1,488**	**26,088**	**280,529**	**20,624**	**1,449**	**30,268**	**329,725**	**1,475**	**34,578**	**1,070**	**145,336**	**387,601**
201	Meat products	3,623	318	4,993	67,602	3,267	341	5,701	77,002	390	7,025	330	17,476	89,391
202	Dairy products	2,724	140	2,553	38,771	2,366	142	3,217	44,755	136	3,595	84	13,855	49,853
203	Preserved fruits and vegetables	(NA)	(NA)	(NA)	(NA)	1,912	209	3,784	36,343	216	4,572	181	22,043	46,806
204	Grain mill products	2,745	108	2,197	31,386	2,610	102	2,704	36,737	103	3,126	71	19,835	47,111
205	Bakery products	(NA)	(NA)	(NA)	(NA)	2,850	217	4,761	23,677	209	5,279	127	16,452	26,539
206	Sugar and confectionery products	1,033	96	1,661	15,576	1,094	90	1,991	18,887	92	2,328	73	10,107	21,959
207	Fats and oils	724	39	774	16,752	595	30	702	15,881	28	744	19	3,815	18,735
208	Beverages	2,584	194	4,244	38,801	2,214	161	4,521	47,327	145	4,591	73	26,839	54,610
209	Miscellaneous foods and kindred products	3,941	158	2,300	23,959	3,716	158	2,887	29,116	156	3,318	114	14,915	32,598
21	**Tobacco products**	**163**	**58**	**1,324**	**16,061**	**138**	**45**	**1,486**	**20,757**	**40**	**1,520**	**29**	**24,484**	**32,032**
211	Cigarettes	14	42	1,094	12,127	11	32	1,486	17,372	27	1,224	20	22,210	27,111
212	Cigars	60	5	59	254	20	3	36	192	3	51	2	201	312
213	Chewing and smoking tobacco	29	3	52	665	29	3	77	1,114	3	88	2	1,203	1,602
214	Tobacco stemming and redrying	60	8	120	3,015	78	7	139	2,079	7	157	5	871	3,008
22	**Textile mill products**	**6,630**	**717**	**9,046**	**47,515**	**6,412**	**672**	**11,410**	**62,786**	**598**	**11,375**	**515**	**26,925**	**65,706**
221	Broadwoven fabric mills, cotton	269	77	965	3,972	301	72	1,260	5,508	66	1,246	59	2,480	5,695
222	Broadwoven fabric mills, manmade	523	141	1,815	8,191	441	88	1,596	8,049	78	1,600	69	3,551	8,315
223	Broadwoven fabric mills, wool	131	13	176	763	119	14	236	1,051	15	296	13	705	1,804
224	Narrow fabric mills	281	18	216	852	277	19	296	1,136	16	291	14	698	1,248
225	Knitting mills	(NA)	(NA)	(NA)	(NA)	2,130	203	2,988	13,531	181	3,022	159	7,244	15,449
226	Textile finishing, except wool	753	58	834	4,972	971	56	1,036	7,042	49	1,046	41	2,641	6,360
227	Carpets and rugs	505	42	603	5,808	477	53	1,028	9,795	49	1,028	38	2,846	8,988
228	Yarn and thread mills	714	109	98	7,036	610	114	1,850	10,277	94	1,670	86	3,684	10,687
229	Miscellaneous textile goods	(NA)	(NA)	(NA)	(NA)	1,086	53	1,109	6,398	50	1,176	38	3,077	7,160
23	**Apparel and other textile products**	**24,391**	**1,189**	**12,129**	**53,388**	**22,872**	**1,081**	**13,904**	**64,243**	**960**	**14,135**	**815**	**33,432**	**65,345**
231	Men's and boys' suits and coats	529	75	878	3,062	347	55	779	2,863	44	743	37	1,400	2,467
232	Men's and boys' furnishings	2,544	299	2,837	12,727	2,195	280	3,246	15,441	252	3,371	222	8,681	15,988
233	Women's and misses' outerwear	10,838	419	4,110	18,225	10,290	349	4,297	19,389	307	4,244	262	9,953	19,433
234	Women's and children's undergarments	755	82	783	3,323	557	68	839	3,738	58	810	49	2,172	3,683

See footnotes at end of table.

No. 1235. Manufactures—Summary, by Industry: 1982, 1987, and 1991

No. 1235. Manufactures—Summary, by Industry: 1982, 1987, and 1991—Continued

[See headnote, page 753]

SIC code	INDUSTRY	1982 Establish-ments	1982 All employees Number (1,000)	1982 All employees Payroll (mil. dol.)	1982 Value of shipments (mil. dol.)	1987 Establish-ments	1987 All employees Number (1,000)	1987 All employees Payroll (mil. dol.)	1987 Value of shipments (mil. dol.)	1991 All employees Number (1,000)	1991 All employees Payroll (mil. dol.)	1991 Produc-tion workers	1991 Value added by manufac-ture (mil. dol.)	1991 Value of shipments (mil. dol.)
23	**Apparel, other textile products—Con.**													
235	Hats, caps, and millinery	419	16	157	522	461	17	204	663	16	228	14	455	801
236	Girls' and children's outerwear	968	71	671	2,711	834	72	826	3,753	59	791	50	1,907	3,579
237	Fur goods	504	3	60	419	380	2	48	423	2	29	1	70	257
238	Miscellaneous apparel and accessories	1,223	50	513	2,118	986	41	518	2,229	37	546	30	1,167	2,244
239	Miscellaneous fabricated textile products	6,611	174	2,120	10,281	6,822	198	3,143	15,744	186	3,373	152	7,627	16,894
24	**Lumber and wood products**	32,984	576	8,445	42,995	33,982	698	12,707	69,747	631	12,738	526	26,995	70,569
241	Logging	11,658	81	1,208	8,274	11,952	86	1,518	10,938	78	1,561	65	4,097	11,434
242	Sawmills and planing mills	7,403	158	2,306	11,132	6,696	180	3,297	19,220	158	3,244	141	6,803	19,409
243	Millwork, plywood, and structural members	6,545	165	2,596	11,683	7,930	240	4,658	22,614	210	4,487	171	8,885	21,448
244	Wood containers	2,250	36	391	1,635	2,216	37	483	2,069	40	634	33	1,203	2,864
245	Wood buildings and mobile homes	1,163	60	880	4,955	1,077	65	1,215	6,575	54	1,106	42	2,173	5,952
249	Miscellaneous Wood Products	3,965	77	1,064	5,255	4,104	90	1,536	8,330	91	1,706	74	3,832	9,462
25	**Furniture and fixtures** [2]	10,003	436	6,084	24,129	11,613	511	9,082	37,462	466	9,489	369	20,669	40,027
251	Household furniture	5,475	263	3,162	12,776	5,606	284	4,452	18,559	259	4,576	217	9,723	19,499
252	Office furniture	700	59	1,051	4,150	986	81	1,790	7,538	66	1,761	48	4,128	7,263
253	Public building and related furniture	413	19	295	1,103	484	22	397	2,088	26	559	20	1,259	3,136
254	Partitions and fixtures	2,148	60	1,025	3,710	2,455	74	1,552	5,537	67	1,622	49	3,210	5,929
259	Miscellaneous furniture and fixtures	1,267	36	551	2,390	2,084	50	892	3,740	48	972	35	2,348	4,200
26	**Paper and allied products**	(NA)	(NA)	(NA)	(NA)	6,342	611	16,860	108,989	621	19,363	477	58,281	128,824
261	Pulp mills	43	17	468	3,110	39	14	535	4,314	17	697	13	2,446	5,329
262	Paper mills	299	129	3,431	20,995	281	129	4,597	28,918	130	5,224	99	15,510	33,344
263	Paperboard mills	222	56	1,502	9,531	199	52	1,859	13,730	51	2,027	39	7,257	15,013
265	Paperboard containers and boxes	2,781	188	3,517	19,192	2,796	194	4,618	25,863	199	5,392	153	11,531	30,577
267	Miscellaneous converted paper products	3,006	213	3,961	26,701	3,027	222	5,251	36,165	224	6,043	173	11,537	44,560
27	**Printing and publishing**	53,406	1,292	22,707	85,797	61,774	1,494	33,440	156,196	1,488	38,742	787	103,771	156,685
271	Newspapers	8,846	402	6,555	21,276	9,079	434	9,022	31,850	428	10,309	145	26,093	33,702
272	Periodicals	3,328	94	1,986	11,478	4,017	110	2,983	17,329	111	3,661	21	13,794	20,345
273	Books	2,811	112	2,090	10,132	2,856	114	2,821	15,876	126	3,700	55	14,071	20,736
274	Miscellaneous publishing	2,057	45	706	2,871	2,376	70	1,513	7,810	65	1,780	23	7,354	9,762
275	Commercial printing	(NA)	(NA)	(NA)	(NA)	36,103	553	12,301	44,786	556	14,135	401	28,892	51,948
276	Manifold business forms	810	50	934	5,059	853	53	1,281	7,397	46	1,269	32	3,840	7,234
277	Greeting cards	154	21	344	1,894	162	22	471	2,911	24	609	13	2,925	3,810
278	Blankbooks and bookbinding	1,487	61	903	2,803	1,545	69	1,265	4,080	70	1,395	54	3,217	4,571
279	Printing trade services	(NA)	(NA)	(NA)	(NA)	4,783	69	1,784	4,157	62	1,884	45	3,584	4,577

See footnotes at end of table.

No. 1235. Manufactures—Summary, by Industry: 1982, 1987, and 1991—Continued

[See headnote, page 753]

SIC code	INDUSTRY	1982				1987				1991				
		Establish-ments	All employees		Value of shipments (mil. dol.)	Establish-ments	All employees		Value of shipments (mil. dol.)	All employees		Produc-tion workers	Value added by manufac-ture (mil. dol.)	Value of shipments (mil. dol.)
			Number [1] (1,000)	Payroll (mil. dol.)			Number [1] (1,000)	Payroll (mil. dol.)		Number [1] (1,000)	Payroll (mil. dol.)			
28	Chemicals and allied products	11,901	873	20,836	170,737	12,109	814	25,016	229,546	846	31,002	477	154,793	292,326
281	Industrial inorganic chemicals	1,365	108	2,795	17,280	1,405	94	3,099	19,774	104	4,085	56	15,724	26,511
282	Plastics materials and synthetics	606	141	3,451	28,428	680	123	4,013	40,851	129	4,889	87	19,673	46,235
283	Drugs	1,281	166	3,966	24,695	1,356	172	5,304	39,263	184	7,198	83	43,245	60,836
284	Soap, cleaners, and toilet goods	2,379	127	2,581	26,031	2,399	119	3,099	34,748	123	3,750	76	25,374	41,854
285	Paints and allied products	1,441	54	1,158	9,162	1,431	55	1,492	12,702	51	1,568	25	6,784	14,255
286	Industrial organic chemicals	969	144	4,005	38,157	961	126	4,541	51,158	127	5,429	75	26,441	64,432
287	Agricultural chemicals	1,127	51	1,156	14,653	973	40	1,171	14,267	41	1,406	25	8,121	18,522
289	Miscellaneous chemical products	2,733	82	1,725	12,330	2,904	85	2,298	16,782	87	2,678	51	9,431	19,682
29	Petroleum and coal products	2,322	152	4,339	208,919	2,254	116	3,996	130,414	113	4,729	73	24,024	158,076
291	Petroleum refining	(NA)	(NA)	(NA)	(NA)	331	75	2,845	118,186	74	3,448	48	19,796	145,392
295	Asphalt paving and roofing materials	1,307	30	629	5,948	1,367	28	786	7,749	26	843	19	2,543	7,233
299	Miscellaneous petroleum and coal products	582	14	312	3,614	556	13	365	4,479	13	438	7	1,685	5,452
30	Rubber and misc. plastics products	13,449	682	11,597	55,416	14,515	831	17,581	86,634	840	20,298	647	50,295	100,668
301	Tires and inner tubes	164	70	1,734	9,340	164	65	2,070	10,427	66	2,286	52	6,654	11,883
302	Rubber and plastics footwear	65	18	197	706	66	11	153	557	12	182	10	384	757
305	Hose and belting and plastics and packing	635	55	999	3,612	693	52	1,159	4,648	53	1,332	39	2,843	5,241
306	Fabricated rubber products, n.e.c.	(NA)	(NA)	(NA)	(NA)	1,573	104	2,245	9,227	98	2,323	75	5,293	10,370
308	Miscellaneous plastics products, n.e.c.	(NA)	(NA)	(NA)	(NA)	12,019	599	11,955	61,775	611	14,176	471	35,121	72,417
31	Leather and leather products	2,735	200	2,219	9,719	2,193	129	1,831	9,082	106	1,753	89	4,293	9,142
311	Leather tanning and finishing	384	20	311	1,753	344	15	292	2,219	12	278	10	710	2,183
313	Footwear cut stock	161	7	81	368	128	5	70	324	5	83	5	182	383
314	Footwear, except rubber	751	121	1,250	5,269	479	71	913	4,073	53	770	46	1,942	3,775
315	Leather gloves and mittens	96	4	37	178	77	3	34	185	3	33	2	58	141
316	Luggage	292	16	194	789	241	11	196	929	13	230	10	598	1,148
317	Handbags and personal leather goods	636	25	271	1,035	529	17	232	942	12	210	10	495	906
319	Leather goods, n.e.c.	415	7	76	327	395	7	95	411	9	149	7	308	607

See footnotes at end of table.

No. 1235. Manufactures—Summary, by Industry: 1982, 1987, and 1991—Continued

[See headnote, page 753]

SIC code	INDUSTRY	1982 Establishments	1982 All employees — Number[1] (1,000)	1982 All employees — Payroll (mil. dol.)	1982 Value of shipments (mil. dol.)	1987 Establishments	1987 All employees — Number[1] (1,000)	1987 All employees — Payroll (mil. dol.)	1987 Value of shipments (mil. dol.)	1991 All employees — Number[1] (1,000)	1991 All employees — Payroll (mil. dol.)	1991 Production workers	1991 Value added by manufacture (mil. dol.)	1991 Value of shipments (mil. dol.)
32	**Stone, clay, and glass products**	**16,545**	**532**	**10,097**	**45,181**	**16,166**	**524**	**12,349**	**61,477**	**476**	**12,612**	**363**	**31,839**	**59,611**
321	Flat glass	69	15	414	1,666	81	15	507	2,549	13	486	11	1,254	2,104
322	Glass and glassware, pressed or blown	459	97	2,032	7,941	522	77	1,959	8,339	67	2,015	57	5,129	8,755
323	Products of purchased glass	1,337	41	696	2,977	1,432	51	1,060	5,429	52	1,243	41	3,312	6,155
324	Cement, hydraulic	237	25	636	3,542		19	599	2,915	16	560	12	1,604	3,778
325	Structural clay products	628	30	491	1,868	598	35	689	2,416	32	705	25	1,758	2,782
326	Pottery and related products	910	37	598	1,762	1,006	38	762		37	820	29		2,559
327	Concrete, gypsum, and plaster products	9,933	167	2,995	14,947	9,814	203	4,632	24,427	180	4,571	129	10,632	22,466
328	Cut stone and stone products	711	11	156	555	745	13	243	841	12	267	10	582	956
329	Miscellaneous nonmetallic mineral products	(NA)	(NA)	(NA)	(NA)	1,753	73	1,898	10,226	67	1,945	49	5,630	10,057
33	**Primary metal industries [2]**	**7,061**	**854**	**20,603**	**104,667**	**6,771**	**701**	**19,777**	**120,248**	**677**	**21,640**	**516**	**46,605**	**132,837**
331	Blast furnace and basic steel products	1,068	366		46,720	1,241	253	8,166	51,815	246	8,976	187	19,685	56,327
332	Iron and steel foundries	1,438	157	3,113	9,642	1,231	130	3,426	10,628	125	3,580	100	6,194	11,172
333	Primary nonferrous metals	161	44	1,307	11,321	169	32	996	10,869	35	1,310	27	3,593	13,838
334	Secondary nonferrous metals	458	19	402	4,852	397	13	312	4,431	13	388	10	815	5,041
335	Nonferrous rolling and drawing	1,022	167	3,636	25,463	1,066	163	4,298	33,282	150	4,602	111	10,956	36,318
336	Nonferrous foundries (castings)	(NA)	(NA)	(NA)	(NA)	1,687	80	1,805	6,315	75	1,873	60	3,454	6,693
34	**Fabricated metal products**	**35,560**	**1,460**	**28,283**	**119,444**	**36,105**	**1,458**	**35,000**	**147,366**	**1,359**	**36,827**	**995**	**76,670**	**157,077**
341	Metal cans and shipping containers	566	59	1,533	12,172	538	48	1,527	12,114	41	1,490	34	3,984	13,642
342	Cutlery, handtools, and hardware	2,238	141	2,585	10,082	2,327	145	3,389	13,481	132	3,420	99	8,156	14,353
343	Plumbing and heating, except electric	1,177	48	821	4,003	828	46	1,005	5,283	42	1,106	29	2,965	5,733
344	Fabricated structural metal products	12,681	422	7,897	34,904	12,579	407	9,042	40,416	379	9,643	269	19,313	42,549
345	Screw machine products, bolts, etc.	2,690	94	1,727	5,834		95	2,270	7,890	91	2,437	69	4,997	8,484
346	Metal forgings and stampings	4,019	236	5,110	20,057	4,062	255	7,235	28,410	232	7,251	182	12,729	27,927
347	Metal services, n.e.c	5,070	97	1,518	5,125	5,251	113	2,167	7,790	110	2,464	86	4,787	8,758
348	Ordnance and accessories, n.e.c	349	79	1,780	4,993	5,374	88	2,458	7,644	69	2,205	39	4,378	6,673
349	Miscellaneous fabricated metal products	6,770	284	5,312	22,274	7,577	262	5,906	24,340	264	6,814	188	15,361	28,959
35	**Industrial machinery and equipment**	**52,912**	**2,189**	**46,911**	**187,896**	**52,135**	**1,844**	**50,553**	**217,670**	**1,774**	**54,983**	**1,101**	**124,235**	**243,479**
351	Engines and turbines	341	112	2,850	13,040	356	87	2,906	14,570	78	2,871	52	7,560	16,608
352	Farm and garden machinery	2,078	114	2,386	13,018	1,804	82	1,917	11,474	90	2,305	64	7,133	15,166
353	Construction and related machinery	3,952	326	7,332	32,038	3,467	188	5,272	24,622	190	5,819	118	12,531	27,727
354	Metalworking machinery	(NA)	(NA)	(NA)	(NA)	11,470	268	7,301	22,004	266	8,192	186	15,515	25,456
355	Special industry machinery	(NA)	(NA)	(NA)	(NA)	4,550	169	4,588	17,096	164	5,377	92	10,876	20,687
356	General industrial machinery	(NA)	(NA)	(NA)	(NA)	3,929	240	6,203	24,121	255	7,527	161	16,832	30,809
357	Computer and office equipment	(NA)	(NA)	(NA)	(NA)	2,134	328	10,668	60,627	265	10,082	90	27,419	58,755
358	Refrigeration and service machinery	1,937	172	3,344	16,450	2,129	190	4,752	23,235	174	4,832	121	11,750	25,064
359	Industrial machinery, n.e.c.	(NA)	(NA)	(NA)	(NA)	22,296	292	6,946	19,921	292	7,977	217	14,621	23,207

See footnotes at end of table.

No. 1235. Manufactures—Summary, by Industry: 1982, 1987, and 1991—Continued

[See headnote, page 753]

SIC code	INDUSTRY	1982 Establishments	1982 All employees Number (1,000)	1982 All employees Payroll (mil. dol.)	1982 Value of shipments (mil. dol.)	1987 Establishments	1987 All employees Number (1,000)	1987 All employees Payroll (mil. dol.)	1987 Value of shipments (mil. dol.)	1991 All employees Number (1,000)	1991 All employees Payroll (mil. dol.)	1991 Production workers	1991 Value added by manufacture (mil. dol.)	1991 Value of shipments (mil. dol.)
36	**Electronics; other electric equip.**	(NA)	(NA)	(NA)	(NA)	15,962	1,565	38,738	171,286	1,427	41,611	896	106,669	197,880
361	Electric distribution equipment	(NA)	(NA)	(NA)	(NA)	766	77	1,791	8,197	70	1,873	49	4,939	9,276
362	Electrical industrial apparatus	(NA)	(NA)	(NA)	(NA)	2,213	166	3,882	15,266	153	4,166	102	9,824	17,754
363	Household appliances	(NA)	(NA)	(NA)	(NA)	480	117	2,642	16,498	104	2,497	84	7,413	17,692
364	Electric lighting and wiring equipment	1,993	159	2,718	12,048	1,986	167	3,732	18,004	144	3,677	105	10,161	18,131
365	Household audio and video equipment	(NA)	(NA)	(NA)	(NA)	854	44	850	7,833	45	1,027	32	3,370	9,823
366	Communications equipment	(NA)	(NA)	(NA)	(NA)	1,437	260	7,537	34,001	238	8,394	109	21,286	37,946
367	Electronic components and accessories	(NA)	(NA)	(NA)	(NA)	5,911	546	13,623	50,258	519	15,477	314	38,650	65,233
369	Misc. electrical equipment and supplies.	(NA)	(NA)	(NA)	(NA)	2,315	188	4,682	21,230	154	4,500	101	11,026	22,025
37	**Transportation equipment**	9,443	1,596	40,812	201,346	10,500	1,817	58,790	332,936	1,634	60,079	1,056	151,979	364,032
371	Motor vehicles and equipment	3,867	616	15,393	112,270	4,422	751	23,910	205,923	653	21,883	519	73,333	206,101
372	Aircraft and parts	1,471	539	14,714	52,027	1,618	596	20,590	77,304	568	21,886	300	49,046	102,381
373	Ship and boat building and repairing	2,566	205	4,326	13,326	2,766	177	4,266	13,857	162	4,504	122	7,959	14,524
374	Railroad equipment	200	35	790	3,457	173	22	631	2,471	26	820	19	1,690	4,450
375	Motorcycles, bicycles, and parts	273	13	225	1,341	246	7	158	1,063	11	277	9	741	1,914
376	Guided missiles, space vehicles, parts	105	146	4,481	14,398	156	214	8,114	26,285	178	7,750	62	17,103	28,965
379	Miscellaneous transportation equipment	961	43	879	4,528	1,119	49	1,122	6,033	36	959	25	2107	5,698
38	**Instruments and related products**	(NA)	(NA)	(NA)	(NA)	10,326	982	28,778	107,325	901	31,797	452	82,536	127,160
381	Search and navigation equipment	(NA)	(NA)	(NA)	(NA)	1,137	369	12,368	36,267	280	11,631	112	23,672	36,213
382	Measuring and controlling devices	(NA)	(NA)	(NA)	(NA)	4,240	285	7,807	26,042	268	9,070	133	20,096	32,263
384	Medical instruments and supplies	2,973	189	3,559	15,133	3,443	204	5,027	22,865	241	7,218	143	21,873	33,596
385	Ophthalmic goods	410	26	409	1,273	494	24	475	1,689	26	627	17	1,645	2,313
386	Photographic equipment and supplies	795	119	3,193	17,038	791	88	2,878	19,241	78	3,044	40	14,603	21,398
387	Watches, clocks, watchcases and parts	237	17	248	1,188	221	12	223	1,221	8	207	6	646	1,377
39	**Misc. manufacturing industries**	15,871	383	5,647	26,891	16,544	374	6,884	32,012	363	7,750	260	19,999	37,131
391	Jewelry, silverware, and plated ware	2,882	50	770	4,379	2,978	50	941	5,554	46	982	32	2,458	5,275
393	Musical instruments	452	18	258	916	425	12	218	814	12	238	9	536	881
394	Toys and sporting goods	2,570	99	1,389	8,256	2,711	89	1,512	8,798	93	1,923	69	6,088	11,343
395	Pens, pencils, office, and art supplies	1,026	32	485	2,372	1,013	29	540	2,536	30	625	21	1,788	3,306
396	Costume jewelry and notions	(NA)	(NA)	(NA)	(NA)	1,020	32	498	2,062	26	527	19	1,286	2,203
399	Miscellaneous manufactures [3]	(NA)	(NA)	(NA)	(NA)	8,397	163	3,174	12,248	157	3,454	111	7,843	14,124
(X)	Administrative and auxiliary [3]	9,676	1,276	38,220	-	9,480	1,234	47,202	-	1,269	61,979	-	-	-

- Represents zero. NA Not applicable. X Not applicable. [1] Represents the average of production workers plus all other employees for the payroll period ended nearest the 15th of March. [2] Includes other industries not shown separately. [3] Manufacturing concerns often reported separately for central offices or auxiliaries which serve the manufacturing establishment of a company, rather than the general public. Separate reports were obtained from such units if at a different location or if they serviced more than one establishment.

Source: U.S. Bureau of the Census, *1987 Census of Manufactures* and *Annual Survey of Manufactures.*

No. 1236. Manufactures—Summary, by Industry; Selected Based on Value Added: 1982, 1987, and 1991

[Data based on various editions of the Standard Industrial Classification (SIC) Manual, published by the Office of Management and Budget; see text, section 27. N.e.c.=Not elsewhere classified. See also Historical Statistics, Colonial Times to 1970, series P 58-67]

SIC code	INDUSTRY	1982 Establish-ments	1982 All employees Number (1,000)	1982 Payroll (mil. dol.)	1982 Value of shipments (mil. dol.)	1987 Establish-ments	1987 All employees Number (1,000)	1987 Payroll (mil. dol.)	1987 Value of shipments (mil. dol.)	1991 All employees Number (1,000)	1991 Payroll (mil. dol.)	1991 Production workers	1991 Value added by manufacture (mil. dol.)	1991 Value of shipments (mil. dol.)
2011	Meat packing plants	1,780	134.4	2,549	44,854	1,434	113.2	2,141	44,991	120.8	2,375	103.3	5,958	49,326
2013	Sausages and other prepared meats	1,311	65.5	1,206	12,278	1,344	79.1	1,619	16,623	79.6	1,833	59.0	5,046	18,361
2015	Poultry slaughtering and processing	532	117.7	1,237	10,471	463	147.7	1,919	14,912	189.6	2,817	168.0	6,473	21,703
2026	Fluid milk	1,190	78.2	1,469	18,736	946	72.4	1,681	20,591	65.5	1,840	32.3	5,656	21,137
2033	Canned fruits and vegetables	715	70.5	1,040	9,283	647	65.6	1,163	11,890	67.3	1,484	57.2	6,859	15,579
2038	Frozen specialties, n.e.c.	(NA)	(NA)	(NA)	(NA)	288	37.5	669	5,624	44.9	876	36.7	4,230	8,428
2043	Cereal breakfast foods	52	15.6	435	4,132	53	16.0	599	6,566	15.7	707	12.7	6,581	8,954
2051	Bread, cake, and related products	2,305	170.7	3,254	13,143	2,357	161.6	3,556	16,202	150.2	3,834	83.0	10,801	17,279
2052	Cookies and crackers	358	45.6	797	4,665	380	45.4	1,010	6,309	49.3	1,247	36.2	4,991	8,022
2064	Candy and other confectionery products	(NA)	(NA)	(NA)	(NA)	685	45.8	900	6,980	49.1	1,121	39.3	4,999	8,746
2082	Malt beverages	109	43.0	1,308	11,183	134	31.9	1,355	13,619	32.4	1,446	23.5	9,037	15,925
2086	Bottled and canned soft drinks	1,626	113.8	2,146	16,808	1,190	95.6	2,277	22,006	81.7	2,210	31.9	9,555	25,191
2087	Flavoring extracts and syrups, n.e.c.	(NA)	11.6	237	4,237	280	9.1	258	4,665	8.1	275	4.6	4,123	5,642
2099	Food preparations, n.e.c.	(NA)	(NA)	(NA)	(NA)	1,658	57.9	1,234	9,787	54.7	1,193	37.5	5,666	11,322
2111	Cigarettes	14	41.5	1,094	12,127	12	32.0	1,110	17,372	26.9	1,561	19.5	22,210	27,111
2411	Logging	11,658	80.8	1,208	8,274	11,936	85.7	1,516	10,880	78.1	1,224	65.4	5,866	11,434
2421	Sawmills and planing mills, general	6,316	131.9	2,020	10,065	5,742	148.2	2,817	17,357	129.5	2,747	116.1	7,485	17,485
2511	Wood household furniture	2,607	125.6	1,403	5,057	2,948	135.8	2,017	7,980	121.4	2,005	103.8	4,169	7,980
2621	Paper mills	299	129.0	3,431	20,995	282	129.1	4,587	28,916	130.3	5,224	99.4	15,510	33,344
2631	Paperboard mills	222	55.6	1,502	9,531	205	52.3	1,859	13,730	50.6	2,027	39.0	7,257	15,013
2653	Corrugated and solid fiber boxes	1,492	94.4	1,862	10,558	1,601	105.8	2,610	16,107	108.7	3,047	79.4	6,064	15,594
2676	Sanitary paper products	138	36.7	863	9,086	133	38.4	1,155	11,698	38.8	1,343	31.1	8,747	18,026
2711	Newspapers	8,846	401.5	6,555	21,276	9,091	434.6	9,025	31,849	428.4	10,387	145.1	26,093	33,702
2721	Periodicals	3,328	94.0	1,986	11,478	4,020	110.0	2,983	17,329	110.6	3,661	20.7	13,794	20,345
2731	Book publishing	2,130	67.1	1,327	7,740	2,298	70.1	1,860	12,620	77.3	3,157	17.1	11,683	16,596
2741	Miscellaneous publishing	2,057	45.3	706	2,871	2,369	69.4	1,513	7,810	65.0	2,514	22.6	7,354	9,762
2752	Commercial printing, lithographic	17,842	311.9	5,746	19,442	24,980	403.0	9,132	32,698	400.1	10,203	290.8	20,952	37,719
2759	Commercial printing, n.e.c.	(NA)	(NA)	(NA)	(NA)	10,796	126.2	2,490	8,973	133.8	3,055	92.1	6,270	10,723
2761	Manifold business forms	810	49.5	934	5,059	853	53.2	1,276	7,359	46.3	1,780	32.2	3,840	7,234
2819	Industrial inorganic chemicals, n.e.c.	645	81.7	2,134	12,060	662	72.2	2,425	13,212	60.5	2,480	41.0	10,612	17,649
2821	Plastics materials and resins	440	54.7	1,434	15,769	480	56.3	2,006	26,246	46.9	1,569	36.7	11,012	29,566
2824	Organic fibers, noncellulosic	70	60.2	1,382	8,263	72	45.7	1,347	10,112	45.0	1,575	35.0	6,119	11,084
2834	Pharmaceutical preparations	683	124.4	3,053	18,998	732	131.6	4,168	32,094	129.1	5,012	59.2	34,978	47,376
2841	Soap and other detergents	723	35.4	827	9,167	764	31.7	956	11,559	36.6	1,221	23.1	8,165	15,233
2842	Polishes and sanitation goods	(NA)	23.0	444	4,614	726	20.6	500	5,594	19.6	573	12.2	3,895	6,172
2844	Toilet preparations	639	60.4	1,102	10,183	694	58.5	1,353	14,593	57.4	1,616	35.6	12,047	17,085
2851	Paints and allied products	1,441	54.1	1,158	9,162	1,426	55.2	1,491	12,701	51.1	1,568	25.2	6,784	14,255
2869	Industrial organic chemicals, n.e.c.	(NA)	(NA)	(NA)	(NA)	699	100.3	3,696	42,189	101.0	4,403	58.4	22,248	53,069
2879	Agricultural chemicals, n.e.c.	330	16.5	404	5,436	277	16.1	518	6,300	16.4	620	9.1	4,951	8,346
2899	Chemical preparations, n.e.c.	1,443	39.7	837	6,344	1,529	37.9	1,021	8,024	39.4	1,202	22.5	4,765	9,176

See footnotes at end of table.

SIC code	INDUSTRY	1982				1987				1991				
		Establish-ments	All employees Number[1] (1,000)	All employees Payroll (mil. dol.)	Value of shipments (mil. dol.)	Establish-ments	All employees Number[1] (1,000)	All employees Payroll (mil. dol.)	Value of shipments (mil. dol.)	All employees Number[1] (1,000)	All employees Payroll (mil. dol.)	Produc-tion workers	Value added by manufac-ture (mil. dol.)	Value of shipments (mil. dol.)
2911	Petroleum refining	(NA)	(NA)	(NA)	(NA)	309	74.6	2,846	118,216	73.9	3,448	47.6	19,796	145,392
3011	Tires and inner tubes	164	70.3	1,734	9,340	163	65.4	2,070	10,427	65.5	2,286	52.4	6,654	11,883
3081	Unsupported plastics film and sheet	(NA)	(NA)	(NA)	(NA)	594	48.4	1,256	8,140	50.5	1,489	36.0	4,246	9,169
3089	Plastics products, n.e.c.	(NA)	(NA)	(NA)	(NA)	8,571	384.7	7,286	33,774	388.9	8,540	301.9	20,121	39,188
3273	Ready-mixed concrete	5,379	81.4	1,475	8,163	5,321	96.9	2,289	12,975	86.1	2,243	62.8	5,170	11,681
3312	Blast furnaces and steel mills	301	295.8	8,678	36,824	342	188.9	6,451	38,663	177.3	6,940	135.3	14,568	40,775
3357	Nonferrous wiredrawing and insulating	440	67.6	1,270	8,217	487	64.9	1,504	10,827	57.1	1,575	41.9	4,313	11,686
3429	Hardware, n.e.c.	1,185	80.1	1,521	5,741	1,240	85.6	2,056	8,175	73.8	1,938	56.2	4,278	8,223
3441	Fabricated structural metal	2,740	103.6	1,990	8,853	2,454	80.9	1,881	8,667	77.0	2,064	54.2	3,900	9,079
3443	Fabricated plate work (boiler shops)	1,929	102.9	2,180	8,225	1,740	74.6	1,842	6,795	77.0	2,127	51.2	4,396	8,684
3444	Sheet metal work	3,795	81.1	1,495	6,854	4,297	100.3	2,237	9,700	94.9	2,411	70.7	4,753	9,961
3465	Automotive stampings	668	90.5	2,293	8,777	713	119.8	3,977	15,252	99.3	3,681	82.1	5,663	13,404
3469	Metal stampings, n.e.c.	2,843	100.4	1,783	6,438	2,815	95.5	2,132		95.0	2,400	71.9	4,811	9,338
3519	Internal combustion engines, n.e.c.	253	79.6	1,979	9,363	278	64.0	2,043	11,123	56.3	1,909	38.9	4,677	11,516
3523	Farm machinery and equipment	1,903	96.1	2,067	10,743	1,634	57.0	1,416	6,880	65.1	1,787	45.4	5,268	10,347
3531	Construction machinery	939	115.5	2,653	11,658	955	81.2	2,429	12,773	81.0	2,563	52.8	5,509	13,351
3544	Special dies, tools, jigs, and fixtures	7,255	115.0	2,293	5,375	7,317	114.4	3,164	7,550	114.0	3,659	87.5	6,281	8,890
3559	Special industry machinery, n.e.c.	(NA)	(NA)	(NA)	(NA)	2,531	83.3	2,286	8,275	83.0	2,778	45.7	5,657	10,543
3571	Electronic computers	(NA)	(NA)	(NA)	(NA)	974	151.9	4,953	33,627	126.0	5,344	38.1	16,878	35,573
3585	Refrigeration and heating equipment	865	120.5	2,393	12,390	892	133.3	3,355	17,027	119.0	3,377	87.1	8,186	18,224
3599	Industrial machinery, n.e.c.	(NA)	(NA)	(NA)	(NA)	21,545	228.4	5,119	13,692	233.0	6,227	178.7	11,205	16,925
3621	Motors and generators	472	84.2	1,546	6,060	1,168	74.6	1,664	6,753	69.7	1,742	51.9	4,037	7,674
3625	Relays and industrial controls	(NA)	(NA)	(NA)	(NA)	469	66.6	1,631	6,101	61.2	1,799	35.3	4,289	7,379
3661	Telephone and telegraph apparatus	(NA)	(NA)	(NA)	(NA)	655	112.3	3,178	17,583	94.1	3,468	46.9	9,503	17,425
3663	Radio and TV communications equip.	(NA)	(NA)	(NA)	(NA)	853	126.0	3,776	14,229	123.4	4,395	53.7	10,339	18,165
3674	Semiconductors and related devices	766	166.5	3,785	12,430	2,900	184.6	5,495	19,795	175.0	6,491	86.2	20,152	29,668
3679	Electronic components, n.e.c.	(NA)	(NA)	(NA)	(NA)		162.6	3,891	15,439	165.4	4,531	101.6	9,513	19,450
3711	Motor vehicles and car bodies	355	240.1	6,822	70,740	413	284.4	10,376	133,346	218.1	9,803	178.5	25,147	133,861
3714	Motor vehicle parts and accessories	2,420	321.4	7,614	36,293	2,807	389.1	11,947	62,007	369.9	12,587	290.5	25,213	63,604
3721	Aircraft	165	275.1	7,744	28,024	155	268.2	9,680	39,093	258.3	10,324	125.3	23,091	58,090
3724	Aircraft engines and engine parts	340	130.7	3,544	13,809	453	139.6	4,814	20,262	122.3	4,822	67.3	12,278	22,746
3728	Aircraft parts and equipment, n.e.c.	966	132.8	3,429	10,193	1,013	187.7	6,088	17,923	187.3	6,740	107.5	13,678	21,544
3731	Ship building and repairing	689	166.7	3,738	10,967	590	120.2	3,218	8,504	120.8	3,680	90.1	6,354	10,849
3761	Guided missiles and space vehicles	29	99.6	3,159	10,219	40	166.7	6,415	21,586	135.8	6,026	45.0	13,551	23,399
3812	Search and navigation equipment	(NA)	(NA)	(NA)	(NA)	1,084	369.4	12,373	36,267	279.8	11,631	112.3	23,672	36,213
3825	Instruments to measure electricity	749	89.7	1,888	6,094	930	85.2	2,477	7,703	69.3	2,497	34.0	5,456	8,240
3841	Surgical and medical instruments	859	56.9	1,000	4,085	1,136	73.1	1,786	7,780	87.7	2,591	53.1	7,432	10,710
3842	Surgical appliances and supplies	1,367	68.8	1,211	5,667	1,500	78.5	1,786	8,533	93.3	2,510	60.6	8,044	12,555
3861	Photographic equipment and supplies	795	119.3	3,193	17,038	787	88.0	2,878	19,241	78.0	3,044	40.0	14,603	21,398

NA Not available.   [1] Represents the average of production workers plus all other employees for the payroll period ended nearest the 15th of the month.

Source: U.S. Bureau of the Census, 1987 Census of Manufactures and Annual Survey of Manufactures.

No. 1237. Manufactures Summary,

[Sum of State totals may not add to U.S. total

	DIVISION AND STATE	1982				1987				
		Establish-ments [1]	All employees [2]		Value of ship-ments [3] (mil. dol.)	Establish-ments [1]	All employees [2]		Value added by manu-facture [4] (mil. dol.)	Value of ship-ments [3] (mil. dol.)
			Num-ber (1,000)	Payroll (mil. dol.)			Num-ber (1,000)	Payroll (mil. dol.)		
1	U.S....	358,061	19,094	379,627	1,960,206	368,897	18,950	475,651	1,165,917	2,475,902
2	Northeast ..	91,102	4,798	95,919	400,767	88,287	4,357	112,222	259,074	483,748
3	N.E........	25,659	1,445	27,603	105,938	26,393	1,350	34,455	78,908	136,989
4	ME......	2,009	110	1,775	8,649	2,172	102	2,192	5,271	10,662
5	NH......	1,981	107	1,792	7,636	2,328	108	2,509	8,189	12,214
6	VT......	1,104	47	863	3,730	1,262	49	1,140	2,543	4,753
7	MA.....	11,017	643	12,353	48,204	11,006	591	15,211	35,770	62,794
8	RI......	2,855	114	1,760	7,652	2,878	112	2,292	4,788	9,166
9	CT......	6,693	424	9,060	30,067	6,747	389	11,111	22,349	37,400
10	M.A......	65,443	3,353	68,316	294,829	61,894	3,007	77,767	180,165	346,759
11	NY	32,651	1,419	29,156	121,469	29,608	1,279	33,916	80,033	145,657
12	NJ	15,126	754	15,845	70,420	14,442	691	18,550	42,527	82,451
13	PA	17,666	1,180	23,315	102,940	17,844	1,038	25,302	57,605	118,651
14	Midwest....	91,318	5,609	117,830	596,245	94,269	5,508	148,994	351,139	787,123
15	E.N.C......	67,378	4,337	92,400	440,702	69,756	4,186	116,148	266,248	590,487
16	OH......	16,960	1,102	24,740	112,278	17,544	1,100	30,765	71,707	158,560
17	IN.......	7,960	585	12,559	63,332	8,641	602	15,757	39,279	83,788
18	IL.......	18,618	1,069	22,681	112,929	18,404	990	26,235	63,350	132,204
19	MI	15,158	884	22,223	99,715	16,010	980	30,628	60,259	146,339
20	WI	8,682	497	10,197	52,448	9,157	514	12,763	31,653	69,596
21	W.N.C.....	23,940	1,272	25,430	155,543	24,513	1,322	32,846	84,891	196,637
22	MN......	6,775	350	7,423	35,321	7,112	374	10,142	23,152	47,604
23	IA.......	3,598	213	4,403	31,397	3,569	206	4,971	14,469	35,409
24	MO......	7,069	406	8,013	41,459	7,290	419	10,390	25,917	59,889
25	ND	587	15	246	2,465	627	15	310	979	2,574
26	SD	748	25	398	3,005	764	28	498	1,476	3,859
27	NE	1,928	92	1,624	15,143	1,876	91	1,938	5,819	16,076
28	KS	3,235	171	3,323	26,753	3,275	189	4,597	12,909	31,056
29	South	99,304	5,819	101,293	647,918	104,500	5,839	128,278	354,380	800,875
30	S.A........	48,855	2,930	48,588	256,625	53,478	3,104	66,893	179,075	373,181
31	DE	632	68	1,743	8,383	673	67	2,091	3,866	10,730
32	MD......	3,883	234	4,859	21,282	4,244	230	5,956	14,020	28,000
33	DC	514	17	394	1,537	486	17	494	1,525	2,128
34	VA	5,568	391	6,649	36,803	6,137	429	9,740	26,857	51,902
35	WV......	1,662	96	2,007	9,869	1,619	84	2,108	5,404	11,561
36	NC	10,133	799	11,717	64,176	10,995	842	16,293	47,007	95,317
37	SC	4,206	368	5,540	27,836	4,534	366	7,324	19,112	41,212
38	GA	8,534	503	7,906	48,056	9,187	570	11,933	33,708	75,709
39	FL	13,723	454	7,773	38,683	15,603	499	10,954	27,574	56,613
40	E.S.C.	18,573	1,241	20,132	119,698	19,718	1,303	26,524	74,296	164,862
41	KY	3,502	247	4,639	29,639	3,693	252	5,865	18,092	41,827
42	TN	6,417	462	7,378	40,777	6,864	485	9,869	27,050	57,753
43	AL	5,528	330	5,234	29,794	5,843	347	6,963	18,652	40,901
44	MS	3,126	202	2,881	19,488	3,318	219	3,827	10,503	24,381
45	W.S.C.	31,876	1,648	32,573	271,595	31,304	1,432	34,861	101,009	262,832
46	AR	3,313	190	2,824	19,747	3,390	206	3,815	10,827	25,308
47	LA	4,107	202	4,304	57,058	3,816	161	4,176	16,426	50,700
48	OK	4,168	197	4,010	23,116	3,728	151	3,629	9,857	24,074
49	TX	20,288	1,059	21,435	171,674	20,370	914	23,241	63,899	162,751
50	West	76,337	3,074	64,587	315,277	81,841	3,246	86,158	201,325	404,325
51	Mountain ...	14,854	556	10,863	56,997	16,479	596	14,689	35,822	73,554
52	MT	1,090	20	379	3,668	1,239	20	426	1,112	3,498
53	ID.......	1,404	48	865	5,370	1,491	53	1,149	3,057	7,005
54	WY	511	10	183	2,558	500	8	180	493	2,074
55	CO	4,406	192	3,983	17,963	4,718	184	4,958	12,046	23,236
56	NM	1,223	33	521	3,815	1,322	35	713	1,653	4,226
57	AZ	3,407	150	3,037	12,907	4,151	184	4,669	11,299	20,758
58	UT	1,962	83	1,539	8,960	2,083	89	2,073	4,883	10,287
59	NV	851	20	356	1,756	975	24	521	1,279	2,470
60	Pacific.....	61,483	2,518	53,724	258,280	65,362	2,650	71,469	165,503	330,771
61	WA	6,788	291	6,681	34,665	7,630	310	8,842	19,016	46,532
62	OR	5,659	185	3,783	17,897	6,353	203	4,767	11,610	25,352
63	CA	47,625	2,005	42,630	199,695	49,930	2,104	57,148	132,638	252,729
64	AK	445	13	270	2,580	427	11	272	834	2,711
65	HI.	966	24	360	3,443	1,022	22	440	1,405	3,448

[1] Includes central administrative offices and auxiliary units. [2] Includes employment and payroll at administrative offices and auxiliary units. *All employees* represents the average of production workers plus all other employees for the payroll period ended nearest the 12th of March. *Production workers* represents the average of the employment for the payroll periods ended nearest the 12th of March, May, August, and November.

by State: 1982 to 1991

because U.S. and State figures were independently derived]

	1990			1991				
	All employees [2]		Value of ship-ments [3] (mil. dol.)	All employees [2]		Value added by manu-facture [4] (mil. dol.)	Value of ship-ments [3] (mil. dol.)	
	Number (1,000)	Payroll (mil. dol.)		Number (1,000)	Payroll (mil. dol.)			
18,840	532,317	2,873,502	18,062	529,019	1,313,829	2,826,207	1
4,002	119,838	519,990	3,719	118,054	268,581	506,762	2
1,215	36,515	141,252	1,112	36,149	77,682	138,645	3
103	2,499	12,477	98	2,451	5,428	11,642	4
92	2,554	9,727	86	2,542	5,647	9,771	5
44	1,236	5,592	43	1,231	3,163	5,786	6
529	16,321	63,796	490	15,843	34,472	61,859	7
101	2,364	9,761	95	2,305	5,140	9,577	8
345	11,541	39,898	339	11,777	23,832	40,010	9
2,787	83,323	378,738	2,607	81,905	190,899	368,117	10
1,150	35,145	154,714	1,054	33,831	81,625	148,403	11
627	20,353	87,498	591	20,371	44,332	85,692	12
1,010	27,826	136,526	962	27,703	64,942	134,022	13
5,553	166,888	902,270	5,352	164,581	393,332	877,220	14
4,169	129,372	669,480	4,006	127,183	292,462	647,237	15
1,085	33,318	177,787	1,045	33,091	78,876	174,928	16
616	18,920	98,619	594	17,755	43,805	97,282	17
1,008	30,515	156,675	976	30,659	70,104	151,925	18
913	31,699	153,386	858	30,757	63,351	143,103	19
548	14,920	83,013	533	14,921	36,328	79,999	20
1,384	37,516	232,790	1,346	37,398	100,860	229,983	21
395	11,790	55,244	386	11,744	25,042	53,303	22
230	6,012	45,927	224	5,967	19,062	44,996	23
423	11,557	67,355	401	11,238	31,803	66,415	24
16	351	3,013	17	385	1,152	3,056	25
30	564	4,533	30	597	1,691	4,508	26
99	2,296	20,370	101	2,337	7,537	21,010	27
191	4,946	36,349	187	5,130	14,573	36,695	28
5,942	146,361	962,574	5,788	148,255	422,967	955,032	29
3,058	74,584	427,439	2,935	74,642	208,337	425,451	30
66	2,486	12,901	62	2,434	4,231	11,934	31
212	6,357	30,679	201	6,271	15,242	29,583	32
14	541	2,152	13	555	1,573	2,057	33
423	10,683	61,042	408	10,680	33,245	61,642	34
82	2,262	12,938	78	2,221	6,009	12,474	35
832	18,315	116,245	802	18,813	59,915	118,206	36
368	8,348	46,734	353	8,349	22,491	47,515	37
564	13,210	83,997	545	13,118	36,576	82,765	38
498	12,382	60,750	473	12,201	29,055	59,275	39
1,384	31,141	200,241	1,366	31,774	90,149	202,695	40
279	7,013	53,777	273	7,001	23,714	53,500	41
504	11,407	67,404	493	11,711	32,499	69,549	42
368	8,194	48,748	363	8,287	21,056	48,449	43
233	4,527	30,313	237	4,775	12,880	31,197	44
1,500	40,636	334,894	1,487	41,839	124,481	326,886	45
219	4,359	30,493	220	4,471	12,826	31,084	46
171	4,812	65,807	175	5,005	22,126	63,382	47
168	4,482	28,010	169	4,637	11,959	28,418	48
943	26,983	210,584	923	27,726	77,570	204,002	49
3,343	99,230	488,669	3,167	98,133	229,029	487,195	50
619	17,039	88,989	610	17,311	43,251	91,468	51
20	450	4,040	20	479	1,093	3,767	52
61	1,508	9,184	61	1,607	3,895	9,810	53
10	248	2,756	10	251	925	2,733	54
180	5,528	27,701	176	5,647	13,704	26,825	55
40	862	5,548	41	927	3,931	8,037	56
181	5,321	22,886	174	5,171	11,551	22,983	57
102	2,494	13,950	102	2,592	6,689	14,492	58
26	628	2,925	26	637	1,463	2,821	59
2,724	82,192	399,680	2,557	80,822	185,778	395,727	60
367	11,344	67,538	354	11,801	24,852	67,978	61
216	5,657	31,073	208	5,644	13,344	30,692	62
2,106	64,352	293,190	1,962	62,521	144,908	289,613	63
14	362	3,676	14	390	1,291	3,639	64
21	477	4,203	19	466	1,383	3,805	65

[3] For definition, see footnote 8, table 1234.   [4] See footnote 7, table 1234.

Source: U.S. Bureau of the Census, *1982* and *1987 Census of Manufactures* and *Annual Survey of Manufactures*.

No. 1238. Average Hourly Earnings of Production Workers in Manufacturing Industries, by State: 1980 to 1993

[In dollars]

DIVISION AND STATE	1980	1985	1987	1988	1989	1990	1991	1992	1993
United States	7.27	9.54	9.91	10.19	10.48	10.83	11.18	11.46	11.76
New England:									
Maine	6.00	8.40	8.77	9.31	9.92	10.59	11.08	11.40	(NA)
New Hampshire	5.87	8.39	9.29	9.97	10.37	10.83	10.84	11.22	11.61
Vermont	6.14	8.41	9.12	9.47	9.99	10.52	11.00	11.52	11.81
Massachusetts	6.51	9.00	9.77	10.40	10.87	11.39	11.81	12.15	12.36
Rhode Island	5.59	7.59	8.20	8.64	9.06	9.45	9.73	9.92	10.22
Connecticut	7.08	9.57	10.46	10.78	11.21	11.53	11.99	12.46	13.01
Middle Atlantic:									
New York	7.18	9.67	10.09	10.43	10.67	11.11	11.43	11.72	11.97
New Jersey	7.31	9.86	10.40	10.86	11.17	11.76	12.17	12.57	12.98
Pennsylvania	7.59	9.57	9.98	10.33	10.66	11.04	11.46	11.78	12.09
East North Central:									
Ohio	8.57	11.38	11.73	12.00	12.26	12.64	13.12	13.49	14.05
Indiana	8.49	(NA)	(NA)	(NA)	11.70	12.03	12.43	12.79	13.17
Illinois	8.02	10.37	10.85	10.98	11.21	11.44	11.68	11.84	12.04
Michigan	9.52	12.64	12.97	13.31	13.51	13.86	14.52	14.81	15.36
Wisconsin	8.03	10.26	10.55	10.61	10.77	11.11	11.47	11.85	12.17
West North Central:									
Minnesota	7.61	10.05	10.37	10.59	10.95	11.23	11.52	11.92	12.23
Iowa	8.67	10.32	10.62	10.56	10.82	11.27	11.62	11.92	12.22
Missouri	7.26	9.57	10.00	10.24	10.49	10.74	10.86	11.24	11.54
North Dakota	6.56	8.05	8.43	8.36	8.80	9.27	9.25	9.60	9.87
South Dakota	6.50	7.43	7.92	8.09	8.30	8.48	8.79	8.84	8.89
Nebraska	7.38	9.02	9.33	9.38	9.53	9.66	9.84	10.22	10.46
Kansas	7.37	9.45	9.97	10.24	10.68	10.94	11.24	11.60	11.99
South Atlantic:									
Delaware	7.58	9.86	10.67	11.49	12.36	12.39	12.20	12.35	13.31
Maryland	7.61	9.73	10.11	10.71	11.19	11.57	11.92	12.50	12.83
District of Columbia	8.46	10.48	10.73	11.10	11.79	12.51	13.05	13.17	13.18
Virginia	6.22	8.51	9.14	9.37	9.69	10.07	10.43	10.62	10.85
West Virginia	8.08	10.24	10.55	10.81	11.17	11.53	11.77	12.11	12.27
North Carolina	5.37	7.29	7.84	8.12	8.42	8.79	9.19	9.49	9.80
South Carolina	5.59	7.61	8.10	8.30	8.54	8.84	9.17	9.48	9.80
Georgia	5.77	8.10	8.49	8.65	8.87	9.17	9.56	9.86	10.08
Florida	5.98	7.86	8.16	8.39	8.67	8.98	9.30	9.59	9.76
East South Central:									
Kentucky	7.34	9.53	10.02	10.16	10.37	10.70	11.00	11.28	11.48
Tennessee	6.08	8.29	8.78	8.96	9.22	9.55	9.92	10.13	10.33
Alabama	6.49	8.48	8.76	8.95	9.10	9.39	9.72	9.99	10.36
Mississippi	5.44	7.22	7.59	7.83	8.03	8.37	8.67	8.91	9.16
West South Central:									
Arkansas	5.71	7.57	7.88	8.07	8.26	8.51	8.81	9.05	9.36
Louisiana	7.74	10.43	10.90	10.94	11.13	11.41	11.86	12.19	12.66
Oklahoma	7.36	9.86	10.14	10.35	10.48	10.73	11.09	11.38	11.41
Texas	7.15	9.41	9.85	9.97	10.25	10.47	10.84	10.92	11.02
Mountain:									
Montana	8.78	10.95	10.61	10.68	11.15	11.51	11.57	12.18	12.38
Idaho	7.55	9.41	9.75	10.00	10.21	10.60	11.11	11.42	11.88
Wyoming	7.01	9.64	9.75	10.27	10.58	10.83	10.98	11.10	11.54
Colorado	7.63	9.52	10.05	10.38	10.44	10.94	11.33	11.32	12.02
New Mexico	5.79	8.41	8.74	8.87	8.74	9.04	9.40	9.68	9.74
Arizona	7.29	9.48	9.97	9.85	9.92	10.21	10.70	10.96	11.07
Utah	7.02	9.64	9.96	10.11	10.14	10.32	10.77	11.09	11.10
Nevada	7.72	9.15	9.76	10.08	10.33	11.05	11.04	11.55	11.65
Pacific:									
Washington	(NA)	11.63	11.73	11.90	12.12	12.61	13.13	13.59	13.97
Oregon	8.65	10.50	10.56	10.60	10.81	11.15	11.53	11.97	12.18
California	7.70	10.12	10.75	10.80	11.16	11.48	11.87	12.19	12.37
Alaska	10.22	12.19	11.79	11.98	12.01	12.46	11.40	10.75	11.14
Hawaii	6.83	8.65	9.30	9.84	10.37	10.99	11.39	11.61	11.98

NA Not available.

Source: U.S. Bureau of Labor Statistics, *Employment and Earnings*, monthly.

No. 1239. Industrial Production Indexes, by Industry: 1970 to 1993

[1987 = 100. Beginning 1988, data based on 1987 Standard Industrial Classification (SIC), earlier years based on 1977 SIC; see text, section 27. See also *Historical Statistics, Colonial Times to 1970*, series P 13 and P 18-39]

SIC code	INDUSTRY	1970	1975	1980	1985	1986	1988	1989	1990	1991	1992	1993
(X)	Total index	61.4	66.3	84.1	94.4	95.3	104.4	106.0	106.0	104.1	106.5	110.9
(X)	**Manufacturing**	56.4	61.1	78.8	91.6	94.3	104.7	106.4	106.1	103.7	106.8	111.7
(X)	**Durable goods**	53.3	56.7	75.7	91.8	93.9	106.6	108.6	107.4	103.9	107.0	114.3
24	Lumber and products	66.7	66.5	76.9	88.0	95.1	100.1	99.4	97.1	90.6	96.5	100.6
25	Furniture and fixtures	55.6	59.4	78.5	88.1	92.5	100.3	101.6	100.1	94.1	97.2	103.2
32	Stone, clay, and glass products ..	71.1	77.8	92.0	93.6	97.1	102.6	102.5	100.3	92.6	95.1	98.6
33	Primary metals	115.2	107.2	110.8	101.8	93.7	108.7	107.2	106.5	98.3	101.7	106.4
34	Fabricated metal products	75.9	76.7	92.5	94.5	93.8	104.2	102.8	99.5	94.9	95.6	99.5
35	Industrial, commercial machinery [1]	32.8	38.1	60.6	86.8	90.3	113.0	117.3	117.6	113.8	123.4	144.1
36	Electrical machinery	40.5	45.1	73.3	93.1	94.3	108.5	111.0	111.4	112.7	115.7	127.5
37	Transportation equipment	55.5	59.7	72.3	91.8	96.9	105.2	109.6	107.0	101.9	102.8	104.2
38	Instruments	38.8	52.4	78.8	95.7	95.1	103.6	104.6	104.9	105.3	105.0	104.0
(X)	**Nondurable goods**	61.1	67.7	83.1	91.5	94.9	102.3	103.7	104.4	103.5	106.5	108.6
20	Foods	64.0	71.4	84.6	94.9	97.4	101.5	102.5	103.7	105.3	107.7	108.6
21	Tobacco products	90.6	97.8	103.6	97.3	95.8	101.8	100.7	100.8	96.3	99.3	91.7
22	Textile mill products	74.4	77.7	92.1	89.7	93.9	98.6	100.3	97.1	96.8	105.6	107.6
26	Paper and products	62.9	65.9	83.1	92.2	97.1	103.1	105.0	105.6	106.2	108.7	112.3
27	Printing and publishing	52.7	53.7	70.3	87.6	90.6	100.9	101.1	100.8	96.9	99.0	101.3
28	Chemicals and products	55.9	69.1	87.8	91.4	94.6	106.0	109.2	111.8	117.4	114.3	117.7
29	Petroleum products	83.9	91.5	99.0	92.6	98.9	101.9	102.3	103.3	101.6	102.7	105.0
30	Rubber and plastics products ..	37.6	47.4	61.7	85.8	90.8	102.6	106.0	107.2	104.5	110.8	115.9
31	Leather and products	208.0	182.5	161.7	112.5	102.6	99.8	99.6	96.0	87.9	86.8	85.0
(X)	**Mining**	100.4	98.0	110.0	109.0	101.0	101.3	100.0	102.0	100.1	98.2	97.2
(X)	**Utilities**	72.9	84.3	95.9	99.5	96.3	105.0	108.7	109.9	112.3	112.0	116.3

X Not applicable. [1] Includes computer equipment.
Source: Board of Governors of the Federal Reserve System, *Federal Reserve Bulletin*, monthly.

No. 1240. Index of Manufacturing Capacity: 1950 to 1993

[1987 output = 100. Annual figures are averages of quarterly data. Capacity represents estimated quantity of output relative to output in 1967 which the *current* stock of plant and equipment in manufacturing industries was capable of producing. Primary processing industries comprise textiles, lumber, paper and pulp, petroleum, rubber, stone, clay, glass, primary metals, fabricated metals, and a portion of chemicals. Advanced processing industries comprise chemical products, food, beverages, tobacco, apparel, furniture, printing and publishing, leather, machinery, transportation equipment, instruments, ordnance, and miscellaneous industry groups]

YEAR	Index of capacity	RELATION OF OUTPUT TO CAPACITY (percent)			YEAR	Index of capacity	RELATION OF OUTPUT TO CAPACITY (percent)		
		All manu-facturing	Primary pro-cessing	Advanced pro-cessing			All manu-facturing	Primary pro-cessing	Advanced pro-cessing
1950........	29	83	88	80	1984........	114	80	80	80
1955........	36	87	92	84	1985........	117	80	80	79
1960........	44	80	80	80	1986........	120	79	81	78
1965........	54	90	91	89	1987........	123	82	85	80
1970........	71	80	80	79	1988........	125	84	87	82
1975........	84	73	73	74	1989........	127	83	86	82
1980........	102	80	78	81	1990........	129	81	84	80
1981........	106	79	78	79	1991........	132	78	80	77
1982........	109	73	69	75	1992........	134	79	82	79
1983........	112	75	75	75	1993........	136	80	84	79

Source: Board of Governors of the Federal Reserve System, *Capacity Utilization In Manufacturing, Mining, Utilities, and Industrial Materials*, G.3., monthly. (Based on data from Federal Reserve Board, Commerce, U.S. Bureau of Labor Statistics, and McGraw-Hill Information Systems Company, New York, NY, and other sources.)

No. 1241. Finances of Manufacturing Corporations: 1970 to 1992

[In billions of dollars. Beginning 1986, data exclude estimates for corporations with less than $250,000 in assets at time of sample selection. Prior years include estimates for corporations in this size category. See table 876 for individual industry data]

ITEM	1970	1980	1982	1983	1984	1985	1986	1987	1988	1989	1990	1991	1992
Net sales	709	1,897	2,039	2,114	2,335	2,331	2,221	2,378	2,596	2,745	2,811	2,761	2,890
Net operating profit	50	129	105	125	159	138	125	159	190	182	173	133	151
Net profit:													
Before taxes	48	145	108	133	166	137	129	173	216	189	160	100	34
After taxes	29	92	71	86	108	88	83	116	155	136	112	68	24
Cash dividends	15	36	41	42	45	46	46	50	57	65	62	60	63
Net income retained in business.	14	58	30	44	63	42	37	66	98	71	49	7	-39

Source: Through 1980, U.S. Federal Trade Commission; thereafter, U.S. Bureau of the Census, *Quarterly Financial Report for Manufacturing, Mining, and Trade Corporations.*

No. 1242. Capital in Manufacturing Establishments: 1980 to 1992

[In billions of dollars, except percent. Data refer to privately owned manufacturing establishments and are based on the capital expenditures data from the Census of Manufactures, the *Annual Survey of Manufactures,* and the inventory investment component of GNP. For details, see source]

ITEM	CURRENT DOLLARS						CONSTANT (1987) DOLLARS					
	1980	1985	1989	1990	1991	1992	1980	1985	1989	1990	1991	1992
Purchases of equipment and structures	79.5	97.7	121.0	128.2	127.7	128.5	102.7	102.1	114.0	118.4	116.4	118.7
Percent equipment	70.5	65.3	68.1	65.9	68.0	70.1	68.6	64.6	68.6	66.8	68.8	71.4
Depreciation (straight line) [1]	54.0	77.5	95.9	101.4	106.1	109.8	71.8	82.7	90.4	93.3	96.1	99.0
Percent equipment	76.4	74.3	73.2	73.0	73.1	73.2	75.5	74.1	73.7	73.6	73.6	73.7
Net investment [2]	25.5	20.2	25.1	26.8	21.6	18.7	30.9	19.4	23.6	25.1	20.3	19.7
Net stock, end of year [1]	976.2	1,237.5	1,498.0	1,576.4	1,599.4	1,626.0	1,221.6	1,285.3	1,372.5	1,402.6	1,418.8	1,435.6
Equipment and structures	666.4	897.7	1,088.3	1,152.7	1,192.1	1,225.1	860.4	949.5	998.7	1,025.7	1,048.2	1,069.7
Percent equipment	62.0	57.7	56.5	56.6	56.7	56.4	61.3	57.8	56.8	56.5	56.4	56.5
Inventories	309.8	339.9	409.7	423.7	407.3	400.9	361.2	335.7	373.9	376.9	370.6	365.9

[1] Depreciation and net stock estimates for equipment and structures are derived using the perpetual inventory method and the straight-line depreciation formula. [2] Represents the difference between purchases and depreciation.

Source: U.S. Bureau of Economic Analysis, *The National Income and Product Accounts of the United States,* volume 2, 1959-88, *Fixed Reproducible Tangible Wealth in the United States, 1925-89,* and *Survey of Current Business,* August and September 1993.

No. 1243. U.S. Share of World Exports of Manufactures: 1980 to 1992

[World exports = exports from the 15 major trading countries: United States, Austria, Belgium-Luxembourg, Canada, Denmark, France, Germany, Italy, Japan, Netherlands, Norway, Sweden, Switzerland, and United Kingdom. Percents are calculated from the values of exports (which are based on current exchange rates) of the 5 commodity groups from each of the 15 countries. Details are reported according to the United Nations Standard International Trade Classification (SITC)]

COMMODITY	TOTAL (bil. dol.)						PERCENT OF WORLD EXPORTS					
	1980	1985	1989	1990	1991	1992	1980	1985	1989	1990	1991	1992
Total [1]	147.2	150.7	275.0	300.3	328.0	349.7	16.8	16.7	17.1	16.3	17.2	17.4
Machinery	57.1	62.7	112.2	119.7	129.8	138.7	21.4	21.4	20.6	20.2	20.0	20.2
Transport equipment	28.9	35.2	55.2	62.9	70.3	76.7	18.3	18.7	17.9	17.6	18.6	18.6
Chemicals	20.8	21.5	38.0	39.5	43.4	44.6	17.9	17.9	18.0	16.6	17.4	16.8
Basic manufactures [2]	23.3	15.0	31.6	33.9	37.8	38.3	10.1	7.9	9.6	9.3	10.4	10.2
Misc. articles [3]	17.0	16.3	38.1	43.1	46.7	51.3	16.0	14.6	17.8	16.8	17.6	18.1

[1] Represents manufactures exports. Excludes mineral fuel products, processed food, fats, oils, firearms of war, and ammunition. [2] Includes semimanufactures of various materials, such as metals, fibers, wood, glass, leather, rubber, and certain finished products of metal. [3] Includes mainly nondurable consumer goods and professional and scientific instruments.

Source: U.S. Dept. of Commerce, International Trade Administration, Office of Trade and Investment Analysis, *Business America,* biweekly; *Market Share Reports,* annual; and unpublished data.

No. 1244. Foreign Direct Investment Position in the United States—Manufacturing: 1991 and 1992

[In millions of dollars. Book value at year end. Covers U.S. firms in which foreign interest or ownership was 10% or more. Minus sign (-) indicates a negative position]

AREA OR COUNTRY	TOTAL [1]		FOOD AND KINDRED PRODUCTS		CHEMICALS AND ALLIED PRODUCTS		PRIMARY AND FABRICATED METALS		MACHINERY	
	1991	1992	1991	1992	1991	1992	1991	1992	1991	1992
All countries [2]	156,586	159,492	23,773	25,898	48,414	50,255	13,164	13,182	28,584	26,381
Canada	16,066	17,313	(D)	(D)	(D)	(D)	1,851	1,840	1,969	2,492
Europe [2]	113,365	113,595	15,237	16,999	42,873	44,218	8,610	8,719	19,994	17,321
France	15,053	14,121	1,362	1,445	4,481	4,321	2,905	2,642	2,723	2,280
Germany	15,466	15,050	-69	-84	8,543	8,495	816	931	3,304	3,039
Netherlands	18,267	21,442	2,368	3,994	7,463	8,581	1,142	1,308	4,614	4,147
United Kingdom	42,259	42,208	8,699	8,540	14,721	16,177	1,818	1,731	3,241	2,471
Sweden	5,189	4,981	-	1	898	1,069	137	173	2,623	2,293
Switzerland	10,927	11,124	2,445	2,438	3,390	3,919	539	691	3,117	2,745
Africa	(D)	(D)	3	3	(D)	(D)	1	-12	8	-2
Latin America	4,639	5,784	310	113	628	1,364	86	-47	-62	-114
Middle East	(D)	(D)	-	-	(D)	(D)	-	-	81	75
Asia and Pacific [2]	22,171	22,461	(D)	(D)	(D)	(D)	2,616	2,682	6,594	6,609
Japan	18,545	19,149	892	943	3,415	3,343	1,656	1,781	5,699	5,805

- Represents or rounds to zero. D Data withheld to avoid disclosure of individual companies. [1] Includes other manufacturing industries not shown separately. [2] Includes other countries not shown separately.

Source: U.S. Bureau of Economic Analysis, *Survey of Current Business,* July 1993.

No. 1245. Employment Related to Manufactured Exports, by Industry: 1980 to 1989

[Total employment related to manufactured exports is the sum of employment directly calculated for the plants shipping the exported product, the supplying industries and service organizations, and the central offices and auxiliaries. For manufacturing industries, employment is limited to paid employees in manufacturing plants, while for nonmanufacturing it includes an estimate for working proprietors and partners]

INDUSTRY	EMPLOYMENT RELATED TO MANUFACTURED EXPORTS						CIVILIAN EMPLOYMENT (1,000)		
	Employees (1,000)			Percent of civilian employment					
	1980	1985	1989	1980	1985	1989	1980	1985	1989
Total	**4,808**	**4,413**	**6,022**	**4.8**	**4.0**	**5.1**	**100,260**	**110,136**	**118,744**
Manufacturing	2,639	2,295	2,949	12.8	12.2	15.5	20,647	18,788	19,042
Nonmanufacturing	2,170	2,118	3,073	2.7	2.3	3.1	79,613	91,348	99,702
Trade	845	949	1,385	4.3	4.3	5.9	19,737	21,999	23,553
Business services	575	227	425	3.3	1.1	1.7	17,245	21,139	24,843
Transportation [1]	305	282	443	4.8	4.6	6.9	6,369	6,155	6,435
Agriculture	144	127	131	4.5	3.7	3.9	3,225	3,423	3,387
Mining	69	50	83	7.3	4.9	11.3	947	1,016	733
Other	233	483	606	0.7	1.3	1.5	32,090	37,616	40,751

[1] Includes communications and utilities.

No. 1246. Manufacturing Establishments—Export-Related Shipments and Employment, 1977 to 1989, and by Industry, 1989

[The export-related employment data do not include the jobs involved in the export of nonmanufactured goods and various services sold to foreign buyers. Thus, jobs in the manufacturing sector that relate to the export of nonmanufactured goods are excluded from the estimates. In addition, all of the indirect exports being reported are domestically produced; that is, they exclude imports. See source for further details on methodology]

SIC [1] code	INDUSTRY	MANUFACTURER'S SHIPMENT VALUE				MANUFACTURING EMPLOYMENT			
		Total [2] (bil. dol.)	Export related		Export related as percent of shipments	Total (1,000)	Export related		Export related as percent of total employment
			Total (bil. dol.)	Direct exports [3] (bil. dol.)			Total (1,000)	Direct exports [4] (1,000)	
(X)	1977	1,358.4	142.4	85.8	10.4	19,590	1,990	1,106	10.2
(X)	1980	1,852.7	249.8	151.2	13.5	20,647	2,639	1,486	12.8
(X)	1981	2,017.5	271.7	164.3	13.4	20,264	2,604	1,486	12.9
(X)	1983	2,055.3	246.4	141.6	12.0	18,737	2,173	1,118	11.6
(X)	1984	2,253.8	268.3	151.0	11.9	19,141	2,179	1,083	11.4
(X)	1985	2,278.9	286.7	156.9	12.6	18,788	2,295	1,083	12.2
(X)	1986	2,260.3	294.3	159.4	13.0	18,371	2,318	1,061	12.6
(X)	1987	2,475.9	378.8	193.6	15.3	18,900	2,771	1,185	14.7
(X)	1988	2,684.7	395.3	242.9	14.7	19,147	2,638	1,412	13.8
(X)	**1989, total . . . .**	**2,793.0**	**460.5**	**287.4**	**16.5**	**19,042**	**2,948**	**1,610**	**15.5**
20	Food and kindred products	364.4	23.5	18.1	6.5	1,459	79	62	5.4
21	Tobacco products	25.8	5.6	4.9	21.8	43	12	10	27.8
22	Textile mill products	67.3	7.4	3.2	10.9	653	66	26	10.1
23	Apparel, other textile products . . .	63.4	3.8	2.6	5.9	1,018	44	28	4.4
24	Lumber and wood products. . . .	74.3	12.2	6.0	16.4	686	88	37	12.8
25	Furniture and fixtures	41.2	1.5	1.0	3.8	508	15	9	3.0
26	Paper and allied products	131.4	17.5	7.6	13.3	630	74	26	11.8
27	Printing and publishing	149.9	11.0	2.7	7.4	1,504	111	22	7.4
28	Chemical and allied products. . . .	278.1	58.0	39.3	20.8	848	169	116	19.9
29	Petroleum and coal products. . . .	143.7	14.7	4.8	10.2	112	10	10	9.2
30	Rubber, misc. plastics products . .	98.4	15.0	5.1	15.2	877	133	43	15.2
31	Leather, leather products	9.9	1.5	1.3	15.4	120	10	9	8.5
32	Stone, clay, glass products	63.6	5.2	2.6	8.2	520	41	20	7.9
33	Primary metal industries	153.0	38.6	9.8	25.2	727	178	38	24.4
34	Fabricated metal products	162.2	22.8	8.3	14.4	1,469	210	72	14.3
35	Machinery, except electric	253.6	69.0	52.0	27.2	1,913	475	336	24.8
36	Electric, electronic equipment . . .	192.6	52.1	33.2	27.1	1,551	435	269	28.0
37	Transportation equipment	366.0	74.8	62.7	20.4	1,805	364	295	20.2
38	Instruments and related products .	118.5	21.6	18.2	18.3	968	182	154	18.8
39	Misc. manufacturing.	35.8	4.8	4.1	13.3	386	42	34	11.0
(X)	Administrative and auxiliary	(X)	(X)	(X)	(X)	1,246	211	(X)	16.9

X Not applicable.   [1] Standard Industrial Classification; see text, section 13.   [2] Includes total domestic and export shipments for all manufacturing establishments.   [3] Includes only the value of manufactured products exported by the producing plants.   [4] Employment is limited to paid employees in manufacturing plants producing the export product. The number of employees related to export shipments was calculated for each establishment, aggregated by industry and by States, and inflated to a level comparable to the plant value of exports reported in the official foreign trade statistics at port value.

Source of tables 1245 and 1246: U.S. Bureau of the Census, *1977* and *1987 Census of Manufactures* and *Annual Survey of Manufactures*.

No. 1247. Export-Related Shipments and Employment of Manufacturing Establishments, by State: 1989

[Export-related figures exclude jobs in the manufacturing sector that are involved in the export of nonmanufactured goods and various services sold to foreign buyers. In addition, all of the indirect exports being reported are domestically produced, that is they exclude imports. Includes central administration and auxiliary office employees]

REGION, DIVISION, AND STATE	MANUFACTURES SHIPMENT VALUE					MANUFACTURING EMPLOYMENT				
	Total (bil. dol.)	Export related			Export related shipments, percent of total	Total (1,000)	Export related			Export related employment, percent of total
		Total (bil. dol.)	Direct exports (bil. dol.)	Supporting exports (bil. dol.)			Total (1,000)	Direct exports (1,000)	Supporting exports (1,000)	
United States	2,793.2	460.8	287.9	173.3	16.5	19,041.2	2,948.7	1,610.7	1,338.0	15.5
Northeast	517.4	83.6	51.7	32.0	16.2	4,168.9	667.2	357.9	309.3	16.0
New England	141.5	28.5	19.2	9.3	20.1	1,265.1	242.9	146.2	96.7	19.2
Maine	12.5	2.1	1.1	1.0	17.1	106.4	15.2	8.0	7.2	14.3
New Hampshire	10.2	1.9	1.2	0.7	18.6	97.8	16.7	8.6	8.1	17.1
Vermont	5.4	1.4	0.9	0.5	24.9	46.6	9.9	6.2	3.7	21.2
Massachusetts	65.2	13.0	9.0	4.0	19.9	561.5	110.0	66.9	43.1	19.6
Rhode Island	9.7	1.7	1.0	0.7	17.0	104.0	18.9	11.7	7.2	18.2
Connecticut	38.5	8.4	6.0	2.4	21.8	348.8	72.2	44.8	27.4	20.7
Middle Atlantic	375.9	55.1	32.5	22.7	14.7	2,903.8	424.3	211.7	212.6	14.6
New York	155.3	25.2	16.6	8.7	16.2	1,207.5	181.6	102.1	79.5	15.0
New Jersey	88.0	10.9	6.1	4.8	12.4	657.9	92.3	39.6	52.7	14.0
Pennsylvania	132.6	19.0	9.8	9.2	14.4	1,038.4	150.4	70.0	80.4	14.5
Midwest	889.2	135.7	83.2	52.6	15.3	5,600.7	857.5	434.1	423.4	15.3
East North Central	664.4	104.8	62.7	42.0	15.8	4,231.5	671.6	333.6	338.0	15.9
Ohio	176.5	30.8	18.8	12.0	17.4	1,100.2	184.7	93.9	90.8	16.8
Indiana	98.0	16.0	8.8	7.2	16.3	626.6	96.8	48.7	48.1	15.4
Illinois	152.0	23.7	13.8	9.8	15.6	1,033.4	158.8	76.5	82.3	15.4
Michigan	156.9	23.7	15.1	8.6	15.1	929.7	154.8	77.2	77.6	16.7
Wisconsin	81.0	10.6	6.2	4.4	13.1	541.6	76.5	37.3	39.2	14.1
West North Central	224.8	30.9	20.5	10.6	13.7	1,369.2	185.9	100.5	85.4	13.6
Minnesota	53.6	8.6	5.7	2.9	16.0	391.4	62.9	33.7	29.2	16.1
Iowa	42.9	5.7	3.8	1.9	13.3	225.3	28.7	16.9	11.8	12.7
Missouri	68.3	9.5	6.2	3.3	13.9	426.0	53.6	26.5	27.1	12.6
North Dakota	2.9	0.5	0.4	0.1	15.9	15.2	1.6	1.0	0.6	10.5
South Dakota	4.4	0.4	0.3	0.2	10.1	28.8	3.3	1.8	1.5	11.5
Nebraska	18.7	1.9	1.2	0.7	10.3	93.8	10.5	5.5	5.0	11.2
Kansas	34.0	4.3	2.9	1.5	12.8	188.7	25.3	15.1	10.2	13.4
South	925.6	144.7	85.4	59.1	15.6	5,924.1	788.1	417.2	370.9	13.3
South Atlantic	419.4	63.4	38.8	24.6	15.1	3,088.3	397.8	206.7	191.1	12.9
Delaware	12.4	1.2	0.6	0.6	9.6	67.9	9.7	2.6	7.1	14.3
Maryland	31.3	4.8	3.0	1.8	15.3	226.2	31.9	17.5	14.4	14.1
District of Columbia	2.2	0.2	0.1	0.1	10.0	14.4	1.3	0.4	0.9	9.0
Virginia	59.4	8.8	5.6	3.2	14.8	424.9	49.1	24.5	24.6	11.6
West Virginia	13.1	2.8	1.5	1.3	21.0	83.2	13.3	5.7	7.6	16.0
North Carolina	113.6	16.7	9.7	7.0	14.7	836.3	102.4	51.7	50.7	12.2
South Carolina	46.5	8.5	5.1	3.4	18.3	370.7	55.5	30.4	25.1	15.0
Georgia	82.8	10.6	6.3	4.3	12.8	568.1	62.0	30.4	31.6	10.9
Florida	58.1	9.8	6.9	2.9	16.9	496.6	72.6	43.5	29.1	14.6
East South Central	192.8	27.8	15.5	12.3	14.4	1,360.8	163.7	82.9	80.8	12.0
Kentucky	49.4	6.9	3.9	3.0	13.9	270.4	34.5	16.4	18.1	12.8
Tennessee	67.0	9.1	5.2	3.9	13.5	499.6	58.6	30.6	28.0	11.7
Alabama	47.2	7.5	3.8	3.7	15.9	364.4	46.9	23.4	23.5	12.9
Mississippi	29.2	4.3	2.6	1.7	14.7	226.4	23.7	12.5	11.2	10.5
West South Central	313.4	53.5	31.1	22.2	17.1	1,475.0	226.6	127.6	99.0	15.4
Arkansas	29.7	3.9	2.1	1.8	13.2	214.4	26.0	13.5	12.5	12.1
Louisiana	59.8	9.4	5.0	4.3	15.6	166.5	19.8	9.5	10.3	11.9
Oklahoma	27.7	3.2	1.6	1.6	11.4	162.1	19.3	9.3	10.0	11.9
Texas	196.2	37.0	22.4	14.5	18.8	932.0	161.5	95.3	66.2	17.3
West	461.0	96.8	67.6	29.6	21.0	3,347.5	635.9	401.5	234.4	19.0
Mountain	84.7	14.4	8.5	6.1	17.0	610.0	99.3	56.1	43.2	16.3
Montana	3.9	0.6	0.2	0.4	15.6	20.7	2.5	0.6	1.9	12.1
Idaho	9.0	1.6	1.0	0.6	17.8	58.1	9.4	5.2	4.2	16.2
Wyoming	2.5	0.2	0.1	0.2	9.4	8.9	0.9	0.3	0.6	10.1
Colorado	26.6	4.0	2.6	1.4	15.1	183.9	29.8	18.5	11.3	16.2
New Mexico	5.2	0.8	0.4	0.5	15.6	38.8	6.0	3.8	2.2	15.5
Arizona	22.3	4.8	2.9	1.9	21.5	180.2	34.4	19.2	15.2	19.1
Utah	12.6	2.0	1.1	0.9	15.7	96.0	13.6	7.2	6.4	14.2
Nevada	2.6	0.4	0.2	0.2	13.2	23.4	2.7	1.3	1.4	11.5
Pacific	376.3	82.4	59.1	23.5	21.9	2,737.5	536.6	345.4	191.2	19.6
Washington	59.4	23.2	20.1	3.1	39.1	361.6	107.7	84.5	23.2	29.8
Oregon	30.8	6.0	3.6	2.5	19.5	217.7	39.4	22.6	16.8	18.1
California	279.2	51.2	33.6	17.6	18.3	2,126.3	380.8	230.7	150.1	17.9
Alaska	3.1	1.5	1.4	0.1	21.5	11.4	6.0	5.6	0.4	52.6
Hawaii	3.8	0.5	0.4	0.2	14.0	20.5	2.7	2.0	0.7	13.2

Source: U.S. Bureau of the Census, *Exports from Manufacturing Establishments* AR89-1.

No. 1248. Manufacturing Technology—Percent of Establishments Using and Planning to Use: 1988

ESTABLISHMENT CHARACTERISTIC	Computer aided design (CAD) or computer aided engineering	Numerically controlled machines	Automated material handling	Automated sensor based inspection or testing	Programmable controllers	Computer control on factory floor	LAN [1] For technical data	LAN [1] For factory use	Inter-company computer network	Design and engineering	Fabrication/machining, assembly	Automated material handling	Automated sensor based inspection or testing	Communication and control
	ESTABLISHMENTS USING SELECTED TECHNOLOGIES					Communication and control				PLANNING TO USE WITHIN 2 YEARS				
Major SIC [2] group:														
34, Fabricated metal products	26.8	32.2	1.8	15.0	26.8	21.1	13.4	11.6	14.9	20.4	14.7	1.3	6.5	38.8
35, Industrial mach. and equip.	43.2	56.7	5.3	18.4	33.9	28.1	18.5	16.3	12.4	30.8	14.9	2.6	8.2	40.3
36, Electronic and other	48.5	34.9	6.7	38.4	38.0	34.5	24.9	21.1	16.2	26.6	21.9	3.3	12.0	49.5
37, Transportation equip.	39.9	37.3	8.0	27.1	32.0	27.4	22.0	18.7	21.7	25.8	20.2	3.5	7.1	36.3
38, Instruments, related prod.	48.9	33.6	5.5	27.6	32.7	32.3	25.8	21.3	13.8	29.7	19.4	2.5	12.0	45.4
Employment size:														
20 to 99	29.8	35.9	1.7	13.8	22.5	18.9	13.1	11.0	9.7	23.3	11.4	1.2	6.2	36.2
100 to 499	54.4	50.0	5.4	31.6	48.1	41.0	25.9	22.9	22.7	32.6	26.9	3.8	13.4	53.0
500 and over	82.6	69.8	37.5	85.8	77.8	68.0	58.6	50.7	41.8	32.6	40.7	10.3	16.0	55.9
Age of plant (years):														
Less than 5	44.4	37.3	3.7	24.7	29.5	27.3	21.3	18.0	11.9	32.0	19.5	1.7	13.4	50.3
5 to 15	42.6	42.3	4.4	24.8	34.5	29.8	21.3	17.4	16.2	28.8	19.9	3.3	9.9	48.1
16 to 30	41.3	48.0	4.7	23.7	34.9	29.0	19.4	17.1	16.6	27.5	17.6	2.2	7.9	45.1
Over 30	43.1	50.0	7.3	24.9	39.0	32.1	20.7	18.7	18.0	27.0	17.0	2.6	7.9	38.5
Manufacturing process:														
Fabrication/machining	31.1	53.5	2.4	20.6	31.2	24.7	13.7	12.2	14.6	24.1	15.6	1.6	9.9	45.1
Assembly	49.9	15.1	7.4	30.5	30.5	32.6	26.2	22.5	18.3	22.9	19.5	3.9	11.0	45.7
Both	47.2	55.0	5.7	25.2	38.7	32.1	21.8	18.8	16.6	33.3	20.1	2.7	9.0	46.0
Neither	18.5	9.6	2.7	14.8	24.6	17.4	15.9	12.1	11.9	13.7	10.9	1.3	6.0	36.3
Market for most products:														
Consumer	27.6	23.9	4.6	21.2	34.5	27.1	16.1	17.2	17.5	21.7	21.3	3.0	10.6	42.3
Commercial	49.1	41.7	6.5	25.9	34.3	33.0	24.4	22.0	16.4	32.1	18.7	2.8	9.8	43.5
Industrial	42.8	49.5	3.9	21.3	34.5	27.6	19.1	15.9	13.6	29.9	16.4	2.2	8.5	45.8
Transportation	45.7	47.9	8.3	35.4	44.3	34.5	24.8	20.4	32.6	34.1	29.9	3.6	11.9	57.0
Government	57.0	62.0	7.9	42.2	39.4	41.0	28.8	22.8	13.9	29.0	20.1	3.7	13.5	51.9
Other	36.6	36.9	4.5	14.6	24.5	24.0	16.7	13.3	12.2	16.6	12.4	1.5	5.4	31.6
Market price for most products:														
Less than $5	28.6	29.0	2.2	27.0	39.3	26.4	16.7	15.1	21.5	25.4	22.1	1.7	13.4	47.6
$5 to $100	33.3	45.1	3.5	25.6	35.7	29.9	16.4	17.7	19.0	28.2	22.1	3.7	11.9	47.1
$101 to $1,000	41.0	51.5	4.5	24.9	31.6	29.6	20.0	16.1	13.7	27.6	18.5	1.9	8.0	47.0
$1,001 to $2,000	50.2	49.2	6.0	25.8	32.1	30.5	22.1	18.5	14.1	29.9	16.9	3.6	10.5	43.3
$2,001 to $10,000	50.9	45.0	4.9	21.2	28.0	30.7	22.0	17.4	11.8	30.7	13.5	2.0	6.7	41.1
Over $10,000	61.8	48.8	9.8	22.2	39.8	31.9	29.9	21.8	14.4	33.5	16.0	3.0	6.0	46.5

[1] Local area network. [2] Standard Industrial Classification; see text, section 13.

Source: U.S. Bureau of the Census, *Current Industrial Reports, Manufacturing Technology, 1988.*

No. 1249. Alcoholic Beverages—Summary: 1980 to 1992

[For 1980-1985, stocks on hand for years ending June 30; later data for years ending September 30. All other items for fiscal years ending in year shown; see text, section 9. Includes Puerto Rico. Excludes imports. See *Historical Statistics, Colonial Times to 1970*, series P 235 for beer and P 236a for distilled spirits]

ITEM	Unit	1980	1985	1987	1988	1989	1990	1991	1992
BEER									
Breweries operated	Number	86	103	120	183	245	286	333	392
Production [1]	Mil. bbl. [2]	193	194	196	197	198	202	204	202
Value of shipments [3]	Mil. dol.	9,362	12,216	13,619	13,871	14,321	15,186	15,925	(NA)
Tax-paid withdrawals	Mil. bbl. [2]	172	175	178	178	179	182	183	182
Stocks on hand	Mil. bbl. [2]	15	14	14	14	14	14	14	14
DISTILLED SPIRITS									
Production facilities operated .	Number	143	117	102	105	140	143	145	143
Warehouses operated	Number	200	214	211	186	260	243	224	236
Production [4]	Mil. tax gal. [5] . .	236	117	90	99	135	122	129	110
Tax-paid withdrawals [6]	Mil. tax gal. [5] .	330	306	271	255	251	251	242	246
Stocks on hand [4]	Mil. tax gal. [5] .	696	588	508	456	456	451	459	400
Bottled for consumption	Mil. wine gal. [7] .	392	371	337	317	312	306	299	304
Whisky: Production [1]	Mil. tax gal. [5] . .	87	65	42	38	75	77	75	67
Stocks on hand	Mil. tax gal. [5] . .	566	467	409	370	361	365	368	309
Bottled for consumption . . .	Mil. wine gal. [7] .	165	138	119	111	109	106	100	101
STILL WINES									
Production [1]	Mil. wine gal. [7] .	982	622	677	538	611	577	478	483
Distilling materials	Mil. wine gal. [7] .	184	148	155	119	122	103	108	134
Tax-paid withdrawals [8]	Mil. wine gal. [7] .	340	414	451	451	464	468	387	387
Stocks on hand [9]	Mil. wine gal. [7] .	486	602	618	570	558	562	539	544
EFFERVESCENT WINES [10]									
Production [1]	Mil. wine gal. [7] .	26.8	32.0	29.2	29.8	30.9	26.9	22.8	24.7
Tax-paid withdrawals	Mil. wine gal. [7] .	24.1	30.9	31.2	29.2	27.0	26.2	24.6	24.1
Stocks on hand	Mil. wine gal. [7] .	11.9	21.3	18.7	18.2	19.4	22.1	20.4	18.8

NA Not available. [1] Production represents total amount removed from fermenters, including distilling material, and includes increase after fermentation (by amelioration, sweetening, and addition of wine spirits). [2] Barrels of 31 wine gallons. [3] Source: U.S. Bureau of the Census, *Census of Manufactures, 1982* and *1987*, and *Annual Survey of Manufactures*. [4] Excludes alcohol produced for industrial use. [5] For spirits of 100 proof or over, a tax gallon is equivalent to the proof gallon; for spirits of less than 100 proof, the tax gallon is equivalent to the wine gallon. A proof gallon is the alcoholic equivalent of a U.S. gallon at 60 degrees F, containing 50 percent of ethyl alcohol by volume. [6] Includes ethyl alcohol. [7] A wine gallon is the U.S. gallon equivalent to the volume of 231 cubic inches. [8] Includes special natural wines. [9] Excludes distilling materials. [10] Includes champagne, other effervescent wines, and artificially carbonated wines.

Source: Except as noted, U.S. Bureau of Alcohol, Tobacco, and Firearms, *Alcohol and Tobacco Summary Statistics*, annual.

No. 1250. Tobacco Products—Production, Consumption, and Expenditures: 1970 to 1992

[Production data are for calendar years. Excludes cigars produced in customs bonded manufacturing warehouses. See also *Historical Statistics, Colonial Times to 1970*, series P 239-241]

ITEM	Unit	1970	1980	1983	1984	1985	1986	1987	1988	1989	1990	1991	1992
PRODUCTION													
Cigarettes	Billions .	583	714	667	669	665	658	689	695	677	710	695	719
Nonfilter tip	Billions .	116	54	43	39	36	33	30	28	24	23	19	18
Regular	Billions .	54	23	19	18	16	15	14	12	11	11	9	9
King	Billions .	62	30	24	21	20	18	16	16	13	12	10	9
Filter tip	Billions .	467	661	625	630	629	625	660	667	654	687	675	701
Long and king	Billions .	362	439	384	380	378	373	397	400	392	417	423	430
Extra long	Billions .	105	222	241	251	252	252	263	267	261	270	253	271
Cigars	Billions .	8	4	4	4	3	3	2	2	2	2	2	2
Tobacco [1]	Mil. lb. .	165	163	162	163	158	147	143	142	141	142	142	141
CONSUMPTION PER PERSON [2]													
Total	Lb. [3] . . .	10	8	7	7	7	7	6	6	6	6	5	5
Cigarettes	1,000 . .	4	4	4	3	3	3	3	3	3	3	3	3
Cigars [4]	Number .	60	24	21	20	18	17	15	14	14	13	12	12
CONSUMER EXPENDITURES													
Total	Mil. dol .	11.5	21.0	28.7	30.7	32.2	33.7	35.4	37.8	40.9	43.8	47.4	48.4
Cigarettes	Mil. dol .	10.4	19.4	26.8	28.8	30.3	31.8	33.6	35.9	38.3	41.6	45.2	45.8
Cigars	Mil. dol .	0.7	0.7	0.7	0.7	0.7	0.7	0.6	0.6	0.7	0.7	0.7	0.6
Other	Mil. dol .	0.4	0.9	1.2	1.2	1.2	1.2	1.3	1.4	1.4	1.5	1.8	2.0

[1] Smoking and chewing tobaccos and snuff output. [2] Based on estimated population 18 years old and over, as of July 1, including Armed Forces abroad. [3] Unstemmed processing weight equivalent. [4] Weighing over 3 pounds per 1,000.

Source: U.S. Dept. of Agriculture, Economic Research Service, *Tobacco Situation and Outlook*, quarterly.

No. 1251. Cotton, Wool, and Manmade Fibers—Consumption, by End-Use: 1988 to 1992

[Represents products manufactured by U.S. mills. Excludes glass fiber]

YEAR	Total (mil. lb.)	COTTON		WOOL		MAN-MADE FIBERS					
								Cellulosic [1]		Noncellulosic [2]	
		Total (mil. lb.)	Percent of end-use	Total (mil. lb.)	Percent of end-use	Total (mil. lb.)	Percent of end-use	Total (mil. lb.)	Percent of end-use	Total (mil. lb.)	Percent of end-use
Total:											
1988	13,532	4,033	29.8	210	1.6	9,289	68.6	613	4.5	8,676	64.1
1989	14,125	4,633	32.8	196	1.4	9,296	65.8	600	4.2	8,696	61.6
1990	14,011	4,699	33.5	185	1.3	9,127	65.2	599	4.3	8,528	60.9
1991	14,421	5,033	34.9	213	1.5	9,175	63.6	557	3.8	8,618	59.8
1992	15,481	5,424	35.0	217	1.4	9,840	63.6	558	3.6	9,282	60.0
Apparel:											
1988	5,164	2,513	48.7	139	2.7	2,512	48.6	276	5.3	2,236	43.3
1989	5,514	2,821	51.2	124	2.2	2,569	46.6	274	5.0	2,295	41.6
1990	5,204	2,897	55.7	118	2.3	2,189	42.0	287	5.5	1,902	36.5
1991	5,451	3,103	56.9	142	2.6	2,206	40.5	270	5.0	1,936	35.5
1992	5,942	3,348	56.3	144	2.4	2,450	41.3	271	4.6	2,179	36.7
Home furnishings:											
1988	2,052	1,079	52.6	19	0.9	954	46.5	130	6.3	824	40.2
1989	2,285	1,339	58.6	19	0.8	927	40.6	123	5.4	804	35.2
1990	2,235	1,325	59.3	14	0.6	896	40.1	104	4.7	792	35.4
1991	2,326	1,428	61.4	11	0.5	887	38.1	97	4.1	790	34.0
1992	2,488	1,566	62.9	11	0.4	911	36.7	96	3.9	815	32.8
Floor coverings:											
1988	3,053	12	0.4	21	0.7	3,020	98.9	1	-	3,019	98.9
1989	2,997	14	0.5	24	0.8	2,959	98.7	1	-	2,958	98.7
1990	3,075	18	0.6	21	0.7	3,036	98.7	-	-	3,036	98.7
1991	2,995	22	0.8	25	0.8	2,948	98.4	-	-	2,948	98.4
1992	3,297	20	0.6	26	0.8	3,251	98.6	-	-	3,251	98.6
Exports of domestic products:											
1988	456	124	27.2	19	4.2	313	68.6	25	5.5	288	63.1
1989	492	135	27.4	20	4.1	337	68.5	27	5.5	310	63.0
1990	532	146	27.4	22	4.1	364	68.5	29	5.5	335	63.0
1991	572	155	27.1	23	4.0	394	68.9	32	5.6	362	63.3
1992	613	164	26.8	23	3.8	426	69.4	34	5.5	392	63.9
Industrial: [3]											
1988	2,807	305	10.9	12	0.5	2,490	88.6	181	6.4	2,309	82.2
1989	2,837	324	11.4	9	0.3	2,504	88.3	175	6.2	2,329	82.1
1990	2,965	313	10.6	10	0.3	2,642	88.1	179	6.0	2,463	83.1
1991	3,077	325	10.6	12	0.4	2,740	89.0	158	5.1	2,582	83.9
1992	3,141	326	10.4	13	0.4	2,802	89.2	157	5.0	2,645	84.2

- Represents or rounds to zero.   [1] Rayon and acetate.   [2] Nylon, polyester, acrylic, and olefin.   [3] Includes consumer-type products.

Source: Fiber Economics Bureau, Inc., Roseland, NJ, *Textile Organon*, monthly, (copyright).

No. 1252. Textiles and Apparel Products—U.S. Exports and Imports: 1991 to 1993

[In millions of dollars. Excludes glass fibers, rubber and leather apparel, and clothing donated for charity. Minus sign (-) indicates deficit]

PRODUCT	EXPORTS			GENERAL IMPORTS			MERCHANDISE TRADE BALANCE		
	1991	1992	1993	1991	1992	1993	1991	1992	1993
Total	8,669	10,120	10,977	33,197	39,070	42,225	-24,528	-28,950	-31,248
Textile yarn fabrics	5,457	5,911	6,025	6,991	7,844	8,438	-1,534	-1,933	-2,413
Textile yarn	1,254	1,179	1,045	831	955	1,146	423	224	-101
Cotton fabric, woven	542	591	641	1,281	1,493	1,552	-739	-902	-911
Woven fabric of manmade textiles	703	825	883	1,106	1,206	1,261	-403	-381	-378
Woven fabric of textile material	141	185	210	677	666	662	-536	-481	-452
Special yarns	1,166	1,335	1,418	724	797	878	442	538	540
Other	1,651	1,796	1,828	2,372	2,727	2,939	-721	-931	-1,111
Apparel	3,212	4,209	4,952	26,206	31,226	33,787	-22,994	-27,017	-28,835

Source: U.S. Bureau of the Census, *U.S. Merchandise Trade: Exports, General Imports, and Imports for Consumption*, Report FT925, monthly.

No. 1253. Iron and Steel Industry—Summary: 1980 to 1992

[For financial data, the universe in 1992 consists of the companies that produced 68 percent of the total reported raw steel production. The financial data represent the operations of the steel segment of the companies. Minus sign (-) indicates net loss]

ITEM	Unit	1980	1984	1985	1986	1987	1988	1989	1990	1991	1992
Steel mill products, apparent supply . . .	Mil. tons [1] . .	95.2	98.9	96.4	90.0	95.9	102.7	96.8	97.8	88.3	95.0
Net shipments	Mil. tons [1] . .	83.9	73.7	73.0	70.3	76.7	83.8	84.1	85.0	78.8	82.2
Exports.	Mil. tons [1] . .	4.1	1.0	1.0	1.0	1.1	2.1	4.6	4.3	6.3	4.3
Imports.	Mil. tons [1] . .	15.5	26.2	24.3	20.7	20.4	20.9	17.3	17.2	15.8	17.1
Scrap consumed	Mil. tons [1] . .	66.6	51.8	53.2	49.7	51.7	56.3	51.7	50.1	50.5	51.9
Scrap inventory.	Mil. tons [1] . .	6.9	4.4	4.0	3.4	3.8	3.5	3.5	3.6	3.7	3.3
Iron and steel products: Exports	Mil. tons [1] . .	5.1	1.7	1.6	1.5	1.7	2.8	5.4	5.3	7.4	5.3
Imports.	Mil. tons [1] . .	17.9	29.5	27.6	24.2	23.8	25.7	22.1	21.9	20.2	21.9
Capacity by steelmaking process	Mil. net tons	153.7	135.3	133.6	127.9	112.2	112.0	115.9	116.7	117.6	113.1
Revenue	Bil. dol.	37.7	30.3	28.4	25.0	27.1	32.7	31.8	30.9	27.1	26.9
Net income	Bil. dol.	0.7	(-Z)	-1.8	-4.1	1.0	-0.6	1.6	0.1	-2.0	-3.8
Stockholders' equity	Bil. dol.	14.5	9.4	6.9	2.4	3.0	2.2	2.1	4.3	2.8	-0.8
Total assets.	Bil. dol.	30.8	26.2	24.0	21.0	21.9	24.2	24.6	28.3	27.4	28.2
Capital expenditures	Bil. dol.	2.7	1.2	1.6	0.9	1.2	1.8	2.3	2.6	2.3	1.8
Working capital ratio [2]	Ratio	1.6	1.4	1.3	1.6	1.5	1.7	1.6	1.6	1.4	1.3
Inventories.	Bil. dol.	4.7	4.2	3.5	3.0	3.4	3.8	4.0	4.7	4.4	4.1
Average employment.	1,000 . .	399	236	208	175	163	169	169	164	146	140
Hours worked.	Million	758	474	419	356	354	363	360	350	304	293
Producer price indexes: [3]											
Iron and steel, total	1982=100 .	90.0	105.3	104.8	101.1	104.6	115.7	119.1	117.2	114.1	111.5
Steel mill products	1982=100 .	86.6	104.7	104.7	99.8	102.3	110.7	114.5	112.1	109.5	106.4
Blast and electric furnace products . .	1982=100 .	97.1	97.3	95.6	94.2	97.1	119.6	129.4	120.1	116.9	115.5
Iron ore	1982=100 .	87.8	101.2	97.5	91.5	84.2	82.8	82.8	83.3	83.6	83.7
Scrap, iron and steel.	1982=100 .	140.9	123.7	112.6	109.6	128.4	177.1	173.7	166.0	147.6	139.2
Foundry and forge shop products . .	1982=100 .	89.7	104.4	105.2	105.2	105.7	109.6	114.6	117.2	119.0	120.1

Z Less than $50 million.   [1] In millions of short tons.   [2] Current assets to current liabilities.   [3] Source: U.S. Bureau of Labor Statistics, *Producer Price Indexes,* monthly and annual.

No. 1254. Raw Steel, Pig Iron, and Ferroalloys Production: 1970 to 1992

[In millions, except percent. *See also Historical Statistics, Colonial Times to 1970,* series P 265-269]

ITEM	1970	1980	1984	1985	1986	1987	1988	1989	1990	1991	1992
Raw steel (net tons):											
World production.	654.2	790.4	782.6	792.9	788.9	811.1	859.2	865.3	848.8	811.1	787.6
U.S. production.	131.5	111.8	92.5	88.3	81.6	89.2	99.9	97.9	98.9	87.9	92.9
Percent of world	20	14	12	11	10	11	12	11	12	11	12
Basic oxygen process. . .	63.3	67.6	52.8	51.9	47.9	52.5	58.0	58.3	58.5	52.7	57.6
Electric.	20.2	31.2	31.4	29.9	30.4	34.0	36.8	35.2	36.9	33.8	35.3
Open hearth	48.0	13.0	8.3	6.4	3.3	2.7	5.1	4.4	3.5	1.4	-
Carbon.	117.4	94.7	79.9	76.7	71.4	78.0	86.8	86.2	86.6	77.9	82.5
Alloy and stainless	14.1	17.1	12.6	11.6	10.2	11.2	13.1	11.7	12.3	10.0	10.4
Pig iron and ferroalloys, production (sh. tons) [1]	93.5	68.7	51.9	50.4	44.0	48.4	55.7	55.9	54.8	48.6	52.2

- Represents or rounds to zero.   [1] For 1970, excludes blast furnace ferroalloys.

No. 1255. Steel Products—Net Shipments, by Market Classes: 1970 to 1992

[In thousands of short tons. Comprises carbon, alloy, and stainless steel]

MARKET CLASS	1970	1980	1985	1987	1988	1989	1990	1991	1992
Total [1]	**90,798**	**83,853**	**73,043**	**76,654**	**83,840**	**84,100**	**84,981**	**78,846**	**82,241**
Automotive.	14,475	12,124	12,950	11,343	12,555	11,763	11,100	10,015	11,092
Steel service centers, distributors.	16,025	16,172	18,439	19,840	21,037	20,769	21,111	19,464	21,328
Construction, incl. maintenance	8,913	8,742	7,900	7,681	8,607	8,318	9,245	9,161	9,536
Containers, packaging, shipping. . . .	7,775	5,551	4,089	4,372	4,421	4,459	4,474	4,278	3,974
Machinery, industrial equipment, tools. .	5,169	4,543	2,271	2,277	2,798	2,409	2,388	1,982	1,951
Steel for converting and processing . . .	3,443	4,117	5,484	7,195	8,492	8,235	9,441	8,265	9,226
Rail transportation.	3,098	3,155	1,061	758	1,146	1,229	1,080	999	1,052
Contractors' products.	4,440	3,148	3,330	3,337	3,495	3,182	2,870	2,306	2,694
Oil and gas industries	3,550	5,371	2,044	1,489	1,477	1,203	1,892	1,425	1,454
Electrical equipment	2,694	2,441	1,869	2,373	2,459	2,449	2,453	2,102	2,136
Appliances, utensils, and cutlery	2,160	1,725	1,466	1,633	1,638	1,721	1,540	1,388	1,503

[1] Includes nonclassified shipments and other classes not shown separately.

Source of tables 1253-1255: American Iron and Steel Institute, Washington, DC, *Annual Statistical Report,* (copyright).

No. 1256. Computer Shipments and Revenues: 1990 to 1992

[Revenue is in if-sold, end-user dollars]

ITEM	FACTORY REVENUE (mil. dol.)			SHIPMENTS (units)		
	1990	1991	1992	1990	1991	1992
United States:						
Supercomputer	788.8	877.6	944.9	531	553	567
Mainframe	12,538.1	9,855.6	8,527.9	3,952	3,434	2,782
Midrange	9,815.8	6,340.3	8,680.3	208,102	178,276	127,406
Workstation	3,147.2	3,474.1	3,722.4	161,488	210,649	230,909
Personal computer	18,660.9	18,428.0	23,531.1	9,848,593	10,182,500	12,544,374
Canada:						
Supercomputer	29.9	29.7	38.0	19	19	25
Mainframe	892.4	771.7	624.8	257	266	156
Midrange	744.3	579.0	648.5	17,832	14,277	9,434
Workstation	225.6	191.1	189.3	12,077	7,996	11,580
Personal computer	1,447.7	1,474.0	2,150.9	857,706	884,378	1,174,984
Western Europe:						
Supercomputer	505.6	554.4	472.5	291	295	263
Mainframe	10,861.9	8,924.2	7,239.6	4,307	4,390	2,291
Midrange	10,061.5	9,892.1	6,452.5	243,340	250,778	151,415
Workstation	2,395.5	2,544.4	2,590.8	121,577	155,249	171,534
Personal computer	14,810.1	14,519.4	16,353.2	7,954,834	8,572,164	9,437,893
Japan:						
Supercomputer	469.9	495.6	448.4	116	141	107
Mainframe	5,697.6	6,242.4	5,382.3	6,222	5,639	3,635
Midrange	5,392.1	5,668.3	4,845.9	231,571	287,640	233,481
Workstation	1,511.6	1,875.5	1,924.5	96,267	123,904	124,519
Personal computer	4,746.0	4,600.8	4,363.7	2,243,500	2,363,000	2,223,810

Source: Dataquest Inc., San Jose, CA, Consolidated Data Base, January 1994.

No. 1257. Microcontrollers and Chip Shipments: 1989 to 1992

ITEM	REVENUE (mil. dol.)				SHIPMENTS (millions of units)			
	1989	1990	1991	1992	1989	1990	1991	1992
Microcontrollers, worldwide	3,262	3,667	4,519	5,958	1,153	1,358	1,592	1,723
8-bit	2,002	2,079	2,618	(NA)	461	563	722	814
4-bit	1,173	1,394	1,598	(NA)	682	777	838	861
16-bit	86	194	303	(NA)	9	17	32	48
32-bit processors	817	1,402	2,456	4,363	9	8	15	30
RISC [1]	(NA)	175	270	305	1	1	2	3
CISC [2]	(NA)	1,227	2,186	4,057	8	7	14	27
256K DRAM [3] chips	2,442	1,322	622	346	780	621	299	193
1-Megabit DRAM chips	5,599	4,229	3,776	2,919	408	665	835	821

NA Not available.   [1] RISC=Reduced Instruction Set Computer.   [2] CISC=Complex Instruction Set Computer.
[3] DRAM=Dynamic Random Access Memory.

Source: Dataquest, Inc., San Jose, CA, unpublished data.

No. 1258. Computers and Industrial Electronics—Shipments: 1982 to 1991

[In millions of dollars]

ITEM	1982	1983	1984	1985	1986	1987	1988	1989	1990	1991
Total	55,639	60,084	73,610	74,247	73,086	79,456	82,022	85,075	84,962	83,959
Computer and peripheral equipment:										
Computers	16,036	17,865	24,401	25,616	26,020	28,975	28,693	28,464	27,559	27,091
Peripheral equipment	18,728	20,844	23,954	23,828	22,195	23,865	25,443	25,729	25,709	25,291
Industrial electronics:										
Controlling, processing equipment	7,363	7,428	8,683	8,719	8,924	9,193	9,861	11,992	12,471	12,105
Testing, measuring equipment	4,695	5,200	6,279	6,008	5,736	6,009	5,807	5,953	5,955	5,768
Nuclear electronic equipment	546	490	480	519	560	601	616	606	651	631
Other electronic equipment	3,869	3,412	4,665	4,530	4,720	5,238	5,588	5,992	5,609	5,539
Electromedical electronic equipment	4,402	4,845	5,148	5,028	4,931	5,576	6,015	6,339	7,010	7,535

Source: Electronic Industries Association, Washington, DC, *Electronic Market Data Book*, annual, (copyright).

No. 1259. Consumer Electronics and Electronic Components—Factory Sales: 1980 to 1991

[In millions of dollars]

PRODUCT	1980	1983	1984	1985	1986	1987	1988	1989	1990	1991
Consumer electronics	10,891	14,560	17,594	23,652	21,480	21,835	22,139	22,340	22,602	21,977
Audio systems [1]	809	630	976	1,372	1,370	1,048	1,225	1,217	1,270	1,264
Car audio.	1,368	1,900	2,500	2,761	3,135	3,523	3,937	4,125	4,292	4,107
Video disc players.	(NA)	81	45	23	26	26	34	50	72	81
Portable audio tape equipment . . .	1,403	1,102	1,191	1,140	1,389	1,469	1,547	1,595	1,645	1,780
Separate audio components	1,424	1,268	913	1,132	1,358	1,715	1,854	1,871	1,935	1,805
Blank audio cassettes	(NA)	234	256	270	300	375	354	367	376	373
Color TV receivers	4,210	5,002	5,538	5,565	6,040	6,303	6,277	6,530	6,247	6,035
Monochrome TV receivers	588	465	419	328	373	341	236	156	132	92
Projection TV	(NA)	268	385	488	529	527	529	478	626	683
VCR decks	621	2,162	3,585	4,739	5,258	3,442	2,848	2,625	2,439	2,454
Camcorders	(NA)	(NA)	(NA)	565	1,280	1,651	1,972	2,007	2,260	2,013
Blank video cassettes	(NA)	580	770	1,055	1,235	1,006	936	923	948	980
Color cameras	(NA)	303	355	228	59	(NA)	(NA)	(NA)	(NA)	(NA)
Home radios	468	565	661	379	408	409	377	379	360	310
Electronic components	25,571	33,856	43,306	39,459	38,829	45,335	50,988	54,937	55,094	55,974
Solid state products.	9,089	12,570	17,032	14,650	14,408	16,819	19,790	22,376	21,507	21,979
Parts.	7,080	8,318	10,155	9,329	9,169	10,664	10,871	10,560	9,976	9,985
Electron tubes	1,744	2,049	2,137	2,055	2,125	2,176	2,289	2,596	2,627	2,564
Other components [2]	7,658	10,919	13,982	13,423	13,121	15,676	18,038	19,405	20,984	21,446

NA Not available. [1] Includes compact and rack systems. [2] Includes sockets, delay lines, loudspeakers, magnetic components, transducers, printed circuit boards, microwave components, assemblies, and parts.

Source: Electronic Industries Association, Washington, DC, *Electronic Market Data Book*, annual, (copyright).

No. 1260. Semiconductors and Related Devices: 1980 to 1992

[In millions of dollars, except percent. Semiconductors and related devices represent SIC 3674]

ITEM	1980	1985	1987	1988	1989	1990	1991	1992
Consumption, North American market [1]	6,053	9,420	12,858	15,844	17,070	16,540	16,990	20,426
Capital expenditures (North America) [2]	1,438	2,629	2,594	3,434	3,875	4,088	3,851	4,132
Percent of sales	22.6	27.9	20.2	21.7	22.7	24.7	22.7	20.2
Japanese capital expenditures as a percent of revenues . .	17.2	40.0	16.0	21.4	23.3	23.4	(NA)	(NA)
R&D (North America)	423	1,159	1,448	1,661	(NA)	(NA)	(NA)	(NA)
Imports, total [3]	2,223	4,870	6,656	9,502	10,758	(NA)	(NA)	(NA)
Integrated circuits	1,909	4,365	6,000	8,683	9,957	(NA)	(NA)	(NA)
Transistors	193	242	318	402	401	(NA)	(NA)	(NA)
Diodes and rectifiers	121	263	338	417	400	(NA)	(NA)	(NA)
Shipments [4]	9,455	15,253	17,929	20,332	23,488	23,978	26,302	25,813
Integrated microcircuits	6,768	10,872	13,300	14,857	16,682	16,372	19,151	18,456
Semiconductor devices, n.e.c. [5]	1,398	2,569	2,586	3,337	4,875	5,584	5,761	5,962
Assets, beginning of year.	4,014	12,200	16,515	(NA)	(NA)	(NA)	(NA)	(NA)
New capital expenditures	1,596	2,832	1,921	2,681	3,132	3,439	2,945	(NA)
Used capital expenditures	40	390	94	56	46	37	108	(NA)
Retirements	230	896	1,442	(NA)	(NA)	(NA)	(NA)	(NA)
Assets, end of year.	5,420	14,526	17,088	(NA)	(NA)	(NA)	(NA)	(NA)
Depreciation charges.	601	1,512	1,719	(NA)	(NA)	(NA)	(NA)	(NA)
Rental payments	74	184	203	(NA)	(NA)	(NA)	(NA)	(NA)

NA Not available. [1] Source: Dataquest Inc., San Jose, CA, unpublished data. Revenue from shipments by all companies into Canada and the United States. [2] Capital expenditures by all companies in Canada and the United States. [3] Imports for consumption. Includes imports not shown separately. [4] Includes items not shown separately. [5] N.e.c.=Not elsewhere classified.

Source: Except as noted, U.S. Bureau of the Census, *Current Industrial Reports*, series MA-36Q; *U.S. Imports, FT 210*, 1980-1988; *Import CD-ROM Disc 1989*; and *Annual Survey of Manufactures*.

No. 1261. Machine Tools—New Orders and Shipments: 1970 to 1993

[In millions of dollars. Data represents total industry volume based on reports from over 200 manufacturers]

YEAR	METAL CUTTING TOOLS					METAL FORMING TOOLS				
	New orders (net)		Shipments		Order backlog, end of period	New orders (net)		Shipments		Order backlog, end of period
	Total	Domestic	Total	Domestic		Total	Domestic	Total	Domestic	
1970.	651	507	993	827	471	261	227	450	412	235
1971.	609	524	672	554	408	252	223	326	286	162
1972.	1,009	877	714	627	702	403	368	304	267	260
1973.	1,825	1,550	1,074	935	1,454	787	717	427	388	621
1974.	2,017	1,716	1,445	1,241	2,025	566	470	585	522	600
1975.	916	781	1,879	1,548	1,062	361	284	573	485	388
1976.	1,662	1,477	1,482	1,270	1,243	541	485	578	474	351
1977.	2,202	1,981	1,651	1,470	1,794	793	729	630	560	515
1978.	3,373	3,043	2,189	1,960	2,981	973	901	825	729	663
1979.	4,495	3,866	2,930	2,606	4,546	1,126	991	947	860	843
1980.	3,885	3,496	3,681	3,206	4,750	870	744	1,011	879	701
1981.	2,228	1,946	4,105	3,552	2,873	717	617	991	824	427
1982.	1,064	890	2,895	2,599	1,043	433	372	710	600	151
1983.	1,152	1,069	1,372	1,200	823	545	489	474	430	222
1984.	1,916	1,700	1,607	1,484	1,132	1,000	932	679	609	542
1985.	1,853	1,652	1,742	1,549	1,243	675	610	803	743	414
1986.	1,544	1,377	1,890	1,685	897	581	507	688	621	307
1987.	1,451	1,294	1,677	1,499	672	667	536	647	538	327
1988.	2,708	2,316	1,575	1,400	1,806	883	749	825	702	386
1989.	1,977	1,723	2,359	2,059	1,423	832	719	837	704	380
1990.	2,070	1,772	2,330	2,004	1,164	894	761	970	851	304
1991.	1,894	1,549	1,872	1,595	1,186	748	546	802	625	251
1992.	1,756	1,532	1,918	1,605	1,025	726	609	678	547	299
1993.	2,237	2,106	2,091	1,883	1,170	945	807	1,043	881	201

Source: The Association For Manufacturing Technology, McLean, VA, *The Economic Handbook of The Machine Tool Industry*, annual, (copyright).

No. 1262. Manufacturers' Shipments, Inventories, and Orders: 1950 to 1992

[In billions of dollars, except ratio. See also *Historical Statistics, Colonial Times to 1970*, series P 74-92]

YEAR	Ship-ments	Invento-ries (Dec. 31) [1]	Ratio of invento-ries to ship-ments [2]	New orders	Unfilled orders (Dec. 31)	YEAR	Ship-ments	Invento-ries (Dec. 31) [1]	Ratio of invento-ries to ship-ments [2]	New orders	Unfilled orders (Dec. 31)
1950.	224	32	1.41	242	41	1972.	756	108	1.58	770	120
1951.	261	39	1.78	287	67	1973.	875	124	1.63	913	158
1952.	270	42	1.71	279	76	1974.	1,018	158	1.86	1,047	187
1953.	298	44	1.90	283	60	1975.	1,039	160	1.77	1,023	171
1954.	280	42	1.71	268	48	1976.	1,186	175	1.66	1,194	180
1955.	318	45	1.63	330	60	1977.	1,358	188	1.58	1,381	202
1956.	333	51	1.74	340	68	1978.	1,523	209	1.55	1,580	259
1957.	345	52	1.90	331	53	1979.	1,727	239	1.61	1,771	303
1958.	327	50	1.75	324	47	1980.	1,853	262	1.61	1,876	326
1959.	363	53	1.68	369	52	1981.	2,018	280	1.74	2,015	323
1960.	371	54	1.79	363	45	1982.	1,960	307	1.91	1,947	309
1961.	371	55	1.67	373	47	1983.	2,071	308	1.80	2,105	343
1962.	400	58	1.76	401	48	1984.	2,288	334	1.78	2,315	370
1963.	421	60	1.66	426	53	1985.	2,334	330	1.72	2,348	384
1964.	448	63	1.62	460	65	1986.	2,336	318	1.66	2,342	390
1965.	492	68	1.58	505	79	1987.	2,476	333	1.64	2,513	427
1966.	538	78	1.70	557	97	1988.	2,682	361	1.64	2,724	469
1967.	558	84	1.71	565	104	1989.	2,793	380	1.66	2,831	507
1968.	603	90	1.76	608	110	1990.	2,874	392	1.66	2,888	522
1969.	642	98	1.81	647	115	1991.	2,826	380	1.64	2,812	508
1970.	634	101	1.91	625	106	1992.	2,934	373	1.55	2,901	475
1971.	671	102	1.76	672	107						

[1] Beginning in 1982, inventories are stated at current cost and are not comparable to the book value estimates for prior years.   [2] Ratio based on December seasonally adjusted data.

Source: U.S. Bureau of the Census, Current Industrial Reports, *Manufacturers' Shipments, Inventories, and Orders: 1982-1992*, series M3; and monthly press releases.

No. 1263. Value of Manufactures Shipments and Inventories, by Industry: 1980 to 1992

[In billions of dollars. Based on 1987 Standard Industrial Classification (SIC). See also *Historical Statistics, Colonial Times to 1970*, series P 74-79]

SIC code	INDUSTRY	1980	1985	1988	1989	1990	1991	1992
(X)	**Shipments**	**1,852.7**	**2,334.5**	**2,682.5**	**2,792.7**	**2,873.5**	**2,826.2**	**2,934.1**
(X)	Durable goods [1]	929.0	1,215.4	1,415.9	1,460.4	1,468.6	1,429.8	1,506.6
32	Stone, clay, and glass products	44.5	55.8	63.1	63.6	63.5	59.6	66.6
33	Primary metals	134.1	112.3	149.1	153.0	146.1	132.8	135.9
34	Fabricated metal products	116.1	143.3	158.8	162.2	163.1	157.1	160.5
35	Industrial machinery and equipment	180.6	218.4	243.3	253.6	256.3	243.5	253.4
351	Engines and turbines₂	13.7	15.1	16.2	16.9	16.6	16.6	16.8
353	Construction, mining [2]	33.6	27.6	27.7	29.5	30.7	27.7	25.2
357	Computer and office equipment.	30.4	60.4	67.6	65.4	65.4	58.8	65.6
36	Electronic and other.	112.9	164.0	186.9	192.3	194.8	197.9	209.4
361-2	Elec. transmission and distribution	20.1	23.8	25.9	27.4	27.9	27.0	27.7
363	Household appliances	12.9	16.1	17.3	18.3	18.0	17.7	18.2
365	Household audio and video equipment	8.5	11.5	8.4	9.1	9.3	9.8	11.0
366	Communications equipment	21.3	35.4	36.1	35.1	38.5	37.9	42.3
367	Electronic components ₁	26.7	42.2	57.0	59.9	60.8	65.2	69.7
37	Transportation equipment [1]	186.5	307.4	354.0	366.0	367.9	364.0	391.3
371	Motor vehicles and parts	104.6	193.4	221.6	225.6	215.0	206.1	235.7
372, 6	Aircraft, missiles, and parts.	58.5	91.3	107.7	113.5	125.2	131.3	128.0
38	Instruments and related products [1]	59.8	96.2	114.5	118.5	123.8	127.2	127.3
382	Measuring and controlling devices	15.7	25.9	28.8	29.6	31.5	32.3	33.6
(X)	Nondurable goods [1]	923.7	1,119.1	1,266.6	1,332.3	1,404.9	1,396.4	1,427.5
20	Food and kindred products [1]	256.2	308.6	351.5	364.4	384.0	387.6	395.0
208	Beverages.	33.0	43.7	49.7	50.1	52.2	54.6	57.3
21	Tobacco products	12.2	18.6	23.8	25.8	29.9	32.0	33.1
22	Textile mill products . . . . . ₁	47.3	54.6	64.8	67.3	66.0	65.7	69.9
26	Paper and allied products [1]	72.6	94.7	122.6	131.4	131.4	128.8	131.3
261-3,6	Paper, pulp, paperboard mill products. . . .	31.5	39.1	54.9	58.1	57.5	53.7	53.5
265	Paperboard containers and boxes	17.2	23.2	28.2	30.5	30.5	30.6	32.5
28	Chemicals and allied products [1]	168.2	204.8	259.7	278.1	288.2	292.3	301.5
281,2,6,8,9	Industrial chemicals.	101.7	114.7	145.5	156.2	157.3	153.9	156.4
283-4	Drugs, soaps, toiletries	41.9	61.3	81.8	88.0	95.2	102.7	110.4
29	Petroleum and coal products	193.0	176.6	131.4	143.7	172.6	158.1	154.7
30	Rubber and plastics products.	49.2	75.6	94.2	98.4	101.4	100.7	103.3
(X)	**Inventories (Dec. 31)**	**261.7**	**329.6**	**361.5**	**380.5**	**392.5**	**379.9**	**373.0**
(X)	Durable goods [1]	171.9	214.0	236.5	250.7	254.5	243.8	232.6
32	Stone, clay, and glass products	5.5	6.9	7.4	7.7	8.1	7.8	7.7
33	Primary metals	23.1	19.8	22.3	22.5	22.3	20.3	19.4
34	Fabricated metal products	19.2	22.5	24.4	24.7	24.1	23.0	22.9
35	Industrial machinery and equipment	40.3	45.6	46.5	48.7	48.0	46.5	44.3
351	Engines and turbines₂	2.6	2.7	3.1	3.0	3.2	3.2	3.2
353	Construction, mining [2]	9.2	7.8	6.6	6.6	6.7	6.4	5.8
357	Computer and office equipment.	8.0	11.5	11.2	11.6	10.4	10.3	9.8
36	Electronic and other.	21.3	29.8	30.7	32.2	31.7	30.6	30.4
361-2	Elec. transmission and distribution	3.9	4.7	4.7	4.7	4.7	4.4	4.2
363	Household appliances	1.8	2.5	2.7	3.0	2.8	2.3	2.2
365	Household audio and video equipment	1.3	1.3	1.0	1.1	1.1	1.1	1.0
366	Communications equipment	5.0	8.0	6.6	7.0	7.1	7.1	7.4
367	Electronic components ₁	5.2	7.5	9.0	9.6	9.5	9.6	9.5
37	Transportation equipment [1]	35.3	51.5	61.4	70.5	75.0	72.0	65.2
371	Motor vehicles and parts	9.6	11.8	12.1	11.8	13.0	12.5	11.3
372, 6	Aircraft, missiles, and parts. . . ₁	21.7	36.2	45.4	54.5	57.6	55.3	49.8
38	Instruments and related products [1]	12.9	21.0	24.3	24.7	24.8	23.6	22.5
382	Measuring and controlling devices	4.2	6.2	6.6	6.9	7.0	6.6	6.5
(X)	Nondurable goods [1] . . . . . . ₁	89.8	115.6	125.0	129.7	138.0	136.2	140.4
20	Food and kindred products [1]	22.4	24.4	27.4	27.7	29.4	29.8	30.0
208	Beverages.	3.8	4.7	4.9	4.9	5.1	5.2	5.3
21	Tobacco products	3.9	6.3	5.5	5.7	6.1	6.5	6.8
22	Textile mill products	6.5	7.2	8.1	8.3	8.4	8.2	8.7
26	Paper and allied products [1]	7.7	10.1	12.4	13.2	13.4	13.4	13.3
261-3,6	Paper, pulp, paperboard mill products. . . .	2.9	3.8	4.4	4.9	5.2	5.5	5.5
265	Paperboard containers and boxes	1.9	2.5	3.3	3.5	3.3	3.3	3.3
28	Chemicals and allied products [1]	19.9	26.0	29.4	30.8	33.2	33.5	34.8
281,2,6,8,9	Industrial chemicals.	10.7	14.0	15.3	16.1	17.6	17.2	17.4
283-4	Drugs, soaps, toiletries	5.9	7.8	9.9	10.3	11.0	11.9	13.0
29	Petroleum and coal products	9.6	13.7	9.0	10.4	13.1	11.3	11.2
30	Rubber and plastics products.	6.3	9.1	11.1	11.4	11.8	11.3	11.9

X Not applicable.　　[1] Includes industries not shown separately.　　[2] Also includes material handling industries.

Source: U.S. Bureau of the Census, Current Industrial Reports, *Manufactures' Shipments, Inventories, and Orders: 1982-1992*, and monthly press releases.

No. 1264. Fiber, Rugs, Carpeting, and Sheets—Shipments: 1986 to 1992

PRODUCT	Unit	1986	1987	1988	1989	1990	1991	1992
All fibers [1]	Mil. lbs. .	677	720	730	743	812	837	(NA)
Raw wool [2][3]	Mil. lbs. .	137	143	133	135	133	152	(NA)
Noils, and fiber [4]	Mil. lbs. .	35	30	24	24	20	21	(NA)
Other fibers. .	Mil. lbs. .	505	548	573	584	659	664	(NA)
Knit fabric production.	Mil. lbs. .	1,757	1,737	1,662	1,935	1,901	1,963	2,081
Rugs, carpet and carpeting.	Mil. dol. .	7,312	7,929	8,417	8,431	8,527	7,980	8,712
Sheets	1,000 doz	15,053	15,361	15,505	15,663	15,408	14,001	15,198
Pillow cases.	1,000 doz	12,372	12,627	12,564	13,089	12,665	11,301	12,523
Terry towels.	1,000 doz	50,182	52,425	47,179	62,741	42,376	43,158	48,789

NA Not available.   [1] Includes man-made fiber top converted from tow without combing. A number of companies were added for 1990 based on information in the 1987 Census of Manufactures. Data were received from these companies for 1990; therefore, the information shown for years prior to 1990 may not be directly comparable. These changes represent approximately 20 percent of the total fibers consumed on the woolen system and worsted combing.   [2] Data are shown on a scoured basis for greasy wool.   [3] Shorn and pulled wool of sheep excludes raw wool consumed in cotton system spinning to avoid disclosing figures for individual companies.   [4] Includes reprocessed and reused wool, mohair, alpaca, vicuna, and other specialty fibers as well as tops and noils consumed in woolen spinning and mohair consumed in worsted combing. Does not include wool tops consumed in cotton system spinning.

Source: U.S. Bureau of the Census, *Current Industrial Reports*, MA22K, MA22Q, and MQ23X, annual.

No. 1265. Glass Containers, Clay Construction Products, and Refractories—Shipments: 1986 to 1992

[In millions of dollars]

PRODUCT	1986	1987	1988	1989	1990	1991	1992
Glass container shipments.	(NA)	282	280	286	285	279	283
Brick shipments [1]	(NA)	(NA)	(NA)	1,088	1,014	985	907
Clay tile shipments [2]	(NA)	(NA)	(NA)	698	687	639	640
Clay pipe and fittings shipments	(NA)	(NA)	(NA)	63	60	33	38
Refractory shipments	1,521	1,682	1,950	2,011	2,003	1,947	1,957
Clay	670	740	814	823	771	784	752
Nonclay.	851	943	1,136	1,188	1,232	1,163	1,205

NA Not available.   [1] Building or common and face bricks.   [2] Floor and wall tile including quarry tile.

Source: U.S. Bureau of the Census, *Current Industrial Reports*, M32G, MQ32D, and MA32C, annual.

No. 1266. Mining and Mineral Processing Equipment—Shipments: 1991 and 1992

Product code	PRODUCT	Number of companies	QUANTITY (units)		VALUE (mil. dol.)	
			1991	1992	1991	1992
3531K	Portable crushing, screening, washing, and combination plants.	17	471	468	64	65
35325	Underground mining machinery [1]	22	1,877	1,293	318	248
35326	Mineral processing and beneficiation equip. [1]	40	5,364	5,310	75	70
35327	Crushing, pulverizing, and screening machinery [2]	40	2,520	2,469	132	135
35328	Drills, mining machinery, n.e.c. [1][3]	20	15,349	12,749	177	162
3533A	Portable drilling rigs and parts	23	(X)	(X)	262	255

X Not applicable.   [1] Excludes parts.   [2] Excludes portables and parts.   [3] n.e.c. = Not elsewhere classified.

Source: U.S. Bureau of the Census, *Current Industrial Reports*, MA35F, annual.

No. 1267. Inorganic Materials and Pharmaceutical Preparations: 1989 to 1992

Product code	PRODUCT	Unit	1989	1990	1991	1992
	INORGANIC FERTILIZERS					
28731 31	Ammonia, synthetic anhydrous:					
	Total production	1,000 sh. tons	16,467	17,003	17,169	18,295
	Shipments	1,000 sh. tons	9,599	10,382	10,002	10,392
	Shipments value	Mil. dol.	1,010	1,072	1,036	1,095
28731 50	Ammonium nitrate, original solution:					
	Total production	1,000 sh. tons	7,871	7,714	7,819	7,833
28731 57	Ammonium sulfate:					
	Total production	1,000 sh. tons	2,384	2,519	2,243	2,391
	Shipments	1,000 sh. tons	2,282	2,529	2,251	2,239
	Shipments value	Mil. dol.	142	130	130	140
28732	Urea (100%):					
	Total production	1,000 sh. tons	8,004	8,217	8,133	8,981
	Shipments	1,000 sh. tons	5,231	5,362	5,432	5,343
	Shipments value	Mil. dol.	625	640	723	696
28731 11	Nitric acid (100%):					
	Total production	1,000 sh. tons	8,349	7,931	7,927	8,043
	Shipments	1,000 sh. tons	743	647	623	670
	Shipments value	Mil. dol.	85	81	82	85
28741 81	Phosphoric acid (100% P2O5):					
28741 85	Total production	1,000 sh. tons	11,736	12,035	12,109	12,792
	Shipments	1,000 sh. tons	4,307	4,170	4,398	4,375
	Shipments value	Mil. dol.	1,300	1,226	1,282	1,170
28193	Sulfuric acid, gross (100%):					
	Total production	1,000 sh. tons	43,301	44,337	43,466	44,860
	Shipments	1,000 sh. tons	11,842	11,879	11,536	11,000
	Shipments value	Mil. dol.	638	589	587	535
28742	Superphosphates and other fertilizer materials (100% P2O5):					
	Total production	1,000 sh. tons	8,362	8,982	9,044	9,712
	Shipments	1,000 sh. tons	8,247	9,016	9,017	9,687
	Shipments value	Mil. dol.	2,449	2,711	2,832	2,522
	INORGANIC CHEMICAL SHIPMENTS					
2812	Alkalies and chlorine	Mil. dol.	2,989	3,187	3,029	2,845
28121	Chlorine (100% Cl)	Mil. dol.	653	478	260	194
28123	Sodium hydroxide (caustic soda)	Mil. dol.	1,989	2,341	2,387	2,192
28125	Other alkalies	Mil. dol.	340	361	375	452
28120 00	Alkalies and chlorine n.s.k.	Mil. dol.	7	7	7	7
2816	Inorganic color pigments	Mil. dol.	2,195	2,261	2,065	2,443
28161 00	Titanium dioxide (composite and pure) (commodity weight)	Mil. dol.	2,059	2,131	1,949	2,316
2819	Inorganic chemicals n.e.c.	Mil. dol.	12,408	13,612	12,817	12,284
28193	Sulfuric acid, gross (new and fortified)	Mil. dol.	638	589	587	535
28194	Inorganic acids, except nitric, phosphoric and sulfuric.	Mil. dol.	588	603	559	491
28195	Aluminum oxide, except natural alumina	Mil. dol.	1,215	1,499	1,081	948
28196	Aluminum compounds	Mil. dol.	577	665	662	576
28197	Potassium and sodium compounds (except bleaches, alkalies, and alums).	Mil. dol.	1,941	1,956	1,892	1,914
28198	Chemical catalytic preparations	Mil. dol.	1,225	1,221	1,238	1,312
28199	Other inorganic chemicals n.e.c.	Mil. dol.	6,018	6,846	6,567	6,288
28190 00	Industrial inorganic chemicals n.s.k.	Mil. dol.	206	232	232	220
28422 00	Household bleaching compounds.	Mil. dol.	723	724	826	852
	PHARMACEUTICAL PREP. SHIPMENTS					
28341	Affecting neoplasms, endocrine systems, and metabolic disease	Mil. dol.	2,507	2,743	2,877	3,179
28342	Acting on the central nervous system and sense organs	Mil. dol.	6,441	7,219	7,431	8,103
28343	Acting on the cardiovascular system.	Mil. dol.	4,875	4,815	4,810	4,877
28344	Acting on the respiratory system	Mil. dol.	3,286	3,724	4,260	5,024
28345	Acting on the digestive system	Mil. dol.	4,363	4,840	5,625	7,050
28346	Acting on the skin	Mil. dol.	1,452	1,558	1,579	1,687
28347	Vitamin, nutrient, and hematinic preps.	Mil. dol.	2,672	2,588	2,787	2,998
28348	Affecting parasitic and infective disease	Mil. dol.	4,936	5,411	6,006	7,060
28349	Pharmaceutical preps. for veterinary use	Mil. dol.	1,071	1,057	1,462	1,350

Source: U.S. Bureau of the Census, *Current Industrial Reports*, MA28A, MA28B, and MA28G, annual.

No. 1268. Engines, Refrigeration and Heating Equipment, and Pumps and Compressors: 1990 to 1992

Product code	PRODUCT	Unit	1990	1991	1992
(X)	Internal combustion engines produced..............	1,000	16,969	16,791	18,928
35191	Gasoline (except outboard, aircraft, and auto).........	1,000	16,326	16,220	18,299
35193	Nonautomotive diesel (except aircraft)..............	1,000	206	184	177
35194	Automotive diesel............................	1,000	433	383	448
35196	Natural gas and LPG..........................	1,000	4	4	4
(X)	Air-conditioning, heating equipment shipments:				
35851	Heat transfer equipment........................	Mil. dol....	4,308	3,925	4,237
35852	Unitary air-conditioners........................	Mil. dol....	3,560	3,533	3,685
35854	Compressors and compressor units	Mil. dol....	2,377	2,317	2,646
3561,3 pt.	Pumps and compressors [1].....................	Mil. dol....	4,797	5,119	5,157
35611	Industrial pumps.............................	Mil. dol....	2,131	2,263	2,202
35613	Domestic water systems........................	Mil. dol....	264	273	280
35615 pt.	Oil well, oilfield, and other pumps (including laboratory pumps)	Mil. dol....	563	597	591
35631	Compressors and vacuum pumps	Mil. dol....	1,839	1,993	2,078

X Not applicable.   [1] Excludes hand pumps, automotive circulating pumps, compressors for icemaking and refrigeration equipment, air conditioning units, and replacements and repair parts for pumps and compressors.

Source: U.S. Bureau of the Census, *Current Industrial Reports*, MA35L, MA35M, and MA35P, annual.

No. 1269. Computers and Office and Accounting Machines—Shipments: 1991 and 1992

Product code	PRODUCT	Number of companies, 1992	QUANTITY (number)		VALUE (mil. dol.)	
			1991	1992	1991	1992
3571	Electronic computers (automatic data processors)..	185	(X)	(X)	26,274	27,190
35713	Large-scale processing equipment [1].........	27	(NA)	79	(NA)	5,536
35714	Medium- and small-scale processing equipment [2]..	38	(NA)	142	(NA)	3,111
35715	Personal computers and workstations..........	77	(NA)	8,469	(NA)	16,024
35716	Portable computers	25	(NA)	1,173	(NA)	1,331
35721	Computer storage devices and equipment	89	3,811	4,679	5,610	6,056
35722	Parts for computer storage devices and subassemblies	26	(X)	(X)	780	1,132
35751	Computer terminals	72	3,282	3,869	1,730	1,698
35752	Parts for computer terminals	21	(X)	(X)	417	209
35771	Computer peripheral equipment, n.e.c.	238	(X)	(X)	7,764	8,478
35784	Calculating and accounting machines	45	(X)	(X)	974	984
35792	Automatic typing and word processing machines ..	5	1,734	2,323	417	465
35795	Mailing, letter handling, addressing machines.....	30	1,116	906	1,125	1,149
35799	Other office machines, n.e.c..............	50	(X)	(X)	518	500
36950	Magnetic and optical recording media..........	57	(X)	(X)	3,894	4,000

NA Not available.   X Not applicable.   [1] 64 megabytes in MINIMUM main memory configuration.   [2] Up to 64 megabytes in MINIMUM main memory configuration.

Source: U.S. Bureau of the Census, *Current Industrial Report*, MA35R, annual.

No. 1270. Metalworking Machinery—Shipments: 1986 to 1992

[In millions of dollars]

Product code	PRODUCT	1986	1987	1988	1989	1990	1991	1992
(X)	Metalworking machinery.......	2,710	2,669	2,858	3,514	3,426	3,172	3,074
(X)	Metal cutting type	1,912	1,781	1,735	2,429	2,371	2,139	2,000
3541A	Machining centers [1]...........	213	218	334	442	437	362	378
3541B	Station type machines	518	300	225	563	502	450	435
3541C	Other metal cutting machine tools [2]..	148	174	165	174	142	196	167
(X)	Metal forming type.............	798	888	1,123	1,086	1,065	1,033	1,074

X Not applicable.   [1] Multi-function numerically controlled machines.   [2] Excludes those designed primarily for home workshops, labs, etc.

Source: U.S. Bureau of the Census, *Current Industrial Reports*, MQ35W, annual.

No. 1271. Switchgear, Switchboard Apparatus, Relays, and Industrial Controls—Shipments: 1987 to 1992

[In millions of dollars]

Product code	PRODUCT	Companies, 1992 (number)	1987	1988	1989	1990	1991	1992
36132	Power circuit breakers	23	373	386	393	388	368	393
36133	Low volt panelboards & dist. boards [1]	117	1,569	1,664	1,747	1,722	1,643	1,613
36134	Fuses and fuse equipment [2]	19	368	390	419	419	409	413
36135	Molded case circuit breakers, 1,000 volts and under.	37	879	948	952	959	917	963
36136	Duct [3]	24	132	152	188	194	184	189
36139	Switchgear, except ducts	121	1,049	1,100	1,319	1,324	1,398	1,375
36251	General purpose and other relays	117	889	873	835	805	772	770
36252	Specific purpose industrial controls.	196	1,732	1,808	1,928	2,020	1,993	2,098
36253	General purpose industrial controls	255	2,403	2,655	2,971	2,912	2,879	2,783
36254	Motor controller accessories [4]	122	429	459	503	452	434	443

[1] Includes other switching and interruption devices, 1,000 volts and below.   [2] Under 2,300 volts, except power distribution cutouts.   [3] Includes plug-in units and accessories, 1,000 volts and under, consisting of enclosed sectionalized prefabricated bus bars rated 20 amperes or more, associated structures and fittings.   [4] Includes parts for industrial controls.

Source: U.S. Bureau of the Census, *Current Industrial Reports*, MA36A, annual.

No. 1272. Selected Industrial Air Pollution Control Equipment—Shipments: 1992

[Quantity in number of units, value in millions of dollars]

Product code	PRODUCT	Number of companies	NEW ORDERS		SHIPMENTS		BACKLOG (Dec. 31)	
			Quantity	Value	Quantity	Value	Quantity	Value
35646	Selected industrial air pollution control equip. . .	100	(X)	781	(X)	713	(X)	754
(X)	Particulate emissions collectors	(X)	(X)	422	(X)	463	(X)	255
35646 51	Electrostatic precipitators.	19	225	124	236	153	86	138
35646 54	Fabric filters	51	43,361	219	42,059	228	5,530	62
35646 55	Mechanical collectors	35	3,674	40	3,597	43	703	18
35646 58	Wet scrubbers	32	1,225	40	1,101	39	690	38
(X)	Gaseous emissions control devices	(X)	(X)	292	(X)	197	(X)	423
35646 70	Catalytic oxidation systems	7	124	22	104	19	66	11
35646 72	Thermal and direct oxidation systems	11	263	31	258	29	62	12
35646 73	Scrubbers (gas absorber)	12	812	34	597	20	302	18
35646 75	Dry flue gas desulfurization systems	9	29	181	28	120	34	339
35646 76	Gas absorbers.	8	46	25	37	9	26	43
35646 79	Other types of industrial air pollution control equip. .	19	(X)	67	(X)	53	(X)	76

X Not applicable.

Source: U.S. Bureau of the Census, *Current Industrial Reports*, MA35J, annual.

No. 1273. Fluid Power Products—Shipments: 1987 to 1992

[In millions of dollars. Includes aerospace]

Product code	PRODUCT	1987	1988	1989	1990	1991	1992
	Fluid power products, incl. aerospace	6,166	6,785	6,915	7,207	6,477	6,249
34921	Hydraulic valves, nonaerospace type	554	615	629	663	606	626
34922	Pneumatic valves, nonaerospace type	392	445	463	458	434	463
34923	Aerospace type hydraulic & pneumatic valves	387	400	451	498	527	439
34924	Fittings for metal and plastic tubing [1]	398	460	505	500	471	455
34925	Hydraulic and pneumatic fittings and couplings for hose (nonaerospace).	605	649	625	620	552	575
34926	Hydraulic and pneumatic hose or tube end fitting and assemblies (aerospace)	250	327	336	394	386	343
34927	Parts for hydraulic & pneumatic valves	183	219	206	209	161	97
35692	Filters for hydraulic and pneumatic fluid power systems	284	310	352	385	410	384
	Hydraulic and pneumatic cylinders etc.:						
35931	Nonaerospace.	794	907	909	941	865	931
35932	Aerospace	637	636	646	636	510	412
35933	Parts for hydraulic and pneumatic cylinders [2]	289	291	281	264	204	169
35941	Hydraulic fluid power pumps and motors	1,052	1,178	1,180	1,240	997	999
35942	Parts for pumps and motors	340	348	333	399	354	356

[1] Used in fluid and power transfer systems (nonaerospace).   [2] Includes parts for actuators, accumulators, cushions, and nonvehicular shock absorbers.

Source: U.S. Bureau of the Census, *Current Industrial Reports*, MA35N, annual.

No. 1274. Selected Instruments and Related Products—Shipments: 1986 to 1992

[In millions of dollars]

Product code	PRODUCT	1986	1987	1988	1989	1990	1991	1992
34918	Automatic regulating and control valves	1,302	1,221	1,262	1,331	1,418	1,537	1,569
34919	Solenoid-operated valves (except nuclear and fluid power transfer)	285	327	338	374	346	360	404
38121	Aeronautical, nautical, and navigational instruments.	1,789	2,270	2,365	2,521	2,518	2,672	2,431
38122	Search & detection, navigation & guidance systems and equipment	29,504	30,911	31,145	30,840	32,420	31,774	30,279
38210	Laboratory apparatus and laboratory furniture [1] . . .	1,330	1,549	1,565	1,698	1,675	1,612	1,681
38220	Controls for monitoring residential and commercial environments and appliance	1,966	2,093	2,207	2,224	1,982	1,982	2,156
38230	Process control instruments	3,895	4,084	4,348	4,743	5,224	5,230	5,408
38242	Integrating and totalizing meters for gas and liquids	526	589	610	647	725	698	721
38243	Counting devices. . . . . ,2.	177	198	193	206	210	226	269
38244	Motor vehicle instruments [2].	197	232	682	637	1,457	1,330	1,395
38251	Integrating instruments, electrical.	403	401	388	401	396	390	426
38252	Test equipment for testing electrical, radio and communication circuits, and motors	5,592	6,144	6,248	6,134	6,156	6,525	6,306
38253	Instruments to measure electricity	617	647	663	620	586	584	548
38260	Analytical, scientific instruments (except optical). . .	2,532	3,046	3,442	4,042	4,412	4,519	4,651
38271	Sighting, tracking, and fire-control equipment, optical.	651	726	609	595	581	547	493
38274	Optical instruments and lenses [3]	1,245	1,215	1,270	1,274	1,252	1,292	1,342
38291	Aircraft engine instruments (except flight)	505	520	505	508	579	682	591
38292	Physical properties and kinematic testing equip. . . .	775	859	894	946	1,012	1,024	1,106
38294	Nuclear radiation detection and monitoring instruments.	587	637	654	606	567	570	581
38295	Commercial, geophysical, meteorological, and general purpose instruments	317	358	1,072	1,035	1,140	1,335	1,353
38296	Surveying and drafting instruments.	230	247	270	270	274	235	266

[1] Beginning 1987, includes laboratory furniture. Prior to 1987, laboratory furniture was included in product class 38296. [2] Beginning 1990, includes some data previously classified in product class 37149, "Other motor vehicle parts and accessories, new, n.e.c." [3] Beginning 1992, product classes 38272, "Binoculars and astonomical instruments," and 38273, "Other optical instruments and lenses" were combined into product class 38274; prior years have been restated to reflect revision.

Source: U.S. Bureau of the Census, *Current Industrial Reports*, MA38B, annual.

No. 1275. Robots—Shipments: 1987 to 1989

[Based on a survey of all known manufacturers of robots, robot accessories, and components. Shipment value represents the net sales price, f.o.b. plant, to the customer or branch to which the products are shipped, net of discounts, allowances, freight charges and returns. A robot is a reprogrammable multifunctional manipulator designed to move materials, parts, tools, or specialized devices through variable programmed motions for the performance of a variety of tasks]

ROBOTS, ACCESSORIES, AND COMPONENTS	QUANTITY (number)			VALUE (mil. dol.)		
	1987	1988	1989	1987	1988	1989
Robots, robot accessories, and components	(X)	(X)	(X)	284	238	256
Robots, complete.	6,037	4,603	2,217	220	164	151
Servo-controlled robots	2,677	2,072	1,840	203	138	136
Point-to-point type:						
Welding, soldering, brazing, and/or cutting (welding type). .	675	304	273	65	32	29
Foundry, forging, and/or heat treating [1]	28	31	34	3	3	9
Assembly for nonelectronic and electronic products	535	296	238	20	8	8
Material handling and/or parts transfer	726	247	162	48	27	26
Continuous-path type:						
Welding, soldering, brazing, and/or cutting.	110	79	31	9	4	2
Spraying, painting, gluing, and/or sealing.	297	292	254	41	30	35
Fettling, grinding, polishing, and/or deburring [2]	306	823	848	17	33	26
Nonservo-controlled robots	215	336	377	17	17	15
Other robots.	3,145	2,195	(3)	9	9	(3)
Robot accessories, subassemblies, etc	(X)	(X)	(X)	65	74	105
Miscellaneous receipts	(X)	(X)	(X)	8	6	3

X Not applicable.   [1] Includes all point-to-point robots, except assembly, material handling, and/or parts transfer. [2] Includes other continuous-path type, not elsewhere classified.   [3] Beginning 1989, data no longer available for other robots which included education hobby, experimental, and nonindustrial robots.

Source: U.S. Bureau of the Census, *Current Industrial Reports*, MA35X(89-1).

Figure 27.1
Distribution of Retail Sales, by Kind of Business: 1980 and 1993

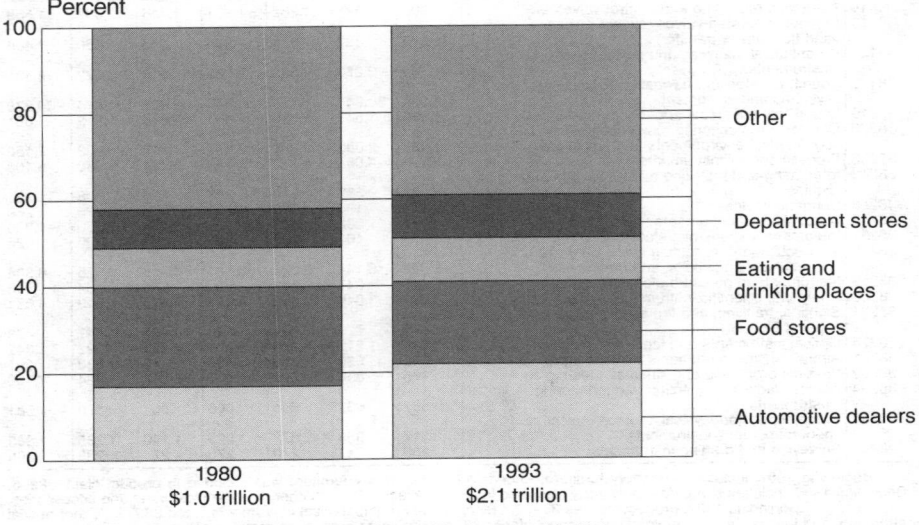

1980
$1.0 trillion

1993
$2.1 trillion

Other

Department stores

Eating and drinking places

Food stores

Automotive dealers

Source: Chart prepared by U.S. Bureau of the Census. For data, see table 1281.

Figure 27.2
Percent of Supermarkets Offering Selected Services and Products: 1990 and 1993

1990
1993

- Scanning checkouts
- Service delicatessen
- Reusable grocery bags
- Accept credit cards
- Self-service delicatessen
- Service meat
- Chilled prepared food
- Automated teller machines (ATM's)
- Pharmacy

Percent

Source: Chart prepared by U.S. Bureau of the Census. For data, see table 1286.

Domestic Trade and Services

This section presents statistics relating to the distributive trades and service industries. Data shown for the trades, classified by kind of business, and for the various categories of services (e.g., personal, business, repair, hotel) cover sales or receipts, establishments, employees, payrolls, and other items. Also included are data for franchised businesses. The principal sources of these data are census reports and survey reports of the Bureau of the Census. Data on gross product in trade and service industries usually appear in the *Survey of Current Business*, issued by the U.S. Bureau of Economic Analysis. Financial data for firms engaged in retail, wholesale, or service activities appear in the annual *Statistics of Income,* published by the Internal Revenue Service.

Censuses.—Censuses of retail trade and wholesale trade have been taken at various intervals since 1929. Limited coverage of the service industries started in 1933. Beginning with the 1967 census, legislation provides for a census of each area to be conducted every 5 years (for years ending in "2" and "7"). The industries covered in the censuses and surveys of business are those classified in three divisions defined in the *Standard Industrial Classification Manual* (see text, section 13). *Retail trade* refers to places of business primarily engaged in selling merchandise for personal or household consumption; *wholesale trade,* to establishments primarily engaged in selling goods to dealers and distributors for resale or to purchasers who buy for business and farm uses; and *services,* to establishments primarily engaged in providing a wide range of services for individuals and for businesses.

Beginning with the 1954 Censuses of Retail Trade and Service Industries, data for nonemployer establishments are included and published separately. The census of wholesale trade excludes establishments with no paid employees. Beginning in 1977, sales taxes and finance charges are excluded from sales (or receipt) figures of the three censuses. In 1982 and prior censuses, the count of

In Brief		
Retail sales, 1993:		
Total		*$2.1 trillion*
Automotive dealers		*$.5 trillion*
Food stores		*$.4 trillion*
Annual receipts of taxable service firms ($ billions):		
	1985	*1992*
Business services	*156*	*303*
Health services	*147*	*285*

establishments represented the number in business at the end of the year. For 1987, the count of establishments represents those in business at any time during 1987.

The 1987 Census of Service Industries includes hospitals whereas the 1982 census did not. For 1987, hospitals operated by governmental organizations are included. Government-operated facilities in other service kind-of-business classifications are excluded from the census. In 1982 and 1987, data were not collected for elementary and secondary schools, colleges and universities, labor unions and similar organizations, and political organizations.

The census of retail trade beginning in 1977, excludes nonemployer direct sellers. Beginning 1982, the census treated each leased department in a store as a separate establishment and classified it according to the kind of business it conducted. In prior years, data for leased departments were consolidated with the data for stores in which they were located.

Current surveys.—Current sample surveys conducted by the Bureau of the Census cover various aspects of the retail and wholesale trade and selected service industries. Its *Monthly Retail Trade Report* contains monthly estimates of sales, inventories, inventory/sales ratios, and sales of organizations operating 11 or more retail stores, for the United States, by kind of business. In addition, monthly retail sales data for census regions and divisions, large States, metropolitan areas, and cities are included. Annual figures on sales, year-end inventories, and sales/inventory ratios, by kind of business, appear in the *Combined Annual and Revised Monthly Retail Trade Report*.

Statistics from the Bureau's monthly wholesale trade survey include national estimates of merchant wholesalers' sales, inventories, and stock-sales ratios by major summary groups—durable and nondurable—and selected kinds of business. Merchant wholesalers are those wholesalers who take title to the goods they sell (e.g., jobbers, exporters, importers, major distributors). These data, based on reports submitted by a sample of firms, appear in the *Monthly Wholesale Trade Report*. Annual figures on sales, sales-inventory ratios, and year-end inventories appear in the *Combined Annual and Revised Monthly Wholesale Trade Report*. The *Service Annual Survey* provides annual estimates of receipts for selected service kinds of

business for the United States as a whole.

For the current sample survey programs, retail trade coverage is the same as for the census; wholesale trade coverage is limited to merchant wholesalers; and selected services coverage is less inclusive than the census.

Estimates obtained from annual and monthly surveys are based on sample data and are not expected to agree exactly with results that would be obtained from a complete census of all establishments. Data include estimates for sampling units not reporting.

Statistical reliability.—For a discussion of statistical collection and estimation, sampling procedures, and measures of statistical reliability applicable to Census Bureau data, see Appendix III.

Historical statistics.—Tabular headnotes provide cross-references, where applicable, to *Historical Statistics of the United States, Colonial Times to 1970.* See Appendix IV.

Figure 27.3
Service Industries—Annual Receipts of Taxable firms: 1985 and 1992

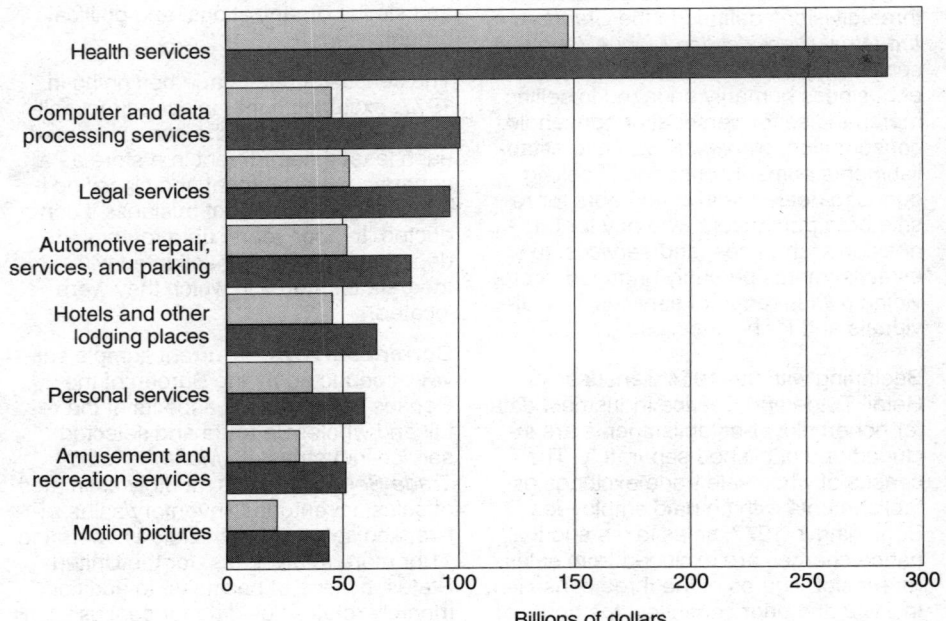

Billions of dollars

Source: Chart prepared by U.S. Bureau of the Census. For data, see table 1305.

No. 1276. Gross Domestic Product in Domestic Trade and Service Industries in Current and Constant (1987) Dollars: 1987 to 1991

[In billions of dollars, except percent. For definition of gross domestic product, see text, section 14. Based on 1987 Standard Industrial Classification]

INDUSTRY	CURRENT DOLLARS				CONSTANT (1987) DOLLARS			
	1987	1989	1990	1991	1987	1989	1990	1991
Wholesale and retail trade	**744.8**	**854.1**	**878.8**	**907.2**	**744.9**	**808.4**	**797.6**	**800.5**
Percent of gross domestic product	16.4	16.3	15.8	15.9	16.4	16.7	16.3	16.5
Wholesale trade.	303.1	351.6	363.0	375.1	303.1	324.5	319.5	326.4
Retail trade.	441.8	502.5	515.7	532.1	441.8	483.9	478.1	474.1
Services.	**782.5**	**948.8**	**1,040.0**	**1,089.8**	**782.5**	**845.7**	**869.4**	**866.7**
Percent of gross domestic product	17.2	18.1	18.8	19.0	17.2	17.5	17.8	17.8
Hotels and other lodging places	42.6	49.3	49.9	52.0	42.6	46.0	45.0	46.9
Personal services.	31.0	35.4	36.3	36.5	31.0	32.2	31.0	29.5
Business services.	141.6	175.5	198.2	201.8	141.6	163.2	172.6	167.9
Auto repair, services, and garages	38.2	42.9	46.2	47.9	38.2	38.2	38.9	38.7
Miscellaneous repair services.	13.7	16.3	17.1	16.1	13.7	16.0	15.9	14.4
Motion pictures	13.7	17.4	18.6	18.4	13.7	15.5	15.5	14.6
Amusement and recreation services	28.1	34.6	40.2	44.0	28.1	31.3	34.6	36.2
Health services	228.9	273.0	304.4	333.0	228.9	233.3	241.4	245.8
Legal services	61.1	73.0	79.6	81.9	61.1	65.7	66.1	64.1
Educational services.	30.3	36.3	38.1	42.5	30.3	32.2	32.1	33.9
Social services, membership organizations	45.7	56.0	60.6	64.8	45.7	52.3	55.0	56.8
Other services.	100.0	130.3	141.3	141.8	100.0	111.1	112.3	109.6
Private households.	7.7	8.9	9.4	9.2	7.7	8.7	8.9	8.2

Source: U.S. Bureau of Economic Analysis, *Survey of Current Business*, November 1993.

No. 1277. Retail Trade—Summary: 1958 to 1987

[1972 through 1982 based on 1972 Standard Industrial Classification (SIC) code; 1987 based on 1987 SIC code. Prior years based on earlier editions of SIC. Comparability of data over time is affected by changes in the SIC code. See also *Historical Statistics, Colonial Times to 1970*, series T 43-47 and T 79-91]

ITEM	Unit	1958	1963	1967	1972	1977	1982	1987
Firms, total [1]	1,000	(NA)	1,532	1,577	1,665	1,567	1,573	1,992
Multiunit establishments [1][2]	1,000	(NA)	240	234	301	343	415	498
Establishments, total [1].	1,000	1,795	1,708	1,763	1,780	1,855	1,923	2,420
With payroll	1,000	1,185	1,206	1,192	1,265	1,304	1,324	1,504
With sales of $1,000,000 or more.	1,000	(NA)	(NA)	(NA)	74	119	193	259
Consumer Price Index: [3]								
All items.	1982-84=100. .	28.9	30.6	33.4	41.8	60.6	96.5	113.6
All commodities.	1982-84=100. .	33.3	34.4	36.8	44.5	64.2	97.0	107.7
Sales	Bil. dol.	200	244	310	457	723	1,066	1,540
By establishments with payroll	Bil. dol.	188	233	295	440	700	1,039	1,493
By multiunit establishments [2]	Bil. dol.	[4]67	90	124	202	341	567	844
Percent of total sales	Percent	33.5	36.6	39.8	44.0	47.1	53.2	56.5
Percent of multiunit sales by 100-or-more establishment multiunits [2][5]	Percent	42.4	43.1	46.7	55.8	55.8	54.5	54.6
In 1982 dollars [6]	Bil. dol.	(NA)	645	764	943	1,054	1,066	1,393
Percent of sales by corporations	Percent	53.0	61.9	67.4	76.4	79.8	84.6	88.9
Per capita sales: [7]								
Current dollars	Dollars	1,156	1,296	1,571	2,186	3,291	4,599	6,328
Constant (1982) dollars [6]	Dollars	(NA)	3,423	3,869	4,508	4,798	4,599	5,722
Sales as percent of personal income	Percent	[4]55.5	52.4	49.3	48.1	46.9	41.5	40.9
Sales, inside metropolitan areas [8]	Bil. dol.	[4]133	170	221	(NA)	552	845	[9]1,230
Percent of total sales	Percent	66.4	69.5	71.4	(NA)	76.3	79.3	[9]82.4
Payroll, entire year	Bil. dol.	21.7	27.6	36.2	55.4	85.9	123.6	177.5
Percent of sales	Percent	[4]11.5	11.3	11.7	12.1	11.9	11.6	11.5
Paid employees, March 12 pay period [10].	1,000	7,942	8,410	9,381	11,221	13,040	14,468	17,780

NA Not available. [1] Through 1982, represents the number of establishments and firms in business at the end of the year. For 1987, represents the number of establishments and firms in business at any time during year. [2] Establishments operated by firms which operate at two or more locations. [3] Source: U.S. Bureau of Labor Statistics, *Monthly Labor Review*. Beginning 1982, CPI-U annual averages, see text, section 14. [4] Excludes Alaska and Hawaii. [5] Prior to 1982, data provided for percent of multiunit sales by 101-or-more establishment units. [6] Based on implicit price deflators for retail sales supplied by U.S. Bureau of Economic Analysis. [7] Based on estimated resident population as of July 1. [8] Through 1982 based on Standard Metropolitan Statistical Area definitions. Data for 1987 based on Metropolitan Statistical Area definitions. See Appendix II. [9] Covers only establishments with payroll. [10] 1958 and 1963 data for week including November 15.

Source: Except as noted, U.S. Bureau of the Census, *U.S. Census of Business: 1958*, vol. I; *1963*, vol. I; *1967*, vol. I; and *Census of Retail Trade, 1972*, RC72-S-1; *1977*, RC77-52; *1982*, RC82-A-52 and RC82-I-1; and *1987*, RC87-A-52, RC87-N-1, and RC87-S-1.

No. 1278. Retail Trade—Establishments, Employees, and Payroll: 1990 and 1991

[Excludes government employees, railroad employees, self-employed persons, etc. For statement on methodology, see Appendix III]

KIND OF BUSINESS	1987 SIC code [1]	ESTABLISHMENTS (1,000)		EMPLOYEES (1,000)		PAYROLL (bil. dol.)	
		1990	1991	1990	1991	1990	1991
Retail trade, total	(G)	1,529.7	1,547.3	19,815	19,600	241.7	247.0
Building materials and garden supplies [2]	52	71.9	71.7	703	685	11.9	12.0
Lumber and other building materials	521	27.5	27.4	403	394	7.5	7.6
Paint, glass, and wallpaper stores.	523	10.2	10.3	54	51	0.9	0.9
Hardware stores	525	19.0	18.9	143	141	1.9	1.9
Retail nurseries and garden stores	526	10.1	10.2	76	72	1.0	1.0
General merchandise stores [2]	53	36.6	36.9	2,135	2,093	22.9	23.4
Department stores	531	10.1	10.2	1,710	1,646	18.3	18.4
Variety stores	533	10.0	9.9	109	99	1.0	0.9
Misc. general merchandise stores.	539	15.0	15.6	310	342	3.6	4.0
Food stores [2]	54	186.1	187.8	3,124	3,114	35.8	37.4
Grocery stores	541	132.5	133.3	2,757	2,748	32.4	33.7
Meat and fish markets	542	9.3	9.2	54	52	0.6	0.7
Retail bakeries	546	19.9	20.8	176	175	1.5	1.6
Automotive dealers and service stations [2] . . .	55	207.3	204.5	2,104	2,006	40.0	39.1
New and used car dealers.	551	26.1	25.8	917	865	23.9	23.1
Used car dealers.	552	14.3	14.7	56	54	1.0	1.0
Auto and home supply stores.	553	43.4	43.7	305	299	5.1	5.2
Gasoline service stations	554	104.8	101.9	701	674	7.5	7.5
Apparel and accessory stores [2]	56	150.2	147.6	1,193	1,194	12.2	12.2
Men's and boys' clothing stores	561	14.7	14.0	108	101	1.5	1.4
Women's clothing stores.	562	50.2	48.8	439	445	4.0	4.0
Women's accessory and specialty stores. .	563	7.7	7.9	46	44	0.5	0.5
Family clothing stores.	565	17.8	18.0	283	293	3.0	3.0
Shoe stores	566	37.4	36.5	206	196	2.2	2.1
Misc. apparel and accessory stores	569	9.1	9.3	47	48	0.5	0.5
Furniture and homefurnishings stores [2]	57	108.1	110.7	749	746	12.3	12.7
Furniture and homefurnishings stores [2] . . .	571	61.1	62.2	430	414	7.2	7.1
Furniture stores	5712	30.8	31.4	245	237	4.3	4.2
Floor covering stores.	5713	13.2	13.5	77	73	1.5	1.5
Misc. homefurnishings stores	5719	13.3	13.6	92	89	1.1	1.1
Household appliance stores. . . . . :	572	10.0	10.0	63	61	1.1	1.1
Radio, television, and computer stores [2] . .	573	34.2	35.8	245	260	3.9	4.4
Radio, TV, and electronic stores	5731	16.5	16.9	120	125	2.1	2.2
Computer and software stores	5734	5.1	6.0	33	40	0.8	1.0
Record and prerecorded tape stores . . .	5735	7.1	7.6	60	64	0.6	0.6
Eating and drinking places [2]	58	402.6	415.2	6,461	6,416	49.6	51.4
Eating places	5812	286.8	280.2	5,700	5,460	43.8	44.0
Drinking places	5813	43.8	41.4	267	251	2.0	2.0
Miscellaneous retail [2]	59	349.0	354.7	2,487	2,504	33.2	34.6
Drug stores and proprietary stores	591	50.0	49.1	593	609	8.3	9.0
Liquor stores.	592	30.8	30.6	141	136	1.6	1.6
Used merchandise stores	593	15.0	16.3	79	83	0.9	1.0
Sporting goods and bicycle shops	5941	21.4	22.2	139	139	1.6	1.7
Book stores	5942	11.7	12.3	86	94	0.8	0.9
Jewelry stores.	5944	26.6	26.4	161	150	2.3	2.2
Hobby, toy, and game shops	5945	9.4	9.6	83	87	0.8	0.9
Gift, novelty, and souvenir shops	5947	29.5	29.6	164	163	1.4	1.4
Sewing, needlework, and piece goods. . . .	5949	8.2	8.2	68	64	0.5	0.5
Catalog and mail-order houses.	5961	7.2	7.4	141	148	2.6	2.8
Merchandising machine operators.	5962	5.1	5.3	76	73	1.3	1.2
Direct selling establishments	5963	8.8	8.7	107	104	1.7	1.6
Fuel dealers	598	12.0	11.8	100	96	2.2	2.1
Florists	5992	25.8	26.5	131	129	1.2	1.2
Optical goods stores	5995	13.2	13.7	66	69	1.1	1.1
Administrative and auxiliary.	(X)	18.0	18.3	860	842	23.7	24.3

X Not applicable. [1] Based on 1987 Standard Industrial Classification; see text, section 13. [2] Includes kinds of business not shown separately.

Source: U.S. Bureau of the Census, *County Business Patterns,* annual.

No. 1279. Retail Trade Establishments—Number, Sales, Payroll, and Employees, by Kind of Business: 1987

[Each kind-of-business classification includes leased departments classified in that kind of business as if they were separate establishments. See *Historical Statistics, Colonial Times to 1970*, series T 79-196 for similar but not comparable data]

KIND OF BUSINESS	1987 SIC code [1]	ALL ESTABLISHMENTS		ESTABLISHMENTS WITH PAYROLL				
		Number [2] (1,000)	Sales (mil. dol.)	Number [2] (1,000)	Sales Total (mil. dol.)	Sales Per establishment ($1,000)	Annual payroll (mil. dol.)	Paid employees [3] (1,000)
Retail trade, total	52	[4]2,420	[4]1,540,263	1,504	1,493,309	993	177,548	17,780
Building materials & garden supplies	52	107	83,454	74	81,487	1,104	9,760	668
Building materials, supply stores	521, 3	51	61,302	38	60,525	1,593	6,929	432
Hardware stores	525	27	11,036	20	10,535	525	1,564	138
Retail nurseries and garden stores	526	21	5,809	11	5,411	506	822	71
Mobile home dealers	527	8	5,307	5	5,015	993	445	27
General merchandise stores	53	57	181,971	35	181,147	5,112	19,586	2,003
Department stores (incl. leased depts.) [5]	531	10	153,679	10	153,679	15,305	(NA)	(NA)
Department stores (excl. leased depts.) [5]	531	10	144,017	10	144,017	14,343	16,365	1,651
Variety stores	533	21	7,134	10	6,762	649	926	121
Misc. general merchandise stores	539	26	30,819	15	30,368	2,029	2,294	231
Food stores [6]	54	290	309,460	191	301,847	1,583	29,819	2,855
Grocery stores	541	197	290,979	138	285,481	2,075	27,084	2,502
Meat and fish markets	542	(NA)	(NA)	11	5,616	494	606	59
Fruit and vegetable markets	543	(NA)	(NA)	3	1,802	551	186	20
Candy, nut, confectionery stores	544	(NA)	(NA)	6	1,182	193	199	31
Retail bakeries	546	31	5,194	22	4,871	224	1,353	185
Automotive dealers [6]	55 ex. 554	194	342,896	103	333,420	3,246	28,688	1,373
New and used car dealers	551	28	280,529	28	280,529	9,906	22,205	940
Used car dealers	552	75	18,295	15	10,849	726	809	55
Auto and home supply stores	553	67	26,622	46	25,460	551	4,152	286
Boat dealers	555	(NA)	(NA)	5	6,824	1,319	620	35
Recreational vehicle dealers	556	(NA)	(NA)	3	5,538	1,842	437	25
Motorcycle dealers	557	(NA)	(NA)	4	3,475	828	382	27
Gasoline service stations	554	137	104,769	115	101,997	889	6,414	702
Apparel and accessory stores [6]	56	197	79,322	149	77,391	518	9,725	1,121
Men's and boys' clothing stores	561	19	9,017	17	8,869	537	1,361	115
Women's clothing specialty stores	562, 3	77	29,208	60	28,531	477	3,519	455
Women's clothing stores	562	64	26,366	52	25,868	495	3,150	419
Children's and infants' wear stores	564	(NA)	(NA)	6	2,101	342	245	37
Family clothing stores	565	27	21,472	18	21,117	1,145	2,362	268
Shoe stores	566	43	14,594	39	14,411	365	1,880	205
Furniture and homefurnishings stores	57	180	78,072	110	74,783	682	9,904	703
Furniture stores	5712	46	26,740	33	25,997	793	3,828	247
Homefurnishings stores	5713, 4, 9	63	17,737	32	16,374	512	2,389	176
Household appliance stores	572	17	8,642	11	8,332	744	953	65
Radio, television, computer stores	573	54	24,953	34	24,080	714	2,734	215
Computer and software stores	5734	8	2,799	4	2,651	687	325	22
Eating and drinking places	58	490	153,462	391	148,776	380	38,582	6,100
Eating places [6]	5812	402	142,627	333	139,282	419	36,633	5,787
Restaurants and lunchrooms	5812 pt.	(NA)	(NA)	155	66,364	429	18,796	2,822
Refreshment places	5812 pt.	(NA)	(NA)	138	56,870	412	13,269	2,352
Drinking places	5813	88	10,834	59	9,495	162	1,950	313
Drug stores and proprietary stores	591	56	54,142	52	53,824	1,031	6,476	574
Miscellaneous retail stores [6]	59 ex. 591	[4]710	[4]152,716	284	138,636	489	18,594	1,682
Liquor stores	592	45	19,826	35	18,597	528	1,454	157
Used merchandise stores	593	89	5,217	15	3,502	236	663	69
Misc. shopping goods stores [6]	594	263	53,777	123	49,460	403	6,481	706
Sporting goods, bicycle shops	5941	50	11,256	22	10,077	467	1,218	121
Book stores	5942	19	5,338	11	5,116	462	581	72
Stationery stores	5943	7	1,942	5	1,814	376	287	27
Jewelry stores	5944	50	12,925	28	11,994	428	1,921	163
Hobby, toy, and game shops	5945	28	7,451	10	7,031	730	614	76
Camera, photo supply stores	5946	6	2,383	4	2,294	605	276	21
Gift, novelty, souvenir shops	5947	79	8,446	32	7,459	231	1,055	151
Sewing, needlework, and piece goods	5949	22	3,138	10	2,836	294	406	65
Nonstore retailers	596	[4]66	[4]34,878	23	33,894	1,470	4,523	318
Catalog and mail-order houses	5961	31	20,765	7	20,347	2,815	1,932	123
Merchandising machine operators	5962	24	6,258	5	5,692	1,074	1,090	74
Direct selling establishments	5963	[4]11	[4]7,855	11	7,855	746	1,501	121
Fuel dealers	598	17	14,503	13	14,198	1,114	1,824	99
Florists	5992	50	5,441	27	4,810	180	1,019	125
Optical goods stores	5995	15	3,480	14	3,415	251	811	54

NA Not available. [1] Based on 1987 Standard Industrial Classification; see text, section 13. [2] Represents the number of establishments in business at any time during year. [3] For pay period including March 12. [4] Excludes nonemployer direct sellers, SIC 5963. [5] Includes sales from catalog order desks. [6] Includes other kinds of businesses, not shown separately.
Source: U.S. Bureau of the Census, *1987 Census of Retail Trade*, RC87-A-52 and RC87-N-1.

No. 1280. Retail Trade Sales—Summary: 1980 to 1993

[Sales and inventories for leased departments and concessions are tabulated in the kind-of-business category of the leased department or concession. Based on Current Business Survey, see Appendix III. Minus sign (-) indicates decrease. See also *Historical Statistics, Colonial Times to 1970*, series T 245, 246, and 255]

YEAR	CURRENT DOLLARS							CONSTANT (1987) DOLLARS [4]		
	Total sales (bil. dol.)	Annual percent change [1]	Per capita [2] (dol.)	Index of sales (1982= 100)	Durable goods (bil. dol.)	Nondurable goods (bil. dol.)		Total sales (bil. dol.)	Annual percent change [1]	Per capita [2] (dol.)
						Total	Dept. stores [3]			
1980	957	6.7	4,213	89.5	299	658	86	1,193	-3.8	5,252
1981	1,039	8.5	4,527	97.1	325	714	96	1,201	0.6	5,232
1982	1,069	3.0	4,616	100.0	336	733	100	1,189	-1.0	5,130
1983	1,170	9.4	5,005	109.4	391	779	109	1,272	7.0	5,440
1984	1,287	10.0	5,457	120.3	454	832	120	1,360	6.9	5,767
1985	1,375	6.8	5,779	128.6	498	877	126	1,420	4.4	5,969
1986	1,450	5.4	6,037	135.6	541	909	134	1,498	5.5	6,240
1987	1,541	6.3	6,361	144.1	576	965	144	1,539	2.7	6,351
1988	1,657	7.5	6,778	155.0	630	1,028	152	1,599	3.9	6,541
1989	1,761	6.3	7,136	164.7	659	1,103	161	1,642	2.7	6,654
1990	1,848	4.9	7,411	172.8	671	1,177	166	1,654	0.7	6,632
1991	1,863	0.8	7,389	174.2	653	1,209	174	1,622	-2.0	6,432
1992	1,959	5.2	7,680	183.2	707	1,252	187	1,673	3.1	6,558
1993	2,082	6.3	8,071	194.7	785	1,297	201	1,758	5.1	6,816

[1] Change from immediate prior year.   [2] Based on Bureau of the Census estimates of resident population as of July 1.
[3] Excludes leased departments.   [4] Source: U.S. Bureau of Economic Analysis, *Survey of Current Business*, monthly; and unpublished data.

No. 1281. Retail Trade—Sales, by Kind of Business: 1980 to 1993

[In billions of dollars. See headnote, table 1280. Based on Current Business Survey, see Appendix III. See also *Historical Statistics, Colonial Times to 1970*, series T 245-271]

KIND OF BUSINESS	1987 SIC code [1]	1980	1985	1988	1989	1990	1991	1992	1993
Retail trade, total		957.4	1,375.0	1,657.3	1,761.4	1,848.4	1,863.0	1,959.1	2,081.6
Durable goods stores, total [2]		299.2	498.1	629.8	658.7	671.3	653.5	707.3	784.6
Automotive dealers	55 exc. 554	164.1	303.2	372.2	385.2	384.6	370.8	403.6	454.4
Motor vehicle, misc. automotive dealers..	551,2,5,6,7,9	146.2	278.0	341.9	353.5	352.1	336.5	367.8	416.9
Motor vehicle dealers	551,2	137.7	263.1	323.6	334.8	333.9	318.7	349.7	400.7
Motor vehicle dealers, franchised	551	130.5	251.6	302.6	310.3	313.8	298.4	328.9	375.1
Auto and home supply stores.	553	18.0	25.2	30.3	31.7	34.3	34.3	35.9	37.6
Building materials and garden supplies...	52	50.8	71.2	91.8	94.1	97.4	95.2	106.0	115.9
Building materials, supply stores.	521,3	35.0	50.8	67.1	68.0	71.3	69.5	77.1	84.6
Hardware stores	525	8.3	10.5	11.8	12.5	12.4	11.9	12.4	12.9
Furniture and homefurnishings stores [2].	57	44.2	68.3	86.3	93.4	94.9	96.3	102.6	113.7
Furniture, homefurnishings stores	571	26.3	38.3	47.9	51.8	51.5	50.8	53.6	57.7
Furniture stores	5712	(NA)	23.9	28.4	32.3	31.4	31.0	32.2	35.7
Floor covering stores.	5713	(NA)	7.9	11.3	11.2	11.5	11.1	11.7	11.7
Household appliance, radio, TV, and computer stores.	5722,31,34	14.0	25.1	31.1	33.9	34.9	36.2	39.3	44.8
Household appliance stores	5722	(NA)	8.4	9.0	9.8	9.5	9.3	9.7	10.2
Radio, TV, and computer stores	5731,34	(NA)	16.7	22.2	24.1	25.4	27.0	29.6	34.7
Sporting goods and bicycle shops	5941	(NA)	8.7	13.0	14.7	15.8	16.2	17.2	19.3
Book stores.	5942	(NA)	4.5	6.0	6.6	7.5	7.8	8.5	9.0
Jewelry stores	5944	(NA)	11.2	14.2	14.2	14.9	14.3	14.7	16.3
Nondurable goods stores, total [2]		658.1	876.9	1,027.5	1,102.7	1,177.1	1,209.4	1,251.8	1,297.0
Apparel and accessory stores [2].	56	49.3	70.2	85.3	92.3	95.7	97.3	104.1	106.1
Men's and boys' clothing stores	561	7.7	8.5	9.5	9.8	9.4	9.0	8.5	8.4
Women's clothing specialty stores	562,3	17.6	26.1	31.1	33.4	34.7	35.4	39.2	39.6
Women's clothing stores	562	15.9	23.6	27.9	30.1	31.5	32.3	35.0	35.5
Family clothing stores.	565	10.8	17.8	23.6	25.8	27.4	29.1	31.1	32.7
Shoe stores	566	10.5	13.1	15.4	17.2	18.0	17.4	18.0	17.7
Drug stores and proprietary stores.	591	31.0	47.0	57.9	63.5	70.8	75.9	78.2	80.9
Eating and drinking places	58	90.1	127.9	167.5	176.8	188.5	194.1	200.6	211.0
Eating places	5812	80.4	117.6	156.5	165.9	176.7	181.8	187.6	198.3
Restaurants, lunchrooms, cafeterias. ...	5812 pt	(NA)	68.2	87.2	91.8	98.2	102.1	104.4	109.0
Refreshment places	5812 pt	(NA)	48.1	66.9	71.2	75.4	76.7	80.4	86.6
Drinking places	5813	(NA)	10.3	11.0	10.9	11.8	12.2	13.0	12.7
Food stores.	54	220.2	285.1	326.6	349.3	372.0	379.3	382.4	392.4
Grocery stores	541	205.6	269.5	308.0	329.7	350.9	357.7	361.8	370.7
Gasoline service stations	554	94.1	113.3	109.7	121.5	136.2	134.1	132.3	133.5
General merchandise stores.	53	109.0	158.6	192.7	206.9	216.5	228.5	248.8	267.0
Department stores [3].	531	85.5	126.4	151.6	160.8	166.2	173.5	187.2	201.2
Variety stores	533	7.8	8.5	7.1	7.2	7.2	7.1	7.7	7.1
Misc. general merchandise stores.	539	15.7	23.8	34.0	38.8	43.0	47.9	53.9	58.7
Liquor stores	592	16.9	19.5	19.8	20.5	22.4	23.3	22.8	21.2
Nonstore retailers	596	22.8	28.3	40.0	42.5	43.7	46.1	50.8	50.5
Catalog and mail-order houses.	5961	(NA)	15.8	23.5	25.1	24.7	27.0	31.1	29.3
Fuel dealers.	598	(NA)	16.8	15.3	15.8	17.4	17.0	17.3	18.6

NA Not available.   [1] Based on 1987 Standard Industrial Classification code; see text, section 13.   [2] Includes kinds of business, not shown separately.   [3] Excludes leased departments.

Source of tables 1280 and 1281: Except as noted, U.S. Bureau of the Census, *Current Business Reports, Combined Annual and Revised Monthly Retail Trade, January 1984 Through December 1993*, (BR/93-RV) and prior issues.

No. 1282. Retail Trade—Sales of Multiunit Organizations, by Kind of Business: 1980 to 1993

[Data based on sales of companies which had 11 or more retail establishments according to the most recent update of multiestablishment files selected with certainty (i.e., their sales size exceeded specified dollar volume cutoffs which varied by kind of business). For details, see source. See also *Historical Statistics, Colonial Times to 1970*, series T 197-219]

KIND OF BUSINESS	1987 SIC code [1]	SALES (bil. dol.) 1980	1985	1990	1991	1992	1993	PERCENT OF TOTAL RETAIL SALES 1980	1990	1993
Total		361.3	520.3	738.0	765.6	811.6	854.4	37.3	39.9	41.0
Durable goods stores		35.2	55.1	98.3	102.1	112.7	124.8	11.4	14.6	15.9
Auto and home supply stores..	553	4.7	5.9	10.7	11.2	12.4	13.4	26.2	31.1	35.7
Nondurable goods stores [2]		326.0	465.2	639.7	663.5	698.9	729.6	49.1	54.3	56.2
General merchandise stores.........	53	101.6	151.4	206.3	216.4	236.0	254.6	90.6	95.3	95.4
Department stores................	531	83.2	124.0	163.2	176.2	184.5	198.6	96.1	98.2	98.7
Variety stores...................	533	6.3	7.0	4.8	4.5	5.3	4.9	80.9	66.6	68.5
Misc. general merchandise stores	539	12.1	20.4	38.2	41.2	46.3	51.1	58.1	88.9	87.0
Food stores.....................	54	119.8	162.5	219.1	226.0	228.0	232.6	54.4	58.9	59.3
Grocery stores.................	541	118.1	160.2	215.7	222.4	224.6	229.3	57.4	61.5	61.9
Apparel and accessory stores [2]	56	21.1	35.9	57.9	60.9	65.5	68.0	42.7	60.5	64.1
Women's clothing specialty stores	562,3	8.3	13.6	20.6	21.9	24.1	24.7	47.1	59.5	62.3
Family clothing	565	(NA)	11.3	20.3	21.9	23.7	25.2	(NA)	74.0	77.2
Shoe stores	566	5.3	7.7	11.8	11.5	12.1	12.3	50.8	65.6	69.4
Eating places...................	5812	22.6	33.8	45.2	44.9	47.2	49.3	28.1	25.6	24.9
Drug stores and proprietary stores	591	16.8	27.9	42.8	46.0	48.4	50.2	54.3	60.4	62.1

NA Not available. [1] Based on 1987 Standard Industrial Classification code; see text, section 13. [2] Includes kinds of business not shown separately.

Source: U.S. Bureau of the Census, *Current Business Reports, Combined Annual and Revised Monthly Retail Trade, January 1984 Through December 1993* (BR/93-RV); and unpublished data.

No. 1283. Retail Trade—Merchandise Inventories and Inventory/Sales Ratios, by Kind of Business: 1990 to 1993

[As of Dec. 31. Includes warehouses. Adjusted for seasonal variations. Sales data also adjusted for holiday, and trading-day differences. See headnote, table 1280]

KIND OF BUSINESS	1987 SIC code [1]	INVENTORIES AT COST [2] (bil. dol.) 1990	1991	1992	1993	INVENTORY/SALES RATIOS 1990	1991	1992	1993
Total		241.1	245.0	253.8	271.6	1.57	1.57	1.50	1.50
Excluding automotive group......		*178.7*	*185.1*	*191.2*	*203.7*	*1.45*	*1.49*	*1.43*	*1.46*
Durable goods stores [3]		121.7	119.7	123.5	135.8	2.26	2.17	1.99	1.91
Building materials and garden supplies....	52	17.6	17.5	18.2	20.6	2.26	2.18	1.96	1.93
Automotive dealers................	55 exc. 554	62.5	59.9	62.7	67.9	2.03	1.90	1.76	1.63
Furniture and homefurnishings stores	57	18.1	18.5	19.1	22.2	2.35	2.29	2.10	2.18
Nondurable goods stores [3]		119.5	125.3	130.3	135.8	1.20	1.24	1.22	1.24
General merchandise stores..........	53	42.5	46.0	48.9	53.1	2.33	2.36	2.30	2.33
Department stores...............	531	33.5	36.2	38.3	41.6	2.40	2.46	2.38	2.41
Food stores......................	54	25.4	26.2	26.4	27.0	0.81	0.83	0.81	0.81
Apparel and accessory stores	56	19.6	20.1	22.1	22.9	2.48	2.51	2.46	2.59

[1] Based on 1987 Standard Industrial Classification code; see text, section 13. [2] Excludes supplies and equipment used in store and warehouse operations that are not for resale. [3] Includes kinds of business not shown separately.

Source: U.S. Bureau of the Census, *Current Business Reports, Combined Annual and Revised Monthly Retail Trade, January 1984 Through December 1993* (BR/93-RV).

No. 1284. Retail Foodstores—Number and Sales, by Type: 1980 to 1992

TYPE OF FOODSTORE	NUMBER [1] (1,000) 1980	1985	1990	1991	1992	SALES [2] (bil. dol.) 1980	1985	1990	1991	1992	PERCENT DISTRIBUTION Number 1980	1992	Sales 1980	1992
Total	253.4	255.9	253.0	251.7	250.4	220.2	285.1	369.8	376.9	384.0	100.0	100.0	100.0	100.0
Grocery stores ...	178.3	177.2	170.1	168.0	165.9	205.6	269.5	348.7	355.3	360.8	70.4	66.3	93.4	94.0
Supermarkets [3] .	26.3	26.2	23.8	23.7	23.4	157.0	201.8	260.1	268.9	274.3	10.4	9.3	71.3	71.4
Convenience stores [4]	35.8	45.4	51.7	50.7	49.9	18.9	33.7	46.5	47.3	48.5	14.1	19.9	8.6	12.6
Superette [5]	116.2	105.6	94.6	93.6	92.6	29.7	34.0	42.1	39.1	38.0	45.9	37.0	13.5	9.9
Specialized food stores [6]	75.0	78.7	83.0	83.7	84.5	14.6	15.5	21.1	21.6	23.2	29.6	33.7	6.6	6.0

[1] Estimated. [2] Includes nonfood items. [3] A grocery store, primarily self-service in operation, providing a full range of departments, and having at least $2.5 million in annual sales in 1985 dollars. [4] A small grocery store selling a limited variety of food and nonfood products, typically open extended hours. [5] A grocery store, primarily self-service in operation, selling a wide variety of food and nonfood products with annual sales below $2.5 million (1985 dollars). [6] Primarily engaged in the retail sale of a single food category such as meat and seafood stores and retail bakeries.
Source: U.S. Dept. of Agriculture, Economic Research Service, *Food Marketing Review*, annual.

No. 1285. Supermarkets—Number and Sales, by Type of Format: 1980 to 1992

[Covers establishments open the entire year. For definition of supermarket, see footnote 3, table 1284]

SUPERMARKET FORMAT	NUMBER			SALES (bil. dol.)				PERCENT DISTRIBUTION			
								Number		Sales	
	1980	1990	1992	1980	1990	1991	1992	1980	1992	1980	1992
Supermarkets, total	26,321	23,813	23,381	157.0	260.1	268.9	274.3	100	100	100	100
Conventional	21,009	12,550	11,323	114.7	90.7	81.8	84.7	80	48	73	31
Superstore [1]	3,150	5,810	6,000	27.8	87.6	91.1	93.3	12	26	18	34
Warehouse [2]	1,670	3,381	3,350	6.6	33.1	35.3	33.1	6	14	4	12
Combination food and drug [3] . . .	475	1,619	2,100	6.3	34.8	46.0	42.3	2	9	4	15
Superwarehouse [4]	7	333	470	1.6	12.6	13.8	13.9	(Z)	2	1	5
Hypermarket [5]	10	120	138	(NA)	1.3	0.9	7.0	(Z)	1	(NA)	3

NA Not available.   Z Less than 0.5 percent.   [1] Contains greater variety of products than conventional supermarkets, including specialty and service departments, and considerable nonfood (general merchandise) products.   [2] Contains limited product variety and fewer services provided, incorporating case lot stocking and shelving practices.   [3] Contains a pharmacy, a nonprescription drug department, and a greater variety of health and beauty aids than that carried by conventional supermarkets.   [4] A larger warehouse store that offers expanded product variety and often service meat, deli, or seafood departments. [5] A very large store offering a greater variety of general merchandise—like clothes, hardware, and seasonal goods—and personal care products than other grocery stores.

Source: U.S. Dept. of Agriculture, Economic Research Service, *Food Marketing Review*, annual.

No. 1286. Percent of Supermarkets Offering Selected Services and Product Lines: 1990 and 1993

[In percent. Based on a sample survey of chain and independent supermarkets and subject to sampling variability; for details, see source]

SERVICE OR PRODUCT LINE OFFERED	TOTAL		CHAINS		INDEPENDENTS	
	1990	1993	1990	1993	1990	1993
Service delicatessen	73	79	76	81	69	77
Service bakery	60	62	66	66	53	55
Hot takeout food	55	55	59	57	49	52
Chilled prepared food	50	46	55	50	42	40
Service meat	42	47	45	47	37	46
Self-service delicatessen	38	50	38	52	39	46
Service fish	33	37	43	47	20	21
Separate cheese department	33	34	43	44	19	20
Salad bar	18	19	22	23	13	13
Plastic grocery bags	88	94	94	97	79	89
Reusable grocery bags	58	61	68	65	44	54
Carryout services	82	82	81	79	84	86
Scanning checkouts	71	85	79	91	61	75
Automated teller machines (ATM's)	20	38	28	46	10	25
Accept credit cards	19	51	23	55	13	44
Accept debit cards	(NA)	31	(NA)	36	(NA)	23
Pharmacy	15	20	22	28	6	8
Home delivery	(NA)	16	(NA)	10	(NA)	25

NA Not available.

Source: Maclean Hunter Media Inc., Stamford, CT, *Progressive Grocer, Annual Report of the Grocery Industry*, (copyright).

No. 1287. Supermarket Shopping—Selected Characteristics: 1990 and 1993

[Based on a sample survey of 500 households and subject to sampling variability; for details, see source]

TYPE OF OUTLET	PERCENT OF HOUSEHOLDS SHOPPING AT OUTLET		AVERAGE NUMBER OF WEEKLY TRIPS		AVERAGE WEEKLY SPENDING (dollars)		NUMBER OF SUPER-MARKETS SHOPPED IN EACH WEEK	PERCENT DISTRIBUTION	
	1990	1993	1990	1993	1990	1993		1990	1993
Supermarket	100	100	2.3	2.1	72.65	71.04	Total	100	100
Convenience store	41	51	2.3	2.5	12.86	11.28	One	31	26
Fast-food restaurant	67	68	1.9	1.9	16.17	17.72	Two	45	48
Mass merchandiser	64	71	1.4	1.4	26.25	28.50	Three	20	20
Wholesale clubs	(NA)	26	(NA)	1.2	(NA)	86.30	Four or more . . .	4	6

NA Not available.

Source: Maclean Hunter Media Inc., Stamford, CT, *Progressive Grocer, Annual Report of the Grocery Industry*, (copyright).

No. 1288. Commercial and Institutional Groups—Food and Drink Sales: 1980 to 1994

[Excludes military. Data refer to sales to consumers of food and alcoholic beverages. Sales are estimated. For details, see source]

TYPE OF GROUP	Number, 1991	SALES (mil. dol.)							
		1980	1985	1989	1990	1991	1992 [1]	1993 [1]	1994 [1]
Total	729,364	119,004	172,787	225,644	237,700	245,418	253,769	263,553	274,029
Commercial foodservice [2][3]	553,739	101,529	151,762	200,583	211,083	217,983	225,454	234,462	244,142
Eating places [2]	344,061	72,276	111,657	146,716	154,227	159,272	165,341	173,848	181,826
Full-service restaurants	165,111	39,307	57,939	72,727	76,072	78,355	80,313	83,102	85,510
Limited-service restaurants [4]	152,936	28,699	47,477	65,775	69,458	71,889	75,627	80,927	86,026
Bars and taverns [5]	37,227	7,785	8,338	8,952	9,212	9,442	9,169	8,875	8,742
Food contractors [2]	15,739	6,818	9,460	13,198	14,149	14,829	15,494	15,740	16,359
Manufacturing and industrial plants	(NA)	2,121	2,721	3,669	3,856	3,918	4,021	3,894	4,014
Colleges and universities	(NA)	1,140	1,738	2,569	2,788	3,072	3,195	3,527	3,756
Lodging places [2]	27,364	6,768	10,557	13,606	14,272	14,601	15,170	15,065	15,463
Hotel restaurants	17,028	4,964	8,986	12,215	12,907	13,281	13,856	13,791	14,205
Motel restaurants	8,628	1,151	975	836	820	790	779	753	738
Retail hosts [2][6]	109,007	3,264	5,254	9,276	9,888	10,380	10,607	11,010	11,441
Department store restaurants	4,980	857	865	925	950	980	(NA)	(NA)	(NA)
Grocery store restaurants [6]	44,966	830	2,074	5,379	5,733	6,013	(NA)	(NA)	(NA)
Gasoline service stations	34,788	492	1,052	1,523	1,681	1,824	(NA)	(NA)	(NA)
Recreation and sports	14,447	1,452	1,972	2,787	2,916	2,949	3,045	3,146	3,237
Institutional foodservice [2]	175,625	17,475	21,025	25,061	26,617	27,436	28,314	29,090	29,887
Employee foodservice	7,636	1,635	1,971	1,994	1,985	1,913	1,876	1,778	1,926
Industrial, commercial organizations	3,012	1,377	1,682	1,641	1,603	1,535	(NA)	(NA)	(NA)
Educational foodservice [2]	96,356	4,610	5,978	7,237	7,671	8,223	8,353	8,977	9,375
Elementary and secondary schools	93,535	2,312	2,919	3,478	3,700	3,878	3,984	4,123	4,265
Hospitals	6,606	6,668	7,104	8,396	8,968	9,018	9,643	9,344	9,447
Miscellaneous [2]	31,568	1,521	2,077	2,677	2,845	2,993	3,041	3,386	3,395
Clubs	10,310	1,056	1,537	1,914	1,993	2,039	(NA)	(NA)	(NA)

NA Not available.   [1] Projection.   [2] Includes other types of groups, not shown separately.   [3] Data for establishments with payroll.   [4] Fast-food restaurants.   [5] For establishments serving food.   [6] Beginning 1989, a portion of delicatessen sales in grocery stores are considered foodservice.

Source: National Restaurant Association, Washington, DC, *Foodservice Numbers: A Statistical Digest for the Foodservice Industry*, 1992; *Foodservice Industry in Review*, annual; and National Restaurant Association *Foodservice Industry Forecast*, December 1993, (copyright).

No. 1289. Motor Vehicle Factory Sales and Retail Sales: 1980 to 1992

[In thousands. See also *Historical Statistics, Colonial Times to 1970*, series Q 148 and 150]

YEAR	1980	1983	1984	1985	1986	1987	1988	1989	1990	1991	1992
Factory sales, total	8,067	9,153	10,696	11,359	10,909	10,907	11,225	10,869	9,769	8,783	9,727
Passenger cars	6,400	6,739	7,621	8,002	7,516	7,085	7,105	6,807	6,050	5,407	5,684
Trucks and buses	1,667	2,414	3,075	3,357	3,393	3,821	4,121	4,062	3,719	3,375	4,042
Retail sales, total	11,466	12,311	14,483	15,724	16,323	15,189	15,679	14,713	14,146	12,539	13,117
Passenger cars (new), total	8,979	9,182	10,390	11,042	11,460	10,277	10,530	9,772	9,300	8,175	8,214
Domestic	6,581	6,795	7,952	8,205	8,215	7,081	7,526	7,073	6,897	6,137	6,277
Imports	2,398	2,387	2,439	2,838	3,245	3,196	3,004	2,699	2,403	2,038	1,938
Trucks (new), total	2,487	3,129	4,093	4,682	4,863	4,912	5,149	4,941	4,846	4,365	4,903
Domestic	2,001	2,658	3,475	3,902	3,921	4,055	4,508	4,403	4,215	3,813	4,481
Imports	486	471	618	780	942	857	641	538	631	551	422

Source: American Automobile Manufacturers Association, Detroit, MI, *AAMA Motor Vehicle Facts and Figures*, annual, (copyright).

No. 1290. Franchised New Car Dealerships—Summary: 1980 to 1992

ITEM	Unit	1980	1984	1985	1986	1987	1988	1989	1990	1991	1992
Dealerships [1]	Number	27,900	24,725	24,725	24,825	25,150	25,025	25,000	24,825	24,200	23,500
Sales	Bil. dol.	130.5	225.9	251.6	270.4	280.5	302.1	309.2	312.1	296.5	320.0
New cars	1,000	8,979	10,393	11,046	11,463	10,225	10,595	9,830	9,296	8,176	8,211
Used vehicles	1,000	9,717	12,410	13,360	13,540	13,260	14,600	14,610	14,180	14,270	15,140
Employment	1,000	745.2	794.8	856.9	896.7	926.0	960.1	956.4	926.4	886.4	876.0
Annual payroll	Bil. dol.	11.0	17.8	20.1	21.7	22.6	24.7	24.4	24.1	23.3	23.7
Advertising expenses	Bil. dol.	1.2	2.1	2.8	3.2	3.7	4.0	3.9	3.6	3.4	3.6
Dealer pretax profits as a percentage of sales	Percent	0.6	2.2	2.2	2.2	1.9	1.7	1.0	1.0	1.0	1.4
Inventory: [2]											
Domestic: [3]											
Total	1,000	1,506	1,413	1,510	1,687	1,710	1,549	1,677	1,450	1,263	1,196
Days' supply	Days	71	55	58	63	74	65	72	66	64	62
Imported: [3]											
Total	1,000	458	216	271	392	567	647	648	597	584	539
Days' supply	Days	55	26	30	37	55	65	70	74	86	83

[1] At beginning of year.   [2] Annual average.   [3] Classification based on where automobiles are produced (i.e., automobiles manufactured by foreign companies but produced in the United States are classified as domestic).

Source: National Automobile Dealers Association, McLean, VA, *NADA Data*, annual.

No. 1291. Domestic and International Franchising—Summary: 1980 to 1991

[Franchising is a form of marketing or distribution in which a parent company customarily grants an individual or a company the right, or privilege, to do business in a prescribed manner over a certain period of time in a specified place. The parent company is termed the franchisor; the receiver of the privilege the franchisee; and the right, or privilege, the franchise]

ITEM	Unit	1980	1983	1984	1985	1986	1987	1988	1989	1990	1991
DOMESTIC [1]											
Number of franchised establishments.	1,000 ..	442	442	444	455	462	479	481	493	521	542
Company-owned [2]	1,000 ..	85	86	87	86	88	89	94	95	97	100
Franchisee-owned	1,000 ..	357	355	357	369	374	390	387	398	424	442
Sales of products and services	Bil. dol.	336	423	492	543	569	599	648	678	714	758
Company-owned [2]	Bil. dol .	47	59	64	68	85	90	98	107	117	127
Franchisee-owned	Bil. dol .	289	364	428	475	484	509	550	570	597	631
Average sales per establishment	$1,000 .	760	958	1,108	1,193	1,231	1,251	1,348	1,376	1,370	1,399
INTERNATIONAL											
U.S. companies operating foreign outlets	Number.	279	305	328	342	354	(NA)	374	(NA)	(NA)	(NA)
Foreign outlets	1,000 ..	20.4	25.7	27.0	30.2	31.6	(NA)	35.0	(NA)	(NA)	(NA)

NA Not available.   [1] Excludes foreign outlets of U.S. companies.   [2] Represents establishments owned by the parent company.

Source: U.S. Dept. of Commerce, International Trade Administration, *Franchising in the Economy, 1986-88*, 1988. Beginning 1988, International Franchise Association Educational Foundation, Inc., Washington, DC, *Franchising in the Economy*, annual.

No. 1292. Domestic Franchising—Number of Establishments and Sales, by Kind of Franchised Business: 1980 to 1991

[See headnote, table 1291, for definition of franchising. Excludes foreign outlets of U.S. companies]

KIND OF FRANCHISED BUSINESS	NUMBER OF ESTABLISHMENTS (1,000)						SALES (bil. dol.)					
	1980	1985	1988	1989	1990	1991	1980	1985	1988	1989	1990	1991
All franchising, total	**442.4**	**455.2**	**480.8**	**492.5**	**521.2**	**542.5**	**336.2**	**543.0**	**648.1**	**677.9**	**713.8**	**757.8**
Auto and truck dealers [1]	29.4	27.5	27.8	26.9	26.8	26.5	143.9	282.6	345.1	351.0	345.9	354.5
Percent	6.6	6.0	5.8	5.5	5.1	4.9	42.8	52.0	53.2	51.8	48.5	46.8
Restaurants (all types)	60.0	73.9	90.3	92.0	99.3	103.3	27.9	47.7	64.3	70.1	77.9	85.5
Percent	13.6	16.2	18.8	18.7	19.1	19.0	8.3	8.8	9.9	10.3	10.9	11.3
Gasoline service stations [1]	158.5	124.6	113.2	111.5	107.5	107.0	94.5	100.8	101.9	109.4	128.6	143.2
Percent	35.8	27.4	23.5	22.6	20.6	19.7	28.1	18.6	15.7	16.1	18.0	18.9
Retailing (nonfood)	35.2	45.1	46.2	50.0	54.4	57.0	10.5	20.6	23.3	26.7	29.3	31.4
Percent	8.0	9.9	9.6	10.2	10.4	10.5	3.1	3.8	3.6	3.9	4.1	4.1
Auto, truck rental services	7.3	11.2	9.5	9.8	10.7	11.1	3.1	5.7	6.6	6.9	7.5	8.0
Automotive products and services [2]	40.2	36.5	34.7	36.2	39.2	42.2	7.1	10.7	11.4	12.5	13.9	15.5
Business aids and services	40.7	49.8	55.6	58.2	64.4	69.5	6.7	12.0	15.7	16.9	18.6	20.8
Employment services	4.4	4.8	6.5	6.6	7.5	8.3	1.6	2.7	4.7	5.0	5.7	6.4
Tax preparation services	9.2	8.1	8.3	8.2	8.3	8.5	0.3	0.4	0.6	0.7	0.7	0.7
Accounting, credit, collection, and general	2.4	2.1	1.7	1.7	1.8	1.9	0.1	0.2	0.2	0.2	0.2	0.2
Real estate [3]	17.3	13.9	15.3	15.8	16.4	18.2	3.6	4.6	5.9	6.2	6.8	7.7
Printing and copying	2.8	4.5	5.9	6.3	6.8	7.4	0.4	0.9	1.5	1.6	1.8	2.0
Other	4.8	16.4	17.9	19.5	23.6	25.3	0.8	3.1	3.0	3.4	3.5	3.8
Construction, home improvement, maintenance, and cleaning	14.3	17.5	22.0	24.1	27.4	30.6	1.5	4.1	5.3	5.8	6.5	7.1
Convenience stores	15.6	15.1	17.2	17.6	17.2	17.3	7.8	10.8	13.9	14.3	14.3	15.0
Educational products and services	3.2	8.2	11.6	11.1	12.5	13.9	0.3	0.8	1.7	1.7	2.0	2.3
Equipment rental services	2.2	2.5	3.0	2.6	2.7	2.9	0.4	0.7	0.7	0.7	0.7	0.8
Food retailing [4]	15.5	18.7	21.6	21.1	24.5	25.4	7.4	10.1	10.2	10.0	11.7	12.2
Hotels and motels [5]	6.4	7.5	9.3	10.1	11.0	11.4	9.5	14.8	19.7	21.6	23.8	26.0
Laundry, dry cleaning services	3.4	2.3	2.3	3.0	3.2	3.5	0.3	0.3	0.3	0.4	0.4	0.5
Recreation, entertainment, travel.	4.6	7.8	8.8	9.8	10.9	11.6	0.5	2.3	3.5	3.5	4.2	4.8
Soft drink bottlers [1][6]	1.9	1.4	0.9	0.8	0.8	0.8	14.4	18.3	22.7	24.6	26.2	28.0
Miscellaneous	3.6	5.5	6.9	7.6	8.4	8.6	0.4	0.9	1.7	2.0	2.3	2.6

[1] Estimated by source on basis of Bureau of the Census and trade association data.   [2] Includes some establishments with significant sales of nonautomotive products such as household appliances, garden supplies, etc.   [3] Gross commissions. [4] Excludes convenience stores.   [5] Includes campgrounds.   [6] Includes soft drinks, fruit drinks and ades, syrups, flavoring agents and bases. Excludes independent private label and contract-filler bottling companies, which accounted for 22 percent of the value of shipments of the total industry in recent years.

Source: U.S. Dept. of Commerce, International Trade Administration, *Franchising in the Economy, 1986-88*, 1988. Beginning 1988, International Franchise Association Educational Foundation, Inc., Washington, DC, *Franchising in the Economy*, annual.

No. 1293. Shopping Centers—Number, Gross Leasable Area, and Retail Sales, by Gross Leasable Area: 1990 to 1993

[As of **December 31.** A shopping center is a group of architecturally unified commercial establishments built on a site that is planned, developed, owned, and managed as an operating unit related in its location, size, and type of shops to the trade area that the unit serves. The unit provides on-site parking in definite relationship to the types and total size of the stores. The data base attempts to include all centers with three or more stores. Estimates are based on a sample of data available on shopping center properties; for details, contact source]

YEAR	Total	GROSS LEASABLE AREA (sq. ft.)					
		Less than 100,001	100,001- 200,000	200,001- 400,000	400,001- 800,000	800,001- 1,000,000	More than 1 million
NUMBER							
1990.	36,515	23,231	8,756	2,781	1,102	288	357
1991.	37,975	23,997	9,226	2,953	1,141	294	364
1992.	38,966	24,578	9,467	3,086	1,170	294	371
1993.	39,633	24,993	9,611	3,166	1,194	295	374
Percent distribution	100.0	63.1	24.2	8.0	3.0	0.7	0.9
Percent change, 1992-93	1.7	1.7	1.5	2.6	2.1	0.3	0.8
GROSS LEASABLE AREA							
1990 (mil. sq. ft.)	4,390	1,125	1,197	734	618	259	457
1991 (mil. sq. ft.)	4,564	1,162	1,258	775	639	264	466
1992 (mil. sq. ft.)	4,679	1,190	1,289	807	653	264	475
1993 (mil. sq. ft.)	4,771	1,214	1,312	834	666	265	479
Percent distribution	100.0	25.4	27.5	17.5	14.0	5.6	10.0
Percent change, 1992-93	2.0	2.0	1.8	3.3	2.0	0.4	0.8
RETAIL SALES							
1990 (bil. dol.)	706.4	205.1	179.5	108.0	91.7	45.1	77.0
1991 (bil. dol.)	716.9	208.3	182.2	109.5	93.0	45.8	78.2
1992 (bil. dol.)	768.2	223.3	195.3	117.2	99.6	49.0	83.8
1993 (bil. dol.)	814.2	236.6	206.9	124.2	105.6	52.0	88.9
Percent distribution	100.0	29.1	25.4	15.3	13.0	6.4	10.9
Percent change, 1992-93	6.0	6.0	6.0	6.0	6.0	6.0	6.1

No. 1294. Shopping Centers—Number, Gross Leasable Area, and Retail Sales, by State: 1993

[See headnote, table 1293. Minus sign (-) indicates decrease]

DIVISION AND STATE	Number	Gross leasable area (mil. sq. ft.)	Retail sales (bil. dol.)	PERCENT CHANGE, 1992-93			DIVISION AND STATE	Number	Gross leasable area (mil. sq. ft.)	Retail sales (bil. dol.)	PERCENT CHANGE, 1992-93		
				Number	Gross leasable area	Retail sales per sq. ft.					Number	Gross leasable area	Retail sales per sq. ft.
U.S .	39,633	4,771	814.2	1.7	2.0	3.9	VA	1,138	147	24.6	1.4	1.9	4.3
							WV	155	21	3.1	0.6	2.0	3.0
N.E	2,296	247	42.2	1.7	1.8	4.7	NC	1,386	146	23.1	2.1	1.8	3.6
ME	189	16	3.1	1.6	1.9	3.6	SC	749	73	12.6	1.6	1.4	4.0
NH	202	21	3.1	2.5	3.3	3.0	GA	1,397	147	25.2	0.9	2.5	3.2
VT	103	7	1.3	-	-	5.7	FL.....	3,044	385	71.4	1.5	1.7	3.9
MA	907	102	17.9	1.5	1.1	5.4	**E.S.C ....**	2,713	293	49.1	1.8	1.9	3.4
RI	184	17	3.0	0.5	1.7	4.2	KY	585	63	11.2	1.7	2.0	3.2
CT	711	85	13.9	2.4	2.3	4.6	TN	1,121	123	18.3	2.2	1.8	3.6
M.A	4,069	568	88.6	3.2	2.7	3.4	AL....	593	69	12.7	1.0	1.7	3.5
NY	1,564	214	35.4	3.4	3.2	2.8	MS	414	38	7.0	2.2	2.3	2.7
NJ	1,012	140	21.6	3.5	2.2	4.6	**W.S.C ....**	4,338	494	101.9	0.4	1.2	4.3
PA	1,493	213	31.6	2.7	2.7	3.2	AR	333	32	6.2	0.3	0.9	4.2
E.N.C	5,831	754	114.7	1.6	1.9	4.0	LA	666	78	15.0	0.9	0.7	4.6
OH	1,539	218	33.4	1.6	2.3	3.5	OK	549	57	11.1	-	-	5.5
IN	835	110	17.3	2.1	1.6	4.0	TX	2,790	328	69.7	0.4	1.6	4.1
IL	1,917	230	32.5	1.2	2.0	4.1	**Mountain .**	2,632	315	57.8	1.7	1.8	4.1
MI	958	125	20.1	1.9	1.5	4.5	MT	91	9	1.6	1.1	3.9	1.4
WI	582	71	11.4	1.7	1.3	4.6	ID	137	16	2.7	5.4	3.8	1.7
W.N.C	2,343	297	51.7	1.6	2.2	3.4	WY	53	6	1.1	-	-	5.7
MN	428	62	11.0	1.7	1.1	4.9	CO	668	86	17.5	0.5	0.2	6.0
IA	272	36	6.0	0.7	2.7	2.7	NM	282	27	5.2	2.2	1.5	4.1
MO	821	101	18.1	1.6	1.0	4.6	AZ	918	108	19.2	1.8	2.2	3.8
ND	80	9	1.7	-	-	5.5	UT	207	29	5.3	1.5	0.3	6.1
SD	51	7	1.0	4.1	3.3	2.0	NV	276	33	5.1	2.6	5.8	0.3
NE	240	32	4.6	3.9	8.4	-2.6	**Pacific ...**	6,526	745	123.8	2.0	2.3	4.2
KS	451	50	9.3	1.1	2.2	3.5	WA	651	85	13.8	2.0	1.1	5.2
S.A	8,885	1,058	184.4	1.5	1.8	3.9	OR	434	49	7.2	1.2	1.4	4.5
DE	124	18	3.3	2.5	1.8	4.2	CA	5,221	587	98.4	2.0	2.3	4.3
MD	826	113	19.7	2.0	1.8	4.6	AK	60	8	1.5	-	-	6.3
DC	66	8	1.4	-	-	5.3	HI	160	16	2.9	4.6	11.1	-4.0

- Represents zero.

Source of tables 1293 and 1294: National Research Bureau, Chicago, IL. Data for 1990 published by Monitor Publishing, Clearwater, FL, in *Monitor Magazine*, November/December 1991, (copyright). Data for 1991 and 1992 published by Communication Channels, Inc., Atlanta, GA, in *Shopping Center World*, March 1993, (copyright). Data for 1993 published by International Council of Shopping Centers in *Shopping Centers Today*, April 1994, (copyright—Blackburn Marketing Services (U.S.), Inc.).

No. 1295. Retail Sales—

[In millions of dollars, except as indicated. Kind-of-business classification based on

REGION, DIVISION, AND STATE	ALL STORES [1]				FOOD STORES				GENERAL MERCHANDISE STORES			
	1991, total	1992 Total	1992 Sales per household [2] Amount (dol.)	1992 Percent change, 1991-92	Total 1991	Total 1992	Supermarkets 1991	Supermarkets 1992	Total 1991	Total 1992	Department stores 1991	Department stores 1992
U.S. . . .	1,821,386	1,964,022	20,710	6.5	370,255	384,574	347,716	360,319	217,494	247,448	173,960	197,069
Northeast .	377,542	399,627	20,994	5.8	81,392	82,080	74,160	74,671	38,815	39,905	31,889	32,791
N.E	110,944	112,745	22,662	1.9	22,367	24,136	20,471	22,060	10,918	11,340	8,689	8,994
ME . . .	10,092	11,450	24,377	14.4	2,299	2,746	2,177	2,593	875	1,013	610	706
NH . . .	11,009	11,978	27,831	7.3	2,314	2,688	2,206	2,555	1,213	1,356	875	970
VT . . .	4,450	5,096	23,571	13.8	1,007	1,220	947	1,145	304	357	212	249
MA . . .	52,090	47,451	21,083	-8.7	10,178	9,810	9,144	8,785	5,232	4,889	4,174	3,887
RI . . .	6,760	7,357	19,330	8.9	1,361	1,564	1,188	1,362	752	835	597	659
CT . . .	26,544	29,412	23,963	11.9	5,208	6,106	4,809	5,621	2,543	2,891	2,221	2,524
M.A . . .	266,598	286,883	20,403	7.4	59,025	57,944	53,689	52,611	27,897	28,564	23,200	23,797
NY . . .	122,446	126,079	18,889	3.0	27,261	25,546	24,345	22,757	12,504	12,166	10,099	9,839
NJ . . .	63,210	67,702	23,987	7.0	13,970	13,658	12,876	12,555	6,161	6,292	5,262	5,384
PA . . .	80,942	93,102	20,401	14.3	17,795	18,739	16,468	17,300	9,231	10,106	7,838	8,574
Midwest . .	432,340	471,615	20,704	7.9	78,561	83,217	73,872	78,006	58,063	63,346	48,105	52,384
E.N.C . .	303,829	330,386	20,775	7.5	53,901	56,972	50,366	53,068	40,347	44,105	34,044	37,122
OH . . .	76,295	81,163	19,463	5.0	14,820	15,347	13,943	14,395	10,490	11,258	8,673	9,277
IN . . .	39,882	41,526	19,641	2.7	6,848	6,950	6,543	6,621	5,084	5,329	4,089	4,255
IL . . .	84,710	94,705	22,192	10.6	14,534	15,741	13,536	14,609	10,332	11,579	8,832	9,875
MI . . .	67,761	73,197	21,043	7.2	11,360	11,951	10,397	10,912	9,988	10,857	8,879	9,645
WI . . .	35,181	39,795	21,253	11.6	6,340	6,982	5,947	6,532	4,452	5,083	3,572	4,071
W.N.C . .	128,510	141,229	20,539	8.7	24,660	26,246	23,505	24,938	17,716	19,240	14,061	15,262
MN . . .	35,160	35,686	20,968	0.2	6,233	6,084	5,909	5,749	5,028	5,019	3,656	3,623
IA . . .	19,512	22,000	20,344	11.2	4,146	4,531	3,986	4,343	2,573	2,881	2,041	2,275
MO . . .	36,428	41,238	20,559	12.4	6,874	7,543	6,603	7,222	5,179	5,807	4,406	4,931
ND . . .	4,670	5,312	21,969	13.0	837	922	806	885	641	725	503	571
SD . . .	4,888	5,608	21,116	13.1	958	1,062	921	1,018	530	603	406	463
NE . . .	10,693	12,112	19,707	11.7	2,105	2,300	1,888	2,052	1,404	1,576	1,139	1,282
KS . . .	17,160	19,273	19,891	10.9	3,506	3,803	3,393	3,668	2,362	2,630	1,910	2,117
South	617,011	666,419	20,160	6.4	128,021	135,470	122,273	128,969	76,591	88,602	60,491	69,814
S.A . .	328,762	357,145	20,704	7.1	65,621	69,557	62,438	65,989	37,894	43,779	30,189	34,785
DE . . .	6,060	6,299	24,473	2.4	1,101	1,117	1,022	1,033	860	954	751	834
MD . . .	36,385	38,205	21,121	4.3	7,004	7,184	6,579	6,729	4,324	4,845	3,470	3,874
DC . . .	3,606	3,553	14,763	0.2	604	583	543	522	327	345	284	301
VA . . .	45,783	53,335	22,415	15.0	9,571	10,879	9,244	10,474	5,170	6,409	4,047	4,999
WV . . .	10,147	10,651	15,299	3.5	2,439	2,488	2,295	2,333	1,490	1,661	1,021	1,127
NC . . .	46,078	50,741	19,326	8.2	9,345	10,019	9,039	9,659	4,789	5,599	3,586	4,182
SC . . .	24,220	25,440	19,426	3.4	5,260	5,375	5,085	5,180	2,584	2,883	1,988	2,221
GA . . .	46,910	49,628	19,933	4.2	9,115	9,404	8,795	9,045	5,820	6,545	4,751	5,324
FL . . .	109,571	119,291	21,919	7.2	21,181	22,510	19,836	21,013	12,530	14,540	10,291	11,923
E.S.C . . .	97,307	105,676	18,203	7.0	19,319	23,652	18,425	22,487	13,760	15,507	10,757	12,103
KY . . .	24,098	25,585	18,129	4.4	5,028	5,988	4,802	5,702	3,448	3,776	2,684	2,930
TN . . .	33,384	38,140	19,921	12.7	6,093	7,885	5,797	7,479	4,744	5,641	3,788	4,491
AL . . .	26,132	27,625	17,808	4.0	5,108	6,141	4,867	5,834	3,479	3,833	2,825	3,110
MS . . .	13,692	14,325	15,435	3.5	3,091	3,638	2,959	3,472	2,089	2,258	1,459	1,573
W.S.C . . .	190,942	203,599	20,356	4.9	43,081	42,261	41,411	40,493	24,937	29,316	19,545	22,927
AR . . .	15,584	15,741	17,194	-0.5	3,381	3,136	3,268	3,021	2,252	2,503	1,885	2,088
LA . . .	28,997	30,736	20,156	4.6	7,423	7,251	7,094	6,907	4,033	4,714	3,040	3,550
OK . . .	20,200	19,879	16,167	-3.1	4,583	4,142	4,382	3,948	2,570	2,793	2,088	2,268
TX . . .	126,161	137,243	21,675	6.9	27,694	27,732	26,667	26,617	16,082	19,307	12,533	15,021
West.	394,494	426,360	21,356	5.9	82,280	83,806	77,411	78,673	44,025	55,595	33,475	42,080
Mt . . .	96,491	109,569	20,426	10.1	21,898	24,748	21,130	23,806	11,441	13,596	8,764	10,389
MT . . .	5,473	6,334	19,917	11.8	1,331	1,538	1,287	1,483	548	664	426	516
ID . . .	6,192	7,064	18,416	9.3	1,488	1,695	1,444	1,640	628	750	482	573
WY . . .	2,794	3,199	18,480	11.7	617	702	604	685	301	361	226	273
CO . . .	25,216	29,137	21,326	11.0	5,401	6,196	5,217	5,965	3,169	3,815	2,521	3,041
NM . . .	9,645	10,934	19,132	11.1	2,096	2,361	2,000	2,246	1,170	1,392	845	1,002
AZ . . .	26,893	30,290	20,673	10.0	6,371	7,159	6,169	6,910	3,153	3,728	2,246	2,640
UT . . .	10,452	11,623	20,589	8.6	2,452	2,704	2,353	2,588	1,313	1,526	1,031	1,187
NV . . .	9,826	10,988	21,054	8.0	2,142	2,392	2,057	2,289	1,159	1,360	989	1,157
Pac	298,003	316,791	21,697	4.6	60,383	59,058	56,281	54,867	32,585	41,999	24,711	31,690
WA . . .	37,717	40,691	20,577	5.1	8,476	8,436	8,116	8,051	4,077	5,343	3,082	4,015
OR . . .	23,262	25,235	21,817	6.0	4,582	4,529	4,312	4,248	3,102	4,018	2,226	2,858
CA . . .	220,871	233,688	21,471	4.4	43,854	42,653	40,600	39,352	23,277	29,864	17,747	22,654
AK . . .	4,740	5,090	24,818	2.6	1,246	1,247	1,209	1,206	601	781	432	571
HI . . .	11,412	12,086	32,008	2.9	2,224	2,194	2,043	2,009	1,527	1,994	1,224	1,593

[1] Includes other types of stores, not shown separately.   [2] Based on number of households as of July 1 as estimated by source. Minus sign (-) indicates decrease.   [3] Includes hardware dealers.   [4] Includes homefurnishings stores.

by Type of Store and State: 1991 and 1992

1987 Standard Industrial Classification code; see text, section 13. Data are estimates]

AUTOMOTIVE DEALERS		EATING AND DRINKING PLACES		GASOLINE SERVICE STATIONS		BUILDING MATERIALS DEALERS [3]		APPAREL AND ACCESSORIES STORES		FURNITURE AND APPLIANCE STORES [4]		REGION, DIVISION, AND STATE
1991	1992	1991	1992	1991	1992	1991	1992	1991	1992	1991	1992	
375,641	398,768	189,190	202,079	128,270	133,727	92,731	103,134	95,346	105,050	89,836	104,906	U.S.
73,946	70,997	38,276	41,823	22,129	23,749	16,810	19,000	22,841	27,680	19,428	19,130	Northeast
22,691	18,570	12,954	13,065	6,801	6,924	5,885	6,382	5,573	6,667	4,925	4,608	N.E
2,063	1,869	1,004	1,143	663	744	649	771	346	469	326	341	ME
2,494	2,202	1,052	1,156	563	614	744	858	430	558	533	536	NH
925	850	493	568	304	347	342	413	171	233	169	179	VT
10,476	7,678	6,774	6,171	2,993	2,716	2,376	2,279	2,859	3,090	2,339	1,964	MA
1,255	1,091	859	936	470	508	337	384	340	438	245	245	RI
5,480	4,879	2,773	3,091	1,809	1,996	1,437	1,678	1,427	1,879	1,312	1,342	CT
51,255	52,427	25,322	28,757	15,328	16,824	10,925	12,617	17,268	21,013	14,503	14,522	M.A
21,203	20,631	12,517	13,565	6,154	6,405	4,936	5,429	8,726	10,174	6,997	6,706	NY
13,354	13,564	5,505	6,263	3,852	4,186	2,481	2,850	4,338	5,311	3,793	3,802	NJ
16,698	18,232	7,300	8,930	5,322	6,234	3,508	4,338	4,204	5,527	3,714	4,013	PA
92,098	102,872	43,143	48,637	37,493	34,631	23,900	24,392	20,579	22,042	19,057	23,371	Midwest
62,483	71,246	30,930	35,164	25,680	21,980	16,615	16,870	15,226	15,955	14,779	17,320	E.N.C
15,863	17,745	7,910	8,804	6,690	5,611	3,958	3,940	3,250	3,331	3,507	4,027	OH
8,593	9,394	3,899	4,243	3,574	2,951	2,432	2,368	1,711	1,714	1,724	1,932	IN
16,501	19,319	8,736	10,174	6,446	5,649	4,244	4,414	5,206	5,583	4,335	5,203	IL
14,693	16,664	6,614	7,474	5,671	4,824	3,855	3,893	3,641	3,781	3,454	4,011	MI
6,833	8,125	3,770	4,469	3,299	2,946	2,127	2,253	1,418	1,546	1,759	2,146	WI
29,615	31,625	12,214	13,473	11,813	12,651	7,286	7,523	5,353	6,087	4,278	6,051	W.N.C
7,519	7,368	3,297	3,343	2,973	2,923	2,215	2,108	1,532	1,603	1,294	1,685	MN
4,582	5,025	1,762	2,000	1,907	2,099	1,063	1,135	797	934	587	857	IA
8,774	9,642	3,587	4,081	3,393	3,744	1,965	2,101	1,482	1,740	1,125	1,648	MO
1,139	1,259	423	485	479	530	286	307	202	238	123	182	ND
1,168	1,301	445	513	527	588	284	306	197	235	142	211	SD
2,373	2,601	1,078	1,224	1,023	1,122	541	576	452	530	418	611	NE
4,061	4,429	1,621	1,828	1,510	1,643	933	989	692	806	589	857	KS
138,702	141,428	59,296	64,421	42,786	47,572	30,786	36,989	30,464	33,546	29,309	36,683	South
71,254	74,681	33,303	36,136	22,419	24,364	18,240	21,932	15,973	18,725	17,074	20,622	S.A
1,240	1,242	547	568	346	360	360	415	267	300	317	366	DE
7,920	8,027	3,516	3,693	2,405	2,533	1,662	1,939	2,015	2,285	1,956	2,287	MD
159	151	865	856	132	131	67	74	334	357	194	213	DC
9,771	11,209	4,275	4,990	3,298	3,844	2,378	3,071	2,185	2,749	2,453	3,174	VA
2,027	2,040	841	880	787	826	633	732	372	421	380	442	WV
9,944	10,528	4,585	5,042	3,215	3,535	3,258	3,961	2,228	2,645	2,546	3,109	NC
4,908	4,956	2,379	2,496	1,899	1,988	1,631	1,888	1,297	1,470	1,203	1,401	SC
9,952	10,135	4,744	5,004	3,500	3,698	2,757	3,235	2,205	2,512	2,319	2,721	GA
25,134	26,393	11,553	12,607	6,837	7,449	5,494	6,617	5,070	5,985	5,707	6,909	FL
22,350	20,339	8,556	9,436	7,268	8,225	5,127	6,222	4,693	4,353	4,306	5,731	E.S.C
4,902	4,327	2,271	2,428	1,954	2,145	1,311	1,545	993	894	1,036	1,337	KY
8,046	7,703	3,031	3,526	2,562	3,060	1,733	2,222	1,627	1,587	1,625	2,275	TN
6,408	5,696	2,198	2,366	1,830	2,021	1,386	1,641	1,468	1,335	1,125	1,459	AL
2,995	2,613	1,056	1,116	922	999	697	814	605	537	519	660	MS
45,097	46,409	17,438	18,850	13,099	14,983	7,419	8,835	9,798	10,468	7,930	10,330	W.S.C
3,839	3,730	1,124	1,145	1,191	1,285	892	1,005	643	646	557	684	AR
5,815	5,939	2,567	2,754	1,943	2,214	1,161	1,377	1,379	1,460	1,161	1,495	LA
5,017	4,768	1,876	1,871	1,398	1,478	790	872	1,056	1,042	805	970	OK
30,426	31,972	11,870	13,081	8,567	10,006	4,576	5,580	6,721	7,321	5,407	7,182	TX
70,896	83,471	48,475	47,198	25,863	27,775	21,234	22,753	21,463	21,781	22,042	25,722	West
18,359	20,994	10,302	12,004	6,936	7,811	5,514	6,255	4,374	4,538	4,765	5,910	Mt
1,000	1,167	613	728	465	534	352	407	232	246	231	293	MT
1,260	1,450	588	689	509	576	409	466	265	277	282	353	ID
509	589	307	360	311	352	156	177	127	133	94	118	WY
4,664	5,401	2,930	3,466	1,704	1,943	1,323	1,522	1,178	1,241	1,317	1,658	CO
1,883	2,155	1,063	1,238	735	825	618	700	446	463	411	511	NM
5,239	5,956	2,787	3,221	1,769	1,984	1,447	1,634	1,114	1,149	1,399	1,723	AZ
1,978	2,210	965	1,097	808	888	588	651	546	552	594	720	UT
1,828	2,066	1,050	1,206	636	708	622	698	467	477	437	535	NV
52,537	62,476	38,173	35,194	18,927	19,964	15,720	16,498	17,089	17,244	17,277	19,812	Pac
6,229	7,531	4,627	4,342	2,552	2,738	2,240	2,392	1,989	2,044	1,964	2,291	WA
4,477	5,369	2,721	2,533	1,566	1,670	1,224	1,298	1,140	1,159	1,146	1,326	OR
39,890	47,236	28,044	25,727	13,916	14,606	11,670	12,182	12,808	12,866	13,607	15,544	CA
550	667	686	643	236	253	244	263	269	275	151	176	AK
1,390	1,673	2,095	1,949	655	698	343	364	883	899	409	475	HI

Source: Market Statistics, New York, NY, *The Survey of Buying Power Data Service*, annual, (copyright).

No. 1296. Retail Trade—Summary of Establishments, by State: 1991

[Covers establishments with payroll. Excludes government employees, railroad employees, self-employed persons, etc. For statement on methodology, see Appendix III. Kind-of-business classification based on 1987 Standard Industrial Classification code; see text, section 13]

DIVISION AND STATE	Establishments (1,000)	Paid employees [1] (1,000)	Annual payroll (mil. dol.)	DIVISION AND STATE	Establishments (1,000)	Paid employees [1] (1,000)	Annual payroll (mil. dol.)	DIVISION AND STATE	Establishments (1,000)	Paid employees [1] (1,000)	Annual payroll (mil. dol.)
U.S. ..	1,547.3	19,600	247,011	IA	20.1	239	2,445	MS	15.5	157	1,670
N.E.	90.6	1,085	14,882	MO	33.2	420	5,010	W.S.C. ...	156.8	1,980	23,683
ME	9.3	96	1,200	ND	5.0	53	522	AR	15.0	161	1,844
NH	8.6	98	1,283	SD	5.6	59	605	LA	22.7	291	3,187
VT	5.2	47	574	NE	11.7	137	1,383	OK	19.5	220	2,370
MA	39.2	511	7,034	KS	16.8	202	2,260	TX	99.5	1,308	16,281
RI....	6.6	72	902	S.A	284.8	3,642	44,517	Mt	87.5	1,118	13,447
CT	21.7	260	3,889	DE	4.8	61	765	MT	6.7	64	688
M.A.	235.0	2,676	37,063	MD	28.9	396	5,588	ID	6.9	74	866
NY	112.5	1,178	17,074	DC	3.8	49	711	WY	3.6	37	405
NJ....	49.6	577	8,800	VA	38.0	509	6,319	CO	22.8	292	3,642
PA	72.9	921	11,189	WV	10.6	117	1,235	NM	9.3	114	1,267
E.N.C ...	250.1	3,452	40,699	NC	45.0	537	6,229	AZ	21.6	303	3,682
OH	64.4	905	10,550	SC	22.9	275	3,035	UT	9.1	130	1,446
IN	33.8	467	5,079	GA	41.2	536	6,400	NV	7.5	104	1,451
IL	65.8	912	11,577	FL	89.6	1,163	14,235	Pac	228.9	3,042	43,602
MI	54.0	746	8,974	E.S.C ...	93.2	1,097	12,249	WA	30.9	396	5,444
WI	32.1	421	4,519	KY	22.6	276	2,936	OR	19.3	243	3,123
W.N.C ...	120.4	1,508	16,869	TN	31.0	384	4,536	CA	167.3	2,248	32,708
MN	28.1	397	4,643	AL	24.1	280	3,107	AK	3.6	39	693
								HI	7.8	116	1,634

[1] For pay period including March 12.
Source: U.S. Bureau of the Census, *County Business Patterns*, annual.

No. 1297. Wholesale Trade—Summary: 1958 to 1987

[Data prior to 1972 based on earlier editions of Standard Industrial Classification (SIC) code. Comparability of data over time is affected by changes in the SIC code; for details, see source. See also *Historical Statistics, Colonial Times to 1970*, series T 43-47, and T 274-279]

ITEM	Unit	1958	1963	1967	1972 [1]	1977 [1]	1982 [1]	1987 [1]	1987 [2]
Firms, total [3]	1,000...	(NA)	232	233	276	289	335	(NA)	364
Establishments, total [3]	1,000...	287	308	311	370	383	435	467	470
With sales of $1,000,000 or more.	1,000...	(NA)	62	75	103	152	(NA)	(NA)	222
Sales, all establishments	Bil. dol..	286	358	459	695	1,258	1,998	2,524	2,525
Merchant wholesalers	Bil. dol..	122	157	206	354	678	1,159	1,477	1,478
Inventories, end of year.	Bil. dol..	14.9	20.1	28.1	45.7	82.3	130.7	(NA)	165.1
Payroll, entire year	Bil. dol..	13.2	18.1	23.9	36.9	58.3	95.2	133.2	133.4
Paid employees, Mar. 12 workweek [4]	1,000...	2,808	3,089	3,519	4,026	4,397	4,985	5,581	5,596

NA Not available.   [1] Based on 1972 SIC code.   [2] Based on 1987 SIC code.   [3] Through 1977 number of firms and establishments in business at end of year; beginning 1982 number of firms and establishments in business at any time during year.   [4] 1958 and 1963 data for workweek including Nov. 15.

No. 1298. Wholesale Trade, by Kind of Business: 1982 and 1987

[Based on 1972 Standard Industrial Classification code; see text, section 13. See *Historical Statistics, Colonial Times to 1970*, series T 274-287 and T 352-369 for similar but not comparable data]

KIND OF BUSINESS	ESTABLISHMENTS [1] (1,000)		SALES (mil. dol.)		ANNUAL PAYROLL (mil. dol.)		PAID EMPLOYEES [2] (1,000)	
	1982	1987	1982	1987	1982	1987	1982	1987
Wholesale trade	435.1	466.7	1,997,895	2,523,688	95,209	133,153	4,985	5,581
Durable goods	267.4	292.8	881,212	1,258,483	57,368	82,248	2,913	3,303
Motor vehicles, automotive equipment	41.1	43.0	187,607	(D)	7,524	(D)	433	(D)
Furniture, home furnishings	13.1	14.5	32,452	48,123	2,367	3,652	126	153
Lumber, construction materials	17.9	19.1	50,694	79,946	3,429	5,476	184	231
Sporting, recreational, photographic goods [3]	7.6	8.9	26,980	40,965	1,646	2,312	85	97
Metals and minerals, except petroleum	10.6	11.1	102,690	114,528	3,359	4,038	148	143
Electrical goods	30.4	35.3	120,062	(D)	7,462	(D)	357	(D)
Hardware, plumbing, heating equipment	21.6	23.1	43,529	57,126	4,051	5,610	217	235
Machinery, equipment, supplies	103.4	114.4	263,309	336,976	24,804	35,612	1,192	1,353
Miscellaneous	21.7	23.4	53,889	75,506	2,726	3,777	171	184
Nondurable goods	167.8	173.9	1,116,683	1,265,205	37,841	50,905	2,072	2,278
Paper, paper products	14.5	16.8	53,493	83,173	3,586	5,202	187	228
Drugs, drug proprietaries [4]	4.0	4.9	33,987	64,280	1,975	2,968	106	120
Apparel, piece goods, notions	15.0	16.9	55,897	81,476	2,897	4,661	144	181
Groceries and related products	40.4	42.1	288,659	380,945	12,269	16,729	674	763
Farm-product raw materials	14.4	12.6	153,419	117,606	1,839	1,847	136	117
Chemicals, allied products	11.2	12.7	76,103	94,620	2,902	3,847	124	131
Petroleum, petroleum products	20.3	16.7	296,995	234,874	3,433	3,658	188	175
Beer, wines, distilled alcoholic beverages	6.7	5.8	42,122	49,433	3,091	3,849	141	146
Miscellaneous	41.2	45.3	116,008	158,800	5,849	8,143	372	417

D Data withheld to avoid disclosure.   [1] Number of establishments in business at any time during the year.   [2] For pay period including March 12.   [3] Includes toys, hobby goods, and supplies.   [4] Includes druggists sundries.
Source of tables 1297 and 1298: U.S. Bureau of the Census, *U.S. Census of Business: 1958*, vol. III; *1963*, vol. IV; *1967*, vol. III; and *Census of Wholesale Trade: 1972*, vol. I; *1977*, WC77-A-52; *1982*, WC82-A-52; and *1987*, WC87-A-52.

No. 1299. Merchant Wholesalers—Summary: 1988 to 1993

[Inventories and stock/sales ratios, as of December, seasonally adjusted. Data reflect latest revision. Based on Current Business Survey; see Appendix III. See *Historical Statistics, Colonial Times to 1970*, series T 280-371, for related sales data]

KIND OF BUSINESS	1987 SIC code [1]	1988	1989	1990	1991	1992	1993
SALES (bil. dol.)							
Merchant wholesalers		**1,622.0**	**1,725.1**	**1,786.3**	**1,762.0**	**1,824.4**	**1,922.6**
Durable goods	**50**	**812.9**	**858.0**	**883.1**	**858.1**	**902.8**	**979.4**
Motor vehicles, parts, and supplies	501	166.4	166.2	172.1	164.5	168.1	176.7
Furniture and homefurnishings	502	30.1	31.9	33.9	32.3	33.2	34.9
Lumber and construction materials	503	62.5	65.1	67.3	63.1	70.2	80.8
Professional and commercial equipment	504	93.5	108.3	112.1	121.0	135.4	150.7
Metals and minerals, except petroleum	505	76.9	75.8	71.2	67.4	65.9	70.0
Electrical goods	506	101.3	114.7	120.0	119.2	123.9	143.2
Hardware, plumbing and heating equipment	507	44.4	47.3	50.2	46.7	48.8	47.1
Machinery, equipment and supplies	508	142.2	156.3	168.5	160.8	167.2	180.9
Miscellaneous durable goods	509	95.4	92.3	87.9	83.1	90.1	95.0
Nondurable goods	**51**	**809.1**	**867.1**	**903.2**	**903.9**	**921.6**	**943.2**
Paper and paper products	511	46.7	50.3	51.2	51.6	54.2	58.8
Drugs, proprietaries, and sundries	512	40.1	44.9	51.1	58.9	66.0	72.8
Apparel, piece goods, and notions	513	53.7	63.1	67.6	68.6	73.4	75.6
Groceries and related products	514	236.0	259.1	272.5	277.0	279.2	289.5
Farm-product raw materials	515	124.2	119.9	108.2	103.2	104.8	96.9
Chemicals and allied products	516	34.2	32.8	35.0	36.8	37.5	38.0
Petroleum and petroleum products	517	118.5	129.2	138.2	125.5	124.4	121.6
Beer, wine, and distilled beverages	518	44.0	46.9	51.7	55.0	54.6	54.4
Miscellaneous nondurable goods	519	111.8	120.7	127.6	128.3	127.6	135.5
INVENTORIES (bil. dol.)							
Merchant wholesalers		**180.5**	**188.6**	**196.9**	**201.5**	**208.8**	**216.6**
Durable goods	**50**	**118.9**	**124.0**	**127.9**	**128.9**	**132.5**	**136.6**
Motor vehicles, parts, and supplies	501	22.5	22.0	23.7	24.3	24.1	24.9
Furniture and homefurnishings	502	4.6	4.7	4.7	4.6	4.9	4.7
Lumber and construction materials	503	5.9	6.3	6.3	6.3	6.9	7.3
Professional and commercial equipment	504	13.0	14.7	15.6	16.5	16.6	16.9
Metals and minerals, except petroleum	505	10.5	10.4	10.0	9.1	8.8	9.9
Electrical goods	506	14.2	15.7	16.4	17.0	18.5	19.0
Hardware, plumbing and heating equipment	507	7.1	7.9	8.1	7.9	8.1	8.3
Machinery, equipment and supplies	508	30.4	31.7	34.0	32.9	33.8	33.2
Miscellaneous durable goods	509	10.6	10.5	9.3	10.3	10.9	12.5
Nondurable goods	**51**	**61.7**	**64.6**	**69.0**	**72.5**	**76.2**	**80.0**
Paper and paper products	511	4.1	4.5	4.9	5.2	5.6	6.2
Drugs, proprietaries, and sundries	512	5.3	5.8	6.3	7.4	8.5	9.9
Apparel, piece goods, and notions	513	8.2	9.9	10.4	10.3	11.7	12.5
Groceries and related products	514	12.8	14.0	14.6	15.5	15.9	16.0
Farm-product raw materials	515	9.2	8.2	8.7	9.0	9.0	10.1
Chemicals and allied products	516	2.9	2.6	2.9	2.9	3.1	3.4
Petroleum and petroleum products	517	3.5	3.5	4.1	4.0	3.9	3.6
Beer, wine, and distilled beverages	518	4.1	4.3	4.6	5.0	4.7	5.0
Miscellaneous nondurable goods	519	11.5	11.7	12.5	13.2	14.0	13.4
STOCK/SALES RATIO							
Merchant wholesalers		**1.28**	**1.28**	**1.32**	**1.36**	**1.34**	**1.34**
Durable goods	**50**	**1.66**	**1.73**	**1.77**	**1.80**	**1.70**	**1.62**
Motor vehicles, parts, and supplies	501	1.57	1.68	1.68	1.80	1.66	1.67
Furniture and homefurnishings	502	1.66	1.74	1.70	1.80	1.62	1.60
Lumber and construction materials	503	1.06	1.19	1.26	1.17	1.07	0.94
Professional and commercial equipment	504	1.53	1.53	1.60	1.54	1.40	1.33
Metals and minerals, except petroleum	505	1.56	1.83	1.66	1.64	1.60	1.64
Electrical goods	506	1.55	1.55	1.70	1.70	1.71	1.51
Hardware, plumbing and heating equipment	507	1.83	1.94	1.91	2.02	2.07	2.07
Machinery, equipment and supplies	508	2.39	2.38	2.46	2.45	2.35	2.10
Miscellaneous durable goods	509	1.35	1.34	1.30	1.51	1.41	1.60
Nondurable goods	**51**	**0.88**	**0.86**	**0.90**	**0.95**	**0.99**	**1.03**
Paper and paper products	511	1.03	1.05	1.17	1.18	1.20	1.20
Drugs, proprietaries, and sundries	512	1.48	1.42	1.44	1.40	1.45	1.58
Apparel, piece goods, and notions	513	1.74	1.71	1.75	1.79	1.72	2.01
Groceries and related products	514	0.59	0.63	0.65	0.67	0.66	0.67
Farm-product raw materials	515	0.89	0.88	1.02	1.09	1.01	1.18
Chemicals and allied products	516	1.06	0.91	0.95	0.96	0.95	1.07
Petroleum and petroleum products	517	0.37	0.29	0.33	0.38	0.39	0.40
Beer, wine, and distilled beverages	518	1.09	1.06	0.97	1.04	1.08	1.15
Miscellaneous nondurable goods	519	1.20	1.10	1.18	1.23	1.44	1.21

[1] Based on 1987 Standard Industrial Classification code; see text, section 13.

Source: U.S. Bureau of the Census, *Current Business Reports, Combined Annual and Revised Monthly Wholesale Trade, January 1987 Through 1993*, (BW/93-RV).

No. 1300. Service Industries—Summary of Establishments, by Tax Status: 1987

[Data for firms subject to Federal income tax cover all establishments, except as noted. Data for firms exempt from Federal income tax cover only establishments with payroll. See *Historical Statistics, Colonial Times to 1970*, series T 391-443, for similar but not comparable data]

KIND OF BUSINESS	1987 SIC code [1]	Establishments [2] (1,000)	Receipts or revenues [3] (mil. dol.)	Annual payroll (mil. dol.)	Paid employees [4] (1,000)	Receipts or revenues per establishment [3] ($1,000)	Annual payroll per employee (dol.)
Firms subject to Federal income tax [5]	(X)	6,254.5	868,343	289,807	16,054.7	474.9	18,051
Hotels, rooming houses, camps, and other lodging places [5][6]	70 ex. 704	85.7	53,630	14,452	1,410.8	1,108.4	10,244
Hotels and motels	701	63.4	51,633	14,135	1,380.2	1,246.1	10,241
Personal services [5]	72	1,037.4	43,247	10,853	1,105.0	169.8	9,822
Laundry, cleaning, and garment services	721	108.6	14,184	4,388	408.3	252.6	10,746
Photographic studios, portrait	722	56.2	2,929	514	50.1	215.6	10,253
Beauty and barber shops	723, 4	407.3	11,990	3,538	390.7	91.0	9,055
Funeral service and crematories	726	22.3	5,668	1,362	82.6	343.7	16,479
Business services [5]	73	1,433.2	188,856	66,456	4,414.4	660.3	15,054
Advertising	731	79.2	16,802	5,537	181.6	830.2	30,493
Credit reporting and collection	732	7.1	4,124	1,415	82.8	[7]582.8	17,078
Mailing, reproduction, stenographic	733	[7]27.2	[7]12,407	3,945	210.6	[7]455.6	18,729
Services to dwellings and other buildings	734	290.4	15,649	6,555	746.0	277.1	8,788
Miscellaneous equipment rental and leasing	735	49.1	15,472	3,579	185.3	592.1	19,319
Personnel supply services	736	43.2	20,336	13,590	1,397.1	824.7	9,727
Computer and data processing services	737	140.5	56,004	19,142	637.4	1,362.7	30,031
Detective agencies and protective services	7381, 2	45.2	9,303	5,040	475.8	697.1	10,594
Automotive repair, services, and parking	75	388.2	58,278	11,690	785.3	340.1	14,886
Automotive rental and leasing, without drivers	751	19.9	16,679	2,366	134.6	1,448.2	17,578
Automobile parking	752	10.5	2,691	491	45.7	283.8	10,751
Automotive repair shops	753	301.3	34,182	7,727	485.6	250.1	15,913
Automotive services, except repair	754	56.4	4,726	1,106	119.4	230.4	9,258
Miscellaneous repair services [5]	76	247.6	24,597	6,416	345.8	318.0	18,551
Electrical repair shops	762	65.7	7,584	2,107	107.4	352.2	19,618
Amusement and recreation services [5][8]	78, 79, 84	467.0	64,524	15,474	1,094.4	579.4	14,139
Motion picture prod., distribution, services	781, 2	37.1	20,778	4,973	171.3	1,771.6	29,029
Motion picture theaters	783	8.6	4,056	584	94.1	511.5	6,211
Video tape rental	784	24.7	2,920	581	79.6	159.7	7,300
Producers, orchestras, entertainers [9]	792	186.9	7,725	1,607	55.2	625.0	29,092
Bowling centers	793	8.3	2,597	702	99.8	380.7	7,039
Commercial sports	794	50.6	5,966	2,047	75.5	1,577.6	27,106
Physical fitness facilities	7991	22.3	2,721	745	104.9	274.2	7,097
Amusement parks	7996	[7]0.7	[7]3,470	820	60.4	[7]4,663.8	13,566
Membership sports and recreation clubs	7997	[7]7.7	[7]3,700	1,173	112.7	[7]483.1	10,403
Health services [5]	80	800.6	196,211	78,820	3,592.5	448.2	21,940
Offices and clinics of doctors of medicine	801	297.7	96,698	43,856	1,131.6	462.7	38,756
Offices and clinics of dentists	802	131.3	25,258	8,760	491.5	230.6	17,822
Offices and clinics of chiropractors	8041	31.4	3,707	900	58.0	163.2	15,504
Offices and clinics of optometrists	8042	23.1	3,755	893	57.9	216.0	15,429
Nursing and personal care facilities	805	38.3	20,570	9,465	961.6	1,495.5	9,843
Hospitals	806	[7]1.4	[7]19,720	6,582	366.5	[7]14,136.2	17,958
Medical and dental laboratories	807	[7]14.8	[7]7,114	2,567	131.8	[7]479.4	19,474
Home health care services	808	[7]5.1	[7]3,024	1,578	184.8	[7]595.3	8,542
Legal services	81	273.2	72,115	26,078	807.6	484.7	32,291
Selected educational services [5]	823, 4, 9	155.9	6,102	1,657	109.4	460.8	15,144
Vocational schools	824	[7]3.7	[7]3,058	1,086	65.3	[7]826.1	16,637
Social services [5]	83	319.5	9,561	2,971	357.3	170.2	8,315
Child day care services	835	248.7	4,284	1,307	199.7	109.8	6,547
Engineering and architectural services	871	195.3	57,051	23,175	747.0	859.8	31,024
Accounting, auditing, and bookkeeping services	872	250.1	26,612	10,204	448.1	350.9	22,768
Research and testing services [10]	873 ex. 8733	[7]12.4	[7]14,184	5,615	222.2	[7]1,144.8	25,266
Management and public relations services	874	418.8	43,381	14,515	551.8	580.4	26,303
Firms exempt from Federal income tax [5]	(X)	175.8	267,490	117,976	6,736.7	1,521.3	17,513
Membership sports and recreation clubs	7997	6.5	3,694	1,467	116.4	564.0	12,607
Museums, botanical, zoological gardens	84	2.7	2,597	778	52.1	961.9	14,933
Nursing and personal care facilities	805	4.1	8,201	4,264	371.5	1,995.5	11,479
Hospitals	806	5.9	172,001	82,342	3,964.1	29,137.9	20,772
Hospitals, excluding government	806	3.8	123,533	55,318	2,773.6	32,508.7	19,945
Social services [5]	83	63.0	31,552	11,617	1,109.5	500.8	10,470
Individual and family social services	832	21.9	8,585	3,629	312.7	392.7	11,606
Job training and related services	833	5.0	3,664	1,741	238.2	732.0	7,307
Residential care	836	10.5	6,125	2,768	240.5	584.8	11,507
Business associations	861	12.3	6,756	1,996	87.5	549.3	22,819
Professional membership organizations	862	5.6	4,110	1,133	49.3	732.6	22,981
Civic, social, and fraternal associations	864	40.4	8,569	2,779	322.9	212.0	8,604
Research and testing services	873	3.2	8,303	3,088	107.8	2,623.5	28,643

X Not applicable. [1] Based on 1987 Standard Industrial Classification; see text, section 13. [2] Represents the number of establishments in business at any time during year. [3] Receipts refer to establishments subject to Federal income tax. Revenues refer to establishments exempt from Federal income tax. [4] For pay period including March 12. [5] Includes other kinds of business, not shown separately. [6] Excludes membership lodging. [7] Covers only establishments with payroll. [8] Includes motion pictures and museums. [9] Excludes motion picture producers. [10] Excludes noncommercial research organizations.

Source: U.S. Bureau of the Census, *1987 Census of Service Industries*, SC87-A-52, SC87-N-1, and SC87-S-4.

No. 1301. Selected Service Industries—Summary: 1982 and 1987

[For establishments with payroll]

KIND OF BUSINESS	1972 SIC code [1]	ESTABLISH-MENTS [2] (1,000)		RECEIPTS OR EXPENSES [3] (mil. dol.)		PAID EMPLOYEES [4] (1,000)	
		1982	1987	1982	1987	1982	1987
Firms subject to Federal income tax [5]	(X)	1,339.2	1,624.6	426,982	752,474	11,106	15,688
Hotels, rooming houses, camps, and other lodging places	70	44.3	46.8	33,215	51,865	1,102	1,411
Personal services	72	179.6	196.1	22,980	35,133	970	1,209
Business services	73	230.1	339.3	106,866	216,807	3,152	5,250
Automotive repair, services, and parking	75	123.6	151.2	30,695	51,423	553	785
Miscellaneous repair services	76	58.2	65.5	14,133	20,838	300	346
Amusement and recreation services [6]	78, 79	73.0	74.3	33,115	52,808	804	929
Health services, except hospitals	80 ex. 806	360.4	405.4	95,610	162,569	2,433	3,226
Legal services	81	122.7	138.2	34,325	66,998	569	808
Selected educational services	823, 4, 9	7.8	10.6	2,400	4,882	68	109
Social services	83	29.7	43.1	3,636	7,330	222	357
Engineering, architectural, surveying services	891	47.6	62.3	34,315	53,563	581	747
Accounting, auditing, and bookkeeping services	893	55.3	69.8	14,596	24,483	330	448
Firms exempt from Federal income tax [5]	(X)	151.6	169.9	54,522	87,448	2,280	2,773
Selected health services	805, 8, 9	10.2	13.2	10,438	19,084	476	684
Social services	83	54.2	63.0	16,455	26,884	904	1,110
Selected membership organizations	861,2,4,9	63.2	68.0	15,093	22,028	493	539

X Not applicable.   [1] Based on 1972 Standard Industrial Classification; see text, section 13.   [2] Number of establishments in business at any time during the year.   [3] Receipts refer to establishments subject to Federal income tax. Expenses refer to establishments exempt from Federal income tax.   [4] For pay period including March 12.   [5] Excludes hospitals. Includes other kinds of business, not shown separately.   [6] Includes motion pictures.

Source: U.S. Bureau of the Census, *1987 Census of Service Industries*, Geographic Area Series, SC87-A-52.

No. 1302. Selected Service Industries—Revenue and Expenses for Tax-Exempt Firms: 1990 to 1992

[**In billions of dollars**. Estimated from a sample of employer firms only]

KIND OF BUSINESS	1987 SIC code [1]	REVENUE			EXPENSES		
		1990	1991	1992	1990	1991	1992
Selected amusement and recreation services [2]	792, 7991, 7997, 7999	8.2	8.5	9.5	8.1	8.5	9.5
Nursing and personal care facilities	805	9.3	10.5	11.7	9.2	10.3	11.5
Hospitals	806	251.9	279.6	302.1	226.6	248.5	270.8
Home health care services	808	3.2	3.9	4.8	3.1	3.6	4.5
Health and allied services, n.e.c.	809	4.6	5.1	6.1	4.6	5.2	5.9
Social services	83	44.6	48.3	52.9	39.8	43.5	47.6
Individual and family social services	8322	12.8	14.2	15.8	12.2	13.7	15.0
Job training and related services	8331	5.1	5.6	6.0	4.8	5.5	5.8
Child day care services	8351	2.9	3.2	3.8	3.0	3.2	3.7
Residential care	8361	8.6	9.3	10.1	8.4	9.2	9.9
Museums, botanical, zoological gardens	84	3.0	3.2	3.4	2.8	3.1	3.2
Selected membership organizations [3]	86 (pt)	34.0	36.1	39.1	29.3	31.8	34.3
Research and testing services	873	12.1	13.0	14.6	11.3	12.3	13.9

[1] Standard Industrial Classification; see text, section 13.   [2] Covers theatrical producers, bands, orchestras, and entertainers (SIC 792); physical fitness facilities (SIC 7991); membership sports and recreation clubs (SIC 7997); and amusement and recreation services, not elsewhere classified (SIC 7999).   [3] Includes business associations (SIC 861); professional membership organizations (SIC 862); civic, social, and fraternal organizations (SIC 864); and other membership organizations, except labor unions and political and religious organizations (SIC 869).

Source: U.S. Bureau of the Census, *Current Business Reports*, Service Annual Survey: 1992 (BS/92).

No. 1303. National Nonprofit Associations—Number, by Type: 1980 to 1993

[Data compiled during last few months of year previous to year shown and the beginning months of year shown]

TYPE	1980	1985	1990	1993	TYPE	1980	1985	1990	1993
Total	14,726	19,121	22,289	22,691	Fraternal, foreign interest, nationality, ethnic	435	492	573	567
Trade, business, commercial	3,118	3,719	3,918	3,837	Religious	797	953	1,172	1,230
Agriculture	677	882	940	1,130	Veteran, hereditary, patriotic	208	281	462	594
Legal, governmental, public admin., military	529	658	792	787	Hobby, avocational	910	1,311	1,475	1,516
Scientific, engineering, tech	1,039	1,270	1,417	1,360	Athletic sports	504	737	840	849
Educational	[1]2,376	[1]2,822	1,291	1,301	Labor unions	235	252	253	247
Cultural	([1])	([1])	1,886	1,897	Chambers of Commerce [2]	105	142	168	169
Social welfare	994	1,450	1,705	1,833	Greek and non-Greek letter societies	318	331	340	339
Health, medical	1,413	1,886	2,227	2,325	Fan clubs	(NA)	(NA)	581	501
Public affairs	1,068	1,935	2,249	2,209					

NA Not available.   [1] Data for cultural associations included with educational associations.   [2] National and binational.

Source: Gale Research Inc., Detroit, MI. Compiled from *Encyclopedia of Associations*, annual, (copyright).

No. 1304. Services—Establishments, Employees, and Payroll: 1990 and 1991

[Covers establishments with payroll. Excludes government employees, railroad employees, self-employed persons, etc. For statement on methodology, see Appendix III]

KIND OF BUSINESS	1987 SIC code [1]	ESTABLISHMENTS (1,000)		EMPLOYEES (1,000)		PAYROLL (bil. dol.)	
		1990	1991	1990	1991	1990	1991
Services, total [2]..............	(I)	**2,059.3**	**2,141.7**	**28,800**	**29,575**	**599.4**	**639.4**
Hotels and other lodging places [2]........	70	50.6	52.6	1,529	1,508	19.1	19.4
Hotels and motels...................	701	39.2	40.9	1,463	1,441	18.3	18.6
Personal services [2]..................	72	186.1	193.9	1,196	1,229	13.5	14.1
Laundry, cleaning, and garment services [2]..	721	50.4	53.0	418	427	5.2	5.4
Coin-operated laundries and cleaning ...	7215	11.1	11.5	45	45	0.4	0.4
Drycleaning plants, except rug	7216	17.6	18.2	148	141	1.6	1.6
Beauty shops.....................	723	76.1	78.6	371	374	3.9	4.0
Funeral service and crematories	726	14.9	15.0	85	85	1.7	1.7
Business services [2].................	73	292.3	309.7	5,119	5,213	98.1	103.0
Advertising......................	731	19.1	20.5	204	205	7.3	7.3
Advertising agencies..............	7311	11.1	11.0	137	132	5.4	5.3
Mailing, reproduction, stenographic......	733	26.2	27.7	233	238	5.1	5.3
Services to buildings...............	734	48.5	52.8	802	807	8.3	8.8
Miscellaneous equipment rental and leasing...................	735	22.6	23.1	209	206	4.9	4.9
Personnel supply services [2]	736	27.0	27.6	1,518	1,527	20.6	21.6
Employment agencies..............	7361	12.8	12.8	247	261	4.3	4.2
Help supply services..............	7363	13.3	14.2	1,210	1,230	15.6	17.0
Computer and data processing services [2]..	737	40.5	43.8	773	799	28.5	30.6
Computer programming services......	7371	12.4	13.2	217	221	8.9	9.5
Data processing and preparation......	7374	6.8	6.8	229	225	6.4	6.7
Miscellaneous business services	738	62.7	70.3	1,093	1,159	17.2	18.3
Detective and armored car services..	7381	9.4	10.2	467	474	5.2	5.4
Automotive repair, services, and parking [2] ...	75	156.6	162.8	877	862	15.2	15.3
Automotive rentals, no drivers.........	751	10.5	10.5	147	141	2.9	2.9
Automotive repair shops [2]...........	753	112.7	117.4	507	498	9.6	9.7
Top and body repair and paint shops....	7532	30.5	31.3	164	156	3.2	3.2
General automotive repair shops.......	7538	54.8	57.4	214	214	3.8	4.0
Automotive services, except repair......	754	18.1	19.4	145	146	1.5	1.6
Miscellaneous repair services............	76	67.4	69.5	403	402	8.7	9.1
Electrical repair shops	762	17.2	17.7	115	115	2.6	2.8
Motion pictures [2]....................	78	35.4	36.8	430	420	8.6	8.4
Motion picture production and services ...	781	9.2	9.6	189	176	5.9	5.8
Video tape rental.................	784	16.4	17.5	103	109	0.8	0.8
Amusement and recreation services [2]	79	75.2	79.8	1,032	1,060	16.1	17.3
Membership sports and recreation clubs ...	7997	13.1	13.6	242	247	3.4	3.7
Health services [2]...................	80	436.7	447.9	8,811	9,202	213.8	234.8
Offices and clinics of medical doctors.....	801	193.6	195.6	1,387	1,454	63.0	68.2
Offices and clinics of dentists	802	104.7	106.4	533	544	11.6	12.3
Offices and clinics of chiropractors.......	8041	22.9	24.6	73	77	1.3	1.5
Offices and clinics of optometrists.......	8042	15.3	15.4	63	64	1.1	1.2
Nursing and personal care facilities	805	19.1	19.6	1,461	1,520	18.6	20.7
Hospitals.....................	806	6.3	6.6	4,325	4,466	99.2	108.5
Medical and dental laboratories	807	14.4	14.7	158	169	3.8	4.3
Home health care services..........	808	7.7	8.2	351	397	4.8	5.9
Legal services.....................	81	142.4	145.9	932	941	36.0	37.3
Educational services [2]................	82	36.0	38.1	1,755	1,819	29.5	31.9
Elementary and secondary schools	821	14.3	14.9	451	470	6.6	7.2
Colleges and universities	822	3.0	3.1	1,082	1,122	19.2	20.8
Social services [2]..................	83	115.6	124.8	1,750	1,862	20.9	23.3
Individual and family services	832	27.6	29.6	408	441	5.6	6.3
Job training and related services	833	6.9	7.3	289	298	2.8	3.0
Child day care services	835	39.0	40.8	405	419	3.4	3.8
Residential care	836	21.0	22.3	417	450	5.4	6.1
Membership organizations [2]............	86	218.2	234.3	1,892	1,968	22.6	24.4
Business associations	861	12.7	13.8	99	98	2.7	2.9
Labor organizations	863	19.2	19.9	176	181	2.7	2.8
Civic and social associations..........	864	40.0	43.4	366	385	3.7	4.1
Religious organizations..............	866	128.8	139.1	1,096	1,143	10.1	11.0
Engineering and management services [2]	87	201.1	213.6	2,473	2,565	79.8	84.5
Engineering services	8711	33.1	34.0	652	652	24.9	25.5
Architectural services..............	8712	15.7	15.8	140	128	4.8	4.4
Accounting, auditing, and bookkeeping	872	67.9	71.3	524	559	13.8	14.9
Research and testing services.........	873	14.9	15.8	393	403	12.3	13.2
Commercial physical research	8731	3.7	4.1	165	167	6.5	7.0
Management services	8741	15.3	16.6	286	307	7.7	8.5
Management consulting services	8742	24.5	27.2	226	244	8.6	9.6

[1] Based on 1987 Standard Industrial Classification; see text, section 13.   [2] Includes kinds of business not shown separately.

Source: U.S. Bureau of the Census, *County Business Patterns*, annual.

No. 1305. Service Industries—Annual Receipts of Taxable Firms: 1985 to 1992

[In billions of dollars. Covers employer and nonemployer firms except as noted. Estimated]

KIND OF BUSINESS	1987 SIC code [1]	1985	1987	1988	1989	1990	1991	1992
Hotels and other lodging places [2]	70	45.4	53.6	57.6	59.0	60.7	60.5	64.6
Hotels and motels	701	43.5	51.6	55.5	56.9	58.5	58.3	62.1
Personal services [3]	72	36.7	43.2	48.4	52.1	55.3	54.5	59.1
Laundry, cleaning, and garment services	721	12.8	14.2	15.5	16.3	17.0	17.2	18.3
Beauty shops	723	9.0	10.6	11.3	12.1	12.1	12.1	13.1
Funeral service and crematories	726	5.2	5.7	6.3	6.5	7.0	7.4	7.9
Business services [3]	73	155.9	188.9	222.4	249.1	276.5	282.1	302.6
Advertising	731	14.9	16.8	18.8	20.0	21.6	20.8	21.9
Advertising agencies	7311	11.1	12.0	13.8	15.0	16.3	15.5	16.3
Credit reporting and collection	732	4.4	5.5	5.6	6.0	6.4	6.5	7.0
Mailing, reproduction, stenographic [3]	733	13.6	16.6	18.4	19.9	21.7	21.5	22.3
Direct mail advertising services	7331	4.4	5.5	6.5	6.8	7.9	7.8	8.5
Commercial art and graphic design	7336	(NA)	(NA)	(NA)	(NA)	6.5	6.5	6.6
Services to dwellings and other buildings	734	13.3	15.6	17.3	19.7	21.3	21.0	21.6
Miscellaneous equipment rental and leasing	735	(NA)	(NA)	(NA)	(NA)	21.6	21.1	21.2
Personnel supply services	736	14.6	20.3	24.3	26.3	28.6	27.8	30.4
Employment agencies	7361	3.4	4.0	5.0	6.1	7.5	7.1	7.6
Help supply services [3]	7363	(NA)	(NA)	(NA)	(NA)	21.1	20.6	22.8
Computer and data processing services [3]	737	45.2	56.0	67.7	77.2	85.8	91.3	100.7
Computer programming services	7371	(NA)	(NA)	(NA)	(NA)	19.0	20.9	22.2
Prepackaged software	7372	(NA)	(NA)	(NA)	(NA)	11.4	12.6	14.5
Computer integrated systems design	7373	(NA)	(NA)	(NA)	(NA)	18.7	19.9	22.0
Data processing and preparation	7374	(NA)	(NA)	(NA)	(NA)	17.9	19.0	20.7
Miscellaneous business services [3]	738	(NA)	(NA)	(NA)	(NA)	69.5	72.2	77.6
Detective, guard, and armored car services	7381	(NA)	(NA)	(NA)	(NA)	9.3	9.9	10.0
Photofinishing laboratories	7384	4.9	5.4	6.0	6.5	6.4	6.8	7.3
Automotive repair, services, and parking [3]	75	51.7	58.3	66.4	71.7	75.0	73.3	79.5
Automotive rentals, no drivers [3]	751	14.6	16.7	19.5	21.1	23.2	22.8	23.5
Truck rental and leasing, without drivers	7513	5.5	6.5	7.6	8.2	8.9	8.4	8.2
Passenger car rental [3]	7514	(NA)	(NA)	(NA)	(NA)	9.7	10.3	11.2
Automotive repair shops [3]	753	30.5	34.2	38.6	41.9	43.4	41.9	46.4
Top & body repair & paint shops	7532	(NA)	(NA)	(NA)	(NA)	13.4	12.7	13.8
General automotive repair shops	7538	(NA)	(NA)	(NA)	(NA)	14.8	13.4	16.0
Automotive services, except repair	754	(NA)	(NA)	(NA)	(NA)	6.2	6.4	7.3
Miscellaneous repair services	76	20.7	24.6	27.8	30.3	33.4	33.1	36.3
Electrical repair shops	762	(NA)	(NA)	(NA)	(NA)	11.1	11.1	11.6
Motion pictures	78	21.6	27.8	31.2	35.0	38.1	41.1	43.8
Motion picture produc., distribution, allied services	781,2	15.1	20.8	22.6	24.7	26.1	28.5	30.6
Motion picture theaters	783	3.8	4.1	4.7	5.7	6.6	7.0	6.9
Video tape rental	784	(NA)	(NA)	(NA)	(NA)	5.4	5.6	6.3
Amusement and recreation services [3]	79	31.2	36.6	40.2	42.2	46.5	46.7	51.1
Producers, orchestras, entertainers	792	6.4	7.7	8.1	7.5	9.2	9.5	10.1
Commercial sports	794	5.0	6.0	6.9	7.9	9.3	9.7	10.6
Professional sports clubs and promoters	7941	(NA)	(NA)	(NA)	(NA)	4.6	5.2	5.9
Health services [3][4]	80	147.4	182.3	203.8	220.1	244.5	262.7	285.0
Offices and clinics of doctors of medicine	801	72.1	90.5	100.8	107.5	117.0	124.5	135.0
Offices and clinics of dentists	802	20.6	24.0	25.6	27.1	28.8	30.0	32.9
Offices and clinics of chiropractors	8041	2.7	3.3	4.0	4.4	4.8	5.0	5.8
Nursing and personal care facilities	805	17.5	20.1	21.4	23.3	26.4	28.8	30.7
Hospitals [3]	806	15.7	19.7	22.6	24.7	28.3	30.7	33.1
General medical and surgical hospitals	8062	(NA)	(NA)	(NA)	(NA)	21.8	23.7	25.8
Psychiatric hospitals	8063	(NA)	(NA)	(NA)	(NA)	5.1	5.4	5.4
Medical laboratories	8071	3.9	5.5	6.6	7.4	8.2	8.8	9.3
Home health care services	808	(NA)	(NA)	(NA)	(NA)	6.2	7.4	8.9
Legal services [4]	81	52.8	67.0	75.2	81.4	88.3	89.5	96.2
Social services [4]	83	(NA)	(NA)	(NA)	(NA)	12.3	13.1	14.4
Residential care	8361	(NA)	(NA)	(NA)	(NA)	4.7	5.3	5.5
Engineering and management services [3]	87	(NA)	(NA)	(NA)	(NA)	190.3	194.9	207.6
Engineering & architectural services [3]	871	49.3	57.1	61.2	70.0	73.6	73.7	75.8
Engineering services	8711	(NA)	(NA)	(NA)	(NA)	58.8	59.7	61.5
Architectural services	8712	(NA)	(NA)	(NA)	(NA)	12.1	11.4	11.8
Accounting, auditing, & bookkeeping	8721	21.2	26.6	29.2	32.2	32.5	33.6	37.0
Research and testing services [5]	873, ex. 8733	(NA)	(NA)	(NA)	(NA)	22.3	22.8	24.7
Commercial physical research	8731	6.0	7.2	8.9	10.3	11.7	11.8	13.0
Management and public relations	874	37.5	43.4	51.5	57.2	61.9	64.8	70.0
Management services	8741	(NA)	(NA)	(NA)	(NA)	20.9	22.1	24.0
Management consulting services	8742	(NA)	(NA)	(NA)	(NA)	25.3	26.1	28.1
Facilities support services	8744	(NA)	(NA)	(NA)	(NA)	6.3	7.0	7.4
Arrangement of passenger transportation	472	6.3	7.3	8.0	8.7	9.0	8.5	9.0
Real estate agents and managers [4]	653	31.3	38.2	42.2	44.1	44.1	43.7	50.2

NA Not available.   [1] Standard Industrial Classification; see text, section 13.   [2] Excludes those on membership basis.   [3] Includes other kinds of businesses, not shown separately.   [4] Covers employer firms only.   [5] Excludes noncommercial research organizations.

Source: U.S. Bureau of the Census, *Current Business Reports, Service Annual Survey: 1992* (BS/92); and unpublished data.

Figure 28.1
U.S. International Transaction Balances: 1970 to 1992

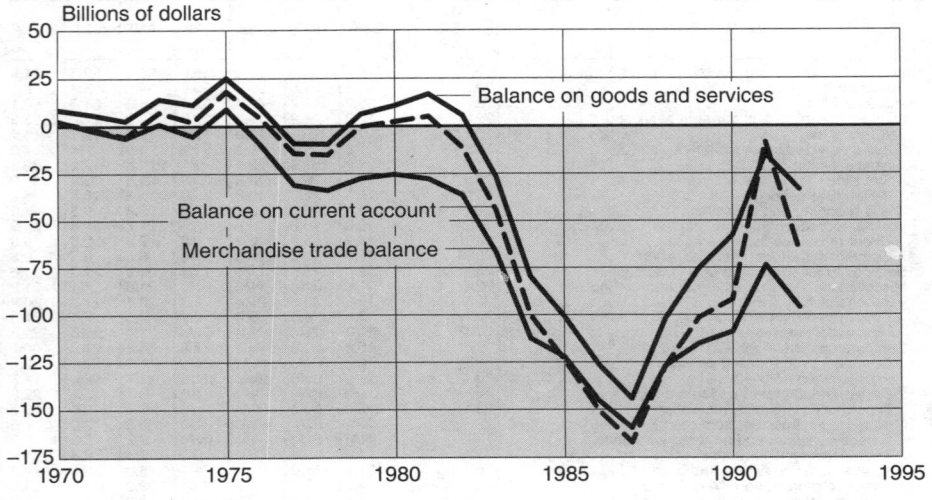

Source: Chart prepared by U.S. Bureau of the Census. For data, see table 1307.

Figure 28.2
Top Purchasers of U.S. Exports and Suppliers of U.S. General Imports: 1992

Total U.S. Exports $448.2 billion

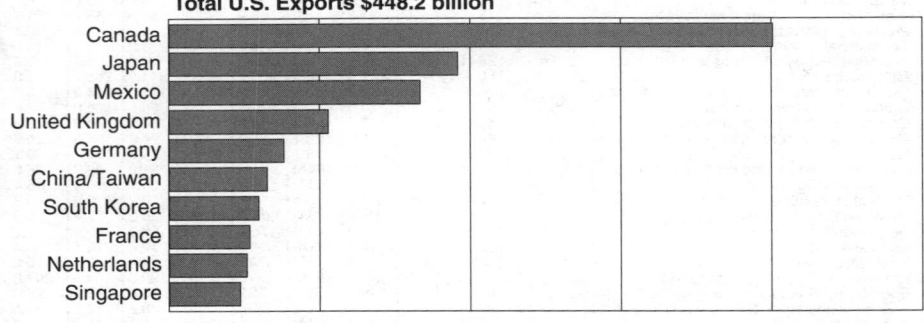

Total U.S. General Imports $532.5 billion

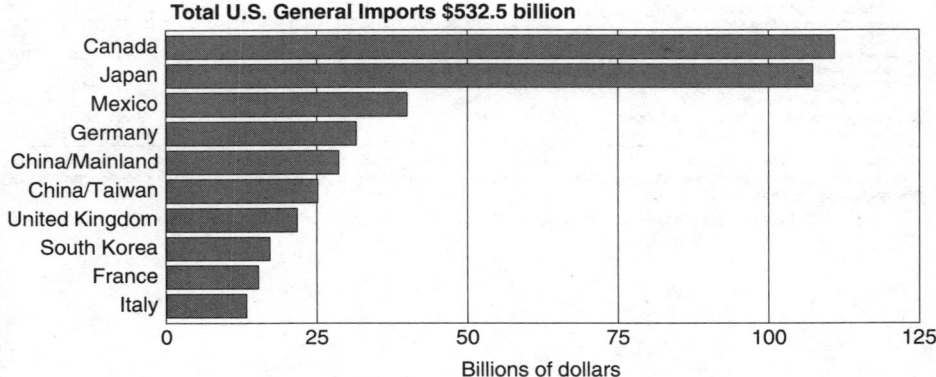

Source: Chart prepared by U.S. Bureau of the Census. For data, see table 1329.

Foreign Commerce and Aid

This section presents data on the flow of goods, services, and capital between the United States and other countries; changes in official reserve assets of the United States; international investments; foreign assistance programs; and import duties.

The Bureau of Economic Analysis publishes current figures on U.S. international transactions and the U.S. international investment position in its monthly *Survey of Current Business.* Statistics for the foreign aid programs are presented by the Agency for International Development (AID) in its annual *U.S. Overseas Loans and Grants and Assistance from International Organizations;* and by the Department of Agriculture in its *Foreign Agricultural Trade of the United States.*

The principal source of merchandise import and export data is the Bureau of the Census. Current data are presented monthly in *U.S. Merchandise Trade,* (beginning 1994, retitled *U.S. International Trade in Goods and Services*) report series FT900, and *U.S. Merchandise Trade: Exports, General Imports, and Imports for Consumption,* report series FT925. The *Bureau of the Census Catalog* and the *Guide to Foreign Trade Statistics* lists the Bureau's monthly and annual reports in this field. In addition, the International Trade Administration and the Bureau of Economic Analysis present summary as well as selected commodity and country data for U.S. foreign trade in the *Overseas Business Reports* and the *Survey of Current Business,* respectively. The merchandise trade data in the latter source include balance of payments adjustments to the Census data. The Treasury Department's *Monthly Treasury Statement of Receipts and Outlays of the United States Government* contains information on import duties.

International accounts.—The international transactions tables (Nos. 1306 to 1308) show, for given time periods, the transfer of goods, services, grants, and financial assets and liabilities between the United States and the rest of the world. The international investment posi-

> ### In Brief
> The U.S. international trade in goods and services ran a deficit of $75.7 billion in 1993 with goods being in deficit $132.6 billion and services in surplus $56.9 billion
>
> Canada was the major source of U.S. imports in 1993 with $111 billion followed closely by Japan, $107 billion, and Mexico a distant third with $40 billion

tion table (No. 1309) presents, for specific dates, the value of U.S. investments abroad and of foreign investments in the United States. The movement of foreign and U.S. capital as presented in the balance of payments is not the only factor affecting the total value of foreign investments. Among the other factors are changes in the valuation of assets or liabilities, including changes in prices of securities, defaults, expropriations, and write-offs.

Direct investment abroad means the ownership or control, directly or indirectly, by one person of 10 percent or more of the voting securities of an incorporated business enterprise or an equivalent interest in an unincorporated business enterprise. Direct investment position is the value of U.S. parents' claims on the equity of, and receivables due from, foreign affiliates, less foreign affiliates' receivables due from their U.S. parents. Income consists of parents' shares in the earnings of their affiliates plus net interest received by parents on intercompany accounts, less withholding taxes on dividends and interest.

Foreign aid.—Foreign assistance is divided into three major categories—grants (military supplies and services and other grants), credits, and other assistance (through net accumulation of foreign currency claims from the sale of agricultural commodities). *Grants* are transfers for which no payment is expected (other than a limited percentage of the foreign currency "counterpart" funds generated by the grant), or which at most involve an obligation on the part of the receiver to extend aid to the United States or other countries to achieve a common objective. *Credits* are loan disbursements or transfers under other agreements which give rise to specific obligations to repay, over a period of years, usually with interest. All known returns to the U.S. Government stemming from grants and credits (reverse grants, returns of grants, and payments of principal) are taken into account in net grants and net credits, but no allowance is made for interest or commissions. *Other assistance* represents the transfer of U.S. farm products in exchange for foreign currencies (plus, since enactment of Public Law 87-128, currency claims from principal and interest collected on credits extended under the farm products program), *less* the Government's disbursements of the currencies as grants, credits, or for purchases. The net acquisition of currencies represents net transfers of resources to foreign countries under the agricultural programs, in addition to those classified as grants or credits.

The basic instrument for extending military aid to friendly nations has been the Mutual Defense Assistance Program authorized by the Congress in 1949. Prior to 1952, economic and technical aid was authorized in the Foreign Assistance Act of 1948, the 1950 Act for International Development, and other legislation which set up programs for specific countries. In 1952, these economic, technical, and military aid programs were combined under the Mutual Security Act, which in turn was followed by the Foreign Assistance Act passed in 1961. Appropriations to provide military assistance were also made in the Department of Defense Appropriation Act (rather than the Foreign Assistance Appropriation Act) beginning in 1966 for certain countries in Southeast Asia and in other legislation concerning program for specific countries (such as Israel). Figures on activity under the Foreign Assistance Act as reported in the *Foreign Grants and Credits* series differ from data published by AID or its immediate predecessors, due largely to differences in reporting, timing, and treatment of particular items.

Exports.—The Bureau of the Census compiles export data primarily from Shipper's Export Declarations required to be filed with customs officials for shipments leaving the United States. They include U.S. exports under mutual security programs and exclude shipments to U.S. Armed Forces for their own use.

The value reported in the export statistics is generally equivalent to a free alongside ship (f.a.s.) value at the U.S. port of export, based on the transaction price, including inland freight, insurance, and other charges incurred in placing the merchandise alongside the carrier at the U.S. port of exportation. This value, as defined, excludes the cost of loading merchandise aboard the exporting carrier and also excludes freight, insurance, and any other charges or transportation and other costs beyond the U.S. port of exportation. The country of destination is defined as the country of ultimate destination or country where the merchandise is to be consumed, further processed, or manufactured, as known to the shipper at the time of exportation. When ultimate destination is not known, the shipment is statistically credited to the last country to which the shipper knows the merchandise will be shipped in the same form as exported.

For certain "low-valued" shipments, the export statistics include estimates based upon selected samples of such shipments. The dollar value of the "low-valued" shipments has varied. For instance, effective January 1987 through September 1989, data are estimated for shipments valued under $1,501; from October 1989 through December 1989, data are estimated for shipments valued under $2,501 to all countries.

Effective January 1990, the United States began substituting Canadian import statistics for U.S. exports to Canada. As a result of the data exchange between the United States and Canada, the United States has adopted the Canadian import exemption level for its export statistics based on shipments to Canada.

Data are estimated for shipments valued under $2,501 to all countries, except Canada, using factors based on the ratios of low-valued shipments to individual country totals. These shipments represent slightly less than 2.5 percent of the monthly value of U.S. exports to those countries. Data are estimated for shipments reported on Canadian import documents which total less than $900 (Canadian). Such shipments represent 2 percent of the monthly value of U.S. exports to Canada.

Prior to 1989, exports were based on Schedule B, Statistical Classification of Domestic and Foreign Commodities Exported from the United States. These statistics were retabulated and published using Schedule E, Standard International Trade Classification, Revision 2. Beginning in 1989, Schedule B classifications were based on the Harmonized System and made to coincide with the Standard International Trade Classification, Revision 3. This revision will affect the comparability of most export series beginning with the 1989 data.

Imports.—The Bureau of the Census compiles import data from various customs forms required to be filed with customs officials. From 1974-1981, data on import values were presented on three bases: The transaction values f.a.s. (free alongside ship) at the foreign port of export, the c.i.f. (cost, insurance, and freight), and the previously reported customs import value (as appraised by the U.S. Customs Service in accordance with legal requirements of the Tariff Act of 1930, as amended). This latter valuation, primarily used for collection of import duties, frequently did not reflect the actual transaction value. Beginning 1982, import data are based on customs values, i.e., the price paid by the buyer to the seller in accordance with the 1979 Trade Agreement Act amendments to the 1930 Tariff Act. For the c.i.f. imports, the new customs value was substituted for the arms-length transaction value used for 1981 and earlier years. The f.a.s. transaction values were discontinued as of January 1982. Country of origin is defined as country where the merchandise was grown, mined, or manufactured. If country of origin is unknown, country of shipment is reported.

Imports are classified either as "General imports" or "Imports for consumption." General imports are a combination of entries for immediate consumption, entries into customs bonded warehouses, and entries into U.S. Foreign Trade Zones, thus generally reflecting total arrivals of merchandise. Imports for consumption are a combination of entries for immediate consumption, withdrawals from warehouses for consumption, and entries of merchandise into U.S. customs territory from U.S. Foreign Trade Zones, thus generally reflecting the total of the commodities entered into U.S. consumption channels.

Since July 1953, the import statistics include estimates, not classified by commodity, for certain low-valued shipments. For instance, from January 1985 through September 1989, import statistics include estimates for shipments valued under $1,001. Effective October 1989, import statistics are fully compiled on shipments valued over $1,250 or, under certain textile programs, for any article which must be reported on a formal entry. Value data for shipments valued under $1,251 and not required to be reported on formal entries are estimated for individual countries using factors based on the ratios of low-valued shipments to individual country totals for past periods. The estimated low-valued shipments generally amount to slightly less than 4 percent of the import total.

Prior to 1989, imports were based on the Tariff Schedule of the United States Annotated. The statistics were retabulated and published using Schedule A, Standard International Trade Classification, Revision 2. Beginning in 1989, the statistics are based on the Harmonized Tariff Schedule of the United States, which coincides with the Standard International Trade Classification, Revision 3. This revision will affect the comparability of most import series beginning with the 1989 data.

Area coverage.—Except as noted, the geographic area covered by the export and import trade statistics is the United States Customs area (includes the 50 States, the District of Columbia and Puerto Rico), the U.S. Virgin Islands (effective January 1981), and U.S. Foreign Trade Zones (effective July 1982). Data for selected tables and total values for 1980, have been revised to reflect the U.S. Virgin Islands' trade with foreign countries, where possible.

No. 1306. U.S. International Transactions, by Type of Transaction: 1980 to 1992

[In millions of dollars. Minus sign (-) indicates debits. See also *Historical Statistics, Colonial Times to 1970,* series U 1-25]

TYPE OF TRANSACTION	1980	1983	1984	1985	1986	1987	1988	1989	1990	1991	1992
Exports of goods and services [1]	344,440	351,613	391,435	380,051	398,583	445,216	550,323	629,468	680,890	704,914	726,948
Merchandise, excl. military [2][3]	224,250	201,799	219,926	215,915	223,344	250,208	320,230	361,697	388,705	415,962	439,272
Foods, feeds, and beverages	36,278	32,091	32,196	24,566	23,522	25,229	33,770	37,429	35,117	35,737	40,114
Industrial supplies and materials	72,088	58,936	64,120	61,159	64,720	70,052	90,019	99,907	105,682	109,977	109,570
Capital goods, except automotive	76,283	71,660	77,007	79,322	82,815	92,707	119,103	139,563	153,279	167,029	176,837
Automotive vehicles and parts	17,443	18,461	22,422	22,945	25,097	27,583	33,397	34,940	36,504	40,045	46,686
Consumer goods (nonfood) [5]	17,751	14,925	15,085	14,593	16,730	20,307	26,981	36,565	42,779	45,944	50,386
Services	47,584	64,199	71,094	73,026	86,241	98,434	110,636	127,080	148,638	163,637	178,503
Transfers under U.S. military agency sales contracts	9,029	12,524	9,969	8,718	8,549	11,106	9,289	8,526	9,833	10,691	10,901
Travel	10,588	10,947	17,320	17,920	20,529	23,718	29,665	36,571	43,418	48,757	54,689
Passenger fares	2,591	3,610	4,058	4,382	5,545	6,966	8,925	10,525	15,140	15,627	16,868
Other transportation	11,618	12,590	13,809	14,674	15,784	17,334	19,456	21,095	22,942	23,625	24,672
Royalties and license fees	7,085	5,745	6,098	6,550	7,927	9,914	11,802	13,064	16,140	17,799	19,626
Other private services	6,276	[6]18,117	19,126	19,904	27,312	28,869	30,835	36,711	40,166	46,444	50,868
U.S. Government misc. services	398	666	714	878	595	526	664	587	668	693	879
Income on U.S. assets abroad	72,606	85,614	100,415	91,110	88,998	96,574	119,456	140,692	143,547	125,315	109,173
Direct investment	37,146	26,528	30,581	29,630	30,850	38,080	50,436	54,490	55,428	49,221	49,606
Other private receipts	32,898	54,255	64,607	55,981	51,735	53,183	62,318	80,567	77,612	67,990	53,139
U.S. Government receipts	2,562	4,832	5,227	5,499	6,413	5,311	6,703	5,635	10,508	8,104	6,428
Imports of goods, services and income	-333,774	-377,495	-469,647	-478,821	-521,937	-585,637	-652,109	-705,005	-738,401	-716,524	-758,036
Merchandise, excl. military [2][3]	-249,750	-268,901	-332,418	-338,088	-368,425	-409,765	-447,189	-477,365	-497,558	-489,398	-535,547
Foods, feeds, and beverages	-18,564	-18,824	-21,879	-21,850	-24,376	-24,809	-24,928	-25,077	-26,653	-26,467	-27,879
Industrial supplies and materials	-132,472	-108,794	-124,109	-114,008	-104,210	-113,746	-122,684	-135,112	-144,831	-132,032	-139,770
Capital goods, except automotive	-31,576	-43,735	-60,367	-61,287	-71,990	-85,128	-102,202	-112,453	-116,040	-120,735	-134,411
Automotive vehicles and parts [4]	-28,257	-43,044	-56,521	-65,905	-78,061	-85,174	-87,947	-87,380	-87,695	-84,941	-91,238
Consumer goods (nonfood) [5]	-34,268	-47,277	-61,094	-66,336	-79,355	-88,824	-96,425	-105,453	-105,294	-108,024	-123,003
Services	-41,491	-54,894	-67,657	-72,859	-79,892	-90,243	-97,930	-101,314	-116,583	-118,341	-123,378
Direct defense expenditures	-10,851	-13,087	-12,516	-13,108	-13,730	-14,918	-15,643	-15,364	-17,651	-16,215	-13,404
Travel	-10,397	-13,149	-22,913	-24,558	-25,913	-29,310	-32,114	-33,418	-37,349	-36,958	-43,534
Passenger Fares	-3,607	-6,003	-5,724	-6,484	-6,554	-7,318	-7,768	-8,258	-10,608	-10,636	-11,781
Other transportation	-11,790	-12,222	-14,843	-15,643	-16,715	-17,788	-19,534	-20,664	-23,401	-23,297	-23,401
Royalties and license fees	-724	-941	-1,164	-1,165	-1,392	-1,844	-2,585	-2,602	-3,133	-3,984	-4,290
Other private services	-2,909	[6][7]-7,924	-8,963	-10,166	-13,901	-17,172	-18,365	-19,137	-22,522	-25,154	-24,707
U.S. Government miscellaneous services	-1,214	-1,568	-1,534	-1,735	-1,686	-1,893	-1,921	-1,871	-1,919	-2,097	-2,262
Income on foreign assets in the United States	-42,532	-53,700	-69,572	-67,875	-73,620	-85,629	-106,991	-126,326	-124,261	-108,886	-99,111
Direct investment	-8,635	-4,206	-8,723	-7,213	-7,058	-7,425	-11,693	-6,643	-1,083	3,675	-404
Other private payments	-21,214	-30,501	-39,694	-37,689	-42,491	-52,913	-65,133	-83,827	-85,308	-73,575	-69,846
U.S. Government payments	-12,684	-18,993	-21,155	-22,972	-24,071	-25,291	-30,164	-35,856	-37,870	-38,986	-38,861
Unilateral transfers (excl. military grants), net	-8,349	-17,741	-20,612	-22,950	-24,176	-23,052	-24,869	-25,606	-32,916	8,028	-31,360
U.S. Government grants	-5,486	-6,469	-8,696	-11,268	-11,867	-10,287	-10,506	-10,773	-17,597	24,487	-13,832
U.S. Government pensions	-1,818	-2,207	-2,159	-2,138	-2,197	-2,221	-2,501	-2,517	-2,945	-3,462	-3,736
Private remittances and other transfers	-1,044	9,066	9,756	9,545	-10,112	-10,544	-11,863	-12,316	-12,374	-12,996	-13,793

TYPE OF TRANSACTION	1980	1983	1984	1985	1986	1987	1988	1989	1990	1991	1992
U.S. assets abroad, net (increase/capital outflow (-))	-86,967	-58,856	-29,224	-34,069	-91,069	-62,402	-92,708	-114,944	-56,321	-62,220	-44,900
U.S. official reserve assets, net	-8,155	-1,196	-3,131	-3,858	312	9,149	-3,912	-25,293	-2,158	5,763	3,901
Special drawing rights	-16	-66	-979	-897	-246	-509	127	-535	-192	-192	2,316
Reserve position in the International Monetary Fund	-1,667	-4,434	-995	908	1,501	2,070	1,025	471	731	-367	-2,692
Foreign currencies	-6,472	3,304	-1,156	-3,869	-942	7,588	-5,064	-25,229	-2,697	6,307	4,277
U.S. Govt. assets, other than official reserve assets, net	-5,162	-5,006	-5,489	-2,821	-2,022	1,006	2,967	1,271	2,304	3,397	-959
U.S. credits and other long-term assets	-9,860	-9,967	-9,599	-7,657	-9,084	-6,506	-7,680	-5,580	-8,417	-12,123	-5,144
Repayments on U.S. credits and other long-term assets [7]	4,456	5,012	4,490	4,719	6,089	7,625	10,370	6,725	10,853	16,522	4,242
U.S. foreign currency holdings and U.S. short-term assets, net	242	-51	-379	117	973	-113	277	126	-131	-1,002	-57
U.S. private assets, net	-73,651	-52,654	-20,605	-27,391	-89,360	-72,556	-91,762	-90,922	-56,467	-71,379	-47,843
Direct investments abroad	-19,222	-4,889	-10,948	-13,401	-17,090	-27,181	-15,448	-28,995	-32,694	-27,135	-35,311
Foreign securities	-3,568	-6,762	-4,756	-7,481	-4,271	-5,251	-7,846	-22,070	-28,765	-45,017	-48,646
U.S. claims on unaffiliated foreigners reported by U.S. nonbanking concerns	-4,023	-11,075	6,226	-5,186	-8,024	1,995	-12,146	11,398	-2,477	5,526	(NA)
U.S. claims reported by U.S. banks, n.i.e. [8]	-46,838	-29,928	-11,127	-1,323	-59,975	-42,119	-56,322	-51,255	7,469	-4,753	32,372
Foreign assets in the U.S., net (increase/capital inflow (+))	58,112	83,380	102,010	130,966	223,191	229,972	219,489	213,693	99,379	66,980	120,400
Foreign official assets in the U.S., net	15,497	5,845	3,140	-1,119	35,648	45,387	39,758	8,489	33,908	18,407	40,307
U.S. Government securities	11,895	6,496	4,703	-1,139	33,150	44,802	43,050	1,532	30,243	17,116	22,358
U.S. Treasury securities	9,708	6,972	4,690	-838	34,364	43,238	41,741	149	29,576	15,815	18,333
Other	2,187	-476	13	-301	-1,214	1,564	1,309	1,383	667	1,301	4,025
Other U.S. Government liabilities	615	602	739	844	2,195	-2,326	-467	146	1,866	1,600	2,469
U.S. liabilities reported by U.S. banks, n.i.e. [8]	-159	545	555	645	1,187	3,918	-319	4,976	3,385	-1,668	16,168
Other foreign official assets	3,145	-1,798	-2,857	-1,469	-884	-1,007	-2,506	1,835	-1,586	1,359	-688
Other foreign assets in the United States, net	42,615	77,534	98,870	132,084	187,542	184,585	179,731	205,204	65,471	48,573	80,093
Direct investments in the United States	16,918	10,457	24,748	20,010	35,623	58,219	57,278	67,872	45,137	11,497	-3,948
U.S. Treasury securities	2,645	8,689	23,001	20,433	3,809	-7,643	20,239	29,618	-2,534	16,241	35,077
U.S. securities other than U.S. Treasury securities	5,457	8,164	12,568	50,962	70,969	42,120	26,353	38,767	1,592	34,918	29,884
U.S. liabilities to unaffiliated foreigners reported by U.S. nonbanking concerns	6,852	-118	4,704	-366	-2,641	2,863	5,626	5,565	4,906	-405	(NA)
U.S. liabilities reported by U.S. banks, n.i.e. [8]	10,743	50,342	33,849	41,045	79,783	89,026	70,235	63,382	16,370	-13,678	14,667
Allocations of special drawing rights	1,152	-	-	-	-	-	-	-	-	-	-
Statistical discrepancy	25,386	19,099	26,038	24,825	15,407	-4,096	-126	2,394	47,370	-1,078	-13,052
Balance on merchandise trade [2]	-25,500	-67,102	-112,492	-122,173	-145,081	-159,557	-126,959	-115,668	-108,853	-73,436	-96,275
Balance on services	6,093	9,306	3,437	167	6,350	8,191	12,707	25,766	32,055	45,296	55,125
Balance on investment income	30,073	31,915	30,843	23,235	15,378	10,945	12,466	14,366	19,287	16,429	10,062
Balance on goods, services, and income	10,666	-25,882	-78,212	-98,771	-123,353	-140,421	-101,787	-75,537	-57,511	-11,710	-31,088
Unilateral transfers, net [1]	-8,349	-17,741	-20,612	-22,950	-24,176	-23,052	-24,869	-25,606	-32,916	8,028	-31,360
Balance on current account	2,317	-43,623	-98,824	-121,721	-147,529	-163,474	-126,656	-101,143	-90,428	-3,682	-62,448

- Represents zero. NA Not available. [1] Excludes transfers of goods and services under U.S. military grant programs. [2] Excludes exports of goods under U.S. military agency sales contracts identified in Census export documents, excludes imports of goods under direct defense expenditures identified in Census import documents, and reflects various other adjustments (for valuation, coverage, and timing) of Census statistics to a balance of payments basis. [3] Includes other end-use items, not shown separately. [4] Includes engines. [5] Excludes automotive. [6] Break in series due to inclusion of new data. [7] Includes sales of foreign obligations to foreigners. [8] Not included elsewhere. [9] Includes foreign currency notes sold to private residents abroad.

See Technical Note in *Survey of Current Business*, June 1979.

Source: U.S. Bureau of Economic Analysis, *Survey of Current Business*, June 1993.

No. 1307. U.S. International Transactions—Summary: 1960 to 1992

[In billions of dollars. Reserve assets are for end of period. Minus sign (-) indicates debits, see headnote, table 1306]

YEAR	Merchandise trade balance[1]	Net investment income	Net military transactions	Net travel and transportation receipts	Other services, net	Balance on goods, services, and income.	Unilateral transfers[1]	Balance on current account	Net foreign assets in U.S.	Net U.S. assets abroad	Net U.S. official reserve assets
1960	4.9	3.4	-1.1	-1.0	0.6	6.9	-4.1	2.8	2.3	-4.1	19.4
1965	5.0	5.4	-0.5	-1.3	1.5	10.0	-4.6	5.4	0.7	-5.7	15.5
1966	3.8	5.0	-1.0	-1.3	1.5	8.0	-5.0	3.0	3.7	-7.3	14.9
1967	3.8	5.3	-1.2	-1.8	1.7	7.9	-5.3	2.6	7.4	-9.8	14.8
1968	0.6	6.0	-0.6	-1.5	1.8	6.2	-5.6	0.6	9.9	-11.0	15.7
1969	0.6	6.0	-0.7	-1.8	2.0	6.1	-5.7	0.4	12.7	-11.6	17.0
1970	2.6	6.2	-0.6	-2.0	2.3	8.5	-6.2	2.3	6.4	-9.3	14.5
1971	-2.3	7.3	0.7	-2.3	2.6	6.0	-7.4	-1.4	23.0	-12.5	12.2
1972	-6.4	8.2	1.1	-3.1	3.0	2.7	-8.5	-5.8	21.5	-14.5	13.2
1973	0.9	12.2	0.7	-3.2	3.4	14.1	-6.9	7.1	18.4	-22.9	14.4
1974	-5.5	15.5	0.2	-3.2	4.2	11.2	-9.2	2.0	34.2	-34.7	15.9
1975	8.9	12.8	1.5	-2.8	4.9	25.2	-7.1	18.1	15.7	-39.7	16.2
1976	-9.5	16.1	0.9	-2.6	5.0	10.0	-5.7	4.3	36.5	-51.3	18.7
1977	-31.1	18.1	1.7	-3.6	5.7	-9.1	-5.2	-14.3	51.3	-34.8	19.3
1978	-33.9	20.4	0.9	-3.6	6.9	-9.4	-5.8	-15.1	64.0	-61.1	18.7
1979	-27.6	30.9	-1.3	-2.9	7.3	6.3	-6.6	-0.3	38.8	-66.1	19.0
1980	-25.5	30.1	-1.8	-1.0	8.9	10.7	-8.3	2.3	58.1	-87.0	26.8
1981	-28.0	32.9	-0.8	0.1	12.6	16.7	-11.7	5.0	83.0	-114.1	30.1
1982	-36.5	29.8	0.1	-1.0	13.2	5.6	-17.1	-11.4	92.4	-122.3	34.0
1983	-67.1	31.1	-0.6	-4.2	14.1	-26.7	-17.7	-44.5	83.4	-58.7	33.7
1984	-112.5	29.5	-2.5	-8.4	14.3	-79.7	-20.6	-100.3	102.0	-29.7	34.9
1985	-122.2	21.2	-4.4	-9.8	14.3	-100.9	-23.0	-123.9	131.0	-34.7	43.2
1986	-145.1	12.8	-5.2	-7.4	18.9	-126.0	-24.2	-150.2	223.2	-91.3	48.5
1987	-159.6	7.7	-3.8	-6.5	17.9	-144.3	-23.1	-167.3	230.0	-61.3	45.8
1988	-127.0	12.6	-6.3	1.5	20.0	-102.2	-25.0	-127.2	219.5	-91.4	47.8
1989	-115.2	14.8	-6.7	5.1	26.6	-75.5	-26.1	-101.6	213.6	-129.3	74.6
1990	-109.0	20.3	-7.8	9.0	29.5	-58.0	-33.8	-91.9	105.2	-44.1	83.3
1991	-73.8	13.0	-5.9	17.9	33.8	-14.9	6.6	-8.3	83.4	-60.0	77.7
1992	-96.1	6.2	-2.8	19.7	39.4	-33.5	-32.9	-66.4	129.6	-51.0	71.3

[1] Excludes military.

Source: U.S. Council of Economic Advisers, *Economic Indicators*, monthly; and *Economic Report of the President*, annual.

No. 1308. U.S. Balances on International Transactions, by Area and Selected Country: 1990 to 1992

[In millions of dollars. Minus sign (-) indicates debits]

AREA OR COUNTRY	1990, BALANCE ON—			1991, BALANCE ON—			1992, BALANCE ON—		
	Merchandise trade[1]	Goods, services, and income	Current account	Merchandise trade[1]	Goods, services, and income	Current account	Merchandise trade[1]	Goods, services, and income	Current account
All areas	-109,033	-58,034	-91,861	-73,802	-14,899	-8,324	-96,138	-33,505	-66,400
Western Europe	2,220	6,710	7,301	14,928	21,060	25,903	3,167	6,383	6,226
European Union	4,929	6,998	8,377	15,588	19,529	25,907	6,728	8,001	8,989
United Kingdom	2,970	-4,118	-3,334	3,257	-6,183	-5,407	2,464	-7,804	-6,928
Eastern Europe	2,071	2,906	1,856	3,039	3,700	1,062	3,653	3,720	2,420
Canada	-9,635	5,770	5,476	-7,107	8,846	8,528	-9,725	4,829	4,507
Latin America, other Western Hemisphere	-10,070	-6,821	-15,073	262	5,944	-4,272	6,200	16,727	8,116
Australia	3,895	7,954	7,894	4,200	6,670	6,592	5,024	8,991	8,911
Japan[2]	-42,564	-38,393	-38,152	-45,040	-36,828	-28,026	-50,513	-43,380	-43,541
Other Asia and Africa	-55,508	-44,751	-63,208	-44,474	-31,153	-18,041	-54,033	-37,813	-51,945
International and unallocated	558	8,593	2,045	390	6,862	-70	89	7,038	-1,094

[1] Adjusted to balance of payments basis; excludes exports under U.S. military sales contracts and imports under direct defense expenditures.   [2] Includes Ryukyu Islands.

Source: U.S. Bureau of Economic Analysis, *Survey of Current Business*, December 1993.

No. 1309. International Investment Position: 1980 to 1992

[In millions of dollars. Estimates for end of year; subject to considerable error due to nature of basic data. See *Historical Statistics, Colonial Times to 1970,* series U 26-39, for similar data]

TYPE OF INVESTMENT	1980	1985	1987	1988	1989	1990	1991	1992
U.S. net international investment position:								
Current cost	392,547	139,056	-34,033	-140,312	-288,516	-291,900	-364,865	-521,331
Market value	(NA)	142,311	46,837	5,415	-128,909	-269,654	-396,402	-611,482
U.S. assets abroad:								
Current cost	936,275	1,252,641	1,557,345	1,697,985	1,856,959	1,924,780	1,998,381	2,003,406
Market value	(NA)	1,244,566	1,640,964	1,860,897	2,114,703	2,018,385	2,152,617	2,113,332
U.S. official reserve assets	171,412	117,930	162,370	144,179	168,714	174,664	159,223	150,307
Gold	155,816	85,834	127,648	107,434	105,164	102,406	92,561	90,040
Special drawing rights	2,610	7,293	10,283	9,637	9,951	10,989	11,240	8,503
Reserve position in IMF.	2,852	11,947	11,349	9,745	9,048	9,076	9,488	11,759
Foreign currencies	10,134	12,856	13,090	17,363	44,551	52,193	45,934	40,005
U.S. Government assets, other	63,865	87,752	88,880	86,117	84,489	82,165	79,148	80,756
U.S. loans and other long-term assets.	62,023	85,814	88,099	85,388	83,903	81,464	77,518	79,061
U.S. foreign currency holdings and short-term assets	1,842	1,938	781	729	586	701	1,630	1,695
U.S. private assets:								
Current cost	700,998	1,046,959	1,306,095	1,467,689	1,603,756	1,667,951	1,760,010	1,772,343
Market value	(NA)	1,038,884	1,389,714	1,630,601	1,861,500	1,761,556	1,914,246	1,882,269
Direct investments abroad:								
Current cost.	396,249	387,183	493,341	515,702	560,017	622,653	655,314	666,346
Market value	(NA)	379,108	576,960	678,614	817,761	716,258	809,550	776,272
Foreign securities.	62,454	112,839	153,716	176,573	216,035	229,279	294,239	327,446
U.S. claims on unaffiliated foreigners [1]	38,429	99,574	109,581	122,187	113,887	120,332	118,570	111,692
U.S. claims reported by U.S. banks [2].	203,866	447,363	549,457	653,227	713,817	695,687	691,887	666,859
Foreign assets in the U.S.								
Current cost	543,728	1,113,585	1,591,378	1,838,297	2,145,475	2,216,680	2,363,246	2,524,737
Market value	(NA)	1,102,255	1,594,127	1,855,482	2,243,612	2,288,039	2,549,019	2,724,814
Foreign official assets in the U.S.	176,062	202,482	283,058	322,036	341,859	375,614	402,103	443,362
U.S. Government securities . .	118,189	145,063	220,548	260,934	[3]	294,983	315,911	335,653
Other U.S. Government liabilities	13,367	15,803	15,667	15,200	15,374	17,530	19,072	21,614
U.S. liabilities reported by U.S. banks [2]	30,381	26,734	31,838	31,520	[3]	39,880	38,396	54,823
Other foreign official assets . .	14,125	14,882	15,005	14,382	[3]	23,221	28,724	31,272
Other foreign assets in the U.S:								
Current cost.	367,666	911,103	1,308,320	1,516,261	1,803,616	1,841,066	1,961,143	2,081,375
Market value	(NA)	899,773	1,311,069	1,533,446	1,901,753	1,912,425	2,146,916	2,281,452
Direct investments:								
Current cost.	125,944	231,326	313,451	374,345	436,597	468,242	487,199	492,270
Market value	(NA)	219,996	316,200	391,530	534,734	539,601	672,972	692,347
U.S. securities other than U.S. Treasury securities	74,114	207,868	341,732	392,292	[3]	468,978	556,279	617,310
U.S. liabilities to unaffiliated foreigners [1]	30,426	29,458	29,818	35,003	40,549	48,006	46,094	46,251
U.S. liabilities reported by U.S. banks [2]	121,069	354,497	540,731	613,744	[3]	693,436	682,065	700,674
U.S. Treasury securities	16,113	87,954	82,588	100,877	[3]	162,404	189,506	224,870

NA Not available.   [1] Reported by U.S. nonbanking concerns.   [2] Not included elsewhere.   [3] Data not available unitl release of the "Foreign Portfolio Investment Survey" results.

Source: U.S. Bureau of Economic Analysis, *Survey of Current Business,* June 1993.

No. 1310. U.S. Reserve Assets: 1980 to 1993

[In billions of dollars. As of end of year, except as indicated]

TYPE	1980	1983	1984	1985	1986	1987	1988	1989	1990	1991	1992	1993
Total	26.8	33.7	34.9	43.2	48.5	45.8	47.8	74.6	83.3	77.7	71.3	73.4
Gold stock [1]	11.2	11.1	11.1	11.1	11.1	11.1	11.1	11.1	11.1	11.1	11.1	11.1
Special drawing rights	2.6	5.0	5.6	7.3	8.4	10.3	9.6	10.0	11.0	11.2	8.5	9.0
Foreign currencies	10.1	6.3	6.7	12.9	17.3	13.1	17.4	44.6	52.2	45.9	40.0	41.5
Reserve position in IMF [2]. . . .	2.9	11.3	11.5	11.9	11.7	11.3	9.7	9.0	9.1	9.5	11.8	11.8

[1] Includes gold in Exchange Stabilization Fund; excludes gold held under earmark at Federal Reserve banks for foreign and international accounts. Beginning 1975, gold assets were valued at $42.22 pursuant to the amending of Section 2 of the Par Value Modification Act, PL-93-110, approved September 21, 1973.   [2] International Monetary Fund.

Source: Board of Governors of the Federal Reserve System, *Federal Reserve Bulletin,* monthly; and Department of the Treasury, *Treasury Bulletin,* monthly.

No. 1311. Foreign Direct Investment Position in the U.S. on a Historical Cost Basis—Value, by Area and Industry: 1980 to 1992

[In millions of dollars. Book value at year end. Covers U.S. firms, including real estate investments in which foreign interest or ownership was 10 percent or more. Minus sign (-) indicates a negative position. See also *Historical Statistics, Colonial Times to 1970*, series U 47-74]

AREA AND INDUSTRY	1980	1984	1985	1986	1987	1988	1989	1990	1991	1992, prel.
All areas [1]	83,046	164,583	184,615	220,414	263,394	314,754	368,924	394,911	414,358	419,526
Petroleum	12,200	25,400	28,270	29,094	37,815	36,006	40,345	42,882	40,196	38,545
Manufacturing	32,993	51,802	59,584	71,963	93,865	122,582	150,949	152,805	156,586	159,492
Finance and insurance	12,027	24,881	27,429	34,978	39,455	44,010	59,597	35,482	44,841	44,992
Trade, wholesale and retail	15,210	31,219	35,873	42,920	45,399	53,590	54,005	60,152	64,347	66,203
Canada	12,162	15,286	17,131	20,318	24,684	26,566	30,370	29,544	37,301	38,997
Petroleum	1,817	1,544	1,589	1,432	1,088	1,181	1,141	1,373	1,413	1,342
Manufacturing	5,227	4,115	4,607	6,108	8,085	9,730	9,766	9,201	16,066	17,313
Finance and insurance	1,612	3,245	4,008	4,283	5,797	5,769	7,356	6,033	7,469	5,494
Europe	54,688	108,211	121,413	144,181	181,006	208,942	239,190	247,320	251,248	248,461
Petroleum	10,137	23,142	25,636	26,139	35,700	33,499	32,649	34,284	31,698	30,015
Manufacturing	21,953	39,083	45,841	56,016	74,300	95,641	118,129	115,831	113,365	113,595
Finance and insurance	8,673	15,945	17,022	21,787	26,336	27,121	33,157	21,310	26,462	26,514
United Kingdom	14,105	38,387	43,555	55,935	75,519	95,698	103,458	98,676	100,386	94,718
Petroleum	-257	10,991	12,155	11,758	17,950	19,522	16,666	15,900	14,355	11,863
Manufacturing	6,159	9,179	11,687	16,500	30,372	41,708	50,166	42,365	42,259	42,208
Finance and insurance	3,350	5,485	6,483	10,163	9,801	11,256	12,790	11,609	11,972	11,275
Netherlands	19,140	33,728	37,056	40,717	46,636	48,128	56,734	64,671	59,355	61,341
Petroleum	9,265	9,981	11,481	(D)	(D)	9,045	10,061	13,267	12,398	12,373
Manufacturing	4,777	12,497	13,351	13,293	15,615	17,843	23,090	24,734	18,267	21,442
Switzerland	5,070	8,146	10,568	12,058	13,772	14,372	18,746	17,674	19,189	19,562
Manufacturing	3,116	4,774	6,881	7,520	6,921	7,613	11,798	10,651	10,927	11,124
Finance and insurance	1,033	(D)	5,425	2,517	3,211	3,506	4,492	4,833	5,360	5,206
Germany [2]	7,596	12,330	14,816	17,250	21,905	25,250	28,386	28,232	28,618	29,205
Manufacturing	3,875	4,389	6,015	7,426	10,298	13,980	15,560	15,718	15,466	15,050
Finance and insurance	1,248	1,902	(D)	1,962	3,442	2,683	3,139	1,652	1,320	2,581
Other Europe [3]	8,777	15,620	15,417	18,221	23,174	25,494	31,866	38,067	43,700	43,635
Petroleum	991	2,080	(D)	(D)	(D)	4,580	4,786	4,835	4,597	5,826
Manufacturing	4,026	7,704	7,907	11,277	11,094	14,497	17,515	22,363	26,446	23,771
Finance and insurance	1,193	(D)	(D)	(D)	2,189	406	2,519	-1,817	-778	-462
Japan	4,723	16,044	19,313	26,824	34,421	51,126	67,268	83,091	92,896	96,743
Other areas	11,472	25,043	26,758	29,091	23,283	28,120	32,096	34,956	32,912	35,325

D Withheld to avoid disclosure of data of individual companies.   [1] Area totals include industries not shown separately. [2] For 1989, includes only the Federal Republic of Germany. For 1990, also includes the former German Democratic Republic (GDR). This change has no effect on the data because, prior to 1990, there were no U.S. affiliates of the former GDR.   [3] Direct investments in 1992 (in millions of dollars): Belgium and Luxembourg, 4,627; France, 22,740; Italy, 2,859; and Sweden, 5,597.
Source: U.S. Bureau of Economic Analysis, *Survey of Current Business*, July 1993, and earlier issues.

No. 1312. U.S. Affiliates of Foreign Companies—Assets, Sales, Employment, Land, Exports, and Imports: 1991

[A U.S. affiliate is a U.S. business enterprise in which one foreign owner (individual, branch, partnership, association, trust, corporation, or government) has a direct or indirect voting interest of 10 percent or more. Universe estimates based on a sample survey of nonbank affiliates with assets, sales, or net income of $10 million or more]

INDUSTRY	Total assets (mil. dol.)	Sales [1] (mil. dol.)	Employ-ment [2] (1,000)	Employee compen-sation (mil. dol.)	GROSS BOOK VALUE (mil. dol.) Plant and equip-ment [3]	Land	Land owned (1,000 acres)	Merchan-dise exports [4] (mil. dol.)	Mer-chandise imports [4] (mil. dol.)
Total	1,743,762	1,174,069	4,809.2	173,911	574,635	60,053	17,479	98,369	179,694
Petroleum	102,052	106,393	142.0	6,753	101,491	3,689	736	3,700	15,911
Manufacturing	448,592	399,936	2,214.8	91,884	231,475	9,875	4,245	39,432	47,983
Chemicals and allied products	144,412	111,268	497.7	24,501	88,138	2,914	810	11,268	9,751
Wholesale trade [5]	173,898	355,565	429.8	17,397	40,890	2,710	439	51,995	112,064
Motor vehicles and auto parts and supplies	53,793	94,616	77.1	3,522	17,117	725	23	5,650	40,279
Farm-product raw materials	9,647	39,512	19.0	644	1,691	350	36	15,146	3,706
Retail trade	51,152	86,689	780.1	13,825	23,400	2,934	70	1,103	2,389
Finance, except banking	377,086	32,124	58.7	5,325	4,239	730	26	5	3
Insurance	302,859	72,910	159.9	6,925	15,428	1,458	151	-	-
Real estate	114,238	16,276	41.9	1,378	68,741	23,140	2,322	7	2
Services	91,006	43,718	597.9	14,853	36,135	6,799	205	346	259
Other	82,879	60,458	384.0	15,572	52,836	8,718	9,286	1,782	1,083

- Represents zero.   [1] Excludes returns, discounts, allowances, and sales and excise taxes.   [2] Average number of full-time and part-time employees.   [3] Includes other property, value of mineral rights owned, and capitalized value of mineral rights leased.   [4] F.a.s. value at port of exportation.   [5] Includes industries not shown separately.
Source: U.S. Bureau of Economic Analysis, *Survey of Current Business*, May 1993, and *Foreign Direct Investment in the United States, Operations of U.S. Affiliates of Foreign Companies*, Preliminary 1991 Estimates and Revised 1990 Estimates.

No. 1313. Foreign Direct Investment in the United States—Gross Book Value and Employment of U.S. Affiliates of Foreign Companies, by State: 1981 and 1991

[A U.S. affiliate is a U.S. business enterprise in which one foreign owner (individual, branch, partnership, association, trust corporation, or government) has a direct or indirect voting interest of 10 percent or more. Universe estimates based on a sample survey of nonbank affiliates with assets, sales, or net income of $10 million or more]

DIVISION, STATE, AND OTHER AREA	GROSS BOOK VALUE OF PROPERTY, PLANT, AND EQUIPMENT (mil. dol.)		TOTAL EMPLOYMENT			MANUFACTURING EMPLOYMENT, 1991	
				1991			
	1981	1991	1981	Total (1,000)	Percent of all businesses	Total (1,000)	Percent of all manufacturing
Total	187,956	634,688	2,416.6	4,809.2	(X)	2,024.4	(X)
United States	178,003	607,624	2,402.3	4,778.0	5.1	2,010.9	10.8
New England	5,686	22,362	143.9	284.5	5.3	115.5	10.1
Maine	1,637	2,235	17.7	26.6	6.1	7.7	8.0
New Hampshire	409	1,738	13.9	28.2	6.7	11.6	11.7
Vermont	315	666	6.0	7.2	3.4	3.4	7.6
Massachusetts	1,712	10,319	55.6	129.2	5.1	54.1	11.1
Rhode Island	359	1,346	9.9	13.6	3.6	6.2	6.6
Connecticut	1,254	6,058	40.8	79.7	5.7	32.5	10.0
Middle Atlantic	20,216	81,353	480.2	809.0	5.7	301.8	11.6
New York	7,892	42,417	210.3	361.8	5.4	99.0	9.3
New Jersey	6,552	20,466	134.9	228.0	7.6	93.0	16.6
Pennsylvania	5,772	18,470	135.0	219.2	4.8	109.8	11.2
East North Central	19,215	81,499	388.6	813.7	5.0	443.3	10.8
Ohio	5,178	22,492	99.9	220.1	5.2	128.2	11.9
Indiana	1,883	14,005	47.0	123.2	5.6	78.9	12.7
Illinois	5,646	25,644	113.6	248.0	5.4	118.5	12.5
Michigan	4,188	13,767	65.9	139.2	4.1	70.9	7.9
Wisconsin	2,320	5,591	62.2	83.2	4.1	46.8	8.5
West North Central	8,400	30,441	112.2	262.0	3.8	116.3	8.4
Minnesota	2,902	12,703	33.0	93.8	5.0	35.0	8.8
Iowa	1,032	3,229	21.6	32.7	3.1	19.4	8.3
Missouri	1,894	6,508	32.6	77.2	3.8	35.6	8.5
North Dakota	1,155	1,206	3.5	3.4	1.6	1.4	7.7
South Dakota	299	588	1.3	4.9	2.0	2.6	7.4
Nebraska	241	949	5.6	16.8	2.7	8.8	8.8
Kansas	877	5,258	14.6	33.2	3.6	13.5	7.3
South Atlantic	33,271	103,640	476.0	938.3	5.7	402.6	13.3
Delaware	1,869	6,176	36.0	41.6	13.7	14.4	20.5
Maryland	2,103	6,519	45.1	76.6	4.4	29.5	15.2
District of Columbia	547	4,192	3.2	11.3	2.7	0.5	3.3
Virginia	3,046	12,008	49.8	117.6	5.1	48.1	11.6
West Virginia	3,992	8,323	35.4	34.7	6.9	18.1	21.6
North Carolina	5,543	16,325	89.0	179.6	6.7	107.3	12.9
South Carolina	5,318	10,861	65.1	105.7	8.3	63.4	17.0
Georgia	4,558	18,571	78.5	159.9	6.4	73.2	13.5
Florida	6,295	20,665	73.9	211.3	4.5	48.1	9.7
East South Central	9,802	34,708	121.7	275.0	5.2	166.8	11.7
Kentucky	1,848	10,521	26.0	69.6	5.6	46.5	16.5
Tennessee	3,747	12,481	57.4	119.6	6.3	70.6	14.0
Alabama	2,776	8,379	27.0	62.0	4.5	34.8	9.1
Mississippi	1,431	3,327	11.3	23.8	3.1	14.9	6.0
West South Central	34,651	87,919	268.5	444.7	4.8	168.4	10.7
Arkansas	636	2,502	17.5	30.1	3.7	17.9	7.6
Louisiana	7,872	19,072	47.0	61.9	4.7	23.1	12.3
Oklahoma	2,760	5,702	25.0	43.2	4.4	17.1	10.1
Texas	23,383	60,643	179.0	309.5	5.1	110.3	11.2
Mountain	12,353	36,146	97.9	203.8	4.1	44.8	7.1
Montana	1,235	2,295	3.0	5.8	2.3	1.3	5.9
Idaho	312	1,000	3.8	12.6	3.7	5.1	8.0
Wyoming	2,144	2,909	4.2	5.5	3.5	0.8	8.5
Colorado	2,369	7,058	24.7	60.9	4.6	12.1	6.5
New Mexico	997	4,599	7.9	14.8	3.3	3.2	7.6
Arizona	2,949	7,824	30.6	56.2	4.4	12.2	6.9
Utah	1,791	4,201	16.8	23.4	3.8	7.0	6.5
Nevada	556	6,260	6.9	24.6	4.3	3.1	11.8
Pacific	34,409	129,554	313.3	747.2	5.1	251.3	9.5
Washington	2,430	9,356	26.0	81.4	4.3	23.3	6.6
Oregon	845	4,495	13.1	41.9	3.9	15.4	7.2
California	20,404	81,842	248.4	555.0	5.0	206.6	10.2
Alaska	(D)	20,149	8.8	13.3	7.6	3.2	17.7
Hawaii	(D)	13,712	17.0	55.6	12.1	2.8	13.6
Puerto Rico	413	1,611	9.5	17.5	(X)	10.1	(X)
Other territories and offshore	7,496	18,445	3.1	9.4	(X)	2.2	(X)
Foreign	2,044	7,008	1.6	4.3	(X)	1.2	(X)

D Withheld to avoid disclosure of data of individual companies.   X Not applicable.

Source: U.S. Bureau of Economic Analysis, *Survey of Current Business*, May 1993, and *Foreign Direct Investment in the United States, Operations of U.S. Affiliates of Foreign Companies*, Preliminary 1991 Estimates and Revised 1990 Estimates.

No. 1314. U.S. Businesses Acquired or Established by Foreign Direct Investors, by Industry of U.S. Business Enterprise: 1991 and 1992

[Foreign direct investment is the ownership or control, directly or indirectly, by one foreign individual branch, partnership, association, trust, corporation, or government of 10 percent or more of the voting securities of a U.S. business enterprise or an equivalent interest in an unincorporated one. Data represent number and full cost of acquisitions of existing U.S. business enterprises, including business segments or operating units of existing U.S. business enterprises and establishments of new enterprises. Investments may be made by the foreign direct investor itself, or indirectly by an existing U.S. affiliate of the foreign direct investor. Covers investments in U.S. business enterprises with assets of over $1 million, or ownership of 200 acres of U.S. land]

INDUSTRY	1991						1992, prel.					
	Investments			Investors			Investments			Investors		
	Total	Acqui-sition	Estab-lish-ments	Total	For-eign direct inves-tors	U.S. affili-ates	Total	Acqui-sition	Estab-lish-ments	Total	For-eign direct inves-tors	U.S. affili-ates
NUMBER OF INVESTMENTS [1] Total........	1,091	561	530	1,220	438	782	690	360	330	732	279	453
Petroleum........	32	23	9	35	6	29	(NA)	(NA)	(NA)	(NA)	(NA)	(NA)
Manufacturing.....	320	264	56	354	124	230	(NA)	(NA)	(NA)	(NA)	(NA)	(NA)
Wholesale trade....	71	42	29	78	29	49	(NA)	(NA)	(NA)	(NA)	(NA)	(NA)
Retail trade......	39	23	16	39	7	32	(NA)	(NA)	(NA)	(NA)	(NA)	(NA)
Banking.........	21	8	13	25	20	5	(NA)	(NA)	(NA)	(NA)	(NA)	(NA)
Finance, except banking........	59	16	43	67	27	40	(NA)	(NA)	(NA)	(NA)	(NA)	(NA)
Insurance........	19	15	4	22	12	10	(NA)	(NA)	(NA)	(NA)	(NA)	(NA)
Real estate.......	306	32	274	348	131	217	(NA)	(NA)	(NA)	(NA)	(NA)	(NA)
Services........	171	107	64	198	63	135	(NA)	(NA)	(NA)	(NA)	(NA)	(NA)
Other [2].........	53	31	22	54	19	35	(NA)	(NA)	(NA)	(NA)	(NA)	(NA)
INVESTMENT OUTLAYS (mil. dol.) Total........	25,538	17,806	7,732	25,538	8,885	16,653	13,469	10,191	3,278	13,469	3,616	9,853
Petroleum........	702	404	298	702	21	681	484	466	18	484	4	480
Manufacturing.....	11,461	9,669	1,792	11,461	4,530	6,930	5,274	4,413	861	5,274	1,708	3,566
Wholesale trade....	623	524	99	623	197	426	605	405	200	605	251	353
Retail trade......	1,605	1,436	170	1,605	(D)	(D)	224	(D)	(D)	224	28	196
Banking.........	482	440	42	482	281	201	55	55	-	55	19	37
Finance, except banking........	2,199	1,399	800	2,199	693	1,506	968	801	167	968	230	738
Insurance........	2,102	1,951	152	2,102	1,255	847	251	(D)	(D)	251	16	235
Real estate.......	3,823	177	3,646	3,823	1,110	2,713	1,937	444	1,493	1,937	798	1,139
Services........	2,256	1,616	641	2,256	239	2,017	1,476	1,179	297	1,476	318	1,158
Other [2].........	284	191	93	284	(D)	(D)	2,195	2,138	57	2,195	245	1,950

- Represents zero.   D Withheld to avoid disclosure of data of individual companies.   NA Not available.   [1] Excludes investments that do not meet asset or acreage criteria in headnote.   [2] Includes agriculture, forestry, and fishing; mining; construction; transportation; and communication and public utilities.
Source: U.S. Bureau of Economic Analysis, *Survey of Current Business*, May 1993, and unpublished data.

No. 1315. U.S. Businesses Acquired by Foreign Direct Investors—Assets, Sales, and Employment, by Industry of U.S. Business Enterprise: 1991 and 1992

[See headnote, table 1314. Minus sign (-) indicates loss]

INDUSTRY	1991					1992				
	Total assets (mil. dol.)	Sales (mil. dol.)	Net income (mil. dol.)	Employ-ment (1,000)	Acres of land owned (1,000)	Total assets (mil. dol.)	Sales (mil. dol.)	Net income (mil. dol.)	Employ-ment (1,000)	Acres of land owned (1,000)
Total........	152,076	52,364	-154	249.0	392.7	30,912	21,661	-62	120.3	121.0
Petroleum..........	1,435	(D)	41	(D)	(D)	612	(D)	71	1.0	0.2
Manufacturing.......	14,786	15,657	-73	100.3	29.0	7,645	9,154	-194	63.0	5.6
Wholesale trade......	1,400	2,632	-10	8.8	0.2	1,339	2,319	91	9.3	0.2
Retail trade.........	(D)	10,765	(D)	69.7	(D)	827	(D)	-136	(D)	(D)
Banking...........	36,785	3,871	-109	13.4	(D)	2,200	87	-12	1.0	(D)
Finance, except banking	13,955	(D)	(D)	3.9	(D)	8,393	(D)	86	(D)	(D)
Insurance..........	(D)	(D)	97	(D)	(D)	2,921	(D)	8	(D)	(D)
Real estate.........	4,805	368	-12	0.6	63.4	2,205	236	-36	0.7	(D)
Services..........	(D)	1,626	25	23.0	15.7	1,224	814	-31	10.4	0.8
Other [1]..........	525	844	(D)	(D)	(D)	3,546	3,658	90	(D)	(D)

D Withheld to avoid disclosure of data of individual companies.   [1] Includes agriculture, forestry, and fishing; mining; construction; transportation; and communication and public utilities.
Source: U.S. Bureau of Economic Analysis, *Survey of Current Business*, May 1993; and unpublished data.

No. 1316. U.S. Direct Investment Position Abroad, by Country: 1980 to 1992

[In millions of dollars. Direct investments represent private enterprises in one country owned or controlled by investors in another country or in the management of which foreign investors have an important role. Negative position occurs when U.S. parent company's liabilities to the foreign affiliate are greater than its equity in, and loans to the foreign affiliate. See also *Historical Statistics, Colonial Times to 1970*, series U 41-46]

COUNTRY	1980	1985	1989	1990	1991	1992			
						Total [1]	Manu-facturing	Petro-leum	Finance [2]
All countries	215,375	230,250	381,781	426,958	460,955	486,670	187,276	55,207	129,546
Canada	45,119	46,909	63,948	69,106	68,853	68,432	33,306	7,945	12,938
Europe [3]	96,287	105,171	189,467	213,368	233,245	239,389	93,733	23,289	67,225
Austria	524	493	962	1,136	1,258	1,365	622	(D)	(Z)
Belgium	6,259	5,038	7,710	9,413	10,607	10,771	5,940	291	2,072
Denmark	1,266	1,281	(D)	1,724	1,813	1,707	315	(D)	351
Finland	188	258	(D)	530	359	322	91	(D)	1
France	9,347	7,643	16,443	18,950	20,798	23,257	13,975	(D)	2,363
Germany [4]	15,415	16,764	23,673	27,480	34,027	35,393	20,951	2,111	4,666
Greece	347	210	210	293	353	429	129	(D)	(D)
Ireland	2,319	3,693	4,665	5,725	6,635	7,229	4,505	119	1,947
Italy	5,397	5,906	11,221	14,076	14,775	13,605	8,821	416	1,589
Luxembourg	652	690	1,560	1,683	1,782	1,863	852	17	779
Netherlands	8,039	7,129	19,160	18,720	19,772	19,114	7,216	1,465	4,931
Norway	1,679	3,215	3,447	4,209	4,349	4,047	291	3,251	123
Portugal	257	237	(D)	892	1,026	1,160	379	(D)	(D)
Spain	2,678	2,281	6,500	7,802	7,992	8,165	5,430	149	166
Sweden	1,474	933	1,297	1,754	2,242	2,033	1,289	38	136
Switzerland	11,280	15,766	21,144	25,151	25,604	28,662	1,508	333	15,917
Turkey	207	234	343	515	529	705	469	(D)	(Z)
United Kingdom	28,460	33,024	67,722	72,343	78,072	77,842	20,328	13,153	32,013
Japan	6,225	9,235	19,911	22,511	24,938	26,213	11,920	4,768	2,707
Australia	7,654	8,772	14,368	14,997	15,795	16,697	6,631	2,691	1,523
New Zealand	579	576	1,062	3,099	2,916	3,008	417	397	195
South Africa	2,350	1,394	699	767	857	871	501	(D)	(D)
Latin America [3]	39,581	28,758	62,145	70,752	76,213	88,860	26,729	4,152	40,521
South America [3]	16,342	17,623	21,806	22,682	24,082	27,185	15,855	2,283	3,528
Argentina	2,540	2,705	2,215	2,479	2,767	3,353	1,633	499	538
Brazil	7,704	8,893	14,025	14,268	14,882	16,114	12,014	668	1,839
Chile	536	88	1,412	1,876	1,916	2,446	257	(D)	1,030
Colombia	1,012	2,148	1,660	1,647	1,627	2,077	699	596	10
Ecuador	322	361	301	278	296	310	88	154	(D)
Peru	1,665	1,243	813	594	522	466	18	(D)	-
Venezuela [3]	1,908	1,588	932	1,063	1,424	1,725	1,069	179	111
Central America [3]	11,013	10,155	17,846	20,259	23,309	25,479	9,824	845	10,863
Costa Rica	303	113	213	239	214	221	253	2	-
Guatemala	229	213	111	129	105	107	80	18	6
Honduras	288	171	251	225	212	184	92	(D)	(D)
Mexico	5,986	5,088	8,264	10,255	12,257	13,330	9,281	(D)	798
Panama	3,170	3,959	8,913	9,257	10,427	11,457	107	694	10,059
Other W. Hemisphere [3]	12,226	980	22,493	27,810	28,822	36,196	1,050	1,024	26,130
Bahamas, The	2,712	3,795	4,577	3,944	3,768	4,566	(D)	407	1,260
Barbados	40	81	141	247	319	507	7	89	62
Bermuda	11,045	13,116	18,297	20,084	23,059	25,799	19	(D)	24,837
Dominican Republic	316	212	(D)	479	572	744	134	(D)	(D)
Jamaica	407	122	383	612	729	850	748	(D)	4
Netherlands Antilles	-4,336	-20,499	-8,378	-4,534	-5,697	-1,939	(D)	(D)	-2,097
Trinidad and Tobago	951	484	(D)	487	507	575	89	(D)	18
U.K. Islands, Caribbean	979	3,490	6,123	5,919	5,112	5,024	-29	53	2,027
Other Africa [3]	3,778	4,497	3,936	3,592	3,584	2,647	459	(D)	(D)
Egypt	1,038	1,926	1,541	1,226	1,239	922	74	735	5
Nigeria [3]	18	44	-42	-407	611	274	63	159	(D)
Middle East [3]	2,163	4,606	3,518	4,007	4,823	5,814	1,742	1,791	1,418
Israel	379	717	827	933	1,014	1,543	960	(D)	327
Saudi Arabia	1,037	2,442	1,655	1,772	2,163	2,503	781	(D)	(D)
United Arab Emirates	384	792	391	404	466	480	(Z)	306	(D)
Other Asia and Pacific [3]	8,505	15,400	20,464	22,980	27,398	32,246	11,839	(D)	(D)
China	-6	311	436	356	431	469	260	91	1
Hong Kong	2,078	3,295	5,412	5,994	6,516	8,544	2,243	385	1,291
India	398	383	(D)	368	410	479	201	(D)	(D)
Indonesia	1,314	4,475	2,771	3,175	3,783	4,278	138	3,686	13
Korea, Republic of	575	743	2,370	2,677	2,862	2,779	1,140	67	165
Malaysia	632	1,140	1,263	1,513	1,711	1,714	747	513	233
Philippines	1,259	1,032	1,107	1,355	1,377	1,565	1,021	(D)	(D)
Singapore	1,204	1,874	2,998	3,183	5,294	6,631	3,460	1,213	369
Taiwan	498	750	1,968	2,214	2,626	2,870	1,806	(D)	158
Thailand	361	1,074	1,511	1,789	2,038	2,459	783	774	(D)
International	3,955	5,428	2,962	2,548	2,331	2,496	-	1,207	-
Addendum: OPEC [5]	*6,090*	*10,383*	*6,217*	*6,947*	*9,398*	*10,255*	*2,142*	*5,146*	*1,209*

- Represents zero. D Suppressed to avoid disclosure of data of individual companies. Z Less than $500,000. [1] Includes industries not shown separately. [2] Includes insurance. [3] Includes countries not shown separately. [4] Prior to 1991, West Germany only. [5] OPEC=Organization of Petroleum Exporting Countries. Includes Algeria, Ecuador, Gabon, Indonesia, Iran, Iraq, Kuwait, Libya, Nigeria, Qatar, Saudi Arabia, United Arab Emirates, and Venezuela.

Source: U.S. Bureau of Economic Analysis, *Survey of Current Business*, July 1993.

No. 1317. U.S. Government Foreign Grants and Credits: 1946 to 1992

[In millions of dollars. "P.L." means Public Law. For explanation of minus sign (-), see headnote, table 1318. See also text, section 29, and *Historical Statistics, Colonial Times to 1970*, series U 75-101]

PROGRAM	1946-1955, total	1956-1965, total	1966-1975, total	1976-1985, total	1988	1989	1990	1991	1992, prel.
Total, net	51,509	49,723	70,368	104,188	8,081	10,041	14,297	-31,897	16,624
Investment in international financial institutions [1]	635	655	2,719	10,432	1,314	1,173	1,301	1,498	1,419
Under assistance programs, net	50,875	49,067	67,649	93,756	6,768	8,868	12,996	-33,395	15,206
Developed countries [2]	35,150	5,834	616	757	-131	63	193	-14,288	1,173
Developing countries [2]	15,725	43,233	67,033	92,998	6,899	8,805	12,804	-19,107	14,032
Net new military grants [2]	14,200	21,564	30,236	14,957	3,576	3,802	6,717	4,221	6,506
Developed countries [2]	8,910	7,931	691	1,369	305	321	551	448	608
Developing countries [2]	5,291	13,633	29,545	13,588	3,271	3,481	6,165	3,773	5,898
Gross new grants [3]	14,434	21,805	30,281	14,993	3,578	3,805	6,721	4,223	6,517
Foreign Assistance Act [3]	13,427	21,769	30,281	14,993	3,578	3,805	6,721	4,223	6,517
Military supplies and services	12,282	20,662	9,802	2,438	92	119	151	468	304
Military assistance, service funded [4]	-	8	18,161	-	-	-	-	-	-
Financing of military purchases [5]	-	-	1,584	10,122	3,185	3,368	6,017	3,365	5,791
Relocation of facilities in Israel	-	-	-	800	-	-	-	-	-
Other special programs	1,145	1,100	734	1,633	301	319	553	390	422
Other	1,007	36	-	-	-	-	-	-	-
Less: Reverse grants and returns.	234	241	45	36	2	3	5	1	11
Other grants, credits, and other assistance (through net accumulation of foreign currency claims)	36,675	27,503	37,413	78,799	3,192	5,067	6,280	-37,617	8,700
Developed countries [2]	26,240	-2,097	-75	-612	-435	-257	-359	-14,736	565
Developing countries [2]	10,434	29,600	37,488	79,411	3,627	5,324	6,639	-22,880	8,135
Net new economic and technical aid grants [6]	27,529	17,675	21,748	43,302	7,231	7,393	10,014	-32,242	8,530
Developed countries [2]	19,424	780	-182	464	72	54	-606	-13,388	867
Developing countries [2]	8,104	16,896	21,929	42,839	7,160	7,340	10,620	-18,854	7,663
Gross new grants [3]	28,769	17,993	22,003	43,311	7,231	7,393	15,531	14,634	9,890
Foreign Assistance Act [3]	17,711	12,189	12,191	31,525	5,559	5,784	6,767	7,071	7,488
Farm products disposals: Foreign currencies, P.L. 83-480 [7]	-	2,048	4,234	186	1	2	(Z)	(Z)	(Z)
Famine and other urgent relief	530	2,704	2,862	5,026	740	614	601	1,185	924
Payment of transportation	-	494	946	1,890	177	113	156	240	130
Food for development loan forgiveness	-	-	-	353	133	7	166	27	54
Supplies to military or trusteeship administration areas.	5,528	132	536	1,246	202	155	50	15	(Z)
Peace Corps	-	232	912	979	151	151	179	178	218
Forgiveness of Foreign Debt	-	-	-	-	-	207	7,220	5,130	57
Other	5,000	194	321	2,106	269	360	391	788	1,019
Less: Reverse grants and returns.	1,240	318	255	9	-	-	-	-	-
Less: Receipts from Persian Gulf partners	-	-	-	-	-	-	5,517	46,876	1,360
Net new credits [8]	8,605	7,025	16,955	35,784	-4,006	-2,325	-3,701	-5,398	170
Developed countries [2]	6,627	-3,207	310	-1,019	-481	-294	255	-1,346	-300
Developing countries [2]	1,978	10,232	16,645	36,803	-3,524	-2,031	-3,955	-4,052	469
New credits	11,958	15,429	37,424	72,193	5,906	3,949	6,658	10,864	5,245
Export-Import Bank Act [3]	4,241	5,257	15,506	22,093	1,060	776	2,515	1,383	2,499
Foreign Assistance Act [3]	1,919	6,196	12,053	35,324	3,473	1,589	2,347	3,619	1,611
Country program loans	1,765	5,722	8,362	10,733	455	396	323	2,937	797
Financing or military purchases	9	247	3,089	24,288	2,989	1,159	1,993	605	690
Social Progress Trust Fund	-	226	487	142	-4	-1	-14	2	5
Other	145	2	116	162	34	36	46	75	119
P.L. 83-480 [7]	48	3,839	7,161	8,142	959	793	869	3,107	476
Loans of foreign currency: To foreign governments	48	3,285	1,843	10	(Z)	(Z)	3	(Z)	(Z)
To private enterprises	-	202	217	16	11	9	36	11	1
Long-term credit sales	-	352	5,101	8,116	948	784	829	3,095	475
P.L. 80-806 [9]	-	-	2,433	5,559	414	790	928	2,756	659
Other	5,750	137	271	1,074	-	-	-	-	-
Less: Principal collections	3,353	8,404	20,469	36,409	9,912	6,274	10,359	16,262	5,076
Export-Import Bank Act [3]	1,787	4,458	9,282	15,221	1,501	1,395	1,834	1,865	2,295
Foreign Assistance Act [3]	38	1,263	3,557	11,234	7,715	3,860	7,355	6,930	1,798
Country program loans	1	944	2,481	4,212	489	744	691	4,732	1,033
Financing of military purchases	2	222	852	6,492	7,193	3,083	6,639	2,161	742
Social Progress Trust Fund	-	9	198	354	15	11	11	20	14
Other	35	88	25	177	18	21	14	17	9
P.L. 83-480 [7]	-	180	3,753	2,923	468	353	578	3,905	373
Loans of foreign currency: To foreign governments	-	111	2,354	551	24	27	31	47	17
To private enterprise	-	43	175	96	1	2	4	8	3
Long-term credit sales	-	27	1,223	2,275	444	325	542	3,850	352
Lend-lease, surplus property, and grant settlements	675	2,001	1,438	386	16	16	16	17	17
P.L. 80-806 [9]	-	-	1,763	4,748	106	548	469	3,440	488
Other	853	501	677	1,897	106	103	107	105	106

See footnotes at end of table.

No. 1317. U.S. Government Foreign Grants and Credits: 1946 to 1992—Continued

[In millions of dollars. See headnote, p. 812]

PROGRAM	1946-1955, total	1956-1965, total	1966-1975, total	1976-1985, total	1988	1989	1990	1991	1992, prel.
Other assistance (through net accumulation of foreign currency claims) [10]	541	2,802	-1,290	-287	-34	-2	-33	23	(Z)
Developed countries [3]	190	330	-203	-56	-26	-17	-7	-3	-2
Developing countries [2]	351	2,472	-1,086	-231	-8	15	-26	26	2
Currency claims acquired.	813	11,498	6,888	1,227	81	64	76	100	31
Sales of farm products.	813	11,170	3,013	114	35	25	13	25	10
Second-stage operations [11]	-	329	3,875	1,113	46	39	63	75	21
Less: Currencies disbursed	*272*	*8,696*	*8,177*	*1,514*	*116*	*66*	*109*	*76*	*31*
Economic grants and credits to purchasing country.	182	6,863	6,238	180	16	10	36	10	1
Other uses.	90	1,833	1,940	1,334	99	56	72	67	30

- Represents zero. Z Less than $500,000. [1] For details, see table 1318. [2] Developed countries include Australia, Canada, Japan, New Zealand, South Africa, all countries listed under "Western Europe" in table 1318, except Portugal, Spain (through 1981), Yugoslavia, and Malta, and all countries listed under "Eastern Europe" in table 1318. Developing countries include all other countries listed in table 1318 (including Spain through 1981). [3] Foreign Assistance Act of 1961 (P.L. 87-195), as amended. Also includes predecessor and related programs. [4] Includes military assistance under Dept. of Defense Appropriation Act, 1966 (P.L. 89-394) and later acts. [5] Includes funds made available under Public Law 93-199 and subsequent legislation to release Israel from its contractual liability to pay for defense articles and services purchased under other legislation. [6] Net new grants are not adjusted for settlements for postwar relief and other grants under agreements, and net new credits exclude prior grants converted into credits, which were as follows: 1946-55, $1,463 million; 1956-65, $491 million; 1972, $994 million. Repayments on these settlements are included in net new credits. [7] Agricultural Trade Development and Assistance Act. [8] Outstanding credits on Dec. 31, 1992, totaled $54,754 million representing net credits extended since organization of Export-Import Bank, Feb. 12, 1934, less chargeoffs and net adjustments due to exchange rates ($2,083 million), and excluding World War I debts. The amount repayable in dollars at U.S. Government option was $53,659 million; the remainder was repayable in foreign currencies, commodities, or services, at the option of the borrowers. [9] Commodity Credit Corporation Charter Act. [10] Equivalent value of currencies still available to be used, including some funds advanced from foreign governments and after loss by exchange rate fluctuation ($1,618 million), was $56 million on Dec. 31, 1992. [11] Includes foreign currencies acquired from triangular trade operations and principal and interest collections on credits, originally extended under P.L. 83-480, which—since enactment of P.L. 87-128—are available for the same purposes as P.L. 83-480 currencies.

Source: U.S. Bureau of Economic Analysis, press releases, and unpublished data.

No. 1318. U.S. Government Foreign Grants and Credits, by Type and Country: 1946 to 1992

[In millions of dollars. See text, section 29. Negative figures (-) occur when the total of grant returns, principal repayments, and/or foreign currencies disbursed by the U.S. Government exceeds new grants and new credits utilized and/or acquisitions of foreign currencies through new sales of farm products. See also *Historical Statistics, Colonial Times to 1970*, series U 75-186]

TYPE AND COUNTRY	1946-1955, total	1956-1965, total	1966-1975, total	1976-1985, total	1988	1989	1990	1991	1992, prel.
Total, net	**51,509**	**49,723**	**70,368**	**104,188**	**8,081**	**10,041**	**14,297**	**-31,897**	**16,624**
Investment in financial institutions	**635**	**655**	**2,719**	**10,432**	**1,314**	**1,173**	**1,301**	**1,498**	**1,419**
African Development Bank.	-	-	-	54	9	7	19	(Z)	9
African Development Fund.	-	-	-	125	40	34	75	78	131
Asian Development Bank.	-	-	110	602	111	160	127	146	86
Inter-American Development Bank	-	300	1,321	2,770	124	97	90	74	128
Special Facility For Sub-Saharan Africa.	-	-	-	-	48	-	-	-	-
International Bank for Reconstruction and Development	635	-	13	353	95	23	61	72	94
International Development Association.	-	320	1,275	6,417	826	852	842	1,051	835
International Finance Corporation .	-	35	-	111	25	-	75	40	25
Inter-American Investment Corporation.	-	-	-	-	13	-	13	(Z)	12
Multilateral Investment Guarantee Agency	-	-	-	-	22	-	-	-	-
European Bank for Reconstruction and Development	-	-	-	-	-	-	-	36	99
Under assistance programs	**50,875**	**49,067**	**67,649**	**93,756**	**6,768**	**8,868**	**12,996**	**-33,395**	**15,206**
Developed Countries.	35,150	5,834	616	757	-131	63	193	-14,288	1,173
Developing Countries.	15,725	43,233	67,033	92,998	6,899	8,805	12,804	-19,107	14,032
Western Europe	**33,067**	**6,752**	**1,004**	**1,626**	**121**	**-247**	**-58**	**-5,859**	**553**
Austria.	1,001	193	-19	34	-9	-11	-10	-19	-1
Belgium and Luxembourg.	1,570	305	17	-46	-9	-9	-9	-3	-
Denmark.	596	276	64	-58	-	-	-	-	-
Finland.	86	-26	-19	21	6	7	-8	-5	-5
France.	8,661	-171	-93	-222	-14	-14	-15	-8	-2
Germany.	3,881	10	-117	-117	-	-1	-338	-6,117	-
Iceland.	34	33	-8	-12	-4	(Z)	(Z)	-	-
Ireland.	146	-16	-51	7	-6	-7	2	-6	-6
Italy.	3,851	1,435	85	133	-28	-28	-30	-14	(Z)
Netherlands.	1,716	322	116	-180	-	-	-	-	-
Norway.	697	362	379	-257	-	-	-	-1	-15
Portugal.	248	241	34	1,003	69	71	56	44	158
Spain.	258	1,203	607	965	-113	-474	-122	-76	-123
Sweden.	107	-20	17	-1	-3	-2	-	-	-
United Kingdom.	7,458	105	-546	-964	-105	-109	-111	-113	-115
Yugoslavia.	1,356	1,151	84	174	-2	11	-39	-55	-21
Other [1] and unspecified.	1,399	1,351	454	1,146	338	320	566	514	682

See footnotes at end of table.

Foreign Commerce and Aid

No. 1318. U.S. Government Foreign Grants and Credits, by Type and Country: 1946 to 1992—Continued

[In millions of dollars. See headnote, p. 813]

COUNTRY	1946-1955, total	1956-1965, total	1966-1975, total	1976-1985, total	1988	1989	1990	1991	1992, prel.
Eastern Europe	823	501	226	1,029	-121	419	954	898	577
Albania	9	-	-	-	-	-	-	12	29
Armenia	(X)	(X)	(X)	(X)	(X)	(X)	(X)	(X)	16
Belarus	(X)	(X)	(X)	(X)	(X)	(X)	(X)	(X)	22
Bulgaria	-	-	-	-	-	-	-	34	29
Czechoslovakia	136	-	-	-5	-	-	(Z)	32	46
Estonia	(X)	(X)	(X)	(X)	(X)	(X)	(X)	(X)	24
Hungary	18	5	-5	6	-	-	1	37	38
Latvia	(X)	(X)	(X)	(X)	(X)	(X)	(X)	(X)	25
Lithuania	(X)	(X)	(X)	(X)	(X)	(X)	(X)	(X)	25
Poland	350	555	-75	1,017	-53	524	919	714	112
Romania	-	-	92	55	-1	-59	64	48	25
Russia	(X)	(X)	(X)	(X)	(X)	(X)	(X)	(X)	47
Soviet Union	292	-59	214	-44	-66	-46	-30	3	(X)
Other and unspecified	17	(Z)	-	-	-	-	-	11	140
Near East and South Asia	4,944	16,828	17,195	50,793	2,128	4,442	6,674	-24,589	7,241
Afghanistan	31	227	185	56	30	76	57	59	70
Bangladesh	-	-	701	1,670	170	138	175	188	136
Cyprus	-	19	20	138	14	19	16	18	10
Egypt	41	1,009	271	13,600	3,490	2,085	4,976	2,508	2,539
Greece	2,026	1,281	905	362	488	306	282	-181	388
India	370	4,890	3,810	1,021	139	73	-8	100	17
Iran	314	1,061	914	-847	-19	-	-	-23	-
Iraq	13	81	-5	5	29	-16	-7	336	9
Israel	390	483	3,760	25,417	-1,826	1,902	4,454	2,029	4,746
Jordan	26	495	618	1,320	-231	161	139	67	118
Kuwait	-	-	-	-	-	-	-2,506	-13,550	-2
Lebanon	15	78	90	233	-7	(Z)	8	5	11
Nepal	3	86	105	177	19	15	20	16	19
Oman	-	-	(Z)	79	9	8	4	3	13
Pakistan	189	3,092	2,048	1,971	389	-387	524	346	89
Saudi Arabia	12	35	23	-20	-	-	-1,614	-13,913	-1,328
Sri Lanka	(Z)	89	153	512	43	43	72	109	53
Syria	1	57	15	262	(Z)	-	(Z)	-	-
Turkey	1,295	3,020	2,703	3,760	-720	-91	367	865	231
United Arab Emirates	-	-	-	-	(Z)	-	-361	-3,709	-
Yemen (Sanaa)	-	40	24	216	33	42	14	(X)	(X)
Yemen	-	-	-	-	-	-	28	19	14
UNRWA [2]	131	274	296	596	54	39	7	76	69
Other and unspecified	85	510	559	264	26	29	27	43	40
Africa	147	2,272	3,610	11,074	1,257	982	1,841	1,485	1,396
Algeria	1	135	263	345	-58	-77	59	-42	-13
Angola	-	-	6	115	2	-13	-15	-4	-30
Benin	-	7	12	44	5	12	5	10	16
Botswana	-	-	35	169	20	15	17	11	8
Burkina	-	5	40	287	18	14	15	32	14
Burundi	-	4	5	62	5	3	18	6	16
Cameroon	-	16	50	150	24	18	42	57	34
Cape Verde	-	-	1	68	6	4	6	7	8
Chad	(Z)	5	20	145	38	15	24	26	32
Ethiopia	13	200	297	310	71	37	54	123	62
Ghana	(Z)	64	203	152	17	46	14	32	28
Guinea	-	58	68	74	19	5	15	22	16
Ivory Coast	-	14	57	57	27	2	25	58	46
Kenya	(Z)	34	76	549	47	56	110	88	75
Lesotho	-	(Z)	27	197	23	19	15	11	14
Liberia	24	139	86	459	27	13	31	64	19
Madagascar	-	7	13	86	21	7	33	31	12
Malawi	-	5	30	56	34	44	34	51	38
Mali	-	12	58	199	50	27	31	44	31
Mauritania	-	1	20	161	11	14	11	6	2
Morocco	7	464	413	948	181	-5	95	98	13
Mozambique	-	-	1	175	56	-48	80	89	61
Niger	-	5	64	223	25	34	33	44	34
Nigeria	(Z)	87	284	267	169	44	156	34	31
Rwanda	-	2	13	91	16	9	13	27	7
Senegal	-	18	48	361	45	46	60	40	37
Sierra Leone	(Z)	22	36	85	8	12	2	11	14

See footnotes at end of table.

No. 1318. U.S. Government Foreign Grants and Credits, by Type and Country: 1946 to 1992—Continued

[In millions of dollars. See headnote, p. 813]

COUNTRY	1946-1955, total	1956-1965, total	1966-1975, total	1976-1985, total	1988	1989	1990	1991	1992, prel.
Africa—Continued									
Somalia	(Z)	42	47	582	62	38	77	11	307
Sudan	-	86	52	1,358	110	118	145	113	11
Swaziland	-	(Z)	8	58	12	11	14	13	12
Tanzania	2	34	123	259	16	16	40	42	28
Togo	-	9	18	60	9	15	10	19	11
Tunisia	2	407	376	563	-175	56	38	5	16
Uganda	-	12	33	40	21	20	43	39	22
Zaire	(Z)	258	342	938	142	72	241	48	33
Zambia	-	1	35	331	18	21	63	50	76
Zimbabwe	-	(Z)	(Z)	271	6	12	10	28	72
Other and unspecified	96	118	350	781	133	157	176	141	185
Far East and Pacific	**9,678**	**16,199**	**34,780**	**9,635**	**304**	**408**	**-124**	**-9,152**	**583**
Australia	-9	-	276	-12	-26	-18	-34	-26	-18
Burma	25	134	43	31	9	1	1	-3	(Z)
Cambodia	28	327	1,771	-	-	-	-	-	-
China: Mainland	-	-	-	49	48	35	71	55	31
Taiwan	1,267	2,681	1,523	648	-8	-7	-7	-8	-7
Hong Kong	3	35	41	11	-8	-8	-8	-	-
Indonesia	246	501	1,390	1,661	-3	36	46	23	81
Japan and Ryukyu Islands	3,267	1,318	-345	-210	-4	-1	-635	-9,377	-30
Laos	37	647	1,868	-	-	-	-	-	-
Malaysia	1	30	86	39	-9	-36	-1	-2	(Z)
New Zealand	3	2	95	-68	-4	-4	-2	-2	-1
Pacific Islands, Trust Territory of the [3]	28	89	488	1,260	138	156	52	16	1
Philippines	1,028	554	729	1,466	418	338	566	391	503
Singapore	-	-	78	110	1	1	2	3	3
South Korea	1,420	4,744	5,426	3,518	-383	-132	-192	-331	-132
Thailand	192	727	996	733	72	12	-19	49	43
Vietnam	244	3,566	19,721	-	-	-	-	-	-
Other and unspecified	1,898	844	595	400	65	36	39	59	111
Western Hemisphere	**1,248**	**5,181**	**6,816**	**9,860**	**1,448**	**1,194**	**2,034**	**1,976**	**2,244**
Argentina	86	342	34	21	16	-6	64	87	90
Bolivia	77	288	270	413	82	131	116	197	174
Brazil	509	1,400	1,518	399	(Z)	-202	260	-21	494
Canada	-1	4	272	317	-50	-30	-41	-50	-38
Chile	100	740	724	-565	11	-46	-32	-40	-56
Colombia	43	446	846	298	-23	29	-29	19	-77
Costa Rica	15	83	103	687	107	143	108	63	23
Dominican Republic	2	184	360	550	52	52	28	25	3
Ecuador	32	131	144	153	47	24	62	26	26
El Salvador	3	56	93	1,681	405	406	303	309	288
Guatemala	23	146	160	270	142	161	96	82	105
Guyana	(Z)	7	71	36	5	8	42	11	9
Haiti	27	75	42	370	41	76	53	69	40
Honduras	6	53	113	801	194	133	223	194	126
Jamaica	16	3	120	643	95	148	108	111	83
Mexico	225	178	305	1,162	62	-100	141	38	-172
Nicaragua	8	67	150	197	(Z)	(Z)	100	395	205
Panama	10	103	210	205	13	8	102	152	193
Paraguay	4	67	86	22	(Z)	1	(Z)	1	(Z)
Peru	55	304	274	757	67	36	87	139	607
Trinidad and Tobago	-	35	21	151	-11	16	5	5	-10
Uruguay	8	90	116	-9	9	-6	-4	-5	-3
Venezuela	6	156	115	-35	-28	-21	-18	-14	-3
Central American Bank for Economic Integration	-	6	121	36	-3	-1	-5	-5	3
Caribbean Development Bank	-	-	8	108	-2	-2	-2	-6	-7
Other [4] and unspecified	-6	218	543	1,193	219	233	268	195	138
Other international organizations and unspecified areas	969	1,335	4,018	9,739	1,629	1,668	1,675	1,846	2,612

- Represents zero. Z Less than $500,000. [1] Includes European Atomic Energy Community, European Coal and Steel Community, European Payments Union, European Productivity Agency, North Atlantic Treaty Organization, and Organization for European Economic Cooperation. [2] United Nations Relief and Works Agency for Palestine refugees. [3] Excludes transactions after October 1986, with Commonwealth of the Northern Mariana Islands; includes transactions with Federated States of Micronesia, Republic of the Marshall Islands, and Republic of Palau. [4] Includes Andean Development Corporation, Eastern Caribbean Central Bank, Inter-American Institute of Agricultural Sciences, Organization of American States, and Pan American Health Organization.

Source: U.S. Bureau of Economic Analysis, press releases; and unpublished data.

No. 1319. U.S. Foreign Economic and Military Aid Programs: 1946 to 1991

[In millions of dollars. For years ending June 30 except, beginning 1977, ending Sept. 30. Economic aid shown here represents U.S. economic aid—not just aid under Foreign Assistance Act. Major components in recent years include AID, Food for Peace, Peace Corps, and paid-in subscriptions to international financial institutions, such as IBRD, and IDB. Cumulative totals for 1946-1991 are true totals net of deobligation; annual figures however, are gross unadjusted program figures. Military aid includes Military Assistance Program (MAP) grants, foreign military credit sales, service-funded programs, and excess defense articles]

PERIOD OR YEAR AND REGION	Total economic and military aid	ECONOMIC AID			MILITARY AID		
		Total	Loans	Grants	Total	Loans	Grants
1946 to 1991, total.........	389,731	243,796	56,003	187,793	145,935	41,488	104,447
1946 to 1952.................	41,661	31,116	8,518	22,598	10,545	-	10,545
1953 to 1961.................	43,358	24,053	5,850	18,203	19,305	161	19,144
1962 to 1969.................	50,254	33,392	15,421	17,972	16,862	1,620	15,242
1970 to 1979.................	65,714	26,902	9,995	16,907	38,812	14,179	24,633
1980 to 1989.................	140,130	92,082	13,740	78,342	48,048	21,884	26,164
1970	6,568	3,676	1,389	2,288	2,892	70	2,822
1975	6,916	4,908	1,679	3,229	2,009	750	1,259
1976	6,412	3,878	1,759	2,119	2,535	1,442	1,093
1976, TQ [1]	2,603	1,931	840	1,091	672	494	178
1977	7,784	5,594	2,083	3,511	2,190	1,411	779
1978	9,014	6,661	2,530	4,131	2,353	1,601	752
1979	13,845	7,120	1,900	5,220	6,725	5,173	1,552
1980	9,695	7,573	1,993	5,580	2,122	1,450	672
1981	10,550	7,305	1,460	5,845	3,245	2,546	699
1982	12,324	8,129	1,454	6,675	4,195	3,084	1,111
1983	14,202	8,603	1,619	6,984	5,599	3,932	1,667
1984	15,524	9,038	1,621	7,417	6,486	4,401	2,085
1985	18,128	12,327	1,579	10,748	5,801	2,365	3,436
1986	16,739	10,900	1,330	9,570	5,839	1,980	3,859
1987	14,488	9,386	1,138	8,248	5,102	953	4,149
1988	13,792	8,961	852	8,109	4,831	763	4,068
1989	14,688	9,860	694	9,166	4,828	410	4,418
1990	15,727	10,834	756	10,078	4,893	404	4,489
1991	16,405	11,623	354	11,269	4,783	428	4,355
Near East and South Asia	7,660	3,628	171	3,457	4,032	370	3,662
East Asia	806	574	14	560	232	25	207
Europe....................	519	415	-	415	104	-	104
Latin America	1,712	1,475	100	1,376	237	23	214
Africa....................	1,394	1,300	66	1,234	94	10	84
Oceania and other	29	28	-	28	-	-	-
Nonregional	4,285	4,201	3	4,198	85	-	85

- Represents zero.   [1] Transition quarter, July-Sept.

No. 1320. U.S. Foreign Military Aid, by Region and Selected Countries: 1985 to 1991

[In millions of dollars. For years ending Sept. 30. Military aid data include Military Assistance Program (MAP) grants, foreign military credit sales, International Military Education and Training, and excess defense articles]

REGION AND COUNTRY	1985	1988	1989	1990	1991	REGION AND COUNTRY	1985	1988	1989	1990	1991
Total	5,801	4,831	4,828	4,893	4,783	Cameroon	5	(Z)	(Z)	-	1
						Djibouti	3	1	1	2	2
Europe.........	531	88	105	89	104	Gabon	(Z)	(Z)	(Z)	-	-
Portugal.......	128	85	103	87	101	Kenya	22	6	16	11	1
Spain.........	403	2	2	2	2	Liberia	13	1	1	-	-
Near East and						Morocco	50	53	53	44	44
South Asia	4,248	4,231	4,202	4,241	4,032	Niger.........	5	1	1	2	2
Egypt.........	1,177	1,302	1,302	1,296	1,302	Somalia.......	34	7	1	1	-
Greece	501	344	351	349	351	Sudan........	46	1	1	1	-
Israel........	1,400	1,800	1,800	1,792	1,800	Tunisia.......	67	28	31	31	12
Jordan........	92	28	12	70	21	Zaire........	8	4	4	4	-
Lebanon	1	(Z)	(Z)	-	-	Latin America [1]...	269	144	164	234	237
Oman	40	(Z)	(Z)	-	3	Colombia	1	4	8	73	50
Pakistan......	326	261	231	230	-	Costa Rica	11	(Z)	(Z)	-	-
Turkey........	704	493	504	501	554	Dominican Rep ..	9	1	1	2	2
Yemen........	6	2	2	2	2	Ecuador.......	7	1	5	1	3
East Asia	416	182	157	152	232	El Salvador.....	136	82	81	81	67
Indonesia.....	34	6	3	2	27	Haiti	1	(Z)	(Z)	1	2
Malaysia......	5	1	1	1	-	Honduras.....	67	41	41	21	34
Philippines	42	128	128	143	203	Jamaica.......	8	(Z)	4	1	2
South Korea	232	2	2	1	1	Panama.......	11	-	-	-	-
Thailand.......	102	46	24	5	1	Peru	9	(Z)	3	2	25
Africa [1]	279	116	118	114	94	Nonregional	58	70	82	63	85
Botswana.....	9	(Z)	1	1	1						

- Represents zero.   Z Less than $500,000.   [1] Includes countries not shown separately.
Source of tables 1319 and 1320: U.S. Agency for International Development, *U.S. Overseas Loans and Grants and Assistance from International Organizations,* annual.

No. 1321. U.S. Foreign Aid—Commitments for Economic Assistance, by Region and Selected Countries: 1985 to 1991

[In millions of dollars. For years ending **Sept. 30**. Falls under economic portion of the Foreign Assistance Act. Data cover commitments for economic and technical assistance by AID. See text, section 29]

REGION AND COUNTRY	1985	1988	1989	1990	1991	REGION AND COUNTRY	1985	1988	1989	1990	1991
Total	8,132	5,705	6,136	6,964	7,668	Lesotho	11	26	10	7	11
						Liberia	60	10	21	-	-
Europe	94	77	54	141	341	Malawi	25	44	21	23	57
Italy	2	-	-	-	-	Mali	32	21	27	21	37
Portugal	80	32	50	39	43	Mauritania	11	4	2	1	1
Spain	12	3	-	-	-	Mauritius	7	15	2	-	3
Near East and South Asia [1]	3,867	2,523	2,562	2,565	3,192	Morocco	38	31	32	31	50
Bangladesh	76	49	53	56	49	Niger	28	35	24	20	28
Cyprus	15	10	20	5	15	Rwanda	19	5	9	12	40
Egypt	1,065	718	817	901	783	Senegal	44	24	49	37	25
Israel	1,950	1,200	1,200	1,195	1,850	Seychelles	2	3	3	3	3
Jordan	100	24	16	4	31	Sierra Leone	(Z)	1	1	1	1
Lebanon	20	5	3	8	9	Somalia	51	10	13	1	1
Nepal	18	12	15	17	24	Sudan	149	17	5	8	2
Oman	20	13	15	13	16	Swaziland	9	16	7	7	9
Pakistan	250	385	265	276	96	Tanzania	(Z)	9	10	9	39
Sri Lanka	35	28	29	21	28	Togo	4	4	4	4	9
Turkey	175	32	60	15	250	Tunisia	23	12	13	14	4
Yemen (Sanaa)	28	22	24	23	3	Uganda	9	25	14	43	45
Regional	23	-	-	12	8	Zaire	36	31	36	31	22
East Asia	313	225	541	482	522	Zambia	42	13	7	17	35
Burma	15	6	-	-	-	Zimbabwe	41	13	29	28	43
Indonesia	72	42	50	48	60	Regional	96	65	110	73	12
Philippines	183	78	347	314	328	**Latin America** [1]	1,506	967	937	1,486	1,075
Thailand	36	25	23	14	3	Belize	23	8	8	6	7
East Asia Regional	7	74	122	106	118	Bolivia	18	38	37	58	100
Africa [1]	900	644	748	666	919	Costa Rica	196	101	115	78	42
Botswana	10	13	9	9	8	Dominican Rep.	126	33	20	18	14
Burkina	8	4	6	4	6	Ecuador	33	15	27	17	16
Burundi	4	6	2	20	15	El Salvador	376	266	253	200	180
Cameroon	24	19	33	22	20	Grenada	11	-	-	-	-
Cape Verde	3	3	3	3	4	Guatemala	76	110	114	86	60
Chad	16	17	16	11	16	Guyana	-	-	-	2	1
Congo	1	1	1	1	1	Haiti	31	31	40	42	51
Djibouti	4	4	3	3	4	Honduras	205	130	53	167	99
						Jamaica	115	40	65	28	27
Equatorial Guinea	1	1	1	1	1	Nicaragua	-	-	4	220	215
Gambia, The	6	4	4	5	15	Panama	74	1	-	396	40
Ghana	2	7	10	15	29	Paraguay	1	1	1	1	1
Guinea	4	18	16	15	31	Peru	38	28	22	22	69
						ROCAP [2]	107	59	48	30	21
Guinea-Bissau	4	1	2	3	4	Regional	30	74	100	88	96
Kenya	40	43	56	36	25	**Nonregional**	1,453	1,269	1,296	1,607	1,598

- Represents zero.   Z Less than $500,000.   [1] Includes countries not shown separately.   [2] Regional programs covering Costa Rica, El Salvador, Guatemala, Honduras, Nicaragua, and Panama.

Source: U.S. Agency for International Development, *U.S. Overseas Loans and Grants and Assistance from International Organizations*, annual; and unpublished data.

No. 1322. U.S. International Trade in Goods and Services: 1992 and 1993

[In millions of dollars. Data presented on a balance of payments basis and will not agree with the following merchandise trade tables 1323 to 1332]

CATEGORY	EXPORTS		IMPORTS		TRADE BALANCE	
	1992	1993	1992	1993	1992	1993
Total	616,924	641,677	657,308	717,402	−40,384	−75,725
Goods	440,361	456,866	536,458	589,441	−96,097	−132,575
Services	176,563	184,811	120,850	127,961	55,713	56,850
Travel	54,284	57,621	39,007	40,564	15,277	17,057
Passenger fares	16,972	16,550	10,608	11,416	6,364	5,134
Other transportation..............	22,704	23,151	23,460	24,502	−756	−1,351
Royalties and license fees..........	19,922	20,398	4,987	4,840	14,935	15,558
Other private services	50,992	54,870	26,625	32,119	24,367	22,751
Direct defense expenditures	10,828	11,413	13,862	12,176	−3,034	−763
U.S. Government miscellaneous services.....	861	808	2,301	2,344	−1,440	−1,536

Source: U.S. Bureau of the Census, *U.S. International Trade in Goods and Services*, series FT-900(93).

No. 1323. U.S. Exports and Imports of Merchandise: 1970 to 1993

[In billions of dollars, except percent. Includes silver ore and bullion; beginning 1974, includes shipments of nonmonetary gold. Data may differ from those shown in other tables due to revisions and inclusion of the Virgin Islands since 1974. For basis of dollar values, see text, section 29. See also *Historical Statistics, Colonial Times to 1970*, series U 190-195 and U 207-212]

YEAR	Merchandise trade balance	EXPORTS [1]					GENERAL IMPORTS [4]				AVERAGE ANNUAL PERCENT CHANGE [5]	
		Total [2]	Domestic				Total [3]	Petroleum	Machinery	Transport equipment	Domestic exports	General imports
			Total [3]	Agricultural	Machinery	Transport equipment						
1970	2.7	42.7	42.0	7.2	11.4	6.5	40.0	2.8	5.3	5.9	14.1	10.8
1971	−2.0	43.5	42.9	7.7	11.6	7.9	45.6	3.3	6.0	7.9	1.9	14.0
1972	−6.4	49.2	48.4	9.4	13.2	8.3	55.6	4.3	7.8	9.6	13.1	21.9
1973	1.3	70.8	69.7	17.7	17.1	10.7	69.5	7.6	10.0	11.1	43.9	25.0
1974	−4.5	98.1	96.5	22.0	23.7	14.5	102.6	24.3	11.6	12.5	38.6	47.6
1975	9.1	107.7	106.1	21.9	28.5	17.2	98.5	24.8	12.0	12.2	9.8	−4.0
1976	−8.3	115.2	113.5	23.0	31.3	18.2	123.5	31.8	15.2	14.6	7.0	25.4
1977	−29.2	121.2	118.9	23.7	32.5	18.5	150.4	41.5	17.7	17.8	5.2	21.8
1978	−31.1	143.7	141.0	29.4	37.0	22.3	174.8	39.1	24.4	23.2	18.6	16.2
1979	−27.6	181.9	178.6	34.8	44.7	25.8	209.5	56.0	28.0	25.6	26.6	19.9
1980	−24.2	220.6	216.5	41.3	55.8	28.8	244.9	77.6	31.9	28.6	21.3	16.9
1981	−27.3	233.7	228.9	43.3	62.9	32.8	261.0	75.6	38.2	31.4	5.9	6.6
1982	−31.8	212.3	207.1	36.6	60.3	23.6	244.0	59.4	39.7	33.6	−9.2	−6.5
1983	−57.5	200.5	196.0	36.1	54.3	28.3	258.0	52.3	47.0	39.2	−5.6	5.7
1984	−107.9	217.9	212.1	37.8	60.3	29.7	325.7	55.9	68.4	50.8	8.7	26.2
1985	−132.1	213.1	206.9	29.2	59.5	34.8	345.3	49.6	75.3	62.0	−2.2	6.0
1986	−152.7	217.3	206.4	26.1	60.4	34.9	370.0	34.1	87.5	74.0	2.0	7.2
1987	−152.1	254.1	243.9	28.6	69.6	39.0	406.2	41.5	99.4	78.4	16.9	9.8
1988	−118.6	322.4	310.0	37.0	88.4	46.7	441.0	38.8	117.3	79.8	26.9	8.6
1989	−109.6	363.8	349.4	40.0	98.3	50.5	473.4	49.1	126.8	79.0	12.8	7.3
1990	−101.7	393.6	375.1	38.7	122.4	32.1	495.3	60.5	134.8	72.4	8.2	4.6
1991	−65.4	421.7	401.1	38.5	139.7	34.9	487.1	50.1	131.8	70.6	7.1	−1.7
1992	−84.5	448.2	425.7	42.2	126.6	36.9	532.7	50.4	148.3	75.5	6.3	9.4
1993	−115.8	464.8	439.3	41.8	136.4	36.6	580.5	49.7	168.7	83.3	3.7	9.0

[1] Includes "Special Category" items and beginning 1974, includes trade of Virgin Islands with foreign countries. F.a.s. value basis. [2] Domestic and foreign exports excluding M.A.P. Grant-Aid shipments, through 1985; 1986 through 1988 include Grant-Aid shipments. [3] Includes commodity groups not shown separately. [4] 1970-73, 1982-91, customs value basis; 1974-81, f.a.s. value basis. Beginning 1974, includes trade of Virgin Islands with foreign countries. [5] 1970, change from 1965; thereafter, from previous year. For explanation of average annual percent change, see Guide to Tabular Presentation.

Source: U.S. Bureau of the Census, 1970-88, *Highlights of U.S. Export and Import Trade*, FT 990, monthly; beginning 1989, *U.S. Merchandise Trade: Export, General Imports, and Imports for Consumption*, series FT 925, monthly.

No. 1324. U.S. Exports and Imports for Consumption of Merchandise, by Major Customs District: 1980 to 1993

[In billions of dollars. Exports are f.a.s. (free alongside ship) value all years; imports are on customs value basis. See also *Historical Statistics, Colonial Times to 1970*, series U 264-273]

CUSTOMS DISTRICT	EXPORTS						IMPORTS FOR CONSUMPTION					
	1980	1985	1990	1991	1992	1993	1980	1985	1990	1991	1992	1993
Total [1]	220.8	213.1	393.0	421.9	447.5	464.9	244.0	343.6	490.6	483.0	525.1	574.9
Anchorage, AK.	1.0	1.3	3.7	4.6	5.1	4.8	0.2	0.2	0.7	0.9	1.3	2.0
Baltimore, MD	9.0	5.5	6.7	8.0	7.7	7.7	6.0	8.8	11.2	10.1	10.8	11.7
Boston, ...	0.8	3.0	5.6	4.3	4.4	4.4	5.0	8.2	12.2	11.8	12.0	11.7
Buffalo, NY	6.3	8.4	15.8	15.7	18.0	19.5	7.4	14.7	19.2	18.7	21.2	24.2
Charleston, SC [2]	3.1	2.9	6.7	7.2	7.3	7.3	1.8	3.3	6.8	6.3	6.6	7.5
Chicago, IL	4.2	5.4	10.2	11.3	11.9	13.2	4.1	11.4	18.3	19.4	22.5	25.1
Cleveland, OH	1.8	2.1	4.0	4.0	4.1	4.4	1.5	3.8	11.3	11.8	13.8	15.5
Dallas/Fort Worth, TX . . .	0.5	1.0	3.4	2.6	3.9	4.2	1.2	2.4	4.8	4.9	5.3	6.3
Detroit, MI	14.6	22.8	35.6	36.0	37.4	44.3	12.7	27.4	37.8	37.6	42.0	47.5
Duluth, MN	1.5	0.9	0.8	0.8	0.9	0.9	3.0	3.0	3.9	3.3	3.6	4.1
El Paso, TX	1.8	2.1	3.9	4.7	6.1	6.5	1.4	2.5	5.0	5.5	6.5	8.1
Great Falls, MT	1.8	1.5	2.4	3.3	3.1	3.5	3.2	4.0	4.7	4.6	4.9	5.7
Honolulu, HI.	0.2	0.4	0.5	0.6	0.6	1.1	1.8	1.6	2.1	1.9	2.1	2.2
Houston/Galveston, TX . . .	15.7	12.5	17.6	20.5	20.2	19.8	20.1	17.3	21.6	19.2	18.7	19.7
Laredo, TX	8.3	7.2	15.2	18.2	21.7	22.7	2.7	4.8	10.0	10.4	11.8	13.7
Los Angeles, CA.	14.8	19.5	42.1	46.0	49.4	48.3	20.0	44.1	64.1	66.4	71.9	79.5
Miami, FL	6.9	6.1	11.2	13.4	16.0	17.1	2.6	4.4	7.1	7.3	8.4	9.4
Milwaukee, WI	0.4	0.2	0.1	0.1	0.1	0.1	0.4	1.0	1.1	1.1	1.2	1.2
Minneapolis, MN.	0.1	0.2	0.9	0.9	1.1	1.1	0.3	1.0	2.0	2.2	2.7	2.5
Mobile, AL [2]	2.6	1.1	1.9	2.2	2.2	2.1	3.0	2.8	3.4	3.3	3.2	3.1
New Orleans, LA	19.5	13.9	18.0	18.8	20.1	19.7	22.5	14.7	24.1	22.3	23.3	24.7
New York, NY	38.9	28.5	50.9	54.6	53.4	58.5	43.4	60.5	68.0	67.4	72.8	75.7
Nogales, AZ	0.8	0.8	2.1	2.2	2.8	3.0	1.2	2.0	4.2	4.4	4.6	5.7
Norfolk, VA [2]	8.0	5.4	11.7	11.5	11.9	11.0	4.7	6.0	7.4	7.4	7.5	7.3
Ogdensburg, NY.	3.8	4.1	7.9	7.5	7.9	7.8	4.6	6.8	9.8	9.9	10.0	11.4
Pembina, ND	2.3	2.2	3.4	4.3	4.3	4.8	3.0	3.2	4.1	4.1	4.5	5.3
Philadelphia, PA	3.2	2.0	4.0	4.4	4.4	4.4	15.6	15.8	18.3	16.1	16.4	16.1
Port Arthur, TX.	2.0	0.8	0.9	0.7	0.8	0.9	9.4	2.7	3.2	2.8	3.1	3.8
Portland, ME	4.3	0.6	1.7	2.1	1.8	2.2	1.6	2.3	4.3	3.8	4.0	4.0
Portland, OR	3.8	3.5	5.8	6.0	7.2	7.4	2.6	3.8	5.6	5.3	5.1	5.7
Providence, RI	2.7	0.1	(Z)	(Z)	(Z)	0.1	1.5	2.3	1.3	1.1	1.1	1.1
San Diego, CA	1.4	1.6	3.4	3.9	4.6	4.6	1.0	1.8	4.3	4.7	5.5	6.2
San Francisco, CA	10.6	11.3	23.1	23.9	27.1	29.5	8.3	15.5	28.0	29.2	33.2	38.8
San Juan, PR.	0.9	1.2	2.5	2.4	2.5	2.7	3.7	4.0	5.4	4.8	5.0	4.9
Savannah, GA	2.4	3.4	7.4	8.4	8.9	8.7	2.2	5.1	9.8	10.1	11.3	12.8
Seattle, WA.	12.0	12.1	32.6	35.0	35.5	35.2	9.2	13.4	20.9	18.9	20.5	21.8
St. Albans, VT	0.7	1.1	4.0	4.1	4.0	3.8	1.6	2.7	5.2	5.2	5.3	5.5
St. Louis, MO.	0.2	0.1	0.3	0.4	0.7	0.3	0.9	1.6	3.0	2.8	3.4	3.9
Tampa, FL.	2.8	2.8	4.3	5.2	5.2	4.7	3.7	6.6	7.0	6.8	7.0	7.3
Virgin Islands of the U.S. . .	0.1	0.1	0.2	0.3	0.1	0.2	4.1	1.7	2.1	1.7	1.8	1.6
Washington, DC	0.3	0.5	1.1	1.6	1.6	1.9	0.4	0.5	0.8	0.7	0.8	0.8
Wilmington, NC	1.3	1.3	3.0	2.8	3.9	3.0	1.1	1.9	3.3	3.4	4.6	5.6

Z Less than $50 million.   [1] Totals shown for exports reflect the value of estimated parcel post and Special Category shipments, and beginning 1990, adjustments for undocumented exports to Canada which are not distributed by customs district. Beginning 1985, the value of bituminous coal exported through Norfolk, VA; Charleston, SC; and Mobile, AL is reflected in the total but not distributed by district.   [2] Beginning 1985, excludes exports of bituminous coal.

Source: U.S. Bureau of the Census, 1980 and 1985, *Highlights of U.S. Export and Import Trade*, FT 990; beginning 1990, *U.S. Merchandise Trade: Selected Highlights*, series FT 920, monthly.

No. 1325. Export and Import Unit Value Indexes—Selected Countries: 1989 to 1993

[Indexes in U.S. dollars, 1985=100. A unit value is an implicit price derived from value and quantity data]

COUNTRY	EXPORT UNIT VALUE					IMPORT UNIT VALUE				
	1989	1990	1991	1992	1993	1989	1990	1991	1992	1993
United States.	112.8	113.9	114.9	115.0	115.5	111.9	115.6	115.6	116.5	115.7
Australia	140.6	140.0	127.7	122.8	115.2	126.8	130.2	131.3	129.3	129.4
Austria	146.2	169.6	159.8	166.3	(NA)	141.0	160.0	156.1	162.9	(NA)
Belgium-Luxembourg	146.3	167.2	160.5	168.1	(NA)	134.9	156.2	150.8	155.0	(NA)
Canada	118.4	119.2	117.1	113.6	112.4	111.9	115.6	116.1	114.7	114.1
Denmark.	146.2	169.9	164.7	172.6	(NA)	136.5	155.8	151.6	155.4	(NA)
France	145.0	167.1	160.8	166.5	(NA)	129.2	148.4	141.8	145.3	(NA)
Germany	155.5	178.9	173.1	182.7	(NA)	133.9	151.9	150.4	154.9	(NA)
Italy	149.8	175.2	174.1	176.6	(NA)	126.5	143.8	137.8	137.9	(NA)
Japan.	143.3	141.9	152.0	162.9	(NA)	107.2	113.2	110.6	109.5	(NA)
Norway.	101.4	116.8	108.0	103.6	(NA)	139.5	155.0	147.2	150.7	(NA)
Sweden	150.9	167.5	165.4	165.6	(NA)	136.5	151.6	147.4	148.7	(NA)
United Kingdom	123.2	138.4	138.5	140.2	(NA)	124.6	138.4	139.1	139.5	(NA)

NA Not available.

Source: International Monetary Fund, Washington, DC, *International Financial Statistics*, monthly.

No. 1326. U.S. Exports, by State of Origin: 1990 to 1993

[In millions of dollars. Exports are on a f.a.s. value basis]

STATE AND OTHER AREAS	1990	1992	1993 Total	1993 Rank	STATE AND OTHER AREAS	1990	1992	1993 Total	1993 Rank
Total......	394,045	448,156	464,767	(X)	MT	229	268	272	49
					NE	693	1,233	1,355	36
U.S.........	315,065	379,263	391,925	(X)	NV	394	507	539	44
AL........	2,834	3,629	3,440	27	NH	973	917	904	42
AK	2,850	3,195	2,512	31	NJ........	7,633	8,955	9,286	13
AZ	3,729	5,109	5,436	21	NM	249	356	434	45
AR	920	1,324	1,353	37	NY	22,072	22,628	28,370	3
CA	44,520	56,307	57,198	1	NC	8,010	10,374	9,889	12
CO	2,274	2,594	3,065	28	ND	360	336	408	46
CT	4,356	5,028	5,519	20	OH	13,378	16,306	17,306	6
DE	1,344	1,508	1,318	39	OK	1,646	1,987	2,101	33
DC	320	344	464	(X)	OR	4,065	4,890	5,273	22
FL........	11,634	14,431	14,239	9	PA	8,491	10,329	10,463	10
GA	5,763	7,652	6,823	16	RI	595	859	893	43
HI	179	206	260	48	SC	3,116	4,222	4515	23
ID........	898	1,076	1,122	40	SD	205	232	254	50
IL........	12,965	15,328	16,424	7	TN	3,746	5,156	5,597	19
IN........	5,273	6,148	7,188	15	TX	32,931	43,553	45,290	2
IA........	2,189	2,476	2,779	29	UT	1,596	2,706	2,367	32
KS	2,113	2,514	2,668	30	VT	1,154	1,314	1,342	38
KY	3,175	3,648	4,212	25	VA	9,333	9,784	9,052	14
LA........	14,199	16,151	14,372	8	WA	24,432	28,041	26,624	4
ME	870	902	1,027	41	WV	1,550	1,746	1,423	35
MD	2,592	3,879	4,376	24	WI........	5,158	6,173	6,769	17
MA	9,501	10,400	10,426	11	WY	264	368	337	47
MI........	18,474	20,414	23,198	5					
MN	5,091	6,137	6,228	18	PR	3,600	3,872	4,073	(X)
MS	1,605	1,963	1,687	34	VI	51	121	150	(X)
MO	3,130	3,664	3,528	26	Other [1]	75,328	64,900	68,619	(X)

X Not applicable.   [1] Includes unreported, not specified, special category, estimated shipments, foreign trade zone, re-exports, and any timing adjustments.

Source: U.S. Bureau of the Census, U.S. Merchandise Trade, series FT 900, December issues.

No. 1327. U.S. Trade in Advanced Technology Products: 1990 to 1993

[In billions of dollars. Exports are f.a.s. value basis and imports are on customs value basis]

PRODUCT CATEGORY	EXPORTS				GENERAL IMPORTS				MERCHANDISE TRADE BALANCE			
	1990	1991	1992	1993	1990	1991	1992	1993	1990	1991	1992	1993
Total................	93.4	100.0	105.1	108.4	59.3	63.1	71.8	81.2	34.1	36.9	33.3	27.2
Advanced materials [1].......	6.4	6.2	0.6	0.7	1.0	1.1	0.4	0.5	5.4	5.1	0.2	0.2
Aerospace.....	37.0	41.9	42.5	37.4	10.7	12.1	12.8	11.6	26.3	29.8	29.7	25.9
Biotechnology [2]	0.6	0.7	0.7	0.8	(Z)	(Z)	(Z)	0.1	0.6	0.7	0.7	0.8
Electronics........... [3]	7.5	8.9	16.5	19.6	11.0	12.4	15.4	19.4	-3.5	-3.5	1.2	0.2
Flexible manufacturing [3]....	3.1	3.3	3.4	4.0	1.7	1.8	1.7	2.2	1.4	1.5	1.7	1.8
Information and communications	31.4	30.7	32.5	36.7	30.2	29.2	33.9	40.1	1.2	1.5	-1.4	-3.4
Life science	4.9	5.5	5.8	6.1	3.4	4.3	4.8	4.7	1.5	1.2	1.1	1.5
Nuclear technology	1.3	1.3	1.5	1.4	(Z)	(Z)	(Z)	(Z)	1.3	1.3	1.5	1.4
Opto-electronics [4]	0.5	0.6	0.6	0.7	1.1	2.0	2.6	2.5	-0.6	-1.4	-2.0	-1.8
Weapons...............	0.7	0.9	0.8	0.7	0.1	0.2	(Z)	0.2	0.6	0.7	0.6	0.6

Z Less than $50 million.   [1] Encompasses recent advances in the development of materials that allow for further development and application of other advanced technologies. Examples are semiconductor materials, optical fiber cable and video discs.   [2] Biotechnology is the medical and industrial application of advanced scientific discoveries in genetics to the creation of new drugs, hormones and other therapeutic items for both agricultural and human use.   [3] Encompasses advances in robotics, numerically—controlled machine tools, and similar products involving industrial automation that allow for greater flexibility to the manufacturing process and reduce the amount of human intervention. Includes robots, numerically controlled machine tools and semiconductor production and assembly machines.   [4] Encompasses electronic products and components that involve the emitting and/or detection of light. Examples of products included are optical scanners, optical disc players, solar cells, photo-sensitive semiconductors and laser printers.

Source: U. S. Bureau of the Census, U. S. Merchandise Trade, series FT 900, December issues.

No. 1328. U.S. Exports and General Imports of Major SITC Commodity Groups—Value, by Area: 1992

[In millions of dollars. SITC=Standard International Trade Classification. Includes nonmonetary gold. Exports are f.a.s. (free alongside ship) transaction value basis; imports are customs value basis]

COMMODITY GROUPS	Total [1]	WESTERN HEMISPHERE		WESTERN EUROPE				ASIA	
		Canada	Mexico	United Kingdom	Germany	France	Italy	Japan	South Korea
Exports, total [1]	448,164	90,594	40,592	22,800	21,249	14,593	8,721	47,813	14,639
Meat and meat preparations	4,233	579	586	27	17	59	13	1,993	247
Fish (except marine mammal) crustaceans, etc., preparations	3,491	370	49	147	20	110	43	2,238	134
Cereals and cereal preparations	12,237	496	985	47	33	44	114	2,315	451
Vegetables and fruit	6,284	2,345	214	289	292	137	67	1,112	90
Feeding stuff for animals not including unmilled cereal	3,665	424	264	123	105	91	60	499	58
Miscellaneous edible products and preparations	1,533	360	112	23	8	50	3	108	35
Tobacco and tobacco manufactures	6,177	21	7	74	315	12	60	1,666	119
Hides, skins, and furskins, raw	1,375	70	135	2	10	11	36	289	580
Oil seeds and oleaginous fruits	4,851	95	510	72	230	69	147	913	248
Cork and wood	5,347	726	289	99	167	43	195	2,617	260
Pulp and waste paper	3,883	280	297	200	277	189	328	661	422
Textile fibers & their wastes (excluding wool tops, etc)	3,118	157	182	61	83	12	99	368	380
Crude fertilizers & crude minerals [2]	1,434	259	74	39	64	20	54	297	77
Metalliferous ores and metal scrap	3,653	926	140	126	73	25	48	567	425
Crude animal and vegetable materials, n.e.s.	1,189	223	133	47	88	28	33	116	35
Coal, coke and briquettes	4,428	559	20	264	40	335	447	532	151
Petroleum, petroleum products, and related materials	6,095	630	892	46	100	77	154	515	551
Organic chemicals	11,141	1,162	816	400	468	257	285	998	521
Inorganic chemicals	4,262	501	277	182	222	99	49	1,142	176
Dyeing, tanning and coloring materials	1,892	535	163	112	49	22	19	105	69
Medicinal and pharmaceutical products	5,447	771	130	294	376	368	445	817	58
Essential oils, etc; toilet, polishing, preparations	2,711	650	205	162	74	66	40	232	59
Fertilizers [3]	2,391	199	78	11	32	46	9	158	78
Plastics in primary forms	7,206	1,434	671	227	200	78	53	459	276
Plastics in nonprimary forms	3,128	868	495	134	149	78	41	187	73
Chemical materials and products, n.e.s.	6,461	1,312	325	284	425	328	168	724	216
Rubber manufactures, n.e.s.	2,560	1,120	328	86	82	37	21	229	27
Cork and wood manufactures other than furniture	1,439	331	224	143	138	14	23	100	61
Paper, paperboard and articles	6,403	1,658	986	234	183	94	106	545	150
Textile yarn, fabrics, made-up articles, n.e.s.	5,911	1,517	712	303	192	89	117	233	132
Nonmetallic mineral manufactures, n.e.s.	4,885	1,270	286	192	144	94	53	342	110
Iron and steel	3,868	1,359	959	110	61	35	41	112	82
Nonferrous metals	5,073	1,344	587	246	127	132	48	1,009	135
Manufactures of metals, n.e.s.	7,286	2,632	1,320	343	277	114	106	416	140
Power generating machinery and equipment	18,485	4,596	1,528	1,195	732	2,381	234	882	705
Machinery specialized for particular industries	17,250	2,933	1,382	807	738	544	302	783	511
Metalworking machinery	3,149	491	443	155	172	97	73	246	250
General industrial machinery, equipment, parts	18,908	5,086	1,905	851	814	538	265	1,046	708
Office machines and automatic data processing machines	30,997	5,025	1,317	3,102	2,884	1,527	598	3,660	532
Telecommunications, sound recording, reproduction apparatus and equipment	12,370	2,103	1,928	619	447	253	257	929	406
Electrical machinery, apparatus, and appliances, n.e.s.	37,561	8,502	5,256	2,146	1,630	860	638	2,660	1,465
Road vehicles (incl. air-cushion vehicles)	38,191	18,271	4,309	472	1,929	376	175	1,573	284
Transport equipment, n.e.s.	38,527	1,826	983	2,712	2,386	1,713	1,219	3,890	1,531
Furniture, bedding, mattresses, etc.	2,600	1,142	628	85	68	41	9	97	11
Articles of apparel and clothing accessories	4,209	341	741	100	79	81	72	519	11
Professional scientific and control instruments and apparatus	14,947	2,070	1,238	1,030	1,248	842	493	1,762	512
Photo apparatus, equipment and optical goods n.e.s.; watch and clocks	4,340	729	295	441	291	295	95	612	46
Miscellaneous manufactured articles	23,324	4,832	1,771	1,793	1,647	789	343	2,431	539
Special transactions and commodities not classified by kind	4,072	1,331	154	142	200	46	25	275	115
Gold, nonmonetary (excluding ores and concentrates	4,142	507	180	1,031	106	354	4	144	19
Shipments under $10,000 and under $1,500 documented exports	10,432	1,803	1,506	689	547	367	185	577	135

See footnotes at end of table.

No. 1328. U.S. Exports and General Imports of Major SITC Commodity Groups—Value, by Area: 1992—Continued

[In millions of dollars. See headnote, page 821]

COMMODITY GROUPS	Total [1]	WESTERN HEMISPHERE		WESTERN EUROPE				ASIA	
		Canada	Mexico	United Kingdom	Germany	France	Italy	Japan	South Korea
Imports, total [1].............	**532,665**	**98,630**	**35,211**	**20,093**	**28,820**	**14,797**	**12,314**	**97,414**	**16,682**
Meat and meat preparations.........	2,722	668	2	-	1	4	7	3	-
Fish (except marine mammal) crustaceans, etc., preps...........	5,657	1,121	250	16	2	8	1	140	108
Vegetables and fruit...............	5,698	277	1,327	8	91	22	33	41	13
Coffee, tea, cocoa, spices manufactures thereof.............	3,209	213	294	28	87	11	20	4	1
Beverages.....................	4,062	591	262	667	186	990	403	33	5
Cork and wood..................	3,970	3,539	178	-	2	1	3	1	-
Pulp and waste paper	2,129	1,793	5	-	5	-	-	-	-
Metalliferous ores and metal scrap.....	3,340	1,016	221	60	24	26	1	22	12
Petroleum, petroleum products, and related materials	50,361	6,518	4,663	1,790	151	245	481	49	104
Gas, natural and manufactured	3,885	3,540	74	6	3	9	1	-	3
Organic chemicals................	9,408	851	306	1,085	1,339	474	423	1,184	87
Inorganic chemicals...............	3,305	1,026	195	308	351	240	68	215	4
Medicinal and pharmaceutical products..	3,810	172	27	673	502	169	219	323	2
Chemical materials and products, n.e.s.	2,622	414	59	245	399	190	37	348	12
Rubber manufactures, n.e.s.	3,727	1,063	71	97	204	165	92	1,002	235
Cork and wood manufactures other than furniture	2,497	939	114	12	29	47	45	8	5
Paper, paperboard and articles	7,998	5,958	134	200	230	146	60	210	61
Textile yarn, fabrics, made-up articles, n.e.s...........	7,844	600	353	284	357	195	512	642	540
Nonmetallic mineral manufactures, n.e.s..	10,172	706	468	489	430	318	552	723	87
Iron and steel..................	9,320	1,922	271	334	727	557	184	1,939	599
Nonferrous metals................	8,513	3,711	411	312	389	126	41	291	4
Manufactures of metals, n.e.s........	9,493	1,345	675	279	595	263	222	1,612	475
Power generating machinery and equipment	15,888	2,416	1,433	2,163	1,669	2,479	239	3,742	93
Machinery specialized for particular industries	11,814	1,068	163	869	2,868	544	771	3,087	66
Metalworking machinery............	3,187	268	12	148	569	47	110	1,292	64
General industrial machinery, equipment, parts	15,520	1,982	981	913	2,226	421	731	4,079	377
Office machines and automatic data processing machines	36,377	2,365	952	1,169	688	348	192	13,993	1,421
Telecommunications, sound recording, reproduction apparatus and equipment .	25,803	1,126	3,560	299	197	161	52	9,237	1,916
Electrical machinery, apparatus and appliances, n.e.s.............	39,710	3,610	5,527	1,102	2,119	625	273	10,736	2,715
Road vehicles (incl air-cushion vehicles) .	75,477	28,112	5,120	755	6,595	654	457	28,952	876
Transport equipment, n.e.s.	8,252	2,224	25	951	246	1,885	498	569	78
Furniture, bedding, mattresses, etc.	5,503	1,269	780	82	148	59	428	174	38
Travel goods, handbags and similar containers................	2,509	16	64	5	14	75	202	6	304
Articles of apparel and clothing accessories	31,226	442	1,183	167	132	182	877	133	2,676
Footwear.....................	10,163	50	212	72	65	48	785	4	1,527
Professional scientific and control instruments and apparatus	7,602	634	821	702	1,123	310	94	1,848	96
Photo apparatus, equipment and optical goods,n.e.s.; watch and clocks......	7,916	347	194	296	365	222	343	3,083	141
Miscellaneous manufactured articles, n.e.s.	28,543	1,555	995	1,307	955	813	1,633	4,458	1,442
Special transactions and commodities not classified by kind	13,134	4,063	1,165	1,094	841	495	248	882	123
Estimate of low valued import transactions	3,947	900	320	222	373	124	105	733	44

- Represents zero.   [1] Includes countries and commodities not shown separately .   [2] Other than fertilizers covered in SITC division 56 (Fertilizers).   [3] Other than crude fertilizers covered in SITC division 272.

Source: U.S. Bureau of the Census, *U.S. Merchandise Trade: Exports, General Imports, and Imports for Consumption*, series FT 927.

No. 1329. U.S. Exports, Imports, and Merchandise Trade Balance, by Country: 1989 to 1993

[In millions of dollars. Includes silver ore and bullion. Country totals include exports of special category commodities, if any. Data include nonmonetary gold and includes trade of Virgin Islands with foreign countries, see footnote 2 for exception. Minus sign (-) denotes an excess of imports over exports. See Historical Statistics, Colonial Times to 1970, series U 317-352, for selected countries]

COUNTRY	EXPORTS, DOMESTIC AND FOREIGN					GENERAL IMPORTS [1]					MERCHANDISE TRADE BALANCE				
	1989	1990	1991	1992	1993	1989	1990	1991	1992	1993	1989	1990	1991	1992	1993
Total [2]	363,812	393,592	421,730	448,164	464,767	473,211	495,311	487,129	532,665	580,511	-109,399	-101,718	-65,399	-84,501	-115,744
Afghanistan	5	4	3	4	10	5	5	5	2	3	(Z)	-1	-2	2	7
Albania	5	10	18	36	34	5	2	3	5	8	(Z)	8	15	31	26
Algeria	756	951	727	688	898	1,829	2,626	2,103	1,586	1,583	-1,074	-1,674	-1,376	-898	-685
Andorra	50	40	17	16	15	(Z)	(Z)	(Z)	(Z)	(Z)	50	40	17	16	15
Angola	97	152	186	158	169	1,929	1,904	1,775	2,303	2,090	-1,832	-1,752	-1,589	-2,145	-1,921
Anguilla	17	15	11	11	14	(Z)	(Z)	1	(Z)	(Z)	17	15	10	11	14
Antigua	74	69	74	68	73	12	4	4	5	15	62	65	70	63	58
Argentina	1,039	1,179	2,045	3,223	3,772	1,391	1,511	1,287	1,256	1,206	-352	-333	758	1,967	2,566
Armenia	(X)	(X)	(X)	25	78	(X)	(X)	(X)	2	1	(X)	(X)	(X)	23	77
Aruba	127	202	235	288	266	1	1	100	212	457	126	201	135	76	-191
Australia	8,331	8,538	8,404	8,876	8,272	3,873	4,447	3,988	3,688	3,294	4,458	4,091	4,416	5,188	4,978
Austria	873	875	1,056	1,256	1,326	1,136	1,318	1,264	1,306	1,411	-263	-444	-208	-50	-85
Azerbaijan	(X)	(X)	(X)	(Z)	37	(X)	(X)	(X)	(Z)	(Z)	(X)	(X)	(X)	(Z)	37
Bahamas, The	772	800	721	712	704	462	509	470	605	348	310	291	252	107	356
Bahrain	489	721	500	489	653	80	81	87	61	97	409	640	413	428	556
Bangladesh	282	181	179	188	245	428	539	524	831	886	-147	-357	-345	-643	-641
Barbados	180	161	166	128	146	46	31	31	31	34	134	130	135	97	112
Belarus	(X)	(X)	(X)	25	92	(X)	(X)	(X)	25	34	(X)	(X)	(X)	(Z)	58
Belgium	8,381	10,318	10,572	9,775	8,876	4,351	4,375	3,929	4,476	5,177	4,029	5,942	6,643	5,299	3,699
Belize	101	105	114	117	136	43	47	45	59	54	58	58	69	58	82
Benin	18	24	26	27	22	11	17	23	10	16	6	6	4	17	6
Bermuda	354	255	233	242	265	11	13	8	6	15	343	242	225	236	250
Bolivia	145	138	192	222	216	118	203	209	162	191	27	-65	-17	60	25
Bosnia-Hercegovina [3]	(X)	(X)	(X)	5	15	(X)	(X)	(X)	9	7	(X)	(X)	(X)	-4	8
Botswana	30	19	31	47	25	17	13	13	13	9	13	6	18	34	16
Brazil	4,804	5,048	6,148	5,751	6,045	8,410	7,898	6,717	7,609	7,466	-3,606	-2,850	-569	-1,858	-1,421
British Virgin Islands	49	60	45	44	46	61	13	2	3	14	-12	47	43	41	32
Brunei	63	143	162	453	478	75	85	26	29	30	-12	58	136	424	448
Bulgaria	181	84	142	85	115	59	47	56	78	159	122	37	86	7	-44
Burkina	10	15	24	13	18	(Z)	1	1	(Z)	(Z)	10	14	23	13	18
Cameroon	35	47	45	57	48	426	147	127	84	101	-391	-100	-82	-27	-53
Canada	78,809	83,674	85,150	90,594	100,177	87,953	91,380	91,064	98,630	110,922	-9,144	-7,707	-5,914	-8,036	-10,745
Cayman Islands	204	183	117	282	179	48	21	18	10	35	155	162	99	272	144
Chad	35	8	14	8	8	(Z)	(Z)	(Z)	3	(Z)	35	8	14	5	8
Chile	1,414	1,664	1,839	2,466	2,605	1,292	1,313	1,302	1,388	1,462	122	351	537	1,078	1,143
China: Mainland	5,755	4,806	6,278	7,418	8,767	11,990	15,237	18,969	25,728	31,535	-6,235	-10,431	-12,691	-18,309	-22,768
China: Taiwan	11,335	11,491	13,182	15,250	16,250	24,313	22,666	23,023	24,596	25,105	-12,978	-11,175	-9,841	-9,346	-8,855
Colombia	1,924	2,029	1,952	3,286	3,229	2,555	3,168	2,736	2,837	3,033	-631	-1,139	-784	449	196
Congo (Brazzaville)	12	90	43	59	27	504	414	410	510	500	-492	-324	-367	-451	-473
Costa Rica	882	986	1,034	1,357	1,547	962	1,005	1,154	1,411	1,542	-81	-19	-120	-54	5
Croatia [3]	(X)	(X)	(X)	91	103	(X)	(X)	(X)	43	106	(X)	(X)	(X)	48	-3
Cyprus	109	129	119	166	138	15	19	12	11	16	94	111	107	155	122
Czechoslovakia	53	91	123	413	(X)	85	87	145	242	(X)	-32	4	-22	171	(X)
Czech Republic	(X)	(X)	(X)	(X)	266	(X)	(X)	(X)	(X)	278	(X)	(X)	(X)	(X)	-12
Denmark	1,051	1,311	1,574	1,473	1,092	1,535	1,678	1,661	1,667	1,664	-484	-367	-87	-194	-572

See footnotes at end of table.

No. 1329. U.S. Exports, Imports, and Merchandise Trade Balance, by Country: 1989 to 1993—Continued

[See headnote, page 823]

COUNTRY	EXPORTS, DOMESTIC AND FOREIGN					GENERAL IMPORTS [1]					MERCHANDISE TRADE BALANCE				
	1989	1990	1991	1992	1993	1989	1990	1991	1992	1993	1989	1990	1991	1992	1993
Djibouti	3	7	10	11	13	(Z)	(Z)	(Z)	(X)	(Z)	3	7	10	11	13
Dominica	33	31	42	34	27	8	9	5	5	6	26	22	37	29	21
Dominican Republic	1,645	1,656	1,743	2,100	2,350	1,646	1,752	2,008	2,372	2,672	-1	-96	-265	-273	-323
East Germany [4]	94	62	(X)	(X)	(X)	139	85	(X)	(X)	(X)	-45	-23	(X)	(X)	(X)
Ecuador	643	678	948	999	1,098	1,474	1,376	1,327	1,343	1,399	-832	-697	-379	-344	-301
Egypt	2,612	2,249	2,720	3,088	2,763	227	398	206	435	613	2,385	1,851	2,514	2,654	2,150
El Salvador	520	554	534	742	869	245	238	303	384	488	275	316	231	358	381
Equatorial Guinea	(Z)	(X)	13	11	3	(Z)	(Z)	(Z)	(Z)	4	(Z)	(X)	13	11	-1
Estonia	(X)	(X)	(X)	59	54	(X)	(X)	(X)	13	20	(X)	(X)	(X)	46	34
Ethiopia	67	157	210	250	137	70	40	14	9	22	-3	117	196	241	115
Federated States of Micronesia	27	25	46	32	25	1	6	5	13	14	26	19	41	19	11
Fiji	22	25	18	59	27	16	34	43	67	69	6	-9	-25	-8	-42
Finland	969	1,126	952	785	847	1,370	1,262	1,085	1,185	1,609	-402	-136	-133	-400	-762
France	11,579	13,665	15,346	14,593	13,267	13,014	13,153	13,333	14,797	15,244	-1,435	511	2,013	-205	-1,977
French Guiana	270	271	150	82	323	5	2	3	4	3	265	269	150	78	320
French Polynesia	70	80	80	82	102	8	20	12	11	9	62	60	68	71	93
Gabon	46	49	85	55	48	437	701	712	921	941	-390	-652	-627	-866	-893
Gambia	10	9	11	10	10	2	2	2	9	9	8	7	9	1	1
Georgia	(X)	(X)	(X)	16	47	(X)	(X)	(X)	7	21	(X)	(X)	(X)	9	26
Germany [4]	16,956	18,760	21,302	21,249	18,957	24,971	28,162	26,137	28,820	28,605	-8,015	-9,402	-4,835	-7,572	-9,648
Ghana	121	140	142	124	215	127	169	152	96	209	-7	-29	-10	27	6
Gibraltar	2	32	10	11	9	1	1	1	2	4	2	31	9	9	5
Greece	697	763	1,039	901	884	473	509	429	370	348	224	255	610	531	536
Greenland	4	6	4	3	3	8	1	4	12	13	-4	5	(Z)	-9	-10
Grenada	28	35	31	24	24	8	8	8	8	8	20	27	23	16	16
Guadeloupe	34	53	83	60	49	2	1	2	1	5	33	52	81	59	44
Guatemala	662	764	945	1,205	1,310	609	794	899	1,081	1,195	53	-31	46	124	115
Guinea	40	43	88	61	59	132	141	138	103	118	-92	-98	-50	-42	-59
Guyana	78	76	86	118	123	56	53	83	102	91	22	23	3	17	32
Haiti	472	477	395	209	221	374	343	284	107	154	97	134	111	102	67
Honduras	515	564	625	811	898	461	491	557	783	915	54	73	68	28	-17
Hong Kong	6,291	6,817	8,137	9,077	9,873	9,722	9,622	9,279	9,793	9,558	-3,431	-2,805	-1,142	-716	315
Hungary	122	156	256	295	434	328	348	367	347	401	-207	-191	-111	-52	33
Iceland	179	232	156	119	147	208	163	209	165	233	-29	69	-53	-46	-86
India	2,458	2,486	1,999	1,917	2,761	3,315	3,197	3,193	3,780	4,551	-857	-711	-1,194	-1,863	-1,790
Indonesia	1,247	1,897	1,892	2,780	2,770	3,529	3,341	3,241	4,530	5,439	-2,282	-1,444	-1,349	-1,750	-2,669
Iran	55	163	528	748	616	7	7	231	(X)	(Z)	47	156	297	747	616
Iraq	1,169	732	(Z)	1	(Z)	2,415	3,008	6	(-)	(-)	-1,246	-2,276	-6	1	(Z)
Ireland	2,483	2,540	2,681	2,862	2,731	1,566	1,756	1,948	2,262	2,520	917	784	733	600	211
Israel	2,827	3,203	3,911	4,077	4,420	1,576	3,313	3,484	3,816	4,426	1,251	-110	427	261	-6
Italy	7,215	7,992	8,570	8,721	6,456	11,933	12,751	11,764	12,314	13,223	-4,718	-4,760	-3,194	-3,593	-6,767
Ivory Coast	79	81	87	87	88	234	200	229	188	178	-155	-121	-142	-100	-90
Jamaica	1,006	943	961	939	1,113	509	569	576	599	720	497	374	385	340	393
Japan	44,494	48,580	48,125	47,813	47,950	93,553	89,684	91,511	97,414	107,268	-49,059	-41,105	-43,386	-49,601	-59,319
Jordan	380	309	219	258	363	8	11	6	18	19	372	298	213	240	344
Kazakhstan	(X)	(X)	(X)	15	68	(X)	(X)	(X)	21	39	(X)	(X)	(X)	-6	29
Kenya	133	116	91	124	117	68	58	69	73	92	65	58	22	51	25
Kiribati	16	19	27	35	31	1	(Z)	1	(Z)	2	14	19	26	35	29

COUNTRY	EXPORTS, DOMESTIC AND FOREIGN					GENERAL IMPORTS [1]					MERCHANDISE TRADE BALANCE				
	1989	1990	1991	1992	1993	1989	1990	1991	1992	1993	1989	1990	1991	1992	1993
Kuwait	853	403	1,228	1,337	1,009	973	569	36	281	1,819	-120	-166	1,192	1,055	-810
Kyrgyzstan	(X)	(X)	(X)	3	18	(X)	(X)	(X)	1	2	(X)	(X)	(X)	2	16
Latvia	(X)	(X)	(X)	55	90	(X)	(X)	(X)	11	23	(X)	(X)	(X)	44	67
Lebanon	94	98	165	311	377	30	24	27	28	27	63	74	138	283	350
Lesotho	4	3	4	3	4	19	25	27	53	56	-15	-22	-24	-50	-52
Liberia	98	44	50	31	20	106	49	9	12	3	-8	-5	41	18	17
Liechtenstein	10	12	10	12	11	(X)	15	21	36	100	(X)	-3	-11	-24	-89
Lithuania	(X)	(X)	(X)	44	57	(X)	(X)	(X)	5	16	(X)	(X)	(X)	39	41
Luxembourg	142	134	217	272	561	218	210	188	227	253	-76	-76	29	45	308
Macao	11	8	10	19	28	654	736	581	721	669	-643	-728	-571	-702	-641
Macedonia [3]	(X)	(X)	(X)	4	11	(X)	(X)	(X)	46	111	(X)	(X)	(X)	-42	-100
Madagascar	7	11	14	4	11	38	42	47	54	43	-30	-30	-33	-47	-32
Malawi	14	14	55	14	16	39	49	73	60	60	-24	-36	-18	-46	-44
Malaysia	2,870	3,425	3,900	4,363	6,065	4,744	5,272	6,102	8,294	10,568	-1,874	-1,847	-2,202	-3,931	-4,504
Mali	11	9	18	11	33	7	3	2	2	1	-12	6	16	10	32
Malta	48	45	57	58	172	60	40	65	91	104	-12	-8	-8	-33	68
Marshall Islands	33	27	38	34	36	3	3	4	8	12	30	25	35	26	24
Martinique	25	34	36	33	32	10	1	1	1	1	15	33	11	31	31
Mauritania	13	15	22	59	19	10	24	11	9	7	2	-9	11	51	12
Mauritius	12	13	15	22	18	159	159	132	136	197	-147	-146	-117	-113	-179
Mexico	24,982	28,279	33,277	40,592	41,636	27,162	30,157	31,130	35,211	39,930	-2,180	-1,878	2,147	5,381	1,706
Moldova	(X)	(X)	(X)	9	31	(X)	(X)	(X)	(Z)	(Z)	(X)	(X)	(X)	9	31
Monaco	4	10	7	6	6	14	13	14	13	16	-9	-3	-7	-6	-10
Morocco	394	495	403	496	602	98	109	154	178	185	296	386	249	318	417
Mozambique	41	50	101	150	40	20	29	23	19	9	21	21	78	130	31
Namibia	13	44	33	34	20	15	33	35	23	22	-2	11	-2	11	-2
Netherlands	11,364	13,022	13,511	13,752	12,839	4,810	4,952	4,811	5,300	5,451	6,554	8,071	8,700	8,452	7,388
Netherlands Antilles	412	543	627	478	523	383	429	647	644	397	29	114	-20	-166	126
New Caledonia	65	34	44	36	23	54	27	20	15	23	11	7	-7	21	-1
New Zealand	1,117	1,135	1,006	1,307	1,247	1,209	1,197	1,209	1,219	1,208	-91	-62	-203	88	39
Nicaragua	2	68	150	185	150	(Z)	15	60	69	126	2	52	91	117	24
Niger	9	12	10	13	16	2	46	5	6	6	7	-34	5	10	10
Nigeria	490	553	831	1,001	891	5,284	5,982	5,168	5,103	5,301	-4,794	-5,429	-4,337	-4,102	-4,410
Norway	1,037	1,281	1,489	1,279	1,212	1,991	1,830	1,624	1,969	1,938	-955	-549	-135	-690	-726
Oman	170	163	202	257	252	117	292	115	186	277	53	-129	87	71	-25
Pakistan	1,134	1,143	950	881	810	523	610	663	865	898	612	533	288	16	-88
Panama	724	869	978	1,103	1,191	268	234	269	254	281	455	635	709	850	910
Papua New Guinea	121	54	96	72	50	29	22	34	64	98	92	32	62	8	-48
Paraguay	168	307	374	415	521	45	51	43	35	50	123	256	331	380	471
Peru	695	772	840	1,005	1,069	814	802	776	739	754	-119	-30	64	267	315
Philippines	2,202	2,471	2,265	2,759	3,529	3,068	3,384	3,471	4,355	4,896	-866	-913	-1,206	-1,597	-1,367
Poland	414	406	459	641	917	387	408	357	375	454	26	-2	102	266	463
Portugal	925	922	792	1,024	735	800	832	695	664	790	125	91	97	360	-55
Qatar	100	115	147	189	166	50	53	30	70	65	50	62	117	119	101
Romania	155	369	209	248	324	354	231	69	87	69	-199	138	140	161	255

See footnotes at end of table.

No. 1329. U.S. Exports, Imports, and Merchandise Trade Balance, by Country: 1989 to 1993—Continued

[See headnote, page 823]

COUNTRY	EXPORTS, DOMESTIC AND FOREIGN					GENERAL IMPORTS[1]					MERCHANDISE TRADE BALANCE				
	1989	1990	1991	1992	1993	1989	1990	1991	1992	1993	1989	1990	1991	1992	1993
Russia	(X)	(X)	(X)	2,112	2,967	(X)	(X)	(X)	481	1,744	(X)	(X)	(X)	1,631	1,223
Saudi Arabia	3,574	4,049	6,557	7,167	6,666	7,157	10,021	10,900	10,371	7,710	-3,583	-5,971	-4,343	-3,204	-1,044
Senegal	69	52	76	80	69	41	6	10	10	8	27	46	66	70	61
Sierra Leone	25	28	25	28	21	53	46	48	61	47	-28	-19	-39	-33	-26
Singapore	7,345	8,023	8,804	9,626	11,676	9,003	9,800	9,957	11,313	12,796	-1,658	-1,778	-1,153	-1,687	-1,120
Slovakia	(X)	(X)	(X)	34	34	(X)	(X)	(X)	2	65	(X)	(X)	(X)	(X)	-31
Somalia	21	12	7	21	31	2	3	3	(Z)	(Z)	21	12	4	18	31
South Africa	1,659	1,732	2,113	2,434	2,197	1,531	1,698	1,728	1,727	1,847	128	34	385	707	350
South Korea	13,459	14,404	15,505	14,639	14,776	19,737	18,485	17,019	16,682	17,123	-6,278	-4,081	-1,514	-2,043	-2,347
Spain	4,796	5,213	5,474	5,537	4,181	3,317	3,311	2,848	3,002	2,813	1,479	1,901	2,626	2,535	1,368
Sri Lanka	143	137	121	178	203	449	538	604	789	1,002	-306	-401	-483	-612	-799
Sudan	81	42	92	53	53	20	16	16	16	12	61	26	82	42	41
Suriname	140	156	134	142	118	74	50	52	46	58	66	106	96	96	60
Sweden	3,139	3,405	3,287	2,844	2,354	4,892	4,937	4,525	4,716	4,532	-1,753	-1,533	-1,238	-1,872	-2,179
Switzerland	4,911	4,943	5,557	4,540	6,804	4,714	5,587	5,576	5,645	5,979	197	-645	-19	-1,105	825
Syria	91	150	209	165	98	98	52	25	42	130	-7	98	184	123	56
Tajikistan	(X)	(X)	(X)	9	12	(X)	(X)	(X)	11	18	(X)	(X)	(X)	7	-6
Tanzania	29	48	35	34	33	53	16	15	11	11	-24	33	20	23	22
Thailand	2,288	2,995	3,753	3,989	3,769	4,380	5,289	6,122	7,529	8,542	-2,091	-2,293	-2,369	-3,540	-4,774
Togo	28	31	24	20	13	3	4	2	6	3	25	27	22	13	10
Trinidad and Tobago	563	428	468	447	529	768	1,020	866	848	803	-205	-592	-398	-401	-274
Tunisia	160	177	172	233	232	55	40	25	48	41	105	137	147	184	191
Turkey	2,003	2,243	2,468	2,735	3,434	1,372	1,183	1,006	1,110	1,196	632	1,061	1,462	1,625	2,238
Turkmenistan	(X)	(X)	(X)	35	46	(X)	(X)	(X)	1	4	(X)	(X)	(X)	34	44
Turks and Caicos Islands	46	39	40	38	22	3	(X)	(X)	(X)	2	43	36	36	32	18
Uganda	23	26	13	15	21	41	15	18	6	10	-17	11	-5	3	11
Ukraine	(X)	(X)	(X)	307	311	(X)	(X)	(X)	89	172	(X)	(X)	(X)	218	139
United Arab Emirates	1,240	1,004	1,455	1,553	1,811	684	889	713	812	727	556	114	742	741	1,084
United Kingdom	20,837	23,490	22,046	22,800	26,376	18,319	20,188	18,413	20,093	21,736	2,518	3,302	3,633	2,707	4,640
Uruguay	134	144	216	231	253	219	206	237	266	266	-85	-62	-21	-35	-13
U.S.S.R. (former)	4,284	3,087	3,579	1,036	(X)	709	1,059	802	187	(X)	3,574	2,028	2,777	849	(X)
Uzbekistan	(X)	(X)	(X)	51	73	(X)	(X)	(X)	(Z)	7	(X)	(X)	(X)	51	66
Venezuela	3,025	3,108	4,656	5,444	4,599	6,771	9,480	8,179	8,181	8,140	-3,746	-6,371	-3,523	-2,737	-3,541
Vietnam	11	7	4	5	10	3	1	1	(2)	1	11	7	4	5	7
Western Samoa	4	5	7	73	318	(2)	(X)	(X)	(X)	1	(2)	5	6	72	9
Yemen, Republic of[3]	80	110	192	321	(X)	260	391	152	41	98	-179	-281	40	281	220
Yugoslavia (former)[3]	499	565	371	167	(X)	799	776	674	225	(X)	-300	-211	-303	-58	(X)
Yugoslavia, Fed. Rep. of[4]	(X)	(X)	(X)	6	1	(X)	(X)	(X)	39	(2)	(X)	(X)	(X)	-33	1
Zaire	122	138	62	33	35	330	325	294	250	238	-208	-187	-232	-218	-203
Zambia	50	80	24	68	42	24	29	42	70	41	26	52	-18	-2	1
Zimbabwe	121	135	53	144	84	127	119	90	106	111	-6	16	-37	38	-27

- Represents zero. Z Less than $500,000. X Not applicable. [1] Imports are on a customs value basis. Exports are f.a.s. value. [2] Includes revisions not carried to area values; therefore, area values will not add to total. [3] Beginning June 1992 trade data were reported for the following countries which were formerly part of Yugoslavia — Croatia, Slovenia, Bosnia-Hercegovina, and Macedonia. The Federal Republic of Yugoslavia, which now includes only Serbia and Montenegro, will continue to be shown as "Yugoslavia (former)." "Yugoslavia (former)" reflects data for the former country and includes data for the period of January through May 1992. [4] Effective October 3, 1990, East Germany ceased to exist as a sovereign state and became a part of West Germany. Accordingly, trade statistics for East Germany reflect trade for January through September 1990. Trade statistics for 1990 for former West Germany reflect this unification beginning with October 1990. Data for Germany reflect the consolidation of the two countries for 1991.

Source: U.S. Bureau of the Census, U.S. Merchandise Trade, series FT 900, monthly.

No. 1330. U.S. Exports and General Imports, by Selected Commodity Groups: 1990 to 1993

[In millions of dollars. N.e.s.=Not elsewhere specified]

COMMODITY GROUP	EXPORTS [1]				GENERAL IMPORTS [2]			
	1990	1991	1992	1993	1990	1991	1992	1993
Total	393,592	421,730	448,164	464,767	495,311	487,129	532,665	580,511
Agricultural commodities	38,723	38,510	42,238	41,821	22,343	22,140	23,375	23,646
Animal feeds	2,868	3,192	3,550	3,478	284	312	337	367
Bulbs	109	113	112	107	162	178	201	217
Cereal flour	686	813	924	1,072	569	641	724	802
Cocoa	38	23	31	39	783	823	774	739
Coffee	12	10	18	32	1,766	1,738	1,563	1,382
Corn	6,195	5,146	4,966	4,463	23	39	69	61
Cotton, raw and linters	2,799	2,514	2,015	1,541	20	16	11	12
Dairy products; eggs	372	455	711	775	501	452	506	544
Furskins, raw	144	107	95	97	78	57	61	59
Grains, unmilled	811	701	894	681	110	112	122	157
Hides and skins	1,612	1,276	1,253	1,189	94	110	124	120
Live animals	514	688	609	519	1,185	1,172	1,437	1,539
Meat and preparations	3,189	3,630	4,208	4,359	2,958	2,908	2,712	2,789
Oils/fats, animal	425	447	497	475	21	29	18	21
Oils/fats, vegetable	665	596	725	738	716	735	955	862
Plants	103	99	135	112	99	105	102	91
Rice	798	754	726	770	72	80	92	106
Seeds	246	274	302	298	119	132	153	154
Soybeans	3,597	3,995	4,463	4,627	15	27	16	22
Sugar	8	12	6	2	848	713	662	606
Tobacco, unmanufactured	1,445	1,430	1,649	1,306	680	989	951	944
Vegetables and fruit	5,015	5,342	5,736	6,010	5,795	5,391	5,698	5,666
Wheat	3,887	3,350	4,503	4,668	80	66	191	213
Other agricultural	3,184	3,546	4,112	4,466	5,365	5,313	5,898	6,173
Manufactured goods	298,236	325,978	347,494	364,346	388,820	392,433	434,349	480,016
ADP equipment, office machinery	24,735	25,979	27,000	27,167	26,862	30,019	36,377	43,182
Airplanes	19,641	24,335	26,286	21,297	2,733	3,347	3,860	3,735
Airplane parts	9,815	10,284	9,366	9,494	3,556	4,046	3,358	2,607
Aluminum	2,857	3,128	2,667	2,312	2,843	2,409	2,540	3,273
Artwork/antiques	2,282	1,239	1,076	952	2,340	1,979	2,087	2,673
Basketware, etc	1,097	1,290	1,522	1,645	1,837	1,911	2,189	2,391
Chemicals, cosmetics	1,964	2,361	2,632	3,043	1,323	1,415	1,711	1,809
Chemicals, dyeing	1,591	1,649	1,871	2,011	1,287	1,416	1,623	1,700
Chemicals, fertilizers	2,578	2,977	2,371	1,799	921	918	952	1,135
Chemicals, inorganic	3,823	4,083	4,123	3,813	3,204	3,297	3,305	3,285
Chemicals, medicinal	4,103	4,609	5,357	5,747	2,491	3,047	3,810	4,133
Chemicals, organic	10,427	10,898	10,993	11,090	7,427	8,133	9,406	9,316
Chemicals, plastics	9,074	10,316	10,258	10,742	3,744	3,784	4,292	4,847
Chemicals, n.e.s.	5,490	6,019	6,265	6,821	2,022	2,122	2,622	2,941
Clothing	2,472	3,215	4,092	4,808	25,622	26,202	31,227	33,787
Copper	1,213	1,328	1,172	1,201	1,774	1,573	1,642	1,736
Electrical machinery	28,406	30,050	32,172	36,639	33,564	35,067	39,710	46,752
Footwear	477	543	603	604	9,564	9,554	10,163	11,176
Furniture and parts	1,605	2,120	2,553	2,771	5,006	4,936	5,503	6,249
Gem diamonds	320	209	369	153	3,974	4,002	4,148	5,099
General industrial machinery	15,828	17,153	18,480	19,519	14,461	14,396	15,520	17,084
Glass	1,087	1,145	1,213	1,321	760	770	850	1,004
Glassware	401	449	496	501	939	937	1,015	1,032
Gold, nonmonetary	2,970	3,279	4,109	9,034	1,081	1,922	1,899	2,015
Iron and steel mill products	3,270	4,211	3,606	3,329	8,805	8,301	8,328	9,040
Lighting, plumbing	680	877	977	1,096	1,233	1,246	1,547	1,764
Metal manufactures, n.e.s.	4,783	5,189	5,513	5,959	6,441	6,372	6,727	7,641
Metalworking machinery	2,759	2,709	3,034	3,262	3,677	3,605	3,187	3,675
Motorcycles, bicycles	935	1,308	1,439	1,438	1,438	1,636	1,913	2,159
Nickel	228	219	196	199	1,102	1,061	797	686
Optical goods	639	713	766	796	1,470	1,484	1,645	1,683
Paper and paperboard	5,004	5,965	6,348	6,472	8,491	8,021	7,998	8,639
Photographic equipment	2,773	2,926	2,950	2,934	3,341	3,641	3,844	4,257
Plastic articles, n.e.s.	1,945	2,240	2,777	2,988	3,138	3,114	3,572	3,935
Platinum	224	311	292	341	1,856	1,659	1,429	1,257
Pottery	71	87	103	110	1,222	1,242	1,404	1,434
Power generating machinery	15,796	16,960	17,995	19,132	14,552	14,195	15,888	17,163
Printed materials	3,164	3,589	3,803	3,982	1,669	1,702	1,875	2,027
Records/magnetic media	3,877	4,267	4,846	5,309	2,531	2,788	3,106	3,444
Rubber articles, n.e.s.	505	579	622	674	650	705	878	1,014
Rubber tires and tubes	1,148	1,274	1,409	1,465	2,591	2,309	2,512	2,736

See footnotes at end of table.

No. 1330. U.S. Exports and General Imports, by Selected SITC Commodity Groups: 1990 to 1993—Continued

[In millions of dollars]

COMMODITY GROUP	EXPORTS [1]				GENERAL IMPORTS [2]			
	1990	1991	1992	1993	1990	1991	1992	1993
Manufactured goods—Continued								
Scientific instruments	12,121	13,499	14,375	15,213	6,206	6,733	7,602	8,452
Ships, boats	1,277	1,155	1,421	978	329	249	319	969
Silver and bullion	163	237	209	202	451	363	449	391
Spacecraft	598	257	270	393	(Z)	-	92	-
Specialized industrial machinery	15,277	16,686	16,689	17,635	12,990	10,864	11,814	13,546
Telecommunications equipment	9,139	9,999	11,248	13,071	22,230	23,446	25,803	27,303
Textile yarn, fabric	4,947	5,482	5,778	5,879	6,424	6,981	7,844	8,438
Toys/games/sporting goods	1,819	2,087	2,437	2,710	9,080	8,821	10,749	11,640
Travel goods	133	159	194	199	2,223	2,346	2,509	2,654
Vehicles/new cars, Canada	6,232	6,195	5,931	6,350	13,348	13,518	13,890	17,655
Vehicles/new cars, Japan	531	496	694	982	19,220	20,422	20,801	21,593
Vehicles/new cars, Other	2,465	3,070	5,095	4,976	12,542	10,813	11,561	12,055
Vehicles/trucks	3,084	3,879	3,706	4,162	8,580	8,293	9,772	10,109
Vehicles/chassis/bodies	207	241	310	372	518	352	338	407
Vehicles/parts	14,463	14,371	16,753	18,958	15,230	14,067	15,838	17,652
Watches/clocks/parts	209	225	208	235	2,247	2,285	2,320	2,549
Wood manufactures	1,222	1,251	1,389	1,476	2,034	1,907	2,410	2,869
Zinc	47	40	38	40	1,017	652	855	735
Other manufactured goods	22,246	24,570	27,031	26,542	30,605	30,042	32,924	35,485
Mineral fuel	**12,233**	**12,081**	**11,254**	**9,736**	**64,661**	**54,056**	**55,256**	**55,582**
Coal	4,636	4,776	4,427	3,198	288	310	419	513
Crude oil	137	33	32	20	43,785	36,902	38,553	38,438
Petroleum preparations	4,072	4,399	4,011	3,922	16,094	12,312	11,277	10,796
Liquified propane/butane	161	253	257	229	808	859	707	952
Natural gas	203	308	353	244	2,328	2,482	3,030	3,391
Electricity	493	44	63	61	463	487	590	662
Other mineral fuels	2,531	2,268	2,111	2,062	895	704	680	831
Selected commodities:								
Fish and preparations	2,801	3,063	3,383	2,985	5,192	5,638	5,657	5,820
Cork, wood, lumber	5,236	5,114	5,314	5,768	3,123	3,057	3,970	5,632
Pulp and waste paper	4,043	3,600	3,859	2,986	2,867	2,163	2,129	1,887
Metal ores; scrap	4,949	4,039	3,470	3,257	3,990	3,561	3,340	3,026
Crude fertilizers	1,266	1,385	1,388	1,345	1,129	982	894	938
Cigarettes	4,757	4,238	4,193	3,926	53	130	271	496
Alcoholic bev. distilled	254	279	344	344	1,725	1,595	1,827	1,737
All other	2,576	2,822	2,801	2,769	1,408	1,375	1,597	1,687
Re-exports	18,517	20,621	22,427	25,563	(X)	(X)	(X)	(X)
Agricultural commodities	848	857	893	888	(X)	(X)	(X)	(X)
Manufactured goods	17,119	19,153	20,977	24,178	(X)	(X)	(X)	(X)
Mineral fuels	151	206	76	80	(X)	(X)	(X)	(X)
Other, re-exports	399	405	481	417	(X)	(X)	(X)	(X)
Timing adjustment	(X)	(X)	(X)	-78	(X)	(X)	(X)	75

- Represents zero.   Z less than $500,000.   X Not applicable.   [1] F.A.S. basis.   [2] Customs value basis.
Source: U.S. Bureau of the Census, *U.S. Merchandise Trade*, series FT 900, Final Reports, and December 1993 issue.

No. 1331. Imports for Consumption—Values and Duties: 1970 to 1993

[Imports are on customs value basis. Beginning 1970, includes silver ores and bullion, and beginning 1980, includes trade of Virgin Islands with foreign countries. For basis of dollar values and for area coverage, see text, section 29. See also *Historical Statistics, Colonial Times to 1970*, series U 207-212]

YEAR	VALUES				Duties calculated [1] (mil. dol.)	RATIO OF DUTIES TO VALUES		Duties per capita [2] (dollar)
	Total (mil. dol.)	Free (mil. dol.)	Dutiable (mil. dol.)	Percent free		Total imports (percent)	Dutiable imports (percent)	
1970	39,756	13,870	25,886	35	2,584	6.5	10.0	12.60
1975	96,516	31,030	65,486	32	3,780	3.9	5.8	17.50
1980	[3]244,007	106,992	132,951	45	7,535	3.1	5.7	33.09
1981	259,012	76,338	182,674	29	8,893	3.4	4.9	38.67
1982	242,340	75,856	166,484	31	8,688	3.6	5.2	37.40
1983	256,679	83,397	173,283	32	9,430	3.7	5.4	40.21
1984	322,989	102,977	220,012	32	12,042	3.7	5.5	50.90
1985	343,553	106,035	237,518	31	13,067	3.8	5.5	54.73
1986	368,657	121,742	246,915	33	13,312	3.6	5.4	55.10
1987	402,066	132,152	269,914	33	13,923	3.5	5.2	57.08
1988	437,140	151,693	285,447	35	15,054	3.4	5.3	61.12
1989	468,012	156,365	311,647	33	16,096	3.4	5.2	64.70
1990	490,554	161,108	329,446	33	16,339	3.3	5.0	65.38
1991	483,028	167,641	315,386	35	16,197	3.4	5.1	64.10
1992	525,091	194,583	330,508	37	17,164	3.3	5.2	67.12
1993	574,863	236,007	338,856	41	18,334	3.2	5.4	70.99

[1] Customs duties (including import excise taxes) calculated on the basis of reports of quantity and value of imports of merchandise entered directly for consumption or withdrawn from bonded customs warehouses.   [2] Based on estimated population including Armed Forces abroad as of July 1.   [3] Total includes revisions not carried to free and dutiable values.
Source: U.S. Bureau of the Census, 1970-1988, *Highlights of U.S. Export and Import Trade*, series FT 990, monthly; beginning 1989, *U.S. Merchandise Trade: Selected Highlights*, series FT 920, and unpublished data.

No. 1332. Domestic Exports and Imports for Consumption of Merchandise, by Selected SIC-Based Product Category: 1985 to 1993

[In millions of dollars. Includes nonmonetary gold]

SIC [1] code	SIC-BASED PRODUCT CATEGORY	1985	1988	1989	1990	1991	1992	1993
(X)	**Domestic exports, total [2]**	**212,961**	**310,346**	**349,433**	**374,537**	**400,842**	**425,377**	**439,282**
(X)	Agricultural, forestry and fishery products	20,074	24,464	27,198	26,225	25,052	26,785	25,324
01	Agricultural products	19,199	21,508	24,142	22,597	21,075	22,633	21,615
02	Livestock and livestock products	735	1,014	821	829	970	871	836
08	Forestry products	122	266	270	281	306	324	276
09	Fish, fresh or chilled; and other marine products [3]	18	1,676	1,965	2,518	2,701	2,959	2,596
(X)	Mineral commodities	6,394	6,559	7,030	7,335	7,442	7,210	5,584
10	Metallic ores and concentrates	686	883	1,247	1,137	1,014	1,084	799
11,12	Bituminous, lignite and anthracite coal	4,465	4,014	4,287	4,513	4,623	4,241	3,090
13	Crude petroleum and natural gas	476	485	490	638	675	737	588
14	Nonmetallic minerals, fuels	767	1,177	1,006	1,047	1,130	1,148	1,107
(X)	Manufactured commodities	175,752	261,755	290,536	330,403	359,635	383,082	400,721
20	Food and kindred products	10,055	14,788	15,205	16,160	17,492	19,761	20,509
21	Tobacco manufactures	1,268	2,901	3,632	5,040	4,574	4,509	4,253
22	Textile mill products	1,462	2,415	2,794	3,635	4,108	4,473	4,687
23	Apparel and related products	1,019	1,824	2,349	2,848	3,679	4,599	5,433
24	Lumber and related products	2,668	5,326	6,050	6,523	6,477	6,802	7,361
25	Furniture and fixtures	483	841	1,011	1,589	2,086	2,518	2,818
26	Paper and allied products	3,886	7,197	8,126	8,631	9,214	9,969	9,457
27	Printing and publishing	1,250	1,996	2,598	3,150	3,590	3,808	4,057
28	Chemicals and allied products	21,797	31,722	35,825	37,806	41,483	41,953	42,742
29	Petroleum and coal products	5,433	3,926	5,019	6,794	7,026	6,403	6,163
30	Rubber and misc. plastics products	2,765	4,412	5,010	6,398	7,049	7,872	8,554
31	Leather and leather products	478	953	1,131	1,388	1,413	1,541	1,536
32	Stone, clay, and glass products	1,792	2,272	2,638	3,295	3,533	3,855	3,844
33	Primary metal products	4,747	12,362	12,110	13,116	15,243	15,105	18,669
34	Fabricated metal products	5,765	8,318	9,117	11,138	11,962	13,265	13,497
35	Machinery, except electrical	37,478	51,803	55,524	61,229	65,300	68,554	72,279
36	Electric and electronic machinery	18,908	27,033	32,718	39,807	42,330	45,992	52,947
37	Transportation equipment	38,024	49,768	56,875	68,113	76,172	82,862	80,196
38	Instruments and related products	8,623	17,160	17,327	19,524	21,699	22,815	24,699
39	Misc. manufactured commodities	1,773	4,443	4,553	4,296	4,621	5,446	5,288
(X)	**Imports for consumption, total [2]**	**343,553**	**437,140**	**468,012**	**490,554**	**483,028**	**525,091**	**574,863**
(X)	Agricultural, forestry and fishery products	12,805	12,759	13,251	12,750	13,148	14,216	15,866
01	Agricultural products	7,483	5,786	6,109	5,925	6,107	6,716	7,839
02	Livestock and livestock products	933	1,235	1,290	1,453	1,501	1,873	2,161
08	Forestry products	830	1,326	1,235	1,015	978	1,088	1,068
09	Fish, fresh or chilled; and other marine products [3]	3,559	4,412	4,617	4,357	4,562	4,540	4,798
(X)	Mineral commodities	39,011	31,540	41,264	51,391	44,581	44,823	45,965
10	Metallic ores and concentrates	1,265	1,126	1,425	1,500	1,244	1,167	1,108
11,12	Bituminous, lignite and anthracite coal	70	65	97	93	112	127	218
13	Crude petroleum and natural gas	35,872	29,573	38,842	48,917	42,415	42,796	43,871
14	Nonmetallic minerals, exc. fuels	1,804	776	900	881	810	734	767
(X)	Manufactured commodities	280,089	379,172	396,903	407,043	406,550	445,127	490,289
20	Food and kindred products	12,521	15,043	15,122	16,564	16,298	17,445	16,090
21	Tobacco manufactures	78	86	88	94	199	285	467
22	Textile mill products	3,616	5,506	7,294	6,807	7,132	7,808	6,161
23	Apparel and related products	15,710	20,890	22,841	24,644	25,497	30,533	35,475
24	Lumber and related products	5,105	5,720	5,848	5,446	5,229	6,700	8,901
25	Furniture and fixtures	3,220	4,796	5,148	5,235	5,130	5,601	6,242
26	Paper and allied products	7,493	11,001	11,880	11,669	10,431	10,382	10,891
27	Printing and publishing	1,200	1,776	1,807	1,849	1,878	2,046	2,211
28	Chemicals and allied products	12,790	18,602	20,118	21,611	22,999	25,849	27,259
29	Petroleum and coal products	18,282	11,027	11,979	14,472	11,097	10,410	9,906
30	Rubber and misc. plastics products	4,721	9,590	9,488	9,731	9,855	11,287	13,053
31	Leather and leather products	7,724	9,578	9,837	10,944	10,714	11,342	11,692
32	Stone, clay, and glass products	4,296	5,921	5,775	5,845	5,558	5,951	6,431
33	Primary metal products	20,439	25,075	25,563	23,232	22,262	22,891	22,772
34	Fabricated metal products	7,754	11,215	11,568	11,608	11,396	12,436	12,941
35	Machinery, except electrical	31,310	50,301	54,051	55,021	55,578	62,274	73,370
36	Electric and electronic machinery	37,951	52,539	55,316	55,736	58,610	65,596	76,869
37	Transportation equipment	65,944	86,717	87,972	89,599	88,004	92,930	102,259
38	Instruments and related products	8,805	15,430	15,364	16,846	18,668	20,338	22,080
39	Misc. manufactured commodities	11,130	18,359	19,844	20,090	20,015	23,025	25,219

X Not applicable.   [1] Standard Industrial Classification.   [2] Includes scrap and waste, used or secondhand merchandise, and manufactured commodities not identified by kind.   [3] Includes frozen and packaged fish.

Source: U.S. Bureau of the Census, 1985 and 1988, *Highlights of U.S. Export and Import Trade*, series FT 990; beginning 1989, *U.S. Merchandise Trade*, series FT 900.

Figure 29.1
Selected Outlying Areas of the United States

Outlying Areas

This section presents summary economic and social statistics for Puerto Rico, Virgin Islands, Guam, American Samoa, and the Northern Mariana Islands.

Primary sources are the decennial censuses of population and housing, and the censuses of agriculture, business, manufactures, and construction (taken every 5 years) conducted by the Bureau of the Census; the annual *Vital Statistics of the United States,* issued by the National Center for Health Statistics; and the annual *Income and Product* of the Puerto Rico Planning Board, San Juan.

Jurisdiction.—The United States gained jurisdiction over these areas as follows:

The islands of *Puerto Rico* and *Guam,* surrendered by Spain to the United States in October 1898, were ceded to the United States by the Treaty of Paris, ratified in 1899. Puerto Rico became a Commonwealth on July 25, 1952, thereby achieving a high degree of local autonomy under its own constitution. The *Virgin Islands,* comprising 50 islands and cays, was purchased by the United States from Denmark in 1917. *American Samoa,* a group of seven islands, was acquired by the United States in accordance with a convention among the United States, Great Britain, and Germany, ratified in 1900 (Swains Island was annexed in 1925).

By an agreement approved by the Security Council and the United States, the Northern Mariana Islands, previously under Japanese mandate, was administered by the United States between 1947 and 1986 under the United Nations trusteeship system. The Northern Mariana Islands became a Commonwealth in 1986. Palau was also part of the trusteeship. Because Palau remained under U.S. jurisdiction in 1990, it was included as part of the 1990 decennial census.

For a brief summary of U.S. territorial development, see table 352.

Censuses.—Because characteristics of the outlying areas differ, the presentation of census data for them is not uniform.

In Brief

Persons per household, 1990:
Puerto Rico	3.3
Virgin Islands	3.1
Guam	4.0
American Samoa	7.0
Northern Mariana Islands	4.6

The 1960 Census of Population covered all of the places listed above except the Northern Mariana Islands (their census was conducted in April 1958 by the Office of the High Commissioner), while the 1960 Census of Housing also excluded American Samoa. The 1970, 1980 and 1990 Censuses of Population and Housing covered all five areas. The 1959, 1969, and 1978 Censuses of Agriculture covered Puerto Rico, American Samoa, Guam, and the Virgin Islands; the 1964, 1974, and 1982 censuses covered the same areas except American Samoa; and the 1969, 1978, and 1987 censuses included the Northern Mariana Islands. Beginning in 1967, Congress authorized the economic censuses, to be taken at 5-year intervals, for years ending in "2" and "7." Prior economic censuses were conducted in Puerto Rico for 1949, 1954, 1958, and 1963 and in Guam and the Virgin Islands for 1958 and 1963. In 1967, the census of construction industries was added for the first time in Puerto Rico; in 1972, Virgin Islands and Guam were covered. For 1982 and 1987, the economic censuses covered the Northern Mariana Islands.

Information in other sections.—In addition to the statistics presented in this section, other data are included as integral parts of many tables showing distribution by States in various sections of the *Abstract.* See "Outlying areas of the United States" in the index. For definition and explanation of terms used, see section 1, Population; section 4, Education; section 23, Agriculture; section 25, Construction and Housing; section 26, Manufactures; and section 27, Domestic Trade and Services.

No. 1333. Estimated Resident Population With Projections: 1950 to 2020

[In thousands. Population data generally are de facto figures for the present territory. Population estimates were derived from information available as of early 1994. See text, section 30, for general comments regarding the data. For details of methodology, coverage, and reliability, see source]

AREA	1950	1960	1970	1980	1990	1994	2000, proj.	2010, proj.	2020, proj.
Puerto Rico	2,218	2,358	2,716	3,206	3,604	3,802	3,838	4,002	4,220
American Samoa	19	20	27	32	47	55	69	85	86
Guam	60	67	86	107	134	150	171	202	230
Virgin Islands	27	33	63	98	101	98	99	107	111
Northern Mariana Islands	6	9	12	17	44	50	57	71	86

Source: U.S. Bureau of the Census, *World Population Profile: 1994*, WP/94.

No. 1334. Population and Median Age, by Sex: 1960 to 1990

[As of **April 1**. For definition of median, see Guide to Tabular Presentation]

AREA AND SEX	POPULATION (1,000)				MEDIAN AGE (years)			
	1960	1970	1980	1990	1960	1970	1980	1990
Puerto Rico	2,349.5	2,712.0	3,196.5	3,522.0	18.5	21.6	24.6	28.4
Male	1,162.8	1,329.9	1,556.7	1,706.0	18.0	20.9	23.7	27.2
Female	1,186.8	1,382.2	1,639.8	1,816.0	18.9	22.2	25.5	29.6
American Samoa	20.1	27.2	32.3	46.8	15.2	16.1	18.8	20.9
Male	10.2	13.7	16.4	24.0	14.6	16.1	18.4	20.6
Female	9.9	13.6	15.9	22.8	15.8	16.1	19.2	21.2
Guam	67.0	85.0	106.0	133.2	20.8	20.4	22.3	25.0
Male	39.2	47.3	55.3	70.9	22.9	21.6	22.4	25.2
Female	27.8	37.7	50.7	62.2	16.5	18.2	22.1	24.9
Virgin Islands	32.1	62.5	96.6	101.8	20.7	23.0	22.5	28.2
Male	15.9	31.3	46.2	49.2	20.3	23.1	21.1	27.1
Female	16.2	31.3	50.4	52.6	21.2	23.0	23.6	29.2
Northern Mariana Islands	(NA)	9.6	16.8	43.3	(NA)	15.2	19.7	27.4
Male	(NA)	4.9	8.8	22.8	(NA)	15.4	20.9	29.9
Female	(NA)	4.7	8.0	20.5	(NA)	15.0	18.5	24.9

NA Not available.

Source: U.S. Bureau of the Census, *Census of Population: 1970*, vol. I, *Characteristics of the Population*, parts 53-58; *1980*, vol. 1, chapter B, *Characteristics of the Population*, parts 53-57a; and *1990*, CPH-1, parts 53A and 55; CPH-6, parts G (Guam), AS (American Samoa), and CNMI (Commonwealth of the Northern Mariana Islands); and Summary Tape File 1A, (Puerto Rico) and Summary Tape File 2 (Virgin Islands).

No. 1335. Population, by Place of Birth and Year of Immigration: 1990

[As of **April 1**]

ITEM	United States	Puerto Rico	Virgin Islands	Guam	American Samoa	Northern Mariana Islands
All persons	**248,709,873**	**3,522,037**	**101,809**	**133,152**	**46,773**	**43,345**
Born in this area	225,695,826	3,200,940	49,839	63,504	25,573	16,752
Percent of total	90.7	90.9	49.0	47.7	54.7	38.6
Born in the United States	225,695,826	229,304	14,246	28,010	3,519	1,271
Born elsewhere [1]	23,014,047	91,793	37,724	41,638	17,681	25,322
Born outside area	23,014,047	321,097	51,970	69,648	21,200	26,593
Year of entry:						
1985 to 1990	5,562,288	104,900	13,765	43,575	9,302	21,984
1980 to 1984	4,222,420	52,487	7,951	8,768	5,025	2,491
1970 to 1979	5,601,860	90,934	12,279	10,994	4,423	1,600
1960 to 1969	3,410,665	58,278	13,072	4,143	1,758	274
Before 1960	4,216,814	14,498	4,903	2,168	692	244

[1] Includes persons born in other outlying areas under United States jurisdiction and persons born abroad with at least one parent who is a United States citizen, as well as foreign born persons.

Source: U.S. Bureau of the Census, *1990 Census of Population and Housing*, Summary Tape File, parts 3C, (United States), 3A and unpublished data, (Puerto Rico), and 3, (Virgin Islands); CPH-L-98, *The Foreign Born Population in the United States, 1990*; *1990 Census of Population and Housing*, CPH-6, parts G (Guam), AS (American Samoa), and CNMI (Commonwealth of the Northern Mariana Islands).

No. 1336. Land Area and Population Characteristics, by Area: 1990

[As of **April 1**. See also table 352 for gross area (land and water). For definition of median, see Guide to Tabular Presentation]

ITEM	United States	Puerto Rico	Virgin Islands	Guam	American Samoa	Northern Mariana Islands
Land area (sq. miles)	3,536,338	3,427	134	210	77	179
Total resident population	**248,709,873**	**3,522,037**	**101,809**	**133,152**	**46,773**	**43,345**
Per square mile	70.3	1,027.9	760.9	637.1	607.4	235.6
Percent increase, 1980-90. . .	9.8	10.2	5.4	25.6	44.8	158.3
Urban	187,053,487	2,508,346	37,885	50,801	15,599	12,151
Rural.	61,656,386	1,013,691	63,924	82,351	31,174	31,194
Male.	121,239,418	1,705,642	49,210	70,945	24,023	22,802
Female	127,470,455	1,816,395	52,599	62,207	22,750	20,543
Males per 100 females	95.1	93.9	93.6	114.0	105.6	111.0
Median age (years)	32.9	28.4	28.2	25.0	20.9	27.4
Male (years)	31.7	27.2	27.1	25.2	20.6	29.9
Female (years).	34.1	29.6	29.2	24.9	21.2	24.9
Marital status, persons						
15 years old and over	195,142,002	2,563,818	72,365	93,200	28,952	33,030
Never married.	52,559,853	711,470	27,539	30,759	11,412	13,810
Married [1]	111,498,578	1,499,449	35,199	54,717	15,958	17,869
Widowed or divorced	31,083,571	352,899	9,627	7,724	1,582	1,351
Households and families:						
Households	91,947,410	1,054,924	32,020	31,373	6,607	6,873
Persons in households	242,012,129	3,487,667	100,488	124,596	46,267	31,856
Persons per household	2.63	3.31	3.14	3.97	7.00	4.63
Families.	64,517,947	886,339	23,012	27,313	6,301	5,312
Husband-wife families	50,708,322	634,872	13,197	21,342	5,153	3,947
Children ever born per						
1,000 females 15 to 44 years . .	1,223	1,512	1,662	1,523	1,757	1,226

[1] For Puerto Rico, includes consensually married couples and for all areas, includes separated couples.

Source: U.S. Bureau of the Census, *1990 Census of Population*, CP-1 parts 1, (United States), 53 (Puerto Rico), 55 (Virgin Islands); *1990 Census of Population and Housing*, CPH-1, parts 53A and 55; CPH-6, parts G (Guam), AS (American Samoa), and CNMI (Commonwealth of the Northern Mariana Islands); and Summary Tape File, parts 3C, (United States), 3A (Puerto Rico), and 3 (Virgin Islands).

No. 1337. Selected Social and Economic Characteristics, by Area: 1990

[As of **April 1**]

CHARACTERISTIC	United States	Puerto Rico	Virgin Islands	Guam	American Samoa	Northern Mariana Islands
EDUCATIONAL ATTAINMENT						
Persons 25 years and over	158,868,436	1,952,297	55,639	66,700	19,570	24,633
Less than 9th grade	16,502,211	691,835	12,908	9,238	3,664	4,285
9th to 12th grade, no diploma.	22,841,507	290,173	11,278	8,602	5,239	4,016
High school graduate	47,642,763	410,559	14,021	22,220	6,253	8,659
Some college or associate degree	39,571,702	281,248	9,011	14,984	3,062	3,818
Bachelor's degree or higher	32,310,253	278,482	8,421	11,656	1,352	3,855
EMPLOYMENT STATUS						
Total persons, 16 years old						
and over.	191,829,271	2,497,078	70,323	90,990	27,991	32,522
In labor force.	125,182,378	1,180,162	47,553	66,138	14,198	26,589
Percent of total	65.3	47.3	67.6	72.7	50.7	81.8
Armed forces	1,708,928	5,486	110	11,952	11	8
Civilian labor force.	123,473,450	1,174,676	47,443	54,186	14,187	26,581
Employed	115,681,202	934,736	44,267	52,144	13,461	25,965
Unemployed	7,792,248	239,940	3,176	2,042	726	616
Percent of civilian labor force.	6.3	20.4	6.7	3.8	5.1	2.3
Not in labor force	66,646,893	1,316,916	22,770	24,852	13,793	5,933
FAMILY INCOME IN 1989						
Families, census year.	65,049,428	889,998	23,012	27,313	6,301	5,312
Percent distribution by income class	100.0	100.0	100.0	100.0	100.0	100.0
Less than $5,000	4.0	25.1	8.8	4.0	11.0	8.2
$5,000 to $9,999.	5.6	24.9	9.5	4.7	19.2	13.9
$10,000 to $14,999	7.2	16.5	12.8	8.3	17.0	13.1
$15,000 to $24,999	16.4	17.5	20.6	21.1	23.6	21.6
$25,000 or more	66.9	16.0	48.3	61.9	29.1	43.2
Median income (dollars)	35,225	9,988	24,036	31,178	15,979	21,275
RESIDENCE IN 1985						
Persons 5 years and over.	230,445,777	3,219,765	92,579	118,055	39,821	39,206
Same house	122,796,970	2,190,479	56,098	54,665	30,759	11,479
Different house in this area	102,540,097	879,691	25,003	24,763	2,763	6,870
Outside area	5,108,710	149,595	11,478	38,627	6,299	20,857
LANGUAGE SPOKEN AT HOME						
Persons 5 years and over.	230,445,777	3,219,765	92,579	118,055	39,821	39,206
Speak only English at home.	198,600,798	(NA)	70,442	44,048	1,203	1,878

NA Not available.

Source: U.S. Bureau of the Census, *1990 Census of Population and Housing*, Summary Tape File, parts 3C, (United States), 3A, and unpublished data, (Puerto Rico), and 3 (Virgin Islands); CPH-L-98, *The Foreign Born Population in the United States: 1990*; *1990 Census of Population and Housing*, CPH-6, parts G (Guam), AS (American Samoa), and CNMI (Commonwealth of the Northern Mariana Islands).

No. 1338. Vital Statistics—Specified Areas: 1960 to 1990

[Births, deaths, and infant deaths by place of residence; marriages and divorces by place of occurrence. Rates for 1960, 1970, 1980, and 1990 based on population enumerated as of **April 1;** for other years, on population estimated as of **July 1**]

AREA AND YEAR	BIRTHS		DEATHS		INFANT DEATHS		MARRIAGES		DIVORCES [3]	
	Number	Rate [1]	Number	Rate [1]	Number	Rate [2]	Number	Rate [1]	Number	Rate [1]
Puerto Rico: 1960	76,314	32.5	15,791	6.7	3,307	43.3	[4]20,212	[4]8.6	5,218	2.2
1970.............	67,628	24.8	18,080	6.7	1,930	28.6	29,905	11.0	9,688	3.6
1980.............	72,986	22.8	20,413	6.4	1,351	18.5	33,167	10.4	15,276	4.8
1985.............	63,547	19.4	23,071	7.0	944	14.9	30,355	9.2	14,686	4.5
1990.............	66,417	18.9	25,957	7.4	888	(NA)	(NA)	(NA)	(NA)	(NA)
Guam: 1965	2,523	32.8	336	4.4	82	32.5	471	6.2	53	0.7
1970.............	2,842	28.8	355	5.8	62	21.6	874	9.9	84	1.0
1980.............	2,945	27.8	393	3.7	43	14.6	(NA)	(NA)	(NA)	(NA)
1985.............	3,049	24.6	415	3.4	35	11.5	(NA)	(NA)	(NA)	(NA)
1990.............	3,839	28.8	520	3.9	31	(NA)	(NA)	(NA)	(NA)	(NA)
Virgin Islands: 1960	1,180	36.8	332	10.3	42	35.6	359	11.1	135	4.2
1970.............	2,898	46.8	469	7.9	72	24.6	1,149	18.4	270	4.3
1980.............	2,504	25.9	504	5.2	61	24.4	1,112	11.5	478	4.9
1985.............	2,375	21.4	506	4.6	42	17.7	1,448	13.1	363	3.3
1990.............	2,267	22.3	480	4.7	33	(NA)	(NA)	(NA)	(NA)	(NA)

NA Not available. [1] Per 1,000 population. [2] Per 1,000 live births. [3] Includes reported annulments. [4] Data are incomplete.

Source: U.S. National Center for Health Statistics, *Vital Statistics of the United States,* annual.

No. 1339. Public Elementary and Secondary Schools, by Areas: 1992

[For school year ending in year shown, unless otherwise indicated]

ITEM	Puerto Rico	Guam	Virgin Islands	American Samoa	ITEM	Puerto Rico	Guam	Virgin Islands	American Samoa
PUBLIC EL/SEC					Teachers.......	37,291	1,699	1,581	671
Enrollment, fall......	642,392	28,244	22,346	13,365	Other support				
Elementary					services staff.....	22,033	1,045	816	405
(kindergarten-									
grade 8)	474,976	20,710	16,675	10,050	Current expenditures [1]				
Secondary (grades					($1,000).........	1,142,863	122,170	119,950	24,946
9-12 and post					Per pupil [2] (dol.) ...	1,779	4,326	5,368	1,867
graduates)	167,416	7,534	5,671	3,315					
Staff, fall.........	67,948	3,157	3,290	1,277	HIGHER				
School district staff .	1,813	7	269	18	EDUCATION				
School staff	44,102	2,105	2,205	854	Enrollment, fall......	158,120	4,845	2,856	1,295

[1] Public elementary and secondary day schools. [2] Annual expenditures per pupil enrolled.

Source: U.S. National Center for Education Statistics, unpublished data.

No. 1340. Federal Direct Payments for Individuals: 1992 and 1993

[**In thousands of dollars.** For fiscal years ending **September 30**]

PROGRAM PAYMENTS	1992				1993			
	Puerto Rico	Guam	Virgin Islands	American Samoa	Puerto Rico	Guam	Virgin Islands	American Samoa
Total	4,086,581	127,067	105,364	16,998	4,483,643	136,608	124,703	18,249
Pell Grants	291,401	1,184	619	326	297,048	1,019	674	377
Medicare: Hospital Insurance ..	255,133	3,103	6,792	-	275,526	3,351	7,335	-
Supplemental medical								
insurance..............	260,308	2,767	4,624	-	257,239	2,734	4,569	-
Social Security:								
Disability insurance	660,884	4,558	7,574	3,019	704,821	4,678	7,996	3,385
Retirement insurance	1,246,085	23,589	37,497	5,114	1,321,392	25,784	40,483	5,283
Survivors insurance	539,050	14,425	13,259	5,093	575,940	14,525	14,058	5,382
Veterans:								
Pension and disability......	311,838	4,124	1,734	1,554	335,243	4,633	3,027	1,781
Education assistance	2,687	73	28	18	2,270	84	22	20
Federal retirement and								
disability	149,771	39,562	6,809	1,767	158,151	49,355	6,987	1,903
Food Stamps..............	[1]996,488	28,458	17,622	-	[1]1,018,582	17,316	19,328	-
Other	369,424	5,224	8,806	107	556,013	13,129	20,224	118

- Represents or rounds to zero. [1] Food stamp program in Puerto Rico was replaced by the Nutritional Assistance Grant Program. Figures shown represent grants to State and local governments, not included in totals.

Source: U.S. Bureau of the Census, *Federal Expenditures by State for Fiscal Year,* annual.

No. 1341. Puerto Rico—Summary: 1970 to 1993

ITEM	Unit	1970	1980	1985	1989	1990	1991	1992	1993
POPULATION									
Total [1]	1,000	2,722	3,184	3,378	3,497	3,528	3,549	3,579	3,621
Persons per family	Number...	4.6	4.3	3.9	3.7	3.7	3.7	3.6	3.6
EDUCATION [2]									
Enrollment, total	1,000	922.6	1,090.9	1,107.9	(NA)	(NA)	(NA)	(NA)	(NA)
Public day school	1,000	672.3	716.1	692.9	660.6	651.2	644.7	642.7	(NA)
Other public	1,000	103.9	149.5	152.0	(NA)	(NA)	(NA)	(NA)	(NA)
Private schools	1,000	89.1	95.2	107.3	137.2	145.8	134.2	(NA)	(NA)
College and university	1,000	57.3	130.1	155.7	156.9	156.1	157.5	157.1	(NA)
Expenses	Mil. dol ...	288.8	825.0	1,171.8	1,564.2	1,686.4	1,759.7	2,039.0	(NA)
As percent of GNP	Percent ...	6.2	7.5	7.8	7.8	7.8	7.7	8.6	(NA)
Public	Mil. dol ...	254.6	612.2	810.2	990.8	1,054.2	1,081.9	1,328.0	(NA)
Private	Mil. dol ...	34.2	212.8	361.6	573.4	644.2	677.8	711.0	(NA)
LABOR FORCE [3]									
Total [4]	1,000	765	907	985	1,108	1,124	1,152	1,170	1,201
Employed [5]	1,000	686	753	774	948	963	977	977	999
Agriculture [6]	1,000	68	38	39	37	36	35	34	34
Manufacturing	1,000	132	143	141	165	168	164	164	168
Trade	1,000	128	138	150	186	185	195	193	201
Government	1,000	106	184	183	219	222	217	219	216
Unemployed	1,000	79	154	211	160	161	175	193	202
Unemployment rate [7]	Rate	10	17	21	14	14	15	17	17
Compensation of employees	Mil. dol ...	2,800	7,200	9,442	12,817	13,639	14,277	15,009	15,918
Avg. compensation	Dollar	4,082	9,563	12,456	14,131	14,854	14,613	15,362	15,934
Salary and wages	Mil. dol ...	2,555	6,290	8,137	10,965	11,681	12,193	12,844	13,618
INCOME [8]									
Personal income:									
Current dollars	Mil. dol ...	3,753	11,002	14,588	19,198	21,105	21,884	22,596	24,090
Constant (1954) dollars	Mil. dol ...	2,654	3,985	4,274	5,200	5,251	5,514	5,636	5,949
Disposable personal income:									
Current dollars	Mil. dol ...	3,565	10,403	13,760	18,170	19,914	20,632	21,222	22,664
Constant (1954) dollars	Mil. dol ...	2,521	3,768	4,032	4,921	5,238	5,198	5,294	5,596
Average family income:									
Current dollars	Dollar	6,366	14,858	16,914	20,416	22,231	22,883	22,824	24,337
Constant (1954) dollars	Dollar	4,503	5,381	4,957	5,530	5,847	5,765	5,693	6,009
BANKING [9]									
Assets	Mil. dol ...	3,322	10,223	21,209	27,179	27,902	27,946	31,564	31,635
TOURISM [8]									
Number of visitors	1,000	1,225.0	2,140.0	2,061.6	3,221.2	3,425.8	3,504.3	3,722.2	3,871.1
Visitor expenditures	Mil. dol ...	235.4	618.7	757.7	1,254.0	1,366.4	1,435.7	1,520.0	1,629.1
Average per visitor	Dollar	192	289	368	389	399	410	408	421
Net income from tourism	Mil. dol ...	89.8	202.2	223.1	372.8	383.3	400.8	420.0	464.7

NA Not available. [1] 1970, 1980, and 1990 enumerated as of April 1; all other years estimated as of July 1. [2] Enrollment for the first school month. Expenses for school year ending in year shown. [3] Annual average of monthly figures. For fiscal years. [4] Beginning 1980, for population 16 years old and over; 1970, for population 14 years and over. [5] Includes other employment not shown separately. [6] Includes forestry and fisheries. [7] Percent unemployed of the labor force. [8] For fiscal years. [9] As of June 30.

Source: Puerto Rico Planning Board, San Juan, PR, *Income and Product*, annual; and *Socioeconomics Statistics*, annual.

No. 1342. Puerto Rico—Employment Status: 1970 to 1993

[In thousands. For 1970, for persons 14 years old and over; beginning 1980, 16 years old and over. Annual averages for calendar years of the civilian noninstitutional population]

EMPLOYMENT STATUS	1970	1980	1985	1988	1989	1990	1991	1992	1993		
									Total	Male	Female
Total	1,743	2,116	2,348	2,420	2,455	2,493	2,528	2,536	2,562	1,186	1,376
In the labor force	777	916	992	1,103	1,115	1,132	1,165	1,170	1,201	735	466
Employed	693	758	776	938	952	971	979	977	999	595	404
Working	657	712	710	848	858	(NA)	(NA)	(NA)	(NA)	(NA)	(NA)
35 hours or more	569	535	508	614	651	(NA)	(NA)	(NA)	(NA)	(NA)	(NA)
Less than 35 hours	88	177	203	234	207	(NA)	(NA)	(NA)	(NA)	(NA)	(NA)
Unemployed	84	156	216	165	163	160	186	193	202	140	62
Percent	10.7	17.0	21.8	15.0	14.6	14.2	16.0	16.5	16.8	19.0	13.3
Not in labor force	966	1,200	1,356	1,317	1,340	1,362	1,363	1,366	1,361	451	910

NA Not available.

Source: Puerto Rico Dept. of Labor and Human Resources, Bureau of Labor Statistics, San Juan, PR.

No. 1343. Puerto Rico—Gross Product and Net Income: 1980 to 1993

[In millions of dollars. For fiscal years ending June 30. Data for 1993 are preliminary]

ITEM	1980	1985	1988	1989	1990	1991	1992	1993
Gross product	11,065	15,002	18,550	19,954	21,619	22,809	23,562	24,991
Agriculture	380	357	399	443	434	449	420	410
Manufacturing	5,306	7,909	10,513	11,133	12,126	12,661	13,392	14,133
Contract construction and mining [1] . . .	369	334	551	662	720	770	797	823
Transportation [2]	1,279	1,709	2,262	2,315	2,468	2,671	2,808	2,948
Trade.	2,273	3,160	4,125	4,376	4,728	4,832	5,049	5,382
Finance, insurance, real estate	1,486	2,547	3,545	3,750	3,896	4,308	4,634	4,763
Services	1,279	1,837	2,505	2,699	3,015	3,322	3,574	3,849
Government	1,897	2,346	2,918	3,187	3,337	3,522	3,672	3,900
Commonwealth.	1,574	1,996	2,506	2,745	2,884	3,044	3,154	3,345
Municipalities	323	350	413	442	453	478	518	555
Rest of the world	-3,372	-5,287	-7,629	-8,313	-8,985	-9,478	-10,442	-10,843
Statistical discrepancy.	166	91	-640	-298	-121	-248	-342	-373
Net income	9,007	12,182	15,699	16,662	17,941	18,927	19,555	20,824
Agriculture	435	410	447	494	486	503	476	468
Manufacturing	4,756	7,117	9,704	10,299	11,277	11,732	12,494	13,183
Mining	9	10	22	24	26	26	26	26
Contract construction	337	309	516	624	679	728	754	781
Transportation [2]	1,022	1,248	1,646	1,681	1,777	1,900	1,964	2,105
Trade.	1,609	2,285	2,942	3,154	3,420	3,485	3,597	3,835
Finance, insurance, and real estate . . .	1,200	2,141	2,978	3,136	3,280	3,609	3,886	4,000
Services	1,114	1,606	2,154	2,377	2,643	2,901	3,128	3,371
Commonwealth Government [3]	1,897	2,346	2,918	3,187	3,337	3,522	3,672	3,900
Rest of the world	-3,372	-5,287	-7,629	-8,313	-8,985	-9,478	-10,442	-10,843

[1] Mining includes only quarries.   [2] Includes other public utilities, and radio and television broadcasting.   [3] Includes public enterprises not elsewhere classified.
Source: Puerto Rico Planning Board, San Juan, PR, *Economic Report of the Governor, 1992-93.*

No. 1344. Puerto Rico—Transfer Payments: 1985 to 1993

[Data represent transfer payments between Federal and State governments and other nonresidents. See headnote, table 1343]

ITEM	1985	1988	1989	1990	1991	1992	1993
Total receipts	3,531	4,073	4,289	4,871	4,973	5,108	5,590
Federal government	3,348	3,840	4,082	4,649	4,708	4,903	5,397
Transfers to individuals [1]	3,283	3,761	4,014	4,577	4,633	4,818	5,303
Veterans benefits.	317	323	337	349	370	383	409
Medicare	220	292	320	368	415	487	517
Old age, disability, survivors.	1,581	1,826	1,940	2,055	2,243	2,315	2,659
Nutritional assistance	780	822	853	880	916	957	975
Industry subsidies	65	80	68	72	75	86	94
U.S. State governments.	17	15	17	18	18	29	33
Other nonresidents.	166	217	191	205	246	175	160
Total payments	1,180	1,524	1,664	1,801	1,857	1,975	2,090
Federal government	1,145	1,512	1,651	1,756	1,840	1,905	2,022
Transfers from individuals	508	692	766	817	864	914	981
Contribution to Medicare	44	70	89	97	101	108	122
Employee contribution for Social Security. .	463	620	675	720	762	805	857
Transfers from industries	13	15	15	16	19	24	26
Unemployment insurance	189	223	237	247	243	209	208
Employer contribution for Social Security. . . .	435	582	633	675	714	758	807
Other nonresidents.	35	11	13	45	17	69	64
Net balance.	2,351	2,550	2,625	3,070	3,116	3,133	3,500
Federal government	2,203	2,328	2,431	2,893	2,869	2,998	3,375
U.S. State governments.	14	14	14	16	15	25	27
Other nonresidents.	134	208	180	162	232	110	98

[1] Includes other receipts and payments not shown separately.
Source: Puerto Rico Planning Board, San Juan, PR, *Economic Report of the Governor, 1991-92.*

No. 1345. Puerto Rico—Merchandise Imports and Exports: 1980 to 1991

[In millions of dollars. Imports are imports for consumption; see text, section 28]

ITEM	1980	1981	1982	1983	1984	1985	1986	1987	1988	1989	1990	1991
Imports.	9,018	9,329	8,167	8,708	10,116	10,162	10,321	11,308	13,096	15,010	16,200	15,079
From U.S. . . .	5,345	5,801	5,300	5,162	5,738	6,130	6,467	7,307	8,788	10,193	10,792	10,306
From other. . .	3,673	3,528	2,867	3,546	4,378	4,032	3,854	4,001	4,308	4,817	5,408	4,773
Exports.	6,576	7,047	8,888	8,242	9,426	11,087	11,854	12,508	14,436	17,455	20,402	21,128
To U.S.	5,643	6,024	7,624	6,936	8,074	9,873	10,524	11,153	12,756	15,334	17,915	18,729
To other	933	1,023	1,264	1,306	1,352	1,214	1,330	1,355	1,680	2,121	2,487	2,399

Source: U.S. Bureau of the Census, *Foreign Commerce and Navigation of the United States,* annual; *U.S. Trade with Puerto Rico and U.S. Possessions, FT 895;* and, through 1988, *Highlights of U.S. Export and Import Trade, FT990;* thereafter, FT990 supplement.

No. 1346. Puerto Rico—Economic Summary, by Industry: 1991

[Excludes employees of establishments totally exempt from the Federal Insurance Contributions Act: government workers, railroad employment jointly covered by Social Security and railroad retirement programs, self-employed persons, domestic service, agriculture production employees, and employees on oceanborne vessels or in foreign countries]

INDUSTRY	1987 SIC code [1]	Total establish-ments	Employment-size class					Employ-ees [2]	Annual payroll (mil. dol.)
			1 to 4	5 to 9	10 to 19	20 to 49	50 or more		
Total [3]	(X)	**35,742**	**21,451**	**5,655**	**3,953**	**2,835**	**1,848**	**560,441**	**7,578.9**
Agricultural services, forestry, and fishing	A	81	54	14	9	3	1	457	5.5
Mining	B	36	6	10	6	8	6	942	11.0
Nonmetallic minerals, except fuels	14	27	3	8	6	7	3	525	6.2
Construction [3]	C	892	343	136	125	125	163	36,486	385.2
General contractors and operative builders	15	363	106	50	48	55	104	23,066	232.1
Special trade contractors	17	460	216	78	67	55	44	9,782	104.5
Manufacturing [3]	D	1,623	346	191	245	297	544	147,082	2,473.6
Food and kindred products	20	223	59	31	38	42	53	17,327	289.7
Textile mill products	22	17	2	1	2	4	8	3,051	36.2
Apparel and other textile products	23	237	30	19	23	40	125	30,362	287.9
Furniture and fixtures	25	88	28	18	21	15	6	1,788	17.6
Paper and allied products	26	40	5	5	10	7	13	1,826	29.0
Printing and publishing	27	147	65	25	27	20	10	3,782	57.7
Chemicals and allied products	28	152	16	17	15	23	81	25,926	705.8
Petroleum and coal products	29	13	-	1	4	1	7	1,277	39.4
Rubber and misc. plastic products	30	82	7	4	17	24	30	5,677	89.8
Leather and leather products	31	28	3	1	5	2	17	6,592	67.0
Stone, clay, and glass products	32	105	22	20	26	27	10	3,236	63.0
Fabricated metal products	34	105	25	13	19	26	22	3,692	49.8
Industrial machinery and equip	35	72	24	11	9	15	13	3,780	69.2
Electronic and other electronic equip	36	105	14	3	4	11	73	18,094	325.0
Instruments and related products	38	67	6	2	6	8	45	13,053	228.1
Transportation and public utilities [3]	E	822	425	141	116	75	65	23,839	449.1
Trucking and warehousing	42	300	167	51	47	22	13	2,985	35.8
Water transportation	44	54	22	6	6	6	14	4,788	69.3
Air transportation	45	72	21	11	13	16	11	2,421	48.7
Transportation services	47	229	159	36	17	12	5	1,845	29.6
Communication	48	99	18	20	27	17	17	10,832	251.6
Electric, gas, and sanitary services	49	13	4	3	-	1	5	703	12.3
Wholesale trade [3]	F	1,876	741	351	343	269	172	34,571	614.5
Durable goods	50	954	363	201	183	139	68	14,819	255.0
Nondurable goods	51	905	374	148	157	124	102	19,271	345.6
Retail trade [3]	G	9,164	4,861	1,873	1,199	872	359	106,239	1,010.1
Building materials, garden supplies	52	555	312	117	65	44	17	4,981	50.4
General merchandise stores	53	410	163	50	59	60	78	17,561	175.2
Food stores	54	1,189	651	186	123	114	115	19,577	163.8
Automotive dealers and service stations	55	1,417	918	300	122	59	18	8,813	100.2
Apparel and accessory stores	56	1,320	521	332	284	163	20	13,605	108.2
Furniture and home furnishings	57	643	373	167	63	37	3	3,919	42.7
Eating and drinking places	58	1,695	815	295	277	258	50	19,818	157.4
Finance, insurance, and real estate [3]	H	1,843	868	346	331	201	97	35,993	652.9
Depository institutions	60	331	64	44	137	62	24	14,314	286.2
Nondepository institutions	61	412	108	120	87	71	26	7,786	116.2
Insurance carriers	63	77	18	13	11	20	15	3,925	83.1
Insurance agents, brokers, and service	64	230	121	45	28	20	16	3,793	75.9
Real estate	65	743	524	117	63	26	13	5,464	63.9
Services [3]	I	7,592	5,020	1,019	661	451	441	123,217	1,435.2
Personal services	72	528	363	85	54	21	5	3,318	27.3
Business services	73	653	286	106	81	62	118	31,110	317.5
Auto repair, services, and parking	75	515	370	83	42	13	7	2,789	29.7
Motion pictures	78	83	34	16	18	6	9	1,334	16.9
Amusement and recreation services	79	135	74	21	20	13	7	1,741	17.5
Health services	80	2,808	2,241	300	131	65	71	29,170	331.8
Legal services	81	724	604	43	49	20	8	3,218	59.3
Education services	82	439	96	61	67	113	102	20,848	243.4
Social services	83	228	93	50	42	17	26	4,539	48.6
Membership organizations	86	501	312	79	47	39	24	5,913	53.3
Engineering and management services	87	582	345	97	62	44	34	7,246	117.6

- Represents or rounds to zero. X Not applicable. [1] 1987 Standard Industrial Classification (SIC) code; see text, section 13. [2] For the pay period including March 12. [3] Includes other establishments not shown separately.

Source: U.S. Bureau of the Census, *County Business Patterns*, 1991.

No. 1347. Puerto Rico, Guam, and Virgin Islands—Agriculture: 1982 and 1987

[1 cuerda=.97 acre. Tons specified are short tons]

ITEM	1982	1987	ITEM	1982	1987	ITEM	Unit	1982 (Amount Harvested [1])	1987 (Amount Harvested [1])	1982 (Sales $1,000)	1987 (Sales $1,000)
PUERTO RICO											
Farms.	21,820	20,245	Tenure of operator: Percent—			Dairy products.	(X)	(X)	(X)	152,126	157,864
Percent—						Poultry [2].	(X)	(X)	(X)	45,945	70,560
Less than 10 cuerdas	45.1	48.7	Full-owners .	79.3	77.5	Coffee	1,000 cwt.[3]	243.9	246.2	39,302	41,786
10 to 19 cuerdas.	20.9	19.5				Cattle and					
			Part-owners .	11.5	13.1	calves	(X)	(X)	(X)	28,579	30,206
20 to 49 cuerdas.	18.0	16.7	Managers . .	1.8	2.3	Sugarcane . . .	1,000 tons	1,462	1,170	26,663	26,643
50 to 99 cuerdas.	7.1	6.7	Tenants. . . .	7.4	7.1	Fruits/nuts . . .	(X)	(X)	(X)	14,060	20,645
100 to 174 cuerdas	3.9	3.7	Avg. farm size- cuerdas—			Pineapples . . .	1,000 tons	44	69	9,534	15,495
175 or more cuerdas	5.0	4.7	Full-owners .	31.1	30.6						
			Part-owners .	99.3	85.7	Hogs	(X)	(X)	(X)	6,903	9,525
Cuerdas in farms	982,457	886,846	Managers . .	122.8	128.0						
			Tenants. . . .	90.9	84.0	Vegetables. . .	Cuerdas. .	6,669	6,179	9,547	8,236
GUAM											
Farms.	297	351	Tenure of operator: Percent—			Chicken eggs .	(X)	(X)	(X)	791.9	651.1
Percent—						Fish.	(X)	(X)	(X)	121.3	235.0
Less than 1 acre .	9.4	6.3	Full-owners . .	62.0	64.1	Cucumbers . . .	1,000 lbs..	623.3	587.1	217.8	233.5
1 to 2 acres	36.0	35.9	Permittees . .	21.9	20.5	Green beans. . .	1,000 lbs..	116.5	303.8	81.7	230.2
3 to 7 acres	28.6	29.1	Tenants. . . .	9.1	4.3	Watermelons . .	1,000 lbs..	400.3	632.6	115.6	178.6
8 or more acres .	26.0	28.8	Part-owners .	5.1	4.6	Tomatoes. . . .	1,000 lbs..	88.0	142.7	64.3	108.6
			Non- permittees .	1.3	6.0	Hogs and pigs.	(X)	(X)	(X)	117.0	106.4
Acres in farms	17,787	13,134	Others.	0.7	0.6						
VIRGIN ISLANDS											
Farms.	259	267	Tenure of operator:			Milk.	(X)	(X)	(X)	922.8	1,042.7
						Cattle and					
Percent—			Percent—			calves	(X)	(X)	(X)	488.6	613.4
Less than 3 acres.	29.0	30.0									
3 to 9 acres	34.7	30.3	Full-owners .	79.9	75.3	Hogs and pigs.	(X)	(X)	(X)	130.0	125.2
10 to 19 acres . .	9.3	12.0	Part-owners .	10.4	13.5						
			Tenants. . . .	9.3	8.6	Tomatoes. . . .	Acres . . .	8	16	33.7	113.7
20 or more acres.	27.0	27.7				Lettuce	Acres . . .	2	8	7.8	49.5
			Managers . .	0.4	2.6	Mangoes	1,000. . . .	205.0	171.1	(D)	44.0
Acres in farms	17,778	17,785				Poultry [2]	(X)	(X)	(X)	315.6	16.8

D Withheld to avoid disclosure of information pertaining to a specific organization or individual.　X Not applicable.
[1] Includes amounts not sold.　[2] Includes poultry products.　[3] Cwt=hundredweight (100 lbs.).
Source: U.S. Bureau of the Census, *1987 Census of Agriculture*, vol. 1, parts 52, 53, and 54.

No. 1348. Guam, Virgin Islands, and Northern Mariana Islands— Economic Summary: 1987

[Sales and payroll in millions of dollars]

ITEM	Guam	Virgin Islands	No. Mariana Islands	ITEM	Guam	Virgin Islands	No. Mariana Islands
Total: Establishments.	1,490	2,604	768	Wholesale trade:			
Sales.	1,510	(D)	374	Establishments	94	84	28
Annual payroll	221	255	57	Sales.	245	211	50
Paid employees [1].	18,582	20,709	9,090	Annual payroll	19	20	2
Unpaid family workers [2]. . . .	371	209	167	Paid employees [1].	1,392	1,322	187
				Unpaid family workers [2]. . . .	6	2	-
Construction: Establishments. .	79	92	72	Retail trade:			
Sales.	127	124	43	Establishments	804	1,311	383
Annual payroll	35	29	12	Sales.	786	703	155
Paid employees [1].	2,705	2,170	2,061	Annual payroll	79	85	14
Unpaid family workers [2]. . . .	1	3	6	Paid employees [1].	7,344	8,529	2,304
Manufacturing:				Unpaid family workers [2]. . . .	273	168	126
Establishments	38	66	39	Services: Establishments	475	1,051	246
Sales.	81	(D)	58	Sales.	271	296	67
Annual payroll	17	44	14	Annual payroll	71	76	16
Paid employees [1].	1,320	2,102	2,257	Paid employees [1].	5,821	6,586	2,281
Unpaid family workers [2]. . . .	1	-	3	Unpaid family workers [2]. . . .	90	36	32

- Represents zero.　D Withheld to avoid disclosure of information pertaining to a specific organization or individual.　[1] For pay period including March 12.　[2] Includes those who worked 15 hours or more during the week including March 12.
Source: U.S. Bureau of the Census, *1987 Economic Census of Outlying Areas*, OAC 87-5 to OAC 87-7.

Comparative International Statistics

This section presents statistics for the world as a whole and for many countries on a comparative basis with the United States. Data are shown for population, births and deaths, social and industrial indicators, finances, agriculture, communication, and military affairs.

Statistics of the individual nations may be found primarily in official national publications, generally in the form of yearbooks, issued by most of the nations at various intervals in their own national languages and expressed in their own or customary units of measure. (For a listing of selected publications, see Guide to Sources.) For handier reference, especially for international comparisons, the Statistical Office of the United Nations compiles data as submitted by member countries and issues a number of international summary publications, generally in English and French. Among these are the *Statistical Yearbook*; the *Demographic Yearbook*; the *Yearbook of International Trade Statistics*; the *Yearbook of National Accounts Statistics: Vol. II, International Tables; Population and Vital Statistics Reports* (quarterly); the *Monthly Bulletin of Statistics*; and the *Energy Statistics Yearbook*. Specialized agencies of the United Nations also issue international summary publications on agricultural, labor, health, and education statistics. Among these are the *Production Yearbook* and *Trade Yearbook* issued by the Food and Agriculture Organization, the *Yearbook of Labour Statistics* issued by the International Labour Office, the *World Health Statistics* issued by the World Health Organization, and the *Statistical Yearbook* issued by the Educational, Scientific, and Cultural Organization.

The Bureau of the Census presents estimates of basic demographic measures for countries and regions of the world in the *World Population Profile* series. The *International Population Statistics Reports*, P90 and P91 series, also present population figures for many foreign countries. Detailed population statistics are also available from the Bureau of the Census' computerized International Data Base.

In Brief

Ten largest countries in 1994: (1,000 persons)

China, Mainland	1,190,431
India	919,903
United States	260,714
Indonesia	200,410
Brazil	158,739
Russia	149,609
Pakistan	128,856
Bangladesh	125,149
Japan	125,107
Nigeria	98,091

The U.S. Arms Control and Disarmament Agency and the International Monetary Fund (IMF) also compile data on international statistics. In its *World Military Expenditures and Arms Transfers,* published annually, the ACDA presents data on various economic indicators, as well as basic military data. Among the topics presented have been military expenditures, gross national product, imports and exports, and armed forces, by region and/or country. The IMF publishes a series of reports relating to financial data. These include *International Financial Statistics, Direction of Trade,* and *Balance of Payments Yearbook,* published in English, French, and Spanish.

Statistical coverage, country names, and classifications.—Problems of space and availability of data limit the number of countries and the extent of statistical coverage shown. The list of countries included is based almost entirely on a list of sovereign nations, dependencies, and areas of special sovereignty published by the U.S. Department of State in *Status of the World's Nations.* Country names are shown here as specified in that publication. In the few cases where a lack of comparability exists between State Department and United Nations' terminology, the State Department's preferences are used.

In recent years, several important changes took place in the status of the world's nations. Two nations, Yemen and Germany, were formed in 1990, each by unification of two formerly separate nations. In the case of Germany, the former German Democratic Republic (East) was subsumed by the Federal Republic of Germany (West). In most cases, data presented in the *Statistical Abstract* are for former West Germany. The Republic of Yemen was formed by union of the former Yemen Arab Republic and the People's Democratic Republic of Yemen. Also in 1990, Namibia finally realized its independence; the United Nations terminated its status as a South African mandate in 1966.

The year 1990 also began a period of turmoil in the former Soviet Union. The independence of three Baltic States—Estonia, Latvia, and Lithuania—was recognized by the central Soviet government in August 1991. The United States established diplomatic relations with the democratically elected governments of the Baltic States in September 1991. In December 1991, the 12 former Soviet republics became separate sovereign nations—Armenia, Azerbaijan, Belarus, Georgia, Kazakhstan, Kyrgyzstan, Moldova, Russia, Tajikistan, Turkmenistan, Ukraine, and Uzbekistan. Eleven of the 12 have formed a Commonwealth of Independent States (Georgia has not joined). Most data presented in the *Statistical Abstract* are for former Soviet Union.

In 1992, the Socialist Federal Republic of Yugoslavia dissolved and none of the successor states represents its continuation. Bosnia and Herzegovina, Croatia, and Slovenia have been formally recognized as independent states by the United States. Macedonia has proclaimed independent statehood, but has not been formally recognized as a state by the U.S. Serbia and Montenegro have asserted the formation of a joint independent state, but this entity has not been formally recognized as a state by the U.S. In addition, on December 31, 1992, at midnight, Czechoslovakia ceased to exist and was succeeded by two separate and independent states, the Czech Republic and Slovakia. The United States formally recognized the Czech Republic and Slovakia as independent states on January 1, 1993. Finally, Eritrea announced its independence from Ethiopia on April 27, 1993. After this announcement, the U.S. recognized Eritrea as an independent state.

The population estimates and projections used in tables 1351-1353 were prepared by the Census Bureau. For each country, the data on population, by age and sex, fertility, mortality, and international migration were evaluated and, where necessary, adjusted for inconsistencies and errors in the data. In most instances, comprehensive projections were made by the component method, resulting in distributions of the population by age and sex, and requiring an assessment of probable future trends of fertility, mortality, and international migration.

Economic associations.—The Organization for European Economic Co-operation (OEEC), a regional grouping of Western European countries established in 1948 for the purpose of harmonizing national economic policies and conditions, was succeeded on September 30, 1961, by the Organization for Economic Cooperation and Development (OECD). The member nations of the OECD are Australia, Austria, Belgium, Canada, Denmark, Finland, France, Germany, Greece, Iceland, Ireland, Italy, Japan, Luxembourg, the Netherlands, New Zealand, Norway, Portugal, Spain, Sweden, Switzerland, Turkey, the United Kingdom, and the United States.

Quality and comparability of the data.— The quality and comparability of the data presented here are affected by a number of factors:

(1) The year for which data are presented may not be the same for all subjects for a particular country, or for a given subject for different countries, though the data shown are the most recent available. All such variations have been noted. The data shown are for calendar years except as otherwise specified.

(2) The bases, methods of estimating, methods of data collection, extent of coverage, precision of definition, scope of territory, and margins of error may vary for different items within a particular country, and for like items for different countries. Footnotes and headnotes to the tables give a few of the major time-period and coverage qualifications attached to the figures; considerably more detail is presented in the source publications. Many of the

measures shown are, at best, merely rough indicators of magnitude.

(3) Figures shown in this section for the United States may not always agree with figures shown in the preceding sections. Disagreements may be attributable to the use of differing original sources, a difference in the definition of geographic limits (the 50 States, conterminous United States only, or the United States including certain outlying areas and possessions), or to possible adjustments made in the U.S. figures by the United Nations or other sources in order to make them more comparable with figures from other countries.

International comparisons of national accounts data.—In order to compare national accounts data for different countries, it is necessary to convert each country's data into a common unit of currency, usually the U.S. dollar. The market exchange rates which are often used in converting national currencies do not necessarily reflect the relative purchasing power in the various countries. It is necessary that the goods and services produced in different countries should be valued consistently if the differences observed are meant to reflect real differences in the volumes of goods and services produced. The use of purchasing power parities (see table 1370) instead of exchange rates is intended to achieve this objective.

The method used to present the data shown in table 1370 is to construct volume measures directly by revaluing the goods and services sold in different countries at a common set of international prices. By dividing the ratio of the gross domestic products of two countries expressed in their own national currencies by the corresponding ratio calculated at constant international prices, it is possible to derive the implied purchasing power parity (PPP) between the two currencies concerned. PPP's show how many units of currency are needed in one country to buy the same amount of goods and services which one unit of currency will buy in the other country. For further information, see *National*

Accounts, Main Aggregates, volume I, issued annually by the Organization for Economic Cooperation and Development, Paris, France.

International Standard Industrial Classification.—The original version of the International Standard Industrial Classification of All Economic Activities (ISIC) was adopted in 1948. Wide use has been made both nationally and internationally in classifying data according to kind of economic activity in the fields of production, employment, national income, and other economic statistics. A number of countries have utilized the ISIC as the basis for devising their industrial classification scheme. Substantial comparability has been attained between the industrial classifications of many other countries, including the United States, and the ISIC by ensuring, as far as practicable, that the categories at detailed levels of classification in national schemes fitted into only one category of the ISIC. For more detail, see Bureau of the Census, *The International Standard Industrial Classification and the U.S. Standard Industrial Classification,* Technical Paper No. 14 and text, section 27. The United Nations, the International Labour Organization, the Food and Agriculture Organization, and other international bodies have utilized the ISIC in publishing and analyzing statistical data. Revisions of the ISIC were issued in 1958, 1968, and 1989.

International maps. A series of regional world maps is provided on pages 842–848. References are included in table 1374 for easy location of individual countries on the maps. The Robinson map projection is used for this series of maps. A map projection is used to portray all or part of the round Earth on a flat surface, but this cannot be done without some distortion. For the Robinson projection, distortion is very low along the Equator and within 45 degrees of the center but is greatest near the poles. For additional information on map projections and maps, please contact the Earth Science Information Center, U.S. Geological Survey, 507 National Center, Reston, VA 22092.

S0

See Inset

Pacific Ocean

S1

Arctic Ocean

Canada

United States

Greenland

Atlantic Ocean

S2

Brazil

S4

S3

Algeria Libya

Mali

Zaire

Sudan

Saudi Arabia

Madagascar

Iran

Kazakhstan

Russia

Mongolia

China, Mainland

India

Japan

Philippines

Arctic Ocean

S5

Pacific Ocean

Indian Ocean

Australia

New Zealand

S6

Inset

Western Samoa

· Kiribati

American Samoa

▸Tonga

Cook Islands

French Polynesia

S2

Arctic Ocean

Faroe Islands

Russia

Sweden

Finland

Norway

Denmark

Estonia

Russia

Latvia

Netherlands

Lithuania

Russia

Ireland

Germany

Poland

Belarus

Isle of Man

United Kingdom

Guernsey

Jersey

Ukraine

France

Romania

San Marino

Serbia

Andorra

Monaco

Italy

Spain

Bulgaria

Albania

Macedonia

Portugal

Gibraltar

Greece

Atlantic Ocean

Netherlands

Belgium

Poland

Germany

Czech Republic

Luxembourg

Slovakia

Liechtenstein

France

Austria

Hungary

Switzerland

Slovenia

Italy

Croatia

Bosnia &
Herzegovina

Serbia

Spain
Morocco
Western
Sahara
Tunisia
Malta
Greece
Cyprus
Lebanon
West Bank
Gaza Strip
Israel
Syria
Iraq
Iran
United
Arab
Emirates
Algeria
Libya
Egypt
Jordan
Kuwait
Bahrain
Qatar
Saudi Arabia
Oman
Yemen
Mauritania
Mali
Niger
Chad
Sudan
Djibouti
Ethiopia
Somalia
Nigeria
Cameroon
Central
African Republic
Uganda
Kenya
Indian
Ocean
Sao Tome &
Principe
Gabon
Congo
Zaire
Rwanda
Burundi
Tanzania
Equatorial Guinea
Seychelles
Comoros
Mayotte
St. Helena
Angola
Zambia
Malawi
Mauritius
Atlantic Ocean
Namibia
Zimbabwe
Mozambique
Reunion
Botswana
Madagascar
Swaziland
South Africa
Lesotho

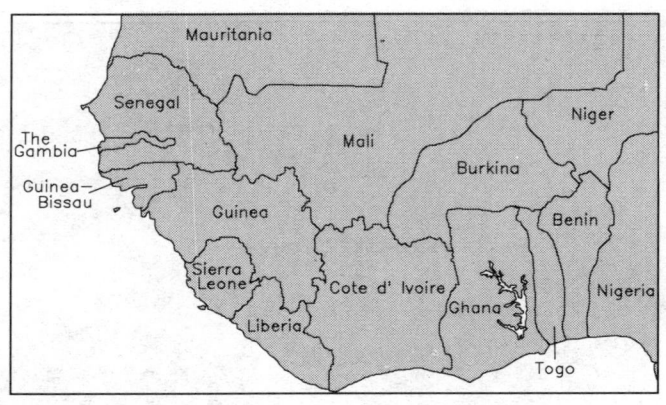

Mauritania
Senegal
Niger
The
Gambia
Mali
Burkina
Guinea-
Bissau
Guinea
Benin
Sierra
Leone
Cote d' Ivoire
Nigeria
Liberia
Ghana
Togo

China, Mainland

China, Taiwan

Macau

Burma   Laos   Hong
Kong

Thailand

Pacific Ocean

Northern
Mariana
Islands

Guam

Marshall
Islands

Trust Ter. of the
Pac. Isl. (Palau)

Federated States
of Micronesia

Kiribati

Papua
New Guinea

Nauru

Indonesia

Solomon
Islands

Tuvalu

Wallis &
Futuna

Indian Ocean

Vanuatu

Fiji

New Caledonia

Australia

New Zealand

Pacific Ocean

Thailand

Philippines

Vietnam

Cambodia

Malaysia

Singapore

Indonesia

Indian Ocean

No. 1349. World Summary: 1980 to 1992

[See text, section 30, for general comments concerning quality of the data]

ITEM	Unit	1980	1985	1986	1987	1988	1989	1990	1991	1992
Population	Millions	4,453	4,850	4,936	5,024	5,112	5,202	5,294	5,384	5,478
Agriculture, forestry, fishing production: [1]										
Barley	Mil. metric tons	156.7	172.7	177.5	175.5	163.3	164.1	177.7	168.1	165.0
Coffee	Mil. metric tons	4.8	5.8	5.2	6.4	5.7	6.0	6.1	6.1	5.8
Corn	Mil. metric tons	397.5	486.9	478.2	450.9	400.4	474.6	479.0	489.9	530.1
Cotton (lint)	Mil. metric tons	13.8	17.4	15.2	16.6	18.3	17.1	18.4	20.7	18.1
Meats	Mil. metric tons	135.9	152.9	157.5	163.0	169.8	172.9	178.2	181.5	184.3
Peanuts (groundnuts)	Mil. metric tons	16.9	20.8	21.4	21.7	25.4	23.1	23.1	23.4	24.2
Rice	Mil. metric tons	398.9	471.0	471.3	464.1	490.8	517.4	520.5	517.8	526.4
Tobacco	Mil. metric tons	5.3	7.0	6.0	6.2	6.8	7.0	7.0	7.5	8.0
Wheat	Mil. metric tons	440.1	499.6	528.6	504.9	500.8	538.5	592.8	546.6	566.3
Wool, greasy	Mil. metric tons	2.8	3.0	3.0	3.1	3.1	3.0	3.1	3.0	2.9
Roundwood	Mil. cubic meters	2,932	3,199	3,305	3,372	3,426	3,455	3,450	(NA)	(NA)
Fish catches	Mil. metric tons	72.0	86.3	92.8	94.4	99.0	100.2	97.4	96.9	(NA)
Industrial production:										
Wine [1]	Mil. metric tons	35.3	29.5	32.2	32.3	27.3	28.5	28.4	26.0	29.6
Sugar [1]	Mil. metric tons	84.4	98.6	101.5	102.5	104.3	105.8	111.3	112.2	117.4
Wheat flour [1]	Mil. metric tons	237.2	270.0	274.4	280.4	288.4	291.7	300.1	305.3	305.9
Coal	Mil. metric tons	2,728	3,161	3,249	3,411	3,488	3,584	3,517	3,453	(NA)
Lignite and brown coal	Mil. metric tons	1,042	1,202	1,219	1,250	1,261	1,282	1,212	1,180	(NA)
Crude petroleum [2]	Bil. bbl.	21.8	19.7	20.5	20.7	21.4	21.8	22.1	21.9	22.0
Natural gas (dry) [2]	Trl. cu. ft	53.1	61.8	63.4	66.3	69.7	72.1	73.7	74.8	75.0
Electricity	Bil. kWh	8,247	9,747	10,055	10,587	11,059	11,505	11,802	12,034	(NA)
Iron ore	Mil. metric tons	841	862	868	890	916	920	921	922	(NA)
Pig iron and ferroalloys	Mil. metric tons	542	507	496	503	504	570	543	505	(NA)
Tin [3]	1,000 metric tons	231	196	191	194	210	242	237	214	(NA)
Crude steel	Mil. metric tons	699	685	671	682	685	777	762	687	(NA)
Cement	Mil. metric tons	872	949	997	1,045	1,109	1,144	1,152	1,135	(NA)
Non-cellulosic fibers [3]	Mil. metric tons	10.0	11.5	11.7	12.4	13.2	13.3	11.6	12.4	(NA)
Sawnwood	Mil. cubic meters	451	468	485	506	508	508	506	458	(NA)
Woodpulp	Mil. metric tons	125.8	135.5	140.9	146.5	151.4	155.6	154.1	154.7	(NA)
Newsprint	Mil. metric tons	25.4	28.2	29.2	30.4	31.8	32.0	32.8	32.4	(NA)
Merchant vessels, launched [3]	Mil. gross tons	13.9	17.3	14.9	9.6	11.8	12.7	14.7	16.7	(NA)
Motor vehicles	Millions	38.9	44.8	45.3	45.9	48.1	48.9	48.1	46.4	(NA)
External trade:										
Imports, c.i.f	Bil. U.S. dollars	2,047	2,028	2,198	2,544	2,908	3,154	3,563	3,514	(NA)
Exports, f.o.b	Bil. U.S. dollars	1,998	1,927	2,121	2,465	2,814	3,037	3,432	3,409	(NA)
Transport:										
Civil aviation, kilometers flown [4]	Millions	9,362	10,565	11,455	12,208	13,026	13,564	14,339	14,167	(NA)
Merchant shipping, freight [5]	Mil. metric tons	3,676	3,362	3,459	3,506	3,692	3,891	(NA)	(NA)	(NA)

NA Not available.   [1] Source: U.S. Department of Agriculture, Economic Research Service, *World Agriculture-Trends and Indicators*.   [2] Source: U.S. Energy Information Administration, *International Energy Annual* and *Annual Energy Review*.   [3] Excludes China: Mainland. Tin and merchant vessels exclude Soviet Republics. For other exclusions, see source.   [4] Scheduled services of members of International Civil Aviation Organization. Excludes Soviet Republics.   [5] Freight loaded.

Source: Except as noted, Statistical Division of the United Nations, New York, NY, *Monthly Bulletin of Statistics*, (copyright).

No. 1350. U.S. Population Abroad, by Country: 1993

[In thousands. As of **October 15, 1992**. Data taken from the annual noncombatant personnel evacuation requirements report, which is used solely to estimate the number of potential U.S. citizen evacuees from a given country in a crisis]

AREA	Resident U.S. citizens [1]	U.S. tourists	AREA	Resident U.S. citizens [1]	U.S. tourists
Argentina	13	11	Italy	104	105
Australia	62	56	Jerusalem	43	20
Canada	296	495	Mexico	539	1,088
Costa Rica	23	21	Netherlands	19	11
Dominican Republic	97	36	Panama	36	2
Egypt	17	11	Portugal	26	28
France	59	89	Saudi Arabia	40	6
Germany	354	1,060	South Korea	30	2
Greece	32	60	Spain	79	155
Hong Kong	24	23	Switzerland	27	29
Ireland	46	86	United Kingdom	255	377
Israel	112	61	Venezuela	24	2

[1] Totals represent broad estimates and may include some non-U.S. citizens, as well as dual nationals.

Source: U.S. Dept. of State, unpublished data.

No. 1351. Population, by Country: 1980 to 2000

[Population data generally are de facto figures for the present territory. Population estimates were derived from information available as of early 1994. See text, section 31, for general comments concerning the data. For details of methodology, coverage, and reliability, see source. Minus sign (-) indicates decrease]

COUNTRY OR AREA	Map reference	MIDYEAR POPULATION (1,000)				Population rank, 1994	ANNUAL RATE OF GROWTH [1] (percent)		Population per sq. mile, 1994
		1980	1990	1994	2000, proj.		1980-1990	1990-2000	
World	S0	4,456,531	5,294,294	5,643,290	6,165,079	(X)	1.7	1.5	112
Afghanistan	S5	14,985	15,332	16,903	25,725	54	0.2	5.2	68
Albania	S3	2,673	3,249	3,374	3,610	125	2.0	1.1	319
Algeria	S4	18,862	25,352	27,895	31,743	37	3.0	2.2	30
Andorra	S3	34	53	64	73	202	4.5	3.3	367
Angola	S4	6,794	8,430	9,804	11,513	75	2.2	3.1	20
Antigua and Barbuda	S1	69	64	65	68	201	-0.7	0.7	381
Argentina	S2	28,237	32,386	33,913	36,202	31	1.4	1.1	32
Armenia	S5	3,115	3,363	3,522	3,685	123	0.8	0.9	306
Aruba	S1	60	64	66	68	200	0.6	0.6	880
Australia	S6	14,616	17,071	18,077	19,386	50	1.6	1.3	6
Austria	S3	7,549	7,718	7,955	8,108	85	0.2	0.5	249
Azerbaijan	S5	6,173	7,216	7,684	8,243	88	1.6	1.3	230
Bahamas, The	S1	210	255	273	298	174	2.0	1.5	70
Bahrain	S4	348	518	586	687	160	4.0	2.8	2,451
Bangladesh	S5	88,077	114,203	125,149	143,548	8	2.6	2.3	2,421
Barbados	S1	252	254	256	260	176	0.1	0.2	1,541
Belarus	S3	9,644	10,248	10,405	10,576	69	0.6	0.3	130
Belgium	S3	9,847	9,962	10,063	10,144	74	0.1	0.2	862
Belize	S1	144	190	209	242	180	2.7	2.4	24
Benin	S4	3,444	4,676	5,342	6,517	100	3.1	3.3	125
Bhutan	S5	1,281	1,585	1,739	1,996	142	2.1	2.3	96
Bolivia	S2	5,470	7,029	7,719	8,801	87	2.5	2.2	18
Bosnia and Herzegovina	S3	4,092	4,517	4,651	4,828	110	1.0	0.7	236
Botswana	S4	903	1,224	1,359	1,554	147	3.0	2.4	6
Brazil	S2	122,830	150,062	158,739	169,543	5	2.0	1.2	49
Brunei	S6	185	254	285	331	173	3.2	2.6	140
Bulgaria	S3	8,844	8,966	8,800	8,742	80	0.1	-0.3	206
Burkina	S4	6,939	9,042	10,135	11,871	72	2.6	2.7	96
Burma	S5	33,578	41,044	44,277	49,300	25	2.0	1.8	174
Burundi	S4	4,138	5,558	6,125	6,939	93	3.0	2.2	618
Cambodia	S5	6,499	8,731	10,265	12,098	71	3.0	3.3	151
Cameroon	S4	8,756	11,697	13,132	15,677	60	2.9	2.9	72
Canada	S1	24,070	26,620	28,114	29,867	35	1.0	1.2	8
Cape Verde	S1	296	375	423	503	165	2.4	2.9	272
Central African Republic	S4	2,269	2,866	3,142	3,511	128	2.3	2.0	13
Chad	S4	4,024	5,024	5,467	6,221	98	2.2	2.1	11
Chile	S2	11,094	13,108	13,951	15,207	58	1.7	1.5	48
China: Mainland	S5	984,736	1,136,626	1,190,431	1,260,154	1	1.4	1.0	331
Taiwan	S5	17,848	20,436	21,299	22,448	42	1.4	0.9	1,710
Colombia	S2	26,580	32,983	35,578	39,172	30	2.2	1.7	89
Comoros	S4	334	460	530	656	161	3.2	3.5	633
Congo	S4	1,620	2,215	2,447	2,784	135	3.1	2.3	19
Costa Rica	S2	2,307	3,031	3,342	3,797	126	2.7	2.3	171
Cote d'Ivoire	S4	8,418	12,399	14,296	17,321	57	3.9	3.4	116
Croatia	S3	4,593	4,686	4,698	4,717	109	0.2	0.1	215
Cuba	S1	9,653	10,622	11,064	11,617	62	1.0	0.9	258
Cyprus	S5	627	702	730	768	156	1.1	0.9	205
Czech Republic	S3	10,289	10,363	10,408	10,607	68	0.1	0.2	215
Denmark	S3	5,123	5,141	5,188	5,255	103	(Z)	0.2	317
Djibouti	S4	279	370	413	454	167	2.8	2.0	49
Dominica	S1	75	83	88	95	195	1.0	1.3	302
Dominican Republic	S1	5,847	7,249	7,826	8,644	86	2.2	1.8	419
Ecuador	S2	8,123	9,806	10,677	11,945	65	1.9	2.0	100
Egypt	S4	42,333	55,883	60,765	67,957	17	2.8	2.0	158
El Salvador	S1	4,655	5,303	5,753	6,459	95	1.3	2.0	719
Equatorial Guinea	S4	256	369	410	478	168	3.7	2.6	38
Eritrea [2]	S4	(NA)	(NA)	(NA)	(NA)	(NA)	(NA)	(NA)	(NA)
Estonia	S3	1,482	1,583	1,617	1,670	144	0.7	0.5	93
Ethiopia [2]	S4	38,967	51,507	58,710	70,340	19	2.8	3.1	138
Fiji	S6	635	738	764	823	154	1.5	1.1	108
Finland	S3	4,780	4,986	5,069	5,153	104	0.4	0.3	43
France	S3	53,870	56,720	57,840	59,354	22	0.5	0.5	275
Gabon	S4	808	1,078	1,139	1,244	149	2.9	1.4	11
Gambia, The	S4	644	848	959	1,154	152	2.8	3.1	248
Georgia	S5	5,048	5,484	5,681	5,925	96	0.8	0.8	211
Germany	S3	78,298	79,357	81,088	82,239	12	0.1	0.4	600
Ghana	S4	10,777	15,195	17,225	20,608	53	3.4	3.0	194
Greece	S3	9,643	10,123	10,565	10,878	66	0.5	0.7	209
Grenada	S2	90	94	94	98	193	0.4	0.4	719
Guatemala	S1	7,232	9,633	10,721	12,408	64	2.9	2.5	256
Guinea	S4	4,320	5,930	6,392	7,372	92	3.2	2.2	67
Guinea-Bissau	S4	789	998	1,098	1,263	151	2.3	2.4	102
Guyana	S2	759	748	729	710	157	-0.2	-0.5	10
Haiti	S1	5,473	6,052	6,491	7,102	91	1.0	1.6	610
Honduras	S1	3,625	4,741	5,315	6,192	101	2.7	2.7	123
Hungary	S3	10,711	10,365	10,319	10,372	70	-0.3	(Z)	289
Iceland	S1	228	255	264	277	175	1.1	0.8	7
India	S5	692,394	852,656	919,903	1,018,105	2	2.1	1.8	801

See footnotes at end of table.

No. 1351. Population, by Country: 1980 to 2000—Continued

[See headnote, page 850]

COUNTRY OR AREA	Map reference	MIDYEAR POPULATION (1,000)				Population rank, 1994	ANNUAL RATE OF GROWTH [1] (percent)		Population per sq. mile, 1994
		1980	1990	1994	2000, proj.		1980-1990	1990-2000	
Indonesia	S6	154,936	187,728	200,410	219,496	4	1.9	1.6	284
Iran	S5	38,810	57,005	65,615	78,350	15	3.8	3.2	104
Iraq	S5	13,233	18,425	19,890	24,731	45	3.3	2.9	119
Ireland	S3	3,401	3,508	3,539	3,627	122	0.3	0.3	133
Israel	S4	3,737	4,303	5,051	5,507	106	1.4	2.5	643
Italy	S3	56,451	57,661	58,138	58,865	20	0.2	0.2	512
Jamaica	S1	2,229	2,466	2,555	2,746	134	1.0	1.1	611
Japan	S5	116,807	123,540	125,107	127,554	9	0.6	0.3	821
Jordan	S4	2,165	3,305	3,961	4,814	118	4.2	3.8	112
Kazakhstan	S5	14,994	16,749	17,268	17,886	52	1.1	0.7	16
Kenya	S4	16,681	24,229	28,241	32,479	34	3.7	2.9	128
Kiribati	S6	58	72	78	87	197	2.1	1.9	281
Kuwait	S5	1,370	2,117	1,819	2,494	141	4.4	1.6	264
Kyrgyzstan	S5	3,623	4,392	4,698	5,119	108	1.9	1.5	61
Laos	S5	3,293	4,191	4,702	5,557	107	2.4	2.8	53
Latvia	S3	2,525	2,693	2,749	2,833	132	0.6	0.5	110
Lebanon	S4	3,137	3,367	3,620	4,115	121	0.7	2.0	917
Lesotho	S4	1,347	1,755	1,944	2,242	140	2.6	2.4	166
Liberia	S4	1,900	2,311	2,973	3,620	129	2.0	4.5	80
Libya	S4	3,119	4,355	5,057	6,294	105	3.3	3.7	7
Liechtenstein	S3	25	29	30	32	214	1.3	1.2	487
Lithuania	S5	3,436	3,727	3,848	4,007	119	0.8	0.7	153
Luxembourg	S3	364	382	402	415	169	0.5	0.8	403
Madagascar	S4	8,700	11,811	13,428	16,232	59	3.1	3.2	60
Malawi	S4	6,128	9,289	9,732	11,045	76	4.2	1.7	268
Malaysia	S6	13,764	17,556	19,283	21,953	46	2.4	2.2	152
Maldives	S5	154	218	252	310	177	3.5	3.5	2,176
Mali	S4	6,728	8,234	9,113	10,911	78	2.0	2.8	19
Malta	S4	364	354	367	382	172	-0.3	0.8	2,959
Mauritania	S4	1,456	1,935	2,193	2,653	138	2.8	3.2	6
Mauritius	S4	964	1,074	1,117	1,194	150	1.1	1.1	1,565
Mexico	S1	68,686	85,121	92,202	102,912	11	2.1	1.9	124
Moldova	S5	3,996	4,389	4,473	4,565	112	0.9	0.4	344
Monaco	S3	27	30	31	32	213	1.2	0.7	40,505
Mongolia	S5	1,662	2,186	2,430	2,826	136	2.7	2.6	4
Morocco	S4	20,457	26,164	28,559	32,189	33	2.5	2.1	166
Mozambique	S4	12,103	14,438	17,346	20,868	51	1.8	3.7	57
Namibia	S4	967	1,387	1,596	1,957	145	3.6	3.4	5
Nauru	S6	8	9	10	11	222	2.0	1.3	1,236
Nepal	S5	15,001	19,104	21,042	24,364	43	2.4	2.4	398
Netherlands	S3	14,144	14,952	15,368	15,801	55	0.6	0.6	1,173
New Zealand	S6	3,113	3,300	3,389	3,476	124	0.6	0.5	33
Nicaragua	S2	2,776	3,617	4,097	4,759	116	2.6	2.7	88
Niger	S4	5,661	7,868	8,972	10,985	79	3.3	3.3	18
Nigeria	S4	65,699	86,551	98,091	118,620	10	2.8	3.2	279
North Korea	S5	17,999	21,412	23,067	25,491	40	1.7	1.7	496
Norway	S3	4,086	4,242	4,315	4,387	113	0.4	0.3	36
Oman	S5	984	1,481	1,701	2,098	143	4.1	3.5	21
Pakistan	S5	85,219	114,842	128,856	148,540	7	3.0	2.6	429
Panama	S2	1,956	2,427	2,630	2,934	133	2.2	1.9	90
Papua New Guinea	S6	2,991	3,823	4,197	4,812	115	2.5	2.3	24
Paraguay	S2	3,379	4,651	5,214	6,104	102	3.2	2.7	34
Peru	S2	17,295	21,879	23,651	26,258	38	2.4	1.8	48
Philippines	S6	50,864	64,405	69,809	77,747	14	2.4	1.9	606
Poland	S3	35,578	38,112	38,655	39,531	29	0.7	0.4	329
Portugal	S3	9,778	10,365	10,524	10,744	67	0.6	0.4	297
Qatar	S5	231	452	513	572	162	6.7	2.4	121
Romania	S5	22,201	23,191	23,181	23,383	39	0.4	0.1	261
Russia	S5	139,045	148,124	149,609	151,460	6	0.6	0.2	23
Rwanda	S4	5,170	7,415	8,374	9,715	84	3.6	2.7	869
St. Kitts and Nevis	S1	44	40	41	43	210	-1.0	0.8	293
St. Lucia	S1	122	142	145	151	186	1.5	0.6	615
St. Vincent and the Grenadines	S1	98	112	115	122	190	1.4	0.8	882
San Marino	S3	21	23	24	25	215	0.8	0.9	1,040
Sao Tome and Principe	S4	94	123	137	159	188	2.7	2.6	369
Saudi Arabia	S4	10,139	16,271	18,197	22,070	48	4.7	3.0	22
Senegal	S4	5,731	7,715	8,731	10,533	82	3.0	3.1	118
Seychelles	S4	65	70	72	75	198	0.6	0.8	410
Sierra Leone	S4	3,315	4,230	4,630	5,421	111	2.4	2.5	167
Singapore	S6	2,414	2,720	2,859	3,025	130	1.2	1.1	11,867
Slovakia	S3	4,966	5,298	5,404	5,585	99	0.6	0.5	112
Slovenia	S3	1,885	1,954	1,972	1,998	139	0.4	0.2	252
Solomon Islands	S6	233	336	386	470	171	3.7	3.4	36
Somalia	S4	5,799	6,753	6,667	9,176	90	1.5	3.1	28
South Africa	S4	30,270	39,535	43,931	51,334	26	2.7	2.6	93
South Korea	S5	38,124	43,237	45,083	47,861	24	1.3	1.0	1,189
Spain	S3	37,488	38,964	39,303	39,972	28	0.4	0.3	204
Sri Lanka	S5	14,900	17,227	18,130	19,377	49	1.5	1.2	725
Sudan	S4	19,064	26,542	29,420	35,236	32	3.3	2.8	32
Suriname	S2	355	398	423	465	166	1.2	1.6	7

See footnotes at end of table.

No. 1351. Population, by Country: 1980 to 2000—Continued
[See headnote, page 850]

COUNTRY OR AREA	Map reference	MIDYEAR POPULATION (1,000)				Population rank, 1994	ANNUAL RATE OF GROWTH [1] (percent)		Population per sq. mile, 1994
		1980	1990	1994	2000, proj.		1980-1990	1990-2000	
Swaziland	S4	607	853	936	1,137	153	3.4	2.9	141
Sweden	S3	8,310	8,559	8,778	8,994	81	0.3	0.5	55
Switzerland	S3	6,385	6,779	7,040	7,268	89	0.6	0.7	458
Syria	S4	8,692	12,762	14,887	18,519	56	3.8	3.7	209
Tajikistan	S5	3,969	5,346	5,995	6,956	94	3.0	2.6	109
Tanzania	S4	18,695	25,155	27,986	32,254	36	3.0	2.5	82
Thailand	S5	47,026	56,220	59,510	63,620	18	1.8	1.2	301
Togo	S4	2,596	3,680	4,255	5,263	114	3.5	3.6	203
Tonga	S0	93	101	105	110	191	0.9	0.8	378
Trinidad and Tobago	S2	1,091	1,271	1,328	1,420	148	1.5	1.1	670
Tunisia	S4	6,452	8,084	8,727	9,599	83	2.3	1.7	145
Turkey	S5	45,121	57,130	62,154	69,624	16	2.4	2.0	209
Turkmenistan	S5	2,875	3,660	3,995	4,474	117	2.4	2.0	21
Tuvalu	S6	7	9	10	11	223	2.0	1.6	979
Uganda	S4	12,252	16,927	19,122	21,358	47	3.2	2.3	248
Ukraine	S5	50,047	51,674	51,847	51,931	23	0.3	(Z)	222
United Arab Emirates	S5	1,000	2,252	2,791	3,582	131	8.1	4.6	86
United Kingdom	S3	56,314	57,418	58,135	58,951	21	0.2	0.3	623
United States	S1	227,726	249,924	260,714	275,327	3	0.9	1.0	74
Uruguay	S2	2,920	3,106	3,199	3,344	127	0.6	0.7	48
Uzbekistan	S5	16,000	20,615	22,609	25,467	41	2.5	2.1	131
Vanuatu	S6	117	154	170	193	184	2.8	2.2	30
Venezuela	S2	14,452	18,776	20,562	23,196	44	2.6	2.1	60
Vietnam	S5	54,234	67,718	73,104	80,533	13	2.2	1.7	582
Western Samoa	S0	155	186	204	235	181	1.8	2.3	186
Yemen	S5	7,324	9,746	11,105	13,603	61	2.9	3.3	54
Zaire	S4	27,954	37,903	42,684	51,413	27	3.0	3.0	49
Zambia	S4	5,638	8,233	9,188	10,625	77	3.8	2.6	32
Zimbabwe	S4	7,298	10,187	10,975	12,013	63	3.3	1.6	74
AREAS OF SPECIAL SOVEREIGNTY AND DEPENDENCIES									
American Samoa	S0	32	47	55	69	206	3.8	3.8	719
Anguilla	S1	7	7	7	7	224	0.5	0.7	201
Bermuda	S1	55	59	61	64	204	0.8	0.8	3,233
British Virgin Islands	S1	11	12	13	14	220	1.1	1.3	222
Cayman Islands	S1	17	27	32	41	211	4.4	4.3	317
Cook Islands	S0	18	18	19	20	216	0.1	1.1	206
Faroe Islands	S3	43	47	48	51	209	0.9	0.7	90
Federated States of Micronesia	S6	77	109	120	133	189	3.4	2.0	444
French Guiana	S2	68	116	139	173	187	5.4	4.0	4
French Polynesia	S0	151	196	215	245	178	2.6	2.2	152
Gaza Strip	S4	454	633	731	898	155	3.3	3.5	4,971
Gibraltar	S3	29	31	32	33	212	0.6	0.5	13,677
Greenland	S1	50	56	57	60	205	1.0	0.8	(Z)
Guadeloupe	S1	327	399	429	460	164	2.0	1.4	631
Guam	S6	107	134	150	171	185	2.3	2.4	716
Guernsey	S3	53	61	64	67	203	1.4	1.0	851
Hong Kong	S5	5,063	5,558	5,549	5,587	97	0.9	0.1	14,531
Isle of Man	S3	64	69	72	76	199	0.7	1.0	317
Jersey	S3	76	84	86	89	196	1.0	0.7	1,905
Macau	S6	318	456	485	516	163	3.6	1.2	78,438
Macedonia [3]	S3	1,893	2,132	2,214	2,324	137	1.2	0.9	223
Marshall Islands	S6	31	46	54	68	207	4.1	3.9	773
Martinique	S1	339	374	392	419	170	1.0	1.2	960
Mayotte [3]	S4	52	80	93	117	194	4.3	3.8	644
Montenegro [3]	S5	579	645	667	696	158	1.1	0.8	125
Montserrat	S1	12	13	13	13	221	0.6	0.3	329
Netherlands Antilles	S2	170	183	186	193	182	0.8	0.5	501
New Caledonia	S6	139	168	181	200	183	1.9	1.7	25
Northern Mariana Islands	S6	17	44	50	57	208	9.7	2.6	270
Puerto Rico	S1	3,206	3,604	3,802	3,838	120	1.2	0.6	1,099
Reunion	S4	507	600	653	730	159	1.7	2.0	677
St. Helena	S4	6	7	7	7	225	0.3	0.3	43
St. Pierre and Miquelon	S1	6	6	7	7	226	0.8	0.8	72
Serbia [3]	S3	9,262	9,883	10,093	10,425	73	0.6	0.5	296
Trust Ter. of the Pac. Isl. (Palau)	S6	13	15	16	18	217	1.3	1.7	93
Turks and Caicos Islands	S1	7	12	14	15	219	4.5	2.7	82
Virgin Islands	S1	98	101	98	99	192	0.4	-0.2	722
Wallis and Futuna	S6	11	14	14	15	218	2.4	1.1	136
West Bank	S4	916	1,275	1,444	1,661	146	3.3	2.6	663
Western Sahara	S4	126	191	212	245	179	4.2	2.5	2

NA Not available. X Not applicable. Z Less than .05 percent or one person per square mile. [1] Computed by the exponential method. For explanation of average annual percent change, see Guide to Tabular Presentation. [2] Eritrea included in Ethiopia totals. [3] The U.S. view is that the Socialist Federal Republic of Yugoslavia has dissolved and no successor state represents its continuation. Macedonia has proclaimed independent statehood, but has not been recognized as a state by the United States. Serbia and Montenegro have asserted the formation of a joint independent state, but this entity has not been recognized by the United States.

Source: U.S. Bureau of the Census, *World Population Profile: 1994.*

No. 1352. Age Distribution, by Country: 1994 and 2000

[In percent. Covers countries with 10 million or more population in 1993]

COUNTRY OR AREA	1994 Under 5 years old	5 to 14 years old	15 to 64 years old	65 years old and over	2000, proj. Under 5 years old	5 to 14 years old	15 to 64 years old	65 years old and over
World	11.3	20.5	61.9	6.3	10.5	20.0	62.7	6.8
Afghanistan	16.8	26.1	54.4	2.7	16.5	26.3	54.5	2.7
Algeria	13.9	27.3	55.1	3.7	12.5	23.9	59.6	3.9
Argentina	9.4	19.0	62.0	9.6	9.1	17.6	63.3	10.0
Australia	7.2	14.5	66.6	11.7	6.8	14.2	67.0	12.0
Bangladesh	14.7	26.1	56.2	3.0	14.1	23.8	59.1	3.1
Belarus	6.7	15.5	65.2	12.6	6.2	14.0	65.4	14.5
Belgium	6.0	11.9	66.3	15.8	5.4	11.8	65.6	17.2
Brazil	10.0	21.8	63.7	4.5	9.3	19.2	66.4	5.2
Burma	12.9	23.4	59.4	4.3	12.1	22.2	61.1	4.6
Cameroon	17.2	27.2	52.2	3.4	17.1	26.5	52.9	3.4
Canada	7.2	13.6	67.1	12.1	6.4	13.6	67.2	12.8
Chile	10.1	19.2	64.2	6.5	9.3	18.3	65.1	7.3
China: Mainland	8.9	17.8	67.3	6.0	7.7	17.3	68.2	6.8
Taiwan	7.9	16.8	68.0	7.3	7.2	14.6	69.8	8.4
Colombia	11.2	21.5	63.0	4.3	9.6	20.3	65.2	5.0
Cote d'Ivoire	19.3	28.2	50.5	2.1	18.7	29.2	49.9	2.3
Cuba	8.4	14.2	68.2	9.2	7.1	15.6	67.4	9.9
Czech Republic	6.3	13.2	67.5	12.9	6.7	12.4	67.4	13.4
Ecuador	12.4	24.1	59.2	4.2	10.9	22.0	62.5	4.5
Egypt	13.0	25.8	57.7	3.4	12.0	22.8	61.6	3.7
Ethiopia	18.5	27.2	51.5	2.8	17.9	27.9	51.4	2.8
France	6.6	12.6	65.4	15.4	6.2	12.8	64.5	16.4
Germany	5.5	10.9	68.2	15.4	5.2	11.1	67.2	16.5
Ghana	18.8	26.5	51.7	3.0	17.7	28.4	50.9	3.0
Greece	5.2	12.5	67.3	15.0	5.3	10.8	66.8	17.1
Guatemala	16.2	27.3	53.1	3.4	14.6	26.6	55.2	3.7
Hungary	6.0	12.4	67.6	14.0	6.4	11.9	66.8	14.9
India	12.8	22.6	60.7	3.9	11.5	21.8	62.3	4.4
Indonesia	11.2	21.9	63.5	3.4	10.5	19.7	65.6	4.3
Iran	18.5	28.2	49.7	3.6	17.5	28.3	50.3	3.9
Iraq	19.2	28.7	49.0	3.1	18.2	28.8	50.2	2.9
Italy	5.1	10.3	68.6	15.9	5.4	10.1	67.0	17.5
Japan	5.0	11.6	69.7	13.7	5.5	10.2	67.8	16.5
Kazakhstan	9.9	20.7	62.6	6.8	8.8	19.2	64.6	7.3
Kenya	18.5	29.7	49.5	2.3	16.9	29.3	51.4	2.4
Madagascar	19.0	27.9	50.0	3.2	18.3	28.3	50.4	3.0
Malaysia	13.5	23.2	59.5	3.8	12.4	23.0	60.6	4.0
Mexico	13.0	24.3	58.5	4.2	11.9	22.8	60.5	4.8
Morocco	13.4	25.4	57.1	4.2	12.1	23.3	60.1	4.6
Mozambique	18.1	26.9	52.5	2.5	17.4	27.4	52.6	2.6
Nepal	16.1	26.7	54.4	2.8	15.5	25.7	55.7	3.0
Netherlands	6.4	11.9	68.4	13.3	5.8	12.3	67.8	14.1
Nigeria	18.1	26.9	52.2	2.9	17.8	26.9	52.3	2.9
North Korea	11.1	18.4	66.4	4.0	10.2	19.2	65.9	4.7
Pakistan	17.5	26.5	52.1	3.9	16.8	26.9	52.5	3.9
Peru	12.0	23.7	60.3	4.0	10.8	21.3	63.4	4.5
Philippines	12.9	24.4	59.0	3.7	11.6	22.5	61.8	4.0
Poland	6.8	16.6	65.6	10.9	6.5	13.9	67.3	12.3
Portugal	5.7	13.1	67.3	14.0	5.8	11.5	67.7	15.1
Romania	6.7	15.0	66.6	11.6	6.6	13.8	65.9	13.6
Russia	6.5	15.8	66.1	11.6	6.1	14.0	67.2	12.6
Saudi Arabia	16.7	24.1	57.0	2.2	16.5	25.7	55.1	2.8
Serbia [1]	7.0	14.9	66.6	11.4	6.9	13.8	65.4	14.0
South Africa	15.1	24.7	56.2	4.0	14.7	24.7	56.5	4.1
South Korea	7.5	16.9	70.4	5.3	7.3	14.4	71.8	6.5
Spain	5.2	12.1	68.0	14.7	5.7	10.5	67.4	16.4
Sri Lanka	9.2	20.4	64.6	5.8	8.3	17.3	67.8	6.6
Sudan	18.2	28.1	51.5	2.2	16.9	27.7	53.1	2.3
Syria	19.3	29.1	48.8	2.8	18.4	29.1	49.7	2.8
Tanzania	18.5	28.3	50.4	2.8	18.1	28.6	50.5	2.8
Thailand	9.6	19.9	65.8	4.7	8.4	17.8	68.0	5.7
Turkey	12.3	22.8	59.9	5.1	11.0	21.5	61.8	5.8
Uganda	19.7	29.3	48.8	2.2	18.6	31.1	48.1	2.3
Ukraine	6.2	14.5	65.5	13.8	6.0	13.1	66.4	14.5
United Kingdom	6.8	12.8	64.6	15.8	6.2	13.2	64.7	15.9
United States	7.6	14.4	65.3	12.7	6.9	14.5	65.9	12.7
Uzbekistan	14.4	25.8	55.2	4.6	12.7	25.1	57.4	4.9
Venezuela	12.5	23.5	59.9	4.2	11.2	21.7	62.4	4.7
Vietnam	13.0	23.9	58.2	4.9	11.2	22.7	60.9	5.2
Yemen	20.3	29.0	48.2	2.6	20.0	29.5	47.9	2.6
Zaire	19.3	28.3	49.7	2.7	19.2	29.0	49.3	2.6
Zimbabwe	16.9	30.2	50.2	2.7	15.0	29.2	53.0	2.7

[1] The U.S. view is that the Socialist Federal Republic of Yugoslavia has dissolved and no successor state represents its continuation. Serbia and Montenegro have asserted the formation of a joint independent state, but this entity has not been recognized by the United States.

Source: U.S. Bureau of the Census, International Data Base.

No. 1353. Vital Statistics, by Country: 1994 and 2000

[Covers countries with 5 million or more population in 1994]

COUNTRY OR AREA	CRUDE BIRTH RATE [1]		CRUDE DEATH RATE [2]		EXPECTATION OF LIFE AT BIRTH (years)		INFANT MORTALITY RATE [3]		TOTAL FERTILITY RATE [4]	
	1994	2000, proj.	1994	2000, proj.	1994	2000, proj.	1994	2000, proj.	1994	2000, proj.
United States	15.2	14.1	8.7	8.8	75.9	76.4	8.1	6.6	2.06	2.07
Afghanistan	43.5	41.6	18.9	16.6	44.9	47.8	155.8	137.5	6.27	5.87
Algeria	29.7	26.5	6.2	5.4	67.7	69.6	52.1	42.2	3.83	3.16
Angola	45.4	42.6	18.6	15.9	45.8	48.9	145.4	125.9	6.48	6.05
Argentina	19.6	19.1	8.6	8.6	71.4	72.3	29.4	26.1	2.68	2.50
Australia	14.3	13.2	7.4	7.4	77.6	78.7	7.3	6.4	1.83	1.80
Austria	11.4	10.1	10.3	10.0	76.7	78.0	7.1	6.2	1.48	1.50
Azerbaijan	23.0	18.5	6.6	6.5	70.9	72.5	34.8	28.7	2.70	2.39
Bangladesh	35.0	32.5	11.7	10.3	55.1	57.5	106.9	93.0	4.47	4.00
Belarus	13.1	12.6	11.2	11.3	70.9	72.2	18.9	16.4	1.88	1.83
Belgium	11.7	10.4	10.3	10.2	77.0	78.2	7.2	6.3	1.62	1.60
Benin	47.7	44.9	14.4	12.0	51.8	54.6	110.1	95.3	6.79	6.32
Bolivia	32.2	28.8	8.4	7.1	63.3	66.3	73.7	57.2	4.21	3.63
Brazil	21.5	19.2	8.6	10.1	62.3	60.9	59.5	47.8	2.44	2.14
Bulgaria	11.7	11.7	11.4	10.9	73.2	75.5	12.0	9.4	1.71	1.70
Burkina	48.4	45.6	18.2	20.3	47.0	41.6	118.3	112.8	6.94	6.48
Burma	28.5	25.9	9.8	8.7	60.0	62.8	63.7	52.4	3.64	3.29
Burundi	44.0	40.9	21.4	21.3	40.3	39.1	113.7	102.2	6.69	6.25
Cambodia	45.1	41.0	16.4	14.3	49.3	51.5	110.6	100.5	5.81	5.81
Cameroon	40.5	40.1	11.4	10.2	57.1	59.4	77.1	67.5	5.84	5.61
Canada	14.1	12.3	7.4	7.7	78.1	79.1	6.9	6.2	1.84	1.80
Chad	42.1	39.7	20.6	18.4	40.8	43.3	131.8	118.6	5.33	5.05
Chile	20.6	19.0	5.5	5.3	74.5	76.4	15.1	11.4	2.50	2.43
China, Mainland	18.1	15.0	7.4	7.0	67.9	70.2	52.1	38.7	1.84	1.80
Taiwan	15.6	14.5	5.6	6.1	75.3	76.4	5.7	5.3	1.81	1.80
Colombia	22.6	19.0	4.8	4.6	72.1	74.2	28.3	21.3	2.47	2.17
Cote d'Ivoire	46.5	43.9	15.0	14.7	48.9	48.5	95.0	83.8	6.67	6.21
Cuba	16.6	13.6	6.5	6.7	76.9	77.8	10.3	9.2	1.83	1.80
Czech Republic	13.2	13.6	11.1	9.9	73.1	75.4	9.3	7.5	1.84	1.80
Denmark	12.5	11.7	11.3	10.7	75.8	77.4	6.9	6.1	1.68	1.70
Dominican Republic	24.9	21.1	6.2	5.6	68.4	70.4	51.5	40.8	2.80	2.42
Ecuador	25.8	22.5	5.7	5.2	70.0	72.0	39.3	31.1	3.08	2.59
Egypt	28.7	26.3	8.9	8.0	60.8	62.7	76.4	65.7	3.77	3.24
El Salvador	32.8	29.5	6.4	5.5	67.0	69.7	40.9	30.9	3.78	3.30
Ethiopia	45.0	42.3	13.9	11.9	52.7	55.4	106.4	92.1	6.81	6.36
Finland	12.4	11.4	9.8	9.7	75.9	77.5	5.3	4.9	1.79	1.80
France	13.1	12.3	9.3	9.3	78.2	79.2	6.6	5.9	1.80	1.80
Georgia	16.1	14.4	8.7	8.9	72.8	74.5	23.4	18.6	2.18	2.05
Germany	11.0	9.8	10.9	10.5	76.3	77.8	6.5	5.7	1.47	1.53
Ghana	44.1	40.5	12.3	10.8	55.5	57.5	83.1	74.8	6.15	5.76
Greece	10.5	10.6	9.3	9.5	77.7	78.8	8.6	7.3	1.45	1.50
Guatemala	35.4	31.2	7.5	6.5	64.4	66.9	53.9	44.6	4.76	4.00
Guinea	44.1	39.9	19.6	16.9	44.1	47.0	139.2	123.7	5.85	5.46
Haiti	39.7	35.0	18.8	18.3	45.1	43.9	108.5	102.2	5.94	5.16
Honduras	35.0	30.3	6.2	5.2	67.6	70.0	45.3	35.4	4.71	3.83
Hong Kong	12.2	11.2	5.9	6.8	80.1	80.6	5.8	5.5	1.37	1.50
Hungary	12.5	12.9	12.7	11.4	71.4	74.1	12.5	9.7	1.83	1.80
India	28.5	24.7	10.3	9.1	58.6	61.4	78.4	65.8	3.48	3.04
Indonesia	24.5	22.5	8.6	8.1	60.7	63.4	67.3	55.4	2.80	2.53
Iran	42.4	39.3	7.8	6.2	65.7	69.0	60.2	45.9	6.33	5.88
Iraq	44.1	40.8	7.3	5.6	65.7	68.7	67.1	50.1	6.71	5.81
Israel	20.6	19.7	6.4	6.3	78.0	78.9	8.6	7.5	2.83	2.66
Italy	10.8	10.9	9.7	10.0	77.6	78.7	7.6	6.6	1.39	1.50
Japan	10.5	11.4	7.3	8.3	79.3	80.0	4.3	4.1	1.55	1.60
Kazakhstan	19.4	18.3	7.9	7.9	68.0	69.6	40.9	34.6	2.44	2.32
Kenya	42.4	37.5	11.7	15.2	53.2	46.4	74.1	72.3	5.91	4.97
Libya	45.3	42.6	8.1	6.9	63.9	66.2	63.4	52.1	6.38	6.00
Madagascar	45.2	42.7	13.4	11.3	54.0	56.7	89.0	77.1	6.68	6.25
Malawi	50.4	46.9	23.2	25.7	39.7	35.2	141.1	134.2	7.43	6.94
Malaysia	28.5	25.6	5.7	5.2	69.2	71.0	25.6	20.9	3.51	3.31
Mali	51.8	49.3	20.4	17.5	45.9	48.8	106.2	95.6	7.33	6.91
Mexico	27.2	24.3	4.7	4.4	72.9	75.0	27.4	20.7	3.17	2.79
Morocco	28.6	25.0	6.3	5.1	68.2	71.8	49.6	32.9	3.83	3.13
Mozambique	45.0	42.1	16.3	14.1	48.5	51.3	128.7	112.8	6.25	5.84
Nepal	37.6	35.6	13.3	11.2	52.5	55.9	83.5	70.1	5.24	4.68
Netherlands	12.6	10.9	8.5	8.6	77.8	78.8	6.1	5.5	1.58	1.50
Niger	55.0	51.7	21.3	18.1	44.6	47.5	111.0	100.3	7.35	7.00
Nigeria	43.5	41.6	12.4	10.1	55.3	59.1	75.0	61.4	6.37	5.95
North Korea	23.8	19.9	5.5	5.4	69.8	71.5	27.7	22.2	2.37	2.21
Pakistan	42.2	39.7	12.4	10.8	57.4	59.7	101.9	90.3	6.43	5.94
Paraguay	32.0	29.1	4.5	4.1	73.3	74.9	25.2	19.6	4.29	3.86
Peru	25.6	22.7	7.0	6.3	65.6	68.1	54.2	42.9	3.11	2.63
Philippines	27.3	24.4	6.9	6.6	65.4	66.9	50.8	44.4	3.35	2.88
Poland	13.4	13.2	9.4	8.7	72.7	75.0	13.1	10.0	1.94	1.80
Portugal	11.7	11.7	9.7	9.5	75.2	76.9	9.5	7.8	1.46	1.50
Romania	13.7	13.5	10.0	9.5	71.7	74.4	19.9	14.3	1.82	1.80
Russia	12.7	12.7	11.3	11.2	68.9	70.5	27.0	22.6	1.83	1.80
Rwanda	49.2	45.9	21.4	23.8	40.3	35.7	118.7	110.2	8.19	7.64
Saudi Arabia	38.3	36.9	5.8	4.9	67.9	71.1	52.1	36.3	6.67	6.43
Senegal	43.2	41.3	12.0	10.0	56.6	59.9	75.7	63.5	6.09	5.71
Serbia [5]	14.4	13.9	8.9	8.7	73.4	75.6	21.4	16.6	2.06	2.01

See footnotes at end of table.

No. 1353. Vital Statistics, by Country: 1994 and 2000—Continued
[See headnote, page 854]

COUNTRY OR AREA	CRUDE BIRTH RATE [1]		CRUDE DEATH RATE [2]		EXPECTATION OF LIFE AT BIRTH (years)		INFANT MORTALITY RATE [3]		TOTAL FERTILITY RATE [4]	
	1994	2000, proj.	1994	2000, proj.	1994	2000, proj.	1994	2000, proj.	1994	2000, proj.
Slovakia	14.6	14.1	9.3	8.5	72.8	75.1	10.4	8.4	1.96	1.80
Somalia	46.0	42.4	13.5	9.8	54.8	61.1	125.8	87.1	7.25	6.53
South Africa	33.6	32.3	7.5	6.9	65.1	67.0	47.1	39.8	4.37	4.23
South Korea	15.7	14.8	6.2	6.4	70.6	72.3	21.7	17.7	1.65	1.70
Spain	11.1	11.6	8.8	9.2	77.7	78.8	6.9	6.1	1.40	1.50
Sri Lanka	18.5	16.9	5.8	5.9	71.9	73.2	21.9	18.7	2.12	1.95
Sudan	42.0	38.8	12.1	10.3	54.3	56.8	79.5	69.2	6.09	5.47
Sweden	13.5	11.5	10.9	10.6	78.3	79.2	5.7	5.2	2.00	1.80
Switzerland	12.2	10.8	9.2	9.1	78.2	79.1	6.5	5.8	1.60	1.60
Syria	43.7	40.5	6.3	5.3	66.5	68.4	42.5	35.2	6.65	6.00
Tajikistan	34.8	30.4	6.7	6.0	68.8	70.5	62.0	52.1	4.62	4.10
Tanzania	45.5	43.6	19.4	22.4	43.3	38.4	109.7	104.3	6.20	5.85
Thailand	19.4	17.2	6.4	8.1	68.4	65.9	37.1	34.3	2.10	1.91
Tunisia	23.4	20.2	5.0	4.7	72.9	74.8	34.1	25.3	2.88	2.33
Turkey	26.0	22.8	5.8	5.1	70.9	73.8	48.8	33.3	3.21	2.78
Uganda	48.8	43.7	23.7	26.3	37.5	33.6	112.2	106.8	6.77	6.24
Ukraine	12.3	12.2	12.6	12.6	70.0	71.2	20.7	18.1	1.82	1.79
United Kingdom	13.4	11.9	10.8	10.3	76.8	78.1	7.2	6.3	1.83	1.80
Uzbekistan	30.0	26.8	6.5	6.0	68.6	70.1	53.2	45.1	3.73	3.37
Venezuela	25.7	22.9	4.6	4.5	73.0	74.4	27.7	22.6	3.05	2.68
Vietnam	27.1	22.9	7.8	7.0	65.4	67.1	45.5	39.9	3.33	2.80
Yemen	50.7	48.3	14.9	12.4	51.5	54.6	112.8	96.5	7.20	6.73
Zaire	48.4	46.1	16.7	15.5	47.4	48.4	110.9	97.9	6.70	6.39
Zambia	46.0	43.2	17.7	23.0	44.2	36.5	85.0	85.3	6.68	6.28
Zimbabwe	37.2	32.3	18.1	20.0	42.1	39.6	74.0	65.9	5.10	4.11

[1] Number of births during 1 year per 1,000 persons (based on midyear population). [2] Number of deaths during 1 year per 1,000 persons (based on midyear population). [3] Number of deaths of children under 1 year of age per 1,000 live births in a calendar year. [4] Average number of children that would be born if all women lived to the end of their childbearing years and, at each year of age, they experienced the birth rates occurring in the specified year. [5] The U.S. view is that the Socialist Federal Republic of Yugoslavia has dissolved and no successor state represents its continuation. Serbia and Montenegro have asserted the formation of a joint independent state, but this entity has not been recognized by the United States.

Source: U.S. Bureau of the Census, International Data Base.

No. 1354. Religious Population of the World: 1993
[In thousands, except percent. Refers to adherents of all religions as defined and enumerated for each of the world's countries in World Encyclopedia (1982), projected to mid-1993, adjusted for recent data]

RELIGION	Total	Percent distribution	Africa	Asia	Latin America	Northern America	Europe	Eurasia [1]	Oceania
Total population	5,575,954	100.0	703,090	3,291,718	474,996	281,986	501,881	294,681	27,602
Christians	1,869,751	33.5	341,208	300,383	443,056	241,147	409,653	111,618	22,686
Roman Catholics	1,042,501	18.7	128,167	130,102	412,366	97,892	260,034	5,711	8,229
Protestants	382,374	6.9	91,070	85,764	17,550	97,176	73,206	10,071	7,537
Orthodox	173,560	3.1	29,771	3,847	1,793	6,062	35,777	95,733	577
Anglicans	75,847	1.4	28,013	744	1,322	7,404	32,629	1	5,734
Other Christians	195,470	3.5	64,187	79,926	10,025	32,614	8,007	102	609
Muslims	1,014,372	18.2	284,844	668,298	1,400	3,332	13,663	42,761	104
Nonreligious [2]	912,874	16.4	2,578	721,113	18,444	24,718	57,542	84,907	3,572
Hindus	751,360	13.5	1,569	746,512	916	1,285	707	2	369
Buddhists	334,002	6.0	22	332,143	561	565	273	412	26
Atheists	241,852	4.3	336	167,217	3,343	1,336	16,669	52,402	549
Chinese folk-religionists [3]	140,956	2.5	14	140,661	76	123	60	1	21
New-religionists [4]	123,765	2.2	22	121,693	550	1,439	50	1	10
Tribal religionists	99,736	1.8	70,000	28,654	971	41	1	-	69
Sikhs	19,853	0.4	28	19,318	8	257	232	1	9
Jews	18,153	0.3	359	6,264	1,132	6,850	1,475	1,973	100
Shamanists	10,854	0.2	1	10,591	1	1	2	257	1
Confucians	6,238	0.1	1	6,204	2	26	2	-	1
Baha'is	5,742	0.1	1,591	2,774	830	370	91	7	79
Jains	3,927	0.1	56	3,847	4	4	15	-	1
Shintoists	3,336	0.1	-	3,332	1	1	1	-	1
Other religionists	19,183	0.3	461	12,714	3,701	491	1,475	337	4

- Represents zero. [1] Source's provisional new term for the former Soviet Union. [2] Persons professing no religion, nonbelievers, agnostics, freethinkers, and dereligionized secularists indifferent to all religion. [3] Followers of traditional Chinese religion (local deities, ancestor veneration, Confucian ethics, Taoism, etc.). [4] Followers of Asiatic 20th-century New Religions, New Religious movements, radical new crisis religions, and non-Christian syncretistic mass religions.

Source: Encyclopaedia Britannica, Inc., Chicago, IL, Britannica Book of the Year. (Reprinted with permission. Copyright.)

Comparative International Statistics

No. 1355. Population, by World's Largest Cities: 1992 to 2000

[When these city projections were prepared in 1985, cities were defined as population clusters of continuous built-up area with a population density of at least 5,000 persons per square mile. Boundaries were determined by examining detailed maps of each city in conjunction with the most recent official population statistics. The aerial expansion of each city was not projected, hence density figures for 1992 are based on areas as of 1985]

CITY AND COUNTRY	Rank	MIDYEAR POPULATION (1,000)			AVERAGE ANNUAL GROWTH RATE (percent)		Area (square miles)	Population per square mile, 199
		1992	1995	2000	1992-1995	1995-2000		
Tokyo-Yokohama, Japan	1	27,540	28,447	29,971	1.1	1.0	1,089	25,290
Mexico City, Mexico	2	21,615	23,913	27,872	3.4	3.1	522	41,408
Sao Paulo, Brazil	3	19,373	21,539	25,354	3.5	3.3	451	42,956
Seoul, South Korea	4	17,334	19,065	21,976	3.2	2.8	342	50,684
New York, United States	**5**	**14,628**	**14,638**	**14,648**	**(Z)**	**(Z)**	**1,274**	**11,482**
Osaka-Kobe-Kyoto, Japan	6	13,919	14,060	14,287	0.3	0.3	495	28,119
Bombay, India	7	12,450	13,532	15,357	2.8	2.5	95	131,051
Calcutta, India	8	12,137	12,885	14,088	2.0	1.8	209	58,073
Rio de Janeiro, Brazil	9	12,009	12,786	14,169	2.1	2.1	260	46,190
Buenos Aires, Argentina	10	11,743	12,232	12,911	1.4	1.1	535	21,950
Manila, Philippines	11	10,554	11,342	12,846	2.4	2.5	188	56,141
Moscow, Russia	12	10,526	10,769	11,121	0.8	0.6	379	27,773
Cairo, Egypt	13	10,372	11,155	12,512	2.4	2.3	104	99,726
Jakarta, Indonesia	14	10,185	11,151	12,804	3.0	2.8	76	134,014
Tehran, Iran	15	10,102	11,681	14,251	4.8	4.0	112	90,198
Los Angeles, United States	**16**	**10,072**	**10,414**	**10,714**	**1.1**	**0.6**	**1,110**	**9,074**
Delhi, India	17	9,243	10,105	11,849	3.0	3.2	138	66,976
London, United Kingdom	18	9,168	8,897	8,574	-1.0	-0.7	874	10,490
Paris, France	19	8,589	8,764	8,803	0.7	0.1	432	19,883
Lagos, Nigeria	20	8,487	9,799	12,528	4.8	4.9	56	151,548
Karachi, Pakistan	21	8,174	9,350	11,299	4.5	3.8	190	43,023
Essen, Germany	22	7,506	7,364	7,239	-0.6	-0.3	704	10,662
Lima, Peru	23	7,028	7,853	9,241	3.7	3.3	120	58,563
Shanghai, China	24	7,000	7,194	7,540	0.9	0.9	78	89,739
Istanbul, Turkey	25	6,937	7,624	8,875	3.2	3.0	165	42,040
Taipei, Taiwan	26	6,924	7,477	8,516	2.6	2.6	138	50,173
Chicago, United States	**27**	**6,493**	**6,541**	**6,568**	**0.2**	**0.1**	**762**	**8,521**
Bogota, Colombia	28	6,176	6,801	7,935	3.2	3.1	79	78,173
Bangkok, Thailand	29	6,088	6,657	7,587	3.0	2.6	102	59,687
Madras, India	30	5,998	6,550	7,384	2.9	2.4	115	52,156
Beijing, China	31	5,791	5,865	5,993	0.4	0.4	151	38,354
Hong Kong, Hong Kong	32	5,762	5,841	5,956	0.5	0.4	23	250,524
Santiago, Chile	33	5,484	5,812	6,294	1.9	1.6	128	42,840
Pusan, South Korea	34	5,161	5,748	6,700	3.6	3.1	54	95,582
Bangalore, India	35	5,080	5,644	6,764	3.5	3.6	50	101,604
Nagoya, Japan	36	4,909	5,017	5,303	0.7	1.1	307	15,990
Tianjin, China	37	4,857	5,041	5,298	1.2	1.0	49	99,121
Milan, Italy	38	4,718	4,795	4,839	0.5	0.2	344	13,714
St. Petersburg, Russia	39	4,645	4,694	4,738	0.4	0.2	139	33,415
Dhaka, Bangladesh	40	4,640	5,296	6,492	4.4	4.1	32	144,991
Madrid, Spain	41	4,577	4,772	5,104	1.4	1.4	66	69,344
Lahore, Pakistan	42	4,475	4,986	5,864	3.6	3.2	57	78,500
Baghdad, Iraq	43	4,358	4,566	5,239	1.6	2.8	97	44,924
Shenyang, China	44	4,323	4,457	4,684	1.0	1.0	39	110,848
Barcelona, Spain	45	4,221	4,492	4,834	2.1	1.5	87	48,521
San Francisco, United States	**46**	**4,005**	**4,104**	**4,214**	**0.8**	**0.5**	**428**	**9,358**
Kinshasa, Zaire	47	3,997	4,520	5,646	4.1	4.5	57	70,130
Manchester, United Kingdom	48	3,984	3,949	3,827	-0.3	-0.6	357	11,159
Philadelphia, United States	**49**	**3,970**	**3,988**	**3,979**	**0.2**	**-0.1**	**471**	**8,429**
Belo Horizonte, Brazil	50	3,920	4,373	5,125	3.6	3.2	79	49,625
Ahmadabad, India	51	3,826	4,200	4,837	3.1	2.8	32	119,555
Hyderabad, India	52	3,787	4,149	4,765	3.0	2.8	88	43,031
Ho Chi Minh City, Vietnam	53	3,725	4,064	4,481	2.9	2.0	31	120,164
Athens, Greece	54	3,613	3,670	3,866	0.5	1.0	116	31,144
Sydney, Australia	55	3,528	3,619	3,708	0.9	0.5	338	10,437
Guadalajara, Mexico	56	3,525	3,839	4,451	2.8	3.0	78	45,192
Miami, United States	**57**	**3,522**	**3,679**	**3,894**	**1.5**	**1.1**	**448**	**7,862**
Surabaya, Indonesia	58	3,327	3,428	3,632	1.0	1.2	43	77,382
Guangzhou, China	59	3,314	3,485	3,652	1.7	0.9	79	41,952
Caracas, Venezuela	60	3,247	3,338	3,435	0.9	0.6	54	60,133
Wuhan, China	61	3,231	3,325	3,495	1.0	1.0	65	49,700
Porto Alegre, Brazil	62	3,220	3,541	4,109	3.2	3.0	231	13,938
Toronto, Canada	63	3,182	3,296	3,296	1.2	0.0	154	20,662
Casablanca, Morocco	64	3,136	3,327	3,795	2.0	2.6	35	89,604
Monterrey, Mexico	65	3,084	3,385	3,974	3.1	3.2	77	40,057
Rome, Italy	66	3,028	3,079	3,129	0.6	0.3	69	43,889
Greater Berlin, Germany	67	3,020	3,018	3,006	(Z)	-0.1	274	11,021
Ankara, Turkey	68	3,000	3,263	3,777	2.8	2.9	55	54,551
Naples, Italy	69	2,996	3,051	3,134	0.6	0.5	62	48,324
Alexandria, Egypt	70	2,981	3,114	3,304	1.5	1.2	35	85,180
Montreal, Canada	71	2,933	2,996	3,071	0.7	0.5	164	17,881
Detroit, United States [1]	**72**	**2,890**	**2,865**	**2,735**	**-0.3**	**-0.9**	**468**	**6,175**
Rangoon, Burma	73	2,876	3,075	3,332	2.2	1.6	47	61,198
Melbourne, Australia	74	2,865	2,946	2,968	0.9	0.2	327	8,763
Dallas, United States	**75**	**2,856**	**2,972**	**3,257**	**1.3**	**1.8**	**419**	**6,817**

Z Less than .05 percent   [1] Includes Windsor, Canada.

Source: U.S. Bureau of the Census, International Data Base.

No. 1356. Percent Distribution of Households, by Type and Country

YEAR	Total	MARRIED-COUPLE [1]			Single parent [2]	One-person	Other [3]
		Total	With children [2]	Without children [2]			
United States:							
1960	100	74	44	30	4	13	8
1970	100	71	40	30	5	17	7
1980	100	61	31	30	8	23	9
1990	100	56	26	30	8	25	11
1991	100	55	26	29	9	25	11
1992	100	55	26	29	9	25	11
Canada:							
1961	100	[4]78	[4]51	[4]27	[4]4	9	[4]9
1971	100	74	47	28	5	13	8
1981	100	67	36	31	5	20	8
1991	100	63	30	33	6	23	9
Japan:							
1960	100	65	49	16	3	17	14
1970	100	64	45	20	2	20	13
1980	100	68	43	26	2	20	10
1990	100	65	33	32	2	23	10
Denmark: [5]							
1976	100	45	24	21	5	(NA)	(NA)
1983	100	44	23	21	5	(NA)	(NA)
1988	100	41	20	21	5	(NA)	(NA)
1989	100	41	20	21	5	(NA)	(NA)
1990	100	40	19	21	5	(NA)	(NA)
1991	100	37	19	18	6	(NA)	(NA)
France:							
1968	100	70	44	27	4	20	5
1975	100	69	42	27	4	22	5
1982	100	67	40	27	4	25	4
1990	100	65	39	26	7	26	2
1991	100	64	38	26	7	27	2
1992	100	64	37	27	7	27	2
Germany: [6]							
1961	100	67	44	22	11	21	2
1970	100	65	42	23	6	27	3
1980	100	61	37	24	7	30	3
1990	100	54	31	23	6	35	4
1991	100	56	32	24	7	34	4
1992	100	55	31	24	7	34	4
Netherlands:							
1961	100	78	55	22	6	12	5
1971	100	74	52	22	5	17	4
1981	100	67	44	23	6	21	6
1985	100	60	39	22	7	28	5
1990 [7]	100	64	36	28	5	30	1
1991	100	64	35	29	5	30	1
1992	100	63	34	29	5	31	1
Sweden:							
1960	100	66	36	31	4	20	10
1970	100	64	30	34	3	25	7
1980	100	58	25	33	3	33	6
1985	100	55	22	33	3	36	6
1990	100	52	20	32	3	40	5
United Kingdom: [8]							
1961	100	74	38	36	2	12	12
1971	100	70	34	35	3	18	9
1981	100	64	31	34	5	22	9
1990	100	61	25	36	6	26	7
1991	100	61	25	36	6	27	6

NA Not available. [1] May include unmarried cohabitating couples. Such couples are explicitly included under married couples in Canada (beginning in 1981) and France. For Sweden, beginning in 1980, all cohabitants are included as married couples, and the figures for 1970 have been adjusted to include all cohabitants. For Denmark, beginning 1983, persons reported separately as living in consensual unions with joint children have been classified here as married couples. In other countries, some unmarried cohabitants are included as married couples, while some are classified under "other households," depending on responses to surveys and censuses. [2] Children are defined as unmarried children living at home according to the following age limits: under 18 years old in the United States, Canada, Japan, Denmark, and the United Kingdom, except that the United Kingdom includes 16- and 17-year-olds only if they are in full-time education; under 25 years old in France; under 16 years old in Sweden; and children of all ages in the Netherlands and Germany. [3] Includes both family and nonfamily households not elsewhere classified. These households comprise, for example, siblings residing together, other households composed of relatives, and households made up of roommates. Some unmarried cohabitating couples may also be included in the "other" group. See footnote 1. [4] Estimated by the U.S. Bureau of Labor Statistics. [5] From family-based statistics. However, one person living alone constitutes a family in Denmark. In this respect, the Danish data are closer to household statistics. [6] Prior to 1991, data are for former West Germany. [7] Beginning 1988, data are not strictly comparable with prior years due to change in source of data. [8] Great Britain only (excludes Northern Ireland).

Source: U.S. Bureau of Labor Statistics, *Monthly Labor Review*, March 1990; and unpublished data.

No. 1357. Marriage and Divorce Rates, by Country: 1970 to 1991

COUNTRY	MARRIAGE RATE PER 1,000 POPULATION, 15 TO 64 YEARS OLD						DIVORCE RATE PER 1,000 MARRIED WOMEN					
	1970	1980	1988	1989	1990	1991	1970	1980	1988	1989	1990	1991
United States [1]	17	16	15	15	15	14	15	23	21	21	21	21
Canada	14	12	11	11	10	10	6	10	12	12	11	11
Denmark	12	8	9	9	9	9	8	11	13	14	13	11
France	12	10	7	8	8	8	3	6	8	8	8	9
Germany [2]	12	9	9	9	9	8	5	6	9	9	8	(NA)
Italy	11	9	8	8	8	8	1	1	2	2	2	2
Japan	14	10	8	8	8	(NA)	4	5	5	5	5	(NA)
Netherlands	15	10	9	9	9	9	3	8	8	8	8	8
Sweden	8	7	8	[3]20	7	7	7	11	11	12	12	12
United Kingdom	14	12	11	11	10	9	[4]5	[4]12	12	13	13	13

NA Not available.   [1] Beginning 1980, includes unlicensed marriages registered in California.   [2] Prior to 1991, data are for former West Germany.   [3] Increase in Swedish marriage rate in 1989 is due to change in inheritance laws which caused many cohabiting couples to marry.   [4] England and Wales only.

No. 1358. Births to Unmarried Women, by Country: 1970 to 1991

[For U.S. figures, beginning 1980, marital status is inferred from a comparison of the childs' and parents' surnames on the birth certificate for those States that do not report on marital status. No estimates are included for misstatements on birth records or failures to register births]

COUNTRY	1970		1980		1990		1991	
	Total live births (1,000)	Percent born to unmarried women	Total live births (1,000)	Percent born to unmarried women	Total live births (1,000)	Percent born to unmarried women	Total live births (1,000)	Percent born to unmarried women
United States	3,731	11	3,612	18	4,158	28	4,111	30
Canada [1]	372	10	360	13	398	24	403	29
Denmark	71	11	57	33	63	46	64	47
France	850	7	800	11	762	30	759	(NA)
Germany [2]	811	6	621	8	727	11	830	15
Italy	902	2	640	4	554	6	556	(NA)
Japan	1,932	1	1,616	1	1,240	1	1,224	(NA)
Netherlands	239	2	181	4	198	11	199	12
Sweden	110	18	97	40	124	47	124	48
United Kingdom	904	8	754	12	799	28	793	30

NA Not available.   [1] 1980 through 1990 data exclude Newfoundland.   [2] Prior to 1991, data are for former West Germany.
Source of tables 1357 and 1358: U.S. Bureau of Labor Statistics, *Monthly Labor Review*, 1990; and unpublished data.

No. 1359. Death Rates, by Cause and Country

[Age-standardized death rate per 100,000 population. For explanation of age-adjustment, see text, section 2. The standard population for this table is the old European standard; see source for details. Deaths classified according to ninth revision of *International Classification of Diseases*; see text, section 2]

COUNTRY	Year	Ischemic heart disease	Cerebrovascular disease	CANCER OF—			Bronchitis,[1] emphysema, asthma	Chronic liver disease and cirrhosis	Motor vehicle traffic accidents	Suicide and self-inflicted injury
				Lung, trachea, bronchus	Stomach	Female breast				
United States	1989	179.8	50.7	56.1	5.5	31.9	9.0	11.6	18.1	12.0
Australia	1988	200.5	77.9	40.4	9.0	29.6	14.6	8.1	17.8	13.3
Austria	1991	154.9	95.4	35.2	17.3	31.1	17.0	27.2	16.0	20.6
Belgium	1987	103.5	75.9	54.8	13.2	37.0	20.8	11.3	18.3	21.2
Bulgaria	1991	231.8	234.3	31.2	20.9	21.5	11.9	14.2	10.1	14.6
Canada	1990	161.3	50.0	54.1	8.0	34.2	8.1	8.8	13.3	12.4
Czechoslovakia	1990	314.4	183.5	53.2	20.1	28.7	21.1	26.1	13.6	18.3
Denmark	1991	196.4	71.3	51.9	8.6	39.3	36.2	13.5	10.6	20.9
Finland	1991	228.4	96.9	32.1	13.1	22.6	15.3	10.6	11.4	28.6
France	1990	61.9	55.4	34.1	9.0	28.1	9.7	17.4	16.8	19.0
Germany	1990	149.2	85.6	36.1	15.9	32.9	22.7	19.4	10.8	13.9
Hungary	1991	244.5	174.2	61.8	23.8	33.4	38.1	55.1	21.9	36.9
Italy	1989	96.2	94.6	43.3	19.3	29.8	23.6	23.8	13.8	6.8
Japan	1991	36.4	84.5	27.1	34.4	9.0	10.7	12.5	10.8	15.0
Netherlands	1990	130.2	67.3	51.7	12.3	38.3	17.1	4.8	8.1	9.3
New Zealand	1989	221.1	81.7	43.4	10.0	38.4	18.9	3.7	21.5	13.8
Norway	1990	187.2	84.4	28.1	11.6	27.3	14.0	5.4	7.4	15.1
Poland	1991	127.0	76.1	52.1	20.2	21.7	24.0	13.1	23.2	14.7
Portugal	1991	86.0	219.9	21.5	26.2	26.7	13.1	27.0	28.2	9.2
Spain	1989	73.0	93.5	32.4	15.9	24.2	9.1	20.2	20.2	7.4
Sweden	1989	186.3	66.7	23.0	9.9	25.2	11.7	6.5	9.4	17.4
Switzerland	1991	107.3	52.9	34.2	9.5	36.1	17.7	9.1	11.6	20.7
United Kingdom:										
England and Wales	1991	208.3	86.9	52.4	12.1	40.2	12.2	5.7	8.1	7.4
Scotland	1991	253.5	111.5	67.4	12.8	38.2	8.3	9.1	9.4	10.0

[1] Chronic and unspecified.
Source: World Health Organization, Geneva, Switzerland, *World Health Statistics Annual*.

No. 1360. Suicide Rates, by Country

[Rate per 100,000 population. Includes deaths resulting indirectly from self-inflicted injuries. Deaths classified according to the ninth revision of the *International Classification of Diseases (I.C.D.)*; see text, section 2]

SEX AND AGE	United States, 1989	Australia, 1988	Austria, 1991	Canada, 1990	Denmark, 1991	France, 1990	Germany,[1] 1990	Italy, 1989	Japan, 1991	Netherlands, 1990	Poland, 1991	Sweden, 1989	United Kingdom,[2] 1991
MALE													
Total[3]	19.9	21.0	34.6	20.4	30.0	29.6	22.4	11.2	20.6	12.3	23.9	26.8	12.1
15 to 24 years old	22.2	27.8	25.7	24.6	12.0	14.1	15.0	5.1	9.1	8.2	15.8	19.8	10.8
25 to 34 years old	24.3	28.2	29.7	29.6	28.0	30.6	21.3	9.9	18.1	15.8	29.1	33.7	17.2
35 to 44 years old	22.8	26.0	42.8	26.7	41.5	37.2	22.2	9.2	21.7	16.2	39.3	31.0	18.7
45 to 54 years old	22.4	24.4	36.6	23.4	44.4	41.1	28.2	13.5	33.5	14.8	44.1	35.4	17.3
55 to 64 years old	24.6	23.8	48.2	22.6	46.2	38.3	31.0	17.1	34.9	16.1	37.4	36.0	12.8
65 to 74 years old	33.0	27.7	64.0	20.7	41.5	47.1	34.6	25.0	32.3	15.4	32.1	34.6	10.8
75 yrs. and over.	54.2	39.8	123.6	32.4	69.4	105.9	72.2	43.6	58.6	34.0	30.4	53.3	17.4
FEMALE													
Total[3]	4.8	5.6	11.6	5.2	15.1	11.1	9.6	4.1	11.8	7.2	4.4	10.6	3.4
15 to 24 years old	4.2	4.5	6.1	5.0	3.6	4.4	4.5	1.6	4.7	3.6	2.4	8.3	2.2
25 to 34 years old	5.6	7.2	7.6	6.4	8.1	9.1	6.9	3.2	8.3	7.2	4.0	12.5	3.2
35 to 44 years old	6.6	7.5	12.4	9.0	14.4	11.8	7.6	3.5	8.9	8.7	6.9	11.4	4.2
45 to 54 years old	7.3	8.2	16.3	7.4	21.7	16.4	11.4	5.1	13.8	10.1	7.7	12.5	4.6
55 to 64 years old	7.3	8.7	16.1	5.4	30.4	18.1	12.8	6.7	16.9	12.1	7.6	16.2	5.3
65 to 74 years old	5.9	7.4	19.2	5.9	32.5	18.5	17.1	8.5	24.0	9.4	7.8	16.8	5.2
75 yrs. and over.	5.9	10.0	26.7	4.2	28.4	25.6	23.7	9.5	43.1	14.9	5.6	13.5	5.6

[1] Former West Germany. [2] England and Wales only. [3] Includes under 15 years old not shown separately.

Source: World Health Organization, Geneva, Switzerland, *World Health Statistics Annual;* and unpublished data.

No. 1361. Health Expenditures, by Country: 1980 to 1991

[G.D.P.=gross domestic product; for explanation, see text, section 14. For explanation of purchasing power parities, see text, section 30]

COUNTRY	TOTAL HEALTH EXPENDITURES						PUBLIC HEALTH EXPENDITURES			
	Percent of gross domestic product					Per capita, 1991, on basis of G.D.P. purchasing power parities	1980		1991	
	1980	1985	1989	1990	1991		Percent of gross domestic product	Percent of total health expenditures	Percent of gross domestic product	Percent of total health expenditures
United States	9.2	10.5	11.6	12.4	13.4	2,867	3.9	42.0	5.9	43.9
Australia	7.3	7.7	7.7	8.2	8.6	1,411	4.6	62.9	5.8	67.8
Austria	7.9	8.1	8.5	8.4	8.6	1,492	5.4	68.8	5.7	67.1
Belgium	6.6	7.4	7.6	7.6	7.9	1,354	5.5	83.4	7.0	88.9
Canada	7.4	8.5	9.0	9.5	10.0	1,917	5.5	74.7	7.2	72.2
Denmark.	6.8	6.3	6.5	6.3	6.5	1,151	5.8	85.2	5.4	81.5
Finland	6.5	7.3	7.4	8.0	9.1	1,420	5.1	79.0	7.4	80.9
France	7.6	8.5	8.7	8.9	9.1	1,656	6.0	78.8	6.8	73.9
Germany[1]	8.4	8.7	8.3	8.3	8.4	1,663	6.3	75.0	6.0	71.8
Greece	4.3	4.9	5.4	5.4	5.2	404	3.6	82.2	[2]4.1	[2]77.0
Iceland	6.4	7.1	8.6	8.3	8.4	1,476	5.7	88.2	7.2	87.0
Ireland	9.2	8.2	6.9	7.0	7.3	844	7.5	82.2	5.6	75.8
Italy	6.9	7.0	7.6	8.1	8.3	1,408	5.6	81.1	6.5	77.5
Japan	6.6	6.5	6.6	6.7	6.8	1,307	4.6	70.8	4.8	70.1
Luxembourg	6.8	6.8	6.9	7.2	7.3	1,476	6.3	92.8	[2]6.6	[2]91.4
Netherlands	8.0	8.0	8.1	8.2	8.4	1,366	6.0	74.7	6.1	73.1
New Zealand.	7.2	6.5	7.2	7.3	7.7	1,047	6.0	83.6	6.1	78.9
Norway.	6.6	6.4	7.4	7.4	7.6	1,305	6.5	98.4	[2]7.3	96.6
Portugal	5.9	7.0	7.2	6.7	6.8	624	4.3	72.4	[2]4.1	[2]61.7
Spain	5.6	5.7	6.3	6.6	6.7	848	4.5	79.9	5.5	82.2
Sweden	9.4	8.8	8.6	8.6	8.6	1,443	8.7	92.5	6.7	78.0
Switzerland	7.3	7.6	7.5	7.8	7.9	1,730	4.9	67.5	5.4	68.3
Turkey	4.0	2.8	3.9	4.0	4.0	142	1.1	27.3	[2]1.4	[2]35.6
United Kingdom	5.8	6.0	6.1	6.2	6.6	1,033	5.2	89.6	5.5	83.3

[1] Former West Germany. [2] 1990 data.

Source: Organization for Economic Cooperation and Development, Paris, France, *OECD Health Data,* 1993; *OECD Health Systems: Facts and Trends,* 1993; and unpublished data.

No. 1362. Education Expenditures, by Country: 1991

[Includes both current and capital expenditures. Public expenditure refers to the spending of public authorities at all levels. Private expenditure refers to the spending of private sources- mainly households, private nonprofit institutions, and firms and businesses. Expenditure per student based on full-time equivalent students enrolled in both public and private schools. Purchasing power parities (PPP's) are the rates of currency conversion that equalize the purchasing power of different countries. This means that a given sum of money, when converted into different currencies at the PPP rates, will buy the same basket of goods and services in all countries. Thus, PPP's are the rates of currency conversion that eliminate differences in price levels between countries. Educational program levels classified according to the International Standard Classification for Education developed by United Nations Educational, Scientific, and Cultural Organization]

COUNTRY	EXPENDITURES AS PERCENT OF GROSS DOMESTIC PRODUCT			PUBLIC EXPENDITURE FOR EDUCATION AS PERCENT OF TOTAL PUBLIC EXPENDITURES	EXPENDITURES PER STUDENT USING PURCHASING POWER PARITIES (U.S. dollars)					
	Total	Public sources	Private		Total	Early childhood education [1]	Primary and secondary			Higher education
							Total	Primary	Secondary [2]	
OECD......	6.4	5.2	1.4	12.8	5,343	2,518	4,571	3,824	5,270	9,326
Australia........	5.5	4.7	0.8	12.6	3,663	(NA)	2,626	(NA)	(NA)	10,934
Austria.........	5.4	5.4	-	10.8	4,730	2,400	4,313	3,573	4,680	6,441
Belgium	5.4	5.4	-	9.5	4,003	2,245	3,635	2,142	5,000	6,235
Canada	7.4	6.7	0.7	13.8	6,191	(NA)	5,004	4,456	5,406	10,415
Denmark........	6.1	6.1	-	10.4	5,524	4,418	4,589	4,060	5,073	7,685
Finland........	6.6	6.1	0.5	14.7	5,370	2,795	4,132	2,754	5,112	7,218
France . [3] [4]	6.0	5.4	0.6	10.6	4,319	2,308	5,432	2,609	6,638	5,871
Germany [3] [4]	5.4	4.0	1.5	8.0	5,588	1,517	2,057	1,598	2,592	6,322
Ireland [5]	5.9	5.5	0.4	(NA)	2,412	1,494	3,433	3,300	3,547	7,047
Japan..........	5.0	3.7	1.3	11.4	4,203	1,962	3,490	2,791	4,071	7,570
Netherlands [4]	5.8	5.6	0.1	9.8	4,277	2,390	4,701	3,885	5,376	9,373
Norway.........	6.8	6.8	-	12.1	5,613	6,286	2,223	2,110	2,364	8,405
Portugal........	5.5	5.5	-	(NA)	2,551	1,506	2,513	1,980	2,835	6,161
Spain [6]	5.6	4.5	1.1	(NA)	2,837	2,073	6,051	5,465	6,627	3,875
Sweden	6.5	6.5	-	10.4	6,151	2,501	6,089	5,447	6,563	8,548
Switzerland [4]	5.4	5.4	-	15.9	6,815	2,017	(NA)	(NA)	504	14,682
Turkey	4.0	4.0	-	(NA)	693	(NA)	3,559	2,794	4,255	2,795
United Kingdom....	5.3	5.3	-	12.5	4,268	2,233	5,555	4,920	6,291	9,621
United States.....	**7.0**	**5.5**	**1.5**	**14.7**	**6,593**	**3,088**	**5,555**	**4,920**	**6,291**	**13,639**

- Represents or rounds to zero.   NA Not available.   [1] Covers young children participating in a program intended to foster learning, and emotional and social development.   [2] Includes general, technical, or vocational education for students. It may either be "terminal" (i.e., preparing students for entry directly into working life) and/or "preparatory" (i.e., preparing students for higher education).   [3] Data for former West Germany.   [4] Provisional.   [5] Private expenditures only include household spending.   [6] Public expenditure is underestimated because a large part of the pension costs are not included.

No. 1363. Educational Attainment, by Country: 1991

[Percent of persons 25 to 64 years old]

COUNTRY	Total	No high school diploma	High school diploma	College or postsecondary degree
Australia [1]	100	44	25	31
Austria	100	33	61	7
Belgium	100	57	24	20
Canada	100	24	36	40
Denmark............	100	39	43	18
Finland.............	100	40	42	18
France	100	49	35	15
Germany	100	18	60	22
Ireland	100	60	24	16
Italy...............	100	72	22	6
Netherlands	100	44	37	20
New Zealand.........	100	44	33	23
Norway.............	100	21	54	25
Portugal............	100	93	3	4
Spain..............	100	78	12	10
Sweden	100	33	44	23
Switzerland	100	19	60	20
Turkey	100	82	11	6
United Kingdom......	100	35	49	16
United States........	**100**	**17**	**47**	**36**

[1] Persons 25 to 69 years old.

Source of tables 1362 and 1363: Organization for Economic Cooperation and Development, Paris, France, *Education at a Glance,* annual, (copyright).

No. 1364. Ratio of Students to Teachers, by Country: 1991

[Public and private education. Educational program levels classified according to the International Standard Classification for Education developed by United Nations Educational, Scientific, and Cultural Organization]

COUNTRY	Early childhood education [1]	Primary	Secondary [2]		
			Total	Lower	Upper
Australia	(NA)	18.5	18.6	(NA)	(NA)
Austria	20.9	10.8	10.0	6.7	17.0
Belgium	17.4	13.5	7.7	(NA)	(NA)
Denmark	13.6	11.1	10.7	9.5	12.4
Finland	(NA)	18.8	(NA)	(NA)	(NA)
France	27.5	22.8	14.0	(NA)	(NA)
Germany [3]	20.8	20.5	16.5	14.9	19.3
Ireland	28.3	26.9	17.2	(NA)	(NA)
Japan	18.9	20.3	17.3	17.5	17.0
Netherlands	21.2	19.7	15.9	(NA)	(NA)
Norway	(NA)	10.8	8.9	8.8	8.9
Portugal	22.2	13.4	11.6	(NA)	(NA)
Spain	24.8	22.0	16.9	18.1	16.0
Sweden	(NA)	10.4	10.7	9.7	11.9
Turkey	16.8	30.4	23.9	51.1	12.7
United Kingdom	27.8	21.5	14.7	17.7	13.2
United States	**(NA)**	**15.2**	**15.5**	**15.7**	**15.2**

NA Not available.   [1] Covers young children participating in a program intended to foster learning, and emotional and social development.   [2] Includes general, technical, or vocational education for students. It may either be "terminal" (i.e., preparing students for entry directly into working life) and/or "preparatory" (i.e., preparing students for higher education).   [3] Data for former West Germany.

Source: Organization for Economic Cooperation and Development, Paris, France, *Education at a Glance*, annual, (copyright).

No. 1365. Unemployment, by Educational Attainment and Country: 1991

[Percent of persons 25 to 64 years of age in the labor force. Education program levels according to the International Standard Classification for Education developed by United Nations Educational, Scientific, and Cultural Organization]

COUNTRY	Total	Early childhood, [1] primary	Secondary [2]		Higher education	
			Lower	Upper	Nonuniversity	University
Australia	7.1	7.8	9.6	6.0	6.6	4.2
Austria	3.4	(NA)	4.8	3.1	(NA)	1.5
Belgium	7.8	19.5	6.6	4.2	2.3	1.7
Canada	9.1	14.6	13.7	9.5	7.8	5.1
Denmark	9.9	(NA)	14.2	9.1	5.7	4.6
Finland	6.6	(NA)	8.6	7.0	2.9	2.1
France	7.8	9.0	11.5	6.6	3.6	3.8
Germany	6.6	(NA)	10.5	6.6	4.6	4.5
Ireland	13.6	24.5	15.8	7.3	4.9	3.4
Italy	6.1	5.1	6.3	7.2	(NA)	5.0
Netherlands	6.1	13.0	6.7	4.9	4.2	4.6
New Zealand	8.1	12.5	7.0	7.4	5.3	4.2
Norway	4.1	(NA)	6.7	4.4	2.3	1.6
Portugal	3.8	4.0	3.6	3.1	0.8	1.8
Spain	12.9	13.0	16.0	12.2	(NA)	9.3
Sweden	2.1	(NA)	2.6	2.3	1.1	1.1
Switzerland	1.4	(NA)	1.3	1.5	0.8	2.2
Turkey	5.7	5.2	9.2	7.2	(NA)	3.1
United Kingdom	7.1	(NA)	10.4	6.5	3.7	3.1
United States	**6.8**	**11.8**	**12.8**	**7.3**	**5.6**	**3.6**

NA Not available.   [1] Covers young children participating in a program intended to foster learning and emotional and social development.   [2] Includes general, technical, or vocational education for students. It may either be "terminal" (i.e., preparing students for entry directly into working life) and/or "preparatory" (i.e., preparing students for higher education).

Source: Organization for Economic Cooperation and Development, Paris, France, *Education at a Glance*, annual, (copyright).

No. 1366. Gross National Product, by Country: 1985 to 1991

[In billions of dollars. For most countries, data for GNP are based on local currencies which are deflated to constant 1991 local currency values before conversion to U.S. dollar equivalents. In general, the rates used for conversion are the 1991 average par/market exchange rates as supplied by the International Bank for Reconstruction and Development]

COUNTRY	CURRENT DOLLARS				CONSTANT (1991) DOLLARS				Per capita (dollars)		
	1985	1989	1990	1991	1985	1989	1990	1991	1985	1990	1991
United States	4,054	5,267	5,543	5,695	5,057	5,714	5,765	5,695	21,140	23,020	22,550
Algeria	34	39	40	41	42	42	41	41	1,890	1,626	1,564
Argentina	95	110	116	130	119	119	120	130	3,920	3,742	3,984
Australia	204	264	274	288	254	286	285	288	16,080	16,690	16,600
Austria	109	139	152	162	136	151	158	162	18,040	20,480	20,760
Bangladesh	14	19	21	23	18	21	22	23	177	192	195
Belgium	131	171	183	196	163	185	191	196	16,530	19,150	19,580
Brazil	287	384	384	404	358	416	399	404	2,596	2,618	2,601
Bulgaria	41	50	¹45	¹37	51	54	¹47	¹37	5,750	¹5,254	¹4,140
Burma ¹	21	22	24	¹22	26	23	25	¹22	692	610	¹531
Canada	402	531	549	563	501	576	571	563	19,890	21,450	20,840
Chile	15	24	26	30	19	26	27	30	1,602	2,085	2,215
China:											
Mainland	774	1,242	1,369	1,528	965	1,347	1,424	1,528	920	1,256	1,327
Taiwan	91	153	168	187	114	166	175	187	5,903	8,551	9,068
Colombia	25	34	37	40	31	37	39	40	1,038	1,173	1,187
Cuba ¹	30	35	34	27	37	38	35	27	3,652	3,314	1,584
Czechoslovakia	98	123	¹124	¹109	122	134	¹129	¹109	7,872	¹8,248	¹6,914
Denmark.	92	112	119	125	114	121	123	125	22,320	24,000	24,230
Egypt	20	27	28	30	25	29	29	30	533	544	543
El Salvador	4	5	5	6	5	5	6	6	1,064	1,060	1,075
Ethiopia	4	6	6	7	6	7	7	7	130	129	124
Finland	88	119	124	120	110	129	129	120	22,480	25,970	24,110
France . . ., ...	817	1,068	1,136	1,191	1,019	1,158	1,182	1,191	18,470	20,840	20,900
Germany ²	1,052	1,346	1,472	1,586	1,313	1,461	1,531	1,586	21,510	24,260	19,830
Ghana	4	5	6	6	5	6	6	6	366	394	401
Greece	50	63	66	69	63	68	68	69	6,317	6,813	6,878
Hungary	53	65	¹63	¹59	66	70	¹65	¹59	6,160	¹6,281	¹5,727
India	156	228	251	263	195	247	261	263	253	306	303
Indonesia	61	90	100	111	76	97	104	111	442	550	577
Iran	77	77	89	100	96	83	92	100	2,067	1,619	1,689
Iraq	33	34	25	13	41	37	26	13	2,617	1,400	705
Israel	37	50	55	62	46	54	57	62	11,680	13,290	13,590
Italy	777	1,014	1,078	1,134	970	1,100	1,121	1,134	16,970	19,440	19,630
Japan.	2,071	2,841	3,117	3,386	2,584	3,082	3,242	3,386	21,400	26,240	27,300
Kenya	5	7	7	8	6	7	7	8	295	318	310
Kuwait ¹	26	33	26	16	32	36	27	16	17,100	12,800	19,510
Madagascar	2	2	3	3	2	3	3	3	236	227	205
Malaysia	23	34	40	45	29	37	41	45	1,835	2,354	2,506
Mexico	195	232	254	276	243	251	264	276	3,079	2,988	3,051
Morocco	16	22	24	27	20	24	25	27	878	987	1,014
Mozambique	1	1	1	1	1	1	1	1	68	73	74
Nepal	2	2	3	3	2	3	3	3	123	137	141
Netherlands	199	252	273	290	248	274	284	290	17,140	19,010	19,310
Nigeria	19	24	26	30	23	26	27	30	227	230	242
North Korea ¹	26	30	30	23	33	33	31	23	1,674	1,443	1,068
Norway	75	91	97	103	94	99	101	103	22,620	23,810	24,150
Pakistan	26	37	40	44	33	40	42	44	328	363	369
Peru.	39	45	45	47	48	49	47	47	2,459	2,147	2,090
Philippines	28	40	44	46	35	44	46	46	615	709	694
Poland	144	175	¹163	¹160	180	190	¹170	¹160	4,841	¹4,456	¹4,185
Portugal	39	55	61	65	48	60	63	65	4,771	6,099	6,251
Romania.	99	113	¹105	¹94	124	123	¹109	¹94	5,455	¹4,705	¹4,064
Saudi Arabia	94	93	109	118	118	101	114	118	8,718	6,982	7,151
South Africa	76	96	100	105	94	104	104	105	2,726	2,629	2,573
South Korea	124	219	249	281	155	237	259	281	3,797	5,997	6,430
Soviet Union	2,118	2,645	2,660	¹2,531	2,642	2,870	2,767	¹2,531	9,475	9,509	¹8,639
Spain	328	454	491	522	409	493	510	522	10,630	13,100	13,370
Sri Lanka	6	7	8	9	7	8	9	9	455	502	518
Sudan	19	25	26	28	24	27	27	28	1,031	1,027	1,016
Sweden	170	216	226	230	213	234	235	230	25,430	27,490	26,900
Switzerland	172	220	233	242	214	239	242	242	32,740	35,920	35,590
Syria	17	19	23	25	21	20	23	25	1,957	1,842	1,909
Tanzania.	2	2	2	2	2	2	2	2	98	95	96
Thailand	43	72	82	92	53	78	86	92	1,028	1,531	1,618
Turkey	62	87	100	105	77	95	104	105	1,518	1,819	1,790
Uganda	2	2	3	3	2	3	3	3	150	158	157
United Kingdom	711	943	985	1,002	887	1,023	1,025	1,002	15,660	17,850	17,400
Venezuela.	33	39	46	53	41	43	48	53	2,378	2,413	2,609
Yugoslavia	91	107	105	(NA)	113	117	109	(NA)	4,892	4,545	(NA)
Zaire	7	9	9	(NA)	8	9	9	(NA)	268	244	(NA)

NA Not available.　　¹ Estimated.　　² Prior to 1991, data are for former West Germany.

Source: U.S. Arms Control and Disarmament Agency, *World Military Expenditures and Arms Transfers,* annual. Data from International Bank for Reconstruction and Development and U.S. Central Intelligence Agency.

No. 1367. Annual Growth Rates of Real Gross Domestic Product, by Country: 1980 to 1995

[Percent change from previous year. Minus sign (-) indicates decline. See also *Historical Statistics, Colonial Times to 1970*, series F 10-16]

COUNTRY	1980	1985	1988	1989	1990	1991	1992	1993	1994	1995
OECD	1.1	3.3	4.4	3.3	2.5	0.8	1.7	1.1	2.1	2.7
United States	-0.5	3.2	3.9	2.5	1.2	-0.7	2.6	2.8	3.1	2.7
Australia	2.5	4.8	4.4	4.6	1.4	-0.8	2.0	2.5	3.1	3.4
Austria	2.9	2.5	4.1	3.8	4.6	3.0	1.5	-0.5	1.0	2.3
Belgium	4.1	0.8	5.0	3.9	3.3	2.1	0.8	-1.2	0.9	2.0
Canada	1.5	4.7	5.0	2.4	-0.2	-1.7	0.7	2.5	3.7	4.1
Denmark	-0.4	4.3	1.2	0.6	2.0	1.2	1.0	0.2	2.5	2.8
Finland	5.3	3.3	5.4	5.4	-	-7.0	-4.0	-2.0	-0.3	2.4
France [1]	1.6	1.9	4.5	4.3	2.5	0.7	1.4	-0.9	1.1	2.7
Germany [1]	1.0	2.0	3.7	3.6	5.7	4.5	2.1	-1.5	0.8	2.2
Greece	1.8	3.1	4.4	3.5	-1.1	3.3	0.9	0.5	0.9	2.1
Iceland	7.0	3.6	-0.3	-0.3	0.5	1.0	-3.7	0.4	-2.0	1.1
Ireland	3.1	3.1	4.2	6.5	9.1	2.6	4.9	2.7	3.1	3.2
Italy	4.1	2.6	4.1	2.9	2.1	1.3	0.9	-0.1	1.7	2.3
Japan	3.6	5.0	6.2	4.7	4.8	4.0	1.3	-0.5	0.5	2.3
Luxembourg	0.8	2.9	5.7	6.7	3.2	3.1	1.8	1.0	1.5	2.3
Netherlands	0.9	2.6	2.6	4.7	4.1	2.1	1.4	-0.2	0.6	2.2
New Zealand	0.4	1.2	3.0	-0.7	0.5	-1.8	0.5	3.0	3.3	3.1
Norway	4.2	5.3	-0.5	0.6	1.7	1.6	3.3	1.6	3.2	3.8
Portugal	4.6	2.8	3.9	5.2	4.4	2.1	1.6	-0.4	2.0	3.1
Spain	1.3	2.6	5.2	4.7	3.6	2.2	0.8	-1.0	0.8	2.6
Sweden	1.7	1.9	2.3	2.4	1.4	-1.7	-1.7	-2.7	1.5	2.2
Switzerland	4.4	3.7	2.9	3.9	2.3	-	-0.1	-0.8	0.8	2.0
Turkey [2]	-1.1	5.1	3.6	2.1	9.1	0.3	5.9	7.0	5.0	4.7
United Kingdom	-1.9	3.8	4.4	2.1	0.5	-2.2	-0.6	2.0	2.9	2.9

- Represents or rounds to zero.   [1] Former West Germany.   [2] Gross national product.

No. 1368. Gross Domestic Product of Selected Countries as Percent of United States: 1970 to 1991

[Comparisons are based on constant (1985) price data converted to U.S. dollars using 1985 exchange rates]

COUNTRY	1970	1975	1980	1981	1982	1983	1984	1985	1986	1987	1988	1989	1990	1991
United States	100	100	100	100	100	100	100	100	100	100	100	100	100	100
OECD Europe [1]	75	78	76	76	78	77	74	74	74	74	73	74	75	77
European Union [1]	65	66	65	65	67	66	63	63	63	63	63	63	65	66
Canada	7	8	8	9	9	8	9	9	9	9	9	9	9	9
France	13	14	14	14	14	14	13	13	13	13	13	13	13	14
Germany [2]	17	16	16	16	16	16	16	15	15	15	15	15	16	17
Japan	27	29	31	32	34	33	33	33	33	34	34	35	37	38
United Kingdom	13	12	12	11	12	12	11	11	12	12	12	12	12	12

[1] For countries, see text, section 30.   [2] Prior to 1990, data are for former West Germany.
Source of tables 1367 and 1368: Organization for Economic Cooperation and Development, Paris, France, *National Accounts*, annual.

No. 1369. Selected International Economic Indicators, by Country: 1980 to 1993

[Data cover gross domestic product (GDP) at market prices. Gross fixed capital formation covers private and government sectors except military. Savings data are calculated by deducting outlays—such as personal consumption expenditures, interest paid, and transfer payments to foreigners—from disposable personal income. Minus (-) indicates decline]

YEAR	United States	France	Germany	Italy	Netherlands	United Kingdom	Japan	Canada
GDP growth rates [1] (constant 1987 prices):								
1980	-0.5	1.6	(NA)	4.1	0.9	-2.2	3.6	1.5
1985	3.2	1.9	(NA)	2.6	2.6	3.8	5.0	4.8
1990	1.2	2.5	(NA)	2.1	4.1	0.4	4.8	-0.2
1991	-0.7	0.8	1.0	1.2	2.1	-2.2	4.3	-1.7
1992	2.6	1.2	2.1	0.7	1.4	-0.6	1.1	0.7
1993	3.0	-1.0	-1.2	-0.7	0.2	1.9	0.1	2.4
Ratio of gross fixed capital formation to GDP (current prices):								
1980	20.4	23.0	(NA)	24.3	21.6	17.9	31.6	23.3
1985	19.4	19.3	(NA)	20.7	19.7	17.0	27.5	19.7
1990	16.8	21.4	(NA)	20.3	20.9	19.4	32.2	21.1
1991	15.4	21.1	23.2	19.7	20.5	16.8	31.8	19.8
1992	15.5	20.0	23.4	19.2	20.4	15.5	30.8	18.9
1993	16.1	18.9	22.7	17.1	19.7	14.9	30.1	18.2
Ratio of savings to disposable personal income:								
1980	7.9	17.6	(NA)	21.9	11.0	13.1	17.9	13.3
1985	6.4	14.0	(NA)	18.9	13.1	10.7	15.6	13.1
1990	4.2	12.5	(NA)	18.4	16.5	8.6	14.1	9.7
1991	4.8	13.1	13.8	18.6	12.5	10.1	14.9	10.1
1992	5.3	13.9	13.9	18.7	13.2	12.3	16.0	10.6
1993	4.0	14.2	13.2	(NA)	(NA)	11.5	(NA)	10.5

NA Not available.   [1] Percent change from previous year.
Source: U.S. Dept. of Commerce, International Trade Administration, Office of Trade and Economic Analysis, based on official statistics of listed countries.

No. 1370. Gross Domestic Product, Using Purchasing Power Parities, by Country: 1970 to 1991

[The goods and services produced in different countries should be valued consistently if the differences observed are meant to reflect real differences in the volumes of goods and services produced. The use of purchasing power parities (PPP) instead of exchange rates is intended to achieve this objective. PPP's show how many units of currency are needed in one country to buy the same amount of goods and services which one unit of currency will buy in the other country. See text, section 30]

COUNTRY	TOTAL (bil. dol.)						PER CAPITA (dollars)					
	1970	1980	1985	1989	1990	1991	1970	1980	1985	1989	1990	1991
OECD, total	2,504	6,962	10,255	13,456	14,349	15,003	3,505	8,927	12,689	16,180	17,133	17,772
OECD Europe [1] .	1,072	2,941	4,184	5,475	5,880	6,180	2,907	7,475	10,359	13,247	14,102	14,720
European Union [1] .	942	2,581	3,648	4,773	5,120	5,393	3,111	8,133	11,346	14,651	15,612	16,378
Australia	45	126	195	257	271	279	3,468	8,597	12,326	15,261	15,887	16,085
Austria	22	65	92	117	128	135	3,004	8,664	12,156	15,401	16,596	17,280
Belgium	30	85	116	151	163	172	3,140	8,637	11,805	15,194	16,301	17,454
Canada	76	243	368	489	507	518	3,571	10,082	14,632	18,629	19,049	19,178
Denmark	17	44	66	80	85	91	3,499	8,563	12,868	15,636	16,567	17,621
Finland	13	38	58	79	82	80	2,873	7,993	11,835	15,853	16,522	15,997
France	178	498	707	920	982	1,040	3,499	9,247	12,785	16,310	17,301	18,227
Germany	223	595	826	1,056	1,158	1,249	3,678	9,660	13,535	17,020	18,307	19,500
Greece	13	41	58	72	75	80	1,442	4,247	5,797	7,176	7,403	7,775
Iceland	1	2	3	4	4	5	2,621	9,040	12,628	16,035	16,662	17,237
Ireland	5	17	25	33	38	41	1,741	4,892	7,014	9,489	10,755	11,507
Italy	159	469	662	866	923	976	2,962	8,317	11,585	15,046	16,012	16,896
Japan	290	919	1,453	1,986	2,180	2,368	2,798	7,871	12,035	16,130	17,645	19,107
Luxembourg	1	3	5	7	8	8	3,772	9,274	13,703	18,657	19,923	21,372
Netherlands	46	125	173	220	239	249	3,534	8,847	11,949	14,821	15,951	16,530
New Zealand	10	25	38	44	46	47	3,443	7,790	11,477	13,175	13,564	13,883
Norway	10	34	52	64	68	72	2,686	8,259	12,610	15,152	16,033	16,904
Portugal	12	40	55	75	82	90	1,465	4,289	5,674	7,694	8,364	9,191
Spain	76	217	306	423	457	496	2,239	5,814	7,953	10,880	11,738	12,719
Sweden	31	75	109	138	145	144	3,788	9,073	13,008	16,188	16,881	16,729
Switzerland	32	74	104	134	143	149	5,088	11,527	15,884	19,911	21,020	21,747
Turkey	21	71	119	167	190	201	597	1,595	2,340	3,017	3,363	3,491
United Kingdom . .	181	447	650	869	911	902	3,256	7,935	11,473	15,177	15,866	15,720
United States . . .	1,012	2,708	4,017	5,205	5,465	5,611	4,933	11,891	16,786	20,920	21,866	22,204

[1] For countries, see text, section 30.
Source: Organization for Economic Cooperation and Development, Paris, France, *National Accounts of OECD Countries*, vol. I, annual.

No. 1371. Food and Beverage Expenditures, by Country: 1990

[Percent of total private consumption expenditures]

COUNTRY	Food	Nonalcoholic beverages	Alcoholic beverages	COUNTRY	Food	Nonalcoholic beverages	Alcoholic beverages
United States . . .	6.9	1.1	1.1	Israel	22.3	2.4	0.7
				Italy	17.9	0.4	1.1
Australia	[1]14.8	(NA)	4.1	Netherlands	13.9	0.6	1.8
Austria	16.5	0.7	2.2	Norway	18.3	1.3	3.0
Belgium	15.5	0.6	1.4	Philippines [3]	52.8	2.4	(NA)
Canada	[1]11.0	(NA)	2.6	Portugal [4]	34.1	0.3	2.0
Denmark	14.9	0.6	3.2	South Africa	27.1	1.5	6.2
Finland	15.6	0.5	4.2	Spain	18.1	0.4	1.2
France	15.7	0.5	2.0	Sweden	14.8	0.6	3.2
Germany	[2]19.5	(NA)	(NA)	Switzerland	17.9	[5]7.0	(NA)
Greece	31.2	1.2	3.0	Thailand	23.5	3.8	4.8
India	51.2	0.1	1.1	United Kingdom . .	10.8	1.0	6.5
Ireland	22.4	1.5	11.8	Venezuela	24.7	3.9	2.6

NA Not available. [1] Food expenditures include nonalcoholic beverages. [2] Food expenditures include all beverages. [3] Data for 1989. [4] Data for 1986. [5] Nonalcoholic beverage expenditures include all beverages.
Source: U.S. Dept. of Agriculture, Economic Research Service. Based on data from the United Nations, New York, NY, *National Accounts Statistics*, annual.

No. 1372. Per Capita Consumption of Meat and Poultry: 1993

[Preliminary. In pounds per capita. Beef, veal, and pork quantities are as of September and in carcass-weight equivalents; poultry quantities are as of July and are on ready-to-cook basis]

COUNTRY	PORK		COUNTRY	POULTRY		COUNTRY	BEEF AND VEAL	
	Quantity	Rank		Quantity	Rank		Quantity	Rank
Denmark	146	1	Hong Kong	100	1	Uruguay	158	1
Belgium-Lux	114	2	Israel	91	2	Argentina	153	2
Poland	112	3	United States	89	3	United States	95	3
Austria	112	4	Singapore	79	4	Canada	80	4
Spain	111	5	Saudi Arabia	71	5	Australia	79	5
Germany	108	6	Canada	63	6	New Zealand	75	6
Hungary	103	7	United Kingdom . . .	61	7	Kazakhstan	65	7
Taiwan	88	8	Australia	57	8	France	63	8
Switzerland	86	9	France	54	9	Russia	62	9
Hong Kong	86	10	Spain	53	10	Switzerland	58	10
United States	67	20						

Source: U.S. Department of Agriculture, Foreign Agricultural Service, *World Poultry Situation* and *World Livestock Situation*, annual.

No. 1373. Percent of Households Owning Selected Appliances, by Country: 1991

APPLIANCE	United States [1]	Bel-gium	Den-mark	France	Ger-many [2]	Italy	Nether-lands	Spain	Sweden	Swit-zerland	United King-dom
Cassette recorder. . . .	(NA)	75	82	76	74	64	81	67	88	82	82
Clothes washer	76	88	76	88	88	96	89	87	72	78	87
Dishwasher.	45	26	26	33	34	18	11	11	31	32	11
Food processor	(NA)	91	83	83	92	48	84	50	77	91	80
Microwave oven. . . .	79	21	14	25	36	6	22	9	37	15	48
Radio.	(NA)	90	98	98	84	92	99	95	93	99	90
Television set, color/mono	99	97	98	94	97	98	95	98	97	93	98
Tumbledrier.	53	39	22	12	17	10	27	5	18	27	32
Vacuum cleaner. . . .	(NA)	92	96	89	96	56	98	29	97	93	98
Video recorder. . . .	(NA)	42	39	35	42	25	50	40	48	41	65

NA Not available.   [1] Represents appliances possessed and generally used by the household (as of November). Source: U.S. Energy Information Administration, *Annual Energy Review*.   [2] Former West Germany.
Source: Except as noted, Euromonitor Publications Limited, London, England, *European Marketing Data and Statistics*, annual, (copyright).

No. 1374. Motor Vehicle Deaths and Vehicle Registrations, by Country

[Deaths are included if they occur within 30 days after the accident, except as noted. Death data must be compared cautiously because of differences in the volume and kinds of traffic, numbers of vehicles, population density, definitions of deaths, and other factors]

COUNTRY	MOTOR VEHICLE TRAFFIC DEATHS			1991 VEHICLE REGISTRATIONS			
				All vehicles		Passenger cars	
	Year	Number	Rate [1]	Number (mil.)	Persons per vehicle	Number (mil.)	Persons per car
Argentina	1989	3,085	9.7	5.8	5.6	4.3	7.5
Australia.	1989	4,210	16.1	9.6	1.7	7.7	2.2
Austria.	1991	1,363	17.4	3.8	2.0	3.1	2.5
Belgium	1987	[2]1,937	[2]19.6	4.4	2.3	3.9	2.5
Bulgaria	1991	929	10.3	1.5	6.1	1.3	6.8
Canada	1990	[3]3,645	[3]13.7	16.8	1.6	13.1	2.1
Chile	1989	941	7.3	1.0	13.0	0.7	19.0
Costa Rica	1989	389	13.2	0.3	12.0	0.2	18.0
Czechoslovakia	1990	2,127	13.6	3.6	4.4	3.3	4.7
Denmark.	1991	598	11.6	1.9	2.7	1.6	3.2
Dominican Republic	1985	557	8.9	0.2	31.0	0.1	53.0
Ecuador	1990	2,049	19.4	0.2	44.0	0.1	134.0
Finland.	1991	589	11.7	2.2	2.3	1.9	2.6
France	1990	[4]10,006	[4]17.6	28.8	2.0	23.8	2.4
Germany	1990	10,578	13.3	40.7	2.0	37.6	2.1
Greece.	1990	2,247	22.3	2.6	3.9	1.8	5.6
Hong Kong	1989	309	5.4	0.4	14.0	0.3	22.0
Hungary	1991	2,313	22.4	2.2	4.7	2.0	5.3
Ireland	1990	456	13.0	1.1	3.3	0.8	4.2
Israel	1989	439	9.7	1.0	4.4	0.8	5.3
Italy	1989	[4]8,717	[4]15.1	30.7	1.9	28.2	2.0
Japan.	1991	14,347	11.7	59.9	2.1	37.1	3.3
Kuwait	1987	343	18.3	0.7	3.1	0.5	4.0
Netherlands	1990	1,290	8.6	6.2	2.4	5.6	2.7
New Zealand.	1989	766	22.9	1.9	1.8	1.6	2.1
Norway.	1990	335	7.9	1.9	2.2	1.6	2.6
Panama	1989	320	13.5	0.2	12.0	0.2	16.0
Paraguay	1987	225	9.6	0.1	44.0	0.1	64.0
Poland	1991	8,643	22.6	7.4	5.1	6.1	6.2
Portugal	1991	2,896	29.4	2.4	4.2	1.8	5.8
Puerto Rico.	1990	548	15.5	1.6	2.3	1.4	2.6
Singapore.	1990	246	9.1	0.4	6.6	0.3	9.7
Sweden	1989	857	10.1	3.9	2.2	3.6	2.4
Switzerland	1991	845	12.4	3.4	2.0	3.1	2.2
Syria	1985	176	1.7	0.3	51.0	0.1	109.0
Thailand.	1987	4,441	8.3	2.7	21.0	0.8	69.0
United States.	**1989**	[3]46,586	[3]18.8	188.4	1.3	143.0	1.7
Uruguay	1990	375	12.1	0.3	10.0	0.2	16.0
Yugoslavia	1990	3,970	16.7	4.5	5.3	3.6	6.6

[1] Deaths per 100,000 population.   [2] Deaths occurring at the accident scene only.   [3] Deaths occurring within 1 year after the accident.   [4] Deaths occurring within 3 days after the accident.
Source: World Health Organization, Geneva, Switzerland, *World Health Statistics*, annual, and unpublished data; and American Automobile Manufactures Association, Inc., Detroit, MI, *AAMA Motor Vehicle Facts & Figures*, annual, (copyright).

No. 1375. Telephones, Newspapers, Television, and Radio, by Country

[See text, section 30, for general comments about the data. For data qualifications for countries, see source]

COUNTRY	Telephone main lines per 100 people, [1] 1992	Cellular telephone subscribers per 100,000 people, [1] 1992	Daily newspaper circulation per 1,000 people, [2] 1990	Television receivers per 1,000 people, [3] 1991	Radio receivers per 1,000 people, [4] 1991
Algeria	4	18	51	74	234
Argentina	11	136	124	220	676
Australia	47	2,510	246	480	1,268
Austria	44	2,188	351	478	617
Belgium	43	615	301	451	769
Brazil	7	20	54	207	386
Bulgaria	26	-	452	252	442
Canada	59	3,727	[5]228	639	1,029
Chile	9	474	455	209	344
China, Mainland	1	15	[6]37	31	182
Taiwan	36	1,850	49	(NA)	(NA)
Colombia	8	25	62	116	177
Costa Rica	11	-	[7]101	140	258
Cuba	3	2	172	163	345
Cyprus	40	1,353	110	144	292
Czechoslovakia	17	32	507	476	872
Denmark	58	3,993	352	536	1,031
Dominican Republic	6	94	32	84	171
Ecuador	5	-	87	84	317
Egypt	4	13	57	116	326
Finland	54	7,028	558	501	997
France	52	568	208	407	888
Germany	44	958	593	556	876
Greece	44	-	[8]139	197	421
Guatemala	2	(NA)	21	52	66
Honduras	2	-	39	73	386
Hong Kong	49	4,023	110	278	667
Hungary	13	226	233	412	596
Iceland	54	5,866	[6]467	319	786
India	1	-	[6]26	35	79
Indonesia	1	19	28	59	146
Iran	5	-	26	63	231
Iraq	(NA)	-	36	72	215
Ireland	31	1,239	169	301	630
Israel	36	696	258	269	470
Italy	41	1,355	108	421	791
Jamaica	7	320	64	131	420
Japan	47	1,260	587	613	907
Kuwait	18	2,589	210	283	343
Lebanon	12	134	117	325	833
Luxembourg	53	287	383	267	632
Malaysia	11	442	140	149	430
Mexico	8	298	133	148	255
Morocco	2	12	13	74	210
Netherlands	49	1,097	[5]647	485	907
New Zealand	45	2,938	324	443	929
Norway	53	6,527	610	423	794
Pakistan	1	12	15	18	90
Panama	10	-	70	166	224
Paraguay	3	33	39	50	171
Peru	3	121	79	98	253
Philippines	1	17	54	44	138
Poland	10	7	128	295	433
Portugal	32	378	39	187	228
Puerto Rico	31	1,428	129	264	710
Russia	15	4	(NA)	(NA)	(NA)
Romania	11	-	[5]158	196	199
Saudi Arabia	10	99	40	266	304
Singapore	42	4,270	282	378	646
South Africa	9	31	35	98	302
South Korea	36	623	277	208	1,001
Spain	35	461	[6]82	400	310
Sweden	68	7,558	525	468	877
Switzerland	61	3,231	456	406	842
Syria	4	-	23	60	255
Thailand	3	431	73	114	191
Trinidad and Tobago	14	101	77	315	492
Tunisia	4	22	37	79	199
Turkey	16	104	71	175	161
United Kingdom	45	2,595	[8]394	434	1,143
United States	**56**	**4,326**	**249**	**814**	**2,118**
Uruguay	16	55	233	231	604
Venezuela	9	101	145	162	447

- Represents or rounds to zero.　NA Not available.　[1] As of December 31.　[2] Publications containing general news and appearing at least 4 times a week; may range in size from a single sheet to 50 or more pages. Circulation data refer to average circulation per issue or number of printed copies per issue and include copies sold outside the country.　[3] Estimated number of sets in use.　[4] Data cover estimated number of receivers in use and apply to all types of receivers for radio broadcasts to the public, including receivers connected to a radio "redistribution system" but excluding television sets.　[5] For 1989.　[6] For 1985.　[7] For 1991.　[8] For 1988.

Source: International Telecommunications Union, Geneva, Switzerland, World Telecom Indicators, (copyright); and United Nations Educational, Scientific, and Cultural Organization, Paris, France, *Statistical Yearbook*, (copyright).

No. 1376. Tax Revenues, by Country: 1980 to 1991

[Covers national and local taxes and Social Security contributions]

COUNTRY	TAX REVENUES, 1991 Total (bil. dol.)	TAX REVENUES, 1991 Per capita (dol.)	PERCENT CHANGE IN TOTAL TAX REVENUE AS EXPRESSED IN NATIONAL CURRENCY [1] 1987	1988	1989	1990	1991	TAX REVENUES AS PERCENT OF GROSS DOMESTIC PRODUCT 1980	1985	1989	1990	1991
Australia	88	5,050	13.8	12.1	8.7	3.0	-3.4	28.4	30.1	30.6	30.8	29.2
Austria	69	8,830	2.8	4.9	4.3	8.4	8.5	41.2	43.1	41.0	41.3	42.1
Belgium	88	8,985	5.3	3.5	4.6	7.4	4.6	44.4	47.9	44.4	44.9	44.9
Canada	221	8,190	13.4	8.2	9.8	5.8	2.8	31.6	33.1	35.5	37.0	37.3
Denmark	63	12,219	6.6	4.8	2.8	0.1	3.5	45.5	49.0	50.7	48.5	48.3
Finland	47	9,366	2.3	18.6	11.3	7.5	-4.9	33.0	37.0	37.4	37.9	37.7
France	528	9,255	6.4	6.0	7.1	5.8	4.6	41.7	44.5	43.7	43.8	44.2
Germany [2]	661	8,279	4.0	4.5	7.7	4.5	23.3	38.2	38.1	38.2	36.8	39.2
Greece	27	2,635	14.6	12.0	11.9	30.3	29.4	29.4	35.1	33.3	36.1	38.3
Ireland	16	4,623	7.5	12.3	1.7	6.2	5.7	34.0	38.0	36.9	36.8	37.5
Italy	457	7,907	9.7	12.9	12.8	13.6	10.4	30.2	34.5	37.9	39.1	39.7
Japan	1,043	8,419	9.3	8.6	8.4	9.9	3.4	25.4	27.6	30.7	31.4	30.9
Luxembourg	5	11,976	6.3	8.0	10.4	7.7	5.4	46.0	50.1	48.2	48.8	48.5
Netherlands	137	9,064	6.5	4.2	-0.2	5.9	10.8	44.7	43.8	44.9	44.6	47.0
New Zealand	15	4,481	23.3	6.0	14.2	-1.1	-3.6	32.9	33.5	38.7	37.3	36.0
Norway	50	11,701	4.8	3.6	2.5	7.1	5.6	47.1	47.6	46.0	46.3	47.1
Portugal	24	2,487	10.4	27.7	20.5	18.2	19.1	28.7	31.6	35.1	34.8	35.6
Spain	183	4,693	18.8	11.8	18.5	10.7	10.3	24.1	28.8	34.6	34.4	34.7
Sweden	126	14,628	14.0	7.8	11.4	11.8	-0.7	49.1	50.4	56.0	56.9	53.2
Switzerland	72	10,489	3.0	7.1	5.4	7.3	4.3	30.8	32.0	31.7	31.5	31.0
Turkey	32	549	57.0	63.6	84.6	85.4	68.0	21.7	19.7	25.4	27.8	29.4
United Kingdom	364	6,341	8.4	12.4	7.8	6.8	2.4	35.3	37.8	36.7	36.7	36.0
United States	1,655	6,550	10.2	6.7	8.2	5.0	3.6	29.3	28.7	29.7	29.5	29.8

[1] Change from previous year. [2] Prior to 1991, data are for former West Germany.

Source: Organization for Economic Cooperation and Development, Paris, France, *Revenue Statistics of OECD Member Countries,* annual.

No. 1377. Percent Distribution of Tax Receipts, by Country: 1980 to 1991

COUNTRY	Total [1]	INCOME AND PROFITS TAXES [2] Total [3]	Individual	Corporate	SOCIAL SECURITY CONTRIBUTIONS Total [4]	Employees	Employers	TAXES ON GOODS AND SERVICES [5] Total [3]	General consumption taxes [6]	Taxes on specific goods, services [7]
United States: 1980	100.0	47.0	36.9	10.2	26.2	10.0	15.5	16.6	6.6	7.8
1990	100.0	43.2	35.8	7.4	29.5	11.6	16.6	16.5	7.6	6.8
1991	100.0	42.2	34.9	7.3	29.8	11.8	16.5	16.8	7.6	7.1
Canada: 1980	100.0	46.6	34.1	11.6	10.5	3.7	6.6	32.6	11.5	13.0
1990	100.0	47.9	40.4	7.0	14.2	4.3	9.7	27.4	14.2	9.8
1991	100.0	46.6	40.7	5.5	15.3	4.8	10.2	27.3	14.1	10.1
France: 1980	100.0	18.1	12.9	5.1	42.7	11.1	28.4	30.4	21.1	8.4
1990	100.0	17.2	11.8	5.3	44.0	13.2	27.2	28.3	18.7	8.6
1991	100.0	18.0	13.5	4.5	43.8	13.0	27.1	27.1	17.8	8.3
Germany [8]: 1980	100.0	35.1	29.6	5.5	34.3	15.3	18.4	27.1	16.6	9.3
1990	100.0	32.4	27.6	4.8	37.5	16.2	19.1	26.7	16.6	9.2
1991	100.0	31.4	27.1	4.3	39.1	17.1	20.1	26.7	16.4	9.3
Italy: 1980	100.0	31.1	23.1	7.8	38.0	6.9	28.4	26.5	15.6	9.7
1990	100.0	36.5	26.3	10.0	32.9	6.3	23.6	28.0	14.7	10.6
1991	100.0	36.1	26.4	9.6	33.0	6.6	23.2	28.1	14.3	11.0
Japan: 1980	100.0	46.1	24.3	21.8	29.1	10.2	14.8	16.3	-	14.1
1990	100.0	48.3	26.8	21.5	29.2	10.9	15.2	13.2	4.2	7.3
1991	100.0	46.9	26.9	20.0	30.1	11.4	15.6	13.5	4.4	7.4
Netherlands: 1980	100.0	32.8	26.3	6.6	38.1	15.7	17.8	25.2	15.8	7.3
1990	100.0	33.5	24.7	7.5	37.4	22.8	7.5	26.4	16.5	7.5
1991	100.0	33.5	26.2	7.3	37.1	22.8	-	25.4	15.6	7.5
Sweden: 1980	100.0	43.5	41.0	2.5	28.8	-	27.6	24.0	13.4	9.2
1990	100.0	41.0	37.9	3.1	27.6	-	25.4	24.6	14.6	9.0
1991	100.0	37.3	34.2	3.1	27.7	-	26.9	26.9	16.7	9.2
United Kingdom: 1980	100.0	38.2	29.8	8.3	16.6	6.7	9.5	29.2	14.4	13.1
1990	100.0	39.6	28.6	11.0	17.2	6.6	10.0	30.1	16.4	12.2
1991	100.0	37.4	28.5	8.9	17.8	6.7	10.4	32.7	18.5	12.8

- Represents zero. [1] Includes property taxes, employer payroll taxes other than Social Security contributions, and miscellaneous taxes, not shown separately. [2] Includes taxes on capital gains. [3] Includes other taxes not shown separately. [4] Includes contributions of self-employed not shown separately. [5] Taxes on the production, sales, transfer, leasing, and delivery of goods and services and rendering of services. [6] Primary value-added and sales taxes. [7] For example, excise taxes on alcohol, tobacco, and gasoline. [8] Prior to 1990, data are for former West Germany.

Source: Organization for Economic Cooperation and Development, Paris, France, *Revenue Statistics of OECD Member Countries,* annual.

No. 1378. Employee-Employer Payroll Tax Rates for Social Security Programs, by Country: 1981 to 1993

[In percent. Covers old-age, disability and survivors insurance, public health or sickness insurance, workers' compensation, unemployment insurance, and family allowance programs]

COUNTRY	ALL SOCIAL SECURITY PROGRAMS					OLD-AGE, DISABILITY, SURVIVORS INSUR.				
	1981	1991	1993			1981	1991	1993		
			Total	Employer	Employee			Total	Employer	Employee
United States ...	17.60	20.50	20.50	12.85	7.65	10.70	12.40	12.40	6.20	6.20
Austria	35.80	[1]39.40	[1]41.00	[2]24.55	16.45	21.10	22.80	22.80	12.55	10.25
Belgium	34.70	39.33	39.33	[2]26.86	13.07	15.11	16.36	16.36	8.85	7.50
Canada	[3]7.92	[3]10.00	[3]13.70	8.20	5.50	3.60	4.60	5.00	2.50	2.50
France	47.55	54.41	49.88	31.61	[4]18.27	13.00	17.00	17.25	8.20	[4]9.05
Germany [5]	34.80	36.16	38.19	19.79	18.40	18.50	17.70	17.50	8.75	8.75
Ireland	14.95	21.70	21.20	13.45	[6]7.75	12.00	18.70	18.70	12.20	[6]6.50
Italy	54.30	55.72	55.59	[7]46.45	9.14	24.46	27.42	28.27	[7]20.13	8.14
Japan	21.41	[8]24.86	[8]24.62	13.39	11.23	10.60	14.50	14.50	7.25	7.25
Luxembourg	34.25	[1]31.78	[1]32.20	[2]14.70	17.50	16.00	16.00	16.00	8.00	8.00
Netherlands	54.85	43.73	46.50	12.94	[9]33.56	32.45	20.25	21.82	-	[9]21.82
Sweden	32.65	34.11	32.31	31.36	0.95	21.15	20.95	19.89	19.89	-
Switzerland	11.90	12.00	12.69	6.89	5.80	9.40	9.60	9.60	4.80	4.80
United Kingdom ..	21.45	21.45	21.40	[10]10.40	[11]11.00	11.00	(NA)	(NA)	(NA)	(NA)

- Represents zero.   NA Not available.   [1] Sickness and maternity refers to wage earners.   [2] Work-injury refers to wage earners.   [3] Excludes work-injury.   [4] Includes 2.4 percent employee tax on all sources of income.   [5] Prior to 1990, data are for former West Germany.   [6] Includes 1 percent tax to finance employment training for youth.   [7] OASDI, work injury, and unemployment refers to industrial workers.   [8] OASDI rate refers to male employees and contributions for employee pension insurance only.   [9] The employed persons' Supplementary Disability Pension Program has been adjusted downward to avoid the distortions that would otherwise occur from taxing only a very narrow band of earnings.   [10] 4.6 to 10.4 percent. Covers all programs.   [11] 2 percent on first 46 pounds per week plus 9% of earnings between 46 and 350 pounds. Covers all programs.
Source: U.S. Social Security Administration, Office of Research and Statistics, *Social Security Programs Throughout the World*, biennial.

No. 1379. Annual Percent Change in Consumer Prices, by Country: 1989 to 1993

[Change from previous year. See text, section 30, for general comments concerning the data. For additional qualifications of the data for individual countries, see source. Minus sign (-) indicates decrease]

COUNTRY	1989	1990	1991	1992	1993	COUNTRY	1989	1990	1991	1992	1993
United States..	5	5	4	3	3	Italy	6	6	6	5	4
Argentina	3,080	2,314	172	25	11	Japan	2	3	3	2	1
Australia	8	7	3	1	2	Mexico	20	27	23	16	10
Austria	3	3	3	4	4	Netherlands ...	4	3	4	4	2
Belgium	3	4	3	2	3	Norway	5	4	3	2	2
Brazil	1,287	2,938	441	1,009	2,148	Peru	3,399	7,482	410	74	49
Canada	5	5	6	2	2	Philippines	12	14	19	9	8
Chile	17	26	22	15	13	Portugal	13	13	11	9	7
France [1]	4	3	3	2	2	South Africa	15	14	15	14	10
Germany [1]	3	3	4	4	4	South Korea ...	6	9	10	6	5
Greece	14	20	20	16	14	Spain	7	7	6	6	5
Guatemala	11	41	33	10	(NA)	Sweden	6	11	9	2	5
India	6	9	14	12	6	Switzerland	3	5	6	4	3
Indonesia	6	8	9	8	10	Turkey	63	60	66	70	66
Iran	22	8	17	23	20	United Kingdom.	8	10	6	4	2
Israel	20	17	19	12	11	Venezuela	84	41	34	31	38

NA Not available.   [1] Prior to July 1990, data for former West Germany.
Source: International Monetary Fund, Washington, DC, *International Financial Statistics*, monthly.

No. 1380. Civilian Employment-Population Ratio and Females as Percent of Total Civilian Employment, by Country: 1980 to 1992

[See headnote, table 1381]

COUNTRY	CIVILIAN EMPLOYMENT-POPULATION RATIO [1]								CIVILIAN EMPLOYMENT, PERCENT FEMALE			
	Women				Men							
	1980	1990	1991	1992	1980	1990	1991	1992	1980	1990	1991	1992
United States..	47.7	54.4	53.7	53.8	72.0	71.9	70.2	69.7	42.4	45.4	45.6	45.7
Australia	41.9	49.3	48.1	47.7	75.1	71.3	68.2	66.6	36.4	41.3	41.8	42.1
Canada	46.2	53.7	52.6	51.6	73.0	69.8	66.7	65.0	39.7	44.7	45.3	45.5
France	40.1	41.5	41.6	[2]41.7	68.6	61.3	60.6	[2]59.6	39.5	43.0	43.3	[2]43.8
Germany [3]	38.9	[2]40.9	[2]41.7	[2]41.9	69.9	[2]65.6	[2]66.4	[2]65.3	39.2	[2]41.2	[2]41.5	[2]42.0
Italy	27.9	[2]29.2	[2]29.6	(NA)	66.0	[2]60.1	[2]60.4	(NA)	31.7	[2]34.7	[2]34.9	(NA)
Japan	45.7	48.0	48.6	48.7	77.9	75.4	75.8	76.1	38.4	40.3	40.4	40.5
Netherlands ...	31.0	(NA)	(NA)	(NA)	74.1	(NA)	(NA)	(NA)	30.2	(NA)	(NA)	(NA)
Sweden	58.0	[2]62.7	[2]61.6	[2]59.4	73.6	[2]71.7	[2]70.3	[2]66.8	45.2	[2]47.8	[2]47.9	[2]48.3
United Kingdom .	44.8	[2]49.7	[2]48.9	[2]48.8	72.8	[2]70.1	[2]67.5	[2]65.0	40.4	[2]43.5	[2]44.1	[2]44.9

NA Not available.   [1] Civilian employment as a percent of the civilian working age population.   [2] Preliminary.   [3] Former West Germany.   [4] Break in series.
Source: U.S. Bureau of Labor Statistics, *Comparative Labor Force Statistics for Ten Countries, 1959-1992*, August 1993.

No. 1381. Civilian Labor Force, Employment, and Unemployment, by Country: 1980 to 1992

[Data based on U.S. labor force definitions adopted in 1967 (see text, section 13) except that minimum age for population base varies as follows: United States, France, Sweden, and United Kingdom, 16 years; Australia, Canada, Japan, Netherlands, and Germany, 15 years; Italy, 14 years]

YEAR	United States	Aus-tralia	Canada	France	Ger-many [1]	Italy	Japan	Nether-lands	Sweden	United Kingdom
Civilian labor force (mil.):										
1980	106.9	6.7	11.6	22.9	27.3	21.1	55.7	5.9	4.3	26.5
1985	115.5	7.3	12.5	23.6	28.0	21.8	58.8	6.2	4.4	27.2
1990	124.8	8.5	13.7	24.3	[2]29.4	[2]22.7	63.0	6.8	4.6	28.5
1991	125.3	8.5	13.8	24.5	[2]29.8	[2,3]22.9	64.3	[2]6.9	4.6	28.4
1992	127.0	8.6	13.8	24.6	[2]30.0	22.8	65.0	[2]6.9	4.5	[2]28.2
Labor force participation rate: [4]										
1980	63.8	62.1	64.1	57.5	54.7	48.2	62.6	55.4	66.9	62.5
1985	64.8	61.6	65.3	56.9	54.7	47.2	62.3	55.5	66.9	62.2
1990	66.4	64.7	67.0	55.5	[2]55.0	[2]47.2	62.6	56.8	68.1	63.9
1991	66.0	64.3	66.3	55.8	[2]55.7	[2,3]47.6	63.2	57.5	[2]67.6	[2]63.4
1992	66.3	64.0	65.5	[2]56.0	[2]55.4	[2]47.3	63.4	[2]57.7	[2]66.1	[2]62.8
Civilian employment (mil.):										
1980	99.3	6.3	10.7	21.4	26.5	20.2	54.6	5.5	4.2	24.7
1985	107.2	6.7	11.2	21.2	26.0	20.5	57.3	5.6	4.3	24.2
1990	117.9	7.9	12.6	22.1	[2]28.0	[2]21.1	61.7	6.3	4.6	26.6
1991	116.9	7.7	12.3	22.1	[2]28.5	[2,3]21.4	62.9	[2]6.4	4.5	25.9
1992	117.6	7.7	12.2	[2]22.0	[2]28.7	[2]21.2	63.6	[2]6.5	4.3	[2]25.4
Employment-population ratio: [5]										
1980	59.2	58.3	59.3	53.8	53.1	46.1	61.3	52.1	65.6	58.1
1985	60.1	56.5	58.5	51.0	50.7	44.4	60.6	50.1	65.0	55.2
1990	62.7	60.2	61.5	50.5	[2]52.2	[2]43.9	61.3	52.5	67.0	59.5
1991	61.6	58.1	59.5	50.4	[2]53.3	[2,3]44.3	61.8	53.5	[2]65.8	[2]57.8
1992	61.4	57.1	58.1	[2]50.2	[2]52.9	[2]43.9	62.0	[2]53.9	[2]63.0	[2]56.5
Unemployment rate:										
1980	7.1	6.1	7.5	6.4	2.8	4.4	2.0	6.0	2.0	7.0
1985	7.2	8.3	10.5	10.5	7.2	6.0	2.6	9.6	2.8	11.2
1990	5.5	6.9	8.1	9.1	[2]5.0	[2]7.0	2.1	7.5	1.5	6.9
1991	6.7	9.6	10.3	9.6	[2]4.3	[2,3]6.9	2.1	7.0	2.6	[2]8.8
1992	7.4	10.8	11.3	10.4	[2]4.6	[2]7.3	2.2	[2]6.6	4.7	[2]10.0
Under 25 years old	14.2	19.4	17.8	(NA)	(NA)	(NA)	4.5	(NA)	11.0	[6]15.4
Teenagers [7]	20.0	24.7	19.7	(NA)	(NA)	(NA)	6.8	(NA)	10.6	[6]16.4
20 to 24 years old	11.3	16.2	16.6	(NA)	(NA)	(NA)	3.9	(NA)	11.1	[6]14.9
25 years old and over	6.1	8.4	9.9	(NA)	(NA)	(NA)	1.8	(NA)	2.8	[6]8.3

NA Not available. [1] Former West Germany. [2] Preliminary. [3] Break in series. [4] Civilian labor force as a percent of the civilian working age population. [5] Civilian employment as a percent of the civilian working age population. [6] Data are for the spring quarter. [7] 16 to 19 years old in the United States, France, Sweden, and the United Kingdom; 15 to 19 years old in Canada, Australia, and Japan; and 14 to 19 years old in Italy and Germany.

Source: U.S. Bureau of Labor Statistics, *Comparative Labor Force Statistics for Ten Countries, 1959-1992*, August 1993, and *Monthly Labor Review*.

No. 1382. Labor Force Participation Rates, by Country: 1980 and 1991

[Participation rates represent percent of population of each specified group in labor force]

COUNTRY AND SEX	15 TO 19 YEARS OLD		20 TO 24 YEARS OLD		25 TO 54 YEARS OLD		55 TO 64 YEARS OLD		65 YEARS AND OVER	
	1980	1991	1980	1991	1980	1991	1980	1991	1980	1991
United States: Male	[1]60.5	53.5	85.7	83.1	93.4	92.3	71.2	66.3	18.3	15.2
Female	[1]52.4	50.2	69.1	70.5	63.8	74.0	41.0	45.0	7.6	8.0
Canada: Male	57.9	55.8	86.3	81.5	94.8	92.5	76.2	62.5	14.8	11.3
Female	52.2	53.8	73.0	75.6	60.1	75.8	33.6	35.6	4.4	3.5
France: Male	25.7	12.3	80.2	62.3	96.4	95.3	68.5	44.5	7.5	3.5
Female	18.3	6.8	67.5	53.7	63.0	73.7	39.7	30.6	3.3	1.5
Italy: Male	33.3	23.2	72.5	69.5	[2]93.1	90.7	[3]39.6	34.9	9.0	5.2
Female	28.9	19.0	57.9	61.2	[2]39.9	49.9	[3]11.0	10.0	2.3	1.6
Japan: Male	17.4	19.1	69.6	72.8	97.0	97.2	85.4	84.5	41.0	38.0
Female	18.5	17.8	70.0	75.6	56.7	65.0	45.3	48.5	15.5	16.6
Sweden: Male	55.3	42.3	84.5	82.8	95.4	94.6	78.7	75.5	14.2	14.7
Female	55.8	47.1	81.6	77.5	82.9	90.5	55.3	66.9	3.7	5.1
United Kingdom: Male	73.6	73.6	86.0	85.7	95.4	93.4	81.6	67.5	10.3	8.4
Female	75.3	70.9	67.9	72.7	63.4	72.9	39.1	39.2	3.6	3.1

[1] Persons 16 to 19 years old. [2] Persons 25 to 59 years old. [3] Persons 60 to 64 years old.

Source: Organization for Economic Cooperation and Development, Paris, France, *Labour Force Statistics*, annual.

No. 1383. Civilian Employment, by Industry and Country: 1980 and 1990

[Data based on U.S. labor force definitions adopted in 1967 except that minimum age for population base varies as follows: United States, France, Sweden, and United Kingdom, 16 years; Australia, Canada, Germany, Japan, and Netherlands, 15 years; Italy, 14 years. Industries based on International Standard Industrial Classification; see text, section 31]

INDUSTRY	United States	Aus-tralia	Canada	France	Ger-many [1]	Italy	Japan	Nether-lands	Sweden	United Kingdom
TOTAL EMPLOYMENT (1,000)										
1980, total..............	99,303	6,284	10,708	21,334	26,486	20,195	54,600	5,520	4,214	25,004
Agriculture, forestry, fishing......	3,529	408	583	1,854	1,373	2,870	5,510	285	237	654
Industry [2].................	29,136	1,818	2,931	7,475	11,373	7,694	19,180	1,642	1,327	9,059
Manufacturing.............	21,942	1,248	2,111	5,495	8,998	5,433	13,630	1,176	1,025	7,081
Services	66,638	4,058	7,194	12,005	13,740	9,631	29,910	3,593	2,650	15,291
Public utilities	1,179	130	124	189	215	(NA)	300	50	36	353
Wholesale and retail trade,										
restaurants and hotels.......	21,339	1,467	2,411	3,413	4,079	3,765	12,980	985	582	4,818
Transport and communication ..	5,619	461	782	1,319	1,572	1,124	3,500	328	295	1,580
Finance, insurance, real estate,										
and business...............	8,351	518	1,018	1,591	1,540	418	3,170	435	283	1,837
Community, social, personal [3]...	30,148	1,452	2,859	5,493	6,335	4,224	9,920	1,794	1,454	6,703
1990, total..............	117,914	7,872	12,572	21,684	27,961	21,074	61,710	6,268	4,560	26,620
Agriculture, forestry, fishing......	3,355	438	531	1,310	966	1,876	4,270	292	174	568
Industry [2].................	29,610	1,895	2,959	6,284	10,893	6,841	20,890	1,620	1,289	7,508
Manufacturing.............	21,184	1,204	2,001	4,612	8,843	[4]4,726	15,010	1,196	961	5,384
Services	84,949	5,539	9,083	14,090	16,102	12,357	36,550	4,356	3,097	18,544
Public utilities	1,292	107	136	204	255	(NA)	300	41	37	292
Wholesale and retail trade,										
restaurants and hotels.......	26,049	1,960	3,014	3,756	4,554	4,467	14,850	1,114	657	5,306
Transport and communication ..	6,307	539	815	1,397	1,622	1,153	3,770	386	320	1,548
Finance, insurance, real estate,										
and business...............	13,346	907	1,457	2,174	2,214	858	5,190	652	396	3,094
Community, social, personal [3]...	37,955	2,028	3,661	6,559	7,458	5,618	12,420	2,162	1,687	7,968
PERCENT DISTRIBUTION										
1980, total..............	100	100	100	100	100	100	100	100	100	100
Agriculture, forestry, fishing......	4	7	5	9	5	14	10	5	6	3
Industry [2].................	29	29	27	35	43	38	35	30	32	36
Services	67	65	67	56	52	48	55	65	63	61
1990, total..............	100	100	100	100	100	100	100	100	100	100
Agriculture, forestry, fishing......	3	6	4	6	4	9	7	5	4	2
Industry [2].................	25	24	24	29	39	33	34	26	28	28
Services	72	70	72	65	58	59	59	70	68	70

NA Not available.   [1] Beginning 1990, data for unified Germany. Prior years for former West Germany.   [2] Includes mining and construction.   [3] Includes public administration, education, health, and recreation services.   [4] Data for 1989.

Source: Bureau of Labor Statistics, *Monthly Labor Review*, October 1993.

No. 1384. Index of Industrial Production, by Country: 1980 to 1992

[Industrial production index measures output in the manufacturing, mining, and electric and gas utilities industries. Minus sign (-) indicates decrease]

COUNTRY	INDEX (1985= 100)							ANNUAL PERCENT CHANGE					
	1980	1987	1988	1989	1990	1991	1992	1986-1987	1987-1988	1988-1989	1989-1990	1990-1991	1991-1992
OECD, total.....	91.4	104.9	110.7	114.2	115.9	115.1	114.4	3.6	5.6	3.2	1.4	-0.6	-0.7
Australia [1]........	87.1	104.0	109.3	115.2	116.4	112.6	112.2	4.9	5.1	5.4	1.0	-3.3	-0.3
Austria..........	92.2	102.1	106.6	112.9	121.6	123.6	122.3	1.0	4.4	6.0	7.7	1.6	-1.1
Belgium [2]........	96.0	103.0	109.7	113.4	117.7	115.3	115.2	2.1	6.5	3.4	3.8	-2.0	-0.1
Canada [2]........	86.2	104.1	109.6	109.4	106.0	102.1	102.5	4.9	5.3	-0.1	-3.1	-3.7	0.4
Finland..........	86.0	106.5	111.1	113.8	114.5	103.3	105.8	4.6	4.3	2.4	0.6	-9.7	2.4
France..........	101.9	102.8	107.7	112.1	114.2	114.2	112.8	1.9	4.7	4.1	1.9	-	-1.2
Germany [3]......	97.2	102.5	106.2	111.5	117.2	120.6	118.3	0.4	3.6	5.0	5.1	2.9	-1.9
Greece..........	92.5	97.5	102.5	104.4	101.9	100.5	99.3	-1.5	5.2	1.8	-2.4	-1.4	-1.2
Ireland..........	78.0	111.3	123.2	137.5	143.9	148.6	162.2	8.9	10.7	11.6	4.7	3.3	9.1
Italy............	103.2	106.6	114.2	118.7	117.9	115.4	113.6	2.6	6.9	3.9	-0.7	-2.1	-1.6
Japan...........	84.4	103.3	114.7	120.3	125.4	127.7	120.4	3.4	11.1	4.8	4.2	1.9	-5.8
Luxembourg	82.3	101.2	110.0	118.6	118.0	118.6	117.4	-0.6	8.7	7.8	-0.5	0.5	-1.0
Netherlands	94.6	101.3	101.3	106.5	109.0	113.2	113.4	1.1	0.1	5.1	2.4	3.8	0.2
Norway..........	82.4	110.0	113.3	124.1	126.3	128.9	137.2	6.6	3.0	9.6	1.7	2.1	6.5
Portugal	84.9	112.0	116.2	124.1	135.2	135.3	132.1	4.4	3.8	6.7	9.0	-	-2.3
Spain...........	96.7	107.9	111.1	116.1	116.1	115.3	112.0	4.6	3.0	4.5	-	-0.7	-2.9
Sweden [4]	90.2	103.0	104.3	108.1	109.3	103.2	99.1	2.5	1.3	3.7	1.1	-5.6	-4.0
Switzerland [5].....	97.0	105.0	112.0	115.0	118.0	119.0	118.0	1.2	6.2	3.0	2.7	0.8	-0.6
United Kingdom ...	92.6	106.5	111.4	113.9	113.4	109.0	108.6	4.0	4.6	2.2	-0.4	-3.9	-0.3
United States.....	89.1	105.9	110.6	112.3	112.3	110.2	112.8	4.9	4.4	1.5	-	-1.9	2.4

- Represents or rounds to zero.   [1] Index of Real Gross Product in industry.   [2] Gross domestic product in industry at factor cost and 1986 prices.   [3] Former West Germany.   [4] Mining and manufacturing.   [5] Excludes mining and quarrying.

Source: Organization for Economic Cooperation and Development, Paris, France, *Main Economic Indicators, Historical Statistics, 1969-1988*, 1990; and *Main Economic Indicators*, monthly.

No. 1385. International Economic Composite Indexes, by Country: 1980 to 1993

[Average annual percent change from previous year; derived from indexes with base 1980=100. The coincident index changes are for calendar years and the leading index changes are for years ending June 30 because they lead the coincident indexes by about 6 months, on average. The G-7 countries are United States, Canada, France, Germany, Italy, United Kingdom, and Japan. Minus sign (-) indicates decrease]

COUNTRY	1980	1983	1984	1985	1986	1987	1988	1989	1990	1991	1992	1993
LEADING INDEX												
Total, 11 countries	2.4	1.6	9.2	2.9	2.0	4.6	7.9	5.0	2.3	-1.2	0.7	1.1
10 countries, excluding U.S.	6.7	0.6	5.9	4.4	1.7	5.1	8.2	5.9	3.3	-0.9	-2.2	-2.1
G-7 countries	2.4	1.6	9.2	2.7	1.9	4.4	7.7	4.9	2.4	-1.2	0.5	0.9
North America	-2.8	2.8	13.9	1.0	2.6	3.7	7.2	3.6	0.7	-1.8	4.8	5.2
United States	-3.3	3.0	14.1	0.8	2.5	3.9	7.3	3.8	1.0	-1.6	5.1	5.4
Canada	3.3	0.6	11.3	4.3	3.0	2.7	6.1	1.0	-2.2	-4.6	0.8	3.8
4 European countries.	2.8	1.2	3.9	2.4	2.2	3.6	3.1	4.2	1.5	0.9	0.8	0.1
France	4.5	0.9	3.8	2.7	1.9	6.1	5.2	6.0	0.5	1.0	2.9	0.3
Germany [1]	2.5	2.0	6.0	2.0	2.9	1.6	3.5	5.2	4.6	3.5	0.4	-1.8
Italy.	3.0	-1.0	0.8	2.7	4.1	4.2	0.6	2.1	0.3	-1.8	-0.3	1.8
United Kingdom	1.0	2.1	3.5	2.2	0.2	3.3	2.0	2.3	-0.8	-1.8	-0.2	1.8
5 Pacific region countries	14.5	-0.2	8.1	7.9	0.7	7.8	16.1	8.6	6.3	-2.7	-6.3	-5.7
Australia	6.3	-3.8	9.1	6.6	2.9	3.4	7.2	5.1	-1.9	-3.2	1.2	3.8
China: Taiwan	4.8	8.0	11.9	6.4	8.2	13.6	14.5	12.3	7.5	1.2	8.0	5.9
Japan	17.2	-0.5	7.9	8.3	-0.4	7.6	17.6	8.9	7.2	-3.2	-8.7	-8.3
South Korea	-2.6	8.1	9.3	4.7	9.8	17.2	13.7	10.0	4.5	3.7	5.2	4.0
New Zealand	1.8	-1.7	6.4	5.3	-1.1	2.8	-1.5	0.8	1.6	-3.1	2.5	4.0
COINCIDENT INDEX												
Total, 11 countries	0.3	1.6	6.0	3.7	3.2	4.1	6.0	4.8	3.6	0.1	0.7	0.2
10 countries, excluding U.S.	2.5	1.2	3.6	3.9	3.5	4.5	6.9	6.4	5.7	2.6	0.5	-1.4
G-7 countries	0.2	1.7	5.8	3.6	2.9	4.0	6.0	4.7	3.5	0.1	0.6	0.1
North America	-2.4	2.3	9.3	3.6	2.6	3.8	4.8	2.4	-	-4.0	0.8	2.9
United States	-2.8	2.4	9.6	3.4	2.5	3.7	4.7	2.3	-0.4	-4.0	0.9	3.0
Canada	2.0	2.0	6.3	5.2	3.5	4.9	5.9	2.7	0.2	-3.7	0.4	2.3
4 European countries.	1.5	0.5	2.2	2.9	3.7	3.8	6.1	6.0	5.6	1.7	-0.2	-2.8
France	1.3	2.0	0.5	1.4	3.9	5.0	8.0	8.7	7.1	2.4	0.6	-1.3
Germany [1]	2.5	-0.5	2.7	3.5	4.3	3.1	3.5	5.4	7.2	5.4	0.2	-4.5
Italy.	5.2	-1.0	3.4	2.5	1.7	1.5	5.2	2.1	4.6	2.1	-1.1	-8.2
United Kingdom	-2.1	1.5	2.6	4.4	3.5	5.2	7.9	5.9	2.3	-4.5	-1.6	1.1
5 Pacific region countries	4.2	2.0	5.3	5.1	3.5	5.2	8.2	7.5	6.7	4.6	1.5	0.1
Australia	5.0	-6.8	9.4	7.4	5.2	3.8	8.3	10.3	0.8	-7.4	-0.9	2.6
China: Taiwan	7.1	7.4	12.0	5.0	10.7	11.6	6.0	6.1	1.8	4.3	5.5	4.2
Japan	4.5	2.3	4.6	4.7	2.6	4.6	8.3	7.4	7.5	5.8	1.4	-0.7
South Korea	-4.3	11.0	9.0	5.5	11.7	13.5	10.6	6.1	9.3	7.9	4.4	3.7
New Zealand	2.0	0.8	3.6	2.1	1.4	1.4	-1.0	-0.4	1.3	-0.9	1.2	3.3

- Represents or rounds to zero. [1] Former West Germany.

Source: Center for International Business Cycle Research, Columbia Business School, New York, NY, *International Economic Indicators*, monthly.

No. 1386. Patents, by Country: 1992

[Includes only U.S. patents granted to residents of areas outside of the United States and its territories]

TOP COUNTRY	Total [1]	Inventions	Designs	TOP COUNTRY	Total [1]	Inventions	Designs
Total, foreign country residents	**48,699**	**45,189**	**3,256**	Netherlands	973	855	66
Japan	23,151	21,925	1,149	Sweden	728	627	98
Germany	7,605	7,311	258	South Korea	586	538	48
France	3,280	3,029	234	Australia	498	410	83
United Kingdom	2,633	2,425	194	Austria	402	370	30
Canada	2,217	1,964	240	Belgium	370	324	43
Italy.	1,446	1,271	172	Finland	380	360	19
Switzerland	1,293	1,196	93	Israel.	350	335	8
China: Taiwan	1,252	1,000	250	Denmark	275	193	77
				Other countries	1,260	1,056	194

[1] Includes patents for botanical plants and reissues, not shown separately.
Source: U.S. Patent and Trademark Office, Technology Assessment and Forecast Data Base.

No. 1387. World's 500 Largest Industrial Corporations, by Country: 1991

[Sales as of December 31, 1991, assets as of company's fiscal year-end. Companies must have derived more than 50% of their sales from manufacturing and/or mining. Sales of consolidated subsidiaries are included and exclude excise taxes collected by manufacturers. Profits are shown after taxes and extraordinary credits or charges]

COUNTRY	Number of companies	Sales ($bil.)	Profits ($bil.)	Assets ($bil.)	Employees (1,000)	COUNTRY	Number of companies	Sales ($bil.)	Profits ($bil.)	Assets ($bil.)	Employees (1,000)
Australia. . . .	9	48	15	671	235	Japan	119	1,097	258	11,827	3,458
Canada	9	49	12	685	289	Netherlands . .	7	58	12	576	405
Finland	5	28	-10	338	95	South Korea .	13	143	14	1,185	547
France.	32	337	75	4,376	1,866	Sweden	14	93	6	1,052	615
Germany . . .	33	473	91	3,998	3,017	Switzerland . .	10	117	53	1,306	754
India	6	27	7	328	966	U.K.	45	477	222	4,831	2,587
Italy.	7	186	7	1,235	851	U.S.	157	1,785	435	20,148	9,045

Source: Time Warner, New York, NY, *The Fortune Directories*, (copyright).

No. 1388. Indexes of Hourly Compensation Costs for Production Workers in Manufacturing, by Country: 1980 to 1992

[United States = 100. Compensation costs include pay for time worked, other direct pay, employer expenditures for legally required insurance programs and contractual and private benefit plans, and for some countries, other labor taxes. Data adjusted for exchange rates. Area averages are trade-weighted to account for differences in countries' relative importance to U.S. trade in manufactured goods. The trade weights used are the sum of U.S. imports of manufactured products for consumption (customs value) and U.S. domestic exports of manufactured products (f.a.s. value) in 1986; see source for detail]

AREA OR COUNTRY	1980	1985	1989	1990	1991	1992	AREA OR COUNTRY	1980	1985	1989	1990	1991	1992
United States	100	100	100	100	100	100	Austria [6]	87	56	95	114	111	122
Total [1]	71	55	83	90	92	96	Belgium.	133	69	108	129	127	136
OECD [2]	84	65	97	105	107	111	Denmark.	110	62	101	120	117	124
Europe [3]	103	63	102	119	118	126	Finland [7]	83	63	116	139	132	116
Asian newly industrial-							France	91	58	88	102	98	104
izing economies [4] . . .	12	12	23	25	27	30	Germany [6][8].	125	74	124	147	145	160
Canada.	88	84	104	107	110	105	Greece	38	28	38	45	44	(NA)
Mexico	22	12	10	11	13	15	Ireland	60	46	67	79	77	82
Australia	85	63	86	86	86	80	Italy	83	59	101	117	117	120
Hong Kong [5]	15	13	19	21	23	24	Luxembourg.	121	59	95	110	(NA)	(NA)
Israel	38	31	54	57	56	(NA)	Netherlands	122	67	105	123	118	128
Japan.	56	49	87	85	93	100	Norway	117	80	128	144	139	143
South Korea.	10	10	23	26	28	30	Portugal	21	12	20	25	27	31
New Zealand	54	34	54	56	54	49	Spain	60	36	62	76	78	83
Singapore	15	19	22	25	28	31	Sweden.	127	74	122	140	142	150
Sri Lanka.	2	2	2	2	(NA)	(NA)	Switzerland	112	74	117	140	139	144
China: Taiwan	10	12	25	26	28	32	United Kingdom	77	48	74	85	88	91

NA Not available. [1] The 25 foreign economies for which 1992 data are available. [2] Canada, Australia, Japan, New Zealand, and the 16 European countries for which 1992 data are available. [3] The 16 European countries for which 1992 data are available. [4] Hong Kong, South Korea, Singapore, and China: Taiwan. [5] Average of selected manufacturing industries. [6] Excludes workers in establishments considered handicraft manufactures (including all printing and publishing and miscellaneous manufacturing in Austria). [7] Includes workers in mining and electrical power plants. [8] Former West Germany.

Source: Bureau of Labor Statistics, *Report 844*, April 1993.

No. 1389. Structure of Manufacturing Industry, by Country: 1980 to 1990

[In percent. Contribution of each industry group to total manufacturing production. Based on International Standard Industrial Classification; see text, section 30, and source. Numbers in parentheses refer to ISIC codes]

COUNTRY	Food (3100)	Textile (3200)	Wood (3300)	Paper (3400)	Chemical (3500)	Nonmetal (3600)	Basic metal (3700)	Machinery (3800)	Other (3900)
United States: 1980 . .	14.5	5.6	2.8	7.7	22.2	2.5	6.8	36.6	1.3
1985	14.1	5.3	2.9	9.1	19.9	2.4	4.5	40.8	1.1
1990	14.5	4.9	3.1	9.9	19.9	2.3	4.7	39.5	1.2
Japan: 1980.	11.3	5.4	3.6	6.2	19.3	3.9	11.4	37.7	1.2
1985	11.0	4.9	2.4	6.1	16.7	3.3	8.5	45.7	1.4
1990	10.2	4.2	2.5	6.6	14.2	3.3	7.4	50.2	1.4
France: 1980	17.0	6.9	3.1	5.6	21.4	3.5	8.4	32.6	1.3
1985	17.6	6.9	2.5	6.5	21.6	3.0	7.3	33.3	1.3
1990	16.5	5.9	2.8	7.4	18.4	3.4	6.5	37.9	1.3
Italy: 1980	12.2	11.4	3.2	4.6	19.7	5.6	10.1	32.5	0.8
1985	12.6	13.5	2.9	5.4	22.5	4.8	9.6	27.8	0.8
1990	(NA)	(NA)	(NA)	(NA)	(NA)	(NA)	(NA)	(NA)	(NA)
Portugal: 1980	18.2	18.9	6.0	6.3	24.5	6.1	2.2	17.6	0.2
1985	19.5	18.5	3.6	6.8	28.5	4.8	3.3	15.0	0.2
1990	(NA)	(NA)	(NA)	(NA)	(NA)	(NA)	(NA)	(NA)	(NA)
Sweden: 1980	13.3	2.6	8.1	13.5	15.3	2.6	8.5	35.8	0.4
1985	13.9	2.1	6.4	13.9	15.5	2.1	7.9	37.9	0.3
1990	(NA)	(NA)	(NA)	(NA)	(NA)	(NA)	(NA)	(NA)	(NA)
United Kingdom: 1980 .	18.6	5.9	2.9	6.8	20.6	3.6	6.8	33.9	0.9
1985	18.7	5.6	2.7	7.5	21.1	3.5	5.8	34.2	0.9
1990	15.8	5.0	3.1	8.7	18.9	3.9	5.4	38.2	1.0
West Germany: 1980. .	12.4	5.4	3.4	4.1	22.9	3.4	7.6	40.3	0.5
1985	12.2	4.8	2.4	4.2	23.7	2.7	6.6	43.1	0.4
1990	11.7	4.4	2.8	4.6	22.9	2.8	5.5	47.5	0.5

NA Not available. [1] Manufacture of food, beverages, and tobacco. [2] Textile, apparel, and leather. [3] Wood products and furniture. [4] Paper, paper products and printing. [5] Chemical products, petroleum, coal, rubber, and plastic products. [6] Nonmetallic mineral products, except petroleum and coal products. [7] Basic metal industries, including iron, steel, and nonferrous metal. [8] Fabricated metal products, machinery and equipment.

Source: Organization for Economic Cooperation and Development, Paris, France, *OECD Industrial Structure Statistics, 1988*; and unpublished data.

No. 1390. Selected Indexes of Manufacturing Activity, by Country: 1970 to 1992

[1982 = 100. Data relate to all employed persons in the United States and Canada; all employees in other countries. Minus sign (-) indicates decrease. For explanation of average annual percent change, see Guide to Tabular Presentation]

INDEX	United States	Bel-gium	Cana-da	Den-mark	France	Ger-many [1]	Italy	Japan	Neth-erlands	Swe-den	United King-dom
Output per hour:											
1970	(NA)	44.3	76.9	57.2	59.6	67.1	54.6	52.0	52.9	69.0	71.3
1980	92.9	87.5	99.9	98.0	90.5	98.5	95.5	92.1	93.9	96.3	90.3
1985	106.8	117.2	119.8	105.0	108.2	113.4	122.3	112.0	118.7	113.2	117.4
1990	122.2	133.9	120.6	107.5	127.2	125.5	141.1	144.5	130.1	124.9	146.3
1991	124.5	136.9	121.4	108.9	127.0	129.2	145.8	150.7	131.3	126.5	151.9
1992	129.9	142.7	126.4	110.4	130.7	129.8	151.2	143.2	132.3	135.5	159.4
Average annual percent change:											
1979-85	2.0	6.1	2.4	2.1	3.1	2.1	5.0	3.9	4.2	3.0	4.4
1985-92	2.8	2.9	0.8	0.7	2.7	2.0	3.1	3.6	1.6	2.6	4.5
1991-92	4.3	4.3	4.2	1.4	2.9	0.5	3.7	-5.0	0.8	7.2	4.9
Compensation per hour, national currency basis: [2]											
1970	(NA)	23.2	28.7	22.3	18.1	34.5	11.6	25.0	27.8	24.4	14.5
1980	83.3	86.3	78.6	83.4	72.7	89.2	70.2	89.0	88.5	84.5	77.9
1985	111.2	122.0	116.8	120.6	129.7	116.3	150.9	110.1	111.5	131.8	127.5
1990	134.7	147.8	146.9	155.1	159.3	148.0	213.3	138.3	123.3	197.5	187.5
1991	141.9	157.2	155.8	161.9	166.1	157.8	236.1	146.3	129.7	215.1	208.5
1992	148.2	164.6	162.2	166.3	171.7	167.3	252.2	153.0	136.7	222.3	226.0
Average annual percent change:											
1979-85	6.9	7.8	8.7	8.1	12.8	5.9	16.7	4.7	4.8	9.6	12.1
1985-92	4.2	4.4	4.8	4.7	4.1	5.3	7.6	4.8	3.0	7.8	8.5
1991-92	4.4	4.6	4.1	2.7	3.4	6.0	6.8	4.6	5.4	3.4	8.4
Real hourly compensation: [2][3]											
1970	(NA)	55.1	77.4	70.1	58.3	62.6	60.3	63.6	63.9	72.6	64.3
1980	97.5	101.0	97.9	102.6	92.2	99.9	96.9	96.0	100.0	103.0	94.9
1985	99.8	101.6	101.8	101.4	103.9	107.9	109.3	103.6	102.7	102.6	109.3
1990	99.4	110.9	102.9	107.5	109.8	128.6	117.3	121.7	109.2	114.4	120.6
1991	100.5	114.1	103.3	109.6	110.8	132.4	121.8	124.7	110.6	114.2	126.6
1992	101.9	116.8	106.0	110.3	111.9	135.0	123.5	128.2	112.4	115.7	132.3
Average annual percent change:											
1979-85	0.1	0.8	0.7	-0.5	2.3	1.8	1.5	1.1	0.3	-0.5	2.9
1985-92	0.3	2.0	0.6	1.2	1.1	3.3	1.8	3.1	1.3	1.7	2.8
1991-92	1.3	2.4	2.6	0.6	1.0	2.0	1.3	2.8	1.7	1.3	4.5
Unit labor costs, national currency:											
1970	(NA)	52.2	37.3	39.0	30.4	51.4	21.3	48.0	52.7	35.3	20.3
1980	89.6	98.7	78.7	85.1	80.3	90.6	73.5	96.7	94.2	87.7	86.3
1985	104.2	104.1	97.6	114.9	119.9	102.6	123.4	98.4	93.9	116.4	108.6
1990	110.3	110.4	121.8	144.2	125.3	117.9	151.2	95.7	94.7	158.1	128.2
1991	114.0	114.9	128.4	148.7	130.7	122.1	161.9	97.1	98.8	170.1	137.2
1992	114.0	115.3	128.3	150.6	131.4	128.8	166.8	106.9	103.3	164.1	141.8
Average annual percent change:											
1979-85	4.9	1.6	6.1	5.9	9.4	3.8	11.1	0.7	0.6	6.4	7.4
1985-92	1.3	1.5	4.0	3.9	1.3	3.3	4.4	1.2	1.4	5.0	3.9
1991-92	0.1	0.4	-	1.3	0.5	5.5	3.0	10.1	4.6	-3.6	3.3
Unit labor costs, U.S. dollar basis: [4]											
1970	(NA)	48.2	44.1	43.4	36.2	34.2	46.0	33.4	38.9	42.8	27.9
1980	89.6	154.7	83.1	126.2	125.2	121.2	116.3	106.7	126.8	130.3	114.8
1985	104.2	80.3	88.2	90.4	87.8	84.6	87.5	102.7	75.6	85.0	80.6
1989	106.6	123.7	120.3	159.0	125.8	148.3	139.5	171.1	117.7	141.9	117.6
1990	110.3	151.2	128.9	194.4	151.3	177.1	170.8	164.4	138.9	167.7	130.8
1991	114.0	153.8	138.3	193.8	152.3	178.5	176.6	179.7	141.0	176.6	138.7
1992	114.0	164.2	131.1	208.2	163.3	200.3	183.3	210.0	157.0	176.9	143.3
Average annual percent change:											
1979-85	4.9	-9.7	3.4	-5.8	-3.4	-4.1	-3.3	-0.8	-7.5	-5.2	-1.0
1985-92	1.3	10.7	5.8	12.6	9.3	13.1	11.1	10.8	11.0	11.0	8.6
1991-92	0.1	6.8	-5.2	7.4	7.2	12.2	3.8	16.8	11.3	0.2	3.3
Employment:											
1970	(NA)	137.7	96.3	119.6	105.4	115.2	97.6	99.9	135.4	114.4	141.9
1980	107.8	109.9	108.4	103.9	105.0	104.9	107.8	98.5	108.1	107.4	117.5
1985	102.3	95.1	103.6	112.4	92.5	97.4	89.8	106.9	96.5	99.7	91.7
1990	101.8	92.9	109.5	112.1	88.6	103.3	89.9	112.0	103.2	95.8	87.0
1991	98.2	92.0	101.7	109.5	87.3	104.9	87.5	116.3	102.5	89.5	80.8
1992	96.2	88.6	97.4	108.2	85.0	103.1	84.0	118.4	101.5	81.2	76.2
Average annual percent change:											
1979-85	-1.4	-2.7	-0.8	1.0	-2.3	-1.1	-2.9	1.7	-2.1	-1.2	-4.9
1985-92	-0.9	-1.0	-0.9	-0.5	-1.2	0.8	-0.9	1.5	0.7	-2.9	-2.6
1991-92	-2.1	-3.8	-4.3	-1.2	-2.6	-1.8	-3.9	1.8	-1.0	-9.2	-5.6
Aggregate hours:											
1970	(NA)	159.9	102.1	132.3	122.0	129.7	107.0	105.9	152.0	131.9	154.9
1980	109.8	110.1	110.8	103.7	111.2	106.3	108.0	99.3	108.1	106.3	118.1
1985	106.7	93.5	106.0	109.8	91.6	95.6	89.0	108.2	93.6	102.2	92.7
1990	106.9	94.4	111.1	106.9	88.4	97.0	93.7	111.2	99.4	99.5	88.1
1991	102.6	92.0	103.1	104.7	86.8	97.5	90.2	112.8	98.5	92.8	80.3
1992	101.5	88.5	99.4	103.8	84.7	95.6	86.6	111.5	97.4	85.9	75.9
Average annual percent change:											
1979-85	-1.2	-3.3	-0.9	0.8	-3.4	-1.8	-3.1	1.8	-2.5	-0.9	-5.3
1985-92	-0.7	-0.8	-0.9	-0.8	-1.1	-	-0.4	0.4	0.6	-2.4	-2.8
1991-92	-1.1	-3.8	-3.6	-0.9	-2.4	-2.0	-4.0	-1.2	-1.2	-7.4	-5.5

- Represents or rounds to zero. NA Not available. [1] Former West Germany. [2] Compensation includes, but real hourly compensation excludes, adjustments for payroll and employment taxes that are not compensation to employees, but are labor costs to employers. [3] Index of hourly compensation divided by the index of consumer prices to adjust for changes in purchasing power. [4] Indexes in national currency adjusted for changes in prevailing exchange rates.

Source: Bureau of Labor Statistics, *Monthly Labor Review*, Dec. 1993, and *News Release* USDL 94-64, Feb. 8, 1994.

No. 1391. Crude Steel Production, by Country: 1980 to 1991
[In million metric tons. Covers both ingots and steel for castings and excludes wrought (puddled) iron]

COUNTRY	1980	1983	1984	1985	1986	1987	1988	1989	1990	1991
World	718.2	672.8	718.3	727.1	721.2	741.2	783.3	785.0	767.0	725.1
United States [1]	101.5	76.8	83.9	80.1	74.0	80.9	91.8	[2]88.9	[2]89.7	79.1
Argentina	2.6	2.8	2.5	2.8	3.1	3.5	3.5	3.9	[2]3.6	[2]3.0
Australia [3]	7.9	5.4	4.6	6.3	6.8	6.2	6.1	6.7	6.7	6.0
Austria	4.6	4.4	4.9	4.7	4.3	4.3	4.4	4.9	[2]4.3	4.1
Belgium	12.3	10.3	11.4	10.8	9.8	9.8	11.3	11.0	11.5	11.3
Brazil	15.3	14.7	18.4	20.5	21.2	22.1	24.6	25.0	20.5	22.6
Bulgaria	2.6	2.8	2.9	2.9	3.0	3.0	2.9	2.9	2.2	2.0
Canada	15.9	12.8	14.7	13.5	14.1	14.7	14.8	[2]15.0	[2]12.2	13.0
China: Mainland	39.0	41.9	45.6	49.5	54.8	58.9	62.1	64.2	68.9	71.0
Czechoslovakia	15.2	15.0	14.8	15.0	15.1	15.4	15.4	15.5	14.8	12.1
Finland	2.5	2.4	2.6	2.5	2.6	2.7	2.8	2.9	2.9	2.9
France	23.2	17.6	19.0	18.8	17.9	17.7	19.1	19.5	19.3	18.7
Germany	51.1	42.9	47.0	48.4	45.1	44.4	49.1	48.9	43.7	41.6
Greece	1.1	0.9	0.9	1.0	1.0	0.9	1.0	1.0	1.0	1.0
Hungary	3.8	3.5	3.6	3.5	3.6	3.5	3.5	3.3	2.9	2.0
India	9.4	10.1	10.3	11.2	11.4	12.3	13.0	12.9	13.0	(NA)
Indonesia [4]	0.4	0.8	1.0	1.2	1.5	1.5	[2]2.0	[2]2.0	[2]2.1	(NA)
Italy	26.5	21.8	24.1	23.9	22.9	22.9	23.9	25.5	25.6	25.3
Japan	111.4	97.2	105.6	105.3	98.3	98.5	105.7	107.9	110.3	109.6
Luxembourg	4.6	3.3	4.0	3.9	3.7	3.3	3.7	3.7	3.6	3.4
Mexico	7.0	6.7	7.3	7.2	7.0	7.2	7.3	7.3	8.2	7.5
Netherlands	5.3	4.5	5.7	5.5	5.3	5.1	5.5	5.7	5.4	5.2
North Korea [2][4]	5.8	6.1	6.5	6.5	6.5	6.5	8.0	8.0	8.0	(NA)
Poland	18.6	16.2	15.2	15.4	16.3	16.3	15.9	13.1	12.2	9.3
Romania	10.7	13.3	15.2	14.6	15.0	14.6	15.1	15.2	10.6	7.8
South Africa	9.1	7.2	7.8	8.6	8.1	9.1	8.8	9.3	8.7	9.4
South Korea	14.4	16.4	17.8	18.6	18.8	19.5	21.3	23.7	24.5	27.9
Soviet Union	147.9	152.5	154.2	154.7	160.6	161.9	163.0	160.1	154.4	(NA)
Spain	12.6	13.3	13.4	14.7	[2]12.1	[2]11.6	[2]11.7	[2]12.6	[2]12.8	12.7
Sweden	4.2	4.2	4.7	4.9	4.7	4.7	4.7	4.8	4.7	[2]4.5	(NA)
Turkey	1.7	3.6	4.1	4.7	6.0	7.0	8.0	7.9	8.4	8.6
United Kingdom	11.3	15.0	15.1	15.7	14.7	17.4	19.0	18.7	17.8	16.5
Venezuela	1.8	2.3	2.8	3.1	3.4	3.7	3.7	3.4	3.1	2.9
Yugoslavia	3.6	4.1	4.2	4.5	4.5	4.4	4.5	4.5	3.6	2.2

NA Not available. [1] Excludes steel for castings made in foundries operated by companies not producing ingots.
[2] Estimated. [3] For year ending June 30. [4] Source: U.S. Bureau of Mines.
Source: Except as noted, Statistical Office of the United Nations, New York, NY, *Statistical Yearbook* and *Industrial Statistics Yearbook*, vol. II, annuals, (copyright).

No. 1392. World Production of Major Mineral Commodities: 1990 to 1993

COUNTRY	Unit	1990	1991	1992, est.	1993, est.	Leading producers, 1992
MINERAL FUELS [1]						
Coal	Mil. metric tons	4,745	4,506	4,527	(NA)	China, United States, Russia
Dry natural gas	Tril. cu. ft.	73.7	74.8	75.0	(NA)	Russia, United States, Canada
Natural gas plant liquids [2]	Mil. barrels [3]	1,728	1,809	1,868	(NA)	United States, Saudi Arabia, Canada
Petroleum, crude	Mil. barrels [3]	22,072	21,938	21,993	(NA)	Saudi Arabia, Russia, United States
Petroleum, refined	Mil. barrels [3]	23,791	23,624	(NA)	(NA)	United States, Russia, Japan (for 1991)
NONMETALLIC MINERALS						
Cement, hydraulic	Mil. metric tons	1,148	1,190	1,254	1,266	China, Japan, United States
Diamond, gem and industrial	1,000 carats	110,919	105,855	107,771	(NA)	Australia, Russia, Botswana
Nitrogen in ammonia	Mil. metric tons	97.1	94.0	92.5	92.5	China, United States, Russia
Phosphate rock	Mil. metric tons	162	150	144	131	United States, China, Morocco
Potash, marketable	Mil. metric tons	27.8	26.1	24.3	22.4	Canada, Belarus, Russia
Salt	Mil. metric tons	184	192	185	185	United States, China, Germany
Sulfur, elemental basis	Mil. metric tons	58.1	55.0	52.4	53.0	United States, Russia, Canada
METALS						
Aluminum [4]	Mil. metric tons	19.3	19.5	19.2	19.0	United States, Russia, Canada
Bauxite, gross weight	Mil. metric tons	108.6	108.2	103.6	101.0	Australia, Guinea, Jamaica
Chromite, gross weight [2]	1,000 metric tons	12,968	13,445	10,896	10,000	Kazakhstan, South Africa, India
Copper, metal content [5]	1,000 metric tons	9,017	9,187	9,290	9,300	Chile, United States, Japan
Gold, metal content	Metric tons	2,133	2,149	2,248	2,290	South Africa, United States, Australia
Iron ore, gross weight [6]	Mil. metric tons	982	956	930	940	China, Brazil, Australia
Lead, metal content [5]	1,000 metric tons	3,353	3,276	3,242	3,200	Australia, United States, China
Manganese ore, gross weight	Mil. metric tons	25.3	21.2	19.9	20.4	Ukraine, China, South Africa
Nickel, metal content [5]	1,000 metric tons	965	949	922	826	Russia, Canada, New Caledonia
Steel, crude	Mil. metric tons	771	736	721	728	Japan, United States, China
Tin, metal content [5]	1,000 metric tons	222	203	179	175	China, Brazil, Indonesia
Zinc, metal content [5]	1,000 metric tons	7,184	7,170	7,137	7,000	Canada, Australia, China

NA Not available. [1] Source: Energy Information Administration, *International Energy Annual.* 1992 data preliminary.
[2] Excludes China: Mainland. [3] 42-gallon barrels. [4] Unalloyed ingot metal. [5] Mine output. [6] Includes iron ore concentrates and iron ore agglomerates.
Source: Except as noted, U.S. Bureau of Mines, *Mineral Commodity Summaries, 1994.*

No. 1393. Energy Consumption and Production, by Country: 1980 to 1991

[See text, section 30, for general comments about the data. For additional data qualifications for countries, see source]

COUNTRY	ENERGY CONSUMED [1] (coal equiv.)				ELECTRIC ENERGY PRODUCTION [2] (bil. kWh)		CRUDE PETROLEUM PRODUCTION [3] (mil. metric tons)		COAL PRODUCTION [4] (mil. metric tons)	
	Total (mil. metric tons)		Per capita (kilograms)							
	1980	1991	1980	1991	1980	1990	1980	1990	1980	1990
World	8,783	10,950	1,626	2,026	8,237	11,771	2,982	3,019	2,728	3,561
United States	2,391	2,727	9,566	10,798	[5]2,354	[5]3,041	424	371	710	[8]854
Algeria	25	27	993	1,044	7	16	47	37	(Z)	[6](Z)
Argentina	50	65	1,537	1,977	40	51	25	25	(Z)	(Z)
Australia	91	127	5,351	7,298	(NA)	155	(NA)	26	(NA)	159
Austria	31	32	4,051	4,195	42	50	1	1	-	-
Bahrain	4	8	8,728	15,608	2	4	2	2	(NA)	(NA)
Bangladesh [7]	4	9	35	77	3	8	(Z)	[6](Z)	(X)	(X)
Belgium	65	69	6,560	6,900	53	71	(X)	(X)	6	[6]1
Brazil	92	121	619	797	139	223	9	33	(NA)	5
Bulgaria	34	29	3,771	3,270	35	41	[6](Z)	(Z)	(Z)	[6](Z)
Burma [9]	2	2	48	55	1	3	2	[6]1	(Z)	[6](Z)
Canada	259	294	9,725	10,903	378	482	70	76	20	38
Chile	11	16	864	1,182	12	18	2	1	1	2
China: Mainland [11]	545	933	481	811	301	621	106	138	596	[10]1,080
Taiwan [11]	39	76	2,126	3,645	(NA)	(NA)	(Z)	(Z)	3	1
Colombia	20	28	627	848	21	35	7	22	4	21
Cuba	14	13	1,288	1,208	10	16	(Z)	[6]1	(X)	(X)
Czechoslovakia	99	89	6,317	5,666	73	89	(Z)	(Z)	[8]28	[6,8]23
Denmark	28	26	5,381	5,084	27	26	(Z)	6	(X)	(X)
Ecuador	6	8	539	757	3	6	10	15	(NA)	(NA)
Egypt	21	38	399	713	19	39	29	44	(X)	(X)
Ethiopia	1	1	16	29	1	1	(X)	(X)	(NA)	(NA)
Finland [12]	27	34	5,497	6,845	[5]39	[5]54	(X)	(X)	(X)	(X)
France [13]	257	311	4,535	5,457	[5]246	[5]420	1	3	[8]20	[8]11
Germany [13]	382	509	6,237	6,375	368	455	[14]5	[14]4	94	[6]76
Greece	20	32	1,998	3,169	23	35	-	[14]1	(X)	(X)
Hong Kong	7	11	1,277	1,920	13	29	(NA)	(NA)	(X)	(X)
Hungary	39	38	3,730	3,574	24	28	2	2	[6]3	[6]2
India [9]	140	290	165	336	119	286	9	33	109	202
Indonesia	36	65	196	348	14	44	78	70	(Z)	7
Iran [15]	46	99	784	1,654	22	56	73	159	[6]1	[6]1
Iraq	11	18	589	970	11	29	130	101	(NA)	(NA)
Ireland	11	14	3,264	4,143	11	15	(X)	(X)	(Z)	(Z)
Israel [16]	9	15	1,895	2,999	13	21	(Z)	(Z)	(X)	(X)
Italy [16]	192	231	3,335	3,998	183	217	2	5	(Z)	(Z)
Japan [17]	455	590	3,684	4,754	578	857	(Z)	1	18	8
Kuwait [17]	12	4	5,605	1,925	9	21	84	60	(NA)	(NA)
Libya	7	20	1,607	4,328	5	19	88	67	(X)	(X)
Malaysia	11	28	632	1,534	10	23	13	30	(X)	(Z)
Mexico	116	162	1,376	1,879	[5]67	[5]122	100	133	7	[6]10
Morocco	7	10	260	384	5	10	(Z)	(Z)	1	1
Netherlands	100	109	6,695	7,248	65	72	1	4	-	-
New Zealand [18]	11	20	3,338	5,838	22	30	(Z)	2	2	2
Nigeria	12	24	110	210	7	10	104	86	(Z)	[6](Z)
North Korea	49	96	2,230	4,308	35	54	(X)	(X)	[6]36	[6]41
Norway [19]	26	29	6,217	6,818	84	122	25	80	(Z)	(Z)
Pakistan [7]	17	35	141	290	15	44	(Z)	3	2	3
Peru	11	10	512	476	10	14	10	7	(Z)	[6](Z)
Philippines	18	26	292	405	18	26	1	(Z)	(Z)	1
Poland	177	121	4,630	3,167	122	136	(Z)	(Z)	193	[6]147
Portugal	13	19	1,268	1,960	15	29	(X)	(X)	(Z)	(Z)
Romania	99	70	4,254	3,025	67	64	12	8	8	[6]5
Saudi Arabia [16]	25	107	1,704	6,922	19	47	496	320	(NA)	(NA)
South Africa [20]	84	107	1,955	2,431	90	167	(X)	(X)	117	176
South Korea	52	130	1,206	2,977	40	119	(X)	(X)	19	17
Soviet Union (former)	1,592	1,867	5,502	6,415	1,294	1,726	603	566	493	543
Spain	88	120	2,270	3,065	109	152	2	1	[8]13	[8]15
Sudan	2	2	60	62	1	1	(X)	(X)	(NA)	(NA)
Sweden	51	59	5,941	6,892	96	146	(Z)	(Z)	(Z)	(Z)
Switzerland [21]	28	32	4,114	4,698	[5]47	56	(X)	(X)	(X)	(X)
Syria	9	14	699	1,100	4	12	9	23	(X)	(X)
Tanzania	1	1	33	38	1	1	(X)	(X)	(Z)	[6](Z)
Thailand	17	46	317	833	15	46	(Z)	1	-	-
Trinidad and Tobago	7	11	6,041	8,400	2	4	11	8	(NA)	(NA)
Tunisia	4	7	510	839	3	6	6	5	(X)	(X)
Turkey	31	59	555	1,036	23	58	2	4	4	3
United Arab Emirates	10	36	6,233	22,379	6	14	83	102	(NA)	(NA)

See footnotes at end of table.

No. 1393. Energy Consumption and Production, by Country: 1980 to 1991—Continued

[See text, section 30, for general comments about the data. For additional data qualifications for countries, see source]

COUNTRY	ENERGY CONSUMED [1] (coal equiv.)				ELECTRIC ENERGY PRODUCTION [2] (bil. kWh)		CRUDE PETROLEUM PRODUCTION [3] (mil. metric tons)		COAL PRODUCTION [4] (mil. metric tons)	
	Total (mil. metric tons)		Per capita (kilograms)							
	1980	1991	1980	1991	1980	1990	1980	1990	1980	1990
United Kingdom	281	309	4,877	5,353	284	319	79	88	[8]130	[8]94
Venezuela.	49	68	2,549	3,429	36	56	115	112	(Z)	2
Vietnam	7	8	103	116	4	9	(X)	3	5	5
Yugoslavia	46	41	1,927	1,731	59	86	4	4	(Z)	(Z)
Zaire	2	2	52	65	4	6	1	[6]1	(Z)	[6](Z)
Zambia.	2	2	279	205	[5]9	8	(X)	(X)	1	(Z)

- Represents or rounds to zero.   NA Not available.   X Not applicable.   Z Less than 500,000 metric tons.   [1] Based on apparent consumption of coal, lignite, petroleum products, natural gas, and hydro, nuclear, and geothermal electricity. [2] Comprises production by utilities generating primarily for public use, and production by industrial establishments generating primarily for own use. Relates to production at generating centers, including station use and transmission losses.   [3] Includes shale oil, but excludes natural gasoline.   [4] Excludes lignite and brown coal, except as noted.   [5] Net production, i.e. excluding station use.   [6] Provisional.   [7] For year ending June of year shown.   [8] Includes recovered slurries.   [9] For year ending April of year shown.   [10] Includes lignite.   [11] Source: U.S. Bureau of the Census. Data from Republic of China publications. 1992 data shown for 1991.   [12] Includes Monaco.   [13] Prior to 1991, data for former West Germany.   [14] Includes inputs other than crude petroleum and natural gas liquids.   [15] For year ending March 20 of year shown.   [16] Includes San Marino.   [17] Includes share of production and consumption in the Neutral Zone.   [18] For year ending March 31 for year shown.   [19] Includes Svalbard and Jan Mayen Islands.   [20] Includes Botswana, Lesotho, Namibia, and Swaziland.   [21] Includes Liechtenstein.

Source: Except as noted, Statistical Office of the United Nations, New York, NY, *Energy Statistics Yearbook*, annual, (copyright).

No. 1394. Selected Petroleum Product Prices, by Country: 1993

[As of January. Includes taxes]

COUNTRY	AUTOMOTIVE FUELS (U.S. dollars per gallon)		RESIDENTIAL (U.S. dollars per gallon)			INDUSTRIAL (U.S. dollars per barrel)	
	Premium gasoline	Diesel fuel	Light fuel oil	Kerosene	Liquified petroleum gases	Light fuel oil	Heavy fuel oil
Argentina	2.60	(NA)	0.92	0.92	(NA)	(NA)	(NA)
Australia [1]	1.83	1.72	(NA)	(NA)	(NA)	(NA)	(NA)
Austria	3.23	2.67	1.47	(NA)	1.82	44.76	45.08
Belgium [1]	3.32	2.34	0.91	(NA)	(NA)	32.04	16.53
Bolivia	2.49	1.42	0.83	0.88	0.46	(NA)	(NA)
Brazil	2.01	1.27	(NA)	1.15	0.46	12.79	6.95
Canada [1]	1.85	1.55	1.12	(NA)	(NA)	26.34	15.72
Chile	1.59	1.26	(NA)	1.01	(NA)	(NA)	22.46
Denmark [1]	3.38	1.92	2.49	(NA)	(NA)	39.96	18.16
El Salvador	1.70	0.89	(NA)	0.87	0.62	40.16	17.67
Finland [1]	3.28	2.26	1.17	(NA)	(NA)	40.18	20.31
France [1]	3.41	2.05	1.44	(NA)	(NA)	42.85	16.29
Germany [1]	3.25	2.20	1.09	(NA)	(NA)	39.75	18.34
Greece [1]	3.27	1.97	1.71	(NA)	(NA)	97.76	20.19
India	2.34	0.80	(NA)	0.33	0.41	26.25	21.14
Indonesia	1.01	0.55	0.40	0.55	(NA)	21.85	21.85
Ireland [1]	3.55	2.70	1.52	(NA)	(NA)	44.48	22.06
Israel	0.68	0.70	(NA)	0.69	(NA)	(NA)	16.29
Italy [1]	3.77	2.52	2.98	(NA)	(NA)	105.19	23.06
Japan.	4.55	2.45	2.45	1.62	7.77	78.48	33.47
Luxembourg [1]	2.48	1.85	0.97	(NA)	(NA)	36.42	17.68
Mexico [1]	[2]1.51	0.89	(NA)	(NA)	(NA)	35.14	11.97
Morocco	[2]2.91	1.73	0.88	(NA)	(NA)	32.77	32.35
Netherlands [1]	3.86	2.28	1.43	(NA)	(NA)	(NA)	25.08
Norway [1]	4.34	1.52	1.65	(NA)	(NA)	56.67	52.55
Pakistan	1.25	0.65	0.52	0.77	(NA)	21.85	27.31
Panama	1.57	1.08	(NA)	1.06	4.37	(NA)	26.68
Peru.	2.28	1.27	(NA)	1.09	(NA)	45.79	29.41
Portugal [1]	3.54	2.48	2.60	(NA)	(NA)	104.07	26.18
Saudi Arabia	(NA)	(NA)	(NA)	(NA)	(NA)	(NA)	(NA)
South Africa	0.67	0.69	(NA)	0.68	(NA)	(NA)	15.71
Spain [1]	3.21	2.24	1.54	(NA)	(NA)	56.20	18.35
Sweden [1]	4.20	2.05	2.03	(NA)	(NA)	35.43	27.29
Switzerland [1]	[2]2.52	2.65	0.83	(NA)	(NA)	31.98	18.85
Taiwan [1]	2.57	1.82	(NA)	(NA)	(NA)	37.24	21.88
Turkey [1]	2.60	1.89	2.01	(NA)	(NA)	(NA)	24.56
United Kingdom [1] . . .	2.77	2.36	0.80	(NA)	(NA)	(NA)	15.29
United States [1]	1.31	0.98	0.94	0.82	0.75	26.34	14.83
Venezuela.	0.29	0.22	(NA)	0.14	(NA)	(NA)	7.04

NA Not available.   [1] Average for January.   [2] Unleaded regular gasoline.

Source: Energy Information Administration, *International Energy Annual*.

No. 1395. Indices of Food Production, by Country: 1980 to 1992

[1979-1981=100. For explanation of average annual percent change, see Guide to Tabular Presentation. Minus sign (-) indicates decrease]

REGION AND COUNTRY	TOTAL FOOD PRODUCTION				Average annual percent change		PER CAPITA FOOD PRODUCTION				Average annual percent change	
	1980	1990	1991	1992	1980-1992	1991-1992	1980	1990	1991	1992	1980-1992	1991-1992
World	99.18	125.69	125.44	128.36	2.1	2.3	99.19	105.62	103.60	104.22	0.4	0.6
Developed countries	98.80	110.86	107.36	108.83	0.8	1.4	98.78	103.50	99.54	100.25	0.1	0.7
United States	95.68	105.60	104.09	114.02	1.5	9.5	95.63	96.15	93.86	101.80	0.5	8.5
Canada	99.27	127.11	127.04	124.25	1.9	-2.2	99.25	114.80	113.09	109.03	0.8	-3.6
Europe	100.99	108.94	108.57	105.83	0.4	-2.5	100.97	105.34	104.58	101.66	0.1	-2.8
Japan	94.52	100.94	93.81	99.36	0.4	5.9	94.49	95.38	88.37	93.43	-0.1	5.7
Oceania	94.65	110.92	110.36	120.79	2.0	9.5	94.71	95.18	93.25	100.24	0.5	7.5
South Africa	96.52	103.55	105.32	81.19	-1.4	-22.9	96.64	80.66	80.10	60.29	-3.9	-24.7
Soviet Union (former)	99.50	121.06	107.65	101.42	0.2	-5.8	99.49	111.38	98.32	91.97	-0.7	-6.5
Developing countries	99.56	140.87	143.93	148.35	3.3	3.1	99.61	114.31	114.43	115.57	1.2	1.0
Africa	99.83	132.66	138.87	134.93	2.5	-2.8	99.82	98.35	99.84	94.08	-0.5	-5.8
China: Mainland	99.29	156.06	160.02	167.74	4.4	4.8	99.32	134.81	136.17	140.65	2.9	3.3
Near East	100.31	133.40	135.41	142.52	2.9	5.3	100.40	99.95	98.52	100.68	0.0	2.2
Far East	99.48	148.19	151.42	157.11	3.8	3.8	99.53	123.06	123.50	125.88	2.0	1.9
India	98.06	148.89	152.30	156.91	3.9	3.0	98.14	121.30	121.70	122.98	1.9	1.1
Latin America	99.37	127.11	128.65	132.49	2.4	3.0	99.39	103.47	102.79	103.94	0.4	1.1
Mexico	99.96	125.92	126.96	134.37	2.5	5.8	100.04	100.01	98.70	102.28	0.2	3.6
Brazil	103.36	132.92	137.31	146.36	2.9	6.6	103.41	108.22	109.90	115.21	0.9	4.8
Argentina	95.25	109.94	112.38	116.80	1.7	3.9	95.22	96.01	96.97	99.60	0.4	2.7

Source: Food and Agriculture Organization of the United Nations, Rome, Italy, FAO AGRISTAT Database.

No. 1396. Wheat, Rice, and Corn—Exports and Imports of 10 Leading Countries: 1980 to 1991

[In millions of dollars. Countries listed are the ten leading exporters or importers in 1991]

LEADING EXPORTERS	EXPORTS			LEADING IMPORTERS	IMPORTS		
	1980	1990	1991		1980	1990	1991
WHEAT				**WHEAT**			
United States	6,376	3,887	3,350	Soviet Union (former)	2,891	2,490	2,553
Canada	3,302	2,863	3,315	Italy	773	1,217	1,685
France	2,110	3,296	2,793	China, Mainland	2,436	2,157	1,460
Australia	2,425	1,971	1,338	Japan	1,236	1,019	920
United Kingdom	260	760	758	Egypt	839	853	620
Argentina	816	871	479	South Korea	367	419	577
Germany	198	504	463	Brazil	1,051	331	550
Greece	27	156	311	Belgium-Luxembourg	360	384	501
Denmark	23	229	211	Spain	71	162	454
Turkey	52	4	204	Indonesia	162	282	366
RICE				**RICE**			
Thailand	953	1,086	1,196	Brazil	99	144	372
United States	1,285	804	756	Iran	209	225	236
Italy	289	357	361	France	154	216	231
Pakistan	422	242	345	United Kingdom	98	209	205
India	173	258	339	Saudi Arabia	230	153	147
Vietnam	10	305	188	Soviet Union (former)	265	119	145
Spain	22	108	171	Malaysia	60	100	127
Belgium-Luxembourg	91	168	152	South Africa	58	87	117
China, Mainland	450	84	152	Belgium-Luxembourg	80	106	108
Australia	145	143	140	Netherlands	93	112	104
CORN				**CORN**			
United States	8,571	6,206	5,147	Japan	2,011	2,295	2,242
France	869	1,854	1,420	Soviet Union (former)	1,508	1,690	1,536
China, Mainland	17	404	864	Taiwan	437	704	736
Argentina	513	329	410	South Korea	376	837	697
Thailand	352	162	153	Netherlands	626	538	532
Hungary	27	51	120	United Kingdom	547	396	398
Greece	-	32	94	Germany	996	486	392
Canada	113	28	93	Belgium-Luxembourg	473	298	323
Germany	39	71	88	Italy	450	363	291
Spain	1	41	86	Spain	668	307	255

- Represents or rounds to zero.

Source: U.S. Dept. of Agriculture, Economic Research Service, World Agriculture-Trends and Indicators.

No. 1397. Wheat, Rice, and Corn Production, by Country: 1980 to 1992

[In thousands of metric tons. Rice data cover paddy. Data for each country pertain to the calendar year in which all or most of the crop was harvested. See text, section 30, for general comments concerning quality of the data]

COUNTRY	WHEAT			RICE			CORN		
	1980	1990	1992	1980	1990	1992	1980	1990	1992
World	440,141	592,811	566,282	398,879	520,549	526,360	397,472	479,008	530,067
Argentina	7,780	11,014	9,685	266	428	695	6,400	5,047	10,699
Australia	10,856	15,066	16,184	613	846	1,128	151	219	210
Austria	1,201	1,404	1,325	(X)	(X)	(X)	1,293	1,620	1,118
Belgium-Luxembourg ...	906	1,347	1,428	(X)	(X)	(X)	39	56	86
Brazil	2,702	3,094	2,796	9,776	7,421	9,962	20,372	21,348	30,557
Burma	91	124	143	13,317	13,969	14,915	166	187	206
Canada	19,292	32,098	29,871	(X)	(X)	(X)	5,753	7,066	4,883
China: Mainland	55,213	98,232	101,594	142,852	191,589	188,290	62,715	97,158	95,760
Egypt	1,736	4,268	4,618	2,382	3,167	3,910	3,231	4,799	5,069
France	906	1,347	1,428	24	125	122	9,365	9,291	14,886
Germany	11,254	15,242	15,542	(X)	(X)	(X)	676	1,552	2,139
Greece	2,970	1,938	2,385	80	99	101	1,279	2,131	2,048
Hungary	6,077	6,198	3,444	24	39	15	6,673	4,500	4,417
India	55,213	98,232	101,594	80,312	111,517	108,011	6,957	8,962	10,400
Indonesia	(X)	(X)	(X)	29,652	45,179	47,700	3,991	6,734	7,996
Iran	5,850	8,012	10,350	1,311	1,981	2,500	60	130	200
Iraq	976	1,196	1,006	167	229	160	60	172	260
Italy	9,156	8,109	8,943	968	1,291	1,284	6,377	5,864	7,679
Japan	583	952	759	12,189	13,124	13,216	4	1	1
Mexico	2,785	3,935	3,626	445	394	361	12,374	14,640	17,003
Pakistan	10,857	14,316	15,684	4,685	4,891	4,674	970	1,185	1,178
South Korea	92	1	1	5,311	7,722	7,835	154	120	92
Soviet Union (former) ...	92,500	101,891	90,037	2,594	2,166	1,969	9,454	9,886	7,319
Sweden	1,193	2,243	1,411	(X)	(X)	(X)	(X)	(X)	(X)
Thailand	-	-	1	17,368	17,193	19,935	2,998	3,722	3,672
United Kingdom	8,470	14,033	14,092	(X)	(X)	(X)	1	(NA)	(NA)
United States	**64,800**	**74,473**	**66,920**	**6,629**	**7,080**	**8,123**	**168,647**	**201,532**	**240,774**
Yugoslavia	5,091	6,359	4,100	42	28	43	9,317	6,724	7,025

- Represents or rounds to zero.   NA Not available.   X Not applicable.

Source: U.S. Department of Agriculture, Economic Research Service, *World Agriculture-Trends and Indicators.*

No. 1398. Fisheries—Commercial Catch, by Country: 1987 to 1991

[In thousands of metric tons, live weight. Catch of fish, crustaceans, mollusks (including weight of shells). Does not include marine mammals and aquatic plants]

COUNTRY	1987	1988	1989	1990	1991	COUNTRY	1987	1988	1989	1990	1991
World	**94,399**	**99,062**	**100,333**	**97,434**	**96,926**	North Korea (est.) ..	1,700	1,700	1,700	1,750	1,700
Canada	1,565	1,610	1,572	1,624	1,529	Norway	1,949	1,839	1,908	1,711	2,095
Chile	4,814	5,209	6,454	5,195	6,002	Peru	4,587	6,641	6,853	6,875	6,944
China: Mainland ...	9,346	10,358	11,219	12,095	13,134	Philippines	1,988	2,010	2,098	2,208	2,311
Denmark	1,706	1,971	1,927	1,517	1,793	South Korea	2,876	2,728	2,833	2,833	2,515
Iceland	1,632	1,759	1,504	1,508	1,051	Soviet Union					
India	2,906	3,125	3,640	3,794	4,036	(former)	11,159	11,332	11,310	10,389	9,216
Indonesia	2,583	2,789	2,948	3,043	3,186	Spain	1,524	1,592	1,559	1,450	1,350
Japan	11,857	11,966	11,173	10,350	9,306	**United States ....**	**5,986**	**5,937**	**5,763**	**5,858**	**5,473**
Mexico	1,419	1,372	1,469	1,400	1,429	Thailand	2,779	2,642	2,699	2,786	3,065

Source: U.S. National Oceanic and Atmospheric Administration, National Marine Fisheries Service, *Fisheries of the United States,* annual. Data from Food and Agricultural Organization of the United Nations, Rome, Italy.

No. 1399. Meat Production, by Country: 1980 to 1993

[In thousands of metric tons, carcass weight. Covers beef and veal (incl. buffalo meat), pork (incl. bacon and ham), mutton and lamb (incl. goat meat), horsemeat, and poultry. Refers to meat from animals slaughtered within the national boundaries irrespective of origin of animals, and relates to commercial and farm slaughter. Excludes lard, tallow, and edible offals. See text, section 30, for general comments concerning the data]

COUNTRY	1980	1990	1993	COUNTRY	1980	1990	1993
World	**135,940**	**178,169**	**185,917**	Italy	3,564	3,950	3,936
				Japan	3,046	3,503	3,378
Argentina	3,622	3,383	3,617	Mexico	2,540	3,478	3,628
Brazil	4,550	6,439	7,545	Soviet Union (former) ..	15,072	19,996	15,566
France	5,455	5,765	6,085	Spain	2,648	3,466	3,701
Germany	6,972	7,292	5,947	United Kingdom	3,070	3,357	2,340
India	2,675	3,723	3,992	**United States ......**	**24,599**	**28,632**	**31,350**

Source: U.S. Department of Agriculture, Economic Research Service, *World Agriculture-Trends and Indicators,* and Food and Agriculture Organization of the United Nations, Rome, Italy, *FAO Production Yearbook, 1992.*

No. 1400. Foreign Trade—Source of Imports and Destination of Exports, by Country: 1992

[In billions of dollars. All exports are f.o.b. (free on board) and all imports are c.i.f. (cost insurance freight) except for United States, Australian, and Canadian imports, which are f.o.b.]

COUNTRY	Total [1]	O.E.C.D. [2]		C.E.E.C.[4]	China: Mainland, Vietnam, North Korea	O.P.E.C. [5]	Other developing countries [6]	Africa	America [7]	Middle East [8]	Far East [9]
		Total	E.E.C. [3]								
IMPORTS											
Australia.	40.8	29.1	8.2	0.1	1.8	1.9	7.7	0.1	0.4	1.1	8.7
Austria.	54.2	45.8	36.8	3.5	0.6	1.1	3.3	1.0	0.5	0.5	2.4
Belgium-Lux	125.0	109.3	92.0	2.1	0.4	3.3	9.9	4.8	1.8	2.9	3.8
Canada	123.1	105.0	12.0	0.4	2.1	1.7	11.6	0.9	4.5	0.7	9.3
Denmark	33.6	29.1	18.0	1.1	0.6	0.2	2.7	0.2	1.0	0.1	1.9
France.	238.8	191.9	142.3	5.5	3.6	9.4	23.8	11.2	5.0	5.7	13.7
Germany	408.5	326.3	212.5	22.5	7.8	9.8	41.8	10.6	9.4	4.2	30.9
Italy.	164.4	127.1	96.7	6.7	2.4	10.1	17.6	11.4	4.0	4.3	8.2
Japan	232.7	112.3	31.4	3.1	18.1	38.9	60.4	3.5	8.3	29.1	75.5
Netherlands	130.4	110.6	85.5	2.2	1.0	6.3	10.3	2.8	2.4	4.6	7.4
Spain.	99.8	78.9	60.6	1.5	1.7	5.9	11.6	6.5	4.4	2.0	6.1
Sweden	49.9	43.4	27.7	1.6	0.8	0.9	3.3	0.4	0.7	0.6	3.0
Switzerland.	65.7	59.5	47.4	0.7	0.6	0.0	4.8	0.7	1.2	0.6	2.9
United Kingdom. .	220.3	183.3	115.0	2.7	1.7	4.9	26.5	4.7	4.2	4.1	19.1
United States . . .	531.3	310.1	94.1	2.0	25.7	33.0	160.6	14.3	68.7	15.7	119.7
EXPORTS											
Australia.	42.4	23.6	5.4	0.2	1.4	2.1	14.3	0.6	0.4	1.0	14.6
Austria.	44.4	35.8	29.4	4.3	0.3	1.3	2.8	0.6	0.4	1.0	1.5
Belgium-Lux	123.0	106.7	92.1	1.7	0.5	2.6	10.7	2.8	1.2	4.3	5.1
Canada	134.9	122.8	9.5	1.2	1.9	1.7	7.2	0.8	2.7	0.8	6.4
Denmark	39.6	34.0	21.5	1.1	0.1	0.8	3.4	0.8	0.9	0.9	1.5
France.	231.8	183.7	145.4	4.8	1.6	9.7	31.9	15.3	8.1	6.2	11.0
Germany	430.4	345.9	234.0	23.9	3.8	14.8	41.3	9.9	9.2	13.0	23.5
Italy.	155.4	120.2	89.8	5.7	1.4	8.0	19.6	6.4	4.4	6.9	8.2
Japan	339.8	184.1	62.8	1.9	12.6	19.0	122.2	6.4	15.1	14.0	117.1
Netherlands	139.0	123.0	105.8	2.7	0.5	3.0	8.9	2.7	1.8	2.6	4.6
Spain.	64.3	53.0	45.8	0.8	0.3	2.3	7.5	3.1	3.1	1.4	1.7
Sweden	56.1	48.5	31.3	1.4	0.4	1.4	4.3	0.7	1.1	1.3	2.8
Switzerland.	65.5	52.4	38.6	1.3	0.5	2.4	9.0	1.2	1.9	2.7	5.6
United Kingdom. .	189.6	152.0	106.2	2.8	0.8	9.3	23.1	6.3	3.1	9.1	13.5
United States . . .	447.5	264.6	102.9	5.5	7.5	21.9	147.7	9.9	75.7	16.9	73.6

[1] Includes other areas not shown separately.   [2] Organization for Economic Cooperation and Development. For member countries, see text, section 30.   [3] European Economic Community comprises Belgium-Luxembourg, Denmark, France, Germany, Greece, Ireland, Italy, Netherlands, Portugal, Spain, and United Kingdom.   [4] Central and Eastern European countries comprises Albania, the Baltic States (Estonia, Latvia, Lithuania), Bulgaria, Czechoslovakia, Hungary, new independent states of the ex-Soviet Union, Poland, and Romania.   [5] Organization of Petroleum Exporting Countries comprises Algeria, Ecuador, Gabon, Iran, Iraq, Kuwait, Libya, Nigeria, Qatar, Saudi Arabia, United Arab Emirates, and Venezuela.   [6] Comprises trade with all countries other than China, North Korea, Vietnam, South Africa, Eastern Europe, and members of OPEC and OECD.   [7] All countries comprising the continent except Canada and the United States.   [8] Comprises Syria, Lebanon, Israel, Gaza Strip, Jordan, Iraq, Saudi Arabia, Yemen, Kuwait, Bahrain, United Arab Emirates, Qatar, Oman, and Iran.   [9] All countries comprising the continent of Asia except Japan, China, North Korea, Vietnam, and those countries listed under Middle East.

Source: Organization for Economic Cooperation and Development, Paris, France. Data derived from Monthly Statistics of Foreign Trade.

No. 1401. Reserve Assets and International Transaction Balances, by Country: 1985 to 1993

[In millions of U.S. dollars. Assets include holdings of convertible foreign currencies, special drawing rights, and reserve position in International Monetary Fund and exclude gold holdings. Minus sign (-) indicates decrease]

COUNTRY	TOTAL RESERVE ASSETS				CURRENT ACCOUNT BALANCE			MERCHANDISE TRADE BALANCE		
	1985	1990	1993 Total	1993 Currency holdings [1]	1985	1990	1992	1985	1990	1992
United States	32,100	72,260	62,350	41,530	122,250	−90,460	−66,380	−122,160	−108,840	−96,140
Algeria	2,819	725	1,475	1,468	1,015	1,420	(NA)	4,223	4,187	(NA)
Argentina	3,273	4,592	14,089	13,636	−952	1,903	−8,381	4,878	8,628	−1,450
Australia	5,768	16,265	11,102	10,470	9,015	−15,099	−10,728	−1,317	366	1,558
Austria	4,767	9,376	14,611	13,866	−273	1,174	−164	−4,406	−7,012	−8,801
Bangladesh	337	629	2,411	2,388	−458	−397	181	−1,287	−1,587	(NA)
Belgium	4,849	12,151	11,415	10,474	669	4,950	5,409	−472	590	215
Brazil	10,605	7,441	30,604	30,602	−273	−3,788	6,275	12,466	10,747	15,525
Burma	34	313	303	303	−206	(NA)	(NA)	−202	(NA)	(NA)
Cameroon	132	26	2	2	−562	−335	(NA)	490	599	(NA)
Canada	2,503	17,845	12,481	10,471	−2,279	−22,172	−23,012	12,574	8,785	8,183
Chile	2,450	6,069	9,640	9,639	−1,328	−598	−583	850	1,273	748
China: Mainland	12,728	29,586	(NA)	(NA)	−11,417	11,997	6,401	−13,123	9,165	5,183
Colombia	1,595	4,212	(NA)	(NA)	−1,809	542	912	−23	1,971	1,233
Cote d'Ivoire	5	4	2	1	64	−1,305	−1,424	1,351	1,327	994
Denmark	5,429	10,591	10,301	9,791	−2,767	1,380	4,700	−764	4,875	7,189
Ecuador	718	839	(NA)	(NA)	114	−166	(NA)	1,294	1,003	(NA)
Egypt	792	2,684	12,904	12,761	−2,166	184	2,812	−5,215	−6,699	−5,501
Finland	3,750	9,644	5,411	4,993	−811	−6,961	−4,943	878	725	3,952
France	26,589	36,778	22,649	20,008	−35	−15,244	4,109	−5,276	−13,673	1,661
Germany [2]	44,380	67,902	77,640	72,727	16,960	46,560	−25,560	28,580	71,630	32,870
Ghana	479	219	(NA)	(NA)	−134	−229	−378	−36	−308	−470
Greece	868	3,412	7,790	7,634	−3,276	−3,537	−2,140	−5,053	−10,178	−11,603
Hungary	2,153	1,070	6,772	6,692	−455	379	352	448	534	−11
India	6,420	1,521	10,199	9,807	−4,177	−7,037	(NA)	−5,616	−5,151	(NA)
Indonesia	4,974	7,459	11,263	10,988	−1,923	−2,988	−3,679	5,822	5,352	6,021
Ireland	2,940	5,223	5,925	5,579	−690	45	2,629	631	3,969	6,804
Israel	3,680	6,275	6,386	6,382	1,120	574	86	−2,364	−3,015	−5,035
Italy	15,595	62,927	27,545	25,140	3,408	−14,420	−25,422	−6,083	616	2,410
Japan	26,719	78,501	98,524	88,720	49,170	35,870	117,640	55,990	63,580	132,400
Kenya	391	205	(NA)	(NA)	−113	−520	−98	−327	−995	−591
Kuwait	5,471	1,952	4,214	3,916	5,150	4,042	−873	5,047	3,540	85
Libya	5,904	5,839	(NA)	(NA)	1,906	2,201	(NA)	4,599	3,777	(NA)
Malaysia	4,912	9,754	27,249	26,814	−613	−918	−1,649	3,577	2,622	3,375
Mexico	4,906	9,863	(NA)	(NA)	1,130	−7,117	−22,811	8,451	−4,433	−20,677
Morocco	115	2,066	3,655	3,579	−891	−200	−427	−1,368	−2,071	−2,736
Nepal	56	295	(NA)	(NA)	−122	−289	−181	−283	−449	−376
Netherlands	10,782	17,484	31,352	29,677	4,190	8,854	6,750	5,393	10,330	10,956
Nigeria	1,667	3,864	(NA)	(NA)	2,566	4,988	2,268	5,616	8,653	4,611
Norway	13,917	15,332	19,622	18,642	3,052	4,023	2,925	4,728	7,761	9,289
Pakistan	807	296	1,197	1,196	−1,080	−1,654	−2,020	−3,230	−2,714	−2,700
Peru	1,842	1,040	3,408	3,407	135	−1,092	−2,080	1,172	340	−567
Philippines	615	924	4,676	4,546	−35	−2,695	−999	−482	−4,020	−4,695
Poland	870	4,492	4,092	3,985	−982	3,067	−3,104	347	3,589	−131
Portugal	1,395	14,485	15,840	15,481	380	−181	−184	−1,504	−6,831	−9,540
Romania	199	373	1,005	1,003	1,381	−3,254	−1,506	1,772	−3,344	−1,194
Saudi Arabia	25,004	11,668	7,435	5,689	−12,932	−4,117	−19,431	7,029	22,756	12,991
Singapore	12,847	27,748	48,361	48,066	−4	1,743	2,929	−2,829	−5,129	−4,900
South Africa	315	1,008	1,020	1,008	2,622	2,253	1,388	5,842	6,338	5,429
South Korea	2,869	14,793	20,500	19,976	−887	−2,172	−4,529	−19	−2,004	−2,146
Spain	11,175	51,228	41,045	39,798	2,851	−16,819	−18,481	−4,171	−29,566	−31,034
Sri Lanka	451	423	1,629	1,601	−419	−298	−451	−523	−473	−715
Sudan	12	11	(NA)	(NA)	155	−369	−506	−139	−322	−597
Sweden	5,793	17,988	19,050	18,372	−1,231	−6,907	−5,229	2,385	3,402	6,672
Switzerland	18,016	29,223	32,635	31,650	6,040	6,942	13,419	−1,561	−6,391	−251
Syria	83	(NA)	(NA)	(NA)	−958	1,762	55	−2,090	2,094	159
Thailand	2,190	13,305	24,473	24,078	−1,537	−7,282	−6,604	−1,332	−6,751	−4,155
Trinidad and Tobago .	1,129	492	(NA)	(NA)	−90	440	122	756	988	666
Turkey	1,056	6,050	(NA)	(NA)	−1,013	−2,625	−943	−2,975	−9,555	−8,191
United Kingdom	12,860	35,850	36,780	34,630	4,136	−31,647	−15,516	−3,850	−32,742	−23,963
Venezuela	10,251	8,321	9,216	8,531	3,327	8,279	−3,365	6,782	10,637	1,689
Yugoslavia	1,095	5,474	(NA)	(NA)	833	−2,364	(NA)	−588	−2,676	(NA)
Zaire	190	219	(NA)	(NA)	−289	−643	(NA)	606	600	(NA)

NA Not available.   [1] Holdings of convertible foreign currencies.   [2] Prior to July 1990, data for former West Germany.

Source: International Monetary Fund, Washington, DC, *International Financial Statistics*, monthly.

No. 1402. Foreign Exchange Rates: 1980 to 1993

[National currency units per dollar, except as noted. Data are averages of certified noon buying rates for cable transfers]

YEAR	Australia [1] (dollar)	Austria (schilling)	Belgium (franc)	Canada (dollar)	China: Taiwan (dollar)	Denmark (krone)	France (franc)	Greece (drachma)	Hong Kong (dollar)
1980	114.00	12.945	29.237	1.1693	36.015	5.6345	4.2250	42.62	4.9760
1981	114.95	15.948	37.194	1.1990	36.849	7.1350	5.4396	55.41	5.5678
1982	101.65	17.060	45.780	1.2344	39.124	8.3443	6.5793	66.87	6.0697
1983	90.14	17.968	51.121	1.2325	40.065	9.1483	7.6203	87.90	7.2569
1984	87.94	20.005	57.749	1.2953	39.633	10.3540	8.7355	112.73	7.8188
1985	70.03	20.676	59.336	1.3658	39.889	10.5980	8.9799	138.40	7.7911
1986	67.09	15.260	44.662	1.3896	37.837	8.0954	6.9256	139.93	7.8037
1987	70.14	12.649	37.357	1.3259	31.756	6.8477	6.0121	135.47	7.7985
1988	78.41	12.357	36.783	1.2306	28.636	6.7411	5.9594	142.00	7.8071
1989	79.19	13.236	39.409	1.1842	26.407	7.3210	6.3802	162.60	7.8008
1990	78.07	11.331	33.424	1.1668	26.918	6.1899	5.4467	158.59	7.7899
1991	75.93	11.686	34.195	1.1460	26.759	6.4038	5.6468	182.63	7.7712
1992	73.52	10.992	32.148	1.2085	25.160	6.0372	5.2935	190.81	7.7402
1993	67.99	11.639	34.581	1.2902	26.416	6.4863	5.6669	229.64	7.7357

	India (rupee)	Ireland [1] (pound)	Italy (lira)	Japan (yen)	Malaysia (ringgit)	Netherlands (guilder)	New Zealand[1] (dollar)	Norway (krone)	Portugal (escudo)
1980	7.887	205.77	856.20	226.63	2.1767	1.9875	97.34	4.9381	50.08
1981	8.681	161.32	1,138.60	220.63	2.3048	2.4998	86.85	5.7430	61.74
1982	9.485	142.05	1,354.00	249.06	2.3395	2.6719	75.10	6.4567	80.10
1983	10.104	124.81	1,519.30	237.55	2.3204	2.8543	66.79	7.3012	111.61
1984	11.348	108.64	1,756.10	237.45	2.3448	3.2083	57.84	8.1596	147.70
1985	12.332	106.62	1,908.90	238.47	2.4806	3.3184	49.75	8.5933	172.07
1986	12.597	134.14	1,491.16	168.35	2.5830	2.4484	52.46	7.3984	149.80
1987	12.943	148.79	1,297.03	144.60	2.5185	2.0263	59.33	6.7408	141.20
1988	13.899	152.49	1,302.39	128.17	2.6189	1.9778	65.56	6.5242	144.26
1989	16.213	141.80	1,372.28	138.07	2.7079	2.1219	59.35	6.9131	157.53
1990	17.492	165.76	1,198.27	145.00	2.7057	1.8215	59.62	6.2541	142.70
1991	22.712	174.70	1,241.28	134.59	2.7503	1.8720	54.03	6.4912	144.77
1992	28.156	170.42	1,232.17	126.78	2.5463	1.7587	53.79	6.2142	135.07
1993	31.291	146.47	1,573.41	111.08	2.5738	1.8585	54.13	7.0979	161.08

	Singapore (dollar)	South Africa (rand)	South Korea (won)	Spain (peseta)	Sweden (krona)	Switzerland (franc)	Thailand (baht)	United Kingdom[1] (pound)	Germany (deutsche mark)
1980	2.1412	0.7796	607.43	71.76	4.2309	1.6772	20.476	232.43	1.8175
1981	2.1053	0.8787	681.03	92.40	5.0659	1.9674	21.731	202.43	2.2632
1982	2.1406	1.0876	731.93	110.09	6.2838	2.0327	23.014	174.80	2.4281
1983	2.1136	1.1146	776.04	143.50	7.6717	2.1006	22.991	151.59	2.5539
1984	2.1325	1.4761	807.91	160.78	8.2706	2.3500	23.582	133.66	2.8455
1985	2.2008	2.2344	861.89	169.98	8.6031	2.4551	27.193	129.74	2.9420
1986	2.1782	2.2919	884.61	140.04	7.1272	1.7979	26.314	146.77	2.1705
1987	2.1059	2.0385	825.93	123.54	6.3468	1.4918	25.774	163.98	1.7981
1988	2.0132	2.2770	734.51	116.52	6.1369	1.4642	25.312	178.13	1.7570
1989	1.9511	2.6214	674.29	118.44	6.4559	1.6369	25.725	163.82	1.8808
1990	1.8134	2.5885	710.64	101.96	5.9231	1.3901	25.609	178.41	1.6166
1991	1.7283	2.7633	736.73	104.01	6.0521	1.4356	25.528	176.74	1.6610
1992	1.6294	2.8524	784.58	102.38	5.8258	1.4064	25.411	176.63	1.5618
1993	1.6158	3.2729	805.75	127.48	7.7956	1.4781	25.333	150.16	1.6545

[1] Value is U.S. cents per unit of foreign currency.

Source: Board of Governors of the Federal Reserve System, *Federal Reserve Bulletin*, monthly.

No. 1403. Exchange Rates—Indexes of Value of Foreign Currency Relative to U.S. Dollar: 1980 to 1992

[1982 = 100]

YEAR	United States	Belgium	Canada	Denmark	France	Germany [1]	Italy	Japan	Netherlands	Norway	Sweden	United Kingdom [1]
1980	100.0	156.8	105.6	148.2	155.9	133.8	158.3	110.4	134.6	130.8	148.6	133.1
1981	100.0	123.6	103.0	116.9	121.0	107.7	118.9	112.9	107.4	112.4	124.0	115.8
1982	100.0	100.0	100.0	100.0	100.0	100.0	100.0	100.0	100.0	100.0	100.0	100.0
1983	100.0	89.5	100.2	91.2	86.3	95.1	89.1	104.8	93.6	88.4	81.9	86.7
1984	100.0	79.3	95.3	80.6	75.3	85.3	77.1	104.9	83.3	79.1	76.0	76.5
1985	100.0	77.2	90.4	78.7	73.3	82.5	70.9	104.4	80.5	75.1	73.0	74.2
1986	100.0	102.5	88.8	103.1	95.0	111.9	90.8	147.9	109.1	87.3	88.2	84.0
1987	100.0	122.5	93.1	121.9	109.4	135.0	104.4	172.2	131.9	95.8	99.0	93.8
1988	100.0	124.5	100.3	123.8	110.4	138.2	104.0	194.3	135.1	99.0	102.4	101.9
1989	100.0	116.2	104.2	114.0	103.1	129.1	98.7	180.4	125.9	93.4	97.3	93.7
1990	100.0	137.0	105.8	134.8	120.8	150.2	113.0	171.8	146.7	103.2	106.1	102.1
1991	100.0	133.9	107.7	130.3	116.5	146.2	109.1	185.1	142.7	99.5	103.8	101.1
1992	100.0	142.4	102.1	138.2	124.3	155.5	109.9	196.5	151.9	103.9	107.9	101.0

[1] Prior to 1991, data for former West Germany.

Source: U.S. Bureau of Labor Statistics, *Monthly Labor Review*, December 1993.

No. 1404. Central Bank Discount Rates, Money Market Rates, and Government Bond Yields, by Country: 1980 to 1994

[In percent per annum. Central bank discount rates refer to the rate at which the monetary authority lends or discounts eligible paper for deposit money banks. **Money market rates** refer to the rate at which short-term borrowings are effected between financial institutions. **Government bond yields** refer to one or more series representing average yields to maturity of government bonds or other bonds that would be indicative of longer term rates]

NATIONAL INTEREST RATE AND YEAR	United States	Canada	Japan	France	Germany [1]	Italy	Netherlands	Sweden	Switzerland	United Kingdom
Central bank discount rates: [2]										
1980	13.00	17.26	7.25	9.50	7.50	16.50	8.00	10.00	3.00	14.00
1985	7.50	9.49	5.00	9.50	4.00	15.00	5.00	10.50	4.00	(3)
1990	6.50	11.78	6.00	9.50	6.00	12.50	7.25	11.50	6.00	(3)
1991	3.50	7.67	4.50	9.50	8.00	12.00	8.50	8.00	7.00	(3)
1992	3.00	7.36	3.25	9.50	8.25	12.00	7.75	10.00	6.00	(3)
1993	3.00	4.11	1.75	9.50	5.75	8.00	5.00	5.00	4.00	(3)
1994, February	3.00	4.00	1.75	9.50	5.25	(NA)	(NA)	4.50	4.00	(3)
Money market rates: [4]										
1980	13.36	13.28	10.93	11.85	9.10	17.17	10.13	12.17	2.29	15.62
1985	8.10	9.57	6.46	9.93	5.20	15.25	6.30	13.85	3.75	10.78
1990	8.10	11.62	7.24	9.85	7.92	12.38	8.29	13.45	8.33	14.68
1991	5.70	7.40	7.46	9.49	8.84	12.18	9.01	11.81	7.73	11.75
1992	3.52	6.79	4.58	10.35	9.42	13.97	9.27	18.42	7.47	9.55
1993	3.02	3.79	3.06	8.75	7.49	10.20	7.10	9.08	4.94	5.60
1994, February	3.25	4.64	2.24	6.39	6.22	(NA)	(NA)	7.63	4.23	(NA)
Government bond yields:										
1980	11.46	12.48	9.22	13.03	8.50	16.11	10.21	11.74	4.77	13.79
1985	10.62	11.04	6.34	10.94	6.87	13.00	7.34	13.09	4.78	10.62
1990	8.55	10.85	7.36	9.96	8.88	11.51	8.92	13.08	6.68	11.08
1991	7.86	9.76	6.53	9.05	8.63	10.10	8.74	10.69	6.35	9.92
1992	7.01	8.77	4.94	8.60	7.96	(NA)	8.10	10.02	5.48	9.15
1993	5.82	7.85	3.69	6.91	6.28	(NA)	6.50	8.54	4.05	7.87
1994, February	5.97	7.33	(NA)	6.13	5.76	(NA)	(NA)	6.94	4.34	(NA)

NA Not available.   [1] Prior to July 1990, data are for former West Germany.   [2] End of period.   [3] Minimum lending rate suspended as of August 20, 1981.   [4] Period averages.

Source: International Monetary Fund, Washington, DC, *International Financial Statistics*, monthly.

No. 1405. External Debt of Eastern European Countries: 1980 to 1992

[In billions of dollars. **Gross debt:** total amount owed. **Commercial debt:** money owed to private institutions or individuals. **Official debt:** money owed to or guaranteed by a foreign government. **Net debt** represents gross debt minus assets held with Western commercial banks]

ITEM	1980	1985	1986	1987	1988	1989	1990	1991	1992
Bulgaria: Gross debt	3.5	3.7	4.9	6.1	8.9	10.2	10.6	12.7	14.2
Commercial debt	3.2	3.1	4.2	5.3	7.0	8.5	8.6	9.8	10.2
Official debt	0.3	0.6	0.7	0.9	1.9	1.7	2.0	2.9	4.0
Net debt	2.7	1.5	3.6	5.0	(NA)	(NA)	(NA)	(NA)	(NA)
Czechoslovakia: Gross debt	4.9	3.8	4.5	5.8	6.1	7.8	8.1	9.4	9.9
Commercial debt	4.1	2.8	3.4	4.5	4.8	5.9	6.1	6.9	7.7
Official debt	0.9	1.0	1.1	1.3	1.3	1.9	2.0	2.5	2.2
Net debt	3.7	2.8	3.3	4.2	(NA)	(NA)	(NA)	(NA)	(NA)
Hungary: Gross debt	9.1	11.8	15.1	17.8	19.6	20.4	21.3	22.7	21.4
Commercial debt	8.8	9.8	12.7	15.0	16.6	17.3	16.4	16.1	14.3
Official debt	0.3	0.8	0.9	1.0	1.2	1.4	1.4	1.7	2.3
IMF/World Bank [1]		1.2	1.5	1.8	1.8	1.7	3.5	4.9	4.8
Net debt	7.0	8.6	12.0	15.5	(NA)	(NA)	(NA)	(NA)	(NA)
Poland: Gross debt	25.0	29.3	33.5	39.2	39.2	40.8	48.5	48.4	47.0
Commercial debt	14.9	10.6	12.1	12.8	15.4	15.3	14.4	16.4	12.1
Official debt	10.1	18.7	21.4	26.4	23.2	24.9	32.8	30.2	30.9
IMF/World Bank [1]	-	-	-	-	0.6	0.6	1.3	1.8	4.0
Net debt	24.4	27.7	31.8	36.2	(NA)	(NA)	(NA)	(NA)	(NA)
Romania: Gross debt	9.4	6.6	6.4	5.1	2.2	0.1	0.9	2.1	2.3
Commercial debt	6.5	2.9	2.7	1.7	0.4	0.1	0.4	0.6	0.6
Official debt	1.7	1.1	1.1	0.8	0.6	-	0.1	0.6	0.7
IMF/World Bank/CEMA bank [1]	1.2	2.6	2.6	2.6	1.2	-	0.4	0.9	1.0
Net debt	9.1	6.4	5.8	4.5	(NA)	(NA)	(NA)	(NA)	(NA)
Russia: [2] Gross debt	20.5	29.0	36.0	40.8	42.4	50.8	53.6	61.0	74.0
Commercial debt	11.0	19.5	25.9	30.1	33.7	40.5	35.6	31.8	38.0
Official debt	9.5	9.5	10.1	10.7	8.7	10.2	18.0	29.2	36.0
Net debt	10.5	15.7	21.1	25.9	26.9	36.3	45.4	(NA)	(NA)

- Represents zero.   NA Not available.   [1] IMF=International Monetary Fund. CEMA=Council for Mutual Economic Assistance.   [2] The debt of the former Soviet Union was assumed by Russia.

Source: U.S. Central Intelligence Agency, *Handbook of International Economic Statistics, 1993;* and unpublished data.

No. 1406. External Public Debt, by Country: 1980 to 1992

[External public debt is defined as debt repayable to external creditors in foreign currency, goods, or services, with an original or extended maturity of more than 1 year, which is a direct obligation of, or has repayment guaranteed by, a public body in the borrowing country. Excludes undisbursed debt (amounts not yet drawn by recipient) and unguaranteed private debt, which for some countries is substantial. Debt contracted for the purchase of military equipment is not usually reported. Debt service payments represent the sum of interest payments and repayments of principal on external public debt]

COUNTRY	TOTAL EXTERNAL PUBLIC DEBT (mil. dol.)							DEBT SERVICE PAYMENTS (mil. dol.)			DEBT SERVICE RATIO [3] (percent)		
				1992									
	1980	1990	1991	Total [1]	Bilateral official	Banks [2]	International organizations	1980	1990	1992	1980	1990	1992
Argentina [4]	10,180	46,906	47,568	46,835	7,555	33,037	5,037	1,987	4,812	3,521	18	32	24
Bangladesh	3,417	11,451	11,961	12,226	4,656	-	7,398	110	516	468	11	26	14
Bolivia	2,181	3,690	3,535	3,693	1,570	225	1,849	290	275	223	28	28	28
Brazil	40,861	83,760	81,476	86,251	16,393	54,609	10,062	8,060	6,345	6,271	35	18	16
Bulgaria	(NA)	9,813	9,987	9,951	1,149	7,150	1,113	(NA)	1,324	264	(NA)	19	4
Cameroon	2,005	4,753	5,026	5,464	3,167	335	1,430	186	301	159	10	12	7
Chile	4,705	10,426	10,071	9,578	855	4,119	4,333	1,375	1,612	1,438	22	15	11
China: Mainland	4,504	45,319	50,551	58,475	10,499	22,087	8,603	930	5,896	8,027	5	10	9
Colombia	4,089	14,671	14,469	13,245	1,948	4,246	5,876	529	3,115	3,445	9	35	32
Congo	1,257	4,203	4,066	3,877	2,604	423	536	71	473	120	7	32	9
Costa Rica	1,700	3,076	3,323	3,207	1,394	593	1,174	206	432	480	17	21	18
Cote d'Ivoire	4,310	10,015	10,634	10,685	5,093	2,491	2,905	870	494	517	24	13	15
Dominican Republic	1,220	3,434	3,751	3,761	1,944	791	869	154	145	280	12	7	11
Ecuador	3,300	9,867	9,951	9,831	2,150	4,763	2,253	559	874	812	19	27	22
Egypt	16,212	34,317	36,098	35,724	28,597	591	3,329	746	2,733	1,995	11	30	12
Ethiopia	688	3,612	3,961	4,168	2,145	91	1,485	34	196	105	6	29	14
Gabon	1,271	3,135	3,180	2,998	2,034	175	349	398	102	334	16	4	13
Ghana	1,161	2,672	2,957	3,096	706	2	2,188	108	180	188	9	18	17
Guatemala	549	2,238	2,233	2,104	846	322	886	45	164	449	3	10	24
Honduras	975	3,400	3,060	3,192	1,167	96	1,801	97	307	347	10	31	32
Hungary [5]	6,416	17,999	19,084	17,836	609	13,189	3,243	1,460	3,750	4,351	14	30	31
India	18,343	59,787	62,855	67,721	17,852	11,221	26,130	1,166	5,145	5,411	9	22	21
Indonesia	15,027	44,966	48,626	49,289	23,683	3,918	16,400	1,763	6,660	7,422	8	22	20
Jamaica	1,421	3,899	3,772	3,596	2,037	263	1,130	206	496	560	15	21	20
Jordan	1,486	7,104	7,546	6,914	3,454	1,644	877	182	532	657	10	21	18
Kenya	2,062	4,671	4,835	4,635	1,298	615	2,509	232	490	325	11	22	14
Madagascar	892	3,673	3,857	3,805	2,154	47	1,391	57	193	73	11	37	16
Malaysia	4,007	12,668	13,983	13,346	2,560	6,895	1,861	376	2,827	2,518	11	8	5
Mali	669	2,345	2,451	2,472	1,400	2	1,068	9	40	32	3	9	5
Mexico	33,915	77,490	79,048	72,219	9,744	43,113	15,537	7,890	7,980	15,253	36	19	33
Morocco	8,325	22,089	20,138	20,332	10,617	3,249	5,313	1,172	1,443	1,857	36	23	21
Nicaragua	1,671	8,245	8,750	8,994	5,974	1,824	1,118	86	9	80	17	2	25
Oman	436	2,399	2,472	2,340	333	1,578	167	223	714	493	6	12	10
Pakistan	8,507	16,502	17,707	18,476	9,205	233	8,764	592	1,363	1,723	20	22	17
Panama	2,271	3,988	3,918	3,770	620	2,394	694	466	141	632	6	3	10
Papua New Guinea	485	1,502	1,592	1,539	343	228	836	61	274	196	6	20	9
Peru	6,218	13,634	15,301	15,417	9,105	3,174	2,085	1,506	179	760	31	4	17
Philippines	6,363	23,885	24,833	26,004	11,703	6,616	6,908	596	2,897	4,394	8	22	25
Poland	(NA)	39,291	44,222	43,034	31,786	9,272	1,167	(NA)	841	1,306	(NA)	4	8
Portugal	6,728	16,994	19,374	21,277	1,357	10,769	3,230	1,024	4,395	4,832	15	19	16
Senegal	1,105	2,950	2,867	2,932	1,292	70	1,528	219	222	121	26	14	8
South Korea	15,933	18,788	22,381	23,919	5,734	10,457	3,327	2,783	4,770	4,589	12	6	5
Sri Lanka	1,227	4,938	5,653	5,607	2,949	264	2,097	84	285	372	6	12	10
Sudan	3,822	9,155	9,220	8,984	5,618	1,472	1,889	102	23	25	12	4	5
Syria	2,918	14,959	14,952	14,341	12,599	-	925	302	1,375	810	12	27	16
Tanzania	1,915	5,586	5,820	6,048	3,611	40	2,194	63	105	169	8	19	31
Thailand	3,943	12,573	13,292	13,238	5,058	3,315	2,925	441	3,297	2,144	5	11	5
Tunisia	3,210	6,708	7,190	7,418	3,189	510	2,848	428	1,216	1,252	13	23	19
Turkey	15,040	38,594	39,181	39,640	7,811	19,807	9,290	1,053	6,439	7,432	29	29	26
Uganda	543	2,231	2,352	2,495	734	84	1,565	36	64	43	11	29	22
Uruguay	1,127	3,009	2,856	3,092	160	1,951	973	198	710	438	12	30	16
Venezuela	10,614	24,509	24,863	25,252	871	19,723	2,727	2,955	4,167	1,807	13	19	11
Yemen	1,453	5,107	5,197	5,341	4,194	80	1,011	35	107	110	10	7	5
Yugoslavia [6]	4,580	12,986	11,640	11,015	3,632	4,725	2,553	617	2,719	968	10	5	8
Zaire	4,261	8,952	9,182	8,895	5,963	520	2,080	397	136	58	5	13	8
Zambia	2,141	4,846	4,975	4,809	2,810	73	1,589	287	173	251	18	6	4
Zimbabwe	696	2,464	2,611	2,782	917	406	967	50	370	468	3	18	21

- Represents or rounds to zero. NA Not available. [1] Includes other types of creditors not shown separately. [2] Includes other private financial institutions. [3] Debt service payments as percent of exports. [4] The increase in debt outstanding from 1980 to 1990 includes the refinancing of short-term private debt by public debt, which matured in 1986-87. [5] Fiscal year basis. [6] The bulk of the debt of Yugoslovian enterprises is reported as nonguaranteed.

Source: The World Bank, Washington, DC, World Debt Tables, periodic.

No. 1407. Net Flow of Financial Resources to Developing Countries: 1980 to 1991

[In billions of U.S. dollars. Net flow covers loans, grants, and grant-like flows minus amortization on loans. Military flows are excluded. Developing countries cover countries designated by Development Assistance Committee (DAC) as developing. Official development assistance covers all flows to developing countries and multilateral institutions provided by official agencies, including State and local governments, or by their executive agencies, which are administered with the promotion of economic development and welfare of developing countries as their main objective and whose financial terms are intended to be concessional in character with grant element of at least 25 percent. Other official flows cover export credits and portfolio investment from the official sector]

ORIGIN AND TYPE OF RESOURCE	1980	1983	1984	1985	1986	1987	1988	1989	1990	1991
DAC countries [1]	75.4	69.8	79.1	45.2	68.8	66.4	85.6	84.4	68.4	(NA)
Official development assistance	27.3	27.6	28.7	29.4	36.7	41.6	48.1	45.7	53.0	56.7
Bilateral grants [2]	14.1	14.2	15.5	17.8	21.1	23.4	26.0	25.9	30.8	34.6
Bilateral loans [3]	4.0	4.4	4.2	4.1	5.2	6.6	7.1	7.1	6.4	6.7
Multilateral contributions [3]	9.2	9.0	9.0	7.5	10.4	11.6	15.0	12.8	15.8	15.4
Other official flows	5.3	4.9	6.2	3.4	2.1	2.0	4.9	5.8	8.9	(NA)
Private flows at market terms	40.4	35.0	41.6	9.4	26.7	18.8	28.3	28.8	1.4	(NA)
Direct investment	10.1	7.8	10.9	6.5	11.0	21.0	25.1	30.1	26.8	(NA)
Private export credits	11.5	5.3	3.5	0.8	-1.7	-2.4	-1.3	5.7	-0.4	(NA)
Portfolio investment	18.7	22.2	27.2	2.1	17.4	0.3	4.4	-7.0	-25.2	(NA)
Private voluntary agencies	2.4	2.3	2.6	2.9	3.3	4.0	4.2	4.0	5.1	(NA)
OPEC [4]	10.8	5.9	3.7	4.1	(NA)	(NA)	(NA)	(NA)	(NA)	(NA)
Official development assistance	9.7	5.0	4.6	3.6	4.7	3.3	2.4	2.4	6.4	2.7
Other official flows	1.1	0.9	-0.9	0.5	(NA)	(NA)	(NA)	(NA)	(NA)	(NA)
Centrally-planned economies: [5]										
Official development assistance	2.6	3.5	3.4	3.6	4.6	5.0	5.0	4.7	-2.2	(NA)
Total net flow to developing countries, by DAC country [1]	75.4	69.8	79.1	45.2	68.8	66.4	85.6	84.4	68.4	(NA)
United States	13.9	23.0	28.6	1.8	18.2	13.8	17.5	16.4	11.1	20.8
Official development assistance	7.1	8.1	8.7	9.4	9.6	8.9	10.1	7.7	11.4	11.3
Bilateral grants [2]	3.0	4.5	5.6	7.3	7.0	6.7	6.5	6.8	8.5	12.1
Bilateral loans [3]	1.4	1.0	0.8	0.9	0.6	0.3	0.3	(Z)	-0.2	-2.7
Multilateral contributions [3]	2.8	2.5	2.3	1.2	2.0	1.9	3.4	0.9	3.0	1.9
Other official flows	1.1	(Z)	1.0	0.2	-0.6	-1.8	1.9	-0.5	-0.4	-0.8
Private flows at market terms	4.3	13.6	17.4	-9.3	7.5	4.4	3.2	7.3	-2.4	7.6
Direct investment	3.4	2.3	4.4	0.9	3.1	8.0	4.2	7.1	7.8	10.5
Private export credits and portfolio investment	0.9	11.2	13.0	-10.2	4.4	-3.6	-1.0	-0.3	-10.1	-2.9
Private voluntary agencies	1.3	1.3	1.5	1.5	1.7	1.6	2.3	1.9	2.5	2.7
Australia	0.9	1.0	1.5	1.2	1.1	0.9	3.6	1.5	1.5	-2.1
Austria	0.3	0.1	0.1	0.2	0.1	0.2	0.3	0.2	0.6	0.7
Belgium	2.9	0.8	3.5	1.3	-0.8	-0.3	1.8	1.5	0.1	1.5
Canada	3.2	2.6	2.8	1.7	1.6	2.5	2.7	2.7	3.2	4.0
Denmark	0.8	1.1	0.6	0.4	0.5	0.9	0.7	0.9	1.1	1.1
Finland	0.2	0.2	0.3	0.3	0.4	0.6	0.8	0.9	1.0	1.0
France	11.6	9.3	8.9	8.9	9.2	8.7	7.2	5.6	6.1	(NA)
Germany [6]	10.6	7.0	6.5	5.8	7.9	8.8	11.8	12.1	13.6	13.1
Ireland	(Z)	(Z)	0.1	0.1	0.1	0.1	0.3	0.1	0.2	0.2
Italy	4.0	3.1	2.3	2.2	2.6	2.0	5.1	5.8	3.2	7.6
Japan	6.8	7.9	11.7	11.6	14.6	20.3	21.2	24.1	18.7	25.0
Netherlands	2.4	2.2	2.0	2.6	2.8	3.2	2.7	2.5	4.0	4.4
New Zealand	0.1	0.1	0.1	0.1	0.1	0.1	0.1	0.1	0.1	0.1
Norway	0.9	0.7	0.6	0.6	0.7	0.9	0.9	0.9	1.2	1.4
Sweden	1.9	1.3	1.3	1.4	1.7	1.8	2.3	2.3	2.8	1.8
Switzerland	2.7	3.3	3.4	2.5	1.4	-1.6	2.0	2.7	4.6	0.8
United Kingdom	12.2	6.1	4.8	2.5	6.7	3.5	4.7	3.4	-4.4	(NA)

NA Not available. Z Less than $50 million. [1] Includes flows to OPEC countries (see footnote 4). Comprises as donors Australia, Austria, Belgium, Canada, Denmark, Finland, France, Ireland, Italy, Japan, Netherlands, New Zealand, Norway, Sweden, Switzerland, United Kingdom, United States, and Germany. [2] Includes "grant-like" flows (i.e., loans repayable in recipients' currencies). [3] Includes capital subscriptions to multilateral organizations in the form of demand instruments as of date of issue. [4] Organization of Petroleum Exporting Countries: Algeria, Ecuador, Gabon, Iran, Iraq, Kuwait, Libya, Nigeria, Qatar, Saudi Arabia, United Arab Emirates, and Venezuela. [5] Bulgaria, Czechoslovakia, Hungary, Poland, Romania, and former Soviet Union. [6] Former West Germany.

Source: Organization for Economic Cooperation and Development, Paris, France, unpublished data.

No. 1408. Per Capita Public and Private Aid to Developing Countries: 1980 to 1991

[In dollars. See headnote, table 1407. Private aid figures exclude government subsidies to voluntary agencies]

COUNTRY	OFFICIAL DEVELOPMENT ASSISTANCE			PRIVATE VOLUNTARY AID			COUNTRY	OFFICIAL DEVELOPMENT ASSISTANCE			PRIVATE VOLUNTARY AID		
	1980	1990	1991	1980	1990	1991		1980	1990	1991	1980	1990	1991
Australia	45	56	61	3	3	6	Japan	29	73	88	(Z)	1	1
Austria	24	51	70	3	4	6	Netherlands	115	170	167	6	16	15
Belgium	60	89	83	5	6	3	New Zealand	23	28	29	2	4	4
Canada	45	93	95	4	10	10	Norway	119	284	276	8	31	30
Denmark	92	228	233	3	6	5	Portugal	(NA)	14	20	(NA)	(NA)	(Z)
Finland	23	170	185	3	7	3	Spain	(NA)	25	30	(NA)	2	1
France	77	127	131	1	3	(NA)	Sweden	116	235	245	7	16	15
Germany [1]	58	100	86	7	12	10	Switzerland	40	111	126	10	17	19
Ireland	9	16	20	-	7	7	United Kingdom	33	46	57	2	6	(NA)
Italy	12	59	59	(Z)	(NA)	(NA)	United States	31	45	45	6	10	11

- Represents or rounds to zero. NA Not available. Z Less than 50 cents. [1] Former West Germany.
Source: Organization for Economic Cooperation and Development, Paris, France, unpublished data.

No. 1409. Military Expenditures, by Country: 1980 to 1991

[In millions of dollars, except as indicated. See also table 546. For most countries, data for expenditures and for GNP were based on local currencies which were deflated to constant 1991 local currency values before conversion to U.S. dollar equivalents. In general, the rates used for conversion are the 1991 average par/market exchange rates as supplied by the International Bank for Reconstruction and Development]

COUNTRY	CURRENT DOLLARS				CONSTANT (1991) DOLLARS					
								1991		
	1980	1985	1990	1991	1980	1985	1990	Total	Per capita (dollars)	Percent of GNP
United States......	144,000	265,800	306,200	280,300	212,100	331,660	318,400	280,300	1,110	5
Algeria [1].........	940	850	812	730	1,385	1,060	845	730	28	2
Argentina.........	1,559	[1]3,621	2,979	2,449	2,296	[1]4,517	3,099	2,449	75	2
Australia.........	3,226	5,445	6,434	7,400	4,753	6,793	6,692	7,400	427	3
Austria.........	820	1,291	1,636	1,667	1,208	1,610	1,701	1,667	213	1
Belgium.........	2,951	4,038	4,486	4,625	4,348	5,038	4,665	4,625	463	2
Brazil...........	1,899	2,356	6,617	5,295	2,799	2,940	6,882	5,295	34	1
Bulgaria [1]......	3,993	5,808	3,887	1,464	5,883	7,246	4,043	1,464	164	4
Canada.........	5,176	9,018	11,610	11,510	7,626	11,250	12,080	11,510	427	2
Chile [2]........	449	636	[1]938	[1]1,010	662	794	[1]976	[1]1,010	[1]76	[1]3
China:										
Mainland [1]......	16,370	39,720	50,310	51,040	24,120	49,560	52,330	51,040	44	3
Taiwan.........	3,222	[1]6,439	[1]9,063	9,748	4,748	[1]8,033	[1]9,426	9,748	472	5
Cuba [2].........	1,140	1,335	1,400	(NA)	1,680	1,666	1,456	(NA)	(NA)	(NA)
Czechoslovakia [1]...	5,249	7,998	4,432	2,804	9,105	9,979	4,610	2,804	179	3
Denmark.........	1,454	2,073	2,535	2,672	2,143	2,587	2,637	2,672	519	2
Egypt [1]........	2,923	2,583	1,083	1,022	4,306	3,223	1,126	1,022	19	3
El Salvador [1]......	120	217	179	171	177	[1]271	186	171	31	3
Finland.........	909	1,502	1,986	2,454	1,339	1,873	2,066	2,454	492	2
France. [3].......	21,230	32,630	40,820	42,430	31,270	40,710	42,450	42,430	744	4
Germany [3].......	22,400	33,630	[1]41,280	[1]39,520	33,000	41,960	[1]42,930	[1]39,520	[1]494	[1]3
Hungary [1]......	1,779	3,482	3,832	3,807	2,621	4,344	3,986	3,807	379	6
India...........	2,832	3,782	1,277	1,261	4,173	4,719	1,328	1,261	122	2
Indonesia........	3,608	5,527	7,487	7,189	5,316	6,895	7,787	7,189	8	3
Iran [1].........	1,093	1,447	1,609	1,732	1,611	1,805	1,674	1,732	9	2
Iraq [1]..........	2,624	5,631	5,213	5,647	3,867	7,026	5,422	5,647	96	6
Israel...........	(NA)	12,470	11,890	9,459	(NA)	15,560	12,370	9,459	528	75
Italy...........	6,654	7,519	6,940	4,992	9,805	9,380	7,218	4,992	1,100	8
Japan...........	10,110	17,150	23,290	24,340	14,900	21,400	24,220	24,340	421	2
	12,330	20,210	30,250	32,560	18,170	25,210	31,460	32,560	263	1
Kuwait.........	892	1,576	[1]13,820	[1]16,740	1,314	1,966	[1]14,380	[1]16,740	19,940	102
Malaysia........	664	[1]873	1,066	1,651	978	[1]1,089	1,109	1,651	92	4
Mexico..........	456	1,282	1,087	[1]1,185	671	1,599	1,131	[1]1,185	[1]13	(Z)
Morocco [1]......	763	(NA)	1,296	1,147	1,124	(NA)	1,348	1,147	44	4
Netherlands......	4,048	5,980	7,155	7,246	5,965	7,461	7,442	7,246	482	3
Nicaragua [1].....	53	254	(NA)	70	78	317	(NA)	70	19	4
Nigeria.........	447	301	193	244	658	376	200	244	2	1
North Korea [1].....	4,380	5,260	5,940	4,660	6,454	6,563	6,178	4,660	214	20
Norway.........	1,320	2,369	3,210	3,288	1,945	2,956	3,339	3,288	769	3
Oman...........	1,059	1,937	1,707	1,450	1,560	2,417	1,775	1,450	945	16
Pakistan........	777	1,650	2,829	2,672	1,145	2,059	2,943	2,672	23	6
Peru [1].........	1,457	2,501	795	506	2,147	[1]3,121	827	506	23	1
Philippines......	501	388	951	947	738	485	989	947	14	2
Poland [1].......	9,644	14,670	8,752	7,362	14,210	18,300	9,103	7,362	192	5
Portugal........	858	1,294	2,020	2,115	1,265	1,614	2,101	2,115	203	3
Romania [1]......	4,587	6,840	3,869	3,747	6,759	8,534	4,024	3,747	162	4
Saudi Arabia.......	14,990	21,340	[1]23,160	[1]35,510	22,090	26,620	[1]24,090	[1]35,510	[1]2,151	[1]30
Singapore........	533	1,250	1,627	2,107	785	1,560	1,692	2,107	764	5
South Africa......	2,563	2,872	[1]4,411	[1]3,839	3,777	3,583	[1]4,587	[1]3,839	[1]95	[1]4
South Korea......	3,821	6,292	10,800	10,580	5,629	7,851	11,240	10,580	242	4
Soviet Union [1].....	198,000	277,200	292,000	260,000	292,000	345,800	303,700	260,000	887	10
Spain..........	4,560	7,943	9,126	9,115	6,719	9,909	9,491	9,115	233	2
Sweden.........	3,257	5,065	6,062	6,432	4,799	6,319	6,305	6,432	751	3
Switzerland......	2,461	4,084	4,826	4,528	3,626	[1]5,095	5,019	4,528	667	2
Syria [1] [2]......	1,936	3,593	3,479	4,526	2,852	[1]4,483	3,618	4,526	342	18
Thailand........	1,011	1,874	2,130	2,438	1,489	2,338	2,215	2,438	43	3
Turkey.........	1,635	2,848	4,985	5,671	2,409	3,554	5,185	5,671	97	5
United Arab Emirates..	1,724	[1]1,901	[1]2,590	[1]4,900	2,541	[1]2,372	[1]2,694	[1]4,900	[1]2,053	[1]16
United Kingdom....	22,080	36,400	40,660	43,200	32,530	45,420	42,290	43,200	750	4
Venezuela.......	317	340	[1]927	1,900	467	424	[1]964	1,900	94	3
Yugoslavia......	1,669	3,339	[1]4,210	(NA)	2,459	4,166	[1]4,379	(NA)	(NA)	(NA)

NA Not available.   Z Less than 0.5 percent.   [1] Estimated.   [2] Data probably omit a major share of total military expenditures, probably including most arms acquisitions.   [3] Prior to 1991, data for former West Germany.

Source: U.S. Arms Control and Disarmament Agency, World Military Expenditures and Arms Transfers, annual.

No. 1410. Armed Forces Personnel, by Country: 1980 to 1991

[Personnel data as of July. Armed Forces refer to active-duty military personnel, including paramilitary forces where those forces resemble regular units in their organization, equipment, training, or mission. Reserve forces are not included]

COUNTRY	ARMED FORCES PERSONNEL (1,000)						ARMED FORCES PER 1,000 POPULATION					
	1980	1985	1988	1989	1990	1991	1980	1985	1988	1989	1990	1991
United States	2,050	2,244	2,246	2,241	2,181	2,115	9.0	9.4	9.1	9.0	8.7	8.4
Algeria	101	170	126	126	126	126	5.4	7.7	5.2	5.1	5.0	4.8
Argentina..............	155	129	95	95	85	70	5.5	4.3	3.0	3.0	2.6	2.2
Australia	71	70	71	70	68	68	4.9	4.4	4.3	4.1	4.0	3.9
Austria	40	40	55	48	43	44	5.3	5.3	7.2	6.3	5.6	5.6
Belgium..............	108	107	110	110	106	101	11.0	10.9	11.1	11.1	10.6	10.1
Brazil	450	496	319	319	295	295	3.7	3.6	2.2	2.1	1.9	1.9
Bulgaria..............	188	189	160	150	129	107	21.2	21.2	17.8	16.6	14.4	12.0
Canada...............	82	83	88	88	87	86	3.4	3.3	3.4	3.3	3.3	3.2
Chile.................	116	124	96	95	95	90	10.5	10.3	7.6	7.4	7.2	6.8
China: Mainland	4,650	4,100	3,783	3,903	3,500	3,200	4.7	3.9	3.4	3.5	3.1	2.8
Taiwan..........	465	440	390	379	405	424	26.1	22.8	19.5	18.7	19.8	20.5
Cuba	220	297	297	297	297	297	22.8	29.4	28.6	28.3	27.9	27.6
Czechoslovakia	190	210	211	175	198	154	12.5	13.5	13.5	11.2	12.6	9.8
Denmark..............	33	29	30	31	31	30	6.4	5.7	5.8	6.0	6.0	5.8
Egypt................	447	466	452	450	434	434	10.7	9.9	8.8	8.6	8.1	7.9
El Salvador	16	48	45	45	55	60	3.4	10.0	8.8	8.6	10.3	11.0
Finland	36	40	40	39	31	32	7.5	8.2	8.1	7.9	6.2	6.4
France	575	563	558	554	550	542	10.7	10.2	10.0	9.8	9.7	9.5
Germany [1].............	490	495	495	503	[2]545	[2]457	8.0	8.1	8.1	8.1	8.6	5.7
Greece	186	201	199	201	201	205	19.3	20.2	19.9	20.1	20.0	20.4
Honduras	14	21	19	19	18	17	3.9	5.0	4.2	4.1	3.7	3.4
Hungary	120	117	117	109	94	87	11.2	11.0	11.2	10.5	9.1	8.4
India................	1,104	1,515	1,362	1,257	1,200	1,200	1.6	2.0	1.7	1.5	1.4	1.4
Indonesia	250	281	284	285	285	285	1.6	1.6	1.6	1.5	1.5	1.5
Iran	305	345	654	604	440	465	7.8	7.5	12.3	11.0	7.7	7.9
Iraq	430	788	1,000	1,000	1,390	475	32.5	50.2	58.4	56.4	75.4	26.5
Israel	196	195	191	191	190	190	52.4	49.6	46.7	46.0	44.2	41.9
Italy	500	504	506	506	493	473	8.9	8.8	8.8	8.8	8.5	6.2
Japan	242	241	245	247	250	250	2.1	2.0	2.0	2.0	2.0	2.0
Kuwait...............	12	16	15	20	7	10	8.8	9.3	7.7	10.0	3.3	11.9
Malaysia	83	[2]106	108	110	114	114	6.0	[2]6.8	6.5	6.4	6.5	6.3
Mexico	120	140	154	154	175	175	1.7	1.8	1.8	1.8	2.0	1.9
Morocco	117	165	195	195	195	195	5.7	7.2	7.9	7.8	7.6	7.5
Netherlands	107	103	107	106	104	104	7.6	7.1	7.2	7.1	7.0	6.9
Nicaragua	24	74	74	65	28	20	8.6	23.5	21.9	18.7	7.7	5.3
Nigeria	150	134	107	107	94	94	1.7	1.3	1.0	0.9	0.8	0.8
North Korea............	700	784	842	1,040	1,200	1,200	38.9	40.0	40.8	49.5	56.0	55.0
Norway...............	40	36	40	43	51	41	9.7	8.7	9.5	10.2	12.0	9.6
Oman................	15	25	27	29	32	29	15.2	20.2	19.3	20.3	21.6	18.9
Pakistan	467	647	645	684	790	803	5.5	6.5	5.9	6.1	6.9	6.8
Peru.................	151	128	111	110	125	123	8.7	6.5	5.3	5.1	5.7	5.5
Philippines............	155	157	105	106	112	112	3.0	2.7	1.7	1.7	1.7	1.7
Poland	408	439	430	350	313	305	11.5	11.8	11.4	9.2	8.2	8.0
Portugal	88	102	104	104	87	86	9.0	10.0	10.1	10.1	8.4	8.3
Qatar	6	[2]7	7	7	11	11	26.0	[2]20.3	16.9	16.1	24.4	23.5
Romania	211	[2]237	220	207	126	201	9.5	[2]10.4	9.5	8.9	5.4	8.7
Saudi Arabia	79	[2]80	84	82	146	191	7.8	[2]5.9	5.4	5.2	9.0	11.6
Singapore	50	59	56	56	55	55	20.7	23.1	21.0	20.7	20.2	20.0
South Africa...........	70	95	100	100	85	80	2.3	2.7	2.7	2.6	2.1	2.0
South Korea...........	600	600	626	647	650	750	15.7	14.7	14.8	15.1	15.0	17.2
Soviet Union (former).......	3,900	3,900	3,900	3,700	3,400	3,000	14.6	14.0	13.6	12.8	11.7	10.2
Spain	356	314	304	277	263	246	9.5	8.2	7.8	7.1	6.7	6.3
Sweden	70	[2]69	65	62	65	63	8.4	[2]8.3	7.7	7.4	7.6	7.4
Switzerland	23	[2]23	23	17	22	22	3.6	[2]3.5	3.5	2.5	3.3	3.2
Syria................	250	402	400	400	408	408	28.8	38.2	33.9	32.7	32.1	30.9
Thailand	234	270	273	273	283	283	5.0	5.2	5.0	4.9	5.1	5.0
Turkey	717	814	847	780	769	804	15.9	16.0	15.5	14.0	13.5	13.8
United Arab Emirates.......	44	44	43	43	66	66	44.0	28.0	21.7	20.3	29.3	27.6
United Kingdom	330	334	324	318	308	301	5.9	5.9	5.7	5.6	5.4	5.2
Venezuela	55	71	73	75	75	73	3.7	4.1	3.9	3.9	3.8	3.6
Vietnam	900	1,000	1,100	1,000	1,000	1,000	16.9	16.9	17.3	15.4	15.1	14.8
Yugoslavia	260	258	229	225	180	169	11.6	11.2	9.7	9.5	7.6	7.1

[1] Prior to 1991, data for former West Germany.   [2] Estimated.

Source: U.S. Arms Control and Disarmament Agency, *World Military Expenditures and Arms Transfers,* annual.

Guide to—Sources of Statistics, State Statistical Abstracts, and Foreign Statistical Abstracts

Alphabetically arranged by subject, this guide contains references to the important primary sources of statistical information for the United States. Secondary sources have been included if the information contained in them is presented in a particularly convenient form or if primary sources are not readily available. Nonrecurrent publications presenting compilations or estimates for years later than 1984 or types of data not available in regular series are also included.

Much valuable information may also be found in State reports (see pp. 920-923) and foreign statistical abstracts (see pp. 924 and 925) and in reports for particular commodities, industries, or similar segments of our economic and social structures, many of which are not included here.

Publications listed under each subject are divided into two main groups: "U.S. Government" and "Other." The location of the publisher of each report is given except for Federal agencies located in Washington, DC. Most Federal publications may be purchased from the Superintendent of Documents, U.S. Government Printing Office, Washington, DC 20402, tel. 202-783-3238, or from Government Printing Office bookstores in certain major cities. In some cases, Federal publications may be obtained from the issuing agency.

Major reports, such as the Census of Population, which consist of many volumes, are listed by their general, all-inclusive titles.

Bureau of the Census Publications

In most cases, separate reports of the most recent censuses are available for each State, subject, industry, etc. Complete information on publications of all the censuses and current surveys conducted by the Bureau of the Census appears in the *Bureau of the Census Catalog*, published annually and available from the Superintendent of Documents.

Abortions—*see* Vital Statistics.

Accidents —*see also* Health; Insurance; and Vital Statistics

U.S. Government

Bureau of Labor Statistics

Evaluating Your Firm's Injury and Illness Record, Construction Industries, Report 776 (1990).

Handbook of Labor Statistics. 1989.

Heatburn Injuries, Bulletin 2358 (1990).

Injuries Involving Longshore Operation, Bulletin 2326 (1989).

Occupational Injuries and Illnesses in the United States by Industry. Annual.

Department of Transportation

Transportation Safety Information Report. Quarterly.

Federal Railroad Administration

Accidents —Con.

U.S. Government —Con.

Accident/Incident Bulletin. Summary, statistics, and analysis of accidents on railroads in the United States. Annual.

Rail-Highway Crossing Accident/Incident and Inventory Bulletin. Annual.

Mine Safety and Health Administration

Informational Reports by Mining Industry: Coal; Metallic Minerals; Nonmetallic Minerals (except stone and coal); Stone, Sand, and Gravel. Annual.

Mine Injuries and Worktime. (Some preliminary data.) Quarterly.

National Center for Health Statistics

Vital Statistics of the United States. Annual.

Volume I, Natality

Volume II, Mortality

Volume III, Marriage and Divorce

National Transportation Safety Board

City Government —see State and Local Government.

Civil Service —see Federal Government; and State and Local Government.

Climate —see also Agriculture

U.S. Government

National Oceanic and Atmospheric Administration

Climatography of the United States, No. 20, Supplement No. 1, Freeze/Frost Data.

Climatography of the United States, No. 81: Monthly Normals of Temperature, Precipitation, and Heating and Cooling Degree Days 1961-90. 1992. Issued by State.

Climatological Data. Issued in sections for States and outlying areas. Monthly with annual summary.

Comparative Climatic Data Through 1992.

General Summary of Tornadoes. Annual.

Hourly Precipitation Data. Monthly with annual summary; for each State.

Local Climatological Data. Monthly with annual summary; for major cities.

Storm Data. Monthly.

Weekly Weather and Crop Bulletin. National summary.

Commerce —see Foreign Commerce; Retail and Wholesale Trade; and Transportation.

Commodity Prices —see also Economic Indexes

U.S. Government

Board of Governors of the Federal Reserve System

Annual Statistical Digest.

Federal Reserve Bulletin. Monthly.

Bureau of Labor Statistics

Consumer Prices: Energy and Food. Monthly.

CPI Detailed Report. Monthly.

Handbook of Labor Statistics. 1989.

Monthly Labor Review.

Producer Price Indexes. Monthly, with annual supplement.

Relative Importance of Components in the Consumer Price Indexes. Annual.

U.S. Import and Export Price Indexes. Monthly.

Department of Agriculture

Agricultural Price Reports. Monthly and annual.

Other

Commodity Research Bureau, a Knight-Ridder Business Information Service, Chicago, IL.

Commodity Year Book Statistical Abstract Service. (Three editions annually.)

CRB Commodity Index Report. Weekly.

CRB Commodity Year Book. Annual.

CRB Futures Chart Service. Weekly.

CRB Infotech.

Commodity Prices —Con.

Other —Con.

Electronic Futures Trend Analyzer. Daily.

Final Markets. End of day.

Futures Market Service. Weekly.

Futures Market Service Fundamental & Technical Commentary. Daily and weekly.

Knight-Ridder News Summaries. Daily

Price Service. Daily

The Blue Line. Daily

Wall Street Journal. (Dow Jones & Co., New York, NY.) Daily except Saturdays, Sundays, and holidays.

Communications —see also Newspapers

U.S. Government

Bureau Of Labor Statistics

Outlook for Technology and Labor in Telephone Communications, Bulletin 2357 (1990).

Federal Communications Commission

Annual Report.

Statistics of Communications Common Carriers. Annual.

Rural Electrification Administration

Annual Statistical Report—Rural Telephone Borrowers.

U.S. Postal Service

Annual Report of the Postmaster General.

Cost and Revenue Analysis. Annual.

Other

John Blair & Company, New York, NY

Statistical Trends in Broadcasting. Annual.

Book Industry Study Group, Inc., New York, NY

Book Industry Trends. Annual.

Reed Publishing USA, Newton, MA

Broadcasting & Cable Market Place. Annual.

Broadcasting Magazine. Weekly.

Corporation for Public Broadcasting, Washington, DC

Average Revenue Profiles for Public Broadcasting Stations. Annual.

Public Broadcasting Income. Annual.

Public Broadcasting Stations' Income from State Governments and State Colleges & Universities Ranked State-By-State. Annual.

Public Broadcasting and You. Annual.

Public Radio and Television Programming Content by Category. Biennial.

Editor & Publisher Co., New York, NY

International Year Book. Annual.

Market Guide. Annual.

Electronic Industries Association, Washington, DC

Electronic Market Data Book. Annual.

Electronic Market Trends. Monthly.

Communications —Con.
Other —Con.
Electronics Foreign Trade. Monthly.

Electronics Foreign Trade 5-Year Summary. Annual.

Radio Advertising Bureau, New York, NY

Radio Facts. Annual.

United States Telephone Association, Washington, DC

Statistics of the Independent Telephone Industry. Annual.

Warren Publishing, Inc., Washington, DC

Cable Action Update. Weekly.

Cable and Station Coverage Atlas. Annual.

Television Action Update. Weekly.

Television and Cable Factbook. Annual.

TV Station & Cable Ownership Directory. Semi-annual.

Construction, Housing, and Real Estate —see also Money and Roads
U.S. Government
Board of Governors of the Federal Reserve System

Annual Statistical Digest.

Federal Reserve Bulletin. Monthly.

Bureau of Census

Census of Construction Industries. Quinquennial. (1987, most recent.)

Census of Housing. Decennial. (1980, most recent.)

Current Construction Reports: Housing Starts, C20 (monthly); New Residential Construction in Selected Metropolitan Statistical Areas, C21 (quarterly); Housing Completions, C22 (monthly); New One-Family Houses Sold and for Sale, C25 (monthly with annual report, Characteristics of New Housing); Price Index of New One-Family Houses Sold, C27 (quarterly); Value of New Construction Put in Place, C30 (monthly with occasional historical supplement); Housing Units Authorized by Building Permits, C40 (monthly and annual); Residential Alterations and Repairs, C50 (quarterly and annual).

Current Housing Reports: Housing Vacancies, H-111 (quarterly and annual); Market Absorption of Apartments, H-130 (quarterly and annual); Characteristics of Apartments Completed, H-131 (annual); Annual Housing Survey, H-150 (series of six biennial reports); Annual Housing Survey—Housing Characteristics for Selected Metropolitan Areas, H-170.

Bureau of Economic Analysis

Business Statistics, 1963-91. 1992.

Fixed Reproducible Tangible Wealth in the United States, 1925-89. 1993.

The National Income and Product Accounts of the United States, 1929-88: Volume I, 1993 and Volume II, 1992.

Survey of Current Business. Monthly.

Construction, Housing, and Real Estate —Con.
U.S. Government —Con.
Bureau of Labor Statistics

Compensation and Working Conditions. Monthly.

Employment and Earnings. Monthly.

Employment, Hours, and Earnings, United States, 1909-90. 1991. Bulletin No. 2370.)

Supplement to Employment and Earnings

Evaluating Your Firm's Injury and Illness Record, Construction Industries Report 776, (1990).

Monthly Labor Review.

Occupational Employment in Mining, Construction, Finance, and Services. 1992. (Bulletin No. 2397.)

Occupational Injuries and Illnesses in the United States by Industry. Annual.

Department of Housing and Urban Development

Survey of Mortgage Lending Activity. Monthly and quarterly press releases.

Department of Veterans Affairs

Loan Guaranty Highlights. Quarterly.

Trend Data 1964-1988.

Energy Information Administration

Residential Energy Consumption Survey: Housing Characteristics. Triennial.

International Trade Administration

Construction Review. Bimonthly.

Office of Thrift Supervision

Annual Report.

Savings and Home Financing Source Book. Annual. Discontinued after 1989.

Other
Dodge, F.W., National Information Services Division, McGraw-Hill Information Systems Co., New York, NY

Dodge Construction Potentials. Monthly.

NATIONAL ASSOCIATION OF REALTORS, Washington, DC

Real Estate Outlook: Market Trends & Insights, Monthly.

Consumer Income and Expenditures, and Personal Income —see also Agriculture; Economic Indexes; Investments; and National Income
U.S. Government
Board of Governors of the Federal Reserve System

Annual Statistical Digest.

Federal Reserve Bulletin. Monthly.

Bureau of the Census

Census of Population. Decennial. (1990, most recent.)

Current Population Reports. (Series on Consumer Income, P60.)

Current Population Reports. (Series on Household Economic Studies, P70.)

Special Studies Reports. (Series on Special Studies, P23.)

Bureau of Economic Analysis

Consumer Income and Expenditures, and Personal Income —Con.

U.S. Government —Con.

Business Statistics, 1963-91. 1992.

Survey of Current Business. Monthly.

Bureau of Labor Statistics

Consumer Expenditure Survey, integrated Diary and Interview Survey data.

Annual press releases.

Consumer Expenditure Survey: 1988-89. 1991. (Bulletin No. 2383.)

Consumer Expenditure Interview Survey. Quarterly.

Congressional Budget Office

The Changing Distribution of Federal Taxes: 1975-1990. October 1987.

Trends in Family Income: 1970-1986. February 1988.

Internal Revenue Service

Statistics of Income.

Individual Income Tax Returns. Annual.

Statistics of Income Bulletin. Quarterly.

National Science Foundation

Characteristics of Recent Science/Engineering Graduates. Detailed Statistical Tables. Biennial.

Science Resources Studies. Data Brief. Frequent.

Social Security Administration

Trends since 1960 In the Economic Status of Aged Men and Women. (Research and Statistics Note No. 3. 1983.)

Other

American Financial Services Association, Washington, DC

AFSA Annual Research Report and Second Mortgage Lending Report on Finance Companies. Annual.

AFSA Annual Research Report and Second Mortgage Lending Report Supplements. Annual.

Finance Facts Yearbook. Annual. (Discontinued in 1988.)

Consumer Prices —*see* Commodity Prices.

Corporations —*see* Business; *and* Manufactures.

Correctional Institutions —*see* Law Enforcement.

Cost of Living —*see* Commodity Prices.

Courts —*see* Law Enforcement.

Crime —*see* Law Enforcement.

Crops —*see* Agriculture.

Deaths —*see* Vital Statistics.

Defense —*see* National Defense.

Divorce —*see* Vital Statistics.

Domestic Trade —*see* Retail and Wholesale Trade; *and* Service Establishments.

Economic Indexes —*see also* Agriculture; Business; Commodity Prices; Manufactures; *and* Science Resources

Economic Indexes —Con.

U.S. Government

Board of Governors of the Federal Reserve System

Annual Statistical Digest.

Federal Reserve Banks. Monthly review published by each Bank with special reference to its own Federal Reserve District.

Federal Reserve Bulletin. Monthly. (Also monthly releases on industrial production indexes.)

Bureau of Economic Analysis

Business Statistics, 1963-91. 1992.

The National Income and Product Accounts of the United States, 1929-88: Volume I, 1993 and Volume II, 1992.

Survey of Current Business. Monthly.

Bureau of Labor Statistics

CPE Detailed Report. Monthly.

Employment Cost Indexes and Levels. Annual.

Producer Price Indexes. Monthly, with annual supplement.

Handbook of Labor Statistics. 1989.

Monthly Labor Review.

Council of Economic Advisers

Economic Indicators. Monthly.

Economic Report of the President. Annual.

Other

The Conference Board, New York, NY

The Conference Board Economic Times. Monthly.

National Bureau of Economic Research, Cambridge, MA

The National Balance Sheet of the United States, 1953-80, by Raymond W. Goldsmith. 1982. (University of Chicago Press, Chicago, IL.)

The U.S. National Income and Product Accounts: Selected Topics, Murray F. Foss, editor. 1982. (Studies in Income and Wealth, No. 47.) (University of Chicago Press, Chicago, IL.)

Education —*see also* Science Resources; *and* Vocational Rehabilitation

U.S. Government

Bureau of the Census

Census of Population. Decennial. (1990, most recent.)

Current Population Reports. (Series on Population Characteristics, P20; and Special Studies, P23.)

Finances of Public School Systems. Annual. (GF No. 10.)

Bureau of Labor Statistics

Educational Attainment of Workers, March 1982-83. 1984. (Bulletin No. 2191.)

Education —Con.
  U.S. Government —Con.
    Women and Minorities in Science and
      Engineering. Report. Biennial.

    Office for Civil Rights
      Racial, Ethnic and Sex Enrollment Data,
        From Institutions of Higher Education.
        Fall 1982. Biennial.
      State and National Summaries of Data
        from the fall 1982 Civil Rights Survey of
        Elementary and Secondary Schools.
        Biennial.

  Other

  American Council on Education, Washing-
    ton, DC
    A Fact Book on Higher Education. Quar-
      terly.
    National Norms for Entering College
      Freshmen. Annual.

  Bowker (R.R.) Company, New Providence,
    NJ
    American Library Directory. Annual.
    Book Publishing Annual. (1985, most re-
      cent.)
    Bowker Annual Library and Book Trade
      Almanac.

  Chronicle of Higher Education, Inc., Wash-
    ington, DC
    Almanac. Annual.

  College Entrance Examination Board, New
    York, NY
    National Report on College-Bound Se-
      niors. Annual.

  National Catholic Educational Association,
    Washington, DC
    Catholic Schools in America. Annual.
    United States Catholic Elementary and
      Secondary Schools. Staffing and Enroll-
      ment. Annual.
    U.S. Catholic Elementary Schools and
      their Finances. Biennial.
    U.S. Catholic Secondary Schools and
      their Finances. Biennial.

  National Education Association, Washington,
    DC
    Estimates of School Statistics. Annual.
    Rankings of the States. Annual.
    Status of the American Public School
      Teacher, 1985-86. Quinquennial.

  Research Associates of Washington, Wash-
    ington, DC
    Inflation Measures for Schools & Col-
      leges. Annual.
    State Profiles: Financing Public Higher
      Education. Annual.

Elections

  U.S. Government

    Bureau of the Census

      Congressional District Data:

Elections —Con.
  U.S. Government —Con.
      1990 Census of Population and
        Housing, 1990 CPH-4, Congres-
        sional Districts of the 103rd Con-
        gress.
      Current Population Reports. (Series P20,
        Voting and Registration in the Election
        of November 19—. Biennial survey; and
        P25, Projections of the Population of
        Voting Age for States: November 19—,
        Biennial projection.)

    Commission on Civil Rights
      New Evidence on School Desegregation.
        1987.
      The Economic Status of Americans of
        Asian Descent. 1988.
      The Economic Status of Americans of
        Southern and Eastern European Ances-
        try. 1986.

    Congress. Clerk of the House
      Statistics of the Presidential and Con-
        gressional Election Years. Biennial.

    Congress. Joint Committee on Printing
      Congressional Directory. Biennial.

  Other

  The Council of State Governments, Lexing-
    ton, KY
    The Book of the States. Biennial.
    State Elective Officials and the Legisla-
      tures. Biennial.
    State Legislative Leadership, Commit-
      tees, and Staff. Biennial.

  Elections Research Center, Chevy Chase
    MD
    America Votes. A handbook of contem-
      porary American election statistics,
      compiled and edited by Richard M.
      Scammon and Alice V. McGillivray. Bi-
      ennial.

  Joint Center for Political and Economic
    Studies, Washington, DC
    Black Elected Officials: A National Ros-
      ter. Annual.

  Michigan, The University of, Center for Po-
    litical Studies, Institute for Social Research,
    Ann Arbor, MI
    National Election Studies Cumulative
      Datafile. Biennial.

  National Association of Latino Elected and
    Appointed Officials, Washington, DC
    National Roster of Hispanic Elected Offi-
      cials. Annual.

  Pharos Books/World Almanac, New York,
    NY
    The World Almanac and Book of Facts.
      Annual.
    World Almanac of U.S. Politics. 1989.
      2nd edition, May 1991.

Electric Utilities —*see* Energy.

Emigration —*see* Immigration.

Employment —*see* Federal Government; Labor;
  and State and Local Government.

Energy —Con.

Other —Con.

Comparative Oil Company Statistics, 1991-1992.

U.S. Council for Energy Awareness, Washington, DC

Electricity from Nuclear Energy: The Economic Context. July 1990.

Electricity from Nuclear Energy. (Map booklet of U.S. Nuclear Power Plants.) 1990-91.

Key Data on Nuclear Energy. July 1990.

U.S. Public Opinion on Nuclear Energy. (Polling reports updated periodically.)

Environment

U.S. Government

Bureau of the Census

Current Industrial Report, Survey of Pollution Abatement Costs and Expenditures, series MA-200.

Council on Environmental Quality

Environmental Quality. Annual.

Environmental Protection Agency

Air Quality Data. Annual.

Cost of Clean Water. Annual.

Federal Certification Test Results for Motor Vehicles. Annual.

Municipal Water Facilities Inventory. Quinquennial.

National Air Pollutant Emission Estimates, 1900-92.

National Air Quality and Emissions Trends Report. 1992.

Needs Survey, Conveyance and Treatment of Municipal Wastewater Summaries of Technical Data. Biennial.

Pesticides Monitoring Journal. Quarterly.

Radiation Data and Reports. Monthly.

Sewage Facility Construction. Annual.

Summary of Water Enforcement Actions Pursued by EPA since December 3, 1970. (Updated continuously.)

Geological Survey

A Statistical Summary of Data from the U.S. Geological Survey's National Water Quality Networks. (Open-File Report 83-533.)

Estimated Use of Water in the United States in 1985. 1987. (Geological Survey Circular 1004.)

Other

The Conservation Foundation, Washington, DC

State of the Environment: A View Toward the Nineties. 1987.

State of the Environment: An Assessment at Mid-Decade. 1984.

State of the Environment. 1982.

Executions —*see* Law Enforcement.

Exports —*see* Foreign Commerce.

Family Characteristics —*see* Population.

Farms and Farm Characteristics —*see* Agriculture.

Federal Government Finances and Employment
—*see also* Elections; Science Resources; *and* State and Local Government

U.S. Government

Board of Governors of the Federal Reserve System

Annual Statistical Digest.

Federal Reserve Bulletin. Monthly.

Bureau of the Census

Federal Expenditures by State for Fiscal Year. Annual.

Bureau of Economic Analysis

Business Statistics, 1963-91. 1992.

Survey of Current Business. Monthly.

Council of Economic Advisers

Economic Indicators. Monthly.

Economic Report of the President. Annual.

Council on Environmental Quality

Environmental Quality. Annual.

Department of Labor

Annual Report of the Secretary.

Department of the Treasury

Consolidated Financial Statements of the United States Government. (Prototype.)

Daily Treasury Statement.

Monthly Statement of the Public Debt of the United States.

Monthly Treasury Statement of Receipts and Outlays of the United States Government.

Statistical Appendix to Annual Report of the Secretary of the Treasury on the State of the Finances Through 1980.

Treasury Bulletin. Monthly through 1982; beginning 1983, quarterly.

United States Government Annual Report and Appendix.

Internal Revenue Service

Annual Report of the Commissioner and Chief Counsel.

Statistics of Income.

Corporation Income Tax Returns. Annual.

Statistics of Income Bulletin. Quarterly.

National Science Foundation

Federal Funds for Research and Development. Detailed Statistical Tables. Annual.

Federal R&D Funding by Budget Function. Report. Annual.

Federal Scientists and Engineers. Detailed Statistical Tables. Annual.

Federal Support to Universities, Colleges, and Nonprofit Institutions. Detailed Statistical Tables. Annual.

Geographic Patterns: R&D in the United States. Special Report. (NSF 89-317.)

International Science and Technology Data Update. Report. Annual.

Foreign Commerce —Con.
U.S. Government —Con.
Waterborne Commerce of the United States (in five parts). Annual.

Bureau of the Census

Summary of U.S. Export and Import Merchandise Trade. Monthly; includes cumulative data. (FT 900.)

Survey of the Origin of Exports of Manufacturing Establishments. Triennial. (Current Industrial Reports M76(AS)-8.)

U.S. Airborne Exports and General Imports. Monthly and annual. (FT 986.)

U.S. Commodity Exports and Imports as Related to Output. Annual. (Series ES 2.)

U.S. Exports of Domestic Merchandise, SIC-Based Products by World Areas. Annual. (FT 610.)

U.S. Exports, Schedule B Commodity by Country. Annual. (FT 446.)

U.S. Exports, Schedule E Commodity by Country. Monthly; includes cumulative data. (FT 410.)

U.S. Exports, Schedule E Commodity Groupings by World Area and Country. Annual. (FT 450.)

U.S. Exports, World Area and Country by Schedule E Commodity Groupings. Annual. (FT 455.)

U.S. General Imports and Imports for Consumption, Schedule A Commodity by Country. Monthly; includes cumulative data. (FT 135.)

U.S. General Imports, Schedule A Commodity Groupings by World Area and Country. Annual. (FT 150.)

U.S. General Imports, World Area by Schedule A Commodity Groupings. Annual. (FT 155.)

U.S. Imports, SIC-Based Products. Annual. (FT 210.)

U.S. Imports for Consumption and General Imports, TSUSA Commodity by Country of Origin. Annual. (FT 246.)

U.S. Trade with Puerto Rico and U.S. Possessions. Monthly and Annual. (FT 800.)

U.S. Waterborne Exports and General Imports. Monthly and Annual. (FT 985.)

Bureau of Economic Analysis

Business Statistics, 1963-91. 1992.

Survey of Current Business. Monthly. (June issue contains detailed data on merchandise trade.)

U.S. Merchandise Trade: Exports and Imports by End-Use Category. Annually.

Department of Agriculture

Foreign Agricultural Trade of the United States (FATUS). Bimonthly with annual supplements on calendar year and fiscal year trade statistics.

World Agricultural Trends and Indicators, 1970-88 Statistical Bulletin No. 781. Annual.

Department of the Treasury

Foreign Commerce —Con.
U.S. Government —Con.
Statistical Appendix to Annual Report of the Secretary of the Treasury on the State of the Finances through 1980.

Energy Information Administration

Annual Energy Review.

Monthly Energy Review.

International Trade Administration

Business America. Monthly. (Issues in March, June, September, and December contain quarterly data on U.S. share of world exports of manufactures.)

Overseas Business Reports. Irregular.

U.S. Foreign Trade Highlight. Annual.

Maritime Administration

Annual Report.

United States Oceanborne Foreign Trade Routes. Annual.

National Science Foundation

International Science and Technology Data Update. Report. Annual.

Science and Engineering Indicators. Report. Biennial.

Science and Technology Pocket Data Book. Report. Annual.

The Science and Technology Resources of Japan: A Comparison With the United States. Special Report. (NSF 88-318.)

The Science and Technology Resources of West Germany: A Comparison with the United States. Special Report. (NSF 86-310.)

Other
Aerospace Industries Association of America, Washington, DC

Exports of Aerospace Products. Quarterly.

Imports of Aerospace Products. Quarterly.

Commodity Research Bureau, New York, NY

Commodity Yearbook. Annual.

Forests and Lumber —see also Economic Indexes
U.S. Government
Bureau of the Census

Census of Manufactures. Quinquennial. (1987, most recent.)

Current Industrial Reports. Monthly, quarterly, and annual series on various industries.

Bureau of Labor Statistics

Technology and Its Impact on Labor in Four Industries. 1986. (Bulletin 2263.)

Forest Service

An Analysis of the Timber Situation in the United States: 1989-2040. 1990.

Forest Resources of the United States, 1992.

Land Areas of the National Forest System. Annual.

Forests and Lumber —Con.

U.S. Government —Con.

The 1993 RPA Timber Assessment Update. Forthcoming.

U.S. Timber Production, Trade, Consumption, and Price Statistics, 1960-88. Annual.

International Trade Administration

Construction Review. Quarterly.

Other

American Forest & Paper Association, Washington, DC

Statistics of Paper, Paperboard, and Wood Pulp. Annual.

Statistical Roundup.

Wood Pulp and Fiber Statistics. Annual.

Gas Utilities —*see* Energy.

Geography —*see also* Environment *and* Public Lands

U.S. Government

Geological Survey

Elevations and Distances in the United States. 1990.

Estimated Use of Water in the United States in 1985. 1988. (Geological Survey Circular 1004.)

National Gazetteer of the United States. 1984. (Issued by State.) (Geological Survey Professional Paper 1200.)

State Hydrologic Unit Maps. 1987. (Geological Survey Water Supply Paper 2294.)

Government —*see* Federal Government; *and* State and Local Government.

Guam —*see* Outlying Areas.

Health Insurance —*see* Insurance.

Health and Medical Care —*see also* Accidents; Environment; Food; Insurance; Social Insurance; *and* Vital Statistics

U.S. Government

Bureau of Labor Statistics

CPI Detailed Report. Monthly.

Employee Benefits in Medium and Large Firms. Biennial.

Employee Benefits in State and Local Governments. Biennial.

Handbook of Labor Statistics. 1989.

Monthly Labor Review.

Centers for Disease Control

Morbidity and Mortality Weekly Report. (HHS Pub. No. CDC 90-8017.)

Department of Agriculture, Food and Nutrition Service

Annual Historical Review:

Food and Nutrition Service Programs.

Food Program Update. Monthly.

Department of Health and Human Services

Annual Report.

Cancer Incidence and Mortality in the United States, 1973-81. Revised November 1984.

Health and Medical Care —Con.

U.S. Government —Con.

Department of Veterans Affairs

Annual Report of The Secretary of Veterans Affairs.

Female Veterans' Usage of VA Hospitalization. July 1987.

Profile of Veterans Administration Extended Care Programs: 1974-1986. July 1987.

Summary of Medical Programs. September 1988. Quarterly.

Trend Data 1964-1988.

Drug Enforcement Administration

Drug Abuse and Law Enforcement Statistics. Irregular.

Health Care Financing Administration

Health Care Financing Program Statistics Medicare and Medicaid data. Annual.

Health Care Financing Research Reports Occasional.

Health Care Financing Review. Quarterly.

National Center for Health Statistics

Health: United States. Annual. (DHHS Pub. No. PHS 86-1232.)

Vital and Health Statistics. (A series of statistical reports covering health-related topics.)

Series 10: Health Interview Survey Statistics. Irregular.

Current Estimates from the Health Interview Survey. Annual.

Series 11: Health and Nutrition Examination Survey Statistics. Irregular.

Series 13: Health Resources Utilization Statistics. Irregular.

National Hospital Discharge Survey: Annual Summary. Annual.

Series 14: Health Resources: Manpower and Facilities Statistics. Irregular.

National Institute on Drug Abuse

High School Senior Survey. 1975-1991.

Substance Abuse and Mental Health Services Administration

Drug Abuse Warning Network. Advance Reports, Annual Report, latest year available 1992.

National Drug and Alcoholism Treatment Unit Survey, latest year available 1992.

National Household Survey on Drug Abuse. Advance Reports, Main Findings, Population Estimates, latest year available 1992.

Social Security Administration

Social Security Bulletin. Quarterly with annual statistical supplement.

Other

American Dental Association, Chicago, IL

Dental Statistics Handbook. Triennial.

Dental Students' Register. Annual.

Health and Medical Care —Con.
  Other —Con.
    Distribution of Dentists in the United
      States by Region and State. Triennial.
    Survey of Dental Practice. Annual.
  American Hospital Association, Chicago, IL
    Hospital Statistics. Annual.
  American Medical Association, Chicago, IL
    Physician Characteristics and Distribution
      in the U.S. Annual.
    Socioeconomic Characteristics of Medical
      Practice. 1993.
    U.S. Medical Licensure Statistics, and
      License Requirements. Annual.
  American Osteopathic Association, Chicago,
    IL
      Yearbook and Directory of Osteopathic
        Physicians. Annual.
  Medical Economics, Montvale, NJ
    Physicians' Earnings and Expenses. Pub-
      lished annually in Medical Economics
      magazine.
  Metropolitan Life Insurance Company, New
    York, NY
      Health and Safety Education.
      Statistical Bulletin. Quarterly.
Hotels —*see* Health.
Hotels —*see* Service Establishments.
Household Appliances —*see* Construction, Hous-
  ing, and Real Estate. Housing—*see* Construction.
Immigration and Naturalization
  U.S. Government
    Department of State, Bureau of Consular
      Affairs
        Report of the Visa Office. Annual. (Dept.
          of State Pub. 8810.)
    Department of Transportation
      Report of Passenger Travel Between the
        United States and Foreign Countries.
        Annual, semiannual, quarterly, monthly.
    Immigration and Naturalization Service
      I&N Reporter. Quarterly.
      Statistical Yearbook of the Immigration
        and Naturalization Service. Annual.
    National Science Foundation
      Foreign Citizens in U.S. Science and En-
        gineering: History, Status, and Outlook.
        Special Report. (NSF 86-305, revised.)
      Foreign Students Account for Most
        Growth in Graduate Science and Engi-
        neering Enrollment. Science Resources
        Studies Highlights. (NSF 88-316.)
      Immigrant Scientists and Engineers. De-
        tailed Statistical Tables. Annual.
      Science and Engineering Doctoral
        Awards Reached Record Highs in
        1990. SRS Data Brief. (NSF 91-308.)
      Survey of Direct U.S. Private Capital In-
        vestment in Research and Develop-
        ment Facilities in Japan. (NSF 91-312)
      Science and Engineering Doctorates. De-
        tailed Statistical Tables. Annual.
  Imports —*see* Foreign Commerce.

Income —*see* Consumer Income; *and* National In-
  come.
Industry —*see* Business; Economic Indexes; *and*
  Manufactures.
Institutions —*see* Education; Health; *and* Law En-
  forcement. **Insurance**—*see also* Social Insur-
  ance
  U.S. Government
    Department of Veterans Affairs
      Annual Report of The Secretary of Veter-
        ans Affairs.
      Government Life Insurance Programs for
        Veterans and Members of the Service.
        Annual.
      Trend Data 1964-1988.
  Other
    American Council of Life Insurance, Wash-
      ington, DC
        Life Insurance Fact Book. Annual.(update
          odd years)
    Health Insurance Association of America,
      Washington, DC
        Source Book of Health Insurance Data.
          Annual (odd years.) Update (even
          years.)
    Insurance Information Institute, New York,
      NY
        Insurance Facts. Annual.
    National Association of Insurance Commis-
      sioners, Washington DC
        Auto Insurance Database Report. De-
          cember 1993.
    The National Underwriter Co., Cincinnati,
      OH
        Statistical Compilation of Annual Statement
          Information for Life/Health Insurance Com-
          panies. 1992.
        Statistical Compilation of Annual Statement
          Information for Property/Casualty Insur-
          ance Companies. 1992.
        Argus Chart. Health insurance company
          financial data. Annual.
        Argus F.C. & S. Chart. Property and liabil-
          ity insurance company financial data.
          Annual.
        Life Rates and Data. Premiums, values,
          dividends, and contract analysis by
          company. Annual.
        Life Reports. Life company financial data.
          Annual.
        Timesaver. Health insurance costs and
          contract analysis by company. Annual.
International Accounts and Aid
  U.S. Government
    Agency for International Development
      U.S. Overseas Loans and Grants and
        Assistance From International Organi-
        zations. Annual.
    Board of Governors of the Federal Reserve
      System
        Annual Statistical Digest.
        Federal Reserve Bulletin. Monthly.

International Statistics —Con.
Other —Con.

Consumer Europe.

Consumer Japan 1993.

Consumer Latin America 1993.

Consumer Southern Europe 1993.

Consumer USA

European Marketing Data and Statistics. Annual.

International Marketing Data and Statistics. Annual.

Food and Agriculture Organization of the United Nations, Rome, Italy

Production Yearbook.

Trade Yearbook.

Yearbook of Fishery Statistics.

Yearbook of Forest Products.

Inter-American Development Bank, Washington, DC

Annual Report.

Economic and Social Progress in Latin America. Annual Survey.

The International Institute for Strategic Studies, London, England

The Military Balance. Annual.

International Labour Office, Geneva, Switzerland

Economically Active Population, Estimates and Projections: 1950-2025, Vols. 1-6. 3rd Edition. 1986.

Yearbook of Labour Statistics. 49th issue. 1989-1990.

International Monetary Fund, Washington, DC

International Financial Statistics. Monthly with annual yearbook.

Jane's Information Group, Coulsdon, UK and Alexandria, VA

Jane's Air-Launched Weapons. (Binder-4 monthly update.)

Jane's All the World's Aircraft. Annual.

Jane's Armour and Artillery. Annual.

Jane's Avionics. Annual.

Jane's Fighting Ships. Annual.

Jane's Infantry Weapons. Annual.

Jane's Merchant Ships. Annual.

Jane's Military Communications. Annual.

Jane's Military Logistics. Annual.

Jane's Military Training Systems. Annual.

Jane's NATO Handbook. Annual.

Jane's Spaceflight Directory. Annual.

Organization for Economic Cooperation and Development, Paris, France

Annual Oil Market Report.

Coal Information. Annual.

Demographic Trends 1950-1990.

Energy Balances of OECD Countries. Annual.

Energy Prices and Taxes. Quarterly.

Energy Statistics. Annual.

International Statistics —Con.
Other —Con.

Financial Market Trends. Triennial.

Financing and Delivering Health Care, 1987.

Food Consumption Statistics. Irregular.

Geographical Distribution of Financial Flows to Developing Countries.

Historical Statistics of Foreign Trade Series A. Annual.

Indicators of Industrial Activity. Quarterly.

Industrial Structure Statistics. Annual.

The Iron and Steel Industry. Annual.

Labour Force Statistics. Annual.

Latest Information on National Accounts of Developing Countries. Annual.

Living Conditions in OECD Countries. 1986.

Main Economic Indicators. Monthly.

Main Science and Technology Indicators. Biennial.

Maritime Transport. Annual.

Measuring Health Care, 1960-1983. 1985.

Meat Balances in OECD Countries. Annual.

Milk and Milk Products Balances in OECD Countries. Annual.

National Accounts of OECD Countries. Annual.

Vol. I: Main Aggregates.

Vol. II: Detailed Tables.

National and International Tourism Statistics. 1974-1985.

OECD Economic Outlook. Bi-annual. Historical Statistics. Annual.

OECD Economic Studies. Annual for member countries.

OECD Employment Outlook. Annual.

OECD Environmental Data-Compendium 1989.

OECD Financial Statistics. Annual (three vols.) and monthly supplements.

OECD Health Data (Diskette)

OECD Health Systems: Facts and Trends.

OECD Microtables on Foreign Trade by Commodities covering Series B (individual reporting countries) and Series C (total reporting countries). Annual from 1977.

OECD Purchasing Power Parities and Real Expenditures, 1985. (January 1988.)

Oil and Gas Information. Annual.

The Pulp and Paper Industry. Annual.

Quarterly Labor Force Statistics.

Quarterly National Accounts.

Quarterly Oil Statistics and Energy Balances.

Revenue Statistics of OECD Member Countries. Annual.

Investments and Securities —Con.

Other —Con.

Financial Aspects of the United States Pension System, Zvi Bodie and John B. Shoven, editors. 1983. (University of Chicago Press, Chicago,IL.)

New York Stock Exchange, Inc., New York, NY

Fact Book. Annual.

Shareownership, 1983, and 1985.

Securities Industry Association, New York, NY

Foreign Activity Report. Quarterly.

Investor Activity Report. Monthly.

Securities Industry Trends. Periodic.

SIA Fact Book. Annual.

Standard and Poor's Corporation, New York, NY

Analyst's Handbook. Annual with monthly cumulative supplements.

Corporation Records. Six basic volumes; News Supplements, daily; Dividend Record, daily, and cumulative monthly and annual.

Daily Stock Price Records. Quarterly.

Security Owner's Stock Guide. Monthly.

Statistical Service. (Security Price Index Record; business and financial basic statistics with monthly supplement.)

Wall Street Journal. (Dow Jones & Co., New York, NY.) Daily except Saturdays, Sundays, and holidays.

Irrigation, Drainage, and Soil Conservation —*see* Agriculture

Juvenile Court —*see* Law Enforcement.

Labor —*see also* Accidents; Business; Economic Indexes; International Statistics; Science Resources; *and* Social Insurance

U.S. Government

Board of Governors of the Federal Reserve System

Annual Statistical Digest.

Federal Reserve Bulletin. Monthly.

Bureau of the Census

Census of Population. Decennial. (1990, most recent.)

County Business Patterns. Annual.

Current Governments Reports: Public Employment, GE No. 1 (annual); City Employment, GE No. 2 (annual); Local Government Employment in Selected Metropolitan Areas and Large Counties, GE No. 3 (annual); County Government Employment, GE No. 4 (annual).

Labor Force Status and Other Characteristics of Persons With a Work Disability: 1981-1988. (Current Population Reports, Special Studies, Series P23-160.) 1989.

Population Profile of the United States. (Biennial Series P23.)

Social Indicators, 1980.

Labor —Con.

U.S. Government —Con.

Women in the American Economy. (Current Population Reports, Special Studies, Series P23, No. 146.) 1987.

Bureau of Justice Statistics and Bureau of the Census

Justice Expenditure and Employment in the U.S. Annual.

Bureau of Labor Statistics

Area Wage Surveys: Selected Metropolitan Areas. Annual.

Bargaining Calendar. Annual.

Compensation and Working Conditions. Monthly.

Employee Benefits in Medium and Large Firms. Biennial.

Employee Benefits in State and Local Governments. Biennial.

Employment and Earnings. Monthly, with annual supplement.

Employment and Earnings Characteristics of Families. Quarterly.

Employment and Wages. Annual.

Employment Cost Index. Quarterly.

Employment, Hours, and Earnings, United States, 1909-90. 1991. (Bulletin 2370.)

Employment in Perspective: Minority Workers. Quarterly.

Employment in Perspective: Women in the Labor Force. Quarterly.

The Employment Situation. Monthly.

Geographic Profile of Employment and Unemployment. Annual.

Handbook of Labor Statistics. 1989.

How Workers Get Their Training. 1985. (Bulletin No. 2226.)

Industry Wage Surveys. (Separate bulletins for selected industries; each industry on a 3- to 5-year cycle.)

Labor Force Statistics Derived from the Current Population Survey, 1948-87. 1988. (Bulletin No. 2307.)

Major Collective Bargaining Settlements. Quarterly.

Major Work Stoppages. Annual.

Mass Layoffs. Annual.

Monthly Labor Review.

Occupational Employment in Manufacturing Industries. 1991. (Bulletin No. 2376.)

Occupational Employment in Mining, Construction, Finance, and Services. 1992. (Bulletin No. 2397.)

Occupational Employment in Selected Nonmanufacturing Industries. 1990. (Bulletin No. 2348.)

Occupational Injuries and Illnesses in the United States, by Industry. Annual.

Occupational Projections and Training Data. Biennial.

Outlook 2000. 1990. (Bulletin No. 2352.)

Labor —Con.

U.S. Government —Con.

Permanent Mass Layoffs and Plant Closings, 1987. 1988. (Bulletin 2310.)

Real Earnings. Monthly.

Revised Seasonally Adjusted Labor Force Statistics, 1978-87. 1988. (Bulletin 2506.)

State and Metropolitan Area Employment and Unemployment. Monthly.

Weekly Earnings of Wage and Salary Workers. Quarterly.

White-Collar Pay. Annual.

Work Experience of the Population. Annual.

Working Woman: A Chartbook. 1991 (Bulletin No. 2385.)

Department of Agriculture

Farm Labor. Monthly.

Department of Labor

Annual Report of the Secretary.

Employment and Training Administration

Employment and Training Report of the President. Annual.

Unemployment Insurance Claims. Weekly.

Interstate Commerce Commission

Monthly Report of Class I Railroad Employees, by Group. (Statement No. 350.)

Wage Statistics of Class I Railroads in the United States. Annual. (Statement No. 300.)

Maritime Administration

Employment Report of United States Flag Merchant Fleet Ocean-going Vessels 1,000 Gross Tons and Over. Annual. (Monthly and quarterly data available from source.)

Seafaring Wage Rates. Biennial.

National Science Foundation

Characteristics of Doctoral Scientists and Engineers in the United States. Detailed Statistical Tables. Biennial.

Characteristics of Recent Science and Engineering Graduates. Detailed Statistical Tables. Biennial.

Immigrant Scientists and Engineers. Detailed Statistical Tables. Annual.

U.S. Scientists and Engineers. Detailed Statistical Tables. Biennial.

U.S. Scientists and Engineers: 1984 Detailed Statistical Tables.

Woman and Minorities in Science and Engineering. Report. Biennial.

Office of Personnel Management

Affirmative Employment Statistics. Biennial. (Even Years.)

Occupations of Federal White-Collar and Blue-Collar Workers. Biennial. (Odd Years.)

Women's Bureau

Labor —Con.

U.S. Government —Con.

Handbook on Women Workers. Periodic.

Other

Aerospace Industries Association of America, Washington, DC

Employment in the Aerospace Industry. Monthly.

Survey of Aerospace Employment. Annual.

The Bureau of National Affairs, Inc., Washington, DC

Basic Patterns in Union Contracts. Annual.

BNA's Employment Outlook. Quarterly.

BNA's Job Absence and Turnover. Quarterly.

Briefing Sessions on Employee Relations Workbook. Annual.

Calendar of Negotiations. Annual.

Directory of U.S. Labor Organizations. Annual.

82 Key Statistics on Work and Family Issues. (The National Report on Work and Family. Special Report No. 9, September 1988.)

National Labor Relations Board Election Statistics. Annual.

NLRB Representation and Decertification Elections Statistics. Quarterly.

101 Key Statistics on Work and Family for the 1990's. (The BNA Special Report Series on Work and Family. Special Report No. 21, September 21, 1989.)

PPF Survey (Personnel Policies Forum.) Three times a year.

Law Enforcement, Courts, and Prisons

U.S. Government

Administrative Office of the United States Courts

Annual Report of the Director ... with, as issued, Reports of the Proceedings of the Judicial Conference of the United States. Includes statistics on Federal Courts.

Calendar Year Reports on Authorized Wiretaps. (State and Federal.)

Federal Court Management Statistics. Annual.

Federal Judicial Workload Statistics. Quarterly.

Bureau of the Census

Census of Population. Decennial. (1990, most recent.)

Bureau of Justice Statistics

American Response to Crime: An Overview of Criminal Justice Systems. December 1983.

Bank Robbery: Federal Offenses and Offenders. August 1984.

Black Victims. April 1990.

Minerals and Metals —Con.

U.S. Government —Con.

Treasury Bulletin. Monthly through 1982; beginning 1983, quarterly.

Energy Information Administration

Annual Energy Review.

Coal Production. Annual.

Domestic Uranium Mining and Milling Industry. Annual.

International Energy Annual.

Monthly Energy Review.

Natural Gas Annual.

Petroleum Supply Annual.

Quarterly Coal Report.

U.S. Crude Oil, Natural Gas, and Natural Gas Liquids Reserves. Annual.

Other

American Bureau of Metal Statistics, Inc., Secaucus, NJ

Non-Ferrous Metal Data.

American Gas Association, Arlington, VA

Gas Facts. Annual.

Year Book.

American Metal Market, New York, NY

Daily Newspapers.

Metal Statistics. Annual.

American Petroleum Institute, Washington, DC

Quarterly Review of Drilling Statistics for the United States.

American Petroleum Institute, Independent Petroleum Association of America, and MidContinent Oil and Gas Association

Joint Association Survey on Drilling Costs. Annual.

Knight-Ridder Financial Publishing-Commodity Research Bureau, Chicago, IL

Commodity Yearbook. Annual.

Independent Petroleum Association of America, Washington, DC

IPAA Weekly Oil Trends.

IPAA Wholesale Oil Prices. Monthly.

The Oil & Natural Gas Producing Industry in Your State. Annual.

U.S. Petroleum Statistics. Semiannual.

McGraw-Hill Publications Co., New York, NY

Engineering and Mining Journal. Monthly.

Keystone Coal Industry Manual. Annual.

National Coal Association, Washington, DC

Coal Data. Annual.

PennWell Publishing Co., Tulsa, OK

Offshore. Monthly.

Oil and Gas Journal. Weekly.

Carl H. Pforzheimer & Co., New York, NY

Comparative Oil Company Statistics, 19911990. Annual.

Money and Banking —see also Construction; Insurance; International Accounts; and Investments

Money and Banking —Con.

U.S. Government

Board of Governors of the Federal Reserve System

Annual Statistical Digest.

Domestic Offices, Commercial Bank Assets and Liabilities Consolidated Report of Condition. Quarterly.

Federal Reserve Bulletin. Monthly.

Flow of Funds Accounts: Seasonally Adjusted and Unadjusted. Z.1(780). Quarterly.

Money Stock, Liquid Assets, and Debt Measures. H.6 (508). Weekly.

Bureau of the Mint

Annual Report of the Director.

Comptroller of the Currency

Quarterly Journal.

Department of the Treasury

Daily Treasury Statement.

Monthly Treasury Statement of Receipts and Outlays of the United States Government.

Statement of United States Currency and Coin. Monthly.

Statistical Appendix to Annual Report of the Secretary of the Treasury on the State of the Finances through 1980.

Treasury Bulletin. Monthly through 1982; beginning 1983, quarterly.

Farm Credit Administration

Annual Report on the Work of the Cooperative Farm Credit System.

Production Credit Association: Summary of Operations. Annual.

Report to the Federal Land Bank Associations. Annual.

Federal Deposit Insurance Corporation

Annual Report.

Data Book-Operating Banks and Branches. Annual.

Historical Statistics on Banking. 1934-1992.

Quarterly Banking Profile.

Statistics on Banking. Annual.

Trust Assets of Insured Commercial Banks. Annual.

National Credit Union Administration

Annual Report.

Yearend Statistics.

Midyear Statistics.

National Credit Union Share Insurance Annual Report.

Office of Thrift Supervision

Annual Report.

Asset and Liability Trends. Annual.

Savings and Home Financing Source Book. Annual. Discontinued after 1989.

Appendix I

Newspapers, Periodicals, and Books —Con.
U.S. Government —Con.
  Census of Manufactures. Quinquennial. (1987, most recent.)
 Library of Congress
  Annual Report.
 The National Library of Medicine (for clinical medical reports)
  Annual Report.
 The National Agricultural Library (for technical agricultural publications)
  Annual Report
Other
 Book Industry Study Group, Inc., New York, NY
  Book Industry Trends. Annual.
 Cahners/Bowker (R.R.) New York, NY
  Library Journal. Bimonthly.
  Publishers Weekly.
  School Library Journal. Monthly.
 Editor & Publisher Co., New York, NY
  International Year Book. Annual.
  Market Guide. Annual.
 Gale Research Inc., Detroit, MI
  Gale Directory of Publications and Broadcast Media. 1994.

Nutrition —*see* Food *and* Health.

Occupation —*see* Labor; Population; *and* Social Insurance.

Outlying Areas —*see also* Foreign Commerce
U.S. Government
 Bureau of the Census
  Census of Agriculture. (1987, most recent.)
  Census of Housing. Decennial. (1990, most recent.)
  Census of Population. Decennial. (1990, most recent.)
  Current Population Reports. (Series on Population Estimates, P25.)
  Economic Censuses of Outlying Areas. Quinquennial. (1987, most recent.)
 Bureau of Mines
  Minerals Yearbook. Annual.
 National Center for Education Statistics
  Digest of Education Statistics. Annual.
  Statistics of Public Elementary and Secondary School Systems. Fall. Annual.
 National Center for Health Statistics
  Vital Statistics of the United States. Annual.
   Volume I, Natality
   Volume II, Mortality
   Volume III, Marriage and Divorce
Other
 Puerto Rico Planning Board, San Juan, PR
  Balance of Payments—Puerto Rico. Annual.
  Economic Report to the Governor. Annual.

Outlying Areas —Con.
Other —Con.
  Income and Product. Annual.
  Socioeconomic Statistics. Annual.

Paper —*see* Forests and Lumber.

Parks —*see* Public Lands.

Pensions —*see* Social Insurance.

Petroleum —*see* Energy *and* Minerals.

Population and Population Characteristics —*see also* Labor *and* Vital Statistics
U.S. Government
 Bureau of the Census
  Census of Population. Decennial. (1990, most recent.)
  Current Population Reports. (Series on Population Characteristics, P20; Special Studies, P23; Population Estimates and Projections, P25; Local Population Estimates, P26; Special Censuses, P28; Consumer Income, P60; and Household Economic Studies, P70.)
 Bureau of Labor Statistics
  Employment and Earnings. Monthly, with annual supplement.
  Handbook of Labor Statistics. 1989.
  Labor Force Statistics Derived From the Current Population Survey, 1948-87. 1988 (Bulletin No. 2307.)
  Monthly Labor Review.
  Outlook 2000. 1990. (Bulletin No. 2352.)
  Work Experience of the Population. Annual.
 Department of Veterans Affairs
  Annual Report of The Secretary of Veterans Affairs.
  Data on Vietnam Era Veterans, 1984.
  Disability Compensation, Pension, and Death Pension Data. Semiannual.
  1987 Survey of Veterans.
  Selected Compensation and Pension Data by State of Residence. Annual.
  State and County Veteran Population. Annual.
  Survey of Female Veterans.
  Veteran Population Data. Semiannual.
 National Science Foundation
  Characteristics of Doctoral Scientists and Engineers in the United States. Detailed Statistical Tables. Biennial.
  Characteristics of Recent Science and Engineering Graduates. Detailed Statistical Tables. Biennial.
  Federal Scientists and Engineers. Detailed Statistical Tables. Annual.
  Immigrant Scientists and Engineers. Detailed Statistical Tables. Annual
  Science and Engineering Doctorates. Detailed Statistical Tables.
  Science and Engineering Personnel. A National Overview. Report. Biennial.

Population and Population Characteristics —Con.

Other

Population Association of America, Washington DC

Demography. Quarterly.

Population Index. (Princeton University, Princeton, NJ, Woodrow Wilson School of Public and International Affairs for the Population Association of America, Inc.) Quarterly.

Postal Service —*see* Communications.

Power —*see* Energy.

Prices —*see* Commodity Prices; *and* Economic Indexes.

Prisons and Prisoners —*see* Law Enforcement.

Public Assistance —*see* Social Insurance.

Public Lands and Park Systems —*see also* Federal Government; *and* Recreation

U.S. Government

Bureau of Land Management

Public Land Statistics. Annual.

General Services Administration

Inventory Report on Real Property Leased to the United States Throughout the World. Annual.

Inventory Report on Real Property Owned by the United States Throughout the World. Annual.

National Park Service

Federal Recreation Fee Report. Annual.

National Park Statistical Abstract. Annual.

Other

National Association of State Park Directors

Annual Information Exchange.

Public Utilities —*see* Communications; Energy; *and* Transportation.

Puerto Rico —*see* Outlying Areas.

Radio —*see* Communications.

Railways —*see* Transportation.

Real Estate —*see* Agriculture; *and* Construction.

Reclamation Projects —*see* Agriculture.

Recreation —*see also* Public Lands

U.S. Government

Bureau of the Census

Census of Transportation. Quinquennial. (1987, most recent.)

Bureau of Economic Analysis

The National Income and Product Accounts of the United States,

1929-82: Statistical Tables. 1986.

Survey of Current Business. Monthly.

Department of Transportation

U.S. International Air Travel Statistics. Annual.

Fish and Wildlife Service

Federal Aid in Fish and Wildlife Restoration. Annual.

Recreation —Con.

U.S. Government —Con.

National Survey of Fishing, Hunting, and Wildlife-Associated Recreation. Quinquennial. (1990 most recent.)

National Endowment for the Arts

Research Division Notes Nos. 3, 4, 5, 10, 13, and 15. 1983-1986.

National Park Service

Federal Recreation Fee Report. Annual.

National Park Statistical Abstract. Annual.

Other

Association of Racing Commissioners International, Inc., Lexington, KY

Statistical Reports on Greyhound Racing in the United States. Annual.

Statistical Reports on Horse Racing in the United States. Annual.

Statistical Reports on Jai Alai in the United States. Annual.

National Golf Foundation, Jupiter, FL

Americans' Attitudes Toward Golf in Their Community.

An Operational Profile of Canadian Golf Facilities.

Golf Consumer Spending and Facility Fees.

Golf Course Operations.

Golf Facilities in Canada.

Golf Facilities in the United States. 1992.

Golf Participation in Canada.

Golf Participation in the United States. 1992.

Golf Travel in the United States. $Maintenance Survey Report.

Stand-Alone Golf Ranges in the United States.

Trends in the Golf Industry 1987-1991.

Women in Golf.

National Marine Manufacturers Association, Chicago, IL

Boating. (A Statistical Report on America's Top Family Sport.) Annual.

State Boat Registration. Annual.

National Sporting Goods Association, Mt. Prospect, IL

The Sporting Goods Market in 1993. Annual.

Sports Participation in 1992. Annual.

Resources for the Future, Inc., Washington, DC

Statistics on Outdoor Recreation. 1984.

Part I: The Record Through 1956

Part II: The Record Since 1956

Religious Bodies

Other

American Jewish Committee and the Jewish Publication Society, New York, NY

American Jewish Year Book.

Glenmary Research Center, Atlanta, GA

Religious Bodies —Con.

Other —Con.

Churches and Church Membership in the United States 1990 by M. Bradley; N.Green, Jr; D. Jones; M.Lynn; and L. McNeil. 1992.

National Council of the Churches of Christ in the U.S.A., New York, NY

Yearbook of American and Canadian Churches. Annual.

Research and Development —see Science Resources.

Retail and Wholesale Trade —see also Commodity Prices; Economic Indexes; and Service Establishments

U.S. Government

Board of Governors of the Federal Reserve System

Annual Statistical Digest

Federal Reserve Bulletin. Monthly.

Bureau of the Census

Annual Retail Trade Report.

Annual Wholesale Trade Report.

Census of Retail Trade. Quinquennial. (1987, most recent.)

Census of Wholesale Trade. Quinquennial. (1987, most recent.)

County Business Patterns. Annual.

Merchant Wholesalers Measures of Value Produced, Capital Expenditures, Depreciable Assets, and Operating Expenses. (1987, most recent.)

Monthly Retail Trade Report. Sales and Inventories.

Monthly Wholesale Trade Report. Sales and Inventories.

Selected Characteristics of Retail Trade-Measures of Value Produced, Capital Expenditures, Depreciable Assets, and Operating Expenses. (1987, most recent.)

Bureau of Economic Analysis

Business Statistics, 1963-91. 1992.

Survey of Current Business. Monthly.

Bureau of Labor Statistics

Compensation and Working Conditions. Monthly

CPI Detailed Report. Monthly.

Employment and Earnings. Monthly, with annual supplement.

Employment, Hours, and Earnings, United States, 1909-90. 1991. (Bulletin No. 2370.)

Handbook of Labor Statistics. 1989.

Monthly Labor Review.

Occupational Employment in Selected Nonmanufacturing Industries. 1990. (Bulletin No. 2348.)

Occupational Injuries and Illnesses in the United States by Industry. Annual.

Producer Price Indexes. Monthly, with annual supplement.

Retail and Wholesale Trade —Con.

U.S. Government —Con.

Productivity Measures for Selected Industries and Government Services. Annual.

Technological Change and Its Labor Impact in Four Industries. 1988. (Bulletin 2316.)

Technology and Labor in Three Service Industries: Utilities, Retail Trade, and Lodging. 1990. (Bulletin 2367.)

International Trade Administration

Franchising in the Economy. Annual. (Last issued 1988.)

U.S. Industrial Outlook. Annual.

Other

Dealerscope Merchandising, Philadelphia, PA

Merchandising. Annual.

Lebhar-Friedman, Inc., New York, NY

Accounting Today. Biweekly.

Apparel Merchandising. Monthly.

Chain Store Age Executive. Census Issue, August 1989. Monthly.

Discount Store News. July 1989, Statistical Issue. Biweekly.

Drug Store News. May 1989, Statistical Issue. Biweekly.

National Home Center News. May 1989, Two Statistical Issues. Biweekly.

Nation's Restaurant News. August 1989, Statistical Issue. Weekly.

Market Statistics, New York, NY

The Survey of Buying Power Data Service. Annual.

National Restaurant Association, Washington, DC

Foodservice Industry Forecast. Annual.

Foodservice Industry in Review. Annual.

Foodservice Market Measure. Monthly in Restaurants USA.

Foodservice Numbers: A Statistical Digest for the Foodservice Industry. 1992.

Restaurant Industry Operations Report. Annual.

Restaurants USA. Monthly.

Survey of Wage Rates for Hourly Employees. Biennial.

Compensation for Salaried Personnel in Foodservice. Triennial.

Roads —see Transportation.

Sales —see Retail and Wholesale Trade.

Savings Institutions —see Money.

Science Resources

U.S. Government

Bureau of the Census

Current Industrial Reports, MA37D. Annual.

Energy Research and Development Administration

The Nuclear Industry. Annual.

Science Resources —Con.
  U.S. Government —Con.
    National Aeronautics and Space Administration
      Annual Procurement Report.
      The Civil Service Work Force.
      Pocket Statistics. Annual.
    National Science Foundation
      A Comparative Analysis of Information on National Industrial R&D Expenditures. Special Report. (NSF 85-311.)
      Academic Research Equipment in Computer Science, Central Computer Facilities and Engineering: 1989.
      Academic Research Equipment and Equipment needs in Selected Science/Engineering Fields: 1989-90.
      Academic Research and Equipment Needs in the Physical Sciences: 1989.
      Academic Science and Engineering: Graduate Enrollment and Support. Detailed Statistical Tables. Annual.
      Academic Science and Engineering: R&D Expenditures. Detailed Statistical Tables. Annual.
      Biotechnology Research and Development Activities in Industry: 1984 and 1985. Special Report. (NSF 87-311.)
      Blacks in Undergraduate Science and Engineering Education, April 1992. Special Report. (NSF 92-305.)
      Characteristics of Doctoral Scientists and Engineers in the United States. Detailed Statistical Tables. Biennial.
      Characteristics of Recent Grads.
      Characteristics of Recent Scientists and Engineers. Detailed Statistical Tables. Biennial.
      Characteristics of Science and Engineering Equipment in Academic Settings: 1989-90.
      Doctoral Scientists and Engineers: A Decade of Change. Special Report. (NSF 88-302.)
      Federal R&D Funding by Budget Function. Report. Annual.
      Federal Funds for Research and Development. Detailed Statistical Tables. Annual.
      Federal Academic R&D Support Increased by 6 Percent Between FYs 1989 and 1990. (NSF 92-328.)
      Federal Support to Universities, Colleges, and Nonprofit Institutions. Detailed Statistical Tables. Annual.
      Geographic Patterns of R&D Expenditures. Special Report. (NSF 89-317.)
      Immigrant Scientists and Engineers. Detailed Statistical Tables. Annual.
      International Science and Technology Data Update. Report. Annual.
      National Patterns of R&D Resources. Report. Annual.
      Planned R&D Expenditures of Major U.S. firms: 1990-91. Special Report. (NSF 91-306.)

Science Resources —Con.
  U.S. Government —Con.
    Research and Development Expenditures of State Government Agencies: Fiscal Years 1987 and 1988. Special Report. (NSF 90-309.)
    Research and Development in Industry. Detailed Statistical Tables. Annual.
    Science and Engineering Degrees. Detailed Statistical Tables. Annual.
    Science and Engineering Degrees, by Race/Ethnicity of Recipients: 1977-90. Detailed Statistical Tables. Annual.
    Science and Engineering Doctorates. Detailed Statistical Tables. Annual.
    Science and Engineering Indicators. Report. Biennial.
    Science and Engineering Personnel: A National Overview. Report. Biennial.
    Science and Technology Pocket Data Book. Report. Annual.
    Science and Technology Resources in U.S. Industry. Special Report. (NSF 88-321.)
    The Science and Technology Resources of Japan: A Comparison with the United States. Special Report. (NSF 88-318.)
    The Science and Technology Resources of West Germany: A Comparison with the United States. Special Report. (NSF 86-310.)
    Scientific and Engineering Research Facilities at Universities and Colleges. Report. Biennial.
    Scientists, Engineers, and Technicians in Manufacturing are Concentrated in High Technology Industries. (NSF 91-321.)
    Scientists, Engineers, and Technicians in Manufacturing Industries. Detailed Statistical Tables. Triennial.
    Scientists, Engineers, and Technicians in Nonmanufacturing Industries. Detailed Statistical Tables. Triennial.
    Scientists, Engineers, and Technicians in Trade and Regulated Industries. Detailed Statistical Tables. Triennial.
    Superconductivity Research and Development Activities in U.S. Industry: 1987 and 1988. Special Report.
    Survey of Direct U.S. Private Capital Investment in Research and Development Facilities in Japan. Special Report. (NSF 91-12.)
    Undergraduate Origins of Recent Science and Engineering Doctorate Recipients. Special Report (NSF 92-332.)
    U.S. Firms Report Real R&D Expenditures Declining in 1991 and 1992. (NSF 92-306.)
    U.S. Scientists and Engineers. Detailed Statistical Tables. Biennial.
    Women and Minorities in Science and Engineering: An Update. Report. Biennial.

Science Resources —Con.

U.S. Government —Con.

Women Continue to Earn Increasing Percentage of Science and Engineering Baccalaureates. (NSF 92-313.)

Patent and Trademark Office

Commissioner of Patents and Trademarks Annual Report.

Technology Assessment and Forecast Reports "All Technologies" and State Country Report. Annual.

Other

National Academy of Sciences, Washington, DC

Science, Engineering, and Humanities Doctorates in the United States. Biennial. Summary Report. Doctorate Recipients from United States Universities. Annual.

Securities —see Investments; and Money. Service Establishments—see also Retail and Wholesale Trade

U.S. Government

Bureau of the Census

Census of Service Industries. Quinquennial. (1987, most recent.)

Motor Freight Transportation and Warehousing Survey. Annual.

Selected Characteristics of Selected Service Industries—Capital Expenditures, Depreciable Assets, and Operating Expenses. (1987, most recent.)

Services Annual Survey Report.

Internal Revenue Service

Statistics of Income. (Annual report on Corporation Income Tax Returns. Periodic compendiums on Studies of International Income and Taxes.)

Statistics of Income Bulletin. Quarterly.

Other

Decker Communications, Inc., New York, NY

Marketing Communications. (Advertising.) Monthly.

Laventhol & Horwath, Philadelphia, PA

The Executive Conference Center: A Statistical and Financial Profile. Annual.

Gaming Industry Study. Annual.

Lifecare Industry. Annual. (Analysis of facilities by size and section of the country for selected financial data, resident census information, and medical costs.)

National Trends of Business in the Lodging Industry. Monthly. (Analysis of nationwide trends in sales, occupancy, and room rates of hotels, motor hotels, and economy lodging facilities.)

Separate reports on the segments of lodging industries. Annuals. (Reports covering economy, all-suite, and resort.)

Securities —Con.

Other —Con.

U.S. Lodging Industry. Annual. (Report on hotel and motor hotel operations.)

Worldwide Lodging Industry. Annual. (Report on international hotel operations.)

Pannell Kerr Forster, Houston, TX

Clubs in Town and Country. Annual.

Trends in the Hotel Industry, International Edition. Annual.

Trends in the Hotel Industry, U.S.A. Edition. Annual.

Social Insurance and Human Services —see also Insurance and Labor

U.S. Government

Bureau of the Census

Census of Governments. Quinquennial. (1987, most recent.)

Consolidated Federal Funds Report. Annual.

Federal Expenditures by State

Volume I County Areas

Volume II Subcounty Areas

Current Population Reports (series P60, Consumer Income.)

Finances of Employee-Retirement Systems of State and Local Governments. Annual. (GF No. 2.)

Finances of Selected Public Employee Retirement Systems. Quarterly. (GR Nos. 1-4.)

Bureau of Labor Statistics

Employee Benefits in Medium and Large Firms. Biennial.

Employee Benefits in State and Local Governments. Biennial.

Department of Health and Human Services

Annual Report.

Income of the Population 55 and Over. 1984.

Department of Labor

Annual Report of the Secretary.

Department of Veterans Affairs

Annual Report of The Secretary of Veterans Affairs.

Government Life Insurance Programs for Veterans and Members of the Services. Annual.

Trend Data 1964-1988.

Employment and Training Administration

Unemployment Insurance Claims. Weekly.

Family Support Administration

Quarterly Public Assistance Statistics. Annual.

Health Care Financing Administration

Health Care Financing Program Statistics. Medicare and Medicaid data. Annual.

Health Care Financing Review. Quarterly.

Office of Personnel Management

Compensation Report. Annual.

Transportation —Con.

U.S. Government —Con.

Large Class I Motor Carriers of Passengers Selected Earnings Data. Quarterly.

Large Class I Motor Carriers of Property Selected Earnings Data. Quarterly.

Quarterly Report.

Transport Statistics in the United States. Issued annually in two separate parts:

Part 1: Railroads

Part 2: Motor Carriers

Maritime Administration

Annual Report.

Employment Report of United States Flag Merchant Fleet Ocean-going Vessels 1,000 Gross Tons and Over. Annual. (Monthly and quarterly data available from source.)

Foreign Flag Merchant Ships Owned by U.S. Parent Companies. Annual.

Maritime Manpower Report. Monthly.

United States Oceanborne Foreign Trade Routes. Annual.

Research and Special Programs Administration

Air Carrier Financial Statistics. Quarterly.

Air Carrier Industry Scheduled Service Traffic Statistics. Quarterly.

Air Carrier Traffic Statistics. Monthly.

Other

Aerospace Industries Association of America, Washington, DC

Aerospace Facts and Figures. Annual.

Net New Orders, Shipments, and Backlog for Jet Transport Aircraft. Quarterly.

Commercial Helicopter Shipments. Quarterly.

Air Transport Association of America, Washington, DC

Air Transport Facts and Figures. Annual.

American Automobile Manufacturers Association, Detroit, MI.

Motor Vehicle Facts and Figures. Annual.

World Motor Vehicle Data. Annual.

American Bureau of Shipping, Paramus, NJ

The Record. Annual with one supplement.

American Public Transit Association, Washington, DC

Transit Fact Book. Annual.

Association of American Railroads, Washington, DC

Analysis of Class I Railroads. Annual.

Cars of Revenue Freight Loaded. Weekly with annual summary.

Freight Commodity Statistics, Class I Railroads in the United States. Annual.

Yearbook of Railroad Facts.

ENO Transportation Foundation, Leesburg, VA

Transportation in America. mid-year, annually with periodic supplements.

Transportation —Con.

Other —Con.

General Aviation Manufacturers Association, Washington, DC

Shipment Report. Quarterly and Annual.

Statistical Databook. Annual.

Lake Carriers' Association, Cleveland, OH

Annual Report.

Monthly Bulk Commodities Report.

Lloyd's Register of Shipping, London, England

Annual Summary of Merchant Ships Completed in the World.

Casualty Return. (Annual statistical summary of all merchant ships totally lost or reported broken up during year.)

Merchant Shipbuilding Returns. (Quarterly Statistical summary of world shipbuilding.)

World Fleet Statistics-December 1992 (A end-year analysis of world merchant fleet.)

National Air Carrier Association, Washington, DC

Annual Report.

Regional Airline Association, Washington, DC

Statistical Reports.

Shipbuilders Council of America, Arlington, VA

Annual Report.

Tanker Advisory Center, Inc., New York, NY

Worldwide Tanker Casualty Returns. Annual.

Travel —see Recreation and Transportation.

Unemployment Insurance —see Labor; and Social Insurance.

Utilities, Public—see Communications; Energy and Transportation.

Veterans —see National Defense; and Population.

Virgin Islands of the United States —see Outlying Areas.

Vital Statistics —see also Accidents; and Health

U.S. Government

Centers for Disease Control, Atlanta, GA

Morbidity and Mortality Weekly Report. Annual summary also.

National Center for Health Statistics

Monthly Vital Statistics Report. Provisional statistics. Annual summary also.

Vital and Health Statistics. (A series of statistical reports covering health-related topics.)

Series 20: Mortality Data. Irregular.

Series 21: Natality, Marriage, and Divorce Data. Irregular.

Series 23: National Survey of Family Growth Statistics. Irregular.

Vital Statistics of the United States. Annual.

Other

The Alan Guttmacher Institute, New York, NY

Guide to State Statistical Abstracts

This bibliography includes the most recent statistical abstracts for States and Puerto Rico published since 1980 plus those that will be issued in late 1994 or early 1995. For some States, a near equivalent has been listed in substitution for, or in addition to, a statistical abstract. All sources contain statistical tables on a variety of subjects for the State as a whole, its component parts, or both. The page counts given for publications are approximate.

Alabama

University of Alabama, Center for Business and Economic Research, P.O. Box 870221, Tuscaloosa 35487
205-348-6191

Economic Abstract of Alabama. 1994. 600 pp.

Alaska

Department of Commerce and Economic Development, Division of Economic Development, P.O. Box 110804, Juneau 99811
907-465-2017

The Alaska Economy Performance Report. 1990-1991

Arizona

University of Arizona, Economic and Business Research, College of Business and Public Administration, McClelland Hall 204 Tucson 85721-0001
602-621-2155 FAX 602-621-2150

Arizona Statistical Abstract: A 1993 Data Handbook. 616 pp.

Arizona Economic Indicators. 52 pp. Biannual.

Arizona's Economy. 20 pp. (Quarterly newsletter and data.)

Arkansas

University of Arkansas at Little Rock, Economic Research, Library 512, Little Rock 72204

Arkansas State and County Economic Data. 9 pp. (Revised annually.)

University of Arkansas at Little Rock, Census State Data Center, Library 508, Little Rock 72204
501-569-8530

Arkansas Statistical Abstract. 650 pp. (Revised biennially.)

California

Department of Finance, 915 L Street, 8th Floor, Sacramento 95814
916-322-2263

California Statistical Abstract, 1994. 216 pp.

Pacific Data Resources, P.O. Box 1922, Santa Barbara 93116-1922
800-422-2546

California Almanac, 6th ed. Biennial. 275 pp.

Colorado

University of Colorado, Business Research Division, Campus Box 420, Boulder 80309
303-492-8227

Statistical Abstract of Colorado, 1987. 600 pp.

Connecticut

Connecticut Department of Economic Development, 865 Brook St., Rocky Hill 06067-3405
1-800-392-2122

Connecticut Market Data. 1994, Approx. 120 pp.

Delaware

Delaware Development Office, P.O. Box 1401, 99 Kings Highway, Dover 19903
302-739-4271

Delaware Data Book, 1993. 141 pp.

University of Delaware Bureau of Economic Research, College of Business and Economics, Newark 19716-2730
302-831-8401

Delaware Economic Report 1993-94. 200 pp. Annual

District of Columbia

Office of Planning, Data Management Division, Presidential Bldg., Suite 500, 415 12th St., N.W. Washington 20004
202-727-6533

1990 Census, Population and Housing for the District of Columbia 72 pp.

1990 Census: Social, Economic and Housing Characteristics. (44 pp. for each of nine volumes).

Socio-Economic Indicators by Census Tract. 221 pp.

Socio-Economic Indicators of Change by Census Tract, 1980-1990. 146 pp.

Office of Policy and Evaluation, Executive Office of the Mayor, 1 Judiciary Square, Suite 1000, 441 4th St., N.W., Washington 20001
202-727-4016

Indices—A Statistical Index to DC Services, Dec. 1993. Annual. 340 pp.

Florida

University of Florida, Bureau of Economic and Business Research, Gainesville 32611-2017
904-392-0171

Florida Statistical Abstract, 1993. 27th ed. 760 pp. Also available on diskette.

National Data Consultants, P.O. Box 6381, Athens, Georgia 30604
706-548-8460

Florida County Perspectives: 1993. Annual. 110 pp.

Georgia

University of Georgia, Selig Center for
Economic Growth,
Terry College of Business,
Athens 30602-6269
706-542-4085

Georgia Statistical Abstract, 1992-93. 1992.
535 pp. 1994-1995 edition will be released
in December 1994.

University of Georgia, College of Agricultural
and Environmental Sciences,
Cooperative Extension Service,
Athens 30602
706-542-8938

The Georgia County Guide. 1994. 13th ed.
Annual. 200 pp.

Office of Planning and Budget,
254 Washington St., S.W.,
Atlanta 30334-8501
404-656-0911

Georgia Descriptions in Data. 1990-91.
249 pp.

Hawaii

Hawaii State Department of Business, and
Economic Development & Tourism,
Research and Economic Analysis Division,
Statistics Branch
P.O. Box 2359,
Honolulu 96804.
Inquiries 808-586-2481;
Copies 808-586-2424

*The State of Hawaii Data Book 1992:
A Statistical Abstract.* 26th ed. 1993.
618 pp.

Idaho

Department of Commerce,
700 West State St., Boise 83720
208-334-2470

County Profiles of Idaho, 1994

Idaho Community Profiles, 1994.

Idaho Facts, 1994.

Idaho Facts Data Book, 1993.

Profile of Rural Idaho 1993.

University of Idaho, Center for Business
Development and Research,
Moscow 83844-3227
208-885-6611

Idaho Statistical Abstract. 1980. 415 pp.
(Out of print.)

Illinois

University of Illinois, Bureau of Economic
and Business Research,
428 Commerce West,
1206 South 6th Street,
Champaign 61820. 217-333-2330

Illinois Statistical Abstract. 1993. 766 pages.

Indiana

Indiana University, Indiana Business
Research Center, School of Business,
801 W. Michigan BS4015
Indianapolis 46202-5151
317-274-2204

Indiana Factbook, 1994-95. 413 pages.

Iowa

Iowa Department of Economic Development
Research Bureau, 200 East Grand Ave.,
Des Moines 50309

1994 Statistical Profile of Iowa.

Kansas

University of Kansas,
Institute for Public Policy and Business
Research,
607 Blake Hall, Lawrence 66045-2960
913-864-3701

Kansas Statistical Abstract, 1992-93.
28th ed. 1994.

Kentucky

Department of Existing Business and Industry,
Capital Plaza Office Tower,
Frankfort 40601
502-564-4886

Kentucky Deskbook of Economic Statistics.
30th ed.

Louisiana

University of New Orleans,
Division of Business and Economic
Research,
New Orleans 70148
504-286-6248

Statistical Abstract of Louisiana.
9th ed. 1994.

Maine

Maine Department of Economic and
Community Development,
State House Station 59, Augusta 04333
207-287-3153

Maine: A Statistical Summary.
(Updated periodically.)

Maryland

Department of Economic and Employment
Development, 217 E. Redwood St.,
Baltimore 21202
Inquiries 410-333-6953;
Copies 410-333-6955

Maryland Statistical Abstract. 1993-94.
274 pp. Biennial.

Massachusetts

Massachusetts Institute for
Social and Economic Research,
128 Thompson Hall,
University of Massachusetts at Amherst
01003
413-5453460
FAX 413-545-3686

*Projected Total Population and Age
Distribution for 2000 and 2005:
Massachusetts Cities and Towns.*
June 1994.

Michigan

Wayne State University, Bureau of Business
Research, School of Business Administration,
Detroit 48202

Michigan Statistical Abstract. 20th ed.
1986-87. 629 pp.

Minnesota

Department of Trade and Economic Development, Business and Community Development Division, 500 Metro Square Building, St. Paul 55101 612-296-8283

Compare Minnesota: An Economic and Statistical Factbook, 1994-95. 165 pp.

Economic Report to the Governor: State of Minnesota, 1992. 148 pp.

Office of State Demographer, Minnesota Planning, 300 Centennial Bldg., St. Paul 55155 612-296-2557

Minnesota Population and Household Estimates, 1993. Available after mid-July on diskette only, in Lotus, dBase or ASCII formats. Summary analysis available in printed form by late fall.

Mississippi

Mississippi State University, College of Business and Industry, Division of Research, Mississippi State 39762. 601-325-3817

Mississippi Statistical Abstract. 1993. 750 pp.

Missouri

University of Missouri, Business and Public Administration Research Center, Columbia 65211. 314-882-4805

Statistical Abstract for Missouri, 1993 Biennial. 280 pp.

Montana

Montana Department of Commerce, Census and Economic Information Center, 1424 9th Ave., Helena 59620 406-444-2896

Statistical Reports from the Montana County Database. (Separate county and State reports; will be available by subject section as well as complete reports by county and State, updated periodically, available in paper and diskette.)

Nebraska

Department of Economic Development, Division of Research, Box 94666, Lincoln 68509. 402-471-3779

Nebraska Statistical Handbook. 1994-1995. 300 pp.

Nevada

Department of Administration, Budget and Planning Division, Capitol Complex, Carson City 89710 702-687-4065

Nevada Statistical Abstract. 1994. Biennial. 405 pp.

New Hampshire

Office of State Planning, 2 1/2 Beacon St., Concord 03301 603-271-2155

Current Estimates and Trends in New Hampshire's Housing Supply. Update: 1992. 32 pp.

1992 Population Estimates for New Hampshire Cities and Towns, New Hampshire Population Projections for Cities and Towns 1990-2015.

New Jersey

New Jersey State Data Center, NJ Department of Labor, CN 388, Trenton 08625-0388 609-984-2593

New Jersey Statistical Factbook, 1992. 115 pp.

New Jersey Source Book, 1993. 156 pp.

New Mexico

University of New Mexico, Bureau of Business and Economic Research, 1920 Lomas N.E. Albuquerque 87131-6021 505-277-2216

County Profiles. 1994. 72 pp. The County Profiles are available from New Mexico Economic Development Department 505-827-0300. They can be accessed on line by dialing 1-800-283-2638 and entering ONESTOP.

New York

Nelson Rockefeller Institute of Government, 411 State Street, Albany 12203-1003 518-443-5522

New York State Statistical Yearbook, 1994. 19th ed. 580 pp.

North Carolina

Office of Governor

Office of State Planning, 116 West Jones Street, Raleigh 27603-8003 919-733-4131

Statistical Abstract of North Carolina Counties, 1991. 6th edition.

North Dakota

University of North Dakota, Bureau of Business and Economic Research, Grand Forks 58202. 701-777-2637

The Statistical Abstract of North Dakota. 1988. 700 pp.

North Dakota Department of Economic Development and Finance 1833 E. Bismarck Expressway, Bismarck 58504 701-221-5300

North Dakota Economic Data Book. 1988. 100 pp. (No longer available.)

Ohio

Department of Development, Office of Statistical Research, P.O. Box 1001, Columbus 43266-0101 614-466-2115

Research Products and Services. (Updated continuously.)

The Ohio State University, School of Public Policy and Management, 1775 College Road, Columbus 43210-1399 614-292-8696

Benchmark Ohio, 1991. Biennial. 300 pp.

Oklahoma

University of Oklahoma, Center for Economic and Management Research, 307 West Brooks Street, Room 4, Norman 73019 405-325-2931

Statistical Abstract of Oklahoma, 1993. Annual. 543 pp.

Oregon

Secretary of State, Room 136,
State Capitol, Salem 97310

Oregon Blue Book. 1993-1994. Biennial.
441 pp. $12.

Pennsylvania

Pennsylvania State Data Center,
Institute of State and Regional Affairs,
Penn State Harrisburg, 777 West Harrisburg
Pike, Middleton Pennsylvania 17057-4898.
717-948-6336

Pennsylvania Statistical Abstract, 1992.
30th ed. 1992. 249 pp.

Rhode Island

Department of Economic Development,
7 Jackson Walkway, Providence 02903
401-277-2601

*Rhode Island 1990 Census of Population
and Housing Summary.* 1990.

The Rhode Island Economy. May 1994.

South Carolina

Budget and Control Board, Office of Research
and Statistical Services,
R. C. Dennis Building, Room 425,
Columbia 29201. 803-734-3780.

South Carolina Statistical Abstract: 1994.
430 pp.

South Dakota

University of South Dakota, State Data Center,
Vermillion 57069 605-677-5287

*Selected Social and Economic
Characteristics.* 550 pp.

1993 South Dakota Community Abstracts.
400 pp.

Tennessee

University of Tennessee, Center for Business
and Economic Research,
Knoxville 37996-4170. 615-9745441

Tennessee Statistical Abstract, 1992-93.
14th ed. 800 pp. Annual.

Texas

Dallas Morning News,
Communications Center,
P.O. Box 655237, Dallas 75265.
214-977-8261

Texas Almanac, 1994-1995. 1993.
672 pp.

University of Texas, Bureau of Business
Research, Austin 78712. 512-471-5180

Texas Fact Book, 1989. 6th ed. 250 pp.

Utah

University of Utah, Bureau of Economic
and Business Research,
401 Kendall D. Garff Building,
Salt Lake City 84112. 801-581-6333

Statistical Abstract of Utah. 1993.
Triennial.

Utah Foundation,
10 West 100 South 323,
Salt Lake City 84101-1544
801-364-1837

Statistical Review of Government in Utah.
1993. 135 pp.

Vermont

Office of Policy and Information,
Department of Employment and Training,
Montpelier 05601
802-828-4202

Demographic and Economic Profiles. Annual

Virginia

University of Virginia, Weldon Cooper
Center for Public Service,
Dynamics Building, 4th Floor, 2015 Ivy Road,
Charlottesville 22903
804-924-3921

Virginia Statistical Abstract, 1994-95.
Biennial. 950 pp.

Washington

Washington State Office of Financial
Management, Forecasting Division
P.O. Box 43113 Olympia, WA 98504-3113
206-753-5617

Washington State Data Book, 1993.
Biennial. 306 pp.

Population Trends for Washington State.
Annual. 48 pp.

West Virginia

West Virginia Chamber of Commerce,
P.O. Box 2789, Charleston 25330
304-342-1115

*West Virginia: Economic-Statistical Profile,
1994.* Biennial. 750 pp.

West Virginia Research League, Inc.,
405 Capitol Street, Suite 414,
Charleston 25301
304-346-9451

Economic Indicators. 1994. 110 pp.

The 1993 Statistical Handbook. 94 pp.

Wisconsin

Wisconsin Legislative Reference Bureau,
P.O. Box 2037, Madison 53701-2037
608-266-0341

1992-1994 Wisconsin Blue Book.
1,000 pp. Biennial. 1994-95 edition will be
published September/October 1995.

Wyoming

Department of Administration and Information,
Division of Economic Analysis,
327 E. Emerson Building, Cheyenne 82002
307-777-7504

The Equality State Almanac 1993. 310 pp.

Puerto Rico

Planning Board, Area of Economic
and Social Planning, Bureau of Economic
Analysis and Bureau of Statistics,
Santurce 00940
809-722-2070

Monthly Economic Indicators. December
1993.

*Historic Series of Employment,
Unemployment and Labor Force, 1992.*

Social Statistics Abstract. 1990.

Socioeconomic Statistics of Puerto Rico.
1992.

Guide to Foreign Statistical Abstracts

This bibliography presents recent statistical abstracts for Mexico, Russia, and member nations of the Organization for Economic Cooperation and Development. All sources contain statistical tables on a variety of subjects for the individual countries. Many of the following publications provide text in English as well as in the national language(s). For further information on these publications, contact the named statistical agency which is responsible for editing the publication.

Austria

Osterreichisches Statistisches Zentralamt, P.O. Box 9000, A-1033 Vienna

Statistisches Handbuch for die Republik Osterreich. Annual. 1993. 599 pp. (In German.)

Australia

Australian Bureau of Statistics, Canberra

Yearbook Australia. Annual. 1994. 869 pp. (In English.)

Belgium

Institut National de Statistique, 44 rue de Louvain, 1000 Brussels

Annuaire statistique de la Belgique. Annual. 1990. 791 pp. (In French and Dutch.)

Canada

Statistics Canada, Ottawa, Ontario, KIA OT6

Canada Yearbook: A review of economic, social and political developments in Canada. 1994. 707 pp. Irregular. (In English and French.)

Croatia

Republika Hrvatska, Republicki Zavod Za Statistiku

Statisticki Ljetopis 1992. 601 pp. (In English and Serbo-Croatian.)

Czech Republic

Czech Statistical Office, Sokolovska 142, 186 04 Praha 8

Statisticka Rocenka Ceske Rpubliky 1993. 441 pp. (In English and Czech.)

Denmark

Danmarks Statistik, Postboks 2550 Seqrogade 11, DK 2100, Copenhagen

Statistical Yearbook. 1993. Annual. 566 pp. (In Danish with English translations of table headings.)

Finland

Central Statistical Office of Finland, Box 504 SF-00101 Helsinki

Statistical Yearbook of Finland. Annual. 1993. 620 pp. (In English, Finnish, and Swedish.)

France

Institut National de la Statistique et des Etudes Economiques, Paris 18, Bld. Adolphe Pinard, 75675 Paris (Cedex 14)

Annuaire Statistique de la France. Annual. 1993. 856 pp. (In French.)

Greece

National Statistical Office, 14-16 Lycourgou St., 101-66 Athens

Concise Statistical Yearbook 1990-91 254 pp. (In English.)

Statistical Yearbook of Greece. Annual. 1989. 535 pp. (plus 7 pages of diagrams). (In English and Greek.)

Iceland

Hagstofa Islands/Statistical Bureau, Hverfisgata 8-10, Reykjavik.

Statistical Abstract of Iceland. 1992. Irregular. 280 pp. (In English and Icelandic.)

Ireland

Central Statistics Office, Earlsfort Terrace, Dublin 2

Statistical Abstract. Annual. 1993. 426 pp. (In English.)

Italy

ISTAT (Istituto Centrale di Statistica), Via Cesare Balbo 16, 00100 Rome

Annuario Statistico Italiano. Annual. 1993 565 pp. (In Italian.)

Japan

Statistics Bureau, Management & Coordination Agency, 19-1 Wakamatsucho, Shinjuku Tokyo 162

Japan Statistical Yearbook. Annual. 1993/94. 871 pp. (In English and Japanese.)

Luxembourg

STATEC (Service Central de la Statistique et des Etudes), P.O. Box 304, L-2013, Luxembourg

Annuaire Statistique. Annual. 1992. 529 pp. (In French.)

Mexico

Instituto Nacional de Estadistica Geografia e Informatica, Avda. Insurgentes Sur No. 795-PH Col. Napoles, Del. Benito Juarez 03810 Mexico, D.F.

Anuario estadistico de los Estados Unidos Mexicanos. Annual. 1992. 610 pp. (In Spanish.)

Netherlands

Centraal Bureau voor de Statistiek. 428 Prinses Beatrixlaan P.O. Box 959, 2270 AZ Voorburg

Statistisch Yearbook 1993. 568 pp. (In Dutch.)

New Zealand

Department of Statistics, Wellington

New Zealand Official Yearbook. Annual.
1992. 484 pp. (In English.)

Norway

Central Bureau of Statistics, Skippergate 15,
P.B. 8131 Dep. N-Oslo 1

Statistical Yearbook. Annual. 1993. 495 pp.
(In English and Norwegian.)

Portugal

INE (Instituto Nacional de Estatistica), Avenida
Antonio Jose de Almeida, P-1078 Lisbon
Codex

Anuario Estatistico: de Portugal. 1992
336 pp. (In Portugese.)

Russia

State Committee of Statistics of Russia,
Moscow

*Russian Federation in the Year 1992.
Statistical Yearbook.* 1993. 645 pp.
(In Russian.)

Slovakia

Statistical Office of the Slovak Republic,
Mileticova 3, 824 67 Bratislava

Statisticka Rocenka Slovensak 1991.
514 pp. (In English and Slovak)

Slovenia

Statistical Office of the Republic of Slovenia,
Vozarski Pot 12, 61000 Ljubljana

Statisticni Letopis Republike Slovenije 1992.
530 pp. (In Slovenian.)

Spain

INE (Instituto Nacional de Estadistica),
Paseo de la Castellana, 183, Madrid 16

Anuario Estadistico de Espana. Annual.
1992. 859 pp. (In Spanish.)

Anuario Estadistico. 1988. (Edicion Manual.)
976 pp.

Sweden

Statistics Sweden, S-11581 Stockholm

Statistical Abstract of Sweden. Annual.
1994. 563 pp.
(In English and Swedish.)

Switzerland

Bundesamt fur Statistik, Hallwylstrasse 15,
CH-3003, Bern

Statistisches Jahrbuch der Schweiz.
Annual. 1994. 448 pp.
(In French and German.)

Turkey

State Institute of Statistics, Prime Ministry,
114 Necatibey Caddesi, Bakanliklar,
Yenisehir, Ankara

Statistical Yearbook of Turkey.
Published on odd numbered years.
1991. 639 pp.
(In English and Turkish.)

Statistical Pocketbook of Turkey.
Published on even numbered years.
1990. 312 pp.
(In English and Turkish.)

United Kingdom

Central Statistical Office,
Great George Street,
London SW1P 3AQ

Annual Abstract of Statistics. Annual.
1991. 349 pp. (In English.)

West Germany

Statistische Bundesamt, Postfach 5528,
6200 Wiesbaden

*Statistisches Jahrbuch fur die
Bundesrepublic Deutschland.* Annual.
1993. 790 pp. (In German.)

Metropolitan Areas: Concepts, Components, and Population

Statistics for metropolitan areas (MA's) shown in the *Statistical Abstract* represent areas designated by the U.S. Office of Management and Budget (OMB) as metropolitan statistical areas (MSA's), consolidated metropolitan statistical areas (CMSA's), and primary metropolitan statistical areas (PMSA's).

The general concept of an MA is that of a core area containing a large population nucleus, together with adjacent communities having a high degree of economic and social integration with that core. Currently defined MA's are based on application of 1990 standards (which appeared in the *Federal Register* on March 30, 1990) to 1990 decennial census data. These MA definitions were announced by OMB effective June 30, 1993.

In this appendix, tables A, B, and C present historical summary information for MA's and nonmetropolitan areas as defined on certain dates. Table E presents geographic components and latest populations for each MSA, CMSA, and PMSA. As of the June 1993 OMB announcement, there were 250 MSA's, and 18 CMSA's comprising 73 PMSA's in the United States. (In addition, there were 3 MSA's, 1 CMSA, and 3 PMSA's in Puerto Rico; MA's in Puerto Rico do not appear in these tables.) Table D presents definitions and data for New England county metropolitan areas (NECMA's), the county-based alternative metropolitan areas for the city- and town-based MSA's and CMSA's of the six New England States.

Standard definitions of metropolitan areas were first issued in 1949 by the then Bureau of the Budget (predecessor of OMB), under the designation "standard metropolitan area" (SMA). The term was changed to "standard metropolitan statistical area" (SMSA) in 1959, and to "metropolitan statistical area" (MSA) in 1983. The current collective term "metropolitan area" (MA) became effective in 1990. OMB has been responsible for the official metropolitan areas since they were first defined, except for the period 1977 to 1981, when they were the responsibility of the Office of Federal Statistical Policy and Standards, Department of Commerce.

The standards for defining metropolitan areas were modified in 1958, 1971, 1975, 1980, and 1990.

Defining MSA's, CMSA's, and PMSA's. The current standards provide that each MSA must include at least: (a) One city with 50,000 or more inhabitants, or (b) A Census Bureau-defined urbanized area (of at least 50,000 inhabitants) and a total metropolitan population of at least 100,000 (75,000 in New England).

Under the standards the county (or counties) that contains the largest city becomes the central county (counties), along with any adjacent counties that have at least 50 percent of their population in the urbanized area surrounding the largest city. Additional "outlying counties" are included in the MSA if they meet specified requirements of commuting to the central counties and other selected requirements of metropolitan character (such as population density and percent urban). In New England, the MSA's are defined in terms of cities and towns rather than counties.

An area that meets these requirements for recognition as an MSA and also has a population of one million or more may be recognized as a CMSA if: 1) separate component areas can be identified within the entire area by meeting statistical criteria specified in the standards, and 2) local opinion indicates there is support for the component areas. If recognized, the component areas are designated PMSA's, and the entire area becomes a CMSA. (PMSA's, like the CMSA's that contain them, are composed of individual or groups of counties outside New England, and cities and towns within New England.) If no PMSA's are recognized, the entire area is designated as an MSA.

The largest city in each MSA/CMSA is designated a "central city," and additional cities qualify if specified requirements are met concerning population size and commuting patterns. The title of each MSA consists of the names of up to three of its central cities and the name of each State into which the MSA extends. However, a central city with less than one-third the population of the area's largest city is not included in an MSA title unless local opinion desires its inclusion. Titles of PMSA's also typically are based on central city names but in certain cases consist of county names. Generally, titles of CMSA's are based on the names of their component PMSA's.

A 1990 census list, CPH-L-145, showing 1990 and 1980 populations for current MA's and their component counties or New England subcounty areas is available through the Statistical Information Office, Population Division, (301) 763-5002. A 1990 census Supplementary Report, 1990 CPH-S-1-1, *Metropolitan Areas as Defined by the Office of Management and Budget, June 30, 1993,* contains extensive population and housing statistics for the current MA's and is available from the U.S. Government Printing Office (GPO) (stock number 003-024-08738-3). Also available from the GPO is the Census Bureau's wall map for the 1993 MA's (stock number 003-024-08740-5).

Defining NECMA's.

Defining NECMA's. The OMB defines NECMA's as a county-based alternative for the city- and town-based New England MSA's and CMSA's. The NECMA for an MSA or CMSA includes: 1) the county containing the first-named city in that MSA/CMSA title (this county may include the first-named cities of other MSA's/CMSA's as well), and 2) each additional county having at least half its population in the MSA's/CMSA's whose first-named cities are in the previously identified county. NECMA's are not identified for individual PMSA's. There are twelve NECMA's, including one for the Boston-Worcester-Lawrence CMSA and one for the portion of the New York-Northern New Jersey-Long Island CMSA in Connecticut.

Central cities of a NECMA are those cities in the NECMA that qualify as central cities of an MSA or a CMSA. NECMA titles derive from names of central cities of MSA's/CMSA's.

Changes in MA definitions over time. Changes in the definitions of MA's since the 1950 census have consisted chiefly of (1) the recognition of new areas as they reached the minimum required city or area population; and (2) the addition of counties or New England cities and towns to existing areas as new census data showed them to qualify. Also, former separate MA's have been merged with other areas, and occasionally territory has been transferred from one MA to another or from an MA to nonmetropolitan territory. The large majority of changes have taken place on the basis of decennial census data, although the MA standards specify the bases for intercensal updates.

Because of these changes in definition, users must be cautious in comparing MA data from different dates. For some purposes, comparisons of data for MA's as defined at given dates may be appropriate. To facilitate constant-area comparisons, data for earlier dates have been revised in tables where possible to reflect the MA boundaries of the more recent date.

In tables A, B, and C below, data are given for MA's as defined for specific dates, thereby indicating the extent of change in population and land area resulting from revisions in definitions.

Table A. Number, Population, and Land Area of MA's as Defined at Specified Dates From 1960 to 1993

[The differences in population shown here for each year within each column of the table result entirely from net expansion of metropolitan territory through changes in the MA definitions. The differences in population over time shown for each MA definition (on the successive lines of the table) result entirely from population changes within that territory, unaffected by changes in MA definitions. The changes in 1990 land area result entirely from net change in MA territory. All data include Alaska and Hawaii and exclude Puerto Rico. Subtraction of any line of the table from the line below will show the net effect of change in population and land area undergone by the MA's as the result of changes in definitions between the specified dates. Such changes may have occurred throughout the period, not on any single date, and may have included reductions in, as well as additions to, MA territory. Census population data through 1980 include corrections made since publication. The area data for the 1960, 1970, and 1980 census definitions of MA's differ from the data published in those censuses because of subsequent remeasurement of land areas and changes in inland water area occurring for the 1990 census]

MA DEFINITION AS OF—	Number of MA's	POPULATION					Land area, 1990 (sq. mi.)
		1960 (April 1)	1970 (April 1)	1980 (April 1)	1990 (April 1)	1992 (July 1)	
1960 census (Nov. 1960)	212	[1]112,885,139	130,982,661	140,793,427	155,088,626	(NA)	308,742
1964 (Aug. 31) [2]	217	115,876,343	134,700,911	145,503,863	160,500,956	(NA)	348,400
1968 (Jan. 31) [3]	230	118,413,604	137,976,252	149,811,057	165,707,672	(NA)	377,042
1970 census (Feb. 28, 1971). . .	243	[4]119,593,498	[5]139,479,806	151,662,221	167,896,646	(NA)	386,241
1974 (Apr. 30) [6]	265	[7]126,613,710	148,198,993	162,753,335	181,125,276	(NA)	490,551
1977 (Dec. 31) [8]	277	127,674,818	149,482,664	164,383,496	182,989,860	(NA)	509,841
1980 census (June 30, 1981) [9] .	318	131,318,714	153,693,762	169,430,623	188,759,597	(NA)	565,288
1983 (June 30)	[10]275	132,633,988	155,411,328	171,776,970	191,634,355	(NA)	559,752
1984 (June 30)	[10]277	132,707,748	155,519,340	171,955,900	191,903,497	(NA)	563,796
1985 (June 30)	[10]280	132,887,134	155,700,823	172,169,456	192,135,964	(NA)	569,816
1986 (June 30)	[10]281	132,977,580	155,805,452	172,304,016	192,314,367	(NA)	571,745
1987 (June 30) [11]	[10]281	133,003,445	155,832,688	172,334,547	192,345,395	(NA)	572,284
1988 (June 30) [12]	[10]282	133,088,400	155,937,275	172,454,948	192,476,951	(NA)	573,560
1989 (June 30) [12]	[10]283	133,233,777	156,084,580	172,601,873	192,618,846	(NA)	574,622
1990 census (June 30, 1990) [12] .	[10]284	133,275,412	156,137,337	172,679,870	192,725,741	(NA)	580,136
1992 (Dec. 31) [12]	[10]268	(NA)	(NA)	176,662,797	197,466,567	202,903,519	669,927
1993 (June 30) [12] [13]	[10]268	(NA)	(NA)	176,892,735	197,724,892	203,172,185	673,057

NA Not available. [1] Corresponds to total MA population for 1960 published in 1960 census (112,885,178), corrected by subtracting population (39) erroneously included in Franklin County, Ohio (Columbus metropolitan area). [2] MA's as defined for the 1963 economic censuses. [3] MA's as defined for the 1967 economic censuses. [4] Corresponds to total 1960 population for 1970 MA's published in 1970 census (119,594,754), corrected by subtracting 1,256 population from Lawrence-Haverhill metropolitan area; this represented an addition to the 1960 population of Andover town made subsequent to the original census tabulations, and therefore not reflected in State or national totals. [5] Corresponds to total MA population for 1970 published in 1970 census (139,418,811), plus net corrections made subsequent to publication. [6] MA's as defined for the 1972 economic censuses. [7] Includes 1960 population (82,833) of Anchorage Census Division, as defined in 1970. [8] MA's as defined for the 1977 economic censuses. [9] MA's as defined for the 1982 economic censuses. [10] MSA's and CMSA's. [11] MA's as defined for the 1987 economic censuses. [12] Data exclude the portion of Sullivan city in Crawford County, MO (1990 population 1,116) added to the St. Louis, MO-IL MSA by congressional action effective Dec. 22, 1987. [13] MA's as defined for the 1992 economic censuses.

Source: U.S. Bureau of the Census, 1960-70, *U.S. Census of Population*, vol. 1; *1980 Census of Population*, vol. 1, chapters A and B and *Supplementary Report, Metropolitan Statistical Areas* (PC80-S1-18); *1990 Census of Population and Housing Data Paper Listing* (CPH-L-10 and CPH-L-118); *1990 Census of Population and Housing, Supplementary Reports, Metropolitan Areas as Defined by the Office of Management and Budget, June 30, 1993*, (1990 CPH-S-1-1); and *Population Paper Listing* (PPL-2).

Table B. Nonmetropolitan Population and Land Area as Defined at Specified Dates From 1960 to 1993

[See headnote for table A. Nonmetropolitan population and land area are equivalent to that portion of the total national population and land area not included within MA's at the dates specified]

METROPOLITAN AREA DEFINITION AS OF—	POPULATION					Land area, 1990 (sq. mi.)
	1960 (April 1)	1970 (April 1)	1980 (April 1)	1990 (April 1)	1992 (July 1)	
1960 census (Nov. 1960)	66,438,036	72,319,370	85,752,378	93,621,247	(NA)	3,231,027
1964 (Aug. 31)	63,446,832	68,601,120	81,041,942	88,208,917	(NA)	3,191,368
1968 (Jan. 31)	60,909,571	65,325,779	76,734,748	83,002,201	(NA)	3,162,726
1970 census (Feb. 28, 1971)	59,729,677	63,822,225	74,883,584	80,813,227	(NA)	3,153,527
1974 (Apr. 30)	52,709,465	55,103,038	63,792,470	67,584,597	(NA)	3,049,218
1977 (Dec. 31)	51,648,357	53,819,367	62,162,309	65,720,013	(NA)	3,029,928
1980 census (June 30, 1981)	48,004,461	49,608,264	57,115,182	59,950,276	(NA)	2,974,481
1983 (June 30)	46,689,187	47,890,703	54,768,835	57,075,518	(NA)	2,980,016
1984 (June 30)	46,615,427	47,782,691	54,589,905	56,806,376	(NA)	2,975,972
1985 (June 30)	46,436,041	47,601,208	54,376,349	56,573,909	(NA)	2,969,952
1986 (June 30)	46,345,595	47,496,579	54,241,789	56,395,506	(NA)	2,968,023
1987 (June 30)	46,319,730	47,469,343	54,211,258	56,364,478	(NA)	2,967,484
1988 (June 30)	46,234,775	47,364,756	54,090,857	56,232,922	(NA)	2,966,208
1989 (June 30)	46,089,398	47,217,451	53,943,932	56,091,027	(NA)	2,965,146
1990 census (June 30, 1990)	46,047,763	47,164,694	53,865,935	55,984,132	(NA)	2,959,632
1992 (Dec. 31)	(NA)	(NA)	49,883,008	51,243,306	52,174,017	2,866,411
1993 (June 30)	(NA)	(NA)	49,649,464	50,984,981	51,905,351	2,863,281

NA Not available.

Table C. Percent of Total U.S. Population and Percent of Land Area Inside MA's as Defined at Specified Dates From 1960 to 1993

[See headnote for table A]

METROPOLITAN AREA DEFINITION AS OF—	PERCENT OF POPULATION					Percent of land area, 1990
	1960 (April 1)	1970 (April 1)	1980 (April 1)	1990 (April 1)	1992 (July 1)	
1960 census (Nov. 1960)	63.0	64.4	62.1	62.4	(NA)	8.7
1964 (Aug. 31)	64.6	66.3	64.2	64.5	(NA)	9.8
1968 (Jan. 31)	66.0	67.9	66.1	66.6	(NA)	10.7
1970 census (Feb. 28, 1971)	66.7	68.6	66.9	67.5	(NA)	10.9
1974 (Apr. 30)	70.6	72.9	71.8	72.8	(NA)	13.9
1977 (Dec. 31)	71.2	73.5	72.6	73.6	(NA)	14.4
1980 census (June 30, 1981)	73.2	75.6	74.8	75.9	(NA)	16.0
1983 (June 30)	74.0	76.4	75.8	77.1	(NA)	15.8
1984 (June 30)	74.0	76.5	75.9	77.2	(NA)	15.9
1985 (June 30)	74.1	76.6	76.0	77.3	(NA)	16.1
1986 (June 30)	74.2	76.6	76.1	77.3	(NA)	16.2
1987 (June 30)	74.2	76.7	76.1	77.3	(NA)	16.2
1988 (June 30)	74.2	76.7	76.1	77.4	(NA)	16.2
1989 (June 30)	74.3	76.8	76.2	77.4	(NA)	16.2
1990 census (June 30, 1990)	74.3	76.8	76.2	77.5	(NA)	16.4
1992 (Dec. 31)	(NA)	(NA)	78.0	79.4	79.5	18.9
1993 (June 30)	(NA)	(NA)	78.1	79.5	79.7	19.0

NA Not available.

Source: U.S. Bureau of the Census, 1960-70, *U.S. Census of Population*, vol. 1; *1980 Census of Population*, vol. 1, chapters A and B and *Supplementary Report, Metropolitan Statistical Areas* (PC80-S1-18); *1990 Census of Population and Housing Data Paper Listing* (CPH-L-10 and CPH-L-118); *1990 Census of Population and Housing, Supplementary Reports, Metropolitan Areas as Defined by the Office of Management and Budget, June 30, 1993*, (1990 CPH-S-1-1); and *Population Paper Listing* (PPL-2).

Table D. New England County Metropolitan Areas (NECMA's)

[In thousands. As of July 1]

NECMA	Population, 1992	NECMA	Population, 1992	NECMA	Population, 1992
Bangor, ME	146	**Burlington, VT**	181	**New London-Norwich, CT**	248
Penobscot County	146	Chittenden County	134	New London County	248
Barnstable-Yarmouth, MA	189	Franklin County	41	**Pittsfield, MA**	137
Barnstable County	189	Grand Isle County	6	Berkshire County	137
Boston-Worcester-Lawrence-		**Hartford, CT**	1,121	**Portland, ME**	244
Lowell-Brockton, MA-NH	5,670	Hartford County	847	Cumberland County	244
Bristol County, MA	507	Middlesex County	145	**Providence-Warwick-**	
Essex County, MA	670	Tolland County	130	**Pawtucket, RI**	915
Middlesex County, MA	1,394	**Lewiston-Auburn, ME**	104	Bristol County	49
Norfolk County, MA	621	Androscoggin County	104	Kent County	162
Plymouth County, MA	440	**New Haven-Bridgeport-**		Providence County	591
Suffolk County, MA	639	**Stamford-Waterbury-**		Washington County	113
Worcester County, MA	708	**Danbury, CT**	1,630	**Springfield, MA**	600
Hillsborough County, NH	340	Fairfield County	829	Hampden County	452
Rockingham County, NH	246	New Haven County	801	Hampshire County	147
Strafford County, NH	105				

Source: U.S. Bureau of the Census, *Population Paper Listing* (PPL-7).

Table E. Metropolitan Areas and Their Components as of June 30, 1993

[Population estimated as of July 1, 1992. All metropolitan areas are arranged alphabetically. For relationship of PMSA's to their CMSA's, see CMSA entry]

	Population, 1992 (1,000)		Population, 1992 (1,000)		Population, 1992 (1,000)
Abilene, TX MSA	121	Cobb County	479	Billings, MT MSA	118
Taylor County	121	Coweta County	60	Yellowstone County	118
Akron, OH PMSA	669	De Kalb County	564	Biloxi-Gulfport-Pascagoula, MS	
Portage County	146	Douglas County	75	MSA	324
Summit County	523	Fayette County	70	Hancock County	33
		Forsyth County	50	Harrison County	170
Albany, GA MSA	115	Fulton County	666	Jackson County	121
Dougherty County	98	Gwinnett County	392		
Lee County	17	Henry County	68	Binghamton, NY MSA	266
		Newton County	45	Broome County	212
Albany-Schenectady-Troy,		Paulding County	47	Tioga County	53
NY MSA	872	Pickens County	15		
Albany County	293	Rockdale County	59	Birmingham, AL MSA	859
Montgomery County	52	Spalding County	56	Blount County	40
Rensselaer County	156	Walton County	41	Jefferson County	658
Saratoga County	188			St. Clair County	53
Schenectady County	150	Atlantic-Cape May, NJ PMSA	326	Shelby County	107
Schoharie County	32	Atlantic County	229		
		Cape May County	97	Bismarck, ND MSA	86
Albuquerque, NM MSA	616			Burleigh County	62
Bernalillo County	499	Augusta-Aiken, GA-SC MSA.	444	Morton County	24
Sandoval County	69	Columbia County, GA.	73		
Valencia County	48	McDuffie County, GA	21	Bloomington, IN MSA	111
		Richmond County, GA	202	Monroe County	111
Alexandria, LA MSA	131	Aiken County, SC	129		
Rapides Parish	131	Edgefield County, SC	19	Bloomington-Normal, IL	
				MSA	133
Allentown-Bethlehem-		Austin-San Marcos, TX MSA.	901	McLean County	133
Easton, PA MSA	606	Bastrop County	40		
Carbon County	58	Caldwell County	27	Boise City, ID MSA	320
Lehigh County	296	Hays County	68	Ada County	223
Northampton County	252	Travis County	613	Canyon County	96
		Williamson County	153		
Altoona, PA MSA	131			Boston, MA-NH PMSA	3,211
Blair County	131	Bakersfield, CA MSA	588	Bristol County, MA (pt.)	94
		Kern County	588	Essex County, MA (pt.)	430
Amarillo, TX MSA	192			Middlesex County, MA (pt.)	1,118
Potter County	100	Baltimore, MD PMSA	2,434	Norfolk County, MA (pt.)	616
Randall County	92	Anne Arundel County	441	Plymouth County, MA (pt.)	224
		Baltimore County	705	Suffolk County, MA	639
Anchorage, AK MSA	246	Carroll County	130	Worcester County, MA (pt.)	82
Anchorage Borough	246	Harford County	195	Rockingham County, NH (pt.)	7
		Howard County	200		
Ann Arbor, MI PMSA	505	Queen Anne's County	35	Boston-Worcester-	
Lenawee County	94	Baltimore city	726	Lawrence, MA-NH-ME-CT	
Livingston County	123			CMSA	5,439
Washtenaw County	288	Bangor, ME MSA	90	Boston, MA-NH PMSA	3,211
		Penobscot County (pt.)	87	Brockton, MA PMSA	236
Anniston, AL MSA	116	Waldo County (pt.)	3	Fitchburg-Leominster, MA PMSA	137
Calhoun County	116			Lawrence, MA-NH PMSA	357
		Barnstable-Yarmouth, MA MSA	137	Lowell, MA-NH PMSA	283
Appleton-Oshkosh-Neenah,		Barnstable County (pt.)	137	Manchester, NH PMSA	175
WI MSA	324			Nashua, NH PMSA	171
Calumet County	35	Baton Rouge, LA MSA	546	New Bedford, MA PMSA	173
Outagamie County	144	Ascension Parish	61	Portsmouth-Rochester, NH-ME	
Winnebago County	145	East Baton Rouge Parish	392	PMSA	219
		Livingston Parish	74	Worcester, MA-CT PMSA	477
Asheville, NC MSA	197	West Baton Rouge Parish	20		
Buncombe County	180			Boulder-Longmont, CO	
Madison County	17	Beaumont-Port Arthur, TX		PMSA	238
		MSA	370	Boulder County	238
Athens, GA MSA	129	Hardin County	43		
Clarke County	88	Jefferson County	243	Brazoria, TX PMSA	204
Madison County	22	Orange County	83	Brazoria County	204
Oconee County	19				
		Bellingham, WA MSA	138	Bremerton, WA PMSA	211
Atlanta, GA MSA	3,143	Whatcom County	138	Kitsap County	211
Barrow County	32				
Bartow County	60	Benton Harbor, MI MSA	161	Bridgeport, CT PMSA	443
Carroll County	74	Berrien County	161	Fairfield County (pt.)	334
Cherokee County	102			New Haven County (pt.)	109
Clayton County	189	Bergen-Passaic, NJ PMSA	1,291		
		Bergen County	835		
		Passaic County	456		

	Popu-lation, 1992 (1,000)
Brockton, MA PMSA	236
Bristol County (pt.)	30
Norfolk County, (pt.)	5
Plymouth County, (pt.)	201
Brownsville-Harlingen, TX MSA	279
Cameron County	279
Bryan-College Station, TX MSA	125
Brazos County	125
Buffalo-Niagara Falls, NY MSA	1,194
Erie County	972
Niagara County	222
Burlington, VT MSA	154
Chittenden County (pt.)	127
Franklin County (pt.)	25
Grand Isle County (pt.)	3
Canton-Massillon, OH MSA	399
Carroll County	27
Stark County	372
Casper, WY MSA	63
Natrona County	63
Cedar Rapids, IA MSA	173
Linn County	173
Champaign-Urbana, IL MSA	175
Champaign County	175
Charleston, WV MSA	253
Kanawha County	208
Putnam County	45
Charleston-North Charleston, SC MSA	529
Berkeley County	136
Charleston County	305
Dorchester County	88
Charlotte-Gastonia-Rock Hill, NC-SC MSA	1,212
Cabarrus County, NC	104
Gaston County, NC	179
Lincoln County, NC	53
Mecklenburg County, NC	538
Rowan County, NC	113
Union County, NC	89
York County, SC	137
Charlottesville, VA MSA	134
Albemarle County	68
Fluvanna County	14
Greene County	12
Charlottesville city	41
Chattanooga, TN-GA MSA	431
Hamilton County, TN	289
Marion County, TN	25
Catoosa County, GA	44
Dade County, GA	13
Walker County, GA	59
Cheyenne, WY MSA	75
Laramie County	75
Chicago, IL PMSA	7,561
Cook County	5,139
DeKalb County	80
Du Page County	816
Grundy County	34
Kane County	334
Kendall County	41
Lake County	541
McHenry County	200
Will County	376

	Popu-lation, 1992 (1,000)
Chicago-Gary-Kenosha, IL-IN-WI CMSA	8,410
Chicago, IL PMSA	7,561
Gary, IN PMSA	617
Kankakee, IL PMSA	99
Kenosha, WI PMSA	134
Chico-Paradise, CA MSA	188
Butte County	188
Cincinnati, OH-KY-IN PMSA	1,560
Brown County, OH	36
Clermont County, OH	158
Hamilton County, OH	872
Warren County, OH	120
Boone County, KY	63
Campbell County, KY	85
Gallatin County, KY	6
Grant County, KY	17
Kenton County, KY	144
Pendleton County, KY	13
Dearborn County, IN	41
Ohio County, IN	5
Cincinnati-Hamilton, OH-KY-IN CMSA	1,865
Cincinnati, OH-KY-IN PMSA	1,560
Hamilton-Middletown, OH PMSA	305
Clarksville-Hopkinsville, TN-KY MSA	178
Montgomery County, TN	110
Christian County, KY	68
Cleveland-Akron, OH CMSA	2,890
Akron, OH PMSA	669
Cleveland-Lorain-Elyria, OH PMSA	2,221
Cleveland-Lorain-Elyria, OH PMSA	2,221
Ashtabula County	101
Cuyahoga County	1,411
Geauga County	83
Lake County	220
Lorain County	277
Medina County	129
Colorado Springs, CO MSA	421
El Paso County	421
Columbia, MO MSA	117
Boone County	117
Columbia, SC MSA	472
Lexington County	178
Richland County	294
Columbus, GA-AL MSA	270
Chattahoochee County, GA.	16
Harris County, GA	18
Muscogee County, GA	186
Russell County, AL	49
Columbus, OH MSA	1,394
Delaware County	71
Fairfield County	109
Franklin County	992
Licking County	132
Madison County	39
Pickaway County	50
Corpus Christi, TX MSA	361
Nueces County	301
San Patricio County	61
Cumberland, MD-WV MSA	102
Allegany County, MD	75
Mineral County, WV	27

	Popu-lation, 1992 (1,000)
Dallas, TX PMSA	2,795
Collin County	291
Dallas County	1,913
Denton County	295
Ellis County	88
Henderson County	60
Hunt County	65
Kaufman County	54
Rockwall County	29
Dallas-Fort Worth, TX CMSA	4,215
Dallas, TX PMSA	2,795
Fort Worth-Arlington, TX PMSA	1,419
Danbury, CT PMSA	196
Fairfield County (pt.)	165
Litchfield County (pt.)	32
Danville, VA MSA	109
Pittsylvania County	56
Danville city	54
Davenport-Moline-Rock Island, IA-IL MSA	356
Scott County, IA	155
Henry County, IL	51
Rock Island County, IL	150
Dayton-Springfield, OH MSA	962
Clark County	148
Greene County	140
Miami County	95
Montgomery County	579
Daytona Beach, FL MSA	422
Flagler County	34
Volusia County	388
Decatur, AL MSA	136
Lawrence County	32
Morgan County	104
Decatur, IL MSA	118
Macon County	118
Denver, CO PMSA	1,715
Adams County	282
Arapahoe County	421
Denver County	484
Douglas County	73
Jefferson County	456
Denver-Boulder-Greeley, CO CMSA	2,089
Boulder-Longmont, CO PMSA	238
Denver, CO PMSA	1,715
Greeley, CO PMSA	136
Des Moines, IA MSA	406
Dallas County	31
Polk County	338
Warren County	37
Detroit, MI PMSA	4,308
Lapeer County	79
Macomb County	728
Monroe County	136
Oakland County	1,119
St. Clair County	150
Wayne County	2,096
Detroit-Ann Arbor-Flint, MI CMSA	5,246
Ann Arbor, MI PMSA	505
Detroit, MI PMSA	4,308
Flint, MI PMSA	434
Dothan, AL MSA	133
Dale County	50
Houston County	83

	Popu- lation, 1992 (1,000)		Popu- lation, 1992 (1,000)		Popu- lation, 1992 (1,000)
Dover, DE MSA	**116**	**Fort Smith, AR-OK MSA**	**181**	**Greenville-Spartanburg-**	
Kent County	116	Crawford County, AR	44	**Anderson, SC MSA**	**853**
		Sebastian County, AR	101	Anderson County	148
Dubuque, IA MSA	**87**	Sequoyah County, OK	35	Cherokee County	46
Dubuque County	87			Greenville County	328
		Fort Walton Beach, FL		Pickens County	99
Duluth, MN-WI MSA	**241**	**MSA**	**153**	Spartanburg County	233
St. Louis County, MN	199	Okaloosa County	153		
Douglas County, WI	42			**Hagerstown, MD PMSA**	**125**
		Fort Wayne, IN MSA	**463**	Washington County	125
Dutchess County, NY PMSA.	**263**	Adams County	31		
Dutchess County	263	Allen County	305	**Hamilton-Middletown, OH**	
		De Kalb County	37	**PMSA**	**305**
Eau Claire, WI MSA	**140**	Huntington County	36	Butler County	305
Chippewa County	53	Wells County	26		
Eau Claire County	87	Whitley County	28	**Harrisburg-Lebanon-**	
				Carlisle, PA MSA	**601**
El Paso, TX MSA	**628**	**Fort Worth-Arlington, TX**		Cumberland County	201
El Paso County	628	**PMSA**	**1,419**	Dauphin County	242
		Hood County	31	Lebanon County	116
Elkhart-Goshen, IN MSA	**159**	Johnson County	100	Perry County	42
Elkhart County	159	Parker County	68		
		Tarrant County	1,220	**Hartford, CT MSA**	**1,156**
Elmira, NY MSA	**95**			Hartford County (pt.)	845
Chemung County	95	**Fresno, CA MSA**	**805**	Litchfield County (pt.)	38
		Fresno County	706	Middlesex County (pt.)	98
Enid, OK MSA	**56**	Madera County	99	New London County (pt.)	18
Garfield County	56			Tolland County (pt.)	129
		Gadsden, AL MSA	**100**	Windham County (pt.)	28
Erie, PA MSA	**280**	Etowah County	100		
Erie County	280			**Hickory-Morganton, NC MSA**	**299**
		Gainesville, FL MSA	**189**	Alexander County	28
Eugene-Springfield, OR		Alachua County	189	Burke County	77
MSA	**291**			Caldwell County	72
Lane County	291	**Galveston-Texas City, TX**		Catawba County	122
		PMSA	**228**		
Evansville-Henderson, IN-KY		Galveston County	228	**Honolulu, HI MSA**	**863**
MSA	**283**			Honolulu County	863
Posey County, IN	26	**Gary, IN PMSA**	**617**		
Vanderburgh County, IN	166	Lake County	482	**Houma, LA MSA**	**187**
Warrick County, IN	47	Porter County	135	Lafourche Parish	87
Henderson County, KY	44			Terrebonne Parish	100
		Glens Falls, NY MSA	**121**		
Fargo-Moorhead, ND-MN		Warren County	60	**Houston, TX PMSA**	**3,530**
MSA	**158**	Washington County	60	Chambers County	21
Cass County, ND	107			Fort Bend County	256
Clay County, MN	51	**Goldsboro, NC MSA**	**108**	Harris County	2,972
		Wayne County	108	Liberty County	55
Fayetteville, NC MSA	**277**			Montgomery County	204
Cumberland County	277	**Grand Forks, ND-MN MSA**	**103**	Waller County	24
		Grand Forks County, ND	71		
Fayetteville-Springdale-		Polk County, MN	32	**Houston-Galveston-**	
Rogers, AR MSA	**226**			**Brazoria, TX CMSA**	**3,962**
Benton County	106	**Grand Rapids-Muskegon-**		Brazoria, TX PMSA	204
Washington County	120	**Holland, MI MSA**	**964**	Galveston-Texas City, TX	
		Allegan County	93	PMSA	228
Fitchburg-Leominster, MA PMSA	**137**	Kent County	512	Houston, TX PMSA	3,530
Middlesex County (pt.)	3	Muskegon County	162		
Worcester County (pt.)	134	Ottawa County	197	**Huntington-Ashland,**	
				WV-KY-OH MSA	**315**
Flint, MI PMSA	**434**			Cabell County, WV	96
Genesee County	434	**Great Falls, MT MSA**	**79**	Wayne County, WV	42
		Cascade County	79	Boyd County, KY	51
Florence, AL MSA	**134**			Carter County, KY	25
Colbert County	52	**Greeley, CO PMSA**	**136**	Greenup County, KY	37
Lauderdale County	82	Weld County	136	Lawrence County, OH	63
Florence, SC MSA	**119**	**Green Bay, WI MSA**	**201**	**Huntsville, AL MSA**	**308**
Florence County	119	Brown County	201	Limestone County	57
				Madison County	251
Fort Collins-Loveland, CO		**Greensboro—Winston-**			
MSA	**198**	**Salem—High Point, NC**		**Indianapolis, IN MSA**	**1,424**
Larimer County	198	**MSA**	**1,078**	Boone County	38
		Alamance County	111	Hamilton County	121
Fort Lauderdale, FL PMSA	**1,301**	Davidson County	130	Hancock County	48
Broward County	1,301	Davie County	28	Hendricks County	79
		Forsyth County	271	Johnson County	93
Fort Myers-Cape Coral, FL		Guilford County	358	Madison County	132
MSA	**352**	Randolph County	110	Marion County	813
Lee County	352	Stokes County	39	Morgan County	59
		Yadkin County	31	Shelby County	41
Fort Pierce-Port St. Lucie,					
FL MSA	**265**	**Greenville, NC MSA**	**112**	**Iowa City, IA MSA**	**98**
Martin County	104	Pitt County	112	Johnson County	98
St. Lucie County	161				

	Popu-lation, 1992 (1,000)
Jackson, MI MSA	152
Jackson County	152
Jackson, MS MSA	405
Hinds County	255
Madison County	58
Rankin County	92
Jackson, TN MSA	80
Madison County	80
Jacksonville, FL MSA	953
Clay County	114
Duval County	701
Nassau County	47
St. Johns County	90
Jacksonville, NC MSA	145
Onslow County	145
Jamestown, NY MSA	142
Chautauqua County	142
Janesville-Beloit, WI MSA	143
Rock County	143
Jersey City, NJ PMSA	555
Hudson County	555
Johnson City-Kingsport-Bristol, TN-VA MSA	445
Carter County, TN	52
Hawkins County, TN	46
Sullivan County, TN	147
Unicoi County, TN	17
Washington County, TN	95
Scott County, VA	23
Washington County, VA	47
Bristol city, VA	18
Johnstown, PA MSA	241
Cambria County	162
Somerset County	79
Joplin, MO MSA	138
Jasper County	92
Newton County	46
Kalamazoo-Battle Creek, MI MSA	436
Calhoun County	138
Kalamazoo County	226
Van Buren County	72
Kankakee, IL PMSA	99
Kankakee County	99
Kansas City, MO-KS MSA	1,617
Cass County, MO	67
Clay County, MO	159
Clinton County, MO	17
Jackson County, MO	634
Lafayette County, MO	31
Platte County, MO	62
Ray County, MO	22
Johnson County, KS	375
Leavenworth County, KS	67
Miami County, KS	24
Wyandotte County, KS	159
Kenosha, WI PMSA	134
Kenosha County	134
Killeen-Temple, TX MSA	255
Bell County	191
Coryell County	64
Knoxville, TN MSA	610
Anderson County	71
Blount County	90
Knox County	348
Loudon County	33
Sevier County	55
Union County	14

	Popu-lation, 1992 (1,000)
Kokomo, IN MSA	99
Howard County	82
Tipton County	16
La Crosse, WI-MN MSA	118
La Crosse County, WI	99
Houston County, MN	19
Lafayette, IN MSA	165
Clinton County	32
Tippecanoe County	133
Lafayette, LA MSA	353
Acadia Parish	56
Lafayette Parish	171
St. Landry Parish	81
St. Martin Parish	45
Lake Charles, LA MSA	172
Calcasieu Parish	172
Lakeland-Winter Haven, FL MSA	419
Polk County	419
Lancaster, PA MSA	434
Lancaster County	434
Lansing-East Lansing, MI MSA	436
Clinton County	59
Eaton County	95
Ingham County	282
Laredo, TX MSA	148
Webb County	148
Las Cruces, NM MSA	147
Dona Ana County	147
Las Vegas, NV-AZ MSA	971
Clark County, NV	846
Nye County, NV	20
Mohave County, AZ	106
Lawrence, KS MSA	85
Douglas County	85
Lawrence, MA-NH PMSA	357
Essex County, MA (pt.)	240
Rockingham County, NH (pt.)	117
Lawton, OK MSA	120
Comanche County	120
Lewiston-Auburn, ME MSA	92
Androscoggin County (pt.)	92
Lexington, KY MSA	420
Bourbon County	19
Clark County	30
Fayette County	233
Jessamine County	32
Madison County	60
Scott County	25
Woodford County	21
Lima, OH MSA	156
Allen County	110
Auglaize County	46
Lincoln, NE MSA	220
Lancaster County	220
Little Rock-North Little Rock, AR MSA	526
Faulkner County	64
Lonoke County	41
Pulaski County	353
Saline County	67
Longview-Marshall, TX MSA	197
Gregg County	108
Harrison County	57
Upshur County	32

	Popu-lation, 1992 (1,000)
Los Angeles-Long Beach, CA PMSA	9,054
Los Angeles County	9,054
Los Angeles-Riverside-Orange County, CA CMSA	15,048
Los Angeles-Long Beach, CA PMSA	9,054
Orange County, CA PMSA	2,485
Riverside-San Bernardino, CA PMSA	2,823
Ventura, CA PMSA	687
Louisville, KY-IN MSA	968
Bullitt County, KY	51
Jefferson County, KY	671
Oldham County, KY	36
Clark County, IN	90
Floyd County, IN	67
Harrison County, IN	31
Scott County, IN	22
Lowell, MA-NH PMSA	283
Middlesex County, MA (pt.)	273
Hillsborough County, NH (pt.)	10
Lubbock, TX MSA	225
Lubbock County	225
Lynchburg, VA MSA	198
Amherst County	29
Bedford County	48
Campbell County	49
Bedford city	6
Lynchburg city	66
Macon, GA MSA	299
Bibb County	152
Houston County	94
Jones County	21
Peach County	22
Twiggs County	10
Madison, WI MSA	380
Dane County	380
Manchester, NH PMSA	175
Hillsborough County (pt.)	133
Merrimack County (pt.)	13
Rockingham County (pt.)	28
Mansfield, OH MSA	175
Crawford County	48
Richland County	128
McAllen-Edinburg-Mission, TX MSA	421
Hidalgo County	421
Medford-Ashland, OR MSA	154
Jackson County	154
Melbourne-Titusville-Palm Bay, FL MSA	426
Brevard County	426
Memphis, TN-AR-MS MSA	1,034
Fayette County, TN	26
Shelby County, TN	845
Tipton County, TN	39
Crittenden County, AR	50
De Soto County, MS	74
Merced, CA MSA	189
Merced County	189
Miami, FL PMSA	2,008
Dade County	2,008
Miami-Fort Lauderdale, FL CMSA	3,309
Fort Lauderdale, FL PMSA	1,301
Miami, FL PMSA	2,008

	Popu-lation, 1992 (1,000)		Popu-lation, 1992 (1,000)		Pop latio 199 (1,00
Middlesex-Somerset-Hunterdon, NJ PMSA	1,047	**New London-Norwich, CT-RI MSA**	284	**Odessa-Midland, TX MSA** . .	2
Hunterdon County	112	Middlesex County, CT (pt.) .	10	Ector County	1
Middlesex County	684	New London County, CT (pt.)	226	Midland County	1
Somerset County	250	Windham County, CT (pt.) .	19	
Milwaukee-Racine, WI CMSA	1,629	Washington County, RI (pt.).	29	**Oklahoma City, OK MSA** . . .	9
Milwaukee-Waukesha, WI				Canadian County	
PMSA	1,450	**New Orleans, LA MSA**	1,303	Cleveland County	1
Racine, WI PMSA	180	Jefferson Parish	458	Logan County	
		Orleans Parish	490	McClain County	
Milwaukee-Waukesha, WI PMSA	1,450	Plaquemines Parish	26	Oklahoma County	6
Milwaukee County	952	St. Bernard Parish	67	Pottawatomie County	5
Ozaukee County	76	St. Charles Parish	44	
Washington County	102	St. James Parish	21	**Olympia, WA PMSA**	1
Waukesha County	320	St. John the Baptist Parish .	41	Thurston County	1
Minneapolis-St. Paul, MN-WI MSA	2,618	St. Tammany Parish	156	**Omaha, NE-IA MSA**	6
Anoka County, MN	259	**New York, NY PMSA**	8,552	Cass County, NE.	
Carver County, MN	52	Bronx County	1,195	Douglas County, NE	4
Chisago County, MN	32	Kings County	2,286	Sarpy County, NE	1
Dakota County, MN	296	New York County	1,489	Washington County, NE . . .	
Hennepin County, MN	1,041	Putnam County	87	Pottawattamie County, IA . .	4
Isanti County, MN	27	Queens County	1,951	
Ramsey County, MN	486	Richmond County	391	**Orange County, CA PMSA** . .	2,4
Scott County, MN	62	Rockland County	271	Orange County	2,4
Sherburne County, MN. . . .	46	Westchester County	882	**Orlando, FL MSA**	1,3
Washington County, MN. . .	158			Lake County	1
Wright County, MN	72	**New York-Northern New Jersey-Long Island, NY-NJ-CT-PA**		Orange County	7
Pierce County, WI	33	**CMSA**	19,670	Osceola County	1
St. Croix County, WI	52	Bergen-Passaic, NJ PMSA .	1,291	Seminole County	3
Mobile, AL MSA	496	Bridgeport, CT PMSA	443	
Baldwin County	106	Danbury, CT PMSA	196	**Owensboro, KY MSA**	
Mobile County	389	Dutchess County, NY PMSA	263	Daviess County	
Modesto, CA MSA	395	Jersey City, NJ PMSA	555	**Panama City, FL MSA**	1
Stanislaus County	395	Middlesex-Somerset-Hunterdon, NJ PMSA	1,047	Bay County	1
Monmouth-Ocean, NJ PMSA	1,004	Monmouth-Ocean, NJ PMSA	1,004	**Parkersburg-Marietta, WV-OH MSA**	1
Monmouth County	566	Nassau-Suffolk, NY PMSA .	2,640	Wood County, WV.	
Ocean County	438	New Haven-Meriden, CT PMSA	527	Washington County, OH. . .	
Monroe, LA MSA	145	New York, NY PMSA	8,552	**Pensacola, FL MSA**	3
Ouachita Parish	145	Newark, NJ PMSA	1,923	Escambia County	2
		Newburgh, NY-PA PMSA . .	348	Santa Rosa County	
Montgomery, AL MSA	304	Stamford-Norwalk, CT PMSA	331	
Autauga County	36	Trenton, NJ PMSA	328	**Peoria-Pekin, IL MSA**	3
Elmore County	53	Waterbury, CT PMSA	222	Peoria County	1
Montgomery County	215			Tazewell County	1
Muncie, IN MSA	120	**Newark, NJ PMSA**	1,923	Woodford County	
Delaware County	120	Essex County	773	**Philadelphia, PA-NJ PMSA** . .	4,9
		Morris County	428	Bucks County, PA	5
Myrtle Beach, SC MSA	152	Sussex County	135	Chester County, PA	3
Horry County	152	Union County	493	Delaware County, PA.	5
		Warren County	94	Montgomery County, PA. . .	6
Naples, FL MSA	165			Philadelphia County, PA . . .	1,5
Collier County	165	**Newburgh, NY-PA PMSA** . . .	348	Burlington County, NJ	3
		Orange County, NY	316	Camden County, NJ.	5
Nashua, NH PMSA	171	Pike County, PA	33	Gloucester County, NJ. . . .	2
Hillsborough County (pt.) . .	171			Salem County, NJ	
		Norfolk-Virginia Beach-Newport News, VA-NC MSA	1,497	
Nashville, TN MSA	1,023	Gloucester County, VA. . . .	31	**Philadelphia-Wilmington-Atlantic City, PA-NJ-DE-MD**	
Cheatham County	29	Isle of Wight County, VA . .	26	**CMSA**	5,9
Davidson County	518	James City County, VA . . .	37	Atlantic-Cape May, NJ PMSA	4,9
Dickson County	37	Mathews County, VA	8	Philadelphia, PA-NJ PMSA .	4,9
Robertson County	44	York County, VA	47	Vineland-Millville-Bridgeton, NJ PMSA	1
Rutherford County	129	Chesapeake city, VA	166	Wilmington-Newark, DE-MD PMSA	5
Sumner County	108	Hampton city, VA	137	
Williamson County	89	Newport News city, VA . . .	177	**Phoenix-Mesa, AZ MSA**	2,3
Wilson County	71	Norfolk city, VA	254	Maricopa County	2,2
		Poquoson city, VA	11	Pinal County	1
Nassau-Suffolk, NY PMSA . .	2,640	Portsmouth city, VA	104	
Nassau County	1,302	Suffolk city, VA	53	**Pine Bluff, AR MSA**	
Suffolk County	1,338	Virginia Beach city, VA . . .	417	Jefferson County	
		Williamsburg city, VA	12	
New Bedford, MA PMSA . . .	173	Currituck County, NC	15	**Pittsburgh, PA MSA**	2,4
Bristol County (pt.)	159			Allegheny County	1,3
Plymouth County (pt.)	14	**Oakland, CA PMSA**	2,148	Beaver County	1
		Alameda County	1,308	Butler County	1
New Haven-Meriden, CT PMSA	527	Contra Costa County	841	Fayette County	1
Middlesex County (pt.) . . .	18			Washington County	2
New Haven County (pt.) . . .	509	**Ocala, FL MSA**	208	Westmoreland County	3
		Marion County	208	

	Popu-lation, 1992 (1,000)
Pittsfield, MA MSA	87
Berkshire County (pt.)	87
Portland, ME MSA	222
Cumberland County (pt.)	202
York County (pt.)	20
Portland-Salem, OR-WA CMSA	1,897
Portland-Vancouver, OR-WA PMSA	1,605
Salem, OR PMSA	292
Portland-Vancouver, OR-WA PMSA	1,605
Clackamas County, OR	297
Columbia County, OR	39
Multnomah County, OR	601
Washington County, OR	338
Yamhill County, OR	69
Clark County, WA	261
Portsmouth-Rochester, NH-ME PMSA	219
Rockingham County, NH (pt.)	84
Strafford County, NH (pt.)	98
York County, ME (pt.)	37
Providence-Fall River-Warwick, RI-MA MSA	1,131
Bristol County, RI	49
Kent County, RI	162
Newport County, RI (pt.)	23
Providence County, RI	591
Washington County, RI (pt.)	82
Bristol County, MA (pt.)	224
Provo-Orem, UT MSA	275
Utah County	275
Pueblo, CO MSA	124
Pueblo County	124
Punta Gorda, FL MSA	119
Charlotte County	119
Racine, WI PMSA	180
Racine County	180
Raleigh-Durham-Chapel Hill, NC MSA	909
Chatham County	40
Durham County	188
Franklin County	38
Johnston County	86
Orange County	100
Wake County	457
Rapid City, SD MSA	85
Pennington County	85
Reading, PA MSA	343
Berks County	343
Redding, CA MSA	158
Shasta County	158
Reno, NV MSA	269
Washoe County	269
Richland-Kennewick-Pasco, WA MSA	161
Benton County	120
Franklin County	41
Richmond-Petersburg, VA MSA	896
Charles City County	6
Chesterfield County	225
Dinwiddie County	20
Goochland County	15
Hanover County	68
Henrico County	223

	Popu-lation, 1992 (1,000)
New Kent County	11
Powhatan County	17
Prince George County	28
Colonial Heights city	16
Hopewell city	24
Petersburg city	40
Richmond city	202
Riverside-San Bernardino, CA PMSA	2,823
Riverside County	1,288
San Bernardino County	1,534
Roanoke, VA MSA	226
Botetourt County	26
Roanoke County	80
Roanoke city	97
Salem city	24
Rochester, MN MSA	110
Olmsted County	110
Rochester, NY MSA	1,081
Genesee County	61
Livingston County	63
Monroe County	724
Ontario County	98
Orleans County	44
Wayne County	91
Rockford, IL MSA	340
Boone County	33
Ogle County	47
Winnebago County	259
Rocky Mount, NC MSA	137
Edgecombe County	56
Nash County	81
Sacramento, CA PMSA	1,419
El Dorado County	138
Placer County	187
Sacramento County	1,093
Sacramento-Yolo, CA CMSA	1,563
Sacramento, CA PMSA	1,419
Yolo, CA PMSA	145
Saginaw-Bay City-Midland, MI MSA	403
Bay County	112
Midland County	78
Saginaw County	212
St. Cloud, MN MSA	153
Benton County	31
Stearns County	121
St. Joseph, MO MSA	98
Andrew County	15
Buchanan County	83
St. Louis, MO-IL MSA	2,519
Franklin County, MO	84
Jefferson County, MO	178
Lincoln County, MO	30
St. Charles County, MO	226
St. Louis County, MO	1,001
Warren County, MO	21
St. Louis city, MO	384
Clinton County, IL	34
Jersey County, IL	21
Madison County, IL	253
Monroe County, IL	23
St. Clair County, IL	263
Salem, OR PMSA	292
Marion County	239
Polk County	53
Salinas, CA MSA	368
Monterey County	368

	Popu-lation, 1992 (1,000)
Salt Lake City-Ogden, UT MSA	1,128
Davis County	200
Salt Lake County	764
Weber County	165
San Angelo, TX MSA	99
Tom Green County	99
San Antonio, TX MSA	1,379
Bexar County	1,233
Comal County	55
Guadalupe County	67
Wilson County	24
San Diego, CA MSA	2,601
San Diego County	2,601
San Francisco, CA PMSA	1,626
Marin County	234
San Francisco County	729
San Mateo County	664
San Francisco-Oakland-San Jose, CA CMSA	6,410
Oakland, CA PMSA	2,148
San Francisco, CA PMSA	1,626
San Jose, CA PMSA	1,529
Santa Cruz-Watsonville, CA PMSA	231
Santa Rosa, CA PMSA	401
Vallejo-Fairfield-Napa, CA PMSA	475
San Jose, CA PMSA	1,529
Santa Clara County	1,529
San Luis Obispo-Atascadero-Paso Robles, CA MSA	221
San Luis Obispo County	221
Santa Barbara-Santa Maria-Lompoc, CA MSA	376
Santa Barbara County	376
Santa Cruz-Watsonville, CA PMSA	231
Santa Cruz County	231
Santa Fe, NM MSA	123
Los Alamos County	18
Santa Fe County	105
Santa Rosa, CA PMSA	401
Sonoma County	401
Sarasota-Bradenton, FL MSA	499
Manatee County	217
Sarasota County	282
Savannah, GA MSA	267
Bryan County	18
Chatham County	222
Effingham County	27
Scranton—Wilkes-Barre—Hazleton, PA MSA	639
Columbia County	63
Lackawanna County	217
Luzerne County	329
Wyoming County	29
Seattle-Bellevue-Everett, WA PMSA	2,124
Island County	65
King County	1,558
Snohomish County	501
Seattle-Tacoma-Bremerton, WA CMSA	3,131
Bremerton, WA PMSA	211
Olympia, WA PMSA	177
Seattle-Bellevue-Everett, WA PMSA	2,124
Tacoma, WA PMSA	620

	Population, 1992 (1,000)
Sharon, PA MSA	122
Mercer County	122
Sheboygan, WI MSA	105
Sheboygan County	105
Sherman-Denison, TX MSA	95
Grayson County	95
Shreveport-Bossier City, LA MSA	374
Bossier Parish	86
Caddo Parish	246
Webster Parish	41
Sioux City, IA-NE MSA	117
Woodbury County, IA	100
Dakota County, NE	17
Sioux Falls, SD MSA	146
Lincoln County	16
Minnehaha County	130
South Bend, IN MSA	251
St. Joseph County	251
Spokane, WA MSA	381
Spokane County	381
Springfield, IL MSA	193
Menard County	11
Sangamon County	181
Springfield, MA MSA	584
Franklin County (pt.)	3
Hampden County (pt.)	441
Hampshire County (pt.)	140
Springfield, MO MSA	276
Christian County	36
Greene County	215
Webster County	24
Stamford-Norwalk, CT PMSA	331
Fairfield County (pt.)	331
State College, PA MSA	127
Centre County	127
Steubenville-Weirton, OH-WV MSA	142
Jefferson County, OH	80
Brooke County, WV	27
Hancock County, WV	35
Stockton-Lodi, CA MSA	504
San Joaquin County	504
Sumter, SC MSA	105
Sumter County	105
Syracuse, NY MSA	752
Cayuga County	83
Madison County	71
Onondaga County	474
Oswego County	125
Tacoma, WA PMSA	620
Pierce County	620
Tallahassee, FL MSA	245
Gadsden County	42
Leon County	203
Tampa-St. Petersburg-Clearwater, FL MSA	2,107
Hernando County	110
Hillsborough County	859
Pasco County	284
Pinellas County	855
Terre Haute, IN MSA	149
Clay County	25
Vermillion County	17
Vigo County	107
Texarkana, TX-Texarkana, AR MSA	121
Bowie County, TX	82
Miller County, AR	39
Toledo, OH MSA	615
Fulton County	40
Lucas County	462
Wood County	114
Topeka, KS MSA	163
Shawnee County	163
Trenton, NJ PMSA	328
Mercer County	328
Tucson, AZ MSA	690
Pima County	690
Tulsa, OK MSA	732
Creek County	62
Osage County	42
Rogers County	58
Tulsa County	520
Wagoner County	50
Tuscaloosa, AL MSA	154
Tuscaloosa County	154
Tyler, TX MSA	154
Smith County	154
Utica-Rome, NY MSA	318
Herkimer County	66
Oneida County	252
Vallejo-Fairfield-Napa, CA PMSA	475
Napa County	113
Solano County	362
Ventura, CA PMSA	687
Ventura County	687
Victoria, TX MSA	77
Victoria County	77
Vineland-Millville-Bridgeton, NJ PMSA	138
Cumberland County	138
Visalia-Tulare-Porterville, CA MSA	331
Tulare County	331
Waco, TX MSA	192
McLennan County	192
Washington, DC-MD-VA-WV PMSA	4,360
District of Columbia	585
Calvert County, MD	57
Charles County, MD	106
Frederick County, MD	160
Montgomery County, MD	781
Prince George's County, MD	751
Arlington County, VA	172
Clarke County, VA	12
Culpeper County, VA	29
Fairfax County, VA	857
Fauquier County, VA	51
King George County, VA	14
Loudoun County, VA	94
Prince William County, VA	230
Spotsylvania County, VA	61
Stafford County, VA	71
Warren County, VA	28
Alexandria city, VA	113
Fairfax city, VA	21
Falls Church city, VA	9
Fredericksburg city, VA	21
Manassas city, VA	30
Manassas Park city, VA	7
Berkeley County, WV	63
Jefferson County, WV	38
Washington-Baltimore, DC-MD-VA-WV CMSA	6,920
Baltimore, MD PMSA	2,434
Hagerstown, MD PMSA	125
Washington, DC-MD-VA-WV PMSA	4,360
Waterbury, CT PMSA	222
Litchfield County (pt.)	39
New Haven County (pt.)	183
Waterloo-Cedar Falls, IA MSA	125
Black Hawk County	125
Wausau, WI MSA	118
Marathon County	118
West Palm Beach-Boca Raton, FL MSA	901
Palm Beach County	901
Wheeling, WV-OH MSA	158
Marshall County, WV	37
Ohio County, WV	50
Belmont County, OH	71
Wichita, KS MSA	501
Butler County	54
Harvey County	31
Sedgwick County	417
Wichita Falls, TX MSA	128
Archer County	8
Wichita County	120
Williamsport, PA MSA	120
Lycoming County	120
Wilmington, NC MSA	182
Brunswick County	54
New Hanover County	128
Wilmington-Newark, DE-MD PMSA	530
New Castle County, DE	455
Cecil County, MD	75
Worcester, MA-CT PMSA	477
Hampden County, MA (pt.)	2
Worcester County, MA (pt.)	466
Windham County, CT (pt.)	9
Yakima, WA MSA	198
Yakima County	198
Yolo, CA PMSA	145
Yolo County	145
York, PA MSA	350
York County	350
Youngstown-Warren, OH MSA	606
Columbiana County	110
Mahoning County	266
Trumbull County	230
Yuba City, CA MSA	130
Sutter County	69
Yuba County	61
Yuma, AZ MSA	118
Yuma County	118

Limitations of the Data

Introduction.—The data presented in this *Statistical Abstract* came from many sources. The sources include not only Federal statistical bureaus and other organizations that collect and issue statistics as their principal activity, but also governmental administrative and regulatory agencies, private research bodies, trade associations, insurance companies, health associations, and private organizations such as the National Education Association and philanthropic foundations. Consequently, the data vary considerably as to reference periods, definitions of terms and, for ongoing series, the number and frequency of time periods for which data are available.

The statistics presented were obtained and tabulated by various means. Some statistics are based on complete enumerations or censuses while others are based on samples. Some information is extracted from records kept for administrative or regulatory purposes (school enrollment, hospital records, securities registration, financial accounts, social security records, income tax returns, etc.), while other information is obtained explicitly for statistical purposes through interviews or by mail. The estimation procedures used vary from highly sophisticated scientific techniques, to crude "informed guesses."

Each set of data relates to a group of individuals or units of interest referred to as the *target universe* or *target population,* or simply as the *universe* or *population.* Prior to data collection the target universe should be clearly defined. For example, if data are to be collected for the universe of households in the United States, it is necessary to define a "household." The target universe may not be completely tractable. Cost and other considerations may restrict data collection to a *survey universe* based on some available list, such list may be inaccurate and out of date. This list is called a *survey frame* or *sampling frame.*

The data in many tables are based on data obtained for all population units, *a census,* or on data obtained for only a portion, or *sample,* of the population units. When the data presented are based on a sample, the sample is usually a scientifically selected *probability sample.* This is a sample selected from a list or sampling frame in such a way that every possible sample has a known chance of selection and usually each unit selected can be assigned a number, greater than zero and less than or equal to one, representing its likelihood or probability of selection.

For large-scale sample surveys, the probability sample of units is often selected as a multistage sample. The first stage of a multistage sample is the selection of a probability sample of large groups of population members, referred to as primary sampling units (PSU's). For example, in a national multistage household sample, PSU's are often counties or groups of counties. The second stage of a multistage sample is the selection, within each PSU selected at the first stage, of smaller groups of population units, referred to as secondary sampling units. In subsequent stages of selection, smaller and smaller nested groups are chosen until the ultimate sample of population units is obtained. To qualify a multistage sample as a probability sample, all stages of sampling must be carried out using probability sampling methods.

Prior to selection at each stage of a multistage (or a single stage) sample, a list of the sampling units or sampling frame for that stage must be obtained. For example, for the first stage of selection of a national household sample, a list of the counties and county groups that form the PSU's must be obtained. For the final stage of selection, lists of households, and sometimes persons within the households, have to be compiled in the field. For surveys of economic entities and for the economic census, the Census Bureau generally uses a frame constructed from the Bureau's Standard Statistical Establishment List (SSEL). The SSEL contains all establishments with payroll in the United States including small single establishment firms as well as large multi-establishment firms.

Wherever the quantities in a table refer to an entire universe, but are constructed from data collected in a sample survey, the table quantities are referred to as *sample estimates*. In constructing a sample estimate, an attempt is made to come as close as is feasible to the corresponding universe quantity that would be obtained from a complete census of the universe. Estimates based on a sample will, however, generally differ from the hypothetical census figures. Two classifications of errors are associated with estimates based on sample surveys: (1) *sampling error*—the error arising from the use of a sample, rather than a census, to estimate population quantities and (2) *nonsampling error*—those errors arising from nonsampling sources. As discussed below, the magnitude of the sampling error for an estimate can usually be estimated from the sample data. However, the magnitude of the nonsampling error for an estimate can rarely be estimated. Consequently, actual error in an estimate exceeds the error that can be estimated.

The particular sample used in a survey is only one of a large number of possible samples of the same size which could have been selected using the same sampling procedure. Estimates derived from the different samples would, in general, differ from each other. The *standard error* (SE) is a measure of the variation among the estimates derived from all possible samples. The standard error is the most commonly used measure of the sampling error of an estimate. Valid estimates of the standard errors of survey estimates can usually be calculated from the data collected in a probability sample. For convenience, the standard error is sometimes expressed as a percent of the estimate and is called the relative standard error or *coefficient of variation* (CV). For example, an estimate of 200 units with an estimated standard error of 10 units has an estimated CV of 5 percent.

A sample estimate and an estimate of its standard error or CV can be used to construct interval estimates that have a prescribed confidence that the interval includes the average of the estimates derived from all possible samples with a known probability. To illustrate, if all possible samples were selected under essentially the same general conditions, and using the same sample design, and if an estimate and its estimated standard error were calculated from each sample, then: 1) Approximately 68% of the intervals from one standard error below the estimate to one standard error above the estimate would include the average estimate derived from all possible samples; 2) approximately 90% of the intervals from 1.6 standard errors below the estimate to 1.6 standard errors above the estimate would include the average estimate derived from all possible samples; and 3) approximately 95% of the intervals from two standard errors below the estimate to two standard errors above the estimate would include the average estimate derived from all possible samples.

Thus, for a particular sample, one can say with the appropriate level of confidence (e.g., 90% or 95%) that the average of all possible samples is included in the constructed interval. Example of a confidence interval: An estimate is 200 units with a standard error of 10 units. An approximately 90% confidence interval (plus or minus 1.6 standard errors) is from 184 to 216.

All surveys and censuses are subject to nonsampling errors. Nonsampling errors are two kinds—*random* and *nonrandom*. Random nonsampling errors arise because of the varying interpretation of questions (by respondents or interviewers) and varying actions of coders, keyers, and other processors. Some randomness is also introduced when respondents must estimate values. These same errors usually have a nonrandom component. Nonrandom nonsampling errors result from total nonresponse (no usable data obtained for a sampled unit), partial or item nonresponse (only a portion of a response may be usable), inability or unwillingness on the part of respondents to provide correct information, difficulty interpreting questions, mistakes in recording or keying data, errors of collection or processing, and coverage problems (overcoverage and undercoverage of the target universe). Random nonresponse errors usually, but not always, result in an understatement of sampling errors and thus an overstatement of the precision of survey estimates. Estimating the magnitude of nonsampling errors would require special experiments or access to independent data and, consequently, the magnitudes are seldom available.

Nearly all types of nonsampling errors that affect surveys also occur in complete censuses. Since surveys can be conducted on a smaller scale than censuses, nonsampling errors can presumably be controlled more tightly. Relatively more funds and effort can perhaps be expended toward eliciting responses, detecting and correcting response error, and reducing processing errors. As a result, survey results can sometimes be more accurate than census results.

To compensate for suspected nonrandom errors, adjustments of the sample estimates are often made. For example, adjustments are frequently made for nonresponse, both total and partial. Adjustments made for either type of nonresponse are often referred to as *imputations*. Imputation for total nonresponse is usually made by substituting for the questionnaire responses of the nonrespondents the "average" questionnaire responses of the respondents. These imputations usually are made separately within various groups of sample members, formed by attempting to place respondents and nonrespondents together that have "similar" design or ancilliary characteristics. Imputation for item nonresponse is usually made by substituting for a missing item the response to that item of a respondent having characteristics that are "similar" to those of the nonrespondent.

For an estimate calculated from a sample survey, the *total error* in the estimate is composed of the sampling error, which can usually be estimated from the sample, and the nonsampling error, which usually cannot be estimated from the sample. The total error present in a population quantity obtained from a complete census is composed of only nonsampling errors. Ideally, estimates of the total error associated with data given in the *Statistical Abstract* tables should be given. However, due to the unavailability of estimates of nonsampling errors, only estimates of the levels of sampling errors, in terms of estimated standard errors or coefficients of variation, are available. To obtain estimates of the estimated standard errors

from the sample of interest, obtain a copy of the referenced report which appears at the end of each table.

Principal data bases.—Beginning below are brief descriptions of 34 of the sample surveys and censuses that provide a substantial portion of the data contained in this *Abstract.*

SECTION 1. POPULATION

Source and Title: Bureau of the Census, *Census of Population*
Tables: See tables citing *Census of Population* in section 1 and also in sections 2, 4, 6, 8, 13, 14, 21, 25, and 29.
Universe, Frequency, and Types of Data: Complete count of U.S. population conducted every 10 years since 1790. Data obtained on number and characteristics of inhabitants.
Type of Data Collection Operation: In 1970, 1980, and 1990 complete census for some items—age, sex, race, marital status, and relationship to household head. In 1970, other items collected from a 5% and a 15% probability (systematic) sample of the population. In 1980, approximately 19% of the housing units were included in the sample; in 1990, approximately 17%.
Data Collection and Imputation Procedures: In 1970, extensive use of mail questionnaires in urban areas; personal interviews in most rural areas. In 1980 and 1990, mail questionnaires were used in even more areas than in 1970, with personal interviews in the remainder. Extensive telephone and personal followup for nonrespondents was done in the censuses. Imputations were made for missing characteristics.
Estimates of Sampling Error: Sampling errors for data are estimated for all items collected by sample and vary by characteristic and geographic area. The CV's for national and State estimates are generally very small.
Other (nonsampling) Errors: Since 1950, evaluation programs have been conducted to provide information on the magnitude of some sources of nonsampling errors such as response bias and undercoverage in each census. Results from the evaluation program for the 1990 census indicate that the net under coverage amounted to about 1.5 to 2 percent of the total resident population.
Sources of Additional Material: U.S. Bureau of the Census, *The Coverage of Population in the 1980 Census,* PHC80-E4; *Content Reinterview Study: Accuracy of Data*

for Selected Population and Housing Characteristics as Measured by Reinterview, PHC80-E2; 1980 Census of Population, vol. 1., (PC80-1), appendixes B, C, and D.

Source and Title: U.S. Bureau of the Census, Current Population Survey (CPS)

Tables: See tables citing Current Population Reports primarily in section 1, but also in sections 2, 3, 4, 8, 12, 13, 14, 18, 23, and 29. Many Bureau of Labor Statistics' (BLS) tables in section 13 are CPS based.

Universe, Frequency, and Types of Data: Nationwide monthly sample survey of civilian noninstitutional population, 15 years old or over, to obtain data on employment, unemployment, and a number of other characteristics.

Type of Data Collection Operation: Multistage probability sample of about 60,000 households in 729 PSU's in 1993. Oversampling in some States and the largest MSA's to improve reliability for those areas of employment data on annual average basis. A continual sample rotation system is used. Households are in sample 4 months, out for 8 months, and in for 4 more. Month-to-month overlap is 75%; year-to-year overlap is 50%.

Data Collection and Imputation Procedures: For first and fifth months that a household is in sample, personal interviews; other months, approximately, 85% of the data collected by phone. Imputation is done for both item and total nonresponse. Adjustment for total nonresponse is done by a predefined cluster of units, by MSA size and residence; for item nonresponse imputation varies by subject matter.

Estimates of Sampling Error: Estimated CV's on national annual averages for labor force, total employment, and nonagricultural employment, 0.2%; for total unemployment and agricultural employment, 1.0% to 2.5%. The estimated CV's for family income and poverty rate for all persons in 1986 are 0.5% and 1.5%, respectively. CV's for subnational areas, such as States, would be larger and would vary by area.

Other (nonsampling) Errors: Estimates of response bias on unemployment are not available, but estimates of unemployment are usually 5% to 9% lower than estimates from reinterviews. Four to 5.0% of sample households unavailable for interviews.

Sources of Additional Material: U.S. Bureau of the Census and Bureau of Labor Statistics, Concepts and Methods Used in Labor Force Statistics from Current Population Survey (Census series P-23, No. 62; BLS Report No. 463) and Bureau of the Census, Current Population Survey (Tech. Paper 40) and Bureau of Labor Statistics,

Employment and Earnings, monthly, Explanatory Notes and Estimates of Error, tables 1-A through 1-H and BLS Handbook of Methods, Chapter 1 (Bulletin 2414.)

SECTION 2. VITAL STATISTICS

Source and Title: U.S. National Center for Health Statistics (NCHS), Vital Registration System

Tables: See tables citing Vital Statistics of the United States; 307 in section 5; and 1338 in section 29.

Universe, Frequency, and Types of Data: Annual data on births and deaths in the United States.

Type of Data Collection Operation: Mortality data based on complete file of death records, except 1972, based on 50% sample. Natality statistics 1951-71, based on 50% sample of birth certificates, except a 20% to 50% in 1967, received by NCHS. Beginning 1972, data from some States received through Vital Statistics Cooperative Program (VSCP) and complete file used; data from other States based on 50% sample. Beginning 1986, all reporting areas participated in the VSCP.

Data Collection and Imputation Procedures: Reports based on records from registration offices of all States, District of Columbia, New York City, Puerto Rico, Virgin Islands, and Guam.

Estimates of Sampling Error: For recent years, CV's for births are small due to large portion of total file in sample (except for very small estimated totals).

Other (nonsampling) Errors: Data on births and deaths believed to be at least 99% complete.

Sources of Additional Material: U.S. National Center for Health Statistics, Vital Statistics of the United States, vol. I and vol. II, annual, and Monthly Vital Statistics Report.

(See section 1 above for information pertaining to tables 102-107.)

SECTION 3. HEALTH AND NUTRITION

Source and Title: U.S. National Center for Health Statistics, National Health Interview Survey (NHIS)

Tables: 174, 175, 198, 201, 203, 207, 208, 212, and 214-217.

Universe, Frequency, and Types of Data: Continuous data collection covering the civilian noninstitutional population to obtain information on personal and demographic characteristics, illnesses, injuries, impairments, and other health topics.

Type of Data Collection Operation: Multistage probability sample of 42,000 households (in 376 PSU's) selected in groups of about four adjacent households.

Data Collection and Imputation Procedures: Personal household interviews with extensive followup of nonrespondents. Data are adjusted for nonresponse by imputation procedure based on "average" characteristics of persons in interviewed households in the same geographic area.

Estimates of Sampling Error: Estimated CV's: For physician visits by males, 1.5%; for workdays lost by males, 3.5%; for persons injured at home, 4.7%.

Other (nonsampling) Errors: Response rate was 95.7% in 1985 for the NHIS.

Sources of Additional Material: U.S. National Center for Health Statistics, "Current Estimates from the National Health Interview Survey, U.S., 1983," Vital and Health Statistics, series 10.

(See section 13 for information pertaining to table 169, section 15 for table 163, and section 27 for table 170.)

SECTION 4. EDUCATION

Source and Title: U.S. Department of Education, National Center for Education Statistics, *Higher Education General Information Survey (HEGIS), Fall Enrollment in Institutions of Higher Education;* beginning 1986, *Integrated Postsecondary Education Data Survey (IPEDS), Fall Enrollment*

Tables: 270, 271, 274 and 275.

Universe, Frequency, and Types of Data: Annual survey of all institutions and branches listed in the *Directory* to obtain data on total enrollment by sex, level of enrollment, type of program, racial/ethnic characteristics (in alternate years) and attendance status of student, and on first-time students.

Type of Data Collection Operation: Complete census.

Data Collection and Imputation Procedures: Survey package is usually mailed in the spring with surveys due at varying dates in the summer and fall; mail and phone followup procedures for nonrespondents. Missing data are imputed by using data of similar institutions.

Estimates of Sampling Error: Not applicable.

Other (nonsampling) Errors: Approximately 87% response rate.

Sources of Additional Material: U.S. Department of Education, National Center for Education Statistics, *Fall Enrollment in Higher Education,* annual.

Source and Title: U.S. Department of Education, National Center for Education Statistics, *Higher Education General Information Survey (HEGIS), Financial Statistics of Institutions of Higher Education;* beginning 1986, *Integrated Postsecondary Education Data Survey (IPEDS), Financial Statistics of Institutions of Higher Education*

Tables: 224, 227, 274, and 277.

Universe, Frequency, and Types of Data: Annual survey of all institutions and branches listed in the *Education Directory, Colleges and Universities* to obtain data on financial status and operations, including current funds revenues, current funds expenditures, and physical plant assets.

Type of Data Collection Operation: Complete census.

Data Collection and Imputation Procedures: Survey package is usually mailed in the spring with surveys due at varying dates in the summer and fall; mail and phone followup procedures for nonrespondents. Missing data are imputed by using data of similar institutions.

Estimates of Sampling Error: Not applicable.

Other (nonsampling) Errors: For 1990, a 87% response rate. Imputed expenditures amounted to about 2.8% of total expenditures.

Sources of Additional Material: U.S. Department of Education, National Center for Education Statistics, *Financial Statistics of Institutions of Higher Education,* annual.

Source and Title: U.S. Department of Education, National Center for Education Statistics, *Higher Education General Information Survey (HEGIS), Degrees and Other Formal Awards Conferred.* Beginning 1986, *Integrated Postsecondary Education Data Survey (IPEDS), Degrees and Other Formal Awards Conferred.*

Tables: 291-296.

Universe, Frequency, and Types of Data: Annual survey of all institutions and branches listed in the *Education Directory, Colleges and Universities* to obtain data on earned degrees and other formal awards, conferred by field of study, level of degree, sex, and by racial/ethnic characteristics (in alternate years).

Type of Data Collection Operation: Complete census.

Data Collection and Imputation Procedures: Survey package is usually mailed in the spring with surveys due at varying dates in the summer and fall; mail and phone followup procedures for nonrespondents. Missing data are imputed by using data of similar institutions.

Estimates of Sampling Error: Not applicable.

Other (nonsampling) Errors: For 1989-90, approximately 92.3% response rate.

Sources of Additional Material: U.S. Department of Education, National Center for Education Statistics, *Earned Degrees Conferred,* annual.

(See sections 1 and 9 for information pertaining to the Bureau of the Census and section 3 above for the National Center for Health Statistics.)

SECTION 5. LAW ENFORCEMENT, COURTS, AND PRISONS

Source and Title: U.S. Federal Bureau of Investigation, *Uniform Crime Reporting (UCR) Program*

Tables: 301-306, 308, 309, 315-317, and 319.

Universe, Frequency, and Types of Data: Monthly reports on the number of criminal offenses that become known to law enforcement agencies. Data are collected on crimes cleared by arrest, by age, sex, and race of offender, and on assaults on law enforcement officers.

Type of Data Collection Operation: Crime statistics are based on reports of crime data submitted either directly to the FBI by contributing law enforcement agencies or through cooperating State UCR programs.

Data Collection and Imputation Procedures: States with UCR programs collect data directly from individual law enforcement agencies and forward reports, prepared in accordance with UCR standards, to FBI. Accuracy and consistency edits are performed by FBI.

Estimates of Sampling Error: Not applicable.

Other (nonsampling) Errors: Coverage of 96% of the population (98% in SMSA's, 93% in "other cities," and 89% in rural areas) by UCR program, though varying number of agencies report. Some error may be present through incorrect reporting.

Sources of Additional Material: U.S. Federal Bureau of Investigation, *Crime in the United States.*

Source and Title: U.S. Bureau of Justice Statistics (BJS), *National Crime Survey*

Tables: 310-314.

Universe, Frequency, and Types of Data: Monthly survey of individuals and households in the United States to obtain data on criminal victimization of those units for compilation of annual estimates.

Type of Data Collection Operation: National probability sample survey of about 50,000 interviewed households in 376 PSU's selected from a list of addresses from the 1980 census, supplemented by new construction permits and an area sample where permits are not required.

Data Collection and Imputation Procedures: Interviews are conducted every 6 months for 3 years for each household in the sample; 8,000 households are interviewed monthly. Personal interviews are used in the first and fifth interviews; the intervening interviews are conducted by telephone whenever possible.

Estimates of Sampling Error: CV's in 1985: 2.2% for crimes of violence; 14.8% for estimate of rape counts; 5.5% for robbery counts; 2.5% for assault counts; 1.4% for personal larceny counts; 2.2% for burglary counts; 1.8% for household larceny; 1.3% for all household crimes; and 4.8% for motor vehicle theft counts.

Other (nonsampling) Errors: Respondent recall errors which may include reporting incidents for other than the reference period; interviewer coding and processing errors; and possible mistaken reporting or classifying of events. Adjustment is made for a household noninterview rate of about 4% and for a smaller within-household noninterview rate.

Sources of Additional Material: U.S. Bureau of Justice Statistics, *Criminal Victimization in the United States,* annual.

(See section 2 for details on table 307 and section 9 for details on table 326.)

SECTION 7. PARKS AND RECREATION

(See section 27 for details on table 395.)

SECTION 8. ELECTIONS

(See section 1 above for information pertaining to tables 447 and 448.)

SECTION 9. STATE AND LOCAL GOVERNMENT FINANCES AND EMPLOYMENT

Source and Title: U.S. Bureau of the Census, *Census of Governments*

Tables: See tables in section 9 citing *Census of Governments.*

Universe, Frequency, and Types of Data: Survey of all governmental units in the United States conducted every 5 years to obtain data on government revenue, expenditures, debt, assets, employment and employee retirement systems, property values, public school systems, and number, size, and structure of governments.

Type of Data Collection Operation: Complete census. List of units derived through classification of government units recently authorized in each State and identification, counting, and classification of existing local governments and public school systems.

Data Collection and Imputation Procedures: Data collected through field and office compilation of financial data from official records and reports for States and large local governments; mail canvass of selected data items, like State tax revenue and employee retirement systems; and collection of local government statistics through central collection arrangements with State governments.

Estimates of Sampling Error: Not applicable.

Other (nonsampling) Errors: Some nonsampling errors may arise due to possible inaccuracies in classification, response, and processing.

Sources of Additional Material: U.S. Bureau of the Census, *Census of Governments, 1987,* various reports, and *State Government Finances in 1990,* GF 90, No. 3.

Source and Title: U.S. Bureau of the Census, *Annual Surveys of State and Local Government*

Tables: See tables citing *Public Employment* and *Governmental Finances* in section 9; table 250 in section 4; table 326 in section 5; and table 586 in section 12.

Universe, Frequency, and Types of Data: Sample survey conducted annually to obtain data on revenue, expenditure, debt, and employment of State and local governments. Universe is all governmental units in the United States (about 83,000).

Type of Data Collection Operation: Sample of about 22,000 units includes all State governments, county governments with 50,000+ population, municipalities and townships with 25,000+ population, all school districts with 10,000+ enrollment in October 1986, and other governments meeting certain criteria; probability sample for remaining units.

Data Collection and Imputation Procedures: Field and office compilation of data from official records and reports for States and large local governments; central collection of local governmental financial data through cooperative agreements with a number of State governments; mail canvass of other units with mail and telephone followups of nonrespondents. Data for nonresponses are imputed from previous year data or obtained from secondary sources, if available.

Estimates of Sampling Error: CV's for estimates of major employment and financial items are generally less than 2% for most States and less than 1.2% for the majority of States.

Other (nonsampling) Errors: Nonresponse rate is less than 15% for number of units. Other possible errors may result from undetected inaccuracies in classification, response, and processing.

Sources of Additional Material: U.S. Bureau of the Census, *Public Employment in 1990,* GE 90, No. 1, *Governmental Finances in 1989-90,* GF 90, No. 5, and *Census of Governments, 1987,* various reports.

SECTION 10. FEDERAL GOVERNMENT

Source and Title: U.S. Internal Revenue Service, *Statistics of Income, Individual Income Tax Returns*
Tables: 521-525.
Universe, Frequency, and Types of Data: Annual study of unaudited individual income tax returns, forms 1040, 1040A, and 1040EZ, filed by U.S. citizens and residents. Data provided on various financial characteristics by size of adjusted gross income, marital status, and by taxable and nontaxable returns. Data by State, based on 100% file, also include returns from 1040NR, filed by nonresident aliens plus certain self-employment tax returns.

Type of Data Collection Operation: Annual stratified probability sample of approximately 125,000 returns broken into sample strata based on the larger of total income or total loss amounts as well as the size of business plus farm receipts. Sampling rates for sample strata varied from .025% to 100%.

Data Collection and Imputation Procedures: Computer selection of sample of tax return records. Data adjusted during editing for incorrect, missing, or inconsistent entries to ensure consistency with other entries on return.

Estimates of Sampling Error: Estimated CV's for tax year 1987: Adjusted gross income less deficit .13%; salaries and wages .20%; and tax-exempt interest received 4.51%. (State data not subject to sampling error.)

Other (nonsampling) Errors: Processing errors and errors arising from the use of tolerance checks for the data.

Sources of Additional Material: U.S. Internal Revenue Service, *Statistics of Income, Individual Income Tax Returns,* annual.

SECTION 12. SOCIAL INSURANCE AND HUMAN SERVICES

Source and Title: U.S. Social Security Administration, *Benefit Data*
Tables: 582 and 583.
Universe, Frequency, and Types of Data: All persons receiving monthly benefits under Title II of Social Security Act. Data on number and amount of benefits paid by type and State.

Type of Data Collection Operation: Data based on administrative records. Data based on 100% files, as well as 10% and 1% sample files.

Data Collection and Imputation Procedures: Records used consist of actions pursuant to applications for benefits, updated by subsequent post-entitlement actions.

Estimates of Sampling Error: Varies by size of estimate and sample file size.

Other (nonsampling) Errors: Processing errors, which are believed to be small.

Sources of Additional Material: U.S. Social Security Administration, *Annual Statistical Supplement to the Social Security Bulletin.*

Source and Title: U.S. Social Security Administration, *Supplemental Security Income (SSI) Program*

Tables: 597-600.

Universe, Frequency, and Types of Data: All eligible aged, blind, or disabled persons receiving SSI benefit payments under SSI program. Data include number of persons receiving federally administered SSI, amounts paid, and State administered supplementation.

Type of Data Collection Operation: Data based on administrative records.

Data Collection and Imputation Procedures: Data adjusted to reflect returned checks and overpayment refunds. For federally administered payments, actual adjusted amounts are used.

Estimates of Sampling Error: Not applicable.

Other (nonsampling) Errors: Processing errors, which are believed to be small.

Sources of Additional Material: U.S. Social Security Administration, *Annual Statistical Supplement to the Social Security Bulletin.*

(See section 1 above for information pertaining to the Current Population Survey, section 3 for information pertaining to the National Center for Health Statistics, and section 9 for information pertaining to Annual Surveys of State and Local Government.)

SECTION 13. LABOR FORCE, EMPLOYMENT, AND EARNINGS

Source and Title: U.S. Bureau of Labor Statistics (BLS), *Current Employment Statistics (CES) Program*

Tables: 654-656, 661; in section 3, table 169; in section 21, table 993; in section 22, table 1055; and in section 24, table 1133.

Universe, Frequency, and Types of Data: Monthly survey covering about 6 million nonagricultural establishments to obtain data on employment, hours, and earnings, by industry.

Type of Data Collection Operation: Sample survey of about 375,000 establishments in March 1993.

Data Collection and Imputation Procedures: Cooperating State agencies mail questionnaires to sample establishments to develop State and local estimates; information is forwarded to BLS where national estimates are prepared.

Estimates of Sampling Error: Estimated CV's for average weekly hours paid, 0.1% and for average hourly earnings, 0.2%.

Other (nonsampling) Errors: Estimates of employment adjusted annually to reflect complete universe. Average adjustment is 0.2%.

Sources of Additional Material: U.S. Bureau of Labor Statistics, *Employment and Earnings,* monthly, Explanatory Notes and Estimates of Error, tables 2-A through 2-G and *BLS Handbook of Methods,* Chapter 2, Bulletin 2414 (Sept. 1992).

(See section 1 above for information pertaining to the Current Population Survey.)

SECTION 14. INCOME, EXPENDITURES, AND WEALTH

(See section 1 above for information pertaining to the Bureau of the Census.)

SECTION 15. PRICES

Source and Title: U.S. Bureau of Labor Statistics (BLS), *Consumer Price Index (CPI)*

Tables: 746-750, 763, 764, and in section 3, table 163.

Universe, Frequency, and Types of Data: Monthly survey of price changes of all types of consumer goods and services purchased by urban wage earners and clerical workers prior to 1978, and urban consumers thereafter. Both indexes continue to be published.

Type of Data Collection Operation: Prior to 1978, sample of various consumer items in 56 urban areas; thereafter, in 85 PSU's, except from January 1987 through March 1988, when 91 areas were sampled.

Data Collection and Imputation Procedures: Prices of consumer items are obtained from about 57,000 housing units, and 19,000 other reporters in 85 areas. Prices of food, fuel, and a few other items are obtained monthly; prices of most other commodities and services are collected every month in the five largest geographic areas and every other month in others.

Estimates of Sampling Error: Estimates of standard errors are not available at present.

Other (nonsampling) Errors: Errors result from inaccurate reporting, difficulties in defining concepts and their operational implementation, and introduction of product quality changes and new products.

Sources of Additional Material: U.S. Bureau of Labor Statistics, *The Consumer Price Index:* 1987 Revision, Report 736, and *BLS Handbook of Methods,* Bulletin 2285.

Source and Title: U.S. Bureau of Labor Statistics, *Producer Price Index (PPI)*

Tables: 746, 753-755, and in section 21, table 1039; in section 24, table 1137; and in section 25, table 1193.

Universe, Frequency, and Types of Data: Monthly survey of producing companies to determine price changes of all commodities produced in the United States for sale in commercial transactions. Data on agriculture, forestry, fishing, manufacturing, mining, gas, electricity, public utilities, and a few services.

Type of Data Collection Operation: Probability sample of approximately 3,100 commodities and about 75,000 quotations per month.

Data Collection and Imputation Procedures: Data are collected by mail. If transaction prices are not supplied, list prices are used. Some prices are obtained from trade publications, organized exchanges, and government agencies. To calculate index, price changes are multiplied by their relative weights based on total net selling value of all commodities in 1982.

Estimates of Sampling Error: Not applicable.

Other (nonsampling) Errors: Not available at present.

Sources of Additional Material: U.S. Bureau of Labor Statistics, *BLS Handbook of Methods,* Bulletin 2285.

SECTION 17. BUSINESS ENTERPRISE

Source and Title: U.S. Internal Revenue Service, *Statistics of Income, Sole Proprietorship Returns* and *Statistics of Income Bulletin*

Tables: 832-835.

Universe, Frequency, and Types of Data: Annual study of unaudited income tax returns of nonfarm sole proprietorships, form 1040 with business schedules. Data provided on various financial characteristics by industry.

Type of Data Collection Operation: Stratified probability sample of approximately 31,000 sole proprietorships for tax year 1990. The sample is classified based on presence or absence of certain business schedules; the larger of total income or loss; and size of business plus farm receipts. Sampling rates vary from .043% to 100%.

Data Collection and Imputation Procedures: Computer selection of sample of tax return records. Data adjusted during editing for incorrect, missing, or inconsistent entries to ensure consistency with other entries on return.

Estimates of Sampling Error: Estimated CV's for tax year 1990 are not available; for 1987 (the latest available): For sole proprietorships, business receipts, 1.66%; net income, (less loss), 1.33%; depreciation 2.17%; interest expense 2.80%; and employee benefit programs 7.55%.

Other (nonsampling) Errors: Processing errors and errors arising from the use of tolerance checks for the data.

Sources of Additional Material: U.S. Internal Revenue Service, *Statistics of Income, Sole Proprietorship Returns* (for years through 1980) and *Statistics of Income Bulletin,* vol. 10, No. 1 (summer 1990).

Source and Title: U.S. Internal Revenue Service, *Statistics of Income, Partnership Returns* and *Statistics of Income Bulletin*

Tables: 832-834, 836, and 837.

Universe, Frequency, and Types of Data: Annual study of unaudited income tax returns of partnerships, Form 1065. Data provided on various financial characteristics by industry.

Type of Data Collection Operation: Stratified probability sample of approximately 28,000 partnership returns from a population of 1,660,000 filed during calendar year 1990. The sample is classified based on combinations of gross receipts, net income or loss, and total assets, and on industry. Sampling rates vary from .04% to 100%.

Data Collection and Imputation Procedures: Computer selection of sample of tax return records. Data are adjusted during editing for incorrect, missing, or inconsistent entries to ensure consistency with other entries on return. Data not available due to regulations are not imputed.

Estimates of Sampling Error: Estimated CV's for tax year 1988 (latest available): For number of partnerships, .51%; business receipts, .78%; net income, 3.03%; net loss, 2.21% and total assets, 1.22%.

Other (nonsampling) Errors: Processing errors and errors arising from the use of tolerance checks for the data.

Sources of Additional Material: U.S. Internal Revenue Service, *Statistics of Income, Partnership Returns* and *Statistics of Income Bulletin,* vol. 10, No. 1 (summer 1990).

Source and Title: U.S. Internal Revenue Service, *Corporation Income Tax Returns*

Tables: 832-834 and 840-842.

Universe, Frequency, and Types of Data:
Annual study of unaudited corporation income tax returns, Forms 1120 and 1120 (A, F, L, PC, REIT, RIC, and S), filed by corporations or businesses legally defined as corporations. Data provided on various financial characteristics by industry and size of total assets, and business receipts.

Type of Data Collection Operation: Stratified probability sample of approximately 85,000 returns for 1987, distributed by sample classes generally based on type of return, size of total assets, size of net income or deficit, and selected business activity. Sampling rates for sample strata varied from .25% to 100%.

Data Collection and Imputation Procedures: Computer selection of sample of tax return records. Data adjusted during editing for incorrect, missing, or inconsistent entries to ensure consistency with other entries on return and to achieve statistical definitions.

Estimates of Sampling Error: Estimated CV's for 1988: Number of returns in subgroups ranged from 1.4% with assets under $100,000, to 0% with assets over $100 mil.; for amount of net income and amount of income tax, .18%

Other (nonsampling) Errors: Processing errors and errors arising from the use of tolerance checks for the data.

Sources of Additional Material: U.S. Internal Revenue Service, *Statistics of Income, Corporation Income Tax Returns,* annual.

SECTION 18. COMMUNICATIONS

(See section 1 for information pertaining to table 889, and section 26 for table 898.)

SECTION 19. ENERGY

Source and Title: U.S. Energy Information Administration, *Residential Energy Consumption Survey*

Tables: 927, 928, 959, and table 1223 in section 25.

Universe, Frequency, and Types of Data: Triennial survey of households and fuel suppliers. Data are obtained on energy-related household characteristics, housing unit characteristics, use of fuels, and energy consumption and expenditures by fuel type.

Type of Data Collection Operation: Probability sample of 7,183 eligible units in 129 PSU's. For responding units, fuel consumption and expenditure data obtained from fuel suppliers to those households.

Data Collection and Imputation Procedures: Personal interviews. Extensive followup of nonrespondents including mail questionnaires for some households. Adjustments for nonrespondents were made in weighting for respondents. Most item nonresponses were imputed.

Estimates of Sampling Error: Estimated CV's for household averages: For consumption, 1.3%; for expenditures, 1.0%; for various fuels, values ranged from 1.4% for electricity to 5.9% for LPG.

Other (nonsampling) Errors: Household response rate of 86.7%. Nonconsumption data were mostly imputed for mail respondents (5.2% of eligible units). Usable responses from fuel suppliers for various fuels ranged from 82.8% for electricity to 55.7% for fuel oil.

Sources of Additional Material: U.S. Energy Information Administration, *Household Energy Consumption and Expenditures, 1987* and *Housing Characteristics,* 1987.

SECTION 21. TRANSPORTATION—LAND

(See section 1 for information pertaining to table 1005, section 13 for table 993, and section 15 for table 1039.)

SECTION 22. TRANSPORTATION—AIR AND WATER

Source and Title: U.S. Bureau of the Census, *Foreign Trade—Export Statistics*

Tables: See Bureau of the Census citations for export statistics in source notes in sections 22 and 28 and also tables 1160, 1161, and 1175 in section 24; and 1345 in section 29.

Universe, Frequency, and Types of Data: The export declarations collected by Customs are processed each month to obtain data on the movement of U.S. merchandise exports to foreign countries. Data obtained include value, quantity, and shipping weight of exports by commodity, country of destination, Customs district of exportation, and mode of transportation.

Type of Data Collection Operation: Shipper's Export Declarations are required to be filed for the exportation of merchandise valued over $1,500. Customs officials collect and transmit the documents to the Bureau of the Census on a flow basis for data compilation. Value data for shipments valued under $1,501 are estimated, based on established percentages of individual country totals.

Data Collection and Imputation Procedures: Statistical copies of Shipper's Export Declarations are received on a daily basis from Customs ports throughout the country and subjected to a monthly processing cycle. They are fully processed to the extent they reflect items valued over $1,500.

Estimates for shipments valued at $1,500 or less are made, based on established percentages of individual country totals.

Estimates of Sampling Error: Not applicable.

Other (nonsampling) Errors: Clerical and complex computer checks intercept most processing errors and minimize otherwise significant reporting errors; other nonsampling errors are caused by undercounting of exports to Canada due to the nonreceipt of some Shipper's Export Declarations.

Sources of Additional Material: U.S. Bureau of the Census, *U.S. Merchandise Trade: Exports, General Imports, and Imports for Consumption, SITC, Commodity by Country*, FT 925.

Source and Title: U.S. Bureau of the Census, *Foreign Trade—Import Statistics*

Tables: See Bureau of the Census citations for import statistics in source notes in sections 22 and 28 and also tables 1160, 1161, and 1175 in section 24; and 1345 in section 29.

Universe, Frequency, and Types of Data: The import entry documents collected by Customs are processed each month to obtain data on the movement of merchandise imported into the United States. Data obtained include value, quantity, and shipping weight by commodity, country of origin, Customs district of entry, and mode of transportation.

Type of Data Collection Operation: Import entry documents are required to be filed for the importation of goods into the United States valued over $1,000 or for articles which must be reported on formal entries. Customs officials collect and transmit statistical copies of the documents to the Bureau of the Census on a flow basis for data compilation. Estimates for shipments valued under $1,001 and not reported on formal entries are based on established percentages of individual country totals.

Data Collection and Imputation Procedures: Statistical copies of import entry documents, received on a daily basis from Customs ports of entry throughout the country, are subjected to a monthly processing cycle. They are fully processed to the extent they reflect items valued at $1,001 and over or items which must be reported on formal entries.

Estimates of Sampling Error: Not applicable.

Other (nonsampling) Errors: Verification of statistical data reporting by Customs officials prior to transmittal and a subsequent program of clerical and computer checks are utilized to hold nonsampling errors arising from reporting and/or processing errors to a minimum.

Sources of Additional Material: U.S. Bureau of the Census, *U.S. Merchandise Trade: Exports, General Imports and Imports for Consumption, SITC, Commodity by Country*, FT 925.

(See section 13 for information pertaining to table 1055.)

SECTION 23. AGRICULTURE

Source and Title: U.S. Department of Agriculture, National Agricultural Statistics Service (NASS), *Basic Area Frame Sample*

Tables: See tables citing NASS in source notes in section 23, which pertain to this or the following two surveys.

Universe, Frequency, and Types of Data: Two annual area sample surveys of U.S. farm operators: June agricultural survey collects data on planted acreage and livestock inventories; and a February Farm Costs and Returns survey that collects data on total farm production, expenses and specific commodity costs of production.

Type of Data Collection Operation: Stratified probability sample of about 16,000 land area units of about 1 sq. mile (range from 0.1 sq. mile in cities to several sq. miles in open grazing areas). Sample includes 60,000 parcels of agricultural land. About 20% of the sample replaced annually.

Data Collection and Imputation Procedures: Data collection is by personal enumeration. Imputation is based on enumerator observation or data reported by respondents having similar agricultural characteristics.

Estimates of Sampling Error: Estimated CV's range from 1% to 2% for regional estimates to 3% to 6% for State estimates of livestock inventories.

Other (nonsampling) Errors: Minimized through rigid quality controls on the collection process and careful review of all reported data.

Sources of Additional Material: U.S. Department of Agriculture, SRS, *Scope and Methods of the Statistical Reporting Service,* (name changed to National Agricultural Statistics Service), Miscellaneous Publication No. 1308, September 1983 (revised).

Source and Title: U.S. Department of Agriculture, National Agricultural Statistics Service (NASS), *Multiple Frame Surveys*

Tables: See tables citing NASS in source notes in section 23, which pertain to this or the following survey.

Universe, Frequency, and Types of Data: Surveys of U.S. farm operators to obtain data on major livestock inventories, selected crop acreages and production, grain stocks, and farm labor characteristics; and to obtain farm economic data for price indexing.

Type of Data Collection Operation: Primary frame is obtained from general or special purpose lists, supplemented by a probability sample of land areas used to estimate for list incompleteness.

Data Collection and Imputation Procedures: Mail, telephone, or personal interviews used for initial data collection. Mail nonrespondent followup by phone and personal interviews. Imputation based on average of respondents.

Estimates of Sampling Error: Estimated CV for number of hired farm workers is about 3%. Estimated CV's range from 1% to 2% for regional estimates to 3% to 6% for State estimates of livestock inventories.

Other (nonsampling) Errors: In addition to above, replicated sampling procedures used to monitor effects of changes in survey procedures.

Sources of Additional Material: U.S. Department of Agriculture, SRS, *Scope and Methods of the Statistical Reporting Service,* (name changed to National Agricultural Statistics Service), Miscellaneous Publication No. 1308, September 1983 (revised).

Source and Title: U.S. Department of Agriculture, National Agricultural Statistics Service (NASS), *Objective Yield Surveys*

Tables: See tables citing NASS in source notes in section 23, which pertain to this or the preceding survey.

Universe, Frequency, and Types of Data: Surveys for data on corn, cotton, potatoes, soybeans, wheat, and rice to forecast and estimate yields.

Type of Data Collection Operation: Random location of plots in probability sample of fields. Fields selected in June from Basic Area Frame Sample (see above).

Data Collection and Imputation Procedures: Enumerators count and measure plant characteristics in sample fields. Production measured from plots at harvest. Harvest loss measured from post harvest gleanings.

Estimates of Sampling Error: CV's for national estimates of production are about 2-3%.

Other (nonsampling) Errors: In addition to above, replicated sampling procedures used to monitor effects of changes in survey procedures.

Sources of Additional Material: U.S. Department of Agriculture, SRS, *Scope and Methods of the Statistical Reporting Service,* (name changed to National Agricultural Statistics Service), Miscellaneous Publication No. 1308, September 1983 (revised).

(See section 1 above for information pertaining to the Census of Population and Current Population Survey.)

SECTION 24. NATURAL RESOURCES

(See section 13 for information pertaining to table 1133, section 15 for table 1137, and section 22 for tables 1160, 1161 and 1175.)

SECTION 25. CONSTRUCTION AND HOUSING

Source and Title: U.S. Bureau of the Census, *Monthly Survey of Construction*
Tables: 1202 and 1204-1206.
Universe, Frequency, and Types of Data: Survey conducted monthly of newly constructed housing units (excluding mobile homes). Data are collected on the start, completion, and sale of housing. (Annual figures are aggregates of monthly estimates.)

Type of Data Collection Operation: Probability sample of housing units obtained from building permits selected from 17,000 places. For nonpermit places, multistage probability sample of new housing units selected in 169 PSU's. In those areas, all roads are canvassed in selected enumeration districts.

Data Collection and Imputation Procedures: Data are obtained by telephone inquiry and field visit.

Estimates of Sampling Error: Estimated CV of 3% to 4% for estimates of national totals, but are as high as 20% for estimated totals of more detailed characteristics, such as housing units in multiunit structures.

Other (nonsampling) Errors: Response rate is over 90% for most items. Nonsampling errors are attributed to definitional problems, differences in interpretation of questions, incorrect reporting, inability to obtain information about all cases in the sample, and processing errors.

Sources of Additional Material: U.S. Bureau of the Census. *Construction Reports,* series C20, *Housing Starts;* C22, *Housing Completions; and* C25, *New One-Family Houses Sold and For Sale.*

Source and Title: U.S. Bureau of the Census, *Value of New Construction Put in Place*
Tables: 1195-1197.
Universe, Frequency, and Types of Data: Survey conducted monthly on total value of all construction put in place in the current

month, both public and private projects. Construction values include costs of materials and labor, contractors' profits, overhead costs, cost of architectural and engineering work, and miscellaneous project costs. (Annual figures are aggregates of monthly estimates.)

Type of Data Collection Operation: Varies by type of activity: Total cost of private one-family houses started each month is distributed into value put in place using fixed patterns of monthly construction progress; using a multistage probability sample, data for private multifamily housing are obtained by mail from owners of multiunit projects. Data for residential additions and alterations are obtained in a quarterly survey measuring expenditures; monthly estimates are interpolated from quarterly data. Estimates of value of private nonhousekeeping, nonresidential buildings, and State and local government construction are obtained by mail from owners (or agents) for a probability sample of projects. Estimates of farm nonresidential construction expenditures are based on U.S. Department of Agriculture annual estimates of construction; public utility estimates are obtained from reports submitted to Federal regulatory agencies and from private utility companies; estimates for all other private construction (nonbuilding) are obtained by phasing F. W. Dodge contract award data; estimates of Federal construction are based on monthly data supplied by Federal agencies.

Data Collection and Imputation Procedures: See "Type of Data Collection Operation." Imputation accounts for approximately 20% of estimated value of construction each month.

Estimates of Sampling Error: CV estimates for private nonresidential building construction range from 3% for estimated value of industrial buildings to 10% for miscellaneous buildings. CV is approximately 2% for total new private nonresidential buildings.

Other (nonsampling) Errors: For directly measured data series based on samples, some nonsampling errors may arise from processing errors, imputations, and misunderstanding of questions. Indirect data series are dependent on the validity of the underlying assumptions and procedures.

Sources of Additional Material: U.S. Bureau of the Census, *Construction Reports,* series C30, *Value of New Construction Put in Place.*

Source and Title: U.S. Bureau of the Census, *Census of Housing*

Tables: See tables citing *Census of Housing* in source notes in section 25.

Universe, Frequency, and Types of Data: Census of all occupied and vacant housing, excluding group quarters, conducted every 10 years as part of the decennial census (see section 1 above) to determine characteristics of U.S. housing.

Type of Data Collection Operation: For 1970, 1980, and 1990, a complete count of some housing items (e.g. Owned or rented, and value). In 1970, other items collected from 5% and 15% probability samples selected from two sets of detailed questions on housing (these two sets having some common items). In 1980, approximately 19% of the housing units were included in the sample; in 1990, approximately 17%.

Data Collection and Imputation Procedures: In 1970, a self-enumeration census using a mail-out/mail-back procedure was used in most areas. In 1980 and 1990, mail questionnaires were used in even more areas than in 1970, with personal interviews in the remainder. Followup for nonrespondents and identification of vacant units done by phone and personal visit.

Estimates of Sampling Error: Sampling errors for data are estimated for all items collected by sample and vary by characteristic and geographic area.

Other (nonsampling) Errors: Evaluation studies for 1980 estimated the underenumeration of occupied housing units at 1.5%. The missed rate in 1980 for all units was 2.6% or approximately 2.3 million units, 1 million of which were vacant housing units.

Sources of Additional Material: U.S. Bureau of the Census, *1980 Census of Population and Housing, The Coverage of Housing in the 1980 Census,* PHC80-E1, July 1985.

Source and Title: U.S. Bureau of the Census, *American Housing Survey*

Tables: See tables citing *American Housing Survey* in source notes.

Universe, Frequency, and Types of Data: Conducted nationally in the fall in odd numbered years to obtain data on the approximately 103 million occupied or vacant housing units in the United States (group quarters are excluded). Data include characteristics of occupied housing units, vacant units, new housing and mobile home units, financial characteristics, recent mover households, housing and neighborhood quality indicators, and energy characteristics.

Type of Data Collection Operation: The national sample was a multistage probability sample with about 51,300 units eligible for interview in 1987. Sample units, selected within 394 PSU's, were surveyed over a 5-month period.

Data Collection and Imputation Procedures: For 1987, the survey was conducted by personal interviews. The interviewers obtained the information from the occupants or, if the unit was vacant, from informed persons such as landlords, rental agents, or knowledgeable neighbors.

Estimates of Sampling Error: For the national sample, illustrations of the S.E. of the estimates are provided in the appendix B of the 1987 report. As an example, the estimated CV is about 0.5% for the estimated percentage of owner occupied units with two persons.

Other (nonsampling) Errors: Response rate was about 97%. Nonsampling errors may result from incorrect or incomplete responses, errors in coding and recording, and processing errors. For the 1985 national sample, approximately 6% of the total housing inventory was not adequately represented by the AHS sample.

Sources of Additional Material: U.S. Bureau of the Census, *Current Housing Reports,* series H-150 and H-170, *American Housing Survey.*

(See section 1 above for information pertaining to the Census of Population, section 15 pertaining to table 1193, and section 19 for table 1223.)

Section 26. MANUFACTURES

Source and Title: U.S. Bureau of the Census, *Census of Manufactures*

Tables: See tables citing *Census of Manufactures* in source notes in section 26 and also table 898 in section 18 and table 1348 in section 29.

Universe, Frequency, and Types of Data: Conducted every 5 years to obtain information on labor, materials, capital input and output characteristics, plant location, and legal form of organization for all plants in the United States with one or more paid employees. Universe was 350,000 manufacturing establishments in 1987.

Type of Data Collection Operation: Complete enumeration of data items obtained from 200,000 firms. Administrative records from Internal Revenue Service and Social Security Administration are used for 150,000 smaller single-location firms, which were determined by various cutoffs based on size and industry.

Data Collection and Imputation Procedures: Five mail and telephone followups for larger nonrespondents. Data for small single-location firms (generally those with fewer than 10 employees) not mailed census questionnaires were estimated from administrative records of IRS and SSA. Data for nonrespondents were imputed from related responses or administrative records from IRS and SSA. Approximately 8% of total value of shipments was represented by fully imputed records in 1987.

Estimates of Sampling Error: Not applicable.

Other (nonsampling) Errors: Based on evaluation studies, estimates of nonsampling errors for 1972 were about 1.3% for estimated total payroll; 2% for total employment; and 1% for value of shipments. Estimates for later years are not available.

Sources of Additional Material: U.S. Bureau of the Census, *1987 Census of Manufactures, Industry Series, Geographic Area Series, and Subject Series.*

Source and Title: U.S. Bureau of the Census, *Annual Survey of Manufactures*

Tables: See tables citing *Annual Survey of Manufactures* in source notes.

Universe, Frequency, and Types of Data: Conducted annually to provide basic measures of manufacturing activity for intercensal years for all manufacturing establishments having one or more paid employees.

Type of Data Collection Operation: Sampling frame is 350,000 establishments in the 1987 Census of Manufactures (see above), supplemented by Social Security Administration lists of new manufacturers and new manufacturing establishments of multi-establishment companies identified annually by the Census Bureau's Company Organization Survey. A probability sample of about 55,000 establishments is selected. All establishments of companies with more than $500 million of manufacturing shipments in 1987 are included with certainty. All establishments with 250+ employees are also included with certainty along with a probability sample of smaller establishments.

Data Collection and Imputation Procedures: Survey is conducted by mail with phone and mail followups of nonrespondents. Imputation (for all nonresponse items) is based on previous year reports, or for new establishments in survey, on industry averages.

Estimates of Sampling Error: Estimated standard errors for number of employees, new expenditure, and for value added totals are given in annual publications. For U.S. level industry statistics, most estimated standard errors are 2% or less, but vary considerably for detailed characteristics.

Other (nonsampling) Errors: Response rate is about 85%. Nonsampling errors include those due to collection, reporting, and transcription errors, many of which are corrected through computer and clerical checks.

Sources of Additional Material: U.S. Bureau of the Census, *Annual Survey of Manufactures*, and Technical Paper 24.

Section 27. DOMESTIC TRADE AND SERVICES

Source and Title: U.S. Bureau of the Census, *Census of Wholesale Trade, Census of Retail Trade, Census of Service Industries*

Tables: See tables citing the above censuses in source notes in section 27 and table 1348 in section 29.

Universe, Frequency, and Types of Data: Conducted every 5 years to obtain data on number of establishments, number of employees, total payroll size, total sales, and other industry-specific statistics. In 1987, the universe was all employer establishments primarily engaged in wholesale trade, and employer and nonemployer establishments in retail trade or service industries.

Type of Data Collection Operation: All wholesale firms with paid employees surveyed; all retail and service large employer firms surveyed (i.e. all employer firms above the payroll size cutoff established to separate large from small employers) plus a 10-percent sample of smaller employer firms. Firms with no employees were not required to file a census return.

Data Collection and Imputation Procedures: Mail questionnaire is utilized with both mail and telephone followups for nonrespondents. Data for nonrespondents and "nonselected" small employer firms in retail trade and service industries are obtained from administrative records of IRS and the Social Security Administration.

Estimates of Sampling Error: Not applicable.

Other (nonsampling) Errors: Response rate in 1987 of 80% for single establishment firms; 83% for multi-establishment firms. Item response ranged from 60% to 90% with higher rates for less detailed questions.

Sources of Additional Material: U.S. Bureau of the Census, Appendix A of *Census of Retail Trade; Census of Service Industries; Census of Wholesale Trade;* and *History of the 1987 Economic Censuses*, April 1992.

Source and Title: U.S. Bureau of the Census, *Current Business Surveys*

Tables: 1280-1283, 1299, 1302, 1305, and table 170 in section 3, table 395 in section 7, and table 995 in section 21.

Universe, Frequency, and Types of Data: Provides monthly estimates of retail sales by kind of business and geographic area, and end-of-month inventories of retail stores; wholesale sales and end-of-month inventories; and annual receipts of selected service industries.

Type of Data Collection Operation: Probability sample of all firms from a list frame and, additionally, for retail and service an area frame. The list frame is the Bureau's Standard Statistical Establishment List (SSEL) updated quarterly for recent birth Employer Identification (EI) Numbers issued by the Internal Revenue Service and assigned a kind-of-business code by the Social Security Administration. The largest firms are included monthly; a sample of others is included every three months on a rotating basis. The area frame covers businesses not subjected to sampling on the list frame.

Data Collection and Imputation Procedures: Data are collected by mail questionnaire with telephone followups for nonrespondents. Imputation made for each nonresponse item and each item failing edit checks.

Estimates of Sampling Error: For the 1989 monthly surveys, CV's are about 0.6% for estimated total retail sales, 1.7% for wholesale sales, 1.3% for wholesale inventories. For dollar volume of receipts, CV's from the *Service Annual Survey* vary by kind of business and range between 1.5% to 15.0%. Sampling errors are shown in monthly publications.

Other (nonsampling) Errors: Imputation rates are about 18% to 23% for monthly retail sales, 20% to 25% for wholesale sales, about 25% to 30% for monthly wholesale inventories and 14% for the *Service Annual Survey*.

Sources of Additional Material: U.S. Bureau of the Census, *Current Business Reports, Monthly Retail Trade, Monthly Wholesale Trade,* and *Service Annual Survey*.

Section 29. OUTLYING AREAS

(See section 1 for information pertaining to tables 1336 and 1337, section 2 for table 1338, section 22 for table 1345, section 26 for table 1348.)

Index to Tables Having Historical Statistics, Colonial Times to 1970 Series

[The most recent historical supplement to the *Statistical Abstract* is the bicentennial edition, *Historical Statistics of the United States, Colonial Times to 1970* (see inside back cover). Listed below are statistical time series (identified by number) appearing in this edition, for which tables in the *Statistical Abstract* present comparable figures. Historical series are listed only where related or comparable data are available for one or more years later than 1970. In a few instances, it may be necessary to combine figures shown in the *Abstract* to obtain totals comparable to the series shown in *Historical Statistics*]

Historical Statistics series	1994 Abstract table number	Historical Statistics series	1994 Abstract table number	Historical Statistics series	1994 Abstract table number	Historical Statistics series	1994 Abstract table number
A		**C**		**H—Con.**		**J—Con.**	
A 6-8	2	C 1-10	54	H 197-229	582	J 26-32	541
A 73-81	11	C 89	5	H 238-242	581	J 33-34	1129
A 119-134	13	C 143-157	6	H 262-270	585	J 85-91	1082
A 143-149	11	C 144	322	H 305-317	590	J 92-103	360
A 158-159	142	C 149-157	7	H 332-345	592	J 110-136	379
A 160-171	59, 60	C 158-160	322	H 346-354	598	J 164-267	379
A 172	26			H 355-367	597	J 268-278	378
A 195	26	**D**		H 392-397	595		
A 197	27			H 398-411	610	**K**	
A 204-209	33	D 11-19	614	H 421-429	223		
A 210-263	351	D 29-41	619	H 442-476	229	K 4-7	1084
A 264-275	40	D 42-48	615	H 494; 499	224	K 16	1087
A 288-319	66	D 49-62	625	H 513-519	224	K 17-18	1083
A 320-334	71	D 85-86	614	H 535-544	257	K 82-113	1081
A 335-349	69	D 87-101	646	H 690-692	274	K 142-146	1080
A 353-358	75	D 116-126	631	H 699-705	274	K 162-173	1078
A 359-371	84	D 127-141	654	H 710	274	K 184-191	1101
		D 142-151	656	H 729-738	277	K 192	1093
B		D 689-704	658	H 747-749	277	K 204-219	1088
		D 802-810	656	H 751-763	291	K 251-255	1106
B 1-5	90	D 877-892	656	H 793-799	86	K 259-260	1093
B 5-10	92			H 806-828	389	K 264-285	1093
B 11	94	**E**		H 829-835	390	K 286-302	1095
B 12-20	92			H 862-864	405	K 344-353	1098
B 20-27	96	E 73-86	753	H 865-870	404	K 358-360	1099
B 28-35	100	E 135-173	747	H 871	405	K 414-429	1103
B 107-115	114			H 872	404	K 486-495	1100
B 116-125	115	**F**		H 874	405	K 496-501	1111
B 136-147	120			H 875-876	401	K 502-505	1114
B 142	90	F 566-594	702	H 877	405	K 506-563	1113
B 149-166	125			H 921-940	420	K 564-569	1122
B 163-165	134	**G**		H 946-951	421	K 575-582	1122
B 167-173	117			H 952-961	301	K 583-594	1121
B 181-192	117	G 1-8	714	H 971-978	307	K 595-601	1126
B 214-217	139	G 16-23	714	H 979-986	135	K 609-623	1127
B 218	143	G 31-138	716	H 987-998	324		
B 221-235	149	G 179-188	721	H 1012-1027	322	**L**	
B 222-232	151	G 190-192	714	H 1028-1062	327		
B 248-261	148	G 197-199	714	H 1063-1078	328	L 10-14	1131
B 262-272	163	G 257-268	723	H 1079-1096	329	L 15-31	1129
B 275-280	171	G 851-856	219	H 1097-1111	330	L 72-86	1134
B 281-290	172	G 881-915	220	H 1135-1140	339	L 87-97	1135
B 291-303	204			H 1155-1167	346	L 98-112	1139
B 305-318	179	**H**				L 113-121	1140
B 331-344	179			**J**		L 122-137	1139
B 359-362	180	H 1-47	572			L 151-170	1145
B 384-387	181	H 57-69	579	J 1-2	352	L 172	1142
B 413-422	179	H 115-124	596	J 3-6	353	L 174	1142
		H 172-185	580	J 10-15	541	L 175	1144

Historical Statistics series	1994 Abstract table number	Historical Statistics series	1994 Abstract table number	Historical Statistics series	1994 Abstract table number	Historical Statistics series	1994 Abstract table number
L—Con.		**Q**		**T**		**X—Con.**	
L 178-191	1142	Q 36-42	993	T 43-47	1277	X 410-417	802
L 192-198	1143	Q 50-51, 55 ...	997	T 79-196	1279	X 444-453	807
L 199-205	1138	Q 69-75	1029	T 197-219	1282	X 454-455	806
L 206-210	1137	Q 90-94	1001	T 245-246	1280	X 474-491	810
L 224-226	1149	Q 136-147	1004	T 245-271	1281	X 492-498	808
L 227-235	1160	Q 148; 150 ...	1289	T 274-287	1298	X 517-530	812
L 229	1149	Q 156-162	1024	T 280-371	1299	X 536-539	822
L 254-261	1148	Q 199-207	1027	T 391-443	1300	X 551-560	797
L 262-293	1150	Q 208	1014	T 444-471	913	X 588-609	780
L 305-310	1153	Q 224-232	1014	T 472-484	912	X 716-724	777
L 312-318	1161	Q 233-234	1003			X 741, 748....	778
L 338-357	1158	Q 238-250	1028			X 756, 761....	778
L 362-365	1159	Q 284-312	1036	**U**		X 821; 835....	770
		Q 319, 330 ...	1036			X 864-878	786
M		Q 332	1038	U 1-25	1306	X 879-889	828
		Q 356-378	1036	U 26-39	1309	X 890-917	826
M 1-12	1165	Q 400-401	1036	U 41-46	1316		
M 13-37	1166	Q 414-416	1072	U 47-74	1311		
M 68-71	1164	Q 438-448	1068	U 75-186	1318		
M 76-92	919	Q 449-458	1070	U 190-195	1323	**Y**	
M 93-126	1190	Q 473-480	1074	U 207-212	1331		
M 127-128	936	Q 487-502	1069	U 264-273	1324	Y 79-83	423
M 143-146	1182	Q 507-517	1067	U 317-352	1329	Y 84-134	426
M 147-161	1187	Q 604-623	1053			Y 135-186	427
M 266-267	1191					Y 189-198	433
M 271-286	1176	**R**		**V**		Y 199-203	434
						Y 204-210	432
N		R 1-12	888	V 1-12	832	Y 211-214	430
		R 31-45	888	V 20-30	846	Y 272-307	493
N 1-29	1196	R 46-70	886	V 42-53	834	Y 308-317	529
N 66-69	1196	R 75-88	886	V 167-183	842	Y 318-331	533
N 78-100	1198	R 106-109	913	V 193-196	842	Y 335-338	509
N 118-137	1194	R 123-126	913	V 197-212	955	Y 339-342	504
N 140-155	1193	R 140-148	891			Y 343-351	505
N 156-163	1202	R 163-171	908			Y 358-373	520
N 170	1202	R 172-186	909	**W**		Y 381-392	840
N 186-191	1227	R 188-191	910			Y 393-411	521
N 238-245	1215	R 191-216	899	W 14, 17, 19 ..	657	Y 412-439	526
N 249-258	1225	R 224-231	904	W 22-25	658	Y 458-460	539
N 273, 276....	791	R 232-243	903	W 30-54	657	Y 472-487	505
				W 62-65	657	Y 505-637	463
P		**S**		W 82-95	907	Y 638-651	468
				W 96-108	857	Y 652-848	463
P 1-12	1234	S 1-14	918	W 109-125	966	Y 710-782	477
P 13	1239	S 32-52	946	W 126	969	Y 787-788	465
P 18-39	1239	S 78-82	946	W 142	968	Y 794	474
P 58-67	1235	S 86-107	946	W 167	977	Y 856-903	558
P 74-92	1262	S 133-146	955			Y 904-916	553
P 93-106	877	S 160-175	956	**X**		Y 943-956	566
P 235, 236a...	1249	S 190-204	962			Y 998-999	569
P 239-241	1250	S 205-218	961	X 114-147	773		
P 265-269	1254			X 192, 229....	770		

Tables Deleted From the 1993 Edition of the Statistical Abstract

Appendix VI
New Tables

Index

NOTE: Index citations refer to table numbers, not page numbers.

NOTE: Index citations refer to table numbers, not page numbers.

NOTE: Index citations refer to table numbers, not page numbers.

NOTE: Index citations refer to table numbers, not page numbers.

NOTE: Index citations refer to table numbers, not page numbers.

NOTE: Index citations refer to table numbers, not page numbers.

NOTE: Index citations refer to table numbers, not page numbers.

NOTE: Index citations refer to table numbers, not page numbers.

NOTE: Index citations refer to table numbers, not page numbers.

NOTE: Index citations refer to table numbers, not page numbers.

NOTE: Index citations refer to table numbers, not page numbers.

Index

NOTE: Index citations refer to table numbers, not page numbers.

NOTE: Index citations refer to table numbers, not page numbers.

NOTE: Index citations refer to table numbers, not page numbers.

NOTE: Index citations refer to table numbers, not page numbers.

NOTE: Index citations refer to table numbers, not page numbers.

NOTE: Index citations refer to table numbers, not page numbers.

NOTE: Index citations refer to table numbers, not page numbers.

NOTE: Index citations refer to table numbers, not page numbers.

NOTE: Index citations refer to table numbers, not page numbers.

NOTE: Index citations refer to table numbers, not page numbers.

NOTE: Index citations refer to table numbers, not page numbers.

NOTE: Index citations refer to table numbers, not page numbers.

NOTE: Index citations refer to table numbers, not page numbers.

NOTE: Index citations refer to table numbers, not page numbers.

NOTE: Index citations refer to table numbers, not page numbers.

NOTE: Index citations refer to table numbers, not page numbers.

NOTE: Index citations refer to table numbers, not page numbers.

NOTE: Index citations refer to table numbers, not page numbers.

NOTE: Index citations refer to table numbers, not page numbers.

NOTE: Index citations refer to table numbers, not page numbers.

NOTE: Index citations refer to table numbers, not page numbers.

NOTE: Index citations refer to table numbers, not page numbers.

996   Index

NOTE: Index citations refer to table numbers, not page numbers.

NOTE: Index citations refer to table numbers, not page numbers.

NOTE: Index citations refer to table numbers, not page numbers.

NOTE: Index citations refer to table numbers, not page numbers.

NOTE: Index citations refer to table numbers, not page numbers.

NOTE: Index citations refer to table numbers, not page numbers.

NOTE: Index citations refer to table numbers, not page numbers.

NOTE: Index citations refer to table numbers, not page numbers.

NOTE: Index citations refer to table numbers, not page numbers.

NOTE: Index citations refer to table numbers, not page numbers.

NOTE: Index citations refer to table numbers, not page numbers.

NOTE: Index citations refer to table numbers, not page numbers.

NOTE: Index citations refer to table numbers, not page numbers.

NOTE: Index citations refer to table numbers, not page numbers.

U.S. Census Bureau Announces

Census Catalog and Guide: 1994

Helps you select from all the products

Every Census Bureau product issued
mid-1988–1993:

- *Reports*
- *Microfiche*
- *Computer tapes*
- *CD-ROM*
- *Floppy disks*
- *Online access*
- *Maps*
- *FAX*

AND

Many statistical publications from other
Federal agencies

Features facts about each product

Topics   Dates
Areas   Prices

Makes finding the right product easy

Title index   Detailed subject index
Guides to statistics from all censuses
and surveys, covering population, housing,
business, construction, and more.

Identifies sources of assistance

1,700 data center organizations
200 Census Bureau data specialists
1,500 depository libraries
Other Federal statistical agencies
5 other directory lists

Superintendent of Documents **Publications** Order Form

*7366

□ **YES,** please send me the following indicated publications:

_____copies of **Census Catalog and Guide: 1994**
at $23, S/N 003-024-08752-9.

The total cost of my order is $_____. Prices include regular domestic postage and handling and are subject to change. International customers please add 25%.

_____
(Company or personal name)   (Please type or print)

_____
(Additional address/attention line)

_____
(Street address)

_____
(City, State, ZIP Code)

_____
(Daytime phone including area code)

_____
(Purchase Order No.)

Charge your order. It's easy!

VISA

MasterCard

P3S

Please Choose Method of Payment:

□ Check payable to the Superintendent of Documents

□ GPO Deposit Account ⬚⬚⬚⬚⬚⬚⬚–⬚

□ VISA or MasterCard Account

⬚⬚⬚⬚⬚⬚⬚⬚⬚⬚⬚⬚⬚⬚⬚⬚⬚⬚⬚⬚⬚

To fax your orders (202) 512−2250

⬚⬚⬚⬚ (Credit card expiration date)

_____
(Authorizing Signature)   6/94

Thank you for your order!

Mail To: Superintendent of Documents
           P.O. Box 371954, Pittsburgh, PA 15250−7954